2001
Britannica Book of the Year

Encyclopædia Britannica, Inc.
Chicago · London · New Delhi · Paris · Seoul · Sydney · Taipei · Tokyo

2001 Britannica Book of the Year

Editorial and design-production services provided by Proof Positive/Farrowlyne Associates, Inc., Evanston, IL.

Photo research provided by Feldman & Associates, Inc.

Library of Congress Catalog Card Number: 38-12082
International Standard Book Number: 0-85229-782-3
International Standard Serial Number: 0068-1156

BRITANNICA BOOK OF THE YEAR

Britannica.com may be accessed on the Internet at http://www.britannica.com.

(Trademark Reg. U.S. Pat. Off.) Printed in U.S.A.

Foreword

Whether or not you celebrated Jan. 1, 2000, as the first day of the new year, century, millennium, or whatnot, the transition from 1999 to 2000 was remarkably smooth and trouble-free. Worries about "Y2K" problems with computers did not materialize, and generally the world continued in its petty pace into the new year.

Happily, no major wars raged during 2000. On the other hand, only fitful progress was made in resolving ongoing violent ethnic, religious, and political struggles in Northern Ireland, Central Africa, Sierra Leone, the Horn of Africa, and Sri Lanka. A very serious degeneration of the situation in Palestine began in the summer and continued through year's end. Central Asian states were traumatized by destabilizing projections of power from Afghanistan. Ethnic differences paralyzed Fiji, while Indonesia seemed threatened with dismemberment resulting from centrifugal nationalist forces.

Still, rays of hope radiated from Korea, where the two halves of a peninsula politically divided for half a century established a dialogue. Kim Dae Jung of South Korea was awarded the Nobel Prize for Peace for his efforts. Changes in government in 2000 seemed, on balance, to favour democracy and stability. New heads of state in Morocco, Syria, and Jordan all made impressive debuts. Vojislav Kostunica sought to mend the tatters of a Yugoslavia rent by Slobodan Milosevic, while the sudden resignation of Alberto Fujimori suggested that Peru, too, might be shaking off its authoritarian past. Somalia moved cautiously in the direction of reestablishing a stable government.

The world was riveted by the spectacle of a U.S. presidential election that was, for a very long time indeed, "too close to call." Legislatures and supreme courts jumped into the fray, and recriminations, vituperations, and calls for revision of the electoral system were legion—a spectacle that will surely colour the new administration's mandate to lead the country and America's authority as an impartial observer of elections elsewhere. Vicente Fox's elevation to president of Mexico was hardly less remarkable, overturning, as it did, 70 years of single-party incumbency. Women politicians captured headlines during the year, notably Tarja Halonen in Finland, Chandrika Kumaratunga in Sri Lanka, and Angela Merkel, whose task it was to rebuild a centre-right in Germany—not to mention the virtual "declaration of independence" by political wives Hillary Rodham Clinton in the U.S. and Cherie Booth in the U.K.

A number of social concerns continued into the new millennium. We have chosen to highlight three in this edition of the *Book of the Year:* the shocking persistence of slavery throughout the world, the difficulty of finding reliable statistics in emotion-charged issues such as, in this case, the gun-control debate in the U.S., and the troubled path of socialized medicine. Some view globalization as a social ill as well, and we have included in this edition a sidebar to help us all understand what is understood by that term.

The inexorable march of the computer continued throughout 2000; in past volumes we have reported on e-commerce and e-trading, among others. This e-year, 2000, could be the one in which e-publishing came into its own—and this topic comes up repeatedly in the "Media" and "Literature" sections of the book—but we decided to focus special attention on another matter of widespread concern, e-privacy.

China has come out as a political and economic superpower, but in 2000 there were signs that Chinese authors were debuting in world literary circles as well. Poet Gao Xingjian was honoured with the Nobel Prize for Literature, while novelist Ha Jin received the PEN/Faulkner Award for his novel *Waiting*.

Though the world economy seemed to be stable-to-growing and there was a remarkable budget surplus in the U.S., nervousness nonetheless prevailed on the stock market over high-tech issues and there was a growing desolation as investors abandoned "dot-com" companies in droves.

The science story of the year was the announcement that the human genome had been all but completely mapped—an accomplishment that will surely rank in importance with the splitting of the atom or the beginning of human exploration of space. The impact on health, medicine, agriculture, and even sciences as remote as anthropology—not to mention the thorny ethical questions that applications of such research raise—will be profound. Other fascinating scientific stories that we cover in the yearbook this year include the remains of early man discovered in a cave in the Caucasus mountains, close-up photos of an asteroid, the continuing squabbles over genetically modified foods, and a new book that is shaking up cultural anthropologists.

At the XXVII Games in Sydney, Australia, 48 world records were set and 928 medals were bestowed on athletes from 199 IOC member countries. Despite troubling instances of poor sportsmanship and, of course, doping, it was all in all a fine spectacle—as IOC Chairman Juan Antonio Samaranch was pleased to proclaim, "the best ever" Games.

Last year Britannica conducted a poll of yearbook customers, and we would like to thank all who took part. Though we found a general level of satisfaction with the yearbook, we have made an effort to improve the product along lines our readers suggested. This year we have reorganized the photos, adding, among other changes, art-quality images to introduce the various major sections, "People of 2000," etc. We have also reinstated the "Calendar," which more of you rely on than we had anticipated! Readers told us that they often turn to Obituaries first. In this volume you will find sketches of personalities who died in 2000 such as entertainers Steve Allen, Gwen Verdon, and Alec Guinness; politicians and statesmen such as Japan's Keizo Obuchi and Syria's Hafez al-Assad; and sports figures including tennis legend Don Budge—to name but a few.

We hope you will also find a number of surprises, here and in other sections of the book, and may be moved to utter an occasional "Oh, I remember him" or "I didn't know she had died!" That's what the *Britannica Book of the Year* should be: a succession of surprises as you (re)discover all the people and events that made 2000 a remarkable year and apprehend the interconnectedness of it all.

Editor

Contents 2001

John McColgan/Alaskan Type I Incident Management Team/Bureau of Land Management, Alaska Fire Service

Dates of 2000

The first year of the new millennium or last year of the old? What was that rule about calculating leap years? Whatever the math, every day of 2000 was filled with events to alter and illuminate our times.

AP/Wide World Photos

January

We are fortunate to be alive at this moment in history. Never before has our nation enjoyed, at once, so much prosperity and social progress with so little internal crisis and so few external threats. Never before have we had such a blessed opportunity—and, therefore, such a profound obligation—to build the more perfect union of our founders' dreams.

U.S. Pres. William J. Clinton in his state of the union message before Congress, January 27

1 The year 2000 arrives safe and sound, without serious computer-related "Y2K" problems that many had anticipated, such as computer breakdowns, interruptions in utility services, banking and billing crises, airplane crashes, and military incidents; the rollover is celebrated by some as the beginning of a new millennium, others will wait a year.

•

Greenwich Electronic Time, a new time standard for the Internet based upon the long-traditional and universally accepted Greenwich Mean Time and Coordinated Universal Time, is launched in London by Prime Minister Tony Blair.

2 ***Rioting and looting break out between majority Muslims and minority Coptic Christians in the village of Al-Kosheh, about 450 km (270 mi) south of Cairo, and more than two dozen deaths are reported; Copts constitute about 10% of the Egyptian population. (Photo below.)***

3 Acting Russian Pres. Vladimir Putin fires Tatyana Dyachenko, daughter of former president Boris Yeltsin; Dyachenko had wielded enormous power in the Kremlin, maintaining links to a number of controversial businessmen, and had organized her father's presidential campaign in 1996.

•

Turkish Pres. Suleyman Demirel officially opens the new Ataturk International Airport, located 24 km (15 mi) west of Istanbul; the terminal building is designed to accommodate 14 million passengers a year and has been constructed with special provisions to withstand earthquakes.

Norbert Schiller

4 Alan Greenspan is nominated by Pres. Bill Clinton for a fourth four-year term as chairman of the Board of Governors of the U.S. Federal Reserve System.

•

In the annual postseason Sugar Bowl, Florida State University defeats Virginia Tech 46–29 and claims the national college football Division I-A championship; other New Year's classic bowl games include the Rose Bowl, the Cotton Bowl, the Citrus Bowl, and the Gator Bowl on January 1; the Orange Bowl and Fiesta Bowl take place on January 2.

5 At least 11 persons, including the woman suicide bomber, die in an explosion in the offices of Sri Lankan Prime Minister Sirimavo Bandaranaike; the unsuccessful assassination attempt on the prime minister is widely believed to be the work of the Liberation Tigers of Tamil Eelam separatist group.

•

Hillary Rodham Clinton formally moves into the house she bought in Chappaqua, N.Y., in order to establish residency in the state and thereby meet the electoral requirements as a candidate for senator from New York; she is the only first lady ever to have moved out of the White House before the end of the president's term.

6 After fleeing his homeland in late December 1999 and crossing the Himalaya Mountains, the 17th Karmapa Lama, Uguen Trinley Dorje, third in the hierarchy of Tibetan Buddhist leaders (after the Dalai and Panchen Lamas), arrives in Dharmshala, India, near the border with Tibet; the motives and circumstances for the defection are not immediately clear.

•

The Canadian Broadcasting Corp., Canada's national television network, is ordered by the state regulatory authority, the Canadian Radio-Television and Telecommunications Commission, to stop broadcasting highly popular foreign-made films during peak viewing hours and concentrate on Canadian program content.

7 In contravention of the North American Free Trade Agreement, U.S. officials announce that they will not permit free access to roads in all states by Mexican trucks and buses, citing safety concerns; some interpret the announcement as a political move aimed at winning support of the Teamsters Union for the presidential candidacy of Vice Pres. Al Gore.

8 The National Society of Film Critics awards are announced; for the first time in the 34-year history of the awards, two films are tied for best-picture honours, *Being John Malkovich* and *Topsy-Turvy.*

9 With almost 92% of voters' support and a 95% turnout, Uzbekistan's Pres. Islam Karimov comfortably, if controversially, wins reelection; he has been president of the Central Asian country since 1991.

•

The IBM Corp. announces that it will develop Internet software to support Linux, the open-source operating system available free to computer programmers, and will set up a Linux software development centre in India.

10 In the largest corporate merger ever—a deal valued at $183 billion—Internet service provider America Online, Inc., announces that it plans to buy the giant media corporation Time Warner, Inc.; AOL chief executive Steve Case would be chairman and Time Warner head Gerald Levin the CEO of the new company. (*See* January 30.)

•

Defying a decision by the U.S. Immigration and Naturalization Service on January 5 that Elián González, a six-year-old Cuban refugee, be returned to his father in Cuba no later than January 14, a circuit court judge in Miami, Fla., grants custody of the youngster to his maternal relatives living in the Miami area. (*See* April 22.)

11 Following a medical examination on January 5, the British government announces that exiled dictator Gen. Augusto Pinochet Ugarte is not fit to stand trial in Spain; Pinochet is charged with 35 counts of human rights violations that took place during his tenure as president of Chile.

•

Two baseball players, Carlton Fisk, a catcher for the Boston Red Sox and the Chicago White Sox, and Tony Pérez, a first baseman for the Cincinnati Reds, are elected to the National Baseball Hall of Fame in Cooperstown, N.Y.; Pérez is the first Cuban to be so honoured.

•

By executive order President Clinton creates three new national monuments—Grand Canyon-Parashant on the north rim of the Grand Canyon and Agua Fria, both in Arizona, and California Coastal, along the coast of California—and extends the territory of a fourth, the Pinnacles National Monument, in California.

12 The government of Turkey announces that it has postponed the scheduled execution of Kurdish rebel leader Abdullah Ocalan; the decision, seen as a political victory for Prime Minister Bulent Ecevit, is apparently linked to scrutiny of Turkey's human rights record and its application to join the European Union. (*See* February 9.)

•

In compliance with a 1999 European Court of Human Rights ruling, Great Britain ends its ban on the service of openly gay men and women in the armed forces.

13 Bill Gates resigns as chief executive officer of Microsoft Corp. and is replaced by Steven Ballmer; Gates continues as chairman and chief architect of software.

•

Park Tae Joon, president of the United Liberal Democrats, is confirmed as prime minister of the Republic of Korea.

14 The Russian government issues a new, tougher national security strategy, replacing one adopted in 1997; the new document criticizes the United States and Western Europe for expansionism and allows for the use of nuclear weapons in war if other methods of resolution have been exhausted.

•

After scientists express concern about possible undesirable ecological consequences of some genetically modified crops (notably threats to the monarch butterfly), the U.S. Environmental Protection Agency places sowing limits on Bt, a type of corn that has been genetically engineered to make the plant resistant to certain types of insects. (*See* January 24.)

•

South Korea announces plans to build a rocket capable of placing a satellite into Earth orbit and to establish a national space program.

15 Zeljko Raznatovic (known by his nom de guerre, "Arkan"), a Serb ultranationalist paramilitary leader and crony of Yugoslav Pres. Slobodan Milosevic, and two others are shot dead by unknown assassins in a downtown Belgrade hotel.

16 In the second round of Chile's presidential elections, Ricardo Lagos Escobar of the centre-left Concertación alliance narrowly defeats Joaquín Lavín Infante of the rightist Alliance for Chile.

•

Two huge British pharmaceutical companies, Glaxo Wellcome PLC and SmithKline Beecham PLC, announce plans to merge on equal terms in a deal worth $75.7 billion; the combined corporation would represent the world's largest pharmaceutical company. (*See* February 7.)

17 Charismatic, which won the 1999 Kentucky Derby and Preakness Stakes thoroughbred horse races but lost his chance to become the first Triple Crown winner in two decades when he broke a leg in the Belmont Stakes, is named 1999 Horse of the Year in Los Angeles.

18 Former German chancellor Helmut Kohl resigns as honorary chairman of his party, the Christian Democratic Union; Kohl and other former top CDU officials have been under formal investigation since January 3 on charges of embezzling state funds. (*See* January 20.)

•

A test of the missile defense system being developed by the U.S. military fails when a rocket launched in the Pacific does not intercept and destroy a mock warhead launched from an air base in California. (*See* July 8.)

19 The UN Security Council endorses the appointment of former South African president Nelson Mandela, originally made in December 1999, to lead the Arusha (Tanz.) peace process toward a settlement of grievances between the sides in Burundi.

•

Retired basketball superstar Michael Jordan announces that he is acquiring part ownership in the Washington Wizards professional basketball team; the Washington, D.C., franchise has not won a championship since 1978.

20 Wolfgang Hüllen, a leading finance official of Germany's Christian Democratic Union, hangs himself as a parliamentary group begins an investigation into illicit payments to the party in the 1990s. (*See* January 18.)

•

The Times (London) reports that scientists have discovered remains of the largest dinosaur yet known, a herbivore about 48–50 m (157–164 ft) in length, in the southern Patagonia region of Argentina; no name has yet been given to the dinosaur.

21 ***Pres. Jamil Mahuad Witt of Ecuador is ousted in a military coup in Quito; the action by a group of middle-ranking army officers follows the occupation of the capital and other large cities by indigenous rights groups such as those pictured in the photo below.* (See *March 9.*)**

AP/Wide World Photos

•

Representatives of 70 countries gathered in Geneva under United Nations auspices agree to ban the use of soldiers under the age of 18 in military conflicts; the final document is a protocol to the 1990 UN Convention on the Rights of the Child.

22 Chinese officials react strongly and negatively to plans to hold a one-day conference on January 23 in Osaka, Japan, on the sensitive issue of the 1937 Nanking (Nanjing) Massacre, in which thousands of residents of the Chinese city were killed, raped, and robbed by invading Japanese troops; the conference promoters had called the 1937 event "the biggest myth of the 20th century."

23 Pres. Hugo Chávez Frías appoints Isaías Rodríguez, a top official in the Constituent Assembly, to the new post of vice president of Venezuela.

•

At the Golden Globe Awards ceremony in Beverly Hills, Calif., the film *American Beauty* wins honours for best drama, best director—Sam Mendes (for his first motion picture), and best screenplay.

24 Delegates from more than 130 countries convene in Montreal to discuss regulation of trade in genetically modified (GM) foods; the group agrees that importing countries should have the right to scientific information about the GM organisms used in a given product and should have the right to refuse to admit GM items into their countries; an agreement, the Cartagena Protocol on Biosafety, is reached on January 29. (*See* January 14.)

•

The U.S. Supreme Court votes 6–3 to uphold a Missouri law that limits the amount of money a person may donate to support a candidate in a state election; the decision is expected to have a significant impact on the national debate about campaign finance issues.

25 Thai special forces overrun a hospital in the town of Ratchaburi that had been occupied on January 24 by 10 members of a Karen rebel group from neighbouring Myanmar (Burma) who held staff and patients hostage; the terrorists, believed to be members of the gang controlled by Johnny and Luther Htoo, 12-year-old twin brothers, are all killed in the government raid.

26 Hans Blix, former director general of the International Atomic Energy Agency, is appointed to lead the United Nations commission to oversee the disarmament of Iraq after the first candidate, another Swedish diplomat, Rolf Ekeus, could not win the support of all Security Council members.

•

Egypt's People's Assembly passes a new law according women the right to divorce their husbands on grounds of incompatibility; the old principle, based on Islamic law, allowed women to divorce only with convincing evidence of mistreatment or other specific circumstances. (*See* March 12.)

•

The International Tennis Hall of Fame in Newport, R.I., announces that its year 2000 honorees are women's tennis legend Martina Navratilova, 1950s Australian star Mal Anderson, and referee and tennis official Robert Kelleher; the three are to be inducted on July 15.

27 Following a decade of vigorous public debate, German officials dedicate a two-hectare (five-acre) parcel of land near the Brandenburg Gate in central Berlin as the site of a national Holocaust memorial; the design of American architect Peter Eisenman is chosen for the project.

28 A U.S. government report concludes that workers making nuclear weapons have been exposed to radiation and chemicals that have led to higher-than-normal rates of cancers and early death; this is the first time the government has acknowledged that people probably contracted cancer from radiation exposure while working in the plants.

•

American Lindsay Davenport wins the Australian Open women's singles tennis championship, defeating defending champion Martina Hingis of Switzerland 6–1, 7–5; in the men's competition on January 30, American Andre Agassi also defeats the defending champion, Russian Yevgeny Kafelnikov, 3–6, 6–3, 6–2, 6–4.

•

Two new subway lines, part of a $2.2 billion project funded largely by the European Union, are opened in Athens. The two new routes are added to an earlier line that links the Plaka district of the Greek capital with the port of Piraeus.

29 Quarterback Joe Montana, Ronnie Lott (who played several positions), defensive end Howie Long, linebacker Dave Wilcox, and Pittsburgh Steelers owner Dan Rooney are named to the American Pro Football Hall of Fame in Canton, Ohio.

•

Awards are announced at the closing gala of the 2000 Sundance Film Festival; the Grand Jury Prize for best dramatic film is split between *Girlfight,* directed by Karyn Kusama, and *You Can Count on Me,* directed by Kenneth Lonergan, while the Grand Jury Prize for best documentary goes to *Long Night's Journey into Day,* directed by Frances Reid and Deborah Hoffmann.

30 In a move that surprises industry observers, the French telecommunications group Vivendi announces an alliance with the British mobile telephone group Vodafone AirTouch PLC, which in turn has tendered a hostile takeover bid for the German company Mannesmann AG (*see* February 3); the new company will be Europe's number one Internet and new-media provider.

•

The St. Louis Rams defeat the Tennessee Titans 23–16 in the professional football Super Bowl XXXIV; Rams quarterback Kurt Warner, who threw passes for a record 414 yd, is voted the game's Most Valuable Player.

31 Two separate reports, one by the Indonesian Commission to Investigate Human Rights Violations in East Timor and the other by the UN Commission of Inquiry into East Timor, find that the Indonesian military cooperated with local pro-Indonesian militia groups in violating the human rights of the East Timorese.

•

Gov. George Ryan of Illinois, citing the large number of death row inmates whose convictions had recently been overturned, declares a moratorium on executions in the state.

February

I am asking for forgiveness for what Germans have done, for myself and my generation, for the sake of our children and grandchildren, whose future I would like to see alongside the children of Israel.

German Pres. Johannes Rau addressing the Israeli Knesset (parliament), February 16, during a state visit

1 Following four months of intensive negotiations, the Austrian People's Party agrees to form a coalition with the Freedom Party of Austria (FPÖ), led by ultranationalist Jörg Haider; the FPÖ's success has clouded Austrian politics, and on January 31 the European Union had threatened to break with Austria if the right-wingers were allowed to participate in the government.

•

Subway and bus workers in France go on strike to protest the first day of the mandated shorter workweek; the government had decreed a maximum 35-hour week in an effort to lower unemployment.

2 The U.S. Federal Trade Commission moves to block the takeover of the Atlantic Richfield Co., a large California-based petroleum company, by the British giant BP Amoco, citing the possibility that the new company would enjoy a dominant economic position on the West Coast.

•

Some 120 Koreans, who had been sent to Sakhalin Island in the 1940s and put to forced labour by Japan and had been trapped there by Cold War politics ever since, return home to South Korea.

3 Vodaphone AirTouch PLC of Great Britain announces plans to acquire Mannesmann AG, Germany's largest mobile phone company; the deal, reportedly worth about $180 billion, would be the largest takeover ever (*see* January 30) and would result in the world's largest telecommunications group.

•

The Ford Motor Co. announces that it will provide each of its 350,000 employees worldwide with a personal computer and unlimited Internet access for $5 per month for three years, after which the computers will belong to the employees.

•

Jill Barad, who had revived the Barbie doll for American toy manufacturer Mattel Inc., resigns as chairman and CEO of the company; she had been one of a very few women to lead a Fortune 500 company.

4 Lord Archer, a prominent British Conservative politician who had campaigned for mayor of London, is expelled from the party for five years for breaches of political ethics and integrity.

•

The U.S. Department of Labor reports that the unemployment rate in the United States for January 2000, adjusted for seasonal variations, is the lowest it has been in 30 years—4%.

5 Several mortar shells land near the presidential palace in Tehran, Iran; a group called the Mujaheddin-e-Khalq says it launched the attack and that the target was Ayatollah Sayyed Ali Khamenei.

•

Violent anti-immigrant riots break out in El Ejido, near Almería, Spain, the centre of a region that has a high percentage of Moroccan agricultural labourers; the violence spreads to nearby towns and continues until February 7.

6 Acting Russian Pres. Vladimir Putin announces that Russian troops have taken Grozny, the capital of the secessionist republic of Chechnya; few expect the guerrilla war to wind down, however, as the Chechen insurgents retreat to the mountainous southern regions of the republic.

•

Tarja Halonen, a Social Democrat and former foreign minister, is elected president of Finland; she is the first woman to hold the position.

•

A long-running strike at the huge National Autonomous University of Mexico, Mexico City, ends after a majority of the students and faculty vote to stop striking and federal police enter the campus and evict the protesters from university buildings.

AP/Wide World Photos

The two-day 2000 world speed-skating championships finish up in Milwaukee, Wis.; the overall winners are Gianni Romme of The Netherlands and Claudia Pechstein of Germany.

7 In the second pharmaceutical megamerger of the year (*see* January 16), the U.S. company Pfizer Inc. announces it will acquire another American firm, Warner-Lambert Co., for nearly $90.3 billion and create the second largest drug company in the world.

Stipe Mesic comfortably wins the second round of the presidential election in Croatia, defeating Drazen Budisa 56% to 44%.

Puerto Rico wins baseball's 30th Caribbean Series with a 13–10 victory over the Dominican Republic; the Puerto Rican team racked up 86 hits during the series, breaking a record that had stood for 47 years.

8 Some of the largest World Wide Web sites, including eBay, CNN, Amazon.com, and E*Trade, are attacked by a hacker and maliciously jammed—closed down—for several hours following a similar attack on Yahoo! a day earlier; in April it is revealed that a main culprit is a 15-year-old youth from Montreal who goes by the Internet name of "Mafiaboy."

Ion Gheorghe Maurer, the communist prime minister of Romania from 1961 to 1974, dies in Bucharest, Rom., at age 97.

9 The Kurdistan Workers' Party (PKK), a major organization seeking independence for the Kurds who live in Turkey, declares an end to its violent activities and calls for its members to work within the Turkish state structure; the PKK leader, Abdullah Ocalan, remains in a Turkish prison sentenced to death for terrorism. (*See* January 12.)

10 Researchers at the European Organization for Nuclear Research (CERN) in Geneva announce that they have recreated in the laboratory the conditions that existed at the beginning of the universe within 10 microseconds after the big bang.

A major space telescope, ASTRO-E, is launched from Japan's Kagoshima Space Center as the third leg of a triangle whose other legs are NASA's Chandra X-Ray Observatory and Europe's XXM-Newton Observatory and whose purpose is to study cosmic X-rays; the telescope is lost when it fails to achieve a sustainable orbit.

11 Self-rule for Northern Ireland, under which power in the province was shared between the Roman Catholic and Protestant factions and which had been instituted a scant two months earlier, is revoked by the British government because of lack of progress in disarmament by the Irish Republican Army.

Cyanide from a gold mine spill on January 30 has killed as much as 90% of the aquatic life in the Somes (Szamos) River in Romania and Hungary and the Tisza River in Hungary before it reaches the Danube River north of Belgrade, Yugos. (Photo left.) (*See *March 10.)

12 A referendum in Zimbabwe on a new constitution that would give aging Pres. Robert Mugabe vastly increased powers is defeated when 55% of those turning out to vote cast their ballots against it; Mugabe has been in power since 1980.

The 10th heads of state and ministerial meeting of the United Nations Conference on Trade and Development, held every four years, opens in Bangkok, with representatives of some 180 countries and organizations in attendance.

In Cleveland, Ohio, Michelle Kwan wins the U.S. figure skating championship women's title for the third time in a row and the fourth time overall; Michael Weiss took the men's title for the second time.

13 Hans von Sponeck, head of the UN "oil for food" humanitarian program in Iraq, resigns, complaining that the UN's efforts are inadequate; the following day Jutta Burghardt, head of the UN World Food Programme in Iraq, resigns as well for the same reasons.

14 NASA's Near Earth Asteroid Rendezvous spacecraft achieves orbit around the asteroid Eros, becoming the first spacecraft ever to orbit an asteroid.

The former powerful head of the Indonesian military forces, General Wiranto, is suspended from his duties by Pres. Abdurrahman Wahid; Wiranto had been accused of human rights abuses in East Timor.

Foreign ministers of the European Union gather in Brussels at the first meeting of a 10-month intergovernmental conference to streamline and rationalize the operation of the EU as its membership expands significantly in coming years.

A series of tornadoes in southwestern Georgia kills at least 18 people and injures more than 100 others.

15 Peacekeeping troops from the United Nations Mission in the Central African Republic leave the country; the UN forces had been in the country since March 1998.

The establishment in the U.S. of the Women's United Soccer Association is announced by Discovery Communications Inc., which led the search for financing; the eight-team league plans to begin play in April 2001.

The top prize in the Westminster Kennel Club Dog Show, the most prestigious competition for dog breeders, is won by Salilyn 'N Erin's Shameless, an English springer spaniel. (Photo below.)

16 Wolfgang Schäuble, head of the Christian Democratic Union, Germany's opposition party, resigns his party posts and acknowledges mishandling of the scandal involving alleged irregularities in party finance under former chancellor Helmut Kohl. (*See* January 20.)

The South Korean *chaebol* (conglomerate) Hyundai Group announces that it will soon open an office in the North Korean capital, Pyongyang, to oversee a construction project; Hyundai is the first southern company to establish an office in North Korea. (*See* February 26.)

17 The United Nations Security Council recommends the Pacific island nation of Tuvalu as the 189th full member of the United Nations.

Following his easy victory in elections in January, Kumba Ialá of the Party for Social Renewal is sworn in as president of Guinea-Bissau.

The U.S. Food and Drug Administration approves Wyeth-Ayerst Laboratories' Prevnar, the first vaccine against invasive pneumococ-

Ashbey Photography

cal diseases for infants and toddlers, including a form of meningitis that kills several hundred children around the world annually.

18 Reformist elements win a large majority in the elections to the sixth Majlis (parliament) in Iran, much strengthening the hand of Pres. Mohammad Khatami.

•

The U.S. Department of Labor announces that the Ford Motor Co. has agreed to a settlement in a suit charging it with widespread discrimination against women and minorities.

19 Shots are exchanged between border patrols from Honduras and Nicaragua in the Gulf of Fonseca area on the Pacific Coast; the maritime border—especially the small island of Cayo Sur—has been in dispute for some time. (*See* March 7.)

•

The first stage of the Red Sea Free Trade Zone, an area encompassing some 26 sq km (10 sq mi) between Port Sudan and Sawakin, is opened by the government of The Sudan.

20 At the concluding ceremonies of the 50th Berlin Film Festival, the American film *Magnolia* is awarded the Golden Bear, the festival's top prize.

•

The 42nd annual Daytona 500 automobile race at Daytona Beach, Fla., is won by Dale Jarrett, the fourth three-time winner of the race, the most important in the NASCAR Winston Cup series.

•

The Winter Goodwill Games at Lake Placid, N.Y., which began February 16, wrap up; among the winners are Great Britain's Alexandra Hamilton in women's skeleton, American Jim Shea, Jr., in men's skeleton, and Latvia's Sandis Prusis and Janis Ozols in two-man bobsled.

21 Three days of violent conflicts begin between Muslims and Christians in the northern Nigerian city of Kaduna after calls for the introduction of Shari'ah (fundamental Islamic law) in Kaduna state; other states in the predominantly Muslim north of the country are in the process of adopting Shari'ah.

•

Some 85,000 people, including the mayor of San Juan, march silently in Puerto Rico's capital to protest the resumption by the U.S. of military bombing exercises on the island of Vieques.

•

Veteran consumer rights advocate Ralph Nader announces that he will seek the nomination of the Green Party for the United States presidency. Nader is expected to draw a larger measure of support than previous third-party contenders have done.

•

Iranian Pres. Mohammad Khatami opens the first subway in Tehran, the capital city, a metropolis of 11 million people.

22 The giant Finnish paper manufacturer Stora Enso Oyj announces that it will acquire Consolidated Papers, Inc., based in Wisconsin, for $3.9 billion plus assumption of $900 million in debts; this is the fourth large acquisition in the paper industry in two weeks.

•

Dileep Nair, a management expert from Singapore, is named to the post of inspector general of the United Nations.

23 The Grammy Awards for excellence in recorded music are presented; the big winner is Carlos Santana, who takes home eight Grammys; Christina Aguilera is named best new artist.

•

A study published in the *Journal of the American Medical Association* indicates a sharp rise between 1991 and 1995 in prescriptions for behaviour-altering drugs for children two to four years of age.

24 Pope John Paul II arrives in Cairo for the first-ever visit by a pontiff to Egypt. (*See* March 20.)

•

Some 60,000 people are evacuated as Mt. Mayon, a volcano north of Legaspi on the Philippine island of Luzon, begins to erupt; an eruption in 1993 killed 77 people.

•

The Chamber of Mines of South Africa announces that gold production in the country has fallen to its lowest level since 1954; the cause is thought to be weak gold prices resulting from restructuring in the mining sector.

25 Bombs explode on a bus that is being transported on a ferry off Mindanao in the Philippines, killing about 40 people.

•

Four New York City police officers are acquitted of all charges in the shooting death in February 1999 of Amadou Diallo, an unarmed immigrant from Guinea; the verdict sets off several days of protest.

26 Fisheries associations in North and South Korea sign an agreement allowing South Korean vessels to fish in North Korean waters. The government of South Korea rejects the agreement on February 28, however. (*See* February 16.)

•

Egypt's People's Assembly votes to extend for an additional three years the state of emergency that has existed in that country since 1981.

•

Mt. Hekla, located in an uninhabited region of Iceland some 120 km (75 mi) from Reykjavík, erupts as thousands of tourists observe.

27 The Limpopo River in southern Africa overflows its banks in the culmination of weeks of heavy rains and disastrous flooding primarily in Mozambique but also in Botswana, South Africa, and Zimbabwe.

28 Prime Minister Pierre-Célestin Rwigema of Rwanda resigns following a series of disagreements with the Transitional National Assembly, the Rwandan legislature.

•

Darryl Strawberry of the New York Yankees is suspended for the entire 2000 baseball season as a result of a blood test that was positive for cocaine; he had previously been suspended in 1999 and 1995.

29 A girl in the first grade is shot and killed by a six-year-old boy in her class in an elementary school in Mount Morris township, near Flint, Mich.

•

Manager Sparky Anderson is named to the National Baseball Hall of Fame, as are Norman ("Turkey") Stearnes, a Negro leagues star, and John ("Bid") McPhee, who played for the Cincinnati Reds in the late 19th century.

March

We are deeply saddened by the behaviour of those who in the course of history have caused these children of yours to suffer, and asking your forgiveness we wish to commit ourselves to genuine brotherhood with the people of the Covenant.

Pope John Paul II, in a prayer at the Western Wall in Jerusalem, March 26

1 In ceremonies in Washington, D.C., the U.S. turns over to Turkey 133 artifacts that had been looted from archaeological sites; some of the items are more than 2,500 years old.

•

The World Wildlife Fund begins a program in which it will work with businesses to help them find practical ways to reduce greenhouse gas emissions; the first companies to join the program are IBM and Johnson & Johnson.

•

The last workers of 11 foreign aid agencies leave The Sudan rather than accede to an ultimatum issued by the rebel Sudan People's Liberation Army, which demanded money and control over the agencies' operations.

2 Great Britain announces that it has decided to drop extradition proceedings against former Chilean dictator Gen. Augusto Pinochet Ugarte because of his poor health; on his return to Chile the following day, however, Pinochet appears to be robust. (*See* January 11.)

•

Team New Zealand, skippered by Russell Coutts, wins the America's Cup yacht race for the second time in a row, defeating the Prada Challenge of Italy in five straight races in the best-five-of-nine regatta. (*See* May 19.)

3 Kevin Uliassi ends his attempt at the first solo around-the-world balloon flight a little past the halfway mark, in Myanmar (Burma).

•

In the face of widespread criticism, Bob Jones University, a fundamentalist Christian institution in Greenville, S.C., abandons its long-standing ban on interracial dating.

4 Hundreds of persons demonstrate in support of a church in Indianapolis, Ind., that refuses to withhold taxes from its employees' paychecks; the church denies the government's authority.

5 ***To the general acclaim of government and private groups unable to cope with abandoned babies, SterniPark e.V., a German nonprofit organization, opens the first "Babyklappe" (baby depository) in Hamburg; unwanted newborns may be left anonymously in the device, similar to a bank deposit receptacle, which provides a heated crib and signals an attendant within a few minutes of the presence of a baby. (Photo below.)***

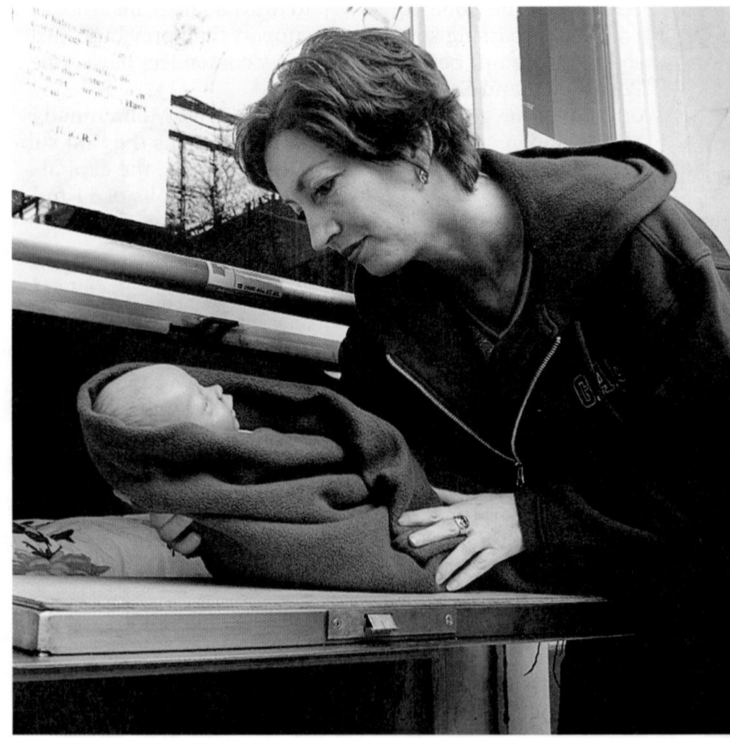

AP/Wide World Photos

•

A Southwest Airlines jet crashes through a fence at the end of the runway in Burbank, Calif.; only minor injuries result.

6 The Rock and Roll Hall of Fame induction ceremonies are held; among those admitted are Eric Clapton, Bonnie Raitt, and James Taylor and the bands Earth, Wind & Fire, the Lovin' Spoonful, and the Moonglows.

•

John Cardinal O'Connor, the Roman Catholic archbishop of New York, is awarded the Congressional Gold Medal, the highest civilian honour awarded by the U.S. Congress; O'Connor dies on May 3, 2000.

•

The first African elephant ever to be born after conception through artificial insemination is born at the Indianapolis Zoo; the mother, 24-year-old Kubwa, has carried the female, which is later named Amali (Swahili for "hope") and which weighs 92 kg (201 lb) at birth, for 22 months.

7 In the series of U.S. primary elections known as "Super Tuesday," the clear choices to emerge are Vice Pres. Al Gore for the Democrats and Texas Gov. George W. Bush for the Republicans. (*See* March 9.)

•

Voters in California support a ban on recognizing gay marriage and reject a campaign finance reform measure; these two items are among the 20 propositions on ballots in the state.

•

Under the auspices of the Organization of American States, Nicaragua and Honduras agree on a joint border patrol, a first step toward resolving a dispute over the two countries' maritime boundaries. (*See* February 19.)

8 The Bosnian town of Brcko, which links the two Serb sections of the nation, is officially established as a "self-governing neutral district," part of neither the Serb Republic nor the Muslim-Croat federation; the event marks the resolution of the last outstanding Bosnian territorial dispute from the Dayton accords.

•

Two rush-hour subway trains collide in Tokyo after one derails; 5 deaths result, and at least 33 are injured.

9 In a desperate attempt to save an economy in free fall, a measure is signed into law that changes Ecuador's currency from the sucre to the U.S. dollar; the rate of exchange is 25,000 sucres to the dollar. (*See* January 21.)

•

Two of the largest German banks, Deutsche Bank AG and Dresdner Bank AG, announce plans to merge and form the largest investment bank in Europe; the plans later fall through, however.

•

As a result of huge victories in primaries held on March 7 by Texas Gov. George W. Bush and Vice Pres. Al Gore, John McCain suspends his campaign for the Republican nomination for president, and Bill Bradley withdraws from the race for the Democratic nomination.

10 Jens Stoltenberg becomes prime minister in Nor way and appoints an all-Socialist government following the resignation announcement on March 9 of the centre coalition of Prime Minister Kjell Magne Bondevik.

•

The National Climatic Data Center reports that winter temperatures in the United States were the warmest on record for the third year in a row.

•

A dam in a Romanian mine breaks, causing spillage of toxic metals into the Vaser River and the rivers fed by it. (*See* February 11.)

11 In what is called the worst mining disaster in decades in Ukraine, a methane-gas explosion in a coal mine kills some 80 workers.

•

Ricardo Lagos Escobar is sworn in as president of Chile, the first Socialist to hold the office since Pres. Salvador Allende Gossens was killed in a coup in 1973. (*See* January 16.)

12 Spanish legislative elections return an absolute majority for the incumbent, Prime Minister José María Aznar López, and his Popular Party; opposition leader Joaquín Almunia resigns his post as head of the Spanish Socialist Workers' Party.

•

Speaking at St. Peter's Basilica in Rome, Pope John Paul II issues an apology for sins committed by Roman Catholics in the past two millennia against Jews, women, indigenous peoples, immigrants, the poor, and the unborn as well as for sins committed "in the service of the truth."

•

Chinese dissident clergyman Ignatius Kung, the former Roman Catholic bishop of Shanghai who spent 30 years in Chinese jails for his beliefs and who was secretly named cardinal in 1979, dies in exile.

•

Hundreds of thousands of Muslims march in Casablanca, Mor., to protest governmental plans to grant increased rights to women, including the right to marry without the consent of a male guardian. (*See* January 26.)

13 The United Nations publishes a report that is critical of a number of African and European countries for ignoring UN sanctions imposed on the National Union for the Total Independence of Angola rebel movement for the sale of diamonds to finance the purchase of arms for use in the Angolan civil war.

•

South African Pres. Thabo Mbeki announces that he has called for the creation of a panel of experts to assess claims by some scientists that AIDS is caused not by the HIV virus but rather by poverty and drug abuse.

•

Dan Marino, quarterback for the Miami Dolphins and the most productive quarterback in National Football League history, announces his retirement.

14 It is announced in London that Ross Stretton, director of the Australian Ballet, will succeed Sir Anthony Dowell as the director of the Royal Ballet for 2000–2001.

•

Doug Swingley of Lincoln, Mont., wins the 28th Iditarod Trail Sled Dog Race, finishing the Anchorage to Nome run in 9 days 58 minutes, which breaks the record he set in 1995.

15 Thailand's new central bankruptcy court declares Thai Petrochemical Industry insolvent; the firm had defaulted on a $3.5 billion loan in 1997.

•

Researchers announce that they have found in China the fossils of what may have been the first primate in the world; the creature, which scientists have named Eosimias, lived 45 million years ago and weighed less than 28 g (one ounce).

16 Two of the three people vying for the position of managing director of the International Monetary Fund withdraw, ensuring the election of Horst Köhler, a German; Köhler is unanimously elected to the post on March 23.

•

Krishna Prasad Bhattarai, the prime minister of Nepal, agrees to resign; on March 20 King Birendra names Girija Prasad Koirala to the post.

•

A judge in Lahore, Pak., sentences Javed Iqbal, who had been found guilty of the murder and mutilation of 100 children, to be executed in the same manner in which he murdered his victims.

17 A fire in the church of the Movement for the Restoration of the Ten Commandments of God in Kanungu, Uganda, kills at least 500 cult members; the tragedy is originally thought to be a mass suicide, but later evidence suggests that the victims were kept in the church involuntarily and some tried to escape.

•

Queen Elizabeth II of Great Britain begins her first state visit to Australia since 1992, four months after a proposal to make Australia a republic was defeated in a referendum.

18 More than half a century of rule by the Kuomintang comes to an end in Taiwan as opposition leader Chen Shui-bian is elected to the presidency; his position favouring Taiwanese independence vexes China, but his pledge to root out corruption in government is popular among the electorate.

19 Abdoulaye Wade wins a second-round election to succeed Abdou Diouf as president of Senegal; he is the third president in the history of independent Senegal, and his victory marks the end of the 40-year rule of the Socialist Party.

•

U.S. Pres. Bill Clinton arrives in New Delhi, his first stop on a weeklong visit in South Asia that takes him to India, Bangladesh, and Pakistan; this is the first visit of a U.S. president to India since 1978.

•

One of the longest private-sector white-collar strikes in U.S. history comes to an end as management and engineers at the Boeing Co., based in Seattle, Wash., approve a new contract.

20 At least 35 Sikhs are massacred in a village in the Indian state of Jammu and Kashmir; the attackers wear Indian army uniforms, but the Indian government claims that the raid is the work of militant Muslim organizations based in Pakistan.

•

France's ParisBourse SA, Belgium's Brussels Exchange, and The Netherlands' Amsterdam Exchange announce that they will merge to become the second largest stock exchange in Europe, Euronext NV. (*See* May 3.)

•

Pope John Paul II begins the third of his historic visits to the Middle East (*see* February 24) in Amman, Jordan, spending the rest of his visit, until March 26, in Israel and Palestinian-administered areas.

21 The U.S. Supreme Court rules that the Food and Drug Administration does not have the authority to regulate tobacco products.

•

More than 150 Kurds are arrested in Turkey for violating the ban on celebrating the Kurdish New Year. (*See* February 9.)

22 At least 50 people are burned to death when a pipeline delivering oil from the Niger River delta region of Nigeria explodes; the poor people were reportedly trying to siphon off fuel from the pipeline.

•

American physicist Freeman Dyson is named winner of the Templeton Prize for Progress in Religion.

•

Former South African president Nelson Mandela rejects assertions published in a history of the British secret service, *MI6: Fifty Years of Special Operations* by Stephen Dorril, that he at one time was an agent of influence for MI6.

23 Pres. Pasteur Bizimungu of Rwanda resigns for personal reasons, and the Supreme Court appoints Vice Pres. Maj. Gen. Paul Kagame to replace him ad interim; Kagame is the first Tutsi to hold this office since the civil war between the Hutu and Tutsi peoples began in 1994. (*See* April 1.)

•

At the summit meeting of the European Union in Lisbon, Port., a free-trade agreement is signed with Mexico; it is the first such agreement between the EU and a Latin American country.

•

The Loloata Understanding, an agreement to establish an autonomous government on the secessionist island of Bougainville, is signed by the president of the Bougainville People's Congress and Papua New Guinea's minister for Bougainville affairs.

•

Daniel Coughlin is appointed chaplain of the U.S. House of Representatives; he is the first Roman Catholic clergyman to hold the post.

24 A judge in São Paulo, Brazil's largest city, orders Celso Pitta, the city's mayor, out of office for alleged corruption; two days later Pitta obtains permission to remain in office pending an appeal of the charges.

•

NASA announces that in order to avoid the risk of an uncontrolled crash and possible casualties and property damage, it will intentionally crash the Compton Gamma Ray Observatory into the ocean because the orbiting observatory's navigation system is damaged.

•

The World Health Organization says that 11% of tuberculosis cases worldwide involve drug-resistant strains of the disease; areas worst hit by the drug-resistant strain are Estonia, Latvia, and parts of Russia and China.

25 ***The Audrey Jones Beck Building, an addition to the Houston Museum of Fine Arts, opens in the Texas city; the new structure, designed by Spanish architect Rafael Moneo, doubles the exhibition space of the museum. (Photo right.)***

26 Vladimir Putin is elected president of Russia with about 53% of the vote; he had served as acting pres-

AP/Wide World Photos

ident since Boris Yeltsin's resignation in December 1999.

•

The Academy Awards are presented, with Billy Crystal as host; big winners are *American Beauty,* Kevin Spacey, Hilary Swank, Michael Caine, and Angelina Jolie.

27 As part of the settlement of a lawsuit brought by a coalition of environmental groups, the U.S. Department of Energy abandons plans to build the nation's first nuclear-waste incinerator in Idaho.

28 The Japanese Diet (parliament) passes legislation raising the retirement age in Japan from 60 to 65 beginning in 2013.

•

Tornadoes touch down in the Texas cities of Fort Worth and Arlington; the twister in Fort Worth rips through downtown, damaging or destroying about 70 commercial buildings and more than 300 homes.

•

Police in Israel recommend that former prime minister Benjamin Netanyahu be indicted for bribery, theft, and obstruction of justice.

29 Astronomers announce that they have detected two planets, about the size of Saturn, orbiting distant stars.

•

The Chicago Cubs play the New York Mets in Tokyo as major league baseball opens the season with its first game ever played outside North America.

30 An article in the journal *Nature* reports the discovery and DNA analysis of clearly dated late Neanderthal remains from a limestone cave in the northern Caucasus Mountains of Russia; the find demonstrates the genetic identity of Neanderthals throughout Europe and supports the theory that the Neanderthals and *Homo sapiens,* modern humans, did not share a common human ancestor.

•

It is reported that Lieut. Gen. Claudia Kennedy, the highest-ranking woman in the U.S. Army, has filed a complaint of sexual harassment against Maj. Gen. Larry G. Smith.

31 Relief agencies of the United Nations report that some 12 million people in Africa, some 8 million of them in Ethiopia, face imminent starvation; they appeal for emergency food aid totaling about $200 million.

•

The Xerox Corp. discloses plans to lay off 5,200 workers, about 5% of its workforce.

•

Hollywood actor Leonardo DiCaprio is tapped to interview U.S. Pres. Bill Clinton for a television show; his selection unleashes a tempest of criticism by professional journalists.

April

The Court concludes that Microsoft maintained its monopoly power by anticompetitive means and attempted to monopolize the Web browser market, both in violation of Section 2 of the Sherman Antitrust Act.

Judge Thomas Penfield Jackson, in his "conclusions of law" at the end of the second phase of the U.S. government's suit against Microsoft Corp., April 3

1 Maj. Gen. Paul Kagame, a Tutsi, is nominated by the Rwandan Patriotic Front to run for president of Rwanda; he has been acting as interim president since Pasteur Bizimungu resigned the post (*see* March 23) and is duly elected to office on April 17.

•

Michelle Kwan wins the women's title at the world figure-skating championships in Nice, France, with a program that includes seven triple jumps; Kwan had captured this title in 1996 and 1998 as well. (*See* February 13.)

2 A cyclone, the third in two months to hit Madagascar, destroys the coastal town of Antalaha.

•

Japanese Prime Minister Keizo Obuchi suffers a stroke and is rushed to a Tokyo hospital; he dies on May 14 after having lain in a coma for 43 days. (*See* April 5.)

•

Zambia's former longtime president, Kenneth Kaunda, officially announces his retirement from politics just a few months before the presidential elections that he was expected to enter.

3 Leaders of the European Union and the Organization of African Unity hold the first African-European summit in Cairo.

•

The Michigan State University Spartans win the NCAA men's Division I basketball tournament by defeating the University of Florida Gators 89–76; the previous day the women's tournament had been won by the University of Connecticut Huskies when they beat the University of Tennessee Lady Volunteers 71–52.

4 The government of South Korea orders some 85% of the country's livestock markets closed in an attempt to end an outbreak of foot-and-mouth disease that had struck livestock in South Korea and Japan in recent days.

•

The United Nations Development Programme issues a report saying that bad government is frequently a major cause of poverty.

•

Waiting, a novel by Chinese émigré writer Ha Jin, wins the 2000 PEN/Faulkner Award for fiction; the book had earlier won the 1999 National Book Award.

5 The Diet (parliament) elects Yoshiro Mori of the Liberal-Democratic Party prime minister of Japan replacing Keizo Obuchi. (*See* April 2.)

•

A computer glitch closes down the London Stock Exchange for nearly eight hours on the last day of Great Britain's fiscal year.

•

The Turkish Grand National Assembly votes down a proposed constitutional amendment that would have allowed a president a second term in office; the measure had been supported by Pres. Suleyman Demirel and Prime Minister Bulent Ecevit.

6 At the end of a 10-week trial beset with controversy, Nawaz Sharif, who had been deposed as prime minister of Pakistan in October 1999, is found guilty of hijacking and terrorism and is sentenced to life imprisonment.

7 The World Health Organization reports that more than two-thirds of the world's nations do not maintain safe blood supplies.

•

Momcilo Krajisnik, a Bosnian Serb leader, appears before an international war crimes tribunal in The Hague to face charges of genocide.

•

In a bid to reduce its dependence on diminishing oil reserves, Oman begins exporting gas; the first shipment, bound for South Korea, is carried out of the port of Qalhat.

8 Pres. Hugo Bánzer Suárez declares a state of emergency in Bolivia after five days of protest, which erupted in Cochabamba over a plan to raise water rates 35%, virtually shut down the country; the water plan is dropped on April 11, but antigovernment protests continue.

9 In the first single-drama production broadcast live on American television in almost 40 years, a revival of *Fail Safe,* the 1964 film by Sidney Lumet, is shown on CBS television; reviews are generally favourable.

•

Eduard Shevardnadze is reelected president of Georgia with what some observers believe is an improbably large margin of victory.

•

The Panhellenic Socialist Movement (Pasok) party of Konstantinos Simitis wins a narrow majority in the Greek parliamentary elections.

•

German race-car driver Michael Schumacher wins the San Marino Grand Prix in his Ferrari, making a clean sweep of the first three events of the season; he had previously won the Australian (March 12) and Brazilian (March 26) Grand Prix races.

•

Fijian golfer Vijay Singh wins the Masters Tournament in Augusta, Ga., with a final score of 10 under par.

10 The winners of the Pulitzer Prizes are announced at Columbia University, New York City; recipients of journalistic awards include the *Washington Post* and the *Denver Post,* and in arts and letters the winners include Jhumpa Lahiri for fiction and Donald Margulies for drama.

•

The British Home Office proposes that pubs be permitted to serve drinks past 11 PM, the cutoff time that has been in effect since World War I.

11 David Irving, a British right-wing historian, loses the lawsuit he brought against Deborah Lipstadt, an American writer; Irving claims that she libeled him by calling him a Holocaust denier in her book *Denying the Holocaust,* but the judge rules that Lipstadt's description of Irving is accurate.

•

The Egyptian government approves the sale of a parcel of land near Cairo for the construction of a private French-language university, which will open in 2001.

12 Prime Minister Andris Skele of Latvia resigns as a result of a disagreement over privatization issues; on April 25 Pres. Vaira Vike-Freiberga names Andris Berzins to replace him.

•

The National Office of Electoral Processes announces that Pres. Alberto K. Fujimori of Peru must face Alejandro Toledo in a runoff election; Toledo's supporters had alleged electoral fraud. (*See* May 28.)

13 Government leaders of the 11-member Council of the Baltic Sea States meet in the Danish town of Kolding; discussions centre on relations with Russia and increasing the prominence of the Baltic region in Europe.

•

The top prize of the International Exhibition of Inventions of Geneva is awarded to the Swedish-made Aqua Barrier, a temporary flood barrier that can be erected easily and quickly. (Photo below.)

International Exhibition of Inventions of Geneva

•

South Africa announces plans to construct a deepwater port at Coega, Eastern Cape province; the port, to be built in 2000, is visualized as the centre of a new industrial zone.

14 Explosions at Ndjili International Airport in Kinshasa, Democratic Republic of the Congo, triggered by a fire of unknown origins in an ammunition dump, kill more than 100 people.

•

The Nasdaq Composite Index, which reflects the performance of a number of mostly high-technology stocks, falls 10% in a single day, the most precipitous drop in three years; the index bounds back by 7% on April 18, however.

15 Scientists in Australia announce the discovery of the fourth largest crater in the world, located near Shark Bay in Western Australia; they believe it may be the result of the impact that caused a mass extinction of terrestrial life.

•

U.S. Pres. Bill Clinton proclaims the creation of the Giant Sequoia National Monument, a 133,000-ha (328,000-ac) area in the Sierra Nevada in California. (*See* July 18.)

•

A new eight-lane highway bridge connecting the cities of Laredo, Texas, and Nuevo Laredo, Mex., across the Rio Grande is formally opened; the route handles about 40% of all merchandise that moves overland across the U.S.-Mexico border.

16 The International Monetary Fund holds its spring meeting in Washington, D.C.; protests, while smaller than those that assembled for the World Trade Organization meeting in Seattle, Wash., in December 1999, nonetheless bring the city to a standstill.

•

The London Marathon is won by Antônio Pinto of Portugal, with a time of 2 hr 6 min 36 sec, and by Tegla Loroupe of Kenya, with the best women's time of 2 hr 24 min 33 sec.

17 Israel informs the United Nations that it will withdraw all its forces from Lebanon by July 7; the action will end its 18-year occupation of an area in southern Lebanon that Israel called a security zone.

•

Dutch architect and author Rem Koolhaas is named the winner of the 2000 Pritzker Architecture Prize; the award is presented in ceremonies in Jerusalem on May 29.

•

Business Week magazine reports that in 1999 the average pay of a corporate chief executive officer rose 17% over 1998 levels and that the average CEO in 1999 received 475 times what the average blue-collar worker was paid.

•

The Boston Marathon is won by Kenyan Elijah Lagat, who just barely beats out Gezahenge Abera of Ethiopia with a time of 2 hr 9 min 47 sec; in the women's race Catherine Ndereba of Ethiopia triumphs with a time of 2 hr 26 min 11 sec.

18 The European Roma Rights Centre files a suit in the European Court of Human Rights in which the government of the Czech Republic is accused of racial discrimination in education; the suit is brought on behalf of 18 Roma (Gypsy) families who say that their children were placed in schools for the mentally deficient because of their race.

•

"Ant Noises," an outrageous new art exhibit that follows up on the 1997 "Sensation" show and features works by Damien Hirst (his* Hymn *is pictured below), Ron Mueck, and Jenny Saville among others, opens for a private showing at London's Saatchi Gallery; it opens to the public on April 20.

19 The Federation Council, the upper house of Russia's parliament, votes to ratify the START-II treaty; the Duma (lower house) had approved the treaty, which called on Russia to halve its strategic arsenal, on April 14.

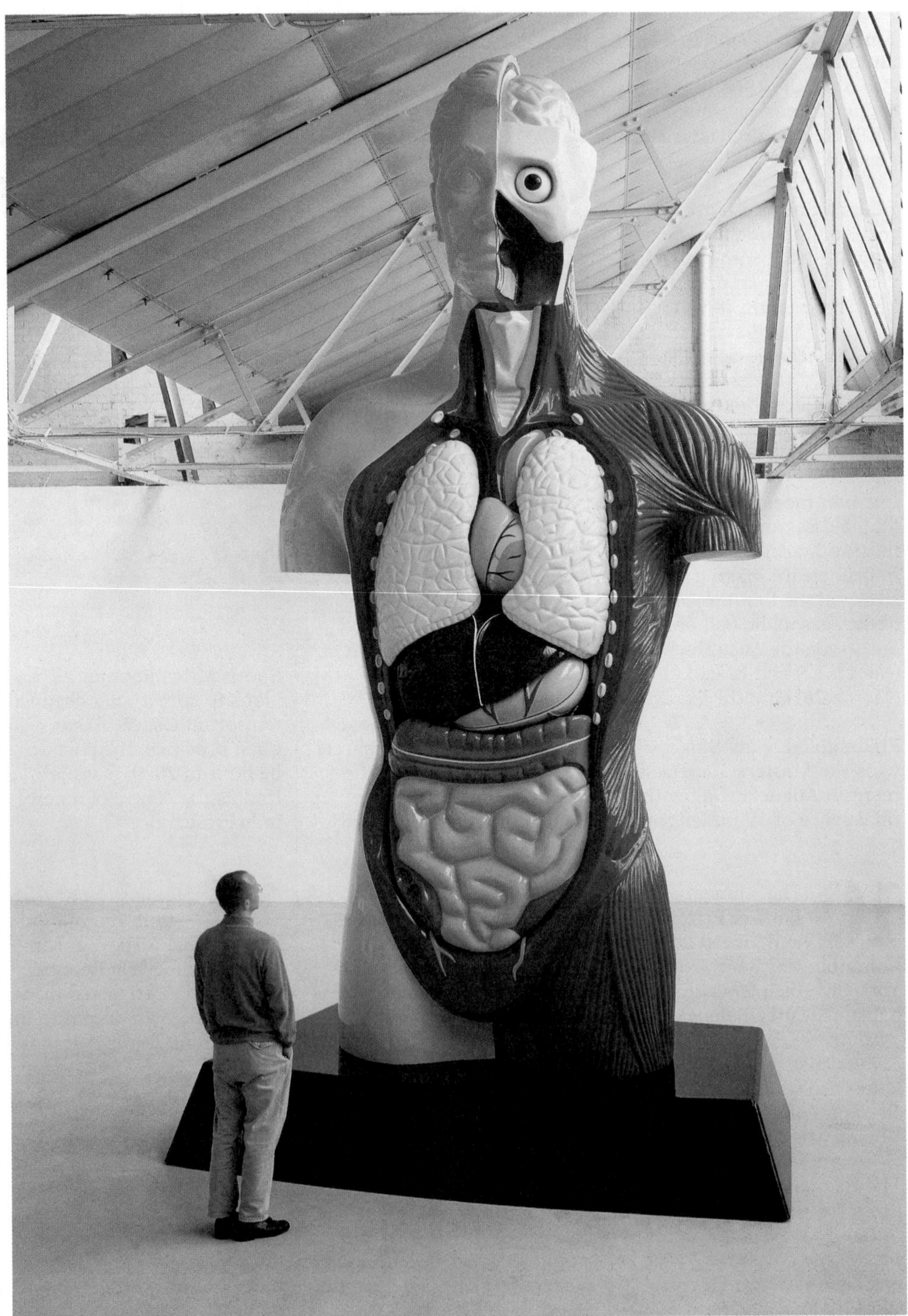

Steven White/Saatchi Gallery

•

A Philippine Airlines Boeing 737 airliner crashes in the Philippines upon its landing approach, killing all 131 people aboard.

•

The Oklahoma City National Memorial, built to commemorate the 168 victims of the 1995 terrorist bombing of the Alfred P. Murrah Federal Building, is officially dedicated.

20 According to a report circulated by the Associated Press, South Korean military and police forces executed at least 2,000 political prisoners early in the Korean War (1950–53).

•

Paleontologists announce that they have discovered the fossilized heart of a dinosaur in a skeleton found in South Dakota; it appears to have four chambers and one aorta, which suggests that dinosaurs may have been warm-blooded.

21 Pakistani leader Gen. Pervaiz Musharraf announces that henceforth "honour killings" of women who are felt to have shamed their families will be legally treated as murders.

•

French automobile manufacturer Renault agrees to purchase Samsung Motors of South Korea for an estimated \$340 million–\$350 million plus \$200 million in debts; Renault acquired a 37% stake in the Japanese carmaker Nissan in 1999.

22 On the first day of official celebrations commemorating the 500th anniversary of the arrival of the Portuguese in Brazil, a "march of the excluded" led by Brazilian Indians is broken up by military police in the town of Pôrto Seguro, Bahia state.

•

Months after the U.S. Immigration and Naturalization Service had ordered the Miami, Fla., relatives of Elián González to return the boy to his Cuban father's custody, agents stage a predawn raid and forcibly return Elián to his father. (*See* January 10 and June 28.)

23 Abu Sayyaf, a Muslim rebel group from the Philippines, takes 21 European and African tourists and Malaysian and Filipino workers hostage on the Malaysian island of Sipitang; Philippine Pres. Joseph Estrada rejects their ransom demands. (*See* August 27.)

•

Fernando Sáenz, the archbishop of San Salvador, asks the El Salvador government to pardon two soldiers who have served 19 years for the rape and murder of three American nuns and a social worker in 1980.

•

In Las Vegas, Nev., Brazilian rider Rodrigo Pessoa wins the World Cup 2000 competition in horse show jumping for a record third year in a row; his mount is the French-bred stallion Baloubet.

24 Seven children are wounded when a gunman fires into a crowd at the main entrance to the National Zoo in Washington, D.C.

25 In the world weight lifting championships, held in Sofia, Bulg., Donka Mincheva of Bulgaria breaks her own world record set in 1999 for the snatch in the women's 48-kg (105.5-lb) division, and Halil Mutlu of Turkey breaks a world record in the clean and jerk in the men's 56-kg (123-lb) class.

•

Small Square in the historic centre of Prague is renamed to honour Franz Kafka; a house in which the author lived was situated on the square.

26 A major exhibit of African art, "Art and Oracle: Spirit Voices of Africa," opens to the public at New York City's Metropolitan Museum of Art; two days earlier the collection had been blessed by a Yoruba priest.

•

Gov. Howard Dean of Vermont signs into law a measure allowing same-sex couples to enter into civil unions that confer the same legal rights as those pertaining to marriage.

27 AT&T sells 360 million shares of tracking stock in a subsidiary, AT&T Wireless Group, in the largest initial public offering of stock in U.S. history.

•

Scientists in France announce that they have successfully used gene therapy to cure three babies born with severe combined immunodeficiency (SCID), which otherwise would have doomed them to live in a sterile, controlled-atmosphere bubble.

28 After the resignation of Prime Minister Massimo D'Alema on April 19, Giuliano Amato is approved for the post by a narrow margin of votes in Parliament, and he sets about forming Italy's 58th government since World War II.

•

The U.S. Department of Justice and 17 states ask Judge Thomas Penfield Jackson to break Microsoft Corp. into two competing companies. (*See* June 7.)

•

A U.S. federal judge agrees with five major music publishers that MP3.com, a company that distributes recorded music free over the Internet, is acting in violation of copyright laws. (*See* July 26.)

29 A Japanese tourist and a tour group bus driver are beaten to death in Todos Santos Cuchumatán, Guat., by a mob of some 500 people who reportedly believe that the tourists planned to steal the villagers' children.

•

A major exhibit titled "Vikings: The North Atlantic Saga" opens at the National Museum of Natural History in Washington, D.C.; the show features 300 items from 29 lenders and will travel to several other cities in the U.S. and Canada.

•

Lennox Lewis of Great Britain knocks out American Michael Grant in the second round of a title fight at Madison Square Garden in New York City and retains the World Boxing Council and International Boxing Federation heavyweight titles.

30 Ceremonies to celebrate the 25th anniversary of the end of the Vietnam War are held at the Reunification Palace in Ho Chi Minh City, Vietnam; in a gesture of goodwill by the government, some 12,000 prisoners are released.

•

Emirates, the airline of the United Arab Emirates, is the first company to buy the Airbus A3XX, the new generation of jumbo jet airliner; an order is placed for 10 of the huge craft. (*See* September 29.)

May

Regardless of whether we grant normal trade status to China, the Chinese market is opening. Someone is going to have the opportunity to sell to this vast new market. The question is who will be there when the door opens?

Dennis Hastert, speaker of the U.S. House of Representatives, in floor debate, May 24

1 Union actors in the United States go on strike against the advertising industry to protest proposed changes in the way they are paid for making television commercials.

•

The National Archaeological Museum of Naples sets a museum record for attendance; the draw is an exhibit of erotic art, most of it from Pompeii, Italy, that is being exhibited to the public essentially for the first time since Pompeii was excavated in the 18th century.

2 U.S. Army Gen. Wesley Clark steps down as commander of NATO forces and is replaced by U.S. Air Force Gen. Joseph Ralston.

•

Archaeologists excavating the ruins of León Viejo, a well-preserved Spanish colonial lowland city in Nicaragua, find the skeleton of Francisco Hernández de Córdoba, the conquistador who established the first two settlements in Nicaragua.

•

Julie Krone becomes the first woman jockey elected to thoroughbred racing's national Hall of Fame; in 1993 she became the first woman to win a Triple Crown race (the Belmont Stakes).

3 The London Stock Exchange announces plans to merge with the Frankfurt, Ger.-based Deutsche Börse AG to form iX, the fourth largest stock exchange in the world; the LSE scotches the agreement on September 12, however. (*See* March 20.)

•

The U.S. Food and Drug Administration announces plans to require that companies notify and receive permission from the FDA before putting genetically altered foods onto the market.

4 London holds its first direct elections for the post of mayor; the winner is Ken Livingstone, an independent left-wing politician.

•

An e-mail virus that started the previous day in Asia sweeps through Europe and North America, forcing major companies and government institutions, including the British Parliament and the U.S. House of Representatives, to shut down their e-mail systems; dubbed the Love Bug, the computer "worm" comes disguised as a love letter. (*See* August 21.)

•

The Nature Conservancy agrees to buy Palmyra, a 275-ha (680-ac) atoll lying 1,693 km (1,052 mi) south of Hawaii, from the family that has owned it since 1922; the group's plans for the area involve ecotourism and protection of the fragile atoll environment.

•

The government of the Australian state of Victoria confirms that the air-conditioning cooling towers of the aquarium in Melbourne are the source of the outbreak of Legionnaire disease that had sickened 81 people since April 27.

5 Ahmet Necdet Sezer, chief justice of the Constitutional Court, is elected president by the Turkish Grand National Assembly.

•

The French Canadian performance troupe Cirque du Soleil releases the IMAX movie *Journey of Man,* made up of acts drawn from the shows *Mystère* and *O.*

6 The 126th running of the Kentucky Derby at Churchill Downs in Louisville, Ky., is won by Fusaichi Pegasus—owned by Fusao Sekiguchi, trained by Neil Drysdale, and ridden by Kent Desormeaux.

•

A new award show, the Classical BRIT Awards for accomplishment in classical music (and marketing) in Great Britain, is broadcast from the Royal Albert Hall in London; pianist Martha Argerich and bass-baritone Bryn Terfel are named female and male Artists of the Year, respectively; *Sacred Arias* by tenor Andrea Bocelli takes Album of the Year honours.

7 Vladimir Putin is sworn in as president of Russia; he promptly appoints Mikhail Kasyanov prime minister. (*See* March 26.)

•

Rwanda says that it will withdraw its troops from the Democratic Republic of the Congo, which raises hopes for an end to the six-nation war.

•

Three members of Emgann, a Breton separatist group, are put under investigation for the bombing on April 19 of a McDonald's restaurant in Quévart, France.

8 It is announced that German and Japanese scientists have decoded the human chromosome 21, which is responsible for the condition known as Down syndrome. (*See* June 26.)

•

The Philadelphia school board adopts a policy requiring all public-school students to wear uniforms to class; it is the first major American city to take this step.

9 Former Louisiana governor Edwin Edwards, together with his son and three associates, is found guilty of conspiracy and racketeering; he had served four terms as governor and had survived more than two dozen criminal investigations before this trial, which began January 10.

•

The biggest lottery jackpot in U.S. history, $366 million, is won by two people, one in Utica, Mich., and one in Lake Zurich, Ill., in the seven-state Big Game.

10 In an important setback for those who seek to patent biological substances and processes, the European Patent Office revokes a U.S. patent granted to the U.S. Department of Agriculture and W.R. Grace & Co. for a preparation derived from the neem tree, native to India and used as a fungicide there for centuries.

•

The United States makes its first report on its compliance with the UN Convention Against Torture, maintaining that, though there are areas of concern, the nation is committed to the elimination of abuse by police officers and other government agents; Amnesty International, however, paints a darker picture of the U.S. record.

11 A baby girl born in New Delhi is officially declared to be the billionth Indian citizen, although the UN says that India already reached this milestone in August 1999.

•

A forest fire in New Mexico roars into the towns of Los Alamos and White Rock, threatening the highly sensitive Los Alamos National Laboratory; the fire was set on May 4 by the National Park Service as a controlled burn to prevent wildfires, but it had blazed out of control by May 5.

•

A new art museum, Tate Modern, is opened in London in the restored Bankside Power Station; it houses some 600 modern paintings and sculptures.

12 The Supreme Court of Pakistan rules that the coup by which Gen. Pervaiz Musharraf seized power in October 1999 was legal and gives Musharraf three years in which to restore democracy.

•

In an interview at the United Nations in New York City, Secretary-General Kofi Annan criticizes the U.S. for its reluctance to participate fully in peacekeeping operations in Africa; he especially regrets Pres. Bill Clinton's reluctance to commit ground troops in areas of distress.

•

Science magazine reports that two skulls found in the Caucasus Mountains in Georgia are 1.7 million years old and may have belonged to members of the human species that first migrated out of Africa.

13 The Vatican reveals the Third Secret of Fátima, ending decades of sometimes fevered speculation; the pope believes the vision, which was revealed to a group of children at Fátima, Port., in 1917 by an apparition of the Virgin Mary, prophesied his attempted assassination in 1981.

•

India's cabinet approves plans to create three new states to be carved from existing states: Uttaranchal, from Uttar Pradesh; Jharkhand, from Bihar; and Chhattisgarh, from Madhya Pradesh; the three states come into being in November.

•

Lara Dutta of India is named Miss Universe 2000 in ceremonies in Nicosia, Cyprus; another Indian, Priyanka Chopra, wins the Miss World title in November.

14 ***On Mother's Day hundreds of thousands of gun-control advocates rally in Washington, D.C., and several other U.S. cities in the Million Mom March. (Photo left.)***

•

The 45th Drama Desk Awards are held in New York City; winning shows include *Copenhagen*, *Contact*, *The Real Thing*, and *Kiss Me, Kate*.

AP/Wide World Photos

15 Street battles between Palestinians and Israeli troops in the West Bank towns of Janin and Ram Allah erupt in shooting; it is the worst gunfire exchange since 1996.

•

The U.S. Supreme Court invalidates a law that had permitted victims of rape and domestic violence to sue their attackers in federal court.

16 The Internet portal Lycos announces that it will be bought by Terra Networks, the Spanish telephone company Telefónica's Internet branch, in a deal that includes a partnership with the German company Bertelsmann AG to create an Internet company with operations in 37 countries.

•

Thomas E. Blanton, Jr., and Bobby Frank Cherry are charged with murder in the 1963 bombing of the 16th Street Baptist Church in Birmingham, Ala.

•

The pop musician who had changed his name to an unpronounceable glyph in 1993 announces that he is henceforth to be known by his previous name, Prince.

17 Two weeks after his forces took 500 UN peacekeepers hostage, rebel leader Foday Sankoh is arrested outside his home in Freetown, Sierra Leone, and turned over to the government.

•

The Turkish soccer team Galatasaray (Istanbul) beats Arsenal of London 4–1 in a penalty shootout to win the Union des Associations Européennes de Football (UEFA) Cup in Copenhagen after a day of violent clashes between supporters of the teams; it is the first time a Turkish team has won a major European trophy.

AP/Wide World Photos

•

Sue, the most complete *Tyrannosaurus rex* fossil ever found, is unveiled at The Field Museum in Chicago; the museum acquired the skeleton, found in 1990 in South Dakota, for $8.4 million at auction.

18 Thousands of protesters clash with police in Belgrade, Yugos., responding to the government's shutdown of opposition-controlled media outlets.

Chris Ferguson, nicknamed "Jesus" because of his beard and shoulder-length hair, wins the 31st annual World Series of Poker in Las Vegas, Nev., and takes away $1.5 million. (Photo above.)

19 A group of gunmen led by businessman George Speight storm Fiji's Parliament and take Prime Minister Mahendra Chaudhry and other officials hostage, declaring that they are staging a coup. (*See* May 29.)

•

New Zealand is shocked to learn that five members of the victorious Team New Zealand, including skipper Russell Coutts, have resigned in order to compete for the next America's Cup with Swiss pharmaceutical heir Ernesto Bertarelli.

•

Egypt holds its first-ever horse endurance race on a nearly 100-km (62-mi) course in the desert; the winner is Falah—ridden by Sheikh Muhammad ibn Rashid al-Maktum, the crown prince of

Dubayy—which finishes with a time of 5 hr 34 min.

20 Cherie Booth, wife of British Prime Minister Tony Blair, gives birth to a 3.1-kg (6-lb 12-oz) baby boy, Leo, the first child to be born to a prime minister in office in more than 150 years.

•

The largest diamond mine in the world is officially opened in northern Botswana; it is expected to increase Botswana's diamond production by 30%.

•

Mt. Cameroon, a volcano located southwest of the Cameroonian capital, Yaoundé, erupts; no casualties are reported, however.

21 Long-delayed local and legislative elections are held in Haiti, where the turnout is estimated at over 50% (compared with 5% in the last legislative election, in 1997); the nation has had no legislature since January 1999.

•

In the Bavarian Alpine village of Oberammergau the 40th showing (since 1634) of the world-famous Passion Play—about the last five days in the life of Jesus Christ—opens; in response to criticism, some of the play's passages that had been considered anti-Semitic have been removed or changed.

•

The Cannes International Film Festival awards ceremony is held; the winner of the Palme d'Or is *Dancer in the Dark,* by Danish director Lars von Trier; its star, the Icelandic singer Björk, wins the best actress award.

22 The U.S. Supreme Court rules that the 1996 Communications Decency Act, requiring that sexually oriented cable programming be completely blocked from nonsubscribers or restricted to the hours between 10 PM and 6 AM, is overly restrictive and in violation of the First Amendment to the Constitution.

•

Celebrations are held in Yemen to mark the 10th anniversary of that country's unification.

23 United Airlines reveals plans to buy US Airways, formerly known as USAir and earlier as Allegheny Airlines, for $11.6 billion; the purchase would make it a dominant carrier in the northeastern United States.

24 In the wake of the collapse of Israel's proxy militia, the South Lebanese Army, Israel withdraws the last of its forces from southern Lebanon six weeks earlier than originally planned.

•

The U.S. House of Representatives approves permanent normal trading status for China, a status Congress had denied China for 20 years.

•

Pres. Rexhep Meidani of Albania visits Kosovo, the first visit ever by an Albanian head of state to the neighbouring Yugoslav province; Kosovo is heavily populated by ethnic Albanians.

25 Croatia becomes the 26th member of the NATO Partnership for Peace program.

•

The Martha Graham Dance Company announces that financial problems have forced it to suspend operations for the foreseeable future.

•

The Israel Festival, featuring art, music, theatre, opera, and dance, opens in Jerusalem.

26 The Biennale of Sydney begins an exhibition of works by 50 influential artists and thinkers, including Gerhard Richter and Yayoi Kusama.

27 Pakistan launches a program to collect income taxes from the 99% of the people who do not pay; it has been estimated that 70% of the Pakistani economy is off the books.

•

A recently rediscovered opera with music by Wolfgang Amadeus Mozart is performed for the first time since 1814; the work, *The Philosopher's Stone,* debuts at the Hampstead and Highgate Festival in London.

•

The U.S. government releases new dietary guidelines, indicating that 9 out of 10 Americans need to improve their eating habits.

28 Under public pressure following exposure of financial misdealings 10 years ago, Israeli Pres. Ezer Weizman announces that he will resign effective July 10.

•

Pres. Alberto K. Fujimori of Peru wins a third term in a runoff election that is widely viewed as fraudulent. (*See* April 12 and September 16.)

•

More than 200,000 people march through downtown Sydney in the biggest civil rights march in Australia's history.

•

Colombian Juan Montoya wins the 84th Indianapolis 500, the first rookie to win the auto race since 1966.

29 Suharto, the former president of Indonesia, is put under house arrest as the government prepares to bring charges of corruption and abuse of power against him. (*See* August 3.)

•

Fiji's military takes over the government and imposes martial law; the deposed president had recently fired Prime Minister Mahendra Chaudhry, who is being held hostage by forces led by George Speight. (*See* May 19.)

•

The Dutch architect Rem Koolhaas is awarded the Pritzker Architecture Prize; his best-known work is Euralille, a multipurpose complex in Lille, France.

30 The local government for Northern Ireland, suspended in February, begins operating again after the Irish Republican Army agrees to put down its weapons and allow inspections.

•

Mou Qizhong, once touted as a model entrepreneur in the Chinese socialist-market economy, is sentenced to life in prison for fraud.

•

Russia's Bolshoi Ballet begins its first American tour in 10 years with a performance of *Romeo and Juliet* at the John F. Kennedy Center for the Performing Arts in Washington, D.C.

31 UNICEF releases a report indicating that up to half of the females worldwide are at one time or another subject to domestic abuse; the report was commissioned as a follow-up to the Fourth World Conference on Women in Beijing in 1995.

•

Hong Kong closes the last of the refugee camps that it had maintained for Vietnamese refugees since 1975, offering the 1,400 people who still reside in the camp Hong Kong residency.

June

When life is reduced to its very essence, we find that we have many genes in common with every species on Earth, and that we're not so different from one another.

J. Craig Venter, at the White House news conference announcing the sequencing of the human genome, June 26

1 After European regulators torpedoed a three-way deal that would have included French aluminum producer Pechiney, Alcan Aluminum Ltd. of Canada announces its impending purchase of Algroup of Switzerland for $4.7 billion; the resulting company would be the world's second largest aluminum company, after Alcoa.

•

Expo 2000, a universal world exposition, opens in Hannover, Ger., to run until October 31; exhibits include a half-underground Ferris wheel and a giant eyeball in which visitors may interact with mechanical rats and pigeons. (*See* July 22.)

2 A group supporting independence for the Indonesian province of Irian Jaya releases a document amounting to a draft constitution for an independent "State of Papua."

•

About 60 small ships, some of which had been used to assist in rescuing British troops from the beaches of Dunkirk, France, during World War II, set sail from Dover, Eng., in a special 60th-anniversary voyage to Dunkirk; the Dunkirk Veterans Association plans to disband on June 30.

•

U.S. Pres. Bill Clinton is awarded the International Charlemagne Prize for his contributions to European unity; the award is conferred by the German city of Aachen, which was the favourite residence of the 8th–9th-century emperor Charlemagne.

3 Archaeologists announce that they have discovered the remains of the ancient Egyptian cities of Herakleion, Canopus, and Menouthis; the ruins are submerged in the Mediterranean Sea.

•

The *Symphony of the Millennium,* composed by 19 people and played by 333 musicians, church bells in 15 area churches, and 2,000 bell ringers in the audience, takes place at St. Joseph's Oratory in Montreal, Que.

4 A magnitude-7.9 earthquake shakes the southeastern part of Sumatra, the second largest island in the Indonesian archipelago; at least 120 people are known to be dead.

•

The Tony Awards are presented in Radio City Music Hall in New York City; recipients include the plays *Copenhagen, Contact, The Real Thing,* and *Kiss Me, Kate* and the actors Jennifer Ehle, Stephen Dillane, Heather Headley, and Brian Stokes Mitchell.

5 Bill Clinton becomes the first U.S. president to address the Russian parliament; before a joint session of the State Duma and the Federation Council in Moscow, he calls for an end to divisiveness between the two countries.

•

Ukraine's Pres. Leonid Kuchma announces that the Chernobyl nuclear power station, site of a catastrophic accident in 1986, will be closed down completely. (*See* December 15.)

6 The British-Dutch corporation Unilever announces that it plans to buy Bestfoods of the United States for $24.3 billion; if approved, the union would create the world's second largest food and consumer products business. (*See* June 25.)

•

Poland's centre-right "Solidarity coalition" government falls after nearly three years in power; a new minority government under Prime Minister Jerzy Buzek is named the following day.

•

The World Bank approves a plan for an oil pipeline to carry oil from the Doba Basin, an oil field under development in southern Chad, through Cameroon to the Atlantic Ocean; environmentalists consider this a dubious choice.

7 In the final decision of the widely watched and publicized case, U.S. District Court Judge Thomas Penfield Jackson orders the Microsoft Corp. to split into two competing entities. (*See* April 28.)

•

As Sri Lanka celebrates its first War Heroes Day, a suicide bomber kills a cabinet minister and 20 other people; it is assumed that the secessionist Liberation Tigers of Tamil Eelam group is behind the attack. (*See* August 3.)

•

A new map of the region of the universe that includes the Milky Way Galaxy is announced; it encompasses a much larger area than have previous maps and appears to confirm the theory of the end of greatness—that is, that there is a limit to how large a cosmic structure can be—as well as other theories of the origin of the universe.

8 Stephen Saunders, the military attaché at the British embassy in Athens, is shot and killed; the attack is blamed on the left-wing terrorist group November 17, which has been blamed for 23 killings since 1975, although no member of the group has ever been arrested.

•

The government of Brazil decrees that same-sex couples who can prove that their relationship is stable may inherit pension and social security benefits from one another; this is the first legal recognition of same-sex relationships in Latin America. (*See* September 12.)

9 Buenos Aires is brought to a virtual standstill as workers stage a nationwide one-day strike to protest the Argentine government's austerity plan.

•

"Food for the Mind," an exhibit of 150 modern paintings and sculptures, opens at the State Gallery of Modern Art in Munich, Ger.; it is part of a collection of 550 pieces recently donated by the Anette and Udo Brandhorst Foundation.

10 Pres. Hafez al-Assad, ruler of Syria since 1971, dies in Damascus; his son, Bashar al-Assad, succeeds him and is inaugurated on July 17.

•

The New Jersey Devils defeat the defending champions, the Dallas Stars, to win the Stanley Cup, the National Hockey League championship; the score of the final game is 2–1.

•

The 132nd running of the Belmont Stakes is won by Commendable ridden by three-time Belmont winning jockey D. Wayne Lukas; neither the winner of the Kentucky Derby, Fusaichi Pegasus, nor the winner of the Preakness, Red Bullet, participates in the race.

•

The Millennium Bridge, a footbridge over the River Thames and the first new span across the river in London in more than a century, formally opens; the weight of the thousands of first-day visitors induces the structure to sway noticeably, which causes some concern among the design engineers, and they close the bridge for repairs on June 12. (See June 30.) (Photo below.)

Reuters NewMedia Inc./Corbis

11 An earthquake of magnitude 6.7 strikes Taiwan; it is considered an aftershock of the quake that killed approximately 2,400 people in September 1999.

•

Brazilian tennis player Gustavo Kuerten wins the French Open, defeating Sweden's Magnus Norman one day after Mary Pierce of France was victorious over Conchita Martínez of Spain in the women's tournament.

12 Officials reveal that, while checking the Los Alamos National Laboratory after forest fires burned near the sensitive facility in May, they discovered that computer hard drives containing weapons data were missing; the drives are mysteriously discovered behind a photocopy machine on June 16.

•

The U.S. Department of Justice agrees to pay $18 million to the estate of Richard Nixon in compensation for the papers and tapes that it seized in 1974 after Nixon resigned the presidency.

•

The Jubilee Line, the newest extension of the London Underground mass transit system, is named the Millennium Building of the Year by the Royal Fine Art Commission Trust; it was designed by architect Roland Paoletti.

13 Pres. Kim Dae Jung of South Korea meets with Kim Jong Il, leader of North Korea, in Pyongyang, North Korea, to begin talks on reunification; it is the first-ever visit of a South Korean leader to North Korea. (*See* June 25.)

•

Pres. Carlo Azeglio Ciampi of Italy pardons Mehmet Ali Agca for his attempted assassination of Pope John Paul II in 1981; Agca is freed from prison in Italy and sent to Turkey to serve time in prison for the murder of a newspaper editor. (*See* May 13.)

14 Bartholomew Ulufa'alu, prime minister of the Solomon Islands, resigns under duress nine days after being kidnapped by the Malaita Eagle Force; the nation has been undergoing ethnic unrest and fighting between natives of Guadalcanal and those of Malaita; on June 30 Parliament elects Manasseh Sogavare to replace Ulufa'alu.

•

Bass PLC, a British brewing and retail corporation, agrees to sell Bass Brewers, together with the trade name Bass, to a Belgian company, Interbrew SA; the sale will make Interbrew the second largest brewer in the world.

15 The government of Germany promises to shut down 19 nuclear power plants over the next 20 years in an agreement supported by the Greens but denounced by the Christian Democrats.

•

An economic survey shows that the number of people living below the poverty level in Pakistan has nearly tripled over the past 10 years.

16 MirCorp, a company that is owned by a Russian space-launch company and a group of foreign investors and that seeks to develop commercial uses for the abandoned space station *Mir,* announces that it plans to send paying customers as tourists to *Mir* beginning in 2001; on November 16, however, Russia reconsiders and elects to crash *Mir* into the Pacific Ocean in February 2001.

NASA/JPL/Malin Space Science Systems

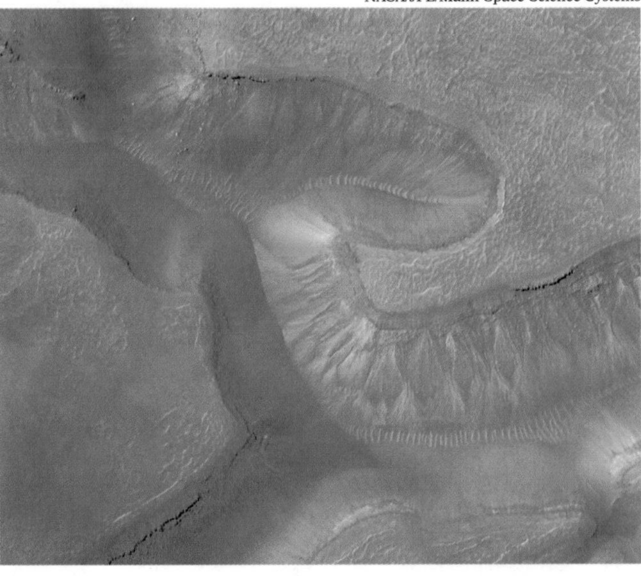

17 An upper-caste militia slaughters 34 lower-caste people in a village in Bihar state, India, where intercaste violence kills scores of people every year.

•

The undefeated Shane Mosley wins the World Boxing Council welterweight boxing title, defeating Oscar de la Hoya in a split decision in Los Angeles.

18 Tiger Woods wins the 100th U.S. Open with a score of 272, 12 under par and 15 strokes ahead of his nearest competitor; this is the largest margin of victory ever in a major golf tournament. (*See* July 23.)

•

The 7th International Exhibition of Architecture, part of the Venice Biennale, opens in that Italian city; with Massimiliano Fuksas as curator, it is the largest and most expensive architecture exhibit ever mounted.

19 British customs officials discover the bodies of 58 Chinese people hidden behind crates of tomatoes in the cargo area of a Dutch truck arriving on a ferry from Belgium; the victims, believed to be illegal immigrants, perished from respiratory failure.

•

The Los Angeles Lakers defeat the Indiana Pacers 116–111, winning the National Basketball Association championship; Shaquille O'Neal is named Most Valuable Player of the series.

20 The facade of the Palais Garnier, the Paris opera house first opened in 1875, is officially unveiled; it is part of a restoration project scheduled to be completed in 2007.

21 The World Health Organization releases a report ranking the health care systems of its member countries; the top five are France, Italy, San Marino, Andorra, and Malta, and the lowest rank is given to Sierra Leone.

•

Thousands rally in Athens to protest a government decision to bar disclosure of religious affiliation on Greek national identification cards.

•

The Oklahoma City National Memorial, built to commemorate the 168 victims of the 1995 terrorist bombing of the Alfred P. Murrah Federal Building, is officially dedicated.

22 ***NASA announces that images from the Mars Global Surveyor suggest that there may be sources of liquid water at or near the surface of Mars. (Photo left.)***

•

For the first time in 15 years, the general public is permitted to observe sunrise at the summer solstice at Stonehenge, a prehistoric monument in England; some 6,000 assorted druids, New Age religionists, and others peacefully celebrate the solstice, although rain obscures view of the sunrise.

23 The Cotonou Agreement, a trade and aid agreement between the European Union and close to 80 less-developed countries, is signed in Cotonou, Benin; the document replaces the 25-year-old Lomé Convention.

•

An oil tanker sinks off the South African coast near Cape Town, spilling hundreds of tons of oil and causing severe damage to the Robben Island nature reserve, home to one of the world's biggest African penguin colonies.

•

In a referendum held in the Dutch part of the Caribbean island of Sint Maarten/Saint Martin, the people vote in favour of withdrawing from the Netherlands Antilles but remaining within The Netherlands.

•

The Experience Music Project, a rock and roll museum designed by architect Frank Gehry, opens in Seattle, Wash., with three days of concerts in six venues.

24 The first International India Film Awards ceremony takes place in the Millennium Dome in London; awards go to the movie *Hum dil de chuke sanam* and to the actors Aishwarya Rai and Sanjay Dutt.

•

The two largest white-led political parties in South Africa, the New National Party and the Democratic Party, merge to form the Democratic Alliance; its membership is primarily white, Coloured (mixed-race), and Indian, but it hopes to attract more black members.

25 Parliamentary elections in Japan result in large gains for the opposition Democratic Party of Japan; the ruling coalition led by the Liberal-Democratic Party barely holds on to its majority. (*See* April 5.)

•

South Korea observes the 50th anniversary of the start of the Korean War with low-key speeches, eschewing the usual military parade and canceling battle reenactments. (*See* June 13 and August 3.)

•

Philip Morris announces plans to buy Nabisco Holdings, which will make it the world's second largest food company, overtaking the planned Unilever-Bestfoods merger. (*See* June 6.)

26 Francis S. Collins, director of the National Institutes of Health's Human Genome Project, and J. Craig Venter, of Celera Genomics, announce that they have essentially completed the sequencing of the human genome.

•

Adrian Nicholas of Great Britain leaps from a height of 3,000 m (10,000 ft) over Mpumalanga, S.Af., using a parachute made according to a design by Leonardo da Vinci some 500 years ago; the device works, which confounds the expectations of most experts.

27 The Joint United Nations Programme on HIV/AIDS issues a report indicating that, at present infection rates, at least two-thirds of 15-year-old boys in the hardest-hit African countries (among them Botswana, Zimbabwe, and South Africa) will eventually die of AIDS.

•

The U.S. Fish and Wildlife Service releases 10 captive-bred Puerto Rican parrots (*Amazona vittata*) into a rain forest in Puerto Rico as part of a program to replenish the population of wild parrots, which number fewer than 50.

28 Elián González arrives back in Cuba, seven months after he was rescued at sea and became the centre of an international drama. (*See* April 22.)

•

The U.S. Supreme Court rules that the Boy Scouts are legally entitled to exclude gay troop leaders from membership in the organization.

•

Indian Prime Minister Atal Bihari Vajpayee meets with Portuguese Prime Minister António Guterres, who is president of the European Council, and the president of the European Commission, Romano Prodi, for the first-ever summit-level talks India has had with the EU.

•

The Western premiere of *Semyon Kotko*, an opera by Sergey Prokofiev (who died in 1953) that had been banned in the U.S.S.R. since it was composed in 1948, takes place in London with the Mariinsky (Kirov) Company under the direction of Valery Gergiev, who has been specializing in the often-neglected works of Soviet-era composers.

29 In a referendum in Uganda, voters choose to retain the nonparty system that has been in place there since 1986.

•

On the Indonesian island of Halmahera about 500 people crowd onto a ferry designed to hold only 250 in an attempt to escape Christian-Muslim violence; the ferry sinks in a storm off Sulawesi, drowning everyone aboard except 10 passengers.

•

American artist Robert Rauschenberg's latest work, *Synapsis Shuffle*, a series of 52 panels that are meant to be reassembled by different people each time the work is exhibited, goes on display at the Whitney Museum of American Art in New York City.

•

IBM Corp. announces a new computer, ASCI White, which it created for the U.S. Department of Energy to simulate nuclear weapons tests; it is the fastest computer in the world.

•

A copy of the Declaration of Independence is auctioned over the Internet by Sotheby's for $8,140,000, the highest price ever in an Internet auction.

30 Sirius Satellite Radio successfully launches its first satellite; the company plans to use it to beam 50 channels of digital radio to paid subscribers throughout the U.S.

•

It is reported that a wooden bridge built in 1207 in Zhejiang province in China has been destroyed in flooding resulting from torrential rains. (*See* June 10.)

July

Today we have shown those at home and abroad that our nation is one of free men and women who believe in the means of democracy and law to achieve progress and solutions to our problems.

Mexican Pres. Ernesto Zedillo Ponce de Léon in his message to the people after his party's loss in the election, July 2

1 The 16.4-km (10.2-mi) series of bridges and tunnels spanning The Sound (Øresund in Danish, Öresund in Swedish), which lies between Copenhagen and Malmö, Swed., is formally opened by Queen Margrethe II of Denmark and King Carl XVI Gustaf of Sweden.

•

A military ceremony marks the closing of France's nuclear testing facility in French Polynesia.

•

Under growing pressure, notably from African American groups, South Carolina removes the Civil War Confederate battle flag from the statehouse; instead, the flag is flown at an adjacent memorial for Confederate soldiers.

2 Vicente Fox Quesada, of the centre-right National Action Party, wins the election for president of Mexico, ending the 71-year domination of the Institutional Revolutionary Party.

AP/Wide World Photos

•

The former communist rulers in Mongolia are returned to power in a landslide election, winning 72 of the 76 contested legislative seats. (*See* July 26.)

•

France, the 1998 world champion, defeats Italy 2–1 in the association football (soccer) Euro 2000 final in Rotterdam, Neth.

3 The Gettysburg National Tower, a privately owned observation tower overlooking Gettysburg National Military Park in Pennsylvania, opened in 1974 and acquired in a lawsuit by the U.S. National Park Service, is demolished as the first step of a plan to restore the site to its Civil War-era appearance.

4 Pattimura University in the city of Ambon in the Moluccas is extensively burned in the continuing civil violence between Muslims and Christians in Indonesia.

•

The "tall ships" sail into New York Harbor; the colourful flotilla of sailing ships includes a full-size replica of the 39-m (129-ft) slave ship* Amistad, *which eventually will be docked at New Haven, Conn., and serve as a museum. (Photo left.)

5 The UN Security Council imposes an 18-month worldwide ban on purchases of diamonds from Sierra Leone, profits from which have been supporting weapons purchases and armed conflict in that West African nation and elsewhere in Africa. (*See* March 13 and July 12.)

•

U.S. Pres. Bill Clinton signs two international agreements, one to prevent children under the age of 18 from being sent to war and the other to prevent children from being sold or traded for purposes such as sexual exploitation or organ harvesting.

6 Twyla Tharp's new troupe, Twyla Tharp Dance, debuts at the American Dance Festival in Durham, N.C., with two premieres, *Surfer at the River Styx* and *Mozart Clarinet Quintet K. 581.*

7 A panel convened by the Organization of African Unity issues a report criticizing France, the United States, the UN Security Council, the Roman Catholic and Anglican churches, and Belgium for having failed to prevent genocide in Rwanda in 1994.

8 The Episcopal Church approves an alliance with the Evangelical Lutheran Church in America (which had approved the agreement in 1999) that involves each church's recognizing the members and sacraments of the other and sharing clergy and resources.

•

The third official test of the proposed U.S. missile defense system fails when a decoy does not deploy and a dummy warhead fails to separate from its booster rocket.

•

The latest novel by J.K. Rowling, *Harry Potter and the Goblet of Fire,* is released in the United States; many bookstores open at midnight and host theme parties for the event, and lines of eager fans of the youthful sorcerer stretch for blocks.

9 American Pete Sampras wins a record-breaking 13th Grand Slam tennis title when he defeats Australian Patrick Rafter at Wimbledon to win the men's All England final for the seventh time; on uly 8 Venus Williams defeats fellow American Lindsay Davenport to become the first African American to win a women's Wimbledon championship since Althea Gibson did so in 1958.

•

Police fire tear gas into the crowd after some fans begin throwing debris on the field at a World Cup qualifying soccer game in Harare, Zimb.; 13 people are trampled to death in the melee that follows.

10 Belfast, N.Ire., comes to a standstill as a result of a protest called by the Protestant loyalists in response to new rules that do not permit the traditional Orange parade to pass through Roman Catholic areas.

•

Pres. Ezer Weizman of Israel resigns three years before the end of his term after reports of financial misdealings were made public. (*See* May 28.)

11 A cattle raid in northern Uganda leaves 63 herders dead; the cattle rustling that is traditional among nomadic herders in the region has become especially deadly in recent years because of the growing number of firearms being brought into the area.

•

The African Methodist Episcopal Church names a female bishop, Vashti Murphy McKenzie, for the first time in its 213-year history.

•

An Israeli expert says that several years of drought have caused a dangerous shortage of water in Israel; a further threat is that the water sources may become contaminated by salt deposits and thereby be rendered useless.

12 In Afghanistan the ruling Taliban agrees to rescind an order forbidding women to hold jobs; the ban had greatly increased the number of women and children begging. (*See* July 28.)

•

Matthew Coon Come, the former grand chief of the Cree Indians of Quebec, is elected head of Canada's Assembly of First Nations.

•

De Beers Consolidated Mines, which controls more than half the world's raw diamonds, announces that henceforth, rather than hoarding diamonds to manipulate prices, it will rely on an advertising-led marketing strategy; in addition, it announces new rules intended to decrease trafficking of diamonds from conflict areas in Africa. (*See* July 5.)

13 In Fiji 18 political hostages, including the former prime minister, Mahendra Chaudhry, are released by rebels after 56 days in captivity. (*See* May 19 and July 26.)

•

Vietnam and the United States sign a trade agreement in Washington, D.C.; President Clinton hails it as "a historic reconciliation."

•

WorldCom and Sprint call off their proposed merger, which, when it was announced in October 1999, was believed to be the largest in history.

14 A freak tornado touches down in Alberta at a popular campground on Pine Lake, killing 12 people and injuring dozens more.

•

Science magazine publishes an analysis of climate data for the past 1,000 years that strongly suggests that human activity is primarily responsible for the sharp global warming of the 20th century.

•

The French national holiday Bastille Day is celebrated with the largest picnic in history; some four million Frenchmen break bread together at nearly 640 km (400 mi) of red-and-white checkered tablecloths stretching from Dunkirk on the English Channel, through Paris, to the Pyrenees Mountains in the south.

15 UN troops rescue 222 Indian peacekeepers and 11 UN military observers who have been held by the rebel Revolutionary United Front since May in Kailahun, Sierra Leone. (*See* August 4.)

16 A pipeline explosion in Warri, Nigeria, kills at least 30 villagers who had been illegally siphoning gas from the line; the explosion occurs less than a week after another, at Adeje, killed more than 250; the practice of puncturing pipelines to steal fuel has resulted in many such disasters in Nigeria.

•

A pipe bursts at the Petrobrás-owned Getúlio Vargas oil refinery in Araucária, Braz., spilling about four million litres (about a million gallons) of oil into a tributary of the Iguaçu River; it is Brazil's worst oil disaster in 25 years.

17 Germany agrees to pay $5 billion to compensate people who were forced into slave labour under the Nazi regime; half of the money will be contributed by industrial concerns and half by the government.

•

Nepal abolishes bonded servitude, freeing some 36,000 serfs, most of whom had been labouring to pay off debts incurred by their forebears; the move comes two days after a massive demonstration against the practice.

•

General Mills, Inc., agrees to buy the Pillsbury Co., a division of Diageo PLC; the resulting company, with about $13 billion in sales annually, would rank fifth among the world's food companies.

18 A bill to end the right of U.S. presidents to create national monuments is defeated in the Senate; President Clinton's commitment of nearly 1.4 million ha (4 million ac) to national monuments has aroused opposition in western states. (*See* April 15 and November 9.)

•

A new dress code permits girls in elementary schools in Tehran to wear colours other than black, brown, or dark blue.

19 The U.S. Export-Import Bank announces a program in which it will offer $1 billion annually in loans to sub-Saharan Africa to be used in the fight against AIDS.

•

At the Somali peace conference that opened May 2 in Arta, Djibouti, delegates declare that the yet-unnamed interim government will be seated in Baidoa, Somalia, pending the rehabilitation of the traditional capital, Mogadishu.

•

In London, Elizabeth the Queen Mother's 100th birthday is officially celebrated with a pageant of 7,000 marchers, floats, singers, dancers, and well-wishers; the "Queen Mum," who won the enduring love of her people during World War II, actually turns 100 on August 4. (Photo right.)

20 Scientists in Princeton, N.J., report that they have induced light waves to travel faster than the speed of light but reassure doubters that this does not contradict Einstein's theory that nothing having mass can exceed the speed of light; it is believed that the technology used could find applications in fibre optics and computer networks.

•

French Prime Minister Lionel Jospin reveals a plan that would gradually bring autonomy to the Mediterranean island of Corsica, which has been the scene of a violent separatist campaign.

21 The annual meeting of the Group of Eight industrialized nations opens in Nago, Okinawa; the three-day summit is preceded by demonstrations by about 27,000 people protesting the American military presence on the Japanese island.

AP/Wide World Photos

•

Scientists at Fermilab's Tevatron particle accelerator in Illinois announce that the tau neutrino, a subatomic particle that is integral to the standard model of particle physics and that has existed only in theory for 25 years, has been detected.

22 The Ottawa Chamber Music Festival, the largest such gathering in the world, opens with a performance by the Beaux Arts Trio; the event will last two weeks and feature 98 concerts.

•

Four hundred Oz fans, many in costume, gather in Bloomington, Ind., to celebrate the 100th anniversary of the publication of L. Frank Baum's beloved fantasy *The Wonderful Wizard of Oz.*

•

Peter Stein's production of Goethe's *Faust,* a spectacle in six parts that cost DM 30 million (about $15 million) to stage and takes 21 hours to complete, opens at Expo 2000 in Hannover, Ger. (*See* June 1.)

23 Côte d'Ivoire votes on a new constitution; the most important changes in the country's basic law would significantly tighten citizenship requirements for presidential candidates. (*See* October 25.)

•

A wildfire that was started by lightning on July 20 in Mesa Verde National Park, Colo., suddenly triples in size, threatening 1,000-year-old Anasazi cliff dwellings in the park.

•

American cyclist Lance Armstrong wins the Tour de France for the second consecutive year.

•

Australian golfer Karrie Webb wins the U.S. Women's Open by five strokes; also, Tiger Woods becomes the youngest player ever to win golf's Grand Slam round of tournaments when he wins the British Open by eight strokes.

24 The Offshore Kazakhstan International Operating Co., a consortium of nine oil companies, confirms that there has been a major oil find, the Kashagan oil field, in the Caspian Sea off Kazakhstan.

•

Portuguese association football (soccer) star Luis Figo is traded from the Barcelona team to Real Madrid for a record $56 million.

25 An Air France Concorde en route from Paris to New York City crashes on takeoff, killing all 109 on board as well as 4 persons on the ground; in 24 years of passenger service, it is the first time one of the supersonic airliners has crashed.

•

President Clinton announces that two weeks of intense negotiations with Israeli Prime Minister Ehud Barak and Palestinian leader Yasir Arafat in an attempt to bring peace to the Middle East have failed.

26 Mongolia's legislature, the Great Hural, elects Nambaryn Enhbayar of the Mongolian People's Revolutionary Party prime minister. (*See* July 2.)

•

Fiji's army arrests coup leader George Speight, claiming that he has not returned the military weapons he stole and that he has made threats against the new president, Ratu Josefa Iloilo. (*See* July 13.)

•

In a flagship copyright case, U.S. Judge Marilyn Patel issues a preliminary injunction ordering Napster, a company that facilitates the free exchange of music files on the Internet, to cease trading copyrighted materials; a court decision on July 28, however, permits Napster to continue operating pending further investigations.

•

As part of the year-long London String of Pearls Millennium Festival, the Royal Opera House presents *The Fleeting Opera* over two nights on barges being towed along the Thames; the audience must walk slowly along the riverbank to see the performance.

27 British Prime Minister Tony Blair announces an extensive plan to revamp the National Health Service over the course of the next 10 years.

•

An article in *The New England Journal of Medicine* says that a rare heart disorder called long-QT syndrome may be responsible for more than one-quarter of sudden infant death syndrome cases.

28 The Taliban orders a complete ban on the growing of the opium poppy, a major cash crop in Afghanistan; in the past the Taliban has said the country could not afford to give up the crop. (*See* July 12.)

•

At Katyn, Russia, a memorial is dedicated to the 4,000 Polish officers who were massacred there by Soviet secret police in 1940.

•

The leftist Italian newspaper *L'Unità,* which first appeared in 1924, publishes its last issue before suspending operations.

•

To foil a murder plot against the mayor, police in Zaragoza, Spain, arrest two people believed to be Basque separatist Euskadi Ta Askatasuna terrorists, but the next day a former Basque provincial governor is assassinated in the town of Tolosa.

29 Joe Montana, Howie Long, Ronnie Lott, Dan Rooney, and Dave Wilcox are inducted into the Pro Football Hall of Fame in Canton, Ohio, in a ceremony attended by 111 of the 136 living hall of famers.

30 In elections in Venezuela, Pres. Hugo Chávez Frías wins reelection under a new constitution that extends his term and dramatically increases the power of the office.

•

An outbreak of dengue fever, a disease borne by mosquitos, causes health authorities in El Salvador to place the nation in a state of high alert.

•

Rubens Barrichello, driving a Ferrari, wins the German Grand Prix at Hockenheim, Ger.; his teammate Michael Schumacher is eliminated in a collision at the first curve of the race.

31 A report published in Colombia says that in the past three years two million Colombians have abandoned the country and that millions more would leave if they could; the reasons for the exodus include the high rates of violence and unemployment.

•

Ninety-five-year-old Stanley Kunitz is named 10th poet laureate of the United States; his 12th book of poetry is scheduled to be released later in the year.

August

All the crew from the 6th, 7th and 8th compartments moved over to the 9th. There are 23 people here. We decided to do this because of the accident. None of us can get to the surface. . . . It's too dark to write here and I'm writing blindly. It seems we have no chance, no more than 10–20 percent. I hope that at least someone will read this.

Excerpts from the note written probably on August 12 or 13 and found on the body of Capt.-Lieut. Dmitry R. Kolesnikov aboard the sunken Russian submarine *Kursk*, as read by Adm. Vladimir Kuroyedov, commander in chief of the Russian navy, to the families of the crew in Murmansk, Russia, in October

1 ***The Steel Dragon 2000, the world's largest roller coaster at 97 m (318 ft) in height, 2.4 km (1.5 mi) in length, and nearly four minutes in duration, opens at Nagashima Spaland, an amusement park in western Japan. (Photo right.)***

•

The *Frankfurter Allgemeine Zeitung,* Germany's newspaper of record, gives up the use of the reformed German that had been agreed to by German-speaking countries in 1996 and returns to publishing in the traditional language.

Toru Yamanaka/AFP World Wide

2 Republican Party delegates, meeting at their national convention in Philadelphia, nominate Texas Gov. George W. Bush and former secretary of defense Richard Cheney as the party's candidates for president and vice president. (*See* August 16.)

•

A number of Chinese citizens, frustrated at their inability to obtain Hong Kong residency permits, set fire to the immigration offices in the special administrative region.

3 The former president of Indonesia, Suharto, is formally charged with corruption. (*See* May 29 and September 28.)

•

An official with South Korea's Ministry of Unification announces plans to rebuild the Pyongyang–Seoul railroad, which had been severed in 1945; ground is broken on September 18. (*See* June 25 and August 15.)

•

Sri Lankan Pres. Chandrika Kumaratunga proposes a new constitution that will give increased autonomy to Tamils in hopes of ending the war with Tamil separatists; she is forced to postpone voting indefinitely on August 8, however. (*See* June 7.)

4 The UN Security Council extends and strengthens the mandate of the peacekeepers in Sierra Leone but does not order more troops, notwithstanding the request for the additional help by the commander of the force. (*See* July 15.)

•

More than 400 new forest fires are ignited by lightning in the western United States on a day during which 70 major fires, 15 of them in Montana, are burning 300,000 ha (747,000 ac) of land. (*See* August 18.)

5 Twenty-two years after authorization was granted to do so, United Nations peacekeepers begin spreading out in force to guard the border between Israel and Lebanon. (*See* May 24.)

•

Chicago-based United Airlines cancels 156 flights because of a shortage of pilots, who, since their contract lapsed in April, have been refusing to work overtime; a tentative settlement of the dispute is reached on August 26.

6 Ayatollah Ali Khamenei orders the Iranian legislature to drop a bill—which had been the centrepiece of the legislation to be considered since the electoral victory of the reformists earlier in 2000—to permit a free press; two days later *Bahar,* the last major reformist newspaper, is ordered closed.

7 The U.S. National Academy of Sciences reports that sites where nuclear bombs were built are likely to remain unacceptably toxic for tens of thousands of years.

•

An agreement is signed between the U.S. government, the state of Michigan, and five Native American tribes to change the fishing method permitted Native Americans in the Great Lakes in northern Michigan; the measure is intended to rebuild fish populations and improve relations between whites and Native Americans.

•

It is announced that by decision of the International Court of Arbitration Andersen Consulting is ordered to pay parent firm Arthur Andersen $1 billion and give up the Andersen name for which it is allowed to become an independent company.

8 A bomb explodes in a pedestrian underpass in Moscow's Pushkin Square at the evening rush hour, killing 12 people; Russian authorities believe it is an act of Chechen terrorism, but Chechen spokesmen deny it.

•

Anwar Ibrahim, the former deputy prime minister and the leader of the opposition to Malaysian Prime Minister Mahathir bin Mohamad, is convicted of sodomy and sentenced to nine years in prison.

•

The Supreme Court of Chile rules that former dictator Augusto Pinochet Ugarte is not entitled to immunity from prosecution, clearing the way for a possible trial. (*See* March 2 and December 1.)

9 Bridgestone/Firestone, Inc., announces the recall of 6.5 million tires, citing a tread-separation problem that has led to 46 deaths to date, though it will take up to a year to replace the tires; the company is faced with 50 lawsuits and a federal investigation relating to the problem.

•

Prices of stock for Eli Lilly and Co. drop 31% following news that patent protection for the firm's top-selling pharmaceutical, the antidepressant Prozac, will end two years sooner than expected; the company can expect to lose billions of dollars in revenue as vastly cheaper generic substitute drugs go on the market.

10 Sirimavo Bandaranaike of Sri Lanka, the world's first female prime minister, retires, and her daughter, Pres. Chandrika Kumaratunga, appoints Ratnasiri Wickramanayake to the post; Bandaranaike dies on October 10.

•

Venezuelan Pres. Hugo Chávez Frías becomes the first head of state to visit Iraq since the Persian Gulf War when he meets with Saddam Hussein in Baghdad; the stop is part of his tour to encourage unity among OPEC countries.

11 Veerappan, a legendary bandit in India, issues a list of new demands to be met before he will release his hostage, the at least equally legendary movie star Rajkumar, whom he kidnapped two weeks previously. (*See* November 15.)

12 The Russian nuclear submarine *Kursk* sinks in the Barents Sea after the hull is damaged by a series of explosions; rescuers finally reach the submarine on August 21 only to find the vessel flooded and all 118 crew members dead.

•

A week after the U.S. National Marine Fisheries Service announced the closure of 260,000 sq km (100,000 sq mi) of the Gulf of Mexico and the Atlantic Ocean to long-line fishing, the Natural Resources Defense Council and SeaWeb release 700 chefs from their pledge not to serve swordfish.

13 Paraguay holds an election to fill the vice presidential post left vacant when Luis María Argaña was assassinated in 1999; results are so close that the winner, Julio César Franco, of the opposition Authentic Radical Liberal Party, is not announced until August 24.

14 In the course of a four-day meeting in Moscow, the Jubilee Bishops' Council of the Russian Orthodox Church votes to canonize Tsar Nicholas II, the last of the Romanov dynasty to have ruled Russia, and his family; they were murdered on the orders of communist officials in 1918.

•

The U.S. Department of Energy reports that natural gas prices have doubled in the past year and forecasts winter heating bills as much as 50% higher than the previous winter's; it warns that heating oil may also experience steep price rises.

15 Two hundred members of families separated by the Korean War are permitted to meet each other for the first time since then, half in South Korea and half in North Korea. (*See* August 3.)

•

Colombian army troops fighting an insurgency in the northwestern Antioquia province fire on an elementary-school hiking trip, killing six children.

•

Muhammad Ibrahim Egal, the president of Somaliland, calls on the United Nations to grant it a special status, given that international recognition of the self-proclaimed republic is unlikely to be forthcoming, so that it can develop separately from Somalia.

16 Democratic Party delegates, meeting at their national convention in Los Angeles, nominate Vice Pres. Al Gore and Joseph Lieberman, senator from Connecticut, as the Democratic candidates for president and vice president of the United States. (*See* August 2.)

•

A band of militant Muslims from Tajikistan, intending to destabilize the government of Uzbekistan, attempts to cross Kyrgyzstan but is held down by Kyrgyz troops in a fierce battle.

17 The Royal Ulster Constabulary holds its final graduation parade; it is to be renamed the Police Service of Northern Ireland and restructured in hopes that it will become a force that is supported by Roman Catholics as well as Protestants.

•

A U.S. federal judge issues a ruling that prohibits the distribution of software that makes it possible to copy digital video discs (DVDs).

18 The People's Consultative Assembly of Indonesia decides to keep the military included as part of the government until 2009.

•

More than 400,000 ha (1,000,000 ac) are on fire in the western region of the United States, more than at any other time since 1910, and Secretary of the Interior Bruce Babbitt warns that the situation is very likely to worsen. (*See* August 4.)

•

Brazilian authorities say a group of 250 Indians living near the border with Peru, who were noticed only when they turned out to protest the creation of a national park on their land, are the Naua tribe, thought to have become extinct in the 1920s.

19 A natural gas pipeline explodes near Carlsbad, N.M., sending a fireball into a nearby campsite and killing 11 people.

•

In the German town of Neubrandenburg three young men, dubbed neo-Nazis in the press, beat a 15-year-old boy to death "out of frustration and boredom."

20 Pope John Paul II celebrates mass for more than two million youths at the close of the six-day World Youth Festival held by the Roman Catholic Church in Rome.

•

As the culmination of the Hungarian celebration of the 1,000th anniversary of their nation, King Stephen I is canonized by the Eastern Orthodox Church; the Roman Catholic Church canonized him more than 900 years ago.

•

Tiger Woods wins his second consecutive Professional Golfers' Association of America championship by one stroke; he is the second player ever to win three major tournaments in one year (the first was Ben Hogan, in 1953).

21 Charges against the Philippine student believed to be responsible for the Love Bug are dropped; the Philippines currently has no law against creating and disseminating such a virus. (*See* May 4.)

22 Japanese automaker Mitsubishi Motors admits it had covered up tens of thousands of consumer complaints since 1977 in order to avoid costly and embarrassing recalls.

•

The *Golden Venture,* an old freighter used to smuggle refugees from China to the United States until it ran aground in 1993, is sunk off the coast of Boca Raton, Fla., to create an artificial reef.

23 In response to widespread anger over his ineffectual leadership, Indonesian Pres. Abdurrahman Wahid revamps his cabinet and signs a decree turning the day-to-day running of the government over to Vice Pres. Megawati Sukarnoputri.

•

A Gulf Air Airbus A320 crashes just before approaching Bahrain International Airport in the capital, Manama, killing all 143 passengers and crew.

24 A record 23.9 cm (9.4 in) of rain fall in Hyderabad, Andhra Pradesh state, India; flooding in the state kills at least 120 people in three days, which brings the total of flood-related deaths in India for the year to 400.

•

The journal *Nature* reports that a team of Finnish scientists has succeeded in creating a stable compound with the element argon, long believed to be inert.

25 Somalia's new legislature, meeting in Arta, Djibouti, elects Abdiqassim Salad Hassan as Somalia's first president in nine years; warlords in Somalia warn that they will not allow this government. (*See* July 19 and October 14.)

•

A report in *Science* magazine says that magnetic readings from the *Galileo* spacecraft suggest that Jupiter's moon Europa has an ocean of liquid water beneath its surface ice.

•

Ceremonies in Weimar, Ger., mark the centenary of Friedrich Nietzsche's death; speakers include the controversial philosopher Peter Sloterdijk and the actress Libgart Schwarz.

26 U.S. Pres. Bill Clinton arrives in Nigeria to meet with Pres. Olusegun Obasanjo and show his support for the new civilian government; during his four-day trip he will also visit Tanzania and Egypt.

•

Sparked by their retiring star, Cynthia Cooper, the Houston Comets defeat the New York Liberty two games to none to take the Women's National Basketball Association championship in Houston, Texas.

•

The team of youngsters from Maracaibo, Venez., defeats the squad from Bellaire, Texas, 3–2 to claim the 2000 baseball Little League World Series in Williamsport, Pa.

AP/Wide World Photos

27 ***A fire breaks out near the top of the world's second tallest free-standing structure, the 540-m (1,772-ft) Ostankino television tower; most TV service to Moscow is knocked out, and three people die in the blaze. (Photo above.)***

•

The Philippine separatist group Abu Sayyaf releases 5 of the 21 hostages it seized from a Malaysian resort (*see* April 23), in addition to a hostage taken later (though it also takes a further hostage); Libya paid ransom for all the released hostages.

28 The Millennium World Peace Summit of Religious and Spiritual Leaders opens at the United Nations; the four-day meeting of some 1,000 religious leaders explores ways for diverse religions to contribute to world peace.

•

Northern Texas experiences its 59th consecutive day without rain; the drought in the state breaks the Dust Bowl record set in 1934 and tied in 1950. (*See* September 23.)

•

The New York Stock Exchange begins listing the prices of seven stocks in dollars and cents; previously all stock was listed in fractions.

•

Der Spiegel reports that the new Duden dictionary of the German language is on sale; included are 5,000 new words, including many from the world of computers, such as the new verbs *downloaden* and *mailen*.

29 Pres. Andrés Pastrana Arango of Colombia says that his country cannot make progress against the production and trafficking of illegal drugs without a large reduction in demand elsewhere in the world.

30 A subway train entering the Notre-Dame de Lorette station in Paris mysteriously keels over and derails; 24 passengers are injured.

•

East Timorese refugees riot in Kupang, the capital of West Timor, on the first anniversary of the vote for independence.

•

Tatarstan, a largely Muslim republic in the Russian Federation, chooses to begin teaching the Tatar language in the Roman rather than the Cyrillic alphabet; the changeover is expected to be completed in 2011.

•

The Supreme Court in Israel rules that a scholar working on the Dead Sea Scrolls has a copyright to his reconstruction of the text of one of the scrolls.

31 Poland marks the 20th anniversary of the founding of Solidarity, originally a trade union and later a political party.

•

The journal *Nature* reports that computer scientists have built a robot that has designed and built other robots.

September

We believe that the central challenge we face today is to ensure that globalization becomes a positive force for all the world's people. For while globalization offers great opportunities, at present its benefits are very unevenly shared, while its costs are unevenly distributed.

United Nations Millennium Declaration
from the General Assembly

1 U.S. Pres. Bill Clinton decides that the technology for building a national missile defense system is insufficiently developed and passes the decision as to whether to proceed with such a system on to his successor in office.

•

The first South American regional summit, attended by 12 heads of state, concludes in Brasília, Braz.

•

TV Breizh, the first television channel to present programming in the Breton language, begins broadcasting in France.

2 Transnistria celebrates the 10th anniversary of its declaration of independence from Moldova with a military parade in the city of Tiraspol; its independence, however, has never been recognized internationally.

•

The four-day World Conference on Assisted Dying, attended by about 500 people from 22 countries, opens in Boston; members of the disabled rights group Not Dead Yet protest outside the venue.

3 Pope John Paul II beatifies five persons, including Pope John XXIII, a popular choice, and Pope Pius IX, whose elevation is criticized by many because of Pius's conservative dogma and alleged anti-Semitism.

•

The governor of Khartoum issues an order banning women in the Sudanese capital from any job in which they come in contact with men, in order to "honour women [and] uphold their lofty status."

•

An earthquake of magnitude 5.2 shakes northern California; its epicentre, under Mt. Veeders near Yountville, is found to lie along a previously unknown fault.

4 Truckers in France blockade fuel depots as they begin a nationwide strike to protest high fuel costs. (*See* September 12.)

•

Israel ends the monopoly of Bezeq, the state-owned company, on domestic telephone and Internet service.

5 To the dismay of members of other faiths, Roman Catholic Church officials in the Vatican issue a pronouncement that salvation is available "fully and only through the Catholic Church." (*See* October 17.)

•

The U.S. State Department releases a report on religious freedom worldwide; it singles out China, Afghanistan, Iraq, Russia, and Israel for criticism.

•

Pres. Alberto Fujimori of Peru decrees a major expansion of Bahuaja-Sonene National Park and creates the adjoining Tambopata National Reserve; as many as 550 bird species and more than 1,200 butterfly species have been recorded in a single locality within the region.

•

The American scooter fad rolls on; the Consumer Product Safety Commission says that the number of scooter-related injuries in the U.S. has increased 700% since May. (Photo right.)

6 The three-day Millennium Summit, attended by more than 150 heads of state or their representatives (the largest group of such notables ever assembled in one place), opens at the United Nations in New York City with an address by Secretary-General Kofi Annan.

•

Tuvalu, a group of nine coral atolls with a population of about 10,000, becomes the 189th member of the United Nations.

•

Three UN workers are beaten to death by pro-Indonesia militiamen in West Timor; the UN High Commissioner for Refugees effectively suspends operations in West Timor.

7 Archaeologists announce that they have discovered a particularly large and splendid Mayan palace hidden in the jungle at the Cancuén site in Guatemala.

•

Two American researchers report in the journal *Nature* that they have found empirical evidence of cannibalism at an early Anasazi site in southwestern Colorado.

8 NASA scientists report that earlier in the season than expected the ozone hole over Antarctica is at its largest yet, 28.5 million sq km (11 million sq mi).

AP/Wide World Photos

•

A ceremony is held in Galveston, Texas, to commemorate the 100th anniversary of the worst natural disaster in U.S. history, the hurricane that killed approximately 6,000 residents of Galveston in 1900.

9 Venus Williams defeats Lindsay Davenport to win the women's competition at the U.S. Open tennis tournament, her second Grand Slam tennis victory in a row; the following day Marat Safin upsets Pete Sampras to take the men's championship.

•

The Filipino rebel group Abu Sayyaf releases the last four of the vacationing Westerners that they had seized at a Malaysian resort in April and held captive; they still hold workers from the resort as well as two journalists and a dozen evangelical Christians whom they abducted later. (*See* April 23.)

•

"Unseen Treasures: Imperial Russia and the New World," an exhibit detailing Russian activities in North America in the 18th and 19th centuries, opens at the Mint Museum of Art in Charlotte, N.C.

10 Completing its 7,485th showing in an 18-year run, the musical *Cats,* written by Andrew Lloyd Webber and directed by Trevor Nunn, closes on Broadway; it was the longest-running Broadway show in history.

•

The Emmy Awards are presented; winners include the television series *Will & Grace* and *The West Wing* and actors Michael J. Fox, James Gandolfini, Patricia Heaton, Sela Ward, Sean Hayes, Richard Schiff, Megan Mullally, and Allison Janney.

•

Indiana University at Bloomington fires Bobby Knight, its controversial head basketball coach, for having assaulted a student; Knight held the position for 29 years and was one of college basketball's most successful coaches ever, despite a succession of charges of truculent and unsportsmanlike behaviour.

•

Hong Kong holds its second legislative election under Chinese rule; observers are struck by the unexpectedly low turnout, which is believed to reflect disillusionment with the political process.

11 Secretary-General Annan tells the UN Security Council that Iraq has refused to allow a group of experts into the country to assess the impact of the economic sanctions imposed on the country since 1990; Iraq complains that its populace is suffering privations but has refused all offers of help.

12 The U.K. is brought to a standstill as protesters effectively put a stop to gasoline deliveries to service stations throughout the country; similar protests against high fuel prices are taking place in Belgium, The Netherlands, Germany, Ireland, Italy, Poland, and Spain. (*See* September 4.)

•

The Dutch parliament passes a law giving status to marriages of same-sex couples equal to that of unions between men and women; gays are said to enjoy more civil rights in The Netherlands than in any other country.

•

Scientists report that extensive searches by primatologists for Miss Waldron's red colobus (*Procolobus badius waldroni*), a monkey of the tropical forests of western Ghana and eastern Côte d'Ivoire, have failed to find any living examples, and they fear it may be extinct; if so, this would be the first primate to have become extinct since the early 1700s.

•

The second of two elephant groups, comprising 15 animals in all, arrives safely at Quicama National Park in Angola; the animals were donated by South Africa to help restock the park, which has been all but emptied of wildlife by the civil war that began in 1975.

13 Chase Manhattan Corp. announces plans to purchase J.P. Morgan & Co. Inc. for more than $35 billion; the resulting company, J.P. Morgan Chase & Co., will be the third largest financial concern in the U.S.

•

The U.S. government agrees to drop 58 of the 59 charges of stealing nuclear weapons secrets under which it had held Wen Ho Lee, an employee of Los Alamos (N.M.)

National Laboratory, for nine months; in the plea agreement Lee pleads guilty to one minor count and, sentenced to time already served, goes free.

14 Premier Cruise Lines, based in Port Canaveral, Fla., abruptly goes out of business; authorities seize three ships mid-cruise, putting at least 1,450 passengers ashore.

15 The Games of the XXVII Olympiad open in Sydney, Australia.

•

The man believed to be the leader of the Basque separatist organization ETA, Ignacio Gracia Arregui, is arrested in Bidart, France.

16 Pres. Alberto K. Fujimori of Peru unexpectedly announces that he will call new elections immediately and will not be a candidate in those elections; he does not, however, specify when they will be held. (*See* May 28 and November 20.)

•

Public transportation in Los Angeles shuts down as the United Transportation Union goes on strike one minute after midnight; hundreds of thousands of people, mostly low-income, rely on the transit system.

•

Istanbul's first new subway in 125 years is inaugurated; the new 24-hour line runs about eight kilometres (five miles) from Taksim Square to the neighbourhood of Levent, making four stops.

•

A delegation from Cuba's National Assembly offers to send Cuban physicians to poor areas of the U.S. and to train 500 poor and minority Americans in medicine in Cuba; the U.S. government makes no response.

17 The winners of the Lasker Awards for medical research are announced: in clinical research, Harvey Alter and Michael Houghton; in basic medical research, Aaron Ciechanover, Avram Hershko, and Alexander Varshavsky; and for special achievement, Sydney Brenner.

18 Betty S. Beene, president of United Way of America since 1997, announces her resignation, effective Jan. 31, 2001; she is displaced in a power struggle between the national United Way and a number of large local chapters of the charitable organization.

•

A Chinese newspaper reports that the army of terra-cotta soldiers in the Qin tomb that was discovered in 1974 could be threatened by mold; a Belgian firm has been hired to combat the problem. (See October 8.) (Photo below.)

•

Ground is broken for a new four-lane highway to run parallel to the new Pyongyang–Seoul railway in Korea. (*See* August 15.)

19 The U.S. Congress passes a bill to give China permanent normal trading status after 20 years of having annually refused to grant such status.

•

U.S. Census Bureau officials say that 67% of households

Bettmann/Corbis

filled out and returned census forms in 2000, which is 2% higher than the previous census, in 1990, and a reversal of a 30-year trend of declining participation.

20 After six years the Whitewater investigation into alleged financial irregularities involving President Clinton and first lady Hillary Rodham Clinton closes; the independent counsel says there is insufficient evidence to charge the Clintons with any wrongdoing.

•

The U.S. Securities and Exchange Commission brings stock fraud charges against a 15-year-old high-school student and reaches an agreement in which the boy is to repay $285,000, the allegedly ill-gotten gains plus interest.

21 Somali Pres. Abdiqassim Salad Hassan meets with warlord Hussein Muhammad Aydid in Surt, Libya, to discuss reconciliation.

•

The final approval from the U.S. National Capital Planning Commission is obtained for architect Friedrich St. Florian's design for the National World War II Memorial, to be built on the National Mall in Washington, D.C.; the ground breaking is scheduled to take place on Veterans Day. (*See* November 11.)

22 The British Court of Appeal issues a ruling that doctors may operate to separate conjoined twins born August 8; though the surgery will kill one of them, it has been determined that they will both die without it; the parents, from Malta, had sought to block the surgery. (*See* November 7.)

•

France permits a charter plane to fly from Paris to Baghdad, in violation of UN sanctions against Iraq, in an apparent attempt to force reconsideration of the flight embargo.

•

The German federal radiation protection authority announces that shipments of spent nuclear fuel will be resumed; plutonium from several German power plants is to be recycled at a plant in La Hague, France.

•

The premiere of *Intolleranza,* a two-act opera with music by Luigi Nono to texts by a variety of writers that includes Bertolt Brecht, Vladimir Mayakovsky, Paul Éluard, and Jean-Paul Sartre, takes place at the Cologne (Ger.) Opera House.

23 A few drops of rain falling just before midnight end a record-shattering 84 days without rain in northern Texas; the more plentiful showers that fall the following day are not enough to end the drought, however. (*See* August 28.)

24 The head of Peru's National Intelligence Service, Vladimiro Montesinos, flees to Panama and requests asylum; he has been missing since September 14, when a video surfaced showing him bribing a legislator to vote for President Fujimori.

•

In a referendum French citizens agree to shorten the presidential term of office from seven to five years; turnout is the lowest for such a vote in decades.

•

Voters in Switzerland reject a proposal to impose a limit on the percentage of the population that may be composed of foreigners.

25 Vojislav Kostunica declares he is the winner of the Yugoslav presidential election held September 24, but the incumbent, Slobodan Milosevic, will not release election results; on September 28 the government-controlled election commission orders a runoff to be held in October. (*See* October 6.)

•

It is reported that dozens of African guest workers, mostly Chadians, have been killed in clashes with Libyans that continue near the town of Az-Zawiyah, in northwestern Libya.

26 A Greek ferryboat runs aground on a well-marked islet in the Aegean Sea and sinks, killing at least 80 passengers; it is later reported that the captain was asleep and most of the crew were watching a sports match at the time.

•

The annual conference of the International Monetary Fund and the World Bank begins in Prague; thousands of protesters attempt to disrupt proceedings but are unsuccessful.

27 Floodwaters wash through the streets of Calcutta, leaving 55,000 people homeless.

•

The heads of state of the 11 members of OPEC meet for the first time since 1975, in Caracas, Venez.

•

A team of researchers reports in the journal *Nature Genetics* that they have discovered the gene associated with the development of type 2 diabetes.

28 Voters in Denmark reject the euro, the common European currency, opting instead to retain the krone as their currency; Denmark is the only European Union country to have offered a referendum on the issue.

•

Corruption charges against former Indonesian president Suharto are dropped and his house arrest is lifted after court-appointed physicians declare him medically unfit to stand trial. (*See* May 29 and August 3.)

•

Israeli statesman Ariel Sharon visits the Temple Mount in Jerusalem and asserts Israeli sovereignty over it; local Palestinians feel this is a provocation and respond with rage.

•

The U.S. Food and Drug Administration announces that it has approved the marketing in the U.S. of RU-486, a prescription pill that will allow a woman to terminate a pregnancy days or even weeks after conception.

29 Aventis CropScience, which grows genetically modified corn (maize) for use in animal feed, agrees to buy back the year's entire crop when it learns that some of its corn was used for making Taco Bell taco shells.

•

Singapore Airlines orders 25 of Airbus Industrie's superjumbo A3XXs, 15 of them on option; the sale is seen as a reversal for the American airplane manufacturer Boeing.

30 John Crosby, who created the Santa Fe (N.M.) Opera and directed it for 43 years, retires; he is succeeded by Richard Gaddes.

•

La Grange, Ga., becomes the first completely wired town in the U.S.; the city project brings free Internet access to all residents, schools, and businesses.

October

I expect support from Europe for the democratic changes in Serbia and for its return to where it has always belonged—Europe.

Vojislav Kostunica, new president of Yugoslavia, on October 13

1 Pope John Paul II canonizes Mother Katharine Drexel, Josephine Bakhita, and Maria Josefa as well as 120 Roman Catholics who were killed in China; China says the new martyr saints were guilty of heinous crimes against the Chinese people.

•

Syria's official newspaper, *Al-Thawra,* publishes a two-page article by Arif Dalila, a leader of Syria's new civil rights movement, that criticizes state control of the economy; the publication of such criticism is unprecedented in the Syrian press.

2 On the eve of the 10th anniversary of German reunification, three Molotov cocktails are thrown at the front of the Jewish synagogue in Düsseldorf, Ger.; the national debate on residual anti-Semitism in Germany is rekindled.

3 Tang Fei, who has served as premier of Taiwan for less than five months, resigns, citing poor health; the following day Pres. Chen Shui-bian appoints Tang's deputy, Chang Chun-hsiung, in his place.

•

The Seimas (legislature) of Lithuania agrees to return to Jewish communities throughout the world hundreds of Torah scrolls found in the country after World War II.

4 A government spokeswoman says the worst floods in over a century have left more than 700,000 people homeless in Bangladesh.

•

Prime Minister Jean Chrétien announces that Mt. Logan, the highest peak in Canada, will henceforth be known as Mt. Pierre Elliott Trudeau, for the recently deceased former prime minister; by October 19, however, protests have caused him to rescind the decision.

5 Responding positively to a challenge from Germany, the European Court of Justice halts a proposed European Union-wide ban on tobacco advertising that was to have taken effect in 2001.

•

Recipients of the "Alternative Nobel Prizes" (officially the Right Livelihood Awards) are announced: Birsel Lemke and Tewolde Egzhiaber, environmentalists from Turkey and Ethiopia, respectively; Munir, an Indonesian human rights activist; and Wes Jackson, an American plant geneticist.

•

The former president and chief executive officer of Sotheby's auction house, Diana D. Brooks, pleads guilty to having fixed commission fees with rival auction house Christie's.

6 The day after a massive popular uprising that caused the opposition to melt away, Yugoslavia's high court declares that opposition leader Vojislav Kostunica is the winner of the presidential election held on September 24, and Slobodan Milosevic resigns. (*See* September 25.)

•

A magnitude-7.3 earthquake strikes near Sakaiminato, Japan; though it is the most powerful earthquake since the devastating Great Hanshin Earthquake in 1995, damage and casualties are relatively low because the epicentre of the earthquake is in a sparsely inhabited area.

7 Grand Duke Jean of Luxembourg, who turned 79 in January, abdicates in favour of his eldest son, Henri; Henri had been serving as his father's "lieutenant-representant" since 1998.

•

The new opera *Dead Man Walking* opens at the San Francisco Opera with music by Jake Heggie and libretto by Terrence McNally; mezzo-soprano Susan Graham stars in the role of Sister Helen Prejean.

•

At the height of its success, the popular American improv-rock band Phish plays its final concert before breaking up for at least the foreseeable future.

•

Davo Karnicar, a ski instructor from Slovenia, becomes the first person in history to ski down Mt. Everest in a single run.

8 Pres. Aleksander Kwasniewski is reelected for a second term in Poland's third presidential election since the fall of communism.

•

Spokesmen from Advanced Cell Technology, a biotechnology company based in Massachusetts, announce that they have cloned an endangered African gaur, which is now being carried by a cow in Iowa.

•

Newspapers report that the largest Buddha image in the world, carved of red sandstone in a cliff in western China, is eroding rapidly as a result of its humid environment and of acid rain. (*See* September 18.)

•

A huge $240 million conference centre for the Church of Jesus Christ of Latter-day Saints formally opens in Salt Lake City, Utah; the centre includes a 21,000-seat auditorium and a 1.6-ha (4-ac) rooftop garden featuring an alpine meadow and hundreds of trees.

9 The Nobel Prize for Physiology or Medicine is awarded to Paul Greengard, Eric R. Kandel, and Arvid Carlsson.

•

During the ongoing violent crisis in Israel, Jews living in the largely Arab-populated town of Nazareth rampage through the streets following Yom Kippur services; in the ensuing melee, two Arabs are killed. (*See* October 12.)

•

David Trimble, first minister of the Northern Ireland Assembly, survives a no-confidence vote brought by a segment of his Ulster Unionist Party that feels that he is too conciliatory toward Sinn Fein.

10 The Nobel Prize for Physics is awarded to Herbert Kroemer, Zhores Alferov, and Jack S. Kilby for work in information technology; the Nobel Prize for Chemistry goes to Alan G. MacDiarmid, Hideki Shirakawa, and Alan J. Heeger.

•

For the first time, South Korean visitors attend the military parade in Pyongyang that celebrates the anniversary of communist rule in North Korea; meanwhile, one of North Korea's top military leaders meets in the White House with Bill Clinton, the first time a U.S. president has ever met with a North Korean official. (*See* October 24.)

11 The Nobel Prize in Economic Sciences is awarded to Americans James J. Heckman and Daniel L. McFadden.

•

The Philippine Congress opens hearings into bribery charges against Pres. Joseph Estrada. (*See* November 13.)

•

The 100th launch of the NASA space shuttle program takes place as* Discovery *is placed into orbit with the final components for the International Space Station; the crew of the station arrives aboard a Russian Soyuz spacecraft on November 2. (Photo below.)

AP/Wide World Photos

•

In a ceremony in London, the International Women of the Year Association awards the title Greatest Woman Achiever of the Century to Russian cosmonaut Valentina Tereshkova, the first woman in space; South African statesman Nelson Mandela is named Leader of the Century.

12 A small boat pulls alongside the USS *Cole,* a U.S. Navy destroyer refueling in the port of Aden, Yemen, and explodes, ripping a 150-sq m (1,600-sq ft) hole in the side of the ship and killing 17 U.S. crew members; no likely activist group claims responsibility.

•

The crisis in Israel escalates when two Israeli soldiers wander into a funeral in the Palestinian city of Ram Allah and are killed by a mob. (*See* October 9.)

•

The Nobel Prize for Literature is awarded to Gao Xingjian, a Chinese-born novelist and playwright.

13 The Nobel Prize for Peace is awarded to Kim Dae Jung, president of South Korea.

•

A U.S. federal court of appeals overturns a district court ruling that U.S. citizens residing in Puerto Rico have the right to vote in the U.S. presidential election; the appeals court rules that an amendment to the Constitution would be required for Puerto Ricans to gain that right.

•

The Basketball Hall of Fame in Springfield, Mass., inducts players Isiah Thomas, Bob McAdoo, and Meadow George ("Meadowlark") Lemon; coaches Pat Summitt, Morgan Wootten, and C.M. Newton; journalist Dave Kindred and broadcaster Hubie Brown; and the inventor of the 24-second shot clock, Danny Biasone.

14 Pres. Abdiqassim Salad Hassan enters Mogadishu, the capital of Somalia, to establish a national government, the first in Somalia since 1991. (*See* August 25.)

•

A Saudi Arabian Airlines jet en route from Jiddah, Saudi Arabia, to London is hijacked by two Saudi civil servants; they are flown to Baghdad, Iraq, where they request political asylum, citing a lack of basic freedoms in Saudi Arabia.

•

Kiribati holds spectacular ceremonies to mark the opening of its new parliament building in the capital on Tarawa atoll.

•

The Rosie the Riveter Memorial, the first national monument to the women who worked on the American home front during World War II, is dedicated in Richmond, Calif., where tens of thousands of women worked in the shipyards.

•

Miss Hawaii, Angela Perez Baraquio, is named Miss America; of Filipino descent, she is the first Asian American woman to win the crown.

AP/Wide World Photos

15 Pro-government candidates win decisively in elections held for the lower house of the legislature in Belarus; opposition candidates had urged a boycott, and Western governments had said that they would not recognize the election.

16 Reports from Cambodia say that 227 people have died there in flooding of the Mekong River; this is in addition to the 319 people in Vietnam reported killed by the floods.

•

Minister Louis Farrakhan of the Nation of Islam leads the Million Family March in Washington, D.C.; the celebration of the family is organized in cooperation with the Unification Church, run by the Rev. Sun Myung Moon, and includes a mass wedding ceremony.

•

The Chevron Corp. announces that it will buy Texaco Inc. for $35.1 billion and create a new company, called ChevronTexaco, that will be the world's fourth largest oil company.

17 The U.K.'s Queen Elizabeth II meets with Pope John Paul II at the Vatican; the meeting is intended to defuse tension between the Anglican and Roman Catholic churches that arose when the Vatican declared the primacy of the Roman Catholic Church. (*See* September 5.)

•

Patrick Roy, goaltender for the Colorado Avalanche hockey team, wins his 448th game, breaking Terry Sawchuk's record, which had stood since 1970 and had been considered unbreakable.

•

In England a high-speed train traveling from London to Leeds derails while traveling around a bend, killing four passengers; the cause appears to be a damaged track.

The World March of Women, which has been holding demonstrations against poverty and violence against women around the world, gathers at Dag Hammarskjöld Plaza in New York City to present petitions to the U.N. (Photo above.)

18 World Health Organization workers begin an intensive effort to discover the origins of an outbreak of Ebola fever in Uganda that began when a woman in the village of Kabede Opong died of the disease on September 17 and that has to date killed some 40 people within a 24-km (15-mi) radius.

•

The Royal Gold Medal for Architecture is presented to American Frank O. Gehry at London's Banqueting House.

19 Former U.S. president Jimmy Carter announces that he feels compelled to sever his ties with the Southern Baptist Convention because of its adoption of increasingly conservative doctrines.

•

The journal *Nature* publishes a report by biologists at West Chester University of Pennsylvania who believe they have revived a 250 million-year-old—10 times older than any other known living organism—bacterium from a crystal of rock salt.

20 A fire destroys a large nightclub in Mexico City, killing at least 20 patrons; the city had earlier sought to shut the club down for safety violations, but the owners, suspected of being involved in organized crime, had obtained injunctions to keep it open.

•

The much-ballyhooed heavyweight boxing match between Mike Tyson and Andrew Golota ends abruptly when Golota quits after the second round; later Golota is hospitalized with a concussion.

21 The leaders of Egypt, Jordan, Morocco, and Tunisia are among the participants who meet in Cairo in the first Arab League summit meeting since 1996.

•

Tantalus, a 10-part, 10 1/2-hour play about the Trojan War staged by the Denver (Colo.) Center Theatre Company, opens at the Denver Center for the Performing Arts.

22 The General Electric Co. agrees to acquire Honeywell International Inc. in a tax-free merger valued at $45 billion, plus assumed debt; the transaction is one of the biggest industrial mergers ever.

•

Turkey requires all residents to stay at home while it conducts a national census by sending census takers door-to-door for the first time.

23 The Avery Fisher Prize, awarded for excellence in instrumental music, is conferred upon Edgar Meyer, a double bassist, and David Shifrin, a clarinetist; at the ceremony they play a duet that Meyer composed for the occasion.

•

Construction magnate Rafiq al-Hariri is named prime minister of Lebanon.

24 The board of directors of AT&T approves a plan to split the company into four entities, each of which would be traded independently; it would be the largest reorganization of the company since it broke apart into regional "Baby Bells" in 1984.

•

U.S. Secretary of State Madeleine Albright concludes two days of meetings with North Korea's leader, Kim Jong Il, in Pyongyang. (*See* October 10.)

•

Veteran comedian, writer, and director Carl Reiner is awarded the Mark Twain Prize of the John F. Kennedy Center for the Performing Arts; previous recipients of the prize, which acknowledges contributions to American humour, were Richard Pryor (1998) and Jonathan Winters (1999).

25 Robert Gueï, military leader of Côte d'Ivoire, flees the country, and Laurent Gbagbo declares victory in presidential elections that were held three days earlier. (*See* July 23 and December 10.)

•

UN Secretary-General Kofi Annan appoints Thoraya Ahmed Obaid of Saudi Arabia director of the UN Population Fund and nominates Ruud Lubbers of The Netherlands to replace Sadako Ogata as UN High Commissioner for Refugees.

•

French and Kenyan scientists unearth the fossilized remains of a group of hominids at Kapsomin, Kenya; the rocks in which they are found are six million years old, so the team believes the fossils could be the oldest hominid remains ever discovered.

26 The New York Yankees beat the New York Mets four games to one to win baseball's World Series (popularly called the Subway Series this year) for the third year in a row.

•

The robot spacecraft NEAR Shoemaker passes within a distance of five kilometres (three miles) from the asteroid 433 Eros and takes detailed pictures of the ancient solid rock body.

•

The European Parliament awards the Sakharov Prize for Freedom of Thought to the citizens group ¡Basta Ya!, which is trying to put an end to Basque separatist terrorism in Spain. (*See* October 30.)

•

China's news agency, Xinhua, reports that archaeologists have found relics in the Three Gorges area that indicate that it was occupied by humans 100,000 years ago, which makes it, and not the valley of the Huang Ho, the cradle of civilization in China.

27 After autonomy talks between Denmark and its dependency the Faroe Islands break down, Faroese Prime Minister Anfinn Kallsberg announces that a referendum on independence will be held in 2001.

•

Gordon Davis is appointed to succeed Nathan Leventhal as the president of the Lincoln Center for the Performing Arts in New York City at the end of the year.

•

For the first time, at a concert near Tel Aviv, the music of German composer Richard Wagner is played in public in Israel; a group of Holocaust survivors protests.

28 Opening ceremonies are held for Dubai Internet City, a free-trade zone in the city of Dubayy, U.A.E., that the crown prince envisions as a major new economy centre in the Middle East.

•

A baseball game is played in Barquisimeto, Venez., between a team of retired Cuban all-stars managed by Fidel Castro and a similar Venezuelan team featuring Pres. Hugo Chávez at first base; Cuba wins 17–6.

29 Volker Braun, a poet from the former East Germany, is awarded the Georg Büchner Prize, considered by many to be the top award in German literature.

•

Local elections in Brazil bring the leftist Workers' Party to power in several major cities, including São Paulo, where party candidate Marta Suplicy is elected mayor.

•

Pres. Ben Mkapa of Tanzania is reelected to a five-year term, and Amani Abeid Karume is elected president of Zanzibar; the elections in Zanzibar, however, are widely viewed as fraudulent.

30 Spanish Supreme Court Judge José Francisco Querol Lombardero, as well as his driver and bodyguard, are killed by a car bomb in Madrid; it is believed that the Basque separatist group Euskadi Ta Askatasuna is responsible. (*See* October 26.)

•

Ferocious storms that began the night before lash European coasts from southern England to Scandinavia, causing several deaths and immense property damage.

31 Stung by French reports that call his country a haven for money launderers, Prince Rainier of Monaco declares that treaties between France and Monaco should be reworked in order to grant full sovereignty to Monaco.

•

Pope John Paul II proclaims Sir Thomas More, an English humanist and statesman who was canonized in 1935, the Roman Catholic patron saint of politicians; More was decapitated in 1535.

November

The American people have now spoken, but it's going to take a little while to determine exactly what they said.

U.S. Pres. Bill Clinton on November 8, the day after the U.S. presidential election and six weeks before the winner was known

1 The General Assembly of the United Nations admits Yugoslavia as a member eight years after ruling that, since four of its six constituent republics had seceded, it had to reapply for membership as a new state.

•

Formal ceremonies mark the beginning of the official celebration of the 200th anniversary of the White House, which was first occupied by U.S. Pres. John Adams in 1800 (Print, right, from 1807.)

Hulton Getty/Stone

2 Chess world champion Garry Kasparov loses his title to a former protégé, Vladimir Kramnik; observers feel that Kasparov's play in the tournament was uncharacteristically weak.

•

Members of an expedition in Turkey announce the discovery of a well-preserved 1,500-year-old wooden ship under the waters of the Black Sea, the fourth find in recent months; researchers are seeking evidence for a theory that the Black Sea was at one time a freshwater lake and was later inundated with salt water.

3 The U.K.'s High Court rules that the involuntary exile of the indigenous population of the Chagos Archipelago by the British government in the late 1960s was illegal and that the people affected may resettle; the islands were evacuated because of their strategic Indian Ocean location.

•

American media giant Viacom Inc. announces that it will buy BET Holdings, the 10th largest African American-owned company in the U.S. and the owner of Black Entertainment Television, for a total of about $3 billion, including assumption of $570 million in debts.

4 Arguably the most extravagant opera production ever takes place when the China Shanghai International Festival of the Arts stages Giuseppe Verdi's *Aïda* in a sports stadium with a cast of thousands as well as elephants, camels, lions, tigers, a panther, and a boa constrictor.

•

Max Nicholson, the father of the British environmental movement, supervises a census of birds in London's Kensington Gardens that he pioneered in 1925; the census's findings show that the number of house sparrows has dropped from 2,603 in 1925 to 8 in 2000.

5 In its biggest electoral victory since 1990, the Sandinista National Liberation Front in Nicaragua wins municipal elections in Managua, the capital; the Sandinista candidate for mayor, Herty Lewites, wins the ballot by a 15% margin.

•

In parliamentary elections in Azerbaijan, the ruling New Azerbaijan Party wins 17 of the 25 contested seats; international observers consider the balloting flawed, however.

•

The body of Emperor Haile Selassie I of Ethiopia, who died—or was killed—in 1975, is ceremonially reburied in a marble tomb in Holy Trinity Cathedral in Addis Ababa.

•

The New York City Marathon is won by Abdel Kader el-Mouaziz of Morocco with a time of 2 hr 10 min 8 sec; Lyudmila Petrova of Russia, with a time of 2 hr 25 min 45 sec, is the first woman across the finish line.

•

Iraqi Airways resumes domestic civilian flights; these flights had been suspended since the Persian Gulf War in 1991.

6 The Anglo-Australian mining group Rio Tinto, Ltd., wins the bidding for Australian diamond-mining concern Ashton Mining, Ltd., against rival De Beers of South Africa.

•

After the U.S. Food and Drug Administration announces that it will seek to end the use in drugs of phenylpropanolamine, which is associated with a slight risk of stroke, manufacturers and pharmacists rush to remove many popular cold remedies from the market.

7 The U.S. presidential election arrives at a statistical tie between Vice Pres. Al Gore and Gov. George W. Bush of Texas; although Gore wins the popular vote nationally, the tally of votes in the electoral college, which legally determines the winner, hinges on Florida, where the results are too close to call. (*See* November 26.)

•

In London the Booker Prize for literature is awarded to Canadian Margaret Atwood for *The Blind Assassin*.

•

Surgeons in Manchester, Eng., separate conjoined twin girls born August 8 to parents from Malta; as expected, the twin that lacked the ability to live on her own dies, but the prognosis for the surviving girl is good. (*See* September 22.)

8 The South Korean conglomerate Daewoo Motor Co. is forced into bankruptcy when creditors, in response to the refusal of labour unions to accept job cuts, halt the cash flow to the company.

•

The director of CERN, the European Organization for Nuclear Research in Geneva, announces that the Large Electron-Positron Collider will be shut down; many believed that the CERN facility provided the best chance to accomplish a top scientific quest, confirming the existence of the Higgs boson, a hypothetical subatomic particle.

•

The French Senate passes a bill, approved by the National Assembly in May, stating that the Ottoman Empire was guilty of genocide against Armenians in 1915; Turkey condemns the move.

9 The General Assembly of the United Nations votes to condemn the U.S. embargo against Cuba for the ninth consecutive year; the margin of votes against the embargo is the largest yet.

•

U.S. Pres. Bill Clinton creates the Vermilion Cliffs National Monument in Arizona north of the Grand Canyon and expands the Craters of the Moon National Monument in Idaho by 267,500 ha (661,000 ac). (*See* July 18 and December 4.)

•

In observance of the anniversary of Kristallnacht, the night of Nazi violence against the Jews in 1938, hundreds of thousands of people march in German cities protesting neo-Nazis and recent attacks on immigrants and synagogues.

•

Ruth Simmons is named president of Brown University, Providence, R.I.; she will be the first African American to head an Ivy League university.

10 In Haiti 16 former soldiers and paramilitary personnel are found guilty of having perpetrated a massacre in the slum of Raboteau in 1994.

•

For the first time, it becomes possible to register Internet domain names in Chinese, Japanese, and Korean.

11 A fire breaks out in a cable car carrying at least 180 skiers through a tunnel to a glacier ski run near Kaprun, Austria; nearly all the passengers are killed.

•

President Clinton, former U.S. senator Bob Dole, and actor Tom Hanks symbolically break ground (by shoveling dirt from a box) for the National World War II Memorial in Washington, D.C.; a court injunction bars actual construction until the arguments of those opposed to the location of the memorial can be heard. (*See* September 11.)

12 OPEC chooses as its new secretary-general Ali Rodríguez Araque, the oil minister of Venezuela.

•

In India the Congress (I) party elects as its leader Sonia Gandhi, widow of former prime minister Rajiv Gandhi, who was assassinated in 1991.

13 The House of Representatives of the Philippines formally impeaches Pres. Joseph Estrada; the four articles of impeachment concern bribery, corruption, violation of public trust, and violation of the constitution. (*See* October 11 and December 7.)

•

Pres. Jiang Zemin of China arrives in Cambodia for the first visit of a Chinese head of state in that country in more than three decades; the previous day he had become the first Chinese president ever to visit Laos.

•

Montenegro, one of the two constituent republics of Yugoslavia, makes the Deutsche Mark the sole legal tender in the republic, replacing Yugoslavia's own currency, the dinar.

14 The city of Pusan, S.Kor., announces plans to build what it believes will be the world's tallest building, Lotte World II, which will be 107 stories and 464.5 m (1,524 ft) tall and house an amusement park; it is scheduled to be completed in 2005.

•

Martin Macwan, founder of the National Campaign on Dalit Human Rights, an Indian organization that supports the rights of Dalits, or untouchables, is honoured by the Human Rights Watch organization; on November 21 Macwan also receives the Robert F. Kennedy Human Rights Award.

•

Joining the wave of panic over "mad cow" disease that has been sweeping Europe for weeks, the French government bans the sale of T-bone steaks; French chefs have been declining to make beef dishes, and Italian municipalities have been banning beef from school menus.

15 The Southern Cross Cable Network, at 30,000 km (18,000 mi) the world's longest fibre-optic cable—connecting Australia, New Zealand, Fiji, and the U.S. state of Hawaii to the West Coast of the United States—goes live.

•

President Clinton arrives in Brunei, the first stop of a farewell tour of Asia; on December 16 he flies to Hanoi; he is the first U.S. president to visit Vietnam since 1969 and the first ever to visit Hanoi.

•

The National Book Awards are presented to Susan Sontag for her fiction work *In America,* Nathaniel Philbrick for his nonfiction book *In the Heart of the Sea,* Lucille Clifton for her poetry collection *Blessing the Boats,* and Gloria Whelan for her young-adult book *Homeless Bird;* science-fiction writer Ray Bradbury is given a medal for distinguished contribution to American letters.

•

Indian movie star Rajkumar, kidnapped by notorious bandit Veerappan on July 30, is released unharmed, though it appears that most of Veerappan's demands have not been met; India rejoices. (See August 11.) (Photo right.)

AP/Wide World Photos

16 The board of the Internet Corporation for Assigned Names and Numbers votes to add seven new possible suffixes for domain names: .biz, for businesses; .coop, for cooperatives; .museum, for museums; .aero, for aviation; .info, for general information; .pro, for professionals; and .name, for individuals; they should be operational in summer 2001.

•

The Acela Express, Amtrak's first high-speed train, makes its inaugural run from Washington, D.C., to Boston in 2 hours 26 minutes.

•

The Coca-Cola Co. settles a racial discrimination lawsuit, agreeing to pay $192.5 million, make broad changes, and allow an outside panel to monitor its behaviour; it is the largest such settlement in history.

17 The Thunderbolt roller coaster at Coney Island, New York City, is demolished; the coaster had been built in 1926 and last operated in 1983.

•

In Colorado a man who killed another man in a skiing accident in 1997 is convicted of criminally negligent homicide; it is the first time a skier has faced criminal charges for such a death.

18 The French government notifies holders of czarist-era Russian government bonds, worthless since the October Revolution in 1917, that they can now redeem those bonds.

•

Ground is broken in Shanghai on a computer-chip factory that is a joint venture between Jiang Mianheng, the son of Chinese Pres. Jiang Zemin, and Winston Wang, the son of the chairman of Taiwan's Formosa Plastics.

19 India announces that it will unilaterally suspend military operations in Kashmir throughout Ramadan, the Muslim holy month.

•

American chef Julia Child is awarded the Legion of Honour by France in a ceremony in Boston.

20 Pres. Alberto Fujimori of Peru faxes a letter of resignation from Tokyo; the following day the legislature refuses to accept his resignation and deposes him instead. (*See* November 22.)

•

The Banco do Estado de São Paulo, Braz., is privatized when Banco Santander Central Hispano wins the auction to buy it for the highest price—some $3.6 billion—ever paid for a state bank in South America.

•

Great Britain's Royal Botanic Gardens, Kew, formally opens the Millennium Seed Bank at Wakehurst Place, West Sussex, with the goal of collecting and conserving seeds from 10% of the world's wild seed-bearing plant species in order to safeguard them against extinction.

21 A group of armed gunmen robs a branch of the National Bank of Egypt in Maragha and flees with more than a quarter million dollars; the bandits fire at random as they drive away, and a total of 13 people die in the raid.

•

More than one-third of the Australian state of New South Wales is covered with mud and water from 13 flooded rivers; the floods are called the worst in the region in 40 years.

•

The United Farm Workers calls off the boycott of California table grapes called in 1984 by union organizer Cesar Chavez, saying the goals of the strike have been met.

•

The U.S. Fish and Wildlife Service announces that it will be unable to add to the endangered species list this year because its resources are tied up defending lawsuits brought by environmentalist groups seeking to create critical habitat designations.

22 Moderate opposition legislator Valentín Paniagua is sworn in as interim president of Peru; he names former UN secretary-general Javier Pérez de Cuellar prime minister. (*See* November 20.)

•

The U.S. Drug Enforcement Administration approves a plan to assess the usefulness of marijuana in relieving pain and increasing appetite in AIDS patients; in the study 60 such patients are to be given government-grown marijuana.

•

A United Nations report sponsored by the World Health Organization and the United Nations Children's Fund says that 40% of the world's people lack basic sanitation and one-sixth of the population has no access to a water supply.

23 The European Court of Human Rights, sitting at Strasbourg, France, rules that Constantine II, former king of Greece, and his family are entitled to compensation for real property seized when he was dethroned in 1974 and his holdings formally confiscated by the government of Greece in 1994.

•

A spokesman for Mozambique says that 82 prisoners died mysteriously on November 21 in the town of Montepuez; many of them had been jailed after antigovernment riots two weeks previously.

24 *Science* magazine reports that scientists from Cornell University, Ithaca, N.Y., have created a working "nanomachine"; a submicroscopic motor powered by organic molecules drives an equally tiny propeller.

•

An attempt by Gen. Ansumane Mane to overthrow his erstwhile partner, Pres. Kumba Ialá of Guinea-Bissau, is suppressed. (*See* November 30.)

25 Slobodan Milosevic is reelected head of the Socialist Party of Serbia; he had emerged from his postelection seclusion only a few days earlier. (*See* October 6.)

•

The UN World Climate Change Conference, meeting in The Hague, ends without agreement after two weeks of negotiation between the U.S. and the European Union on greenhouse gas issues.

26 Florida Secretary of State Katherine Harris certifies that George W. Bush has won the presidential election in that state by a margin of 537 out of approximately 6,000,000 votes cast, taking Florida's 25 electoral votes; Al Gore immediately contests the count. (*See* November 7 and December 8.)

•

Haitian elections draw a light turnout and a boycott by the opposition, and they are neither financed nor observed by the international community; on November 29 former president Jean-Bertrand Aristide is declared the winner, with a margin of almost 92%.

•

The electorate in Switzerland votes overwhelmingly against cutting spending on the traditionally neutral country's unusually large military.

27 In elections in Canada, Prime Minister Jean Chrétien and his Liberal Party beat out the rightist Canadian Alliance, led by Stockwell Day; it is the first time since World War II that a prime minister has won a third consecutive election.

•

The giant General Electric Co. announces that Jeffrey Immelt, head of GE Medical Systems, will succeed Jack Welch as president and CEO when Welch retires in April 2001.

•

The Lærdal Tunnel, at 24.5 km (15.2 mi) the world's longest, opens to traffic in Norway, allowing travelers to go from Oslo to Bergen without traversing mountains.

28 Israeli Prime Minister Ehud Barak surprises opponents in the Knesset (parliament), who are preparing to vote him out, by calling for new elections.

•

French composer Pierre Boulez is awarded the 2001 Grawemeyer Award for Music Composition of the University of Louisville, Ky., for his chamber piece *Sur incises;* the award is considered the top international music composition prize.

29 It is reported that novelist Stephen King has decided to suspend serialization of *The Plant,* which he had been publishing on his World Wide Web site and asking readers to pay for on the honour system; a diminishing number of people, King says, have been making the requested payment.

•

The Coca-Cola Co. formally donates 50 years of television advertising and related materials to the Library of Congress as part of the observance of the library's bicentennial.

30 Gen. Ansumane Mane, the leader of the opposition in Guinea-Bissau as well as a former president, is killed in a scuffle with government troops north of Bissau, the capital. (*See* November 24.)

•

A spokesman for the municipality of Bethlehem says the city is canceling its traditional Christmas celebration owing to the ongoing violence between Israelis and Palestinians; previously Bethlehem had expected a record number of tourists this year.

•

The KunstHaus in Vienna opens an exhibit of the work of Friedensreich Hundertwasser entitled "Hated—Built—Loved: From Utopia to Reality," which includes some 20 scale models of the architect's international projects; Hundertwasser, famed for his iconoclastic, fairy-tale structures, died in February 2000.

•

Queen Elizabeth II of the United Kingdom names her daughter, Princess Anne, Lady of the Order of the Thistle because of her close ties to Scotland.

December

He who wins by injustice may dominate the present day, but history will always judge him to be a shameful loser. There can be no exception.

Kim Dae Jung, on accepting the Nobel Prize for Peace in Oslo, December 10

1 Vicente Fox Quesada is inaugurated as president of Mexico, ending the dominance of the Institutional Revolutionary Party, which had ruled since 1929.

•

Chinese officials confirm rumours that Gao Changli, the minister of justice, was removed from office in the past week; they make no comments on the reports that say Gao is under investigation for corruption.

•

Charges of kidnappings are brought against former Chilean dictator Augusto Pinochet Ugarte, and his arrest is ordered in Chile. (*See* August 8.)

•

The U.S. Army announces that it has destroyed the last of the chemical weapons stockpiled on Johnston Island, a coral reef about 1,330 km (825 mi) southwest of Hawaii, and has begun a three-year cleanup of the depot.

•

Civil rights pioneer Rosa Parks attends a ceremony opening the Rosa Parks Library and Museum in Montgomery, Ala., and she is awarded the first Governor's Medal of Honor for Extraordinary Courage.

2 Indonesian troops open fire on independence supporters in the secessionist province of Irian Jaya (West Papua). (*See* June 2.)

•

The popular and highly successful alternative rock band Smashing Pumpkins holds its last concert, in Chicago, before breaking up after 13 years together.

3 The annual Kennedy Center Honors Gala celebrates the artistic contributions of tenor Plácido Domingo, rocker Chuck Berry, actress Angela Lansbury, dancer Mikhail Baryshnikov, and actor Clint Eastwood.

•

Brazilian Gustavo Kuerten wins the Masters Cup in Lisbon and thereby attains the number one tennis ranking for the year.

•

Sandra Baldwin is elected president of the U.S. Olympic Committee; she is the first woman to hold this position.

4 PepsiCo Inc. concludes a deal to purchase the Quaker Oats Co. for about $13.4 billion in stock; the deal brings the popular sports drink Gatorade to PepsiCo, a leader in carbonated beverage brands as well as the owner of Tropicana juices and Lipton teas.

•

U.S. Pres. Bill Clinton creates the Northwestern Hawaiian Islands Coral Reef Ecosystem Reserve, at 341,360 sq km (131,800 sq mi)—all underwater—the largest nature reserve in the nation. (*See* November 9.)

5 Pentagon investigators conclude that large numbers of unarmed Korean civilians were killed by U.S. forces at No Gun Ri in 1950, although the exact number killed and the reason for the incident remain unclear.

6 The French Internet service provider Wanadoo (a unit of France Télécom) agrees to buy the troubled British Internet service provider Freeserve to create the second largest such company in Europe.

•

At a time when many nations around the world are lowering their spending on defense, Australia plans to increase defense spending in light of the increased peacekeeping role being played in the Pacific region by Australian armed forces.

•

Mei Xiang and Tian Tian, two giant pandas on long-term loan from China, arrive at the National Zoological Park in Washington, D.C.

•

Queen Elizabeth II formally opens the Great Court, the redesigned centre of the British Museum in London.

7 *Nature* magazine reports that a study of mitochondrial DNA from 53 people of diverse ethnic and geographic backgrounds indicates that the human race originated in Africa and that migration from Africa did not begin until 52,000 years ago.

•

The impeachment trial of Philippine Pres. Joseph Estrada opens in the Senate chamber in a suburb of Manila. (*See* November 13.)

•

Officials in California declare a stage-three power alert, the first ever in the state, as electricity reserves drop to dangerous levels.

•

Construction begins on the Millennium Ribble Link, the first canal to be built in England in 150 years; the 6.5-km (4-mi) canal will have nine locks and link the Lancaster Canal with the River Ribble.

•

The 45th annual Asia-Pacific Film Festival opens in Hanoi, Vietnam; 450 delegates from 17 countries are in attendance to view 57 films entered into competition.

8 The Florida Supreme Court rules that ballots in some Florida counties must be hand counted in order to determine the winner of the U.S. presidential election in Florida and thus the winner of Florida's electoral college votes, necessary to win the presidency; Republican candidate George W. Bush appeals the decision. (*See* November 26 and December 12.)

•

An attack by a member of an outlawed fundamentalist Muslim sect kills 20 people at Friday prayers at a mosque in Khartoum, The Sudan.

•

The Russian parliament votes to restore the old Soviet national anthem with new lyrics as the new national anthem of Russia to replace the wordless song by Mikhail Glinka that has been the Russian national anthem since 1990; the change becomes official on December 30.

9 Prime Minister Ehud Barak announces his resignation, forcing new elections in Israel, probably in early February 2001.

•

The Heisman Trophy goes to Chris Weinke, a quarterback for the Florida State University Seminoles; the 28-year-old is the oldest player ever to win the trophy.

10 The Nobel Prizes are presented in ceremonies in Stockholm and Oslo.

•

In parliamentary elections in Côte d'Ivoire, the Ivorian Popular Party, the party of Pres. Laurent Gbagbo, wins 96 of the 225 seats; a boycott by Alassane Ouattara's Rally of Republicans party means that the seats for representatives of the Muslim north will remain vacant. (*See* October 25.)

•

In a runoff presidential election, former president Ion Iliescu of the leftist Social Democratic Party of Romania handily defeats Corneliu Vadim Tudor of the nationalist extremist Greater Romania Party; Tudor characterizes the results as "a victory of the Antichrist."

•

Spain clinches its first-ever Davis Cup international team tennis championship, knocking off Australia three matches to one (with a dead fifth match not played).

•

Former prime minister Mohammed Nawaz Sharif, who had been convicted of abuse of power as well as kidnapping and hijacking in connection with the coup in Pakistan in 1999, is released from prison and flown into exile in Saudi Arabia. (*See* April 6.)

11 Parliamentary elections in Trinidad and Tobago result in a narrow victory for the United National Congress, the party of Prime Minister Basdeo Panday.

•

Zinedine Zidane, a French midfielder who plays for Juventus of Turin, Italy, is named Player of the Year by FIFA, the world association football (soccer) governing body; the Algerian-born Zidane won the award in 1998 as well.

•

Alex Rodriguez, shortstop for the Texas Rangers professional baseball team, nails down the largest contract in sports history; the team agrees to pay him $252 million over a 10-year period, more than doubling the previous record contract (Kevin Garnett of basketball's Minnesota Timberwolves in 1997).

12 ***In a complex and divided decision, the U.S. Supreme Court rules that, though Florida ballots should be hand counted, there are inadequate standards for such a count and there is insufficient time in which to perform it; in effect, the decision grants victory in the presidential election to George W. Bush. (See December 8 and December 18.) (Photo below.)***

William Philpott/Archive Photos

•

In Algiers Ethiopian Prime Minister Meles Zenawi and Eritrean Pres. Isaias Afwerki sign a treaty to end their countries' destructive two-year border war; UN Secretary-General Kofi Annan and U.S. Secretary of State Madeleine Albright are among the observers.

•

Spanish novelist, critic, and newspaper columnist Francisco Umbral is named the 2000 recipient of the Cervantes Prize, the highest honour in Spanish-language letters.

•

General Motors announces plans to phase out production of the Oldsmobile; first produced in 1897, Oldsmobile is the oldest American automobile brand.

13 It is announced in Washington that an international 22-member team has discovered the source of the Amazon River, Carhuasanta Creek on Nevado Mismi mountain in Peru, some 6,400 km (4,000 mi) from its mouth on the Atlantic Ocean.

•

The U.S. Equal Employment Opportunity Commission rules that employers that provide insurance coverage for preventive medicines should also provide coverage for contraceptive drugs and devices.

•

Patrick McEnroe replaces his brother, John, as captain of the American Davis Cup tennis team.

14 Russian Pres. Vladimir Putin pardons Edmond Pope, an American businessman who on December 6 had been sentenced to 20 years in prison for espionage.

•

Minister of Culture and Islamic Guidance Ataollah Mohajerani, known for having liberalized press and artistic freedoms in Iran, is removed from office.

15 On the order of Ukrainian Pres. Leonid Kuchma, the Chernobyl nuclear station is powered down and officially closed. (*See* June 5.)

•

Botanists in Australia report that they have found a stand of "living fossil" trees of the genus *Eidothea* in a remote area about 640 km (400 mi) north of Sydney; a similar discovery of a different genus of trees also believed to be unchanged since prehistoric times was reported in the Blue Mountains west of Sydney in 1994.

•

The Academy of American Poets announces that the Wallace Stevens Award for poetry will be given to Frank Bidart.

16 George W. Bush names retired general Colin Powell to be his secretary of state when he takes office as president of the United States in January; if confirmed, Powell will be the first African American to hold that post.

•

The Mousetrap, the longest-running play in England, is performed for the 20,000th time; based on an Agatha Christie story, the play opened in the West End in 1952 and has employed 318 actors in the eight roles in the play.

•

The findings of the *Galileo* spacecraft that suggest that there is water under ice on Jupiter's moon Ganymede are reported to the American Geophysical Union; previous findings had suggested the presence of water on Europa and Callisto.

17 Two Teamsters local unions ratify contracts with the *Detroit News* and the *Detroit Free Press*, ending a dispute that lasted five and one-half years.

18 Members of the electoral college from Nevada have the honour of formally electing George W. Bush to the U.S. presidency when they bring the total electoral vote cast for the Republican candidate to 271, one more than needed for victory. (*See* December 12.)

•

Popocatépetl, a volcano near Mexico City, produces what observers believe is its biggest eruption in centuries and the fourth major eruption in the past 5,000 years.

•

Aetna Inc., the biggest health insurance company in the United States, announces plans to raise premiums, drop two million customers, and lay off 5,000 workers; on the same day, the Gillette Co. announces plans to close eight factories and lay off 8% of its workforce in January 2001.

19 The UN Security Council imposes a harsh embargo on the Taliban, the de facto rulers of Afghanistan; Secretary-General Kofi Annan and aid workers in Afghanistan, both UN-affiliated and private, oppose the move.

•

The Guatemalan legislature approves a plan to use the U.S. dollar in everyday business while keeping the quetzal as the official currency of the country.

•

Airbus Industrie's A380 superjumbo jet program is formally launched in Toulouse, France; the double-decker aircraft will be the largest passenger plane in the air, seating up to 555 passengers in cruise-ship-style luxury. (Photo below.)

APF Worldwide

20 Indian authorities announce plans to extend the unilateral Ramadan cease-fire in Kashmir for another month; Pakistan responds by announcing a partial withdrawal of its troops in the area.

•

U.S. Pres. Bill Clinton issues rules that require that medical providers obtain the consent of patients before releasing medical information pertaining to those patients.

•

The second Charles Ives Living award, the largest award for musical composition, is given to Chen Yi, a prolific Chinese-born American composer; recipients of the award are required to forswear employment other than composition for a three-year period.

21 Military contractor Northrop Grumman agrees to buy Litton Industries, a builder of military ships and information systems.

•

Zimbabwe's Supreme Court rules that Pres. Robert Mugabe must produce a workable plan for land reform within six months, indicating that, while land redistribution is necessary, simply seizing the land from the owners is unconstitutional.

22 The World Bank and the International Monetary Fund announce that the world's industrial powers, including the United States, Japan, and many European countries, have agreed to forgive the debts of 22 of the world's poorest countries.

•

Three American teenagers, sons of U.S. Army personnel stationed in Germany, are convicted of murder in Hessen, Ger., for a February incident in which they dropped rocks from a pedestrian overpass onto a highway in Darmstadt, killing two motorists.

23 The United Nations completes the first major reform of its budget in nearly 30 years; one of the changes reduces the percentage of both the administrative and the peacekeeping budgets that the U.S. is responsible for.

24 Viswanathan Anand of India defeats Aleksey Shirov of Spain to become the Fédération Internationale des Échecs world champion, replacing Aleksandr Khalifman in the position, in Tehran; Anand declines to say whether he plans to play Vladimir Kramnik, who became the Brain Games Network world champion in November.

•

On Christmas Eve in Bethlehem, Manger Square is dark and the new hotels almost empty; tourism, the major industry in the West Bank Israeli town, has been choked off since October, when the Israeli army sealed the area.

25 A partial eclipse of the Sun is visible throughout most of North America; there will not be another Christmas Day solar eclipse until 2307.

•

Pres. Jiang Zemin of China and Pres. Tran Duc Luong of Vietnam sign an agreement demarcating the border between the countries in the Gulf of Tonkin, the culmination of years of negotiation.

26 Thailand's new official anticorruption commission rules that the leading candidate for the January 2001 elections for prime minister has engaged in financial wrongdoing; the following day a member of the commission itself resigns after admitting failure to disclose assets.

•

The Seventh World Zoroastrian Congress opens with two days of athletic contests followed by five days of meetings and educational and arts programs in Houston, Texas; it is the first time the world congress has taken place outside Asia.

•

An employee of Edgewater Technology Inc. in Wakefield, Mass., murders seven of his fellow employees in a workplace rampage.

27 Muslims worldwide begin the three-day celebration of Eid al-Fitr, the end of Ramadan.

•

Peru's legislature passes a law to change the legislative system from one of all at-large representatives to one of representation based on geographic districts.

•

Hockey Hall of Fame member Mario Lemieux, one of the best players in the game, returns to the ice as the player-owner of the Pittsburgh Penguins for the first time since his retirement on April 27, 1997; he scores one goal and makes two assists.

28 Montgomery Ward & Co., Inc., an icon in American catalog sales and retailing since its beginnings in 1872, announces that it will close its 250 remaining stores and file for bankruptcy.

•

In a runoff election necessitated by the results of the election held December 7 in Ghana, John Agyekum Kufuor defeats John Atta Mills, the candidate supported by Jerry Rawlings, for the presidency; Rawlings had held power since 1982.

•

At the end of a three-day meeting in Tehran, top military leaders from Russia and Iran agree on an expanded military and security cooperation agreement; relations between the two countries had been cool and low-key since the 1979 Islamic Revolution in Iran.

•

The U.S. Census Bureau reports that the population of the United States topped 281 million in 2000, with the fastest growth rate recorded in the South and West.

29 In a suburb of Tehran, a soccer brawl spreads off the fields and into the streets, resulting in damage to 250 buses and the arrest of at least 60 people; one team owner blames increased soccer violence on the ban on women's attendance at soccer games.

30 In the third session of a closed-door trial in Tehran, a former head of internal security, Mostafa Kazemi, confesses to having masterminded the killings of dissident writers and intellectuals.

•

The biggest meeting of the philosophical community, the three-day annual meeting of the American Philosophical Association, Eastern Division, attended by some 3,000 philosophers, wraps up in New York City.

31 Five bombs go off in scattered locations around Manila, killing at least 14 people.

•

After a full year of utterly failing to live up to its publicity, the Millennium Dome in Greenwich, London, closes.

Disasters

The following list records the **MAJOR DISASTERS** that occured in 2000. Events included in this feature involved the loss of **15 OR MORE LIVES** and/or significant damage to property.

Aviation

January 13, Off the coast of Libya. A twin-engine jet en route from Tripoli to Marsa al-Burayqah, Libya, plunged into the sea about 10 km (6 mi) short of its destination; 22 of the 41 persons aboard the craft were killed.

January 30, Off the coast of Côte d'Ivoire. A Kenya Airways jet bound for Lagos, Nigeria, went down in the Atlantic Ocean shortly after takeoff from Abidjan, Côte d'Ivoire; 169 persons died, and 10 persons survived the crash.

January 31, Off the coast of southern California. En route from Puerto Vallarta, Mex., to San Francisco, Alaska Airlines Flight 261 plummeted into the Pacific Ocean; all 88 persons aboard the MD-83 jetliner were killed.

Early February, Lubango, Angola. An overloaded military helicopter that was carrying 37 persons, well over its capacity, crashed soon after takeoff and burst into flames; at least 30 persons perished.

March 30, Near Anuradhapura, Sri Lanka. While attempting to land, an air force plane crashed after one of its engines caught fire; 36 soldiers and 4 crew members died.

April 8, Marana, Ariz. A U.S. Marine Corps V-22 Osprey tilt-rotor aircraft carrying 19 persons crashed on a training mission while landing at an airfield; there were no survivors.

April 19, Near Davao, Phil. In what was the worst aviation disaster in the history of the Philippines, a Boeing 737-200 slammed into a coconut plantation on Samal Island, killing all 131 persons aboard; while there was no immediate word on what caused the crash, the airliner apparently encountered foggy conditions as it was making its approach to the airport in Davao.

May 21, Near Wilkes-Barre, Pa. A twin-engine charter plane en route from Atlantic City, N.J., to Wilkes-Barre with 19 persons on board crashed after both engines failed; there were no survivors.

June 22, Central China. While flying through a thunderstorm, a Chinese airliner was struck by lightning and went down in Hubei province; all 42 persons aboard the craft were killed.

July 8, Southern Mexico. After encountering bad weather, a passenger plane crashed in a heavily wooded area in Chiapas state; all 19 persons on board died.

July 17, Patna, India. A Boeing 737-200 crashed into houses during its second landing attempt at Patna, killing 51 persons aboard the craft and 4 on the ground; 7 persons on the plane survived.

July 21, Near St. Petersburg. A Russian air force helicopter crashed in a military airfield shortly after takeoff; 19 persons died.

July 25, Near Paris. A Concorde jet en route from Paris to New York City suffered engine failure shortly after takeoff, burst into flames, and crashed into a small hotel and restaurant; all 109 persons on board, including 100 passengers and 9 crew members, died; 4 people on the ground were also killed.

July 27, Western Nepal. A small passenger plane carrying 25 persons crashed while attempting to land in bad weather; there were no survivors.

August 12, Kasai-Occidental province, Democratic Republic of the Congo. An airliner developed engine problems after takeoff and crashed, killing 26 persons.

August 23, Off the coast of Bahrain. An Airbus A320 en route from Cairo to Manama, Bahrain, crashed into the Persian Gulf after one of its engines caught fire; all 143 persons aboard the plane were killed.

September 16, Sri Lanka. An air force helicopter en route from Colombo to Amparai crashed into a hill and exploded; 15 persons were killed, including Sri Lankan Ports Minister M.H.M. Ashraff.

October 25, Western Georgia. A Russian military plane with 75 persons aboard crashed into a mountain while attempting to land in bad weather; there were no survivors.

October 31, Taipei, Taiwan. A Singapore Airlines jumbo jet with 179 persons aboard crashed while taking off and burst into flames; 82 persons died.

October 31 and November 15, Angola. Two Soviet-built Antonov planes crashed in separate incidents; on October 31 an Antonov An-26 crashed in a remote jungle area shortly after takeoff, killing all 48 persons aboard; on November 15 an Antonov An-24 slammed into a field after takeoff and exploded, killing at least 40 persons.

Fires and Explosions

February–March, Southern Nigeria. On February 7 a group of people in the village of Ogwe were illegally siphoning off fuel from an oil pipeline when a young man in the crowd struck a match, igniting an explosion that claimed the lives of at least 15 persons. In a similar incident on March 22, a large number of people were sabotaging an oil pipeline in Isioma when the pipeline caught fire, killing at least 50 persons.

March 9, Tuvalu. A fire in a locked dormitory of a boarding school on Vaitupu atoll claimed the lives of at least 17 schoolgirls and one of the school's female staff members.

March 28, Guangdong province, China. An explosion at a cigarette lighter factory claimed the lives of 17 persons.

Fire trails from the engine of a Concorde jet on July 25 at Charles de Gaulle Airport near Paris; the plane crashed shortly after takeoff.

AP/Wide World Photos

March 29, Henan province, China. A fire swept through a pornographic movie theatre whose front doors had been locked with a steel grille to prevent police from entering; of those persons trapped inside, at least 74 perished.

April 14, Kinshasa, Democratic Republic of the Congo. A series of explosions occurred at a military fuel and munitions depot located at the airport in Kinshasa; 109 persons were killed, and more than 200 were injured; as to what caused the blasts, there were conflicting accounts, including reports of a warehouse fire, sabotage by political dissidents, and a military plane crash.

May 13, Enschede, Neth. A fire broke out inside a large fireworks warehouse, setting off multiple explosions that killed at least 20 persons, injured some 950, and destroyed more than 400 homes in a nearby residential area; the owners of the warehouse were later arrested and charged with safety violations.

Late June, Jiangmen, China. A fire that began in a fireworks factory set off an explosion and spread to two other factories; 30 persons died, and 200 were injured.

Mid-July, Southern Nigeria. In two separate incidents, one in the city of Warri and the other in the village of Adeje, persons intent on stealing fuel ruptured an oil pipeline and triggered deadly explosions; at least 30 persons were killed in Warri, and more than 250 died at Adeje.

July 19, Tileran, Costa Rica. A fire, apparently caused by a short circuit, engulfed a retirement home, claiming the lives of 17 persons.

August 4, Jiangxi province, China. A blast in an apartment building where illegal fireworks were produced claimed the lives of at least 27 persons and injured 26 others.

September 8, Urumqi, China. A truck carrying explosives intended for disposal blew up on a highway, killing more than 60 persons and damaging more than 20 other vehicles and houses nearby.

October 20, Mexico City. An early-morning fire swept through one of the largest nightclubs in the city, destroying the building and claiming the lives of at least 20 persons; the fire apparently was ignited by short circuits in the nightclub's electrical system.

November 11, Near Kaprun, Austria. A fire in an Alpine mountain tunnel claimed the lives of at least 155 skiers who were traveling through the tunnel in a cable car; investigators suspected that the cable car may have caught fire before it entered the tunnel, but the cause of the fire was unclear.

November 30, Near Apapa, Nigeria. A group of people were collecting fuel from a ruptured pipeline when the liquid exploded into flames; between 30 and 60 persons died.

December 25, Luoyang, China. A fire swept through a crowded dance hall on the fourth floor of a commercial building, killing 309 persons; the disaster occurred one week after the building had failed a safety inspection.

Marine

January 16, Off the coast of the Dominican Republic. An overcrowded fishing boat, apparently bound for Puerto Rico with Dominican migrants aboard, capsized in the Mona Passage; at least 16 persons died.

February 12, Lake Albert, Eastern Africa. At least 45 persons lost their lives when a boat capsized on the lake, which borders Uganda and the Democratic Republic of the Congo.

Mid-March, Southern Bangladesh. An overcrowded ferry sank in the Sandhya River, killing at least 17 persons.

Late March, Nowshera, Pak. A boat being pulled by a cable across the Kabul River overturned after the cable snapped in strong winds; at least 22 persons drowned, and 12 were missing and feared dead.

April 12, Southern Philippines. A cargo boat overloaded with passengers capsized off Jolo island; of the more than 200 persons aboard, at least 143 perished.

April 19, Southeastern Nigeria. A boat carrying some 500 persons, more than twice its capacity, sank on the Nembe River; all aboard were feared dead.

April 30, Off the coast of Tarifa, Spain. A small boat overloaded with passengers from Morocco who apparently were intent on entering Spain illegally sank in the Straits of Gibraltar; at least 20 persons died.

May 2, Eastern Bangladesh. In separate incidents on the Meghna River, two ferries sank after being caught in a storm; at least 73 persons died, and more than 100 were missing.

May 7, Eastern Indonesia. Large waves capsized an overcrowded ferry off the coast of Ambon island; at least 41 persons were killed.

June 22, Sichuan province, China. A ferry carrying some 221 passengers, more than twice its capacity, overturned on the Chang Jiang (Yangtze River) after striking rocks in heavy fog; more than 100 persons died.

June 29, Eastern Indonesia. A ferry overloaded with passengers fleeing fighting between Christians and Muslims in the Maluku Islands sank in heavy seas; of the some 500 persons aboard, only 10 survived.

Mid-July, Madhya Pradesh state, India. A ferry overturned during a storm on the Talperu River, killing at least 20 persons.

July 27, Near Dhaka, Bangladesh. A small ferry collided with a larger boat on the Buriganga River and sank; at least 50 persons lost their lives.

August 5, Off the coast of Nigeria. A boat overloaded with Nigerian traders bound for Cameroon capsized in a storm; at least 40 persons died.

August 12, Off the northern coast of Russia. A Russian nuclear submarine with 118 crew members on board suddenly plunged to the floor of the Barents Sea about 56 km (35 mi) offshore; Russian officials cited a collision as the cause of the accident, though Western experts believed a series of catastrophic explosions occurred in the submarine's torpedo bay; days later a team of Norwegian and British divers were able to open the rear escape hatch but found that the entire vessel had been flooded; there were no survivors.

August 23, Near Sinjah, The Sudan. An overloaded boat capsized on the Nile River; as many as 50 persons, mostly schoolchildren, were feared drowned.

September 4, Northwestern Uganda. A boat carrying about 50 passengers capsized on Lake Albert; 37 persons were missing and presumed dead.

September 26, Off the coast of Paros, Greece. A ferry en route from Athens to the island of Lipsoi struck a rocky outcrop and sank; at least 80 persons perished; the ship's captain, who admitted having been asleep before the collision, and four crew members were later arrested and charged with manslaughter.

October 21, Lake Malawi, Malawi. An overloaded boat capsized and sank during a storm; at least 17 persons drowned.

Mid-December, Off the northern coast of Australia. Two boats transporting more than 160 suspected illegal immigrants from Indonesia to Australia sank in stormy seas; all aboard the two vessels were feared drowned.

December 29, Southeastern Bangladesh. A collision in dense fog between two ferries on the Meghna River claimed the lives of at least 150 persons.

Mining and Construction

Early March, Near Koidu–New Sembehun, Sierra Leone. The collapse of an illegal diamond mine claimed the lives of some 150 persons.

March 11, Krasnodon, Ukraine. A powerful methane-gas explosion in the Barakova coal mine killed 82 miners; authorities stated that safety violations were to blame for the blast; the accident was the worst mining disaster in Ukraine since 1980.

Mid-June, China. In Sichuan province on June 16, a gas explosion in a mine claimed the lives of seven miners, and gas fumes killed five others who were attempting to rescue them. A day later in Henan province, another gas explosion occurred in a coal mine; seven miners died, and seven were missing.

July 19, Alexandria, Egypt. A six-story clothing factory collapsed after a fire, killing at least 15 persons and injuring 38.

September 2, Near Agra, India. A locomotive shed collapsed as it was being demolished, killing more than 25 persons, most of them workers at the site.

September 27, Guizhou province, China. A huge gas explosion ripped through a coal mine, killing some 150 miners.

Early October, Khogiani, Afg. The roof of a mud house where a wedding was taking place collapsed, killing at least 42 persons and injuring 15.

November 5, Jilin province, China. A gas explosion at a coal mine left 13 miners dead and 18 missing and feared dead.

November 26, Northern China. A gas explosion at a coal mine claimed the lives of 51 miners.

December 11, Guangxi province, China. A gold mine collapsed, killing at least 15 persons and injuring 4.

Natural

Early January, Northern India. A cold wave that swept across the Gangetic Plain left as many as 341 persons dead, including at least 211 in Bihar state.

Early January, Southeastern Brazil. Heavy rains triggered floods and landslides that claimed the lives of at least 28 persons, including 13 in Rio de Janeiro state, and left tens of thousands homeless.

January 20–23, Eastern Australia. A heat wave brought blistering temperatures to

Queensland state; 22 persons died, and more than 100 were hospitalized.

Late January–mid-March, Southern Africa. Torrential rains produced some of the worst flooding in the region in more than four decades. The hardest-hit country was Mozambique, where floods washed away some 200,000 homes before Cyclone Eline—with winds of up to 260 km/h (162 mph)—brought new rains on February 22. By mid-March the country's official death toll stood at 492, and countless others were missing. Eline moved on to strike Madagascar, which was also hit by Tropical Storm Gloria on March 4–5; the storms left at least 137 persons dead and some 500,000 homeless on the island. Other affected areas included South Africa's Northern and Mpumalanga provinces, where floods had claimed the lives of at least 70 persons by the end of February. Thousands of persons were also left homeless in Zimbabwe, Namibia, and southern Botswana.

Mid-February, Bangladesh. A cold wave accompanied by heavy fog swept across the country; 65 persons, most of whom were elderly, died.

February 14, Georgia. A series of tornadoes wreaked havoc in the southwestern portion of the U.S. state, claiming the lives of 18 persons, injuring more than 100, and damaging hundreds of homes and businesses.

May 4, Central Indonesia. An earthquake of magnitude 6.5 caused severe damage across Central Sulawesi province and Peleng and Banggai islands; the earthquake was followed by tidal waves, which flattened a number of coastal villages; at least 40 persons were killed, and some 15,000 homes and other buildings were destroyed.

Mid-May, West Timor, Indon. Severe floods caused by a combination of monsoon rain and a tidal surge claimed the lives of at least 140 persons and left some 20,000 homeless.

May 21, Southern Colombia. Flooding and mud slides were blamed in the deaths of at least 21 persons.

June 4, Sumatra, Indon. A magnitude-7.9 earthquake hit the southwestern part of the island; at least 120 persons were killed, and some 25,000 were left homeless.

Mid-June, Northeastern India. Heavy monsoon rains triggered floods that killed at least 20 persons in Assam and Arunachal Pradesh states.

Early July, Southeastern Europe. A heat wave scorched the region as hot air masses moved north from the Sahara desert; more than 50 persons died throughout the region.

July 12, Near Mumbai (Bombay). After days of heavy rain, a landslide destroyed a slum settlement north of the city; at least 80 persons died.

July 13, Shaanxi province, China. A huge mud slide buried numerous houses and knocked out electrical power in 10 towns; at least 119 persons died, and 29 were missing.

Mid-July, India. Heavy rains in Maharashtra, Gujarat, and Andhra Pradesh states produced floods that left some 140 persons dead.

July 21, Northern Vietnam. Landslides claimed the lives of at least 20 persons.

Late July–early August, Northeastern Brazil. Days of torrential rain caused mud slides that killed at least 56 persons and forced more than 100,000 from their homes.

Jay Directo/AFP Worldwide

Rescuers retrieve a body from the massive garbage dump that avalanched on a cluster of homes in Manila on July 10.

Late July–early October, Vietnam, Laos, and Cambodia. Unseasonably early and heavy monsoon rains contributed to the worst flooding in the Mekong Delta in 40 years; by October 8 at least 315 persons had died, among whom 232 were children.

August 22–23, East Asia. Two deadly storms wreaked havoc on the region; on August 22 Tropical Storm Kaemi killed 14 persons in Vietnam; a day later Typhoon Bilis claimed the lives of at least 11 persons and injured 80 others.

August 22–24, Southern India. Heavy rains and flooding in Andhra Pradesh state killed at least 70 persons, including 13 in Hyderabad, the state capital.

September 1, Southern China. Typhoon Maria swept through Guangdong and Hunan provinces; the storm claimed the lives of at least 47 persons and caused some $175 million in damage.

September–October, India and Bangladesh. Heavy monsoon rains set off widespread flooding in India's West Bengal state and in southwestern Bangladesh; more than 900 persons were killed in India, and some 150 persons died and about 5 million were left homeless in Bangladesh.

September 10, Southern Italy. A mud slide brought on by flash floods destroyed a campsite in the Calabria region; 11 persons were killed, and 4 were missing and feared dead.

Mid-September, Guatemala. Floods and mud slides occurred throughout the country after days of torrential rain; at least 19 persons lost their lives.

Mid-October, Italian and Swiss Alps. Extremely heavy rains set off floods and landslides in the mountainous region; at least 35 persons were killed.

Late October–November, Southeast Asia. Torrential monsoon rains triggered floods and landslides across the region; by the end of November, at least 119 persons had died in Indonesia, at least 51 had died in Malaysia, and some 20 persons had perished in Thailand.

November 1–2, Taiwan. Typhoon Xangsane triggered the worst flooding on the island in 30 years; the storm, which produced winds of up to 145 km/h (90 mph), pounded the island for two days; at least 58 persons died, and another 31 were missing.

November 3, Northern Philippines. Landslides and floods set off by Typhoon Bebinca claimed the lives of 40 persons, and at least 13 others were missing.

Early December, Northern Tanzania. The heaviest rains in eight years set off floods that killed at least 30 persons and left more than 600 homeless.

Railroad

January 4, Near Rena, Nor. In one of the worst railroad disasters in Norway's history, two passenger trains traveling at about 90 km/h (55 mph) collided head-on as they rounded a curve; 17 persons were confirmed dead, and several were missing.

March 1, Near Ksar el-Kebir, Mor. A collision between a passenger train and a vehicle transporting farm workers at a railway crossing claimed the lives of at least 35 persons.

August 20, Near Nairobi, Kenya. Nine train cars—six of them carrying liquefied gas—became detached from a freight train and derailed, igniting an explosion in which 25 persons were killed.

October 11, Near Hwange, Zimb. A passenger train en route to Victoria Falls collided with a train transporting goods to Bulawayo; 15 persons lost their lives.

December 2, Northern India. The end cars of a freight train derailed and strayed into the path of an oncoming passenger train; as many as 43 persons perished.

Traffic

January 1, Fujian province, China. A bus rear-ended a truck hauling steel bars, which punctured the front of the bus upon collision; 22 persons died, and 29 were injured.

January 2, Southern Peru. A crowded bus left a mountain road and plummeted some 150 m (495 ft) into a ravine; at least 29 persons perished, and 7 others were injured.

January 4, Near Quito, Ecuador. A bus fell off a mountain road into a ravine about 40 km (25 mi) east of Quito; at least 15 persons died, and 30 were injured.

January 10, Central Malawi. A truck transporting some 40 mourners and the coffin of a dead child was struck head-on by another vehicle near a one-lane bridge, then plummeted into the Kaombe River; at least 15 persons lost their lives, including the mother, grandmother, and siblings of the deceased child.

January 12, Near Pouso Redondo, Braz. A double-decker tourist bus collided head-on with another bus in heavy fog on a mountain highway; the collision started a pileup involving several other cars. At least 42 persons died, and 50 were injured.

January 13, Near Cairo. A collision between two buses claimed the lives of 21 persons and injured 19.

January 23, Near Queenstown, S.Af. A crowded bus veered from a rain-slickened highway and overturned, killing at least 30 persons.

Late January, Punjab state, India. A truck overturned and hit two oncoming cars; 18 persons died.

January 31, Near Bhansali, India. A bus traveling in the lower Himalayas went out of control and dropped into a gorge; 31 persons died.

February 14, Central Vietnam. A collision between two buses sent one careening into a river; 17 of the 73 persons on board were confirmed dead.

February 19, Near Huancayo, Peru. A bus smashed through the barriers of a narrow, rain-slickened bridge in the Andes and landed in a river; 31 persons died, and 15 were injured.

March 6, Near Coronel Oviedo, Paraguay. A collision between a bus and a truck loaded with bricks claimed the lives of at least 32 persons.

March 6, Sindh province, Pak. An overcrowded bus careened off a road and landed in a ravine; at least 52 persons were killed, and 24 were injured.

March 17, Leogane, Haiti. A collision between a bus and a truck claimed the lives of 18 persons.

March 29, Near Kericho, Kenya. A head-on collision between two buses occurred after one bus swerved to avoid a pothole and crossed into the lane of the other, oncoming bus; at least 101 persons died.

April 3, Near Miracatu, Braz. A container fell off a truck and struck a bus on the Regis Bitencourt Highway; 18 persons were killed.

April 15, Central Guatemala. A bus overloaded with passengers overturned in a curve on a mountainous road in Sacatepéquez department; at least 30 persons died.

April 19/20, Near Mtito Andei, Kenya. An overcrowded bus collided head-on with a truck, killing 69 persons and injuring 30.

April 23, Northern Honduras. A tourist bus crashed in Rio Lindo after a brake failure; at least 22 persons died, and 60 were injured.

May 8, Dandipur, India. A bus crowded with passengers, some sitting on the roof, swerved off the road to avoid hitting an oncoming truck and plummeted into a canal; 20 persons died, and 50 were injured.

May 13, Bosnia and Herzegovina. A bus carrying Muslim worshipers from Zenica to a prayer gathering in Buna fell off a bridge into the Bosna River after smashing through a guardrail; 43 persons perished, and 11 were injured.

June 5, Jammu and Kashmir, India. A bus careened off a mountain road and plunged into the Chenab River near the village of Thatri; at least 30 persons died, and 15 were injured.

June 12, Abia state, Nigeria. A collision involving an oil tanker and two buses claimed the lives of 30 persons.

June 29, Near Nazret, Eth. At least 60 persons died when a bus en route from Addis Ababa to Harer crashed in a ravine.

July 6, Southeastern Morocco. A collision between a truck and a passenger bus killed at least 19 persons and injured 20.

July 6, Near Soria, Spain. A truck hauling livestock swerved out of control and collided head-on with a chartered bus filled with teenagers heading to summer camp; at least 27 persons died.

July 14, Near Kimchon, S.Kor. A pileup involving three school buses and a truck occurred on a rain-slickened highway and claimed the lives of more than 20 persons, at least 14 of whom were students.

July 17, Southern Egypt. A minibus collided with a car, and the two vehicles were then slammed by a truck; 18 persons died, and at least 15 were injured.

August 12, Near Bordj Bou Arreridj, Alg. A collision between an oil truck and a bus killed 22 persons.

August 22, Sarawak state, Malaysia. After colliding with a car, a truck went out of control and then slammed into a bus; at least 15 persons died.

August 24, Eastern Kenya. A bus that was reportedly overloaded with passengers and traveling at a high speed fell from a bridge into a river near the town of Meru; at least 37 persons died, and 19 were injured.

August 28, Edea, Cameroon. A bus ran off a road and rolled several times after its driver attempted to pass a truck; 15 persons died, and 30 were seriously injured.

September 5, Southwestern Rwanda. Brake failure caused a bus to slam into a stopped truck; 39 persons died, and more than 80 were injured.

September 10, West Bengal state, India. A bus plummeted into a river after its driver lost control of the vehicle; at least 20 persons lost their lives.

October 14, Central Turkey. A head-on collision between two buses claimed the lives of 19 persons and injured 29.

November 4, Southwestern Nigeria. An oil tanker truck slammed into a line of cars stopped at a police checkpoint and burst into flames; at least 200 persons died.

November 13, Near Jahanian, Pak. A head-on collision between two buses killed 40 persons and injured at least 17; one of the buses had apparently swerved to avoid hitting a cyclist.

Mid-November, Northern Egypt. A bus collided with a tractor and overturned in an irrigation canal; as many as 30 persons were believed dead.

November 23, Southern Nigeria. A bus fell from a bridge into a river, killing 60 persons.

Late November, Northern Thailand. A bus swerved from a four-lane highway and fell into a ditch; at least 20 persons were killed, and 15 were injured.

December 14, Western Saudi Arabia. After a bus and a truck collided head-on, both vehicles caught fire; 26 persons perished.

December 19, Himachal Pradesh state, India. A truck plunged down a mountain gorge, killing some 50 persons.

December 24, Central Bolivia. A collision between two buses claimed the lives of 17 persons and injured 48.

Miscellaneous

February, Southern Bangladesh. At least 40 persons died and some 100 others became ill after drinking a brew of contaminated homemade liquor.

Late March, Krishnanagar, India. At least 18 persons died after drinking illegally brewed liquor that was apparently contaminated with methyl alcohol.

June 19, Dover, Eng. British customs officials discovered the bodies of 58 illegal Chinese immigrants who had suffocated in an airtight compartment of a Dutch-registered truck that had arrived on a ferry from Belgium; two persons were found alive inside the compartment. The driver of the truck was charged with 58 counts of manslaughter, and Dutch authorities brought charges against several others.

July 10, Manila. Heavy rain from a typhoon caused a massive garbage dump to avalanche on a shantytown known as the "Promised Land"; by mid-July 196 persons had been confirmed dead, and hundreds were still missing.

September 1, Pucallpa, Peru. At least 15 persons died and 14 were hospitalized after they drank cocktails tainted with rubbing alcohol.

October, El Salvador. In numerous incidents throughout the country, at least 119 persons lost their lives after drinking liquor contaminated with methyl alcohol.

Mid-November, Nairobi, Kenya. At least 34 persons died and some 112 were hospitalized after they drank contaminated homemade liquor.

People of 2000

A year is really about people–politicians who contend for every last vote, entertainers and sports figures who make us laugh and cheer, cry and gasp, scientists who extend the edges of our knowledge. . . . Here are some of the people who gave substance, interest, and colour to the year 2000.

Courtesy of Cheryl Hatch

Nobel Prizes

The **2000 NOBEL PRIZES** were awarded in ceremonies on **DECEMBER 10** in **OSLO** (the Prize for Peace) by the Norwegian Nobel Committee and **STOCKHOLM** (the remaining prizes) by **KING CARL XVI GUSTAF** of Sweden.

PRIZE FOR PEACE

The 2000 Nobel Prize for Peace was awarded to South Korean Pres. Kim Dae Jung, who had spent much of his life in a struggle to transform his homeland. In making the announcement, the Norwegian Nobel Committee cited his contributions to "democracy and human rights in South Korea and in East Asia in general, and for peace and reconciliation with North Korea in particular." For decades Kim had fought for a more democratic government in South Korea, and he made improved relations with the North a principal goal of his administration. As president he instituted a "sunshine" policy that allowed South Koreans to visit relatives in the North, and he also eased the rules on investment by South Koreans there. In 1998 direct talks between the two countries resumed for the first time in four years, and in June 2000 Kim accepted an invitation to Pyongyang, the capital of North Korea, to meet his counterpart, Kim Jong Il. It was the first meeting between the leaders of the two countries, still technically at war, since the Korean War of 1950–53.

Kim was born on Dec. 3, 1925, in Mokp'o, S.Kor. He graduated from the Mokp'o School of Commerce in 1943 and then worked for a Japanese-owned company and also briefly published a newspaper. He was captured by communist forces in the Korean War but escaped. An advocate of a Western-style pluralistic democracy, he opposed the one-party rule of Pres. Syngman Rhee during the 1950s. In 1961 he won the first of six terms in the National Assembly, and during the decade he became an outspoken critic of the harsh regime of Pres. Park Chung Hee. In 1970 Kim became head of the Korean Democratic Party, and in 1971 he ran unsuccessfully against Park in the presidential election. The Korean Central Intelligence Agency abducted him from a hotel in Tokyo in 1973, and he was spared death only through pressure from Japan and the U.S. He spent much of the following decade under arrest and in prison, at times under sentence of death, until in 1982 he was allowed to go in exile to the U.S. for medical treatment. Kim returned to South Korea in 1985 and ran again for president in 1987 and 1992. In 1995 he founded the National Congress for New Politics, and in 1997 he won election as president of South Korea, the first opposition candidate ever to do so.

AFP Worldwide

Kim Dae Jung

Kim, a devout Roman Catholic, had spent half a century as a dissident in South Korea, supporting democratic values and improved relations with the North even when his views put him in mortal danger. For his patience and persistence and for his lack of recrimination against those at whose hands he had suffered, he was sometimes compared to South African apartheid foe Nelson Mandela. The change in relationship toward the North, for which Kim had often been ridiculed, seemed to bear fruit. Following his meeting with Kim Jong Il, head of what was sometimes called the world's last Stalinist state, the two countries marched together in the ceremonies of the 2000 Summer Olympic Games, arranged further visits between separated families, and agreed to restore severed rail links. Further, in October U.S. Secretary of State Madeleine K. Albright made a trip to Pyongyang. Thus, Kim's policy appeared to be defusing one of the tensest and most dangerous situations in the world. (ROBERT RAUCH)

PRIZE FOR ECONOMICS

The Nobel Memorial Prize in Economic Sciences was awarded in 2000 to James J. Heckman and Daniel L. McFadden, two Americans who developed theories and methods that resolved some of the problems associated with the analysis of microdata. Their contributions to econometrics (the application of mathematical and statistical techniques to economic problems) and microeconomics (the interface between economics and statistics) provided essential tools for economists and other social scientists.

Heckman received the Nobel award for his "development of theory and methods for analyzing selective samples." He found a solution to a major problem encountered in microeconomic studies; e.g., a sample—in which all members shared a common characteristic or attribute—might not represent the underlying population because of rules governing data collection. Selection problems can arise, for example, when a government study of the relationship between wages and working hours relies on observable data while ignoring other factors, including individual choice. Heckman, who had a reputation as the world's leading researcher on the microevaluation of labour-market programs, devised various methods to deal with such sample-selection problems. The best known of these was the Heckman correction (known as Heckit method or Heckman lamda), which consisted of a simple and easily applied two-stage method. In order to gauge the relationship between wages and working hours by using observable data, Heckman proposed that a model based on economic theory be formulated to establish the probability of working. The result generated by this model could then be used to predict the probability for each individual. This would be treated as an additional variable in stage two, when the probability was factored into the calculation.

McFadden, working in a related area, received the Nobel award for his "development of theory and methods for analyzing discrete choice." Much of his work was done in the 1970s, and his seminal contribution to conditional logit analysis came in 1974. Previously, the value of microdata in empirical studies was often undermined because the data reflected a limited number of alternatives upon which individual choices were made in, for example, buying a house or selecting a mode of travel to work. In traditional demand analysis only a continuous (or measurable) variable could be used to represent individual choice, which made it inappropriate for studying discrete-choice behaviour. McFadden developed statistical methods that could easily be applied to the needs of society. His econometric discrete-choice analysis became an essential component in studying individual-choice behaviour. McFadden's models were applied to studies of labour-force participation, public transport systems, health care, housing (for the elderly in particular), and the environment and thereby enabled a greater understanding of the human choices that could influence the success or failure of public-policy decisions.

Heckman was born April 19, 1944, in Chicago and was educated at Colorado College (B.A. 1965) and Princeton University (M.A. 1968, Ph.D. 1971). He joined the faculty of the University of Chicago, where he was an associate professor (1973–77) and professor (from 1977) of economics. In 1989 he received an honorary M.A. from Yale University, where he served as professor of both economics (1988–90) and statistics (1990). He also acted as a research associate at the U.S. National Bureau of Economic Research (1971–85 and from 1987) and held associate editorships of the *Journal of Econometrics* (1977–83), the *Journal of Labor Economics* (from 1982), and *The Review of Economics and Statistics* (from 1994). Heckman was awarded the John Bates Clark medal by the American Economics Association in 1983.

McFadden was born on July 29, 1937, in Raleigh, N.C., and was educated at the University of Minnesota at Minneapolis (B.S. 1957, Ph.D. 1962). He taught economics (1963–79) at the University of California, Berkeley, where he became professor of economics in 1968. From 1978 he was on the faculty at the Massachusetts Institute of Technology, where he also held (1984–91) the James R. Killian Chair and was director (1986–88) of the Statistics Center. In 1990 McFadden returned to Berkeley and held several prestigious positions, including the E. Morris Cox Chair. That same year he was also the Sherman Fairchild Distinguished Scholar while a visiting professor at the California Institute of Technology, Pasadena. He was editor of the *Journal of Statistical Physics* (1968–70) and the Econometric Society monographs (1980–83) and was on the editorial boards of several academic journals. (JANET H. CLARK)

PRIZE FOR LITERATURE

AP/Wide World Photos

Gao Xingjian

Chinese émigré writer Gao Xingjian was awarded the 2000 Nobel Prize for Literature for "an oeuvre of universal validity, bitter insights and linguistic ingenuity, which has opened new paths for the Chinese novel and drama." Gao, the first Chinese-language writer to win the award, was a respected novelist, playwright, translator, and critic whose works had been banned in his native country since the late 1980s. He was also renowned both as a stage director and as an artist. Subjected to persistent harassment from government authorities, Gao left China in 1987 and settled in France as a political refugee. He became a French citizen and took up residence in the Paris suburb of Bagnolet.

Gao was born on Jan. 4, 1940, in Ganzhou, Jiangxi province. He was educated in state schools and from 1957 to 1962 attended the Beijing Foreign Languages Institute, where he earned a degree in French. Persecuted as an intellectual during the repression of the Cultural Revolution (1966–76), Gao was forced to destroy his early writings and was later sent to a reeducation camp, enduring nearly six years of hard labour. Afterward, Gao was assigned by the government to work at the Foreign Languages Press. He then became a translator in the Chinese Writers Association, but he was unable to publish his work or travel abroad until 1979.

Gao emerged in the early 1980s as an innovative and provocative voice in contemporary Chinese literature. He first gained critical recognition with the publication in 1980 of the novella *Hanye zhong de xingchen* ("Stars on a Cold Night"). This was followed by the controversial literary study *Xiandai xiaoshuo jiqiao chutan* (1981; "A Preliminary Discussion of the Art of Modern Fiction").

In 1981 Gao became a resident playwright with the Beijing People's Art Theater, and in 1982 he saw the premiere of his first play, *Juedui xinhao* (*Alarm Signal*, 1996), written in collaboration with Liu Huiyuan and published in *Gao Xingjian xiju ji* (1985; "Collected Dramatic Works of Gao

Xingjian"). Merging elements of traditional Chinese opera and drama with the influence of Western modernism, Gao created a body of work that earned praise and acclaim as well as disapproval and censure. His second and most celebrated play, *Chezhan* (1983; *The Bus Stop,* 1996, also translated as *Bus Stop,* 1998), incorporated various techniques of avant-garde European theatre. It premiered in June 1983 and was openly condemned as "intellectual pollution" by Communist Party officials. Gao continued to explore the boundaries of experimental drama with plays such as *Yeren* (1985; *Wild Man,* 1990), *Dubai* (1985; "Soliloquy"), and most notably *Bi'an* (1986; *The Other Side,* 1997, also translated as *The Other Shore,* 1999). Deemed counterrevolutionary by authorities, the play was stopped after 10 performances, and Gao was placed under surveillance. In part to avoid further reprisal, Gao embarked on a 10-month walking tour of the forest and mountain regions of Sichuan province, following the course of the Chang Jiang (Yangtze River). For Gao the journey was both a spiritual and an artistic pilgrimage that became the basis for his first novel, *Lingshan* (1989; *Soul Mountain,* 2000), a masterful tour de force. He later produced another novel, *Yige ren de shengjing* (1999; to be published in 2001 as *One Man's Bible*).

Gao, who wrote in both French and Chinese, was the recipient in 1992 of the title of Chevalier of the Order of Arts and Letters by the French Ministry of Culture. Following the publication of his play *Taowang* (1989; *Fugitives,* 1993), set against the backdrop of the brutal suppression in 1989 of student demonstrations in Tiananmen Square, Gao was declared persona non grata by the Chinese regime, and his works were banned. Other plays included *Sheng si jie* (1991; *Between Life and Death*), *Duihua yu fanjie* (1992; *Dialogue and Rebuttal*), *Yeyou shen* (1993; *Nocturnal Wanderer*), and *Zhoumo sichongzou* (1995; *Weekend Quartet*), translated by Gilbert C.F. Fung and collected in *The Other Shore: Plays by Gao Xingjian* (1999).

As cited by the Swedish Academy, "In the writing of Gao Xingjian literature is born anew from the struggle of the individual to survive the history of the masses. He is a perspicacious skeptic who makes no claim to be able to explain the world." In search of meaning through personal expression, Gao asserted that only as a writer and as an artist had he found reaffirmation of his own existence. (STEVEN R. SERAFIN)

PRIZE FOR CHEMISTRY

It was once common knowledge that plastics—polymeric materials that can be molded or shaped—are fundamentally different from metals in their properties. Plastics, for example, are used around the copper wires in power cords because their insulating characteristics protect people from electric shocks and equipment from short circuits. In the 1970s the three scientists who shared the 2000 Nobel Prize for Chemistry turned that idea upside down. Alan G. MacDiarmid of the University of Pennsylvania, Hideki Shirakawa of the University of Tsukuba, Japan, and Alan J. Heeger of the University of California, Santa Barbara (UCSB), showed that certain plastics can be chemically modified to conduct electricity almost as readily as metals.

The discovery of electrically conductive polymers provided insights into the nature of polymers and electrical conductivity and opened up new fields of chemical and physical research. The materials, which are light in weight and can be fabricated as films, found practical applications as well. By the end of the 20th century, conductive polymers were used in, or were being developed for, corrosion inhibitors, antistatic coatings on photographic film, "smart" windows that automatically darkened in strong sunlight to keep buildings cool, light-emitting diodes, flexible solar cells, displays for mobile telephones and other small electronic devices, and thin wall-sized, roll-up computer displays.

MacDiarmid was born April 14, 1927, in Masterton, N.Z. He earned Ph.D.'s in chemistry from the University of Wisconsin at Madison in 1953 and the University of Cambridge in 1955. He then joined the faculty of the University of Pennsylvania, becoming full professor in 1964 and Blanchard Professor of Chemistry in 1988. Shirakawa was born Aug. 20, 1936, in Tokyo. He earned a Ph.D. from the Tokyo Institute of Technology in 1966. That same year he joined the faculty of the Institute of Materials Science at the University of Tsukuba, where he became professor of chemistry in 1982. Heeger was born Jan. 22, 1936, in Sioux City, Iowa. After receiving a Ph.D. in physics from the University of California, Berkeley, in 1961, he taught and conducted research at the University of Pennsylvania until 1982, when he became professor at UCSB and director of its Institute for Polymers and Organic Solids. In 1990 Heeger founded the UNIAX Corp. to develop and manufacture light-emitting displays based on conducting polymers.

Heeger, MacDiarmid, and Shirakawa carried out their prizewinning work while studying polyacetylene, a polymer that was known to exist as a black powder. In 1974, at the University of Tsukuba, Shirakawa and associates serendipitously synthesized polyacetylene in the form of a silvery film. Although the material had a distinct metallic appearance, it still behaved as an insulator. The following year Shirakawa discussed his discovery with MacDiarmid during the latter's visit to Japan. In 1977 the two men and Heeger, collaborating at the University of Pennsylvania, exposed polyacetylene to iodine vapour. Their strategy was to introduce impurities into the polymer much as in the doping process used to tailor the conductive properties of semiconductors. Doping with iodine increased polyacetylene's electrical conductivity by a factor of 10 million, which made it as conductive as some metals.

Scientists later discovered other conductive polymers, including some that emit light when electrically stimulated, and established the key properties of the group. Polymers consist of molecules—acetylene molecules (HC≡CH) in the case of polyacetylene—linked together into long chains. To be conductive, a polymer must have so-called conjugated double bonds along its carbon-atom backbone. Conjugation means that the bonds between carbon atoms alternate, with one single bond followed by one double bond (–C=C–C=C–). In addition, the material must contain charge carriers in the form of extra electrons or of locations that lack an electron (called holes). The impurity atoms, or dopants, in the conductive polymer provide the electrons or holes. When an electric current is applied to the polymer, it can flow either by movement of the negatively charged electrons or by migration of the holes, which behave as positively charged particles.

Scientists looked forward to the future application of conductive polymers in the emerging field of molecular electronics, where the materials could give rise to a new generation of plastic electronic devices. "In the future, we will be able to produce transistors and other electronic components consisting of individual molecules—which will dramatically increase the speed and reduce the size of our computers," stated the Royal Swedish Academy of Sciences, which awarded the chemistry prize. "A computer corresponding to what we now carry around in our bags would suddenly fit inside a watch."

(MICHAEL WOODS)

PRIZE FOR PHYSICS

Three scientists whose pioneering work laid the foundations for the modern era of silicon microchips, computers, and information technology won the 2000 Nobel Prize for Physics. The Royal Swedish Academy of Sciences awarded half of the prize jointly to Herbert Kroemer of the University of California, Santa Barbara (UCSB), and Zhores Alferov (Zhores Ivanovich Alfyorov) of the A.F. Ioffe Physico-Technical Institute, St. Petersburg. The other half went to Jack S. Kilby of Texas Instruments Inc., Dallas, Texas.

"Two simple but fundamental requirements are put on a modern information system," stated the Swedish Academy in its award announcement. "It must be fast, so that large volumes of information can be transferred in a short time. The user's apparatus must be small so that there is room for it in offices, homes, briefcases or pockets." Kroemer, Alferov, and Kilby invented the technology to meet those requirements, the Academy asserted.

Kroemer was born Aug. 25, 1928, in Weimar, Ger., and received a Ph.D. in theoretical physics in 1952 from Georg August University of Göttingen, Ger. His early employment included stints at RCA Laboratories, Princeton, N.J. (1954–57), and Varian Associates, Palo Alto, Calif. (1959–66), where he did much of his prizewinning work. In 1968 Kroemer became professor of electrical engineering at the University of Colorado at Boulder, and he moved to UCSB in 1976. Alferov was born March 15, 1930, in Vitebsk in the Soviet republic of Belorussia (now Belarus). He received a doctorate in physics and mathematics in 1970 from the A.F. Ioffe Physico-Technical Institute, with which he had been associated since 1953. Alferov became director of the institute in 1987.

Kroemer and Alferov were cited for their work in the 1950s and '60s to develop fast optoelectronic and microelectronic components made from semiconductor heterostructures. Most computer chips and other semiconductor components are made from one kind of material, such as silicon, that has been chemically modified, or doped, to change its electronic characteristics. As the term suggests, heterostructure semiconductors are made of layers of different materials, such as gallium arsenide and aluminum gallium arsenide.

In 1957, while working at RCA, Kroemer carried out theoretical calculations showing that a heterostructure transistor would be superior to a conventional transistor, especially for certain high-frequency uses and other applications. Scientists later showed that he was correct—heterostructure transistors can operate at frequencies 100 times higher than the best conventional transistors, and they also work better as amplifiers. Alferov's research team in the Soviet Union applied Kroemer's theory, developing the first practical heterostructure electronic device in 1966 and then pioneering electronic components made from heterostructures. One of them was the first heterostructure laser, which both Kroemer and Alferov had proposed independently in 1963. This invention led to a technological breakthrough by the end of the decade—heterostructure solid-state lasers that could operate continuously at room temperature. These lasers made fibre-optic communication possible.

The Nobel citation emphasized the many uses of heterostructure devices in everyday life. Laser diodes in compact disc audio and video players and CD-ROM computer drives, for instance, relied on semiconductor heterostructures. Heterostructure devices also were used in communications satellites, cellular telephone communications, bar code readers, and light-emitting diodes used in auto brake lights, control-panel indicators, and other products.

Kilby was born Nov. 8, 1923, in Jefferson City, Mo. In 1950, while working as a circuit designer, he earned a master's degree in electrical engineering from the University of Wisconsin at Madison. In 1958 he joined Texas Instruments, where he remained until 1970, when he took a leave of absence to pursue independent research. From 1978 to 1984 he was distinguished professor of electrical engineering at Texas A&M University at College Station.

Kilby received his half of the physics prize for his role in inventing the integrated circuit, or microchip. A microchip is a tiny sliver of semiconduc-

Jack S. Kilby, Herbert Kroemer, and Zhores I. Alferov

AP/Wide World Photos

tor, typically silicon, that contains thousands or millions of microscopic transistors, resistors, and other electronic components. All are designed to work in an integrated fashion as amplifiers, computer processors and memories, and other components that underpin the microelectronics revolution.

When Kilby began his prizewinning work, the conventional transistor already was the limiting factor in computer advances. Transistors, invented in 1947, were in many ways superior to vacuum tubes, but thousands had to be soldered together with resistors, capacitors, and other discrete components on printed circuit boards. By the early 1950s scientists were discussing a solution to this complexity—manufacturing all the circuit components as a single package.

As a new employee at Texas Instruments in 1958, Kilby had earned no vacation and spent the summer working almost alone in the laboratory. During that period he demonstrated that it was possible to fabricate all the different components of a circuit from silicon. The next year Kilby filed a patent for his idea of miniaturized electronic circuits. As the Swedish Academy pointed out, another young engineer, Robert Noyce, then of Fairchild Semiconductor Corp., also had demonstrated the practical possibility of an integrated circuit at about the same time. Kilby, however, was first with a patent application. Kilby later coinvented the pocket calculator, the first common use of an integrated circuit. (MICHAEL WOODS)

PRIZE FOR PHYSIOLOGY OR MEDICINE

The 2000 Nobel Prize for Physiology or Medicine was awarded to Arvid Carlsson of Göteborg (Swed.) University, Paul Greengard of Rockefeller University, New York City, and Eric Kandel of Columbia University, New York City. Their seminal investigations clarified the way in which brain cells transmit signals to each other both in healthy people and in individuals with common neurological and mental illnesses. As was noted by the Nobel Assembly at the Karolinska Institute in Stockholm, which awarded the medicine prizes, these findings resulted in the development of new drugs for treatment of Parkinson disease and other disorders.

Carlsson was born Jan. 25, 1923, in Uppsala, Swed. He received his medical degree in 1951 from the University of Lund, Swed., where he subsequently held teaching positions. In 1959 he became professor of pharmacology at Göteborg University. Greengard, born Dec. 11, 1925, in New York City, received a Ph.D. in 1953 from Johns Hopkins University, Baltimore, Md. Following postgraduate work, he was employed with Geigy Research Laboratories, Ardsley, N.Y. (1959–67), and held professorships at Albert Einstein College of Medicine, New York City (1961–70), and Yale University (1968–83). In 1983 he became professor and head of the Laboratory of Molecular and Cellular Neuroscience at Rockefeller University. Kandel, born Nov. 7, 1929, in Vienna, received his medical degree in 1956 from New York University's School of Medicine. Following residency in psychiatry and employment at Harvard University, he served as associate professor at New York University (1965–74). Beginning in 1974 Kandel held a series of professorships at Columbia University, where he also directed that institution's Center for Neurobiology and Behavior until 1983.

In the human brain more than 100 billion nerve cells, or neurons, exchange chemical signals at synapses—points where two cells make contact—in a process called synaptic transmission. Neurons transmit their signals via chemical compounds, neurotransmitters, that travel across the synapse. The neurotransmitter delivers the signal by contacting receptor sites on the surface of the receiving cell. The receiving cell then must change the exterior signal into an internal message to which it can respond. The process of converting exterior signals into internal action is termed signal transduction.

In the late 1950s Carlsson carried out pioneering studies establishing that the molecule dopamine is an important neurotransmitter in the brain. Scientists previously had thought that dopamine worked only indirectly, by causing brain cells to make another neurotransmitter, noradrenaline. Using a sensitive test for dopamine that he devised, Carlsson detected particularly high levels of the compound in areas of the brain that controlled walking and other voluntary movements. In animal experiments he showed that depletion of dopamine impairs the ability to move. When Carlsson treated dopamine-depleted animals with the substance L-dopa, which the brain uses to make dopamine, the symptoms disappeared, and the animals moved normally again.

Carlsson and others recognized that the animal symptoms were similar to those in Parkinson disease patients. As a result, L-dopa was employed as a treatment for Parkinson disease, eventually becoming the single most important medication for the disease. Carlsson's work also contributed to an understanding of the relationship between neurotransmitters and mental states such as clinical depression, which led to the introduction of new antidepressant drugs, including Prozac.

The Nobel Assembly honoured Greengard for having discovered how dopamine and other neurotransmitters work in the nervous system. When he began his prizewinning work in the late 1960s, scientists recognized dopamine, noradrenaline, and serotonin as key neurotransmitters in a signaling process called slow synaptic transmission. Greengard showed that slow synaptic transmission involves a chemical reaction called protein phosphorylation. In that reaction a phosphate molecule is linked to a protein, changing the protein's function. Greengard worked out the signal-transduction pathway that begins with dopamine. When dopamine attaches to receptors in a neuron's outer membrane, it causes a rise in a second messenger, cyclic AMP. This molecule, in turn, activates an enzyme that adds phosphate molecules to other proteins in the neuron. Protein phosphorylation can affect the neuron in different ways, including its sensitivity to being triggered to fire off nerve signals.

Kandel's award-winning research revealed the role of synaptic transmission in learning and memory. He used a simple experimental model, the sea slug *Aplysia*, which has only about 20,000 nerve cells, many of them very large and easy to study. The sea slug also has a protective reflex to guard its gills, which Kandel used to study basic learning mechanisms.

The sea-slug experiments—combined with later research in mice—established that, in the words of the Nobel Assembly, "our memory can be said to be 'located in the synapses' and changes in synaptic function are central, when different types of memories are formed." Kandel's research showed that weak stimuli give rise to certain chemical changes in synapses; these changes are the basis for short-term memory, which lasts minutes to hours. Stronger stimuli cause different synaptic changes, which result in a form of long-term memory that can remain for weeks. (MICHAEL WOODS)

Biographies

The **SUBJECTS** of these biographies are the people who in the editors' opinions captured the **IMAGINATION** of the world in 2000—the most **INTERESTING** and/or **IMPORTANT PERSONALITIES** of the year.

Abu Zayd, Nasr Hamid

Even five years after he was declared an apostate by a high court, ordered to divorce his wife, and, in effect, forced out of his homeland, Egyptian academic Nasr Hamid Abu Zayd continued to serve as a focal point for those concerned with the human and civil rights excesses of Islamic fundamentalism in 2000. Abu Zayd's case was often mentioned in the same breath as those of Indian-born author Salman Rushdie and Bangladeshi feminist Taslima Nasrin, both also unable to return to their homelands because their writings had been declared insulting to Islam.

Abu Zayd was born in Tanta, Egypt, in the Nile Delta on Oct. 7, 1943. He attended Cairo University and received his Ph.D. in Arabic and Islamic studies in 1981. He wrote his doctoral thesis on the Andalusian-born Sufi Ibn al-ʿArabi (1165–1240), a mystic and philosopher who wrote in a multicultural (Provençal, Latin, and Arabic) and multireligious (Judaic, Christian, and Islamic) environment that he sought to reconcile in a universal love. Abu Zayd's thesis was published as *The Philosophy of Hermeneutics* in Beirut in 1983.

From his studies Abu Zayd realized the importance of sociocultural factors in the interpretation of the Qur'an and took the point that interpretation is human, not divine, into his own beliefs. Abu Zayd observed how Islam was being interpreted by fundamentalists in Egypt and elsewhere in ways that served political ends, a position he opposed in his 1992 book *Naqd al-khitab al-dini* ("Critique of Religious Discourse"). When in that same year he applied for promotion to full professor at Cairo University, the tenure committee split. One of Abu Zayd's colleagues resorted to the pulpit of a mosque in Cairo to denounce him as an apostate for his writings. The Abu Zayd case became a cause célèbre among Muslim fundamentalists, and even the newspaper of the ruling National Democratic Party called for his expulsion from the university and execution as a heretic. On June 14, 1995, a Cairo court ruled that Abu Zayd had to divorce his wife, Ibtihal Yunis, a teacher of French culture at Cairo University, because he was a heretic and therefore a non-Muslim, and a Muslim woman could not be married to a non-Muslim man. The Court of Cassation upheld the ruling in 1996. Fearful for their lives, the couple fled Egypt and settled in The Netherlands. As his case continued to draw attention from international human rights organizations, Abu Zayd followed academic pursuits at the State University of Leiden, Neth., lectured throughout Europe and the U.S., and served on the editorial board for two forthcoming volumes of the *Encyclopaedia of the Qur'an*. (MARIUS K. DEEB)

Amis, Martin

The publication in May 2000 of Martin Amis's long-anticipated memoir, *Experience,* was greeted with enthusiasm by most literary critics on both sides of the Atlantic. Hitherto, few had questioned Amis's stature as a writer of brilliance and biting satire, but some had found his prodigious cleverness lacking at times in emotional depth. Most reviewers agreed, however, that the pages of *Experience* resounded with a new candour and thoughtfulness. As an autobiography and a riveting portrait of an unusual family—particularly, the depiction of his close relationship with his late father, novelist Kingsley Amis—the book was hailed as not just "entertaining" and "gossip-rich" but also "fine," "affecting," and "profound." Amis himself explained that he always knew he would be compelled to commemorate his father, who had leapt to international fame with the publication of *Lucky Jim* (1954) when Martin was five: "He was a writer and I am a writer; it feels like a duty to describe our case—a literary curiosity."

Martin Louis Amis was born on Aug. 25, 1949, in Oxford, Eng., and was the godson of poet Philip Larkin. Despite having had literary influences, Amis was dismissed from school; his intellect was termed "unexceptional." He went on, however, to graduate from Exeter College, Oxford, in 1971 with first-class honours in English. After a brief stint as a book reviewer, Amis joined the *Times Literary Supplement,* and he soon became its fiction and poetry editor. He then moved to the *New Statesman,* where he became literary editor. His first novel, *The Rachel Papers* (1973), won the Somerset Maugham Award and was followed by eight more novels and several short stories.

Amis, the father of two sons by his first marriage to American philosopher Antonia Phillips and of two daughters by his second marriage to writer Isabel Fonseca, discovered in 1995 that he had a third daughter, Delilah Seale, from an affair two decades earlier. In *Experience* he describes meeting his 19-year-old daughter for the first time: there were "hugs and kisses for the girl with my face."

His life, magnified by his extroverted nature, was much documented by the press. He acknowledged the rancour with which some fellow writers and journalists judged his glittering career: "I'm like the son of the lord of manor, in that I took over the estate . . . by right of birth, whereas everyone else has had to struggle." His style had been frequently imitated but rarely matched. Such novels as *Other People* (1981), *Money* (1984), and *London Fields* (1989) showcased his virtuoso storytelling technique but also revealed a dark side. Amis's characters inhabited a frightening world, where selfishness and avidity had caused humanity to teeter on the edge of disaster. Regardless of his birthright, Amis's continuing reputation as a doyen of English letters had been secured with his endlessly inventive, highly readable prose. (SIOBHAN DOWD)

Assad, Bashar al-

On July 17, 2000, Bashar al-Assad was inaugurated president of Syria. The 34-year-old ophthalmologist, described as intellectual and soft-spoken, was elected to the office for a seven-year term after the death on June 10 of his father, Hafez al-Assad, who had ruled Syria since 1971. In his inaugural speech the new president emphasized the need to modernize the nation's economy, which was mostly government-controlled and was heavily dependent on oil exports. He also continued his father's hard-line approach in regard to recovering for Syria the Golan Heights region, which had been lost to Israel in the 1967 Arab-Israeli War.

Assad was born Sept. 11, 1965, in Damascus, the capital of Syria. He studied medicine at the University of Damascus and graduated as a general practitioner in 1988. He then trained to become an ophthalmologist at a Damascus military hospital and in 1992 moved to London to continue his studies. In 1994 his older brother, Basil, who had been designated his father's heir apparent, was killed in an automobile accident, and Bashar was summoned to return to Syria to take his brother's place. He was sent to a military academy north of Damascus to receive the requisite training for becoming the nation's president and eventually gained the rank of colonel in the elite Presidential Guard. Assad also took over his brother's position as head of

left: Knut Simon Photography; right: AP/Wide World Photos

the Syrian Computing Society and made it his goal to increase the use of computers in his nation. In 1999 he traveled to France, Saudi Arabia, Oman, and Jordan to meet with the leaders of those countries. On June 18, soon after the death of his father, Assad was appointed secretary-general of the ruling Ba'th Party, and two days later the party congress nominated him as its candidate for the presidency. The national legislature approved the nomination on June 27, and on July 10, running unopposed, Assad gained the approval of 97.29% of those who voted. Among his first moves as president was to announce that, unlike his father, he did not want to see pictures of himself on public and private buildings throughout Syria. In his inaugural address he stated that he would not support policies that might threaten the dominance of the Ba'th Party and that freedom of expression should be encouraged but in the form of "positive criticism" of government policies. Rejecting democracy as practiced in other countries, Assad declared, "We have to have our own democracy to match our history and culture, arising from the needs of our people and our reality." (DAVID R. CALHOUN)

Berezovsky, Boris

When Russian Pres. Boris Yeltsin resigned, Russian tycoon Boris Berezovsky lost his status as a Kremlin insider and one of Russia's most powerful men. Yeltsin's successor, Vladimir Putin, came to power in 2000 promising to "liquidate the oligarchs as a class." By year's end Berezovsky had been ousted from Kremlin circles and was facing a criminal investigation into his business affairs.

Berezovsky had epitomized the "oligarchs," the small group of Russians who had made their fortunes in the chaotic last years of the U.S.S.R. and parlayed their wealth into political power in the new, capitalist Russia. In 1996 Berezovsky had boasted that he and six other financiers controlled 50% of the Russian economy.

Boris Abramovich Berezovsky was born Jan. 23, 1946, in Moscow and was the only son of a nurse and a builder. He studied electronics and computer science; completed his postgraduate studies in 1975, and earned his doctorate in decision-making theory in 1983. Thereafter he worked on information management at an institute of the Academy of Sciences of the U.S.S.R. In 1991 he became a corresponding member of the Russian Academy of Sciences.

Berezovsky founded his business empire in the last years of the Soviet Union. The economic liberalization launched by Soviet leader Mikhail Gorbachev legalized small-scale private enterprise and made it possible for enterprising Soviet businessmen to privatize the profitable parts of their state-owned businesses. They could also exploit the gap between the controlled prices set by the state and the prices Soviet-produced goods could fetch on the free market. Berezovsky typified these "new Russians." He had worked as a consultant on information management to AvtoVaz, Inc., the largest Soviet car producer. In 1989 Berezovsky used these contacts to set up LogoVaz, the U.S.S.R.'s first capitalist car dealership. LogoVaz bought cars at the state-set price for cars intended for export and sold them at the much higher price such cars could fetch inside Russia. The profits enabled Berezovsky to expand his interests into oil and banking. His cultivation of Yeltsin's bodyguard and of Yeltsin's daughter gave Berezovsky an entrée into the Kremlin. As a result, he won financial control of the former Soviet state airline, Aeroflot, and of Russian Public Television (ORT), Russia's main television channel.

In 1996 Berezovsky helped bankroll Yeltsin's reelection as president. He was rewarded with political appointments, first as deputy secretary of the Security Council in 1996 and then in 1998 as executive secretary of the Commonwealth of Independent States. Under his management, ORT supported first Yeltsin and then Yeltsin's designated successor, Vladimir Putin.

Putin's determination to reassert state control soon brought him into conflict with Berezovsky. Accusing Putin of returning to totalitarianism, Berezovsky announced the formation of a "constructive opposition." He complained that the Kremlin had threatened him with imprisonment unless he surrendered control of ORT. Instead, Berezovsky transferred his shares to a handpicked group of writers and journalists. During the summer a long-standing investigation into Berezovsky's handling of Aeroflot's finances was revived. In December, Berezovsky announced that he was establishing a multimillion-dollar foundation to promote the development of civil society in Russia. At year's end observers were divided. Though some saw Berezovsky's fall from power as permanent, others warned that it was too early to rule him out, since he would retain his influence in Russian politics through his shareholders at ORT.

(EDITOR)

Booth, Cherie

Until 1997, when the Labour Party's victory in the U.K. general election propelled her into Downing Street as the wife of the incoming prime minister, Tony Blair, British barrister Cherie Booth was normally referred to by her married name. After her husband's election, however, she reclaimed her maiden name to emphasize her determination to pursue an independent professional career; she became the first spouse of a British prime minister to maintain a career of her own. In 2000 she also became the first woman in over 150 years to give birth while her husband was serving as prime minister. On May 20, at the age of 45, Booth became a mother for the fourth time when Leo Blair was born.

Booth was born on Sept. 23, 1954, in Bury, Lancashire. Both of her parents, Anthony Booth and Gale Smith, were actors, socialists, and Roman Catholics. Life became significantly harder when her father left her mother in the early 1960s. Though he went on to become a well-known comedy actor through the long-running BBC television series *Till Death Do Us Part,* his private life dissolved into alcoholism, womanizing, and debt, and Smith and her children never benefited materially from his acting success. Cherie Booth attended Roman Catholic schools near Liverpool and subsequently studied law at the London School of Economics.

In 1976 Booth was offered a "pupillage" (trainee position) with a group of lawyers headed by Derry Irvine (he was subsequently made a life peer and in 1997 was appointed lord chancellor). It was there that she met Blair, who was hired at the same time she was. Blair and Booth married in 1980, by which time both were active in the Labour Party, though she was

Cherie Booth, Q.C., with her husband, Prime Minister Tony Blair, and their son Leo Blair

Mary McCartney
REUTERS/Corbis

widely regarded as the more radical of the two. Both stood for Parliament in the general election of 1983. Whereas he won a traditional Labour constituency in the north of England, she came in third in a normally Conservative part of Kent, southeast of London.

As her husband's political career flourished, Booth dedicated herself to the law. She specialized in public-law issues, such as workers' rights and sex-discrimination cases. Following Blair's election as Labour Party leader in 1994, the couple decided that she should continue her career but refrain from becoming a "political" wife in the manner of Hillary Rodham Clinton, wife of U.S. Pres. Bill Clinton. Booth was appointed a queen's counsel, or senior barrister, in 1995. Following Labour's return to government in 1997, she continued to fight public-law cases, which occasionally required her to argue in court against the government led by her husband. The only political topic on which she spoke publicly concerned the incorporation of the European Convention on Human Rights into British law, a cause she strongly supported and on which she commanded a considerable amount of professional authority. In 2000 Booth helped to set up Matrix, a new firm of London lawyers specializing in human rights cases.

(PETER KELLNER)

Brosnan, Pierce

Although the James Bond film franchise was approaching 40 years of age, the adventures of the suave Agent 007 were more popular than ever in 2000, thanks to Irish actor Pierce Brosnan, the most recent Bond incarnation in a long line of handsome leading men. The latest Bond film, *The World Is Not Enough* (1999), was the 19th in the series, and it did more than $30 million in business during its first weekend, the most for any Bond film.

Pierce Brendan Brosnan was born May 16, 1953, in County Meath, Ire. His father left home shortly thereafter, so he was raised by relatives after his mother left to work in England. At age 15 Brosnan set out on his own in London to be an actor. He joined a theatre group and later studied at the Drama Centre of London. He married actress Cassandra Harris, and when the two moved to the U.S., Harris landed a role in the 1981 Bond film *For Your Eyes Only.* Brosnan became a rising star with his role in the NBC television detective series *Remington Steele,* but when he was chosen as the successor to Roger Moore as Agent 007 in 1986, his NBC contract prevented him from accepting, and Timothy Dalton took the role instead. Brosnan continued to take on television and film roles and in 1991 dealt with the loss of his wife, who died after a four-year battle with ovarian cancer.

Meanwhile, Dalton's two Bond films were seen as relative failures, and the series was in need of a saviour. In 1994 Brosnan finally had his chance—he was signed to a contract as the fifth James Bond for three films, with an option for a fourth. His first film, *GoldenEye,* made more than $350 million worldwide, the most ever for a Bond film. The second, *Tomorrow Never Dies,* scored record grosses for a Bond film in the U.S. Brosnan brought out the human side of the Bond character, and the series producers sought to emphasize that in *The World Is Not Enough.* Brosnan's Bond was vulnerable, almost fallible.

Although he might have been tiring of the role after making the second film, Brosnan seemed to be hinting in early 2000 that he would stick around to make a fourth. Still, he sought to expand his repertoire and took advantage of his popularity to choose new projects. In 1999 he produced and starred in a remake of the 1968 film *The Thomas Crown Affair,* and he had plans to produce more of his own films.

(ANTHONY G. CRAINE)

Browne, Sir John

With its $27 billion acquisition of Atlantic Richfield Co. in 2000, BP Amoco became the world's second largest producer of oil and natural gas. At the helm of the ever-growing energy giant was chief executive officer Sir John Browne, a shy, private, unmarried man who lived with his mother and was known for his long work hours and unflagging loyalty to the company that had employed him for more than 30 years. Browne's personal life, daring deals, and calls for environmentally sound business practices made him an odd and highly recognizable character within the oil industry. When Browne took charge of British Petroleum (BP) in 1995, it was a company that had no clear direction and had just raised itself from debt. Browne laid out a plan to expand BP and, in the process, protect it from fluctuating oil prices while grabbing a larger share of the market for natural gas, which increased in demand as producers reacted to consumers' wishes for cleaner alternatives to oil.

Browne first made waves in 1997 when he abandoned the oil industry's customary resistance to more environmentally friendly production procedures. He later promised to see that BP cut its emission of greenhouse gases by 10% by 2010. In 1999 BP Amoco began a plan to power 200 of its retail outlets by using solar panels. Although some environmentalists were skeptical, Browne said that he was responding to the wishes of consumers, who, he believed, would continue demanding cleaner alternatives to fossil fuel. He backed this up in April 1999 by spending $45 million for a controlling interest in Solarex and thereby making BP Amoco the world's largest solar-energy concern. He also created a major commotion in the petroleum industry in August 1998 when he announced BP's $57 billion agreement to merge with Amoco, which effectively eliminated one competitor while sending industry giants Exxon, Mobil, Texaco, and Chevron scrambling to attempt their own mergers in response.

Edmund John Phillip Browne was born on Feb. 20, 1948, in Hamburg, Ger. At the suggestion of his father, who worked for BP, he took a position with the firm in 1966 as an apprentice while studying at the University of Cambridge, where he earned a degree in physics. He later received a business degree from Stanford University and held various positions at BP in exploration and production before becoming group treasurer and chief executive officer of BP Finance International in 1984. He became CEO of the Standard Oil Co. after it merged with BP in 1987, and he continued his climb up the BP management ladder until he was named CEO in 1995. Browne was knighted in 1998.

(ANTHONY G. CRAINE)

Bush, George W.

As a result of the vote held on Nov. 7, 2000, Republican George W. Bush, governor of Texas, was elected the 43rd president of the U.S. He defeated the Democratic candidate, Al Gore (*q.v.*), the country's vice president. It was the closest presidential election in more than a century, with Gore winning the popular vote by more than 500,000 out of some 105,000,000 ballots cast but with Bush taking the electoral college 271–266. The electoral count was not settled until December, after political and legal disputes over the results in Florida. Bush was especially strong in suburban, small town, and rural areas in Southern and Western states. His father, George Bush, had served as the 41st U.S. president (1989–93), and with his election George W. Bush thus became the second son of a president to be elected to the office, the first having been John Quincy Adams, the 6th U.S. president (1825–29), the son of John Adams, the 2nd president (1797–1801).

Bush was born on July 6, 1946, in New Haven, Conn., to a politically active family. Not only did his father have a long career in government, but his grandfather Prescott Bush was a U.S. senator from Connecticut (1952–62). The younger Bush grew up mostly in Texas. He graduated from Yale University (B.A., 1968) and Harvard Business School (M.B.A., 1975). Beginning in the mid-1970s he worked in the oil business in Midland, Texas, and for a time he owned his own company. In 1978 he lost a bid for a seat in the U.S. House of Representatives. He later worked for his father, and in 1989 he was the managing partner of a group that bought the Texas Rangers baseball team. In 1994 he was elected governor of Texas, the first son of a U.S. president to win a governorship, and in 1998 he was reelected. As governor he presided over changes in the state's welfare system and an increase in spending on schools.

Bush announced his candidacy for president on June 12, 1999, advocating what he called "compassionate conservatism." He raised record amounts of campaign money and gained the endorsements of prominent Republican officeholders. His principal rival was U.S. Sen. John McCain of Arizona, known particularly as an advocate of campaign finance reform. McCain upset Bush in the first primary, held on Feb. 1, 2000, in New Hampshire, but by March 7, so-called Super Tuesday, when Bush took 9 of 13 contests, it was clear that he would win the nomination.

During the primaries Bush courted right-wing Republicans, but with his choice of Richard B. Cheney (*q.v.*), who had been his father's secretary of defense, as his running mate, he tied his

opposite page, far left: AP/Wide World Photos; above: MGM/Liaison Agency

President-elect George W. Bush

Reuters/Archive Photos

candidacy more closely to the party's mainstream and then moved farther toward the centre. Bush's campaign proposals included large tax cuts and a partial privatization of Social Security. Although some people criticized his lack of experience at the national level—particularly in foreign affairs—and even questioned his competence, he did better than expected in debates with Gore, and he projected an easygoing manner that was popular among large groups of voters. (ROBERT RAUCH)

Case, Steve

During the closing months of 1999, Steve Case, the boyish-looking 41-year-old cofounder and CEO of Internet service provider (ISP) America Online, Inc. (AOL), initiated talks that would result in the largest corporate merger in history and the coming of age of the "dot-com" industry of Internet-related businesses. His effort resulted in the January 2000 announcement that AOL would purchase entertainment behemoth Time Warner Inc. in a $183 billion deal. The move marked the latest and largest step in Case's steady path toward fulfilling a nearly 20-year-old vision of what an on-line service could be—a vision that, not so long before, few shared with the man who had become one of the most powerful executives in the world.

Stephen M. Case was born Aug. 21, 1958, in Honolulu. His father was a corporate lawyer, his mother a teacher, and from a young age Case and his brother Dan—later a millionaire venture capitalist—began devising business opportunities for themselves. After graduating (1981) from Williams College, Williamstown, Mass., with a degree in political science, Case held positions in the marketing departments of Procter & Gamble and Pizza Hut. Not long after buying his first computer and discovering the world of on-line computing, Case took a marketing position in 1983 with Control Video Corp., a start-up company that planned to offer consumers downloadable video-game software via telephone lines. The plan failed, but the company—at Case's suggestion—regrouped and, under the name Quantum Computer Services, began providing an on-line network for users of Commodore 64 computers. Case foresaw an information-delivery service for computer users not unlike those that were being offered by Prodigy and CompuServe. His idea was to make the service far more user-friendly and more widely available. Quantum, using a friendly graphical interface originally developed by Apple Computer, Inc., became America Online in 1991 and confounded its critics by steadily outpacing all other on-line services in number of subscribers.

By the end of 1999, Case had built AOL into the world's largest ISP, engineered AOL's takeover of rival CompuServe and of World Wide Web-browser company Netscape Communications, and arranged deals that would ensure delivery of AOL services via satellite television, palmtop computers, and wireless telephones. Throughout, he seemed unaffected by ego; steady, unassuming, and simple, he surrounded himself with capable managers and built a reputation for loyalty. As the merger unfolded, he suggested that Time Warner CEO Gerald M. Levin assume the top position of the newly created AOL Time Warner. As he moved ahead with his plans in 2000, Case appeared to be writing his own chapter in the history of communications technology.

(ANTHONY G. CRAINE)

Chalayan, Hussein

The 2000 autumn-winter ready-to-wear show staged by Hussein Chalayan at Sadler's Wells, an east London dance theatre, was such a critical hit that it propelled the 30-year-old Turkish Cypriot designer to the designation of British Designer of the Year—for the second consecutive year—by the British Fashion Council. The audience compared his presentation with performance art. Chalayan's stage set consisted of modernist furniture—just four chairs and a circular coffee table set up at the foot of his catwalk. Throughout the show, models wearing his signature elegant, skillfully designed ensembles—floral-sprigged tops and skirts and black coats made of layered fabric and edged in white—moved by these pieces. At the finale of the show, a model approached the table, removed an inner wood ring from it, and stepped into the table; the furniture piece was instantly fashioned as a skirt.

By blending such clever theatrics with his beautiful designs, Chalayan became known as one of fashion's most intellectual designers. In a previous season he had dressed a troupe of models in traditional female Muslim headdresses but left their bodies naked. His presentation outraged the Muslim community, of which he was a member, but attracted the attention of the press. At another show models wore metal prongs that twisted their facial expressions into screams. In explaining his penchant for going to such stylistic extremes, Chalayan said simply, "Fashion is so transient. I am trying to give my work constant development, both conceptually and aesthetically." Unlike the designers whose catwalk theatrics overshadowed their clothes, Chalayan's work was remembered as clearly as his avant-garde styling. Shortly after his autumn-winter show, the London department store Harvey Nichols stocked his work for the first time. Although there was speculation that Chalayan would succeed Jil Sander as design director of her former company—which she sold to the Prada group—as the year drew to a close, Chalayan was still based in London designing his own line as well as knitwear for TSE New York.

Chalayan was born Huseyin Chaglayan on Aug. 12, 1970, in Nicosia, Cyprus, to Muslim parents. He moved to London with his family while still a child. After graduating from the prestigious British design college Central Saint Martin's College of Art and Design, London, he established his own independent design label in 1993. Chalayan's big break came soon thereafter when a collection that he developed was presented during London Fashion Week. His Fashion Week debut was critically acclaimed, as were his subsequent shows, which often fea-

bottom left: Stan Honda/AFP Worldwide

Gavin Smith/Frank Spooner Pictures Ltd.

Designer of the Year Hussein Chalayan

tured body-inhibiting designs—such as his cocoon dress, a sleeveless creation that bound the arms of its wearer to the sides of the body but provided slits for the release of the hands. In 1995 he won a design competition sponsored by the Absolut Vodka distillers. Two years later the Victoria and Albert Museum included his creations in an exhibition entitled "The Cutting Edge: 50 Years of British Fashion," and that same year his aubergine-coloured silk beaded gown was chosen as the dress of the year by the Museum of Costume in Bath.

(BRONWYN COSGRAVE)

Chambers, John T.

"The Internet will change companies, industries, and products in ways we can't even imagine. These changes will take place at speeds we have never seen before. If a company does not move rapidly, they will get left behind." So spoke John T. Chambers, president and chief executive officer of Cisco Systems, Inc., and in that role he made sure that his company moved at speeds necessary not only to maintain its position but also to far outstrip competitors. Since becoming head of Cisco in 1995, he had led the computer networking equipment firm to a more than 10-fold increase in annual revenues and a growth of 1,700%. By 2000 it was the third largest company in the world, behind the General Electric Co. and Microsoft Corp., and in January of that year *Business Week* magazine, which had dubbed Chambers "Mr. Internet," placed him on its list of the world's top 25 executives for the third time.

John Thomas Chambers was born in Cleveland, Ohio, on Aug. 23, 1949, and grew up in Charleston, W.Va. He gained a bachelor's degree in business and a law degree from West Virginia University as well as an M.B.A. in finance and management from Indiana University at Bloomington. He began his business career at IBM Corp. in 1976, and after six years there he moved to Wang Computers. During his eight-year tenure at Wang, he had to lay off 5,000 employees, and he later said, "I'll do anything to avoid that again." Chambers joined Cisco in 1991 as senior vice president of worldwide operations at a time when the firm had annual sales of $70 million. By 2000 annual revenue was estimated at $14 billion. One share of Cisco stock bought for $18 in 1990 was worth about $14,000 some 10 years later.

Chambers made it clear that he did not intend to let Cisco rest on its laurels as the world's chief provider of routers, the powerful network computers that sort the information packets that speed data through the Internet. Although the firm continued to improve the speed and capacity of the routers so that they could process one billion bits of information per second, Chambers had loftier goals. He viewed the future as a time when "data, voice, and video will be delivered over a single connection in our homes." With that in mind, he had engineered the acquisition of more than 60 companies since 1994, aiming to broaden Cisco's expertise and range of products. One area that he planned for Cisco to enter was the telecommunications business; he believed that Cisco's data networks would eventually become the world's leading voice networks. As a leader, Chambers had this credo: "Never ask your employees to do something you wouldn't be willing to do yourself." In keeping with that policy, the man named "the best boss in America" by the *20/20* television program had an office that was described as "austere and tiny as that of an entry-level programmer," and he and his top executives flew coach class and had no reserved parking spaces at Cisco's San Jose, Calif., headquarters.

(DAVID R. CALHOUN)

Chen Shui-bian

Despite strong warnings from the leaders of China not to vote a pro-independence candidate into power, Taiwanese voters did just that on March 18, 2000, electing opposition leader Chen Shui-bian as president of Taiwan. A former mayor of Taipei, Chen was an ambitious, tough-talking politician best known for advocating independence for his country. Only days before the election, he described Taiwan as a "sovereign country" and "not a part of the People's Republic of China"—an assertion that predictably infuriated Beijing. Nevertheless, Chen's bold words struck a responsive chord at home, as did his attacks on the corruption-plagued Kuomintang (KMT), Taiwan's ruling party. Garnering nearly 40% of the votes in a three-way race for president, Chen notched a landmark victory that decisively ended 55 years of unbroken KMT rule.

Born into a poor farming family on Feb. 18, 1951, in Tainan county, Taiwan, Chen distinguished himself early through academic performance. He won a scholarship to National Taiwan University, Taipei, and graduated with highest honours from its law school. Entering private practice in the mid-1970s, he became one of the island's leading attorneys. His first encounter with politics came when he defended eight anti-KMT protesters who had been charged with sedition. Chen lost the case, but thereafter his name was linked with the opposition movement. He ran for public office in 1981, winning a seat on the Taipei City Council.

In the mid-1980s Chen spent eight months in prison on charges of libeling a KMT official. He subsequently joined the pro-independence Democratic Progressive Party (DPP) and advanced through the party ranks. A member of the DPP Central Standing Committee from 1987 to 1989, Chen later served (1989–94) in the Taiwanese legislature before running successfully for mayor of Taipei. As mayor from 1994 to 1998, he delivered on campaign promises to fight government corruption, crack down on the city's sex industry, reduce crime, alleviate traffic problems, and raise Taipei's international profile. In pursuing his agenda, however, Chen often employed a heavy-handed, autocratic style, which ultimately turned off supporters and galvanized his enemies. He suffered a bitter defeat in his bid for reelection.

The defeat freed Chen to pursue the DPP's presidential nomination in 2000 and, according to his advisers, taught him the value of striking a more conciliatory tone as a politician. Chen's rhetoric on Taiwanese independence remained firm, but following his historic victory on March 18, he was quick to state his desire to "reduce the tensions" between Taiwan and China. During his inaugural address, he declared that he would not pursue independence while in office as long as China refrained from threatening to invade the island. In a significant overture in June, Chen proposed a summit meeting between the leaders of the two countries to discuss cross-strait relations. (SHERMAN HOLLAR)

Cheney, Richard B.

When Texas oil executive Richard B. Cheney took the job of heading a search committee to find a running mate for George W. Bush (*q.v.*), few suspected that he himself would end up the Republican vice presidential candidate. On July 25, 2000, however, Bush announced that Cheney was his choice. What he brought to the ticket was experience in national government and in foreign affairs, both of which Bush lacked. Cheney's campaign appearances, which included attacks on what he called the "big government" policies of Al Gore (*q.v.*), were effective among many voters and helped the Republican ticket win a narrow victory.

Cheney was born on Jan. 30, 1941, in Lincoln, Neb., but he grew up in Casper, Wyo. He entered Yale University in 1959 but failed to graduate. Cheney then earned B.A. (1965) and M.A. (1966) degrees in political science from the University of Wyoming and did work toward a doctorate at the University of Wisconsin at Madison. In 1968 he went to Washington, D.C., as a congressional fellow, and beginning in 1969 he worked in the administration of Pres. Richard Nixon. In 1974 Cheney became deputy chief of staff and in 1975 chief of staff for Pres. Gerald Ford. In 1978 he was elected from Wyoming to the first of six terms in the House of Representatives, and by 1988 he had risen to become the Republican whip. In the House he took conservative positions on issues, in particular opposing abortion, gun control, and environmental regulation. From 1989 to 1993 he was secretary of defense in the administration of Pres. George Bush and presided over reductions in the military following the breakup of the Soviet Union. Cheney also oversaw military operations in Panama and was the principal strategist of Operation Desert Storm in the Middle East. After President Bush lost his reelection bid in 1992, Cheney left government to become a fellow at the American Enterprise Institute. In 1995 he became the chairman and CEO of the Halliburton Co., a firm in Dallas, Texas, engaged in the oil-services industry and in construction.

Beginning in 1978 Cheney suffered three mild heart attacks, and he underwent quadruple-bypass surgery in 1988. Doctors pronounced him fit to participate in a national campaign and to serve as vice president, and his medical condition did not become an issue. Two weeks after the election, however, he suffered another mild heart attack, but he quickly resumed his duties in assisting in transition plans. There were signs that he would play a very active role in a Bush administration. (ROBERT RAUCH)

Vice president-elect Richard B. Cheney

AP/Wide World Photos

Cher

During a career that spanned well over three decades, Cher had made so many comebacks that, barring her "infomercial years," one might argue that the American singer and actress was never really gone. In 2000 she staged yet another return, this time taking home her first Grammy Award for the hit dance single "Believe." By early 2000 the song had become a number one hit in over 20 countries, and in the United Kingdom it became the top-selling single of all time by a female artist. This came on the heels of her first well-received film performance in years in *Tea with Mussolini* (1999), and it seemed that in 2000 Cher was once again back on top.

Cher was born Cherilyn Sarkisian on May 20, 1946, in El Centro, Calif. At age 16 she moved to Los Angeles, where she met Sonny Bono, whom she married in 1964. The couple began singing together, and their first big pop hit came in 1965 with "I Got You Babe," which sold over three million copies. The duo went on to score a number of hits, but by the late 1960s their popularity had begun to fade. A jump start came in 1971 with a television show, *The Sonny and Cher Comedy Hour,* which ran until 1974 and at its peak drew more than 30 million viewers weekly. During this time Cher's solo career flourished with hits such as "Half Breed" and "Gypsies, Tramps, and Thieves." Cher and Sonny divorced in 1974, and her later television efforts, both with and without Sonny, never matched their earlier success.

The 1980s were boom years for both her film and her music careers. Cher left the successful nightclub act she had cultivated in the late 1970s and early '80s to revisit an earlier interest in acting. She appeared in the Broadway and film versions of *Come Back to the Five and Dime, Jimmy Dean, Jimmy Dean* (1982) and, on the basis of her solid performance, was cast in a supporting role in *Silkwood* (1983), for which she received an Academy Award nomination. She made a number of other film appearances and was recognized for her outstanding performance as the mother of a disfigured teen in *Mask* (1985). In 1988 she won an Academy Award for her starring role as an Italian-American widow in the romantic comedy *Moonstruck* (1987). In the late 1980s she also had two successful albums—*Cher* (1987), featuring the hit single "I Found Someone," and *Heart of Stone* (1989), whose "If I Could Turn Back Time" also topped the charts. Cher's music career, which had waned by the mid-1990s, made a sharp turnaround with the late 1998 release of *Believe.* In 1998 Cher published the autobiographical *The First Time.*

(SANDRA LANGENECKERT)

Collins, Francis

On June 26, 2000, scientists gathered in Washington, D.C., accompanied by U.S. Pres. Bill Clinton, to announce that the sequencing of the DNA in the human genetic map had been completed through the combined effort of a public research consortium and a private company. The breakthrough was hailed as the first step toward helping doctors diagnose, treat, and even prevent thousands of illnesses caused by genetic disorders. One of the primary players in the work that led to the historic announcement was Francis Collins, director of the National Human Genome

Research Institute. Though he had come under fire for waging a well-publicized feud with J. Craig Venter, his counterpart in the private sector, Collins had led the government-backed effort, known as the Human Genome Project (HGP), since 1993, steering the effort through years of lean funding and increasing critical scrutiny.

Francis Sellers Collins was born on April 14, 1950, in Staunton, Va. Homeschooled by his mother for much of his young life, Collins took an early interest in science. He received his B.S. from the University of Virginia (1970), went on to Yale University to earn his M.S. and Ph.D. (1974), and earned his M.D. (1977) at the University of North Carolina at Chapel Hill. In 1984 Collins joined the staff of the University of Michigan at Ann Arbor as an assistant professor. His work at Michigan would earn him the reputation as one of the world's foremost genetics researchers. In 1989 he announced

Human genome researcher Francis Collins

Photo Courtesy of National Human Genome Research Institute, National Institutes of Health

the discovery of the gene that causes cystic fibrosis. The following year a Collins-led team found the gene that causes neurofibromatosis, a genetic disorder that generates the growth of tumours. He also served as a leading researcher in a collaboration of six laboratories that in 1993 uncovered the gene that causes Huntington chorea, a neurological disease.

In 1993 Collins, by then a full professor, left Michigan to take the post as head of the National Institutes of Health's sector of the HGP, which had originated three years earlier with a stated goal of completing the sequencing project in 15 years at a cost of $3 billion by coordinating the work of a number of leading academic research centres around the country, in collaboration with the U.S. Department of Energy and the Wellcome Trust of London. Known as a team player driven by a sincere interest in successful research that could help humanity, Collins was an obvious choice for the job, and he willingly took a sizable pay cut to participate in a historic project.

The necessity of a government effort was questioned when a rival operation, Celera Genomics, emerged in 1998 and appeared to be working even faster than the HGP at sequencing DNA. Headed by Venter, a former National Institutes of Health scientist, Celera had devised its own, quicker method—though some scientists, Collins among them, questioned the accuracy of the work. Collins successfully thwarted attempts to merge the public effort with the private endeavours, but in the end the two sides came together to announce the completion of the project.

A devout Christian, Collins freely expressed the awe he experienced as a leader in the uncloaking of one of the mysteries of life. As concerns arose about the moral and ethical implications of the research he had conducted, Collins actively cautioned against misuse of genetic information. At congressional hearings in July, Collins urged the passage of federal law to set guidelines on how individuals' genetic information could be handled. "The potential for mischief is quite great," he said.

(ANTHONY G. CRAINE)

Coutts, Russell

To celebrate his 38th birthday, on March 1, 2000, yachtsman Russell Coutts tied a 97-year-old record when he skippered Team New Zealand to its ninth straight winning race with him at the helm in the America's Cup sailing competition. The first five consecutive wins had come when he led the Kiwis' stunning sweep of the U.S. in 1995, his nation's first America's Cup triumph and only the second Cup victory by a non-U.S. team. His four victories in 2000 were over the Italian Prada team in its sleek yacht *Luna Rossa* and came in the defenders' home waters off New Zealand's North Island. The Kiwis easily overcame the Italians' fast starts, but Coutts waited until the fourth race to introduce a secret weapon—a new, light "code zero" headsail, designed for light winds. He appeared poised to lead the yacht *Black Magic* to the first-ever America's Cup defense by non-Americans, but instead of setting a personal record, Coutts had another surprise for the sailing world. In the fifth race of the best-five-of-nine series, he yielded command of the *Black Magic* to his backup helmsman, 26-year-old Dean Barker, who rose to the challenge by leading the crew to a comfortable 48-second win. Afterward, Barker credited Coutts with the victory, "All the hard work's been done by Russell."

After the Cup victory and a hero's welcome in a nation where sailing was a leading sport, Coutts remained in the spotlight by joining his design-team leader, Tom Schnackenberg, and tactician Brad Butterworth in taking over the administration of Team New Zealand, replacing yachting legend Sir Peter Blake. Securing and paying a team of yacht designers as well as a crew of sailors, negotiating broadcasting rights, finding sponsorship, and otherwise attending to the details of operating Team New Zealand became the responsibility of Coutts and his two partners. An even bigger surprise was in store, however, when Coutts and Butterworth quit Team New Zealand in May and signed an agreement with Swiss billionaire and avid yachtsman Ernesto Bertarelli to prepare a team from Switzerland to challenge for the next America's Cup, to be held in 2003.

Coutts was born March 1, 1962, and won his first regatta when he was nine years old, steering a 2.13-m (7-ft) wooden dinghy off the windy coast of Dunedin, South Island. Nine years later he became the single-handed world youth champion, and in 1984 he won an Olympic gold medal in the Finn class. He was with the national team when it finished third in the 1992 America's Cup challenge, but the next year he was rated the number one match racer in the world. In the 1990s he compiled an extraordinary series of international victories, including the Nippon Cup, the Bermuda Cup, and the World Match Racing championships, along with the 1995 America's Cup. Coutts was named MBE in 1985 and advanced to CBE 10 years later. (JOHN LITWEILER)

Curtis, Christopher Paul

In 2000 author Christopher Paul Curtis was still basking in the limelight after having received the highest form of recognition of his profession, and he did it after publishing only his second book. The 46-year-old author of young people's literature won the 1999 Newbery Medal, awarded by the American Library Association (ALA) to the author of the outstanding children's book published in the U.S., for *Bud, Not Buddy.* Curtis also was the winner of the Coretta Scott King Award, the ALA's prize for outstanding contribution by an African American writer. The honours were special milestones on a long journey for Curtis, a late starter who had always loved to write but did not become an author until he received some prodding from his wife and a little help from his children.

Curtis was born in Flint, Mich., on May 10, 1954. His father, a chiropodist, was eventually forced to take a job in an auto assembly plant for a better salary. After high school Curtis followed his father into the auto plant, earning money to pay for his part-time enrollment at the University of Michigan's Flint campus. Curtis married Kaysandra Sookram, a nurse from Trinidad, who, recalling the letters she received during their courtship, was convinced that he could be a writer. She encouraged him in 1993 to take a year off to concentrate on writing while she supported the family. Curtis spent his days at a children's library writing and editing in longhand. In the evenings his son, Steven, would type the manuscript into a computer. It was during that year that Curtis wrote his first book, *The Watsons Go to Birmingham—1963.* An early draft of the book won a Jules Hopwood Prize from the University of Michigan. Published by Delacorte Press in 1995, the book merited a Newbery Honor Award in 1996.

The Watsons Go to Birmingham—1963 is the story of an African American family from Flint that travels to the South during the days of the civil rights movement. Told from the perspective of a 10-year-old boy, the book starts out as a comic adventure but turns darker and more tragic as the family is exposed to, and changed by, the ugliness of racial tensions in Birmingham, Ala. *Bud, Not Buddy* is also narrated by a 10-year-old, a motherless boy in search of his unknown father. Curtis did not intend to write specifically for children, but he felt that his stories were best told from a child's perspective. The characters' experiences were often coloured by events from Curtis's own life, and the tales were told in a fresh, original voice that appealed to young readers. The Newbery Medal made Curtis's work even more popular, as was evidenced by the ascent of *Bud, Not Buddy* in sales. Although the book ranked well over 5,000 on the sales chart of a popular on-line bookseller before the award was announced, the following day it jumped to the top 10. (ANTHONY G. CRAINE)

Canadian opposition leader Stockwell Day

Reuters NewMedia Inc./Corbis

Day, Stockwell

On March 28, 2000, Albertan politician Stockwell Day announced that he would enter the race to head the newly formed Canadian Reform Conservative Alliance (CRCA). The group succeeded the Reform Party, founded by Preston Manning in 1987 and headed by him, and most observers presumed that Manning would assume the leadership of the new party. The younger and more charismatic Day captured the imagination of the membership, however, and in a runoff election on July 8 took 63% of the votes. He quickly moved to close ranks with Manning supporters, and on September 11 won a seat in Parliament from a riding in British Columbia, thus becoming leader of the opposition to the Liberal government of Prime Minister Jean Chrétien.

Day was born on Aug. 16, 1950, in Barrie, Ont. He grew up in Montreal and in Ottawa, where he attended high school. He then lived in a number of other provinces and held various jobs, including work as a deckhand on a trawler and as an administrator of a religious school. He briefly attended the University of Victoria, B.C., and became a lay minister in a Pentecostal church. Beginning in 1986, he represented the town of Red Deer in the Alberta legislature, and he held a number of cabinet positions in the Progressive Conservative provincial government. During this time he helped enact a number of policy shifts, including a reduction in government expenditures, a single-rate income tax, and welfare reform.

In his campaign for the leadership of the CRCA, Day advocated a program of traditional conservatism combined with the stance of the religious right. He proposed a reduction in the role of the federal government, limiting it to national defense, foreign affairs, monetary policy, and the regulation of financial institutions, trade, and criminal law. He advocated a looser federation of provinces, an arrangement that he believed could accommodate Quebec separatists. Day proposed a flat-rate income tax along with an increase in spending on defense and on health care, although he said that some health services should be privatized, and he favoured government support for religious schools. He advocated dropping the government's gun registry while being tougher on convicted criminals and illegal immigrants. Day supported capital punishment and opposed abortion and the expansion of homosexual rights, although he said that the electorate should decide such matters.

Joe Clark, leader of the Progressive Conservatives, the other principal party on the right, remained adamantly opposed to reconciliation with Day, and it was the Liberals and not the CRCA that picked up most of the support from Progressive Conservative defectors. Although the CRCA was Canada's largest party in terms of membership, polls indicated continuing widespread support for the Liberals.

(ROBERT RAUCH)

De Bruijn, Inge

Four years after having nearly quit swimming altogether, Inge de Bruijn of The Netherlands turned in a phenomenal performance at the Olympic Games in 2000. De Bruijn won gold medals in the 100-m butterfly, the 100-m freestyle, and the 50-m freestyle in Sydney, Australia, and set new world records in each of these events. She also earned a silver medal as part of the Dutch 4 × 100-m freestyle relay team. Although she qualified for the Dutch Olympic team in 1996, de Bruijn was asked to leave the squad because of her bad attitude. By her own admission, she was suffering from burnout that affected her approach to competitive swimming, but she later regretted missing the Games. She went on to find a new coach, new equipment, and a rigorous new training regimen, and she was able to turn her career around.

De Bruijn was born on Aug. 24, 1973, in Barendrecht, Neth. She began swimming at age 7 and participated in her first international meet at age 12. She joined swimming's elite when she took four medals at the 1991 European championships in Athens. Food poisoning almost forced her to miss the 1992 Olympic Games in Barcelona, Spain, but she competed and finished eighth in the 50-m freestyle and ninth in the 100-m butterfly. As the 1996 Games approached, however, de Bruijn's enthusiasm for swimming was waning. Even after making the national team, she skipped practices or showed up late. Jacco Verhaeren, her coach and boyfriend, asked her to leave the team.

In 1997 de Bruijn began training under noted swimming coach Paul Bergen. The workouts he tailored for her involved weight lifting and other strength exercises as well as swimming. The regimen did not yield immediate results, but at the 1999 European championships, de Bruijn began showing new signs of life, taking two gold medals and setting a European record in the 100-m butterfly. Then, in the spring and summer leading up to the 2000 Games, she went on a furious winning streak. By the time the Sydney Games began, de Bruijn held world records in the 50- and 100-m freestyle and the 50- and 100-m butterfly events. As had been the case with other women swimmers, de Bruijn's surprising success at the relatively advanced age of 26 brought with it suspicions of the use of performance-enhancing drugs. De Bruijn, who had never failed a drug test, denied the allegations and attributed her success to coaching, training, and the use of new swimwear that had been proved to improve her times as well as those of other swimmers. (ANTHONY G. CRAINE)

DiCaprio, Leonardo

After a two-year absence from the big screen, American actor Leonardo DiCaprio made his much-anticipated return to theatres in 2000, starring in *The Beach*, a dark film about a young backpacker's search for paradise. It was the first movie he chose to do after *Titanic* (1997) vaulted him to international stardom, and it was in sharp contrast to the sentimental romance set aboard the doomed ocean liner. Though flooded with offers to appear in blockbusters and other mainstream fare after *Titanic*, DiCaprio instead embraced roles that featured the complex and unconventional characters that

below left: AP/Wide World Photos

had come to define his career. While *The Beach*'s mixed reviews and less-than-titanic performance at the box office might have ended DiCaprio's reign as "king of the world," his daring choice of roles and innate talent placed him among acting's elite. In late 2000 he began work on his next film, Martin Scorsese's *Gangs of New York,* a period piece about gangsters in New York City in the mid-1800s.

Leonardo Wilhelm DiCaprio was born on Nov. 11, 1974, in Los Angeles. He first acted at the age of five, performing on the children's television show *Romper Room,* and as a teenager made numerous commercials and educational films. In 1988 he began appearing on a series of television shows, including *The New Lassie* and *Santa Barbara,* and in 1991 he landed a recurring role on *Growing Pains.* That year he also made his big-screen debut in *Critters 3,* a low-budget horror film. DiCaprio's breakthrough came in 1992 when he beat out 400 other hopefuls to act opposite Robert De Niro in *This Boy's Life* (1993). DiCaprio earned rave reviews, and for his next film, *What's Eating Gilbert Grape* (1993), he received an Academy Award nomination for his realistic portrayal of a mentally disabled teenager. Several independent movies followed, including *The Basketball Diaries* (1995) and *Total Eclipse* (1995), which focused on poet Arthur Rimbaud's homosexual relationship with Paul Verlaine. Although the films had little success at the box office, they proved DiCaprio a fearless and gifted actor.

In the mid-1990s DiCaprio began to attract a wider audience with more mainstream movies. He became a teen heartthrob after starring in *William Shakespeare's Romeo and Juliet* (1996), a modern retelling of the classic love story, and with the release of *Titanic,* he was firmly established as a leading man. His good looks and his poignant portrayal of Jack Dawson, a penniless artist who falls in love with an upper-class passenger, helped make *Titanic* the highest-grossing film ever. One of the most sought-after actors in Hollywood, he proved his star power by propelling *The Man in the Iron Mask* (1998), a movie made before the release of *Titanic,* to box-office success despite mixed reviews. Described as an avid partygoer in the media, DiCaprio parodied his reputation in Woody Allen's *Celebrity* (1998). In 2000 he recast his public image as that of an environmental activist, hosting Earth Day festivities and interviewing U.S. Pres. Bill Clinton for a television special on global warming. (AMY TIKKANEN)

Dirie, Waris

Having in her lifetime gone from Somalian nomad to international supermodel, Waris Dirie continued in 2000 to exert her influence as an activist in the fight against female genital mutilation (FGM; also called female circumcision). The statuesque model, who had undergone the procedure at about age five, overcame personal and cultural barriers to speak openly about it during a 1996 magazine interview. Her celebrity status helped to catapult the topic into the public eye, and in 1997 she was appointed the United Nations Population Fund's special ambassador for the elimination of FGM. In this capacity she traveled and spoke extensively, vigorously pursuing her goal of preventing future generations of women from suffering as she had.

The World Health Organization estimated that more than 130 million girls and women had undergone some form of FGM. While it was also performed in the Middle East and Asia, FGM was most prevalent in Africa; in Dirie's native Somalia the procedure was performed on an estimated 98% of women. Dirie experienced the most extreme form, called infibulation, in which all or part of the external genitalia is cut off and the vagina stitched up, with only a small, and often insufficient, opening left for the passage of bodily fluids. Dirie's procedure was performed under primitive and unsanitary conditions without anesthesia, and she was forced to endure excruciating pain and both short- and long-term complications.

Dirie was one of 12 children born in the Somalian desert into a large nomadic family. She was probably born sometime in the late 1960s, but her exact age was unknown, as no birth records were kept. Much of her childhood was focused on tending to the family's herd and obtaining enough food and water to survive. She ran away from home in her early teens to avoid an arranged marriage, embarking on a long and treacherous journey that took her through the desert to Mogadishu and from there eventually to London to serve as a maid in the home of an uncle who was beginning a term as an ambassador there. When his tenure ended, Dirie elected to stay in London illegally. She was illiterate, but she found work in the kitchen at a fast-food restaurant and a room at the YMCA, and she took classes to learn to read and write English. In 1983 she contacted a photographer who had earlier approached her on the street about modeling. The photos he took launched her career, and she went on to appear on the runways of Paris, Milan, and New York and in top fashion magazines such as *Elle, Glamour,* and *Vogue.* She recounted her dramatic transformation, as well as her experience with FGM, in her autobiography *Desert Flower: The Extraordinary Journey of a Desert Nomad* (1998). (SANDRA LANGENECKERT)

Dyson, Freeman

While advances in genetic research made commercial trafficking in genetic material a distinct possibility, one prominent voice led the call for caution. Freeman Dyson, a British-born American physicist, issued a warning upon receiving the 2000 Templeton Prize for Progress in Religion. He speculated that such activity could lead to "a splitting of humanity into hereditary castes," a situation that would amount to the human race's regressing back to a society of masters and slaves. "No matter how strongly we believe in the virtues of the free market economy, the free market must not extend to human genes."

Dyson had made a career out of encouraging a symbiosis between science and religion, emphasizing the importance of having both points of view complement each other so that advances in technology could be implemented in ways that were moral and ethical. He had also advocated using technological advances in ways that would span economic and social gaps. The alternative, he said, was profit-driven research that merely created "toys for the rich."

Dyson was born on Dec. 15, 1923, in Crowthorne, Berkshire, Eng. He received a degree in mathematics from the University of Cambridge in 1945 after having taken time out from his studies to work as a civilian statistician for the Royal Air Force during World War II. Graduate studies at Cambridge, the University of Birmingham, Eng., and Cornell University, Ithaca, N.Y., followed, and he returned to Cornell to teach in 1951. From there Dyson moved on in 1953 to the Institute for Advanced Study in Princeton, N.J., where he remained professor emeritus in 2000.

In addition to encouraging a conscientious approach to scientific progress, Dyson was also known for having the ability to relate scientific principles to the layperson. His 1979 autobiography, *Disturbing the Universe,* was praised as an accessible account of the mind of a scientist. Other books included *Weapons and Hope* (1984), a study of nuclear weapons; *Origins of Life* (1985); *Infinite in All Directions* (1988); and *Imagined Worlds* (1998). He also published articles in *Scientific American* and other periodicals. His projections for the future offered a hopeful vision of what scientific progress could achieve, including exploration and colonization of space and the search for intelligent life elsewhere in the universe. In the 1950s he was a member of the Orion Project research team that developed a working model of a spacecraft meant to carry humans to Mars.

A fellow of the Royal Society (U.K.) and a member of the National Academy of Sciences (U.S.), Dyson received in 1996 the Lewis Thomas Prize, awarded to scientists for artistic achievements. He had also been awarded the Wolf Prize in physics in 1981. (ANTHONY G. CRAINE)

Edwards, Jorge

On April 24, 2000, King Juan Carlos of Spain presented the Cervantes Prize, the highest honour in Spanish-language literature, to Chilean writer Jorge Edwards. In his acceptance speech Edwards, the first Chilean to win the prize, remarked, "I never calculated the consequences of this calling in the beginning. It was an accidental path."

Edwards was born July 29, 1931, in Santiago, Chile. He studied law and philosophy at the University of Chile and earned a law degree in 1958. During his student years he published a collection of short stories, *El patio* (1952). In its portrayal of the alienation of a young man of the middle class, it was a noteworthy break from the prevailing national literary tradition, which emphasized the rural aspects of Chilean life.

After graduation Edwards entered Chile's diplomatic corps and began a dual career as a government official and a writer. In 1959 his government sent him to the U.S. to study political science at Princeton University. While there, he wrote *Gente de la ciudad* (1961), a view of the dehumanizing effects of oppressive bureau-

above: United Nations

cracy. He then went to Paris, where he served until 1967 as secretary of the Chilean embassy and representative for European affairs. During those years he wrote his first novel, *El peso de la noche* (1965), in which he described Chilean society as authoritarian with rigid social norms. Also in Paris he wrote *Las máscaras* (1967), a collection of short stories in which he broke away from social realism and raised the question of the limits between reality and fantasy, and *Temas y variaciones* (1969), short stories dealing with such subjects as self-destruction, isolation, anguish, and the desire for utopia.

Returning to Chile in 1967, Edwards served as the nation's chairman of the Department of Eastern Affairs, often negotiating relations with socialist countries. He worked briefly in the Chilean embassy in Peru and in 1970 was sent to Cuba by Chile's first socialist president, Salvador Allende, with the mission of reinstating relations between the two countries. Edwards recounted his experiences there in *Persona non grata* (1973), which became his best-known book. In it he sharply criticized the regime of Cuban Pres. Fidel Castro, describing in detail the harassment of writers and the imprisonment of intellectuals and claiming that the only efficient aspect of Cuban society was the government secret police. Because of these views, Edwards was asked to leave Cuba in 1971. He served as assistant to the Chilean ambassador to France, but in 1973 he was expelled from the diplomatic corps by Chile's right-wing dictator Gen. Augusto Pinochet Ugarte, who had overthrown Allende in a military coup. Edwards then lived in Spain and Chile, where he continued to write. Among his works during that time were *El museo de cera* (1981), a novel that revealed his feelings about the conditions in Chile during the Pinochet regime, and *Adios, poeta—* (1990), a study of Cuban poet and diplomat Pablo Neruda. (DAVID R. CALHOUN)

Eminem

Hip-hop MC Eminem had a very full year in 2000. Along with releasing the fastest-selling album in the history of rap—*The Marshall Mathers LP*— he was sued by both his mother (for the second time) and his wife, was charged with carrying a concealed weapon (twice) and with assault, and filed for divorce. A white performer who had won acceptance in an art form dominated by African Americans, Eminem was revered by some critics, who praised his mastery of rhyme, but reviled by others, who accused him of misogyny and homophobia.

Marshall Bruce Mathers III was born in St. Joseph, Mo., in 1973. Within a year his father left the family. Living largely on welfare, Mathers, his mother, and his half-brother bounced back and forth between Kansas City, Mo., and Detroit and finally settled in Detroit's predominantly black east side. According to Mathers, he and his brother were abused by their mother. Perennially the "new kid," he was frequently the victim of bullies at school. When unexcused absences kept him in the ninth grade for the third year, Mathers quit school, determined to make it in hip-hop music.

At age 14 he had begun rapping in Detroit clubs and, as Eminem, made a name for himself in the hip-hop underground. His first album, *Infinite* (1996), sold poorly, however, and he continued working at menial jobs. When Eminem finished second in the freestyle category at the 1997 Rap Olympics in Los Angeles, he came to the attention of Dr. Dre, founding member of pioneering gangsta rappers N.W.A. and the head of Aftermath records. By this time Eminem had developed the persona of the inhibitionless Slim Shady, who gave voice to Eminem's id in often vulgar and violent lyrics. With Dr. Dre as his producer and mentor, Eminem released *The Slim Shady LP* early in 1999. Benefiting from the inventive channel-surfing video for the hit song "My Name Is" and the instant street credibility of Dr. Dre's involvement, the album went multiplatinum, and Eminem won two Grammy Awards and four MTV Video Music Awards.

Grounded in his life experience but seemingly reflecting a troubled psyche, Eminem's songs outraged many, including gay and lesbian groups and the attorney general of Ontario, who in October 2000 sought to block Eminem's entrance into Canada because his songs "advocate . . . physical, graphic violence against women." Still, supporters praised Eminem for "keeping it real," and the performer asserted that young people understood the humour behind his vitriol. His tumultuous relationship with his wife, Kim, was chronicled in songs in which he rapped about killing her. In June 2000 Eminem was charged with assault when he allegedly pistol-whipped a man he saw kissing her. Soon after the incident she attempted suicide. Eminem later filed for divorce; Kim won custody of their daughter; and they settled the $10 million lawsuit she had brought against him. His mother also sued him for defaming her in song and interviews. Meanwhile, Eminem scaled the pop charts. (JEFF WALLENFELDT)

Henny Ray Abrams/AFP Worldwide

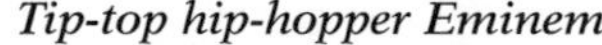

Tip-top hip-hopper Eminem

Enhbayar, Nambaryn

Nambaryn Enhbayar, the chairman since 1997 of the Mongolian People's Revolutionary Party (MPRP), was appointed Mongolia's new prime minister on July 26, 2000, following the landslide election victory of the MPRP. With a view toward modernizing the MPRP, Enhbayar had cut the party's ties to its communist past, turned it into a democratic socialist party, and pointed it along the road of market reform. He had visited Washington, London, Paris, Beijing, and other capitals and established contacts with world leaders ranging from British Prime Minister Tony Blair to the Dalai Lama, the exiled religious and political leader of Tibet. Enhbayar also envisaged an important role for Mongolia's Lamaist religion in reestablishing traditional moral values.

Enhbayar was born on June 1, 1958, in the Mongolian capital, Ulaanbaatar, and he graduated in 1980 from what is now known as the Maksim Gorky Institute of World Literature in Moscow. After returning home, he worked as a translator and an editor for the committee of the Mongolian Union of Writers until 1983, when he became head of the union's foreign relations department. He was elected vice president of the Mongolian Translators' Association in 1990, and in November of that year he was appointed chief deputy chairman of the Mongolian Culture and Art Development Committee (formerly the Ministry of Culture), a post he held for some 18 months.

Enhbayar's political career took off in June 1992 when, standing as a candidate for the MPRP, he won the seat for Ulaanbaatar Suhbaatar 23 constituency in the State Great Hural (national assembly) elections. He was appointed minister of culture in August 1992 and served in the government of Prime Minister Puntsagiyn Jasray for four years. In October 1992 he was elected to the MPRP Little Hural (the former Central Committee).

Enhbayar replaced Budragchaagiyn Dash-Yondon as secretary-general of the MPRP in July 1996 and was reelected at the party's 22nd Congress in February 1997, but he was effectively demoted following Natsagiyn Bagabandi's election to the newly created post of MPRP chairman. Bagabandi was elected president of Mongolia in May 1997, however, and a month later Enhbayar took over the MPRP chairmanship. He did not stand in the 1996 general elections but returned to the Great Hural in August 1997 after winning the by-election in Bagabandi's Zavhan 21 constituency. Enhbayar was reelected to the Great Hural on July 2, 2000, this time for Ulaanbaatar Bayangol 65 constituency, with a majority of over 6,000 votes. Before becoming prime minister, Enhbayar also acted as an adviser to the Asian Development Bank. (ALAN J.K. SANDERS)

Fleming, Renée

American soprano Renée Fleming continued to command the heights of the opera world in 2000, winning wide acclaim with the recording *Strauss Heroines,* which she made in collaboration with a number of colleagues. She was praised for the beauty and richness of her voice and for the thought and sensitivity she brought to the texts. Although Fleming had come to be known particularly as a singer of Richard Strauss, her repertoire was extraordinarily broad, spanning three centuries and ranging from Handel and Mozart through 19th-century bel canto to the works of a number of contemporary composers.

Fleming was born on Feb. 14, 1959, in Indiana, Pa., but she grew up in Rochester, N.Y., where her parents taught music in high school. She began music lessons as a young child and as a college student had success as a jazz vocalist. In 1981 she graduated from the State University of New York College at Potsdam with a degree in music education. She continued her studies at the Eastman School of Music at the University of Rochester, N.Y., and from 1983 to 1987 studied at the Juilliard School's American Opera Center in New York City, where Beverley Johnson was among her teachers. She spent 1984–85 on a Fulbright fellowship in West Germany, where she studied with Arleen Augér and, in a master class, with Elisabeth Schwarzkopf. Prior to performing, Fleming always experienced anxiety, and after her return from Europe she suffered such a severe loss of confidence that she was forced to withdraw from the stage. She quickly recovered, however, and she made her professional debut in Salzburg, Austria, in 1986. Two years later she won the Metropolitan Opera National Council Auditions and in 1989 the George London Award. The following year she received the Richard Tucker Award. From this point her career took off, and she was soon in demand at the world's most prestigious opera houses.

Among Fleming's roles were Fiordiligi in Mozart's *Così fan tutte,* Marguerite in Gounod's *Faust,* Ellen Orford in Benjamin Britten's *Peter Grimes,* and the title characters in Handel's *Alcina,* Massenet's *Manon,* and Carlisle Floyd's *Susannah.* She sang the world premieres of the countess in John Corigliano's *The Ghost of Versailles* (1991), of Madam de Tourvel in Conrad Susa's *The Dangerous Liaisons* (1994), and of Blanche DuBois in André Previn's *A Streetcar Named Desire* (1998). Fleming won perhaps her most lavish praise for her performances as the Marschallin in Strauss's *Der Rosenkavalier,* with a number of critics counting her among the very best ever to have sung the role. Fleming recorded extensively, and the recording of Dvorak's *Rusalka,* in which she sang the title role, won *Gramophone* Awards in 1999 as the best opera recording and the Record of the Year. (ROBERT RAUCH)

Fox Quesada, Vicente

In elections on July 2, 2000, Vicente Fox Quesada was elected president of Mexico and thereby ended 71 uninterrupted years of rule by the Institutional Revolutionary Party (PRI). As the candidate of the centre-right National Action Party (PAN), Fox won approximately 43% of the vote to 36% for PRI candidate Francisco Labastida Ochoa and 16.5% for Cuauhtémoc Cárdenas Solórzano of the leftist Democratic Revolutionary Party (PRD). After his election Fox, at one time president of the Mexican subsidiary of the Coca-Cola Co., said that he planned to run a "businesslike" administration and that "the main problem of Mexico is development . . . growth of the economy, it's getting the jobs that we need, it's sharing the income, redistributing income." He also pledged to end the cronyism that had been prevalent in PRI administrations, saying he would "make sure we get the best men and best women this country has for each of the positions. It's a little bit like we do it in companies."

Fox was born July 2, 1942, in Mexico City and was raised on a 445-ha (1,100-ac) ranch in the central Mexican state of Guanajuato. The ranch had been purchased by his paternal grandfather, an immigrant from Ireland. Fox's mother was born in Spain; at one time having a foreign-born parent would have barred Fox from seeking the presidency. A Roman Catholic, Fox was educated at the Jesuit Ibero-American University in Mexico City. After graduation he did postgraduate studies at Harvard University before working as a salesman for the Mexican unit of Coca-Cola. In 1971 he was transferred to the company's office in Mexico City, where he quickly rose in the firm to serve as its chief executive in Mexico from 1975 to 1979. In recalling that period in his life, Fox said, "What I hated most about those years at Coca-Cola was the time I had to spend dithering with the government." In 1979 Coca-Cola offered Fox a promotion to become head of its Latin American operations, but because this would have required him to live in Miami, Fla., he resigned and moved back to Guanajuato with his brothers. Mexico's difficult economy during the 1980s convinced Fox that the country needed new leadership. In 1988, as a PAN candidate, he ran for a seat in the Chamber of Deputies, the lower house of Mexico's legislature, and was elected. After serving one term he ran for governor of Guanajuato but lost in an election during which charges of fraud were made. In 1995 he again ran for governor and was elected.

During the sometimes stormy presidential campaign, the almost 2-m (6-ft 5-in)-tall Fox lashed out at Labastida, calling him "shorty" and ridiculing him as an "errand boy" for the PRI. After the election Fox broke precedent by apologizing in person to Labastida and other opponents he had criticized. (DAVID R. CALHOUN)

Garnier, Jean-Pierre

On Jan. 17, 2000, two of the world's largest pharmaceutical companies, SmithKline Beecham PLC and Glaxo Wellcome PLC, announced that they were merging. The two British giants had tried to join forces in 1998, but the deal had fallen through largely because of a disagreement over who would head the combined firm. This time around, the companies agreed that there was only one man suitable for the position—French business executive Jean-Pierre Garnier. Without him, according to industry observers, the merger that produced Glaxo SmithKline could not have been achieved.

Garnier was born on Oct. 31, 1947, in France and was the son of an advertising executive. He studied at Louis Pasteur University, Strasbourg, France, where he earned a master's degree in pharmaceutical science and a Ph.D. in pharmacology. In 1974, as a Fulbright scholar at Stanford University, Garnier obtained a master's degree in business administration. Beginning his business career in the U.S., he quickly achieved success. From 1975 to 1990 he worked for the pharmaceutical firm Schering-Plough Corp., holding various management positions before becoming director of the firm's U.S. operations. In 1990 Garnier made the move to SmithKline Beecham, where he was named president of the company's North American pharmaceutical business. He was elected to SmithKline Beecham's board of directors in 1992 and was appointed chief operating officer of the company in 1995. In recognition of his accomplishments, Garnier was made a Chevalier of the Legion of Honour in 1997. Two years later he was named chief executive officer designate of SmithKline Beecham after the firm's longtime CEO, Jan Leschly, announced plans to step down.

Garnier was known as a calm, levelheaded, and highly disciplined executive—traits that had served him well throughout his career. He was also praised by many in the industry for his rare blend of experience and skills in the fields of both marketing and science. What made him even more attractive as a candidate to lead Glaxo SmithKline was his preference for employing a consensual style of management, which involved taking into account the views of employees before making strategic decisions. Garnier's style was expected to help smooth the process of merging two huge and—in many respects—markedly different firms. Whereas Glaxo had in the past focused primarily on selling prescription medicines, SmithKline had emphasized over-the-counter drugs and consumer health products. Garnier indicated his desire to find a proper balance and to exploit the resources of both companies.

(DAVID R. CALHOUN)

Gellar, Sarah Michelle

In recent years a number of American television shows that catered to the youth market had emerged, with varying degrees of success. In 2000, however, one stood out as a notable winner in the eyes of both the public and the critics, *Buffy the Vampire Slayer* starring Sarah Michelle Gellar. By combining action-adventure elements, supernatural themes, a strong female lead, wry humour, and ideas of special interest to young people, *Buffy the Vampire Slayer* (a spin-off of the 1992 motion picture of the same name) extended its appeal across the age spectrum. This success was due in no small part to Gellar, who portrayed Buffy's strength and plucky determination as well as her teenage conflicts and vulnerabilities.

Gellar was born on April 14, 1977, in New York City. Her show-business career began when, at the age of four, she was eating in a

left: AP/Wide World Photos; right: Gerry Penny/AFP Worldwide

local restaurant and was noticed by an agent. A few weeks later she began work in her first motion picture, the made-for-TV *An Invasion of Privacy* (1983). Such other projects as the films *Over the Brooklyn Bridge* (1984) and *Funny Farm* (1988), an appearance on the television series *Spenser: For Hire* in 1986, hostess duties on the TV talk show *Girl Talk* (1989), and the role of the young Jacqueline Bouvier Kennedy in the TV miniseries *A Woman Named Jackie* (1991) followed, as did Broadway roles in *The Widow Claire* (1986) and *Jake's Women* (1992). Gellar began attracting fans with a role in the teen soap opera *Swans Crossing* (1991), and she gained more popularity—as well as a 1995 Emmy Award—for her work (1993–95) in the soap opera *All My Children.* During these years she also competed as an ice skater, worked as a model, appeared in dozens of TV commercials, and studied tae kwon do—a martial art that she put to good use as Buffy.

In 1997 Gellar made her first appearance as the slayer—the chosen one destined to do battle with an assortment of demons, vampires, werewolves, and the like that threatened the fictional town of Sunnydale, Calif. The show spawned a spin-off, *Angel,* and both were renewed for the 2000–01 season. When not working on *Buffy,* Gellar added more films to her list of credits—among them the teenage thrillers *I Know What You Did Last Summer* (1997) and *Scream 2* (1997), the romantic comedy *Simply Irresistible* (1999), and *Cruel Intentions* (1999), a youthful reworking of *Dangerous Liaisons* with Gellar as the seductive villain. In 2000 she starred in *Harvard Man,* which was scheduled for release in 2001. (BARBARA WHITNEY)

Googoosh

In 2000 Iranian pop singer Googoosh made a major comeback, performing in public for the first time in 20 years. On a world tour that began in North America, she sang old favourites as well as a few selections from her new compact disc (CD), *Zoroaster,* to packed stadiums, affording Iranian immigrants the opportunity to see one of their most popular musical icons for the first time since Iran's 1979 Islamic revolution. It was an emotionally charged return that reportedly left audiences in tears.

Googoosh was born in 1950 in Tehran. Her legal name was Faegheh Atashin, but she was called "Googoosh" from birth. She began singing and acting at a young age, performing with her father, an entertainer, when she was a toddler and making her first film at age seven. In the 1970s Googoosh was at the height of her film and music career and was widely emulated by Iranian women; in addition to listening to her music, they copied her clothing (miniskirts) and her short haircut (the "Googooshy"). The 1979 revolution, however, brought a number of cultural restrictions; women were no longer allowed to sing in public, and pop music was banned completely. Most performers chose to leave the country rather than be silenced, but Googoosh, who was visiting the United States at the time of the revolution, elected to return home within a few months despite the possibility of persecution or even execution. She was jailed briefly but was not harmed. After her release she reportedly lived in seclusion.

Pop icon Googoosh

Lucy Nicholson/AFP Worldwide

In the decades in which Googoosh was publicly silent, her music was not. Bootleg recordings and videos were readily available in Iran, and many found their way into the hands of the younger generation. Googoosh acquired a number of fans among those who had never had the freedom to purchase one of her CDs legally or hear her perform live.

Following the election of Pres. Mohammad Khatami in 1997, many restrictions began to be lifted. Some women (Googoosh was not among them) were once again allowed to sing in public to all-female audiences, and, while distributing pop music was still officially illegal, possession of it was allowed. Googoosh finally was granted a passport and allowed to leave the country for the first time since the revolution, and she made plans to tour and to work on a film with her husband, director Masud Kimiai. Islamic fundamentalists, however, vehemently opposed the tour, and it remained to be seen whether she would ever again be able to perform for fans in her native country. (SANDRA LANGENECKERT)

Gore, Albert A., Jr.

In the voting held on Nov. 7, 2000, Democrat Albert A. Gore, Jr., the country's vice president, lost his bid for the U.S. presidency to Republican George W. Bush (*q.v.*), governor of Texas. It was the closest presidential election in more than 100 years. Although Gore won the popular contest by more than 500,000 votes out of some 105,000,000 cast, he lost the electoral college 271–266. The final electoral vote, which hinged on disputes over the outcome in Florida, was not determined until December. Gore ran strongly in urban and industrial areas, and he won a number of states on the East and West coasts and in the Great Lakes region. He was hurt in some areas by Green Party candidate Ralph Nader (*q.v.*).

Gore was born on March 31, 1948, in Washington, D.C., to a prominent political family. His father, Albert Gore, Sr., represented Tennessee for seven terms in the U.S. House and for three terms in the U.S. Senate. After the son earned a B.A. (1969) from Harvard University, he volunteered for the draft and served as a U.S. Army reporter in Vietnam. He then worked as a reporter and editor for the *Nashville Tennessean* and also studied theology and law at Vanderbilt University, Nashville. In 1976 he was elected to the first of four terms in the U.S. House of Representatives, and in 1984 he was elected to the Senate. Gore made an unsuccessful bid for the Democratic nomination for president in 1988, but he won reelection to the Senate in 1990. In Congress Gore was known for developing expertise in such matters as technology and arms control, and his book on environmental issues, *Earth in the Balance,* was published in 1992. That same year Bill Clinton chose Gore as his running mate, and as vice president he took an active role in decision making.

On June 16, 1999, Gore formally announced his candidacy for the Democratic nomination, and he had the support of the party establishment. Nonetheless, former U.S. senator Bill Bradley of New Jersey took more liberal positions on many issues and mounted a strong challenge. By March 7, however, the date of Super Tuesday, Gore had won all 16 state contests, and it was clear that he would get the nomination.

With the aid of running mate U.S. Sen. Joseph I. Lieberman (*q.v.*) of Connecticut, Gore tried to distance himself from the scandals of the Clinton administration, but he continued to face allegations that he had engaged in illegal fund-raising activities and over the years had taken inconsis-

AP/Wide World Photos

Democratic presidential candidate Al Gore

tent positions on issues. Gore's policy proposals included targeted tax cuts and the use of budget surpluses to pay down the national debt. Although he campaigned from the centre, there was a populist element to his proposals, which he said were designed to benefit "working people." He was not successful, however, in taking credit for the economic boom of the Clinton-Gore administration, and despite his reputation as a debater, his performances against Bush were not strong. Polls indicated that a majority of voters agreed with Gore's positions on major issues and considered him the more knowledgeable and capable of the candidates, but it also was widely agreed that his was a poorly managed campaign. (ROBERT RAUCH)

Greenspan, Alan
On Jan. 4, 2000, economist Alan Greenspan was nominated by Pres. Bill Clinton to a fourth four-year term as chairman of the Board of Governors of the U.S. Federal Reserve System (Fed). In a bipartisan vote on February 3, the U.S. Senate overwhelmingly confirmed the nomination. Thus, the fiscally conservative chairman, a staunch advocate of deregulation and balanced budgets as well as a determined foe of inflation, continued to wield enormous power over the U.S. economy. He was commonly given a major share of the credit for the economic expansion that began in March 1991 and that on Feb. 1, 2000, officially became the longest in U.S. history. In addition, his influence on global finance was so extensive that in September 1999 *The Sunday Times* named him one of the three most powerful people in the British Isles.

During the years of his chairmanship, Greenspan became known for his decisive use of monetary policy to steer the economy between the hazards of inflation and recession. When the Dow Jones Industrial Average fell a record 508 points on Oct. 19, 1987, shortly after he took command at the Fed, he acted quickly to ensure liquidity in the markets, but he moved too slowly to prevent the U.S. from falling into a recession in 1990. When Asian countries underwent a financial crisis and an economic downturn beginning in 1997, he lowered U.S. interest rates in 1998 in order to cushion the economy. As the Asian economies recovered and the U.S. economy continued its solid expansion, he then began a series of interest-rate hikes in June 1999 that continued into 2000. His justification for these increases included what he called "unsustainable" rates of growth in the U.S. economy, the lowest unemployment rates in three decades, and "overextended" stocks, particularly among technology issues, and he spoke publicly about the "wealth effect" of booming stock prices. Given the extraordinarily high rates of growth in productivity and the lack of apparent inflation, however, some observers argued that Greenspan's policies were unnecessary or even might be counterproductive. Nonetheless, by mid-2000 the chairman's moves seemed to be having the effects he wanted, with signs that the economy was slowing and that the stock market had become less speculative.

Greenspan was born on March 6, 1926, in New York City. He received B.S. (1948), M.A. (1950), and Ph.D. (1977) degrees in economics from New York University and was a disciple of the writer Ayn Rand, who was known for advocating laissez-faire capitalism. From 1958 Greenspan headed his own consulting firm. He then entered the public sector as an adviser to Pres. Richard Nixon (1968–74) and went on to be chairman of the Council of Economic Advisers (1974–77) and chairman of the National Commission on Social Security Reform (1981–83). He also served on other advisory boards and on the boards of a number of private companies. In 1987 Pres. Ronald Reagan nominated him to succeed Paul A. Volcker as chairman of the Fed. (ROBERT RAUCH)

Halonen, Tarja
On March 1, 2000, Tarja Halonen was inaugurated as president of Finland, the first woman to have won that office. The candidate of the left-wing Social Democratic Party (SDP), she had defeated on February 6 former prime minister Esko Aho of the Centre Party in the closely contested (51.6–48.4%) second round of Finland's two-stage election process. She had prevailed by a wider margin in the first round of voting, held on January 16, winning 40% of the electorate to 34.4% for Aho. While Halonen's strongest support came from urban and female voters, she made inroads among other constituencies as well, in part by emphasizing her experience as Finland's minister of foreign affairs, a post she had held since 1995.

Halonen was born on Dec. 24, 1943, in Helsinki. As a student at the University of Helsinki, she served (1969–70) as social affairs secretary and general secretary of the National Union of Finnish Students. After earning a degree in law in 1970, she began her professional career as an attorney with the Central Organization of Finnish Trade Unions.

Halonen entered politics in 1974, when she became parliamentary secretary to Prime Minister Kalevi Sorsa. She held the job until Sorsa left office in 1975. Halonen later became chair of the Finnish National Organization for Sexual Equality. From 1977 to 1996 she was a member of the Helsinki City Council, and in 1979 she was elected to Parliament as a candidate of the SDP. While retaining her parliamentary seat, Halonen broadened her experience in domestic and international politics by holding a number of Cabinet posts. Before her appointment as foreign affairs minister, she had served as minister of social affairs and health (1987–90), minister for Nordic cooperation (1989–91), and minister of justice (1990–91).

On the day of Halonen's inauguration as president, a new constitution for Finland went into effect. It reduced the powers of the president and emphasized the position of Parliament as the strongest body in the government. The most notable changes concerned domestic policy; for example, Parliament was given the power to choose the prime minister, a responsibility formerly discharged by the president. The president, however, retained considerable powers in foreign policy, the area of Halonen's greatest strength. The previous constitution had stated that "Finland's relations with foreign states are determined by the president." The new document specified that "Finland's foreign policy is headed by the president in conjunction with the Council of Ministers." Halonen was expected to continue Finland's pro-European Union policies, but she had voiced her opposition to the idea of Finnish membership in NATO. (DAVID R. CALHOUN)

Jacq, Christian
"Life was so monotonous." So begins *Nefer the Silent*, the first volume of *The Stone of Light*, a series of historical novels about the artists who created the legendary tombs of the Egyptian pharaohs and the soldiers who guarded the treasures stored there. Life, however, had been anything but monotonous for Christian Jacq, the book's best-selling French author, who launched the series *La Pierre de lumière* in March 2000 with *Néfer le silencieux*, which had an initial printing of 1.5 million copies; the book was available worldwide in 22 languages. The second volume, known in English as *The Wise Woman*, followed in September, and the concluding two installments were scheduled for publication in 2001.

Earlier Jacq had created a sensation in the publishing industry with his five-volume biographical epic about Ramses II, the pharaoh who ruled Egypt from 1279 to 1213 BC. The *Ramses* books, which were first released in installments in France in 1995 and 1996, touched off a passion there for all things Egyptian. By 2000 the popular series had sold 11 million copies in 29 countries, and Jacq was crowned the "pharaoh of publishing."

Best-selling Egyptologist Christian Jacq

Paco Torrente/AFP Worldwide

Jacq was born in Paris in 1947 and became fascinated with Egyptology as a teenager after reading Jacques Pirenne's *Histoire de la civilisation de l'Egypte ancienne.* After earning his doctorate in Egyptian studies from the Sorbonne, Jacq pursued a career of scholarship. His first published works were serious, straightforward histories that earned him recognition from the French Academy. Jacq published his first successful novel, *Champollion l'Egyptien,* in 1987. His fiction did not receive much critical attention at first, and when it did, critics often dismissed his works as romantic potboilers, a blend of soap opera and fantasy, laced with a few historical details. Jacq persevered, however, determined to share the enthusiasm and awe he felt for Egypt with as wide an audience as possible. With the *Ramses* series—titled, in English, *The Son of Light, The Eternal Temple, The Battle of Kadesh, The Lady of Abu Simbel,* and *Under the Western Acacia*—he achieved just that. Millions of readers were enthralled by the work, an episodic story filled with battles, magic, sex, and adventure. Fans lined up outside bookstores as each new volume was released, and Jacq was given much of the credit for the 100% increase in the number of French tourists traveling to Egypt.

Besides promoting Egypt's splendour, Jacq was dedicated to preserving the physical record of Egypt's past. To meet that challenge, he founded the Ramses Institute in Paris to register and photograph Egypt's endangered archaeological sites. (AMY R. TAO)

Jahn, Helmut

With the opening in 2000 of the Sony Center in Berlin's Potsdamer Platz, German architect Helmut Jahn showed that at age 60 he had not lost any of his flair for the dramatic, an attribute that had fueled his rise to prominence in the 1980s as a young star of the international architectural scene. The Sony Center—a seven-building, at least $800 million complex made up of an office tower, residences, and retail and entertainment space—was Jahn's most grandiose project to date. Characterized by a glass sheathing that made the buildings appear to be lacking outside walls, the Sony Center displayed an attention to functionality that marked Jahn's return to a simpler style. After having made a name for himself by designing a series of distinctive—some would call them "cartoonish"—Postmodern buildings throughout much of his career, Jahn had earned the nickname "Flash Gordon."

Jahn was born on Jan. 4, 1940, in Nürnberg, Ger. His decision to pursue architecture as a career came when, as a young man, he witnessed the rebuilding of Nürnberg, which had been bombed extensively during World War II. He studied (1960–65) at the Technische Hochschule in Munich before leaving for the United States to spend a year at the Illinois Institute of Technology in Chicago, where Ludwig Mies van der Rohe was propounding his "less is more" philosophy, which heavily influenced the construction of spare steel-and-glass skyscrapers during the late 20th century. Jahn became a disciple of Mies, and after he joined C.F. Murphy Associates in Chicago in 1967, much of his work bore the mark of the master's teachings—functional structures based on what were thought to be rational, objective principles. Early works included the McCormick Place convention centre in Chicago (1970) and Kemper Arena (1974) and the Kansas City Convention Center (1976), both in Kansas City, Mo.

Jahn became head of Murphy/Jahn Associates in 1982 and, during the office-building boom of the 1980s, carved his niche, working in Chicago and other parts of the U.S. He began to take the glass-and-steel approach in a different, less-restrictive direction, making use of light, colour, and space in an attempt to place structures within the context of their locale or their purpose. His most prominent work, the James R. Thompson Center in Chicago's Loop, would have a significant impact on the public's perception of Jahn and his style. The futuristic government office tower—with its massive central blue-glass-covered rotunda devoted to enhancing the building's some 7,400 sq m (80,000 sq ft) of retail space—did not receive entirely favourable reviews locally. The reputation of the building—and of Jahn himself—took another battering when the air-conditioning system malfunctioned. Jahn claimed, however, that it was this building that had attracted many overseas clients to him. After 1985 most of his significant work was done in Europe, where he said the attitude toward architecture had become much more adventurous and interesting than in the U.S. His next big project was the Max, a bank building in Frankfurt, Ger., that was being billed as a "transparent skyscraper."

(ANTHONY G. CRAINE)

Jin, Ha

Chinese American writer Ha Jin won the PEN/Faulkner Award for fiction in 2000 for his novel *Waiting.* When, a year earlier, the novel had won the 1999 National Book Award, critics noted that in certain respects the choice was an unusual one. Jin's first language was not English, and *Waiting* was his first full-length novel. Further, it was a story not about assimilation into American culture but rather about the difficulties of life in Chinese society. Yet the book was popular with both critics and readers, who found Jin's plain, unadorned prose an effective vehicle for his story. And like all of his fiction, the novel dealt with basic human concerns in a way reminiscent of writers such as Anton Chekhov and Nikolay Gogol, whom Jin cited as influences.

Xuefei Jin (he used Ha Jin as a pen name) was born on Feb. 21, 1956, in Jinzhou, Liaoning province. His father was a member of the army, and the son had only a brief, incomplete education before the schools closed in 1966 at the beginning of the Cultural Revolution. At age 14 Jin joined the army and was sent to the northern border with the Soviet Union. After the army he worked as a railway telegraph operator and began to learn English by listening to the radio. When the schools reopened, he attended Heilongjiang University, Harbin, from which he graduated in 1981 with a degree in English. Jin earned a master's degree in American literature from Shandong University, Qingdao, in 1984, and the following year he entered Brandeis University, Waltham, Mass. He received a doctorate in 1992 and became a professor of creative writing at Emory University, Atlanta, Ga., in 1993. He did all of his writing in the United States and all in English, in which he felt that he had found his voice.

Before he published fiction, Jin published poems, which he collected in two volumes, *Between Silences* (1990) and *Facing Shadows* (1996). His volume of army stories, *Ocean of Words* (1996), received the PEN/Hemingway Award in 1997, and his second book of stories, *Under the Red Flag* (1997), which told of life during the Cultural Revolution, won the Flannery O'Connor Award for Short Fiction. Individual stories also took a number of other prizes. The novella *In the Pond,* which was published in 1998, depicted factory life in a small Chinese town through the sometimes comical tug-of-war between a worker and party officials. In *Waiting* a doctor who took a traditional wife but then fell in love with a nurse was forced to wait the prescribed 18 years before he could obtain a divorce. As with much of Jin's fiction, the novel illustrated the tension between the individual and the family, the modern and the traditional, and feeling and duty. (ROBERT RAUCH)

Jones, Marion

In September 2000 American track-and-field (athletics) phenomenon Marion Jones became the first woman in history to win five track-and-field medals (three gold and two bronze) at a single Olympic Games. Though quite a remarkable accomplishment, the feat was overshadowed by the fact that Jones, a driven 25-year-old Olympic rookie, had failed to complete her much-publicized mission—to take home from the Games in Sydney, Australia, five gold medals, one in each of her events.

Jones was born on Oct. 12, 1975, in Los Angeles. Her father left the family when she was very young, but her mother worked hard to help her children succeed. The family moved several times during Jones's adolescence so that the future track star would be able to compete on choice junior-high and high-school teams. By the time she was 12, the strong-willed Jones, nicknamed "hard nails," was competing internationally; in 1992 she won a place as an alternate on the U.S. Olympic track team but declined the invitation. She also became an accomplished basketball player, winning California's Division I Player of the Year award in 1993.

Jones attended the University of North Carolina at Chapel Hill on a basketball scholarship but also ran track, her first love. After two highly successful years on the Carolina basketball team, Jones quit the squad in 1996 to try for a spot on the U.S. Olympic track team, but she was thwarted by a foot injury. She then returned to basketball for a third and final season, and she received the MVP award of the 1997 Atlantic Coast Conference Tournament. After graduating that spring with a degree in communications and journalism, Jones rededi-

AP/Wide World Photos

AP/Wide World Photos

Multi-medalist Marion Jones

cated herself to track. She was introduced to track coach Trevor Graham by her future husband, champion shot-putter C.J. Hunter.

In a three-year time span, Jones's rise in track and field had been meteoric. After only a few months of training with Graham, Jones gained the title of "world's fastest woman" in 1997 by winning the 100 m with a time of 10.83 sec at the world championship in Athens. The following year she became the first American woman to be ranked number one in three track-and-field events simultaneously—the 100 m, the 200 m, and the long jump. In 2000 she won Olympic gold medals in the 100 m (10.75 sec), the 200 m (21.84 sec), and the 4 × 400-m relay (3 min 22.62 sec); she claimed bronze medals in the long jump and the 4 × 100-m relay.

(SHANDA SILER)

Köhler, Horst

On March 23, 2000, after months of international wrangling, German banker Horst Köhler was named the managing director and chairman of the executive board of the International Monetary Fund (IMF), a UN agency established in 1944 to secure international monetary cooperation, stabilize exchange rates, and expand international liquidity. His accession was due in large part to the determination of Germany's chancellor, Gerhard Schröder, that—for the first time—a German should head the IMF. Schröder's first choice for the post, Caio Koch-Weser, the nation's deputy finance minister, was rejected by the United States because he did not meet "the criteria of maximum stature who would be able to command support from around the world." Undaunted by the rejection of Koch-Weser, Schröder embarked on a vigorous and ultimately successful campaign to persuade other European nations, some of which had their own candidates for the post, to line up behind Köhler.

Köhler was born on Feb. 22, 1943, in Skierbieszow, Pol. As the Soviet army advanced into Poland during World War II, his family fled to East Germany; they escaped to the West in 1953. Köhler earned a doctorate in economics and political sciences in West Germany from the Eberhard-Karl University of Tübingen and served (1969–76) as a scientific research assistant at the university's Institute for Applied Economic Research before joining the German government. In the early 1990s, as a member of the Finance Ministry, he played an important role in the economic planning for German reunification and also helped provide aid to Russia after the breakup of the Soviet Union. His major achievement at the time, however, was as Germany's lead official in the difficult negotiations that led to the Maastricht Treaty in 1991, which formed the foundation of European financial and monetary union.

In 1993 Köhler became the head of the national association of German savings banks, and in 1998 he was chosen to run the European Bank for Reconstruction and Development (EBRD). In that capacity he helped shift the EBRD's priorities away from large infrastructure projects and toward support for small businesses. He also succeeded in improving the EBRD's finances. In 1998 the bank lost $252.8 million, but in 1999 it earned a profit of $41 million. As head of the IMF, Köhler faced many critics of former IMF policies. In the U.S., for example, both Congress and the Clinton administration strongly urged the IMF to follow more "hard-line" economic principles while undertaking its task of rescuing financially troubled nations. Recent IMF "rescue packages" were assailed as being ineffective (Russia), causing undue hardship (Indonesia), and failing to punish banks and investors adequately for risky investments (South Korea).

(DAVID R. CALHOUN)

Kostunica, Vojislav

When on Oct. 7, 2000, Vojislav Kostunica was sworn in as president of Yugoslavia, it was the culmination of two weeks of dramatic developments. Results from the elections held on September 24 showed that Kostunica, the candidate of the 18-member coalition known as the Democratic Opposition of Serbia, had defeated Pres. Slobodan Milosevic. The Milosevic government, however, was unwilling to accept defeat, claiming that Kostunica had not received a majority of the votes and that a runoff would thus be necessary. Citizens took to the streets; workers went on strike; and on October 5 protesters set fire to the parliament building in Belgrade. When it became clear that he was being abandoned by government agencies, including the police, Milosevic announced on October 6 that he would step down. Kostunica and his supporters then began to assume the control of key ministries and institutions and to undertake the governing of Yugoslavia.

Kostunica was born on March 24, 1944, in Belgrade, Yugos. He graduated from the University of Belgrade Law School in 1966 and earned a master's degree in 1970. In 1974 he was fired as a lecturer at the university for supporting a colleague who had spoken out against a constitutional change instituted by Yugoslav Pres. Josip Broz Tito, and he refused an offer from Milosevic in 1989 to be rehired. In 1976 he earned a doctorate from an academic institute, and in 1981 he translated *The Federalist* papers into Serbo-Croatian. Throughout his career Kostunica was an advocate of free speech, the rule of law, and an independent judiciary, and he was committed to Serbian nationalism.

With opposition leader Zoran Djindjic, Kostunica founded the Democratic Party in 1989. He split with Djindjic in 1992, however, to form the Democratic Party of Serbia. Kostunica was a member of the Serbian parliament from 1990 to 1997. Although he opposed the policies of Milosevic, Kostunica denounced NATO for its bombing of Serbia in 1999 and criticized the international tribunal at The Hague, which had indicted Milosevic and other Serbian leaders for war crimes, as an instrument of U.S. foreign policy. Upon taking office, he rejected vindictive moves against Milosevic and his supporters. On October 16 his government reached a power-sharing agreement with the Socialist Party of Serbia, the party of Milosevic, which would continue to control that republic's parliament until elections were held on December 23. Kostunica was less successful in his initial dealings with the republic of Montenegro, which had officially boycotted the September elections and which was demanding greater autonomy within the Yugoslav federation. Although the new government was faced with an economy in ruins and a society permeated by corruption, the election of Kostunica gave hope that Yugoslavia would be reintegrated into the community of European nations.

(ROBERT RAUCH)

Krall, Diana

The golden girl of jazz at the 2000 Grammy Awards was Diana Krall, whose CD *When I Look in Your Eyes* not only won the prize for best jazz vocal performance but also received the first Album of the Year nomination for a jazz album in many years. Singer-pianist-arranger Krall's album, her sixth, was understated compared with most contemporary hits. In an era of song-belt-ing pop divas, pounding rhythms, electric instruments, and busy, high-volume productions, she sang in an unforced contralto voice that was often sultry and always swinging. She did not scat or offer virtuoso displays of vocal technique or drama. Her accompaniment was spare—a cool jazz rhythm section featuring her own piano, occasionally augmented by discreet string-orchestra backgrounds. The settings were perfect for her intimate portrayals of the subtleties of romantic feelings and for her whimsical humour, too. The songs she interpreted were notable for their intelligence and subtlety—crafty love songs by old masters such as Irving Berlin and Cole Porter and witty modern tunes such as "Popsicle Toes" by Michael Franks and Nat King Cole's version of "Frim Fram Sauce." Krall's charm worked on pop as well as jazz record buyers, and shortly after her Grammy, the album zoomed up *Billboard*'s Hot 100 chart. In March she bagged the Canadian Juno Award for best vocal jazz album.

Krall was performing on a special millennium cruise to Antarctica when her double Grammy nomination was announced; the cruise and the honours were the two latest triumphs in a career that began to skyrocket in the mid-1990s. Krall was born on Nov. 16, 1964, in Nanaimo, B.C. She frequently credited her musical family for stimulating her career, and in girlhood she began playing classical piano, singing in a church choir, and learning to play and sing the Fats Waller songs in her father's record collection. She began playing piano professionally at age 15 and used scholarships to study at Berklee College of Music in Boston and privately with jazz pianist Jimmy Rowles; it was Rowles who urged her to emphasize her singing skills. Years of performing on the U.S. East and West coasts and in Toronto preceded her first recording in 1993. There was a period when, according to Krall, "I wasn't really able to pay my rent," but in 1995 she recorded the album that was her breakthrough to jazz fame: *All for You,* a tribute to an earlier singer-pianist, Nat King Cole; it spent over a year on the jazz best-seller lists. As Krall's 1997 album *Love Scenes* was selling a half million copies worldwide, the New York glamour magazines and Hollywood were noticing the tall and slender blonde beauty. She appeared in photo spreads in *Vanity Fair* and *Glamour,* and the covers and inside liners of *When I Look in Your Eyes* featured photos of Krall in DKNY and Donna Karan designer clothing. While most jazz stars never appear on American television or in movies, Krall sang on episodes of *Melrose Place* and in three films by Clint Eastwood, who directed the video for her song "Why Should I Care?" Her glamorous image went with the sophisticated songs she chose for her repertoire. Yet perhaps because of her fashion photos and her hobnobbing with Hollywood stars, the response from jazz critics to Krall was mixed. The singer, however, insisted on the purity of her motives: "I'm excited about the music. I play it with integrity and I don't compromise my vision. I approach it from an artistic perspective." (JOHN LITWEILER)

AP/Wide World Photos

Jazz's golden girl, Diana Krall

Kurzweil, Raymond

In March 2000 American computer scientist Raymond Kurzweil was awarded the U.S. National Medal of Technology in recognition of his many innovations. Already well known in scientific circles, Kurzweil increasingly was attracting the attention of the general public with his daring prognostications about how technology would shape the future. His book *The Age of Spiritual Machines* (1999) presented a vision of the 21st century as a time when computer technology would have advanced far enough to allow machines to operate on a level equivalent to that of the human brain. Computers, he predicted, would make complex decisions, appreciate beauty, and even experience emotions. Moreover, Kurzweil believed that as humans transferred the information in their brains to computers, the distinction between person and machine would become blurred.

Kurzweil was born on Feb. 12, 1948, in Queens, N.Y. As a teenager he earned first prize in the International Science Fair—and an appearance on the television show *I've Got a Secret*—with a computer program that could write music that mimicked the styles of great composers. The program marked the beginning of his career-long attempt to re-create pattern recognition, or the ability to find order in complex data. It was Kurzweil's belief that pattern recognition formed the basis of human thought.

As a student at the Massachusetts Institute of Technology (MIT), Kurzweil created a computer program that helped high-school students choose a college to attend. He then sold the service to a publisher for $100,000 plus royalties. He graduated from MIT in 1970, and four years later he established Kurzweil Computer Products, Inc., which developed technology that allowed computers to read text printed in any typestyle. Under Kurzweil's direction, the company also pioneered a flatbed scanner and a text-to-speech synthesizer and used all three inventions to build a reading machine for the blind. A commercial version of the machine was developed, which led to the eventual sale of the company to the Xerox Corp. A friendship with musician Stevie Wonder led Kurzweil next to launch a business that created professional-quality music synthesizers. That venture was later sold to the Korean instrument manufacturer Young Chang.

In 1987 another Kurzweil company spawned the first commercial speech-recognition system and was sold to a concern that later teamed with the Microsoft Corp. to market speech-recognition software for personal computers. In the late 1990s yet another Kurzweil firm produced software that used artificial intelligence for a variety of purposes, including financial analysis and the training of doctors. Somehow Kurzweil found time away from starting businesses to launch a successful writing career. Before *The Age of Spiritual Machines* came *The Age of Intelligent Machines* (1990), which anticipated the explosion in popularity of the Internet. Kurzweil also wrote *The 10% Solution for a Healthy Life* (1993), which detailed a diet that he had used to help cure himself of diabetes.

(ANTHONY G. CRAINE)

Kwan, Michelle

At the 2000 world championships on April 1 in Nice, France, American figure skater Michelle Kwan proved to the world what determination was all about. Although she already had two world championships to her credit, she had had a less-than-stellar season—having lost several major international competitions—and was being written off by many critics, who cited the distractions caused by her studies at the University of California, Los Angeles, and the challenge posed by an upcoming crop of young teenagers with a dazzling mastery of technical skills. She managed to win the U.S. women's championship, but she still had to face such formidable opponents as the Russians Mariya Butyrskaya, the defending world champion, and Irina Slutskaya, who had been left off her country's world team a year earlier but, newly energized, had recently become European champion. Indeed, going into the final free skate, Kwan found herself only in third place. At that point, however, she pulled out all the stops. Skating her technically challenging program—with its seven triple jumps, including the difficult triple toe–triple toe combination—with a new abandon enhancing her customary superb artistry, Kwan took command of the ice and decisively snared her third world championship.

Kwan, whose Chinese name was Kwan Shan Wing, was born on July 7, 1980, in Torrance, Calif. She began skating at the age of five and from the outset was determined to be a champion. When she was 12, her eagerness to advance prompted her to take the test for advancing to the senior level on the sly—while her coach, Frank Carroll, was out of town—and at 13 she captured public attention by landing the alternate spot on the U.S. Olympic team. A year later she placed fourth at the world championships, and in 1996, sporting a new, more grown-up look, she won her first world championship. Although the pressures of being champion, combined with a growth spurt that added both height and weight, sent Kwan into a slump the following year, she still

World champion Michelle Kwan

Pascal Guyot/AFP Worldwide

finished a close runner-up to new superkid Tara Lipinski at the 1997 world championships, and the stage was set for a public rivalry in the battle for the gold medal at the 1998 Olympic Games in Nagano, Japan. Kwan defeated Lipinski at the 1998 U.S. championships, was favoured to win the Olympic title, and was in the lead after the short program but, despite high marks for her long program, was second to an inspired Lipinski. With her usual optimism, however, she stated that she won the silver, not that she lost the gold, and she came back the following month to win her second world championship, though her win was somewhat diminished by the absence of Lipinski, who turned professional, from the competition. At the 1999 U.S. championships, Kwan again took the gold, and she took the silver medal at the world championships.

In her autobiography, *Michelle Kwan, Heart of a Champion* (1997), Kwan reiterated her motto: "Work hard, be yourself, and have fun." She was planning for that motto to help take her to victory in the next Winter Olympics, to be held in 2002 in Salt Lake City, Utah.

(BARBARA WHITNEY)

Lagos Escobar, Ricardo

On March 11, 2000, economist and political leader Ricardo Lagos Escobar was inaugurated as president of Chile. The first socialist to hold the office since Salvador Allende Gossens, he was an outspoken opponent of Gen. Augusto Pinochet Ugarte, who had overthrown the Marxist Allende in a military coup in 1973. The new president had a distinguished career both in Chile and abroad in public affairs and as a teacher.

Lagos was born on March 2, 1938, in Santiago, Chile. He earned a degree in law from the University of Chile in 1960 and a doctorate in economics from Duke University, Durham, N.C., in 1966. He taught economics and held administrative posts at the University of Chile from 1967 to 1972. In 1973, shortly before the coup against him, Allende appointed Lagos to be Chile's ambassador to the Soviet Union. After the coup Lagos lived in exile in the United States, teaching at the University of North Carolina at Chapel Hill in 1974–75, and from 1978 to 1984 he served as an economist with the United Nations. After he returned to Chile, he became president (1983–84) of the Democratic Alliance, a group in opposition to Pinochet. The military regime briefly jailed Lagos without charges in 1987, and in that same year he founded the Party for Democracy. From 1990 to 1992 he was minister of education under Pinochet's successor, Pres. Patricio Aylwin Azócar, and in 1994–98 was minister of public works under Pres. Eduardo Frei Ruiz-Tagle. In 1999, winning 70% of the vote, he became the presidential candidate of Concertación, a coalition that included the Socialists and the Christian Democrats.

In the general election Lagos faced another economist, Joaquín Lavín, a rightist who had served as a Planning Ministry official under Pinochet. Much of the campaign centred on practical social and economic issues, although Lagos also advocated changes to what some critics called the Pinochet constitution. Overall, however, both candidates campaigned as relative moderates. They also agreed that as president they would not block any attempt to prosecute Pinochet, an action that would once again open deep divisions within Chilean society. In the initial balloting, held on Dec. 12, 1999, each candidate took roughly 48% of the votes. Because the constitution required a majority, a runoff was required. Lagos won the second round of balloting, held on Jan. 16, 2000, with just over 51% of the votes. It was the strongest showing by the right since the end of military rule in 1990 and, in light of the esteem in which Lagos was held, an unexpectedly weak showing for the ruling coalition. (ROBERT RAUCH)

Li Ka-shing

Topping *Asiaweek* magazine's 2000 list of Asia's 50 most powerful people was Li Ka-shing, a billionaire who took "old economy" money and parlayed it into a "new economy" juggernaut. Nicknamed "Superman" by the regional media because of his uncanny ability to pull off a succession of profitable deals, Li inspired loyalty among stockholders, who had come to expect every Li-inspired venture to be a sure thing. Although he began building his fortune in Hong Kong, Li had substantial holdings worldwide, and his ties with top leaders in his native China gave him an inside track in gaining a foothold in that country's burgeoning markets.

Li was born into a poor family on June 13, 1928, in Chaozhou, Guangdong province, China. Japanese invasions forced the family to leave the mainland for Hong Kong in 1940. Without much formal education, Li began his career in Hong Kong as a salesman and eventually formed a company, Cheung Kong, that manufactured plastics. Business boomed throughout the 1950s when Cheung Kong began making artificial flowers and exporting them to the U.S. As the firm prospered, Li began to acquire property at a rate that, by the late 1970s, made him Hong Kong's leading private developer.

In 1979 he became the first Chinese businessman to buy one of the large British-owned local trading companies when he purchased a controlling interest in Hutchison Whampoa. Under his leadership, Hutchison emerged as the world's largest independent operator of ports; the company also bought out Husky Oil in Canada and set up mobile-phone operations in Australia, Europe, and the U.S. Among Li's other ventures was an Internet service, Tom.com, that proved highly popular in China.

Characteristic of Li's approach to business was the way Hutchison made money in the mobile-phone business in the U.K. After getting a foot in the door by investing in a money-losing phone operation called Rabbit, Hutchison launched a service called Orange that it later sold for $14.6 billion. Shortly thereafter, Hutchison jumped back into the telecom business in the U.K., acquiring a license for a wireless Internet service. For Li, making money involved identifying lucrative technologies before they became lucrative, investing in them, and then selling when the properties hit peak value.

Li's ties with high-ranking officials in China and Hong Kong benefitted his business but prompted criticism. After his son was kidnapped in 1996, the culprit was caught by mainland police and executed, which led many to speculate that Li had gone above local Hong Kong police and sought help at the highest levels of China's government. Li's attempt to influence the political climate in Hong Kong by threatening to cancel a major development also resulted in a backlash. In the U.S. some members of Congress worried that Li's ties to Chinese leaders made his ownership of ports at both ends of the Panama Canal a security risk. (ANTHONY G. CRAINE)

Lieberman, Joseph I.

The announcement on Aug. 7, 2000, that U.S. Sen. Joseph I. Lieberman of Connecticut had been chosen by Al Gore (*q.v.*) as his vice presidential running mate on the Democratic ticket was seen as a bold decision, and it was met with widespread approval. Lieberman was an Orthodox Jew whose religious beliefs had a pervasive influence on his life and work, and he was the first Jew on the national ticket of a ma-

above right: Peter Parks/AFP Worldwide

jor U.S. political party. He had been the first Democratic senator to criticize Pres. Bill Clinton publicly for his behaviour in the Monica Lewinsky affair, although he later voted against removing Clinton from office. It was thought that one of the benefits of Lieberman's candidacy would be to help distance the Democratic ticket from the scandals of the Clinton administration. Although he proved to be an effective campaigner and helped to build support among the party's traditional base, the ticket narrowly lost the election. Lieberman, however, also appeared on the Connecticut ballot for reelection to the Senate, a contest he won easily.

Lieberman was born on Feb. 24, 1942, in Stamford, Conn. He earned B.A. (1964) and LL.B. (1967) degrees from Yale University. During the 1960s he was active in the civil rights movement, and he practiced law briefly. In 1970, in a campaign in which Clinton, then a student at Yale, served as a volunteer, Lieberman was elected to the Connecticut Senate, and he was majority leader from 1975 to 1981. In 1980 Lieberman was defeated in a bid for a seat in the U.S. House of Representatives, but two years later he was elected Connecticut attorney general. In 1988 he won election to the U.S. Senate, becoming the first Orthodox Jew to sit in that body, and he was reelected in 1994. Lieberman, who served as the chairman of the Democratic Leadership Council, took a generally centrist stance. Although he supported Democratic positions on issues such as campaign finance reform, abortion rights, and gun control, he broke ranks with his party by advocating school vouchers, cuts in capital gains taxes, and limits on liability awards. He was the author of five books, including the memoir *In Praise of Public Life* (2000), which he wrote with Michael D'Orso.

Early in the campaign Lieberman was criticized for a speech in which he called for a greater role for religion in public life. The Anti-Defamation League as well as many individuals said that his remarks violated the spirit of the principle of separation of church and state. Nonetheless, he continued to emphasize the importance of morality in government at the same time that he promoted the Democratic platform. (ROBERT RAUCH)

Democratic vice presidential candidate Joseph I. Lieberman

Livingstone, Ken

Constitutional history was made on May 4, 2000, when Londoners voted for British politician Ken Livingstone to be their mayor—it was the first time that a direct election had been held to fill any executive post in the U.K. Previously, all positions, from council leader to prime minister, had been filled indirectly, usually by the leader of the party with the greatest number of elected representatives. The other unusual feature of Livingstone's election was that he won as an independent—a rare achievement in a country in which politicians without a party base usually sank without a trace.

Kenneth Livingstone was born on June 17, 1945, in Lambeth, an inner London borough. He left school at 17 and started work as a laboratory technician. By his early 20s he was an active Labour Party member. He was elected to the Lambeth Borough Council in 1971 and to the Greater London Council (GLC) in 1973. Between 1977 and 1981, when the GLC was run by members of the Conservative Party, Livingstone led a left-wing faction within Labour's group in the GLC. In the GLC elections of May 1981, Labour won a majority. Livingstone immediately challenged the party's moderate GLC leader, Andrew McIntosh, who had led the party to victory. Backed by a majority of Labour GLC councillors, Livingstone took over the running of the council.

Margaret Thatcher, then the U.K.'s Conservative prime minister, was appalled by the left-wing domination of a number of cities, including London. She took action when Livingstone, popularly dubbed "Red Ken," sought to intervene in national controversies (for example, by inviting to London leading members of Sinn Fein, the Irish Republican Army's political wing). Thatcher abolished the big metropolitan councils, including the GLC. She achieved her goal in 1986 but at the price of turning Livingstone from "the most odious man in Britain," as one newspaper described him in 1981, into a political martyr.

Livingstone entered the House of Commons in 1987 as the Labour MP for the northwest London seat of Brent East, but he was shunned by successive Labour leaders because of his left-wing views. His chance to reclaim real power came after 1997, when the incoming Labour government redeemed its pledge to restore a citywide authority to London. This time the government decided to establish a directly elected mayor. Although Livingstone was the preferred choice of 60% of Labour Party members in London, he lost the mayoral primary contest to Frank Dobson, who enjoyed the backing of most London Labour MPs and trade union officials who, together, commanded two-thirds of the party's electoral college. Condemning the result as a fix, Livingstone left the party, stood as an independent, and won a convincing victory. He gained support from voters across the political spectrum by describing himself as a "London nationalist," rather than a left-wing socialist, and by promising to work closely with his political rivals and with London's business community—a promise he kept during his early months in office. (PETER KELLNER)

McLachlin, Beverley

On Jan. 12, 2000, 71 years after the Supreme Court of Canada ruled that women were not "persons," Beverley McLachlin was sworn in as the court's first woman chief justice. In her inaugural address McLachlin stated that the court would be dealing with difficult cases in such areas as child pornography, gun registry, mercy killing, computer crime, and Internet copyrights. She also promised that the court would not act in isolation, declaring, "We understand that our decisions, while true to the law and its traditions, do not stand in abstraction from society. They affect real people in life. They have consequences." The dynamic McLachlin replaced Antonio Lamer, who resigned after a decade as chief justice.

McLachlin was born Sept. 7, 1943, near Pincher Creek, Alta. In recalling her childhood on a farm in Alberta, she said, "We didn't have much money. We struggled, but we lived on land we loved and, like so many Canadian farm families, we did whatever was required to make a living from it." Educated at the University of Alberta, she earned a B.A. in 1964 and an M.A. in philosophy and a law degree in 1968. She practiced law with several firms in Alberta and British Columbia from 1969 to 1975 and served as a professor of law at the University of British Columbia from 1974 to 1981. In 1981 McLachlin was appointed to the Supreme Court of British Columbia, and in 1985 she was named to the Court of Appeal of that province. She was appointed chief justice of the Supreme Court of British Columbia in 1988 and in 1989 took her seat as a justice of the Supreme Court of Canada. McLachlin brought to the bench skills as an able administrator as well as a fluency in English and French; she was also a prolific writer. Her fellow justices praised McLachlin for her ability to blend theoretical principles of the law with practical applications for Canadians and predicted that she would be a strong and effective leader of the nation's highest court. (DAVID R. CALHOUN)

McMahon, Vince

American wrestling promoter Vince McMahon took his act to the gridiron in 2000 when he challenged the National Football League (NFL) to a showdown. Looking to end the NFL's stranglehold on the sport, the president of the World Wrestling Federation (WWF) announced the creation of the Extreme Football League (XFL). While many questioned the move, citing the failure of past ventures to compete with the NFL, McMahon displayed the bravado and marketing muscle that had turned the WWF into a billion-dollar industry, watched by some 10 million–20 million viewers weekly. Slamming the NFL as dull and the "No Fun League," he promised a faster and more entertaining (though, unlike the WWF, unscripted) sport with no-holds-barred access, including microphones in the huddles and helmet cameras. In March McMahon signed a broadcast contract with NBC

left: AP/Wide World Photos; above: UK Press/Liaison Agency

worth more than $30 million, and he later inked a deal with UPN. While the gridiron rumble was not scheduled to begin until February 2001, when the XFL would kick off in eight cities, many were already placing bets that McMahon's venture would be successful.

Vincent Kennedy McMahon, Jr., was born on Aug. 24, 1945, in Pinehurst, N.C., the son of a wrestling promoter. In the 1970s he began working as a ringside announcer for his father's business, Capital Wrestling Corp. (later renamed the World Wrestling Federation), and in 1982 he bought the company. McMahon displayed a brash ambition and innate promotional ability that would become his trademark. Creating a unique blend of sports and entertainment, he added rock and roll, celebrities, and outrageously scripted matches, and he molded wrestlers into child-friendly stars. Outside the ring he lured performers away from rival companies and broke the long-standing regionalism of wrestling organizations as he took his eastern-based business national. Although McMahon made many enemies, his bold changes revolutionized the sport and moved it into the mainstream. WWF cable shows and live events were hits, and by the mid-1980s the WWF was the leading wrestling group.

In the early 1990s McMahon encountered difficulties as the WWF was rocked by charges of steroid use and sexual misconduct. In addition, the National Wrestling Alliance (later bought by media magnate Ted Turner and renamed World Championship Wrestling [WCW]) experienced a resurgence, and its cable shows soon surpassed those of the WWF in numbers of viewers. McMahon responded by hiring new writers to create soap-opera story lines. Skimpily clad female wrestlers became prominent, as did "colourful language" (profanity) and "sign language" (obscene gestures). Although critics, parents in particular, complained of excessive sex and vulgarity, audiences roared their approval. By the late 1990s the WWF's programs, including *Raw Is War* and *SmackDown!*, had double the ratings of those of the WCW and dominated cable programming. McMahon had turned the WWF into a national obsession, complete with books, video games, action figures, magazines, and pay-per-view events, such as *Wrestlemania*. In 1999 he took the company public, raising $170 million in its initial offering. (AMY TIKKANEN)

Sports promoter Vince McMahon

Marcy, Geoffrey W.

One day in 1983, American astronomer Geoffrey Marcy announced to colleagues that he planned to search for planets in other solar systems. His fellow astronomers thought him foolish to spend time on what they considered a futile pursuit. No one was sure such planets existed, and even if they did, scientists had no instruments with which to see them. Marcy was undaunted, however, and by 2000 he and his research team at San Francisco State University had detected 19 planets orbiting stars other than the Sun—nearly two-thirds of the total number of "extrasolar" planets hitherto discovered.

Marcy was born on Sept. 29, 1954, in St. Clair Shores, Mich., and grew up in southern California. His parents bought him a telescope when he was 14, and, according to his mother, it "vanished into his room immediately." In 1982 he earned a Ph.D. in astronomy and astrophysics from the University of California, Santa Cruz. From 1982 to 1984 Marcy was a Carnegie fellow at the Carnegie Institution of Washington, D.C. After deciding to devote himself to his search for extrasolar planets, he moved on to a professorship at San Francisco State, where he recruited a graduate student, Paul Butler, to help him develop instrumentation that would be sensitive enough to indicate the presence of such faraway objects. Marcy realized that no telescope would be powerful enough to see such a planet directly, but he thought that a large planet might exert enough gravitational force on its star that the star would move slightly, a motion that Marcy called a "wobble." This motion, he predicted, would reveal itself as a slight shift in the wavelengths of light traveling from the star to the Earth. Eventually Marcy and Butler developed a light analyzer that could detect these shifts.

Using this technique, two Swiss scientists, Michel Mayor and Didier Queloz, in 1995 became the first astronomers to detect a planet circling a star outside the Earth's solar system. Marcy confirmed their discovery, and the following year he and Butler discovered two more extrasolar planets. A succession of similar discoveries followed. In 1999 Marcy found a star with a wobble that suggested a huge planet would pass directly in front of the star and thereby block some of the star's light, and on November 7 of that year one of his colleagues noted a 1.7% decline in the brightness of the star at exactly the time Marcy had predicted. As a reward for his groundbreaking research, Marcy was appointed a professor of astronomy at the University of California, Berkeley, and accepted an invitation to head the university's proposed Center for Integrative Planetary Studies. In addition, in April 2000 he was named California Scientist of the Year.

(DAVID R. CALHOUN)

Margulis, Lynn

At a White House ceremony on March 14, 2000, Pres. Bill Clinton presented the U.S. National Medal of Science to eminent microbiologist Lynn Margulis, one of 12 distinguished recipients. She was cited "for her outstanding contributions to understanding of the development, structure, and evolution of living things, for inspiring new research in the biological, climatological, geological and planetary sciences, and for her extraordinary abilities as a teacher and communicator of science to the public."

Margulis was born in Chicago on March 5, 1938. Intellectually precocious, she graduated with an A.B. from the University of Chicago in 1957. She earned her M.S. in zoology and genetics from the University of Wisconsin at Madison in 1960 and her Ph.D. in genetics from the University of California, Berkeley, in 1965. She joined the biology department of Boston University in 1966 and taught there until 1988, when she was named distinguished university professor in the department of botany at the University of Massachusetts at Amherst. She retained that title when her affiliation at the university changed to the department of biology in 1993 and then to the department of geosciences in 1997.

Throughout most of her career, Margulis was considered a radical by peers who pursued traditional Darwinian "survival of the fittest" approaches to biology. Her ideas, which focused on symbiosis—a living arrangement of two different organisms in an association that can be beneficial or unfavourable—were frequently greeted with skepticism and even hostility. Among her most important work was the development of the serial endosymbiotic theory of the origin of cells, which posits that eukaryotic cells (cells with nuclei) evolved from the symbiotic merger of nonnucleated bacteria that had previously existed independently. In this theory mitochondria and chloroplasts, two major organelles of eukaryotic cells, are descendants of once free-living bacterial species. She explained the concept in her first book, *Origin of Eukaryotic Cells* (1970). At the time, her theory

above: Duomo/Corbis; right: Paul Schnaittacher/Department of Geosciences

was regarded as far-fetched, but it has since been widely accepted. She elaborated in her 1981 classic, *Symbiosis in Cell Evolution* (second edition, 1993), proposing that another symbiotic merger of cells with bacteria—this time spirochetes, a type of bacterium that undulates rapidly—developed into the internal transportation system of the nucleated cell. This hypothesis, which also met with much professional resistance, remained the subject of much of Margulis's research work into 2000.

Another area of interest for Margulis was her long collaboration with British scientist James Lovelock on the controversial Gaia hypothesis. This proposes that the Earth can be viewed as a single self-regulating organism—that is, a complex entity whose living and inorganic elements are interdependent and whose life-forms actively modify the environment to maintain hospitable conditions.

Margulis was elected to the National Academy of Sciences in 1983 and was one of three American members of the Russian Academy of Natural Sciences. She held honorary doctorates from several universities and was awarded the William Procter Prize of Sigma Xi, the international research society, in 1999. Margulis was the author of several popular books on science (many co-written with her son Dorion Sagan), as well as more than 130 other technical works.

(AMY R. TAO)

Mendes, Sam

In March 2000 British director Sam Mendes won the Academy Award for best director for his work on the widely acclaimed and commercially successful film *American Beauty,* a satire that attempted to expose the seamy underbelly of life in modern American suburbia. He was also named best director by the Los Angeles Film Critics Association, the Directors Guild of America, and the Golden Globe awards for *American Beauty,* and the film also won an Oscar for star Kevin Spacey (*q.v.*). On the surface, Mendes, who had never made a film before, seemed an unlikely winner. Although he was a newcomer to Hollywood, he had long before forged a successful career on the British stage.

Samuel Alexander Mendes was born Aug. 1, 1965, in Reading, Eng. His mother, a writer of children's fiction, and father, a university professor, divorced when he was five. He attended the University of Cambridge, where he formed a theatre company with playwright Tim Firth. After graduating in 1987 with first-class honours in English, he landed a job at the Chichester (Eng.) Festival Theatre, and when the director of a production of *London Assurance* walked out, Mendes was summoned to take over. The play was a hit and moved to London's West End, where Mendes quickly made a name for himself, directing Dame Judi Dench in *The Cherry Orchard.* Stints with the Royal Shakespeare Company and the Royal National Theatre followed.

In 1992 Mendes took over as artistic director of London's nonprofit Donmar Warehouse Theatre and transformed it from a stop for visiting productions to a starting point for new productions. A series of successes followed as Mendes's reputation attracted big-name actors to the low-paying, 250-seat venue. Celebrated productions such as *Cabaret* (1993) and *The Glass Menagerie* (1995) catapulted Mendes to further fame, and he had similar success in 1998 when he took *Cabaret* and *Othello* to New York. In 1998 Mendes directed film star Nicole Kidman's London stage debut in a provocative rendition of David Hare's *The Blue Room.*

It was Steven Spielberg who offered Mendes the chance to try his hand on screen. The legendary director-producer had seen Mendes's productions of *Oliver!* and *Cabaret,* and he handed the script of *American Beauty* to Mendes over lunch. Filming got off to a rocky start when Mendes decided after three days that he had taken the wrong approach. He convinced the studio that it was worth the expense to reshoot, and the film went on to win the Academy Award for best picture.

After winning the Oscar, Mendes formed his own production company with backing from Spielberg's DreamWorks studio. He turned down a multifilm offer from DreamWorks, however, preferring to focus on the theatre, from which moviemaking had forced him to take a two-year hiatus. In May he announced plans to return to the Donmar with a World War I drama by a little-known author. In June it was revealed that Mendes had been appointed CBE for his contributions to drama.

(ANTHONY G. CRAINE)

Merkel, Angela

On April 10, 2000, Angela Merkel was elected head of Germany's conservative Christian Democratic Union (CDU). She took the job at a critical juncture in the history of the CDU; not only had the party lost power in 1998 after the 16-year incumbency of Chancellor Helmut Kohl, but the party was in tatters as the worst setback in its history, a campaign-finance scandal affecting the topmost echelons of the party, unfolded in late 1999 and early 2000.

In many ways Merkel seemed an ideal new leader. She was born Angela Dorothea Kasner on July 17, 1954, in Hamburg, West Germany, but moved with her family to East Germany so that her father, a Protestant pastor, could work in his native Brandenburg. She completed a doctorate in physics in Leipzig in 1978, moved to East Berlin, and accepted a job in the Academy of Sciences as a quantum chemist. She joined the democratic opposition in East Germany, called the Democratic Breakthrough, and became its press secretary in February 1990. She moved to the CDU the following August and was elected with a direct mandate (as opposed to party list mandate) as a Bundestag (lower house of parliament) deputy in December of that year. Kohl quickly recognized her political skill and made her minister of family affairs, senior citizens, women, and youth (1991–94) and minister of environment, conservation, and reactor safety (1994–98).

Merkel's visibility and popularity with the German public rose quickly. She distanced herself from Kohl—a one-time patron, who had dubbed her fondly "das Mädchen" ("that girl")—by writing a newspaper article in 1999 calling for an investigation into the party financing scandal. She led the charge of CDU members who begged Kohl to do right by his party by naming names to end the scandal and begin the healing process.

Still, Merkel's political jockeying earned her enemies among Kohl loyalists in the CDU. She was controversial in other ways as well—not only was she the first woman to serve as CDU head, she was also the first non-Catholic, a divorcée (and remarried earlier in 2000 to Joachim Sauer, a scientist), the first CDU leader from the former East Germany, and the first from the party's liberal wing, which proved particularly problematic for the CDU's sister party in Bavaria, the ultraconservative Christian Social Union.

Merkel's dual challenge was to overcome the CDU scandal and to unite the party behind her. She suffered a major defeat in mid-July when her party failed to stop a tax-reform law in the Bundesrat (upper house of parliament). After the vote Merkel, known for her poker face and nerves of steel, offered the following comment: "This is the first and last time this will happen to me." Many pundits believed her. By year's end Merkel was still struggling to find a foothold and soothe party infighting.

(SUZANNE M. CROW)

Mesic, Stipe

The election of Stipe Mesic as president of the Republic of Croatia on Feb. 7, 2000, was a turning point for the country, which had been run on a very tight rein by Pres. Franjo Tudjman since independence in 1991. Mesic's political biography was characterized by dramatic falls from political privilege and uncanny reemergence to public prominence, capped by his unexpected election as president following Tudjman's death in late 1999. Croatia, which had been something of an international pariah state, seemed on the brink of a new era.

Mesic was born Stjepan Mesic into a World War II partisan family in the small town of Orahovica, Croatia (Kingdom of Yugoslavia), on Dec. 24, 1934. He earned a degree in law from the University of Zagreb, after which he returned to his hometown in eastern Croatia and served as mayor. In 1971, however, the Yugoslav communist authorities jailed him as a counterrevolutionary for supporting the "Croatian Spring," a liberal nationalist awakening. He spent a year in the harsh Croatian Stara Gradiska political prison camp. Afterward, as a political outcast, Mesic continued to suffer personal difficulties and focused his energies on serving as general manager of a small architectural firm in Zagreb.

In 1989 he again became active in oppositionist politics, joining Tudjman and other antiregime dissidents, and became secretary of the new pro-independence and nationalist Croatian Democratic Union (HDZ), which won power the following year. Mesic was appointed president of the new government and represented Croatia at the federal Yugoslav level, having the distinction of serving as the last president of the large Yugoslav Federation. He resigned on

AP/Wide World Photos

Dec. 5, 1991, following attacks on Croatia by the Serb-dominated Yugoslav armed forces. Upon the creation of an independent Croatian state, Mesic became president of the parliament.

By 1994 Mesic had broken with Tudjman over the issue of Bosnia and Herzegovina. Thus, he began another period of political wandering. He failed in an attempt to forge a new party among HDZ dissidents, and in 1997 he joined the small Croatian National Party (HNS) and soon became its vice president. In 1999 the HNS joined other opposition parties to contest parliamentary elections that resulted in the HDZ's defeat. In the presidential elections called after Tudjman's death, Mesic (who had failed to win his own parliamentary seat) ran an antiestablishment campaign and won a 56–44% victory over the Croatian Social-Liberal Party–Social Democratic Party coalition candidate in the second round of balloting. His folksy and populist campaign, as well as his well-honed political instincts, struck a chord with an electorate tired of government corruption and abuse of authority.

Facing a fractious six-party coalition government, President Mesic promised to reduce the powers of the presidency, scale back the intelligence services, reform a corrupt privatization process, restore friendly ties with Croatia's neighbours, and integrate Croatia into NATO and European institutions. (MAX PRIMORAC)

Mori, Yoshiro

After Japanese Prime Minister Keizo Obuchi suffered a crippling stroke on April 2, 2000, Yoshiro Mori, secretary-general of the long-ruling Liberal-Democratic Party (LDP), succeeded him. In a speech to the Japanese Diet (legislature) on April 7, Mori stated that his government would work for the "rebirth of Japan," making it "a nation that engenders the trust of the world." Critics, however, contended that Mori remained dedicated to the large-scale spending on public works that was generally believed to have played a role in Japan's decade-long economic decline.

In his first few months in office, Mori was unable to negate such criticism. On June 25 he witnessed a resounding defeat for the LDP in elections for the House of Representatives, the lower house of the Diet. The LDP won 233 of the 480 seats in the House, down from the 271 it had held in the previous session, and was thereby forced for the first time to rely on two small coalition partners, the New Komeito and the New Conservative Party, to gain a legislative majority. Citing comments by Mori that seemed to echo Japan's aggressively nationalistic past and his advice to undecided voters to "sleep away" the election, many Japanese blamed the prime minister for the LDP's defeat. Though reappointed prime minister in July, Mori faced a no-confidence vote in November. He narrowly survived the motion. In December, in an effort to raise his approval ratings, Mori reshuffled his cabinet.

Mori was born on July 14, 1937, in Neagari, Ishikawa prefecture, Japan. Both his father and his grandfather had served as mayor of the town. Mori attended Waseda University, Tokyo, where he graduated in 1959 with a degree in commerce. In 1960 he went to work at the newspaper *Sankei Shimbun,* where he came in contact with many of Japan's business leaders. Mori began his political career in 1962 as secretary to a Diet member. In 1969 he ran as an independent for a House seat and was elected. He then joined the LDP and was reelected nine times.

In 1983–84 Mori served as minister of education under Prime Minister Yasuhiro Nakasone. In 1989 he was connected with the so-called Recruit scandal, in which high-ranking LDP officials were said to have accepted discounted shares in the Recruit Co. in exchange for political favours. Although Mori reportedly earned a profit of almost $1 million when he sold his Recruit shares, prosecutors determined that there was no evidence on which to charge him. Mori served as chairman of the LDP's Policy Research Council in 1991–92 and as minister of international trade and industry in 1992–93. In 1993 he was appointed secretary-general of the LDP, the party's second highest post, and he held other party and government positions from 1995 to 1998. When Obuchi became prime minister in 1998, Mori again was named LDP secretary-general, which put him in position to succeed Obuchi. Despite the LDP's poor performance in the June 2000 parliamentary elections, Mori was reconfirmed as prime minister by the Diet on July 4, and he appointed a new cabinet the same day. (DAVID R. CALHOUN)

Mugabe, Robert

During the first six months of 2000, Pres. Robert Mugabe of Zimbabwe suffered two political setbacks. In a referendum held on February 12–13, voters turned down a proposal for a new constitution that would have expanded his powers. In addition, in the June 24–25 parliamentary elections, the president's party, the Zimbabwe African National Union–Patriotic Front (ZANU-PF), won only 62 of the 120 contested seats, with the opposition Movement for Democratic Change taking 57 and the ZANU-Ndonga capturing one. In the previous election, ZANU-PF had won all but two seats.

Shortly after the February referendum, veterans of the Zimbabwean war for independence began to move onto white-owned farms. They did so with the approval of Mugabe, and law-enforcement officials generally refused to intercede, even when ordered to do so by the courts. Violence ensued, with people on both sides losing their lives. A constitutional amendment passed by the legislature on April 6 allowed Mugabe on May 24 to amend the 1992 Land Acquisition Act, which provided for the takeover of white-owned farms without compensation to the owners for the land, although payment would be made for existing structures. The property was to be redistributed to landless blacks. Meanwhile, the economy deteriorated further, with inflation running at 60% and unemployment at more than 50%, and some observers believed that Mugabe promoted the farm takeovers to distract attention from the country's problems as well as to institute long-promised land reform.

Robert Gabriel Mugabe was born on Feb. 21, 1924, in Kutama, then in Southern Rhodesia. He received an education from the Jesuits and at age 17 became a teacher in a mission school. He then studied at the University of Fort Hare, Alice, S.Af., where he received a B.A. degree in 1951 and where he was introduced to Marxist thought. During the 1950s he taught in Southern Rhodesia and Northern Rhodesia (now Zambia) and in Ghana, and he joined the Zimbabwe African People's Union (ZAPU), the nationalist movement of Joshua Nkomo. In 1963 Mugabe helped form ZANU, a breakaway group. He was arrested by the Rhodesian white colonial government in 1964 and during 10 years in detention took correspondence courses from the University of London, receiving degrees in law and administration. Upon release he went into exile, primarily in Mozambique, where he headed nationalist guerrilla forces. He participated in the talks with Rhodesia that resulted in independence for Zimbabwe, and following elections in April 1980 he became prime minister.

Initially, Mugabe ran a tolerant regime, including black opponents as well as whites in the government, and he spent money on schools and health clinics. Increasingly, however, his government became corrupt, with opposition often brutally suppressed. In 1987 he effectively made Zimbabwe a one-party state under ZANU-PF and assumed the position of president. As much as half of the arable land in Zimbabwe was owned by some 4,000 white farmers, and although the farms supplied most of the country's exports, Mugabe had often threatened to seize them. (ROBERT RAUCH)

Murphy-O'Connor, Cormac

In 2000 Cormac Murphy-O'Connor, formerly the bishop of Arundel and Brighton, succeeded the late Basil Cardinal Hume as leader of Great Britain's four million Roman Catholics. In the months following his installation as archbishop of Westminster in March, Murphy-O'Connor showed that he would not shy away from tackling controversial issues. In an interview with *The Guardian* in May, the archbishop stated that priests who had accepted celibacy when they were ordained should keep that vow; he also stated that marriage was not incompatible with the priesthood. "I would not rule it out," he said of the possibility of ordaining married priests. "The matter will come up again." In a church in which priests were still expected to remain celibate for life, Murphy-O'Connor's statements prompted criticism from some quarters.

A few months later the archbishop publicly acknowledged that he had made a mistake in the 1980s in appointing Father Michael Hill chaplain to Gatwick Airport near London despite allegations at the time that the priest was a pedophile. Hill was convicted of nine sex attacks and jailed from 1997 to September

left: Yuri Kadobnov/AFP Worldwide; right: Odd Andersen/AFP Worldwide

2000. Shortly after Hill's release, Murphy-O'Connor appointed a committee to recommend ways in which child sex abuse by priests could be prevented.

In yet another controversy the Vatican provoked outrage from other church leaders by issuing a declaration in September proclaiming the Roman Catholic Church the only "instrument for the salvation of all humanity." The archbishop subsequently attempted to allay the anger of clergies of other faiths by stating that the document did not represent a change in the church's position on ecumenism. "Certainly no slight is intended by its comments regarding other Christian communities," he said.

Murphy-O'Connor was born on Aug. 24, 1932, in Reading, Berkshire, Eng. In his family three uncles and two brothers were priests. Murphy-O'Connor was ordained in 1956, and after serving parishes in Portsmouth and Fareham, he became director of vocations for the diocese of Portsmouth. In 1966 he was named private secretary and chaplain to Bishop Derek Worlock, and in 1971 he was appointed rector of the English College in Rome. In that position he hosted Anglican Archbishop Donald Coggan of Canterbury during a historic visit to Pope Paul VI in 1977.

After Murphy-O'Connor was appointed bishop of Arundel and Brighton at the end of 1977, he gained a reputation as a champion of ecumenism. He became cochairman of the Anglican–Roman Catholic International Commission in 1982 and chairman of the British Catholic bishops' Committee for Christian Unity in 1983. Anglican Archbishop George Carey of Canterbury awarded him the first Lambeth doctorate in divinity given to a Roman Catholic bishop since the Reformation. Murphy-O'Connor's book *The Family of the Church* was published in 1984. (DARRELL J. TURNER)

Musharraf, Pervaiz

As he completed his first year as chief executive of the military government of Pakistan, Gen. Pervaiz Musharraf continued in 2000 to take a hard line on a number of policies, including the country's efforts to develop nuclear weapons. He had a brief and inconclusive meeting on various issues, including terrorism, with U.S. Pres. Bill Clinton in Islamabad, Pak., on March 25. On April 6 the government won a guilty verdict on charges of hijacking and terrorism against Mohammed Nawaz Sharif, the former prime minister whom Musharraf had deposed. After having dismissed members of the Supreme Court who refused to sign an oath not to challenge the decisions of the military government, the general agreed to accept the court's decision on May 12 that civil rule was to be reestablished within three years. In September he spoke at the UN Millennium Summit on Pakistan's continuing dispute with India over the future of Jammu and Kashmir.

Musharraf's father was a civil servant in British India, and the son was born in New Delhi on Aug. 11, 1943. The family fled to Karachi, Pak., in 1947 when Pakistan was separated from India. The father worked for the new Pakistani government, and the boy grew up in Karachi, getting a secondary education there and then attending college in Lahore. In 1964 he joined the army, beginning a 35-year career as a professional soldier. He fought in Pakistan's 1965 and 1971 wars with India and was awarded a medal for bravery in the 1965 conflict. He later graduated from the Army Command and Staff College in Quetta, and he attended Britain's Royal College of Defence Studies. Musharraf served in infantry, artillery, and commando units and rose through the ranks. He taught at the Army Command and Staff College and at Pakistan's National Defence College in Rawalpindi. In October 1998 Sharif appointed Musharraf to the post of chief of the army. The general supported the Pakistani invasion of Indian-held territory in Jammu and Kashmir in the summer of 1999 and, like other members of the military, was angered by Sharif's decision to accept a U.S.-sponsored accord for a withdrawal.

Discord between the prime minister and the army grew, and on Oct. 12, 1999, Sharif dismissed Musharraf while the general was on a visit to Sri Lanka. Sharif tried to prevent Musharraf from returning to Pakistan by refusing permission for the plane carrying him to land at the Karachi airport. At this point the army took control of key government agencies and deposed Sharif, with Musharraf becoming the head of a military government. Although he promised an eventual return to civilian rule, his first steps included suspension of the constitution and the dissolution of the parliament. He established a National Security Council, with both military and civilian members, to run the country but in March 2000 said that elections for local councils would begin in December. (ROBERT RAUCH)

Mutlu, Halil

It seemed to many in 2000 that the only challenges left for Turkish weight-lifting champion Halil Mutlu to face were those created by the man himself. Though standing a diminutive 1.5 m (4 ft 11 in) and weighing 56 kg (123 lb), the "Little Dynamo" had loomed large over the weight-lifting stage and in the Turkish imagination for nearly a decade. Having placed first in every major international competition in which he had participated since 1996, Mutlu accomplished what adoring fans and leery opponents alike fully expected him to do—he donned his cloak of invincibility and won gold medals at the 1999 world championships, the 2000 European championships, and the 2000 Olympic Games in Sydney, Australia. Though Mutlu consistently emerged victorious, his matches continued to hold an air of suspense; he repeatedly broke his own world records in the process.

He was born Huben Hubenov on July 14, 1973, to Turkish parents in Postnik, Bulg. He defected to Turkey in 1989 in the footsteps of fellow ethnic Turk and weight-lifting great Naim Suleymanoglu, who had left Bulgaria three years earlier to escape the government's "Bulgarization" of the Turkish minority. After the move he changed his name to Mutlu from Hubenov to reaffirm his Turkish heritage, and he became a member of the renowned weight-lifting team in Ankara. At the age of 18, Mutlu began competitive weight lifting, and he placed fifth in the 54-kg weight division at the 1992 Olympic Games in Barcelona, Spain. Two years later he swept both the European championships and the world championships, and he subsequently missed placing first in only one international competition (Chinese lifter Zhang Xianseng bested him at the 1995 world championships). At the 1996 Olympic Games in Atlanta, Ga., he set an Olympic record when he won gold. In 1999 Mutlu, who had set more than 20 world records during his career, was named Turkey's Best Sportsman of the Year. He set three world records at the 2000 Olympic Games in Sydney: one in the snatch (138 kg), one in the clean and jerk (167.5 kg), and one for the total weight lifted (305 kg).

Mutlu's phenomenal achievements resulted in superstar status for him in his adopted

"Little Dynamo" Halil Mutlu

AP/Wide World Photos

homeland, where weight lifting was big business. His athletic prowess also led to his being compared to the legendary Suleymanoglu, his teammate and idol. Though the two had similar stories, were roughly equal in size, and had both won Olympic gold, Mutlu believed that there was not a comparison to be made between Suleymanoglu—"the greatest weight lifter"—and his biggest fan. (SHANDA SILER)

Nader, Ralph

Running as the candidate of the Green Party, American consumer advocate Ralph Nader won fewer than 3% of the votes cast in the U.S. presidential election held on Nov. 7, 2000, but as it turned out, he was crucial to the outcome. He took far more votes from the Democratic candidate, Vice Pres. Al Gore, than from the Republican, Texas Gov. George W. Bush, and in two states, Florida and New Hampshire, Nader's total votes far exceeded Bush's winning margins. Without Nader on the ballot, it was argued, Gore might well have carried the two states, either one of which would have given him a majority in the electoral college.

Nader was born on Feb. 27, 1934, to Lebanese immigrants in Winsted, Conn. He graduated with honours from Princeton University in 1955 and from Harvard Law School in 1958. After a short period in private practice, he moved to Washington, D.C., in 1963 and in 1964 began a brief stint in the U.S. Department of Labor, during which he worked on automobile safety. His 1965 best-selling book, *Unsafe at Any Speed,* helped lead to passage of the National Traffic and Motor Vehicle Safety Act of 1966. It was only the first of a long series of issues Nader took up, including food processing, the use of pesticides, pension reform, and global trade. Earning a living largely from royalties from his writing and from speaking fees, he was assisted by a staff known as Nader's Raiders. In 1971 he founded Public Citizen, which coordinated his activities, and over the years he was credited with having influenced the establishment of a number of government agencies, including the Occupational Safety and Health Administration and the Environmental Protection Agency. His advocacy also was important in passage of the Freedom of Information Act of 1974. Perhaps more than any other single person, he became identified with the consumer protection movement of the late 20th century, and many safeguards that came to be taken for granted—such as manufacturers' recalls of defective products and standards for food safety—originated with or were influenced by his work.

In the campaign, along with denouncing what he called "corporate welfare," Nader advocated public financing of elections, universal health care, large cuts in military spending, better mass transit, and increases in the minimum wage. He justified his campaign, his second as the Green Party candidate, by arguing that both Gore and Bush were beholden to corporate interests and that the differences between them were insignificant. Dismissing those who warned that he was helping to elect a president opposed to the principles for which he stood, he said that people should vote their consciences, but many of the Democrats who over the years had supported his reforms felt betrayed by a spoiler. (ROBERT RAUCH)

Green Party presidential contender Ralph Nader

AP/World Wide Photos

Newman, Randy

Although he had been called the greatest living American songwriter, by his own reckoning Randy Newman had only 40,000 fans. As a recording artist, he had always been more popular with critics than with consumers, and his greatest success had come from writing scores and songs for motion pictures, which had brought him 13 Academy Award nominations, including three in 1999 and one in 2000, for *Toy Story II.*

The son of a doctor with a roster of celebrity patients, Randall Stuart Newman was born on Nov. 28, 1943, in Los Angeles and was part of a remarkable musical family. He began music lessons early, not only formally but also at the studios of Liberty Records, owned by the father of his lifelong friend Lenny Waronker, and on movie soundstages with his uncle Alfred Newman, one of Hollywood's most honoured composers. (Two other uncles, Lionel and Emil Newman, were also film composers, as were his cousins Thomas and David.) In 1960, encouraged by Waronker (later his producer), Newman began writing for Liberty's publishing arm, and he continued churning out pop songs after abandoning his musical studies at the University of California, Los Angeles. During this period Newman's songs included "I Think It's Going to Rain Today," recorded by Judy Collins, and "Momma Told Me Not to Come," which became a hit single for Three Dog Night.

His debut album as a performer, *Randy Newman* (1968), however, sold fewer than 5,000 copies. The follow-up, *12 Songs* (1970), again sold poorly but was critically acclaimed, as were *Randy Newman Live* (1971), *Sail Away* (1972), and *Good Old Boys* (1974), the last a meditation on the American South that sprang from his childhood memories of New Orleans. In 1977 Newman released his most commercially successful album, *Little Criminals,* with the hit song "Short People," a frequently misunderstood indictment of bigotry. *Born Again* followed in 1979; *Trouble in Paradise* (1983) sold better and featured "I Love L.A." (one of Newman's many odes to American cities), a jaded take on Los Angeles that was nonetheless embraced as a boosterist anthem for the city. Increasingly, Newman focused on his more lucrative contributions to films, including Oscar-nominated compositions for *Ragtime* (1981), *The Natural* (1984), *Parenthood* (1989), and *Toy Story* (1995). In 1999 he received three nominations—for *A Bug's Life, Babe: Pig in the City,* and *Pleasantville.*

A gifted pianist, Newman was equally influenced by the shuffles of Fats Domino and the orchestral music of George Gershwin and Aaron Copland, a fact that was evident both in his film scores and in his arrangements. In Newman's songs plainspoken lyrics belie layers of subversive meaning, while misanthropic cynicism and dark humour mask a well of compassion and pain due partly to his severely crossed eyes, which required several childhood operations, and partly to his perceived outsider status as a (nonpracticing) Jew. In 1988 Newman released the uncharacteristically autobiographical *Land of Dreams;* that work was followed by a reworking of *Faust* (1995), which was later staged as a musical, and another more personal album, *Bad Love* (1999). Despite his legendary procrastination—and his lack of an Oscar—in 2000 Newman continued to turn out classic American music. (JEFF WALLENFELDT)

O'Neal, Shaquille

Before 2000, Los Angeles Lakers centre Shaquille O'Neal—a 2.16-m (7-ft 1-in), 143-kg (315-lb) giant of a man who, nonetheless, was a remarkably agile athlete and a great leaper—had averaged 27.5 points and 12.4 rebounds per game, had made regular appearances in the National Basketball Association (NBA) All-Star game, and had been named in 1996 to the league's list of its 50 greatest players of all time. O'Neal had not, however, won a championship—a fact that fueled the perception that he cared more about himself than his teams. In 2000 O'Neal finally answered his critics by leading the Lakers to the NBA title and becoming only the third player in history to be named the Most Valuable Player of the regular season, the All-Star game, and the finals in the same season.

As early as his freshman year at Louisiana State University (LSU) in 1989, O'Neal was expected by fans and journalists to become one of the game's great players; many of those same observers, however, seemed to resent his presence and revel in his failures. The failures included a number of early exits from the NBA postseason by O'Neal's teams—including the 1994–95 Orlando Magic, which was swept in four games by the Houston Rockets in the finals. The resentment was inspired by a number of factors, including the league's overwrought attempts to promote O'Neal as its marquee player and O'Neal's own self-promotion, which included rap albums and a feature film, *Kazaam* (1996), the story of a rapping genie.

Shaquille Rashaun O'Neal was born on March 6, 1972, in Newark, N.J. As a high-school senior in San Antonio, Texas, he attracted the attention of college recruiters when his team won the state championship. After being named the Consensus College

MVP Shaquille O'Neal

Mike Fiala/Liaison Agency

Player of the Year as a junior at LSU, O'Neal opted for the NBA draft and was taken with the first pick by Orlando. In 2000 he earned his degree from LSU.

Named NBA Rookie of the Year in 1992–93, O'Neal led the Magic to a 41–41 record—20 wins better than the previous season. Two years later O'Neal won the scoring title and led Orlando to the finals against Houston. After Houston's sweep of the Magic, O'Neal developed a reputation for losing big games. Opposing teams purposely fouled him, knowing that he was less likely to make free throws than to score a field goal. He joined the Lakers in 1996, and although he continued to dominate on offense, his teams also continued to disappoint in the play-offs. That changed in 1999–2000 when new Lakers coach Phil Jackson transformed O'Neal. At Jackson's urging, O'Neal became more of a team player, paying special attention to his defense, rebounding, and free-throw shooting. The result was that the most dominating player in the game won his first championship since high school. (ANTHONY G. CRAINE)

Pelevin, Viktor

The reputation of the Russian writer Viktor Pelevin continued to grow among readers in the West in 2000. *Buddha's Little Finger,* the English translation of his novel *Chapayev i pustota* (1996), appeared during the year, and a number of articles about him turned up in the popular press. His depiction of the grotesqueries and absurdities of contemporary life in his country, of its anarchy and corruption and of the despair of its citizens, was especially popular among young Russians. His 1999 novel, which was published in Russian under the English title *Generation "P"* and which depicted politics as the creation of television advertising, was an enormous best-seller.

Viktor Olegovich Pelevin was born in Moscow on Nov. 22, 1962, the son of a military officer and a state economist. He had a technical education and worked briefly as a journalist and as an advertising copywriter. Although he projected a somewhat antic image reminiscent of the American beats of the 1950s, he also was a reclusive man who practiced Buddhist meditation as a way of withdrawing from the chaos of the life around him. His fiction was in the tradition of such Russian writers as Nikolay Gogol, Maksim Gorky, and Mikhail Bulgakov. Pelevin himself cited Bulgakov, Franz Kafka, and William S. Burroughs as among his influences. Pelevin was held in disdain by the official literary establishment, which looked upon his works as lacking gravity, and he lived wholly outside Russian literary society. Nonetheless, his works sometimes took awards, including the Russian Booker Prizes for *Siny fonar* (1991; *The Blue Lantern and Other Stories,* 1997) and *Problema vervolka v sredney polose* (1994; *A Werewolf Problem in Central Russia and Other Stories,* 1998). In addition, his works were wildly popular among young Russian readers, who saw in them unerring portraits of their own lives, and they were highly regarded in the non-Russian literary world, which saw in them a continuation of the tradition of Russian protest literature.

Among the first of Pelevin's works to be published in English was his novel *Zhyoltaya strela* (1993), which appeared in 1994 as *The Yellow Arrow.* In the novel a train that seemed not to have started from any point or to be going anywhere carried passengers who continued the sometimes bizarre routines of their lives. *Omon Ra* (1992; published in English under the same title in 1996), was a surreal exposé of the Soviet space program during the Leonid Brezhnev years. Also in 1996 there appeared *The Life of Insects* (*Zhizn nasekomykh,* 1993), a novel set in a decaying resort on the Black Sea in which two Russians and an American live alternately as humans and insects and thereby learn valuable lessons—for example, as dung beetles, about how to manage in life. (ROBERT RAUCH)

Philbin, Regis

In 2000 television personality and game-show host Regis Philbin sparked a resurgence in television game shows and in the process became the biggest winner of all. With his unabashed enthusiasm and Everyman quality—at times he mispronounced answers—Philbin helped make *Who Wants to Be a Millionaire?* a phenomenon in the United States and turned "Is that your final answer?" into a national catchphrase. Based on the British program of the same name, *Millionaire* debuted in American homes in 1999 and touched off a flurry of rival quiz shows. None of the challengers, however, could match its level of success. *Millionaire* dominated ratings, averaging some 28 million viewers per episode, and made ABC the most-watched network on television. It also established Philbin as one of the small screen's most popular personalities, and in March 2000 it was announced that he had been given a new contract, reported to be worth nearly $20 million a year, to remain with the program. In addition, Philbin kept his day job, cohosting *Live! With Regis and Kathie Lee.* After Kathie Lee Gifford left the program in July, Philbin continued the popular morning talk show.

Born on Aug. 25, 1934, in New York City, Regis Francis Xavier Philbin was an avid weight lifter as a teenager; he later boxed while attending the University of Notre Dame, from which he graduated in 1953 with a degree in sociology. After a short stint with the U.S. Navy, Philbin settled in Los Angeles and found work in the television industry as a stagehand and later as a news writer. He soon moved in front of the camera and in 1961 began hosting *The Regis Philbin Show,* a late-night program that was nationally syndicated during the 1964–65 season as *That Regis Philbin Show.* After appearing as an announcer and sidekick on *The Joey Bishop Show* (1967–69), Philbin helmed a series of programs, including *A.M. Los Angeles* (1975–81), before becoming cohost in 1983 of New York City's *The Morning Show.* Ratings of the struggling show began to climb, and, with the addition of Kathie Lee Gifford in 1985, *Morning* became a huge success. Much of its popularity centred on the on-air chemistry between Philbin and Gifford. The duo's unscripted banter during the opening chat sequence was a highlight of the show, and Philbin became noted for his comical complaining and crankiness. In 1988 the program was nationally syndicated as *Live! With Regis and Kathie Lee.* Focusing on celebrity interviews and home-oriented advice, *Live* attracted one of the fastest-growing American talk-show audiences in the early 1990s.

A confessed workaholic, Philbin also appeared in movies and on television sitcoms. He was coauthor of several cookbooks with Gifford, and a memoir, *I'm Only One Man!* (1996). A regular guest on *Late Show with David Letterman,* he also became one of that program's guest hosts. (AMY TIKKANEN)

Premji, Azim

One of the world's richest men (*The Sunday Times* of London, in its "Rich List 2000," ranked him third in March) was virtually unknown outside his own country. That man, Azim Premji, was chairman of the Wipro Corp., a Bangalore, India-based conglomerate. Thanks to wild increases in technology stocks, Wipro's value had skyrocketed in the late 1990s. The surge, however, was much more than simply the result of outside forces inflating the value of the company. Wipro was once a modest family-owned cooking-oil-producing concern, but Premji had transformed it into an information technology powerhouse. Eschewing Indian industrial tradition, he ventured out of the country's protected economy and into the global marketplace. Whereas traditionally most fortunes in India were based on ownership of land and factories used to produce domestically consumed goods, Premji's wealth was derived from the value of Wipro's stock and the firm's success in foreign markets. The company's market capitalization rose from $67 million in 1990 to more than $4 billion in early 2000. Although Wipro's value slipped later in the year, Premji remained among the world's richest entrepreneurs. In October American Depository shares of Wipro made a modest debut on the New York Stock Exchange.

Azim Hasham Premji was born in Bombay (now Mumbai) on July 24, 1945. That same year his father founded Western Indian Vegetable Products Ltd., which produced *vanaspati,* a widely used hydrogenated shortening. Three years later colonial India was partitioned into mainly Hindu India and Muslim Pakistan, but the Premjis, a Muslim family, chose to remain in India. Premji had nearly completed his degree in engineering at Stanford University in 1966 when his father died unexpectedly. The son returned to India to take the reins of the family business and immediately began to diversify, delving into consumer products such as soap, shoes, and lightbulbs as well as hydraulic cylinders. The company was renamed Wipro in 1977.

Premji's big break came in 1979 after IBM was asked to leave the country, a protectionist move by the Indian government that would ultimately lead to Wipro's success in the global market. Premji steered Wipro toward the computer business. Wipro established a number of successful international partnerships in the 1980s to help it build computer hardware for sale in India, but it was software development that made the firm so lucrative. Premji built a reputation for hiring the best people and providing them with unparalleled training, and he took advantage of India's large pool of well-educated software developers who were willing to work for much less money than their American counterparts could demand. Wipro concentrated on developing custom software for export, primarily to the U.S. Despite his vast personal wealth, Premji was known for his modesty and lack of extravagance. He preferred to fly economy class, and he drove an economy car that did not have its own special parking space at Wipro headquarters. His reputation was that of a highly ethical entrepreneur whose operation stood as a model for other Indian firms. (ANTHONY G. CRAINE)

Rist, Pipilotti

As art critics proclaimed, 2000 was the year that Swiss video installation artist Pipilotti Rist "arrived." The year marked her first solo debut at two major North American venues, the Museum of Fine Arts in Montreal and the Luhring Augustine Gallery in New York City. Rist had been described as "emerging" ever since she won the Premio 2000 Prize at the Venice Biennale in 1997; in March 2000, however, the Toronto *Globe and Mail* newspaper reported that it was "time to change that designation," as "her promise is clearly being filled." The year marked a flurry of media interest in her provocative, often humorous, but always stylish work, and she was dubbed "the irreverent icon of the multimedia world" and "the siren of the 21st century." Her stature was underpinned by her role as artistic director of Expo Schweiz 01, the megasize world exhibition planned for 2001 in Neuchâtel, Switz.

Born Charlotte Rist on June 21, 1962, in the Swiss village of Grabs, she later changed her name to Pipilotti, a fusion of the energetic larger-than-life storybook heroine Pippi Longstocking and her own nickname, Lotti. She attended the Institute of Applied Arts in Vienna and the School of Design in Basel, Switz., where her first experiments were with animated cartoons and scenery for pop music concerts. She also played drums and bass in an all-girl rock band, Les Reines Prochaines ("The Next Queens"). By the late 1980s she was producing vivid and slickly made videos; in her earliest production, *I'm Not the Girl Who Misses Much* (1986), Rist starred as a hysterical blonde bobbing around in a revealing black dress. Following her first exhibition in 1989, her credits included shows at Chicago's Museum of Contemporary Art, Amsterdam's Stedelijk Museum, and Berlin's National Gallery. In 1998, as one of six finalists for the Hugo Boss Prize, her *Sip My Ocean* (1996) was shown at the Guggenheim Museum SoHo in New York City.

She was renowned for bridging the gulf between popular culture and art and for fusing the various art disciplines. Her work drew deliberately on MTV-style pop music videos, but she added a reflective element of her own—she described pain and innocence as two favoured themes. "Art is already the ultimate multidisciplinary field," she commented, a medium through which she could explore the "feelings and emotions of telling stories." Her installations captured the many contradictions and anxieties of modern society. In *Ever Is Over All* (1997), she skips down a street smashing windshields on cars with a flowerlike wand while a policewoman looks on benignly. For *Selfless in a Bath of Lava* (1994), she removed a knot from a wooden floorboard in the P.S.1 gallery space in downtown Manhattan and installed in its place a tiny video screen on which ran indefinitely a minuscule filmed version of herself, shrieking to be let out. (SIOBHAN DOWD)

Rivaldo

Another Brazilian athlete was crowned king of association football (soccer) when, on Jan. 24, 2000, a Fédération Internationale de Football Association (FIFA) poll named Rivaldo Player of the Year for 1999. The 140 national team

Regenfrau (I Am Called a Plant), *video projection on a kitchen unit by Pipilotti Rist, 2000*

above: Sebastian D'Souza/AFP Worldwide; right: Courtesy of the artist, Luhiring Augustine and Hauser & Wirth, Zurich

coaches who voted in the poll gave Rivaldo more than 535 points, compared with 194 for the second-ranked player, David Beckham. Rivaldo was the third Brazilian to have been so honoured since the mid-1990s, following the two other "R's": Romario (1994) and Ronaldo (1996, 1997).

Rivaldo Vitor Borba Ferreira was born on April 19, 1972, into a working-class family in Recife, Braz. Like many poor Brazilian youths, he took up football at an early age. In 1989 he made his club debut with Paulista. After playing with other clubs (Santa Cruz, Mogi-Mirim, and Corinthians), the 1.86-m (6-ft 1-in), 73-kg (161-lb) midfielder-striker joined the Palmeiras team, which won Brazil's national championship in 1994. Two years later Rivaldo scored 20 goals in a 16-game hot streak for Deportivo de la Coruña, and he led Brazil's bronze-medal-winning team at the 1996 Summer Olympic Games in Atlanta, Ga. He moved across the Atlantic to Spain in 1997 after the Barcelona club spent $25.7 million to obtain him as a replacement for Ronaldo, who had transferred to another team. That year Rivaldo helped Barcelona conquer the Spanish League, a feat the team repeated in 1999. In 1997 and 1998 he was the league's top scorer. For his efforts in the 1998 World Cup—Rivaldo led Brazil to the World Cup final, which Brazil lost to France 3–0—he was named to FIFA's all-star team. In 1999 he keyed Brazil's successful bid to capture the Copa América (South American championship).

A fearsome free kicker and an excellent dribbler, Rivaldo traditionally worked the left side of the field, though increasingly over the years he had added other positions to his game. Despite his obvious striking prowess, many observers believed Rivaldo still had room for improvement. He sometimes appeared to lack control while hitting headers in traffic, and he was not as effective as other players inside the penalty area. At times he had also been criticized for his individual style of play, which had exacerbated conflicts with his coach at Barcelona, Louis Van Gaal. Nonetheless, Rivaldo repeatedly had proved himself to be an exceptionally talented player, and as he continued to concentrate on the finer points of his game, the world was sure to be watching for what greater goals he had in store. (STEPHEN P. DAVIS)

Player of the Year Rivaldo
Patrick Hertzog

Roberts, Julia

In 2000—10 years after she first captured the limelight with her starring role opposite Richard Gere in the box-office hit *Pretty Woman*—American actress Julia Roberts, the veteran of some 25 films, became the highest-paid female Hollywood star ever. She commanded $20 million, a figure heretofore paid only to male leads, for her starring role in *Erin Brockovich* (2000), the real-life story of a law-office clerk who helped the citizens of a California town win a multimillion-dollar settlement against a utility company for health problems caused by the company's pollution of their drinking water.

Julia Fiona Roberts was born on Oct. 28, 1967, in Smyrna, Ga., a suburb of Atlanta. Although her parents briefly ran an actors' workshop when she was a child, Roberts had no acting experience or formal training when she moved to New York City after high school to pursue a career in show business. Although she signed with a modeling agency upon her arrival in New York, she never landed any jobs. Her first film role turned up after she was recommended by her older brother, actor Eric Roberts, for a bit part as his on-screen sister in *Blood Red* (1988), a drama set in the late 1800s. Her career took off quickly; she next made a television appearance and had a role in a cable television movie before securing her first leading part in *Mystic Pizza* (1988). She portrayed one of three young women working in a pizzeria in a small Connecticut town; audiences were captivated by Roberts, with her long, curly auburn hair and wide, toothy grin. Her work in this film led to a place in the star-studded cast of *Steel Magnolias* (1989), in which she worked with such veteran actresses as Shirley MacLaine, Olympia Dukakis, and Sally Field. Roberts received a Golden Globe Award and an Academy Award nomination for best supporting actress for her heartrending portrayal of Field's diabetic daughter. Her performance in *Pretty Woman*, an upbeat comedy about a romance between a prostitute and a business tycoon, made Roberts a household name and earned her a second Golden Globe and a second Oscar nomination.

She continued to work steadily throughout the 1990s, starring in such films as *Flatliners* (1990); *Sleeping with the Enemy* (1991); *The Pelican Brief* (1993); *Something to Talk About* (1995); *Mary Reilly* (1996), for which she was paid a then-record $10 million; *My Best Friend's Wedding* (1997); and *Stepmom* (1998), for which she also served as executive producer. Her personal life, however, including a highly publicized short-lived marriage to singer Lyle Lovett, sometimes overshadowed her career. All of that changed in 1999 with the release of two popular romantic comedies, *Notting Hill* and *Runaway Bride*, the latter of which reteamed her with Gere. Roberts, who had at least two more films in production in 2000, also launched her own production company, Shoelace Productions. (SANDRA LANGENECKERT)

Santana, Carlos

By winning three Latin Grammys and nine Grammy Awards—including Album of the Year for *Supernatural* and Song of the Year for "Smooth"—Latino rocker Carlos Santana staged a comeback of millennial proportions in 2000. At age 52 he fell somewhere between youthful phenoms Ricky Martin and Jennifer Lopez at one end of the new wave of Latin pop music and the Cuban elder statesmen of *The Buena Vista Social Club* at the other. Supported by such collaborators as pop rocker Rob Thomas of Matchbox 20, hip-hop luminary Lauryn Hill, fellow guitarist Eric Clapton, and former Arista Records head Clive Davis, Santana crafted a pop gem.

Santana was born on July 20, 1947, in Autlán de Navarro, Mex., and began playing the violin at age five; by age eight, however, he had switched to the guitar. As a teenager he played in bands in Tijuana, Mex., where he was exposed not only to the local Norteño music but to blues, especially to guitarists T-Bone Walker and B.B. King. Although his family moved to San Francisco in the 1960s, Santana returned frequently to Tijuana. Influenced by the San Francisco Bay Area's burgeoning rock scene, in 1966 he formed the Santana Blues Band, which came to the attention of rock music impresario Bill Graham. The band began performing at the legendary club Fillmore West and, though

Multi-Grammy winner Santana
AP/Wide World Photos

largely unknown, triumphed at the Woodstock Festival in 1969.

Signed to Columbia, Santana ("Blues Band" had been dropped from the band's name) released a series of hit albums that infused rock with a Latin feel rooted in Afro-Cuban rhythms and that centred on Carlos's extraordinary lead-guitar playing, characterized by the distinctive sustaining of individual notes that became his trademark. *Santana,* featuring the top-10 hit "Evil Ways," peaked at number four on the album charts in 1969; *Abraxas,* with the hits "Black Magic Woman" and "Oye Como Va," reached number one the next year. *Santana III* (1971) and *Caravanserai* (1972) followed. Over the next two decades, however, the group's output was more uneven—and less commercially successful—as Santana led ever-shifting personnel toward a jazz-rock fusion that reflected his admiration for Miles Davis and John Coltrane and resulted in collaborations with jazz artists such as Buddy Miles, Stanley Clarke, and John McLaughlin. Having earlier shown an interest in the philosophy of Sri Chimnoy, Santana became a born-again Christian in 1992. Meditation and mysticism became central to his life, and Santana began to see himself as a musical shaman whose pursuit of songs that offered hope and healing culminated in *Supernatural.* In 1998 Santana's lasting contribution was marked by his group's induction into the Rock and Roll Hall of Fame. (JEFF WALLENFELDT)

Savon, Felix

Cuban heavyweight boxer Felix Savon won his third Olympic gold medal with a 21–13 decision over Russia's Sultanakhmed Ibragimov at the 2000 Olympic Games in Sydney, Australia. Savon became only the third fighter in history to win three gold medals and the second to win all three in the same weight class. His performance, and much of his career leading up to it, bore a striking resemblance to that of his countryman heavyweight Teófilo Stevenson, who 20 years earlier—at the 1980 Olympics in Moscow—vanquished a Russian to become the first boxer to win gold three times in the same weight class. Like Stevenson in 1980, Savon entered the 2000 Games with a fading reputation after having dominated the sport for many years—he was no longer the overwhelming favourite to win the gold. With blood flowing from a cut under his eye suffered during his semifinal match with German Sebastian Köber, Savon withstood a late attack by Ibragimov to win the title.

Félix Savón Fabré was born on April 22, 1967, in San Vicente, Cuba. He rose to prominence in 1985 when he won the heavyweight title at the world junior championships. A year later he won the world championship, a feat he would repeat five more times (1989, 1991, 1993, 1995, and 1997), and he claimed Olympic titles in 1992 and 1996. He complemented those titles with first-place finishes in the Pan American Games (1987, 1991, and 1995) and the Goodwill Games (1990, 1994, and 1998). His first sign of weakness came in the final match of the world championships in 1997, where he was soundly defeated by Rustam Chagayev of Uzbekistan. Chagayev, however, was later disqualified because of violations of his amateur status, and Savon was awarded the victory. Savon was scheduled to fight in the final of the 1999 world championships, but he pulled out of the match after the Cuban delegation claimed it had been the victim of several questionable decisions during the competition.

At 1.96 m (6 ft 5 in) and 91 kg (201 lbs), Savon had the power to crush opponents. Just as Stevenson had done a generation before, Savon shunned the professional circuit entirely. Politics also played a role in Savon's career. Whereas Stevenson never had a shot at a fourth gold medal, owing to Cuba's boycott of the 1984 Games, Savon would almost certainly have won his fourth gold in Sydney, but a Cuban boycott in 1988 kept him out of the Games when he was at the height of his powers. An International Amateur Boxing Association rule prohibiting amateur boxers from competing beyond their 34th birthday meant that Savon faced retirement in 2001. (ANTHONY G. CRAINE)

Sherman, Cindy

In 2000 American photographer Cindy Sherman continued to reinvent herself and her art after having been declared in 1999 one of the 25 most influential artists of the 20th century by *ARTnews* magazine. Her staged photography, in which she occupied centre stage, evoked disquieting and provocative images of popular culture in the realm of advertising, television programming, film, and fashion. In March the Gagosian Gallery in Beverly Hills showed her most recent work, a collection of self-portraits in which she posed as Hollywood women with overblown makeup and silicone implants. Critics found the show one of her most disturbing and poignant to date.

Courtesy of Cindy Sherman and Metro Pictures

Cindy Sherman in a stylish photographic "self-portrait"

Cynthia Morris Sherman was born on Jan. 19, 1954, in Glen Ridge, N.J., but when she was three her family moved to Long Island, N.Y. As a child, she loved dressing up in old clothes and constantly drew pictures, often of scenes on television. She graduated from the State University of New York at Buffalo in 1976 with a degree in photography and moved to New York City shortly thereafter after being awarded a National Endowment for the Arts grant in 1977.

For the next four years, she worked at Artists Space, while simultaneously developing her first wave of photographic art—portraits of herself or her friends masquerading as a small-town librarian, a hitchhiker, or various movie stars, such as Sophia Loren, Liza Minelli, and Marilyn Monroe. Photographs in which she portrayed stereotypical characters in seemingly familiar settings formed Sherman's first series, *Untitled Film Stills.* The collection, taken between 1978 and 1980, was printed in 10 sets, and virtually overnight her reputation was established. In 1982 her *Centerfolds* show at Metro Pictures Gallery brought her international acclaim, and she received invitations to exhibit at the Stedelijk Museum in The Netherlands and Documenta 7 in Germany. Other notable shows included *Sex Pictures,* which employed an assortment of body parts from medical dummies; *Pink Robes; Fashion; Fairy Tales; Disasters;* and an untitled exhibit, featuring the mangled parts of plastic dolls disjointed from their bodies.

Sherman's "setup" photography—in which the artist and viewer engage with fictional tableaus where all is not what it seems—also inspired a generation of younger artists. Whatever the elements in her chosen scenario—whether mutilated dolls, a parody of a movie star, or a sly takeoff of a famous painting—the result was usually one of enigmatic pathos. She explored stereotypes of women, drawing heavily but critically from such popular sources as television soap operas. Over the years her work ranged from outrageous eroticism to harrowing images of decay.

Her now legendary *Untitled Film Stills* became some of the most highly sought-after objects in the field of photographic art; in 1996 the Museum of Modern Art in New York City purchased the only complete collection of 69 stills for a price of what sources claimed was over $1,000,000; in 1999 one still, originally priced at $50, fetched more than $200,000 at Christie's auction house. Sherman was the recipient of a Guggenheim Fellowship and a MacArthur Foundation "genius" grant, and her images were shown in major retrospectives at the Whitney Museum of American Art in New York City and the Museum of Contemporary Art in Los Angeles. In addition, her work was included in some of the world's most prestigious collections of modern art, including those held by London's Tate Gallery and New York City's Metropolitan Museum of Art. (SIOBHAN DOWD)

Spacey, Kevin

For his masterful performance as a frustrated husband and father in the dark comedy *American Beauty,* American actor Kevin Spacey was presented with the 2000 Academy Award for best actor. The role was a significant departure for Spacey, who had been known primarily for his skillful portrayals of bad guys. He had, for example, won a 1991 Tony Award for featured actor for his performance as the mobster Uncle Louie in *Lost in Yonkers* and a 1996 Oscar for best supporting actor for his portrayal of a double-talking con man in *The Usual Suspects*. In *American Beauty*, however, Spacey was allowed to explore a quite different character. His ability to show the alienation and vulnerability of his character, Lester Burnham—a middle-class family man obsessed with a beautiful classmate of his teenage daughter—brought Spacey enthusiastic critical acclaim as well as widespread popular recognition.

Kevin Spacey Fowler was born on July 26, 1959, in South Orange, N.J. His family moved frequently, and young Kevin had difficulty finding his way in life. Feelings of being an outsider sometimes resulted in misbehaviour, and he was expelled from California's Northridge Military Academy, where his parents had sent him in hopes he would gain some discipline. At Chatsworth High School in Los Angeles, Spacey was steered toward drama classes and finally found his direction; he appeared in numerous school productions and exploited his talent for impersonation by performing in comedy clubs. Following graduation he attended Los Angeles Valley College for a while, but in 1979 he moved to New York City and enrolled at the Juilliard School there. After two years Spacey felt that he was ready to move on and soon made his professional debut in a small part in Shakespeare's *Henry IV, Part I*. He took a job with the New York Shakespeare Festival as an assistant to the festival's founder and director, Joseph Papp, but after witnessing Spacey's performance in an "off-off-off-Broadway" production, Papp fired him so that Spacey would be compelled to intensify his search for acting jobs. In 1982 Spacey made his Broadway debut in Henrik Ibsen's *Ghosts*. Notable roles in *Hurlyburly* (1985) and *Long Day's Journey into Night* (1986) followed, as did appearances in the films *Heartburn* (1986) and *Working Girl* (1988) and in several 1988 episodes of the television series *Wiseguy*.

Following his theatrical success in *Lost in Yonkers*, Spacey earned praise for his performances in such films as *Glengarry Glen Ross* (1992), *Swimming with Sharks* (1994), *Seven* (1995), *A Time to Kill* (1996), and, especially, *L.A. Confidential* (1997). In 1998 Spacey returned to the stage and received the *Evening Standard*, London Theatre Critics' Circle, and Laurence Olivier best actor awards for his performance as Hickey in Eugene O'Neill's *The Iceman Cometh*.

Spacey maintained a busy acting schedule in 2000. He released *The Big Kahuna*, finished shooting *Pay It Forward*, and was scheduled to star in the film adaptation of author E. Annie Proulx's award-winning 1993 novel *The Shipping News*. (BARBARA WHITNEY)

Oscar winners Kevin Spacey (left) and Sam Mendes (q.v.)

Scott Nelson/AFP Worldwide

Speight, George

Declaring that he was defending the rights of indigenous Fijians against the increasing power of the country's ethnic Indian minority, George Speight led a small group of armed men to the Parliament building in the capital, Suva, on May 19, 2000, and took Prime Minister Mahendra Chaudhry and about 40 other legislators hostage. Speight and his followers then demanded that Fiji's constitution be replaced so that ethnic Indians would be excluded from government, amnesty be granted to those who had participated in the coup, and he and his supporters have a voice in choosing the new government. All of these conditions were met on July 9 under the terms of an amnesty accord reached between Fiji's military and the rebels, who carried through on their promise to release the hostages. On July 26, however, Speight was arrested and taken into custody. The amnesty agreement was later declared invalid because the military commander had signed "under duress."

Speight was born in Naivicula, a small village in Fiji's Tailevu province. His mother was an indigenous Fijian. His father was a well-to-do farmer of Fijian-European descent who later became a member of Parliament. Speight studied marketing in Australia and later earned bachelor's and master's degrees in business from Andrews University, Berrien Springs, Mich. After completing his education, he worked in Australia as a marketer for an insurance company and as a computer salesman.

Speight returned to Fiji in 1996, at a time when his father was a senior member in the government. Largely through his father's influence, he became chairman of Fiji Pine, Ltd., and Fiji Hardwood Corp., Ltd.—two companies engaged in Fiji's lucrative timber business. In May 1999 the government was defeated in the election that brought ethnic Indian Chaudhry and his Fiji Labour Party to power. With his father out of office, Speight lost much of his political clout and, partly as a result, was fired as chairman of the two timber companies in 1999. He also lost his job as a local managing director of the insurance brokering firm Heath Fiji, Ltd., having been blamed for financial irregularities at the company.

Soon after Speight was arrested, his supporters created incidents of civil disorder in many parts of Fiji and clashed with the army. After complaining that he and others had been assaulted by soldiers while in custody, Speight pleaded not guilty to charges of unlawful assembly and failing to disarm. In August Speight and 16 of his followers were also charged with treason. (DAVID R. CALHOUN)

Straw, Jack

Following his appointment as the U.K.'s home secretary in 1997, British politician Jack Straw proved hard to characterize. Though liberal and reformist in some respects, he was conservative and authoritarian in other ways. Nevertheless, by 2000 he had managed to acquire a reputation for competence that had eluded many of his predecessors.

Born on Aug. 3, 1946, in Essex, Jack Straw belonged to the generation of 1960s student radical activists and became president of the U.K.'s National Union of Students in 1969. Unlike many of his contemporaries, however, he steered well clear of "alternative" lifestyles; one of his first causes was opposition to the use of all illegal drugs, including cannabis. He trained to be a barrister and then worked as a special adviser to Labour Party cabinet ministers Barbara Castle (1974–76) and Peter Shore (1976–77). After a brief stint as a television researcher, Straw entered Parliament in 1979 as MP for Castle's former seat of Blackburn, Lancashire. He rose steadily through Labour's rank and was elected to the party's opposition shadow cabinet in 1987. During the 1980s he moved from being a traditional left-winger to becoming a more centrist modernizer. He was the first leading member of the Labour Party to propose that it repeal its socialist commitment—Clause Four of the party's constitution—to the state control of industry. In 1994 Straw managed Tony Blair's successful campaign to be elected party leader; one of Blair's first acts on becoming leader was to win the party's agreement to rewrite Clause Four.

Following Labour's election victory in 1997, Straw was appointed home secretary. He quick-

top: AP/Wide World Photos

ly established his progressive credentials by setting up an inquiry into charges of racism in the London police force, promoting the incorporation of the European Convention on Human Rights into British law, and refusing to allow the former Chilean head of state, Gen. Augusto Pinochet Ugarte, to return home following Pinochet's October 1998 arrest in London. (The arrest followed a request by the Spanish government that Pinochet be extradited to Spain to face charges of murder. He was allowed to return to Chile in March 2000 when a panel of doctors advised that he was unfit to face trial.)

Straw upset many progressives, however, by initiating legislation to withdraw the right of some defendants to be tried by a jury, introducing harsher requirements for people going to Great Britain to seek political asylum, diluting Labour's pre-1997 election promise to establish a freedom of information law, and resisting calls to decriminalize the consumption of "soft" drugs. The drugs issue caused Straw some embarrassment in December 1997 when his own 17-year-old son, William, was arrested in London for selling cannabis. Straw commanded widespread sympathy when it transpired that William had been the victim of entrapment by a newspaper and that as soon as the paper confronted the home secretary with its story, ahead of publication, he took his son to the police to confess what had happened.

(PETER KELLNER)

Suzuki, Ichiro

By 2000 Ichiro Suzuki had established himself as the best baseball player in Japan and had begun his quest for stardom in the U.S. A speedy left-handed-hitting right fielder for the Orix BlueWave of Japan's Pacific League (PL), Suzuki spent two weeks in the Seattle Mariners' 1999 spring-training camp in Peoria, Ariz., as part of a U.S.-Japan player exchange. A Japanese player in an American lineup was no longer quite the rarity it once had been; several Japanese pitchers had crossed the Pacific to play in the major leagues. Suzuki became the first nonpitcher to make the transition when he signed a three-year contract with the Mariners in November 2000. Because pitchers in the U.S. threw harder than their Japanese counterparts, some observers believed that Japanese hitters would struggle at the plate. Suzuki, however, had been rewriting the record books in Japan since 1994. No Japanese hitter stood a better chance in the U.S. than he.

Suzuki was born on Oct. 22, 1973, in Aichi, Japan, and took to baseball at an early age. Upon finishing high school, he was drafted by the BlueWave. He saw limited action during his first two seasons because his manager disliked the young player's unorthodox batting style—a sort of pendulum motion created by kicking the front foot back and then striding forward with the swing. In 1994 a new manager gave Suzuki a starting spot on the team and let him swing the way he liked. He responded in amazing fashion, lifting his batting average to .400 during the season and finishing at .385—the second best batting mark in the history of Japanese baseball. He collected 210 hits, a record for one season. Through 2000 he had won seven consecutive PL batting titles, posted a career average of .353, and led his team to two PL pennants. At 1.8 m (5 ft 11 in) and 70 kg (155 lb), he was not a power hitter, but his speed and bat control were unmatched. He was also considered among the top outfielders, with the strongest, most accurate throwing arm in the league.

Suzuki represented a new type of Japanese ballplayer. In addition to his unusual swing, he bucked the conservative baseball establishment in other ways. Unlike other players, he wore his first name, rather than his last, on the back of his uniform. He commanded the highest annual salary in history ($4.2 million) and parlayed his unrivaled popularity into lucrative product endorsements. Whether he could carry his success to American ball fields was a question that remained unanswered by the time he left Arizona. Dehydration had limited his playing time, and he had one hit in six at-bats. Critics felt his motion-intensive batting style would fail against faster pitching, but Suzuki left the U.S. expressing hopes of a return. His contract with the BlueWave was to end after the 2001 baseball season, when he would surely be seeking new challenges. (ANTHONY G. CRAINE)

Tavener, Sir John

As thousands ushered in the year 2000 under London's Millennium Dome, John Tavener's choral composition *A New Beginning* was premiered. The piece set the tone for the evening's magnificent festivities and served to acknowledge Tavener's standing as Great Britain's most popular living composer. The choice of his music to celebrate and welcome the future was a bit ironic; unlike most of his contemporaries, Tavener, who was knighted in January 2000, was influenced by some distinctly nonmodern sources—sacred and spiritual texts. Although some critics dismissed his work as lightweight ("holy muzak," reported *The Guardian* newspaper), he was widely considered a composer who could succeed in making classical music accessible to the masses.

Significant Tavener works that brought praise and widespread approval throughout the 1980s and '90s included such pieces as *Orthodox Vigil Service, Akathist of Thanksgiving,* and *The Protecting Veil,* a piece for solo cello and strings popularized by renowned cellists, including Steven Isserlis and Yo-Yo Ma. Other works included *Resurrection,* a large-scale choral piece, and *Mary of Egypt,* an opera. Tavener's *Song for Athene* was played during the funeral of Diana, princess of Wales. Another of his choral works, *Fall and Resurrection,* premiered in the first days of 2000 to mark the new year.

Tavener was born on Jan. 28, 1944, in London. He composed music as early as the age of three and learned to play piano and organ. He attended the Royal Academy of Music, London, where his instructors included the composers David Lumsdaine and Sir Lennox Berkeley. Tavener made his first significant mark with *The Whale,* an avant-garde cantata that received a

Composer Sir John Tavener

popular debut at the London Sinfonietta in 1968. Tavener was soon befriended by the rock group the Beatles, whose record label, Apple, issued a recording of the piece. Always spiritual in content, Tavener's style became even more inwardly focused after he joined the Russian Orthodox Church in 1977. He suffered a stroke at age 36 and in 1991 was diagnosed with Marfan syndrome, a genetic disorder affecting the connective tissues. Tavener acknowledged that these events further strengthened his commitment to his faith and his commitment to expressing it through music. He likened composing to prayer, and he said he thought of himself as more of a conduit to the spiritual world than a composer. His spiritual mentor, Mother Thekla, an abbess at an Orthodox monastery in North Yorkshire, was also his librettist. Tavener's music hewed more to Eastern than to Western styles, drawing from Russian, Byzantine, and Greek influences. (ANTHONY G. CRAINE)

Thani, Sheikh Hamad ibn Khalifah ath-

By 2000, in the five years since Sheikh Hamad ibn Khalifah ath-Thani had overthrown his father and become emir of Qatar, he had instituted a number of policies that had transformed the smallest of the Middle Eastern counties. He moved to allow Qatar's 600,000 residents to participate more actively in the government and to promote greater equality for women. After becoming ruler he announced plans to establish an elected parliament, appointed a committee to draft a permanent constitution, largely abolished censorship of the press, and in 1999 held the country's first open general elections for a municipal council. For the first time, women not only were allowed to vote but, even more revolutionary, were also allowed to run for office.

One reform that thrust Qatar into the international spotlight was the establishment in 1996 of the country's satellite television network, Al Jazeera ("The Peninsula"). The network, which was guaranteed government financial backing for its first five years, was likened to an "Arab CNN." It created a rare forum for uncensored news and debate, much to the delight of its viewers and to the displeasure of many Arab rulers. Some leaders, finding their policies under attack, on occasion

left: John G. Mabanglo/AFP Worldwide; top right: Clive Barda/Performing Arts Library; bottom right: Alessandro Bianchi/AFP Worldwide

moved to block their residents' access to the programming. Guests on the popular live call-in show *Opposite Direction* debated radically different viewpoints on sensitive subjects, and some sessions became so heated that guests walked off the set in mid-broadcast. By 2000 Al Jazeera's programming was seen 24 hours a day in over 20 countries, and the network was a leading source for Arab-language news.

Hamad was born in 1950 in Doha, Qatar, into a family that at the time had ruled the country for a century. His father, Sheikh Khalifah ibn Hamad ath-Thani, became Qatar's leader in 1972, just months after the country had won independence from Great Britain. Hamad, who was educated in Qatar and in England at the Royal Military Academy at Sandhurst, became a lieutenant colonel in Qatar's military after graduating in 1971. He was promoted in 1975 to major general and commander in chief of the armed forces, and in 1977 he became minister of defense as well as heir apparent to the throne. Following the 1990–91 Persian Gulf War, Hamad was, for most purposes, leading the country, and in 1995 he staged a coup and ousted his father while the latter was traveling outside the country. Hamad himself survived a number of subsequent coup attempts and succeeded in returning to the government a portion of the estimated $3 billion–$7 billion in gas and oil profits his father had held in personal bank accounts. (SANDRA LANGENECKERT)

Wade, Abdoulaye

Following four unsuccessful attempts to gain high office, on April 1, 2000, Senegalese Democratic Party (PDS) leader Abdoulaye Wade was sworn in as Senegal's third president; his election signaled a major power shift in the country, which had been ruled by the Socialist Party (PS) since gaining independence from France in 1960. In the first round of elections on February 27, Wade secured only about 31% of the vote, whereas incumbent PS leader Abdou Diouf captured 41%. In the second round on March 19, however, Wade scored an overwhelming victory in the country's first-ever runoff election.

Wade was born on May 29, 1926, in the town of Kébémer, between Dakar and St. Louis in the Louga region. He was educated in Senegal and France, and in 1970 he earned a Ph.D. from the faculty of law and economics of the Sorbonne. After practicing law in France, he returned to Senegal and became a professor at the University of Dakar and later served as dean of its Faculty of Law and Economics. In 1974 Wade launched the PDS in opposition to Léopold Sédar Senghor, and four years later he won a seat in the National Assembly. He rapidly became the focal point of the then fledgling opposition movement. That same year he unsuccessfully ran against Senghor in the presidential election. He made a second bid in the 1988 presidential election, this time losing to Senghor's handpicked successor, Diouf. In 1988 Wade lost again to the incumbent in a disputed contest that created civil unrest that arose from the manner in which that election was conducted. Diouf offered Wade a post in his government to calm the situation, and Wade served as senior minister of state for 18 months before resigning to protest Diouf's various policies. He ran against Diouf again in 1993 but received only 32% of the vote. Later that year Wade was imprisoned briefly by Diouf on charges of endangering the security of the state, but Wade was nonetheless invited to rejoin the cabinet in his former position in March 1995. He resigned in March 1998 to prepare for a fifth presidential bid.

As president, Wade faced major problems; he had to find the means to deliver on his campaign promises to improve literacy levels, raise health standards, and alleviate poverty, as well as address the deteriorating economic situation of the country at large. In addition, he had to deal with the country's huge international debt resulting from severe balance of payments problems. Among his first actions was to ask merchants to lower the price of rice, the country's staple food. He was expected to distance himself somewhat from France and to seek much closer ties with the United States. (NANCY ELLEN LAWLER)

Walsh, Courtney

On March 27, 2000, appropriately enough at Sabina Park cricket ground in his hometown of Kingston, Jam., Courtney Walsh became the highest wicket-taker in Test history. The victim, Henry Olonga of Zimbabwe, was the 435th of Walsh's distinguished career, and when he had achieved the feat, the tall Jamaican with the ready smile and extraordinary stamina stooped down to kiss the ground, sending the whole island into carnival.

Courtney Andrew Walsh was born in Kingston on Oct. 30, 1962, and made his first-class debut for Jamaica in 1982. His Test career began in Perth, Australia, in 1984, but it was not until four years later that he became a regular member of the West Indies pace attack, forming, with Curtley Ambrose, a formidable fast-bowling partnership that reaped a total of 752 wickets in 94 Tests and sustained the side through triumph and, more recently, rapid decline. While Ambrose was metronomically accurate, Walsh was instinctively aggressive, always probing the mental and physical weaknesses of batsmen and never allowing them to settle into a rhythm. His stock delivery, the one he relied on for his wickets, was a wicked leg-cutter, bowled with an awkward flailing action that defied the coaching books. As he grew older, however, his ability to bowl fast all the time diminished. In response, he developed a devastating slower ball and a deceptive inswinger. By 2000 he had become the complete fast bowler and only the third man to reach 400 Test wickets. Yet the most formidable quality Walsh displayed was his stamina. He very rarely missed a Test match through injury, often bowled long spells during the day, and was always willing to go back for more.

A quiet, intelligent, and dedicated man, Walsh first captained his country on a tour of India in 1994. As the permanent captain in 1996, he led the West Indies to victories over India and New Zealand, but after a 3–0 series defeat by Pakistan, he lost the captaincy contentiously to Brian Lara. The handover could have caused a riot in Lara's first Test as captain, which was to be played against England in Kingston. Though his pride was deeply hurt, Walsh defused any anger among his supporters by accompanying Lara onto the field with his arm around the new captain. In August 2000, to mark his last Test in England, the home team formed a guard of honour for Walsh and Ambrose, who had announced his plans to retire. Indeed, Walsh was a particular favourite of English crowds in general and most particularly in Gloucestershire, the unfashionable county for which he had played so devotedly since 1984. There was speculation that Walsh, who turned 38 at the end of October, would join his partner in retirement, but he agreed to tour Australia one final time in search of the elusive wickets that would make him the first bowler in history to reach 500 Test wickets. (ANDREW LONGMORE)

Premier wicket-taker Courtney Walsh

Warner, Kurt

With 1 minute 54 seconds left to play and the score tied 16–16 in Super Bowl XXXIV on Jan. 30, 2000, St. Louis Rams quarterback Kurt Warner lofted a 73-yd touchdown pass to wide receiver Isaac Bruce. The play led to a 23–16 victory for the Rams over the Tennessee Titans and was a fitting climax to a storybook year for the 28-year-old Warner, who only a few years before had been working as a stock boy at an Iowa grocery store. In the Super Bowl, which came at the end of Warner's first season as a starting quarterback in the National Football League (NFL), he completed 24 of 45 passes for a record 414 yd, including two touchdowns, and threw no interceptions in the game. His performance earned him the Bowl's Most Valuable Player (MVP) award. He had already been voted the league's MVP, having led the Rams to a 13–3 regular-season record. With 41 touchdown passes, he joined Dan Marino as the only NFL players to have surpassed the 40 mark in a single season.

Warner was born on June 22, 1971, in Burlington, Iowa. Unable to land a football scholarship to a Division I college, he attended the University of Northern Iowa, where he did not become a first-string player until his fifth and final year. After an unsuccessful tryout with the NFL's Green Bay Packers in 1994, he played football in the Arena Football League with the Iowa Barnstormers from 1995 to 1997. Between seasons, in order to support his wife and three children and to be free to work out during the day, he stocked grocery shelves at night for $5.50 an hour. In 1998 he signed with the Amsterdam Admirals of NFL Europe. Starting all 10 games for the Admirals that season, he led the league in passing with 2,101 yd.

He was called up by St. Louis for the 1998–99 NFL season and spent the year as a backup quarterback, starting only in the final game of the team's 4–12 season. When first-string quarterback Trent Green injured his knee during the 1999 preseason, Warner became the team's starter. His phenomenal performance thereafter seemed to stun everyone except Rams coach Dick Vermeil and Warner himself. "It is not a fairy tale," said Vermeil, who praised Warner's persistence. "[Warner] has a willingness to accept coaching and criticism and was willing to work and play a subordinate role until he got the opportunity and then took advantage of it." For his part, Warner credited the support of his family and his deep Christian faith for helping him through the tough times. Speaking after the Super Bowl, he also thanked those in the Rams organization, stating, "Everybody—the players, the coaches—their belief in me has been tremendous." (DAVID R. CALHOUN)

Webb, Karrie

While she was in no immediate danger of being mobbed by throngs of admirers, reporters, and photographers, Australian golfer Karrie Webb gained a reputation in 2000 as the women's tour's answer to Tiger Woods. She began the year with three straight tournament victories—one short of Nancy Lopez's record of four wins in a row—and went on to win two majors, the Nabisco Championship and the U.S. Women's Open. By shooting a 6-under-par 282 to take the U.S. Women's Open title in July, the 25-year-old Webb claimed the largest single tournament prize ($500,000, plus a $250,000 bonus) in Ladies Professional Golf Association (LPGA) history and earned enough points to qualify for enshrinement in the LPGA Hall of Fame (though she was not eligible for induction until she had played 10 years on the tour). She needed only to win the LPGA championship to become the youngest woman ever to win all four of the modern-day majors—and she had until 2009 to do so.

Webb was born on Dec. 21, 1974, in Ayr, Queen., Australia, and began playing golf at the age of eight. By her early teens she was competing exclusively against top local men players. Turning professional in 1994, she joined the Women's Professional Golfers' European Tour. The following year she won the Women's British Open, her last win before joining the LPGA tour in 1996.

In just her second LPGA tournament, Webb demonstrated the mental toughness of a veteran, defeating Martha Nause and Jane Geddes on the fourth hole of a sudden-death play-off. Shortly thereafter, Webb began her assault on golf's record books, collecting tournament titles at a dizzying pace. Three more tournament victories, along with 12 top-five finishes, led her to a single-season earnings record of $1,002,000—the first time that a rookie on either the men's or the women's tour had reached the million-dollar mark. Webb capped her incredible debut season by winning the LPGA Rookie of the Year award.

In 1997 Webb shot a career-low 63 en route to her second victory at the Women's British Open in three years. She collected two other wins and led the tour with a scoring average of 70. With two tournament victories and 20 top-20 finishes in 1998, Webb passed the $2 million mark in career earnings.

Like Woods, Webb continued to exceed expectations, putting together another amazing season in 1999: six tournament titles (including her first major at the du Maurier Classic), 22 top-10 finishes, and record-setting numbers in both scoring average (69.43) and single-season earnings ($1,591,959). (ANTHONY G. CRAINE)

Williams, Serena and Venus

The Williams sisters, Serena and Venus, emerged in 2000 as the most formidable duo in women's tennis. The year was particularly special for Venus, who won the first Grand Slam singles title of her career at Wimbledon—after having beaten Serena in the semifinal—and went on to triumph at the U.S. Open and the Olympic Games in Sydney, Australia. Venus became only the second player to capture Wimbledon, the U.S. Open, and the Olympic singles titles in the same year. Together, she and Serena also made history in the doubles event; their resounding 6–1, 6–1 Olympic finals victory over the Dutch team of Kristie Boogert and Miriam Oremans made them the first sisters to win a gold medal in doubles.

Venus was born on June 17, 1980, in Lynwood, Calif. Serena was born on Sept. 26, 1981, in Saginaw, Mich. Each was introduced to tennis at age four by their father, Richard, whose stated goal was to raise them to be champions. The sisters' unlikely ascent began on shoddy public courts in Los Angeles. By age 10 Venus had attracted national media attention, and both sisters played exhibition matches against leading professionals before they reached their teens. In 1991 the family moved to Florida, where Venus and Serena were enrolled in a tennis academy.

Venus turned professional in 1994, shortly after her 14th birthday. Her first big performance was in 1997, when she became the first unseeded U.S. Open women's finalist in the open era, but she lost 6–0, 6–4 to Martina Hingis. Serena's professional debut came in 1995, and in 1997, in only her fifth professional tournament, she upended Mary Pierce (ranked number seven) and Monica Seles (ranked fourth) at the Ameritech Cup in Chicago to become the lowest-ranked player (304) ever to have beaten two top-10 players in the same tournament.

Expectations for the sisters began to grow quickly. Richard made brash statements to the media about his talented daughters, who both signed multimillion-dollar endorsement deals. Not until late in the 1999 season, however, did the promise become reality. Serena, much to the private dismay of her older sister, took the U.S. Open singles title—the first Grand Slam win for a Williams. While there was no animosity between the siblings, Venus felt that she had failed by not being the first to win a big tournament. Although Richard hinted early in 2000 that Venus might be ready to retire from the sport, her triumphs later in the year seemed to indicate that she would continue to play tennis competitively. (ANTHONY G. CRAINE)

The winning Williams sisters, Venus and Serena

above: AP/Wide World Photos; right: AP/Wide World Photos

Obituaries

In 2000 **THE WORLD LOST** many **LEADERS,** pathfinders, newsmakers, **HEROES, CULTURAL ICONS,** and rogues. The pages below **RECAPTURE THE LIVES** and accomplishments of **THOSE WE REMEMBER BEST.**

Abram, Morris Berthold, American lawyer and civil and human rights advocate (b. June 19, 1918, Fitzgerald, Ga.—d. March 16, 2000, Geneva, Switz.), fought a 14-year battle all the way to the U.S. Supreme Court to overthrow a Georgia electoral rule that gave ballots cast by rural voters, most of whom were white, greater strength than those cast by urban, mostly black, voters. The Supreme Court's landmark 1963 declaration that the rule was unconstitutional struck a blow against segregation and upheld the principle of one voter, one vote. Abram graduated (1938) summa cum laude from the University of Georgia and was selected to be a Rhodes scholar, but Great Britain's entrance into World War II temporarily halted his plans to attend the University of Oxford. He instead enrolled in the University of Chicago Law School. Following graduation (1940) and military service, however, Abram did attend Oxford and earned bachelor's (1948) and master's (1953) degrees. Abram began his struggle against the Georgia electoral rule in 1949 and himself fell victim to it when, running on a desegregation platform, he failed in an attempt to become a Democratic Party nominee in the 1953 congressional election even though he carried a populous urban county. In 1961 Pres. John F. Kennedy appointed Abram the first general counsel to the Peace Corps, and he went on to serve on commissions and panels under four more presidents. He also served as national president of the American Jewish Committee (1963–68), chairman of the United Negro College Fund (1970–79), chairman of the National Conference on Soviet Jewry (1983–88), and chairman of the Conference of Presidents of Major Jewish Organizations (1986–88). Abram was a partner at the law firm of Paul, Weiss, Rifkind, Wharton & Garrison from 1963 until 1983, except for two turbulent years (1968–70) during which he served as president of Brandeis University, Waltham, Mass., and in 1993 he became counsel to that law firm. Also in 1993, with Edgar M. Bronfman, Abram cofounded UN Watch, and he served as its chairman until his death. His autobiography, *The Day Is Short,* was published in 1982.

Adderley, Nathaniel ("Nat"), American cornetist-songwriter (b. Nov. 25, 1931, Tampa, Fla.—d. Jan. 2, 2000, Lakeland, Fla.), became a star in the 1959–75 quintet headed by his older brother, Cannonball Adderley, which was probably the most popular "soul jazz" group of its era. Although he began playing the trumpet in his teens, Nat switched in 1950 to the somewhat smaller cornet, playing it in the U.S. Army band that his brother led. After a year with Lionel Hampton's big band (1954–55), he played in Cannonball's first quintet (1956–57), then toured widely with J.J. Johnson's group and the Woody Herman band. Formed at the height of the popularity of hard bop, the second quintet, the Cannonball Adderley Quintet, in which Nat's warm, lyric improvising contrasted with his brother's flaring alto saxophone solos, was a success from the beginning. Meanwhile, Nat introduced his best-known tune, "Work Song," on one of his own albums in 1960; the song soon became a standard—Herb Alpert made a hit recording of it—and Nat's blues-drenched songs, including "Jive Samba" and "Sermonette," also became hits for Cannonball's group. The brothers collaborated on a musical about the mythical African American railroad man John Henry, originally recorded as "Big Man" (1975) and staged as *Shout Up a Morning* (1986). After Cannonball's death, Nat's retirement was only temporary; from 1976 he led his own groups, which usually included a Cannonball-styled altoist. A favourite of audiences, in part for his good-humoured presentation, and of fellow musicians, Nat played on nearly 100 albums as a leader and sideman. Diabetes led to the amputation of a leg (1997), which effectively ended his career.

Jazz cornetist and songwriter Nat Adderley

Derrick A.Thomas; Dat's Jazz/Corbis

Albert, Carl Bert, American politician (b. May 10, 1908, McAlester, Okla.—d. Feb. 4, 2000, McAlester), served as speaker of the U.S. House of Representatives from 1971 to 1976. He twice stood briefly next in line for the presidency—in 1973 after Spiro Agnew resigned as vice president and again in 1974 after the resignation of Pres. Richard M. Nixon. During his three decades (1946–76) in Congress, Albert played a key role in many behind-the-scenes negotiations and was instrumental in helping pass historic civil rights legislation during the presidency of Lyndon B. Johnson.

Alcock, George Eric Deacon, British schoolteacher and amateur astronomer (b. Aug. 28, 1912, Peterborough, Cambridgeshire, Eng.—d. Dec. 15, 2000, England), was ranked as one of the world's finest amateur astronomers; his 10 major discoveries exceeded the previous record of 8 discoveries made by 18th-century English astronomer Caroline Herschel. Despite the notorious vagaries of English weather, between 1959 and 1991 Alcock was credited with the identification of five novas (exploding stars) and five comets, notably Comet Alcock 1959 IV, Comet Alcock 1959 VI, and 1983 VII IRAS-

Araki-Alcock, which he spotted on May 3, 1983, with 15 × 80-power binoculars through his bedroom window. Alcock, an avid stargazer from childhood, was also noted for his prodigious memory of star patterns and his exceptional ability to detect fine detail. He was made an MBE in 1979; in 1987 asteroid 3174 Alcock was named in his honour. A biography, *Under an English Heaven: The Life of George Alcock,* was published in 1996.

Alla Rakha Khan (Alla Rakha Qureshi), Indian musician (b. April 29, 1919, Phagwal, Jammu province, India—d. Feb. 3, 2000, Mumbai [Bombay], India), was a maestro of the tabla, small drums used in classical Indian music, and was the first tabla player to give solo concerts. Alla Rakha, who was awarded the honorific *ustad* ("master"), supplemented his virtuoso classical performances with occasional work in jazz, on the radio, and as music director for Hindi and Punjabi motion pictures. In the 1940s he began working with sitarist Ravi Shankar, and they later performed together in the West, including joint appearances at the Royal Festival Hall in London in 1958, the 1967 Monterey (Calif.) Pop Festival, and the legendary 1969 Woodstock Music Festival.

John Werner/Moment Records

Tabla virtuoso Alla Rakha Khan

Allen, Stephen Valentine Patrick William (Steve), American entertainer, composer, and author (b. Dec. 26, 1921, New York, N.Y.—d. Oct. 30, 2000, Encino, Calif.), was a prolific, versatile, creative, and influential modern-day renaissance man. Although he could be considered to have made his greatest impact when he created and hosted what became *The Tonight Show*—the mold for television talk shows—he also composed thousands of songs (his best known: "This Could Be the Start of Something Big"), recorded about 40 albums, wrote newspaper columns and more than 50 books, engaged in political activism, and appeared in films (most notably, 1955's *The Benny Goodman Story*), in television variety and quiz shows and dramas, and on the Broadway stage. Allen's parents were vaudeville entertainers, and he often traveled with his mother when she toured after his father's death. He therefore attended a number of schools before they settled in Phoenix, Ariz., to ease his asthma. Allen attended Drake University, Des Moines, Iowa, and Arizona State Teachers College but dropped out and became a radio disc jockey and entertainer. Though drafted into World War II military service in 1943, he was released after a few months because of his asthma and returned to radio, first back in Phoenix and then in Los Angeles. His talent for humorous ad-libbing made him an audience favourite, and in 1950 he was given *The Steve Allen Show* on CBS television in New York City. In 1953 he began hosting a local NBC late-night talk show, *Tonight*, which became a network show the following year and was named *The Tonight Show*. Before Allen left the show in 1957, he instituted such present-day staples of late-night TV shows as the opening monologue, man-in-the-street interviews, and zany stunts. In the meantime, in 1956 Allen had begun a second incarnation of *The Steve Allen Show* on Sunday nights in competition with the popular *Maverick* and *The Ed Sullivan Show*. It ran until 1961. A third incarnation ran from 1962 to 1964 in syndication, and *The Steve Allen Comedy Hour* appeared in the early 1980s. Of all Allen's creations, he was most proud of the Emmy Award-winning series *Meeting of Minds*, which ran on the Public Broadcasting Service from 1977 to 1981. In it, actors portrayed famous persons from various eras engaging in roundtable discussions of philosophy and important issues, with Allen as moderator. In recent years Allen had taken up a crusade against the vulgarity he saw as increasingly permeating popular culture, and at the time of his death he was finishing work on his 54th book, *Vulgarians at the Gate*.

Amarnath, Lala (Nanik Bhardwaj Amarnath), Indian cricketer (b. Sept. 11, 1911, Lahore, India—d. Aug. 5, 2000, New Delhi, India), was a popular and flamboyant all-rounder and the first cricket captain of independent India after partition. In a solid first-class career (1929–64) Amarnath, a right-handed batsman and medium-pace bowler, made 10,323 runs (average 41.62), including 31 centuries, and took 457 wickets, despite his unusual wrong-foot delivery. Between 1933 and 1952 he played in 24 Test matches (15 as captain), scoring 878 runs (average 24.38) and capturing 45 wickets. He achieved status as a national hero overnight on Dec. 17, 1933, when he scored 118 runs against England in his Test debut—his only Test century and the first ever by an Indian batsman. Amarnath's three sons were also successful cricketers, with two, Surinder and Mohinder, representing India at Test level.

Amichai, Yehuda, Israeli poet (b. May 3, 1924, Würzburg, Ger.—d. Sept. 22, 2000, Jerusalem, Israel), wrote in Hebrew and combined the ancient Jewish poetic tradition with elements of Modernism, including colloquial language and references to various aspects of 20th-century life. He was a patriot who was sometimes critical of Israeli militarism, and he championed the individual in a collectivist society. Frequently called the national poet of Israel, he was extraordinarily popular, and his collections of poetry were best-sellers. He also published novels, plays, short stories, children's books, and essays. He was born Yehuda Pfeuffer, but his family changed its name to Amichai (Hebrew for "my people lives") when it immigrated to Jerusalem in 1936. Amichai served in North Africa in the Jewish Brigade of the British army during World War II, and it was at this time that he first read T.S. Eliot and W.H. Auden. Both had profound effects on his poetics, and he later became a friend of Auden. After the war he joined the Zionist underground, and he fought in the Arab-Israeli wars of 1948, 1956, and 1973. In the mid-1950s he graduated from the Hebrew University of Jerusalem, where he studied literature and biblical studies and where he later taught. His first collection of poetry, *Akhshav u-ve-yamim aherim* ("Now and in Other Days"), was published in 1955. Some critics considered his final collection, *Patuah sagur patuah* (1998; *Open Closed Open,* 2000), to be his masterpiece. Amichai's works were translated into many other languages, often through the influence of poet friends such as Ted Hughes who were admirers of his work, and he traveled widely to give readings, particularly in the U.S. He received a number of honours and was often nominated for the Nobel Prize for Literature.

Anhalt, Edward, American screenwriter and motion picture producer (b. March 28, 1914, New York, N.Y.—d. Sept. 3, 2000, Los Angeles, Calif.), won Academy Awards for best screenplay for *Panic in the Streets* (1950; co-written with his wife, Edna Anhalt) and *Becket* (1964); he was especially skilled at adapting stage plays and works of literature for the movies and, in addition to *Becket,* counted *The Member of the Wedding* (1952), *Luther* (1973), *The Man in the Glass Booth* (1975), and *The Holcroft Covenant* (1985) among those credits.

Antley, Chris, American jockey (b. Jan. 6, 1966, Fort Lauderdale, Fla.—found dead Dec. 2, 2000, Pasadena, Calif.), won a total of 3,480 races in his career, including the Kentucky Derby in 1991 and 1999. Antley quickly established himself as one of the world's leading jockeys after making his professional debut in 1985; two years later, he became the first jockey ever to win nine races in a single day. In 1999 he rode Charismatic to victory in the Preakness Stakes as well as in the Kentucky Derby but fell short of capturing the

left: Bettmann/Corbis; right: Ariel Jerozolimski/AFP Worldwide

Triple Crown when Charismatic pulled up lame and finished third in the Belmont Stakes. Antley was found dead in his home after suffering what authorities described as a severe head trauma probably caused by falling down while under the influence of drugs.

Archer, Violet Balestreri, Canadian composer (b. April 24, 1913, Montreal, Que.—d. Feb. 21, 2000, Ottawa, Ont.), was an accomplished musician whose large body of work encompassed a variety of genres. She was also a highly regarded musical educator. After studying composition at McGill University, Montreal, and Yale University, Archer began a long teaching career, which included stints at North Texas State College from 1950 to 1953 and the University of Oklahoma from 1953 to 1961. She returned to Canada in 1962, where she taught theory and composition at the University of Alberta until her retirement from teaching in 1978. Although Archer's compositions never attained widespread popularity, they were critically acclaimed, and by the time of her death, interest in her work was growing. Her compositions included, most notably, the virtuosic *Piano Concerto No. 1* (1956), the comic opera *Sganarelle* (1973), and *Evocations* (1987), a piano and orchestral work inspired by Inuit and Tsimshian melodies. Archer was appointed a Member of the Order of Canada in 1983.

Arguedas Mendieta, Antonio, Bolivian political leader (b. 1929?, Bolivia—d. Feb. 22, 2000, La Paz, Bol.), rose to become Bolivia's minister of the interior during the 1964–69 military dictatorship of Gen. René Barrientos; recruited by the U.S. Central Intelligence Agency in 1965, he aided efforts to defeat a guerrilla group in eastern Bolivia led by Che Guevara. Following the capture and execution of Guevara in 1967, Arguedas became disenchanted with the Barrientos regime and secretly arranged for copies of Guevara's diaries to be smuggled to Cuba; the subsequent publication of the diaries, which detailed the relentless pursuit of the guerrilla leader by Bolivian special forces, was perceived as a major embarrassment for Barrientos. Fearful of being exposed, Arguedas fled to Chile and eventually to Cuba, where he spent most of the 1970s. He later returned to Bolivia, and by the late 1990s he had reportedly become a terrorist. He died when a bomb he was carrying exploded.

Arkan (Zeljko Raznatovic), Serbian paramilitary leader (b. April 17, 1952, Brezice, Slovenia—d. Jan. 15, 2000, Belgrade, Yugos.), was head of the Serbian Volunteer Guard, a paramilitary force known as the Tigers that was accused of committing atrocities during the wars in Croatia and Bosnia and Herzegovina in the first half of the 1990s. While still a teenager, he allegedly became a hit man for the Yugoslav secret police. During the 1970s and early 1980s, he was involved in criminal activities across Western Europe, including bank and jewelry theft. Despite a number of convictions, he managed to escape from jails in Belgium, The Netherlands, and Germany. By 1990 he had begun organizing the Tigers. Among the force's alleged crimes were the massacre of more than 250 Croat civilians during a siege of Vukovar in eastern Croatia in 1991 and the slaughter of some 1,000 Muslims in the eastern Bosnian towns of Bijeljina and Zvornik the following year. Celebrated as a hero among Serbs, Arkan was elected to the Serbian parliament in 1992 and launched the ultranationalist Serbian Unity Party. In 1997 the UN's International War Crimes Tribunal indicted him for crimes against humanity. He was shot dead by masked gunmen in the lobby of the Intercontinental Hotel in Belgrade.

Arkan, the Tiger

2287/Liaison Agency

Arron, Henck (Alphonsus Eugène), Surinamese politician (b. April 25, 1936, Paramaribo, Dutch Guiana [now Suriname]—d. Dec. 4, 2000, Alphen aan den Rijn, Neth.), served as prime minister (1973–80) of Suriname and was instrumental in leading the nation to independence from The Netherlands. Arron worked as a banker before entering politics in 1963. He was elected to the Staten (Surinamese legislature) that year as a member of the Suriname National Party (NPS), and he became the party's leader in 1970. The NPS was composed mainly of Creoles (Surinamese of African descent), and it favoured independence from The Netherlands. Under Arron's guidance, the NPS won the elections of 1973, and he became prime minister. He secured independence for Suriname in 1975 after two years of negotiations with The Netherlands. Arron was reelected in 1977, but his efforts to stem Suriname's calamitous economic decline following independence were unsuccessful; a high rate of unemployment was a major cause of his downfall. A coup was staged by discontented junior army officers in February 1980. Arron was arrested and was released in 1981, after which he returned for a time to his banking activities. Elections in 1987 ousted the military regime, and Arron became vice president, but the government was again deposed by the military in 1990. Declining health forced Arron to leave politics shortly thereafter. He died of a heart attack while visiting The Netherlands.

Assad, Hafez al-, Syrian head of state (b. Oct. 6, 1930, Qardaha, Syria—d. June 10, 2000, Damascus, Syria), as president of Syria from 1971 until his death, brought stability to the country and established it as a powerful presence in the Middle East. In 1946 Assad joined the Syrian wing of the Ba'th Party as a student activist. He graduated from the Syrian Military Academy at Hims in 1955 and became an air force pilot. Stationed in Egypt from 1959 to 1961, he and other military officers formed a secret committee and plotted to seize power in Damascus. After the Ba'thists took control of the Syrian government in 1963, Assad became commander of the air force. In 1966, having taken part in a coup that overthrew the civilian leadership of the party and sent its founders into exile, he became minister of defense. After Syria lost the Golan Heights to Israel in the Six-Day War (June 1967), Assad engaged in a protracted power struggle with Salah al-Jadid—chief of staff of the armed forces, Assad's political mentor, and effective leader of Syria. In November 1970 Assad assumed power, arresting Jadid and other members of the government. He became prime minister and in 1971 was elected president. With Soviet aid, Assad set about building up the Syrian military. Political dissenters were eliminated by arrest, torture, and execution. A new alliance with Egypt culminated in a surprise attack on Israel in October 1973, but Egypt's unexpected cessation of hostilities exposed Syria to military defeat. In 1976, with Lebanon racked by a civil war, Assad dispatched several divisions to that country and secured their permanent presence there as part of a peacekeeping force sponsored by the Arab League. After Israel's invasion and occupation of southern Lebanon in 1982–85, Assad was able to reassert control of the country, eventually compelling Lebanese Christians to accept constitutional changes granting Muslims equal representation in the government. In the 1980s he supported Iran in its war against Iraq, and he readily joined the U.S.-led alliance against Iraq in the Persian Gulf War of 1990–91. This cooperation resulted in more cordial relations with Western governments, which previously had condemned his alleged sponsorship of radical Palestinian and Muslim terrorist groups based in Lebanon and Syria. Assad sought to establish peaceful relations with Israel in the mid-1990s, but his repeated call for the return of the Golan Heights stalled the talks. In 1998 he cultivated closer ties with Iraq in light of Israel's growing strategic partnership with Turkey. Assad's death from heart failure set off days of national mourning in Syria.

Auriol, Jacqueline-Marie-Thérèse-Suzanne, French pilot (b. Nov. 5, 1917, Challans, France—d. Feb. 12, 2000, Paris, France), overcame a near-fatal 1949 crash, numerous operations to repair her shattered face, and the reservations of her powerful father-in-law, French Pres. Vincent Auriol, to become one of France's most successful test pilots in the 1950s. Between 1951 and her retirement in 1963, she competed with American Jacqueline Cochran for the title of fastest woman in the world, setting five world records and finishing her career second to

Cochran with a top speed of 2,029 km/h (1,261 mph). Auriol was made an officer of the Legion of Honour and published her autobiography, *Vivre et voler,* in 1968.

Austin, Henry Wilfred ("Bunny"), British tennis player (b. Aug. 26, 1906, London, Eng.—d. Aug. 26, 2000, Coulsdon, Surrey, Eng.), was one of the world's highest-ranked players in the 1930s, twice a finalist at the All-England (Wimbledon) Championships (1932 and 1938), and a pivotal member of the British team that won four consecutive Davis Cups (1933–36), but he was best known as the first player to break with tradition (in 1932) and appear on court in shorts instead of the conventional white flannel trousers.

Autant-Lara, Claude (Claude Autant), French motion picture director (b. Aug. 5, 1903, Luzarches, France—d. Feb. 5, 2000, Antibes, France), was one of the world's leading directors in the post-World War II era, winning international acclaim with his classic film *Le Diable au corps* (1947). Educated in London and Paris, he first found work in the movie industry as a set decorator for Marcel L'Herbier's *Le Carnaval des vérités* (1919). Autant-Lara's first short film, *Faits divers* (1923), was made while he was an assistant director to René Clair. Later he worked in Hollywood directing French versions of American movies. It was not until 1933, however, that he directed his first feature, *Ciboulette.* Two films that Autant-Lara completed in 1942—*Le Mariage de chiffon* and *Lettres d'amour*—prefigured his work in *Le Diable au corps.* Adapted from a novel by Raymond Radiguet, *Le Diable au corps* was the story of an adolescent boy's affair with a married woman whose husband was away at war. Both its subject matter and its antiwar, antiestablishment sentiments made it Autant-Lara's most popular—and most controversial—film. In the 1950s Autant-Lara's preference for literary adaptations and his emphasis on psychological realism, tight scripting, and carefully delivered dialogue fell out of fashion. He nonetheless continued to make motion pictures, directing his last film, *Gloria,* in 1977. In the late 1980s he again stirred controversy, this time in the world of politics. He became a member of the far-right National Front and was elected to the European Parliament in 1989. That same year, after a magazine quoted several of his anti-Semitic remarks, he resigned his seat.

Baarova, Lida, Czech actress (b. 1914, Prague, Austro-Hungarian Empire [now Czech Rep.]—d. Oct. 27, 2000, Salzburg, Austria), appeared in a number of successful German films in the 1930s, including *Barcarole* (1935) and *Die Stunde der Versuchung* (1936), but her career was damaged by her affair with Nazi minister of propaganda Joseph Goebbels. The affair ended when Adolf Hitler refused to give Goebbels permission to divorce his wife and marry Baarova. After the war she was suspected of being a Nazi spy and spent two years in jail. She later returned to acting and appeared in Spanish and Italian films, including Federico Fellini's *I vitelloni* (1953).

Baden Powell (Roberto Baden Powell Aquino), Brazilian guitarist and composer (b. Aug. 6, 1937, Varre-e-Sai, Braz.—d. Sept. 26, 2000, Rio de Janeiro, Braz.), helped popularize the bossa nova ("new trend"), a romantic, sensual style of the 1950s and '60s that was created from a fusion of the samba, a Brazilian dance music, and cool jazz. He came from a musical family, and his father, who was a troop leader, named his son for Robert S.S. Baden-Powell, the British founder of the Boy Scouts. The boy was a child prodigy and was playing on Rádio Nacìonal by the age of eight. Beginning in his early teens Baden Powell played professionally. In the mid-1950s he met Antônio Carlos Jobim, one of the best known of the bossa nova composers; he encouraged Baden Powell to devote himself to the new music. Perhaps Baden Powell's most distinctive contribution to the bossa nova style was the incorporation of African influences, derived from his study of African rituals in Brazil. In 1964 he moved to Europe, first to Paris and later to West Germany, and he subsequently recorded with such jazz musicians as Stan Getz, Herbie Mann, and Stéphane Grappelli. Baden Powell returned to Brazil in 1988 and later underwent a religious conversion that led him to stop performing certain of his compositions. "Deve Ser Amor" and "Samba Triste" were his first major hits. More than 50 of his compositions were written in collaboration with the poet Vinícius de Moraes. These included "Samba de Benção," used on the sound track of Claude Lelouch's 1966 film *Un Homme et une femme* (*A Man and a Woman*), "Berimbau," "Samba em Preludio," and "Bom Dia, Amigo."

Bandaranaike, Sirimavo Ratwatte Dias, Sri Lankan political leader (b. April 17, 1916, Ratnapura, Ceylon [now Sri Lanka]—d. Oct. 10, 2000, Gampaha, Sri Lanka), became in 1960 the first woman in the world to serve as a prime minister. She was a member of a family dynasty that dominated Sri Lankan politics in the last half of the 20th century. Born Sirimavo Ratwatte, she married S.W.R.D. Bandaranaike, an official in the United National Party (UNP), in 1940. Her husband formed the nationalist Sri Lanka Freedom Party (SLFP) in 1951 and became prime minister in 1956. Three years later he was assassinated, and in the following year his widow replaced him, serving as prime minister from 1960 to 1965. She became a leader in the movement of nonaligned nations in the 1960s. During a second term, from 1970 to 1977, Bandaranaike moved to the left and nationalized a number of industries and institutions. She used the military to put down a Marxist uprising, transformed the country (renamed Sri Lanka in 1972) into a republic with an executive presidency, favoured Buddhism, and made Sinhalese the official language. These last acts further angered the Tamil-speaking Hindu minority and helped lead to a bloody civil war beginning in the early 1980s. In 1980 she was expelled from Parliament and banned from holding office for seven years, although her rights were restored in 1986. She lost a bid for the presidency in 1988, but her younger daughter, Chandrika Kumaratunga, who succeeded her as head of the SLFP, won the office in 1994 and appointed her mother prime minister, by this time a largely ceremonial post. Bandaranaike's son, Anura, defected to the opposition UNP when his sister took over the SLFP. Bandaranaike, suffering from ill health, resigned her post in August 2000 and died shortly after voting in parliamentary elections.

Barbosa Lima Sobrinho, Alexandre José, Brazilian journalist and politician (b. Jan. 22, 1897, Recife, Braz.—d. July 16, 2000, Rio de Janeiro, Braz.), was a longtime columnist for the daily newspaper *Jornal do Brasil* and head of the Brazilian Press Association for more than 25 years. After graduating from law school in 1917, Barbosa Lima went to work for *Jornal do Brasil.* He became the paper's editor in chief in 1926, the same year he assumed the leadership of the Brazilian Press Association. A socialist, Barbosa Lima was a leading critic of Brazil's military dictatorships and an outspoken advocate of measures to improve the social conditions of the country's workers. He also used his position to fight censorship and defend press freedom. Barbosa Lima made a number of forays into politics, serving as governor of the state of Pernambuco in the late 1940s and later serving three terms in Congress. In 1973 he ran unsuccessfully for vice president on a ticket headed by opposition leader Ulysses Guimarães. Barbosa Lima's most significant political contribution came in 1992, however, when he helped organize a petition calling for the impeachment of Pres. Fernando Collor, who resigned amid corruption charges after impeachment proceedings began. By the end of his long career, Barbosa Lima had published more than 50 books and some 5,000 newspaper articles, the last of which appeared in *Jornal do Brasil* on the day he died. Pres. Fernando Henrique Cardoso declared three days of national mourning following Barbosa Lima's death.

Barcelona, countess of (Doña María de las Mercedes Cristina Gennara Isabella Luisa Carolina Victoria de Borbón y Orléans), Spanish royal (b. Dec. 23, 1910, Madrid, Spain—d. Jan. 2, 2000, Lanzarote, Canary Islands), was the mother of King Juan Carlos I and the wife of Don Juan de Borbón, who was compelled by strongman Gen. Francisco Franco to renounce his claim to the Spanish throne in favour of his son. Doña María, much admired for her charm and diplomacy, was credited with working behind the scenes to reconcile her husband and son.

top: AP/Wide World Photos; bottom: AP/Wide World Photos

Bartali, Gino, Italian cyclist (b. July 18, 1914, Ponte a Ema, near Florence, Italy—d. May 5, 2000, Ponte a Ema), became a national hero and helped unite Italy during a period of political upheaval when he won the 1948 Tour de France 10 years after he had first won cycling's premier event; despite having his 20-year career (1935–54) interrupted by World War II, the "Iron Man of Tuscany" won more than 180 other races, including the Giro d'Italia (three times), the Milan–San Remo race (four times), the Tour of Switzerland (twice), the Tour of Lombardy (three times), and the Italian national championships (four times).

Bartel, Paul, American director, screenwriter, and actor (b. Aug. 6, 1938, Brooklyn, N.Y.—d. May 13, 2000, New York, N.Y.), was perhaps best remembered for creating and starring in the black comedy *Eating Raoul* (1982), a cult classic that featured Paul and Mary Bland, a married couple who murder swingers by beating them over the head with a frying pan before robbing them. Bartel's quirky humour was reflected in such car-crash films as *Death Race 2000* (1975) and *Cannonball* (1976), the erotic shorts *The Secret Cinema* (1966) and *Naughty Nurse* (1969), and *Private Parts* (1972), his first feature film. He stole the show portraying a director bent on sensationalizing productions ("spice up the crucifixion scene") in Joe Dante's *Hollywood Boulevard* (1976) and had bit parts in such films as *The Usual Suspects* (1995), *Basquiat* (1996), and *Billy's Hollywood Screen Kiss* (1998). His last role was as Osric in an adaptation of *Hamlet* (2000).

Baskin, Leonard, American sculptor and graphic artist (b. Aug. 15, 1922, New Brunswick, N.J.—d. June 3, 2000, Northampton, Mass.), was a master sculptor, wood-carver, and etcher who achieved prominence with his bleak but impressive portrayals of the human figure. After studying in the U.S. and Europe, Baskin held his first one-man show in New York City in 1939. He taught at Smith College, Northampton, Mass., from 1953 to 1974 and at Hampshire College, Amherst, Mass., from 1984 to 1994. Baskin designed monumental figures in bronze, limestone, wood, and relief. He often portrayed artists (*Blake,* 1955; *Barlach Dead,* 1959), scenes of death (*Hanged Man,* 1956), and biblical subjects (*Prodigal Son,* 1976; *Ruth and Naomi,* 1978). Baskin imbued his representations of the human figure with qualities of spiritual death, decay, and vulnerability, which he felt characterized the condition of humankind in the 20th century. In his woodcuts he developed a distinctively wiry and nervous linearity; *Man of Peace* (1952) and *Everyman* were among his best-known woodcuts. Baskin used many of his woodcuts and etchings to illustrate books printed by Gehenna Press, which he owned. Several of his sculptures were also used in public memorials, including the Holocaust Memorial, Ann Arbor, Mich., dedicated in 1994, and the Franklin Delano Roosevelt Memorial, Washington, D.C., dedicated in 1997. Among his numerous honours, Baskin was presented the Gold Medal of the National Academy of Arts and Letters in 1969.

Bassani, Giorgio, Italian writer and editor (b. March 4, 1916, Bologna, Italy—d. April 13, 2000, Rome, Italy), skillfully presented the plight of Jews of the Ferrara community in Fascist-era Italy in his award-winning 1962 novel *Il giardino dei Finzi-Contini* (*The Garden of the Finzi-Continis,* 1965). Wildly popular, the book was translated into several languages and made into a movie that won the 1971 Academy Award for best foreign film. *Il giardino dei Finzi-Contini* was not, however, Bassani's only claim to fame. He won Italy's Strega Prize in 1956 for his short-story collection *Cinque storie ferraresi* (*Five Stories of Ferrara,* 1971). While working as an editor at the Feltrinelli publishing company, he secured the manuscript for Giuseppe Tomasi di Lampedusa's celebrated *Il gattopardo* (1958; *The Leopard,* 1960), a novel that other publishers had rejected because they thought the story was too old-fashioned. Besides his notable contributions to literature, Bassani also led an active public life. In 1955 he worked together with other Italian intellectuals to found Italia Nostra, an environmental protection and historic preservation society. From 1957 to 1967 he acted as vice president of RAI, the Italian national broadcasting network.

Bell, Ken, Canadian photographer (b. July 30, 1914, Toronto, Ont.—d. June 26, 2000, Gibsons, B.C.), was one of Canada's most accomplished photographers. Bell documented Canada's participation in World War II while serving in the Canadian Army Film and Photo Unit; his war pictures were housed permanently at the National Archives of Canada in Ottawa. After the war, Bell freelanced for numerous Canadian publications, including the news magazine *Maclean's.* He also served as the official photographer of the National Ballet of Canada. Bell published many books, including *The Way We Were* (1988) and, with historian Desmond Morton, *The Royal Canadian Military Institute—100 Years, 1890–1990* (1990). Bell twice won the Professional Photographers of Canada's Photographer of the Year Award, in 1965 and 1966, and received the Canadian Association of Photographers and Illustrators Lifetime Achievement Award in 1986.

Beneke, Tex (Gordon Beneke), American musician and band leader (b. Feb. 12, 1914, Fort Worth, Texas—d. May 30, 2000, Costa Mesa, Calif.), played tenor saxophone solos in a Coleman Hawkins-inspired manner, sang hit songs such as "I Got a Gal in Kalamazoo" and "Chattanooga Choo Choo," and appeared in the films *Sun Valley Serenade* (1941) and *Orchestra Wives* (1942) with the most popular of all swing bands, the Glenn Miller Orchestra during 1938–42; after Miller's death, Beneke briefly led the Miller ghost band, before fronting from 1950 his own big band, which played in a Miller-derived style.

Benson, (Dorothy) Mary, South African writer and antiapartheid activist (b. Dec. 8, 1919, Pretoria, S.Af.—d. June 20, 2000, London, Eng.), rejected her privileged upbringing as a white in South Africa to campaign against her country's racial policies. She was a cofounder and secretary (1952–56) of the London-based antiapartheid Africa Bureau and secretary (1957) of the defense fund set up for Nelson Mandela and others. Benson, who lived in voluntary exile in London from the mid-1960s, was also the author of a history of the African National Congress, the authorized biography *Nelson Mandela* (1986), and a candid auto-

Master sculptor and graphic artist Leonard Baskin

AP/Wide World Photos

biography, *A Far Cry: The Making of a South African* (1989).

Bertolucci, Attilio, Italian poet, critic, and translator (b. Nov. 18, 1911, San Lazzaro di Parma, Italy—d. June 14, 2000, Rome, Italy), created lyrical verse that was often based on the details of his family's life and especially his childhood. A sense of anxiety, which was present in the writer's own personality, was a common element in his poetry. Born to farmers, he published his first volume of poems—*Sirio* (1929)—when he was not yet 18 years old. He studied law at the University of Parma (1931–35) but did not graduate and then took art history classes at the University of Bologna (1935–38). To support himself and his family, he taught, reviewed films and other arts for newspapers, worked in radio and television and in publishing, and contributed to a number of magazines. In 1951 there appeared *La capanna indiana* (1951), a collection dealing with the search for privacy in a difficult world; it won the Viareggio Prize. *La camera da letto,* first published in 1984, won Bertolucci a second Viareggio Prize when it was released in an expanded version in 1988. An autobiographical account of his family in verse, it became his best-known work, and the poet read it aloud on a seven-hour television program. Other major volumes of poetry included *Fuochi in novembre* (1934) and *Viaggio d'inverno* (1971). Translations by Charles Tomlinson published in *Selected Poems* in 1993 helped introduce Bertolucci to English readers. As a translator himself, he was partial to the work of such French writers as Charles Baudelaire and Marcel Proust and to a number of British and American writers, especially Thomas Hardy. Both of Bertolucci's sons, Bernardo and Giuseppe, became successful filmmakers.

Blee, David Henry, American intelligence officer (b. Nov. 20, 1916, San Francisco, Calif.—d. Aug. 4, 2000, Bethesda, Md.), was a master spy (1947–85) in the CIA (and its wartime forerunner, the Office of Strategic Services) and was noted for his deft decision making. While serving as CIA station chief in India, Blee took the initiative in 1965 to spirit away Svetlana Stalin, the Soviet dictator's daughter, after she asked for asylum at the American Embassy; his action came while Washington was considering her request. He then became the CIA chief of the Near East Division, which undertook espionage in the Middle East. Blee played a crucial role in reviving the counterintelligence activities of the agency's Soviet Division after he was placed in charge of the unit in 1971; he diplomatically countered the measures of the erratic chief of counterintelligence, James Jesus Angleton—who believed that virtually all Soviet defectors were spies—and began recruiting Soviet operatives. In 1976 Blee became deputy director of operations. He retired from the CIA in 1985, just before the defection to the Soviet Union of CIA agent Edward Lee Howard and the later revelations that double agent Aldrich Ames had exposed at least 10 American operatives in the U.S.S.R., which compromised much of what Blee had accomplished.

Bloch, Konrad Emil, German-born American biochemist (b. Jan. 21, 1912, Neisse, Ger. [now Nysa, Pol.]—d. Oct. 15, 2000, Burlington, Mass.), conducted research to determine how the body creates cholesterol, work that earned him a share, together with Feodor Lynen, of the 1964 Nobel Prize for Physiology or Medicine. Bloch's studies helped to reveal that cholesterol, a substance that occurs naturally in cells, results from the biosynthesis of acetic acid. The discovery led to a heightened awareness of cholesterol's role in some circulatory diseases and to the development of drugs that lowered cholesterol in the blood. Bloch earned a degree (1934) in chemical engineering from the Technische Hochschule, Munich, Ger. Nazi oppression kept Bloch, a Jew, from continuing his studies, so he first went to Switzerland and, in 1936, to the U.S., where he earned a doctorate in biochemistry at Columbia University, New York City. His cholesterol studies began at Columbia, and in 1942, along with David Rittenberg, he noted that a series of 30 or more chemical reactions took place in transforming acetic acid into cholesterol. He moved to the University of Chicago, where he served as a professor (1946–54) before being named the Higgins Professor of Biochemistry at Harvard University; he held the post until his retirement in 1982. Bloch also served as a professor in the School of Public Health at Harvard (1979–84) and was chairman of the biochemistry department (1968–72). He was also the author of *Blondes in Venetian Paintings, the Nine-Banded Armadillo, and Other Essays in Biochemistry* (1994). Bloch was awarded the National Medal of Science in 1988.

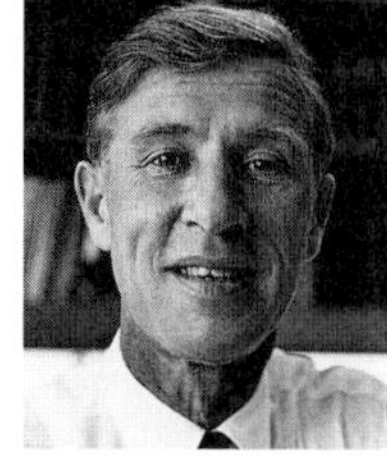

Bettmann/Corbis

Boon, Alan Wheatley, British book editor (b. Sept. 28, 1913, London, Eng.—d. July 29, 2000, Leicester, Eng.), built Mills & Boon, a small family publishing house cofounded by his father in 1909, into a byword for the genre of formulaic romantic novels that made the company's fortune. While relinquishing the financial end of the business to his brother, Boon devised a strict editorial formula for the escapist romantic fiction that Mills & Boon published, mainly in softcover format. He personally guided a stable of some 150 freelance women writers and continued to work after the firm was sold in 1971 to the Canadian publisher Harlequin Books. By 2000 tens of millions of Mills & Boon paperback novels were being sold in 26 languages in at least 100 markets.

Borge, Victor (Børge Rosenbaum), Danish-born American pianist and comedian (b. Jan. 3, 1909, Copenhagen, Den.—d. Dec. 23, 2000, Greenwich, Conn.), was known worldwide for his irrepressible humour, which combined deadpan delivery, clever wordplay, satire, irreverence, and physical comedy and which, when coupled with his extraordinary musicianship, sustained him through a more than 70-year performing career. His trademark bits—including his "phonetic punctuation," in which he read a story but used a sound for each punctuation mark, and his "inflated language," in which each number or homonym of a number became the next-higher number (*wonderful* became *twoderful,* etc.)—never lost their power to entertain. Borge's mother began teaching him piano when he was three, and it was soon apparent that he was a prodigy. While in his teens, he studied on scholarship at the Copenhagen Music Conservatory, and he later studied in Vienna and Berlin. On the way to becoming a concert pianist, however, Borge discovered his flair for comedy and his ability to respect the music while skewering the pomposity often present in the world of musicians. He also made Adolf Hitler a target of his satire, despite the danger that he, being Jewish, faced. Luckily, Borge was performing in Stockholm when the Nazis invaded Den-

AP/Wide World Photos

Pianist and comedian Victor Borge

mark in 1940, and he soon was able to flee to the U.S. He began performing on radio in 1941 and by 1945 had his own show; his Carnegie Hall debut came that same year. Appearances in nightclubs, on other concert stages, and on television followed, as did his one-man show, *Comedy in Music*, which ran for 849 performances in 1953–56 and set a Broadway record for a solo show. Borge continued performing throughout the rest of his life. In addition, in 1963 he helped create the Thanks to Scandinavia Foundation, which funded scholarships for Scandinavian students in gratitude for the aid many Scandinavians gave to Jews during the Holocaust. He wrote, with Robert Sherman, the books *My Favorite Intermissions* (1971) and *Victor Borge's My Favorite Comedies in Music* (1980). Borge was knighted by five European countries and in 1999 was a recipient of a Kennedy Center Honor.

Bourguiba, Habib Ben Ali, Tunisian politician (b. Aug. 3, 1903?, Al-Munastir, Tun.—d. April 6, 2000, Al-Munastir), led Tunisia in its effort to win independence from France and afterward served as his country's first president. Trained as a lawyer, Bourguiba helped found a nationalist political party, the Neo-Destour, in the 1930s that was dedicated to ending French colonial rule and securing Tunisian independence. Although Bourguiba was imprisoned by French authorities in 1934–36, 1938–42, and 1952–55, attempts by the French to suppress the Neo-Destour were unsuccessful. After France granted full independence to Tunisia on March 20, 1956, Bourguiba was hailed as a national hero and soon ascended to power. He was elected president on July 25, 1957. During his 30 years in office, he modernized Tunisia and introduced numerous secular reforms, including granting women the right to vote and abolishing the practice of polygamy. His reforms and largely pro-Western views angered other Arab and Muslim countries. In the early 1970s, Bourguiba's call for a "just and lasting peace" with Israel further increased his regional unpopularity, but he eventually countered his critics by giving refuge to the Palestine Liberation Organization in 1982. Although he had been declared president for life in 1975, he was ousted in a bloodless coup in November 1987 after he allegedly showed signs of senility. He spent his remaining years confined to his palace in Al-Munastir.

Bowers, Edgar, American poet (b. March 2, 1924, Rome, Ga.—d. Feb. 4, 2000, San Francisco, Calif.), was a masterful poet who addressed in formalist verse such universal themes as beauty and faith. After serving in the U.S. Army's Counter Intelligence Corps during World War II, he earned a Ph.D. in English at Stanford University, where he studied under the critic and poet Yvor Winters. Bowers's early work, including *The Form of Loss* (1956), his first book of poetry, was strongly influenced by Winters, who stressed adherence to traditional poetic forms and the use of rhyme. From 1958 to 1991 Bowers taught English at several American universities, spending most of his career at the University of California, Santa Barbara. His collection *For Louis Pasteur* (1989) won the Bollingen Prize for Poetry. Bowers's *Collected Poems* appeared in 1997.

Bradbury, Sir Malcolm Stanley, British author, critic, and university professor (b. Sept. 7, 1932, Sheffield, Eng.—d. Nov. 27, 2000, Norwich, Eng.), wrote novels, literary criticism, biographies, short stories, and plays and served for more than 35 years on the faculties of three British universities. Considered one of the finest contemporary satirists, he often focused on academia in such novels as *Eating People Is Wrong* (1959), *Stepping Westward* (1965), and *The History Man* (1975). In the latter, regarded by many as his best novel, he satirized the academic environment of the 1960s in the person of a left-wing college lecturer for whom teaching was primarily a means of manipulating the minds of his students. Bradbury's later novels included *Rates of Exchange* (1983), *Doctor Criminale* (1992), and *To the Hermitage* (2000). Among his other works were the collection of short stories *Who Do You Think You Are?* (1976), *The Social Context of Modern English Literature* (1971), *Modernism* (1976; coedited with James McFarlane), *The Modern American Novel* (1983), and *The Modern British Novel* (1993). He also wrote many studies of literary figures and adapted for television works by such authors as Alison Lurie and Kingsley Amis. Bradbury gained his undergraduate degree in English from University College, Leicester (now University of Leicester), in 1953 and earned a doctorate in American Studies at the University of Manchester in 1962. He began his teaching career at the University of Hull in 1959, and he taught English at the University of Birmingham from 1962 to 1965. From 1965 until his retirement in 1995, he served as professor of American Studies at the University of East Anglia; there, in 1970, he developed Britain's first master's-level program in creative writing. Among his students were Ian McEwan and Kazuo Ishiguro, both of whom later won Britain's Booker Prize.

Brandys, Kazimierz, Polish novelist and essayist (b. Oct. 27, 1916, Lodz, Pol., Russian Empire—d. March 11, 2000, Paris, France), spent his career as a writer documenting life in Poland prior to, during, and following World War II. Shortly before the war, Brandys earned a law degree (1939) from the University of Warsaw, and in 1945 he joined the editorial board of the Marxist weekly *Kúznica* ("The Forge"). Although a Jew, Brandys escaped Nazi detection by securing falsified documents. He lived in the Polish side of Warsaw and was a survivor of the 1944 Warsaw uprising. His first novel, *Drewniany koń* (1946; "The Wooden Horse"), recounted the hardship faced by the Polish intelligentsia under the Nazis. After the war he joined the Communist Party, and his works reflected this ideology. His early novels were considered prime examples of the Socialist Realism genre, and one of them, *Miasto niepokonane* (1946; "The Invincible City") won the government's highest literary award; a poignant narrative about wartime Warsaw, it was translated into several languages. His most celebrated work in this genre was probably *Obywatele* (1954; "Citizens"), which dealt with high-school vigilantes. After becoming disaffected with the Communists, Brandys penned a number of revisionist works, notably *Matka Królów* (1957; *Sons and Comrades*, 1961), before leaving the party in 1966. His later works, like the earlier ones, explored the impact that history had on the individual and centred on themes of love, death, the uncertainties of life, solitude, and God. During the 1970s Brandys began to experiment. His *Wariacje pocztowe* (1972; "Postal Variations") was a series of letters—spanning the 18th to the 20th century—penned by successive generations of a family. The novel, a literary masterpiece, was highly stylized and written in distinctive idioms. Brandys was a founding member during the 1970s of the unerground journal *Zapis* ("The Record"), which featured his essays on life in Warsaw. These were later compiled and formed the basis for Brandys's most defining multivolume work, *Miesiące* ("Months"), a series of diaries. Volume one, translated into English as *A Warsaw Diary, 1978–1981* (1983), was followed by an abridged version of volume three: *Paris, New York: 1982– 1984* (1988). Volume four covered the years 1985 to 1987.

Brooks, Gwendolyn Elizabeth, American writer (b. June 7, 1917, Topeka, Kan.—d. Dec. 3, 2000, Chicago, Ill.), was a Pulitzer Prize-winning poet and author who spoke of and to the everyday struggles and triumphs of African Americans during a distinguished literary career that spanned more than half a century. Her dedication to teaching was evidenced by a lifetime spent visiting young people in schools, holding public readings, and supporting community arts initiatives. Brooks, who grew up on Chicago's South Side, revealed a precocious talent for writing poetry; at age 11 she began submitting her work to local newspapers. During her teens she became a regular contributor to the *Chicago Defender,* at that time the most influential black newspaper in the U.S. After graduating (1936) from Woodrow Wilson Junior College (now Kennedy-King College) in Chicago, Brooks did clerical work until shortly after her marriage in 1939 to Henry Blakely, a fellow writer and poet. In 1945 Harper & Bros. (later Harper & Row and now HarperCollins) published her first volume of poetry, *A Street in Bronzeville,* which chronicled black life on the South Side. In 1946 she was the recipient of a Guggenheim fellowship and a $1,000 award from the American Academy of Arts and Letters, recognitions that further established her reputation. When her second collection, *Annie Allen* (1949), was awarded the Pulitzer Prize, Brooks became the first African American poet to receive this honour. In this work, Brooks told the story of a black girl coming of age in Chicago and introduced her own innovation in poetic form, the sonnet-ballad. The novel that followed, *Maud Martha* (1953), had a similar storyline, but it did not garner the praise that her poetry continued to elicit. Poems that appeared in *The Bean Eaters* (1960) and *Selected Poems* (1963)

AP/Wide World Photos

Bettmann/Corbis

Pulitzer Prize-winning poet Gwendolyn Brooks

showed that Brooks's social consciousness had broadened beyond the South Side to include the injustices experienced by blacks everywhere in the U.S. Brooks began to lose her mainstream appeal as her poetic participation in the civil rights movement of the 1960s prompted her to leave her longtime publisher Harper & Row and move to the smaller, black-owned Broadside Press. Brooks was able, however, to achieve her goal of making her work more affordable and, by extension, more accessible. With Broadside and, later, with Third World Press, she published more than two dozen volumes of poetry and prose, including the autobiographical works *Report from Part One* (1972) and *Report from Part Two* (1996). Brooks succeeded Carl Sandburg as poet laureate of Illinois in 1968 and received lifetime achievement awards from the National Endowment for the Arts (1989) and the National Book Foundation (1994). During her career, she was the recipient of more than 50 honorary degrees, but renown was never her aim. She simply wanted "to be clean of heart, clear of mind, and claiming of what is right and just."

Brower, David Ross, American environmentalist (b. July 1, 1912, Berkeley, Calif.—d. Nov. 5, 2000, Berkeley), spent nearly 70 years in his effort to protect wilderness areas in the United States. He was involved with such groups as the Sierra Club, Friends of the Earth, the League of Conservation Voters, and the Earth Island Institute, and his work resulted in the creation of the Kings Canyon, North Cascades, and Redwood national parks and the Point Reyes and Cape Cod national seashores; protection of the Grand Canyon and Dinosaur National Monument from dams; passage (1964) of the Wilderness Act; and innumerable other environmental-protection victories. When Brower was eight years old, he began taking his recently blinded mother on walks in the Berkeley Hills, and he attributed his interest in the beauty of nature in part to having had to serve as the eyes for someone else. He graduated from high school at age 16, attended the University of California, Berkeley, for two years, until 1931, and in 1933 joined the Sierra Club. Brower went to work for Yosemite National Park two years later and in his six years there ascended its mountain peaks scores of times; he also was able to put his superior climbing skills to good use during his World War II army service both as instructor and in combat. Upon leaving the army, he returned to the job he had held before the war, editing for the University of California Press, and in 1952 he became executive director of the Sierra Club, a position he held until 1969. During Brower's tenure, the club became a powerful activist organization and saw its membership grow from 7,000 to 77,000, but there were disagreements over the level of activism, and he felt pressured to leave office. He thereupon formed the Friends of the Earth and served as its chairman until disagreements with its board caused him to be dismissed in 1984. Although he was reinstated soon thereafter, he resigned in 1986 and returned to the Sierra Club, whose board he had rejoined in 1982. That same year, he founded the Earth Island Institute in San Francisco to back worldwide conservation projects. Brower remained on the Sierra Club's board until 1998. His autobiography, *For Earth's Sake: The Life and Times of David Brower,* was published in 1990.

Budge, John Donald ("Don"), American tennis player (b. June 13, 1915, Oakland, Calif.—d. Jan. 26, 2000, Scranton, Pa.), won the four major tennis tournaments—Wimbledon and the championships of Australia, France, and the United States—in 1938 to become the sport's first Grand Slam winner. More interested in football and baseball than tennis as a boy, he was eventually persuaded by his brother, Lloyd, to pursue tennis seriously. He won the first tournament he entered, capturing the California state boys' singles title in 1930. Tall and thin and possessed of exceptional stamina, he was a graceful athlete, though one who employed an aggressive style of play, attacking opponents with his backhand—which hitherto had been considered mainly a defensive stroke—as well as his powerful serve. He represented the U.S. in Davis Cup competition four times (1935–38), winning 25 of 29 matches and leading the U.S. team to the Davis Cup title in 1937 with a memorable five-set come-from-behind victory over German tennis ace Gottfried von Cramm. At Wimbledon in 1937 and again in 1938, he won the singles, the men's doubles (with Gene Mako), and the mixed doubles (with Alice Marbles). He also won four U.S. Open titles: two singles (1937–38) and two men's doubles (1936 and 1938, with Mako). The feat he achieved in 1938—sweeping all four major tennis titles in a single year—was not reproduced until 1962, when Rod Laver recorded the first of his two Grand Slams. Budge turned professional in 1939, the same year his influential book, *Budge on Tennis,* was published. His career was interrupted in 1942 when he entered the U.S. Army Air Corps, but he returned to competition in 1946. He retired from playing in 1954 and for the next three decades operated a tennis camp in Maryland. He was inducted into the National Lawn Tennis Association Hall of Fame in 1964 and was later selected by *Tennis* magazine as one of the 20 greatest players of the 20th century.

Bueno, Rodrigo Alejandro, Argentine singer (b. May 24, 1973, Rosario, Arg.—d. June 24, 2000, Berazategui, near Buenos Aires, Arg.), was known simply as "Rodrigo" or popularly as "El Potro" ("the Stallion"); his popularity in *cuarteto,* a form of music popular with working-class and poor Argentines, had skyrocketed just a few months previously such that his was a top act and his compact discs became instant bestsellers. He died in a car crash at night while returning from a concert in La Plata under circumstances that many fans found suspicious; he had an elevated blood alcohol level, and his body was thrown from the car although the passengers—including his ex-wife and infant son—were relatively unharmed in the crash. Rodrigo's death occasioned massive outpourings of grief (including the suicides of four teenage girls) and a huge jump in sales of his albums. Media reports often mentioned Rodrigo's friend and sometime artistic mentor, the association football (soccer) player Diego Maradona, and referred to the death—65 years earlier to the day—of another musician of the people, tango king Carlos Gardel.

Buero Vallejo, Antonio, Spanish playwright (b. Sept. 29, 1916, Guadalajara, Spain—d. April 28, 2000, Madrid, Spain), was the country's best-known and most important dramatist in the second half of the 20th century. He was studying art in Madrid when the Spanish Civil War began in 1936, and he left school to become a medical orderly in the Republican Army. At the end of the war he was imprisoned and sentenced to death (the Nationalists had earlier killed his father), but his death sentence was commuted. When he was released from prison in 1946, he decided to stay in Spain and oppose the regime of Francisco Franco through his writing. Using allegory and myth and, particularly in his later plays, events and personages from history, he created dramas that portrayed the oppressive political situation of Spain, and they usually, but not always, got past the government's censors. A number of his characters were blind, deaf, or insane or suffered from other disabilities, a device he used to comment on both the political and the human situation. His second play, *Historia de una escalera,* won the Lope de Vega prize in 1949. It was followed by some 30 additional plays, including *Hoy es fiesta* (1956) and *El concierto de San Ovidio* (1962). He also translated the works of other playwrights, including those of Bertolt Brecht, and published writings on art and artists. In 1971 he was given membership in the Royal Spanish Academy, and in 1986 he won the Cervantes Prize, the highest literary award in Spain. He was the first playwright ever to be so honoured.

Bundy, William P., U.S. presidential adviser (b. Sept. 24, 1917, Washington, D.C.—d. Oct. 6, 2000, Princeton, N.J.), was one of the foremost architects of the U.S. policy in Vietnam. He and his younger brother, McGeorge, who was national security adviser in the administrations of John F. Kennedy and Lyndon B. Johnson, were the sons of parents from prominent Boston families. William graduated from Yale University in 1939 with a B.A. in history and in 1940 earned an M.A. in history from Harvard University. He left Harvard Law School in 1941 to enlist in the Army Signal Corps and served in England in intelligence, for which he received the Legion of Merit and was made a member of the Order of the British Empire. He received his law degree in 1947 and worked for a private firm until 1951, when he entered government service preparing estimates for the Central Intelligence Agency. In 1960 he served as the staff director of the Commission on National Goals, appointed by Pres. Dwight D. Eisenhower, which in the following decade influenced civil rights laws and poverty programs as well as policy on women in the workforce. In 1961 Bundy moved to the Department of Defense and in 1964 to the Department of State, becoming assistant secretary for Far Eastern affairs. Although he at first reportedly argued against escalation of the fighting in Vietnam and even proposed withdrawal, he later refused to support those who took a dovish position. He left government in 1969 to teach at the Massachusetts Institute of Technology, where he became a target for antiwar protesters who once tried to bomb his office. In 1972 he became editor of the journal *Foreign Affairs* and beginning in the mid-1980s taught part-time at Princeton University. His book *A Tangled Web* (1998) was a critique of the foreign policy of Pres. Richard M. Nixon.

Bury, John, British set designer (b. Jan. 27, 1925, Aberystwyth, Cardiganshire [now Dyfed], Eng.—d. Nov. 12, 2000, Burleigh, Gloucestershire, Eng.), was head of design for the Royal Shakespeare Company from 1965 to 1968 and for the Royal National Theatre from 1973 to 1985. He also created sets for the Royal Opera House and the Glyndebourne Festival Opera. Bury's bold, stylized sets—which often incorporated such materials as metal, glass, and brick and featured dramatic architectural structures—were a radical departure from the painted, decorative sets that had characterized traditional British theatre. In 1981 he won Tony Awards for best set design and best lighting for the Broadway production of Peter Shaffer's *Amadeus.* Bury was made an OBE in 1979.

Canby, Vincent, American journalist (b. July 27, 1924, Chicago, Ill.—d. Oct. 15, 2000, New York, N.Y.), as senior film critic for the *New York Times,* delivered thousands of highly influential reviews and feature articles in prose noted for its conversational tone and wry wit. Canby joined the newspaper in 1965, becoming the senior film critic in 1969, but switched to theatre criticism in 1993. Noted for a tireless devotion to his craft, Canby often used his vacation time to write novels and plays.

Cartland, Dame (Mary) Barbara Hamilton, British author (b. July 9, 1901, Edgbaston, Birmingham, Eng.—d. May 21, 2000, near Hatfield, Hertfordshire, Eng.), had a seven-decade-long career during which she wrote 723 books, sometimes at a rate of one every two weeks. Her works—most of them romance novels—sold more than a billion copies and were translated into some three dozen languages. Sales of her books broke records for 18 years and gained her the title of world's best-selling author in *The Guinness Book of Records.* Widely acknowledged as the queen of romance, Cartland created works peopled with virginal heroines and dashing, magnetic heroes who experienced great passion—but ripped no bodices—as they underwent intense trials, described in florid prose, on their way to their story's inevitable happy ending. She was also known for her copious use of makeup, for the pink frocks that dominated her wardrobe, for the fact that she was the step-grandmother of Diana, princess of Wales, and for having given herself the longest entry in *Who's Who* by listing all her books. Cartland had a finishing school education at Malvern Girls College and Abbey House, Netley Abbey, in Hampshire, and began her writing career by providing social gossip items to the *Daily Express.* She advanced to writing the stories herself and in 1925 published her first novel, *Jigsaw.* In 1927 Cartland married Alexander McCorquodale after having reportedly turned down proposals from at least four dozen other men. The marriage did not last, however, and in 1936 she married McCorquodale's cousin Hugh, with whom she remained until his death in 1963. Besides writing romance novels—which sported such titles as *Again This Rapture* (1947), *The Tears of Love* (1975), *Revenge of the Heart* (1984), and *The Haunted Heart* (1990)—as well as biographies and other nonfiction works on a range of subjects from diet and health to marriage and motherhood to stately homes, Cartland engaged in a number of social crusades. During World War II she organized the donation of hundreds of secondhand wedding dresses so that service brides might be married in white, and she later campaigned for rights for Gypsies. In 1991 Cartland was created DBE, an honour to which she had long aspired.

Cashin, Bonnie, American fashion designer (b. Sept. 28, 1915, Oakland, Calif.—d. Feb. 3, 2000, New York, N.Y.), was a highly influential innovator who created loose-fitting sportswear and light, layered clothes. She first designed sportswear for the fashion house Adler & Adler from 1937 to 1943. Working for Twentieth Century Fox from 1944 to 1949, Cashin created clothes for some 60 films, including *Laura* (1944) and *The Keys of the Kingdom* (1944). She started her own company, Bonnie Cashin Designs, in 1952 and was one of the world's most prominent designers during the following two decades. In 1972 Cashin was inducted into the Coty American Fashion Critics Hall of Fame.

Cassidy, Frederic Gomes, Jamaican-born American lexicographer (b. Oct. 10, 1907, Kingston, Jam.—d. June 14, 2000, Madison, Wis.), was a leading authority on American folk language; he edited the comprehensive *Dictionary of American Regional English.* In 1939, a year after receiving his Ph.D. from the University of Michigan at Ann Arbor, Cassidy joined the faculty of the University of Wisconsin at Madison, where he spent the duration of his career. He published two books on the language of his native Jamaica, *Jamaica Talk: Three Hundred Years of the English in Jamaica* (1961) and the *Dictionary of Jamaican English* (1967), while beginning work on the *Dictionary of American Regional English.* The first volume of the dictionary appeared in 1985. At the time of Cassidy's death, three volumes had been published, and work on a fourth was in progress.

Chaban-Delmas, Jacques (Jacques Michel Pierre Delmas),French French politician and Resistance fighter (b. March 7, 1915, Paris, France—d. Nov. 10, 2000, Paris), served as prime minister of France from 1969 to 1972. As a left-wing member of the conservative Gaullist Party, he attempted as prime minister to create a "new society," in which the government would

top: Abilio Lope/Corbis; bottom: AFP Worldwide

undertake a program of social justice and the trade unions would play a major role in the national economy. These efforts, however, were not supported by the more conservative Gaullists, who persuaded Pres. Georges Pompidou to force Chaban-Delmas to resign. He was educated at the École Libre des Sciences Politiques in Paris and joined the Resistance in 1940 after the German occupation of France; he became the chief liaison officer for northern France between Gen. Charles de Gaulle's provisional government in exile and the Nazi-installed Vichy regime. For his service he was rewarded by de Gaulle with a promotion to brigadier general; at 29 he was the youngest man to achieve that rank. During the war Delmas took the code name of Chaban, which he later legally added to his name. After the war he entered politics, an arena in which his military record and personal charm served him well. In 1947 he was elected mayor of Bordeaux, an office he held until 1995. He held several cabinet posts during the 1950s and thrice served (1958–69, 1978–81, and 1986–88) as president of the National Assembly. Chaban-Delmas also wrote seven books, including a biography of de Gaulle.

Chatrier, Philippe, French tennis player, sportswriter, and sports administrator (b. Feb. 2, 1928, Créteil, France—d. June 22, 2000, Dinard, France), as head of the French tennis federation (1973–93) and the International Tennis Federation (1977–91) and a member of the International Olympic Committee (from 1990), was instrumental in the introduction (1968) of the "open" format (in which amateurs and professionals play in the same tournaments), the resurgence of the French Open, and the return of tennis to the Olympic Games in the 1980s. Chatrier was the French junior champion in 1945, a member (1948–50) and later the nonplaying captain (1969–72) of his nation's Davis Cup team, and founding editor of *Tennis de France* magazine.

Christian, Barbara, Caribbean American educator and critic (b. Dec. 12, 1943, St. Thomas, U.S. Virgin Islands—d. June 25, 2000, Berkeley, Calif.), was a noted professor of African American studies and a leading figure in the field of modern literary feminism. Educated at Marquette University, Milwaukee, Wis. (B.A., 1963), and Columbia University, New York City (M.A., 1964; Ph.D., 1970), Christian taught at the City College of the City University of New York from 1965 to 1970. From 1971 until her death she was a professor at the University of California, Berkeley, where she helped found the university's department of African American studies. A prolific author and editor, Christian first attracted widespread attention with her 1980 book, *Black Women Novelists: The Development of a Tradition, 1892–1976,* in which she discussed such important writers as Nella Larsen and Zora Neale Hurston. Among Christian's other published works were *Teaching Guide to Accompany Black Foremothers* (1980); *Black Feminist Criticism: Perspectives on Black Women Writers* (1985), a work emphasizing literary, textual analysis of fiction by black women; *From the Inside Out: Afro-American Women's Literary Tradition and the State* (1987); and *Alice Walker's "The Color Purple" and Other Works: A Critical Commentary* (1987). In addition, Christian contributed to *Black Expression* (1969; edited by Addison Gayle) and to the journals *The Black Scholar* and *Journal of Ethnic Studies,* and she coedited works such as *Female Subjects in Black and White: Race, Psychoanalysis, Feminism* (1997).

Jane Scherr/University of California, Berkeley

Claiborne, Craig, American food critic (b. Sept. 4, 1920, Sunflower, Miss.—d. Jan. 22, 2000, New York, N.Y.), was food editor of the *New York Times* from 1957 to 1986; he introduced millions of readers to classical French cuisine and began the widely imitated practice of using a rating system in his restaurant reviews; he was also the author of more than 20 books, including the best-selling *New York Times Cook Book;* his autobiography, *A Feast Made for Laughter,* appeared in 1982.

Clarke, Sir Cyril Astley, British physician and scientist (b. Aug. 22, 1907, Leicester, Eng.—d. Nov. 21, 2000, Hoylake, Cheshire, Eng.), helped develop a vaccine against erythroblastosis fetalis (also known as Rh hemolytic disease of the newborn)—a potentially fatal complication that may occur when a fetus and its mother have incompatible blood Rh factors. Clarke was also noted for his work on genetic mutations in the peppered moth; his research supported the evolutionary theory of natural selection. In 1965 he was appointed professor of medicine at the University of Liverpool. Clarke served as president of the Royal College of Physicians from 1972 to 1977, and he directed the college's research unit from 1983 to 1988. He was knighted in 1974.

Coetsee, Hendrik Jacobus ("Kobie"), South African politician (b. April 19, 1931, Ladybrand, Orange Free State, S.Af.—d. July 29, 2000, Bloemfontein, S.Af.), was the pragmatic minister of justice, police, and prisons (1980–94) under South African presidents P.W. Botha and F.W. de Klerk. Coetsee, who first met with imprisoned antiapartheid leader Nelson Mandela in 1985, was credited with initiating official talks four years later between Mandela and Botha and then between Mandela and de Klerk after Botha's resignation. In 1994, after Mandela's election as president of an African National Congress-led government, Coetsee was named president of the South African Senate.

Coggan, (Frederick) Donald, Baron, British cleric (b. Oct. 9, 1909, London, Eng.—d. May 17, 2000, near Winchester, Eng.), served as Anglican archbishop of Canterbury from 1974 to 1980; a prominent theologian and educator, he was the first Evangelical Anglican to become spiritual leader of the Church of England in more than a century. Educated at the University of Cambridge (B.A., 1931) and ordained in 1935, Coggan taught Semitic languages at the University of Manchester from 1931 to 1934 and at Wycliffe College, Toronto, from 1937 to 1944. It was during this period that he allied himself with the Evangelicals, a group within the church known for its missionary zeal. Principal of the London College of Divinity from 1944 to 1956, he was consecrated bishop of Bradford in 1956. He was elevated to archbishop of York in 1961 and succeeded Michael Ramsey as archbishop of Canterbury 13 years later. As spiritual leader of the church, Coggan was noted for his progressive views. He was the first archbishop of Canterbury to support the ordination of women; the church eventually admitted women to the priesthood in 1994. He also used his background in Semitic study to foster relations between Christians and Jews, and he publicly denounced racial intolerance and nuclear arms. Coggan was elevated to a life peerage in 1980. Among his numerous writings were *The Ministry of the Word* (1945), *The Glory of God* (1950), *Stewards of Grace* (1958), *Christian Priorities* (1963), *Convictions* (1975), *The Name Above All Names* (1981), and *Mission to the World* (1982). He also served on the panel of scholars who produced The New English Bible and The Revised English Bible.

Cohen, Alexander Henry, American theatrical producer (b. July 24, 1920, New York, N.Y.—d. April 22, 2000, New York), provided financial backing for more than 100 shows on Broadway and the West End theatre district in London. Using money inherited from his father, Cohen began producing shows in the 1940s, achieving his first success with the hit drama *Angel Street* (1941), starring Vincent Price. Among Cohen's other notable successes were the 1964 production of *Hamlet,* starring Richard Burton, and the 1967 production of Harold Pinter's *The Homecoming.* In 1967 Cohen also produced the first telecast of the Tony Awards ceremony. His last production, *Waiting in the Wings,* starring Lauren Bacall, opened on Broadway in December 1999.

Coley, Doris (Doris Kenner-Jackson), American singer (b. Aug. 2, 1941, Goldsboro, N.C.—d. Feb. 4, 2000, Sacramento, Calif.), was one of the Shirelles, the all-girl pop group that created a sensation in the late 1950s and early '60s with a string of hits that included "Tonight's the Night" (1960), "Mama Said" (1961), and "Baby It's You" (1962). As a teenager, she and three of her classmates at Passaic (N.J.) High School won a talent show with the song "I Met Him on a Sunday," which led to a recording contract. In 1958 the song became the group's first record to enter the charts. Coley was the lead vocalist on the Shirelles' 1959 hit "Dedicated to the One I Love." Another hit, "Will You Love Me Tomorrow," became the first number one record by an African American female group. After breaking up in 1968, the group reunited for several performances in the 1970s, and in 1996 the Shirelles were inducted into the Rock and Roll Hall of Fame.

Comfort, Alex, British writer (b. Feb. 10, 1920, London, Eng.—d. March 26, 2000, Northamptonshire, Eng.), was, to his chagrin, primarily identified as the author of *The Joy of Sex: A Gourmet Guide to Lovemaking* (1972); the book was the free-love generation's homage to the *Kama-sutra.* Complete with line drawings featuring a merely "ordinary-looking" couple, *Joy* eased the anxieties of even those most embarrassed to explore the possibility that sex could actually be fun and got whole nations into the act when the groundbreaking work was translated into two dozen languages. This was no small feat for a book that was reportedly written in only two weeks' time by a professed amateur. A lucid and engaging writer, Comfort published his first book, *The Silver River* (1938), at the age of 18 and went on to write 50 more books, including novels, volumes of poetry, and scientific texts on physiology, biology, and aging. Comfort, a pacifist, protested the indiscriminate bombing of Germany during World War II and was a member of the Campaign for Nuclear Disarmament. In addition, he earned three academic degrees and held a variety of academic and medical posts at respected institutions in England and in California.

Cooke, Marvel Jackson, American journalist (b. 1903?, Mankato, Minn.—d. Nov. 29, 2000, New York, N.Y.), wrote for such black publications as *The Crisis,* the *Amsterdam News,* and the *People's Voice* before becoming the first African American woman to serve (1949–52) as a reporter for a mainstream white-owned newspaper, the *Daily Compass;* among her work for that paper was a series, "I Was a Slave," that exposed the chronic underpayment of domestic day labourers. She later worked for a number of left-leaning organizations.

Cooney, Barbara, American children's author and illustrator (b. Aug. 6, 1917, New York, N.Y.—d. March 10, 2000, Portland, Maine), was a literary star in the world of children's publishing who wrote or illustrated 110 books in a career that spanned six decades. Born into a family of artists, she received formal training at the Art Students League in New York City before publishing her first book, *King of Wrecked Island* (1941). In 1959 Cooney was awarded the Caldecott Medal for children's book illustration for *The Chanticleer and the Fox,* her adaptation of a story from Chaucer's *The Canterbury Tales.* She received a second Caldecott Medal in 1980 for her illustrations for poet Donald Hall's *Ox-Cart Man.* Cooney's 1982 work, *Miss Rumphius,* won the National Book Award for children's picture books. *Basket Moon,* her last book, appeared in 1999.

Cooper, Harry ("Lighthorse Harry"), American professional golfer (b. Aug. 6, 1904, England—d. Oct. 18, 2000, White Plains, N.Y.) was ranked 13th on the all-time victories list (31 triumphs) of the Professional Golfers' Association tour but never won any of the sport's major titles. After his playing days, Cooper continued as an instructor until age 93, when he was believed to be the oldest active teaching professional.

Cormier, Robert Edmund, American children's writer (b. Jan. 17, 1925, Leominster, Mass.—d. Nov. 2, 2000, Boston, Mass.), was an award-winning journalist for the *Fitchburg* (Mass.) *Sentinel* before making his name as one of the first writers to explore the darker realms of teenage life in such works as *The Chocolate War* (1974), the controversial story about the abuse heaped on a Roman Catholic schoolchild who refuses to sell chocolate bars; *I Am the Cheese* (1977), a look at the torturous imprisonment and psychiatric examination of a youth; and *The Bumblebee Flies Anyway* (1983), a morbid view of terminally ill children in an experimental hospital. His last work, *Frenchtown Summer* (1999), was an unexpectedly warmhearted story about the relationship between a father and son.

Cowdrey, (Michael) Colin (Lord Cowdrey of Tonbridge), British cricket player and administrator (b. Dec. 24, 1932, Putumala, India—d. Dec. 5, 2000, Angmering, West Sussex, Eng.), was one of England's finest batsmen and the first player to represent his country in more than 100 Test matches. Cowdrey was still a schoolboy at Tonbridge and then at Brasenose College, Oxford, when he began playing for Kent, which he captained from 1957 to 1971. He scored 42,719 first-class runs (average 42.89), including 107 centuries; his highest score was 307 against South Australia in 1962. He made his Test debut against Australia in 1954 and played in 114 Test matches (27 as captain), becoming England's fourth-highest run-scorer in Test history with 7,624 runs (average 44.06), including 22 centuries and 120 catches, an English record. In 1957 against the West Indies he scored a record fourth-wicket partnership of 411 runs with Peter May. In 1963 against the West Indies he famously returned to the crease to finish the match, despite having suffered a broken arm. Cowdrey was unexpectedly called up in 1975 at age 42 to play Australia in his final Test appearance; he retired from Kent the next year. He later served as president of the Marylebone Cricket Club (1986–87) and chairman of the International Cricket Conference (1986–87; 1989–93). Two of his sons also played for Kent, and one, Chris, played for England. Cowdrey was made CBE in 1972, awarded a knighthood in 1992, and granted a life peerage in 1997.

Cranston, Alan, American politician (b. June 19, 1914, Palo Alto, Calif.—d. Dec. 31, 2000, Los Altos, Calif.), served as a Democratic U.S. senator from California from 1969 until 1993, by which time his reputation had been clouded by his intervention with federal regulators on behalf of Charles Keating, president of one of the banks at the centre of the savings and loan scandal in the early 1990s. He had briefly been a presidential candidate in 1983–84, with arms control as his focus, and after leaving the Senate continued to promote that cause, becoming chairman of the Gorbachev Foundation USA think tank.

Craxi, Bettino Benedetto, Italian politician (b. Feb. 24, 1934, Milan, Italy—d. Jan. 19, 2000, Hammamet, Tun.), was Italy's first Socialist prime minister; elected to successive terms (1983–87), he was also the country's longest-serving prime minister of the post-World War II years. He joined the Socialist Youth Movement in his late teens and became a member of the Italian Socialist Party's central committee in 1957. He was elected to a seat in the national Chamber of Deputies in 1968 and became a deputy secretary of the Socialist Party in 1970. After the Socialists performed badly in the 1976 general elections, Craxi became the party's general secretary. He proceeded to unite the faction-ridden party, committed it to moderate social and economic policies, and tried to dissociate it from the much larger Communist Party. Under his leadership the Socialists were members in five of Italy's six coalition governments from 1980 to 1983. His decision to pull out of the Christian Democrat-led coalition in April 1983 provoked general elections in June that resulted in his being invited to form a government. He formed a coalition government with the Christian Democrats and several small, moderate parties. As prime minister he pursued anti-inflationary fiscal policies and steered a pro-American course in foreign affairs. He formed a new coalition government in 1986 but resigned in early 1987. In February 1993 multiple charges of political corruption forced Craxi, who denied the allegations, to resign his post as party leader. He left Italy for Tunisia later that year. The government continued to investigate charges against him, and in 1994 he was twice sentenced in absentia to prison terms resulting from some of these charges.

Cuccia, Enrico, Italian banker (b. Nov. 24, 1907, Rome, Italy—d. June 23, 2000, Milan, Italy), as the cofounder (1946), managing director (1946–82), and honorary chairman (after he was forced to retire in 1982) of Mediobanca SpA, Italy's first—and for a time only—merchant bank, orchestrated many of the nation's biggest business deals and was instrumental in the transformation of Italy's depressed industrial sector after World War II.

Cunningham, Emory Orgustus, American publisher (b. March 17, 1921, Kansas, Ala.—d. Jan. 24, 2000, Birmingham, Ala.), founded *Southern Living* magazine in 1966, a publication that highlighted the hospitality of the American South and was credited with increasing appreciation of the region's culture. In 1985 he sold *Southern Living*'s holding company, Southern Progress Corp., to Time Inc. for $480 million.

Cunningham, Sir Josias, Northern Irish politician (b. Jan. 20, 1934, County Antrim, N.Ire.—d. Aug. 9, 2000, Belfast, N.Ire.), was a key figure for more than 25 years in the Ulster Unionist Party (UUP), Northern Ireland's largest Protestant political party, and was president of the UUP's governing body, the Ulster Unionist Council, from 1991. A moderate who was skilled at behind-the-scenes negotiations, he was considered instrumental in finalizing in early 2000 the power-sharing arrangement with Sinn Fein, the political arm of the Irish Republican Army. Cunningham, who was knighted in the 2000 New Year's Honours List, died in an automobile accident.

Daniel, (Elbert) Clifton, Jr., American journalist and newspaper editor (b. Sept. 19, 1912, Zebulon, N.C.—d. Feb. 21, 2000, New York, N.Y.), served as managing editor of the *New York Times* from 1964 to 1969 and as its Washington, D.C., bureau chief from 1973 to 1976. Daniel began his long career at the *Times* in 1944 as a foreign correspondent, distinguishing himself in assignments in wartime Europe and, later, in the Middle East and Asia. His coverage of the Soviet Union in 1954–55 earned him an Overseas Press Club Award. In 1956, the same year that he married Margaret Truman—the only child of former president Harry S. Truman—Daniel returned to the U.S. to work in the home office of the *Times.* As managing editor, he enlivened the newspaper's style, in part by increasing the number of feature articles and expanding society and arts coverage. He was a commentator on the *Times*-owned radio station, WQXR, from 1969 to 1973. Following his retirement from journalism in 1977, Daniel edited the book *Chronicle of the 20th Century* (1987), which became a best-seller.

Dard, Frédéric Charles Antoine, French novelist (b. June 29, 1921, Bourgoin-Jallieu, France—d. June 6, 2000, Bonnefontaine, Switz.), wrote mainly "hard-boiled" detective novels, notable for their ribald humour and their inventive, often racy, vocabulary. Although Dard wrote under several pseudonyms, more than half of his output, which totaled some 300 books, featured Paris police superintendent San-Antonio and his sidekick, Inspector Bérurier. The series included the illustrated *L'histoire de France vue par San-Antonio* (1965); *Dictionnaire San-Antonio* (1993), an extensive lexicon and glossary; and his final novel, *Napoléon Pommier* (2000), published shortly before his death.

Davies, Donald Watts, British computer scientist (b. June 7, 1924, Treorchy, Wales—d. May 28, 2000, Esher, Eng.), helped lay the groundwork for the Internet in the 1960s when he devised a more efficient method of computer communications known as packet switching, a technique in which each data stream is broken into discrete, easily conveyed blocks, or packets, of data that can be electronically transmitted between remote computers and then reassembled into a coherent message.

Davis, Marc, American cartoonist (b. March 30, 1913, Bakersfield, Calif.—d. Jan. 12, 2000, Glendale, Calif.), was an animator for Walt Disney Studios from 1935 to 1978 and helped create the title characters for such classic Disney films as *Snow White and the Seven Dwarfs* (1937), *Cinderella* (1950), *Alice in Wonderland* (1951), and *Sleeping Beauty* (1959).

Day, Sir Robin, British broadcast journalist (b. Oct. 24, 1923, London, Eng.—d. Aug. 7, 2000, London), gained the label "grand inquisitor" for his technique in political interviews, in which he asked pointed questions and probed relentlessly for nonevasive answers, in contrast to the then-traditional gentle, deferential manner of asking only expected questions. Especially on the two BBC programs most associated with him—*Panorama* (1959–72) and *Question Time* (1979–89)—wearing his trademark polka-dot bow tie, pin-striped suit, and oversize horn-rimmed glasses, he tenaciously but courteously took charge of his interviews and knowledgeably quizzed political leaders in such a way that, while his subjects were often uncomfortable, his audience was enlightened and delighted. Following service in the Royal Artillery (1943–47), Day read law (1947–51) at St. Edmund Hall, Oxford, where in 1950 he served as president of the Oxford Union. He was called to the bar in 1952 but the next year went into journalism, traveling to the U.S. for the British Information Services. Following his return to London, Day worked as a freelance broadcaster and as a BBC radio producer before joining (1955) Independent Television News. He left ITN in 1959 to run for a seat in Parliament, which he did not win, and then rejoined the BBC. In 1979 Day also began presenting the BBC radio program *The World at One,* with which he remained until 1987. He ended his active career in 1989 but appeared on the BBC's *Breakfast News* during the 1992 and 1997 election campaigns. Among Day's books were the autobiographical *Day by Day: A Dose of My Own Hemlock* (1975) and *Grand Inquisitor* (1989), the latter of which became a best-seller. He was knighted in 1981.

de Camp, L(yon) Sprague, American writer (b. Nov. 27, 1907, New York, N.Y.—d. Nov. 6, 2000, Plano, Texas), wrote more than 100 science-fiction and fantasy books. He began his writing career in the late 1930s as a contributor to *Astounding Stories,* the influential science-fiction magazine edited by John W. Campbell. De Camp's best-known novels were *The Incomplete Enchanter* (1940), written with Fletcher Pratt, and *Lest Darkness Fall* (1941). He also wrote nonfiction works, including *Great Cities of the Ancient World* (1972). De Camp received a Grand Master Award from the Science Fiction and Fantasy Writers of America in 1978.

Dewar, Donald Campbell, U.K. statesman (b. Aug. 21, 1937, Glasgow, Scot.—d. Oct. 11, 2000, Edinburgh, Scot.), was for many years a leading proponent of Scottish devolution; he saw his desire become reality and in the process became first minister of Scotland's first Parliament in almost 300 years. A witty, brilliant man known for his exceptional debating skill, Dewar garnered respect from his Labour Party peers, as well as from the opposition, owing to his devotion to civil service and 26 years of service as a member of the U.K. Parliament. His standing, his geniality, and his characteristic moderation made him the ideal candidate to work out the difficulties of Scottish devolution, and he came to be known in Scotland as the "Father of the Nation," a title that he immediately tried to downplay. Dewar attended Glasgow Academy and studied law at the University of Glasgow. In 1966 he entered Parliament as MP for Aberdeen South, a seat he lost in the 1970 election. Dewar practiced law until 1978, when he won election as MP in the Glasgow Garscadden by-election. He served as shadow Scottish secretary in the 1980s. In 1992 he was named shadow social services secretary, and he later took the post of chief whip. Prime Minister Tony Blair named him Scottish secretary after Labour won the 1997 general election. Dewar then went to work on drafting the bill that would create a Scottish Parliament. Although some opponents found the proposal too nationalistic, Dewar saw his job through, and in July 1999 he reached the peak of his political career when he opened the Scottish Parliament as first minister. His brief time in the post was marked by turmoil that led many to believe that the man who created the Parliament was not necessarily the right one to lead it, but through it all he remained one of his country's most trusted and beloved public servants.

Dufresne, Jean-V., Canadian journalist (b. July 15, 1930, Montreal, Que.?—d. Sept. 16, 2000, Montreal), had a nearly 50-year career during which he wrote for almost all the leading Quebec newspapers, both French and English, as well as appeared on radio and television; he twice served as managing editor of *Le Magazine Maclean* (later *L'Actualité*) and from 1990 until his retirement in 1996 was a columnist for *Le Journal de Montreal.* He was honoured with the Jules Fournier Prize in 1989.

Durack, Elizabeth, Australian painter (b. July 6, 1915, Perth, Australia—d. May 25, 2000, Perth), created oil paintings using Aboriginal themes, a variety of artistic techniques, and natural materials and drew international applause beginning in the 1960s. In the 1990s many of her paintings were shown as authentic Aboriginal art created by a young man named Eddie Burrup, but she was caught up in a

Scottish nationalist Donald Dewar

Reuters NewMedia Inc./Corbis

national furor in 1997 when her professional alter ego was revealed at her request. Durack defended her use of Burrup as an artistic persona, a stand supported by many in the Aboriginal community. She was appointed OBE in 1966 and CMG in 1982.

Dury, Ian, British singer, songwriter, and actor (b. May 12, 1942, Upminster, Essex, Eng.—d. March 27, 2000, Hampstead, North London, Eng.), was celebrated as a pioneer of British punk rock. A veteran of the early 1970s pub-rock scene with his first band, Kilburn and the High Roads, Dury founded the Blockheads in 1977. Dury and the Blockheads became punk-rock icons with such hit songs as "Sex & Drugs & Rock & Roll," "Hit Me with Your Rhythm Stick," and "Reasons to Be Cheerful (Part Three)." After the group broke up in the early 1980s, he worked as a solo performer, actor, and television presenter, even during his unsuccessful five-year battle with cancer. Throughout his career, Dury, who had been crippled by polio at age seven, used his celebrity status to campaign for UNICEF, the disabled, and polio vaccination in the Third World.

Edelstein, David Norton, American judge (b. Feb. 16, 1910, New York, N.Y.—d. Aug. 19, 2000, New York), spent 43 years (1952–95) presiding over the U.S. Department of Justice's antitrust action against IBM, considered one of the most important antitrust proceedings in modern judicial history, and was involved since 1988 in the landmark *United States* v. *International Brotherhood of Teamsters* lawsuit. Before he was ordered off the IBM case in 1995—owing to a ruling by a federal appeals court that questioned his impartiality—Edelstein had signed a consent order in 1956 under which IBM had agreed to modify some of its practices. In the case of the Teamsters union, Edelstein worked doggedly to rid the union of corruption; he sanctioned a 1998 review board decision to oust former union president Ron Carey, he paved the way for James P. Hoffa to accede to the union presidency in 1999, and shortly before his death, outlined rules for 2001 elections. Edelstein, who was appointed to the bench in 1951 by Pres. Harry Truman, was still hearing cases at the time of his death.

Elchibey, Abulfaz (Abulfaz Kadyrgula ogly Aliyev), Azerbaijani historian and nationalist leader (b. June 7, 1938, Keleki, Nakhichevan A.S.S.R, U.S.S.R.—d. Aug. 22, 2000, Ankara, Turkey), was a leading anti-Soviet dissident and cofounder (1989) of the nationalist Azerbaijan Popular Front, before becoming the first democratically elected president of newly independent Azerbaijan in June 1992. He proved to be an ineffectual president, however, and after one year he was ousted in favour of former Azerbaijan Communist Party leader Heydar Aliyev. Elchibey, who had previously worked as an Arab philologist and a history professor, published more than 50 books on such subjects as philosophy, history, and religion.

Epstein, Julius J., American screenwriter (b. Aug. 22, 1909, New York, N.Y.—d. Dec. 30, 2000, Los Angeles, Calif.), had a long career, most noted for the adaptation—in partnership with his twin brother, Philip, and others—of the unproduced play *Everybody Comes to Rick's* that became the screenplay for the film *Casablanca* (1942), for which its team of writers won an Academy Award. Following his brother's death (1952), he continued writing, garnering two more Oscar nominations and, in 1998, a Los Angeles Film Critics Association career achievement award.

Fairbanks, Douglas Elton Ulman, Jr., American actor, socialite, and businessman (b. Dec. 9, 1909, New York, N.Y.—d. May 7, 2000, New York), had a successful film career before moving on to meritorious World War II service and later pursuing business interests and acting as executive producer and host of a television show as well as giving support to a number of charitable, artistic, diplomatic, and educational enterprises. The son of silent-screen swashbuckling hero Douglas Fairbanks, Sr., he managed to create his own image despite playing a few similar roles himself, in part by using his urbane charm and good looks to help him gain social position. Fairbanks began his film career early, in 1923, in *Stephen Steps Out*, and followed that with such vehicles as *Stella Dallas* (1925), *A Woman of Affairs* (1928), and *The Power of the Press* (1928), all silent films. He also occasionally appeared on the Los Angeles stage. His career gained momentum with the introduction of sound to motion pictures and with the publicity surrounding his marriage to Joan Crawford in 1929—and the end of the marriage four years later—and he tallied such successes as *The Dawn Patrol* (1930), *Little Caesar* (1930), *Morning Glory* (1933), *The Prisoner of Zenda* (1937), and *Gunga Din* (1939). During World War II Fairbanks served in the U.S. Navy with such distinction that he received a number of awards, including an honorary knighthood (1949) from the British king, George VI, for his contribution to joint Anglo-American operations. Following the war he spent much of his time in England and made only a few films. Instead, he concentrated on charitable and social concerns in addition to producing and acting in selected episodes of a British television anthology drama series, *Douglas Fairbanks Presents*, during the 1950s. In the 1970s Fairbanks returned to the U.S. to live. Besides seeing to his business interests, he toured in plays such as *My Fair Lady* and *The Pleasure of His Company* and appeared in his final film, *Ghost Story* (1981). Fairbanks also took pride in his writing; in addition to publishing poetry, stories, and articles in a number of prestigious magazines, he produced two volumes of memoirs, *The Salad Days* (1988) and *A Hell of a War* (1993).

Fanning, Katherine Woodruff ("Kay"), American journalist (b. Oct. 18, 1927, Joliet, Ill.—d. Oct. 19, 2000, Boston, Mass.), was a relative latecomer to her profession but rose to become one of the most highly respected and influential figures in her field. Considered a pioneer, she helped the *Anchorage Daily News* grow to be Alaska's largest newspaper and a Pulitzer Prize winner, became the first female editor of *The Christian Science Monitor*, and was the first woman to serve as president of the American Society of Newspaper Editors. Having graduated from Smith College, Northampton, Mass., in 1949 and from 1950 to 1963 been married to department store heir and *Chicago Sun-Times* publisher Marshall Field IV, she moved to Alaska in 1965, took a low-level job at the *Anchorage Daily News*, and, employing the knowledge of journalism she gained during her marriage, worked her way up to the position of reporter. In 1966 she married Larry Fanning, and the couple bought the *Daily News* the following year. Under their leadership the paper was transformed into an arm of investigative journalism, a path Fanning continued after her husband's death in 1971. With her as editor and publisher, it raised its daily circulation from 12,000 to 50,000 and in 1976 won the Pulitzer for a 15-part series that exposed Teamsters Union activities during the construction of the Alaska oil pipeline. Fanning sold the *Daily News* in 1983 and moved to Boston, where she became editor of *The Christian Science Monitor*. By the time she left five years later, in protest against budget cuts, she had built the paper into one of national importance, noted for its quality of international news coverage. Fanning thereafter spent a year at Harvard University's Institute of Politics, until 1993 was an adjunct professor at Boston University, and served as president of the American Society of Newspaper Editors and as a board member of the *Boston Globe*, the Associated Press, and the Pulitzer Prize organization.

Farnsworth, Richard, American actor and film stuntman (b. Sept. 1, 1920, Los Angeles, Calif.—d. Oct. 6, 2000, Lincoln, N.M.), was twice nominated for an Academy Award. Known mostly for his roles in westerns, Farnsworth brought a simple honesty to the characters he portrayed. He began his film career as a horse-riding stuntman in 1937. His first substantial movie role came in *Comes a Horseman* (1978). It landed him an Oscar nomination for best supporting actor and his first starring role in *The Grey Fox* (1982). At age 79, he became the oldest best actor nominee for his role in *The Straight Story* (1999).

Favaloro, René Gerónimo, Argentine heart surgeon (b. July 14, 1923, La Plata, Arg.—d. July 29, 2000, Buenos Aires, Arg.), performed the first documented coronary bypass operation and was the first surgeon to perform successful heart-transplant surgery in Argentina. Favaloro earned a degree in medicine from the National University of La Plata in 1948; he worked as a doctor in the province of La Pampa before moving to the U.S. in 1962 to study thoracic and cardiovascular surgery at the Cleveland (Ohio) Clinic. In 1967, while working at the Cleveland Clinic, Favaloro successfully performed bypass surgery on a 51-year-old woman; the procedure involved hooking the patient to an artificial heart-lung machine, removing a saphenous vein from her leg, and using the vein to form a bypass around blockages in her heart. In 1972 Favaloro returned to Argentina, where he specialized in heart transplant surgery and later established a medical institute—the Favaloro Foundation—in Buenos Aires to promote cardiological research. After Favaloro's death, a suicide, Argentine Pres. Fernando de la Rúa declared a national day of mourning.

Ferré, Sister M. Isolina, Puerto Rican Roman Catholic nun (b. 1914, Ponce, Puerto Rico—d. Aug. 3, 2000, Ponce), used her family's influence as wealthy owners of two leading Puerto Rican newspapers as well as their political power to establish charitable clinics, youth centres, and educational and empowerment establishments in Puerto Rico, New York City, and the Appalachia area in the eastern U.S. Ferré took her vows in 1935 and joined the Missionary Servants of the Most Blessed Trinity. Armed with training in sociology from Fordham University, Bronx, N.Y., and prepared to draw on her Puerto Rican heritage, Ferré successfully mediated wars in the Bronx between feuding Puerto Rican gangs. Her role as a peacemaker and as a crusader for the impoverished earned Ferré numerous awards, including the 1989 Albert Schweitzer Prize for Humanitarianism and the 1999 U.S. Presidential Medal of Freedom, the nation's highest civilian award.

Fitzgerald, Penelope Mary Knox, British novelist and biographer (b. Dec. 17, 1916, Lincoln, Eng.—d. April 28, 2000, London, Eng.), was noted for her economical yet evocative, witty, and intricate works, which often concerned the efforts of her characters to cope with their life circumstances. Although she did not begin writing until she was in her late 50s, she published nine novels and three biographies and was honoured with some of literature's top awards. Fitzgerald attended boarding school at Wycombe Abbey in High Wycombe, Buckinghamshire, and took first-class honours at Somerville College, Oxford. Following graduation (1939) she worked at the Ministry of Food and at the BBC, and in 1941 she married Desmond Fitzgerald. After she and her husband edited the short-lived literary-political journal *World Review* in the early 1950s, she managed a bookstore and then taught English at the Italia Conti stage school in London. Fitzgerald's first two books, the biographies *Edward Burne-Jones* and *The Knox Brothers,* appeared in 1975 and 1977, respectively, and later in 1977 she published her first novel, *The Golden Child,* which she wrote to entertain her husband, who was ill. A number of her early works of fiction, including *The Bookshop* (1978), *Offshore* (1979), *Human Voices* (1980), and *At Freddie's* (1982), drew on her own experiences; *Offshore,* which was inspired by the time she spent living on a houseboat, was awarded the Booker Prize. Fitzgerald produced another biography, *Charlotte Mew and Her Friends* (1984), and then returned to fiction. Her later novels—*Innocence* (1986), *The Beginning of Spring* (1988), and *The Gate of Angels* (1990)—were historical in nature. Fitzgerald's last novel, *The Blue Flower* (1995), was prompted by a visit she made to a church in Bonn, Ger., and the hymns she heard there by the Romantic poet Novalis. For that book she was given the National Book Critics Circle Award in 1998, the first non-American to be so honoured. A collection of Fitzgerald's stories, *The Means of Escape,* was published posthumously.

Foran, Thomas Aquinas, American lawyer (b. Jan. 11, 1924, Chicago, Ill.—d. Aug. 6, 2000, Lake Forest, Ill.), served as the combative chief prosecutor in the sensational case of the "Chicago Seven," a group of prominent radicals—Lee Weiner, David Dellinger, Jerry Rubin, Tom Hayden, John Froines, Rennie Davis, and Abbie Hoffman—who were charged with crossing state lines with intent to incite riots at the 1968 Democratic national convention in Chicago. Though Foran won convictions against five of the defendants, they never served prison time; an appeals court overturned the convictions. Foran, a 1950 graduate of the University of Detroit School of Law, was a founder in 1957 of the Chicago law firm Foran & Schultz and was the tenacious prosecutor of more than 150 organized crime figures.

Fowler, Henry Hamill, American government official (b. Sept. 5, 1908, Roanoke, Va.—d. Jan. 3, 2000, Alexandria, Va.), created Special Drawing Rights, a reserve currency sometimes called "paper gold," while serving as U.S. secretary of the treasury (1965–68) under Pres. Lyndon B. Johnson; he had previously served as treasury undersecretary (1961–64) and as head of the Defense Production Administration during the Korean War (1950–53). After leaving his cabinet post, he headed Goldman Sachs International Corp. (1969–84); he remained a limited partner at the investment firm until 1999.

Freund, Gisèle, German-born French photographer (b. Dec. 19, 1908?, Berlin, Ger.—d. March 31, 2000, Paris, France), was noted especially for her portraits of the cultural elite of France and for her service as François Mitterrand's official photographer following his election (1981) as president of France. Unlike the prevailing photographers of the time, she worked in colour, saying it was "closer to life." As a student in Frankfurt, Ger., Freund was engaged in the struggle against the rise of Nazism and in 1933 was forced to flee Germany to avoid arrest. She settled in Paris and studied at the Sorbonne for a doctorate, which was awarded in 1936. She had already become established as a photojournalist and was freelancing for leading news magazines, and Paris bookseller Adrienne Monnier published her dissertation as a book, *La Photographie en France au 19ᵉ siècle* (1936). Monnier became Freund's friend, mentor, and companion and introduced her to Parisian intellectuals, including the subject of one of her most famous photographs, André Malraux. The Nazi invasion of France forced Freund to flee again, and she went to Argentina. Following the end of World War II, she worked in Mexico before returning (1952) to Paris. Robert Capa invited Freund to join the cooperative agency Magnum Photos but later (1954) dismissed her because her inclusion on the blacklist of the communist-hunting Sen. Joseph McCarthy made Capa fearful for the agency's future in the U.S. Freund's career continued until the mid-1980s, when she gave up photography in favour of another interest—reading. Among the numerous books Freund produced were *James Joyce in Paris: His Final Years* (1965), *Le Monde et ma camera* (1970; *The World in My Camera,* 1974), and *Photographie et société* (1974), and she garnered such awards as the Grand Prix National des Arts. Freund was made an Officer of Arts and Letters in 1982 and chevalier of the Legion of Honour in 1983.

Friedrich, Götz, German opera director and administrator (b. Aug. 4, 1930, Naumburg, Ger.—d. Dec. 12, 2000, Berlin, Ger.), combined creative passion, innovation, and artistic perfectionism as principal director (1972–81) at the Hamburg Staatsoper; principal producer (1977–81) at London's Royal Opera House, Covent Garden; and general manager and principal director (from 1981) of the Deutsche Oper Berlin. Friedrich began his career in 1953 as assistant to Walter Felsenstein at the Komische Oper in East Berlin and rose to director of production there in 1968. In 1972 he defected to West Germany. While simultaneously holding posts in Hamburg and London, Friedrich also directed operas throughout Western Europe and the U.S., including productions of Richard Wagner's *Tannhäuser* and *Parsifal* at the Bayreuth Festival and the world premiere of Luciano Berio's *Un re in ascolta* at the Salzburg Festival.

Fryer, Robert, American theatrical and film producer (b. Dec. 18, 1920, Washington, D.C.—d. May 28, 2000, Los Angeles, Calif.), staged some of Broadway's most popular productions from the 1950s to the 1980s. Fryer got his start on Broadway in 1951 as a co-producer, with George Abbott, of *A Tree Grows in Brooklyn.* He went on to produce such hits as *Wonderful Town* (1958), *Sweet Charity* (1966), *Chicago* (1975), and *Merrily We Roll Along* (1981). His Broadway shows won a total of 37 Tony Awards. Fryer also produced a number of well-known films, including *The Prime of Miss Jean Brodie* (1969), *The Boys from Brazil* (1978), and *The Shining* (1980).

Fyodorov, Svyatoslav Nikolayevich, Russian eye surgeon (b. Aug. 8, 1927, Proskurov, Ukrainian S.S.R. [now Khmelnytskyy, Ukraine], U.S.S.R.—d. June 2, 2000, near Moscow, Russia), developed (1974) radial keratotomy, the first surgical procedure to correct myopia using tiny, precise incisions near the cornea of the eye. Although the technique was later supplanted by laser surgery, tens of thousands of patients were operated on at Mikrokhirurgiya Glaza, Fyodorov's eye microsurgery institute in Moscow, and at medical centres throughout the world. Fyodorov, who also developed (1973) a surgical treatment for glaucoma, was elected to the Russian Duma (parliament) in 1995 and ran unsuccessfully for president in 1996.

Patrick Kovarik/AFP Worldwide

Gassman, Vittorio, Italian actor and director (b. Sept. 1, 1922, Genoa, Italy—d. June 29, 2000, Rome, Italy), epitomized the quintessential Italian leading man—"tall, dark, and handsome"—but his conventional good looks sometimes obscured his talent and versatility in both comic and serious roles. Gassman studied at the Academy of Dramatic Art in Rome and made his professional stage debut in 1943. By the time he made his screen debut in 1946, he had appeared in more than 40 productions of classic plays by Shakespeare, Aeschylus, Ibsen, Tennessee Williams, and others. He later formed a traveling repertory theatre company and performed in Europe and South America. Gassman made a brief foray to Hollywood in the 1950s and occasionally worked in English-language movies throughout his career. He was best known, however, for such Italian films as *Riso amaro* (1948; *Bitter Rice*), a powerful melodrama that marked his entry to the international cinema; the comic tour de force *I soliti ignoti* (1958; *Big Deal on Madonna Street*); *La grande guerra* (1959; *The Great War*); and *Il sorpasso* (1962; *The Easy Life,* 1963). In 1975 he won the Cannes Film Festival's award for best actor for *Profumo di donna* (later remade as *Scent of a Woman* [1992] with American actor Al Pacino). Gassman won the Golden Lion award for lifetime achievement at the Venice Film Festival in 1996 and Spain's Prince of Asturias prize in 1997.

Gaucher, Yves, Canadian abstract artist (b. Jan. 3, 1934, Montreal, Que.—d. Sept. 8, 2000, Montreal), was a painter, printmaker, and collagist who was best known for creating massive monochromatic paintings, many of them inspired by atonal music; late in his life a shoulder injury and other health concerns caused him to scale back the size of his works, and he returned to his earlier pursuit of producing collages.

Gault, Henri André Paul Victor, French food critic (b. Nov. 4, 1929, Pacy-sur-Eure, France—d. July 9, 2000, Saint-Sulpice-en-Pareds, France), collaborated with Christian Millau on the *Guide Gault-Millau*, an annual restaurant guide founded in 1969 as a rival for the already well-established Michelin guidebook. In 1973 *Gault-Millau* coined the term *nouvelle cuisine* to describe the lighter, more artistically designed cooking technique that was then challenging classic French haute cuisine, and the two men consistently championed the chefs who specialized in it. Gault, who also wrote other, more specific food guides, became a restaurant consultant after splitting with Millau in 1985.

Gennaro, Peter, American dancer and choreographer (b. Nov. 23, 1919, Metairie, La.—d. Sept. 28, 2000, New York, N.Y.), gained public attention as a member of the trio who danced the Bob Fosse number "Steam Heat" in the Broadway production *The Pajama Game* (1954), sustained that attention with the "Mu Cha Cha" number with Judy Holliday in *Bells Are Ringing* (1956), and went on to further acclaim for his Broadway, television, and film performances and choreography. By the time he was four Gennaro was already winning dance competitions. He pursued dance training throughout his school years, and during World War II, after enlisting in the army and ending up in India as a result of a mix-up, he was recruited into an entertainment group and performed for the troops as a dancer. After the war Gennaro worked briefly at his father's bar but then moved to New York City. There he studied at the American Theater Wing and at the Katherine Dunham School, and in 1947 he secured a job in the chorus of the San Carlo Opera Company. Gennaro's Broadway debut came in 1948 in the chorus of *Make Mine Manhattan.* Dancing roles in such shows as *Kiss Me, Kate* (1948), *Arms and the Girl* (1950), and *Guys and Dolls* (1950) followed, and he also branched out into teaching dance to other professional performers. Gennaro began choreographing shows with the musical *Seventh Heaven* (1955) and in 1956 assisted Jerome Robbins on *West Side Story,* creating most of the "America" number and the Sharks' dance-at-the-gym routines. Later Broadway choreographic efforts included the Pulitzer Prize-winning *Fiorello!* (1959), which garnered him his first Tony Award nomination; *The Unsinkable Molly Brown* (1960), the 1964 movie version of which he also choreographed; *Mr. President* (1962); *Bajour* (1964); *Irene* (1973); and *Annie* (1977), for which he won a Tony. Gennaro amassed extensive television credits in the 1950s and '60s—among them the *Kraft Music Hall, The Ed Sullivan Show, Your Hit Parade,* and *The Steve Allen Show,* on many of which he appeared with the Peter Gennaro Dancers—and between 1974 and 1980 he staged the spectacular shows at New York City's Radio City Music Hall.

Gertz, Elmer, American lawyer, teacher, and writer (b. Sept. 14, 1906, Chicago, Ill.—d. April 27, 2000, Chicago), was a champion of civil rights—working for fairness in access to housing, battling against police brutality, and shepherding a strong bill of rights into the Illinois constitution—and figured prominently in some of the most famous court cases of the second half of the 20th century. Gertz represented such high-profile clients as Nathan Leopold in his quest for parole after he had served over 30 years of a life sentence for the 1924 "thrill" murder of Bobby Franks, Henry Miller in his struggle against censorship of his 1934 novel, *Tropic of Cancer,* after it was accused of being obscene, and Jack Ruby in his bid to have his murder conviction overturned on the grounds that his case had been tainted by pretrial publicity regarding his shooting of Lee Harvey Oswald—the accused assassin of Pres. John F. Kennedy. Gertz was educated at the University of Chicago, earning a bachelor's degree (1928) and a law degree (1930), and practiced law at a prominent Chicago law firm. He came to public attention in 1958 with his successful argument that Leopold had been rehabilitated and deserved parole. In the 1960s, in addition to his victory in the Supreme Court in the Miller case and his gaining Ruby the right to a retrial (Ruby died in jail before he could be retried), Gertz was responsible for another landmark Supreme Court decision—that in murder trials potential jurors could not be excluded solely on the basis of their opposition to the death penalty. Although Gertz was a champion of freedom of the press, he himself became a principal in a notable case in 1969 when a John Birch Society publication accused him of being a communist after he represented a family who sued a Chicago police officer. The Supreme Court's 1983 decision extended to public figures the protection that private citizens enjoyed against attacks on their reputations. With that case, Gertz succeeded in redefining libel law.

Giedroyc, Jerzy, Russian-born Polish editor and publisher (b. July 27, 1906, Minsk, Russia [now in Belarus]—d. Sept. 14, 2000, Paris, France), saw the political value of literature and, while living in Warsaw, founded (1929) the right-wing magazine *Bunt Mlodych* ("The Rebellion of the Young"), which later (1937) became *Polityka.* He left Poland when the Germans invaded (1939), and he eventually settled in Paris, where he founded a publishing company and became (1947) a founding editor of the anticommunist magazine *Kultura;* through these two enterprises he distributed the writings of dissident Polish intellectuals.

Gielgud, Sir (Arthur) John, British actor, producer, and director (b. April 14, 1904, London, Eng.—d. May 21, 2000, near Aylesbury, Buckinghamshire, Eng.), was widely regarded as one of the modern era's finest interpreters of Shakespeare's verse and was renowned for his elegant bearing and for the unsurpassed artistry of his exquisite speaking voice. Along with his contemporaries and frequent costars Ralph Richardson and Laurence Olivier, Gielgud defined Shakespearean acting in the 20th century. The grandnephew of noted British actress Ellen Terry, Gielgud studied at the Royal Academy of Dramatic Art and made his stage debut in 1921. He was 25 when he first appeared in *Hamlet* (1929) at the Old Vic. Critic James Agate singled out Gielgud's performance as the melancholy prince as "the high water mark of English Shakespearean acting in our time." Speaking some of Shakespeare's most beautiful verse as Richard II in his own production of Gordon Daviot's *Richard of Bordeaux* (1933), Gielgud established himself as a West End star. He alternated with Olivier in the roles of Romeo and Mercutio in a celebrated 1935 production of *Romeo and Juliet;* played Lear, Prospero, and Benedick among other Shakespearean parts; performed in classics by Oscar Wilde and Anton Chekhov; and worked as Noël Coward's understudy (an experience he later credited with improving his comic timing). From 1959 he toured extensively with his acclaimed one-man show, *Ages of Man,* in which he performed passages from Shakespeare. He spent much of the 1960s directing, including a 1964 staging of *Hamlet*, starring Richard Burton, and Hugh

HO/Reuters/Archive Photos

O Sullivan Tim/Spooner/Liaison Agency

Shakespearean Sir John Gielgud

Wheeler's comedy *Big Fish, Little Fish,* for which he won a Tony Award as best director in 1961. Gielgud eventually tackled modern theatre, appearing in Edward Albee's *Tiny Alice* (1964) and opposite Richardson in David Storey's *Home* (1970) and Harold Pinter's *No Man's Land* (1975). Gielgud's motion picture career began in 1925 and included acclaimed turns as Cassius in *Julius Caesar* (1953), Clarence in Olivier's *Richard III* (1955), and Henry IV in Orson Welles's *Chimes at Midnight* (1966). After receiving an Academy Award nomination for *Becket* (1964), Gielgud won an Oscar for best supporting actor for his hilarious portrayal of the supercilious butler in *Arthur* (1981). Another comic gem was his performance in the television adaptation of Evelyn Waugh's *Brideshead Revisited* (1982). Gielgud published two autobiographies, *Early Stages* (1939) and *An Actor and His Time* (1979), and two collections of essays, *Stage Directions* (1963) and *Distinguished Company* (1972). His final stage appearance was in Hugh Whitemore's *Best of Friends* in 1988. Three years later he captured his portrayal of Prospero in his last major film, *Prospero's Books.* Gielgud's final performance was in David Mamet's screen version of Samuel Beckett's *Catastrophe* a month before his death. Gielgud was knighted in 1953, made a Companion of Honour in 1977, and named to the Order of Merit in 1996.

Gilruth, Robert Rowe, American aeronautical engineer and administrator (b. Oct. 8, 1913, Nashwauk, Minn.—d. Aug. 17, 2000, Charlottesville, Va.), oversaw the Mercury, Gemini, and Apollo projects and thus had enormous influence on the U.S. manned space program. He was interested in aeronautics and astronomy as a boy and received two degrees, in 1935 and 1936, from the University of Minnesota at Minneapolis in aeronautical engineering. Gilruth also became knowledgeable in materials science, which would later be important in his work in the space program. In 1937 he joined the National Advisory Committee for Aeronautics, the predecessor of the National Aeronautics and Space Administration (NASA), where he did research on the behaviour of vehicles traveling at supersonic speeds and on rocket-powered aircraft. He also helped develop a launch range on the Atlantic coast of Virginia. In 1958 Gilruth was made director of NASA's Space Task Group and given the mandate to develop a manned space program. He oversaw the development of virtually all aspects of Project Mercury, which in 1961 put the first American into space, and then managed the Gemini and Apollo programs, which in 1969 put the first astronaut on the Moon. It was Gilruth who promoted a nondirect method of reaching the Moon by orbiting a spacecraft around it and then lowering a module from the craft to the surface. In 1961 he became the first director of the Manned Spacecraft Center (later the Lyndon B. Johnson Space Center) in Houston, Texas, and he served in that position until 1972 and retired in 1973. Gilruth received many honours, including membership in the National Space Hall of Fame and the President's Award for Distinguished Federal Civilian Service.

Golshiri, Hushang, Iranian writer and political activist (b. 1936/37, Esfahan, Iran—d. June 5, 2000, Tehran, Iran), was a prominent figure in Persian secular literature, but his fiction was banned inside Iran from 1979; his significant works, most of which were smuggled out of Iran and published elsewhere, included *Shazdeye Ehtejab* (1968; *"Prince Ehtejab"*), *Shah-e siyah-pushan* (*King of the Benighted,* 1990), and *Jen-Nameh* (1998; *"The Book of the Genies"*). Golshiri, who was a founding member of the Iranian Writers' Association (IWA), was one of the 134 Iranian writers to sign a 1994 declaration on intellectual freedom. In 1999 Golshiri and the IWA received Erich Maria Remarque awards for their efforts "to promote democracy and human rights."

Goodman, Louis Sanford, American pharmacologist (b. Aug. 27, 1906, Portland, Ore.—d. Nov. 19, 2000, Salt Lake City, Utah), was credited with developing the first effective anticancer chemotherapy. During World War II Goodman had been studying chemical warfare agents when he discovered that nitrogen mustard could be effective in treating cancer. In 1946 he published the first paper on the use of nitrogen mustard as an anticancer drug. Goodman also wrote, with Alfred Gilman, an influential textbook, *The Pharmacological Basis of Therapeutics,* first published in 1941. The textbook was in its ninth edition at the time of Goodman's death.

Gorey, Edward St. John, American illustrator and writer (b. Feb. 22, 1925, Chicago, Ill.—d. April 15, 2000, Hyannis, Mass.), created meticulous black-and-white crosshatched drawings to accompany both other authors' works and his own eerie and macabre yet witty gothic stories, which featured pale, haunted characters facing bizarre fates in bleak settings. He wrote at least 90 books and illustrated some 60 others—many of them under such anagrammatic pseudonyms as Ogdred Weary, Drew Dogyear, Dogear Wryde, and Mrs. Regera Dowdy—as well as designing the opening animated sequence for PBS's *Mystery* program and costumes and sets for the 1977 Broadway production of *Dracula.* He won the 1978 Tony Award for that show's costumes. Gorey took art classes at the Art Institute of Chicago and, following World War II military service, attended Harvard University, graduating in 1950. He worked in Boston illustrating book jackets before moving to New York City, where he worked in Doubleday & Co.'s art department, staying after hours to create his own books. When he could not find a publisher, he started Fantod Press to print them, beginning with *The Unstrung Harp* (1953), and sold them to stores directly. Such works as *The Doubtful Guest* (1957), about a strange penguin-like being that moves into a mansion and shows no sign of leaving, attracted praise from Edmund Wilson in *The New Yorker* magazine in

Gothic illustrator Edward Gorey

AP/Wide World Photos

1959 and led to illustration commissions for Gorey. He continued producing his own works as well, publishing such future classics as *The Hapless Child* (1961), the illustrated alphabet *The Gashlycrumb Tinies* (1962), and *The Wuggly Ump* (1963). Gorey—a fan of ballet, especially dances choreographed by George Balanchine—made it a point to attend every home performance of the New York City Ballet until Balanchine's death in 1983 and featured the ballet in some of his books, among them *The Gilded Bat* (1966) and *The Lavender Leotard* (1973). His works were anthologized in *Amphigorey* (1972), *Amphigorey Too* (1975), and *Amphigorey Also* (1983) and were dramatized in a number of adaptations, including *Gorey Stories* (1978) and *The Vinegar Works* (1989). Gorey moved to Cape Cod, Mass., in the 1980s and, in addition to publishing such works as *The Raging Tide: Or, the Black Doll's Imbroglio* (1987) and *The Headless Bust: A Melancholy Meditation on the False Millennium* (1999), began directing revues based on his works.

Grant, Bernard Alexander Montgomery ("Bernie"), Guyanese-born British politician (b. Feb. 17, 1944, Georgetown, British Guiana [now Guyana]—d. April 8, 2000, London, Eng.), was a firebrand leftist, outspoken trade-union activist, and prominent campaigner for minority rights in his position as a member (1978–88) and the first black leader of a local British council authority (1985–87) and as a backbench Labour Party MP (from 1987).

Greco, José, Italian-born flamenco dancer (b. Dec. 23, 1918, Montorio nei Frentani, Italy—d. Dec. 31, 2000, Lancaster, Pa.), came to be considered the world's greatest Spanish dancer—through appearances onstage, in films, on television, and, between 1952 and 1973, on tours with his troupe, the José Greco Dance Company—and was credited with having helped meld flamenco with traditional ballet. The Spanish government knighted him in 1962.

Greene, Harold Herman (Heinz Gruenhaus), German-born American federal judge (b. February 1923, Frankfurt, Ger.—d. Jan. 29, 2000, Washington, D.C.), presided over the 1983–84 antitrust suit that split telephone giant AT&T into seven regional companies. As a young lawyer, he worked (1957–65) under Attorney General Robert Kennedy in the Department of Justice, helping draft the legislation that eventually became the Civil Rights Act of 1964 and the Voting Rights Act of 1965. He was appointed to the U.S. District Court for the District of Columbia in 1978 by Pres. Jimmy Carter. His ruling in the AT&T case transformed the field of telecommunications by bringing competition to the industry. In 1990 he also presided over former national security adviser John Poindexter's Iran-contra trial, ordering former president Ronald Reagan to testify as a witness—the first time a U.S. president had been compelled to testify in a case that pertained to his own administration.

Groza, Lou ("The Toe"), American professional football player (b. Jan. 25, 1924, Martins Ferry, Ohio—d. Nov. 29, 2000, Middleburgh Heights, Ohio), was regarded as one of football's greatest placekickers. An offensive lineman as well as a placekicker, he played with the Cleveland Browns of the All-America Football Conference and, subsequently, of the National Football League, from 1946 to 1967. One of the most memorable moments in NFL history came in 1950 when Groza kicked a 16-yd field goal with 28 sec left in the NFL championship game to give the Browns a 30–28 victory over the Los Angeles Rams. Groza retired with 1,349 NFL points—a franchise record that remained unbroken at the time of his death. In 1974 he was inducted into the Pro Football Hall of Fame.

Flamenco dancer extraordinaire José Greco

Hulton-Deutsch Collection/Corbis

Guinness, Sir Alec (Alec Guinness de Cuffe), British actor (b. April 2, 1914, Mary- lebone, London, Eng —d. Aug. 5, 2000, Midhurst, West Sussex, Eng.), was one of the 20th century's best-known, most distinguished, and most versatile stage and screen performers. Although his style was low-key and economical—he so disappeared into his characters that he was often unrecognized in public—he had a quiet intensity that was all the more powerful for being unostentatious and that thereby aided him in inhabiting his characters. Guinness had an impoverished childhood and never knew who his father was. After leaving school at the age of 18, he took a job at a London advertising agency. At the same time, as he had enjoyed the acting he had done in school, he began taking acting lessons. Guinness made his professional stage debut in *Libel!* (1934) in a nonspeaking part and soon thereafter was cast in three small parts in *Queer Cargo* (1934) and then as Osric and the Third Player in John Gielgud's (*q.v.*) production of *Hamlet*. That year he also made his film debut as an extra in *Evensong*. He continued working with Gielgud and also performed with Tyrone Guthrie. After service in the Royal Navy during World War II, Guinness resumed his stage career and pursued film work, finding success as two Charles Dickens characters, Herbert Pocket in David Lean's *Great Expectations* (1946) and Fagin in Lean's *Oliver Twist* (1948). In 1949 he began his association with the Ealing Studios comedies that gained him an international following. In his first Ealing film, *Kind Hearts and Coronets,* he played eight members of a family successively—and amusingly—"done in" by a fortune-seeking relative. Other Ealing comedies included *The Lavender Hill Mob* (1951), *The Man in the White Suit* (1951), and *The Ladykillers* (1955). Guinness returned to Lean for *The Bridge on the River Kwai* (1957), for which he was rewarded with a best actor Academy Award, and further collaborated with him on *Lawrence of Arabia* (1962), *Doctor Zhivago* (1965), and *A Passage to India* (1984). Others of his best films were *The Horse's Mouth* (1958) and *Tunes of Glory* (1960), and in 1977 came one of his most famous—and possibly his least favourite—roles, Obi-Wan Kenobi in *Star Wars,* a role he reprised in the following two films of that series. Throughout the years Guinness continued to perform on stage and also triumphed on television as George Smiley in two miniseries based on John le Carré's works, *Tinker, Tailor, Soldier, Spy* (1979) and *Smiley's People* (1982), and in 1987 he returned to Dickens for another notable screen role, William Dorrit in *Little Dorrit.* In 1980 Guinness was awarded a second Oscar, an honorary one for his contribution to the art of screen acting. He recorded his memories in his books *Blessings in Disguise* (1985), *My Name Escapes Me: The Diary of a Retiring Actor* (1996), and *A Positively Last Appearance* (1999). Guinness was made CBE in 1955, was knighted in 1959, and was named a Companion of Honour in 1994.

Lynn Goldsmith/Corbis

Gulda, Friedrich, Austrian pianist and composer (b. May 16, 1930, Vienna, Austria—d. Jan. 27, 2000, Weissenbach, Austria), was noted for his renditions of the classical repertoire (including Bach, Beethoven, Mozart, Schubert, and Debussy), his improvisatory jazz interpretations, and his eccentricities, which included jazz improvisations in the middle of classical pieces and the release in March 1999 of his own obituary so that he could perform at a "resurrection party."

Gwyn, Sandra, Canadian journalist (b. May 17, 1935, St. John's, Nfd.—d. May 26, 2000, Toronto, Ont.), passionately championed her native province of Newfoundland in writings for *Saturday Night* magazine that heralded the work of its sons and daughters; Gwyn also gained critical acclaim as a social historian with two insightful books: *The Private Capital: Ambition and Love in the Age of Macdonald and Laurier* (1984), for which she won the 1984 Governor General's Award for nonfiction, and *Tapestry of War: A Private View of Canadians in the Great War* (1992). On her last birthday, Gwyn was presented with the Order of Canada.

Gyngell, Bruce, Australian-born television executive (b. July 8, 1929, Melbourne, Australia—d. Sept. 7, 2000, London, Eng.), had a 50-year career that took him from being the first face seen on Australian TV to being managing director of three British ITV franchises, one of which—the breakfast channel TV-am—he turned from impending bankruptcy in 1984 into one of the world's most profitable.

Halberstam, Solomon ("Shlomo"), Polish-born American religious leader (b. 1907, Bobowa, Pol.—d. Aug. 2, 2000, New York, N.Y.), emigrated in the late 1940s to New York, where in Borough Park, a section of Brooklyn, he became the leader of the Bobov sect, a Hasidic group whose numbers had been greatly reduced by the Holocaust. Halberstam's father, Ben Zion, had led the Bobovers in Poland before he perished in a death camp. Halberstam lost most of his family in the Holocaust, including his wife, but managed to survive together with a son. Though he briefly lost his faith, Grand Rabbi Halberstam had a charismatic personality, and he inspired others to join him in reestablishing the community; like his father, he enjoyed singing and dancing, and the latter was showcased in the documentary *A Life Apart: Hasidism in America* (1997). Besides establishing the Hasidic centre in Brooklyn, Halberstam founded a settlement in Bat Yam, Israel, home to some 100 families. Halberstam, who was fond of using parables or maxims in his teachings, collected his discourses in such periodicals as *Shaarei Zion* (1960), *Etz Havvim* (1965), and *Kerem Shlomo* (1978). In the two-volume *Kedushat Zion* (1967 and 1976) he collected the discourses of his father.

Hall, Sir Arnold Alexander, British aeronautical engineer and administrator (b. April 23, 1915, Liverpool, Eng.—d. Jan. 9, 2000, Dorney, Berkshire, Eng.), was instrumental in determining the cause of several deadly crashes (1953–54) of the de Havilland Comet 1 and subsequently correcting design flaws in the aircraft, which flew British Overseas Airways Corp.'s first regular scheduled transatlantic jet service in 1958. Hall joined the powerful aircraft manufacturer Hawker Siddeley Group PLC in 1955 and succeeded Sir Thomas Sopwith as chairman (1967–86); in the 1970s he allied Hawker Siddeley with France and Germany in the construction of Airbus aircraft, despite official British government misgivings about the project. Hall was made a fellow of the Royal Society in 1953 and was knighted in 1954.

Hall, Gus (Arvo Kusta Halberg), American political organizer (b. Oct. 8, 1910, Iron, Minn.—d. Oct. 13, 2000, New York, N.Y.), was for over 40 years the leader of the Communist Party of the United States of America. Although his activities led to his imprisonment for much of the 1950s, he later—in the four elections from 1972 to 1984—was his party's candidate for the U.S. presidency. Hall was the son of members of the militant Industrial Workers of the World, and he had their radical ideas reinforced by the harsh life he experienced while working in a logging camp, the first job he held after leaving school following eighth grade. His father had joined the Communist Party at its inception in 1919 and in 1927 recruited Hall. Hall studied at the V.I. Lenin Institute (renamed the Marx-Engels-Lenin Institute) in Moscow from 1931 to 1933. After returning to the U.S., he engaged in union organizing activities, occasionally getting arrested for his zealous efforts, and in 1937 he became a full-time party officer. Following World War II navy service, Hall joined the party's national executive board. In 1949 he and 10 other party leaders were convicted of conspiring to overthrow the government by force and were sentenced to five years' imprisonment. Free on bail during an appeal, Hall and three others fled to Mexico when the appeal was rejected in 1951. Their freedom lasted only three months, however, and Hall's sentence was extended; he was incarcerated in the Leavenworth, Kan., federal penitentiary until 1957. Upon his release, Hall—having gained hero status—began a quest for the party's leadership position, to which he was elected in 1959. He began making annual trips to Moscow, which he continued until the end of Soviet communism, and was awarded the U.S.S.R.'s highest medal, the Order of Lenin. Although the party's adherence to its faith in Soviet-style communism kept it apart from the new left and its membership dwindled steadily, Hall never wavered from his political beliefs and continued to consider the downfall of capitalism inevitable.

Hamilton, William Donald ("Bill") British evolutionary biologist (b. Aug. 1, 1936, Cairo, Egypt—d. March 7, 2000, Oxford, Eng.), was one of the most influential evolutionary biologists and a leader of the so-called second Darwinian revolution—the attempt by 20th-century scientists to unify the principles of natural selection with a modern understanding of genetics. Hamilton became a skilled field naturalist at an early age. After completing undergraduate work at the University of Cambridge, he pursued a Ph.D. in genetics, enrolling jointly at University College, London, and the London School of Economics and Political Science. In 1964, while still a graduate student, Hamilton published a series of papers that laid the foundation for the field of sociobiology. In these papers, he explained why many species of animals—in apparent opposition to the struggle for the survival of the fittest—display altruistic behaviour. His theory, known as kin selection, stated that animals make altruistic self-sacrifices, usually for the benefit of relatives, in order to help propagate their own genes and, thus, their behaviour is understandable from a Darwinian perspective. Hamilton later tackled the question of why most species reproduce sexually rather than asexually; his controversial conclusion was that sexual reproduction, by allowing organisms to adapt more rapidly, increased their chances of fending off parasites. From 1964 to 1977 Hamilton was a lecturer at Imperial College, London, and from 1978 to 1984 he was professor of evolutionary biology at the University of Michigan at Ann Arbor. Thereafter he served as Royal Society Research Professor at the University of Oxford. Fond of fieldwork, he made many trips to South America and Africa to collect insect specimens. He died of complications from malaria, which he had contracted during an expedition to the Congo Basin.

Harsanyi, John Charles, Hungarian-born American economist and philosopher (b. May 29, 1920, Budapest, Hung.—d. Aug. 9, 2000, Berkeley, Calif.), shared the 1994 Nobel Memorial Prize in Economic Sciences for his work in game theory. As a secondary school student, he won a national prize in mathematics, but he studied pharmacology so that he could help in his father's business. He narrowly escaped being sent to a forced-labour camp by the Nazis in 1944. After World War II he returned to the Technical University of Budapest, where he earned a doctorate in philosophy in 1947. Harsanyi taught sociology at the university for a year but was dismissed because of his anti-Marxist views. In 1950 he escaped to Austria and then went to Australia, where in 1953 he received an M.A. in economics from the University of Sydney. In 1954 he became a lecturer at the University of Queensland in Brisbane, and in 1956 he entered Stanford University, where he gained a Ph.D. in 1959. After teaching at the Australian National University in Canberra and at Wayne State University in Detroit, in 1964 he became a

left: Herwig Prammer Reuters/Corbis; right: Jane Scherr Photography

professor in the business school at the University of California, Berkeley, and in 1966 he became professor of economics. He built on the work of John F. Nash, one of his fellow recipients of the Nobel Prize, by extending game theory so that it could be applied to situations in which people had little knowledge of their competitors' intentions. With Reinhard Selten, the third recipient of the prize, he published *A General Theory of Equilibrium Selection in Games* (1988). Other books included *Essays on Ethics, Social Behavior and Scientific Explanation* (1976) and *Papers in Game Theory* (1982). He was a member of the American Academy of Arts and Sciences.

Hartling, Poul, Danish politician and diplomat (b. Aug. 14, 1914, Copenhagen, Den.—d. April 30, 2000, Copenhagen), was the longtime leader of the Danish Liberal Party, foreign minister (1968–71), and prime minister (1973–75) of Denmark before leaving politics to serve two terms as United Nations High Commissioner for Refugees (1978–85); Hartling accepted the Nobel Prize for Peace on behalf of the Office of the United Nations High Commissioner for Refugees in 1981.

Hartshorne, Charles, U.S. philosopher and theologian (b. June 5, 1897, Kittanning, Pa.—d. Oct. 10, 2000, Austin, Texas), developed what was called process philosophy, in which reality was held to be endless change. In this system God was conceived of not as an omnipotent, omniscient creator, as in traditional Judeo-Christian thought, but rather as a part of the evolving cosmos and as a being who responded to the changes that were taking place. Hartshorne entered Haverford (Pa.) College in 1915 but left in 1917 to join the Army Medical Corps. He took a supply of philosophy books with him to the front in France. After World War I he entered Harvard University, earning B.A. (1921), M.A. (1922), and Ph.D. (1923) degrees, and he then studied in Germany with the philosopher Martin Heidegger. Among his teachers at Harvard was Alfred North Whitehead, whose thought was an influence on Hartshorne's own philosophical system. He was also influenced by the thought of the American philosopher Charles Sanders Peirce, whose papers he edited with Paul Weiss. From 1928 to 1955 Hartshorne taught philosophy and theology at the University of Chicago and from 1955 to 1962 at Emory University, Atlanta, Ga. He then taught at the University of Texas at Austin until his retirement in 1976. He also held short-term appointments at a number of other universities. Among his more than 20 books were *The Philosophy and Psychology of Sensation* (1934), *Beyond Humanism* (1937), *The Divine Relativity* (1948), *Reality as Social Process* (1953), *The Logic of Perfection* (1962), *Omnipotence and Other Theological Mistakes* (1983), and *Creativity in American Philosophy* (1984). His 1973 book, *Born to Sing,* demonstrated his expertise in ornithology. He received a number of honorary degrees and served (1948–49) as president of the American Philosophical Association.

Has, Wojciech Jerzy, Polish filmmaker (b. April 1, 1925, Krakow, Pol.—d. Oct. 3, 2000, Lodz, Pol.), won an international following with his surrealist epic *The Saragossa Manuscript* (1964). After graduating from the Krakow Film Institute in 1946, Has spent 10 years as a documentary filmmaker before making his first feature film, *The Noose* (1958). One of his later films, *The Sandglass* (1973), won the Jury Prize at Cannes. He served as director of the Lodz Film School from 1990 to 1996.

Hawkins, Screamin' Jay (Jalacy J. Hawkins), American blues singer (b. July 18, 1929, Cleveland, Ohio—d. Feb. 12, 2000, Neuilly-sur-Seine, France), was acclaimed as much for his outrageous onstage antics and the groans, grunts, and screams that accompanied his music as for the songs themselves, the most famous of which was "I Put a Spell on You"; he also appeared in the films *Mystery Train* (1989), *A Rage in Harlem* (1991), and others, and in 1998 the Rhythm & Blues Foundation honoured him with its Pioneer Award.

Haza, Ofra, Israeli singer (b. Nov. 19, 1957, Tel Aviv, Israel—d. Feb. 23, 2000, Tel Aviv), achieved international stardom by setting traditional Jewish-Yemenite song lyrics to Western-style disco-pop arrangements. Discovered at the age of 12 by Bezalel Aloni, who became her manager, Haza recorded a number of albums that enjoyed gold and platinum sales in Israel before releasing her first international album, *Yemenite Songs,* in 1985. After the album topped the charts in Europe and Asia, it was released to wide acclaim in the U.S. in 1987, and Haza toured the U.S. the following year. Onstage she was energetic and colourful, often donning exotic Middle Eastern costumes for performances. She was a guest vocalist on many European and American records, including ones by Paula Abdul and Thomas Dolby. Her album *Shaday* won the New Music Award for International Album of the Year in 1989, and her 1992 album *Kirya,* on which Lou Reed and Iggy Pop made guest appearances, was nominated for a Grammy Award. In 1994 Haza gave a memorable performance at the Nobel Peace Prize ceremony in Oslo for Yitzhak Rabin, Shimon Peres, and Yasir Arafat. She again attracted attention in 1998 when she sang the theme song for the hit animated film *The Prince of Egypt.* During her career she made a total of 16 gold or platinum albums. Her death set off days of national mourning in Israel. It was later reported that Haza had died of complications from AIDS.

Carraro/Liaison Agency

Israeli popular singer Ofra Haza

Hearst, Randolph Apperson, American publishing executive (b. Dec. 2, 1915, New York, N.Y.—d. Dec. 18, 2000, New York), was the last surviving son of newspaper tycoon William Randolph Hearst and served the family's media interests for more than 30 years, including acting as chairman of the board from 1973 to 1996, but found himself most in the public eye when his daughter, Patricia Hearst, was kidnapped (1974) by the Symbionese Liberation Army guerrilla group, subsequently participated in a bank robbery the group staged, and was later captured, tried, and imprisoned.

Hébert, Anne, Canadian novelist, poet, and playwright (b. Aug. 1, 1916, Ste-Catherine-de-Fossambault, Que.—d. Jan. 22, 2000, Montreal, Que.), spent much of her career in France crafting powerful verse and novels that were marked by an extreme violence and evoked the loneliness and isolation of her adolescence in Quebec that were the result of spells of scarlet fever, pleurisy, and appendicitis. Hébert's first volume of poetry, *Les Songes en équilibre,* appeared in 1942 and was followed by *Le Tombeau des rois* (1953) and *Mystère de la parole* (1960), the latter two of which showed her progression into a mature poet. Her eight novels, seven of which were set in the rural Quebec of her childhood, penetrated the human psyche and explored difficulties of loving and the violence that seems to be an inevitable part of the human condition. Hébert's first book of prose, *Le Torrent* (1950), was a collection of tales that centred on a young boy and his punitive relationship with his mother; though shocking in nature, it became a classic. Many of her other works presented a child or an adolescent as the central figure and featured the wildflowers, birds, rivers, and isolated farmhouses that were rooted in her childhood. *Kamouraska* (1970; filmed in 1973 by Claude Jutra), considered the best of her Quebec-based novels, was a tightly woven masterpiece of suspense and won France's Prix de Libraires. Other novels included *Les Enfants du sabbat* (1975), a tale of sorcery; *Héloïse* (1980), a horror story about ghost vampires in the Paris subway; *Les Fous de Bassan* (1982; winner of France's Prix Fémina), about the disappearance and murder of two teenage girls; and *Un Habit de lumière* (1999), her last. Hébert was honoured with the Governor General's Award three times (1960, 1975, and 1992) and was the recipient of the Molson Prize in 1967. In 1997 she returned from France to reside in Montreal.

Hejduk, John Quentin, American architect and educator (b. July 19, 1929, New York, N.Y. —d. July 3, 2000, New York), attracted attention with austere designs that were often intended to evoke dark psychological states or to explore the relationship between public and private space. After studying at the Cooper Union for the Advancement of Science and Art, New York City, and the University of Cincinnati, Ohio, Hejduk earned his M.A. from Harvard University's Graduate School of Design in 1953. He taught briefly at the University of Texas at Austin before returning to New York City in 1956 to work for a number of leading architects, including I.M. Pei. Hejduk began teaching at Cooper Union in 1964; in 1975 he became a dean of the school, a position he held until his retirement in 2000. Among his notable works were the Berlin Tower and Garden Apartments (1988) and his redesign of Cooper Union's Foundation Building (1975). The bulk of Hejduk's work, however, consisted of theoretical projects, which he executed in the form of intricate, poetic drawings. Hejduk's drawings were collected in 21 published books, including *Mask of Medusa: Works 1947–1983* (1985).

Henning, Douglas James ("Doug"), Canadian magician (b. May 3, 1947, Winnipeg, Man.— d. Feb. 7, 2000, Los Angeles, Calif.), helped revive interest in magic with his traveling act and a series of Broadway shows and television specials in the 1970s and early '80s. He was a master magician who reprised many of the sensational escape acts of Harry Houdini, his idol. Henning also brought a lighthearted approach to his craft, interjecting comedy into shows he typically performed while wearing a tie-dyed T-shirt and jumpsuit. *The Magic Show,* a musical in which Henning mixed magic with rock music, opened on Broadway in 1974 and ran for four years. He returned to Broadway in the musical *Merlin* (1983) and a solo show, *Doug Henning and His World of Magic* (1984). His television specials, which aired yearly from 1975 to 1982, garnered one Emmy Award and seven Emmy nominations. He quit magic in the mid-1980s to devote himself to transcendental meditation.

Gary Bernstein/Liaison Agency

Master illusionist Doug Henning

Henri, Adrian Maurice, British poet and artist (b. April 10, 1932, Birkenhead, Cheshire [now Merseyside], Eng.—d. Dec. 20, 2000, Liverpool, Eng.), was one of the three "Merseybeat" poets who gained renown when their works were published in *The Mersey Sound* (1967), which remained a best-seller. He was primarily a painter, however, and he also led the Liverpool Scene rock and poetry band, taught, and wrote children's books and stage and television plays.

Herling-Grudzinski, Gustaw, Polish-born writer (b. May 20, 1919, Kielce, Pol.—d. July 4, 2000, Naples, Italy), wrote novels, short stories, diaries, and critical essays but was best known for *Inny Swiat* (1953; first published in London in English as *A World Apart* in 1951), a stirring memoir of the time he spent as a prisoner in a Soviet labour camp during 1940–42. Herling-Grudzinski, who also published under the name Gustaw Herling, went into self-exile after World War II and later co-founded *Kultura,* a Polish-language cultural periodical for Polish émigrés.

Hernández, Amalia, Mexican folk dancer and choreographer (b. 1917, Mexico City, Mex.—d. Nov. 4, 2000, Mexico City), was founder of the internationally renowned Ballet Folklórico de México. Although she was trained in classical ballet, Hernández decided to specialize in native Mexican dance. She founded the Ballet Folklórico in 1952, and under her leadership the company became the largest and most widely respected Mexican dance company in the world. She choreographed more than 40 ballets that incorporated local dance traditions from some 60 regions of Mexico.

Hinton, Milton John, American jazz artist and photographer (b. June 23, 1910, Vicksburg, Miss.—d. Dec. 19, 2000, Queens, N.Y.), was among the great jazz bassists during a career that lasted nearly 70 years; he began performing in groups before the advent of swing, starred in Cab Calloway's popular big band, and eventually became a marathon man in recording studios, playing on an estimated 600 jazz albums as well as in another 600 nonjazz sessions. Hinton grew up in Chicago, where he began studying violin at Wendell Phillips High School, a hotbed of young jazz talent; he then played bass in Chicago bands and toured with violinist Eddie South before joining Calloway in 1936. Hinton's full tone and rhythmic vigour propelled the powerful Calloway big band and Calloway's small groups until 1951; at the height of the swing era Hinton also appeared on all-star recordings with Billie Holiday and Lionel Hampton, among others. Hinton later played with Louis Armstrong's All-Stars and with Count Basie before becoming one of the first black musicians in a television network orchestra; in 1954 comedian Jackie Gleason insisted on Hinton for his weekly CBS show. That position led, in turn, to Hinton's playing in a multitude of recording sessions—often three sessions a day—for his swing, harmonic sophistication, and refined sensitivity led him to adapt quickly to the differing demands of Dixieland, swing, bop, blues, and popular music. When the New York studio scene declined in the 1960s, he began touring internationally to jazz clubs and festivals and with stars such as Pearl Bailey, Barbra Streisand, and Bing Crosby. He also taught in New York City's Hunter and Baruch colleges and conducted interviews with historic jazz figures for the National Endowment for the Arts oral-history program. During most of his musical career he was an exceptional photographer as well, and hundreds of his candid pictures of jazz musicians were published in *Bass Line* (1988), his vivid autobiography, and in the photo collection *OverTime* (1991); both were completed in collaboration with David G. Berger, Hinton's former student.

Hirst, Ivan, British army officer (b. March 1, 1916, Saddleworth, Yorkshire, Eng.—d. March 10, 2000, Marsden, West Yorkshire, Eng.), was credited with resurrecting post-World War II German heavy industry when he retooled Volkswagen's bombed-out factory in Wolfsburg, Ger., convinced the British military to order 20,000 vehicles for local use, and began producing the homely, noisy, little "people's car" that came to be known as the Beetle.

Holt, Bertha Marian, American children's advocate (b. Feb. 5, 1904, Des Moines, Iowa—d. July 24, 2000, Creswell, Ore.), together with her husband, Harry, founded Holt International Children's Services, a Eugene, Ore.-based agency that specialized in international adoptions. After having six children of their own, the Holts were deeply moved by a film depicting abandoned Amerasian children in South Korean orphanages. The Baptist couple, believing that these orphans were the responsibility of Americans, decided to adopt eight Korean children. As a result of their efforts to facilitate foreign adoptions, the U.S. Congress passed the 1955 Bill for Relief of Certain War Orphans. This paved the way for the Holts to adopt four boys and four girls from South Korea and to place more than 30,000 children from 15 countries in American homes. Even after the death in 1964 of her husband, "Grandma" Holt remained committed to the agency's mission. She traveled extensively, worked to improve conditions in orphanages, and petitioned other countries to establish adoption programs. She was named National Mother of the Year in 1966 by Pres. Lyndon B. Johnson, received South Korea's Order of Civil Merit, Mugunghwa Medal, in 1995, and was awarded the Kiwanis World Service Medal in 2000.

Homme, Robert, American-born Canadian television personality (b. 1919? Stoughton, Wis.—d. May 2, 2000, Grafton, Ont.), delighted children and adults alike as the star of the long-running Canadian television show *The Friendly Giant* (1958–85), which first aired in the U.S. Homme's brainchild offered children

15 minutes of entertainment centred on a single theme, employing a book or music, or both. His low-key style was enhanced by his two sidekicks: hand puppets Rusty the Rooster and Jerome the Giraffe. In 1998 Homme was awarded the Order of Canada.

Hooper, Fred William, American thoroughbred horse owner and breeder (b. Oct. 6, 1897, Cleveland, Ga.—d. Aug. 4, 2000, Ocala, Fla.), was the indomitable head for 38 years of the Montgomery, Ala.-based Hooper Construction Co., one of the major contractors in the Southeast, and used his wealth from that enterprise to establish Hooper Farms, which, in addition to developing at that time the largest herd of purebred Hereford cattle in the nation, bred or raced more than 100 thoroughbred winners of stake races. The pinnacle of Hooper's horse-racing career came in 1945, when the first thoroughbred he purchased, Hoop Jr., convincingly won the Kentucky Derby. In 1966 Hooper retired from construction and relocated his horse and cattle farm to Ocala. Besides serving as a founder and president of the Florida Thoroughbred Breeders' and Owners' Association, he was one of the first proprietors to import Latin American jockeys, notably such inductees into the Racing Hall of Fame as Jorge Velásquez and Laffit Pincay, Jr. Hooper was the recipient of Eclipse Awards for outstanding breeder in 1975 and 1982 and of an Eclipse Award of Merit in 1991, the highest honour in thoroughbred racing.

Hope, A(lec) D(erwent), Australian poet, writer, and teacher (b. July 21, 1907, Cooma, N.S.W., Australia—d. July 13, 2000, Canberra, Australia), was considered by many to have been nonpareil among Australian poets of his generation. Combining classical form with modernist, often sexually frank content, Hope created rich and powerful verse that inspired moral disgust in some and awe in others. Although Hope had written verse throughout his life, his first collection of poems, *The Wandering Islands* (1955), was not published until he was 48 years old. Other volumes followed, and in the late 1960s Hope retired from a distinguished academic career in which he had played an instrumental role in the creation of the country's first degree program in Australian literature. Hope was also known for his thoughtful essays and unmercifully harsh literary critiques, both of which were collected in part in *The Cave and the Spring* (1965), *A Midsummer Eve's Dream* (1970), and *Native Companions* (1974). The recipient of numerous awards and recognitions, Hope was made an OBE in 1972 and a Companion of the Order of Australia in 1981.

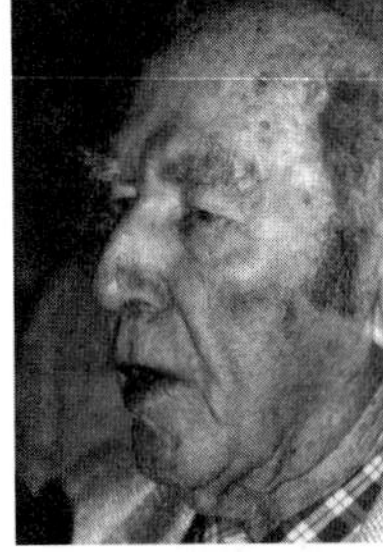
ANU Photography

Hope, Claude, American horticulturist (b. May 10, 1907, Sweetwater, Texas—d. July 14, 2000, Dulce Nombre de Jesús, Costa Rica), transformed North American gardens with the introduction of impatiens, flowering annuals that flourished in shady conditions and later became the number one bedding plant in the U.S. Hope discovered the plants in Costa Rica, where he found them growing wild and spindly. Following years of breeding and hybridizing, he was successful in the 1960s in producing compact plants with profuse blooms. At the time of his death, there were some 900 species of impatiens. Hope first became enamoured with Costa Rica during a brief stint there while serving in the army in World War II. After the war Hope made his home in Costa Rica and established the PanAmerican Seed Co. In 1953 he founded Linda Vista, S.A., which became one of the world's largest flower-seed producers.

Hovhaness, Alan, American composer (b. March 8, 1911, Somerville, Mass.—d. June 21, 2000, Seattle, Wash.), combined Western and Eastern elements to create music that was a synthesis of the earthly and the mystical and spiritual. His music, which often employed unusual instruments, was lyrical and frequently characterized by complex rhythms. The emphasis was on melody rather than complex harmony or development, and the music sometimes included controlled improvisation, what the composer called "Spirit Murmur." It stood outside the mainstream, and some critics called it simple and repetitious; however, many listeners found the music accessible, and it was widely recorded. Hovhaness, who was the son of an Armenian father and a Scottish mother, was born Alan Vaness Chakmakjian, but he changed his name to honour his maternal grandfather. Using his own system of notation, he began composing at the age of four. He attended Tufts University (1929–32), Medford, Mass., and the New England Conservatory of Music (1932–34), Boston, and he later studied with Bohuslav Martinu. From 1948 to 1951 Hovhaness taught at the Boston Conservatory of Music. He became interested in Armenian religious music, which led to explorations of other Middle Eastern and Asian music, including that of India, where he went in 1959 on a Fulbright fellowship. In 1966 he became composer in residence with the Seattle (Wash.) Symphony Orchestra. He composed an estimated 500 works in addition to the 1,000 or more early pieces he destroyed in 1943. His compositions included operas and ballets, piano pieces, chamber works, and orchestral pieces, including 67 symphonies and works for various combinations of voices and instruments with orchestra. Among his best-known works were the piano concerto *Lousadzak* (1944; "The Coming of Light"), Symphony no. 2 (1955; *Mysterious Mountain*), and Symphony no. 6 (1959; *Celestial Gate*). The orchestral work *And God Created Great Whales* (1970) included taped sounds of humpback whales.

Howard, Jean (Ernestine Hill), American actress and celebrity photographer (b. Oct. 13, 1910, Longview, Texas—d. March 20, 2000, Beverly Hills, Calif.), was an actress in films of the 1930s and '40s and later became a prominent socialite and a noted photographer of Hollywood's glamour set. She started in show business as a chorus girl, appearing in Florenz Ziegfeld's Broadway musical *Whoopee* in 1930 and Ziegfeld's last *Follies* (1931). A screen test led to a Metro-Goldwyn-Mayer contract and roles in such movies as *The Prizefighter and the Lady* (1933), *Broadway to Hollywood* (1933), and *Claudia* (1943). After her marriage to film producer Charles K. Feldman in 1934, Howard increasingly devoted her time and attention to hosting parties, where she snapped pictures of the famous stars who regularly attended, including Marlene Dietrich, Tyrone Power, Clark Gable, and Marilyn Monroe. In the 1950s a few of her photos appeared in the magazines *Life* and *Vogue*. She later compiled her photos into two highly praised picture books, *Jean Howard's Hollywood: A Photo Memoir* (1989) and *Travels with Cole Porter* (1991).

Hundertwasser, Friedensreich (Friedrich Stowasser), Austrian artist and architect (b. Dec. 15, 1928, Vienna, Austria—d. Feb. 19, 2000, on board the *Queen Elizabeth II* at sea), substituted asymmetry, undulating swirls, and labyrinthine spirals for straight vertical and horizontal lines, which he asserted were "the rotten foundation of our doomed civilisation." He incorporated bright, contrasting colours, elaborate ornamentation, asymmetrical, organic forms, and natural vegetation in both his artwork and his buildings, notably the Hundertwasserhaus, a residential block in Vienna that opened in 1986. Hundertwasser, who expressed his unconventional views in the 1958 "Mouldiness Manifesto," was admitted to the Art Club of Vienna in 1951 and awarded the Austrian State Prize in 1980.

Ingrid (Princess Ingrid Victoria Sofia Louise Margareta), Swedish-born Danish royal (b. March 28, 1910, Stockholm, Swed.—d. Nov. 7, 2000, Fredensborg, Den.), was queen of Denmark from 1947 to 1972, after which she was known as Queen Mother Ingrid. Ingrid was the only daughter of King Gustaf VI Adolf of Sweden. In 1935 she married Crown Prince Frederik, who 12 years later ascended the Danish throne as King Frederik IX. Ingrid's casual style helped endear her to the Danish public, and she was highly popular as queen. After her husband died in 1972 and her eldest daughter, Margrethe, became queen, Ingrid remained visible in the public eye. At the time of her death, she was a patron to some 40 social welfare organizations.

Ioanna, Queen (Giovanna Elisabetta Antonia Romana Maria), Bulgarian royal (b. Nov. 13, 1907, Rome, Italy—d. Feb. 26, 2000, Estoril, Port.), as the daughter of the last king of Italy, Victor Emmanuel III; the wife of King Boris III of Bulgaria; and the mother of Bulgaria's last king, Simeon II, was at the centre of regional politics during the 1930s and '40s. Although her marriage to King Boris was attended by several Fascist government ministers, including Benito Mussolini, Ioanna opposed Bulgaria's official support of Nazi Germany

Bettmann/Corbis

Queen Ioanna with her husband King Boris III of Bulgaria and their children Prince Simeon and Princess Marie-Louise

and reportedly helped many Bulgarian Jews escape to safety. She fled into exile with her two children in 1946, three years after the death of her husband, who was rumoured to have been poisoned during a visit to Germany.

Jack, Beau (Sidney Walker), American boxer (b. April 1, 1921, Augusta, Ga.—d. Feb. 9, 2000, Miami, Fla.), was twice world lightweight champion (1942, 1943) and was one of the main attractions at Madison Square Garden in New York City during the 1940s. A shoeshine boy in his youth, he got his first taste of boxing by participating in Southern "battle royals"—an outlawed form of boxing in which black fighters fought blindfolded in a ring before white audiences. He made his professional debut in 1940. A relentless puncher with extraordinary stamina, he first captured the world lightweight title with a three-round knockout of Tippy Larkin at the Garden in December 1942. He lost to Bob Montgomery in May 1943 but avenged the defeat in a return bout in November 1943. In all, Jack headlined boxing events at the Garden a total of 21 times, more than any other fighter of his era. Financially impoverished in later life, he settled in Miami, where he returned to shining shoes and tutored boxers at the famed Fifth Street Gym. He also became an outspoken advocate of a pension plan for boxers.

Jafri, Ali Sardar, Indian poet (b. Nov. 29, 1913, Balrampur, Uttar Pradesh, India—d. Aug. 1, 2000, Mumbai [Bombay], India), crafted progressive Urdu-language verse that expressed both his vehement anti-imperialist sentiments and his passion for social justice and religious tolerance. Jafri, whose many honours included the Jnanpith Award in 1998, published several volumes of poetry, as well as short stories, autobiographical essays, translations, literary criticism, and two plays. He also produced documentary films for television and the cinema.

Jandl, Ernst, Austrian poet (b. Aug. 1, 1925, Vienna, Austria—d. June 9, 2000, Vienna), crafted "sound poetry" that relied on linguistic experimentation, word fragmentation, surrealist elements, and sardonic humour to express his anti-Nazi sentiments as well as his profound personal pessimism. Jandl was often linked with the Vienna Group, whose concrete poetry employed graphic patterns and other typographical elements to convey meaning. His best-known works included the volume *Laut und Luise* (1966) and the 1962 poem "Heldenplatz."

Ji Pengfei, Chinese diplomat (b. 1910, Linyi, Shanxi province, China—d. Feb. 10, 2000, Beijing, China), served from 1982 to 1990 as director of Hong Kong and Macau affairs in the State Council, playing a lead role in the negotiations with Britain over the return of Hong Kong to Chinese sovereignty. He was also chairman of the committee that drafted the Basic Law, the constitution governing the relationship between Hong Kong and the Chinese mainland. As a young man, he participated in the Long March, the historic trek of the Chinese Communists in 1934–35 that resulted in the relocation of the Communist revolutionary base from southeastern China to northwestern China and in the emergence of Mao Zedong as the undisputed party leader. Mao appointed Ji ambassador to East Germany in 1950, a post he held for five years. He served as China's vice foreign minister from 1955 to 1972 and as foreign minister from 1972 to 1974. He retired from public life after the Basic Law was approved in 1990.

Jones, Jonah (Robert Elliott Jones), American jazz musician (b. Dec. 31, 1909, Louisville, Ky.—d. April 30, 2000, New York, N.Y.), played Louis Armstrong-inspired trumpet in swing bands, recorded with Billie Holiday and Teddy Wilson among others, and was a longtime sideman with Cab Calloway; in the late 1950s Jones became famous for his melodic solos, which were showcased on such albums as *Muted Jazz* (1957), *Swingin' on Broadway* (1957), and *Jumpin' with Jonah* (1958), all featuring his own quartet.

Kane, Gil (Eli Katz), Latvian-born American comic book artist (b. April 6, 1926, Riga, Latvia—d. Jan. 31, 2000, Miami, Fla.), became a legend during his more than half-century-long career. His innovative and dramatic style and technique brought new life and vibrancy to such superheroes as Spider-Man, Green Lantern, Captain Marvel, the Incredible Hulk, and the Atom during what was known as the silver age of comics, and he was the creator of such characters as Morbius the Living Vampire and Iron Fist. Kane moved to the U.S. with his parents when he was three years old. He became enthralled by the coloured comic pages in the Sunday newspapers and by comic books after they came on the market in 1933, and when he was a teenager, he took a job erasing pencil lines and drawing borders for the comic publisher MLJ. He also worked briefly for the Jack Binder Agency and for DC Comics before serving (1944–45) in World War II. Returning to DC following his 19 months in the army, Kane worked on a variety of comics, adding to his skills and responsibilities. He also freelanced for numerous other companies. In the late 1950s came the revival of the superhero characters from what had been known as the golden age of comics, and Kane, with Green Lantern, began the work that would lead to his being considered one of the silver age's most important influences on action comics. Over the next several years he added a number of other titles and worked also for Marvel, King, and Tower comics, among others. Whenever possible, despite the huge amount of work he produced, Kane inked his own drawings rather than leave the work for assistants, as most comic book artists did, in order to maintain the integrity of his designs. Besides comic books, Kane also published two graphic novels that he wrote and illustrated, *His Name Is Savage* (1968) and *Blackmark* (1971), drew his newspaper comic strip creation *Star Hawks* from 1977 to 1981, illustrated such items as paperback books and records, and co-wrote the novel *Excalibur!* (1980, with John Jakes). During the 1980s Kane worked on animated television series, notably *Superman,* and his projects in the 1990s included comic book adaptations of Richard Wagner's *The Ring of the Nibelung* (1990, with Roy Thomas) and of the motion picture *Jurassic Park* (1993).

Karski, Jan (Jan Kozielewski), Polish-born Resistance hero (b. April 24, 1914, Lodz, Pol.—d.

July 13, 2000, Washington, D.C.), as a member of the Polish Resistance during World War II, endured considerable hardship to infiltrate the Warsaw Ghetto and Nazi concentration camps and report back to Allied leaders on the persecution of Polish Jews. Few believed his findings, however, and little immediate action was taken. Karski published *Story of a Secret State* in 1944 and later lectured on government and international relations at Georgetown University, Washington, D.C.

Kedrova, Lila (Elizabeth Kedrova), Russian-born character actress (b. 1918/19?, Petrograd [now St. Petersburg], Russia—d. Feb. 16, 2000, Sault Ste. Marie, Ont.), was an accomplished stage and screen actress in Europe, Canada, and Hollywood but never fully escaped from being associated with her best-known role as the tragic courtesan Mme Hortense, a part that won her an Academy Award for best actress in a supporting role for the 1964 motion picture *Zorba the Greek* (her first English-language film) and a Tony Award for the musical adaptation, *Zorba*, on Broadway two decades later. Kedrova also won a French César award (1955) for her performance as a drug addict in the film *Razzia sur la chnouf* and an *Evening Standard* award (1968) for her portrayal of Mme Ranevskaya in *The Cherry Orchard* on the London stage.

Keenan, Philip Childs, American astronomer (b. March 31, 1908, Bellevue, Pa.—d. April 20, 2000, Columbus, Ohio), developed with fellow astronomer William Wilson Morgan the influential MK (for Morgan Keenan) system for classifying stars by their luminosity and spectral type. In 1932 Keenan earned his Ph.D. in astronomy from the University of Chicago, where he was an instructor from 1936 to 1942. In 1943 he and Morgan published *An Atlas of Stellar Spectra, with an Outline of Spectral Classification.* This work formed the basis for the MK system, which facilitated efforts by scientists to classify stars. From 1946 to 1976 Keenan was professor of astronomy at Ohio State University at Columbus. A prolific researcher, he had an unusually long publishing career, producing his first professional paper in 1929, on the colour of the Moon during eclipses, and his last paper in 1999, on the distances of stars from the Earth.

Kieser, Ellwood Eugene ("Bud"), American clergyman and film producer (b. March 27, 1929, Philadelphia, Pa.—d. Sept. 16, 2000, Los Angeles, Calif.), was the Roman Catholic priest who founded (1960) Paulist Productions, the nonprofit company that produced the public-service television series *Insight,* which during its 23-year run (1960–83) won six Emmy Awards. He also established the annual Humanitas Prize and produced such films as *Romero* (1989) and *Entertaining Angels: The Dorothy Day Story* (1996).

King, Pee Wee (Julius Frank Anthony Kuczynski), American bandleader and songwriter (b. Feb. 18, 1914, Milwaukee, Wis.—d. March 7, 2000, Louisville, Ky.), was an innovative and colourful figure in country music who co-wrote the classic hit "Tennessee Waltz." The son of Polish immigrants, he learned fiddle and accordion at an early age and by his teens led his own polka band. In 1934 he joined Gene Autry's show as an accordion player with the Log Cabin Boys. After Autry left for Hollywood in 1936, King formed a band, naming it the Golden West Cowboys. The band was invited to join the Grand Ole Opry in 1937, and King was credited with introducing nontraditional instruments, such as drums and electric guitars, to the Opry stage. With Redd Stewart, the lead vocalist of the Cowboys, he wrote "Tennessee Waltz" in 1947. Recorded by Patti Page in 1950, the song became one of country music's most popular hits, selling more than five million copies worldwide. King went on to record several other hits, including "Bonaparte's Retreat" (1950) and "Slow Poke" (1951). He was inducted into the Country Music Hall of Fame in 1974.

Kirby, Durward, American broadcaster and actor (b. Aug. 24, 1912, Covington, Ky.—d. March 15, 2000, Fort Myers, Fla.), parlayed his success as a radio announcer in the 1930s into a long and varied career in television. He first achieved popularity during his broadcasting stints at radio stations in Indianapolis, Ind.; Cincinnati, Ohio; and Chicago before the outbreak of World War II. After serving in the navy during the war, Kirby worked exclusively in television. He was an announcer and a comic performer on *The Garry Moore Show,* a variety program, in 1950–51, 1958–64, and 1966–67. He also served as a cohost of the popular show *Candid Camera* from 1961 to 1966. Kirby later took intermittent broadcasting assignments until his retirement from television in 1973.

Kirchschläger, Rudolf, Austrian politician and diplomat (b. March 20, 1915, Obermühl, Upper Austria, Austria-Hungary—d. March 30, 2000, Vienna, Austria), attained international respect for himself and his country as a judge and international lawyer, a signatory of the Austrian State Treaty (May 1955) that reestablished Austria's sovereignty after World War II, coauthor of the Austrian Neutrality Act (October 1955), envoy to Czechoslovakia (1967–70), and foreign minister (1970–74) before serving two terms (1974–86) as president of Austria.

Kleindienst, Richard Gordon, American government official and attorney (b. Aug. 5, 1923, Winslow, Ariz.—d. Feb. 3, 2000, Prescott, Ariz.), served as U.S. attorney general under Pres. Richard Nixon from 1972 to 1973; he resigned his post during the Watergate scandal and later pleaded guilty to an unrelated misdemeanour charge for having not testified accurately during his Senate confirmation hearing. He was sentenced to 30 days in jail and fined $100 (both suspended), after which he returned to private law practice in his native Arizona.

Klemperer, Werner, German-born American actor (b. March 22, 1920, Cologne, Ger.—d. Dec. 6, 2000, New York, N.Y.), earned fame for his portrayal of Nazi Colonel Klink, a bumbling German prison-camp commandant, on the hit television sitcom *Hogan's Heroes* (1965–71). A Jewish refugee from Nazi Germany, Klemperer settled in the U.S. in the 1930s. After serving in the U.S. Army during World War II, he studied acting and appeared in a number of films, including *Flight to Hong Kong* (1956), *The Goddess* (1958), *Judgment at Nuremberg* (1961), and *Operation Eichmann* (1961). In later years he performed as a narrator with American symphony orchestras; he also earned a Tony Award nomination for his work in the 1988 Broadway revival of the musical *Cabaret.*

Koltanowski, George, Belgian-born American chess master and author (b. Sept. 17, 1903, Antwerp, Belg.—d. Feb. 5, 2000, San Francisco, Calif.), was a prominent player on the international chess circuit during the 1920s and '30s but was most famous for his skill at playing chess while blindfolded. In 1937 he set a world record in blindfold chess when he played 34 games simultaneously, winning 24 and drawing 10; he set another world record in 1960 when he played 56 consecutive games while blindfolded, winning every game. From 1948 until his death, he was a chess correspondent for the *San Francisco Chronicle,* contributing more than 19,000 columns. In addition, he wrote 18 books on chess. He served (1976–78) as president of the U.S. Chess Federation, and in 1986 he was inducted into the U.S. Chess Federation Hall of Fame. The Fédération Internationale des Échecs, chess's world ruling body, made him an honorary grandmaster in 1988.

Kray, Reginald ("Reggie"), British gangster (b. Oct. 24, 1933, London, Eng.—d. Oct. 1, 2000, Thorpe St. Andrew, Norfolk, Eng.), was the last of the three notorious Kray brothers, who in the 1950s and '60s, though ruthless and brutal, became Cockney legends as Robin Hood-style folk heroes; even after being imprisoned, they were glamorized in the media, films, songs, and theatre.

Kung, Ignatius Cardinal (Gong Pinmei), Chinese prelate (b. Aug. 2, 1901, Shanghai, China—d. March 12, 2000, Stamford, Conn.), spent 30 years in Chinese prisons for his opposition to state control of religion and became China's best-known Christian dissident. Born into a Roman Catholic family, he studied for the priesthood and was ordained in 1930. Appointed bishop of Shanghai in 1949—only days after the establishment of the People's Republic of China—Kung was the first native Chinese to hold that post. He found himself increasingly at odds with the policies of China's communist government, and in

left: Hulton-Deutsch Collection/Corbis; right: AP/Wide World Photos

1955, after his repeated refusals to denounce the pope and adhere to the state-run Patriotic Catholic Association, he was arrested, tried, and sentenced to life in prison for leading a "counterrevolutionary clique under the cloak of religion." He was released to house arrest in 1985. Two years later he was freed from house arrest and the next year went to the U.S. to seek medical treatment, eventually settling with family members in Connecticut. In a private audience with Pope John Paul II in Rome in 1988, he learned that the pope had secretly named him a cardinal in 1979. The appointment was made public in May 1991. Kung was never allowed to return to China. During his last years, he was involved in running the Cardinal Kung Foundation, a human rights organization devoted to helping Roman Catholics in China.

Lamarr, Hedy (Hedwig Eva Maria Kiesler), Austrian-born American actress (b. Nov. 9, 1913, Vienna, Austria—d. Jan. 19, 2000, Orlando, Fla.), possessed such a combination of exotic glamour and sex appeal that she was labeled the movie world's most beautiful woman. Although she appeared opposite many of Hollywood's most famous male stars, her films were not highly regarded, and she never came to be considered to have much acting ability; she was remembered instead for her looks and her romantic liaisons, which included six marriages and divorces. Lamarr appeared in a few German-language films and stage productions before the Czech film *Extase* (1933; *Ecstasy*), with her steamy love scene and nude swimming sequence, gained her international notoriety after being denounced by the pope and banned in many countries. She moved to the U.S. in 1937 and made her Hollywood debut the following year in *Algiers*. Although that film was a hit, Lamarr's roles in such films as *Lady of the Tropics* (1939), *I Take This Woman* (1940), *Boom Town* (1940), and *White Cargo* (1942) were not well received. The performance she rated her best came in *Tortilla Flat* (1942), but it too failed to become a hit. Lamarr's femme fatale image finally found an appropriate vehicle in *Samson and Delilah* (1949), and it became her biggest box-office triumph, but she was unable to repeat that success in the films that followed, which included *Copper Canyon* (1950) and *My Favorite Spy* (1951). Her last film, *The Female Animal*, was released in 1958. Lamarr garnered headlines twice in her later life, in 1966 and 1991, when she was arrested on suspicion of shoplifting. She was cleared of the charges in both incidents. A lesser-known side of Lamarr was her intelligence; in 1942 she and composer George Antheil were granted a patent for a device that could prevent the jamming of radio signals. The military finally put it to use in 1962, during the Cuban missile crisis. During the 1980s versions of it found a home in cellular phone technology, but the patent had lapsed in 1959, and Lamarr did not benefit from its application. She was, however, honoured by the Electronic Frontier Foundation in 1996.

Reuters NewMedia Inc./Corbis

Hedy Lamarr as Delilah

Lamb, Sir Larry (Sir Albert Lamb), British newspaper editor (b. July 15, 1929, Fitzwilliam, Yorkshire, Eng.—d. May 18, 2000, London, Eng.), was credited with inventing modern British tabloid journalism when he transformed *The Sun*, a respectable broadsheet newspaper with a falling circulation, into Great Britain's most popular daily with a circulation of more than four million. During his tenure (1969–81) as editor of *The Sun*, Lamb inaugurated the tabloid format, mixed serious journalism with sensationalism, increased coverage of sports and entertainment news, added circulation-boosting contests and serialized fiction, and introduced the infamous topless "Page Three Girl." He was knighted in 1980.

Landry, Thomas Wade ("Tom"), American football coach (b. Sept. 11, 1924, Mission, Texas—d. Feb. 12, 2000, Dallas, Texas), coached the Dallas Cowboys from 1960 to 1989, leading the team to 20 postseason victories—the most in National Football League (NFL) history—five Super Bowl appearances, and two Super Bowl wins (1972, 1978). He began his NFL coaching career after having played six seasons (1950–55) as a defensive back and punter for the New York Giants. He served as the Giants' defensive coordinator from 1956 to 1959 before becoming head coach at Dallas. A stoic man who was famous for pacing the sidelines in a business suit and fedora, Landry was also one of professional football's greatest innovators. He was responsible for inventing two defenses (the 4-3 and the flex) as well as for reviving the shotgun offensive formation. His 270 career victories were the third most in NFL history. After the end of the 1988–89 season, Cowboys fans were shocked when businessman Jerry Jones bought the team and fired Landry the same day. To honour the coach, the city of Dallas later sponsored a Hats Off to Tom Landry Day, an event that attracted some 100,000 people. Landry was inducted into the Pro Football Hall of Fame in 1990.

Bettmann/Corbis

Lardner, Ringgold Wilmer, Jr. ("Ring"), American screenwriter (b. Aug. 19, 1915, Chicago, Ill.—d. Oct. 31, 2000, New York, N.Y.), not only was the last surviving son of writer Ring Lardner but also was the last surviving member of the blacklisted film screenwriters, producers, and directors known as the Hollywood Ten. He had shared (with Michael Kanin) an Academy Award for the screenplay for *Woman of the Year* (1942) and came back from the blacklisting to win another, for *M*A*S*H* (1970). Lardner studied at Princeton University and the Anglo-American Institute of Moscow State University and, upon his return to New York, became (1935) a reporter for the *New York Daily Mirror*. Soon thereafter he moved to Hollywood to take charge of publicity work for producer David O. Selznick, and around that same time he joined the Communist Party. By 1937 Lardner had made uncredited contributions to the scripts of the 1937 films *Nothing Sacred* and *A Star Is Born*. His next efforts, the screenplays of three minor films, were credited, however, and in 1941 he and Kanin wrote *Woman of the Year*. Following World War II army service, Lardner added to his credits a number of films, including *The Cross of Lorraine* (1943), *Tomorrow the World* (1944), *Cloak and Dagger* (1946), and *Forever Amber* (1947). Then, however, he was summoned before the House Un-American Activities Committee and was asked if he had ever been a member of the Communist Party. Feeling that the committee had no right to question him about his political beliefs, Lardner replied, "I could answer the question exactly the way you want, but if I did, I would hate myself in the morning." He lost his job and subsequently spent nine months in prison for contempt of Congress. Following his imprisonment, Lardner had difficulty finding work because of the blacklisting and had to use pseudonyms. He worked on such films as *Virgin Island* (1958) and *The Cardinal* (1963) and the British television series *The Adventures of Robin Hood* (1955–60) before—beginning with the film *The Cincinnati Kid* (1965)—he was able once again to be credited under his own name. Another of his later screenplays was that for *The Greatest* (1977), which starred heavyweight boxing champion Muhammad Ali as himself. Lardner then concentrated more on writing books, among which was his autobiography, *I'd Hate Myself in the Morning*, published in late 2000.

Laurin, Lucien, Canadian-born American horse trainer (b. Jan. 11, 1912, Joliette, Que.—d. June 26, 2000, Key Largo, Fla.), was one of horse racing's foremost trainers. During a career that spanned nearly five decades, Laurin trained a total of 36 stakes winners, including Secretariat, who in 1973 became the first horse to capture the U.S. Triple Crown since Citation in 1948. Laurin was a successful jockey, winning 161 races, before becoming a trainer in 1942. In the early 1970s, as head trainer at Meadow Stable in Doswell, Va., Laurin won five Triple Crown races with Riva Ridge—the 1972 Kentucky Derby and Belmont Stakes champion—and Secretariat. He was inducted into the Racing Hall of Fame in 1977. Laurin retired from training in 1976 but returned to the sport in 1983, remaining active as a trainer until 1990.

Lawrence, Jacob, American painter (b. Sept. 7, 1917, Atlantic City, N.J.—d. June 9, 2000, Seattle, Wash.), portrayed scenes of African American life and history with vivid, stylized realism. At the age of 13 Lawrence moved with his family to the Harlem section of New York City. At free art classes offered by the Utopia Children's Center, he showed a talent for creating lively, decorative masks, a motif that would later figure strongly in his narrative painting. At the Harlem Art Workshop in 1932, he studied under artist Charles H. Alston, who became his mentor. Gouache and tempera were Lawrence's characteristic mediums. His use of sombre browns and black for shadows and outlines in an otherwise vibrant palette lent his work a distinctive overtone. His best-known works were his series on historical or social themes, including the landmark 60-painting epic *Migration of the Negro* (1941), *Life in Harlem* (1942), and *War* (1947). In 1964, while living in Nigeria, Lawrence painted scenes of local life. His later works included a powerful series on the struggles of African Americans during the era of desegregation. From 1971 to 1986 he was a professor of art at the University of Washington at Seattle. Lawrence was awarded the U.S. National Medal of the Arts in 1990.

LeClercq, Tanaquil, French-born American ballet dancer (b. Oct. 2, 1929, Paris, France—d. Dec. 31, 2000, New York, N.Y.), was one of the original members of Ballet Society, the forerunner of the New York City Ballet (NYCB), and had a musicality, wit, and sleek, long-limbed look that enhanced her extraordinary abilities and made her an ideal muse for choreographer George Balanchine, to whom she was married from 1952 to 1969. At the peak of her career, however, she contracted polio and was left paralyzed below the waist. Ironically, in 1946, in a ballet that had only one performance, *Resurgence*—choreographed by Balanchine for a March of Dimes benefit—LeClercq had portrayed a dancer menaced by the evil Polio, danced by Balanchine. At the age of seven, LeClercq began studying ballet with former Bolshoi Ballet star Mikhail Mordkin, and in 1941 she won a scholarship to Balanchine's School of American Ballet, where in 1945 he cast her in student performances of *Symphonie Concertante* and *Elegie*. She joined Ballet Society when it was founded in 1946 and remained a principal dancer when in 1948 it became NYCB. Creating roles in such ballets as *The Four Temperaments* (1946), *Bourrée fantasque* (1949), and *La Valse* (1951), LeClercq secured her reputation as an ideal interpreter of Balanchine's works. She also shone in the ballets of a variety of other choreographers, among them Merce Cunningham (*The Seasons* [1947]), Frederick Ashton (*Illuminations* [1950]), and, especially, Jerome Robbins (*Age of Anxiety* [1950], *Ballade* [1952], *Afternoon of a Faun* [1953], and *The Concert* [1956]). Robbins cut a solo from *The Concert* when, after being stricken with polio in Europe in 1956 while on tour with NYCB, LeClercq could no longer dance it. LeClercq remained active in the world of dance, however, teaching (1974–82) at the Dance Theatre of Harlem's school and frequently attending NYCB performances. She also wrote the books *Mourka: The Autobiography of a Cat* (1964) and *The Ballet Cook Book* (1967). In 1998, on the opening night of NYCB's 50th anniversary season, LeClercq was honoured with a tribute to her as a founding member and as a legend.

Lemon, Robert Granville ("Bob"), American baseball player (b. Sept. 22, 1920, San Bernardino, Calif.—d. Jan. 11, 2000, Long Beach, Calif.), was one of the most successful pitchers in the 1940s and '50s. He played as an outfielder and third baseman in the minor leagues from 1938 to 1940 and was brought up to the major leagues by the Cleveland Indians as a third baseman in 1941. Military service during World War II interrupted his baseball career, and he returned to the Indians in 1946. Doubts about his hitting ability and the fact that his throws had a natural sinking effect led coaches to try him as a pitcher. He was immediately successful, compiling an 11–5 record in 1947. In 1948 he threw a no-hitter against the Detroit Tigers, was 20–14 in 43 pitching appearances, and won two games in the Indians' World Series triumph over the Boston Braves. A strong, dependable pitcher known for his sinking fastball, Lemon won 20 or more games in a season seven times between 1948 and 1956. He became a capable pinch hitter as well, compiling 31 career hits in 109 pinch-hit appearances. Injuries forced him to retire in 1958 with a 207–128 pitching record and 1,277 career strikeouts. He later turned to coaching, earning the Manager of the Year award in 1971 with the Kansas City Royals. He succeeded Billy Martin as manager of the New York Yankees in 1978 and led the team to a World Series title over the Los Angeles Dodgers that year. Martin was brought back as manager in 1979, and Lemon was reassigned as a scout for the team. He again served as Yankees manager from 1981 to 1982. Lemon was inducted into the National Baseball Hall of Fame in 1976.

Levi, Edward Hirsch, American lawyer and educator (b. June 16, 1911, Chicago, Ill.—d. March 7, 2000, Chicago), as U.S. attorney general under Pres. Gerald Ford from 1975 to 1977, he helped restore public confidence in the Department of Justice following the Watergate scandal. Before his service in Washington, he held numerous posts at the University of Chicago, including dean of the law school (1950–62), university provost (1962–68), and president of the university (1968–75). He returned to the university in 1977, teaching law until his retirement in 1984. Among Levi's publications, his 1949 work *An Introduction to Legal Reasoning* was regarded as a classic and became required reading at many American law schools.

Liebowitz, Jacob S. ("Jack"), Ukrainian-born American comic-book publisher (b. Oct. 10, 1900, Proskurov [now Khmelnytskyy], Ukraine —d. Dec. 11, 2000, Great Neck, N.Y.), sowed the seeds for what would become DC Comics when, in partnership with Harry Donenfeld, he created (1937) the comic-book series Detective Comics, which two years later launched the Batman line. In another of his series, Action Comics, the popular superhero Superman debuted (1938) after Liebowitz acquired the rights and licensing royalties from that character's two creators, a move that was ultimately worth millions of dollars to him; the two creators, however, were finally granted additional money in 1978, after many years of litigation.

Lindsay, John Vliet, American politician (b. Nov. 24, 1921, New York, N.Y.—d. Dec. 19, 2000, Hilton Head Island, S.C.), served in the U.S. House of Representatives from 1959 to 1965 and as mayor of New York City from 1966 to 1973, first as a Republican but from 1971 as a Democrat; in 1972 he was a candidate for the

Prima ballerina Tanaquil LeClercq

Genevieve Naylor/Corbis

Democratic presidential nomination. Faced with the turbulence of civil-rights and antiwar demonstrations during his terms as mayor, he defused much of the tension by appearing in the streets and talking with the people. After leaving office, Lindsay practiced law, made an unsuccessful attempt (1980) at a Senate nomination, acted as a political commentator on television, and wrote a number of books.

Lindt, Auguste Rudolph, Swiss diplomat (b. Aug. 5, 1905, Bern, Switz.—d. April 15/16, 2000, Switzerland), as the United Nations High Commissioner for Refugees (1956–60) provided assistance for refugees fleeing Hungary after Soviet intervention there in 1956 and for Algerian refugees in North Africa the next year; Lindt, who had trained as a lawyer and worked as a foreign correspondent for several European newspapers, was Switzerland's permanent observer to the UN (1953–56) and, after he left his UN post, served as his country's ambassador to the U.S., the U.S.S.R., Mongolia, India, and Nepal.

Linville, Lawrence Labon ("Larry"), American actor (b. Sept. 29, 1939, Ojai, Calif.—d. April 10, 2000, New York, N.Y.), was best known for his portrayal of the hapless, neurotic army surgeon Maj. Frank Burns on the hit television series *M*A*S*H*. After training (1959–61) at the Royal Academy of Dramatic Art in London, Linville spent eight years as a stage actor before embarking on a career in television. In the late 1960s and early '70s he appeared in such series as *Bonanza; Marcus Welby, M.D.;* and *Cannon* before landing the role of Burns in *M*A*S*H* in 1972. Linville, whose character hilariously pursued Nurse "Hot Lips" Houlihan and was the constant butt of pranks by his tentmates, helped make *M*A*S*H* one of the most successful series in television history. He left the show in 1977. In the 1980s Linville had supporting roles in a number of films and made appearances on such television shows as *Lou Grant* and *Murder, She Wrote.* He returned to the stage in the Broadway play *Travels with My Aunt* in 1995.

London, Julie (Julie Peck), American singer and actress (b. Sept. 26, 1926, Santa Rosa, Calif.—d. Oct. 18, 2000, Los Angeles, Calif.), had a sultry, sophisticated look and a smoky voice that gained her pinup status and enhanced her success in films and as a torch singer in the 1940s and '50s. "Cry Me a River"—a single from the first of her 32 albums, *Julie Is Her Name* (1955)—sold over three million copies and remained the song most associated with her. From 1972 to 1977 London achieved new popularity with her role as Nurse Dixie McCall in the American television series *Emergency!*

MacColl, Kirsty, British singer and songwriter (b. Oct. 10, 1959, Croydon, Surrey, Eng.—d. Dec. 18, 2000, Cozumel, Mex.), had a two-decade-long career during which she had her greatest solo success with the witty "There's a Guy Works Down the Chip Shop (Swears He's Elvis)" in 1981 and accompanied Shane MacGowan on "Fairytale of New York," which was a hit for the Pogues in 1987. Among the other songs she wrote was "They Don't Know," which she sang on her first record in 1979 and which was later a hit in a recording by Tracey Ullman.

MacLehose of Beoch, Crawford Murray MacLehose, Baron, British diplomat (b. Oct. 16, 1917, Glasgow, Scot.—d. May 27, 2000, Ayrshire, Scot.), as the 25th governor of Hong Kong (1971–82), presided over the transformation of the British colony from a small, regional trading post into one of Asia's biggest economic powerhouses. A career diplomat and Chinese-language scholar, MacLehose fought corruption in Hong Kong; improved local social welfare services, housing, and public transportation; and cultivated better relations with China, but he believed that introducing democracy in the colony would be counterproductive in light of the impending 1997 handover to Beijing. He was knighted in 1971 and made a life peer in 1982.

MacNelly, Jeffrey Kenneth ("Jeff"), American cartoonist (b. Sept. 17, 1947, New York, N.Y. —d. June 8, 2000, Baltimore, Md.), won three Pulitzer Prizes for his editorial cartoons and created the popular daily comic strip *Shoe.* After graduating (1965) from Phillips Academy, Andover, Mass., MacNelly attended the University of North Carolina at Chapel Hill, where he contributed cartoons to the student newspaper. He also drew cartoons for a local newspaper, the *Chapel Hill Weekly;* the editor, Jim Shumaker, would become the inspiration for the character of P. Martin Shoemaker in *Shoe.* Leaving college without taking a degree, MacNelly joined the Richmond (Va.) *News Leader* in 1970, and only 16 months later, in 1972, he won the first of his Pulitzer Prizes. In 1977 he began drawing *Shoe,* which portrayed a group of humorous, often sarcastic, birds who ran a newspaper; the comic strip was highly successful, eventually appearing in about 1,000 newspapers. MacNelly won his second Pulitzer in 1978, while still at the *News Leader.* He joined the *Chicago Tribune* in 1982, earning his third Pulitzer three years later. Beginning in 1987, he drew illustrations for the syndicated column of humorist Dave Barry, and, from 1993 to 1997, he drew the one-panel comic strip *Pluggers.* MacNelly was also twice the recipient of the National Cartoonists Society's Reuben Award for cartoonist of the year, in 1978 and 1979.

Chris Cassat

Maggio, Michael John, American stage director (b. July 3, 1951, Chicago, Ill.—d. Aug. 19, 2000, Chicago), gained a national reputation as one of the most talented in his field. Besides directing more than 50 plays at such venues as Chicago's Goodman Theatre, the New York Shakespeare Festival, the Guthrie Theater in Minneapolis, Minn., and the Seattle (Wash.) Repertory Theatre, he served as artistic director of Northlight Theatre in Evanston, Ill. (1984–87), associate artistic director of the Goodman (from 1987), and dean of the Theatre School at DePaul University in Chicago (from 1999). Afflicted with cystic fibrosis, he underwent a rare double lung transplant in 1991 that saved his life and gave him nearly 10 more years in which to pursue his creative endeavours; complications from that procedure, however, ultimately took his life.

Marais, Jacob Albertus ("Jaap"), South African politician (b. Nov. 2, 1922, Vryburg, S.Af.—d. Aug. 8, 2000, Pretoria, S.Af.), was a formidable orator, unrepentant white supremacist, and lifelong supporter of the South African racial segregation policy known as apartheid. As the cofounder (1969) and chairman (from 1977) of the radical right-wing Reconstituted National Party, Marais never wavered in his relentless fight for a return to white rule in South Africa.

Marca-Relli, Conrad (Corrado Marcarelli), American artist (b. June 5, 1913, Boston, Mass. —d. Aug. 29, 2000, Parma, Italy), was said to have raised the status of collage to collectible high art; his Abstract Expressionist collages initially were patchworks that were then painted, but he later incorporated other materials such as plastics and metals.

Marchand, Nancy, American actress (b. June 19, 1928, Buffalo, N.Y.—d. June 18, 2000, Stratford, Conn.), was an award-winning actress whose work on television—most notably her roles as an aristocratic newspaper publisher on *Lou Grant* and as the domineering matriarch of a Mafia family on *The Sopranos*—earned her fame and critical praise. Marchand began her career on the stage, appearing in a number of Broadway and Off-Broadway productions during the 1950s before winning an Obie Award for her work in *The Balcony* (1960). She appeared on *Lou Grant* from 1977 to 1982, winning four consecutive Emmy Awards. In 1999 she won a Golden Globe Award for her performance on *The Sopranos.* Marchand also appeared in several films, including *The Bostonians* (1984), *The Naked Gun* (1988), and *Sabrina* (1995).

Martin, Don Edward, American cartoonist (b. May 18, 1931, Passaic, N.J.—d. Jan. 6, 2000, Miami, Fla.), was renowned for the slapstick style and "sick" humour of the drawings he made for over 30 years as *Mad* magazine's "maddest" artist. His hapless wild-haired, odd-looking characters generally found themselves in unfortunate circumstances that led to some grotesque misfortune, which would be punctuated with an inventive onomatopoeic sound, such as "SKROINK," "FOINSAPP," "SPLOP," "SPADATSCH," or "POIT." He carried that whimsy into his everyday life also; his automobile license plate sported the exclamation "SHTOINK." Martin studied at the Newark (N.J.) School of Fine and Industrial Art for three years, received a degree in fine arts from the Pennsylvania Academy of the Fine Arts, and in the mid-1950s began drawing for *Mad.* He remained with that magazine until 1987, when a disagreement with its publisher over reprint rights led to his joining the staff of *Cracked,* a rival magazine. Martin's style was influenced by Hiëronymus Bosch's characters, Warner Brothers cartoons' mania and energy, and caricaturist Al Hirschfeld's elegant line, and his work in turn influenced that of such cartoonists as Robert Crumb and Gary Larson. Martin began to publish paperback collections of his previously unpublished cartoons in 1962, with *Mad's Maddest Artist Don Martin Steps Out!*, and more than seven million copies were subsequently sold. Such volumes as *Mad's Maddest Artist Don Martin Bounces Back* (1963), *Don Martin Drops 13 Stories!* (1965), and *Mad's Don Martin Carries On* (1973) went through multiple printings. Martin later also issued greeting cards and calendars.

Martín Gaite, Carmen, Spanish writer (b. 1925, Salamanca, Spain—d. July 22, 2000, Madrid, Spain), was a member of the group of Social Realist novelists that arose in Spain in the 1950s, but she departed from her more conventional contemporaries as she infused many of her works with greater psychological depth and with elements drawn from folk legends, fables, and fairy tales. In addition to novels, short stories, critical essays, poetry, and translations, she wrote several children's books and a philosophical thesis on 18th-century Spanish love customs. Martín Gaite won numerous awards, notably the Nadal Prize for *Entre visillos* (1958; *Behind the Curtains,* 1990), the Prince of Asturias Prize for Literature in 1988, and the National Prize for Literature in 1978 and 1994; at the time of her death, she was one of only two female members of the Spanish Royal Academy.

Matthau, Walter (Walter Matuschanskayasky), American character actor (b. Oct. 1, 1920, New York, N.Y.—d. July 1, 2000, Santa Monica, Calif.), had a versatility that allowed him to portray such characters as bums, criminals, rich snobs, and even leads in romantic comedies, but, by using his stooped, gangly frame, his growling voice, and a craggy countenance described as a "bloodhound face," he enhanced his impeccable comic instincts and thereby became one of his generation's most successful comedians. Among his most notable roles were those in the eight films he starred in with his best friend, Jack Lemmon—from *The Fortune Cookie* (1966), for which he won an Academy Award for best supporting actor, and *The Odd Couple* (1968) to *Grumpy Old Men* (1993), *Grumpier Old Men* (1995), and *The Odd Couple II* (1998)—and that partnership came to be considered one of Hollywood's funniest. Matthau grew up in the poverty of New York City's Lower East Side and at age 11 began selling refreshments in Yiddish theatres, where he was careful to study the performers and eventually appeared in small parts. Following military service during World War II, he studied in New York City at the New School for Social Research's Dramatic Workshop and began performing in summer stock. Portraying an aged bishop, Matthau made his Broadway debut in 1948 in *Anne of the Thousand Days,* and he went on to appear in shows such as *Twilight Walk* (1951), a revival of *Guys and Dolls* (1955), *Will Success Spoil Rock Hunter?* (1955), *Once More with Feeling* (1958), and *A Shot in the Dark* (1961), for which he won his first Tony Award. In the meantime, he had appeared in films such as *The Kentuckian* (1955), *A Face in the Crowd* (1957), *Slaughter on Tenth Avenue* (1957), *King Creole* (1958), and *Strangers When We Meet* (1960). Matthau truly came into his own with the character of Oscar Madison in *The Odd Couple,* a role created for him by playwright Neil Simon. First in the Broadway play (1965)—for which he won another Tony Award—and then in the movie adaptation, Matthau brought his charming irascibility to the part and made being a slob endearing. He went on to star in other films: *A New Leaf* (1971), *Charley Varrick* (1973), *The Sunshine Boys* (1975), *The Bad News Bears* (1976), *The Grass Harp* (1995; directed by his son Charles Matthau), and *I'm Not Rappaport* (1996). Matthau's final film was *Hanging Up* (2000).

AP/Wide World Photos

Veteran character actor Walter Matthau

Matthews, Sir Stanley, British association football (soccer) player (b. Feb. 1, 1915, Hanley, Stoke-on-Trent, Staffordshire, Eng.—d. Feb. 23, 2000, Newcastle-under-Lyme, Staffordshire), became a legendary sports figure over an astonishing 34-year career that included more than 700 league and cup appearances for Stoke City (1932–47, 1961–65) and Blackpool (1947–61) and 54 international matches for England (1934–57). Matthews, known as the "wizard of dribble" for his dazzling footwork, was the first English player named European Footballer of the Year (an honour he garnered twice) and the first footballer to receive a knighthood. The son of a barber and veteran boxer who instilled in his son his own respect for physical fitness, Matthews joined Stoke City as an office assistant at age 15 and made his debut as a player at 17. His slight 1.75-m (5-ft 9-in) frame and self-effacing charm off the field belied his exceptional speed and ballhandling skill, and within two years he had been selected for the national side. He quickly became a crowd favourite, but he failed to win a national title until 1953 when, at age 38, he led Blackpool to the Football Association Cup championship. Matthews was appointed CBE in 1957 and was knighted in 1965, one month before he made his last professional appearance at age 50. An autobiography, *The Stanley Matthews Story,* was published in 1960.

Maurer, Ion Gheorghe, Romanian politician (b. Sept. 23, 1902, Bucharest, Rom.—d. Feb. 8, 2000, Bucharest), as a member of the then-illegal Communist Party from 1936, was interned for antigovernment activities during World War II but, after the postwar replacement of the Romanian monarchy with a communist-led government, rose in influence, eventually serving as foreign minister (1957–58), titular head of state (1958–61), and prime minister (1961–74). Maurer, who was widely regarded as a moderate, retired in 1974, an action generally attributed to his disapproval of Pres. Nicolae Ceausescu's increasingly autocratic policies.

Maxwell, William Keepers, Jr., American editor and writer (b. Aug. 16, 1908, Lincoln, Ill.—d. July 31, 2000, New York, N.Y.), as a fiction editor at *The New Yorker* magazine, spent some four decades collaborating with, encouraging, and polishing the prose of some of the most notable writers of the 20th century, among them John Updike, Mary McCarthy, J.D. Salinger, John Cheever, Vladimir Nabokov, Eudora Welty, Isaac Bashevis Singer, and John O'Hara. In addition, he wrote a number of books, including six novels, three collections of short stories, and a volume of essays and reviews, much of which was informed by the death of his mother during the influenza epidemic of 1918–19, when he was 10 years old. Maxwell was educated at the University of Illinois at Urbana-Champaign (B.A., 1930) and Harvard University (M.A., 1931) and then taught at Illinois for two years. With one novel, *Bright Center of Heaven* (1934), to his credit and a second one begun, he moved (1936) to New York City. In order to continue writing, he secured part-time work at *The New Yorker,* at first in the art department but then, after a few months, as a fiction and poetry editor. Maxwell was known for his sensitivity to the writer's own voice and sought only to make the works clear and unconvoluted, and he found that his attention to other authors' works also helped him in his own writing. His later novels were *They Came like Swallows* (1937), *The Folded Leaf* (1945), *Time Will Darken It* (1948), *The Chateau* (1961), and *So Long, See You Tomorrow* (1980), the last of which won the American Book Award. Other books included the children's fantasy *The Heavenly Tenants* (1946); the short-story collections *The Old Man at the Railroad Crossing and Other Tales* (1966), *Over by the River, and Other Stories* (1977), and *Billie Dyer and Other Stories* (1992); the memoir *Ancestors* (1971); and the essay collection *The Outermost Dream* (1989). His stories were also collected in *All the Days and Nights* (1995).

Merrick, David (David Margulois), American theatrical producer (b. Nov. 27, 1912, St. Louis, Mo.—d. April 25, 2000, London, Eng.), staged many of the most commercially and critically successful plays in the American theatre during the late 1950s and '60s. Merrick's superior talent for generating publicity earned him the nickname "The Abominable Showman." For the musical *Fanny* (1954), Merrick's first major success, he employed established talents Joshua Logan as director and Ezio Pinza as the star of the production; the advertising campaign for the show used television, radio, and full-page newspaper advertisements, all Broadway firsts. Publicity included sophomoric "Have You Seen Fanny?" stickers attached to men's room mirrors and a nude statue of the show's belly dancer stealthily installed in Central Park's poet's corner. This, combined with Merrick's legal background, which helped him draft an advantageous theatre rental agreement, enabled *Fanny* to enjoy the largest weekly operating profits Broadway had seen. Merrick's 88 eclectic productions included musicals, such as *Gypsy* (1959) and *42nd Street* (1980); dramas, notably John Osborne's *The Entertainer* (1958) and Peter Brook's production of *Marat/Sade* (1965); and comedies, including Tom Stoppard's *Travesties* (1975) and Woody Allen's *Don't Drink the Water* (1966). In 1983 Merrick suffered a stroke that left him virtually speechless and immobile, limiting but not altogether curtailing his producing activity. His revivals of the musicals *Oh, Kay!* (1990) and *State Fair* (1996) were financial failures. Merrick's mentor, Herman Shumlin, once summed up Merrick's career as "a milestone in our modern theatre, where the exploitation of plays has become a lost art."

Mickelson, Siegfried ("Sig"), American broadcasting executive (b. May 24, 1913, Clinton, Minn.—d. March 24, 2000, San Diego, Calif.), as the first president of CBS's television news operation, pioneered many of the techniques of television news presentation, such as the use of anchormen, and was responsible for launching the career of Walter Cronkite. Mickelson joined CBS in 1943, organizing a radio news department in Minneapolis, Minn. He was put in charge of CBS's news division in 1951, and a year later he selected Cronkite to anchor the network's coverage of the 1952 presidential conventions. Mickelson was also responsible for hiring reporter Fred Friendly and teaming him with legendary correspondent Edward R. Murrow on the successful CBS documentary series *See It Now.* In 1954, with Mickelson's support, Friendly and Murrow broadcast an exposé on Sen. Joseph McCarthy that helped to turn the tide of public opinion against the controversial senator. Mickelson remained at CBS until 1961. He served as director of Time-Life Broadcasting from 1961 to 1970 and later held teaching posts at Northwestern University, Evanston, Ill.; Louisiana State University at Baton Rouge; and San Diego State University. From 1975 to 1978 Mickelson headed Radio Free Europe and Radio Liberty, combining the two into a single public corporation in 1976. His book *From Whistle Stop to Sound Bite: Four Decades of Politics and Television* appeared in 1989.

Mielke, Erich, East German government minister (b. Dec. 28, 1907, Berlin, Ger.—d. May 22, 2000, Berlin), was the long-time head (1957–89) of the German Democratic Republic's dreaded ministry of state security (Stasi), a secret police and espionage agency that scrutinized every aspect of East German domestic life, persecuted and arrested suspected dissidents, and ruthlessly suppressed all forms of dissent through a network of tens of thousands of official operatives and civilian informants, many of whom were forced to spy on their families and friends. In 1993 Mielke was deemed physically unfit to stand trial for his actions as director of the Stasi, but he served two years in prison (1993–95) for the 1931 murder of two police officers.

Miller, Merton Howard, American economist (b. May 16, 1923, Boston, Mass.—d. June 3, 2000, Chicago, Ill.), pioneered the field of capital asset theory; along with Harry M. Markowitz and William F. Sharpe, Miller was awarded the Nobel Prize for Economics in 1990. Educated at Harvard University (B.A., 1944) and Johns Hopkins University, Baltimore, Md. (Ph.D., 1952), Miller taught at the Carnegie Institute of Technology (now Carnegie Mellon University), Pittsburgh, Pa., until 1961. He was a professor of finance at the University of Chicago's Graduate School of Business Administration from 1961 to 1993. Miller's work was based on the work of Markowitz (whose portfolio theory established that wealth can best be invested in assets that vary in terms of risk and expected return) and Sharpe (who developed the capital asset pricing model to explain how securities prices reflect risks and potential returns). With his colleague Franco Modigliani, who received the Nobel Prize for Economics in 1985, Miller created the Modigliani-Miller theorem to explain the relationship between a company's capital asset structure and dividend policy and its market value and cost of capital. The theorem demonstrated that how a company funds its activities is less important than the profitability of those activities. Miller was recognized as one of the most important developers of theoretical and empirical analysis in the field of corporate finance. He was also noted for his work as a director of the Chicago Mercantile Exchange and the Chicago Board of Trade.

Mir, Pedro, Dominican poet (b. June 3, 1913, San Pedro de Macorís, Dom.Rep.—d. July 11, 2000, Santo Domingo, Dom.Rep.), was national poet of the Dominican Republic from 1982 until his death. His poems celebrated the working class and examined aspects of his country's painful past, including colonialism, slavery, and dictatorship. By his mid-30s Mir had developed a prominent literary reputation. His social commentary, however, angered Dominican dictator Rafael Trujillo, and Mir was forced into exile in 1947. He spent the next 15 years in Cuba (where he published perhaps his best-known poetry collection, *Hay un país en el mundo,* in 1949), Mexico, and the Soviet Union. Mir returned to the Dominican Republic in 1962, a few months after Trujillo's assassination. He continued his prolific writing career, publishing essays and novels as well as poems. He was awarded the Dominican National Prize for History in 1975 and was appointed national poet seven years later. In 1993 Mir also received the National Prize for Literature for lifetime achievement.

Mitchell, Dame Roma Flinders, Australian jurist (b. Oct. 2, 1913, Adelaide, Australia—d. March 5, 2000, Adelaide), was a lifelong advocate of rights for women, Aboriginals, and the disabled as well as a pioneer in holding numerous official positions that had previously been exclusively male. Mitchell, who received her law degree from the University of Adelaide in 1934 and practiced law in her native South Australia, was the first woman in Australia to be named a queen's counsel (1962), the first woman sworn in as a state Supreme Court justice (in South Australia; 1965), the inaugural chairman of the Australian Human Rights Commission (1981–86), the first nonroyal woman to serve as chancellor of an Australian university (at her alma mater; 1983–90), and the first female state governor (South Australia; 1991–96). Mitchell also successfully campaigned for the right to have women sworn in on Australian juries and chaired the committee that issued the influential five-volume Mitchell report on penal reform in the 1970s. She was made CBE in 1971, Dame Commander in 1982, a Companion of the Order of Australia in 1991, and Commander of the Royal Victorian Order in January 2000.

Mitra, Ramon, Philippine politician (b. 1928, Palawan, Phil.—d. March 20, 2000, Manila, Phil.), was a prominent politician, a pro-democracy activist, and an outspoken critic of the 1966–86 regime of Philippine Pres. Ferdinand Marcos. After working as a journalist and diplomat, Mitra served in the House of Representatives in the 1960s and was elected to the Senate in 1971. After Marcos imposed martial law in the Philippines in 1972, Mitra was imprisoned along with other opposition figures. He gained his release in the early 1980s and was elected to the House of Representatives again in 1984. Two years later, after Marcos was forced into exile, Mitra was appointed minister of agriculture by Marcos's successor, Corazon Aquino. In 1992 Mitra lost a bid for the presidency, but in 1998 he returned to the political spotlight as a key supporter of Joseph Estrada's successful presidential campaign. Estrada rewarded Mitra by naming him president of the state-owned Philippine National Oil Corp., a post Mitra held until his death from liver cancer.

Mladenov, Petar Toshev, Bulgarian politician (b. Aug. 22, 1936, Toshevtsi, Bulg.—d. May 31, 2000, Sofia, Bulg.), served as Bulgaria's foreign minister for 18 years (1971–89) until he engineered the bloodless overthrow of Pres. Todor Zhivkov, who had ruled with an iron fist for 35 years. As the new president from Nov. 10,

Bettmann/Corbis

1989, Mladenov supported numerous reforms, including the repudiation of Zhivkov's anti-Turkish policies and the holding of multiparty elections in June 1990, but he was forced to resign from office soon after those elections.

Montgomery, George (George Montgomery Letz), American actor (b. Aug. 29, 1916, Brady, Mont.—d. Dec. 12, 2000, Rancho Mirage, Calif.), brought his rugged handsomeness to some 87 films and a number of television series during a six-decade career. Best known for his roles in westerns, he also appeared in romantic comedies and musicals. Montgomery grew up on a farm, and the skills he gained there, such as handling horses, later proved useful to his performing career. After a year at the University of Montana, where he studied interior design, he moved to Hollywood and soon became a stuntman and played small parts in westerns, *The Singing Vagabond* (1935) and *Springtime in the Rockies* (1937) among them. The 15-chapter serial *The Lone Ranger* (1938) gave him his first major role, and he went on to be featured in such films as *The Cisco Kid and the Lady* (1940), *Ten Gentlemen from West Point* (1942), *Roxie Hart* (1942), and *Coney Island* (1943). After having romanced several prominent actresses, Montgomery married singer Dinah Shore in 1943. Following World War II service in the army air corps, which he entered in 1943, Montgomery returned to movies in *Three Little Girls in Blue* (1946), and in 1947 he played detective Philip Marlowe in *The Brasher Doubloon* (released in the U.K. as *The High Window*). Montgomery thereafter appeared mostly in low-budget westerns and war movies, and he starred for two years (1958–59) in the TV series *Cimarron City*. He also directed a few action films. Montgomery found himself in the headlines in 1963 when, after he and Shore had divorced, he was shot by a housemaid who objected to his socializing with glamour girls. Since the 1940s Montgomery had done carpentry and set and prop construction, and he later became a painter and sculptor; those interests generally occupied him in his later years.

Morgan, (Anthony) John, British journalist (b. May 28, 1959, Sunderland, Eng.—d. July 9, 2000, London, Eng.), became a popular arbiter of modern British etiquette, dress, and manners despite having come from a working-class Scottish background and having had no formal training. The impeccably dapper Morgan was associate fashion editor for *The Guardian* newspaper for a short time in the mid-1980s, style editor for *Gentleman's Quarterly* (*GQ*) magazine from 1988, and, most recently, the author of a weekly advice column in *The Times* (London) newspaper. He also edited the best-selling *Debrett's New Guide to Etiquette and Modern Manners* (1996) and *The Times Book of Modern Manners* (2000). Morgan was found dead on the pavement outside his apartment building, an apparent suicide.

Mulligan, Richard, American actor (b. Nov. 13, 1932, New York, N.Y.—d. Sept. 26, 2000, Los Angeles, Calif.), had a 40-year career during which he appeared in numerous films, including *Little Big Man* (1970) and *S.O.B.* (1981), and Broadway plays, including *How the Other Half Loves* (1971), but achieved his greatest renown in television series with his portrayals of Burt Campbell on *Soap* (1977–81) and Dr. Harry Watson on *Empty Nest* (1988–95). He won Emmy Awards in 1980 and 1989.

Myers, George Carleton, American sociology and demographics educator (b. April 8, 1931, Brooklyn, N.Y.—d. Aug. 10, 2000, Burnsville, N.C.), was the founding director in 1972 of the Center for Demographic Studies at Duke University, Durham, N.C. During his 25-year tenure there, he was at the forefront of analyzing and compiling statistics on the aging population worldwide. Besides serving as a consultant to government agencies, Myers was coordinator for the Committee of Centers of Populations Research, the International Network on Health Expectancy, and the population activities segment of the United Nations Economic Commission for Europe. In addition to earning a B.A. (1953) from Yale University, Myers gained a Ph.D. (1963) from the University of Washington; he wrote or co-wrote more than 100 publications dealing with demographic trends and was the editor of various professional journals on aging and gerontology.

Nagako, Dowager Empress, Japanese royal (b. March 6, 1903, Tokyo, Japan—d. June 16, 2000, Tokyo), was the consort of Emperor Hirohito and the mother of Emperor Akihito. The eldest daughter of Prince Kunihiko—a nobleman of a collateral clan of the Japanese Imperial family—Nagako at age 14 was chosen by Hirohito to be his intended bride. The two were married on Jan. 26, 1924. In 1926, upon the death of his father, Hirohito became emperor. Nagako's first responsibility as empress was to produce a male heir. After bearing four daughters, she succeeded, giving birth to Crown Prince Akihito on Dec. 23, 1933. Although seldom seen in public, Nagako became a beloved figure in Japan. She wrote numerous letters of condolence to bereaved families during World War II and later devoted herself to several charities. She was also known as an accomplished painter, poet, and musician. In 1973, at the age of 70, Nagako became Japan's longest-reigning empress, and in 1995—six years after the death of her husband—she became the longest-living dowager empress in Japanese history.

Nash, N. Richard (Nathan Richard Nusbaum), American playwright, screenwriter, and novelist (b. June 7, 1913, Philadelphia, Pa.—d. Dec. 11, 2000, New York, N.Y.), found his greatest success with *The Rainmaker*, which was a Broadway drama (1954) and a film (1956), was translated into some 40 languages, and was made into the musical *110 in the Shade* (1963). He also wrote the screenplay for *Porgy and Bess* (1959); wrote the books for Broadway musicals, including *Wildcat* (1960), which he also produced; and published such novels as *East Wind, Rain* (1977).

Nasution, Abdul, Indonesian politician (b. Dec. 3, 1918, Kotanopan, North Sumatra, Dutch East Indies—d. Sept. 6, 2000, Jakarta, Indon.), was a leader in winning (1949) Indonesian independence from The Netherlands and thereafter served in a number of capacities, including defense minister (1959–66). He missed an opportunity to seize power when he was the only survivor among a group of seven generals targeted during an uprising (1965) against President Sukarno; instead, General Suharto took over, and Nasution became a critic of his authoritarian rule.

Neel, James Van Gundia, American geneticist (b. March 22, 1915, Hamilton, Ohio—d. Feb. 1, 2000, Ann Arbor, Mich.), was a pioneer in the field of genetics; his studies provided evidence of the genetic basis of numerous diseases, including sickle-cell anemia. In the late 1940s, as acting director of field studies for the National Research Council's Atomic Bomb Casualty Commission, he led studies of the effects of radiation on survivors of the atomic bombings of Hiroshima and Nagasaki, Japan. Later, at the University of Michigan at Ann Arbor in 1956, he founded one of the nation's first departments of human genetics.

Néel, Louis-Eugène-Félix, French physicist (b. Nov. 22, 1904, Lyon, France—d. Nov. 17, 2000, Brive-la-Gaillarde, France), shared the 1970 Nobel Prize for Physics for his discoveries concerning new forms of magnetism. His findings led to applications ranging from the development of improved computer memory units to paleomagnetic techniques for establishing the age of fossils. In 1932 he discovered antiferromagnetism, a condition in some solids in which alternating groups of atoms align their electrons in opposite directions, thereby neutralizing the net magnetic effect. In his work on magnetic oxides (known as ferrites in the late 1940s), Néel found that the magnetic fields associated with individual atoms spontaneously align themselves either in the same direction, as in ferromagnetism, or are paired off in opposite directions, as in antiferromagnetism. Consequently, such ferromagnetic materials generally exhibit weaker strength than do the purely ferromagnetic solids, such as metallic iron. Ferrite crystals are essential ingredients in snooper paint, which allows stealth aircraft to be undetectable by radar. Néel served as a professor of science at the University of Strasbourg from 1937 to 1945 and at the University of Grenoble from 1945 to 1976; he was the founder and a former director of the Centre for Nuclear Studies in Grenoble.

Newman, William Stein, American musicologist and educator (b. April 6, 1912, Cleveland, Ohio—d. April 27, 2000, Chapel Hill, N.C.), was a leading historian of music who in 1963 published a seminal three-volume work, *The History of the Sonata* (*The Sonata in the Baroque Era, The Sonata in the Classical Era*, and *The Sonata Since Beethoven*). Newman earned a Ph.D. in musicology from the Cleveland (Ohio) Institute of Music in 1939. After service in World War II, he joined the faculty of the University of North Carolina at Chapel Hill, where he was a professor of music from 1945 to 1977. Newman published another influential work, *Beethoven on Beethoven: Playing His Piano Music His Way*, in 1988.

Nicholas, Harold Lloyd, American dancer (b. March 21/27, 1921, Winston-Salem, N.C.—d. July 3, 2000, New York, N.Y.), along with his older brother, Fayard, constituted the Nicholas Brothers dance team. In vaudeville shows and nightclubs, on Broadway and television, and especially in motion pictures, they combined elements of ballet, jazz, and acrobatics with tap in their routines to produce displays of dazzling virtuosity, which they called "classical tap." In their most famous number—the dance to "Jumpin' Jive" in the movie *Stormy Weather* (1943), the brothers descended a staircase by alternately jumping over each other's head in full splits and landing, still in splits, on the step below. Nicholas began performing as a dancer at age five when he, his brother, and his sister, Dorothy—as the Nicholas Kids—appeared in black vaudeville houses in Philadelphia, and the brothers debuted professionally in 1930 on the *Horn & Hardart Kiddie Hour* radio show. The brothers went on to bookings at the Lafayette Theater and the Cotton Club in New York City's Harlem and made their movie debut in the short film *Pie Pie Blackbird* (1932). Discovery by Samuel Goldwyn led to roles in such films as *Kid Millions* (1934), *The Big Broadcast of 1936* (1935), *Down Argentine Way* (1940), and *Tin Pan Alley* (1940). They also appeared in *The Ziegfeld Follies of 1936* on Broadway, in the London revue *Blackbirds of 1936,* and in the stage musicals *Babes in Arms* (1937) and *St. Louis Woman* (1946). Because of segregation restrictions in Southern states, whites did not perform in movie scenes with blacks, and films were arranged so that black performers' numbers could be easily cut before the films were shown in the South. In *The Pirate* (1948), however, which was the brothers' last film together, they broke the colour barrier by dancing with Gene Kelly in the "Be a Clown" number. Nicholas moved to France in 1950 and embarked on a solo career that took him throughout Europe and North Africa. In the mid-1960s he returned to the U.S., and by the end of the decade, with his brother's performing career winding down, Nicholas was once again appearing solo. He had roles in such Broadway shows as *Sophisticated Ladies* (1982) and the touring musical *The Tap Dance Kid* (1985) and in the films *Uptown Saturday Night* (1974) and *Tap* (1989). The Nicholas Brothers were recipients of Kennedy Center Honors in 1991 and in 1992 were the subject of a documentary film, *The Nicholas Brothers: We Sing and We Dance.*

Nitzsche, Bernard Alfred ("Jack"), American musician, songwriter, and arranger (b. April 22, 1937, Chicago, Ill.—d. Aug. 25, 2000, Hollywood, Calif.), not only worked with record producer Phil Spector (for whom he developed the "wall of sound"), and such musicians as the Rolling Stones, Neil Young, and Miles Davis—producing, creating musical arrangements for, and playing on many of their recordings—but also had his own hit instrumental record, "The Lonely Surfer" (1963), and scored some 35 films. He received Academy Award nominations for his scores for *One Flew over the Cuckoo's Nest* (1975) and *An Officer and a Gentleman* (1982) and—along with Buffy Sainte-Marie and Will Jennings—won the best song Oscar for "Up Where We Belong," the theme song of the latter film.

Nzo, Alfred Baphethuxolo, South African black nationalist and statesman (b. June 19, 1925, Benoni, S.Af.—d. Jan. 13, 2000, Johannesburg, S.Af.), served as secretary-general of the African National Congress (ANC) from 1969 to 1991 and as South Africa's first foreign minister in the postapartheid era. Active in the ANC from the early 1950s, he was arrested in 1963 for organizing antigovernment protests and was exiled the following year. Nzo represented the ANC in Egypt and India before being elected secretary-general and relocating the organization's headquarters to Tanzania and returned to South Africa after the ban on the ANC was lifted in 1990. He served as foreign minister under Pres. Nelson Mandela from 1994 to 1999.

O'Brian, Patrick (Richard Patrick Russ), British novelist and biographer (b. Dec. 12, 1914, near London, Eng.—d. Jan. 2, 2000, Dublin, Ire.), wrote a highly acclaimed series of historical novels on the Napoleonic-era British Royal Navy as well as biographies of Pablo Picasso and 18th-century naturalist Sir Joseph Banks. Between 1969 and 1998 he published 20 novels set during the Napoleonic Wars and featuring Jack Aubrey, a British naval officer, and Stephen Maturin, an Irish-Catalan physician and Aubrey's friend. The series made O'Brian a literary celebrity. A reclusive man who purposely distorted his personal history (for years he claimed to be Irish and Catholic), he was unmasked by journalists in 1998 as the son of an English mother and a physician of German-Jewish descent. Since 1949 he had lived mostly in the village of Collioure in southwestern France. Aside from the Aubrey-Maturin books, he published several literary novels, including *Three Bear Witness* (1952). *Pablo Ruiz Picasso: A Biography* appeared in 1976 and *Joseph Banks, a Life* in 1987. O'Brian was made CBE in 1995.

O'Connor, John Joseph Cardinal, American prelate (b. Jan. 15, 1920, Philadelphia, Pa.—d. May 3, 2000, New York, N.Y.), served as the archbishop of New York from 1984 until his death and was regarded as the Vatican's leading spokesman in the U.S. An ardent traditionalist, he was an outspoken defender of Roman Catholic teaching on sexual and moral ethics; his staunch opposition to abortion often brought him into conflict with prominent politicians. Born into a working-class family, O'Connor resolved early in life to become a priest and studied at the St. Charles Borromeo Seminary in Philadelphia. He was ordained in 1945 and later earned a Ph.D. from Georgetown University, Washington, D.C. In 1952 he joined the U.S. Navy as a military chaplain, ministering to soldiers in both the Korean War and the Vietnam War. He published a book, *A Chaplain Looks at Vietnam,* in 1968 and eventually rose to become the U.S. Navy's chief of chaplains before retiring from the military—with the rank of rear admiral—in 1979. He served (1979–83) as auxiliary bishop of New York to Terence Cardinal Cooke before being appointed bishop of Scranton, Pa., in May 1983. In January 1984 he was appointed archbishop of New York by Pope John Paul II and was elevated to cardinal a year later. O'Connor began to make frequent public pronouncements outlining his conservative views and was soon at loggerheads with politicians who supported abortion rights, such as New York Gov. Mario Cuomo and New York City Mayor Ed Koch. In 1990 the cardinal provoked an outcry when he stated that Catholics who were in favour of abortion should be excommunicated. Although O'Connor's conservative positions were often criticized by gay and women's rights lobbies as well as by pro-choice activists, he was applauded in liberal circles for his steadfast opposition to the death penalty, immigration controls, and cuts in welfare programs. He also won support for advocating workers' rights, leading efforts toward Catholic-Jewish reconciliation, and reaching out to African Americans. Despite the public controversies he was involved in, O'Connor was known as cheerful and outgoing, and he developed friendships with many of his former adversaries, including Koch, with whom he wrote a popular book, *His Eminence and Hizzoner* (1989). In March 2000 O'Connor was awarded a U.S. Congressional Gold Medal.

Obuchi, Keizo, Japanese politician (b. June 25, 1937, Nakanojo, Japan—d. May 14, 2000, Tokyo, Japan), served as prime minister of Japan from July 1998 until just before his death and was responsible for instituting policies that sparked Japan's economic recovery in the wake of the Asian financial crisis. The son of a politician, Obuchi earned a degree in English literature from Waseda University, Tokyo, in 1962. The following year, at age 26, he became the youngest person ever elected to the Diet (parliament), winning the seat his father had held in the Diet's lower house. Retaining his seat in 11 subsequent elections, Obuchi built a reputation as a congenial party functionary adept at forging behind-the-scenes compromises between competing political factions. In 1973 he served as deputy director general in the prime minister's office, and in 1987 he was named chief cabinet secretary. He also rose steadily through the ranks of the ruling Liberal-Democratic Party (LDP), serving as deputy secretary-general (1984) and secretary-general (1991). He was appointed foreign minister by Prime Minister Ryutaro Hashimoto in 1997. A year later he replaced Hashimoto, who was forced to resign as prime minister following the LDP's stunning losses in elections to the upper house of the Diet. Obuchi also assumed the presidency of the LDP. Although as foreign minister he had been perceived as bland and undistinguished—pundits dubbed him "Mr.

left: AP/Wide World Photos; right: AP/Wide World Photos

Average" and described him as "about as exciting as cold pizza"—Obuchi moved quickly to win the confidence of Japanese citizens, assembling a credible cabinet and vowing decisive action to pull the country out of its worst economic crisis in decades. He first addressed the formidable problems facing Japan's banking sector. After a frustrating two months in office, Obuchi was able to win parliamentary approval of crucial bills to bail out banks saddled with bad loans. In other efforts to jump-start the Japanese economy, he drastically cut income taxes and significantly expanded the budget. Obuchi's stimulus package had the intended effect—by July 1999 Japan's gross domestic product had begun to expand again after months of decline. Obuchi's approval ratings soared, though by the time of his death support for his administration had slipped as the economic recovery slowed. He died six weeks after suffering a stroke that left him comatose.

Oliphant, Sir Mark (Marcus Laurence Elwin Oliphant), Australian physicist (b. Oct. 8, 1901, Adelaide, Australia—d. July 14, 2000, Canberra, Australia), was an esteemed specialist in high-energy physics at the University of Cambridge's Cavendish Laboratory, where he had won a scholarship in 1927. Oliphant was also Poynting Professor of Physics at the University of Birmingham, Eng. (1937–50), and a co-discoverer (1934) of tritium with Ernest Rutherford and Paul Harteck, and he directed the team (1939) that developed the cavity magnetron used in advanced microwave radar. Having been a member of the British team that split the atom in 1932, he went to the U.S. in 1943 to work on the Manhattan Project, the joint undertaking that designed and built the first atomic bombs. Oliphant later fiercely opposed the dropping of the atomic bombs on Japan and the nuclear proliferation that followed, but he endorsed research into atomic energy. After World War II he returned to Australia, where he served as director of the research school of physical sciences at the Australian National University (ANU), Canberra (1950–63), president of the Australian Academy of Science (1954–57), and professor of physics of ionized gases at the Institute of Advanced Studies at ANU (1964–67). He was made a fellow of the Royal Society in 1937, knighted in 1959, and appointed a Companion of the Order of Australia in 1977. From 1971 to 1976 Oliphant also held the post of governor of South Australia.

Oppenheimer, Harry Frederick, South African businessman (b. Oct. 28, 1908, Kimberley, S.Af.—d. Aug. 19, 2000, Johannesburg, S.Af.), as the enormously wealthy chairman of the Anglo American Corp. (1957–82) and De Beers Consolidated Mines, Ltd. (1957–84), controlled one of the world's largest suppliers of diamonds, gold, platinum, coal, and other strategic mineral resources. The complex family conglomerate, which he had inherited from his father, also included banking, real estate, and other industrial concerns. Although Oppenheimer was often criticized for the working conditions of his nonwhite employees, he remained an outspoken opponent of the racial segregation policy known as apartheid and a supporter of labour unions, education, and improved housing for blacks.

Padilla, Heberto, Cuban poet (b. Jan. 20, 1932, Puerta de Golpe, Pinar del Río province, Cuba—d. Sept. 25, 2000, Auburn, Ala.), rose to international prominence in 1971 as a symbol of intellectual repression under the regime of Fidel Castro after his criticism of the government resulted in his imprisonment and in the banning of his works in Cuba. This course of events, known worldwide as the "Padilla Affair," began in 1968 when Padilla's volume of poetry *Fuera del juego* was awarded Cuba's highest literary prize by the state-sponsored Union of Cuban Writers and Artists. The government was so upset by the award that an appendix denouncing the work as counterrevolutionary was added to the book by its publisher. From that point on, Padilla was under constant state surveillance, and he was later arrested when it was discovered that he was writing yet another inflammatory book. Soon thereafter, Padilla was forced to read a 4,000-word confession of his "crimes" on television; it was a statement so obviously written by someone else that many prominent intellectuals the world over who had been supporters of the Cuban Revolution turned away from Castro and banded together in protest of Padilla's treatment. After being released from prison, Padilla was kept under virtual house arrest until he was granted permission in 1980 to move to the U.S. There, Padilla held various academic posts and published many other works, including several volumes of poetry, the novel *En mi jardín pastan los héroes* (1981; *Heroes Are Grazing in My Garden,* 1984), and *La mala memoria* (1989; *Self-Portrait of the Other,* 1990), an autobiographical portrait of his life under Castro. His works have been translated into 14 languages.

Pais, Abraham, Dutch-born American physicist and science historian (b. May 19, 1918, Amsterdam, Neth.—d. July 28, 2000, Copenhagen, Den.), was a prominent theoretical physicist who in later life wrote widely acclaimed biographies of Albert Einstein and Niels Bohr. Pais earned a Ph.D. in physics from the University of Amsterdam in 1941. A Jew, he was forced into hiding after Germany overtook The Netherlands during World War II and was briefly imprisoned in 1945. After the war Pais worked at the Institute of Theoretical Physics, Copenhagen, where he was an assistant to Bohr; later he was recruited to work at the Institute for Advanced Study, Princeton, N.J., where he met Einstein. Pais's work involved studying the behaviour of subatomic particles. In 1952 he explained a process he termed "associated production," by which certain particles are produced rapidly but decay slowly, and in 1955, with colleague Murray Gell-Mann, he published a theoretical paper on the laws of quantum mechanics that led physicists James Cronin and Val Fitch to conduct experiments in 1964 that won them a Nobel Prize. Pais joined the faculty of Rockefeller University, New York City, in 1963; he was appointed professor emeritus at the university in 1988. His biography of Einstein, entitled *Subtle Is the Lord* and considered by some critics to be the best biography of the scientist ever written, appeared in 1982. His book on Bohr, *Niels Bohr's Times: In Physics, Philosophy, and Polity,* was published in 1991. Among Pais's other works were *Einstein Lived Here: Essays for the Layman* (1994), *A Tale of Two Continents: A Physicist's Life in a Turbulent World* (1997), and *The Genius of Science: A Portrait Gallery of Twentieth-Century Physicists* (2000).

Palmer, Bruce, American four-star general and U.S. Army vice chief of staff (b. April 13, 1913, Austin, Texas—d. Oct. 10, 2000, Alexandria, Va.), was the author of *The 25-Year War: America's Military Role in Vietnam* (1984), which went against conventional wisdom regarding the strategy of the Joint Chiefs of Staff to win the Vietnam War. In his book, Palmer claimed that the Joint Chiefs were never able to define the role of the United States in Southeast Asia and, thus, could not devise a strategy. Palmer served as deputy commanding general of American troops in South Vietnam and was for a time considered a leading candidate to succeed Gen. William C. Westmoreland as commander, a post that was given instead to Gen. Creighton W. Abrams.

Papineau-Couture, Jean, Canadian composer (b. Nov. 12, 1916, Outremont, Que.—d. Aug. 11, 2000, Montreal, Que.), was one of the country's foremost contemporary music composers and was highly influential as a teacher at the Collège Jean-de-Brébeuf, the Conservatoire de musique de Montréal, and the University of Montreal, where he served (1968–73) as dean before retiring as professor in 1985. Among his students at the latter were composers Jacques Hétu, François Morel, and André Prévost. Papineau-Couture had an abiding interest in acoustics and developed a class dedicated to its study. Among his major works were *Étude in B-flat Minor* for piano (1945), *Psaume CL* (1954), and five works titled *Pièce concertante* (1957–63). Papineau-Couture was a founding member and president of the Canadian Music Centre and served other musical bodies in that capacity. Among his numerous awards were the 1962 Prix de musique Calixa-Lavallée and the Canadian Music Council Medal (1973), and he had bestowed upon him the title of Grand Officer of the Ordre du Québec in 1989; in 1994 he was the recipient of the Governor-General's Performing Arts Award.

Paulson, Allen, American racehorse owner and businessman (b. April 22, 1922, Clinton, Iowa—d. July 19, 2000, La Jolla, Calif.), owned a number of highly successful racehorses, most notably Cigar, which in 1996 tied legendary racehorse Citation's record of 16 victories in a row. Trained as an aviation mechanic, Paulson founded his own company, Gulfstream Aerospace, in 1978 and turned it into a leading producer of private jets. He began breeding racehorses in the early 1980s. His stable went on to produce 32 Breeders' Cup runners and 8 champions, including Arazi in 1991. Nevertheless, none of Paulson's horses was more successful than Cigar, which was twice voted Horse of the Year (1995–96) and earned more prize money—$9.9 million—than any other racehorse in history.

Paz García, Policarpo, Honduran politician and military leader (b. Dec. 7, 1932, Goascorán, Honduras—d. April 16, 2000, Tegucigalpa, Honduras), was the last military ruler of Honduras. As an infantry officer, Paz distinguished himself in his country's so-called Soccer War (a conflict touched off by a riot at a soccer match) with El Salvador in 1969, turning back an enemy offensive in southern Honduras. In late 1978, after he was appointed commander of the Honduran armed forces, he staged a bloodless coup that toppled the military regime of Gen. Juan Alberto Melgar Castro. Paz ruled Honduras until 1980, when he permitted elections for a civilian government to be held. He headed a transitional government until 1982, then handed power over to the civilian president, Roberto Suazo Córdova, before retiring from public life. The handover marked the end of nearly 20 years of continuous military rule in Honduras.

Pentland, Barbara Lally, Canadian composer (b. Jan. 2, 1912, Winnipeg, Man.—d. Feb. 5, 2000, Vancouver, B.C.), was one of Canada's first avant-garde composers. She studied at the Juilliard School of Music in New York City and the Berkshire (Mass.) Music Center. Pentland taught composition and theory at the Toronto Conservatory of Music from 1943 to 1949 and at the University of British Columbia from 1949 to 1963. Her music was influenced by, among other modern composers, Paul Hindemith, Igor Stravinsky, and Anton Webern. Among Pentland's notable compositions were *Studies in Line* (1941), *Concerto for Violin and Small Orchestra* (1942), *Symphony for Ten Parts* (1957), *News* (1970), and *Disasters of the Sun* (1976). She was made a Member of the Order of Canada in 1989.

Perkins, Charles Nelson, Australian civil servant and activist (b. June 16, 1936, Alice Springs, N.Terr.—d. Oct. 18, 2000, Sydney, N.S.W.), was the first indigenous Australian to head a government department and the most influential figure in the Aboriginal fight for civil rights; he was often compared to U.S. civil rights leader the Rev. Martin Luther King, Jr. Perkins began his struggle to publicize and address the unfair treatment of indigenous peoples in the mid-1960s, when he accompanied white students on "freedom rides" through the outback of New South Wales. The rides, inspired by similar activities in the U.S.'s segregated South, generated a great deal of publicity, as did a related effort to secure the right of Aboriginal children to swim in public pools in the town of Bourke. He devoted the rest of his life to the cause, becoming a lightning rod for controversy. A mixed-race Aboriginal, Perkins was sent at age 10 to a school for Aboriginal boys in Adelaide. His talent as an association football (soccer) player attracted the attention of clubs in the U.K., where he became the first Aboriginal to play professionally. He returned to Australia in 1959 and, six years later, became one of the first Australian Aboriginal university graduates when he earned an arts degree from the University of Sydney. That same year Perkins formed the Foundation for Aboriginal Affairs, which was a driving force behind the campaign that helped pass a 1967 referendum that gave the federal government authority to legislate justice for Aboriginals. In 1969 Perkins joined the government's Aboriginal Affairs Department of Western Australia as a researcher, and he worked his way up to department secretary in 1984. Unlike most government officials, however, he continued his activist work and was sometimes criticized publicly by his own department. He was forced to resign his position in 1988 following a scandal involving the funding of an Aboriginal social club, but he was later cleared of any charges of wrongdoing. Although he was a member of the group that helped Sydney make its successful bid for the 2000 Olympic Games, he also used the Olympics to stage his last campaigns against racism, threatening that there could be widespread civil unrest among the Aboriginal population during the Games, though he later retracted his statements, which many considered inflammatory.

Civil rights defender Charles Perkins

Matthew McKee/Corbis

Peters, (Elizabeth) Jean, American actress (b. Oct. 15, 1926, Canton, Ohio—d. Oct. 13, 2000, La Jolla, Calif.), appeared in leading roles in several films in the 1940s and '50s—among them *Captain from Castile* (1947), *Pickup on South Street* (1953), *Three Coins in the Fountain* (1954), and *A Man Called Peter* (1955), her last—but was more notable to the public for her relationship with (beginning in 1946) and marriage to (1957–71) eccentric, reclusive billionaire Howard Hughes. She was said to have agreed, as part of her divorce settlement, not to appear in films as long as Hughes was alive and never to divulge details of their marriage. Peters later performed in a few television shows.

Petty, Lee, American race-car driver (b. March 14, 1914, Level Cross, N.C.—d. April 5, 2000, Greensboro, N.C.), was a three-time National Association for Stock Car Auto Racing (NASCAR) Grand National champion, winner of the first Daytona 500, and the patriarch of a stock-car racing dynasty that included his legendary son, Richard. Beginning his racing career in 1949—two years after NASCAR was founded—Petty quickly established himself as one of his sport's early stars. He went on to win a total of 54 NASCAR races, including the inaugural Daytona 500 in 1959. He won NASCAR Grand National titles in 1954, 1958, and 1959. After his retirement from professional racing in the early 1960s, he oversaw the family business, Petty Enterprises, which became the winningest team in stock-car racing history.

Pham Van Dong, Vietnamese revolutionary (b. March 1, 1906, Quang Ngai province, Annam [now Vietnam]—d. April 29, 2000, Hanoi, Vietnam), was an architect of Vietnam's communist revolution; he was prime minister of the Democratic Republic of Vietnam (North Vietnam) from 1955 to 1976 and of the Socialist Republic of Vietnam (reunified Vietnam) from 1976 to 1987. The son of a Confucian scholar, Dong joined Ho Chi Minh's Vietnamese Revolutionary Youth Association in the 1920s. He was arrested by the French authorities for being a communist organizer in 1929 and spent seven years in prison. In 1941 Dong, who had become one of Ho's most trusted advisers, helped Ho found the Viet Minh, a communist-dominated organization dedicated to ending French colonial rule in Vietnam. After Viet Minh guerrillas finally succeeded in defeating the French in 1954, Vietnam was partitioned and Dong was appointed prime minister of the North. As prime minister, Dong served as the North's principal spokesman during the Vietnam War and headed the government of the reunified Vietnam after the war was over. In the 1970s and '80s Dong firmly opposed attempts to implement liberal economic reforms, but his obstinate stance only contributed to mounting pressure on him to step down. He did so in 1987, in later years serving as a government adviser.

Pindling, Sir Lynden Oscar, Bahamian politician (b. March 22, 1930, Nassau, Bahamas, British West Indies—d. Aug. 26, 2000, Nassau, Bahamas), served as prime minister of The Bahamas for more than 25 years. He guided the nation from 1967 (when it was still

top: Keystone Collection/Hulton Getty Historical Archive/Liaison Agency; bottom: AP/Wide World Photos

a British colony) through its transition to independence in 1973 and over long years of burgeoning tourism and economic growth (during which he won reelection five times). Pindling's tenure ended when he and the Progressive Liberal Party he had cofounded in 1953 were defeated in the 1992 general elections amid economic decline and unproven accusations of official corruption and of taking bribes from illegal drug traffickers.

Powell, Anthony Dymoke, British writer (b. Dec. 21, 1905, London, Eng.—d. March 28, 2000, near Frome, Somerset, Eng.), was the author of one of the most highly regarded post-World War II literary creations, the 12-volume series *A Dance to the Music of Time* (1951–75). In this million-word masterpiece, with its hundreds of characters, he satirically chronicled the lives of a group of upper-middle-class schoolmates from the beginning of World War I through the early 1970s, observing the relationships between his books' inhabitants and the effects that life's unpredictability had on their character. He came to be called the "English Proust." Powell was educated at Eton College and at Balliol College, Oxford, and upon graduation (1926) went to work at the Duckworth publishing firm. His first book, *Afternoon Men* (1931), was published by that firm, as were his three subsequent offerings—*Venusberg* (1932), *From a View to a Death* (1933), and *Agents and Patients* (1936). Powell became a film scriptwriter for Warner Brothers in 1936 and spent a few months in Hollywood in 1937, and around that same time he began writing book reviews for London newspapers. His next book, *What's Become of Waring?*, was published in 1939. Powell served in the Welch Regiment and then in the Intelligence Corps during World War II, and afterward he returned to journalism, serving on the staffs of *The Times Literary Supplement* and *Punch* magazine and writing book reviews for *The Daily Telegraph*. In 1948 he published the biography *John Aubrey and His Friends*, and in 1951 came *A Question of Upbringing*, the first volume of *A Dance to the Music of Time*. Following the publication of the series' final volume, *Hearing Secret Harmonies* (1975), Powell produced such works as the four-volume collection of memoirs *To Keep the Ball Rolling* (1976–82), the novel *The Fisher King* (1986), the collections of reviews *Miscellaneous Verdicts* (1990) and *Under Review* (1992), and three volumes of diaries entitled *Journals* (1995–97). Powell was made CBE in 1956, was offered a knighthood in 1973 but refused it, and was appointed a Companion of Honour in 1988.

Puente, Tito (Ernest Anthony Puente, Jr.), American bandleader and percussionist (b. April 20, 1923, New York, N.Y.—d. May 31, 2000, New York), joked and mugged as he played vibraphone and timbales (paired, high-pitched drums) with infectious energy, and rose to fame with 1950s mambo dance hits; nicknamed the "King of Mambo," he became a major figure by joining the melodies of jazz to the bravura showmanship of Latin music. The son of immigrants from Puerto Rico, he grew up in New York's Barrio, or Spanish Harlem, and became a professional musician when he was 13. After an apprenticeship in the historic Machito Orchestra, he served in the navy during World War II and formed his own 10-piece band in 1947. The fashion for mambo music soon followed, centred in New York City's Palladium Ballroom, where the bands of Puente, Tito Rodriguez, and Perez Prado excited crowds of dancers; "It is not music for a funeral parlor," he said. Puente added to his repertoire other Latin and Afro-Cuban rhythms, including cha-cha, merengue, bossa nova, and salsa; songs such as "Babarabatiri," "Ran Kan Kan," and "Oye Como Va" fueled his fame. The most popular among the Latin musicians he introduced to American audiences was singer Celia Cruz, after she defected from Cuba in 1961. Always influenced by big-band jazz—"I start off writing a straight jazz arrangement, then I just add a Latin rhythm section," he said—Puente performed with jazz stars, including George Shearing and Woody Herman, as well as with many stars of Latin music and, in later years, with symphony orchestras. Of the approximately 120 albums that he recorded, 5 won Grammy Awards, including *Mambo Birdland* in 2000. Almost to the end, he led his band on an unusually active schedule, playing 200–300 engagements a year throughout the world. He also performed in several films, including *Radio Days* (1987) and *The Mambo Kings* (1992).

Janet Sommer/Archive Photos

King of Mambo Tito Puente

Purdy, Alfred Wellington ("Al"), Canadian poet (b. Dec. 30, 1918, Wooler, Ont.—d. April 21, 2000, Sidney, B.C.), was one of the leading Canadian poets of the 20th century. Purdy captured the loneliness and quiet grandeur of the Canadian landscape in his work, which included a novel (*A Splinter in the Heart* [1990]), an autobiography (*Reaching for the Beaufort Sea* [1993]), nine collections of essays, and more than 30 volumes of poetry. Purdy, a high-school dropout, published his first volume of poetry in 1944 when he was serving in the Royal Canadian Air Force. It was not until the 1960s, however, that he was able to support his family on earnings from his poetry and freelance journalism. Purdy's poems ranged from the mundane to the sublime. He often wrote of his native eastern Ontario, of the members of Canada's working class—farmers, lumberjacks—and of life's frustrations and sorrows. He was a two-time recipient of Canada's highest literary prize, the Governor General's Award for Poetry—first in 1965 for *The Cariboo Horses* and later, in 1986, for *Collected Poems*. Purdy's final collection of poems, *Beyond Remembering*, was published posthumously.

Quilico, Louis, Canadian opera singer (b. Jan. 14, 1925, Montreal, Que.—d. July 15, 2000, Toronto, Ont.), was an acclaimed baritone who sang more than 80 opera roles during a career that spanned nearly five decades. As a young man, Quilico won a scholarship to study at the Conservatorio di Musica Santa Cecilia in Rome. He later attended the Montreal Conservatory and the Mannes College of Music, New York City, before making his professional debut at the Opera Guild of Montreal in 1954. The following year Quilico was a winner of the Metropolitan Opera Auditions of the Air, though he did not debut at the Met until 1972. He sang at the Met for 25 consecutive years, giving nearly 300 performances for the company, and he also appeared at prominent opera houses in Paris, Vienna, Florence, and Buenos Aires, Arg. Quilico specialized in Italian and French Romantic roles and was particularly admired for his performance in the title role of Giuseppe Verdi's *Rigoletto*, which he sang more than 500 times. He was named a Companion of the Order of Canada in 1974.

Quine, Willard Van Orman, American logician and philosopher (b. June 25, 1908, Akron, Ohio—d. Dec. 25, 2000, Boston, Mass.), was a major figure in Anglo-American analytic philosophy. Quine majored in mathematics at Oberlin (Ohio) College (1926–30) before earning his Ph.D. (1932) in philosophy from Harvard University; his dissertation in symbolic logic was supervised by Alfred North Whitehead. In 1932–33 Quine traveled as a Sheldon traveling fellow to Vienna, Prague, and Warsaw, where he met logicians Alfred Tarski and Kurt Gödel, as well as Rudolf Carnap, Moritz Schlick, and other members of the Vienna Circle of logical positivists, whose ideas achieved great influence in Great Britain and the U.S. After three years as a junior fellow at Harvard, Quine joined the faculty in 1936, and, except for the years he served (1942–46) in the U.S. Navy, where he deciphered German submarine codes, he remained there until he retired in 1978. Quine's early writings were on logic, but he turned to more general philosophical concerns in the late 1940s. His 1951 paper "Two Dogmas of Empiricism" attacked the distinction between analytic statements (whose truth depends on the synonymy of the terms in it) and synthetic statements (whose truth depends on correspondence with experience), which was accepted by logical positivists and other analytic philosophers. Quine argued that synonymy cannot be established independently of analyticity, and that the distinction therefore collapses. Consequently, all statements are dependent on experience. The paper established his reputation, and its conclusion reflected Quine's thoroughgoing empiricism, in which even the most abstract statements of logic, mathematics, and philosophy must ultimately be tested by experience. Among his many books were *Mathematical Logic* (1940), *From a Logical Point of View* (1953), *Word and Object* (1960), and his autobiography, *The Time of My Life* (1985).

Rabin, Leah (Leah Schlossberg), German-born Israeli consort and peace activist (b. April 8, 1928, Königsberg, Ger. [now Kaliningrad, Russia]—d. Nov. 12, 2000, Tel Aviv, Israel), was the wife of former Israeli prime minister Yitzhak Rabin, who was assassinated in 1995. She grew up in Tel Aviv and met her husband while both were serving in the Palmach, a Jewish militia unit. The two were married during the Arab-Israeli war of 1948–49. Leah Rabin was an outspoken supporter of her husband, who served as prime minister in 1974–77 and, after his return to office in 1992, led Israel toward peace with its Palestinian and Arab neighbours. After his murder by a right-wing Jewish activist, Leah Rabin campaigned internationally for the peace process that her husband had promoted.

Rampal, Jean-Pierre, French flutist (b. Jan. 7, 1922, Marseilles, France—d. May 20, 2000, Paris, France), was considered the preeminent performer on the instrument in the 20th century. A brilliant virtuoso, he made more than 400 recordings and was credited with restoring the flute to its position as a popular solo instrument. Rampal took lessons from his father, who taught at the local conservatory. He then entered medical school but during World War II, to escape conscription by the Germans, went underground and left Marseilles for Paris. He studied at the Paris Conservatory, where he took a first prize in flute, and at the end of the war began his career. He gave recitals throughout Europe, entered into a long collaboration with the pianist and harpsichordist Robert Veyron-Lacroix, became principal flutist with the Paris Opera, and in the late 1950s made his first tours to the United States and Canada. He made 100–150 appearances a year, both with orchestras and chamber groups and as a soloist. Although he was closely identified with the music of the baroque and classical periods, he also played 20th-century as well as nonclassical and non-Western music. His recording of Claude Bolling's *Suite for Flute and Jazz Piano* remained on the U.S. *Billboard* charts for 10 years, and he is considered to have paved the way for what became known as classical crossover. Rampal taught at the Paris Conservatory, and he also took up conducting and became active in recovering and editing forgotten works for the flute. He played a gold-plated instrument made in 1869. His autobiography, *Music, My Love,* was published in 1989.

Rankin, John Morris, Canadian musician (b. April 28, 1959, Mabou, Cape Breton Island, N.S.—d. Jan. 16, 2000, near Inverness, Cape Breton Island), was a master fiddler and pianist who, as leader of the Rankins, a musical group made up of members of his family, helped revive interest in North American Celtic music and culture; a child prodigy who was featured in the 1973 documentary film *The Vanishing Cape Breton Fiddler,* he went on to achieve stardom with the tradition-oriented Rankins, who sold two million albums and won five Juno Awards; he died when his truck skidded off a coastal highway into the Gulf of St. Lawrence.

Rausing, Gad Anders, Swedish industrialist (b. May 19, 1922, Bromma, near Stockholm, Swed.—d. Jan. 28, 2000, Lausanne, Switz.), was the son of the developer of a sealed, laminated paperboard beverage box that did not require refrigeration and thus revolutionized the milk and juice industries. Rausing (with his younger brother, Hans) built the family business, Tetra Pak (later Tetra Laval Group), from a small Scandinavian concern into one of the world's largest food-container companies, with a worldwide near monopoly in drinks packaging, and amassed a personal fortune estimated at some $9 billion. He was also an avid archaeologist and a member of the Royal Swedish Academy of Letters, History and Antiquities.

Raymond, Claude, Haitian general (b. 1929—d. Feb. 9, 2000, Port-au-Prince, Haiti), was army chief of staff under Haitian dictator François ("Papa Doc") Duvalier and defense and interior minister under Duvalier's son and successor, Jean-Claude ("Baby Doc") Duvalier. After the younger Duvalier was forced into exile in 1986, Raymond tried to run for president, but electoral officials rejected him as a candidate. Raymond, who was accused of having overseen the election-day massacre of voters on Nov. 29, 1987, was arrested in July 1996 on suspicion of plotting to overthrow the elected government. He was imprisoned and held without trial, despite insufficient evidence, international protests, and three Haitian court orders for his release.

Reed, Janet, American dancer (b. Sept. 15, 1916, Tolo, Ore.—d. Feb. 28, 2000, Seattle, Wash.), was noted not only for her technique but also for her charm, vivacity, and flair for comedy, all of which were especially well showcased in the ballets *Fancy Free* and *Interplay.* During her performing career, from the late 1930s through the '50s, she danced with such companies as the San Francisco Ballet, Ballet Theatre (now American Ballet Theatre), and New York City Ballet, as well as on Broadway; she later served as NYCB's ballet mistress, and in 1974 she aided in the founding of Seattle's Pacific Northwest Ballet, which she served as artistic director for the following two years.

Janet Reed in The Nutcracker

New York City Ballet Co.

Reeves, Steven, American bodybuilder and actor (b. Jan. 21, 1926, Glasgow, Mont.—d. May 1, 2000, Escondido, Calif.), reigned as Mr. America of 1947, Mr. World (1948), and Mr. Universe (1950) before parlaying his spectacular physique into a bonanza at the box office. The first of his 18 films, the Italian *Le fatiche di Ercole* (1957), was dubbed into English, titled *Hercules* (1959), and set the stage for a series of swashbuckling sword-and-sandal epics that showcased Reeves as a heroic strongman. Other Italian American hits included *Diavolo bianco* (1959; *The White Warrior,* 1961), *Gli ultimi giorni di Pompeii* (1959; *The Last Days of Pompeii,* 1960), *Il terrore dei barbari* (1959; *Goliath and the Barbarians,* 1960), and *La battaglia di Maratona* (1959; *The Giant of Marathon,* 1960). Although Reeves was reportedly the highest-paid actor in Europe in 1967, he retired two years later to an estate in California, where he raised horses.

Rembar, Charles, American lawyer (b. March 12, 1915, Oceanport, N.J.—d. Oct. 24, 2000, Bronx, N.Y.), successfully defended the publishers of such celebrated books as *Lady Chatterley's Lover* (1928), *Tropic of Cancer* (France, 1934; U.S., 1961) and *Fanny Hill* (1748–49) in some of the foremost censorship battles waged in the U.S. After winning the *Fanny Hill* case before the U.S. Supreme Court, which ruled that the book was protected under the First Amendment, Rembar was hailed as a pathfinder; no other book was ever again judged to be obscene in U.S. courts. Rembar's anticensorship campaign began when Norman Mailer, his cousin, asked him to defend the earthy language in one of his works. Rembar recounted his constitutional encounters in *The End of Obscenity* (1968), for which he won the George Polk Memorial Award in journalism in 1969.

Rettig Guissen, Raúl, Chilean lawyer and statesman (b. May 26, 1909, Temuco, Chile—d. April 30, 2000, Santiago, Chile), headed the Truth and Reconciliation Commission responsible for investigating human rights abuses in Chile during the 1974–90 regime of Gen. Augusto Pinochet Ugarte. Rettig had served as a senator and ambassador before being appointed to lead the commission in 1990. The nine-member panel published its findings—known as the Rettig report—in 1991, concluding that at least 3,197 persons were killed or disappeared during Pinochet's rule.

Riabouchinska, Tatiana (Tatyana Ryabushinskaya), Russian-born dancer and teacher (b. May 23, 1917, Moscow, Russia—d. Aug. 24, 2000, Los Angeles, Calif.), was the oldest of the "baby ballerinas," the three teenage dancers who in the 1930s captured public attention and attracted an audience to the Ballet Russe de Monte Carlo, the company formed to fill the gap left by the dissolution of the renowned Ballets Russes following the death of impresario Sergey Diaghilev in 1929. She was known for her speed,

Hulton-Deutsch Collection/Corbis

Ballerina Tatiana Riabouchinska

her light, delicate style, her musicality, and her sensitive interpretation of roles. To many, however, she was also known in a completely different light—as the "model" for the hippopotamus ballerina in the Walt Disney animated film *Fantasia* (1940), whose artists had made rehearsal sketches of her. Riabouchinska escaped from Russia with family members during the Russian Revolution and settled in Paris. She was performing with a variety show, the *Chauve Souris,* when George Balanchine discovered her and signed her for the Ballet Russe, with which she danced from 1932 to 1942 and again in 1947. Among her most notable roles for the company were the Child in *Jeux d'enfants,* the Mistress of Ceremonies in *Cotillon,* the title role in *Le Coq d'or,* the Florentine Beauty in *Paganini,* Frivolity in *Les Présages,* and the Prelude in *Les Sylphides.* In another of her most famous roles, the Romantic Girl in *Graduation Ball,* she was partnered by the ballet's choreographer, David Lichine, whom she married in 1943. The couple made a number of guest appearances internationally over the following years—during which Riabouchinska added the title roles in the classics *La Sylphide* and *Giselle* to the list of her more memorable triumphs—and in 1953 moved to California and opened a ballet school in Beverly Hills. For a few years they attempted to found a permanent Los Angeles-based ballet company, but they were unable to attract sufficient financial support. Riabouchinska continued teaching ballet until a few hours before her death.

Richard, (Joseph Henri) Maurice ("the Rocket"), Canadian ice hockey player (b. Aug. 4, 1921, Montreal, Que.—d. May 27, 2000, Montreal), skated with electrifying passion, as a star of the Montreal Canadiens dynasty that won eight National Hockey League championship Stanley Cups in the 1940s and '50s. The first player to score 500 goals, the left-handed Richard skated on right wing, attacking opponents' goal nets with speed, an accurate backhand shot, and blazing black eyes—"crazy eyes," according to his Detroit rival Gordie Howe, who maintained that Richard "set the standard to chase, and that was the scoring and also his total ability." Over 18 seasons Richard's aggressive play made him a hero among French Canadians. Opposing teams sent their roughest players to hack, slash, or trip him—anything to stop him; his retaliating led to his gaining a reputation for having a hot temper. In 1955, when he was suspended from playing because of fighting, fans in Montreal rioted, and the destruction did not end until after he broadcast an appeal for calm the next day. The son of a former semiprofessional hockey player, Richard broke in with the Canadiens in 1942, and in the next season, with 32 goals, he led his team to the Stanley Cup. In his third season he scored 50 goals in 50 games and set a record that was not broken until 1981. Altogether he led the league in scoring five times; in 1947, after scoring 45 goals, he was awarded the Hart Memorial Trophy for most valuable player. Meanwhile, the Canadiens won additional Stanley Cups in 1946 and 1953; by the time the star-studded Canadiens won their extraordinary five Stanley Cups in a row (1956–60), Maurice and his brother Henri Richard ("the Pocket Rocket") were teammates. Maurice scored a total of 544 goals and 965 points in 978 regular-season games, and an additional 82 goals in 133 playoff games. Dignitaries, including Canadian Prime Minister Jean Chrétien and former prime minister Brian Mulroney, joined the throng at Notre Dame Basilica in Montreal for Richard's funeral, which was broadcast live on national television networks. Richard was admitted to the Hockey Hall of Fame in 1961, and during the 1998–99 season the NHL instituted a trophy for the leading goalscorer bearing his name.

Richards, Beah, American actress (b. July 12, 1926, Vicksburg, Miss.—d. Sept. 14, 2000, Vicksburg), had a more than 50-year career in film and on stage and television; her television honours included a CableACE Award (1987) for *As Summers Die* on HBO and Emmy Awards for appearances on *Frank's Place* (1988) and *The Practice* (2000). Among her films were *Guess Who's Coming to Dinner* (1967) and *Beloved* (1998).

Robards, Jason Nelson, American actor (b. July 26, 1922, Chicago, Ill.—d. Dec. 26, 2000, Bridgeport, Conn.), was one of the most distinguished and well-respected stage and screen performers of the second half of the 20th century. He was especially noted for his interpretations of roles in the plays of Eugene O'Neill and was credited with having enhanced O'Neill's reputation and having helped secure his position in theatrical history. Robards enlisted in the navy in 1939 after graduating from high school. He was serving in the South Pacific when the U.S. entered World War II, participated in 13 major engagements, and was awarded the Navy Cross. Following the war—at the urging of his father, actor Jason Robards, Sr.—he enrolled (1946) at the American Academy of Dramatic Arts in New York City. Robards took a number of odd jobs while seeking to launch his acting career and had a few small parts in stage productions, and in 1953 director José Quintero gave him a lead role in an Off-Broadway play, *American Gothic.* His career did not take off, however, until Quintero offered Robards a small part in a 1956 revival of O'Neill's *The Iceman Cometh.* When the lead role of Hickey had not been cast, Robards asked to read for it, and by the time he had finished one monologue, it was clear that he could totally inhabit the role. That production made Robards a star and began the revival of O'Neill's reputation. Robards and Quintero further collaborated on Broadway productions of the O'Neill plays *Long Day's Journey into Night* (1956), *Hughie* (1964), *A Moon for the Misbegotten* (1973), and *A Touch of the Poet* (1977), and Robards revisited some of those roles in later revivals. Robards also starred in such Broadway hits as *The Disenchanted* (1958), for which he won a Tony Award in 1959; *Toys in the Attic* (1960); *A Thousand Clowns* (1962); *After the Fall* (1964); and *No Man's Land* (1994). While live theatre was his first love, Robards also had an extensive film and television career. Among his motion pictures were film versions of two of his Broadway successes, *Long Day's Journey into Night* (1962) and *A Thousand Clowns* (1965), and two for which he won Academy Awards for best supporting actor, *All the President's Men* (1976) and *Julia* (1977). Other notable film performances came in *The Night They Raided Minsky's* (1968), *Melvin and Howard* (1980), *Philadelphia* (1993), and *Magnolia* (1999). Robards was presented the National Medal of Arts in 1997 and a Kennedy Center Honor in 1999.

AP/Wide World Photos

Roosevelt, Kermit ("Kim"), American intelligence officer (b. 1916, Buenos Aires, Arg.—d. June 8, 2000, Cockeysville, Md.), as director of the Central Intelligence Agency's (CIA's) Near East and Africa division, he orchestrated the 1953 coup that overthrew Iranian Prime Minister Mohammad Mosaddeq and brought Mohammad Reza Shah Pahlavi to power. Roosevelt was a grandson of U.S. Pres. Theodore Roosevelt and a distant cousin of Pres. Franklin D. Roosevelt. Educated at Harvard University, he joined the Office of Strategic Services—the forerunner of the CIA—during World War II. The operation he directed in Iran in 1953 was the CIA's first successful overthrow of a foreign government. Roosevelt later wrote a book about his experience, *Countercoup: The Struggle for the Control of Iran* (1979). After leaving the CIA in 1958, he worked for several American corporations with business in the Middle East and as a lobbyist representing foreign governments in Washington.

Rotimi, Ola (Emmanuel Gladstone Olawale Rotimi), Nigerian playwright and director (b. April 13, 1938, Sapele, Nigeria—d. Aug. 18, 2000, Ile-Ife, Nigeria), was trained in the Western theatre tradition but incorporated into his predominately English-language plays traditional Nigerian cultural forms, including ethnic dances and indigenous languages. His works often presented figures or incidents of historical importance in Nigeria in an effort to highlight the relevance of the past to contemporary issues. A Nigerian government scholarship took Rotimi in 1959 to the United States, where he studied fine arts at Boston University and writing at the school of drama at Yale University. While at Boston and Yale, he wrote his first two plays, *To Stir the God of Iron* (1963) and *Our Husband Has Gone Mad Again* (1966). After earning a master's degree from Yale, Rotimi returned to Nigeria, lecturing first at what became Obafemi Awolowo University in Ile-Ife and later at the University of Port Harcourt. During this time, he wrote several plays, including the acclaimed *The Gods Are Not to Blame* (1968), a retelling of the Oedipus story; *Ovonramwen Nogbaisi* (1971), about the last ruler of the Benin empire; and *Hopes of the Living Dead* (1985), which recounted Nigerian choral composer Ikoli Harcourt Whyte's fight for equal rights for lepers. Rotimi had taught at Macalester College in St. Paul, Minn., until he returned home to Nigeria shortly before his death.

Rowan, Carl Thomas, American journalist, writer, and radio and television commentator (b. Aug. 11, 1925, Ravenscroft, Tenn.—d. Sept. 23, 2000, Washington, D.C.), was one of the first African American officers in the U.S. Navy during World War II, broke colour barriers at the State Department when he served as a deputy assistant secretary of state in the administration of Pres. John F. Kennedy, and from 1965 wrote newspaper columns, usually concerned with race relations, that came to be syndicated to 60 newspapers thrice weekly. He was also a panelist on the weekly television show *Inside Washington* (originally *Agronsky and Company*) from 1967 to 1996 and wrote eight books.

Runcie of Cuddesdon, Robert Alexander Kennedy Runcie, Baron, British cleric (b. Oct. 2, 1921, Liverpool, Eng.—d. July 11, 2000, St. Albans, Eng.), was archbishop of Canterbury from 1980 to 1991; as spiritual leader of the Church of England, he often stirred controversy with his outspoken views on the British royal family and the government of Prime Minister Margaret Thatcher. Runcie earned a scholarship to the University of Oxford but left after his freshman year to serve as a tank officer in the Scots Guards during World War II. After the war, he returned to Oxford, took a degree in Greats, with first-class honours, and was ordained in 1951. A number of academic positions followed; he served as a dean of the University of Cambridge and, from 1960 to 1969, was principal of Cuddesdon Theological College, near Oxford. Runcie was consecrated bishop of St. Albans in 1970. As cochairman of the Anglican-Orthodox Joint Doctrinal Commission from 1973 to 1980, he traveled widely in Eastern Europe, meeting with Orthodox leaders in an effort to improve relations between the two churches. As archbishop of Canterbury, Runcie conducted the 1981 wedding of Charles, prince of Wales, and Diana Spencer, but he later publicly criticized the two, calling their union an "arranged" one. Runcie also angered the Thatcher government by denouncing Britain's nuclear buildup and accusing the government of neglecting the poor. Thatcher's successor, Prime Minister John Major, made Runcie a life peer in 1991. Among Runcie's publications were *Seasons of the Spirit* (1983), *One Light for One World* (1988), and *The Unity We Seek* (1989).

Adam Woolfitt/Corbis

Runciman, Sir Steven (James Cochran Stevenson Runciman), British historian (b. July 7, 1903, Northumberland, Eng.—d. Nov. 1, 2000, Radway, Eng.), was a leading expert on the history of the Byzantine Empire and the Crusades. His three-volume work, *A History of the Crusades,* was published in 1951–54 to wide acclaim and was followed by *The Fall of Constantinople, 1453* (1965), another highly praised work. Runciman served as a lecturer at the University of Cambridge from 1932 to 1938 and as a professor of Byzantine art and history at the University of Istanbul from 1942 to 1945, but for most of his life he was an independent scholar. *A Traveller's Alphabet,* a memoir, appeared in 1991. Runciman was knighted in 1958.

Sainsbury, Sir Robert James, British grocer and arts patron (b. Oct. 24, 1906, London, Eng. —d. April 2, 2000, London), was joint manager of Sainsbury's grocery business with his older brother, Alan (later Lord Sainsbury), but he made his personal mark as an art collector and philanthropist, championing such contemporary artists as Henry Moore, Alberto Giacometti, and Francis Bacon. Sainsbury served as trustee (1959–73), vice-chairman (1967–69), and chairman (1969–73) of the Tate Gallery, and in 1973 he donated his large art collection to the University of East Anglia's Sainsbury Centre for Visual Arts in Norwich, which he commissioned from architect Norman Foster and later expanded. Sainsbury was knighted for his contributions to the arts in 1967.

Salam, Saeb Salim, Lebanese politician and statesman (b. Jan 17, 1905, Beirut, Lebanon—d. Jan. 21, 2000, Beirut), was a prominent Sunni Muslim and Arab nationalist who served as his nation's prime minister six times between 1952 and 1973 (once for only four days) and worked for Muslim-Christian reconciliation during and after the Lebanese civil war (1975–76).

Sasaki, Hideo, American landscape architect and educator (b. Nov. 25, 1919, Reedley, Calif.—d. Aug. 30, 2000, Walnut Creek, Calif.), pioneered a collaborative approach to design. His work on the Deere & Company headquarters in Moline, Ill., helped define the modern corporate office park.

Sautet, Claude, French motion picture director (b. Feb. 23, 1924, Montrouge, near Paris, France —d. July 22, 2000, Paris), specialized in exploring the intimate lives of the contemporary French bourgeoisie, notably in such films as *Les Choses de la vie* (1969; *The Things of Life*), *César et Rosalie* (1972; *César and Rosalie*), and the Academy Award-nominated *Une Histoire simple* (1978; *A Simple Story*). Sautet twice won the César Award in France for best director, for *Un Coeur en hiver* (1992; *A Heart in Winter*) and *Nelly et Monsieur Arnaud* (1995).

Schindler, Alexander Moshe, German-born American rabbi (b. Oct. 4, 1925, Munich, Ger.—d. Nov. 15, 2000, Westport, Conn.), was president (1973–96) of the Union of American Hebrew Congregations (UAHC), Reform Judaism's main governing body. Fleeing Nazi Germany with his family, he arrived in the U.S. at the age of 12. After serving with the U.S. Army during World War II, during which he earned a Purple Heart and a Bronze Star for bravery, he studied at the City College of New York and Hebrew Union College, New York City; he was ordained in 1953. As president of the UAHC, Schindler was praised for developing an outreach program in 1978 to attract non-Jews to Judaism and draw non-observant Jews back to the faith. He also supported the rights of gay and lesbian Jews to become rabbis.

Schmirler, Sandra, Canadian curler (b. June 11, 1963, Biggar, Sask.—d. March 2, 2000, Regina, Sask.), was captain of the Canadian women's curling team that won a gold medal at the 1998 Winter Olympics—the first Olympics in which curling was a medal sport. Before Schmirler and her Olympic teammates Jan Betker, Joan McCusker, and Marcia Gudereit captured the gold medal, they won three world championships (1993–94, 1997). In 1999 Schmirler was inducted into the Canadian Curling Hall of Fame. One of Canada's most popular sports figures, she was admired for her outgoing personality as well as her athletic skill. Her appearance at a news conference three weeks before her death from cancer attracted widespread media attention.

Schulz, Charles Monroe ("Sparky"), American cartoonist (b. Nov. 26, 1922, Minneapolis, Minn.—d. Feb. 12, 2000, Santa Rosa, Calif.), spent nearly half a century creating *Peanuts,* a simple comic strip that reflected the humour, fantasies, and anxieties in the lives of a group of

John Burgess/Press Democrat/Liaison Agency

Charles Schulz and friends

children, and made it one of the most popular in the world. The antics of the perennially frustrated roundheaded Charlie Brown and his friends—notably his sister, Sally; the fussbudget Lucy; Lucy's philosophical brother Linus, whose security blanket added a term to the English language; the piano-playing Beethoven fan Schroeder; and the sandal-wearing nonstudent Peppermint Patty—as well as Snoopy, his imaginative pet dog, appeared in more than 20 languages in over 2,600 newspapers in some 75 countries and were enjoyed by 355 million readers. Schulz's nickname came from the comic strip *Barney Google,* one of whose characters was the horse Spark Plug, and when he was a young child, Schulz knew he wanted cartoons also to give him a career. He practiced by copying the work of established cartoonists, and when he was 15, one of his drawings was printed in the "Ripley's Believe It or Not!" newspaper feature. Ironically, his high-school yearbook rejected his cartoons. Following high school, Schulz studied cartooning through a correspondence course offered by Art Instruction Inc. in Minneapolis. He then was drafted into the army for World War II service, and upon leaving the military he had a variety of jobs, including correcting students' work for Art Instruction, lettering comics in the Roman Catholic publication *Timeless Topix,* and drawing the *Li'l Folks* cartoon for the *St. Paul* (Minn.) *Pioneer Press. The Saturday Evening Post* also published some of his cartoons. In 1950 United Features Syndicate accepted the *Li'l Folks* strip but changed its name to *Peanuts,* a name Schulz disliked. At first only a handful of newspapers printed the strip, but by 1958 it was running in over 400. *Peanuts* also gave rise to huge amounts of related merchandise—including calendars, greeting cards, dolls, clothes, and hundreds of books—as well as such animated television specials as the Emmy Award-winning "A Charlie Brown Christmas" (1965) and "It's the Great Pumpkin, Charlie Brown" (1966) and the stage musical *You're a Good Man, Charlie Brown* (1967). Snoopy became NASA's official mascot, and in 1969 the Apollo 10 mission's Lunar Module was named "Snoopy" and the Command Module "Charlie Brown." Among Schulz's honours were the National Cartoonists Society's Reuben Award (1955 and 1964) and the National Education Association's School Bell Award (1960). Schulz, who had been battling colon cancer and had announced his retirement, scheduled his final original strip for Sunday, February 13. His death came on the eve of that strip, which was a signed farewell.

Segal, George, American sculptor (b. Nov. 26, 1924, New York, N.Y.—d. June 11, 2000, South Brunswick, N.J.), was one of the world's most influential and innovative sculptors during the second half of the 20th century. He was best known for his monochromatic, cast plaster figures, which he often situated in environments of mundane furnishings and objects. Educated at Cooper Union, New York, N.Y.; the Pratt Institute of Design, Brooklyn, N.Y.; New York University (B.S., 1950); and Rutgers University, New Brunswick, N.J. (M.F.A., 1963), Segal began his artistic career as an abstract painter. In the late 1950s he was associated with members of the burgeoning Pop art movement. Segal's sculptures, however, cast from living models and outfitted with the bland commercial props of the Pop idiom, were distinguished from that characteristically ironic movement by a mute, ghostly anguish. His casting technique, in which a live model was wrapped in strips of plaster-soaked cheesecloth, imparted a rough texture and a minimum of surface detail to the figures, thus heightening the sense of anonymity and isolation. Among his notable works were *The Butcher Shop* (1965), *The Truck* (1966), *The Laundromat* (1966–67), and *Hot Dog Stand* (1978). From the late 1970s Segal devoted much of his time to creating large sculptures for public memorials, including three—*Depression Breadline, Fireside Chat,* and *Appalachian Farm Couple 1936*—for the Franklin Delano Roosevelt Memorial in Washington, D.C., dedicated in 1997. Segal was awarded the National Medal of the Arts in 1999.

Shamlu, Ahmad, Iranian poet (b. Dec. 12, 1925, Tehran, Iran—d. July 24, 2000, Tehran), defied the conventional restrictions of formal Persian poetry in favour of heartfelt free-flowing verse that displayed his secular nationalism and his passion for political freedom and social justice. A fierce opponent of both the shah and the repressive Islamic Revolution that deposed him, Shamlu was briefly imprisoned under the shah and was treated with contempt by the Islamic regime; his books were officially banned but were privately circulated in Iran among admirers of his work.

Shapiro, Karl (Jay), American poet and critic (b. Nov. 10, 1913, Baltimore, Md.—d. May 14, 2000, New York, N.Y.), won attention early in his career as a writer of technically accomplished verse but later, particularly after he attacked the modernist movement in poetry, suffered from neglect. He attended the University of Virginia, the Peabody (music) Institute, and Johns Hopkins University, the latter two in Baltimore, but did not graduate. *V-Letter and Other Poems* (1944), written in New Guinea while he was a solider in the U.S. Army during World War II and the recipient of lavish praise from reviewers, won the Pulitzer Prize for Poetry in 1945. The volume included one of his most anthologized poems, "Elegy for a Dead Soldier." In 1946–47 he was consultant in poetry at the Library of Congress, and he edited *Poetry* magazine from 1950 to 1956 and then, for nearly a decade, the Nebraska-based *Prairie Schooner.* After teaching briefly at Johns Hopkins and at the Chicago campus of the University of Illinois, he spent two decades at the University of California, Davis. Among his many honours was the 1969 Bollingen Prize, and he twice received a Guggenheim fellowship. His criticism of poets like T.S. Eliot and Ezra Pound, sometimes in biting, even mocking, terms, coupled with an anti-intellectualist stance and the adoption of the prose poem and other antimodernist forms, put him in disfavour during the latter part of his life. He nonetheless maintained the exuberant, irreverent spirit for which he had long been known. Among his volumes of poetry were *Poems of a Jew* (1958), *The Bourgeois Poet* (1964), *Collected Poems, 1940–1978* (1978), and *New & Selected Poems, 1940–86* (1987).

Shumsky, Oscar, American violinist, conductor, and teacher (b. March 23, 1917, Philadelphia, Pa.—d. July 24, 2000, Rye, N.Y.), was a virtuoso violinist and one of the 20th century's greatest interpreters of Bach, Mozart, and Brahms. He played the violin from the age of three, and at age eight he began studying under renowned Hungarian-born violinist Leopold Auer. Later Shumsky studied under one of Auer's star pupils, Efrem Zimbalist. In the late 1930s and early '40s, Shumsky was a member of the internationally acclaimed NBC Symphony and Primrose Quartet. He also embarked on a solo career, which was interrupted by service in the U.S. Navy during World War II. Shumsky eventually tired of the commercial demands placed on soloists, and from the early 1950s he gave concerts only sporadically. Instead, he turned his attention to conducting and, especially, to teaching. Shumsky conducted, among other orchestras, the San Francisco Symphony and Canada's National Festival Orchestra. He held teaching posts at the Curtis Institute of Music, Philadelphia; the Juilliard School, New York City; and Yale University. A revival of interest in Shumsky's work occurred in the 1980s, ignited in part by a series of triumphant performances the violinist made in Europe in 1981. He also gave four enthusiastically received concerts with the Philadelphia Orchestra in 1987.

Simon, William Edward, American investment banker and government official (b. Nov. 27, 1927, Paterson, N.J.—d. June 3, 2000, Santa Barbara, Calif.), served as U.S. treasury secretary during the administrations of presidents Richard Nixon and Gerald Ford. Simon was a partner at the investment firm of Salomon Brothers when Nixon appointed him head of the Federal Energy Office in 1973; as "energy czar," Simon was credited with easing public fears during the Arab oil embargo of the early 1970s. He was later named treasury secretary under Nixon and retained the post for the duration of the Ford administration, returning to Wall Street in 1977. During the 1980s Simon formed his own investment firm and pioneered the "leveraged buyout"—the strategy of borrowing money to buy undervalued companies and then selling them for a profit. He also served (1980–84) as president of the U.S. Olympic Committee, leading efforts to raise the $90 million in funds necessary to stage the 1984 Olympic Games in Los Angeles. In 1991 Simon was inducted into the U.S. Olympic Hall of Fame.

Sithole, Ndabaningi, Zimbabwean clergyman and nationalist leader (b. July 31, 1920, Nyamandhlovu, Matabeleland, Rhodesia [now Zimbabwe]—d. Dec. 12, 2000, Philadelphia, Pa.), was an intellectual force within the Zimbabwean nationalist movement; cofounder (1961), with Joshua Nkomo, of the Zimbabwe African Peoples' Union (ZAPU); and then cofounder (1963), with Robert Mugabe, and president of the breakaway Zimbabwe

Bettmann/Corbis

African National Union (ZANU). Sithole trained as a teacher and was ordained a minister before entering politics in 1960. An advocate of armed struggle against white minority rule, he was twice imprisoned (1965–74; 1975), during which time Mugabe took control of ZANU. Sithole was elected to parliament in 1979, but he was widely criticized for his cooperation with the white regime during the nation's transition from Rhodesia to Zimbabwe. He lost his seat in the 1980 election that brought Mugabe to power as president. After living in self-imposed exile in the U.S. (1983–91), Sithole returned home and in 1995 was again elected to parliament as head of a new party, ZANU-Ndonga. In 1997 he was convicted of plotting to assassinate Mugabe and sentenced to two years in jail, but in 2000 he was permitted to go to the U.S. for medical treatment. Sithole's most influential book, *African Nationalism,* was published in 1959.

Smith, Michael, British-born Canadian biochemist (b. April 26, 1932, Blackpool, Lancashire, Eng.—d. Oct. 5, 2000, Vancouver, B.C.), won the 1993 Nobel Prize for Chemistry for the development of oligonucleotide-based site-directed mutagenesis, a technique for introducing precise changes (mutations) into genes through the hybridization of chemically synthesized sequences of DNA. The technique involved the preparation of a short piece of single-stranded DNA (an oligonucleotide) containing the desired alteration in the base sequence of the gene of interest, and it took advantage of Smith's discovery that the altered oligonucleotide, when mixed with the complementary strand of the gene, would still bind to, or hybridize with, the strand at the proper location, forming a short stretch of double-stranded DNA. When the hybridized DNA was placed in a suitable host organism, the bound oligonucleotide served as a primer for new DNA replication, using the complementary strand as a template. The result was a complete gene containing the altered sequence. The procedure, which allowed scientists to modify as well as study DNA and the proteins that they encode, was considered to hold enormous practical implications, including the development of new treatments for diseases through gene therapy and the production of bioengineered food. Smith shared the Nobel Prize with Kary B. Mullis, an American chemist who developed the polymerase chain reaction, another tool of genetic engineering. Smith entered the University of Manchester (England) in 1950 and earned a Ph.D. in 1956. In the same year he moved to Canada to work for the British Columbia Research Council. In 1966 he began teaching at the University of British Columbia, an affiliation that lasted more than 30 years. In 1987 Smith founded and became director of the university's biotechnology laboratory, and he also helped found Zymos (later ZymoGenetics Inc.), a biotechnology company. On his retirement in 1997 he became director of the Genome Sequence Centre at the Cancer Agency. He gave half of his Nobel Prize money to support research in schizophrenia and the rest to support science education for women and for elementary schoolteachers.

Smith, Wilfred Cantwell, Canadian theologian (b. July 21, 1916, Toronto, Ont.—d. Feb. 7, 2000, Toronto), was a scholar of Islam and comparative religions who encouraged dialogue and the interchange of ideas between faiths. He earned a doctorate in Islamic studies from Princeton University in 1948, and in 1949 he began teaching at McGill University, Montreal, where he founded the Institute of Islamic Studies. Smith later served (1964–1973) as director of Harvard University's Center for the Study of World Religions. He returned to Canada in 1973, establishing a department of comparative religion at Dalhousie University in Nova Scotia. He became a senior research associate at the University of Toronto following his retirement from teaching in 1984. Among his numerous books were *Islam in Modern History* (1957) and *Towards a World Theology* (1981). Smith was appointed an Officer of the Order of Canada in January 2000.

Sobchak, Anatoly Aleksandrovich, Russian politician and legal scholar (b. Aug. 10, 1937, Leningrad, Russian S.F.S.R., U.S.S.R. (now St. Petersburg, Russia)—d. Feb. 20, 2000, Svetlogorsk, Kaliningrad oblast, Russia), as mayor of Leningrad, the country's second largest city, was a leading political figure in the events surrounding the collapse of the Soviet Union and the establishment of a democratic Russia. Although born in Leningrad, Sobchak grew up in the eastern Siberian city of Chita. He returned to Leningrad in the mid-1950s and earned a law degree, after which he practiced law in Stavropol, the southern Russian city where Mikhail Gorbachev was rising in power and influence. Sobchak completed advanced legal studies in Leningrad and was appointed (1983) the first professor of economic law at Leningrad State University. He was briefly a member of the Communist Party and served (1989–91) in the U.S.S.R.'s newly democratized parliament, the Congress of People's Deputies. Gaining widespread popularity for his liberal views, incisive speaking style, and trenchant critiques of old-style politics and politicians (he reportedly once reduced Premier Nikolay Ryzhkov to tears on television), Sobchak was elected mayor of Leningrad in 1991. In the dramatic events of the anti-Gorbachev coup attempt in August 1991, Sobchak played a key role in Leningrad by defusing tensions among the local police and military leaders, persuading the pro-coup Leningrad garrison troops to remain outside the city, and rallying the civilian population in defiance of the coup leaders. Shortly after the communist regime collapsed at the end of 1991, Sobchak made the highly symbolic move of reinstating the city's pre-World War I name, St. Petersburg. In 1993 Pres. Boris Yeltsin availed himself of Sobchak's legal expertise by inviting him to draft a new constitution with a strong presidential model. Meanwhile, back in St. Petersburg, Sobchak's star was falling as popular expectations outstripped his ability to resolve vital economic issues and battle the rising level of crime and graft. He himself was accused of political improprieties, and he decisively lost his bid for reelection as mayor in 1996. Ill with a heart condition and hounded by his political opponents, Sobchak traveled to France for medical treatment in 1997, a stay that turned into self-imposed political exile. In 1999, after Vladimir Putin—Sobchak's former student and political protégé in St. Petersburg—became head of the Federal Security Bureau, Sobchak returned home. He seemed poised for a personal political comeback when he died of a heart attack while on a campaign trip for Putin.

AP/Wide World Photos

Leningrad politician Anatoly Sobchak

Soffen, Gerald Alan, American biologist (b. Feb. 7, 1926, Cleveland, Ohio—d. Nov. 22, 2000, Washington, D.C.), was the chief scientist for the Viking 1 and 2 missions to Mars. After earning a Ph.D. in biology from Princeton University in 1961, Soffen joined the National Aeronautics and Space Administration. He became the driving force behind NASA's efforts to search for life on Mars. He was disappointed when the Viking space probes, after landing on the surface of Mars in 1976, did not detect any signs of life on the planet, but he speculated that Martian life should not be ruled out completely until it was possible to explore all of the areas of Mars where evidence of water had been found. In 1983 Soffen went to work at NASA's Goddard Space Flight Center in Greenbelt, Md., and in 1990 he formed Goddard's University Programs Office to help strengthen the relationship between NASA's research groups and the academic community.

Sokolow, Anna, American dancer, choreographer, and teacher (b. Feb. 9, 1910, Hartford, Conn.—d. March 29, 2000, New York, N.Y.), created influential dramatic modern-dance works that often reflected the loneliness and alienation engendered by contemporary urban life and that often were punctuated with confrontational glares that the dancers directed at the audience. She taught and choreographed internationally, and her dances found expression in a number of prominent companies, as well as in musical theatre. Sokolow received her early dance training in a cultural centre on New York City's Lower East Side—Martha Graham was one of her teachers—and she later also studied ballet. She danced with Graham's company from 1930 to 1938 and during part of that time also had her own troupe, the Dance Unit. In 1939 she traveled to Mexico to perform and stayed on long enough to found a company. She returned there often, and in 1953 she also began visiting Israel to advise, teach, and choreograph. Perhaps Sokolow's best-known work was *Rooms* (1955), in which chairs served as symbols of the characters' isolation. With *Rooms* she became the first modern-dance choreographer to have a work presented on national television, and the dance also appeared in the short film *Rooms* (1966). Among the musicals that featured Sokolow's choreography were *Street Scene* (1947), *Regina* (1949), *Candide* (1956), and the Off-Broadway *Hair* (1967), although she withdrew from *Hair* before its opening. Sokolow continued working well into the 1990s and directed her own company in New York City, the Players' Project, choreographing for it works such as *September Sonnet* (1995).

Son Sann, Cambodian politician (b. Oct. 5, 1911, Phnom Penh, Cambodia—d. Dec. 19, 2000, Paris, France), served as Cambodia's prime minister under Prince Norodom Sihanouk from 1967 to 1968 but went into exile in Paris when Sihanouk was overthrown in 1970; during the brutal rule of the Khmer Rouge (1975–79), he helped organize the opposition to that regime. When the Vietnamese then invaded and occupied his country, Son Sann returned to Southeast Asia, formed and served as prime minister of an opposing coalition government that the UN recognized as legitimate, and helped negotiate the 1991 peace treaty.

Staples, Roebuck ("Pops"), American gospel singer (b. Dec. 28, 1915, Winona, Miss.—d. Dec. 19, 2000, Dolton, Ill.), formed (1948) and headed the resilient Staple Singers, which featured his children; the group performed in Chicago churches before recording rhythm-and-blues hits ("Uncloudy Day," "Stand By Me") in the 1950s, social-awareness songs such as "Why? (Am I Treated So Bad)" in the '60s, and soul music ("Respect Yourself," "I'll Take You There") in the '70s; Staples's bass voice, as lead singer, and his tremolo-rich guitar gave the group—which was inducted into the Rock and Roll Hall of Fame in 1999—its distinctive sound. Staples's solo career flourished with two albums, *Peace to the Neighborhood* (1992) and *Father Father* (1994), for which he won a Grammy Award.

Statham, (John) Brian ("George," "the Whippet"), British cricketer (b. June 17, 1930, Gorton, near Manchester, Eng.—d. June 11, 2000, Manchester), was one of England's finest fast bowlers, renowned for his extraordinary accuracy and consistency. In his long playing career for Lancashire (1950–68, captain 1965–67) and England (1951–65), Statham took 2,260 wickets (average 16.36), including 252 in 70 Test matches (average 24.84), and achieved 100 or more wickets in a season 13 times, with a season high of 139 in 1959. Statham formed a successful partnership with Frank Tyson in the early 1950s but reached the top of his form in a remarkable partnership with the more flamboyant Fred Trueman. After retiring from the game in 1968, Statham served Lancashire as a committee member (1970–95) and president (1997–98); he was appointed CBE in 1966.

Stebbins, George Ledyard, Jr., American botanist and geneticist (b. Jan. 6, 1906, Lawrence, N.Y.—d. Jan. 19, 2000, Davis, Calif.), was a pioneer in the field of evolutionary biology and the first scientist to artificially produce a new species of plant that was capable of thriving under natural conditions. He was educated at Harvard University (Ph.D., 1931) and then taught biology at Colgate University, Hamilton, N.Y., and the University of California, Berkeley. In 1950 he transferred to the Davis campus of the University of California, where he founded the department of genetics. He was credited with being one of the biologists responsible for applying the modern synthetic theory of evolution—which integrates such processes as natural selection, gene mutation and recombination, changes in structure and number of chromosomes, and reproductive isolation—to higher organisms. The publication of Stebbins's *Variation and Evolution in Plants* (1950) established him as the first biologist to have applied this theory to plant evolution. Working with several species of flowering plants, Stebbins and a colleague, Ernest B. Babcock, studied polyploid plants, new plant species that originated from a spontaneous doubling of the chromosomes of existing species. When a technique was developed for doubling a plant's chromosomal number artificially, Stebbins used it to produce polyploids from several species of wild grass, of which the new species *Ehrharta erecta* was established in a natural environment in 1944. Stebbins's numerous later books included the influential *Processes of Organic Evolution* (1966).

Stevens, Craig (Gail Shikles, Jr.), American actor (b. July 8, 1918, Liberty, Mo.—d. May 10, 2000, Los Angeles, Calif.), appeared in a number of forgettable films before creating the debonair yet hard-boiled title character in the popular television series *Peter Gunn* (1958– 61). Stevens reprised his TV role for the film *Gunn* (1967) and later appeared on Broadway, in cameos on TV, and in the Blake Edwards film *S.O.B.* (1981), his last screen role.

Suárez Goméz, Roberto, Bolivian drug trafficker (b. 1932, Trinidad, Bol.—d. July 20, 2000, Santa Cruz, Bol.), nicknamed the "king of cocaine," was one of the world's most notorious drug kingpins. Born into a wealthy and socially prominent family, Suárez seemed to have little motive for entering the drug trade. Nevertheless, by the mid-1970s he had begun to recruit Bolivian coca producers into "the Corporation"—an organization that, under Suárez's leadership, became a major supplier for the Medellín drug cartel of Colombia. In 1980 Suárez backed a military coup that toppled the Bolivian government; in return, he received political protection for his enterprise, and he quickly amassed a fortune that at its peak was estimated at $400 million. Unlike others in his trade, Suárez courted publicity, meeting frequently with the media and making ostentatious displays of philanthropy. These actions made him a target, however, and in the late 1980s, after civilian government had been restored in Bolivia, Suárez lost his grip on power. He was convicted on drug charges in absentia in 1988. Arrested a year later, Suárez eventually served 7 years of a 15-year prison sentence.

Subramaniam, C(hidambaram), Indian politician (b. Jan. 30, 1910, Pollachi, near Coimbatore, Tamil Nadu, India—d. Nov. 7, 2000, Chennai [formerly Madras], India), was commonly referred to as the "Father of the Green Revolution" after he introduced a new variety of wheat seed that transformed Indian agriculture and helped the country achieve self-sufficiency in grain production. Subramaniam received a degree in physics from Presidency College, University of Madras, and a law degree from Madras Law College. In the early 1940s he was imprisoned by the British authorities, and after India gained independence (1947) he was a member of the Constituent Assembly that drafted the Indian constitution. Subramaniam was elected to the Lok Sabha (lower house of parliament), held various ministerial offices in Madras state and in the national cabinet, served (1990–93) as governor of Maharashtra state, and published a multivolume autobiography, *Hand of Destiny* (1993). In 1998 he was awarded the Bharat Ratna, India's highest civilian honour.

Sunal, Kemal, Turkish actor (b. Nov. 11, 1944, Istanbul, Turkey—d. July 3, 2000, Istanbul), delighted audiences on television and in more than 80 Turkish motion pictures, particularly in a long-running series of homey situation comedies; his enormous popularity was evident when the name of one of his most lovable film personae, Saban the Cow, entered the Turkish slang vocabulary to signify a well-meaning fool. His last film, *Propaganda* (1999), however, was perceived as a shift to somewhat more serious themes. Sunal, who had a lifelong fear of flying, suffered a heart attack after being persuaded to board an airplane in Istanbul; his funeral, which drew thousands of mourners, was broadcast live on Turkish television.

Swanton, E(rnest) W(illiam) ("Jim"), British sportswriter and broadcaster (b. Feb. 11, 1907, Forest Hill, London, Eng.—d. Jan. 22, 2000, Canterbury, Kent, Eng.), was one of England's most respected and influential cricket authori-

left: Hunt Institute for Botanical Documentation; right: Dinodia Picture Agency

ties for more than 70 years. Except for his years of military service during World War II (which included 3½ years interned in a Japanese prison camp), Swanton reported on cricket throughout his life, as a radio and television commentator for the BBC (1934–75) and as a writer for the *Evening Standard* (1927–39), as cricket correspondent for the *Daily Telegraph* (daily from 1946 to 1975 and as a regular contributor thereafter), and as editorial director of *The Cricketer* magazine (1967–88). Swanton, who also reported on rugby until 1964, was a founding member of the Cricket Writers' Club and the author or editor of numerous books on the sport. He was made OBE in 1965 and advanced to CBE in 1994.

Takeshita, Noboru, Japanese politician (b. Feb. 26, 1924, Shimane prefecture, Japan —d. June 19, 2000, Tokyo, Japan), was prime minister of Japan from November 1987 to June 1989, at which time he resigned because of his involvement in an influence-peddling scandal. The son of a sake brewer, Takeshita graduated from Waseda University, Tokyo, in 1947, after which he taught high school for four years. He served seven years on the Shimane prefectural council before being elected to the lower house of the Diet (parliament) in 1958; it was the first of 11 consecutive terms. His first ministerial post was as chief cabinet secretary in 1971; he later became minister of construction and was minister of finance in 1979–80 and 1982–86. He was secretary-general of the ruling Liberal-Democratic Party (LDP) in 1986–87. In November 1987 Takeshita was handpicked for the post of president of the LDP by his predecessor, Prime Minister Yasuhiro Nakasone; following his selection as LDP president, Takeshita became prime minister of Japan. As prime minister, Takeshita garnered support for the passage of a new national sales tax. In April 1988 he publicly disclosed that he and several aides had been among those politicians who had received stocks, donations, and loans from Recruit Co., Ltd., a Japanese telecommunications firm that had made large financial contributions to many politicians in the hope of obtaining governmental favours. Deepening public dissatisfaction with Takeshita's involvement in the scandal prompted him on April 25, 1989, to announce his intention to resign. He left office the following June, but, despite his departure from the public spotlight, he continued to wield considerable influence in the world of Japanese politics until his death.

Tanaka, Toyoichi, Japanese-born American biophysicist (b. Jan. 4, 1946, Nagaoka, Japan—d. May 20, 2000, Wellesley, Mass.), conducted experiments in 1978 with mixtures of polymers and fluids while serving on the faculty of the Massachusetts Institute of Technology and created "smart gels," so called because they expanded and contracted or changed colour when exposed to even slight variations of temperature, light, magnetism, or electricity. These properties made them ideal for a number of important applications in such fields as chemistry, medicine, and agriculture. When certain gels are exposed to electricity, for example, their large changes in volume (as much as 1,000-fold) allow them to act as artificial muscles. Smart gels also have uses in the cleanup of oil spills (as the cross-linked polymer networks in the gel grow and shrink, they act as giant sponges). Tanaka, who was educated (B.S., 1968; M.A., 1970; and D.Sc., 1973) at the University of Tokyo, was the recipient of numerous awards for his work, including the 1996 Discover Award and the 1993 Vinci d'Excellence Prize. He was the founder of GelMed Inc., Gel Sciences Inc., and Buyo-Buyo, Inc.

Thomas, Bill (William Thomas Petersen), American costume designer (b. Oct. 13, 1921, Chicago, Ill.—d. May 30, 2000, Beverly Hills, Calif.), created costumes for more than 300 films. Thomas received 10 Academy Award nominations for best costume design. After studying at the University of Southern California and the Chouinard Art Institute, Los Angeles, he served in the Army Air Corps during World War II and provided fashions for United Service Organizations shows. After the war he was an apprentice designer at Metro-Goldwyn-Mayer from 1947 to 1949 and later worked for Universal Studios and Walt Disney Productions. Thomas and fellow designer Valles shared the Oscar for best costume design for their work on *Spartacus* (1960). Among other films for which Thomas received Oscar nominations were *Toys in the Attic* (1963), *Ship of Fools* (1965), and *Bedknobs and Broomsticks* (1971).

Thomas, Derrick, American football player (b. Jan. 1, 1967, Miami, Fla.—d. Feb. 8, 2000, Miami), was a star linebacker for the National Football League's Kansas City Chiefs from 1989 to 2000, earning All-Pro honours nine times and ranking ninth on the NFL's career sack list with 126.5. He also held the NFL record for most sacks in a single game (seven). One of the NFL's most popular players, he was noted for his charity work, and in 1992 he was designated one of Pres. George H.W. Bush's "thousand points of light," an honour accorded to outstanding volunteers. He died from a blood clot he developed after being involved in an automobile accident that left him paralyzed.

Thomas, R(onald) S(tuart), Welsh clergyman and poet (b. March 29, 1913, Cardiff, Glamorgan [now South Glamorgan], Wales—d. Sept. 25, 2000, Llanfairynghornwy, Gwynedd, Wales), wrote about the land and its people and about religious faith in the modern world. His poetry was austere and wholly lacking in sentimentality, but it was sometimes lyrical and often witty. He had an anglicized upbringing in Holyhead and was educated at the University College of North Wales in Bangor, where he earned a B.A. in classics in 1935. He studied theology at St. Michael's College, Llandaff, in Cardiff and was ordained a priest in the Church in Wales in 1937. His first appointments were in the borderland, but he later served churches in the west and north of Wales, in the heart of the nationalist movement. It was not until he was in his late 20s that he began to learn Welsh, and his poetry was written in English. His few writings in Welsh were in prose, primarily autobiographical essays collected in *Neb* (1985; "Nobody") and published in English translation in 1997 as *Autobiographies*. His earlier poems, collected in volumes such as *The Stones of the Field* (1946), *Song at the Year's Turning* (1955), and *Tares* (1961), were largely concerned with life on Welsh hill farms, with many employing the persona Iago Prytherch. Thomas vehemently opposed the English influence on Wales, but he was equally critical of the Welsh neglect of their own culture. Later collections, including *Laboratories of the Spirit* (1975), *Mass for Hard Times* (1992), and *No Truce with the Furies* (1995), showed a heightened concern with religious and philosophical matters. He also edited the works of other poets. Honours included the Queen's Gold Medal for Poetry in 1964 and the Cheltenham Prize in 1993, and in 1996 the Welsh Academy nominated him for the Nobel Prize for Literature.

Thompson, Homer Armstrong, Canadian-born American archaeologist (b. Sept. 7, 1906, Devlin, Ont.—d. May 7, 2000, Hightstown, N.J.), as acting deputy (1931–47) and field director (1947–67) of the American excavation of the Agora, the civic centre of ancient Athens, conducted painstaking and laborious research to unearth the site and restore its landscaping with plants used in ancient gardens. After studying the classics and earning an undergraduate degree from the University of British Columbia, Thompson completed graduate studies at the University of Michigan, where Benjamin Dean Merritt introduced him to the Agora project. In addition, Thompson unearthed the Pnyx, the meeting site of the Athenian assembly; reconstructed the Stoa of Attalus, a huge colonnade situated on the east side of the area; and wrote a definitive work on the tholos, which served as a dining hall for the Athenian Senate. From 1947 to 1977 he was professor of classical archaeology at the Institute for Advanced Study, Princeton, N.J.

Titov, Gherman Stepanovich, Russian cosmonaut (b. Sept. 11, 1935, Verkhneye Zhilino, Russia, U.S.S.R. —d. Sept. 20, 2000, Moscow, Russia), as pilot of the Vostok 2 spacecraft on its Aug. 6–7, 1961, orbital flight of 25 hours 18 minutes, was the second human to orbit the Earth. He was the first person to orbit more than once, the first to spend more than a day in space, and the first to sleep in space, and in 2000 he still held the distinction of having been the youngest to go into space. In addition, though

left: Junji Kurokawa/AFP Worldwide; right: AP/Wide World Photos

he jubilantly called out his radio identification, "I am Eagle," during his flight, he shortly thereafter became the first to suffer the nausea of space sickness. Titov graduated from the Stalingrad Flying Academy as a jet fighter pilot in 1957 and in 1960 was chosen for cosmonaut training. During his training an engineering proposal he made gained him the Order of Lenin, and he was named backup cosmonaut for the first spaceflight, which Yury Gagarin made on April 12, 1961. Following Titov's flight, the only one he made, he was named a Hero of the Soviet Union and awarded a second Order of Lenin. He served as a deputy of the Supreme Soviet during 1962–70, and in 1968 he graduated from the Zhukovsky Air Force Engineering Academy. He thereafter worked on the design and research aspects of the space program, and in 1975 he became a major general. By the time he retired in 1992, he had attained the rank of colonel general. Titov then entered politics and in 1995 ran successfully on the Communist Party ticket for a seat in the State Duma; he did not run for reelection in 1999. A crater on the far side of the Moon was named for Titov to commemorate his accomplishments.

Tranter, Nigel Godwin, Scottish historian and novelist (b. Nov. 23, 1909, Glasgow, Scot.—d. Jan. 9, 2000, Gullane, East Lothian, Scot.), published more than 130 historical novels, romances, biographies, histories, children's books, and architectural studies on Scottish castles. Although most of Tranter's books were derived from Scottish history and traditions, he also wrote a series of Western novels under the pen name Nye Tredgold. He was appointed OBE in 1983.

Trevor, Claire (Claire Wemlinger), American actress (b. March 8, 1909?, Bensonhurst, Long Island, N.Y.—d. April 8, 2000, Newport Beach, Calif.), appeared in dozens of motion pictures during her half-century-long career, often as a tough-talking though vulnerable and kind-hearted floozy. Films of the 1930s and '40s provided many of her most notable roles, among them a prostitute in *Stagecoach* (1939); a duplicitous gold digger in *Murder, My Sweet* (1944); and sadistic gangster Edward G. Robinson's mistress, a pathetic liquor-craving nightclub singer, in *Key Largo* (1948), for which she was awarded a best supporting actress Academy Award. Following studies in New York City at Columbia University and the American Academy of Dramatic Arts, Trevor began performing in repertory theatre and short films. In 1932 she made her Broadway debut in *Whistling in the Dark*, and the following year she appeared in *The Party's Over.* Later in 1933 she made her feature film debut in *Life in the Raw.* Notable among the many other films she made in the mid-1930s were *Dante's Inferno* (1935); *Dead End* (1937), which gained her her first Oscar nomination; and *The Amazing Dr. Clitterhouse* (1938), and from 1937 to 1940 she also performed on the radio drama *Big Town*. Among Trevor's later films were *Johnny Angel* (1945); *The High and the Mighty* (1954), for which she received her third Oscar nomination; *Marjorie Morningstar* (1958); *How to Murder Your Wife* (1965); and *Kiss Me Goodbye* (1982), her final film. Trevor occasionally returned to the stage, and she also made a number of television appearances. For one of her TV performances, in a revival of *Dodsworth* (1956), she was honoured with an Emmy Award.

Trout, Robert (Robert Albert Blondheim), American broadcast journalist (b. Oct. 15, 1909, Washington, D.C.—d. Nov. 14, 2000, New York, N.Y.), helped create the role of news anchor. Trout got his start in journalism as a news announcer for radio station WJSV in Alexandria, Va. When Columbia Broadcasting System (CBS) bought WJSV in 1932, he joined the team that became "Murrow's boys," a select group of reporters led by CBS foreign correspondent Edward R. Murrow. Trout worked with Murrow throughout the late 1930s and World War II. On March 13, 1938, Trout anchored the first live radio newscast to combine reports from cities around the world. After the war, he continued to work for CBS in both radio and television. In later years he was a commentator for the National Public Radio program *All Things Considered*.

Trudeau, Pierre Elliott, Canadian politician (b. Oct 18, 1919, Montreal, Que.—d. Sept. 28, 2000, Montreal), was a charming, flamboyant, charismatic, and cosmopolitan leader who brought glamour and excitement to Canadian politics while overseeing a number of the most momentous changes in the country in the latter half of the 20th century. Under his guidance both English and French were established as official languages by the Official Languages Act of 1969, diplomatic relations with China were established in 1970, a referendum on Quebec separation was defeated in 1980, and formal independence from Great Britain was achieved in 1982, with a new constitution that included a charter of rights. Trudeau's style and flamboyance were especially apparent in his social life, where he was known for the succession of celebrities and starlets with whom he appeared in public, and in 1971 he married former flower child Margaret Sinclair, at 22 less than half his age. They separated in 1977, after the birth of three sons, and divorced in 1984. Trudeau studied at Montreal's Collège Jean-de-Brébeuf and at the University of Montreal, from which he earned a law degree in 1943. He was called to the bar that same year. He went on to earn a master's degree in political economy from Harvard University in 1945 and studied further at such institutions as the École des Sciences Politiques in Paris and the London School of Economics before returning home, where he worked in the Privy Council Office in Ottawa, practiced law, and helped found (1950) the radical monthly *Cité libre.* Trudeau served (1961–65) as an assistant professor of law at the University of Montreal and in 1965, as a member of the Liberal Party, was elected to the House of Commons. Two years later he was named minister of justice in the cabinet of Prime Minister Lester Pearson. In 1968, when Pearson announced that he would resign, Trudeau campaigned for and won the party leadership and subsequently became prime minister. In holding that office

AFP/Corbis

Statesman Pierre Elliott Trudeau

until 1984, except for nine months in 1979–80, he became the longest-serving post-World War II Western leader. In 1999 a Canadian Press–Broadcast News poll named Trudeau Canada's Newsmaker of the Century.

Tukey, John Wilder, American statistician (b. June 16, 1915, New Bedford, Mass.—d. July 26, 2000, New Brunswick, N.J.), was a renowned statistician and researcher who was credited with having coined the terms *software* and *bit.* Tukey was educated at Brown University, Providence, R.I., and Princeton University; he founded Princeton's statistics department in 1965 and remained on the university's faculty for the duration of his career. In an article that was published in the *American Mathematical Monthly* in 1958, he introduced the word *software* to describe programs on which electronic calculators ran. In 1970, while working as a researcher for AT&T's Bell Laboratories, Tukey first used the word *bit* as an abbreviation for *binary digit.* He later served as a consultant for the Educational Testing Service, Xerox Corp., and Merck & Co. He was also a noted public commentator on social and environmental topics, attracting attention with his criticism of Alfred C. Kinsey's research on sexual behaviour—which Tukey believed was seriously flawed—and his warnings that aerosol spray cans damaged the ozone layer. From 1960 to 1980 Tukey helped design election polls for NBC.

Tunström, Göran, Swedish novelist, poet, and playwright (b. 1937, Sunne, Swed.—d. Feb. 5, 2000, Stockholm, Swed.), was widely regarded as Sweden's foremost contemporary author. His largely autobiographical works were sensitive explorations of childhood, family relationships, and the struggle to transcend grief. He published his first book, a poetry collection entitled

Sophie Bassouls/Corbis/Sygma

Inringning, in 1958. It was not until the 1970s, however, that he established his literary reputation with a trilogy of novels set in his native Sunne: *De heliga geograferna* (1973), *Guddöttrarna* (1975), and *Prästungen* (1976). He later published *Juloratoriet* (1983; *The Christmas Oratorio,* 1995); perhaps his best-known novel, the book won Tunström the Nordic Literature Prize and was made into a film in 1996. Among his other notable works were the novels *Ökenbrevet* (1978) and *Tjuven* (1986) and the play *Chang Eng* (1987).

Turner, Albert, American civil rights activist (b. Feb. 29, 1936, Marion, Ala.—d. April 13, 2000, Selma, Ala.), was a leader in the civil rights movement in the American South and an adviser to Martin Luther King, Jr. Turner was the Southern Christian Leadership Conference's field secretary in Alabama at the height of the movement and helped organize the historic voting-rights march from Selma to Montgomery, Ala., on March 7, 1965. In later years he served as a Perry county (Ala.) commissioner.

Turrentine, Stanley William, American jazz musician (b. April 5, 1934, Pittsburgh, Pa.—d. Sept. 12, 2000, New York, N.Y.), played tenor saxophone with a rich, hearty sound and a flair for blues phrasing that made him a popular favourite for four decades. Turrentine originally played cello but at the age of 11 took up the tenor saxophone. In his apprentice years he played in rhythm-and-blues groups with Earl Bostic and Ray Charles and in jazz groups, notably with Tadd Dameron. After serving in the army, Turrentine joined his older brother, trumpeter Tommy, in Max Roach's quintet. From 1960, Turrentine's saxophone playing—an original adaptation of Illinois Jacquet's style—proved invigorating in hard-bop recordings led by Horace Parlan and Duke Jordan, among others. His solos in organist Jimmy Smith's hit "soul jazz" albums such as *Midnight Special* and *Back at the Chicken Shack* led to his own "soul jazz" success. Turrentine's reputation grew with his own Blue Note albums, especially with *That's Where It's At* and *Joyride,* and he regularly appeared with his then-wife, "soul jazz" organist Shirley Scott. An increasing fascination with pop and rock material led to a series of crossover albums that began in 1970 with *Sugar* and continued throughout the decade. While his fusion music recordings made him a star, he retained his potency as a straightforward jazz improviser as well, and in the 1980s and '90s he alternated successfully between the jazz and jazz-rock idioms.

Francis Wolff/Corbis

Soul-jazz saxophonist Stanley Turrentine

Uglow, Euan Ernest Richard, British painter (b. March 10, 1932, London, Eng.—d. Aug. 31, 2000, London), was a representational artist appreciated as much for the painstaking perfectionism that he applied to his work as for his impersonal, carefully structured nudes and still lifes. Although Uglow's work was not widely seen—he seldom produced more than two paintings a year and often laboured over one canvas for several months—in 2000 he was identified as "one of Britain's 15 most significant artists" in a show by photographer Lord Snowdon honouring the opening of the new Tate Modern museum.

Vadim, Roger (Roger Vadim [or Vladimir] Plemiannikov), French filmmaker (b. Jan. 26, 1928, Paris, France—d. Feb. 11, 2000, Paris), showcased the appreciation of beautiful women that defined his personal life by featuring them in his professional life—about 25 motion pictures over his 40-year career. He was perhaps best known for discovering Brigitte Bardot, who became the first of his five wives, and starring her in his first film, *Et Dieu créa la femme* (1956; *And God Created Woman;* U.K. title, *And Woman Was Created*). That film broke new ground for "acceptable" eroticism in film, made Bardot a sex symbol, and set the stage for the French New Wave of the late 1950s and '60s. Vadim at first intended to become an actor, then tried journalism, and finally became an assistant movie director and television director. He met Bardot when she was in her mid-teens, and they were married in 1952, when she was 18. Vadim wrote a few screenplays for her, but her films had little impact until he made her a star with his film directorial debut. He made another motion picture for her, *Les Bijoutiers du clair de lune* (1957; *The Night Heaven Fell;* U.K. title, *Heaven Fell That Night*), but by that time their marriage had ended. Vadim's next marriage was to Annette Stroyberg, whom he starred in a modern-dress version of *Les Liaisons dangereuses* (1959; *Dangerous Love Affairs*) and in *Et mourir de plaisir* (1960; *Blood and Roses;* also released as *To Die with Pleasure*), and he then entered a relationship with Catherine Deneuve, who starred in his *Le Vice et la vertu* (1962; *Vice and Virtue*). Vadim starred his third wife, Jane Fonda, in another of his most famous films, the cult classic *Barbarella* (1968), which was his last commercial success. He thereafter worked mostly in television. Vadim's last two marriages were to heiress Catherine Schneider and actress Marie-Christine Barrault. Vadim was also the author of a number of books in which he revealed details of his life, including *Memoires du diable* (1975; *Memoirs of the Devil,* 1976), *L'Ange affame* (1982; *The Hungry Angel,* 1983), and *D'une étoile à l'autre* (1986; *Bardot Deneuve Fonda: My Life with the Three Most Beautiful Women in the World,* 1986).

Valente, José Angel, Spanish poet (b. April 25, 1929, Orense, Galicia, Spain—d. July 18, 2000, Geneva, Switz.), was highly regarded for his verse as well as his criticism and translations. One of the principal Spanish poets of the last half of the 20th century, he had a highly individual voice. His verse was both lyrical and philosophical, but in later years it became less

Roger Vadim, well-married filmmaker

top: Ballesteros/AFP Worldwide; bottom: Martine Peccoux/Liaison Agency

direct and more complex. Although he sometimes wrote of life in modern Spain under Francisco Franco, he tended to favour matters such as loneliness and death over overtly political subjects. Valente wrote in Galician as well as Spanish. He earned a degree in Romance languages from the University of Madrid in 1953 and then taught at the University of Oxford, where he gained a master's degree, and at the University of California, Irvine. Living in exile from the 1950s until 1986, he was a translator (1958–80) for the World Health Organization in Geneva and worked (1980–86) for UNESCO in Paris. *A modo de esperanza* (1955) was the first of his more than 20 volumes of poetry. Among later volumes were *Presentación y memorial para un monumento* (1970), featuring poems on the individual in modern society, and *No amanece el cantor* (1992), involving series of opposites such as darkness and light. Valente won many literary prizes, including the National Poetry Prize in 1992, and he was twice awarded the Premio de la Crítica, for *Poemas a Lázaro* (1960) and for *Tres lecciones de tinieblas* (1980). *Obra poética* appeared in 1999. He translated the work of a number of European poets into Spanish, and many of his own poems were translated into other languages.

Varney, James ("Jim"), American comedian (b. June 15, 1949, Lexington, Ky.—d. Feb. 10, 2000, White House, Tenn.), starred in numerous television commercials and nine films as Ernest P. Worrell, a dim-witted Southern handyman who provoked laughter with the catchphrase "KnowhutImean, Vern?" The first of the Ernest films, *Ernest Goes to Camp,* appeared in 1987. Varney later starred as Jed Clampett in the movie *The Beverly Hillbillies* (1993) and was the voice of Slinky Dog in *Toy Story* (1995) and *Toy Story 2* (1999).

Verdon, Gwyneth Evelyn ("Gwen"), American dancer and actress (b. Jan. 13, 1925, Culver City, Calif.—d. Oct. 18, 2000, Woodstock, Vt.), was the quintessential stage musical star, considered by many to have been the best Broadway dancer ever. She was highly regarded not only for her dancing but also for the depth she brought to the characters she portrayed, and she was especially noted for her collaboration with choreographer Bob Fosse in his innovative works. Verdon's mother had been a dancer, and Verdon began studying dance when she was a young child, partially as a means of strengthening her illness-weakened legs. By age six she was performing as "the fastest little tapper in the world." She began dancing in a repertory company at age 15 and in a nightclub the following year, but she married at 17 and gave up dancing until the marriage ended five years later. Verdon made her musical-comedy debut in *Bonanza Bound* (1947), which closed before reaching Broadway. Her Broadway debut came in 1950 in *Alive and Kicking,* and she began appearing in specialty dance numbers in films, including *On the Riviera* (1951), as well as coaching film stars in movement. She returned to Broadway in 1953 to be a featured dancer in *Can-Can,* stopped the show with a dazzling performance of her biggest number, and won her first Tony Award. In 1955 Verdon began her association with Fosse when she was given her first starring role, the Devil's temptress assistant Lola, in *Damn Yankees,* for which she won another Tony. She also played that role in the show's 1958 film adaptation. Her next stage musicals were *New Girl in Town* (1957), for which she was co-winner of a Tony, and *Redhead* (1959), which garnered her a fourth Tony; both shows featured Fosse choreography, and he also directed the latter. Verdon and Fosse were married in 1960, and not until 1966—in *Sweet Charity*—did she return to the stage. Verdon and Fosse separated in 1971 but never divorced, and they remained friends and collaborators until his death in 1987. They worked together on her next Broadway hit, *Chicago* (1975)—in which Verdon's character was one she had long wanted to portray, Roxie Hart—and on Fosse's musical *Dancin'* (1978), film *All That Jazz* (1979), and revival of *Sweet Charity* (1987). After ending her dancing career, Verdon concentrated on acting; she appeared on television in numerous series and in the made-for-TV film *Legs* (1983) and in such motion pictures as *The Cotton Club* (1984), the two *Cocoon* movies (1985 and 1988), and *Alice* (1990). In 1999 she served as artistic adviser for the retrospective *Fosse.*

Musical-comedy star Gwen Verdon

Vogt, A(lfred) E(lton) van, Canadian-born American science-fiction writer (b. April 26, 1912, Winnipeg, Man.—d. Jan. 26, 2000, Los Angeles, Calif.), was one of the most prominent writers during science fiction's golden age—the period from 1939 to 1951, when the work of such notable talents as van Vogt, Robert A. Heinlein, and Isaac Asimov appeared in the field's leading magazine, John W. Campbell's *Astounding Science Fiction.* After getting his start as a writer by selling "confession" stories to pulp magazines and writing plays for Canadian radio, van Vogt turned to science fiction. His first story, "Black Destroyer," which appeared in Campbell's publication in 1939, came to be regarded as a classic and later was cited as the inspiration for the *Alien* film series. Among the 85 novels and short-story collections that followed were a number of other classics, including *Slan* (1946), *The World of Null-A* (1948), and *The Weapon Shops of Isher* (1951). These works were distinctive for their vivid imagery and fast-moving narratives. In 1996 van Vogt was one of four inaugural inductees in the Science Fiction and Fantasy Hall of Fame and received a special award for lifetime achievement from the World Science Fiction Convention.

Walker, Jack, British industrialist (b. May 19, 1929, Blackburn, Lancashire, Eng.—d. Aug. 17, 2000, Isle of Jersey), made millions in the steel industry and in aviation, then used his fortune to elevate the Blackburn Rovers, the local association football (soccer) team he had supported since childhood, from the obscurity of the Second Division to the 1995 Premier League title. Walker spent some £60 million ($80 million) on stadium improvements and new players, brought in a top-notch manager in Kenny Dalglish, and in 1992 paid a then-record £3.2 million ($4.6 million) for Alan Shearer, one of England's finest forwards. The gamble paid off in 1995 when Blackburn won its first championship since 1914, but the team's success was short-lived and the Rovers were again relegated to the Second Division in 1999.

Ware, Lancelot Lionel, British barrister (b. June 5, 1915, Mitcham, Surrey, Eng.—d. Aug. 15, 2000, Surrey), was cofounder (1946), with Australian barrister Roland Berrill, of Mensa, an international society for intellectually gifted people, which they originally called the High IQ Club. Ware, apparently disillusioned with the group's infighting and low membership of about 150, dropped out in 1950 to concentrate on his legal career. The faltering society was successfully resurrected by Victor Serebriakoff (*q.v.*) in 1954, however, and Ware rejoined in 1961.

Weber, Joseph, American physicist (b. May 17, 1919, Paterson, N.J.—d. Sept. 30, 2000, Pittsburgh, Pa.), pioneered research that led to the development of lasers and the detection of gravitational waves. Weber was the first to articulate the possibility of molecules, in an energetic state, amplifying coherent light—the basic principle behind the operation of a laser. He gave the first known public address on lasers in 1952. Those who built the first lasers, however, were credited with the discovery and were awarded a 1964 Nobel Prize. The son of Eastern European immigrants, Weber originally spoke Yiddish but lost his ability to speak after being hit by a bus at the age of five. Upon regaining his speech, he had adopted his speech therapist's middle-American accent, leading Weber's family to nickname him "Yankee." He graduated from the U.S. Naval Academy in 1940 and served in the navy, surviving a 1942 Japanese attack that sank the aircraft carrier *Lexington* in the Coral Sea. He left the navy in 1948 to serve as a professor of electrical engineering at the University of

Bettmann/Corbis

Maryland at College Park, where he remained until his retirement in 1989. In 1951 he earned his doctorate from the Catholic University of America, Washington, D.C., and two years later wrote his first scientific paper, on microwaves. His work led to the development of the maser (microwave amplification by the stimulated emission of radiation) and later of the laser. Weber went on to try to uncover a way to detect gravitational waves, which Albert Einstein described in his theory of relativity. The waves, said to result from disturbances in the cosmos, could alter the size of space and matter. He built a device that consisted of aluminum bars, weighing more than a ton, insulated against vibration and equipped with special sensors. Though he claimed that his device detected gravitational waves, creating a stir in the scientific community in the late 1960s, Weber was never able to provide conclusive proof of his findings. His early work in the field, however, has been credited as a direct catalyst for all subsequent efforts to detect the waves, including the creation of a $300 million observatory.

Wechsler, Herbert, American lawyer and legal scholar (b. Dec. 4, 1909, New York, N.Y.—d. April 26, 2000, New York), as director of the American Law Institute, he created a model penal code, completed in 1962, that helped state legislatures achieve greater consistency in their criminal laws. He was also noted for his successful defense of the *New York Times* before the U.S. Supreme Court in the 1964 libel case *New York Times* v. *Sullivan;* swayed by Wechsler's arguments, the court found that public officials must prove that libelous statements were made "with actual malice" in order to win damages. A professor at Columbia Law School from 1933 to 1978, Wechsler was a highly influential legal scholar whose 1953 casebook, *The Federal Courts and the Federal System,* co-written with Henry Melvin Hart, became a standard legal text.

Weinstein, Louis, American physician (b. Feb. 26, 1908, Bridgeport, Conn.—d. March 16, 2000, Newton, Mass.), pioneered treatments for infectious diseases and was a prominent medical educator. He earned his medical degree in 1943 from Boston University and served as the university's chief of infectious diseases from 1947 to 1957. He moved to Tufts University School of Medicine, Boston, in 1957, where he served as chief of infectious diseases until his retirement in 1975. Aside from Weinstein's highly influential career as a professor of medicine, he was responsible for introducing numerous antibiotic treatments, warning the medical community of drug resistance to antibiotic therapy, and establishing hospital units to treat infectious diseases. In addition, he was praised for his role in fighting the polio epidemics in New England in 1949 and 1955. After his retirement, he served as chairman of an advisory committee to the Centers for Disease Control and Prevention.

Werner, Ruth (Ursula Ruth Kuczynski), German-born Soviet espionage agent and writer (b. May 15, 1907, Berlin, Ger.—d. July 7, 2000, Berlin), was a committed communist who operated as a spy for the Soviet Union in China, Nazi Germany, Switzerland, and England beginning in about 1930. Using the code name Sonya, she gathered and transmitted classified intelligence to Moscow, including technical information supplied by the German-born British physicist Klaus Fuchs about the Manhattan Project's research into the atomic bomb. After World War II she settled in East Germany, where she took the pen name Ruth Werner and became a celebrated writer of short stories, novels, and an autobiography, *Sonja's Rapport* (1977; *Sonya's Report,* 1991).

Wessely, Paula, Austrian actress (b. Jan. 20, 1907, Vienna, Austria—d. May 11, 2000, Vienna), reigned as Austria's most distinguished and beloved stage and screen actress almost from her debut at the Vienna Volkstheater in 1924 until her retirement in 1987; although she was castigated for her appearance in the anti-Semitic 1941 Nazi-propaganda film *Heimkehr* ("Homecoming")—an act for which she later expressed regret—Wessely's popularity never waned, and she established a glittering post-World War II career, primarily at the Vienna Burgtheater.

Wicki, Bernhard, motion picture actor and director of German-language films (b. Oct. 28, 1919, Sankt Pölten, Austria—d. Jan. 5, 2000, Munich, Ger.), was best known outside West Germany for his powerful antiwar film *Die Brücke* (1959; *The Bridge*), which received a Golden Globe Award and an Academy Award nomination, and his last film, *Das Spinnennetz* (1989; *The Spider's Web*). Wicki, who was born to Swiss-Hungarian parents and held Swiss citizenship, also directed two American motion pictures, *The Visit* (1964) and *Morituri* (1965), and the German sections of the international World War II epic *The Longest Day* (1962).

Widdowson, Elsie May, British nutritionist (b. Oct. 21, 1906, London, Eng.—d. June 14, 2000, Cambridge, Eng.), who, in collaboration with her longtime research partner, Robert A. McCance, guided the British government's World War II food rationing program. Widdowson and McCance documented the nutritional content of thousands of foods; advocated fortifying food (notably bread) with iron, vitamins, and calcium (the latter derived from chalk when other forms of calcium were unavailable); and did extensive research into the effects of dietary deprivation, including the surprising benefits of an extremely low-calorie, near-starvation diet. Their 1940 book, *The Chemical Composition of Foods,* became a classic in the field of nutrition and was revised several times. Widdowson, who received doctorates in chemistry at the Imperial College, London, and the Courtauld Institute of Biochemistry, London, also studied neonatal and children's nutritional needs and advised the British government on the nutritional needs of concentration camp survivors and German war orphans. She was a member of the research staff at the University of Cambridge (1938–72); served as president of the Nutrition Society (1977–80), the Neonatal Society (1978–81), and the British Nutrition Foundation (1986–96); and was elected (1976) a Fellow of the Royal Society. Widdowson was made a CBE in 1979 and a Companion of Honour in 1993. In 1999 she attended the dedication of the Elsie Widdowson Laboratory for human nutrition research at Cambridge.

Wiggins, J(ames) Russell, American journalist, newspaper editor, and statesman (b. Dec. 4, 1904, Luverne, Minn.—d. Nov. 12, 2000, Brooklin, Maine), helped transform the *Washington Post* from a relatively obscure newspaper into one that had an influential voice in national affairs; he was an editor at the *Post* from 1947 to 1968, when he left to become the U.S. ambassador to the United Nations. Wiggins served as ambassador for four months, before beginning a 30-year career as editor of the *Ellsworth American,* a Maine weekly newspaper.

Wilcox, Desmond John, British television executive and documentarian (b. May 21, 1931, Welwyn Garden City, Hertfordshire, Eng.—d. Sept. 6, 2000, London, Eng.), made memorable television documentaries noted for their humanitarian aspects, among them *Americans* (1979) and, especially, *The Boy David* (1983), part of his BBC series *The Visit* (1982–91). Over 10 years' time—on the BBC series and its ITV revival (1993–94)—he followed the story of David, a Peruvian boy facially disfigured by disease, who was adopted and treated by a Scottish plastic surgeon.

Williams, Hosea, American civil rights leader and politician (b. Jan. 5, 1926, Attapulgus, Ga.—d. Nov. 16, 2000, Atlanta, Ga.), was a major figure in the struggle against segregation and served as organizer and advance man with the Rev. Martin Luther King, Jr. He helped lead such demonstrations as the "Bloody Sunday" march in Selma, Ala., in 1965, during which marchers seeking voting rights for African Americans were tear-gassed and brutally beaten, and he was present when King was assassinated in Memphis, Tenn., in 1968. Williams had a difficult childhood and in his teens was, as he put it, a "thug and gangster." After holding a series of odd jobs, he lied about his age and joined the army after the U.S. entered World War II. Seriously wounded, he spent over a year in a British hospital before returning home and completing his education—a high-school diploma at age 23, followed by a bachelor's degree from Morris Brown College, Atlanta, and a master's degree in chemistry from Atlanta University (now Clark Atlanta University). While working for the Department of Agriculture in Savannah, Ga.—the first federally employed

left: Jan Chlebik/Imperial College; right: AP/Wide World Photos

black research chemist in the South—Williams became involved in the civil rights movement, in part as a result of having been nearly fatally beaten by a white mob years earlier when he drank from the only water fountain in an Americus, Ga., bus station and also in part because of his distress when his children could not join white children spinning on the stools of a segregated lunch counter. He became active in the National Association for the Advancement of Colored People and worked his way up through the ranks but was denied a position on its board because his parents had not married. Williams then (1963) joined King at the Southern Christian Leadership Conference (SCLC), and by the following year he was helping run it. He traveled to numerous cities in the South, recruiting and organizing volunteers, teaching them the techniques of nonviolent demonstrations, leading them on marches, and otherwise paving the way for King and his associates Andrew Young and Jesse Jackson. Williams was ousted from the SCLC in the late 1970s in a power struggle but had already entered politics by running successfully for the Georgia state legislature, in which he served from 1974 to 1985. In 1984 he made an unsuccessful run for a U.S. Senate seat, and in 1985 he was elected to a term on the Atlanta City Council. In 1989 he lost a bid to be mayor of Atlanta, and he thereafter served for several years as a county commissioner. Although Williams's later years were troubled by numerous traffic arrests and erratic behaviour, he continued working to help the poor and homeless.

Willmott, Peter, British sociologist (b. Sept. 18, 1923, Oxford, Eng.—d. April 8, 2000, London, Eng.), examined patterns of kinship and the changing networks of familial relationships found in contemporary urban Great Britain and published a series of books—many of them prepared with his frequent collaborator, Michael (later Lord) Young—that influenced official Labour Party economic and social policies; Willmott and Young's most notable studies included *Family and Kinship in East London* (1957), *Family and Class in a London Suburb* (1960), and *The Symmetrical Family* (1973).

Activist Hazel Wolf

Natalie Fobes/Corbis

Wilson, Robert Rathbun, American physicist (b. March 4, 1914, Frontier, Wyo.—d. Jan. 16, 2000, Ithaca, N.Y.), was one of the leading scientists on the Manhattan Project, working closely with Enrico Fermi on experiments that led to the development of the atomic bomb; a noted researcher in particle physics, he later served (1967–78) as the first director of the Fermi National Accelerator Laboratory (Fermilab) in Batavia, Ill., overseeing the building of the world's most powerful particle accelerator.

Windsor, Marie (Emily Marie Bertelsen), American actress (b. Dec. 11, 1919, Marysvale, Utah—d. Dec. 10, 2000, Beverly Hills, Calif.), portrayed strong but often unsavoury women in most of her more than 70 films and was known as the "queen of the B's"—a title she wore proudly—because of the many B films, including *Cat Women of the Moon* (1954) and *Swamp Women* (1955), in which she appeared. She was, however, best remembered for her first film as star, *The Narrow Margin* (1952), as well as such film noir classics as *Force of Evil* (1948) and *The Killing* (1956). She later branched out into television, and she also served for many years on the board of the Screen Actors Guild.

Wolf, Hazel, Canadian-born American environmentalist (b. March 10, 1898, Victoria, B.C.—d. Jan. 19, 2000, Port Angeles, Wash.), was a longtime advocate for environmental causes. After moving to the U.S. from Canada in 1923, she worked on behalf of the rights of immigrants and became a member of the Communist Party (she left the party during World War II); she later was involved in struggles over civil rights and labour issues. Her environmental activism began in the early 1960s, after she had joined the National Audubon Society, and she became a noted speaker. She was profiled in Studs Terkel's book *Coming of Age: The Story of Our Century by Those Who've Lived It* (1995), and in 1997 she was awarded the National Audubon Society's Medal of Excellence.

Wright, Judith, Australian poet and writer (b. May 31, 1915, Armidale, N.S.W.—d. June 25, 2000, Canberra, A.C.T.), published more than 50 books drawing on life in her native country, but she also developed an international reputation. Her poetry, largely written in traditional forms, showed great technical skill. Beginning in the 1960s she became prominent as a conservationist, decrying the despoliation of the land, and as an advocate, among other things, of land rights for Aboriginals. Wright's parents ran a sheep and cattle station, and she was educated at home and at the New England Girls' School in Armidale. She studied at the University of Sydney and in 1937–38 traveled in England and Europe. Returning to Australia, she helped run the family farm during World War II. She then worked as a statistician at the University of Queensland, Brisbane, where she was involved in publishing the journal *Meanjin*, and her poems began to appear in various magazines. From 1949 she was a lecturer at Australian universities, and in 1967 she became a tutor at the University of Queensland. Her first two volumes of poetry, which are usually considered her best, were *The Moving Image* (1946), devoted to the land and farm life, and *Woman to Man* (1949), about women and female sexuality. In 1959 she published *The Generations of Men*, a prose work based on the diaries of her grandfather. *Preoccupations in Australian Poetry* (1965) was among her critical writings, and she edited several anthologies of verse. She also wrote a number of books for children. In 1992 she was the first Australian to be awarded the Queen's Gold Medal for Poetry. The first volume of her autobiography, *Half a Lifetime*, was published in 1999, and she was working on the second volume at the time of her death.

Xie Bingying (Hsieh Ping-ying), Chinese writer (b. 1906, Hunan province, China—d. Jan. 5, 2000, San Francisco, Calif.), was highly regarded for her autobiographical works that challenged traditional Chinese feminine identity. In 1926, in order to avoid an arranged marriage, she became a "girl soldier" in the Nationalist Army; her first book, *War Diary* (1928), recounted her experiences helping Chinese combat troops battle warlords in eastern China. In 1937, after working as a teacher and a freelance journalist for several years, she again served as a soldier, fighting with Chinese troops against invading Japanese forces. Her second book, *Girl Rebel: The Autobiography of Hsieh Ping-ying*, was published in the U.S. in 1940. After World War II she moved to Taiwan, where she continued to teach and write. She eventually settled in San Francisco.

Yanofsky, Daniel Abraham ("Abe"), Polish-born Canadian chess master (b. March 25, 1926, Brody, Pol.—d. March 5, 2000, Winnipeg, Man.), was Canada's first chess grandmaster and an eight-time national champion. He was a chess prodigy who, by the age of 12, was champion of Manitoba. In 1939, as Canada's second-ranking player, he participated in the Chess Olympiad in Buenos Aires, Arg., scoring a remarkable 85% in his first international tournament. Yanofsky captured the first of his eight Canadian championships in 1941. He later embarked on a playing tour of Europe, winning a memorable match against future world champion Mikhail Botvinnik in 1946, but eventually opted to pursue a law career rather than play chess full-time. In 1953, while studying law at the University of Oxford, Yanofsky won the British championship. He qualified as a grandmaster—the highest title in chess—in 1964. By that time he had established a successful law practice and also entered politics, winning election as mayor of the Winnipeg suburb of West Kildonan. From 1970 to 1986 he served on the Winnipeg City Council and was credited with bringing the Pan American Chess Championships to Winnipeg in 1974. Yanofsky was awarded the Order of Canada in 1972.

Yates, Paula, British television presenter (b. April 24, 1959, Colwyn Bay, Wales—d. Sept. 17, 2000, London, Eng.), was a co-presenter on the music show *The Tube* (1982–87) and on *The Big Breakfast* (from 1992) but was perhaps better known for the celebrity status gained by her marriage to singer Bob Geldof, which ended in 1996, and her subsequent relationship with rock star Michael Hutchence, who was found hanged in 1997. Her unexpected death was attributed to a heroin overdose.

Yefremov, Oleg Nikolayevich, Russian actor and theatre director (b. Oct. 1, 1927, Moscow, U.S.S.R.—d. May 24, 2000, Moscow, Russia), was one of his country's finest and most influential directors; Yefremov championed new, young playwrights as well as offered classics by Anton Chekhov and others, first as the founding head (1957–70) of the Sovremennik ("Contemporary") Theatre-Studio and then as artistic director of the famed Moscow Art Theatre (1970–87), founded by Konstantin Stanislavsky, and its spin-off Moscow Chekhov Art Theatre (1987–2000). As an actor Yefremov made several successful movies, but he was best known for his stage work, including his final appearance in Aleksandr Pushkin's *Boris Godunov* in 1994. Yefremov's funeral was attended by Russian Pres. Vladimir Putin and other dignitaries; he was buried in Moscow's Novodevichy Cemetery near Stanislavsky.

Young, Loretta (Gretchen Michaela Young), American actress (b. Jan. 6, 1913, Salt Lake City, Utah—d. Aug. 12, 2000, Los Angeles, Calif.), brought beauty and grace to her performances in more than 90 motion pictures, most of them in the 1930s and '40s, and to her role as the glamorous hostess and star of her television series in the 1950s and early '60s. She was perhaps best known for her twirling entrances as she displayed her designer gowns during the introduction to her weekly TV drama. At age three Young moved to Los Angeles with her mother and sisters after her parents' marriage broke up, and the young girls soon began appearing in movies as extras or in small parts. When she was 14, she managed to snare a part in the film *Naughty but Nice* (1927) that was originally intended for her sister Polly Ann, and her career blossomed. A small role in *The Whip Woman* (1928) was followed by Young's first lead, in *Laugh, Clown, Laugh* (1928), and her first talking picture, *The Squall* (1929). Over the next several years, she was paired with a number of Hollywood's leading men, including Douglas Fairbanks, Jr. (in such films as *The Careless Age* [1929] and *Loose Ankles* [1930]), James Cagney (*Taxi!* [1932]), Spencer Tracy (*A Man's Castle* [1933]), Ronald Colman (*Clive of India* [1935]), Clark Gable (*The Call of the Wild* [1935]), Tyrone Power (*Ladies in Love* [1936]), and Cary Grant and David Niven (*The Bishop's Wife* [1947]). Young also became known for her romances with some of those matinee idols, most notably Gable, by whom she had a daughter, although that fact was not acknowledged until many years later. Other films included *The Farmer's Daughter* (1947), for which she won a best actress Academy Award; *Come to the Stable* (1949), for which she received an Oscar nomination; and *Cause for Alarm* (1951). From 1953 to 1961 Young presented her anthology series, at first titled *A Letter to Loretta* but then changed to *The Loretta Young Show*. She won three Emmy Awards for best actress—in 1954, 1956, and 1959—and thereby became the first actress to win both an Oscar and an Emmy. The show returned in 1962–63 as *The New Loretta Young Show*. Young then virtually retired from show business and devoted herself mostly to charitable works, although she returned for the television movies *Christmas Eve* (1986) and *Lady in a Corner* (1989). Her memoirs, *The Things I Had to Learn*, appeared in 1961.

Zalygin, Sergey Pavlovich, Russian writer and editor (b. Dec. 6, 1913, Durasovka, Russia—d. April 19, 2000, Moscow, Russia), was a respected Soviet novelist and the first non-Communist Party editor in chief of the monthly literary magazine *Novy Mir;* during Zalygin's tenure (1986–98) at *Novy Mir* he took advantage of Pres. Mikhail Gorbachev's glasnost policy and published many previously banned writings, including Boris Pasternak's *Dr. Zhivago,* works by Vladimir Nabokov and Joseph Brodsky, and, after a long struggle with the censors, Aleksandr Solzhenitsyn's *The Gulag Archipelago.*

Zatopek, Emil, Czech long-distance runner (b. Sept. 19, 1922, Koprivnice, Czech.—d. Nov. 21/22, 2000, Prague, Czech Rep.), won at the 1952 Olympic Games the 5,000 m, 10,000 m, and marathon, a feat never achieved before or since. At the same time, he set Olympic records in the 5,000 m and 10,000 m and ran the marathon in Olympic record time; it was his first marathon. Zatopek also won a gold medal in the 10,000 m at the 1948 Olympics and from 1948 to 1954 won an unprecedented 38 consecutive 10,000-m races. During his career he set 18 world records at distances ranging from 5,000 m to 30,000 m, and he was the first to run the 10,000 m in less than 29 minutes. Zatopek began running at the age of 18 and trained intensively while serving in the Czechoslovak army. He retired as a runner in 1958 and later fell out of favour with his government for criticizing the 1968 Soviet-led invasion of Czechoslovakia.

AFP Worldwide

Long-distance champion Emil Zatopek

Zuʻbi, Mahmud az-, Syrian politician (b. 1938, Khirbat al-Ghazalah, Syria—d. May 21, 2000, near Damascus, Syria), was a loyal ally of Pres. Hafez al-Assad (*q.v.*) and served his country as speaker of the People's Assembly (1981–87) and as prime minister from November 1987 until March 2000 when he resigned amid charges of economic mismanagement and corruption. Zuʻbi, who was also expelled from the ruling Baʻth Party, was still under investigation at the time of his death. He reportedly shot himself.

Zumwalt, Elmo Russell, Jr. ("Bud"), admiral (ret.), U.S. Navy (b. Nov. 29, 1920, San Francisco, Calif.—d. Jan. 2, 2000, Durham, N.C.), was responsible for implementing a variety of reforms while serving as the U.S. Navy's chief of naval operations from 1970 to 1974; he was also noted for his decision during the Vietnam War to spray the jungles of the Mekong Delta with the defoliant Agent Orange. After graduating (1942) from the U.S. Naval Academy, he served on a destroyer during World War II, earning a Bronze Star for valour in the Battle of Leyte Gulf in 1944. During the Korean War he served on the battleship *Wisconsin.* In 1965, at the age of 44, he became the youngest officer to attain the rank of rear admiral. In 1968 he was named the commander of naval forces in Vietnam, and two years later he assumed the U.S. Navy's highest command as chief of naval operations. He immediately set about instituting reforms, which included permitting women to serve on ships and ending racial discrimination in housing for navy personnel. He believed his order to spray the Vietnam jungles with Agent Orange inadvertently led to the death from cancer in 1988 of his son, Elmo Zumwalt III, who commanded a navy patrol boat during the war. The two co-wrote a book, *My Father, My Son* (1986), about their Vietnam experiences. The admiral retired from military service in 1974 and later led efforts for more research into the deadly effects of Agent Orange. In 1998 he was awarded the Presidential Medal of Freedom, the highest civilian award in the U.S.

left: Bettmann/Corbis; right: Evening Standard/Hulton Getty Historical Archive/Liaison Agency

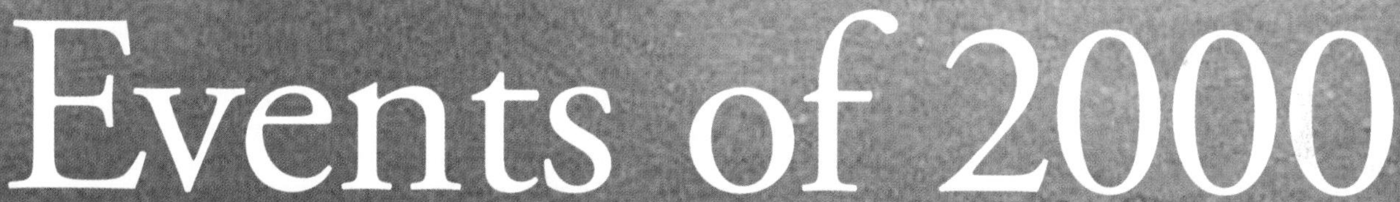

Events of 2000

Ghetto Fabulous, the Iberian lynx, globalization, *American Beauty,* the Million Mom March, Yanomami, dimpled chads, the *Kursk,* e-books, *Aïda*–these things, among many others, were history in 2000.

AP/Wide World Photos

Agriculture and Food Supplies

STARVATION, genetically modified organisms, **"MAD COW" DISEASE,** and **WEATHER-RELATED PROBLEMS** all captured **HEADLINES** in the year 2000 and **RAISED QUESTIONS** about the world's **FOOD SUPPLY.**

NATIONAL AND INTERNATIONAL ISSUES

Food Production. Agricultural markets throughout the world enjoyed ample supplies and low prices in 2000. Though total agricultural and food production was about 1% greater than in 1999, global per capita food production was slightly lower than in 1999. (*See* Table I.) Both developed and less-developed countries (LDCs) experienced increased output. For developed nations the output increase was greater than their population increase, so per capita production rose. The output increase in the LDCs was not as great as the population increase, and, consequently, per capita output fell.

Production did not increase in two areas of the world. Countries undergoing the transition from centrally planned to market economies in the former Soviet Union and Eastern Europe continued to experience low output, only 70% of the 1989–91 totals. Little recovery was evident in 2000. Those states were hindered by agricultural bottlenecks due to poor infrastructure, weak credit markets, underdeveloped input and land markets, weak macroeconomic performance, and incomplete privatization.

Countries in sub-Saharan Africa had experienced production difficulties during the 1990s, and that pattern continued in 2000. Some economies expanded their total output but suffered from declining per capita production. Other countries experienced declines in both total and per capita output. Dry weather occurred in some areas, including Kenya and Ethiopia. Mozambique experienced catastrophic flooding. Output in many countries in central Africa fell, owing to man-made causes, including environmental degradation, war, inadequate economic development, and rapid population growth.

Food Aid. With several countries experiencing stagnant or declining production, food aid continued to be critical. (*See* TABLE II.) Shipments of cereals for aid were lower in 1999–2000 than in the previous year but were well above the levels recorded in the mid-1990s, when global food supplies were tight. The United States remained the largest donor, followed by the European Union (EU). The U.S. also registered the largest increase in shipments compared with the mid-1990s. During that time the U.S.

Table I. Selected Indexes of World Agricultural and Food Production (1989–91 = 100)

	Total agricultural production					Total food production					Per capita food production				
Region and country	1996	1997	1998	1999	2000	1996	1997	1998	1999	2000	1996	1997	1998	1999	2000
Developed countries	**97.4**	**98.8**	**98.1**	**99.6**	**101.2**	**98.1**	**99.5**	**99.0**	**100.5**	**102.0**	**95.4**	**96.4**	**95.6**	**96.6**	**97.8**
Australia	117.4	118.8	124.1	124.8	125.4	130.5	129.6	136.5	137.8	138.7	121.4	119.4	124.5	124.4	124.0
Canada	117.4	116.6	123.5	131.8	130.9	117.4	116.4	123.2	131.8	131.4	109.0	107.0	112.1	118.8	117.2
European Union	101.9	102.0	102.0	104.0	104.0	101.9	101.9	101.9	103.8	103.9	99.8	99.6	99.4	101.2	101.2
Japan	95.3	94.7	91.6	92.0	92.3	95.9	95.2	92.0	92.5	92.8	94.2	93.3	90.0	90.3	90.4
South Africa	100.6	100.7	95.5	100.8	105.5	103.0	103.6	97.9	103.1	108.8	91.8	90.8	84.6	87.9	91.6
Transition countries	71.5	72.4	68.3	69.0	69.6	72.6	73.5	69.0	70.0	70.4	72.3	73.3	69.0	69.8	70.2
United States	114.6	118.8	119.5	121.1	125.6	114.4	118.6	120.8	121.8	126.2	107.9	110.9	112.0	112.0	115.2
Less-developed countries	**127.0**	**130.9**	**134.2**	**137.2**	**138.5**	**128.6**	**132.6**	**136.7**	**140.0**	**141.2**	**115.9**	**117.5**	**119.2**	**120.2**	**119.3**
Argentina	119.3	121.7	132.8	134.4	134.1	121.0	124.4	136.1	138.7	138.8	111.8	113.5	122.6	123.4	122.0
Bangladesh	109.5	111.6	111.8	115.0	115.0	109.8	111.3	111.6	115.9	115.9	99.7	99.4	97.9	99.9	98.2
Brazil	125.3	128.2	129.2	136.6	137.5	128.4	131.7	131.7	139.2	139.4	117.6	119.0	117.5	122.5	121.2
China	143.7	153.1	158.8	162.7	165.4	147.3	156.3	164.5	169.2	171.9	138.0	145.1	151.3	154.2	155.4
Congo, Dem. Rep. of the	94.8	93.7	93.5	90.3	88.0	95.1	94.5	94.7	91.8	89.7	76.1	73.7	72.1	68.3	65.0
Egypt	136.2	143.6	139.9	147.2	149.7	137.6	145.5	143.6	151.1	153.7	122.1	126.6	122.6	126.6	126.5
Ethiopia	124.3	125.6	118.1	124.1	121.0	125.5	126.9	118.8	125.2	122.0	106.5	105.0	95.8	98.5	93.6
India	118.8	121.5	121.4	125.8	125.8	118.6	122.0	121.5	126.2	126.2	106.2	107.4	105.2	107.6	105.9
Indonesia	122.2	119.3	117.6	119.4	119.8	122.5	119.7	117.7	119.6	119.9	111.7	107.6	104.3	104.5	103.3
Malaysia	118.3	119.1	117.3	123.6	123.7	125.9	128.6	127.8	137.2	137.4	109.4	109.5	106.6	112.3	110.3
Mexico	117.0	121.7	123.2	126.5	130.7	117.1	122.6	124.2	128.4	132.7	105.1	108.3	107.9	109.8	111.7
Nigeria	139.5	142.8	148.9	153.1	153.1	140.0	143.3	149.4	153.6	153.6	120.3	120.1	122.4	122.8	120.0
Philippines	122.8	128.6	118.8	129.4	131.5	124.6	130.5	120.3	131.3	133.5	108.2	111.0	100.1	107.1	106.7
Turkey	109.7	109.0	115.9	111.1	111.1	110.1	108.3	116.4	111.3	111.3	99.1	95.8	101.3	95.3	93.8
Venezuela	110.7	118.3	114.8	115.9	115.4	111.9	120.0	116.6	117.7	117.6	97.8	102.7	97.8	96.8	94.9
Vietnam	136.9	143.6	150.1	160.8	163.4	134.1	138.9	145.6	155.4	155.5	119.0	121.3	125.2	131.7	129.9
World	**113.6**	**116.4**	**117.9**	**120.2**	**121.6**	**114.6**	**117.3**	**119.3**	**121.8**	**123.1**	**105.0**	**106.1**	**106.5**	**107.3**	**107.1**

Source: World Wide Web site for UN Food and Agriculture Organization: <http://apps.fao.org> (Dec. 5, 2000).

shipped approximately 6 million tons, but in 1998 and 1999 the U.S. provided 10 million–11 million tons. Other donors also increased shipments but had more stable commitments, so the increases were not as large. The large rise in U.S. shipments occurred as global supplies increased. This produced criticism by other donors that the U.S. was using food aid primarily to raise farm prices rather than to fight hunger.

Food aid was provided to Ethiopia as drought and the war with Eritrea threatened many with starvation. Unrest in Angola and other countries in central and southern Africa created food-assistance needs. North Korea received food aid from the U.S. and other donor nations. Traditional recipients such as Bangladesh also continued to obtain aid. The catastrophic flooding in Mozambique in February resulted in a large relief effort to that nation. Russia emerged as the single largest recipient of U.S. food aid, receiving $217 million, because of its problems with the transition to a market economy.

World Trade Organization (WTO). In late 1999 representatives of 135 nations gathered in Seattle, Wash., to launch new trade-liberalization negotiations. The meeting failed to establish a new round of comprehensive negotiations, but talks on agriculture mandated by the Uruguay Round began.

Little progress on agricultural issues was made. The U.S. called for the elimination of export subsidies, reduced farm support, improved market access, and tighter rules for government trading agencies. The Cairns Group of "nonsubsidizing" countries held many of the same views as the U.S. but with some critical differences. Cairns Group members (Argentina, Australia, Brazil, Canada, Chile, Colombia, Fiji, Indonesia, Malaysia, New Zealand, Paraguay, Philippines, South Africa, Thailand, and Uruguay) took a broader view of the policies that could be considered export subsidies by including export credit and credit guarantee programs. European states, Japan, and South Korea supported continued large subsidies to agriculture, arguing that farming provides such nonmarket benefits as environmental protection, rural development, landscape preservation, and food security.

China's entry into the WTO became more likely in 2000. In late 1999 the U.S. and China reached agreement on Chinese policy reforms required for membership. China agreed to convert nontariff barriers to tariffs and to reduce barriers by 2005 and also allowed private trading firms to have larger shares in international trade. During the summer after much debate the U.S. Congress ratified the agreement. The EU also completed an agreement with China to facilitate WTO membership.

European Union Expansion. Negotiations to expand the EU to include Central and Eastern European states continued, with agriculture one of the most sensitive areas. The EU expansion under existing farm policy would cause large increases in farm program costs, which in 2000 represented about half of the EU's budget. In many Central and Eastern European countries, farming was a substantial share of the economy and a large employer of labour. For countries with limited abilities to support farmers, competition with subsidized EU farmers would be difficult. Access to EU subsidies would provide more balanced competition and inject large subsidies into a critical sector for those economies.

Genetically Modified Organisms (GMOs). Trade in agricultural products containing genetically modified material continued to be controversial. Europeans resisted consuming genetically altered food products and staged mass protests against those products. Consumer concerns about GMOs in food also increased in many other countries, including Japan, Australia, and Canada. New labeling requirements for GMO food were adopted. In the U.S. the Gerber and Heinz companies announced that they would not use genetically modified material in baby food, and other food product manufacturers quit using farm commodities containing GMOs.

In January an international agreement on trade in food with GMOs was reached in Montreal. The Cartagena Protocol on Biosafety allowed a nation to ban imports of a genetically modified product if it believed that there was insufficient scientific evidence of the product's safety. The agreement also included rules on transportation and labeling. The effectiveness of the protocol in bridging the interests of advocates and opponents of GMO foods was disputed, however.

Instances of GMO contamination of the American corn crop were reported in autumn 2000. StarLink was a genetically modified variety of corn approved in the U.S. for animal feed but not for human food because of potential human allergic reactions. Some countries, such as Japan, did not allow StarLink for any use. StarLink was to be segregated from other varieties when grown and marketed. Tests on American food products, notably taco shells, however, revealed traces of the variety. It was also found in export shipments to Japan. Products were recalled, and efforts to find the source of the contamination were begun. Exports of American corn were disrupted. Tracing StarLink corn through the marketing system proved impossible. Evidence of contamination of other corn emerged, as pollen from StarLink had drifted into other fields, and StarLink corn became mixed with other corn. Some estimated that up to half of the Iowa corn crop was thus contaminated, even though StarLink accounted for only 1% of the state's planted crop. (*See* Special Report.)

Livestock Diseases. Two important livestock diseases affected agriculture during the year. Foot-and-mouth disease outbreaks occurred in Argentina, Brazil, South Korea, and Japan and resulted in herd slaughter and the banning of fresh meat exports to disease-free markets. Fresh meat exports were diverted to lower-priced markets or sold as cooked meat.

Bovine spongiform encephalopathy (BSE) appeared in continental European nations. The disease, sometimes called "mad cow" disease, had first appeared in British cattle in the 1980s. At first it was believed that BSE could not be passed to humans, so infected beef was allowed to enter the food system. In the mid-1990s, however, a potential link to a fatal human ailment, Creutzfeldt-Jakob disease, caused a severe reduction in demand for beef and a ban on British beef and cattle exports. In late 2000 BSE-infected cattle appeared in France, Germany, Por tugal, and Spain. Demand for beef plunged. The EU introduced policies to halt the further spread of the disease and to provide emergency aid to cattle farmers.

Trade Disputes. Ongoing trade disputes burdened the international food system. The U.S. and the EU were unable to resolve differences over the EU ban on hormone-treated beef and the restrictive EU import policy for bananas. At the end of 2000, those policies remained in effect, as did the U.S. retaliatory duties. U.S. trade law allowed for the retaliatory duties to rotate among commodities, a process called "carousel" retaliation. The U.S. government, however, decided against rotating the duties, which angered U.S. agricultural interests.

The U.S. and the international community maintained embargoes prohibiting the exports of goods to several countries. Agricultural interests in the U.S. opposed those restrictions and lobbied for their removal, with some success.

Improved relations with North Korea and that nation's urgent food needs resulted in further food-aid shipments from the U.S. The 40-year embargo by the U.S. against Cuba was eased in the case of food. UN sanctions against several nations, including Yugoslavia, Iraq, and Libya, were softened during the year as well.

Table II. Shipment of Food Aid in Cereals[1]
In 000,000 metric tons

Region and country	1996–97	1997–98	1998–99	1999–2000
Australia	170	296	267	264
Canada	373	384	332	349
European Union	1,099	890	1,572	1,324
Japan	292	356	936	303
Norway	32	45	65	48
Switzerland	43	42	37	40
United States	2,273	2,787	6,390	6,693
Others	1,323	1,441	1,435	1,207
Total	5,605	6,241	11,034	10,228
To LIFDC[2]	4,487	5,267	7,908	6,779
Sub-Saharan Africa	1,871	2,172	2,532	2,555
To other countries	1,118	974	3,126	3,449

[1]July–June years. [2]Low-income food-deficit countries.
Source: World Wide Web site for UN Food and Agriculture Organization: <http://apps.fao.org> (Dec. 11, 2000).

GLOBAL MARKETS IN 2000

Grains, Oilseeds, and Livestock. World grain production in the 2000 crop year was lower than in 1999. A major cause of the reduced output was drought in China. World wheat production fell 1.2% to 580 million tons, the lowest output since the 1995 crop. Coarse grains production declined 2%, also the smallest crop since 1995. Rice production fell 1.1%, the first decline since 1993.

The reduced outputs of wheat and coarse grains were reflected in trade as both worldwide wheat trade and coarse grains trade fell about 3%. In contrast, rice trade remained constant. Despite falling output and reduced trade, global wheat consumption expanded slightly; consequently, there was a 13% reduction in ending stocks. Coarse grains consumption also expanded, and stocks were reduced. For rice the expansion in trade was less than the reduction in output. Use rose, and ending stocks fell. The tighter global supply and the increase in consumption caused a slight improvement in wheat and coarse grains prices, yet price levels remained low. Rice prices weakened slightly.

World oilseed production expanded 1.2% and set a new record. Output had increased 35% since the 1991 crop. The U.S. harvested a huge soybean crop, and soybean production in Argentina and Brazil was also large. Oilseed trade fell 1.5%, and ending stocks were 8% lower. Oilseed meal and vegetable oil outputs rose, and trade remained about the same as in the 1999 crop year. Increased production allowed an expansion of meal and oil use. With reduced global stocks, farm prices for soybeans improved compared with the 1999 crop.

World meat production expanded in 2000. Beef output by major trading nations rose by 1.4% to 49.6 million tons. That increase matched the rise in consumption, so world beef trade remained at the record levels observed in 1999. A similar situation occurred for pork. World production rose 1.5%. Trade in pork was slightly lower in 2000 compared with 1999 but remained well above the levels observed in 1996, 1997, and 1998. Both world production and trade of poultry meat expanded in 2000. Output increased about 2.7%, and trade was 5% higher. The expanded output and trade resulted in an increase of 2.9% in consumption. Cow milk production rose more than 1%. Butter production and exports were higher, and cheese output rose 2%. Nonfat dry milk production was more than 2% above the 1999 level.

Tropical Products. World sugar production for 2000–01 (the 2000 crop) declined 7% from the record output of 1999–2000. As consumption continued to grow, world ending stocks fell. Global sugar trade at 33.2 million tons was below the 1999 record level of 35.5 million tons. A drought in Brazil caused output to fall by 4.1 million tons. Increases in China and the EU were not sufficient to offset that decline. Owing to the tighter global supply and the increase in consumption, prices were slightly higher.

Coffee production in 2000 was 9% above the 1999 level as most major producers increased their output. During the El Niño–La Niña years, production was hurt by weather, including excessive rain in Central America and droughts in parts of Africa. Coffee prices dropped and in New York City they reached six-year lows. In May the Association of Coffee Producing Countries elected to reduce export supplies by 20% in order to boost prices. Members of the International Coffee Organization agreed to a new six-year international coffee agreement, scheduled to start in the fall of 2001. The agreement would strengthen international cooperation, promote coffee consumption, and assist with technology transfer.

World cocoa production rose more than 6% in 2000. Brazil, Côte d'Ivoire, and Ecuador experienced production increases. Most other nations had outputs similar to those in 1999.

(PHILIP L. PAARLBERG)

Harald M. Valderhaug

The Atlantic Dawn, *the world's largest-capacity fishing vessel, was launched in September 2000.*

FISHERIES

The finalized figures for world fish catch during 1998, the latest year for which figures were available, were confirmed by the UN Food and Agriculture Organization (FAO) at 86.3 million metric tons. The figure was lower than the estimate of 87.8 million metric tons published in late 1999. The result was a 7.8% decrease from the 1997 figure of 93.6 million metric tons of fish caught and reversed the trend that had been observed since 1991 of a steady climb in catch totals.

China again took an increasing share of the total catch with 17.2 million metric tons, a 9.6% increase over the 1997 figure and a massive 300% rise in the 10 years since 1989. Following three years of stability in catch, Japan (in second place) fell from 5.9 million metric tons in 1997 to 5,260,000 metric tons in 1998. The El Niño weather pattern in the Pacific Ocean had a drastic effect on the anchovy resources off Peru, which registered a drop from 7,870,000 metric tons in 1997 to 4,340,000 metric tons in 1998. Figures for 1999, however, showed that the resources had recovered strongly, with a total of 8.5 million metric tons recorded, and forecasts for the 2000 catch were even higher. Reductions in catch during 1997 were also recorded for Chile, which suffered from the effects of El Niño, as well as for South Korea, Iceland, Denmark, and Mexico. None of the top 25 countries except China showed a strong increase for the year.

Aquaculture contributed an additional 30.9 million metric tons for a total marine production of 117.2 million metric tons in 1998. China continued as the world leader, with aquaculture production of 20.8 million metric tons, an increase from 19.3 million metric tons in 1997.

During 2000 the FAO produced a projection of world fishery production in 2010. Estimates ranged between 107 million and 144 million metric tons; it was likely that about 30 million metric tons would be reduced to fish meal and oil for nonfood use. An estimated 74 million to 114 million metric tons would be made available for human consumption. It was expected that most of the increase in fish production would come from aquaculture. The contribution from capture fisheries would depend on further development and the effectiveness of fisheries management. According to the FAO, if management of currently overfished stocks was improved, there could be an increase of between 5 million and 10 million metric tons; continued overfishing, however, would result in decreasing production. Poaching, too, continued to be a problem, notably in Antarctic waters. (*See* WORLD AFFAIRS: Antarctica.)

The world's largest-capacity fishing vessel, which was launched in September 2000, arrived at its home port on the west coast of Ireland. The *Atlantic Dawn,* built at a cost of £50 million (about $75 million), was capable of freezing and storing a massive 7,000 metric tons of whole frozen pelagic fish on three decks of holds. The vessel was 144 m (472 ft) long, with a beam of 24.3 m (80 ft) and a carrying capacity estimated to be some 2,000 metric tons greater than its nearest rival. To keep such a vessel economical, the designers built it to be as flexible as possible and to be able to fish worldwide either as a pelagic trawler or by utilizing purse seine techniques. The *Atlantic Dawn* was scheduled to begin fishing for sardinella, mackerel, and horse mackerel in West African waters off the coast of Mauritania.

(MARTIN GILL)

Nominal Catches of Fish by Principal 50 Producers

Country	1997 production (metric tons)	1998 production (metric tons)
China	15,722,344	17,229,957
Japan	5,916,155	5,259,089
United States	4,983,468	4,708,980
Russia	4,661,853	4,454,759
Peru	7,869,871	4,338,437
Indonesia	3,791,025	3,698,850
Chile	5,811,567	3,265,306
India	3,517,084	3,214,765
Thailand	2,877,622	2,900,320
Norway	2,856,017	2,850,428
South Korea	2,204,047	2,026,934
Philippines	1,805,806	1,827,971
Iceland	2,205,944	1,681,951
Denmark	1,826,852	1,557,335
Mexico	1,489,020	1,181,402
Malaysia	1,172,922	1,153,719
Vietnam	1,078,668	1,130,660
Argentina	1,351,066	1,128,823
Spain	1,143,122	1,106,557
Taiwan	1,038,048	1,076,288
Canada	963,492	995,011
United Kingdom	886,269	919,905
Myanmar (Burma)	830,346	872,971
Bangladesh	829,426	839,141
Brazil	744,585	760,000
Morocco	783,615	708,332
New Zealand	596,017	635,711
Pakistan	589,731	596,980
South Africa	514,453	558,832
Netherlands	451,799	536,626
France	567,476	536,254
Venezuela	463,215	506,177
Turkey	459,153	487,200
Ukraine	373,005	462,308
Ghana	446,788	442,692
Senegal	506,966	425,766
Sweden	357,406	410,886
Faroe Islands	329,736	376,270
Iran	349,921	366,853
Egypt	345,220	365,580
Namibia	279,484	352,188
Tanzania	356,960	348,000
World Total	**93,619,100**	**86,299,400**

Source: UN Food and Agriculture Organization.

Genetically Modified Foods: The Political Debate

by Norman Myers

By 2000 genetically modified (GM) foods had created a political furor in many parts of the world. Those on one side of the controversy argued that GM foods could represent one of the biggest advances ever achieved in farming, while those in opposition believed that GM foods could trigger a wide variety of serious environmental and health problems. The scientific evidence supporting either view was far from complete and might not become so without field trials extending over several crop seasons. Public opinion remained deeply divided, sometimes bitterly so.

The stakes are high, with huge sums invested by giant agribusinesses in the research and development of such foods. The result is a combustible mix of fact and fiction, opinion and prejudice, and governments pitted against one another in one of the most acrimonious policy debates in decades.

The main proponents of GM foods are Americans, and the main skeptics are Europeans. American farmers have long planted GM crops and are by far the world's largest exporters of GM foods. Only in recent years have they encountered widespread analyses of the crops' benefits and drawbacks. Europe, by contrast, grows only small amounts of GM crops but has become the site of large-scale resistance.

The question that arises is why GM foods generate such strident reactions. Certain of their benefits are beyond doubt. According to a July 2000 report by Europe's leading scientific body, the Royal Society of London, together with the U.S. National Academy of Sciences and five other leading academies, GM crops resist pests, grow in salty soils, and produce food that is both more nutritious and more stable in storage. Nor is there any doubt about the urgent need for more bountiful farming when humankind is likely to increase its numbers by nearly two billion people within another two decades.

A crop at the centre of the controversy is oilseed rape. In many parts of Europe, it is often the third most popular crop, after wheat and barley. The oil is used in up to 60% of processed foods, from bread and pizzas to cookies and ice cream. It has been commercially important in Europe for centuries but has become popular in North America (where it is known as canola) only since World War II, when it was grown for use as a lubricant.

Oilseed rape was one of the first crops to be genetically modified for herbicide tolerance. It has several wild relatives in Europe, such as wild radish and wild turnip. Because the GM plants are resistant to herbicides and there is a possibility that some of these plants could crossbreed with wild relatives and thereby create weeds immune to herbicides, farmers could, according to the critics, witness the emergence of unkillable superweeds. Other concerns include the fact that pollen from corn modified to kill corn borer pests might sometimes land on neighbouring milkweed plants, where it could kill butterfly caterpillars.

Scientists for the most part have been guardedly in favour of GM farming or have at least been neutral. Invariably, however, they register a strong proviso: that there should be sufficiently comprehensive field trials, over however long a time is necessary, to demonstrate that GM crops are safe in terms of both the environment and public health. In March full-scale trials were approved for three GM crops across England and in Scotland: up to 25 fields of oilseed rape, up to 25 fields of corn, and 30 fields of mixed sugar and fodder beets. The fields are to be monitored regularly to check the spread of pollen, the effects on mammals and birds, and the potential threat of weeds. Conclusive results might not become available for several seasons.

Environmental activists have been less optimistic than the scientists. In Great Britain Friends of the Earth declared that GM crops are "scientifically nonsensical," while Greenpeace termed them "a potential tragedy" and "genetic tyranny with almost complete absence of public consultation." To demonstrate its concerns, Greenpeace ripped up entire fields of GM corn before the plants could produce pollen to be blown into other fields.

Genetically modified corn plants grow at a greenhouse near Slater, Iowa.

AP/Wide World Photos

There is also a more philosophical objection, exemplified by Britain's Prince Charles. He believes that humans should not meddle with basic processes of life itself. GM crops, he maintains, betray "the sacred trust between mankind and our Creator." He inveighs against "the artificial and uncontained transfer of genes between species of plants and animals." Assertions such as these have engendered deep-seated concerns among many people, concerns that mostly have little to do with strict science. Many European consumers remain suspicious about science in the food arena after the recent dioxin-in-poultry scare in Belgium and the "mad cow" disease outbreak in Britain and elsewhere, even though neither of these problems had anything to do with genetic engineering.

Equally to the point, Europeans are united in their view that biotechnologies should not be controlled by giant agribusinesses, most of which are American. Companies such as the Monsanto

Co. have invested hundreds of millions of dollars in research and development of GM crops. Global sales of GM crop products grew from $75 million in 1995 to $1.5 billion in 1998 and could reach $25 billion by 2010. Although genetic modification and release of GM foods are closely regulated in Europe, there are few overarching bodies (as opposed to specialist committees) to monitor the impact of GM crops on agriculture generally and to consider the cumulative effects of such crops.

Conversely, Americans insist that their country has the highest food-safety standards in the world and that the new products have been thoroughly analyzed and approved by the U.S. Department of Agriculture, the Environmental Protection Agency, and the Food and Drug Administration. They also point out that for a number of years Americans have been eating large amounts of genetically modified foods without suffering any apparent adverse effects. In addition, Americans protest against Europe's "artificial" trade barriers that limit imports of agricultural products, as evidenced by Europe's 1998 refusal to allow entry of certain genetically modified corn varieties, costing American farmers some $200 million in lost sales.

Finally, a major concern in 2000 centred on public trust in both the scientists and the agribusiness leaders. Without greater public support, the GM industry in Europe is likely to remain undeveloped. Opinion polls consistently show that more than 80% of the public there do not want GM foods. As a result, many European food producers and suppliers alike are working to reduce or eradicate GM organisms in the food chain. They will almost certainly continue to do so until policy decisions on the GM issue are seen to be taken in light of reliable, comprehensive, and objective information—a resource that is in short supply thus far. Fortunately, product labeling, a critically important measure, is becoming widespread in Europe and is becoming more common in the U.S.

In response to this challenge, GM advocates need to improve their communications if public opinion is to be convinced that the advantages outweigh the risks. Efforts should be made to listen to, as well as speak to, the public. The issue is one not only of the public's understanding of science but also of scientists' understanding of the public.

Norman Myers is a consultant scientist in environment and development and a visiting fellow of Green College, Oxford.

On May 25, as policemen in Genoa, Italy, block access to an area where an international biotechnology conference is being held, one of thousands of protesters against genetically modified foods prepares to march in a massive demonstration.

Rodney White/NYT Pictures

Anthropology and Archaeology

Surprisingly recent ages for **NEANDERTHAL** remains from Russia and Croatia indicated that these early humans were **STILL PRESENT LESS THAN 30,000 YEARS AGO.** One of the **WORLD'S OLDEST CITIES** was unearthed in northeastern **SYRIA.** A fresh theory was offered to explain the **MYSTERIOUS NAZCA LINES** of Peru.

ANTHROPOLOGY

Physical Anthropology. In 2000 an international research team published a molecular analysis of mitochondrial DNA extracted from the rib of an approximately 29,000-year-old Neanderthal infant. (Mitochondria are DNA-containing cytoplasmic components of cells that play an essential role in the conversion of the energy of foodstuffs into the energy used for cellular activities.) The specimen was recovered from Mezmaiskaya Cave in the northern Caucasus region of Russia, one of the easternmost Neanderthal sites. When the DNA fragment, consisting of 345 base pairs, was compared with the same region sequenced in 1997 from a specimen found in the Feldhofer Cave in Germany, only 12 differences (3.48%) were found. This close genetic relationship provided invaluable corroboration for the authenticity of the previously reported, but undated, Neanderthal sequence from Germany. The infant's DNA exhibited 22 differences from the standard human (Anderson) reference sequence for modern human mitochondrial DNA, whereas the Feldhofer Cave specimen contained 27 differences with respect to the Anderson sequence. Nineteen of these differences were shared by the two Neanderthals, and subsequent analysis placed them in a clade (lineage) distinct from modern humans. The age of the most recent common ancestor of the mitochondrial DNA molecules of the two Neanderthal specimens was estimated to be 151,000–352,000 years, a range concordant with dates derived from the paleontological record for the emergence of the Neanderthal lineage. Overall, the results supported the out-of-Africa theory for the origin of modern humans rather than the multiregional hypothesis.

The surprisingly recent radiocarbon date (29,195 [±965] years ago) on collagen derived from the Neanderthal infant lent credence to the assertion that Neanderthals and modern humans overlapped throughout much of Europe for thousands of years. An international team also recently redated two important Neanderthal specimens from Vindija Cave in Croatia. The new radiocarbon dates of 29,080 (±400) and 28,020 (±360) years ago from a mandible and a parietal bone of different individuals provided additional confirmation of previous claims, based on sites in Spain and Portugal, that some Neanderthal populations were still present less than 30,000 years ago, well after the first definitive evidence of modern human skeletal structure in Europe (at approximately 32,000 years ago).

The extreme simplicity of stone tools found at the Dmanisi site (right)—very similar to earlier tools found in the Rift Valley of Africa (left)—helped anthropologists to revise their theories of why early man moved out of Africa.

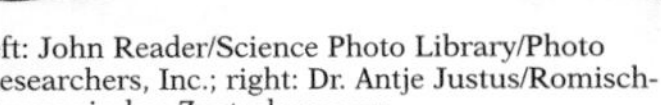

left: John Reader/Science Photo Library/Photo Researchers, Inc.; right: Dr. Antje Justus/Romisch-Germanisches Zentralmuseum

Dmanisi, Georgia, captured the paleoanthropological spotlight when two partial hominid crania dated to about 1.7 million years ago documented what may have been the first migration of the genus *Homo* out of Africa. The site had previously yielded a hominid mandible in 1991 and a metatarsal bone in 1997; however, the taxonomic affinities of the two specimens as well as their dating were uncertain. The new skeletal material, along with more than 1,000 simple stone artifacts and new geochronological and paleomagnetic data, were combined by an international group of scholars to suggest the following scenario. Shortly after the first appearance of *Homo ergaster* (also called African *Homo erectus*) about 1.9 million years ago, a population of these hominids moved out of Africa via the Levantine corridor (near the eastern end of the Mediterranean Sea) and continued in a northeasterly direction, eventually arriving in Dmanisi between the Black and Caspian seas.

Structurally, the Dmanisi remains closely resembled the 1.6 million-year-old Kenyan fossil known as the Nariokotome boy. The larger of the two Georgian specimens was an almost complete adult male calvarium (skullcap) with a cranial capacity of 780 cc (47.6 cu in), while the slightly smaller but more extensively preserved cranium, thought to be from an adolescent female, yielded an estimate of 650 cc (39.7 cu in). Perhaps the biggest surprise came not from the African morphology of the specimens but rather from the extreme simplicity of the associated artifacts. The tools consisted of flakes, scrapers, and choppers made entirely from local basalt sources, using a technology similar to that employed in East Africa as early as 2.4 million years ago. Consequently, a major implication of the cultural remains was that biological changes rather than new tools may have prompted early global colonization by *Homo*. Once *H. ergaster* achieved larger body size and once brain size exceeded that of the australopithecines, the forests of Africa were quickly left behind. It is possible that after Dmanisi these hominids moved eastward to Asia, where simple chopping tools predominated for more than a million years and where their descendants gave rise to Asian *H. erectus.*

The apolipoprotein (a complex molecule that combines fat and protein) E locus provided a clear example of natural selection in action during the last 300,000 years of human evolutionary history. An American-Finnish collaboration traced the genealogical history of a potentially deadly human gene. Although humans exhibited three different alleles at this locus (designated E2, E3, and E4), their closest living relative, the chimpanzee, had only the medically dangerous E4 allele. (An allele is any one of two or more genes that may occur alternatively at a given site [locus] on a chromosome.) The E4 allele was already known to increase the risk of cardiovascular disease and Alzheimer disease in humans. The ancestral E4 allele associated with elevated lipid levels was detected in only 13.5% of the chromosomes taken from an ethnically diverse set of four human populations, whereas the much more favourable E3 allele had a frequency of 79.7% among the 96 individuals sequenced at this locus on chromosome 19. Thus, the E4 allele inherited from humans' apelike common ancestor with the chimpanzee was hypothesized to be undergoing a rapid replacement throughout the world's populations by the medically far less dangerous E3 allele under the influence of natural selection.

June 26, 2000, was a historic day in the annals of human biology and physical anthropology. It marked the joint announcement—by Francis Collins (*see* BIOGRAPHIES), leader of a publicly funded international consortium of genome scientists, and by J. Craig Venter, president of Celera Genomics—of the final assembly of two working drafts of the human genome sequence. The actual data were posted on the Internet as a public database <www.ncbi.nlm.nih.gov/genome/guide>. (*See* LIFE SCIENCES: *Special Report.*) (STEPHEN L. ZEGURA)

Cultural Anthropology. As it entered the new millennium, cultural anthropology, after a decade of questioning its subdisciplinary character (specifically versus physical anthropology) and its role in understanding major trends in the contemporary world, had undergone changes that culminated in clear directions for the future. Among current concerns were ethnographic methods in anthropology, violence and war, race and ethnicity, the public face and role of anthropology, cross-national immigration and identity, the anthropological code of ethics, the environment, and human rights. In addition, core topics such as kinship were being revisited.

The shift from an earlier focus on discourse, gender, and postmodernist writing was reflected in American Anthropological Association Distinguished Lectures (for example, Sidney Mintz) and in major publications (most prominently, *Handbook of Methods in Cultural Anthropology,* edited by H. Russell Bernard, an updating of the 1970 methodological "bible" edited by Raoul Naroll and Ronald Cohen). The Sidney Mintz distinguished lecture of 1996 was published in *Current Anthropology* in 2000, and the *Handbook of Methods,* a major 1998 hardcover reference volume of 19 chapters by anthropologists actively engaged in research, was reissued in paperback during the year and was thus made more accessible for classroom teaching and research.

Both publications were trendsetting and pathbreaking. This was welcomed in a field that had become saturated with nonempirical works on, among other subjects, women and gender (especially on women in the Middle East)—works that were influenced more by premises from area, women's, and cultural studies than by anthropology. Some had adopted strong anticulture postmodernist postures that questioned ethnographic authority and stressed multiple "voices." Discourse scholarship (originating in art, literary, and cultural studies) examined text without understanding its context and words without ethnography.

Reaction against this trend was strong, some of it ironically by non-Western scholars who challenged its fundamental humanist claim and objected to its implications of Western superiority. Most prominent was the discussion by Ziauddin Sardar, who wrote: "Colonialism has already drained much of the wealth of the 'Third World,' [and now] postmodernism appropriates the last resources . . . its traditions, spiritualities, cultural property, ideas and notions . . . the new imperialism." This challenged the presumed claim that a humanistic quality inheres in certain human domains, such as oratory and dance performance, but not in others, such as alliance and kinship practices. Mintz's lecture-publication reaffirmed field-gathered ethnographic data. Beyond this, it recalled earlier anthropology with its applications and impact beyond academia, adopting unpopular postures in defense of the legitimacy of traditional ways of life and cultural practices.

The recent posture against culture and generalization, which denied people's individuality and the particularity of cultures, was compellingly critiqued in the above-mentioned *Handbook of Methods.* Stripped of identity, people become homogenized and globalized actors in a large machine of economy and postmodernity. The volume was timely in topic and current and comprehensive in the range of subjects covered; it embraced qualitative and quantitative approaches and visual and archival methods, from epistemology to ethics to visual anthropology and much more. The chapter on visual anthropology reflected the growing importance of the visual as a tool for analysis and a source of data. The *Handbook* was favourably reviewed as authoritative on the methods of anthropological research (systematic collecting and interpreting of human behaviour in natural settings) by experts on fieldwork in anthropology and also was regarded as serious about the ethnographic enterprise.

As to public issues, an international conference was organized by universities in Sweden and Denmark to which international scholars were invited to discuss the impact of legal immigration from less-developed (particularly Islamic) countries to the welfare states of Scandinavia. The rapid shift in population demographics became an urgent subject, intersecting cultural anthropology with public policy. The growing presence of Muslim immigrants in predominantly Lutheran scandinavia was changing the sociocultural landscape of that area. This trend drew attention to the need of anthropological understanding of Islam and Muslim life.

The publication in November of *Darkness in El Dorado: How Scientists and Journalists Devastated the Amazon* by freelance journalist Patrick Tierney produced a major crisis in anthropology. Advance proofs of the book precipitated sensationalized stories critical of the Yanomami project, a series of studies among the indigenous Yanomami people of Venezuela and Brazil that began with genetic research conducted in 1968, funded in part by the U.S. Atomic Energy Commission and led by the late James V. Neel of the University of Michigan at Ann Arbor. Also on the project team were anthropologist Napoleon A. Chagnon of the University of California, Santa Barbara (now retired), who had worked with the Yanomami since 1964, and, later, filmmaker Timothy Asch. Tierney's allegations included improper use by Neel and his team of a vaccine purported to have resulted in a devastating measles epidemic among the Yanomami. Subsequent expert investigations refuted these and many other claims, and by year's end the credibility of Tierney's own research was being called into question.

A second aspect of the controversy involved accuracy and representation of data, specifically Chagnon's depiction of the Yanomami as a fierce and violent people. Concerns over scientific accuracy were not new (for example, more discussion of the controversy over Margaret Mead's classic work in Samoa was reported in *Current Anthropology*'s August–October 2000 issue). In the current case, this longstanding intramural debate among anthropologists was further muddied by external factors, including an old dispute between Chagnon and local missionaries and the sometimes violent relations between Brazilian gold miners and the Yanomami. On the bright side, out of this crisis in cultural anthropology emerged a needed debate on ethical accountability in field research, informed consent by studied populations, and the role of the revised Code of Ethics drafted by the American Anthropological Association in 1998.

(FADWA EL GUINDI)

Hilti Foundation/Franck Goddio/Discovery Channel/Photographer: Christoph Gerigk

A black stone head from the Late Dynastic Period was among the artifacts discovered during an underwater archaeological survey of a site off the northern coast of Egypt in 2000.

ARCHAEOLOGY

Eastern Hemisphere. The year 2000 proved fruitful for Old World archaeology. A joint Syrian-American expedition uncovered what was purported to be one of the world's oldest cities, a more than 5,500-year-old urban centre at Tell Hamoukar in northeastern Syria near the Iraqi border. At the site, located on an ancient trade route between Nineveh and Aleppo, archaeologists identified what may be a Late Chalcolithic (about 3500 BC) mud-brick city wall, 3 m (10 ft) high and 4 m (13 ft) wide, and excavated a group of mud-brick dwellings complete with ovens. Also recovered were more than 80 bone stamp seals carved with animals such as leopards, lions, rabbits, fish, bears, birds, and dogs; 15 seal impressions; and thousands of beads. The presence of a Late Chalcolithic city in Syria challenged the generally accepted view that urban centres first developed in ancient Sumer (present-day southern Iraq) following the invention of writing during the Uruk period (about 3200 BC). It would appear that Tell Hamoukar developed well before the invention of writing and before the appearance of several other criteria thought of as marking "civilization."

An underwater archaeological survey of the Mediterranean just a few kilometres off Egypt's north coast revealed the remains of two 2,500-year-old cities, possibly the suburbs of Canopus with the districts of Menouthis and Iraklion, which served as trading hubs in the Late Dynastic Period. Among the well-preserved remains were temple structures with statues of Isis, Sarapis, and Osiris associated with royal heads of pharaohs; port facilities; fallen monuments; inscriptions; ceramics; and late Islamic and Byzantine jewelry and coins, all embedded in the seafloor less than 10 m (33 ft) below the water's surface.

A controversial find was the so-called Tomb of Osiris on the Giza Plateau in Egypt. Thought by some to be an Osirion, a cenotaph dedicated to Egypt's master of the underworld and god of fertility, the four-pillared rock-hewn grotto, 30 m (98 ft) below the Giza Plateau, may simply have been another shaft tomb belonging to royalty of the Late Dynastic Period.

Pits containing the remains of sacrificed dogs at the 5,500-year-old settlement of Botai in north-central Kazakhstan may shed light on ritual practices recorded in the Rigveda, written c. 1000 BC. In the epic, dogs serve as guardians of the gate into the afterlife, which was believed to lie to the west. The bodies of at least 15 dogs, similar in stature and cranial features to Samoyeds, had been deposited in small pits in or near the western walls of houses. Each pit contained between one and six dogs, along with the skulls of horses.

Thirteen 2,500-year-old carved stelae (stone pillars) of a type never seen before in Anatolia or the Middle East were found at Hakkari, a small town in Turkey near the border with Iran and Iraq. Hewn from a hard local stone, the stelae ranged from about 75 cm (28 in) to more than 3 m (10 ft) in height. They may depict rulers of Hubushkia, a kingdom centred on the headwaters of the Great Zap River that appears in the Assyrian annals of the 10th and 9th centuries BC.

In China a walled city about 3,300 years old was unearthed at Anyang. Known as Huanbei Shang City, the site, covering approximately 465 ha (1,160 ac) and surrounded by rammed earthen walls, dates to the Middle Shang Period (about 1450–1250 BC), a time little understood in Chinese history. Oracle-bone inscriptions placed the last Shang capital at a site known as Yinxu, about 1.5 km (1 mi) southwest of Huanbei Shang City. Scholars believed the newly found site may have been the city of Xiang, which, according to historical sources, served as the capital of the Shang Empire prior to the founding of Yinxu.

A large cache of gold and silver bangles, gold beads, and agate and onyx beads, dating to the Harappan Period (2600–1900 BC) and of a type known from the Indus Valley sites of Harappa and Mohenjo-daro in Pakistan and Lothal, Rakhigarhi, and Dholavira in India, was discovered by villagers in the city of Mandi some 150 km (90 mi) east of New Delhi. The finds extended the known reach of the Indus Valley civilization beyond its previously known cultural area of eastern Pakistan and western India.

Excavations in Britain yielded a number of important finds, including a large cache of Roman coins found in a farmer's field near Glastonbury, Eng. The hoard comprised more than 9,200 coins, most of which were silver denarii, common coins equivalent to pennies in Roman times. The coins spanned the period from Mark Antony (31–30 BC) to Severus Alexander (AD 222–235), with the latest coin dating to about AD 224. The hoard was unusual in that many of the coins dated from the early part of the 3rd century, a relatively calm and prosperous period of Roman rule in Britain. Most Roman hoards found in Britain date from the end of the Roman period, the late 4th and early 5th centuries, when political instability prompted people to hide their wealth.

What was hailed as the best-preserved Iron Age settlement in Britain was found on the southern tip of Mainland, Shetland Islands. Occupied from about 200 BC to AD 800, the site consisted of a massive round stone watchtower approximately 15 m (50 ft) in diameter and 3–4 m (12–15 ft) high, surrounded by well-preserved buildings, some still bearing traces of yellow plastered walls. The tower was an Iron Age status symbol for the ruling elite, which suggested that the site was a centre of considerable wealth.

Ongoing construction and development in Italy laid bare more of the country's ancient past. In Rome walls and foundations belonging to a villa from about AD 150 were found during construction of a tunnel leading to a large parking garage beneath the Vatican, and the remains of the Imperial Roman port, once used to receive and warehouse goods arriving from Ostia on the coast, came to light during excavations prior to the building of a streetcar station at Trastevere on the Tiber River. Port remains included warehouses, workshops, offices, and baths adorned with mosaics depicting sea creatures and marine life, as well as numerous amphorae, ceramics, coins, and oil lamps dating to the 2nd through the 4th century AD.

A submarine crew searching for the wreckage of an airplane piloted by Antoine Saint-Exupéry, author of *The Little Prince,* discovered the wreck of a 6th–5th-century BC Etruscan ship off the coast of southern France. Found off the coast of the Hyères Islands near Toulon, the ship was carrying a varied cargo, which included amphorae possibly filled with wine, olive oil, or garum, a fermented fish sauce, and a shipment of tile. Only three Etruscan wrecks had ever been recovered, all plundered and poorly preserved.

(ANGELA M.H. SCHUSTER)

Western Hemisphere. The debate over the date of the first human settlement of the Americas continued unabated in 2000. A few new discoveries appeared to support a pre-Clovis culture settlement more than 13,000 years ago. The Topper site on South Carolina's Savannah River was originally thought to be a Clovis site of about 11,500 BC, but test pits sunk below the Paleo-Indian occupation level revealed small stone flakes and tools of an apparent pre-Clovis type more than one metre (3.3 ft) lower. The artifacts included tiny microblades and a scraping tool, which excavator Albert Goodyear considered unique to southeastern North America but reminiscent of Stone Age tools from Siberia. As of late 2000, the occupation level remained undated but was possibly up to 18,000 years old, one of the earliest known records of human occupation in the Western Hemisphere.

Maya archaeology continued to yield spectacular discoveries. A Maya lord named Ukit-Kan Lek ("Snake Gourd") ruled over the ceremonial centre of Ek Balam in Mexico's northern Yucatán between AD 790 and 835. In 1999 archaeologist Victor Castillo unearthed Snake Gourd's grave under a limestone pyramid, which was built atop at least four earlier buildings. Twenty-two ceramic vessels lay in the burial chamber, one bearing the lord's name, together with fine jade fragments, obsidian (volcanic glass) blades, and inscribed conch shells.

The spectacular Nazca lines of southern coastal Peru had generated controversy for generations. The Nazca were farmers, fisherfolk, and expert weavers, and their pots and textiles revealed complex religious beliefs. They lived on the fringes of the Pampa de Ingenio, a desert with all the potential of a fine sketch pad. There they swept away the topsoil of fine sand and small stones to form in the white alluvium an intricate web of lines and figures too large to be fully viewed from the ground. High above the desert in a helicopter, one can see lines, some as wide as an airport runway, that extend for kilometres across valleys and low hills. Others radiate from hubs. Some lines coalesce into giant birds, monkeys, a whale, spiders, even plants, but those who created them never saw them in their entirety. Why, then, did people without airplanes draw such lines and figures? Were the lines a giant astronomical observatory or a huge religious monument?

Astroarchaeologists Anthony Aveni and Gary Urton, in an effort to answer those questions, mapped more than 62 raylike hubs of lines and measured the orientation of 762 straight lines near Nazca, some up to 13 km (8 mi) long. Aveni and Urton plotted the orientations on a computer and found that many of them pointed to the point on the horizon where the Sun appears during those critical days in early November when runoff first flows into coastal rivers from the Andes Mountains. Thousands of Nazca potsherds, crude shelter remains, and cairns litter the lines, the latter serving as markers for people walking the alignments. Aveni concluded that the Nazca lines were pathways, maintained, swept, and ritually cleansed by local kin groups as an important part of ritual activity surrounding the arrival of water on the pampa. A nearby ceremonial centre, Cahuachi, forms a complex of mounds, cemeteries, and shrines, which face toward the pampa and its pathways. Also nearby, water bubbles to the surface year-round. Nazca art from Cahuachi and other locations emphasizes masked performances by priests and mythical beings, part of the ceremonies that surrounded the first appearance of life-giving mountain water. Aveni's research thus pointed to a close connection between the lines in the desert and the water that nourished crops and people along the Pacific.

Brazil's Amazon Basin was among the archaeologically least-known regions of the world. Recently, caves in Amapá state on the Maracá River, a tributary of the Amazon, yielded ceramic funerary urns, used by local peoples between the 5th and 15th centuries AD. The now sparsely occupied area was densely populated 1,500 years ago. The finely made urns, about 0.75 m (2.5 ft) high, were modeled in the form of seated male and female figures and placed on benches, a privilege reserved for shamans and chiefs. The urns contained defleshed bones from corpses that were exposed until the flesh had decayed and then were laid to rest in deep caverns. The Maracá finds were unique and dated to a period before the region was depopulated by European contact and infectious diseases.

While reexamining the excavated bones of colonists from Jamestown, Va., the earliest permanent English settlement in the New World, biological anthropologist Doug Owsley of the Smithsonian Institution discovered that five of the skeletons were those of Africans. The five died in their early 20s to mid-40s, and, as they had not been buried on their backs with their hands at their sides and heads to the west—the European fashion at the time—they were originally thought to be Native Americans. One of them displayed an advanced case of syphilis, which had affected every bone in his body. Judging from the bullet hole in his head, he was killed to put him out of his misery. Owsley's discovery confirmed that Europeans, Native Americans, and African slaves were all present at Jamestown.

In a fascinating piece of archaeological detective work, British Museum scientists determined that a copper breastplate owned by late-19th-century Pacific Northwest coast Native American chief Neghicum-gee was made not of native copper but of English ore. His intricately decorated breastplate was an important status symbol, one of many "coppers" that linked individuals to the remote past of their ancestors. Neghicum-gee's copper contained unusually high quantities of bismuth, a heavy element that occurs in large amounts only in Cornish copper from southwestern England, where it was smelted between 1700 and 1850. The scientists believed it was quite possible that the copper was made from ore traded with trappers or whalers decades before the Spaniards and Capt. James Cook arrived in the area in 1774 and 1777.

On Nov. 29, 1864, more than 700 soldiers of a volunteer Colorado militia unit attacked a Cheyenne and Arapaho Native American encampment at Sand Creek in southeastern Colorado. Ignoring the American flag, peace signals, and a white flag, they slaughtered at least 150 old men, women, and children while most of the men were out hunting.

Although the general location of the massacre was known through oral tradition to the descendants of the victims, it was only when an archaeological survey was carried out that the actual location was found, about a kilometre and a half (about a mile) north of where historical evidence said it was. The archaeologists found 5.4-kg (12-lb) cannonballs, the type used by the Colorado soldiers in their surprise attack, and artifacts that matched well with records of goods given to the Native Americans and found at sites of equivalent age. The Sand Creek research confirmed the essential truth of Native American oral traditions and thus allowed them to be used as archaeological tools. (BRIAN FAGAN)

A large tree-shaped design in a desert of southern coastal Peru forms part of the spectacular Nazca lines.

Roman Soumar/Corbis

Architecture and Civil Engineering

Two broad architectural trends—**GREEN ARCHITECTURE** and **THE GROWING ROLE OF COMPUTERS**—seemed more important in 2000 than any individual architect or new building.

ARCHITECTURE

Green Architecture was a worldwide movement that was dedicated to constructing buildings that were designed to be kind to the environment. These environmentally friendly structures were sparing in their use of water and energy, and they emitted little of the greenhouse-gas emissions that contributed to global warming. Though the green movement was strongest in Europe, it had begun to gain advocates in the United States as well. In March the Architectural League of New York sponsored an exhibition that embodied the movement. "Ten Shades of Green" showcased eight European buildings, an Australian building, and four American houses. Through new technologies some of the buildings generated more energy than they consumed. Writing on the show, British critic Peter Buchanan remarked, "Soon no building will be considered first-rate if it is not also green." Green attitudes were also a factor in the revival of older cities, especially in the United States, owing to the fact that densely populated cities consumed less energy per capita than did suburban and rural areas. A standout among the many notable examples of green design in Europe was a building for the Dutch Institute for Forestry and Nature Research by architects Behnisch, Behnisch & Partner. In lieu of mechanical ventilation, a system of gardens, which was interwoven among the offices, provided fresh air and insulation.

The other major architectural trend was the increasing use of computers to influence the appearance of buildings. By working with the aid of computers, architects and builders were able to create buildings of almost any shape. The result was a trend toward what some called biomorphic or Blob Design. The architects who embraced this new trend were nicknamed "Blobmeisters." An example of this conceptual phenomenon was the Experience Music Project (EMP), the new rock-and-roll museum in Seattle, Wash. Designed by American Frank O. Gehry, whom many considered the world's most influential architect, and funded by software billionaire Paul Allen, the EMP consisted of huge muffinlike shapes covered in reflective metal skin, some of which changed colour as museum patrons moved around them. The Venice Biennale of Architecture exhibit was dominated by biomorphs, including the U.S. pavilion designed by Blobmeister Greg Lynn of California and others. In Venice the natural shapelessness of this kind of architecture was emphasized by video projections on many of the surfaces, which suggested that the architecture of the future might be more virtual than solid.

Awards. Dutch architect Rem Koolhaas was the recipient of the Pritzker Architecture Prize, the world's top award for architecture. Koolhaas was best known for his irreverent and influential thinking and writing in such books as *Delirious New York* (1994) and *S, M, L, X* (1998) rather than for any of his individual buildings. He argued that architecture should not be an elitist art and that architects should accept and collaborate with the realities of globalization and international commerce. British architect Richard Rogers received the Praemium Imperiale, which was offered by the Japan Art Association. Rogers was known as the co-designer of the Pompidou Centre in Paris and the architect of the Lloyds Building in London. The biannual Mies van der Rohe Prize for Latin American architecture, which is awarded to a building rather than to an architect, went to the State Pinoteca in São Paulo, Braz. Michael Graves won the Gold Medal of the American Institute of Architects (AIA), which, like the Pritzker, is for lifetime achievement. Graves, who is generally regarded as a Postmodernist, has revived themes from the architecture of different eras of the past. Among his notable works are the public library in San Juan Capistrano, Calif.; two hotels at Disney World in Florida; the Humana Building in Louisville, Ky.; and The Netherlands Ministry of Health, Welfare and Sport at The Hague. Graves also produced tableware and other household objects. (*See* ART, ANTIQUES, AND COLLECTIONS: *Special Report.*) The AIA's 25-Year Award, for a building that has proved its merit over time, went to the Smith House in Darien, Conn., designed by Richard Meier. The AIA also announced 38 winners of its annual Honor Awards. Among the more prominent recipients were Meier's Getty Center in Los Angeles; Bernard Tschumi's Le Fresnoy National Studio for Contemporary Arts in Tourcoing, France; Beyer Blinder Belle restoration architects' renovation of Grand Central Terminal in New York City; and Cesar Pelli's Kuala Lumpur City Centre in Malaysia. Samuel Mockbee—an Alabama architect and cofounder in 1993 of Auburn University's Rural Studio, a program in which students experienced hands-on architectural design by building housing in a poor Alabama county—won a MacArthur Foundation fellowship. Jane Jacobs—urban planner and author of many books, including the classic *The Death and Life of Great American Cities* (1961), which was described by the *New York Times* as "perhaps the most influential single work in the history of planning"—was the recipient in November of the second Vincent Scully Prize.

Civic Buildings. The design elements in new airports made them the most noticeable type of civic structure of the year. Many of the new facilities sought to reflect the excitement of flight in swooping architectural shapes, as well as to provide shopping, hotels, and offices for travelers. Among them were the enormous Kuala Lumpur International Airport in Malaysia, by Japanese architect Kisho Kurokawa; the Shanghai-Pudong International Airport in China, by Aéroports de Paris Architectes et Ingénieurs; and the Sondica Airport in Bilbao, Spain, by internationally known

Ted Thai/Timepix

architect-engineer Santiago Calatrava. In New York City the spectacular Rose Center for Earth and Space, a planetarium at the American Museum of Natural History, was in the form of a huge luminous sphere and proved a popular and critical success. The architect was the Polshek Partnership, a New York firm that was again in the news when its design for a presidential library in Little Rock, Ark., for Pres. Bill Clinton was unveiled in December.

In London the largest single space ever enclosed, the Millennium Dome by Richard Rogers, was filled with commercial exhibits that attracted few visitors. Also in London, Sir Norman Foster's pedestrian Millennium Bridge across the River Thames had to be closed two days after it opened because it swayed too much.

The Oklahoma City (Okla.) Memorial, commemorating the 1995 terrorist bombing of a U.S. federal building, opened to acclaim in April. In Sydney, Australia, a vast complex of new buildings for the Olympics was praised for its plan—by American landscape architect George Hargreaves—but received less acclaim for the architecture of the individual buildings.

Cultural Buildings. The most widely noted new museum of the year was the Tate Modern in London. There Swiss architects Herzog & de Meuron transformed a vast brick 1965 riverfront power plant into a new museum for international modern art. The architects left much of the huge interior space open, as a setting for large works of art; several floors of new galleries, shops, and restaurants were inserted elsewhere in the building.

In Houston, Texas, Spanish architect Rafael Moneo added a major new wing to the Museum of Fine Arts, earlier portions of which were designed by the great modernist Ludwig Mies van der Rohe. Moneo's design was a rather Spartan box of limestone on the outside, leading to a mix of traditional and modern motifs on the inside, with much natural light provided by skylights.

In Los Angeles the long-delayed Walt Disney Concert Hall, by Gehry, was at last under construction, while in New York an astonishing Gehry design for a branch of the Guggenheim Museum received the backing of the city's mayor. Reminiscent of Gehry's famed Guggenheim branch in Bilbao, the New York design was conceived as swirling shapes of titanium, which would appear to float above the water of the East River like a cloud. The original New York Guggenheim—a landmark design by Frank Lloyd Wright—will hold collections of art prior to 1945 if the new building, budgeted at almost $700 million, is built. The Polshek Partnership completed a new entrance to the Brooklyn Museum of Art. Its asymmetrical design contrasts with the classical symmetry of the century-old main structure.

The Rose Center for Earth and Space, a planetarium at the American Museum of Natural History designed by the Polshek Partnership, glowing in the New York City night.

Commercial Buildings. Easily the most spectacular new commercial building to be completed during the year was the Burj al Arab (also known as the Arabian Tower) in Dubayy, U.A.E. The 60-story hotel, which was sited on an artificial island, was the tallest in the world at 320 m (1,053 ft) and was intended to attract visitors by the sheer drama of its architecture, which rose from the sea like the curve of a scimitar. At night computerized lighting transformed the building into a huge kinetic light show. The minimum guest rate of $900 per night was seen as an added attraction; visitors would stay at the hotel merely to show that they could afford to. The interior of the structure was no less spectacular; it featured a 183-m (600-ft) atrium, the world's tallest, and luxurious rooms that provided a breathtaking view of Dubayy and the Persian Gulf. The architect for the building was Tom Wright of the British firm WS Atkins, an offshore engineering consultancy that also served as the site architect.

In Shanghai the Jin Mao Tower outdid the Burj al Arab in one respect. Its 31 uppermost floors formed a hotel that was even loftier than Burj. The hotel floors achieved their height by resting on 52 floors of office space in a 420-m (1,377-ft) tower designed by the American firm Skidmore, Owings & Merrill.

Equally dramatic, but in a more avant-garde style, was the Alpe-Adria Centre for the Hypo Bank in Klagenfurt, Austria, by American Thom Mayne of the firm Morphosis. This banking headquarters was constructed in such a way that wings of the building seemed to crash into one another like boxcars in a train wreck. Like the work of the Blobmeisters, the structure was made possible by the use of computers in design and construction. In New York the LVMH Tower, by French architect Christian de Portzamparc, featured a glass facade that looked like transparent pleated drapery.

Exhibitions. London's Victoria and Albert Museum presented "Art Nouveau 1890–1914," which traced the Art Nouveau style in art and architecture through Paris; Brussels; Glasgow, Scot.; Munich, Ger.; Vienna; and elsewhere. The Cooper-Hewitt National Design Museum in New York opened "Design Culture Now," the first of the planned triennial National Design exhibitions. On display were everything from motorcycles and typefaces to houses and computers, many of which were flexible or adaptable to different shapes and functions. Some referred to them as "blobjects."

In Hannover, Ger., Expo 2000, the latest world's fair, drew disappointing crowds but included national pavilions by major architects: Peter Zumthor (Switzerland), Ricardo Legorreta (Mexico), Álvaro Siza (Portugal), and Shigeru Ban (Japan)—the latter was built mostly of paper in keeping with the Expo's theme of environmentalism.

Preservation. Two early landmarks of American Modernism, both originally built as office towers, took on new life as hotels. The PSFS Building (1932; also known as the Philadelphia Savings Fund Society Building and the Philadelphia Saving Fund Building) was purchased, refurbished, and tranformed by the Loews Corp. into a hotel, and the Reliance Building in Chicago (1895) became the Hotel Burnham, named after the original architect, Daniel Burnham. The remarkable but much altered Art and Architecture Building (1963) at Yale University by Paul Rudolph underwent the first stages of a restoration intended to return it to its original form.

In New York a controversy arose over whether to save the Huntington Hartford Gallery (1964) on Columbus Circle, an early effort in white marble by Edward Durell Stone that was meant to recapture a kind of lacy prettiness that had been expunged from architecture by the Modern movement. In Kosovo, a Serbian province in Yugoslavia, an international effort was under way, on a small scale, to plan for the reconstruction of some of the many landmark buildings destroyed by the civil conflicts of the 1990s.

On the Drawing Boards. The new projects under way were more often than not developed on computer screens rather than on drawing boards. Daniel Libeskind, designer of the Jewish

Museum in Berlin, was named architect of an addition to the Denver (Colo.) Art Museum. A proposed new pavilion for the Liberty Bell in Philadelphia was designed by Bohlin Cywinski Jackson. Kallmann McKinnell & Wood of Boston was chosen to design the Blanton Museum of Art in Austin, Texas, after conservative trustees rejected an earlier design by Herzog & de Meuron. A design competition for a Martin Luther King Memorial, on a site near the Franklin Delano Roosevelt Memorial in Washington, D.C., was won by ROMA Design Group of San Francisco. Renzo Piano of Italy won a four-firm competition to design a New York Times tower in New York after Gehry, the favourite, unexpectedly withdrew. The World War II Memorial in Washington, D.C., a competition-winning design by Friederich St. Florian, received final approvals from government agencies but still faced lawsuits from citizens' groups concerned about its site on the Mall between the Lincoln Memorial and the Washington Monument.

Deaths. Among the losses to the architectural community were Italian writer and professor Bruno Zevi, an advocate of "organic" architecture that would be free from overly rational geometries; Edward Logue, American city planner and public-housing developer; Christian Norberg-Shultz, a Norwegian philosopher of architecture who sought in many books to define the essential meanings of architecture; Hideo Sasaki (*see* OBITUARIES), a pioneering American landscape architect; James Marston Fitch, the virtual founder of the contemporary American architectural preservation movement and a powerful advocate of environmentally responsive architecture; and John Hejduk, author of influential theoretical designs and dean for 25 years of the Cooper Union school of architecture in New York City.

(ROBERT CAMPBELL)

The Burj al Arab (also known as the Arabian Tower) in Dubayy, U.A.E., a new 60-story hotel sited on an artificial island.

AFP/Worldwide

Notable Civil Engineering Projects (in work or completed, 2000)

Name	Location		Year of completion	Notes
Airports		**Terminal area (sq m)**		
Inchon International	Inchon, South Korea (near Seoul)	369,000	2001	Landfill between islands; may be northeast Asia hub
Athens International	Spata, Greece	209,000	2001	Europe's biggest airport project
JFK Int'l (new terminal)	Queens, New York City, N.Y.	140,000	2001	Connected by 13.5 km light rail to Manhattan by 2003
S.F. Int'l (new int'l terminal)	San Francisco, Calif.	120,000	2000	Opened December 10; 7-story bldg.; largest int'l terminal in N. Am.
Ataturk Int'l (new terminal)	Istanbul, Turkey	?	2000	Opened January 10; will withstand force 8.5 earthquake
Aqueduct		**Length (m)**		
Great Man-Made River (phase 2)	Libyan interior to Tripoli area	1,650,000	2001	Vast pipeline system transferring water from Saharan aquifers; phase 1 to Benghazi area (1983–93); phase 2 begun 1990
Bridges		**Length (main span; m)**		
Carquinez (#3)	Crockett, Calif.–Vallejo, Calif.	728	?	Begun 2000; first major U.S. suspension bridge since 1965
Rion Antirion	Patrai, Greece (across Gulf of Corinth)	560	2005	Multicable-stayed; complex deepwater foundations
Yongjong Grand	Inchon, South Korea	500	2000	World's first two-story, self-anchored suspension bridge
Øresund	Copenhagen, Denmark–Malmö, Sweden	490	2000	Opened July 1; 16.4 km road/rail link; tunnel, artificial island, bridge
Wadi Leban	Riyadh Ring Road, Saudi Arabia	405	2000	First cable-stayed bridge in Saudi Arabia
William Natcher	Owensboro, Ky.–near Rockport, Ind.	365	2002	To be longest cable-stayed bridge over U.S. inland waterway
Rosario–Victoria	Rosario to Victoria, Argentina	350	2002	Bridges/viaducts across 59-km wide Paraná wetlands
Al-Firdan	Al-Firdan, Egypt	?	2000	Longest (640 m) movable steel bridge in world; spans Suez Canal
Buildings		**Height (m)**		
Lotte World II	Pusan, South Korea	464.5	2005	Begun December 2000; will be world's tallest
Shanghai World Financial Centre	Shanghai, China	460?	?	Ground broken in 1997; construction on hold
Taipei Financial Centre	Taipei, Taiwan	448	2003	Begun 1999; will be world's second tallest to rooftop (with spire, 508 m)
Two International Finance Centre	Hong Kong, China	420	2003	Begun 2000; to be world's fourth tallest building
Fairwell International Centre	Xiamen, China	397	2002	Construction begun in March 1998
Plaza Rakyat	Kuala Lumpur, Malaysia	382	?	Will be tallest reinforced-concrete complex; construction delayed
Emirates Tower One	Dubayy, U.A.E.	350	2000	World's ninth tallest building
Migdal (Tower) Egged	Tel Aviv, Israel	326	2003	Begun July 2000
Torre Generali	Panama City, Panama	318	2003	Begun mid-2000; will be Latin America's tallest building
City		**Area (ha)**		
Putrajaya	near Kuala Lumpur, Malaysia	4,400	2005	Planned national capital begun 1996; first staff moved in June 1999
Dams		**Crest length (m)**		
Eastside Reservoir: East/Dam	Hemet, Calif.	3,380	2000	Dedicated March 18; almost doubles southern California's surface storage capacity; reservoir's new name is Diamond Valley Lake
Eastside Reservoir: West/Dam	Hemet, Calif.	2,736	2000	
Birecik Dam	Euphrates River, Turkey (30 km from Syria)	2,507	2000	Begun 1996; last major dam on Euphrates in Turkey
Three Gorges	west of Yichang, China	1,983	2009	World's largest hydroelectric project; begun 1993
Xiaolangdi	Huang Ho (Yellow River), China	1,667	2000	Hydroelectricity (from January 2000) and flood control
San Roque Multi-Purpose	Agno River, Luzon, Philippines	1,100	2002	Irrigation and flood control; tallest earth-and-rock fill dam in Asia
Mohale (Lesotho Highlands Water Project, phase 1B)	Maluti Mountains, Lesotho–South Africa	600	2001	Begun 1989; phase 1A inaugurated 1998 (first transfer of water to S.Af.); expect second transfer of water in 2003
Sardar Sarovar Project	Narmada River, Madhya Pradesh, India	?	?	Irrigation for Gujarat, electricity; construction halted 1995, reapproved 2000
Highway		**Length (km)**		
Indus Highway	Karachi–Peshawar, Pakistan	1,225	?	61% complete as of October 2000
Railways (Heavy)		**Length (km)**		
Guangdong–Hainan	Zhanjiang, China–southern tip of Hainan	568	?	Begun September 2000; rail with container ship; mostly completed 2002
Western coastal Libya	Tripoli area	191	2003	Begun 2000; built by China; additional lines planned
Trans-Isthmus	Colón–Panama City, Panama	89	2000	Inaugurated in February; full operation will be delayed
Kyongui (reconnection)	Munsan, S.Kor.–Kaesong, N.Kor.	24	2001	Begun September 2000; complete 499 km connection by 2001
Railways (High Speed)		**Length (km)**		
Kyongbu	Seoul–Pusan, South Korea	412	2004	Connects two largest cities; first stretch inaugurated December 1999
German High Speed (third line)	Frankfurt–Cologne, Germany	226	2001	Connects Ruhr to Frankfurt International Airport
Italy High Speed (second line)	Rome–Naples, Italy	222	2004	Begun 1994; part of planned 1,300-km high-speed network
Belgium High Speed	Brussels–Liège, Belgium	95	2002	Extension to Cologne, Germany, planned for 2005
Acela Express	Boston, Mass.–Washington, D.C.	?	2000	First scheduled service in December; maximum speed is 240 km/hr
Subways/Metros/Light Rails		**Length (m)**		
Oporto Light Rail	Oporto, Portugal	70,000	2003	Europe's largest total rail system project; first line to be opened in 2001
Copenhagen Metro	Copenhagen, Denmark	22,000	2001–04	Line 1: 2001; most extensive driverless system in world
Athens Subway (parts of lines 2 + 3)	Athens, Greece	18,200	2000	21 new stations; scheduled extensions through 2004
Tren Urbano (phase 1)	San Juan, P.R.	17,200	2002	Bayamón (western suburbs) to north San Juan; 60% elevated
Manila Light Rail	Manila, Philippines	16,800	2000	Built over congested auto routes; from Quezon City to central Manila
Hudson–Bergen Light Rail	Bayonne to Jersey City, N.J.	12,000	2000	Opened in April; future extension to Hoboken (in 2002) and Weehawken
Tehran Subway	Tehran, Iran	9,400	2000	First in Persian Gulf; central city to western suburb; extensions planned
Istanbul Subway (phase 1)	Istanbul, Turkey	7,500	2000	For congested old city north of Golden Horn; extension planned
Tunnels		**Length (m)**		
Apennine Range tunnels (9)	Bologna–Florence, Italy (high-speed railway)	66,000	2006	Begun 1996; longest tunnel, 18.6 km; tunnels to cover 90% of railway
Lærdal	Lærdal–Aurland, Norway	24,500	2000	World's longest road tunnel; last key road link between Oslo and Bergen
Qinling	between Xi'an and Ankang, China	18,457	1999	World's ninth largest railway tunnel; railway to open in 2001
A86 Ring Road	around Paris, France	17,700	2006	Two tunnels (to east [10,100 m], to west [7,600 m])
Pinglin Highway	near Taipei, Taiwan	12,900	2003	Twin tunnels under Sheuhshan Range; Taipei-I-lan expressway link
Oslofjord Connection	Drøbak, Norway (30 km south of Oslo)	7,230	2000	First tunnel between two heavily populated sides of Oslofjord
Anton Anderson Memorial	Whittier, Alaska	4,000	2000	North America's longest road tunnel and new piggyback rail link between Anchorage, Alaska, and Seattle, Wash.; opened in June
Øresund	Copenhagen, Denmark–Malmö, Sweden	3,750	2000	Twin tunnels; world-record immersed tube
Urban Developments		**Area (sq m)**		
Potsdamer Platz	Berlin, Germany	620,000	2000	19 buildings including Helmut Jahn-designed, seven-building Sony Centre
Central Artery/Tunnel	Boston, Mass.		2004	Extremely complex highway/tunnel/bridge project begun in 1991
Miscellaneous		**Area (sq m)**		
Steel Dragon roller coaster	Nagashima (near Nagoya), Japan		2000	Opened August 1; tallest, longest, fastest in world, and tallest first drop

1 m=3.28 ft; 1 km=0.62 mi; 1 ha=2.47 ac

Art, Antiques, and Collections

The year 2000 saw the opening of the new **TATE MODERN** and exhibits by Alice Neel, Nam June Paik, and James Nachtwey. **RECORD AUCTION PRICES** were paid for art works and collectibles, notably a rare self-portrait by **FRIDA KAHLO** and a 1933 **PATEK PHILLIPE** pocket watch.

PAINTING AND SCULPTURE

There were two important opportunities in 2000 to view contemporary work in New York City. An exhibit focused on broader American production, and another show concentrated specifically on activities of artists in New York. The latter, "Greater New York: New Art in New York Now," was organized at P.S.1 Contemporary Art Center and intended to showcase the best of art in all mediums created in the city that was still considered the most important place for artists to live and produce work. Among the participants who made painting their focus were Inka Essenhigh, Ellen Gallagher, and Brad Kahlhamer. Jeff Gauntt's architecturally inspired work and James Siena's small abstractions were also shown. Cecily Brown and Giles Lyon both made large-scale gestural abstract paintings. Lyon's works were intended to suggest visually the profusion of influences and stimuli that bombarded the spectator in everyday life. The everyday was rendered in sculptural terms by Rob de Mar, whose sculptures depicted small segments of landscapes mounted to walls or often situated atop slender poles, which forced the viewer literally to take a different perspective on the environment and his work. DeMar cut wood into the shapes of mountains, trees, and fragments of roadways and covered these forms with velvety flocking material, rendering the materials of the environment with abbreviated accuracy. E.V. Day's sculptures involved an element of the destructive in their execution. Her materials included, most memorably, blow-up sex dolls, which were inflated to the point that they exploded. The remaining pink vinyl fragments were suspended from floor and ceiling by taut stainless-steel wires.

Day was one of several artists whose work could be seen at both P.S.1 and the Whitney Biennial. The Biennial aimed to present the broader aspect of artistic practices in the United States. A curatorial team of experts put together by Maxwell Anderson, director of the Whitney Museum of American Art, selected 27 artists who it believed best represented the existing state of American art. The exhibition had a substantial video, film, and, for the first time, Internet component, but painting and sculpture were also represented by such significant artists as John Currin, Robert Gober, Joseph Marioni, Josiah McElheny, Sarah Sze, Richard Tuttle, and Lisa Yuskavage.

Several painters focused on the human figure. Kurt Kauper's series (also part of the Whitney Biennial), *Diva Fictions*, comprised full-length portraits of imaginary opera stars. The series, highly realistic in style yet representing individuals who had never actually existed outside the frame of these works, derived its power from the symbolic, between high artificiality and intense realism. Neo Rauch relied on such sources as 1950s and '60s advertising, propaganda, or popular magazine imagery that he encountered while growing up in East Germany. Rauch situated his figures in uneasy juxtapositions, and his vignettes—which played on nostalgia and the disruption of the seemingly routine—were uneasy and ambiguous.

Polly Apfelbaum exhibited new work in Los Angeles for the first time in several years. Her pieces—made from hand-cut pieces of bright-coloured dyed-velvet fabric arranged in circular patterns on the gallery floor and around the perimeter of the exhibition space—blurred the boundaries between painting and sculpture. Another artist whose work questioned standard definitions of mediums was Jeremy Blake, who referred to his craft as painting, although technically he did not apply paint to canvas. His digital video disc "paintings" of projected computerized light allowed the varied aspects of the medium, flatness as well as depth, to emerge and be seen simultaneously.

Tom Friedman transformed everyday materials—sugar cubes, hair, fuzz, and Play-Doh—into art objects. Among his works were his self-portrait carved into an aspirin, a pair of identically wrinkled pieces of paper, and a sculpture constructed from 30,000 toothpicks. These labour-intensive and humorous pieces made allusions to process-oriented art and conceptual practices. Lucky DeBellevue also used "humble" and often unexpected materials for his sculptural works. Bright-coloured pipe cleaners were densely woven into pyramids and organic moundlike shapes, and plastic compact-disc storage racks stuffed with foam tubes were wrought into objects with a deliberately low-key sensibility. A more traditional rendition of sculpture, at least in terms of function if not form, was the much-anticipated Holocaust Memorial by British sculptress Rachel Whiteread. The memorial was unveiled at its Vienna site in late October, although Whiteread had completed her design in 1996. The large reinforced concrete sculpture was characteristic of Whiteread's other projects in that it represented the interior

Among the sculptures created by Tom Friedman from everyday objects was this untitled piece, constructed from 30,000 toothpicks.

Oren Slor/Feature Inc., NY

of a room essentially turned inside out. In this case it was the space of a library; the spines of the books were facing inward so that the volumes became part of the sculpture itself. The structure was intended to represent a library symbolically and to suggest the "immaterial heritage of Judaism."

In London one of the most exciting art-world events was the opening of the new Tate Modern in London. The enormous space renovated by the museum—a redesigned and adapted power station on the South Bank of the River Thames—provided a spectacular location for three monumental works by American sculptor Louise Bourgeois. Three 9-m (30-ft) steel towers entitled *I Do, I Undo, I Redo* (1999–2000) were installed in the Tate's 152-m (500-ft)-long by 30-m (100-ft)-high Turbine Hall. Adjacent to the towers was one of Bourgeois's enormous 10.7-m (35-ft)-high spider sculptures. Visitors were invited to climb the spiral staircases on the towers, each of which supported a platform with chairs surrounded by a series of large swivel mirrors that were intended to provoke heightened contemplation and conversation about the viewers and their surrounding space.

The impact of technological discoveries on creativity and artistic practices was the object of "Paradise Now: Picturing the Genetic Revolution" at New York's alternative exhibition space Exit Art. Curated by Marvin Heiferman and Carole Kismaric, this exhibition was a chronicle of 39 artists' reactions to social, personal, and ethical implications of cloning and of the biotechnical alteration of foods and animal and human bodies. It spoke to the controversy surrounding the amount of control humans have over their genetic makeup in the wake of the completion of the Human Genome Project. (*See* LIFE SCIENCES: *Special Report.*) Some "works" included tanks containing donor sperm and eggs, a vast computer printout of the human genome sequence hanging from the ceiling and ending in a large stack on the floor, and plastic containers holding frogs that were being bred. More traditional mediums were represented, such as Alexis Rockman's painting depicting a genetically modified barnyard in which an enormous drooling pig containing human organs was flanked by a basket of pillow-sized tomatoes and the neatly squared-off body of a cow. The show elicited equal parts of optimism and paranoia.

For a dose of pure romance, there was Swiss artist Ugo Rondinone's New York solo debut. "Love Invents Us" featured his "target" paintings, which achieved Op-art visual effects, and a group of stylistically unrelated black-and-white photographs. The centrepiece was a room-sized video installation, *It's Late and the Wind Carries a Faint Sound . . .* (1999–2000), a montage of different repeated filmic images of people engaged in repetitive motions such as swimming and dancing, accompanied by a haunting sound track sung by the artist, who repeated the refrain, "Everyday sunshine."

(MEGHAN DAILEY)

ART EXHIBITIONS

Some of the most significant exhibitions of 2000 focused on single artists. One of the most important of these monographic retrospectives recognized American painter Alice Neel. The show was organized by the Philadelphia Museum of Art and debuted at the Whitney Museum of American Art, New York City. It was the first comprehensive exhibition of Neel's output and featured 75 works, including cityscapes and still lifes among her famous portraits. In the 1930s, early in her career, Neel was an artist with the Works Progress Administration, and she worked as a figurative painter for decades before attaining recognition for her portraits, which depicted those closest to her with an unflinching, canny, and insightful eye.

Sol LeWitt was featured at the San Francisco Museum of Modern Art in another much-anticipated solo exhibition. The focus was on LeWitt's signa-

Alice Neel's **Woman and Three Children** *(1982) was among the paintings featured in a retrospective of Neel's work organized by the Philadelphia Museum of Art in 2000.*

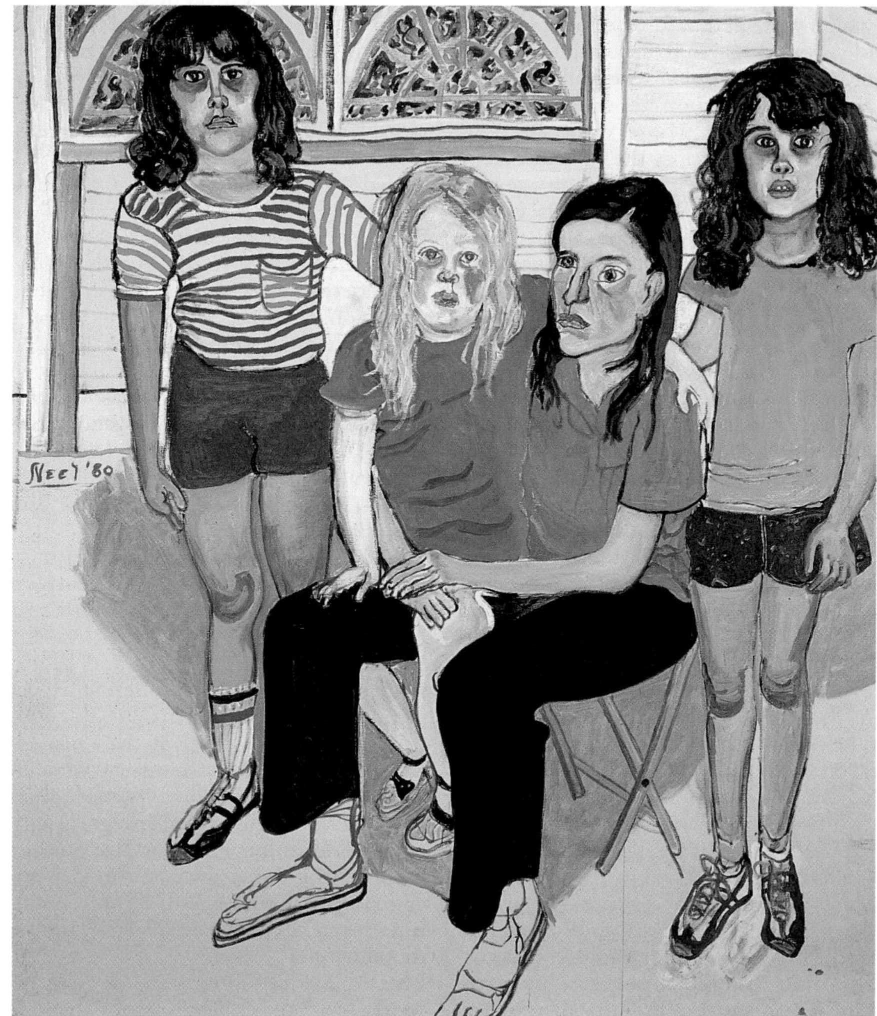

ture wall drawings—works executed directly on the wall in pencil, crayon, ink washes, and, recently, acrylic paint. Many of these, as well as LeWitt's works on paper and "structures" (his preferred term for sculptural works) dating from the past 40 years, were shown in this traveling exhibition.

Wayne Thiebaud, another artist who came of age in the 1950s, was featured in Texas at the Modern Art Museum of Fort Worth, which held the most comprehensive overview of the California artist's career to date. Over 100 works were shown, including Thiebaud's signature Pop art-inspired still lifes of sliced cakes and pies as well as his later San Francisco cityscapes.

"Amazons in the Drawing Room: The Art of Romaine Brooks" at the National Museum of Women in the Arts in Washington, D.C., was the result of a steady reassessment of Brooks, an American expatriate known as much for her unconventional life as her art. This survey focused on her portraiture and more general artistic interests, which were tied to ideas about personal identity, class, and sexuality. Another independent woman who had exerted a profound impact on her cultural milieu was Yoko Ono, whose work was featured in New York at the Japan Society, Ono's first major American venue. Included were her early Fluxus works, installations, films, photographs, and unique musical output, which was captured on a compact disc produced especially for the occasion.

Video artist Nam June Paik was the subject of a retrospective at the Solomon R. Guggenheim Museum, New York City. This spectacular show included a laser waterfall in the museum's rotunda and many of his installations, which reflected on the ways in which electronic media, particularly television, impacted aesthetics and perceptions of art in the world at large.

There was no shortage of historical surveys in 2000, one of which looked back at the turn of the last century. "1900: Art at the Crossroads" appeared at London's Royal Academy of Arts. The exhibition was inspired by the 1900 "Exposition Universelle" in Paris, where many of the approximately 250 paintings and sculptures were first exhibited. To indicate the vast range of styles being practiced at the time, 1900 was arranged by genre—Portraits, Bathers and Nudes, and Interiors and Still-Lifes, among other categories—and offered a chance to (re)-consider them both at the turn of the last century and at the dawning of the new millennium.

Another nod to the 1900 Paris exposition was the Victoria and Albert Museum's "Art Nouveau 1890–1914," which gathered an impressive number of objects rendered in the sensuous fin de siècle design mode—jewelry, furniture, and glassware among them—produced mostly between 1890 and World War I. The show was also on view at the National Gallery of Art, Washington, D.C., where additional objects were added. The lure of the exotic was explored in "Noble Dreams, Wicked Pleasures: Orientalism in America, 1870–1930," a traveling exhibition that unraveled the fascination with so-called Oriental art and cultures and featured nearly 100 works at the Sterling and Francine Clark Art Institute, Williamstown, Mass. Paintings by John Singer Sargent and Frederic Edwin Church were included, as well as examples of popular culture, the decorative arts, and photographs.

"Taoism and the Arts of China" at the Art Institute of Chicago was a consideration of the undeniable overlap between the philosophical-religious force of Taoism and the visual arts; the exhibit included calligraphy, books, and textiles. The Portland (Ore.) Art Museum presented "Stroganoff: The Palace and Collections of a Russian Noble Family" in cooperation with the State Hermitage Museum, St. Petersburg. For the show, masterworks were reassembled from the collections of one of imperial Russia's most influential families (more than 230 objects, many of which never had been seen outside Russia), and the exhibit included a selection of Russian icons from the Stroganoff School and 18th-century French paintings by Élisabeth Vigée-Lebrun, Antoine Watteau, and Jean-Baptiste Greuze.

"The Triumph of French Painting," which debuted at the Philbrook Museum in Tulsa, Okla., focused on the 19th century and its notable painters—Eugène Delacroix, Claude Monet, and Henri Matisse among them. A different aspect of Europe was revealed in "The Splendor of 18th-Century Rome" at the Philadelphia Museum of Art. On display were an unprecedented 380 works by more than 160 artists, including paintings, sculpture, works on paper, decorative objects, architectural renderings, and models inspired by Rome and its treasured antiquities and Renaissance and Baroque monuments.

Several exhibitions were devoted to works from the collections of Giuseppe Panza di Biumo. The Guggenheim Museum, Bilbao, Spain; the Peggy Guggenheim Collection, Venice; and the Museum of Contemporary Art (MOCA), Los Angeles, all exhibited Panza works. Many site-specific sculptures by artists of the 1960s and '70s were housed at the Villa Panza in Varese, Italy, which opened to the public in 2000. The Panza holdings included some of the most important works of Abstract Expressionism, Pop art, minimalism, and postminimalism by artists such as Carl Andre, Franz Kline, Robert Rauschenberg, James Rosenquist, Robert Irwin, and Richard Serra. These exhibitions were intended to celebrate the prescient vision and generosity of the Panzas.

An eclectic group of exhibitions were shown in European museums, including "Samuel Beckett/Bruce Nauman" at the Kunsthalle Wein (Vienna), which explored the conceptual connections between playwright and writer Beckett and Nauman's activities as a contemporary artist via their respectively radical considerations of space and relentless questioning of perception and the human condition. Since the early 1970s, artist Adrian Piper had been addressing similar notions of selfhood but focusing on racial and gender stereotyping in her personal, often performance-driven work. Piper's uncompromising text-based photographs, videos, and drawings were the subject of a show at the Fine Arts Gallery, University of Maryland at Baltimore. Also, "MEDI(t)Ations," a presentation of nearly all of Piper's audio and video works, was shown at the MOCA. The MOCA was the site of the first major retrospective devoted to influential California artist Paul McCarthy. McCarthy had produced some of the most provocative and challenging performance and installation work of the past two decades, much of it in European collections; this venue provided a significant opportunity to see his output in the U.S.

Ed Ruscha, perhaps the quintessential West Coast artist, was given a retrospective at the Hirshhorn Museum and Sculpture Garden in Washington, D.C. Ruscha's witty post-Pop gestures in the form of books of photographs (such as the iconic *Twentysix Gasoline Stations* of 1963) and paintings incorporating logos and words anticipated the issues of originality and seriality that would become the preoccupation of Conceptual artists in the 1960s, '70s, and beyond. (MEGHAN DAILEY)

James Nachtwey/Magnum Photos

An image from the "James Nachtwey: Testimony" exhibition.

PHOTOGRAPHY

Despite a roller-coaster stock market and rising interest rates, photography auctions continued to reflect what might seem, in U.S. Federal Reserve Board Chairman Alan Greenspan's words, "irrational exuberance." In late 1999 at Sotheby's New York, Charles Sheeler's *Criss-Crossed Conveyors, Ford Plant* commanded a whopping $607,500, establishing a world auction record for one of his photographs. Alfred Stieglitz's *From the Back Window, 291, New York, 1915* did the same for him with a price of $420,500. Gustave Le Gray's *Grand Vague—Sète* topped both figures when it sold for $840,370 at Sotheby's London. In 2000, top sales at Christie's included $314,000 for *Cello Study, 1926* by André Kertész and *The Terminal, New York, 1892* by Stieglitz, setting a world auction record for this work at $215,000.

The Internet's explosive growth continued to expand the alternative ways available to buy, sell, view, research, and enjoy photographs. Among an abundance of eye-boggling World Wide Web sites was Corbis—The Place for Pictures on the Internet (www.corbis.com). The site provided a way to dip into the enormous photographic collection acquired by Microsoft chairman Bill Gates from thousands of sources, including the famous Bettmann Archive. Newly featured among a wide array of Corbis's products and services was "The Living Lens: 75 of the Most Intriguing Photographs of the 20th Century," chosen from Bettmann. Described as "museum-quality" photographs, they were available for purchase on-line in a limited edition of 250 prints of each photograph at unusually affordable prices.

George Eastman House in Rochester, N.Y., showed "Migrations: Humanity in Transition," a visually and emotionally powerful exhibition of black-and-white images by Brazilian-born Sebastião Salgado. Taken in some 40 countries during the 1990s, Salgado's latest "photographic investigation," as he called his projects, explored the growing, wretched plight of migrant workers and refugees worldwide. His compassionate but unsparing vision and elegantly graphic images continued to establish him as a modern master of documentary photography.

Photojournalist James Nachtwey continued to win acclaim for his coverage of contemporary warfare. His exhibition "James Nachtwey: Testimony" at the International Center of Photography in New York City, however, was not about war itself but about its catastrophic impact on civilians. The photographs were taken during the 1990s as Nachtwey witnessed atrocities and their aftermath in Romania, Somalia, Bosnia and Herzegovina, Rwanda, Zaire (now the Democratic Republic of the Congo), and Chechnya, Russia. Large-format colour and black-and-white prints pictured a hell on Earth in harrowing, sometimes gruesome images in which the distinction between living and dead became blurred. The J. Paul Getty Museum in Los Angeles opened "The Man in the Street: Eugène Atget in Paris." The exhibit explored Atget's richly inclusive vision as he documented his beloved city with a tripod-mounted view camera and glass-plate negatives from about 1897 to 1927.

New York City's Museum of Modern Art presented "Making Choices," the second installment of "MoMA2000," a blockbuster millennial celebration of modern art in all media. Focusing on the years 1920 to 1960, it included a series of 24 exhibits exploring the "contentions and vital complexities of modern art's middle years." Four shows were exclusively devoted to photographers—"Walker Evans & Company," "Man Ray, Photographer," "The Observer: Cartier-Bresson After the War," and "Ideal Motif: Stieglitz, Weston, Adams, and Callahan"—while a number of other exhibitions in the series also included photographs. The art of the artless snapshot provided the theme for a delightful exhibition, "Other Pictures: Vernacular Photographs from the Thomas Walther Collection," at New York's Metropolitan Museum of Art. The 90 or so black-and-white images were made by anonymous amateurs from about 1910 to 1960 and gathered by well-known collector Walther from images found in family albums, dusty shoe boxes, and flea markets. Cocurator Mia Fineman called them the "crème-de-la-snapshot. . . . Each one is a little lure for the imagination, an enticement, a revelation." Also at the Met, a retrospective "Walker Evans" exhibition surveyed, for the first time in its full scope and mostly in vintage prints, this photographer's influential body of work from the late 1920s to 1974. It traced the course of the "certain severity, rigor, or simplicity, directness, clarity" that Evans so successfully achieved in his photographs, from his early New York City street scenes, through his Depression-era images for the U.S. Farm Security Administration and his book *Let Us Now Praise Famous Men* (1941), to his later work for *Fortune* magazine.

Organized by the Aperture Foundation and opening at the Philadelphia Museum of Art, "Mary Ellen Mark: Photographs" was this highly acclaimed photographer's first major exhibition to focus exclusively on her American work. Included were some 140 black-and-white photographs, many never before exhibited. Mark's compassionate but astringently unsentimental vision gave a panorama of sad, funny, and disturbing views of contemporary American lifestyles from documentary projects such as "Streetwise," "Beauty Pageants," "Rural Poverty," "Texas Rodeos," and "Spring Break."

"Without Sanctuary: Lynching Photography in America" at the New-York Historical Society aroused shocked attention with tormenting postcard images from a dark side of American social history when, between 1882 and 1968, an estimated 4,742 blacks were killed by lynch mobs. Collected over a period of 15 years by James E. Allen and John Littlefield, the pictures showed the corpses of sometimes mutilated victims hanging from a tree branch or makeshift gallows, often in front of a large crowd of onlookers that includes children. The postcards had been sold as popular mementos of these "hideous spectacles" that, according to Allen, left "even the dead victims without sanctuary." Appearing at the Gagosian Gallery in Beverly Hills, Calif., was Cindy Sherman's (*see* BIOGRAPHIES) most recent collection of staged self-portraiture. Her elaborately costumed and histrionically posed depictions of Hollywood women offered provocative commentary on film, glamour, artificiality, and social clichés.

The 2000 Pulitzer Prize for spot news photography went to the photo staff of the *Denver* (Colo.) *Rocky Mountain News* for its coverage of the 1999 shootings at Columbine High School. Carol Guzy, Michael Williamson, and Lucian Perkins of the *Washington* (D.C.) *Post* won the Pulitzer for feature photography with their photographs of fleeing Kosovar refugees. At the 57th Annual Pictures of the Year contest, sponsored by the National Press Photographers Association and the University of Missouri School of Journalism, John Stanmeyer of SABA Press Photos/*Time* magazine received the Magazine Photographer of the Year award, while Rob Finch of the *Beacon-News*/Copley Chicago Newspapers was named Newspaper Photographer of the Year. The International Center of Photography Infinity Awards included presentations to Nachtwey for photojournalism for the third time and Helmut Newton for *SUMO* (2000), a massive book of his controversial, often voyeuristic images of famous personalities and models. The 2000 W. Eugene Smith Grant in Humanistic Photography went to Brenda Ann Kenncally and the two W. Eugene Smith Fellowship Grants to Nigel Dickenson and Francesco Zizola. The Howard Chapnick Grant for the Advancement of Photojournalism was awarded to David J. Spear.

(ARTHUR GOLDSMITH)

ART AUCTIONS AND SALES

Defying all expectations, the art market in 2000 sustained substantial growth over 1999. Major auction houses Christie's and Sotheby's, however, came under scrutiny for commission fixing, and they agreed in September to pay $512 million to settle a civil suit against them. Bolstered by a bull stock market and increased consumer wealth, the auction houses continued to see record prices for high-quality works of art, through both traditional auction venues and transactions conducted via the Internet. In January 2000 Sotheby's launched Sothebys.com, an e-commerce art and antiques World Wide Web site that achieved $31,000,000 in sales in its first six months, a total punctuated by the $8,140,000 sale of a rare first printing of the *Declaration of Independence,* by far the most expensive item ever auctioned on-line. Although Christie's opted not to conduct auctions on Christies.com, the auction house greatly expanded its on-line capabilities by hosting live Webcasts of its important auctions.

In the sale of Old Master paintings held in New York City, Christie's achieved $39,290,500, its highest total in 10 years. The high seller was Canaletto's *The Grand Canal Venice, Looking East from Campo di San Vio,* which went for $6,602,500. Records were also established for artists Giovanni Battista, Carracci, and Carlo Maratta. In May Christie's New York offered the single-owner Karl Lagerfeld Collection, which fetched $7,217,121. Christie's London in July offered one of the most important drawings ever to appear at auction; *Study for the Risen Christ* by Michelangelo Buonarroti realized $12,378,500.

Reaching a sale total of $47,482,575, the Old Master auction at Sotheby's included Peter Paul Rubens's *Portrait of a Man as the God Mars,* which fetched $8,252,500 and set a record for the artist. *The Rebuke of Adam and Eve* by Domenichino also set a record at $3,302,500.

The sales of Impressionist and Modern art and Contemporary art at both auction houses were resoundingly successful. At Sotheby's New York in May, the totals for these sales were the second highest in 10 years, with Impressionist art earning a staggering $140,354,000, earmarked by the sale of Claude Monet's *Le Portail (Soleil),* which fetched $24,205,750. An Henri Matisse sculpture entitled *La Serpentine–Femme à la stele–l'araignee* sold for a record $14,030,750, the highest price paid for a sculpture at auction.

Reclining Venus 1985, by Fernando Botero, courtesy, Marlborough Gallery, New York/Christie's Images NY

Fernando Botero's **Reclining Venus** *was auctioned at Christie's New York in June.*

Christie's New York set a world auction record in May with the sale of Gustave Caillebotte's *L'Homme au balcon,* which commanded $14.3 million in a sale that earned $104.5 million. Monet's *Nympheas* reached $20.9 million, the highest bid of the evening.

Sotheby's London Impressionist sale in June totaled $80,327,040 and was underscored by Edgar Degas's *Petit danseuse de quatorze ans,* which sold for $11,547,740 and established a European record at auction for a sculpture. In June Christie's London sold Paul Cézanne's *Still Life with Fruit* for $18.2 million.

In its sale of 20th-century art, Christie's New York set 15 auction records in a sale totaling $14.5 million. The apex of the auction was Sigmar Polke's atypical dot painting *Zwei Frauen,* which realized $1,650,000. In its sale of 20th-century art, Christie's offered Pablo Picasso's *Nature morte aux tulipes,* which achieved $28.6 million. Also in May, Sotheby's New York held a robust sale of Contemporary art. The highlight was a 1956 painting by Mark Rothko, *Yellow over Purple,* which sold for $14,305,750, an unprecedented price for this artist at auction.

The June sale at Sotheby's London gave way to eight new auction records for Contemporary artists, including one for Gerald Richter, whose *Martha* set a record for an abstract painting when it realized £443,500 (about $643,075). The Christie's June sale in London earned $8.9 million.

In New York Sotheby's American paintings, drawings, and sculpture sale in May totaled $38,497,075. The sale was highlighted by 10 lots that realized winning bids of more than $1,000,000, notably Ralph Albert Blakelock's *Indian Encampment Along the Snake River,* which fetched $3,525,750 and set an artist record. Christie's American paintings sale earned $33,164,800, the highest total for this category in the auction house's history. Highlighting the sale was Frederic Edwin Church's *Mount Newport on Mount Desert Island* for $4,186,000.

At Sotheby's New York sales of Latin American art on May 31 and June 1, a record was achieved for a rare self-portrait by Frida Kahlo, which sold for $5,065,750 and established the highest auction price ever paid for a work by a woman artist. The June sale at Christie's New York of Latin American paintings realized $8,984,757 and gave rise to seven auction records, including the $468,000 brought for Fernando Botero's sculpture *Reclining Venus.*

Both Christie's and Sotheby's boasted strong results in the worldwide jewelry market. In May Christie's New York sale of magnificent jewels totaled $19.3 million. The top lot was a 27.49-carat ring, which went for $1,381,000. Christie's Hong Kong had the best sale results of the spring series with Magnificent Jewellery I: The Far Eastern Collector and Magnificent Jewellery II: Tradition and Innovation Jewels Without Reserve, which together realized $36.3 million. Sotheby's New York offered the private collection of Mr. and Mrs. Lloyd H. Smith, which commanded $19,986,472. The spring jewelry sale in Geneva totaled $32,229,427, owing in large part to the sale of the magnificent jewels of Marie Vergottis, whose sapphire and diamond necklace sold for $1,035,450.

Sales in antiquities brought Sotheby's the highest total for a various-owner sale in the auction house's history; the June sale realized $9.5 million. The bronze head of an athlete—a rare Roman copy of a lost original by Greek sculptor Lysippos—stole the show and sold for $4.5 million, a record price for a classical antiquity at auction.

At Sotheby's New York in June was the sale of the items from the shipwrecked SS *Central America.* The cache aboard this treasure ship, recovered after 132 years, consisted primarily of gold bars and coins. The sale brought $5,567,815; an 18,779.9-g (663.6-oz) gold bar made by Kellogg and Humbert, Assayers, San Francisco, fetched $265,000.

Christie's achieved impressive sales results for books and manuscripts and in New York set a world record for a printed book with the $8,802,500 sale of John James Audubon's *The Birds of America: From Original Drawings by John James Audubon.* Christie's London sold the private library of William Foyle for $18.9 million, the highest European price ever realized for such a collection. Sotheby's London attained great success with the sale of the 16th-century *Book of Hours,* illustrated by Renaissance illuminator Simon Bening, for £2,610,500 (about $3,785,000). (AMY TODD MIDDLETON)

ANTIQUES AND COLLECTIBLES

The Internet continued to influence the prices paid for antiques and collectibles, but major shops, shopping malls, and regular auctions remained the most important barometers of sales in 2000. Regional auction houses were enjoying astounding results for important examples of folk art, toys, Arts and Crafts furniture and accessories, and art pottery. The sales of ordinary 1950s and '60s furniture were slow, however. Although ignored 25 years earlier, Arts and Crafts and art pottery were in demand at every price point, from $10 table runners to $900,000 tables. High-style pieces made after 1950 were popular even though many of these items were still being made. There was less buyer interest in clocks and 18th-century porcelains than in the past, but a record price was paid at auction for a watch—$11,002,500, for a 1933 18-carat gold Patek Philippe pocket watch with 24 complications—special features such as a calendar, dual power source, or central alarm.

(continued on page 170)

SPECIAL REPORT

Design for the Third Millennium

by Patrick Coyne

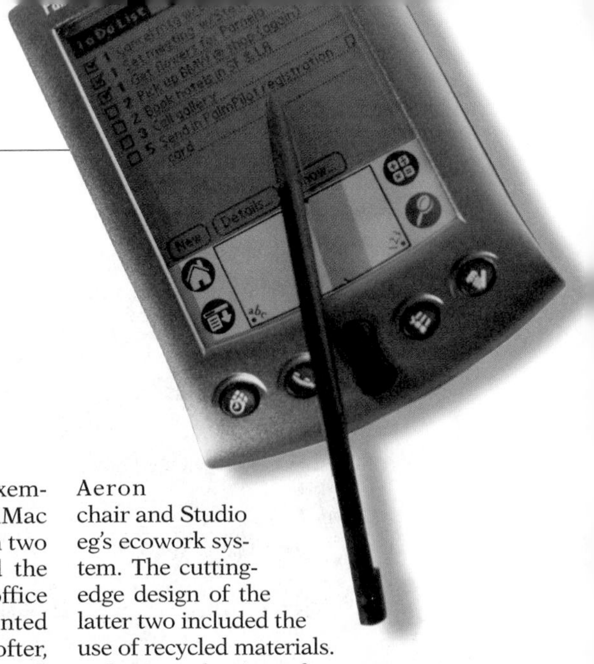

At the turn of the millennium, new product design—both functional and visually striking—was being showcased in homes around the world, defined the look of cars, and offered innovative styles for the products used for office or household work. Design not only reflected the current culture but also harkened back to the past as well as showing the promise of times to come—a future embodied in metallic, luminescent, and translucent objects that were also fluid, organic, humanistic, and often whimsical. The product that best exemplified this vision was the Apple iMac personal computer, which, less than two years after its introduction, paved the way for a flood of other home and office products similarly encased in tinted translucent plastic. The iMac's softer, rounder form was also incorporated into the design of such unglamorous everyday objects as the Umbra Garbino wastebasket, Michael Graves's toilet brush for Target, and OXO's Good Grips kitchen tools.

Sleek car designs beckoned to the future, while others embraced the past, notably the new Volkswagen Beetle, the Chrysler PT Cruiser, and the Ford Thunderbird. The office landscape was changing too as the regulation cubicle and padded chair were being banished by Herman Miller's Resolve office system and Aeron chair and Studio eg's ecowork system. The cutting-edge design of the latter two included the use of recycled materials.

The introduction of new handheld technology also had an effect on design. Products such as the Motorola Talkabout, Nokia's brightly coloured cellular phones, and the Palm VII personal digital assistant were developed with the use of existing design trends, but they represented an early glimpse of the wireless revolution that could eventually connect the workplace

(clockwise from far left) The Chrysler PT Cruiser; the Palm VII personal digital assistant; the Motorola Talkabout; Umbra Garbino wastebasket; Michael Graves's toilet brush for Target.

(clockwise from far left) AP/Wide World Photos; Matthew Klein/Corbis; photo provided by Motorola; Umbra, Inc. <www.umbra.com>; Kristine A. Strom

to the home as well as owners to their possessions and ultimately people to one another. The biggest impact on product design and daily life, however, probably would come from the continued miniaturization of new technology.

Patrick Coyne is editor and designer of* Communication Arts *magazine.

(continued from page 167)

The biggest surprise of the year was the sums paid for folk art, notably the $195,500 fetched at auction in Bedford, N.Y., for a 33-cm (13-in)-long early-19th-century paint-decorated box. Other impressive folk art sales included a miniature Pennsylvania painted blanket chest dated 1777, $220,000; a hooked rug with stars and stripes, $46,000; and an 1857 American carved game board painted with flags, $46,000. A 1917 sleeping Canada goose decoy by Elmer Crowell made $684,500.

Lamps, especially those with glass shades, continued to sell well. Three Pairpoint puffy table lamps set records: a Lilac lamp, $145,600; an Orange Tree lamp, $60,480; and a Begonia lamp, $67,200. A Tiffany Poppy table lamp went for $123,200, a Handel Peacock table lamp brought $56,000, and a Tiffany Daffodil lamp sold for a record $67,200.

Toys remained popular, especially tin banks, trucks, and cars; mechanical toys sold for high but not record prices. Records were established for British lead soldiers. A Boy Scout display set of 44 pieces auctioned for $2,912, and a soldier set of British army infantry officers made in the 1940s went for $5,264. A prototype Hot Wheels hot pink Volkswagen Beach Bomb with rear-loaded surfboards sold for $72,000, and a full-size (c. 1891) Ohio Diamond Frame safety bicycle auctioned for $164,820. A signed 1937 first edition of Dr. Seuss's *And to Think That I Saw It on Mulberry Street,* his first children's book, sold for $8,625.

Sports memorabilia sales slowed. A Babe Ruth-signed baseball fetched $76,020, and a baseball autographed by Pope John Paul II in 1987 was auctioned for $33,979. The famous Honus Wagner baseball card that sold for $640,500 in 1996 commanded $1,265,000 in 2000.

Unusual collectibles set records, including a 1954 Superman tin lunch box with a thermos, which brought $11,500, and a 1905 Vermont license plate with a white number 9 on a blue plate made $14,850. The sale of a *Titanic* lunch menu dated April 14, 1912, commanded $74,750. Collectors were also buying old computers; a component of ENIAC, the first general-purpose digital computer (constructed in 1946) sold for $79,500.

Prices continued to soar for American art pottery. The Cowan Pottery jazz bowl designed in the 1930s by Victor Schreckengost for Eleanor Roosevelt sold for $121,000. A Newcomb College high-glaze vase—15 cm (6 in) high and made c. 1907 by Leona Nicholson—set a record at $82,500. A 46-cm (18-in)-high Teco vase with green and charcoal glaze brought $66,000 at auction.

An English George III lady's secretary bookcase by Thomas Weeks (c. 1800) auctioned in New York for a record $167,500, and a cabinet made in 1679 set an American furniture record when it went for $2,422,500. Records for 18th-century furniture were also set: $2,862,500 for a Cornelius Stevenson Chippendale mahogany card table, $1,432,500 for a John Cadwalader Chippendale mahogany side chair, and $910,000 for a pair of Chippendale carved mahogany game tables. Although record prices were paid for Arts and Crafts furniture toward the end of 1999, none of the high prices paid in 2000 were records. Eames furniture rarities set records: the DTW-3 three-dowel-leg dining table, $10,350; a wall unit ESU-421-C, $70,700; and a set of six DKR-1 dining chairs, $10,063. The one-of-a-kind prototype DCW armchair went for $107,000. (RALPH AND TERRY KOVEL)

Antiques & Collecting Magazine

Vintage toys continued to sell well in 2000; these vinyl Beatles dolls were traded in August on buynsellit.com, an Internet auction site.

Computers and Information Systems

MICROSOFT'S legal troubles dominated computer news in 2000, as did the decline of **DOT-COM COMPANIES** that for the most part did not earn any money; the music industry was pitted against **NAPSTER,** while **WIRELESS INTERNET ACCESS** emerged as the latest trend.

Microsoft. Microsoft lost its hard-fought antitrust case when a federal judge, siding with the U.S. Department of Justice (DOJ), ruled that Microsoft was guilty of anticompetitive behaviour. The key event in the case, in which the federal government and 19 states were plaintiffs, was the June ruling by U.S. District Court Judge Thomas Penfield Jackson that Microsoft had violated the Sherman Antitrust Act, the nation's main antitrust law, by anticompetitive actions that were intended to maintain Microsoft's monopoly on the operating system (OS) software used to run the vast majority of personal computers (PCs). Jackson ordered that Microsoft be split into two companies. One would be in charge of Microsoft's Windows OS, and the other would be responsible for other software and Internet business. The ruling also put restrictions on Microsoft's conduct.

Denying it had violated the law, Microsoft characterized the judge's ruling as likely to "undermine our high-tech economy, hurt consumers, make computers harder to use, and impact thousands of other companies and employees throughout the high-tech industry."

Microsoft opponents, such as Sun Microsystems, Inc., applauded the ruling. Sun had long maintained that Microsoft used unfair tactics to keep competitors' products from running on computers using Windows OS. The decision also was lauded by the former CEO of Netscape Communications Corp., the once-dominant Web-browser company acquired by America Online (AOL) in 1998 after having suffered from what Netscape officials maintained were unfair Microsoft marketing tactics.

The Microsoft ruling was not surprising, since the judge had issued findings of fact in late 1999 that Microsoft had misused its monopoly power to the detriment of competitors and consumers. Jackson said after his ruling that he had decided to split up the world's largest software company because of what he described as "Microsoft's intransigence" in the court case. The judge said Microsoft was "unwilling to accept the notion that it broke the law or accede to an order amending its conduct." Microsoft criticized the judge for speaking publicly about the case, but Jackson said he had acted properly.

Jackson put his order to break up Microsoft on hold until all appeals had been completed. The judge then proposed a "fast track" handling of the appeal that would have taken the case directly to the U.S. Supreme Court, but the Supreme Court declined. As a result, the case was referred to a federal appeals court, a process that put off further rulings until at least 2001. The appeals court could rule in the case or return it to Jackson for additional court proceedings. It addition, it was unclear whether the appeals court would have the final say in the case or whether Microsoft's fate ultimately would be decided by the Supreme Court.

The shifting of the case to the appeals court, which Microsoft had sought in its court pleadings and the DOJ had opposed, was widely viewed as at least a temporary victory for the software giant. Many believed that the delay caused by the appeals process meant that the final outcome of the case could be changed by shifts in software industry competitive conditions or by a change in Washington politics following the November presidential election.

Microsoft faced another legal setback in December when it reached a settlement on a case filed in 1992 by thousands of temporary workers hired after 1986. The company agreed to pay $97 million to some 8,000–12,000 "permatemps," long-term workers who claimed they had been denied company benefits such as health care and pensions because they had been hired through temporary agencies. Microsoft had altered its hiring policies in 1997.

On a high note, Microsoft introduced its newest OS, Windows 2000, during the year. Microsoft chairman Bill Gates called it "the most ambitious software project ever done" and said that creating Windows 2000 had required 5,000 technical people, $2 billion, and 750,000 people to test early versions of the software.

High-Tech Stocks. The recent economic boom had been fueled largely by technology companies, but a sharp drop in technology stock prices in April 2000 sent shockwaves through the dot-com and e-commerce communities, where stock market valuations and not profits had provided the fuel for growth. By late in the year, the stock prices of even some of the most promising Internet firms were down 50–90% from a year earlier.

The decline in the stock market resulted in postponements of public stock offerings, which in the past had seemed a foolproof way for Internet start-up companies to raise cash. Venture capital money also became harder to find. Venture capitalists had been willing to pour huge amounts of money into start-up Internet companies when they could recover their investments through the soaring stock market. When technology stocks were at their peak, venture capitalists often could sell stock in start-ups for much more than they paid for it. When the stock prices declined, however, the venture capitalists became much more careful about supporting companies that had no profits in sight.

The setbacks for the Internet firms also had ripple effects. Employees whose long-term compensation was tied to stock options of those firms saw that incentive decline. Companies that sold hardware and software to dot-com and e-commerce companies found that many start-up companies could no longer afford expensive capital spending.

Lars Ulrich (centre) of the rock band Metallica trades words with Napster chief executive officer Hank Barry during a Senate Judiciary Committee hearing in Washington, D.C., on July 11.

AP/Wide World Photos

Napster. A court fight of another sort resulted from the activities of Napster, the high-profile music-sharing Web site, and it pitted the music industry against Internet file sharing. Napster's peer-to-peer networking technology allowed thousands of people simultaneously to share the contents of their computer hard drives in order to exchange music, much of it copyrighted, in the form of compressed MP3 files, which could then be played on an MP3 player or a PC. Napster said it had more than 30 million users.

The Recording Industry Association of America (RIAA), which represented record labels, music publishers, and artists, sued Napster for allegedly contributing to copyright infringement on a huge scale. Some musicians also took swipes at Napster, including the band Metallica and rap artist Dr. Dre, who searched for people downloading their songs and demanded they be removed from the service. In addition, Metallica sued some universities where students downloaded songs from Napster.

The Napster case occurred at the same time that another music site, MP3.com, lost a court case brought by Universal Music Group. MP3.com, facing damages of as much as $250 million for maintaining an archive of digital music on its Web site without legal permission, in November agreed to pay U niversal $53.4 million. The difference between Napster and MP3.com, however, was that Napster did not maintain a music archive, since the music resided on the computers of its users.

Napster's court defense against the RIAA was based partly on the groundbreaking Betamax case, in which members of the motion picture and television industries sued Sony Corp. over its development of video recorders. In January 1984 the U.S. Supreme Court had declined to ban the videocassette recorder, even if it was used for copying movies protected by copyright, on the grounds that it had substantial "noninfringing" uses as well. Napster also argued that the Audio Home Recording Act of 1992 protected the rights of consumers to share music as long as they did not make money from it.

Initially, neither argument made much headway in federal court. A district court judge in San Francisco issued a preliminary injunction that ordered Napster to stop its users from trading copyrighted songs pending the outcome of the trial. Napster said it could not comply without shutting down, since it was impossible to tell which music was copyrighted. Two federal appeals court judges stayed the preliminary injunction pending the outcome of an appeal by Napster.

At year's end the U.S. Court of Appeals for the Ninth Circuit had not decided the case, but a new development hinted at a solution for the controversy. German media giant Bertelsmann AG said it would join with Napster and offer subscription-based music downloads, which would thereby ensure that musicians were paid. In return, Bertelsmann agreed to drop its lawsuit against Napster, leaving the rest of the music industry to pursue the court case on its own. In any event, there was speculation that other methods of sharing music over the Internet would survive the court case, since they did not depend on central computer servers as Napster did.

Publicity about the case had made an overnight celebrity out of Shawn Fanning, the programmer who created Napster in 1999 when he was a college freshman. The publicity also served to increase sharply the number of people using Napster. In September Internet tracking firm Media Metrix said the number of people using Napster had quadrupled in five months. The music industry took note and began tentative steps to sell music over the Internet, something that had not been widely tried before.

Many experts suggested that the ramifications of Internet file sharing were enormous and that Hollywood movies might be the next digital product to be freely exchanged. One of the first dot-com companies to enable users to share movies, Scour, Inc., was caught in an even worse position than Napster. Sued by both the recording and the motion picture industries, it filed for bankruptcy but continued to operate.

A Norwegian teenager became embroiled in another type of copyright controversy when he developed a computer program that cracked the security codes on digital video discs (DVDs) used to distribute theatrical movies. The Hollywood movie industry and a DVD copyright organization sought to use the federal courts to prevent other people from distributing the software over the Internet.

Wireless Developments. The Web went wireless in 2000. Web-enabled digital wireless telephones and PDAs were developed that could use special browsing software to download information such as news stories, stock prices, driving directions, and business phone directories. The functions of Web phones were limited, however. Receiving an e-mail was feasible, but sending one was an arduous process because of the small telephone keypad. The phones had slower modem speeds than desktop PCs and therefore were limited to text-only content (downloading graphics from the Web would be too time-consuming), and because the phones could effectively access only those Web sites that were formatted for their tiny screens, Web phones initially accessed only a small part of the Internet. Experts promised that wireless phones and PDAs would become more attractive as their screens improved in clarity and their modem speeds increased. It also appeared that there would be more crossover wireless devices with features of both phones and PDAs.

Acceptance of wireless Web phones appeared to be broader in Europe and Japan, where computer access to the Internet was relatively expensive, than it was in the U.S., where PCs were more widely available and Internet access costs were lower. In the U.S. the first target market for wireless Web phones was mobile professionals, although they also were being offered to consumers. In other countries the phones were used more for personal use, particularly for sending text messages, such as real-time instant messaging.

Bullish pundits predicted that Web phones eventually would become the main way of connecting to the Internet, but toward the end of the year, wireless phone service providers and manufacturers registered awareness that some projections had been too optimistic. In addition, there was concern about how much money the wireless phone service providers would have to spend on government auctions of wireless broadcast spectrum in order to provide higher-speed wireless access in the future.

In the U.S., PDAs and other handheld computers, some of which included add-on modems and telephones, grew in popularity with businesspeople and consumers. The most popular units came from Palm, Inc.; Handspring; and Microsoft (which made the operating system Windows CE for handhelds but left device manufacturing up to other firms). Palm, formerly a unit of 3Com Corp., was spun off as a separate company in early 2000 and had its initial public stock offering (IPO) in March. Handspring, which was started by two founders of Palm and marketed handhelds based on the Palm OS, had its IPO in June.

Computer Hardware. Unit sales of personal computers continued to grow in 2000, although more slowly than in the past. It was projected that American market growth would reach just over 12% for the year. Prices continued to decline, with the average selling price projected to be $1,000 when accessories were included.

Some saw signs that the PC market might be reaching saturation, even though 40% or more of American households still did not own a computer. Dell Computer Corp., the largest manufacturer of Windows-based PCs, warned that demand for PCs was less than expected. Microchip manufacturer Intel Corp. concurred, although other PC makers said they expected no shortfall in sales. Some analysts predicted the PC market would become largely a replacement business. Other observers suggested that the worldwide market, where about 435 million PCs had been installed, remained largely untapped. They predicted that several times that many PCs might eventually be sold. In addition to a dearth of new buyers, some analysts attributed slower PC sales to a weak euro currency in Europe and to slow adoption of Microsoft's new Windows 2000 operating system.

Apple Computer Corp., which wowed the industry in 1998–99 with its award-winning designs and its financial comeback, suffered a slowdown in demand for its popular iMac and initially disappointing sales of its highly touted new G4 Cube in the latter half of 2000 that left it falling short of newly lowered Wall Street revenue projections. The company announced price cuts and a hiring freeze. Earlier in the year, Apple had introduced for beta testing an early version of its long-awaited new operating system, the Mac OS X, which was expected to increase demand for Apple computers when the final version was introduced in 2001.

While it initially was believed that PCs would face competition from low-priced Internet appliances, which would offer Internet access and little else, those fears appeared to have been exaggerated. The appliances did not sell particularly well, partly because they were nearly as expensive as low-priced PCs. Proponents of the appliances said that once more households had high-speed broadband Internet connections, Internet appliances would be more appealing.

Apple Computer's G4 Cube debuted in 2000.

Peter Belanger and R.J. Muna

The hottest new computer accessory of 2000 was the "CD burner," a recordable compact disc (CD) drive, the popularity of which was fueled by the ability of consumers to download free music from the Internet. The burners, more properly called CD-recordable (CD-R) and CD-rewriteable (CD-RW) drives, could then be used to create new music CDs that could be played on a standard CD music player. The drives also could be used to copy existing music CDs onto new discs and to store other kinds of computer data on high-capacity 650-megabyte computer CD-ROMs. By year's end many new PCs came with the drives already built in.

A shortage of electronic parts affected the profits of many manufacturers during the year. Makers of computers, cell phones, and other electronic products were affected. Among the components in short supply were memory chips and the liquid crystal displays used in computer screens.

The Internet. As use of the Internet continued its rapid growth, privacy and security became major concerns in 2000. There were changes in the demographics of people who used the Internet and new studies about the "digital divide"—the gulf between those with access to the Net and those without. There also were major shifts in the still-new world of e-commerce.

Fear of losing privacy was the number one concern of most people who went on-line, as well as the chief worry of a majority of those who chose not to go on-line at all, according to a survey of American Internet users by the Center for Communication Policy at the University of California, Los Angeles. The amount of trust people had in the Internet was linked to the amount of time they spent using it, the survey showed. Those who had not purchased goods or services on-line were almost all concerned about the security of their credit card information. A series of corporate actions and events on the Internet in 2000 highlighted privacy concerns. (*See* Special Report.)

Another broad privacy issue involved the right of dissidents to criticize corporations on the Internet, which had become a place where grievances were freely aired. Some corporations said the Internet provided an unfair forum in which their reputations could be damaged, and they were willing to use lawsuits to force the operators of Web sites to disclose the real identities of anonymous critics who posted commentaries on their pages. Civil libertarians argued that using lawsuits to identify critics was a way of stopping on-line free speech and dampening the Internet's potential as a place where ideas could be freely discussed.

The security risks of using the Internet became apparent in February when hackers launched a series of "denial of service" attacks that immobilized the computer servers at some well-known corporate Web sites and some universities. Denial of service attacks involved flooding a server with countless ostensibly innocent requests for a response and thereby rendering it useless. A series of virus attacks also were launched by hackers early in the year, some of them causing billions of dollars in damage to computers around the world.

The apparently coordinated denial of service attacks in February showcased the vulnerability of the Internet to disruption. They began with an attack on Yahoo.com, then continued with attacks on e-commerce sites Amazon.com, eBay.com, Buy.com, and etrade.com and news media sites CNN.com and ZDNet.com. Experts said the hackers commandeered other computers around the Internet to host the time-delayed messages used in the attacks. At a predetermined time, software planted on those computers launched the attacks and bombarded the target Web sites with messages that jammed their servers. A Canadian youth later was arrested and charged with being part of a group that coordinated the attacks; he pleaded innocent to the charges.

While the attacks were disruptive, experts said they were not technically difficult to achieve and, because of the structure of the Internet, would be hard to defend against in the future. By year's end, an Internet industry group was developing a list of "best practices" on how to respond when under a denial of service attack.

In May computers around the world were struck by the "I Love You" virus, which was transmitted by e-mail. The name came from the subject line on the e-mail, which presumably enticed people to open the e-mail and thereby set in motion its destructive activities. The virus attacked and destroyed certain types of computer files, including files containing electronic photographs. The virus, which began its rampage in Hong Kong, also spread by mailing copies of itself to the computers of people listed in a victim's electronic address book.

Worldwide damages for what became known as the "Love Bug" virus were estimated at several billion dollars. An international search for the perpetrator traced the virus to the Philippines, where a 24-year-old college dropout was arrested but later was released on the grounds that the evidence against him was insufficient. The Philippine government, concluding its laws were inadequate to cover computer crime, passed new legislation to cover that area of the law.

The Internet also was the vehicle for other types of crimes—some old, some new. A 15-year-old New Jersey boy was caught in an Internet stock-manipulation scheme that earned him more than $270,000. A 16-year-old from Miami became the first juvenile hacker sentenced to jail in the U.S. after he on several occasions broke into computer systems at the Department of Defense and NASA. A stock-market day trader in Houston, Texas, was arrested after he allegedly posted a fake news release on the Internet that caused a decline in the stock price of Lucent Technologies. In October hackers broke into Microsoft's corporate network and allegedly viewed the source code for some Microsoft programs. Microsoft said that, while no damage was done, it was an act of industrial espionage.

Sometimes crime not only did not pay, it was also expensive. The operators of a group of pornography Web sites who

Filipino college dropout Onel de Guzman, who claimed his release of the "I Love You" computer virus was accidental, faces questions from the media on May 11 in Manila.

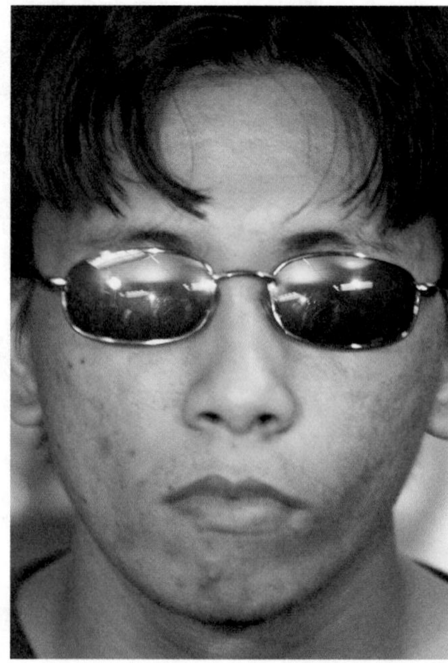

AP/Wide World Photos

were found to have fraudulently billed more than 700,000 credit card holders were fined $37.5 million in a Los Angeles federal court. Two men and a woman who operated half a dozen adult-content Web sites were found to have bought credit card account information from a California bank, then initiated fake charges to some of the cardholders.

Western Union disclosed that a technical error had made its cash-transfer Web site vulnerable, and a hacker had downloaded the credit card and debit card numbers of about 15,700 customers. Western Union advised the customers to cancel their cards. A hacker tried to extort $100,000 from Internet music seller CD Universe by threatening to release some of the 300,000 customer credit card files he claimed to have copied from the company's Web site. CD Universe refused to pay the blackmail, and the hacker posted some of the stolen credit card information on the Internet.

The Internet Corporation for Assigned Names and Numbers (ICANN) began in August to accept proposals for new Web site suffixes that would expand the list of names available for Internet addresses. It was believed that new top-level domain names, in addition to existing suffixes such as .net, .org, and .com, would make it possible to add many new Web site names. In November ICANN's board of directors, after debating a list of close to 200 domain names submitted by numerous organizations, voted in favour of seven new suffixes—.aero (for aviation sites), .biz (businesses), .coop (cooperatives), .info (general information), .museum (museums), .name (individuals), and .pro (professionals such as doctors). There were some complaints from applicants whose suggested names had been rejected, and registry agreements were still to be worked out, but the new names were expected to begin appearing in 2001.

New ways of browsing the Web also came into play with the arrival of "voice portals" that let people obtain Web information by speaking into a telephone. Users of the services could obtain news, sports scores, stock prices, and directory information. About 30 companies offered the service, using colourful names such as Tellme, BeVocal, and Quack.com. The number of companies offering free Internet access service increased in 2000, but the availability of free access did not make major inroads against for-pay service. One reason may have been that free services often required users to view advertisements and to allow their on-line surfing habits to be tracked for advertising purposes. Providers of free service counted on advertising revenues to pay their operating costs. Freeserve, the U.K.'s largest Internet service provider, which began in 1998 as a free service in which customers paid only phone charges, introduced flat-rate, unmetred service in May. At year's end, however, financial setbacks forced the sale of the company to Wanadoo, a branch of France Télécom, for a fraction of its previous value.

Internet telephony sites, which allowed people to place free long-distance phone calls from their computers by using the Internet instead of the conventional telephone network, remained more of a curiosity than a threat to the telephone companies. One reason may have been the long lag times that could be introduced into a conversation if packets of voice data became stalled on the busy Internet. Experts said that planned improvements eventually would give voice packets priority over other data and thus reduce the lag time in Net-based telephone conversations.

In the U.S. a study by Nielsen/NetRatings found that blue-collar workers spent their on-line time at home, while professional people went on-line mostly at work. While the study highlighted the differences in Net use between people in different income brackets and job types, it also was said to be an indication that Internet use had become more pervasive. Another study, by Media Metrix, indicated that low-income households, defined as at or below $25,000 in annual income, were the fastest-growing segment of Internet users. In addition, women were becoming a greater force on the Internet, a trend that was forcing e-commerce sites to cater to their tastes. Several studies showed that women accounted for half of the Web audience, and some showed there were more women than men. A survey by the Office for National Statistics found that 32% of all households in the U.K. had Internet access at home, with the total rising to 45% when access at work was included. While this was lower than in the U.S., it exceeded that of most of Britain's European neighbours.

The reach of high-speed cable modem and telephone digital subscriber line (DSL) services continued to grow. While dial-up phone-line connections to the Internet continued to predominate, the high-speed services with their always-on connections were favoured by businesses and by consumers who downloaded large data files, MP3 music files, or video. On the horizon was a wireless form of high-speed Internet access called multichannel multipoint distribution service; customers would have receivers and transmitters on the outside of their homes or office buildings to connect to the Net.

E-Commerce. The growing impatience on Wall Street with profitless e-commerce firms led some Web-based companies to change their strategies. The most successful raised their prices or sought useful alliances. The less successful underwent layoffs, consolidations, and retrenchments. E-commerce, however, continued to grow, and experts projected that on-line advertising, another source of revenue for e-commerce firms, would increase sharply in the next few years. Meanwhile, traditional bricks-and-mortar companies continued to try to extend their reach with on-line marketing.

Raising prices represented a sharp change of strategy for e-commerce companies, which tended to underprice their bricks-and-mortar competitors by up to 15%, largely because their operating costs were lower and they had taken a long-term view of achieving profitability. Raising prices was seen as a way to help profitability at a time when venture capitalists and other investors no longer wanted to support profitless firms, a decision tied to the decline in technology stock prices. E-commerce companies raised prices in several forms: reduced discounts, higher shipping charges, and more narrowly aimed promotional prices.

Corporate cutbacks became common. On-line firms such as home furnishings site Living.com, drugstore More.com, and eSprocket, an on-line marketplace for used metal-working machinery, laid off staff in an effort to maintain viability. Even big players were affected. Brokerage firm Merrill Lynch closed two Web sites aimed at consumer purchases, Shopmerrill.com and Merrill-auctions.com, as part of a retrenchment. Other firms were acquired by competitors for a fraction of the stock valuations they had held only a few months before.

Meanwhile, bricks-and-mortar companies turned to the Internet to boost sales, both on-line and in their retail outlets, and to increase customer awareness. Kmart, the second largest American discount retailer, offered free Internet accounts through its BlueLight.com e-commerce site. Despite the slowing of on-line retail sales at midyear, expectations were that they would continue to grow. Forrester Research predicted that on-line sales could account for more than 7% of all retail sales by 2004. Web advertising was also projected to increase. A study by Veronis Suhler, an investment banking firm, predicted that Internet advertising would increase at nearly a 40% compound annual growth rate and would exceed $24 billion by 2004.

U.S. Pres. Bill Clinton signed into law a bill that gave legal status to electronic signatures and thus allowed electronic contracts to be finalized on-line. The law recognized as legal a signature that was electronically entered into a computer, then transmitted over the Internet. It was presumed the law would result in consumers' signing electronic contracts for bank loans and other types of transactions.

Some new e-commerce ventures were controversial. Orbitz, an on-line travel agency started by five airlines (American, Continental, Delta, Northwest, and United), postponed its start from September 2000 until mid-2001, apparently because of complaints from travel agents. Orbitz invested in a new search engine that could more effectively seek the optimum fare and offered some fares available only through airline Web sites. Some travel agencies worried they would not be able to offer the same fares. A complaint filed by the Association of Retail Travel Agents resulted in a congressional hearing on whether the Orbitz site was an antitrust issue. Orbitz argued that the start up was delayed in part owing to complicated new technology.

Car sales on the Internet heated up, especially as Amazon.com announced it would sell cars. Amazon buyers could configure the vehicle of their choice, get a price quote, and put down a deposit with a credit card, although the vehicles actually would be purchased from a car dealership. Earlier in the year, Autobytel.com began selling cars by acting as a broker between shoppers and car dealers. Car manufacturers also expressed interest in selling over the Internet. Meanwhile, U.S. federal regulators agreed to let five large automakers buy supplies through a single business-to-business Web site.

The issue of Internet taxes continued to be a hot topic. While no new U.S. taxes on the Internet were created, the U.S. General Accounting Office estimated that states and cities would lose somewhere between $300 million and $3.8 billion in tax revenue as a result of sales over the Internet. The wide range of the estimate was attributed to difficulties in tracking Internet sales.

Acquisitions and Mergers. Thanks to the high-flying stock market of early 2000, some acquisitions paid for with stock carried huge valuations. The grandest acquisition of all was AOL's plan to buy entertainment firm Time Warner in an exchange of stock. The deal was valued at $183 billion when it was announced by AOL's ambitious CEO, Steve Case (*see* BIOGRAPHIES) in January. In March AOL was active again, buying out Bertelsmann's interest in AOL Europe and AOL Australia in a deal said to be worth between $6,500,000,000 and $8,250,000,000.

The merged AOL Time Warner, with its on-line, media, and entertainment properties, promised to be a powerful giant; some called the planned acquisition the most significant deal ever struck in the Internet business. That was precisely what worried regulators. By October the European Commission had approved the merger, then revalued downward to $165 billion, but antitrust regulators in Washington, D.C., had proved harder to convince. While the Europeans had been concerned mainly about stopping the merged companies from controlling on-line music distribution, the U.S. Federal Trade Commission was concerned that the combined companies would be the biggest provider of on-line services in the nation and also would own one of the country's largest cable TV networks. Though these regulatory concerns delayed completion of the deal in 2000, it was likely to be completed in January 2001.

Other big mergers and acquisitions included the January announcement that JDS Uniphase Corp. would acquire E-TEK Dynamics, Inc., in an all-stock deal worth roughly $15 billion. In February software firm Computer Associates International, Inc., planned to acquire Sterling Software for about $4 billion in stock; both firms were strong in storage-management technology. A deal that fell apart was the plan of Corel Corp., a proponent of the Linux OS, to acquire Inprise/Borland Corp., a maker of Linux software tools, in an all-stock deal that in early 2000 was valued at more than $1 billion. When Corel's stock price declined, the deal was canceled. VeriSign, Inc., which dealt with Internet security, said in March that it would buy Network Solutions, which handled the registration of Web site names, for $21 billion in stock.

In May Internet portal Web site Lycos was purchased by Terra Networks SA, the Internet unit of Spanish telephone firm Telefónica, in a $12.5 billion exchange of stock. Educational publisher Pearson PLC in July paid $2.5 billion in cash for National Computer Systems, Inc., which provided school software and managed information for the U.S. Census Bureau. In August Phone.com, a wireless Internet service provider, and Software.com, a maker of Internet messaging software, said they would merge in a stock deal worth $6.4 billion. AT&T paid $1.4 billion in cash in August for a 32% stake in Net2Phone, an Internet telephony firm. Broadcom Corp., which made chips for accessing broadband telecommunications networks, said in August that it would pay $1.2 billion in stock to acquire Silicon Spice, Inc., which made chips that enabled voice, video, and data to travel over a single network.

Despite some national security concerns, the U.S. allowed Nippon Telegraph and Telephone Corp. to purchase Verio, Inc., a Colorado-based Internet service provider, for $5.5 billion. Verio linked a number of large American corporations to the Internet, and there were concerns that the Japanese might be able to obtain classified information if the U.S. tapped Internet communications through Verio during an investigation.

Late in the year it was disclosed that computer hardware manufacturer Hewlett-Packard Co. was discussing the purchase of PricewaterhouseCoopers's management and information technology consulting practice for an estimated $17 billion–$18 billion in cash and stock. (In 2000 Hewlett-Packard also named Carly Fiorina board chairman following her first year as president and CEO. She was one of the few women to be a top executive in the computer field.) In October two makers of computer hard disks prepared to merge to form the world's largest disk-drive firm. Maxtor Corp. said it would buy Quantum Corp.'s hard-disk-drive group in a stock exchange valued at $2.3 billion.

Other Developments. In consumer electronics the biggest event of the year was the frustrating introduction in the United States of Sony's PlayStation 2 video game machine. Plagued by component shortages, Sony could deliver only half as many of the units as planned for the October introduction. That resulted in long lines of would-be buyers, and many gamers were disappointed when stores ran out of the machines on the first day they were available. The shortfall led to speculation that Sega Enterprise Ltd.'s competing Dreamcast video game machine would prosper during the 2000 holiday season and that new game machines due out

AP/Wide World Photos

In October an employee of Sony Computer Entertainment demonstrates the PlayStation 2 "Gran Turismo 3," a racing simulation game with realistic tactile effects.

from Nintendo and Microsoft in 2001 might have an easier time competing against Sony than had been thought. Despite the popularity of video games, critics of the game industry continue to oppose its marketing of violent games. An industry-devised ratings system aimed at keeping some of the more violent games out of the hands of young teenagers failed to allay those concerns.

A study critical of computer use in public schools said the billions of dollars spent on computers and Internet access should go instead for educational needs such as more teachers. The report by the Alliance for Childhood said that American public schools had spent more than $27 billion on computers and related technology over the previous five years, even though there was not much research to show what impact they were having on education. Others urged more computer use by everyone. In an effort to promote computer literacy among its employees, Ford Motor Co. said all of its 350,000 workers around the world would be offered a desktop computer with unlimited Internet access for $5 a month. As plants and factories grew more automated, companies such as Ford expressed concern that they needed employees who were familiar with computers. (STEVE ALEXANDER)

Microelectronics. Projected worldwide sales of semiconductors grew 37% to $205 billion in 2000, according to the Semiconductor Industry Association (SIA). This was the first time sales had exceeded $200 billion. The industry expected to see growth of 22% in 2001 to $249 billion and to $319 billion within three years. Sales of communications solutions for data networking, broadband, wireless, and optoelectronics as well as continued demand for personal computers (PCs) contributed to the record number. The optoelectronics category, including laser devices and image sensors, grew 68% in 2000 to $10 billion and was projected to be $19 billion by 2003. The market for programmable logic devices was expected to grow at a compound annual rate of 17% through 2003. The market for digital signal processors (DSPs), fueled by the use of DSPs in MP3 music players, digital cameras, digital video (or versatile) discs, camcorders, colour printers, and video games, grew 48% to $6 billion, and the microcontroller market rose 35% to $19 billion. Flash memory, the fastest-growing market segment, grew 13% in 2000 to $10 billion and was projected to increase to $23 billion by 2003. The microprocessors usually found in PCs and imbedded applications grew at an 11% rate, with sales of $30 billion. The PC market was expected to increase only 6% in 2001; over the next three years, it was likely to become a $39 billion market. Dynamic random access memory was a big growth area, up 48% to $31 billion.

The Americas (North and South) increased sales 34% in 2000 and at $64 billion continued to lead the world markets. This was expected to become a $96 billion market by 2003. The Asia-Pacific region (Singapore, South Korea, Taiwan, and India) was the fastest-growing microchip market, up 41% in 2000 to $52 billion. The Asia-Pacific market was expected to increase to $85 billion by 2003. The Japan market increased 42% to $46 billion and was projected to reach $72 billion in sales by 2003, while the European market, up 33% to $42 billion, was expected to rise to $66 billion. The SIA pointed out that 10 years earlier the two largest markets, the U.S. and Japan, had constituted about two-thirds of the global semiconductor market. By 2000, however, the Americas and Asia-Pacific constituted less than 60% of that market.

Intel Corp., the world's largest chip manufacturer, signed a $1.5 billion deal to supply flash memory to Telefon AB L.M. Ericsson over the next three years. To meet demand, Intel bought two facilities from Rockwell International Corp. in Colorado Springs, Colo., and planned to build another facility in Chandler, Ariz. The shortage of Intel's Pentium III processors continued well into the year. On July 31 Intel introduced the world's fastest chip, a 1.13-GHz (gigahertz) version of its Pentium III processor, but the company promptly recalled all 10,000 of those shipped because of design problems and announced it would reintroduce the chip in the second quarter of 2001. The Pentium 4, a 32-bit chip formerly code-named Willamette, was introduced in November. Running at 1.4 GHz and 1.5 GHz, it consisted of 42 million transistors. Intel planned to retire the Pentium III processor at the end of 2001. Intel also tested Itanium, a 64-bit chip running at 800 MHz and designed to be used in high-end servers and workstations. In October Intel canceled plans for the lower-end Timna chip.

Advanced Micro Devices, Inc. (AMD), the world's second largest chip company, with a 17% market share, signed a $400 million deal in January to supply flash memory to Samsung Electronics Co. Ltd. for use in its mobile telephones. Unlike Intel, AMD beat analysts' predictions for its third quarter with revenues of $1.2 billion, double 1999's third quarter. The quarterly profit was $219 million versus a loss of $99 million in 1999. After the recall of Intel's 1.13-GHz chip, AMD's 1.2-GHz Athlon became the new speed leader.

A new microprocessor manufacturer, Transmeta Corp., began producing its

(continued on page 180)

SPECIAL REPORT

Invasion of Privacy on the Internet

by Jeffrey Rosen

In the year 2000 concerns about privacy in cyberspace became an issue of international debate. As reading and writing, health care and shopping, and sex and gossip increasingly took place in cyberspace, citizens around the world seemed concerned that the most intimate details of their daily lives were being monitored, searched, recorded, stored, and often misinterpreted when taken out of context. For many, the greatest threats to privacy came not from state agents but from the architecture of e-commerce itself, which was based, in unprecedented ways, on the recording and exchange of intimate personal information. In 2000 the new threats to privacy were crystallized by the activities of DoubleClick, Inc.

For a few years DoubleClick, the Internet's largest advertising company, had been compiling detailed information on the browsing habits of millions of World Wide Web users by placing "cookie" files on computer hard drives. Cookies are electronic footprints that allow Web sites and advertising networks to monitor people's on-line movements with telescopic precision—including the search terms people enter as well as the articles they skim and how long they spend skimming them. As long as users were confident that their virtual identities were not being linked to their actual identities, many were happy to accept DoubleClick cookies in exchange for the convenience of navigating the Web more efficiently.

Then in November 1999 DoubleClick bought Abacus Direct, which held a database of names, addresses, and information about the off-line buying habits of 90 million households compiled from the largest direct-mail catalogs and retailers in the nation. Two months later DoubleClick began compiling profiles linking individuals' actual names and addresses to Abacus's detailed records of their on-line and off-line purchases. Suddenly, shopping that once seemed anonymous was being archived in personally identifiable dossiers.

Under pressure from privacy advocates and dot-com investors, DoubleClick announced in March 2000 that it would postpone its profiling scheme until the U.S. government and the e-commerce industry had agreed on privacy standards. The retreat of DoubleClick might seem like a victory for privacy, but it was only an early battle in a much larger war—one in which many observers expected privacy to be vanquished.

"You already have zero privacy—get over it," Scott McNealy, the CEO of Sun Microsystems, memorably remarked in 1999 in response to a question at a product show at which Sun introduced a new interactive technology called Jini. Sun's cheerful Web site promised to usher in the "networked home" of the future, in which the company's "gateway" software would operate "like a congenial party host inside the home to help consumer appliances communicate intelligently with each other and with outside networks." In this chatty new world of electronic networking, a household's refrigerator and coffeemaker could talk to a television, and all three could be monitored from the office computer. The incessant information exchanged by these gossiping appliances might, of course, generate detailed records of the most intimate details of their owners' daily lives.

New evidence seemed to emerge daily to support McNealy's grim verdict about the triumph of on-line surveillance technology over privacy. A survey of nearly a thousand large companies conducted by the American Management Association in 2000 found that more than half the large American firms surveyed monitored the Internet connections of their employees. Two-thirds of the firms monitored e-mail messages, computer files, or telephone conversations, up from only 35% three years earlier. Some companies used Orwellian computer software with names like Spector, Assentor, or Investigator that originally was available for as little as $99 and could monitor and record every keystroke on the computer with video-like precision. These virtual snoops could also be programmed to screen all incoming and outgoing e-mail for forbidden words and phrases—such as those involving racism, body parts, or the name of the boss—and then forward suspicious messages to a supervisor for review.

Changes in the delivery of books, music, and television were extending these technologies of surveillance beyond the office, blurring the boundaries between work and home. Amazon.com was criticized in 1999 for a feature that used postal codes and Internet domain names to identify the most popular books purchased on-line by employees at prominent corporations. In 2000 Amazon created further controversy by changing its privacy policy without warning and announcing that it would no longer permit customers to block the sharing of personal data.

The same technologies that made it possible to download digitally stored books, compact discs, and movies directly onto computer hard drives would soon make it possible for publishers and entertainment companies to record and monitor each individual's browsing habits with unsettling specificity. "Snitchware" programs could regulate not only which books an individual read but also how many times he or she read them, charging different royalties on the basis of whether parts of the book were copied or forwarded to a friend.

Television, too, was being redesigned to create precise records of viewing habits. A new electronic device known as a personal video recorder made it possible to store up to 30 hours of television programs; it also enabled viewers to skip commercials and to create their own program lineups. One model,

TiVo, established viewer profiles that it then used to make viewing suggestions and to record future shows.

There was also growing concern about Globally Unique Identifiers, or GUIDs, that made it possible to link every document, e-mail message, and on-line chat room posting with the real-world identity of the individual who created it. In effect, GUIDs are a kind of serial number that can be linked with a person's name and e-mail address when he or she registers on-line for a product or service.

In November 1999 RealJukebox, one of the most popular Internet music players, with reportedly 45 million registered users, became a focus of media attention when privacy advocates noted that the player could relay information to its parent company, RealNetworks, about the files that each user downloaded, and that this could then be matched with a unique identification number that pinpointed the identity of the user. RealNetworks insisted that the company had never, in fact, matched the GUIDs with the data about music preferences. Nevertheless, hours after the media outcry began, RealNetworks disabled the GUIDs to avoid a DoubleClick-like public relations debacle.

Even some software products such as Microsoft Corp.'s Word 97 and PowerPoint 97 embedded unique identifiers into every document. Soon all documents created electronically might have invisible markings that could be traced back to the author or recipient.

Americans increasingly seemed to agree that Congress should save them from the worst excesses of on-line profiling. In a *Business Week* magazine poll conducted in March, 57% of the respondents said that the government should pass laws regulating how personal information could be collected and used on the Internet. The European Union, for example, adopted the principle that information gathered for one purpose could not be sold or disclosed for another purpose without the consent of the individual concerned. The United States declined to adopt similar protection, even in light of evidence that bankrupt dot-coms, such as Toysmart, were being sold to other companies eager to sell personal data that had been collected on the condition that it not be disclosed.

Efforts to pass comprehensive privacy legislation in the U.S. had long been thwarted by a political reality: the beneficiaries of privacy—everyone, in the abstract—were anonymous and diffuse, while the corporate opponents of privacy were well organized and well heeled. For this reason many privacy advocates were putting more emphasis on privacy-enhancing technologies, such as those offered by Montreal-based Zero-Knowledge.com and others, that made it possible for an individual to cover his or her electronic tracks by, for example, browsing the Web and sending e-mails anonymously or pseudonymously.

At a computer industry trade show that took place in December 2000, keynote speaker and IBM Corp. Chairman and CEO Louis Gerstner addressed the electronic privacy issue, declaring it the "paramount" Internet-related concern.

There is no single solution to the erosion of privacy in cyberspace, no single law that can be proposed or single technology that can be invented to stop the profilers and surveillants in their tracks. The battle for privacy must be fought on many fronts—legal, political, and technological—and each new assault must be vigilantly resisted as it occurs. There is nothing inevitable about the erosion of privacy in cyberspace, just as there is nothing inevitable about its reconstruction. We have the ability to rebuild some of the private spaces we have lost. What we need now is the will to do so.

Jeffrey Rosen is an associate professor at the George Washington University Law School and author of The Unwanted Gaze: The Destruction of Privacy in America *(Random House, 2000). Part of this report is adopted from his article "The Eroded Self," which first appeared in* The New York Times Magazine.

photo credit: Ricco

(continued from page 177)
Crusoe family of low-power microchips for mobile computers. The chip, which ran both the Linux and Windows operating systems, used an advanced power-management feature that could throttle back power and scale performance dynamically with a software application running. Fujitsu, Ltd., and the Sony Corp. announced plans to use the Crusoe chip in some of their notebook computers.

Lucent Technologies Inc. announced it would spin off its Microelectronics Group in 2001. This would allow the new concern, named Agere Systems Inc. in December, to sell chips to any company. Motorola, Inc., China's biggest foreign investor ($3.4 billion), announced plans to spend $1.9 billion to expand its electronic chip and cellular phone production in Tianjin, China. In April Motorola announced the purchase of a $2 billion facility in Dunfermline, Scot. The plant, which was built by the Hyundai Motor Co. of South Korea in 1997 but never opened, would be Motorola's largest microchip-fabricating facility in Europe.

Telecommunications. In June 2000 the U.S. Federal Communications Commission (FCC) approved AT&T Corp.'s $44 billion purchase of MediaOne Group, Inc. Along with the company's purchase of Tele-Communications, Inc. (TCI), in 1999, this further increased AT&T's presence in the cable television market. The FCC also required that AT&T meet the 30% ownership limits for cable providers.

On October 25 AT&T announced its intention to split into four separate companies. With AT&T's consumer long-distance voice service in a rapid decline and stagnant growth in its business services unit, the company's chairman, C. Michael Armstrong, abandoned his vision of one-stop shopping for telephone, cable, and Internet services. The four new publicly traded companies would provide business services, consumer services, wireless, and broadband (cable). In 1996 AT&T had split into three companies—Lucent Technologies, NCR, and AT&T.

On November 1 WorldCom, Inc., the nation's second largest long-distance phone company, announced its own restructuring. This would create two tracking stocks and separate business customers and data and Internet services from the consumer long-distance business, which would be renamed MCI. A proposed merger of WorldCom and Sprint, the third largest long-distance provider, was blocked by the U.S. Department of Justice on the grounds that it would reduce competition in the telecommunications industry. Rebounding from the failed Sprint merger, WorldCom announced it would acquire voice and data network operator Intermedia Communications Inc. and a controlling interest in Digex, Inc., a World Wide Web site hosting operation, for $6 billion.

Lucent (the former AT&T equipment manufacturer), which was plagued by a falling stock price, failure to meet forecasts, component shortages, and a product line that had not kept up with the fast-changing technology, replaced its CEO, Richard McGinn, with its original CEO, Henry Schacht, until a permanent replacement could be found. Lucent spun off Enterprise Networks Group, the division that provided office telephone equipment, during the year and formed Avaya, Inc. Lucent was also proceeding with plans to spin off the microelectronics division into a separate company.

Iridium LLC, the bankrupt $5 billion satellite communications system backed by Motorola, Inc., was purchased for $25 million by a group headed by former Pan Am executive Dan Colussy. Prior to the sale's approval, there were plans to decommission the 66 satellites already launched and dispose of them by using the reentry heat of the atmosphere.

Owing to industry consolidation and an FCC ruling allowing only one wireless phone license in any market, two new major wireless companies were formed. Verizon was formed from the cellular resources of Bell Atlantic Corp., British-based Vodafone AirTouch PLC, and GTE Corp., which had bought Ameritech Cellular when Ameritech Corp. was purchased by SBC Communications, Inc., in 1999. Verizon had 25 million customers in 96 major markets and joined AT&T Wireless, Sprint PCS, Nextel Communications, Inc., and newly formed Cingular Wireless for nationwide service. Cingular, an $8 billion company with 19 million customers, was formed in 2000 by merging the wireless services of SBC (CellularOne) and BellSouth Corp. In August Verizon purchased digital subscriber line (DSL) provider NorthPoint Communications Group, Inc., for $800 million and broadband-data provider OnePoint Communications for $250 million.

In July the FCC authorized a new nationwide three-digit code, 511, to be used for telephone numbers that provide traffic reports and travel information. The FCC also decreed that all telephone companies had to provide local number portability, the option to keep one's telephone number when switching service providers, for wireline phones by the end of 2000 and for wireless phones by 2002.

The U.S. Supreme Court upheld an appeals court ruling that would allow telephone companies to use customer information to market other services to their customers without their consent. This decision was contrary to FCC rules implementing the 1996 Telecommunications Act. In May the FCC and AT&T announced lower long-distance telephone bills made possible by reducing access charges that long-distance carriers paid to local telephone companies. At the same time, AT&T filed with the FCC for other rate increases. Owing to a deluge of consumer complaints, however, AT&T backed off and deferred the rate hikes. After the FCC received 2,900 complaints, WorldCom agreed to pay $3.5 million for "slamming"—switching customers' long-distance provider without their permission.

Vodafone acquired the German firm Mannesmann AG in May for $170 billion in stock. This constituted the world's largest corporate takeover. The agreement headed off a potential hostile takeover by Vodafone and created the world's largest mobile communications company. Japan's largest mobile phone company, NTT DoCoMo, Inc., attempted to purchase VoiceStream Wireless Corp., the eighth largest provider in the U.S., but was outbid by Deutsche Telekom AG, which offered over $50 billion for the company. Mexican telecommunications giant Teléfonos de México requested the overturn of a ruling by Mexico's federal telecommunications regulators (Cofetel) that reduced by 63% the interconnection fees the company's competitors were required to pay for international calls originating or terminating in Mexico.

As the Internet and wireless telephony began to merge, mobile phone giants Motorola, Sweden-based Ericsson, and Nokia of Finland announced plans to develop standards jointly for the security of electronic transactions over mobile devices. In May the European Commission created the Wireless Strategic Initiative, a consortium of four leading telecommunications suppliers in Europe—Ericsson, Nokia, Australia-based Alcatel, and Siemens AG of Germany—to develop and test new prototypes for advanced wireless communications systems. After meeting with an international think tank, the consortium partners in December invited other companies to join them in a Wireless World Research Forum to be held in 2001. (THOMAS E. KROLL)

Earth Sciences

New reports on **SNOWBALL EARTH** and continental collisions captured the attention of earth scientists in 2000, while the world struggled with devastating **EARTHQUAKES** in Turkey, a volcanic eruption in Mexico, and extreme weather events influenced by the end of the **LA NIÑA** cycle.

GEOLOGY AND GEOCHEMISTRY

In 2000 Joseph L. Kirschvink (California Institute of Technology) published a novel report (with six coauthors from the U.S. and South Africa) relating the end of the 2.4 billion-year "Snowball Earth" to global geochemistry and major episodes in the history of life. He had originated the Snowball Earth concept about a decade earlier and by 2000 had evidence for two periods when the Earth was completely glaciated, covered with ice like a snowball, at about 2.4 billion and 600 million to 800 million years ago. The evidence includes measurements of the Earth's ancient magnetic field preserved in old rocks, which indicate the near-equatorial latitude of rock formations known to indicate the presence of ice. There is a 45-m (147.6-ft)-thick layer of manganese ore in the Kalahari Desert with an age corresponding to the end of the 2.4 billion-year Snowball Earth period, and the report proposed that its deposition was caused by the rapid and massive change in global climate as the snowball melted.

Most primitive organisms had been wiped out as the freeze developed on a global scale. The ice-covered oceans, separated from oxygen by thick sea ice, became reducing agents and therefore dissolved more metals. Carbon dioxide from increased volcanic activity is a candidate for cause of the eventual global warming, creating a greenhouse effect by preventing much of the Sun's radiation from escaping into space. As the ice melted, the dissolved metals and most other essential nutrients for photosynthesis were available for the hungry blue-green algae that had escaped extinction, and the algae bloom released enough oxygen to cause a cascade of chemical reactions. The global warming associated with oxidizing conditions led to the precipitation from seawater of iron and carbonates, producing characteristic rock masses known as banded iron formations and postglacial cap carbonates (limestones deposited above glacial rock deposits). The oxygen spike, in effect, led to a "rusting" of the iron and manganese. The manganese precipitation involved large quantities of oxygen, and these geochemical changes may have forced the organisms to mutate in such a way that they were protected from the changing chemical environment. Kirschvink suggested that the organisms may have adapted the enzyme known as superoxide dismutase to compensate for the changes. The enzyme and its evolutionary history were well known to biologists, but this was the first time a global climatic change had been suggested as a cause of the enzyme's diversification.

Much attention had been devoted to tracking the history of continental migration, with evidence for the formation of supercontinent Pangaea being firmly based on ocean-floor magnetic anomalies. Information about the assembly of the previous supercontinent of Rodinia was more speculative. I.W.D. Dalziel at the University of Texas at Austin and two coauthors in 2000 presented testable evidence for the hypothesis that Rodinia formed by the amalgamation of four separate continental entities along three boundaries, which are belts of mountain formation between 1.2 billion and 1 billion years ago. C.R. Scotese at the University of Texas at Arlington and his colleagues had devoted 20 years to the PALEOMAP Project, with the goal of illustrating the plate tectonic development of oceans and continents and their changing dis-

Joseph L. Kirschvink discusses his Snowball Earth concept on the campus of the California Institute of Technology where he works.

Robert Paz/Caltech

tribution during the past 1.1 billion years. The project also generated maps showing plate tectonics in the far future, illustrating the formation of the next supercontinent of "Pangaea Ultima." The results were made available on a World Wide Web site, <www.scotese.com>, in an atlas of full-colour paleogeographic maps showing ancient mountain ranges, active plate boundaries, and the extent of paleoclimatic belts. In addition, the site provided many animations, including how the continental configuration could change over the next 250 million years.

Development of plate tectonic theory after the 1960s demonstrated with precision how the continental masses drifted across the Earth during the past 250 million years, but understanding the origin and evolution of the continents remained a major objective. Several reports published during 2000 demonstrated the power of geochemical data produced by the measurement of isotope ratios by mass spectrometers to advance the understanding of the structure and evolution of continents. Three examples outlined below are the continental growth of southern Africa and the current collision between India and Asia as generators of major fault systems, and huge sedimentary fans accumulated from the erosion products of the Himalayas.

Evidence about continental origins involving the birth and death and erosion of successive mountain ranges is found in the oldest, stabilized parts of the continents, called cratons. The origin and history of the craton in South Africa was recently described in considerable detail in a report by R.W. Carlson (Carnegie Institution of Washington) and 16 coauthors from the U.S., Great Britain, and South Africa. This integrated investigation illustrated the necessity for a multidisciplinary approach involving geology, geochemistry, and geophysics for the comprehension of processes in the Earth sciences. The geology of the shallow crust of the craton was very well known. Hundreds of kimberlites (a rare, deep-seated kind of volcanic eruption) brought rock samples of upper mantle and lower crust (xenoliths) through cylindrical pipes to the Earth's surface. High-resolution measurements of isotopes of uranium-lead and rhenium-osmium systems on many samples revealed a long, complex history. Rocks of the upper mantle have ages of 3.5 billion to 3.3 billion years, and the craton was stabilized about 3 billion years ago. Mantle rocks formed during that time interval included subducted materials from plate margins around the continent, and these became attached to the continent through time, creating a stable block of lithosphere. The craton consists of crust and a thick section of the underlying mantle.

The Indian subcontinent collided with Asia about 50 million years ago, and the continued convergence of these masses at a rate of about five centimetres (two inches) per year has elevated the huge area to an average height of about five kilometres (three miles). This continental collision provided a natural laboratory for the study of the plate tectonic forces that generate continents. An example is a series of huge strike-slip faults in northern Tibet where blocks of the Earth's crust slide past one another. There are two competing models: Do these faults define major discontinuities to depths of 100 km (60 mi), through the crust and into the upper mantle, or are they relatively shallow features playing a secondary role to displacements in a more fluid (but solid) lithosphere? Geophysicists Rick Ryerson, Jerome Van der Woerd, Bob Finkel, and Marc Caffee at Lawrence Livermore National Laboratory, Livermore, Calif., with collaborators from Los Angeles, Paris, and Beijing, made the first-ever measurements of the rates of long-term movement along these large faults in order to characterize their large-scale behaviour. Specific fault breaks (tectonic offsets) were first identified from satellite images with a resolution of 10 m (33 ft). Sensitive accelerator mass spectrometry made it possible to measure very low levels of the nuclides Be_{10} and Al_{26}, which provided dates for the surfaces exposed by faulting. Slip rates can be calculated from those ages. The first stage of the research suggested that the northern portion of the Tibetan plateau had been uplifted by successive episodes of eastward fault propagation coupled with the uplift of young mountain ranges. The Livermore data indicated that the models representing the lithosphere as fluid might be flawed.

The Himalayan mountains are being eroded rapidly. The products of erosion have been deposited into the huge submarine sedimentary fans on either side of India—the eastern Bengal Fan and the western Indus Fan. The Bengal Fan is fed by the Ganges and Brahmaputra rivers, which deliver sediments derived from the high Himalayas along much of the mountain range. This fan is swamped by material from the rapidly unroofing Himalayas, which has occurred during the past 20 million years. The material and structure of the Indus Fan had been investigated by deep-ocean drilling. Its age had been debated for a decade, with one view being that the fan was formed as a response to the high Himalayan uplift and unroofing starting about 20 million years ago. The sequence of sediments deposited on the Indus Fan yields information on the uplift and erosion of the western Himalayas, as described in a 2000 report by Peter D. Clift (Woods Hole [Mass.] Oceanographic Institution) and six coauthors from the U.S., Germany, and Pakistan. The erosion sequence is more readily isolated than for the sediments of the Bengal Fan. Modern microbeam mass spectrometry is capable of measuring the very small amounts of lead occurring in feldspars eroded and transported from the mountains. Clift and his colleagues characterized various parts of the Himalayas in terms of their lead isotope ratios and then measured the lead isotopes in feldspars from sediment cores drilled from the Indus Fan. The significant observation was that the mineral grains were derived from the northwestern regions, and none were derived from the Indian plate. These results, together with new seismic studies of fan structure, suggested that the Indus River and fan system were initiated soon after the India-Asia collision, about 55 million years ago. These results demonstrated that different sedimentary fans may provide quite different images of evolving mountain ranges, which is important when determining the history of ancient deposits that are contemporaneous with mountain-building episodes.

(PETER J. WYLLIE)

GEOPHYSICS

During 2000 scientists reported on several societally relevant strong earthquakes that took place late in the previous year. On Sept. 21, 1999, a magnitude-7.6 quake occurred on the Chelungpu thrust fault in central Taiwan, killing more than 2,300 people. The earthquake produced tremendous surface slip, offsetting man-made structures vertically as much as 10 m (33 ft). Because the Taiwan Central Weather Bureau had recently completed installation of the most densely instrumented strong-ground-motion network in the world, scientists were able to determine the location and magnitude of the earthquake less than two minutes after it happened. Indeed, the network provided a wealth of digital data on the quake for seismology and earthquake engineering studies.

On Oct. 16, 1999, an earthquake of magnitude 7.1 occurred within the eastern California shear zone (ECSZ) in a sparsely populated area (Hector Mine) of the Mojave Desert east-southeast of Barstow, rupturing 45 km (28 mi) of faults. Twelve minor foreshocks were recorded in the 12 hours preceding the main shock, and 2,500 aftershocks were recorded in the succeeding two weeks. Although people in Los Angeles felt the earthquake, damage and disruption were minimal.

In a preliminary report, scientists from the U.S. Geological Survey (USGS), Southern California Earthquake Center, and California Division of Mines and Geology observed that the Hector Mine earthquake involved rupture on two previously studied faults, the Bullion and Lavic Lake faults. Much of the fault zone had been buried by young stream deposits and had not experienced significant offset during the past 10,000 years. As was the case for other parts of the ECSZ, the rate of movement along these faults was slow (less than one millimetre [0.04 in] per year), which explained its long period of inactivity during the Holocene Epoch (the past 10,000 years). By analyzing satellite imagery data of the Mojave Desert before and after the Hector Mine earthquake, scientists from the Scripps Institution of Oceanography and the USGS mapped the surface deformation. They found that the locations of the aftershocks delineated the entire rupture zone and that maximum slip (offset) along the main rupture was as high as 7 m (23 ft), compared with 5.2 m (17 ft) estimated from ground-based observations.

Two strong earthquakes near Istanbul—one of magnitude 7.4 on Aug. 17, 1999, and the other of magnitude 7.1 on Nov. 12, 1999—together killed 18,000 people, destroyed 15,400 buildings and structures, and resulted in $10 billion–$25 billion in damage. The first event, with an epicentre southwest of the city of Izmit, was the most recent manifestation of a westerly progression of major earthquakes along the North Anatolian Fault that had begun in 1939. The Istanbul region had been struck and heavily damaged by 12 major earthquakes in the past 15 centuries, which attested to the significant earthquake hazard there. Stress-induced triggering and rupturing was considered to be the mechanism for the west-

The Popocatépetl volcano in central Mexico spews lava and ashes on December 19.

AP/Wide World Photos

erly propagation of these earthquakes. Seismologists at the USGS studied the time-dependent effect of stress transfer to adjacent faults following the Izmit event. From this they estimated that the next large quake or quakes in the region had a 62% (±15%) probability of occurring during the next 30 years and a 32% (±12%) probability during the next decade.

The Hawaii Scientific Drilling Project (HSDP), involving an international team of scientists from dozens of universities and institutions, was focused on drilling into the buried lava flows constituting Mauna Loa volcano on the island of Hawaii. Begun in 1999, the first phase of drilling, to a depth of 3,109 m (10,201 ft), was accomplished. The goal of the second phase was to reach 5,500–6,100 m (18,000–20,000 ft). Temperature measurements in the borehole revealed that temperature decreases with depth and that variations in temperature are affected by hydrologic factors. From analyses of drill core samples, in conjunction with geophysical well-logging and downhole measurements, HSDP scientists expected to learn more about mantle plumes—upwellings of hot, solid mantle material, perhaps originating from the thermal boundary layer at the mantle-core boundary (3,000 km [1,860 mi] deep)—that accounted for the creation of the Hawaiian Islands volcanic chain. Other objectives of the HSDP were to investigate variations in mantle geochemistry and the intensity and polarity of Earth's magnetic field during the formation of the Hawaiian volcanoes.

Geodetic measurements making use of the satellite-based Global Positioning System (GPS) continued to aid in geophysical studies of earthquakes, volcanoes, tectonic plate motion, and related dynamic phenomena at the Earth's surface (for example, vertical movements of the crust caused by the growth or shrinkage of large ice sheets) and in its interior (for example, in subduction zones). Using GPS observations made before and after the Izmit earthquake of 1999, scientists from the Massachusetts Institute of Technology and the University of California, Berkeley, and their collaborators from Turkey and France estimated the distribution slip along the earthquake rupture during and after the event, which led to a better understanding of the seismic zone. Such studies could also help assess the potential for neighbouring faults to generate future earthquakes.

Volcanic activity, magma transport, and seismic tremors under and around volcanoes are interrelated. Volcanoes often deform prior to eruption. Studies of volcanoes continued to be enhanced by seismological techniques in conjunction with the use of tiltmeters, leveling instruments, and the GPS. Using GPS measurements and seismic data from earthquake swarms, scientists from Stanford University and the University of Tokyo estimated the space-time evolution of a propagating magma-filled crack off the Izu Peninsula, Japan, and provided improved understanding of magma transport through the brittle crust and of the cause of volcanic seismicity.

Results from continuous GPS monitoring of the eruptive event of Jan. 30, 1997, on the east rift zone of Hawaii's Kilauea volcano by scientists from Stanford University, the USGS, and the University of Hawaii provided unprecedented insight into the spatial and temporal behaviour of a volcanic eruption. Models based on GPS data showed the rift opening eight hours prior to the eruption. Absence of precursory inflation of the summit led the investigators to reject magma storage in favour of pressure buildup as the cause of the eruption. Other, non-GPS types of studies involving simultaneous measurements of deformation and gravity also can be used to identify magma-chamber processes prior to the onset of the conventional precursors of eruptions.

Collaborating scientists from France, Spain, and Italy produced detailed internal imagery of Italy's Mt. Etna volcano through the use of a set of arrival times of seismic waves from local earthquakes. The data were collected by a dense array of temporarily emplaced three-component seismographs. The study revealed a body of intrusive material of magmatic origin under the southern part of Valle del Bove, on Etna's eastern flank, above the basement rock 6 km (3.7 mi) below sea level. Velocity changes in the seismic waves passing through the body signified the presence of magmatic melt and partial melt.

Sandwiched between Earth's crust and molten outer core is the mantle, which continued to be a major topic of debate in geophysics. The mantle makes up 83% of Earth's volume and consists of solid ferromagnesian silicate rock, heated by the outer core and its own radioactive decay. Circulation of the mantle is the driving force for the motion of the tectonic plates, which causes mountain building and earthquakes. Several seismic and geochemical-petrologic modeling studies have continued to address the issues of whole-mantle and two-layer circulation in the mantle. On the basis of results from recent seismological studies, researchers at the University of Arizona and the University of California, Berkeley, reported highly anomalous structures—modeled as "fuzzy" patches roughly 5–50 km (3–30 mi) thick—at the base of the mantle (about 2,900 km [1,800 mi] deep). The patches, which appeared to exhibit a wide range of increased density (as much as 60%), were inferred as being contamination of the deep mantle by the outer core. Such patches may represent zones of intense chemical and physical interaction at the mantle-core boundary. (MURLI H. MANGHNANI)

METEOROLOGY AND CLIMATE

Many of the unusual climate and weather events during 2000 were influenced by the ongoing La Niña over the Pacific Ocean, characterized by below-normal sea-surface temperatures over the eastern and central equatorial Pacific and somewhat warmer-than-normal temperatures over much of the western Pacific. Although La Niña began to weaken noticeably during the spring and summer, its impact was felt over many areas into the early fall. Greater-than-usual rainfall occurred over much of the western Pacific and Indian Ocean basins, with enhanced tropical storm activity affecting Australia, southeastern Africa, and the southern Indian Ocean during the first several months of the year. With the advent of summer in the Northern Hemisphere, the area of heavy monsoon rains and tropical storm activity shifted northward, and numerous tropical storms and typhoons produced periods of torrential rains and flooding over southeastern Asia, China, the Korean peninsula, and Japan.

One of the effects of La Niña on the United States was relatively wet weather over the western part of the country during the first three months of the year as the jet stream repeatedly steered Pacific storms into northern California and Oregon. Except for a brief period of cold and snow over the southern and middle Atlantic states in late January and early February, storms avoided much of the remainder of the country. The winter and early spring period was the warmest on record in many areas. Drought continuing from 1999 affected inland areas

NOAA Photo Library

A satellite image shows a large area in the southwestern U.S. affected by wildfires in the Los Alamos, N.M., area in May.

of the Northeast and much of the Midwest early in the year, but as the La Niña-influenced circulation steered most storms across southern Canada and the northern U.S., the driest areas shifted southward to the southeast and Gulf Coast regions.

Later in the summer the extreme drought conditions and record heat had a severe impact on agriculture and water supplies in Texas and the southern Great Plains. Areas to the west of the Continental Divide became progressively drier throughout the summer, and, although the southwestern U.S. monsoon started earlier than usual in June, it yielded little rainfall during July and much of August. Its circulation pattern steered mid-level moisture northward and caused numerous "dry" thunderstorms. These storms produced little rainfall but much lightning over the western part of the country and led to many wildfires that contributed to the worst fire season in 50 years over a large area expanding northward and westward from New Mexico in May to Montana and the West Coast states by the end of the summer.

The late summer drought and heat set many new all-time records over Texas, Oklahoma, and some adjacent states. Some areas of northern Texas went nearly three months without measurable rain, the longest such period on record for more than 100 years. Maximum temperatures in the triple-digit range were observed nearly every day in August over parts of Texas and Oklahoma, and drought and heat matched or exceeded records set in 1913 and in 1934 and 1936 during the Dust Bowl era. Records were set in several locations in Texas, Oklahoma, and Arkansas in late August and early September, with values exceeding 43.3 °C (110 °F) at several locations.

To the north and east of the areas of heat and drought, temperatures were cooler than normal, and rainfall was normal or greater, which produced a good year for crops in parts of the nation's important Midwestern agricultural areas. Nebraska, however, suffered drought-induced economic losses totaling more than $1 billion. Over much of the Northeast, it was one of the coolest summers in many years.

As in most recent years, the Atlantic hurricane season (June–November) got off to a late start, with the first storm not developing until early August. As had been forecast because of the lingering effects of La Niña, the season became somewhat more active than normal, with 14 named tropical storms, of which eight became hurricanes. Most remained away from the U.S.; three attained major (category 3 or higher) intensity. None caused significant damage to the U.S., and two of the storms brought welcome rains to parts of the southeastern drought area.

The first several months of the year were stormy and wet over much of western and northern Europe, but abnormally warm and dry weather developed over much of northern Africa, southeastern Europe, and the Middle East in the spring and most of the summer. Temperatures soared to well over 40 °C (104 °F) over those areas during the summer months, with severe adverse impacts on agriculture and health. A maximum of 40.8 °C (105 °F) in Jerusalem recorded in late July was the highest there in more than 100 years. Several damaging storms brought strong winds and floods to parts of western and southern Europe during October and November.

The weather was abnormally wet over southeastern Africa during the first several months of the year, partly from the effects of tropical storms from the Indian Ocean. In February an intense cyclone brought disastrous flooding rains to Mozambique and parts of neighbouring countries, killing hundreds and leaving thousands, including entire villages, homeless. Abnormally wet conditions, some due to tropical cyclones and at times accompanied by unseasonably cool weather, also prevailed over much of Australia during the first half of the year, especially in the northern and western portions of the island continent.

In South America the first three months of the year were unusually wet over much of Colombia and western Venezuela. Abnormal summer heat developed over central and southeastern parts of the continent during January. Periods of abnormally heavy rainfall occurred over central and southern parts of South America during much of the first seven months of the year, augmented by strong storms from the Pacific affecting Chile during the winter season. Unusually cold weather developed during July and brought subfreezing temperatures to much of the southern part of the continent. (JOHN J. KELLY, JR.)

Economic Affairs

With Y2K fears at an end, the **WORLD ECONOMY** experienced its **FASTEST GROWTH** for more than a decade in 2000. **STOCK INVESTORS,** however, had a **VOLATILE RIDE,** as the nine-year-old **U.S. BULL MARKET**—especially among the **HIGH-FLYING HIGH-TECH STOCKS**—came to an **END.**

The year 2000 got off to a good start and ended on a positive note. Overall, the world economy experienced its fastest growth for more than a decade, and the prospects were for only a modest slowdown in 2001. As the year began, widespread predictions of disruption or even chaos being caused by Y2K problems, or the "Millennium Bug," proved ill-founded. In the first few months of 2000, it was evident that the economic momentum, largely driven by American consumer demand, was building up. In much of the world, including the U.S., the growth rate had peaked by midyear, after which there was a slowdown.

The International Monetary Fund (IMF) projected that real output would rise 4.7% in the year 2000, compared with an actual increase of 3.4% in 1999. The rate was by far the fastest since 1988 (4.6%) and took place against a background of volatile oil and stock markets. Despite inflationary pressures in some parts of the world, consumer prices were kept under control, helped by tight monetary policies. Consumer prices in the transition countries rose by 18.3%, well down from the 43.8% rate in 1999. In the economically advanced countries, consumer prices rose a modest 2.3%, up from 1.4% in 1999, when there were fears of deflation. These fears were realized in Japan, where there was a fractional fall. Inflation in less-developed countries (LDCs) moderated slightly to an average 6.2%, which was inflated by more excessive rates in a few countries.

As usual, growth in the LDCs was faster (5.6%) than in the advanced countries (4.2%). Although the difference between the two rates widened from 1999 (0.6 percentage point), it was modest compared with the early 1990s. In those years the LDCs were expanding at between two and four times the rate of the advanced countries, a reflection of the dynamic expansion in many Asian economies.

The U.S. continued to provide a strong market for world exports and output growth, as it had done since the Asian financial crisis began in July 1997. In 2000, however, there was also buoyant demand from Europe and the transition countries. Japan's modest recovery, too, made a contribution. The slowdown in the U.S. economy was a growing cause of concern. The country had been spending beyond its capacity and means. To meet the shortfall, it was relying on credit and a huge flow of imports. Despite the slowdown, there were no signs of an easing in the burgeoning U.S. current-account deficit, which ended the year at around $450 billion, well above that of the year before. In November, imports unexpectedly rose sharply, which caused a record one-month deficit of $34 billion. The fear was that a sudden change in sentiment, such as one that might be prompted by a further escalation of oil prices, would cause a hard landing with a sharp slowdown in inflows of foreign direct investment (FDI) and foreign share buying with turbulence in world financial markets. The close and contested finish to the U.S.

Table I. Real Gross Domestic Products of Selected OECD Countries
% annual change

Country	1996	1997	1998	1999	2000[1]
United States	3.6	4.4	4.4	4.2	5.2
Japan	5.1	1.6	−2.5	0.2	1.9
Germany	0.8	1.4	2.1	1.6	3.0
France	1.1	1.9	3.2	2.9	3.3
Italy	1.1	1.8	1.5	1.4	2.8
United Kingdom	2.6	3.5	2.6	2.2	3.0
Canada	1.5	4.4	3.3	4.5	4.8
All developed countries	3.2	3.5	2.5	3.0	4.3
Seven major countries above	3.0	3.2	2.5	2.9	3.9
European Union	1.7	2.5	2.7	2.4	3.4

[1]Estimated.
Note: Seasonally adjusted at annual rates.
Sources: OECD, *Economic Outlook,* November 2000 (provisional); International Monetary Fund, *World Economic Outlook,* October 2000.

Table II. Standardized Unemployment Rates in Selected Developed Countries
% of total labour force

Country	1996	1997	1998	1999	2000[1]
United States	5.4	4.9	4.5	4.2	4.0
Japan	3.4	3.4	4.1	4.7	4.7
Germany	8.6	9.5	8.9	8.3	7.7
France	12.3	12.4	11.8	11.1	9.7
Italy	11.7	11.8	11.9	11.5	10.8
United Kingdom	7.9	6.5	5.9	6.0	5.5
Canada	9.6	9.1	8.3	7.6	6.7
All developed countries	7.3	7.0	6.8	6.7	6.2
Seven major countries above	6.7	6.4	6.2	6.0	5.7
European Union	10.7	10.4	9.8	9.1	8.2

[1]Projected.
Source: OECD, *Economic Outlook,* November 2000 (provisional).

presidential election was not perceived as threatening a negative effect in the coming year. Any fiscal stimulus carried little risk of the economy's overheating. Given a parallel weakening in the euro-zone economies, the dollar was not expected to fall dramatically.

An increasing influence on international production was FDI. The strong desire of many nations and companies to participate in and benefit from globalization was reflected in changes in the regulatory environments of most countries to smooth the path for foreign investors. In 1999, of the 140 regulatory changes in investment conditions made by 60 countries, only 9 were less favourable to FDI. Global FDI outflows were expected to exceed $1 trillion in 2000, 20% more than in 1999. The number of transnational companies rose to 63,000, with 690,000 foreign affiliates whose sales, at $14 billion, were nearly twice global exports. The number of workers employed by affiliates was growing rapidly and by the year 2000 had reached 41 million.

Cross-border mergers and acquisitions (M&As) continued to account for a high proportion of FDI, reaching $720 billion in 1999. Most of these were acquisitions between firms in the same industry. Where a corporate objective was to build a strong position in a new market, it was often considered quicker and simpler to buy an established company and with it acquire instant local knowledge and contacts. Because these deals involved a transfer of ownership and assets into foreign hands, however, acquisitions were often the targets for local opposition from nationalistic groups and the press, whether in advanced or less-developed countries. The alternative to an M&A was to set up a new operation in a little-known location, which might take too long in the current highly competitive environment. In the manufacturing sector, the focus of most worldwide M&A activity was automobiles, pharmaceuticals and chemicals, and food, beverages, and tobacco. In these industries economies of scale could be achieved and synergies exploited. There also were numerous cross-border bank mergers. (See *Banking*, below.)

Most acquisitions continued to be in the advanced countries, although the share of M&A activity in the LDCs was steadily rising. The U.S. was the most attractive single FDI destination, and in 1999 acquisitions in the U.S. by foreign investors reached $233 billion. In the European Union (EU) the rate of takeover activity accelerated to $344 billion, much of it intra-European deals driven by the introduction of the euro in January 1999. Latin America, mainly attracted by privatizations in Argentina and Brazil, led activity in LDCs. Asian firms, notably those in Singapore, were actively buying companies in the less-developed world. While still recovering from the earlier financial crisis, South Korea saw foreign acquisitions that exceeded $9 billion in 1999. The largest buyers of foreign enterprises were from the U.K., followed by Germany and France.

NATIONAL ECONOMIC POLICIES

The IMF projected a rise in gross domestic product (GDP) of the advanced economies—which included the industrialized countries, the 11 EU members that made up the euro zone, and the newly industrializing countries (NICs) such as South Korea, Taiwan, and Singapore—of 4.2%, compared with an actual outturn of 3.2% in 1999.

United States. The U.S. proved once again to be the dynamo for world growth, with output projected to increase 5.2%. (*See* TABLE I.) This was the fastest rate among the industrialized countries and reflected an acceleration from 4.2% in 1999. The country was experiencing its longest period of continuing growth on record—the expansion had begun in 1991. Much of the strength of the U.S. performance could be attributed to the flexibility of American labour and product markets. Over the years, labour productivity had been increased by the strong inflow of investment.

Consumer spending accounted for two-thirds of economic output, and there were good reasons for the consumer confidence that was stimulating the economic growth. Unemployment remained low during the year, and job opportunities kept increasing. (*See* TABLE II.)

As the year 2000 drew to a close, there were definite indications of a slowdown. The signs were not of the long-predicted and feared recession—with its global implications—but rather of a hoped-for "soft landing." The first half of the year was one of phenomenal growth, with GDP rising by 5.6%. In the third quarter, however, output slowed dramatically to less than 2.5%. The signs of a slowdown were widely welcomed, quelling fears that the economy was overheating. The Federal Reserve (Fed) raised interest rates three times in early 2000 but left the Fed funds target rate unchanged at 6.5% in November, as it had in the June, August, and October meetings. Although rates remained steady in December, there were signs that the Fed was changing its stance on inflation. Fed chairman Alan Greenspan (*see* BIOGRAPHIES) hinted that a rate cut might be possible in early 2001.

United Kingdom. Growth in the U.K. was robust in the year 2000, with output expected to rise at least 3%, which

Inflation Rate
(percentage change from December to December)

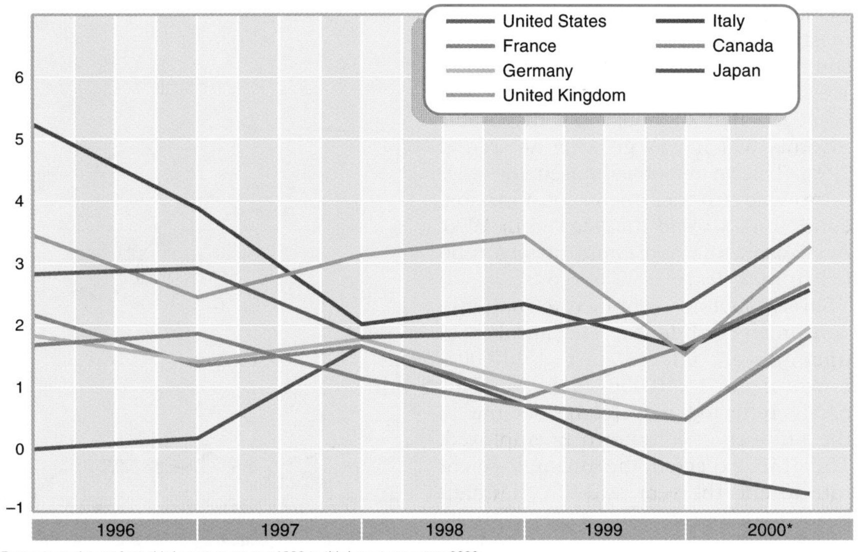

*Percentage change from third quarter average 1999 to third quarter average 2000.
Source: International Monetary Fund, *International Financial Statistics*.

Industrial Production
semiannual averages: 1995 = 100

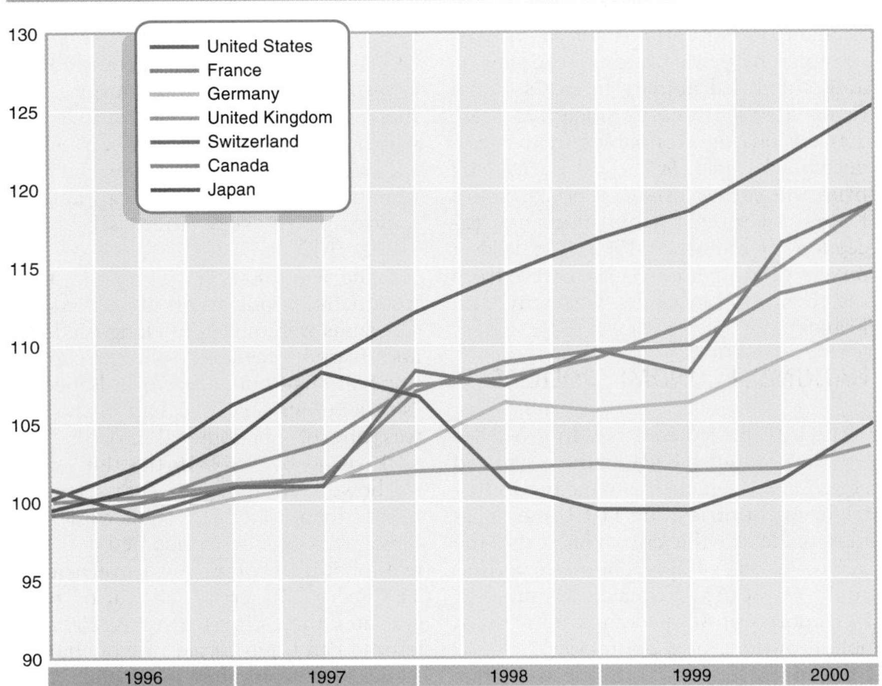

Source: International Monetary Fund, *International Financial Statistics*.

reflected a sharp acceleration on the 2.1% increase of 1999. (*See* TABLE I.) Since 1992, when sterling was withdrawn from the European exchange-rate mechanism, the country had been experiencing its longest period of sustained growth since World War II. The increasing economic output, helped by sterling's relative strength against the euro, pushed the U.K. into fourth place among the world's largest economies, after the U.S., Japan, and Germany.

Once again, growth was led by domestic demand. At 3.6%, household consumption rose at a slower pace than in 1999 (4.3%). Nevertheless, the rate still exceeded that of household disposable income, which was growing at around 2.5%. This meant that households were borrowing to fuel their consumption, continuing a trend that started in 1996. As a result, the household savings ratio fell from 5.1% in 1999 to 3.6%.

Several factors combined to maintain consumer confidence. The number of unemployed fell to just 1,000,000, down from 1,250,000 in 1999. This partly reflected a welcome decline in the number of long-term unemployed. The IMF expected the unemployment rate to end the year at 3.9% (claimant basis), compared with 4.3% in 1999. This was the lowest rate among the industrialized countries. (*See* TABLE II.)

Despite the tighter labour-market conditions, which disguised some serious skills shortages, wage and price inflation were modest. Fears that the economy was overheating and that higher oil prices would increase the rate of inflation proved ill-founded. There was little evidence to suggest that producers were passing on the higher cost of oil, possibly because the stronger pound reduced the cost of other imported input, and the inflation rate in 2000 was expected to be around 2%, slightly below the 2.3% rise in 1999.

Japan. During the year the Japanese economic performance was mixed, but it was recovering from a recession that caused a decline in output in 1998 and only a modest rise of 0.3% in 1999. (*See* TABLE I.) Growth in 2000 was expected to be 1.5–2%. The year began well, with quarter-on-quarter output increasing by 2.4% in the first three months; after a seasonal correction taking into account the fact that 2000 was a leap year, it probably would be nearer 1.5%. April to June saw a further 1% rise (4.2% annualized), but there was a slowdown in the second half of the year.

Although the recovery was patchy, it was sufficient for the Bank of Japan (BOJ) to raise its call rate (the target interest rate on uncollateralized overnight call loans) from virtually zero to 0.25%. This brought to an end the 18-month emergency "zero interest-rate policy" (known as the ZIRP), which had been introduced in the face of sluggish private demand and fears that the economy was on the verge of a serious deflationary spiral. The ZIRP had ef-

Interest Rates: Short-term
three-month money market rates

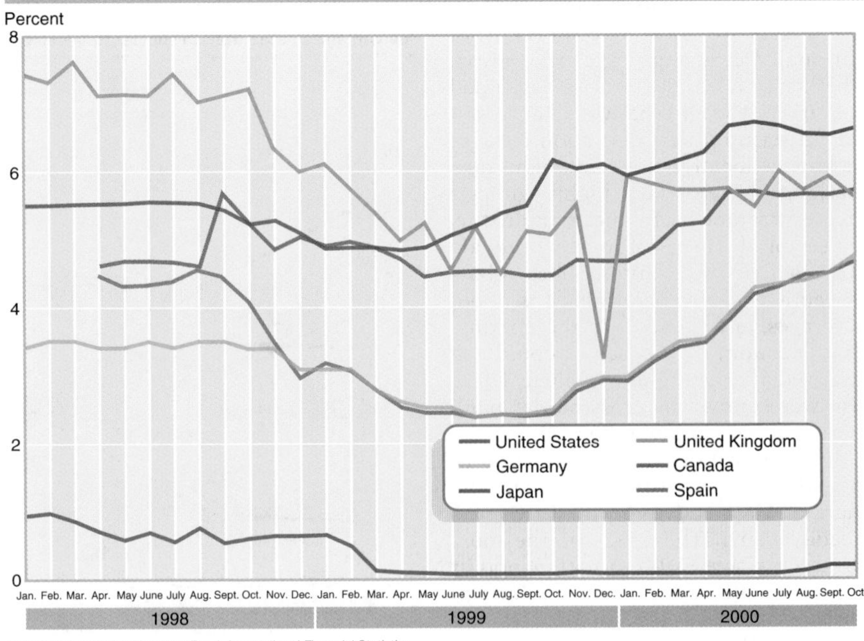

Source: International Monetary Fund, *International Financial Statistics*.

fectively prevented market speculation on higher future interest rates and a stock market meltdown. The interest-rate move was not unexpected and had no adverse consequences in the financial markets. Interest rates remained extremely low for the prevailing business conditions.

Labour-market conditions were improving, with the unemployment rate stabilizing at 4.6%–4.7% (October) and a rising trend in the number of job vacancies. (*See* TABLE II.) An emerging problem, however, was the mismatch of skills to jobs, which was curbing employment growth. For the first time in two years, wages were rising, largely because of overtime worked, and bonus payments increased in the summer. The rate of inflation was not an issue, since consumer prices were expected to rise by less than 1% over the year.

Euro Zone. The IMF forecast that growth in the euro zone, or euro area, would reach 3.5% in 2000, following a better-than-expected 2.4% in 1999. (*See* TABLE I.) The expansion was being helped by increasing weakness of the euro, which made exports more competitive at a time of strengthening global demand. A high point of 3.7% (year on year) was reached in the second quarter, after which demand and output moderated and growth of closer to 3% was more likely.

Several factors influenced confidence and economic performance in the second half of the year. Possibly the most significant factor was the effect of rising oil prices, which was made more damaging by the weakness of the euro against the U.S. dollar and other currencies. While this made exports much more competitive, the higher cost of imports was causing consumer prices to rise faster and real incomes to fall. The economic consequences were made worse by Europe-wide oil blockades staged in protest against the increases in gasoline and diesel oil prices. Another factor was the series of interest-rate hikes imposed by the European Central Bank (ECB) between November 1999 and October 2000, with rates rising from 2.5% to 4.75%.

The differences in individual country performances were less marked than in 1999, except in the case of Ireland, which once again grew fastest, with GDP up 8.7% following much faster growth than expected in 1999 (9.9%). All other euro-zone countries saw either similar or faster expansion than in 1999.

Interest Rates: Long-term

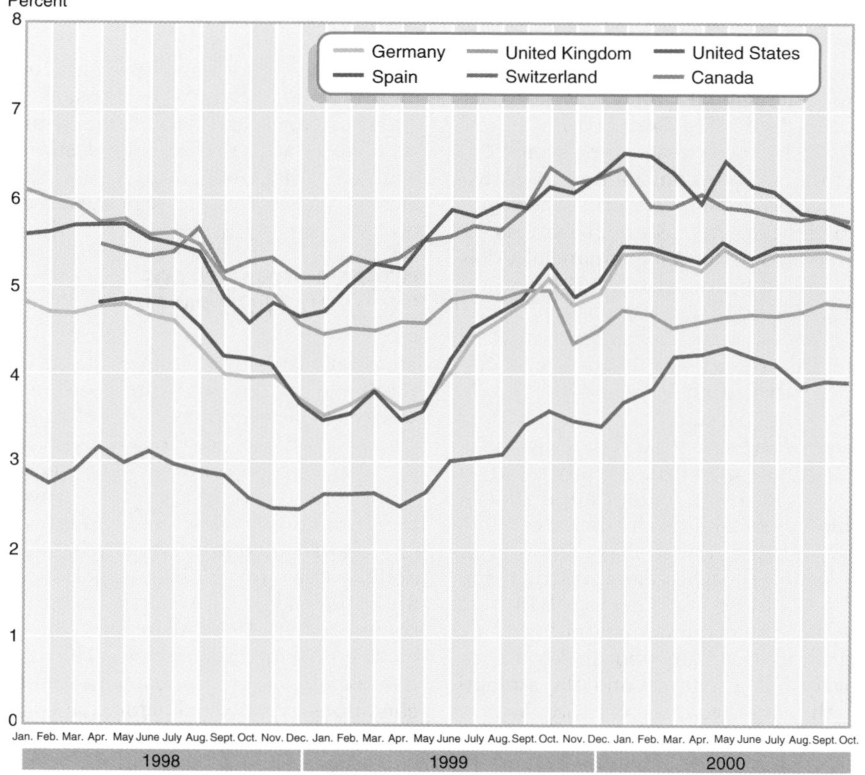

Source: International Monetary Fund, *International Financial Statistics*.

AP/Wide World Photos

Danish newspapers show a disappointed Prime Minister Poul Nyrup Rasmussen as well as a triumphant Pia Kjaersgaard, who led the campaign against adopting the euro.

France again led the major industrial country members, with growth of 3.5% (2.9% in 1999), and was followed by Italy, with 3.1% (1.4%). Germany, the region's biggest economy, was forecast by the IMF to expand 2.9% (1.6%). As the year drew to a close, however, a more marked slowdown than expected made this look overly optimistic. The other countries surged ahead, led by Luxembourg 5.1% (5.2%), Finland 5% (4%), and Spain 4.1% (3.7%). The Netherlands and Belgium both anticipated growth of 3.9% (3.6% and 2.5%, respectively). Greece, Portugal, and Austria each grew by around 3.5%.

More marked were the differences in inflation rates, which were exacerbated by the requirement for a single euro-zone interest rate. Ireland suffered most with 4.8%, and many others were between 2% and 3%. In Germany the year-on-year inflation rate reached 2.4% in October, and producer prices reached their highest level for 18 years. In France too the ECB's 2% ceiling, or "tolerance level," was being exceeded. The ECB was expected to raise interest rates to defend this limit early in 2001.

Table III. Changes in Output in Less-Developed Countries
% annual change in real gross domestic product

Area	1996	1997	1998	1999	2000[1]
All less-developed countries	6.5	5.7	3.5	3.8	5.6
Regional groups					
Africa	5.7	2.8	3.1	2.2	3.4
Asia	8.3	6.5	4.1	5.9	6.7
Middle East and Europe	4.5	5.1	3.1	0.8	4.7
Western Hemisphere	3.6	5.4	2.2	0.3	4.3
Countries in transition	–0.5	1.6	–0.8	2.4	4.9

[1]Projected.
Source: International Monetary Fund, *World Economic Outlook*, October 2000.

Table IV. Changes in Consumer Prices in Less-Developed Countries
% change from preceding year

Area	1996	1997	1998	1999	2000[1]
All less-developed countries	15.3	9.7	10.1	6.6	6.2
Regional groups					
Africa	30.2	13.6	9.1	11.8	12.7
Asia	8.3	4.7	7.5	2.4	2.4
Middle East and Europe	26.9	25.4	25.3	20.4	17.4
Western Hemisphere	21.6	13.4	10.2	9.3	8.9

[1]Projected.
Source: International Monetary Fund, *World Economic Outlook*, October 2000.

The stronger economic activity brought a welcome decline in unemployment. The unemployment rate fell during the year from 9% in 1999 to an estimated 8.3% in 2000. While all countries experienced falling rates, in many they remained high. In Belgium, Germany, Greece, and Italy, for example, between 8% and 15% of the labour forces were without jobs. (*See* TABLE II.)

The Former Centrally Planned Economies. Recovery from the 1998 financial crisis was well under way in 2000, and average growth in the region was 4% to 5%. The recovery was broad-based and helped by the strength of the global economy, particularly the buoyant EU. Higher oil and gas prices stimulated faster growth in Russia and other oil-rich countries in the Commonwealth of Independent States. While output in the Russian economy was expected to expand by more than 7% as a result of higher energy prices, any acceleration in the rate of future growth was likely to be handicapped by continuing slow progress toward structural reform. Inflation, too, was again accelerating, and in December prices were up 20% from a year earlier.

Output by the group of countries destined to join the EU rose 4.1% after a 0.3% decline in 1999. Stronger exports and continuing structural reforms helped boost output, which was led by Hungary (5.5%) and Poland (5%)—with both countries experiencing record GDP rises, in excess of 6%, in the first quarter. Unemployment continued to increase in nearly all countries as it had done throughout the decade of transition. A high level of unemployment was an expected result of the shift of labour from the overmanned state sector to a more efficient private sector.

Less-Developed Countries. The IMF projected an acceleration in the rate of growth in output of the LDCs to 5.6%, compared with 3.8% in 1999. While there continued to be wide disparities between individual country performances, regional differences were less than in 1999. (*See* TABLE III.)

As in previous years, the Asian LDCs were the major contributors to growth in the less-developed world. The region experienced the fastest growth as recovery from the Asian financial crisis, which had begun in July 1997, got well under way. Expansion was projected at 6.7%, compared with 5.9% in 1999. In China the economy remained buoyant, with output expected to rise by 7.5%, compared with 7.1% in 1999. Much of the activity was in anticipation of China's pending membership in the World Trade Organization (WTO), which necessitated further economic liberalization, the modernization of inefficient industries, and restructuring of the Chinese financial sector. In India the rise in economic output was expected to exceed 6%, boosted by the recovery of agriculture and the strength of the high-tech sector. (*See* WORLD AFFAIRS: *India:* Sidebar.)

In Africa, GDP was expected to increase from 2.2% in 1999 to 3.4%. Individual country performances were mixed. In South Africa, the region's largest economy, the finance minister announced that growth in the current fiscal year had been revised down from 3.6% at the time of the February budget to 2.6%. This was because of the loss of agricultural output due to flooding and the contagion effect of uncertainty in global financial markets. The rand weakened, largely as a result of the turbulence in Zimbabwe, the only African country to suffer a fall in output (–6%) and an excessive rate of inflation.

Several countries in sub-Saharan Africa were being helped by a resumption of IMF funding. Most unexpected was a $1 billion IMF standby credit granted to Nigeria in August that raised the country's financial status. Nigeria and Algeria had the advantage of increased oil prices, which boosted their public finances. Several countries, including Côte d'Ivoire, Eritrea, and the Democratic Republic of the Congo, had their economies disrupted by political events or war.

In Latin America the recovery from the emerging market crisis in 1997–98 was expected to be between 4% and 4.5%. Although growth was being fueled by exports to the U.S., there was also a revival of consumer demand. The region generally was vulnerable to fluctuations in commodity prices, and Mexico, Venezuela, and Colombia benefited from higher oil prices.

Economic performances during 2000 in the Middle East were boosted by higher oil and gas prices. A major preoccupation was the Israeli-Palestinian conflict, which intensified in October. Overall growth in the region was expected to be 4–5%.

INTERNATIONAL TRADE, EXCHANGE, AND PAYMENTS

International Trade. The increase in the volume of world trade in goods and services nearly doubled to 10%, compared with a faster-than-expected increase of 5.3% in 1999. This meant that the difference in the rate of growth in production (4.7%) and trade was much wider than in previous years. The dollar rise in global exports, at $7,497,000,000,000, was just under 9% compared with 1999. All regions actively participated in the upsurge. The year marked a return to the buoyant trading conditions experienced before the Asian financial crisis. The economic recovery in Western Europe and Latin America, combined with the continuing recovery

Globalization—Why All the Fuss?

In 2000 the media were full of references to globalization of the economy, communications—even politics and military affairs. Large crowds turned out to protest meetings such as that of the World Trade Organization (WTO) in Seattle, Wash., in 1999 or called attention to International Monetary Fund (IMF) policies in granting loans to struggling economies. What were these protests all about?

Globalization is a phenomenon involving the integration of economies, cultures, governmental policies, and political movements around the world. Internationalization is nothing new. Many of the large empires and religious movements represented forms of globalization. Trade and investment between countries have promoted interdependence of the world's economies for centuries. What is now called globalization, however, represents an exponential acceleration of the integration process. As early as 1962 the Canadian visionary Marshall McLuhan wrote that the electronic age was turning all humanity into a "global tribe," and the term *global village* is attributed to him.

Nowadays, the larger corporations organize production on a worldwide scale. Each step in the value-added chain, from research and development to processing of raw materials, production of parts, assembly of components, and marketing of the final product, is carried out in the most advantageous geographic location, regardless of where corporate headquarters are located or where the final good is sold. The globalization of markets means increasingly that similar goods are sold around the world for similar prices. The highly integrated financial and commodity markets see price movements in one part of the world instantaneously reflected in other major markets.

The BBC, CNN, MTV, and the Internet have accelerated the integration of global culture. Teenagers around the world watch the same videos, listen to the same music, and wear the same clothes. At the same time, television audiences in virtually all countries watch the same major events, listen to the same financial forecasts, and see the same three-minute glimpses of ecological disasters.

As globalization proceeds, the economic welfare of individuals is increasingly impacted by global market forces beyond the control of nation states and international institutions outside the domestic political process. Institutions such as the WTO and the IMF have become the target of criticism and protests from all sides. Some observers believe that too many economic decisions have been delegated to these institutions; others believe they should be given greater responsibility for solving the world's social and environmental problems. Some complain that they are secretive and unresponsive to civil society, while others worry about the loss of national sovereignty when citizen groups influence decision making in these institutions directly rather than indirectly through national governments.

Clearly, the reality of globalization has outstripped the ability of the world population to understand its implications and the ability of governments to cope with its consequences. At the same time, the ceding of economic power to global actors and international institutions has outstripped the development of appropriate global political structures. As a result, probably many more years of public confusion and unfocused protests can be expected as the stable new global world order takes shape. (GEZA FEKETEKUTY)

in Asia and strong growth in demand from the buoyant U.S. economy, helped to fuel the global expansion. World fuel exports increased 8% in volume terms but, because of higher prices, jumped by 46% in value terms. Sales of manufactured goods rose by 14% over 1999, while primary products (excluding fuel) increased by 11%.

In volume terms both the advanced and less-developed countries showed similar increases. The advanced countries provided strong growth markets. The U.S. and Canada increased imports by 13% (7.6% in 1999). Euro-zone imports rose 8.9% (6.3%), while imports to the U.K. rose 8.2% (7.6%). Japan bought 6.8% more than in 1999 (5.9%). Strong economic recovery in the NICs stimulated 14.1% more imports (8.3%).

In value terms, however, the rise in the rate of exports by the LDCs more than doubled to over 20%, and imports accelerated from a 1.5% annual increase to 15% in 2000. At the same time, the LDCs' share of world exports was increasing and reached 27.5% in 1999, compared with 17% in 1990. This rise reflected their greater manufacturing capability. Nevertheless, many LDCs remained extremely vulnerable to changes in commodity prices. In 2000 nonfuel primary commodity export prices showed a modest overall rise after four years of decline, largely because of the recovery in metals prices.

Unusually, the most rapid rise in exports was from Africa, where the increase was a record 25.6% (7.2% in 1999). The rise from sub-Saharan Africa was 22.8% (5.6%); imports increased by 9% after two years of decline. Asian exports rose 14% in dollar terms (14%), while the 17.3% growth in imports reflected the strong recovery in many Asian countries. Trade in the Middle East largely reflected higher oil prices, with exports rising 37% and imports up 15% after a 2.7% decline in 1999. Latin America's exports were up sharply at 18%, while imports rose 14% following a 6% contraction in 1999.

Regionalism. Although the concept of globalization was firmly established and the general thrust of many small as well as large businesses was to support it, the trend toward greater regionalism persisted. Membership of the WTO grew to 140 countries in 2000, and, with China expected to join early in 2001, the WTO was representative of most of the world's governments and people. Its prime goal was the liberalization of world trade in goods and services, which was compatible with, and essential to, globalization. (*See* Sidebar.) At the same time, regional trading arrangements with integration objectives and their built-in preferences and rules were proliferating. Global and regional interests were not always compatible, however, and this contributed to the WTO's difficulty in launching a new trade policy. There was also a risk that some of the world's poorest countries would be excluded if regional arrangements took precedence over the WTO. With 170 regional agreements in existence and another 70 under discussion, there were signs that the regional versus global debate was developing.

Established regional groups continued to work toward closer internal cooperation and expansion. After months of tense negotiations, the EU and the African, Caribbean, and Pacific (ACP) group signed a 20-year partnership agreement on June 23 in Cotonou, Benin. The Cotonou Agreement replaced the 25-year-old Lomé Conventions, the last of which, Lomé IV, expired in February. There were accusations that the EU was using the trade provisions of the WTO, to which the EU and 55 of the ACP's 77 members also belonged, to override the old agreement. ACP Secretary-General Jean-Robert Goulongana, however, claimed that the final accord would smooth the integration of the ACP member states into the world economy and benefit globalization.

In November government representatives of the 10 members of the Association of Southeast Asian Nations (ASEAN) held an informal summit in Singapore, which was also attended by China, Japan, and South Korea. An e-ASEAN Framework Agreement was signed under which a collective effort would be made to plug ASEAN into the global networked economy in order to increase ASEAN's global competitiveness. At the meeting China indicated its willingness to establish trading links with ASEAN or establish a free-trade zone between China and ASEAN; ASEAN was due to implement its free-trade agreement in 2002. Significantly, the China proposal was developed further and culminated in the idea of a free-trade zone for the entire region.

Exchange and Interest Rates. Once again the main focus of international interest was on the value of the euro against the dollar, as it had been since the euro's launch on Jan. 1, 1999. In early January 2000 the euro rose above the $1.03 level, having dipped below parity late in 1999. Thereafter it exhibited the same weaknesses as it had in its launch year, and, notwithstanding some volatility, the overall trend was downward. In the final weeks of the year, the euro's exchange rate was fluctuating at around 85 cents = €1, but it finished the year at about 94 cents. The euro also declined rapidly against the Japanese yen over the year, falling from a 1999 average of ¥121 = €1 to ¥93 in the last quarter of 2000. It strengthened slightly to end the year at ¥107.

The ECB announced in its January 2000 report that no direct intervention had been made to influence the euro's exchange rate. It admitted that the weakness of the euro had exacerbated inflation in the euro zone because of high oil prices. At the same time, the report gave details of the procedures to be followed if intervention did take place. Markets were not impressed, and when the decline persisted, the ECB on March 16 began a series of interest-rate rises. By April 27 the euro had fallen to new lows against all currencies, and there were fears that inflation would exceed the ECB's 2% limit. Markets responded briefly to a third rise in May, and the euro appreciated strongly against sterling and the dollar. Following a further 50 basis-point rise in June, however, the euro began to slip back again. Yet another interest rate rise at the end of August failed to stem the fall. On September 22 the ECB led a coordinated international intervention to prevent a fall below 85 cents; this was followed by another rise in interest rates on October 5. Confidence was dented further by a statement from ECB Pres. Wim Duisenberg that further intervention would not be appropriate. Nevertheless, the ECB continued to intervene with little success.

In Japan the BOJ began intervening in the market at the end of 1999 and in 2000 to prevent the yen from rising above 100 to the U.S. dollar; it saw the yen's continuing strength as a threat to Japan's fragile recovery. Despite the BOJ's interventions, the yen came under continuing pressure in the first quarter as confidence in the economy increased. Pressure was particularly acute against the euro, with the yen reaching record levels in March—a pattern that continued throughout the year. The lifting of the 18-month emergency zero-rate measure in August made little impact on the markets. In the last few months of the year, the yen was trading in a narrow band, dipping briefly after a no-confidence vote in the government on November 20, which, though it did not pass, was perceived as having left the country with a weak prime minister. The yen ended the year at 114 to the dollar.

In Australasia deteriorating economic conditions led to currency weakness and prompted increases in interest rates, but the currencies remained vulnerable to the strength of the U.S. dollar. In South Africa the inflationary pressure exerted by high fuel prices led to an increase of 25 basis points in the key repo rate in mid-October. This was not reflected in higher bank lending rates, however, for fear of dampening business confidence.

Japanese Prime Minister Yoshiro Mori (facing left in foreground) attends a meeting during the ASEAN summit in Singapore on November 24.

AP/Wide World Photos

Payments. As was predicted in 1999, the overall current account of the balance of payments in the advanced economies moved into deficit following six years of surplus. The deficit continued in 2000, rising to a projected $176 billion, compared with $134.2 billion in 1999. As in 1999, the negative cause of the overall deficit was the U.S. with its own deficit of around $420 billion, well up on the $331.5 billion of 1999.

Among the major Group of Seven industrial countries, only the U.S. and the U.K. had significant deficits. In the U.K. the deficit rose modestly to $20.9 billion ($17.8 billion in 1999). In Germany there was a dramatic fall from $19.8 billion to $3.7 billion. Of the other advanced European countries, only Spain ($12.6 billion), Austria ($5.8 billion), Greece ($5.7 billion), and Portugal ($11 billion) had deficits. Most other European countries were in surplus, led by France ($35.7 billion), Switzerland ($24.2 billion), Belgium/Luxembourg ($22.9 billion), and Norway ($22.6 billion). The euro zone remained in surplus despite the increased cost of imports.

The Japanese surplus remained high and was expected to exceed the 1999 level of $109 billion. Exports, particularly of semiconductors and office machinery destined for Asia, grew strongly. Trade with China was burgeoning and, at $38 billion in the first half of the year, was running 38% up on the same year-earlier period. In Australia and New Zealand there were falls from the record deficits of 1999 to $18.6 billion ($22.5 billion) and $3.2 billion ($4.4 billion), respectively.

All four of the Asian NICs had surpluses, led by Singapore with $22.1 billion ($21.3 billion). In South Korea the surplus fell sharply from $25 billion, which reflected the higher cost of fuel imports. In Taiwan there was a slight fall to $6.6 billion, while Hong Kong's rose to $11.2 billion ($9.3 billion).

The overall current account of the LDCs was expected to move into surplus for the first time in many years. The improvement from a deficit of $24.1 billion in 1999 to a $21.1 billion surplus reflected the higher oil prices. The 1999 surplus of $3.8 billion in the Middle East jumped to $43.9 billion. Improved commodity prices and agricultural output shrank the deficit of Africa from $16.8 billion to $3.6 billion. The Latin American deficit was little changed at $58.7 billion. In Asia the surplus fell from $45.2 billion to $39.4 billion because of the higher fuel costs.

Indebtedness of the LDC countries rose by a modest 1% to $2,068,000,000,000. Short-term debt, which accounted for 18% of the total, fell to $270 billion ($299 billion). Latin America, with $775 billion, remained by far the most heavily indebted region.

As a share of exports of trade and services, regional indebtedness fell from 164% to 140%. By this measure all areas improved, with Latin America's share falling from 260% to 225%, followed by Africa at 193% (from 237%) and the Middle East, which, with its debt falling from 122.5% to 94%, improved its relative position to third place. Asian debt fell from 104% to 99%. (IEIS)

STOCK EXCHANGES

The year 2000 opened to one anticlimax—the failure of the "Millennium Bug" to attend the party—and ended with another—the failure of the American electorate to be unequivocal in its choice of president. Throughout the intervening months, stock markets worldwide were highly volatile, dominated by speculation on the economic outlook for the United States and the tensions between "old economy" and "new economy" businesses. The vast disparity of price-earnings (p/e) ratios in the information technology (IT) sector compared with all other sectors was the single most influential factor in world market sentiment. According to the International Monetary Fund (IMF), this marked divergence, or bifurcation, of the stock prices of IT and non-IT sectors had been developing since the mid-1990s. What was newer was the growing market capitalization of the IT sector worldwide and the greater internationalization of capital markets. Those led to closer cross-border correlation of stock prices, particularly IT stock prices. The increased weight of IT stocks in national indexes amplified any general market volatility and left markets around the world highly sensitive to events, particularly in the U.S., the home country of most IT companies that operated internationally. Macroeconomic expectations exerted greater influence on the markets than before.

Investors' nervousness was heightened by rising oil prices, a falling euro, and, from late summer, the threat of war in the Middle East. The main victim of bearish sentiment had been the technology media and telecommunications subsector, the star of 1999, tarnished in the first quarter of 2000 by the high-profile collapse of some Internet, or "dot-com," companies. The aftershock of these collapses reverberated through the year, compounded by fears that many telecommunications companies might have paid too much for third-generation mobile telephony licenses. The technology-dominated National Association of Securities Dealers automated quotations (Nasdaq) composite index peaked on March 10 and by late November had fallen by 45.4%—more than the Dow Jones Industrial Average (DJIA) fell in the crash of 1987 but still leaving many high-tech companies at exceptionally high valuations unjustified by their profits.

As early as June some of the tech stocks that had entered the U.K.'s *Financial Times* Stock Exchange 100 (FTSE 100) index in March were out again because their valuations no longer met index criteria and old economy stocks had returned to favour. Against this background came moves, led in September by the U.S. company Dow Jones, to recalculate the weightings of stocks in global indexes to reflect the real number of "free float" shares that investors could buy and sell. Shares tied up in corporate cross holdings, privately or government held, would no longer count in the company's market capitalization. The likely effect was that investors would seek to avoid companies with low free floats, many of them high-grade blue-chip firms, particularly in Europe and Asia but also in the U.S.

The main concern of investors, however, was the long steady fall in share prices across sectors and regions. By

Financial Times Industrial Ordinary Share Index
Annual averages, 1977–2000

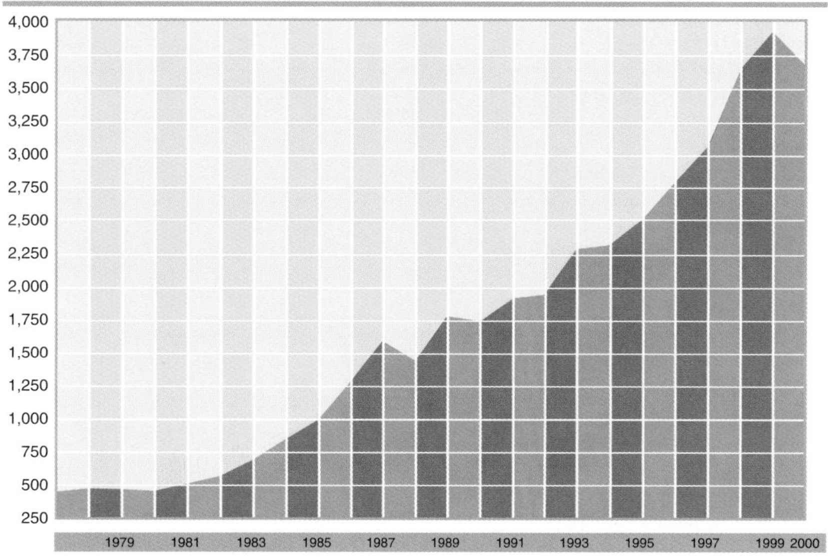

Source: *Financial Times.*

year's end the Morgan Stanley Capital International World Index had lost some 14%. (*See* TABLE V.) (IEIS)

United States. The longest bull market in history, with market indexes achieving unprecedented gains and trading volumes since it began in 1991, came to an end after peaking in March 2000. By the end of the year, all of the major indexes were down significantly. (*See* TABLE VI.) The DJIA slid 6.18%; the broader Standard & Poor's index of 500 stocks (S&P 500) was down 10.14%; and the Nasdaq composite index, heavily weighted with IT stocks, sank 39.29%. The Russell 2000, which represented mostly smaller capitalization (small-cap) stocks, was down only 4.2%, while the broad-based Wilshire 5000 fell 11.85%. The last time that all of those indexes had experienced no growth on an annual basis was 1981. Of the major indexes only the energy-heavy American Stock Exchange (AMEX) eked out a gain of 2.37%. The few big winners included indexes of financial stocks and utilities. Many top blue-chip stocks also were down, including AT&T, Lucent Technologies, and Microsoft Corp. Pharmaceutical companies such as Merck, Pfizer, and Eli Lilly, on the other hand, were up.

Adverse changes in the economy accounted for much of the market decline during the year. During the third quarter the economy grew at an annualized rate of 2.4%, less than half the second quarter's growth rate of 5.6%. Capital spending was down, while concerns about corporate earnings and a continued rise in oil prices and weakness of the euro were factors leading to investors' apprehensions about the short-term stock market prospects. The index of industrial production, which climbed steadily during the first three quarters of 2000, dipped by 0.1% in October. Business inventories in September were growing at their slowest pace in nearly two years. Personal income fell 0.2% in October, the slowest rate in six months. The Conference Board's Index of Leading Indicators declined irregularly between January and year's end.

The DJIA fluctuated between an all-time high of 11,722.98 in mid-January and a low of 9796.03 in March, after which it climbed to above 11,000 in April and then drifted irregularly throughout the remainder of the year. The Dow was down 9.4% at the end of November, which signaled its worst year since 1977, when it fell 17.3%. It strengthened slightly in the final days of the year to close at 10,786.85. The Nasdaq composite index, which ended 1999 at 4069.31, set monthly highs or lows six times in the first nine months of 2000—three monthly record gains and three monthly record losses—before plummeting in the final quarter to close at 2470.52. The 39.29% drop for the year was the Nasdaq's worst ever and was well greater than the 35.1% loss the index suffered in 1974.

Electronic communications networks (ECNs), automated trading systems that disseminated orders to third parties and dealers and executed such orders within the network itself, grew in importance in 2000. The nine registered ECNs, which focused on other brokers and institutional investors, captured approximately 26% of the volume of Nasdaq trading, and the expectation was that this ratio would rise to 50%. The networks' share of New York Stock Exchange (NYSE) volume was only 4% in 2000. During the year the Pacific Exchange (PCX) in Los Angeles merged with one ECN, Archipelago, to convert to an all-electronic system, closing down its trading floor. The ultimate goal was to create a fully electronic national stock exchange for NYSE, AMEX, and Nasdaq stocks.

Over half of all U.S. households owned stock either directly or indirectly through pension and mutual funds, by far the largest proportion ever. On-line trading accounts rose to 18 million by midyear. Trading volume and margin debt were on the rise. On-line stock-fraud cases also were up sharply, with the Internet replacing the brokerage "boiler rooms" of the past. The Securities and Exchange Commission (SEC) caseload nearly doubled during the year.

Net purchases of American stocks by foreign portfolio investors rose to more than $150 billion in 2000, a record high. Venture capital flows continued strong in 2000, although at a slower pace than 1999. More than $15 billion was invested by venture capitalists each quarter in the year 2000. More than 14 venture capital firms each raised upwards of $1 billion, with IT start-ups favoured.

Investor confidence gradually shifted during 2000 from optimistic to cautious, with concerns about a slowing economy. The initial public offering (IPO) market continued strong but was more selective than in previous years. New issues attracted $57 billion on 325 separate issues through August, up 59% over 1999's volume. Another 117 IPOs worth some $23 billion were issued in the remainder of the year.

Table V. Selected Major World Stock Market Indexes[1]

Country and Index	2000 range[2] High	2000 range[2] Low	Year-end close	Percent change from 12/31/99
Australia, Sydney All Ordinaries	3330	2920	3155	0
Belgium, Brussels BEL20	3311	2532	3024	–9
Brazil, Bovespa	18,951	13,287	15,259	–11
Canada, Toronto Composite	11,389	8114	8934	6
Finland, HEX General	18,331	10,506	13,034	–11
France, Paris CAC 40	6922	5450	5926	–1
Germany, Frankfurt Xetra DAX	8065	6201	6434	–8
Hong Kong, Hang Seng	18,302	13,723	15,096	–11
Ireland, ISEQ Overall	5941	4781	5723	14
Italy, Milan Banca Comm. Ital.	2182	1666	1916	5
Japan, Nikkei Average	20,833	13,423	13,786	–27
Mexico, IPC	8320	5232	5652	–21
Netherlands, The, CBS All Share	997	850	897	–4
Philippines, Manila Composite	2153	1251	1495	–30
Singapore, SES All-Singapore	696	487	502	–25
South Africa, Johannesburg Industrials	10,196	7433	8084	–12
South Korea, Composite Index	1059	501	505	–51
Spain, Madrid Stock Exchange	1146	858	881	–13
Sweden, Affarsvarlden General	6961	4731	4830	–12
Switzerland, SBC General	5770	4686	5621	12
Taiwan, Weighted Price	10,202	4615	4744	–44
Thailand, Bangkok SET	498	251	269	–44
United Kingdom, FT-SE 100	6798	5995	6223	–10
United States, Dow Jones Industrials	11,723	9796	10,788	–6
World, MS Capital International	1455	1179	1215	–14

[1]Index numbers are rounded. [2]Based on daily closing price.
Source: *Financial Times.*

During the third quarter, IPO issuance rose 24% to $18.2 billion from $14.7 billion for the same period of 1999. Follow-on issuance by already public companies rose 55% to $27.2 billion from the corresponding earlier period. Although the number of completed deals was down from 1999, the amount raised hit a record owing to numerous large $1 billion-plus IPOs that came out in 2000. More money was raised by IPOs in the first nine months of 2000 than in all of 1999. Among the major mergers of the year were General Electric's acquisition of Honeywell International for $45.2 billion and Chevron's acquisition of Texaco for $35.9 billion. The biggest deal, the $165 billion merger of Internet provider America Online, Inc., and media giant Time Warner, Inc., announced in January 2000, was still awaiting government approval at year's end.

Interest rates generally rose during the year, although the Federal Reserve (Fed) held official rates steady after announcing its sixth straight increase in May. At the end of November, key rates included the prime rate at 9.5% (7.75% a year earlier), the discount rate at 6% (4.5%), and the federal funds rate at 6.62% (5.58%). Three-month Treasury bills were 6.02% (5.08%); six-month Treasury bills were 5.89% (5.32%); and 10-year Treasury notes stood at 5.47% (4.16%). The 30-year Treasury bond, however, was 5.61%, down from 6.32%.

Volume on the NYSE for the first 11 months of 2000 was 239,539,935,000, up 29% from the 1999 figure of 185,369,204,000. The record for one day was 1,512,000,000, set April 4, 2000. Of the 3,999 stocks listed on the NYSE, 2,337 advanced in 2000, while 1,623 declined and only 39 were unchanged. Short interest hit a record on the Big Board through mid-November, betting on a market decline. The level of short sales not yet closed out, known as "short interest," rose 2.2% to 4,591,354,587 in the month ended November 15 from 4,494,751,764 one month earlier. A membership seat on the NYSE sold for $2 million on September 15. At the end of September, an exchange seat was bid at $1,750,000 and offered for sale at $6.5 million. Despite its rank as the world's largest centralized bond-trading exchange, the NYSE gave consideration to selling its bond-trading exchange at year-end 2000. Approximately 78% of NYSE bond volume was in straight fixed-income securities, with the rest in convertible bonds.

The stocks in the AMEX performed well in the first nine months of 2000, closing at 967.92, up 10.3% for the year to date. Although the AMEX slid in the final quarter to finish at 897.75, it was the only major index to end the year in the plus column. Of the 1,104 issues listed, 401 advanced, 665 declined, and 38 remained unchanged. Volume for the first 11 months was 11,902,736,000, up 26% from 7,335,678,000 in the corresponding period of 1999.

The dot-com "bubble" burst in 2000, and the average issue on the Nasdaq,

Table VI. Selected U.S. Stock Market Indexes[1]

	2000 range[2] High	2000 range[2] Low	Year-end close	Percent change from 12/31/99
Dow Jones Averages				
30 Industrials	11,723	9796	10,787	–6
20 Transportation	2981	2264	2947	–1
15 Utilities	416	274	412	46
65 Composite	3324	2752	3317	3
Standard & Poor's				
500 Index	1527	1265	1320	–10
Industrials	1918	1468	1528	–17
Utilities	353	221	351	55
Others				
NYSE Composite	678	576	657	1
Nasdaq Composite	5049	2333	2471	–39
Amex Composite	1036	847	898	2
Russell 2000	606	444	484	–4

[1]Index numbers are rounded. [2]Based on daily closing price.
Sources: *Financial Times, Wall Street Journal.*

New York Stock Exchange Composite Index, 2000 stock prices (Dec. 31, 1965 = 100)

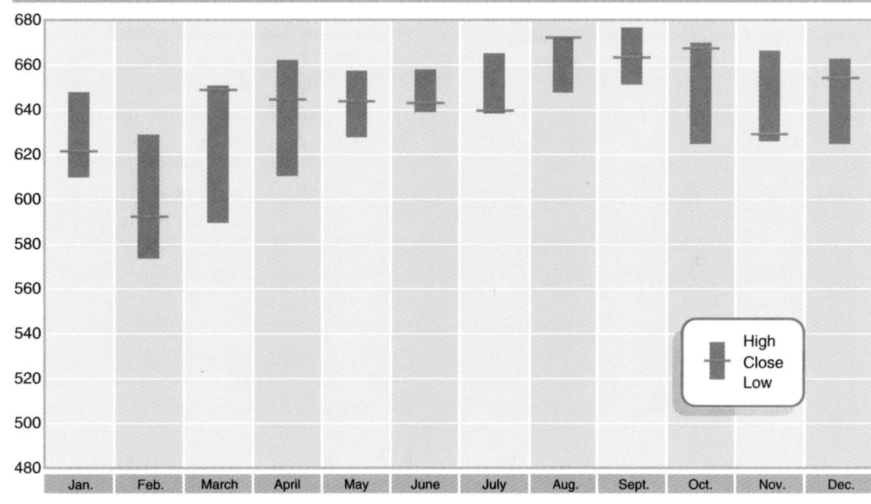

Average daily share volume in thousands of shares

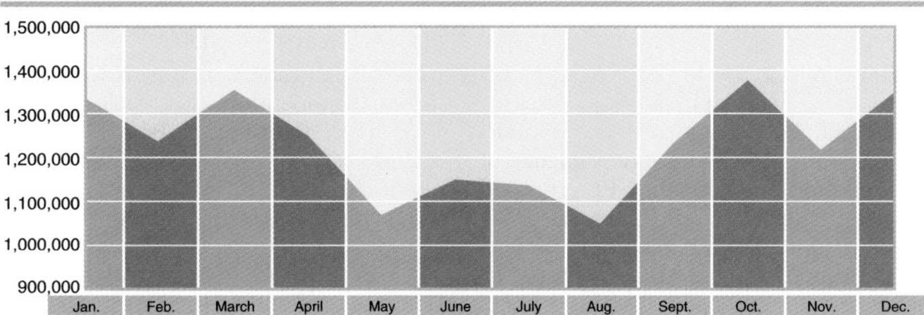

Sources: *Barron's National Business and Financial Weekly; The Wall Street Journal.*

AP/Wide World Photos

A man watches falling Nasdaq stock quotes in New York City's Times Square on December 20.

where most high-tech stocks were listed, was down 50% from its 52-week high at the end of November. The index plunged an additional 22.9% in November, its worst month since the crash in October 1987, and, despite a short rally, it fell even farther in December. After surging 40% in 1998 and 86% in 1999, the index fell sharply from its March all-time high of 5048.62 to end at 4069.31. Despite the overall plunge, 1,917 of the 6,765 Nasdaq stocks gained for the year, with 3,816 down and 48 unchanged. Volume on Nasdaq during the first 11 months of 2000 was 391,796,171,000, up 66.8% from 234,800,067,000 in November 1999.

Stock mutual funds attracted a net $231 billion in the first seven months of 2000. Net investments made into stock mutual funds peaked in February at $55 billion and then fell sharply to about $20 billion in May and under $20 billion by November. According to the Investment Company Institute, ownership of mutual funds reached a new peak in August 2000 to a record 50.6 million U.S. households. A year earlier the figure had been 47.4%, or 48.4 million households. Bond mutual funds sustained the strongest net outflows since 1994. First-quarter outflows were nearly $15 billion, with further declines during subsequent quarters. In order to ensure independence of mutual fund directors, the SEC proposed that a majority of directors be independent and disclose their investments in the funds on whose boards they sat.

The S&P 500 closed 1999 at 1469.2, peaked above 1500 in March 2000, and then drifted irregularly downward to close 2000 at 1320.28. The p/e ratio, based on expected earnings as reported by analysts, was 25.3 in January but then drifted down to 21.4 in the fourth quarter. This was the lowest p/e ratio for this index since October 1998.

Treasury bonds returned 13.9% and Treasury bills 3.9% for the year, both outstripping the 2.2% return from stocks, according to Ibbotson Associates. Convertible bonds set a record, with more than $40 billion being issued in the year 2000. Weak economic data helped push bond prices up. Bond yields fell to 15-month lows in August. The spread between U.S. high-yield bonds and 10-year Treasuries in percentage points rose steeply from 5% to more than 7% during the year. Concerns about the default risk and the flotation of record volumes of new debt issues accounted for much of the change. Disappointing corporate profits resulted in the downgrading of investment-grade bonds. Antitrust regulators launched an investigation of on-line bond-trading and foreign exchange systems owned by several of Wall Street's biggest securities firms to examine whether the trading platforms were used to limit competition.

A seat on the Chicago Board of Trade (CBOT) sold for $355,000 in 2000, down nearly $100,000 to a 20-year low. After topping out at $642,000 on April 14, the value of a CBOT seat had fallen nearly 45% by mid-August, a record low. Demutualization of the Chicago Mercantile Exchange resulted in a material downsizing in the layers of governance. More than 200 committees shrank to 14 during the year. The New York Mercantile Exchange also made the move to demutualization as a result of a favourable Internal Revenue Service ruling. With more than 10 million employees having unrestricted stock options, there were concerns about whether insider trading could be adequately regulated. The Commodity Futures Trading Commission filed a number of enforcement cases alleging that promoters used the Internet to claim that they had earned enormous profits from nearly fail-safe commodities-trading formulas.

The National Association of Securities Dealers (NASD) was very active in 2000. Through August, investors filed 152 margin-related arbitration claims with NASD Dispute Resolution, Inc., a unit of the NASD. That was up from 117 margin claims in all of 1999 and just 44 a year earlier. Nasdaq aggressively pursued market share in 2000. Among its major changes since its creation in 1971 was a proposal to establish "SuperMontage," a proposed new trading platform. SuperMontage would make Nasdaq more of a conventional stock exchange and less a network of market makers who quote prices at which they will trade with investors. Nasdaq's practice was to show each market maker's best price; under the new plan it would show up to three of a participant's best bids and offers. Opposition came from the ECNs, which contended that the system would discriminate against them and aggressively opposed SuperMontage.

The SEC also was very active in 2000, with initiatives to more aggressive enforcement of the securities laws. The SEC attempted to resolve the issue of auditor-consultant conflicts of interest by prohibiting auditors from representing the same companies for which they did audits. Accountants responded by spinning off their consulting arms. PricewaterhouseCoopers LLP, the largest accounting firm, negotiated to sell its consultancy to Hewlett-Packard Co. Ernst & Young LLP, the second largest accounting firm, sold its consulting arm in May. Audit failures provoked the interest by the SEC, which sought to have publicly traded companies disclose consulting fees paid to their auditors.

The U.S. Department of Justice and the SEC reported that the four major options exchanges—the Chicago Board Options Exchange, the AMEX, the PCX, and the Philadelphia Stock Exchange—signed a consent decree and accepted censure from the SEC but did not admit any wrongdoing. These exchanges were charged with restraint of competition by not seeking to trade options already traded on other exchanges. The SEC took steps to restrain selective disclosure of nonpublic information to selected persons and approved a move toward demutualization of the exchanges, following the move by the NASD to privatize. On June 13, 2000, the SEC ordered the exchanges and the Nasdaq market to submit a plan to phase in decimal pricing for listed stocks and certain options. The argument for decimal pricing was that it would be advantageous for international trading and would lower transaction costs owing to narrower spreads than were customary under the fractions quotation method common in the U.S. The first 13 U.S. stocks—seven on the NYSE and six on the AMEX—began trading in decimals on August 28.

Canada. The Canadian stock market had a positive year in 2000, with the Toronto Stock Exchange's index of 300 issues (TSE 300) up well above the previous year's high. In early December the index closed at 9230.59 for a 9.71% rise for the year to date, although it had slipped to 8933.70 (6.18%) by year's end. The Dow Jones Global Index for Canada showed a gain through August of 32.7% on a year-to-date basis. During the second half of the year, the market lost some of its momentum as the index plunged by 8.1% in one day with a sell-off of its biggest single component, Nortel Networks. Nortel accounted for almost one-third of the Toronto market's capitalization. Trading was halted at midday on August 25 owing to the overwhelming volume of trading.

Foreign investors swarmed into the Canadian market in 2000, according to Statistics Canada, a government agency. Foreign investors bought a total of Can$33 billion (U.S. $22.3 billion) of Canadian stocks in the first half of the year alone, compared with about Can$35 billion for the previous three full years combined. A Canadian shareholder study, sponsored by the TSE, found that 49% of adult Canadians directly or indirectly owned shares. This was a sharp increase from previous studies conducted in 1996 and 1989, which had indicated 37% and 23%, respectively. Share owners moved to on-line trading in substantial numbers. The growth rate in on-line trading was projected at 45% by year's end.

Trading volumes on Canadian stock exchanges in 2000 were 50% higher than in the previous year, with high-tech stocks leading the way. Canadian banks recorded higher-than-expected fiscal earnings, and this led to strong market activity. Among the most active issues on the TSE were Bank of Nova Scotia, Bank of Montreal, BCE Inc., Bombardier Inc., JDS Uniphase Canada Ltd., Nortel, Royal Bank of Canada, Seagram, Thomson Corp., and Toronto Dominion Bank.

The Canadian brokerage industry reported a nine-month operating profit of $2.8 billion, according to the Investment Dealers Association of Canada. This was more than double the year-earlier figure. The Canadian Venture Exchange (CDNX), a marriage of the Vancouver and Alberta exchanges, celebrated its first full year in operation. The CDNX, with nearly 2,300 companies listed, was down 34% from its peak of 4526.06, set on March 20. Computer problems halted trading for several hours on November 28. Technical problems also interrupted trading at the TSE, which was forced to close several

New York Stock Exchange Common Stock Index Closing Prices
Stock prices (Dec. 31, 1965 = 50)

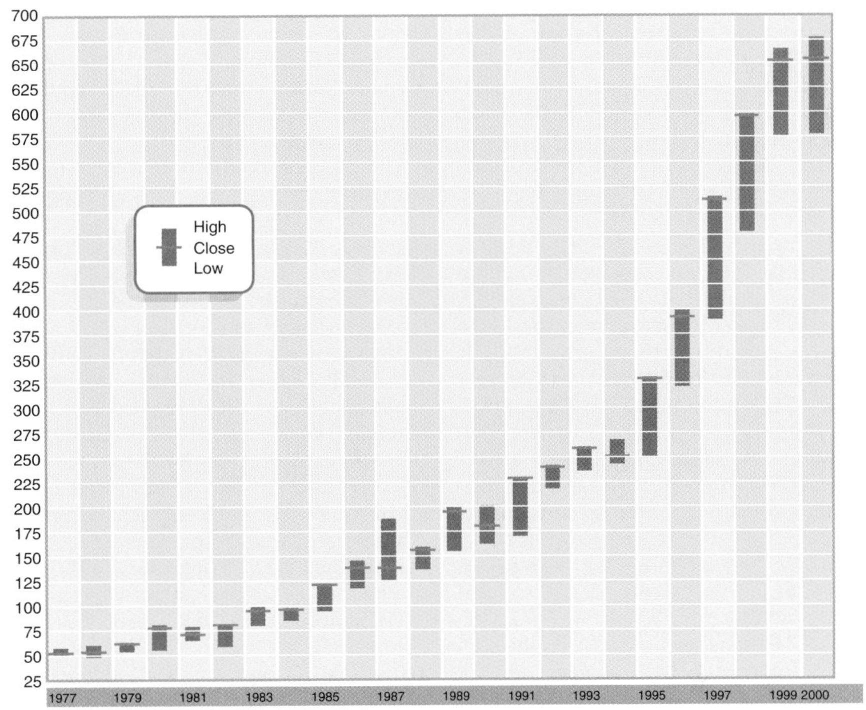

Number of shares sold
In billions of shares

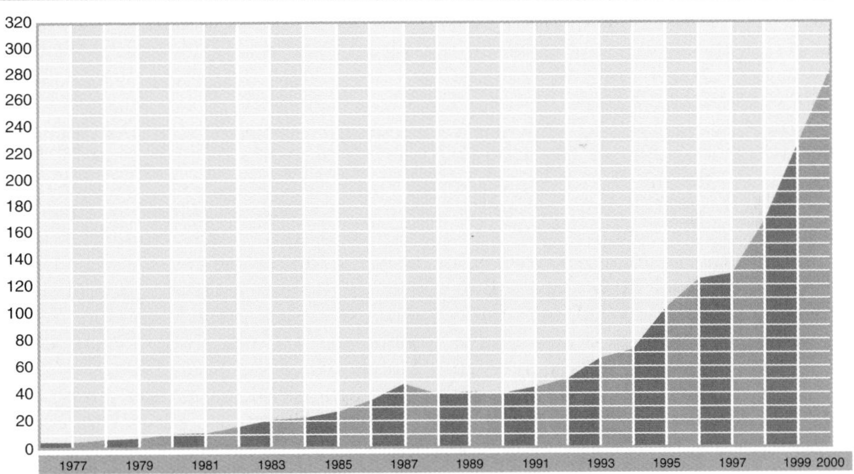

Sources: *Barron's National Business and Financial Weekly; The Wall Street Journal.*

times during the year. Nasdaq launched the first phase of Nasdaq Canada from its base in Montreal, in cooperation with the Montreal Stock Exchange.

The TSE index climbed to a 52-week high at the end of August, led by technology and energy shares, with Canadian banks also delivering strong performances. During November the TSE 100 at 559.43 was up 37.1%, the TSE 200 was up 14.2% to 492.05, and the TSE 300 was up 33.4% to 9024.43. By September oil- and gas-related issues had depressed the market and reduced the year-to-date gains in stock prices of major corporations, though the TSE 300 ended the year up 6.18%. On December 5 the TSE posted its second biggest one-day gain ever, climbing 3.74% on news that the U.S. might cut interest rates.

Canadian interest rates trended upward in 2000, with three-month money-market rates at 5.63% in November, up from 4.73% a year earlier. The prime rate was 7.5%; two-year government bonds were at 5.63%; and 10-year government bonds were down slightly to 5.55%, versus 6.14% a year earlier. Corporate bonds averaged 7.18%.

(IRVING PFEFFER)

Western Europe. The power of the American market continued generally to suck investment capital out of Western Europe, where economic performance undershot expectations and the euro continued to fall. Following the first quarter correction in IT stocks, mergers and acquisitions continued to generate some stock market activity. Outstanding among these was the British Vodafone Group's takeover of German telecommunications company Mannesmann. This was the world's biggest hostile bid and the first to succeed in Germany, Europe's largest economy. Mannesmann was made vulnerable to attack by the 60% foreign ownership of its shares—an indication of the growing equity culture in Western Europe.

The increasing European passion for equities received a reality check before the end of the first quarter. Technology media and telecom stocks plummeted as investors became aware of how long they would take to show profits. Germany's Nemax 50 Index halved in value between March and October. Dramatic stock market declines around the world on November 13 appeared to result not only from uncertainty surrounding the U.S. presidential election but also from worse-than-expected results from technology company Hewlett-Packard. By year-end 2000 the London FTSE 100 had fallen 10.2% and Germany's Frankfurt DAX was down about 7.5%, while the Paris Bourse's CAC 40 had slipped less than 1%. Rising consumer prices, an uptick in unemployment in France, failure to keep inflation below the European Central Bank's target rate of 2%, and the continuing decline of the euro all sapped confidence.

The IT-stock bubble burst early in the year, but the technological and logistic shakeout in the stock exchange companies took longer. Members of the London Stock Exchange (LSE) voted to demutualize on March 15 and pursued cross-border mergers with other European exchanges, principally Germany's Deutsche Börse. The merger of the LSE with Deutsche Börse to form International Exchanges (iX) was announced on May 3, with each former exchange to hold 50% of the new one. It was expected to form the biggest stock market in Europe. The practical and technical problems facing the iX venture, however, were enough to sow widespread doubt that LSE shareholders would support the merger. The Swedish technology company OM Group, owner of the OM Stockholm Exchange, entered a hostile $1.2 billion bid for the LSE on September 12, forcing the 200-year-old London exchange to withdraw the merger plans. LSE shareholders rejected the OM bid in November, but new partnership deals were under discussion with Nasdaq, Euronext, and the merged Paris, Brussels, and Amsterdam exchanges.

The year began with more liquidity (investors' cash) available than U.K. brokers, at least, could cope with. On-line brokerages were swamped with business as the small investors' appetite, particularly for Internet stocks, continued into the new year. An estimated 10% of share deals were being made on-line. Sentiment turned decisively negative in March when the U.S. Supreme Court ruled against Microsoft after a long battle over antitrust law. Flows into equity mutual funds generally slowed, shrinking the revenues of the new on-line brokerages that had expanded with the dot-com stocks bubble. In Europe the outlook for equities was almost unanimously bearish, although indexes in a few countries, notably Ireland and Switzerland, managed to show gains. (*See* TABLE V.)

Other Countries. Global trends powered by the U.S. economy dominated stock market behaviour in every region, but the high correlation of technology stock price fluctuations between Asia and the U.S. posed particular problems for Asia. Through their development of high-technology business, Asian markets had been directly exposed to the developed world's market fluctuations and to the increased influence of stock price fluctuations on the international capital flows. Any serious correction was likely to cut output in Asia more than in other regions.

The effect of oil price rises on the more oil-dependent countries of Asia and the reemergence of structural financial problems and political instability also added to stock market volatility. China, where the stock market looked set to end the year 50% up in dollar terms, was among the countries struggling most to pay the increased price of oil. The bill to China was predicted by the International Energy Agency to rise by around 250% by the end of the year.

Between mid-September and mid-October, the Philippine peso fell 8.1% following political scandal and government failure to contain debt. The currency strengthened again in November only on news of Pres. Joseph Estrada's impeachment on corruption charges, including price manipulation at the Philippine Stock Exchange. Most Asian stock exchanges also rose on this news, but political, economic, and fiscal problems remained for most countries. Even in Taiwan, where the financial status had appeared relatively sound, a financial crisis was looming by the end of the year. Between March and November the stock market fell by 35%. The Taiwanese government had been buying publicly traded equities in an attempt to shore up share prices, producing a flight of foreign capital from the Taipei stock market.

On Latin American stock markets, share prices were rising sharply at the beginning of the year, but investors later suffered the less-positive effects of market globalization. Some of the most actively traded shares were in companies sought by foreign owners, particularly large Spanish firms, and others were being traded in the U.S. Plans for the privatization of former state-run industries also added to the problem when large tranches of shares were sold to single buyers, often foreign consortia. The result was that there were fewer shares for local markets to trade. In local currency terms the Bovespa, the stock exchange in São Paulo, Braz., had hardly grown over two years.

Another globalization effect emerged when on May 3 Nasdaq announced plans to create the first "global digital stock market." In June shares of Japanese companies started trading on Nasdaq

Japan, a joint venture between Nasdaq and the Japanese Internet company Softbank. At the end of July, Nasdaq began exploratory discussions with representatives of 10 Middle Eastern stock exchanges. In the rush to go global, the Tokyo Stock Exchange began talks with the NYSE on creating a 24-hour global stock market. Analysts warned, however, that the problem with multiple currencies and their variable exchange rates was just one of several practical and technical obstacles to 24-hour trading.

Commodity Prices. The potential for the price of one staple commodity—oil—to destabilize world markets entered the realm of folk memory. In the 1970s similar rises ushered in a bear market in equities that lasted more than a decade. In February 1999 prices for Brent crude dipped below $10 a barrel. By Sept. 7, 2000, however, the price had hit a 10-year high of $35 a barrel; it later topped $37, setting off popular unrest across Europe against rising prices and the levels of taxation on fuel.

OPEC producers had been trying since March to raise the price to around $25 a barrel, but control over output had been too imprecise to achieve a measured and gradual rise. The price dropped back toward $30, only to spike up above $32 again in early October following freezing weather in the U.S. and growing Middle East tension. In response the U.S. government sanctioned the release of 30 million bbl of oil from its strategic reserve. The IMF estimated that prices sustained at 20% higher than in the first half of 2000 would reduce output by about 0.2 percentage points in major industrialized countries and as much as 0.4 percentage points in Asia. OPEC announced in November that it would no longer try to peg back the oil price, because an impending glut would send prices falling sharply over the next 12 months. The problem, it claimed, was not shortage of oil but shortage of refinery capacity and stocks. At the root of anxiety however, was the fact that, apart from a few OPEC members, most oil producers were operating at close to maximum output capacity. They had little incentive to invest in expanding capacity if the aim of this expansion was to cut prices and thus lower their own income.

While black gold dominated the news, the yellow metal kind failed to record the price rises predicted for it a year before. In July 1999 the price of gold had hit a 20-year low of $255 an ounce when the IMF announced plans to sell 300 tons of gold to aid international debt-relief programs. Following representations from the gold-producing countries, 15 European central banks agreed to restrict sales of official reserves to a total of 2,000 tons over the forthcoming five years. The gold price, having spiked up to $295 an ounce in December 1999, drifted back down to remain at around $273 for much of 2000, dipping to $264 on November 14.

In many nonfuel commodity markets, particularly in agricultural commodities, the level of prices remained low compared with 1997 pre-Asian crisis prices. In the wake of recovery, improved supplies had kept prices in check, but a further difficulty was the slow pace at which producers were able to adjust to changed conditions. For example, coffee, cocoa, and sugar carried high fixed costs that made it potentially profitable to harvest in the short term, even when prices were below production costs. Rising stocks might then also restrain prices.

Price increases were less than expected in most metals and industrial commodities, given the rise in global demand, for similar reasons. Only nickel attained a price increase above its average price in 1995–97. (IEIS)

BANKING

Industrywide consolidation, including significant cross-border transactions involving European banks and American securities firms, continued to reshape the global banking and financial services landscape in 2000. At the same time, however, enactment of sweeping financial modernization legislation in the United States did not trigger significant merger activity between banks and insurers—combinations that had previously been prohibited under federal banking law but had become permissible under the Gramm-Leach-Bliley (GLB) Act, which was enacted in November 1999 and became effective in March 2000.

The year's most dramatic merger transaction came in mid-September with the announcement that the Chase Manhattan Corp. had agreed to buy J.P. Morgan & Co. through an exchange of shares valued at the time at approximately $36 billion. The merger agreement between the American banking giants followed earlier rumours of a trans-Atlantic combination of Morgan and Germany's Deutsche Bank AG, which had completed the purchase of the Bankers Trust Corp. in 1999. In Germany merger talks between Deutsche Bank and Dresdner Bank AG and later between Dresdner and Commerzbank AG were announced and then called off. In December a proposed government-backed merger of Kookmin Bank and Housing & Commercial Bank in South Korea triggered massive protests and nationwide strikes by unionized bank employees.

Though each deal was only a third of the value of the Chase-Morgan merger, the acquisitions of Wall Street securities firms Donaldson, Lufkin & Jenrette (for about $13 billion) and PaineWebber Inc.

Exchange rates of major currencies to U.S.$, 2000

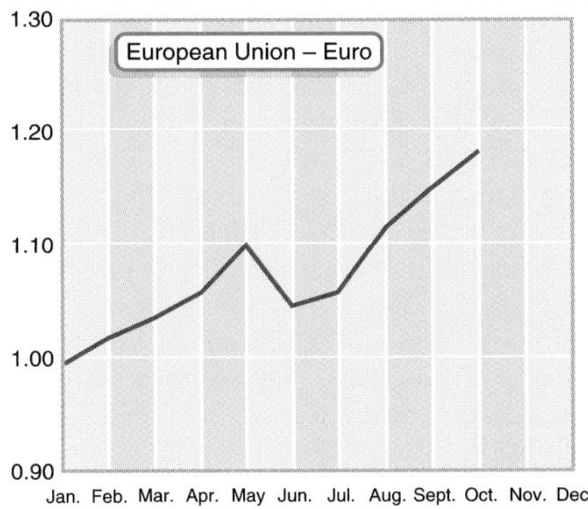

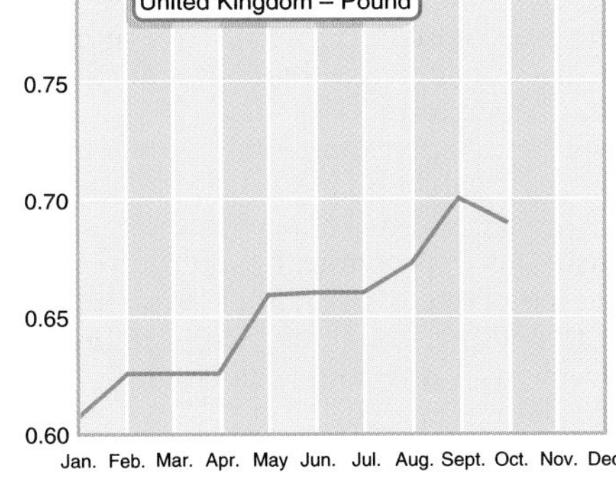

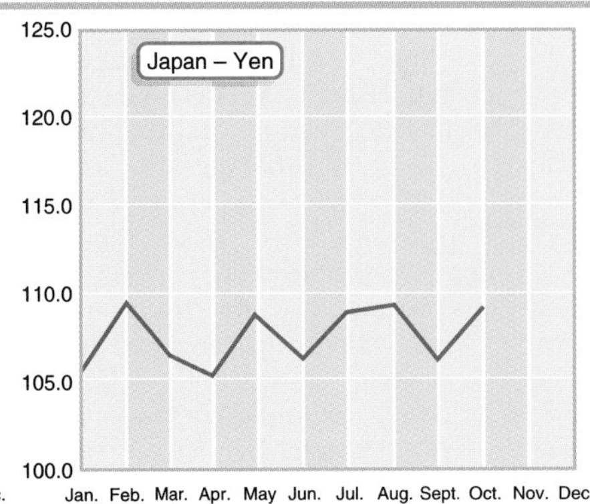

Source: International Monetary Fund, *International Financial Statistics.*

(for $11.8 billion) by Swiss banking giants Credit Suisse Group and UBS AG, respectively, stood out among the year's cross-border transactions, which further underscored the fact that competitive strategies were being driven by a reach for massive size and global scale. The MeritaNordbanken Group, created in 1997 by the merger of Finland's Merita Bank PLC and Nordbanken AB of Sweden, continued to expand across Scandinavia. Early in 2000 the bank purchased Unidanmark of Denmark, and in October the newly renamed Nordic Baltic Holding Group (NBH) announced the acquisition of Norway's Christiania Bank. The series of cross-border transactions made NBH, to be renamed Nordea AB, the region's largest financial institution.

Apart from the ongoing global consolidation, one of the most significant developments in 2000 was also the most anticlimactic—the smooth transition to the new year without any of the feared "Y2K" computer meltdowns. Indeed, there were strong indications that the intensive efforts by banks and other financial institutions around the world to renovate and test their systems and develop contingency plans for the year 2000 "millennium bug" yielded a number of important collateral benefits, including a better understanding and increased enhancement of their information technology systems and improvements in their business continuity planning.

Another development with important ramifications for the international financial markets in 2000 was the implementation of the euro, the single currency adopted by the 11 European Union (EU) members that then constituted the Economic and Monetary Union (EMU). Although the euro's trading value had declined since its inception on Jan. 1, 1999, the operational transition to the euro appeared to have been accomplished smoothly. Much work still remained to prepare consumers in EMU countries for the transition to the ultimate disappearance of their local currencies in favour of euro banknotes and coins as legal tender for cash transactions. This final stage was scheduled to occur by Jan. 1, 2002.

Meanwhile, a number of countries continued to grapple with the question of how to reform their domestic regulatory systems to enable them to meet the challenges presented by the formation of complex financial groups engaged in a diverse array of activities both at home and abroad. For example, Japan established a new Financial Services Agency, which would assume the responsibilities previously exercised by three agencies: the Financial Supervisory Agency, the Financial System Planning Bureau of the Ministry of Finance, and, when its mandate expired in January 2001, the Financial Reconstruction Commission.

Reviews of existing regulatory and supervisory relationships were also under way in South Africa and Switzerland, while Belgium and The Netherlands were striving to strengthen cooperation between existing authorities. Elsewhere, significant changes in the allocation of supervisory responsibilities within the financial sector were legislated in Latvia, where a new Financial and Capital Market Commission was due to assume responsibility for consolidated supervision of the financial system on July 1, 2001; in Turkey, which had vested bank-supervisory authority in a new Banking Regulation and Supervision Agency; and in Venezuela, where a Financial Regulation Board had been established to oversee the financial system. The global trend clearly was in the direction of some form of "umbrella" oversight, but there remained as yet no international consensus on what governmental authority or authorities should exercise this responsibility.

In the United States the Federal Reserve Board (Fed) was vested with statutory responsibility for oversight of financial holding companies established under the GLB Act. Culminating the 20-year effort to pass comprehensive financial-modernization legislation, the GLB Act repealed provisions of the Glass-Steagall Act that for more than six decades had restricted affiliations between commercial and investment banks. Unlike Glass-Steagall, the GLB Act permitted financial holding companies to own commercial banks and engage—through separate nonbank subsidiaries—in securities underwriting, insurance underwriting, merchant banking, and other types of financial activities. The appropriate primary bank regulators (including the Office of the Comptroller of the Currency in the case of national banks and the state banking agencies in the case of state-chartered banks) and functional regulators (such as the Securities and Exchange Commission in the case of securities broker-dealers and state insurance commissioners in the case of insurance companies) would oversee the component operations of a financial holding company, with umbrella oversight of the consolidated group entrusted to the Fed.

The GLB Act provided that international banks might qualify as financial holding companies if, among other conditions, they met a capital standard "comparable" to the "well-capitalized" standard applicable to American bank subsidiaries of domestic financial holding companies, which included both risk-based and leverage measures. The act further directed that this comparable standard be applied by the Fed "giving due regard to the principle of national treatment and equality of competitive opportunity." As originally announced by the Fed in January, the comparable-capital standard for international banks included both risk-based and leverage tests, notwithstanding that a substantial number of international banks operating in the U.S. were not subject to a leverage test under their home country's capital standards. In response to the very strong concerns raised by the international banking community and governmental authorities in other countries regarding the inclusion of a leverage test as part of the comparable-capital standard, the Fed in December removed the leverage test from the numerical criteria applied to international banks. Instead, it added the leverage ratio to the list of other factors it might take into account in assessing an international bank's capital. Other factors included the composition of a bank's capital and the rating of its long-term debt. Under this revised approach, the comparable-capital standard was applied on the basis of numerical criteria limited to an international bank's risk-based capital ratios determined in accordance with the internationally agreed-upon Basel risk-based standards.

There were a number of other significant developments occurring in global financial markets during 2000. Deposit insurance schemes were strengthened in several countries, notably France, Ireland, and Japan. A number of countries, including Brazil, China, Panama, and Turkey, instituted changes to enhance their banks' practices regarding classification of assets and loan loss provisions. Measures to improve banks' assessment of their country risks were introduced in Latvia and The Netherlands, while efforts to promote risk-management practices within banks in general were initiated in India and Israel. Corporate governance issues received increasing attention in several jurisdictions, including Australia, Hong Kong, and Singapore. Reforms in accounting and financial-reporting practices to bring them up to the level of international standards were adopted in Bahrain, the Philippines, and South Africa.

One theme common to many countries was the extensive effort under way to adapt banking and other financial services to developments in the "new economy"—for example, initiatives to promote Internet payment systems and virtual banking. Although exclusively on-line banks faltered, many traditional brick-and-mortar financial institutions increased their on-line components. The EU issued a directive establishing the legal framework for electronic signatures, while similar legislation was enacted in several countries, notably Australia, Colombia, and the U.S. The EU also took the lead in authorizing nonbanks to issue electronic money through the formation of electronic money institutions.

Action was taken, or was under consideration, in a number of countries to combat money laundering. Legislation prohibiting money laundering was introduced in Israel, while in other countries, including Italy and Japan, measures were enacted to expand the list of predicate crimes that could give rise to money-laundering violations. Actions to enhance the effectiveness of suspicious-activity reporting were instituted in Canada and Colombia. At the international level, the Financial Action Task Force on Money Laundering in June 2000 issued a report identifying 15 jurisdictions where the existing measures to combat money laundering were deemed to be inadequate. The 15 locations—which included such high-profile offshore financial centres as The Bahamas, the Cayman Islands, Dominica, Israel, Liechtenstein, the Philippines, and Russia—were described as "non-cooperative in the fight against money laundering." An additional 14 jurisdictions had been investigated. Just days before the report was released, six jurisdictions (Bermuda, the Caymans, Cyprus, Malta, Mauritius, and San Marino) issued letters offering to eliminate by the end of 2005 practices that had made them offshore tax havens.

Privatization of banks continued in a number of countries, including the Czech Republic and Poland. In Brazil the privatization of a list of large-scale government-owned assets was completed when Banco Santander Central Hispano SA, which already owned banks in 12 Latin American countries, won the auction to buy the state-run Banco do Estado de São Paulo SA, or Banespa, for a record price of nearly $3.6 billion. (LAWRENCE R. UHLICK)

BUSINESS OVERVIEW

The year 2000 was likely to be best remembered for hosting a changing of the guard in the business world. Stumbling was the "new economy" of technology start-ups, Internet sites operating without profits, and media-telecommunications companies; surging were some of the high elders of the "old economy": energy providers and a number of traditional manufacturers.

For the American stock market, the ebullience that marked the late 1990s seemed to have dissipated, as evidenced by the volatile stock performances of such New Economy icons as the Intel Corp. and Amazon.com. The cooling off of once red-hot areas such as telecommunications and technology contributed to poor performances in such areas as growth mutual funds and the high-yield corporate bond market.

Real gross domestic product growth for the U.S. was projected to be 4.3% for 2000, up slightly from 4.2% in 1999, but a slowdown in the second half of the year portended a reduced rate for 2001. Job growth was vigorous for much of the year, and the unemployment rate hovered at a 4% average, down from 4.2% in 1999. Wage growth was modest, while core inflation remained about 2.5%, and the unadjusted Consumer Price Index rose to 3.4%, partly because of rising oil prices.

The most vigorous performances came from some of the most traditional business sectors, especially the energy market. Out of fashion for much of the previous decade, energy companies showed a stunning return to form, in many cases posting record or near-record earnings. One of the most crucial influences was the spike in oil prices throughout 2000, with a year high for crude oil in September of $37.20 per barrel and a high of $1.68 per gallon for gasoline in June.

The top global firms in oil and gas—ExxonMobil Corp., BP Amoco PLC, Royal Dutch/Shell Group, Texaco Inc., and Chevron Corp. (the latter two set to merge early in 2001)—controlled a growing majority of the worldwide oil market. Such consolidation was likely to be echoed in the natural gas market in the near future, as analysts expected the current dozen major players to begin merging. Improving efficiencies and, most of all, high oil prices caused all major oil providers to exceed fiscal expectations. ExxonMobil, for example, earned $4,500,000,000 in the third quarter of 2000, up 105% from the third quarter of 1999. Chevron more than doubled its third-quarter net income, increasing to $1,531,000,000 while its proposed acquisition Texaco posted a record income of $798,000,000, up 106% from the same period in 1999.

Such influx of new profits allowed the major oil firms to expand their research and exploration-production operations as well as set the stage for further industry consolidation. Investors showed a preference for the top global companies at the expense of those with smaller capitalization; thus, the stock value of ExxonMobil was valued at more than 20 times earnings, while that of second-tier Phillips Petroleum Co. was only 11 times earnings. The lopsided situation gave more buying power to the top companies and seemed likely to provide them with further means to raid their less-valued counterparts in 2001.

The situation was muddier in the utilities sector, which continued to undergo a massive reorganization made necessary by the regulatory reforms of the previous few years. States in the U.S. ranging from California to New Jersey had broken up their former utility monopolies in the late 1990s, and this created at times a bewildering array of new utilities contending for market share. In many cases a former monopoly decided to split its businesses; for example, Consolidated Edison Co. moved out of the energy-production business, selling its power plants to new companies, in favour of the merchant power distribution market, in which utilities sell bulk power to buyers located across the U.S.

Some deregulation agreements eventually hindered the performances of the former monopolies. California utilities such as Pacific Gas & Electric and Edison International were caught in a fiscal bind, as their deregulation agreements had frozen the rates at which the companies could charge consumers, which caused considerable financial problems when the utilities were confronted with increases in oil and gas prices. The U.S. Federal Energy Regulation Commission in November ruled that the utilities could expand their methods of buying bulk power as a way to keep the companies solvent.

The confusion and volatility of the U.S. utility market also presented an opportunity for international power companies to begin incursions into North America. Such former national monopolies as Scottish Power and Italy's ENEL SpA, which had limited customer bases in Europe, saw the potential to win market shares in the U.S. and Latin America as a significant way to expand their growth.

The American auto industry experienced a mixed year during which most major car manufacturers posted healthy growth rates while at times being hob-

AP/Wide World Photos

Hyundai automobiles from South Korea sit in a storage yard in Newark, N.J.

bled by negative outside influences. The industry's light vehicle sales totaled about 18 million shipped for the year, said to be a new industry record. The growth of imports of new car and noncommercial light trucks was, however, just as impressive. While American manufacturers exported $40.2 billion of road vehicles in the first nine months of 2000, imports for the same period totaled about $106.4 billion. During the first nine months, imports from Germany increased 15.2%, those from Japan rose 15.9%, and, most notably, Korean imports increased 48.5%.

The surge in imports helped the Toyota Motor Corp., the Nissan Motor Co., and the Honda Motor Co., Inc., to post their best production rates in three years. Toyota, for example, increased its North American exports by 15.7% at mid-2000 but believed that increase would lessen to about 8% by the end of its fiscal year in March 2001.

The heightened presence of foreign competitors caused difficulties for American auto manufacturers. The Ford Motor Co. increased its total revenues by 9% to $127.5 billion for the first nine months of 2000, but its net income declined. Ford was also hurt by public relations damage from its association with Bridgestone/Firestone, Inc., which in August recalled 6.5 million tires after defective tires were blamed for a number of fatalities. The great majority of the tires in question had been equipped on the automaker's popular Ford Explorers.

Even worse was the lot of DaimlerChrysler AG. The merged company, which was considered in 1998 a herald of future North American–European supermergers, posted a $512 million operating loss for the third quarter of 2000 and saw its stock lose $60 billion in value from a $108 per share high in January 1999. DaimlerChrysler's production in North America declined by about 100,000 vehicles in the first three quarters of 2000, and the company began idling plants in late 2000.

Aerospace companies had a successful year overall. The American aerospace industry booked $32.4 billion in firm orders in June, shattering the previous record of $20.7 billion set in November 1997. Orders for the first half of 2000 totaled $85.4 billion, up from $62.6 billion in the first half of 1999. The recovery of the Asian markets helped increase export orders, although a strike at the Boeing Co. in early 2000 depressed exports in the first quarter. Manufacturers were also heartened by NASA's announcement in October of a long-term strategy for the exploration of Mars, which would result in expenditures of $500 million per year for the next five years.

The improved health of the industry generated a number of mergers, perhaps the most significant being the General Electric Co.'s $45 billion acquisition of Honeywell International Inc. Honeywell's space avionics division gives GE a foothold in space transportation, an area in which it had previously had no direct involvement. The Northwest Airlines Corp. and Continental Airlines, Inc., also explored a merger, but it was contested by the U.S. government in late 2000.

The metals industries contended with surging imports, a drawdown of inventories by spot purchasers, and a spike in natural gas prices. Steel companies were faced with the difficult equation of rising energy costs cutting into whatever increases in demand they received, although most top manufacturers still posted gains. For example, the U.S. Steel Group, the largest U.S. steelmaker, had third-quarter revenues of $1,430,000,000, up from $1,340,000,000 in the same period of 1999 despite a decline in steel shipments to 2.6 million tons for the quarter from 2.8 million a year earlier.

Steel production in the U.S. through late October totaled 94.8 million tons at a capability utilization rate of 88.3%, a 12% increase from the 85 million tons produced during the same period of 1999, when the capability utilization rate was 80.5%. Much of the industry's growth came from increased shipments to service centres, construction enterprises, and oil and gas manufacturers, while shipments to the automotive, industrial equipment, and appliance industries were down for the year.

For aluminum a strong first half was followed by slower third and fourth quarters, with declines in construction, forging, and fastener businesses caused by weakening demand. The leading worldwide aluminum producer, Alcoa Inc., posted net income of $1.1 billion for the first nine months of 2000, up 53% from the same period in 1999, but said that continued high energy costs seemed likely to be a constraint on future growth.

Gold-mining producers continued to be disappointed by poor prices. Although the price of gold had risen to $340 per ounce in late 1999 owing to an accord by 15 European central banks to limit gold sales and trading, prices sank back to the $260–$270-per-ounce range for much of 2000. The strength of the U.S. dollar throughout the year made dollar-denominated precious metals such as gold more expensive to international gold buyers, and there was also a decline in gold investments from traditional buyers in such nations as India and China.

The forest products industry experienced a dichotomy in 2000. Pulp prices soared, while lumber prices greatly deteriorated, and this created a situation in which companies increased their lumber production for the sole purpose of creating pulp. Prices for northern bleached softwood kraft—the benchmark grade of pulp—were $710 per ton in October, up from $600-per-ton average prices earlier in the year. Meanwhile, lumber prices fell roughly 31% compared with 1999, reaching $270 per 1,000 bd ft, while production at Western sawmills rose 2.6% to 22.1 billion bd ft in the first seven months of 2000. The situation created a good fiscal climate for such leading firms as the Georgia-Pacific Corp., Weyerhaeuser, and International Paper, which had contracts to supply lumber to construction shops such as Home Depot. International Paper, for example, registered a 21% increase in revenue during the first nine months of 2000.

The strong economy and overall low mortgage rates helped home builders experience one of their healthiest years of the last decade. Economists expected 2000 to post a near-record 5,970,000 homes sold during the year. The construction market experienced some cooling, however. Spending on residential construction fell at an annual rate of 9.2% in the third quarter, the first decline in a year, and, while housing starts began robustly with 1.7 million in January, they fell to a rough average of 1.5 million in the latter months. The manufactured housing industry was not as solid, as many of the top lenders of subprime mortgages and manufactured housing loans came under scrutiny. Conseco, Inc., a leader in mobile home lending, suffered a $489 million net loss in the third quarter alone.

There were a number of industries, however, that encountered trouble in 2000. The textile industry had a grim year, with many of the top American textile manufacturers, including Burlington Industries, Guilford Mills, Inc., and Galey & Lord, experiencing declines in revenues and thus being forced to undertake major personnel layoffs. The woes were in part due to a continued emphasis on business casual clothing in the American workplace at the expense of suits, as even such Wall Street firms as Goldman Sachs and J.P. Morgan had moved to a business casual dress code. The trade deficit continued to worsen for American textiles; apparel imports rose 14% to $37.9 billion, and textile imports were up 15% to $9.8 billion during the first eight months of 2000. Meanwhile, American apparel exports increased only 2.2% although textile mill product exports rose dramatically by 16%.

Many companies in the imaging/copying business suffered, in part owing to softening demand as well as to the growing use of digital alternatives to their products; this trend gave the edge to such Asian companies as Canon Inc. The traditional business of such manufacturers as the Polaroid Corp., the Eastman Kodak Co., Lexmark International, Inc., and Pitney Bowes Inc. suffered, but one of the most adversely affected was the Xerox Corp. Xerox, which experienced a net loss of $167 million in the third quarter alone and did not expect to recover until mid-2001, planned to hold a fire sale for its operations, including ventures in Japan and China and its highly regarded research center in Palo Alto, Calif.

The increase in oil and gas prices was felt yet again in the chemicals industry, where many major firms experienced business declines owing to higher operating expenses. E.I. du Pont de Nemours and Co., the largest worldwide chemical company, served as a case in point. The firm's decision to sell its oil subsidiary, Conoco, in 1999 may have hurt it in 2000, as one of DuPont's major problems was contending with ballooning operating expenses caused by high oil and gas costs. DuPont's operating earnings fell by 14% in the third quarter of 2000 alone.

DuPont was not alone in its woes. The Union Carbide Corp., the Rohm and Haas Co., and the PolyOne Corp., among others, struggled in 2000 as energy costs rose and the weak euro caused export sales to Europe to slow. The Dow Chemical Co. during the year mounted a challenge to DuPont's supremacy through its proposed takeover of Union Carbide, as well as by going against the industry grain by posting record sales increases. Raising its sales prices helped Dow avoid being submerged by energy cost increases.

Two industries—pharmaceuticals and tobacco—were perhaps the most affected by government actions in 2000, though with vastly different results. The large pharmaceutical companies became one of the cornerstones of Vice Pres. Al Gore's presidential campaign when Gore charged the manufacturers with spending too much on advertising and overcharging consumers. Sentiment in the U.S. Congress also ran against the interests of pharmaceutical manufacturers. In July legislation was passed to reduce restrictions on imported drugs, considered a loss for American pharmaceuticals' lobbying interests. Legislation was also considered that would greatly expand Medicare coverage for seniors, in some cases putting one-half of prescriptions under price controls. Both Gore and rival presidential candidate Texas Gov. George W. Bush supported some measure of prescription drug relief.

The top pharmaceutical companies, however, continued to prosper despite the political attacks. Pfizer Inc., the American Home Products Corp., and the Schering-Plough Corp. posted solid increases in earnings on the strength of their prescription drug businesses. Pfizer, for example, had a 31% earnings increase in the third quarter, helped by the popularity of such products as Viagra and cholesterol fighter Lipitor.

Along with threats of government action, however, was a rising threat by generic pharmaceuticals. Generics worked to whittle away at drug monopolies held by the large companies, often beating their rival's legal challenges. For example, a federal district court in August approved Barr Laboratories' plan to market a generic alternative to Eli Lilly and Co.'s Prozac, starting in 2001. The decision gave generics the green light to go after such popular drugs as AstraZeneca International's Prilosec and the Bristol-Meyers Squibb Co.'s Glucophage. Generic pharmaceutical manufacturers also received a boost via Congress, as legislation introduced in September was designed to streamline the federal approval process for generics.

Ironically, perhaps the most reviled industry of the previous decade experienced a healthy year overall. Tobacco companies, especially industry leaders R.J. Reynolds Tobacco Co. and Phillip Morris Co., began a recovery in 2000 after a decade in which the once-invulnerable industry endured a series of legal challenges that culminated in the $206 billion settlement in November 1998 between tobacco manufacturers and 46 states. As the year progressed, it became clear that the major tobacco companies had been able to stem the tide against further legal action as well as increase their revenues.

The U.S. Supreme Court ruled in March that Congress had not empowered the Food and Drug Administration to regulate tobacco, and legislation introduced subsequently to give the FDA such powers stalled in Congress. In addition, tobacco companies won several significant consumer lawsuits throughout the year in which states had tried to gain punitive damages. The companies also were in better fiscal shape, as R.J. Reynolds posted an 8% increase in income from continuing operations for the first nine months and Phillip Morris's profits were up 15% at the end of the third quarter.

The cigarette companies were not home free, however. The impact of tax-influenced price increases was felt, as manufacturers had to raise prices by 13 cents per pack in January and again by 6 cents in July. There was also a growing discomfort about the long-term potential for tobacco companies, which resulted in their stocks' becoming less favoured by a number of investors. For example, the U.S.'s largest pension fund, the California Public Employees' Retirement System, voted to divest its $560 million of tobacco stock holdings.

Consequently, it appeared that even the healthiest of industries had an inevitable downside during 2000, influenced by such factors as rising energy costs and general market uncertainty about Internet technology. Market analysts and investors concluded, however, that the return to form by such disparate industries as oil drillers and tobacco manufacturers showed that traditional industries may not be as appealing as those in high-tech enterprises, but they often are more rewarding.

(CHRISTOPHER O'LEARY)

Education

Noteworthy during 2000 were efforts to improve **SCHOOLING**, inequitable educational **OPPORTUNITIES**, controversies concerning the **TESTING** of teachers, strategies for **FINANCING** higher education, innovations in **DISTANCE EDUCATION**, and the **POLITICAL ACTIVITIES** of university students.

Primary and Secondary Education. During April the 1,500 delegates from 181 countries attending the World Education Forum in Dakar, Senegal, assessed the past 10 years of progress toward the goal of universal primary schooling that had been set at the 1990 World Conference on Education for All in Thailand and also established new goals for the future. The 10-year assessment revealed that whereas some progress toward universal education had been achieved, the 1990 dream of schooling for everyone had not been realized. An estimated 113 million children (mostly girls) still had no access to primary education; 880 million adults were illiterate; gender discrimination continued to permeate education systems; and the quality of learning often fell short of the needs of societies. Goals that Forum delegates aspired to reach by 2015 included providing all children free, compulsory primary schooling of good quality; achieving gender equality in educational opportunities in both primary and secondary schools; and reducing adult illiteracy by 50%.

A study by the Organisation for Economic Co-operation and Development (OECD) summarized the condition of education for two-thirds of the world's population. The report included 29 OECD member nations and 16 nonmembers. Twenty-five of the OECD nations were located in Europe and North America; the remaining four nations were Australia, Japan, New Zealand, and South Korea. The nonmember group included China, India, Russia, and a variety of less-developed countries in Africa, South America, and Southeast Asia. The report identified the following trends:

During the 1990s the average number of years a five-year-old child would spend in school in OECD countries rose from 15.1 to 16.4; the number varied widely, however, from 9.7 years in Turkey to 12.2 years in Mexico, 16.8 in the United States, 17.1 in the United Kingdom, and 20 in Australia.

By the end of the decade, the average adult within the age range of 25 to 64 had participated for more than one year in continuing education.

In the year 2000 approximately 40% of young people could look forward to entering a postsecondary-school program leading to the equivalent of at least a bachelor's degree. Near the close of the 1990s, about one-third of students who entered higher education in OECD countries left before earning a degree. Survival rates ranged from over 80% in Japan and the U.K. to 63% in the U.S.; 55% or less in Austria, France, Portugal, and Turkey; and 35% in Italy.

In many OECD countries teachers were among the most highly educated workers, but their salaries after 15 years of experience were generally lower than the average earnings of other university graduates.

Another OECD report, *Literacy in the Information Age,* compared 20 nations in terms of the reading and calculating skills of people between ages 16 and 65. Literacy was judged on a five-level scale ranging from "very poor" (level one) to "higher-order information processing skills" (levels four and five). The report concluded that in the countries studied, "between one-quarter and three-quarters of adults fail to achieve literacy Level 3, considered by experts as a suitable minimum skill level for coping with the demands of modern life and work." Participants from Nordic countries (Denmark, Finland, Norway, and Sweden) had some of the highest scores. The five lowest-scoring nations were Chile, Poland, Slovenia, Ireland, and Hungary. A separate study conducted in the U.K. estimated that 24% of British adults were both functionally illiterate and functionally innumerate (unable to perform simple mathematical functions).

Attempts to improve the quality of education assumed a variety of forms. The U.S. charter-school movement, which provided public funding for independently operated schools, continued to expand. At the beginning of the 1998–99 school year, more than 250,000 students were enrolled in 1,605 schools in 30 states and the District of Columbia; 90% of the schools used student achievement

Hispanic students practice writing essays in Spanish in their classroom at Saul Martinez Elementary School in Mecca, Calif.

AP/Wide World Photos

tests and other measures to reflect the effectiveness of their programs. Although more than 70% of charter schools were newly created institutions, in 11 of the 36 states with existing charter laws, private schools were allowed to become publicly financed charter institutions.

There was an increase in support for U.S. voucher programs that offered public funds to finance attendance by children at any school chosen by their parents. During the year, 25 states introduced new voucher legislation. At the same time, the number of American children who were home schoolers reached an estimated 1,500,000, an increase from 700,000 in 1995.

The Ugandan government's Universal Primary Education program, launched in 1996, was well on its way toward its goal of enrolling all primary-aged children in school by 2003. Enrollment had grown from 2.3 million in 1996 to 6.5 million by 2000, with much of the increase due to increased government financing, the help of such nongovernmental organizations as World Vision, and the donation by parents of their labour for constructing and maintaining buildings.

Russian educational leaders voiced fears about the future of the nation's prestigious mathematics and physics secondary schools. The special schools, established in the 1960s and 1970s at the urging of the Soviet Union's leading scientists, had proved successful in preparing youths for distinguished careers in science. Since the dissolution of the Soviet Union, however, the schools' viability had been threatened by a variety of problems, including shortages of funds, public disillusionment with science's contribution to the quality of life, fewer bright students' choosing science as a field of study, the emigration of talented Russian scientists, and the establishment of new "special schools" that were generally considered inferior copies of the originals.

In Nepal the Rugmark Foundation continued to provide hostels for youngsters who had formerly been among the estimated 2,000 children working in carpet factories that sold their products to Western nations. The hostels, with aid from UNICEF, provided children with living quarters and education. The Nepalese government, in a further move to reduce the exploitation of the young, announced plans to outlaw the employment of children in factories.

Fearing that harmful side effects might result from hyperactive preschool children's taking such calming drugs as Ritalin and Prozac, the U.S. government prepared a guidebook for parents and teachers that described proper ways to treat young children who suffered from emotional and behavioral disorders. The U.S. Food and Drug Administration also required drug companies to apply new labels to psychiatric drugs, informing physicians of proper dosages for children. In addition, drug companies would receive directions on how best to conduct research on hyperactivity and attention-deficit medications.

The issue of educational equity attracted attention in Hungary, China, and Great Britain. Hungary's inadequate educational provisions for Roma (Gypsy) children were blamed on the majority population's faulty perception of their culture. (The Roma made up 5% of the population.) Critics charged that an inordinate number of Roma children were placed in classes for the mentally disabled because school personnel failed to recognize the children's actual learning potential. A program initiated by the Zsambek Catholic Faculty of Teacher Training was designed to help teachers understand Romany cultural characteristics so that Gypsy pupils would not be seen as inferior simply because of their social background.

Western analysts estimated that despite Chinese government regulations intended to keep peasants on the farm, during recent years 200 million–300 million people had moved to urban centres in search of employment. By living in illegal settlements on the outskirts of cities, the migrants failed to qualify for government-supported schooling. Consequently, they created their own primary schools, using volunteer teachers who were paid a small wage out of tuition fees. In 2000, when an estimated 100 such schools were operating on the fringes of Beijing, government officials decided to alter the existing regulations and begin supporting migrant schools.

In the U.K the expenditure on education would rise by 5.4% each year between 2001 and 2004, reaching a total increase of almost £12 billion (£1= about $1.45). Each primary school would receive up to £40,000 annually and each secondary school up to £70,000. Nearly 200,000 teachers applied for the plan's £2,000 performance-related pay (PRP) for teachers whose students scored high on exams. Teachers unions denounced the PRP program, claiming it would adversely affect the recruitment and retention of teachers.

National and regional plans for testing students and their teachers proliferated. The Vietnamese Ministry of Education and Training prepared the nation's first large-scale educational survey, focusing on the fifth grade in more than 3,000 schools that were chosen to represent all 61 of the nation's provinces. Both pupils' and teachers' skills in reading comprehension and mathematics were scheduled for testing in early 2001, with questionnaires to be filled out by pupils, teachers, and administrators in order to reveal conditions in children's lives that affected their school success.

In Canada's province of Ontario, Premier Mike Harris proposed to raise the level of students' learning by testing all 100,000 of Ontario's teachers. The task of designing and implementing his proposal within the following few months was assigned to the Ontario College of Teachers, Toronto. The plan reached a stalemate when the college responded with a 100-page report summarizing the problems of trying to improve students' learning by testing teachers. The report suggested that better preservice education, guidance for new teachers, and mandatory in-service professional development would yield greater student achievement than would testing in-service teachers.

The American Federation of Teachers, the second largest teachers union in the U.S., with nearly one million members, advocated testing aspiring educators as a way of improving student achievement. The National Education Association, the largest teachers union, opposed the plan, claiming that testing would interfere with existing efforts to raise standards during the current nationwide shortage of teachers.

In response to news that the average achievement-test scores of 4.7 million California students remained below the U.S. national average, the California Department of Education reported that when the scores of the state's one million students from non-English-speaking backgrounds were set aside, the scores of the remaining English-proficient students were above the national average. Whereas the national sample had included only 1.8% of students from homes where English was spoken either little or not at all, California's testing had included 25% of such students. Officials also noted that after the state in 1998 eliminated nearly all bilingual education programs in favour of English-immersion plans for immigrant children, the test scores of such students improved.

AFP Worldwide

Striking and nonstriking students at Mexico City's National Autonomous University clash in late January.

Higher Education. Universities and colleges in the U.S. profited from the country's strong economy. The government's large tax-income surplus emboldened Congress to vote more than $1 billion in special-project funds to be divided among institutions in the U.S. and its territories. The allotment exceeded the 1999 total by 31%. Colleges and universities also experienced growing success with fund-raising campaigns, particularly in their efforts to attract major contributors.

Russia's largest bank, Sberbank, announced plans to offer students loans to pay the tuition costs that had become an increasingly important requirement for attending college. An estimated 1.1 million of the nation's 4 million college and university students would be paying for their education during the current year. Sberbank Pres. Andrey Kazmin said that $53.8 million had been designated for the low-interest-loan program, with each loan sufficient to cover 70% of a student's educational expenses.

In addition to their fund-raising, some U.S. institutions were attempting to lower the expense of certain programs. To reduce the annual $10 million cost of remedial classes, the 22-campus California State University system (359,000 students) adopted the dual approach of requiring entering students to become competent in basic English and mathematics skills within one year or be subject to dismissal and helping secondary schools prepare students to pass university placement exams. In recent years nearly half of the entering freshmen had needed remedial studies in English or math. University officials hoped to cut that number to 10% by 2007.

The California legislature in September set up the nation's largest state-financed college scholarship program in the U.S., a plan providing at least $1.2 billion annually to pay tuition and other costs for all low-income students with a grade point average of at least C and all middle-income students with an average of B or higher. "Low income" was defined as annual earnings of $33,700 or less for a family of four and "middle-income" as $64,100 or less for a family of four. Grants would begin during the 2001–02 academic year.

Distance-education programs continued to multiply. In India, where only about 6.5% of high-school graduates entered higher education, compared with 30% in developed nations, additional distance-education programs were being created to meet the huge demand for college degrees. By 2000, 63 of India's more than 200 universities furnished distance courses via the mail, radio, television, and computer networks.

The U.S. Army intended to spend $600 million during the next six years to furnish laptop computers and distance-learning courses to all of its soldiers, a plan that potentially would produce one million distance-education students. The program was designed to improve the army's image and its ability to attract new recruits.

With a start-up fund of $129 million, the British government established a University for Industry, which planned to focus on teaching vocational skills. The university's operating base would be 178 existing local learning centres, a number soon to be expanded to 250. Students would be able to access most courses through the World Wide Web. The initial course offerings were in the fields of accounting, information technology, and business management.

Concern in China over rote-memorization instructional practices in the nation's 56 programs offering master's degrees in business administration inspired innovative educators to import business-education methods from Europe and the United States that emphasized the flexible problem-solving skills needed by real-life managers. Typical of the cooperative ventures was the China Europe International Business School in Shanghai, funded jointly by the city government and the European Union. Another was Shanghai's Center for Business Skills Development, affiliated with Thunderbird, the American Graduate School of International Management, in Glendale, Ariz.

In March the Canadian Association of University Teachers sent a letter to Prime Minister Jean Chrétien denouncing a 60-page report—titled *Public Investments in University Research—Reaping the Benefits*—that was published by Industry Canada, a federal government agency. The report had urged professors to focus their research on developing goods and services useful in the marketplace. The report also had recommended that professors' efforts to commercialize their research be recognized in tenure and promotion decisions. Association representatives contended that adopting such a policy would violate professors' freedom of inquiry and be devastating to many traditional fields of knowledge.

Student political activities created difficulties for officials in Yugoslavia, Israel, Mexico, Iran, and the U.S. A Yugoslav organization named Otpor (Serbian for "resistance") was created in 1998 by 15 students at the University of Belgrade. Within two years it had expanded to 126 chapters nationwide with nearly 30,000 members, most of them students dedicated to the organization's primary aim, the nonviolent removal of Slobodan Milosevic as Yugoslavia's president. During 2000, when police and Milosevic supporters discovered that detaining and interrogating Otpor members failed to stop the resistance movement, they increasingly administered violent beatings.

After several relatively peaceful years for student groups on Israel's university campuses, violent demonstrations that pitted Arabs against Jews and university administrators broke out in April at the University of Haifa. The troubles soon spread to other campuses. Arab students, who accounted for 18% of Haifa's enrollment, claimed that the university administration had violated their right of free speech and had refused to permit the teaching of some courses in Arabic rather than Hebrew, even though Arabic was one of the nation's official languages. Jewish students accused Arab politicians, and particularly those in the Communist Party, of inciting the demonstrations.

A 9½-month student strike at Mexico City's prestigious National Autonomous University ended in February when police removed 745 activists from the campus so that classes for the institution's 270,000 students could resume. Although many of the strikers' demands had been met, the more basic question of the university's proper role in Mexican society remained unsettled. The question was: Should the institution's primary aim be to emphasize academic excellence and research or to fulfill the ideal of providing education for everyone who sought it?

In July police in Iran's capital, Tehran, used tear gas to disperse flower-bearing pro-democracy Iranian students who marched in peaceful protest on the anniversary of a 1999 bloody police attack on a university dormitory. Demonstrators who failed to leave the streets were later pursued by several hundred right-wing vigilantes armed with clubs and electrical cables. Observers suggested that the police action was an attempt by conservative Islamic religious forces to intimidate supporters of Pres. Mohammad Khatami's social reforms.

In the U.S., representatives of the Students of Color Coalition seized the offices of Michigamua, a traditionally exclusive club at the University of Michigan at Ann Arbor, where they found Native American artifacts and photos of Michigamua members engaged in rituals employing Native American regalia. The Students of Color charged that the club had violated a 1989 agreement to cease using Native American customs in their ceremonies. Students of Color Coalition members demanded that the artifacts be returned to the Native Americans and that the university revoke its association with Michigamua. (R. MURRAY THOMAS)

The Environment

Rising **FUEL PRICES,** global warming, uncontrollable **FOREST FIRES,** and the transportation of **SPENT NUCLEAR FUEL** were among the major environmental concerns of 2000. **WILDLIFE CONSERVATION EFFORTS** also made headlines, as did a pair of young **GIANT PANDAS.**

INTERNATIONAL ACTIVITIES

On Feb. 3, 2000, the European Parliament passed the second reading of the end-of-life vehicles directive, and on May 23 a committee of diplomats and members of the Parliament agreed to its terms. The directive would require automobile manufacturers to pay all or a significant part of the cost of scrapping cars.

On July 4 the European Court of Justice in The Hague imposed daily fines on Greece for continuing to use a landfill site in the Chania area of Crete in breach of two waste-management directives. The Greek government was ordered to pay €20,000 (€1=about $0.84) a day from July 4 until it complied with the law. Greece agreed to the judgment and set a target date at the end of November. By that time the total fine was nearly €3 million.

Popular protests against high taxes on gasoline (petrol) and diesel fuel erupted across the European Union (EU) in September. The U.K. was the country most seriously affected. Freight haulers and farmers blockaded oil refineries and managed to prevent most gasoline and diesel supplies from reaching gas stations and public services such as hospitals. The blockade caused panic buying that emptied gasoline stations within days and almost brought the country to a standstill. People then began buying in food stores, creating local shortages. On September 26 about 7,000 German drivers blocked the central thoroughfare to the Brandenburg Gate in Berlin, but they left a lane free for public transportation.

NATIONAL DEVELOPMENTS

China. On August 8 the Xinhua News Agency reported that the Shenyang Smeltery had been closed in June because of the pollution it caused. The factory, in northeastern China, was said to have been discharging 74,000 tons of sulfur dioxide and 67 tons of heavy metals each year. It affected about 50 sq km (20 sq mi) of Shenyang, once one of the 10 most polluted cities in the world, and accounted for about 42% of the sulfur dioxide in the city. The smeltery was founded in 1936 and refined gold, silver, copper, lead, and zinc. In the 1980s it was among the top 500 government-owned enterprises.

Germany. At a meeting on January 15, the Social Democratic and Green parties moved a step closer to agreement on the operating limit for nuclear power stations. Talks between the government and industry had remained suspended pending agreement between the coalition partners. On June 23 at a meeting in Münster, the Greens approved the deal that had been agreed upon between the government and the power companies. This allowed nuclear plants to operate at full power for an average of 30 years; because the plants did not always operate at full power, however, their average lifetimes would be about 35 years, an average of 5 years shorter than they would have been without the new limit. Production limits were specified for each station, but to maximize operating efficiency, companies were allowed to switch those amounts among stations. Consequently, it was impossible to say when each station would close or when the last one would close. The government undertook not to introduce taxes or other economic measures that would harm the industry and not to strengthen safety standards.

On September 22 the federal radiation protection authority announced that shipments of spent nuclear fuel were to be resumed. Eight shipments of the fuel would be allowed during 2000, traveling from the power stations at Stade, Biblis, and Philippsburg to the La Hague reprocessing plant in France. The industry had requested 54 shipments by the end of 2001. The safety regulations were tightened, and plant operators agreed that all plutonium derived from reprocessing would be recycled to prevent it from accumulating.

An opinion poll published on June 30 found that 94% of the population ranked the environment as important and 71% said they would pay higher taxes to improve environmental protection. About 85% said they considered nuclear power to be dangerous and wished it to be phased out as quickly as possible.

Norway. On March 9 the Norwegian government became the first in the world to fall over a global-warming issue. Coalition Prime Minister Kjell Magne Bondevik lost a vote of confidence in the Storting (parliament) arising from his opposition to building gas-fired power stations.

The Norwegian government argued that the new stations would release too much carbon dioxide and that the project should be postponed until cleansing technology had been developed. The Conservative and Labour opposition favoured the plan, maintaining that there was no other way to meet the demand for electricity.

The national statistics agency reported in September that collecting, sorting, cleaning, and transporting household waste for recycling consumed at least 100 gigawatt-hours of power annually, equal to half the output from a proposed new power station. Householders in the survey reported they spent almost 30 minutes and used 50 litres (13 gal) of water each week preparing their rubbish for collection.

Russia. Pres. Vladimir Putin abolished the State Committee for Environmental Protection in May. It had been responsible for monitoring all aspects of the environment except for nuclear safety and had replaced the Federal Environment Ministry in 1996. Its responsibilities were transferred to the Ministry of Natural Resources.

Sweden. On August 16 the government postponed the closing of the Barsebäck 2 nuclear reactor, previously scheduled for July 2001. Industry Minister Björn Rosengren said that the country would be unable to make up the resulting shortfall quickly enough by increasing renewable energy capacity. Barsebäck 1 closed in November 1999.

Brushing aside protests over fuel prices, the government in its proposed 2001 budget announced on September 20 that it would increase the tax on diesel fuel by SKr 0.10 (SKr 1=about U.S. $0.10) per litre, raising the price by 3%. The carbon dioxide emission tax was to increase by 15% and the tax on electricity by SKr 0.018 per kilowatt-hour. These were part of a proposed increase of SKr 3.3 billion in environmental taxation, amounting to just over 10% of the final "green tax" target of SKr 30 billion. The increases were offset by reduced employment taxes, including a SKr 12.5 billion reduction in the income tax. Sales taxes on public transportation would be halved to 6% and spending on environmental research and rehabilitation increased by SKr 360 billion.

Thailand. It was reported in February that five people had been hospitalized in Bangkok after they were exposed to radiation leaking from a cylinder containing scrap metal that had been sold to a recycling yard on the city's outskirts. Two workers who handled the metal cylinder were in comas, and the man who sold it suffered radiation burns to his hands. The owner of the scrap yard and another worker were also taken to a hospital. After searching for 11 hours, staff from the Thai atomic research centre found the cylinder. It contained cobalt-60. This was said to be the first radioactive leak ever to have occurred in Thailand.

United States. On January 21 the Earth Liberation Front, a radical environmental group, sent faxes to the Associated Press and several newspapers claiming responsibility for a fire on New Year's Eve that did $400,000 worth of damage in the Agriculture Hall at Michigan State University (MSU). The group said that Catherine Ives, director of the MSU Agricultural Biotechnology Support Project, whose office was one of those damaged in the fire, directed a program aimed at persuading less-developed countries to adopt genetically modified crops. On March 13 a group claiming to be from the Animal Liberation Front broke into a Wisconsin warehouse, placed incendiary devices against propane tanks, set the timers, and departed. Later, they claimed to have burned down the refrigerated warehouse, which contained gourmet dog food. The devices malfunctioned, however, and the attack failed.

On June 12 the Environmental Protection Agency (EPA) claimed that dioxins were 10 times more likely to cause cancer than had previously been believed, creating a 0.1–1% risk in the most exposed individuals, such as those eating a diet high in animal fat. The agency also upgraded dioxins from "probable" to "known" carcinogens. Some scientists, however, said that the estimate was "unbelievable." The EPA also said that exposure to dioxins among the population had fallen significantly since the 1980s and was still falling and that there were no indications of ill effects.

ENVIRONMENTAL ISSUES

Climate Change. The sixth conference of parties to the UN Framework Convention on Climate Change was held in November at The Hague. A week of official preparatory talks took place in Bonn, Ger., in June. These centred on accounting methods for assessing greenhouse gases, rules for liability for emissions, and mechanisms for ensuring compliance.

The draft of the third assessment report by the Intergovernmental Panel on Climate Change (operating under World Meteorological Organization and United Nations auspices), scheduled for final publication in 2001, was released in April. The draft revealed that three of the past five years had been the warmest on instrumental record—which went back 140 years—and that 1,000-year tree-ring data had shown the abrupt 20th-century warming to be unique. The report identified a human-induced warming of 0.6 °C (1.08 °F) over the past century but noted that there had been little progress in projecting the future of greenhouse warming because of the many uncertainties about climate models, cloud behaviour, and the changing use of fossil fuels. The report continued to estimate a warming of 2.5 °C (4.5 °F; range 1.5–4.5 °C [2.7–8.1 °F]) from a doubling of carbon dioxide. It also included estimates of the amount of carbon that might be absorbed by changes in land use. The special scientific report on the effects of land use was approved in May by delegates from more than 100 countries attending a meeting in Montreal.

A report by an 11-member panel of the National Research Council (the research arm of the U.S. National Academy of

Sciences complex), published in January, said there was no doubt that temperatures had risen worldwide in the previous 20 years despite the fact that data from satellites and high-altitude balloons had detected little or no warming. The panel found unanimously that although the upper-atmosphere data were reliable, they did not call the ground-based data into question. It found a warming of 0.25–0.4 °C (0.45–0.72 °F) from 1979 to 1999, compared with 0.4–0.8 °C (0.72–1.44 °F) over the past century. The panel said, however, that this did not necessarily mean the warming was caused by greenhouse gases or would continue.

On January 18 the World Bank announced at The Hague the first global market-based project aimed at reducing greenhouse gas emissions and at promoting better technologies in less-developed countries. The project was to be funded by the governments of Finland, Sweden, Norway, and The Netherlands, each contributing $10 million, as well as by several companies, each of which would contribute $5 million. The Bank would act as broker and aimed at a price of about $15 per ton of carbon.

Air Pollution. Up to 500 fires raging in March in the forests of Sumatra, one of the major islands comprising Indonesia, produced clouds of smoke that drifted toward Malaysia and threatened to repeat the major pollution that affected much of Southeast Asia in 1997. Hundreds of hectares of national park and plantation forest were burned. Many of the fires were set deliberately to clear land for cultivation.

In March the U.S. Environmental Protection Agency issued new pollution-control standards covering hydrocarbon emissions from handheld tools such as chain saws and garden trimmers. The standards applied only to newly purchased items with engines of 25 hp or less.

A study by Jonathan Levy and John D. Spengler reported in May that emissions from power stations in Massachusetts could be linked to 43,000 asthma attacks and an estimated 159 premature deaths each year. The com-

The Salem Harbor Station power plant in Salem, Mass., whose owner, Pacific Gas and Electric Co., agreed to cut emissions after a study in May suggested that emissions from such plants were linked to asthma and premature deaths.

Salem Harbor Station, Salem, Massachusetts

panies owning the two plants in question agreed to cut emissions, as did four other plants. Nitrogen oxide and sulfur dioxide emissions would be cut by 50% by 2003, and carbon dioxide and soot would also be reduced.

Marine Pollution. In March the European Commission, supported by all 15 member states as well as by nonmember Norway, persuaded the Marine Environment Protection Committee of the International Maritime Organization to designate the North Sea a low-sulfur-fuel zone. This would require ships in the sea to use fuels containing no more than 1.5% sulfur rather than the 4.5% permitted globally. The Commission said that this should at least halve North Sea sulfur dioxide emissions from the approximately 460,000 metric tons released in 1990. The change would come into effect when at least half the world's fleet had ratified an annex to the Marpol Convention. Panama, with 16.5% of the fleet, and the EU and two applicant countries, Malta and Cyprus, with 20% between them favoured the change, but Liberia and some other countries remained unconvinced.

The annual meeting of the Ospar Convention was held in Copenhagen in June. Great Britain and France were isolated when other nations called for an end to the reprocessing of spent nuclear reactor fuel, although a few days before the meeting began, British Environment Minister Michael Meacher outlined plans to reduce radioactive discharges by 85% by 2020. The meeting ended on June 30, having made significant progress toward implementing a 1998 agreement to reduce pollution dramatically over a 20-year period.

In December 1999 a Maltese-registered tanker carrying fuel oil from Rotterdam, Neth., to Leghorn, Italy, broke in two in severe storms 69 km (43 mi) off the coast of Brittany, France, spilling 11.4 million litres (1 litre=0.26 gal) of heavy fuel oil (10,000 of the 30,000 tons it was carrying). The oil soiled more than 400 km (250 mi) of the coast and polluted oyster beds. Both halves of the 24-year-old vessel sank, with about 20,000 tons of oil still on board. A preliminary report said the ship's structure might have been faulty and criticized the owners and an Italian company responsible for safety checks on the ship. In its official report, a French government committee joined with the European Commission in calling for stricter safety standards, saying ships carrying "black" products (fuel oil, tar, and crude oil) should be subject to the same safety requirements as those carrying "white" products (naphtha, kerosene, and gasoline). The operation to pump oil from the two halves of the tanker was completed on July 30, and the cleanup, paid for by TotalFina, was completed by the end of September.

Freshwater Pollution. On January 30 a tailings-containment dam failed at the Aurul gold tailings retreatment mine near Baia Mare, Rom. The mine tailings contained an estimated 480,000 oz of gold and 2,200,000 oz of silver. Esmeralda Exploration Ltd., an Australian company based in Perth, owned 50% of the mine and operated it, and the Romanian state-owned company Remin owned the other 50%. Esmeralda Exploration placed itself in voluntary liquidation in order to fend off legal actions. About 100,000 cu m (3,530,000 cu ft) of water contaminated with high concentrations of cyanide as well as large quantities of heavy metals were released into the Lapus River. Cyanide is used in separating gold from the surrounding rock. The contamination fed into the Somes (becoming the Szamos when it crossed into Hungary) and Tisza rivers and from there into the Danube River east of Novi Sad, Yugos., and thereby affected Hungary and Serbia before returning to Romania. It reached the Serbian border on February 10, and by February 16 the cyanide concentration in the Danube in Romania was four times higher than permitted EU levels and almost 20 times higher than the levels permitted in Romania. More cyanide escaped some days later, carried by melting snow, and polluted seven wells in the village of Bozanta Mare, near the mine. As the cyanide moved downstream, city authorities shut down water pumps. The cities of Turnu Magurele and Zimnicea had to rely on wells.

On March 7, after no dead fish had been found over a period of 24 hours, the Hungarian authorities lifted a water-quality alert on the Tisza River. Life was returning to the Tisza by June as fishermen dumped tiny fish into the water. All the species originally present were being introduced, and it was expected that they would survive. (See *Wildlife Conservation*, below.)

At about midnight on January 18, a pipeline began leaking oil from the Reduc oil refinery in Brazil, a property of the government-owned company Petrobrás. The oil flowed into Guanabara Bay, contaminating about 14,000 ha (35,000 ac) of mangrove swamps and causing damage to birds, shellfish, and fish. In all, 1.3 million litres were spilled. State environmental officials said that the Petrobrás pipelines were old and poorly maintained.

On August 15 three chemical company executives and 19 employees were charged in Taipei, Taiwan, with dumping dimethyl benzene solvent into the Kao-p'ing River, the principal source of drinking water in southern Taiwan. The water supply had been shut down after three men were caught dumping the solvent into the river from a tanker holding more than 100 tons. The Shengli Chemical Co., under contract to the Eternal Chemical Co., was alleged to have dumped 13,500 tons of waste solvent into the river since 1987.

Genetically Modified Foods. On January 29 representatives from about 130 countries agreed in Montreal on the text of rules governing trade in genetically modified organisms. The agreement would become the Cartagena Protocol on Biosafety (after the city in Colombia where an earlier set of negotiations had ended inconclusively) to the 1992 UN Convention on Biological Diversity and would come into force when 50 parties had ratified it. Representatives of more than 60 countries signed the protocol on May 24, at the end of the UN Convention on Biological Diversity in Nairobi, Kenya. (*See* AGRICULTURE AND FOOD SUPPLIES *Special Report.*)

(MICHAEL ALLABY)

WILDLIFE CONSERVATION

As a result of captive breeding and conservation efforts, breeding populations of the black-footed ferret (*Mustela nigripes*) had by 2000 returned to the wild in the Rocky Mountains region of the U.S. The ferret's ultimate fate would, however, depend on that of its prey—prairie dogs. Only one of the five species of prairie dogs was listed as threatened, but all had experienced reductions in their ranges. The black-tailed prairie dog had suffered a 98% reduction in range in 100 years and was being assessed for possible listing as endangered.

After primates had survived a century with no extinctions, 25 species of apes, monkeys, lemurs, and other primates were at risk of disappearing forever, according to a report released January 10. The main causes for the declines were forest destruction and hunting. Intensifying conflict in the Democratic Republic of the Congo (DRC) threatened bonobos (*Pan paniscus*), which lived only in central DRC; these and other apes fell prey to troops and refugees.

BBC Wild

An Iberian lynx prowls Doñana National Park in southern Spain. Fewer than 1,000 of the species remain, and, for the first time, tuberculosis has been diagnosed in the population.

About 200 tons of fish were killed in January and February as a result of the mine-spill accident in Romania before the 50-km (30-mi)-long pulse of cyanide and heavy metals spilled into the Danube River in northern Yugoslavia, killing still more fish. It may have been the worst-ever case of water pollution in Eastern and Central Europe. Two fish species found only in the upper Tisza may have been pushed to the brink of extinction, and prospects were bleak for other wild species, including white-tailed eagles and otters. (See *Environmental Issues: Freshwater Pollution* above.)

Although a survey of coral reefs off Belize in the Caribbean Sea in February found no signs of recovery from the bleaching caused by the El Niño event of 1997–98, some coral reefs in the Indian and Pacific oceans seemed to be recovering more quickly than expected, possibly owing to the unexpected survival of juvenile coral. The reefs would, however, need a decade or more of undisturbed growth to recover completely, and this was not likely, because repeated bleaching was forecast to accompany the projected global warming. Rising carbon dioxide levels may also cripple coral reefs by dissolving in sea water and reacting with carbonate, reducing the availability of carbonate to corals, which need it to build their skeletons.

Tuberculosis was diagnosed for the first time in an Iberian lynx in Doñana National Park in southern Spain, and fears were raised for the fewer than 1,000 remaining Iberian lynxes, most of which lived in the park. Wild boar and fallow deer in the area were also infected, and it was suspected that cattle in the park were harbouring the disease.

The 1,000th giant tortoise (*Geochelone elephantopus hoodensis*) to be repatriated to its native Galápagos island of Española was released in March, a milestone in the breeding program started by the Charles Darwin Research Station in 1963, when only 14 individuals remained. Attention was now being given to many other threatened tortoise species in the archipelago.

A 10-year study of Pacific leatherback turtles suggested that they were nearing extinction. The population that nested at Playa Grande, Costa Rica, fell from 1,367 in 1988 to 117 in 1998, and by 2004 there could be fewer than 50. Net fishing off the coast of South America was thought to be catching and killing the turtles accidentally.

At the Convention on International Trade in Endangered Species of Wild Fauna and Flora (CITES) meeting in Nairobi, Kenya, in April, it was decided that the ban on regular international trade in elephant ivory should continue and that in the future the issue should be decided by two new bodies established to monitor the illegal killing of elephants and to keep tabs on ivory seizures. Along with 13 other plants, the African tree *Prunus africana* was given protection by CITES. In order to supply the pharmaceutical trade, this species was being felled much faster than it was being replaced and could be extinct within a decade. On April 22 the discovery of two new marmoset species—*Callithrix manicorensis* and *Callithrix acariensis*—in northwestern Brazil was announced. Another 10 new species of monkey, 5 new birds, 1 deer, and 1 peccary were also discovered in the region and awaited scientific description.

In May it was reported that orangutans were now restricted to the shrinking forests of Borneo and Sumatra; without urgent action they could be extinct in the wild within 20 years because of large-scale habitat destruction for logging and agriculture. A plan was launched to save the species, and there was optimism because International Monetary Fund loans to Indonesia were forbidding extensions to oil palm plantations and loans to loggers.

Increasing human presence and influence on land use were putting many tropical forest fragments in immediate danger of collapse if new conservation measures were not enacted quickly. Small isolated fragments were unable to sustain their original biodiversity and needed to be connected across broad landscapes. Researchers in July stated that a combination of interacting factors, including forest fragmentation, logging, and El Niño-driven drought, altered the extent of forest fires and thereby caused forest ecosystems to break down and regional climates to change.

On September 5 Pres. Alberto Fujimori of Peru decreed protection of one of the most biologically important ecosystems in the world. The size of Bahuaja-Sonene National Park was doubled to cover more than 1.1 million ha (1 ha=2.47 ac) in the rich Amazonian lowland forests at the base of the Andes Mountains, and the adjoining 254,000-ha Tambopata National Reserve, as well as a 262,000-ha buffer zone, was created. As many as 550 bird species and more than 1,200 butterfly species had been recorded in just one of the region's localities. A consortium of oil and gas companies that had held exploratory drilling rights had recently relinquished the area incorporated into the park.

A viral infectious disease, possibly transmitted through infected battery-hen carcasses, was believed to be the cause of the mysterious and catastrophic decline in vultures in northern India, which had started a decade earlier. One species, the common white-backed vulture (*Gyps bengalensis*), had been virtually wiped out in some areas, and captive breeding of the birds was being considered. (JACQUI M. MORRIS)

ZOOS

The gathering of tracking data by zoos had by 2000 become, depending on the animal involved, greatly simplified. For example, Mike Loomis of the North Carolina Zoological Park tracked African elephants in Cameroon, David St. Aubin of the Mystic (Conn.) Aquarium tracked beluga whales in the Canadian Arctic, Molly Lutcavage of the New England Aquarium in Boston used pop-up tags to track bluefin tuna in the North Atlantic, and Scott Pfaff of the Riverbanks Zoological Park and Botanical Gardens in Columbia, S.C., tracked a local population of eastern diamondback rattlesnakes. The Outreach Program at the Baltimore (Md.) Zoo engaged 900 local students to help track wild eastern box turtles by means of radio telemetry. At the New England Aquarium, a display next to a tank containing a harbour seal depicted a real-time tracking of a wild harbour seal moving between Ireland and Scotland and thus immediately linked the captive world to the wild one.

One of the most significant and gratifying pursuits of zoos and aquariums was the rehabilitation and postrelease tracking of marine mammals and turtles. In 1999 a pair of juvenile long-finned pilot whales had become stranded on the eastern shore of Cape Cod, Massachusetts. The staffs from the New England Aquarium and the Cape Cod Stranding Network were able to respond quickly before the animals could become seriously hurt by abrasion and exposure in the surf. From Cape Cod the animals were transported by truck to the Aquatic Animal Study Center at Mystic Aquarium. The centre was designed specifically for quarantine and intensive care of cetaceans and other marine mammals. Following the whales' arrival, physical examinations revealed evidence of bacterial infection in one animal but little beyond dehydration and stress in the other. Both were later returned to the waters of the western North Atlantic. Each animal carried on its dorsal fin a specially fitted Global Positioning System satellite tag and instrument pack designed to transmit data revealing dive patterns and locations to any of four polar orbiting satellites. A flow of electrical current through seawater prevented signal transmission so long as the unit was underwater; an air break at the surface initiated uplink. Within 24 hours, Mystic had received its first set of transmission data from the tags; some 115 days later, more than 30,000 uplink signals had been received, longer than any other pilot whales (and most other cetaceans) had been continuously monitored. The data continued to indicate that both animals remained together and were swimming and diving consistently.

During the winter of 1999–2000, sea turtles in large numbers had washed ashore on Cape Cod beaches. Ultimately, the live turtles were transported to Boston's New England Aquarium. Nearly all of them were subsequently relocated to aquariums and marine animal hospitals from Boston to Florida, and they later were released.

Since 1994 the Zoological Society of San Diego, Calif., in conjunction with the Australian Koala Foundation, had been organizing teams of representatives from interested zoos to assist in collecting field data in Australia with regard to koala habitat utilization and tree species preferences. The data were then analyzed to develop regional models of habitat use by koalas and subsequently to complete further the computerized "Koala Habitat Atlas." In 2000 two field expeditions were offered to zoo representatives interested in participating in this koala-conservation effort.

In June 1999 the U.S. Fish and Wildlife Service and the City of New Orleans embarked on an exciting new pilot program when the New Orleans mayor and the deputy assistant director of refuges signed the U.S.'s first Urban Conservation Treaty for Migratory Birds. With the help of the Bayou Sauvage National Wildlife Refuge and the

Carla M. Cataldi/AP/Wide World Photos

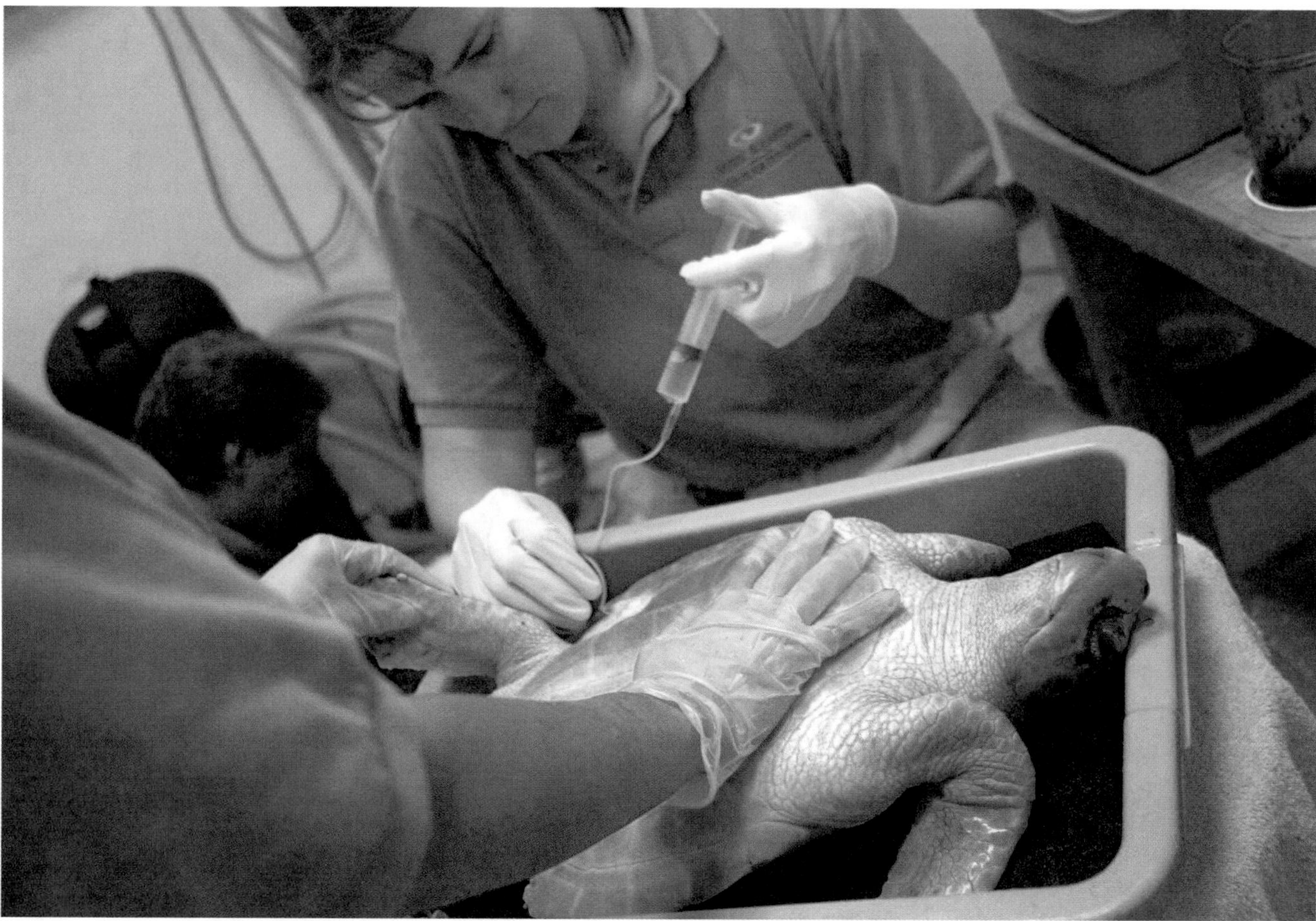

A veterinary intern at Mystic (Conn.) Aquarium administers fluids to a sea turtle in June.

Audubon Institute's Louisiana Nature Center, New Orleans began emphasizing the value of cities as sanctuaries for wildlife and exploring ways to enhance parks, gardens, and median areas for the benefit of birds. The mayor of Chicago signed the treaty in March 2000.

On March 6, 2000, the first African elephant conceived by artificial insemination was born at the Indianapolis (Ind.) Zoo. By July the baby girl, named Amali (a Swahili word meaning "hope"), was a thriving 180-kg (400-lb) toddler. With the numbers of wild elephants dropping sharply in recent years and the level of natural births far below the rate needed to maintain the population, it had become an urgent matter to develop new ways to produce these animals.

In April the government of China approved the sending of a pair of giant pandas to the National Zoological Park in Washington, D.C., for breeding purposes. In return, the Smithsonian Institution, which operated the zoo, agreed to donate $1 million per year to China for 10 years for panda research and conservation projects, including protecting Chinese forests. Mei Xiang, a two-year-old female, and Tian Tian, a three-year-old male, were sent from the China Research and Conservation Center for the Giant Panda in Wolong, Sichuan province, and arrived in Washington on December 6. The pair brings the panda population in U.S. institutions to seven: three at the San Diego, Calif., Zoo and two at Zoo Atlanta in Georgia. (ALAN H. SHOEMAKER)

GARDENING

In 2000 home gardeners continued to purchase plants rather than grow them from seed. In addition, buyers grouped annuals, perennials, grasses, and even tender shrubs together in the landscape or planted them together in a container. There was an increase in the number of gardeners who favoured container gardening, as well as the vegetative rather than seed propagation of both container and bedding plants. Though vegetative propagation had been limited to cultivars not available from seed, such as *Lantana, Abutilon, Scaevola,* and *Bacopa* (Sutera), vegetatively propagated petunias, verbena, and snapdragons began to appear.

All-America Rose Selections (AARS) named three winners for the 2001 season. Glowing Peace—a descendant of Peace, one of the world's best-known roses—was hybridized by the House of Meilland of France from parents Sun King and Roxanne. The plants grew to 1.2 m (1 m=3.3 ft) in height and were 0.9 m in width, with nearly 8-cm (1 cm =0.4 in) blooms that were coloured yellow and cantaloupe-orange above glossy, deep-green foliage that turned burgundy in fall. Slightly smaller was *floribunda* AARS winner Marmalade Skies, at 0.9 m high and across, with green satiny foliage and clusters of between five and eight 6–8-cm tangerine-orange double flowers on each stem. This stellar rose—developed by Meilland from a combination of Parador, Patricia, and Tamango—was judged excellent for hedging. The first miniature rose to win since 1993 was Sun Sprinkles, a disease-resistant upright, rounded, plant with dark green, glossy foliage. Having a height of only 45–60 cm made Sun Sprinkles ideal for edging or containers. The bright yellow 5-cm double blossoms were moderately fragrant, with an odour of spice and musk. Sun Sprinkles was hybridized by John Walden and introduced by Bear Creek Gardens of the U.S.

In an effort to build consumer enthusiasm for new plant introductions, seed-industry associations continued to promote award competitions. Interspecific hybrid Zinnia Profusion White, bred by Sakata Seed of Japan for both professional and amateur bedding and container plantings, was chosen to receive a Gold Medal award from both All-America Selections (AAS) and the European flower-testing organization Fleuroselect. Zinnia Profusion White—an open-pollinated diploid annual at 30 cm in height and width, with lance-shaped green leaves and 5-cm single white ray petals crowned by raised orange discs—was also found to be highly resistant to mildew (*Erysiphe* species).

Nicotiana x sanderae Avalon Bright Pink, bred for bedding and container use by Floranova of the U.K., also won awards from both organizations—a Gold Medal from Fleuroselect and a bedding-plant award from AAS. It was a very compact F_1 hybrid annual with a height of 25 cm and diameter of 30 cm. The star-shaped flowers were 4–5 cm in diameter, with five petals and a unique pale-pink colour with a darker pink edge. *Nicotiana* Avalon Bright Pink bloomed only 90 days from sowing, resisted summer heat well, and continued to bloom without deadheading until frost.

Two other plants that received AAS bedding plant awards were *Portulaca* F_1 hybrid Margarita Rosita from Waller Genetics of the U.S. and *Eustoma* F_1 hybrid Forever Blue from the multinational Pan American Seed. Margarita Rosita was a mounding *Portulaca;* it stood 8–10 cm and spread 30–35 cm. The plants, which had fleshy leaves and semidouble rose flowers 3–4 cm across, were highly heat- and drought-tolerant. *Eustoma* Forever Blue had a novel basal branching habit that made it more dense than normal *Lisianthus* and was submitted for a utility patent, which was far more difficult to obtain and more restrictive than a plant patent. Forever Blue reached 30 cm in height and nearly the same in width and bore warm blue 6-cm single flowers atop small shield-shaped foliage.

AAS awarded one flower award for the 2001 season—to Sunflower (*Helianthus*) Ring of Fire, bred by Benary Samenzucht of Germany. The late-blooming plants stood 120–150 cm, spread 60–90 cm, and after approximately 120 days displayed a distinct bicolour pattern, with a deep red ring between the golden outer petal colour and the chocolate-brown centres.

Among the All-America Rose Selections for the 2001 season was the hybrid grandiflora Glowing Peace.

Courtesy of The Conrad-Pyle Company

Four vegetables were recognized by AAS for their garden performance in a range of American gardening regions. Hybrid Sweet Corn Honey Select from Rogers (Novartis) of the U.S. was chosen for its enhanced flavour and ease of growth. The 20-cm-long, 5-cm-diameter ears matured in just under 80 days with 18–20 rows of yellow kernels. Honey Select—which contained 75% supersweet genes (which would normally require isolation from other corn varieties) and 25% sugar-enhanced genes (which did not require isolation)—could be grown adjacent to other sweet corns and could withstand a long storage period without losing its flavour.

Jolly, a new hybrid cluster tomato from Known-You Seed of Taiwan, was awarded a 2001 AAS vegetable award. The peach-shaped pink fruits weighed 40–45 g (1.4–1.5 oz) and were borne in clusters of 9 to 14 on vigorous indeterminate plants about 70–75 days after transplanting when the plants were trellised and pruned.

Seminis Vegetable Seeds of California earned a vegetable award for Giant Marconi, a hybrid pepper. Introduced as an improved Italian-type grilling pepper, Giant Marconi bore 15–20-cm elongated fruits that were ready for green harvest about 72 days after transplanting. The fruits, if left on the 75-cm plants, matured to red up to a month later. The plants were resistant to both potato and tobacco viruses.

For the first time, an onion won an AAS award. Hybrid Onion Super Star, a globular white onion from Seminis, was chosen for its wide adaptability to daylight. The bulbs were resistant to pink root.

In the U.S. leading on-line retailer GARDEN.COM ceased operations after failing to secure additional financing, and the nonprofit National Gardening Association (NGA) ceased publication of *National Gardening,* its for-profit magazine. In addition, the NGA sold to mySEASONS.com—the on-line marketing arm of Foster and Gallagher's stable of horticultural retailers—all rights to the magazine's content as well as to the content of its World Wide Web site, <http://www.garden.org>. Then MySEASONS.com created a Web site—<http://www.NationalGardening.com>—that incorporated the content from garden.org.

(SHEPHERD OGDEN)

Fashions

The roaring stock market inspired such opulent looks as **PARK AVENUE PRINCESS, PALM BITCH,** and **GHETTO FABULOUS.**

Reuters NewMedia Inc/Corbis

Michael Kors's "Palm Bitch" look featured brown leather hot pants, a matching jacket, and a knit tank top.

The fashion industry witnessed a changing of the guard in 2000. Legendary 20th-century designers Bill Blass and Yves Saint Laurent retired and were replaced by younger faces. American Steven Slowik—who had designed ready-to-wear fashions for Salvatore Ferragamo in Florence before becoming an independent designer in Paris—succeeded Blass, but his 2000 spring-summer collection was a critical failure. Gucci designer Tom Ford took over the reins at Saint Laurent, where he would design both menswear and the women's ready-to-wear line Rive Gauche. Alber Elbaz, Rive Gauche's former designer, moved to Milan and took over as head designer at Krizia. Saint Laurent's menswear designer Hedi Slimane, who had successfully reestablished and popularized the company's menswear in the 1990s, moved to head up menswear design at Christian Dior. Jil Sander resigned as chairman of her company in January and sold 75% of her stock to the Prada group, which later purchased Azzedine Alaia, famous in the 1980s for its body-hugging lycra dresses.

A shift also took place among prominent women at the forefront of style. The front-row seats at New York fashion shows were filled with young, stylish Manhattan socialites, notably sisters Aerin and Jane Lauder (granddaughters of beauty mogul Estée Lauder), Alexandra and Erin Lind, Samantha and Serena Boardman, Lulu de Kwiatkowski, and the Miller sisters: Pia Getty, Alexandra von Fürstenberg, and Princess Marie-Chantal of Greece. Their presence overshadowed that of elder American fashion icons Nan Kempner, Nancy Kissinger, Betsey Bloomingdale, and Pat Buckley.

A contingent of designers produced pieces for both spring-summer and autumn-winter that seemed directly inspired by this so-called Park Avenue Princess look. Ralph Lauren, Calvin Klein, and Valentino all produced crisp and sophisticated yet sexy and luxurious wardrobe staples, perfect for luncheon—trousers, skirts, shirtdresses, and day coats in solid colours such as white and red. Established designers Carolina Herrera—who in midsummer opened her first shop on Madison Avenue in New York City—and Oscar de la Renta (named Womenswear Designer of the Year by the Council of Fashion Designers of America [CFDA]) succeeded in presenting modern collections that appealed to both younger and older socialites. In Great Britain, Hussein Chalayan (*see* BIOGRAPHIES) was named Designer of the Year for the second consecutive year.

It was Michael Kors, however, who best captured the neoconservative zeitgeist with his spring-summer collection Palm Bitch, a humorous take on the styles that the young rich wore while vacationing in Palm Beach, Fla. The look featured skimpy bikinis and bright acid-yellow

Reuters/Jonathan Evans/Archive Photos

Alexander McQueen's red feather dress debuted in September during London Fashion Week.

and *uber*-lime silk shirts, as well as matching head scarves. Kors continued the rich-bitch theme for the spring-summer collection of Celine, the French Moët Hennessy Louis Vuitton-owned line of which he was creative director, but he added a European twist by including such items as tie-dyed silk-denim jeans that were inspired by the French seaside resort town Saint-Tropez. Kors's collection and the jet-set chic current that filtered through spring-summer fashion—Louis Vuitton produced a signature beach towel, Versace made rhinestone-rimmed sunglasses, and Burberry unveiled its first bikini in the company's signature plaid—were a direct response to the bull market and the long-term economic boom in the West. Increasingly, women were wearing expensive jewelry with casual daytime clothes. In Tokyo, Paris, and London, Cartier opened a string of "casual-style" shops, where the atmosphere was meant to be relaxed and no item exceeded £15,000 (about $21,750).

European designers adopted their own interpretation of the refined, conservative look. Sincere chic, a ladylike theme, dominated Miuccia Prada's spring-summer collection, which included demure silk pussycat-bow blouses with matching pleated skirts and cardigan sweaters. Prada's theme proved influential. Her large bowling-bag-style handbag became an instant best-seller and was quickly copied by retailers, who successfully sold their own much-less-expensive versions.

For autumn-winter a group of international designers—Narciso Rodriguez, Clements Ribeiro, Max Mara, Alberta Ferretti, Marcus Lupfer, and Turssardi—all produced ladylike clothes such as 1950s- and '60s-inspired dresses, tweed suits, and blouse and skirt ensembles. Such styles, particularly Prada's, drew heavily on vintage clothing, increasingly sought after from such specialized vintage vendors as Kenny Valenti in New York and Vent in London. Most designer ladylike styles and accessories—such as Gucci's classic Chanel-inspired sling backs and Jackie Onassis-style coats and Michael Kors's Barbara Bush-like multilayer pearl necklace created by Janis Savitt—were produced with a definite modern feeling. Gucci's pumps featured high, slim heels, and its coats were accessorized with dark sunglasses and psychedelic head scarves.

Although the new uptown style was a dominant look, it was countered by an urban downtown cool look—an inventive style that merged art with fashion. British *Vogue* defined the look as featuring battered fabrics, tight stonewashed denim, baseball caps, and fake designer tracksuits worn with cheap stilettos. At the forefront of the downtown cool generation was Chloë Sevigny, whose film role as a young woman who falls in love with a lesbian in the controversial *Boys Don't Cry* thrust her into the media spotlight. American *Vogue* columnist Andre Leon Talley praised her unique style and singled her out as a new fashion icon and perhaps "the new postmodern grunge Audrey Hepburn."

Austrian designer Helmut Lang, who in 1997 had moved his business from Paris to New York, launched the first art-inspired fragrance of the 21st century, an eponymous perfume—one for men and another for women. As with fashion's neoconservative look, both established labels and younger designers experimented with the downtown aesthetic. For Chanel's autumn-winter collection, Karl Lagerfeld fashioned a handbag from distressed denim, and for Christian Dior's spring-summer couture show, John Galliano took inspiration from street urchins. Meanwhile, in New York, Miguel Adrover, a 34-year-old Spanish self-taught designer who had worked briefly for Alexander McQueen, debuted his inventive spring-summer collection—highlighted by a day coat made from cotton ticking taken from the mattress of his neighbour, the late Quentin Crisp—which won him the respect of fashion critics as well as the CFDA's Perry Ellis Award for Women's Wear.

At the forefront of London's young fashion scene was a group of friends and colleagues: Luella Bartley, Katie Grand, Liberty Ross, and Giles Deacon. Bartley, a former *Vogue* fashion writer, followed her promising 1999 debut with a 2000 spring-summer collection that personified the new London girl look—pink gingham shirts and shrunken kilts paired with striped ankle socks and Converse sneakers. Her friend Grand, a stylist and fashion director for the British youth magazine *The Face*, promoted Bartley's work in *Pop*, a new arts-meets-fashion magazine that Grand launched in September as editor. Ross, a young British model who was hailed in Britain as the next Kate Moss, was also found on the pages of *Pop*; in addition, she modeled for Luella and fronted advertising campaigns for Burberry and Emanuel Ungaro. Meanwhile, Deacon, a young London-based designer, was appointed creative director of the Italian leather goods label Bottega Veneta. Deacon succeeded in updating the company's signature style—woven leather—with a more modern design aesthetic. Formerly tacky sun visors were reworked in ostentatious crocodile skin, and the shell suit was retooled as sensuous casual wear in the most expensive supple leather. Deacon's footwear for autumn-winter—kitten-heeled two-tone pumps and red leather baggy boots—were found on the most fashionable feet, just as Marc Jacobs's stitched flat-heeled shoes and low-heeled sling backs were in the summer.

Style-conscious teenage girls emerged as the new affluent free spenders. Their role models were blonde pop singers such as Britney Spears and Christina Aguilera. Meanwhile, supermodels Christy Turlington, who launched an Ayurvedic skin-care line, Sundari, and Claudia Schiffer, who publicly romanced her playboy boyfriend, Tim Jeffries, reestablished their modeling careers as 30-something role models. When the first issue of *Teen Vogue* was published in September, the *New York Times* newspaper noted that "the upward-striving teenager is now more than ever the target of luxury marketers who once focused strictly on adults." Making inroads into the teenage market were Chanel, Ralph Lauren (who introduced his first teenage scent, Ralph), Lancôme, and Versace. Teenage shoppers boosted sales at upscale shops around the world. *Fortune* magazine reported that Spanish international clothing retailer Zara, which specialized in manufactured copies of designer clothes, reported sales of $2 billion, which represented a profit gain of 34%. The Gap, meanwhile, opened its biggest shop in the world on Regent Street in London.

African American style icons, once relegated to the sidelines of style, emerged as major industry players. Music producer and rapper Sean ("Puff Daddy") Combs introduced Sean John, his first ready-to-wear line for men and women during the 2000 autumn-winter fashion week in New York. His collection responded to the popularity of Ghetto Fabulous—a unisex look that promoted the overt luxury that he, his girlfriend, actress and singer Jennifer Lopez, and black female musicians Mary J. Blige, Lil' Kim, and the trio TLC had established. The Ghetto Fabulous look popularized labels such as Versace, Tommy Hilfiger, Dolce & Gabbana, Roberto Cavalli, and Galliano's designs for Christian Dior, as well as copious amounts of chunky real gold and diamond jewelry and fur of rare breeds, such as chinchilla. Motorola's answer to the look was a diamond-encrusted mobile phone, which retailed for $25,000. Logomania—a look that overtly displayed designer initials on clothes, jewelry, and accessories such as handbags and shoes—was the fashion industry's take on Ghetto Fabulous and was popularized in the 2000 spring-summer collections by Gucci, Marc Jacobs for Louis Vuitton, and Galliano at Dior.

(BRONWYN COSGRAVE)

Sean ("Puff Daddy") Combs presented the Sean John line and showcased the "Ghetto Fabulous" look with a "hot" black leather jacket.

Reuters NewMedia Inc/Corbis

Health and Disease

There are very few years in which a single achievement in medicine **OVERSHADOWS** all others. Such a year was 2000, however, and such an achievement was the sequencing of the **ENTIRE HUMAN GENOME.**

At a June 26 White House ceremony marking the occasion, Francis Collins (*see* BIOGRAPHIES), who led the international, publicly funded Human Genome Project, said, "This is a milestone in biology unlike any other." J. Craig Venter, head of Celera Genomics, a private company that entered the genome race in 1998, looked ahead: "It's my belief that the basic knowledge that we are providing the world will have a profound impact on the human condition." Whether one considered the sequencing of the genome to be the end of a colossal project or the beginning of a new science of human beings, there was no question that it would revolutionize medicine. (*See* LIFE SCIENCES: *Special Report.*)

Infectious Diseases. Across the globe there were outbreaks of old and new infectious diseases. They included Ebola hemorrhagic fever in Uganda; cholera in at least 15 African countries, Afghanistan, and Micronesia; dengue fever in Paraguay; leptospirosis in Canada and France; yellow fever in Liberia; measles in Ireland; Legionnaire disease in Australia; polio in China; variant Creutzfeld-Jakob disease in France, the U.K., and Ireland; and hantavirus in Panama.

Malaria, long a scourge of the tropical world, was increasing at a rate of about 130 million new cases a year. Some 90% of cases were in Africa, where in the late 1990s close to one million children were dying of the mosquitoborne disease annually. In April the World Health Organization (WHO) convened the first sub-Saharan African summit on malaria, for which leading health economists prepared an eye-opening report on the true costs of the disease. The authors calculated not only the direct medical costs and short-term losses of economic growth and productivity but also the devastating longer-run losses to tourism, foreign investment, and commerce, and they factored in the social and emotional costs of pain and suffering. Their analysis showed that controlling malaria in Africa would save "in the dozens of billions of dollars per year" in a matter of just a few years. The summit ended with a pledge of nearly $750 million in extra funds to fight the disease. The outpouring of cash, which came from the World Bank and several wealthy countries, was earmarked for the already established Roll Back Malaria program, which had the ambitious goal of cutting the incidence of malaria in Africa in half by 2010.

Another mosquitoborne disease, the West Nile virus, made a comeback in the northeastern U.S. in mid-2000, after having first appeared in the Western Hemisphere a year earlier. The West Nile virus normally circulates between birds and mosquitoes and is capable of infecting humans and other mammals. At its most virulent, the virus causes inflammation of the brain and spinal cord (meningoencephalitis) and death. In the 1999 outbreak, 62 people were infected and 5 died, all in the New York City area. The sweep of the 2000 outbreak was broader—infected birds and mosquitoes were found in New York, Connecticut, New Jersey, Massachusetts, and Maryland—but the toll on humans was comparatively mild. Twelve people were hospitalized with serious nervous system infections, and one person died.

A far more significant West Nile virus outbreak occurred in Israel, where the virus was in familiar territory. In late September Israeli health authorities declared an epidemic when it appeared that thousands of people were suffering from symptoms of the disease and at least 12 had died.

Antimicrobial Drug Resistance. For many years disease authorities around the world had been warning that antimicrobial drugs employed to treat common infections were becoming increasingly ineffectual, which was allowing the comeback of previously conquered diseases and the emergence of virulent new infections. A WHO report issued during the year documented the extent to which infectious diseases, including malaria, tuberculosis (TB), AIDS, pneumonia, and diarrheal diseases, were "arrayed in the increasingly impenetrable armour of antimicrobial resistance." It noted that in less-developed countries antibiotics and other antimicrobial agents tended to be underused or misused but that in developed countries they were notoriously overused. The report recommended that access to these drugs be widened to include the world's poorest people, but at the same time it stressed that antibiotics should be reserved "to treat only those diseases for which they are specifically required."

On a positive note, a Centers for Disease Control and Prevention (CDC) survey showed that in the late 1990s American doctors were writing 34% fewer prescriptions for antibiotics for children than they had at the beginning of the decade. This finding suggested that physicians were getting the message that antibiotics are not effective for colds and other viral illnesses and that inappropriate use promotes resistant bacteria.

One tactic in the battle against antimicrobial resistance was investment in the development of new antibiotics. In April the U.S. Food and Drug Administration (FDA) approved a long-awaited drug, linezolid (Zyvox), the first in a new class of antibiotics, the oxazolidinones. Zyvox was designed to stop bacteria very early in the reproduction process. The FDA specifically approved the drug for use in adults with severe hospital-acquired infections. Welcomed as it was, Zyvox was not a magic bullet; even before it came on the market, physicians had encountered at least 15 cases of infection resistant to it.

In order to surmount the growing problem of multidrug-resistant TB, an alliance of researchers and drug companies announced plans to accelerate development of fast-acting TB drugs. Standard TB drugs must be taken for six to nine months to eradicate the infection. Many patients, however, were failing to take the complete course, and the TB organisms were thus allowed to survive and grow resistant to available medications. Having drugs that could wipe out the infection in a shorter period would be a huge boon to the world, where each day more than 5,000 people died from TB and as many as eight million new people were infected.

Vaccine Developments. An immunization against herpes simplex 2 (genital herpes) was tested in medical centres in the U.S., Canada, Australia, New Zealand, Italy, and the U.K. To the surprise of the investigators, it was highly effective in women but not in men. The trials involved couples in which one member had herpes and the other did not. Experts said that once the herpes vaccine was on the market, it would have the greatest impact if it was given to prepubescent girls.

The first vaccine against the varicella-zoster virus, which causes chicken pox and shingles, was approved in 1995 and subsequently was administered to more than 10 million American children. In 2000, researchers studying children in Los Angeles county reported that chicken pox cases had fallen 80% between 1995 and 1999. The vaccine protected not only those children who received it but many children who did not—a phenomenon known as herd immunity. When there were large numbers of immunized individuals in a community, the chances that those who remained susceptible would come in contact with a contagious case were sharply reduced.

In 2000 Alzheimer disease affected about 12 million people in the world. That number could reach 22 million by 2025 unless effective means of prevention or cure were found. Scientists began the first human trials of a vaccine intended to prevent the accumulation in the brain of amyloid plaques, a hallmark of the disease.

HIV and AIDS. In July more than 12,000 attendees gathered in Durban, S.Af., for the 13th International AIDS Conference. The setting could not have been more poignant—70% of the world's 34 million AIDS cases were in sub-Saharan Africa, where life expectancy would be reduced to about 30 years by the year 2010 unless dramatic steps were taken. Prior to the start of the conference, 5,228 physicians and scientists from 84 countries signed a manifesto called the Durban Declaration. Its message was that "the evidence that AIDS is caused by HIV-1 or HIV-2 is clear-cut, exhaustive and unambiguous." The declaration was in anticipation of the opening remarks of South African Pres. Thabo Mbeki, who had previously expressed doubts whether HIV was the cause of AIDS. At the conference he questioned whether Western treatments were appropriate for African AIDS. "We are just trying to find solutions that are situated to South Africa, the southern Africa region, and the continent as a whole," Mbeki told the delegates. The closing speech was delivered by South Africa's former president Nelson Mandela, who urged the delegates to rise above their differences and not be distracted from the main course—that is, stepping up efforts to stop the spread of HIV.

Sobering statistics indicated that HIV infections and AIDS were spreading rapidly in Eastern Europe, the Caribbean, China, and India. In the U.S., public health practitioners were alarmed by a surge in new cases among homosexual men in San Francisco. That rise was attributed to complacency, brought about in part by the availability of effective treatments. A global HIV/AIDS surveillance report issued by WHO and the UNAIDS program at the end of 2000 indicated that for the first time the incidence of new infections in sub-Saharan Africa had stabilized rather than increased. That good news, however, was offset by the increase in the number of people in the region suffering and dying from AIDS. The same report estimated that the number of AIDS deaths worldwide since the beginning of the pandemic (in the early 1980s) was 21.8 million.

On the clinical front, a study reported in the journal *Nature* found that some people with HIV who began highly aggressive antiretroviral therapy very soon after their diagnosis could take a "holiday" from the drugs. Although their viral levels rose with the cessation of the drugs, their immune systems seemed to

AP/Wide World Photos

South African Pres. Thabo Mbeki delivers a controversial opening address at the 13th International AIDS Conference, held in Durban, S.Af., in July.

keep severe illnesses at bay. This suggested that in the future people with AIDS would be able to have "structured treatment interruptions" from complicated and expensive drug regimens.

British scientists started trials of a vaccine against the strain of HIV most prevalent in Africa. If the vaccine proved safe for the first recipients—18 volunteers in the U.K.—wider trials were expected to begin in Nairobi, Kenya, within a year. Another HIV vaccine trial involving 2,500 volunteers began in Thailand; this was the first large-scale clinical trial of an AIDS vaccine in a less-developed country. Vaccines were considered the single intervention most likely to alter the frightening course of the AIDS pandemic, and in 2000 more than 70 different vaccines were being tested.

New Treatments. In 2000 stroke disabled at least 570,000 people in the U.S. alone. Until recently little could be done for the paralysis and loss of function that typically occur. For one thing, it had long been thought that the adult brain was not capable of regeneration. During the year researchers in Birmingham, Ala., and Jena, Ger., helped prove that regeneration was possible even years after a stroke. The scientists tested a technique called constraint-induced-movement therapy in 13 patients with paralyzed arms. The treatment required exercising the disabled arm a full six hours a day for several weeks. Immediately following the therapy, images of the brain showed that nerve connections on distinct areas of brain circuitry had almost doubled; six months later the changes were still evident. The subjects regained about 75% of the use of their arms.

Another treatment for stroke involved patients using a "robotic arm" for about an hour a day to do exercises, such as connecting dots on a computer screen. Those who worked with the robotic aid gained twice as much arm movement as stroke patients who had traditional physical therapy.

A quite different stroke therapy enabled 42% of patients who received infusions of ancrod—a substance derived from Malaysian pit vipers—to regain "favorable functional status." To be effective the snake venom had to be given within three hours of the onset of the attack.

Canadian researchers developed a unique islet-cell transplant technique that eliminated the need for insulin injections in seven persons with poorly controlled type I (insulin-dependent) diabetes. The achievement was so impressive that *The New England Journal of Medicine* posted the paper describing the work on the Internet nearly two months prior to its scheduled publication.

In April the FDA approved two new nondrug treatments for gastroesophageal reflux disease, a severe, persistent form of heartburn. The treatments repaired the actual cause of the problem, a faulty muscular valve (lower esophageal sphincter) between the esophagus and stomach. Both treatments were minimally invasive and were performed by means of a tube that was positioned in the throat. One placed stitches in the sphincter; the other seared it with radio-frequency energy. The procedures enhanced the valve's barrier function, thereby preventing the reflux of bile and stomach acid into the esophagus. In August the American Heart Association revised its guidelines for giving emergency cardiopulmonary resuscitation (CPR), making it easier for the layperson to perform and increasing the chances that the victim would survive. The streamlined approach no longer recommended that bystanders take time to check for a pulse in a cardiac arrest victim. It was more important to begin the lifesaving steps without delay: 15 chest compressions alternated with two mouth-to-mouth breaths—until emergency defibrillation could be administered.

An especially promising study found that the drug interferon beta-1a (Avonex) could delay the development of established, clinically definite multiple sclerosis (MS), a disease that gradually destroys the myelin covering of nerve fibres. The trial, carried out in the U.S. and Canada, involved people who had experienced a single, isolated neurological event suggestive of MS—for example, weakness of a limb or a visual disturbance. Interferon beta-1a previously had been available for people with diagnosed MS. Avonex's manufacturer, Biogen, Inc., sought FDA approval for expanded use of the drug. An approved cancer drug, mitoxandrone (Novantrone), was approved for treating patients with advanced or chronic MS. The drug was found to reduce the number of relapses and help patients keep their mobility longer.

Investigators in Germany had impressive early results from a novel vaccine-like treatment given to 17 patients with advanced kidney cancer. The treatment used cells from the patients' own tumours that were fused with immune-system cells from healthy donors. Four patients had been cancer-free for at least 11 months, and two others had tumour shrinkage of more than 50%. In an experimental protocol in the U.S., 15 patients with advanced kidney cancer received a transplant of cancer-fighting cells from the immune system of a sibling. Nine patients were still alive after more than a year, and in four subjects all signs of the cancer were gone. In others, tumours shrank by more than half.

A treatment already available to women in 15 countries around the world finally became available to women in the U.S. late in the year. The so-called abortion pill—RU-486, or mifepristone—was approved in late September and was on the market before the end of the year, selling under the brand name Mifeprex. Owing to strict regulations imposed by the FDA on the use of mifepristone, many U.S. doctors opted not to dispense it.

Drugs Off the Market. Troglitazone (Rezulin), a prescription drug used to treat type 2 diabetes, was removed from the market in March because of its potential to cause severe liver toxicity. Two newly approved diabetes drugs, rosiglitazone (Avandia) and pioglitazone (Actos), offered the same benefits without the risk.

In November the FDA asked manufacturers of hundreds of widely sold over-the-counter appetite suppressants, decongestants, cold and cough remedies containing phenylpropanolamine (PPA) to stop marketing them. PPA was linked to a slight but significant risk of stroke in women. Among the products pulled from store shelves were various forms of Contac, Alka-Seltzer, Acutrim, Dexatrim, Robitussin, and Triaminic. The FDA was taking steps to ban PPA as an ingredient in all drug products.

A drug for irritable bowel syndrome in women, Lotronex (alosetron), was approved in February. In late June, after cases of serious intestinal problems were reported in some women taking the drug, the FDA required pharmacists to distribute a "medication guide" that warned patients directly about the risks. In November the manufacturer voluntarily withdrew Lotronex from the market, at which point 70 cases of adverse effects and 5 deaths had been reported.

Colorectal Cancer. In March Katie Couric, cohost of the NBC morning show *Today,* took a camera crew to her doctor's office, where, under mild sedation, she underwent a colonoscopy examination before millions of television viewers. Couric's husband had died of colon cancer in 1998, and her goal was to convince viewers of the importance of screening. The procedure involved in-

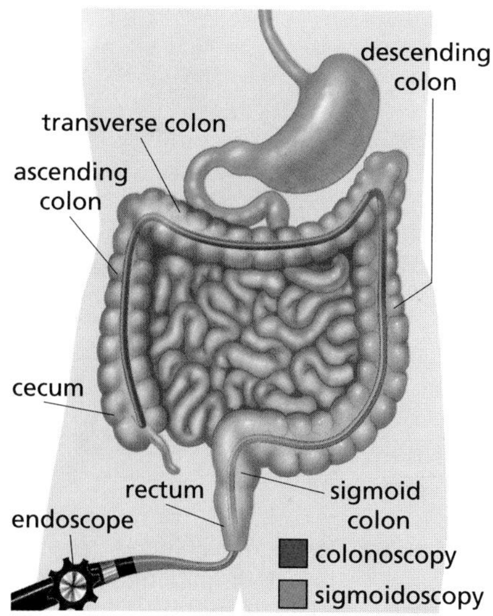

A comparison of the portions of the colon examined through sigmoidoscopy and colonoscopy.

sertion of a flexible lighted tube through the rectum into the colon; video technology enabled the doctor to see the entire lining of the approximately 150-cm (60-in)-long large intestine.

Two studies published in July found that colonoscopy was a far more reliable way to detect cancerous lesions and precancerous polyps than the recommended preliminary screening procedure, sigmoidoscopy (which allows the doctor to see only inside the rectum and lower colon). The studies suggested that as many as half of all cancerous lesions in the upper portion of the colon were missed by routine sigmoidoscopy. An editorial commenting on the findings compared "relying on flexible sigmoidoscopy" to "performing mammography of one breast" and called for insurers to cover the cost of the far-better screening method for colorectal cancer. At the end of the year the results of an 18-year study showed that the simplest test for colon cancer—an occult fecal blood screen—which detects traces of the blood in the stool, had the potential to reduce the rate of colorectal cancer by as much as 20%. In mid-November the FDA approved a laser system that improves a physician's ability to distinguish small harmless growths from precancerous growths in the colon. The device can be used during sigmoidoscopy or colonoscopy.

Alternative Medicine. According to the *Nutrition Business Journal,* the U.S. public was expected to spend an estimated $15.7 billion on herbal products, vitamins, minerals, and other dietary supplements in 2000. Although the FDA did not require manufacturers of these products to establish their safety or efficacy before marketing them, ConsumerLab.com, a private company, began assessing hundreds of products sold to the public for the purpose of promoting health and wellness. Its evaluations were published on the company's World Wide Web site, <www.consumerlab.com>.

A review of 20 herbal preparations purportedly containing the stimulant ephedra (also known as ma huang) was published in the *American Journal of Health-System Pharmacy* in May. The products were found to contain anywhere from 0% to 154% of the amount of ephedra listed on the label, and considerable variation was found between lots of the same product. A report later in the year linked ephedra in dietary supplements to 10 deaths and 13 cases of permanent disability.

At least 21 million people in the U.S. alone suffered from osteoarthritis, characterized by stiffness, pain, inflammation in the joints, and often some degree of debilitation. When a best-selling book published in 1997 claimed that glucosamine and chondroitin were a "cure" for arthritis, the medical establishment was profoundly skeptical. Despite the lack of scientific evidence that the substances—both natural components of cartilage—worked millions of arthritis sufferers began using them either separately or combined. Boston University researchers analyzed the results of 15 studies on chondroitin and glucosamine. They found that glucosamine (extracted commercially from crustacean shells) was by itself moderately effective in relieving symptoms, while chondroitin (made from cow, pig, or shark cartilage) offered more significant relief. A problem, however, was that most chondroitin products on the market were of unreliable quality. The side effects of both were fewer and milder than those associated with standard arthritis pain relievers.

During the year the *Washington Post* carried out the first survey in the U.S. on the illness and death associated with the growing use of supplements. Among other things, the survey found that poison-control centres in many states were seeing a dramatic increase in the number of adverse reactions caused by supplements, including ephedra, Saint-John's-wort, melatonin, and ginseng; that people taking products containing ephedra or its derivatives for weight loss or extra energy experienced adverse effects ranging from jitteriness to chest pains, insomnia, addiction, stroke, and death; and that children increasingly were being given supplements and suffering adverse reactions. The survey revealed rampant abuse of body-building supplements like gamma-hydroxybutyrate, or GHB, which was held responsible for hundreds of hospital and poison-centre visits and several deaths. Dangerous contaminants such as mercury, arsenic, and lead were found in supplements, especially in herbal products from Asia.

Health Systems. The first assessment ever attempted of the world's health systems was published by WHO in June. Countries whose systems were ranked highest (on the basis of five indicators) included France, Italy, San Marino, Andorra, Malta, Singapore, Spain, Oman, Austria, and Japan. The WHO assessment, titled *The World Health Report 2000—Health Systems: Improving Performance*, found wide variation in the performance of health systems, even among countries with similar levels of income and expenditures on health. Other key findings were that the vast majority of countries were underutilizing available resources and that poorly performing health systems had profound effects on the poorest people, often driving them deeper into poverty. It was not surprising that the lowest-ranking systems were in sub-Saharan Africa. The U.S., which of all countries spent the highest proportion of its gross domestic product on health, received the highest ranking for one indicator—the availability of resources. Overall, however, the country ranked 37th out of 191 countries evaluated. (*See* Special Report.)

Stem Cell Research. In August the U.S. National Institutes of Health released new rules governing the use of human stem cells in medical research. Stem cells are undifferentiated cells that can be coaxed to grow into various types of specific cells and thus have great potential for the repair of damaged or defective tissues and organs. The rules stipulated that federally funded researchers could work with embryonic stem cells but that the cells had to come from excess frozen embryos (those already destined for destruction) obtained from private fertility centres. Prior to the release of the guidelines, American researchers had been experimenting with stem cells derived from adult organs. Although adult stem cells had distinct therapeutic possibilities, they were sometimes difficult to isolate and purify, and they had less capacity to proliferate than embryonic cells. The biomedical research comunity, therefore, enthusiastically welcomed the ruling. (ELLEN BERNSTEIN)

SPECIAL REPORT

Socialized Medicine's Aches and Pains

by Bryan Christie

After a detailed examination by the World Health Organization (WHO) to assess the standards, responsiveness, and effectiveness of health systems in 191 countries, France was judged to have the best health care service in the world. The first-ever analysis of the world's health systems, published in *The World Health Report 2000,* produced some surprising findings and revealed wide variations in performance. The United States, which spent more than any other nation on health care, was ranked 37th and trailed countries such as Colombia and Morocco, which had much lower levels of health spending. Italy, Spain, Oman, Austria, and Japan all captured spots in the top 10, whereas many African countries—dragged down by the high death rates caused by the AIDS epidemic—were among the poorest performers. The publication of the report came at a time when health systems around the world faced ever-increasing pressures. The triple effect of an aging population, which placed additional demands on health services; of medical advances, which produced new and usually more expensive drugs and treatments; and of a public with high expectations of what medicine could achieve—all combined to push up costs, particularly in countries in the developed world.

The strains produced by these pressures were seen most clearly in "socialized medicine," nationally funded health systems such as Great Britain's National Health Service (NHS). Many countries voiced concern over long waiting lists for treatment and deteriorating standards of care, but state-controlled budgets proved incapable of providing the level of care people expected. As a result, serious doubts were being raised about the ability of socialized medicine to provide what was seen by many as the civilized answer to health care provision in the 21st century.

In Norway protests were staged in June outside the Storting (parliament) following a decision to raise charges for patients who saw their family doctor. Such charges had risen 40% in three years. In The Netherlands the government appointed a task force to report on the future of the Dutch health system as concern mounted about lengthening waiting lists, shortages in health staff, and budget restrictions. Following the deaths of several patients awaiting surgery, the Spanish government ordered that additional operating sessions be scheduled to reduce hospital waiting lists. In an attempt to control the ever-escalating budget for medication, the government in Spain also proposed an end to free prescription drugs for old-age pensioners. Doctors working in public hospitals in Israel imposed a series of sanctions over 18 weeks in an effort to gain a pay increase. The dispute led to the cancellation of 30,000 nonemergency operations and ended when the doctors accepted a 13% salary increase. The physicians also were given guarantees that a national review would be conducted of public medicine, including the possibility of allowing private medical services in public hospitals. Though France was judged to have the best health system in the world, that ranking did not make the country immune from these problems. Hospital staff staged demonstrations in February to protest staff shortages and budget restrictions.

Meanwhile, Canadians were increasingly dissatisfied with their publicly funded health system—which was also plagued with long waiting lists—especially when Canadians could see that just across the border Americans were being treated much more quickly. A report published by the Canadian Institute for Health Information—*Health Care in Canada 2000: A First Annual Report*—revealed that more and more Canadians were dissatisfied, and it noted that between 1987 and 1997 the proportion of those who felt that the system could work properly after only minor changes were made fell from 56% to 20%. Problems included delays in treating seriously ill patients, extreme overcrowding of hospital emergency services, and shortages of staff and vital equipment. Canadian Prime Minister Jean Chrétien responded to concerns that the country's health system was failing by announcing a 35% increase in spending over the next five years. The Can$23.4 billion (about U.S. $15.6 billion) increase was welcomed, although there were warnings that even more money would be needed in the future.

A similar solution had been fashioned in the U.K., where the NHS received the biggest funding increase in its history following widespread concern about the system's viability. The U.K. had some of the poorest cancer-survival rates, employed fewer medical specialists, and had a lower use of new drugs and medical technologies than most of its European neighbours. The NHS, which the British once believed was the envy of the world for establishing free access to high-quality health care for all, had been exhibiting all the signs of terminal decline. Owing to hospitals' inability to cope with demand during winter peaks, operations were canceled and waiting lists became lengthier. Expensive drugs were denied to those who needed them, and deteriorating standards of care were recorded across the country. These criticisms persuaded the British government to fund an extra £20 billion (about U.S. $30 billion) over the next five years to bring spending more into line with the European average.

"The essence of a satisfactory health system is that the rich and the poor are treated alike, that poverty is not a disability and wealth is not an advantage." This was the view of Aneurin Bevan, the British politician who helped create the NHS in 1948. His vision also led to the expansion of socialized medicine, which raised money through taxes or social security contributions to pay for health care for all. It was never imagined, however, that equity would mean that everyone would suffer from the same deteriorating level of service and that reality would force a call for change. Though additional funding seemed likely to solve the existing problems in the U.K. and Canada in the short term, an escalation in costs could obliterate a long-term solution. For that reason, the British Medical Association embarked on a wide-ranging review of future funding options for the NHS.

Socialized medicine was not the only system with problems. The U.S. was considered the Jekyll and Hyde of modern health care. It offered the best level of health care provision in the world, but in a system in which millions of uninsured people feared the consequences of falling ill. The WHO report found that the U.S. had the most responsive health service in the world and provided the most prompt attention, but when the fairness of the financing of health care was considered, it ranked 55th of the 191 countries.

The U.S., which spent almost twice as much as most European countries on health care, also found a need to reduce costs. The U.S. left cost containment to the marketplace, which over the past 20 years had led to the development of health maintenance organizations (HMOs). Although HMOs were privately run for-profit organizations, they worked in a similar fashion to socialized medicine, the state-run systems. HMOs provided medical care to large populations within tightly controlled budgets and often employed the doctors and nurses that supplied care. The persistent difficulty of meeting financial targets as demand for services constantly grew was demonstrated when Harvard Pilgrim Health Care, the largest HMO in New England, went into receivership earlier in the year. It was one of a number of failures among HMOs in recent years.

Americans also became increasingly angry at restrictions placed on their access to health care and accused some HMOs of denying them the care they needed. The problem was highlighted in June when the U.S. Supreme Court ruled against a woman who sued her HMO for failing to provide the best possible care. Cynthia Herdrich suffered a ruptured appendix days after she went to her HMO doctor complaining of abdominal pain. Herdrich had to wait eight days for the test at an HMO-affiliated hospital more than 80 km (50 mi) away. Her appendix ruptured prior to the test, and she won a $35,000 malpractice suit against the doctor and sued the HMO in a federal court. She claimed the arrangement that allowed doctors to keep a share of the HMO's profits gave them an incentive to act in their own interests rather than those of patients. The Supreme Court threw out the claim, however, and cited that "no HMO could survive without some incentive connecting physician reward with treatment rationing."

In *The World Health Report 2000,* WHO explained the complexity of adopting a single health care model. "The world is currently experimenting with many variants and there is no clear way to proceed." WHO did, however, consider systems that funded health services through prepayment schemes such as taxes, insurance, or social security preferable to those that relied on patients' paying the costs of treatment when illness struck. The report stated that governments worldwide should embrace the "new universalism"—the establishment of essential services that would be available to all citizens—but cautioned, "Clearly limits exist on what governments can finance and on what services they can deliver. . . . If services are to be provided for all, then not all services can be provided."

Bryan Christie is a freelance medical writer working in Edinburgh; he is a regular contributor to the British Medical Journal *and to other medical publications in the U.K.*

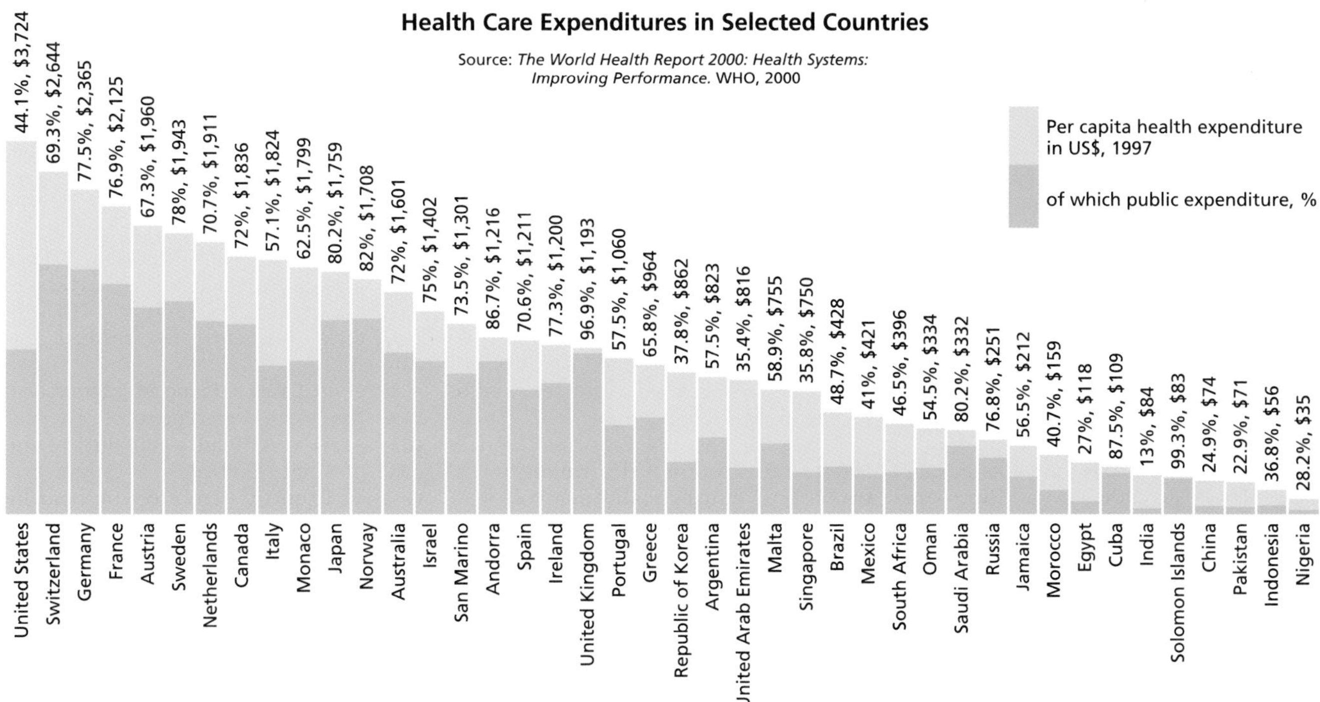

Law, Crime, and Law Enforcement

Among the topics claiming attention in law and crime in 2000 were **HUMAN RIGHTS** and **WAR CRIMES,** the **MICROSOFT** and **NAPSTER** cases, **TERRORISM,** and, of course deciding the **U.S. PRESIDENTIAL ELECTION.**

INTERNATIONAL LAW

International law continued to evolve in the areas of human rights, international security, and trade. In addition, the pressures of globalization and the consequences of the expanding web of international agreements shaped state interactions throughout 2000. (*See* ECONOMIC AFFAIRS: *Sidebar.*)

International Courts, War Crimes, and Human Rights. Caribbean states voted to establish a Caribbean Court of Justice, which would join three existing permanent international courts: the International Court of Justice (ICJ), the European Court of Justice, and the European Court of Human Rights (ECHR). The ICJ heard cases on India's 1999 downing of a Pakistani aircraft and a request from the Democratic Republic of the Congo (DRC) that Uganda withdraw from its territory. The court determined that it had no jurisdiction in the India-Pakistan dispute. In Congo's petition the ICJ bowed to Resolution 1304 of the United Nations Security Council, which demanded that Uganda and others retreat from the DRC.

The ECHR heard several cases against Turkey concerning its human rights record. The court in 1999 had ruled against Great Britain by declaring a ban on gays in the military a violation of the right to privacy.

States continued to make amends for World War II-era crimes. Germany established the $4.8 billion Remembrance, Responsibility and the Future Foundation to address all Nazi-era claims against German companies, particularly those that had employed slave labour. Similarly, a Japanese company agreed to establish a fund for descendants of Chinese who had been forced into slave labour during the Japanese occupation. A $1,250,000,000 fund was set up in Switzerland to reimburse people who had lost assets in Swiss banks, had been slave labourers for Swiss companies, or had been refused asylum in Switzerland. The Marshall Islands Nuclear Claims Tribunal granted $341 million to the people of Enewetak atoll, who were displaced from 1947 to 1980 and returned to find vast stretches of their land contaminated. The payment topped a $150 million fund the U.S. provided to settle claims arising from the nuclear-testing program conducted on the islands from 1948 through 1958.

The International Criminal Tribunal for the Former Yugoslavia produced its assessment of the 1999 NATO bombing of Yugoslavia. It determined that NATO did not cause "excessive" environmental damage and had selected noncivilian targets as much as "reasonably possible." The tribunal continued to await the arrest of indicted war criminals Radovan Karadzic and Slobodan Milosevic, former leaders of Bosnia and Herzegovina and of Yugoslavia, respectively. Dragan Nikolic, commander of the Susica prison camp in Bosnia, was apprehended in April.

The International Criminal Tribunal for Rwanda (ICTR) tried six cases and heard two appeals. The appeal of former prime minister Jean Kambanda's 1998 sentence to life in prison was dismissed in October. Georges Ruggiu, a former journalist, pleaded guilty to having incited genocide and received a 12-year sentence.

In October the UN Security Council adopted Resolution 1315, calling for a tribunal to punish Foday Sankoh and his followers for atrocities committed during their continuing rebel campaign in Sierra Leone. A tribunal was also being established for Cambodia. To avoid continued ad hoc international tribunal formation, states had voted in 1998 to establish a permanent International Criminal Court (ICC). By Dec. 31, 2000, 139 states had signed and 27 states had ratified the ICC treaty, which required 60 ratifications before it came into force. On the last day of the year U.S. Pres. Bill Clinton unexpectedly added the U.S. as a treaty signatory. Although no international tribunal was expected, in mid-December the UN Transitional Administration in East Timor indicted several Indonesians for war crimes.

A number of former government officials accused of human rights violations in their home countries faced prosecution elsewhere. In 1998 former Chilean dictator Gen. Augusto Pinochet Ugarte was arrested in Britain on a Spanish warrant. In March 2000 the British ruled that his health made him unfit to stand trial, and he was flown back to Chile. Following a Chilean Supreme Court ruling stripping Pinochet of the prosecutorial immunity he had enjoyed in Chile since 1978, a Chilean court indicted Pinochet on kidnapping charges and placed him under house arrest. The arrest was overturned on the grounds that Pinochet had not been questioned. The court-ordered questioning and mental health evaluation were to begin on Jan. 7, 2001, but the former dictator was refusing to cooperate.

In February the exiled dictator of Chad, Hissène Habré, was indicted and arrested in Senegal and charged with crimes against humanity. In July the charges were dismissed on the grounds that Senegal was not the proper venue. The dismissal was under appeal, and Chadians brought additional charges against Habré. Spain sought the extradition of Argentine Ricardo Miguel Cavallo, who was accused of torture in Argentina during the military's 1976–83 rule. Cavallo was arrested in Mexico in August.

U.S. Court Cases Relating to International Law. American awareness of international law was heightened during the case of Elián González, a Cuban boy rescued from the sea after the boat he was on sank, killing his mother, who had been trying to escape to the United States. Relatives in the U.S. had asked that he be granted asylum, but the court ruled that a six-year-old could not understand the request. Given the boy's close relationship with his father in Cuba and no imminent danger to him

AP/Wide World Photos

On April 22 U.S. federal agents in Miami remove six-year-old Elián González from the arms of one of the fishermen who rescued the boy after a failed ocean crossing from Cuba.

if he returned, the court decreed that the U.S. had to abide by the father's wishes and return him to Cuba.

In *Crosby* v. *National Foreign Trade Council,* the U.S. Supreme Court upheld a lower-court ruling that a Massachusetts law forbidding trade with Myanmar (Burma) was unconstitutional under the Supremacy Clause because it interfered with a similar national law.

Other Notable Events and International Legislation. The U.S. agreed to normalize trade relations with China permanently upon the latter's accession to the World Trade Organization (WTO). The U.S. lost two cases brought by the European Union (EU) in the WTO, which illustrated the difficulties of harmonizing national and international laws. The EU imposed sanctions against Austria after a coalition government was formed in February that included Jörg Haider's ultranationalist Freedom Party. The EU lifted sanctions in September but continued to monitor Austrian actions.

The first cases under the Internet Corporation for Assigned Names and Numbers (ICANN)'s new Uniform Domain Name Dispute Resolution Policy (UDNDRP) were settled in 2000, including those brought by the World Wrestling Federation and actress Julia Roberts. President Clinton signed an executive order stating that the U.S. would not enforce intellectual property rights concerning patented AIDS drugs in cases where infringements made the drugs available less expensively in sub-Saharan African nations.

In January more than 130 countries signed the Cartagena Protocol on Biosafety, which required notification if any transported material had been genetically modified. Two protocols were added to the Convention on the Rights of the Child. The first required states to stop forced recruitment of children under 18 into armed conflict. The second called for states to make child pornography and prostitution criminal offenses.

(VICTORIA C. WILLIAMS)

COURT DECISIONS

The United States courts decided a number of important and controversial cases during 2000, but none that would be recalled with such scrutiny and passion as the ones involving the election of the 43rd American president. The closest U.S. presidential election in modern history, the race between Democrat Al Gore and Republican George W. Bush hinged on the outcome in Florida. With less than 0.5% of the vote separating the candidates, an automatic recount was triggered. As Bush's winning margin dwindled, methods were sought to determine the intent of voters who filed disqualified ballots in a number of traditionally Democratic counties; the Republicans, meanwhile, fought to bar recounts and objected staunchly to any human determination of voters' intentions. There were also disputes over the discretionary authority of the Florida secretary of state, and a spate of trial court rulings as well as two decisions by the Florida Supreme Court transferred what would have been political questions into justiciable disputes or, as some would say, politicized Florida's legal system. Finally, in a decision every bit as divided as public opinion, the U.S. Supreme Court ruled 5–4 on December 12 that the manual recount of ballots required by the Flordia Supreme Court was unconstitutional, effectively determining the winner. George W. Bush claimed Florida's 25 votes in the Electoral College and the victory in the 2000 election.

The U.S. Supreme Court also addressed such contentious issues as abortion rights, the First Amendment freedoms of speech and association, church-state relations, and criminal law. To that list the court added a selection of cases dealing with federalism as well as newly ripe issues involving governmental regulation and public health.

One of the distinguishing characteristics of these cases was that they did not appear to have been selected for the purpose of promulgating doctrinal changes in the law. The Supreme Court's decisions reflected a pattern of predictability and ideological moderation. In the pair of cases involving laws pertaining to abortion, the court expanded procreative freedom on two fronts. By striking down a Nebraska law criminalizing "partial-birth" abortions, the authority of women and their physicians to make procedural decisions free from an undue burden imposed by the state was upheld in *Stenberg* v. *Carhart.* Furthering the rights of those seeking to procure an abortion, in *Hill* v. *Colorado* the court upheld a law restricting protests in the immediate vicinity of abortion clinics. Balancing the First Amendment rights of protesters and the privacy rights of women, the court reasoned "private citizens have always retained the power to decide for themselves what they wish to read, and within limits, what oral messages they want to consider. This statute simply empowers private citizens entering a health care facility with the ability to prevent a speaker, who is within eight feet and advancing, from communicating a message they do not wish to hear."

Falling more squarely under the rubric of association rights were a pair of cases involving the deliberate exclusion of gays from the Boy Scouts and the constitutionality of California's "blanket primary." The common denominator of these cases was a presumed right to permit organizational exclusivity. In *Boy Scouts of America* v. *Dale,* the court ruled 5–4 that application of New Jersey's public accommodations law, designed in part to prohibit discrimination based upon sexual orientation, constituted a violation of the Boy Scouts' freedom of expressive association. Arguing that retaining James Dale—an openly gay Scout leader—would "significantly burden the organization's right to oppose or disfavor homosexual conduct," Chief Justice William Rehnquist blunted what he called the "severe intrusion" of public law into the private organization's values and rules. In *California Democratic Party* v. *Jones,* the court declared unconstitutional Proposition 198, a 1996 law that permitted voters to choose among all candidates regardless of party affiliation in the state's primary election. Rebuking the argument that the law serves the compelling state interest of promoting, inter alia, fairness, participation, choice, and privacy, the court supported the party's right of exclusive association and participation, proffering that "in no area is the political association's right to exclude more important than in the process of selecting its nominee."

In another set of First Amendment cases, the court addressed the controversial subject of church-state relations. Forging an accommodationist path in *Mitchell* v. *Helms,* the court upheld Chapter 2 of the Education Consolidation and Improvement Act of 1981, which provided equipment and materials funding for public and private schools alike. Reasoning that the law results in neither governmental indoctrination nor decisions made by reference to religion, Justice Clarence Thomas wrote that the allocation of funds to parochial schools under Chapter 2 could not be construed as a "law respecting an establishment of religion." In *Santa Fe Independent School District* v. *Doe,* which involved the practice of an elected student council chaplain broadcasting over the intercom a prayer at the beginning of every varsity football game, however, the court adopted a separationist position on the establishment clause. In striking down the school district's policy, the court explained that such invocations could not be regarded as "private speech," and that despite the majoritarian process of electing the student council chaplain, the school's policy "does nothing to protect minority views but rather places the students who hold such views at the mercy of the majority."

In the area of criminal law, the court reiterated its objection to enhanced penalties for hate crimes in *Apprendi* v. *New Jersey,* prohibited random drug checkpoints in *Indianapolis* v. *Edmond,* and, perhaps most significantly, stabilized what appeared to be the eroding foundation of "Miranda warnings"—statement rights guaranteed to the criminally accused—in *Dickerson* v. *United States.* Despite a heated dissent from Justice Antonin Scalia, the court ruled that Miranda rights were, in fact, constitutional rights and therefore could not be denied through legislation passed by Congress.

The court also addressed a number of cases involving federalism and governmental regulation. In two important rulings it limited states' rights. In holding that state law must yield to federal law in the conduct of foreign policy in *Crosby* v. *National Foreign Trade Council,* the Supreme Court struck down a Massachusetts law barring state entities from conducting business with Myanmar (Burma) because it conflicted with an act of Congress. In *Reno* v. *Condon,* the court upheld the Driver's Privacy Protection Act of 1994, which restricted states from disclosing drivers' personal information without their consent. On regulatory policy, the court addressed what Justice Sandra Day O'Connor called "one of the most troubling public health problems facing our Nation today"—tobacco use. In what would likely become a central case in the field of administrative law, the court in *Food and Drug Administration* v. *Brown & Williamson Tobacco Corp.* disallowed FDA regulation of tobacco. Because Congress had clearly "precluded the FDA from asserting jurisdiction to regulate tobacco products," the agency could not, under the rubric of the Food, Drug, and Cosmetics Act, regulate cigarettes as delivery devices for the drug nicotine.

In the emerging field of "cyberlaw," the dominant cases addressed by the lower strata of the federal judiciary involved the Microsoft Corp. and Napster, Inc. Concluding that Microsoft violated antitrust laws, District of Columbia District Judge Thomas Penfield Jackson called for the divestiture of the software giant, effectively splitting the company's operation in two. On July 26, U.S. Judge Marilyn Hall Patel of the Northern District of California ordered Napster, the Internet start-up company that facilitated free on-line music trading, to shut down its World Wide Web site. A stay of injunction from the Ninth Circuit Court of Appeals followed two days later. The German-based Bertelsmann AG, which was suing Napster, offered to drop its suit—and encouraged other plaintiffs to do so as well—and merge with Napster to provide a fee-based operation that would solve the company's legal problems through negotiated settlement rather than litigation. (BRIAN SMENTKOWSKI)

CRIME

Terrorism. In its latest review of patterns of global terrorism, the U.S. Department of State in 2000 reported an encouraging and sharp decrease in the number of deaths and injuries caused by terrorist attacks. During 1999, 233 persons were killed and 706 wounded, compared with 741 deaths and 5,952 injuries in 1998. For the first time the review also identified South Asia, in addition to the Middle East, as a major hub of international terrorism. Both Pakistan and Afghanistan were accused of providing continuing support to international terrorists, including the notorious group led by Osama bin Laden, the alleged mastermind behind the 1998 bombings of U.S. embassies in East Africa.

In the Middle East, in the midst of escalating violence between Israelis and Arabs, suicide bombers carried out a deadly attack on October 12 against a U.S. Navy ship in the Yemeni port of Aden. The USS *Cole,* a modern missile-armed destroyer, was crippled by an explosion that ripped a huge hole in its hull and left 17 sailors dead and 39 wounded. The suicide mission appeared to have been launched from a small boat. As a massive investigation

National Security News Service/AFP Worldwide

A suspected terrorist attack on October 12 left a gaping hole in the side of the USS* Cole *and claimed the lives of 17 sailors.

got under way to identify the attackers, officials stated that no credible claim of responsibility had been made.

A spate of bombings and kidnappings in the Philippines, Malaysia, and Indonesia during the year prompted rising concern about the terrorist threat in Southeast Asia and, in particular, from Muslim extremist groups. In April one of those groups, the Abu Sayyaf, seized 21 hostages from a tourist diving resort in Malaysia and then held them captive on the Philippine island of Jolo, 900 km (565 mi) south of Manila in the Sulu Sea. The kidnappers demanded substantial ransoms for their captives, who included a number of foreign tourists. As negotiations continued for the release of the hostages, the Libyan government and others were reported to have paid as much as $15 million to secure the freedom of the foreign captives.

According to terrorism experts, such kidnappings were part of a growing global industry. An authoritative insurance industry survey reported that in 1999, 1,789 kidnappings for ransom occurred worldwide, almost all in the top 10 high-risk countries, led by Colombia, Mexico, and Brazil.

Drug Trafficking. A World Bank study published in June reported that rebel groups involved in conflicts throughout the world were more often motivated by the pursuit of lucrative commodities such as drugs and diamonds than they were by political, religious, or other goals. The study, which reviewed 47 civil wars that took place from Afghanistan to Zimbabwe between 1960 and 1999, found that the single biggest risk factor for the outbreak of conflict was a nation's economic dependence on commodities and an eagerness to profit from them. In Colombia, for example, the Revolutionary Armed Forces of Colombia (FARC), the country's largest rebel group, was said in reality to be a huge narcotics organization maintaining a force of 12,000 paid workers and fighters paid for by $700 million in annual drug-trafficking revenues.

In August, during a brief visit to Colombia, U.S. Pres. Bill Clinton reinforced the commitment of the U.S. to assisting that nation in retaking control of the nearly half of its territory lost to rebel groups such as the FARC. This commitment included $1.3 billion in mostly military aid approved by the U.S. Congress. U.S. officials estimated that 90% of the cocaine and much of the heroin consumed in the U.S. originated in or passed through Colombia.

Law-enforcement officials in both Europe and North America reported record seizures throughout the year of the so-called mood-enhancing "hug drug" ecstasy, or 3, 4-methylenedioxymethamphetamine (MDMA), as it was known scientifically. It was thought that at least 80% of all of the world's ecstasy was produced in clandestine urban laboratories established in The Netherlands.

Murder and Other Violence. The violent crime rate declined by more than 10% in the U.S. in 1999, the largest one-year drop reported in the 26-year history of the U.S. Department of Justice's largest crime survey. The survey figures—which were released in August and compiled from interviews with some 77,000 American households as well as from other collected data—confirmed preliminary FBI figures released in May for the same year that revealed a 7% decrease in the violent crime category comprising murder, forcible rape, robbery, and aggravated assault. The survey was the broadest measure of crime, as it was compiled from interviews throughout the U.S. with more than 77,000 people and collected data not only on crimes reported to police but also on the large number that went unreported. The FBI data were based on reports made to 17,000 police agencies throughout the U.S. In 1999 only 44% of violent crimes were reported to the police.

Despite the national traumas of mass shootings in schools, offices, and other public places in recent years, gun control advocates in the U.S. continued to have to battle for tougher laws against an entrenched and still powerful pro-gun lobby in the U.S. Congress. (*See* SPECIAL REPORT: *The U.S. Gun-Control Debate: A Critical Look.*) In May tens of thousands of people marched in Washington, D.C., and other cities across the country to demand that guns be licensed and registered and that their sales be strictly controlled. The march followed several gun-related incidents, including the fatal handgun shooting by a six-year-old boy of a fellow first-grader at an elementary school in a suburb of Flint, Mich., in February and the nonfatal shooting of seven young children at the National Zoo in Washington, D.C., in April by a 16-year-old boy armed with a handgun.

In Uganda authorities struggled to cope with a mass murder investigation involving approximately 900 victims who were members of an obscure religious cult known as the Movement for the Restoration of the Ten Commandments of God. At least 500 members of the apocalyptic sect were found burned to death in a fire at the cult's headquarters in Kanungu on March 17. (*See* RELIGION.)

War Crimes. Following the historic agreement in 1998 among 120 nations to adopt a treaty establishing an International Criminal Court (ICC) under the auspices of the UN, further consensus was reached among those nations in June on the elements of the crimes and the rules of evidence and procedure to be utilized by the ICC. Under the terms of the treaty, the Rome Statute, the creation of the ICC remained dependent upon its ratification by at least 60 nations. By late 2000 more than 20 ratifications had occurred. If established, the ICC would be a permanent court investigating and bringing to justice individuals who committed the most serious violations of international humanitarian law such as genocide, war crimes, and crimes against humanity.

In March the International Criminal Tribunal for the Former Yugoslavia sentenced a former Bosnian Croat general, Tihomir Blaskic, to 45 years in prison for having orchestrated ethnic cleansing during the 1992–95 Bosnian war. The sentence was the most severe punishment imposed by the tribunal to date.

White Collar Crime, Corruption, and Fraud. A survey commissioned by Transparency International (TI), a Berlin-based nongovernmental organization established to expose and prevent corruption, found that only 25% of the 779 multinational business executives who were questioned thought that corruption in their country of residence had diminished during the previous five years. The survey findings, released by TI in January, came despite the existence of a 20-year-old U.S. law prohibiting corrupt practices abroad and a new international convention outlawing bribery. The survey also found that government officials were most likely to accept or extort bribes in exchange for contracts in the construction and defense industries. In a separate report published in September, TI named Nigeria as the world's most corrupt country among 90 nations assessed for their levels of administrative probity. The five Nordic countries, led by Finland, along with Singapore, New Zealand, and Canada, were ranked the eight cleanest national administrative environments. The U.S. was ranked 14th.

In September an Indonesian court dismissed a landmark corruption case brought by that nation's first democratically elected government, led by Pres. Abdurrahman Wahid, against former Indonesian president Suharto. The court

SPECIAL REPORT

The U.S. Gun-Control Debate: A Critical Look

by Iain Murray

In 2000—a year that witnessed the antigun Million Mom March in Washington, D.C., as well as surging membership in the pro-gun National Rifle Association (NRA)—the issue of gun control was at the forefront of American political debate. Two facts define the poles of the controversy. On the one hand is the Second Amendment to the U.S. Constitution, which states: "A well regulated Militia, being necessary to the security of a free State, the right of the people to keep and bear arms, shall not be infringed." The exact meaning of the Second Amendment has been debated, but few people would argue that an outright ban on firearms would be possible as long as this text stands. On the other hand is the indisputably high rate of gun-related homicide in the U.S., both in absolute terms and in comparison with other industrialized countries. Each side of the gun-control debate has busied itself with gathering data to support the pro- or antigun stance. The evidence they have presented, however, is not as clear-cut as each side has suggested.

Through use of misleading definitions, advocates on both sides of the debate have distorted some data. The organizers of the Million Mom March, for example, made much of the figure of "12 children who die every single day from gunfire." This figure holds true only if persons aged 15–19 are counted as children. Deaths in this group usually occur because of older teenagers' involvement in distinctly unchildlike activities, such as drug-related crime. Using a more usual definition of children—aged 14 or below—1.7 children die daily from gun violence, and the number drops to 1.3 when suicides are excluded.

Pro-gun lobbyists, meanwhile, made much of the "defensive use" of guns, but the order-of-magnitude range of scientific findings makes these arguments suspect as well. Advocates argue that if more crimes are foiled by citizens defending themselves with guns than are committed by criminals using guns, then possession of firearms may actually provide a net benefit to society. Statistics from a U.S. Department of Justice (DOJ) survey, however, suggested that guns are used defensively in this sense only about 100,000 times a year, compared with 400,000-plus criminal gun uses. Other surveys indicated much higher levels of defensive firearm use. The figure of 2.5 million defensive uses a year proposed by Florida State University professor Gary Kleck was seized on by gun rights advocates such as the NRA. A more recent study undertaken by Philip J. Cook and Jens Ludwig for the National Institute of Justice, a government agency in Washington, D.C., estimated that 1.5 million owners used their guns defensively at least once a year. Kleck and others explained their high figures by pointing out that merely displaying or referring to the weapon can often deter a crime. Cook and Ludwig argued that surveys like this are vulnerable to "false positives"—cases, for example, when the person being interviewed remembers that an incident had taken place in the past but assigns it, erroneously, to the year about which the pollster is asking. Researchers such as Cook and Ludwig suspect that the truth lies somewhere in between the "official" DOJ figures and those of Kleck.

In addition to the careful research of academics such as Kleck, Cook, and Ludwig, advocacy groups also produced their own data, sometimes lacking in statistical rigour. In the U.S. the Brady Law, a measure implemented in February 1994, enforced a nationwide series of background checks of potential gun buyers. In July 2000 the Center to Prevent Handgun Violence (CPHV) issued a report that claimed the Brady Law had significantly reduced the number of homicides nationwide. About a week later, however, the *Journal of the American Medical Association* published a study (once again by Cook and Ludwig) that found that the introduction of background checks had not reduced homicide rates or overall suicide rates. What happened is that the CPHV researchers constructed a set of figures for what *could* have been the level of violent crime after 1993 and then attributed the negative difference to the Brady Law. The Cook-Ludwig study, on the other hand, compared the numbers of gun-related deaths in states that previously had background check programs with those in states that introduced the checks after February 1994 and found no significant difference between the two sets of figures. In other words, the Cook-Ludwig study employed a "control" (states where the Brady Law was essentially already in effect), while the CPHV study had no such basis for comparison. Cook and Ludwig admit that their study is not the end of the matter—further work needs to be done, they say, in assessing the Brady Law's impact on interstate gun traffic and other factors. Nevertheless, it is clear that the matter is not as simple as the CPHV study suggests.

The work of Yale University economist John Lott has also stirred controversy. His 1998 book *More Guns, Less Crime* summarized extremely detailed research into what happens when states (most famously Florida) liberalize laws

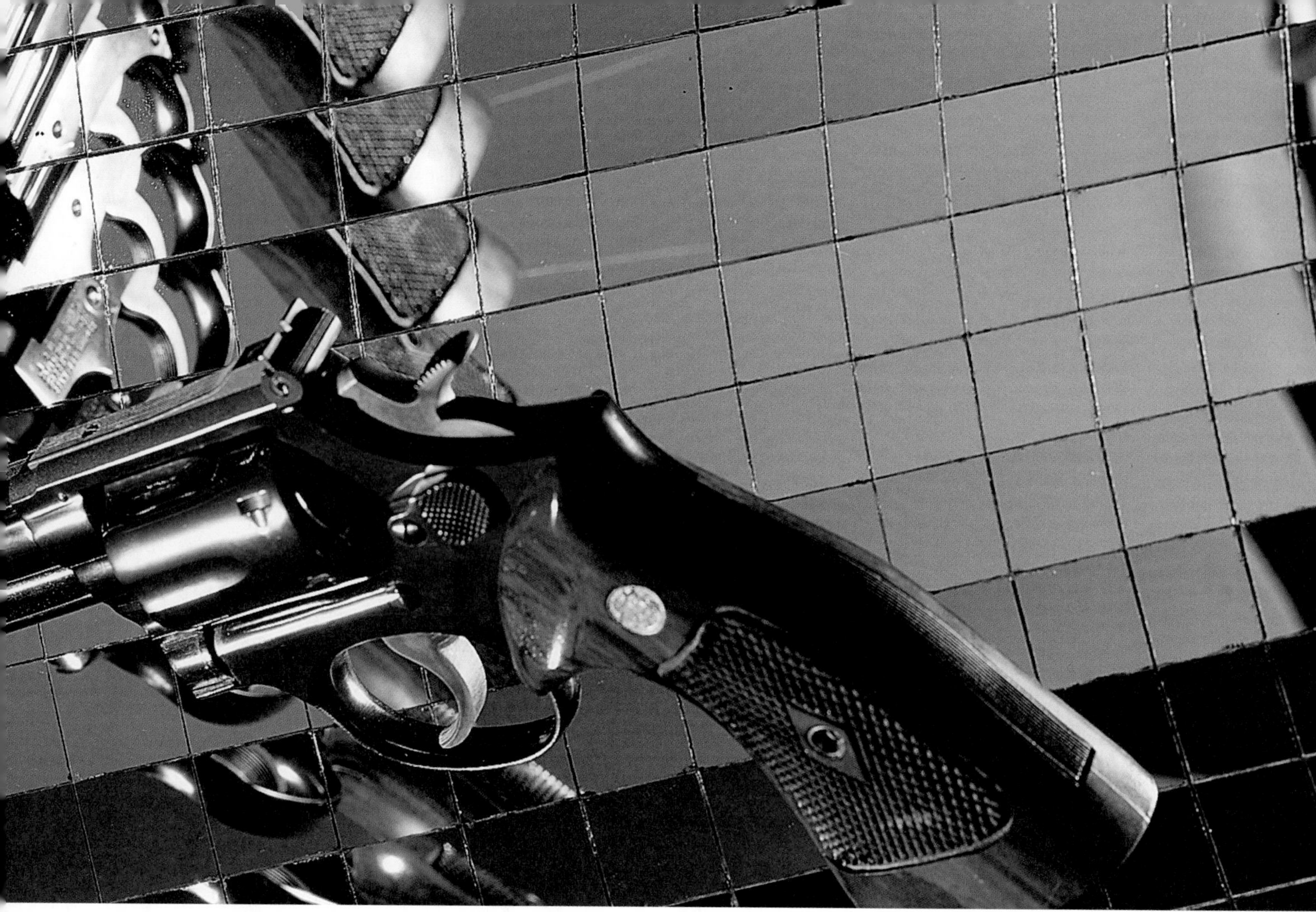

François Robert

to allow citizens to carry concealed weapons. He concluded that states that adopted such laws experienced significant declines in crime that could not be attributed to other factors, such as demographic changes, new policing methods, or tougher sentences. Many researchers, including Ludwig, attacked this work for supposed methodological weaknesses, and Lott's work came under intense scrutiny. Repeatedly he refined his data to control for a very large number of influencing factors. He could therefore counter all of the methodological criticisms, although many researchers remain unconvinced.

While the academic jury was still out, Lott's work was seen by both sides in the gun-control debate almost as a litmus test—if you were pro-gun, you believed Lott's findings; if you were pro-gun control, you dismissed them. The level of contention is so high that acceptance of a set of data by one side often means a knee-jerk rejection by the other. The research of U.S. government agencies should be objective enough to be acceptable to both sides, yet some data produced by the U.S. Department of Health and Human Services have been criticized for being biased in favour of gun control. As Cook said, "Many of the basic statistics about guns are in wide disagreement with each other depending on which source you go to. That's been a real puzzle to people who are trying to understand what's going on." The result is that the debate over gun control is dominated by interested parties who "cherry pick" data to suit their arguments.

The media are often not very critical of the statistics they are presented with either. With a vested interest both in reporting crime stories and in recording the views of those proposing solutions, the media often provide a platform for those who link gun ownership causally to gun homicide. The conservative Media Research Center found that from 1997 to 1999 television news stories "advocating more gun control outnumbered stories opposing gun control by 357 to 36. . . . (Another 260 were neutral.)" Probably understandably, newspapers, especially those based in the large metropolitan areas that suffered the most during the gun-homicide boom of the early 1990s, often adopted an editorial policy in favour of gun control and were more willing to accept numbers proposed by gun-control advocates on trust. Even so, the figures of pro-gun groups were sometimes conveyed uncritically as well. During the Million Mom March, members of the pro-gun group Second Amendment Sisters were quoted in the press as stating that "every day 550 rapes, 1,100 murders, and 5,200 other violent crimes are prevented just by showing a handgun," but these numbers, which derive from Kleck's work, are themselves disputable.

The gun-control issue in the United States is extraordinarily complex. Careful, scientific research and truthful, well-founded statistics can be the means to shed light on the root causes of firearm misuse and crime as well as other pressing social problems. Society will best be served when the general population and especially the public's chief source of information, the media, adopt a responsible approach and critical skepticism toward the claims of the parties at interest.

Iain Murray is a senior analyst at the Statistical Assessment Service, a nonpartisan, nonprofit research organization located in Washington, D.C.. The service is devoted to the accurate use of scientific and social research in public-policy debate.

ruled that Suharto, 79, was medically unfit to stand trial on charges that he embezzled $570 million in state funds during his 32-year dictatorial rule, which ended in 1998 amid economic collapse and widespread civil unrest. Suharto, along with his six children, was believed to have stolen billions of dollars from Indonesia through an elaborate network of family-related business arrangements.

In China an ongoing campaign against corruption at the top levels of the ruling Communist Party resulted in the conviction and execution in March of a senior official for taking bribes worth more than $600,000. The official, Hu Changqing, a former deputy governor of a province, was the highest-ranking person to have been put to death for corruption since the communists seized power in China in 1949.

In the U.S. a survey conducted by the Computer Security Institute and released in March estimated that computer fraud and theft were responsible for an estimated $10 billion in losses during 1999. This figure, almost double that of the previous year, was said to be a reflection of the vast increase in the use of the Internet.

Law Enforcement. In May the highly influential Group of Seven nations, together with Russia, convened the first international gathering of law-enforcement agencies, business leaders, and government officials to combat the problems of computer crime. The meeting followed the release on May 4 of a computer virus, dubbed the Love Bug, that crippled e-mail systems around the globe and other high-profile on-line frauds that demonstrated both the technical flaws of the Internet and the legal vacuum in which it still operated. Critics claimed that computer crime could be fought more effectively by technical innovation, education of users about security risks, and better use of existing laws.

Federal law-enforcement officials in the U.S. came under sustained criticism during the year for their handling of the controversial investigation and prosecution of a Taiwanese American scientist, Wen Ho Lee, who was accused of having stolen secrets from the Los Alamos (N.M.) National Laboratory, where he worked. Lee, who was arrested and indicted in December 1999 on 59 felony counts of mishandling classified information, was held in harsh conditions under solitary confinement and without bail until his release in September following his agreement with prosecutors to plead guilty to just one of those counts. Justifying the plea bargain, FBI Director Louis Freeh testified before Congress that national security concerns prompted the agreement, preventing sensitive information about nuclear secrets from being disclosed in open court and securing Lee's cooperation in revealing what had happened to the material he had downloaded at work onto a portable computer.

In Great Britain a nearly four-month-long sensational trial and subsequent conviction of the nation's most prolific serial killer raised serious concerns about the handling of the case by local police and medical authorities. In January Harold Shipman, a well-respected general practitioner, was sentenced to life imprisonment for having murdered 15 elderly women patients by injecting them with fatal doses of morphine. Following the conviction, the Greater Manchester Police disclosed that they had investigated a total of 136 suspicious deaths involving Shipman's patients during a 15-year period. It was also revealed that despite warnings from survivors and other physicians about the striking rate of deaths among Shipman's patients, neither the medical establishment nor the police had detected the murders for years.

In Brazil human rights groups claimed in February that civil and military police in Latin America's most populous nation had participated in at least 2,500 killings since 1997. Most of those killed were thieves or drug dealers, and many had been tortured or mutilated before being shot in the head at close range. The allegations drew renewed attention to a long-standing problem in Brazil, where corrupt police preyed on impoverished communities, often in collaboration with politicians and businessmen who used the poorly trained and low-paid officers as neighbourhood vigilantes or enforcers in drug trafficking. (*See also* SOCIAL PROTECTION: *Special Report:* Slavery in the 21st Century.) (DUNCAN CHAPPELL)

PRISONS AND PENOLOGY

The prison populations of most countries continued to rise in 2000. Of the worldwide total of 8.6 million persons who were either untried or not yet sentenced, approximately half was accounted for by the United States, Russia, and China. Although the U.S. total exceeded two million for the first time, the 3.4% rate of growth during 1999 was half the annual average achieved during the previous 10 years. Only the U.S. and Russia had prison population rates of about 700 per 100,000 inhabitants. England and Wales were at the midpoint on the world list with rates of 125, while China's rate was 110. One-third of the countries had rates of 150 or higher, and almost all of them were in southern Africa, the Caribbean, former Soviet Central Asia, and Central and Eastern Europe.

In May, Russian authorities, celebrating the 55th anniversary of the defeat of Germany, authorized the release of 120,000 prisoners. This measure, however, provided only marginal and temporary relief for the crowded conditions (Butyrsky Prison in Moscow, two centuries old, held 5,500 persons in cells designed for 2,500) and for the tuberculosis epidemic among the nation's prisoners, described by Médecins Sans Frontières (Doctors Without Borders) as a threat to world health. In South Korea 3,586 prisoners were released to mark the anniversary of liberation from Japan's colonial rule in 1945, and in Pakistan, 20,000 persons were released. Amnesties were also under consideration in Belarus, Uzbekistan, and Italy.

In many parts of the world, prison conditions reached new depths of degradation and despair. In South Africa (where the rise in untried prisoners was especially sharp), many prisons, including juvenile institutions, remained grossly overcrowded. In Thailand 200,000 persons were being held in facilities designed for 80,000, and severe overcrowding and explosive conditions were reported across much of Latin America. In the Czech Republic, with 24,000 prisoners held in facilities designed for 19,500, a widespread hunger strike drew attention to deteriorating conditions. In Brazil troops put down a riot at the juvenile Tauape Detention Centre in May, and in the following months at a prison in Curitiba, guards were taken hostage during two riots that focused on crowded conditions. At Lurigancho, Peru's largest prison, five prisoners were killed in a riot during which court delays and crowding (6,000 persons against a capacity of 1,500) were cited as aggravating issues. The U.S. Department of Justice found that there had been beatings and other forms of abuse of inmates by guards at the Jena Juvenile Justice Center in Louisiana; it was run by the Wackenhut Corrections Corp., which managed penal institutions with a total of almost 41,000 beds in North America, Europe, Australia, and Africa.

DEATH PENALTY

By mid-2000, 108 countries, more than half the world's total, had abolished the death penalty in law or practice; 87 countries retained the death penalty for ordinary crimes and 12 for crimes under military law or for crimes committed in exceptional circumstances. Four abolitionist countries had reintroduced the death penalty since 1985, but by 2000 only one of those, the Philippines, had carried out executions. The UN's Second Optional Protocol to the International Covenant on Civil and Political Rights (which provides for the total abolition of the death penalty) had by 2000 been ratified by 43 member states and signed by 7 others. The U.S., which had ratified the Covenant but with reservations in regard to the death penalty provisions, seemed likely to find itself under increasing international pressure on that issue. In April the UN Commission on Human Rights voted 27–13 (countries voting against included China, the U.S., Cuba, Rwanda, Indonesia, Pakistan, India, and Japan) to condemn capital punishment.

Executions were resumed in Qatar after a 12-year lull. The number of executions was greatest in China (where over 1,000 took place in 1999, more than the combined figure for the rest of the world), Saudi Arabia, Iran, the Democratic Republic of the Congo, and the U.S. (where 85 persons—13 fewer than in 1999—were executed in 2000). Anxieties that innocent people had received the death penalty led the governor of Illinois in January to declare a moratorium on executions in the state until he could be sure that no innocent person would meet that fate.

(ANDREW RUTHERFORD)

Anti-death penalty activists march outside the State Capitol in Austin, Texas, on June 19 to protest the scheduled execution of convicted murderer Gary Graham.

Edward A. Ornelas/San Antonio Express News/Liaison Agency

Libraries and Museums

TORNADOES, flooding, **PRESERVATION,** restoration, and **INTERNET ACCESS** were among the issues concerning **LIBRARIES** and **MUSEUMS** during the year; several new **EYE-POPPING** facilities were opened, **THEFT** was a problem, and **CLAIMS** were made by **HOLOCAUST** and other wartime **SURVIVORS** for materials seized as **SPOILS OF WAR.**

LIBRARIES

Two important roles of libraries—as repositories of knowledge and as keepers of culture—were highlighted in the year 2000. Libraries collected vast quantities of written materials that ranged from incunabula to digital information.

Parents and politicians in the U.S. continued to voice concerns over children's access to inappropriate material in libraries. Once again, legislation was introduced in the U.S. Congress that would require the schools and libraries receiving federal "e-rate" subsidies for Internet connections to install filtering software that would block access to World Wide Web sites containing sexually explicit content. Voters in Holland, Mich., drew national attention in February when they defeated (55% to 45%) a ballot proposal that would have required the city to withhold funding from the Herrick District Library unless the library installed filters on all of its public Internet workstations.

King Juan Carlos I of Spain launched a bilingual Web site—<http://lcweb.loc.gov/rr/hispanic/frontiers/meetingeng.html>—developed jointly by the National Library of Spain and the U.S. Library of Congress. The latter, which celebrated its 200th birthday on April 24, was cautioned in July by the National Research Council to act quickly to "address strategy, management, funding, and staffing issues that threaten to render the institution second rate among today's digital libraries."

Libraries increasingly scanned print materials into digital form to make them accessible worldwide; some nations, however, clearly feared losing control of information and communication. At the National Library of China, some 24 million pages of printed information were now available on-line, but in October the Chinese government issued draconian new Internet policies that forbade, among other things, spreading rumours and hurting China's "reputation." Meanwhile, friends and colleagues in the U.S. used the Internet to help secure the release from a Chinese prison of Song Yongyi, a librarian at Dickinson College, Carlisle, Pa. He had been imprisoned for nearly six months by Chinese authorities on charges of illegally gathering documents on behalf of foreign interests. He was released on January 28 and became a U.S. citizen on February 20.

The Shanghai Library completed restoration of some 30,000 ancient rubbings from stone inscriptions that illuminated life in China. In Berlin the handwritten scores of many of Johann Sebastian Bach's greatest works were turning to dust as the country commemorated the 250th anniversary of the composer's death. Analysis of the documents showed that the ink Bach used was extremely acidic. Cooperative efforts by the State Library in Berlin, IBM Corp., and eight other institutions produced a digital preservation Web site—<www.bachdigital.org>.

A number of claims were made during the year concerning library materials seized as spoils of war. An Italian archbishop renewed a request that the British Library (BL) return a 12th-century manuscript looted from a cathedral near Naples during World War II. Monks at the Monastery of St. Catherine

AP/Wide World Photos

U.S. Sen. Jay Rockefeller visits a library in Paw Paw, W.Va., population 500, where federal money is being used to bring Internet access to rural areas.

on Mt. Sinai, Egypt, were demanding the return from the BL of the Codex Sinaiticus, the oldest-existing New Testament in the world. Ethiopian scholars were pressing a number of British libraries to return manuscripts, jewelry, religious icons, and other artifacts taken by British troops in 1868. A parliamentary commission was studying the claim. Johns Hopkins University, Baltimore, Md., returned a section of a 9th-century edition of the Qur'an written in gold leaf to its original home in Turkey. Parts of the Gold Qur'an had disappeared after 1756, and the section was bequeathed to Johns Hopkins in 1942. According to Elan Steinberg, executive director of the World Jewish Congress, some 186,000 books confiscated by the Nazis were given in 1951 to various Austrian libraries. Documents discovered in the State Archives in Vienna revealed that the Austrian government authorized this distribution.

Valuable library materials were stolen, too. Thefts from university libraries in Poland, Russia, and Ukraine in recent years were attributed in 2000 to an "international book mafia." The gang was known as the Astronomers because many of the books stolen were works by astronomers Nicolaus Copernicus and Ptolemy; Interpol believed the gang was Russian, and journalists speculated that the thefts were being commissioned by a fanatic collector.

A tornado that on March 28 struck downtown Fort Worth, Texas, caused $1.2 million in damage to the exterior and some $400,000 to the interior of the city's recently renovated Central Library. Catastrophic flooding soaked some 100,000 volumes at the North Dakota State University library in the early hours of June 20; damage totaled at least $5 million.

In January the Seattle, Wash.-based Bill & Melinda Gates Foundation donated $2.5 million to the Canadian province of British Columbia for computer equipment; the gift also included $1 million of software. In August Microsoft Corp. cofounder Paul Allen donated $20 million to the Seattle Public Library, earmarking $15 million for books and other materials and $5 million to go toward building a children's centre in the new central library.

The Friends of Cuban Libraries, an anti-Castro group based in the U.S., reported that some 30 independent libraries had opened in Cuba and offered access to books banned by the government. The caretakers of these collections were reportedly subjected to "systematic persecution," although it was not clear if this was because of book-related problems or oppositionist activities. Meanwhile, the British government planned to spend £252 million (about $380 million) to equip libraries, pubs, and soccer clubs with computers and Internet connections in a move to extend the Internet to the "information underclass."

A number of new libraries opened in 2000. In Israel, at Yad Vashem, a new archive and library containing the world's largest collection of Holocaust material opened. In Sarawak, Malaysian officials greeted the millennium by opening the Sarawak State Library, a state-of-the-art information technology centre. American Vietnam veteran William J. Kelly, Jr., financed a new library that opened in the southern province of Binh Phuoc, Vietnam.

(GORDON FLAGG; THOMAS GAUGHAN)

MUSEUMS

The opening of several new museums around the world highlighted 2000. Bankside Power Station in London was transformed into the new Tate Modern, which housed the modern collection of the Tate Gallery; the structure was designed by Swiss architects Herzog & de Meuron. In Germany the last new federal museum opened in Greifswald; the Pommersches Landesmuseum was charged with interpreting Pomerania's history and culture. The inaugural exhibition at the Jewish Museum Berlin, designed by Daniel Libeskind, was postponed until 2001. Greece announced a new design competition for a museum to be built at the foot of the Acropolis in Athens and to be opened in time for the 2004 Athens Olympics. At the end of 2000, Italy planned to open a Mafia documentation centre in Sicily that was meant to break the code of silence surrounding organized crime. Thirty years after it was conceived, the Salvador Allende Museum of Solidarity opened in Santiago, Chile.

Part of the stuffed body of a 19th-century Bushman is displayed in Gaborone, Botswana, in October after being returned by the Darder Museum of Natural History in Banyoles, Catalonia, Spain.

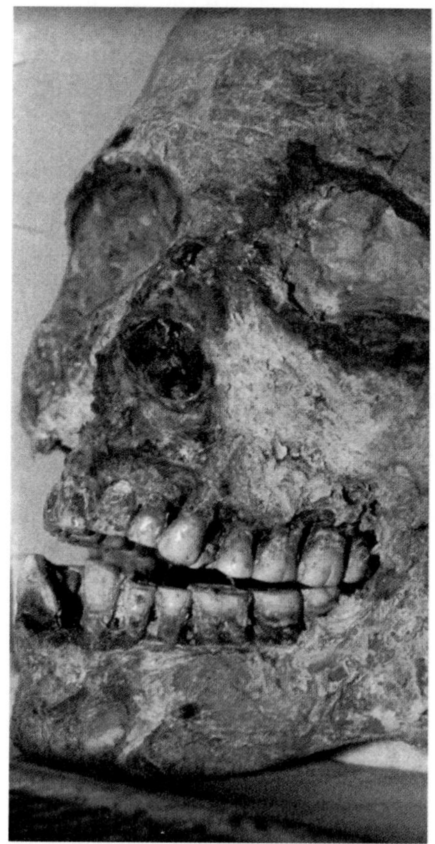

Reuters NewMedia Inc./Corbis

After having been closed for a decade, the Iraq Museum in Baghdad reopened after the reinstallation of some 10,000 of the approximately 250,000 artifacts that had been crated and stored during the Gulf War. The national museum in Kabul, Afg., also reopened briefly for the first time after years of civil war. A 1993 rocket attack had destroyed the building, and its contents had been looted by mujahideen. The oldest gallery in England, the Dulwich Picture Gallery in London, was reopened in the spring after months of extensive renovations. Rome's Pinacoteca Capitolina resumed operations after a restoration and reorganization increased its available space. The Louvre opened its new galleries of Africa, Asia, Oceania, and the Americas and for the first time displayed art from sub-Saharan Africa.

An alliance struck between the Solomon R. Guggenheim Foundation and the State Hermitage Museum focused on the renovation of space at the Hermitage for exhibitions from the Guggenheim and the lending of works from the Hermitage for the Guggenheim's future space on the East River in New York City as well as for other museums. The two institutions would also collaborate on the opening of a small museum in Las Vegas, Nev. Another joint venture, between the Museum of Modern Art in New York and the Tate Gallery, would result in a new, for-profit World Wide Web site from which the two institutions would sell goods and services.

Holocaust survivors or their heirs continued to make claims for objects in European museums. At a gathering in Vilnius, Lithuania, 37 governments agreed to make every reasonable effort to achieve the restitution of cultural assets looted during World War II. Ten national museums in the United Kingdom posted and continually updated a list of works whose Holocaust-era ownership histories were incomplete; German museums and such American museums as the Art Institute of Chicago; the Denver Art Museum; the Museum of Fine Arts, Boston; the National Gallery of Art, Washington, D.C.; and the North Carolina Museum of Art, Raleigh, took similar steps. In compliance with a 1998 law, Austrian museums examined their collections for Nazi booty. Images of those items for which owners could not be located would be posted on the Internet. The Czech Republic passed a law that would allow property confiscated by the Nazis to be returned, including material held in national museums. Russia passed a law that would permit victims of the Nazi regime or Russia's wartime allies to seek the return of looted art; this measure did not include, however, the lifting of a prohibition against the return of material taken by the Soviet Union from Germany or German citizens. Armenia, on the other hand, returned thousands of objects that the Red Army had taken from libraries and museums in Germany.

Some museums were victims of theft, while others welcomed returned goods. Claude Monet's painting *The Beach at Pourville* was stolen from the National Gallery in Poznan, Pol., and a reproduction was put in its place. Thieves filched Paul Cézanne's painting *Auvers-sur-Oise* after breaking into the University of Oxford's Ashmolean Museum of Art and Archaeology. A stolen Enigma machine, used to break Nazi codes during World War II, was anonymously sent to a U.K. newscaster, who returned it to Bletchley Park, the home of Great Britain's wartime code breakers. It was missing several rotors, however. The Darder Museum of Natural History in Banyoles, Catalonia, Spain, returned the stuffed body of a 19th-century Bushman to Botswana after officials deemed the display (on view from 1916 to 1997) inappropriate. The Berlin Museum returned to Nepal a stone idol of Uma-Maheshwor, an 800-year-old stone relief stolen 18 years earlier.

During 2000 an estimated $1.9 billion was spent on new museums and expansions in the U.S., ranging from Frank O. Gehry's $100 million Experience Music Project in Seattle, Wash., to the $1.2 million National D-Day Museum in New Orleans. Among the projects were the expansion of the $210 million Frederick Phineas and Sandra Priest Rose Center for Earth and Space at the American Museum of Natural History in New York City and the creation of a $2.5 million children's garden at the Winterthur (Del.) Museum.

American museums boasted 865 million visits in 2000, up from the 600 million annual visits in the late 1980s. Increased scrutiny was therefore placed on these institutions, especially regarding ethical issues. Concerns both inside and outside museum groups prompted the museum community, led by the American Association of Museums, to produce ethical guidelines on the exhibition of borrowed objects.

(BARRY SZCZESNY; HELEN J. WECHSLER)

Life Sciences

An **ACHIEVEMENT OF PROFOUND SIGNIFICANCE** in 2000 was the completion of a rough draft of the **SEQUENCE OF THE HUMAN GENOME.** Scientists' observation of a pervasive **DECLINE IN REPTILE POPULATIONS** suggested that a **WORLDWIDE CRISIS** was in progress. **DEBATE** continued over the **ENVIRONMENTAL AND HEALTH EFFECTS** of **GENETICALLY MODIFIED CROP PLANTS.**

ZOOLOGY

Research on animals in 2000 ranged from tiny hummingbirds to the giant extinct moas, delved into the evolutionary responses of prey to predators, and focused on dolphins to gain insight into the development of language. Issues in conservation biology continued to dominate concerns about wildlife on a global scale.

Dolphins were considered to be among the most intelligent of nonhuman animals because of their large brains, their advanced social behaviour, and their ability—observed in captivity—to communicate with each other by whistling. A study by Vincent M. Janik of the University of St. Andrews, Scot., provided evidence that dolphin whistles are used for social communication between individuals in the wild. Captive dolphins previously had been documented to repeat underwater whistles immediately upon first hearing them and to develop individualized signature whistles with distinctive frequency patterns. To test the effectiveness of whistle communication in wild dolphins while avoiding observer effects, Janik analyzed recordings of hydrophones that had been placed in an area inhabited by groups of bottle-nosed dolphins (*Tursiops truncatus*) in the Kessock Channel of Moray Firth, Scotland. More than 1,700 whistles were recorded in instances when an average of 10 dolphins were in the vicinity. Of the total number of recorded whistles, Janik was able to pinpoint the exact location for 991 of them by means of direction-finding techniques. From an analysis of whistle timing and location, he was able to identify cases in which whistles had received responding whistles from dolphins in other locations. Whistle matching, in which one dolphin responded immediately by repeating the signature whistle of another dolphin, was documented in 39 instances. The average distance between animals was 179 m (587 ft), and the maximum signature whistle and response observed between two animals was 579 m (2,000 ft). Imitating the vocalizations of other individuals was considered a key step in the evolution of language among humans. Because, other than humans, no land mammals were known to imitate sounds, study of the communication mechanisms and vocal interactions between dolphins offered a valuable opportunity to gain new perspectives on the origin of language and vocal learning.

The presence of predators was known to be responsible for the evolution of certain traits, including a variety of behavioral and morphological mechanisms of defense, in prey organisms. Ann V. Hedrick of the University of California, Davis, conducted experiments on field crickets (*Gryllus integer*) to test the assumption of evolutionary models that the fitness advantage conferred to males that exhibit conspicuous female-attracting behaviour is offset by their greater risk of predation. Male crickets attract female mates by calling, and the length of time that different individuals call is genetically inherited. Female field crickets generally select male mates with the longest calling times. Predators of field crickets, which include mice, birds, lizards, and toads, are able to locate calling crickets by their sound, as are parasitoid flies that deposit their larvae on crickets. Consequently, individual crickets having longer periods of calling are more likely to attract female crickets but also are at greater risk of being located by predators and parasitoids. In experiments designed to compare how male crickets having different call lengths responded to predators, Hedrick used two measures of predator avoidance—the length of time before a male left a protected shelter after exposure to a predator and the length of time before it began to call again. The study demonstrated that males exhibiting the most conspicuous and effective behaviour to attract mates also were the most cautious in their response to predatory threats. This result contradicted the assumption that the males that are most ostentatious and thus most alluring to females necessarily suffer the greatest cost from predation.

Rick A. Relyea and Earl E. Werner of the University of Michigan at Ann Arbor observed a morphological response of prey to the presence of predators that suggested an adaptive process. The predators in this case were larval dragonflies of the genus *Anax*, and the prey were tadpoles of four species of frogs of the genus *Rana*. In each of the prey species of frogs, the investigators observed an ability to alter morphological development that depended on whether dragonfly predators were present. To assess morphological change in individual tadpoles, they conducted computerized image analysis of tail-fin, body, and tail-muscle measurements. For each of the four species of frogs, tadpoles reared with dragonfly predators showed significant morphological differences from those raised without predators present, which indicated a potential for plasticity in body shape for each species. (By contrast, the normal rates of growth and development of the tadpoles of each species were not affected by predator presence.) Many of the changes noted by the investigators, such as the development of deeper tail fins that increase swimming speed, previously had been shown to be effective antipredator mechanisms that could possibly have adaptive value.

Among the various ways that morphological differences within a species can be expressed is sexual dimorphism, in which members of the two sexes vary in body size or proportions and appearances of body parts. Charles Darwin gave three possible explanations for the evolution of sexual dimorphism. Two are sexual selection (selection for traits that improve mating success) and fecundity selection (selection for traits that increase reproductive output); in each case a reproductive advantage accrues to a particular sex. Examples of both are apparent in many species. Ethan J. Temeles

National Audobon Society/Photo Researchers, Inc.

The bills of the female and male carib hummingbird (left and right, respectively) show differences attributed to ecological causation.

and colleagues of Amherst (Mass.) College provided evidence in purple-throated carib hummingbirds (*Eulampis jugularis*) for Darwin's third, rarely documented explanation of sexual dimorphism—ecological causation. The carib hummingbirds on the island of St. Lucia in the West Indies pollinate two plant species, *Heliconia caribaea* and *H. bihai,* from which they obtain nectar. Male hummingbirds are larger and have longer wings than females, but the bills of females are more than 30% longer and are curved downward at twice the angle of the males' bills. In a census of foraging hummingbirds, all of 15 males were observed to feed on *H. caribaea,* compared with only 7 of 18 females, presumably owing to males' defending their territories. Instead, females fed primarily on *H. bihai.* The two flower species differ in floral structure, with the bills and feeding times of males being more compatible with *H. caribaea* and those of females with *H. bihai.* The investigators concluded that the evolution of bill dimorphism had been driven by responses to specialization for the different flower types. In a comparison of wing length to bill length among purple-throated carib hummingbirds and several of their close relatives, no reliable pattern was apparent that might have been expected from phylogenetic similarity, which suggested that sexual dimorphism in bill length had been influenced by behaviour or ecology of the species.

Zoological conservation continued as an important issue for a variety of animal groups and species. R.N. Holdaway of Palaecol Research, Christchurch, N.Z., and Christopher Jacomb of the Canterbury Museum, Christchurch, examined information relating to the extinction of 11 species of moas, the enormous flightless birds formerly indigenous to New Zealand. The study provided the disquieting revelation that the elimination of all species had probably been completed within a century from the time of arrival in New Zealand of the Polynesian ancestors of the Maori, possibly as late as the 13th century. The investigators used human colonization rates and the human exploitation of birds, habitat loss, and numbers of birds initially present to develop simulation models to estimate the rates of decline. In order not to underestimate the time necessary for extinction to have occurred, the most conservative figures were used for each variable. Even when only 100 original colonists and a large original population of 160,000 moas were assumed and when the environmental impact of habitat loss was discounted, none of the models yielded a span of more than 160 years between the arrival of the Polynesians and the extinction of the birds. From a conservation perspective, it was significant that a small number of original colonists exploiting a long-lived animal species with a low reproductive rate could cause adult mortality rates high enough to render extinct a major portion of a region's fauna in a relatively short time.

The applicability of the moa study to modern species was reinforced with the report by investigators from the University of Georgia's Savannah River Ecology Laboratory, Aiken, S.C., that documented the decline of representatives of all major groups of reptiles on all continents within the past century. As had been reported previously for amphibians, many reptile populations were unquestionably declining in size and abundance on a global scale. When coupled with the problems experienced by amphibians, the evidence suggested that a worldwide crisis was in progress. The causes of declines for both reptiles and amphibians were known with certainty in many instances and were suspect in many more, the six most commonly identified threats being habitat loss and degradation, introduced invasive species, environmental pollution, disease and parasitism, unsustainable commercialization, and global climate change. The study emphasized that the decline and disappearance of populations of reptiles and amphibians or, in some instances, of entire species can occur with little awareness even by biologists. The threats to these animals, as well as to other wildlife, had to be viewed as a serious worldwide situation not only by scientists but also by the general public and government policy makers. (J. WHITFIELD GIBBONS)

BOTANY

The potential dangers of genetically modified (GM) plants continued to be debated in 2000. The issue grew increasingly heated in both Western Europe and the U.S. as concerns were expressed about the effects of the plants on the environment and human health. Policy makers in Europe set new restrictions on how far away from conventional crops GM crops undergoing field trials had to be grown to prevent transfer of GM plant pollen, but these limits were later shown to be highly suspect as to their effectiveness. Results of the first large-scale study of the flow of genetic material from GM oilseed rape to its wild relatives suggested that hybridization between crops and weeds is rare but that it does occur. Alarm was also raised over the accidental planting of GM oilseed rape on several farms in Europe. That the problem of inadvertent mixing could be widespread was suggested by results of a random sampling conducted by a company that screened for GM material. Genetic ID of Fairfield, Iowa, found that more than half the samples of conventional seed taken from American distributors contained some GM seeds.

Another controversy continued to brew over so-called GM terminator seeds. These seeds can give rise to only one generation of plants; the next-generation seeds are sterile. Poor farmers in the less-developed world saw this technology as a serious economic threat because they relied on saving some seeds from their crop for the next year's planting. In August the U.S. Department of Agriculture (USDA) announced that it would sanction the terminator technology, albeit with conditions to guard against environmental damage—for example, from cross-pollination with conventional crops, which might then become sterile. (The USDA was a joint patent holder of terminator technology, but it also regulated the engineered seeds to ensure that they were safe enough to be field-tested and sold commercially.) Biotechnology protesters vehemently opposed the decision.

Despite significant biological and ethical concerns, the potential benefits of GM crops remained tantalizing. During the year a gene that helps determine the size of fruit in tomato plants was identified by Anne Frary, Steven Tanksley, and colleagues of Cornell University, Ithaca, N.Y.—the first time that a gene for a quantitative trait such as height or weight had been found in plants. Because related genes exist in many other plant species, the discovery could lead to the genetic engineering of giant fruit, vegetables, or grain and the development of small wild plants into new, larger crops.

GM crops also had considerable potential to be tailored into products having therapeutic and health benefits. In September Charles Arntzen of Cornell University reported that his team had genetically engineered a vaccine into tomatoes and bananas that could wipe out hepatitis B and thus potentially save hundreds of thousands of lives each year. The edible vaccine awaited a license from the USDA to allow the plants to be grown commercially. (*See* AGRICULTURE: *Special Report.*)

The excitement surrounding GM research had a tendency to overshadow significant conventional plant-breeding work. A team at the John Innes Centre, Norwich, Eng., announced in May at an Institute of Food Research seminar in London that it had bred a "superbroccoli" by crossing ordinary broccoli with a wild relative that contains 10 times as much sulforaphane, a compound that helps neutralize cancer-causing substances in the human digestive tract. USDA researcher David Garvin and colleagues also pinpointed the gene in a strain of barley that allows it to tolerate high levels of aluminum in the soil. Aluminum toxicity blights half the world's arable land, and the discovery opened up the possibility of breeding aluminum tolerance into other crops and thus exploiting huge barren tracts.

Fascinating insights were gained into the ways that plants fight off insect attacks. Whereas plants suffering damage by insects were known to release airborne chemicals to attract natural predators of the pests, lima bean plants under attack by mites also switch on the defenses of neighbouring plants to attract predators. A team led by Gen-ichiro Arimura of the Bio-oriented Technology Research Advancement Institution in Tokyo found that three volatile terpenoids released by the besieged plants turn on the defense genes of their neighbours. These chemicals potentially could be used in new "natural" forms of crop protection. Plants also were found to use astonishing defenses against insect eggs laid on the plants. A new class of compounds called bruchins was discovered in pea weevils during their egg-laying activity on pea plants. The chemicals switch on a gene in the plants that causes them to surround the weevil's eggs with small tumourlike growths, which impede the larvae after they hatch.

For the first time, the explosive fertilization of a flower was observed. After a pollen grain lands on a flower's stigma, it germinates, sending a growing pollen tube down the style. When the pollen tube enters the flower's embryo sac, it thrusts between the two sterile, synergid cells located on either side of the egg, ruptures its tip, and releases its gametes. Tetsuya Higashiyama of the University of Tokyo and colleagues recorded the pollen tube exploding, discharging its contents at a flow rate some 50 times higher than the cytoplasmic flow observed in the tube prior to discharge, and instantly pulverizing one of the synergid cells.

Assumptions about how trees respond to global warming and elevated atmospheric carbon dioxide were proving more complex than first thought. A study of tree growth in Alaska revealed that higher mean temperatures in the past century had caused drought and stress. This finding upset calculations that the northern forests would absorb some of the additional carbon dioxide being blamed for the rise in world temperatures. The British government's Hadley Centre for Climate Prediction and Research near London warned that global warming could wipe out a third of the Amazon rain forest by the end of the 21st century owing to rising temperatures and drought.

Efforts to conserve plant species from extinction relied increasingly on storing seeds in seed banks, but disturbing evidence uncovered some alarming shortcomings with these banks. According to Stefano Padulosi of the International Plant Genetic Resources Institute in Rome, of 5,300 species of food plants collected worldwide, more than half had only a single sample left in a seed bank, even though each species may have hundreds or thousands of varieties. Many collections were being destroyed by seed banks short of money, especially in less-developed countries. Many of the stored seeds were also losing their viability. Either the seeds needed to be sown every few years and fresh seed collected, or they had to be stored in deep-freeze facilities. Most seed banks, however, did not have freezers. (PAUL SIMONS)

MOLECULAR BIOLOGY

Among the landmarks of human achievement, a major milestone was reported in 2000—the completion of a rough draft of the sequence of the human nuclear genome. This tome consists of more than three billion characters, arranged as linear sets of carefully ordered nucleic acid bases. The accomplishment was of profound significance and promised revolutionary advances not only in biology and medicine but also in the way humans perceive themselves. (*See* Special Report.)

Atherosclerosis as an Inflammatory Disease. Atherosclerosis is an insidious vascular disease in which lesions, called plaques, form inside arteries and gradually occlude them. The plaques are composed of variable proportions

Kent Loeffler/Cornell University Genetics & Development Dept.

A wild tomato fruit is dwarfed by a tomato from a cultivar bred for giant fruit. One of the genes responsible for tomato fruit size was found during the year.

Joyce Naltchayan/AFP Worldwide

U.S. Pres. Bill Clinton stands with J. Craig Venter (left) and Francis Collins (right) during ceremonies to announce the completion of a working draft of the sequence of the human genome, a milestone in genetic research.

of smooth muscle, collagen, platelets, and lipids. The high lipid content of plaques, principally cholesterol, as well as the correlation of high levels of cholesterol in the blood plasma with the incidence of atherosclerosis, indicated that lowering blood levels of cholesterol should be beneficial in preventing or limiting plaque formation. Indeed, it was amply demonstrated that lowering circulating cholesterol, by means of drugs that inhibit cholesterol synthesis in the body or by lowered dietary intake of lipids and cholesterol, decreases the incidence and severity of atherosclerosis.

As the principal cause of heart attacks, strokes, and circulatory insufficiencies, atherosclerosis remained under active investigation. Work in the late 1990s led to the view that plaque formation may be a response to chronic inflammation of the innermost arterial layer. This inflammation could be initiated by microbial or viral infection, or it could be due to damage to the artery's fragile endothelial lining caused by turbulent blood flow. Whatever the cause, it was becoming clear that treatment aimed at diminishing inflammation could be a new and effective means of treating atherosclerosis.

Mice that are genetically prone to atherosclerosis and that are fed a diet rich in cholesterol develop the disease. These animals have proved useful in studies aimed at revealing the role of inflammation. Results obtained with such mice during the year demonstrated that decreasing inflammation—either by crippling a gene whose protein product plays a key role in inflammation or by inactivating that product with a specific antibody—reduces the formation and development of atherosclerotic plaques and also increases the structural stability of existing plaques by raising their content of collagen. Unstable plaques in large arteries can break down under the constant pounding of blood. Fragments released from such plaques are swept along with the blood flow until they lodge in and occlude a smaller artery. If this occlusion happens in the brain, it causes a stroke; if in the heart, a heart attack. The increase in understanding the causes of atherosclerosis to encompass the role of inflammation promised to lead to new and more effective methods of treatment and prevention.

Cryptochrome Resets the Biological Clock. Circadian rhythms are patterns of biological activity and rest attuned to the 24-hour day, and they are seen in virtually all animals and plants. These rhythms are controlled by biological clocks that are not perfect timekeepers—in the prolonged absence of external clues, they tend to drift and need to be reset. What serves to reset many biological clocks is light—specifically, blue light. That is why jet lag, or the lack of concordance of an individual's biological clock with the new environs, can be helped by exposure to sunlight. The ability of light to set the clock presupposes a pigment to absorb that light and to respond to it by some chemical change.

In studies carried out in the past few years, the clock-setting pigment, a protein called cryptochrome, was found in the eyes of humans, in the brains of fruit flies, in plants, and even in unicellular cyanobacteria (blue-green algae). In mutant organisms with specific defects in cryptochrome, blue light fails to reset the circadian rhythms, which drift with respect to the 24-hour day. As reported in 2000 in a review of cryptochrome research by Aziz Sancar of the University of North Carolina School of Medicine, Chapel Hill, the amino-acid sequence of cryptochrome was found to have a close structural similarity to the protein photolyase. The two proteins also share the same two light-harnessing, pigmented prosthetic groups (nonprotein portions of the molecule)—one called a flavin and the other a pterin. It is the protein portion of each molecule, however, that dictates the particular use that will be made of the absorbed light energy. In the case of photolyase, the energy is used to reverse a specific kind of damage done to DNA by exposure to ultraviolet light. In the case of cryptochrome, the energy of blue light is somehow used to signal the nervous system to reset the biological clock. Just how that signal operates remained to be determined.

Evolution of a Defense Molecule in Plants. Plants, being subject to attack by disease organisms and insects and other herbivores, have evolved a large array of defenses. Indeed, it was estimated that about 15% of plant genes code for products dedicated to defense. Chitinase is one of those defensive proteins. Its specific target is chitin, a structural polysaccharide (complex sugar) made of subunits derived from glucose. Chitin is abundant in the cell walls of fungi and in the exoskeletons of insects, crustaceans, and other arthropods. The chitinase produced by plants defends against disease-causing fungi by breaking the chemical bonds that join the subunits of chitin. The fungi, in turn, have evolved countermeasures in the form of proteins that inhibit chitinase, and the plants have responded by modifying chitinase in a way that diminishes its susceptibility to inhibition by the fungal proteins.

This scenario of the coevolution of plant defenses and countermeasures had led to the expectation that chitinase must have evolved at a high rate. This was affirmed by the work of J.G. Bishop of the Max Planck Institute for Chemical Ecology, Jena, Ger., and colleagues, who compared the chitinases

The Human Genome: The Ultimate Road Map

by Judith L. Fridovich-Keil

Certain to rank among the all-time landmarks of human technical achievement, the completion of a rough draft of the sequence of the human nuclear genome was announced in June 2000. Its significance and ramifications for science and society are both broad and profound, and, as with any empowering technical advance, the challenge that now faces humanity, both as individuals and as a global community, is to determine how to use that power wisely.

BSIP Agency/Index Stock Imagery

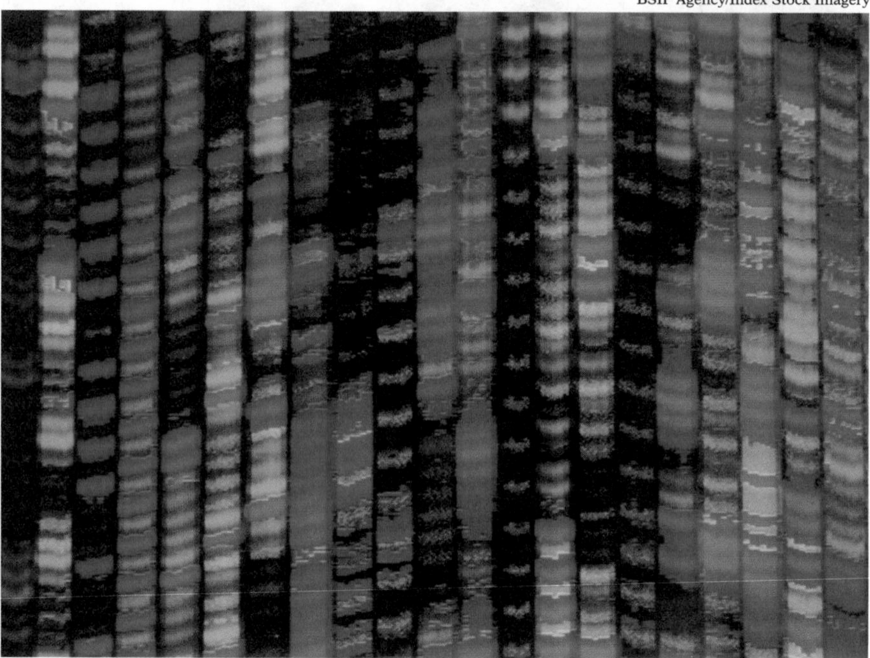

Part of the human genome.

Mendel's Legacy. Human genetics is but one small piece of the much larger field of classical and molecular genetics, which often is said to have begun with the work of the Austrian monk Gregor Mendel in the mid-1800s. Mendel studied the garden pea, exploring in quantitative terms the transmission of sharply defined traits such as plant height, seed colour, and seed texture from one generation to the next. Although Mendel knew nothing about the modern concepts of genes and chromosomes, he deduced from observations that each parent plant carries a pair of determining units for each trait studied, that one trait unit can sometimes dominate the other, and that the units are transmitted as some kind of physical entities from parent to offspring during reproduction. (The pairs of trait units are now recognized to be corresponding genes on paired chromosomes.) The major conclusions of Mendel's studies represented a dramatic break with the mainstream thought of the time and are often summarized as Mendel's laws. His first law is that the paired trait units separate, or segregate, during the formation of gametes (sex cells)—that is, an offspring inherits from a parent either one trait unit or the other, but not both. The second law, which Mendel derived from experiments in which he studied the simultaneous inheritance of different traits, is that the units for the traits assort independently—that is, the unit an offspring inherits for one trait is independent of the unit it inherits for another trait.

It is now recognized that Mendel's laws have many exceptions and that, in fact, they represent only a subset of the whole process of genetic inheritance. Nevertheless, in both peas and humans, they still explain the pattern and frequency of transmission for a large number of genetic traits, including many common human diseases such as cystic fibrosis and sickle-cell anemia. Subsequent work in the 1900s by numerous researchers, using model organisms ranging from fruit flies to corn to viruses that infect bacteria, provided a more comprehensive view of the complexities of genetic transmission. In addition, their studies took the first steps toward a molecular explanation of genetic observations, including the discovery that deoxyribonucleic acid (DNA) and ribonucleic acid (RNA)—long strands built of molecular subunits called nucleotides chained end to end—constitute the genetic material in all living things. In 1953 James Watson and Francis Crick proposed a structure for DNA—a double helix of intertwined nucleotide strands. This event marks what many consider the birth of modern molecular genetics.

Genes and Genomes. In simplified terms, a single gene in a given organism is the set of instructions for making a molecular product. The product may be one of the many macromolecules necessary for the development and life of that organism or one of the components necessary for the maintenance, expression, and propagation of the instruction set itself. The gene uses a chemical code in which the instructions are written, and those instructions are heritable—they can be passed from one generation to the next, which thereby explains Mendel's observations. In physical terms, a gene is a discrete stretch of nucleotides within a DNA or RNA molecule. Each nucleotide contains a chemical "base"—guanine, adenine, thymine, or cytosine (represented as G, A, T, and C, respectively) for the DNA genes of human beings and other organisms. It is the specific sequence of these bases that defines the information contained in the gene and that is ultimately translated into a final product, most often a protein. The protein may have a structural role, or it may serve as a catalyst to promote the formation of other macromolecules, including carbohydrates and lipids. Some functional products of genes are themselves nucleic acids, demonstrating the power and versatility of these molecules.

The genome is the entire coded genetic blueprint of an organism, the full set of genetic instructions for making all of the molecules that constitute it. In the case of humans, the genome is composed of more than three billion pairs of bases, which have been copied and passed on letter by letter with gradual modification and expansion for more than a billion years since life began. The vast majority of the human genome exists as enormously long DNA molecules that reside in the form of 23 pairs of elaborately packaged chromosomes in the nucleus of each cell. The goal of the current genome effort has been the sequencing of the bases in this nuclear portion of the genome and a physical mapping of their location on the chromosomes. Another tiny, but nonetheless essential, chromosome exists outside the nucleus, in cellular organelles called mitochondria. The sequence of the human mitochondrial chromosome has already been described.

Race to the Finish. By the 1980s the base sequence of a large number of genes had been determined through many individual contributions, providing much crucial information to biology and medicine. Nevertheless, the vast majority of the human genome was still unexplored territory. Scientists, politicians, ethicists, and others debated, hotly at times, the merits, risks, and relative costs of sequencing the entire human genome in one concerted undertaking. Was it a feasible goal? Was it worth the billions of public dollars that it would inevitably take away from traditional biomedical research? Despite the controversy, the U.S. Department of Energy and the National Institutes of Health (NIH) pushed forward with an ambitious plan and in 1990 launched what became known as the Human Genome Project. Fortunately, the effort was soon joined by scientists from around the globe. Moreover, a series of technical leaps, both in the biochemical sequencing process itself and in the computer hardware and software used to track and analyze the constituent sequences, enabled such rapid progress that the project eventually drew ahead of schedule.

Technological advance, however, was only one of the forces spurring the pace of discovery. In 1998 a private-sector enterprise, Celera Genomics, headed by former NIH scientist J. Craig Venter, entered the race in the final lap, challenging the publicly funded Human Genome Project, led by geneticist Francis Collins. (*See* BIOGRAPHIES.) At the heart of the competition was the issue of money, especially control over potential patents on the genome sequence, considered by most a pharmaceutical treasure trove. Although the legal and marketplace aspects remained unclear, in the 11th hour the once bitter rivals pulled a surprise move and joined forces to some extent, speeding completion of the rough draft sequence, which represented the first stage of the project.

The Tasks Ahead. It is tempting to think that once the full sequence, or code, of an organism's genome is known, scientists will immediately understand all the inner workings of that organism. The reality is that, although scientists may be empowered, they are not yet enabled. They must still locate all the functional genes in the genome, determine what products they make, and learn what those products do. Their situation is in many ways similar to having all of the words of a foreign language written in a list but without spaces, punctuation, or definitions. Being able to see the letters—or even the words—is only the beginning. Fundamentally, the job of research must now shift from one of gathering data to one of understanding it.

It is also important to recognize that the term *the human genome* is somewhat misleading, because there is no single genome sequence that defines everyone. No two humans other than identical twins share identical genomes. For the rest, although the genomes are more than 99% identical, each is unique. The recently published human genome sequence that has been posted on the Internet as a public database, <www.ncbi.nlm.nih.gov/genome/guide>, is but one "flavour" of normal. The DNA that was sequenced in the project was derived from real people, and real people, even though they are healthy, carry hidden in their genomes not only many neutral polymorphisms, or base sequence variations, but also potentially serious recessive mutations masked by dominant counterparts. Thus, it is likely that some of the sequences currently published as "normal" are, in fact, not. Clearly, a comparison of sequences derived from a spectrum of healthy individuals will be needed to determine what should be included in the normal range.

Implications for Biomedicine. Public availability of the complete human genome represents a defining moment for both biomedical research and medical practice. The genome database will speed identification of genes implicated in a variety of genetic diseases and thus enable more objective and accurate diagnosis, in some cases even before the onset of clinical symptoms.

With regard to prognosis, as more disease-related genes are identified and their mutations pinpointed in the genomes of affected individuals, the information can be combined with information about corresponding clinical outcomes to find correlations between specific gene sequences and outcomes. Such correlations for a given disorder can help guide research into the underlying mechanisms and predict the future severity of symptoms in a given patient. For newly diagnosed individuals and their families, this information can be invaluable in coping with the present symptoms and in planning for the future.

Finally, knowledge of the normal functions of genes associated with disease and the mutations that impair those functions can enable a more rational approach to treatment. Although gene therapy is seen as the ultimate application of human genome research to the treatment of many genetic disorders ranging from cystic fibrosis to cancer, genetic knowledge of a disease can benefit even conventional, symptomatic therapies—for example, by helping to define the disease state in a given individual as benign or aggressive.

Judith L. Fridovich-Keil is an associate professor in the department of genetics, Emory University School of Medicine, Atlanta, Ga.

of related species of plants and documented changes in their amino-acid sequences. The finding added to an appreciation of how selection pressure by predators or disease agents drives the coevolution of prey or host species.

(IRWIN FRIDOVICH)

PALEONTOLOGY

Studies in paleontology during 2000 offered intriguing new information on topics ranging from the origins of fish and feathers to long-term evolutionary patterns in marine communities. Until very recently, little was known about the origin of vertebrates. While the Cambrian Period marked the beginning of an explosive evolutionary radiation among the major groups of invertebrates with hard parts, fish were absent from this first phase of rapid diversification of multicelled animals. Recently described finds from the Early Cambrian Chengjiang beds of China, however, included delicate small fossils that revealed vertebrate-like skulls, gills, and muscles. These specimens pushed the known origin of vertebrates back by as much as 50 million years; previously, the oldest known fish were from the Late Cambrian.

Bony fish were the most diverse group (greatest number of species) of vertebrates, yet few fossils have been found that offer details of their origin and subsequent split into the ray-finned and lobe-finned clades. (A clade is a single lineage composed of a common ancestor and all of its descendants.) A recent paper published by a paleontologist from the Chinese Academy of Sciences' Institute of Vertebrate Paleontology and Paleoanthropology in Beijing, however, extended the fossil record of bony fishes back to the boundary of the Silurian and Devonian periods, about 408 million years ago. Unlike previous early bony-fish fossils, the Chinese specimen included a mixture of lobe-finned and ray-finned features and thus could provide insight into the origin of bony fish from more primitive types of fish. A second study on early bony fish described the most primitive braincase ever found of a ray-finned fish. This 400 million-year-old specimen from southeastern Australia exhibited primitive features previously unknown from any bony-fish fossils, including an opening for a cartilaginous eyestalk.

The featherlike appendages of a 220 million-year-old fossil, **Longisquama insignis,** *suggested the reptile might be an ancestor of modern birds.*

John Ruben/Oregon State University

A controversial paper published in June again raised the issue of feathered reptiles and the origin of birds. After having been housed in a Russian research institute for decades, a 220 million-year-old fossil of a reptile named *Longisquama insignis* was reevaluated by a group of Russian and American scientists and determined to have had featherlike appendages. The scientists further suggested that the mouse-sized creature could have been an ancestor of modern birds. Because *Longisquama* was not a dinosaur and may not even have been an archosaur (a larger group that includes some primitive reptiles as well as dinosaurs, crocodiles, and pterosaurs), this suggestion conflicted with the prevailing idea supported by most paleontologists that birds evolved from theropods (carnivorous dinosaurs, including *Tyrannosaurus*). Critics of the study claimed that the structures described may not have been feathers at all but could instead have been indicative of large membranous scales. They also argued that even if the structures were feathers or featherlike, other birdlike features were not present in this primitive reptile. A complete analysis that included all of the important derived features of birds continued to place them with the theropod dinosaurs.

A third specimen of the much-debated feathered theropod dinosaur, *Caudipteryx,* was described during the year by a scientist at the Institute of Vertebrate Paleontology and Paleoanthropology. Although the specimen lacked a head, the report indicated that it had well-preserved feather impressions and that the skeleton was much better preserved than those of the two earlier specimens described in 1998. The study claimed that although the specimen exhibited some new bird features that were generally not found in theropods, such as an appendage on the foot for perching, it also had 16 dinosaur-like characteristics previously unknown in *Caudipteryx.* Though many seemed convinced that these findings added new strength to the view that dinosaurs and birds are related, others questioned whether this animal had true avian feathers.

A study of 12 articulated ornithomimid dinosaur skeletons discovered in 1997 in the Cretaceous Ulansuhai Formation in China revealed some startling new information about the diet of ornithomimids. Although ornithomimids were toothless, they clearly were theropod dinosaurs; consequently, it was long assumed that they were probably toothless carnivores, feeding on small prey much like modern carnivorous birds. These new skeletons, however, had preserved masses of gastroliths inside the rib cage of each animal. Gastroliths are commonly known as "stomach stones," and they have also been found in the rib cages of many of the large sauropod dinosaurs, such as *Apatosaurus.* The presence of gastroliths suggested that ornithomimids, like the sauropods, were herbivorous rather than carnivorous. The gastroliths function as a grinding mechanism in the stomach to aid in the digestion of coarse plant material. Many modern herbivorous birds use fine-grained gravel in a similar fashion.

Investigators described an oviraptorosaur from Mongolia with a pygostyle, which suggested that this small theropod dinosaur may have had a tail fan of elongate feathers. The pygostyle, comprising several fused vertebrae at the end of the tail, is typically found only in birds. Because other features, however, place oviraptorosaurs at some distance from the origin of birds, the investigators suggested that this structure originated independently in the two groups.

A recent study by a researcher at the National Geological Museum of China and others described *Jeholodens jenkinsi,* the most complete skeleton of a triconodont ever found. Members of the order Triconodonta were among the earliest (Late Triassic Epoch, 230 million to 208 million years ago) mammals known from the fossil record. They represent a clade much more primitive than even the modern egg-laying monotremes. *Jeholodens* exhibited predominantly primitive characteristics, but the structure of its shoulder was somewhat similar to that of more advanced mammal groups. This feature of *Jeholodens* apparently evolved independently of the advanced shoulder of modern mammals.

Those Bones Named Sue

On May 17, 2000, Chicago's Field Museum of Natural History unveiled a display extraordinary not only for what it was—the largest (12.8 m [42 ft] long), most complete, and best-preserved *Tyrannosaurus rex* skeleton ever discovered—but also for its unlikely name, Sue. The approximately 67 million-year-old fossil, named in honour of Susan Hendrickson, who discovered it on Aug. 12, 1990, had made a difficult, decade-long journey to its new home, a journey that began on South Dakota's Cheyenne River Sioux reservation. Hendrickson and Peter Larson, of the Black Hills Institute for Geological Research, were prospecting there on a cattle ranch owned by Maurice Williams, who was one-fourth Native American and whose land was held in trust by the U.S. government for tax-relief purposes. Larson paid Williams $5,000 for the right to excavate the skeleton, had it shipped to the institute's Hill City, S.D., headquarters for restoration, and planned to build a museum to showcase it.

As news traveled about the discovery, however, Larson began receiving sizable offers for it, and Williams, the Cheyenne River Sioux, and the federal government began to raise questions about its legal ownership and to seek its return. After federal agents seized the bones in 1992 on the grounds that government permission had not been granted for the removal of the fossil from federal lands, a convoluted battle for custody ensued. A U.S. district court ruled in April 1993 that the fossil was to remain property of the trust, and in October 1994 the U.S. Supreme Court let that ruling stand. Sue was to be the property of Williams and the Bureau of Indian Affairs (BIA).

The BIA gave Williams permission to sell Sue and suggested that the fossil be auctioned, a controversial move in the eyes of many scientists, who feared the commercialization and possible private collection of scientifically important specimens. Nevertheless, in 1996 Sotheby's was chosen to conduct the sale, which was held on Oct. 4, 1997, with nine bidders in the running. After only about eight minutes, the Field Museum—backed by McDonald's Corp., Walt Disney World Resorts, and the California State University system—emerged the winner, purchasing Sue for $8,362,500. Disney was to be given a replica for exhibition at Walt Disney World, and McDonald's was to get two replicas that would be taken on tour. The remainder of Sue's preparation for display was carried out in the museum's McDonald's Fossil Preparation Laboratory in full view of spectators. Because the dinosaur's 1.5-m (5-ft)-long skull was too heavy (272 kg [600 lb]) for the skeleton to support, a life-size cast was used, while the actual head was displayed on the museum's second-floor balcony, where visitors could get a close-up view. (BARBARA WHITNEY)

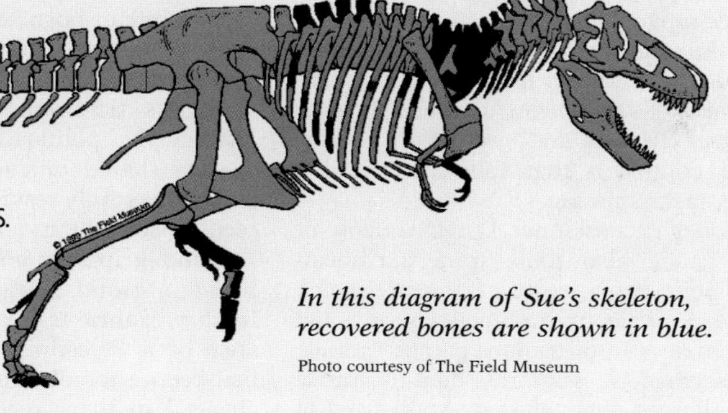

In this diagram of Sue's skeleton, recovered bones are shown in blue.

Photo courtesy of The Field Museum

A primitive, limbed fossil snake from the Middle East was reported during the year in the journal *Science*. This 95 million-year-old fossil found in carbonate deposits near Jerusalem preserved portions of the hind limb, including the tibia, fibula, metatarsals, and phalanges. This species, *Haasiophis terrasanctus*, appears to be evolutionarily near the time when snakes evolved from their limbed predecessors. Loss of limbs is an event that may have occurred more than once during the evolution of snakes in the Late Cretaceous.

The extinctions of large terrestrial mammals and birds during the Quaternary Period (1.6 million years ago to the present) have long been a subject of debate among paleontologists. Contrasting theories blame the extinction on either dramatic climatic change or hunting by primitive human groups. A new study of the fossil record of a large flightless bird from Australia provided new evidence that climate was not a factor in these extinctions. The disappearance of this bird occurred approximately 50,000 years ago, a time when humans first arrived in Australia but not a time of major climate change.

Owing to the poor nature of the hominid fossil record, little has been known about the origin of bipedalism in hominids. A report published during the year on specimens of *Australopithecus anamensis* and *A. afarensis* indicated that those primitive hominids retained the specialized wrist structure and function associated with knuckle-walking primates. Because *Australopithecus* was clearly a hominid, this suggested that bipedalism evolved from knuckle-walking ancestors.

The fossil record often shows that when a new superior group of organisms arises, older, more primitive groups cannot compete and are quickly driven to extinction. Several paleontologists, however, reported that evolutionary patterns in bryozoans suggest that survival of the fittest does not necessarily require extinction of the less fit. They contended that the older cyclostome bryozoans coexisted with the newer cheilostomes for tens of millions of years during the Mesozoic Era until the mass extinction at the end of the Cretaceous Period 66.4 million years ago dramatically reduced the diversity of both groups. It was only then that the more advanced cheilostomes were able to significantly surpass the diversity level of the cyclostomes, which did not rebound from the extinction.

A recent analysis of long-term evolutionary patterns claimed that major changes in marine communities since the beginning of the Phanerozoic Eon about 540 million years ago correlated with increased diversity in terrestrial communities. This was one of the first studies to link diversity trends in terrestrial and marine organisms.

(WILLIAM R. HAMMER)

Literature

Captivating readers in 2000 were **CONFESSIONAL** works, **FANTASTIC** books, the continuing exploits of the fictional wizard **HARRY POTTER**, digital books on the **INTERNET**, and historical tomes marking landmark **ANNIVERSARIES**.

The brightest literary star of the year 2000 came out of South America, but flashes of incandescent brilliance appeared in other areas of the world as well. With *La fiesta del chivo,* Mario Vargas Llosa of Peru produced what many readers considered Latin America's finest novel ever. Interweaving three separate narratives in a series of alternating chapters, Vargas Llosa chronicled the 31-year reign and ultimate demise of Dominican Republic dictator Rafael Trujillo and evoked the chaos and confusion that followed Trujillo's 1961 assassination.

Nobel Prize winner Derek Walcott of St. Lucia also took up a Caribbean theme in his book-length poem *Tiepolo's Hound.* Walcott examined his own life and that of Impressionist painter Camille Pissarro. The volume's dual narrative highlighted their shared experiences of exile and artistic achievement as well as the cultural influences of Europe and the West Indies, which created a certain division in each of them.

Russian author Viktor Pelevin (*see* BIOGRAPHIES) led a banner year in Eastern European fiction with his wildly imaginative novel *Buddha's Little Finger,* a hallucinatory recasting of the life of the legendary Bolshevik commander Vasily Chapayev as told by a time-traveling asylum inmate.

Acclaimed Hungarian author György ("George") Konrád brought out *Stonedial,* a striking work that combined elements of the intellectual teaser and whodunit with the more expansive tapestry of a historical novel covering the years from World War II through the early 1990s.

Chinese novelist Mo Yan—famed for the scathing satire and historical sweep of such works as *Red Sorghum* (1993) and *The Garlic Ballads* (1995)—produced an even more stunning novel, the savage and hallucinatory farce *The Republic of Wine.* Following alarming reports of widespread corruption and infanticidal cannibalism in the province of Liquorland, Communist Party officials dispatch a special investigator to the scene, but he himself soon falls prey to debauchery and mental breakdown and fails to survive the province's insidiously pervasive (and wildly funny) destructive tendencies.

Sri Lankan-born Canadian writer Michael Ondaatje published *Anil's Ghost,* a superb novel set in his native country during its vicious mid-1980s civil war. Though the politically tinged murder mystery that dominates the main plotline is never fully resolved, the novel succeeds beautifully in all other aspects.

In the gripping novel *In Search of Walid Masoud,* Arab author Jabra Ibrahim Jabra tracked the disappearance of a Palestinian intellectual who had been a member of an organization engaged in the armed struggle against Israel. The author artfully used a lengthy but disconnected tape recording of jumbled utterances to compose a series of revealing monologues that together produced a penetrating study of both individual and national character.

(WILLIAM RIGGAN)

ENGLISH

United Kingdom. Although many critics complained that 2000 was a thin year for fiction, a number of literary debuts showed promise. The most remarkable one was that of Zadie Smith, whose *White Teeth* was a panoramic and germane tale addressing issues of ethnic and cultural hybridity in northwestern London. The novel, which sold robustly, was penned by Smith while she was a student at the University of Cambridge and was greeted enthusiastically for its ambitious scope.

Another promising newcomer was Jason Cowley. He was hyped on the cover of his *Unknown Pleasures* as a "cool, edgy new voice," but *The Literary Review,* though praising his book for its feverish readability, found his style more old-fashioned, with "more than a hint" of Graham Greene. Meanwhile Kristin Kenway's *Precious Thing,* an acerbic tale of a disillusioned anarchist in search of love, was compared to Martin Amis's debut novel, *The Rachel Papers* (1973). Among the most praised fictional titles of the year were two collections of short stories. *Equal Love* by Peter Ho Davies was hailed as a "feat of ventriloquism." Though the stories' themes were unexceptional (a funeral, a hospital visit, or marital problems), they were infused with a graceful quirkiness that lifted them above the mundane. The nine stories in Anita Desai's *Diamond Dust* constituted an unsentimental examination of overlapping cultures; in one of the most striking, "Winterscape," two old Indian widows visiting Canada see snow for the first time. Another novel singled out for particular praise was John Banville's *Eclipse,* about an actor whose career ends when he dies on stage.

Other offerings from more established fiction writers were met with varying levels of enthusiasm. Will Self's third novel, *How the Dead Live*—about the death of a middle-aged woman from cancer—showed more humanity than his glitteringly clever earlier books, but some critics found it, like many other novels of the year, too long at 404 pages. Michèle Roberts's *The Looking Glass,* an exuberant tale of an orphan's way through the world, examined the complexity of feminine needs and projected desires. Doris Lessing, entering her ninth decade, delivered *Ben, in the World*—a sequel to her best-selling *The Fifth Child,* published 12 years earlier—but most agreed that it failed to match the forcefulness of its predecessor.

Besides the aforementioned, other Booker Prize hopefuls included Julian Barnes, A.S. Byatt, Muriel Spark, and Fay Weldon, but they were passed over in favour of four somewhat obscure authors. Three of those four short-listed had together sold only 553 copies of their works. Only Kazuo Ishiguro and Margaret Atwood were instantly recognizable. *The Observer* newspaper noted that all the selections had strong narratives and predicted that the millennial shortlist would prove a turning point away from the more innovatory offerings of past years.

Nevertheless, the clear favourite—the bookmakers put it as an odds-on winner at two-to-one—was *The Blind Assassin* by Atwood, the doyenne of Canadian fiction. A structurally baroque account of an elderly woman looking back on her life and her relationship with a long-dead novelist sister, the book welded together themes of rivalry, female fulfillment, politics, and history. Ishiguro's *When We Were Orphans*—a detective story set in 1930s England, where the sleuth investigated the disappearance of his own parents—was the second odds-on favourite. Critics found in these pages the assurance displayed in Ishiguro's earlier winner, *The Remains of the Day* (1989). Though the lesser-known works were ranked as outsiders, many fancied *The Hiding Place* by Trezza Azzopardi. The only debut novel on the shortlist, it was narrated by a gambler's daughter from the Maltese community living in the Welsh town of Cardiff in the 1960s. Michael Collins, at 36, was the youngest writer represented. His third novel, *The Keepers of Truth,* was a story about a burnt-out local reporter in the U.S. Midwest. Matthew Kneale's *English Passengers,* a historical novel about a 19th-century voyage to Tasmania, was given only a six-to-one chance, while Brian O'Doherty's *The Deposition of Father McGreevy* (1999) was judged least likely to win. The latter was a tale of rural Ireland narrated by a defrocked priest.

Atwood, who had been short-listed three times earlier (*The Handmaid's Tale* [1985], *Cat's Eye* [1988], and *Alias Grace* [1996]), was victorious. Simon Jenkins, the chairman of the judges, declared that the panel had agreed that her book was "far reaching, dramatic and structurally superb," demonstrating Atwood's "poet's eye for both telling detail and psychological truth."

The winner of the Orange Prize for Fiction, awarded annually to a woman novelist, was Linda Grant for her *When I Lived in Modern Times.* The work told of a Soho hairdresser who travels to 1940s Palestine to become a citizen of the new country of Israel at its formation. Soon after she was announced as the unanimous choice of the judges, she faced accusations of plagiarism. A.J. Sherman claimed that she had overly relied on his academic study *Mandate Days* (1997) for her period detail and for certain passages. Although Sherman dismissed the allegations, Grant and her publisher, Granta Books, agreed to acknowledge his book in future editions.

The world's richest literary prize, the International IMPAC Dublin Literary Award, worth £Ir 100,000 (about $120,000), went to Nicola Barker, the 34-year-old author of *Wide Open* (1998). This novel dealt with a group of mismatched individuals struggling to live on a remote island amid a backdrop of startlingly funny Magic Realism. The judges praised the book's "razor-sharp comic sensibility and flawless structure."

The Carnegie Medal, a major award for a children's or young-adult book, went to Aidan Chambers for *Postcards from No Man's Land* (1999). Owing to the frank treatment of such themes as adultery, homosexuality, and euthanasia, the choice surprised some. The author, a 65-year-old former monk, defended his outspokenness: "At 15 people . . . are very interested in thinking about important questions for the first time. . . . I refuse to sell young people short by compromising on language or subject matter."

Whitbread winner Seamus Heaney

AFP/Worldwide

The other children's author to capture headlines was J.K. Rowling. Her *Harry Potter and the Goblet of Fire,* the fourth in the blockbuster series, appeared amid a frenzy of advance publicity and anticipation. Its publisher, Bloomsbury, arranged a special tour for Rowling upon a steam-engine train dubbed "Hogwarts Express," the name of the magic train in the story. Despite her phenomenal commercial success, the author narrowly missed winning the Whitbread Book of the Year Award for *Harry Potter and the Prisoner of Azkaban* (1999). The judges were reportedly divided between Rowling and poet Seamus Heaney, whose translation and adaptation of the Old English epic *Beowulf* (1999) had been rapturously received by the critics. One of the judges, biographer Anthony Holden, commented, "Potter is charming, but I think it's derivative, traditional and not particularly well-written, and to compare it to Heaney is absurd." Another judge, writer Robert Harris, countered that it was time to close the gap between the "arbiters of literary taste" and the reading public. After a 5-to-4 vote, the award, worth £21,000 (about $34,000), went to Heaney. Former model Jerry Hall, whose appointment as a judge had been interpreted as a gesture toward acknowledging popular taste, voted with the Heaney faction.

Martin Amis (*see* BIOGRAPHIES) released one of the most discussed nonfiction titles, his long-anticipated memoir, *Experience.* It was praised as both "entertaining" and "profound." There were accusations, however, that Amis had affected to be closer than in fact he was to his cousin Lucy Partington, who had been famously kidnapped and murdered in 1973. Nevertheless, the book was deemed a success both as an autobiography and as a depiction of Amis's close relationship with his late father, novelist Kingsley Amis.

Another major autobiography was Max Hastings's *Going to the Wars,* a portrait of decades of war reporting in Northern Ireland, Biafra, Indochina, Jordan, and the Falkland Islands (Islas Malvinas). Anecdotal rather than analytic, it was praised for casting some fresh light on how modern-day wars had been fought. World War II continued to provide fodder for more scholarly questioning. Eric A. Johnson's massive *Nazi Terror: The Gestapo, Jews, and Ordinary Germans* (1999) reappraised the extent to which "ordinary Germans" could be held jointly responsible for the genocide of Jews in the Nazi camps. He concluded that most citizens were not as terrorized by the Gestapo as had been assumed and could have known what was really happening to those transported to the camps; on the other hand, he warned that their culpability and lack of moral concern might be found in any society where there was deeply embedded hostility "to those perceived as outsiders." William Shawcross, meanwhile, questioned whether the United Nations had the ability to prevent such atrocities in the future. His *Deliver Us from Evil: Warlords & Peacekeepers in a World of Endless Conflict* concluded that the mushrooming of horrific local wars, refugees, and mass killings would be addressed effectively only if the UN's Charter could be fully realized.

History was a recurring theme of the year, dominated by Simon Schama's epic *A History of Britain: At the Edge of the World?: 3000 BC–AD 1603,* the first of two volumes accompanying a highly successful BBC documentary series and described as "magnificent" by *The Guardian.* Philip Wilkinson's *What Did the Romans Do for Us?* was published to complement another BBC documentary series and discussed the legacy (including bridges, roads, decorative arts, and cuisine) of the 400-year Roman occupation of Great Britain. Another major best-seller was the paperback edition of *The Isles: A History* by Norman Davies. It challenged the anglocentricity of other such histories and stressed the importance of the influence of Wales, Scotland, and Ireland on the British Isles as a whole. *The Times* (London) hailed it as a masterwork, declaring it a "tract for the times."

Among the biographies was a scrupulously researched account by Claire Harman of Fanny Burney, the novelist whom Virginia Woolf once described as the "mother of English fiction." Burney's long and illustrious life straddled the 18th and 19th centuries, but her biographer had to sift through a plethora of rumour and gossip—some of it engendered by Burney herself—in order to present a faithful portrait. Janet Todd in *Mary Wollstonecraft: A Revolutionary Life* similarly dispensed with myth when she disregarded the heroine worship that had surfaced in hindsight for the author of *A Vindication of the Rights of Women* (1792) and dispassionately conveyed a woman who was far from perfect. *Samuel Pepys* by Stephen Coote was said to be the first life portrait of the famous Restoration diarist in a generation and depicted Pepys's relationship with his contemporaries, including architect Christopher Wren. A more unusual offering was Peter Ackroyd's remarkable *London: A Biography;* the author explained that the city was for him a "living organism" and thus not a subject of mere history or geography.

Among the literary figures who died were Dame Barbara Cartland, the best-selling author of popular romantic fiction, and Penelope Fitzgerald, a novelist of quiet incisiveness who in 1999 had won a PEN award for lifetime achievement. (*See* OBITUARIES.)

(SIOBHAN DOWD)

United States. In 2000 it was the year of the great hype about the electronic book, the e-book, or whatever other catchy phrases Internet technologists and their publisher partners used to refer to work that appeared on the Internet rather than in a book-bound format. In addition, such genres as fiction, poetry, and nonfiction became known as electronic "content." It was the year that novelist Stephen King pulled an old manuscript out of his reject drawer, offered it as a serial on the Internet for a dollar or two per chapter, and drew thousands of subscribers. It was also a year in which some of the finest novelists went on writing well and publishing in the traditional fashion.

Philip Roth, for example, brought out *The Human Stain*—the third volume in his contemporary American trilogy, a bruising, bawdy, and finally rather magisterial novel about identity and race, freedom of thought, and sexual repression—in which his by-now-ubiquitous narrator Nathan Zuckerman tells a story as powerful as anything Roth had ever told. John Updike worked at no less a level of accomplishment, turning out two works of fiction in a year—the ingenious *Gertrude and Claudius,* a moving retelling of the Hamlet story from the point of view of the troubled Dane's parents, and the story collection *Licks of Love,* in which Updike treated the American readership to a novella-length coda about the late Rabbit Angstrom (the protagonist in his tetralogy) and his heirs.

Other masters produced new work, some of it flawed, such as *Ravelstein,* Saul Bellow's fictional version of the life of teacher and philosopher Allan Bloom; Evan S. Connell's bloodstained pseudo-chronicle of the Crusades, *Deus Lo Volt!;* and E.L. Doctorow's avowedly modernist but not entirely successful novel *City of God.* Joyce Carol Oates's version of the Marilyn Monroe story, a 700-plus-page novel called *Blonde,* also received mixed reviews. Herbert Gold's newest San Francisco novel, *Daughter Mine,* reprised themes of family and paternity and showcased the veteran writer's skill, in his own seriocomic way. In his novel *The Married Man,* Edmund White returned to his by-now-familiar material of love and death among the American and European homosexual middle class.

Family played a central role in a number of effective works of fiction by younger writers. In Jayne Anne Phillips's moving *MotherKind,* a married woman and mother cares for her dying female parent. In *What Remains,* Nicholas Delbanco turned a fictional memoir into a moving story of trans-Atlantic cross-currents in a Jewish family based in London. Susan Richards Shreve deployed dark comedy in *Plum & Jaggers,* in which a group of children, orphaned after a terrorist bombing, turn to theatre for therapy. Though not tragic, a rather bittersweet tone was heard both in Charles Baxter's novel, *The Feast of Love,* set in Ann Arbor, Mich., and in Cornelia Nixon's stories, set mainly in Chicago, that made up the novel *Angels Go Naked.*

The Amazing Adventures of Kavalier & Clay, Michael Chabon's wonderfully entertaining third novel, recounted the education of a couple of wonder boys in the burgeoning comic-book industry during the early 1940s.

A number of other novels had historical themes. In *The Heartsong of Charging Elk,* James Welch took an obscure historical incident—that of a Sioux warrior who finds himself marooned in Marseille while traveling in France with Buffalo Bill's Wild West show—and turned it into a story with great cumulative power. Josephine Humphreys turned to life among the mixed-blood Native Americans of North Carolina during the Civil War to create a lovely historical texture in the narrative voice of *Nowhere Else on Earth.* In *Harry Gold,* Millicent Dillon elaborated on the private life of one of the famous spies for the Soviet Union in the 1950s.

It was also an interesting year for first novels. Veteran story writer Molly Giles debuted as a novelist with her biting,

Author and biography subject Saul Bellow

AP/Wide World Photos

ironic fiction in *Iron Shoes,* the story of a late-blooming California librarian who is both tightly bound to and at odds with her eccentric, ailing mother. Kate Wheeler, a onetime PEN/Faulkner nominee for her first collection of stories, signed in with an impressive first novel, *When Mountains Walked,* set in contemporary Peru. Porter Shreve carried on the literary efforts of his family into the second generation when he came out with his well-received first book, *The Obituary Writer,* in which a young staff writer in search of a place in the world of journalism stumbles on some troubling news. Lucinda Rosenfeld's *What She Saw in Roger Mancuso, Günter Hopstock, Jason Barry Gold, Spitty Clark, Jack Geezo, Humphrey Fung, Claude Duvet, Bruce Bledstone, Kevin McFeeley, Arnold Allen, Pablo Miles, Anonymous 1–4, Nobody 5–8, Neil Schmertz, and Bo Pierce*—the quirky, erotic, and ultimately quite charming novel about a New Jersey girl's entry into the world of love, sex, and work—met with mostly favourable reviews. The most successful experiment of the year was Los Angeles writer Mark Z. Danielewski's horror novel, *House of Leaves.*

Many of the most interesting and appealing works of nonfiction came in the form of autobiography, memoir, and biography. Among the memoirs, magazine editor Dave Eggers's *A Heartbreaking Work of Staggering Genius* was the most highly publicized and, for the most part, extremely well received. *Leap,* an unconventional prose meditation on life and art, came from Terry Tempest Williams. *A Life in the Twentieth Century* by Arthur M. Schlesinger, Jr., was probably the most interesting of mainstream work. Lauren Slater's *Lying* had a certain subversive appeal on the subject of looking back on one's life.

Doris Grumbach took a long view of her literary past in *The Pleasure of Their Company,* and novelist Larry Woiwode signed in with the first volume of his memoir, *What I Think I Did,* the title of which was a play on the title of his first novel, *What I'm Going to Do, I Think* (1969).

King, fresh from a roadside accident in which he nearly lost his life, combined autobiography and his thoughts on the making of fiction in *On Writing: A Memoir of the Craft.* Poet Maxine Kumin reported about her near-fatal horseback-riding accident in *Inside the Halo and Beyond.* The late Sylvia Plath was represented by *The Unabridged Journals of Sylvia Plath, 1950–1962,* edited by Karen V. Kukil. Prizewinning poet C.K. Williams told of family bitterness in his memoir, *Misgivings.* In *Miles and Me,* poet Quincy Troupe looked back on his encounters with great jazz musician Miles Davis.

Among literary biographies, James Atlas's *Bellow* was first among equals, at least as far as the interest it stirred. A mix of straightforward biography and shorthand literary criticism, the book was a warts-and-all account of the life and work of Saul Bellow, the Nobel Prize-winning octogenarian. In light of some of the gossip included about Bellow's sex life and marital problems, Bellow probably wished that he had never given his consent to the project. Since most of the subjects of David Laskin's *Partisans: Marriage, Politics, and Betrayal Among the New York Intellectuals* were dead, they could not feel the uneasiness that Bellow had to be suffering. *The New Yorker*'s former editor Frances Kiernan released *Seeing Mary Plain: A Life of Mary McCarthy,* a gathering of mostly oral testimony on the life of the once enormously popular novelist. Journalist Michael Herr was appreciative and affectionate toward Stanley Kubrick in *Kubrick,* his short tribute to the recently deceased motion picture director. Among other literary memorabilia, Bonnie Kime Scott edited the *Selected Letters of Rebecca West,* and John F. Callahan and Albert Murray edited *Trading Twelves: The Selected Letters of Ralph Ellison and Albert Murray.*

Historian David Levering Lewis published *W.E.B. Du Bois: The Fight for Equality and the American Century, 1919–1963,* the second installment of the biography; Lewis had won an array of prizes for the first volume. One of the best-known American socialist organizers in the second half of the 20th century served as the subject of Maurice Isserman's *The Other American: The Life of Michael Harrington. American Moderns: Bohemian New York and the Creation of a New Century* was Christine Stansell's interesting subject. Alice Kaplan produced *The Collaborator: The Trial & Execution of Robert Brasillach.*

It was a grand year for poetry; both the outgoing and incoming U.S. poet laureates brought out new books. Robert Pinsky published *Jersey Rain:* "It spends itself regardless into the ocean./ It stains and scours and makes things dark or bright:/ Sweat of the moon, a shroud of benediction,/ The chilly liquefaction of day to night,// The Jersey rain, my rain soaks all as one . . . ," and Stanley Kunitz, named poet laureate in July, released *The Collected Poems.*

C.K. Williams published *Repair* (1999), John Ashbery brought out *Your Name Here,* Yusef Komunyakaa offered *Talking Dirty to the Gods,* and Jay Wright weighed in with *Transfigurations,* his collected poems. Among other collections were Stanley Plumly's *Now That My Father Lies Down Beside Me: New & Selected Poems, 1970–2000* and August Kleinzahler's *Live from the Hong Kong Nile Club: Poems, 1975–1990:* "Drifting, drifting, a single gull between sky and earth,/ He said of himself, alone at night on the Yangtze,/ Bent grasses and gentle wind./ And asked where his name was/ Among the poets./ No answer, moon's disk on the great river." Also emerging on the scene were Charles Wright's *Negative Blue: Selected Later Poems* and two volumes by Gjertrud Schnackenberg, *Supernatural Love: Poems 1976–1992* and *The Throne of Labdacus.*

A large group of accomplished lyric poets brought out new volumes, including Richard Tillinghast (*Six Mile Mountain*), Lawrence Raab (*The Probable World*), MacArthur fellowship winner Anne Carson (*Men in the Off Hours*), Michael Collier (*The Ledge*), and Lloyd Schwartz (*Cairo Traffic*). The literary world mourned the loss in December of Pulitzer Prize-winning poet Gwendolyn Brooks. (*See* OBITUARIES.)

It was a fecund year for unorthodox literary criticism. Novelist Nicholas Delbanco included a novella on themes out of Ernest Hemingway's life among the essays in his collection, *The Lost Suitcase: Reflections on the Literary Life.* Joan Acocella created an expanded version in book form of her provocative essay for *The New Yorker* in *Willa Cather and the Politics of Criticism.* In *For Rabbit, with Love and Squalor,* novelist Anne Roiphe featured essays on male characters in contemporary American literature, such as Updike's Rabbit Angstrom and Richard Ford's Frank Bascombe, with whom she became enamoured, she explained, as she read. Harold Bloom focused on *How to Read and Why,* and Kumin was reflective in *Always Beginning: Essays on a Life in Poetry.* In *Canon and Creativity: Modern Writing and the Authority of Scripture,* Robert Alter looked to the Bible as a template for modern literature. David Rosenberg also looked to Hebraic texts as his focus in *Dreams of Being Eaten Alive: The Literary Core of the Kabbalah.* Cynthia Ozick took a temperately Old Testament tone in *Quarrel & Quandary,* a collection of her recent critical essays. Experimental writer Carole Maso encouraged readers and writers to *Break Every Rule.*

A bit more conventional was *Updike: America's Man of Letters,* William H. Pritchard's intelligent critical assessment of John Updike, one of the deans of contemporary literature. Art critic Arthur C. Danto collected his pieces from *The Nation* magazine in *The Madonna of the Future.* Eric Bentley's collection *What Is Theatre?* (2nd edition) gathered criticism and reviews from 1944 to 1967. Poet Mark Strand joined in with *The Weather of Words: Poetic Invention.* Michigan poet Thomas Lynch, a mortician by profession, wrote about art and life in *Bodies in Motion and at Rest.*

Short-story writer Jhumpa Lahiri captured two awards, the Pulitzer Prize for fiction and the PEN/Hemingway Award for first fiction. C.K. Williams won the Pulitzer for poetry. *Embracing Defeat* (1999) by John W. Dower, a study of Japan in the aftermath of World War II, took the general nonfiction Pulitzer. Ha Jin (*see* BIOGRAPHIES) won the PEN/Faulkner Award for Fiction. The PEN/Malamud Award for Excellence in the Short Story went to Ann Beattie and Nathan Englander. (ALAN CHEUSE)

David Draper Clark

Double gold winner David Malouf

Canada. Ghosts of many kinds enlivened Canada's fictional offerings of 2000. In Michael Ondaatje's *Anil's Ghost,* it is one of the many victims of Sri Lanka's interminable guerrilla war whom Anil, a forensic anthropologist, seeks to rescue from anonymity. In Margaret Atwood's *The Blind Assassin,* the younger sister, a long-ago suicide, bedevils the elder as the latter spins interlocking anecdotes of deceit and betrayal arising from their love for the same man. In Susan Musgrave's *Cargo of Orchids,* a blackly funny and bleakly honest account of one woman's sojourn to death row, the haunting is by the ghost of what might have been. Spirits of mythic proportions inform Eden Robinson's first novel, *Monkey Beach,* about a young native woman grappling with the death of her beloved brother amid the shifting mists of the British Columbia coast. In Steven Heighton's *The Shadow Boxer,* the ghosts of the doomed freighter *Edmund Fitzgerald* serve as companions to a young man seeking to find his own way in a deserted lighthouse on the shore of Lake Superior. The presence hovering over Elizabeth Hay's *A Student of Weather* is still alive, but no less potent; in another tale of sibling betrayal, two sisters compete for the same sweet fellow.

Flight and denial were also common themes. In Catherine Bush's *The Rules of Engagement,* a young woman flees into exile to avoid discovering the outcome of a duel fought over her. In *Burridge Unbound* by Alan Cumyn, a survivor of terrorism returns to the place of his incarceration, and Fred Stenson's *The Trade* encompasses a host of fugitives—from the law, civilization, or themselves—forced to face the cold realities of the northern fur trade. Anita Rau Badami dealt with several levels of denial in *The Hero's Walk,* in which an old man, suddenly responsible for his young granddaughter, must face a future foreign to him, his family, and his caste. *Mercy Among the Children* by David Adams Richards presented the consequences of a pact with God as not entirely unlike those arising from a pact with the devil.

Short fiction naturally spawned a number of diverse works. In Carol Shields's *Dressing Up for the Carnival,* a high-class midway was full of familiar yet unique people. Luck in all of its manifestations—good, bad, and indifferent—attends an engagingly eclectic assortment of individuals in the late Matt Cohen's *Getting Lucky.* In Lynn Coady's *Play the Monster Blind,* the cultures of the coasts of Canada were revealed through the idiosyncratic excesses of their inhabitants. Terence Young's *Rhymes with Useless* was a mixed bag of ordinary families coping in their separate ways with an extraordinary world. The first collection by Madeline Sonik, *Drying the Bones,* featured a series of investigations into and beyond the obvious.

Though Al Purdy, one of Canada's major poets, died in April (*see* OBITUARIES), his voice lives on in the posthumously published *Beyond Remembering: The Collected Poems.* Another death, that of Patrick Lane's mother, informed his latest collection, *The Bare Plum of Winter Rain.* The death of Charles Lillard, poet and husband, was mourned in Rhonda Batchelor's *Weather Report.* Winona Baker expressed the essence of life's transient seasons through haiku in *Even a Stone Breathes.* Although death was not ignored, a lighter note was struck in bill bissett's *b leev abul char ak trs.* In *Ruin & Beauty: New and Selected Poems,* Patricia Young explored the necessary contradictions at the heart of life, a concept that also animated *A Pair of Scissors,* Sharon Thesen's examination of how opposites work against each other to create something new. For Don McKay in *Another Gravity,* it was the contrariness of nature and the ambivalence of human nature that formed the dramas of people's lives. George Bowering, in *His Life: A Poem,* spins his timeless meditations on the rotations of solstice and equinox. *What the Small Day Cannot Hold: Collected Poems 1970–1985* summed up Musgrave's mordant take on life in the late 20th century. (ELIZABETH WOODS)

Other Literature in English. In addition to hosting the 2000 Summer Olympic Games, Australia laid claim to English-language writers who accomplished literary feats of Olympic proportion during the year. Leading the way was poet and novelist David Malouf, who released

Dream Stuff, a collection of short stories, before taking home the gold twice by winning both the Neustadt International Prize for Literature and the Lannan Prize for fiction. Close behind were Thea Astley, who garnered the Miles Franklin Award for the fourth time (this time for her novel *Drylands* [1999]), and Lily Brett, whose novel *Too Many Men* (1999) received the Commonwealth Prize for Best Book in Southeast Asia and the South Pacific. Other highlights included works by such well-established authors as Colleen McCullough (*Morgan's Run*), Frank Moorhouse (*Dark Palace*), and poet Les Murray (*Conscious and Verbal* [1999]), as well as by newcomer Ben Rice with his first novel, *Pobby and Dingan.*

In nearby New Zealand, Kapka Kassabova's novel *Reconnaissance* (1999) won the regional Commonwealth Prize for Best First Book, while veteran authors C.K. Stead (*Talking About O'Dwyer* [1999]) and Fleur Adcock (*Poems: 1960–2000*) had important new books as well. Michael King published *Wrestling with the Angel,* his biography on the remarkable life of novelist Janet Frame.

Africa offered its usual fare of outstanding works in English, including Chinua Achebe's *Home and Exile,* in which he provided a personal account of his intellectual and writing life; it was the Nigerian's first book in 13 years. Achebe was widely considered the patriarch of the modern African novel. Poet, fiction writer, and critic Tanure Ojaide brought out a selection of poems spanning more than three decades, *Invoking the Warrior Spirit* (1998), in which the eponymous warrior is the poet himself at battle within his troubled Nigeria. Countryman Funso Aiyejina received the Commonwealth Prize for Best First Book in Africa for his collection *The Legend of the Rockhills and Other Stories* (1999), and South African J.M. Coetzee continued his commercial and critical success by winning the top Commonwealth Writers Prize for 2000 for *Disgrace* (1999). Master storyteller André Brink released *The Rights of Desire,* a fictional meditation on aging and love, loneliness and fulfillment, guilt and innocence, and loss.

Also noteworthy was the publication of *Yesterday, Tomorrow: Voices from the Somali Diaspora* (1999) by the much-heralded Somalian exiled writer Nuruddin Farah, along with outstanding fiction debuts from Ugandan-born Moses Isegawa (*Abyssinian Chronicles*) and South African-born Sindiwe Magona (*Mother to Mother* [1998]), both of whom also lived in exile. Drawing on his own experience of exile in Europe and Africa and going home to an emerging democracy still trying to define itself, Mandla Langa of South Africa offered *The Memory of Stones,* his most ambitious work to date. The memory of Ken Saro-Wiwa of Nigeria was kept alive with the publication of the critical anthology *Before I Am Hanged: Ken Saro-Wiwa—Literature, Politics, and Dissent,* edited by Onookome Okome. Dambudzo Marechera of Zimbabwe was remembered with the posthumous release of his poetry collection *Cemetery of Mind.*

(DAVID DRAPER CLARK)

GERMANIC

German. Wolfgang Hilbig's 2000 novel *Das Provisorium*—the author's first major work since *"ICH"* (1993), his masterful literary examination of the East German Stasi (secret police)—was an anguished, moving autobiographical account of the life of an East German writer who, unable to live productively in the communist state, descends into alcoholism and moves to West Germany. There he leads a peripatetic and problematic existence, moving from town to town while continuously forced by western expectations to play the role of the persecuted East German writer. Hilbig depicted realistically and without euphemism his protagonist's inability to leave behind the German Democratic Republic (GDR), his failed relationships with women, his foreignness in the provisional world of the German west, and his desperate addiction to alcohol.

Brigitte Kronauer's magnificent novel *Teufelsbrück* was a complex and ambitious examination of love and desire as well as a celebration of the sensuous qualities of language and literature. Set in a Hamburg milieu depicted in realistic, sensuous detail, the novel tells the story of the triangular relationship between two women and the much-sought-after man with whom they are both romantically involved.

Dieter Wellershoff's novel *Der Liebeswunsch* also was about a romantic triangle—this time between two men and a woman who has married one of the men after first having had an affair with the other. Into this established triangle of experienced and somewhat jaded adults enters a young female student who longs for pure romantic rapture, no matter what the risks, and whose longing ultimately leads to her demise; her character simultaneously highlights the hypocrisy and compromises of the other, more mature characters.

The Austrian writer Josef Haslinger published his second novel, *Das Vaterspiel,* five years after the appearance of his remarkably successful political thriller *Opernball.* The main character of *Das Vaterspiel* was Rupert Kramer, who rebels bitterly against the politics and viewpoints of his father, an opportunistic and financially successful socialist. The son ultimately creates and markets a computer game, the patricidal theme of which provides the title for the novel. Interspersed with Kramer's story is that of a Lithuanian Jewish immigrant to the United States who has survived the

Autobiographical novelist Wolfgang Hilbig

Gezett Foto

Holocaust. His life intersects with that of Kramer's after Kramer—who has gone to the United States to pursue a love interest as well as to work further on his computer game—discovers a war criminal hiding in a basement on Long Island, N.Y.

The Swiss writer Ulrich Schmid also published a novel with a trans-Atlantic political theme—*Der Zar von Brooklyn,* a powerful thriller about the Russian mafia in New York City and the transformation into a criminal of its main character, a young journalist from Moscow. The novel also touched on many of the problems of Russia itself after the demise of communism.

Bernhard Schlink followed up his 1995 international best-selling novel *Der Vorleser* with *Liebesfluchten,* a well-received and popular short-story collection. As the title suggested, most of the seven stories in the collection revolved around the theme of love and escape, particularly the perceived inability of men to give and receive love. As in *Der Vorleser,* some of Schlink's stories delved into the problems both of the German past and of a younger generation coming to terms with it. Another literary work dealing with the themes of love, retreat, loss, and politics was Michael Kumpfmüller's novel *Hampels Fluchten,* the picaresque story of a sexual and political adventurer who travels from East Germany to West Germany and back again, fleeing various personal and political failures.

David Wagner's first novel, *Meine nachtblaue Hose,* was the story of a young West German man seeking, together with the woman of his affections, to remember a childhood in the Federal Republic of Germany (West Germany) that, together with the GDR, came to a kind of end in 1989–90. The work was an attempt to interpret the present and past for a generation of West Germans whose world, the author seemed to suggest, was radically transformed by national reunification. Maxim Biller's first novel, *Die Tochter,* was a reflection on German and Jewish identity in contemporary Europe, whereas Ralf Bönt's second novel, *Gold,* was a bitter, sarcastic account of life in Berlin, the reunified German capital. Doris Dörrie's first novel, *Was machen wir jetzt?,* was a compassionate portrait of middle age and personal decline. The young Swiss writer Zoë Jenny's second novel, *Der Ruf des Muschelhorns,* was an account of loneliness and betrayal. German writer Susanne Riedel's debut novel, *Kains Töchter,* was a sensational and improbable account of family anger and hatred. Finally, Botho Strauss's *Das Partikular,* a collection of short prose, dealt with problems of love and individuality in the contemporary world.

(STEPHEN BROCKMANN)

Netherlandic. Dutch literature raised its public profile in the media during 2000, with well-received works by both new and established writers. In addition, Dutch literature in translation continued to find a welcome audience in various foreign markets.

In January, on the first annual Nationale Gedichtendag ("National Day of Poetry"), Gerrit Komrij was named the first Dutch poet laureate, a position created by the Poetry International festival, the newspaper *NRC Handelsblad,* and NPS-TV. Komrij stated that he intended to publish at least four times annually a poem commenting on an event of national significance. Meanwhile, he wrote on such tragic and controversial matters as the involvement of Dutch peacekeepers in Srebrenica, Bosnia and Herzegovina, and a major disaster in Enschede, Neth. (*See* WORLD AFFAIRS: *The Netherlands.*) The poetry-reading public also voted Hendrik Marsman's famous "Herinnering aan Holland" its favourite Dutch poem.

Poet laureate Gerrit Komrij

Hollandse Hoogte

Eva Gerlach (a pseudonym for Margaret Dijkstra) was awarded the P.C. Hooftprijs in honour of her oeuvre, 10 volumes of poetry, which was praised for its sophisticated linguistic simplicity. The prize citation stated that "Gerlach's poems read like magical incantations: attempts to create an order in language which does not exist, or is invisible, in reality."

Thomas Rosenboom's novel *Publieke werken* (1999), lauded for its literary style and thematic sophistication, won the Libris Literatuur Prijs for the best novel of the year. Rosenboom had previously won for *Gewassen vlees* (1994).

The Generale Bank Literatuurprijs was known once again as the AKO Literatuurprijs, owing to a change in funding, and the latter was awarded to Arnon Grunberg for *Fantoompijn,* the story of a failed writer's great loneliness and unfulfilled dreams. Grunberg caused controversy by "accepting" the award on live television via e-mail from his home in New York, rather than appearing in person.

Grunberg was also the suspected author of *De geschiedenis van mijn kaalheid,* which was published under the name Marek van der Jagt. The novel, which allegedly bore stylistic resemblance to Grunberg's work, was awarded the Anton Wachterprijs for best debut. Grunberg had received that prize in 1994 for *Blauwe maandagen;* the fact that the prize was not collected led to lively discussions in the media.

(JOLANDA VANDERWAL TAYLOR)

Danish. During 2000 Danish writers and poets explored new themes and modes of expression; created memorable characters, settings, and scenes; and plumbed the depths of emotion, meaning, and memory. In Vibeke Grønfeldt's novel *Det rigtige* (1999), combative Ena Jakobsen struggles to preserve her family's past in a dying village. Arthur Krasilnikoff's *Nattens rygrad* (1999) delves into the past of the Kalahari *raconteur* Kanta and that of his people. In Cæcilie Lassen's *Trio* (1999), three Russian trapeze artists escape an ominous past in Moscow only to reencounter it in Copenhagen. Naja Marie Aidt's collection of poems *Rejse for en fremmed* (1999) interweaves the historical Joan the Mad (1479–1555) with a modern woman's search for identity. Tradition as well as past loves and losses also figured importantly in several novels. In Anne Marie Løn's *Kærlighedens rum,* a casual acquaintance of the narrator, Edith Moreau, reveals a happy, secret love affair spanning 25 years. Morten Sabroe's *Den spanske Gæst* focuses on young Ingeborg's love affair with a transient Spanish visitor and on their son, Arthur, the village outsider. In Anne Marie Ejnæs's *Theas færd* (1999), the title character breaks with tradition to follow her own path. Emma, the protagonist of Karen Fastrup's debut novel, *Brønden,* works on restoring both church frescoes in Lisbon and her connections to the past. The stories in Jan Sonnergaard's *Sidste søndag i oktober* record the passage of time and the loss of love for the aging characters from *Radiator* (1997).

Imaginary worlds were also explored. Vagn Lundbye's collection of novellas *Syv vidnesbyrd om vor Herre Jesu Kristi latter* (1999) interweaves mystery and the magic in personal connection. In Janne Teller's richly satiric *Odins ø* (1999), Old Odin discovers an island beyond time. In Per Helge Sørensen's crime novel *Mailstorm,* a student witnesses an Internet murder with serious ramifications. F.P. Jac created a new poetry of joie de vivre in *Fugl føniks ajour* (1999).

For the second straight year, a Danish poet—this time, Henrik Nordbrandt, author of *Drømmebroer* (1998)—won the Nordic Council Literary Prize. Anne Marie Têtevide's *Mellem himlen og verden* received the Royal Library Prize for Medieval Novel, and Svend Åge Madsen's *Genspejlet* (1999) captured Danish Radio's Novel Award. Bent Haller's *Ispigen og andre fortællinger* (1998) received the Nordic Children's Book Prize.

(LANAE HJORTSVANG ISAACSON)

Norwegian. In Norway a generational shift occurred when more than 20 young writers made their literary debuts in 2000. Many of them experimented with language and genre, notably Hans Christian Grønn, whose *Det som er strengt* was an encyclopaedic collection of anecdotes and jargon entries. Henrik H. Langeland aroused controversy with *Requiem,* a pastiche of Marcel Proust's writing. Kristin Valla borrowed from Latin American magic realism in her promising literary bow, *Muskat,* and literary rebel Tore Renberg incorporated science fiction in his latest novel, *En god tid.*

The realist novel, however, continued to dominate. Themes often focused on the dysfunctional family, such as veteran author Vigdis Hjorth's *Hva er det med mor,* which chronicled a daughter's life with an alcoholic mother. In Hanne Ørstavik's third novel, *Tiden det tar,* she showed how childhood wounds affect adulthood. *Frøken Snehvit* by Knut Faldbakken told a disturbing story about puberty and abuse. Jonny Halberg's lauded novel *Flommen* portrayed dysfunctional families in a community struck by a flood. Two of the nominees for the Brage Prize, Cecilie Enger (*Brødrene Henriksen*) and Per Petterson (*I kjølvannet*), wrote about the loss of a parent. In the prizewinning *I kjølvannet,* Petterson used a tragic passenger-ferry accident as the setting.

Gunnar Staalesen completed his well-received trilogy with *1999. Aftensang,* which was both a social chronicle and a detective story. Women mystery writers continued to assert their preeminence and exhibit keen psychological insight, as was evidenced in prizewinning Karin Fossum's *Elskede Poona* and Pernille Rygg's *Det gyldne snitt.* Though overlooked in the past, Jon Fosse (*Morgon og kveld*) and Jan Kjærstad (*Oppdageren* [1999]) were both nominated for the 2001 Nordic Council Literature Prize.

Despite heated discussions on the merits of the biographical genre, numerous biographies were welcomed, including Jo and Tordis Ørjasæter's *Nini Roll Anker* and Knut Hendriksen's *Ole Bull.*

Stein Mehren, the grand old man of poetry, delighted with *Ark,* and young debutante Hege Woxen impressed with her volume of poetry, *Gjemsel med korte dager.* Håvard Rem published his poetry collection, *Tekstmeldinger,* as text messages for cell phones. Ingvar Ambjørnsen was the first Norwegian to publish a novel (*Dronningen sover*) on the Internet prior to its release in bookstores.

(ANNE G. SABO)

Swedish. Several important books published in Sweden in 2000 kept readers off balance with rapid developments, impassioned feelings, or forces hard to explain in rational ways. The well-established realistic tradition had to skirmish with a wave of subjectiveness that took varied literary forms. As Sweden adapted to its membership in the European Union, literary regionalism flourished.

In Kerstin Ekman's *Urminnes tecken,* harsh northern Sweden was portrayed with detailed realism but was inhabited by archaic creatures not yet, or perhaps never to be, human. Gunnar D. Hansson molded poems and documents, authentic and fake, to a most special rural and learned west-coast blend of past and present in *Förlusten av Norge.* Lars

Jakobson established himself as one of the most interesting younger novelists with *I den röda damens slott,* in which documentary material and science-fiction elements interfered with the story of a man's quest for both a lost father and boyhood.

Mainstream authors such as Theodor Kallifatides, Barbara Voors, and Maria Küchen tried their hands at crime writing. Inspired, perhaps, by a chance to win the Poloni Prize—which was awarded "to a promising female Swedish crime writer"—women wrote 40% of the year's fictional crime works, a considerable increase. Åsa Nilsonne's *Kyskhetsbältet* won the prize, and former winners Liza Marklund and Aino Trosell successfully returned with *Paradiset* and *Om hjärtat ännu slår,* respectively.

Kerstin Thorvall in *Jag minns alla mina älskare och hur de brukade ta på mig* and Carina Rydberg in *Djävulsformeln* used personal love experiences in such a blunt way that the documentary drive turned into its opposite, strong—and transparent—debatable subjectiveness.

Several promising first novels appeared. Cecilia Bornäs rewrote the story of Tarzan from Jane's point of view in *Jag Jane* (1999). Lotta Lotass thematically united four intermingled stories that dwelt mythically on arctic coldness in *Kallkällan.* Poet Mikael Niemi returned to the 1960s with his first novel, *Populärmusik från Vittula,* which cleverly, affectionately, and artistically showed the confrontation of old and modern life in a small town on the far border with Finland. (IMMI LUNDIN)

FRENCH

France. In 2000 the two trends that had for years most strongly marked French literature continued to affirm their hold—the genre of autobiofiction, by which authors novelize portions of their lives, and *déprimisme,* the thematic choice by which authors dwell on the failures of French society.

Fernando Arrabal published one of the year's most moving autobiofictions *Porté disparu,* which recounted the author's own childhood bereft of his father, who had been arrested in 1936 by Francisco Franco's police. The most poignant part of the novel occurs when the author discovers letters written by his mother, who, comfortable with her new, bourgeois life, repeatedly and successfully begged the government to keep her husband interred in prisons and asylums. Frédéric-Yves Jeannet in his autobiofictional *Charité* writes of the loss of his mother, from whom he had been estranged for 20 years. Interweaving childhood memories and present-day realities, Jeannet tried to reconstitute the past and, thus, his identity.

Martin Bureau/AFP Worldwide

Prix Fémina laureate Camille Laurens

Hélène Cixous offered *Les Rêveries de la femme sauvage,* another installment of her recent autobiofictional work; this time she concentrated on the enigma posed by her youth in Algeria, where she was born, but to which, because of her French citizenship, she had always remained a foreigner.

The anguished quest for self-identity was also the subject of Richard Morgiève's two autobiofictional works, *Ma vie folle,* in which the author recounted his orphaned childhood and his attempt to construct an identity without the guidance of adults, and *Ton corps,* in which Morgiève, beginning with his own body, tries to pick up the shattered pieces of his life after his wife abandons him.

Déprimisme, the almost morbid fixation with society's ills, was expressed in a number of works. Régis Jauffret's *Fragments de la vie des gens* presented 56 vignettes of the various miseries married life can cause. In the bitter satire of Eric Laurrent's *Dehors,* the protagonist leaves his wife for a life of sexual adventure, only to fall from one grotesque romantic encounter to the next as he plunges into degeneration in a society devoid of meaning. In Yves Pagès's *Petites natures mortes au travail, déprimisme* washes over the modern working world with 23 vignettes that show people brought low by their petty and demoralizing jobs and that belie the rosy picture painted by politicians boasting the recent decline in unemployment.

Emmanuel Carrère wrote *L'Adversaire,* a *déprimiste* biofiction, which chronicled the life of Jean-Claude Romand, who had murdered his entire family in 1993. Without trying to explain Romand's crime, Carrère traced his progression from his first successful lie, that of acceptance into medical school, to his full-blown life of fiction as he passed himself off as a doctor while embezzling his friends' money. Carrère exposed a society in which appearances are more important than reality and may, when threatened, become as deadly as fact.

Three authors published novels that, though marked by *déprimisme,* nonetheless lightened the overwhelming gloom of the year's works. In *Les Belles Âmes,* Lydie Salvayre joyfully attacked the hypocrisy of many who professed sympathy for the disadvantaged. Taking part in a European tour organized to visit the poor in their natural habitats, the slum safarigoers are ridiculed by their own words—from the writer wishing to remain in touch with street culture to the well-off socialists eager to finally see the poor up close to the businessman seeking a humbler replacement for the wife he has just divorced. No one escapes mockery until the group is finally abandoned at the side of the road by a guide who can stand no more. Linda Lê injected the hope of redemption in *Les Aubes,* in which a young man, blinded after a suicide attempt, finally begins to heal with the help of three inspiring women—the first embodying love, the second purity, and the third poetic resistance. Finally, Pascal Quignard's tender *Terrasse à Rome* tells the story of a 17th-century engraver who, horribly scarred when a romantic rival throws etching acid at his face, is abandoned by his love, whom he spends the rest of his life reproducing in his art. The engraver, who scratches light from inky darkness, meets his opposite mirror image in a painter who sees the world as a play of light and colour, a difference as much in philosophy as in art that is the foundation for a lifelong friendship.

The Prix Goncourt went to the biofiction *Ingrid Caven,* in which Jean-Jacques Schuhl recounts the story of a German singer and of the glitzy debauchery of the 1970s art world. Côte d'Ivoirian writer Ahmadou Kourouma, famous for his recasting of French to African rhythms, won the Prix Renaudot for his *Allah n'est pas obligé,* in which the 10-year- old narrator tries to make sense of the insanity of wars in Liberia and Sierra Leone while wandering through those countries, machine gun in hand. The Prix Fémina was awarded to Camille Laurens's *Dans ces bras-là,* in which the heroine tries to understand the effect men, from her father to lovers, have had on her with the help of the analyst she hopes will learn to love her for what she truly is. Yann Apperry won the Prix Médicis for his *Diabolus in musica,* the story of a musician's quest for perfect orchestral symmetry. (VINCENT AURORA)

Canada. Like most of the Western world, French Canada was swept by the Harry Potter craze in 2000. Potter was the central character in a popular series of books by British author J.K. Rowling. At one point the English version of Rowling's latest offering was the best-selling book in the French bookstore chain Renaud-Bray. Though the province of Quebec might be politically distinct from the rest of Canada, its reading habits were alarmingly global. In a year without a dominating homegrown title, the most popular works ranged from television personality Daniel Pinard's recipe books to the Dalai Lama's universal wisdom.

There were few standout works worth noting. A book that broke with French Canada's obsession with itself, however, was Gil Courtemanche's *Un Dimanche à la piscine à Kigali,* a novel set in Rwanda. Longtime journalist Courtemanche followed in Graham Greene's footsteps to create a popular work that distinguished itself on the literary scene.

The intersection of politics and culture again resulted in a shelfful of books. This time Daniel Poliquin checked in with *Le Roman colonial,* an essay that served notice that nationalism was a retrogressive force in Quebec. Poliquin provoked the ire of a good number of commentators, which was his intent. Another Franco-Ontario writer, Jean-Marc Dalpé, won the country's top French-language fiction prize, the Governor-General's Award, for his novel *Un Vent se lève qui éparpille* (1999), a story that mixed poetry and naturalism to portray life in northern Ontario.

A surprising success was *Un Parfum de cèdre* (1999), the French version of Ann-Marie MacDonald's *Fall on Your Knees* (1996). Translations of books between Canada's two official languages are usually not rewarded with commercial success, but MacDonald's family saga set in Atlantic Canada proved that the country's two solitudes could touch each other. The year was marked by the loss of two very different writers—the much-loved novelist and poet Anne Hébert (*see* OBITUARIES) and beatnik-style poet Denis Vanier. (DAVID HOMEL)

ITALIAN

Two major Italian writers died during 2000—Attilio Bertolucci and Giorgio Bassani. (*See* OBITUARIES.) Bertolucci was one of the most intense and accessible poets of the 20th century. At the centre of his verse was the landscape of his native region, the Po valley, the city of Parma, and his own family life. Bassani, the Jewish novelist and poet from Ferrara, was the author of *Il giardino dei Finzi-Contini* (1962), which chronicled the plight of an aristocratic Jewish family under Fascism; it was one of the most highly cherished and esteemed modern Italian novels.

While most writers were busy building their World Wide Web sites, new books seemed to be quite traditional and tame. The popular success of Andrea Camilleri's detective stories, both new and old, continued unabated. One of the most widely acclaimed books was Fosco Maraini's autobiographical work *Case, amori, universi* (1999). A writer, anthropologist, teacher, and tireless explorer of distant cultures, Maraini transposed in fictional form the many and diverse experiences of a life spent mainly in the Far East. It was a rich tapestry of both different cultures and worlds beautifully woven together by a very expert hand.

More immediately historical was *N,* Ernesto Ferrero's novel about Napoleon Bonaparte. In the work, written in the form of a diary, Napoleon's librarian recounts, with an initial contempt that eventually turns to compassion, the 300 days spent by the emperor as both king and prisoner of the island of Elba. The narrator's vivid imagination transformed historical minutiae into the stuff of a compelling novel. A rigorous documentation also inspired the 20 charming Russian tales of Serena Vitale's *La casa di ghiaccio.* Equally well researched was Melania G. Mazzucco's *Lei così amata,* an elaborate portrait, part documentary and part fictional, of Annemarie Schwarzenbach (1908–42), the writer, archaeologist, photographer, and journalist with whom so many men and women, including Thomas Mann's twin children, Klaus and Erika, fell desperately in love.

Several novels explored the joys and pains of family relationships. The protagonist of Sandro Veronesi's *La forza del passato* discovers that his dead father—a general in the army and ostensibly a mediocre man and bigot—was in fact a KGB spy. This revelation destroys for the son all other certainties about himself and his family and compels him to review and rewrite his entire life. In Domenico Starnone's novel *Via Gemito,* set in Naples, a son remembers how his father—a would-be painter who must settle for a career as a rail worker—took out his frustrations on his wife and children. Though told in such a way as to express a son's hatred for a violent father, the story ultimately revealed the persistence of filial love and made memorable the very person it set out to condemn to oblivion. Against the contemporary myths of forever healthy and athletic bodies, *Nati due volte* by Giuseppe Pontiggia praised

Teller of Russian tales Serena Vitale

Jerry Bauer Photography

the virtue and beauty of physical weakness. In this novel a father teaches his disabled son how to accept his condition and live "normally"; in the process, the father discovers a new and more authentic way of life for himself. In Giorgio Pressburger's *Di vento e di fuoco,* four women write a series of letters, faxes, and e-mail messages to a fifth woman who is about to have a baby. The correspondence revolves around the pregnant woman's dead father, a man the four writers loved and by whom they were all loved. The death in 1968 of this troubled, restless, and mysterious man who survived the Holocaust signals the beginning of the new baby's journey through life.

Andrea De Carlo's *Nel momento* (1999) was a love story of sorts—a detailed diary of self-discovery and of a newfound love following the protagonist's fall from a horse. Quite popular was Sveva Casati Modignani's *Vaniglia e cioccolato,* in which the aptly named Penelope finally abandons her husband, after his umpteenth affair, to find self-respect and happiness with someone else.

Social satire was strong, albeit at the margins of the literary scene. In Ermanno Cavazzoni's *Cirenaica* (1999), the protagonist travels by train to a station in an unspecified "lowland," where he is besieged by hordes of pseudorelatives who quickly relieve him of all his possessions. Equally surreal was Maurizio Salabelle's *Il caso del contabile* (1999), in which an accountant lives in a superficially ordinary world, which conceals a madness that suddenly explodes and just as suddenly is absorbed. Most surreal, fierce, and comical of all was *Spiriti,* by the very popular Stefano Benni; it was a visionary portrait of a mad, fantastic, and futuristic society—a fusion of Italy and the U.S., called Usitalia.

Pithy and humorous sketches that were part of Carlo Emilio Gadda's unfinished novel were published from recently discovered notebooks from the 1930s with the title *Un fulmine sul 220.*

(LINO PERTILE)

SPANISH

Spain. In a bold experiment, the first of its kind in Spanish publishing, the Madrid-based publisher Alfaguara in 2000 offered the complete text of *El oro del rey*—the fourth installment of Arturo Pérez-Reverte's immensely popular Capitán Alatriste series of adventure novels set in Spain's convulsive 17th century—as a downloadable file available on the Internet for 30 days prior to its release in conventional book form. Confounding highbrow critics who look askance at readers' unquenchable thirst for punchy escapist fiction, Pérez-Reverte enjoyed phenomenal success all year with *La carta esférica,* a convoluted historical thriller unrelated to his now-famous Alatriste series. In contrast, Luis Goytisolo's *Diario de 360°,* a conjoining of semimetanovelistic cultural essays and personal aperçus, structured in the form of a diary, drew lavish critical praise and was hailed as Goytisolo's best work since his ambitious tetralogy, *Antagonía* (1973–76). Another senior novelist, José Luis Sampedro, startled readers with the radically ambiguous title of his latest work, *El amante lesbiano,* an erotically charged first-person reverie that inveighed against the repressive "normalcies" of gender and identity in contemporary society. Similarly antiauthoritarian but less reverent in tone was Juan Goytisolo's *Carajicomedia,* which chronicled the successive reincarnations of a 16th-century homosexual priest.

Jerry Bauer Photography

Internet adventure novelist Arturo Pérez-Reverte

Opera as a metaphor for life, and vice versa, was the subject of Álvaro del Amo's *Los melómanos,* while in *La sombra del ángel* Marina Mayoral looked at life as narrative process. Manuel Vicent invoked a variety of master painters in *La novia de Matisse,* a joyful novelistic allegory that celebrated the thaumaturgic effects of fine art upon those who knew how and where to look. Isaac Montero denounced Basque terrorism in *La fuga del mar,* and Rafael Chirbes's *La caída de Madrid* offered a bristling moral portrait of Spanish society on the eve of Francisco Franco's death in 1975.

Spain's most lucrative literary award, the Planeta Prize, went to the popular veteran journalist Maruja Torres for *Mientras vivimos,* a sentimental cliff-hanger with feminist overtones, set in contemporary Barcelona, in which three solitary and dissatisfied women, all related but belonging to different generations, exploit the subtle dynamics of their friendship to find the missing pieces in the interlocking puzzles of their lives. Besides publishing *Las palabras de la vida,* a well-received collection of 17 autobiographical and fictional sketches, Luis Mateo Díez received both the Critics' Prize and the National Narrative Award for *La ruina del cielo* (1999), a beautifully wrought story of death and memory among the inhabitants of Celama, an imaginary rural setting reminiscent of the author's native León. Lorenzo Silva's *El alquimista impaciente,* a story of two Civil Guards assigned to investigate a crime, won the venerable Nadal Prize; and the highest distinction in Hispanic letters worldwide, the Cervantes Prize, went to the Spanish novelist, essayist, and literary critic Francisco Umbral.

The literary world lost three major writers: novelist Carmen Martín Gaite, poet José Ángel Valente, and playwright Antonio Buero Vallejo. (*See* OBITUARIES.)

(ROGER L. UTT)

Latin America. The year 2000 seemed to inspire numerous celebrated writers in Latin America to reflect on times past as well as on their own unique histories, struggles, and diverse cultures.

Mario Vargas Llosa of Peru published *La fiesta del Chivo,* an indictment of institutionalized dictatorship and the reign (1930–61) of the infamous Dominican dictator Rafael Leónidas Trujillo, nicknamed "El Chivo."

Carlos Fuentes of Mexico released what editors called "the novel of novels." *Los cinco soles de México* uniquely combined elements of the novel, short story, essay, and theatre. Fuentes covered Mexico's history from the ancient Aztec civilization to such current events as the indigenous uprising in Chiapas and the end of the Institutional Revolutionary Party's political monopoly.

Ernesto Sábato of Argentina broke a more than 25-year silence with *La resistencia,* which was first released as an e-novel on the Internet before being issued as a bound volume. Sábato reflected on the sociopolitical concerns of his earlier novels and, with a certain urgency, warned against the modern rush for progress, success, and material wealth.

Isabel Allende of Chile released *Retrato en sepia,* which presented a parallel history of Chile from 1862 to 1910 with that of a female photographer whose art form reveals the real truth hidden behind strict social traditions. A similar historical theme characterized a new novel by another Chilean writer, Virginia Vidal. *Javiera Carrera, madre de la patria* recounted—through actual letters, manuscripts, and conversations—the important role played by Javiera Carrera in the 1811 struggle for national independence from Spain.

Julia Álvarez of the Dominican Republic published her second feminist historical novel, *In the Name of Salomé,* a fictional elaboration of the story of Salomé Ureña de Henríquez, a 19th-century poet and educator who fought for the intellectual emancipation of women and contributed significantly to political awareness.

Chilean author Jorge Edwards (*see* BIOGRAPHIES), who in an April ceremony was presented the prestigious Cervantes Prize, produced a new novel, *El sueño de la historia.* The narrative wove two periods of Chilean history—the last years of colonial Chile and the final years of the dictatorship of Gen. Augusto Pinochet Ugarte.

Carlos Gamerro of Argentina returned to the 19th-century pampa for the setting of his new novel, *El sueño del señor juez,* which recounted the barbaric conditions of the gauchos and the indigenous population caught in civil wars and their fates at the hands of arbitrary authority.

In his new novel *Viaje a los olivos,* Gerardo Cham of Mexico re-created a lost part of Hispanic history by imagining the life of the first Mestizo born in Spain, the offspring of one of the first Native Americans taken from the colonies by Christopher Columbus after the 1492 conquest.

The 1982 Falkland Islands/Islas Malvinas war served as the backdrop for a debut novel by Edgardo Russo of Argentina. *Guerra conyugal* followed the personal story of a writer in Buenos Aires whose journalism involves him in the danger and intrigue of national politics.

Ignacio Padilla of Mexico claimed the 2000 Primavera de Novela Prize for *Amphitryon,* a narrative set on a German train during World War I. Two men, a soldier, and a porter agree over a chess game to change identities.

Many Latin American writers adhered to more universal themes. From Venezuela, Gisela Kozak Rovero published *Rapsodia,* a narrative re-creation of the language, music, rhythm, and poetry of Caracas. Cuban-born Puerto Rican Mayra Montero released *Púrpura profundo,* an erotic Caribbean novel framed in the atmosphere of classical symphonies. Priscilla Gac-Artigas of Puerto Rico published *Melina, conversaciones con el ser que serás,* a story of motherhood. Hernán Lara Zavala produced another collection of short stories, *Después del amor y otros cuentos.* Argentine novelist Pablo Toledo won the 2000 Clarín Prize for the suspenseful *Se esconde tras los ojos,* which followed the story of a politician, a financier, a model, and a photographer from behind the lens of the latter's camera. Luis Felipe Castillo of Venezuela published a detective novel, *Como olas del mar que hubo,* and Hernán Garrido-Lecca of Peru produced a collection of stories, *Benedicto Sabayachi y la mujer Stradivarius.* Peruvian novelist Jaime Bayly returned to his favourite topic in *Los amigos que perdí,* his sixth novel—personal anguish over success, old friends, and confused sexuality.

After more than two decades of a repressive political atmosphere, Chile began to recover its rich literary reputation. Enrique Lafourcade published *Otro baile en París,* a story about a four-year-old child, her grandfather, and a cat; the story was reminiscent of the imaginative works of British author Lewis Carroll. Other notable Chilean works included Hernán Rivera Letelier's *Los trenes se van al purgatorio;* Germán Marín's *Idola,* a thriller about the adventures of a man arriving in Santiago after a devastating earthquake; and Marco Antonio de la Parra's *Novelas enanas,* a psychological novel about characters who cannot remember their past. (M.J. FENWICK)

PORTUGUESE

Portugal. António Lobo Antunes, a perennially strong candidate for the Nobel Prize for Literature, was awarded in 2000 the Great Prize for Fiction by the Association of Portuguese Writers for *Exortação aos crocodilos* (1999); it was the second time that he had won this prize. His novel, a subtle yet complex piece of work, featured the free association of events in a narrative that was directed by the soundings of memory and told in the discontinuity of time and thereby became a tale of multilayered meaning. The characters in the story were shown working out a program of rebellion against democratic institutions. Though Antunes often embraced the "terrorism" of the left as a theme, this time he dealt with the "terrorism" of the right. His characters were generally unpleasant, but in this novel their humanity was shown in a more tangible way than before. Antunes's style also underwent a change; his narrative tone was less acerbic, and his writing was gaining an unprecedented poetic quality.

These narrative features were very much in evidence in his latest novel, *Não entres tão depressa nessa noite escura,* the title of which was a paraphrase of Welsh poet Dylan Thomas's poem entitled "Do Not Go Gentle into That Good Night." The purity of language was suited to the subject matter of the novel, which was structured on the basis of the seven days of the creation. By using this method, the author entered the realm of the universal and produced a fable of human life with a deep literary resonance.

Hélia Correia published a new version of her 1996 novel, *Insânia*. All the events in the story were seen and recounted by a child who appears in a Portuguese village and vanishes in the end in the same mysterious way that she arrived. The means of registering the flashes of the unconscious were subtle, and the innocence of the reader was tested and teased in an original narrative that made compelling reading. (L.S. REBELO)

Jerry Bauer Photography

Two-time winner of the Great Prize for Fiction António Lobo Antunes

Brazil. In 2000 the most notable literary celebration of the 500th anniversary of the discovery of Brazil was the revival of major works of Brazilian theatre, ranging from plays by 19th-century dramatists to Oswald de Andrade's revolutionary *O rei da vela* (1937) to contemporary works. (*See* WORLD AFFAIRS: *Brazil:* Sidebar.)

Several important critical studies appeared. Marcelo Ridenti's *Em busca do povo brasileiro: artistas da revolução, do CPC à era da TV* dealt with the continuing effects of the highly politicized culture of the 1960s and '70s. American critic David S. George reconsidered the fate of the Brazilian theatre of the 1980s and '90s in *Flash & Crash Days: Brazilian Theatre in the Postdictatorship Period.* Maria Antonieta Pereira's *No fim do texto: a obra de Rubem Fonseca* examined Fonseca's characters within the context of "barbarous humanism." Luis Alberto Brandão Santos's *Um olho de vidro* was a critical evaluation of the literary achievement of the highly regarded novelist Sérgio Sant'Anna. In late 1999 Yudith Rosenbaum published *Metamorfoses do mal: uma leitura de Clarice Lispector,* in which she studied sadism as an important element in Lispector's fiction. Donaldo Schüler and Linara Ferreira Pavani organized *Gregório de Matos: texto e hipertexto,* a collection of essays reconsidering the colonial poet's works from a sociopolitical perspective. Marisa Lajolo's *Monteiro Lobato* sought to distinguish Lobato's seemingly divergent literary styles—the premodernism of his children's literature and the traditionalist conservatism of his regionalist stories.

The growth of Internet sites dedicated to Brazilian letters and literary criticism was another highlight of the year. A new electronic publisher based in Paris, <www.00h00.com> (called Zero Hour), began to publish digital books of Brazilian and Portuguese literature. RBL Editora (<http://members.tripod.com/~lfilipe>) published all genres of literature as well as literary criticism. The Network of Brazilian Women Writers (Rede de Escritoras Brasileiras) featured younger women authors on its World Wide Web site: <http://rebra.org>. João Ubaldo Ribeiro, one of Brazil's most eminent writers, published his new novel, *Miséria e grandeza do amor de Benedita,* as an electronic book (e-book). This e-book could be read on a personal computer screen or on a portable wireless computer. Discussion groups dedicated to Brazilian literature and sites featuring specific authors were also developed during the year.

Highly esteemed literary scholar and critic Afrânio Coutinho died in August. Coutinho had organized the landmark *A literatura no Brasil* (3 vol., 1955–59), which introduced the "new criticism" movement into Brazilian letters.

(IRWIN STERN)

RUSSIAN

The most important and widely discussed phenomenon affecting Russian literature in 2000 was the burgeoning Internet. With financial backing from the Soros Foundation, which had helped support Russia's post-Soviet culture, the Russian literati established both a presence on the Internet and one of the world's most organized, vital, and interesting forms of this fledgling culture. The Internet, as elsewhere, worked in two directions; both centripetally—consolidating the dominant role played by the Russian "thick journals" (among them *Novy mir, Znamya,* and *Oktyabr*) by placing them on a single or closely linked group of sites (i.e.,<www.infoart.ru/magazine/index.htm>)—and centrifugally, that is to say serving as a portal beyond the "centre," into cyberspace, where one could find a bewildering array of individual sites, home pages, and chat rooms. The major literary magazines used the World Wide Web to battle the twin problems of imperfect book distribution and general material impoverishment that still plagued Russian literary culture. Sergey Kostyrenko, the editor of *Novy mir,* published a monthly roundup on the Web that served as catalyst, critic, and guide to this outstanding phenomenon.

In strictly literary terms the year 2000, although perhaps not epochal, did see the arrival in bookstores of many new and interesting books and witnessed a marked improvement in the realm of literary criticism. In Russian poetry the single most important publication was probably Viktor Sosnora's brilliant book *Kuda poshyol? I gde okno?* (1999; "Whither Gone? And Where's the Window?"), which broke a 15-year poetic silence (Sosnora had been writing phantasmagoric prose during his absence from publishing) and for which he was honoured with the Apollon Grigoryev prize. Sergey Gandlevsky's *Konspekt* (1999; "Summary"), which received the Northern Palmyra prize, was remarkable for its subtle traditionalism and finely honed, if somewhat sentimental, perceptions. Less subtly but nevertheless brilliantly, the young Moscow poet Maksim Amelin in *Dubia* (1999) demonstrated his ability as a versifier in the classical tradition. More quietly, Mikhail Ayzenberg in *Za krasnymi vorotami* ("Beyond the Red Gates") continued his crepuscular meditations, while the young Dmitry Vodennikov in his English-titled *Holiday* (1999) led his readers on a brilliantly realized, desperately lighthearted lyrical-fantastic journey of the soul. Other noteworthy authors who published books of poetry included Semyon Lipkin, Vitaly Kalpidi, Bella Akhmadulina, Yaroslav Mogutin, Polina Barskova, and Arkady Dragomoshchenko, Russia's leading "language poet," whose massive *Opisanie* ("Description") contains poems from his nearly-35-year career.

Khristoforov Valery/Photo ITAR-TASS

Sergey Gandlevsky (left), winner of the Northern Palmyra prize, with playwright Ivan Savelyev

After the previous year's two prose bombshells—*Generation "P"* by Viktor Pelevin (*see* BIOGRAPHIES) and *Goluboye salo* ("Blue Lard") by Vladimir Sorokin—the year's prose marked if not a return to "normalcy" at least a turn toward lyricism, history, and storytelling. This was evident from the shortlist of Russian Booker Prize finalists, almost all of whom were in their 40s: Valery Zalotukha with his timely *Posledny kommunist* ("The Last Communist"); poet Nikolay Kononov with his disturbing yet highly lyrical novel of childhood, *Pokhorony kuznechika* ("The Grasshopper's Funeral"); Svetlana Shenbrunn with her own rather different novel of childhood, *Rozy i khrizantemi* ("Roses and Chrysanthemums"); Marina Paley with her brooding, philosophical *Lanch* ("Lunch"); Aleksey Slapovsky with *Den deneg* ("Money Day"); and Mikhail Shishkin, the winner, with his historical and fantastic *Vzyatie Izmaila* ("The Taking of Izmail"). At the same time, such disparate contemporary Russian "classics" as Lyudmila Petrushevskaya, Andrey Bitov, Viktor Yerofeyev, and Viktor Astafyev appeared with new works, as did radical avant-gardist Pavel Peppershteyn and the more lyrical Postmodernist Aleksandr Ilyanen. Pavel Krusanov's *Ukus angela* ("The Angel's Bite") demonstrated the possibilities of serious literary fantasy, while Vladislav Otroshenko combined a rich, almost Gogolian prose style with Borgesian fantasy in his long-awaited volume of various genres of prose, entitled *Persona vne dostovernosti* ("A Person Not to Be Trusted").

Russian literary criticism remained fiercely polemical; Andrey Nemzer, Alla Latynina, and Pavel Basinsky defended various forms of "tradition" on one side, while Vyacheslav Kuritsyn, Aleksandr Skidan, and Mark Lipovetsky advocated a more Postmodern view on the other. Other critics of note who published widely and interestingly included Karen Stepanyan, Viktor Toporov, Oleg Dark, Valery Shubinsky, Nikita Yeliseyev, and Mariya Remizova. The brightest spot in Russian criticism was probably the appearance of two new excellent magazines in St. Petersburg, *Novaya russkaya kniga* ("The New Russian Book"), edited by Gleb Morev, and *Peterburgsky knizhny vestnik* ("The Petersburg Literary Herald"), edited by Aleksey Vinogradov. Both were in large measure devoted to reviewing new books and discussing the current literary climate in Russia. They joined *Ex libris* and, to a lesser extent, *Literaturnaya gazeta* and *Kommersant* as general book-review centres, whose role in the culture of reading could not be overestimated.

(THOMAS EPSTEIN)

EASTERN EUROPEAN

Writing in the journal Plamak ("Flame"), Bulgarian poet Georgi Konstantinov used the term *vnezapnoto pokolenie* ("the unexpected generation") to describe poets born in the 1960s and '70s who were grappling with the moral and ideological vacuum of postcommunist society such as prevailed in the Balkans in the last years of the 20th century. In recent decades the Serbian literary scene—which had produced about 5,000 new titles a year, including more than 100 novels—had been dominated by Postmodernist metafiction, but in 2000 several other works gained attention. They included *Druid iz Sindiduna* (1998; "Druid from Sindidun"), the third novel by exotic writer Vladislav Bajac; *Pošto Beograd* (1999; "How Much Is Belgrade"), a collection of 15 stories by the prominent traditionalist Serbian writer Moma Dimić; and *Mexico*, the new war diary that Vladimir Arsenijević wrote during the NATO bombing of Yugoslavia.

A collection of poems by Kalin Donkov, *Sabudi me vchera* ("Wake Me Yesterday"), was viewed as the best Bulgarian book of the year. Besides several excellent recent works by Anton Donchev, other books that captured the limelight included *Vlakat, v koyto patuvame* ("The Train We're Traveling On"), the new novel by Stefan Poptonev, and *Kogato Gospod khodashe po zemyata* ("When God Walked the Earth") by Nikola Radev.

Postmodern writer Zoran Ferić won Croatia's Djalski Literature Award (named for Croatian novelist Ksaver Sandor Djalski, 1854–1935) for his novel *Andjeo u ofsajdu* ("An Angel, Offsides"), and feminist writer Julijana Matanović found great success with *Bilješka o piscu* ("Note About the Author"). Established poet Vesna Parun came out with a collection, *Političko valentinovo* ("A Political Valentine").

Change of the System, the first anthology of short stories and a new genre for Macedonian literature, was edited by Richard Gaughran and Zoran Ančevski and published in English and Macedonian. Aleksandar Prokopiev released his intimate diary, *77 Antiuputstva za lična upotreba* ("77 Anti-Instructions for Personal Use"), while Tomislav Osmanli published a play, *Zvezdite nad Skopje* ("The Stars over Skopje"), about problems of transition in contemporary society.

Perhaps the best collection of poetry in Slovenia was *Krogi na vodi* ("Circles on the Water") by Peter Semolič, who had won a top national poetry award in 1997. The best-received novels were by two writers, one middle-aged and the other young: *Mačja kuga* ("Cat Plague") by Maja Novak and *Pasji tango* ("Dog Tango") by Aleš Čar. An important collection assembled by Slovak editor Stanislava Chrobáková, *100 Years of Slovak Literature*, was presented in both Slovene and English at the Vilenica Literary Festival.

British academic John Keane published *Vaclav Havel: A Political Tragedy in Six Acts* (1999), the first full-length biography of the playwright who had become president of Czechoslovakia and later the Czech Republic. The work concentrated more on Havel's politics than on his art. Meanwhile, at the end of 1999, Havel had brought out his complete works in a self-published edition titled *Spisy* ("Works").

Flora Brovina, an Albanian-language poet and writer from Priština, Kosovo, was selected in April as a recipient—together with Chinese writer Xue Deyun, both in absentia—of the PEN/Barbara Goldsmith Freedom-to-Write Award. Brovina, a pediatrician by profession and organizer of the League of Albanian Women in Kosovo, was rounded up by government paramilitary troops in April 1999, charged with "terrorist acts," and sentenced in December 1999 to 12 years in prison. She was released from prison on Nov. 1, 2000, less than a month after Vojislav Kostunica took office as the new president of Yugoslavia.

Two major Polish literary figures died during the year. Novelist Kazimierz Brandys, whose examination of the 20th-century history of his homeland culminated in the four-volume collection of diaries *Miesiące* (1980; volume 4, 1984; "Months," which first appeared in English as *A Warsaw Diary, 1978–1981* [1983]), died in March. Gustaw Herling-Grudzinski, an émigré novelist and essayist best known for his *A World Apart* (1951), published in Polish as *Inny swiat* in 1953, died in Italy in July. (*See* OBITUARIES.)

(DIMITAR ANAKIEV; EDITOR)

JEWISH

Hebrew. The year 2000 was yet another year of illusory prosperity in Hebrew literature. Though bookstores were filled with new novels and collections of short stories, most of these new works failed to achieve significant literary stature.

The main events in Hebrew fiction were the publication of Ronit Matalon's *Sarah, Sarah* and of Mira Magen's *Beshokhvi uvekumi, isha* ("Love, After All"). The two separate subplots of *Sarah, Sarah* carefully examined the intricate connections between the personal and the political in contemporary Israel. Magen's novel richly depicted the tensions of a single mother torn between her sense of responsibility to her son and her attempts to find new love. Other notable novels included Jonathan Ben Nahum's *Indianapolis* (1999), Yoel Hoffmann's *Halev hu Katmandu* ("The Heart Is Katmandu"), Gail Hareven's *She'ahava nafshi* ("My True Love"), and Ruth Almog's *Ha'agam hapnimi* ("The Inner Lake"). Several works by veteran writers failed to match previous achievements. Among them were Aharon Appelfeld's *Masa el hahoref* ("A Journey into Winter"), Aharon Megged's *Persephona zokheret* ("Persephone Remembers"), David Grossman's *Mishehu larutz ito* ("Someone to Run With"), Zeruya Shlev's *Ba'al ve'isa* ("Husband and Wife"), and Savyon Liebrecht's *Nashim mitokh katalog* ("Mail-Order Women"). Noteworthy short-story collections included Yossel Birstein's *Sipurim rokdim birhovot Erushala'yim* ("Stories Dancing in the Streets of Jerusalem") and Orly Castel-Bloom's *Radikalim hofshiyeem* ("Free Radicals"). First books of prose that gained attention were Joshua Sobol's *Shtika* ("Silence"), Amir Guttfreund's *Sho'ah Shelanu* ("Our Holocaust"), and Avraham Balaban's *Shiv'ah* ("Mourning").

Notable books of poetry included Israel Pincas's *Kol hashirim* ("Collected Poems"), Meir Wieseltier's *Shirim iti'yeem* ("Slow Poems"), Gad Kaynar's *Dgimat neshima* ("Breath Sampling"), Tamir Greenberg's *A'l hanefesh hatzme'ah* ("The Thirsty Soul"), and Agi Mishol's *Mahberet hahalomot* ("The Dream Notebook").

Among the works of literary scholarship were Shmuel Werses's *S.Y. Agnon kipshuto* ("S.Y. Agnon Literally") and Benjamin Harshav's *Shirat hatehia ha'ivrit* ("Hebrew Renaissance Poetry"). Chaya Shacham studied Israeli female poetry in *Nashim umaseikhot* ("Women and Masks"); Avidov Lipsker examined the poetry of Avraham Broides in *La'amal yulad* ("Born unto Trouble"); and Ziva Shamir's *Lintiva hane'elam* ("A Track of Her Own") followed the traces of Hayyim Nahman Bialik's secret affair with Ira Jan, as they are implicitly conveyed in his work. Leading Hebrew poet Yehuda Amichai died in September. (*See* OBITUARIES.)

(AVRAHAM BALABAN)

Yiddish. A highlight in Yiddish literature in 2000 was poet and essayist Aleksander Shpiglblat's compelling and personally revealing memoir, *Durkhn shpaktiv fun a zeyger-makher* ("Through the Lens of a Watchmaker"), a lamentation documenting the experience of one family prior to and during World War II in Câmpulung, Bukovina, Shpiglblat's birthplace.

Heshl Klepfish's *Mitn blik af tsurik: yidish mizrekh-eyrope: kiyem un gerangl* ("A Glance at the Past: Jewish Eastern Europe: Continuity and Struggle") was an engaging and intelligent overview full of the complexities and contradictions of that obliterated community.

Rivke Kosman explored the vagaries and social ambiguities of clothing in the Jewish community from the times of ancient Israel to the present day in *Kleyder makht layt* ("Clothes Make the Man"). Her systematic study demonstrated the multivalent role clothing, chosen or imposed, had played in the creation of identity and status.

Yosl Birshteyn's novel, *A ponem in di volkns* ("A Face in the Clouds"), was a compelling tale of a journey from Poland through China featuring an epistolary ménage à trois, impacted by loneliness, fidelity, and friendship. Yekhiel Shraybman's 50 historical vignettes, *Yetsire un libe: khumesh-noveln, naye miniaturn* ("Creativity and Love: Biblical Short Stories, New Miniatures")—from a series of epochs of long ago—were illustrated and presented in absorbing contemporary guise.

Novelist Ronit Matalon

Henry Holt & Company

Rivke Basman penned a lyrically musical collection of some 70 poems, *Di draytsente sho* ("The Thirteenth Hour"), which was finely tuned and employed powerful poetic imagery. As before, she circled the question of personal belief.

Children's literature in Yiddish was enriched by three volumes, two of them published in Germany and inspired by French and German authors: *Der kleyner prints* ("The Little Prince") was a splendid version of Antoine de Saint-Exupéry's *Le Petit Prince* (1943), and *Shmuel un Shmerke* was a sendup of *Max und Moritz; Vini der pu* ("Winnie the Pooh"), was published in the U.S.

On the scholarly front, Mordkhe Schaechter, the most eminent Yiddish scholar of his generation, published *Der eynheytlekher yidisher oysleyg* (1999; "The Standardized Yiddish Orthography"), including an extensive essay on the history (and rules) of the standardized Yiddish spelling.

The first issue of the new quarterly *Toplpunkt* ("Colon") appeared in Israel. Edited by poet Yankev Beser, it focused on original contemporary writing and art. (THOMAS E. BIRD)

TURKISH

Turkish literary offerings were slim in 2000. Notably absent were new novels by such prominent figures as Yaşar Kemal, Orhan Pamuk, and Adalet Ağaoğlu. Pamuk attracted attention by serving as a general editor for Fyodor Dostoyevsky's complete works in Turkish translation. The publication in the United Kingdom of *The Other Side of the Mountain,* the English version of Erendiz Atasü's *Dağin öteki yüzü,* was greeted as a salutatory event.

Though an otherwise lacklustre year for fiction, 2000 saw the appearance of two fascinating works—Nazlı Eray's *Ayışığı sofrası* ("Table Set for Moonlight"), with its lyrical flights of imagination, and *Acı bilgi: fugue sanatı uzerine bir roman denemesi* ("Bitter Knowledge: An Experimental Novel on the Art of the Fugue"), the first novel by the distinguished poet-essayist Enis Batur, arguably Turkey's most prolific writer. Batur also published books of poetry and critical essays during the year.

Poetry seemed dormant—except for the reprintings of the complete poetry of Fazıl Hüsnü Dağlarca and İlhan Berk, an impressive crop of poems in literary magazines, and a handful of laudable collections. The year's most remarkable book of poems came from Özdemir İnce: *Evren ağacı* ("Tree of the Universe"), a highly effective attempt at creating a modern mythology.

The coveted poetry prize of the daily *Cumhuriyet,* which also published an influential weekly book supplement, went to Sennur Sezer. The Aydın Doğan Foundation Prize—which had been awarded in the three previous years to authors of a work of fiction, a book on social studies, and a photographic tome—was given this time to the "best poetic achievement of the 1990s." The recipient was eminent poet Melih Cevdet Anday, also renowned as a playwright, novelist, essayist, and translator.

Criticism had a golden year. Comparative literature professor Jale Parla published her magnum opus, *Don Kişot'tan bugüne roman* ("From *Don Quixote* to the Modern Novel"), a splendid analysis of fiction as well as the Turkish novel. The late Adnan Benk's provocative critical essays were collected in two hefty volumes, and İnce published a remarkable book of critical essays entitled *Şiirde devrim* ("Revolution in Poetry").

A succès d'estime was *Eski dostlar* ("Old Friends") by Hıfzı Topuz, whose novels based on late Ottoman history had been very popular in recent years.

The country mourned the death of Mîna Urgan, renowned professor and translator of English literature; her two autobiographies had enjoyed great success in the late 1990s.

(TALAT SAIT HALMAN)

PERSIAN

In 2000 the Persian-speaking world lost several important figures, notably prominent exiled poet Nader Naderpur; Ahmad Shamlu, the leading Iranian poet living in Iran; Feraydun Moshiri, a poet with popular appeal; and Hushang Golshiri, the most influential novelist and short-story writer of his generation. In Tajikistan two veteran poets of the first rank died, Mumen Qano'at and Loy'eq Sher-Ali. Their departure portended not just a generational but an epochal transition.

The year's most notable aesthetic surprise was a collection of poems by Iranian filmmaker Abbas Kiarostami. *Hamrāh bā bād* ("Walking with the Wind") was a collection of haikulike compositions that offered a fresh, kinetic look at nature and human society in complete and willful disregard of rhyme and metre and with a deceptively simple diction that seemed to defy any native sense of poetry.

Connected at times by the presence of such unconventional poetic personages as a spider, a scarecrow, and a group of nuns, the book stood in an oblique relation to the entire canon of modernist Persian poetry.

Three notable novels published in Iran were among a rich crop of fresh titles whose publication appeared to have been facilitated by a more tolerant official attitude toward literary expression. Hossein Sanapur's *Nimeh-ye ghayeb* ("The Absent Half") and Ja'far Modarres-Sadeqi's *Shah-kelid* (1999; "Master Key") explored themes central in contemporary Iranian society yet insufficiently examined in the heavily political literature of the past two decades. Ahmad Mahmud's two-volume novel *Derakht-e anjir-e ma'abed* (1993; "The Temples' Fig Tree") was judged the year's most important novel. Published in Germany by expatriate writer Abbas Ma'rufi was *Feraydun seh pesar dasht* ("Feraydun Had Three Sons"), which offered a fresh examination of the roots of discord in Iranian society through a perceptive fictional retelling of the mythical king Feraydun's division of the world among his three sons.

In Tajikistan and elsewhere in Central Asia, signs of renewed literary activity emerged. In September the commemorative event held in honour of slain encyclopaedist and literary historian Academician Muhammad Osemi (Osemov) provided an occasion for the country's poets and fiction writers to offer, for the first time, samples of their most recent unpublished work. In Tashkent, Uzbekistan, fresh attempts were undertaken to establish a Persian publishing enterprise. Unbridled violence and near total disregard of matters cultural continued to keep literary developments in Afghanistan hidden from view.

(AHMAD KARIMI-HAKKAK)

ARABIC

Arab intellectuals were preoccupied in 2000 with globalization, and the dubious nature of that phenomenon was questioned in two Egyptian novels, Gamīl 'Atiyyah Ibrāhīm's *Khizānat al-kalām* ("The Coffer of Words") and Amīn al-'Ayyūtī's *Khamriyyah.* Whereas Ibrāhīm relied on dramatic events to convey his message, 'Ayyūtī used humour. (*See* ECONOMIC AFFAIRS: *Sidebar.*)

Increasingly, writers relied on history as a framework for their fiction. Historical novels by 'Abd al-Raḥmān Munīf, Ahdaf Soueif, and Salwá Bakr assessed the impact of Western culture on the Arab world. Both Munīf's trilogy *Arḍ al-sawād* (1999; "The Arable Land") and Soueif's *The Map of Love* (1999)—which tracked the beginnings of Zionism during the Ottoman Empire—depicted and deplored the manipulation of their countries by the West. Bakr's *Al-Bashmūrī II* was a sequel to *Al-Bashmūrī* (1998) and harkened to the Abbasid period. Khairī Shalabī's *Ṣāliḥ ḥaiṣah* ("Saleh Flight") was set against the backdrop of the British mandate in Egypt.

Some Arab writers remained close to their roots and were motivated by a desire to act locally and think globally. This appeared to be the spirit animating Aḥmad al-Tawfīq's novel *Al-sayl* (1998; "The Flood"), in which positive and negative human emotions were played out in a rural environment. Similarly, Youssouf Amine Elalamy's *Les Clandestins* tackled illegal immigration across the Strait of Gibraltar and other forms of clandestine activities. In *Ni fleurs ni couronnes* by Souad Bahéchar, women controlled the action. Laylá Abū Zayd released another autobiographical novel, *Al-faṣl al-akhīr* (*The Last Chapter*), remarkable for its great fluidity of style. 'Abd al-Karīm Ghallāb devoted *Al-Qāhirah tabūḥu bi-asrāriha* ("Cairo Reveals Its Secrets") to his impressions and observations during a visit to the city after a 50-year absence. Muhammad Shukrī published *Wujūh* ("Faces"), the third volume of his autobiography.

The surprise of the year was the publication of *La Ceinture* by Ahmed Abodeḥmān, the first novel ever published in French by a Saudi writer. The book evoked the drastic change that had occurred in his village following the discovery of oil.

The reediting of the Syrian Ḥaydar Ḥaydar's *Walīmah li a'shāb al-baḥr* (1983; "Banquet for Seaweeds") by the Egyptian Ministry of Culture created a controversy when objections were raised against the work's religious and moral content.

The vibrant literary production in Algeria reflected writers' deep need to share their experiences. While many wrote testimonies in which they vented their anger and sorrow, others managed to transcend reality and produce fictional narratives chronicling the absurdities of their contemporary history. Youcef Zirem's *L'Âme de Sabrina* and 'Abd al-Malik Murtād's *Marāyā mutashaẓẓiyyah* ("Splintered Mirrors") adopted this approach. Published posthumously was Tahar Djaout's *Le Dernier été de la raison* (1999); Djaout was assassinated in 1993. Al-Ṭāhir Waṭṭār attempted to convey the nonsensical nature of that horror in *Al-Walī al-Ṭāhir ya'ūdu ilā maqāmihi* ("Saint Tāhir Returns to His Holy Abode"). Yamina Méchakra broke a long silence with *Arris* (1999), a novel concerned with the question of identity.

AFP Worldwide

Novelist and cancer patient Jamāl al-Ghīṭānī

Mahmūd Darwīsh evoked his brush with death during heart surgery in *Jidāriyah* ("The Mural"), and Jamāl al-Ghīṭānī's fight against cancer was the subject of *Muqārabat al-abad* ("Proximity to Eternity").

In *DANSKO*, Ghāzī al-Qusaybī recounted the behind-the-scene plots for the choice of the UNESCO director, a position he coveted. The social problems of Egypt's working classes, set against the backdrop of Anwar al-Sādāt's rule, informed Ibrāhīm Aṣlān's *'Aṣāfīr al-Nīl* (1999; "Nile Sparrows") and Muhammad al-Bisāṭī's *Layālin ukhrā* ("Other Nights").

In Mauritania, Aḥmad ibn 'Abd al-Qādir concerned himself with his country's social history in his novel *Al-'uyūn al-shākhiṣa* ("The Fixed Eyes").

Two Egyptians were recognized—Idwar al-Kharrāṭ was honoured with a State Merit Award and a collection of articles, *Idwār al-Kharrāt, mughāmir ḥattā al-nihāyan* ("Edouard el-Kharrat, an Adventurer to the End"), for his 70th birthday, and Aḥlām Mustaghānimī received the Naguib Mahfouz Prize. Syria lost novelist Hānī al-Rāhib.

(AIDA A. BAMIA)

CHINESE

The 2000 Nobel Prize for Literature went to Gao Xingjian, a Chinese novelist and playwright who had lived in France since 1987. (*See* NOBEL PRIZES.) Gao, whose works had been banned in his native country because of their social and political criticism, was the first Chinese-born author to win the prize. The reaction from the Chinese literati was ambivalent. The spokesperson of the China Writers Association commented that "this is not a selection based on literature but on politics." Some observers argued that there were many writers in both China and Taiwan whose works were more significant than those of Gao. Others disagreed and voiced confidence in the Nobel judges' knowledge of Chinese literature. Many in China were simply happy that the prizewinner was a compatriot, no matter what Gao's political views were.

Another Chinese writer in exile received a major literary award. Ha Jin, who immigrated to the U.S. in 1985, won the 2000 PEN/Faulkner Award, the largest prize for a work of fiction, for his first English-language novel, *Waiting* (1999). (*See* BIOGRAPHIES.) The novel, which had won the National Book Award in 1999, told the story of an army doctor in China who falls in love with a nurse during the Cultural Revolution but who vacillates about asking his traditional village wife for a divorce.

The Mao Dun Literature Awards for fiction, given every four years, were announced on October 19. The awards were given to Tibetan writer Ah Lai's *Chen'ai luo ding* (1999; "When the Dust Settles"), female author Wang Anyi's *Chang hen ge* (1999; "Song of Everlasting Sorrow"), Zhang Ping's *Jueze* ("Hard Choice"), and Wang Xufeng's *Nanfang you jiamu* ("Fine Tree Possessed in Southland") and *Buye zhi hou* ("Delightful Marquis to Break Drowsiness"), the first two books of his trilogy *Charen Sanbuqu* ("Trilogy of Tea Men"). Ah Lai's novel told the story of a Tibetan chieftain. Wang Anyi's book described the daily life of urban Shanghai residents. Zhang Ping's *Jueze* depicted a city mayor fighting against corruption, and Wang Xufeng's novels painted the rise and fall of a tea merchant family.

There were two excellent novels published in China in 2000. The first was Ye Guangcen's *Caisangzi,* which portrayed the lives of the descendants of a former Manchu royal family. The novel was characterized by its distinctive structure. The book's title was taken from the name of a poem written by Nalan Xingde during the Qing dynasty; the name of each chapter of the novel was taken from each line of the poem; and the final meaning of the novel fitted into the poem's artistic conception. The other notable novel was Wang Meng's *Kuanghuan de jijie* ("The Carnival Season"). This work used harmoniously mixed techniques to portray a group of energetic and enthusiastic men and women in their 60s and 70s. Presenting readers with the characters' different living situations, the book described their happiness and grief, sincerity and hypocrisy, losses and hopes, and awakenings and acts of forgiveness.

In other news affecting the Chinese literary world, the government cracked down on a Hong Kong-based poets organization in November; three leaders of the organization were arrested after authorities discovered that dissident writers had been invited to a conference planned for November 6–11 in Guangxi province. (QIAN ZHONGWEN)

JAPANESE

Two Korean-Japanese writers captured centre stage in 2000; the first was Gengetsu, who won the Akutagawa Prize, Japan's top literary award for new writers. His *Kage no sumika* ("House in Shadow") featured a young newspaperman who writes an article about his encounter with an old man—a one-handed Korean-Japanese man living in a decrepit "Korean Town" slum in Osaka. The column reminds the people in the town of the time when they were conscripted as Japanese.

Korean-Japanese writer and former Akutagawa Prize winner Miri Yū wrote about her years with her married boyfriend, his death, and their child in *Inochi* ("Life"), one of the best-selling nonfiction works of the year. The book, which revealed details about many of the living, aroused controversy over privacy issues.

Chiya Fujino's *Natsu no yakusoku* ("Promise in Summer"), a story of adolescence, also won an Akutagawa Prize. Fujino was a male writer who had elected to live as a woman after suffering from a gender-identity disorder. Two other Akutagawa Prize winners were selected for the second half of the year; Kō Machida won for his story about a young ruffian in *Kiregire* ("Snatches") and Hisaki Matsuura for *Hana kutashi* ("Rotten Flower"), which chronicled a day in the life of an unemployed middle-aged man.

Leading fiction writer Haruki Murakami published the short-story collection *Kami no kodomotachi wa mina odoru* ("All the Children of God Dance"). All six stories were inspired by the 1995 Great Hanshin Earthquake, which killed more than 6,000 persons in Kobe, where Murakami grew up. Unlike his former work *Andāguraundo* (1997; "Underground")—in which he interviewed survivors of the 1995 mass murder by the religious group AUM Shinrikyo—this time he tried to express the depth of anguish without using firsthand accounts. Though the stories were well constructed, some criticized Murakami for having failed to look the disaster in the face.

Other best-selling fictions were Banana Yoshimoto's *Furin to Nanbei* ("Affairs and South America") and *Karada wa zenbu shitteiru* ("Body Knows All"), Nobuko Takagi's *Hyakunen no yogen* ("One Hundred Years of Prophecy"), and Ryū Murakami's *Kibō no kuni no ekusodasu* ("Exodus in a Country of Hope").

In literary criticism, Kōjin Karatani published *Rinri 21* ("Ethics 21"). Basing his thoughts upon the philosophical teachings of Immanuel Kant, Karatani put them forth on a number of subjects, including liberty and responsibility. Kazuya Fukuda evaluated 100 contemporary Japanese authors and their 574 stories in *Sakka no neuchi* ("Value of Writers").

The Tanizaki Jun'icherō Prize went to Noboru Tsujihara's *Yūdōtei enmoku* ("Dreams of Yudotei Enmoku"), a story told by and titled after the name of a *rakugo* comic storyteller, and to Ryū Murakami's *Kyōseichū* ("Symbiotic Worm"), a tale about a young man who is programmed to root out mankind. The Yomiuri Prize for Literature for fiction was awarded to Yasutaka Tsutsui's *Watashi no guranpa* (1999; "My Grandpa") and to Taku Miki's *Hadashi to kaigara* (1999; "Naked Feet and Seashell"). The Yasunari Kawabata Literary Prize went to Shun Medoruma's *Mabuigumi* (1999; "Giving Life") and Keiko Iwasaka's *Ame nochi ame?* ("Rain Afterwards Rain?").

Popular contemporary authors Tomie Ōhara, Komimasa Tanaka, and Sumie Tanaka all died during the year.

(YOSHIHIKO KAZAMARU)

Mathematics and Physical Sciences

Scientists reported intriguing evidence for **FLOWING WATER ON MARS** in the relatively recent past and announced the synthesis of perhaps the **WORLD'S MOST POWERFUL EXPLOSIVE.** The growing **INTERNATIONAL SPACE STATION** received its first **PERMANENT CREW.**

MATHEMATICS

In August 2000 the American Mathematical Society convoked a weeklong meeting in Los Angeles devoted to "Mathematical Challenges of the 21st Century." The gathering featured 30 plenary speakers, including eight winners of the quadrennial Fields Medal, a distinction comparable to a Nobel Prize. In assembling at the start of the new century, the participants jointly undertook a task analogous to one accomplished by a single person 100 years earlier. At the Second International Congress of Mathematicians in Paris in August 1900, the leading mathematician of the day, David Hilbert of the University of Göttingen, Ger., had set out a list of 23 "future problems of mathematics." The list included not only specific problems but also whole programs of research. Some of Hilbert's problems were completely solved in the 20th century, but others led to prolonged, intense effort and to the development of entire fields of mathematics.

The talks in Los Angeles included topics of applied mathematics that could not have been imagined in Hilbert's day—for example, the physics of computation, the complexity of biology, computational molecular biology, models of perception and inference, quantum computing and quantum information theory, and the mathematical aspects of quantum fields and strings. Other topics, such as geometry and its relation to physics, partial differential equations, and fluid mechanics, were ones that Hilbert would have found familiar. Just as Hilbert could not have anticipated all the themes of mathematical progress for 100 years into the future, mathematicians at the 2000 conference expected that the emphases within their subject would be reshaped by society and the ways that it applied mathematics.

The reputation and cachet of Hilbert, together with the compactness of his list, were enough to spur mathematical effort for most of the 20th century. On the other hand, major monetary rewards for the solution of specific problems in mathematics were few. The Wolfskehl Prize, offered in 1908 for the resolution of Fermat's last theorem, amounted to $50,000 when it was awarded in 1995 to Andrew Wiles of Princeton University. The Beal Prize of $50,000 was offered in 1998 for the proof of the Beal conjecture—that is, apart from the case of squares, no two powers of integers sum to another power, unless at least two of the integers have a common factor. Unlike Nobel Prizes, which include a monetary award of about $1 million each, the Fields Medal in mathematics carried only a small award—Can$15,000, or about U.S. $9,900.

A major development in 2000 was the offer of $1 million each for the solution of some famous problems. In March, as a promotion for a fictional work about a mathematician, publishers Faber and Faber Ltd. and Bloomsbury Publishing offered $1 million for a proof of Goldbach's conjecture—that every even integer greater than 2 is the sum of two prime numbers. The limited time (the offer was to expire in March 2002) would likely be too short to stimulate the needed effort.

More perduring prizes were offered in May by the Clay Mathematics Institute (CMI), Cambridge, Mass., which designated a $7 million prize fund for the solution of seven mathematical "Millennium Prize Problems" ($1 million each), with no time limit. The aim was to "increase the visibility of mathematics among the general public." Three of the problems were widely known among mathematicians: P versus NP (are there more efficient algorithms for time-consuming computations?), the Poincaré conjecture (if every loop on a compact three-dimensional manifold can be shrunk to a point, is the manifold topologically equivalent to a sphere?), and the Riemann hypothesis (all zeros of the Riemann zeta function lie on a specific line). The other four were in narrower fields and involved specialized knowledge and terminology: the existence of solutions for the Navier-Stokes equations (descriptions of the motions of fluids), the Hodge conjecture (algebraic geometry), the existence of Yang-Mills fields (quantum field theory and particle physics), and the Birch and Swinnerton-Dyer conjecture (elliptic curves).

Hilbert tried to steer mathematics in directions that he regarded as important. The new prizes concentrated on specific isolated problems in already-developed areas of mathematics. Nevertheless, as was noted at the May prize announcement by Wiles, a member of CMI's Scientific Advisory Board, "The mathematical future is by no means limited to these problems. There is a whole new world of mathematics out there, waiting to be discovered."

(PAUL J. CAMPBELL)

CHEMISTRY

Organic Chemistry. After more than a decade of effort, University of Chicago organic chemists in 2000 reported the synthesis of a compound that could prove to be the world's most powerful nonnuclear explosive. Octanitrocubane ($C_8[NO_2]_8$) has a molecular structure once regarded as impossible to synthesize—eight carbon atoms tightly arranged in the shape of a cube, with a nitro group (NO_2) projecting outward from each carbon.

Philip Eaton and colleagues created octanitrocubane's nitro-less parent, cubane (C_8H_8), in 1964. Later, he and others began the daunting task of replacing each hydrogen atom with a nitro group. Octanitrocubane's highly strained 90° bonds, which store large amounts of energy, and its eight oxygen-rich nitro groups accounted for the expectations of its explosive power. Eaton's team had yet to synthesize enough octanitrocubane for an actual test, but its density (a measure of explosive power)—about 2 g/cc—suggested that it could be extraordinarily potent. Trinitrotoluene (TNT), in contrast, has a density of 1.53 g/cc; HMX, a powerful military explosive, has a density of 1.89 g/cc. Eaton pointed out that the research yielded many new insights into the processes underlying chemical bonding. His group also had indications that cubane derivatives interact with enzymes involved in Parkinson disease and so could have therapeutic applications.

Oligosaccharides are carbohydrates made of a relatively small number of units of simple sugars, or monosaccharides. These large molecules play important roles in many health-related biological processes, including viral and bacterial infections, cancer, autoimmune diseases, and rejection of transplanted organs. Researchers wanted to use oligosaccharides in the diagnosis, treatment, and prevention of diseases, but, because of the great difficulty involved in synthesizing specific oligosaccharides in the laboratory, the potential for these compounds in medicine remained unfulfilled. Conventional synthesis techniques were labour-intensive, requiring specialized knowledge and great chemical skill.

Peter H. Seeberger and associates at the Massachusetts Institute of Technology reported the development of an automated oligosaccharide synthesizer that could ease those difficulties. Their device was a modified version of the automated synthesizer that revolutionized the synthesis of peptides. Peptides are chains of amino acids—the building blocks of antibiotics, many hormones, and other medically important substances.

The oligosaccharide synthesizer linked together monosaccharides. It fed monosaccharide units into a reaction chamber, added programmed amounts of solvents and reagents, and maintained the necessary chemical conditions for the synthesis. Seeberger described one experiment in which it took just 19 hours to synthesize a certain heptasaccharide (a seven-unit oligosaccharide), with an overall yield of 42%. Manual synthesis of the same heptasaccharide took 14 days and had an overall yield of just 9%. Seeberger emphasized, however, that additional developmental work would be needed to transform the machine into a commercial instrument widely available to chemists.

Nuclear Chemistry. The periodic table of elements lays out the building blocks of matter into families based on the arrangement of electrons in each element's reactive outer electron shell. Although the table has been highly accurate in predicting the properties of new or as-yet-undiscovered elements from the properties of known family members, theorists believed that it might not work as well for extremely heavy elements that lie beyond uranium on the table. The heavier an element, the faster the movement of its electrons around the nucleus. According to Einstein's theory of relativity, the electrons in a very massive element may move fast enough to show effects that would give the element weird properties. Elements 105 and 106—dubnium and seaborgium, respectively—showed hints of such unusual behaviour, and many nuclear chemists suspected that element 107, bohrium, would exhibit a more pronounced strangeness.

Andreas Türler of the Paul Scherrer Institute, Villigen, Switz., and co-workers reported that relativistic effects do not alter bohrium's predicted properties. Türler and associates synthesized a bohrium isotope, bohrium-267, that has a half-life of 17 seconds. It was long enough for ultrafast chemical analysis to show that bohrium's reactivity and other properties are identical to those predicted by the periodic table. How heavy, then, must an element be for relativistic effects to appear? Türler cited the major difficulty in searching for answers—the short half-lives of many superheavy elements, which often are in the range of fractions of a second, do not allow enough time for chemical analysis.

Applied Chemistry. Polyolefins account for more than half of the 170 million metric tons of polymers or plastics produced around the world each year. Polyolefins, which include polyethylene and polypropylene, find use in food packaging, textiles, patio furniture, and a wide assortment of other everyday products. Demand for polyolefins was growing as new applications were found and as plastics replaced metal, glass, concrete, and other traditional materials.

Robert H. Grubbs and associates of the California Institute of Technology (Caltech) reported the development of a new family of nickel-based catalysts that could simplify production of polyolefins. The catalysts also could permit synthesis of whole new kinds of "designer" plastics with desirable properties. Existing catalysts for making plastics were far from ideal. They demanded extremely clean starting materials as well as cocatalysts in order to grow polymers properly. In addition, they did not tolerate the presence of heteroatoms—that is, atoms such as oxygen, nitrogen, and sulfur within the ring structures of the starting materials. The Caltech team's catalysts, however, did not need a cocatalyst and tolerated less-pure starting materials and heteroatoms. They could polymerize ethylene in the presence of functional additives such as ethers, ketones, esters, alcohols, amines, and water. By altering the functional groups, chemists would be able to design polymers with a wide variety of desired mechanical, electrical, and optical properties.

Radioactive nuclear waste from weapons, commercial power reactors, and other sources was accumulating in industrial countries around the world. The waste caused concern because of uncertainty over the best way of isolating it from the environment. Nuclear waste may have to be stored for centuries just for the most dangerous radioactive components to decay. The waste-storage containers used in the U.S. had a design life of about 100 years, rather than the thousands of years that were required of long-term storage media. Current research into long-term storage focused on first encapsulating the waste in a radiation-resistant solid material before putting it into a container for underground entombment in a geologically stable formation.

A research team headed by Kurt E. Sickafus of Los Alamos (N.M.) National Laboratory reported a new family of ceramic materials that appeared virtually impervious to the damaging effects of radiation. The compounds, a class of complex oxides having the crystal structure of the mineral fluorite (CaF_2), could be the ideal materials in which to encapsulate and store plutonium and other radioactive wastes for long periods. Radiation gradually knocks atoms out of their normal positions in the crystalline structure of materials, which causes them to deteriorate. Sickafus's group developed a fluorite-structured oxide of erbium, zirconium, and oxygen ($Er_2Zr_2O_7$) that showed strong resistance to radiation-induced deterioration. They believed that related compounds that would be even more radiation-resistant could be developed by the use of $Er_2Zr_2O_7$ as a model.

Shortly after the first synthesis of plutonium in 1940, chemists realized that the new element, which eventually would be used in nuclear weapons, could exist in several oxidation states. Evidence suggested that plutonium dioxide (PuO_2) was the most chemically stable oxide. It seemed to remain stable under a wide range of conditions, including temperatures approaching 2,000 °C (about 3,600 °F). Belief in the stability of PuO_2 went unchallenged for more than 50 years and led to its use in commercial nuclear reactor fuels in Russia and Western Europe and to steps toward similar use in Japan and the U.S. In addition, PuO_2 was the form in which plutonium from dismantled nuclear weapons would be stored.

John M. Haschke and associates at Los Alamos National Laboratory reported during the year that PuO_2 is less stable than previously believed. Their results showed that water can slowly oxidize solid crystalline PuO_2 to a phase that can contain greater than 25% of the plutonium atoms in a higher oxidation state, with gradual release of explosive hydrogen gas. This new phase, represented as PuO_{2+x}, is stable only to 350 °C (about 660 °F). In addition, it is relatively water-soluble, which raised the possibility that plutonium that comes into contact with water in underground storage facilities could migrate into groundwater supplies.

"Green" Chemistry. Supercritical carbon dioxide (CO_2) continued to receive attention as a possible "green solvent." Green solvents are nontoxic compounds, environmentally friendly alternatives to the organic solvents used in many important industrial processes, including the manufacture of medicines, textiles, and plastics. Supercriticality occurs in gases such as CO_2 when they are taken above specific conditions of temperature and pressure (the critical point). Supercritical CO_2 has fluidlike properties somewhere between gases and liquids and a combination of desirable characteristics from both states. Although supercriticality was known to enhance the solvent capacity of CO_2, supercritical CO_2 remained a feeble solvent for many substances of interest. Special solubility-enhancing additives called CO_2-philes and very high pressures were employed to make supercritical CO_2 an industrially useful solvent, but the high cost of these measures was limiting its potential.

Eric J. Beckman's group at the University of Pittsburgh (Pa.) reported synthesis of a series of CO_2-phile compounds called poly(ether-carbonate)s that dissolve in CO_2 at lower pressures and could make the use of supercritical CO_2 a more economically feasible process. The compounds are co-polymers—chainlike molecules made from repeating units of two or more simpler compounds—and they can be prepared from inexpensive starting materials such as propylene oxide. Beckman found that the co-polymers performed substantially better than traditional CO_2-philes, which contained expensive fluorocarbon compounds. (MICHAEL WOODS)

PHYSICS

Particle Physics. The standard model, the mathematical theory that describes all of the known elementary particles and their interactions, predicts the existence of 12 kinds of matter particles, or fermions. Until 2000 all but one had been observed, the exception being the tau neutrino. Neutrinos are the most enigmatic of the fermions, interacting so weakly with other matter that they are incredibly difficult to observe. Three kinds of neutrinos were believed to exist—the electron neutrino, the muon neutrino, and the tau neutrino—each named after the particle with which it interacts.

Although indirect evidence for the existence of the tau neutrino had been found, only during the year did an international team of physicists working at the DONUT (Direct Observation of the Nu Tau) experiment at the Fermi National Accelerator Laboratory (Fermilab) near Chicago report the first direct evidence. The physicists' strategy was based on observations of the way the other two neutrinos interact with matter. Electron neutrinos striking a matter target were known to produce electrons, whereas muon neutrinos under the same conditions produced muons. In the DONUT experiment, a beam of highly accelerated protons bombarded a tungsten target, creating the anticipated tau neutrinos among the spray of particle debris from the collisions. The neutrinos were sent through thick iron plates, where on very rare occasions a tau neutrino interacted with an iron nucleus, producing a tau particle. The tau was detected, along with its decay products, in layers of photographic emulsion sandwiched between the plates. In all, four taus were found, enough for the DONUT team to be confident of the results.

Six of the fermions in the standard model are particles known as quarks. Two of them, the up quark and the down quark, make up the protons and neutrons, or nucleons, that constitute the nuclei of familiar matter. Under the low-energy conditions prevalent in the universe today, quarks are confined within the nucleons, bound together by the exchange of particles called gluons. It was postulated that, in the first few microseconds after the big bang, however, quarks and gluons existed free as a hot jumble of particles called a quark-gluon plasma. As the plasma cooled, it condensed into the ordinary nucleons and other quark-containing particles presently observed.

In February physicists at the European Laboratory for Particle Physics (CERN) near Geneva reported what they claimed was compelling evidence for the creation of a new state of matter having many of the expected features of a quark-gluon plasma. The observations were made in collisions between lead ions that had been accelerated to extremely high energies and lead atoms in a stationary target. It was expected that a pair of interacting lead nuclei, each containing more than 200 protons and neutrons, would become so hot and dense that the nucleons would melt fleetingly into a soup of their building blocks. The CERN results were the most recent in a long quest by laboratories in both Europe and the U.S. to achieve the conditions needed to create a true quark-gluon plasma. Some physicists contended that unambiguous confirmation of its production would have to await results from the Relativistic Heavy Ion Collider (RHIC), which went into operation in mid-

Henning Weber/University of Frankfurt

Colliding masses of protons and neutrons (white spheres) melt into a hot quark-gluon plasma (coloured spheres) in this computer graphic from CERN.

year at Brookhaven National Laboratory, Upton, N.Y. RHIC would collide two counterrotating beams of gold ions to achieve a total collision energy several times higher—and thus significantly higher temperatures and densities—than achieved at CERN.

Solid-State Physics. New frontiers in solid-state physics were being opened by the development of semiconductor quantum dots. These are isolated groups of atoms, numbering approximately 1,000 to 1,000,000, in the crystalline lattice of a semiconductor, with the dimensions of a single dot measured in nanometres (billionths of a metre). The atoms are coupled quantum mechanically so that electrons in the dot can exist only in a limited number of energy states, much as they do in association with single atoms. The dot can be thought of as a giant artificial atom having light-absorption and emission properties that can be tailored to various uses. Consequently, quantum dots were being investigated in applications ranging from the conversion of sunlight into electricity to new kinds of lasers. Researchers at Toshiba Research Europe Ltd., Cambridge, Eng., and the University of Cambridge, for example, announced the development of photodetectors based on quantum-dot construction that were capable of detecting single photons. Unlike present single-photon detectors, these did not rely on high voltages or electron avalanche effects and could be made small and robust. Applications could include astronomical spectroscopy, optical communication, and quantum computing.

Lasers and Light. Lasers had become increasingly powerful since the first one was demonstrated in 1960. During the year independent groups of physicists at the Lawrence Livermore National Laboratory, Livermore, Calif., and the Rutherford Appleton Laboratory, Chilton, Eng., reported using two of the world's most powerful lasers to induce fission in uranium nuclei. Each laser, the Petawatt laser in the U.S. and the Vulcan laser in England, could deliver a light pulse with an intensity exceeding a quintillion (10^{18}) watts per square centimetre. In both experiments the powerful electric field associated with the laser pulse accelerated electrons nearly to the speed of light over a microscopic distance, whereupon they collided with the nuclei of heavy atoms. In decelerating from the collisions, the electrons shed their excess energy in the form of energetic gamma rays, which then struck samples of uranium-238. In a process called photonuclear fission, the gamma rays destabilized some of the uranium nuclei, causing them to split. Although laser-induced fission would not seem to be a practical source of nuclear energy (more energy is needed to power the laser than is released in the fission process), the achievements improved the prospects of using lasers to induce and study a variety of nuclear processes.

A development of definite practical significance was reported by scientists at Lucent Technologies's Bell Laboratories, Murray Hill, N.J., who devised the first electrically powered semiconductor laser based on an organic material. Their feat could open the way to the development of cheaper lasers that emit light over a wide range of frequencies, including visible colours. Conventional semiconductor lasers, which were used in a vast array of applications from compact-disc players to fibre-optic communications, were made of metallic elements that required handling in expensive facilities similar to those needed for silicon-chip manufacture and were somewhat limited in their range of colours.

The Bell Labs organic laser employed a high-purity crystal of tetracene placed between two different kinds of field-effect transistors (FETs). When a voltage was applied to the FETs, one device sent negative charges (electrons) into the crystal, and the other created positive charges (holes, or electron vacancies). As electrons and holes combined, they emitted photons that triggered the lasing process, which resulted in a yellow-green light pulse. Despite the apparent requirement for high-purity organic crystals, refinements in manufacturing processes could eventually make organic lasers quite economical. Substitution of other organic materials for tetracene should allow a range of lasers of different colours.

The propagation of light continued to be a topic of interest long after A.A. Michelson and E.W. Morley discovered in the 1880s that the speed of light is independent of Earth's motion through space. Their result ultimately led Albert Einstein to postulate in 1905 in his special theory of relativity that the speed of light in a vacuum is a fundamental constant. Astronomer Kenneth Brecher of Boston University carried out a rigorous test of that postulate during the year, confirming that any variation in the speed of light due to the velocity of the source, if it exists at all, must be smaller than one part in 10^{20}. Brecher studied cosmically distant violent explosions known as gamma-ray bursts, hundreds of which were detected every year by Earth-orbiting astronomical satellites as brief pulses of high-energy radiation. He reasoned that, if the matter that emits the gamma rays in such an explosion is flying at high speed in many different directions, then any effect imposed on the speed of the radiation by the different velocities of the source would create a speed dispersion in the observed radiation coming from a burst. This dispersion would be manifested in the burst's light curve, the way that the burst brightened and dimmed over time. Analyzing the light curves from a number of these phenomena, however, Brecher found no such effect.

Reports of two experiments had physicists debating and carefully restating the meaning of the speed of light as a fundamental speed limit, a necessary part of the theory of relativity. Anedio Ranfagni and co-workers at the Electromagnetic Wave Research Institute of the Italian National Research Council, Florence, succeeded in sending microwave-frequency radiation through air at a speed somewhat faster than that of light by modulating a microwave pulse. At the NEC Research Institute, Princeton, N.J., Lijun Wang pushed the speed of a pulse of visible light much higher than the speed of light in a vacuum by propagating it through a chamber filled with optically excited cesium gas. Such results were not necessarily in contradiction with relativity theory, but they demanded a more careful consideration of what defines the transfer of information by a light beam. If information could travel faster than the speed of light in a way that allowed it to be interpreted and used, it would, in essence, be a preview of the future that could be used to alter the present. It would violate the principle of causality, in which an effect must follow the cause. (DAVID G.C. JONES)

ASTRONOMY

Solar System. In 2000 the search for places in the solar system other than Earth with conditions hospitable enough for life gained support from recent studies of images taken by NASA's Mars Global Surveyor spacecraft, which went into orbit around the planet in 1997. High-resolution photographs of some of Mars's coldest regions revealed surface features suggesting that liquid water may have flowed just beneath the Martian surface, occasionally bursting through the walls of craters and valleys to run down and form gullies like those caused by water erosion on Earth. Michael Malin and Kenneth Edgett of Malin Space Science Systems, San Diego, Calif., who reported the results, found that, of more than 50,000 photographs taken by Surveyor, some 150 revealed the presence of as many as 120 such features. Remarkably, the features were found at high Martian latitudes, where the temperature is much colder than at the planet's equator. Furthermore, from the lack of visible subsequent erosion or small craters in the vicinity, the gullies appeared to be no more than a million years old. Because of the low atmospheric pressure on Mars, any liquid water appearing on the surface should have quickly evaporated. In addition, if subsurface water was present, the cold Martian crust should have kept it in the form of solid ice. Therefore, questions were raised concerning Malin and Edgett's interpretation of the Surveyor images. Nonetheless, they sparked renewed interest in looking for life on Mars even at high latitudes.

NEAR (Near Earth Asteroid Rendezvous)

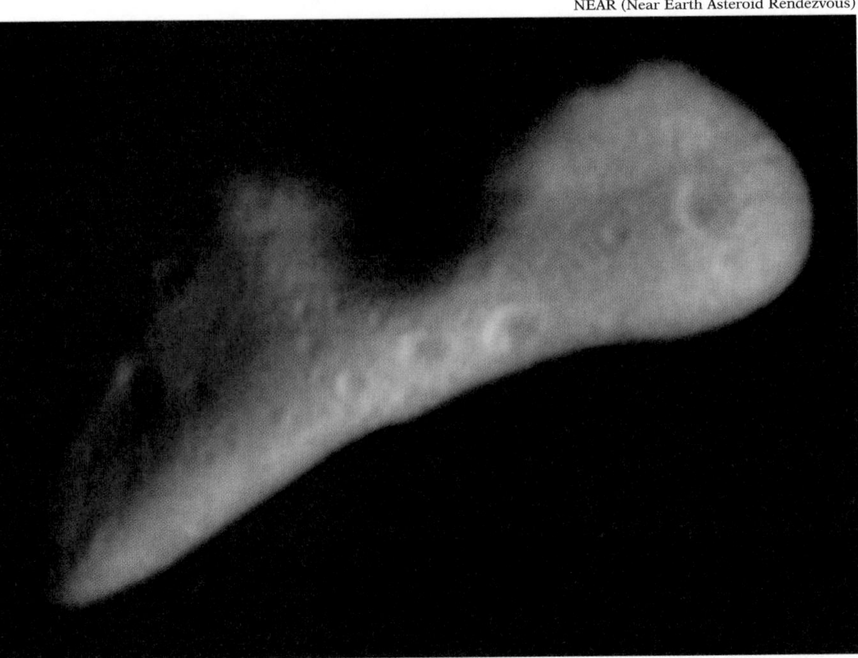

This color image of Eros was taken by the Near Earth Asteroid Rendezvous spacecraft on February 12, two days before it began orbiting the asteroid.

After a four-year trip, the Near Earth Asteroid Rendezvous (NEAR) spacecraft reached its final destination. Its target was 433 Eros, the largest of the near-Earth asteroids—i.e., asteroids that can pass inside the orbit of Mars. Arriving at Eros on February 14 (appropriately, Valentine's Day), NEAR became the first spacecraft to be placed in a gravitationally bound orbit around an asteroid. It immediately began a yearlong survey that included taking photographic images, making X-ray and gamma-ray spectroscopic measurements, conducting magnetic-field studies, and collecting other data from the object. The earliest images showed Eros to be elongated, some 33 × 15 km (about 20 × 9 mi), and riddled with craters. With a density about that of Earth's crust, Eros appeared to be a solid object, not just a gravel pile. By year's end NEAR Shoemaker (the spacecraft had been renamed to honour the late planetary scientist Eugene Shoemaker) was maneuvered to within five kilometres (three miles) of Eros, where it revealed a wealth of surface detail, including boulders as small as 1.4 m (4.6 ft) across. Taken together, the pictures and other data showed Eros to be a primitive object, seemingly unchanged since the birth of the solar system except for its surface, which was cratered and crushed into rubble by billions of years of meteoritic impacts.

The year included a host of discoveries of new solar system objects. Astronomers using the Spacewatch telescope on Kitt Peak, Arizona, concluded that a previously reported asteroid, which they had discovered, was actually a moon of Jupiter, the 17th known. The tiny object, which revolves in orbit some 24 million km (15 million mi) from Jupiter in about two Earth years, does so in a direction opposite that of the other Jovian moons. Astronomers thus concluded that it probably was an asteroid that had been captured by Jupiter's enormous gravitational pull, rather than an original moon formed along with the planet itself. Brett Gladman of the Centre National de la Recherche Scientifique in France and an international team of astronomers, using telescopes in Chile and Hawaii, discovered four new moons for Saturn. This brought the total number of known Saturnian moons to 22, surpassing the 21 moons discovered to date for the planet Uranus. Like the recently discovered moon of Jupiter, the new moons of Saturn are small—only some 10–50 km (6–30 mi) across—and appear to have been captured. Taken together, these new discoveries should help clarify the way in which planets capture asteroids. At year's end Charles Baltay of Yale University and collaborators announced the discovery of a minor planet that orbits the Sun between Neptune and Pluto in a period of 243 years. The object, designated 2000 EB173, is about 650 km (400 mi) across, roughly a fourth the size of Pluto. Although there were at least 300 objects known to orbit in the trans-Neptunian region called the Kuiper belt, this was by far the largest other than Pluto itself.

Stars. The search for planets around stars other than the Sun had accelerated since they were first detected in 1995. Found by looking at the small changes that they induce in the motion of their parent stars, nine new extrasolar planets were reported in the latter part of 2000 by three independent groups of astronomers. This brought the total number discovered to date to about 50. One of the new objects, discovered by William Cochran of the University of Texas McDonald Observatory and collaborators, was the nearest extrasolar planet found to date. It revolves around the star Epsilon Eridani, which lies at a distance from Earth of only about 10.5 light-years, in an orbit that furnishes a wide angular separation distance and so may provide the best opportunity for direct observation of an extrasolar planet in the future. Another exciting extrasolar planetary discovery was one announced by a team led by Michel Mayor of Geneva Observatory. The astronomers detected a planet having a mass that may be only about 0.15 that of Jupiter, or about 50 times the mass of Earth. Furthermore, they showed that the planet is one of at least two planets orbiting the star HD 83443—only the second star other than the Sun known to have two or more planets.

Life on Earth depends on the existence of a wide variety of chemical elements. Hydrogen is thought to have originated in the big bang, and light elements such as carbon and oxygen can be synthesized in the normal course of stellar evolution. Heavy elements up to iron have been theorized to originate only in the centres of massive stars near the end of their evolution and then be spewed into space in supernova explosions at their death. (Elements heavier than iron can be formed only during a supernova explosion itself.) Following its launch into Earth orbit in July 1999, the Chandra X-ray Observatory (named in honour of the astrophysicist Subrahmanyan Chandrasekhar) was trained on a number of supernova remnants, including Cassiopeia A (Cas A), the remnant of a star that exploded in 1680. During the year the Chandra team, after studying the Cas A observations, reported the first unequivocal detection of newly formed iron in a supernova remnant. Much to the team's surprise, however, the iron was detected in gaseous knots rapidly expanding away in the outer regions of the remnant, far beyond the regions where lighter elements such as silicon were found. How the explosion managed to eject the iron (formed at the centre of the dying star) beyond the silicon (formed at shallower depths than the iron) remained a mystery.

Galaxies and Cosmology. During the year the Chandra observatory also made major contributions to studies of distant galaxies. For nearly 40 years, ever since the first X-ray detectors were flown above Earth's X-ray–absorbing atmosphere, astronomers had been puzzled by a uniform glow of X-rays coming from all directions. The radiation, with energies ranging from 1,000 to 100,000 times that of optical light, did not appear to arise from identifiable objects, and it was initially thought to be radiated by energetic particles filling space. Chandra's high-angular-resolution capability, however, allowed the radiation to be resolved into its sources. The team making the observations, headed by Richard Mushotzky of NASA Goddard Space Flight Center, Greenbelt, Md., reported that about 80% of this so-called X-ray background radiation was produced by roughly 70 million discrete sources uniformly spread over the sky. About one-third of the detected sources appeared to be galaxies lying at great distances from Earth and so were being observed as they existed in the very early universe. At the centre of each galaxy was thought to be a massive black hole accreting gas from its surroundings. As the gas fell in, it heated up and radiated X-rays. Many of these X-ray–emitting galaxies had not yet been detected at optical wavelengths, possibly because they were formed early enough in the history of the universe that their relative optical and X-ray emissions were quite different from those typically found in nearby (and, hence, older-appearing) galaxies.

The universe is thought to have originated with a hot, explosive event—the big bang. As the universe expanded and cooled, a faint background radiation was left over, which can be detected today as microwave radiation filling the sky. Unlike the X-ray background discussed above, the microwave background radiation comes from the gas that occupied the universe before galaxies were formed. Nevertheless, at some later time that very gas coalesced to form the galaxies seen today. Therefore, the lumps or fluctuations in the density of the universe that gave rise to galaxies also should have caused fluctuations in the brightness of the cosmic microwave background. Two balloonborne experiments recently were flown high above most of Earth's obscuring atmosphere to look for these "ripples" from space. One, called Boomerang (Balloon Observations of Millimetric Extragalactic Radiation and Geophysics), was launched from the South Pole; the other, called Maxima (Millimeter Anistropy Experiment Imaging Array), was launched from Texas. Both detected intensity fluctuations in the microwave background radiation that can be attributed to primordial sound waves, or density fluctuations throughout space. These variations appeared to fit well with a model of the universe that is topologically "flat" and will expand forever, although at year's end the correct cosmological model still remained very much an open question.

(KENNETH BRECHER)

Earth Perihelion and Aphelion, 2001	
Jan. 4	Perihelion, 147,097,600 km (91,402,000 mi) from the Sun
July 4	Aphelion, 152,087,500 km (94,502,600 mi) from the Sun
Equinoxes and Solstices, 2001	
March 20	Vernal equinox, 13:31[1]
June 21	Summer solstice, 07:38[1]
Sept. 22	Autumnal equinox, 23:04[1]
Dec. 21	Winter solstice, 19:21[1]
Eclipses, 2001	
Jan. 9	Moon, total (begins 17:43[1]), the beginning visible in northern regions (including northern Canada, Alaska, Greenland, northern Europe), most of Africa, Australia; the end visible in northeastern North America, northeastern South America, the Indian Ocean, the western Philippine Sea.
June 21	Sun, total (begins 09:33[1]), the beginning visible near the coast of Uruguay in south Atlantic; the end visible southeast of Madagascar.
July 5	Moon, partial (begins 12:11[1]), the beginning visible in Antarctica, Australia, New Zealand, southeastern Asia, the Pacific and Indian oceans; the end visible in Antarctica, Australia, most of Asia, eastern Africa, the Indian Ocean.
Dec. 14	Sun, annular (begins 18:03[1]), the beginning visible in the northern Pacific Ocean (northwest of Hawaiian Islands); the end visible in the southern Caribbean Sea between Colombia and Cuba.
Dec. 30	Moon, penumbral (begins 08:25[1]), the beginning visible in North, Central, and South America (except eastern coast), northwestern Europe, northeast Asia, the Pacific Ocean; the end visible in North America, northern Central America, Indonesia, Australia, New Zealand, most of the Pacific Ocean.

[1]Universal time.
Source: *The Astronomical Almanac for the Year 2001* (2000).

SPACE EXPLORATION

Manned Spaceflight. The ongoing assembly in orbit of the International Space Station (ISS) and the beginning of its permanent human occupancy constituted the dominant story of 2000 in space exploration. In July the Russian Space Agency, using a Proton rocket, finally launched the ISS's long-awaited Zvezda service module, which had been held up for two years by political and financial problems in Russia. Its docking with the first linked pair of modules already in orbit—Zarya and Unity—allowed the U.S. to start a series of space shuttle launches to add American-built elements, which would be followed by laboratory modules from Europe and Japan. Zvezda, based on the core module for Russia's *Mir* space station, would act as the control centre and living quarters for initial space station crews.

NASA conducted four space shuttle missions in support of ISS operations during the year. Most carried cargoes and crews to outfit the station. Following the addition of Zvezda, the next crucial element for the ISS was NASA's Z1 truss, which was delivered by shuttle in mid-October. Mounted on Unity, Z1 was an exterior framework designed to allow the first set of giant solar arrays and batteries to be attached to the ISS for early power. At the end of October, the first three-man crew, an American and two Russians, was launched from Russia aboard a Soyuz-TM spacecraft. They

NASA Public Affairs Image Collection

Astronauts mounted giant solar arrays to the International Space Station during a series of spacewalks in early December.

would stay for four months and be relieved by a three-person crew carried up by shuttle. From that time forward, the ISS was to be continuously occupied throughout its service life. In early December, in a series of spacewalks, shuttle astronauts successfully mounted the solar arrays to the Z1 truss and connected them electrically to the growing station. They also performed a minor repair to one blanket of solar cells that had not properly deployed. Also during the year, NASA continued its flight tests of the X-38, a demonstrator for the Crew Return Vehicle, which would be the ISS lifeboat.

One space shuttle flight was unrelated to the ISS. Launched in February, STS-99 carried out the Shuttle Radar Topography Mission cosponsored by NASA and the National Imagery and Mapping Agency. The payload comprised a large radar antenna in the payload bay and a smaller element deployed on a 60-m (197-ft) boom; together the two devices operated in the synthetic-aperture mode to produce the effect of a much larger antenna. The mission mapped the elevation of about 80% of the world's landmass—120 million sq km (46 million sq mi)—at resolutions of 10–20 m (33–66 ft).

Reversing its actions of the previous year to shut down the aging *Mir* space station, Russia entered into a leasing agreement with the Dutch-based MirCorp to reopen the station for commercial operations, plans for which included a *Mir* version of the *Survivor* TV show. Between February and October, a Soyuz-TM crew and three Progress tanker loads of supplies were sent to refurbish the station and stabilize its orbit. By year's end, however, financial support for the private venture appeared to be drying up, and *Mir* was scheduled for reentry in early 2001 after its 15th anniversary (the first module had been launched in February 1986).

China continued with plans to become the third country capable of launching humans into space. At year's end it made final preparations for a second unmanned flight test of Shenzhou, a spacecraft that appeared to be based on Russia's Soyuz, although the launcher used was China's Long March 2F rocket. The first test flight had been carried out in 1999. China also announced that it was considering human missions to the Moon.

Space Probes. The loss in late 1999 of the Mars Polar Lander and its two onboard miniprobes badly stung NASA and forced the agency to reassess its Mars exploration strategy. The Mars Polar Lander was to land December 3 near the Martian south pole, but contact was lost during atmospheric entry and never reestablished. In March 2000 investigators reported that, because of a software fault, the onboard computer probably interpreted the jolt from the extension of the landing legs as the landing signal itself and shut off the engines prematurely, when the craft was still more than 40 m (132 ft) above the surface. Following this debacle, NASA restructured its unmanned Mars exploration program and decided to fly simpler missions based on the air-bag lander and rover technology from the highly successful Mars Pathfinder and Sojourner mission of 1997.

Other probes in deep space fared better. The Near Earth Asteroid Rendezvous (NEAR) spacecraft settled into orbit around asteroid 433 Eros on February 14, following an opportunity missed the year before because of a software problem. This time all went well—NEAR returned a series of stunning close-up images, and ground controllers started tightening its orbit for an eventual impact with the tumbling, potato-shaped asteroid. (See *Astronomy*, above.)

The Galileo spacecraft, in orbit around Jupiter since late 1995, completed its official extended mission to study Jupiter's large ice-covered moon Europa, but it continued operating. Galileo data hinted at the possibility that liquid water lies under the ice plates that cover Europa, making it a potential harbour for life. NASA planned to direct Galileo to burn up in Jupiter's atmosphere rather than risk the chance of its crashing on and contaminating Europa when the spacecraft's fuel ran out. Jupiter was visited on December 30 by the Cassini mission to Saturn when the spacecraft, which had been launched in October 1997, flew by for a gravity assist.

During the year the Stardust spacecraft, launched in early 1999, completed the first part of its mission, exposing its ultrapure dust-collection panels to capture grains of interstellar dust. Another set of panels was to collect dust grains from Comet Wild-2 in 2004. The spacecraft was scheduled to return to Earth in 2006, when it would drop its samples for a soft landing. The Ulysses international solar polar mission probe, launched in 1990, began its second passage of the Sun's south polar region late in the year, at a time in the Sun's 11-year sunspot cycle when activity was at its highest. Between 1994 and 1996 Ulysses had observed the Sun during the relatively quiescent part of its cycle. NASA's Pluto-Kuiper Express, planned as the first flyby of the only planet in the solar system not yet explored by a spacecraft, was canceled owing to rising costs and emphasis on a new mission to explore Europa.

Unmanned Satellites. Scientists studying the plasmas (ionized gases) that fill space inside Earth's magnetic field received two significant new tools with the launches of four of the European Space Agency's Cluster spacecraft and of NASA's Imager for Magnetopause-to-Aurora Global Exploration (IMAGE) spacecraft. The original set of Cluster spacecraft was lost in the disastrous June 1996 first launch of the Ariane 5 rocket, which veered off course and had to be destroyed. European scientists developed a new set, partly from spare components, which was launched from Kazakhstan in pairs atop Soyuz launchers on July 16 and August 9. Each of the four satellites carried an identical set of instruments to measure changes in plasma across small distances as the spacecraft flew in formation. A different view of the magnetosphere was provided by IMAGE, launched March 25, which used radio probes and special ultraviolet imager instruments to map the otherwise invisible magnetosphere as it changed during solar activity.

The astrophysics community lost one of its Great Observatories for Space Astrophysics on June 4 when the Compton Gamma Ray Observatory was deliberately guided by NASA into a controlled reentry. Although the science payload was working perfectly, the spacecraft's attitude control system was starting to fail. Rather than risk an uncontrolled reentry and despite protests that an alternative control method was available, NASA ordered the spacecraft destroyed. The year also saw the launch of an increased number of miniature satellites. Microsats, nanosats, and picosats—ranging in mass down to less than a kilogram (about two pounds)—employed advanced technologies in electronics and other disciplines. Quite often, they were built by university students to get them involved in space activities at a relatively low cost. Space engineers expected that large numbers of small, inexpensive satellites would play a larger role in space exploration and utilization.

Launch Vehicles. The future of the commercial single-stage-to-orbit VentureStar Reusable Launch Vehicle (RLV) grew uncertain as its X-33 subscale demonstrator craft was almost canceled during the year. Although most of the X-33's systems—including its revolutionary aerospike engine, which achieved a record 290-second firing—had done well in development and tests, the program as a whole continued to fall behind schedule. A serious failure in late 1999 was the rupture of a lightweight composite-structure liquid-hydrogen tank. After deciding that the technology was beyond its grasp, NASA's X-33 team elected to proceed with an aluminum tank. The first of 13 test flights of the X-33 was set for 2003, about three years late. NASA's other RLV test rocket, the smaller, aircraft-launched X-34, was rolled out in 1999 and prepared for its first flight tests. It would demonstrate a number of new technologies, including a Fastrac rocket engine partly based on commercial components.

In August Boeing Co. finally achieved success with its Delta III launcher, which had failed to orbit commercial payloads in August 1998 and May 1999. The Delta III was based on the reliable Delta II but had a wider first stage and new solid boosters. Boeing conducted the third launch, which carried a dummy satellite, to restore user confidence. The company also prepared for the first launch, scheduled for 2001, of its Delta IV, which employed a low-cost engine derived from the space shuttle's main engine. In May Lockheed Martin Corp. launched its first Atlas III, which used Russian-built rocket engines. Both the Delta IV and Atlas III were developed under the U.S. Air Force's Evolved Expendable Launch Vehicle program, which aimed to reduce space launch costs by at least 25% over current systems. (DAVE DOOLING)

Launches in support of human space flight, 2000

Country	Flight	Crew[1]	Dates	Mission/payload
Russia	Progress	—	February 1	*Mir* supplies
U.S.	STS-99, *Endeavour*	Kevin R. Kregel Dominic L. Pudwill Gorie Janet L. Kavandi Janice E. Voss Mamoru Mohri Gerhard P.J. Thiele	February 11–22	Shuttle Radar Topography Mission
Russia	Soyuz-TM 30	Sergey V. Zalyotin Aleksandr Yu. Kaleri	April 4–June 16	*Mir* repairs/refurbishment
Russia	Progress	—	April 25	*Mir* supplies
U.S.	STS-101, *Atlantis*	James D. Halsell, Jr. Scott J. Horowitz Mary Ellen Weber Jeffrey N. Williams James S. Voss Susan J. Helms Yury V. Usachyov	May 19–29	ISS outfitting and repair
Russia	Zvezda	—	July 12	Zvezda service module for ISS
Russia	Progress	—	August 6	ISS supplies
U.S.	STS-106, *Atlantis*	Terrence W. Wilcutt Scott D. Altman Daniel C. Burbank Edward T. Lu Richard A. Mastracchio Yury I. Malenchenko Boris V. Morukov	September 8–20	ISS outfitting
Russia	Progress	—	September 30	ISS supplies
U.S.	STS-92, *Discovery*	Brian Duffy Pamela A. Melroy Koichi Wakata Leroy Chiao Peter J.K. Wisoff Michael E. Lopez-Alegria William S. McArthur	October 11–24	ISS outfitting, including Z1 truss and mating adapter
Russia/U.S.	Soyuz-TM 31	Yury P. Gidzenko Sergey K. Krikalyov Bill Shepherd[2]	October 31	first ISS habitation crew
Russia	Progress	—	October 20	*Mir* supplies
U.S.	STS-97, *Endeavour*	Brent W. Jett Michael J. Bloomfield Joseph R. Tanner Carlos I. Noriega Marc Garneau	November 30–December 11	ISS outfitting, including photovoltaic module (solar panels and batteries)
Russia	Progress	—	December 12	ISS supplies

[1] Commander and pilot (or flight engineer for Soyuz) are listed first.
[2] Shepherd is ISS commander.

Media and Publishing

While *Survivor*, a "reality" television series, **RIVETED** viewers, readers began scanning **ELECTRONIC BOOKS** and gravitating toward the **INTERNET**, which they found a **TREASURY** of information. Newspapers lost some of their best talent to **ON-LINE START-UPS** and worried about **FREEDOM OF THE PRESS** issues. Magazines, on the other hand, **REJOICED** over **SOARING ADVERTISING REVENUES.**

TELEVISION

Rather than battle it out with the Internet, the television industry in 2000 opted for high-profile mergers. Meanwhile, however, the technology needed to deliver the benefits of interactive TV to consumers had not yet been fully developed.

Organization. Two large-scale mergers kept European and U.S. regulatory agencies busy. The European Commission allowed Time Warner Inc. to proceed with its $165 billion merger with America Online, Inc. (AOL). The U.S. Federal Trade Commission (FTC) was, however, slower to approve the merger, which would result in a company that would be one of the largest cable TV networks in the U.S. as well as the biggest provider of on-line services. AOL pledged to sever ties with Bertelsmann AG, the German media conglomerate that owned 50% of AOL Europe. In December the FTC approved the deal after first receiving assurances that the new alliance would not be used to limit competition.

Earlier, the $34 billion acquisition of Canada's Seagram Co. Ltd. by French conglomerate Vivendi was approved following concessions by both companies to dilute their combined business in entertainment and telecommunications. Vivendi controlled Canal+ pay-TV, a telephone company, and the Havas publishing business. Seagram owned Universal music and film studios. As a result of the merger, Vivendi Universal owned an archive of 9,000 movies and 27,000 TV shows.

Rupert Murdoch's News Corp. acquired the 21% share of Gemstar–TV Guide International, Inc., that was held by cable company Liberty Media Corp. News Corp. already owned 22% of Gemstar, publisher of TV guides and inventor of VCR Plus+, which allowed users to record programs by using a simple code. Murdoch also was strengthening his position to buy DIRECTV Inc., the largest satellite-TV group in the U.S.

German media magnate Leo Kirch expanded his pay-TV's capital base by selling 3.2% to Saudi Prince al-Waleed ibn Talal ibn Abdul-Aziz and 2.76% to Capital Research & Management Co., a Los Angeles-based fund manager. The prince and Capital already were investors in KirchMedia, KirchGruppe's free TV. KirchPayTV operated in Germany and Austria and owned 40% of Swiss pay-TV station Teleclub AG.

Philippine cable TV operator Sky Vision Corp. entered into a $100 million joint venture with Yes Television of the U.K., providing video-on-demand service and nationwide interactive TV. Commercial service included access to hundreds of movies, music videos, children's programs, travel services, sports features, and television comedies and dramas.

With most of the American networks already part of giant corporations, the year's only network ownership change came when the Viacom Inc. entertainment conglomerate increased its stake in UPN, the fifth most popular network, from half to full ownership. In addition to control of two of the seven broadcast television networks, the move gave Viacom ownership of dozens of television stations throughout the U.S.

Viacom also completed its purchase of the CBS television network during 2000. In November it added the cable channel Black Entertainment Television to its roster, buying the parent BET Holdings II, Inc., for $3 billion. The purchase in effect gave Viacom, already in charge of MTV and VH1, control of popular music on American cable television. While some observers decried the loss of one more independent voice in television, others were optimistic that BET's program offerings under Viacom would improve.

Further signs of the trend toward consolidation came when NBC announced that it would rebroadcast its *Nightly News with Tom Brokaw* on stations of the upstart PAX TV network, in which NBC owned a 32% stake. The move, designed to draw maximum audience to the newscast, angered NBC's affiliates, which did not want their own network sending viewers elsewhere. Although the protest caused the network to cancel the plan, the episode signaled further erosion in the relationship between networks and their local affiliates.

Networks became increasingly concerned about rising programming costs and the threat represented by cable. The rate of cable penetration leveled off between May 1999 and May 2000 at about 68% of American homes, but cable continued to increase its audience share, while that of network TV continued to decline. Such moves as NBC had planned with PAX would allow the network to get more bang for its programming buck. Similarly, ABC angered its affiliates by announcing plans to start a cable channel using the network's soap operas.

In its battle for people's attention with home computers and the Internet, television overall got a boost when a November report from Nielsen Media Research showed that TV usage had remained stable over a one-year period in homes that also had computers and World Wide Web access. Earlier in the year Nielsen had reported that, despite the increased competition, television viewing levels were at an all-time high. Nielsen said in January that the average U.S. household kept its TV set on for eight hours 11 minutes per day.

Programming. The broadcasting of the 2000 Summer Olympic Games in Sydney, Australia, was tape-delayed for as long as 24 hours by NBC (which paid $705 million for exclusive broadcast rights) owing to the great time difference between the U.S. and Australia. The International Olympic Committee banned radio play-by-play, live video, and dot-com journalists, even those from ESPN.com and SportsLine.com. Web broadcasts had to be done by TV affiliates.

The Fédération Internationale de Volley Ball agreed to a $400 million, 10-year TV and sponsorship deal with five companies. The next world competitions were scheduled for 2002. Fox Sports struck a $2.5 billion, six-year deal with U.S. Major League Baseball, extending its contract to air play-off and World Series games beginning in 2001. On its first night broadcast over Viacom's newly acquired TNN cable TV network, World Wrestling Federation (WWF) Entertainment, Inc. weighed in as TNN's highest-rated premiere and the highest-rated entertainment in the network's 17-year history. More important, the WWF succeeded in attracting viewers of interest to advertisers, according to Nielsen Media Research.

To protect young viewers, Brazil required stations to rate all programs and indicate on-screen throughout each show whether it contained sex or violence. Programs dealing openly with sex could be aired only between midnight and 5 AM.

During the historic summit between North and South Korea in the North Korean capital of Pyongyang, television coverage of the city was tightly controlled. South Korean media could file only pool reports and were barred from interviewing ordinary people. Street scenes were filmed from moving vehicles.

Lázaro González and his family sued Fox Family Channel for its broadcast of *The Elian Gonzales Story.* Lawyers said that the TV movie did not accurately reflect what happened while Elián lived with Lázaro and his family in Miami, Fla.'s Little Havana.

Serbian state TV was overrun by opposition forces on October 5 following massive objections to the claims to the election by Yugoslav Pres. Slobodan Milosevic. The following day three government-owned TV stations, three state-owned radio networks, and Politika, a powerful media house run by an ally of Milosevic's wife, declared their loyalty to opposition presidential candidate Vojislav Kostunica. (*See* BIOGRAPHIES.)

In Russia Vladimir Gusinsky, owner of Media-Most, Russia's only independent national media empire, and a frequent critic of the Russian government, was imprisoned for fraud, a charge later dropped. At the sinking of the Russian nuclear submarine *Kursk* and the loss of all of its crew, Arkady Momontov from state-owned RTR television essentially followed the military line (including suggestions, never substantiated, that a foreign vessel may have been involved), while Gusinsky's NTV broadcast stories that contradicted official pronouncements. Boris Berezovsky (*see* BIOGRAPHIES), one of Russia's best-known and most controversial businessmen, disclosed that he had been pressured to give up his 49% stake in Russian Public Television (ORT), a state-controlled TV station, after its "unsatisfactory" coverage of the *Kursk* incident. The government owned 51% of ORT, Russia's most-watched channel. Berezovsky said that he planned to transfer his shares to members of the intelligentsia to prevent the station from becoming a government propaganda organ.

Liberia detained four members of Britain's Channel Four for espionage. They were accused of filming in areas where they were not permitted to work. An apology from the chairman of Channel Four secured their release.

On July 22, as thousands watched on TV, three men and a woman, all construction workers, were swept away by currents of Pachang Creek in southern Taiwan. The tragedy sparked a media frenzy questioning government responsiveness to public needs. Cable TV in New Delhi ceased transmission of 70 channels to upwards of 800,000 homes to protest a new law banning tobacco and liquor commercials and pornographic films.

CNN International launched *ebizasia,* a weekly program on how the new economy was affecting Asia.

At CNBC in October, Karuna Shinso replaced Dalton Tanonaka as anchor of CNN's two prime-time daily news programs produced in Hong Kong. They were *Asian Edition,* transmitted to a worldwide audience of 151 million households, and *Asia Tonight,* aired to CNN viewers in Asia-Pacific.

According to Nielsen Media Research based on third-quarter results, CNBC, for the first time in its 11-year history, became the highest-rated news and information network on American cable TV, ending CNN's long reign and crowning the efforts of three-year president Bill Bolster. Under Bolster, advertising rates had risen more than threefold and profits had more than doubled.

The biggest story in American television during 2000 happened, uncharacteristically, during the summer. The runaway success of the reality series–game show hybrid *Survivor* (CBS) took televi-

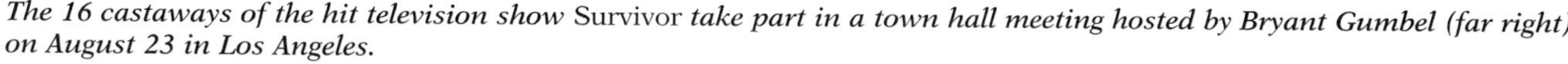

The 16 castaways of the hit television show Survivor *take part in a town hall meeting hosted by Bryant Gumbel (far right) on August 23 in Los Angeles.*

AP/Wide World Photos

sion experts by surprise. Tens of millions of viewers stayed home on summer Wednesday nights to see the taped account of a band of American voluntary castaways on a South Pacific island voting one peer per week off the island until the survivor claimed a $1 million prize. The 13-week program's finale in August drew more than 51 million viewers, a record for a summer program and a viewership number second during the year only to the January broadcast of the National Football League's Super Bowl. The winner was Rhode Island corporate trainer Richard Hatch, who made no secret of his cunning during the show's taping. Most of the castaways became minor celebrities, appearing on talk shows and guest-starring in network series.

The success of *Survivor* prompted the other networks to hurry to acquire rights to their own "reality" shows, a genre pioneered by the cable network MTV's long-running *Real World* series and characterized by nonactors in unscripted situations. At the year's end, however, no other such program had gained popularity. The *Survivor* sequel, set in the Australian Outback, was slated for broadcast beginning in January 2001.

Based on a Swedish television concept, *Survivor* was American network television's second successive successful summertime launch of an idea imported from European TV. The previous summer had seen ABC introduce the U.S. version of the British game show *Who Wants to Be a Millionaire?* Eventually telecast four nights per week by ABC, that series, hosted by American talk-show veteran Regis Philbin (*see* BIOGRAPHIES), went on to become the sensation of the 1999–2000 television season, claiming at season's end in May the three top slots among the year's most popular series. (The *Survivor* broadcasts took place outside the traditional television season.)

The popularity of *Millionaire* led ABC past previous winner CBS to a victory in the 1999–2000 season. Up some 15% from the previous season, ABC won in both the overall households category, averaging about 9.4 million, and in the advertiser-coveted 18–49-year-old demographic group. NBC, which had won the ratings battle through much of the 1990s, finished in a second-place tie with CBS, although it was comfortably ahead of CBS among the 18–49 group.

After its Olympic telecasts from Sydney, featuring no events presented live, were seen by small audiences compared with those of past Olympics, NBC opened the new season in trouble, canceling two of its new series before the end of one month. NBC's juggernaut Thursday night prime-time lineup continued to be popular, accounting for the network's continued lead in the key demographic group, but at a heavy price. After paying a record $13 million per episode for the hospital drama *ER*, it agreed in May to pay each of the six stars of the hit situation comedy *Friends* $750,000 per episode.

As the 2000–01 season began, it was CBS, however, that seemed to be gaining ground. Many of its new series, including a situation comedy starring the movie actress and cabaret performer Bette Midler (*Bette*), drew relatively large audiences quickly. As of early November, the network was second in overall viewers and had pulled into a tie with the Fox network for third place among the 18–49 group.

At ABC the network news department's ambitious globe-spanning turn-of-the-millennium broadcast as 1999 turned into 2000 had been a success. As the new season began, however, *Millionaire*'s hold on the audience was beginning to slip, and the network scrambled to develop more traditional programming. Like NBC, ABC had cut back on its heavy reliance on prime-time news magazines, and with no new reality series taking hold, ABC needed new situation comedies and dramas.

Rupert Murdoch's Fox Network, the fourth of the so-called "Big Four," continued its pattern of executive tumult. Amid declining ratings, early in the year it let go of head programmer Doug Herzog, who had been brought in from cable's Comedy Central the previous year. Herzog left on the schedule one of the brightest new programs of the 2000 calendar year, the razor-sharp family comedy *Malcolm in the Middle.*

At the more recent upstart networks, UPN, powered by a Thursday-night professional wrestling program and a target audience of young men, surpassed the ratings garnered by the WB network, with its target of young women. UPN's average of roughly 2.7 million households during the 1999–2000 season represented a 35% gain over the previous year. The WB, meanwhile, lost 19%, in large measure because its programming stopped running on national cable via Chicago-based "superstation" WGN.

The Emmy Awards, television's highest honours, were won, in a change from tradition, by relatively young shows. A change in voting procedures allowed a wider range of members of the National Academy of Television Arts and Sciences to participate. The beneficiaries were, as best drama, NBC's *The West Wing,* a series about an idealized Democratic White House from playwright and screenwriter Aaron Sorkin, and, as best comedy, NBC's *Will & Grace,* a snappy pop culture-savvy half-hour show about a friendship between a gay man and straight woman.

Responding to protests in 1999 over a lack of ethnic diversity in their new prime-time programs, several of the networks as 2000 began formally agreed to increase variety in their programming. They especially sought to attract a better ethnic mix in their executive ranks in the belief that this would lead to more diversity in their programming.

Technology. Japan's Sakura and Sanwa banks began providing TV banking services on digital broadcasting satellite screens in December. Four of Japan's largest electronic companies—Matsushita, Toshiba, Sony, and Hitachi—joined forces to create an industry standard for set-top boxes and programming for digital TV. Sony unveiled Airboard, which could be a conventional TV, video monitor, and Internet terminal, with the liquid-crystal display doubling as a touch screen.

French telecommunications equipment maker Alcatel and U.S. internet software company Oracle Corp. began building a joint technology platform that was called Thirdspace. The new technology would allow telecommunications companies to offer interactive TV.

Trading in stocks of the Italian Internet TV company Freedomland, which operated in Italy, Britain, and Spain, was suspended for false accounting and rigging of its stock price just as Virgilio Degiovanni, its chairman and founder, was scheduled to announce expansion plans. Degiovanni resigned as CEO in October.

Microsoft Corp. introduced the Solo2 chip to operate its WebTV interactive television service. To be manufactured by Toshiba, the Solo2 chip debuted in UltimateTV, Microsoft's answer to AOLTV. Failure to deliver the chip on time, however, forced Microsoft's customer, the Netherlands-based United Pan-Europe Communications N.V.—Europe's largest cable operator, with 8.4 million subscribers—to buy from Liberate Technologies just as Britain's second largest cable operator, Telewest Communications PLC, had done earlier.

Dot-com advertising, which swept through the U.S. during the year, altered buying patterns of traditional advertisers. Radio and TV advertising was expected to be soft during the last quarter of 2000 and the first quarter of 2001.

RADIO

On September 12 Washington, D.C.-based WorldSpace Corp. introduced satellite technology in Asia to provide an array of radio channels. CEO Noah Samara hoped that WorldSpace would do for radio what satellite and cable had done for TV. Late in 1999 WorldSpace had launched satellite-radio broadcasting services in Africa. From Egypt to South Africa, WorldSpace eventually provided more than 40 channels of music, entertainment, news, and educational programming. International content providers included the BBC, Bloomberg LP, CNN International, and MTV Asia's music programs in English, French, and local languages. Asian content providers included India's Menon Impex Ltd., Broadcasting Network Thailand, and Manila Broadcasting Corp.

The U.S. Federal Communications Commission (FCC) licensed two companies to broadcast digitally—Sirius Satellite Radio, Inc., and XM Satellite Radio, Inc. Each company raced to launch its own satellite, set up digital radio studios, and establish ties with automobile manufacturers. In 2001 Sirius expected to be available in all Daimler-Chrysler and Ford models and XM in General Motors and Honda models. Digital satellite car radios promised to deliver 100 channels with a clear signal from coast to coast.

Motorola unveiled its hands-free prototype called iRadio, which enabled drivers to download on-line music, real-time traffic reports, audio books, voice mail, and news and weather reports. This was achieved by means of satellite, digital, cellular, and FM sideband technologies.

Launching of the wireless radio technology called Bluetooth was delayed. Technical challenges had been underestimated, and subsequent compatibility problems between Bluetooth products made by different manufacturers were not beginning to be fixed until late in the year.

In U.S. radio the aftereffects of the past several years' massive consolidations continued to be felt. That path had been paved with federal deregulation in 1996, which lifted rules that had kept one company from owning more than 40 stations. Massive buying and selling frenzies resulted, and in 2000 one of those companies experienced the dark side of the rush to acquire. The nation's third largest station owner, Cumulus Media Inc. of Milwaukee, Wis., struggled to regain control of its more than 300-station empire after admitting to errors in earnings reports and suffering a more than 80% drop in its stock price. In three years the company had grown from nothing, taking on massive debt in the process. Meanwhile, the U.S. Federal Communications Commission approved the merger of the nation's two largest station owners, Clear Channel Communications, Inc., and AMFM Inc., conditional on the divestiture of 122 of the new entity's almost 1,300 American stations. As an example of what this concentration meant in one city, the 14 stations owned in Chicago by Clear Channel and Viacom's Infinity Broadcasting Corp., the nation's third largest station owner, collected nearly two-thirds of the region's radio advertising dollars.

Reuters NewMedia Inc./Corbis

Controversial radio talk-show host Dr. Laura Schlessinger is shown during a taping of her new television talk program.

Partly in response to the cry for more diversity in radio broadcasting, the FCC began moving in 2000 on a controversial plan to license about 1,000 noncommercial, "low-power" radio stations nationwide. The National Association of Broadcasters filed suit to block the plan, claiming the signals of between 10 and 100 w each would interfere with the signals of existing stations. The FCC disputed that claim.

In radio programming the popular syndicated commentator Paul Harvey signed a 10-year contract to continue his relationship with ABC Radio Networks. Harvey, heard six days a week on more than 1,200 stations in the U.S., was 82. Popular but controversial syndicated radio talk-show host Laura Schlessinger launched a television talk program, *Dr. Laura,* in September, but it was struggling to draw viewers. In November the CBS-owned stations announced that they were moving her show to late nights or dropping it altogether. Advertisers on Schlessinger's radio and TV programs had been targeted by activists in response to remarks she made condemning homosexuality.

(RAMONA MONETTE SARGAN FLORES; STEVE JOHNSON)

NEWSPAPERS

Freedom of the press was a major issue throughout the world in 2000. Panama's newspapers began the year by celebrating the end of two laws that limited press freedom. The nation's new president, Mireya Moscoso, signed an order ending a requirement that journalists be licensed and ending the imposition of a $2,500 fine for reporting that discredited the government. Iranian newspapers were not so fortunate. During a two-month period, Iranian courts ordered the closing of 19 newspapers for publishing stories that violated Islamic principles. Three journalists were imprisoned on such charges as insulting Islam. A newly elected parliament, dominated by reformers, failed to end a campaign against the press when Iran's leader Ayatollah Sayyed Ali Khamenei killed a bill that would have allowed limited press freedom. By August the last major reform newspaper, *Bahar,* had been forced to close.

In China 27 newspapers were punished for having published stories that officials said contained political errors and fabrications. No details were released about the punishments or how many of the newspapers were shut down. In Malaysia the government cut the publishing schedule of the opposition newspaper, run by the fundamentalist Pan-Malaysian Islamic Party, from twice a week to twice a month.

The *Swazi Observer,* one of the leading newspapers in Swaziland, was closed by the government after the newspaper reported about conflicts between King Mswati III's cabinet ministers. In Angola Pres. José Eduardo dos Santos's government proposed that journalists who published news that attacked his government be jailed for two to eight years. This followed a government campaign against the media, including the arrest and intimidation of foreign journalists. In Zambia the government charged 11 journalists with espionage after the independent daily *The Post* reported that Zambia was not prepared to deal with an attack from Angola.

The changing nature of the newspaper business led to closings, sales, mergers, and investment in the Internet. *L'Unità,* once a major left-wing newspaper in Italy, closed. The newspaper was $33 million in debt and had a declining circulation of about 50,000.

As content-rich newspapers moved to develop on-line communities of readers, publishers invested in the Internet, regarding it as a publishing tool with low overhead and no printing costs. In the U.K., for example, industry leader Trinity Mirror PLC invested £150 million (£1=about $1.45) in Internet operations. Newsquest PLC, controlled by the Gannett Co. of the U.S., launched Fish4, a World Wide Web site that featured listings for home and automobile sales along with job openings. Clients included such newspaper groups as Trinity Mirror and Regional Independent Media. London's *Financial Times* expanded its Web product, FT.com, and posted 1999 revenues of £6 million. The television and publishing group United News & Media announced a £370 million investment in the Internet.

In the U.K., newspaper groups fought to control the regional newspaper business as they sought to lower costs and create larger advertising bases. Trinity Mirror paid £285 million for Southnews, a London-based publisher that owned the *Croydon Advertiser* and the *Harrow Leader.* For £444 million Gannett bought Newscom, which published the Southampton *Southern Daily Echo,* among other titles. Trinity Mirror sold the *Belfast Telegraph* for £300 million to Independent News & Media, a Dublin-based chain that controlled most of the daily newspapers in Ireland.

Major changes took place in Canada, where convergence—the combination of print, Internet, and television journalism—ruled. CanWest Global Communications purchased the Canadian newspapers owned by Hollinger, the international media group controlled by Conrad Black, owner of the *Daily Telegraph* and the *Chicago Sun-Times,* for Can$3.2 billion (about U.S. $2.3 billion) in cash and shares.

With an eye toward building an Internet empire, the Thomson Corp. of Canada announced in February that it would sell 54 of its 55 daily newspapers and all of its more than 75 nondaily newspapers in the U.S. and Canada. By midsummer Thomson had sold all but one of its American daily newspapers: Gannett bought 21 of them with a combined circulation of 466,000 for $1,125,000,000; Community Newspaper Holdings, Inc., of Alabama paid $455,000,000 for 17 dailies with a combined circulation of 260,000, which gave it a total of 112 newspapers with a combined circulation of 1,100,000; and Media General bought five dailies and six weekly newspapers for $237,000,000. Gannett also acquired Central Newspapers, Inc., for $2,600,000,000. The deal included the *Arizona Republic* and the *Indianapolis* (Ind.) *Star,* the flagship newspapers of the Pulliam family, owners of Central.

Another dynasty to fall was the Chandler family, which had controlled the *Los Angeles Times* since 1882. In March the Tribune Co., publisher of the *Chicago Tribune,* announced a record-setting $6,460,000,000 deal for the purchase of the Times Mirror Co., which included the Los Angeles newspaper. Total assets of the new company exceeded $11.7 billion. Executives of the Tribune Co. said that the merger would allow them to converge the content of the newspapers with television, cable, and Internet operations. The new company had a nationwide newspaper circulation of 3.6 million (third highest in the nation); its television stations broadcast to more than 38.4 million homes; and its Internet news outlet received more than 3.4 million visitors each month.

Mark Schoofs of the **Village Voice** *talks on the phone from the weekly newspaper's offices in New York City on April 10 after learning that he had been awarded the Pulitzer Prize for international reporting for his series on the AIDS crisis in Africa.*

AP/Wide World Photos

Gannett, the largest chain by readership, owned 99 newspapers, including the nation's largest, *USA Today,* with a combined circulation of about 7.8 million. The 31 newspapers of the second largest chain, Knight Ridder, had a combined daily circulation of four million.

In San Francisco a federal judge ruled in July that the Hearst Corp.'s $660 million purchase of the *San Francisco Chronicle* did not violate antitrust laws. He also allowed the sale of Hearst's *San Francisco Examiner* to the Fang family, publishers of a dozen free newspapers in the San Francisco Bay Area. The *Chronicle*'s circulation of 464,943 was more than four times that of the *Examiner.* To rid itself of the *Examiner,* Hearst agreed to pay as much as $66 million of Fang's expenses for three years.

In May the *Denver Post,* owned by MediaNews Group, and the *Denver Rocky Mountain News,* both in Colorado and owned by E.W. Scripps Co., entered a joint operating agreement that merged advertising sales, production, and distribution, while the editorial departments remained independent. The *News* had lost $123 million since 1990 in its circulation war with the *Post.* If approved, each paper would publish a separate edition Monday through Friday, the *Post* would publish a Sunday joint edition, and the *News* would publish a Saturday newspaper. The Denver arrangement would be the first American joint operating agreement in 11 years. The two newspapers together employed more than 3,600 people.

Each of the Denver newspapers won a Pulitzer Prize for coverage of the tragedy at Columbine High School in Littleton, Colo., in 1999 that left 12 students, one teacher, and two student gunmen dead. The *Post* was honoured in the breaking news category, and the *News* won for breaking news photography. Other Pulitzer Prize winners included Mark Schoofs of the *Village Voice,* an alternative weekly published in New York City. He spent six months in Africa researching the AIDS epidemic by visiting remote villages and documenting the devastation there.

The Internet continued to have a great effect on newspapers. In a study by Middleberg & Associates, a public relations and marketing agency, about two-thirds of American print reporters revealed that they were on-line continuously, looking for information. About two-thirds said they used the Internet to read publications on-line, and almost 90% said that they used the Internet to research stories.

Two major newspapers complained about a talent drain to on-line publications. The *Philadelphia Inquirer* said that it lost six reporters to Web sites such as CNN's, while the *San Jose* (Calif.) *Mercury News* complained that it had lost 11 people to Internet companies. For many newspapers the Internet was a revenue loser, with Knight Ridder, Tribune, the *New York Times,* and McClatchy Newspapers reporting losses ranging from $8 million to $20 million a year on their Internet products.

On July 4 the *Hartford* (Conn.) *Courant* apologized in a front-page story for having made a profit during the 1700s and 1800s on advertisements for the sale and recapture of runaway slaves. The newspaper, the longest continuously published daily newspaper in the U.S., was founded in 1764. Such ads were common in newspapers of the time, when slavery was legal in many states.

In February cartoonist Charles M. Schulz, creator of *Peanuts,* a syndicated strip that ran in 75 countries, died of colon cancer a few hours before his last Sunday cartoon ran. It carried a signed farewell: "Charlie Brown, Snoopy, Linus, Lucy . . . how can I ever forget them. . . ." Jeff MacNelly, a syndicated editorial cartoonist who won three Pulitzer Prizes, also died during the year. The *New York Times* said he "was regarded as one of the nation's foremost political cartoonists, a profession that calls for the combined talents of artist, social critic, political analyst and humorist." (*See* OBITUARIES.)

In a survey of press freedom in the U.S., the First Amendment Center reported that 51% of respondents believed the press had too much freedom and 20% said that the government should be allowed to approve what newspapers publish. When asked to name one of the five freedoms guaranteed by the First Amendment of the U.S. Constitution—freedoms of press, speech, religion, and to assemble and to petition the government—37% could not do so.

(GLEN BLESKE)

MAGAZINES

American magazine advertising revenues surpassed $10 billion during the first nine months of 2000, up 16.4% over 1999. Nina Link, the president of the Magazine Publishers of America, commented that the extraordinary results also extended to dot-com advertising, which "has shown phenomenal growth this year so far with a 320 percent increase year to date." Modest circulation gains in 1999 were fueled largely by growth among smaller, niche magazines; some of the magazines with the highest circulation experienced declines. Spending on magazine advertising reportedly increased 6% worldwide in 1999 to $40 billion.

Magazines reportedly took in 12.9% of the worldwide expenditure for advertising in 1999, compared with 13.9% in 1988. Media ad spending on magazines ranged from a high of 52% in India to less than 2% in Uruguay and Venezuela. American magazines averaged 12% of total media ad spending.

The American magazine with the fastest-growing readership in 1999 was *Maxim,* a "beer-and-babe" title targeted to men; it doubled its 1999 circulation to 2.1 million over 1998 and had increased its readership fourfold (from an initial base of 450,000) since its 1997 launch. Growth in the competitive men's category, however, was mixed. Though *GQ, Men's Journal,* and *Men's Fitness* averaged more than 10% circulation gains in 1999, *Playboy, Penthouse,* and *Men's Health* all lost ground.

New magazine launches in 1999 totaled 864, down from 1,065 in 1998; it was only the second time since 1986 that a decrease had been recorded. The largest category among the new launches was media personalities, with 108 titles, followed by sports with 95.

Time Inc. ended publication of its 64-year-old *Life* magazine in May 2000, explaining that the monthly's advertising base was no longer strong enough to maintain it. The company planned to keep the brand alive, however, by expanding its presence on the World Wide Web and publishing commemorative issues of *Life* to mark important milestones. Among many other magazines that ceased publication were *Mirabella,* a fashion magazine, and two sports-related ones: *Sport* and *Women's Sports & Fitness.*

Two magazines celebrated milestone anniversaries. *Harper's* mounted yearlong festivities in honour of its 150th anniversary, and *The New Yorker* marked its 75th anniversary in print.

Making their debut were two American magazines geared toward women: *O: The Oprah Magazine,* which offered self-help articles as well as recipes and musings of television star Oprah Winfrey, and *Real Simple,* a heavily illustrated magazine dedicated to "streamlining, refining and distilling" women's lives.

Courtesy of Harpo Inc.

O: The Oprah Magazine *debuted in 2000.*

Publishers Clearing House paid more than $18 million to various U.S. states to settle claims that it had used misleading sweepstakes promotions. The settlement placed several restrictions on company promotions, including preventing it from putting "you-are-a-winner" statements on its mailings unless equal prominence was given to qualifying conditions.

Americans reportedly spent more time reading in 2000 compared with 1999. The time that consumers spent watching television, listening to radio, and using the Internet all decreased, but their time spent reading increased by an average of 29% across all print media, and magazines led the way with a 39% increase.

Inside.com, which covered the media and entertainment industries, joined several other on-line magazines in launching a print publication. "One of the things we've discovered about the Web is that it's an incredibly fast way to build up an audience," said Michael Hirschorn, Inside.com editor and former editor of *Spin*. Another World Wide Web-to-print launch in 2000 was *Space.com Illustrated,* from Space.com, run by former CNN anchor Lou Dobbs. *World Magazine Trends* reported that in the U.S., "Internet publishing and the new media are not viewed as threats to print but rather as complements, which offer great potential for magazine brand extensions and transactions."

The Chinese government's decision to ban English-language names and logos on magazines created worries among foreign publishers. Fairchild Publications terminated its licensing agreement to publish its fashion magazine *W* in China owing to the restrictions. Most American publishers disguised their covers with logo-free wraparounds. China also tightened its law on Internet firms and issued new regulations in October.

A 2000 survey of 4,585 Japanese households revealed that 24.4% of those in the market for a personal computer used magazines as their chief information source when they went to purchase a PC. The percentage relying on television was 7.6%, followed by newspapers with 5.9%.

In an effort to control the press, the Russian Press Ministry declared that all magazines and newspapers in the country had to be licensed. Per R. Mortensen, president of the London-based International Federation of the Periodical Press, joined 10 other delegates of the Russian Press Freedom Support group, which represented six leading international free-press organizations, to express the international media community's deep concern over what it considered a serious deterioration of press freedom in Russia.

(DAVID E. SUMNER)

BOOK PUBLISHING

In 2000 the worldwide buzz in book publishing was "e-publishing"—the publication of books in various electronic formats, usually together with paper-and-ink books but sometimes exclusively in "cyberpublished" versions. American suspense novelist Stephen King, for example, serialized his short novel *The Plant*—ironically about a vine that threatens to take over a publishing house—on his World Wide Web site. King asked each fan to send in one dollar after downloading the newest chapter; if enough readers did not do so, King said, he would discontinue the postings. King maintained that the novel had attracted a half million readers and grossed about $600,000 before he suspended postings late in the year. Several top American publishers—including Time Warner, Random House, Simon & Schuster, Modern Library, and McGraw-Hill—announced their intention to embark upon e-publishing. The International eBook Awards, with a top prize of $100,000 and five $10,000 awards, were given out for the first time in Frankfurt (Ger.) during the annual book fair held there in October.

Hardware and software manufacturers contended to develop universal standards for reading devices onto which e-books could be downloaded from a Web site or read from a portable storage medium. The Microsoft Reader software was popular for hand-held devices, while Acrobat from Adobe Systems Inc. was the choice for reading on desktop or laptop computers. Thomson Multimedia introduced a new line of dedicated hand-held readers in September starting at $300.

Publishers in the U.K. were busy digitizing the content of their backlists for the new e-book readers as well. The question of whether established publishers would be obliged by agents to negotiate separately for e-rights on new books was under negotiation—publishers feared that their titles in print would face direct competition from the same titles in e-format. The European Commission proposed that a value-added tax be levied on e-books, whereas printed books currently carried either zero or reduced VAT rates in European Union member states.

Web sites were being developed to market publishing rights on-line. Houghton Mifflin Co., which brought out the fourth edition of its *American Heritage Dictionary of the English Language,* was equally interested in licensing the new dictionary to Web sites and other electronic users. Creating an efficient on-line distribution network was increasingly a requisite for survival; Wolters Kluwer saw its stock tumble by more than 25% in March because of its lack of a viable Internet strategy. Reed Elsevier's purchase in June of eLogic, an applications service provider, signaled that new approaches were needed. Bertelsmann AG agreed to pay $250 million to AOL to be its "preferred provider of media content and e-commerce" for a four-year period. AOL, in turn, took out an option to buy Bertelsmann's 50% stake in AOL Europe and AOL Australia after 2002. Bertelsmann also rolled up Internet interests such as BOL.com and its 40% stake in BarnesandNoble.com into a new e-commerce group.

Publishers' eyes were riveted on the legal attack to shut down Napster, the company that provided the opportunity to download recorded music from the Internet without observing copyrights. (*See* COMPUTERS AND INFORMATION SYSTEMS.) In *Tasini* v. *The New York Times,* a group representing the interests of freelance writers brought suit against the New York Times Co. and other large publishers, alleging copyright violation because of the publications' resale to electronic databases of materials that had been provided by the authors for onetime print use.

The restructuring and merger activity at Bertelsmann, including the splitting up of Bertelsmann Buch, led to major changes in the list of top 10 publishers by domestic sales in Germany. New entrants included BertelsmannSpringer (first), Verlagsgruppe Bertelsmann (third), Süddeutscher Verlag Hüthig (fifth), and Weltbild (eighth). The legitimacy of retail price-fixing in Germany was reconfirmed in February. A separate fixed-price law modeled on the French *loi Lang* came into effect in Austria for an initial five-year period. Because 80% of Austrian books were imported from Germany and German publishers feared the potential for cheap reimports, the latter were also covered by the new law if the reimport was intended solely to undercut fixed prices in Germany. LION.cc, an on-line site belonging to Libro, initially challenged the latter aspect of the new law by offering 20% discounts but four weeks later withdrew the offer after German publishers cut off supplies. The European Commission then began investigating two issues: whether German publishers had colluded in boycotting Libro and whether Libro's restoration of fixed prices was an illegal restriction of competition.

At the end of April, the Danish Competition Council ruled that book prices would be liberalized, with fixed prices permitted for first editions but not for new editions or reprints. It also ruled that beginning on Jan. 1, 2001, the monopoly of booksellers over the sale of books would be abolished for titles priced over 155 kroner ($18).

In February British Butterworths Tolley agreed to buy Eclipse Group Ltd. Nelvana Ltd., an animation house based in Toronto, announced plans in April to buy Klutz Inc., a California children's book publisher, for $74 million. In March Pearson bought troubled Dorling Kindersley (DK), which had heavily overstocked *Star Wars*-related publications, for roughly $460 million. Pearson then axed DK's CD-ROM publishing division and set up its own digital-media division. Scholastic Inc. acquired Grolier, Inc., a major publisher and direct-mail marketer of children's reference books and encyclopaedias, for about $400 million in June. That same month British publisher David & Charles accepted an offer from American F&W Publications, and Bloomsbury paid $25 million for A&C Black. HarperCollins bought Fourth Estate in July, while in August there were rumours of links between Bertelsmann and Reader's Digest. In March it was announced that the two largest American book clubs, the Literary Guild (controlled by Bertelsmann) and the Book-of-the-Month Club (of Time Inc.), would be combining efforts. Also during the year, Pearson agreed to pay $129 million for the U.S.-based FamilyEducation Network.

J.K. Rowling's fourth best-seller in the Harry Potter series of books about a youthful magician swept markets around the world. *Harry Potter and the Goblet of Fire* sold half of its one million initial printing on its first day in German bookstores. In March American novelist Nancy K. Stouffer filed suit against Rowling and American publisher Scholastic Inc., as well as movie and toy companies that stood to profit from the phenomenon, charging that plots, characters, and language in the Potter books had been taken from her 1984 work *The Legend of Rah and Muggles*. Judging that the books presented witchcraft in too positive a light, a school district in Zeeland, Mich., sought to ban them in elementary and middle schools.

AP/Wide World Photos

A handheld e-book reader using Microsoft Reader software displays a list of popular titles.

The 2000 Pulitzer Prize for Fiction was awarded to *Interpreter of Maladies* by Jhumpa Lahiri, while the general nonfiction prize went to John W. Dower's *Embracing Defeat: Japan in the Wake of World War II*, the 1999 National Book Award winner. The NBA fiction prize went to *In America* by Susan Sontag, and the nonfiction award went to Nathaniel Philbrick's *In the Heart of the Sea: The Tragedy of the Whaleship Essex*. The National Book Foundation Medal for Distinguished Contribution to American Letters was awarded to science-fiction writer Ray Bradbury. In children's literature, the Newbery Medal went to *Bud, Not Buddy* by Christopher Paul Curtis (*see* BIOGRAPHIES), and the Caldecott Medal for illustration went to *Joseph Had a Little Overcoat* by Simms Taback. *Waiting* by Ha Jin (*see* BIOGRAPHIES), the 1999 NBA fiction winner, was awarded the PEN/Faulkner Award. According to *Publishers Weekly*, the top hardcover fiction best-sellers in 1999 were *The Testament* by John Grisham (2,475,000 copies sold) and *Hannibal* by Thomas Harris (1,550,000); the nonfiction leaders were *Tuesdays with Morrie* (1997) by Mitch Albom (2,500,000) and *The Greatest Generation* (1998) by Tom Brokaw (1,968,597).

(PETER CURWEN; EDITOR)

Military Affairs

In 2000 the fall from power of Pres. Slobodan Milosevic in **YUGOSLAVIA** and the unprecedented high-level contacts between senior officials of **NORTH** and **SOUTH KOREA** eased tensions in these two often volatile regions. **ISRAELI-PALESTINIAN** relations sharply deteriorated, however, which raised the prospect of another Arab-Israeli war.

Wars between nations and within nations convulsed a large swath of Africa stretching across the continent from Ethiopia to Sierra Leone. Efforts continued to be made to keep children from serving as combatants throughout the world. In May the UN adopted an optional protocol to the Convention on the Rights of the Child that set 18 as the minimum age for combat service. By the end of the year, 75 states had signed the protocol, and 3 had ratified it; 10 ratifications were needed for the protocol to enter into force. Pres. Bill Clinton signed the protocol in July even though the U.S. had never ratified the convention itself. More than 37,000 military personnel and civilian police from 88 countries were involved in the 15 UN peacekeeping operations in place around the world. In addition, the UN was involved in another 14 political and peace-building missions, 8 of which were in Africa.

Arms Control and Disarmament. After years of procrastination the Russian government in April ratified both the 1993 Strategic Arms Reduction Talks II (START-II) treaty and the Comprehensive Test Ban Treaty. The former action opened the way for the U.S. and Russia to begin negotiations on a START-III treaty aimed at making further cuts in the two countries' strategic nuclear arsenals. Little progress was made in these talks, however, as the Russians remained concerned that American efforts to develop a national missile defense system would undermine the Anti-Ballistic Missile (ABM) Treaty, a document that the Russians insisted was the

Under the protocol established by the UN Convention on the Rights of the Child, which set the minimum age of combatants as 18, this 14-year-old soldier in the Sierra Leone army would be prohibited from taking part in warfare.

AP/Wide World Photos

foundation for all nuclear arms control. When the signatories of the Nuclear Non-proliferation Treaty (NPT) met in April and May for their mandated five-year Review Conference, the avowed nuclear weapons states—the U.S., the U.K., France, Russia, and China—renewed an "unequivocal undertaking" to reduce and eventually eliminate their nuclear weapons without setting a timetable for these endeavours. The conference called upon India, Pakistan, and Israel—all possessing nuclear weapons—to join the NPT as nonnuclear weapons states. At the conference, UN Secretary-General Kofi Annan warned that the multilateral disarmament machinery had "started to rust" because of an "apparent lack of political will to use it."

The group monitoring the implementation of the 1997 convention that banned antipersonnel land mines reported in October that while the international trade in these weapons had been halted, their use continued. New land-mine victims had been reported in 71 countries. The UN estimated that 27 people were killed and 41 seriously injured by land mines each day.

The Ukrainian Rada (parliament) in March ratified the 1992 Open Skies Treaty and thus left Russia, Belarus, and Kyrgyzstan as the only signatories yet to approve it. Russia and Belarus had to ratify the treaty before it could enter into effect. The Russian parliament continued to charge that the treaty was not in Russia's national interest.

United States. The end of the Cold War notwithstanding, American military forces continued to be called upon to meet an unprecedented number of overseas commitments. Military leaders warned that the maintenance, training, and modernization of the armed forces had suffered in order to pay for these heavy commitments. In September the members of the U.S. Joint Chiefs of Staff told Congress that the armed forces needed a significant increase in spending in the years ahead in order to maintain American military supremacy. The chiefs of the navy and air force called for their services to receive $20 billion–$30 billion more each year, while the other service heads pressed for similar if smaller increases.

With the regular armed forces stretched thin, reserve and national guard units played an increased role in operations around the world. The army announced plans to align the eight National Guard divisions with active-duty army corps to more fully integrate them with the active-duty force. While all four services met their active-duty enlistment goals for the first time in several years, the army, navy, and air force reserves fell short in their recruitment efforts. The increased demands on the guard and reserves were cited as one of the main reasons for this shortfall. Army leaders were also disturbed by the high number of middle-grade officers leaving the service.

In August Pres. Bill Clinton signed the $287.5 billion defense appropriations bill for fiscal year 2001. An increase of $17.5 billion over the previous year, the appropriations bill was also $3.2 billion higher than requested by the administration. While providing full funding for such modernization programs as the F-22 fighter, the CVN-77 nuclear-powered aircraft carrier, and continued work on a national missile defense system, the bill provided less money than requested for the Joint Strike Fighter and the proposed LPD-17 amphibious ship program. The rival Joint Strike Fighter concept demonstrators, one built by the Boeing Co. and the other by the Lockheed Martin Corp., made their maiden flights later in the year. Clinton also complained that Congress had made significant cuts in the Cooperative Threat Reduction Program and several other foreign military cooperation initiatives. He singled out as troubling the failure to fund the chemical weapons destruction facility at Shchuchye, Russia, which he said was vital to American security and international nonproliferation efforts. In October Clinton signed the $309.9 billion fiscal year 2001 defense authorization bill despite his misgivings about several of its provisions.

Following several unsuccessful tests of components of the proposed national missile defense system, President Clinton in September announced that he would leave to his successor the decision on whether to deploy the system. Critics charged that the technology in the proposed system was fundamentally flawed. On a brighter note, the army demonstrated that a directed-energy weapon could shoot down a short-range ballistic rocket. On June 6 the U.S. Army's Tactical High Energy Laser destroyed a Katyusha rocket in flight. The system detonated the rocket's high-explosive warhead with its deuterium fluoride chemical laser weapon.

More than 4,600 military personnel were assigned to help fight forest fires in the Western states during the summer. In July, because of a vaccine shortage, the Pentagon was forced to cut back its controversial program to vaccinate all military personnel against anthrax. Social issues in the military once again made the headlines. Charges of sexual misconduct reached the highest ranks of the army when that service's highest-ranking female officer, Lieut. Gen. Claudia Kennedy, revealed that a fellow general had made inappropriate sexual contact with her in 1996. The Pentagon's "don't ask, don't tell" policy regarding homosexuals in uniform continued to be much criticized. Following a report in March that found that antigay behaviour was commonplace in the military, the Department of Defense in July launched an education program seeking to eliminate it. An American soldier was sentenced to life imprisonment for the killing of an 11-year-old ethnic Albanian girl in Kosovo, and a subsequent army study revealed that some U.S. peacekeepers in Kosovo were not properly trained for their noncombat roles.

NATO. Nine European states—Albania, Bulgaria, Estonia, Latvia, Lithuania, Macedonia, Romania, Slovakia, and Slovenia—actively sought NATO membership, but NATO Secretary-General Lord Robertson announced in May that there would be no new members before 2002. That month Croatia became the 46th member of the NATO-sponsored Partnership for Peace, and U.S. Air Force Gen. Joseph Ralston took command of the Supreme Headquarters Allied Powers Europe. The historical animosities between NATO members Greece and Turkey erupted once again during a NATO military exercise in the Aegean Sea in October, which prompted Greece to withdraw its forces from the maneuvers. Spain held its last draft lottery, and the Spanish military was to be an all-volunteer force by the end of 2001. Several other European states reduced the terms conscripts had to serve in the armed forces.

United Kingdom. Bowing to a ruling by the European Court of Human Rights, the British government in January ended its ban on service in the armed forces by openly gay men and women. The Ministry of Defence (MoD) issued a new code of social conduct for military personnel reflecting this change. As an interim measure to bolster its aging airlift fleet, the MoD announced in September that it would lease four American C-17 airlifters. Earlier in the year Secretary of State for Defence Geoffrey Hoon had announced that the U.K. would ultimately purchase 25 A400M military transports being developed by the Airbus Military Co. Commitments from six other European nations for an additional 200 aircraft indicated that the international program would go ahead. All 12 of the Royal Navy's attack submarines were withdrawn from service to inspect for and correct faults in their reactor cooling systems.

France. In July the contract was awarded for the construction of a fourth Le Triomphant-class nuclear-powered ballistic missile submarine, to be named *Le Terrible.* It would be armed with the M51 ballistic missile due to enter service in 2008. Sea trials for the nuclear-powered aircraft carrier *Charles de Gaulle* were postponed after it broke a propeller in November. The *Charles de Gaulle* replaced the *Foch,* which was sold to Brazil. In October the government announced that women would be able to serve in virtually any post in the army, except in the Foreign Legion.

Germany. In May Defense Minister Rudolf Scharping announced a major overhaul of the Bundeswehr, noting that it was still structured for Cold War scenarios and was not particularly suited for its contemporary crisis-management commitments. His plan called for 2003 troop levels to be reduced 70,000 to 255,000 and the defense budget to be cut by 2.6%. Only 77,000 conscripts would be in the military, while all the armed forces would be open to female volunteers.

The Balkans. The Kosovo Force (KFOR), the NATO-led international force sent into Yugoslavia to enforce the fragile peace in Kosovo, a Serbian province in Yugoslavia, marked its first anniversary in June, and most observers believed this international military presence would be required for years to come. During the year KFOR reached its full strength of 50,000 men and women. Nearly 42,500 troops from more than 30 countries were deployed in the province, and another 7,500 provided rear support through contingents based in Macedonia, Albania, and Greece. From April until October, KFOR was commanded by Headquarters Eurocorps. A significant part of the Eurocorps staff moved from Strasbourg, France, to the KFOR Headquarters in Pristina, Kosovo; this marked the first time that NATO had entrusted command of an external operation to a unit that was not a part of its own integrated military structure. Thirty-three nations, of which 15 were not members of NATO, continued to provide troops to the Stabilization Force (SFOR) in neighbouring Bosnia and Herzegovina. A restructuring plan aimed to reduce SFOR from some 32,000 troops to approximately 20,000.

Turkey. In February the Kurdistan Workers' Party announced that it was ending its war for self-rule within Turkey and instead would pursue its aims by peaceful means. Fighting subsided in the country's southeastern provinces. In April, however, more than 5,000 Turkish troops, backed by jet fighters and combat helicopters, made another incursion into northern Iraq to combat Kurdish rebels there. In September a Turkish court acquitted journalist Nadire Mater of charges that she had insulted the military in a book about the war against Kurdish separatists. Dissatisfied with the high bids from contractors, Turkey postponed several major procurement programs. The largest was an estimated $7 billion contest to provide 1,000 new main battle tanks, the country's most expensive defense purchase, which was put on hold in April.

Russia and the Commonwealth of Independent States. As the year began, the Russian military was engaged in another full-scale war to regain control over the breakaway republic of Chechnya. This time it was more successful than in 1995–96. The offensive that had begun the previous September reduced the Chechen capital, Grozny, to rubble, and by mid-March the Russians had claimed victory. Bitter fighting continued, however, in the mountainous south of the republic, and the Russian military admitted that it was unable to pacify the entire region. Ambushes and hit-and-run raids by the Chechen guerrillas inflicted casualties on Russian forces throughout the rest of the year. Military officials acknowledged that nearly 2,500 Russian servicemen had been killed and more than 7,000 wounded in this second war in Chechnya.

In early August the nuclear-powered missile submarine *Kursk,* one of the newest in the navy, sank in the Barents Sea with the loss of all 118 crewmen. The vessel had been participating in an exercise of the Northern Fleet. While the Russians maintained that the *Kursk* had sunk after colliding with a foreign submarine, Western intelligence services postulated that the ship had gone down following an onboard accident with one of its weapons. Although the submarine lay in relatively shallow water not far from its home port, the Russian navy was unable to mount an effective rescue operation. More than one week after the sinking, Norwegian and British divers were able to enter the submarine and confirm that all aboard had perished. The contradictory and often inaccurate information on the incident released by the navy and the government provoked an unprecedented public outcry.

Russia's relations with NATO remained strained owing to the latter's criticism of Russian actions in Chechnya and Russia's continued unhappiness with NATO policies in the Balkans. The Ministry of Defense announced that it would not participate in any military exercises during the year that took place within the framework of NATO's Partnership for Peace. In April acting president Vladimir Putin approved a new security doctrine, one that turned away from increased openness and cooperation with the West.

Russia's two most senior military leaders engaged in a public row over the best way to reform the Russian military. Gen. Anatoly Kvashnin, the chief of the General Staff, emphasized the conventional forces in his reform plan, one that would slash the number of strategic nuclear weapons and end the independent status of the Strategic Missile Troops (SMT). Defense Minister Igor Sergeyev, a former head of the SMT, argued that the SMT was in better shape than any of the other services and to downgrade it would highlight Russia's loss of superpower status. Neither man was a clear winner when the Russian Security Council in August decided to make major cuts in all the armed forces. The military was to be cut by 350,000 personnel by 2003, which would leave a total of 850,000 men and women in uniform. The Ground Forces were scheduled for the largest reduction, some 180,000 troops, but the SMT would also be reduced and eventually merged with the air force. Other sources indicated that the "power agencies"—the 12 departments that fielded armed forces of one kind or another—would lose 600,000 troops over the next five years.

The government pledged to increase defense spending in the 2001 budget to 218,940,000,000 rubles (about $7,500,-000,000). The SMT conducted the first test of the mobile version of the Topol-M intercontinental ballistic missiles, but experts said that serial production might be delayed for as long as 10 years. With few domestic contracts, Russian defense plants continued to rely on foreign sales to survive. In October the Russians signed a series of multimillion-dollar arms contracts with India involving jet fighters, main battle tanks, and the former Soviet aircraft carrier *Admiral Gorshkov.*

Militant Islamic fighters operating in the mountainous region where Kyrgyzstan, Tajikistan, and Uzbekistan shared common borders continued to worry the governments in the region. In August hundreds of the militants, many believed to have come originally from Afghanistan, crossed into Uzbekistan and Kyrgyzstan from Tajikistan. Such incursions led Uzbekistan to mine parts of its border with Tajikistan. On October 11 the presidents of the six member states of the 1992 Commonwealth of Independent States (CIS) Collective Security Treaty (Russia, Armenia, Belarus, Kazakhstan, Kyrgyzstan, and Tajikistan) signed an agreement pledging to create a joint rapid-reaction force to go to the aid of any member threatened by external aggression or terrorism. As the Taliban forces in Afghanistan approached the border with Tajikistan, which was defended by Russian army and border troops, fears rose that the civil war in Afghanistan could expand into an international conflict. The Russians pledged to defend Tajikistan in accordance with the CIS treaty.

Middle East and North Africa. Peace talks between Israel and Syria were broken off in January when the two sides could not agree on the future of the Golan Heights. Israel ended its 18-year occupation of southern Lebanon in May. In July President Clinton invited Israeli Prime Minister Ehud Barak and Palestinian leader Yasir Arafat to Camp David, Maryland, for peace talks. Although the participants were said to have been close to a historic agreement, the talks finally broke off after 15 days over the status of Jerusalem. In late September the whole peace process began to unravel. Israelis and Palestinians clashed first in Jerusalem at an ancient site both regarded as holy, and the violence quickly spread to the West Bank and Gaza Strip, which prompted UN Secretary-General Kofi Annan to warn that the region was close to "an all-out war." On October 7 the conflict widened to the Lebanese-Israeli border, where Hezbollah militants abducted three Israeli soldiers. After two Israeli soldiers were lynched in the West Bank town of Ram Allah on October 12, Israeli combat helicopters attacked Palestinian headquarters in Ram Allah and Gaza City. The Middle East violence spread to U.S. forces that same day when terrorists conducted a suicide attack against the guided-missile destroyer USS *Cole* as it prepared to refuel in Aden, Yemen. Seventeen sailors were killed in the blast, and another 39 were injured.

The UN assembled another weapons-inspection team to verify that Iraq was free of chemical, biological, and nuclear arms, but Iraq refused to allow the team entry. In December 1999 the UN had said it would suspend its economic sanctions against Iraq if Iraq would cooperate with the new team. The U.S. and the U.K. continued to enforce the no-fly zones in the north and south of Iraq. During 2000 Iran conducted several successful tests of the Shahab-3 intermediate-range ballistic missile. The 1,300-km (800-mi)-range missile was believed to be based on North Korea's No Dong ballistic missile.

South and Central Asia. Pakistan's chief executive, Gen. Pervaiz Musharraf (*see* BIOGRAPHIES), in September offered to sign a no-war pact with India and join in a mutual reduction of forces, but the Indians did not accept his proposals.

The opposition forces of Ahmad Shah Masoud continued to frustrate the Taliban Islamic militia's effort to seize control of all of Afghanistan, but their resistance seemed to be waning. In September the Taliban seized one of Masoud's last strongholds, the northern provincial capital Taloqan. Further Taliban gains took them to within a few kilometres of the border with Tajikistan.

Sri Lanka's 17-year-long civil war showed little signs of abating. The separatist Liberation Tigers of Tamil Eelam mounted a major offensive in April in which they seized Elephant Pass, the gateway to the Jaffna Peninsula. While unable to capture Jaffna City, they inflicted heavy casualties on the Sri Lankan government troops. In October they shot down a government Mi-24 helicopter gunship and damaged another in an offensive to seize the government military base of Nagarkovil on the eastern coast of the Jaffna Peninsula.

East and Southeast Asia, Oceania. In what was seen as an effort to influence the March presidential elections in Taiwan, China threatened to use force to retake Taiwan should the Taiwanese continue to postpone unification talks. The threat prompted warnings from the U.S. and the deployment of an American aircraft carrier to the region. A Chinese government policy paper on national defense issues released in October blamed the Taiwanese government and the U.S. for the military tension in the region and repeated the threat of force to reunite Taiwan with the People's Republic.

Long branded a rogue regime and a major threat to peace and security in the region, North Korea made a number of peaceful gestures toward both South Korea and the U.S. These included a meeting of the leaders of both Koreas and a visit to Washington by Vice-Marshal Jo Myong Rok, first vice-chairman of North Korea's National Defense Commission (NDC), who met with President Clinton. This was followed by a visit to North Korea by U.S. Secretary of State Madeleine Albright. During this visit Kim Jong Il, the chairman of the NDC, pledged that North Korea would conduct no further launches of its Taepodong long-range ballistic missile if it received aid in launching satellites. The U.S. and North Korea failed to reach an agreement, however, following later bilateral talks on this subject.

To provide security and maintain law and order, the UN deployed a force of about 8,000 military personnel and over 1,400 civilian police to East Timor as that country made its transition to independence following years of Indonesian rule. One of the force's main tasks was to prevent pro-Indonesian East Timorese militiamen from infiltrating back into East Timor from the Indonesian province of West Timor. As a result, that 170-km (105-mi) border became one of the most heavily defended in Southeast Asia. Philippine armed forces battled Muslim separatist guerrillas claiming that they were fighting for an independent Islamic state in the impoverished southern Philippines. Early in the year, government troops and members of the Moro Islamic Liberation Front repeatedly clashsed on the island of Mindanao. In September the government conducted a major assault, backed by fighters and helicopter gunships, to free a number of hostages held for ransom by rebels on the island of Jolo.

Caribbean and Latin America. In a bloodless coup the military in Ecuador in January overthrew the president and installed the country's vice president in his stead. In Colombia the drug war and the civil war became even more closely linked. Forces of the rebel Revolutionary Armed Forces of Colombia (FARC) became bolder and more successful, routing government troops in May and again in October. The U.S. pledged to provide $1.3 billion in military equipment and training to enable Colombian soldiers to seize the drug-producing plantations that were often protected by FARC and other insurgents. In late September the U.S. suspended support and training for two Colombian army brigades because of allegations of human rights abuses. The next month the government dismissed 89 officers and 299 soldiers it accused of misconduct.

Africa South of the Sahara. Repercussions from the 1994 genocide in Rwanda continued to convulse Central Africa,

AP/Wide World Photos

A Portuguese member of the UN peacekeeping force in East Timor patrols a street outside the National Council of Timorese Resistance headquarters in Dili on August 21.

nowhere worse than in the Democratic Republic of the Congo. There the 1999 Lusaka cease-fire agreement had little effect, and troops from six countries as well as numerous indigenous and foreign rebel groups continued to tear the country apart. While the UN authorized a military peacekeeping mission of more than 5,000 troops, Pres. Laurent Kabila balked at allowing them to deploy. In late August he approved their deployment, but at the end of the year only a few hundred were in place. In June troops from Rwanda and Uganda, once allies in the struggle to oust Kabila, fought for control of the strategic northeastern city of Kisangani. Several UN-brokered cease-fires failed, and troops from both countries finally evacuated the city. Flouting the cease-fire, Kabila in July began an offensive in Équateur province against the rebel Movement for the Liberation of Congo. After some initial successes, his forces were driven out of the town of Dongo in September. A peace agreement was also of little value in neighbouring Burundi. An agreement signed in September aimed at ending the seven years of war between Tutsi and Hutu did not stop the killing as Hutu rebels continued to clash with government soldiers.

The civil war in Sierra Leone entered its ninth year—and one in which UN peacekeepers suffered several embarrassing setbacks. In January the rebel Revolutionary United Front (RUF) stepped up its attacks on civilians and also captured and disarmed several UN peacekeepers. When the RUF marched on the capital, Freetown, in May, Great Britain, the former colonial power, sent a naval-marine task force to evacuate foreign nationals from the country. On May 19 the UN Security Council raised the authorized strength of the mission in Sierra Leone to 13,000, which made it the largest current UN peacekeeping operation. That month the RUF detained some 500 UN soldiers. Some were soon released, but 233 UN peacekeepers and military observers were held until they could be rescued in July following heavy fighting. In late August, 12 members of a British military training unit assisting the Sierra Leone army were captured by a rebel group calling themselves the West Side Boys. Five were released, but after mock executions of the others were held, British special forces mounted a dramatic operation in mid-September to rescue the remaining hostages. The government and the RUF signed a cease-fire in November, opening the way for further direct talks. Rebel groups were active in the border areas of Liberia and Guinea. Guinea charged the RUF from neighbouring Sierra Leone of having been involved in rebel attacks on the border town of Macenta in September, while Liberian officials accused Guinea of having been behind the rebel attack on the northern town of Zorzor in October.

Following a lull of more than a year in its border war with Eritrea, Ethiopia began an offensive in May after negotiations to revive the Organization of African Unity (OAU) peace plan had collapsed. Under pressure, Eritrea withdrew from Ethiopian territory near Zela Ambesa that it had held for nearly two years. The UN Security Council imposed an arms embargo on the two countries in an effort to restart the peace negotiations. Ethiopian forces advanced into Eritrea, and Ethiopian jets bombed targets near Asmara and Massawa. Having recovered all its territory, Ethiopia on May 31 declared the border war over but renewed its offensive early in June. On June 18 the foreign ministers of both countries signed a preliminary cease-fire agreement after accepting the OAU peace plan. That included a UN peacekeeping mission to monitor the cease-fire and the Ethiopian withdrawal from Eritrean territory. The leaders of the two countries signed a peace agreement on December 12.

(DOUGLAS L. CLARKE)

Performing Arts

The year **2000** was a **RICH ONE** for the performing arts, with offerings such as the extravagant staging of ***AÏDA* IN SHANGHAI,** critically acclaimed **BALLETS** in the newly rebuilt **ROYAL OPERA HOUSE** in London, and innovative **MUSICAL-THEATRE** performances in the U.S. Popular entertainers **BRITNEY SPEARS,** the **DIXIE CHICKS,** and **EMINEM** also attracted attention—and stirred controversy.

MUSIC

Classical Music. A tidal wave of anniversary observances characterized classical music in 2000. The centennials of the births of composers Aaron Copland and Kurt Weill were celebrated with festivals, and the anniversaries of the deaths of two giants were commemorated: composer Johann Sebastian Bach's 250th anniversary and conductor Leonard Bernstein's 10th. The 50th observation of the birth of another composer, Gioacchino Rossini, born on Feb. 29, 1792, was made during the leap year. Though the centennial of the death of Giuseppe Verdi was not until 2001, many opera companies designed their 2000–01 season as a Verdi year.

Two of the world's leading orchestras, the Vienna Symphony and the Philadelphia Orchestra, celebrated their centennials at home and on tour. Boston's Symphony Hall marked its 100th anniversary with a festival. In Vermont the Marlboro Music Festival celebrated its 50th anniversary, and Sony Classical records issued a set of two compact discs (CDs) of archival recordings featuring pianist and festival founder Rudolf Serkin.

Two of the most important events in the history of Western music were recognized with anniversaries—the 300th anniversary of the invention of the piano and the 400th anniversary of the invention of opera. Though both of these were developed over a period of years, the year 2000 was chosen to mark these milestones.

A flamethrower hurls a ball of fire during the spectacular staging of Giuseppe Verdi's Aïda *in Shanghai.*

Liu Jin/AFP Worldwide

The most spectacular CD celebration of the piano anniversary was the 200-disc collection *Great Pianists of the 20th Century.* A particularly notable festival was held at the Smithsonian Institution in Washington, D.C., in conjunction with an exhibit titled "Piano 300: Celebrating Three Centuries of People and Pianos." Highlighting the festivities were classical and jazz performances by recent winners of top piano competitions in the U.S., including Christopher Basso, winner of the Van Cliburn International Piano Competition for Outstanding Amateurs; Ning An, triumphant in both the Sixth American National Chopin Piano Competition and the 1999 Queen Elizabeth Music Competition; and Eric Lewis, winner of the 1999 Thelonious Monk International Jazz Piano Competition. In addition, a daylong piano film seminar featured films and discussions on Glenn Gould, Sviatoslav Richter, Serkin, and Arthur Rubinstein.

Two notable productions were staged of *Aïda,* the grandest of Verdi's grand operas. In Detroit, as a prelude to a yearlong Verdi festival, the Michigan Opera Theatre offered a minimalist production that omitted the usual expensive pageantry, including scenery and costumes. *Aïda in Concert* starred Luciano Pavarotti in the leading role of Radames. In Shanghai, however, *Aïda* received what was described as the most extravagant production ever given to it or any other opera. A cast of 2,116 in the triumphal scene featured not only 1,650 Egyptian legionnaires portrayed by People's Liberation Army soldiers but also elephants, camels, lions, tigers, a panther, and a boa constrictor. The famous Grand March was repeated three times to accompany the long marching line, and the libretto was modified to give the opera a happy ending. Large video screens were provided for the audience of some 50,000 in a sports stadium, and the performance was produced for television.

In the summer of 2000, an opera staged essentially for TV reached American screens. *La Traviata from Paris* was filmed in such locations as the Hotel Boisgelin, the Petit-Palais, and Le Hameau de la Reine, a rustic retreat at Versailles, France, once used by Marie-Antoinette.

Opera entered its fifth century with remarkable vigour. At least 27 world premieres were scheduled for the 2000–01 season. In Finland 16 new operas by Finnish composers had premieres in 2000. Premieres by American companies included Jake Heggie's *Dead Man Walking,* performed by the San Francisco Opera; Diedre Murray's *Fangs* and Randy Weiner's *Swimming with Watermelons,* both played by New York's Music-Theatre Group; and Minoru Miki's *The Tale of Genji,* performed by the Opera Theatre of Saint Louis (Mo.). Elsewhere, the most unusual debut was that of *The Age of Dreams,* a trilogy produced by Finland's Savonlinna Opera Festival. The three librettos, "Now and Forever," "Maria's Love," and "The Book of Secrets," were all written by Paavo Rintala, but the music was provided by three different composers—Herman Rechberger, Olli Kortekangas, and Kalevi Aho.

Other notable new operas included José Luis Turina's *Don Quijote in Barcelona* at the Gran Teatre del Liceu in Barcelona, Spain, and Aulis Sallinen's *King Lear* at the Finnish National Opera. Tobias Picker's *Thérèse Raquin,* based on Émile Zola's novel of the same title, was scheduled for production in the 2001–02 season. *Muhammad Ali*—based on the life of the former world heavyweight boxing champion—was completed by John Duffy with a libretto by sportswriter Robert Lipsyte, but it was still awaiting a production company. *Il Giocatore,* composed by Joyce Whitelaw with a libretto by Eddie Orton, premiered in Berkeley, Calif., and featured an Italian golfer playing in Scotland; the action was a metaphor for the relationship of the British Isles to Europe's "new economy."

Probably the year's most unusual operatic subject was that of *Parthenogenesis*—a 40-minute music-theatre piece based on a persistent but presumably mythic bit of urban folklore—about a young woman who asexually gives birth to a daughter in Germany during World War II. Rowan Williams, the Anglican archbishop of Wales, collaborated with composer James MacMillan and poet-librettist Michael Symmons Roberts on this opera.

The Glyndebourne Touring Opera company, based in the U.K., enraged some of its older patrons and intrigued some of its younger ones with a modernized production of Giacomo Puccini's *La Bohème;* principal male characters Marcello and Rodolfo were shown using cocaine.

The English National Opera implemented a new cost-cutting idea—use of the same basic set for all 10 of its Italian opera productions in the 2000–01 season—operas as varied as Puccini's *Manon Lescaut,* Verdi's *Nabucco,* Claudio Monteverdi's *The Coronation of Poppea,* and Gioacchino Rossini's *The Turk in Italy.*

The Houston (Texas) Grand Opera embarked on a program to produce digital audio and video recordings of new operas it had premiered. Houston had commissioned more new works than any other major American company and had been discouraged by the fact that record labels showed little interest in the material. After paying production costs, the company would offer the finished products to recording companies and possibly distribute them via the Internet.

Though opera was dubbed the "hottest ticket" in an otherwise diminishing classical-music market, one perennial opera-related attraction seemed to be waning. The "Three Tenors" extravaganzas starring José Carreras, Plácido Domingo, and Luciano Pavarotti began to run into buyer resistance after having played to enormous audiences in arenas and football stadiums for a decade and having charged up to $600 for a ticket. One concert was canceled owing to insufficient ticket sales, and the future of such concerts seemed uncertain.

For Domingo, however, the future looked bright. He became the first male opera singer to receive the Kennedy Center Honors for lifetime achievement since its inception 23 years earlier. Six women singers had received the award: Marian Anderson, Marilyn Horne, Jessye Norman, Leontyne Price, Beverly Sills, and Risë Stevens. Domingo took on new administrative responsibilities as the artistic director of the Los Angeles Opera—a position that he already had and continued to hold at the Washington (D.C.) Opera. His conducting career also continued, notably with *Il trovatore* in Washington, and he sang critically acclaimed performances in some demanding Wagnerian roles—Parsifal in Washington and Siegmund in Bayreuth, Ger. In addition, he made his American debut as a song recitalist in Chicago, with Daniel Barenboim as his pianist.

Gramophone Award winners included Antonio Pappanos, music director designate of the Royal Opera House, Covent Garden; sopranos Barbara Bonney and Angela Gheorghiu; tenor Carlo Bergonzi; composer Elliott Carter; and conductor Sir Simon Rattle. Rattle was honoured three times; his recording of Karol Szymanowski's *King Roger* took the Opera award, and his recording of Gustav Mahler's *Symphony No. 10* won both the orchestral award and the Record of the Year citation.

The persona of Leonard Bernstein seemed vigorously present, despite his demise a decade earlier. More than 50 Internet pages were devoted to him, including an official page, <www.leonardbernstein.com>, with links to many other pages, notably <http://memory.loc.gov/ammem/lbhtml/lbhome.html>, the Library of Congress page. The Sony record label released *The Bernstein Century,* a massive reissue of his records; Deutsche Grammophon reissued recordings of his freelance conducting performances, most notably his extraordinary work with the Vienna Philharmonic, as well as its most recent memorial production—*Lenny: The Legend Lives On,* a wide-ranging and low-priced six-CD collection; and the New York Philharmonic issued *Bernstein Live!,* a limited-edition set of 10 CDs that contained the first commercial release of 33 performances taped between 1956 and 1981.

Bach's work had a similar vitality. Several record companies issued complete or near-complete recordings of his surviving works, and an Internet site, the Bach Digital Project, was set up to provide a database with his manuscripts and other documents in a format easily accessible worldwide: <www. bachdigital.org>.

Michael Kaiser, who had successfully brought the Royal Opera House, Covent Garden, through a series of financial and artistic crises, accepted the presidency of the John F. Kennedy Center for the Performing Arts in Washington, D.C. Kent Nagano, a native of California who had been working largely in Europe, was appointed principal guest conductor of the Los Angeles Opera, beginning in July 2001. Nagano, former artistic director of the Opéra National de Lyon, would remain the music director of the Deutsche Symphonie in Berlin. In other notable appointments, Vladimir Jurowski was chosen to succeed Andrew Davis as music director of the Glyndebourne Festival Opera, East Sussex, Eng. After the post of royal harpist to the prince of Wales had gone unfilled for more than a century, Great Britain's Prince Charles appointed Catrin Finch, a 20-year-old native of Wales. Grant Llewellyn, another native of Wales, was appointed artistic director of the Handel & Haydn Society of Boston and was to begin July 1, 2001. He would succeed Christopher Hogwood, who had led the organization for 15 years and would continue his association as conductor laureate. Kurt Masur, music director of the New York Philharmonic since 1991, was to succeed Charles Dutoit as music director of the Orchestre National de France in the 2001–02 season. Masur had also served as the principal conductor of the London Philharmonic Orchestra in the 2000–01 season. Itzhak Perlman was appointed principal guest conductor of the Detroit Symphony Orchestra for three seasons. He would conduct (and occasionally play violin solos) in Detroit for three weeks each season. Yury Temirkanov began his tenure as music director of the Baltimore (Md.) Symphony Orchestra. Zarin Mehta, brother of conductor Zubin Mehta, was appointed executive director of the New York Philharmonic, which was finding it difficult to fill Masur's vacated post of music director. Riccardo Muti considered an offer but declined. The shortage of suitable candidates was exacerbated by the fact that both the Boston Symphony Orchestra and the Philadelphia Orchestra were also looking for new music directors. In addition, all three orchestras traditionally seemed to rule out women applicants or those native to the U.S.

Among the most prominent deaths were those of French flutist Jean-Pierre Rampal; American composer Alan Hovhaness; Canadian composers Violet Archer, Jean Papineau-Couture, and Barbara Pentland; Austrian bass-baritone Walter Berry; Canadian baritone Louis Quilico; Austrian pianist and composer Friedrich Gulda; American musicologist and educator William Stein Newman; and American violinist Oscar Shumsky. (*See* OBITUARIES.) Other notable losses included American critic and musicologist Henry Pleasants, American recorder virtuoso Bernard Krainis, Belgian soprano Suzanne Danco, Scottish composer Iain Hamilton, American conductor Richard Dufallo, Irish tenor Frank Patterson, Boston radio station WGBH-FM host and producer Robert J. Lurtsema, Italian tenor Cesare Valletti, Finnish bass-baritone Kim Borg, British baritone Roy Henderson, British trumpeter Philip Jones, and American conductor Margaret Harris, who had been the first black woman to conduct the symphony orchestras of Chicago, Detroit, and Los Angeles, among other cities.

(JOSEPH MCLELLAN)

Rahav Segev/Photopass

Pianist Danilo Perez fused jazz and Latin music in his performances.

Jazz. In January 2000, 84-year-old composer Oleg Lundstrem assumed the podium at a concert in Moscow to direct what was believed to be the world's longest-surviving jazz band. Lundstrem's group, formed in 1934 in Harbin, Manchuria, survived a decade in Shanghai during the Japanese occupation of World War II and another in Kazan, U.S.S.R., at a time when Soviet policy condemned jazz as "decadent music."

Jazz was adapted to local music and took root in Latin America, Africa, Europe, and Asia. Musicians such as Hugh Masekela, Bheki Mseleku, and Zim Ngqwana continued to fuse jazz and the popular *kwela* music of South Africa. They were among the top musicians in a parade of Africans who on March 31 and April 1 joined American and European headliners, including Roy Hargrove, Herbie Hancock, Courtney Pine, and Johnny Griffin, at the North Sea Jazz Festival in Cape Town. Ngqwana, who led a sextet from South Africa and Madagascar on its first American tour, proved an especially potent free-jazz alto saxophonist. The North Sea Jazz Festival in The Hague celebrated its 25th anniversary in July by again offering the world's largest weekend jazz blast—220 concerts featuring a worldwide contingent of jazz musicians performing on 16 stages.

Though most of the best international varieties of jazz were heard at European festivals, two theatrical Dutch bands—the Willem Breuker Kollektief and the ICP Orchestra—made U.S. tours. Composer Breuker's antic crew mingled jazz, pop, classical music, Kurt Weill songs, and vaudeville in frantic, often satiric shows. The humour of the ICP Orchestra, though sometimes ripe, was subordinate to improvisation and thoughtful interpretation of the compositions of Misha Mengelberg. American saxophonist Ken Vandermark financed a coast-to-coast tour led by explosive tenor saxophonist Peter Brötzmann, who, together with his 12-member high-energy band of American, German, and Danish improvisers, personified German free-jazz expressionism. The Italian Instabile Orchestra also made its U.S. debut, alternating grand orchestrations and free improvisation at the Chicago Jazz Festival.

Jazz and Latin music remained the most popular of international fusions.

One American favourite was pianist Danilo Perez, who was named a cultural ambassador by his native Panama. The senior Latin jazz veteran was 79-year-old Chico O'Farrill, who composed for top bands and experienced a renewal; with his big band, which played every Monday at New York City's Birdland nightclub, he revived his noted early works "Aztec Suite" and "Afro-Cuban Jazz Suite" in the album *Carambola.* Newer to American audiences was the band ¡Cubanismo!, led by Jesús Alemañy, and jazz singer Claudia Acuña, whose *Wind from the South* included standards and songs from her native Chile.

These international jazz fusions underscored the paucity of organic developments in American jazz. The parade of young lions, youthful virtuosos who became famous by reviving bop and swing styles, slowed to a standstill. In their place appeared a few new youths, such as pianist Jason Moran. Moran stood out for his original sense of melodic line, as evidenced in his album *Facing Left.* Moran's frequent associates included young, ornate vibraphonist Stefon Harris and alto saxophonist Greg Osby, who invented a style with hip-hop flavouring but proved more effective as a straightforward lyric artist. New York composer Maria Schneider—who led her big band in an album of moody colours, *Allegresse*—conducted at Carnegie Hall the Gil Evans–Miles Davis orchestra scores of *Sketches of Spain* and *Porgy and Bess* at New York's JVC Festival. Trumpeter Dave Douglas, named Jazz Artist of the Year in *Down Beat* magazine's critics poll, toured steadily with his own groups, composed *Rapture to Leon James* for the Trisha Brown Dance Company, and offered his first recording on a major label, *Soul on Soul,* a tribute to Mary Lou Williams.

Tito Puente's final album was a collaboration with fellow bandleader Eddie Palmieri, *Masterpiece/Obra Maestra.* Among other important recordings was the New York Art Quartet's fiery *35th Reunion,* with vivid readings by poet Amiri Baraka. The quartet's trombonist Roswell Rudd went on to reunite with another old partner, soprano saxman Steve Lacy, in *Monk's Dream.* Composer Edward Wilkerson led his Eight Bold Souls in *Last Option,* and lyric tenor saxophonist Fred Anderson offered *The Milwaukee Tapes.* Milestone issued an eight-CD box set of pianist Bill Evans's last nightclub engagement, *The Last Waltz.* From the era when live recording was still new came three historic Carnegie Hall concerts: the Benny Goodman band *At Carnegie Hall 1938, Complete;* the Woody Herman band *At Carnegie Hall, 1946;* and *From Spirituals to Swing,* 1938–39 concerts with Count Basie's band, the Goodman sextet, James P. Johnson, and leading blues and gospel music performers. All three sets included performances previously unavailable on record. Other reissues included Ornette Coleman's *Complete Science Fiction Sessions* and boxed sets of *The Complete Columbia Recordings of Miles Davis with John Coltrane,* on both CD and LP.

New books of 2000 included a profusely illustrated history, *Jazz: The First Century,* edited by John Edward Hasse; Nick Catalano's biography *Clifford Brown: The Life and Art of the Legendary Jazz Trumpeter;* and a reference work, *The Oxford Companion to Jazz.* Among the year's deaths were cornetist Nat Adderley, bandleaders Puente and Tex Beneke, trumpeter Jonah Jones, tenor saxophonist Stanley Turrentine, Brazilian bossa nova guitarist Baden Powell (*see* OBITUARIES), Japanese saxophonist Sleepy Matsumoto, singers Jeanne Lee and Teri Thornton, trombonists Al Grey and Britt Woodman, trumpeter Willie Cook, and drummer Gus Johnson.

(JOHN LITWEILER)

AP/Wide World Photos

Popular. Teen pop, much of it generated by alumni of *The Mickey Mouse Club,* continued to dominate American popular music in 2000. Male vocal harmony quintet 'N Sync, including former Mouseketeers Chasez and Justin Timberlake, saw eager fans snap up 2.4 million copies of *No Strings Attached,* its second album. In April the album went platinum after one million copies were shipped (by August it went nine times platinum—9 million copies).

In May Britney Spears, another former cast member of *The Mickey Mouse Club,* sold—during the first week of its release—1.3 million copies of her second album, *Oops! . . . I Did It Again,* a mix of sentimental ballads and rhythm-driven dance pop. Inspired by her success, record labels signed other young women, among them former Mouseketeer Christina Aguilera, who triumphed over Spears by winning the Grammy for best new artist. In late November the Backstreet Boys released their third album, *Black & Blue,* reportedly with an initial shipment of six million copies, a record. Madonna reemerged as a pop music force with a new album. *Music,* a mix of vibrant dance beats, hip-hop rhythms, and trippy guitars and synthesizers, debuted at number one on *Billboard's* album chart; it was Madonna's first number one album in more than 10 years.

Latin music continued to gain in popularity; sales of CDs reportedly jumped 16% from midyear 1999 to midyear 2000. The Latin Academy of Recording Arts and Sciences, the Latin arm of the National Academy of Recording Arts and Sciences, staged the first Latin Grammys on national television. Aguilera performed on the show and released a Spanish-language album the same week. Crooner Luis Miguel, rock-pop group Maná, and veteran rock guitarist Carlos Santana (*see* BIOGRAPHIES) each won three awards. "Corazón Espinado," a collaboration between Santana and Maná, received the Latin Grammy for Record of the Year.

Earlier, at the Grammy Awards, Santana had won eight Grammys, tying a record set in 1983 by Michael Jackson. His victories included Record of the Year for "Smooth," a collaboration with rock singer Rob Thomas of Matchbox Twenty, and Album of the Year, for *Supernatural* (1999), which went platinum. "Smooth" was also named Song of the Year, earning a Grammy for songwriters Itaal Shur and Thomas.

Hip-hop artist Eminem (*see* BIOGRAPHIES) released his second album,

The Dixie Chicks perform at the Country Music Association awards show in Nashville, Tenn., on October 4.

The Marshall Mathers LP. The recording stirred controversy among gay rights groups, feminists, and parents owing to its graphic content, but it also earned accolades from some critics for its mix of humour and dark, disturbing violence. A white rap specialist, Eminem recorded the album with production help from black rapper Dr. Dre, a.k.a. Andre Young. Amid the furor over its contents, the album sold 1,760,000 copies in its first week of release and stayed at the top of *Billboard's* pop "album chart for eight weeks. Eminem's debut album, *The Slim Shady LP,* won a Grammy for best rap album, and "My Name Is," a track from the album, was named best rap solo performance. A video clip for "The Real Slim Shady," a track from *The Marshall Mathers LP,* was named best video and best male video at the MTV Video Music Awards.

The Dixie Chicks—Natalie Maines, Emily Robison, and Martie Seidel—rose to superstar status in the country music world. The group was named Entertainer of the Year by the Country Music Association and picked up Grammys for best country album and best country vocal by a duo or group. The trio also embarked on its first North American tour as headliners.

New technology enabled Napster Inc., a California company, to pioneer a peer-to-peer file-sharing program that allowed computer-savvy music enthusiasts to exchange recordings. (*See* COMPUTERS AND INFORMATION SYSTEMS.) The Recording Industry Association of America filed suit against Napster, calling the company "a haven for music piracy on an unprecedented scale." In April Metallica took legal action against the company. More than 100 of the group's recordings, including five versions of an unreleased track, had appeared on the World Wide Web site. Dr. Dre also sued Napster, but rap-rock band Limp Bizkit accepted tour sponsorship from the company for a 10-date summer tour. On October 31 Napster and BMG parent Bertelsmann announced that they had formed a strategic alliance to develop an "industry-accepted" version of the free file-sharing service, which would include a monthly membership fee of about five dollars as well as compensation for rights holders.

In 2000 the barriers continued to break down between various styles of pop music. Audiences continued to show an interest in music from different parts of the world, and performers from countries as diverse as Venezuela, Mali, and Mexico all made their musical mark.

The most pervasive global music continued to be salsa, rumba, and other dance styles emanating from Latin America. The global Latin music boom had been sparked in part by the success of the elderly Cuban veterans of the Buena Vista Social Club, who continued to tour and release solo albums (most notably pianist Rubén González with his compact disc [CD] *Chanchullo*). Other Cubans enjoying success included trumpeter Jesús Alemañy, who teamed up with veteran New Orleans musicians to record *Mardi Gras Mambo,* which revived the musical links that had been broken between Havana and New Orleans at the start of the Cuban Revolution.

The Latin music boom led to a revival of interest in other veterans, all of whom toured Europe—from the highly political Panamanian singer Rubén Blades to the Argentine singers Victor Heredia and León Gieco, who used their ballads to protest against the military regime in Argentina. Gieco was dubbed the "Bob Dylan of Argentina" owing to his political stance and his use of the harmonica. Susana Baca of Peru was hailed as a "new world music diva" with the release of *Eco de sombros,* an exquisite gentle selection of Afro-Peruvian songs.

There were also fine performances from young newcomers from Latin America. Argentina's 20-year-old singer Soledad mixed political lyrics and folk songs with a dance routine that was worthy of Madonna, and she made an impressive debut in London. From Venezuela the young band Los Amigos Invisibles mixed salsa, cha-cha, and other Latin dance styles with Western funk, disco, and pop influences. Meanwhile, in Mexico there was an impressive showing by Los de Abajo, which fused local styles with an enthusiasm akin to the punk and ska revivals.

In Great Britain bands such as Sidestepper and De Lata, the latter dominated by the exquisite vocals of Brazilian singer Liliana Chachian, mixed Colombian dance music with rhythm-and-blues riffs. Elsewhere British pop continued to fragment into different styles. The most successful newcomer was 19-year-old rhythm-and-blues and garage-music star Craig David, whose cool, gently soulful dance songs and ballads won him a series of awards at the influential MOBO (Music of Black Origin) award ceremony. It was also a good year for the Anglo-Bengali band Joi, whose album *We Are Three* mixed dance rhythms with traditional songs

Pop Goes the Country?

As the 21st century dawned, country music—fueled by the unprecedented crossover success of Garth Brooks, Shania Twain, LeAnn Rimes, Faith Hill, Tim McGraw, and the Dixie Chicks—remained more popular than ever. Still, industry-wide sales fell somewhat from the dizzying heights of the mid-1990s, and critics complained that Nashville's Music Row establishment had squandered country's soul. Rock riffs and rhythms and pop polish from a generation of performers more influenced by the Eagles than by Hank Williams left country traditionalist Randy Travis commenting, "We're supposed to be in the business of country music, so let's hear some."

The first time that country went pop was in the late 1950s when legendary guitarist-producer Chet Atkins attracted a wider audience with the "Nashville sound" by adding "sweetening" strings and vocal choruses to recordings by Eddy Arnold and Jim Reeves, among others. Billy Sherrill employed dense arrangements reminiscent of producer Phil Spector to create 1960s hits for Charlie Rich and Tammy Wynette; pop vocalists such as Olivia Newton-John and John Denver "went country" in the 1970s; and in the 1980s the crossover hits that capitalized on the popularity of the film sound track of *Urban Cowboy* became for many country purists the epitome of pop pandering.

The stars' appearances as well as their masterful exploitation of music videos helped too to contribute to recent country crossover success as much, perhaps, as did musical mainstreaming. Cover girls Twain and Hill promoted cosmetics; the seductive Dixie Chicks (Natalie Maines, Martie Seidel, and Emily Robison) sported hip hairstyles and wardrobes; and Brooks, McGraw, and newcomer Brad Paisley were photogenic hunks.

Beginning in the early 1990s, some of the most roots-oriented country music came not from Nashville but from alt.country (named for the Internet's role in its proliferation), a movement that combined the do-it-yourself aesthetics of alternative rock with the song forms, instrumentation, and vocals of traditional country. Steel guitars and fiddles were moved to the background in Nashville, but twang thrived in St. Louis, Mo., the stomping ground of the pioneering band Uncle Tupelo, whose Jay Farrar and Jeff Tweedy went on to form the influential groups Son Volt and Wilco, respectively. Nearby, in Festus, Mo., the Bottle Rockets were launched, and in Minneapolis, Minn., the Jayhawks took off, while Steve Earle made the journey from Texas to Nashville and then to prison before returning to the music scene. The independent label Bloodshot Records, founded in 1994, made Chicago the mecca for "insurgent country" artists such as Robbie Fulks, Freakwater (with the distinctive close harmonies of Janet Beveridge Bean and Catherine Ann Irwin), cowpunk godfather Alejandro Escovedo, and the Handsome Family (Brett and Rennie Sparks), whose modern Midwestern gothic tales borrowed from the Appalachian tradition. The scene's cornerstones were Tweedy and Welsh expatriate Jon Langford of the Waco Brothers, who long ago had led the erstwhile British punk band the Mekons toward honky-tonk. Meanwhile, back in Music City, BR5-49 and Lambchop produced Nashville sounds that subverted proven pop and traditional formulas.

(JEFF WALLENFELDT)

recorded in Bangladesh. There was continued experimentation from Eliza Carthy, Britain's most successful young folk-music performer; she spent much of the year touring with Joan Baez and released *Angels and Cigarettes*, her first album of strong, mostly self-written pop songs.

Established veteran British musicians also produced some surprises. Robert Plant, best known as Led Zeppelin's singer, formed a new band, Priory of Brion. Joining the new group was guitarist Kevyn Gammond, with whom Plant had once performed in the pre-Zeppelin days. Instead of playing in large venues, however, the band made unannounced appearances in small halls or folk festivals and performed a selection of Plant's favourite songs from the 1960s. Van Morrison also returned to his earliest musical roots and influences. He recorded an album of skiffle songs with Lonnie Donegan, the hero of the 1950s British skiffle movement, before recording an album of old country and rhythm-and-blues songs with Linda Gail Lewis, sister of Jerry Lee Lewis. The year also marked the death of Ian Dury (*see* OBITUARIES), one of the most original British performers of the post-punk era; his songs had combined punk energy with humour and elements of the British music-hall tradition.

After more than a 20-year absence from the stage, Iranian pop diva Googoosh (*see* BIOGRAPHIES) made a comeback—in North America—and released a new CD, *Zoroaster;* she had been forbidden to perform in public in her homeland following the 1979 Islamic revolution.

In Africa the commercial success of the year was *Joko*, the new album by the well-established Senegalese singer Youssou N'Dour, who matched his fine vocals with a series of percussive songs influenced by local Senegalese rhythms as well as elements of soul, reggae, and rap. The African newcomer of the year was Rokia Traoré of Mali, who mixed a frantic dance routine with songs that matched her own acoustic guitar work against the inspired playing by her band of the *n'goni* (traditional African lute).

(JAY ORR; ROBIN DENSELOW)

DANCE

North America. With the exception of David Parson's choreographic direction for New York City's daylong New Year's Eve celebration in Times Square, the year 2000 did little to spur creative energy in the dance world. Ballet seemed to dominate the year, whereas modern dance appeared somewhat more down than up. When 70-year-old American modern dance great Paul Taylor was asked in an interview for *Dance Magazine* to ponder the essence of his modern field, he begged off, claiming to have "no idea what modern dance was any longer." He remained the creative force behind the Paul Taylor Dance Co., however, which premiered *Arabesque* at the Opéra Garnier in Paris before returning to New York to perform the ballet at City Center.

A major motion picture about ballet, *Center Stage*, dwelt on youthful Sturm und Drang as played out in the pressure-cooker atmosphere of a ballet school and company. The film featured dancers from American Ballet Theatre

(ABT); Ethan Stiefel starred as a "bad boy," and Sascha Radetsky was a "nice guy." Unfortunately, owing to illness, the greatly gifted Stiefel had to sit out ABT's New York City spring season. Celebrating its 60th year, ABT ushered in its season with a brand new and gorgeous-looking production of Tchaikovsky's perennial favourite *Swan Lake,* which was reasonably well staged by artistic director Kevin McKenzie and prettily designed by Zack Brown. Principal dancer Susan Jaffe marked her 25th year with ABT, and male principal dancers Vladimir Malakhov, Julio Bocca, José Manuel Carreño, and Angel Corella shone, as did the fast-rising Marcelo Gomes and two especially gifted young American women, Gillian Murphy and Michele Wiles.

New York City Ballet (NYCB) offered a premiere by choreographer Twyla Tharp, *The Beethoven Seventh,* which proved thrilling. Other new works were not quite as good; the troupe's semiannual "Diamond Project" ballets, new works made primarily with the support of the Irene Diamond Fund, were mostly unmemorable.

In addition to creating *The Brahms/ Haydn Variations,* a new ballet for ABT, Tharp started up a new company of her own after a more than 10-year hiatus; Twyla Tharp Dance performed two of her newest offerings, *Surfer at the Styx* and *Mozart Clarinet Quintet K.581,* at the American Dance Festival (ADF). The latter commissioned Trisha Brown, Mark Morris, Mark Dendy, Doug Varone, Ann Carlson, and Jane Comfort for its modern-dance-focused summer fare, sponsored by the Doris Duke Charitable Foundation (DDCF). Pilobolus, the perennially popular communal creative troupe, received the ADF's prestigious Scripps Award and played a monthlong season at the Joyce Theater in New York City, where its sidekick and smaller offshoot, Pilobolus Too, also gained some attention.

In Washington, D.C., the John F. Kennedy Center for the Performing Arts, under the direction of Charles and Stephanie Reinhart (who also ran the ADF), put on an ambitious George Balanchine celebration; six dance organizations presented 14 Balanchine ballets over two weeks. Represented there were several companies now run by and/or originally founded by dancers who worked under Balanchine. These included an ad hoc ensemble directed by Suzanne Farrell, San Francisco Ballet, Miami (Fla.) City Ballet, and Pennsylvania (Philadelphia) Ballet. The series also featured Joffrey Ballet of Chicago, as well as an ensemble of dancers from Moscow's Bolshoi Ballet. Earlier in the year, after a protracted hiatus, the Bolshoi had toured nationally and showed off some its newest, most stellar dancers, notably the young Svetlana Lunkina and Maria Aleksandrova. The Eifman Ballet of St. Petersburg made a U.S. tour that featured Boris Eifman's fulsome and florid dramatic productions, led by *Russian Hamlet,* his newest work. In June alumni from various manifestations of Russian-based ballet companies outside Russia, all variously named or identified during the 20th century as Ballet Russe, held a reunion in New Orleans. Birmingham Royal Ballet, newly reconstituted as a separate entity from the London-based Royal Ballet, played New York City and Chicago for the first time under David Bintley and offered a mostly all-Bintley repertory, including *Edward II,* a two-act ballet that carried a warning: "parental guidance advised."

U.S. ballet companies continued to evolve and in some cases change. The

Arch Higgins (left) and Benjamin Millepied of New York City Ballet dance in choreographer Twyla Tharp's **The Beethoven Seventh.**

Paul Kolnik Photography

fledgling Carolina Ballet gained attention for the multiact *Carmen,* produced by Robert Weiss; Pacific Northwest Ballet (PNB) hosted the taping of a video for the Balanchine Foundation. The *Interpreters Archive* video documented North Carolina School of the Arts teacher (and former Balanchine ballerina) Melissa Hayden coaching PNB dancers in three of her former roles. Houston (Texas) Ballet's (HB's) Ben Stevenson established himself as a choreographer of narrative spectacle with his new *Cleopatra,* made especially for ballerina Lauren Anderson. Boston Ballet (BB) also staged *Cleopatra* following the HB premiere performances and by year's end had offered *The Four Seasons,* another ballet by NYCB "permanent guest choreographer" Christopher Wheeldon. In advance of the 2001 departure of BB artistic director Anna-Marie Holmes, British-born Maina Gielgud was named to replace her. Fernando Bujones announced plans to stress the classical repertory as he assumed the reins of Southern Ballet Theater of Orlando, Fla. Danish-born Ib Andersen took over Phoenix's Ballet Arizona during a grave financial crisis. Former Dance Theatre of Harlem (DTH) ballerina Karen Brown became director of the Oakland (Calif.) Ballet. DTH played two weeks in New York City, featuring its own performances of Balanchine ballets. The perennially funny and highly popular New York City-based all-male travesty company Les Ballets Trockadero de Monte Carlo toured widely and played a sold-out run at the Joyce Theater.

The Alvin Ailey American Dance Theater toured extensively and became a highlight of Lincoln Center Festival 2000 with a new production of *Ailey's Blues Suite.* Avant-garde veteran choreographer Trisha Brown offered one of the year's several jazz commissions, funded by the DDCF, and ballet-dancer-turned-modernist Mikhail Baryshnikov featured works by Brown in his *Past Forward,* a performance project for the White Oak Dance Project (WODP); he also brought out from retirement dance-making iconoclast Yvonne Rainer, whose *After Many a Summer Dies the Swan* proved how enchanting and effective 1960s-style plainness could still be. The WODP also presented a new solo for Baryshnikov by Mark Morris, whose company toured widely and whose new staging of the Virgil Thomson–Gertrude Stein collaboration, *Four Saints in Three Acts,* played in Berkeley, Calif., after its premiere in London.

Casting a pall over much of the modernist activity was the artistic battle and stalemate over the legacy of Martha Graham. Midyear the company's board voted to suspend operations of the Martha Graham Dance Company (MGDC) and school, owing to financial problems and disagreements with Ron Protas, the heir to Graham's corpus of work and head of the Graham Trust. The lack of cooperation on both sides led to the cancellation of performances and the circulation of a letter that petitioned the dance world to refuse to mount or present any of Graham's dances until an agreement could be reached with Protas ensuring the existence of the MGDC and school. As a result of the MGDC's cancellation of a season at the Joyce Theater, the Merce Cunningham Dance Co. gained an extra New York City season. Meanwhile, the Joffrey kept to its plan to stage *Appalachian Spring,* a Graham classic.

The nearly 75-year-old monthly periodical *Dance Magazine* spent its first year in newly relocated quarters in Oakland, Calif., turning out shinier and somewhat more hip issues under the editorship of Janice Berman. Meanwhile, *Pointe,* a brand-new dance glossy specifically dedicated to ballet, started up in New York City.

Much of the dance news in Canada focused on the legal action taken against the National Ballet of Canada (NBC) by dancer Kimberly Glasco, who was dismissed from the company by its artistic director, James Kudelka. When the much-publicized disagreement was settled out of court with a monetary award, the greater questions of "cause" and contractual dancer rights ultimately went unresolved. Major productions of the NBC's year included the staging of Balanchine's evening-long *Jewels* as well as a new staging of Igor Stravinksy's *Firebird* by Kudelka. Les Grands Ballets Canadiens added "de Montréal" to its official name as it proceeded under the direction of the newly arrived Gradimir Pankov. The eighth edition of the Canada Dance Festival was held in Ottawa in June.

Among the deaths in the dance world were choreographers Lucas Hoving, Anna Sokolow, Peter Gennaro (*see* OBITUARIES), and Fred Kelley; dancers Tanaquil LeClercq (*see* OBITUARIES), Janet Reed, Harold Nicholas, and Gwen Verdon (*see* OBITUARIES); dancers and choreographers Greg Reynolds and José Greco; costumer Suzanne Gallo; and composer Lucia Dlugoszewski.

(ROBERT GRESKOVIC)

Europe. Although many European dance companies created new works for the new millennium, others looked to the past with revivals and reworkings of some of the staple works of the 20th century. Particularly favoured were the ballets created for Sergey Diaghilev's company. The works, though over 70 years old, still held a fascination for modern choreographers and audiences.

In London the Royal Ballet settled into the newly rebuilt Royal Opera House, which proved a major attraction. Highlights of the repertory were a Diaghilev program, including the company's first performances of reconstructions of Vaslav Nijinsky's *L'Après-midi d'un faune* and *Jeux* and a controversial revival of Sir Frederick Ashton's ballet *Marguerite and Armand,* in which French guests Sylvie Guillem and Nicholas Le Riche starred in the roles created by Dame Margot Fonteyn and Rudolf Nureyev; hitherto the parts never had been danced by anyone else. The new opera house included a small studio theatre, which allowed the company to stage a short season of new works during the summer. Ross Stretton, director of the Australian Ballet, was appointed to succeed Sir Anthony Dowell as artistic director beginning in the 2000–01 season, and music director Andrea Quinn resigned to take an equivalent post with New York City Ballet. The Birmingham Royal Ballet—which remained homeless while its base theatre, the Hippodrome, was refurbished—moved to another Birmingham venue for a short Ashton festival, which featured an important revival of *Dante Sonata,* not seen since 1950.

English National Ballet's third in-the-round production, a version of *The Sleeping Beauty* with choreography by director Derek Deane, was less well received than its predecessors. The company, which had severe financial problems, canceled plans for another new work by Deane and lost leading dancer Tamara Rojo, who joined the Royal Ballet. Scottish Ballet, under its new director, Robert North, gave the first performance of the full-length *Aladdin,* with choreography by Robert Cohan. Stefano Giannetti, appointed director of Northern Ballet Theatre in 1999, resigned to return to Italy after staging his full-length *Great Expectations* for the company.

On the modern dance scene, Adventures in Motion Pictures (AMP) premiered director Matthew Bourne's latest work, *The Car Man.* Based on Georges

The Birmingham Royal Ballet dancers perform a revival of Sir Frederick Ashton's Dante Sonata.

Dee Conway

Bizet's score for *Carmen* but with a very different story, the piece was greatly admired by AMP's growing audience, although several critics found its dance content rather thin. The company had found a permanent home at London's Old Vic Theatre, once the cradle of the infant Royal Ballet. DV8 took its new work, *Can We Afford This,* to the Queen Elizabeth Hall in London after its first performances at the Olympic Games in Sydney, Australia; Siobhan Davies's most recent piece, *Of Oil and Water,* was seen at the Sadler's Wells Theatre.

Companies visiting Great Britain included the Mark Morris Dance Group, which gave the world premiere of Morris's production of Virgil Thomson's opera *Four Saints in Three Acts,* and the Mariinsky Ballet (touring under its former name, Kirov), which gave five weeks of performances at the Royal Opera House. Good reviews and continuing interest in the new theatre resulted in sold-out houses; as a result, several performances were added to the original schedule. The Béjart Ballet Lausanne gave its first London performance in several years at the Sadler's Wells Theatre, and the Universal Ballet of Korea was seen there during its first-ever visit to the U.K.

The Opéra Garnier, principal home of the Paris Opéra Ballet, also completed a refurbishment during the year. The company revived Rudolf Nureyev's productions of *Raymonda* and *Cinderella;* additions to the repertoire were a new work, *Appartement* by Mats Ek, and the company's first performances of George Balanchine's *Jewels*. Meanwhile, in The Netherlands Jiri Kylian celebrated his 25th anniversary with Nederlands Dans Theater by creating *Arcimboldo 2000,* a show for all three of the NDT companies.

A highlight of the year was the Royal Danish Ballet's Bournonville Week, held in January and featuring five of the surviving masterpieces of its great choreographer August Bournonville. Most controversial was a revival of *The Kermesse in Bruges* with a reorchestrated score and a completely new interpolated divertissement, neither of which pleased the critics. Peter Schaufuss also mounted a new production of *Kermesse* for his own company in Holstebro, Den. Copenhagen hosted the first Chinese staging of a complete Bournonville ballet when the National Ballet of China danced *La Sylphide* in the Tivoli Gardens; the company's artistic director, Zhao Rubeng, indicated that he intended to add more works from the international classical repertory.

Elisabetta Terabust was appointed artistic director of the MaggioDanza in Florence, and English former dancer Patricia Ruanne was given a two-year contract as director of the ballet company of La Scala in Milan. The Milanese group had earlier become the first outside the Royal Ballet to produce Ashton's *Ondine,* with frequent guest dancer Alessandra Ferri in the title role, partnered by Adam Cooper. The ballet troupe in Naples appropriately revived Bournonville's *Napoli,* with Copenhagen-trained guest dancer Johan Kobborg in the lead; meanwhile, in Rome, Amedeo Amodio produced a new version of *Coppélia*. The Zürich Opera Ballet in Switzerland also attracted attention by showing a new version of Sergey Prokofiev's *Cinderella* by director Heinz Spoerli.

German companies toured in the East. The Bavarian State Ballet completed a visit to India; at home it had produced rechoreographed versions of two of Diaghilev's most famous ballets, *Petrushka* and *The Rite of Spring;* later in the year Sir Kenneth MacMillan's *Manon* entered the repertory. Prior to a tour of China, the Stuttgart Ballet gave its first performances of Ashton's *La Fille mal gardée,* featuring leading dancers chosen from among those in the younger ranks of the company. The revival was so successful that two extra performances were scheduled to meet public demand. The Hamburg Ballet showed a new piece by director John Neumeier that was based on the life of Nijinsky, and in Düsseldorf the Deutsche Oper Ballet performed Prokofiev's *Romeo and Juliet,* which was updated to a 1930s setting by Yuri Vamos. Plans for the amalgamation of the three ballet companies in Berlin were still under discussion.

The Mariinsky Ballet in St. Petersburg also put on a new production of *Petrushka,* modeled after the version by Leonid Leontyev; some claimed that Leontyev's version was a more-accurate representation of Michel Fokine's original than was the version known in the West. It also gave its first performances of *Jewels,* which was much acclaimed by critics and audiences in London during the summer. The company's leading ballerina, Altynay Asylmuratova, was elected artistic director of the Vaganova Academy, and many expected that she would greatly cut down on her stage appearances. The most important news from Moscow was the summary dismissal of Bolshoi Theatre chief Vladimir Vasilyev, former star dancer of the Bolshoi Ballet, on the order of Pres. Vladimir Putin; ballet director Aleksey Fadeyechev was also dismissed. Vasilyev was replaced by conductor Gennady Rozhdestvensky and Fadeyechev by another dancer, Boris Akimov. The ballet company made a successful tour in the United States and during the spring gave the first performance of Pierre Lacotte's reconstruction of Marius Petipa's first successful ballet, *Pharaoh's Daughter*. Several productions planned for the 2000–01 season were canceled on Rozhdestvensky's orders.

Deaths during the year included those of June Brae, a dancer with the Sadler's Wells Ballet in the 1930s and '40s; Jeremy James, a choreographer just beginning to make a name for himself; and Russian émigré Tatiana Riabouchinska, one of the "baby ballerinas" of the Ballet Russe de Monte Carlo in the 1930s. (*See* OBITUARIES.) (JANE SIMPSON)

THEATRE

Great Britain and Ireland. Headlines about Lord Lloyd-Webber dominated British theatre news stories during 2000. His Really Useful Group acquired the group of Stoll Moss Theatres—a third of all the West End houses—for £87.5 million (about $126.9 million), in partnership with a venture-capitalist city firm, NatWest Equity Partners.

The acquisition meant that Lord Lloyd-Webber was, in effect, the new landlord of the Theatre Royal Drury Lane, where *The Witches of Eastwick,* the new musical production of his great rival, Sir Cameron Mackintosh, was being presented. The musical was a witty version of both John Updike's novel and the subsequent film, with Ian McShane in the satanic Jack Nicholson role and Lucie Arnaz, Joanna Riding, and Maria Friedman playing the three bored housewives. The book, lyrics, and music by young American authors John Dempsey and Dana P. Rowe were serviceable and enjoyable without being terribly exciting. The first act ended with the three witches flying high into the roof of the theatre above the main floor and almost into the upper level. Otherwise, the musical's content was distinctly earthbound, though the prospects for commercial success seemed stronger than for *Martin Guerre,* Sir Cameron's last major production.

Lord Lloyd-Webber himself refurbished one of his newly acquired theatres, the Cambridge, and unveiled his latest show, *The Beautiful Game,* with book and lyrics by the popular comedy writer Ben Elton. The show followed the fortunes of a soccer team in Northern Ireland at the start of the recent Troubles in 1969. In the end the Cup Final hero was an Irish Republican Army murderer.

Lord Lloyd-Webber could scarcely have dreamed up a more unlikely subject; he took his audience where they almost certainly did not want to go. His score, however, was acclaimed as one of his best by most critics, with its chants, anthems, simple love songs, and a rousing showstopping ballad, "Our Kind of Love," which was a reworking of a Puccinian aria he had originally composed for a possible sequel to *The Phantom of the Opera*. The musical was given a bleak, hard-hitting production by Robert Carsen, who usually worked in opera houses, and some brilliant soccer-style choreography by Meryl Tankard, formerly a star of the Pina Bausch Tanztheater Wuppertal.

It was a busy year all around for new musicals, though none matched the former two. *Lautrec* was a dismal retelling of the life story of diminutive French painter Henri de Toulouse-Lautrec; *Hard Times* was a jolly, not unskilled version of Charles Dickens's least enjoyable novel; and *La Cava* was a strange medieval pageant, starring Oliver Tobias, in which listening to the music was the aural equivalent of chewing cardboard. *Notre-Dame de Paris* was not really a musical but a Gallic rock concert with some striking designs and muscular choreography. *The King and I* settled happily into the Palladium with Elaine Paige at the top of her form as the governess amid sumptuous designs that looked as though the king of Siam lived in a luxuriously appointed scarlet Indian restaurant.

The other musical highlights were provided by Matthew Bourne and his company Adventures in Motion Pictures, which started the year by reprising its gorgeous *Swan Lake* at the Dominion and ended it by opening a rather less-successful but still steamily impressive version of Georges Bizet's *Carmen, The Car Man,* at the Old Vic. *The Car Man,* described as an autoerotic experience, was relocated to a garage in the American Midwest and owed much to both film versions of *The Postman Always Rings Twice* as well as to Elvis Presley's *Jailhouse Rock.*

Elsewhere in the West End, film stars took to the stage. Kathleen Turner gave a blistering, moving performance as the alcoholic Mrs. Robinson in Terry Johnson's new stage version of *The Graduate.* She was succeeded in the role, however, by model Jerry Hall, famous for her marriage to and divorce from rock star Mick Jagger. Although Hall looked great, she failed to muster any inner life for her character. Donald Sutherland, hardly bothering to act, dropped by in a poor mystery play, *Enigmatic Variations,* and then London braced itself for Darryl Hannah in *The Seven Year Itch,* Jessica Lange in *Long Day's Journey into Night,* and Macaulay Culkin in *Madame Melville,* a new play by Richard Nelson.

The surprise hit was *Stones in His Pockets* by Marie Jones, in which two unknown Irish actors, Sean Campion and Conleth Hill, played two extras on a film set in rural Ireland as well as performing the roles of the leading lady, the director, and the rest of the cast. It has been said that theatre, in the end, is about two bare boards and a passion. So it proved here, in an evening of hilarity and delight that they played to packed audiences all year. The success of the play renewed confidence not just in the discernment of West End audiences but also in the art of theatre itself. Equally encouraging was the Almeida Theatre's presentation in the West End of Nicholas Wright's *Cressida,* in which Sir Michael Gambon gave a glorious performance as a manager of boy actors on the Elizabethan stage. Sir Michael returned triumphantly later in the year in *The Caretaker* by Harold Pinter, part of the playwright's 70th birthday celebrations.

The Almeida also colonized a large warehouse in Shoreditch, nearer the East End, for its Shakespearean double whammy: Ralph Fiennes in the title roles of *Richard II* and *Coriolanus.* They were fairly conventional productions made exciting by their setting, and the whole venture had a pleasing European feel about it, with patrons trekking into unknown territory by car and then wandering around a huge welcoming bar and coffee counter area before entering the Gainsborough Studios themselves, the site of the making of many famous British movies, notably Alfred Hitchcock's *The Lady Vanishes.* Fiennes was in fine vocal form as Shakespeare's contrasting titans. In its Islington, North London, headquarters, the Almeida also offered a riveting production of Neil LaBute's *Bash; Celebration,* a short new piece by Pinter that was set in a swish London restaurant and produced on the same bill as his first play, *The Room;* a persuasive revival by Sir Richard Eyre of Jean-Paul Sartre's *Les Mains sales* called *The Novice;* a less-persuasive British premiere of Arthur Miller's *Mr. Peters' Connections;* and a poetic British premiere of Yasmina Reza's inconsequential first play, *Conversations After a Burial,* starring Claire Bloom.

The other small London powerhouse, the Donmar Warehouse in Covent Garden, maintained its standards with Matthew Warchus's exemplary revival of David Mamet's *American Buffalo* with William H. Macy; a searing production by Michael Grandage of Peter Nichols's brilliant comedy of adultery, *Passion Play;* a beautiful new look at Tennessee Williams's *Orpheus Descending* with Helen Mirren and newcomer Stuart Townsend and directed by Nicholas Hytner; and *To the Green Fields Beyond,* a new play by Nick Whitby about a World War I tank division in the French woods, directed by Oscar-winning Sam Mendes (*see* BIOGRAPHIES), who was still at the helm of the Donmar despite the lure of Hollywood.

Overall, the Royal National Theatre (RNT) had a slightly less-successful year. Its new work record under Trevor Nunn had been patchy but was partly redeemed by the ingenious Sir Alan Ayckbourn's *House* and *Garden,* two plays in one, performed simultaneously by the same cast in two separate venues. Actors played a scene and then dashed next door to join another one. In a usual scenario, marriages were falling apart on the day of the local village fete. The RNT also aimed high with David Edgar's *Albert Speer,* based on Gitta Sereny's magisterial book about Adolf Hitler's architect. Alex Jennings played the title role, and Roger Allam was an unforgettable Hitler. Nunn's production was panoramic without being as memorable as his more Dickensian spectacles. Nunn hit his stride once more with an elegiac, beautifully acted Anton Chekhov play, *The Cherry Orchard.* In the small Cottesloe the audience was ringed on three sides of the acting area around Vanessa Redgrave as Ranevskaya, her own brother Corin as her stage brother Gayev, and Allam, who again caught the eye as the upstart estate manager Lopakhin.

Simon Russell Beale played a tubby *Hamlet* for the National and made of him a lonely mama's boy with a quick and racing mind. John Caird's production expunged the Fortinbras scenes and set the action, gloomily, in a dark castle littered with luggage trunks and strewn with candles. The other notable RNT revival was Howard Davies's production of Arthur Miller's first Broadway success, *All My Sons,* in which Julie Walters returned triumphantly to the stage after a nine-year absence and James Hazeldine played the guilty airplane-engine manufacturer.

The Royal Shakespeare Company in Stratford-upon-Avon embarked on a program that featured all of Shakespeare's history plays—from *Richard II* to *Richard III*—for the third time in its own history. Owing to either a lack of coherent vision or a fashionably Postmodern eclecticism, the plays were presented in different styles and on different scales by different directors. An all-white modern-dress chamber production of *Richard II* (with Samuel West as the poet king) was followed by the teeming *Henry IV* plays in traditional costume in the Swan Theatre. Desmond Barrit was a tumultuous Falstaff, and William Houston emerged as a genuine new star, taking his humorous, energetic Prince Hal forward to the main Stratford stage as the most exciting King Henry V since Kenneth Branagh.

The Royal Court reopened its refurbished theatre in February with Conor McPherson's *Dublin Carol,* a gloomy play about an Irish alcoholic. There followed equally gloomy and not very good plays by Jim Cartwright (*Hard Fruit*) and Martin Crimp (*The Country,* with Juliet Stevenson) before Sir David Hare came to the rescue with *My Zinc Bed,* a scintillating comedy about addiction and dependency. A triangular relationship developed between an Internet entrepreneur, his young wife, and a poet who had come to interview the entrepreneur for a newspaper. Sir David's own brilliant production drew compelling performances from Tom Wilkinson, Julia Ormond, and Steven Mackintosh.

The Globe at Southwark had another good year, with Vanessa Redgrave eccentrically playing Prospero in *The Tempest* and Mark Rylance thrilling the open-air spectators as *Hamlet.* Across town the Open Air Theatre in Regent's Park enjoyed the most critically successful season in its recent history with beautiful productions of *Much Ado About Nothing, A Midsummer Night's Dream,* and Gilbert and Sullivan's *The Pirates of Penzance.* In the regional theatre the places to watch were the Sheffield Crucible, the West Yorkshire Playhouse, the Newcastle Playhouse, the Glasgow Citizens, and, after a fallow period, the Bristol Old Vic. The medieval mystery plays were presented for the first time inside the York Minster. Barrie Rutter's Northern Broadsides, based in Halifax, West Yorkshire, gave the rumbustious premiere of *Alcestis,* a version of the *Euripides* play by Ted Hughes, Great Britain's late poet laureate. The Chichester Festival Theatre revived George Bernard Shaw's *Heartbreak House* with Joss Ackland as Captain Shotover and Ayckbourn's *A Small Family Business,* a brilliant family farce that slid into malpractice and criminality.

The Edinburgh Festival mounted a wonderful dance program alongside a sexy version of Molière's *Don Juan* from Ingmar Bergman's Royal Dramatic Theatre of Stockholm and a controversial four-hour translation by Frank McGuinness of Ramón María del Valle-Inclán's *Barbaric Comedies.* This rollicking, crude tale of pillage and rape—and a lot worse—was co-presented by the Dublin Theatre Festival, which did not flinch from shocking the locals with it at the Abbey Theatre.

Joan Marcus Photography

(From left) Blair Brown, Philip Bosco, and Michael Crumpsty appear in the Broadway production of Copenhagen.

Outside the festival the Abbey also presented a lovely new Tom Murphy play, *The House.* At the Gaiety Theatre indomitable Dublin impresario Noel Pearson gave actor Stephen Rea his head with a daringly modernized production of Sean O'Casey's *The Plough and the Stars.* The audience hated it, just as they had the first time it appeared in 1926. (MICHAEL COVENEY)

U.S. and Canada. Whither the American musical? No answer to that well-worn question was forthcoming in the theatrical year 2000, but it was a topic on many minds. The puzzlement escalated to the level of feverish debate at Tony Awards time, when *Contact*—an episodic dance drama with no singing, little dialogue, and (in an alarming development for the Broadway musicians union) a prerecorded score—shut out its more easily categorizable competition for the top musical awards. The Lincoln Center Theater Company production, a vehicle for Susan Stroman's witty and emotion-drenched choreography, had critics as well as Tony voters stammering for superlatives, but its win as best musical served to confirm traditionalists' fears that the art form as they had known it was up for grabs.

Musical-theatre developments outside New York served only to confirm their trepidations. On the West Coast, major musical projects were fashioned from the unlikeliest of raw materials. At San Francisco's American Conservatory Theater, experimental director Martha Clarke, known for bringing to life in her pieces such esoteric stuff as the paintings of Hiëronymus Bosch and Giovanni Battista Tiepolo (*The Garden of Earthly Delights* and *Vienna: Lusthaus,* respectively), made a bid for mass appeal by using the 1952 Hollywood movie *Hans Christian Andersen* as the template for an extravagant entertainment with avant-garde trimmings. The movie's sunny Frank Loesser songs ("Wonderful Copenhagen") mixed sometimes uneasily with the dark psychological themes of Sebastian Barry's book and with Clarke's signature flying choreography to create a one-of-a-kind musical that was likely, after some retooling, to be widely seen. Composer Philip Glass and director JoAnne Akalaitis, his collaborator and former wife, based *In the Penal Colony,* the chamber work they debuted to general acclaim at Seattle, Wash.'s A

Contemporary Theatre, on a brooding story by Franz Kafka.

The actor-centred Steppenwolf Theatre Company of Chicago also tested the musical-theatre waters. Ensemble member Tina Landau directed composer Mike Reid's *The Ballad of Little Jo,* based on a 1993 film, about the fate of a woman who makes her way in the American West of the late 1800s by disguising herself as a man. Like Landau's earlier *Floyd Collins,* created with composer Adam Guettel, *Little Jo* had a quasi-operatic style and musical eclecticism that was likely to be influential.

The old guard of the musical theatre was represented, perhaps ironically, by the artist who had broken the mold a generation (or two) earlier, 70-year-old Stephen Sondheim. *Saturday Night,* a straightforward romantic musical written in the 1950s when Sondheim was 24, arrived for the first time in New York after stagings in London and Chicago and was praised for its peppy score and for having captured the ambiance of Depression-era Flatbush, Brooklyn. Two other musicals of identical title, *The Wild Party,* kicked up a storm of publicity by facing off at major New York nonprofit theatres, but neither was a critical success. Composer Andrew Lippa's Manhattan Theatre Club version of the louche Jazz-Age poem by Joseph Moncure March fared somewhat better than Michael John LaChiusa and George C. Wolfe's adaptation at the New York Shakespeare Festival (NYSF) Public Theater; the latter, studded with such big names as Mandy Patinkin and Eartha Kitt and overweight with production values, lost an estimated $5 million and led to open speculation about artistic director Wolfe's ability to keep the NYSF financially afloat.

On the nonmusical front, the most interesting plays of the year dealt with hot-button social issues. Provocative newcomer Rebecca Gilman, whose work had been praised in London and Chicago, garnered national attention with the Lincoln Center Theater production of *Spinning into Butter,* a daring riff on racial attitudes in academia. Antigay violence was the theme of *The Laramie Project,* a powerful docudrama created by Moisés Kaufman and his Tectonic Theater Project on the heels of the sensational murder of gay college student Matthew Shepard in Laramie, Wyo. Kaufman and his collaborators based their drama on hundreds of interviews conducted in the weeks and months after the killing. This sad, gripping work debuted at the Denver (Colo.) Center Theatre Company, with many of the citizens of nearby Laramie who were depicted on stage in attendance on opening night.

One of the most produced—and most provocative—works of the year was also based on interviews: Eve Ensler's *The Vagina Monologues.* After running 15 months Off-Broadway, the play, a catalog of women's attitudes about their bodies and sexuality, received productions across the country and reached mass audiences not usually receptive to such progressive fare. Originally performed by the author herself, the play gained steam when film and television figures such as Calista Flockhart, Claire Danes, and Whoopi Goldberg joined the cast.

Michael Frayn's talky drama about nuclear physics, *Copenhagen,* was an unlikely crowd pleaser on Broadway, winning the year's best-play Tony. Another British drama, Tom Stoppard's melancholy memory play about A.E. Housman, *The Invention of Love,* had considerable impact on the American scene in well-received productions in San Francisco, directed by Carey Perloff; Philadelphia, directed by Blanka Zizka; Chicago, directed by Charles Newell; and, late in the season, at Lincoln Center Theater in New York, directed by Jack O'Brien.

Iconic Sam Shepard made a long-overdue arrival on Broadway: the cowboy playwright's corrosive 1980 comic drama *True West,* about a pair of combative brothers and their elusive aspirations, was given a sizzling revival with independent film figures Philip Seymour Hoffman and John C. Reilly alternating in the roles. The revolving casting was not just a stunt; it contributed to the play's gleeful absurdity and its central theme of identity confusion. Late in the year Shepard's latest play, a family drama called *The Late Henry Moss,* opened at San Francisco's Magic Theatre, with such high-voltage stars as Nick Nolte, Sean Penn, and Woody Harrelson in the cast.

African American theatre experienced a feeling of crisis. Financial trouble forced the Crossroads Theatre Company of New Brunswick, N.J., which had won the Tony Award for outstanding regional theatre just two seasons earlier, to close its doors, at least temporarily. The African Grove Institute for the Arts, an advocacy organization founded by outspoken playwright August Wilson and two professors from Dartmouth College, Hanover, N.H., worked to improve conditions by providing support and resources for independent black producing organizations.

Another behind-the-scenes shift occurred when more than 200 leaders from the commercial and nonprofit theatre sectors met during the summer at Harvard University to discuss past animosities and the potential for cooperation. The gathering, called Act II, marked the first time in 26 years that the two branches of the American theatre had engaged in structured conversation, and it revealed a landscape greatly changed by such now-commonplace interactions as nonprofit-to-commercial transfers, commercial "enhancement" of productions with transfer potential, and the sharing of artists between theatre worlds.

On the Canadian scene, a pair of musical blockbusters—the West End import *Mamma Mia!,* fashioned around the prefab melodies of the disco-era megagroup Abba, and Disney's ubiquitous *The Lion King*—kept Toronto box offices busy. Perhaps the most artistically interesting development was the wide visibility of *The Overcoat*—a grand-scale dance drama, conceived and directed by Morris Panych and Wendy Gorling—based on Nikolay Gogol's story about a downtrodden man who finds a coat that makes him a king. The play swept eight of Vancouver's local theatre awards in 1997 before finally making its way across Canada in 2000 and carrying with it a cast of 22 and a two-story set weighing more than 10 tons.

Robert Lepage, the presiding genius of the Canadian avant-garde, debuted an important new work, *The Far Side of the Moon,* at the du Maurier World Stage, Toronto's biennial festival of international theatre. The piece explored the narcissism of the space race between the U.S. and the Soviet Union through the lens of sibling psychology. In a sensitive solo performance, Lepage played two brothers, one successful and vain, the other eccentric and unconventional; utilizing his signature special effects, he fashioned a resonant connection between the personal rivalry of the characters and the political rivalry of nations.

Among the losses to the theatre community were a pair of legendary Broadway producers, David Merrick and Alexander H. Cohen; veteran Chicago director Michael Maggio and the promising 38-year-old director of *Wit,* Derek Anson Jones; and actors Nancy Marchand, Gwen Verdon, Richard Mulligan, and Beah Richards. (*See* OBITUARIES.) (JIM O'QUINN)

MOTION PICTURES

Actor Russell Crowe (centre, with shield) appears in a scene from **Gladiator.**

Buitendijk, Jaap/Dreamworks/Universal/Kobal Collection

Generally, the dawn of the new century found world cinema at one of the most stagnant periods of its history. Almost no film of 2000 from any country dazzled viewers with its originality or seemed to herald a new era or proclaim a new talent. Film themes seemed narrow in range, universally and obsessively repetitive.

Perhaps the artistic uncertainty reflected a fundamental economic revolution that had far-reaching implications for the relationship between filmmakers and their audience and ultimately, without doubt, for the future content and use of the moving image. More clearly than ever before, the motion picture was in transition from a public, theatrical medium to a private home entertainment. Huge increases in the video market, as the popularity of the digital versatile disc (DVD) soared, confirmed the changed economies of production and distribution in Hollywood and the rest of the world. In the United States, while video sales and rentals totaled close to $20 billion, gross domestic box-office revenues slipped to $7.5 billion. The top-grossing video film was Disney's *Tarzan,* which earned $268 million in this form—$96 million more than it had earned in theatres during its original release.

United States. Among the year's outstanding box-office winners were *Mission: Impossible 2,* a formulaic sequel to a film that was in itself inspired by a 1960s television series; Ron Howard's charmless adaptation of a classic children's book, *Dr. Seuss' How the Grinch Stole Christmas;* Keenen Ivory Wayans's audaciously gross parody of schlock-horor films and other teenage delights, *Scary Movie;* and Michael Higney's latest sequel to the hugely popular Japanese animation series, *Pokémon: The Movie 2000,* which exploited a massive juvenile enthusiasm.

Films that earned critical as well as commercial success notably included Ridley Scott's sumptuous *Gladiator.* In *Cast Away* director Robert Zemeckis and producer-star Tom Hanks aimed to recapture the mythical quality of their earlier *Forrest Gump,* giving Hanks the role of a modern Robinson Crusoe, an executive cast away on a desert island and discovering the means of spiritual as well as physical survival. Neil LaBute's *Nurse Betty* was an original and eccentric story about a young woman traumatized by her husband's murder and, while being pursued by her husband's former killers, retreating into the fantasy of becoming a soap opera heroine.

Michael Almereyda's *Hamlet* was a bold, sometimes pretentious, but still compelling updating of Shakespeare to a digital-focused 2000 New York. Philip Kaufman's *Quills* offered a stylish and witty adaptation of Doug Wright's play about the Marquis de Sade's incarceration in the asylum of Charenton.

In 2000 comedy appeared as one of Hollywood's strongest genres. Playwright David Mamet's seventh film, *State and Main,* was a winning screwball affair about the impact of a film crew upon a small New England town. The Coen brothers' *O Brother, Where Art Thou?* was a peripatetic period comedy, with nods to Homer's *Odyssey,* about three escapees from a chain gang in the Depression-era Deep South. Lasse Hallström's *Chocolat,* from a novel by Joanne Harris, was a winning social-moral comedy about the transformation of a staid French village when a young woman opens a chocolate shop, with all its seductions and temptations. Curtis Hanson's version of Michael Chabon's novel *Wonder Boys,* adapted by Steve Kloves, became a stylish screwball comedy about a college professor facing mid-life crisis and creative block.

The annual Sundance Festival showed independent filmmaking to be more buoyant than in recent years. Co-winner of the festival's Grand Jury Prize, Kenneth Lonergan's *You Can Count on Me* was a finely observed drama of the complex relationships of a mature brother and sister. Writer-director Karyn Kusama's *Girlfight* brilliantly and delicately traced the sociological and psychological issues involved in the decision of a spirited near-delinquent Latino girl (an outstanding performance by newcomer Michelle Rodriguez) to make her way in the male-dominated world of boxing. Jenniphr Goodman made an endearing character comedy about an overweight Don Juan, *The Tao of Steve.*

Recent events and people inspired a number of major films. Steven Soderbergh's *Erin Brockovich* starred Julia Roberts in the real-life role of a rough-tongued working-class woman inspired to take on big-business interests in an ecological cause. Later in the year Soderbergh completed a second film, *Traffic,* a docudrama on the drug trade and the conduct of the war against it. Roger Donaldson's *Thirteen Days* chronicled the Cuban missile crisis. Wolfgang Petersen, with his penchant for dramatizing actual events, depicted the struggles of a group of Massachusetts fishermen against the great storm of 1991—*The Perfect Storm.* In *Almost Famous* Cameron Crowe nostalgically described his days as a teenage rock critic.

British Isles. In the U.K. the outstanding commercial and critical successes of the year were Stephen Daldry's *Billy Elliott,* a sometimes touching tale of a boy from a tough mining district who sets out to be a ballet dancer; Peter Lord and Nick Park's vigorous animation feature *Chicken Run;* and Nigel Cole's *Saving*

Grace, returning to older styles of British comedy with the story of a green-fingered widow (Brenda Blethyn) who becomes a successful cannabis farmer. The best literary adaptations were Terence Davies's version of Edith Wharton's *The House of Mirth,* about a young woman looking for a husband in early-20th-century New York, and Marleen Gorris's *The Luzhin Defence,* from Vladimir Nabokov's novel about a Russian chess wizard at Lake Como in 1929.

In Ireland Pat Murphy directed *Nora,* the story of James Joyce's life with the former servant Nora Barnacle, while John Mackenzie's *When the Sky Falls* was based on the life of Dublin investigative journalist Veronica Guerin, murdered in 1996. Stephen Frears's *Liam* offered a child's-eye view of the lives of a Dublin Catholic family in the depressed and politically turbulent 1930s.

Australia and New Zealand. The record-breaking Australian box-office success was *The Wog Boy,* a broad comedy about ethnic life conceived and acted by Nick Giannopoulos and directed by Aleksi Vellis. In *Innocence* Dutch-born Paul Cox returned to his early theme of ageless love with a touching, passionate story of a couple who resume an affair after a separation of 45 years. The most memorable film of the year from New Zealand was Vanessa Alexander's first feature film, *Magik and Rose,* a charming, accomplished movie about two girl friends eager to become mothers.

France. Even while national production saw its share of the home market dropping to little over 30%—about half the money earned by American films—France maintained a good standard of commercial production, with a predominance of thrillers and social comedies. While some of the most costly and ambitious films—most notably the period drama *Vatel,* an Anglo-French coproduction directed by Roland Joffé—failed to recoup their costs, a runaway success at the box office was the action comedy sequel *Taxi 2,* directed by Gérard Krawczyk. Other notable commercial successes were Mathieu Kassovitz's thriller *Les Rivières pourpres;* Agnes Jaoui's social comedy *Le Goût des autres* (1999), chronicling the interaction of an actress, a businessman, a bodyguard, and a barmaid; Dominick Moll's eerie thriller *Harry, un ami qui vous veut du bien;* Gérard Jugnot's comedy *Meilleur espoir féminin* (*Most Promising Young Actress*), and Fabien Onteniente's comedy *Jet Set.*

Of France's true *auteurs,* Claude Chabrol, in *Merci pour le chocolat* (*Night Cap*), transformed a 1940s novel by Charlotte Armstrong into a mischievously satiric thriller, set in a rich Swiss industrialist family. One of the most idiosyncratic young directors, François Ozon, adapted an early play by German filmmaker R.W. Fassbinder as *Gouttes d'eau sur pierres brûlantes* (1999). While respecting the four-act structure and four-person cast of the original, Ozon gave his material dazzling cinematic touches. Ozon followed this with the no-less-excellent *Sous le sable,* tracing the progress of the grief and fantasies of a woman suddenly widowed (an outstanding performance by Charlotte Rampling).

Italy. Italian production grew as producers aimed at an international market with co-productions and English-language pictures. One of the biggest box-office hits of the year was Silvio Soldino's *Pane e tulipani* (*Bread and Tulips*), the heartening story of a neglected wife who discovers a fulfilling new bohemian way of life away from her insensitive family. Another notable film in a generally undistinguished year was Marco Tullio Giordana's *I cento passi* (*The Hundred Steps*), about a young Sicilian who rejects his family's Mafioso traditions to become a communist.

Germany. The status of immigrants continued to provide a rich subject for German filmmakers. Roland Suso Richter's *Eine handvoll Gras* (*A Handful of Grass*) told the story of a Hamburg cab driver who befriends a Turkish urchin. Frieder Schlaich's disturbing *Otomo* (1999), based on a true news item, chronicled the last day of a man beaten down and finally killed by racist oppression in the city of Stuttgart. Yuksel Yavuz's *Aprilkinder* (*April Children;* 1999) was a drama about a family of Kurdish immigrants in Hamburg, the generation gap exacerbated by transplantation and new influences.

Among established directors the best work came from Jan Schütte, whose *Abschied: Brechts letzter Sommer* was a fascinating re-creation of a day in the late life of Bertolt Brecht, surrounded by friends and lovers, with the threat of the authoritarian East German state always hovering. Volker Schlöndorff's *Die Stille nach dem Schuss* (*The Legends of Rita;* 1999) was an edgy realist political drama about a 1970s woman terrorist who defects to East Germany only to find new disillusionment.

Spain and Portugal. Spain maintained a substantial popular production. Notable films included José Luis Garci's *Una historia de entonces* (*You're the One*), the story of an aspiring woman writer in the 1940s who returns to her home village after the death of her lover; Álex de la Iglesia's high-spirited comic group portrait of the denizens of a rundown old Madrid tenement, *La comunidad;* and Agustín Villaronga's *El mar,* a striking if overheated melodrama of religion, sexuality, and the heritage of violence from the civil war, set in a tuberculosis hospital in the 1940s.

In Portugal Manoel de Oliveira, at 91 unchallenged as the world's oldest filmmaker, audaciously adapted the collected sermons of the 17th-century priest and missionary Antonio Viera to achieve a demanding but often touching portrayal of faith, in *Palavra e utopia.* More recent historical events inspired José Nascimiento's *Tarde demais* (*Too Late*), a re-creation of the dramas surrounding the real-life catastrophe of a fishing boat sinking in the Tagus River; and the directorial debut of the actress Maria de Medeiros, *Capitães de Abril* (*Captains of April*), about the events of April 25, 1974, when a military coup overthrew Portugal's fascist regime.

Northern Europe. Scandinavia had one of Europe's major successes in the Danish-Swedish-French co-production *Dancer in the Dark,* directed by the Danish enfant terrible Lars von Trier. Conceived as a musical tragedy and starring the Icelandic pop singer Björk, it had an overcooked melodrama whose harvest of international praise and prizes seemed exaggerated. Meanwhile, von Trier's associate in the self-publicizing "Dogme 95" group, Kristian Levring, made a watchable drama, *The King Is Alive,* about a group of bus tourists stranded in the Namibian desert and distracting themselves by putting on a performance of *King Lear.*

In Sweden the actress Liv Ullman filmed a script by Ingmar Bergman, *Trolösa,* in which an old filmmaker, not by chance called Bergman, recollects relationships destroyed by sexual infidelity. Roy Andersson's *Sångerfrån andra våningen* (*Songs from the Second Floor*) offered an absurdist journey, made up of 46 disconnected episodes.

The Finnish directors Anastasia Lapsui and Markku Lehmuskallio explored the legends and tales of magic and myth from the Nenets people in the north of Russia in *Seitsemän laulua tundralta* (*Seven Songs from the Tundra;* 1999). In Iceland, Fridrik Thor Fridriksson's *Englar al heimsins* (*Angels of the Universe*) related the adventures and torments of a sensitive artist. The Norwegian director Stein Leikanger's *Da jeg traff Jesus . . . med sprettert* (*Odd Little Man*) portrayed the tough childhood days of the jazz poet Odd Børretzen.

Eastern Europe. *Safe Sex* (1999), a low-budget and undistinguished sketch comedy about the sexual problems of a group of Athenians, written and directed by Thanasis Papathanasiou and Michalis Reppas, proved the biggest box-office success in the history of Greek cinema.

The most notable international successes of the year in Hungary were Janos Szasz's fine documentary *A Holocaust szemei* (*Eyes of the Holocaust*) and Bela Tarr's characteristic visionary fantasy of elusive political import *Werkmeister Harmoniek* (*Werkmeister Harmonies*), set in a dismal village that is incited to passive revolt. Domestic successes were Frigyes Godros's *Glamour,* which related the changing fortunes of a Budapest family of shopkeepers through the 20th century, and Barna Kabay's popular success with an updating of one of the country's biggest hits of the 1930s, the social comedy *Hippolyt* (1999), about a cultivated butler in the house of a newly rich family.

The collapse and corruption of Russian society continued to provide themes for that country's filmmakers and were toughly dramatized in Stanislav Govorukhin's *Voroshilovsky strelok* (1999), about an old man's revenge on the rapists of his granddaughter when the authorities turn a blind eye.

In sharp contrast was Aleksandr Proskin's *Russky bunt,* a satisfying, if surprisingly traditional adaptation of Aleksandr Pushkin's *The Captain's Daughter*. The cult avant-garde director Aleksandr Sokurov turned to documentary with *Dolce,* a portrait of the Japanese writer Toshio Shimao, mostly reflected through his aged widow, Miho.

From Georgia, Nana Dzhordzhadze's *27 Missing Kisses* related charmingly the encounters of a summer holiday when a teenager and his father are both enchanted by the same 14-year-old girl. The first feature film from Azerbaijan, *Sari gyalin* (*Yellow Bride;* 1999), directed by the documentarist Yaver Rzayev, was a black comedy set during the Armenian-Azerbaijan conflict of 1988 and relating the story of the alliance of two soldiers from opposing sides.

In other parts of Eastern Europe, film production remained sporadic as film industries struggled to revive after years of official subsidy and control. Among the more interesting films to emerge—all looking back to the past—were *Krajinka* by Martin Sulik of Slovakia, which chronicled the changing life of a small Slovak village from the 1920s to the 1970s; the Czech Republic's Jan Hrebejk's *Musime si pomahat* (*Divided We Fall*), the story of a couple sheltering their Jewish neighbour in the last days of the World War II German occupation; and the Croatian Vinko Bresan's *Marsal,* a fantasy about a small Adriatic port bothered by the ghost of the former Yugoslav leader Josip Broz Tito. From Yugoslavia, Ljubisa Samardzic's *Nebeska udica* (*Sky Hook;* 1999) related the struggles of a group of young Belgraders to rebuild their basketball court, destroyed by the NATO bombings.

Middle East. The explosion of creative cinema in Iran seemed attributable mostly to the influence of the gifted, still comparatively young, directors Abbas Kiarostami and Mohsen Makhmalbaf. A Kiarostami alumnus, Jafar Pahani, followed his gentle debut film, *Badkonake sefid* (*The White Balloon;* 1996) with *Dayereh* (*The Circle*), a powerful picture of the oppression of women in Iran's patriarchy, examined through a number of simply told stories. In *Djomeh* another former Kiarostami assistant, Hassan Yektapanah, treated the problems of a young Afghan refugee facing the racism and oppressive customs of an Iranian village. Makhmalbaf's prodigy daughter, Samira, followed her teenage debut, *Sib* (1998), with an equally finely observed story of two itinerant teachers and their encounters in the troubled border region joining Iran and Iraq, *Takhte siah* (*Blackboard*).

Japan. Japanese production in 2000 was marked by nostalgia. With *Doraheita* (1999), the 85-year-old Kon Ichikawa realized a script written 30 years earlier as a joint project with directors Akira Kurosawa, Keisuke Kinoshita, and Masaki Kobayashi. The story, from Shugoro Yamamoto's novel *Diary of a Town Magistrate,* tells of a samurai who poses as a drunken playboy in order to root out some gangsters. Kaneto Shindo—at 88 second only to Portugal's Manoel de Oliveira as the world's oldest working director—made a lively biographical film, *Sammon yakusha,* of the character actor Taiji Tonoyama, who appeared in many of Shindo's films and in private life was a notorious alcoholic and womanizer. A younger veteran, Nagisa Oshima, explored the theme of homosexual love among 19th-century samurai in the handsome *Gohatto* (*Taboo;* 1999).

In contrast to these retrospective works, an outstanding first film by Akira Ogata, *Dokuritsu shonen gasshoudan* (*Boy's Choir;* 1999), was the story of two friends in an orphanage whose lives are conditioned by the political eruptions of the 1970s outside their school and by their growing consciousness of the ephemeral nature of the talent they cherish as ambitious boy sopranos. Almost four hours long and in black and white, Shinji Ayoama's *Eureka* was a powerful portrayal of the traumas of the aftermath of a fatal hijacking incident.

Chinese-language films. While commercial production flourished in ever-increasing variety in China, Zhang Yimou made a small, quiet masterpiece in *Wo de fu qin mu qin* (*The Road Home;* 1999), a poignant chronicle of a lifelong love between a village teacher and his peasant wife. Also notable was Sun Zhou's *Piao liang ma ma* (*Breaking the Silence;* 1999), portraying a single mother living in Beijing and struggling to educate her deaf son. The best of the reviving production of Singapore was Kelvin Tong and Jasmine Ng's *Eating Air* (1999), a spirited study of the dreams and realities of a fecklessly drifting young generation.

Hong Kong production seemed unaffected by the return to China, as effective comedy, crime, and adventure films proliferated. The island's major international success of the year was Wong Kar Wai's *In the Mood for Love,* the story of a love affair between two married people in 1960s Hong Kong. *Xilu xiang* (*Little Cheung;* 1999) completed Fruit Chan's trilogy, set at the time of the handover of Hong Kong, and observed the changing life and the inevitable adjustments through the eyes of the two children of an ordinary family.

After establishing an outstanding career in Hollywood, Ang Lee returned to Taiwan to direct a spectacular magic and martial arts drama *Wo hu zang long* (*Crouching Tiger, Hidden Dragon*), which became one of Taiwan's biggest international hits. Another leading Taiwanese director, Edward Yang, returned brilliantly to form with *Yi yi* (*A One and a Two*), which surveyed a whole milieu through the midlife crisis of a businessman.

India. Established Indian directors dealt with topical themes. Buddhadev Dasgupta's *Uttara* (*The Wrestlers*) examined the effects of Hindu fundamentalism on a quiet Bengali community. Shyam Benegal's *Samar* (*Conflict;* 1999) looked at the abuse of "untouchability" obliquely,

INTERNATIONAL FILM AWARDS 2000

Golden Globes, awarded in Beverly Hills, California, in January 2000

Best motion picture drama	*American Beauty* (U.S.; director, Sam Mendes)
Best musical or comedy	*Toy Story 2* (U.S.; directors, Ash Brannon, John Lasseter, Lee Unkrich)
Best director	Sam Mendes (*American Beauty,* U.S.)
Best actress, drama	Hilary Swank (*Boys Don't Cry,* U.S.)
Best actor, drama	Denzel Washington (*The Hurricane,* U.S.)
Best actress, musical or comedy	Janet McTeer (*Tumbleweeds,* U.S.)
Best actor, musical or comedy	Jim Carrey (*Man on the Moon,* U.S.)
Best foreign-language film	*Todo sobre mi madre* (Spain/France; director, Pedro Almodóvar)

Sundance Film Festival, awarded in Park City, Utah, in January 2000

Grand Jury Prize, dramatic film	*Girlfight* (U.S.; director, Karyn Kusama); *You Can Count on Me* (U.S.; director, Kenneth Lonergan)
Grand Jury Prize, documentary	*Long Night's Journey into Day* (U.S.; directors, Frances Reid, Deborah Hoffmann)
Audience Award, dramatic film	*Two Family House* (U.S.; director Raymond De Felitta)
Audience Award, documentary	*Dark Days* (U.S.; director, Marc Singer)
Best director, dramatic	Karyn Kusama (*Girlfight,* U.S.)
Best director, documentary	Rob Epstein, Jeffrey Friedman (*Paragraph 175,* U.K./Germany/U.S.)

Berlin International Film Festival, awarded in February 2000

Golden Berlin Bear	*Magnolia* (U.S.; director, Paul Thomas Anderson)
Jury Grand Prize	*Wode fuqin muqin* (*The Road Home*) (China; director, Zhang Yimou)
Special Jury Prize	*The Million Dollar Hotel* (Germany/U.K./U.S.; director, Wim Wenders)
Best director	Milos Forman (*Man on the Moon,* U.S.)
Best actress	Bibiana Beglau, Nadja Uhl (*Die Stille nach dem Schuss* [*The Legends of Rita*], Germany)
Best actor	Denzel Washington (*The Hurricane,* U.S.)
International Film Critics Prize	*La Chambre de magiciennes* (France; director, Claude Miller)

Césars (France), awarded in February 2000

Best film	*Vénus Beauté (Institut)* (France; director, Tonie Marshall)
Best director	Tonie Marshall (*Vénus Beauté [Institut],* France)
Best actress	Karin Viard (*Haut les coeurs!,* France)
Best actor	Daniel Auteuil (*La Fille sur le pont,* France)
Best first film	*Voyages* (France/Poland; director, Emmanuel Finkiel)

Academy of Motion Picture Arts and Sciences (Oscars, U.S.), awarded in Los Angeles in March 2000

Best film	*American Beauty* (U.S.; director, Sam Mendes)
Best director	Sam Mendes (*American Beauty,* U.S.)
Best actress	Hilary Swank (*Boys Don't Cry,* U.S.)
Best actor	Kevin Spacey (*American Beauty,* U.S.)
Best supporting actress	Angelina Jolie (*Girl, Interrupted,* U.S.)
Best supporting actor	Michael Caine (*The Cider House Rules,* U.S.)
Best foreign-language film	*Todo sobre mi madre* (Spain/France; director, Pedro Almodóvar)

British Academy of Film and Television Arts, awarded in London in April 2000

Best film	*American Beauty* (U.S.; director, Sam Mendes)
Alexander Korda Award for Outstanding British Film	*East Is East* (director, Damien O'Donnell; producer, Leslee Udwin)
Best director	Pedro Almodóvar (*Todo sobre mi madre,* Spain/France)
Best actress	Annette Bening (*American Beauty,* U.S.)
Best actor	Kevin Spacey (*American Beauty,* U.S.)
Best supporting actress	Maggie Smith (*Tea with Mussolini,* Italy/U.K.)
Best supporting actor	Jude Law (*The Talented Mr. Ripley,* U.S.)
Best foreign-language film	*Todo sobre mi madre* (Spain/France; director, Pedro Almodóvar)

Cannes International Film Festival, France, awarded in May 2000

Palme d'Or	*Dancer in the Dark* (Denmark; director, Lars von Trier)
Grand Jury Prize	*Guizi laile* (*Devils on the Doorstep*) (China; director, Jiang Wen)
Special Jury Prize	*Sånger från andra våningen* (*Songs from the Second Floor*) (Denmark/Norway/Sweden; director, Roy Andersson); *Takhte siah* (*Blackboards*) (Iran/Italy/Japan; director, Samira Makhmalbaf)
Best director	Edward Yang (*Yi Yi* (*A One and A Two*), Taiwan/Japan)
Best actress	Björk (*Dancer in the Dark,* Denmark)
Best actor	Tony Leung Chiu Wai (*In the Mood for Love,* France/Hong Kong)
Caméra d'Or	*Djomeh* (Iran; director, Hassan Yektapanah); *Zamani baraye masti asbha* (*A Time for Drunken Horses*) (France/Iran; director, Bahman Ghobadi)

Locarno International Film Festival, Switzerland, awarded in August 2000

Golden Leopard	*Baba* (*Father*) (China; director, Wang Shuo)
Silver Leopard	*Xilu xiang* (*Little Cheung*) (Hong Kong; director, Fruit Chan); *Manila* (Germany; director, Romuald Karmakar)
Best actress	Sabine Timoteo (*L'Amour, l'argent, l'amour,* Germany)
Best actor	the ensemble of *Der Überfall* (*Hold-Up*) (Austria)

Montreal World Film Festival, awarded in September 2000

Best film (Grand Prix of the Americas)	*Le Goût des autres* (France; director, Agnès Jaoui); *Innocence* (Australia; director, Paul Cox)
Best actress	Gong Li (*Pioliang Mama* [*Breaking the Silence*], China); Isabelle Huppert (*Merci pour le chocolat* [*Nightcap*], France)
Best actor	Mark Ruffalo (*You Can Count on Me,* U.S.)
Best director	Silvio Caiozzi (*Coronación* [*Coronation*], Chile)
Special Grand Prix of the Jury	*Buye kafur, atre yas* (Iran; director, Bahman Farmanara)
Best screenplay	Pupi and Antonio Avati (*La via degli angeli,* Italy)

Toronto International Film Festival, awarded in September 2000

Best Canadian feature film	*Waydowntown* (director, Gary Burns)
Best Canadian first feature	*La Moitié gauche du frigo* (*The Left-Hand Side of the Fridge*) (director, Philippe Falardeau)
Best Canadian short film	*Le Chapeau* (director, Michèle Cournoyer)
International Film Critics' Prize	*Bangkok Dangerous* (Thailand; directors, Oxide and Danny Pang)
People's Choice Award	*Wo hu zang long* (*Crouching Tiger, Hidden Dragon*) (China/Hong Kong/Taiwan/U.S.; director, Ang Lee)

Venice Film Festival, Italy, awarded in September 2000

Golden Lion	*Dayerah* (*The Circle*) (Iran/Italy; director, Jafar Panahi)
Grand Jury Prize	*Before Night Falls* (U.S.; director, Julian Schnabel)
Volpi Cup, best actress	Rose Byrne (*The Goddess of 1967,* Australia)
Volpi Cup, best actor	Javier Bardem (*Before Night Falls,* U.S.)
Silver Lion, best direction	Buddhadev Dasgupta (*Uttara* [*The Wrestlers*], India)
International Film Critics' Prize	*Dayerah* (*The Circle*) (Iran/Italy; director, Jafar Panahi); *Thomas est amoureux* (*Thomas in Love*) (Belgium/France; director, Pierre-Paul Renders
Marcello Mastroianni prize for young actor or actress	Megan Burns (*Liam,* U.K.)

Chicago International Film Festival, awarded in October 2000

Best feature film	*Amores perros* (*Love's a Bitch*) (Mexico; director, Alejandro González Iñárritu)
Special Jury Prize	*Zamani baraye masti asbha* (*A Time for Drunken Horses*) (France/Iran; director, Bahman Ghobadi)
Best director	Clara Law (*The Goddess of 1967,* Australia)
Best actress	Hannelore Elsner (*Die Unberührbare* [*No Place to Go*], Germany)
Best actor	Emilio Echevarría, Gaël García Bernal (*Amores perros* [*Love's a Bitch*], Mexico)
International Film Critics Prize	*Krámpack* (Spain; director, Cesc Gay); *Nichiyobi wa owaranai* (*Sunday's Dream*) (Japan; director, Yoichiro Takahashi)

San Sebastián International Film Festival, Spain, awarded in September 2000

Best film	*La perdición de los hombres* (*The Ruination of Men*) (Mexico/Spain; director, Arturo Ripstein)
Special Jury Prize	*Paria* (France; director, Nicolas Klotz)
Best director	Reza Parsa (*Före stormen* [*Before the Storm*], Sweden)
Best actress	Carmen Maura (*La comunidad,* Spain)
Best actor	Gianfranco Brero (*Tinta roja* [*Red Ink*], Peru/Spain)
Best photography	Nicola Pecorini (*Harrison's Flowers,* France)

Vancouver International Film Festival, Canada, awarded in October 2000

Rogers Award, Best Western Canadian Screenplay	*Waydowntown* (Gary Burns, James Martin)
NFB Award (documentary feature)	*Just, Melvin* (U.S.; director, James Ronald Whitney)
Telefilm Canada Award for Best Western Canadian Feature	*No More Monkeys Jumpin' on the Bed* (director, Ross Weber)
Telefilm Canada Award for Best Western Canadian Short Film	*Evirati* (director, Simon Capet)
Dragons and Tigers Award for Young Cinema	*Fah talai jone* (Thailand; director, Wisit Sasanatieng)
Most Popular Canadian Film	*Waydowntown* (director, Gary Burns)

European Film Awards, awarded in Paris, December 2000

Best European film	*Dancer in the Dark* (Denmark; director, Lars von Trier)
Best European actress	Björk (*Dancer in the Dark,* Denmark)
Best European actor	Sergi Lopez (*Harry, un ami qui vous veut du bien* [*Harry, He's Here to Help*], France)

Animé

Over the past two decades, animé has become the worldwide term for Japanese-style animation, be it for television, feature-length film, or direct-to-video release. Animé differs from Western animation in form, themes, structure, and, most important, philosophical concepts and codes. Because animé primarily is meant for domestic Japanese consumption, it pays little heed to the fact that many narrative and pictorial conventions or cultural and philosophical references are peculiar to Japan and, therefore, risk misinterpretation. For example, the omnipresent "Bambi-like" eyes of animé characters are seen in the West as merely cute, rather than as multifaceted "windows to the soul," as they would be in Japan.

Western animation is aimed mainly at children and juveniles and has a very limited thematic scope, notably fairy tales, funny animals, and humour. This is the focus for much of animé as well—after all, that is where the money is. Animé goes farther, however, running the gamut from cute children's cartoons to adult fantasy, crime, action, romance, science fiction, and even pornography. Animé, in other words, realizes much more of the potential of animation, even though the West had a head start by at least 25 years.

Modern animé began in 1956 with the Toei Animation Co. and got its biggest push in 1961, when Osamu Tezuka, the undisputed giant of modern *manga* (Japanese comics), founded Mushi Productions to develop animation for the new TV industry. His successful children's series *Tetsuwan Atom* (*Astroboy*) and *Jangaru taitei* (*Kimba the White Lion*) found their way to the U.S. and France. After a slow start in the late 1970s with "rewritten" and censored imports of juvenile science-fiction TV series such as *Uchu senkan Yamato* (*Star Blazers,* or *Space Cruiser Yamato*) and *Chojiku yosai Macross* (*Robotech*), animé became quite common in the Western youth market. Recent success stories such as *Sailor Moon, Pokémon,* and *Dragonball Z* are but the highly visible tip of the iceberg. In addition, many Western TV cartoons have been outsourced to Japan, with noticeable effects on style. These forms of animé, in fact, have become so common that they hardly are perceived as animé any longer.

The first adult animé to reach a wider Western audience was *Akira* (1988), an apocalyptic science-fiction feature-length film based on director Katsuhiro Otomo's *manga* series of the same name. Western imports of animé still are dominated by science fiction, fantasy, and violent action aimed mainly at young male adults. The "female" genres of animé, however, such as romance, soap operas, and humour—most of which also have had a high action quotient—commanded a larger market share in Japan. Up to the late 1990s, Western reception of animé had been restricted to a dedicated cult audience. In 1996, however, the Disney Studios struck a deal with Studio Ghibli to distribute all of Hayao Miyazaki's films, such as the much-anticipated *Mononoke Hime* (*Princess Mononoke,* 1997), and this should, finally, open the Western mainstream market to adult forms of animé.

(HORST SCHRÖDER)

The title character in Hayao Miyazaki's animated film epic **Princess Mononoke,** *which was one of the highest-grossing films in Japanese history.*
AFP Worldwide

through the adventures of a film crew trying to make a film on the subject.

Rituparno Ghosh followed in the path of fellow-Bengali director the late Satyajit Ray with *Bariwali* (*Lady of the House;* 1999), a poignant portrait of a woman whose fiancé died from a snakebite on the eve of their wedding and whose solitude is briefly relieved when a film company moves into her home.

Latin America. The film industries of Latin America were mostly dedicated to supplying the local market, and comparatively little filtered through to an international audience. One of the rare international figures was the Mexican Arturo Ripstein, who completed two films of quality in 2000. *Así es la vida* (*Such Is Life*) was a modern version of Medea, set in a contemporary poor urban community and shot with great technical invention that made use of digital video techniques. *La perdición de los hombres* (*The Ruination of Men*) was a black comedy about the murder of a bigamist.

Other notable Latin American films of the year were, from Brazil, the directorial debut of the actress Florinda Bolkan with an elegant and talented portrait of an upper-middle-class family, *Eu nio conhecia Tururu* (*I Didn't Know Tuturu*); and Andrucha Waddington's *Eu, tu, eles,* relating with charm the daily adventures of a poor woman coping with her three husbands and their respective sons.

(DAVID ROBINSON)

Nontheatrical Films. Makers of nontheatrical films continued to set a fast creative pace in 2000. A comedy by Florida State University students Kelsey Scott and Robert McCaffrey won eight first-place awards. *The Buse* (rhymes with muse) is a whimsical tale of two spirits. Another student production, *The Letter,* was an evocative, beautiful, yet gruesome film about the removal of a cancerous breast without anesthesia in France in 1811. Based on a letter from Fanny Burney to her sister, it was produced in Australia by Anne Delaney and was named best overall film at the Columbus (Ohio) International Film & Video Festival.

Generations: The Story of Ketel One Vodka, an industrial film by Pieter-Rim de Kroon of The Netherlands, traced one family's secret-formula vodka business beginning in 1691 through 10 generations. It won prizes in France, The Netherlands, and the U.S. along with the IVCA Award in London for music and photography. (THOMAS W. HOPE)

Religion

INTERFAITH RELATIONS took centre stage in the world of religion during 2000 as faith groups came into **CONFLICT** in some situations and found themselves making **BREAKTHROUGHS** in **COOPERATION** in others. **SAME-SEX UNIONS** and **THE ROLE OF WOMEN** sparked internal conflicts in some traditions, and the **RELATIONSHIP** between religion and government **CHALLENGED** both sides on several fronts.

Interfaith Relations. More than 1,000 religious leaders from around the world gathered at United Nations headquarters in New York City in August for a four-day Millennium World Peace Summit. While sharing common perspectives on issues such as peace and the environment, Hindus and Catholics clashed at the summit over the Roman Catholic Church's evangelistic efforts in India. In June more than 300 representatives of 39 faith groups assembled in Pittsburgh, Pa., to sign the charter of the United Religions Initiative, an effort to build world peace through interfaith cooperation at the grass roots.

More than 160 Jewish leaders issued a statement in September calling on Jews to affirm their joint heritage with Christians while acknowledging a "humanly irreconcilable difference" between the two faiths. The statement came a few days after the Vatican drew dismay from leaders of other churches and religious groups by issuing *Dominus Iesus,* a 14-page declaration calling the Roman Catholic Church the only "instrument for the salvation of all humanity." Earlier in September, Jewish leaders had protested the beatification of Pope Pius IX, who in the mid-1800s had confined Jews to a walled ghetto in Rome, stripped them of property, and adopted a six-year-old boy whom papal guards had abducted from his Italian Jewish parents, raising him to be a priest.

Despite these developments, Pope John Paul II took several major initiatives toward interfaith understanding during the year. In February he became the first pope to visit predominantly Islamic Egypt, denouncing violence in the name of religion as "an offense against God." At a service of penance in Rome in March, he made an unprecedented appeal for forgiveness for acts of violence committed by Christians against followers of other religions and expressed forgiveness for such acts taken against Christians. Later in March, on a trip to Israel, he visited the Yad Vashem memorial to Holocaust victims and expressed sadness at "hatred, acts of persecution and displays of anti-Semitism directed against the Jews by Christians at any time and in any place." The visit to Israel also marked the first papal meeting with the two chief rabbis of the Jewish state, in the chief rabbinate's headquarters in Jerusalem. After hearing a request from the mufti, the chief Muslim cleric of Jerusalem, to oppose "the Israeli occupation" of the holy city, John Paul said, "Jerusalem has always been revered by Jews, Christians and Muslims." That comment came a month after leaders of the Vatican and the Palestine Liberation Organization signed an agreement condemning "unilateral decisions and actions altering the specific character and status" of Jerusalem.

Sectarian Violence. A visit in September by Israeli politician Ariel Sharon to the Noble Sanctuary of Palestinian Muslims in Jerusalem touched off weeks of violence between Palestinians and Israelis. Sharon planted an Israeli flag on the site, where Muslims believe Muhammad ascended to heaven and which Jews revere as the Temple Mount. Violent Hindu attacks against Christian churches, missionaries, and schools in India, including the fatal beating of a Franciscan priest in Uttar Pradesh, prompted Prime Minister Atal Bihari Vajpayee to meet with a delegation of Roman Catholic bishops in June to assure them of the government's commitment to protecting the rights of "all minorities" in India. Hundreds of people were killed in battles between Christians and Muslims in Indonesia and Nigeria during the year, and a series of Christmas eve bombings of churches in Indonesia killed 18 people. A panel formed by the Organization of African Unity criticized Roman Catholic, Anglican, and French government leaders for having failed to use "their unique moral position among the overwhelmingly Christian population" of Rwanda to denounce the ethnic hatred that led to the deaths of 500,000 people there in 1994. Buddhist leaders in Sri Lanka urged the army to fight harder against the Liberation Tigers of Tamil Eelam, a guerrilla movement fighting on behalf of the largely Hindu Tamil minority against the majority Buddhist Sinhalese.

In contrast, leaders of the Muslim, Orthodox, and Roman Catholic communities in the Serbian province of Kosovo set up a joint council to promote democracy and human rights. North America's growing religious diversity was reflected in the listing of Buddhist, Muslim, Jewish, and other non-Christian groups for the first time ever in the *Yearbook of American & Canadian Churches* in its 2000 edition.

Ecumenism. Ecumenical Patriarch Bartholomew I, spiritual leader of the world's Orthodox Christians, joined with leaders of 14 Orthodox churches in December in calling for an end to the rift between Eastern and Western Christendom that began with the Great Schism of 1054. Their proclamation was signed in the Byzantine-era Church

Pope John Paul II blesses a mother and child during the opening ceremony of the Jubilee of Families Holy Year celebration in the Vatican's St. Peter's Square on October 14.

AP/Wide World Photos

of Hagia Sophia in Iznik, Turkey, the site of the ancient city of Nicaea, where the Nicene Creed was issued in 325.

Representatives of 22 churches attended a service in Rome in January celebrating the start of the Roman Catholic Holy Year. Some Protestant leaders stayed away, however, to protest its connection with indulgences, the Catholic practice of remitting punishment for sins in exchange for prayer and repentance. In May clergy from 18 churches helped officiate at a service in Rome commemorating thousands of 20th-century Christian martyrs. At a meeting of the Society for Pentecostal Studies in Kirkland, Wash., in March, Pentecostal and Roman Catholic scholars asked for forgiveness for sins that members of each group had committed against the other.

At its triennial General Convention in Denver, Colo., in July, the Episcopal Church approved the mutual recognition of members and clergy with the Evangelical Lutheran Church in America. This marked the first time the Episcopal Church had agreed that clergy of another denomination could preside at its services. The National Council of the Churches of Christ in the U.S.A. (NCC) authorized a plan to explore creating a new organization that would include representatives of all major branches of Christianity in the United States. The ecumenical body also granted financial independence to its relief and development agency, Church World Service. The National Association of Evangelicals (NAE) changed its bylaws to allow churches that were members of other cooperative organizations to have dual membership with the NAE. The Reformed Church in America, which already held membership in the NCC, became the first denomination to seek dual membership in the NAE.

Homosexuals. Moves to approve homosexual clergy and same-sex unions stirred disagreements in several religious groups. In a statement released in January, more than 800 religious leaders urged all faiths to approve such developments. Meeting in Greensboro, N.C., in March, the rabbinical arm of Reform Judaism declared that same-sex unions were "worthy of affirmation through appropriate Jewish ritual." The move was denounced by leaders of the Conservative and Orthodox movements of Judaism.

In Singapore in January, six Anglican bishops consecrated as bishops two U.S. Episcopal priests who opposed such developments in their church. The Episcopal presiding bishop, Frank T. Griswold III, denounced the consecrations of the Rev. Charles H. Murphy III and the Rev. John H. Rodgers, Jr., and the Anglican archbishop of Canterbury, George Carey, refused to recognize them. At its convention in July, the Episcopal Church declared support for same-sex relationships while defeating a call to create special ceremonies to recognize them. The quadrennial General Conference of the United Methodist Church voted in May in Cleveland, Ohio, to retain a policy forbidding "practicing homosexuals" from becoming ministers, but more than 300 delegates to the denomination's New England Annual Conference signed a declaration a month later promising to conduct same-sex unions and to welcome homosexuals into the ministry. In New Zealand about 2,000 people left that country's Methodist Church, charging that it had strayed from biblical teachings against homosexuality. Despite the opposition of 7 of the country's 11 bishops, the Oslo diocese of Norway's state Lutheran Church appointed to a parish a homosexual priest living openly with another man.

The highest court of the Presbyterian Church (U.S.A.) ruled in May that clergy may conduct same-sex union ceremonies as long as they are not regarded as marriages. A month later the church's annual General Assembly in Long Beach, Calif., approved a resolution to ban same-sex unions and sent it to the denomination's 173 regional presbyteries for approval. The Greater Milwaukee (Wis.) Synod of the Evangelical Lutheran Church in America approved blessings for same-sex unions at its meeting in May. In June the United Church of Christ announced that it had created a scholarship fund for homosexuals who wanted to enter the ministry. In so doing, it became the first Christian denomination actively to promote the ordination of gay clergy.

Women in the Church. Women enjoyed some breakthroughs and suffered some setbacks in the quest to improve their status in religious groups. A key breakthrough came in Cincinnati, Ohio, in July when the oldest black church body in the U.S., the 213-year-old African Methodist Episcopal Church, elected the Rev. Vashti McKenzie of Baltimore, Md., its first female bishop. Her election was the culmination of a 20-year effort by women to attain that status in the denomination. Two other women who gained prominence in religious circles were Nancy Heisey, a professor at Eastern Mennonite University in Harrisonburg, Va., who became the first woman elected president of the Mennonite World Conference, and Anne Graham Lotz, daughter of evangelist Billy Graham, who was the only woman to address a plenary session at a gathering of 10,000 evangelists from 209 countries in Amsterdam in August.

The Southern Baptist Convention declared at its annual meeting in June in Orlando, Fla., that "the office of pastor is limited to men as qualified by Scripture." Although the statement represented the thinking of Southern Baptist leaders, it was not binding on the denomination's congregations, which had ordained 1,600 women. The Southern Baptist action prompted the Presbyterian Church (U.S.A.) General Assembly to express "Christian concern for and solidarity with women who are being denied the exercise of their pastoral gifts." Nonetheless, a smaller denomination, the Presbyterian Church in America, said at its General Assembly in June in Tampa, Fla., that women may teach but not preach. The Episcopal General Convention criticized the dioceses of Fort Worth, Texas; San Joaquin, Calif.; and Quincy, Ill., for refusing to obey church law allowing women to be ordained and established a process to bring them into compliance by 2002. A women's task force of the World Evangelical Fellowship issued a statement in June on domestic violence in which it said that "sinful practices are being ignored, tolerated, sometimes even perpetuated in the church as well as society at large."

Jews in Israel debated whether women should have the same rights as men to conduct worship services at the Western Wall in Jerusalem. The Israeli Supreme Court ruled in May that they had this right, but the nation's parliament subsequently gave preliminary approval to a bill to punish women with seven years in prison if they acted on the court ruling. In August Iran announced that six Islamic jurists had issued a decree allowing women to lead other women in worship for the first time in the history of Shi'ite Islam.

Church, State, Law, and Politics. China came into conflict with the U.S. and the Vatican for its treatment of religious groups. In September, in a report that Chinese authorities denounced as a fabrication, the U.S. State Department charged that China had persecuted members of minority faiths, Tibetan Buddhists, and the banned Falun Gong spiritual movement. Also in September, Roger Cardinal Etchegaray became the

AP/Wide World Photos

The Karmapa Lama (centre) smiles during a ceremony held in Dharmshala, India, to mark the 60th anniversary of the Dalai Lama's enthronement.

first Vatican-based cardinal to say a public mass in China since the communist revolution in 1949. He lodged what he called an "energetic protest" with Chinese authorities over the arrests of Catholic bishops loyal to Pope John Paul II. China's Ministry of Foreign Affairs, in turn, denounced the Vatican's decision to canonize Chinese Christian martyrs on October 1, the 51st anniversary of communist rule. A protest that day by members of the Falun Gong movement forced the brief closure of much of Tiananmen Square in Beijing.

The 14-year-old Gyalwa Karmapa Lama, the third most important spiritual figure in Tibetan Buddhism, fled China on foot across the Himalayas in January to arrive in Dharmshala, the northern Indian city that served as the capital of Tibet's exiled Buddhist leadership. His flight was significant both because he was the first Buddhist figure revered as the reincarnation of a holy person to be recognized by China's communist leaders and because his Kagyu school was the most influential Tibetan Buddhist movement outside Tibet. Organizers of the peace summit at the United Nations elected not to invite the exiled Dalai Lama, the winner of the 1989 Nobel Prize for Peace, for fear of offending China, a move that was denounced by fellow Nobel peace laureate Anglican Archbishop Desmond Tutu of South Africa. A message from the Dalai Lama was read to the conference.

The opening in September of a Jewish community centre in Moscow by Russian Pres. Vladimir Putin drew widespread attention for its significance in a country that had experienced centuries of government-sponsored anti-Semitism. The gesture also stirred controversy, however, because the new centre on the site of the Marina Roshcha Synagogue was built by the Chabad Lubavich movement, which had won Putin's support over other, less conservative branches of Judaism. The Lubavitch-led Federation of Jewish Communities received Kremlin recognition as the official voice of Jews in Russia. Earlier in the year the federation named Lubavich Rabbi Berl Lazar as chief rabbi of Russia, apparently ousting Rabbi Adolf Shayevich, who had held the post for a decade.

A plan by the Greek government to remove religion from state identity cards raised the ire of the Greek Orthodox Church, whose leaders denounced it as a threat to the church's unique status in the country. An estimated 130,000 demonstrators gathered in the central square in Athens in June to criticize the move as Archbishop Christodoulous called on church members to "save our faith." Judicial authorities in Iran closed at least 12 newspapers and magazines in April for publishing material that "disparaged Islam." In May Saudi Arabian Minister of Justice Abdallah ibn Muhammad ibn Ibrahim ash-Sheikh condemned people who claimed that the nation's practice of Islamic law, or Shari'ah, did not guarantee human rights, calling such critics "the enemies of God, religion and humanity."

In the United States, Pres. Bill Clinton signed a law requiring local officials to give preferred treatment to religious groups when their buildings and assemblies come into conflict with zoning boards. The U.S. Supreme Court ruled 6–3 in June in *Santa Fe Independent School District* v. *Doe* that public-school officials could not sponsor a group prayer or encourage a student to deliver a religious message at a school event. In another case that month, *Mitchell* v. *Helms,* the high court ruled 6–3 that tax money could be used to buy computers and other instructional materials that would be loaned to religious schools. In April a federal appeals court struck down the state motto of Ohio, "With God, all things are possible," saying it was a government endorsement of Christianity.

Also in Florida, prosecutors dropped charges against the Church of Scientology in the 1995 death of Lisa McPherson, who had been under the church's care, after the medical examiner determined that her death was accidental.

The Rev. Daniel Coughlin of Chicago became the first Roman Catholic priest to be appointed chaplain of the U.S. House of Representatives. The appointment in March by House Speaker Dennis Hastert followed a controversy in which Hastert and Majority Leader Dick Armey had picked a Presbyterian minister as the next chaplain despite the recommendation by a bipartisan committee favouring another Catholic priest for the post. In September Venkatachalapathi Samuldrala of Parma, Ohio, became the first Hindu ever to deliver an invocation in the House. Democratic vice presidential nominee Joseph Lieberman (*see* BI-

Worldwide Adherents of All Religions by Six Continental Areas, Mid-2000

	Africa	Asia	Europe	Latin America	Northern America	Oceania	World	%	Number of Countries
Christians	**360,232,000**	**312,849,000**	**559,643,000**	**481,102,000**	**260,624,000**	**25,110,000**	**1,999,560,000**	**33.0**	**238**
Affiliated Christians	335,116,000	307,288,000	536,832,000	475,659,000	212,167,000	21,375,000	1,888,437,000	31.2	238
Roman Catholics	120,386,000	110,480,000	285,978,000	461,220,000	71,035,000	8,228,000	1,057,327,000	17.5	235
Protestants	89,001,000	49,967,000	77,529,000	48,132,000	69,978,000	7,392,000	341,999,000	5.6	233
Orthodox	35,304,000	14,113,000	158,105,000	558,000	6,342,000	706,000	215,128,000	3.6	135
Anglicans	42,542,000	727,000	26,637,000	1,090,000	3,244,000	5,409,000	79,649,000	1.3	166
Other Christians	86,268,000	157,218,000	29,288,000	46,301,000	90,769,000	1,966,000	411,810,000	6.8	223
Unaffiliated Christians	25,116,000	5,561,000	22,811,000	5,443,000	48,458,000	3,735,000	111,124,000	1.8	236
Non-Christians	**424,213,000**	**3,369,701,000**	**169,244,000**	**38,036,000**	**49,007,000**	**5,283,000**	**4,055,484,000**	**67.0**	**238**
Atheists	420,000	121,945,000	22,922,000	2,757,000	1,680,000	365,000	150,089,000	2.5	161
Baha'is	1,733,000	3,475,000	130,000	873,000	786,000	110,000	7,107,000	0.1	218
Buddhists	134,000	354,651,000	1,547,000	647,000	2,701,000	301,000	359,981,000	5.9	126
Chinese folk religionists	32,000	383,408,000	255,000	194,000	854,000	64,000	384,807,000	6.4	89
Confucianists	0	6,264,000	11,000	0	0	24,000	6,299,000	0.1	15
Ethnic religionists	96,805,000	128,298,000	1,263,000	1,288,000	444,000	268,000	228,366,000	3.8	142
Hindus	2,351,000	805,120,000	1,416,000	768,000	1,327,000	355,000	811,337,000	13.4	114
Jains	66,000	4,145,000	0	0	7,000	0	4,218,000	0.1	10
Jews	214,000	4,429,000	2,527,000	1,142,000	6,024,000	97,000	14,433,000	0.2	134
Mandeans	0	39,000	0	0	0	0	39,000	0.0	2
Muslims	317,374,000	832,879,000	31,566,000	1,672,000	4,450,000	301,000	1,188,242,000	19.6	204
New-Religionists	28,000	100,639,000	158,000	623,000	842,000	66,000	102,356,000	1.7	60
Shintoists	0	2,699,000	0	7,000	56,000	0	2,762,000	0.0	8
Sikhs	53,000	22,421,000	239,000	0	528,000	18,000	23,259,000	0.4	34
Spiritists	3,000	2,000	133,000	12,039,000	151,000	7,000	12,335,000	0.2	55
Zoroastrians	1,000	2,463,000	1,000	0	78,000	1,000	2,544,000	0.0	24
Other religionists	5,092,000	611,262,000	107,076,000	16,026,000	29,079,000	3,306,000	771,841,000	12.7	76
Nonreligious	5,024,000	608,594,000	106,841,000	15,928,000	28,473,000	3,298,000	768,158,000	12.7	236
Total population	**784,445,000**	**3,682,550,000**	**728,887,000**	**519,138,000**	**309,631,000**	**30,393,000**	**6,055,044,000**	**100.0**	**238**

Continents. These follow current UN demographic terminology, which now divides the world into the six major areas shown above. *See* United Nations, *World Population Prospects: The 1998 Revision* (New York: UN, 1999), with populations of all continents, regions, and countries covering the period 1950–2050. Note that "Asia" now includes the former Soviet Central Asian states and "Europe" now includes all of Russia extending eastward to Vladivostok, the Sea of Japan, and the Bering Strait.
Countries. The last column enumerates sovereign and nonsovereign countries in which each religion or religious grouping has a numerically significant and organized following.
Adherents. As defined in the 1948 Universal Declaration of Human Rights, a person's religion is what he or she says it is. Totals are enumerated for each of the world's 238 countries following the methodology of the *World Christian Encyclopedia,* 2nd ed. (2000), using recent censuses, polls, literature, and other data.
Christians. Followers of Jesus Christ affiliated with churches (church members, including children: 1,888,437,000) plus persons professing in censuses or polls to be Christians though not so affiliated. Figures for the subgroups of Christians do not add up to the totals in the first line because some Christians adhere to more than one denomination.
Other Christians. This term in the table denotes Catholics (non-Roman), marginal Protestants, independents, postdenominationalists, crypto-Christians, and adherents of African, Asian, Black, and Latin American indigenous churches.
Atheists. Persons professing atheism, skepticism, disbelief, or irreligion, including the antireligious (opposed to all religion).
Buddhists. 56% Mahayana, 38% Theravada (Hinayana), 6% Tantrayana (Lamaism).
Chinese folk-religionists. Followers of traditional Chinese religion (local deities, ancestor veneration, Confucian ethics, Taoism, universism, divination, and some Buddhist elements).
Confucianists. Non-Chinese followers of Confucius and Confucianism, mostly Koreans in Korea.
Ethnic religionists. Followers of local, tribal, animistic, or shamanistic religions.
Hindus. 70% Vaishnavites, 25% Shaivites, 2% neo-Hindus and reform Hindus.
Jews. Adherents of Judaism. For detailed data on "core" Jewish population, *see* the annual "World Jewish Populations" article in the American Jewish Committee's *American Jewish Year Book.*
Muslims. 83% Sunnites, 16% Shi'ites, 1% other schools. Until 1990 the Muslims in the former U.S.S.R. who had embraced communism were not included as Muslims in this table. After the collapse of communism in 1990–91, these Muslims were once again enumerated as Muslims if they had returned to Islamic profession and practice.
New-Religionists. Followers of Asian 20th-century New Religions, New Religious movements, radical new crisis religions, and non-Christian syncretistic mass religions, all founded since 1800 and most since 1945.
Other religionists. Including 70 minor world religions and more than 10,000 national or local religions and a large number of spiritist religions, New Age religions, quasi religions, pseudoreligions, parareligions, religious or mystic systems, and religious and semireligious brotherhoods of numerous varieties.
Nonreligious. Persons professing no religion, nonbelievers, agnostics, freethinkers, or dereligionized secularists indifferent to all religion.
Total Population. UN medium variant figures for mid-2000, as given in *World Population Prospects: The 1998 Revision.*

OGRAPHIES), the first Jewish candidate on a major national ticket, stirred criticism from leaders of groups including Americans United for Separation of Church and State and the Anti-Defamation League for stating in August at a black church in Detroit that "there must be a place for faith in America's public life."

Cults. At least 500 members of a Ugandan group called the Movement for the Restoration of the Ten Commandments were found dead in several locations after having been killed by fire, poisoning, and strangulation. It appeared that the group's founder, former Roman Catholic catechist Joseph Kibwetere, and its "prophetess," Credonia Mwerinde, had carried out the murders and then had escaped. A public commission in Japan ruled in January that the AUM Shinrikyo (Supreme Truth) sect that killed 12 people in a nerve gas attack in the Tokyo subway in 1995 continued to pose a threat to society and would be put under surveillance for up to three years. The group announced that it was changing its name to Aleph, the first letter of the Hebrew alphabet.

Places and Personalities. A 21,000-seat conference centre opened in Salt Lake City, Utah, in April by the Church of Jesus Christ of Latter-day Saints was believed to be the largest dedicated space for worship in the world. The church opened its 100th temple, and its worldwide membership passed 11 million during the year. Meanwhile, the Reorganized Church of Jesus Christ of

Religious Adherents in the United States of America, AD 1900–2000

	Year 1900	%	mid-1970	%	mid-1990	%	Annual Change, 1990–1995 Natural	Conversion	Total	Rate (%)	mid-1995	%	mid-2000	%
Christians	**73,270,000**	**96.4**	**191,182,000**	**91.0**	**217,719,000**	**85.7**	**2,218,400**	**-245,000**	**1,973,400**	**0.89**	**227,586,000**	**85.2**	**235,742,000**	**84.6**
Affiliated Christians	54,425,000	71.6	153,299,000	73.0	175,820,000	69.2	1,791,400	-107,000	1,684,400	0.94	184,242,000	69.0	191,828,000	68.8
Roman Catholics	10,775,000	14.2	48,305,000	23.0	56,500,000	22.2	575,700	-532,700	43,000	0.08	56,715,000	21.2	58,000,000	20.8
Protestants	35,000,000	46.1	58,568,000	27.9	60,216,000	23.7	613,500	-151,700	461,800	0.76	62,525,000	23.4	64,570,000	23.2
Anglicans	1,600,000	2.1	3,196,000	1.5	2,450,000	1.0	25,000	-26,000	-1,000	-0.04	2,445,000	0.9	2,400,000	0.9
Orthodox	400,000	0.5	4,163,000	2.0	5,150,000	2.0	52,500	11,900	64,400	1.22	5,472,000	2.0	5,762,000	2.1
Independents	5,850,000	7.7	35,645,000	17.0	66,900,000	26.3	681,600	527,000	1,208,600	1.74	72,943,000	27.3	78,550,000	28.2
Marginal Christians	800,000	1.1	6,126,000	2.9	8,940,000	3.5	91,100	21,300	112,400	1.23	9,502,000	3.6	10,080,000	3.6
Multiple affiliation	0	0.0	-2,704,000	-1.3	-24,336,000	-9.6	-248,000	43,200	-204,800	0.83	-25,360,000	-9.5	-27,534,000	-9.9
Evangelicals	*32,068,000*	*42.2*	*31,516,000*	*15.0*	*37,349,000*	*14.7*	*380,600*	*12,400*	*393,000*	*1.03*	*39,314,000*	*14.7*	*40,640,000*	*14.6*
evangelicals	*11,000,000*	*14.5*	*45,500,000*	*21.7*	*87,656,000*	*34.5*	*893,100*	*267,100*	*1,160,200*	*1.29*	*93,457,000*	*35.0*	*98,662,000*	*35.4*
Unaffiliated Christians	18,845,000	24.8	37,883,000	18.0	41,899,000	16.5	426,900	-137,900	289,000	0.68	43,344,000	16.2	43,914,000	15.8
Non-Christians	**2,725,000**	**3.6**	**18,929,000**	**9.0**	**36,357,000**	**14.3**	**370,400**	**245,000**	**615,400**	**1.64**	**39,434,000**	**14.8**	**42,915,000**	**15.4**
Atheists	1,000	0.0	200,000	0.1	770,000	0.3	7,800	28,200	36,000	4.29	950,000	0.4	1,150,000	0.4
Baha'is	3,000	0.0	138,000	0.1	600,000	0.2	6,100	10,300	16,400	2.60	682,000	0.3	753,000	0.3
Buddhists	30,000	0.0	200,000	0.1	1,880,000	0.7	19,200	34,800	54,000	2.72	2,150,000	0.8	2,450,000	0.9
Chinese folk religionists	70,000	0.1	90,000	0.0	76,000	0.0	800	-600	200	0.26	77,000	0.0	78,000	0.0
Hindus	1,000	0.0	100,000	0.0	750,000	0.3	7,600	28,400	36,000	4.40	930,000	0.3	1,032,000	0.4
Jews	1,500,000	2.0	6,700,000	3.2	5,535,000	2.2	56,400	-43,400	13,000	0.23	5,600,000	2.1	5,621,000	2.0
Muslims	10,000	0.0	800,000	0.4	3,560,000	1.4	36,300	16,700	53,000	1.45	3,825,000	1.4	4,132,000	1.5
Black Muslims	0	0.0	200,000	0.1	1,250,000	0.5	12,700	17,300	30,000	2.29	1,400,000	0.5	1,650,000	0.6
New-Religionists	0	0.0	110,000	0.1	575,000	0.2	5,900	17,100	23,000	3.71	690,000	0.3	811,000	0.3
Sikhs	0	0.0	1,000	0.0	160,000	0.1	1,600	4,800	6,400	3.71	192,000	0.1	234,000	0.1
Ethnic religionists	100,000	0.1	70,000	0.0	280,000	0.1	2,900	18,500	21,400	6.69	387,000	0.1	435,000	0.2
Other religionists	10,000	0.0	450,000	0.2	757,000	0.3	7,700	1,100	8,800	1.1	801,000	0.3	1,141,000	0.4
Nonreligious	1,000,000	1.3	10,070,000	4.8	21,414,000	8.4	218,200	129,000	347,200	1.57	23,150,000	8.7	25,078,000	9.0
Total population	**75,995,000**	**100.0**	**210,111,000**	**100.0**	**254,076,000**	**100.0**	**2,807,000**	**129,000**	**2,936,000**	**1.00**	**267,020,000**	**100.0**	**278,657,000**	**100.0**

Methodology. This table extracts and analyzes a microcosm of the world religion table. It depicts the United States, the country with the largest number of adherents to Christianity, the world's largest religion. Statistics at five points in time across the 20th century are presented. Each religion's *Annual change* is also analyzed by *Natural* increase (births minus deaths, plus immigrants minus emigrants) per year and *Conversion* increase (new converts minus new defectors) per year, which together constitute the *Total* increase per year. *Rate* increase is then computed as percentage per year.

Structure. Vertically the table lists 27 major religious categories. The major religions (including nonreligion) in the U.S. are listed with largest (Christians) first and Other religionists and Nonreligious last. Indented names of groups in the "Adherents" column are subcategories of the groups above them and are also counted in these unindented totals, so they should not be added twice into the column total. Figures in italics draw adherents from all categories of Christians above and so cannot be added together with them. Figures for Christians in 1970, 1990, and 1995 are built upon detailed head counts by churches, often to the last digit. Totals are then rounded to the nearest 1,000. Because of rounding, the corresponding percentage figures may sometimes not total exactly 100%. Figures for AD 2000 are projections based on current trends.

Christians. All persons who profess publicly to follow Jesus Christ as Lord and Saviour. This category is subdivided into **Affiliated Christians** (church members) and **Unaffiliated** (nominal) **Christians** (professing Christians not affiliated with any church). *See also* the note on Christians to the world religion table above.

Evangelicals/evangelicals. These two designations—italicized and enumerated separately here—cut across all of the six Christian traditions listed above and should be considered separately from them. **Evangelicals** are Protestant churches, agencies, and individuals that call themselves by this term (for example, members of the National Organization of Evangelicals); they usually emphasize 5 or more of 7, 9, or 21 fundamental doctrines (salvation by faith, personal acceptance, verbal inspiration of Scripture, depravity of man, Virgin Birth, miracles of Christ, atonement, evangelism, Second Advent, et al.). The **evangelicals** are Christians from all traditions who are committed to the evangel (gospel) and involved in personal witness and mission in the world.

Independents. Members of churches and networks that regard themselves as postdenominationalist and neo-apostolic and thus independent of historic, organized, institutionalized, denominationalist Christianity.

Marginal Christians. Members of denominations on the margins of organized mainstream Christianity (Mormons, Jehovah's Witnesses, Christian Science, Religious Science).

Non-Christians. Followers of non-Christian religions or, in the case of **Nonreligious**, no religion.

Jews. Core Jewish population relating to Judaism, excluding Jewish persons professing a different religion.

Other categories. Definitions are as given above under the world religion table.

(DAVID B. BARRETT; TODD M. JOHNSON)

Latter-day Saints voted to change its name to Community of Christ. Louis Farrakhan, leader of the Nation of Islam, publicly reconciled in February with W. Deen Mohammed, leader of the Muslim American Society and son of the late Elijah Muhammad. Farrakhan later apologized to Attallah Shabazz, the eldest daughter of Malcolm X, for any role he may have played in prompting Nation of Islam followers to assassinate her father in 1965. The first crematorium in North America designed specifically for Sikhs and Hindus opened in Delta, B.C. The $6 million facility was large enough to permit up to 2,000 people to watch a corpse burn to ashes.

Doctrine. Several religious groups grappled with doctrinal matters during the year. In October former U.S. president Jimmy Carter severed his ties to the denomination because of what he called its "increasingly rigid" doctrines, and the Baptist General Convention of Texas, the denomination's largest statewide body, voted to cut $5 million from its support of seminaries and other Southern Baptist agencies. The Alliance of Baptists, which was formed in 1987 by Southern Baptist dissidents, became the 36th member communion of the National Council of Churches in November. The Southern Baptist Convention revised its statement of faith, the Baptist Faith and Message, for the first time since 1963, replacing the assertion that Jesus is "the criterion by which the Bible is to be interpreted" with a statement that "all Scripture is a testimony to Christ, who is himself the focus of divine revelation." A new rule adopted by Jehovah's Witness leaders said that members who accepted blood transfusions would no longer be actively excommunicated, or "disfellowshipped," but would be judged to have voluntarily "disassociated" themselves from the group.

The Evangelical Alliance of the United Kingdom issued a report declaring that the reality of hell as a place of eternal punishment is "the dominant understanding" among evangelical Christians. At the same time, it acknowledged a growing belief among evangelicals in "conditionalism," according to which sinners would be annihilated after judgment. The General Assembly of the Presbyterian Church in America declared that differences of opinion on the length of days of the creation were "acceptable as long as the full historicity of the Creation account is accepted." In May the Vatican announced that the so-called Third Secret of Fátima, revealed to three shepherd children by the Virgin Mary in Portugal in 1917, was a prophecy of a "time of tribulation" for Christianity and the attempted assassination of the pope in 1981.

John Paul II's beatifications of two of his predecessors, Pius IX and John XXIII, brought the total in his 22-year papacy to more than 1,700—the largest number of any pope. In August leaders of the Russian Orthodox Church bestowed sainthood on the nation's last tsar, Nicholas II, his wife and five children, and more than 800 other 20th-century martyrs.

At a conference on the nature of God, held in February at Oregon State University (OSU), seven speakers from three religious traditions described the developing image of a God who was mystical rather than supernatural. According to OSU religion professor Marcus Borg, "They described God as a presence that pervades everything." Freeman J. Dyson, a professor emeritus at the Institute for Advanced Study in Princeton, N.J., was awarded the $948,000 Templeton Prize for Progress in Religion for his writing on the meaning of science and its relation to other disciplines, including religion and ethics. (*See* BIOGRAPHIES.)

(DARRELL J. TURNER)

AP/Wide World Photos

Muslim pilgrims perform afternoon prayers in the shadow of the Grand Mosque in Mecca, Saudi Arabia, on March 13.

Social Protection

Major issues receiving attention in 2000 included the debate over **SOCIAL SECURITY** in the U.S., concern about Canada's strained **HEALTH CARE SYSTEM**, international indictments against **WAR CRIMINALS**, and the plights of **REFUGEES** around the globe.

BENEFITS AND PROGRAMS

In 2000 many countries were concerned about the long-term stability of the various social protection programs. Public debate, reform proposals, and actual reforms were guided by this concern. The pros and cons of the involvement of private elements in public social protection schemes were discussed, and governments and social security administrators continued their efforts to modernize schemes. New approaches, including new technology, were used to improve welfare delivery and to promote fairness and opportunity.

North America. Election-year pressures in 2000 generally dictated social protection activity in the United States. Though a torrent of proposals and much debate occurred, lawmakers postponed passing most new legislation in the partisan-divided Congress.

Two of the strongest threads in the social safety net—Social Security and Medicare—were among the top issues of the presidential campaign; candidates pushed ideas that reflected their respective parties' views of public versus private responsibility. Both Medicare and Social Security received good news early in the year when new projections indicated that they were in better financial shape than had been thought. Trustees of the Medicare Hospital Insurance Trust Fund estimated that Medicare would be solvent until 2023, eight years longer than they reported previously. It was the longest solvency projection for Medicare since 1975. Social Security trustees extended the solvency projection from 2034 to 2037; even if no action was taken, Social Security would be able to pay all promised benefits until 2037 and 72% of promised benefits after that date. Behind the revised projections were the continued strong economy and, in the case of Medicare, government efforts to contain costs and eliminate waste and fraud. Despite the improved outlook, both programs continued to face problems, especially as 76 million baby boomers headed into retirement over the next few decades, with increased life expectancy and soaring health care costs. Social Security, for example, would begin paying out more in benefits than it received from payroll taxes in 2015, and Medicare was expected to reach that tipping point in 2010.

The better-than-expected outlook did not halt all efforts in Congress to make changes in the programs. The most significant new legislation was a repeal of the earnings limit for Social Security recipients over age 65. By an overwhelming vote, Congress ended the practice of deferring Social Security benefits for people aged 65 through 69 who continued to work and earned more than a defined threshold of income each year.

Aside from this, however, most action took place on the presidential campaign trail. Texas Gov. George W. Bush, the Republican nominee, proposed a major shift in Social Security from a program of government-guaranteed benefits to one in which private markets and investment risks would be involved. The Bush plan would allow young workers to divert some of their payroll taxes into private savings accounts through which they could invest in stocks and bonds.

Democratic nominee Vice Pres. Al Gore supported a less-radical change in which the federal government would match contributions from eligible individuals with tax credits that varied according to a person's income. Gore proposed to use excess payroll tax revenue—an estimated $2.4 trillion over 10 years—to pay down the national debt, arguing that this would bolster the economy and make it easier to meet future Social Security needs. A number of bipartisan groups also recommended moving toward private accounts, but most plans guaranteed a minimum benefit to make sure that recipients did not fall into poverty. Still others suggested dealing with the looming threat to Social Security's solvency by raising the retirement age and/or payroll taxes or by lowering benefits. The retirement age was already slated to rise from 65 to 67 in slow incremental stages.

When it came to Medicare, both major party candidates offered plans to deal with a widely recognized shortcoming in the program—the lack of coverage for prescription drugs, which was the fastest-growing form of health care costs in the United States. Almost one-third of Medicare recipients had no drug coverage; the other two-thirds bought private insurance or received drug coverage through Medicaid (the federal-state health care program for the poor) or "medigap" plans that supplemented Medicare.

As with Social Security, the Republican plan would involve the private sector, creating a system in which private insurance companies competed with the government to provide coverage for beneficiaries. The elderly could use government subsidies to purchase government-approved private insurance, including drug coverage, or stay in Medicare. The plan proposed by the Democrats earmarked $253 billion over 10 years to add prescription drug benefits to Medicare.

Another continuing health care issue was how to help those who had no health insurance. The U.S. Census Bureau reported that after rising for 11 years, the number of people who lacked health insurance fell from 16.3% of the population in 1998 to 15.5% in 1999, primarily as a result of government programs such as Medicaid and the State Children's Health Insurance Program (SCHIP) for youngsters whose families could not afford private insurance but made too much money to qualify for Medicaid. That left, however, an estimated 42.6 million Americans, including about 10 million children, without insurance. A report released by the Institute of Medicine, part of the National Research Council, warned that health care assistance for the poor provided through sources such as local clinics, public hospitals, and charitable organizations was overburdened and

AP/Wide World Photos

During a news conference on July 25, Mississippi Gov. Ronnie Musgrove announces plans to enroll more than 85,000 eligible children in a free health insurance program.

underfunded and could collapse without more money and attention. Gore proposed spending $146 billion over 10 years to expand SCHIP. Bush's solution was to use $75 billion over the same period for tax credits to help people buy private insurance. Congress considered some legislation dealing with the uninsured, but most of it did not pass.

As welfare reform marked its fourth anniversary, the Department of Health and Human Services reported that the rolls continued to shrink—to 2.4 million families at the end of 1999, compared with 2.7 million at the start of that year; the number had stood at 4.6 million when the overhaul was enacted in 1996. The report revealed that for the third straight year every state had met standards required by law for the proportion of welfare recipients who were working or preparing for a job. Independent studies found that those left on the rolls increasingly were minorities and children who did not live with their parents.

With Congress slow to move in the social welfare field, Pres. Bill Clinton took some actions on his own. To combat the tight housing market in big cities, he announced that the federal government would increase the value of subsidies given to low-income renters under the "Section 8" housing program, one of the government's largest housing programs, serving three million households. The Department of Housing and Urban Development reported that a record 5.4 million low-income renters paid more than half their incomes for rent or lived in "seriously distressed" housing.

Clinton also announced help for community and faith-based organizations to expand facilities where teenage mothers could receive support. The government reported that teen birthrates were down in 1999 for the eighth straight year—dropping to 49.6 births per 1,000 women aged 15 to 19, the lowest level in the 60 years the data had been kept.

There was other encouraging news about the segment of the population at whom most social programs were aimed. A Census Bureau report in September noted a decline in the percentage of Americans living in poverty. According to the report, 2.2 million households moved above the poverty level (defined as $17,029 for a family of four) in 1999, and the proportion of those living in poverty fell from 12.7% in 1998 to 11.8% in 1999—the lowest point in more than two decades. Seven states and the District of Columbia registered declines in poverty population, while none had a statistically significant rise. A separate study by the National Center for Children in Poverty, a nonpartisan research centre at Columbia University, New York City, found that the child poverty rate fell significantly in a few states. It also revealed, however, that in most states and in the country as a whole, child poverty was higher in 1998—the last year for which figures were available—than in 1979.

In Canada too the main concern was the country's strained health care system. After nearly a year of wrangling about financing and reforming health care, federal and provincial ministers agreed on a plan in September. Under the compromise, the federal government would restore more than Can$5 billion (Can$1.48=$1) a year in contributions to health and social programs by 2005, bringing its transfers to $21 billion annually. In addition, Ottawa would provide Can$1 billion for medical equipment and Can$800 million for health care reform. Federal transfer payments to the provinces had been cut in 1995 in an effort to eliminate the deficit, and this caused the Canada Health and Social Transfer block fund to fall to Can$11 billion in 1996. The debate over what to do included a push by Health Minister Allan Rock for a new home-care program that would relieve hospitals. In the end, the ministers settled for a plan that gave provinces more money to keep the existing system going and did not change federal and state jurisdictions. For their part, provinces gave up demands for automatic yearly increases tied to economic factors. In another area Canada's employment insurance rules were altered to extend parental leave from 10 to 35 weeks. The benefits were available to either the mother or the father.

Europe. Concern about the long-term financial viability of Belgium's old-age scheme led the Belgian budget minister to propose creating a reserve fund for the partial financing of social security retirement pensions. In Ireland legislation was introduced to establish a National Pensions Reserve Fund to partially fund the future cost of pensions. Ireland also discussed the creation of personal retirement savings accounts.

In Slovenia legislation paved the way for the establishment of second- and third-pillar pension schemes; meanwhile, the existing system underwent a major reform to stabilize it for the future. A voluntary pension-fund program could not be implemented as planned in Lithuania owing to inadequate funds to set up a regulatory regime. In Croatia a pension law enacted in June delayed the implementation of the reform process that had been put in place in May 1999. It was considered that extra time was needed to build the necessary infrastructure for the replacement of the existing pay-as-you-go system with a three-pillar system that would include voluntary forms of saving.

In Germany tax-reform legislation—which had been considered a precondition for pension reform—was enacted in July and substantially reduced personal and company taxes. Consensus was not yet reached, however, on a proposed pension reform that would introduce a funded pension component. Tax reform in Austria created new opportunities for taxpayers to add a tax-efficient third pillar to their old-age provision, such as a voluntary supplementary insurance within the framework of the statutory pension scheme. A new flat-rate tax plan, designed to combat tax evasion by strengthening the collection process, was signed into law in Russia. The Tax Ministry was given the authority to assess a single social tax, including payments to the state-operated retirement, unemployment, and health insurance programs. Previously these programs had been administered by separate entities that collected their own contributions.

The future of the entire social security system was heatedly debated in France among the social partners. Throughout much of the year, MEDEF, the employers federation, threatened to withdraw from the comanagement of the country's social protection programs. It sought changes that would make French companies more competitive in world markets and protested against certain regulations in relation to the introduction of a 35-hour workweek. The situation became particularly difficult when in July the government refused to ratify an agreement between the employers federation and the two main private-sector unions concerning a radical reform of unemployment insurance; an appeal was denied in August. The large public-sector unions would not sign the agreement, and the government was concerned about the creation of a "two-speed" unemployment insurance, in which a distinction would be made between people who easily found a new job and those who were penalized for refusing unattractive job offers.

Many European countries also attempted to contain costs to keep health systems viable. Liechtenstein made it mandatory for health insurers to offer their clients a "family doctor system," in which people who limited their free choice of doctor and agreed to see the family physician first would pay reduced insurance premiums. The Hungarian National Assembly passed a health-reform plan involving privatization. The first step would be to allow Hungary's family doctors to buy their practices. Germany's Health Reform 2000 turned out less comprehensive than initially intended. It proved impossible to reach agreement on such points as the overall budget and organizational reform of the associations regrouping physicians under the social health insurance system. The main changes were in entitlement to benefits and compulsory insurance and contributions. In addition, the federal Ministry of Health was empowered to give out a list of prescription-approved medicines. In The Netherlands, system stability was sought by an increase in the insurance base. The social health insurance that covered employees was extended in January to the self-employed. (*See also* HEALTH AND DISEASE: *Special Report.*)

Industrialized Asia and the Pacific. Australia began overhauling its welfare system. Following consultations across the country, a Reference Group on Welfare Reform proposed the establish-

AP/Wide World Photos

A warehouse worker turns a wheel of Beaufort cheese in St. Sorlin d'Arves, France. French trade union members were concerned about their unemployment insurance in 2000.

ment of a system with the following features: individualized service delivery; a simpler income support structure that would be more responsive to individual needs and circumstances; incentives and targeted assistance to encourage and enable participation; social partnerships, including a role for employers and communities; and mutual obligations, with sanctions applied, as a last resort, to noncomplying income-support recipients. The Australian government also continued its efforts to reduce future spending on public health care. Under a Lifetime Health Cover program, favourable premiums were offered beginning in July to people who took out insurance for treatment in private hospitals; low premiums were guaranteed for life if the insurance was uninterrupted.

A management-consolidation process in the health sector in South Korea culminated in July; the National Health Insurance Corp. became the sole insurer in the national health insurance system. At its peak the system had been operated by 500 insurers who separately took care of the health insurance needs of different types of workers.

New Zealand reversed its policy on workers' compensation. Less than one year after the workers' compensation market had been privatized, the state Accident Rehabilitation and Compensation Insurance Corporation (ACC) was reinstated as the sole provider of workplace accident insurance. The Accredited Employers Programme was also revived; under that plan larger employers with good injury-prevention records and rehabilitation systems could accrue some of the risk themselves, in return for cheaper ACC levies.

Beginning in April, Japan embarked on another reform of its pension system. The main objective of the new reform, which would be implemented in stages, was to ensure that the existing public pension system could be maintained in the future while at the same time avoiding a sharp increase in contributions. It was decided, inter alia, to reduce benefits, to make workers between 65 and 69 years of age pay contributions beginning in 2002, to gradually raise the retirement age from 60 to 65 (between the years 2013 and 2025 for men and between 2018 and 2030 for women), and to increase the government subsidy to the National Pension scheme.

Emerging and Less-Developed Countries. An unfavourable economic environment led to financial imbalances and adversely affected a number of social protection systems in Africa and Asia. Nonetheless, reform efforts were made to extend benefits and coverage and to provide better service delivery.

In Cameroon—where some 10% of the population was covered by a system providing old-age, disability, and survivors' benefits, as well as family allowances and benefits in the event of occupational accidents and diseases—authorities discussed ways in which to extend coverage. Measures included the introduction of new insurance branches and, in the area of pension insurance, a movement toward a mixed system—pay-as-you-go coupled with funding. With inflation running above 50%, Zimbabwe had plans to raise the contribution ceiling under the Pension and Other Benefits Scheme so that benefits could also be adapted. The South African Ministry of Labour introduced a draft law to broaden the insurance base and extend the benefits paid by the Unemployment Insurance Fund.

Minimum pensions payable under the Employees Old-Age Benefits Institution were increased by almost 50% in Pakistan. The Social Security Organization of Iran started to systematically assess its health care centres to improve services and contain costs.

The Gulf States began requiring expatriates to contribute to the health care system. Kuwait implemented legislation to this effect starting in February. In Bahrain the government was studying ways in which to recover the full cost of health services provided to foreigners. Saudi Arabia announced that its new compulsory health insurance scheme for foreigners would come into effect in early 2001.

The Latin American countries continued to experiment with totally or partially privatized retirement pensions. In Chile the introduction of "Second Funds" under the Pension Fund Administrators (AFPs) was announced. These were aimed at older AFP members (people within 10 years of retirement age) who were seeking more stable investments. Second Funds' assets were to be invested only in medium-term fixed-interest securities. Ecuador was considering introducing a mixed-pension scheme, partly pay-as-you-go and partly capital funded, with mandatory participation in both components. In Venezuela, where a 1998 framework law that paved the way for the privatization of the country's social security system had never been implemented, the establishment of a mixed system was also discussed, but not before a large budget had been set aside in January to help sustain and restore the Venezuelan Social Security Institute.

(CHRISTIANE KUPTSCH;
DAVID M. MAZIE)

HUMAN RIGHTS

Major issues receiving attention during 2000 were criminal accountability, gender-based abuses, self-determination of minority groups, and economic and social rights in the context of growing demands for changes in the loan and trade policies of international financial institutions in regard to the less-developed world. Particularly notable were two newly emerging approaches and methods for human rights enforcement. First, the criminal proceedings in the United Kingdom and Spain against former Pres. Augusto Pinochet Ugarte of Chile helped to establish the principle that every nation in the world, not just the specially constituted international criminal tribunals, was authorized to take legal action against torturers and other major human rights abusers. Second, mass public demonstrations in the U.S. and Europe protesting the financial practices of the World Bank and other international lending and trade-regulation institutions focused significant worldwide attention, for the first time, on economic and social aspects of human rights.

War Crimes and Crimes Against Humanity. War crimes and other major human rights abuses and the accompanying principle of "universal jurisdiction"—the responsibility of every nation to ensure that torturers and other persecutors are prosecuted and punished—were prominently featured in human rights developments throughout the year. Building on the international criminal indictments against war criminals engaged in ethnic cleansing and genocide in Bosnia and Herzegovina and Rwanda in recent years, the international community expanded the concept of criminal accountability by applying it to the abuses that occurred in Kosovo (a province of Serbia, Yugos.), East Timor (a former Indonesian province under UN administration), Cambodia, and Sierra Leone and by proceeding toward the establishment of a permanent International Criminal Court to provide criminal penalties for major abuses wherever they might occur in the future.

The movement in support of criminal accountability also received substantial support from the decision by the Law

Lords of the U.K.'s House of Lords that Pinochet was subject to criminal extradition to Spain for acts of torture and other atrocities committed during his regime. The Pinochet decision set in motion a new method for holding human rights abusers accountable—the initiation of criminal proceedings by individual governments under international human rights treaties, such as the Convention Against Torture, without requiring the establishment of special international criminal tribunals. As a result of the Pinochet precedent, criminal cases against human rights abusers were filed (or considered) in a number of countries during the year, including the prosecution in Senegal of the former dictator of Chad, Hissène Habré; the arrest in Mexico of Ricardo Miguel Cavallo, who supervised a "torture chamber" in Argentina during the period of Argentina's military dictatorship; and the continued investigation of former Argentine dictator Jorge Videla and nine other leaders of the "dirty war" in that country.

Notable with regard to the development of criminal accountability was the upholding of the first official verdict by an international court (the International Criminal Tribunal for the Former Yugoslavia) that rape and other gender-based abuses occurring in the context of situations of armed conflict can constitute crimes against humanity. Anto Furundzija, a commander of a Bosnian Croat military police unit, had been convicted in 1998 of having failed to intervene to stop a knife-wielding subordinate from torturing and raping a female prisoner. The concept that those types of gender-based sexual abuses are war crimes was also embodied in the statutes of the International Criminal Tribunals for the former Yugoslavia and for Rwanda and in the future International Criminal Court, which would be formally established following ratification by 60 countries.

Equally groundbreaking in criminal accountability efforts was the first subpoena issued against Western armed forces by a war crimes tribunal. The International Criminal Tribunal for the Former Yugoslavia summoned U.S. Army Chief of Staff Gen. Eric Shinseki, former commander of the NATO forces in Bosnia and Herzegovina, to a pending hearing to inquire into unlawful arrest and abductions of suspected war criminals, while the World Court was asked to look at possible war crimes and crimes against humanity relating to alleged NATO bombings of Serbian civilian targets in connection with the Kosovo campaign.

Reuters NewMedia Inc./Corbis

Accused serial killer Javed Iqbal (centre) listens to court proceedings in Lahore, Pak., on March 16.

Minority Rights and Self-Determination. The growing trend of minority groups toward demanding increased autonomy and perhaps even self-determination and independence from their home governments continued to escalate throughout the year, with particularly important developments in Chechnya (the breakaway Russian republic), Kosovo, Nigeria, and The Sudan.

Chechnya renewed its battle for independence from Russia, begun in 1991 when the Soviet Union dissolved. An uneasy truce in 1996 was broken in the summer of 1999 when Chechen guerrillas launched an attack on a neighbouring province. Russia responded with a harsh military crackdown. The UN Human Rights Commission criticized Russia for "widespread and flagrant" human rights abuses committed during its most recent military campaign in Chechnya, abuses that involved "disproportionate and indiscriminate use of Russian military force, including attacks against civilians."

Kosovo, which had become the focus of massive armed conflict and human rights violations in 1999, began the slow process of recovery and movement in the direction of greater autonomy. Elections on October 28 represented the first time that the 90% ethnic Albanian population of Kosovo had been able to select its own representative government.

Nigeria experienced a growing religious conflict between the Muslim population in the northern part of the country and the predominantly Christian south. As part of a movement to reassert Islamic identity under the newly democratic government of Nigeria, eight mainly Muslim states in the northern part of the country began enforcing strict religious laws, which, among other things, barred women from working outside the home, forbade the sale or consumption of alcohol, and imposed strict penalties for violations. These developments ignited Muslim-Christian fighting in both the north and the south that killed hundreds of people and threatened Nigeria's 15-month-old democratic government of Pres. Olusegun Obasanjo. Christians in the north became concerned that they would not be allowed to practice their religion.

The Sudan, the site of a brutal and long-lasting civil war accompanied by human rights abuses, found itself subject to an even more savagely abusive conflict in the latter part of 2000. The predominantly Arabic and Muslim government began subjecting the civilian population of southern Sudan, made up primarily of black African Dinka and Nuer peoples, to almost daily aerial bombardments, aimed at denying the opposition military forces food and supplies. International humanitarian efforts in the south also became targets of attack. In addition, the Sudanese government threatened to cut off UN-sponsored humanitarian relief flights

(continued on page 312)

SPECIAL REPORT

Slavery

in the 21st Century

by Charles A. Jacobs

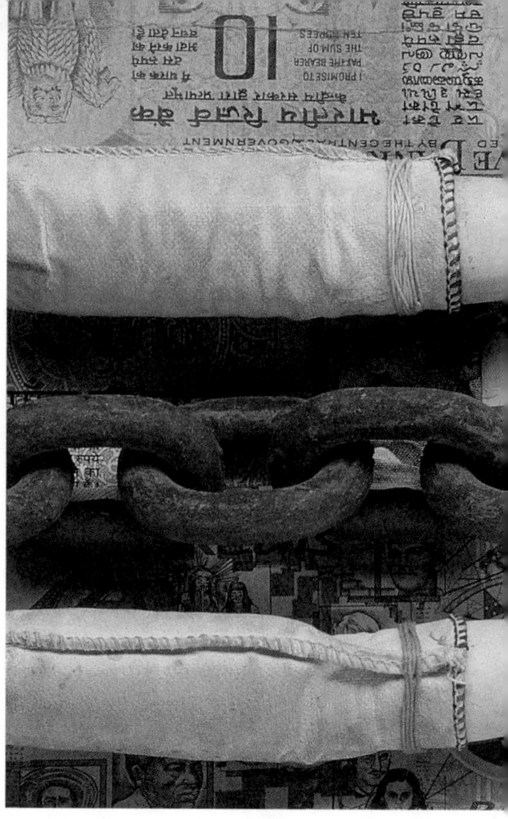

In the midst of the worldwide economic boom, reports documenting modern-day slavery come from every corner of the globe. From Bangladesh to Brazil, from India to The Sudan, and even in the U.S., there are more people enslaved today than ever before in human history. Slavery—defined strictly as forced labour for little or no pay under the threat of violence—engulfs, by conservative estimates, 27 million people.

Hidden at the underbelly of thriving global markets and often contributing to the general wealth and comfort of people around the world, contemporary slavery takes myriad forms, though most are different from the classic pattern known to Americans. The more notable—though by no means the only—cases of modern-day slavery include chattel slavery in Mauritania and The Sudan, debt bondage in Asia, and human trafficking worldwide.

Chattel Slavery in Mauritania and The Sudan. In the northwestern African country of Mauritania, chattel slavery—the owning and trading of humans—never ended. The oldest and most traditional form of slavery, chattel slavery is a vestige of the trans-Saharan slave trade in black Africans. Beginning in the 13th century, Arab-Berber raiders descended upon Mauritania's indigenous African tribes, abducted women and children, and then bred a new caste of slaves.

The raids had long ceased by 2000, but the *bedein* (white Arab masters), who disdained physical work, still hold *haratine* (black African slaves) as property. *Haratine* mothers do not own their own children; they are instead passed down through their master's estate. Slaves are bought and sold, given as wedding gifts, and traded for camels, trucks, or guns. The enslaved perform domestic work, haul water, and shepherd cattle.

El Hor (literally, "the Free"), an underground antislavery group run by former slaves, estimates that there may be as many as one million *haratine*. Hundreds of thousands more are believed to be serving nomadic *bedein* masters in Mali and Senegal, two countries that border Mauritania, and there have been reports of *haratine* being sold to masters in several Gulf states.

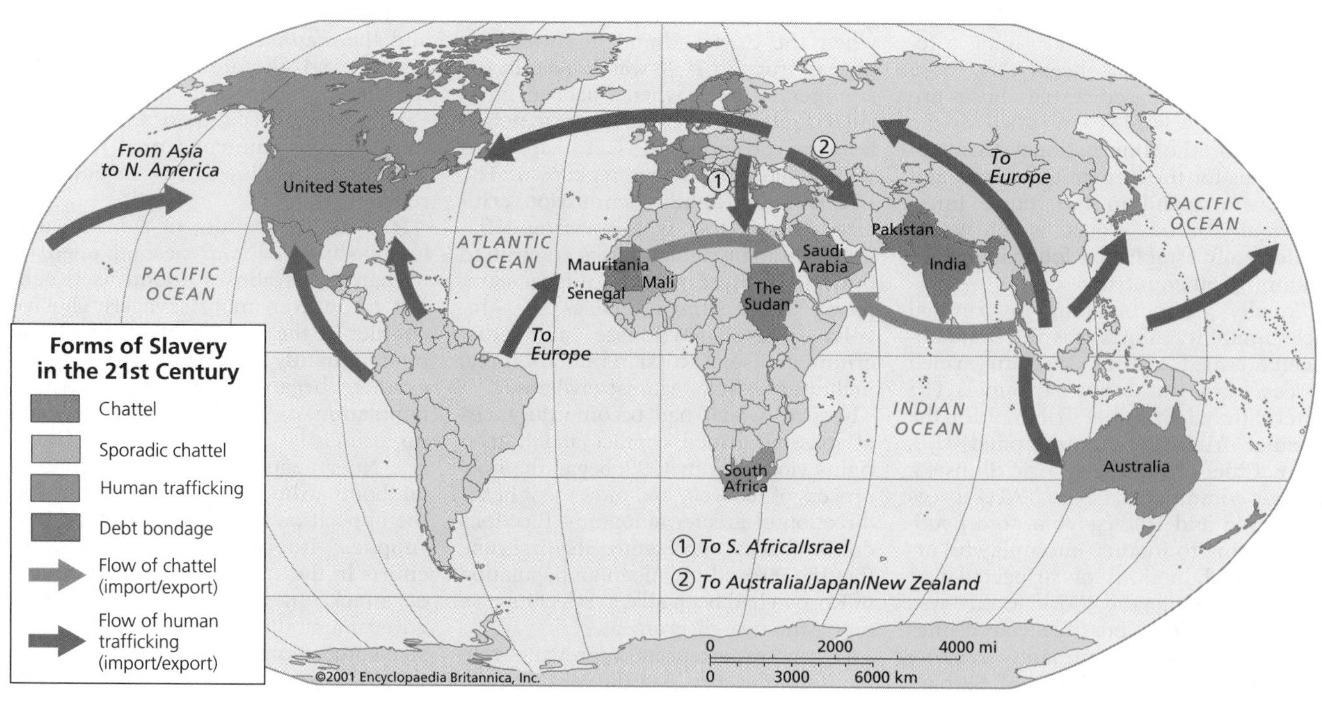

François Robert

In The Sudan, Africa's largest country in area, the black slave trade was rekindled in a brutal civil-religious conflict between Arab Muslims in the northern part of the country and African peoples in the south, who were predominantly Christians and practitioners of traditional faiths. In 1989 the fundamentalist National Islamic Front overthrew the government in Khartoum and declared a jihad, or holy war, to impose Koranic law in the south. As part of its war effort, Arab militia stormed southern villages, killed the men, and abducted the women and children. The captives were transported north, kept by the militiamen, or traded, sometimes in what the UN Special Rapporteur described as "modern-day slave markets."

One of those children taken into bondage was Francis Bok. One day when he was seven years old, his mother sent him to the market to sell the family's rice and beans. Several hundred Arabs on horseback attacked and killed many in the market. Francis was put in a donkey basket along with two little girls and taken north. He was given to a family as their slave. He was beaten with sticks daily and cursed as *abid*—"black slave" in Arabic. He was forced to live with goats and cows because, he was told, "You are an animal, like them." He was given putrid food and forced to eat it at gunpoint, to the laughter of his masters. Francis tried to escape three times. He was tortured after his first two attempts and tied with rope so that he could not move for a week. After 10 years in captivity, he finally escaped and made his way to Khartoum and then to Egypt, from which the UN sent him to the U.S. for resettlement. By 2000 he was working with the American Anti-Slavery Group in Boston to raise awareness about the plight of his people, and he testified before the U.S. Senate Foreign Relations Committee on the abuses.

Debt Bondage: Human Beings as Collateral. The most pervasive form of contemporary slavery is debt bondage, an age-old system that afflicts the poorest of the poor. In India, Pakistan, and Nepal, peasants have fallen into debt bondage from time immemorial. When a crop failed, the family breadwinner fell ill, or other circumstances arose such that people had no other choice but starvation, they borrowed money to stave off death. In return, as they had no assets, they pledged themselves.

People became bonded labourers when they leased, pawned, or sold themselves or family members to landlords or masters in return for having taken on a debt. Ostensibly, the debt could be paid off over time, but the masters charged outrageous interest and added to the debt by charging for food, medicine, and shelter. People were also born into bondage, assuming a debt taken on generations before by an unknown family member who had fallen on hard times.

Today an estimated 10 million to 15 million persons in India live in various forms of debt bondage. Millions of agricultural workers are bonded farm labourers. Much of what the bonded workers produce is exported overseas. For example, some of the tea Americans drink comes from slaves in India's Assam state. Jewelry, bricks, timber, stone, sugar, rugs, and cloth—all are produced by bonded labourers in South Asia.

Trafficking in Humans. In an illicit international trade that is beginning to rival drug trafficking, humans are being smuggled around the world to serve as slaves. New studies estimated that at least 700,000 people are trafficked each year, often by small crime syndicates. Victims are typically women, who are lured, abducted, or forced to work as prostitutes. Trafficking in humans illustrates the truly global nature of contemporary slavery. It is entirely possible for Thai women to find themselves enslaved in Paris and for Sri Lankan women to end up in bondage in New York City.

According to a CIA report published in November 1999, as many as 50,000 women and children were trafficked into the U.S. over the previous 12-month span. The report estimated that approximately 30,000 people, most of whom were women and children, were trafficked annually into the U.S. from Southeast Asia; another 10,000 came from Latin America, 4,000 from Eastern Europe and newly independent states, and 1,000 from various other regions. In one notable case, more than 50 illegal Thai immigrants were forced to sew clothing (bound for top-name retailers) in a Los Angeles sweatshop surrounded by guards and barbed wire.

The Neo-Abolitionist Movement. Former slaves such as Francis Bok represent the face of the new antislavery movement. Abolitionist groups are increasingly giving survivors of slavery a platform to tell their stories and to demand action. These survivors offer compelling testimony that inspires people of all ethnic, religious, and political backgrounds. Though, unlike in the past, abolitionists do not need to win the moral argument against slavery, the task of mobilizing the international community to address contemporary slavery seriously remains a daunting task.

Charles A. Jacobs is president of the American Anti-Slavery Group, based in Boston.

(continued from page 309)
and thereby placed thousands of civilians at risk of starvation. These abuses, together with alleged support for terrorism, resulted in The Sudan's being denied the seat in the UN Security Council that it had been slated to fill.

Economic and Social Rights. Human rights advocates, especially those in the less-developed world, urged that more attention be paid to the economic aspects of the issue. They maintained that the emerging principle of "universality" demanded that equal attention be paid to economic and social concerns, such as the right to health care, food, housing, and employment; they also stressed that violations in these areas that were occurring in the Western democracies should be addressed—that the focus should not remain almost exclusively on abuses in the less-developed nations.

In 2000, for the first time in an international context, a consistent effort was made to bring attention to a major concern in regard to economic and social rights. Public demonstrations were organized to criticize the policies and practices of the major international financial and trade-regulation agencies, such as the International Monetary Fund (IMF), the World Bank, and the World Trade Organization (WTO). Questions were raised as to whether they, and the industrialized governments of the developed world that support and control them, were doing enough to provide assistance to less-developed nations to help them meet the basic economic needs of their people and to advance economically. Advocates urged the World Bank, the IMF, the WTO, and other international institutions and their member countries to forgive or substantially reduce up to $220 billion in international loan debts that had been accumulated by poor countries that needed the funds to feed, house, and employ their own citizens. Less-developed countries also sought the lowering of trade barriers so as to give them more favourable treatment in selling their resources abroad and in obtaining products from industrialized nations at lower cost. Demonstrations began at the WTO meetings in Seattle, Wash., in November 1999, continued at IMF and World Bank meetings in Washington, D.C., in April 2000, and culminated with protests at the World Economic Forum in Melbourne, Australia, on September 11 and at the Prague Summit Meeting of the World Bank and IMF on September 26.

(MORTON SKLAR)

REFUGEES AND INTERNATIONAL MIGRATION

The number of refugees and persons of concern to the Office of the United Nations High Commissioner for Refugees (UNHCR) around the world increased slightly, from 21.5 million in 1998 to 22.3 million in 1999. The latter figure represented one out of every 269 people on Earth. Slightly more than half of them were women, and some 41% were children under 18 years old. This figure, however, did not reflect the dramatic and massive humanitarian crises that occurred during 1999. Systematic violations of human rights, failed peace negotiations or implementation of peace accords, internal strife, and, ultimately, war forced large numbers of people to flee their homes. In the case of East Timor (a former Portuguese colony that had been invaded by Indonesia in 1975) and Kosovo (a province of Serbia within Yugoslavia), the rapid exodus was reversed in a matter of months, but those displaced returned only to find their homes destroyed and the infrastructure damaged so severely that it was inadequate to support them.

Despite resurgent worldwide conflicts, solutions to refugee situations continued to be found. Repatriation remained the preferred solution in many situations, and more than 1.6 million refugees returned to their homes during 1999. Often, however, they returned to uncertainty or uneasy peace. Resettlement also continued to offer solutions for many refugees, frequently the most vulnerable. In 1999, 45,000 refugees were resettled in third countries. Several South American countries opened up as destination points for a limited number of resettled refugees. Although less frequently an option, local integration provided some refugee groups with limited opportunities to start new lives. In southern Mexico 20,000 Guatemalan refugees were expected to be fully integrated in the country and to become self-sufficient in the course of 2000. Elsewhere, however, solutions remained elusive and resulted in protracted refugee displacement that in some cases spanned decades, such as cases involving refugees from Afghanistan.

Although a cease-fire agreement was signed in May 1999, the situation in Sierra Leone remained tense. It was believed that some 2.5 million people (half of the country's population) remained beyond the reach of relief assistance. Security incidents in the area provoked the flight of over 11,000 Sierra Leonean refugees to safer parts in the south of the country. The northern part of neighbouring Liberia continued to be volatile; 8,000 Liberians left their homes for Guinea. Nevertheless, UNHCR assisted in the repatriation of nearly 38,000 Liberian refugees in 1999. Guinea hosted the largest refugee population in the West African region; care and assistance were being provided to more than half a million refugees there. The Central African Republic also received large numbers of refugees, primarily from the neighbouring Democratic Republic of the Congo (DRC).

In the Great Lakes region of Africa, despite the signing in July and August 1999 of the Lusaka cease-fire agreement between the warring parties in the DRC, the situation continued to be tense, and the potential for population movements remained high. Since the resurgence of conflict in the country in 1998, 95,000 Congolese refugees had fled to camps in Tanzania and another 25,000 to camps in Zambia. Despite continuing difficulties in Rwanda, UNHCR supported the return of over 38,000 Rwandans in 1999. At the start of 2000, Tanzania hosted more than 480,000 refugees from Burundi, the DRC, and Rwanda. In Burundi security remained precarious, and there were heightened concerns over the possibility of refugee spillover into other countries. Of the more than 300,000 refugees who had crossed into Tanzania, some 50,000 had fled between October 1999 and February 2000.

The two-year border war between Ethiopia and Eritrea had rendered thousands of civilians homeless and, in some cases, stateless. The signing of a cease-fire agreement in June 2000 led to the reopening of the border between the two countries and thereby allowed UNHCR to begin the repatriation of some 100,000 Eritrean refugees in The Sudan. UNHCR also continued to facilitate the return of Somali refugees from Djibouti, Ethiopia, and Kenya to areas considered to be safe in northwestern and northeastern Somalia. Some 70,000 refugees returned from Ethiopia and additional groups, mostly from Kenya, returned to northeastern Somalia, including 820 refugees who were airlifted from camps in Kenya.

Growing numbers of refugees and internally displaced persons (IDPs) fled intensified fighting as the 26-year war in Angola continued. Almost 20% of the inhabitants were estimated to have fled to safer areas within Angola and to countries in the region over the past several years. By August 2000 the number of IDPs was estimated at over 2.6 million. Tens of thousands of refugees also crossed into Namibia, Zambia, and the DRC.

In South America a deterioration of the Colombian conflict during 1999 led not only to massive forced displacement within the country but also to cross-border movements. An influx of some 4,000 Colombians into Venezuela and Panama raised concerns about the potential for future cross-border movements. An estimated 1,100,000 people had been displaced within Colombia, nearly 600,000 of them in the past two years.

The continuation of the armed conflict between Sri Lankan authorities and the separatist Liberation Tigers of Tamil Eelam led to further population displacements in Sri Lanka's northern provinces. By August 2000 an estimated 700,000 persons had been displaced within the country. Another 70,000 Sri Lankan refugees remained in camps in India; their repatriation hinged on a resolution of the conflict. Elsewhere in Asia, the state of 100,000 Karen and Karenni refugees from Myanmar (Burma) located in 11 camps along the border between Thailand and Myanmar remained unresolved. Some 98,000 Bhutanese refugees in eastern Nepal awaited a durable solution to their plight as the two governments entered into discussions on the modalities for their return. The saga of the Vietnamese boat people in Hong Kong came to an end in February 2000 when authorities there granted the right of abode to the remaining 1,400 Vietnamese refugees and so-called nonnationals who had begun fleeing to countries in Southeast Asia at the end of the 1980s.

The eruption of violence in East Timor following the announcement of the results of the August 1999 referendum on independence provoked the displacement of 75% of the population. Some 500,000 persons were displaced inside East Timor and another estimated 200,000 fled to West Timor and other areas of Indonesia. By mid-March 2000 over 150,000 persons had returned to East Timor from Indonesia and elsewhere. Militia groups in West Timor, however, held large numbers of refugees virtual hostage and restricted access to humanitarian agencies and the distribution of aid. Three UNHCR field-workers were brutally slain in the town of Atambua in West Timor in September 2000 by a gang of militia members. UNHCR and other humanitarian agencies withdrew their operations following the killings and left the remaining refugees to an unknown fate.

Following the new outbreak of violence within the Russian separatist republic of Chechnya in October 1999, more than 200,000 people fled into neighbouring republics, particularly Ingushetia; thousands of others escaped into Georgia and farther afield to Kazakhstan. Though several thousand Chechens returned home to parts of Chechnya under Russian control, many left again owing to continuing insecurity, the destruction of their homes, and the poor state of the general infrastructure. As of March 2000 UNHCR was providing assistance to approximately 180,000 displaced persons in Ingushetia, consisting mainly of women and children. The majority were expected to return home in the near future.

In the Balkan region a dramatic turnaround occurred following the return of ethnic Albanians to Kosovo in July 1999. Ethnic Serbs and other minorities in the province found themselves targets of attacks and persecution, and many were forced to flee. Between July 1999 and July 2000, 210,000 Serbs, Roma (Gypsies), and other ethnic non-Albanians fled in advance of the returning Albanians or were later forced to leave Kosovo. In Croatia some 10,000 Croatian Serbs (including IDPs as well as refugees) returned to their homes during the first half of 2000, almost as many as during all of 1999. Refugee returns to Bosnia and Herzegovina were also accelerated; 20,000 refugees returned to their prewar homes during the first six months of 2000.

More than a decade after the Soviet withdrawal from Afghanistan, millions of Afghan refugees continued to find refuge in camps and villages in Pakistan and Iran. In 1999 some 100,000 Afghan refugees returning from Pakistan and Iran were assisted by UNHCR. Repatriation continued throughout 2000 but was tempered by fresh displacements of people as a result of war and drought. According to respective government figures, 1.3 million refugees remained in Pakistan and more than 1.2 million remained in Iran. Afghans were the largest refugee group in the world.

(UNHCR)

Civilians in Sierra Leone flee toward the capital, Freetown, in early May to escape rebels of the Revolutionary United Front who were terrorizing rural areas in the eastern part of the country.

Issouf Sanogo/AFP Worldwide

Sports and Games

The Summer **OLYMPIC GAMES** were at the centre of attention in the world of sports in 2000, but in non-Olympic sports, standouts such as golfers **TIGER WOODS** and **KARRIE WEBB** and football quarterback **KURT WARNER** also attracted worldwide interest.

Scandals involving the International Olympic Committee (IOC) and its site-selection process gave way to goodwill as the 2000 Summer Olympics in Sydney, Australia, focused attention on the athletes themselves. Among the more heartening stories was that of Australian Cathy Freeman, the Aboriginal track star who lit the Olympic flame in the opening ceremony. Freeman came to symbolize the island nation's hopes while at the same time bringing to the fore historical injustices levied on its indigenous people. She triumphed in the 400-m race, her specialty event, winning gold with a time of 49.11 sec.

Allegations of improprieties and outright misconduct in the selection of Salt Lake City, Utah, as the site of the 2002 Olympic Winter Games led the IOC to revamp its host city selection procedure radically. A two-phase process was created to winnow candidates down to six cities that demonstrated the highest ability in meeting a broad spectrum of criteria. A selection college was created to vet applicants and determine the final winner in the bid process. Visits by IOC members to the host city and the acceptance of "gifts" to IOC members were explicitly prohibited under the new rules. The new procedures were approved by the IOC in December 1999 and would be used in the selection of sites for 2008 and beyond.

The IOC also took steps to master the sports doping problem, a perennial issue in international sports that proved especially troublesome in the wake of drug raids that had taken place prior to and during the 1998 Tour de France cycling race. The IOC convened the World Conference on Doping in Sport in Lausanne, Switz., in February 1999. That conference resulted in the creation of the World Anti-Doping Agency, which was charged with implementing more stringent drug testing of international athletes. At the 2000 Tour, won by American Lance Armstrong for the second successive year, three cyclists were expelled. Prior to the Sydney Olympics, athletes in 27 different sports in 82 nations were subjected to random out-of-competition testing. All told, 70 athletes tested positive for banned drugs before or during the Olympic Games.

Second only to the Olympics among the year's sports stories was the continued domination of American golfer Tiger Woods, who solidified his reputation as one of the greatest golfers ever by winning the U.S. Open in June, the British Open in July, and the Professional Golfers' Association of America (PGA) championship in August. Woods joined Ben Hogan as one of only two professional golfers to win three majors in a season. Australian Karrie Webb (*see* BIOGRAPHIES) had similar success on the Ladies Professional Golf Association tour.

In January 2000 American football fans were treated to an exceptionally competitive championship game as the St. Louis (Mo.) Rams, led by quarterback Kurt Warner, defeated the Tennessee Titans in Super Bowl XXXIV. Warner earned the Most Valuable Player award after passing for 414 yd in the game. (*See* BIOGRAPHIES.)

(GAVIN FORBES EHRINGER)

ARCHERY

At the 2000 Olympic Games in Sydney, Australia, archery provided two different stories—one of continuing domination by a women's team and another of a rising new star in his home country. Wind on the second day of the 70 m (1 m = 3.28 ft) qualifying rounds was the only negative during the six-day event, which ended on September 22.

South Korea completely dominated the women's competition. Yun Mi Jin won the gold, besting her teammates Kim Nam Soon and Kim Soo Nyung by 107–106 and 107–105, respectively, on a 12-arrow match worth 120 points. The same three joined forces to defeat Ukraine 251–239 in the team final, and Germany won the women's team bronze.

Australian Simon Fairweather rose above all comers to win the men's gold medal after having finished outside the top 10 in the two previous Olympics. In Sydney, Fairweather, who had worked with a South Korean coach since 1996, shot consistently throughout the qualifying and elimination rounds and defeated American Vic Wunderle 113–106 in the gold-medal round. Wietse Van Alten of The Netherlands downed Magnus Petersson of Sweden for the bronze. South Korea won more gold when its men's team beat Italy 255–247 for the gold medal. The American squad of Wunderle, Richard ("Butch") Johnson, and Rodney White tied with Russia for third and won the bronze medal in a shoot-off 29–26.

In the U.S. the 116th National Archery Association national outdoor target championships were held in Canton, Mich. Johnson won the recurve title, with Wunderle and Jay Barrs finishing second and third, respectively. The men's compound winner was Dave Cousins, followed by Rich Freitas and Jeff McNail. In the ladies' recurve division, Karen Scavotto won over Janet Dykman and Denise Parker. The women's compound victor was Christie Bisco; Mary Zorn took second place just one point ahead of Michelle Ragsdale. At the National Field Archery Association outdoor national championships in Darrington, Wash., Cousins was the winner in pro freestyle, Becky Pearson won in pro female freestyle, and Steve Gibbs prevailed in the pro freestyle limited division. (LARRY WISE)

AUTOMOBILE RACING

Grand Prix Racing. Michael Schumacher made Grand Prix racing history in 2000 by becoming the first man in 21 years to win the drivers' world championship at the wheel of one of Italy's scarlet Ferraris. For the 31-year-old German ace, this was his third and hardest-won title crown, the culmination of five years of dogged and persistent struggle since he joined the most famous team in the Formula One (F1) business in 1996. On his way to the championship, Schumacher won 9 of the season's 17 races, more than double the total of his key rival, Mika Hakkinen—champion in 1998 and 1999—who managed just four wins for the McLaren-Mercedes team. The remaining races also fell to those two leading teams, with British driver David Coulthard winning three for McLaren and Brazil's Rubens Barrichello, Schumacher's new teammate from the start of the 2000 season, scoring his maiden F1 success with a victory in the German Grand Prix.

Ferrari's convincing return to the F1 front line—and its second consecutive constructor's championship—was a vindication for the entire team, headed by French sporting director Jean Todt, who first joined the team in 1993 and who shaped, planned, and cajoled the whole operation, progressively reinventing Ferrari as an F1 force over a grueling seven-year period. While Ferrari's top engineers Ross Brawn and Rory Byrne built a formidable technical armoury, however, it was unlikely they could have done it without Schumacher, who showed himself uniquely capable of turning situations to his advantage.

Ultimately the McLaren team was thwarted in its efforts to carry Hakkinen to his third straight drivers' championship. Despite this, Hakkinen emerged stronger than ever before as the one man Schumacher clearly respected and knew would definitely give as good as he got. Coulthard did well enough, but somehow he never quite emerged as the potential title threat anticipated in the middle of the year.

Among the also-rans, there was much gloom and precious little promise. The most impressive member of the supporting cast was the BMW Williams team, which showed both a promising new Munich, Ger.-built V10 engine and a dramatic young British talent in the form of Jenson Button. In his first F1 season, Button demonstrated huge talent and assurance for a 20-year-old novice. British American Racing also emerged as a credible F1 operation; a new partnership with Honda helped 1997 champion driver Jacques Villeneuve and the Brackley, Eng.-based team to go up a gear. In doing so they successfully buried dire memories of their awful 1999 season with Supertec power.

There were three key disappointments on the F1 scene, each failing to make a mark for very different reasons. The

AP/Wide World Photos

Michael Schumacher of Germany steers his Ferrari to victory at the Japanese Grand Prix on October 8.

Jordan team, which should have been challenging Williams, had a level of mechanical unreliability that was desperate. Jaguar struggled to make sense of the F1 business with a deficient car, initially unreliable engines, and a management structure caught trying to learn the intricacies of the Grand Prix game while at the same time fighting fires on every business front. Prost was engaged in political battles with its unsympathetic engine partner, Peugeot, which was intent on quitting at the end of the year.

In many ways the biggest single development in 2000 was the return of F1 racing to the U.S. for the first time in nine years. This time, however, the race did not take place between concrete barriers lining the streets of Phoenix, Ariz. (the last American venue to hold an F1 race), but rather occurred on a spectacularly adapted road circuit incorporating a banked corner of the famous Indianapolis (Ind.) Motor Speedway. The inaugural race was a huge success, thanks in part to F1 power broker Bernie Ecclestone's deal with Speedway president Tony George, which was expected to ensure F1's continued presence in Indiana on an open-ended basis. It was uncertain how long it would take to educate American spectators, accustomed to all-action sports with plenty of scoring, to appreciate the strategic "chessboard" philosophy behind contemporary F1 pit-stop racing. Ironically, there was concern that F1's reappearance in the U.S. might leave the Championship Auto Racing Teams single-seater series, which offered consistently great racing and a diversity of venues ranging from street circuit to superspeedway to regular road track, at something of a commercial disadvantage.

(ALAN HENRY)

U.S. Auto Racing. In 2000 the Indianapolis Motor Speedway complex, the site of three major races sanctioned by disparate series, could lay claim to being the epicentre of U.S. automobile racing. With the inaugural race on its purpose-built F1 road course, the venue hosted the U.S. Grand Prix, the Indy Racing League (IRL) Indianapolis 500, and the National Association for Stock Car Auto Racing (NASCAR) Brickyard 400.

The Indy 500, held on May 28, was won by Juan Montoya of Colombia for the Target/Chip Ganassi team, which competed mainly in the rival Championship Auto Racing Teams (CART) single-seater series. Montoya edged the IRL's Buddy Lazier by 7.184 sec at an average speed of 167.607 mph. Montoya and third-place finisher Eliseo Salazar of Chile drove Oldsmobile-powered G-Force chassis, while Lazier drove an Olds-powered Dallara. The top qualifying speed of 223.471 mph was set by defending IRL points champion Greg Ray. Montoya, who planned to defect to F1 racing in 2001, led for

167 of the race's 200 laps. Competitors said Montoya's pit stops were as much as four seconds faster than their own.

In August Bobby Labonte, in a Joe Gibbs Pontiac, won the Brickyard 400, part of the 34-race NASCAR Winston Cup series. Labonte, averaging 155.912 mph, bested Ford's Rusty Wallace by 4.23 sec. Bill Elliott, also in a Ford, finished third. The U.S. Grand Prix in September was the final jewel in Indy Speedway owner Tony George's crown. Michael Schumacher of Germany, driving a Ferrari, won on the new 2.606-mi course, which incorporated part of the famed banked 2.5-mi Indy oval. Each of the three races drew more than 200,000 spectators.

CART, which left a gap in its schedule so its members could attempt the Indianapolis 500, offered $13,632,500 in purse money over its 20-race FedEx series, which traveled to four countries outside the U.S. As in 1999, the championship came down to the Marlboro 500 finale in California. In a weather-hampered contest, Gil de Ferran, driving a Honda-powered Reynard, won the series points championship by finishing third behind his main challenger, fellow Brazilian Christian Fittipaldi, in a Ford Lola.

Lazier won the IRL's Northern Light season championship for Indy single seaters by finishing fourth in the season finale at Texas Motor Speedway. That was all he needed to do to vanquish Canada's Scott Goodyear, who won in an Oldsmobile-powered Dallara. Infiniti's Eddie Cheever, Jr., was third on the season and second in the race, which was the fastest in series history (175.276-mph average over 500 mi).

In the Winston Cup series, 1999 champion Dale Jarrett won the February classic, the Daytona (Fla.) 500, starting from the pole position in a Robert Yates Ford Taurus. The car, which had virtually been rebuilt overnight after a crash in practice the day before, led four other Fords over the finish line as the race ended under caution. Jeff Burton was second and Elliott third. Jarrett, who won $1,277,975 plus an additional $1,000,000 bonus for the Daytona victory—a NASCAR record payout—averaged 155.669 mph. Labonte won the season championship and more than $4,000,000, including $831,225 for winning the Brickyard 400. Labonte led a Pontiac resurgence that edged Chevrolet for second place behind Ford for the manufacturer's title. Seven-time Winston Cup points champion Dale Earnhardt finished second on the season. The top 38 Winston Cup drivers earned at least $1,000,000 on the season.

The NASCAR circuit suffered a double blow early in the year. Lee Petty—three-time champion driver and founder of a four-generation dynasty of stock-car drivers that included his son Richard, grandson Kyle, and great-grandson Adam Petty—died in April at age 86. (*See* OBITUARIES.) Less than six weeks later, 19-year-old Adam Petty, who had made his professional racing debut in 1998, was killed in a crash during a practice run in New Hampshire.

(ROBERT J. FENDELL)

Rallies and Other Races. In the world rally championship circuit, Tommi Mäkinen (Mitsubishi) of Finland won his second consecutive Rally of Monte Carlo in January 2000, but he failed to win another race all season and was unable to capture his fifth straight overall world rally title. In Australia in November, after Mäkinen had crossed the finish first, it was discovered that his car's turbocharger did not comply with regulations of the Fédération Internationale de l'Automobile. The noncompliance was ruled a mistake, but Mäkinen was disqualified in favour of another Finn, Marcus Grönholm (Peugeot). It was Grönholm's fourth win of the season. British driver Richard Burns (Subaru), who was second overall to Mäkinen in 1999, also had four wins in 2000. His victory in the season-ending Rally of Great Britain, however, was not enough to hold off Grönholm, who won his first overall title by only five points, 65–60. Peugeot (111 points) won the manufacturer's title over Ford (91) and Subaru (88).

In June Audi dominated the Le Mans 24-Hour Grand Prix d'Endurance in France, finishing 1–2–3. The winning Audi R8, driven by Frank Biela of Germany, Tom Kristensen of Denmark, and Emmanuele Pirro of Italy, completed 368 laps, or 5,007.988 km (3,111.82 mi). The second-place Audi team of Scotland's Allan McNish and his French co-drivers, Stephane Ortelli and Laurent Aiello, finished one lap back. McNish, Ortelli, and Aiello had won the 1998 race for Porsche.

The two American road racing classics were sanctioned by rival groups. The Rolex 24 Hours of Daytona, put on by the Grand American Road Racing Association, recorded the closest finish in the race's 38-year history as production-based Grand Touring vehicles dominated. A Team Oreca Dodge Viper GTSR driven by Olivier Beretta and Dominique Dupuy of France and Karl Wendlinger of Austria bested a Chevrolet Corvette by 30.879 sec. After a 50-year hiatus, Cadillac reentered racing, finishing cars in 13th and 14th place.

In the 48th annual Superflo 12 Hours of Sebring (Fla.), the jewel of the 12-race American Le Mans endurance series, the Audi R8 team finished 1–2 overall—39.11 sec apart—with the winner averaging 110.692 mph. A lap behind was a BMW V12.

(MELINDA C. SHEPHERD)

BADMINTON

Once again, Chinese badminton players—especially the women—captured most of the important events of the year. Although China had been the sport's powerhouse in recent years, its domination was raised to a new level in 2000.

At the All-England Championships in March, Xia Xuanze of China posted four consecutive upsets to win the men's singles title. In the final Xia defeated Taufik Hidayat, an Indonesian teenager who was hoping to become the youngest men's singles champion of the open era. The women's singles final saw Gong Zhichao of China win her first title in two years with a final-round victory over compatriot Dai Yun.

The Thomas Cup and the Uber Cup, team events for men and women, respectively, featured China in both finals. This event was the first time since 1990 that the Chinese men had advanced to the championship round; the Indonesian men's team beat China 3–0, however. The women's competition saw the appearance of Denmark in the final for the first time since 1960, but in the best-of-five match final, the Chinese women won easily 3–0.

China's medal haul at the 2000 Olympics in Sydney, Australia, paled its performances at the 1996 Games in Atlanta, Ga. In Atlanta China won four medals, only one of which was gold. In Sydney, however, the final tally was eight: four gold, one silver, and three bronze. Ji Xinpeng, seeded seventh, was the giant killer of the men's singles event, scoring numerous upsets on his way to victory. After eliminating the top-seeded Hidayat and the world top-ranked Peter Gade Christensen of Denmark, Ji beat the second-seeded Hendrawan, also of Indonesia, to claim the gold medal.

In the women's final China's Gong Zhichao rallied from behind to beat current world champion Camilla Martin of Denmark. The Chinese women's doubles team of Ge Fei and Gu Jun, virtually unbeatable over the past four years, defended the title they won in Atlanta. The women's doubles competition marked the first time a country had taken gold, silver, and bronze in an Olympic badminton event. Chinese players also won the mixed doubles title, while the remaining gold medal went to the Indonesian men's doubles team of Tony Gunawan and Chandra Wijaya.

(DONN GOBBIE)

BASEBALL

With the opening of new ballparks in Detroit, San Francisco, and Houston, Texas, in 2000 major league baseball established a single-season attendance record of 72,748,970, surpassing the previous record set in 1998. The season opened March 29 in Tokyo, with the Chicago Cubs defeating the New York Mets 5–3 at the Tokyo Dome; the Mets retaliated with a 5–1 victory the next day. The two-game series marked the first time regular-season competition had been staged outside North America.

World Series. The American League (AL) New York Yankees earned their third consecutive championship and their fourth in five years by defeating the National League (NL) Mets 4–2 at Shea Stadium, the Mets' home field, in game five of the World Series on October 26. The Yankees thus captured the best-four-of-seven series 4–1. It was the first New York intracity "Subway Series" since 1956, when the Yankees beat the Brooklyn Dodgers four games to three. Twice before, the Yankee franchise had won at least three consecutive World Series (1936–39, 1949–53). The only other team to have done so was the Oakland A's in 1972–74.

In game one of the World Series at Yankee Stadium on October 21, the Yankees defeated the Mets 4–3 in 12 innings. The game lasted 4 hours 51 minutes, the longest in World Series history. With the victory the Yankees also broke the existing mark of 12 consecutive World Series triumphs established by the Yankees in 1927–32. José Vizcaino ended game one by lashing a first-pitch, bases-loaded, two-out single off Turk Wendell before a crowd of 55,913. Mike Stanton, the third Yankee reliever after starter Andy Pettitte, pitched two scoreless innings and received credit for the win. Wendell, the fifth Met reliever after starter Al Leiter, was the loser.

In game two at Yankee Stadium on October 22, the Yankees amassed a 6–0 lead and survived a five-run uprising by the Mets in the top of the ninth inning against Jeff Nelson and Mariano Rivera, the Yankees' ace relief pitcher. Roger Clemens, who struck out nine and allowed only two hits through eight innings, earned the 6–5 victory for the Yankees before 56,059 fans. Mike Hampton was the losing pitcher. Clemens was involved in a controversial incident in the top of the first inning when Mike Piazza, the Mets' star catcher, who had been hit in the head by a Clemens pitch during a regular-season game, broke his bat while swinging at a pitch. The ball trickled foul, but the barrel end of the bat sailed toward the mound. Clemens grabbed it and threw it in the direction of Piazza, who was running toward first base. Piazza took steps toward Clemens, and players from both dugouts emptied onto the field. No one was officially ejected, but Clemens later was fined $50,000 for his conduct.

On October 24 the Series moved to Shea Stadium before a crowd of 55,299, and the Mets responded with a 4–2 conquest. Orlando Hernández of the Yankees pitched well, striking out 12 in 7$^1/_3$ innings, but he incurred his first postseason loss ever after eight career victories. John Franco, the third of four Mets relievers, was credited with the win in game three.

The Yankees responded in game four with a 3–2 victory on October 25 to seize a 3–1 lead in the series. The Yankees' hot-hitting shortstop, Derek Jeter, opened the game with a first-pitch home run off Bobby J. Jones. The Yankees scored single runs in the sec-

After defeating the New York Mets in the final game of the World Series on October 26, the New York Yankees celebrate their third consecutive world title.

AP/Wide World Photos

ond and third innings, then held on as four relief pitchers for starter Denny Neagle yielded just two hits in the last $4^{1}/_{3}$ innings. Nelson, the third of five Yankee pitchers, received the victory.

The Yankees clinched their 26th World Series championship by scoring two runs in the top of the ninth inning of game five to break a 2–2 tie. With two out, Jorge Posada walked and Scott Brosius singled. Luis Sojo singled through the middle against Leiter, scoring Posada. When the throw toward home plate from centre fielder Jay Payton hit Posada and careened into foul territory, Brosius scored on the error. Stanton, in relief of starter Pettitte, was credited with his second victory of the series, while Rivera worked a scoreless ninth for his second save. The Yankees registered early runs on home runs by Bernie Williams and Jeter, who batted .409 for five games with two home runs and six runs batted in and was selected Most Valuable Player (MVP) of the series.

Play-offs. The Yankees had won their 37th pennant on October 17 by defeating the Seattle Mariners 9–7 at Yankee Stadium to capture the American League Championship Series (ALCS) four games to two. The Yankees, down 4–0 in the fourth inning of game six, exploded for six runs in the seventh inning. The rally was highlighted by David Justice's three-run home run in support of Hernández, the winning pitcher. Justice, who had been acquired by the Yankees from the Cleveland Indians during the season, was voted MVP of the ALCS.

The Mariners opened the best-of-seven series by defeating the Yankees 2–0 in New York on October 10. The Yankees tied the series at home on October 11 by routing the Mariners 7–1. The Yankees were losing 1–0 entering their half of the eighth inning when they scored their first runs of the series. In game three at Seattle, Pettitte pitched the Yankees to an 8–2 triumph. Clemens then took the mound for New York in game four and silenced the Mariners 5–0 with a one-hit complete game featuring 15 strikeouts. Al Martin's seventh-inning double was the only Seattle hit. The Mariners won game five at Seattle 6–2 on a five-run fifth inning keyed by home runs from John Olerud and Edgar Martínez.

The Mets captured the NL pennant on October 16 with a 7–0 rout of the St. Louis Cardinals at Shea Stadium to claim the National League Championship Series (NLCS) four games to one. The Mets staged three-run rallies in the first and fourth innings to support Hampton, who worked a complete-game three-hit performance for the Mets, striking out eight. Hampton, a left-hander acquired from the Houston Astros before the season, recorded two victories in the NLCS and was voted its MVP.

In the opener of the NLCS at St. Louis on October 11, Hampton pitched seven shutout innings for the Mets, who scored twice in the first inning and romped 6–2. In game two at St. Louis, Payton singled in the winning run in the ninth inning to provide the Mets with a 6–5 victory. Rick Ankiel, a rookie left-hander who had thrown five wild pitches in one inning during the Cardinals' division series against the Atlanta Braves, threw two more against the Mets. The Cardinals, however, trounced the Mets in game three at New York 8–2. They collected 14 hits toward their first victory in the series, but the Mets gained a 3–1 lead in the series the next day by beating the Cardinals 10–6.

In the NL division series, the Cardinals, who finished first in the Central division with a 95–67 record, swept the Braves (95–67), who were East division champions by scores of 7–5, 10–4, and 7–1 and were in the play-offs for the ninth consecutive year. The San Francisco Giants (97–65), champions of the West, were eliminated in four games by the Mets (94–68), who posted the best record of any second-place team and thus earned a wild-card berth in the play-offs. After the Giants won the opener 5–1, the Mets won the next three games 5–4, 3–2, and 4–0, the last on a one-hitter by Jones.

The Yankees (87–74) lost 15 of their last 18 games in the regular season and won the AL East division by only $2^{1}/_{2}$ games over the Boston Red Sox. In the division series the Yankees were extended to five games by Oakland (91–70), winners of the West division. The A's won the first game 5–3, lost the next two by 4–0 and 4–2, then routed the Yankees 11–1. In the deciding game the Yankees scored six runs in the first inning and held on to win 7–5. Seattle (91–71), which claimed the AL wild-card entry just a half game behind the A's, swept the Central division champion Chicago White Sox (95–67) in three games, 7–4, 5–2, and 2–1.

Individual Accomplishments. With Mark McGwire of the Cardinals injured for much of the season, it was left to Sammy Sosa of the Cubs to continue the home-run barrage. He did not disappoint, hitting 50 to lead the major leagues and join McGwire and Babe Ruth as the only players to reach that plateau in three straight seasons. Troy Glaus of the Anaheim Angels led the AL with 47.

Todd Helton of the Colorado Rockies led the NL in batting average (.372) and runs batted in (147). Nomar Garciaparra of the Red Sox led the AL with a .372 average, and Martinez of the Mariners set the pace in runs batted in with 145. Tom Glavine led the NL pitching with 21 victories; Tim Hudson of Oakland and David Wells of Toronto each had 20 wins in the AL, where Boston's Pedro Martínez was otherwise dominant, posting 18 victories, a 1.74 earned run average, and 284 strikeouts. Randy Johnson of the NL Arizona Diamondbacks led both leagues in strikeouts with 347.

No pitcher threw a no-hitter during the regular season, and no managers were dismissed, although several were let go at season's end. Brent Mayne, a catcher for Colorado, became the first position player in 32 years to win a game. He came in to pitch the 12th inning of a game against the Braves on August 22, yielded no runs, and received credit for the victory when the Rockies scored in the bottom of the 12th to beat Atlanta 7–6.

Little League World Series. Maracaibo, Venez., won the Little League World Series by defeating Bellaire, Texas, 3–2 in Williamsport, Pa., on August 26. Maracaibo jumped to a 2–0 lead in the first inning behind Rubén Mavarez, who pitched a four-hitter and struck out six as Venezuela won its second championship in six years.

(ROBERT VERDI)

Latin America. The 2000 Caribbean Series was held in the Dominican Republic on February 2–7. The Santurce Crabbers (Los Cangrejeros), representing Puerto Rico, were undefeated with a 6–0 record. The runner-up Eagles (Aguilas Cibaeñas), the Dominican entry, were 4–2, while Mexico (Navojoa Mayos) and Venezuela (Zulia Eagles) tied for last place with 1–5 records.

Santiago de Cuba won its second consecutive Cuban championship. It set a new regular-season record by winning 62 of 90 games and then went undefeated in the 11 play-off games, triumphing over Camagüey, Granma, and Pinar del Río. The Cuban national team, however, which had won gold medals in the 1992 and 1996 Olympic Games, had to settle for a silver medal after losing the title match to the United States 4–0 at the 2000 Games in Sydney, Australia.

The Mexico City Tigers defeated the Mexico City Red Devils four games to

AP/Wide World Photos

Eduardo Pérez (left) is congratulated by teammate José Vidró after scoring a run to put Puerto Rico up 3–0 over the Dominican Republic during the 2000 Caribbean Series.

one in the championship series of the Mexican League. It was the Tigers' seventh league title.

Cuban third baseman Tony Pérez, whose batting helped lead the Cincinnati Reds to four National League pennants in the 1970s, became the seventh Latin American player (and the second Cuban after Martin Dihigo) to be selected to the National Baseball Hall of Fame in Cooperstown, N.Y.

(MILTON JAMAIL)

Japan. The Yomiuri Giants of the Central League (CL) beat the defending champion Fukuoka Daiei Hawks of the Pacific League (PL) four games to two in the 2000 Japan Series. The Giants claimed their 19th Japan Series title and their first since 1994. The 2000 series drew special attention because the teams were managed by two Japanese baseball legends, Shigeo Nagashima for the Giants and Sadaharu Oh for the Hawks. In 1965–73 Nagashima and Oh, batting third and fourth, had led the Giants to nine consecutive championship titles.

Giants slugger Hideki Matsui was named the Most Valuable Player (MVP) for both the Japan Series and the CL's 135-game regular season. Matsui won two of the CL's hitting titles with 42 home runs and 108 runs batted in. The Giants also got a boost from three left-handed starting pitchers, Kimiyasu Kudo (12–5), Darrell May (12–7), and Hisanori Takahashi (9–6), all of whom had joined the team in 2000. Tatsuhiko Kinjo of the Yokohama BayStars, who had the league's best batting average, .346, was named the CL Rookie of the Year.

In the PL, Nobuhiko Matsunaka of the Hawks—with a batting average of .312, 33 home runs, and 106 runs batted in—was named league MVP for his solid performance. Ichiro Suzuki (*see* BIOGRAPHIES) of the Orix BlueWave won his seventh PL batting title with a .387 average. Suzuki later signed a contract to play in the U.S., joining Kazuhiro Sasaki, the American League's 2000 Rookie of the Year, on the Seattle Mariners' roster.

(HIROKI NODA)

BASKETBALL

United States. *Professional.* Led by centre Shaquille O'Neal (*see* BIOGRAPHIES) and coach Phil Jackson, the Los Angeles Lakers dominated the National Basketball Association (NBA) in the year 2000. The 2.16-m (7-ft 1-in), 143-kg (315-lb) O'Neal proved to be an unstoppable force, averaging 38 points and 16.7 rebounds per game during the NBA finals, which the Lakers won by defeating the Indiana Pacers. Under Jackson's tutelage, O'Neal, who was voted Most Valuable Player for the regular season, the All-Star game, and the finals, became more of a team player and in doing so emerged to the point where he could now be compared to such NBA giants as Wilt Chamberlain, Bill Russell, and Kareem Abdul-Jabbar. The Pacers did not go quietly in the finals, however, but put up a fierce battle before falling to the Lakers in six games. In the pivotal fifth game in Indianapolis, Ind., O'Neal fouled out in overtime, but his 21-year-old teammate Kobe Bryant stepped up to hit three clutch baskets to seal a 120–118 Los Angeles victory and take what proved to be an insurmountable lead of three games to one.

The rival coaches also played starring roles in the finals. Jackson, who had rocketed to fame as coach of the Michael Jordan-led Chicago Bulls, earned his seventh NBA title and proved that his ability was not grounded by the absence of Jordan on the roster. In a major blow to the world of professional basketball, Pacers coach Larry Bird, who as a player for the Boston Celtics in the 1980s had helped the NBA achieve unprecedented popularity, announced before the finals began that he would step down whether or not his team won the title. A man of his word, as always, Bird retired at the end of the season. Rookie coach Glenn ("Doc") Rivers of the Orlando Magic upset Jackson and Bird to win the Coach of the Year award.

In women's basketball the Houston Comets won their fourth consecutive Women's National Basketball Association (WNBA) championship by sweeping the New York Liberty two games to none in the best-of-three final series. Houston's one-two punch—Sheryl Swoopes and Cynthia Cooper—tallied 32 of the Comets' last 36 points in the clincher. Just when it seemed the Liberty would force a third game, Cooper stunned the crowd with a three-point basket to tie the game only seconds before the end of regulation play, and the Comets pulled away in overtime. Houston joined the NBA's Boston Celtics as the only professional basketball teams to have won four consecutive titles.

College. On April 3, 2000—21 years after legendary guard Earvin ("Magic") Johnson led the school to its first National Collegiate Athletic Association basketball championship—Michigan State University captured its second NCAA title with a resounding 89–76 victory over

Reuters NewMedia Inc./Corbis

Houston Comets guard Cynthia Cooper (right) leaps over New York Liberty's Vickie Johnson for a shot during the Comets' 79–73 victory in the decisive WNBA championship game.

the University of Florida. This time Michigan State was led by another outstanding playmaker, Mateen Cleaves, a spirited 1.9-m (6-ft 2-in) point guard. Cleaves, who had taken Johnson's advice to return for his senior year before entering the NBA draft, lifted the Spartans with an emotional effort in the first half of the championship game. Early in the second half, however, he limped off the floor with a twisted right ankle. Florida trailed only 50–44 at that juncture, but a dramatic comeback was not to be. Cleaves eventually returned to help his teammates lock up the game, and the Spartans closed out their spectacular 32–7 season.

In the season's aftermath major controversy swirled around Indiana University basketball coach Bobby Knight. On May 15 the university's president, Myles Brand, concluded a seven-week investigation of the coach that had been triggered by former player Neil Reed's accusation that Knight had choked him during a 1997 practice. Reed's charges were bolstered by a videotape that showed Knight momentarily grabbing the player's neck. Knight, who had been involved in a number of outbursts over the years—including a notorious 1985 incident in which he flung a chair across the court during a game—was suspended for three games and forced to agree to a "zero-tolerance" policy that stated that he would lose his job if any outbursts occurred in the future.

Knight, who had coached at Indiana for 29 years, did not last long under the agreement. On September 10 he was fired for what Brand said were violations of the policy guidelines. The firing came in the wake of an incident in which Knight grabbed a student by the arm and allegedly cursed at him after the student had greeted him informally.

The Knight firing was not the only coaching bombshell of 2000. North Carolina head coach Bill Guthridge announced his surprising decision to step down after leading his team to the NCAA Final Four twice since taking over the reins from Dean Smith in 1997. Guthridge's departure supposedly left the door open for Roy Williams of Kansas, who once played at North Carolina and remained a favourite among many Tar Heels fans. In the end, however, Williams decided to stay at Kansas, and another former Tar Heel player, Matt Doherty—fresh from a sensational head coaching debut at Notre Dame—left the Fighting Irish to return to his alma mater. Mike Brey moved from Delaware to fill the Notre Dame vacancy, and Lon Kruger, who had rebuilt Illinois into a Big Ten Conference contender, defected to the Atlanta Hawks of the NBA, with Tulsa's Bill Self taking over the reins of the Illini.

In women's college basketball Connecticut, ranked number one, routed number two Tennessee by a score of 71–52 for the Huskies' first NCAA championship since 1995. That Connecticut and Tennessee were the tournament finalists surprised no one, although Connecticut's margin of victory astounded most followers of the fast-growing women's game.

Tennessee, used to dominating all comers, managed only 10 points in the opening half of the title showdown. A swarming Connecticut defense limited Tamika Catchings, the NCAA women's Player of the Year, to five points in those decisive 20 minutes, and Tennessee was unable to mount a serious second-half threat. The loss thwarted coach Pat Summitt's bid to lead Tennessee to an unprecedented seventh NCAA crown.

(ROBERT G. LOGAN)

AFP/Corbis

Mindaugas Timinskas of Lithuania drives past Vince Carter of the U.S. in the Olympic men's basketball semifinal game in Sydney, Australia.

International. The world technical commission of the International Basketball Federation (FIBA) met in Munich, Ger., in June 2000 and confirmed rule changes, which were implemented around the world after the Olympic Games concluded in October. In the future all games were to be played in four quarters of 10 minutes' duration (rather than two halves of 20 minutes); the shot clock (the time within which a team must shoot when it gains possession of the ball) was reduced from 30 seconds to 24 seconds; and the time allowed for a team to get the ball from its back court into the front court was reduced from 10 to 8 seconds. The FIBA also introduced the free circulation of players for international club competition.

Without doubt the highlight of the year on the court was the staging of the Games of the XXVII Olympiad in Sydney, Australia. Twelve teams contested each basketball tournament, men's and women's, with the United States looking to retain both titles. This they did, but not as easily as some observers had expected. The American men pipped Lithuania by only two points (85–83) in their semifinal and then beat France 85–75 in an enthralling final. The French, who defeated the Australians 76–52 in the semifinals, secured their highest Olympic placing since they won silver in the 1948 Games in London. The American women had a slightly easier ride to gold, beating South Korea 78–65 in the semifinal and then topping Australia comfortably in the final 76–54.

In the major European basketball events of 2000, the young men's competition was won by Slovenia, runners-up in the previous competition in 1998, which defeated Israel in the final. The young women's title was won by Russia, with the Czech Republic finishing in second place. France and Russia captured the championships in the junior men's and junior women's championships, respectively. Sagesse (Lebanon) won the 11th Asian Basketball Confederation Champions Cup for men. The South American Champions Cup for men, which was contested in Venezuela, produced victory for the home team Trotamundos.

The major club competition during the 1999–2000 European season, the men's EuroLeague, was won by Panathinaikos BSA (Greece). AEK Athens (Greece) lifted the European Saporta Cup; Limoges CSP (France) took the European Korac Cup; and SCP Ruzomberok (Slovakia) retained the women's EuroLeague title. The Ronchetti Cup went to Italy, with Lavezzini Basket of Parma defeating the 1999 winner, Sandra Gran Canaria (Spain).

(MARK HANNEN)

BILLIARD GAMES

Carom Billiards. The Billiards Worldcup Association (BWA) World Cup final standings for 1999 saw Dick Jaspers of The Netherlands on top with 200 points. South Korean-born Sang Chun Lee of New York City was second with 190 points.

In January 2000 the carom specialists headed to The Netherlands for the International Dutch Open, where Jaspers defeated 1999 world champion Torbjörn Blomdahl of Sweden 3–1 in the final. Jaspers amassed 290 points in 156 innings and averaged 1.859 points per inning, with a high run of 14. Jaspers also picked up 36 world ranking points. Blomdahl scored 226 points in 155 innings, with an average of 1.458.

Spotted balls were used for the first time in the Dutch Open. For better viewing, the white and yellow balls were provided with six red dots. A time clock was also introduced. Both players had a starting time of 150 seconds, with another 30 seconds per shot added. The time a player used was then subtracted, and if a player used up all of his or her time he or she lost the set. In a final-16 match, Jaspers lost his first set to countryman Ad Koorevarr when he used up all of his time.

The first World Cup event of 2000 was held in Bogotá, Colom., in May. Blomdahl once again was a bridesmaid, losing to Turkish star Semih Sayginer 3–2 in the final. Sayginer averaged 1.404, with a high run of 7. Jaspers finished ninth, while Sang Chun Lee, who had captured his 11th consecutive U.S. three-cushion championship one month earlier, lost in the final 16.

Pocket Billiards. Team U.S.A., led by Johnny Archer, defended its title in the Mosconi Cup in London. The American squad trounced Team Europe 12–7 to capture its fifth title in six years. Archer, the 1999 U.S. Open champion, sealed the match with a 5–2 victory over six-time world snooker champion Steve Davis of England.

Billiards Digest named the 50 greatest players of the century. The top five were Willie Hoppe, Willie Mosconi, Ralph Greenleaf, Alfredo de Oro, and Mike Sigel. Current stars Allison Fisher of England and Archer were ranked 18th and 31st, respectively.

A jury in North Carolina awarded the Professional Billiards Tour (PBT) $886,000 for breach of contract in its lawsuit against the R.J. Reynolds Tobacco Co. Two other charges of fraud and unfair trade practices were earlier thrown out for lack of evidence. Don Mackey, PBT commissioner, announced that plans were under way for an "active" 2001 pool season.

A German player captured the Billiard Congress of America (BCA) U.S. Open straight pool championship for the third time in four years. Ralf Souquet pocketed $15,000 for his 150–95 victory over Ch'ien Ming-wei of Taiwan. Fisher trounced Loree Jon Jones 100–37 in the ladies' section to also cash out for $15,000.

The Steve Mizerak Senior Tour attracted 69 players to Tampa, Fla., in March for the Senior Masters. Nick Varner prevailed over Jim Rempe 13–11 to claim top honours. The tour later announced that the Senior Tour championship scheduled for October had been canceled.

Russel Stuart of Canada announced that he had set up the USA Billiards Tour and the Challenger Circuit to qualify pocket billiard players for several large purse events in 2001. Dan Basovich defeated Buddy Hall in the first event, held in Florida. Two events were canceled—one in Tulsa, Okla., and the other in Atlanta, Ga.—almost immediately. Finnish champion Mika Immonen prevailed in the Nashville, Tenn., stop, while Efren Reyes of the Philippines came out on top at the Baltimore, Md., event. On May 2, USA Billiards announced that the remainder of the tour was being postponed pending "a complete review of the tour, including sponsorship and player participation."

In the Women's Professional Billiard Association (WPBA), Fisher was elected president of the players' association and continued to show her influence on the table as well. In the first four tournaments of the year, Fisher was victorious in two—the WPBA nationals and the San Diego Classic—and reached the finals in the other two, losing to former world snooker champion Karen Corr in Valley Forge, Pa., and being edged by Gerda Hofstatter in the BCA Open event in Las Vegas, Nev. Corr defeated Helena Thornfeldt to capture the Baltimore stop on the WPBA tour in August.

Ninety-six players from 23 countries descended on Cardiff, Wales, in July for the World Pool–Billiard Association world nine-ball championships. Chao Fong-pang of Taiwan trounced the Mexican Ismael Paez 17–6 to take the title and a check for $60,000—the largest prize in pool. Paez received $30,000. The champion also received a reported $90,000 bonus from the Taiwanese government. Americans Earl Strickland and Cory Duel finished third and fourth, respectively, and pocketed $15,000 each. Former snooker champion Davis was the story of the week-long tournament. After barely advancing out of his round-robin bracket, Davis knocked out three former world pool champions before Duel sent him packing in the final-eight bracket.

The 10th annual International Challenge of Champions followed on the heels of the world championships, with eight invited players dueling it out for the sole prize of $50,000. In a reversal of the previous year's final, German Oliver Ortmann defeated defending champion Francisco Bustamante in a one-game tiebreaker. Ortmann became the only two-time winner of this prestigious event.

Reyes pocketed $30,000 with his victory in the Camel Pro 8-Ball Championship in August; Immonen earned $20,000 for his second-place finish. Strickland captured his fifth U.S. Open nine-ball title and $50,000 in winnings in September with an 11–5 victory over Takeshi Okumura of Japan. A record field of 286 players entered the tournament, with defending champion Archer ending up in a 7th place tie.

Snooker. Mark Williams defeated Matthew Stevens 18–16 in the event's first all-Welsh final to claim the 1999–2000 world professional snooker championship. Stevens held a 13–7 lead before the reigning U.K. and Thailand international champion reeled off seven of the next eight frames. Williams, a losing semifinalist in 1999, pocketed £240,000 (about $360,000), while Stevens earned £140,000 ($212,000). Williams, who also took over the number one ranking for the next season, had trailed John Higgins of Scotland 15–11 in his semifinal match, then stormed back for a 17–15 victory. Stevens reached the final with a 17–12 win over Joe Swail of Northern Ireland. Scottish defending champion Stephen Hendry lost 10–7 to England's Stuart Bingham in round one.

Ajeya Prabraker defeated Tom Kollins 5–3 to claim the 2000 U.S. snooker championship. In a battle of former snooker professionals, Kirk Stevens defeated Bob Chaperon to take the Canadian title. All four players qualified for the International Billiards and Snooker Federation amateur world championships in Changchun, China, in October. The tournament winner, 19-year-old Stephen Maguire of Scotland, was banned from IBSF events for three years for allegedly damaging his hotel room. (BILL BRADLEY)

BOBSLEDDING AND LUGE

Bobsledding. The inaugural Winter Goodwill Games took place in February 2000 in Lake Placid, N.Y., and saw Sandis Prusis and Janis Ozols of Latvia take the two-man bobsled title with a combined time of 3 min 49.13 sec. Andre Lange and Lars Behrendt of Germany placed second, and Americans Brian Shimer and Pavle Jovanovic were third.

American Jim Shea, Jr., the 1999 skeleton world champion, claimed the skeleton gold medal at the Games, followed by American Chris Soule and Kazuhiro Koshi of Japan. Alexandra Hamilton of Great Britain recorded the fastest time for the women (4 min 11.22 sec) to take the gold medal. Maya Bieri of Switzerland and Michelle Kelly of Canada won the silver and bronze medals, respectively.

The 1999–2000 World Cup season consisted of seven stops in Italy, France, Switzerland, and Germany. Drivers earned points in three categories: two-man, four-man, and combined standings. Switzerland took the top three spots in the two-man division, with Christian Reich and Urs Aeberhard leading the way with 224 points. Sleds piloted by Reto Götschi (209) and Marcel Rohner (205) followed. Switzerland also captured the four-man title with Rohner's team on top with 224 points. Prusis was second with 192 points, followed by Pierre Lueders of Canada with 181 points.

Steffi Hanzlik and Andy Böhme of Germany won the women's and men's titles at the world skeleton championships, which were held in Igls, Austria, in February. Gregor Stähl of Switzerland finished second to Böhme, while Canada's Melissa Hollingsworth took the silver in the ladies' event.

The world junior bobsled championships were also held in February, at Olympic Park in Calgary, Alta. Switzerland's Martin Annen and Beat Hefti recorded the fastest combined time (1 min 52.65 sec). Annen later piloted his four-man team to victory with a time of 1 min 50.16 sec.

Luge. International luge racing returned to Lake Placid at the Goodwill Games with a world-class field competing on a new $24 million track. Americans Mark Gimmette and Brian Martin captured the doubles gold medal, finishing five-thousandths of a second ahead of Germany's Steffen Skel and Steffen Woller. Italy's Armin Zoeggeler captured the men's singles gold medal. The women's crown went to Germany's Sylke Otto, with her teammate Silke Kraushaar taking second. Iluta Gaile of Latvia was third.

In doubles competition Germany's Patric Leitner and Alexander Resch raced to titles in the 2000 European and world championships. Leitner and Resch also finished on top in the World Cup luge doubles. Ten points back in second place in the final World Cup standings were Skel and Woller.

Women's singles continued to be dominated by Germans, who took the top three spots in the World Cup standings. Otto won four of the seven races and claimed the gold medal. Kraushaar, the 1998 Olympic gold medalist and defending World Cup overall winner, was second. Barbara Niedernhuber finished third.

In men's singles Zoeggeler won the first five World Cup events to take the overall title. Jens Müller of Germany was four points back in second, followed by his teammate, the legendary three-time Olympic champion Georg Hackl.

(BILL BRADLEY)

BOWLING

World Tenpins. The number of national federations affiliated with the Fédération Internationale des Quilleurs (FIQ), the world governing body of the sport of bowling, reached 122 in the year 2000. This growing popularity was reflected in continued calls for the sport's inclusion in the Olympic Games.

The FIQ world championships, held in Abu Dhabi, U.A.E., in November 1999, were the major competition in the 1999–2000 bowling season and the most attended event of the FIQ's 47-year history. A record number of 345 male and 255 female competitors represented 67 countries at the 16-day tournament. The championships were held in the ultramodern $24 million Khalifa International Bowling Stadium, built and financed by the emirate for the championships. If the number of competitors was the highest in FIQ history, so was the scoring as 25 new records were established. During the preceding 45-year history of the world championships, only one perfect 300 game had been recorded—by American Rick Steelsmith in Helsinki, Fin., in 1987. In Abu Dhabi his achievement was matched by four men and the first woman ever, South Korean Cha Mi Jung. Another memorable match was in men's doubles, with a 599 game rolled by Colombia's Jaime Andrés Gómez (300) and Jaime Monroy (299). Australia topped the list of gold medals won with three (women's doubles, all events, and masters). Two were won by South Korea (women's trios and team) and Sweden (men's doubles and team), while Belgium (men's singles), Finland (men's trios), Norway (men's all events), Qatar (men's masters), and the U.S. (women's singles) won one gold each. In all, the 36 medals were shared by 15 countries.

The host country, which won no medals, was praised for a well-run event, despite the increasing difficulty and expense of organizing the international tournament. Meanwhile, the men's masters champion, Ahmed Shaheen of Qatar, gave a warning to the bowling world of what could be expected from future Gulf region competitors. Just a month earlier he had won the 35th AMF Bowling World Cup in Las Vegas, Nev. The World Cup had been the most important international singles tournament since it was created in 1965, and in Las Vegas the field included bowlers from 79 countries.

(YRJÖ SARAHETE)

Professional Bowlers Association

Jason Couch competes in a Professional Bowlers Association tournament.

U.S. Tenpins. An indication of the status of tenpin bowling in the U.S. was the headline "Membership Decline Slows" in the Sept. 7, 2000, issue of *Bowling Newsline,* the official publication of the combined men's American Bowling Congress (ABC) and the Women's International Bowling Congress (WIBC). The story celebrated the fact that during the 1999–2000 season the two organizations (which together sought to register all league bowlers), in combination with the Young American Bowling Alliance (which registered younger bowlers), had lost 4.5% of their members. This was the lowest decrease in a decade and left the groups with a combined total of 3,756,651 paid members.

The decrease was generally believed to reflect a reduction in the number of bowlers who chose to commit to a specific number of weeks, often as many as 35, required for league membership, rather than dissatisfaction with the ABC or WIBC. Some observers attributed part of the decline in bowling's popularity to the rapid rise in the number of ABC/WIBC-sanctioned perfect games and other high scores. Whereas a 300 game was once regarded as an outstanding achievement, the total of perfect-score awards in 1999–2000 was 41,473 (with 39,470 rolled by men). Observers were nearly unanimous in their opinion that improvement in the manufacture of bowling balls was the chief cause. The record-high scores set at the 2000 ABC tournament in Albuquerque, N.M., and especially the WIBC tournament in Reno, Nev., seemed to confirm this trend.

A positive element in the tenpin scene was the purchase of the financially troubled Professional Bowlers Association (PBA) in March by a group of high-tech entrepreneurs. The new owners were former Microsoft Corp. vice president Chris Peters, who had hoped to become a pro bowler himself a few years earlier; Mike Slade, former chairman and CEO of Starwave Corp.; and Rob Glaser, CEO of RealNetworks, Inc. The PBA, formerly a nonprofit group, would henceforth be operated as a profit-making corporation, with heavy use of the Internet for promotion.

Meanwhile, the seldom-publicized Professional Women's Bowling Association (PWBA) continued to flourish. Despite small prize money—the PWBA's leading money winner in 1999, Wendy Macpherson, earned $86,265—a core of about 40 full-time participants competed regularly. The PWBA announced that all of its 23 tournaments in 2001 would be carried on delayed broadcast by the ESPN2 cable television network.

In February Norm Duke narrowly defeated his neighbour and close friend Jason Couch to take the PBA national championship. Couch took his revenge in November, however, winning his second consecutive PBA Tournament of Champions, the first bowler ever to successfully defend that title. Duke finished third. (JOHN J. ARCHIBALD)

BOXING

In 2000, problems outside the ring overshadowed what was an excellent year for boxing in terms of competitive matches. (See Sidebar.) The first in a series of outstanding bouts was between World Boxing Council (WBC) junior featherweight (super bantamweight) champion Erik Morales (Mex.) and challenger Marco Antonio Barrera (Mex.) on February 19 in Las Vegas, Nev. After 12 rounds of virtually nonstop punching, Morales won a controversial split decision. The next exceptional bout came on March 3, when former International Boxing Federation (IBF) welterweight champion Felix Trinidad (P.R.) successfully moved up in weight to the junior middleweight (super welterweight) division by winning the World Boxing Association (WBA) title with a unanimous 12-round decision over 1996 Olympic gold medalist David Reid (U.S.) in Las Vegas. In another top-notch bout, held on April 15 in Las Vegas, IBF junior middleweight champion Fernando Vargas (U.S.) scored the most impressive victory of his career, winning a 12-round decision over former WBA welterweight champion Ike Quartey (Ghana). The hard-fought unification bout between Trinidad and Vargas took place on December 2 in Las Vegas. Trinidad knocked down his previously unbeaten opponent twice in the first round and three times in the 12th to add the IBF belt to his WBA title.

Oscar de la Hoya (U.S.), boxing's biggest attraction outside the heavyweight division, continued to have difficulties both inside and outside the ring. He won his first match of the year, scoring a seventh-round knockout of Derrell Coley (U.S.) on February 26 at Madison Square Garden in New York City. In his only other match, de la Hoya lost a 12-round decision to Shane Mosley (U.S.) for the vacant WBC welterweight title on June 17 in Los Angeles. It was a superb, hard-fought fight, with approximately 580,000 households purchasing the television pay-per-view. Shortly after the loss to Mosley, de la Hoya brought a lawsuit against his longtime promoter, Bob Arum, seeking to break their contract. Arum filed a countersuit.

By beating de la Hoya, the undefeated Mosley, a former IBF lightweight champion, gained recognition as one of the sport's very best fighters. In his first WBC welterweight title defense, Mosley stopped challenger Antonio Diaz (U.S.) with a sixth-round knockout.

WBC and IBF heavyweight champion Lennox Lewis (U.K.) bolstered his recognition as the best heavyweight in the world with a trio of successful title defenses. On April 29 he knocked out previously undefeated Michael Grant (U.S.) in the second round of a bout held in Madison Square Garden; on July 15 in London he scored a second-round knockout of Francois Botha (S.Af.); and on November 11 in Las Vegas he punctuated his excellent year by defeating David Tua (N.Z.) with a 12-round unanimous decision. The vacant WBA heavyweight title, which had been stripped from Lewis because he refused to defend against little-known John Ruiz (U.S.), was won by former WBA and IBF champion Evander Holyfield (U.S.), who scored an unpopular 12-round decision over Ruiz on August 12 in Las Vegas.

Advised by the Nevada State Athletic Commission to take his act elsewhere following a series of controversial performances in Las Vegas, former heavyweight champion Mike Tyson (U.S.) had his first two bouts of the year overseas. On January 29 he tallied a second-round knockout of Julius Francis (U.K.) in Manchester, Eng., and on June 24 he scored a first-round technical knockout over Lou Savarese (U.S.) in Glasgow, Scot. The latter fight was highlighted by Tyson's refusal to stop punching after referee John Coyle (U.K.) stopped the fight. Tyson pushed Coyle to the floor and kept hitting Savarese until the referee regained his feet and restored order. Tyson was subsequently fined $187,500 by the British Boxing Board of Control for his misconduct. Tyson returned to the United States for his third fight of the year, scoring a third-round technical knockout of Andrew Golota (Pol.) on October 20 in Auburn Hills, Mich., near Detroit.

Roy Jones, Jr. (U.S.), boxing's only unified champion, defended the WBC, WBA, and IBF light heavyweight title belts three times. On January 15, in the first boxing show ever held at New York City's Radio City Music Hall, he

Knocking Out Corruption in Boxing

Boxing was called the sporting world's "red light district" for a good reason—it had been a haven for corruption since the bare-knuckle days when bouts were fought in saloons, on barges, and in remote fields, far from the prying eye of the authorities. Although professional boxing had been legal throughout most of the world for 100 years, corruption continued to be one of the sport's biggest problems. Instead of the fixed fights of bygone eras, however, most modern scandals involved rigged rankings of boxers by the various ratings organizations and unscrupulous business practices on the part of governing bodies, promoters, and managers. There were two significant initiatives during 2000 intended to rid professional boxing in the U.S. of corruption—one judicial, the other legislative—but there was still uncertainty about whether these measures could salvage the sport's shaky reputation.

On April 11 Robert W. Lee, Sr., the founder and former president of the International Boxing Federation (IBF), and his son, Robert W. Lee, Jr., went on trial in federal court in Newark, N.J., accused of taking $338,000 in bribes to manipulate the organization's rankings. During the highly publicized trial, prominent boxing promoters Bob Arum, Cedric Kushner, and Dino Duva testified that they had paid thousands of dollars to IBF functionaries to obtain favourable rankings for the boxers they promoted. The government's star witness was Colin Douglas Beavers, the former IBF ratings chairman, who had been secretly helping the FBI since May 1997 and had made dozens of audio recordings of his conversations with Lee, Sr. On August 17 the jury acquitted Lee, Sr., of all the major bribery and racketeering charges but convicted him on counts of money laundering, tax evasion, and interstate travel to aid racketeering. His son was acquitted of all charges.

In the aftermath of the trial, Arum was fined $125,000 by the Nevada State Athletic Commission and put on six months of probation for "conduct detrimental to unarmed combat." Kushner was also fined $100,000 by the New York State Athletic Commission.

On the legislative side, the Muhammad Ali Boxing Reform Act was signed into law by Pres. Bill Clinton on May 26. The long-awaited legislation placed a one-year limit on the length of a boxer's contract with a promoter and banned the coercion of rights from top-ranked mandatory challengers. It also prohibited financial relationships between promoters and managers, barred managers or promoters from making improper payments to ratings organizations, and required ratings organizations both to disclose all charges they imposed on boxers and to publicly explain the reasons for their often-controversial ratings decisions. Promoters were required to disclose their contracts with boxers to state athletic commissions and to inform commissions of any charges or fees they were taking out of a boxer's earnings. Under the act, which was to be enforced by those commissions, state attorneys general could initiate civil actions and injunctions, while boxers could bring private actions. (NIGEL COLLINS)

won a 12-round decision over David Telesco (U.S.). On May 13 he scored an 11th-round technical knockout of Richard Hall (Jam.) in a bout held in Indianapolis, Ind. In his final bout of the year, Jones scored an 11th-round technical knockout of Eric Harding (U.S.) in New Orleans.

In a rematch of 1999's best action fight, Paulie Ayala (U.S.) again won a 12-round decision over Johnny Tapia (U.S.). While highly competitive, the featherweight bout, which took place on October 7 in Las Vegas, was not quite as exciting as their first encounter, but the close decision was more controversial than the first. After both fights Tapia accused the judges of being influenced by the fact that Ayala was under contract to promoter Bob Arum, whose company, Top Rank, Inc., was accused of corruption in Nevada and New Jersey. Tapia's charges, however, were not substantiated.

British boxer Lennox Lewis (right) punishes David Tua during the sixth round of their heavyweight championship bout in Las Vegas, Nev., on November 11.

AP/Wide World Photos

The most significant occurrence in women's boxing took place on February 6 in Scranton, Pa., when Jacqui Frazier-Lyde, the daughter of former heavyweight champion Joe Frazier, turned pro with a first-round knockout of Teela Reese. Frazier-Lyde, a practicing attorney, hoped to procure a match with one of Muhammad Ali's daughters, Laila Ali, who had turned pro in 1999.

At the Olympic Games in Sydney, Australia, Cuban boxers won 4 of the 12 gold medals at stake. Six-time amateur heavyweight world champion Félix Savón Fabré of Cuba collected his third consecutive Olympic gold. (*See* BIOGRAPHIES.) (NIGEL COLLINS)

CHESS

The parallel but entirely separate realms of the Fédération Internationale des Échecs (FIDE), the world ruling body founded in 1924, and former FIDE champion Garry Kasparov of Russia continued in 2000. FIDE made further attempts to come closer to the International Olympic Committee (IOC) in what looked like an attempt to reinforce its legitimacy and its right to organize the world individual championship. Kasparov, who split with FIDE in 1993, spent many months anticipating a title match with the Indian star Viswanathan Anand, then agreed to entrust the arrangement of such a contest to yet another new organization, the Brain Games Network (BGN). Anand, however, would not agree to such a match.

So there was no repeat of the Kasparov-Anand match held in New York City in 1995. In its place London-based backers of BGN arranged a 16-game match between Kasparov and Vladimir Kramnik for October and November 2000. Kramnik's midyear displacement of Anand in second place on the ratings list made this a logical step, but the gap of five years between Kasparov's matches was reminiscent of pre-1945 when Emanuel Lasker, José Raúl Capablanca, and Alexander Alekhine were reluctant to play matches against logical contenders.

Kramnik pulled off a great surprise by beating Kasparov, who had dominated world chess for 15 years. Kramnik, a 25-year-old from the Russian town of Tuapse, wedged between the Black Sea and the Caucasus Mountains, came out the winner on November 2 by scoring 2 wins, no losses, and 13 draws. Kasparov, at age 37, seemed almost unrecognizable. After the match he pointed to Kramnik's adoption of a new opening repertoire as the reason for his failure. Kasparov had felt obliged to work 10 hours a day on rest days in an attempt to counter such innovations as the Berlin Defense to the dreaded Ruy Lopez opening and suffered from a sort of burnout after the first few games. It certainly was unprecedented for Kasparov to offer to call it a draw after only 11 and 14 moves as he did in the 7th and 13th games, respectively. It was the first time since the Lasker-Capablanca match of 1921 that a defending champion had failed to win a single game. (*See* game diagram.)

These developments took place against the background of fewer international tournaments and the financial strains that induced FIDE to set up a commercial arm, the initial business plan of which seemed rather optimistic. The IOC connection brought in the spectre of drug tests, which many leading players resented. Jan Timman, the leading Dutch player of the past 25 years, stated his intention not to cooperate. Grandmasters were generally skeptical about the availability of performance-enhancing drugs for chess, but the drinking of a cup of coffee during play, a traditional feature of the game at all levels, seemed threatened should the proposed testing program go ahead.

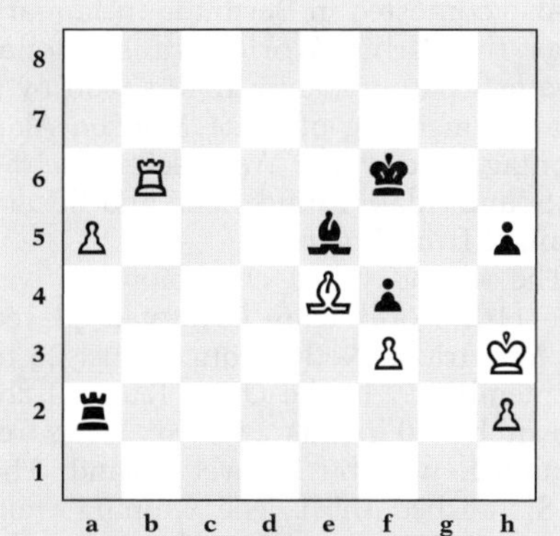

A sign of Garry Kasparov's bad form in the match came as early as the second game. Vladimir Kramnik, White, has just checked Kasparov's king with his rook. After 39 Rb5-b6+, Kasparov moved his king the wrong way by 39 . . . Kf6-e7?, and after 40 Be4-d5, Black had to resign in view of the double threat of 41 Bd5xa2 and 41 Rb6-e6+. Instead, 39 . . . Kg7 would give chances of putting up a long resistance due to the drawing propensity of the opposite-coloured bishops.

Meanwhile, many local clubs and short tournaments played at a rate of more than one game a day found their popularity diminished by the spread of Internet play. The controversial aspect of computer development was crystallized at the Dutch Championship on May 7–19 when Paul van der Sterren announced in advance that he would lose by default rather than meet the computer, and some other competitors played far below their best against it. Loek van Wely defeated it, however, using the slow buildup of a close game, which exploited one of the few remaining advantages human players had over computers, and took the Dutch title with 8.5 points from 11 games. The computer program Fritz SSS scored seven points to share third–fifth place, though van der Sterren came in third on a tiebreaker.

FIDE announced that it would not in the future rate events in which computers took part. The controversy over inflated ratings achieved in Myanmar (Burma) by results attained within too small a pool of players to be valid was mitigated. Every player from that country had 100 rating points deducted in the July 1 list.

Kasparov repeated his feat of 1999 by winning the three strongest tournaments of the year at Wijk aan Zee, Neth.; Linares, Spain (jointly with Kramnik); and Sarajevo, Bosnia and Herzegovina, before coming in second to Anand at the Frankfurt (Ger.) Chess Classic on June 22–25. Anand took the official FIDE world title in December, beating Aleksey Shirov of Spain $3^1/_2$–$^1/_2$ in the six-game final. Xie Jun of China retained her FIDE title with a win over compatriot Qin Karying.

(BERNARD CAFFERTY)

CONTRACT BRIDGE

Two world championship tournaments took place during 2000, the first time that had happened since 1976. The Bermuda Bowl is normally played in odd-numbered years, but because Bermuda requested to host the 50th anniversary competition, the World Bridge Federation (WBF) agreed to postpone the 1999 event to January 2000. In the final the United States defeated Brazil 506–288. The second U.S. entry finished third. The winning team comprised Nick Nickell, Richard Freeman, Eric Rodwell, Jeff Meckstroth, Bob Hamman, and Paul Soloway, with Sidney Lazard the nonplaying captain.

The controversy for the year was reserved for the Venice Cup, also contested in Bermuda at the same time. In this championship tournament for women, The Netherlands beat the U.S. by an official score of 249.75–249.25. The fractions arose because the U.S. was fined 2.5 points more than was The Netherlands for slow play. Also, the U.S. had received a three-point start by virtue of winning the preliminary match between the two teams. Therefore, at the table, over the 128 deals of the final, The Netherlands won by one point. However, those who agreed with the carryover formula from the earlier stages considered this the first world title decided by a slow-play penalty. Denmark finished third. The winning team comprised Marijke van der Pas, Bep Vriend, Jet Pasman, Anneke Simons, Wietske van Zwol, and Martine Verbeek, with Ed Franken the nonplaying captain.

There are many personalities from other fields who play bridge. Most do not win titles, or even try to, but one who may entertain such hopes is the Swedish golfer Jesper Parnevik. He was the declarer of this deal during a social game in his American hometown of Boca Raton, Fla.

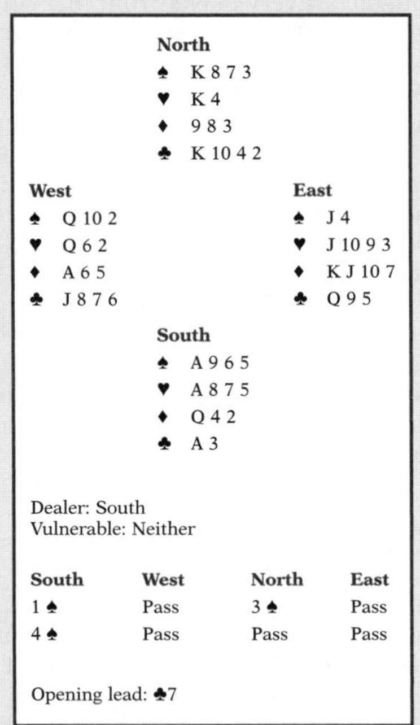

It looks as if Parnevik must lose one spade and three diamond tricks, but watch what happened. After winning in hand with the ♣A, declarer drew two rounds of trumps, cashed dummy's ♣K and ♥K, then played a heart to his ace. Having run out of top tricks, Parnevik ruffed a heart in the dummy and a club in his hand, giving this end-position:

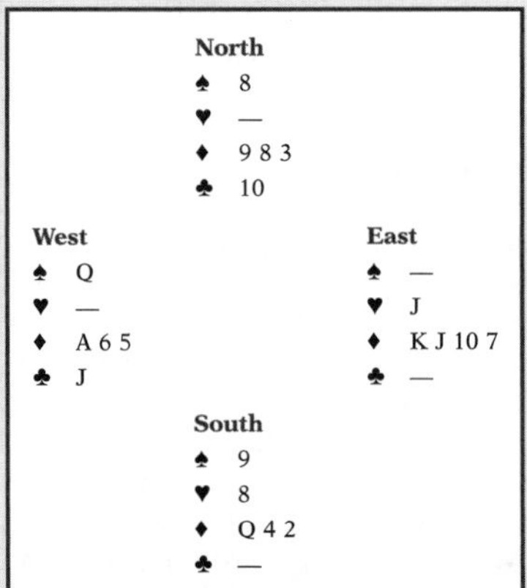

Parnevik led the ♥8, and West, multinational champion Larry Cohen, was caught in a sort of three-suit squeeze including trumps. If he ruffed, one of dummy's diamond losers would be discarded. If he pitched a diamond, dummy would ruff, and a club ruff in hand would be declarer's 10th trick. So West discarded the ♣J, hoping declarer would not realize this made dummy's ♣10 high. However, Parnevik made no mistake. He ruffed the ♥8 and discarded a diamond on the ♣10. The defense's four tricks had shrunk to three: one spade and two diamonds.

Also contested in Bermuda in January was the Orbis World Transnational Teams Championship. It was won by a team consisting of Rose Meltzer, Alan Sontag, and Peter Weichsel from the U.S. and Adam Zmudzinski and Cezary Balicki from Poland.

The second world championship was the 11th World Team Olympiad, played in Maastricht, Neth., from August 26 to September 9. In the Open Teams, Italy, down by 10 points with six deals remaining, won by 20 over Poland. The U.S. finished third. The winning team comprised Norberto Bocchi, Dano deFalco, Giorgio Duboin, Guido Ferraro, Lorenzo Lauria, and Alfredo Versace, with Carlo Mosca the nonplaying captain. The women's event was won by the U.S., which had a comfortable victory by 32 points over Canada. Third was Germany. The winners were Mildred Breed, Petra Hamman, Joan Jackson, Robin Klar, Shawn Quinn, and Peggy Sutherlin, with Bob Hamman the nonplaying captain.

After a one-year hiatus 15,513 pairs from 61 countries competed in the Worldwide Bridge Contest, played throughout the world June 2–3. There was, however, a difference from the tournaments of previous years. Instead of players' receiving the match point score instantly, all results were sent over the Internet to Anna Gudge and Mark Newton in England. Their software scored each deal on a worldwide basis, giving top marks of more than 10,000 match points and using the European 2 and 1 method rather than the American 1 and ½. The highest scores were obtained on June 2 by E. Raffa and L. Treta from Italy (with 204,996.11 match points, or 73.38%) and on June 3 by Le Lin and Luo Wenchan from China (with 75.23%).

In the secondary events the United States won the Seniors, represented by Stevie Robinson, John Mohan, Dan Morse, John Sutherlin, Bobby Wolff, and Kit Woolsey. The Transnational Mixed Teams was won by Irina Levitina, Jill Meyers, John Mohan, Sam Lev (all U.S.), Piotr Gawrys (Poland), and Migry Zur-Campanile (Israel), with Pinhas Romik (Israel) the nonplaying captain. A team from France was second and Austria third. The University Teams was won by Austria: Andreas Gloyer, Arno Lindermann, Bernd Saurer, and Martin Schifko, with Hannelore Thomasberger the nonplaying captain. Italy was second and Denmark third.

Bridge was now recognized as a sport by the International Olympic Committee (IOC), which planned to make bridge part of the Winter Olympics. Consequently, bridge players now had to satisfy IOC regulations. Therefore, players in the semifinals and finals at both world championships were chosen at random for drug testing. It is unclear whether anabolic steroids would be of any benefit to a bridge player, but, like chess players, many drink several cups of coffee while playing, which puts them in danger of exceeding the caffeine limit. (PHILLIP ALDER)

CRICKET

The 1999–2000 cricket year was dominated not by events on the field but by the betting scandal surrounding the South African captain, Wessel Johannes ("Hansie") Cronje, who admitted that he had taken money from bookmakers to influence the outcome of international matches. The scandal broke in early April 2000 when a transcript of a taped conversation, allegedly between Cronje and an Indian bookmaker, was released by Indian police investigating claims of match fixing. Having initially denied that the voice on the tape was his, Cronje later admitted that he had received a sum between $10,000 and $15,000 for providing "forecasts and information," but he resolutely denied actually fixing the results of matches. He was sacked immediately as South African captain and replaced by Shaun Pollock, but cricket's reputation was not so easily cleansed.

In the wake of Cronje's revelations, the whole of cricket came under suspicion. Among the matches subject to investigation was the final Test between England and South Africa at Centurion, S.Af., in January, which ended in a narrow win for England after Cronje unexpectedly set up a final-day declaration following three days of rain, thus officially forfeiting one innings of play for each side and allowing England a chance to win rather than accept the anticipated draw. Several well-known players, including former captains of India and Pakistan, were implicated in the scandal, and the report released by Justice Malik Qayyum in Pakistan found no evidence of "planned match fixing" by the Pakistani team. The Pakistan Cricket Board, acting on the judge's recommendation, banned captain Salim Malik for life.

The International Cricket Council reacted to the crisis by announcing five-year bans for anyone involved in match fixing and by setting up an independent commission of inquiry to be chaired

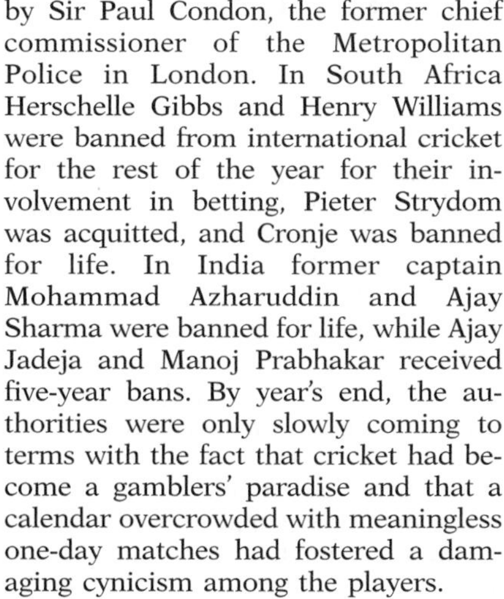

by Sir Paul Condon, the former chief commissioner of the Metropolitan Police in London. In South Africa Herschelle Gibbs and Henry Williams were banned from international cricket for the rest of the year for their involvement in betting, Pieter Strydom was acquitted, and Cronje was banned for life. In India former captain Mohammad Azharuddin and Ajay Sharma were banned for life, while Ajay Jadeja and Manoj Prabhakar received five-year bans. By year's end, the authorities were only slowly coming to terms with the fact that cricket had become a gamblers' paradise and that a calendar overcrowded with meaningless one-day matches had fostered a damaging cynicism among the players.

Reuters NewMedia Inc./Corbis

At the Oval in London on September 3, West Indies cricketers Curtly Ambrose (left) and Courtney Walsh (right) leave the field together for the last time in a Test series.

In the midst of the crisis, there was some excellent cricket played. Australia carried all before it, beating Zimbabwe, Pakistan, India, and New Zealand and setting up a sequence of 10 straight Test victories during the season. The most remarkable of Australia's victories came in November 1999 in the second Test against Pakistan in Hobart, Australia. Set 369 to make in 180 overs, Australia was 126 for 5 when Adam Gilchrist joined Justin Langer. Together the pair put on 238 for the sixth wicket (Langer 127, Gilchrist 149 not out) to guide Australia to the third highest score in the fourth innings to win a Test.

England's fortunes fluctuated as ever, with a series defeat by South Africa followed by a highly successful summer under a new coach, Duncan Fletcher of Zimbabwe, including series victories over Zimbabwe and, for the first time in 31 years, West Indies. Michael Atherton and Alec Stewart both played their 100th Test for England at Old Trafford, Manchester, Eng., in August, joining only five other England cricketers to reach that milestone. Atherton, in particular, enjoyed a fine series against the West Indies, scoring a century and 83 in the final Test to set up England's 3–1 series win, which turned on a thrilling victory for the home side in the second Test at Lord's, London.

The West Indies's Courtney Walsh (*see* BIOGRAPHIES) became the highest wicket-taker in Test history in March when he took his 435th Test wicket in the second Test against Zimbabwe in his native Jamaica. He added to the record with another 48 Test wickets, including 34 against England, before the end of the season. Curtly Ambrose, with whom Walsh had opened the West Indies bowling for the past decade, retired from cricket after the final Test against England at the Oval, London. In the previous Test he had taken his 400th Test wicket. On the final day at the Oval when Walsh and Ambrose came out to bat, the England players formed a guard of honour and clapped the West Indian pair all the way to the wicket.

Meanwhile, the West Indies's Brian Lara suffered an indifferent year, losing the captaincy and dropping out of the game for a short period. Jimmy Adams proved an astute replacement as captain, but only the discovery of Ramnaresh Sarwan, a batsman of genuine ability, gave the once-dominant West Indians a glimpse of hope for the future. Australia, on the other hand, had no such worries. An already formidable pace attack was strengthened by the addition of Brett Lee from New South Wales, who took 13 wickets in his first two Tests against India.

In England Surrey retained its county championship title comfortably, while unheralded Gloucestershire completed a remarkable four-timer of Lord's cup final successes by winning the Benson & Hedges and NatWest one-day trophies. Western Australia won the Mercantile Mutual one-day cup in Australia, Boland surprisingly won the 45-over night series in South Africa, and Jamaica won the Busta Cup in the West Indies. In 2000 cricket lost two of the sport's greats, fast bowler Brian Statham and batsman Colin Cowdrey. (*See* OBITUARIES.)

(ANDREW LONGMORE)

CURLING

International curling provided a nearly clean sweep for Canada in 2000 as Canadian teams captured four of six world titles and settled for silver in two others. The country's on-ice success stood in counterpoint to the death in March of Canadian skip Sandra Schmirler (*see* OBITUARIES), a three-time world champion and the first woman ever to win an Olympic gold medal for curling. Her funeral in Saskatchewan was nationally televised.

Canada, which had not won a women's world championship since Schmirler last turned the trick in 1997, returned to form in Glasgow, Scot., in April when Kelley Law of Richmond, B.C., defeated Switzerland's Luiza Ebnother 7–6 in the final. Norway won the women's bronze by defeating host Scotland. The remaining women's teams, in order, were Sweden, Denmark, Germany, the United States, Japan, and France.

Greg McAulay of New Westminster, B.C., completed the Glasgow sweep for Canada by beating Peter Lindholm of Sweden 9–4. It was McAulay's first world championship, while Lindholm was appearing in his third final in four years—with one victory to his credit in 1997. Canada was the only country to sweep both men's and women's world crowns in one year, a feat it had now accomplished nine times. Finland defeated the U.S. for the men's bronze medal. Rounding out the men's field, in order, were Denmark, Switzerland, Norway, Scotland, France, and Japan.

Canadian dominance continued at the world junior championships in Geising, Ger., where the Canadian men beat Switzerland for the gold and the Canadian women finished second to Sweden. In the inaugural world senior curling championship, also in Glasgow, Canadian men won gold over Scotland, while Scotland prevailed over Canada in the women's final. (BRUCE CHEADLE)

Reuters NewMedia Inc./Corbis

Riding a conventional-frame bicycle at the 2000 world track championships in Manchester, Eng., Chris Boardman of Great Britain pedals his way toward a new world one-hour record in October.

CYCLING

On the recommendation of its management committee, which introduced design restrictions on bicycles in 1996, the Union Cycliste Internationale decided as of Oct. 1, 2000, to return the world one-hour record to Belgian rider Eddy Merckx, who had covered 49.431 km (1 km=0.62 mi) in Mexico in 1972 on a bicycle of standard design. Merckx's record had stood until 1984, when it was broken by Francesco Moser of Italy using aerodynamic disc wheels. British cyclist Chris Boardman's distance of 56.375 km, set in 1996 using the subsequently banned extended-arm "Superman" riding position, was reclassified as a world's best hour performance. Boardman reclaimed the one-hour record, however, on October 27 at the 2000 world track championships in Manchester, Eng., when he covered a distance of 49.441 km riding an officially approved, conventional-frame bicycle.

New tests aimed at detecting the use of the human hormone erythropoietin (EPO) were developed in France and Australia. Plans to use the French test on urine samples at the Tour de France, the premier event on the international calendar, were shelved after consultation with legal and medical experts, but it was decided to freeze all samples taken in daily tests and retest them for EPO at a later date. Three riders were expelled from the Tour before the start when health checks revealed hematocrit levels—the functional level of red blood cells as a percentage of total blood plasma—above 50%, the level at which it was considered safe to race. The International Olympic Committee adopted both the French test and an Australian-developed blood test for the Olympic Games in Sydney in September.

The Tour de France was won by Lance Armstrong for the second successive year. The American rider finished 6 min 2 sec ahead of Germany's Jan Ullrich after 21 stages and 3,662 km of racing. Armstrong took the overall lead on stage 10, the first mountain stage (in the Pyrenees). He lost time to his major rivals in the final Alpine stage but sealed his overall victory by winning the 19th stage, a 58.5-km time trial. Armstrong was clearly the strongest rider in the field and silenced the critics who said that the absence in 1999 of Ullrich (the 1997 winner) and Marco Pantani (the 1998 winner), both of whom were present this time, had detracted from his first victory.

Two world track records were broken at the Olympic Games. Germany produced the first sub-four minute ride in the four-man 4,000-m team pursuit, beating Ukraine in the final in 3 min 59.71 sec. Leontien Zijlaard-van Moorsel of The Netherlands set a new record of 3 min 30.816 sec in the women's 3,000-m pursuit, winning the gold medal at that distance and later adding the road-time-trial and road-race titles.

(JOHN R. WILKINSON)

EQUESTRIAN SPORTS

Thoroughbred Racing. *United States.* The National Thoroughbred Racing Association (NTRA), an organization of racetracks, owners, breeders, off-track betting organizations, and sales companies, showed signs of collapsing late in 2000 when 22 U.S. racetracks announced their intentions to withdraw their support. The NTRA was formed in 1998 to create comprehensive marketing strategies for the sport and increase media exposure of thoroughbred racing. The rebel tracks, which represented more than a quarter of the NTRA's racetrack members, supplied annual membership fees totaling more than $2 million to the organization. Organizers of the withdrawal cited dissatisfaction with the NTRA and some of its policies. Talks among international racing officials that were intended to create a new global lobbying and marketing organization were initiated in a July meeting in Great Britain by racing groups from North America, Europe, Asia, and Australia.

Arlington International Racecourse, near Chicago, reopened in May after a hiatus of more than two years and revived the popular Arlington Million, which was run on August 19. Midway through its summer racing season, however, the racecourse was acquired by Churchill Downs, Inc., in a merger agreement that made Arlington's owner and chairman, Richard L. Duchossois, Churchill's largest stockholder. Citing what he perceived as an unfavourable economic and political environment in Illinois, Duchossois had closed his track's doors after the completion of its 1997 racing season. In early 1999 the Illinois General Assembly had passed legislation that provided tax breaks and other incentives for the state's horse racing tracks and paved the way for Arlington's grand reopening. In addition to Arlington, other tracks that had been taken over by Churchill Downs, Inc., included Ellis Park (in Kentucky), Hoosier Park (Indiana), Calder Race Course (Florida), and Hollywood Park (California).

Thoroughbred racing's answer to the popularity of electronic gaming devices (slot machines) came in January at Oaklawn Park in Hot Springs, Ark., with the debut of "Instant Racing," a pari-mutuel game that allowed a bettor to wager on 50,000 archived horse races. Oaklawn averaged $23,000 daily on Instant Racing machines during its 52-day season, providing the revenue for two purse increases at the track for the first time in five years.

New York City Off-Track Betting (OTB) announced in July that the city of New York was soliciting bids for its purchase and/or management. Interested parties included Churchill Downs, Inc., Frank Stronach (chairman of Magna Entertainment, Inc., which owned six racetracks around the country, including Gulfstream Park in Hallandale, Fla., and Santa Anita in Arcadia, Calif.), Greenwood Racing, Inc. (Philadelphia Park), and the New York Racing Association. New York City OTB topped $1 billion in handle for only the second time in its history during its fiscal year ending June 30.

Fusaichi Pegasus, owned by Japanese entrepreneur Fusao Sekiguchi, won the 126th Kentucky Derby on May 6 at Churchill Downs. He started as the prohibitive 1–5 betting favourite in the Preakness Stakes two weeks later but finished second to Red Bullet, ending any hope for a Triple Crown winner in 2000. The Belmont Stakes, won by Commendable, was the first Belmont in 30 years that did not include either the Kentucky Derby or Preakness winner. Commendable's victory gave trainer D. Wayne Lukas a record-tying 13th victory in a Triple Crown classic.

In the final race of his career, Fusaichi Pegasus finished a disappointing sixth as the 6–5 favourite in America's richest race, the $4,690,000 Breeders' Cup Classic at Churchill Downs on November 4, sending the vote for Horse of the Year honours up for grabs. It was announced in June that Irish conglomerate Coolmore Stud had reached a tentative agreement to purchase the breeding rights to Fusaichi Pegasus for a world-record sum reported to be between $60 million and $70 million.

Jockey Julie Krone, who retired in April 1999, in 2000 became the first woman to be inducted into the Racing Hall of Fame. Krone, who won 3,545 races including the 1993 Belmont Stakes aboard Colonial Affair, was the only female jockey ever to win a classic stake race. Laffit Pincay, Jr., who in 1999 surpassed the legendary Bill Shoemaker as the all-time leading jockey, logged another milestone as the first jockey to reach 9,000 wins. The 53-year-old Panamanian accomplished the feat in flamboyant style when he rode five stake winners on October 28 at Santa Anita.

Several important figures in U.S. horse racing died during the year. Canadian-born Hall of Fame trainer Lucien Laurin died in June. Fred W. Hooper, who bred more than 100 stakes winners, died in August. Allen Paulson, who bred and owned two-time Horse of the Year Cigar and other stakes winners, died of cancer. Jockey Chris Antley was found dead on December 2. (*See* OBITUARIES.) Hubert "Sonny" Hine, trainer of 1998 Horse of the Year Skip Away, died in March.

(JOHN G. BROKOPP)

AP/Wide World Photos

Jockey Frankie Dettori blows kisses to the crowd after crossing the finish line atop Dubai Millennium to win the $6 million Dubayy World Cup in March.

Thoroughbred Racing. *International.* In 2000 Europe enjoyed one of those years when there was not only a strong group of top-class horses but also most of them—with the unfortunate exception of Dubai Millennium—competed throughout the season. Montjeu, Petrushka, and Sinndar each succeeded in gaining Group 1 victories in England, France, and Ireland. Giant's Causeway, later named the European Horse of the Year, won five consecutive Group 1 races between June 20 and September 9 and was never out of the first two finishers in 10 appearances.

Dubai Millennium had ended 1999 with a pair of Group 1 successes at a mile distance. He returned in March 2000 with two flamboyant triumphs at 1¼ mi on the dirt at Nad al Sheba Racecourse in Dubayy, U.A.E., winning each by a wide margin and in course-record time. With jockey Frankie Dettori aboard, he led most of the way to win the world's richest race, the $6 million Dubayy World Cup, by six lengths over the American-trained Behrens. The winner's owner, Sheikh Mohammad al-Maktoum, head of the Godolphin stable, had anticipated the victory two years earlier when he changed his promising young colt's name from Yareek to Dubai Millennium.

Dubai Millennium ran only once more, ridden by Jerry Bailey in place of the injured Dettori, in the Prince of Wales's Stakes, a race newly promoted to Group 1 status, at Great Britain's Royal Ascot on June 21. Bailey employed the same tactics to win by eight lengths over the German-trained Sumitas. Dubai Millennium's career ended when he fractured a bone in his right hind leg at exercise on August 5. He was successfully operated on and retired to Dalham Hall Stud, Newmarket, Suffolk, Eng. Giant's Causeway, Montjeu, and Sinndar also retired to stud in Ireland at the end of the year.

August 5 was also the day on which Dettori returned to action, with wins on both his mounts at Newmarket. He had been injured on June 1 when a light plane carrying him and colleague Ray Cochrane crashed on takeoff at Newmarket, killing the pilot. Cochrane returned to action first, but a racing fall caused him to retire in the autumn. Both he and Dettori admitted that they had hurried back too quickly.

Kieren Fallon, the reigning British champion jockey, was unable to return before the end of the season after injuring his left shoulder in a four-horse accident at Ascot on June 21. He required complex surgery to repair severed nerves. In his absence Kevin Darley, the leading apprentice in 1978, won his first British championship. Darley's finest moment came in the Queen Elizabeth II Stakes at Ascot on September 23. He rode Observatory to a half-length victory over Giant's Causeway, who was attempting to become the first horse in Europe, since Mill Reef in 1971–72, to win six consecutive Group 1 races.

Irish jockey John Murtagh benefited most from Fallon's absence. Murtagh won the Epsom Derby, the Irish Derby, and the Prix de l'Arc de Triomphe in Paris on the Irish-trained Sinndar. The Aga Khan's home-bred colt was one of the best Derby winners of recent years and crowned his career with a defeat of two top-class French fillies, Egyptband and Volvoreta, in the Arc.

Montjeu was dominant in the first half of the season and was an impressive winner of the King George VI and Queen Elizabeth Diamond Stakes in July. The French-trained colt ended the season with three defeats, however, in the Arc (in which he started as the favourite but finished fourth), the Dubayy Champion

Stakes, and the Breeders' Cup Turf. Kalanisi, who had missed most of 1999, improved all season and ended by winning the Dubayy Champion and Breeders' Cup Turf, ridden by Murtagh each time.

Fifth behind Montjeu in the King George VI and Queen Elizabeth Diamond Stakes was the Japanese horse Air Shakur, who had been beaten by a nose by Agnes Flight in the Tokyo Yushun (Japanese Derby) two months earlier. He went home to win the Kikuka Sho (Japanese St. Leger) in October. More successful in Europe was Agnes World. He won the Prix de l'Abbaye de Longchamp in Paris in October 1999 and returned in 2000 to win the July Cup at Newmarket, becoming the first Japanese-trained winner of a Group 1 race in England.

Sunline, a New Zealand-bred five-year-old mare, set a new Australasian earnings record when she won the Southern Hemisphere's richest weight-for-age race, the Cox Plate, for the second year. She scored by seven lengths ahead of Diatribe, winner of the Caulfield Cup seven days earlier. Brew, bottom weight in a field of 22, went off at odds of 14–1 but triumphed by two lengths over runner-up Yippyio in the Melbourne Cup before a record crowd of 121,015. The six-year-old gelding was ridden by 20-year-old Kerrin McEvoy, who had completed his jockey apprenticeship less than a week earlier. (ROBERT W. CARTER)

Harness Racing. While it was unlikely that the pacing gelding Gallo Blue Chip would win any beauty contests, the raw-boned, three-year-old bay won plenty of races and money while dominating the sport of harness racing in 2000. Gallo Blue Chip won million-dollar events in both Canada and the United States during the summer and became the richest harness horse in a single season with earnings of $2,428,816.

The champion pacer was trained by 30-year-old Mark Ford and owned by Martin Scharf of Lawrence, N.Y., who purchased Gallo Blue Chip as a two-year-old in August 1999 after the horse had won his first several starts. It was obvious that Scharf made a good buy when Gallo Blue Chip went unbeaten in eight starts in 1999.

In 2000 Gallo Blue Chip won the $1 million North America Cup at Woodbine Racecourse in Toronto in late June and three weeks later took the $1,150,000 Meadowlands Pace in New Jersey. Favoured to win the Little Brown Jug in September, Gallo Blue Chip ran into a hot opponent in Astreos that day and finished second after a three-heat duel. He gained revenge by defeating Astreos twice in October, in the Tattersalls Pace and the Breeders Crown. French-Canadian driving ace Daniel Dube, who was in the sulky for most of Gallo Blue Chip's wins, marveled at the horse's durability late in the season. "The other horses are tired," Dube said. "This horse doesn't get tired."

The best North American trotters in 2000 were the seven-year-old mare Moni Maker and her rival, Magician, a five-year-old gelding. Moni Maker had reigned as Horse of the Year in 1998 and 1999, and she capped her career by winning the $500,000 Nat Ray at the Meadowlands in August and the $500,000 Trot Mondial at the Hippodrome in Montreal in September. She had to play second fiddle to Magician, however, in the $1 million Breeders Crown at the Meadowlands in July. Magician dominated the trotting scene at the Meadowlands for most of the season and bankrolled more than $1.2 million.

Moni Maker retired with 67 wins in 105 lifetime starts and career earnings of $5,589,256; she was the richest standardbred in history and the richest mare of any breed. She won at 28 tracks in seven countries at distances ranging from 1 mi to 1⅝ mi (1 mi=1.6 km). In her final public appearance, Moni Maker traded her sulky for a saddle and was ridden to a record mile by Hall of Fame thoroughbred jockey Julie Krone. They were paired for a time trial at the historic Red Mile oval in Lexington-Fayette, Ky., and covered the mile in 1:54⅕, breaking the record for a trotter under saddle by more than four seconds.

Trotting's greatest classic, the Hambletonian, celebrated its 75th anniversary in 2000. Yankee Paco coasted to victory despite racing on the outside the entire mile. He was the first Canadian-sired winner in Hambletonian history.

The European trotting season started in January with General du Pommeau winning the Prix d'Amerique in France impressively, but when he traveled to Sweden in late May for the Elitlopp ("Elite Race"), he was soundly defeated by the Swedish-bred gelding Victory Tilly. The five-year-old Victory Tilly, driven by six-time Elitlopp winner Stig H. Johansson, won several more races during the season, including the Oslo Grand Prix, and finished the year with winnings of more than $1 million.

The Inter-Dominion pacing championship in Melbourne, Australia, the most important harness racing event in the Southern Hemisphere, went to Shakamaker in February after the prerace favourite, New Zealand star pacer Courage Under Fire, broke stride at the start. (DEAN A. HOFFMAN)

Steeplechasing. Papillon, owned by American Betty Maxwell Moran, landed a great Irish gamble in the 2000 English Grand National. Ted and Ruby Walsh, respectively the Irish father (trainer) and son (jockey) team responsible for Papillon's win, followed up with Commanche Court in the Irish Grand National 16 days later. Istabraq, also Irish-trained, became the fifth horse to win three Champion Hurdles, while Looks Like Trouble won the Cheltenham Gold Cup. In November Al Capone II, the most popular steeplechaser in France, failed in his attempt to win the Prix La Haye Jousselin for the eighth consecutive year and was retired. His conqueror was First Gold, who had run third to Vieux Beaufai in the Grand Steeplechase de Paris in May. (ROBERT W. CARTER)

Show Jumping and Dressage. Riders from The Netherlands and Germany dominated the equestrian competition at the 2000 Olympic Games in Sydney, Australia. Jeroen Dubbeldam, riding Sjiem, won the show jumping gold medal after a jump-off with his Dutch compatriot Albert Voorn and Khaled al Eid from Saudi Arabia. Brazil's Rodrigo Pessoa, who had won the world's richest contest, the Du Maurier Grand Prix at Calgary, Alta., on Gandini Lianos a few weeks earlier, was expected to prevail in Sydney with Baloubet du Rouet. His mount refused at the eighth fence, however, and was eliminated. The pair did lead Brazil to the bronze behind Germany and Switzerland in the team event.

Anky van Grunsven of The Netherlands rode Gestion Bonfire to win the individual dressage ahead of Germany's Isabell Werth and Gigolo, the combination that had beaten her at the 1996 Games in Atlanta, Ga. Both horses were aged 17 and were retired after the Olympics. Germany dominated the team competition, followed by The Netherlands and the U.S. It was the German team's fifth consecutive gold medal in dressage and its eighth in the past 10 Olympics.

American David O'Connor, riding Custom Made, led throughout the individual three-day event. Andrew Hoy of Australia took the silver, and Mark Todd of New Zealand, the Olympic champion in 1984 and 1988, settled for the bronze in his final competition. Australia won its third consecutive three-day team gold. The

U.K. and U.S. captured silver and bronze, respectively. (ROBERT W. CARTER)

Polo. The 2000 U.S. high-handicap season, played in Florida from January to March, was divided in two leagues that played simultaneously in West Palm Beach and Boca Raton. Grants Farm (composed of Billy Busch, Jeff Blake, Héctor Galindo, and Sugar Erskine) obtained the Gold Cup of the Americas, defeating Excalibur (with Argentines Adolfo Cambiaso and Bartolomé Castagnola) 13–10 in the final. Meanwhile, John Goodman's Isla Carroll (with brothers Ignacio and Eduardo Heguy) defeated Coca Cola 9–8 to win the U.S. Polo Association Gold Cup in Boca Raton. Outback, led by Cambiaso with a woman—Sunny Hale—as a teammate, gained the U.S. Open for the second straight year, outclassing Everglades in the decisive encounter.

In the English season, from May to July, Geebung (with Argentines Cambiaso and Bautista Heguy as its best men) demonstrated its power, demolishing its rivals to obtain the most important tournaments: the Queen's and Gold cups. Argentina won the traditional Coronation Cup, beating the English quartet 10–9 in an extra chukker. Woodchester was the champion of the Gold Cup, held from August to September in Sotogrande, Spain. Local team Santa María defeated Geebung for the Silver Cup.

In Argentina, where the highest-level polo in the world is played, Indios Chapaleufú II, consisting of brothers Alberto, Jr., Ignacio, and Eduardo Heguy with Milo Fernández Araujo, won the Argentine Open, defeating Cambiaso's La Dolfina 16–13 in the final. In the Hurlingham Open, however, La Dolfina took revenge and demolished the earlier victors 17–13 to gain the championship. In April Gonzalo Heguy, son of Horacio Heguy, Sr., died at the age of 35 in a car accident in Argentina. Gonzalo had won the Argentine Open five times, playing with his brothers Marcos, Bautista, and Horacio, Jr., for Indios Chapaleufú.

(JORGE ADRIÁN ANDRADES)

FENCING

The Olympic Games in Sydney, Australia, dominated fencing during 2000. The presentation of the sport in Sydney proved to be the best yet at world level, especially the preliminary rounds. Forty-three nations were represented, and although the traditionally strong Europeans and Russians took the lion's share of medals, South Korea and China were not far behind. The U.S. and Japan were unlucky not to do better, and Australia also showed good form. The South Koreans took their first-ever Olympic gold medal in fencing with a win in the men's individual foil. In the individual events no fencer who won a gold medal at the 1996 Olympics in Atlanta, Ga., successfully defended a title, and many competitors who were expected to reach the medals round were eliminated early. This was a function of the relatively small number of entries allowed at each weapon and the lack of a seeding round. The Fédération Internationale d'Escrime (FIE), the world governing body, intended to keep Olympic selection procedures under review.

The new transparent mask, although authorized for use in Sydney, was not compulsory owing to problems with the product from some manufacturers, and most fencers continued to use the mesh mask. Although tests demonstrated that the clear section of the new mask was safe, weaknesses were identified at the joins in some masks. The FIE formed a special commission to coordinate the testing and introduction of clear masks. A problem also was encountered with the new wireless scoring equipment. Although used successfully at sabre in both the Olympic test event and the women's world sabre championships in Budapest, occasional interference problems were experienced when the equipment was used with other weapons, especially épée.

Four new federations—Senegal, Malta, Algeria, and Burkina Faso—were admitted to the FIE in 2000, which took the total to 104. A new school for coaches opened in Dakar, Senegal, joining the existing one in Johannesburg, S.Af., from which the first promising results were emerging. (GRAHAM MORRISON)

FIELD HOCKEY

At the 2000 Olympic Games in Sydney, Australia, The Netherlands defended the title it had captured in Atlanta, Ga., in 1996 and thereby became the second country to have won back-to-back gold medals, after India, which had won six straight Olympic titles (1928–56). A similar feat was achieved by the Australian women, who won their second consecutive gold and their third in five appearances (they won their first gold in 1988).

The men's finalists, the world champion Netherlands and South Korea, were in danger of not even making the semifinals. A shocking defeat for Germany by Great Britain helped the Dutch top pool A on goal aggregate, despite a loss to Pakistan. In pool B India needed a win against Poland, but a 1–1 draw sealed India's fate, and South Korea, which had a 2–0 pool-match verdict over India, went on to beat Pakistan in the semifinal.

A hat trick by the Dutch captain, Stephan Veen, was the final's highlight. He scored once more in the penalty shoot-out after the teams tied 3–3 despite extra time of 15 minutes. The Dutch won 5–4, profiting from a miss by South Korea's Song Seung Tae. Australia retained the bronze it won in Atlanta by beating Pakistan 6–3. Argentina, which placed eighth, was included as a substitute for South Africa, which became eligible to participate as the winner of the All Africa Games. The National Olympic Committee of South Africa had refused the team permission to join the Games, on the basis of an assessment that the possibility of the men's finishing above the ninth spot was remote.

The "Hockeyroos," as the Australian women were referred to, enjoyed an overwhelming superiority in individual craft and teamwork. Led by the seasoned midfielder Rechelle Hawkes, Australia beat Argentina (3–1), a first-time finalist. The Netherlands earned a bronze by besting Spain 2–0.

The executive board of the sport's international governing body, the Féderation Internationale de Hockey (FIH), accepted the need to restructure and presented the report for approval to the FIH Congress in Paris on November 25. The FIH secretary-general, Els van Breda Vriesman, was nominated to the International Olympic Committee Evaluation Commission for the 2008 Olympiad. Veen and Alyson Annan of Australia were chosen as the players of the year for 2000. (S. THYAGARAJAN)

FOOTBALL

Association Football (Soccer). *Europe.* France emphasized its domination of international association football (soccer) events by adding the 2000 European championship title to the World Cup success it had achieved in 1998. Euro 2000, which was held in Belgium and The Netherlands, was the sport's first major tournament to be staged in two countries, and there was a high standard of play from many of the finalists.

Italy provided France's opposition in the final, staged in Rotterdam, Neth., on July 2, and proved a worthy adversary despite a contrasting style. While the

French used one lone, mobile striker and relied on relentless waves of support from midfield, the Italians stuck to three central defenders and a reinforced blanket of five in midfield, leaving two attackers to forage up front. There was also a distinct difference in the composition of the two teams. While Italy had only home-based players in its lineup, France fielded no fewer than 9 "mercenaries" in its starting 11—players who plied their professional trade in other countries.

In the semifinals France beat Portugal 2–1 with a penalty goal in sudden-death overtime. The Italians had to play for much of their semifinal game against The Netherlands with 10 men, following a dismissal just after half an hour's play. The Dutch missed two penalties during normal time, but Italy survived and won the subsequent penalty shoot-out 3–1.

In the final the Italians were noticeably tired after their marathon with The Netherlands, but they coped well enough with the first-half onslaught from the French and took the lead in the 55th minute following the best move of the match. Francesco Totti, finding no space ahead of him, cleverly back-heeled the ball to Gianluca Pessotto, whose cross was side-footed in by Marco Delvecchio.

The Italians then squandered several opportunities to add to the lead, and France's manager, Roger Lemerre, was forced to use his three substitutes in an effort to wrest the initiative from Italy. It proved an inspired decision. With the game in injury time, one of the replacements, Sylvain Wiltord, latched onto a misheaded clearance, cut in from the left, and fired into the far corner. In the 103rd minute the other two substitutes combined for the sudden-death winner in overtime as Robert Pires crossed the ball for David Trézéguet to produce an unstoppable, spectacular volley. There was some consolation for Italy in winning the under-21 championship, but France was not to be denied another honour, taking the under-18 title.

On May 24 Paris was the venue for the final of the Champions League European Cup. In an all-Spanish affair, Real Madrid convincingly beat Valencia 3–0 in front of 78,759 spectators. Fernando Morientes, who was playing only because of a slight injury to the Brazilian Savio (Savio Bortolini Pimentel), headed Real into a 39th-minute lead from a short right-wing cross by Michel Salgado. In the 67th minute the Valencia defense failed to clear the ball, and Steve McManaman volleyed the second goal. Eight minutes later Raúl (Raúl González Blanco) ran unchallenged from the halfway line for the third score. It was Real's eighth championship in the competition.

In contrast, in the Union des Associations Européennes de Football (UEFA) Cup final, held in Copenhagen a week earlier in front of 38,919 spectators, Galatasaray became the first Turkish team to win a major European trophy when it beat England's Arsenal 4–1 on penalties following a low-key goalless draw. The Turkish side played for all but two minutes of overtime without Gheorghe Hagi, the Romanian playmaker, who was sent off for punching Arsenal's Tony Adams. Galatasaray's first-leg semifinal against Leeds United had been marred by the death of two English supporters in rioting in Istanbul the day before the match.

In domestic football the high and low points both came in Ukraine. Dynamo Kiev won its eighth consecutive Ukrainian national championship and was undefeated in the 30 games played, dropping just six points (in three draws), while Zirka Kirovograd finished at the bottom and failed to win one match. Spain's Real Club Deportivo of La Coruña won its first national title in its 94-year history. Thanks to goal difference, Bayern Munich retained the Bundesliga crown in Germany on the last day of the season.

In France there was a surprise in the cup tournament when Calais, a team composed entirely of amateur players with full-time occupations outside football, reached the final and then lost 2–1 to Nantes. In Scotland a 3–1 defeat on its own ground for Celtic in an early round against Inverness Caledonian Thistle (elected to the Scottish League as recently as 1994) produced immediate reaction. This sensational defeat cost the jobs of the entire Celtic coaching staff. Celtic's longtime Glasgow rivals, the Rangers, achieved that team's 49th championship and its 11th title in 12 years. The Rangers also won the Scottish Cup for the 29th time. Manchester United won the English Premier League for the sixth time since the league's formation in 1992. The leading scorer in Europe was Mario Jardel of Porto in Portugal with 38 league goals.

The Fédération Internationale de Football Association (FIFA), the world governing body, came under severe criticism after the voting to choose the host nation for the 2006 World Cup. South Africa, the favourite, was edged out in the final count in favour of Germany. The New Zealand representative, thought likely to be voting for the South Africans, abstained amid alleged offers of bribery and threats on his life. The African bloc blamed Asia and broke off relations with it. England, which had been convinced of the strength of its own bid, spent about $16 million of taxpayers' money on what was considered to be a poorly organized campaign and blamed fan violence by English hooligans at the start of the Euro 2000 championship for its failure.

Meanwhile, FIFA membership continued to grow, with the admission of Bhutan bringing the total up to 204 coun-

Philippe Huguen/AFP Worldwide

French team captain Didier Deschamps holds up the Euro 2000 association football (soccer) championship trophy after France took the title by defeating Italy 2–1 on July 2.

tries. A record number of 198 members entered the 2002 World Cup, scheduled to be held in Japan and South Korea, but the possibility that two of the games would be staged in North Korea was not substantiated.

More problems for the authorities came when the European Union (EU) insisted that the transfer system be severely restricted, with players over 24 years of age being allowed to move without payment of a fee. This represented the greatest threat yet to a professional sport for which the transfer system had been a cornerstone for more than a century. Thus, the record deal in Spain that took Portuguese midfielder Luis Figo from Barcelona to Real Madrid for about $56 million in July seemed likely to stay the record. His move came after Hernan Crespo's transfer in Italy from Parma to Lazio for about $55 million.

Escalating salaries in Western Europe were chiefly sustained by money from television and other communications. The highest paid player, at about $130,000 a week, was reputed to be 1999 European and World Footballer of the Year Rivaldo Vitor Borba Ferreira—Barcelona's Brazilian midfielder known simply as Rivaldo. (*See* BIOGRAPHIES.) If the EU's proposals went through, the principal beneficiaries would be players and their agents.

Another contentious issue concerned FIFA's wish to introduce a coordinated international match calendar specifying dates upon which all first-class fixtures would be played. Four weeks would be set aside for holidays, with another four weeks for preseason training. On the basis of two matches per week, this would leave 76 match dates—46 for national league and cup matches, 16 for continental club competitions, and 12 for national team matches including friendlies, with a further two dates in reserve.

(JACK ROLLIN)

The Americas. Brazil's long reign as number one in Latin American association football (soccer) came to an end in 2000. Although it beat Argentina 3–1 at home in the first round of the South American zone's World Cup qualifying group, the year ended with Argentina leading the group comfortably by five points after 10 of the 18 games had been played.

The continent's most important club competition, the Libertadores de América Cup, was also won by an Argentine club, Boca Juniors, which went on to beat Real Madrid 2–1 in the annual Intercontinental Cup between the champions of South America and Europe. Brazil was not quite eclipsed, however, as Corinthians of São Paulo defeated Rio de Janeiro's Vasco da Gama 4–3 in the inaugural world club championship in January. The Mercosur Cup—a made-for-television tournament between leading clubs from part of the continent—had an all-Brazilian final for the third consecutive year, with Palmeiras losing to Vasco da Gama 4–3. The similarly organized Merconorte Cup had an all-Colombian final for the third straight year, with Atlético Nacional taking the title in a two-legged final 0–0, 2–0 over Millonarios.

Brazil had other problems off the field. Brazilian football authorities and clubs were being investigated by the country's legislature for tax evasion and dubious contracts, while its national championship could not be held in 2000 because a small club (Gama), in order to avoid relegation in 1999, had gone to court complaining of unfair practices.

Otherwise, the continent's most popular game had three main worries—escalating hooligan violence in many countries, the continued exodus of leading stars to Europe, notably Brazil's 1999 World Player of the Year, Rivaldo (*see* BIOGRAPHIES), and the bankruptcy of many clubs. Some clubs faced bitterly fought takeovers by investors and other dire consequences. In Brazil, Corinthians' star players were sold after the team won the world club championship.

In February Canada pulled off a major upset, overcoming Colombia 2–0 to win the men's CONCACAF Gold Cup. The U.S. women remained strong, topping Brazil 1–0 in the women's Gold Cup in July after having overpowered Canada 4–0 in the U.S. Cup in May.

The Kansas City Wizards (16–7) won the team's first U.S. Major League Soccer (MLS) championship, defeating the Chicago Fire (17–9) 1–0 in the MLS Cup on October 15. The Wizards' goalkeeper, 31-year-old Tony Meola, was named Most Valuable Player for the final, as well as being chosen the regular season's MVP, best goalkeeper, and Comeback Player of the Year. In February the Women's United Soccer Association announced an eight-team U.S. women's professional league to begin playing in April 2001. (ERIC WEIL)

U.S. Football. *College.* The University of Oklahoma won its seventh national championship of U.S. college football and its first since 1985 by defeating Florida State University 13–2 in the Orange Bowl at Miami, Fla., on Jan. 3, 2001. Big 12 Conference champion Oklahoma, with a 13–0 record, held scoreless a Florida State offense that led Division I-A of the National Collegiate Athletic Association (NCAA) in the regular season with 384 yd passing and 549 total yards per game while ranking third with 42.4 points. The two teams' quarterbacks each won Player of the Year awards, with Chris Weinke of Florida State winning the prestigious Heisman Trophy and Josh Heupel of Oklahoma winning the Associated Press (AP) and Walter Camp Foundation awards. Purdue quarterback Drew Brees won the Maxwell Award.

Oklahoma, the only undefeated I-A team in the regular season, was the third consecutive undisputed champion under the Bowl Championship Series (BCS) format, which determined the championship game's opponents on the basis of two established news media polls and eight computerized rankings. Identifying the title game's contenders, however, generated controversy for the second time in three BCS seasons. The polls' second-ranked team, Big East champion University of Miami (11–1), had defeated Atlantic Coast champion Florida State (11–2) during the regular season, which prompted BCS chairman John Swofford to propose that future computer rankings give more value to head-to-head games and less value to high margins of victory.

The final writers' and coaches' polls agreed only through three places, with Miami second after its 37–20 Sugar Bowl victory over Southeastern Conference champion Florida (10–3), and Pacific-10 cochampion Washington (11–1) third after its 34–24 Rose Bowl victory over Big Ten cochampion Purdue (8–4). The coaches ranked Florida State fourth, but the writers ended Florida State's 13-year streak of top-four finishes in their AP poll by selecting Oregon State, which defeated Notre Dame (9–3) by a score of 41–9 in the Fiesta Bowl. The writers' 6th through 10th spots went to Virginia Tech (11–1), Oregon (10–2), Nebraska (10–2), Cotton Bowl winner Kansas State (11–3), and Florida. The coaches' poll dropped Oregon from 7th to 9th and replaced Florida with Michigan (9–3) at 10th. Oregon and Oregon State were the other Pacific-10 cochampions, and Northwestern and Michigan the others in the Big Ten. Other I-A conference winners were Colorado State (10–2) in the Mountain West, Louisville (9–3) in Conference USA, Boise State (10–2) in the Big West, and Marshall (8–5) in the Mid-American, while Texas Christian (10–2) and Texas–El Paso (8–4) tied for the Western Athletic championship.

AP/Wide World Photos

Oklahoma coach Bob Stoops is drenched by his players after the Sooners defeated Florida State 13–2 in the Orange Bowl on Jan. 3, 2001, to capture U.S. college football's national championship.

Weinke, Heupel, and Brees each led Division I-A in quarterbacking categories, Weinke with 4,167 yd passing, Heupel with a .647 completion percentage, and Brees with 358.1 yd per game of total offense. Weinke also won the Davey O'Brien Award for quarterbacks. Bart Hendricks of Boise State led all quarterbacks with an efficiency rating of 170.6 points, 35 touchdowns, 10.1% of his passes for touchdowns, and 9.69 yd per attempt. Boise State was the scoring leader with 44.9 points per game and Nebraska the rushing leader with 349.3 yd per game. Individual scoring leader Lee Suggs had 28 touchdowns for Virginia Tech, and the receiving leaders were James Jordan with 109 catches for Louisiana Tech, Lee Mays with 15 touchdowns for Texas–El Paso, Fred Biletnikoff Award winner Antonio Bryant with 130.2 yd per game for Pittsburgh, and Marvin Minnis with 1,340 total yards in Florida State's longer schedule. LaDanian Tomlinson won the Doak Walker Award and his second-straight rushing crown with 2,158 yd for Texas Christian, which also was the national defensive leader with per-game yields of 245 total yards and 9.6 points allowed.

Florida State defensive end Jamal Reynolds won the Vince Lombardi Award as the best lineman, and Tennessee defensive lineman John Henderson won the Outland Trophy for interior linemen. Akron's Dwight Smith and Louisville's Anthony Floyd were the interception leaders with 10 apiece, while Jamar Fletcher of Wisconsin won the Jim Thorpe Award for defensive backs. Miami linebacker Dan Morgan won the Chuck Bednarik Award for defensive players and the Dick Butkus Award for linebackers. Cincinnati kicker Jonathan Ruffin won the Lou Groza Award with his division-high 26 field goals, but Nick Calaycay of Boise State had the highest percentage, .938 on 15 for 16. Wisconsin punter Kevin Stemke won the Ray Guy Award.

Professional. In the National Football League (NFL), the American Football Conference (AFC) Baltimore Ravens (formerly the Cleveland Browns) crushed the National Football Conference (NFC) New York Giants 34–7 in Super Bowl XXXV on Jan. 28, 2001, in Tampa, Fla. The Ravens' defense, led by middle linebacker Ray Lewis, who was named the game's Most Valuable Player (MVP), held the Giants to only 149 net yards (66 yd rushing). Baltimore's defense also had upset Denver 21–3 in the "wild-card" play-off game, Tennessee 24–10 in the division championship, and Oakland 16–3 in the AFC championship. The Giants had shocked Minnesota 41–0 in the NFC championship match-up.

The defending champion St. Louis Rams were eliminated in the first round of the play-offs by New Orleans, which also won the NFC West division and improved by seven games from 1999, the league's best gain. None of the 1999 division winners defended their crowns successfully, and three of the six did not even qualify for the play-offs. The Giants won the NFC, Minnesota topped the NFC Central, Miami claimed the AFC East, Tennessee won the AFC Central, and Oakland captured the AFC West. The wild-card play-off teams with the best runner-up records were Indianapolis, Baltimore, and Denver in the AFC and St. Louis, Tampa Bay, and Philadelphia in the NFC. Not since 1986, before the play-off pool expanded from 10 teams to 12, had all NFL play-off teams won at least 10 games. The season's worst declines from the previous year were seven games by San Diego and Jacksonville, which, along with Washington and Seattle, fell from a division championship out of the play-offs.

Baltimore broke the record for fewest points allowed in a 16-game regular season with 165 (10.3 per game) and also led NFL defenses by giving up only 60.6 yd rushing per game and taking away 49 interceptions and fumbles, part of its league-best turnover differential of plus-23. Baltimore's Ray Lewis was the league's Defensive Player of the Year. Tennessee's defensive yield of 151.4 yd passing and 238.3 total yards per game helped it become the only team to win at least 11 games in consecutive seasons. Darren Sharper's nine interceptions for Green Bay led the league, as did the 17 sacks by La'Roi Glover of New Orleans.

St. Louis set a record with 7,075 yd on offense (442.2 per game) and also led the league with 327 yd passing per game. NFL MVP Marshall Faulk sparked the Rams with 26 touchdowns, which set a record even though he missed two games with an injury. Terrell Owens of San Francisco broke Tom Fears's 50-year-old record by catching 20 passes in one game, and Corey Dillon of Cincinnati broke Walter Payton's 23-year-old record by running for 278 yd in a game.

The passing leaders were Denver's Brian Griese with a 102.9 efficiency rating and a league-low 1.2% of his passes intercepted, St. Louis's Kurt Warner (*see* BIOGRAPHIES) with 9.88 yd per attempt, Minnesota's Daunte Culpepper with 7% of his passes resulting in touchdowns, and Indianapolis's Peyton Manning with 4,413 yd and 33 touchdowns, which tied Culpepper. Griese completed the first father-son pair to lead the league in passing efficiency, following Bob Griese, who had an 87.8 rating for Miami in 1977. Among receivers, Carolina's Muhsin Muhammad and Indianapolis's Marvin Harrison led with 102 catches, Minnesota's Randy Moss scored 15 touchdowns, and St. Louis's Torry Holt gained a total of 1,635 yd and an average of 19.9 yd per catch.

The Rhine Fire (7–3) defeated the Scottish Claymores (6–4) by a score of 13–10 in Frankfurt, Ger., on June 25 for the championship of NFL Europe. The Orlando Predators (11–3) won the

Arena Football League championship with a game-ending field goal for a 41–38 victory over the Nashville Kats (9–5) in ArenaBowl XIV on August 20 in Orlando, Fla. (KEVIN M. LAMB)

Canadian Football. The British Columbia Lions won the 2000 Canadian Football League (CFL) championship by defeating the Montreal Alouettes 28–26 in the Grey Cup on November 26 at Calgary, Alta., becoming the first champion in the Cup's 88 years with a losing won-lost-tied record in the regular season (8–10–0). The Lions led all CFL offenses during the season with averages of 139.2 yd rushing, 316.8 yd passing, and 436.7 total net yd per game, and then won play-off games against Western Division champion Calgary (12–5–1) and Eastern Division champion Montreal (12–6).

Lions quarterback Damon Allen led the league with 4,840 yd passing and finished the season with career CFL records of 3,588 completions, 6,480 attempts, and 50,789 yd. Kicker Lui Passaglia set a field-goal percentage record of .909 (40 for 44) in the last of his 25 seasons with British Columbia, retiring at age 46 with CFL records for points (3,984), field goals (875), and punting and kickoff yardage.

Calgary quarterback Dave Dickenson was the league's Most Outstanding Player with a record of 114.1 passing efficiency points and league highs of 36 touchdown passes and a .643 completion percentage. His teammate, receiver Allen Pitts, set career records of 966 catches, 14,891 yd, and 117 touchdowns. Montreal running back Mike Pringle led the league with 1,778 yd rushing and 19 touchdowns, another record. Curtis Marsh of Saskatchewan had league highs of 102 catches and 1,560 yd receiving. Most Outstanding Defensive Player Joe Montford of Hamilton had 20 quarterback sacks. (KEVIN M. LAMB)

Quarterback Damon Allen of the B.C. Lions hoists the Grey Cup on November 26.

AP/Wide World Photos

Australian Football. Essendon—the invincibles. That was the cry at the finish of the 2000 Australian Football League (AFL) season as Essendon swept to its 16th premiership. It was a season that belonged to Essendon in every way as the Bombers maintained top position on the ladder after every round, lost only one of their 22 home and away games (in round 21), and then raced through the three finals. In the Grand Final Essendon beat Melbourne (which had failed to qualify for the play-offs in 1999) 19.21 (135) to 11.9 (75) before a crowd of 96,249 at the Melbourne Cricket Ground. It was Essendon coach Kevin Sheedy's fourth premiership since he started in the position in 1981.

Essendon's chief goalkicker Matthew Lloyd kicked 94 goals in the home and away rounds to gain the Coleman Medal and then booted a further 15 goals in the finals to finish with a season total of 109. Shane Woewodin won the Brownlow Medal as the best and fairest player in the competition, while James Hird earned the Norm Smith Medal as best player in the Grand Final. Wayne Carey, the captain of the North Melbourne Kangaroos, was named captain of the All-Australian team, and Paul Hasleby of the Fremantle Dockers was voted the best rookie, winning the Norwich Union AFL Rising Star Award. (GREG HOBBS)

Rugby Football. Following their Rugby Union World Cup triumph in 1999, the Australians silenced any remaining critics by claiming the Tri-Nations series in August 2000, with wins over South Africa and New Zealand. The Australian side, however, was in something of a rebuilding phase. The last match in the Tri-Nations marked the final international appearances of centre Jason Little after representing Australia in 75 matches, flanker David Wilson (79 international matches), and prop Richard Harry (37), all of whom retired from international rugby, along with injured centre Tim Horan (80).

England's Rugby Union side struck a decisive blow for the Northern Hemisphere in June, winning on South African soil for the first time in six years. The 27–22 victory was built around the outstanding form of England's young outside half Jonny Wilkinson, who scored all 27 points. England arrived in South Africa after having lost the Grand Slam (earned by winning all five matches in the tournament) in the Six Nations with a dramatic defeat in the tournament's last match at Scotland. Scotland's Duncan Hodge scored a converted second-half try and four penalties to snatch victory from England. England—despite that single defeat—won the Six Nations (formerly the Five Nations) championship. France finished second, with Ireland third, Wales fourth, Scotland fifth, and Italy (the event's newest member) sixth.

The Heineken (European) Cup again was won by an English team, Northampton, following Bath's victory in 1998. For Northampton this was its first trophy in its 120-year history, with Paul Grayson kicking all nine points in their 9–8 victory over Ireland's Munster. Leicester was the English champion for the second year running. Other domestic honours went to Wasps (Tetley's Bitter [English] Cup), Cardiff (Welsh/Scottish League champion), Llanelli (Welsh Cup), Heriot's (Scottish premiership champion), Boroughmuir (Scottish Cup), St. Mary's College (Irish champion), and Stade Français (French champion).

In the Southern Hemisphere, Todd Blackadder's climb to be captain of New Zealand was confirmed when he led the Canterbury Crusaders to the Super 12 championship, beating Australia's finest provincial side, ACT Brumbies, 20–19, in the final. In South Africa the national coach, Nick Mallett, resigned and left Harry Viljoen to take the Springboks to Europe and Argentina on tour. In October Western Province won South Africa's provincial Currie Cup with a solid 25–15 victory over archrival Natal.

New Zealand took the first World Sevens series title from Fiji. Off the field, Rugby Union renewed its campaign to be accepted as an Olympic sport in 2008.

In Rugby League, St. Helens repeated as the European Super League champion with a 29–16 victory over the Wigan Warriors in the final at Old Trafford in Manchester, Eng., on October 14. The Brisbane Broncos won its fifth premiership in the Australian National Rugby League, vanquishing the Sydney Roosters 14–6 in the grand final on August 27 before 92,277 fans. (PAUL MORGAN)

GOLF

The achievements of one man would mean the year 2000 would always be remembered in golf. Eldrick ("Tiger") Woods matched Ben Hogan's previously unique feat of winning three of the sport's four major championships in one season (1953). En route, he joined Hogan, Gene Sarazen, Gary Player, and Jack Nicklaus as the only players to record at least one victory in each of the four majors—the Masters, U.S. Open, British Open, and Professional Golfers' Association of America (PGA) championship—during their careers. At 24, Woods was also the youngest man to complete the set. It was not only the fact that Woods won the U.S. and British opens and the PGA championship that made it such an unforgettable summer, it was also the manner of his successes.

The 100th U.S. Open at Pebble Beach in Monterey, Calif., was always going to be an emotion-charged occasion in the absence of defending champion Payne Stewart, who was killed along with five others in an airplane accident in October 1999. Woods, however, having mourned the loss of his close friend, registered the widest margin of victory in the entire 140-year history of major championship golf.

Golf phenomenon Tiger Woods poses with the Wanamaker Trophy after claiming the PGA championship in August.

AP/Wide World Photos

No one had ever finished the event in double figures under par, but the world's number-one player—he was untouchable in that position all year—completed the 72 holes in a 12-under-par aggregate of 272, a massive 15 strokes ahead of joint runners-up Ernie Els of South Africa and Miguel Ángel Jiménez of Spain. The previous record margin was the 13 shots by which Tom Morris, Sr., had won the 1862 British Open, and the 272 total equalled the U.S. Open record of Nicklaus in 1980 and Lee Janzen in 1993, both on a par 70 course while Pebble Beach was par 71.

With victories behind him in the 1997 Masters (itself by a tournament record 12 strokes and with a record aggregate) and the 1999 PGA championship, Woods traveled to the British Open at St. Andrews in Fife, Scot., with the opportunity to complete his career Grand Slam. He did not lead from start to finish as he had at Pebble Beach, but after trailing Els by one shot following a first-round 67 he proved himself in a class of his own once more. By adding scores of 66, 67, and 69, Woods, in only his 14th major as a professional, became champion by 8 strokes with a total of 269. Since the Old Course had a par of 72, he was the first player to reach 19 under par in major history.

As a consequence, there had never been a stronger favourite than Woods was for the PGA championship, held at the Valhalla Golf Club in Louisville, Ky. He duly won again, but only after a tremendous battle with his fellow Californian Bob May. Woods threw down the gauntlet with opening rounds of 66 and 67, but the unfancied 31-year-old May, without a single U.S. PGA tour victory to his name, closed with three successive 66s. When May holed a 5.5-m (18-ft) birdie putt on the final green, Woods needed to follow him in from 1.8 m (6 ft) to force a play-off. Showing enormous strength of character, he did. Both players had played the last nine holes in 31, and at 18 under par both had broken the championship record. Previously there would have been a sudden-death shootout, but a three-hole play-off had been introduced. Woods, after sinking a 6.1-m (20-ft) putt on the first hole for yet another birdie, held on (a touch fortuitously perhaps after his drive at the last hole disappeared into the bushes but came out again) to win by one stroke.

May had done the sport a great service by rising to the challenge of the man who had been threatening to dominate in a way never seen in golf before. A week later, however, Woods won the World Golf Championship NEC Invitational at the Firestone Country Club in Akron, Ohio, by 11 strokes. His preeminence was reflected in the signing of a five-year endorsement contract with clothes and ball manufacturer Nike worth an estimated $100 million, believed to be the highest ever agreed upon for an individual sportsman.

It was easy to forget that in the first major championship of the year, the Masters at the Augusta National Golf Club in Augusta, Ga., Woods had finished "only" fifth, six strokes behind winner Vijay Singh. The 37-year-old Fijian, who had his first major victory at the 1998 PGA, finished with a 10-under-par total of 278, three better than Els. The South African was also joint second in the British Open (along with Denmark's Thomas Bjorn), giving him the distinction of being runner-up in the first three majors of the season.

Not surprisingly, Woods, with six other PGA tour victories, shattered all previous records in topping the PGA tour money list with $9,188,321, making him the biggest money-winner in golf history with over $23 million. On top of that he partnered with David Duval as the U.S. retained the World Cup with a three-stroke triumph over Argentina and helped the U.S. to a crushing victory over the international side in the Presidents Cup at the Robert Trent Jones course in Lake Manassas, Va., in October. Having lost the previous encounter by a nine-point margin in Melbourne, Australia, in 1998, the U.S. won the opening session 5–0 and went on to record a 21½–10½ success.

The U.S. also won the Eisenhower Trophy world men's amateur championship by an overwhelming 16-stroke margin at the Sporting Club Berlin in September, and the Curtis Cup women's amateur trophy, beating Great Britain and Ireland 10–8 at Ganton in Yorkshire, Eng., in June. The Solheim Cup was lost for only the second time, with Europe's women professionals defeating the Americans 14½–11½ at Loch Lomond, Scot. The match sparked controversy when Sweden's Annika Sörenstam holed a chip at the 13th hole of her four-ball match but was asked to replay the shot for playing out of turn. Americans Kelly Robbins and Pat Hurst, along with U.S. captain Pat Bradley, initiated the dispute and the letter of the law was applied, but it left Sörenstam in tears and a nasty taste in everyone's mouth.

The women's scene had something of its own "Tiger" in Australian Karrie Webb (*see* BIOGRAPHIES), who as well as being a clear winner of the Ladies Professional Golf Association tour with $1,876,853 captured two majors—the Nabisco Championship by 10 strokes at Mission Hills Country Club in Rancho Mirage, Calif., and most coveted of all, the U.S. Women's Open by 5 at the Merit Club in Libertyville, Ill. At the Nabisco event, however, Webb had to share top billing with 13-year-old Thai amateur Aree Song Wongluekiet, who was lying a remarkable joint 3rd with a round to go before slipping back to finish 10th.

In Europe the men's tour was won by England's Lee Westwood, who won five times in ending the seven-year reign of Colin Montgomerie of Scotland. The European women's circuit was won by Sörenstam, narrowly topping her fellow Swede Sophie Gustafson, for whom the highlight of the year was a two-stroke victory in the Weetabix British Women's Open at Royal Birkdale in Southport, Eng., in August. That championship was scheduled to become one of the four women's majors in 2001 after the Canadian ban on cigarette sponsorship brought an end to the du Maurier Classic following Meg Mallon's one-shot win at the Royal Ottawa Golf Club.

The increasing strength of golf across the continent of Europe was illustrated by France's win in the Espirito Santo women's world amateur team championship at the Sporting Club Berlin in August, the British amateur championship victory of Finland's Mikko Ilonen in June, and Spain's successful defense of the Alfred Dunhill Cup at St. Andrews in October. Age was shown as no barrier to winning when 66-year-old Englishman Neil Coles won on the European seniors tour to join American legend Sam Snead as the only two players to capture professional titles in six different decades.

Off the course, the debate among ruling bodies about whether to curb technological advances in club and ball manufacture continued unresolved. The U.S. Golf Association banned a number of drivers because of the so-called spring-like effect of the clubfaces, but Scotland's Royal and Ancient Golf Club of St. Andrews, the organization that governed the sport in the rest of the world, deemed no action necessary. The lack of uniformity between the two bodies was considered undesirable by both, but no solution was in sight. (MARK GARROD)

GYMNASTICS

At the 2000 Olympic Games in Sydney, Australia, China claimed its first Olympic gymnastics men's team gold medal with a score of 231.919. Ukraine, bronze medalists at the 1996 Games, won the silver (230.306), while Russia took the bronze (230.019). Russian Aleksey Nemov earned the Olympic all-around title with 58.474 points. China's Yang Wei won the silver, and Ukraine's Oleksandr Beresh received the bronze. During the men's event finals, the six gold medals went to athletes from six different countries. Igors Vihrovs of Latvia won the floor exercise, Romania's Marius Urzica won on the pommel horse, Szilveszter Csollany from Hungary earned the rings title, Spain's Gervasio Deferr prevailed in the vault, and China's Li Xiaopeng won on the parallel bars. Nemov and Benjamin Varonian of France tied for first on the horizontal bar with a score of 9.787, but Nemov won through a complex official tiebreaking system and earned the gold.

Romania came from behind in the women's team competition to win the title with a score of 154.608. Russia, which had dominated the team event with 10 Olympic titles as the Soviet Union (including its 1992 win as the "unified team"), earned the silver medal. China captured the bronze. Controversy surrounded the women's all-around competition when it was discovered that the vault had been set 5 cm (about 2 in) too low during the first two rotations, which led to a fifth round of competition for those gymnasts who elected to repeat the event. Some competitors, notably 1997 world champion Svetlana Khorkina of Russia, were unable to recover their form and fared badly in later rotations. Romania's Andreea Raducan earned the all-around gold, scoring 38.893, followed by her teammates Simona Amanar and Maria Olaru who took the silver and bronze, respectively. Days later, however, Raducan was stripped of her all-around gold medal (but was allowed to keep her team gold) because she tested positive for the banned stimulant pseudo-ephedrine—an ingredient found in cold medicine that was prescribed to her by her team doctor. This pushed Amanar into first place, Olaru into second, and China's Liu Xuan into third. In the women's event finals competition, Russia's Yelena Zamolodchikova won the vault and floor exercise, and Liu won the balance beam. Khorkina recovered to prevail in her signature event, the uneven bars.

In the first-ever Olympic trampoline competition, Russia's Irina Karavayeva and Aleksandr Moskalenko won their respective titles. In the rhythmic gymnastics competition, Yuliya Barsukova of Russia earned the individual gold, while in the group competition Russia and Belarus tied at 39.50. A tiebreaking procedure awarded the gold to Russia, the reigning world champions.

(LUAN PESZEK)

Russian gymnast Svetlana Khorkina competes in the uneven bars at the 2000 Summer Olympic Games.

AP/Wide World Photos

ICE HOCKEY

North America. The National Hockey League (NHL) suffered a surplus of uninspiring games and players lost to injury during the 1999–2000 regular season, but once the Stanley Cup play-offs got under way, the league delivered some of the most thrilling contests ever witnessed, including several that were determined only after they went into sudden-death overtime. Among the latter, the New Jersey Devils' 2–1 victory over the Dallas Stars on June 10, 2000, typified the intensity of the play-off season and brought it to a dramatic conclusion at Dallas's Reunion Arena. The game had been extended 8 minutes 20 seconds into its second overtime session when Jason Arnott scored the game-winning goal on a deflected wrist shot that gave the Devils the series four games to two and their second Stanley Cup in six years. Two nights earlier, in game five at the Continental Airlines Arena in East Rutherford, N.J., the defending champion Stars had avoided elimination with a 1–0 victory; Mike Modano's winning goal came at 6 minutes 21 seconds of the third overtime period.

The Devils tied a postseason team record with 10 road victories in the play-offs. Devils' defenseman Scott Stevens captured the Conn Smythe Trophy as the Most Valuable Player (MVP) of the 2000 play-offs. Some observers called Stevens a dubious choice, because he was cheered not for any particular offensive play but for knocking five opposing players out of action. The most noteworthy victim of Stevens's aggression was Eric Lindros, the Philadelphia Flyers centre, who suffered his sixth career concussion when the Devils enforcer leveled him with a vicious hit in a May 26 play-off game. By season's end it had yet to be determined if Lindros's career was finished as well.

The Devils' timely championship delivered an ecstatic good-bye to the game from team owner John McMullen, who had earlier agreed to sell his team to the consortium that owned the New York Yankees and the New Jersey Nets. The Devils' front office similarly received kudos for making one of the boldest moves of the year—firing coach Robbie Ftorek and replacing him with Larry Robinson when only eight games remained on the regular-season schedule. Robinson's positive impact on the slumping Devils was immediate, and the team's success soon followed. Among the 28 teams that contested the 82-game regular season before the play-offs began, the surprising St. Louis Blues led the league in victories (51) and points (114) to capture their division by a six-point margin over runner-up Detroit (48 wins). Philadelphia (105 points), Washington and Dallas (102 each), Toronto (100), and Colorado (96) were the other division champions who advanced to the 16-team play-offs. Dallas reached the Stanley Cup finals for the second straight season by beating Edmonton and San Jose, each by four games to one, before ousting Colorado in the Western Conference final series four games to three. The Devils qualified for the Stanley Cup showdown by sweeping Florida in four games, beating Toronto four games to two, and rebounding to take the Eastern Conference title by defeating the Flyers four games to three. It was in the Philadelphia matchup that New Jersey became the first team since 1967 to come back to win after a one–three deficit in games.

New Jersey's defensive mastery, led by veteran goalie Martin Brodeur, surfaced early in the play-offs. When the Devils clinched the semifinal series with a 3–0 victory on May 8, they allowed Toronto only six shots, the fewest given up in any NHL game in 33 years. In the final game of the championship series, the Devils held the Stars without a shot through the first 16 minutes of the first period, but neither the excitement of the Stanley Cup final series nor the suspense of the overtime games made any great impact on the NHL television ratings, which remained unimpressive. Financial problems also plagued the NHL's Canadian-based franchises in 1999–2000, and players throughout the league complained about the quality of ice, especially in arenas in the South.

AP/Wide World Photos

Martin Prochazka of the Czech Republic scores against Slovakian goalkeeper Jan Lasak during the world ice hockey championship game in St. Petersburg.

In the 50th NHL All-Star game at Toronto on February 6, the World team notched a 9–4 victory over North America, thanks to a three-goal performance by Pavel Bure, the Russian right wing of the Florida Panthers. Bure, who also had an assist, claimed the game's MVP honours.

Hockey lost one of its legendary talents on May 27 when Maurice ("the Rocket") Richard died of cancer at the age of 78. (*See* OBITUARIES.) One of the NHL's great scorers and an intense competitor, Richard led the Montreal Canadiens to eight Stanley Cups during 18 seasons with the team. He was the first player to score 50 goals in a season and 500 in a career.

International. Extending the trend they established in 1999, the men's team from the Czech Republic and the Canadian women's team dominated their respective international ice hockey opposition once again in 2000. Each team finished its season as a world champion in what was a recurrent achievement for both organizations.

The Czech Republic men repeated as world ice hockey champions on May 14 with a 5–3 victory over Slovakia at the St. Petersburg Ice Palace. It was the third world title in five years for the Czechs, who beat Finland for the gold medal in 1999, and the fifth straight loss by the Slovakians to their former countrymen in an international tournament. The Czechs advanced to the gold-medal game by beating Latvia 3–1 in the quarterfinal round and Canada 2–1 in the semifinals. Slovakia, competing for the fifth time as an independent nation at the world championships, reached the finals with a 4–1 quarterfinal victory that knocked the U.S. out of contention and a 3–1 semifinal win over Finland.

The Czechs struck for the gold early on, taking a 3–0 lead in the first period on goals by Michal Sykora, Tomas Vlasak, and Martin Prochazka, then survived a late Slovak rally. Robert Reichel, who scored the winning goal to get the Czech Republic past Canada, rallied again to score an insurance goal with 1 minute 2 seconds left to play. Slovakia had 33 shots on goal, but Roman Cechmanek, the Czech goalkeeper, had 30 saves to outplay Jan Lasak, his Slovakian counterpart, who allowed the five scores on only 15 shots on goal. The Players of the Game were Vlasak of the Czech Republic and Lubos Bartecko of Slovakia.

Team Canada took the women's world championship with a 3–2 overtime victory over the U.S. at Mississauga, Ont., on April 9. It marked the sixth straight world championship gold medal for the Canadians, not counting the 1998 Olympic Games in Nagano, Japan, where they lost the title game to the U.S.

At Mississauga, the U.S. women took a 2–0 lead in the second period on goals by Tricia Dunn and Karen Bye but could not contain Canada's Jayna Hefford in the late going. She scored twice in the third period to leave the game deadlocked at the end of regulation play. The game-winning goal came 6 minutes 50 seconds into overtime when Nancy Drolet picked a loose puck, circled around, and slammed home a shot that beat Sara DeCosta, the American goalie. It was a disappointing swan song for the U.S. team, which started the tournament by routing the Russians 15–0.

On January 4 in Skellefteå, Swed., the Czech Republic captured its first gold medal in the world junior ice hockey tournament, beating Russia in the first final ever decided by a shoot-out. The Czechs got a goal each in the tie-breaking shoot-out format from Libor Pivko and Milan Kraft after the Russians had gone one-up on a goal by Yevgeny Muratov, the team's leading scorer in the tournament. The game was scoreless after its first 80 minutes.

The Russians might have tied it on the final attempt in the shoot-out, but Yevgeny Federov was stopped by Zdenek Smid only seconds before the Czechs began to celebrate their newfound success at the junior level. Russia's silver medal was its 21st since 1977.

The highlight contest of the Skoda Auto European Hockey League (EHL) season was played on February 6 at Lugano, Switz. Andrey Razin, a 27-year-old centre, scored his first two goals of the season in a 3-minute 58-second span to give Metallurg Magnitogorsk a 2–0 victory over Czech Sparta Praha for its second consecutive EHL championship. Metallurg goalie Igor Karpenko had 29 saves on 29 shots on goal for the Russian champions. TPS Turku, the entry from Finland, routed hometown favourite Lugano 6–1 to take the bronze medal.

(RON REID)

ICE SKATING

Figure Skating. Russian athletes, who dominated figure skating throughout the late 1990s, slipped appreciably in 2000, a season in which American Michelle Kwan (*see* BIOGRAPHIES) quashed rumours of her decline by winning her third and least-expected world championship.

The Russian slump was hardly noticeable early in the year. At the European championships in Vienna in February, Yelena Berezhnaya and Anton Sikharulidze came back from second place after their short routine to win the European pairs title, the fifth in succession by a Russian team. Mariya Petrova and Aleksey Tikhonov, the defending champions from Russia, led after the short program but wound up as the silver medalists after Petrova abandoned a triple jump in the opening of the long program, a costly major error.

Yevgeny Plushchenko ended the two-year reign of his Russian countryman Aleksey Yagudin by winning the men's free-skating program. Plushchenko, age 17, completed a quadruple jump and eight triples to finish as the first-place choice of all nine judges and the second youngest European champion in history. Yagudin, the two-time world and European champion, was not at his best after having sustained a broken bone in training on January 25. Dmytro Dmytrenko of Ukraine, in his finest finish since he won the men's 1993 title, took third place.

Irina Slutskaya defeated Mariya Butyrskaya, her Russian compatriot and the defending champion. Each woman hit six triple jumps in the long program, but the judges unanimously selected Slutskaya, who won her third European title and her first since 1997. It was a redemptive victory for Slutskaya, who had failed to make the Russian team in 1999 and almost quit the sport. Viktoriya Volchkova finished third to complete a Russian women's sweep for the second straight year.

Marina Anissina and Gwendal Peizerat of France ended Russia's three-year gold-medal run by winning the ice-dancing title, partly because the defending champions, Anzhelika Krylova and Oleg Ovsyannikov, did not compete. Barbara Fusar-Poli and Maurizio Margaglio took

Patrick Kovarik/AFP Worldwide

French figure skaters Marina Anissina and Gwendal Peizerat perform their winning free-dance routine during the European figure skating championships on February 11 in Vienna.

the silver medal, the first team from Italy to score that high in the championships. The bronze medal went to Margarita Drobiazko and Povilas Vanagas of Lithuania. It marked the first time since 1968 that Russia failed to medal in ice dancing.

Kwan captured her fourth U.S. championship at Cleveland, Ohio, on February 12, surviving a fall in both her short and long programs in a repeat of the cautious approach that cost her a gold medal in the 1998 Winter Olympic Games. None of Kwan's rivals, however, was experienced enough to capitalize on her vulnerability. Sasha Cohen, age 15, took the silver medal, while 14-year-old Sarah Hughes skated a more demanding program than Kwan's but finished third.

The men's competition produced one for the record book when Timothy Goebel landed three quadruple jumps and thereby became the first American to land a quadruple jump in the national championships. Goebel, however, lost to defending champion Michael Weiss, whose challenging routine was superior in terms of spins, footwork, and drama and included eight triple jumps. Weiss's artistic marks included a perfect 6.0, the first of his career. Goebel captured the silver, while Trifun Zivanovic, the 1999 silver medalist, took the bronze.

Kyoko Ina, twice U.S. national pairs champion with her previous partner, Jason Dungjen, returned to the top of the podium with her partner of only two years, John Zimmerman. Naomi Lang and Peter Tchernyshev retained the U.S. ice-dancing title.

Kwan was the biggest story of the world championship competition, held in Nice, France, from March 26 through April 2. Third after the completion of her short program, Kwan rebounded with her finest performance in two years to capture the women's title with one of the most demanding programs of her career. Slutskaya and Butyrskaya finished second and third, respectively. Yagudin, healthier than he had been a month earlier, took his third consecutive men's championship as Canadian Elvis Stojko, the 1997 world champion, and Weiss finished second and third, respectively. Petrova and Tikhonov took the pairs gold medal, with 1999 silver medalists Shen Xue and Zhao Hongbo of China second. Two-time champions Berezhnaya and Sikharulidze had been barred from the event after Berezhnaya tested positive for a banned stimulant. Anissina and Peizerat topped their rivals in the ice-dance competition.

Speed Skating. Among the highlights of the 1999–2000 speed-skating season, Canada's Jeremy Wotherspoon broke the world record for 500 m on January 29, the same day he captured his third World Cup title at Calgary, Alta. Wotherspoon set the 500-m record at 34.63 sec and covered the title-clinching 1,000-m race in 1 min 8.96 sec. The latter mark barely missed the world record of 1 min 8.49 sec he had set 16 days earlier in the Canadian sprint championships.

Speed skater Gianni Romme of The Netherlands topped the season's final World Cup standings in the 5,000-m and 10,000-m distances and succeeded in lowering the world record for the shorter event to 6 min 18.72 sec. Romme also led the final overall standings at the world speed-skating championships contested in February in Milwaukee, Wis., where he finished as the men's overall champion after winning the 10,000-m title by almost 17 seconds. Ids Postma, the 1998 winner, and defending champion Rintje Ritsma finished second and third, respectively, for a Dutch medals sweep.

Eight-time world champion Gunda Niemann-Stirnemann shattered her own world standard for the women's 3,000 m at Calgary on January 30, finishing in 4 min 0.51 sec, more than a full second below the former record. Two weeks earlier, at Hamar, Nor., she had improved the world record for 5,000 m to 6 min 56.84 sec. It was the third straight season in which the 33-year-old Niemann-Stirnemann had broken the world mark in the 5,000 m. It was not enough to retain the world title, however, as her German compatriot Claudia Pechstein took the women's all-around championship at Milwaukee, capturing the 3,000-m gold medal and finishing second in both the 1,500-m and 5,000-m finals.

At the world short-track speed-skating championships at Sheffield, Eng., in March, China finished atop the standings with 6 of the 12 gold medals. South Korea was second and Canada third. Ryoung Min of South Korea captured the men's title to wind up an impressive season in which he also took the overall world junior title and finished third in the World Cup standings. China's Yang Yang (A) defended her title in the women's competition for her fourth straight world championship and won the 1,000-m and 1,500-m finals.

(RON REID)

JUDO

Judo in the year 2000 was highlighted by the Olympic Games in Sydney, Australia. Japan led the winners with four golds, while China, Cuba, and France collected two each. A sharp controversy erupted over the results of the men's over-100-kg final between David Douillet of France and Shinichi Shinohara of Japan after different winners were indicated by the two corner judges. The referee voted for Douillet—the eventual winner. The Japanese officially protested the decision to the International Judo Federation, but the appeal was denied. Meanwhile, Ryoko Tamura of Japan took the women's 48-kg category to finally capture her first Olympic gold after getting silver medals in the last two Games.

The new year got under way with the 2000 Paris Tournament, February 12–13, with *judoka* from seven different countries winning gold medals on the first day. By the end of the competition, however, the Japanese had won four golds and the French hosts three. Cuba came out ahead in the Munich Open Judo Tournament, February 26–27, by winning four matches to three each for host Germany and Japan. On April 29 at Tokyo's Nippon Budokan, Shinohara won the prestigious All-Japan judo championships—the only major world tournament without weight classes. In the Asian judo championships at Osaka, Japan, May 26–28, Japan won nine titles, but Sun Fuming of China took the women's open title. (ANDY ADAMS)

Ryoko Tamura of Japan (left) and Lyudmyla Lusnikova of Ukraine go head over heels during their Olympic finals judo match on September 16.

AP/Wide World Photos

RODEO

The plans of Steve Hatchell, commissioner of the Professional Rodeo Cowboys Association, to create a series of televised rodeo competitions featuring the sport's elite competitors commenced with the first Wrangler Pro Rodeo Tour in 2000. Tour qualifiers were drawn from the final rounds of select rodeos and accumulated points in order to qualify for two finale championship events, one held in Las Vegas, Nev., and the other in Mesquite, Texas. In future years, the 10,000-member organization hoped to move production in-house to create its own pro tour competitions, with exclusive events in major metropolitan areas.

Joe Beaver of Huntsville, Texas, was the big winner at the $4.5 million National Finals Rodeo (NFR), held December 1–10 in Las Vegas. Beaver and his team-roping partner, Bret Gould of Pollok, Texas, earned more money than any other team ropers at the NFR—$68,845 each—and topped off the event with a 10th-round win in 4.2 sec. Beaver's team-roping earnings, combined with his calf-roping earnings, helped him overcome a $47,000 deficit in the all-around title race prior to the NFR. (World titles in professional rodeo, including the all-around title, are based on regular-season arena earnings plus money made at the season-ending NFR.)

Fred Whitfield of Hockley, Texas, 1999's all-around champ, successfully defended his calf-roping world championship. Whitfield clinched the title in the final round by roping and tying his calf in 8.1 sec. Had he been a fraction of a second slower, he would have lost the title. All told, Whitfield claimed $194,936, a margin of just $2,693 over second-place calf roper Brent Lewis.

Billy Etbauer of Ree Heights, S.D., claimed his fourth saddle-bronc-riding title of the decade with total earnings of $183,448. Team ropers Rich Skelton of Llano, Texas, and Speed Williams of Jacksonville, Fla., snared their fourth straight team-roping championship with earnings of $170,680.

Barrel racer Kappy Allen, a 42-year-old attorney from Austin, Texas, upset 10-time world champion Charmayne James of Gustine, Texas, closing an almost $47,000 gap going into the competition to claim her first world title with $145,204. Other first-time world champions for 2000 included bareback rider Jeffrey Collins of Redfield, Kan. ($165,305), and steer wrestler Frank Thompson of Cheyenne, Wyo. ($141,400). Bull rider and NFR rookie Cody Hancock of Taylor, Ariz., rose from 15th place to first place in the world title race, becoming only the second man in NFR history to go from the bottom ranking in an event to the number-one slot. His earnings totaled $139,583. (GAVIN FORBES EHRINGER)

ROWING

Although the highlight for world rowing in 2000 was undoubtedly the Olympic Games, held in September in Sydney, Australia, the sport was dominated for much of the year by the pre-Olympic buildup in the World Cup series. Introduced in 1997, this series provided an unprecedented opportunity every year for countries to reach their final crew selections under international racing conditions. The 24 titles at stake in 2000 (14 in the Olympics and 10 non-Olympic events in the world championships) were shared among 14 nations; Great Britain topped the overall table with four wins.

At the Olympics Great Britain and France both won two titles in the men's events, while Romania with three wins and a double triumph by Germany highlighted the women's classes. In a high standard of racing, 6 of the 14 events were decided by only a fraction of a second. Great Britain won the closest men's final—in coxless fours—by only 0.38 sec over Italy. This enabled crew member Steve Redgrave to become the first person to win a gold medal in an endurance sport at five successive Olympics. At year's end it was revealed that Redgrave, who had announced he was retiring from competition, was to be knighted in 2001.

Australia, the Olympic host, was foiled in the eights and lightweight coxless fours by only a few feet by Great Britain and France, respectively. In the coxless pairs the U.S., which led for much of the race, lost to a memorable storming breakaway by the French, with Australia squeezing into third place. Only the photo-finish camera could separate Belarus from Bulgaria by 0.01 sec in women's single sculls, while Romania held off Germany in women's eights by 0.31 sec. The four remaining men's gold medals went to Italy, Poland, Slovenia, and two-time world champion Rob Waddell of New Zealand, who won his first Olympic title in the single sculls.

At the world championships in Zagreb, Croatia, Great Britain and the U.S. each won twice, while the other winners represented Belarus, Canada, the Czech Republic, Finland, Germany, and Japan. At junior level the 14 winners were Germany (5), Belarus (2), and Italy (2), with one each going to Australia, Bulgaria, France, Romania, and the U.S. In the Nations Cup—the under-23 world championships—in Copenhagen, Great Britain scored four wins, Denmark and Germany took three titles each, and the remainder went to Austria, Estonia, Poland, Romania, Russia, Switzerland, the U.S., and Yugoslavia.

At the 151st Henley Royal Regatta in England, Redgrave won his 19th Henley medal. Eight trophies went overseas, extending the total since 1892 to more than 300. The U.S. triumphed four times in eight—in the Ladies' Challenge Plate (Brown University, Providence, R.I.), Temple Challenge Cup (Yale University), Henley Prize (University of Washington), and Princess Elizabeth Challenge Cup (St. Joseph's Preparatory School, Philadelphia, Pa.)—while Aquil Abdullah (Princeton Training Center) captured the Diamond Challenge Sculls after missing Olympic selection by one foot. The Grand Challenge Cup (eights) went to Australia, The Netherlands (ASR Nereus & DSR Laga) recorded its first win in the Queen Mother Challenge Cup (quadruple sculls), and Denmark (Denmarks Rowing Center) took the Double Sculls trophy.

In the final of the World Cup series held in Munich, Ger.; Vienna; and Lucerne, Switz., titleholder Germany (143 points) remained undefeated, but Australia (100 points) deposed Great Britain (93 points) from second place for the first time.

Oxford, after an epic power struggle, broke the run of seven Cambridge wins in the 146th University Boat Race to reduce the loser's overall lead in the series to 76–69. (KEITH L. OSBORNE)

SAILING (YACHTING)

The America's Cup, held off Auckland, N.Z., and the Olympic Regatta in Sydney, Australia, dominated sailing in 2000. The Louis Vuitton Challenger Series for the America's Cup, which had begun in late 1999, attracted 11 challengers, including five from the U.S. An initial round-robin series of match races (in which every competitor sails against every other competitor) was conducted, eliminating five of the teams. The remaining six then raced in another round-robin. The last

AP/Wide World Photos

Team New Zealand's **Black Magic** *(bottom) sails away from Italy's* **Luna Rossa** *during the America's Cup.*

two survivors, Italy's team Prada and the U.S.'s AmericaOne, sailed an exciting final round to determine which challenger would meet the defending Team New Zealand's *Black Magic*. In the best-of-nine race final Prada's *Luna Rossa* narrowly defeated AmericaOne 5–4, ensuring that for the first time in the event's 149-year history, there would be no American yacht in the America's Cup.

After the close racing of the elimination series, the actual races for the America's Cup were somewhat anticlimactic. In the best-of-nine race series, which began on February 19, skipper Russell Coutts (*see* BIOGRAPHIES) and the sleek black New Zealand boat handily dispatched the Italian challenger in five straight races. New Zealand was never seriously challenged by the *Luna Rossa* under skipper Francesco de Angelis, showing perhaps superior design and indisputably superior skill and precision of evolution. In the months that followed, however, proud Kiwis were distressed to learn that some of their America's Cup heroes, including Coutts, were being drawn away to foreign syndicates, lured by unparalleled salary offerings.

The Olympic Regatta was held in and just outside of Sydney Harbour during the Olympic Games in September, with 402 sailors, ranging in age from 18 to 58 years and hailing from 69 nations, participating in the 11 events. Dominating the national results, Great Britain's team earned three gold and two silver medals. Australia was just behind, with two golds, one silver, and one bronze.

In offshore racing, New Zealand won the Kenwood Cup in Hawaii, and the Volvo 60 *Nokia* set a new record in the Sydney–Hobart race, completing the 630 nautical miles (1 nm=1.85 km) in 1 day 19 hr 48 min at an average speed of more than 14 knots, to take some 18 hours off the previous mark. Other new marks set in 2000 included a new 24-hr distance mark of 625 nm (average 26 knots) by *Club Med*, a mega-catamaran, and a new Victoria–Maui race record by *Grand Illusion* of 9 days 2 hr 8 min 27 sec, taking 17 hours off the previous record.

At the other end of the speed spectrum, in the Cruising Club of America's Newport–Bermuda Race the highest-rated boat in the fleet (i.e., the boat predicted by the handicap to take the longest to sail the course) won the coveted Lighthouse Trophy awarded to the best corrected-time finisher in the cruiser-racer divisions. The faster boats got down the 635-nm course quickly but ran headlong into a high-pressure weather system that resulted in near-calm conditions. While the leaders struggled for every one of the last 100 nm, the smaller and slower boats continued the passage, catching up as the high began to move and light air finally filled in. The whole fleet finished within hours of the first boats, and the corrected-time results in each class were a nearly complete inversion of the handicap order, with the slowest (predicted) boats on top and the fastest (predicted) boats on the bottom of the order. The winner was *Restless*, a 35-year-old Rhodes 41 owned and skippered by Eric Crawford. In the previous Bermuda Race, Crawford had to motor the last 200 nm to Bermuda in order to attend the prize-giving ceremony scheduled a week after the start of the race. In 2000, however, he won it all.

(JOHN B. BONDS)

SKIING

Alpine Skiing. Austria's Hermann Maier swept three individual men's Alpine World Cup titles and claimed a historic overall World Cup championship in 2000. The 1998 Olympic gold medalist had already sewn up the overall and supergiant slalom (super G) victories prior to the World Cup finale in Bormio, Italy, in March, and yet he won the final super G in astounding fashion, surpassing his nearest competitor by two seconds—a World Cup record. Having already destroyed Swiss skier Paul Accola's regular-season points record of 1,699, Maier rode the win to reach the magical 2,000-point mark. The previous day Maier had claimed his first World Cup downhill crown with a second-place finish behind teammate Hannes Trinkl.

Austrians dominated the giant slalom (GS) and super G leader boards at the men's finals, finishing one-two-three in both events. Norwegian Kjetil André Aamodt, the men's overall champion in 1994, claimed the slalom championship on the strength of a sixth-place finish on the final day of the season. Daron Rahlves became the first American man since 1984 to win back-to-back World Cup downhills when he won two races in 24 hours on the 1994 Olympic course in Kvitfjell, Nor.

Austria's Renate Götschl already had won the World Cup super G crown before going to Bormio, but she clinched the title as overall women's champion when she won the final super G race of the winter. Götschl's teammate Michaela Dorfmeister clinched the World Cup GS title. Slovenia's Spela Pretnar captured the women's slalom World Cup with four wins during the season. It was the first World Cup crown for Pretnar, who had considered retiring after the 1999 season. American Kristina Koznick won the last two World Cup slalom races, the only U.S. women's victories of the season.

In the women's World Cup downhill standings, Götschl was narrowly defeated by Germany's Regina Häusl, who surpassed the Austrian by a scant five points. The World Cup win was bittersweet for Häusl; as she crossed the finish line of the final race, she fell hard, broke her leg, and had to be evacuated to a hospital. Amazingly, Häusl failed to

AP/Wide World Photos

Austrian skier Hermann Maier takes a curve on his way to winning the World Cup men's super G title in Bormio, Italy, on March 16.

claim a single downhill victory in 1999–2000, winning the World Cup on the strength of five second-place finishes.

Nordic Skiing. Bente Martinsen of Norway retained the women's cross-country championship, dislodging Kristina Smigun of Estonia from the top ranking with a win in the 5-km classic race at the World Cup finals in Santa Caterina, Italy. German-born Johann Mühlegg of Spain earned the men's overall cross country championship.

In ski jumping Martin Schmitt of Germany set a record with 11 World Cup victories—including four weekends in which he won both events—to capture his second consecutive World Cup title. On the final weekend of the season in Planica, Slovenia, the world distance record was reset twice during a ski-flying competition. Austria's Thomas Hörl set a world record in practice, with a 224.5-m (736-ft) leap. Two days later his teammate Andreas Goldberger soared 225 m (738 ft) in competition. Samppa Lajunen of Finland won the men's Nordic combined title, upending two-time champion Bjarte Engen Vik of Norway.

Freestyle Skiing. Australia's Jacqui Cooper dominated the aerials competition with wins at four of the seven World Cup events and claimed the women's aerials World Cup title. Tied for first place in the men's aerials competition going into the finals, Aleksey Grishin of Belarus, who won the first two World Cup matches of the season, fell to Canada's Nicholas Fontaine, who won the finale and claimed the title.

Janne Lahtela of Finland claimed his second World Cup moguls championship and his first in dual moguls by winning the final competitions. The duals win was controversial, however. Canada's Stéphane Rochon, who led the standings going into the finals, lost his second-round match to Finland's Sami Mustonen after missing his start. The Canadian's protest was rejected, and when Lahtela won the event he also clinched the title. Ann Batelle of the U.S. won her second straight moguls title and was runner-up to Norway's Kari Traa for the dual moguls crown.

Snowboarding. With an astounding eight wins in parallel slalom, including a victory shared with teammate Nicholas Huet at the World Cup finals held on March 18 in Livigno, Italy, Matthieu Bozzetto of France claimed the men's overall World Cup championship. Stefan Kaltschütz of Austria, the 1999 GS champion, defended his number one ranking with four podium finishes during the eight-event season.

Margherita Pirini celebrated her GS title on home soil after winning three World Cup events, beating out France's Karine Ruby. Manuela Riegler of Austria earned the women's overall championship.

In halfpipe Thomas Johansson of Sweden claimed top honours despite missing the last three World Cup competitions owing to injury. After winning five World Cup halfpipe competitions, Tricia Byrnes of the U.S. elected not to compete at Livigno and lost a chance for her second straight title. Sabine Wehr-Hasler of Germany moved ahead of Byrnes in World Cup points on the strength of her winning performance at the finals. (GAVIN FORBES EHRINGER)

SQUASH

Squash players worldwide watched the 2000 Olympic Games in Sydney, Australia, wondering why the sport still had not secured a place on the program, despite lobbying by the World Squash Federation. That disappointment aside, it was a busy and progressive year in squash.

The British Open was notable for a panoply of surprises. World number-one-ranked Peter Nicol of Scotland withdrew with a shin injury, seemingly leaving the field clear for Canadian titleholder Jonathon Power, but he and the rest of the top nine seeds contrived early exits. It was left to the 10th seed, 25-year-old Welshman David Evans, to keep his composure and beat Australian Paul Price, seeded 14th, in the final. The top women's seed, Cassie Campion of England, also succumbed tamely, a victim of a dead leg that turned out to be a trapped back nerve. In her absence, the British title went for the second year to New Zealander Leilani Joyce.

Joyce was expected to win her first World Open title in Edinburgh in November. She reached match ball comfortably in the final against Australian Carol Owens but squandered the opportunity and amazingly lost the next three games and with them the title. Players from a record-equaling 22 nations then traveled to Sheffield, Eng., where the host nation beat Australia to take the women's team title for the first time since 1990. The men's World Open fell victim to a lack of sponsorship, but a five-year deal was announced that would take future stagings to India.

At the junior level the world under-19 men's championships were held in Milan. The individual title went to Kareem Darwish of Egypt, while England snatched the team title from Egypt in an outstanding final.

The most significant partnership of the year was the $10 million injection of support for the women's World Grand Prix for eight years. There was also movement toward the worldwide introduction of 6% larger squash balls for all levels of play in 2002.

(ANDREW SHELLEY)

SWIMMING

In most Olympic years swimming world records fall in profusion, but never before as in 2000. In part, this was owing to the large number of high-level international meets held during the year. In part, it was owing to the decision two years earlier by the Fédération Internationale de Natation Amateur (FINA), the sport's international governing body, to sanction world records in the 50-m backstroke, breaststroke, and butterfly in both long-course (50-m pool) and short-course (25-m pool) competitions, and in the 100-m individual medley in short course. These events were not included in Olympic competition, and until 2000 the records were considered "soft." FINA added the 50-m sprints as well as the 800-m freestyle for men and the 1,500-m freestyle for women to the world championship program beginning in 2001. Still, no one foresaw the orgy of record breaking that took place in 2000 as 20 long-course and even more short-course world marks were shattered. A total of 13 of these new world records were established at the Olympic Games in Sydney, Australia.

The most impressive of the new world marks were turned in by Dutch swimmer Inge de Bruijn (*see* BIOGRAPHIES), who repeatedly lowered global time standards in four events between May and September, triggering the almost inevitable accusations of drug use. De Bruijn began her spree in May at the Speedo Super Grand Prix meet in Sheffield, Eng., setting world records in the 50-m and 100-m freestyle and the 50-m and 100-m butterfly. In the 100-m butterfly, her time of 56.69 sec hacked an unprecedented 1.19 sec off the record set in 1999 by American Jenny Thompson, who had broken Mary T. Meagher's mark of 57.93 sec set 18 years earlier. In Sydney de Bruijn earned Olympic gold medals in the 50-m and 100-m freestyle and the 100-m butterfly, resetting the world records in all three events. At year's end she was selected as the female World Swimmer of the Year by *Swimming World* magazine.

Thompson finished the Games with 10 career medals in three Olympiads (including eight golds in relay events), the most ever for a woman Olympic swimmer. American Brooke Bennett enhanced her credentials as the world's distance queen, winning the 400-m freestyle and repeating as Olympic champion in the 800-m; Romania's Diana Mocanu became her nation's first swimming gold medalist as she swept both backstroke events; and Ukraine's Yana Klochkova took both the 200-m and 400-m individual medley. In perhaps the Games' biggest upset, the unheralded Misty Hyman of the U.S. beat Australia's Susie O'Neill in the women's 200-m butterfly in Olympic record time. O'Neill, the world-record holder and defending Olympic champion, had not lost a 200-m butterfly race in six years.

De Bruijn's teammate at the Eindhoven Swim Club in The Netherlands, Pieter van den Hoogenband, was voted the male World Swimmer of the Year, marking the first time two Dutch swimmers had been accorded the honour. Van den Hoogenband defeated two seemingly invincible world-record holders: Russia's Aleksandr Popov in the 100-m freestyle and Australia's Ian Thorpe ("the Thorpedo") in the 200-m freestyle. In the process, "Hoogie" lowered the world records in both events.

Ukrainian-born American Lenny Krayzelburg, the world-record holder in the backstroke, took both dorsal events as expected, then added a third gold leading off the U.S.'s medley relay. Italy's Domenico Fioravanti pulled off major upsets in both breaststroke races. In the 50-m freestyle, Americans Gary Hall, Jr., and Anthony Ervin, teammates at the Phoenix (Ariz.) Swim Club, tied for the gold with van den Hoogenband in third.

American swimmers Anthony Ervin (left) and Gary Hall, Jr., show off the gold medals they won when they tied for first place in the Olympic men's 50-m freestyle event.

AP/Wide World Photos

American Neil Walker and Sweden's Therese Alshammar were the outstanding swimmers at the World Short-Course Championships, held in Athens in March. Walker won three individual events, all in world-record time, while Alshammar set global standards in the two women's freestyle sprints.

With record breaking almost commonplace, the drugs issue was never far below the surface in 2000. In July FINA announced that China's Wu Yanyan, the world-record holder in the women's 200-m individual medley, had tested positive for steroids. Two weeks before the Olympics, China cut four swimmers from its team, including sprint star Shan Ying, ostensibly after they returned positive doping tests. Romania's Cezar Badita tested positive for steroids in May and was given a provisional suspension by FINA that allowed him to compete in Sydney, where he made the final in the 400-m individual medley. In October it was revealed that Italy's Massimiliano Rosolino, who won three medals in Sydney, had returned an extraordinarily high reading for human growth hormone—more than 15 times the normal level—in a June test. Rosolino denied any wrongdoing and threatened to sue his detractors.

Controversy also swirled around the new, high-tech bodysuits introduced by several swimsuit manufacturers amid unconfirmed reports that they reduced water resistance significantly. Although such performance enhancement is strictly prohibited under FINA rules, FINA had approved the suits for competition in October 1999. A statistical study conducted by Joel Stager of the Human Performance Laboratories at Indiana University at Bloomington and published in *Swimming Technique* indicated that the suits apparently conferred no advantage to swimmers wearing them.

Diving. As expected, China dominated the diving competition at the Olympic Games, winning five of the eight events contested and finishing second in the other three. Veterans Fu Mingxia and Xiong Ni led the way for the Chinese, who finished with five gold and five silver medals. Russia was a distant second with two gold, one silver, and two bronze medals.

Fu took the women's 3-m springboard by almost 12 points over her training partner, Guo Jingjing, to win her fourth gold medal in her third Olympics. The victory made her the first female diver to win gold at three consecutive Olympics. In perhaps the biggest upset of the competition, American Laura Wilkinson, in fifth place after the semifinals, won the gold in the women's 10-m platform with a magnificent final three dives. China's Li Na, the favourite, finished with the silver, less than two points behind Wilkinson and less than two ahead of Anne Montminy of Canada.

In the men's 3-m springboard Xiong moved into the lead on the final dive, edging Mexico's Fernando Platas by only 0.30. Russia's Dmitry Sautin, who led until the final dive, was third. Sautin, the defending Olympic champion in the 10-m platform, managed only to win a bronze in that event, finishing well behind China's Tian Liang and Hu Jia.

Synchronized diving made its initial Olympic appearance in Sydney, with duos from China and Russia splitting the four gold medals. Russia's Vera Ilyina and Yuliya Pakhalina took the women's 3-m synchro, upsetting Fu and Guo. In the 10-m event, China's Sang Xue and Li emerged victorious over Canada's Emilie Heymans and Montminy. Australia won its first Olympic medal in women's diving when Loudy Tourky and Rebecca Gilmore finished third.

The men's 3-m synchronized gold went to Xiong and Xiao Hailiang, who dominated the competition, easily defeating Sautin and Aleksandr Dobroskok by 35 points. Australia's Robert Newbery and Dean Pullar gave the host nation its second bronze of the competition. Sautin finally struck gold when he teamed up with Igor Lukashin to win the men's 10-m synchronized event, six points ahead of Tian and Hu.

Synchronized Swimming. Russia's Olga Brusnikina and Mariya Kiseleva, the 1999 World Cup champions, brought Russia its first Olympic synchronized swimming title at the Sydney Games. The Russian pair received 9 out of a possible 10 perfect scores of 10 to amass a total of 99.580 points and win the duet title. Japan's Miya Tachibana and Miho Takeda finished with the silver, as they had at the 1998 world championships, and Virginie Dedieu and Myriam Lignot of France repeated their world-championship bronze performance. Russia also emerged triumphant in the team competition. Japan was second and Canada third.

In September, in a surprise decision, FINA amended its rules to allow men to participate in the duet competition beginning with the 2002 World Cup.

(PHILLIP WHITTEN)

TABLE TENNIS

At the world team championships in Kuala Lumpur, Malaysia, held Feb. 19–26, 2000, the Chinese women, who had lost the title only once in the last quarter century, again dominated play. In the final they defeated a Taiwanese team led by the Pro Tour grand final winner, Chen Jing. The Chinese men, however, lost their title, held since 1995, to their Swedish arch rivals, among whom were former world champions Jan-Ove Waldner and Jörgen Persson.

At the 2000 Olympic Games in Sydney, Australia, the Chinese team reigned supreme. World women's singles and doubles champion Wang Nan won two gold medals, defeating her doubles partner, Li Ju, in the singles final. Taiwan's Chen won the bronze. In the men's singles Kong Linghui bested Waldner to capture the gold medal, and Liu Guoliang, the current world singles champion and 1996 Olympic gold medalist, took the bronze. The China Open champion, Wang Liqin, paired with Yan Sen to defeat Kong and Liu in the men's doubles.

On October 1 the International Table Tennis Federation (ITTF), in an effort to reduce the speed and spin of the ball and so increase the length of the points, changed from the traditional 38-mm (1.5-in) to the new 40-mm (1.6-in) ball in all its tournaments. The ITTF's approximately 185 member countries were expected to follow suit in their major domestic competitions. (TIM BOGGAN)

TENNIS

In 2000, 24-year-old Brazilian Gustavo Kuerten came of age as a competitor of the highest order, becoming the first South American man ever to finish a season as the number-one ranked player on the official Association of Tennis Professionals (ATP) computer. Kuerten's 2000 campaign featured impressive triumphs at the French Open in June and at the elite Tennis Masters Cup in Lisbon in December. A flamboyant shotmaker and demonstrative performer, he displayed a growing awareness of his immense potential, earning a genuine respect from all of his leading rivals. So, too, did Marat Safin, a dynamic 20-year-old Russian who secured no fewer than seven tournament titles, including a spectacular run at the U.S. Open.

While Kuerten and Safin brought a new energy and diversity to top-level tennis, a pair of enduring American men stood up ably for the old guard of the game. Andre Agassi took the Australian Open crown in convincing fashion to record a sixth career Grand Slam championship. More significantly, Pete Sampras came through at Wimbledon, sealing a men's record 13th Grand Slam singles title in the process.

Many other familiar players emerged as victors at the Grand Slam events. Among the women, Lindsay Davenport of the U.S. was the winner of the Australian Open, and Mary Pierce of France took the top honour in the French Open at Roland Garros. Venus Williams burst into brilliance in claiming the Wimbledon and U.S. Open titles as well as the singles gold medal at the Olympic Games in Sydney, Australia. Williams and her equally dynamic younger sister, Serena, also captured the Wimbledon and Olympic doubles titles. (*See* BIOGRAPHIES.) Although Switzerland's strategically savvy Martina Hingis failed to secure a major title, she surpassed all of her adversaries with nine tournament victories, prize-money earnings of $3,457,049, and her third number-one world ranking in four years. Setting the prize-money pace among the men was Kuerten with $4,701,610.

Australian Open. Seeking a fourth consecutive singles crown in Melbourne, Hingis could not contain an inspired Davenport, who overwhelmed the top-seeded Hingis 6–1, 7–5 in the final despite squandering four straight games after building a commanding 5–1 second-set lead. In garnering the third major tournament win of her career, the number 2 seed Davenport did not drop a set in seven matches.

Agassi was competing with unwavering intensity as he moved persuasively through the field in Melbourne. The top seed conceded only one set on his way to a gripping semifinal confrontation with Sampras. Agassi had lost 17 of his previous 28 career meetings with his countryman—including four of their five showdowns in 1999—but he prevailed this time 6–4, 3–6, 6–7 (7–0), 7–6 (5), 6–1, despite 37 aces from Sampras. Boosted by that big win, Agassi cast aside the defending champion, Yevgeny Kafelnikov of Russia, 3–6, 6–3, 6–2, 6–4 in the final. Remarkably, Agassi did not win another tournament during the rest of 2000.

AP/Wide World Photos

Mary Pierce of France exults after beating top-seeded Martina Hingis of Switzerland in the semifinals of the French Open tennis tournament on June 8.

French Open. A much more seasoned and accomplished player than he had been when he captured the world's premier clay-court event three years earlier, Kuerten was well-prepared this time. He had reached the final of the Italian Open and had won the German Open en route to Roland Garros, and his self-conviction was evident all through the fortnight in Paris. In the most compelling major men's final of the year, Kuerten, the number 5 seed, ousted number 3 seed Magnus Norman of Sweden 6–2, 6–3, 2–6, 7–6 (8–6). Recouping boldly from 4–5, 15–40 down in the fourth set, Norman saved 10 match points before bowing as both players tested each other in tense exchanges from the baseline. Kuerten survived strenuous five-set confrontations with Kafelnikov in the quarterfinals and with the sturdy Spaniard Juan Carlos Ferrero in the semifinals.

Pierce became the first Frenchwoman since Françoise Durr in 1967 to prevail at Roland Garros. The 25-year-old took apart Spain's Conchita Martínez 6–2, 7–5 in a lacklustre final after lifting her game to loftier levels in the previous two rounds. The number 6 seed battled gamely from behind to beat three-time former titlist Monica Seles of the U.S. 4–6, 6–3, 6–4 in the quarterfinals and then removed the top-seeded Hingis 6–4, 5–7, 6–2 in a suspenseful semifinal.

The formidable Australian team of Todd Woodbridge and Mark Woodforde captured their first French Open doubles title in 2000. The win made the pair the only doubles players in history to achieve all four Grand Slams, the Olympic gold medal, the world championship, and the Davis Cup.

Wimbledon. In sweeping his seventh singles title in eight years on the lawns of the All-England Club, Sampras played through most of the fortnight in intense pain. Suffering with an inflamed tendon just above his ankle, Sampras could not practice in between matches after his second-round contest with Karol Kucera. Driven by deep pride and a keen sense of history, Sampras overcame his adverse circumstances. For the fifth time in his seven Wimbledon final-round appearances, he did not lose his serve, reviving to defeat two-time U.S. Open champion Patrick Rafter of Australia 6–7 (10–12), 7–6 (7–5), 6–4, 6–2 in a rain-delayed battle ending in near darkness. At long last, the 28-year-old American broke the record he had shared with Australian Roy Emerson for men's major tournament victories. With his parents in the stands watching him win a Grand Slam crown for the first time, Sampras briefly held his head in his hands and cried in a rare display of public emotion. In doubles, Woodbridge and Woodforde captured their 6th Wimbledon and 11th Grand Slam title.

Venus Williams had been away from tennis from November 1999 until May with tendonitis in both wrists. She was appearing in only her fourth event of 2000 and had not advanced beyond the quarterfinals anywhere else. At age 20, the number 5 seed was ready to make her move on a crucial stage, however, and she did just that. In the final, Williams upended defending champion Davenport 6–3, 7–6 (7–3) to claim her first major crown. Williams was the first African American woman to win at the All-England Club since Althea Gibson in 1958. In a much-heralded semifinal, Venus defeated her sister Serena 6–2, 7–6 (7–3) in only the third singles match ever between sisters at Wimbledon and the first since "open" tennis began in 1968.

U.S. Open. After losing 11 of his first 16 matches in 2000, Safin had raised his game markedly thereafter and came into New York seeded sixth. He was considered by most authorities as a prime candidate to take the U.S. title, but no one was quite prepared for the breathtaking display he gave in dismantling four-time winner and number 4 seed Sampras 6–4, 6–3, 6–3. In his first major final, Safin was a maestro on the tennis court, almost impeccable on serve and off the ground, refusing to drop his delivery even once in three sets. No Russian had ever ruled at the U.S. championships before the charismatic Safin prevailed on the hard courts at the National Tennis Center. After surviving back-to-back five-set skirmishes with the Italian 35-year-old left-hander Gianluca Pozzi and the Frenchman Sebastien Grosjean in the second and third rounds, Safin never looked back.

Venus Williams's breakthrough at Wimbledon lifted her confidence to a new level. On her path to the U.S. Open, she picked up three more tournament wins on the hard-court circuit. That set the stage for her second consecutive major tournament victory. Once more, her victim in the final was the number 2 seed Davenport. Davenport built a 4–1, two service-break lead over Williams in the opening set but did not exploit that opportunity. Williams won five games in a row to take the set, then completed a 6–4, 7–5 triumph in style. The third-seeded Venus was on the edge of elimination in the semifinals when she took on Hingis. The top seed was two points away from ousting Venus at 5–3 in the final set, but Williams struck back convincingly to beat the Swiss star 4–6, 6–3, 7–5.

Other Events. Kuerten played the match of his career to crush Agassi 6–4, 6–4, 6–4 in the final of the Tennis Masters Cup (formerly the ATP Tour world championship and the Compaq Grand Slam Cup) in Lisbon. By taking this tournament reserved for only the game's eight best players, Kuerten moved past Safin to claim the number-one ranking for the year. Hingis won the season-ending Chase Championships with a hard-fought 6–7 (5–7), 6–4, 6–4 win over Seles in the final at New York City's Madison Square Garden.

Spain was victorious for the first time ever in the Davis Cup in December. In the final on clay in Barcelona, Ferrero won the decisive match over the enterprising Lleyton Hewitt of Australia in four sets as King Juan Carlos I and

Queen Sofia cheered him on. A month earlier, the Spanish women lost the Fed Cup final to the U.S. Led by veterans Davenport, Seles, and a resurgent Jennifer Capriati, the Americans defeated Martínez, Arantxa Sánchez-Vicario, and company 5–0 in Las Vegas, Nev., in November. At the Olympics, Kafelnikov won the men's singles gold medal, while Sebastien Lareau and Daniel Nestor of Canada bested Woodbridge and Woodforde, the defending gold medalists.

Jim Courier—the world's top-ranked player in 1992—retired after 13 years as a professional. The 29-year-old American captured four Grand Slam events during his distinguished career. The volatile John McEnroe stepped aside as U.S. Davis Cup captain after only one year, lamenting that he had failed in his goal to inspire Sampras and Agassi to make full commitments to the revered international team competition. McEnroe was succeeded by his younger brother, Patrick, a former player of lesser stature perhaps, but one perhaps better suited to the demands of the job. (STEVE FLINK)

TRACK AND FIELD SPORTS (ATHLETICS)

Olympic dreams danced in the heads of top track and field competitors in 2000, and the effect of many athletes holding their best efforts in abeyance for the Games, held in late September in Sydney, Australia, was noticeable throughout the season.

Olympic Games. Superlative head-to-head competition ruled over record setting at the Sydney Olympics, the first since 1948 in which no world records were broken. Despite the dearth of global marks—attributable to cooler weather and, some would speculate, tightened drug testing—new Olympic records were established in six events: the men's 1,500 m, the 20-km walk, and the javelin and the women's 5,000 m, 10,000 m, and marathon. Three new events were added to the women's program: the pole vault, the hammer throw, and the 20-km walk, which replaced the 10-km walk.

Leading the way was American Marion Jones. (*See* BIOGRAPHIES.) In her first Olympics, the 24-year-old Jones became the first track and field athlete ever to win five medals in events on the modern program. Jones's effort fell short of her goal of winning five golds, but she won the 100 m, the 200 m, and the 4 × 400-m relay and collected bronze medals in the long jump and the 4 × 100-m relay.

In the third round of the long jump, Jones leaped 6.92 m (22 ft 8½ in), inferior to Heike Drechsler of Germany's 6.99 m (22 ft 11¼ in) and equal to the best of Fiona May of Italy. Jones's tie with May was broken on the basis of May's superior second best jump. Jones fouled her remaining three efforts. The swift, sure passing of the Bahamian and Jamaican teams proved too much for the U.S. in the 4 × 100-m relay, and although Jones made up ground on the final leg, The Bahamas won in a season-leading 41.95 sec, with Jamaica timed in 42.13 sec and the U.S. in 42.20. Forty-year-old Merlene Ottey, the anchor runner for Jamaica, won her eighth Olympic medal, a record women's total in track and field.

U.S. male sprinters made history. World-record holder Maurice Greene won the 100 m in 9.87 sec, a metre ahead of his training partner Ato Boldon of Trinidad (9.99 sec) and Obadele Thompson of Barbados (10.04 sec). Michael Johnson became the first man to win two Olympic 400-m titles. Greene and Johnson did not meet in the 200-m final, however. That hoped-for prospect was dashed two months earlier when both athletes pulled up injured in the 200 m at the U.S. Olympic Trials and failed to qualify at that distance.

For emotional impact no champion rivaled Cathy Freeman in the women's 400 m. For four years the aboriginal Australian, who finished second in the 400 m at the 1996 Olympics in Atlanta, Ga., had carried the hopes of her people and her nation. Freeman lit the Olympic torch during Sydney's opening ceremony. In her 400-m final, she lit up the homestretch to win in 49.11 sec before an Olympic-record crowd of 112,524 screaming spectators.

Noah Ngeny of Kenya, age 21, had run hot on the heels of 1,500-m and mile world-record holder Hicham El Guerrouj of Morocco for two seasons. In the 1,500-m final in Sydney, Ngeny charged past El Guerrouj in the last 50 m to win in an Olympic-record 3 min 32.07 sec. The devastated El Guerrouj (3 min 32.32 sec) had waited four years for the race, in which he hoped to make up for having fallen in 1996. In running races of 800 m and longer African-born men took all the medals except the 800-m gold, which was captured by Nils Schumann of Germany.

The men's 10,000 m developed as a rematch between Ethiopia's Haile Gebrselassie and Kenya's Paul Tergat, gold and silver medalists, respectively, in Atlanta and the two fastest men ever in the event. Tension built for 24 of 25

Olivier Morin/AFP Worldwide

American Stacy Dragila rises toward the bar during the Olympic women's pole vault final.

laps until Tergat, in what he said would be his last track race, sprinted ahead 250 m from the finish. With a lean into the finish, Gebrselassie managed to defend his title by a mere 0.09 sec.

Javelin thrower Jan Zelezny of the Czech Republic won in his third consecutive Olympics. Atlanta silver medalist Steve Backley threw an Olympic-record 89.95 m (294 ft 9 in) but saw his hopes crushed when Zelezny, who had not won a major title since 1996, answered with an Olympic record of his own, 90.17 m (295 ft 10 in).

Polish racewalker Robert Korzeniowski was the only man to win two individual events. He crossed the line in the 20-km race 4 sec behind Mexico's Bernardo Segura. It was not until Segura was on a cell phone receiving congratulations from Mexican Pres. Ernesto Zedillo that officials delivered the disqualifying red card for illegal technique. That gave the gold to Korzeniowski, whose time of 1 hr 18 min 59 sec was an Olympic record. Later Korzeniowski won the 50-km walk in 3 hr 42 min 22 sec.

Drug-testing developments played a part in Sydney. Ottey's participation had been in doubt since a positive test for the banned drug nandrolone in 1999, but the International Amateur Athletic Federation (IAAF) overthrew the test result on technical grounds and lifted her two-year suspension before the Games. After her 100-m victory, Jones had to cope with news that her husband, world-champion shot-putter C.J. Hunter, was under investigation for four positive nandrolone tests earlier in the year. Hunter professed his innocence. Women's hammer throw world-record holder Mihaela Melinte of Romania was allowed onto the field for her qualifying round and then promptly escorted off. Melinte, it turned out, had tested positive earlier in the year.

After the International Olympic Committee announced a new test would be used in Sydney for the previously undetectable endurance-boosting hormone erythropoietin (EPO), Chinese officials canceled the Olympic trips of athletes in several sports, including six distance runners trained by coach Ma Junren. Officials admitted that most of these athletes had tested positive for banned drugs.

While no IAAF drug-testing official disputed the validity of high jump world-record holder Javier Sotomayor's positive test for cocaine in 1999, the IAAF Council nonetheless lifted the Cuban's suspension in August, citing an otherwise clean record. Reports later surfaced that at least one out-of-competition test on Sotomayor in 2000 was cocaine-positive, but since the drug was only proscribed during competition, the Council was not informed. Free to compete, Sotomayor placed second in Sydney's high jump.

Men's International Competition. Wilson Kipketer of Denmark, holder of the indoor and outdoor world records for 800 m, broke the indoor 1,000-m standard in Stuttgart, Ger., in February, racing the distance in 2 min 15.25 sec. That cut just 0.01 sec from the previous record, set by Noureddine Morceli of Algeria in 1992. Two weeks later in Birmingham, Eng., Kipketer lowered the mark to 2 min 14.96 sec. In Pretoria, S.Af., in March Johnson broke the world record for the rarely run 300 m, running 30.85 sec, a 0.63 sec improvement. Thin, high-altitude air in Pretoria helped Johnson, and a video showed he ran the second 100 m of the race in a mind-boggling 9.43 sec.

The IAAF's Golden League and Grand Prix series of meets played second fiddle to Sydney. The Golden League's jackpot was reduced from its former $1 million to 50 kg (110 lb) of gold, and athletes were given the reduced task of winning at five of the seven meets, rather than at all seven, in order to share in that prize. Greene and El Guerrouj won five times, but each skipped the Grand Prix final, held in Doha, Qatar, on October 5. El Guerrouj cited injury, and Greene claimed fatigue. The overall men's Grand Prix title thus went to 400-m hurdler Angelo Taylor of the U.S.

Women's International Competition. Polevaulter Stacy Dragila, who won the inaugural Olympic competition in her event in September, set indoor world records of 4.61 m (15 ft 1½ in) and 4.62 m (15 ft 1¾ in) in February and March, respectively. In May she also elevated the outdoor record to the latter height. Two weeks later, Dragila cleared 4.70 m (15 ft 5 in) in an exhibition on a beach, unacceptable for record purposes due to the use of a raised wooden runway. She won the U.S. Olympic Trials, however, with a new record of 4.63 m (15 ft 2¼ in).

Specifications were changed for the women's javelin effective in 1999, with the centre of gravity moved forward so the spears would always land point first. Recognition of world records with the new implement began in January 2000. Norway's Trine Hattestad raised the record twice, to 68.22 m (223 ft 10 in) in Rome in June and to 69.48 m (227 ft 11 in) in Oslo in July.

With Greene and El Guerrouj out of the Grand Prix final, that left Hattestad, 100-m hurdler Gail Devers of the U.S., and Russian long jumper Tatyana Kotova to share in the Golden League's 50 kg (110 lb) of gold. As the women's overall Grand Prix champion, Hattestad earned an additional $200,000 in Qatar, edging out Jones.

Cross Country and Marathon Running. As the year began, 11 of the 12 fastest marathon times ever had been run in either 1998 or 1999. Not surprisingly, given that many athletes chose to focus primarily on Olympic gold rather than on fast times, the pace slowed slightly in 2000. The only man to add his name to the all-time top-10 list was Antônio Pinto. The 34-year-old Portuguese won the London Marathon in April with a time of 2 hr 6 min 36 sec.

In October Khalid Khannouchi returned to the Chicago Marathon, where he had set a world record in 1999, and won in 2 hr 7 min 1 sec, which became the third-fastest time of the year. In May the Moroccan-born Khannouchi had acquired U.S. citizenship, but due to injuries he was forced to withdraw from the U.S. Olympic Trials race just days before it was run. He was thus ineligible to run in the Olympics.

At the Olympics, an Ethiopian man was victorious for the first time since 1968. Gezahenge Abera, at age 22 the youngest Olympic marathon champion ever, finished in 2 hr 10 min 11 sec. Naoko Takahashi reigned in the women's marathon and became the first Japanese woman to win Olympic gold in track and field. Her time of 2 hr 23 min 14 sec in Sydney broke the Olympic record by an astounding 1 min 38 sec.

At the world cross country championships in Vilamoura, Port., Kenya won four of six team crowns in the various divisions, but Tergat failed to win a sixth consecutive long-course title. He placed third, just 2 sec behind winner Mohamed Mourhit of Belgium. In the women's long-course competition, Derartu Tulu of Ethiopia won for the third time and led her country to its second straight women's team title. (SIEG LINDSTROM)

VOLLEYBALL

One dynasty continued in the world of volleyball, while another fell short in its quest for gold, at the 2000 Olympic Games in Sydney, Australia. The Cuban women's team won the Olympic gold medal for a record third successive Olympiad by defeating Russia in a dramatic five-set match. The Russians led the match two sets to none before the powerful and talented Cubans, led by Regla Torres and Regla Bell, won the final three games en route to victory. Brazil downed the U.S. for its second straight Olympic bronze medal. Meanwhile, Yugoslavia, the bronze medal winner at the 1996 Games in Atlanta, Ga., claimed its first Olympic gold medal in men's volleyball. It defeated Russia in three straight games after upsetting three-time defending world champion Italy 3–0 in the semifinals. Both victories avenged preliminary-round losses. Italy, the 1996 Olympic silver medalists, downed Argentina to garner the men's bronze medal.

In the second Olympic appearance for beach volleyball, Dain Blanton and Eric Fonoimoana of the U.S. captured their first-ever international title when they upset Zé Marco de Melo and Ricardo Santos of Brazil 12–11, 12–9 to win an Olympic gold medal. Jörg Ahmann and Axel Hager of Germany won the bronze medal for the initial Olympic volleyball medal for Germany. Natalie Cook and Kerri Pottharst of Australia (1996 Olympic bronze medal winners) claimed the women's gold following a 12–11, 12–10 triumph over Adriana Behar and Shelda Bede of Brazil, while Sandra Pires and Adriana Samuel of Brazil collected the bronze. The Sydney Olympics drew 180,000 spectators to set a record for the most fans ever at a beach volleyball tournament.

The $10 million men's World League was captured by Italy for the eighth time in 11 years. The women's World Grand Prix in August proved to be a preview for the Olympics, as Cuba won the eight-team tournament, followed by Russia and Brazil. (RICH WANNINGER)

WEIGHT LIFTING

The weight lifting competition of the Games of the XXVII Olympiad was held in the Sydney Convention Centre in Sydney, Australia, in September 2000. For the first time in the history of the Olympic Games women weight lifters officially participated. The International Weightlifting Federation only allowed a maximum of four women athletes from each country to compete. A total of 247 athletes entered the competition: 162 men representing 63 countries in eight weight classes and 85 women from 47 countries in seven weight classes.

China topped the rankings with seven medals (five gold, one silver, and one bronze), followed by Greece with five (two gold, two silver, and one bronze), Iran (two gold), Bulgaria (one gold and two silver), and the U.S. (one gold and one bronze). Superheavyweight Hossein Rezazadeh of Iran won the overall Olympic champion title with a 472.5 kg (1,041.7 lb) overall total, a new world and Olympic record. He defeated Olympic champion Andrey Chemerkin of Russia. Three-time world champion Halil Mutlu of Turkey, called the "Little Dynamo," won his second Olympic gold and broke his own world records in the 56-kg class. (*See* BIOGRAPHIES.) American Tara Nott captured the first Olympic gold medal awarded for women's weight lifting, in the 48-kg category.

Nine world records, 17 Olympic records, and 7 junior world records were broken in the men's competition. Seventeen world records, 17 Olympic records, and three junior world records were broken in the women's event.

(DRAGOMIR CIOROSLAN)

WRESTLING

Freestyle and Greco-Roman. The highlight in wrestling at the 2000 Olympic Games in Sydney, Australia, was the win of unheralded U.S. Greco-Roman wrestler Rulon Gardner over previously unbeaten Aleksandr Karelin of Russia in the superheavyweight division. Karelin, considered the greatest Greco-Roman wrestler of all time, was attempting to win his fourth Olympic gold to go with his nine world championship titles. He had never lost in international competition and had not been scored upon in a decade. Gardner won a one-point decision, which came when Karelin broke his grip after the wrestlers were placed in a clinch at the beginning of the second period. Russia was the unofficial team champion with two golds; the remaining five gold medals went to South Korea, Bulgaria, Cuba, Turkey, and Sweden.

In freestyle the U.S. failed to gain a gold medal on the mats for the first time since 1968, but a drug disqualification of Germany's 1994 world champion, Alexander Leipold, at 76 kg (167.5 lb) gave American Brandon Slay the gold. Russia claimed the unofficial team title with five medals, including four golds. The United States was second with four medals. Azerbaijan, Iran, and Canada each took one gold.

The U.S. defeated Iran 17–11 and Russia 22–9 to claim the XXVIII World Cup of freestyle wrestling in Fairfax, Va., in February 2000. Iran upset Russia 17–15 to finish second in the team competition, while Cuba was fourth. In March the University of Iowa claimed its sixth straight National Collegiate Athletic Association wrestling championship—its 20th NCAA title since 1975.

(JOHN HOKE)

Sumo. In 2000, for the first time since his heyday in 1993, the 31-year-old, Hawaiian-born *yokozuna* (grand champion) Akebono captured the *yusho* (championship) of more than one tournament during the year, winning the titles of both the Nagoya Basho in July and the Kyushu Basho in November. Three others won their first *yusho* ever, with *sekiwake* (junior champion) Musoyama taking the New Year's tournament (Hatsu Basho) in January, number 14 *maegashira* (senior wrestler) Takatoriki coming through in March to grab the Haru Basho, and *sekiwake* Kaio winning the Natsu (summer) Basho in May. Both Musoyama and Kaio were promoted to sumo's second highest rank of *ozeki* (champion) at the end of the basho following their respective victories. At age 32, Takatoriki was the lowest ranked sumo wrestler in history to win the championship. The remaining Aki Basho in September was captured by *yokozuna* Musashimaru, marking the eighth title for the 29-year-old, Samoan-born *rikishi.*

In other developments, 29-year-old *yokozuna* Wakanohana retired in the first week of the March tournament, less than two years after his promotion to the top rank. He had won five titles but failed to win a *yusho* as a *yokozuna.* Other retirements were announced by 32-year-old Kotonishiki, the only *maegashira* in history to win two championships (in September 1991 and November 1998), and 38-year-old Mitoizumi.

(ANDY ADAMS)

AP/Wide World Photos

Chinese weight lifter Ding Meiyuan secures an Olympic gold medal with her lift in the clean and jerk event.

SPECIAL REPORT

Games of the XXVII Olympiad

by Melinda C. Shepherd

From Sept. 15 to Oct. 1, 2000, Sydney, Australia, played host to the world as the site of the Games of the XXVII Olympiad. Despite initial concerns about protests by native Aboriginal Australians—and amid the financial scandals that plagued the International Olympic Committee and several other host cities—Sydney's festivities were pronounced "the best Olympic Games ever" by IOC Pres. Juan António Samaranch. Nearly 11,000 accredited athletes, representing 199 IOC member-states, participated; in addition, three athletes from the UN dependency of East Timor competed as individuals. At the spectacular opening ceremony, during which Aboriginal Australian runner Cathy Freeman lit the Olympic flame, North and South Koreans marched together under one flag for the first time (they later competed for their separate countries).

A record 928 Olympic medals were awarded in 300 events (168 for men, 120 for women, and 12 mixed), with 80 countries gaining at least one medal. U.S. athletes won the most medals, 97, followed by competitors from Russia (88), China (59), Australia (58), and Germany (57). A total of 48 world records were broken or equaled, 15 of them in swimming and 27 in weight lifting. Several events were contested at the Olympics for the first time in 2000, including men's and women's taekwondo, trampoline, triathlon, and synchronized diving. Other new women's events included weight lifting, modern pentathlon, and pole vaulting.

As in past Olympics, drugs cast a shadow over Sydney. At least 40 members of China's national team withdrew or were dropped before the Games. An athlete and an Olympic official were denied entry to the Games when they were caught with banned substances in their possession. In two of the biggest drug-related stories, freestyle wrestler Alexander Leipold of Germany tested positive for steroids and was stripped of his gold medal, and Romanian gymnast Andreea Raducan lost her all-around gold after it was discovered that she had taken a nonprescription cold medicine that contained a banned ingredient.

Aboriginal and non-Aboriginal performers enact a scene from Australian history during the opening ceremony of the Olympic Games in Sydney on September 15.

AP/Wide World Photos

Despite falling short of her declared aim to win five gold medals, American sprinter Marion Jones (*see* BIOGRAPHIES) captured three gold and two bronze. In the pool American Jenny Thompson won 4 medals to bring her career total to 10 (8 gold), a record for any woman swimmer and for an American woman in any Olympic sport, while Australian favourite Ian Thorpe gained 3 gold and 2 silver medals. Two Dutch swimmers unexpectedly triumphed—Pieter van den Hoogenband and Inge de Bruijn. (*See* BIOGRAPHIES.) Other prominent athletes included diminutive Turkish weight lifter Halil Mutlu (*see* BIOGRAPHIES); British rower Steven Redgrave, who won his fifth consecutive gold; and Cuban heavyweight boxer Felix Savon (*see* BIOGRAPHIES), who captured his third straight. In perhaps the biggest upset of the Games, American Greco-Roman wrestler Rulon Gardner defeated Aleksandr Karelin; the almost legendary Russian had not lost a bout since 1987.

Melinda C. Shepherd is associate editor of Encyclopædia Britannica Yearbooks.

OLYMPIC CHAMPIONS, 2000 SUMMER GAMES, SYDNEY

Archery

Event	Men	Women
Individual	S. Fairweather (Austl.)	Yun Mi Jin (S.Kor.)
Team	South Korea	South Korea

Badminton

Class	Winner
Men's singles	Ji Xinpeng (China)
Men's doubles	T. Gunawan/C. Wijaya (Indon.)
Women's singles	Gong Zhichao (China)
Women's doubles	Ge Fei/Gu Jun (China)
Mixed doubles	Zhang Jun/Gao Ling (China)

Baseball

Winning Team	United States

Basketball

Men	United States	**Women**	United States

Boxing

Class	Winner	Class	Winner
48-kg class	B. Asloum (Fr.)	67-kg class	O. Saitov (Russia)
51-kg class	W. Ponlid (Thai.)	71-kg class	Y. Ibraimov (Kazakh.)
54-kg class	G. Rigondeaux Ortiz (Cuba)	75-kg class	J. Gutiérrez (Cuba)
57-kg class	B. Sattarkhanov (Kazakh.)	81-kg class	A. Lebziak (Russia)
60-kg class	M. Kindelan (Cuba)	91-kg class	F. Savon (Cuba)
63.5-kg class	M. Abdullayev (Uzbek.)	91+-kg class	A. Harrison (U.K.)

Canoeing—Men

Event	Winner	Time
500-m kayak singles	K. Holman (Nor.)	1 min 57.84 sec
1,000-m kayak singles	K. Holman (Nor.)	3 min 33.26 sec
500-m kayak pairs	Z. Kammerer/B. Storcz (Hung.)	1 min 47.05 sec
1,000-m kayak pairs	B. Bonomi/A. Rossi (Italy)	3 min 14.46 sec
1,000 kayak fours	Hungary	2 min 55.18 sec
Slalom kayak singles	T. Schmidt (Ger.)	217.25 pt
500-m Canadian singles	G. Kolonics (Hung.)	2 min 24.81 sec
1,000-m Canadian singles	A. Dittmer (Ger.)	3 min 54.37 sec
500-m Canadian pairs	F. Novak/I. Pulai (Hung.)	1 min 51.28 sec
1,000-m Canadian pairs	F. Popescu/M. Pricop (Rom.)	3 min 37.35 sec
Slalom Canadian singles	T. Estanguet (Fr.)	231.87 pt
Slalom Canadian pairs	Pa. Hochschorner/ Pe. Hochschorner (Slvk.)	237.74 pt

Canoeing—Women

Event	Winner	Time
500-m kayak singles	J. Idem Guerrini (Italy)	2 min 13.84 sec
500-m kayak pairs	B. Fischer/K. Wagner (Ger.)	1 min 56.99 sec
500-m kayak fours	Germany	1 min 34.53 sec
Slalom kayak singles	S. Hilgertova (Cz.Rep.)	247.04 pt

Cycling—Men

Event	Winner	Time
Road race	J. Ullrich (Ger.)	5 hr 29 min 08 sec
Individual time trial	V. Yekimov (Russia)	57 min 40.420 sec
1-km time trial	J. Queally (U.K.)	1 min 1.609 sec
Individual pursuit	R. Bartko (Ger.)	4 min 18.515 sec[2]
Team pursuit	Germany	3 min 59.710 sec[1]
Sprint	M. Nothstein (U.S.)	
Olympic sprint	France	44.233 sec
Points race	J. Llaneras (Spain)	
Madison	Australia	
Keirin	F. Rousseau (Fr.)	11.020 sec
Mountain bike	M. Martinez (Fr.)	2 hr 9 min 2.50 sec

Cycling—Women

Event	Winner	Time
Road race	L. Zijlaard-van Moorsel (Neth.)	3 hr 6 min 31 sec
Individual time trial	L. Zijlaard-van Moorsel (Neth.)	42 min 0.781 sec
500-m time trial	F. Ballanger (Fr.)	34.140 sec
Individual pursuit	L. Zijlaard-van Moorsel (Neth.)	3 min 33.360 sec
Sprint	F. Ballanger (Fr.)	
Points race	A. Bellutti (Italy)	
Mountain bike	P. Pezzo (Italy)	1 hr 49 min 24.38 sec

Diving—Men

Event	Winner	Score
3-m springboard	Xiong Ni (China)	708.72 pt
10-m platform	Tian Liang (China)	724.53 pt
3-m synchronized	Xiao Hailiang/Xiong Ni (China)	365.58 pt
10-m synchronized	I. Lukashin/D. Sautin (Russia)	365.04 pt

Diving—Women

Event	Winner	Score
3-m springboard	Fu Mingxia (China)	609.42 pt
10-m platform	L. Wilkinson (U.S.)	543.75 pt
3-m synchronized	V. Ilyina/Y. Pakhalina (Russia)	332.64 pt
10-m synchronized	Li Na/Sang Xue (China)	345.12 pt

Equestrian

Event	Individual	Team
3-day event	D. O'Connor (U.S.)	Australia
Dressage	A. Van Grunsven (Neth.)	Germany
Jumping	J. Dubbeldam (Neth.)	Germany

Fencing

Event	Men	Women
Individual foil	Kim Young Ho (S.Kor.)	V. Vezzali (Italy)
Team foil	France	Italy
Individual épée	P. Kolobkov (Russia)	T. Nagy (Hung.)
Team épée	Italy	Russia
Individual sabre	M.C. Covaliu (Rom.)	
Team sabre	Russia	

Field Hockey

Men	Netherlands	**Women**	Australia

Gymnastics—Men

Event	Winner	Score
Team	China	231.919 pt
All-around	A. Nemov (Russia)	58.474 pt
Floor exercise	I. Vihrovs (Latvia)	9.812 pt
Vault	G. Deferr (Spain)	9.712 pt
Pommel horse	M. Urzica (Rom.)	9.862 pt
Rings	S. Csollany (Hung.)	9.850 pt
Parallel bars	Li Xiaopeng (China)	9.825 pt
Horizontal bar	A. Nemov (Russia)	9.787 pt
Trampoline	A. Moskalenko (Russia)	41.70 pt

Gymnastics—Women

Event	Winner	Score
Team	Romania	154.608 pt
All-around	S. Amanar (Rom.)	38.642 pt
Floor exercise	Ye. Zamolodchikova (Russia)	9.850 pt
Vault	Ye. Zamolodchikova (Russia)	9.731 pt
Uneven bars	S. Khorkina (Russia)	9.862 pt
Balance beam	Liu Xuan (China)	9.825 pt
Trampoline	I. Karavayeva (Russia)	38.90 pt
Indiv. rhythmic	Yu. Barsukova (Russia)	39.632 pt
Team rhythmic	Russia	39.500 pt

Handball

Men	Russia	Women	Denmark

Judo—Men[3]

Class	Winner
60-kg class	T. Nomura (Japan)
66-kg class	H. Ozkan (Tur.)
73-kg class	G. Maddaloni (Italy)
81-kg class	M. Takimoto (Japan)
90-kg class	M. Huizinga (Neth.)
100-kg class	K. Inoue (Japan)
100+-kg class	D. Douillet (Fr.)

Judo—Women[3]

Class	Winner
48-kg class	R. Tamura (Japan)
52-kg class	L. Verdecia (Cuba)
57-kg class	I. Fernández (Spain)
63-kg class	S. Vandenhende (Fr.)
70-kg class	S. Veranes (Cuba)
78-kg class	Tang Lin (China)
78+-kg class	Yuan Hua (China)

Modern Pentathlon

Men	D. Satkovsky (Russia)	Women	S. Cook (U.K.)

Rowing—Men

Event	Winner	Time
Single sculls	R. Waddell (N.Z.)	6 min 48.90 sec
Double sculls	I. Cop/L. Spik (Slvn.)	6 min 16.63 sec
Quadruple sculls	Italy	5 min 45.56 sec
Coxless pairs	M. Andrieux/J.-C. Rolland (Fr.)	6 min 32.97 sec
Coxless fours	United Kingdom	5 min 56.24 sec
Eights	United Kingdom	5 min 33.08 sec
Lightweight double sculls	T. Kucharski/R. Sycz (Pol.)	6 min 21.75 sec
Lightweight fours	France	6 min 1.68 sec

Rowing—Women

Event	Winner	Time
Single sculls	Ye. Karsten (Bela.)	7 min 28.14 sec
Double sculls	K. Boron/J. Thieme (Ger.)	6 min 55.44 sec
Quadruple sculls	Germany	6 min 19.58 sec
Coxless pairs	G. Damian/D. Ignat (Rom.)	7 min 11.00 sec
Eights	Romania	6 min 6.44 sec
Lightweight double sculls	A. Alupei/C. Burcica (Rom.)	7 min 2.64 sec

Shooting—Men

Event	Winner	Score
Rapid-fire pistol	S. Alifirenko (Russia)	687.6 pt
Free pistol	T. Kiryakov (Bulg.)	666.0 pt
Air pistol	F. Dumoulin (Fr.)	688.9 pt[2]
10-m running target	Yang Ling (China)	681.1 pt
Small-bore rifle, 3 pos.	R. Debevec (Slvn.)	1,275.1 pt[2]
Small-bore rifle, prone	J. Edman (Swed.)	701.3 pt
Air rifle	Cai Yalin (China)	696.4 pt[2]
Trap	M. Diamond (Austl.)	147.0 pt
Double trap	R. Faulds (U.K.)	187.0 pt
Skeet	M. Milchev (Ukr.)	150.0 pt[1]

Shooting—Women

Event	Winner	Score
Pistol	M. Grozdeva (Bulg.)	690.3 pt[2]
Air pistol	Tao Luna (China)	488.2 pt
Small-bore rifle, 3 pos.	R. Mauer-Rozanska (Pol.)	684.6 pt
Air rifle	N. Johnson (U.S.)	497.7 pt
Trap	D. Gudzineviciute (Lith.)	93.0 pt
Double trap	P. Hansen (Swed.)	148.0 pt[2]
Skeet	Z. Meftakhetdinova (Azer.)	98.0 pt[2]

Soccer (Association Football)

Men	Cameroon	Women	Norway

Softball

Winning Team	United States

Swimming—Men

Event	Winner	Time
50-m freestyle	A. Ervin (U.S.); G. Hall (U.S.)[4]	21.98 sec
100-m freestyle	P. Van den Hoogenband (Neth.)	48.30 sec
200-m freestyle	P. Van den Hoogenband (Neth.)	1 min 45.35 sec[1]
400-m freestyle	I. Thorpe (Austl.)	3 min 40.59 sec[1]
1,500-m freestyle	G. Hackett (Austl.)	14 min 48.33 sec
100-m backstroke	L. Krayzelburg (U.S.)	53.72 sec[2]
200-m backstroke	L. Krayzelburg (U.S.)	1 min 56.76 sec[2]
100-m breaststroke	D. Fioravanti (Italy)	1 min 0.46 sec[2]
200-m breaststroke	D. Fioravanti (Italy)	2 min 10.87 sec
100-m butterfly	L. Frölander (Swed.)	52.00 sec
200-m butterfly	T. Malchow (U.S.)	1 min 55.35 sec[2]
200-m individual medley	M. Rosolino (Italy)	1 min 58.98 sec[2]
400-m individual medley	T. Dolan (U.S.)	4 min 11.76 sec[1]
4 × 100-m freestyle relay	Australia	3 min 13.67 sec[1]
4 × 200-m freestyle relay	Australia	7 min 7.05 sec[1]
4 × 100-m medley relay	United States	3 min 33.73 sec[1]

Swimming—Women

Event	Winner	Time
50-m freestyle	I. de Bruijn (Neth.)	24.32 sec
100-m freestyle	I. de Bruijn (Neth.)	53.83 sec
200-m freestyle	S. O'Neill (Austl.)	1 min 58.24 sec
400-m freestyle	B. Bennett (U.S.)	4 min 5.80 sec
800-m freestyle	B. Bennett (U.S.)	8 min 19.67 sec[2]
100-m backstroke	D. Mocanu (Rom.)	1 min 0.21 sec[2]
200-m backstroke	D. Mocanu (Rom.)	2 min 8.16 sec
100-m breaststroke	M. Quann (U.S.)	1 min 7.05 sec
200-m breaststroke	A. Kovacs (Hung.)	2 min 24.35 sec
100-m butterfly	I. de Bruijn (Neth.)	56.61 sec[1]
200-m butterfly	M. Hyman (U.S.)	2 min 5.88 sec[2]
200-m individual medley	Ya. Klochkova (Ukr.)	2 min 10.68 sec[2]
400-m individual medley	Ya. Klochkova (Ukr.)	4 min 33.59 sec[1]
4 × 100-m freestyle relay	United States	3 min 36.61 sec[1]
4 × 200-m freestyle relay	United States	7 min 57.80 sec[2]
4 × 100-m medley relay	United States	3 min 58.30 sec[1]
Synchronized duet	O. Brusnikina/M. Kiseleva (Russia)	99.580 pt
Synchronized team	Russia	99.146 pt

Table Tennis

Event	Winner
Men's singles	Kong Linghui (China)
Men's doubles	Wang Liqin/Yan Sen (China)
Women's singles	Wang Nan (China)
Women's doubles	Li Ju/Wang Nan (China)

Taekwondo—Men

Class	Winner
58-kg class	M. Mouroutsos (Greece)
68-kg class	S. Lopez (U.S.)
80-kg class	A. Matos Fuentes (Cuba)
80+-kg class	Kim Kyong Hun (S.Kor.)

Taekwondo—Women

Class	Winner
49-kg class	L. Burns (Austl.)
57-kg class	Jung Jae Eun (S.Kor.)
67-kg class	Lee Sun Hee (S.Kor.)
67+-kg class	Chen Zhong (China)

Tennis

Event	Winner
Men's singles	Ye. Kafelnikov (Russia)
Men's doubles	S. Lareau/D. Nestor (Can.)
Women's singles	V. Williams (U.S.)
Women's doubles	S. Williams/V. Williams (U.S.)

Track and Field (Athletics)—Men

Event	Winner	Time/Score
100 m	M. Greene (U.S.)	9.87 sec
200 m	K. Kenteris (Greece)	20.09 sec
400 m	M. Johnson (U.S.)	43.84 sec
4 × 100-m relay	United States	37.61 sec
4 × 400-m relay	United States	2 min 56.35 sec
800 m	N. Schumann (Ger.)	1 min 45.08 sec
1,500 m	N. Ngeny (Kenya)	3 min 32.07 sec[2]
5,000 m	M. Wolde (Eth.)	13 min 35.49 sec
10,000 m	H. Gebrselassie (Eth.)	27 min 18.20 sec
Marathon	G. Abera (Eth.)	2 hr 10 min 11 sec
110-m hurdles	A. García (Cuba)	13.00 sec
400-m hurdles	A. Taylor (U.S.)	47.50 sec
Steeplechase	R. Kosgei (Kenya)	8 min 21.43 sec
20-km walk	R. Korzeniowski (Pol.)	1 hr 18 min 59 sec[2]
50-km walk	R. Korzeniowski (Pol.)	3 hr 42 min 22 sec
High jump	S. Klyugin (Russia)	2.35 m
Long jump	I. Pedroso (Cuba)	8.55 m
Triple jump	J. Edwards (U.K.)	17.71 m
Pole vault	N. Hysong (U.S.)	5.90 m
Shot put	A. Harju (Fin.)	21.29 m
Discus throw	V. Alekna (Lith.)	69.30 m
Javelin throw	J. Zelezny (Cz.Rep.)	90.17 m[2]
Hammer throw	S. Ziolkowski (Pol.)	80.02 m
Decathlon	E. Nool (Est.)	8,641 pt

Track and Field (Athletics)—Women

Event	Winner	Time/Score
100 m	M. Jones (U.S.)	10.75 sec
200 m	M. Jones (U.S.)	21.84 sec
400 m	C. Freeman (Austl.)	49.11 sec
4 × 100-m relay	Bahamas	41.95 sec
4 × 400-m relay	United States	3 min 22.62 sec
800 m	M. Mutola (Mozam.)	1 min 56.15 sec
1,500 m	N. Mérah-Benida (Alg.)	4 min 5.10 sec
5,000 m	G. Szabo (Rom.)	14 min 40.79 sec[2]
10,000 m	D. Tulu (Eth.)	30 min 17.49 sec[2]
Marathon	N. Takahashi (Japan)	2 hr 23 min 14 sec[2]
100-m hurdles	O. Shishigina (Kazakh.)	12.65 sec
400-m hurdles	I. Privalova (Russia)	53.02 sec
20-km walk	Wang Liping (China)	1 hr 29 min 5 sec
High jump	Ye. Yelesina (Russia)	2.01 m
Long jump	H. Drechsler (Ger.)	6.99 m
Triple jump	T. Marinova (Bulg.)	15.20 m
Pole vault	S. Dragila (U.S.)	4.60 m
Shot put	Ya. Korolchik (Bela.)	20.56 m
Discus throw	E. Zvereva (Bela.)	68.40 m
Javelin throw	T. Hattestad (Nor.)	68.91 m
Hammer throw	K. Skolimowska (Pol.)	71.16 m
Heptathlon	D. Lewis (U.K.)	6,584 pt

Triathlon

Men		Women	
Men	S. Whitfield (Can.)	Women	B. McMahon (Switz.)

Volleyball

Event	Men	Women
Beach	D. Blanton/ E. Fonoimoana (U.S.)	N. Cook/K. Pottharst (Austl.)
Indoor	Yugoslavia	Cuba

Water Polo

Men		Women	
Men	Hungary	Women	Australia

Weightlifting—Men[3]

Class	Winner	Weight
56-kg class	H. Mutlu (Tur.)	305.0 kg[1]
62-kg class	N. Pechalov (Cro.)	325.0 kg[2]
69-kg class	G. Boevski (Bulg.)	357.5 kg[2]
77-kg class	Zhan Xugang (China)	367.5 kg
85-kg class	P. Dimas (Greece)	390.0 kg
94-kg class	A. Kakiasvilis (Greece)	405.0 kg
105-kg class	H. Tavakoli (Iran)	425.0 kg
105+-kg class	H. Rezazadeh (Iran)	472.5 kg[1]

Weightlifting—Women[3]

Class	Winner	Weight
48-kg class	T. Nott (U.S.)	185.0 kg
53-kg class	Yang Xia (China)	225.0 kg[1]
58-kg class	S. Jiménez Mendívil (Mex.)	222.5 kg
63-kg class	Chen Xiaomin (China)	242.5 kg[1]
69-kg class	Lin Weining (China)	242.5 kg
75-kg class	M.I. Urrutia (Colom.)	245.0 kg
75+-kg class	Ding Meiyuan (China)	300.0 kg[1]

Wrestling[3]

Class	Freestyle	Greco-Roman
54-kg class	N. Abdullayev (Azer.)	Sim Kwon Ho (S.Kor.)
58-kg class	A.R. Dabier (Iran)	A. Nazaryan (Bulg.)
63-kg class	M. Umakhanov (Russia)	V. Samurgashev (Russia)
69-kg class	D. Igali (Can.)	F. Azcuy (Cuba)
76-kg class	B. Slay (U.S.)	M. Kardanov (Russia)
85-kg class	A. Saytyev (Russia)	H. Yerlikaya (Tur.)
97-kg class	S. Murtasaliyev (Russia)	M. Ljungberg (Swed.)
130-kg class	D. Musulbes (Russia)	R. Gardner (U.S.)

Yachting

Event	Winner	Event	Winner
Men's 470	Australia	49er (open)	Finland
Women's 470	Australia	Laser (open)	B. Ainslie (U.K.)
Men's Mistral	C. Sieber (Austria)	Soling (open)	Denmark
Women's Mistral	A. Sensini (Italy)	Star (open)	United States
Men's Finn	I. Percy (U.K.)	Tornado (open)	Austria
Women's Europe	S. Robertson (U.K.)		

[1]World record. [2]Olympic record. [3]New weight classes introduced in 2000. [4]Tied.

Francois-Xavier Marit/AFP Worldwide

Cameroon players celebrate their victory over Spain in the Olympic soccer (association football) final.

Sporting Record

ARCHERY

FITA Outdoor World Target Archery Championships*

Year	Men's individual Winner	Points	Men's team Winner	Points
1995	Lee Kyung Chul (S.Kor.)	109	South Korea	255
1997	Kim Kyung Ho (S.Kor.)	108	South Korea	254
1999	Hong Sung Chil (S.Kor.)	115	Italy	252

Year	Women's individual Winner	Points	Women's team Winner	Points
1995	N. Valeyeva (Moldova)	113	South Korea	247
1997	Kim Du Ri (S.Kor.)	105	South Korea	242
1999	Lee Eun Kyung (S.Kor.)	115	Italy	240

*Olympic (recurve) division.

Juan Montoya celebrates after winning the Indianapolis 500 on May 28.

AP/Wide World Photos

AUTOMOBILE RACING

Formula One Grand Prix Race Results, 2000

Race	Driver	Winner's time (hr:min:sec)
Australian GP	M. Schumacher	1:34:01.987
Brazilian GP	M. Schumacher	1:31:35.271
San Marino GP	M. Schumacher	1:31:39.776
British GP	D. Coulthard	1:28:50.108
Spanish GP	M. Hakkinen	1:33:55.390
European GP	M. Schumacher	1:42:00.307
Monaco GP	D. Coulthard	1:49:28.213
Canadian GP	M. Schumacher	1:41:12.313
French GP	D. Coulthard	1:38:05.538
Austrian GP	M. Hakkinen	1:28:15.818
German GP	R. Barrichello	1:25:34.418
Hungarian GP	M. Hakkinen	1:45:33.869
Belgian GP	M. Hakkinen	1:28:14.494
Italian GP	M. Schumacher	1:27:31.638
United States GP	M. Schumacher	1:36:30.883
Japanese GP	M. Schumacher	1:29:53.435
Malaysian GP	M. Schumacher	1:35:54.235

WORLD DRIVERS' CHAMPIONSHIP: Schumacher 108 points, Hakkinen 89 points, Coulthard 73 points.
CONSTRUCTORS' CHAMPIONSHIP: Ferrari 170 points, McLaren/Mercedes 152 points, Williams/BMW 36 points.

International Cup for Formula One Manufacturers

Year	Car	Year	Car
1995	Benetton/Renault	1998	McLaren/Mercedes
1996	Williams/Renault	1999	Ferrari
1997	Williams/Renault	**2000**	**Ferrari**

World Championship of Drivers

Year	Winner	Car
1998	M. Hakkinen (Fin.)	McLaren/Mercedes
1999	M. Hakkinen (Fin.)	McLaren/Mercedes
2000	**M. Schumacher (Ger.)**	**Ferrari**

Le Mans 24-Hour Grand Prix d'Endurance

Year	Car	Drivers
1998	Porsche GT1	A. McNish, L. Aiello, S. Ortelli
1999	BMW V12 LMR	Y. Dalmas, P. Martini, J. Winkelhock
2000	**Audi R8**	**F. Biela, T. Kristensen, E. Pirro**

Indy Car Champions*

Year	Driver
1998	A. Zanardi
1999	J. Montoya
2000	**G. de Ferran**

*CART champion.

Monte-Carlo Rally

Year	Car	Driver
1998	Toyota Corolla	C. Sainz (Spain)
1999	Mitsubishi Lancer	T. Mäkinen (Fin.)
2000	**Mitsubishi Lancer**	**T. Mäkinen (Fin.)**

Indianapolis 500

Year	Winner	Avg. speed in mph
1998	E. Cheever, Jr.	145.155
1999	K. Brack	153.176
2000	**J. Montoya**	**167.607**

National Association for Stock Car Auto Racing (NASCAR) Winston Cup Champions

Year	Winner
1998	J. Gordon
1999	D. Jarrett
2000	**B. Labonte**

BADMINTON

All-England Championships—Singles

Year	Men	Women
1998	Sun Jun (China)	Ye. Zhaoying (China)
1999	P. Gade Christensen (Den.)	Ye. Zhaoying (China)
2000	**Xia Xuanze (China)**	**Gong Zhichao (China)**

Uber Cup (women)

Year	Winner	Runner-up
1995–96	Indonesia	China
1997–98	China	Indonesia
1999–2000	**China**	**Denmark**

Thomas Cup (men)

Year	Winner	Runner-up
1995–96	Indonesia	Denmark
1997–98	Indonesia	Malaysia
1999–2000	**Indonesia**	**China**

World Badminton Championships

Year	Men's singles	Women's singles	Men's doubles	Women's doubles
1995	H. Arbi (Indon.)	Ye. Zhaoying (China)	R. Subagja, R. Mainaky (Indon.)	Gil Young Ah, Jang Hye Ock (S.Kor.)
1997	P. Rasmussen (Den.)	Ye. Zhaoying (China)	B. Sigit, C. Wijaya (Indon.)	Ge Fei, Gu Jun (China)
1999	Sun Jun (China)	C. Martin (Den.)	Kim Dong Moon, Ha Tae Kwon (S.Kor.)	Ge Fei, Gu Jun (China)

BASEBALL

Final Major League Standings, 2000

AMERICAN LEAGUE

East Division

Club	W.	L.	G.B.
*New York	87	74	—
Boston	85	77	2½
Toronto	83	79	4½
Baltimore	74	88	13½
Tampa Bay	69	92	18

Central Division

Club	W.	L.	G.B.
*Chicago	95	67	—
Cleveland	90	72	5
Detroit	79	83	16
Kansas City	77	85	18
Minnesota	69	93	26

West Division

Club	W.	L.	G.B.
*Oakland	91	70	—
*Seattle	91	71	½
Anaheim	82	80	9½
Texas	71	91	20½

NATIONAL LEAGUE

East Division

Club	W.	L.	G.B.
*Atlanta	95	67	—
*New York	94	68	1
Florida	79	82	15½
Montreal	67	95	28
Philadelphia	65	97	30

Central Division

Club	W.	L.	G.B.
*St. Louis	95	67	—
Cincinnati	85	77	10
Milwaukee	73	89	22
Houston	72	90	23
Pittsburgh	69	93	26
Chicago	65	97	30

West Division

Club	W.	L.	G.B.
*San Francisco	97	65	—
Los Angeles	86	76	11
Arizona	85	77	12
Colorado	82	80	15
San Diego	76	86	21

*Gained play-off berth.

Caribbean Series

Year	Winning team	Country
1998	Northern Eagles	Dominican Republic
1999	Licey Tigers	Dominican Republic
2000	**Santurce Crabbers**	**Puerto Rico**

World Series*

Year	Winning team	Losing team	Results
1998	New York Yankees (AL)	San Diego Padres (NL)	4–0
1999	New York Yankees (AL)	Atlanta Braves (NL)	4–0
2000	**New York Yankees (AL)**	**New York Mets (NL)**	**4–1**

*AL—American League; NL—National League.

Japan Series*

Year	Winning team	Losing team	Results
1998	Yokohama BayStars (CL)	Seibu Lions (PL)	4–2
1999	Fukuoka Daiei Hawks (PL)	Chunichi Dragons (CL)	4–1
2000	**Yomiuri Giants (CL)**	**Fukuoka Daiei Hawks (PL)**	**4–2**

*CL—Central League; PL—Pacific League.

BASKETBALL

NBA Final Standings, 1999–2000

EASTERN CONFERENCE

Atlantic Division

Team	Won	Lost
*Miami	52	30
*New York	50	32
*Philadelphia	49	33
Orlando	41	41
Boston	35	47
New Jersey	31	51
Washington	29	53

Central Division

Team	Won	Lost
*Indiana	56	26
*Charlotte	49	33
*Toronto	45	37
*Detroit	42	40
*Milwaukee	42	40
Cleveland	32	50
Atlanta	28	54
Chicago	17	65

WESTERN CONFERENCE

Midwest Division

Team	Won	Lost
*Utah	55	27
*San Antonio	53	29
*Minnesota	50	32
Dallas	40	42
Denver	35	47
Houston	34	48
Vancouver	22	60

Pacific Division

Team	Won	Lost
*L.A. Lakers	67	15
*Portland	59	23
*Phoenix	53	29
*Seattle	45	37
*Sacramento	44	38
Golden State	19	63
L.A. Clippers	15	67

*Gained play-off berth.

National Basketball Association (NBA) Championship

Season	Winner	Runner-up	Results
1997–98	Chicago Bulls	Utah Jazz	4–2
1998–99	San Antonio Spurs	New York Knicks	4–1
1999–2000	**Los Angeles Lakers**	**Indiana Pacers**	**4–2**

Women's National Basketball Association (WNBA) Championship

Season	Winner	Runner-up	Results
1997–98	Houston Comets	Phoenix Mercury	2–1
1998–99	Houston Comets	New York Liberty	2–1
1999–2000	**Houston Comets**	**New York Liberty**	**2–0**

Division I National Collegiate Athletic Association (NCAA) Championship—Men

Year	Winner	Runner-up	Score
1998	Kentucky	Utah	78–69
1999	Connecticut	Duke	77–74
2000	**Michigan State**	**Florida**	**89–76**

Division I National Collegiate Athletic Association (NCAA) Championship—Women

Year	Winner	Runner-up	Score
1998	Tennessee	Louisiana Tech	93–75
1999	Purdue	Duke	62–45
2000	**Connecticut**	**Tennessee**	**71–52**

National Invitation Tournament (NIT) Championship

Year	Winner	Runner-up	Score
1998	Minnesota	Penn State	79–72
1999	California	Clemson	61–60
2000	**Wake Forest**	**Notre Dame**	**71–61**

World Basketball Championship—Men

Year	Winner	Runner-up
1996	United States	Yugoslavia
1998	Yugoslavia	Russia
2000	**United States**	**France**

World Basketball Championship—Women

Year	Winner	Runner-up
1996	United States	Brazil
1998	United States	Russia
2000	**United States**	**Australia**

BILLIARD GAMES

World Three-Cushion Championship

Year	Winner
1997	D. Jaspers (Neth.)
1998	T. Blomdahl (Swed.)
1999	**D. Jaspers (Neth.)**

WPA World Nine-Ball Championships

Year	Men's champion
1998	K. Takahashi (Japan)
1999	N. Varner (U.S.)
2000	**Fong Pang Chao (Taiwan)**
Year	**Women's champion**
1998	A. Fisher (U.K.)
1999	Lu Shin-Mei (Taiwan)
2000	**J. Kelly (Ire.)**

World Professional Snooker Championship

Year	Winner	Year	Winner
1995	S. Hendry	1998	J. Higgins
1996	S. Hendry	1999	S. Hendry
1997	K. Doherty	**2000**	**M. Williams**

BOWLING

ABC Bowling Championships—Regular Divisions

Year	Singles	Score	All-events	Score
1998	J. Gaines	814	C. Barnes	2,151
1999	D. Winter	825	T. Jones	2,158
2000	**G. Hein**	**811**	**R. Daniels**	**2,181**

WIBC Bowling Championships—Classic Division

Year	Singles	Score	All-events	Score
1998	N. Glandon	714	L. Johnson	1,989
1999	N. Gianulias	746	H. Mizobuchi	2,065
2000	**C. Krasner**	**729**	**C. Dorin-Ballard**	**2,147**

Professional Bowlers Association (PBA) Tournament of Champions

Year	Champion	Year	Champion
1995	M. Aulby	1998	B. Goebel
1996	D. D'Entremont	1999	J. Couch
1997	J. Gant	**2000**	**J. Couch**

FIQ World Bowling Championships—Men

Year	Singles	Pairs	Triples	Team (fives)
1991	Ying Chieh Ma (Taiwan)	United States	United States	Taiwan
1995	M. Doi (Can.)	Sweden	Netherlands	Netherlands
1999	G. Verbruggen (Belg.)	Sweden	Finland	Sweden

FIQ World Bowling Championships—Women

Year	Singles	Pairs	Triples	Team (fives)
1991	M. Beckel (Ger.)	Japan	Canada	South Korea
1995	D. Ship (Can.)	Thailand	Australia	Finland
1999	K. Kulick (U.S.)	Australia	South Korea	South Korea

BOXING

World Heavyweight Champions No Weight Limit

WBA

Lennox Lewis (U.K.; 11/13/99)
stripped of title in 2000
Evander Holyfield (U.S.; 8/12/00)

WBC

Lennox Lewis (U.K.; 2/7/97)

IBF

Lennox Lewis (U.K.; 11/13/99)

World Cruiserweight Champions Top Weight 195 Pounds

WBA

Fabrice Tiozzo (Fr.; 11/8/97)
Virgil Hill (U.S.; 12/9/00)

WBC

Juan Carlos Gómez (Cuba; 2/21/98)

IBF

Vassily Jirov (Kazak.; 6/5/99)

World Light Heavyweight Champions Top Weight 175 Pounds

WBA

Roy Jones, Jr. (U.S.; 7/18/98)

WBC

Roy Jones, Jr. (U.S.; 8/7/97)

IBF

Roy Jones, Jr. (U.S.; 6/5/99)

World Super Middleweight Champions Top Weight 168 Pounds

WBA

Byron Mitchell (U.S.; 6/12/99)
Bruno Girard (Fr.; 4/8/00)

WBC

Markus Beyer (Ger.; 10/23/99)
Glenn Catley (U.K.; 5/6/00)
Dingaan Thobela (S.Af.; 9/1/00)
Davey Hilton (Can.; 12/15/00)

IBF

Sven Ottke (Ger.; 10/24/98)

World Middleweight Champions Top Weight 160 Pounds

WBA

William Joppy (U.S.; 1/31/98)

WBC

Keith Holmes (U.S.; 4/24/99)

IBF

Bernard Hopkins (U.S.; 4/29/95)

World Junior Middleweight Champions Top Weight 154 Pounds (also called super welterweight)

WBA

David Reid (U.S.; 3/6/99)
Felix Trinidad (P.R.; 3/3/00)

WBC

Javier Castillejo (Spain; 1/29/99)

IBF

Fernando Vargas (U.S.; 12/12/98)
Felix Trinidad (P.R.; 12/2/00)

BOXING (continued)

World Welterweight Champions
Top Weight 147 Pounds

WBA

James Page (U.S.; 10/10/98)
stripped of title in 2000

WBC

Felix Trinidad (P.R.; 9/18/99)
gave up title in 2000
Oscar de la Hoya (U.S.; 3/20/00)
Shane Mosley (U.S.; 6/17/00)

IBF

Felix Trinidad (P.R.; 6/19/93)
gave up title in 2000

World Junior Welterweight Champions
Top Weight 140 Pounds
(also called super lightweight)

WBA

Sharmba Mitchell (U.S.; 10/10/98)

WBC

Kostya Tszyu (Austl.; 8/21/99)

IBF

Terronn Millett (U.S.; 2/20/99)
stripped of title in 2000
Zab Judah (U.S.; 2/12/00)

World Lightweight Champions
Top Weight 135 Pounds

WBA

Gilberto Serrano (Venez.; 11/13/99)
Takanori Hatakeyama (Japan; 6/11/00)

WBC

Steve Johnston (U.S.; 2/27/99)
Jose Luis Castillo (Mex.; 6/17/00)

IBF

Paul Spadafora (U.S.; 8/20/99)

World Junior Lightweight Champions
Top Weight 130 Pounds
(also called super featherweight)

WBA

Jong Kwon Baek (S.Kor.; 10/31/99)
Joel Casamayor (Cuba; 5/21/00)

WBC

Floyd Mayweather (U.S.; 10/3/98)

IBF

Diego Corrales (U.S.; 10/23/99)
gave up title in 2000
Steve Forbes (U.S.; 12/3/00)

World Featherweight Champions
Top Weight 126 Pounds

WBA

Freddie Norwood (U.S.; 5/29/99)
Derrick Gainer (U.S.; 9/9/00)

WBC

Naseem Hamed (U.K.; 10/22/99)
stripped of title in 1999
Gustavo Espadas (Mex.; 4/14/00)

IBF

Paul Ingle (U.K.; 11/13/99)
Mbulelo Botile (S.Af.; 12/16/00)

World Junior Featherweight Champions
Top Weight 122 Pounds
(also called super bantamweight)

WBA

Nestor Garza (Mex.; 12/12/98)
Clarence Adams (U.S.; 3/4/00)

WBC

Erik Morales (Mex.; 9/6/97)
gave up title in 2000
Willie Jorrin (U.S.; 9/9/00)

IBF

Lehlohonolo Ledwaba (S.Af.; 5/29/99)

World Bantamweight Champions
Top Weight 118 Pounds

WBA

Paulie Ayala (U.S.; 6/26/99)

WBC

Veeraphol Sahaprom (Thai.; 12/29/98)

IBF

Tim Austin (U.S.; 7/19/97)

World Junior Bantamweight Champions
Top Weight 115 Pounds
(also called super flyweight)

WBA

Hideki Todaka (Japan; 7/31/99)
Leo Gamez (Venez.; 10/9/00)

WBC

Cho In Joo (S.Kor.; 8/29/98)
Masanori Tokuyama (Japan; 8/27/00)

IBF

Mark Johnson (U.S.; 4/24/99)
stripped of title in 2000
Felix Machado (Venez.; 7/22/00)

World Flyweight Champions
Top Weight 112 Pounds

WBA

Sornpichai Kratchingdaeng (Thai.; 9/3/99)
Eric Morel (U.S.; 8/5/00)

WBC

Medgeon Singsurat (Thai.; 9/17/99)
Malcolm Tunacao (Phil.; 5/19/00)

IBF

Irene Pacheco (Colom.; 4/10/99)

World Junior Flyweight Champions
Top Weight 108 Pounds

WBA

Pichitnoi Siriwat (Thai.; 12/3/96)
vacant
Bebis Mendoza (Colom.; 8/12/00)

WBC

Choi Yo Sam (S.Kor.; 10/17/99)

IBF

Ricardo López (Mex.; 10/2/99)

World Mini-flyweight Champions
Top Weight 105 Pounds
(also called strawweight)

WBA

Noel Arambulet (Venez.; 10/9/99)
stripped of title in 2000
Joma Gamboa (Phil.; 8/20/00)
Keitaro Hoshino (Japan; 12/6/00)

WBC

Wande Chareon (Thai.; 5/4/99)
Jose Antonio Aguirre (Mex.; 2/11/00)

IBF

Zolani Petelo (S.Af.; 12/27/97)
vacant

Evander Holyfield (right) and John Ruiz exchange blows during their WBA heavyweight championship bout on August 12 in Las Vegas, Nev.

John Gurzinski/AFP Worldwide

CHESS

World Chess Championship Matches—Men*

Year	Winner	Runner-up
1998	A. Karpov (Russia)	V. Anand (India)
1999	A. Khalifman (Russia)	V. Akopyan (Arm.)
2000	**V. Kramnik (Russia)**	**G. Kasparov (Russia)**

*FIDE-sanctioned championship until 2000.

World Chess Championship Matches—Women*

Year	Winner	Runner-up
1993	Xie Jun (China)	N. Ioseliani (Georgia)
1996	Z. Polgar (Hung.)†	Xie Jun (China)
1999	Xie Jun (China)	A. Galyamova (Russia)

*FIDE-sanctioned championship. †Stripped of title in 1999.

FIDE Olympiad—Men

Year	Winner	Runner-up
1996	Russia	Ukraine
1998	Russia	United States
2000	**Russia**	**Germany**

FIDE Olympiad—Women

Year	Winner	Runner-up
1996	Georgia	China
1998	China	Russia
2000	**China**	**Georgia**

AFP Worldwide

Vladimir Kramnik of Russia, playing against compatriot Garry Kasparov, stares at his pieces in the 15th game of the world chess championship on November 2 in London.

CONTRACT BRIDGE

World Team Olympiad

Year	Open winner	Open runner-up	Women's winner	Women's runner-up
1992	France	United States	Austria	United Kingdom
1996	France	Indonesia	United States	China
2000	**Italy**	**Poland**	**United States**	**Canada**

Bermuda Bowl

Year	Winner	Runner-up
1995	United States	Canada
1997	France	United States
2000	**United States**	**Brazil**

World Contract Bridge Pair Championship

Year	Open winners	Women's winners	Mixed winners
1994	Marcin Lesniewski, Marek Szymanowski (Pol.)	Carla Arnolds, Bep Vriend (Neth.)	Danuta Hocheker, Apolinare Kowalski (Pol.)
1998	Michal Kwiecien, Jacek Pszczola (Pol.)	Jill Meyers, Shawn Quinn (U.S.)	Enza Rossano, Antonio Vivaldi (Italy)

CRICKET

All-Time First-Class Test Cricket Standings (as of Sept. 30, 2000)

	England			Australia			South Africa			West Indies			New Zealand		
	Wins	Draws	Losses	W	D	L	W	D	L	W	D	L	W	D	L
England *v.*	—	—	—	93	86	117	50	47	23	31	43*	52	37	39	6
Australia *v.*	117	86	93	—	—	—	34	17	14	37	22†	31	18	12	7
South Africa *v.*	23	47	50	14	17	34	—	—	—	5	0	1	13	8	3
West Indies *v.*	52	43*	31	31	22†	37	1	0	5	—	—	—	10	14	6
New Zealand *v.*	6	39	37	7	12	18	3	8	13	6	14	10	—	—	—
India *v.*	14	38	32	11	18†	28	2	4	6	7	35	28	14	20*	7
Pakistan *v.*	9	32	14	11	17	18	1	1	2	10	14	13	18	16	5
Sri Lanka *v.*	2	1	3	1	5	7	1	3	4	0	2	1	4	7	7
Zimbabwe *v.*	0	3	1	0	0	1	0	0	3	0	0	2	0	5	5

	India			Pakistan			Sri Lanka			Zimbabwe		
	W	D	L	W	D	L	W	D	L	W	D	L
England *v.*	32	36	14	14	32	9	3	1	2	1	3	0
Australia *v.*	28	18†	11	18	17	11	7	5	1	1	0	0
South Africa *v.*	6	4	2	2	1	1	4	3	1	3	0	0
West Indies *v.*	28	35	7	13	14	10	1	2	0	2	0	0
New Zealand *v.*	7	20*	14	5	16	18	7	7	4	5	5	0
India *v.*	—	—	—	5	33	9	7	12	1	1	1	1
Pakistan *v.*	9	33	5	—	—	—	13	9*	5	6	5*	2
Sri Lanka *v.*	1	12	7	5	9*	13	—	—	—	5	5	0
Zimbabwe *v.*	1	1	1	2	5*	6	0	5	5	—	—	—

*Including one match abandoned. †Including one tie.

Cricket World Cup

Year	Result			
1992	Pakistan	249–6	England	227
1996	Sri Lanka	245–3	Australia	241
1999	Australia	133–2	Pakistan	132

CRICKET (continued)

Test Match Results, October 1999–September 2000

Host/Ground	Date	Scores	Result
India/Chandigarh	Oct. 10–14	India 83 and 505 for 3 dec; N.Z. 215 and 251 for 7	Match drawn
India/Kanpur	Oct. 22–25	N.Z. 256 and 155; India 330 and 83 for 2	India won by 8 wickets
India/Ahmedabad	Oct. 29–Nov. 2	India 583 and 148 for 5 dec; N.Z. 308 and 252 for 2	Match drawn; India won series 1–0
Zimb./Harare	Oct. 14–17	Zimb. 194 and 232; Austl. 422 and 5 for 0	Austl. won by 10 wickets
S.Af./Bloemfontein	Oct. 29–Nov. 1	Zimb. 192 and 212; S.Af. 417	S.Af. won by an innings and 13 runs
Zimb./Harare	Nov. 11–14	Zimb. 102 and 141; S.Af. 462 for 9 dec	S.Af. won by an innings and 219 runs; S.Af. won series 2–0
Austl./Brisbane	Nov. 5–9	Pak. 367 and 281; Austl. 575 and 74 for 0	Austl. won by 10 wickets
Austl./Hobart	Nov. 18–22	Pak. 222 and 392; Austl. 246 and 369 for 6	Austl. won by 4 wickets
Austl./Perth	Nov. 26–28	Pak. 155 and 276; Austl. 451	Austl. won by an innings and 20 runs; Austl. won series 3–0
Zimb./Bulawayo	Nov. 18–22	Zimb. 286 and 136 for 3; SriL. 428	Match drawn
Zimb./Harare	Nov. 26–30	Zimb. 174 and 292; SriL. 432 and 38 for 4	SriL. won by 6 wickets
Zimb./Harare	Dec. 4–8	Zimb. 218 and 197 for 7 dec; SriL. 231 and 36 for 1	Match drawn; SriL. won series 1–0
S.Af./Johannesburg	Nov. 25–28	Eng. 122 and 260; S.Af. 403 for 9 dec	S.Af. won by an innings and 21 runs
S.Af./Port Elizabeth	Dec. 9–13	S.Af. 450 and 224 for 4 dec; Eng. 373 and 153 for 6	Match drawn
S.Af./Durban	Dec. 26–30	Eng. 366 for 9 dec; S.Af. 156 and 572 for 7	Match drawn
S.Af./Cape Town	Jan. 2–5	Eng. 258 and 126; S.Af. 421	S.Af. won by an innings and 37 runs
S.Af./Centurion	Jan. 14–18	S.Af. 248 for 8 dec (second innings forfeited); Eng. (first innings forfeited) 251 for 8	Eng. won by 2 wickets; S.Af. won series 2–1
Austl./Adelaide	Dec. 10–14	Austl. 441 and 239 for 8 dec; India 285 and 110	Austl. won by 285 runs
Austl./Melbourne	Dec. 26–30	Austl. 405 and 208 for 5 dec; India 238 and 195	Austl. won by 180 runs
Austl./Sydney	Jan. 2–4	India 150 and 261; Austl. 552 for 5 dec	Austl. won by an innings and 141 runs; Austl. won series 3–0
N.Z./Hamilton	Dec. 16–20	W.Ind. 365 and 97; N.Z. 393 and 70 for 1	N.Z. won by 9 wickets
N.Z./Wellington	Dec. 26–29	N.Z. 518 for 9 dec; W.Ind. 179 and 234	N.Z. won by an innings and 105 runs; N.Z. won series 2–0
India/Mumbai	Feb. 24–26	India 225 and 113; S.Af. 176 and 164 for 6	S.Af. won by 4 wickets
India/Bangalore	March 2–6	India 158 and 250; S.Af. 479	S.Af. won by an innings and 71 runs; S.Af. won series 2–0
Pak./Rawalpindi	Feb. 26–March 1	Pak. 182 and 390; SriL. 353 and 220 for 8	SriL. won by 2 wickets
Pak./Peshawar	March 5–9	SriL. 268 and 224; Pak. 199 and 236	SriL. won by 57 runs
Pak./Karachi	March 12–15	Pak. 256 and 421; SriL. 227 and 228	Pak. won by 222 runs; SriL. won series 2–1
W.Ind./Trinidad	March 16–20	W.Ind. 187 and 147; Zimb. 236 and 63	W.Ind. won by 35 runs
W.Ind./Jamaica	March 24–28	Zimb. 308 and 102; W.Ind. 339 and 75 for 0	W.Ind. won by 10 wickets; W.Ind. won series 2–0
N.Z./Auckland	March 11–15	Austl. 214 and 229; N.Z. 163 and 218	Austl. won by 62 runs
N.Z./Wellington	March 24–27	N.Z. 298 and 294; Austl. 419 and 177 for 4	Austl. won by 6 wickets
N.Z./Hamilton	March 31–April 3	N.Z. 232 and 229; Austl. 252 and 212 for 4	Austl. won by 6 wickets; Austl. won series 3–0
W.Ind./Guyana	May 5–9	Pak. 288; W.Ind. 222 for 7	Match drawn
W.Ind./Barbados	May 18–22	Pak. 253 and 419 for 9 dec; W.Ind. 398 and 132 for 4	Match drawn
W.Ind./Antigua	May 25–29	Pak. 269 and 219; W.Ind. 273 and 216 for 9	W.Ind. won by 1 wicket; W.Ind. won series 1–0
Eng./London (Lord's)	May 18–21	Zimb. 83 and 123; Eng. 415	Eng. won by an innings and 209 runs
Eng./Nottingham	June 1–5	Eng. 374 and 147; Zimb. 285 for 4 dec and 25 for 1	Match drawn; Eng. won series 1–0
SriL./Colombo	June 14–17	SriL. 273 and 123; Pak. 266 and 131 for 5	Pak. won by 5 wickets
SriL./Galle	June 21–24	SriL. 181 and 256; Pak. 600 for 8 dec	Pak. won by an innings and 163 runs
SriL./Kandy	June 28–July 2	SriL. 467 for 5	Match abandoned (rain); Pak. won series 2–0
Eng./Birmingham	June 15–17	Eng. 179 and 125; W.Ind. 397	W.Ind. won by an innings and 93 runs
Eng./London (Lord's)	June 29–July 1	W.Ind. 267 and 54; Eng. 134 and 191 for 8	Eng. won by 2 wickets
Eng./Manchester	Aug. 3–7	W.Ind. 157 and 438 for 7 dec; Eng. 303 and 80 for 1	Match drawn
Eng./Leeds	Aug. 17–18	W.Ind. 172 and 61; Eng. 272	Eng. won by an innings and 39 runs
Eng./London (The Oval)	Aug. 31–Sept. 4	Eng. 281 and 217; W.Ind. 125 and 215	Eng. won by 158 runs; Eng. won series 3–1
SriL./Galle	July 20–23	SriL. 522; S.Af. 238 and 269	SriL. won by an innings and 15 runs
SriL./Kandy	July 30–Aug. 2	S.Af. 253 and 231; SriL. 308 and 169	S.Af. won by 7 runs
SriL./Colombo	Aug. 6–10	S.Af. 279 and 241 for 9 dec; SriL. 258 and 195 for 4	Match drawn; Series drawn 1–1
Zimb./Bulawayo	Sept. 12–16	Zimb. 350 and 119; N.Z. 338 and 132 for 3	N.Z. won by 7 wickets
Zimb./Harare	Sept. 19–23	N.Z. 465 and 74 for 2; Zimb. 166 and 370	N.Z. won by 8 wickets; N.Z. won series 2–0

CURLING

World Curling Championship—Men

Year	Winner	Runner-up
1998	Canada	Sweden
1999	Scotland	Canada
2000	**Canada**	**Sweden**

World Curling Championship—Women

Year	Winner	Runner-up
1998	Sweden	Denmark
1999	Sweden	United States
2000	**Canada**	**Switzerland**

CYCLING

Cycling Champions, 2000

Event	Winner	Country
WORLD CHAMPIONS—TRACK		
Men		
Sprint	J. Van Eijden	Germany
Individual pursuit	J. Lehmann	Germany
Kilometre time trial	A. Tournant	France
40-km points	J. Llaneras	Spain
Team pursuit	S. Siedler, D. Becke, G. Fulst, J. Lehmann	Germany
Keirin	F. Magne	France
Olympic sprint	L. Gane, F. Rousseau, A. Tournant	France
60-km Madison	S. Steinweg, E. Weispfennig	Germany
Women		
Sprint	N. Markovnichenko	Belarus
Individual pursuit	Y. McGregor	Great Britain
500-m time trial	N. Markovnichenko	Belarus
25-km points	M. Clignet	France
WORLD CHAMPIONS—ROAD		
Men		
Individual road race	R. Vainsteins	Latvia
Individual time trial	S. Honchar	Ukraine
Women		
Individual road race	Z. Stahurskaia	Belarus
Individual time trial	M. Holden	United States
WORLD CHAMPION—CYCLO-CROSS		
Men	R. Groenendaal	Netherlands
Women	H. Kupfernagel	Germany
WORLD CHAMPIONS—MOUNTAIN BIKES		
Men		
Cross-country	M. Martinez	France
Downhill	M. Rockwell	United States
Women		
Cross-country	M. Fullana	Spain
Downhill	A.-C. Chausson	France
MAJOR ELITE ROAD-RACE WINNERS		
Tour de France	L. Armstrong	United States
Tour of Italy	S. Garzelli	Italy
Tour of Spain	R. Heras	Spain
Tour of Switzerland	O. Camenzind	Switzerland
Milan–San Remo	E. Zabel	Germany
Tour of Flanders	A. Tchmil	Belgium
Paris–Roubaix	J. Museeuw	Belgium
Liège–Bastogne–Liège	P. Bettini	Italy
Amstel Gold	E. Zabel	Germany
San Sebastian Classic	E. Dekker	Netherlands
HEW–Cyclassics Cup	G. Missaglia	Italy
Zurich Championship	L. Dufaux	Switzerland
Paris–Tours	A. Tafi	Italy
Paris–Nice	A. Klöden	Germany
Ghent–Wevelgem	G. Van Bondt	Belgium
Flèche Wallonne	F. Casagrande	Italy
Tour of Romandie	P. Savoldelli	Italy
Dauphiné Libéré	T. Hamilton	United States
Tirreno–Adriatico	A. Olano	Spain
Tour of Catalonia	R. Rumsas	Lithuania

Tour de France

Year	Winner	Kilometres
1998	M. Pantani (Italy)	3,831
1999	L. Armstrong (U.S.)	3,687
2000	**L. Armstrong (U.S.)**	**3,663**

EQUESTRIAN SPORTS

The Kentucky Derby

Year	Horse	Jockey
1998	Real Quiet	K. Desormeaux
1999	Charismatic	C. Antley
2000	**Fusaichi Pegasus**	**K. Desormeaux**

2,000 Guineas

Year	Horse	Jockey
1998	King of Kings	M. Kinane
1999	Island Sands	L. Dettori
2000	**King's Best**	**K. Fallon**

The Preakness Stakes

Year	Horse	Jockey
1998	Real Quiet	K. Desormeaux
1999	Charismatic	C. Antley
2000	**Red Bullet**	**J. Bailey**

The Derby

Year	Horse	Jockey
1998	High-Rise	O. Peslier
1999	Oath	K. Fallon
2000	**Sinndar**	**J. Murtagh**

The Belmont Stakes

Year	Horse	Jockey
1998	Victory Gallop	G. Stevens
1999	Lemon Drop Kid	J. Santos
2000	**Commendable**	**P. Day**

The St. Leger

Year	Horse	Jockey
1998	Nedawi	J. Reid
1999	Mutafaweq	R. Hills
2000	**Millenary**	**R. Quinn**

EQUESTRIAN SPORTS (continued)

Triple Crown Champions—U.S.

Year	Horse
1973	Secretariat
1977	Seattle Slew
1978	Affirmed

Triple Crown Champions—British

Year	Winner
1918	Gainsborough
1935	Bahram
1970	Nijinsky

Melbourne Cup

Year	Horse	Jockey
1998	Jezabeel	C. Munce
1999	Rogan Josh	J. Marshall
2000	**Brew**	**K. McEvoy**

The Hambletonian Trot

Year	Horse	Driver
1998	Muscles Yankee	J. Campbell
1999	Self Possessed	M. Lachance
2000	**Yankee Paco**	**T. Ritchie**

Major Thoroughbred Race Winners, 2000

Race	Won by	Jockey
United States		
Acorn	Finder's Fee	J. Velazquez
Alabama Stakes	Jostle	M. Smith
Apple Blossom	Heritage of Gold	S. Sellers
Arlington Million	Chester House	J. Bailey
Ashland Stakes	Rings a Chime	S. Sellers
Beldame	Riboletta	C. McCarron
Belmont	Commendable	P. Day
Beverly D.	Snow Polina	J. Bailey
Blue Grass Stakes	High Yield	P. Day
Breeders' Cup Juvenile	Macho Uno	J. Bailey
Breeders' Cup Juvenile Fillies	Caressing	J. Velazquez
Breeders' Cup Sprint	Kona Gold	A. Solis
Breeders' Cup Mile	War Chant	G. Stevens
Breeders' Cup Distaff	Spain	V. Espinosa
Breeders' Cup Turf	Kalanisi	J. Murtagh
Breeders' Cup Filly and Mare Turf	Perfect Sting	J. Bailey
Breeders' Cup Classic	Tiznow	C. McCarron
Champagne	AP Valentine	J. Chavez
Charles Wittingham Handicap	White Heart	K. Desormeaux
Cigar Mile Handicap	El Corredor	J. Bailey
Coaching Club American Oaks	Jostle	M. Smith
Donn Handicap	Stephen Got Even	S. Sellers
Eddie Read	Ladies Din	K. Desormeaux
Florida Derby	Hal's Hope	R. Velez
Flower Bowl Invitational	Colstar	J.-L. Samyn
Futurity	Burning Roma	R. Wilson
Gulfstream Park Handicap	Behrens	J. Chavez
Haskell Invitational	Dixie Union	A. Solis
Hollywood Derby	Brahms	P. Day
Hollywood Futurity	Point Given	G. Stevens
Hollywood Gold Cup	Early Pioneer	V. Espinoza
Hollywood Starlet	I Believe In You	A. Solis
Hollywood Turf Cup	Bienamado	C. McCarron
Hopeful Stakes	Yonaguska*	J. Bailey
	City Zip*	J. Santos
Jockey Club Gold Cup	Albert the Great	J. Chavez
Kentucky Derby	Fusaichi Pegasus	K. Desormeaux
Kentucky Oaks	Secret Status	P. Day
Man o' War	Fantastic Light	J. Bailey
Matriarch Stakes	Tout Charmant	C. McCarron
Matron	Raging Fever	J. Bailey
Metropolitan	Yankee Victor	H. Castillo, Jr.
Mother Goose	Secret Status	P. Day
Oaklawn Handicap	K One King	C. Borel
Pacific Classic	Skimming	G. Gomez
Pimlico Special	Golden Missile	K. Desormeaux
Preakness	Red Bullet	J. Bailey
Queen Elizabeth II Challenge Cup	Collect the Cash	S. Sellers
Santa Anita Derby	The Deputy	C. McCarron
Santa Anita Handicap	General Challenge	C. Nakatani
Secretariat Stakes	Ciro	M. Kinane
Spinaway Stakes	Stormy Pick	J. Ferrer
Spinster	Plenty of Light	G. Gomez
Super Derby	Tiznow	C. McCarron
Travers	Unshaded	S. Sellers
Turf Classic	Manndar	C. Nakatani
United Nations Handicap	Down the Aisle	R. Davis
Whitney	Lemon Drop Kid	E. Prado
Woodward	Lemon Drop Kid	E. Prado
Yellow Ribbon Stakes	Tranquility Lake	E. Delahoussaye

*Dead heat.

Race	Won by	Jockey
England		
One Thousand Guineas	Lahan	R. Hills
Two Thousand Guineas	King's Best	K. Fallon
Derby	Sinndar	J. Murtagh
Oaks	Love Divine	R. Quinn
St. Leger	Millenary	R. Quinn
Coronation Cup	Daliapour	K. Fallon
Ascot Gold Cup	Kayf Tara	M. Kinane
Coral-Eclipse Stakes	Giant's Causeway	G. Duffield
King George VI and Queen Elizabeth Diamond Stakes	Montjeu	M. Kinane
Sussex Stakes	Giant's Causeway	M. Kinane
Juddmonte International Stakes	Giant's Causeway	M. Kinane
Dubayy Champion Stakes	Kalanisi	J. Murtagh
France		
Poule d'Essai des Poulains	Bachir	L. Dettori
Poule d'Essai des Pouliches	Bluemamba	T. Jarnet
Prix du Jockey-Club	Holding Court	P. Robinson
Prix de Diane	Egyptband	O. Doleuze
Prix Royal-Oak	Amilynx	O. Peslier
Prix Ganay	Indian Danehill	O. Peslier
Prix Jacques Le Marois	Muhtathir	L. Dettori
Grand Prix de Paris	Beat Hollow	R. Quinn
Grand Prix de Saint-Cloud	Montjeu	C. Asmussen
Prix Vermeille	Volvoreta	M. Kinane
Prix de l'Arc de Triomphe	Sinndar	J. Murtagh
Grand Criterium	Okawango	O. Doleuze
Ireland		
Irish Two Thousand Guineas	Bachir	L. Dettori
Irish One Thousand Guineas	Crimplene	P. Robinson
Irish Derby	Sinndar	J. Murtagh
Irish Oaks	Petrushka	J. Murtagh
Irish St. Leger	Arctic Owl	D. Harrison
Irish Champion Stakes	Giant's Causeway	M. Kinane
Italy		
Derby Italiano	Kallisto	A. Boschert
Gran Premio del Jockey Club	Golden Snake	P. Eddery
Germany		
Deutsches Derby	Samum	A. Starke
Grosser Preis von Baden	Samum	A. Starke
Europa Preis	Golden Snake	D. Bonilla
Australia		
Melbourne Cup	Brew	K. McEvoy
Cox Plate	Sunline	G. Childs
Caulfield Cup	Diatribe	J. Cassidy
United Arab Emirates		
Dubayy World Cup	Dubai Millennium	L. Dettori
Japan		
Japan Cup	T.M. Opera O	R. Wada

FENCING

World Fencing Championships—Men

Year	Individual			Team		
	Foil	Épée	Sabre	Foil	Épée	Sabre
1998	S. Golubitsky (Ukr.)	H. Obry (Fr.)	L. Tarantino (Italy)	Poland	Hungary	Hungary
1999	S. Golubitsky (Ukr.)	A. Schmitt (Ger.)	D. Touya (Fr.)	France	France	France
2000	**Kim Young Ho (S.Kor.)**	**P. Kolobkov (Russia)**	**M.C. Covaliu (Rom.)**	**France**	**Italy**	**Russia**

World Fencing Championships—Women

Year	Individual			Team		
	Foil	Épée	Sabre	Foil	Épée	Sabre
1998	S. Bau (Ger.)	L. Flessel (Fr.)		Italy	France	
1999	V. Vezzali (Italy)	L. Flessel-Colovic (Fr.)	E. Jemaeva (Azer.)	Germany	Hungary	Italy
2000	**V. Vezzali (Italy)**	**T. Nagy (Hung.)**		**Italy**	**Russia**	

FIELD HOCKEY

World Cup Field Hockey Championship—Men

Year	Winner	Runner-up
1990	Netherlands	Pakistan
1994	Pakistan	Netherlands
1998	Netherlands	Spain

World Cup Field Hockey Championship—Women

Year	Winner	Runner-up
1990	Netherlands	Australia
1994	Australia	Argentina
1998	Australia	Netherlands

FOOTBALL

FIFA World Cup—Men

Year	Result			
1990	West Germany	1	Argentina	0
1994	Brazil*	0	Italy	0
1998	France	3	Brazil	0

*Won on penalty kicks.

FIFA World Cup—Women

Year	Result			
1991	United States	2	Norway	1
1995	Norway	2	Germany	0
1999	United States*	0	China	0

*Won on penalty kicks.

Association Football National Champions, 2000

Nation	League Winners	Cup Winners
Albania	SK Tirana	Teuta
Andorra	Constelacio	Constelacio
Argentina	River Plate	
Armenia	Shirak	Mika
Austria	Innsbruck	Graz AK
Azerbaijan	Shamkir	Kopaz
Belarus	BATE Borisov	Slavia
Belgium	Anderlecht	Genk
Bolivia	Blooming	
Brazil	Corinthians	Palmeiras
Bulgaria	Levski	Levski
Chile	Universidad de Chile	
Colombia	Atlético Nacional	
Croatia	Dynamo Zagreb	Hajduk Split
Cyprus	Anorthosis	Omonia
Czech Republic	Sparta Prague	Liberec
Denmark	Herfolge	Viborg
Ecuador	LDU Quito	
England	Manchester United	Chelsea
Estonia	Levadia	Levadia
Faroe Islands	KI Klaksvik	KI Klaksvik
Finland	Haka	Jokerit
France	Monaco	Nantes
Georgia	Torpedo Kutaisi	Lokomotivi
Germany	Bayern Munich	Bayern Munich
Greece	Olympiakos	AEK Athens
Hungary	Dunaferr	MTK
Iceland	KR Reykjavik	KR Reykjavik
Ireland	Shelbourne	Shelbourne
Israel	Hapoel Tel Aviv	Hapoel Tel Aviv
Italy	Lazio	Lazio
Latvia	Skonto Riga	Skonto Riga
Liechtenstein	(no league)	Vaduz
Lithuania	Kaunas	Ekranes
Luxembourg	Dudelange	Jeunesse Esch
Macedonia	Sloga	Sloga
Malta	Birkirkara	Sliema Wanderers
Moldova	Zimbru Chisinau	Constructorul
Netherlands	PSV Eindhoven	Roda
Northern Ireland	Linfield	Glentoran
Norway	Rosenborg	Rosenborg
Paraguay	Olimpia	
Peru	Universitario	
Poland	Polonia	Amica
Portugal	Sporting	Porto
Romania	Dinamo	Dinamo
Russia	Spartak Moscow	Lokomotiv Moscow
San Marino	Folgore	Tre Penne
Scotland	Rangers	Rangers
Slovakia	Inter	Inter
Slovenia	Maribor	Olimpija
Spain	La Coruña	Espanyol
Sweden	Helsingborg	Orgryte
Switzerland	St. Gallen	Zurich
Turkey	Galatasaray	Galatasaray
Ukraine	Dynamo Kiev	Dynamo Kiev
Uruguay	Nacional	
Venezuela	Tachira	
Wales	TNS	Bangor City
Yugoslavia	Red Star Belgrade	Red Star Belgrade

FOOTBALL (continued)

European Cup-Winners' Cup

Season	Result			
1997–98	Chelsea (Eng.)	1	Stuttgart (Ger.)	0
1998–99	Lazio (Italy)	2	Real Mallorca (Spain)	1
1999–2000	**event no longer held**			

European Cup of Champion Clubs

Season	Result			
1997–98	Real Madrid	1	Juventus (Italy)	0
1998–99	Manchester United (Eng.)	2	Bayern Munich (Ger.)	1
1999–2000	**Real Madrid**	**3**	**Valencia (Spain)**	**0**

Libertadores de América Cup

Year	Winner (country)	Runner-up (country)	Scores
1998	Vasco da Gama (Braz.)	Barcelona (Ecua.)	2–0, 2–1
1999	Palmeiras (Braz.)	Deportiva Cali (Colom.)	0–1, 2–1, 4–3*
2000	**Boca Juniors (Arg.)**	**Palmeiras (Braz.)**	**2–2, 0–0, 4–2***

*Winner determined in penalty shootout.

U.S. College Football National Champions

Season	Champion
1998–99	Tennessee
1999–2000	Florida State
2000–01	**Oklahoma**

Fiesta Bowl

Season	Result			
1998–99	Tennessee	23	Florida State	16
1999–2000	Nebraska	31	Tennessee	21
2000–01	**Oregon State**	**41**	**Notre Dame**	**9**

Rose Bowl

Season	Result			
1998–99	Wisconsin	38	UCLA	31
1999–2000	Wisconsin	17	Stanford	9
2000–01	**Washington**	**34**	**Purdue**	**24**

Orange Bowl

Season	Result			
1998–99	Florida	31	Syracuse	10
1999–2000	Michigan	35	Alabama	34
2000–01	**Oklahoma**	**13**	**Florida State**	**2**

Cotton Bowl

Season	Result			
1998–99	Texas	38	Mississippi State	11
1999–2000	Arkansas	27	Texas	6
2000–01	**Kansas State**	**35**	**Tennessee**	**21**

Sugar Bowl

Season	Result			
1998–99	Ohio State	24	Texas A&M	14
1999–2000	Florida State	46	Virginia Tech	29
2000–01	**Miami**	**37**	**Florida**	**20**

NFL Final Standings, 2000

AMERICAN CONFERENCE

Eastern Division

	W	L	T
*Miami	11	5	0
*Indianapolis	10	6	0
New York Jets	9	7	0
Buffalo	8	8	0
New England	5	11	0

Central Division

	W	L	T
*Tennessee	13	3	0
*Baltimore	12	4	0
Pittsburgh	9	7	0
Jacksonville	7	9	0
Cincinnati	4	12	0
Cleveland	3	13	0

Western Division

	W	L	T
*Oakland	12	4	0
*Denver	11	5	0
Kansas City	7	9	0
Seattle	6	10	0
San Diego	1	15	0

NATIONAL CONFERENCE

Eastern Division

	W	L	T
*New York Giants	12	4	0
*Philadelphia	11	5	0
Washington	8	8	0
Dallas	5	11	0
Arizona	3	13	0

Central Division

	W	L	T
*Minnesota	11	5	0
*Tampa Bay	10	6	0
Green Bay	9	7	0
Detroit	9	7	0
Chicago	5	11	0

Western Division

	W	L	T
*New Orleans	10	6	0
*St. Louis	10	6	0
Carolina	7	9	0
San Francisco	6	10	0
Atlanta	4	12	0

*Qualified for play-offs.

Super Bowl

	Season	Result			
XXXIII	1998–99	Denver Broncos (AFC)	34	Atlanta Falcons (NFC)	19
XXXIV	1999–2000	St. Louis Rams (NFC)	23	Tennessee Titans (AFC)	16
XXXV	**2000–01**	**Baltimore Ravens (AFC)**	**34**	**New York Giants (NFC)**	**7**

Grey Cup*

Year	Result			
1998	Calgary Stampeders (WD)	26	Hamilton Tiger-Cats (ED)	24
1999	Hamilton Tiger-Cats (ED)	32	Calgary Stampeders (WD)	21
2000	**British Columbia Lions (WD)**	**28**	**Montreal Alouettes (ED)**	**26**

*ED—Eastern Division; WD—Western Division.

AFL Final Standings, 2000 (League ladder after round 22)

Team*	W	L	D	Points
Essendon	21	1	0	84
Carlton	16	6	0	64
Melbourne	14	8	0	56
Kangaroos	14	8	0	56
Geelong	12	9	1	50
Brisbane	12	10	0	48
Western Bulldogs	12	10	0	48
Hawthorn	12	10	0	48

*Teams that qualified for play-offs.

FOOTBALL (continued)

Record of International Rugby Union Test Matches 1871 to Aug. 31, 2000

	England			Scotland			Ireland			Wales			British Isles*		
	Wins	Draws	Losses	Wins	Draws	Losses	Wins	Draws	Losses	Wins	Draws	Losses	Wins	Draws	Losses
England *v.*				59	17	39	65	8	38	44	12	48			
Scotland *v.*	39	17	59				59	1	45	44	2	56			
Ireland *v.*	38	8	65	45	1	59				37	6	59			
Wales *v.*	48	12	44	56	2	44	59	6	37						
British Isles* *v.*															
South Africa *v.*	11	1	6	8	0	3	11	1	1	11	1	1	19	4	10
New Zealand *v.*	17	1	4	20	2	0	13	1	0	14	0	3	23	2	6
Australia *v.*	16	1	7	11	0	7	13	0	6	11	0	8	2	0	8
France *v.*	28	7	40	35	3	32	42	5	25	31	3	39			

	South Africa			New Zealand			Australia			France		
	Wins	Draws	Losses	Wins	Draws	Losses	Wins	Draws	Losses	Wins	Draws	Losses
England *v.*	6	1	11	4	1	17	7	1	16	40	7	28
Scotland *v.*	3	0	8	0	2	20	7	0	11	32	3	35
Ireland *v.*	1	1	11	0	1	13	6	0	13	25	5	42
Wales *v.*	1	1	11	3	0	14	8	0	11	39	3	31
British Isles* *v.*	10	4	19	6	2	23	8	0	2			
South Africa *v.*				25	3	23	26	0	14	18	5	5
New Zealand *v.*	23	3	25				71	5	31	24	0	8
Australia *v.*	14	0	26	31	5	71				10	2	13
France *v.*	5	5	18	8	0	24	13	2	10			

*The British Isles ("British Lions") is a combined team from the four "Home Unions" (England, Ireland, Scotland, and Wales).

Rugby Union World Cup

Year	Result			
1991	Australia	12	England	6
1995	South Africa	15	New Zealand	12
1999	Australia	35	France	12

Rugby League World Cup

Year	Result			
1992	Australia	10	Great Britain	6
1995	Australia	16	England	8
2000	**Australia**	**40**	**New Zealand**	**12**

Five Nations Championship*

Year	Result
1998	France†
1999	Scotland
2000	**England**

*Six Nations from 2000.
†Grand Slam winner.

Gerry Penny/AFP Worldwide

Australia's Darren Britt (in midair) is tackled by members of the New Zealand team during the Rugby League World Cup final on November 25.

GOLF

British Open Tournament (men)

Year	Winner
1998	M. O'Meara (U.S.)
1999	P. Lawrie (Scot.)
2000	**T. Woods (U.S.)**

United States Open Championship (men)

Year	Winner
1998	L. Janzen (U.S.)
1999	P. Stewart (U.S.)
2000	**T. Woods (U.S.)**

Masters Tournament

Year	Winner
1998	M. O'Meara (U.S.)
1999	J.-M. Olazábal (Spain)
2000	**V. Singh (Fiji)**

U.S. Professional Golfers' Association (PGA) Championship

Year	Winner
1998	V. Singh (Fiji)
1999	T. Woods (U.S.)
2000	**T. Woods (U.S.)**

British Amateur Championship (men)

Year	Winner
1998	S. Garcia (Spain)
1999	G. Storm (U.K.)
2000	**M. Ilonen (Fin.)**

United States Amateur Championship (men)

Year	Winner
1998	H. Kuehne (U.S.)
1999	D. Gossett (U.S.)
2000	**J. Quinney (U.S.)**

Women's British Open Championship

Year	Winner
1998	S. Steinhauer (U.S.)
1999	S. Steinhauer (U.S.)
2000	**S. Gustafson (Swed.)**

Ladies' British Amateur Championship

Year	Winner
1998	K. Rostron (U.K.)
1999	M. Monnet (Fr.)
2000	**R. Hudson (U.K.)**

United States Women's Open Championship

Year	Winner
1998	Pak Se Ri (S.Kor.)
1999	J. Inkster (U.S.)
2000	**K. Webb (Austl.)**

United States Women's Amateur Championship

Year	Winner
1998	G. Park (U.S.)
1999	D. Delasin (U.S.)
2000	**M. Newton (U.S.)**

Ladies Professional Golf Association (LPGA) Championship

Year	Winner
1998	Pak Se Ri (S.Kor.)
1999	J. Inkster (U.S.)
2000	**J. Inkster (U.S.)**

Walker Cup (men; amateur)

Year	Result
1995	Britain and Ireland 14, United States 10
1997	United States 18, Britain and Ireland 6
1999	Britain and Ireland 15, United States 9

GOLF (continued)

Ryder Cup (men; professional)

Year	Result
1995	Europe 14½, United States 13½
1997	Europe 14½, United States 13½
1999	United States 14½, Europe 13½

World Cup (men; professional)

Year	Winner
1998	England (N. Faldo and D. Carter)
1999	United States (T. Woods and M. O'Meara)
2000	**United States (T. Woods and D. Duval)**

Curtis Cup (women; amateur)

Year	Result
1996	Britain and Ireland 11½, United States 6½
1998	United States 10, Britain and Ireland 8
2000	**United States 10, Britain and Ireland 8**

GYMNASTICS

World Gymnastics Championships—Men

Year	All-around team	All-around individual	Horizontal bar	Parallel bars
1997	China	I. Ivankov (Bela.)	J. Tanskanen (Fin.)	Zhang Jinjing (China)
1999	China	N. Krukov (Russia)	J. Carballo (Spain)	Lee Joo Hyung (S.Kor.)
2000	**China**	**A. Nemov (Russia)**	**A. Nemov (Russia)**	**Li Xiaopeng (China)**
Year	**Pommel horse**	**Rings**	**Vault**	**Floor exercise**
1997	V. Belenki (Ger.)	Y. Chechi (Italy)	S. Fedorchenko (Kazak.)	A. Nemov (Russia)
1999	A. Nemov (Russia)	Dong Zhen (China)	Li Xiaopeng (China)	A. Nemov (Russia)
2000	**M. Urzica (Rom.)**	**S. Csollany (Hung.)**	**G. Deferr (Spain)**	**I. Vihrons (Latvia)**

World Gymnastics Championships—Women

Year	All-around team	All-around individual	Balance beam
1997	Romania	S. Khorkina (Russia)	G. Gogean (Rom.)
1999	Romania	M. Olaru (Rom.)	Ling Jie (China)
2000	**Romania**	**S. Amanar (Rom.)**	**Liu Xuan (China)**
Year	**Uneven parallel bars**	**Vault**	**Floor exercise**
1997	S. Khorkina (Russia)	S. Amanar (Rom.)	G. Gogean (Rom.)
1999	S. Khorkina (Russia)	Ye. Zamolodchikova (Russia)	A. Raducan (Rom.)
2000	**S. Khorkina (Russia)**	**Ye. Zamolodchikova (Russia)**	**Ye. Zamolodchikova (Russia)**

ICE HOCKEY

NHL Final Standings, 2000

EASTERN CONFERENCE

Northeast Division

	W	L	T
*Toronto	45	30	7
*Ottawa	41	30	11
*Buffalo	35	36	11
Montreal	35	38	9
Boston	24	39	19

Atlantic Division

	W	L	T
*Philadelphia	45	25	12
*New Jersey	45	29	8
*Pittsburgh	37	37	8
New York Rangers	29	41	12
New York Islanders	24	49	9

Southeast Division

	W	L	T
*Washington	44	26	12
*Florida	43	33	6
Carolina	37	35	10
Tampa Bay	19	54	9
Atlanta	14	61	7

WESTERN CONFERENCE

Central Division

	W	L	T
*St. Louis	51	20	11
*Detroit	48	24	10
Chicago	33	39	10
Nashville	28	47	7

Northwest Division

	W	L	T
*Colorado	42	29	11
*Edmonton	32	34	16
Vancouver	30	37	15
Calgary	31	41	10

Pacific Division

	W	L	T
*Dallas	43	29	10
*Los Angeles	39	31	12
*Phoenix	39	35	8
*San Jose	35	37	10
Anaheim	34	36	12

*Qualified for play-offs.

The Stanley Cup

Season	Winner	Runner-up	Games
1997–98	Detroit Red Wings	Washington Capitals	4–0
1998–99	Dallas Stars	Buffalo Sabres	4–2
1999–2000	**New Jersey Devils**	**Dallas Stars**	**4–2**

World Ice Hockey Championship—Men

Year	Winner
1998	Sweden
1999	Czech Republic
2000	**Czech Republic**

World Ice Hockey Championship—Women

Year	Winner
1998	Canada
1999	Canada
2000	**Canada**

ICE SKATING

World Figure Skating Champions—Men

Year	Winner
1998	A. Yagudin (Russia)
1999	A. Yagudin (Russia)
2000	**A. Yagudin (Russia)**

World Figure Skating Champions—Women

Year	Winner
1998	M. Kwan (U.S.)
1999	M. Butyrskaya (Russia)
2000	**M. Kwan (U.S.)**

World Figure Skating Champions—Pairs

Year	Winners
1998	Ye. Berezhnaya, A. Sikharulidze (Russia)
1999	Ye. Berezhnaya, A. Sikharulidze (Russia)
2000	**M. Petrova, A. Tikhonov (Russia)**

World Ice Dancing Champions

Year	Winners
1998	A. Krylova, O. Ovsyannikov (Russia)
1999	A. Krylova, O. Ovsyannikov (Russia)
2000	**M. Anissina, G. Peizerat (France)**

World Ice Speed-Skating Records Set in 2000 on Major Tracks

Event	Name	Country	Time
MEN			
500 m	Jeremy Wotherspoon	Canada	34.63 sec
1,000 m	Jeremy Wotherspoon	Canada	1 min 08.49 sec
	Jeremy Wotherspoon	Canada	1 min 08.35 sec
1,500 m	Jakko Jan Leeuwangh	Netherlands	1 min 45.56 sec
3,000 m	Steven Elm	Canada	3 min 43.76 sec
	Gianni Romme	Netherlands	3 min 42.75 sec*
5,000 m	Gianni Romme	Netherlands	6 min 18.72 sec
10,000 m	Gianni Romme	Netherlands	13 min 03.40 sec*
WOMEN			
3,000 m	Gunda Niemann-Stirnemann	Germany	4 min 00.51 sec
5,000 m	Gunda Niemann-Stirnemann	Germany	6 min 56.84 sec
	Gunda Niemann-Stirnemann	Germany	6 min 55.34 sec*

*Subject to ISU ratification.

World Ice Speed-Skating Records Set in 2000 on Short Tracks

Event	Name	Country	Time
MEN			
500 m	Jeffrey Scholten	Canada	41.742 sec
1,000 m	Jeffrey Scholten	Canada	1 min 26.970 sec
1,500 m	Andrew Quinn	Canada	2 min 15.495 sec
WOMEN			
500 m	Evgenia Radanova	Bulgaria	44.415 sec
	Evgenia Radanova	Bulgaria	43.873 sec*
3,000 m	Choi Eun Kyung	S.Korea	5 min 01.976 sec

*Subject to ISU ratification.

World All-Around Speed-Skating Champions—Men

Year	Winner
1998	I. Postma (Neth.)
1999	R. Ritsma (Neth.)
2000	**G. Romme (Neth.)**

World All-Around Speed-Skating Champions—Women

Year	Winner
1998	G. Niemann-Stirnemann (Ger.)
1999	G. Niemann-Stirnemann (Ger.)
2000	**C. Pechstein (Ger.)**

World Speed-Skating Sprint Championships

Year	Men	Women
1998	J. Bos (Neth.)	C. LeMay Doan (Can.)
1999	J. Wotherspoon (Can.)	M. Garbrecht (Ger.)
2000	**J. Wotherspoon (Can.)**	**M. Garbrecht (Ger.)**

World Short-Track Speed-Skating Championships—Overall Winners

Year	Men	Women
1998	M. Gagnon (Can.)	Yang Yang (A) (China)
1999	Li Jianjun (China)	Yang Yang (A) (China)
2000	**Ryoung Min (S.Kor.)**	**Yang Yang (A) (China)**

JUDO

World Judo Championships—Men*

Year	Open weights	60 kg	65 kg (66 kg)	71 kg (73 kg)
1995	D. Douillet (Fr.)	N. Ojeguine (Russia)	U. Quellmalz (Ger.)	D. Hideshima (Japan)
1997	R. Kubacki (Pol.)	T. Nomura (Japan)	Kim Hyuk (S.Kor.)	K. Nakamura (Japan)
1999	S. Shinohara (Japan)	M. Poulot (Cuba)	L. Benboudaoud (Fr.)	J. Pedro (U.S.)
Year	**78 kg (81 kg)**	**86 kg (90 kg)**	**95 kg (100 kg)**	**+95 kg (+100 kg)**
1995	T. Koga (Japan)	Chun Ki Young (S.Kor.)	P. Nastula (Pol.)	D. Douillet (Fr.)
1997	Cho In Chul (S.Kor.)	Jeon Ki Young (S.Kor.)	P. Nastula (Pol.)	D. Douillet (Fr.)
1999	G. Randall (U.K.)	H. Yoshida (Japan)	K. Inoue (Japan)	S. Shinohara (Japan)

*Figures in parentheses represent new weight classes established in 1999.

World Judo Championships—Women*

Year	Open weights	48 kg	52 kg	56 kg (57 kg)
1995	M. van der Lee (Neth.)	R. Tamura (Japan)	M.-C. Restoux (Fr.)	D. González (Cuba)
1997	D. Beltran (Cuba)	R. Tamura (Japan)	M.-C. Restoux (Fr.)	I. Fernández (Spain)
1999	D. Beltran (Cuba)	R. Tamura (Japan)	N. Narasaki (Japan)	D. González (Cuba)
Year	**61 kg (63 kg)**	**66 kg (70 kg)**	**72 kg (78 kg)**	**+72 kg (+78 kg)**
1995	Jung Sung Sook (S.Kor.)	Cho Min Sun (S.Kor.)	C. Luna (Cuba)	A. Seriese (Neth.)
1997	S. Vandenhende (Fr.)	K. Howey (U.K.)	N. Anno (Japan)	C. Cicot (Fr.)
1999	K. Maeda (Japan)	S. Veranes (Cuba)	N. Anno (Japan)	B. Maksymow (Pol.)

*Figures in parentheses represent new weight classes established in 1999.

RODEO

Men's World All-Around Rodeo Championship

Year	Winner	Year	Winner
1995	J. Beaver	1998	T. Murray
1996	J. Beaver	1999	F. Whitfield
1997	D. Mortensen	**2000**	**J. Beaver**

ROWING

World Rowing Championships—Men

Year	Single sculls	Min:sec	Double sculls	Min:sec	Coxed pairs	Min:sec
1998	R. Waddell (N.Z.)	6:39.65	S. Volkert, A. Hajek (Ger.)	6:13.20	N. Green, J. Tomkins (Austl.)	6:45.01
1999	R. Waddell (N.Z.)	6:36.68	L. Spik, I. Cop (Slvn.)	6:04.37	J. Neil, P. Henry (U.S.)	6:48.56
2000	**R. Waddell (N.Z.)**	**6:48.90**	**L. Spik, I. Cop (Slvn.)**	**6:16.63**	**K. Borcherding, M. Guerrieri (U.S.)**	**7:07.15**

Year	Coxless pairs	Min:sec	Coxed fours	Min:sec	Coxless fours	Min:sec	Eights	Min:sec
1998	R. Sens, D. Kirchhoff (Ger.)	6:22.32	Australia	6:09.43	Great Britain	5:48.06	United States	5:38.78
1999	D. Ginn, J. Tomkins (Austl.)	6:19.00	United States	6:38.31	Great Britain	5:48.57	United States	6:01.58
2000	**M. Andrieux, J.-C. Rolland (Fr.)**	**6:32.97**	**Great Britain**	**6:16.82**	**Great Britain**	**5:56.24**	**Great Britain**	**5:33.08**

World Rowing Championships—Women

Year	Single sculls	Min:sec	Double sculls	Min:sec	Quadruple sculls	Min:sec
1998	I. Fedotova (Russia)	7:25.09	M. Batten, G. Lindsay (Gt.Brit.)	6:48.85	Germany	6:24.38
1999	Ye. Karsten (Bela.)	7:11.68	J. Thieme, K. Boron (Ger.)	6:41.98	Germany	7:06.53
2000	**Ye. Karsten (Bela.)**	**7:28.14**	**J. Thieme, K. Boron (Ger.)**	**6:55.44**	**Germany**	**6:19.58**

Year	Coxless pairs	Min:sec	Coxless fours	Min:sec	Eights	Min:sec
1998	E. Robinson, A. Korn (Can.)	7:05.19	Ukraine	6:30.63	Romania	6:14.62
1999	E. Robinson, T. Luke (Can.)	7:00.85	Belarus	6:26.25	Romania	6:47.66
2000	**G. Damian, D. Ignat (Rom.)**	**7:11.00**	**Belarus**	**6:44.90**	**Romania**	**6:06.44**

The Diamond Challenge Sculls

Year	Winner	Min:sec
1998	J. Koven (U.S.)	7:56
1999	M. Hacker (Ger.)	7:59
2000	**A.H. Abdullah (U.S.)**	**8:12**

Grand Challenge Cup

Year	Winner	Min:sec
1998	Hansa Dortmund and Berlin, Ger.	6:18
1999	Hansa Dortmund and Berlin, Ger.	6:15
2000	**Institute of Sport, Australia**	**6:19**

British rower Steve Redgrave (foreground) powers his team toward a gold medal in the coxless four competition at the 2000 Olympic Games in Sydney, Australia.

Thomas Coex/AFP Worldwide

SAILING (YACHTING)

America's Cup

Year	Winning yacht	Owner	Skipper	Losing yacht	Owner
1992	*America*³ (U.S.)	America³ Foundation	B. Koch	*Il Moro di Venezia* (Italy)	Compagnia della Vela di Venezia
1995	*Black Magic* (N.Z.)	P. Blake and Team New Zealand	R. Coutts	*Young America*	Pact 95 syndicate
2000	***Black Magic* (N.Z.)**	**Team New Zealand**	**R. Coutts**	***Luna Rossa* (Italy)**	**Prada Challenge**

World Class Boat Champions, 2000

Class	Winner	Country
Europe	K. Roug	Denmark
Finn	M. Kusznierewicz	Poland
2.4 Metre	S. Berlin	Sweden
470 (men)	T. King/M. Turnbull	Australia
470 (women)	S. Bekatorou/E. Tsoulfa	Greece
Etchells 22	C. Miles	Australia
Hobie 16	H. Bride/T. Bride	Tahiti
Laser	R. Scheidt	Brazil
Mistral (men)	N. Kaklamanakis	Greece
Mistral (women)	A. Sensini	Italy
J/24	B. Read	United States
Optimist	S. Fantela	Croatia
Soling	Madrigali/Healy/Jordan	United States
Star	M. Reynolds/M. Liljedahl	United States
Tornado	R. Gaebler/R. Schwall	Germany

Admiral's Cup

Year	Winning team
1995	Italy
1997	United States
1999	Netherlands

Bermuda Race

Year	Winning yacht	Owner
1996	*Boomerang*	G. Coumantaros
1998	*Kodiak*	L. Ecclestone
2000	***Restless***	**E. Crawford**

Transpacific Race

Year	Winning yacht	Owner
1995	*Merlin*	D. Sinclair
1997	*Ralphie*	J. Montgomery
1999	*Grand Illusion*	J. McDowell

SKIING

World Alpine Skiing Championships—Slalom

Year	Men's slalom	Men's giant slalom	Men's supergiant	Women's slalom	Women's giant slalom	Women's supergiant
1997	T. Stiansen (Nor.)	M. von Grünigen (Switz.)	A. Skaardal (Nor.)	D. Compagnoni (Italy)	D. Compagnoni (Italy)	I. Kostner (Italy)
1998	H.-P. Buraas (Nor.)	H. Maier (Austria)	H. Maier (Austria)	H. Gerg (Ger.)	D. Compagnoni (Italy)	P. Street (U.S.)
1999	K. Palander (Fin.)	L. Kjus (Nor.)	L. Kjus (Nor.)* H. Maier (Austria)*	Z. Steggall (Austl.)	A. Meissnitzer (Austria)	A. Meissnitzer (Austria)

*Tie.

World Alpine Skiing Championships—Downhill

Year	Men	Women
1997	B. Kernen (Switz.)	H. Lindh (U.S.)
1998	J.-L. Cretier (Fr.)	K. Seizinger (Ger.)
1999	H. Maier (Austria)	R. Götschl (Austria)

World Alpine Skiing Championships—Combined

Year	Men	Women
1997	K.A. Aamodt (Nor.)	R. Götschl (Austria)
1998	M. Reiter (Austria)	K. Seizinger (Ger.)
1999	K.A. Aamodt (Nor.)	P. Wiberg (Swed.)

Alpine World Cup

Year	Men	Women
1998	H. Maier (Austria)	K. Seizinger (Ger.)
1999	L. Kjus (Nor.)	A. Meissnitzer (Austria)
2000	**H. Maier (Austria)**	**R. Götschl (Austria)**

World Nordic Skiing Championships—Men

Year	10-km	15-km	30-km	50-km	Relay
1997	B. Dæhlie (Nor.)	B. Dæhlie (Nor.)	A. Prokurorov (Russia)	M. Myllyla (Fin.)	Norway
1998	B. Dæhlie (Nor.)	T. Alsgaard (Nor.)	M. Myllyla (Fin.)	B. Dæhlie (Nor.)	Norway
1999	M. Myllyla (Fin.)	T. Alsgaard (Nor.)	M. Myllyla (Fin.)	M. Myllyla (Fin.)	Austria

World Nordic Skiing Championships—Women

Year	5-km	10-km	15-km	30-km	Relay
1997	Ye. Vyalbe (Russia)	Ye. Vyalbe (Russia)	Ye. Vyalbe (Russia)	Ye. Vyalbe (Russia)	Russia
1998	L. Lazutina (Russia)	L. Lazutina (Russia)	O. Danilova (Russia)	Yu. Chepalova (Russia)	Russia
1999	B. Martinsen (Nor.)	S. Belmondo (Italy)	S. Belmondo (Italy)	L. Lazutina (Russia)	Russia

World Nordic Skiing Championships—Ski Jump

Year	90-m hill	120-m hill	Team jump	Combined (7.5-km)	Combined (15-km)	Team combined
1997	J. Ahonen (Fin.)	M. Harada (Japan)	Finland		K. Ogiwara (Japan)	Norway
1998	J. Soininen (Fin.)	K. Funaki (Japan)	Japan		B.E. Vik (Nor.)	Norway
1999	K. Funaki (Japan)	M. Schmitt (Ger.)	Germany	B.E. Vik (Nor.)	B.E. Vik (Nor.)	Finland

Nordic World Cup

Year	Men	Women
1998	T. Alsgaard (Nor.)	L. Lazutina (Russia)
1999	B. Dæhlie (Nor.)	B. Martinsen (Nor.)
2000	**J. Mühlegg (Spain)**	**B. Martinsen (Nor.)**

Bente Martinsen of Norway competes in the Nordic World Cup on March 17.

AP/Wide World Photos

SQUASH

World Open Championship—Men

Year	Winner
1998	J. Power (Can.)
1999	P. Nicol (Scot.)
2000	**not held**

World Open Championship—Women

Year	Winner
1998	S. Fitz-Gerald (Austl.)
1999	C. Campion (Eng.)
2000	**C. Owens (Austl.)**

British Open Championship—Men

Year	Winner
1997–98	P. Nicol (Scot.)
1998–99	J. Power (Can.)
1999–2000	**D. Evans (Wales)**

British Open Championship—Women

Year	Winner
1997–98	M. Martin (Austl.)
1998–99	L. Joyce (N.Z.)
1999–2000	**L. Joyce (N.Z.)**

SWIMMING

World Swimming Records Set in 2000 in 25-m Pools

Event	Name	Country	Time
MEN			
50-m freestyle	Roland Schoeman	South Africa	21.28 sec
	Anthony Ervin	United States	21.21 sec
200-m freestyle	Ian Thorpe	Australia	1 min 42.54 sec
	Ian Thorpe	Australia	1 min 41.10 sec
50-m backstroke	Matt Welsh	Australia	24.11 sec
	Neil Walker	United States	24.04 sec
	Neil Walker	United States	23.42 sec
100-m backstroke	Lenny Krayzelburg	United States	51.28 sec
	Neil Walker	United States	50.75 sec
200-m backstroke	Lenny Krayzelburg	United States	1 min 52.43 sec
	Matt Welsh	Australia	1 min 51.62 sec
100-m breaststroke	Roman Sludnov	Russia	58.51 sec
	Ed Moses	United States	57.66 sec
200-m breaststroke	Roman Sludnov	Russia	2 min 07.59 sec
	Ed Moses	United States	2 min 06.40 sec
50-m butterfly	Lars Frölander	Sweden	23.19 sec
	Michael Klim	Australia	23.11 sec
100-m butterfly	Lars Frölander	Sweden	50.59 sec
	Lars Frölander	Sweden	50.44 sec
100-m individual medley	Neil Walker	United States	52.79 sec
4 x 50-m freestyle relay*	Auburn University	United States	1 min 24.83 sec
4 x 100-m freestyle relay	Sweden National Team	Sweden	3 min 09.57 sec
4 x 200-m freestyle relay	U.S. National Team	United States	7 min 01.33 sec
WOMEN			
50-m freestyle	Therese Alshammar	Sweden	23.59 sec
100-m freestyle	Therese Alshammar	Sweden	52.17 sec
50-m backstroke	Haley Cope	United States	27.25 sec
50-m butterfly	Anna-Karin Kammerling	Sweden	25.60 sec
100-m butterfly	Jenny Thompson	United States	56.80 sec
	Jenny Thompson	United States	56.56 sec
200-m butterfly	Susie O'Neill	Australia	2 min 04.16 sec
4 x 50-m medley relay*	Univ. of California	United States	1 min 49.23 sec
	Sweden National Team	Sweden	1 min 48.31 sec
4 x 100-m medley relay	Univ. of Georgia	United States	3 min 57.46 sec
4 x 50-m freestyle relay*	Sweden National Team	Sweden	1 min 38.21 sec
4 x 200-m freestyle relay	U.K. National Team	United Kingdom	7 min 49.11 sec

*Not an officially ratified event; best performance on record.

World Swimming Records Set in 2000 in 50-m Pools

Event	Name	Country	Time
MEN			
50-m freestyle	Aleksandr Popov	Russia	21.64 sec
100-m freestyle	Michael Klim	Australia	48.18 sec
	Pieter van den Hoogenband	Netherlands	47.84 sec
200-m freestyle	Ian Thorpe	Australia	1 min 45.69 sec
	Ian Thorpe	Australia	1 min 45.51 sec
	Pieter van den Hoogenband	Netherlands	1 min 45.35 sec
400-m freestyle	Ian Thorpe	Australia	3 min 41.33 sec
	Ian Thorpe	Australia	3 min 40.59 sec
100-m breaststroke	Roman Sludnov	Russia	1 min 00.36 sec
50-m butterfly	Geoff Huegill	Australia	23.60 sec
200-m butterfly	Tom Malchow	United States	1 min 55.18 sec
400-m individual medley	Tom Dolan	United States	4 min 11.76 sec
4 x 100-m medley relay	U.S. Olympic Team	United States	3 min 33.73 sec
4 x 100-m freestyle relay	Australia Olympic Team	Australia	3 min 13.67 sec
4 x 200-m freestyle relay	Australia Olympic Team	Australia	7 min 07.05 sec
WOMEN			
50-m freestyle	Inge de Bruijn	Netherlands	24.48 sec
	Inge de Bruijn	Netherlands	24.39 sec
	Inge de Bruijn	Netherlands	24.13 sec
100-m freestyle	Inge de Bruijn	Netherlands	53.80 sec
	Inge de Bruijn	Netherlands	53.77 sec
50-m backstroke	Nina Zhivanevskaya	Spain	28.69 sec
	Mai Nakamura	Japan	28.67 sec
	Sandra Völker	Germany	28.25 sec
50-m butterfly	Inge de Bruijn	Netherlands	25.83 sec
	Inge de Bruijn	Netherlands	25.64 sec
100-m butterly	Inge de Bruijn	Netherlands	56.69 sec
	Inge de Bruijn	Netherlands	56.64 sec
	Inge de Bruijn	Netherlands	56.61 sec
200-m butterfly	Susie O'Neill	Australia	2 min 05.81 sec
400-m individual medley	Yana Klochkova	Ukraine	4 min 33.59 sec
4 x 100-m medley relay	U.S. Olympic Team	United States	3 min 58.30 sec
4 x 100-m freestyle relay	U.S. Olympic Team	United States	3 min 36.61 sec

World Swimming and Diving Championships—Men

	Freestyle				
Year	**50 m**	**100 m**	**200 m**	**400 m**	**1,500 m**
1991	T. Jager (U.S.)	M. Biondi (U.S.)	G. Lamberti (Italy)	J. Hoffmann (Ger.)	J. Hoffmann (Ger.)
1994	A. Popov (Russia)	A. Popov (Russia)	A. Kasvio (Fin.)	K. Perkins (Austl.)	K. Perkins (Austl.)
1998	B. Pilczuk (U.S.)	A. Popov (Russia)	M. Klim (Austl.)	I. Thorpe (Austl.)	G. Hackett (Austl.)

	Backstroke		**Breaststroke**		**Butterfly**	
	100 m	**200 m**	**100 m**	**200 m**	**100 m**	**200 m**
1991	J. Rouse (U.S.)	M. López Zubero (Spain)	N. Rozsa (Hung.)	M. Barrowman (U.S.)	A. Nesty (Suriname)	M. Stewart (U.S.)
1994	M. López Zubero (Spain)	V. Selkov (Russia)	N. Rozsa (Hung.)	N. Rozsa (Hung.)	R. Szukala (Pol.)	D. Pankratov (Russia)
1998	L. Krayzelburg (U.S.)	L. Krayzelburg (U.S.)	F. De Burghgraeve (Belg.)	K. Grote (U.S.)	M. Klim (Austl.)	D. Silantyev (Ukr.)

	Individual medley		**Team relays**		
	200 m	**400 m**	**4 × 100-m freestyle**	**4 × 200-m freestyle**	**4 × 100-m medley**
1991	T. Darnyi (Hung.)	T. Darnyi (Hung.)	United States	Germany	United States
1994	J. Sievinen (Fin.)	T. Dolan (U.S.)	United States	Sweden	United States
1998	M. Wouda (Neth.)	T. Dolan (U.S.)	United States	Australia	Australia

	Diving				
	1-m springboard	**3-m springboard**	**Platform**	**3-m synchronized**	**10-m synchronized**
1991	E. Jongejans (Neth.)	K. Ferguson (U.S.)	Sun Shuwei (China)		
1994	E. Stewart (Zimb.)	Yu Zhuocheng (China)	D. Sautin (Russia)		
1998	Yu Zhuocheng (China)	D. Sautin (Russia)	D. Sautin (Russia)	China	China

SWIMMING (continued)

World Swimming and Diving Championships—Women

Year	Freestyle 50 m	100 m	200 m	400 m	800 m	
1991	Zhuang Yong (China)	N. Haislett (U.S.)	H. Lewis (Austl.)	J. Evans (U.S.)	J. Evans (U.S.)	
1994	Le Jingyi (China)	Le Jingyi (China)	F. van Almsick (Ger.)	Yang Aihua (China)	J. Evans (U.S.)	
1998	A. Van Dyken (U.S.)	J. Thompson (U.S.)	C. Poll (C.Rica)	Chen Yan (China)	B. Bennett (U.S.)	
	Backstroke		**Breaststroke**		**Butterfly**	
	100 m	**200 m**	**100 m**	**200 m**	**100 m**	**200 m**
1991	K. Egerszegi (Hung.)	K. Egerszegi (Hung.)	L. Frame (Austl.)	E. Volkova (U.S.S.R.)	Qian Hong (China)	S. Sanders (U.S.)
1994	He Cihong (China)	He Cihong (China)	S. Riley (Austl.)	S. Riley (Austl.)	Liu Limin (China)	Liu Limin (China)
1998	L. Maurer (U.S.)	R. Maracineanu (Fr.)	K. Kowal (U.S.)	A. Kovacs (Hung.)	J. Thompson (U.S.)	S. O'Neill (Austl.)
	Individual medley		**Team relays**			
	200 m	**400 m**	**4 × 100-m freestyle**	**4 × 200-m freestyle**	**4 × 100-m medley**	
1991	Lin Li (China)	Lin Li (China)	United States	Germany	United States	
1994	Lu Bin (China)	Dai Guohong (China)	China	China	China	
1998	Wu Yanyan (China)	Chen Yan (China)	United States	Germany	United States	
	Diving					
	1-m springboard	**3-m springboard**	**Platform**	**3-m synchronized**	**10-m synchronized**	
1991	Gao Min (China)	Gao Min (China)	Fu Mingxia (China)			
1994	Chen Lixia (China)	Tan Shuping (China)	Fu Mingxia (China)			
1998	I. Lashko (Russia)	Y. Pakhalina (Russia)	O. Zhupina (Ukr.)	Russia	Ukraine	

TABLE TENNIS

2000 Table Tennis World Rankings*

Men	Women
1. Kong Linghui (China)	1. Wang Nan (China)
2. Wang Liqin (China)	2. Li Ju (China)
3. Liu Guoliang (China)	3. Chen Jing (Taiwan)
4. Vladimir Samsonov (Bela.)	4. Sun Jin (China)
5. Jan-Ove Waldner (Swed.)	5. Yang Ying (China)

*ITTF ranking as of October 2000.

World Table Tennis Championships—Men

Year	St. Bride's Vase (singles)	Iran Cup (doubles)	Swaythling Cup (team)
1997	J.-O. Waldner (Swed.)	Kong Linghui, Liu Guoliang (China)	China
1999	Liu Guoliang (China)	Kong Linghui, Liu Guoliang (China)	not held
2000	**not held**	**not held**	**Sweden**

Table Tennis World Cup

Year	Men
1998	J. Rosskopf (Ger.)
1999	V. Samsonov (Bela.)
2000	**Ma Lin (China)**
Year	**Women**
1998	Wang Nan (China)
1999	Wang Nan (China)
2000	**Li Ju (China)**

World Table Tennis Championships—Women

Year	G. Geist Prize (singles)	W.J. Pope Trophy (doubles)	Corbillon Cup (team)
1997	Deng Yaping (China)	Deng Yaping, Yang Ying (China)	China
1999	Wang Nan (China)	Wang Nan, Li Ju (China)	not held
2000	**not held**	**not held**	**China**

World Table Tennis Championships—Mixed

Year	Heydusek Prize
1995	Wang Tao, Liu Wei (China)
1997	Liu Guoliang, Wu Na (China)
1999	Ma Lin, Zhang Yingying (China)

TENNIS

Australian Open Tennis Championships—Singles

Year	Men	Women
1998	P. Korda (Cz.Rep.)	M. Hingis (Switz.)
1999	Ye. Kafelnikov (Russia)	M. Hingis (Switz.)
2000	**A. Agassi (U.S.)**	**L. Davenport (U.S.)**

Australian Open Tennis Championships—Doubles

Year	Men	Women
1998	J. Bjorkman, J. Eltingh	M. Hingis, M. Lucic
1999	J. Bjorkman, P. Rafter	M. Hingis, A. Kournikova
2000	**E. Ferreira, R. Leach**	**L. Raymond, R. Stubbs**

French Open Tennis Championships—Singles

Year	Men	Women
1998	C. Moya (Spain)	A. Sánchez Vicario (Spain)
1999	A. Agassi (U.S.)	S. Graf (Ger.)
2000	**G. Kuerten (Braz.)**	**M. Pierce (Fr.)**

French Open Tennis Championships—Doubles

Year	Men	Women
1998	J. Eltingh, P. Haarhuis	M. Hingis, J. Novotna
1999	M. Bhupathi, L. Paes	S. Williams, V. Williams
2000	**T. Woodbridge, M. Woodforde**	**M. Hingis, M. Pierce**

TENNIS (continued)

All-England (Wimbledon) Tennis Championships—Singles

Year	Men	Women
1998	P. Sampras (U.S.)	J. Novotna (Cz.Rep.)
1999	P. Sampras (U.S.)	L. Davenport (U.S.)
2000	**P. Sampras (U.S.)**	**V. Williams (U.S.)**

All-England (Wimbledon) Tennis Championships—Doubles

Year	Men	Women
1998	J. Eltingh, P. Haarhuis	M. Hingis, J. Novotna
1999	M. Bhupathi, L. Paes	L. Davenport, C. Morariu
2000	**T. Woodbridge, M. Woodforde**	**S. Williams, V. Williams**

United States Open Tennis Championships—Singles

Year	Men	Women
1998	P. Rafter (Austl.)	L. Davenport (U.S.)
1999	A. Agassi (U.S.)	S. Williams (U.S.)
2000	**M. Safin (Russia)**	**V. Williams (U.S.)**

United States Open Tennis Championships—Doubles

Year	Men	Women
1998	S. Stolle, C. Suk	M. Hingis, J. Novotna
1999	S. Lareau, A. O'Brien	S. Williams, V. Williams
2000	**L. Hewitt, M. Mirnyi**	**J. Halard Decugis, A. Sugiyama**

Davis Cup (men)

Year	Winner	Runner-up	Results
1998	Sweden	Italy	4–1
1999	Australia	France	3–2
2000	**Spain**	**Australia**	**3–1**

Fed Cup (women)

Year	Winner	Runner-up	Results
1998	Spain	Switzerland	3–2
1999	United States	Russia	4–1
2000	**United States**	**Spain**	**5–0**

TRACK AND FIELD SPORTS (ATHLETICS)

World Track and Field Championships—Men

Event	1997	1999
100 m	M. Greene (U.S.)	M. Greene (U.S.)
200 m	A. Boldon (Trin.)	M. Greene (U.S.)
400 m	M. Johnson (U.S.)	M. Johnson (U.S.)
800 m	W. Kipketer (Den.)	W. Kipketer (Den.)
1,500 m	H. El Guerrouj (Mor.)	H. El Guerrouj (Mor.)
5,000 m	D. Komen (Kenya)	S. Hissou (Mor.)
10,000 m	H. Gebrselassie (Eth.)	H. Gebrselassie (Eth.)
steeplechase	W.B. Kipketer (Kenya)	C. Koskei (Kenya)
110-m hurdles	A. Johnson (U.S.)	C. Jackson (U.K.)
400-m hurdles	S. Diagana (Fr.)	F. Mori (Italy)
marathon	A. Antón (Spain)	A. Antón (Spain)
20-km walk	D. García (Mex.)	I. Markov (Russia)
50-km walk	R. Korzeniowski (Pol.)	G. Skurygin (Russia)
4 × 100-m relay	Canada (R. Esmie, G. Gilbert, B. Surin, D. Bailey)	United States (J. Drummond, T. Montgomery, B. Lewis, M. Greene)
4 × 400-m relay	United States (J. Young, A. Pettigrew, C. Jones, T. Washington)	United States (J. Davis, A. Pettigrew, A. Taylor, M. Johnson)
high jump	J. Sotomayor (Cuba)	V. Voronin (Russia)
pole vault	S. Bubka (Ukr.)	M. Tarasov (Russia)
long jump	I. Pedroso (Cuba)	I. Pedroso (Cuba)
triple jump	Y. Quesada (Cuba)	C.M. Friedek (Ger.)
shot put	J. Godina (U.S.)	C.J. Hunter (U.S.)
discus throw	L. Riedel (Ger.)	A. Washington (U.S.)
hammer throw	H. Weis (Ger.)	K. Kobs (Ger.)
javelin throw	M. Corbett (S.Af.)	A. Parviainen (Fin.)
decathlon	T. Dvorak (Cz.Rep.)	T. Dvorak (Cz.Rep.)

2000 World Indoor Records—Men

Event	Competitor and country	Performance
1,000 m	Wilson Kipketer (Den.)	2 min 15.25 sec
	Wilson Kipketer (Den.)	
2 mi*	Hailu Mekkonen (Eth.)	
4 x 800-m relay	United States (Joey Woody, Karl Paranya, Rich Kenah, David Krummenacker)	

*Not an officially ratified event; best performance on record.

2000 World Outdoor Records—Men

Event	Competitor and country	Performance
300 m*	Michael Johnson (U.S.)	30.85 sec
300-m hurdles*	Chris Rawlinson (U.K.)	34.59 sec

*Not an officially ratified event; best performance on record.

IAAF World Cup—Men

	100 metre	200 metre	400 metre	800 metre	1,500 metre
1992	L. Christie (Gr.Brit.)	R. Caetano da Silva (Amer.)	S. Bada (Africa)	D. Sharpe (U.K.)	M. Suleiman (Asia)
1994	L. Christie (Gr.Brit.)	J. Regis (Gr.Brit.)	A. Pettigrew (U.S.)	M. Everett (U.S.)	N. Morceli (Africa)
1998	O. Thompson (Amer.)	F. Fredericks (Africa)	I. Thomas (Gr.Brit.)	N. Schumann (Ger.)	L. Rotich (Africa)
	3,000 metre	**5,000 metre**	**10,000 metre**	**Steeplechase**	**110-m hurdles**
1992	—	F. Bayesa (Africa)	A. Abebe (Africa)	P. Barkutwo (Africa)	C. Jackson (U.K.)
1994	—	B. Lahlafi (Africa)	K. Skah (Africa)	M. Kiptanui (Africa)	T. Jarrett (Gr.Brit.)
1998	D. Baumann (Ger.)	D. Komen (Africa)	—	D. Kallabis (Ger.)	F. Balzer (Ger.)
	400-m hurdles	**4 × 100-m relays**	**4 × 400-m relays**	**Triple jump**	**High jump**
1992	S. Matete (Africa)	United States	Africa	J. Edwards (U.K.)	Y. Sergeyenko (UT)
1994	S. Matete (Africa)	Great Britain	Great Britain	Y. Quesada (Amer.)	J. Sotomayor (Amer.)
1998	S. Matete (Africa)	Great Britain	United States	C. Friedek (Ger.)	C. Austin (U.S.)

TRACK AND FIELD SPORTS (ATHLETICS) (continued)

IAAF World Cup—Men (continued)

	Pole vault	Long jump	Shot put	Discus throw	Hammer throw
1992	I. Potapovich (UT)	I. Pedroso (Amer.)	M. Stulce (U.S.)	T. Washington (U.S.)	T. Gecsek (Europe)
1994	O. Brits (Africa)	F. Salle (Gr.Brit.)	C.J. Hunter (U.S.)	V. Dubrovshchik (Europe)	A. Abduvaliyev (Asia)
1998	M. Tarasov (Europe)	I. Pedroso (Amer.)	J. Godina (U.S.)	V. Alekna (Europe)	T. Gecsek (Europe)

	Javelin throw	Team
1992	J. Zelezny (Europe)	Africa
1994	S. Backley (Gr.Brit.)	Africa
1998	S. Backley (Gr.Brit.)	—

World Track and Field Championships—Women

Event	1997	1999
100 m	M. Jones (U.S.)	M. Jones (U.S.)
200 m	Z. Pintusevich (Ukr.)	I. Miller (U.S.)
400 m	C. Freeman (Austl.)	C. Freeman (Austl.)
800 m	A. Quirot (Cuba)	L. Formanova (Cz.Rep.)
1,500 m	C. Sacramento (Port.)	S. Masterkova (Russia)
5,000 m	G. Szabo (Rom.)	G. Szabo (Rom.)
10,000 m	S. Barsosio (Kenya)	G. Wami (Eth.)
100-m hurdles	L. Engquist (Swed.)	G. Devers (U.S.)
400-m hurdles	N. Bidouane (Mor.)	D. Pernía (Cuba)
marathon	H. Suzuki (Japan)	Jong Song Ok (N.Kor.)
10-km walk	A. Sidoti (Italy)	
20-km walk		Liu Hongyu (China)
4 × 100-m relay	United States (C. Gaines, M. Jones, I. Miller, G. Devers)	Bahamas (S. Fynes, C. Sturrup, P. Davis, D. Ferguson)
4 × 400-m relay	Germany (A. Feller, U. Rohlander, A. Rucker, G. Breuer)	Russia (T. Chebykina, S. Goncharenko, O. Kotlyarova, N. Nazarova)
high jump	H. Haugland (Nor.)	I. Babakova (Ukr.)
pole vault		S. Dragila (U.S.)
long jump	L. Galkina (Russia)	N. Montalvo (Spain)
triple jump	S. Kasparkova (Cz.Rep.)	P. Tsiamita (Greece)
shot put	A. Kumbernuss (Ger.)	A. Kumbernuss (Ger.)
discus throw	B. Faumuina (N.Z.)	F. Dietzsch (Ger.)
hammer throw		M. Melinte (Rom.)
javelin throw	T. Hattestad (Nor.)	M. Tzelili (Greece)
heptathlon	S. Braun (Ger.)	E. Barber (Fr.)

2000 World Indoor Records—Women

Event	Competitor and country	Performance
Pole vault	Stacy Dragila (U.S.)	4.57 m (15 ft 0 in)
	Stacy Dragila (U.S.)	4.61 m (15 ft 1½ in)
	Stacy Dragila (U.S.)	4.62 m (15 ft 1¾ in)

2000 World Outdoor Records—Women

Event	Competitor and country	Performance
Steeplechase*	Cristina Casandra (Rom.) Cristina Casandra (Rom.)	9 min 43.64 sec 9 min 40.20 sec
20 km walk	Kristina Saltanovic (Lith.) Rossella Giordano (Italy)	1 hr 35 min 23.7 sec 1 hr 30 min 48.3 sec
4 x 200-m relay	United States (LaTasha Jenkins, LaTasha Colander-Richardson, Nanceen Perry, Marion Jones)	1 min 27.46 sec
4 x 1,500-m relay*	Australia (Natalie Harvey, Georgie Clarke, Kate Richardson, Sarah Jamieson)	17 min 09.75 sec
Pole vault	Stacy Dragila (U.S.)	4.62 m (15 ft 1¾ in)
	Stacy Dragila (U.S.)	4.63 m (15 ft 2¼ in)
Javelin throw*	Trine Hattestad (Nor.)	68.22 m (223 ft 10 in)
	Trine Hattestad (Nor.)	69.48 m (227 ft 11 in)

*Not an officially ratified event; best performance on record.

IAAF World Cup—Women

	100 metre	200 metre	400 metre	800 metre	1,500 metre
1992	N. Voronova (UT)	M.-J. Pérec (Europe)	J. Miles (U.S.)	M. Mutola (Africa)	Y. Podkopayeva (UT)
1994	I. Privalova (Europe)	M. Ottey (Amer.)	I. Privalova (Europe)	M. Mutola (Africa)	H. Boulmerka (Africa)
1998	M. Jones (U.S.)	M. Jones (U.S.)	F. Ogunkoya (Africa)	M. Mutola (Africa)	S. Masterkova (Russia)

	3,000 metre	5,000 metre	10,000 metre	100-m hurdles	400-m hurdles
1992	D. Tulu (Africa)	—	D. Tulu (Africa)	A. López (Amer.)	S. Farmer-Patrick (U.S.)
1994	Y. Murray (Gr.Brit.)	—	E. Meyer (Africa)	A. López (Amer.)	S. Gunnell (Gr.Brit.)
1998	G. Szabo (Europe)	S. O'Sullivan (Europe)	—	G. Alozie (Africa)	N. Bidouane (Africa)

	4 × 100-m relays	4 × 400-m relays	Triple jump	High jump	Long jump
1992	Asia	Americas	—	I. Quintero (Amer.)	H. Drechsler (Ger.)
1994	Africa	Great Britain	A. Biryukova (Europe)	B. Bilac (Europe)	I. Kravets (Europe)
1998	United States	Germany	O. Vasdeki (Europe)	M. Iagar-Dinescu (Europe)	H. Drechsler (Ger.)

	Shot put	Discus throw	Javelin throw	Team
1992	B. Laza (Amer.)	M. Marten (Amer.)	T. Sanderson (U.K.)	Unified Team
1994	Zhihong Huang (Asia)	I. Wyludda (Europe)	T. Hattestad (Europe)	Europe
1998	V. Pavlysh (Europe)	F. Dietzsch (Ger.)	J. Stone (Oceania)	—

World Cross Country Championships—Men

Year	Individual	Team
1998	P. Tergat (Kenya)	Kenya
1999	P. Tergat (Kenya)	Kenya
2000	**M. Mourhit (Belg.)**	**Kenya**

World Cross Country Championships—Women

Year	Individual	Team
1998	S. O'Sullivan (Ire.)	Morocco
1999	G. Wami (Eth.)	Ethiopia
2000	**D. Tulu (Eth.)**	**Ethiopia**

TRACK AND FIELD SPORTS (ATHLETICS) (continued)

Boston Marathon

Year	Men	h:min:s
1998	M. Tanui (Kenya)	2:07:34
1999	J. Chebet (Kenya)	2:09:52
2000	**E. Lagat (Kenya)**	**2:09:47**
Year	**Women**	**h:min:s**
1998	F. Roba (Eth.)	2:23:21
1999	F. Roba (Eth.)	2:23:25
2000	**C. Ndereba (Kenya)**	**2:26:11**

New York City Marathon

Year	Men	h:min:s
1998	J. Kagwe (Kenya)	2:08:45
1999	J. Chebet (Kenya)	2:09:14
2000	**A. El Mouaziz (Mor.)**	**2:10:09**
Year	**Women**	**h:min:s**
1998	F. Fiacconi (Italy)	2:25:17
1999	A. Fernández (Mex.)	2:25:06
2000	**L. Petrova (Russia)**	**2:25:45**

VOLLEYBALL

World Volleyball Championships

Year	Men	Women
1996	Netherlands	Cuba
1998	Italy	Cuba
2000	**Yugoslavia**	**Cuba**

WEIGHT LIFTING

World Weight Lifting Champions, 2000

Weight class	Winner and country	Performance
MEN		
56 kg (123 lb)	Halil Mutlu (Turkey)	305 kg (672.4 lb)
62 kg (136.5 lb)	Nikolay Pechalov (Croatia)	325 kg (716.5 lb)
69 kg (152 lb)	Galabin Boevski (Bulgaria)	357.5 kg (788.2 lb)
77 kg (169.5 lb)	Zhan Xugang (China)	367.5 kg (810.2 lb)
85 kg (187 lb)	Pyrros Dimas (Greece)	390 kg (859.8 lb)
94 kg (207 lb)	Akakios Kakiasvilis (Greece)	405 kg (892.9 lb)
105 kg (231 lb)	Hossein Tavakoli (Iran)	425 kg (936.9 lb)
+105 kg (+231 lb)	Hossein Rezazadeh (Iran)	472.5 kg (1,041.7 lb)
WOMEN		
48 kg (105.5 lb)	Tara Nott (United States)	185 kg (407.8 lb)
53 kg (116.5 lb)	Yang Xia (China)	225 kg (496 lb)
58 kg (127.5 lb)	Soraya Jimenez Mendivil (Mexico)	222.5 kg (490.5 lb)
63 kg (138.5 lb)	Chen Xiaomin (China)	242.5 kg (534.6 lb)
69 kg (152 lb)	Lin Weining (China)	242.5 kg (534.6 lb)
75 kg (165 lb)	Maria Isabel Urrutia (Colombia)	245 kg (540.1 lb)
+75 kg (+165 lb)	Ding Meiyuan (China)	300 kg (661.4 lb)

Rulon Gardner of the U.S. wipes away tears as he stands atop the medal stand following his upset win over legendary Russian wrestler Aleksandr Karelin (left) in the Olympic Greco-Roman wrestling final.

AP/Wide World Photos

WRESTLING

World Wrestling Championships—Freestyle

Year	54 kg	58 kg	63 kg	69 kg
1998	S. Henson (U.S.)	A.R. Dabier (Iran)	S. Barzakov (Bulg.)	A. Gevorkian (Arm.)
1999	Kim Woo Yong (S.Kor.)	H. Dogan (Tur.)	E. Tedeyev (Ukr.)	D. Igali (Can.)
2000	**N. Abdullayev (Azer.)**	**A.R. Dabier (Iran)**	**M. Umakhanov (Russia)**	**D. Igali (Can.)**
Year	**76 kg**	**85 kg**	**97 kg**	**130 kg**
1998	A. Saytyev (Russia)	A.R. Heydari (Iran)	A. Jadidi (Iran)	A. Rodríguez (Cuba)
1999	A. Saytyev (Russia)	Y. Romero (Cuba)	S. Murtasaliyev (Russia)	S. Neal (U.S.)
2000	**B. Slay (U.S.)**	**A. Saytyev (Russia)**	**S. Murtasaliyev (Russia)**	**D. Musulbes (Russia)**

World Wrestling Championships—Greco-Roman Style

Year	54 kg	58 kg	63 kg	69 kg
1998	Sim Kwon Ho (S.Kor.)	Kim In Sub (S.Kor.)	M. Manukyan (Kazakh.)	A. Tretyakov (Russia)
1999	L. Rivas (Cuba)	Kim In Sub (S.Kor.)	M. Manukyan (Kazakh.)	Son Sang Pil (S.Kor.)
2000	**Sim Kwon Ho (S.Kor.)**	**A. Nazaryan (Bulg.)**	**V. Samurgashev (Russia)**	**F. Azcuy (Cuba)**
Year	**76 kg**	**85 kg**	**97 kg**	**130 kg**
1998	B. Bayseytov (Kazakh.)	A. Menshikov (Russia)	G. Koguashvili (Russia)	A. Karelin (Russia)
1999	N. Avluca (Tur.)	L. Mendez (Cuba)	G. Koguashvili (Russia)	A. Karelin (Russia)
2000	**M. Kardanov (Russia)**	**H. Yerlikaya (Tur.)**	**M. Ljungberg (Swed.)**	**R. Gardner (U.S.)**

2000 Sumo Tournament Champions

Tournament	Location	Winner	Winner's record
Hatsu Basho (New Year's tournament)	Tokyo	Musoyama	13–2
Haru Basho (spring tournament)	Osaka	Takatoriki	13–2
Natsu Basho (summer tournament)	Tokyo	Kaio	14–1
Nagoya Basho (Nagoya tournament)	Nagoya	Akebono	13–2
Aki Basho (autumn tournament)	Tokyo	Musashimaru	14–1
Kyushu Basho (Kyushu tournament)	Fukuoka	Akebono	14–1

The World in 2000

New governments brought new hopes for many countries. Violence continued in a number of spots around the world, roke out in several places, but seemed to be ubsiding in others–the world in 2000 continued o spin on much the same axis as always. . . .

World Affairs

THE YEAR 2000 was an eventful one in world affairs. **THE MIDDLE EAST PEACE PROCESS** degenerated into **VIOLENT CLASHES,** and an unprecedented **SUMMIT MEETING** between the leaders of **NORTH AND SOUTH KOREA** occurred. In the U.S. the presidential election—**THE CLOSEST IN MORE THAN A CENTURY**—dominated the headlines. New presidents were also elected in **RUSSIA, MEXICO, AND YUGOSLAVIA.**

UNITED NATIONS

When U.S. Sen. Jesse Helms, one of the UN's severest critics, addressed the UN Security Council on Jan. 20, 2000, his words struck most delegates as hostile: "If the United Nations respects the sovereign rights of the American people, and serves them as an effective instrument of diplomacy, it will earn and deserve their respect and support. But a United Nations that seeks to impose its presumed authority on the American people, without their consent, begs for confrontation and . . . eventual U.S. withdrawal." Americans, Helms said, were moving away from "supranational institutions" and wanted no part of "utopian" international arrangements. Nearly every member of the Council rebutted Helms after he had finished. Ambassador Alain Dejammet of France remarked, "We hear you, but the idea in this house is that others must be heard as well."

After Helms praised the "Reagan doctrine" for bringing freedom and democracy to the world without UN help or approval, Ambassador Martin Andjaba of Namibia rejoined that the doctrine had denied independence to Namibia, supported apartheid in South Africa, empowered the UNITA rebel movement in Angola, and caused suffering in Africa. Others criticized Helms for equating treaties with loss of sovereignty and for presuming that the U.S. could decide unilaterally whether to pay its UN dues.

On March 30 Security Council members visited Washington, D.C., and condemned the "ambivalent" leadership in the U.S. and its restrictions on UN finances. Replying to charges that the UN was an overbloated bureaucracy, Canadian Ambassador Robert R. Fowler responded that the UN Secretariat numbered only 8,000, while the U.S. Congress had 30,000 employees. "We have overlap and duplication," he said, "and so do you." In May the U.S. General Accounting Office praised Secretary-General Kofi Annan's administration for having improved UN management and placed the responsibility for many UN shortcomings upon the General Assembly's vague directives, resulting from the inability of member states to agree.

In early April Annan laid out an "absurdly ambitious" program for a millennium assembly. Besides reiterating the need for environmental protection, military interventions to halt genocide and mass murder, and curbs on the proliferation of weapons of mass destruction, Annan praised imaginative efforts that states, nongovernmental organizations, and the private sector were making to fight poverty and disease. He challenged UN members to cut in half the number of those people whose income was less than a dollar a day and who did not have safe drinking water. He endorsed a World Bank goal to improve the lives of 100 million slum dwellers by 2020 and suggested cooperation with the pharmaceuticals industry to develop an affordable vaccine against AIDS and to reduce HIV infection rates among young adults by 25% in 10 years. He acknowledged that corrupt and authoritarian governments opposed these goals, but he hoped that developed countries would help by dropping trade barriers against exports from less-developed countries. He proposed that the UN establish an Information Technology Service to train less-developed countries to use the Internet for quick access to current medical information. Many of Annan's proposals were adopted at the September 6–8 UN Millennium Summit in New York, the largest gathering of national leaders ever held. Annan praised their response to the summit's agenda—to chart a new course for humanity.

War Crimes. On January 31 UN investigators implicated Indonesia's military command and militia in a systematic campaign of terror and killings in East Timor (a former Indonesian province) in 1999 and recommended establishing an international tribunal to prosecute them. Indonesia insisted that it could conduct its own trials. Annan said that if Indonesia could conduct hearings and a trial fairly, there might be no need for an international tribunal, but on November 23 Mary Robinson, high commissioner for human rights, said that she had not ruled out convening an international tribunal if Indonesia did not follow through.

After long negotiations Cambodia and the UN compromised on April 29 to create an international court to try former Khmer Rouge leaders. In addition, foreign judges would be allowed to bring independent indictments. On May 24 the UN conceded to Cambodia the right to appoint one of two prosecutors, either of whom would be allowed to proceed with a case unless a five-judge panel (three appointed by Cambodia, two by the UN) objected.

In May Annan endorsed the concept of an international criminal court, based on a treaty signed in Rome in July 1998, and on June 9 France became the first Security Council member to ratify the agreement. Altogether 139 states had signed the treaty. On December 31, the last day on which the draft treaty was open to signature, both the U.S. and Israel signed, thus making it possible for them to participate in revising the text.

Though the Security Council voted unanimously on August 14 to establish a war crimes tribunal for Sierra Leone, it was left to Secretary-General Annan to recommend the details governing the court and to decide upon its composition and functions. The final plan, sent to the Security Council on October 5, gave the tribunal jurisdiction over anyone 15 or older but classified those between the ages of 15 and 18 as juvenile offenders, to be tried by a separate chamber and, if found guilty, to be sentenced to community service and to have arrangements made for foster care, training, and other forms of rehabilitation.

Health. The Security Council met on January 10 to discuss for the first time a worldwide health epidemic, AIDS. It asked the U.S. Congress to appropriate $150 million for AIDS research and prevention programs in Africa. On November 24 the UN calculated that 21.8 million people had died from AIDS and that an additional 36.1 million were infected with the HIV virus.

Carol Bellamy, the director of UNICEF, in mid-July called on countries and international institutions to launch a "war of liberation" against HIV in southern Africa, where 24.5 million of the 34 million carriers of the HIV virus lived.

Human Rights. After the U.S. stopped opposing the proposal to set 18 as the minimum age for sending soldiers into combat, negotiators in Geneva agreed on January 21 to prohibit the use of child soldiers in war. Signatories could continue recruiting young people at the age of 17 but would take "all feasible measures" to keep them out of combat until they reached 18. The protocol would also prohibit the drafting of persons younger than 18 and raise the minimum age for volunteers to above 15.

Australia was so offended by criticisms from several UN committees concerned that the country's 430,000 Aboriginals suffered discrimination in employment, housing, health care, and education that it undertook an internal review of the UN committee system in March; in August it announced restrictions on visits to Australia by representatives of UN human rights bodies and refused to sign a UN convention aimed at eliminating discrimination against women.

Iraq. The Iraqi government said on January 12 that inspectors from the International Atomic Energy Agency (IAEA) might visit the country to check on its uranium stockpiles. The inspections were the first since December 1998, when Iraq had refused to comply with laws and allow any further inspections. Later in the month Annan named Hans Blix, former head of the IAEA, to head a new Monitoring, Verification and Inspection Commission for Iraq. Iraq received the news without protest but did not promise any cooperation with the commission, and at year's end the commission's inspectors still had not been admitted into Iraq.

The Security Council voted unanimously on March 31 to allow Iraq to import $1.2 billion in spare parts and other equipment in 2000 to rehabilitate its oil industry and to allow more oil to be pumped efficiently and safely, which thereby would enable Iraq to pay for civilian goods and public-service projects. The Security Council's sanctions committee also drafted four lists (food, pharmaceuticals, educational material, and agricultural equipment) that Iraq might purchase without committee review, although UN officials would still oversee and approve all of the purchases made by Iraq.

On June 8 the Security Council extended the "oil for food" program but refused to adopt a Chinese and Russian amendment that called sanctions the sole cause of Iraq's economic hardships. The majority of the Council pointed out that Iraq had received $8.4 billion from oil sales over the previous six months and possibly hundreds of millions more from illegally smuggled oil, and Annan said that Iraq had enough money to mitigate civilian hardships if it chose to do so. The Council dispatched an assessment team to study the condition of the people, but Iraq refused to admit it. Holes in the UN embargo against Iraq appeared with greater frequency toward the end of the year as more and more states made flights to Baghdad. Annan and Iraqi officials held "frank" conversations in Qatar during meetings of the Organization of the Islamic Conference (November 12–14) as part of an effort to break the deadlock between the UN and Iraq.

Afghanistan. A report by the UN Office for Drug Control and Crime Prevention revealed that Afghanistan was not only the largest opium producer in the world but was becoming a major heroin man-

UN Secretary-General Kofi Annan (centre) poses with Palestinian leader Yasir Arafat (left) and Japanese Prime Minister Yoshiro Mori (right) for photographers during the Millennium Summit in New York City on September 7.

AP/Wide World Photos

ufacturer and was thereby contributing to a rise in addiction throughout the region. In July, however, the Taliban decreed that farming poppies for heroin production was "unislamic." The ban coincided with a UN decision to close its drug-control program in Afghanistan for lack of funding.

Kosovo. On June 12 Bernard Kouchner, UN administrator in Kosovo (a province of Serbia, Yugos.), called the first year of the UN Mission in Kosovo a success, although the hatred between Serbs and Albanians there had greatly interfered with efforts to establish a civil administration. The UN had coordinated the work of the 300 private and government organizations that had provided emergency shelter, food, health care, and transport to nearly a million Kosovo Albanian refugees who had returned from exile. On October 28, 6,000 UN and local police joined NATO forces to prevent violence during the first genuinely free local elections that Kosovo had ever enjoyed. Kouchner resigned on December 8 and was succeeded by Hans Haekkerup, Denmark's defense minister.

Peacekeeping. On February 23 the 19-nation peacekeeping force under Australian leadership that had taken control of East Timor on Sept. 20, 1999, turned over its responsibilities to a UN force. A UN civilian administration was already operating as a transitional government, and in August the UN began to appoint local leaders to important posts and to train citizens in becoming public employees.

On May 12 Secretary-General Annan said that UN peacekeeping activities needed the kind of help that the U.S. was no longer willing to provide. The U.S. was offering only to transport troops to places where they were needed, but the UN declined these offers because the U.S. rate was three times that of commercial transport.

After negotiations that started in the beginning of the year, officials of the Democratic Republic of the Congo agreed on November 27 to allow a UN observer mission to function in the country until a peacekeeping mission could take over.

On November 28 Annan told the General Assembly that the UN should terminate its mission in Haiti because the political situation there was too unstable.

Eritrea-Ethiopia. Fighting between Eritrea and Ethiopia stopped after two years as both countries prepared to sign a cease-fire agreement on June 18 that provided a role for the UN in a 25-km (15.5-mi)-wide buffer zone in Eritrean territory. An independent commission was charged with establishing a definitive border between the two countries. In order to help ensure the safe deployment of a peacekeeping force, the UN authorized an unexploded landmine survey in September. The two nations signed a treaty brokered by the Organization of African Unity on December 12, which put an end to the fighting.

Treaties. After deciding that it could protect its nuclear installations effectively with other weapons, Russia announced on March 10 that it would sign the 1996 treaty banning the antipersonnel land mines that its troops had used widely in Chechnya. At a meeting in Geneva of the signatories to the global weapons pact, the United States proposed strengthening the provisions on land mines to extend restrictions to mines dropped from the air and to antivehicle mines in addition to antipersonnel mines. The proposals, however, would not come into force before December 2001.

Disarmament. In January the General Assembly adopted a resolution calling on states to preserve and strengthen the Anti-Ballistic Missile Treaty and to resist pressures to build antimissile systems; the United States had indicated a desire to build such a system. The Assembly met on April 24 to discuss the issues, and Annan said that a missile-defense system "could well lead to a new arms race." The Organization for the Prohibition of Chemical Weapons announced in mid-May that it had given Russia until April 2002 to begin destroying its 40,000-ton arsenal of chemical weapons. The U.S., which held the second largest stockpile, had already destroyed 17% of its 32,000 tons. At the end of a monitoring conference of more than 185 nations on May 20, the five original atomic powers agreed for the first time to the unequivocal (as opposed to the ultimate) elimination of nuclear arms. Annan called the decision "a significant step forward in humanity's pursuit of a more peaceful world."

On the other hand, Muhammad al Baradei, director-general of the IAEA, declared that the U.S. Senate's rejection in 1999 of the proposed treaty banning nuclear tests had led authorities in other countries to believe that the United States was turning away from multilateral arms-control solutions. Many countries were questioning why they should accept new burdens if the U.S. was rejecting nuclear disarmament.

(RICHARD N. SWIFT)

COMMONWEALTH OF NATIONS

Politically turbulent events in several member countries in 2000 tested the Commonwealth of Nations' rules on democracy and good governance. These tumultuous times coincided with the arrival on April 3, 2000, of Don McKinnon, the new Commonwealth secretary-general and former foreign minister of New Zealand. Two of the upheavals were in his own region—in Fiji the seizure of Prime Minister Mahendra Chaudhry and military takeover and in the Solomon Islands the ousting of Prime Minister Bartholemew Ulufa'alu. On May 24 McKinnon visited Fiji and saw Chaudhry in captivity.

The Commonwealth Ministerial Action Group (CMAG) of eight foreign ministers met on June 6 in London and, as with Pakistan eight months earlier, suspended Fiji "from the councils of the Commonwealth." Since the parliament in the Solomon Islands had elected a new prime minister, no action was taken there.

Simultaneously, the land-reform crisis led to serious violence in Zimbabwe and strained relations with Great Britain. McKinnon held talks with Zimbabwean Pres. Robert Mugabe, who soon afterward proclaimed a date for parliamentary elections. A 44-member Commonwealth observer group, however, led by former Nigerian head of state Gen. Abdulsalam Abubakar, found serious fault with polling conduct there, especially in widespread intimidation that preceded voting.

McKinnon also faced problems with Pakistan, which failed to convince him that civilian rule would return within the Commonwealth timetable. Under rules the Commonwealth had adopted in 1995 to deal with the overthrow of a democratically elected member government, a two-year time limit was laid down; for Pakistan this meant a deadline of October 2001. In August McKinnon met in Islamabad, Pak., with military ruler Pervaiz Musharraf, who outlined a democracy program targeted to 2002. CMAG queried the timetable during a September 15 meeting in New York with Pakistani Foreign Minister Abdul Sattar. That same day CMAG interviewed Fiji's Chaudhry and his successor, Laisenia Qarase.

On all of these issues—and in the case of the Sierra Leone civil war—the Commonwealth approach necessarily varied. Though the 1995 rules had approached the issue of some Commonwealth intervention in internal affairs, a

AP/Wide World Photos

Don McKinnon, the new Commonwealth secretary-general, fields questions from reporters upon his arrival in mid-May in Harare, Zimb., where he was to hold talks with Zimbabwean Pres. Robert Mugabe.

fine line had to be drawn; in Zimbabwe's case the Commonwealth had no mandate to intervene in a situation in which the government was flouting the law. The adoption of tighter rules was deferred and referred to a group of 10 heads of government set up in 1999 to chart the future role of the Commonwealth. The 10 met for a preliminary review on September 5.

The Commonwealth had already set an example internationally by putting an end to the attendance of military leaders at its meetings. The Organization of African Unity followed suit, and the Organization of American States was formulating similar rules. During the UN Millennium Summit, held in New York in September, McKinnon also appealed to the UN to suspend countries in which leaders had taken power undemocratically.

The Commonwealth successfully sensitized the World Bank to the problems of small states. On September 25 a joint task force convened in Prague at the first annual Small States Forum sponsored by the Bank and the Commonwealth Secretariat.

At the September 19–21 Commonwealth meeting of finance ministers in Malta, many small states vented anger at attempts by the Organisation for Economic Co-operation and Development to impose economic sanctions by July 2001 on 20 Commonwealth countries operating offshore financial centres unless they complied with OECD tax rules. Those countries insisted that as sovereign states they reserved the right to impose their own tax regimes.

The ministers also renewed attempts to speed debt repayment, a matter that, owing to Commonwealth pressure led by successive British governments, had begun to pay off; only 10 countries still qualified for relief, however.

(DEREK INGRAM)

EUROPEAN UNION

No year in the life of the European Union (EU) would be complete without a combination of grand visions and short-term crises. The year 2000 had more than its fair share of both.

Having set the euro—the new European currency—on its way at the start of 1999, Europe's leaders found themselves on the threshold of the new millennium casting around for a fresh challenge to maintain the EU's momentum. By the middle of 2000 they were talking confidently of the EU's becoming a "superpower" to rival the U.S.

The year opened with Germany, France, and Great Britain turning their attention to the task of expanding Europe's boundaries eastward into lands that just a decade earlier were under communist rule. At the same time, France and Germany were eager to establish ways of preventing a wider Europe from diverting attention from their plans for deeper political and economic integration.

Such grandiose preoccupations were soon put to one side, however, by events in Austria. Following national elections a government coalition was formed between the conservative Austrian People's Party, led by Wolfgang Schüssel, and the far-right Freedom Party, whose leader and pivotal figure was the controversial populist Jörg Haider. Haider's past expressions of sympathy for some Nazi policies of the 1930s and 1940s, coupled with his anti-immigration rhetoric and hostility to EU enlargement, triggered panic in Europe's capitals. In a gesture of disapproval unprecedented in the EU's history, Austria's 14 EU partners froze bilateral contacts with Austria as the world expressed fears that far-right racist views were being rendered respectable by the new government in Vienna.

Austria threatened to take its revenge by blocking EU measures, including the ongoing intergovernmental conference to reform its institutions before enlargement of the organization. The crisis dragged on until September, when a team of "wise men" appointed by the EU to examine the conduct of the Austrian government and to assess the political character of the Freedom Party found no evidence that the new coalition had strayed from "European common values."

Events in Austria were far from the only worries for EU leaders. By early May the euro had slid to record new lows against the dollar. Economists and analysts blamed structurally rigid European economies and the unwillingness of governments to push through unpopular reforms as well as the strength of the U.S. economy.

Even advisers to Gerhard Schröder, the German chancellor, openly expressed concern about the euro's loss in value with less than two years to go before euro notes and coins were to be introduced. Talk began about the need for the European Central Bank to organize coordinated intervention to prop up the euro and also about the long-term need to rid Europe of some of its structural economic rigidities.

The euro's slump was to be an enduring theme of the year. It was a factor seized upon by "Euroskeptics" in Denmark, where a referendum on September 28 narrowly rejected adoption of the single currency. As they had done in 1992 when they voted against the Maastricht Treaty, the people of Denmark showed that they were not frightened to go it alone within the EU and to resist the headlong rush toward economic and political union that was being driven particularly vigorously from Germany and France. The referendum's result also demonstrated to the U.K. and Sweden, which remained outside the single currency, that there was nothing inevitable about adoption of the euro.

The Danish vote added to the growing belief that perhaps the political elites were pushing the integration project too fast for the people. Europe's leaders were yet again faced with their classic dilemma—that of maintaining sufficient pace in building Europe while also bringing the citizens on board.

These dilemmas had been addressed in May in a controversial speech by Germany's foreign minister, Joschka Fischer, an enthusiastic pro-European integrationist. In it he tackled the question of how to reconcile his equal passions for a wider EU and for the need to deepen political integration and to construct truly democratic structures at Europe's heart. With the problems of Europe's so-called democratic deficit uppermost in his mind, Fischer floated the idea of a fully fledged European government, with an elected EU president, a written constitution, and a second chamber composed of politicians from the national parliaments of the member states. While recognizing the need for nation-states to survive, he intended to ensure that, at least among the EU's most committed members, closer political and economic ties would be built on stronger democratic foundations.

In September similar worries that the EU was out of touch with the public mood prompted Günther Verheugen, the EU's commissioner for enlargement, to suggest that Germany (his nation) consider holding a referendum on the expansion of the EU. He argued that the euro had been introduced "behind the backs of the population" and that such mistakes should not be made again.

From midyear onward the EU's ambitions to run its own defense and foreign policy were also creating tensions between those holding the highest offices in these two key policy fields. There were rumours of friction between Javier Solana, the former secretary-general of NATO who became the high representative for EU common foreign and security policy at the start of the year, and Chris Patten, the ex-governor of Hong Kong, in charge of external relations at the European Commission, the EU's civil service. In September Romano Prodi, the Commission president, admitted that dividing foreign policy between two such heavy hitters did not work. "The EU cannot continue to have its foreign policy split in two; one for external aid, and the other for defense," he said. "With this dualism, Europe cannot go forward." It was another sign that Europe's overarching ambitions to widen its responsibilities lacked the tried-and-tested backup common to institutions of longer standing.

Internally, Neil Kinnock battled to introduce the most extensive modernization of the European Commission in its 43-year history. In spite of strong opposition from the Commission's staff unions, he pressed ahead with plans to tighten up staff training and discipline and also proposed a "whistle-blowers" charter to encourage employees to report instances of fraud and corruption. It had been just such a whistle-blower, Paul van Buitenen, who in 1999 had prompted internal auditing probes that eventually led to the mass resignation of the Commission at that time.

Similarly, as the euro continued to drop in value, serious questions were being asked as to whether the institutions and personnel put in place to run the new currency were capable of doing so. Many European politicians argued that the euro could work only if the individual countries better coordinated their economic policies.

All the while, however, as the everyday problems of running the EU appeared to mount, plans were advancing to admit 13 new countries into the organization—10 former communist countries plus Malta, Cyprus, and Turkey. In November, with the applicants eager to hear when they would be allowed to join, the European Commission issued a long-awaited road map setting out an informal timetable by means of which the 12 Eastern European and Mediterranean candidate nations, plus Turkey, which was farther behind in line, might hope to gain entry.

Prodi announced that the detailed negotiations on terms of entry with the more prepared nations, including Hungary, Poland, the Czech Republic, Estonia, Cyprus, and Malta, should be concluded by the end of 2002. Under an optimistic scenario this could mean that those countries would be EU members before the next elections to the European Parliament in 2004. Most observers, however, thought 2005 to be a more likely date.

At the same time, Prodi made it clear that the timetable would slip if leaders failed to agree on a new sharing of power in an enlarged EU at the approaching summit in Nice, France, in December. Issues addressed included the number of votes each country would wield after enlargement of the European Council (the supreme decision-making body), areas over which countries would maintain their right to a national veto, and the number of commissioners a country would be allowed to send to the Commission in Brussels. Equally thorny was the question of how to allow some groups of member nations to press ahead with integration faster than others.

As ever, the more cautious member nations, such as the U.K. and Denmark, wanted to retain the right to veto policies with which they disagreed, while the more ambitious integrationists—France, Germany, Italy, Spain, Belgium, The Netherlands, and Luxembourg—insisted that almost all vetoes should be disallowed if the EU were to continue functioning with a membership of more than 25. Though the issues stated for discussion were highly inflammatory subjects, Prodi warned that it was time to bang heads together. "The whole momentum of enlargement will be lost if we don't have momentum in Nice," he said.

As it turned out, national interest prevailed over European ones in Nice. Leaders emerged uncertain as to whether they had compromised enough to allow preparations for an enlargement to proceed effectively. Many vetoes, for example over taxation policy, were retained. Some damage was also done to Franco-German relations, after France refused to allow an increase in Germany's voting weight to reflect that nation's post-reunification population increase.

Some progress was made, however. The relative voting strengths of the 12 applicant countries already in negotiations to join the EU were determined. Moreover, there was strong support for the first entrants to be admitted in time to take part in elections to the European Parliament in 2004.

Nice was a typical European summit ending a typical European year—long on vision, but short on nitty-gritty agreement on how to reach ambitious objectives. Nonetheless, the determination to increase the EU's membership to 27 countries has been established beyond doubt even if all the finer details on how to run such a large club had yet to be hammered out. (EMMA TUCKER)

MULTINATIONAL AND REGIONAL ORGANIZATIONS

Members of the Association of Southeast Asian Nations (Brunei, Cambodia, Indonesia, Laos, Malaysia, Myanmar [Burma], the Philippines, Singapore, Thailand, and Vietnam) worried during 2000 about the growing destabilizing influence of Myanmar's heroin trade and growing AIDS population, which adversely affected India, China, and Vietnam. ASEAN ministers met in Thailand on July 24–25 to consider the problems caused by Japan's continuation of business with Myanmar despite a 1977 boycott.

The day after its annual meeting, ASEAN foreign ministers met with their counterparts from China, Japan, and South Korea to allay ASEAN fears stemming from the contrast between the political, religious, and separatist conflicts in Indonesia; the instability and tension in other parts of Southeast Asia; and the muted differences between China and Japan and those of North and South Korea. ASEAN members also worried because Northeast Asia was advancing more quickly than Southeast Asia in such areas as communications, information technology, and electronic commerce. Nonetheless, the delegates affirmed their countries' commitment to developing a free-trade area despite some members' desire to protect sensitive industries. They agreed, however, to allow countries that were "experiencing real difficulties" to withdraw sensitive sectors temporarily from the free-trade agreement.

During meetings held with ASEAN foreign ministers and foreign ministers representing 10 of the region's major trading partners, U.S. Secretary of State Madeleine Albright warned that the rapid spread of HIV and AIDS in the region was the greatest danger to the area's health and security. It was suggested that the ASEAN governments were not facing up to the dangers involved. The UN had reported that the region had 1.3 million new cases of HIV infection during 1999.

Leaders of the Asia-Pacific Economic Cooperation forum agreed on November 16 that in 2001 they would begin negotiations to eliminate trade barriers and continue the efforts disrupted in Seattle, Wash., in 1999. They did not address such substantive issues as the fears among less-developed countries (LDCs) that the U.S. would impose labour and environmental standards that would undercut the competitiveness of poorer nations. (*See* ECONOMIC AFFAIRS: *Sidebar.*)

An independent panel of the Organization of African Unity (OAU) agreed on July 7 that nations and institutions—such as Belgium, France, the UN, the U.S., and the Roman Catholic and Anglican churches—that had failed to prevent or stop the 1994 genocide that had killed up to 800,000 people in Rwanda should pay "significant" reparations. The panel asked UN Secretary-General Kofi Annan to establish a commission to designate the countries that owed Rwanda compensation and asked creditors to cancel Rwanda's international debts. The OAU declined to send observers to the presidential election in Côte d'Ivoire on October 22, fearing that its presence would legitimize an undemocratic process that barred most challengers to military ruler Gen. Robert Gueï.

Annan met with representatives of members of the Economic Community of West African States (Burkina Faso, The Gambia, Guinea, Ghana, Liberia, Mali, Nigeria, Senegal, and Sierra Leone) on September 11 to seek their help in defusing tensions between Guinea and Liberia. He reported that innocent villagers on Guinea's border with Liberia and Sierra Leone were being injured and killed as they fled the fighting in Sierra Leone.

Leaders of LDCs in the Group of 77 (now 133) met in Havana in mid-April looking for ways to persuade the major economic powers to share their wealth. The group urged the UN to promote more economic development and technology transfers to the poorer countries of the world.

The observation team organized by the Organization of American States charged in May that the Peruvian electoral process could hardly be considered fair or free; tally sheets and ballots had disappeared in the first round of the election.

On July 23 the group of leading industrialized countries and Russia praised the recent growth of the global economy and pledged to tackle the root causes of poverty. The members sought reforms to expand investment in LDCs. The group's communiqué called for wealthy countries to maximize the benefits of information technology and make them available to all. All nations were urged to work to defeat AIDS, tuberculosis, and malaria and to make a commitment to achieve gender equality in schooling by 2005 and universal primary education by 2015.

The Arab League met over the weekend of October 21–22 in its first summit meeting in four years and issued a statement accusing Israel of having committed atrocities against Palestinians over the previous three weeks. It urged the UN to establish a war crimes tribunal to judge Israeli actions, asked the Security Council and General Assembly to provide protection for the Palestinians under Israeli occupation, called for Israel to accede to the Nuclear Non-proliferation Treaty, and pledged funds to assist the Palestinian economy. The members decided to limit contact with Israel; though formal diplomatic contacts would continue, trade and political exchanges would be curtailed. (RICHARD N. SWIFT)

DEPENDENT STATES

Europe and the Atlantic. In March 2000 negotiations between Denmark and the Faroe Islands on Faroese secession appeared to be at an impasse. Copenhagen rejected a Faroese plan in which Danish bloc subsidies, which made up as much as one-third of the protectorate's budget, would be "gradually eliminated" over 15 years. Denmark said it would not oppose independence for the Faroes but would provide financial subsidies for no more than four years after separation. Advocates of independence said that the money might be made up through the sale of publicly owned property and offshore oil drilling. There also were reports that the Faroese government had amassed a large budget surplus. In November Faroese leader Anfinn Kallsberg announced that a referendum on sovereignty would be held in April 2001.

A Danish newspaper reported in August that an unexploded hydrogen bomb had been located in the wreckage of an American B-52 that crashed and sank off Greenland in 1968. U.S. and Danish authorities denied the report, claiming that all weapons aboard the bomber had been accounted for. In July NASA scientists reported that Greenland's ice cap was shrinking at a net rate of 51 cu km (12.2 cu mi) of ice per year.

Dependent States[1]

Australia	United Kingdom
Christmas Island	Anguilla
Cocos (Keeling) Islands	Bermuda
Norfolk Island	British Virgin Islands
Denmark	Cayman Islands
Faroe Islands	Falkland Islands
Greenland	Gibraltar
France	Guernsey
French Guiana	Isle of Man
French Polynesia	Jersey
Guadeloupe	Montserrat
Martinique	Pitcairn Island
Mayotte	Saint Helena Tristan da Cunha
New Caledonia	Turks and Caicos Islands
Réunion	**United Nations**
Saint Pierre and Miquelon	East Timor
Wallis and Futuna	**United States**
Netherlands, The	American Samoa
Aruba	Guam
Netherlands Antilles	Northern Mariana Islands
New Zealand	Puerto Rico
Cook Islands	Virgin Islands (of the U.S.)
Niue	
Tokelau	

[1]Excludes territories (1) to which Antarctic Treaty is applicable in whole or in part, (2) without permanent civilian population, (3) without internationally recognized civilian government (Western Sahara), or (4) representing unadjudicated unilateral or multilateral territorial claims.

In July the European Court of Human Rights refused to review a case concerning two Argentine sailors killed during the 1982 Falkland Islands/Islas Malvinas war between Argentina and the U.K. The court ruled that the lawsuit, which had been filed in June by relatives of the sailors seeking compensation from the British government, was made outside the legal time limits. On September 1, presidents of 12 South American countries convened at a regional summit in Brasília, Braz., reiterated their support for Argentina's long-standing claim to the islands.

In Gibraltar Chief Minister Peter Caruana was reelected in February by a vote of approximately 58–41% over his more radical predecessor, Joe Bossano. Caruana's Gibraltar Social Democrats won 8 of the 15 elected seats in the House of Assembly; Bossano's Gibraltar Socialist Labour alliance captured the remaining 7. In April the U.K. and Spain reached a landmark agreement that would permit Gibraltar-issued identity cards to be recognized as valid travel documents within the European Union and would allow Gibraltarian financial authorities to implement EU directives. Caruana later claimed that, despite the agreement and the improvements made to end smuggling in the colony, relations with Spain showed no improvement.

A British nuclear submarine, HMS *Tireless*, limped into Gibraltar's port in May with a coolant leak in the propulsion system. Local protesters demanded that the submarine be removed to the U.K. for repairs, but the Royal Navy issued assurances that there was no chance of radiation leakage. At year's end, repairs still had not begun on the crippled *Tireless*.

Caribbean and Bermuda. The use of live ordnance in bombing practice by U.S. Navy pilots on the island of Vieques remained a contentious issue throughout 2000 in the U.S. Commonwealth of Puerto Rico. Pres. Bill Clinton had temporarily halted bombing in 1999 after one civilian was killed by accident and four others injured. News that the bombing might be resumed brought an estimated 85,000 people out into the streets in February to demonstrate their disapproval; 55 protesters cut their way into Vieques base in May. Four members of the Puerto Rican Independence Party who had refused to post $1,000 bail bonds after being accused of trespass at Vieques were released from prison in September. Environmentalists and other concerned individuals moved to file a restraining order when bombing recommenced in October.

The fact that the Financial Stability Forum ranked Bermuda only in category two (countries said to be in need of remedial action) on its list of offshore financial jurisdictions in May did not seem to disturb investors. The Bermuda Monetary Authority reported that in the first six months of 2000 alone, 1,093 applications were received for the establishment of new companies and partnerships, compared with 699 for the same period in 1999. Companies involved in Internet commerce were said to account for a large proportion of the applicants.

In the Cayman Islands, another well-known offshore financial centre, the government was unsuccessful in persuading the Financial Action Task Force (FATF) to remove it from the "blacklist" of countries around the world deemed "uncooperative" in money-laundering matters. At a meeting with FATF officials in Spain in October, the Caymans was "commended" for its legislative efforts but told it would continue to be monitored.

British Virgin Islands Chief Minister Ralph O'Neal dismissed his deputy, Eileene Parsons, in July, claiming that she had been part of a "coup" plot by the opposition against his administration. Parsons promptly quit the governing Virgin Islands Party and joined the recently formed National Development Party.

Having suffered an inexorable loss of population over the five years following the initial eruption of the Soufrière Hills volcano in 1995, Montserrat began to attract back residents during 2000, though the volcano showed little sign of stabilizing. The number of inhabitants rose to about 5,000 at midyear, compared with 3,400 in 1998; the number had stood at 11,000 in 1995. In June 68.9% of those participating in a referendum in St. Maarten indicated preference for the island's becoming a separate entity within The Netherlands rather than remaining part of the Netherlands Antilles federation. Aruba had chosen this path 14 years earlier, but the Dutch government promptly quashed any hope of St. Maarten's following suit by declaring the idea to be "out of the question."

French Pres. Jacques Chirac gave a clear hint in March that the hitherto highly centralized relationship between Paris and French overseas departments (DOMs) might be relaxed in favour of a looser arrangement. He said that the era of "uniform status" was over and that DOMs such as Martinique and Guadeloupe might enjoy more local control in the future.

Pacific. In the Commonwealth of the Northern Mariana Islands, major concerns over relations with the U.S. and the state of the local economy came together over the status of the Marianas' $1 billion garment industry. Some 90% of the Marianas population comprise foreign migrant labour, mostly Filipino and Chinese. Under a 1986 agreement, the garment industry was exempt from U.S. tariffs, minimum wages, and immigration standards; was permitted to use a "Made in the USA" label; and had free access to the U.S. market. The industry generated nearly $80 million a year for the local government, $42 million in users' charges, and $17 million in income taxes. Against the protests of local businesses, the U.S. was considering legislation that would apply tighter controls.

An initiative to recall Guam Gov. Carl Gutierrez over budget difficulties in the legislature failed for lack of a Senate majority. The development of Anderson Air Force Base as a forward operational location for long-range bombers was completed; cruise missiles had not previously been located at Anderson, the first such missile deployment outside the continental U.S. Late in the year the U.S. Army announced it had destroyed the last chemical weapons stored on Johnston Atoll, where chemical munitions had been stockpiled since 1971.

After years of litigation the California Appeals Court upheld a lower court ruling that awarded the government of American Samoa damages of $48 million against unpaid insurance claims arising from Typhoon Val in 1991. Additional punitive damages of $82 million originally awarded were rejected on appeal. American Samoa's $199 million budget for 2001 was approved by Gov. Tauese Sunia; additional funds of $33 million were provided by the U.S. government.

In October New Caledonia was host to the South Pacific Festival of Arts, attended by 27 Pacific nations. The occasion marked the further emergence of New Caledonia into a regional role following the signing of the 1998 peace accords between Caucasian settlers and their Francophone political allies and Kanaks (the indigenous people), who were pro-independence. Also following from the accords were the appointment of an ombudsman to mediate disputes between the government and its citizens and the government's announcement of a "social pact" to address issues of employment and the provision of social services. The economy, heavily dependent on nickel exports, showed strong growth.

French Polynesia's left-wing politicians continued to seek an inquiry into the economic, social, and environmental repercussions of the nuclear-testing program carried out in the territory for 35 years until the facilities were dismantled in 1996. During 1997–99 the territory experienced strong tourism growth of 26%, with current visitor numbers over 90,000 a year, almost half from Europe and one-third from North America.

Niue's government canvassed opinions on the country's constitutional future and found that about 70% favoured the status quo and 24% endorsed full integration with New Zealand; only 7% favoured full independence for the island with its resident population of 1,865. The budget for the year was approved at $NZ20 million (U.S. $8 million).

In the Cook Islands tourism showed growth as a consequence of political instability in Fiji and because of the weak Australian and New Zealand dollars against the U.S. dollar. Tourist numbers for 2000 were on track to exceed the previous record of 57,000 visitors set in 1994. Following international criticism of the Cook Islands offshore banking system, a Money Laundering Authority was established to provide greater surveillance and control over foreign companies conducting transactions through the Cook Islands banking system.

Indian Ocean and East Timor. In 2000 East Timor began its first full year under the auspices of the UN Transitional Administration for East Timor (UNTAET), which had taken control after the territory's referendum on independence in August 1999 triggered bloodshed. Tens of thousands of East Timorese who had fled the fighting remained in squalid refugee camps in Indonesian-controlled West Timor. At least 100,000 refugees had returned to East Timor, but continuing violence and intimidation by pro-Indonesian militia had prevented many more from returning. In December the UN indicted 11 suspects for crimes against humanity committed during the postreferendum violence. Although nine of those charged were in custody, two were still being sought, notably Lieut. Sayful Anwar of the Indonesian special forces.

In July the National Consultative Council (NCC) announced the formation of a provisional coalition government composed of half East Timorese and half UNTAET officials. A new 36-member National Council (NC) was approved in October to replace the NCC. Xanana Gusmão, president of the National Council of Timorese Resistance (CNRT), was elected president at the NC's first session on October 23. José Ramos-Horta, CNRT vice president and co-winner of the Nobel Prize for Peace in 1996, was named foreign minister. Sergio Vieira de Mello of Brazil, the special representative of the secretary-general and transitional administrator for East Timor, reported that elections for the territory's first independent government could be held in late 2001.

Residents of Mayotte voted 73–27% in a July 2 referendum on changing the island's status from that of a "territorial collectivity" to a "departmental collectivity" with closer links to France. Comoros, from which Mayotte had acrimoniously separated in the mid-1970s, denounced the referendum's results and reiterated its claim to the island. In October the French National Assembly voted to split the island of Réunion into two separate departments in January 2001.

On November 3 the U.K.'s High Court ruled that the Ilois, the former population of the Chagos Archipelago, or British Indian Ocean Territory (BIOT), had been unlawfully expelled from the 65-island group. Between 1967 and 1973 the U.K. had relocated the Ilois to Mauritius and the Seychelles more than 1,600 km (1,000 mi) away as part of an agreement with the U.S. to build an American military base on Diego Garcia, the BIOT's largest atoll. The lawsuit had been brought before the High Court in July 2000. The court's ruling was a major setback for the British Foreign Office, which had opposed the Ilois' return. Foreign Secretary Robin Cook announced that the British government would not appeal the decision, however, and the Ilois, who by 2000 numbered some 5,000 people, would be allowed to return to all the islands except Diego Garcia, which remained under U.S. control.

(BARRIE MACDONALD; DAVID RENWICK; MELINDA C. SHEPHERD)

East Timorese children watch a UN helicopter take off from a beach in Dili on February 16.
AP/Wide World Photos

ANTARCTICA

Ice averaging 2,160 m (7,085 ft) in thickness covers more than about 98% of the continent of Antarctica, which has an area of 14 million sq km (5.4 million sq mi). There is no indigenous human population, and there is no land-based industry. Human activity consists mainly of scientific research. The 44-nation Antarctic Treaty is the managerial mechanism for the region south of latitude 60° S, which includes all of Antarctica. The treaty reserves the area for peaceful purposes, encourages cooperation in science, prescribes environmental protection, allows inspections to verify adherence, and defers the issue of territorial sovereignty.

The ocean around Antarctica experienced its fifth year of widespread poaching of Patagonian toothfish in 2000. The international Commission for the Conservation of Antarctic Marine Living Resources said that illegal, unregulated, and unreported fishers took 6,546 metric tons of the fish, while others said that this amount was a large underestimate because 9,000 metric tons of the fish, worth $45 million, passed through Port Louis, Mauritius, during the first nine months of 2000. (Legal fishers took 25,994 metric tons.) The species was sometimes marketed as deep sea bass or Chilean sea bass. (*See also* AGRICULTURE AND FISHERIES: *Fisheries.*)

Efforts to stop the illegal fishing included an attempt to end Port Louis's reputation as the main pirate port. The Antarctic Commission set up a paper trail, tracing catches from hook to market, that was claimed to be the most restrictive ever imposed to protect a high seas fishery. The illegal activity also had a high human cost; the Spanish-registered pirate fishing vessel *Amur* foundered on October 9 during severe weather, drowning 14 of the crew of 40; in two years an estimated 61 people had died in three vessels that sank while pursuing toothfish illegally.

An estimated 68,000 seabirds died trying to feed on bait hanging from longline hooks set out by the illegal fishers. This was an unsustainable mortality for the albatross, giant petrels, and white-chinned petrels that breed in the area.

Antarctic Treaty negotiators worked toward ensuring that polluters paid for environmental damage in Antarctica. Liability, which some saw as a missing link in the protection of Antarctica, had been set aside as too difficult when the treaty nations approved the landmark Protocol on Environmental Protection in 1991. While environmental accidents in Antarctica were infrequent, a large fuel spill had occurred in 1989 when the Argentine ship *Bahía Paraíso* ran aground, losing some 600,000 litres (about 160,000 gal) of fuel, of which only about two-thirds was recovered. Further progress on liability awaited an Antarctic Treaty consultative meeting planned for St. Petersburg in 2001.

Tourism increased, with 13,193 people visiting Antarctica in the 1999–2000 Antarctic summer, compared with 10,013 the previous season and 9,604 the year before. Most visitors were seaborne, arriving in 24 ships that made 143 voyages. U.S. citizens accounted for more than half of the visitors, according to the International Association of Antarctica Tour Operators and the U.S. National Science Foundation.

Sir Ernest Shackleton's historic 1916 crossing of the South Atlantic island of South Georgia was retraced twice in 2000. Three mountaineers completed the journey over three days in mid-April following a six-day trek by the Shackleton 2000 expedition after its reenactment of Shackleton's open-boat journey from the Antarctic Peninsula to South Georgia.

A boom in prices for Antarctic memorabilia was confirmed at an April auction with a record £93,950 (about $148,000) paid for a single item—the 1912 journal of surgeon Murray Levick, a member of Capt. Robert Scott's stranded party. The auction included a copy of *Aurora Australis,* the hand-published book of articles, poems, and sketches that Shackleton's British Antarctic Expedition produced at Cape Evans in 1908. A private buyer paid £37,600 (about $59,000).

American scientists comparing modern and historic weather data found that Scott's party may have perished from unusually extreme cold during its attempted return from the South Pole in 1912. Scott wrote in his final message to the public that "our wreck is certainly due to this sudden advent of severe weather." Speculation about the reasons for the failure had varied, and such causes as the party's reliance on ponies, poor diet, and unfamiliarity with skis had been considered.

The first evidence of life in Lake Vostok, 3,600 m (11,800 ft) below the East Antarctic Ice Sheet, was claimed on the basis of two investigations of ice cores from 120 m (395 ft) above the suspected water level. The studies suggested that despite the fact that it had been isolated from the atmosphere for hundreds of thousands of years, the lake could support a microbial population. On the basis of these findings, published in *Science,* researchers believed that microbes could thrive in other hostile places in the solar system. They determined that Lake Vostok is a terrestrial analogue to Europa, a frozen moon of Jupiter. (*See* MATHEMATICS AND PHYSICAL SCIENCES: *Space Exploration.*) A separate study also found live bacteria in snow at the South Pole, a discovery that confirmed that life on Earth persisted in the most hostile of climates.

University of Florida geologists revealed evidence that the Antarctic Ice Sheet was massively unstable as recently as the last glacial advance in North America, which occurred about 20,000 years ago. Sediments from southern Atlantic Ocean bottom sites contained large grains of Antarctic quartz and other fragments that icebergs had transported north. The study, published in *Science,* was believed to demonstrate for the first time that instability in parts of that ice sheet coincided with warming in the Northern Hemisphere.

Circumpolar ballooning experiments of the 1990s yielded their biggest payoff yet in 2000: evidence was gathered that the universe is geometrically flat. Images collected above Antarctica in 1998 by an ultrasensitive telescope aboard a balloon at the edge of the atmosphere appeared

"Regulatory Fish Encyclopeaid," Office of Seafood and Office of Regulatory Affairs, Food and Drug Administration, 1993–2001. <http://vm.cfsan.fda.gov/~frf/rfe0.html>

Patagonian toothfish (deep sea bass or Chilean sea bass) was a major target for commercial fishing—and poaching—in Antarctic waters during the year.

in the journal *Nature* in 2000. The journal said of its cover feature, "Columbus may have proved the Earth is round, but cosmologists have had the last word: the universe is flat." The evidence was shown in a map of tiny variations in cosmic microwave background radiation—ancient radiation that remained after the Big Bang. The variations revealed that this violent expansion flattened the geometry of space.

(GUY G. GUTHRIDGE)

ARCTIC REGIONS

The Arctic regions may be defined in physical terms (astronomical [north of the Arctic Circle, latitude 66° 30' N], climatic [above the 10 °C (50 °F) July isotherm], or vegetational [above the northern limit of the tree line]) or in human terms (the territory inhabited by the circumpolar cultures—Inuit [Eskimo] and Aleut in North America and Russia, Saami [Lapp] in northern Scandinavia and Russia, and 29 other peoples of the Russian North, Siberia, and East Asia). No single national sovereignty or treaty regime governs the region, which includes portions of seven countries: Canada, the United States, Russia, Finland, Sweden, Norway, and Greenland (part of Denmark). The Arctic Ocean, 14,090,000 sq km (5,440,000 sq mi) in area, constitutes about two-thirds of the region. The land area consists of permanent ice cap, tundra, or taiga. The population (2000 est.) of peoples belonging to the circumpolar cultures is 375,000. International organizations concerned with the Arctic include the Arctic Council, two institutions of the Barents Euro-Arctic Region, and the Indigenous Peoples' Secretariat. International scientific cooperation of the Arctic is the focus of the International Arctic Research Center of the University of Alaska at Fairbanks.

After more than two decades, oil and natural gas companies, governments, and some indigenous groups were in 2000 once again enthusiastic about developing the petroleum resources of northern Alaska and Canada. In the mid-1970s, citing uncertainties about the environment and unsettled land claims, a public commission headed by British Columbia Supreme Court Justice Thomas Berger had derailed plans to establish a pipeline corridor extending from the Beaufort Sea down the Mackenzie River valley to southern markets in the U.S. An alternative pipeline proposal was suggested that would have brought Alaska's Prudhoe Bay natural gas down the Alaska Highway to be joined to a connecting pipeline along the Dempster Highway in the Yukon and the Northwest Territories. This spur line eventually would have tapped into gas reserves from the Mackenzie delta. Canada's National Energy Board had approved this alternative in July 1977.

In 2000 the economics of natural gas markets and improved pipeline technology appeared to make the 1970s projects more viable than at any time in the past. Conventional gas reserves in other areas were in decline, and energy prices were at record high levels. Technology had also advanced to such an extent that a pipeline could be built at a fraction of its cost in the late 1970s and provide greater gas throughput. In addition, the settlement of land claims in the areas affected by the pipeline in Alaska and in the Mackenzie River valley offered many opportunities for the indigenous inhabitants to participate in the potential benefits of oil and gas development. Producers in the U.S. and Canada were also speculating that a pipeline would spur new exploration activities that would lead to the discovery of enormous additional natural gas reserves. By April the U.S. Federal Trade Commission had also approved the $27.6 billion purchase of the Atlantic Richfield Co. by BP Amoco PLC. As part of the deal, BP Amoco nearly doubled its share of Prudhoe Bay's natural gas, which gave the company a greater incentive to develop this huge resource.

In May a yearlong round of government-to-government meetings began between Alaska's 227 federally recognized tribes to define the roles and responsibilities of tribes and state agencies. Tribal sovereignty advocates had lobbied for recognition in Alaska for more than a decade. Alaska tribes had long sought more authority and influence over a range of issues, including law enforcement, education, and the environment.

Vigorous debate continued on the opening of the Arctic Natural Wildlife Refuge (ANWR) to oil exploration and development. The ANWR, about eight million hectares (1 ha=2.47 ac) in area, was established as part of the Alaska National Interest Lands Conservation Act, signed into law by U.S. Pres. Jimmy Carter in 1980. Although the act was one of the nation's most sweeping pieces of conservation legislation, the ANWR's 607,287-ha coastal plain (known by its technical designation as the 1002 area) was not protected from future oil exploration. Conservation groups and the local Gwich'in Indians claimed that the area is precious for wildlife and as an Arctic ecosystem and that oil production would disrupt the 129,000-strong Porcupine Caribou Herd, the Indians' main source of food.

In October the United States and Russia initialed an agreement that would help preserve the polar bear population, estimated between 22,000 and 28,000 worldwide. Quotas were established for subsistence hunting by native tribes in Alaska and the Chukchi okrug of Siberia.

Throughout the year press reports, research studies, and indigenous knowledge confirmed that climate change was already reworking the Arctic landscape and affecting the lives of its inhabitants. Average temperatures in some parts of the Canadian North were rising at a rate of about 1 °C (1.8 °F) each decade. Glaciers were in retreat. In July the Associated Press reported that a warming climate was melting more than 50,000 billion tons of water a year from the Greenland ice sheet. This was adding to a 23-cm (9-in) rise in sea level throughout the world during the past century and was increasing the risk of coastal flooding. Scientists also reported a thinning of the polar ice cap. Arctic pack ice was melting so rapidly that predictions were that it might be possible within a few decades to use the legendary Northwest Passage routinely as a shortcut between the Atlantic and Pacific oceans.

The climate change could result in the eventual extinction of plants and animals or their permanent forced migration to find other suitable habitats. In some areas it was expected that in order to survive species would have to move 10 times faster than they did during the last ice age.

In September the *Toronto Globe and Mail* reported that RAO Norilsk Nickel, the world's largest nickel-mining company, had announced a restructuring of its vast mining operations in Siberia. Already supplying about 40% of the world's palladium and about 20% of its platinum and nickel, Norilsk was undertaking a $3.5 billion program to modernize its mining assets by 2010. Because of high commodity prices, the company was expected to generate a surplus cash flow of $3 billion in 2000.

Pursuant to the results of a Canadian-Russian feasibility study released in October, commercial airlines were expected to begin flying nonstop over the North Pole through Canadian-Russian airspace sometime during 2001. The polar air routes were expected to save North American airlines bound for Asia millions of dollars annually, which would result in lower ticket prices and save passengers thousands of hours in flying time.

(KENNETH DE LA BARRE)

AFGHANISTAN

Area: 652,225 sq km (251,825 sq mi)
Population (2000 est.): 25,889,000 (including Afghan refugees estimated to number about 1,100,000 in Pakistan and more than 1,200,000 in Iran)
Capital: Kabul
Chief of state: de facto Taliban Supreme Leader (Amir-ul-Momenin), Mullah Mohammad Omar
Head of government: de facto Taliban council leader, Mullah Mohammad Rabbani

The Taliban regime in Afghanistan further marginalized armed opposition during 2000, but the uncompromising severity of its fundamentalist Islamic view of society resulted in continued economic stagnation and international isolation. Facing economic and climatic disaster, Afghan citizens were denied both the benefits of normal commerce and much-needed international assistance.

Clashes between Taliban and opposition forces occurred throughout the year. In September the anti-Taliban militia of Ahmad Shah Masoud was compelled to withdraw from Taloqan, capital of the northeastern province of Takhar. The significance of this Taliban advance was twofold. The area was traditionally home to many of Afghanistan's ethnic Tajiks, which meant that victory here by the Taliban, who were mostly Pashtuns, had an ethnic dimension. Takhar and its capital also straddled supply routes from Tajikistan to the Panjshir Valley, where Masoud had directed resistance to Taliban authority just as he had earlier resisted occupying Soviet forces. Masoud's long success in holding out against the Taliban was grounded in the reluctance of Afghanistan's large Tajik minority, together with other non-Pashtun ethnic groups, to accept domination by Afghanistan's Pashtun majority.

Diplomatic efforts by neighbouring countries and international organizations to find a peaceful solution went on throughout 2000, mostly without visible results. In February the UN secretary-general's personal representative to Afghanistan met with many leading Afghans, including Burhanuddin Rabbani, the Afghan president ousted by the Taliban in 1996 but still recognized by the UN. The Organization of the Islamic Conference sponsored indirect discussions between Taliban and anti-Taliban representatives in Jiddah, Saudi Arabia, in March and May, but the only agreement was on prisoner exchanges. Iran, which supported the anti-Taliban groups, and Pakistan, a Taliban ally, found several occasions to discuss a settlement. Perhaps most active were the Muslim republics of Central Asia, whose governments were especially vulnerable to destabilization from a strong fundamentalist regime in Afghanistan. The Taliban's open sympathy for Chechen separatism kept Russia wary as well. A special envoy of Turkmenistan's Pres. Saparmurad Niyazov met with Masoud in Tajikistan and with Taliban Supreme Leader (Amir-ul-Momenin) Mullah Mohammad Omar in the southern city of Kandahar.

The Taliban remained uncompromising on basic issues, however. Representatives said they were prepared to talk about a broad-based government but insisted that the role of Mullah Omar was not negotiable. Taliban officials repeatedly demanded that they be given Afghanistan's UN seat, but there was no indication they were willing to surrender suspected international terrorist Osama bin Laden to international justice. Rabbani seemed to confirm Afghanistan's international reputation when he told the UN Millennium Summit in September that "foreign interference" had "turned our land into a terrorist training camp, a center for drug smugglers and a base for spilling instability."

Afghanistan's economy, disrupted by more than 20 years of fighting, might have been expected to show signs of recovery under the relative stability in Kabul and the 90% of the country controlled by the Taliban, but little progress was visible. The official Taliban policy discouraging the participation of women in public life further slowed economic activity. Already forbidden to study and banned from most employment, women—including all female civil servants and teachers—were subjected to mass layoffs in April. In July employment by foreign aid agencies was put off-limits to women.

Sanctions invoked by the United Nations in November 1999 in an effort to have bin Laden turned over to the U.S. or a third country also hindered the economy. Afghanistan's foreign assets were frozen, and international air traffic to and from the country was banned. One result was the loss of income from fruit production, traditionally one of the country's important exports.

Overwhelmingly dependent on agriculture, Afghanistan's economy faced calamity when the worst drought in three decades continued into a second year. By midsummer the entire arid wheat crop, well over half the irrigated crops, and 60–80% of livestock had been lost in the southern provinces. Some relief came in early November, when heavy rains fell over large parts of the country. (STEPHEN SEGO)

ALBANIA

Area: 28,748 sq km (11,100 sq mi)
Population (2000 est.): 3,490,000 (not including about 650,000 Albanians living abroad)
Capital: Tirana
Chief of state: President Rexhep Meidani
Head of government: Prime Minister Ilir Meta

Albania's political life in 2000 was dominated by the rivalry between the governing Alliance for the State coalition, led by the Socialist Party, and the opposition, dominated by the Democratic Party of former president Sali Berisha. Throughout the year the opposition focused attention on rallying support for its candidates in local elections on October 1 and 15. They accused the Alliance for the State of corruption and smuggling, charges that the coalition dismissed. The Alliance, for its part, highlighted its efforts to combat corruption through institutional reforms. The most significant success in administrative reform had come with the passage of a new law on the civil service on Nov. 11, 1999, designed to stop the practice of political appointments and to increase the independence and integrity of career civil servants. Implementation of the law and the creation of a workable institutional framework occupied much of the year.

In addition to its reform efforts, the government could point to a significant increase in infrastructure development in Albania, most notably those projects that were financed within the Stability Pact for South Eastern Europe, the 28-nation agreement signed in 1999 to restore peace, stability, and prosperity to the region. Under the "quick start" package launched in March, Albania received about €112 million (about $109 million) for the rehabilitation of roads, railroads, harbours, power and water lines, and the airport in Tirana, the capital. The Stability Pact earmarked an additional €320 million (about $311 million) for near-term infrastructure projects to be implemented.

In municipal elections held in October, the Socialist Party won in 50 municipalities and 218 communities, whereas the Democrats won only in 80 municipalities and 11 communities after calling for a partial boycott of the vote in the runoff. Two municipalities and 17 communities went to smaller parties and independent candidates.

The Stability Pact also dominated Albania's foreign-policy agenda. Numerous projects designed to enhance cooperation between Albania and other southeastern European countries in the fields of human rights, democracy, and security were launched. Pres. Rexhep Meidani traveled to Kosovo on May 24, the first visit ever by an Albanian head of state to that heavily ethnic Albanian-populated province in Yugoslavia. Meidani emphasized Albania's commitment to the creation of "a Europe of the regions" (that is, rather than a continent based on traditional nation-states) and spoke against the desirability of creating a "Greater Albania" that would include ethnic Albanians in neighbouring countries, while stressing the need for closer regional and European integration.

Following the election in October of Vojislav Kostunica as president of Yugoslavia, Albanian Foreign Minister Paskal Milo made the resumption of regular bilateral relations dependent on Serbia freeing Kosovo Albanian prisoners and recognizing its responsibility for crimes against humanity in the Kosovo war.

(FABIAN SCHMIDT)

ALGERIA

Area: 2,381,741 sq km (919,595 sq mi)
Population (2000 est.): 30,554,000
Capital: Algiers
Chief of state: President Abdelaziz Bouteflika
Head of government: Prime Ministers Ahmed Benbitour and, from August 27, Ali Benflis

The year 2000 opened on a high note for Algerian Pres. Abdelaziz Bouteflika as the 600-strong Army of Islamic Salvation and an additional 1,500 militants from other clandestine Islamic groups surrendered under a six-month partial amnesty that ended on January 13. The eight-year-long struggle between the Algerian army and the clandestine Islamist opposition—which had begun after legislative elections were aborted in January 1992 to prevent a victory by the Islamic Salvation Front (FIS)—appeared to be over. Within six months, however, the violence again escalated around the capital. Two groups—the remnants of the Armed Islamic Group and a new group, the Groupe Salafiyyiste de Dawa et Djihad—continued to attract supporters.

President Bouteflika had other troubles too. He lost key army support after relations with Morocco worsened (see *Morocco*, below), and he was roundly attacked in the press by leading army generals. Bouteflika's attempt to restructure the army command in February resulted only in the removal of his predecessor's supporters in charge of the police and coastal defense. The government that he had appointed in December 1999 collapsed in August, and former prime minister Ahmed Benbitour accused Bouteflika of contravening the constitution with his controversial privatization proposals. In the new government—led by Ali Benflis—Abdelaziz Belkhadem replaced Youcef Yousfi as foreign minister, Gen. Larbi Belkhair became presidential adviser, and Gen. Mohamed Touati became presidential adviser for military affairs, appointments that emphasized the army's stranglehold on government.

Army opposition to extending the amnesty blocked Bouteflika's plans for a general amnesty during the year. Governmental opposition to reconciliation with the remnants of the FIS was underlined by Interior Minister Yazid Zerhouni's refusal in May to allow the registration of a new political party that would be led by veteran politician and alleged FIS sympathizer Taleb Ibrahimi.

Bouteflika's domestic problems were eased slightly by his official visit to France in June, only the second by an Algerian president since 1962. He met with Pres. Jacques Chirac, addressed the French National Assembly, and obtained a $60 million debt-swap arrangement and the promise of cooperation on defense issues. In July Prime Minister José María Aznar López of Spain made an official visit to Algeria—the first ever by a Spanish leader.

The rise in world oil prices increased budgetary revenues by 16%. Early in the year foreign debt dropped by 7% to $28,310,000,000. Unemployment, however, continued to rise; it stood at 2.6 million at the end of 1998 and was expected to reach 4 million by the end of 2000 as privatization programs began to exact an impact. Inadequate rainfall also meant that Algeria's heavy dependence on imported food continued;

UN High Commissioner for Refugees Sadako Ogata (left) listens to the remarks of Albanian Pres. Rexhep Meidani (right) during a panel discussion on the crisis in Kosovo.

Alessandro Della Valle/AFP Worldwide

AP/Wide World Photos

Algerian Pres. Abdelaziz Bouteflika (left) shakes hands with French Prime Minister Lionel Jospin before their meeting in Paris on June 15.

two-thirds of the demand for cereal was met through imports.

Following the December 30 parliamentary or Council of the Nation by-elections, the National Democratic Rally of former Algerian president Liamine Zeroual kept its majority in the Council by winning 36 of the 48 contested seats and securing a total of 76 seats. The National Liberation Front obtained 13 seats, the Socialist Forces Front gained 4 seats, and the Movement for a Peaceful Society captured 3 seats. (GEORGE JOFFÉ)

ANDORRA

Area: 468 sq km (181 sq mi)
Population (2000 est.): 66,700
Capital: Andorra la Vella
Chiefs of state: Co-princes of Andorra, the president of France and the bishop of Urgell, Spain
Head of government: Chief Executive Marc Forné Molné

Andorra, which had historically been a haven for smugglers, especially traffickers in illegal cigarettes, came under scrutiny during the year. In 2000 concern about smuggling prompted a crackdown by the antifraud office of the European Union (EU), during which the possibility of bringing suit against several American cigarette manufacturers was raised. In order to circumvent tax dodgers, the EU proposed a plan to withhold taxes up front from interest paid into nonresidents' bank accounts and to do away with banking secrecy laws in Andorra, Switzerland, and other countries. Other, more recent types of crime were also shadowing the valleys of the Pyrenees. In February a network of money launderers for a Colombian drug cartel selling cocaine in Great Britain and Spain was broken up by Spanish police; some of the laundered money was found in banks in Andorra.

The World Health Organization (WHO) announced in June that Andorra ranked 10th in the world in the number of years (72.3) a person could be expected to live in full health. Japan was the healthiest country, with an expected 74.5 years of good health, while Sierra Leone, at 25.9 years, was at the bottom of the list. In WHO's study of the world's health care systems, Andorra ranked fourth.

(ANNE ROBY)

ANGOLA

Area: 1,246,700 sq km (481,354 sq mi)
Population (2000 est.): 10,145,000 (excluding more than 300,000 refugees in the Democratic Republic of the Congo and Zambia)
Capital: Luanda
Chief of state and head of government: President José Eduardo dos Santos

Government forces engaged in combat with National Union for the Total Independence of Angola (UNITA) rebels began 2000 in a strong position, having recently captured the rebel headquarters at Jamba, near the Namibian border, and having forced their opponents into remote, sparsely populated parts of the country. Namibia also became involved in the fighting on behalf of the government, though not without opposition from human rights campaigners in that country and protests from South Africa, which was concerned by the prospect of instability creeping nearer its borders. Early government successes in the campaign were followed by a UNITA counteroffensive in March. Government forces responded with vigorous ground and air attacks, which gave rise to protests from Zambia that its borders had been violated.

The government also struck at UNITA's lifeline, the illicit sale of diamonds, by a January 31 decree that declared that all diamond transactions had to be made through a new state-controlled company, Ascorp. The difficulty of making this control effective was highlighted by a UN report, published on March 13, that criticized seven African countries, together with Belgium and Bulgaria, for breaking sanctions imposed on UNITA. (*See* Sidebar.)

An increase of 1,600% in the price of motor fuel was announced in February and resulted in an immediate rise in the cost of food and public transportation; the cost increases led to an unprecedented demonstration in Luanda on March 11. On April 5, however, the government announced that it had signed

Diamonds: Fuel for Conflict

In 1998 the UN Security Council imposed an embargo on diamonds from areas held by the National Union for the Total Independence of Angola (UNITA). A Council report in March 2000 claimed, however, that significant numbers of UNITA diamonds continued to reach world markets. The report implicated De Beers Consolidated Mines, Ltd., the Anglo–South Africa company that controlled about 60% of the global trade in rough diamonds. The report also criticized the world's largest diamond market, in Antwerp, Belg., for not verifying the origin of the diamonds traded there. In the Angola conflict, which originated during the Cold War, the government funded its military with oil revenues, whereas UNITA resorted to diamonds.

Diamonds also fueled the fighting in the Democratic Republic of the Congo. That conflict continued the 19th-century scramble for Africa, but with African nations now trying to control Congo's vast natural resources. Lucrative diamond concessions were given to companies tied to Zimbabwean military officers, including close associates of Zimbabwe Pres. Robert Mugabe. Zimbabwe was the strongest backer of Congo Pres. Laurent Kabila, who was also thought to have personally benefited from diamond deals. Both Uganda and Rwanda, the main supporters of Congo's anti-Kabila rebels, purportedly profited from diamond mines under rebel control.

More than those conflicts, however, the war in Sierra Leone directed world attention to the destructive role of diamonds. Following the collapse of a fragile peace in May, the Revolutionary United Front (RUF) renewed its battle against the government of Pres. Ahmad Tejan Kabbah. Investigations by the UN and other organizations revealed a network that brought weapons, chiefly from Bulgaria and Ukraine, into Sierra Leone. Often transactions involved the direct exchange of diamonds for arms. Investigators also presented evidence that stones from RUF areas reached diamond-cutting centres in Belgium and Israel. In July the UN Security Council banned the trading of all diamonds from RUF Sierra Leone. Credible allegations emerged that RUF diamonds and weapons passed through Liberia with the cooperation of Liberian Pres. Charles Taylor, a close associate of RUF leader Foday Sankoh. Such transshipments made the UN embargo virtually impossible to enforce.

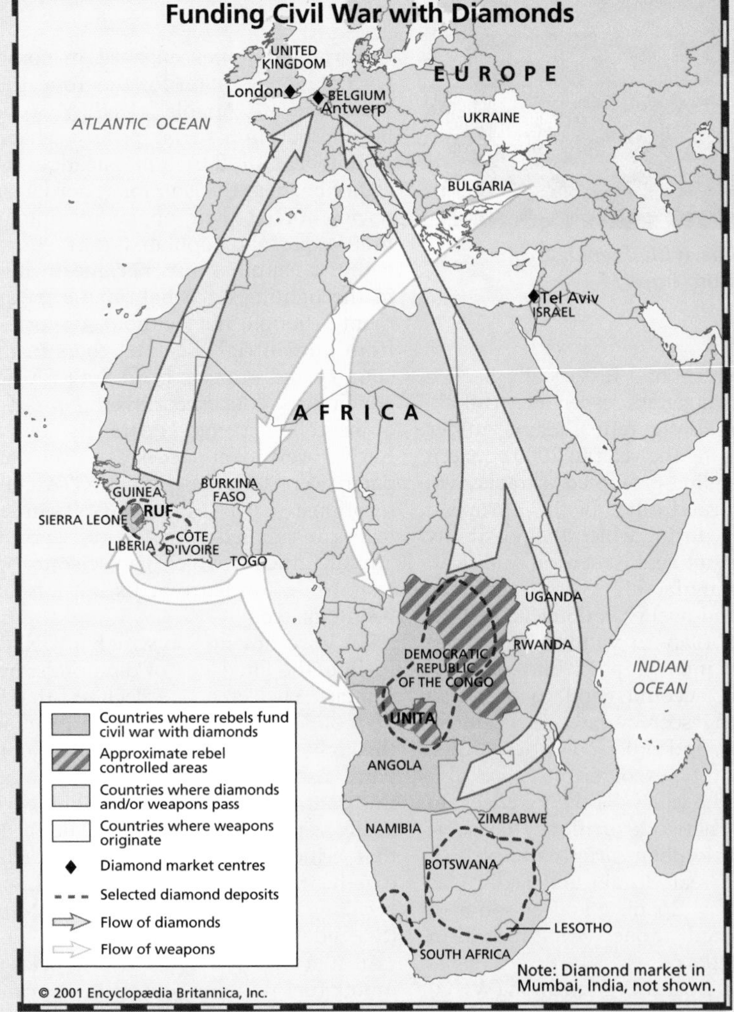

The diamond industry feared that public revulsion against so-called blood diamonds would lead to a general boycott of the gems. De Beers pledged in July that it would buy no diamonds from rebel groups. Despite those efforts, considerable difficulties remained. Once a diamond was polished, for example, there was no way to identify its origin definitively. Also, corruption in many diamond-producing countries allowed smugglers to launder embargoed stones through legitimate channels.

(MATTHEW A. CENZER)

V. Lohuizen/ROPI

Workers labour at a diamond mine in Sierra Leone.

a nine-month economic monitoring agreement with the International Monetary Fund, which, it was hoped, would prepare the way for an IMF loan by the end of the year. The implementation of the agreement was, however, fraught with problems. In spite of greatly enhanced revenues from the sale of oil, due both to increased output and to the rise in world prices, the Angolan people in general saw little improvement in their standard of living. While a handful of leading figures enjoyed considerable wealth, the majority of the population continued to live in poverty, and vested interests did all in their power to block reforms.

In August, in an attempt to improve the situation, the National Assembly supported a government proposal to increase public spending, but the finance minister, Joachim David, felt compelled to point out that, with such a high proportion of the country's revenue committed to the war against UNITA, the economy was in a grave condition. Inflation continued to rise, and the IMF thought it necessary to urge the government to make greater efforts to carry out the reforms called for in the agreement. (KENNETH INGHAM)

ANTIGUA AND BARBUDA

Area: 442 sq km (171 sq mi)
Population (2000 est.): 71,000 (including evacuees from Montserrat)
Capital: Saint John's
Chief of state: Queen Elizabeth II, represented by Governor-General James Carlisle
Head of government: Prime Minister Lester Bird

In 2000 Antigua and Barbuda became, in the words of its prime minister, Lester Bird, "a more reliable partner" in the battle against money laundering and drug trafficking in the Caribbean by updating parts of its anti-money-laundering legislation during the early months of the year. This was followed in April by the signing of a letter of commitment to minimum regulatory standards as approved by the United Nations Offshore Forum.

Despite these initiatives, however, Antigua and Barbuda did not escape being included in the Organisation for Economic Co-operation and Development's blacklist, issued in June, of 15 Caribbean countries allegedly operating "harmful tax regimes." This unflattering categorization incensed the government. Local businessmen, for their part, were upset with John St. Luce, the finance minister, for introducing a 2% turnover tax in his budget in March. The tourism industry was most concerned, claiming that the tax would make Antigua and Barbuda an even more expensive destination than it already was. (DAVID RENWICK)

ARGENTINA

Area: 2,780,092 sq km (1,073,400 sq mi)
Population (2000 est.): 37,032,000
Capital: Buenos Aires
Head of state: President Fernando de la Rúa, assisted by Ministerial Coordinator Chrystian Colombo

On Dec. 10, 1999, Fernando de la Rúa assumed office as president of Argentina, marking the end of Carlos Saúl Menem's 10-year tenure. The Alliance (composed of de la Rúa's Radical Civic Union [UCR], the Front for a Country in Solidarity [Frepaso], and several smaller parties) held a plurality of the seats in the Chamber of Deputies but remained a minority in the Senate, where Menem's Justicialist Party (PJ; also known as the Peronist Party) continued to hold an absolute majority.

The de la Rúa administration inherited a larger-than-expected fiscal deficit as well as a country immersed in a nearly year-and-a-half-long recession. The government's first major policy initiative was a significant tax increase in late December 1999, which, among other things, raised the sales tax on selected consumer goods and services—for example, soft drinks, mineral water, champagne, cellular phone calls, new cars, interurban bus transport—and increased the income tax rate for the wealthiest segment of the population. For example, while those workers earning $2,000 or less a month were unaffected by the tax hike, those earning $3,500 a month suffered a nearly 200% increase.

The only noteworthy electoral contest in 2000 was the May 7 mayoral election in Buenos Aires. In this election the Alliance's Aníbal Ibarra (Frepaso) handily defeated Domingo Cavallo, the candidate supported by Cavallo's Action for the Republic, Gustavo Beliz's New Leadership, and a large number of Peronists. Ibarra garnered 49% of the vote to Cavallo's 33%, and Cavallo withdrew from a scheduled runoff election. The Alliance's share of seats in the Buenos Aires legislature fell, however, from 62% to 40%.

Fabian Gredillas/AFP Worldwide

Angry over Argentina's rising unemployment rate, members of the Headquarters of Argentine Workers march in the city of Rosario in July.

On May 11 the de la Rúa administration obtained the passage of an important labour law reform designed to reduce the costs associated with hiring (and firing) workers in Argentina. In August this legislative victory came back to haunt the government as allegations emerged that senior government officials had bribed several PJ and UCR senators to obtain the law's passage.

At the end of May, under increasing fiscal pressure, the de la Rúa government announced an important budget cut consisting primarily of a 12% salary reduction for national government public employees earning a monthly salary between $1,000 and $6,500 (15% for those earning above $6,500). The legislation also included other measures such as voluntary early retirement for national public employees and the reduction of some specific federal pensions; because of legal complications as well as political pressure, most of the pension reductions were not carried out. In December the International Monetary Fund announced that it would assist Argentina in reducing its rising debt burden by promising an aid package of up to $39.7 billion.

The months of August, September, and October brought additional bad news for the government as the May unemployment figures were released, the government and independent economists revised their economic growth projections for 2000, and the vice president resigned. The unemployment rate in May was 15.4%, up from 13.8% in October 1999 and 14.5% in May 1999. At the same time, the country had yet to emerge from its recession, with estimates of the 2000 gross domestic product growth rate falling from a January high of 4% to between 0.5% and 1% in October. The projected annual inflation rate was –1%. In October Vice President Carlos ("Chacho") Alvarez, a Frepaso leader, abruptly resigned due in part to disagreements with the direction of the de la Rúa government. In a national poll conducted by MORI Argentina in September, 43% of those surveyed considered unemployment to be the number one problem facing the country, followed by corruption (29%), the recession (9%), education (9%), and crime (3%).

Argentina continued to have disagreements with Brazil related to auto production within the Southern Cone Common Market (Mercosur) as well as over the import/export of specific agricultural products such as chicken and sugar. Argentina's dispute with the U.S. over pharmaceutical patents was sent to the World Trade Organization and thus was not a subject of bilateral discussion for most of the year. In June President de la Rúa made an official visit to the U.S., where he met with Pres. Bill Clinton. In July a new U.S. ambassador finally arrived in Argentina; the office had been vacant since December 1996, much to the dismay of most Argentine officials.

Despite the fact that the 2003 presidential election was more than three years away, by mid-2000 the most prominent PJ candidates (José Manuel de la Sota, governor of Córdoba; Carlos Reutemann, governor of Santa Fe; and Carlos Ruckauf, governor of Buenos Aires) were already jockeying for position within the party and among the electorate. Although none of the three had attained status as the favourite, de la Sota benefited from the success thus far of his innovative economic program in Córdoba, while Ruckauf enjoyed a very positive public image as well as governed the country's largest province.

(MARK P. JONES)

ARMENIA

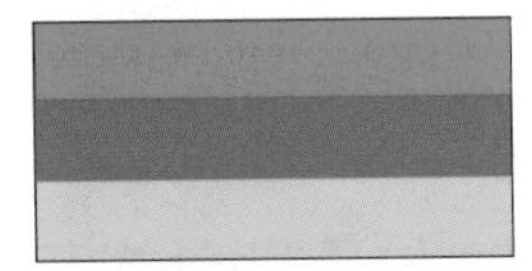

Area: 29,743 sq km (11,484 sq mi). Some 12–15% of neighbouring Azerbaijan (including the 4,400-sq km [1,700-sq mi] disputed region of Nagorno-Karabakh [Armenian: Artsakh]) has been under Armenian control since 1993.
Population (2000 est.): officially 3,810,000; actually about 3,000,000 (plus 150,000 in Nagorno-Karabakh)
Capital: Yerevan
Chief of state: President Robert Kocharyan
Head of government: Prime Ministers Aram Sarkisyan and, from May 12, Andranik Markaryan

The suspicion and mutual hostility generated by the shootings in the National Assembly on Oct. 27, 1999, poisoned relations between Armenian Pres. Robert Kocharyan and the government of Aram Sarkisyan during the early months of 2000. In late February Sarkisyan reshuffled his cabinet and thereby secured the cooperation of opposition parties represented in the National Assembly. Mutual recriminations over the investigation into the killing continued until Kocharyan finally fired Sarkisyan in May and appointed as his successor Andranik Markaryan, leader of the Republican Party of Armenia parliament faction, the senior partner within Miasnutiun.

That appointment alienated the Republican Party's coalition partner, the People's Party of Armenia, whose chairman, Stepan Demirchyan, repeatedly rejected Markaryan's demand that the People's Party accept shared responsibility for implementing the government's program. Demirchyan met with the head of the National Unity Party, Artashes Geghamyan, in August but failed to reach an agreement on possible cooperation. Geghamyan called repeatedly for the resignation of Markaryan's cabinet and pre-term elections.

In late September, on the initiative of the Republican Party, the National Assembly narrowly voted for the removal as its speaker of People's Party member Armen Khachatryan, thereby further exacerbating tensions between the Republican and People's parties. The case was referred to the Constitutional Court, however, which ruled that the vote was invalid and reinstated Khachatryan.

Kocharyan traveled to France in October for a previously unannounced medical examination, after which his staff denied that the 46-year-old president was suffering from a heart ailment.

Ties with Russia remained central to Armenia's foreign policy. Serzh Sarkisyan, who was named defense minister in Markaryan's cabinet, made a high-profile visit to Moscow in June, which engendered speculation that Kocharyan intended to appoint him prime minister in place of Markaryan. In September, Kocharyan and Russian Pres. Vladimir Putin signed a declaration on cooperation in the 21st century. The Council of Europe, of which Armenia had been a guest member since 1996, voted in June to accept Armenia into full membership.

(ELIZABETH FULLER)

AUSTRALIA

Area: 7,692,030 sq km (2,969,910 sq mi)
Population (2000 est.): 19,165,000
Capital: Canberra
Chief of state: Queen Elizabeth II, represented by Governor-General Sir William Deane
Head of government: Prime Minister John Howard

Domestic Affairs. In September 2000 Australia staged its second Olympic Games of the modern era (and its first since Melbourne played host in 1956) in Sydney. In the Olympic torch relay, which preceded the Games for several weeks, the Olympic flame was carried around Australia from Uluru to Sydney, even spending three minutes underwater along the Great Barrier Reef. The heroic images of runner Cathy Freeman holding aloft the Olympic flame and the overwhelming success of Australian athletes at the Games blotted out the initial public disappointment with the performance of the Australian members of the International Olympic Committee and the administrative skills of those responsible for organizing the Games.

Despite Prime Minister John Howard's attempts to implement what he called "practical reconciliation" in the face of expected Aboriginal protests during the 2000 Olympics, Aboriginal issues often took centre stage throughout the year. In the lead-up to the Games, several events signaled the importance of Aboriginal questions in the minds of Australians. In May a "walk for reconciliation" across Sydney Harbour Bridge was overwhelmingly successful in demonstrating a groundswell of support for an apology to Aboriginals for past injustices. The scheduled events, however, emphasized the irreconcilable differences between Aboriginals and Howard, who refused to walk across the bridge or to issue the desired apology. On the eve of the Olympics, Aboriginal activist Charles Perkins, the commissioner for sport for the Aboriginal and Torres Strait Islander Commission, promised that there would be large Aboriginal protests during the Games. Freeman, a gold medal winner and Australia's most high-profile Aboriginal Olympic athlete, added fuel to the fire by complaining in the London press before the Games that the federal government had been insensitive in its treatment of "the stolen generation," the name given to the numerous Aboriginal children taken from their parents and forcibly assimilated as recently as the 1960s. In the event, the Olympics were a huge success, serious protests failed to materialize, and the popular support for Freeman signaled a possible easing of racial tensions. Less than three weeks after the Olympics Perkins died and was accorded a state funeral, including an official wake at the Sydney Opera House. (*See* OBITUARIES.)

The Games did have the effect of diverting criticism away from the government's handling of illegal immigrants. A small group, mostly from Afghanistan and Iraq, proved a continual headache for Immigration Minister Philip Ruddock. In June about 500 illegal immigrants escaped from the Woomera detention centre in South Australia, made their way to the town centre, and chanted that the conditions in the detention centre and the delays in processing their applications for temporary asylum were unacceptable. Ruddock released videos to Australian embassies for distribution overseas. The videos showed shark attacks, snakes, and crocodiles. Ruddock defended the video, commenting, "If you come in a boat and land at Cape York and think you're going to land in a place which is hospitable, you may well find that you could be taken by a crocodile!" In August about 80 illegal immigrants held at the Woomera Centre rioted. They destroyed buildings, and water cannons and tear gas were used to stop the turmoil.

The Economy. In 2000 the Australian economy continued to improve despite record high prices for fuel and a very weak currency. The *Australian* newspaper commented that the weakness of the Australian dollar in spite of a strong domestic economy was "baffling." There was strong economic growth; inflation remained low; and unemployment became less of a problem for policy makers. The trend line in unemployment as measured by the Australian Bureau of Statistics midyear was 6.5%. A similar trend line for gross domestic product ran at 4.4%, while inflation in June stood at 3.2%.

In May Treasurer Peter Costello introduced a national budget for the coming year that was based on a surplus of $A 2.8 billion ($A 1=about U.S. $0.58 in midyear 2000). The surplus, which was derived from the expected sale of mobile phone airspace, allowed Costello to drop the $A 900 million Timor Tax even before it was implemented. The Timor Tax was due to be paid by Australians earning $A 50,000 or more to defray the $A 1 billion cost of Australia's military commitment to East Timor. Funding to indigenous Australians was increased to a record $A 2.3 billion to be spent on health care, housing, education, and unemployment compensation. The government also prepared for possible legal liabilities over native title claims for damages. The government spent a modest $A 52.1 million to build detention centres for illegal immigrants and spent more for added immigration officers in the Middle East and Asia. It decided to tackle the problem of Afghan and Iraqi refugees by providing resettlement funds to allow people to remain in key transit countries en route to Australia.

The major change to the Australian economy was the introduction of a goods and services tax (GST) on July 1. Set at 10% and not applied to certain foods, the GST was offset by the abolition of a range of wholesale sales taxes. In the months leading up to the introduction of the new tax, public opinion turned against the government. Amendments to the legislation resulted in exemptions being given to particular groups and interests. Unperturbed, Howard declared that the new tax was good for Australia and fundamentally fair. Pre-GST activity saw what was called "a frenzy of spending," particularly in the construction industry.

Farmers in the state of New South Wales bemoaned the wettest November on record, as their fields were inundated with muddy floodwaters from 13 rivers that had burst their banks. Also washed away in the floodwaters were livestock and the hopes of farmers who had battled five years of agricultural woes, including droughts, floods, crop disease, and low prices. The estimated damage to crops was $A 500 million. Associated rural businesses that depended on farmers for their livelihoods also suffered losses.

Foreign Affairs. Regional instability caused major problems for Australian foreign-policy makers. The financial cost of deployment in East Timor led to caution about possible involvement in expensive military operations when Fiji and the Solomon Islands suffered breakdowns of law and order. In a wide-ranging reassessment of Australia's global strategic position, the government decided to spend more on defense. During July and August there were 28 public meetings, at which taxpayers were invited to present their views on plans to reequip the aging fleet of F-111 bombers and F/A-18 fighter aircraft and to outfit future warships to replace guided-missile frigates due to end their useful life in 2013.

Normalization of relations with India was extended following Howard's visit to that country in July. During a meeting with Indian Prime Minister Atal Bihari Vajpayee, Howard noted that Australia

AP/Wide World Photos

Australian Aboriginal sprinter Cathy Freeman displays the torch she used to light the Olympic flame during the opening ceremony of the Summer Olympics in Sydney, Australia, on September 15.

and India both shared concern about the Fiji crisis and the arbitrary removal of Fijian Prime Minister Mahendra Chaudhry from office. Howard also agreed to resume defense cooperation with India and to exchange defense attachés, withdrawn in the aftermath of India's 1998 nuclear tests.

Stressing his commitment to the monarchy and Australian loyalty to the British crown, Howard visited the U.K. in July on a trip to celebrate the centenary of the British government's decision to grant the Australian colonies the right to amalgamate to form the federated Commonwealth of Australia. Accompanied by four former Australian prime ministers, Howard received considerable criticism from home for wasting taxpayers' money on the journey just at the time when a new taxation system was being implemented. Matters were made worse when British Prime Minister Tony Blair in the House of Commons confused Australian soldiers with American servicemen during his speech of welcome to Howard.

Australia reacted defensively against criticism from the UN human rights committees. The government took a tough response to the UN, saying that unless it desisted from its unwarranted comments on Australia, Canberra would consider cutting ties with the whole UN treaty committee system. The government's stand was supported by Denis Burke, the Northern Territory chief minister, who had been in the firing line because of the Northern Territory's mandatory sentencing regime.

(A.R.G. GRIFFITHS)

AUSTRIA

Area: 83,858 sq km (32,378 sq mi)
Population (2000 est.): 8,091,000
Capital: Vienna
Chief of state: President Thomas Klestil
Head of government: Chancellors Viktor Klima and, from February 4, Wolfgang Schüssel

In its post-World War II history, Austria had rarely had such an eventful year as 2000. Following the inconclusive general election in October 1999, negotiations between the centre-left and centre-right coalition partners dragged on into early 2000. Contrary to expectations, the two parties, which had been in power since 1986, failed to renew their partnership.

Talks finally broke down in late January, and the conservative Austrian

People's Party (ÖVP) quickly agreed to enter into coalition with the populist right-wing Freedom Party (FPÖ). The participation in government of the FPÖ, and especially of party leader Jörg Haider, provoked an unexpectedly strong reaction at home and abroad. Domestically, the ÖVP's erstwhile partner, the Social Democratic Party of Austria (SPÖ), and others reacted angrily to the inclusion in government of the FPÖ, which had been considered too extremist to participate. Frequent outbursts by FPÖ members expressing anti-immigrant sentiments and lightly veiled admiration of Nazism gained the party notoriety in Europe and beyond.

Widespread street demonstrations ensued. Although these protests were peaceful and dwindled within weeks, they heralded the beginnings of a more adversarial style of politics in Austria, with the new right-leaning coalition set against the centre-left SPÖ and the Green Party.

International opprobrium was heaped upon the new government, and concerns for the civil and political liberties of some groups in Austrian society were voiced. A number of European governments seemed to fear that right-wing populists in their own countries would get a boost from the successes of the FPÖ. This possibility in part underlay the decision of Austria's 14 European Union (EU) partners to impose bilateral diplomatic sanctions. Although no action was taken by the EU itself, Austria found itself diplomatically isolated. Most Austrians, including many of those opposed to the new government, resented the sanctions; indeed, Austria's ostracism by its allies muted internal opposition to the new government as a sense of national victimhood developed. The sanctions also gave Freedom Party populists a rare chance to set the political agenda. (Since that party's entrance into the government, the more experienced ÖVP had led the way on a number of other major issues.)

While the government worked furiously abroad to have the sanctions lifted, the FPÖ pushed for a consultative referendum that would demonstrate that the citizens stood behind the government and against the sanctions. The referendum was canceled, however, after the sanctions were lifted on September 12. A report by an international team of experts had found that Austria was not guilty of mistreating its minorities or anyone else.

In the coming months, domestic politics normalized, and the more mundane issues of budget cuts and industrial relations came to the fore. Although Austria's position on the EU had not officially changed, the sanctions episode left a bad taste, and the country seemed likely to take a more cautious, less enthusiastic view toward future cooperation with some of its EU partners. By December disenchantment with EU membership prompted 100,000 Austrians to sign a petition that called for a referendum on whether Austria should quit the EU.

The turmoil in the spring and summer had no discernible effect on Austria's booming economy. With their gross domestic product expanding by an estimated 3.3%, its strongest performance in years, Austrians enjoyed a rosy combination of low unemployment, rapidly growing exports, and relatively subdued inflation. On almost any scale, Austria was one of the best-performing economies in the EU in 2000. Predictably, economic policy shifted to the right as the new government found its stride, although the changes were hardly radical. Committing to balancing the budget by 2002—a year earlier than anticipated, promising pension and welfare reform, and pledging less state involvement in various sectors of the economy, the new government shook up Austria in more ways than one. (DAN O'BRIEN)

AZERBAIJAN

Area: 86,600 sq km (33,400 sq mi), including the 5,500-sq km (2,100-sq mi) exclave of Nakhichevan and the 4,400-sq km (1,700-sq mi) disputed region (with Armenia) of Nagorno-Karabakh
Population (2000 est.): 8,051,000
Capital: Baku
Head of state and government: President Heydar Aliyev, assisted by Prime Minister Artur Rasizade

Politics in Azerbaijan in 2000 centred on the November 5 parliamentary elections. Talks in the spring between the government, opposition parties, and the Office for Democratic Institutions and Human Rights of the Organization for Security and Cooperation in Europe (OSCE) resulted in amendments that rendered the draft election legislation more democratic but preserved the authorities' control over electoral commissions at all levels.

The opposition showed less cohesion than it had during the presidential election campaign of 1998. Former president Abulfaz Elchibey's death of cancer in August (*see* OBITUARIES) precipitated the split of his Azerbaijan Popular Front Party into two factions, and differences between them led to the collapse in October of the 10-party opposition Democratic Congress.

An abortive aircraft hijacking in August served as the pretext for the arrest of Rauf Arifoglu, editor of the opposition Musavat party's newspaper; he was released on bail six weeks later. Musavat and seven other opposition parties were initially refused registration to contend the parliamentary ballot, but in early October, under pressure from the U.S. government, Pres. Heydar Aliyev ordered that ban lifted. The poll was nonetheless marred by numerous violations, and candidates from the ruling Yeni Azerbaycan party or independents loyal to the authorities won over 100 of the 125 mandates. Contrary to expectations, however, President Aliyev's son Ilham was not elected speaker of the new legislature. Almost all opposition candidates who won election decided to boycott the new legislature, and the opposition convened demonstrations in Baku and several other cities on November 18 to protest the falsification and demand repeat elections. The Council of Europe would review its June decision to accept Azerbaijan into full membership after repeat elections were held in 11 constituencies on Jan. 7, 2001.

Neither five meetings between Aliyev and his Armenian counterpart, Robert Kocharyan, nor continuing mediation by the OSCE's Minsk Group yielded progress toward resolving the Karabakh conflict. The unrecognized enclave's president, Arkady Gukasyan, was severely injured in an assassination attempt in March. Throughout the year Azerbaijan repeatedly signaled its desire to improve relations with Moscow, agreeing to increase the amount of Azerbaijani oil exported via Russia.

The failing health of 77-year-old Pres. Heydar Aliyev, who underwent cataract surgery in the U.S. in February and whose return to an American clinic in September provoked rumours of his death, remained a concern.

(ELIZABETH FULLER)

BAHAMAS, THE

Area: 13,939 sq km (5,382 sq mi)
Population (2000 est.): 295,000
Capital: Nassau
Chief of state: Queen Elizabeth II, represented by Governor-General Orville Turnquest
Head of government: Prime Minister Hubert Ingraham

The highly successful offshore financial sector of The Bahamas was rocked to its foundations twice in June 2000, once when the Paris-based Organisation for Economic Co-operation and Development (OECD) included the country in a list of world centres practicing so-called harmful tax competition and also when the Financial Action Task Force, an arm of the OECD, accused it, along with other countries, of not taking sufficient action against money launderers.

The Free National Movement government of Prime Minister Hubert Ingraham was galvanized into unexpected action by these accusations and announced to stunned bankers that it would substantially relax its traditional secrecy laws to permit The Bahamas to cooperate with other jurisdictions in identifying funds that were the fruit of criminal activity, such as drug trafficking. Such secrecy had been maintained for decades and had facilitated the country's emergence as one of the world's leading offshore financial havens. Ingraham also said that The Bahamas would enter into a Tax Information Exchange Agreement with the U.S., something that Washington had been pressing it to do for some time.

Former prime minister Sir Lynden Pindling died in August. (See OBITUARIES.)

(DAVID RENWICK)

BAHRAIN

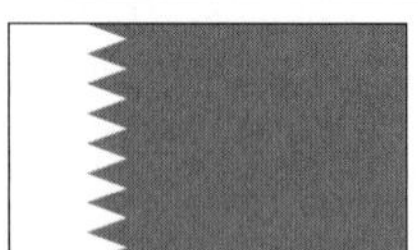

Area: 694 sq km (268 sq mi)
Population (2000 est.): 691,000
Capital: Manama
Chief of state: Emir Hamad ibn Isa al-Khalifah
Head of government: Prime Minister Khalifah ibn Sulman al-Khalifah

In an attempt to decrease tensions between the government and the opposition, Emir Hamad ibn Isa al-Khalifah announced on Dec. 16, 1999, some steps toward reform. He promised to revive the Municipal Council and to give not only Bahraini men but also women the right to vote for its members. He also assured Bahrainis of a freer press and agreed to grant Bahraini nationality to anyone "qualified" to obtain it. In February 2000 Bahraini citizenship was granted to some 650 of the over 20,000 stateless people living in Bahrain, most of them Shi'ite Muslims of Iranian origin. In the spring the Bahrain government also promised to conduct an election for the Consultative Council by the year 2004; all existing Council members had been appointed by the emir.

The ongoing border dispute between Bahrain and Qatar over the Hawar Islands—which were believed to have rich reserves of natural gas—had been sent in 1991 to the International Court of Justice in The Hague; in late June the court began its final deliberations on the matter. Despite the border dispute, both Bahrain and Qatar worked to improve relations, and at the beginning of 2000 the two countries agreed to establish full diplomatic relations and exchange ambassadors for the first time in history. The two countries formed a bilateral committee, headed by the crown prince of each country, to consolidate their relationship.

(LOUAY BAHRY)

BANGLADESH

Area: 147,570 sq km (56,977 sq mi)
Population (2000 est.): 129,194,000
Capital: Dhaka
Chief of state: President Shahabuddin Ahmed
Head of government: Prime Minister Sheikh Hasina Wajed

The stalemate in politics that prevailed in Bangladesh in 1999 continued in 2000. The opposition made a brief appearance at one session of Parliament in a move to save its membership, which, under the constitution, would be nullified after a continued unexplained absence of 90 days. If anything, the relationship between the government and the opposition worsened; the latter was subjected to increased police and legal action as well as to frequent personal attacks, which became sharper and cruder.

In February the controversial Public Safety Act (PSA), which gave an already powerful police force the power to make discretionary arrests, came into effect. The positive feature of the PSA was that cases would be tried and settled within a three-to-four-month time frame, compared with taking years in ordinary courts. The most dangerous feature of the PSA—later dropped—was that those awaiting trial would be held in prison without bail. Under tremendous public opposition, media criticism, and behind-the-scenes pressure from Pres. Shahabuddin Ahmed, the government slightly softened the PSA a few months after passing it into law. By year's end, however, the PSA had made no visible impact on the rising crime rate. The most embarrassing factor was the direct involvement in criminal activities by some ruling-party stalwarts and some district-level leaders who became Mafia-style dons of several district towns.

The most positive diplomatic development of the year was the first-ever visit by a U.S. president to Bangladesh. In March Pres. Bill Clinton arrived for a day trip in the first leg of his South Asia tour. U.S.-Bangladesh relations were further strengthened in October when Prime Minister Sheikh Hasina Wajed visited the U.S.

In a landmark decision the Parliamentary Standing Committee on the Ministry of Defense recommended the revocation of the 1981 court-martial judgment against 37 army officers, 13 of whom had been hanged. They were convicted of the assassination of then president Ziaur Rahman, founder of the Bangladesh Nationalist Party, which was the archrival of the ruling Awami League. The judgment was declared "illegal" and in "violation of both the constitution and Bangladesh Army Act."

The best news came from the agricultural sector. The highest-ever *aman* rice harvest (10.1 million metric tons)—followed by another record *boro* rice harvest—kept the economy afloat and helped to contain inflation around 3.8%. The economy was severely strained by a massive Tk 25 billion (51 taka=$1) revenue shortfall that increased the fiscal deficit by 5.3%. In addition, government expenditures exceeded the budgeted amount by Tk 5 billion. As a result, the government was forced to borrow from the banking system a record Tk 39,340,000,000. In

AP/Wide World Photos

At the U.S. embassy in Dhaka, Bangladesh, on March 20, Pres. Bill Clinton visits with a group of people from the village of Joypura.

August the taka was devalued by 6%, the largest devaluation since 1975. Shortly thereafter, petroleum prices rose about 15%. Direct foreign investment dropped from $308 million in 1998 to $150 million in 1999.

(MAHFUZ ANAM)

BARBADOS

Area: 430 sq km (166 sq mi)
Population (2000 est.): 267,000
Capital: Bridgetown
Chief of state: Queen Elizabeth II, represented by Governor-General Sir Clifford Husbands
Head of government: Prime Minister Owen Arthur

The House of Assembly took an important step toward modernizing Barbados's constitution—inherited in 1966 from Great Britain at the time of independence—when in May 2000 it considered recommendations made by a Constitution Review Commission chaired by former Barbados foreign minister Sir Henry Forde. The panel recommended that the country adopt a republican form of government—similar to the one in Trinidad and Tobago—with a nonexecutive president elected by the House of Assembly and the Senate and proposed the establishment of a parliamentary integrity commission that would help minimize corruption by receiving declarations of incomes, assets, and liabilities of parliamentarians.

In May the Financial Stability Forum (FSF), an offshoot of the Paris-based Organisation for Economic Co-operation and Development, placed Barbados in group two on its list of offshore centres graded according to the degree of supervision exercised by the authorities over banks and other offshore financial institutions. The group two grading meant that Barbados could improve its supervisory regime. Barbadian Prime Minister Owen Arthur condemned the FSF and insisted that it did not possess the "legal authority" to prepare any such grading system.

(DAVID RENWICK)

BELARUS

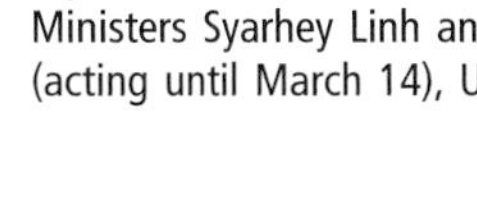

Area: 207,595 sq km (80,153 sq mi)
Population (2000 est.): 9,989,000
Capital: Minsk
Head of state and government: President Alyaksandr G. Lukashenka, assisted by Prime Ministers Syarhey Linh and, from February 18 (acting until March 14), Uladzimir Yarmoshyn

The year 2000 in Belarus was dominated by political conflict centred on the parliamentary elections of October 15. On January 31 the upper chamber, the Council of the Republic, passed a new electoral code. The opposition, using the forum of the Coordinated Council of Democratic Forces, objected

AP/Wide World Photos

With a relief of Vladimir Lenin looming in the background, a woman in Minsk, Belarus, casts her vote in the elections for the Chamber of Representatives in October.

to the acceptance of the code without debate. Further, it insisted, in line with requests from the Organization for Security and Cooperation in Europe (OSCE), that international recognition of the election results be predicated on these and other conditions: application of international electoral standards, apportioning of real authority to the existing parliament, an end to political persecution, and access by the opposition to the official media.

None of these conditions was met, and the opposition divided over whether to participate. The Liberal Democrats and the Communists opted in, while some 58 opposition figures resolved to participate in the elections on an individual basis. Of this number, however, only 17 were permitted by the electoral commission to stand. Neither the OSCE's "limited technical assessment mission," the European Union, nor the U.S. recognized the elections as democratic. Official results over two rounds indicated turnouts of 60.6% and 52%, respectively, and 97 of the 110 seats were filled by October 29.

The year was marked by attacks on the unofficial press and opposition figures. Though a Freedom March-2 took place peacefully in Minsk on March 15, conflict occurred during a demonstration 10 days later commemorating the anniversary of the founding of the Belarusian Democratic Republic in 1918. Members of the Belarusian Popular Front and about 40 journalists (including Russian TV crews) were detained and beaten. Facing international protests, Pres. Alyaksandr Lukashenka dismissed Interior Minister Yury Sivakau, replacing him with Mikhail Udovikau. A U.S. Helsinki Commission hearing in March condemned Belarus for its infringements on human rights.

Prime Minister Syarhey Linh was dismissed on February 18, and Russian-born Uladzimir Yarmoshyn was appointed to replace him. A week later Belarus and Russia signed an agreement to coordinate their foreign policy in 2000 and 2001. In April Lukashenka announced plans for a 300,000-strong joint army with Russia in the face of the eastward expansion of NATO. The Belarusian national bank also approved in February a draft agreement to develop a single currency using the Russian ruble in Belarus. In general, however, the new Russian president, Vladimir Putin, appeared reluctant to expand the current terms of the Russia-Belarus Union.

Lukashenka in April reiterated his reliance on the collective farm system despite a disastrous harvest in 1999. Severe May frosts again depleted the sown area of grain. The Belarusian Federation of Trade Unions announced in April that 47% of Belarusians were living below the official poverty line. Although gross domestic product rose by 4% (compared with 1999) in the first half of 2000, these gains were offset by an approximately 54% rise in consumer prices as well as foreign debts of $290 million (mostly owed to Russia for imports of gas). In January the exchange rate for the Belarusian rubel was fixed at the street rate (about 1,020 to the dollar), which ended the system of multiple exchange rates.

(DAVID R. MARPLES)

BELGIUM

Area: 30,528 sq km (11,787 sq mi)
Population (2000 est.): 10,249,000
Capital: Brussels
Chief of state: King Albert II
Head of government: Prime Minister Guy Verhofstadt

The six parties in Belgium's coalition government consolidated their positions in local elections in October 2000. Substantial gains were also made by Flemish ultranationalist Vlaams Blok, which polled one-third of the votes in the second city, Antwerp, and scored well in several other towns. The main losers in the elections, which were the first in which European Union resident nationals could vote, were the two Social Christian parties, the moderate Flemish nationalist Volksunie, and the extreme right-wing francophone Front National, which all but disappeared. Political parties in Flanders combined to keep the Vlaams Blok out of every municipal authority. Relations in the federal government coalition were strained when the Socialists reversed some earlier local alliances in the Brussels region, and French-speaking Liberals were robbed of a handful of mayoral posts as a result. The most prominent victim of the switch was Liberal Brussels mayor François-Xavier de Donnea, who was replaced by Freddy Thielemans, a Socialist.

Early in the year the government announced a general amnesty to legalize illegal immigrants who had resided in Belgium for six years, or five years if they had school-age children. It was overwhelmed by the response, however, when more than 50,000 took up the offer, and it was not expected to regularize their status before spring 2001.

The persona of Marc Dutroux continued to cast a shadow over Belgium. Although arrested in August 1996 and charged with the kidnapping, imprisonment, and murder of several young girls, he was unlikely to be brought to trial before 2001. In June 2000 he was given a five-year prison sentence and a BF 80,000 (BFI=about $0.02) fine for offenses he committed—assaulting a policeman, theft with violence, and threatening behaviour—when he briefly escaped custody in April 1998. Belgium's judicial system received a blow when the European Court of Human Rights ruled in June that five members of the French-speaking Socialist Party, including former defense minister Guy Coëme, had not received a fair trial when the country's highest court convicted them on corruption charges in 1996.

Belgium's corporate landscape continued to change. Interbrew, the country's leading brewer, went on an acquisition binge. In May it purchased the British company Whitbread's brewing interests for BF 27 billion, in the process adding labels such as Murphy's Irish Stout and Boddingtons to its own brands of Stella Artois and Leffe. Then, Interbrew purchased Bass Brewers, the U.K.'s second largest beer company, for BF 145 billion. The takeovers propelled the Louvain-based company from fifth to second place behind the American group Anheuser-Busch in the world brewing stakes. The year ended on a more downbeat note, however, when the European Commission accused the company, in collaboration with other Belgian brewers, of illegal anticompetitive behaviour between 1993 and 1998.

Belgium's $20 million diamond industry came under attack by the UN for doing little to curb the illegal diamond trade. Some 85% of the worldwide rough-diamond trade was conducted in Antwerp, where traders were allegedly flouting a UN embargo on so-called conflict diamonds being sold by Angolan rebels to stage their civil war. (See ANGOLA: Sidebar.)

SAirGroup, the parent company of Swissair, planned to increase its stake in Sabena, Belgium's national airline, from 49.5% to 85% in a deal that represented the first takeover of a European national airline by a foreign company. The merger forged ahead after almost 70% of the Swiss electorate voted in a referendum for closer links to the European Union. In the fall, GIB, Belgium's biggest retailer, sold its GB supermarket and hypermarket chain to France's Carrefour for €670 million (about $625 million).

The way was paved for the biggest fraud trial in Belgium's history when 10 senior officials of the Luxembourg-based KB Lux, a sister bank of the Belgian KBC, were indicted in April on charges of fiscal fraud, money laundering, falsifying documents, and belonging to a criminal organization. The alleged offenses were thought to have cost Belgium between BF 20 billion and BF 50 billion in lost taxes. (RORY WATSON)

BELIZE

Area: 22,965 sq km (8,867 sq mi)
Population (2000 est.): 253,000
Capital: Belmopan
Chief of state: Queen Elizabeth II, represented by Governor-General Colville Young
Head of government: Prime Minister Said Musa

Increased tourist arrivals boosted Belize's tourism industry by more than 27% during a six-month period in 2000. Over Bz$4.6 million ($2.3 million) were earmarked for tourism publicity and marketing. Efforts were made to promote tourism, including the renovation of the airport, but at the same time, steps were taken in the conservation and protection of Mayan archaeological sites and the barrier reef.

Military units from the Guatemalan Armed Forces and the Belize Defence Force met in July to discuss coordination of military activities and reduction of tension at border areas. In addition, a program to exchange cash for guns was spearheaded by religious institutions and the media in an effort to get guns off the street. The weapons were subsequently dismantled and destroyed in public.

In March the governing People's United Party (PUP) won all seven seats in the municipal elections. The PUP retained control of six of the nation's seven municipalities, which gave them a total of 51 seats; the opposition United Democratic Party had 5.

Prime Minister Said Musa honoured the Right Honourable George Cadle Price, a former prime minister, with Belize's highest government award. Recognized as father of the nation and architect of its independence, Price received the National Hero of Belize gold medal.

On October 2–3 Hurricane Keith battered the offshore resorts of Caye

Caulker and San Pedro on Ambergris Caye and caused damages estimated at more than $200 million. Belize City, in the north of the country, was declared a disaster area, and flash floods in the hinterland resulted in the evacuation of numerous villages. Fortunately, the tourist sector was affected only minimally.

(INES PARKER)

BENIN

Area: 114,760 sq km (44,300 sq mi)
Population (2000 est.): 6,396,000
Capital: Porto-Novo (executive and ministerial offices remain in Cotonou)
Head of state and government: President Mathieu Kérékou

As Benin marked its 40th year of independence in 2000, its beleaguered economy showed little signs of improving. Despite a slightly improved growth in gross domestic product, the impact of rampant inflation, low world prices for Benin's exports, and rapid population expansion left well over half of the country's people living below the UN poverty line. In January the World Bank approved a $30 million credit for export-diversification and income-support programs, but this did little to offset the effects of huge price increases in petroleum and other basic products.

On July 3 Benin hosted a conference in Cotonou attended by delegates from the European Union (EU), Africa, the Caribbean, and the Pacific. The event followed the June 23 signing with the EU of a new economic development agreement that replaced the Lomé Convention of 1990.

On July 13 police broke up a demonstration by 2,000 workers who attempted to march on the presidential palace to protest the steep rise in oil prices. The march was halted, reportedly to protect Libyan leader Col. Muammar al-Qaddafi, who was in Cotonou on a two-day state visit.

Hubert Koutoukou Maga, the first president (1960–63) of independent Dahomey (renamed Benin in 1975), died in May. Maga was ousted in a 1963 coup, but he returned to power in 1970 as part of a triumverate that ruled until it was toppled in 1972.

(NANCY ELLEN LAWLER)

BHUTAN

Area: 47,000 sq km (18,150 sq mi)
Population (2000 est.): 667,000 (excluding 96,000 refugees in Nepal)
Capital: Thimphu
Head of state: Druk Gyalpo (King) Jigme Singye Wangchuk
Head of government: Chairman of the Cabinet Lyonpo Jigmi Yozer Thinley

There was some shifting of posts in the cabinet in mid-2000 with Lyonpo Yeshey Zimba's appointment as chairman, but the younger generation of cabinet members appointed in 1999 continued in office. The good working relationship between the cabinet, the National Assembly, and King Jigme Singye Wangchuk continued, and the process of establishing a more decentralized district and local administrative system also progressed.

The most serious domestic and external policy issue involved the establishment of numerous armed bases in southeastern Bhutan by an Assamese insurrection force that ignored Bhutan's order that it withdraw back into India. Bhutan and India were reportedly negotiating a joint military operation against this force. Bhutan also continued its dialogue with Nepal over the Bhutanese refugee issue.

Per capita income continued to grow at an impressive 12.5% estimate in 2000, but for the first time in recent years there were some job shortages for Bhutan's graduating classes. (LEO E. ROSE)

BOLIVIA

Area: 1,098,581 sq km (424,164 sq mi)
Population (2000 est.): 8,328,700
Capitals: La Paz (administrative) and Sucre (judicial)
Head of state and government: President Hugo Bánzer Suárez

Bolivian Pres. Hugo Bánzer Suárez faced the severest test of his five-year term when unrest over the privatization of water services in Cochabamba, the nation's third largest city, erupted into a nationwide protest in April 2000. The government had turned over the deteriorating water system to the Aguas del Tunari consortium, which included British, American, Italian, Spanish, and Bolivian interests. After water rates were increased to pay for improvements, mass demonstrations paralyzed Cochabamba. Farmers angered by a new law regulating the use of wells joined the protests, followed by teachers and other labour unionists. Roads were blocked in much of the country. Police in La Paz and Santa Cruz de la Sierra mutinied and were quickly granted pay increases.

Bánzer declared a state of emergency on April 8. At least five people, including an army captain, were killed in clashes between protesters and security forces. Coca growers joined the protest to demand an end to the forcible eradication of illegal plantations. The government agreed to halt the Aguas del Tunari project, revise the well law, and release arrested demonstrators. The state of emergency was lifted on April 20. Five days later Bánzer replaced his finance and defense ministers.

The government continued its war on the illegal drug trade. Eradication and crop-substitution schemes reduced the area planted in coca, the raw material for cocaine. Some farmers accepted incentives to switch to bananas, palm hearts, and other crops, but others refused and denounced plans for a U.S-supported military base in the Chaparé region. Protests by farmers and teachers in September and October again forced Bánzer to rescind government initiatives. Minister of Foreign Affairs Javier Murillo de la Rocha said crop eradication had shrunk the economy by $500 million. In March Bánzer announced an emergency plan to deal with the impact of crop eradication, widespread flooding, and slumping commodity prices. The plan included a $500 million loan fund for farmers and manufacturers, a separate loan scheme to finance low-income housing, and the elimination of a tax on imported capital goods.

Exports from January to July totaled $699 million, up 14% over the same period in 1999. Natural gas, soybeans, zinc, and silver accounted for most of the increase. The government continued to pin its hopes on gas exports, and Bánzer announced in March that Bolivia's estimated natural gas reserves had doubled. The Bolivia-Brazil gas pipeline was extended to Pôrto Alegre, Braz., and connections to more Bolivian gas fields were planned. (PAUL KNOX)

AP/Wide World Photos

Bolivian narcotics agents incinerate confiscated cocaine in the nation's mountainous western region in January.

BOSNIA AND HERZEGOVINA

Area: 51,129 sq km (19,741 sq mi)
Population (2000 est.): 3,836,000, excluding more than 300,000 refugees in adjacent countries and Western Europe
Capital: Sarajevo
Heads of state: Tripartite presidency headed by Ante Jelavic, Alija Izetbegovic from February 14, and, from October 14, Zivko Radisic
Heads of government: Cochairmen of the Council of Ministers (co-prime ministers) Haris Silajdzic and Svetozar Mihajlovic; Prime Ministers Spasoje Tusevljak from June 6 and, from October 18, Martin Raguz

In 2000, five years after the implementation of the Dayton Peace Agreement, progress toward rebuilding Bosnia and Herzegovina continued but at a chronically slow and dismal pace. Economically, rampant unemployment and corruption persisted, and the worst drought in nearly 50 years fueled social unrest in the country. Labour leaders resorted increasingly to strikes in attempts to obtain workers' back pay. As the economy neared collapse, experts expressed deep concern over the plight of the majority of workers. According to government data, though the average monthly food bill for a family of four was $234, average monthly wages were about half that amount. Some observers continued to blame the black-market economy—which accounted for as much as 70% of the country's gross domestic product—for the multitude of socioeconomic problems. While much of the over $5 billion in reconstruction funds donated by the international community had put people to work and laid the groundwork for prosperity, Bosnia's transition to a free-market economy remained stalled.

International aid to support the return of Bosnian refugees to their former homes was of limited help. Some refugees were acting on their own initiative and without any international assistance. According to estimates by the NATO-led Stabilization Force in Bosnia and Herzegovina, only about 5% of all the refugees and displaced persons created by the war had returned to their prewar places of residence since 1996. Politically, municipal and general elections produced encouraging results. Overall, the voting was free of violence and more open and fair than in any previous election. The recent voter trend toward moderate parties continued, with the most impressive performance coming from the nonnationalist, Muslim-led Social Democrats, who outpolled the Party of Democratic Action in many areas.

In the November general elections moderates fared somewhat better than in the previous general election (1998) and were now poised to influence the formation of governments in the two constituent entities the Muslim-Croat Federation and the Bosnian Serb Republic. Their performance, however, did not fulfill the expectations of international officials, nor did the replacement of strongmen Franjo Tudjman in Croatia and Slobodan Milosevic in Yugoslavia by moderates find much resonance in Bosnia and Herzegovina. Many of the country's Serbs and Croats remained loyal to their narrowly nationalist parties. Mirko Sarovic, the candidate of the hard-line Serbian Democratic Party, won the presidency of the Bosnian Serb Republic over the Western-backed incumbent moderate Milorad Dodik.

(MILAN ANDREJEVICH)

BOTSWANA

Area: 581,730 sq km (224,607 sq mi)
Population (2000 est.): 1,576,000
Capital: Gaborone
Head of state and government: President Festus Mogae

The most notable event in 2000 was the return to Botswana of a 200-year-old corpse known as "El Negro." It was stolen from its fresh grave by two French taxidermists in about 1830 and had been displayed in a Spanish museum from 1916 to 1997. On Oct. 5, 2000, the remains were interred in a Gaborone public park. (*See* LIBRARIES AND MUSEUMS: *Museums*.)

Botswana continued in 2000 to enjoy a remarkably stable liberal democracy with solid growth, a by-product of the October 1999 elections that had confirmed the mandate of the Botswana Democratic Party (BDP) under Pres. Festus Mogae. The parliamentary opposition, however, was further fragmented into competing factions. A long unexplained leave of absence by Ian Khama, Mogae's ally and vice president, ended in August; Khama returned to office with enhanced powers to improve interministerial coordination and financial accountability of national development projects. Khama's main rival in the BDP, Ponatshego Kedikilwe, had removed himself from the cabinet to the parliamentary back benches in June.

In foreign affairs Botswana retained close ties with South Africa, but relations with other neighbours were tense, espe-

Jason Laure´

A worker polishes diamonds in one of the plants run by Teemane Manufacturing Co. in Botswana.

cially with Zimbabwe, which sought to establish a regional freight monopoly by impeding rail traffic from South Africa via Botswana. An unofficial embargo, imposed in July 1999, was lifted in March when the new link was washed out by floods but was reimposed in June.

In February creditors foreclosed on Botswana's largest manufacturing industry, the new Hyundai and Volvo vehicle assembly plant in Gaborone, owned by a Zimbabwean involved in mining in the Democratic Republic of the Congo. The loss, however, was more than compensated for by the 44% rise in Botswana's diamond production during the first six months. Although "conflict diamonds" from other African countries proved controversial, peaceful Botswana profited from the rising market driven by the boom in the U.S. Foreign currency reserves stood at $6 billion at midyear. (See ANGOLA: Sidebar, above.) (NEIL PARSONS)

BRAZIL

Area: 8,547,404 sq km (3,300,171 sq mi)
Population (2000 est.): 166,113,000
Capital: Brasília
Head of state and government: President Fernando Henrique Cardoso

In Brazil the year 2000 began with escalating political crises just as the country was preparing to commemorate its 500-year anniversary. (See Sidebar.) On January 18 Pres. Fernando Henrique Cardoso fired Élcio Álvares, Brazil's first civilian minister of defense, owing to fallout from a December 1999 luncheon of 600 current and former military officers in Rio de Janeiro. At the luncheon—which was held in support of Air Force Comdt. Brig. Walter Bräuer, who had been sacked by Álvares after alleging that the minister was involved in drug trafficking—many in attendance sharply criticized the Cardoso administration. Cardoso was angered by Álvares's failure to take action or make any public statement regarding the event. The controversy subsided after Cardoso appointed former government legal counsel Geraldo Quintão the new minister of defense. Quintão was sworn in on January 24.

During a special session of Congress in January, the federal government moved quickly to pass the Fiscal Responsibility Law (FRL). With municipal elections looming in October, Cardoso signed the FRL into law in May. The FRL capped government salaries, set fines for officeholders who violated those ceilings, prohibited state governors from increasing budgets unless there was a rise in tax revenues, and excluded the federal government from bailing out states and municipalities.

February brought resolutions to some of the fiduciary fiascoes of 1999. Gov. Itamar Franco of Minas Gerais ended his state's 13-month moratorium on debt payments by making final payments on Eurobonds and rescheduling debt obligations to the federal government. Also, former central bank president Francisco Lopes was indicted for having used public resources for personal gain during the January 1999 devaluation when the central bank sold currency to small private banks at privileged rates.

Just as the legislative session opened on February 15 with Cardoso's Brazilian Social Democratic Party (PSDB) leading the largest party bloc, debate ensued over raising the minimum wage. In late March Cardoso issued a decree raising the monthly minimum salary from 136 reais to 151 reais (1 real=about $0.51). The federal government later passed legislation permitting state and municipal governments to make upward adjustments.

On March 24 Mayor Celso Pitta of São Paulo was thrown out of office by the São Paulo regional court after testimony from his ex-wife. She provided evidence that he used 800,000 reais to buy votes on the city council in order to prevent his impeachment. The Supreme Justice Tribunal in Brasília, however, paved the way for Pitta to be reinstated after ruling that only the city council could remove him from office. Court battles over his status continued throughout the year, but Pitta remained in office.

Cardoso's most troubling scandal of 2000 emerged on April 24 when Judge Nicolau dos Santos Neto fled authorities after a warrant for his arrest had been issued. Santos Neto was charged with siphoning off 169 million reais intended for construction of the regional courthouse of São Paulo. The judge's telephone records led investigators to former secretary-general of the presidency Eduardo Jorge Caldas Pereira. As manager of Cardoso's 1998 reelection campaign, Caldas Pereira allegedly had used his influence to lobby for disbursements for the courthouse. Payments were made to Santos Neto and businessman Luis Estevão, who was elected senator in 1998. For his role in the courthouse scam, the Senate stripped Estevão of his seat and revoked his parliamentary immunity and political rights for 15 1/2 years.

After Caldas Pereira gave testimony to Congress on August 3, plans to move forward with a parliamentary board of inquiry started to lose momentum. On September 13 the committee charged with investigating the scandal dissolved until after the October elections. Nevertheless, faced with the mounting pressures from recent scandals, Cardoso on August 21 launched Transparent Brazil, an anticorruption pack-

Brazil's 500th Anniversary: The Paradox of Celebration

On April 22, 1500, Portuguese explorer Pedro Álvares Cabral, while on a voyage tracing Vasco da Gama's 1497–99 water route to India, sighted the mainland of South America after having strayed far west of his course. He landed near the present-day city of Pôrto Seguro, Braz., held a Roman Catholic mass, and promptly claimed the region—which he called Ilha de Vera Cruz ("Island of the True Cross")—for the Portuguese crown. The new possession was later given the name Brazil, after *pau-brasil,* a valuable red dyewood that grew there in abundance.

Five hundred years later, on April 22, 2000, the scene at Pôrto Seguro would not be so fluid. While Brazilian Pres. Fernando Henrique Cardoso and Portuguese Pres. Jorge Sampaio celebrated the anniversary of Cabral's landing along with government officials and invited guests, scores of peaceful demonstrators who were prevented from entering the city rallied outside to protest the commemoration of an event that for many had marked the beginning of exclusion, slavery, and extermination. The protests were the culmination of weeks of unrest. In early April state police tore down a monument of indigenous resistance constructed by the Pataxó Indians for the 2000 Conference of Indigenous Peoples and Organizations of Brazil in the reservation of Coroa Vermelha. Authorities later sealed off Pôrto Seguro, blocking access even to local residents and tourists in order to contain any movement that might threaten the official events.

On April 22 more than 6,000 policemen and army troops were on alert. That morning over 5,000 people, including 2,000 Indians, marched from Coroa Vermelha to Pôrto Seguro in a countercommemoration they dubbed "Brazil—the Other 500 Years." The demonstrators, among whom were also members of Brazil's landless movement, trade unions, the Roman Catholic church, and Afro-Brazilian organizations, were met at the municipal border by 300 state policemen, who used tear gas and rubber bullets to prevent their entrance into the city. While no one was reported to have been seriously injured, more than 140 persons were arrested.

Repercussions from the unrest were felt throughout the Brazilian government. Rafael Greca de Macedo, Brazil's minister of tourism and sport, resigned. The president of the National Foundation of the Indian, Carlos Frederico Mares, also resigned. President Cardoso made reference to the country's paradoxical celebrations of 500 years that privileged some at the expense of others by addressing the nation's "rediscovery." He asserted that the commemorations "provide us with three distinct moments: a reflective look at our five centuries of history, a critical analysis of the present, and a discussion of the paths that we shall follow for the construction of a Brazil with equality, liberty, and fraternity." Many Brazilians believed that a more appropriate celebration would commemorate the founding of the Republic of Brazil in 1889. (JOHN CHARLES CUTTINO)

age designed to better monitor public spending and improve public service by instituting a code of ethics.

The rift between Cardoso and Gov. Itamar Franco heightened in September when Franco failed to deter members of the landless movement from occupying a 1,100-ha (2,700-ac) farm owned by the Cardoso family in Minas Gerais. For the second time since May, the farm was surrounded as the movement launched a national offensive to occupy farmland and seek liberation of the 2,150,000,000 reais budgeted by the federal government for land reform. More than 300 federal policemen and elite army troops were called to the farm. On September 14, after issuing Cardoso a 12-hour ultimatum for removing federal troops, Franco obtained a Supreme Court injunction ordering the troops to leave. Supreme Court Minister Nelson Jobim delayed the ruling, however, and on September 15 the landless left the area.

The Brazilian economy showed mixed signs of improvement. The stock market hit an all-time high early in the year, closing at 18,053 on January 17. The central bank's open-market committee continued its policy of gradually reducing the interest rate, lowering it in several rate declinations from 19.5% in January to 16.5% in June, where it remained unchanged through mid-November—its lowest level since 1986. The central bank also eased credit restrictions by lowering the compulsory reserves of bank deposits it held from 65% to 45%. Inflation was expected to remain within the range of 6–8% agreed upon with the International Monetary Fund. Despite the country's improving monetary policy, in 1999—the latest year for which statistics were available—average per capita income shrank 5.5% and taxation as a share of gross domestic product reached 30.3%, up from 29.9% in 1998. (JOHN CHARLES CUTTINO)

BRUNEI

Area: 5,765 sq km (2,226 sq mi)
Population (2000 est.): 336,000
Capital: Bandar Seri Begawan
Head of state and government: Sultan and Prime Minister Haji Hassanal Bolkiah Mu'izzaddin Waddaulah

The house of Hassanal Bolkiah, sultan of Brunei Darussalam, began 2000 in disarray, owing mostly to finances. The Asian financial crisis had exacted a heavy toll on the government's stock portfolio and other investments. Good fiscal health was at the crux of Brunei's political, social, and economic stability and ensured the continuation of its high living standards.

The royal family itself was under intense scrutiny. The monarch's once much-favoured youngest brother, former finance minister Prince Jefri Bolkiah, returned from exile to face charges stemming from the misuse of state funds as head of the powerful Brunei Investment Agency (BIA). He was sued by the state for having misused over $15 billion from the government coffers and was accused of "improper withdrawal and the use of substantial funds." Although maintaining that he was a victim of a conspiracy contrived by Muslim conservatives, by mid-May he had reached an out-of-court settlement; he would hand over to the government local and overseas property, businesses, and other assets. It was widely believed that during Jefri's tenure, the value of BIA's investment fund had diminished from $110 billion to $40 billion.

On a positive note, the sultanate on November 12–13 hosted the summit of the Asia-Pacific Economic Cooperation (APEC), the first time an international gathering of this kind had been held there. In addition, the price for oil reached its highest level in 10 years.

(ALEXANDRA A. SENO)

BULGARIA

Area: 110,994 sq km (42,855 sq mi)
Population (2000 est.): 8,172,000
Capital: Sofia
Chief of state: President Petar Stoyanov
Head of government: Prime Minister Ivan Kostov

Reuters New Media Inc./Corbis

Bulgarian Prime Minister Ivan Kostov, whose administration faced allegations of corruption during the year, appears at a session of the National Assembly in Sofia on April 21.

In April 2000 the government of Prime Minister Ivan Kostov was embarrassed by allegations of corruption. Protesting his own innocence, an official spokesman for the government, Mihail Mihailov, resigned, but further incriminating revelations followed. On June 9 Bulgaria's chief negotiator with the European Union (EU) was required to resign after being accused of financial irregularities. By this time the National Assembly had enacted legislation requiring all senior officials to reveal their incomes and expenses.

Further embarrassments for the government came during the summer when listening devices were discovered in the home of the prosecutor general. The government insisted that they had been planted in 1994 and never used. On August 18 Bulgaria ordered the expulsion of five foreign businessmen, four of them Russians, who were said to be involved in money laundering and to have connections with international criminal organizations.

The actions against the Russians prompted a demand from Moscow for information on the evidence against them. The Bulgarian minister for foreign affairs rebuffed her Russian counterpart, reminding him that the Warsaw Pact no longer existed. Another dispute during the year between Bulgaria and Russia was occasioned by the latter's failure to abide by the terms of an agreement to pay off some of its $100 million debt to Bulgaria with spare parts for fighter airplanes. In the wake of the incident, the Bulgarians were considering the purchase of F-16 fighters from the United States.

Bulgaria and Libya also had a serious dispute. Five nurses and one doctor from Bulgaria were accused of having deliberately infected 393 children with the HIV virus in a Banghazi, Libya, hospital. If they were tried and convicted, the Bulgarians could face the death penalty. Pleas from Pres. Petar Stoyanov and intervention from Russia secured a postponement of the trial until November. The Bulgarians' cause was not helped by injudicious comments from their minister of justice, who told the press he could predict the outcome of the trial "in a white country" but not in Libya.

In July the Paris Club of creditor nations agreed in principle to a partial conversion of Bulgaria's external debt into investment. In August the German finance minister warned aspiring nations that they could not join the EU until their economies were prepared for competition. The pain of such preparation was shown when Bulgaria enacted measures to comply with European veterinary regulations, which led to a marked fall in meat production.

(RICHARD J. CRAMPTON)

BURKINA FASO

Area: 274,400 sq km (105,946 sq mi)
Population (2000 est.): 11,946,000
Capital: Ouagadougou
Chief of state: President Blaise Compaoré
Head of government: Prime Minister Kadré Désiré Ouédraogo and, from November 7, Ernest Paramanga Yonli

Repercussions from the December 1998 murder of journalist Norbert Zongo continued to dominate the political landscape in Burkina Faso in 2000. Zongo had been investigating the January 1998 murder of David Ouédraogo in connection with the alleged theft of about CFAF 20 million (about $26,900) from the home of Pres. Blaise Compaoré's brother, François. On August 19 three of the five soldiers on trial for Ouédraogo's murder were convicted.

In his New Year's Eve message to the nation, President Compaoré promised to institute electoral reforms. Protests continued, however, and in early June police used tear gas to disperse a student demonstration at the University of Ouagadougou, which was closed temporarily by the government in July before being shuttered indefinitely in October. Secondary schoolteachers, along with 1,800 students, boycotted the annual baccalaureate exams in July. Additional demands by students for an increase in grants and living allowances led to a delay in the opening of the academic year.

In municipal elections held on September 24, 25 parties contested seats, and the ruling Congress for Democracy and Progress won 802 of the 1,100 seats available. The opposition Alliance for Democracy and Federation/African Democratic Rally secured 133 and the Union for Democracy and Federation 49.

In an effort to help President Compaoré accelerate political and social reforms, the government of Prime Minister Kadré Désiré Ouédraogo resigned on November 6. The following day Compaoré appointed Ernest Paramanga Yonli the new prime minister.

The World Bank announced in July that Burkina Faso, the third poorest nation in the world, would receive $700 million for debt relief.

(NANCY ELLEN LAWLER)

BURUNDI

Area: 27,816 sq km (10,740 sq mi)
Population (2000 est.): 6,055,000 (including 800,000 refugees in Tanzania)
Capital: Bujumbura
Head of state and government: President Pierre Buyoya

Seven years of war between the nation's Tutsi-dominated army and Hutu rebels had by 2000 devastated Burundi; the fighting had claimed the lives of more than 200,000 people. In September 1999 the government had forced an estimated 350,000 people, mostly Hutu civilians, into so-called regroupment camps, claiming that the relocation was to protect them from rebel attacks. Hutu organizations and international humanitarian groups condemned the camps. Many people in the camps were at risk from famine, and in March the World Food Programme began emergency relief operations.

Efforts to end the conflict continued throughout the year. In February peace talks resumed in Arusha, Tanz., with former South African president Nelson Mandela serving as mediator. Nineteen groups, including the main Tutsi and Hutu political parties, participated, but the two major armed rebel forces did not. In June Pres. Pierre Buyoya agreed to key concessions, including the closing of the regroupment camps and ethnic integration of the army. Several Tutsi groups opposed the concessions, and Buyoya cautioned that Tutsi extremists in the army might attempt a coup. On August 28, 14 of the 19 groups that attended the Arusha talks signed a draft agreement. Although the holdout Tutsi parties eventually signed the agreement, some observers claimed that it had little chance of success. Several important provisions, such as the composition of a proposed transitional government, were not finalized.

Despite the draft agreement, cease-fire talks collapsed in September when two rebel leaders refused to participate. As preconditions for a cease-fire, they demanded the release of political prisoners, accelerated closing of the regroupment camps, and assurances of a role in any transitional government. Later in September, fighting between the army and rebel forces escalated.

The civil war had a devastating effect on the country's economy. In April the World Bank approved a $35 million emergency loan. International donors also promised extensive economic aid should the forces in Burundi peacefully settle the civil war.

(MATTHEW A. CENZER)

CAMBODIA

Area: 181,035 sq km (69,898 sq mi)
Population (2000 est.): 12,371,000
Capital: Phnom Penh
Chief of state: King Norodom Sihanouk
Head of government: Prime Minister Hun Sen

The possibility of seeing the surviving leaders of Cambodia's brutal Khmer Rouge answer for widespread atrocities committed by the regime seemed to grow more remote in 2000. The creation of a UN-brokered war crimes tribunal seemed perpetually forthcoming. Even after the international body drafted plans to enact the tribunal, various events held up the process. Although opposition leaders voiced strong support for the tribunal, the Cambodian government—which included a number of former Khmer Rouge members—continued to insist on controlling the proposed proceedings. At one point the framework hammered together by the UN in August did not get tabled for ratification in Cambodia's National Assembly before the legislature went on a 50-day recess in September. A signed agreement and finer details could not be negotiated until the UN draft had been passed. The visit of Chinese Pres. Jiang Zemin to Cambodia in November also complicated matters. Because China had supported the Khmer Rouge in the past, government leaders deemed it diplomatically inappropriate to have the Khmer Rouge issue on the top of the official agenda just when a historic summit was to take place.

One high-profile criminal case involving a former Khmer Rouge leader did go to court during the year, however. Chhouk Rin was acquitted of murder and kidnapping charges in July. In 1994 he had led an ambush of a train in the southern village of Phnom Vour, during which 13 Cambodian passengers were killed and three Western tourists were kidnapped. The tourists—natives of France, Great Britain, and Australia—were later executed after attempts to extract a ransom had failed. The French, British, and Australian governments had actively exerted pressure on Phnom Penh to prosecute Chhouk Rin, but in a highly controversial decision, a judge freed him on what amounted to a technicality. A law passed in 1994 granted amnesty to all Khmer Rouge members

Former Khmer Rouge leader Chhouk Rin, who faced murder and kidnapping charges stemming from the ambush of a train in southern Cambodia in 1994, addresses the court during his trial in Phnom Penh in July.

Reuters NewMedia Inc./Corbis

who defected to the government side within six months, and because Chhouk Rin had done so, the judge ruled that he had immunity under the law.

The economic picture in Cambodia was calm, though the riel remained weak. Tourism was a bright spot as the number of foreign visitors rose to 400,000. Inflation was stable, and gross domestic product growth was projected at 4%. Cambodia's application to join the World Trade Organization was under consideration during the year, and many observers expected it to be approved.

(ALEXANDRA A. SENO)

CAMEROON

Area: 475,442 sq km (183,569 sq mi)
Population (2000 est.): 15,422,000
Capital: Yaoundé
Chief of state: President Paul Biya
Head of government: Prime Minister Peter Mafany Musonge

An International Monetary Fund (IMF) mission visited Cameroon in February 2000 to review the country's structural adjustment plan. Although the three-year plan was achieving some success, the IMF, along with the World Bank, was apparently dissatisfied with the management of the state oil revenues derived from the estimated five million tons of petroleum produced annually. Logging companies registered strong complaints about the impact of new legislation that required the processing of 70% of lumber before it was exported. The government insisted, however, that the partial ban on the export of unprocessed logs had already created 6,000 new jobs in sawmills. On June 6 the World Bank approved a $3.7 billion pipeline project that would move oil from Chad to Cameroon's coast; Cameroon was expected to gain $20 million annually in transit fees. Environmentalists opposed the project, however, claiming that one of the world's last large tropical forests would be severely damaged and that it would have a highly detrimental effect on the lives of nomadic herders.

In December 1999 members of the separatist Southern Cameroon National Council (SCNC) had seized a local radio station in Buea and aired an appeal for independence for the Anglophone area. Six weeks later Prime Minister Peter Musonge made an unscheduled visit to the region and appealed to the SCNC to preserve peace and to seek an acceptable solution to the perennial strife between Anglophone and Francophone Cameroon.

In mid-August gendarmes crossed the border into Taraba state in neighbouring Nigeria, where they arrested several Nigerian citizens. The Cameroonian consul in Cross River state, Nigeria, recommended that joint border patrols be instituted in order to prevent further clashes over illegal immigration.

In September Cameroonians celebrated nationwide after their soccer team defeated Spain 7–5 to win the gold medal in the Olympic Games. It was the nation's first-ever Olympic gold.

(NANCY ELLEN LAWLER)

CANADA

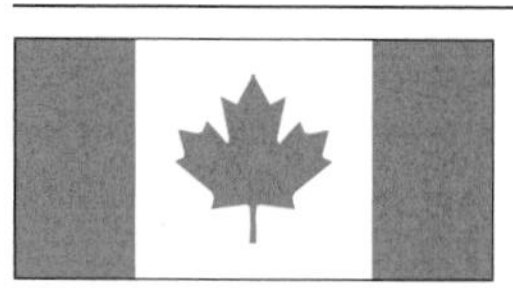

Area: 9,970,610 sq km (3,849,674 sq mi)
Population (2000 est.): 30,770,000
Capital: Ottawa
Chief of state: Queen Elizabeth II, represented by Governor-General Adrienne Clarkson
Head of government: Prime Minister Jean Chrétien

Domestic Affairs. Canadians went to the polls on Nov. 27, 2000, to give a resounding vote of confidence to the Liberal Party government of Prime Minister Jean Chrétien. A five-week campaign saw Chrétien win a third majority in the House of Commons, the first time this had happened in Canada since 1945. First winning office in 1993, the Liberals had taken 177 seats and 41% of the popular vote. A second election in 1997 had seen their standing reduced to 155 seats, but in the 2000 election they rebounded to 172 seats in a 301-seat legislature, again with 41% of the vote.

The result represented a personal victory for Chrétien, who had called the election in spite of the misgivings of some of his party colleagues. Elections in Canada were normally held after a government had been in office for at least four years; to call one after three and a half years risked rousing the wrath of the electorate. There were no large issues to be decided, but Chrétien, a wily campaigner who had been in politics since 1963, decided that the time was ripe for an appeal to the voters. His judgment was confirmed to an extent beyond the forecasts of most commentators. The Liberal Party retained its massive grip on Canada's largest province, Ontario, where it won 100 of the province's 103 seats. In Quebec, where Chrétien was not popular, the party made extensive gains. It won a larger popular vote than the separatist party, the Bloc Québécois (BQ), for the first time in a generation. In the Atlantic provinces, where they had been rebuffed in 1997, the Liberals made substantial gains. Only in the Western provinces, the main centre of opposition, did the party fall short, winning only 13 of the region's 91 seats. For the first time since taking office, the Liberals held seats in every province of Canada as well as in the three territories.

Chrétien's sweeping victory was a bitter blow to the political forces of the right, which had spent the previous year endeavouring to consolidate. The objective had been defined and carried out by Preston Manning, leader of the Reform Party. Manning had sought to broaden the party's appeal. In particular he wished to make inroads into the Liberal dominance in vote-rich Ontario. At a Reform Party convention held on January 29, Manning persuaded members of his party to merge themselves into a new organization, the Canadian Alliance. He had then called for a leadership review, thereby putting his position as party leader on the line. After a number of telephone polls, another Albertan, Stockwell Day, was elected leader of the Canadian Alliance. (*See* BIOGRAPHIES.)

The 49-year-old Day was a fresh face in Canadian federal politics. He had been a Progressive Conservative Party (PCP) member of the Alberta legislature since 1986, holding a number of ministerial positions, most recently that of Provincial Treasurer. There he had successfully balanced the province's books, enabling Alberta to become the first Canadian province to declare a surplus. He was a strong believer in the equality of the provinces, rejecting any form of special status for Quebec. Favouring a more limited role for government, he advocated lower taxes and a reduction of the national debt. Coming from an evangelical Christian background, he held conservative views on abortion and gay rights, although he insisted he would not attempt to impose his personal views on the new party. Personable and energetic, he was bilingual, a rare trait among politicians from the West. Chosen party leader in July, he entered Parliament in September, sitting for an electoral district in British Columbia.

In spite of a vigorous campaign, the Canadian Alliance failed to make the breakthrough in Ontario the party desired. It won only two seats, both in districts close to the national capital, Ottawa. It was shut out of Quebec and the Atlantic provinces. In the West it maintained the dominant position the Reform Party had won, taking 66 of the region's 91 seats. In every region of Canada it increased its share of the popular vote, winning 25%. The PCP, a historic national party, had crumbled badly after its years in office in the 1980s under Brian Mulroney. It had found a new leader in 1998, former prime minister Joe Clark, but Clark had hesitated for two years before entering Parliament in September 2000. Both Manning and Day had urged Clark to join his party with theirs, but Clark had rejected their overtures. Although Clark was personally respected, his party lost further ground in the election. Many Conservatives in English-speaking Canada threw their support behind the Alliance, while in Quebec's French-speaking areas PCP members drifted away to support Liberal candidates. The party had elected 20 members in 1997; it elected only 12 in 2000 (only one in Quebec). Clark won a seat in Calgary, Alberta, an accomplishment in a province where the Alliance reigned supreme but the long-term future of the party was very much in doubt. Canada's left-of-centre party, the New Democratic Party, won only 13 seats across the country.

The election's greatest surprise was the poll results in Quebec. The separatist party, the Bloc Québécois (BQ), saw its support decline. In 1993 it had won 54 of Quebec's 75 seats and had become the official opposition in the Commons. In 1997 it had lost that standing but had still elected 44 members. In 2000 it carried only 38 seats. The Liberals had always been strong in English-speaking districts around Montreal; now they made gains in French-speaking areas. Some of the Bloc's wastage was caused by the unpopularity of its counterpart, the Parti Québécois government of Quebec, which had been forcing smaller municipalities to amalgamate against their will. It also appeared that the cause of separation was losing momentum in Quebec.

The Liberal Party's success was due to several factors. A strong economy, combined with a federal budget surplus for several years, was a principal one. The Liberals had taken over the Alliance's plan for tax relief and had offered cuts in a range of taxes in two budgets released earlier in the year. The government had also put more funds into health care, after having previously reduced support in order to balance the books. It had taken a firmer line on Quebec separatism, laying down more precise terms for the achievement of Quebec's independence.

Election 2000 was not an edifying campaign. Chrétien had caught his opponents off-guard by calling an early election. The Alliance, he claimed, had a hidden agenda that would weaken the authority of the national government. Forced on the defensive from the beginning, the party found it difficult to put forward its own policies. The prime minister dominated the campaign, and, although his opponents attacked him for the mismanagement of public funds, for arrogance, and for lack of vision, they were unable to throw him off his stride. In the end, the victory was Chrétien's, and with it he quelled all questions within his party about his leadership.

The federal government took a strong stand in laying down the terms under which Quebec would be allowed to hold a referendum on independence. The legislation, called the Clarity Act, was based on an opinion of the Supreme Court handed down in 1998. The federal government would not be obliged to negotiate secession, the court stated, unless Quebec voters by a clear majority chose independence. The Clarity Act provided that the House of Commons would have to approve the terms of any future referendum.

The Clarity Act aroused strong opposition from the separatist BQ, which denounced it as an unacceptable intervention into Quebec's affairs. In the country as a whole, opinion polls gave the measure broad support. Even in Quebec the act received endorsement from 58% of voters. The Clarity Act was approved in the Commons on March 15. The separatists in Parliament fought bitterly to the end, proposing more than 400 amendments in an attempt to sabotage the measure.

During the year support for separatism continued to decline in Quebec, reaching its lowest level in five years. Quebec's separatist leader, Premier Lucien Bouchard—who had previously stated that he would not hold another referendum until "winning conditions" emerged—announced that with a balanced budget and an improving economy, those conditions had been achieved. He refused to give a date for another referendum but made it plain that the referendum remained a priority.

Canadians were increasingly concerned during 2000 with the state of their health care system, long a source of national pride. In a system established more than 30 years earlier, medical care in Canada, costing about $80 billion annually, was paid for by the federal and provincial governments. The provincial governments argued that cuts in federal grants for health care had seriously limited their ability to meet the growing demand for health services. After the Liberals took office in 1993, they reduced federal transfers to the provinces for health care, social welfare, and postsecondary education. This action was taken in an effort to achieve a balanced federal budget. Although the amount of funding was gradually increased, the provinces contended that the low level of federal support meant that the federal government had no right to lay down conditions for the operation of the national system.

A bill allowing for a larger measure of private participation in the health service was introduced in Alberta by the PCP government. It became a flash point for the worries of many Canadians over the future of their prized public health plan. The federal government took strong exception to the Alberta arrangements, branding them a violation of the Canada Health Act. This document, the cornerstone of health care in Canada, established general principles governing the operation of the national scheme.

A conference between Prime Minister Chrétien and the first ministers of the provinces and territories on September 11 made a start in increasing federal funds for health care. Chrétien agreed to enrich grants to the provinces for health and social programs by Can$23.4 billion (Can$1.48=$1) over the next five years. This represented a 35% increase in federal support. The outlay included a Can$2.3 billion onetime payment for new medical equipment. The provinces claimed that the funding increase was not large enough, but they resisted a national accounting to measure the delivery of health care, preferring to issue their own reports. It was clear that more fine-tuning would be required for ensuring the smooth running of Canada's single-payer health system.

Finance Minister Paul Martin presented his seventh budget on February

On May 2 in Edmonton, Alta., protesters demonstrate against a bill allowing for a larger measure of private health care.
AP/Wide World Photos

28. It was a "good news budget," offering the first tax-rate cuts in 12 years. In addition, Martin eliminated the impact of bracket creep, by means of which inflation constantly pushed taxpayers into higher brackets. A budget surplus, which had first been experienced in 1997, would continue to grow and was expected to reach between Can$7 billion and Can$9 billion for fiscal year 2000–01.

On October 18, just before the election call, Martin brought forward a midyear budget update. With revenues strong and the surplus growing, Martin doubled the tax cuts announced in February. Countering Canadian Alliance promises, he announced tax reductions of $100 billion over the next five years.

On September 28 Pierre Trudeau, prime minister of Canada in 1968–79 and 1980–84, died in Montreal. (*See* OBITUARIES.)

The Economy. Surging growth marked the Canadian economy in 2000. Every aspect, from real output to personal incomes, recorded increases that returned levels to those reached in 1990, at the start of the recession. For the first time, Canada joined the "trillion-dollar club," those countries that achieved gross domestic product (the value of all goods and services produced in a country in a given year) of more than Can$1 trillion. Economic growth in 2000 was expected to be almost 5%.

Fuel prices, which had increased by 64% since March 1999, sparked a disturbing rise in inflation. In October the consumer price index (inflation rate) stood at 2.8%. Unemployment remained steady at 6.9% in November.

International Affairs. Foreign Affairs Minister Lloyd Axworthy continued to urge new thinking on nuclear arms. He labeled NATO's strategic policies outdated, stating that they had been enunciated in 1989, while the Cold War was still a crucial condition. He was disturbed by the $19 billion plan by the U.S. to build ground-based interceptor rockets to destroy incoming missiles over North America.

Whereas Axworthy expressed doubts about the American plans for missile defense, the Canadian military showed itself eager to cooperate in hemispheric security. A Can$637 million project was unveiled to establish a surveillance system to keep watch on objects in outer space. This scheme would complement the North American Aerospace Defense Command (NORAD), established by the U.S. and Canada 42 years earlier. In May NORAD was renewed for five more years. The renewal was signed one year in advance, presumably to prevent the joint air defense from becoming involved in a possible controversy over the missile shield plan.

Although a nonpermanent member of the UN Security Council, Canada presided over that body in April. One subject of discussion, brought forward by Robert Fowler, Canada's UN ambassador, attracted worldwide attention. It was the sale of rough diamonds by such African countries as Angola and Sierra Leone to support violent civil wars there. Fowler carried out fact-finding missions and in July persuaded the Security Council to impose a ban on the export or purchase of rough diamonds from those countries. Their govern-

The Vikings of 2000

In the year 2000, descendants of the Vikings achieved what their ancestors had failed to do a millennium earlier—conquer the eastern Canadian province of Newfoundland. Instead of using swords, spears, and shields, the latter-day Norsemen used songs, sagas, and a fleet of graceful replica ships to win over the people of this rocky island, where Vikings led by Leif Eriksson briefly settled in about AD 1000.

Capt. Gunnar Eggertsson, an Icelander and a direct descendant of Leif Eriksson, would never forget emerging from the fog, storms, and towering icebergs of the North Atlantic at the spot his ancestors had so hastily left. "L'Anse aux Meadows was a very special place. There we saw the houses that had been there since the year 1000, and we also saw the houses where people live that were like the houses we build in Iceland today," he said.

More than 15,000 people climbed the rocks and gathered in the grassy reaches of L'Anse aux Meadows on July 28. Watched by millions of television viewers, choirs sang Norse songs, and the sleek Viking replica ship *Íslendingur* and a flotilla of other Norse boats danced over the waves, re-creating the arrival of the first Europeans from Iceland a thousand years earlier.

L'Anse aux Meadows, located on the northern tip of western Newfoundland, was the only authenticated North American Viking settlement. Sod huts and a wide array of relics were discovered in 1961 by archaeologists Helge and Anne Stine Ingstad, who were led to the site by a local fisherman. The sheltered meadow became a United Nations heritage site featuring reconstructed sod huts and displays of Norse artifacts.

The Vikings spent three or four years in the land they called Vinland, sailing as far south as the Gulf of Maine, seeking timber and a location for a new colony. According to the Norse sagas, the local aboriginal people, whom the Vikings called *skrælings,* or wretches, then drove them back to Iceland. A thousand years later some native leaders joined the celebrations.

Newfoundlanders, most of whom proudly boasted of having saltwater in their veins, clamoured for a chance to sail with the nine-person *Íslendingur* crew during its tour of the province and to work as actors at the re-creation of a Viking village built near L'Anse aux Meadows. The Newfoundland Museum staged a huge traveling exhibit of Viking and native artifacts to tell the story of the first contact between Europeans and the native people of North America. Plays and concerts also played to packed audiences as actors and singers retold the ancient tale. (KEVIN COX)

The replica Viking ship Íslendingur *began its voyage from Iceland to North America on June 17, marking 1000 years since Leif Eriksson became the first European to set foot on the continent.*

AP/Wide World Photos

ments were urged to issue certificates of origin for diamonds that had been exported through legitimate channels. Fowler also took his case to the World Diamond Congress in Antwerp, Belg., in mid-July. The Congress, governing the almost $7 billion rough-diamond industry, agreed to lay down a set of controls prohibiting traffic in "blood diamonds." (*See* ANGOLA: *Sidebar.*)

(DAVID M.L. FARR)

CAPE VERDE

Area: 4,033 sq km (1,557 sq mi)
Population (2000 est.): 401,000
Capital: Praia
Chief of state: President Antonio Mascarenhas Monteiro
Head of government: Prime Ministers Carlos Veiga and, from July 29, António Gualberto do Rosário

The World Bank and International Monetary Fund structural-adjustment programs had profound implications for national politics in Cape Verde in 2000. Designed to help attract foreign investment, the government's privatization program—especially the privatization of the state petroleum company Enacol—was strongly criticized by the main opposition party, the former ruling African Party for the Independence of Cape Verde, as well as by some members of the ruling Movement for Democracy.

In July Prime Minister Carlos Veiga resigned and became a presidential candidate for the 2001 elections; he was replaced by his deputy, António Gualberto do Rosário. When the ruling party split, a new party emerged; the Democratic Renovation Party, headed by former Praia town councillor Jacinto Santos, began campaigning for the legislative elections, also due in early 2001.

A July visit by the new Senegalese president, Abdoulaye Wade (*see* BIOGRAPHIES), helped cement relations with that country, and closer ties were established with Angola. Diplomatic relations with China were strengthened during the year, as Cape Verde expressed support for the reunification of Taiwan and China.

(CHRISTOPHER SAUNDERS)

CENTRAL AFRICAN REPUBLIC

Area: 622,436 sq km (240,324 sq mi)
Population (2000 est.): 3,513,000
Capital: Bangui
Chief of state: President Ange-Félix Patassé
Head of government: Prime Minister Anicet Georges Dologuélé

The remaining 430 members of the United Nations Mission in the Central African Republic, an approximately 1,350-strong peacekeeping operation, withdrew from the Central African Republic on Feb. 15, 2000, some four months after it had originally been scheduled to complete its withdrawal. Conditions in the capital remained tense, however, exacerbated by a growing fuel shortage, a wave of violent crime, and rumours that the army was poised to overthrow the government.

In early July opposition parties demanded the resignation of Pres. Ange-Félix Patassé and the establishment of a government of national unity. In response, Patassé announced plans to facilitate a reconciliation by bringing together representatives of the various political and economic factions, but a conference date was not announced. In December thousands of civil servants went on strike in Bangui, protesting against 29 months of unpaid salaries.

On January 10 the government of the neighbouring Democratic Republic of the Congo accused authorities in the Central African Republic of allowing Ugandan-backed rebels the use of its territory as a staging point for guerrilla raids. Following a regional summit of the Community of Sahelian-Saharan States in February, the Central African Republic and 10 other members signed a security charter that would guarantee each of them territorial integrity.

Prime Minister Anicet Dologuélé headed a delegation to the United Nations on May 15–16 and met with representatives of donor governments and nongovernmental organizations to discuss rescue efforts for the country's battered economy. The priorities identified included reform of security forces, reduction in the size of the army, and expansion of the country's economic base. Donors agreed to provide aid of only $33 million.

(NANCY ELLEN LAWLER)

CHAD

Area: 1,284,000 sq km (495,755 sq mi)
Population (2000 est.): 8,425,000
Capital: N'Djamena
Chief of state: President Lieut. Gen. Idriss Déby
Head of government: Prime Minister Nagoum Yamassoum

The main issue in 2000 was whether construction of a giant oil-development project, which would link the Doba Basin in the south of Chad to the sea via a pipeline through Cameroon, would go ahead as planned. In November 1999 both French oil group Elf, which held a 20% stake in the project, and Anglo-Dutch Shell, which had a 40% stake, withdrew their support. When the Malaysian state oil firm Petronas took a 35% share, however, the project was finally approved—after 10 years of planning—in June 2000 by the World Bank, despite loud protests from environmentalists and human rights groups. The support of the U.S. government was crucial in the Bank's decision to lend some $193 million of the $3.7 billion needed. Barring further delays, oil was expected to begin flowing in 2004.

Besides the government's inability to deal with corruption, the most serious threat to the project was the continued rebellion in the northern Tibesti region, led by former defense minister Yossouf Togoimi. In February some of Pres. Idriss Déby's presidential guard surrendered to Togoimi. As chair of the Community of the Sahelian-Saharan States, Déby appealed to Togoimi to lay down his arms. Déby was unable to suppress the rebellion. In addition, other elements involved in armed resistance to Déby's government formed a coordinating council based in Libreville, Gabon. Trouble erupted in March when Chadian troops occupied two potentially oil-rich islands belonging to Nigeria in the waters of Lake Chad. The charges of torture and brutality brought by a Senegalese court in May against exiled former Chadian dictator Hissène Habré were dropped inexplicably in July.

At a meeting in N'Djamena President Déby along with Pres. Olusegan Obasanjo of Nigeria and Pres. Tandja Mama-

AP/Wide World Photos

Pres. Idriss Déby of Chad (in sunglasses) presides over the official launch of a $3.7 billion oil development project in the country's southern Doba Basin on October 18.

dou of Niger agreed to take steps to halt the 30-year decline in the water level of Lake Chad.

(CHRISTOPHER SAUNDERS)

CHILE

Area: 756,626 sq km (292,135 sq mi)
Population (2000 est.): 15,211,000
Capitals: Santiago (national) and Valparaíso (legislative)
Head of state and government: Presidents Eduardo Frei Ruiz-Tagle and, from March 11, Ricardo Lagos Escobar

Two dramatic events in 2000 each marked watersheds in Chilean history—the election of Concertación coalition candidate Ricardo Lagos Escobar (*see* BIOGRAPHIES) as president and the return of Gen. Augusto Pinochet Ugarte after 16 months' detention in Great Britain while awaiting possible extradition to Spain for alleged human rights abuses. On Jan. 16, 2000, Lagos won a hard-fought contest in the election runoff against Joaquín Lavín Infante, the candidate of the right-wing parties; he captured 51.3% of the vote to Lavín's 48.7% and became the third consecutive Concertación president as well as the first socialist president since Salvador Allende in 1970.

General Pinochet's return to Chile came after a January medical exam that led to the conclusion that he was not medically fit to stand trial. British Home Secretary Jack Straw announced that he was "minded" to allow Pinochet to return to Chile on medical, humanitarian grounds; after a final round of appeals, Pinochet landed in Chile on March 3 and brought the twin issues of human rights and civil-military relations to centre stage. On August 8 the Supreme Court, in a 14–6 vote, ratified the appeals court's earlier decision granting Judge Juan Guzman Tapia's request to withdraw Pinochet's lifetime senatorial immunity. Guzman, who was presiding over a burgeoning number of human rights charges against Pinochet (177 by November), was joined in his quest for prosecution by the Argentinean courts in late October. They requested the extradition of seven men, including Pinochet and Gen. Manuel Contreras, former head of the Directorate of National Intelligence, for alleged participation in the 1974 assassination of former Chilean army commander Gen. Carlos Prats and his wife Sofia Cuthbert in Buenos Aires. In November the Chilean courts, mindful that Chilean law excused only the mentally incompetent from trial, ordered both mental and neurological medical tests for Pinochet before proceeding further. In December the Courts of Appeals ruled that Pinochet should be examined in a military hospital before facing trial. Another judicial investigation into the 1982 death of labour leader Tucapel Jimenez led to the first arrest of an active-duty army general, Hernán Ramírez Hald. Meanwhile, the U.S. release of formerly secret documents demonstrated U.S. complicity in repressive military activities, including CIA payments to Contreras during 1974–77 and knowledge about military dictatorships' efforts to assist each other in eliminating political opponents.

As president, Lagos named a record number of women to high governmental posts, selected a grassroots activist to head the state environmental agenda, and demanded from his cabinet truthfulness and accountability, the latter through specific performance targets. His legislative agenda included revising the old labour code, providing better health care, increasing the minimum wage, and enacting constitutional reforms. He also assumed a high profile internationally, including attending the Asian Pacific Economic Cooperation meetings in November and negotiating conditions for Mercosur entry with Uruguay. At home, Lagos had to deal with charges of corruption against government officials who had served under former president Eduardo Frei, particularly Christian Democrats, which tarnished the Concertación image, and with a slow economic recovery from recession. The October 29 municipal elections were the first electoral measure of Lagos's popularity and of the political impact of the Lavín candidacy. The results allowed both the Concertación and the right-wing Alliance for Chile to claim victory. While the Concertación maintained its majority hold, winning 52.1% to 40.1%, it lost control of mayoralties in a number of major cities. Santiago was the most significant loss, where defeated presidential candidate Joaquin Lavin easily bested Marta Larraechea, Frei's wife, 61% to 29%.

The economy recovered in 2000, as Chile posted a positive gross domestic product growth rate of 5.5% and a positive balance of trade, spurred by a 20% increase in the export sector and rising copper prices. The slow appreciation of the undervalued dollar to 570 pesos did not hinder exports. Other signs were less optimistic. The economy slowed in the second half of the year. Unemployment remained stubbornly high, rising to 10.7% in the third quarter. The 4.5% inflation rate, while still low, was higher than forecast due to rising oil prices.

(LOIS HECHT OPPENHEIM)

CHINA

Area: 9,572,900 sq km (3,696,100 sq mi), including Tibet and excluding Taiwan (See *Taiwan,* below.)
Population (2000 est., excluding Taiwan): 1,265,207,000
Capital: Beijing
Chief of state: President Jiang Zemin
Head of government: Premier Zhu Rongji

China entered the year 2000 encumbered with a 19th-century ideology and a mid-20th-century industrial plant but was nevertheless determined to become one of the world's leading powers in the 21st century. There was good reason to suppose that such an ambitious goal lay within reach. During the course of the year, however, the Chinese government found itself struggling with a number of long-standing problems. Among them were managing the increasingly complex economy, curbing corruption, maintaining domestic order, keeping pressure on Taiwan, and preventing further deterioration in relations with the U.S. Even as Pres. Jiang Zemin focused on establishing his historical legacy, the celebratory mood of 1999—when the Communist Party of China (CPC) marked its 50th year in power—gave way to more sober, though still mostly optimistic, assessments of the future.

Politics and the Economy. Since Deng Xiaoping's break with the Maoist command economy in the 1980s, pervasive corruption had been the handmaiden of economic reform in China. Rejecting the approach afforded by an open press and a competitive political system, the government and the CPC renewed their joint assault on corruption through a series of high-profile trials that targeted officials just below the top echelons of power. In September, Cheng Kejie, former Guangxi provincial governor and vice-chairman of the Standing Committee of the National People's Congress, was executed after being convicted of having accepted nearly $5 million in bribes and having illegally sold state land. His mistress, Li Ping, received a life sentence for her role in the scandal. The official *People's Daily* newspaper thundered, "There is no place for corrupt elements to hide in the party," and "all citizens are equal before the law." Each of these propositions had yet to be consistently demonstrated.

An even more massive corruption scandal involving billions of dollars and some 200 officials wound its way through the courts of coastal Fujian province. The former vice-minister of public security, Li Jizhou, and the former police chief, vice-mayor, and head of the customs service in Xiamen city were among the accused. Earlier, the former vice-governors of Jiangxi and Guangxi provinces were executed for corruption. In May, Mou Qizhong, once publicly lauded as a leading Chinese entrepreneur, was sentenced to life imprisonment for financial fraud. The National Audit Office instituted a new policy of routinely inspecting the accounts of all retiring high-ranking officials for evidence of financial improprieties. At the popular level, an exhibition showcasing successful government efforts to combat corruption drew large crowds in Beijing. These campaigns signified renewed strength within the CPC of old- and new-guard leftists who viewed corruption as an inevitable consequence of Deng-era capitalist reforms, of which they disapproved.

Two years before his scheduled retirement from the state presidency in 2003, Jiang Zemin, who also doubled as CPC general secretary and chair of the party's Central Military Commission, attempted to burnish his reputation as a party theorist by enunciating the so-called Three Represents. Jiang asserted that the CPC had always represented three essential concerns: China's development needs, the country's advanced culture, and the fundamental interests of the vast majority of the Chinese people. This was an unsubtle expression of Jiang's determination to justify the party's exclusive hold on power in a society that in so many ways had already outgrown the restrictive framework of party rule. While further promoting Hu Jintao as his designated successor, Jiang also favoured CPC Organization Department chief Zeng Qinghong, who was expected to become a member of the inner Political Bureau Standing Committee in 2002. Meanwhile, Jiang appointed three younger generals, Cao Gangchuan, Guo Boxiong, and Xu Caihou, to take over day-to-day management of the armed forces from the elderly Zhang Wannian and Chi Haotian.

Political and religious repression continued to be a hallmark of Jiang's administration. Beneath their facade of self-assurance, government officials were anxious about social stability. For years one locus of unrest had been Xinjiang province, where a militant minority among the nine million Uygurs, a Turkic-speaking Muslim people, had resorted to force in their campaign to overturn Chinese rule. With sporadic violence continuing in Xinjiang, Beijing initiated a massive effort in March to accelerate the economic development of China's vast western region, including not only Xinjiang but also Tibet, Sichuan province, and several other economically depressed provinces. The western development project shifted state investment priorities away from the prosperous coastal provinces to the lagging interior, where poverty remained a major problem. Even if these long-term efforts succeeded, they would not necessarily undercut separatist appeals, which fed on religious and cultural grievances no less than on economic ones. Meanwhile, Tibet continued to bear the brunt of heavy-handed Chinese rule as restrictions on Tibetan Buddhism and Tibetan culture were tightened. The Dalai Lama charged that Beijing was pursuing a policy of cultural genocide. In January Beijing suffered a major humiliation with the spectacular flight to India of the young Karmapa Lama, who was received by the Dalai Lama and allowed to remain in India despite Chinese protests. Beijing had counted on the previously docile Karmapa Lama to help it implement its Tibetan policy.

Beijing's crackdown on Falun Gong, a spiritual movement that blended elements of Buddhism and Taoism with meditation and exercise, continued into its second year. Braving certain arrest, groups of Falun Gong followers periodically practiced their faith in Beijing's Tiananmen Square and were quickly taken into custody. Human rights groups estimated that at least 57 Falun Gong members had died in prison. The government also proscribed the activities of similar groups, including Zhong Gong, whose charismatic leader, Zhang Hongbao, sought political asylum in the American territory of Guam, from which Beijing sought unsuccessfully to extradite him on criminal charges. Evangelical Christians and Roman Catholics loyal to the Vatican were other targets of repression. Eighty-one-year-old Bishop Zeng Jingmu, released in 1998 after 30 years in prison, was rearrested in September for his continued refusal to recognize the authority of the state-controlled Roman Catholic Church. Beijing, reacting sourly to the Vatican's intention to canonize 130 Chinese Catholics martyred between 1648 and 1930, charged that most of them had been imperialist agents and deserved to die. In sum, a rising tide of religious faith lapped at the porous foundations of communist rule as a significant portion of the population looked to a variety of homegrown and domesticated foreign religions for spiritual fulfillment. The arrest, in separate incidents, of two visiting U.S.-based Chinese intellectuals—Song Yongyi, a research librarian, and Bei Ling, a well-known poet and editor—provoked twin storms of international criticism. Both were released and allowed to return to the U.S.

Chinese authorities wrestled too with the question of how to control traffic on the information highway as the number of Internet users in China, doubling every six months, rose to 15 million by midyear. In addition to blocking the World Wide Web sites of overseas human rights organizations and selected foreign newspapers, the Ministry of State Security shut down the New Culture Forum, a dissident Web site. The ministry also arrested Huang Qi, founder of China's first human rights Web site, and Jiang Shihua, operator of an Internet cafe in Sichuan, for having posted articles critical of the CPC.

As China's population—growing by 10 million annually—approached the 1.3 billion mark, authorities reaffirmed the one-child policy, which, they claimed, had prevented at least 250 million births over the past 20 years. Widespread evasion of this policy persisted in rural areas, although not in the cities. The difficulty of policing the vast rural reaches of China was underscored by a campaign to stop the selling of rural women and girls into prostitution. Tens of thousands of such unfortunates were kidnapped annually or hoodwinked with false promises of urban factory employment. Thousands of boys were likewise kidnapped and coerced into becoming pickpockets under the harsh control of professional criminals. According to its own experts, China had been slow to address the growing problem of AIDS and sexually transmitted diseases, which had been increasing at an annual rate of 30% for a few years. Sex education was still very limited, and few resources had been invested in promoting safe sexual practices. Lax procedures for collecting and processing blood donations had contributed to the spread of AIDS, as had widespread addiction to opiates and needle-sharing among drug addicts.

Both an immediate and a long-term threat to China's prosperity was the country's growing water crisis. China was endowed with only one-quarter of the world's per capita average of water resources, and the demands that agriculture, industry, and a growing urban population put on water supplies had already led to severe depletion of groundwater levels, conflicts between upstream and downstream consumers, and theft of water by desperate farmers. Perhaps a fifth or more of the country's water supply was wasted through inefficient irrigation systems, antiquated delivery systems, and the lack of realistic pricing systems for water resources.

Spurred once again by large-scale state investment in infrastructure development and robust export performance, the economy did better than expected, growing at around 8.1% through the first half of the year. This was one percentage point higher than the growth of 1999. In March Beijing announced its renewed intention to run a large deficit in order to stimulate the economy. The proceeds from a $12.5 billion bond issue were to be allocated to infrastructural development, 70% of which would go to the underdeveloped west; expenditures on social welfare would double.

Slack consumer demand persisted as the reduction or termination of government housing, medical, and education subsidies to urban dwellers caused people to focus on long-term security rather than on current spending. Nevertheless, the two-year-plus deflationary period came to an end, and the consumer price index showed a modest 0.1% rise by midyear. In Shanghai, Beijing, and other major cities, the more affluent urbanites invested in privately owned apartments, co-ops, and consumer durables. Foreign currency reserves increased to $158.4 billion at midyear from $150.6 billion a year earlier. Significant growth occurred in e-commerce as young Chinese entrepreneurs, handsomely bankrolled by foreign investors, explored the possibilities of the new economic frontier.

The strains of transition away from an economy dominated by state-owned enterprises to a competitive market economy were manifested in numerous, sometimes violent, protests by workers who had gone unpaid for months or were facing layoffs. In February 20,000 factory workers rioted in Liaoning province after a molybdenum mine was shut down, and in August irate workers briefly took six American managers hostage when their factory was threatened with closure. Similarly, thousands of farmers in Jiangxi violently protested low commodity prices and high taxes, smashing local government offices and attacking the homes of the rich. In a number of cases, troops were called out to put down protests.

Foreign Relations. China's campaign to earn membership in the World Trade Organization (WTO) took a giant step forward in 2000. After prolonged wrangling across partisan lines, the U.S. Congress approved the granting of permanent normal trade relations (PNTR) to China. The administration of Pres. Bill Clinton and the American business community strongly supported PNTR;

labour, human rights, and environmental groups opposed them. In China, as in the U.S. and elsewhere, critics of economic globalization decried the loss of national economic sovereignty and claimed that membership in the WTO—which they viewed as an instrument of foreign, particularly American, capitalism—would harm domestic interests. Nevertheless, China was expected to join the WTO in 2001.

U.S.-China relations recovered partially from the crisis occasioned by the May 1999 NATO bombing of the Chinese embassy in Belgrade, Yugos., but mutual suspicion remained the keynote. The victory of Chen Shui-bian (*see* BIOGRAPHIES), a pro-independence candidate, in Taiwan's March 2000 presidential election renewed the question of what position Washington would take in the event of a direct clash between Beijing and Taipei. China strongly warned the U.S. to keep out of its domestic affairs, including management of the Taiwan issue. Beijing refused Chen's olive branch of unconditional discussions, insisting that he first pledge unequivocal support for Beijing's version of the One China principle. This Chen refused to do. While issuing numerous threats, Beijing did not, however, resort to military exercises or missile tests, as it had four years earlier during Taiwan's first direct presidential election.

North Korean chief of state Kim Jong Il (left) shakes hands with Chinese Pres. Jiang Zemin at the Great Hall of the People in Beijing on May 30.

AP/Wide World Photos

Prior to the June 2000 North-South Korean summit meeting in Pyongyang, Beijing welcomed North Korean leader Kim Jong Il for three days of consultation with President Jiang, National People's Congress Chairman Li Peng, Premier Zhu Rongji, and other top leaders. The meetings were viewed as an indication of China's interest in a peaceful resolution to the intra-Korean conflict.

Relations with Japan remained barely satisfactory as Japanese officials complained about Chinese maritime maneuvers and seabed exploration in Japanese territorial waters. In October Premier Zhu Rongji made an official six-day visit to Japan.

In July Russian Pres. Vladimir Putin visited Beijing, where he and Jiang jointly condemned U.S. proposals for national and Asian theatre missile defense systems, which the Russians and Chinese perceived as violations of the 1972 antiballistic missile treaty. China threatened to significantly upgrade its own nuclear weapons program if Washington went ahead with the proposals. President Clinton opted in September to leave the matter in the hands of his successor, a decision that placated Beijing in the short run. Meanwhile, China pursued an active agenda in the Middle East as well as in Asia and Europe via trade, diplomatic dialogue, and high-level visits.

A narrow loser in its earlier bid to host the 2000 Summer Games, China renewed its effort to bring the Olympics to Beijing, setting its sights on 2008. Beijing made the International Olympic Committee's five-city shortlist, and Chinese officials had high hopes for taking the prize. Authorities in Beijing undertook the "greenification" of their dusty and polluted metropolis by expanding park space, planting trees and grass, and banning the use of coal for cooking and heating. The first positive results were already in evidence by year's end. (STEVEN I. LEVINE)

COLOMBIA

Area: 1,141,568 sq km (440,762 sq mi)
Population (2000 est.): 42,299,000
Capital: Santafé de Bogotá, D.C.
Head of state and government: President Andrés Pastrana Arango

Political turmoil continued on two fronts in Colombia during 2000. Conflict between the executive and legislative branches of the government was fueled by a corruption scandal, and the long-standing battle between the government and leftist guerrilla groups continued virtually unabated. Although these problems contributed to a delay in the government's implementation of restructuring plans mandated by the International Monetary Fund (IMF), the country's economic performance was modestly positive.

In mid-March a corruption scandal broke involving several high-ranking legislators, who were accused of giving more than 500 questionable contracts—amounting to about $3 million—in exchange for political favours. Those implicated in the scandal included members of the coalition supporting Pres. Andrés Pastrana Arango. The president quickly went on the offensive, demanding the resignation of three legislators, including the speaker of the House. Within two weeks Pastrana submitted a draft of a reform referendum to Congress. The proposed reforms included, among other things, dissolving Congress and replacing it with a smaller legislature, barring elected officials from using substitutes to fill their seats while they pursued other activities, publishing congressional votes, and holding new elections. The ambitious package was clearly a political miscalculation on Pastrana's part. Legislators immediately countered that new presidential elections should be held, and the overwhelming opposition in Congress led the president to withdraw his proposal. As part of the political fallout surrounding the failed reform effort, Pastrana was forced to reshuffle his cabinet, and his presidential approval ratings plummeted to about 20%.

Resolution of the violent struggle with leftist guerrilla groups was not on the horizon in 2000. The government agreed to give the National Liberation Army (ELN) de facto control over three municipalities while the guerrilla group negotiated a peace accord with government and civilian representatives. The agreement met with vociferous opposition from locals, who were perhaps encouraged by right-wing paramilitaries. As negotiations continued, the largest of the paramilitary groups, the United Self-Defense Forces of Colombia (AUC), launched a major offensive against the ELN. The guerrillas complained that the AUC was receiving support from the Colombian military. A much larger "demilitarized" zone in the southern part of the country was controlled by the leftist Revolutionary Armed Forces of Colombia (FARC), which used the area to recruit and train members and to raise financial support through the drug trade and kidnappings. In June the U.S. Congress approved $1.3 billion in mostly military aid for Colombia as part of an international aid package worth $7.5 billion. While it was hoped that the aid would encourage the FARC to take peace talks more seriously, many observers expected it to lead to escalating violence in the short run as the guerrillas sought to strengthen their positions in the event that peace talks ever became particularly substantive.

After a recession in 1999 in which the economy shrank by nearly 5%, gross domestic product (GDP) growth in the 2.5–3% range was expected for 2000. The government delayed in addressing its deficit-spending tendencies and was unlikely to hit the target it had promised the IMF—a deficit equal to 3.6% of GDP. IMF support for the Pastrana administration was likely to continue, however. Both the inflation and the unemployment rates were expected to drop, though only by a point or two, and the growth rate was expected to increase slightly in 2001.

(BRIAN F. CRISP)

COMOROS

Area: 1,862 sq km (719 sq mi), excluding the 375-sq km (145-sq mi) island of Mayotte, a de facto dependency of France since 1976
Population (2000 est.): 578,000 (excluding 156,000 on Mayotte)
Capital: Moroni
Chief of state and head of government: Col. Azali Assoumani

In January 2000 the separatist Anjouan government held a referendum on an Organization of African Unity (OAU)-brokered agreement that would end the secession crisis by granting the three Comoros islands (Grande Comore, Anjouan, and Mohéli) a measure of autonomy. Amid accusations of fraud and other irregularities at the nonsecret ballot box, about 95% of the electorate supported the Anjouan government's refusal to sign. As a result, the OAU imposed sanctions on the breakaway island. In late March soldiers mounted an unsuccessful coup against federal Pres. Azali Assoumani, the 19th attempted coup since independence in 1975. In July the OAU Council of Ministers endorsed military intervention to end Anjouan's secession. By August the secessionists and the federal government had signed an agreement to replace the federal constitution with a looser confederation within 18 months. Observers and Comoros residents were skeptical of the arrangement, and in September the Anjouan government began cracking down on opponents of the reunification deal.

In March World Bank and International Monetary Fund officials began talks with the government to activate previously frozen loans and aid projects. They cited the government's implementation of a short-term economic plan and restructured civil service. A cholera outbreak that struck Anjouan in April and then spread to Grande Comore subsided in June.

(MATTHEW A. CENZER)

CONGO, DEMOCRATIC REPUBLIC OF THE (THE FORMER ZAIRE)

Area: 2,344,858 sq km (905,354 sq mi)
Population (2000 est.): 51,965,000
Capital: Kinshasa (executive and ministerial); Lubumbashi (legislative from August 2000)
Head of state and government: President Laurent-Désiré Kabila

In January 2000 a special meeting of the UN Security Council—attended by the leaders of the Democratic Republic of the Congo (DRC), Uganda, Rwanda, Zimbabwe, Angola, and Namibia—attempted to resolve the conflict in the DRC between government forces, aided by troops from Zimbabwe, Angola, and

Namibia, and rebels backed by Ugandan and Rwandan soldiers; the fighting had continued despite the cease-fire agreement signed in Lusaka, Zambia, in July 1999. The Security Council's efforts were frustrated, however, by DRC Pres. Laurent Kabila's demand that all Ugandan and Rwandan troops be withdrawn unconditionally from his country and the counterstatement from Rwanda that withdrawal would be conditional upon adequate measures being taken to protect the security of its borders from incursions from the DRC. Mistrust and intransigence of that kind, together with intermittent fighting between the opposing forces, bedeviled successive attempts by the UN and by neighbouring African countries to bring peace to the Congo. In November fighting intensified, and Eric Silwamba, Zambia's presidential affairs minister, declared that the peace effort was nearing collapse.

In February the UN Security Council agreed to send a 5,537-strong peace-monitoring force to the DRC. On April 8, after two months of renewed hostilities in which charges of aggression were made by all sides, the opposing forces agreed to a new cease-fire, to commence on April 14, with all groups retaining their existing positions for three months in order to allow the peace-monitoring force to deploy among them. Early in May a Security Council delegation led by Richard Holbrooke, the U.S. permanent representative at the UN, arrived in the DRC to check whether the cease-fire would hold sufficiently to allow the peace-monitoring force to operate effectively. Fighting broke out again between Ugandan and Rwandan forces, but by May 22 they had agreed to withdraw their troops 100 km (60 mi) from the much-fought-over town of Kisangani.

President Kabila himself refused to accept the deployment of any peacekeepers—a démarche that he shortly afterward withdrew—when leaders of neighbouring African countries made a further attempt to revive the July 1999 agreement at a meeting in Lusaka in mid-August. Kabila, however, made it clear he would no longer accept any accord that threatened his power. This threw into doubt the prospect of any renewal of the Security Council's mandate for a peace-monitoring force.

In yet another attempt to put a stop to the fighting, UN Secretary-General Kofi Annan appointed Gen. Abdulsalam Abubakar of Nigeria as a special envoy to the DRC to try to enlist the cooperation of Kabila. A few days later Kabila inaugurated a transitional parliament, but once again there were doubts about its effectiveness.

During the year President Kabila shuffled his cabinet twice. The first time, in September, was a minor reorganization. The second occasion, however, in November, was a major restructuring. Deputy Minister of Economy, Commerce, and Industry Jean Amisi Kalondaya was elevated to finance minister, replacing Mawampanga Mwana Nanga (held responsible by many for the country's economic collapse following the 1997 ouster of dictator Mobutu Sese Seko); Mawampanga was assigned to the newly created Ministry of Fisheries and Livestock; and Human Rights Minister Leonard She Okitundu replaced controversial foreign minister Abdoulaye Yerodia Ndombasi, who had made disparaging comments about Tutsi-led rebels and, as a result, had an arrest warrant issued against him by a Belgian judge for inciting ethnic hatred.

(KENNETH INGHAM)

Bodies of dead soldiers lie in a street in Kisangani, Dem. Rep. of Congo, patrolled by Rwandan troops on June 11.

Emmanuel Goujon/AFP Worldwide

CONGO, REPUBLIC OF THE

Area: 342,000 sq km (132,047 sq mi)
Population (2000 est.): 2,831,000
Capital: Brazzaville
Head of state and government: President Denis Sassou-Nguesso

Efforts to stabilize affairs in the aftermath of the Republic of the Congo's civil war achieved some success during 2000. On Dec. 29, 1999, representatives of the army had signed a new truce with rebel groups that were backing either exiled former president Pascal Lissouba or longtime opposition leader Bernard Kolelas. A pledge was made to open a national dialogue. Further progress was signaled when on March 20 a delegation from the army flew into the southwestern district of Zanaga, a centre of support for Lissouba, for new talks. This defused rumours of a military invasion of the area, although another rebel leader, Frederic Bintsangou of the National Resistance Council, issued a statement calling for the withdrawal of all foreign troops before he would join the peace process. In late November the government began drafting a new constitution.

Rebuilding the oil-rich country's shattered economy after three years of civil war remained a high priority. On January 6 the national legislature approved a new budget of $1,060,000,000, an increase of 23% over the previous year. Approximately 60% of the anticipated revenues were projected to come from the petroleum sector. Much of the increase was earmarked for capital investment and for the rebuilding of infrastructure badly damaged during the war. The entire Congo-Ocean Railway was officially reopened on August 15, the 40th anniversary of independence from France. It had been closed for 23 months. (NANCY ELLEN LAWLER)

COSTA RICA

Area: 51,100 sq km (19,730 sq mi)
Population (2000 est.): 3,644,000
Capital: San José
Head of state and government: President Miguel Angel Rodríguez Echeverría

There was good news and bad news for Costa Rica in 2000. The good news was economic; the bad was political. The economy, which had been recovering steadily since its negative performance in 1996, grew at an estimated pace of 4.7% in 2000. Moreover, inflation was reduced to about 9%, the lowest rate since 1993. Capping the good economic news was the successful lobbying effort by Pres. Miguel Angel Rodríguez during his May visit to Washington, D.C., to widen access to American markets for Costa Rican goods. The hope was that greater access to markets for textile and leather goods would create more than 5,000 new jobs and increase exports by $100 million.

Ironically, efforts by the Rodríguez administration to sustain long-term economic growth triggered an onslaught of labour actions and popular protests. The year began with demonstrations by teachers demanding that the government not renege on a 1997 agreement guaranteeing them overtime pay for the expansion of the school year from 195 to 200 days. The greatest civil unrest came in March and April, however, with protests against the approval of the "Energy Combo" legislation, a package of three bills designed to modernize the Costa Rican Electricity Institute (ICE) in the areas of energy and telecommunications. ICE is a state monopoly that had extended electric and telephone service to nearly all areas of the country but had been criticized for inefficiency. The bill was strongly supported by the country's two main political parties but opposed by minor parties. During the largest demonstrations in Costa Rica in 30 years, charges were made that the bill was filled with potential for a division of spoils between the two main parties. Although the government eventually agreed to table the legislation and to set up a bipartisan committee to review its provisions, the Supreme Court on April 18 declared the bill unconstitutional.

(MITCHELL A. SELIGSON)

CÔTE D'IVOIRE

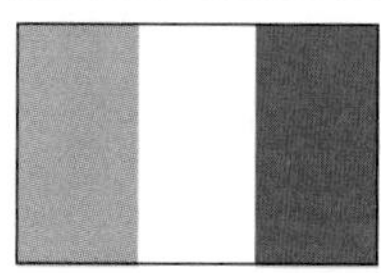

Area: 322,463 sq km (124,504 sq mi)
Population (2000 est.): 15,981,000
Seats of government: predominantly Abidjan; some ministries have relocated to Yamoussoukro
Chiefs of state: Brig. Gen. Robert Gueï and, from October 26, President Laurent Gbagbo
Head of government: Prime Ministers Daniel Kablan Duncan and Seydou Elimane Diarra from May 18, and, from October 27, Affi N'Guessan

Brig. Gen. Robert Gueï, head of the military junta that overthrew Pres. Henri Konan Bédié in a bloodless coup on Christmas Eve 1999, was himself the target of a failed military assassination attempt on Sept. 18, 2000.

On January 12 the newly formed coalition government that included former prime minister Alassane Ouattara's Rally of Republicans (RDR) was further strengthened when four members of Laurent Gbagbo's Ivorian Popular Front (FPI) agreed to join the cabinet. The new government pledged to tackle corruption, reduce administrative costs, boost the flagging coffee and cocoa sectors, and restore civilian rule by October. In a July referendum voters approved a new constitution that included a last-minute addition requiring that both parents of presidential candidates be Ivorian. The clause was widely interpreted as another means of preventing Ouattara, whose mother was said to be Burkinabe, from contesting the October presidential elections.

Protests against the government continued, and tensions remained particularly high in Abidjan. Despite the lifting in May of a ban on political meetings, three journalists from an independent newspaper were arrested on May 16 following publication of an article critical of Gueï. In a May 18 cabinet reshuffle, eight army officers were appointed to office; all but one minister of Ouattara's RDR were dropped, however. Rumours of a new coup swept the country on June 22, causing panic and sporadic looting. Soldiers demanding the payment of a promised bonus mutinied on July 5; Abidjan, Bouaké, and Korhogo were virtually shut down in the two-day crisis, during which a news photographer in Bouaké and several others reportedly were killed. Despite earlier promises that he would withdraw from government following the October 22 elections, Gueï announced in August that he would run for president as an independent.

In the highly volatile event, Gueï, though losing to opponent Laurent Gbagbo, attempted to remain in office by halting the vote count. Violence swept the country as Gbagbo supporters staged a popular revolt; Gueï went into hiding, and Gbagbo assumed office. Another uprising occurred when followers loyal to Ouattara clashed with Gbagbo supporters. Following a week of unrest, in which about 50 opposition leaders were massacred, soldiers and police returned to their barracks. Gbagbo later gave his consent for an international inquiry into the killings.

On October 26 Gbagbo was installed as president, and the following day he named a new prime minister, Affi N'Guessan, the minister of industry and tourism in the outgoing regime. Meanwhile, Ouattara, who had initially refused to support the new government, pledged not to block its formation.

Gueï reemerged in November and instructed the military to support the new government, which hinted that it would not seek prosecution for human rights abuses committed during Gueï's tenure.

When parliamentary elections were held in December, Ouattara was again blocked from participating. More than 20,000 people demonstrated, and at least 20 persons were killed. Both the UN and the European Union condemned his exclusion. Of the 225 parliamentary seats, the FPI captured 96, the Democratic Party of Côte d'Ivoire won 77, independents held 16, and 28 were left vacant, awaiting elections in the northern constituencies.

In early January Gueï suspended payments to foreign creditors but assured them that the measure was only temporary. By January 27 the government had repaid the last of the approximately $30 million of European Union money that had mysteriously "disappeared" under the old regime. Nevertheless, owing to the volatile political situation, major donors refused to renew most assistance to the country. (NANCY ELLEN LAWLER)

CROATIA

Area: 56,542 sq km (21,831 sq mi)
Population (2000 est.): 4,282,000
Capital: Zagreb
Chief of state: Acting Presidents Vlatko Pavletic and, from February 2 to 18, Zlatko Tomcic; President from February 18, Stipe Mesic
Head of government: Prime Ministers Zlatko Matesa and, from January 27, Ivica Racan

AP/Wide World Photos

A day before his inauguration as president of Croatia, Stipe Mesic (left) welcomes Italian Prime Minister Massimo D'Alema (right) in his office in Zagreb.

In 2000 the defeat of Croatia's ruling Croatian Democratic Union (HDZ), which had firmly governed the former Yugoslav republic since independence in 1991, was a watershed in the country's relations with the international community and signaled the beginning of real, if difficult, domestic reforms.

On January 3 a coalition of six opposition political parties led by the centre-left Social Democratic Party of Croatia (SDP) and the centre-right Croatian Social-Liberal Party (HSLS) swept the parliamentary elections, taking 71 of 151 seats (including 6 seats reserved for Croats living abroad). In the February 7 presidential elections to replace Franjo Tudjman, who had died the previous December, the HDZ candidate failed to reach the second round. The SDP-HSLS joint candidate, Drazen Budisa, a prominent dissident jailed by the communist authorities in the 1970s, ran against the former high-ranking HDZ official Stipe Mesic. (*See* BIOGRAPHIES.) Unexpectedly, Mesic won by a wide margin, 56% to 44%.

The liberal opposition's victory opened new opportunities for Croatia's integration into Western institutions, a process that had been frozen by international dissatisfaction with the former regime. Changes came quickly. On January 24 the European Union announced that it was putting in place a joint EU-Croatia Consultative Task Force to guide the development of relations. President Mesic's first official foreign visit took place in March to neighbouring Bosnia and Herzegovina, where the stage was set for several agreements on border and customs issues, ending the former frostiness in their relations. In May, Croatia became the newest member of NATO's Partnership for Peace program, and on November 30 it became the 139th member of the World Trade Organization. Mesic visited Washington, D.C., in August, and U.S. and Croatian naval forces conducted joint military exercises along the Dalmatian coast in September.

Croatia's new government played a difficult balancing act, on the one hand trying to cooperate with the International Criminal Tribunal for the Former Yugoslavia, which sought justice for crimes committed by Croatian armed forces against minority Serbs during the war, and, on the other, trying to keep veterans organizations happy by not calling into question the legitimacy of the country's war of independence. During early September, Croatian authorities arrested dozens of persons, including military officers, for crimes ranging from wartime atrocities to drug trafficking. President Mesic forcibly retired seven generals for publicly criticizing the government's crackdown on suspected war criminals.

Living conditions worsened as the government sought to rationalize the economy, shutting down unprofitable state firms and cutting back subsidies to enterprises. Unemployment rose to 22%. While the important tourism revenues increased substantially over the previous year, nearly reaching the prewar level of $4 billion, and although inflation was checked at 6%, the economy as a whole could generate a growth rate of only about 3.0%. In a drive against the endemic corruption, the new government jailed a former minister of tourism, Ivan Herak, for having embezzled ministry funds. In November Nevenka Tudjman, the daughter of the deceased president Franjo Tudjman, was charged with graft, stemming from a $1.1 million scheme. A formal indictment had not been made, however. Nonetheless, hamstrung by a dysfunctional court system and internal political bickering, the government made little headway against other fraudulent privatization schemes, which were estimated to have cost the state nearly $2 billion. This, coupled with an inability to attract new loans and foreign investment, led to increased public frustration with the worsening standard of living. (MAX PRIMORAC)

CUBA

Area: 110,861 sq km (42,804 sq mi)
Population (2000 est.): 11,148,000
Capital: Havana
Head of state and government: President of the Council of State and President of the Council of Ministers Fidel Castro Ruz

Politics in Cuba in the year 2000 was largely dominated by the plight of a six-year-old. In November 1999 Elián González was rescued off the coast of Florida and taken aboard a U.S. Coast Guard vessel after a failed ocean crossing from Cuba during which his mother and 10 others had drowned. A highly politicized custody battle followed between the boy's Miami, Fla., relatives and his father in Cuba. The case was not resolved until June 28, 2000, when the U.S. Supreme Court refused to issue an order that would keep him in the country. Accompanied by his father, who had been allowed to travel to the U.S., the boy flew home to Cuba that same day.

The "Elián case" had an extraordinary impact in both Cuba and the U.S. The Cuban government viewed the boy's return as a major victory. Cuban officials, including Pres. Fidel Castro, used the opportunity to demand the end of the long-standing embargo and to denounce the "influence of the powerful Cuban-American community on U.S. policy toward Cuba." The case also had a more subtle effect on the island. After months of televised debates during which the pros and cons of the American legal system were analyzed—sometimes in excruciating detail—Cubans had the chance to see for themselves how democracy worked.

Activity in the U.S. Congress during the year promised to have a strong impact on American-Cuban relations. After months of debate, on October 6, Republican negotiators in Congress agreed on a plan to allow for the sale of medicine to Cuba for the first time in nearly four decades. Intense lobbying by agribusinesses and the easing of restrictions on American trade smoothed the way for legislative approval. Nevertheless, the bill drew intense criticism because of restrictions added by Cuban-American lawmakers. Anti-Castro groups were able to win new limitations on travel to Cuba as well as prohibitions on U.S. government credit and private financing for any transactions. The cash-strapped Cuban government vowed they would not buy any food from the U.S. under the restrictions. Despite this, the bill passed through Congress handily, however, and was signed into law on October 28.

The Cuban economy grew for a sixth consecutive year despite high oil prices and weak export markets for sugar. Real gross domestic product (GDP) growth for 1999 was 6.2%. Early estimates for GDP growth in 2000 varied from 4.5% to 5.5%. The figure for the first half of the year was calculated at 7.7%. The growth was largely attributed to a 6% jump in tourism and a 7% increase in Cuba's sugar harvest.

Though the government fell short of attracting its target of two million visitors for 2000, tourism continued to be the driving force behind the economy and one of the biggest earners of hard currency. The United Nations Economic Commission for Latin America estimated that Cuba garnered $2.6 billion in gross earnings from tourism for the year, up from $2.2 billion in 1999. In preparation for a continuing influx, Cuba was investing heavily in infrastructure, including building new hotels and roads. Foreign investment was expected to play a major role in this endeavour. New deals in 2000 included a $10.6 million agreement between Leisure Canada and Cuban partner Gran Caribe Hotels to begin construction on a resort and golf course. The year also saw the merger of two Cuban tourism giants, Cubanacan and CIMEX. The alliance was intended to bolster the already considerable presence of the two government-operated firms in the tourism industry.

In its 2000 report Amnesty International stated that at least 13 people were executed in Cuba during 1999 and that at least nine people remained under sentence of death on the island. There were also reports of the persecution and imprisonment of journalists. Cuban officials arrested three Swedish journalists on August 29 and deported them on the 31st. They were accused of breaking the law by using tourist visas to come to Cuba and then engaging in journalistic work. The three reportedly met with Cuban independent journalists at a workshop on freedom of the press.

(ANA JULIA JATAR)

CYPRUS

Area: 9,251 sq km (3,572 sq mi) for the entire island; the area of the Turkish Republic of Northern Cyprus (TRNC), proclaimed unilaterally (1983) in the occupied northern third of the island, 3,355 sq km (1,295 sq mi)
Population (2000 est.): island 865,000; TRNC only, 192,000 (including recent Turkish settlers and Turkish military)
Capital: Lefkosia/Lefkosa (also known as Nicosia)
Head(s) of state and government: President Glafcos Clerides; of the TRNC, President Rauf Denktash

Turkish-Cypriot leader Rauf Denktash (left) is welcomed by Turkish Prime Minister Bulent Ecevit for talks in Istanbul in August.

AFP/Corbis

In 2000 the leaders of the two Cyprus governments each met challenges. The Greek Cyprus president, Glafcos Clerides, endured surgery but recovered quickly. Rauf Denktash, his Turkish Cyprus counterpart, was reelected.

Tension between the Greek and Turkish sectors continued, but so did dialogue. In UN-organized "proximity talks" leaders of the two sides, though not in direct contact, discussed security, property, and territory. Religious visits by both sides across the border continued and led to agreements to restore shrines under UN auspices. UN-sponsored talks did not yield an agreement on the island's division, however.

Greek Cypriots looked to the UN, the European Union, and Third World nations for support. Their Turkish counterparts sought allies in the Islamic world and the Turkic nations of Central Asia. Negotiations to gain EU membership continued, and the EU did not make resolution of the Greek-Turkish problem a precondition for membership. Accession was forecast for 2001.

The economy of Greek Cyprus continued to grow in 2000, particularly in regard to tourist arrivals, but inflation and balance of trade deficits caused concern. Turkish Cyprus experienced economic crisis sparked by the failure of several major banks and the consequent loss of depositors' savings. Measures to deal with the issue, with Turkish aid, included transfer of the failed banks to the government, plans for reimbursement of uninsured savers, and possible prosecution of those responsible.

(GEORGE H. KELLING)

CZECH REPUBLIC

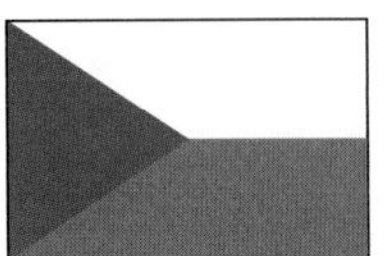

Area: 78,866 sq km (30,450 sq mi)
Population (2000 est.): 10,273,000
Capital: Prague
Chief of state: President Vaclav Havel
Head of government: Prime Minister Milos Zeman

Although the year 2000 brought some improvement, the Czech political and economic situation continued to be rather shaky. On January 26 the ruling Social Democrats (CSSD) and opposition Civic Democratic Party (ODS) agreed to strengthen their "opposition agreement" that had come into force after the June 1998 parliamentary elections and the changes provided for increased cooperation on the state budget, electoral reform, and preparations for accession to the European Union (EU). The international community welcomed the pact, since it ensured more political stability and ended the threat that the CSSD minority government would fall, but it drew criticism from other opposition parties, from Pres. Vaclav Havel, and from within the CSSD itself.

After two failed attempts, the 2000 state budget was finally approved in early March. ODS support, however, was conditional on a cabinet reshuffle. In February Bohumil Fiser was named health minister, taking over from temporary caretaker Vladimir Spidla, a deputy prime minister. Four more ministers lost their posts after the approval of the budget; Transport and Communications Minister Antonin Peltram was replaced with Jaromir Schling, Local Development Minister Jaromir Cisar with Petr Lachnit, Interior Minister Vaclav Grulich with Stanislav Gross, and Minister Without Portfolio Jaroslav Basta with Karel Brezina. Trust in the cabinet began to grow after the reshuffle, and an opinion poll released in September showed that the CSSD was back on top for the first time since April 1999.

The strengthened "opposition agreement" also led the parliament to alter the electoral law and to approve constitutional changes to reduce presidential powers. The new electoral legislation introduced elements of the "first- past-the-post" system and was thought to favour the CSSD and ODS. After a presidential veto of the law was overridden in July, Havel filed a complaint with the Constitutional Court. In any case, some opinion polls showed that four smaller centre-right opposition parties, which in late September signed an agreement to run as a coalition in 2002, would win elections even under the new electoral law.

The ODS and the CSSD also tried to change the law on the Czech National Bank (CNB), and critics argued that the legislation would allow for political interference. Havel vetoed the bill in late October, and the bank's governor, Josef Tosovsky, resigned the following day. In late November a crisis emerged between Havel and the government when the president appointed Zdenek Tuma as the CNB's new governor without getting Zeman's countersignature.

The country's new administrative setup came into force in January, and the 13 regional assemblies were chosen in elections on November 12. Senate elections also took place that day, and the CSSD experienced a bitter defeat in both polls. In fact, the CSSD and ODS lost their majority status in the Senate, calling into question the future of the "opposition agreement."

In other political news, in late February Karel Kuhnl was elected chairman of the Freedom Union, one of the key partners in the four-party opposition coalition. In March the leadership of the secret services was taken over by Prime Minister Milos Zeman and two cabinet ministers. In late May the parliament approved a law to restore Jewish property confiscated after the Nazi occupation.

On the economic front, the Czech Republic finally emerged from two years of recession, and growth in gross domestic product was expected to reach 2–2.7% despite a summer drought that damaged the country's agricultural production. Unemployment was expected to grow to 9.2% by year's end, while annual inflation was predicted at 3.3–3.8%.

Throughout the year the Czech banking sector was the most problematic area of the economy. In February the government announced plans to bail out the troubled Komercni Banka, the country's biggest bank, and a majority share of Ceska Sporitelna was sold to Austria's Erste Bank. In mid-June the ailing IPB bank was placed under forced administration as masked police officers occupied its Prague headquarters, an act that triggered criticism from the Japanese firm Nomura International PLC, which had purchased the bank in 1997.

In September an International Monetary Fund/World Bank annual meeting was held in Prague, and the city became the site of major environmentalist and antiglobalization protests. (*See* ECONOMIC AFFAIRS: *Sidebar.*) Tensions with Austria heated up when the Czech Republic's Temelin nuclear power plant approached completion and underwent test runs in October. The plant, built according to a 1987 Soviet design, was situated only 50 km (30 mi) from the border with Austria, a nuclear-free country since 1978. At one point the Austrians had threatened to obstruct the accession of the Czech Republic into the European Union (EU) if it persisted with the plant. In December the Czechs agreed to have an EU team inspect the facility before it went operational.

(SHARON FISHER)

DENMARK

Area: 43,096 sq km (16,639 sq mi)
Population (2000 est.): 5,339,000
Capital: Copenhagen
Chief of state: Queen Margrethe II
Head of government: Prime Minister Poul Nyrup Rasmussen

After a closely fought six-month campaign, Danes delivered a bruising blow to the euro, the European Union's (EU's) beleaguered single currency. On Sept. 28, 2000, a national referendum was held in which participation in the European Economic and Monetary Union (EMU) was voted down by a resounding 53–47%.

The "no" vote—which split Danes into two almost equal camps—came in defiance of Prime Minister Poul Nyrup Rasmussen's seven-year-old Social Democrat-led government, a majority of parliamentary parties, the central bank, industry, commerce, the media, and the establishment, all of which had strongly urged a "yes" vote. Bemused analysts attributed the rejection of the measure to several factors, including a feel-good factor at a time of economic upturn, which made a change of currency seem superfluous. Denmark's "no" to the euro also stirred up memories of 1992, when Danes triggered a Europe-wide crisis by rejecting the Maastricht Treaty. This time finance markets had braced for a rejection, and the EU and the euro were scarcely rocked.

Political analysts observed that the rejection had no impact on the EMU but that Denmark could become a difficult EU partner when the EU carried out reforms necessary to take in new Central and Eastern European members in 2001. The rejection was also seen as delaying similar votes on euro participation in the two other EMU outsider member nations, the U.K. and Sweden.

In October Prime Minister Rasmussen stressed Copenhagen's determination to work for a speedy EU enlargement and pursue constructive pro-EU policies. He also pledged that any referenda exempting Denmark from European cooperation would be in the distant future. Denmark would also keep its local krone currency pegged tightly to the EU's single currency—the krone was fixed to the euro with a plus/minus 2.25% fluctuation band.

On the economic home front, the upturn in prosperity continued. Inflation was moderate; unemployment was forecast at 5.3% for 2000, a 25-year low; and current account, foreign trade, and state budget surpluses, as well as purchasing power, were at an all-time high. On July 1 Queen Margrethe II of Denmark and King Carl XVI Gustaf of Sweden opened the 16.4-km (10.2-mi) Øresund Fixed Link, a more than $3 billion road-railway tunnel-bridge project that linked Copenhagen with the Swedish city of Malmö.

Independence talks between Denmark and its North Atlantic province—the Faroe Islands—were deadlocked, and a September referendum on the issue was postponed until April 2001. The failure of test drilling to find oil or gas off the coast of Arctic Greenland put a damper on devolution plans of the vast island's home-rule government. In the summer Greenland celebrated the 1,000th anniversary of its conversion to Christianity by Norse explorer Leif Eriksson the Lucky and of his voyage of discovery to Vinland. (*See* CANADA: *Sidebar,* above.)

In November Denmark was plunged into a state of mourning following the death of much-loved Swedish-born Queen Ingred, who died quietly in her sleep. (*See* OBITUARIES.)

(CHRISTOPHER FOLLETT)

DJIBOUTI

Area: 23,200 sq km (8,950 sq mi)
Population (2000 est.): 451,000
Capital: Djibouti
Chief of state and head of government: President Ismail Omar Guelleh, assisted by Prime Minister Barkat Gourad Hamadou

In February 2000 the government of Djibouti and rebels of the Front for the Restoration of Unity and Democracy (FRUD) signed an agreement to end fighting that had begun in 1991. FRUD chairman Ahmad Dini Ahmad returned from nine years of exile and pledged to turn the movement into a peaceful political party.

In March Djibouti reestablished diplomatic relations with Eritrea; they had been suspended in 1998 amid Eritrean claims that arms shipments bound for Ethiopia had passed through the port of Djibouti. Pres. Ismail Omar Guelleh assumed the role of regional peacemaker in March when he hosted talks aimed at finding a settlement to the conflict in Somalia. When the dialogue ended in August, a transitional Somali National Assembly based in Djibouti had been established. Although Guelleh's efforts drew praise from the UN, the Organization of African Unity, and many foreign governments, some Somali faction leaders boycotted the talks and accused Guelleh of pursuing a regional-power agenda.

In April the UN pledged nearly $7 million to upgrade Djibouti's port and road facilities. The already-busy port was the major transit point for relief aid to some 12.4 million people threatened by severe drought in northeastern Africa. An estimated 150,000 people affected by drought in Djibouti received emergency assistance from the UN World Food Programme.

(MATTHEW A. CENZER)

DOMINICA

Area: 750 sq km (290 sq mi)
Population (2000 est.): 76,300
Capital: Roseau
Chief of state: President Vernon Shaw
Head of government: Prime Ministers Edison James, Roosevelt Douglas from February 7 to October 1, and, from October 1, Pierre Charles

Although the Dominica Labour Party (DLP) fell short of capturing an overall majority in the Jan. 31, 2000, general election, winning 10 of the 21 seats in the House of Assembly, it was able to form a government by persuading the Dominica Freedom Party, which obtained two seats, to join forces. DLP leader Roosevelt ("Rosie") Douglas, a veteran politician with a left-wing reputation, became the new prime minister.

The new administration called a halt in February to the controversial "economic citizenship" program, under which Dominican passports were granted to foreigners—most of them from East Asia and many of whom turned out to be of questionable character—but the practice was reinstituted in April.

Also in February the government announced that it would conduct preliminary investigations into allegations of corruption and maladministration by the previous regime, headed by the United Workers' Party. On October 1 Prime Minister Douglas, who had vowed to deal with such matters, suffered a fatal heart attack; Communications and Works Minister Pierre Charles became prime minister. Charles also assumed the portfolios of foreign affairs, legal affairs, and national security, held by Douglas. Reginald Austrie was assigned the communications and works portfolio.

In July Finance Minister Ambrose George presented an EC$354.2 million 2000–01 budget (EC$1=U.S. $2.71), EC$121.3 million of which would be devoted to capital development projects.

(DAVID RENWICK)

DOMINICAN REPUBLIC

Area: 48,671 sq km (18,792 sq mi)
Population (2000 est.): 8,443,000
Capital: Santo Domingo
Head of state and government: Presidents Leonel Fernández Reyna and, from August 16, Hipólito Mejía Dominguez

Hipólito Mejía Dominguez (right), the newly elected president of the Dominican Republic, appears at a news conference with his vice presidential running mate, Milagros Ortiz Bosch.

The central event in the Dominican Republic was the election on May 16, 2000, of Hipólito Mejía Dominguez to the presidency. Apart from an unsuccessful attempt by computer hackers to manipulate the election commission's tabulations, the election was probably the cleanest in the country's history and brought to office the Dominican Revolutionary Party, which had last been in power in 1986 and was deprived of office in 1994 owing to election irregularities.

Although Mejía roundly defeated his opponents—Danilo Medina of the incumbent Dominican Liberation Party and former president Joaquín Balaguer of the Social Christian Reformist Party—he narrowly missed achieving the 50% majority vote necessary to avoid a runoff. Predictions that Medina and Balaguer would form a coalition in a bid to defeat Mejía failed to materialize. Balaguer, the infirm nonagenarian and seven-time president, formally acknowledged Mejía's victory, which thus encouraged Medina to concede. At his inauguration in August Mejía promised that he would govern "from a glass house, with transparency."

Economic growth continued to exceed expectations. For the fourth consecutive year, the country enjoyed one of the most robust surges of growth in Latin America. Gross domestic product expanded by about 10% in the first six months, with strength particularly in construction, tourism, free-trade zones, nickel mining, and telecommunications. In addition, inflation was within targeted limits. Notwithstanding economic prosperity, Mejía was committed to bridging the gulf between the well-off and the estimated 44% of those at the poverty level. In his campaign he had included policies to revitalize the agricultural industry and rehabilitate ramshackle educational and health systems.

Mejía also pressed international donors to develop a coordinated aid package to address the chronically difficult and unstable relationship with Haiti, the Dominican Republic's impoverished neighbour.

(JOHN W. GRAHAM)

AP/Wide World Photos

ECUADOR

Area: 272,045 sq km (105,037 sq mi), including the 8,010-sq km (3,093-sq mi) Galápagos Islands
Population (2000 est.): 12,646,000 (Galápagos Islands, about 16,000)
Capital: Quito
Chief of state and head of government: Presidents Jamil Mahuad Witt and, from January 22, Gustavo Noboa Bejarano

Political upheaval and the controversial adoption of the United States dollar as Ecuador's currency dominated events in 2000. The year began with the corruption-plagued economy in chaos following bank failures, crop losses, and a foreign-debt default. Unpopular Pres. Jamil Mahuad announced early in January that later in the year the dollar would replace the sucre (25,000 sucres=about $1), the sagging national currency. Indian, labour, and student groups assailed this "dollarization," saying that it would benefit only the rich and bind Ecuador to U.S. monetary policy.

On January 21, Indian protesters aided by middle-ranking military officers stormed the National Congress building in Quito and proclaimed a new government, led by a junta composed of Indian leader Antonio Vargas, army Col. Lucio Gutiérrez, and former Supreme Court president Carlos Solórzano. Troops escorted Mahuad from the presidential palace, but the military high command moved immediately to block a full-scale insurrection. Gen. Carlos Mendoza, the armed forces chief of staff, replaced Gutiérrez in the junta, but within hours he announced that it would be scrapped and that Vice Pres. Gustavo Noboa would assume the presidency. The U.S. and several Latin American countries had argued strongly for the preservation of constitutional order.

After Noboa's announcement that the currency conversion to the dollar would go forward, Ecuador reached an agreement with multilateral lenders in March on a three-year $2,045,000,000 loan package, which included a promise to cut fuel-price subsidies. In August most private foreign creditors accepted Ecuador's offer to exchange about $6,500,000,000 of defaulted debt for $3,950,000,000 in new bonds. Noboa planned a balanced budget for 2001 and promised to open the electricity and oil sectors to private investment. Rising crude oil prices brought the prospect of increased revenue from Ecuador's chief export, and the tourist industry received a boost as activity subsided in the Tungurahua volcano.

The economy appeared to have calmed somewhat by mid-September, when the dollar became the only legal circulating currency. Indian groups demonstrated against conversion to the dollar, privatization, and an agreement allowing the U.S. to use the air base at Manta for anti-drug-trafficking operations. Authorities feared a spillover of violence from Colombia after fighting there drove hundreds of refugees into Ecuador in October. (PAUL KNOX)

EGYPT

Area: 997,739 sq km (385,229 sq mi)
Population (2000 est.): 65,871,000
Capital: Cairo
Chief of state: President Hosni Mubarak
Head of government: Prime Minister Atef Ebeid

Egypt during 2000 witnessed six important developments. First, on February 24 Pope John Paul II made his first visit ever to Egypt. Although the vast majority of the estimated 10 million Christians in Egypt belonged to the Coptic Orthodox Church, the pope's visit boosted the morale of the Christian community, which continued to suffer from violence at the hands of Islamic fundamentalists and from discrimination at the hands of the Egyptian authorities. In hopes of dispelling the image of his country as lacking in religious freedom, Pres. Hosni Mubarak welcomed the pope's visit enthusiastically.

The second major development took place on June 30, when the Egyptian-American sociologist Saad al-Din Ibrahim, who taught at the American University in Cairo, was arrested and imprisoned by the Egyptian government, accused of receiving funds from the European Union and of espionage for the U.S. Ibrahim was serving as director of a leading research institute, the Ibn Khaldun Center for Development Studies, which was actively fighting for human rights to be granted to women, minorities, and political prisoners. The Egyptian authorities closed down the institute and arrested its 27 staff members. Under pressure from the U.S., Ibrahim and some of his colleagues were freed on bail on August 10, but the research institute was not allowed to reopen. Ibrahim vowed after his release to continue to fight for democracy: "Nothing will deter me from what I was doing, even a trial by a security court. I am doing nothing wrong, except if [prosecutors] believe that defending democracy and human rights is a crime." The government-controlled newspaper *Akhbar al-Yawm* stated that Ibrahim, through his news conferences and interviews following his release, was "leading a comic and funny play whose lone star deserves to be stoned."

In the year's third major development, President Mubarak remained active in the peace process. It was on Mubarak's urging that U.S. Pres. Bill Clinton met with Syrian Pres. Hafez al-Assad (*see* OBITUARIES) in Geneva on March 26. During March 27–29 Mubarak visited the U.S., where he met with President Clinton and congressional leaders. To keep the peace process alive, Mubarak received Palestinian leader Yasir Arafat many times and met with Israeli Prime Minister Ehud Barak on July 10, prior to the convening by President Clinton of the Israeli-Palestinian Camp David conference, which eventually failed. Clinton made a brief visit to Egypt on August 29 to consult with Mubarak on the peace process. When violence erupted between the Palestinians and the Israelis, President Mubarak hosted a conference during October 16–17, in the town of Sharm ash-Shaykh, which Clinton convened and which was attended by Barak and Arafat. The agreements reached there between the Israelis and the Palestinians to halt the violence were, however, not implemented. The most positive role was played by Egypt during the Arab summit, held October 21–22 and attended by representatives from 22 Arab countries. Mubarak judiciously steered the conference away from the positions taken by hard-line Islamist governments in an effort to highlight regional peace and to emphasize that an Israeli-Palestinian agreement was a "primary objective" for the benefit of the whole region.

A fourth major development during the year was an effort to emphasize the Mediterranean cultural dimension of Egypt. In this regard Suzanne Mubarak, the wife of the president, held a banquet at the Library of Congress in Washington, D.C., on March 27 to promote the newly established Bibliotheca Alexandrina. This was an attempt to revive the Alexandria library that had been established in the 3rd century BC and that had for seven centuries remained the world's greatest library.

Fifth, the Egyptian government held parliamentary elections during October and November. Amid charges that the voting was rigged and notwithstanding several violent clashes between protesters and the police, Mubarak's National Democratic Party won a large majority (388 of the 454 seats) in the new People's Assembly. Sixth and finally, Fuad Saraj al-Din, the charismatic president of the New Wafd Party, the main liberal opposition party, died on August 9 at the age of 89. (MARIUS K. DEEB)

Pope John Paul II (left) sits with Coptic Orthodox Pope Shenouda III during a meeting at Shenouda's residence in Cairo on February 24.

AP/Wide World Photos

EL SALVADOR

Area: 21,041 sq km (8,124 sq mi)
Population (2000 est.): 6,123,000
Capital: San Salvador
Head of state and government: President Francisco Flores Pérez

The year 2000 opened in El Salvador with protests and strikes amid a sluggish economy. Although Pres. Francisco Flores Pérez promised to improve the standard of living, create jobs, and arrest the high crime rate, little progress was made toward these goals. About 50% of the population still lived in extreme poverty. A mosquitoborne dengue fever epidemic plagued the country by midyear, and violent crime and kidnapping rose along with popular criticism of the new National Civilian Police (PNC) force. A four-month strike by health care and social security workers ended in March when Flores agreed not to privatize the health care system.

A low voter turnout (35%) in the March legislative elections reflected rising disenchantment with the right-wing National Republic Alliance (ARENA). Though the leftist Farabundo Martí National Liberation Front (FMLN) won 31 seats and ARENA captured 29, the FMLN fell short of an absolute majority when the National Conciliation Party (PCN) took 14 seats and other parties 10. An alliance between ARENA and the PCN provided a working majority of 43 votes, which prevented the FMLN from gaining the presidency of the Legislative Assembly. The FMLN—which governed 65% of the population at the local level—also won 78 mayorships, including reelection of Héctor Silva in San Salvador.

On July 7 the Assembly ratified (49–35) an agreement that would allow the U.S. to establish an antinarcotics base at the Comalapa National Airport. The Assembly also approved U.S. training of the PNC for antidrug activities and ratified a constitutional amendment allowing Salvadorans to be extradited to the U.S.

In June El Salvador signed a free-trade agreement with Mexico, Guatemala, and Honduras. Foreign aid, investment, and substantial remittances from Salvadorans in the U.S. to friends and family back in El Salvador were important in enabling El Salvador to maintain its low inflation and a stable currency. In November El Salvador announced that it would adopt the U.S. dollar as its currency. The colón, the local currency, would also remain legal tender. The move drew favourable reactions from the United States Treasury Department and the International Monetary Fund. The government continued to privatize government-owned services, and the telephone company and geothermal generating plants came under the control of foreigners. Credit from the World Bank, the Central American Bank for Economic Integration, the Inter-American Development Bank, and nongovernmental organizations benefited the financial sector and helped build El Salvador's infrastructure but also increased the foreign debt. With increasing exports, however, economic indicators for 2000 pointed toward an economic growth in excess of 3%, and increased economic activity resulted in greater sales tax revenues for the government.

(RALPH LEE WOODWARD, JR.)

EQUATORIAL GUINEA

Area: 28,051 sq km (10,831 sq mi)
Population (2000 est.): 474,000
Capital: Malabo; announced capital designate: Bata
Chief of state: President Brig. Gen. Teodoro Obiang Nguema Mbasogo
Head of government: Prime Minister Angel Serafin Seriche Dougan

Equatorial Guinea in 2000 continued to be affected dramatically by an oil boom, fueled by new discoveries in the Gulf of Guinea. No oil was produced there for some time yet by 2000 more than 130,000 bbl a day were being produced, and this was expected to double once the new field, La Ceiba, drilled by the U.S. company Triton Energy, came fully onstream. There were hopes of new finds in deeper waters off the mainland. The oil discoveries produced maritime boundary disputes with Nigeria and Gabon. An agreement signed with Nigeria in August held out some promise that the disputes with that country could be resolved amicably.

The municipal elections held at the end of May were boycotted by the main opposition parties—the Convergence for Social Democracy, the Popular Union, and the Democratic and Progressive Alliance. The ruling Democratic Party of Equatorial Guinea therefore scored an overwhelming victory, and the opposition lost the mayorship of Malabo, which had been won in the 1995 elections. As political tensions increased, some claimed that the president's clan was unduly enriching itself with the oil money.

(CHRISTOPHER SAUNDERS)

ERITREA

Area: 121,144 sq km (46,774 sq mi)
Population (2000 est.): 4,136,000 (including nearly 350,000 refugees in The Sudan)
Capital: Asmara
Head of state and government: President Isaias Afwerki

In 2000 Eritrea entered its eighth year of existence as a sovereign state and saw good prospects for the resolution of the border dispute with Ethiopia, which had erupted in mid-1998. The conflict had plunged the young nation into a costly war that had resulted in numerous deaths and the displacement of hundreds of thousands of civilians. The 1999 military stalemate was broken when in May 2000 Ethiopia began an occupation of previously undisputed areas in western and central Eritrea. Eritrean defense forces withdrew rapidly from areas vulnerable to concerted Ethiopian air and land attacks. Ethiopian armed forces consolidated their control over disputed territories such as Badme and Zala Ambessa and occupied previously uncontested areas such as Barentu, Sen'afe, and Shambiko. Multiple-track diplomatic activities increased and were accompanied by reports of human rights violations in Ethiopian-occupied areas. In July the United Nations Mission in Ethiopia and Eritrea (UNMEE) was established and authorized to deploy 4,200 peacekeeping forces. UNMEE would monitor the cessation of hostilities, ensure the observance of mutually agreed-on security commitments, and coordinate and provide technical assistance for humanitarian mine-action activities. By December UNMEE personnel had opened up secure corridors between the two countries, and a formal

An Eritrean artillery unit fires at Ethiopian positions near Ede Della, 85 km (53 mi) south of Asmara, on May 30.
AP/Wide World Photos

comprehensive peace accord was signed on December 12 in Algiers.

The cautious optimism generated by UNMEE's successful deployment was accompanied by the first public articulation of dissatisfaction with the transitional People's Front for Democracy and Justice regime. In September members of the National Assembly held a meeting in Asmara and openly criticized existing national and local governance procedures. The reformists underscored the need for an accountable and transparent government and called for the implementation of the constitution that had been ratified in May 1997. In early October the National Assembly announced that national elections would be scheduled for December 2001. This official announcement, heralding change from within, was followed by a letter addressed to Pres. Isaias Afwerki—by a group of 13 citizens as well as members of the Eritrean diaspora—echoing the parliamentarians' demand for constitutional governance. Critics questioned the timing of the demands for reform while the nation was at war, while proponents argued that the rule of law need not remain hostage to "external" threats. Dubbed the "Berlin Manifesto" (because the drafting meeting was held in Berlin), this document broke the political establishment's prevailing culture of silence.

(RUTH IYOB)

ESTONIA

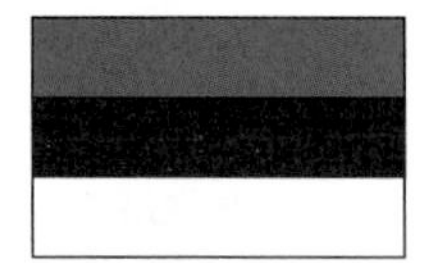

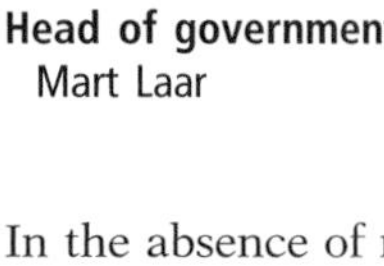

Area: 45,227 sq km (17,462 sq mi)
Population (2000 est.): 1,435,000 (disregarding March 2000 preliminary census results)
Capital: Tallinn
Chief of state: President Lennart Meri
Head of government: Prime Minister Mart Laar

In the absence of national or local elections in 2000, political life in Estonia focused on constitutional issues, especially relations between the president and the parliament. Although the constitution of 1992 envisioned a figurehead executive, Lennart Meri, Estonia's charismatic and popular president during the 1990s, had sought to enhance the powers of the office. The issue came to a head once again in June over Meri's dismissal of the head of Estonia's armed forces without consultation with the parliament. In August the parliament narrowly approved the step, but there were also renewed calls for legislation clearly defining presidential powers.

Following a sluggish performance in the previous year, the Estonian economy showed robust growth during 2000, which suggested that the country had finally recovered from the impact of the Russian financial crisis of 1998. Tourism continued to expand rapidly and accounted for about one-sixth of the country's gross domestic product. The year's most emotional economic issue was the sale of a 49% share of Estonia's main power plants to the U.S.-based NRG Energy, Inc., which raised questions of energy dependence and foreign control. Estonia's first demographic census since regaining independence in 1991, conducted in March and April, confirmed the continuing decline and aging of the population, although the birthrate finally showed a slight upward trend in both

1999 and 2000. Controversy also surrounded the census because the overall count was considerably less than previous official estimates.

Estonia made little concrete progress toward joining the European Union or NATO, although the European Commission's November report called Estonia one of the front-runners for EU membership. Many current EU members appeared increasingly hesitant at the prospect of integrating 12 new candidate members in the near future, and the exposed geopolitical location of Estonia, Latvia, and Lithuania gave some NATO countries pause. Public opinion polls indicated considerable volatility in the sentiments of the population regarding membership in those two organizations. (TOIVO U. RAUN)

ETHIOPIA

Area: 1,133,882 sq km (437,794 sq mi)
Population (2000 est.): 64,117,000
Capital: Addis Ababa
Chief of state: President Negasso Gidada
Head of government: Prime Minister Meles Zenawi

The year 2000 began with a standoff in Ethiopia's border war with Eritrea. Both countries used the lull in the fighting to train troops and purchase military supplies. Disagreements over the Organization of African Unity's peace initiative—specifically, how the disputed areas would be governed once a cease-fire took effect—led to a breakdown of peace talks in May. Ethiopia was adamant that the countries return to the status quo prior to May 1998, when the war began. Preempting any further negotiations, the Ethiopian army launched an offensive on May 12. The army pushed deep into the territory held by Eritrea and within two weeks had reclaimed all contested land. Immediately following the offensive, the UN Security Council voted to ban sales and deliveries of all arms and military equipment to both countries for 12 months. A cease-fire between the two countries was signed on June 18. The UN established a mission to monitor the cease-fire and deployed 4,200 troops in a buffer zone between the two countries while the border was being demarcated. Relations between Ethiopia and Eritrea remained strained until the two nations signed a peace agreement on December 12 that effectively ended the conflict.

The military offensive on May 12 was immediately followed by elections for the national legislature on May 14. A national dialogue regarding issues of land tenure and economic development was evident in the campaigning. Voter-registration difficulties were noted in determining which people of Eritrean descent should be counted as citizens and allowed to vote. The detention of political candidates in the southern areas of Ethiopia was also reported. The governing Ethiopian People's Revolutionary Democratic Front was predicted to win a majority of the 548 seats, and it did so easily, facing no opposition in approximately half the contests.

Drought threatened to turn to famine early in the year as the *belg,* or small rains, failed for the third consecutive year. Conditions were particularly bad in the Somali region of the Ogaden, where many children, older people, and livestock died. The potential for famine dissipated, however, owing to government and international response and in spite of the relative insecurity of the area. The main rainy season arrived on time, alleviating much of the threat of famine in the country for the upcoming year.

The real economic growth rate for 1999 was 0%. International coffee prices continued to decline, which resulted in decreased foreign exchange revenue. Military spending drained government resources in the early part of the year. The International Monetary Fund and the U.S. had discontinued aid to Ethiopia because of excessive military spending; in September, however, the World Bank agreed to resume its program, and other donors were expected to follow the Bank's lead. The government reported significant growth in the small industry sector in response to ongoing market reforms.

(SANDRA F. JOIREMAN)

FIJI

Area: 18,272 sq km (7,055 sq mi)
Population (2000 est.): 819,000
Capital: Suva
Chief of state: Presidents Ratu Sir Kamisese Mara and, from July 18 (interim), Ratu Josefa Iloilo
Head of government: Prime Ministers Mahendra Chaudhry and, from July 28 (interim), Laisenia Qarase

On May 19, 2000, the Fijian government was overthrown in a civilian coup. Dozens of hostages were taken, including Prime Minister Mahendra Chaudhry and 17 others, who were

Fijian Parliament Secretary Mary Chapman (right) surveys one of the ransacked parliamentary offices where hostages were held by coup leader George Speight and his followers for 56 days.

AP/Wide World Photos

held for 56 days in the parliamentary complex. The coup was led by George Speight, a failed businessman who had ties to radical ethnic Fijian groups. (*See* BIOGRAPHIES.) Among the demands of Speight and his followers was that Fiji's constitution be replaced so that Indo-Fijians (descendants of indentured labourers taken to Fiji from India in the colonial period) would be excluded from the government. Elected only a year earlier, the Chaudhry government had alienated ethnic Fijians because it was dominated by Indo-Fijians, despite the fact that Indo-Fijians made up only 44% of the country's population.

The army, whose troops were almost exclusively ethnic Fijian, nevertheless played a central role in negotiating the accord that ended the coup peacefully. Under the terms of the accord, amnesty was granted to those who had participated in the coup, and the last of the hostages were released on July 13. Two weeks later, however, Speight and his rebels were arrested; the amnesty agreement was later declared invalid because the military failed to hand over its weapons and the hostage standoff meant the army commander had signed "under duress." In August Speight and 12 others were charged with treason; all remained in custody awaiting trial. In November Justice Tony Gates of Fiji's High Court ruled that the 1997 constitution, which had been discarded by the military after the May coup, was still in force. As a result, Gates declared that the military-installed interim government had no legitimacy. He urged Parliament to convene to hammer out the issue.

Political instability caused a sharp drop in tourism, and the sugar harvest was disrupted. Because of the threat of international trade sanctions, Fiji's garment industry also suffered. An estimated 7,500 jobs were lost in the months following the coup.

(BARRIE MACDONALD)

FINLAND

Area: 338,145 sq km (130,559 sq mi)
Population (2000 est.): 5,178,000
Capital: Helsinki
Chief of state: Presidents Martti Ahtisaari and, from March 1, Tarja Halonen
Head of government: Prime Minister Paavo Lipponen

In February 2000 Tarja Halonen (*see* BIOGRAPHIES) of the left-wing Social Democratic Party was elected Finland's first woman president. Although known in her youthful political days as "Red Tarja," she later served (1995–2000) as an orthodox foreign minister. Upon her presidential inauguration on March 1, a new constitution came into force that somewhat reduced her powers. A key change was that Parliament would choose the prime minister; Halonen, however, would wield considerable power in foreign affairs, one of her areas of expertise.

At a news conference in Russia following talks with Pres. Vladimir Putin in Moscow, Halonen responded firmly to his curt refusal to discuss the return of Karelia, an area Finland lost to the Soviet Union during World War II; although she said that Finland would not press Russia on the issue, she indicated that the matter was not closed. Finnish authorities deplored border-guard reductions on Russia's side of the 1,269-km (788-mi) frontier. Concern was endemic among Finns, who worried that refugees from an unstable Russia might pour into their sparsely populated country.

There was minor racial tension within the country during the year with a few refugees, mainly Somalis. Although polls indicated that most citizens in Finland still opposed joining NATO—and Moscow would view its joining as an affront—Finland was prepared to offer troops to the European Union.

The nation was shocked by a World Health Organization report that ranked Finland 31st in the world in its provision of health care. A senior commentator wrote that complacency about welfare was a state religion among Nordics. In another poll, this one about corruption, Finland ranked first—as the least corrupt country in the world.

Finland rated extremely well globally in the area of high technology industry; leading the field was Nokia Corp., one of the foremost mobile-phone makers in the world. Prime Minister Paavo Lipponen conjectured that the high-tech industry could one day push unemployment below 7%. Investment in research and development remained massive, but the Organisation for Eeonomic Co-operation and Development again criticized Finland for the rigidity of its traditional labour markets. The overall tax rate was high—at 47%—and the national debt was almost 50% of gross domestic product.

(EDWARD SUMMERHILL)

FRANCE

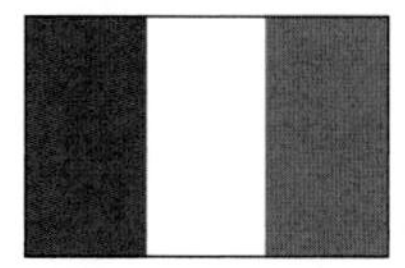

Area: 543,965 sq km (210,026 sq mi)
Population (2000 est.): 58,835,000
Capital: Paris
Chief of state: President Jacques Chirac
Head of government: Prime Minister Lionel Jospin

In Europe the year 2000 was a prestigious one for France. The national football team capped its World Cup success of 1998 by winning the Euro 2000 championship. As president of the European Union in the second half of the year, France steered difficult negotiations on the reform of the EU's institutions to a successful conclusion at the summit meeting in the French city of Nice in December. In its parallel role as president of the Western European Union defense organization, France oversaw moves to create a European rapid reaction force for peacekeeping and crisis management, independent, if need be, of NATO.

At home there were also some major advances. The long-overdue reduction in the presidential term from seven years to five years was approved in a September 24 referendum. Corsica was offered an autonomy deal that constituted the first real crack in France's overcentralized state. The government also started to reverse the tax increases imposed during the 1990s to prepare France for European monetary union.

Each of these developments, however, had possible drawbacks. Shortening the presidential term could actually increase the power of the president over a legislature already seen as weak. The Corsica plan fueled fears of similar demands for autonomy from Basques or Bretons on the mainland, which the government was not prepared to grant. Finally, the tax cuts sparked protest blockades by truck drivers disappointed that the government did not also cut fuel taxes.

Politics. The main political tasks for Lionel Jospin, the Socialist Party prime minister, were to keep his coalition together and to maintain some semblance of reform without alienating lobbies seen as necessary to his expected challenge to Jacques Chirac, the Gaullist president, in the presidential election in 2002. The tasks proved dif-

Corbis/Sygma

Corsican nationalists demonstrate in France; in July the government agreed to grant the Mediterranean island limited autonomy.

ficult. The first ministerial casualties of the year came on March 27, when Christian Sautter was replaced by Laurent Fabius as finance minister and Claude Allegre by Jack Lang as education minister. Sautter had never seemed more than an interim figure, but Allegre was a longtime friend of Jospin. Nonetheless, Allegre had committed the political error of arousing the ire of teachers unions with his reform plans. For his part Sautter had provoked street demonstrations by his own tax agents against his proposal to make changes in the assessment and collection of taxes.

To shore up his government, Jospin decided that it was necessary to bring in Fabius, a longtime rival and former prime minister, and Lang, who had previous experience in the tricky job of running France's Education Ministry. At the end of August, Jospin lost his interior minister, Jean-Pierre Chevenement, who led a small party allied to the Socialists, and replaced him with Daniel Vaillant. Resigning for the third time in his checkered career, Chevenement considered that the deal Jospin had offered Corsican nationalists smacked of appeasement and violated the principle of the indivisibility of the republic and the equality of all within it. Jospin's plan was to give the Mediterranean island, wracked for years by violent nationalist agitation, the right to adapt legislation and eventually, by 2004, the right to originate some of its own laws. In September Jospin came close to losing another minister, Dominique Voynet, the leader of the Greens, who threatened to resign if the prime minister made too many concessions to demonstrators against fuel tax increases. Another ministerial departure took place in October, however, when Martine Aubry, the social affairs minister, who was ranked second behind Jospin in the government, quit to concentrate her efforts on becoming mayor of the northern city of Lille in the 2001 municipal elections.

President Chirac faced fewer problems in maintaining order within his centre-right political forces, partly because they had already suffered considerable fragmentation since their 1997 defeat by Jospin and his left-wing allies. The president did, however, receive a blow in January when the Gaullist Rally for the Republic (RPR), which he had founded, helped to block judicial reforms he had championed. This demonstrated the RPR's independence under its new leader, Michele Alliot-Marie, the first woman to lead a major French party. Chirac—who was mayor of Paris for 18 years before he became president—gained some relief, however, from a court ruling in February that the ongoing investigations into corrupt practices within the Paris city hall could not be extended to him, on the ground that a sitting president was immune from prosecution on any charge except high treason. Magistrates, nonetheless, continued to probe allegations that the city administration had been used as an arm of the Gaullist party; the mayor's wife, Xaviere Tiberi, was put under investigation for drumming up phantom votes for elections. To distance itself, the RPR expelled the mayor, Jean Tiberi. In a consolation to all of France's mainstream parties, Jean-Marie Le Pen, who led a faction of the far-right National Front movement, was ruled in February to be ineligible for one year to sit in the Provence regional council following his conviction for violence during the 1997 election.

Chirac did a U-turn on the question of shortening the presidential term to five years, which in 1999 he had flatly ruled out. The issue had long been debated, with opposition to change coming mainly from the Gaullist right.

When, however, former president Valéry Giscard d'Estaing raised the idea again in May and was backed by Jospin, Chirac quickly succumbed. He appeared to calculate that a shorter presidential term would increase his chances of winning reelection in 2002. The shortening of the presidential term to five years was decisively approved in a vote of 73.21% to 26.79%, though the turnout of 30% of the electorate was very low.

The Economy. France's economic boom continued, with a growth rate of over 3% that at last pushed the country's jobless rate down to below 10% of the workforce. Helped by the weak euro, exports expanded, as did investment abroad. Among major foreign acquisitions by French companies were France Telecom's purchase of Britain's Orange mobile telephone business, the Alcatel telecommunications equipment group's purchase of Canada's Newbridge Networks, and Vivendi's takeover of Seagram of Canada, which, through control of Universal Studios, gave it the world's biggest collection of music rights. French employers were not so happy with their own government. They complained about the imposition of the 35-hour standard workweek that took effect on February 1 for medium- and large-sized companies.

The healthy state of public finances generated by the economy's expansion led, indirectly, to problems for the government. When it announced in early September how it planned to use its revenue surplus, the government was ready with a corporate tax reduction for business and with some cuts in general income taxes; there was, however, no reduction in fuel taxes just as the oil-producing countries were beginning to increase the price of crude. Disappointed in their expectation that they too would benefit from tax cuts, some workers took direct action. Fishermen blockaded ports, and truckers and farmers blocked oil refineries and depots throughout the country. Jospin was under pressure from his Green coalition partners to maintain taxes on fuel, but he found enough concessions to placate the protesters.

In a wider sense the protests were symptomatic of a Gallic revulsion against globalization, epitomized in the person of José Bové. By leading a rampage against a McDonald's restaurant in 1999, Bové, a sheep farmer, had become something of a folk hero to those urging a stand against global market forces. (*See* ECONOMIC AFFAIRS: *Sidebar*, above.) For the damage he caused, he went on trial in June, and in September he found the martyrdom he sought in a three-month prison sentence. McDonald's also found itself a target when one of its stores in Brittany was bombed in April, and a female employee was killed. Breton nationalists were suspected of the crime.

Foreign Policy. The increasing tension between Chirac and Jospin led to problems in foreign policy. Eager to demonstrate that foreign policy was not the exclusive domain of the president, Jospin paid a visit in February to Israel, where his characterization of Hezbollah guerrillas in Lebanon as "terrorists" led to his being stoned by Palestinians on the West Bank. Shocked not so much by the stoning but rather by the prime minister's audacity in unilaterally altering the long-standing pro-Arab tilt to French policy, Chirac summoned Jospin to a disciplinary meeting on his return, but the prime minister refused to attend.

On the more central issue of European policy, the two men stayed more in tune and focused on making France's EU presidency a success.

The culmination of this came at the Nice summit, which proved to be the EU's longest and most bitter round of negotiations. The meeting lasted four days and one night—December 7–11. The Treaty of Nice was designed to streamline EU institutions and decision making in advance of accepting new members, mainly small- and medium-sized countries from Eastern Europe, in the years to come.

While nominally playing the role of neutral chairman, President Chirac succeeded in promoting French interests. He ensured that changes in the voting weights in the Council of Ministers favoured large states over small ones, while at the same time insisting on France's voting parity with more populous Germany. He helped extend the practice of taking decisions by majority vote to more areas of EU activity, but he ensured the maintenance of unanimity (and therefore the possibility of national veto) on audiovisual broadcasting and culture, issues of special sensitivity to France. France also supported the treaty agreement for subgroups of EU states to pursue faster integration in certain areas if they so desired. The only concession that France and other larger states made during the negotiations was to agree to forego their right eventually to nominate a second commissioner to the EU's European Commission in Brussels.

Leaders of several small states complained about Chirac's tactics, accusing him of bullying. The French president proved by his vigorous defense of national interests, however, a claim that he had made earlier in the year—that his vision of the EU was a union of European states rather than a "united states of Europe." (DAVID BUCHAN)

GABON

Area: 267,667 sq km (103,347 sq mi)
Population (2000 est.): 1,208,000
Capital: Libreville
Chief of state: President Omar Bongo
Head of government: Prime Minister Jean-François Ntoutoume-Emane

Eight African nations conducted French-sponsored military exercises in Gabon in January 2000. This was designed as a preliminary step toward creating a rapid-reaction peace force to be deployed to rescue and protect refugees in the case of ethnic conflict of the severity of that experienced in Rwanda in 1999. Soldiers from Burundi, Cameroon, Chad, the Republic of the Congo, the Central African Republic, Equatorial Guinea, Gabon, and São Tomé and Príncipe were to constitute a force of 700 men equipped with surplus French army equipment. During a July meeting of the Organization of African Unity, Pres. Omar Bongo demanded reform of that body, with a greater emphasis on reconciliation and mediation rather than on punitive measures such as the imposition of boycotts.

In late 1999 the government announced plans for the privatization of the posts and telecommunications sector and thereby triggered a prolonged strike by union members. In January top officials of the International Monetary Fund met with African leaders in Libreville. In the wide-ranging talks, priority was given to establishing a means to achieve real economic growth and the reduction of poverty.

On August 30 Defense Minister Ali Bongo launched a new campaign to deport illegal aliens. The opposition Congress for Democracy and Justice closed its second convention on September 10 by calling on the government to ensure that all future elections were free and open.

(NANCY ELLEN LAWLER)

GAMBIA, THE

Area: 10,689 sq km (4,127 sq mi)
Population (2000 est.): 1,367,000
Capital: Banjul
Head of state and government: President Col. Yahya Jammeh

The peaceful change of government by electoral means in neighbouring Senegal in March 2000 encouraged the political opposition in The Gambia. In January and again in June, the police announced that they had foiled coup attempts against Pres. Yahya Jammeh. In April a demonstration in Banjul called by the Gambia Students' Union to protest the torture and murder of a secondary-school pupil by members of the fire brigade turned violent. The paramilitaries opened fire, and at least 12 people were killed. In July, Ousainou Darboe, the leader of the main opposition United Democratic Party, was campaigning in the east of the country for upcoming November local elections when a supporter of the ruling Alliance for Patriotic Reorientation and Construction was killed. Darboe and 23 other members of his party were charged with murder and put on trial.

Relations with Senegal, which nearly surrounds The Gambia, deteriorated after the new government came to power there. A border dispute led to a closing of the border for a time. When Abdoulaye Wade, the new Senegalese president, criticized The Gambia for receiving arms from Libya, The Gambia stopped its mediation efforts in Senegal's Casamance dispute, though later in the year it temporarily resumed its role as mediator. A wing of the separatist Movement of Democratic Forces of Casamance was based in The Gambia, and Senegalese nationals made up an estimated 350,000 of The Gambia's population.

On November 21 Gambian security chiefs apprehended and detained Valentine Strasser, the former head (1992–96) of a Sierra Leonean military junta, who had failed to inform authorities of his arrival as was the custom with former visiting heads of state. Strasser, who was viewed as a potential threat to The Gambia's security, had first entered the country on October 27 but was turned away by immigration authorities and sent back to Britain, where he had been studying since his ouster. British immigration officials, in turn, denied him entry back into that country and returned him to The Gambia, where officials considered Strasser's deportation to Sierra Leone. (CHRISTOPHER SAUNDERS)

GEORGIA

Area: 69,700 sq km (26,911 sq mi)
Population (2000 est.): 5,020,000
Capital: T'bilisi
Head of state and government: President Eduard Shevardnadze, assisted by Secretaries of State Vazha Lortkipanidze and, from May 11, Giorgi Arsenishvili

Political stability and solutions to Georgia's conflicts in Abkhazia and South Ossetia remained elusive throughout 2000. Of 17 would-be candidates, only 7 succeeded in registering to contest the April 9 presidential election, which the incumbent president, Eduard Shevardnadze, won with 79.8% of the vote. Former Georgian Communist Party first secretary Dzhumber Patiashvili came in second with 16.7%. Another candidate from the opposition All-Georgian Union of Revival, Adjar leader Aslan Abashidze, withdrew his candidacy on the eve of the poll.

Shevardnadze named former regional administrator Giorgi Arsenishvili minister of state and reappointed most outgoing ministers to his new government. In late summer a dozen Parliament deputies, including several Parliament committee chairs, quit the majority Citizens' Union of Georgia faction.

Civil violence continued to be a problem. Two UN officials were abducted in Abkhazia's Kodori gorge in early June, but they were released several days later. Three Red Cross personnel were simi-

Refugee children from Chechnya congregate outdoors in the Georgian village of Djokola in January.

AP/Wide World Photos

larly kidnapped near the Chechen border in August, but they too were later freed. In July, Col. Akaki Eliava, who had led an abortive insurrection in western Georgia in October 1998, was detained and then shot dead by police. Former finance minister Guram Absandze, charged with involvement in the failed February 1998 attempt to kill Shevardnadze, escaped with 11 fellow inmates from a T'bilisi prison in October but was recaptured 11 days later.

In late November thousands of T'bilisi residents took to the streets to protest the reduction of already limited electricity supplies to their homes. Shevardnadze blamed those shortages on corrupt officials, having earlier called for resolute measures to eradicate corruption.

In July, Abkhaz and Georgian representatives signed a protocol on measures to stabilize the situation in southern Abkhazia, a move that angered those hard-liners who had fled Abkhazia in 1992–93. Later that month Russia's representative to the UN Security Council declined to endorse the new UN draft peace proposal for Abkhazia.

Relations with Russia remained tense owing to Moscow's repeated accusations that Georgia was allowing Chechen fighters to maintain bases on and supply routes across Georgia's territory and owing to Russia's related decision to introduce a visa requirement from persons entering Russia from Georgia as of December 5. As agreed in November 1999, however, Moscow began withdrawing surplus military equipment from one base near T'bilisi in early August and sent more hardware from a second base in southern Georgia to Armenia in October.

(ELIZABETH FULLER)

GERMANY

Area: 357,021 sq km (137,847 sq mi)
Population (2000 est.): 82,207,000
Capital: Berlin; some ministries remain in Bonn
Chief of state: President Johannes Rau
Head of government: Chancellor Gerhard Schröder

In many ways the Federal Republic of Germany experienced the end of an era in 2000. The move of the seat of government from Bonn to Berlin was completed, and the 10th anniversary of German unification was celebrated. Perhaps the most striking change came with the strengthening profile of the Social Democratic Party of Germany (SPD)–Green government. Whereas the socialist-environmentalist alliance, formerly perennially in opposition, had appeared ill at ease during its first two years in power, 2000 saw the team put in place by Chancellor Gerhard Schröder in the fall of 1998 come into its own. The passage of landmark economic legislation strengthened the government's credibility, as did the slight upturn in the economy. The relative absence of the opposition Christian Democratic Union (CDU), which was struggling with party-financing scandals and a leadership crisis that left the party crippled and self-absorbed rather than taking the lead on the issues of concern to the electorate, further enhanced the presence of the "Red-Green" coalition. It was also the end of an era in terms of world affairs as Germany began to emerge from its self-imposed policy of containment and into greater responsibility in its dealings with other world powers, NATO, the European Union (EU), and the United Nations.

Domestic Affairs. The domestic political scene was dominated during the year by the uproar surrounding CDU financing. News of the scandal affecting the second largest political party came to light in late 1999. Helmut Kohl had left the chancellorship in 1998 after 16 successful years in office, retiring as something of a national hero, so his rapid fall from grace was both a disappointment and an embarrassment to the nation. The events attracted unprecedented media attention by German standards. Kohl refused to name the party's secret financiers, who, he acknowledged, had anonymously provided some DM 2 million (about $1.2 million) in funding between 1993 and 1998. One major casualty of the scandal was party chief Wolfgang Schäuble, Kohl's longtime protégé, who had taken over the CDU in 1998. On February 16 Schäuble announced his intention to give up leadership of the party as well as his position as whip of the CDU faction in the Bundestag (second house of parliament) after it came out that he had personally accepted a briefcase containing more than DM 100,000 (DM 1 equaled about $1.62 in 1993) in cash in the early 1990s from arms dealer Karlheinz Schreiber. Schäuble had earlier denied even knowing Schreiber.

A succession of revelations and rumours throughout the early months of the year kept the story bubbling in the media. Kohl steadfastly refused to name the donors of the illegal funds, asserting that his word of honour was more precious than the law. Kohl gave up his ceremonial chairmanship of the CDU but refused to yield his seat in the Bundestag, where his obduracy soon began to impede the party's desire to put the scandal in the past and get down to the business of legislating. Awkward questions were raised as well by Kohl's planned participation in ceremonies in October commemorating the 10th anniversary of German unification. Ultimately he chose not to attend after the issue had been debated within the party and examined minutely in the media for months on end.

The CDU's troubles detracted attention from pressing policy issues, such as reforming the Bundeswehr (armed forces) to keep pace with post-Cold War defense requirements. This issue, together with the related political, economic, social, and foreign policy dimensions, was studied by an independent 21-member commission appointed by Schröder and headed by former president Richard von Weizsäcker. The commission's report, released on May 23, concluded that "the Bundeswehr has no future in its current structure" because it had produced a surplus of manpower but a shortage of operational forces. The commission recommended that the size of the conscript pool be reduced and that the Bundeswehr be reduced in size over a 10-year period from a peacetime force of about 320,000 to 240,000.

Defense Minister Rudolf Scharping disagreed with some aspects of the report, including the overall target size of the force and the reduction in the number of conscripts. Proponents of universal military service argued that democracy depended on the armed forces' representing a broad cross section of German society. In addition, they pointed out, approximately 50% of the professional military found its way into the Bundeswehr through conscription. Scharping's proposal to maintain a peacetime armed force of 255,000 was accepted by the cabinet in June, with the Greens, who favoured abolishing conscription altogether, dissenting. At a conference of business leaders on May 4, Schröder and Scharping proposed partial privatization of the military. They stressed the importance of modern management methods and said that projected savings would be reinvested in the Bundeswehr to ensure its readiness to meet NATO responsibilities.

Another issue closely related to belt-tightening was the question of continuing subsidies for the development of eastern Germany. A report by the Ifo Institute, a prominent think tank for political and economic research, argued that unification had not yielded economic reunification of the two Germanies, even 10 years and many billions of Deutsche Marks later. Growth in the east had been stagnant since 1996. On the eve of the 10th-anniversary celebrations, in a paid advertisement in a major newspaper, the rhetoric of a 1996 speech by ex-communist politicians from the former East Germany was replayed with heavy irony: "German unity will be completed when the special judicial treatment of the east Germans ends, when wages in the east and west are the same, when there are as many east German homeowners on the island of Sylt as west Germans on the island of Rügen [popular vacation resorts], when an east German can be elected premier of a west German state—and no one in east or west finds this the least bit remarkable."

Economic imbalance was also a factor in the higher incidence of right-wing extremism in eastern Germany than in the west. To cope with the backlash against the presence of foreigners in Germany, Interior Minister Otto Schily announced the creation of a national commission to root out the causes of xenophobia. Schröder made far-right extremism a top theme during a 40-stop tour he made in eastern Germany in late August and early September, although he was careful not to single out easterners as the sole perpetrators—anti-Semitic attacks in Düsseldorf in July and October were just two examples of right-wing violence in western Germany.

Likewise, efforts continued in Germany to cope with the country's Nazi past. A joint public and private foundation called Remembrance, Responsibility and the Future was created in July to supplement existing restitution arrangements for forced labourers and other victims of Nazism with up to $5 billion in funds. Many forced labourers had been impressed into service in Eastern Europe and were not Jewish, factors that had excluded them from sharing in about $100 billion in compensation that Germany had already paid out since World War II. The creation of Remembrance, Responsibility and the Future capped nearly two years of international negotiations under pressure from the U.S. that class-action suits might be filed on behalf of victims of Nazism.

The Economy. Following the passage of a landmark tax-reform bill in July, Schröder exclaimed, "The term *German disease* now belongs to the past. This is a good day for Germany's reputation in the world." Efforts to change the tax system had been under way since 1990. The victory was all the sweeter considering that the chamber in which the coalition received the majority of votes, the Bundesrat, was the one in which it had lost its majority in 1999. Furthermore, it was the same body in which the SPD had used its majority in previous years to block the tax-reform bills of the Kohl government. The SPD managed to have its way by offering inducements to defect and vote for the SPD-Green bill to state governments of Bremen (ruled by an SPD/CDU coalition), Berlin (ruled by a CDU/SPD coalition), and Brandenburg (ruled by an SPD/CDU coalition). In the end, the Schröder government won in a vote of 41–28, even though it needed only 35 votes. The law, which was scheduled to take effect on Jan. 1, 2001, created DM 50 billion (about $22 billion) in tax breaks through the year 2005. Bundesrat passage came only after an overnight session of cajoling, in which the coalition managed to wring out concessions. The bill was touted as a key to attracting more investment in Germany by harmonizing the tax-rate

Wolfgang Schäuble, Christian Democratic Union party leader, resigned his post on February 16 after he and his longtime mentor, former chancellor Helmut Kohl (shown in the background), were involved in a financial scandal.

Michael Jung/AFP Worldwide

structure with those of other industrialized nations. The bill lowered the top personal income tax rate to 42%, down from 51%, and the corporate tax rate to 25%, down from 40%. The decision to eliminate the tax on sales of corporations (set to start in 2002) was welcomed by industry as a step that would make sweeping corporate restructuring possible. German business leaders had viewed this tax—set at about 50%—as punitive.

The second item on the landmark reform agenda was pension reform. The projections were compelling: if in 2000 there were 47 retirees for every 100 members of the workforce, by 2050, it was projected, there would be 104 retirees for every 100 workers. The challenge posed by these demographic trends, one that the SPD-Green government had inherited from its predecessors of the Kohl era, was to find the right balance and timing for increasing pension contributions and reducing pension payments. Reaching agreement within the SPD and Green coalition was a feat in itself, accomplished only after an all-night session ending November 14. During December the coalition tinkered with draft legislation to make it more acceptable to the opposition, but by the end of the year it was still too early to schedule a vote for this long-sought piece of legislation.

The unemployment rate, while still high at over 9%, dropped in August to its lowest level since 1995. The reduction in unemployment, however, was registered primarily in the former West German states. The rates in eastern and western Germany remained critically far apart; in August the unemployment figures were 17% in the east but only 7.4% in the west.

The sustained weakness of the Deutsche Mark and the euro was troubling. The new European currency had been launched on Jan. 1, 1999, at an exchange rate of about $1.17 to the euro amid boasts by European statesmen that it would rival the U.S. dollar in strength and stability. It traded at well under $0.90 for much of the year. Rather than try to talk up the euro, Schröder affected disinterest in September, for which the market rewarded him with an all-time low. As signs of U.S. economic weakness became evident in December, the euro showed signs of modest recovery.

The "Green Card"—the English-language term that Germans used to name a plan to provide visas to 20,000 foreign computer engineers urgently needed to augment the country's high-tech labour force—attracted much attention during the year. Germany had a high unemployment rate, and fully 9% of the population of the country was already defined as foreigners, so this was a question that occasioned intense economic and social debates. The law passed in the parliament in July, however, and within the first month, 1,360 work permits were granted to computer specialists from India, Russia, Ukraine, the Baltic states, and Romania. They were hired primarily by smaller German companies.

Two ecological issues figured prominently in the German economy during the year. First was the "eco-tax," a law that had entered into force in April 1999 and called for taxes on gasoline to rise by 6 pfennigs a litre (about 10 cents a gallon) each year until 2003. Steep fuel-price rises in 2000 reignited opposition. Demonstrations, especially among truckers, put pressure on the coalition to backtrack on the eco-tax, but the government held its ground, insisting that the revenues would finance important ecological projects designed for the long-term well-being of Germany. Second, after nearly two years of tumultuous debate, the government decided in June that the commercial use of nuclear power in Germany would end within 20 years. The timetable was disappointing to the Greens, who had fought for a much earlier end to nuclear power.

Foreign Affairs. The question of enlarging the EU came to a boil in May following an address by Joschka Fischer, who spoke, however, not as German foreign minister but as a private citizen. His message was that Europe needed to be closer to its citizens. Fischer proposed a second chamber, a senate, for the European Parliament that would represent the national legislatures of member states. In addition, he urged reforms of the European Commission, suggesting that instead of commissioners being appointed by national governments, they should be actual members of national governments or people directly elected to the position of commissioner by national electorates.

In September Günter Verheugen, EU commissioner for enlargement, mused about the possibility of putting the question of EU expansion to the German people in the form of a referendum. This was controversial because the constitutionality of referenda had been long debated in the Federal Republic of Germany (they were often used during the Nazi period). Verheugen opened up the question of the right of a citizen of an EU member state to participate directly in EU decisions—a right Germans had not enjoyed, for example, in the voting on the single European currency, although the electorates in France and other European countries did express their will.

Greater German participation in world affairs was at the heart of Schröder's speech before the UN at the Millennium Summit in September. He reiterated in plain terms his country's wish to assume a seat on the UN Security Council, stating that "should the number of permanent members be increased Germany would be prepared to shoulder this responsibility." This marked the continuation of Germany's persistent pursuit of more responsibility in the UN, a policy in keeping with Germany's leading role in Europe and engagement in humanitarian support in the world's crisis zones and poorer areas.

The Society. The move of the central government to Berlin was completed in late September, just before the 10th anniversary celebrations of the reunification, when the Bundesrat settled into a renovated 100-year-old palace near Potsdamer Platz. The Bundestag had moved into its spectacular new domed building in 1999. At the end of October parliament finally approved a budget for the controversial memorial to Holocaust victims, designed by New York architect Peter Eisenman, to be constructed in the capital near the Brandenburg Gate. Meanwhile, in Hanover, Expo 2000, Germany's first-ever world's fair, completed its five-month run of culture, technology, environmentalism, and fun for the family, attracting some 18.1 million visitors.

In late November Germany's first case of an animal infected with bovine spongiform encephalopathy (BSE; or mad-cow disease) was reported by the Agriculture Ministry amid a series of similar acknowledgments by health officials in other European countries. When a second German case surfaced a few days later and with public confidence in beef thoroughly shaken, Chancellor Schröder called for a Europe-wide ban on meat-based animal feeds.

In early December the Bundesrat ratified a law that gave same-sex couples full legal standing. Beginning in 2001 gay and lesbian couples in Germany would be able to register their relationships and enjoy the same inheritance and tenant rights as heterosexual couples.

(SUZANNE CROW)

GHANA

Area: 238,533 sq km (92,098 sq mi)
Population (2000 est.): 19,534,000
Capital: Accra
Head of state and government: Chairman of the Provisional National Defense Council and President Jerry John Rawlings

Politics in Ghana during 2000 were dominated by campaigning for December's presidential and parliamentary elections. Pres. Jerry Rawlings was constitutionally prohibited from running for reelection, and his National Democratic Congress (NDC) party nominated Vice Pres. John Evans Atta Mills. The leading challenger was the New Patriotic Party (NPP), led by John Kufuor. Another opposition party, the National Reform Party, broke away from the NDC and nominated former Rawlings associate Augustus Obuadum Tanoh for president. Opposition candidates charged the NDC government with rampant corruption and economic mismanagement.

In the parliamentary elections held on December 7, the NPP captured 100 of the 200 seats, compared with 92 for the NDC. In the presidential race, contested the same day, neither candidate was able to score an outright victory; Kufuor won 48.4% of the vote, and Mills garnered 44.8%. With neither candidate receiving the required 50% of the vote, a runoff was scheduled for December 28. In the event, Kufuor scored an upset victory over Mills, this time commanding 57% of the vote, compared with 43% for Mills. On December 29 Mills conceded, and offered his cooperation in the transition to a new government. It was the first such peaceful handover of power by elected offficials since independence in 1957. Voter turnout was high—about 85% of the 10.7 million registered voters went to the polls.

Economic news was dominated by the plunge in the value of the cedi. The Ghanaian currency traded at 3,500 to U.S. $1 in January but had fallen to 6,700 to the dollar by September. The government blamed its economic woes on declining world prices for cocoa and gold, which together accounted for approximately 70% of Ghana's export earnings.

Ghana continued to play a leading role in the drive for West African integration. Meeting in Accra in April, the leaders of Ghana, The Gambia, Guinea, Liberia, Nigeria, and Sierra Leone or their representatives pledged to work toward a currency union by 2003. Ghana and Nigeria pursued an even faster track toward integration, announcing their intention to establish a free-trade zone.

(MATTHEW A. CENZER)

GREECE

Area: 131,957 sq km (50,949 sq mi)
Population (2000 est.): 10,562,000
Capital: Athens
Chief of state: President Konstantinos Stephanopoulos
Head of government: Prime Minister Konstantinos Simitis

On Feb. 8, 2000, the Greek Parliament reelected Pres. Konstantinos (Kostis) Stephanopoulos with 269 of the 300 votes. It was the first time since the restoration of democracy in 1974 that the head of state had been elected with votes coming from both of the leading parties, the Panhellenic Socialist Movement (Pasok) and the centre-right New Democracy (ND).

On April 9 Greek citizens elected a new Parliament. These elections, which took place 24 weeks before the mandate of the previous Parliament expired, were the most closely contested in decades. In the end, the ruling Pasok of Prime Minister Konstantinos (Kostas) Simitis came out on top with 43.8% of the vote, narrowly beating the ND with 42.7%. The Greek electoral system favoured the biggest party at the expense of the runner-up, so Pasok received 158 seats in the new Parliament, while the ND had to content itself with 125. Of the smaller parties, the hard-line Communist Party of Greece received 5.5% of the vote and 11 seats, while the Progressive Left Coalition won 3.2% and 6 seats. The leftist-populist Democratic Social Movement with 2.7% failed to meet the 3% threshold and lost its representation in Parliament.

Following the elections Simitis extensively reshuffled his government. Of the 43 ministers and deputy ministers in the resulting cabinet, 15 were new. Simitis, however, left the key positions of foreign affairs, defense, finance and economics, and interior and public administration unchanged. Former foreign minister Theodoros Pangalos and former interior minister Alexandros (Alekos) Papadopoulos, each of whom had resigned in early 1999 after the arrest of Kurdish rebel leader Abdullah Ocalan, returned to the government as culture minister and health minister, respectively.

On March 9 Greece formally applied for entry into the European Economic and Monetary Union (EMU), announcing that it was meeting the organization's main criteria. On May 3 the European Commission recommended that Greece be accepted into the EMU as the 12th member. Finally, on June 19, the leaders of the European Union member nations at their summit in Sintra, Port., formally accepted Greece's entry into the EMU as of Jan. 1, 2001. This decision was a major success for Simitis and his finance and economics minister, Ioannis Papantoniou, who over recent years had pursued a strict and often unpopular stabilization and austerity policy in order to prepare Greece for entry into the euro zone.

Throughout the late spring and summer of 2000, Greek society was divided over whether a citizen's religious affiliation should be marked on his or her identity card. The government in May decided to back a decision by the government-appointed Authority for the Protection of Personal Data to remove, among other data, religion from ID cards. The Greek Orthodox Church responded by launching a nationwide campaign against the decision, saying that Orthodoxy was an integral part of Greek national identity. The church held mass rallies attended by hundreds of thousands, but the government refused to yield. After its initial strategy had failed, the church decided to start collecting signatures for what it described as an "informal referendum" on the issue.

In foreign relations a further warming of relations between Greece and Turkey took place during the year, although none of the fundamental differences dividing the two countries was resolved. On January 19 Greek Foreign Minister Georgios Papandreou embarked on a four-day visit to Turkey, the first official visit of a Greek foreign minister since 1962. During that visit the two sides signed four cooperation agreements. During a visit of Turkish Foreign Minister Ismail Cem to Athens in early February, another five agreements were signed. In May Turkish soldiers for the first time in more than 25 years participated in military exercises on Greek territory, but relations soured in October when the two sides argued over sovereignty rights in the eastern Aegean during a NATO exercise.

Terrorist attacks continued to leave their mark on Greece. In the worst incident in 2000, Britain's military attaché in Greece, Brig. Stephen Saunders, was assassinated by terrorists of the November 17 group on June 8 while he was driving to work.

On September 26 the *Express Samina,* one of the oldest ferries still in service in the Aegean Sea, sank after hitting a reef off the island of Páros. At least 80 people were killed in Greece's worst maritime accident in over 30 years. As a consequence of this disaster and two smaller incidents in the following days, the Merchant Marine Ministry on September 30 revoked the licenses of 56 ferries operating in Greek waters.

(STEFAN KRAUSE)

GRENADA

Area: 344 sq km (133 sq mi)
Population (2000 est.): 102,000
Capital: Saint George's
Chief of state: Queen Elizabeth II, represented by Governor-General Daniel Williams
Head of government: Prime Minister Keith Mitchell

In March 2000 Phyllis Coard—who along with her husband, Bernard Coard, and 15 others serving life sentences for the 1983 murder of former Grenadan prime minister Maurice Bishop and many of his close supporters—was temporarily released from prison and allowed to seek treatment in her native Jamaica for colon cancer.

In April the government appointed a Truth and Reconciliation Commission—patterned after a similar body in South Africa that investigated apartheid-era crimes—to inquire into the cataclysmic political events that had occurred on the island from January 1976 to December 1991. The period covered the last years of the controversial government of the late Sir Eric Gairy, his forcible removal from office in 1979, and the subsequent rule of the Bishop regime, which came to grief at the hands of its own extreme left-wing element. The lengthy trial and conviction of Bernard Coard and his co-conspirators would also be part of the commission's brief.

After being sacked from the cabinet, Michael Baptiste—a junior agriculture minister in the New National Party government—became an opposition of one in Parliament in June.

A diplomatic furor of sorts erupted in September when China's ambassador to Trinidad and Tobago was deported hours after arriving in Grenada, which still recognized Taiwan as the legitimate Chinese government.

(DAVID RENWICK)

GUATEMALA

Area: 108,889 sq km (42,042 sq mi)
Population (2000 est.): 11,385,000
Capital: Guatemala City
Head of state and government: President Álvaro Arzú Irigoyen and, from January 14, Alfonso Portillo Cabrera

Taking office as president of Guatemala on Jan. 14, 2000, Alfonso Portillo Cabrera of the Guatemalan Republican Front (FRG) promised to reduce the army's power and to revitalize the economy. More than 75% of the population continued to live in poverty, however, and, despite Portillo's efforts to curb it, the military remained strong. In Guatemala City five persons died in protests against increased bus fares in April. In September a scandal involving manipulation of an alcohol tax bill by Congress president Efraín Rios Montt brought new problems to the FRG.

Death threats, kidnappings, assassinations, and intimidation of judges by right-wing paramilitary groups continued to trouble Guatemala. Nobel Prize winner Rigoberta Menchú and Guatemalan human rights organizations filed a class-action suit before a Spanish court against Rios Montt and seven other Guatemalan military and civilian officials for alleged crimes relating to the 1980 burning of the Spanish embassy in Guatemala City, during which 39 Guatemalans died. Soon afterward victims of human rights abuses filed cases in Guatemalan courts. Three military officers were arrested and charged with the 1998 assassination of human rights activist Bishop Juan Gerardi Conedera.

In July, Portillo ordered the army to assist the police in combating crime. Fearing for their safety, he also sent

Guatemalan Pres. Alfonso Portillo Cabrera (centre) and his wife, Evelyn (far left), receive blessings from Mayan priests on January 14, the day of Portillo's inauguration.

AP/Wide World Photos

some members of his own family to Canada, a move that hardly inspired public confidence. Some wealthy families also left the country, but perhaps more significant was the very large emigration of poorer Guatemalans, who moved to Mexico and the United States. Their remittances to friends and relations in Guatemala were second only to coffee in total value to the nation's economy. In late December Guatemala announced that the U.S. dollar as well as other foreign currencies could be used along with the quetzal, the official currency.

Under a pact with the U.S. to combat drug trafficking, on April 18 three helicopters and 450 U.S. soldiers, pilots, technicians, and special agents arrived in Guatemala to begin operations. In June, Guatemala signed a free-trade agreement with Mexico, El Salvador, and Honduras. Meanwhile, the Guatemalan government continued its claim to more than half the territory of Belize, calling on the latter to accept international arbitration of the dispute.

(RALPH LEE WOODWARD, JR.)

GUINEA

Area: 245,857 sq km (94,926 sq mi)
Population (2000 est.): 7,466,000 (including nearly 600,000 refugees from Liberia and Sierra Leone)
Capital: Conakry
Head of state and government: President Gen. Lansana Conté, assisted by Prime Minister Lamine Sidimé

In Guinea the year 2000 opened inauspiciously when within the first few days of the new year, Muslim and Christian villagers belonging to different factions of the Tora people clashed over disputed farmland in Korneseredou, western Balizia. At least 30 people were killed, and scores of houses were burned in the fighting.

On January 18 Pres. Lansana Conté ordered the retirement of powerful police chief Fode Moussa Sylla after 32 years on the force, and eight days later Conté sacked five cabinet ministers. Pressure from the International Monetary Fund to trim the nation's wage bill was thought to have been the motivation behind the government's decision to announce the retirement of 900 civil servants.

Tensions between Guinea and Liberia escalated throughout the year. Armed dissidents based in Guinea, whom Liberian Pres. Charles Taylor believed were backed by Conté, attacked a town in northern Liberia in July, the third such incident in less than a year. In the first week of September, Liberian troops crossed into Guinea and killed more than 40 people in the town of Musadu. An attack on the Guinean village of Macenta on the night of September 17 resulted in 51 more deaths, including that of a Togolese employee for the UN High Commissioner for Refugees. Another UN aid worker was kidnapped in the raid but was rescued after several days. The Organization of African Unity called for negotiations between the two countries and dispatched special envoy Kingsley Mamabolo to evaluate the situation. Border clashes continued throughout the year.

After several postponements, the trial began in April of Rally of the Guinean People (RPG) opposition leader Alpha Condé. He had been arrested on Dec. 15, 1998, one day after losing the presidential elections to Conté. He was found guilty, along with seven co-defendants, of having attacked the state's authority and territorial integrity and was sentenced to five years in prison.

(NANCY ELLEN LAWLER)

GUINEA-BISSAU

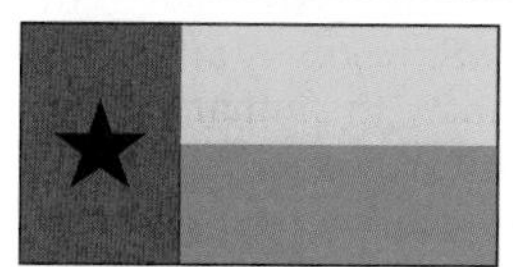

Area: 36,125 sq km (13,948 sq mi)
Population (2000 est.): 1,286,000
Capital: Bissau
Chief of state: Acting President Malam Bacai Sanhá and, from February 17, President Kumba Ialá (Yalla)
Head of government: Prime Ministers Francisco José Fadul and, from February 19, Caetano N'Tchama

In national elections in November 1999, the Party for Social Renewal (PRS) defeated the African Party for the Independence of Guinea-Bissau and Cape Verde (PAIGC), which had been in power since independence. With the aid of the Guinea-Bissau Resistance–Bah Fatah Movement, the PRS secured a majority in the National People's Assembly. In a runoff presidential election in January 2000, Kumba Ialá of the PRS defeated the incumbent, Malam Bacai Sanhá, by 72% to 28% of the votes cast, and he began a five-year term on February 17. His council of ministers included no members of the PAIGC; the post of prime minister went to Caetano N'Tchama of the PRS, previously minister of the interior. In late November junta leader Gen. Ansumane Mane staged an unsuccessful uprising against the government; he was shot dead in a scuffle with loyalist soldiers on November 30.

The international community welcomed the return to democracy and a constitutional order and the peaceful transfer of power. The arrest and detention in harsh conditions in May of two journalists and the most outspoken political critic of the new government led to much criticism, however, not only by Amnesty International and others outside the country but also by members of the National People's Assembly, who accused the prime minister of acting illegally and condoning gross abuse of human rights.

(CHRISTOPHER SAUNDERS)

GUYANA

Area: 215,083 sq km (83,044 sq mi)
Population (2000 est.): 792,000
Capital: Georgetown
Chief of state: President Bharrat Jagdeo
Head of government: Prime Minister Sam Hinds

Guyana finally pulled in line with the majority of its Caribbean Community and Common Market colleagues in February 2000 when it passed a bill making money laundering a specific criminal offense.

The National Assembly took an important step in April toward ensuring that the upcoming general election—postponed from January 2001 to March—would be seen as fair to all parties by creating an independent seven-member Elections Commission. The former chief of staff of the Guyana armed forces, Maj. Gen. Joe Singh, was later named chairman.

In May the government signed an agreement with Beal Aerospace Technologies,

AP/Wide World Photos

Pres. Bharrat Jagdeo of Guyana listens to proceedings during a July 5 Caricom meeting on the border dispute between Guyana and Suriname.

an American company, for the development of a space-satellite-launching project in a 404-sq km (156-sq mi) area in the Essequibo region. The deal was promptly "deplored" by the Venezuelan government, which had a historic claim to the area, on the grounds that a U.S. military base was part of the arrangement. Later in the year Pres. Bharrat Jagdeo soothed Venezuelan Pres. Hugo Chávez Frías by pointing out that the space station had no military intent.

In June, just before drilling was about to begin on a promising oil concession, gunboats from Suriname evicted a drilling rig from waters Guyana regarded as its own. (DAVID RENWICK)

HAITI

Area: 27,700 sq km (10,695 sq mi)
Population (2000 est.): 6,868,000
Capital: Port-au-Prince
Chief of state and government: President René Préval, assisted by Prime Minister Jacques-Édouard Alexis

Long-delayed parliamentary elections to fill 10,000 local and legislative positions began on May 21, 2000, and involved two rounds. The Lavalas Family party of former president Jean-Bertrand Aristide won 18 of the 19 Senate seats, 72 of the 82 contested seats in the Chamber of Deputies, and 80% of Haiti's 133 city halls. Millions of Haitians risked their lives to vote in the country's first democratic election in years. Soon afterward, however, international observers and Haiti's own Provisional Electoral Council charged that the vote count for 10 of the Senate seats was flawed. Despite the threats of international donors to withdraw financial aid if the government did not have runoff elections, Pres. René Préval declared the results official, and the 10 senators were sworn into office. With the legitimacy of the new Parliament in question, the U.S. and other countries decided to withdraw their support for the November 26 presidential elections, in which Aristide was returned to power. The Provisional Electoral Council reported that Aristide won 92% of the vote. Voter turnout was about 68%. Most opposition parties had withdrawn from the contest. Nine additional Senate seats were also filled in the November elections.

Political instability increased considerably throughout the year. The Haitian National Police was in disarray. It had at most 6,200 members and was the government's only security force for a country of nearly 6.9 million people. Because of its displeasure over the election results, the U.S. ended its assistance to the police. The last U.S. troops stationed in Haiti left the country in January.

Nearly all U.S. aid to Haiti was suspended. In addition, the Haitian economy found itself in its worst condition in years as a result of a spending binge by the government, higher petroleum prices, and political turmoil. Remittances by Haitians living abroad, particularly in the U.S.—estimated between $400 million and $1 billion annually—constituted one of the biggest sources of dollars for Haiti. The apparel industry and the construction sector were strong throughout the year, and some meagre investment was made in wireless communications. A privatization program that would have been useful in attracting new investment by making infrastructure upgrades in such run-down state-owned facilities as the port, the airport, and telephone and electric companies was abandoned.

The economic situation had some foreign policy implications. The government had to deal with the problems created by the many Haitians who took to the sea in overcrowded boats to try to reach the southern coast of the U.S. (JEAN-CLAUDE GARCIA-ZAMOR)

HONDURAS

Area: 112,492 sq km (43,433 sq mi)
Population (2000 est.): 6,490,000
Capital: Tegucigalpa
Head of state and government: President Carlos Roberto Flores Facussé

Throughout 2000 Honduras continued to rebuild from the destruction caused by Hurricane Mitch in October 1998. The country received a positive evaluation for its progress from the Consultative Group for the Reconstruction and Transformation of Central America,

Orlando Sierra/AFP Worldwide

which represented about 40 donor nations and international organizations. Boosting that evaluation was an economy that showed its first signs of recovery since the hurricane hit.

Honduras became the second Latin American country to qualify for debt relief under the Heavily Indebted Poor Countries program. The program allowed the World Bank, the International Monetary Fund, the Inter-American Development Bank, and the Central American Bank of Economic Integration to forgive portions of Honduras's debt and work to restructure other debts. In May the government moved to cut spending by announcing a mass layoff in the public sector.

On June 29 Honduras, along with El Salvador and Guatemala, signed a free-trade agreement with Mexico after eight years of negotiations. The treaty was set to take effect on Jan. 1, 2001, when 57% of Mexico's exports and 65% of the three other countries' exports would become duty-free. Duties on the remainder of exports would be lifted over 12 years.

In February a border dispute with Nicaragua became violent. The tension began in late 1999 when Honduras endorsed Colombian sovereignty over Caribbean waters and islands claimed by Nicaragua. Nicaragua retaliated by imposing trade sanctions on Honduras and bringing a lawsuit about the border demarcation to the World Court. In February 2000 the dispute expanded to include the question of fishing rights in the Gulf of Fonseca on the Pacific side of the isthmus. The suit was expected to take years to resolve. On March 7 the countries' foreign ministers signed a pact to prevent acts of aggression and coordinate boat patrols and military operations against drug traffickers. Nevertheless, Nicaragua continued its trade sanctions; in return, Honduras applied sanctions against Nicaraguan goods on March 25.

(MICHELLE M. TAYLOR-ROBINSON)

Residents of a Honduran village destroyed by Hurricane Mitch in 1998 return to the site of their former homes on March 12, 2000, after the village was rebuilt.

HUNGARY

Area: 93,030 sq km (35,919 sq mi)
Population (2000 est.): 10,022,000
Capital: Budapest
Chief of state: Presidents Arpad Goncz and, from August 4, Ferenc Madl
Head of government: Prime Minister Viktor Orban

The year 2000 was one of relative political stability and balanced economic growth in Hungary. The government, however, because of its arrogant communication style and seemingly permanent campaign to demonize the opposition, received increasingly bad press. In polls taken during the fall, the former governing Hungarian Socialist Party overtook the governing Federation of Young Democrats (Fidesz) in voter strength. The two parties' popularity stood at 43% and 33%, respectively.

Relations between the Fidesz-led coalition government and the opposition worsened in the National Assembly, where the two seemed to have abandoned all attempts at consensus-seeking politics. Also, a top-level political scandal involving both the government and the opposition erupted. As a follow-up episode to the oil scandal in 1996, in which attempts were made to link high government officials with the Hungarian oil mafia, new testimony by a criminal-turned-crown-witness led the National Assembly's oil scandal investigating committee to accuse a number of former and current top-level politicians of involvement.

Among the important new legislation passed in 2000 were a law on conflicts of interest of local government representatives and an amendment to a law concerning the screening of public officials for possible cooperation with the corrupt communist regime. The amendment increased the number of those liable for screening from 900 to 17,000 and for the first time prescribed compulsory screening of past activities for judges, prosecutors, and even media editors. The law was criticized by the opposition for including the media and for not covering church representatives.

After 10 years as president, Arpad Goncz, the country's most popular politician, left the political scene at the end of his second term. The National

Assembly elected as his replacement Ferenc Madl, who had been an unsuccessful presidential candidate in 1995. His election came on the third round of voting on June 6. Madl, who did not hold any party membership, was a former law professor and had been a minister of education and culture in the first democratically elected government of Hungary.

After a 10-year tenure and two years before the end of his mandate, independent Chief Prosecutor Kalman Gyorgyi unexpectedly quit, saying that his position had become overly politicized under the current leadership. Studies showed that the country's journalists also complained about the increase of political pressure on the media.

Hungary's economy continued to boom, registering a growth in gross domestic product of 5.5%, up from 4% in 1999. The Ministry of Economic Affairs authorized planning to begin on a large-scale development project named after 19th-century reformer Istvan Szechenyi; the project was to focus on highway and real estate development. The government was criticized for pushing through a politically motivated and unprecedented two-year budget and for its failure to curb inflation, which only dropped a half point, from 10% in 1999 to 9.5% in 2000, despite the tight fiscal policy of the Central Bank. Investments continued to grow.

On August 20 the country celebrated the millennium of its founding by King Stephen I in 1000. At the centre of a controversy, however, was the sacred crown of St. Stephen, given to him by Pope Sylvester II, which had been housed in a national museum until it was moved to the National Assembly for a celebratory ceremony. Opposition leaders questioned the suitability of the transfer and wondered why a king's crown was used to represent the country's new era of democracy. Hungary also gained international headlines for an environmental catastrophe that occurred on its territory in February. Originating from a gold mine in Romania, a cyanide spill severely polluted the Tisza and Szamos rivers, spreading into the Danube in Yugoslavia and seriously damaging the biosphere. Hungary sued the mining company for $110 million.

Negotiations for entry into the European Union slowed after the EU in the fall of 1999 included six more countries (in addition to the original six) in the accession discussions. Prime Minister Viktor Orban repeatedly criticized the EU for its delay. (ZSOFIA SZILAGYI)

ICELAND

Area: 102,819 sq km (39,699 sq mi)
Population (2000 est.): 280,000
Capital: Reykjavík
Chief of state: President Ólafur Ragnar Grímsson
Head of government: Prime Minister Davíd Oddsson

Iceland continued to enjoy economic growth in 2000. Gross domestic product was expected to increase by about 3.5%, bringing total economic growth to 26% since 1996. Unlike earlier expansions, this one was not based on fisheries. Instead, biotechnology, software, and telecommunications were prominent contributors to growth. Inflation became pronounced, rising to a 5–6% annual rate in 2000.

In 1999 a nationwide debate had raged over the planned flooding of a migratory bird habitat at Eyjabakkar, in the northeastern part of the country, for the reservoir of a hydroelectric dam. In the spring of 2000, the uproar ended when a compromise was reached—the habitat would be spared and the reservoir moved to a nearby location, Kárahnjúkar.

Iceland's best-known volcano, Mt. Hekla, erupted on February 26. The eruption was brief, lasting only four days, and there was no significant damage because the emission of pumice and lava was scant. Two large earthquakes took place in southwestern Iceland on June 17 and June 21, both reaching a magnitude of 6.6. Several buildings were destroyed, but there was no loss of life.

In recent years the allocation of fishing quotas had been a source of controversy. Fishing-boat owners were allocated free catch quotas on the basis of their actual catch in the early 1980s. In turn, they could sell the quota on the open market. Critics opposed the allocation at no cost and the consequent windfall profit in case of subsequent quota sales. A government-appointed commission concluded that quotas should in the future no longer be allocated for free.

Iceland sold its genealogical database that had records dating back 1,000 years to DeCode, a U.S. firm, in the hope that the detailed records would provide clues for the possible cure of diseases.

(BJÖRN MATTHÍASSON)

INDIA

Area: 3,165,596 sq km (1,222,243 sq mi)
Population (2000 est.): 1,014,004,000
Capital: New Delhi
Chief of state: President Kocheril Raman Narayanan
Head of government: Prime Minister Atal Bihari Vajpayee

In 2000 India's ruling National Democratic Alliance (NDA) consolidated its hold on power in spite of dissension within the Bharatiya Janata Party (BJP)—the NDA's major constituent—discord between some of the alliance partners, and concern over the ill health of Prime Minister Atal Bihari Vajpayee. Economic liberalization was stepped up. An exchange of visits by U.S. Pres. Bill Clinton and Vajpayee led to a new warmth in Indo-U.S. relations. The visit of Russian Pres. Vladimir Putin renewed the tradition of close ties between New Delhi and Moscow.

Domestic Affairs. Three new states came into being in India during the year: Chhattisgarh (on November 1), Uttaranchal (on November 8), and Jharkhand (on November 15). They were carved out of three large states—Madhya Pradesh, Uttar Pradesh, and Bihar, respectively. Bills enabling the formation of the three new states were adopted by both houses of Parliament with virtual unanimity.

Elections to the legislative assemblies of the states of Bihar, Haryana, Manipur, and Orissa were held. In Bihar the victorious NDA candidate for chief minister, Nitish Kumar, was unable to form a government and resigned his post after only seven days in office. Former Bihar chief minister Rabri Devi of the Rashtriya Janata Dal returned for a third term. In Orissa the BJP–Biju Janata Dal coalition swept the polls and formed a government under Naveen Patnaik; the Congress (I) party, which had held power, was routed. In Haryana the BJP–Indian National Lok Dal coalition, led by Om Prakash Chautala, retained power. In Manipur the Congress was displaced by a coalition headed by Wahengbam Nipamacha Singh.

Two other states had new chief ministers in October. In Uttar Pradesh the BJP asked Rajnath Singh to take over from Ram Prakash Gupta. In Goa the

BJP withdrew its support from coalition chief minister Francisco Sardinha and formed a government of its own headed by Manohar Parrikar. In November, Jyoti Basu of the Communist Party of India (Marxist) stepped down from the chief ministership of West Bengal after holding that office continuously for 23 years and was succeeded by Buddhadeb Bhattacharya of the same party.

Jammu and Kashmir continued to be a source of contention between India and its neighbours. The state was convulsed by the activities of militants during the year. Hundreds of civilians were killed in terrorist attacks, including about 30 Hindu pilgrims bound for the holy temple in Amarnath on August 1. The government's efforts to open negotiations with the militants did not make headway. Leaders of the All-Party Hurriyat Conference were released from prison in May. The separatist Hizbul Mujahideen made an offer of cease-fire in July but abruptly withdrew it. When Pakistani Chief Executive Gen. Pervaiz Musharraf offered to hold talks on Jammu and Kashmir, New Delhi replied that there should "first be total cessation of Pakistani-sponsored terrorism." In late December Prime Minister Vajpayee announced that he would extend a unilateral cease-fire in Kashmir by an additional month and that he would begin to take "exploratory steps" to revive peace talks with Pakistan. In response, Pakistan withdrew its troops from the Line of Control, which separated the two countries.

P.V. Narasimha Rao, India's prime minister from 1991 to 1996, and Buta Singh, a former home minister, were found guilty by a special court on September 29 of having bribed Lok Sabha (House of the People) members in order to survive a vote of no confidence in 1993. Both received three-year prison sentences on October 12. Later the Delhi High Court suspended the sentence and permitted them to appeal. H.K.L. Bhagat, a former central minister, was cleared of involvement in anti-Sikh violence that had followed the assassination of Indira Gandhi in 1984. On September 30 a 13-year-old boy, Sudarshan Hansda, was sentenced to 14 years in prison for his part in the 1999 murders of an Australian missionary, Graham Staines, and his two young sons in Orissa state. The trial of 14 others charged in the murders was in progress.

The Supreme Court, in a major judgement delivered in October, rejected the petition of environmentalists and permitted the Sardar Sarovar Dam across the Narmada River to be raised to a height of 90 m (295 ft) initially and 138 m (453 ft) eventually. Work on the dam had been halted in 1995 when a petition by the Narmada Bachao Aandolan (Save Narmada Movement) was filed.

Raveendran/AFP Worldwide

A member of the Centre of Indian Trade Unions wields a banner during a demonstration in New Delhi against the government's privatization program.

The Economy. The economy took a downturn in 2000. A report of the International Monetary Fund, *World Economic Outlook*, estimated India's gross domestic product growth rate at 6.7%, but the government's own Central Statistical Organization placed GDP growth even lower, at 5.8% during the April–June quarter. The annual inflation rate stood at 6.92% at the end of October. The steep rise in international oil prices compelled the government to announce substantial increases in the prices of petroleum products. The foreign exchange reserves at the end of September stood at $35 billion.

The government's budget for 2000–01, presented on February 29, contained proposals to collect Rs 69 billion (1 Rs=about $0.02) by way of additional taxes. India had an overall fiscal deficit of Rs 1.1 trillion, or 5.1% of GDP. The total allocation for development plans was Rs 1.2 trillion. Allocation for defense was Rs 585.9 billion, an increase of 21% over the previous year.

In May the government announced its intention to divest up to 60% of its hold-

India's Computer Revolution

In May 2000 India's lower house of parliament, the Lok Sabha (House of the People), passed the Information Technology Bill to boost e-commerce and Internet-related business in the country. The bill provided a legal framework for e-commerce, legalized digital documents, and created a police task force to deal with the unsavoury fallout of India's computer revolution—cyber crime. The bill was another milestone in India's journey toward becoming a key player in the knowledge economy, a journey that started with the 5th-century Indian mathematician Aryabhata I's introduction of the concept of zero, the basis of all programming.

At the nucleus of the computer revolution were the major metropolitan cities, notably Mumbai (Bombay) and Chennai (Madras), and the silicon triangle of Bangalore, Pune, and Hyderabad. With the help of these cities, India exported an estimated $4 billion worth of software to the West. Wipro Ltd., a conglomerate based in Bangalore, was identified as India's third largest information technology (IT) company, and Wipro's chairman, Azim H. Premji (*see* BIOGRAPHIES), was listed as one of the world's richest men.

Unlike the Industrial Revolution, which benefited only India's urban elite, the knowledge revolution by 2000 had permeated all sections of Indian society. In a clutch of villages in Madhya Pradesh, an intranet connected rural cyber cafés, allowing villagers access to computerized land records. Project Gyandoot ("Messenger of Knowledge") helped farmers get the best prices for their produce from nearby markets such as Indore and Mumbai. Another wired village, Nayla, Rajasthan, used the Internet in social development schemes, an innovation that impressed U.S. Pres. Bill Clinton during his March 2000 visit to India.

What powered the computer revolution was India's intellectual capital—an over four million-strong technically trained workforce fluent in English—and a 10–12-hour time difference that ensured round-the-clock productivity for North American and European countries outsourcing their software requirements. The low cost of labour and high quality of software capabilities in India spawned such IT-enabled services as call centres, medical transcription, animation, back-office operations, and revenue accounting.

According to India's Ministry of Information Technology, the software industry was projected to export $6 billion worth of software by 2001, and it hoped to reach a stunning $10 billion by 2002. Indian software was expected to be a $5.7 billion industry in 1999–2000. In December 1999 a report commissioned by the National Association of Software and Service Companies predicted that by the year 2008 software and services would contribute more than 7.5% of India's overall gross domestic product growth, with IT exports accounting for 35% of the country's total exports.

The watershed year of this revolution was 1998, when such Indian companies as Infosys and Satyam Infoway emerged as world players as fears over computer problems on Jan. 1, 2000, and preparations for the European Union's new currency unit, the euro, increased demand for Indian software programmers. The Hyderabad Information Technology Engineering Consultancy (Hi-Tec City) in Hyderabad powered the growth of this computer mecca, nicknamed Cyberabad. American companies such as Texas Instruments, Microsoft, IBM, Oracle, Motorola, and GE Capital established operations in India, including software-development centres.

(SHALAKA PARADKAR)

ings in Air-India; the move was seen as a first step toward eventual privatization of the country's state-owned airline. The government also announced that it would reduce its holdings to 26% in three key public-sector enterprises, Indo-Burmah Petroleum, the State Trading Corporation, and the Minerals and Metals Trading Corporation. The same month, the Department of Telecommunications was converted into a corporation, Bharat Sanchar Nigam Limited, as a step toward disinvestment. Domestic long-distance telephony was thrown open to private-sector competition, with up to 49% foreign equity. The government also announced the opening up of international telephony to private-sector competition in 2002, two years ahead of schedule. An Information Technology Bill, giving a legal framework for electronic commerce, was passed in May. (*See* COMPUTERS AND INFORMATION SYSTEMS: *Sidebar*, above.)

Foreign Relations. The diplomatic highlights of the year were the visits to India by President Clinton in March and President Putin in October and Prime Minister Vajpayee's own visit to the U.S. in September. As a result, Indo-U.S. relations were at their best in 50 years, while India's traditional friendship with Russia was reinforced. Clinton and Vajpayee issued a statement in New Delhi outlining their "shared vision of a closer and qualitatively new relationship for shaping a future of peace, prosperity, democracy, pluralism and freedom." Later, in their joint statement in Washington, D.C., they expressed their desire for a continuing institutional dialogue between the two countries. India reaffirmed its moratorium on nuclear explosive tests until the Comprehensive Test Ban Treaty came into effect. There was considerable satisfaction in India that the U.S. had a better appreciation of the threat that India faced from externally sponsored terrorism. During his American visit Vajpayee addressed a joint session of the U.S. Congress as well as the millennium session of heads of state and government at the UN headquarters in New York City.

During President Putin's visit, a declaration of strategic partnership for the new century was signed, and the two countries agreed to work for a multipolar world and to combat terrorism. In addition, a series of agreements were signed to provide for cooperation in defense production, nuclear energy, and information technology. One of the pacts provided for Russia to supply India with 310 T-90 tanks, to enable licensed production in India of 140 Sukhoy fighter aircraft, to lease four TU-22 bombers, and to give an aircraft carrier that would be refitted at India's cost. The two countries were also to set up a joint working group on Afghanistan. Addressing the Indian Parliament, Putin emphasized cooperation to combat terrorism and endorsed the Indian position that the country's dispute with Pakistan over Jammu and Kashmir state should be settled bilaterally without external intervention. India decided to withdraw its troops from the UN peacekeeping force in Sierra Leone. (H.Y. SHARADA PRASAD)

INDONESIA

Area: 1,922,570 sq km (742,308 sq mi)
Population (2000 est.): 209,342,000
Capital: Jakarta
Head of state and government: President Abdurrahman Wahid

AP/Wide World Photos

An Indonesian soldier stands guard above a village in Maluku province devastated by fighting between Muslims and Christians.

When he was elected in October 1999, Indonesian Pres. Abdurrahman Wahid chose a cabinet that included all of Indonesia's major political forces: the nationalist Indonesian Democratic Party of Struggle (PDI-P), the former ruling party Golkar, Muslim-linked parties, and the military. Wahid's tenacious attempt to consolidate power, and the resulting political tug-of-war, provided much of the drama in Indonesia in 2000, even as the country's myriad political, economic, and social problems remained unsolved. The instability marred Indonesia's first year of multiparty, civilian-led democracy and returned some advantage to the once-dominant military.

The religious strife that surged again in late 1999 between Muslims and Christians in the eastern province of Maluku preceded the year's first high-profile political battle. Wahid's senior political minister, former armed forces chief General Wiranto—Wahid's rival for influence over the military—unsuccessfully sought to impose martial law on the region. Meanwhile, Muslim political leader Amien Rais—chairman of the People's Consultative Assembly, Indonesia's highest legislative body—led a January 7 protest in Jakarta against Wahid's perceived inaction. On January 31 a government commission report implicated 33 people, including Wiranto, as responsible for the post-1999 referendum violence in East Timor, largely wrought by Indonesian soldiers and military-backed militias. The president seized the opportunity to suspend the general from the cabinet on February 14.

Wiranto's suspension was followed by a military reshuffle that saw the rise of younger, more reformist officers. Despite alienating military conservatives as well as the Muslim parties that had backed him for the presidency, Wahid, boosted by his reputation as a pro-democracy figure, initially held the advantage. He ran into trouble, however, on April 25, the day after he replaced PDI-P and Golkar cabinet ministers with officials close to him. The move angered members of the two largest parties, including Vice Pres. Megawati Sukarnoputri, leader of the PDI-P.

Local media reported in May that Wahid's masseur, claiming to be the president's personal assistant, had bilked $4 million from Bulog, the former state food-distribution monopoly, by claiming that the president needed the funds to calm the separatist province of Aceh. In explaining the scandal, Wahid inadvertently created another by revealing that he had received $2 million for Aceh from the sultan of Brunei without reporting it to the government. The sackings and the scandals—coupled with impatience at Wahid's frequent foreign trips (in his first eight months in office, he spent about two of them traveling abroad), his erratic leadership style, and his strategy of sidelining political parties—led the parliament to file a motion summoning him for an official explanation. When Wahid faced the parliament on July 20, he insisted that the body had no constitutional right to question him. His hard-line stance seemed to endanger his position before the August 7–18 annual Assembly session.

Wahid failed to prevent a backlash by military conservatives, who on July 31 replaced the officers who had been appointed during the post-Wiranto reshuffle. The Assembly also made concessions to the armed forces by allowing them to retain their 38 unelected seats until 2009. Wahid, however, was able to defuse any attempt to unseat him by declaring on August 9 that he would hand over day-to-day duties to Megawati. Two weeks later Wahid appeared to renege on his pledge by forming a cabinet packed with his aides, none linked to Golkar or PDI-P, and issuing a decree that gave little actual authority to Megawati. Opposition to Wahid hardened in the legislature. On August 28 the parliament voted overwhelmingly to launch investigations into the Bulog and Brunei scandals.

Later in the year the nation's attention turned to the trial of former president Suharto, who was accused of having enriched himself and his family during his more than three decades of rule. Citing poor health, he failed to appear on August 31, the trial's opening day. On September 28 the court acquitted him of all charges, considering him medically unfit to stand trial. The verdict triggered violent clashes in the capital and highlighted the government's mixed record in enforcing justice. A number of high-profile investigations launched in 2000 into prior human rights violations by the military produced few results, although on September 1 the attorney general's office named 19 possible suspects in murders in East Timor.

Although political infighting cast a shadow on the currency, which had weakened 20% by September, the economy recovered 4.17% in the first six months of 2000, mostly on the back of private consumption. In August the government finished issuing bonds to recapitalize the country's beleaguered banking system, an effort that had contributed some $75.8 billion to Indonesia's estimated $144 billion debt. As the year progressed, public criticism mounted over the Indonesian Bank Restructuring Agency's concessions to large local corporations in settling their bad debts.

The security situation worsened, despite the signing of a "humanitarian pause" on May 12 between separatist Free Aceh Movement rebels and the government. The Maluku conflict encouraged the formation of radical religious militia both in Maluku and on Java. In Aceh violations of the cease-fire by both sides were reported, while religious-tinged unrest similar to Maluku's erupted on the island of Celebes. On September 6 armed militia members killed three UN staff members working with East Timorese refugees in Indonesian West Timor. The incident underlined Jakarta's inability to pacify the paramilitaries as well as its slow pace in repatriating refugees to East Timor. On September 13 a bombing at the Jakarta Stock Exchange claimed the lives of 15 persons. Days later Wahid ordered the arrest of Suharto's youngest son, Tommy, who had been convicted in a corruption case. In October, however, Wahid held a secret meeting with Tommy, raising fears that he would set Tommy free in exchange for the return of some of Suharto's allegedly ill-gotten billions.

(JOSÉ MANUEL TESORO)

IRAN

Area: 1,633,841 sq km (630,830 sq mi)
Population (2000 est.): 62,704,000 (excluding more than 1,200,000 Afghan refugees and about 500,000 Iraqi refugees)
Capital: Tehran
Supreme political and religious authority: *Rahbar* (Spiritual Leader) Ayatollah Sayyed Ali Khamenei
Head of state and government: President Mohammad Khatami

On Feb. 18, 2000, more than 80% of the Iranian electorate voted in the first round of the election for members of the national legislature. In principle, with 75% of the elected deputies claiming adherence to the reformist group, Iranians had voted for more dynamic economic change and faster political liberalization. The only clear-cut outcome, however, was that the reformists as a whole won a majority of seats in the legislature but, divided among some 18 factions, represented a far from united front against the hard-liners. Even after the second round of the elections on May 5, when 66 seats were filled, there remained unsettled questions of validation of those elected—particularly to the 30 seats in Tehran itself—by the conservative-dominated Council of Guardians. When the legislature convened on May 27, 41 seats had not yet been allocated. Hojatolislam Ali Akbar Hashemi Rafsanjani, a former president of Iran, finished last in the elections for Tehran, resigned from the legislature, and thereby abandoned his bid to become speaker of the new assembly. The post of speaker was taken instead by Hojatolislam Mehdi Karrubi, a candidate slightly left of centre in his ideological stance, who had politically strong vested interests in the Association of Combatant Clergy party and economically in the powerful Shahid ("Martyrs") Foundation.

President Khatami ultimately obtained a legislature that would be oriented toward liberal policies but would not be unified as a coherent political force. The president's brother was appointed both second vice-speaker and head of the main reformist group of deputies. Even so, the hard-liners were content with having a sympathetic speaker, a first deputy speaker from their own ranks, and perhaps the most single-minded grouping of deputies in the assembly; consequently, the reformists faced a struggle to make headway with their proposed legislative program. Opening the new legislative session, President Khatami urged the deputies to move quickly to salvage the country's sagging economy and to establish social justice.

Political violence persisted, with the presidential palace and other targets being hit by mortar fire on February 5. In the wake of the legislative elections, there was on March 12 an unsuccessful assassination attempt made on Saeed Hajjarian, an important supporter of President Khatami; his loss would have been a blow to the reformists. As disruptive and threatening was a simultaneous burgeoning of attacks by hard-line extremists on those newspapers and journals published by reformists. In mid-December liberal culture minister Ataollah Mohajerani resigned, which was viewed as a possible fatal blow to reform. Despite changes in the judiciary, the intimidation of the free-thinking press by hard-line groups and parts of the security services diminished only slightly during the year.

The trial of 13 Iranian Jews, detained in 1999 on charges of espionage, took place without major adverse international repercussions. Three of the accused were freed on bail before the judicial proceedings began on April 13 in Shiraz. Judgment was given on July 1, when prison sentences of 4–13 years (later reduced) were handed down to 10 of the defendants, while 3 were acquitted. There was concern voiced in France and elsewhere in Europe that the trial was conducted behind closed doors, and U.S. Pres. Bill Clinton expressed deep unhappiness about the trial and its outcome.

Activity in foreign relations was vigorous but was not highly rewarded. Links with the U.S. improved with a loosening of U.S. economic sanctions in March and a visit to New York City by President Khatami in early September, but no major breakthrough toward a final lifting of U.S. sanctions was apparent. Khatami visited China with a delegation of 170 senior officials June 22–26, which led to the signing of agreements on energy, industry, and tourism. He also made a successful formal visit to Germany in July, which helped to increase recognition of the Iranian regime in the European Union as a whole. Iran's regional difficulties with Turkey, Iraq, and Afghanistan did not lessen perceptibly. Iranian contacts with Russia were notably more frigid as a result of conflicting policies on Chechnya, the Caspian basin, and Central Asia.

The buoyancy of the Iranian economy was much aided by growth in oil revenues during the year as unit oil prices rose on the international market. The first $3 billion of income in excess of the budget forecast was channeled into a fund to stabilize the country's foreign reserves in the event of a future fall in oil income. Any additional income was to be used to fund development projects. Long-term economic reforms such as privatization and an opening up of the domestic market, however, remained in need of urgent attention.

(KEITH S. MCLACHLAN)

IRAQ

Area: 435,052 sq km (167,975 sq mi)
Population (2000 est.): 22,676,000
Capital: Baghdad
Head of state and government: President and Prime Minister Saddam Hussein

After lengthy discussions the UN Security Council finally passed Resolution 1284 on Iraq in December 1999. It promised a temporary suspension of economic sanctions on Iraq for four months (renewable) if Iraq demonstrated "cooperation" on all aspects of the UN-mandated program to dismantle its weapons of mass destruction and agreed to the readmission of UN arms inspectors. There were important differences in the Security Council between France, Russia, and China on the one hand and the U.S. and Great Britain on the other over the definition of *cooperation* and implementation of the program should Iraq accept the resolution. A new UN agency, the United Nations Monitoring, Verification and Inspection Commission, was formed to replace the former inspection team, which had left Iraq in December 1998 on the eve of U.S. and British air strikes against Baghdad. Hans Blix of Sweden was appointed to head the commission. Iraq, however, refused to allow the return of arms inspectors if sanctions, which had been imposed on Iraq when that country invaded Kuwait in August 1990, were not completely abolished. Throughout the year American and British airplanes continued to fly over Iraqi territory and to bombard radio and surface-to-air missile sites in the no-fly zones. These raids left casualties among Iraqi military and civilians.

During 2000 UN sanctions on Iraq gradually eroded in practice as hundreds of businessmen and foreign government officials traveled to Baghdad to conclude trade deals with the Iraqi government. Illegal smuggling into Iraq also intensified. Between September and December several European and Arab planes landed at Saddam International Airport in Baghdad. Some of them landed without prior UN approval in defiance of the air-travel ban on Iraq. A railroad link between Iraq and Syria resumed service after some 19 years of interruption.

During the first nine months of the year, relations between Iraq and Iran continued to deteriorate. On several occasions Baghdad was struck by rockets that caused civilian casualties. One such attack, on March 22, struck a residential apartment building, leaving 4 civilians dead and about 40 injured. Iraq accused Iranian agents of launching the missiles and held the Iranian government responsible. For its part the Iranian government accused the Iraqis of helping the Mujaheddin-e-Khalq, an exiled Iranian opposition group with military bases in Iraq that had made frequent cross-border attacks inside Iran. Iran launched car bomb and missile attacks against Mujaheddin bases in Iraq.

Iran and Iraq continued to exchange prisoners of war still held in captivity from the Iran-Iraq War (1980–90). During the year Iran released some 3,300 Iraqi prisoners of war, although each country continued to accuse the other of holding more. Relations between the two countries took a step forward in September, however, when Iranian Pres. Mohammad Khatami met with Iraqi Vice Pres. Taha Yasin Ramadhan during the summit meeting of OPEC in Caracas, Venez. The meeting raised expectations that both countries would begin to address long-standing problems between them.

In September a renewed crisis occurred between Iraq and Kuwait, causing a further deterioration of relations between the two countries. Iraq accused Kuwait of "stealing" oil from fields in southern Iraq and threatened to take unspecified measures against Kuwait. Kuwait denied the Iraqi charges. The crisis prompted the U.S. to declare, on September 15, that it would use military force if Iraq attacked Kuwait.

Relations between Iraq and four other Arab countries in the Persian Gulf region—Qatar, Bahrain, the United Arab Emirates, and Oman—improved during the year. Three of those four countries (Oman never closed its doors) reopened their embassies in Baghdad as a first step toward enhancing trade with Iraq. A maritime link between Doha (Qatar) and Iraq was inaugurated in October. Later in October Iraq for the first time in 10 years was invited to a summit meeting of the Arab League, called in response to the outbreak of violence between Israelis and Palestinians.

Iraq made considerable economic gains from oil sales during the year; its gross income from oil was estimated at $18 billion–$20 billion in 2000. Iraq was allowed to sell oil under a UN-sponsored "oil for food" program that permitted the nation to use the oil revenues to buy food, medicine, and other items that could not be used for military purposes. Since 1996, when the oil for food program went into effect, Iraq had sold more than $37 billion in oil. The nation had made deductions for a fund to compensate victims of the 1990 invasion of Kuwait and had paid set-asides for programs in Kurdish areas. Baghdad, however, had been left with $19 billion from the UN program to buy civilian goods. Although a wide range of items were available in Iraqi markets, they remained beyond the reach of the Iraqi general public because of their high prices. The country also experienced further deterioration of its agricultural production. One reason was a lower level of water downstream in the Tigris and Euphrates rivers owing to dams built by Turkey and Syria on the upstream sections. A second factor was a lack of rainfall in the country for a second consecutive year. The drought forced thousands of Iraqi farmers to abandon their parched land.

(LOUAY BAHRY)

IRELAND

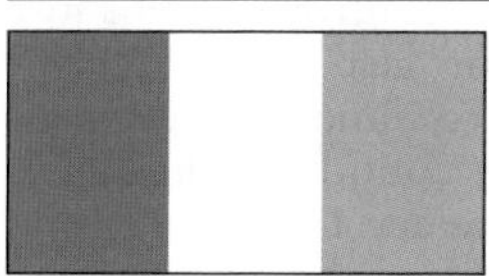

Area: 70,273 sq km (27,133 sq mi)
Population (2000 est.): 3,783,000
Capital: Dublin
Chief of state: President Mary McAleese
Head of government: Prime Minister Bertie Ahern

The continuing growth of the Irish economy resulted in an optimistic start to 2000. A record budget surplus of £Ir 1.1 billion (£Ir 1=about $1.10) enabled the minister of finance to introduce welcome tax cuts in his annual budget. In June record export figures exceeding £Ir 6 billion provided indications that economic growth was continuing to surpass the most optimistic expectations. From 1993 to 2000 gross national product grew by 57%. It also appeared that the export boom was speeding up and that the economy was growing by about 13% annually. An increase in inflation toward the end of the year caused concern, however, with predictions by the central bank that inflation would average at least 4% in 2001, almost twice the government's forecast and well above the European average. Rising inflation was reflected in spiraling house prices and growing wage demands, which were putting at risk the Programme for Prosperity and Fairness that had been negotiated with the social partners (labour unions, management, and farming organizations) earlier in the year. It was also feared that inflation might diminish the attractiveness of Ireland as a location for foreign investment.

The prosperity created during the past few years had its downside. For example, because of staff shortages health agencies could not meet the demands being placed upon them, and recruitment of nurses and physicians from India and the Philippines was being actively pursued.

Increased traffic, especially in Dublin, was causing chaos, to which the government responded with plans for a light-rail and subway system to relieve the congestion. The projected cost of this ambitious 16-year project had by late 2000 already risen from £Ir 8 billion to £Ir 14 billion; the private sector was being asked to bankroll up to half of the expense, which would lessen the burden on taxpayers. The overall planning was beset by controversy, not just over funding but also about aboveground and underground services. With one-third of the country's population located in the greater Dublin area, its future transportation needs emerged during the year as the most difficult of all political problems.

The various tribunals set up to investigate tax and banking irregularities continued their painstaking work during the year. There was public outrage when it was discovered that large payments had been made to a number of politicians as bribes for their support for applications involving the rezoning of land for development. The Moriarty tribunal attracted particular interest, involving as it did the appearance of former prime minister Charles Haughey in the late summer. Investigators had discovered that Haughey had received substantial sums of money from prominent businesspeople when he was in office. He was unable to account for this, pleading loss of memory and poor health. Testimony showed that when Haughey was elected prime minister in 1979, he owed the Allied Irish Bank more than $1.3 million. Within weeks, Haughey was able to pay back more than $930,000 to the bank; one prominent property developer testified that he gave Haughey as much as $475,000 during this time. Further scandals were uncovered by the parliamentary investigatory body, the Public Accounts Committee, which revealed massive tax evasion by the country's banking system and by private individuals using illegal offshore accounts. Restitution was made by the banks.

The coalition government of Fianna Fail and the Progressive Democrats suffered a major and quite unexpected political setback during the summer. They made a highly controversial attempt to appoint a former Supreme Court judge to the board of the European Investment Bank. The judge, who had been forced to resign over charges of direct interference in the course of justice, eventually withdrew his name, but the damage to the government was immense, resulting, according to opinion polls, in a significant drop in support, which reached its lowest level since the coalition took office.

Government support for the Northern Ireland peace process continued to be directed largely by a coalition involving Sinn Fein and the Social Democratic and Labour Party that offered little support for the leader of the Ulster Unionist Party, David Trimble. He found himself in an increasingly difficult position as supporters turned away from a process that remained hampered by illegal hidden arms in both Northern Ireland and the republic.

In early December the coalition government, acknowledging union concerns about the impact of rising inflation on working-class wages, reached an agreement with labour leaders to raise increases in pay rates by 3% over two years. The accord was expected to help defuse threats of strikes by public sector workers in Ireland. A wide-ranging existing pact limited increases to 5.5% a year until 2002; the new rates would add 2% in April 2001 and another 1% in April 2002. (MAVIS ARNOLD)

Chief executive Patricia Byrne stands outside the National Technological Park in Limerick, Ireland, a centre for a growing number of high-tech and knowledge-based firms.

AP/Wide World Photos

ISRAEL

Area: 21,671 sq km (8,367 sq mi), including the Golan Heights and disputed East Jerusalem, excluding the Emerging Palestinian Autonomous Areas
Population (2000 est.): 6,107,000
Capital: Jerusalem is the proclaimed capital of Israel (since Jan. 23, 1950) and the actual seat of government, but recognition has generally been withheld by the international community
Chief of state: Presidents Ezer Weizman, Avraham Burg (interim) from July 12, and, from August 1, Moshe Katzav
Head of government: Prime Minister Ehud Barak

The Emerging Palestinian Autonomous Areas (the West Bank and the Gaza Strip)
Total area: West Bank 5,900 sq km (2,270 sq mi), of which (as of March 2000) 342 sq km is under Palestinian administration, 3,369 sq km under Israeli administration, and 2,189 sq km under joint administration; Gaza Strip 363 sq km (140 sq mi), of which about 236 sq km is under Palestinian administration and about 127 sq km under Israeli administration
Population (2000 est.): West Bank 1,949,000, including 1,772,000 Arabs and 177,000 Jews; Gaza Strip 1,147,000, including 1,141,000 Arabs and 6,000 Jews
Principal administrative centres: Ram Allah and Gaza
Head of government: President Yasir Arafat

Peacemaking between Israel and the Palestinians moved tantalizingly close to a final agreement in 2000 but then degenerated into violent clashes when the two sides failed to agree on sovereignty over their holy sites in Jerusalem. A 15-day summit under U.S. auspices at the U.S. president's Camp David retreat in Maryland broke up on July 25 over the Jerusalem issue. Attempts to find a solution for the holy Temple Mount—which Jews claim as the site of their biblical temple and which Muslims call Al-Haram al-Sharif, the site of the Prophet Muhammad's ascension to heaven—continued until late September. On September 28, in a highly publicized attempt to emphasize Israeli sovereignty, government opposition leader Ariel Sharon paid a visit to the site, sparking widespread rioting in the Palestinian-controlled areas and among Israeli Arabs in Israel.

The unequal fighting between Israeli soldiers and stone-throwing Palestinian youths, the latter backed up by Palestinian National Authority Pres. Yasir Arafat's Tanzim militia firing light weapons, enabled the Palestinians to gain considerable support and sympathy throughout the world. More than 150 Palestinians were killed in the first month of fighting, a quarter of them children. The Palestinians accused the Israeli army of brutality; Israel accused the Palestinians of cynically exposing children to cross fire for propaganda purposes.

Incensed at Israel's handling of the riots and concerned about the angry demonstrations in their own countries, Arab leaders gathered in Cairo on October 21 for their first summit in four years. They issued a communiqué strongly criticizing Israel and calling on Arab nations to downgrade their relations with the Jewish state. Morocco, Tunisia, and Oman closed down low-level missions, and Egypt recalled its ambassador. The Arab states, however, stopped short of economic sanctions or military intervention against Israel.

Israeli leaders charged that Arafat, unhappy about elements in the peace package, was trying to internationalize the conflict and to render the American facilitating role less central. Some observers argued that the main stumbling block was not Jerusalem but the Palestinian refugees and that for historic and emotional reasons it was difficult for Arafat to declare an end of the conflict with less than a full resolution of that highly complex issue.

After his government received an additional 6.1% of the West Bank on March 21, Arafat was in full or partial control of 42.9% of that area, and there was speculation that, on the crest of the new uprising, he would make the unilateral declaration of Palestinian statehood that he had postponed several times. Israeli Prime Minister Ehud Barak warned that if he did, Israel would establish the borders between Israel and the Palestinian state unilaterally.

The Palestinians had been swayed into believing they could force Israel to end its occupation of the West Bank and Gaza by Israel's unilateral pullback from Lebanon in the face of determined resistance by Hezbollah militiamen. Israel's 18-year-long occupation of southern Lebanon ended on May 24, when it withdrew the last of its troops from its self-declared security zone. The withdrawal followed a 1999 campaign promise by Barak to pull the troops out.

In early January it seemed as though Barak might be able to achieve a negotiated withdrawal from Lebanon in peace talks with Syria in Shepherdstown, W.Va. The Syrians, however, continued to insist on an Israeli commitment to withdraw from the Golan Heights, while Israel wanted Syrian commitments in regard to security arrangements and normalization. To break the deadlock, U.S. Pres. Bill Clinton and Syrian Pres. Hafez al-Assad met in Geneva on March 26, but they made little headway. The talks focused on control of the northeastern coast of the Sea of Galilee. Assad insisted on a share of the water, a demand the Israelis rejected out of hand.

Barak's foreign policy and its attendant failures eroded his position at home. He began the year with a comfortable coalition majority of 68 in the 120-member Knesset (parliament), but his determination to take the peace process forward antagonized his more hawkish coalition partners. In addition, constant friction between the secular Meretz party, which controlled the Education Ministry, and the ultra-Orthodox Shas party, which demanded more funding and greater autonomy for its network of religious schools, sapped the coalition's strength.

In early July Shas, the National Religious Party, and Yisrael ba-Aliyah left the coalition, accusing Barak of being ready to concede too much to the Palestinians. Meretz, which supported Barak's peace moves, had already withdrawn from the government over its differences with Shas, and after Barak returned from Camp David, Foreign Minister David Levy resigned, pulling his Gesher party out of the coalition. Barak was then left with a minority coalition of only 40 Knesset members.

On May 28, following allegations that he had received more than $300,000 from two millionaire businessmen friends, Pres. Ezer Weizman announced that he intended to step down in July. The attorney general decided not to prosecute because of the seven-year time lapse since the gifts had been accepted. Elections for a new president took place in the Knesset on July 31, and in a surprising result, indicative of the weakness of Barak's governing coalition, Likud's Moshe Katzav defeated One Israel's elder statesman, Shimon Peres, by 63 votes to 57.

A millennium visit to the holy land in March by Pope John Paul II helped to further reconciliation between Christians and Jews. At Yad Vashem, Israel's

AP/Wide World Photos

Israeli troops handcuff a Palestinian who had scuffled with Jewish settlers in the West Bank on August 19.

memorial to the Holocaust, the pope expressed deep sorrow for acts of persecution and anti-Semitism "against the Jews by Christians at any time and in any place." Prime Minister Barak called the pope's visit to Yad Vashem "a climax of this historic journey of healing," and said that Israelis appreciated the pope's "noble act most profoundly."

In the second half of 2000, there were signs that Israel was emerging from its long economic slump. The rate of economic growth, which had fallen to just 2% in each of the previous two years, doubled, and there were a number of spectacular high-tech and export successes. Labour-intensive enterprises continued to close, however, so unemployment remained high at more than 8%. The Palestinian uprising hurt tourism, and there were fears that it would frighten investors. David Klein, who replaced Jacob Frenkel as governor of the Bank of Israel in January, continued his predecessor's tight monetary policy and kept inflation for the year at record lows. (LESLIE D. SUSSER)

ITALY

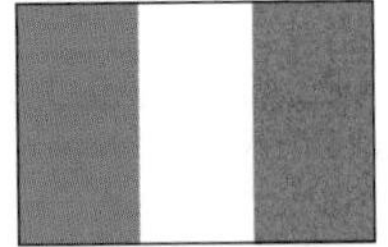

Area: 301,337 sq km (116,347 sq mi)
Population (2000 est.): 57,723,000
Capital: Rome
Chief of state: President Carlo Azeglio Ciampi
Head of government: Prime Ministers Massimo D'Alema until April 19 and, from April 26, Giuliano Amato

Italy's ruling centre-left coalition alliance suffered a severe election setback in the year 2000 and changed its leader as a result. Illegal immigration continued to cause Italians concern, and throughout the year millions of Christian pilgrims converged on Rome to celebrate a special Great Jubilee of the Year 2000, proclaimed by Pope John Paul II to coincide with the beginning of the new millennium.

In the elections, held in April, Italians were called upon for the first time to choose new presidents for 15 of the country's 20 regions. The contests were mainly seen as a dress rehearsal for the general elections scheduled for 2001. The two major contestants were a fractured centre-left so-called Olive Tree alliance led by Prime Minister Massimo D'Alema and a centre-right lineup named the House of Freedoms. At its head was media magnate Silvio Berlusconi. A readmitted ally was Umberto Bossi's Northern League, which claimed greater autonomy for the north.

Berlusconi and his allies won 8 of the 15 regions and gained control of the entire north of Italy. The press called the results "an earthquake," and D'Alema subsequently resigned, although he was not constitutionally obliged to do so. He had earlier tacitly agreed to see the election as a referendum on his government.

Pres. Carlo Azeglio Ciampi then called upon Giuliano Amato, D'Alema's treasury minister and a former prime minister, to form a new government, and Amato's new 24-man team obtained in record time and by a narrow margin a vote of confidence in the Chamber of Deputies; the vote was 319–298 with 5 abstentions. Amato then declared that one aim of his government would be electoral reform, acknowledged by all parties as a necessity to lessen the chronic fragmentation of Italian politics. In May a referendum on the reform issue was invalidated for lack of the required quorum of 50% of the eligible voters plus one. Of the 32% who did vote on a proposal to abolish the election of 25% of the deputies by the proportional system, 82% voted to do so. Thereafter, President Ciampi urged the Chamber of Deputies to legislate reform, but its attempts foundered. In September Amato proposed that the centre-left be led up to the 2001 election not by himself but by the personable 46-year-old mayor of Rome, Francesco Rutelli.

What concerned Italians more than electoral reform, however, was what some termed the biggest influx of immigrants into Italy since the fall of the Roman Empire, though the Interior Ministry said that illegal landings in Italy by boat dropped by more than 50% in 2000, a decline ascribed to more effective policing. Despite the widespread concern, official figures showed that Italy, where immigration was a relatively new phenomenon, housed nearly five times fewer non-Europeans than did Germany or The Netherlands, a total of some 1,500,000 legal and an estimated 400,000 illegal immigrants. Italy's anti-Mafia commission reported that most of the illegal immigrants were smuggled in return for payment by Italian, Albanian, and Turkish Mafia gangs. The biggest drop in new illegal immigrants was among those who were dashed across the Adriatic Sea from Albania to the southeastern "heel" of Italy aboard fast rubber dinghies. By October the gangs had transported some 14,000, a decrease of two-thirds from the previous year. By contrast, there was a fivefold increase, to about 5,000, of destitute immigrants landed on Italy's "toe," Calabria, by rusty cargo vessels limping in from Turkey, their holds packed with "escapees" from the Middle East and Asia. Seeking political asylum, nearly 9,000 Kurds reached Italy in such a way during the year. Illegal immigrants increased by 40% in Sicily, and additional numbers entered Italy by land from Slovenia.

The Italian press estimated that immigrants made up about one-third of Italy's prison population, and Interior Minister Enzo Bianco acknowledged that Mafia gangs controlled 80% of the prostitution in Italy, a trade calculated to be plied by some 25,000 women mainly from Eastern Europe and Africa. The government, however, stressed the need for immigrants to beef up a dwindling labour force and to counterbalance a zero population growth and therefore raised the year's legal quota of such workers by 93,000.

The climax of the Jubilee Year 2000 in a Rome specially renovated for the occasion came in August, when an estimated two million young people invaded the capital for World Youth Day, celebrated in a huge open space far from the city centre in the presence of the pope. Lively controversy had earlier arisen over public attempts by the Vatican to cancel an international gay pride march in Rome on the grounds of its being "inopportune" during the Jubilee Year. Nonetheless, the parade was staged in July after a gentle government affirmation of tolerance in a secular nation, and the organizers estimated that more than 200,000 marchers attended.

In June President Ciampi pardoned Mehmet Ali Agca, the Turk who in 1981 shot at and wounded Pope John Paul II. His release followed a letter of pardon from the pope and a Turkish extradition request. Agca was flown to Turkey.

In September a swollen torrent heavy with mud swept away a campsite in Calabria, killing at least 12 people, some of whom were disabled. Disaster struck despite earlier warnings of the danger of the site. A month later heavy and prolonged rains led to disastrous flooding in much of northern Italy; a number of rivers, including the Po River, burst their banks. Towns were submerged, communications were paralyzed, numerous landslides occurred, bridges were washed out, and at least 25 persons lost their lives. Prime Minister Amato attributed the tragedy partly to global warming.

Early in the year Italy announced that it was opening diplomatic relations with North Korea. Although several European countries, including Sweden, Denmark, Finland, Austria, and Portugal had earlier taken that step, Italy became the first member of the Group of Seven industrial nations to do so. Italian government officials indicated that they had informed the U.S. and South Korea of their overtures to the North Koreans in advance of the announcement and emphasized the need for Western nations to help North Korea end its isolation.

(DEREK WILSON)

JAMAICA

Area:10,991 sq km (4,244 sq mi)
Population (2000 est.): 2,619,000
Capital: Kingston
Chief of state: Queen Elizabeth II, represented by Governor-General Sir Howard Cooke
Head of government: Prime Minister Percival J. Patterson

Prime Minister Percival Patterson informed Jamaicans in April 2000 that the country would not enter into another borrowing relationship with the International Monetary Fund (IMF). The government did, however, ask the IMF to "monitor" its economic and financial policies for the next two fiscal years, a service the fund performed for many of its members.

Jamaica's key commodity, sugar, made a production comeback during the year, with 216,282 metric tons harvested by the time the crop closed in July. The total for the previous year was 204,188 metric tons.

The government responded to public concern over an increase in crime by establishing a specialized police unit in September; it was expected to target gang leaders and armed criminals as a first priority. At least 677 people had been murdered in Jamaica during the year. Multimillionaire hotel owner Gordon Stewart, probably the country's best-known businessman internationally, even called on the government to resign if it could not handle the situation.

The government announced in September that it would set up a national commission to review whether the use of marijuana should be decriminalized under certain conditions. Jamaica was a major Caribbean grower and exporter of the drug, which also contributed to the local crime problem.

Jamaicans were excited over the performance of their athletes in the 2000 Olympic Games in Sydney, Australia. Lorraine Graham claimed two silver medals, finishing second in the women's 400-m dash and 4 × 400-m relay. Tanya Lawrence edged out fellow Jamaican Merlene Ottey to win the bronze medal in the women's 100-m dash. Ottey, who had competed in five previous Olympics, added to her medal total as a member of Jamaica's silver-medal-winning 4 × 100-m relay team. (DAVID RENWICK)

JAPAN

Area: 377,819 sq km (145,877 sq mi)
Population (2000 est.): 126,920,000
Capital: Tokyo
Chief of state: Emperor Akihito
Head of government: Prime Minister Keizo Obuchi and, from April 5, Yoshiro Mori

Domestic Affairs. When Japanese Prime Minister Keizo Obuchi formally opened the 147th session of the Diet (parliament) on Jan. 28, 2000, he delivered his address to a half-empty chamber. The day before, the long-ruling Liberal-Democratic Party (LDP) had rammed through legislation that reduced by 20 the number of seats in the lower house. In protest, opposition parties boycotted Obuchi's speech, and the Liberal Party later decided to leave the governing coalition.

Among other problems for the government were the activities of a former LDP member. In April 1999 Shintaro Ishihara, running as an independent, won the election for governor of Tokyo. In 2000 he urged several controversial actions, including altering the constitution in order vastly to expand the Japanese military and acquire nuclear arms. Moreover, facing a formidable debt problem in Tokyo, he proposed a heavy tax on banks with headquarters in the capital. Although his tax would have been legal under the constitution, national ministries moved to block the plan.

To make matters worse, Ishihara was widely quoted as doubting the occurrence of the Nanking Massacre—the mass killing and ravaging of Chinese citizens by soldiers of the Japanese Imperial Army after its seizure of Nanjing (Nanking), China, in December 1937. Ishihara caused further outrage with his bizarre remark that Korean and Chinese immigrants (he used the derogatory wartime term *sangokujin* to describe them) were apt to cause disturbances after an earthquake. He offered an apology but added that "illegal residents" were "very troublesome."

On April 2 Obuchi suffered a stroke that left him comatose; he died six weeks later. (*See* OBITUARIES.) Three days after Obuchi's stroke, the Diet approved as his successor Yoshiro Mori, secretary-general of the LDP. (*See* BIOGRAPHIES.) Faced with sagging public support, Mori dissolved the lower house of the Diet and called for new elections. In the elections held on June 25, the LDP managed to win only 233 of the 480 seats in the lower house—down from the 271 it had held in the previous session—and was thus forced into an awkward alliance with two smaller parties, the New Komeito and the New Conservative Party, in order to gain a legislative majority.

On a happier note, Fusae Ota became the first Japanese woman to win a gubernatorial election. On February 6 Ota, a former official in the Ministry of International Trade and Industry, was elected governor of Osaka. Two months later Yoshiko Shiotani, who had the support of the LDP, became the second Japanese woman to become a governor when she won the post in the city of Kumamoto.

Japan mourned the loss of Dowager Empress Nagako, who died on June 16 at the age of 97. She was the longest-living dowager empress in Japanese history. (*See* OBITUARIES.)

Much of the nation's attention was focused on disasters during the year. On March 31 and April 1, Mt. Usu, a volcano on Hokkaido, Japan's northernmost island, erupted to spew ash over a wide area. Fortunately, some 11,000 residents of nearby villages had been evacuated days before. On August 30, after some 60 days of seismic activity, Mt. Oyama on Miyake Island—only 193 km (120 mi) south of Tokyo—erupted. The eruption was accompanied by a minor earthquake that struck the island's Ako and Tsubota districts; several jolts were felt in the capital as well. Nearly 4,000 inhabitants of Miyake Island were evacuated.

The Economy. On February 29 the LDP-led coalition chalked up one victory. Its budget for fiscal year 2000 (through March 2001) passed the lower house against stiff opposition. The budget increased spending to about $800 billion to combat the lingering recession. The budget cleared the upper house on March 17 in record time. Before that, however, the government announced that it planned to borrow about $76 billion directly from banks to meet its obligations to local governments. Normally such loans were funded by bonds, a less-expensive method. In any case, some observers predicted that the gross public debt could reach 130% of gross domestic product (GDP) by March 31, 2001.

A stubborn recession meant that the economy was in urgent need of additional priming. The Nomura Research Institute estimated that in the last quarter of 1999, Japan's economy had contracted 1.4% since the previous quarter. The decline translated into an annualized reduction of 5.6% in GDP. Average monthly spending by households had fallen by 1.2% in 1999, down for the seventh consecutive year.

In February 2000, however, industrial production rose 3%. In March a further glimmer of hope was provided by the Economic Planning Agency chief,

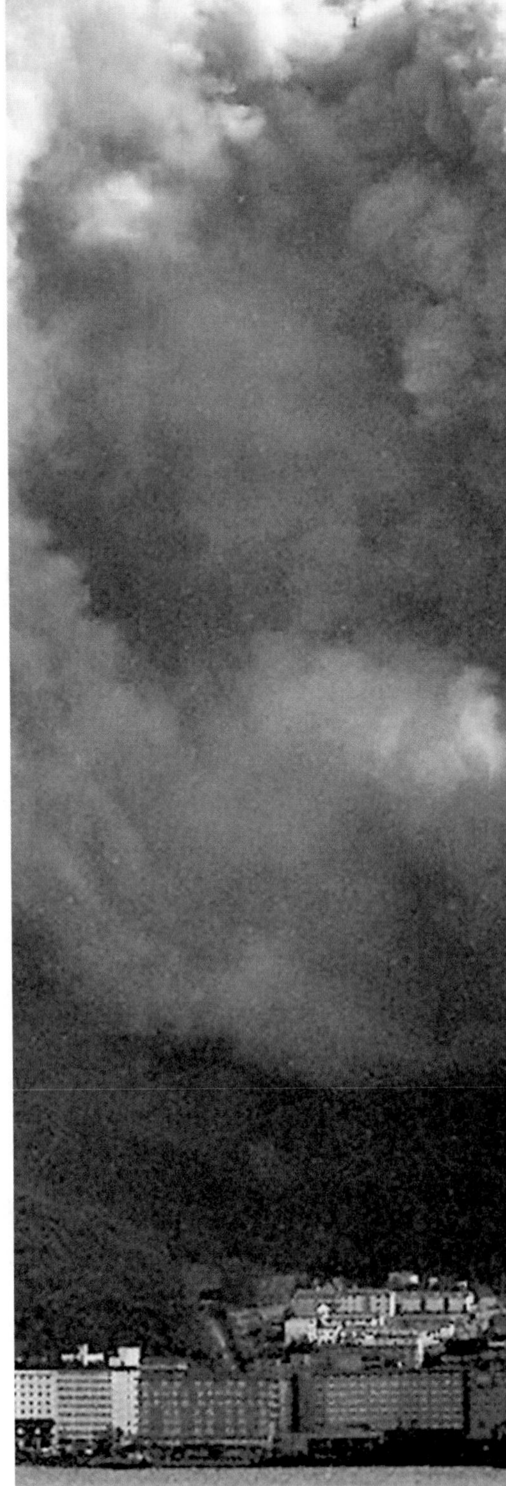

On the Japanese island of Hokkaido, the Mount Usu volcano spews ash-laden smoke in April.

AP/Wide World Photos

Taichi Sakaiya, who predicted that the economy would grow by about 2% from April 1, 2001. Masaru Hayami, governor of the Bank of Japan, was more cautious, noting that there had been no self-sustained recovery in consumer or corporate capital spending.

In July three major banks reached an agreement to consolidate their firms into one holding company. When merged in April 2001, Toyo Trust and Banking, the Sanwa Bank, and the Tokai Bank would become the third wealthiest private banking institution in the world, with about $1 trillion in assets.

Employment data continued to cause concern. Among advanced industrial nations, Japan had often been able to boast of low unemployment rates. By the end of 1999, however, unemployment had climbed to 4.7%—the highest since such data were first compiled in 1953. The rate remained at 4.7% in January 2000 (4.8% for men and 4.5% for women). Inflation was less of a problem. The consumer price index fell by a record 0.3% in 1999.

The impact of the electronic revolution was felt in various quarters. On April 3 the Bank of Japan's quarterly business survey, *Tankan,* reported that big corporations had begun to invest heavily in information technology. According to the Ministry of Posts and Telecommunications and a Japanese research company, InfoCom, by 2001 Japan would become the world's largest user of the Internet. On June 7 the Tokyo Stock Exchange announced plans to enable electronic transactions to be made 24 hours a day.

On August 11 the Bank of Japan raised interest rates for the first time in a decade. The rate was increased to 0.25%. The bank thus defied most government officials, who pressed to keep the rate near zero. The step revealed the independence of the central bank and its belief that the recession was ending.

Foreign Affairs. The Group of Eight (G-8) summit on July 21–23 on Okinawa dominated Japanese foreign policy during the year. On July 8 finance ministers issued reports from meetings that were a prelude to the summit. The reports noted the explosion of information technology and called for reform of the international financial system. A second set of reports emerged from meetings of foreign ministers, and they stressed the need to prevent regional conflicts in part by reforming UN peacekeeping procedures. One report emphasized the importance of reducing tensions between North and South Korea.

While taking a recess from the Israeli-Palestinian negotiations at Camp David, Maryland, U.S. Pres. Bill Clinton arrived on Okinawa on July 21. He was the first president to visit the island since its reversion to Japan in 1972. He stopped first in the city of Itoman for a memorial service dedicated to the more than 200,000 Americans, Japanese, and others who died in 1945 in the Battle of Okinawa. During his stay Clinton promised "to reduce our footprint on this island."

The climax of the summit came with the issue of a communiqué entitled "Okinawa 2000" by the heads of state. This document called for reorganization of the UN, especially the Security Council (Japan was still not a permanent member). It also proposed the establishment of a digital opportunity task force to address what the Japanese called "the digital divide" between developed and less-developed areas.

By the close of the G-8 summit, the main criticism of the Japanese was that their government had spent $750 million in hosting the conference. Moreover, many Okinawa residents were restive over the American involvement in mounting the meetings. In December 1999 Washington had offered Tokyo $1 billion for the reconstruction of the city of Nago, where much of the summit took place. American military officers hoped eventually to construct a new heliport there. A U.S. air base at Futenma (farther south) had been closed as a result of protests from Japanese living nearby. Okinawa, which makes up less than 1% of Japan's geographic area, had 75% of the U.S. military bases in the country and hosted two-thirds of the American troops based in Japan.

In other foreign policy issues, Prime Minister Mori met with Russian Pres. Vladimir Putin in St. Petersburg on April 29. Their otherwise cordial exchange was shadowed by an incident in an area under lingering dispute. On April 21 a Russian coast guard vessel had fired on a Japanese fishing vessel near small islands between Hokkaido and the Russian-held Kuril Islands. The islets, long claimed by Japan, had been occupied by Russian forces since World War II. Tokyo continued to press for the return of what the Japanese called the Northern Territories and to make way for a formal peace treaty, delayed since 1945. During their meeting Mori briefed Putin on the upcoming Okinawa summit, which Putin later attended, and both expressed the desire to resolve the territorial claim by the end of the year. On September 5, however, while Putin was in Tokyo for additional talks with Mori, he rejected the claim of Japanese sovereignty over the islands and thus demolished hopes for signing a peace treaty in 2000.

During the year Japan and the U.S. continued their difficult negotiations on trade. In January the U.S. International Trade Commission ruled that steel-plate imports from Japan were being priced below cost of production. This cleared the way for imposition of punitive dumping duties. On March 23 in Tokyo, Japanese and American negotiators suspended talks on deregulation of Japan's telecommunications market. Washington had demanded a reduction in fees to connect to the Nippon Telegraph and Telephone (NTT) system. It was pointed out that NTT, a former state monopoly, still controlled 99% of local phone traffic. After nine days of intense negotiations, on July 19 the U.S. and Japan reached an agreement to cut linking costs by about 40% over three years.

In May Mori made the obligatory trip to Washington. He offered President Clinton opinions on information technology; the president, in turn, repeated his demand for deregulation in communications. In July Japan sent six ships to the northwestern Pacific on whale-hunting expeditions. Their targets were minke, Bryde's, and sperm whales. The Japanese argued that international conventions allowed such hunts, provided that the mission was to conduct scientific research. Critics pointed out that once the Japanese catches were examined, the whale meat was resold in Japan at high prices to distributors and expensive restaurants. U.S. Secretary of State Madeleine Albright stated that the U.S. was "deeply troubled" by the expansion of whaling. On September 13 President Clinton announced that Japanese fishermen might be expelled from American waters and additional sanctions could be imposed in coming months.

Japan's relations with China were shaped by American policy. Like Washington, Tokyo had formal relations with Beijing and agreed that there was but one China. The Japanese insisted that a solution to the status of Taiwan had to be peaceful. To the consternation of Chinese officials, Japan agreed with the U.S. on joint guidelines to defend undefined "areas surrounding Japan." The Chinese believed those areas included Taiwan.

Japanese retained commercial interests in Taiwan. Indeed, lively trade made its way through the island and Hong Kong to China. Big corporations were fascinated by the size of the potential market on the mainland. On May 29 Japan's largest carmaker, the Toyota Motor Corp., announced that the Chinese government had authorized the formation of a joint venture with China's Tianjin Automobile Xiali Corp. Toyota planned to open a plant in Tianjin by 2002. Total investment in the company would be about $100 million. Toyota was the third Japanese auto company to link with Chinese firms, following the Suzuki Motor Corp. and the Honda Motor Co. Tianjin Xiali was already producing a compact car, known as the Charade, in Japan.

An equally difficult situation marked Japan's ties with the Korean peninsula. Tokyo had established formal ties with Seoul. Only informal contact was sporadically maintained with Pyongyang. On April 5, after eight years of silence, talks regarding the possible normalization of Japan's relations with North Korea opened in Pyongyang, albeit on shaky ground. North Korean negotiators insisted that Japan first apologize for the occupation of the peninsula from

1910 to 1945 and, further, discuss compensation for the occupation. Japan's chief representative repeated Japan's 1995 apology to its neighbours for wartime aggression but refused to offer compensation, then went on to counter by citing other issues: the North's missile buildup and suspected nuclear weapons program as well as its reported abduction of Japanese nationals. The two sides suspended negotiations. After the slight thaw in contacts between Seoul and Pyongyang, talks in Tokyo in late August between Japan and North Korea resulted once again in the entrenchment of positions and another suspension of negotiations.

During the year Japan took the lead in expanding an unusual regional bloc. On April 22 delegates from 16 countries and territories in the South Pacific gathered in Miyazaki. The Pacific Islands Forum (PIF) represented an array of islands ranging from Palau and Micronesia to Samoa and Kiribati and included such nations as Australia and New Zealand. PIF chairman Kuniwo Nakamura of Palau and Prime Minister Mori welcomed the group, which urged the responsible management of natural resources and attention to environmental problems in the South Pacific.

(ARDATH W. BURKS)

JORDAN

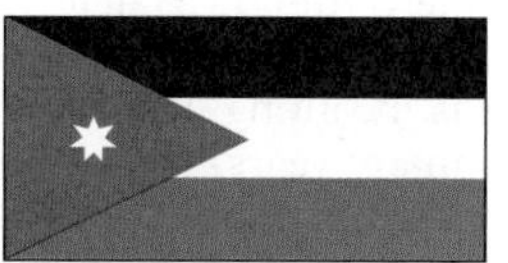

Area: 89,342 sq km (34,495 sq mi)
Population (2000 est.): 4,982,000 (including about 1,500,000 Palestinian refugees, most of whom hold Jordanian citizenship)
Capital: Amman
Head of state and government: King Abdullah II, assisted by Prime Ministers 'Abd al-Rauf al-Rawabdeh and, from June 19, 'Ali Abu al-Raghib

Jordan's King Abdullah II pursued an active foreign policy in 2000, seeking to advance the peace process between Israel and the Palestinians and consolidating Jordan's bilateral relations with major powers in the Middle East. On February 6 the king received the Palestinian leader Yasir Arafat, and on April 23 Abdullah made his first visit to Israel, where he sought to maintain the strong ties that his late father, King Hussein, had developed with that nation. He received Israeli Prime Minister Ehud Barak on July 8. Jordan renewed its trade protocol with Israel on January 12, and the industrial zone that had been established by the two countries was by that time employing some 5,000 people.

King Abdullah made numerous visits to Egypt in an attempt to show support for the peace negotiations and also to consolidate relations with that country. On February 19 Jordan and Egypt decided to abolish customs duties on their trade in a gradual manner and to complete the process in two years. The king visited Saudi Arabia on May 13 and October 14 and thereby further enhanced the already strong ties between the two countries. Accompanied by Queen Rania, Abdullah visited Morocco during March 9–11, and he made another visit to Morocco on July 30 to attend the first anniversary of Moroccan King Muhammad VI's accession to the throne.

Abdullah developed excellent relations with Syria. He visited Damascus on May 21 and later attended the funeral of Syrian Pres. Hafez al-Assad, who died on June 10. (*See* OBITUARIES.) When Bashar al-Assad was selected as Syria's new president, the king visited Damascus on July 19 to congratulate him.

During a visit to the U.S. on June 6–8, Abdullah engaged in talks with American officials on a free-trade agreement between Jordan and the U.S. On October 24 he visited the U.S. to sign the agreement.

On June 19 a new Jordanian cabinet of 29 members was formed, headed by 'Ali Abu al-Raghib, with a mandate to move more effectively in the direction of privatization and economic development; the rate of growth of the Jordanian economy had been only 2% annually. The new prime minister had a strong private-sector background, having served as president of the Jordanian Construction Contractors Association.

(MARIUS K. DEEB)

KAZAKHSTAN

Area: 2,724,900 sq km (1,052,090 sq mi)
Population (2000 est.): 14,913,000
Capital: Astana
Head of state and government: President Nursultan Nazarbayev, assisted by Prime Minister Kasymzhomart Tokayev

Although in 2000 Kazakhstan was affected only indirectly by the activities of Islamic militants elsewhere in the region, the government was deeply concerned about the potential for destabilization by Muslim extremists, particularly in the southern part of the country. At the end of January, Kazakhstan joined Russia and the Central Asian states (except Turkmenistan) in drafting a program to combat international terrorism. Pres. Nursultan Nazarbayev characterized religious and political extremism, the illegal drug trade, and armed conflicts in neighbouring countries as the major threats to Kazakhstan's security. Help was sought from the international community to stop the drug trade in narcotics, principally narcotics from Afghanistan transiting across Kazakh territory.

In July the president announced that defense spending would be doubled in 2001. The following month the Kazakh Ministry of Defense held counterterrorism exercises in the south and stepped up the military presence on the border with Kyrgyzstan. Later in the year, however, a military expert noted that Kazakh forces were not trained to fight a guerrilla war in the mountains and that the border guards were worse equipped than were the militants who had invaded the neighbouring countries.

In response to declining foreign investor interest in Kazakhstan, in April President Nazarbayev lifted the oil export quotas. These quotas had been imposed in 1999 to ensure supplies to domestic refineries, but they had irritated Western firms operating in the country. In the same month, the leadership called for improved investment incentives and the development of high-tech industry. Kazakhstan was able to pay off its International Monetary Fund loans seven years early and announced plans to export more oil via Russian pipelines.

In October Kazakhstan joined the Russian Federation, Belarus, Kyrgyzstan, and Tajikistan in forming a Eurasian Economic Union to replace a nonfunctioning customs union set up by the five countries. The new union started its activities by seeking to harmonize tax laws and customs codes among its members.

Relations between the government and the independent information media remained tense as the president called on the media to stop criticizing the state authorities and to engage in more responsible reporting. Nazarbayev promised visiting U.S. Secretary

Yuri Kochetkov/AFP Worldwide

U.S. Secretary of State Madeleine Albright is greeted by Kazakh Pres. Nursultan Nazarbayev in Astana on April 15.

of State Madeleine Albright that freedom of the media would be respected, but Kazakhstan was later criticized by U.S. officials for continued government harassment of the media. In June a group of ethnic Russians who had been charged with plotting to set up an independent Russian state in northeastern Kazakhstan were given prison sentences of up to 18 years.

(BESS BROWN)

KENYA

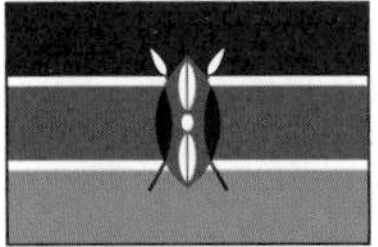

Area: 582,646 sq km (224,961 sq mi)
Population (2000 est.): 30,340,000
Capital: Nairobi
Head of state and government: President Daniel arap Moi

Corruption in high places remained a dominant theme in Kenya throughout 2000. In January the government responded to the damning report on the Coffee Board of Kenya (CBK) contained in the audit ordered by Richard Leakey as Head of the Public Service by replacing almost every one of the board's members. There was, however, stiff resistance from some of the large-scale coffee farmers, who had benefited from the corrupt practices of the board. Small farmers, on the other hand, stepped up their campaign to end the CBK's monopoly on marketing, which they hoped would attract government support. An additional report, made public on February 24, indicated that the Kenya Tea Development Authority had been guilty of similar corrupt practices, claiming that for 10 years the authority had been systematically plundering the farmers' earnings.

Leakey's team was not uniformly successful in its campaign. Although it was able to curtail the powers of senior civil servants, bringing about the retirement of several of them, a proposal by the permanent secretary in the president's office responsible for provincial administration that chiefs and subchiefs be abolished was blocked by the president himself under pressure from Leakey's opponents. Similarly, an announcement by Leakey that there would be a reduction in the size of the army and police was declared null and void by an anonymous army officer.

The budget presented in June by the finance minister, Chris Okemo—based upon a stern analysis of the economic and social crisis—nevertheless appeared to confirm the government's intention to crack down on corruption and to stimulate growth in the economy. Observers remained skeptical of the government's ability to achieve its objectives, but late in July the International Monetary Fund (IMF) seemed to have been sufficiently impressed by Leakey's endeavours and the government's response to resume its aid program to Kenya, though subject to more rigorous conditions than had been imposed on any other country. Among its stipulations was the requirement that government ministers, including the president himself, MPs, senior civil servants, and the spouses of all, declare their assets and liabilities every year. In addition, the IMF declared that there had to be a law to ensure that public figures suspected of corruption were prosecuted and that IMF officials conducted a weekly inspection of Kenya's central bank's balance sheet.

The regulations were unpopular among the country's elite but were recognized as essential if additional aid from bilateral donors was to be forthcoming. Opposition critics, however, believed they did not go far enough and called for a check upon the assets of other members of leaders' families and on companies owned under other names.

Almost immediately, the IMF felt it necessary to review its restrictions because of the crisis resulting from the worst drought in many years. Kenya as a result had to import a large proportion of its food and also suffered curtailed power supplies throughout the country. In addition, fighting broke out among some of the pastoralists in the north over scarce water supplies for their animals.

In May, echoing events in Zimbabwe, an MP, Stephen Ndichu, caused consternation in the government and among white landowners by calling for the redistribution of idle land to landless Africans. This coincided with the occupation of a few white-owned farms by squatters. Moi, himself a large-scale landowner, responded firmly, stating that the government would defend private property.

Kenyan athletes turned in stellar performances during the 2000 Olympic Games in Sydney, Australia, continuing their dominance in the long-distance events. Kenyans won the men's 1,500-m race and took first and second in the 3,000-m steeplechase.

(KENNETH INGHAM)

KIRIBATI

Area: 811 sq km (313 sq mi)
Population (2000 est.): 92,000
Capital: Bairiki, on Tarawa
Head of state and government: President Teburoro Tito

In October 2000, in anticipation of hosting the Pacific Islands Forum (formerly the South Pacific Forum), Kiribati completed construction of its new parliamentary complex. The Forum, a meeting of heads of government of 16 countries in the region, including Australia and New Zealand, adopted the Biketawa Declaration, which addressed issues of political instability in the region; established criteria of democratic government for membership in the Forum; and drew attention to the costs of poor governance and ethnic tension. Prompted by disturbances during the year in Solomon Islands and a civilian coup in Fiji, the Forum thus moved from its 30-year history of "the pacific way," which involved decision making by consensus and the avoidance of conflict.

On the economic front Kiribati continued to draw financial assistance from traditional donors—regional powerhouses Australia, New Zealand, and Japan—for a wide range of enterprises that included a rural solar electrification project. Japan also contributed $22 million for the four-year development of the port of Betio. Kiribati also signed an agreement that would allow Japan to build at Kiritimati (Christmas Island) a landing strip and related infrastructure for unmanned space shuttles that were being developed as part of a space transportation project.

(BARRIE MACDONALD)

KOREA, DEMOCRATIC PEOPLE'S REPUBLIC OF

Area: 122,762 sq km (47,399 sq mi)
Population (2000 est.): 21,688,000
Capital: Pyongyang
Chief of state: Chairman of the National Defense Commission Kim Jong Il
Head of government: Chairman of the Council of Ministers (Premier) Hong Sang Nam

In the year 2000 images that once seemed inconceivable superseded each other one after another on the Korean peninsula. The most arresting was the scene at Pyongyang's airport on June 13 when South Korean Pres. Kim Dae Jung (*see* NOBEL PRIZES) stepped onto the tarmac and grasped the hand of the North

AP/Wide World Photos

North Korea's Kim Jung Il (left) and South Korea's Kim Dae Jung chat at a banquet during their historic meeting in Pyongyang in June.

Korean chief of state, Kim Jong Il, who then led President Kim before an honour guard and accompanied him in a limousine for the journey to the state guest house. It was the first time that a South Korean president had visited North Korea and the first time that the reclusive Kim Jong Il had gone to the airport to greet a visitor.

An unprecedented summit meeting followed, after which change continued at a breakneck pace. In August 100 North Koreans traveled to Seoul for a reunion with long-lost family members, while 100 South Koreans arrived in Pyongyang. For many in both delegations, it was the first time in 50 years—since the Korean War divided their peninsula into two hostile nations—that they had seen relatives who were on the other side of the border. In September 63 North Koreans who had been held in South Korean prisons as spies and political prisoners, some for more than 40 years, were allowed to return to their homeland. Also in September the North and South Korean Olympic teams joined together during the opening ceremonies of the 2000 Summer Games in Sydney, Australia. The athletes marched into the stadium under a single flag showing a map of Korea, although they competed as separate teams.

On October 9 Kim Jong Il's second in command, Vice Marshall Jo Myong Rok, arrived in Washington, D.C. While at the White House the following day, Jo wore his full-dress army uniform—an action that many observers interpreted as a sign that the diplomatic meeting had the full support of North Korea's military. Later in the month U.S. Secretary of State Madeleine Albright visited Pyongyang, where she met with Kim and accompanied him to a lavish celebration at a sports stadium that featured some 100,000 performers. These high-profile visits were set against the backdrop of a major diplomatic offensive; North Korea reestablished relations with Western nations Italy and Australia and opened a consulate in Hong Kong. Some observers predicted that, if the trend continued, North Korea would eventually normalize relations with Japan and the U.S. and that reunification with South Korea was a possibility.

North Korea's economy continued to sputter along. Grain production was projected to decline about 23% from the previous year. The drop meant that the North would continue to be dependent upon international assistance, despite signs that the worst of the country's famine was over. (TODD CROWELL)

KOREA, REPUBLIC OF

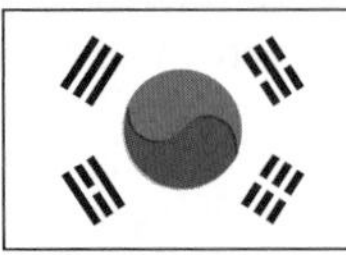

Area: 99,373 sq km (38,368 sq mi)
Population (2000 est.): 47,275,000
Capital: Seoul
Head of state and government: President Kim Dae Jung

Millions of South Koreans gathered around their television sets on Oct. 13, 2000, to hear the news that their president, Kim Dae Jung, had been awarded the Nobel Prize for Peace. (*See* NOBEL PRIZES.) Kim was praised by the Norwegian Nobel Committee for his decades-long fight for democracy and for "his visit to North Korea [which] gave impetus to a process which has reduced tensions between the two countries. There may now be hope that the Cold War will also come to an end in Korea."

The Nobel citation referred to the summit meeting between Kim and the leader of North Korea, Kim Jong Il, in Pyongyang on June 13–15. This historic meeting was seen as a vindication of the South Korean president's "sunshine" policy of reconciliation with the North. At times it had looked as if the policy was having little or no effect. All South Korea seemed to get in return for gestures such as allowing the Hyundai Group to open a tourist destination in North Korea were submarine incursions and missile tests. Kim persisted, however, despite the North's provocations.

A major breakthrough might have been his March 9 speech in Berlin, in which Kim stated Seoul's willingness to assist North Korea economically and called for direct government-to-government talks. After the summit, events moved quickly. Work began on a rail link between the two countries; Northern political prisoners held in the South since the end of the war were allowed to go home; and the defense ministers of the two countries met on the southern island of Cheju.

While Kim basked in the glow of international approval, some of his own people were less enthusiastic about his administration. The announcement of the summit three days before the April 13 midterm National Assembly elections did not give Kim's party the bounce he had expected. His newly styled Millennium Democratic Party won more seats than it had previously held but still came in second to the opposition Grand National Party, which came very close to obtaining a majority. Kim's erstwhile ally, the United Liberal Democrats, lost badly and was reduced to 17 seats.

South Korea's economy continued its strong recovery from the financial crisis of 1997. Though gross domestic product had grown by 13% in the second half of 1999, growth was anticipated to slow down to a more sustainable 7% to 10% during 2000. Foreign exchange reserves exceeded $80 billion, up sharply from the low of $7 billion two years earlier, and unemployment receded from its peak of more than 8% to less than 5%.

Some of the nation's largest business conglomerates, known as *chaebol,* were not so healthy. Daewoo and Hyundai suffered from large debts. American auto manufacturer Ford pulled out of a deal to buy the car division of Daewoo. A public feud over succession at Hyundai underscored the need for more corporate transparency. The controversy erupted after Hyundai's founder, Chung Ju Yung, ordered the transfer of the chairman of one subdivision to another Hyundai company even though Chung was no longer on the board of directors. President Kim was faulted in some quarters for not doing enough to reform and restructure the nation's economy.

(TODD CROWELL)

KUWAIT

Area: 17,818 sq km (6,880 sq mi)
Population (2000 est.): 1,984,000
Capital: Kuwait City
Head of state and government: Emir Sheikh Jabir al-Ahmad al-Jabir as-Sabah, assisted by Prime Minister Crown Prince Sheikh Saad al-Abdullah as-Salim as-Sabah

Ten years after the Iraqi invasion, Kuwait's security in 2000 remained questionable. Renewed Israeli-Palestinian conflict, coupled with long-standing domestic criticism of high-cost Kuwaiti arms purchases from the U.S., eroded domestic support for the strategic status quo. More than 600 Kuwaitis remained prisoners in Iraq, while the September decision of the UN Compensation Commission to award $15.9 billion to Kuwait for damage to its oil industry brought renewed Iraqi accusations and threats.

Within Kuwait economic restructuring continued to be difficult. Health care charges to expatriates were initiated in April. The government also considered assessing fees on employers and foreign workers to fund subsidies and unemployment compensation payments to Kuwaitis who, faced by rising unemployment and a bloated civil service, agree to take jobs in the private sector. Kuwait's social security system faced bankruptcy as the result of overly generous policies on retirement, such as allowing mothers to retire with full benefits after only 15 working years. Economically, higher oil prices eased pressure on the Kuwaiti government to force additional economic restructuring measures through the National Assembly.

The local economy remained stagnant. Oil revenues provided more than 90% of government income and nearly half of gross national product. Kuwait's dependence on oil exports explained the government's eagerness to readmit foreign companies as partners in order to attract needed capital and to offset some of the risks of a planned rapid expansion of oil-production capacity from fields located near the border with Iraq. The nation's refining capacity suffered constriction during the year as the result of two refinery explosions in June.

Domestically, Kuwaitis continued to debate the role of women in society. Despite support for increased rights for women from Kuwait's emir, the National Assembly in June approved by a large margin a measure requiring that any private colleges or universities established in Kuwait be gender segregated, as the national university was required by law to be by September 2001.

(MARY ANN TÉTREAULT)

KYRGYZSTAN

Area: 199,900 sq km (77,200 sq mi)
Population (2000 est.): 4,895,000
Capital: Bishkek
Head of state and government: President Askar Akayev, assisted by Prime Minister Amangeldy Muraliyev

In 2000 Kyrgyzstan again found itself in conflict with Uzbek Islamic militants based in Tajikistan and Afghanistan who sought to reach Uzbekistan's Fergana Valley by crossing Kyrgyz territory. In February the Kyrgyz government announced increased security on its southern border after Uzbek militant leader Juma Namangoni was sighted in Tajikistan. By July half the Kyrgyz army was reported to be deployed on the Tajik border. Fighting started at the beginning of August, and additional Kyrgyz troops were sent to the southern border region. On August 20 Kyrgyz Pres. Askar Akayev hosted a summit of Central Asian heads of state to discuss common measures against terrorism. Kyrgyzstan called for air strikes against militant bases in Tajikistan, but the other Central Asians were unwilling to agree. Subsequently, the Russian Federation provided military assistance to Kyrgyzstan to help stop the incursions.

At the beginning of the year, political life in Kyrgyzstan was dominated by the two rounds of parliamentary elections, in February and March. The opposition Communist Party received the most votes, followed by the Union of Democratic Forces and the Democratic Women's Party. All the deputies from the Democratic Women's Party were later disqualified on technical grounds, though the party had the president's support.

International observers criticized the elections as falling short of international standards, owing at least in part to interference by government officials. The exclusion of one prominent opposition activist from the second round and the failure of opposition leader Feliks Kulov to gain a parliamentary seat resulted in popular demonstrations. These intensified when Kulov was arrested for alleged actions when he had been national security minister. Prominent human rights activists were subject to severe government harassment because of their roles in the protests; the office of the Kyrgyz Committee for Human Rights was sealed, and its leader fled the country.

Kulov was acquitted in August after a closed trial, and he announced his intention to run for president against incumbent Akayev in the election at the end of October. Kulov was refused registration as a presidential candidate because he was unwilling to undergo a test of his knowledge of the Kyrgyz language. Several other potential candidates, including the Communist Party candidate, failed the test and complained that it had been invented by the Central Electoral Commission as a way of excluding credible opponents of the incumbent president, whose own candidacy violated the constitutional limit of two terms in office. Kulov was widely regarded as the most likely to prevail over President Akayev. (BESS BROWN)

LAOS

Area: 236,800 sq km (91,429 sq mi)
Population (2000 est.): 5,497,000
Capital: Vientiane (Viangchan)
Chief of state: President Khamtai Siphandon
Head of government: Prime Minister Sisavath Keobounphanh

A spate of bombings beginning March 30, 2000, at a restaurant in Vientiane and continuing throughout the year caused much puzzled speculation in Laos. No organization claimed responsibility for the acts, and the government blamed no rebel groups. This led to unverified suspicions that rival factions within the secretive top leadership were engaged in a struggle for power. Tellingly, the 25th anniversaries of events leading to the 1975 communist takeover were allowed to pass with little fanfare. The explosions, mostly causing only minor injuries, were at public places, including the capital's main post office, market, bus terminal, and airport.

On September 28 a quasi curfew after midnight was imposed. Tourism in the country was inevitably affected, especially given that 2000 had been designated "Visit Laos Year," with a target of one million visitors and $100 million in revenue. On July 3 a bizarre attack on a southern border post, involving hired gunmen from Thailand, caused a furor on both sides of the border. Six of the raiders were killed and 28 arrested by Thai police as they fled into Thailand.

The Paris-based royal family, led by Prince Regent Sauryavong Savang and his nephew, heir apparent Crown Prince Soulivong Savang, began assuming a higher profile during the year. They had talks with U.S. congressional leaders in advance of a U.S. Congressional Forum on Laos in June and were received at the French Foreign Ministry in September for the first time since their exile.

Rob Elliott/AFP Worldwide

A Laotian woman in traditional costume marches in a parade on National Day, December 2, in Vientiane.

Khamxay Souphanouvong, a government minister and son of the late Laotian president Prince Souphanouvong, was absent from his duties beginning in April, and though the government insisted that nothing was amiss, Thai authorities implied that he was seeking political asylum there. By early December, Souphanouvong had not returned to Laos.

Though not as badly hit as neighbouring Vietnam and Cambodia, Laos suffered from record flooding of the Mekong River basin in September. The UN World Food Programme pledged aid to 30,000 farming people from among the 100,000 whose crops had been lost in the inundation of 25,000 ha (61,750 ac) of rice paddies. These and other economic problems were addressed at a plenary session of the Lao People's Revolutionary Party in mid-September. Ambitious plans for improving literacy, hygiene, communications, energy, and transportation were outlined. Most foreign analysts, however, considered the proposed timescale unrealistic. With a chronically unstable kip, skepticism also greeted the government's claim in October that inflation in Laos was down to 10% and the country was on course for gross domestic product growth of 6% for the year.

(ROBERT WOODROW)

LATVIA

Area: 64,589 sq km (24,938 sq mi)
Population (July 1, 2000, estimate, based on 2000 census): 2,369,000
Capital: Riga
Chief of state: President Vaira Vike-Freiberga
Head of government: Prime Ministers Andris Skele and, from May 5, Andris Berzins

The 10th anniversary of the May 4, 1990, declaration on restoring the Republic of Latvia, originally proclaimed in 1918, encouraged both retrospection and contemplation of the future in 2000. The nation continued to examine the period of occupation by the U.S.S.R. and Nazi Germany. International conferences on the Holocaust were held in Riga in February and October. In March a group of Latvian veterans who had fought with the German forces (including the Waffen-SS) against the Soviet occupiers assembled to lay flowers at the foot of the Monument of Liberty. The Saeima (parliament) rejected a draft law on claiming compensation from Russia for the losses incurred under Soviet occupation. The Simon Wiesenthal Center complained of delays in bringing to trial two Australian citizens of Latvian origin accused of direct involvement in the Holocaust. Russia denounced Latvia's sentencing of Soviet partisans for crimes against humanity and offered them Russian citizenship.

In November Latvia assumed the rotating presidency of the Council of Europe. Membership negotiations with the European Union and the implementation of NATO's membership action plan progressed well. Russia opposed Latvia's intention to join NATO and claimed that Latvia discriminated against its large Russian-speaking population. The census of March 31 recorded Latvia's population at 2,375,300, or 10.9% less than in 1989. The decline stemmed mainly from the return of Soviet citizens to their homelands and the aging of Latvia's population. The Latvian share of the population rose from 52% to 57.6%, while the Russian portion dropped from 34% to 29.6%.

Domestic politics were turbulent early in the year as leading public figures had to contend with allegations of corruption, disrespect for the law, and sexual abuse of minors. Prime Minister Andris Skele resigned on April 12 and was succeeded by the popular mayor of Riga, Andris Berzins. The economy continued to recover. Gross domestic product was expected to grow by 5% in 2000, compared with 0.1% in 1999.

(DZINTRA BUNGS)

LEBANON

Area: 10,400 sq km (4,016 sq mi)
Population (2000 est.): 3,578,000 (excluding Palestinian refugees estimated to number more than 350,000)
Capital: Beirut
Chief of state: President Gen. Émile Lahoud
Head of government: Prime Ministers Salim al-Hoss and, from October 23, Rafiq al-Hariri

Lebanon experienced an especially eventful year in 2000. Israel unconditionally withdrew its forces from occupied Lebanese territory in the south at the end of May in accordance with UN Resolution 425 of 1978. The 2,500-strong South Lebanese Army that was armed and funded by Israel and acted as its proxy along the borders collapsed almost immediately. Although many of its members initially fled to Israel, most of them by the end of the year had returned home, surrendered to Lebanese authorities, and undergone military trial. It took until July to verify the withdrawal line to the general satisfaction of the Lebanese government. At the year's end two issues remained outstanding: Israel's release of Lebanese civilian prisoners and members of Hezbollah, Lebanon's main resistance force in the south, and the question of sovereignty over the Sheba' farms, a stretch of 200 sq km (77 sq mi) that Lebanon maintained was part of the south, while Israel and the UN considered it as part of the Golan Heights that belonged to Syria and maintained that its status should await future negotiations between Syria and Israel. A third important related issue was the resistance of the Lebanese government, backed by Syria, to the pressures exerted by both the UN and the U.S. to deploy the Lebanese army in the liberated southern areas and thus put an end to any further possible activities by Hezbollah either there or south of the Lebanese border. Lebanon said that it would not do so unless Israel evacuated the Sheba' farms and released all of its Lebanese prisoners. This stance prompted the Western governments to put on hold any financial help they were prepared to grant Lebanon to rebuild its southern region. The issue became more complicated in October when Hezbollah captured three Israeli soldiers at the Sheba' farms and an Israeli intelligence colonel in a separate episode.

In domestic politics the year was no less eventful. After the Israeli evacuation of the south, the Christian Maronite patriarch called for a similar step by the Syrian army. Because of Lebanon's close relations with Syria, little came of this call. The most important political development was the election for members of the National Assembly in August and September. Its significant result was the overwhelming support captured by former prime minister Rafiq al-Hariri, who was at odds with both Pres. Gen. Émile Lahoud and Prime Minister Salim al-Hoss. The latter even lost his seat in the National Assembly. The main winners in the new National Assembly were the Movement of the Deprived party in the south, Hariri's followers in the capital, and Druze leader Walid Junbulat in Mount Lebanon.

The outgoing government had been unable to improve the economic situation in the country. With debt servicing accounting for 45–50% of the budget and the salaries of Lebanon's 160,000 public employees an additional 35%, the government was unable to accomplish much. (MAHMOUD HADDAD)

Israeli tanks patrol a South Lebanese Army base near the Israeli-Lebanese border in May.

AP/Wide World Photos

LESOTHO

Area: 30,355 sq km (11,720 sq mi)
Population (2000 est.): 2,143,000
Capital: Maseru
Chief of state: King Letsie III
Head of government: Prime Minister Bathuel Pakalitha Mosisili

Political stagnation continued in Lesotho throughout 2000. Prime Minister Bathuel Pakalitha Mosisili's Lesotho Congress for Democracy (LCD) government remained in power, while the Interim Political Authority (IPA), on which sat representatives of all political parties, debated alternative electoral systems. Arbitration failed to resolve the impasse, and a political stalemate set in with the LCD arguing again for a "winner-take-all" election system despite having earlier agreed to the IPA's proposal for a mixed system that would include elements of proportional representation. As the end of the 18-month election preparation period approached in May, a sense of crisis developed. Opposition parties called on the king to intervene and create a government of national unity. After intense diplomatic activity the opposition parties accepted that the election had to be postponed, though they continued to blame the LCD and Parliament for this. In return for assurances that the electoral system would be changed, they also agreed that the LCD could remain in office. Stating that there was now no time for an election in 2000, the prime minister announced that it would be held between March and May 2001, but the likelihood of following this timetable appeared remote. Lesotho continued to benefit from the sale of its water to South Africa under the giant Highlands Water Project, which was being funded in part by the World Bank.

In one of the brighter stories of 2000, Lesotho's 36-year-old King Letsie III ended years of family and public concern when he took a bride, Karabo Motsoeneng, a commoner. The Roman Catholic wedding was held on February 18 in the national sports stadium and

was witnessed by thousands of the king's subjects as well as dignitaries from several African countries.
(CHRISTOPHER SAUNDERS)

LIBERIA

Area: 97,754 sq km (37,743 sq mi)
Population (2000 est.): 3,164,000
Capital: Monrovia
Head of state and government: President Charles Taylor

Relations between Liberia and Western governments remained tense in 2000. In March Pres. Charles Taylor reacted angrily to a U.S. State Department report critical of his regime's human rights record. He accused the U.S. of undermining his government. In June the European Union suspended aid to Liberia following British charges that Taylor's government facilitated the diamonds-for-arms trade of Sierra Leone's rebels. (*See* ANGOLA: *Sidebar,* above.) The U.S. imposed diplomatic sanctions and travel restrictions on Taylor and his associates in October. Taylor denied all charges, and in October the UN began to investigate the matter.

Throughout the year the government continued to battle rebels in the north of the country, especially in Lofa county. The government declared a state of emergency in the region and dispatched additional troops. They blamed the fighting, which escalated in July, on exiled former faction leaders Alhaji G.V. Kromah and Roosevelt Johnson. Liberia accused Guinea of supporting the rebel attack on the town of Voinjama. In September Liberia charged that the Guinean army had attacked northern towns, using heavy artillery. Guinea initially denied the charges and accused Liberia of armed incursions into its territory. In mid-October Guinea's interior minister said that the two nations were effectively at war and announced plans to arm Guinean villages along the border. The Economic Community of West African States attempted unsuccessfully to mediate the tensions between Liberia and Guinea.

In August the Liberian government arrested four journalists of Britain's Channel Four and charged them with espionage. This action brought a storm of protests from journalists, foreign governments, and international organizations. After intense pressure the Liberian government released the journalists.
(MATTHEW A. CENZER)

LIBYA

Area: 1,757,000 sq km (678,400 sq mi)
Population (2000 est.): 5,115,000
Capital: Tripoli (policy-making body and many secretariats intermittently meet in Surt)
Chief of state: (de facto) Col. Muammar al-Qaddafi; (nominal) Secretary of the General People's Congress Zentani Muhammad az-Zentani
Head of government: Secretaries of the General People's Committee (Prime Ministers) Muhammad Ahmad al-Manqush and, from March 1, Mubarak Abdallah al-Shamikh

With the 1992 UN trade sanctions lifted in 1999, Libya in 2000 rapidly renewed its worldwide links. The U.S. kept most sanctions in place but abandoned those on the export of food and medicine to Libya. The U.S. was unlikely to lift its sanctions before the conclusion of the trial of the two Libyan nationals accused of the December 1988 downing of a PanAm jetliner over Lockerbie, Scot. The trial began on May 3 in The Netherlands, a compromise venue agreed to by the Libyan, U.S., and U.K. governments to enable the proceedings to be held in a neutral place under Scottish law. The prosecution encountered problems in making its technical case because an important witness, the director of the Swiss manufacturer of the bomb's fuses, proved unreliable.

Col. Muammar al-Qaddafi received visits from Middle Eastern leaders throughout the year. Egyptian Pres. Hosni Mubarak called on Qaddafi in late July to discuss the Middle East peace process after the failed Camp David talks earlier in the month. In October the Arab League met in an emergency session in Egypt in response to the escalating violence between the Israelis and Palestinians. Denouncing what it described as the league's feeble response to the violence, the Libyan delegation walked out of the conference after six hours.

Qaddafi continued to make prominent his wish to strengthen his relations with African and European countries. By agreeing to pay the ransoms, Libya played a prominent role in negotiating the release in September of European tourists taken hostage by militants in Malaysia.

On March 1 Qaddafi announced sweeping changes in Libya's government structure. He dismissed the prime minister and foreign minister and abolished 12 ministries. The functions of the ministries were taken over by provincial and municipal bodies. Evidence of the Libyan leader's fear of internal opposition was revealed by the summary execution of three Islamist militants extradited from Jordan in the first week of April. (J.A. ALLAN)

LIECHTENSTEIN

Area: 160 sq km (62 sq mi)
Population (2000 est.): 32,600
Capital: Vaduz
Chief of state: Prince Hans Adam II
Head of government: Mario Frick

"The principality of Liechtenstein faces the biggest domestic and foreign political crisis since World War II," Prince Hans Adam II declared to his people during the country's National Day celebrations on Aug. 15, 2000. Allegations that the principality was a haven for money laundering by Latin American drug cartels, Russian gangsters, and the Italian Mafia first surfaced in November 1999 in the German magazine *Der Spiegel* and were based on a German intelligence service report. The government of Liechtenstein appointed a special prosecutor from Austria, Kurt Spitzer, to lead the investigation. By June eight people had been arrested, including a member of the parliament, a brother of the country's highest-ranking judge, and a brother of the deputy chief of government.

In his report, issued on August 31, Spitzer found particular problems with Liechtenstein's judicial system, where criminal cases remained unprocessed for years, but the special prosecutor stated that the country itself was no more guilty of money laundering than the rest of Europe. Nevertheless, Liechtenstein re-

AP/Wide World Photos

Liechtenstein's Prince Hans Adam II (right) and Prince Alois, his son, toast each other in front of Vaduz Castle in celebration of National Day on August 15.

mained the only European nation on an Organisation for Economic Co-operation and Development task force's blacklist of 15 countries accused of failure to cooperate in the international fight against money laundering. (ANNE ROBY)

LITHUANIA

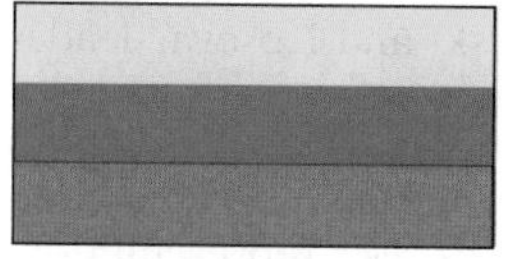

Area: 65,300 sq km (25,212 sq mi)
Population (2000 est.): 3,697,000
Capital: Vilnius
Chief of state: President Valdas Adamkus
Head of government: Prime Ministers Andrius Kubilius and, from October 26, Rolandas Paksas

In 2000 Lithuania continued along the path of strengthening its independence. A desovietization law was passed by the Seimas, the unicameral parliament, on June 27, and a delegation was to be formed by the end of the year to begin negotiations with Russia about gaining reparations for 50 years of Soviet occupation of Lithuania. An international congress for the investigation into communist crimes was also held in Vilnius in the summer.

Following the general election on October 8, a coalition government was formed by the moderate right Liberal Union and the populist left New Union (Social Liberals)—this because the Social Democratic coalition (Lithuania Democratic Labour Party and the Social Democratic Party), which together won a majority, 51 of 141 Seimas seats, were unable to form a ruling coalition. Thus, the Liberal Union and the New Union were joined by Centre Union and Moderate Christian Democrats—with a total of 67 seats—made up the new ruling coalition. Liberal Union leader Rolandas Paksas became prime minister, while New Union leader Arturas Paulaskas was elected chairman of the Seimas.

The country was on a sound economic track, and gross domestic product grew by more than 2%. Foreign direct investment amounted to $2,058,400,000, or $557 per capita, at the end of the first quarter. Foreign trade increased in the first five months of the year—exports and imports by 26.8% and 10.2%, respectively.

Lithuania moved resolutely to fulfill its chief foreign policy objective, closer integration into European institutions. On February 15 accession negotiations formally began at the European Union in Brussels. On May 19 Lithuania, a candidate for the second wave of enlargement of NATO, led the prospective new member states in signing the Vilnius statement, which called upon the NATO members to tender an invitation to join at the organization's next summit in 2002. (DARIUS FURMONAVIČIUS)

LUXEMBOURG

Area: 2,586 sq km (999 sq mi)
Population (2000 est.): 439,000
Capital: Luxembourg
Chief of state: Grand Dukes Jean and, from October 7, Henri
Head of government: Prime Minister Jean-Claude Juncker

Luxembourg celebrated a new chief of state as Crown Prince Henri was sworn in as the new grand duke by the parliament on October 7. His father, Grand Duke Jean, formally abdicated at the age of 79 to hand responsibility over to his son. Henri began his official duties on October 9 with visits to Paris, where he met with French Pres. Jacques Chirac and Prime Minister Lionel Jospin, and then to Berlin, where he met with German Pres. Johannes Rau and Chancellor Gerhard Schröder. The country also welcomed the news that Prince William, the youngest son of Grand Duke Jean, regained consciousness in early October. He had been in a coma since September 10, when he incurred serious injuries in a car crash near Paris.

The crime rate in Luxembourg had been so low that the country had been considering closing its only prison because it was usually standing empty. The quiet was broken on May 31, however, when a gunman with a history of mental illness took hostage some 40 children and teachers at a day-care centre, demanding money and an airplane to fly him to Libya. After a 30-hour standoff, police stormed the centre, shot and wounded the gunman, and rescued the children and their teachers.

In May Luxembourg announced that it was freezing eight accounts containing more than $600 million belonging to the late Nigerian dictator Gen. Sani Abacha and was referring the case to the current Nigerian government, which believed that billions of dollars had been embezzled and smuggled abroad. (ANNE ROBY)

Alexander Joe/AFP Worldwide

Victims of Tropical Storm Gloria gather outside a church in Andapa, Madagascar, one of the many villages in the country left in ruins by the storm.

MACEDONIA

Area: 25,713 sq km (9,928 sq mi)
Population (2000 est.): 2,041,000
Capital: Skopje
Chief of state: President Boris Trajkovski
Head of government: Prime Minister Ljubco Georgievski

For Macedonia the year 2000 brought relative political consolidation, but the country's economy remained a source of concern. On July 27 the cabinet was reduced from 27 to 17 members. In the new group Prime Minister Ljubco Georgievski and seven ministers belonged to the Internal Macedonian Revolutionary Organization–Democratic Party for Macedonian National Unity (VMRO-DPMNE), while the Democratic Alternative (DA) and the Democratic Party of Albanians (DPA) had five and four members, respectively, including one deputy prime minister each.

On August 25 eight parliamentary deputies of VMRO-DPMNE defected to the newly formed VMRO–True Macedonian Reform Option (VMRO), although two later reversed their decision. The deputies' move was followed by mob scenes outside their houses, demonstrations that many believed were orchestrated. Claims by the VMRO-VMRO that more deputies would join failed to materialize after the party's poor showing in the local elections.

Local elections were held on September 10 and 24. The opposition tried to turn them into a referendum on the government and to force general elections, but the results were inconclusive. The opposition won more votes than the VMRO-DPMNE/DA coalition, but the ruling parties won most of the runoffs, especially in rural areas, and secured a majority of the mayoralties. The elections were marred by a high number of irregularities and by violent incidents in which at least one person was killed. On November 23 the DA left the government. Prime Minister Georgievski managed to put together a new coalition by including the Liberal Party and a number of independent members of the parliament.

Interethnic relations remained tense. On January 11 three policemen were killed in the ethnic Albanian village of Aracinovo, allegedly the centre of a smuggling network. On March 31 four Macedonian soldiers were abducted on the border with Kosovo (Yugos.); they were freed only after Macedonian authorities released on bail an ethnic Albanian wanted for murder. Throughout the year a number of serious incidents took place on the Kosovo border.

No breakthrough was reached with Greece on the issue of Macedonia's name. Relations with Bulgaria remained good but were overshadowed by a decision of Bulgaria's Constitutional Court to ban an ethnic Macedonian party. On May 27 Georgievski and Kosovar leader Hashim Thaqi held talks on future cooperation and the possible opening in the respective capitals, Skopje and Pristina, of offices for representation. This was received badly by Yugoslavia, as were allegations that Belgrade's ambassador to Macedonia was meddling in the country's internal affairs. On November 24, on the sidelines of the Zagreb summit meeting, Macedonia and the European Union signed the Stabilization and Association Agreement.

In September the Macedonian government started returning to its former owners property that had been nationalized by the communist regime. In April the majority of Stopanska Banka, the country's largest bank, was opened to international investors. On the whole, however, the economic situation remained precarious as the government found no solutions for high unemployment or measures to deal with the biggest loss-making enterprises.

(STEFAN KRAUSE)

MADAGASCAR

Area: 587,041 sq km (226,658 sq mi)
Population (2000 est.): 15,506,000
Capital: Antananarivo
Chief of state and head of government: President Didier Ratsiraka, assisted by Prime Minister Tantely Andrianarivo

In early 2000 northeastern Madagascar was hard hit by a series of cyclones and tropical storms. As a result of Cyclone Eline and Tropical Storm Gloria in February and Cyclone Hudah in April, more than 100 people were killed, large numbers of people lost their homes, and much agricultural land was destroyed. Tens of thousands moved to the capital, Antananarivo, to join others living on the streets in abject poverty. The storms were also blamed for intensifying a long-running cholera epidemic that had killed more than 1,000. Then in September the south of the island was severely afffected by drought and thousands more died.

The country's total debt, which had tripled during the past two decades, rose to more than $4 billion in 2000. More than twice as much was spent on debt servicing as on national health and education combined, and more than one-third of the money received in grants was paid back in debt service. The infant mortality rate remained among the highest in the world, and investment in infrastructure was so low that during the rainy season many parts of the country were accessible only by air. Madagascar was supposed to benefit from the international initiatives to relieve the debt burden on Heavily Indebted Poor Countries, but there was little significant relief; in July, however, Germany announced that it was canceling DM 52 million (about $25 million) of the country's outstanding debt.

In August the first announcement of candidacy was made for the presidential elections scheduled for 2001. In late December Jean-Eugène Voninahitsy, the vice president of Madagascar's national assembly, was imprisoned for defaming Pres. Didier Ratsiraka, among other charges. Voninahitsy had sharply criticized Ratsiraka for his plan to collect tolls at floating bridges that were used to replace bridges destroyed by the cyclones. (CHRISTOPHER SAUNDERS)

MALAWI

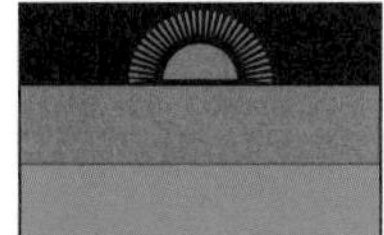

Area: 118,484 sq km (45,747 sq mi)
Population (2000 est.): 10,386,000
Capital: Lilongwe (legislative, ministerial, and financial), Blantyre (executive and judicial)
Head of state and government: President Bakili Muluzi

Malawi was applauded by outside observers for promptly providing two of its three helicopters to assist in rescue operations in neighbouring Mozambique, where floods devastated southern districts in February 2000.

That month a court case was brought against the government by the opposition, which claimed that the 1999 elections had been rigged. The opposition appeared to have the support of an independent monitoring group, which in its report accused the government of serious procedural shortcomings, including media manipulation and conducting of a disinformation operation. The makeup of a new cabinet appointed on March 1 prompted the opposition to criticize Pres. Bakili Muluzi for favouring appointees from the south of the country, where he had greater support.

In October, however, the president dismissed the entire cabinet after a Public Accounts Committee report implicated that ministers and members of parliament were involved in large-scale corruption. Meanwhile, women's rights activists accused male members of main political parties of intimidating women interested in standing for election as councillors in the November 21 local government elections.

In August the Australian company Paladin Resources announced that it had started preliminary development work on Malawi's first uranium mine. It was hoped that mining would begin in 2003. (KENNETH INGHAM)

MALAYSIA

Area: 329,735 sq km (127,311 sq mi)
Population (2000 est.): 23,260,000
Capital: Kuala Lumpur; head of government office in Putrajaya (the future planned capital) from 1999
Chief of state: *Yang di-Pertuan Agong* (Paramount Ruler) Tuanku Ja'afar ibni al-Marhum Tuanku Abdul Rahman
Head of government: Prime Minister Dato Seri Mahathir bin Mohamad

The year 2000 in Malaysia saw the conclusion of the sensational trial of Anwar Ibrahim, the former protégé of Prime Minister Dato Seri Mahathir bin Mohamad who had been fired as deputy prime minister and finance

Supporters of former Malaysian deputy prime minister Anwar Ibrahim rally on January 25 outside a courthouse in Kuala Lumpur where Anwar faced sodomy charges.

AP/Wide World Photos

minister in September 1998 and later arrested on sexual misconduct and sodomy charges. The judge refused Anwar's lawyers' requests that Mahathir be summoned to testify, and the trial came to an abrupt end in August. Anwar was found guilty on three charges of sodomy and was sentenced to nine years in prison. The few protests that followed were swiftly squashed by police. Continuing to maintain his innocence, Anwar claimed that the charges had been fraudulently concocted because he had fallen out of favour with Mahathir and the prime minister feared an electoral challenge within the ruling United Malays National Organization (UMNO).

In May the UMNO held its triennial party elections. The polls had been put off for a year to prevent Anwar's supporters from gaining an upper hand. Mahathir and his allies succeeded in curtailing the campaign of another former finance minister, Tengku Razaleigh Hamzah, who had challenged Mahathir for the UMNO leadership in 1987 and narrowly lost. Still, the party elected three former Anwar allies—Najib Razak, Muhammad Taib, and Muhyiddin Yassin—as vice presidents. The UMNO and the Malay community at large remained deeply divided between those who supported Anwar and those who opposed him.

In October Mahathir and his allies proposed key amendments to the UMNO constitution that would replace the current electoral college system that elected the party's president, his deputy, and the Supreme Council with a much larger, more representative electoral college. This was seen as yet another attempt to reduce the influence of Anwar and his allies within the UMNO. Following a popular revolt in the party's ranks, Mahathir backtracked and diluted most of the amendments just before they were put to vote.

Malaysia's economy continued to recover in 2000, with gross domestic product (GDP) growth at about 8%, up from 5.8% in 1999. As the world's third largest exporter of semiconductors, Malaysia benefited from a robust demand for electronics components from manufacturers of personal computers and telecommunications equipment. Toward the end of the year, however, there were signs that the demand for semiconductors and other electronics components was dramatically slowing. As a net exporter of oil, Malaysia also benefited from higher oil prices during the year, though higher government oil revenues were not enough to push Malaysia's chronic budget deficit into a surplus.

The budget deficit remained a high 5% of Malaysia's total GDP. Malaysia stuck with its capital control measures throughout the year; the government kept the nation's currency pegged artificially low to the U.S. dollar to boost exports. In October the government announced that it would remove a 10% levy on foreign portfolio investments in order to improve lacklustre foreign interest in Malaysia's stock market.

(ASSIF A. SHAMEEN)

MALDIVES

Area: 298 sq km (115 sq mi)
Population (2000 est.): 285,000
Capital: Male
Head of state and government: President Maumoon Abdul Gayoom

Maldives Pres. Maumoon Abdul Gayoom began the year by presenting the 2000 government budget to the Majlis (parliament); the president noted that the budget was balanced and economic progress was satisfactory. Total proposed government expenditure was Rf 2,991,049,432 (about $254,000,000). The biggest outlays were earmarked for the development of social services such as education and for improvement in the quality of general services.

On October 16, World Food Day, the president urged the country to become more self-sufficient in food production. Much of the country's food requirements had been met by imports. A development project to increase the growth of banana trees in Maldives was under way, as were plans for easier access to fertilizers and an increase in agricultural workers.

Deputy Minister Aneesa Ahmed of the Ministry of Women's Affairs and Social Security urged women to expand the scope of their economic activities. There were two government programs under which women could obtain small business loans. She pointed out that most of the women's businesses involved either cooking or sewing and encouraged women to explore other types of work.

(ANNE ROBY)

MALI

Area: 1,248,574 sq km (482,077 sq mi)
Population (2000 est.): 10,686,000
Capital: Bamako
Chief of state: President Alpha Oumar Konaré
Head of government: Prime Ministers Ibrahim Boubacar Keita and, from February 15, Mande Sidibe

Mali's 40th year of independence brought little in the way of good economic news. Sharp price drops in the international cotton market, the country's largest export crop, caused government revenues to drop by nearly 4%, and the 2000 budget deficit was expected to rise by more than one-third, despite a planned reduction in public spending. In addition, various strikes hit the capital, Bamako, during the year as bus drivers, police, and members of the national telecommunication union walked out over a range of issues, including high transport license fees, promotions, privatization, and general living conditions.

Despite the passage of laws designed to preserve Mali's dwindling forest reserves, the rate of deforestation continued to accelerate; about 99% of the country's energy needs were fueled by wood. Only the gold-mining sector showed signs of increased productivity. Reserves in the newly discovered Morila mines were expected to provide over $90 million to the state over 14 years.

On July 25 Belgium agreed to provide Mali with an interest-free loan for the construction of two high-voltage generators to help ease the perennial energy crisis in Bamako. In early September the World Bank and the International Monetary Fund agreed to reduce Mali's international debt. Pres. Alpha Oumar Konaré met with French Pres. Jacques Chirac in Paris on September 25 to discuss, among other issues, the cancellation of Mali's debt to France. In September the French Development Agency agreed to provide an additional subsidy for rural road improvements. Education Minister Moustapha Dicko announced in October a government drive to recruit 2,500 elementary and secondary schoolteachers. Only 26% of students passed the 2000 baccalaureate exams, down from 33% in 1999.

(NANCY ELLEN LAWLER)

MALTA

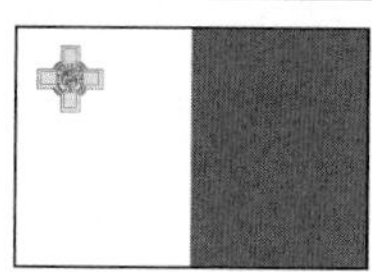

Area: 316 sq km (122 sq mi)
Population (2000 est.): 382,000
Capital: Valletta
Chief of state: President Guido de Marco
Head of government: Prime Minister Eddie Fenech Adami

After Malta had fulfilled the criteria to become a member of the European Union in 1999, formal membership talks were inaugurated in Brussels on Feb. 15, 2000, and continued throughout the year. On October 4 the European Parliament approved a resolution for Malta's application by an overwhelming majority. Malta also met the preconditions for inclusion in the first round of EU enlargement. The Labour Party, however, remained opposed to accession.

Malta's economy showed signs of improvement. During the second quarter of the year, its gross domestic product grew by 3.9% compared with the same period in 1999, and the gross national product rose by 6.4%. In August the percentage of the registered unemployed went down to 4.5% from 5.5% a year earlier.

The World Health Organization ranked Malta fifth in its evaluation of health care systems in 191 countries. The budget for health care was increased to 69.4 million Maltese liri (1 Maltese lira=about $2.30) from 63.3 million Maltese liri in 1999.

Tax enforcement was stepped up to assuage the government's main headache—the budget deficit, which over a two-year period had been brought down by about 50 million Maltese liri. Minister of Finance John Dalli declared in October that efforts would be intensified to collect more revenue through existing taxation.

(ALBERT GANADO)

MARSHALL ISLANDS

Area: 181 sq km (70 sq mi)
Population (2000 est.): 51,600
Capital: Majuro
Head of state and government: Presidents Imata Kabua and, from January 10, Kessai Note

After being elected unanimously by the Nitijela (legislative assembly), Kessai Note took the oath of office as president of Marshall Islands on Jan. 10, 2000. Note's government, which immediately delivered its first budget, was committed to a program of restoring transparency and credibility in the government.

Marshall Islands continued to grapple with major issues concerning its relationship with the U.S., focusing on accountability for the expenditure of $1 billion under the first 15-year Compact of Free Association between the two governments, which was to end in 2001, and negotiations concerning the compact's renewal. Critical to the outcome of financial negotiations would be assessments undertaken by the Asian Development Bank and late-summer talks between the two governments on economic issues. Through a petition to the U.S. Congress, the government sought an additional $2.7 billion in compensation for the consequences and implications of nuclear testing in the islands during the 1940s and 1950s, including funds for a cleanup on Enewetak atoll and for medical facilities and services for 50 years.

(BARRIE MACDONALD)

MAURITANIA

Area: 1,030,700 sq km (398,000 sq mi)
Population (2000 est.): 2,668,000
Capital: Nouakchott
Chief of state: President Col. Maaouya Ould Sidi Ahmad Taya
Head of government: Prime Minister Cheikh El Afia Ould Mohamed Khouna

Mauritania's staggering international debt received some promises of reduction during 2000 when it qualified for the Heavily Indebted Poor Countries, a project of the International Monetary Fund and the World Bank. The G-7 group of wealthy nations announced on July 21 that Mauritania, along with six other sub-Saharan African countries, was eligible for a share of a new $15 billion debt-reduction program. The government took steps toward developing its mineral resources when it granted two exploration permits to enable a Canadian mining company to prospect for gold and strategic metals in the Akchar region.

The offshore fishing industry continued to struggle with the problem of foreign competitors within its territorial

Fishing boats and nets are arranged on the beach in Mauritania.

Bernard and Catherine Desjeux/Corbis

waters. Fishing accounted for 65% of export earnings and constituted 40% of the national budget. A complete ban on commercial fishing during the breeding season of September and October was announced on August 31. The results, however, proved disappointing, as the area had been overfished for many years. Pres. Abdoulaye Wade of Senegal paid a state visit to Mauritania in late June. On the agenda was the controversial fossil valley land reclamation project along the Sénégal River, which Mauritania charged would cause the drying up of land on its side of the river. Wade agreed to abandon the project.

(NANCY ELLEN LAWLER)

MAURITIUS

Area: 2,040 sq km (788 sq mi)
Population (2000 est.): 1,184,000
Capital: Port Louis
Chief of state: President Cassam Uteem
Head of government: Prime Ministers Navin Ramgoolam and, from September 17, Sir Anerood Jugnauth

On Sept. 11, 2000, Mauritians voted in legislative elections. The Mauritius Labour Party of Prime Minister Navin Ramgoolam and its smaller partner, the Mauritian Party of Xavier Duval, faced an opposition alliance of the Mauritian Militant Movement (MMM) and the Mauritian Socialist Movement (MSM). The opposition won a sweeping victory, taking 54 of the 62 legislative seats. Under the opposition parties' agreement, MSM leader Sir Anerood Jugnauth would serve as prime minister for three years, and MMM leader Paul Berenger would then take over for the remaining two years of the government's term. Berenger would be the first prime minister since independence in 1968 who was not from the island's Hindu community. The opposition victory was attributed to anger over corruption scandals involving Labour Party officials.

The Mauritian rupee fell against major currencies early in the year, and in September the new government announced measures to halt its decline. The country's trade deficit rose, a fact widely attributed to the weak sugar crop in 1999 and the high oil prices in 2000.

(MATTHEW A. CENZER)

Vicente Fox speaks during his presidential inauguration ceremony in Mexico City on December 1.

MEXICO

Area: 1,958,201 sq km (756,066 sq mi)
Population (2000 est.): 98,881,000
Capital: Mexico City
Head of state and government: Presidents Ernesto Zedillo Ponce de León and, from December 1, Vicente Fox Quesada

The triumph in the July 2, 2000, presidential election of Vicente Fox Quesada (*see* BIOGRAPHIES) was the single most important event in Mexico during the year. His dramatic victory ended the Institutional Revolutionary Party's (PRI's) 71-year-long dominance in national government and marked the beginning of a new political era.

By mobilizing unexpectedly broad support behind the Alliance for Change coalition (an alliance of the centre-right National Action Party [PAN] and the Mexican Green Ecologist Party [PVEM]), Fox won by a landslide over PRI candidate Francisco Labastida Ochoa. The official tally gave Fox 42.5% of the votes against Labastida's 36.1%. The three-time presidential candidate, Cuauhtémoc Cárdenas Solórzano, heading the Alliance for Mexico coalition (an alliance of the centre-left Party of the Democratic Revolution [PRD], the Labour Party [PT], the Convergence for Democracy [CD], the Nationalist Society Party [PSN], and the Social Alliance Party [PAS]), trailed with 16.6%.

Several factors contributed to this outcome. The charismatic Fox, a former governor of the state of Guanajuato, proved to be the most effective campaigner, with the most powerful message. He argued that Mexico could not consolidate democracy without changing the party in national power. He asserted, moreover, that Mexico's problems demanded new leadership

AP/Wide World Photos

and a fresh approach. On this basis, Fox was able to win support from across the sociopolitical spectrum and in all parts of the country. Many PRD sympathizers voted for Fox in a strategic bid to oust the PRI.

The Federal Electoral Institute, which had been independent of government control since 1996, worked to ensure a fair election. An up-to-date voter registry was created, and government agencies' use of public resources to support particular parties and candidates was constrained, though not completely eliminated. Confident that their ballots would be counted accurately, Mexican voters went to the polls and voiced their frustrations with the country's economic instability, corruption in government, and tradition of impunity for the elite.

The election's outcome deeply shocked both the PRI and the PRD. Although Pres. Ernesto Zedillo won international praise for his immediate public recognition of Fox's electoral triumph and for his statesmanlike pledge to work closely with the incoming administration to ensure a smooth transfer of power on December 1, many traditional elements within the PRI blamed Zedillo for the party's unprecedented defeat. The PRI remained a potentially powerful force—with a large bloc of votes in the national Congress, control over the majority of state and municipal governments, and strong support among some social groups—but the party faced a prolonged internal leadership crisis and a difficult transition to its new role as opposition party.

One of the most interesting elections took place in the southern state of Chiapas, an impoverished area that had experienced several years of conflict between government forces and the rebel Zapatista National Liberation Army. Elected as state governor was Pablo Salazar Mendiguchía, who was supported by a coalition of eight parties in opposition to the PRI, which had long governed the area. One of Salazar's first acts as governor was to order the state's attorney general to review the cases of all those who claimed to be Zapatista political prisoners and to suspend the sentences of those charged with political crimes.

Similarly, the PRD suffered major reverses, especially in the size of its legislative bloc in the Congress. Although the election of Andrés Manuel López Obrador as head of the Federal District government allowed the party to maintain control over a key political base, the PRD was also placed on the political defensive.

Fox's most daunting task was expected to be forging a working coalition behind his programmatic agenda. This would be difficult because no party held a majority in either chamber of the new Mexican Congress. The 500 seats in the federal Chamber of Deputies were distributed among the PAN (206), PRI (211), PRD (49), PVEM (17), PT (8), CD (4), PSN (3), and PAS (2). Similarly, in the federal Senate the 128 seats were distributed among the PRI (60), PAN (46), PRD (16), PVEM (5), and CD (1). Under these circumstances, the success of Fox's reform program would depend centrally on coalition building. Constitutional reform initiatives, which require a two-thirds majority vote, would be especially subject to veto by Fox's political opponents.

Because the PAN shared a number of macroeconomic objectives with the PRI, Fox's administration was not expected to radically alter national economic policy. Fox was committed to new investments in public education, however. He also stated the goal of creating 1,350,000 new jobs in the formal sector each year. Observers believed Fox would, moreover, pursue policies beneficial to small and medium-sized firms.

One unresolved question was whether the transfer of power from the PRI to the PAN would be accompanied by the economic instability that had bedeviled Mexico at the end of several previous presidencies. The country's overall economic situation at the end of the Zedillo administration was quite favourable, with inflation-adjusted gross domestic product rising by approximately 7.9% in 2000 and with gradually falling inflation and interest rates. Zedillo also took a number of steps—including maintaining tight fiscal discipline, accumulating substantial foreign exchange reserves, reducing short-term debt obligations, and arranging for emergency lines of international credit—to avoid a repetition of the country's devastating 1994–95 financial crisis. Nevertheless, the financial sector's continued weakness and the uncertainties inevitably associated with a historic political transition remained elements of concern.

(KEVIN J. MIDDLEBROOK)

MICRONESIA, FEDERATED STATES OF

Area: 701 sq km (271 sq mi)
Population (2000 est.): 118,000
Capital: Palikir, on Pohnpei
Head of state and government: President Leo A. Falcam

A cholera outbreak in Pohnpei caused 19 deaths and affected more than 3,000 people before subsiding in September 2000. The Federated States of Micronesia (FSM) government placed restrictions on movement and on the transport of goods and began vaccinating all members of the population over two years of age.

With assistance from the International Monetary Fund and the Asian Development Bank, the government remained focused on a reform agenda for the public sector and public service and also on implementing the strategy developed at a 1999 economic summit. Gross domestic product increased by

2% in 1999, and GDP growth of 3% was anticipated for 2000. Under a bilateral arrangement with Japan, funds would be provided for the development of the Tebetik fishing port in Pohnpei.

In U.S. congressional hearings into the FSM's 1986 Compact of Free Association with the U.S., the General Accounting Office's testimony suggested FSM irresponsibility and the lack of accountability in its expenditure of $1,080,000,000 in Compact funds. In its renewal negotiations, the FSM sought $84 million annually and an additional $20 million annually to be paid to a trust fund until local revenue and trust income could cover the country's expenditures.

During the year Pres. Leo A. Falcam led delegations to Israel, with which the FSM had developed a close working relationship at the UN, and to China, where he reaffirmed the FSM's commitment to a single-China policy.
(BARRIE MACDONALD)

MOLDOVA

Area: 33,700 sq km (13,000 sq mi)
Population (2000 est.): 4,298,000
Capital: Chisinau
Chief of state: President Petru Lucinschi
Head of government: Prime Minister Dumitru Braghis

A turning point in Moldova's post-Soviet history was marked on July 5, 2000, when an overwhelming majority in Parliament passed an amendment to the 1994 constitution transforming the country from a semipresidential into a parliamentary republic. Parliament's decision came largely as a response to Pres. Petru Lucinschi's long-standing efforts to install a full-fledged presidential system. Lucinschi vetoed the law and continued to press for a nationwide referendum to decide which system was preferred but to no avail. Late in the year Parliament tried three times to elect a new president but failed in each effort to muster at least 61 votes for any of the candidates. On December 31 President Lucinschi signed a decree that would dissolve the present Parliament in two weeks. Elections for a new Parliament were scheduled for Feb. 25, 2001.

Moldovan Pres. Petru Lucinschi (right) chats with Russian Pres. Vladimir Putin before the start of their official talks in Chisinau on June 17.

AFP Worldwide

The Communist-dominated Parliament was the scene of perpetual rearrangements, including an ad hoc alliance between Communist, centrist, and right-wing deputies that on April 17 rejected a bill to privatize the country's wine and tobacco industries. Since that bill was among the key conditions established by the International Monetary Fund and the World Bank for resuming the granting of credit to the nation, its rejection deprived Moldova of badly needed loans, and the economic situation remained precarious. This led to social tension and even open conflict.

Moldova's main diplomatic partner remained Russia. The latter committed itself to the withdrawal of its troops and military equipment from Moldova's breakaway Transnistria region before the end of 2002. Russia failed, however, to present a final timetable for the operation, while it insisted that the withdrawal be related to a political solution of the Transnistria conflict. Following a visit to Chisinau on June 16–17, new Russian Pres. Vladimir Putin decided to set up a state commission for Transnistria headed by former prime minister Yevgeny Primakov. In August Primakov proposed a peace plan structured around the idea of confederation, an idea rejected—for different reasons—by both Moldova and Transnistria.
(DAN IONESCU)

MONACO

Area: 1.95 sq km (0.75 sq mi)
Population (2000 est.): 31,700
Chief of state: Prince Rainier III
Head of government: Ministers of State Michel Leveque and, from January 5, Patrick Leclercq

Monaco expressed concern as Prince Rainier III underwent two lung operations in February 2000, which followed heart surgery on Dec. 16, 1999.

A report from the French Parliament's investigation of financial crimes in Europe in June called Monaco a money-laundering paradise. It accused the principality of having willfully devised such lax banking laws—including a guarantee of anonymity—that officials could not cooperate in the international fight against money laundering even if they desired to do so. The report stated that Monaco had 10 times more bank accounts than residents and that its request to join the Council of Europe and the 16-nation euro zone was unlikely to succeed without substantial changes. Responding to the accusations, Monaco threatened to break with France and "endow the principality with full sovereignty."

On June 30, after weeks of denial, Prince Ernst August of Hanover apologized for urinating on the Turkish pavilion at the Expo 2000 world's fair in Hannover, Ger., saying it was "not a conscious act." The prince had attended the fair with his wife, Princess Caroline, her father, Prince Rainier III, and her brother, Prince Albert. (ANNE ROBY)

MONGOLIA

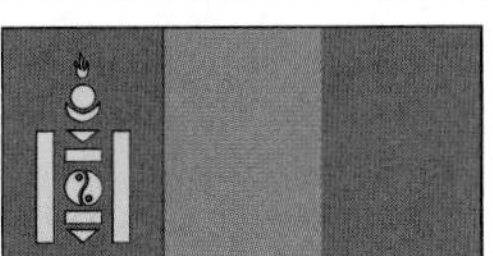

Area: 1,564,116 sq km (603,909 sq mi)
Population (2000 est.): 2,399,000
Capital: Ulaanbaatar
Chief of state: President Natsagiyn Bagabandi
Head of government: Prime Ministers Rinchinnyamyn Amarjargal and, from July 26, Nambaryn Enhbayar

The Mongolian People's Revolutionary Party (MPRP) achieved a landslide victory in the elections to the Mongolian Great Hural (parliament) on July 2, 2000, taking 72 of the 76 seats. The MPRP, a reformed communist party with democratic socialist inclinations, won over 50% of the votes nationwide. The four other seats went to former prime minister Janlavyn Narantsatsralt of the Mongolian National Democratic Party (MNDP); to businessman Badarchiyn Erdenebat, chairman of the Mongolian Democratic New Socialist Party (MDNSP); to the murdered democracy leader Zorig's sister, Sanjaasurengiyn Oyuun, who had left the MNDP to set up the Civil Will (Irgeniy Zorig) Party; and to an Independent, Lamjavyn Gundalay.

On polling day 603 candidates representing 13 parties and 3 coalitions had stood for election. The MNDP, in alliance with the Mongolian Religious Democratic Party, received 13% of votes nationwide, while Erdenebat's MDNSP achieved 10.7%. The MNDP's coalition partner in the 1996 elections, the Mongolian Social Democratic Party, standing alone, managed only 8.9% and won no seats; Great Hural Speaker Radnaasumbereliyn Gonchigdorj thereby lost his base for challenging for the presidency in 2001.

On July 19 the first session of the Great Hural elected a new speaker, Lhamsurengiyn Enebish, secretary-general of the MPRP. The appointment of the MPRP's nominee for prime minister, party Chairman Nambaryn Enhbayar, was delayed by Pres. Natsagiyn Bagabandi, who insisted first on debating the legality of amendments to the Mongolian constitution adopted by the Great Hural in December 1999, which he had vetoed. Annulment of one amendment, allowing members of the Great Hural to serve concurrently as cabinet members, would have prevented Enhbayar from taking up his post. Finally, Enhbayar was appointed prime minister on July 26, and the amendments remained in force pending a Great Hural debate and full session of the Constitutional Court. Enhbayar's cabinet was appointed on August 9. Gonchigdorj's party joined with the MDNP and three smaller parties on December 6 to form a new Democratic Party. (ALAN J.K. SANDERS)

MOROCCO

Area: 710,850 sq km (274,461 sq mi), including the 252,120-sq km (97,344-sq mi) area of the disputed Western Sahara annexation
Population (2000 est.): 29,067,000, of which Western Sahara 245,000
Capital: Rabat
Head of state and government: King Muhammad VI, assisted by Prime Minister 'Abd ar-Rahman Youssoufi

Morocco in 2000 continued to be dogged by the twin problems of the Western Sahara and a sluggish economy. Nonetheless, the new king, Muhammad VI, sought a series of bold social initiatives to begin the process of fundamental social and political reform. The UN Security Council in January and again on four other occasions reluctantly renewed the mandate for the peacekeeping force in the Western Sahara. Relations with Algeria, which had been poisoned by the Western Sahara issue, improved slightly after the Euro-African summit in Cairo despite threats in May by the Polisario Front independence movement in Western Sahara to breach the ceasefire. The two countries agreed to cooperate over border security after Algerian Islamists threatened a Moroccan border village in midyear. The Polisario Front in December released 201 Moroccan soldiers that it had captured 25 years previously at the start of the conflict over the Western Sahara; 1,481 Moroccans remained prisoners of the Polisario Front.

The king's proposals during the year for a new family code that would have outlawed polygamy and given women greater equality with men and guarantees of political participation met with furious opposition. Morocco's Islamist movements organized a 500,000-strong demonstration against the proposals on March 12 in Casablanca, compared with a 40,000-strong demonstration in support of them in Rabat. Nevertheless, Morocco's veteran Islamist leader, Abdesalam Yassine, was released from house arrest after 11 years in mid-May. In December police in Rabat arrested dozens of peaceful demonstrators, who were demanding the legalization of their outlawed Muslim fundamentalist group, Al Adl Wal Ihsane.

The problems facing the government continued, with unemployment heading the list, followed by the ongoing drought. About $350 million was provided for drought relief in the June–December budget, which anticipated a budget deficit of 1% of gross domestic product, 3% growth of GDP, and inflation at only 2.3%. Grain production fell by 50% to 1,820,000 metric tons, and 5,200,000 tons had to be imported during the year. Good economic news emerged in August, when oil was discovered in commercial quantities at Talsint, close to the border with Algeria, which raised hopes that Morocco's domestic needs, 160,00 bbl per day, would be met. King Muhammad VI in late March made his first official trip abroad, to France, where he sought French support for full partnership status within the European Union. (GEORFE JOFFÉ)

MOZAMBIQUE

Area: 812,379 sq km (313,661 sq mi)
Population (2000 est.): 19,105,000
Capital: Maputo
Head of state and government: President Joaquim Chissano, assisted by Prime Minister Pascoal Mocumbi

The slow but steady improvement in the economy of Mozambique received a serious setback in February 2000, when the worst rains in more than 40 years resulted in flooding that devastated the southern provinces of Maputo, Gaza, and Inhambane. This was accompanied almost immediately by the arrival of Cyclone Eline, which crossed the shore in the neighbourhood of Beira and thus compounded the havoc created by the floods. Some 600 people were killed, and an estimated one million more were rendered homeless; 10% of the country's cultivated area was damaged, and one-third of the corn crop was destroyed. Although the floods did not affect the agriculturally more productive northern regions, the estimate of growth in the economy, which had been expected to be of the order of between 8% and 10% for the year, had to be reduced by 2.3%.

The opposition Mozambique National Resistance (Renamo), defeated by the Mozambique Liberation Front (Frelimo) in the elections in December 1999, tried to regain lost ground by accusing Pres. Joaquim Chissano of the responsibility for what many regarded as the tardy arrival of aid from some quarters because of his slowness in requesting external assistance. Later, police arrested eight members of Renamo on charges of inciting people to commit acts of civil disobedience as part of their continuing protest against the election result. Early in November some 40 people, most of whom supported Renamo, were killed in clashes with the police in northern Mozambique. In December President Chissano and Renamo leader Afonso Dhlakama met to discuss the strife between the government and Renamo; it was their first meeting in more than a year.

In mid-March the Southern African Development Community, chaired by Mozambique, called upon the donor community to cancel Mozambique's debts totally. The Paris Club of creditor nations responded by canceling debt service payments pending the reduction of the debt due during the second phase of debt cancellation, which came into effect later in the year. The World Bank and the International Monetary Fund on April 12 also agreed to waive the whole of the debt service for the next 12 months and nine days later approved a credit of $30 million as a contribution to flood relief. As a further step the government approached donors at a meeting in Rome on May 3 with a request for aid amounting to $450 million to assist in reconstruction; donors responded with a total of $452.9 million.

In June Billiton's Mozal aluminum smelter began production. It was expected to reach full operations capacity by early 2001 at a cost appreciably below the original estimate of $1.3 billion.

(KENNETH INGHAM)

MYANMAR (BURMA)

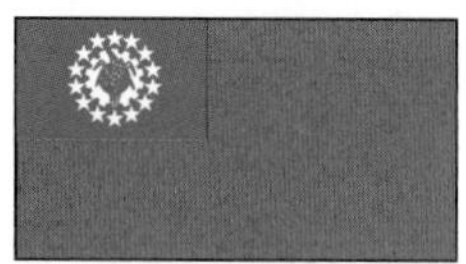

Area: 676,577 sq km (261,228 sq mi)
Population (2000 est.): 41,735,000
Capital: Yangon (Rangoon)
Head of state and government: Chairman of the State Peace and Development Council Gen. Than Shwe

Ten years after Myanmar's ruling military regime nullified the decisive 1990 national election victory of the opposition National League for Democracy, the power struggle between the regime and the NLD continued to dominate the country's political affairs. Early in 2000 NLD leader Daw Aung San Suu Kyi announced that her party would not recognize any constitution devised by the government or any state-run elections. The regime's harassment of Suu Kyi and her followers subsequently escalated. The most notable incident came in late August, when Suu Kyi attempted to leave Yangon to attend a party meeting and authorities stopped her two-car caravan just outside the capital. Refusing to return to Yangon, she and 14 supporters camped out in the cars for nine days before troops transported them back to the capital. The government later accused the NLD of provoking the confrontation. Suu Kyi, in response, condemned the regime for denying her the freedom to travel within her own country.

In September the regime detained NLD deputy leader Tin Oo and eight other NLD members for two weeks. Meanwhile, Suu Kyi was confined to her home in Yangon. Suu Kyi emerged from her confinement vowing to continue challenging Myanmar's military rulers. She made a second attempt to travel outside the capital late in the month when she tried to board a train bound for Mandalay, but authorities refused to issue her a ticket. Days later the UN special envoy to Myanmar, Razali Ismail, met with both Suu Kyi and military leaders during his four-day visit to the country. Despite his attempts to reconcile differences between the two sides, it was certain that the NLD leader's movements would remain heavily restricted.

The government was successful in eliminating the threat posed by the Karen rebel group God's Army during the year. The guerrillas, led by 12-year-old twin brothers Johnny and Luther Htoo—who were considered by their followers to be the reincarnations of ancient Karen warriors—allegedly took part in seizing a hospital along the Thai border on January 24. The jungle base of God's Army was overrun by Myanmar government forces on January 27, although the Htoo brothers managed to elude capture. By midyear it had been reported that the twins were living in a Karen village in Myanmar near the Thai border and had decided, for the time being, to lay down their arms.

Sanctions and embargoes imposed on Myanmar by Western countries continued to stymie development. Sharp criticism of the military regime came from Great Britain, which urged Premier Oil, a British-owned exploration company, to drop its $200 million stake in a gas project in Myanmar. In April a British official described the regime as "disgraceful" and cited its alleged record of killings, forced labour, control of the media, and repression of minorities.

(EDITOR)

NAMIBIA

Area: 825,118 sq km (318,580 sq mi)
Population (2000 est.): 1,771,000
Capital: Windhoek
Chief of state and head of government: President Sam Nujoma, assisted by Prime Minister Hage Geingob

AFP Worldwide

Early in the year Namibian policemen hunt for Angolan rebels in the village of Rundu, near the Angolan border.

Having been reelected with 77% of the vote in December 1999, Pres. Sam Nujoma in 2000 began his third term of office, made possible by an amendment to the constitution. The newly established Congress of Democrats, led by Ben Ulenga, won enough seats in the election for the National Assembly to take over from the Democratic Turnhalle Alliance as the main opposition party, and its members livened up proceedings in the new legislature. They criticized both Namibia's continuing military involvement in the Democratic Republic of the Congo, involvement that had led both Germany and Finland to scale down aid to Namibia, and the authoritarian practices of the government. There was an outcry when the minister of home affairs said that gay people should be "eliminated."

Instability continued in the north of the country throughout much of the year. Nujoma's decision in late 1999 to allow the Angolan armed forces to operate from Namibian soil meant that Namibia became embroiled in the Angolan civil war. Angolan rebels carried out numerous attacks in the Kavango region of Namibia, and tourism in the north, already hard hit by the conflict in late 1999 over the secessionist activities in the northeast Caprivi Corridor, virtually dried up. A number of alleged Angolan rebels were detained without trial south of Windhoek.

Reacting to the Zimbabwe land crisis of early 2000, the Namibian parliament approved legislation designed to speed up land redistribution. President Nujoma continued to support his controversial plan for a dam and hydroelectric project on the Kunene River despite new evidence that the Kudu gas field in the south would be a more valuable source of power.

(CHRISTOPHER SAUNDERS)

NAURU

Area: 21.2 sq km (8.2 sq mi)
Population (2000 est.): 11,800
Capital: Government offices in Yaren district
Head of state and government: Presidents Rene Harris and, from April 20, Bernard Dowiyogo

On April 8, 2000, some 4,000 Nauruans voted in a general election. Rene Harris was reelected president by Parliament on April 13, but he resigned on April 20 after failing to form a government. He was replaced on that same day by Bernard Dowiyogo. Shortly after taking office, Dowiyogo vowed to combat money laundering by taking steps to reform and improve Nauru's offshore banking regime. Following reports that criminals were using the country's offshore banking facilities, Dowiyogo stressed that he and his countrymen did not approve of such activities and welcomed assistance from the United States to develop a system that would conform to international standards. Nauru had been identified by the Organisation for Economic Co-operation and Development as a tax haven practicing such harmful tax competition that it would merit international sanctions.

President Dowiyogo became the first head of state to declare support for the independence of the Indonesian province of West Papua (Irian Jaya). He called on members of the Asia-Pacific Parliamentary Union meeting in Nauru in May to support West Papuan independence. (A.R.G. GRIFFITHS)

NEPAL

Area: 147,181 sq km (56,827 sq mi)
Population (2000 est.): 24,702,000
Capital: Kathmandu
Head of state: King Birendra Bir Bikram Shah Dev
Head of government: Prime Ministers Krishna Prasad Bhattarai and, from March 22, Girija Prasad Koirala

Girija Prasad Koirala replaced K.P. Bhattarai as prime minister of Nepal in March, though the Nepali Congress Party (NCP), which held a majority in Parliament, retained control over the central government throughout 2000. The most serious threat to the NCP cabinet came from the bitter infighting between the Koirala, Bhattarai, and Deuba NCP party factions, but they resolved their disputes. The seven other political parties with representation in Parliament were critical of the Koirala government but lacked the power to vote it out of office.

Though posing no threat to the government, perhaps the most serious internal problem in Nepal was the "People's War" that had been launched by a small "Maoist" faction of the communist movement in the midwestern hill area and that since 1996 had resulted in more than 2,000 casualties. In July the government responded to ongoing protests and abolished bonded labour in the nation; some 36,000 serfs were subsequently freed.

Relations with India were the most critical foreign policy issue. Nepal's economy showed few signs of improvement and was heavily dependent upon expanding the Nepal-Indian economic relationship, particularly through cooperative development of Nepal's vast water-storage and hydropower capacities. (LEO E. ROSE)

NETHERLANDS, THE

Area: 41,526 sq km (16,033 sq mi)
Population (2000 est.): 15,896,000
Capital: Amsterdam; seat of government, The Hague
Chief of state: Queen Beatrix
Head of government: Prime Minister Wim Kok

The economic ascent of The Netherlands continued in 2000. The 2001 budget presented by the government in September was the first since 1950 to show a surplus (when budgeted, rather than after the fact, as were those for 1999 and 2000). It featured substantially raised expenditures in such categories as education, research, health care, and infrastructure plus roughly 7 billion guilders ($2.8 billion) for tax relief and 20 billion guilders ($7.9 billion) to pay down the national debt at an accelerated rate.

On May 13 the nation was shocked when the city of Enschede suffered one of the largest disasters in The Netherlands since World War II. An explosion in a fireworks warehouse and the subsequent fire left at least 21 people dead and nearly 1,000 injured. Some 400 houses were destroyed, and many more were damaged. An investigation into the causes was ongoing, but it appeared likely that hazardous materials had been stored on the premises without a permit.

Several politicians attempted during the year to launch a reevaluation of the role of the monarch in Dutch government. It was generally accepted that Queen Beatrix chose not to exert all the influence that she was granted by law, and the questioners suggested that at least this more limited practice should become a matter of legislation and that perhaps the role of the monarch should officially be made purely ceremonial. The proposal was rejected for various reasons, including an unwillingness to change a system that was perceived to be working well, a sense of historical connection with the House of Orange since the 16th century as a symbol of national unity and identity, and the general popularity of the queen and the crown prince.

Two landmark pieces of legislation were passed late in the year. In November the parliament voted to allow physicians to end the lives of seriously ill patients who have asked to die. The Netherlands thus became the first country to legalize mercy killing and doctor-assisted suicide. In December the government gave final approval to laws that allow same-sex couples to marry and to adopt children. Dutch laws on gays were believed to be the most liberal in Europe.

The discovery by British Customs and Excise of 58 deceased illegal migrants in a Dutch truck intensified discussions of the role and treatment of migrants. The related issue of the status of immigrants in The Netherlands and the question of how the nation could be a more fully multicultural society also remained important topics of debate. The government aimed to offer more courses in Dutch language and citizenship to improve immigrants' opportunities for integration.

The year was a significant one for Dutch-Japanese relations. Both countries celebrated the 400th anniversary of the first arrival in Japan of a Dutch trading ship. As The Netherlands, particularly those citizens with ties to Indonesia, also memorialized the 55th anniversary of the Japanese capitulation that ended World War II in Asia, Japanese Prime Minister Yoshiro Mori expressed apologies on behalf of the Japanese people.

Dutch athletes took home 25 medals from the Olympic Games in Sydney, Australia, significantly more than they had on any previous occasion. (*See* BIOGRAPHIES: *Inge de Bruijn*.) The record had been 19 at the Games in Amsterdam in 1928. In October protesters against globalization demonstrated in Amsterdam during a conference there attended by the president of the World Bank. (*See* ECONOMIC AFFAIRS: *Sidebar.*)

(JOLANDA VANDERWAL TAYLOR)

NEW ZEALAND

Area: 270,534 sq km (104,454 sq mi)
Population (2000 est.): 3,835,000
Capital: Wellington
Chief of state: Queen Elizabeth II, represented by Governor-General Sir Michael Hardie-Boys
Head of government: Prime Minister Helen Clark

A bizarre coup engineered in Fiji by the islands' indigenous chiefs against mainly Indians who had gained political footholds dominated headlines in New Zealand from May 19, 2000. Also noteworthy for the nation were elections in the Indonesian territory of Timor that gave power to East Timor separatists. Together, these Pacific eruptions focused attention in New Zealand on the country's long-running debate on defense forces that it might need in the southern oceans. Its new Labour Party government, in a maze of shifting internal political alliances, probably found more voter support for its backing of army reequipment at the expense of the air force and navy spending than it did in any of the other issues. New Zealand soldiers in East Timor, upholding UN intervention alongside the Australians, were the year's main heroes.

The soldiers, however, could do little to dislodge the year's spotlight from a record fall of the New Zealand dollar accompanied by a Reserve Bank caution that the country could either export its way out of trouble or slow down consumption in order to take the pressure off inflation. (The exchange rate stabilized at about NZ$43.01 to the U.S. dollar by December 15.) Business confidence declined accordingly. In response, Helen Clark, in her first full year as prime minister, claimed that the Labour Party had delivered what it promised in regard to fairer labour laws, saving native forests, and scrapping F-16 fighter planes wanted only by the air force.

Clark kept her political alliances intact through a number of crises, the most controversial being the sacking of her minister of Maori affairs for offenses al-

Helen Clark, prime minister of New Zealand, hoists a banner at a parade on March 4 to celebrate Team New Zealand's victory in the America's Cup sailing competition.

William West/AFP Worldwide

leged to have occurred many years earlier. She retained the support of her deputy, Jim Anderton, leader of a party that was itself an alliance of small parties. Other key supporters included Finance Minister Michael Cullen, Foreign Minister Phil Goff, and State Services Minister Trevor Mallard.

Three years after National Party leader Jim Bolger and the balance of power holder at that time, Winston Peters (New Zealand First), took nine weeks to draft a 60-plus-page alliance agreement, Clark and Anderton took only nine days to produce a 1 1/2 page document that would see their alliance through at least its first year. The agreement was based on creation of a standing coalition management committee comprising the two leaders, deputies, and whips. Intrigues were never in short supply during the year, but Clark's inner circle remained staunch.

Commenting on a budget that allocated NZ$55 million (about US$22 million) for research and development and also for economic trade and development and NZ$1.2 billion (about US$480 million) for social policies, the prime minister characterized it as "balanced and moderate," as had been promised. She also reminded New Zealanders that they had voted for a "change of direction, not for a revolution." By October prospects for alliances on legislative initiatives included one with the official opposition National Party on an issue that had been elusive for decades—a parliamentary joint approach to the treatment of retirees in a country top-heavy with the elderly.

Two other women, each of whom moved up from the bench of the High Court, gained prominence in New Zealand during the year. They were Justice Sian Elias, who was appointed chief justice of the court, and Justice Dame Silvia Cartwright, who in April 2001 would become governor-general.

(JOHN A. KELLEHER)

NICARAGUA

Area: 131,812 sq km (50,893 sq mi)
Population (2000 est.): 4,813,000
Capital: Managua
Head of state and government: President Arnoldo Alemán Lacayo

Though gross domestic product growth for 2000 was projected at over 5%, income distribution remained very unequal in Nicaragua. High unemployment among the impoverished majority was only partly offset by an estimated $600 million in remittances from relatives living abroad.

In January members of the opposition Sandinista National Liberation Front (FSLN) and the ruling Constitutionalist Liberal Party (PLC) used their majority in the National Assembly to give final passage to constitutional and electoral-law changes implementing a controversial 1999 "pact" between the leaders of those two ostensibly polar-opposite parties. As a result, they packed the Supreme Court, the Office of the Comptroller General (CGR), and the Supreme Electoral Council (CSE). These and other changes protected the personal interests of FSLN leader Daniel Ortega Saavedra and PLC Pres. Arnoldo Alemán Lacayo and made it very difficult for other parties to qualify to compete in upcoming municipal elections. It was also unlikely that Ortega would be held responsible for sexually abusing his stepdaughter, as had been charged, or that Alemán would again face the type of corruption charges brought by a once-independent CGR in 1999.

Throughout 2000 flagrant corruption by PLC officeholders went essentially unnoticed by the CGR, and the CSE worked to disqualify apparently legitimate registration efforts by other parties. Though the Conservative Party of Nicaragua (PCN) escaped these maneuvers—reportedly at U.S. insistence—Pedro Solorzano, its popular candidate for mayor of Managua, was disqualified through redistricting.

Reaction to the pact and corruption was strong. Ortega and Alemán scored poorly in opinion polls, and the international donor community admonished the government and refused to grant Nicaragua preferential debt-repayment status under the Heavily Indebted Poor Countries initiative for which it was otherwise qualified.

A significant drop in voter participation in the November 5 municipal elections reflected citizen disillusionment. Though FSLN victories in Managua and many other important cities demonstrated the surprising endurance of the party, poor PLC showings and PCN victories in Granada and other localities signaled a desire among the Nicaraguan electorate for change.

(THOMAS W. WALKER)

NIGER

Area: 1,267,000 sq km (489,000 sq mi)
Population (2000 est.): 10,076,000
Capital: Niamey
Head of state and government: President Tandja Mamadou, assisted by Prime Minister Hama Amadou

Niger's financial crisis deepened during 2000, particularly as a result of the sharp declines in world prices for its primary export, uranium. The political turmoil that followed the two military coups in four years did little to facilitate economic recovery. On January 5 Pres. Tandja Mamadou installed a new 24-member government and called for an emergency plan to revitalize the country's economy. Priority was to be given first to the payment of long-standing salary arrears to civil servants, whose frequent strikes had virtually paralyzed the government, and second to the provision of substantial increases in funding for schools and universities. Internal debt repayments were suspended on January 21 and were to be dealt with separately under the new government's budget. On January 30 three civil service unions rejected plans to pay them only basic wages and to withhold supplementary benefits. When the government promised to pay at least one month's salary arrears, teachers returned to work on January 25 after a three-month strike. Truck drivers went on strike in August, demanding higher wages. The strike, which halted the movement of goods in the country for more than two weeks, was settled on September 1.

Foreign aid, cut off since the April 1999 military coup, resumed as donors signaled their approval of the return to civil rule. On July 25 Niger announced that it had received $10 million from Nigeria to help stabilize democracy. The International Monetary Fund agreed in September to provide CFAF 55 billion (about $74 million) for a three-year poverty-reduction program.

Although rainfall was below average during the year, the country managed to have a reasonable harvest. More than half of Niger was already virtual desert, and an additional 30% was at risk unless rapid reforestation took place. (NANCY ELLEN LAWLER)

NIGERIA

Area: 923,768 sq km (356,669 sq mi)
Population (2000 est.): 123,338,000
Capital: Abuja; judiciary and some ministries remain in Lagos, the former capital
Head of state and government: President Olusegun Obasanjo

During 2000 Pres. Olusegun Obasanjo took a variety of steps to secure Nigeria's transition to democracy. Chief among these were reform of the military and the curbing of government corruption. President Obasanjo, himself a former general, continued to force the retirement of officers who had held political positions under previous military governments. In June he signed an anticorruption law that provided a seven-year prison term for officials convicted of corruption. The law also provided for an independent prosecutor should the president or other senior officials be accused of corruption. In August the third-ranked person in government, Senate Pres. Chuba Okadigbo, was impeached following charges that he had been involved in corruption scandals.

In September Obasanjo swore in members of the Independent Corrupt Practices and Other Related Offences Commission, a permanent watchdog group. They were charged with reviewing government contracts signed by the previous military administration and with trying to recover money stolen by former officials. Ongoing investigations had already located more than $1 billion looted by former president Sani Abacha and his family and associates. Some members of the legislature opposed the commission and the new law. They charged that in this and other actions, Obasanjo had centralized too much power in the hands of the executive at the expense of the legislature.

On August 26 U.S. Pres. Bill Clinton arrived in Abuja for a two-day visit. He praised the country's commitment to democracy and pledged additional U.S. support. Coincident with Clinton's visit was the arrival of the first contingent of U.S. troops sent to train Nigerian soldiers for peacekeeping in Sierra Leone. Another promise of the visit was increased economic ties between the two countries. In one manifestation of this, an American company signed deals to rebuild Nigeria's electricity generation and distribution capabilities. Obasanjo's administration made the restoration of Nigeria's crumbling physical infrastructure a priority. In response to chronic electricity shortages in March, the president fired the entire board of the National Electric Power Authority and appointed a supervisory group that reported directly to him.

Relations between Christians and Muslims remained tense as more northern states adopted the Shari'ah; by late 2000 nine states had adopted the Islamic legal code. Although Shari'ah applied only to Muslims, many Christians opposed its imposition. Riots between supporters and opponents of Shari'ah flared in Kaduna and other northern cities during February and March. Official figures put the death toll at 400, although unconfirmed reports claimed that as many as 1,000 died. In October rioting spread to Lagos, where more than 100 were killed. Throughout the year many Christians fled northern areas that had adopted the Shari'ah, while many Muslims moved into these same areas.

Tensions also remained high in the Niger Delta region. Although it was the centre of the country's oil industry, the delta remained among the poorest areas of Nigeria. Late in 1999 Obasanjo had ordered a military crackdown on antigovernment activists there. In September he visited the area and pledged a more equitable distribution of the oil industry's wealth.

During the year there were several serious oil-pipeline explosions in the southern part of the country. These blasts, which killed more than 300 people, were thought to have been caused by people trying to steal fuel by tapping into the pipes.

In August the International Monetary Fund approved a $1 billion standby credit, and the World Bank took steps toward implementing a $3 billion loan. Both the IMF and the World Bank had frozen relations with Nigeria under the country's military rulers.

(MATTHEW A. CENZER)

A Nigerian youth on July 12 flees the site of a deadly oil pipeline explosion, which was triggered when persons intent on stealing fuel ruptured the pipeline near the village of Oviri-Court.

AP/Wide World Photos

NORWAY

Area: 323,758 sq km (125,004 sq mi)
Population (2000 est.): 4,487,000
Capital: Oslo
Chief of state: King Harald V
Head of government: Prime Ministers Kjell Magne Bondevik and, from March 17, Jens Stoltenberg

On March 10, 2000, Prime Minister Kjell Magne Bondevik officially resigned from office, one day after his government lost a vote of confidence in Parliament. Bondevik and his supporters wanted to delay the construction of Norway's first natural gas-fired power plants until new technology could be developed that would reduce air pollution. The opposition, however, favoured immediate construction and won the vote 81–71. One week later Jens Stoltenberg of the Norwegian Labour Party was named the new prime minister.

After some months of weaker performance in 1999, Norway resumed its economic growth in 2000. Gross national product increased about 3% and the unemployment rate stabilized at about 3.2%. Wage negotiations resulted in an average rise of 3.5%. Two public sectors (teachers, nurses) received a 5% increase, after government intervention.

Prices in the global oil market influenced the Norwegian economy and political life in a dramatic way. The spot price per barrel of Brent Blend rose from approximately $25 before midsummer to well above $30 in the autumn, and it remained there. Even if oil production was not increased, government income from the booming oil market climbed much higher than had been predicted in the national budget. In June the nation's offshore oil workers went on strike, demanding the right to retire at 57 rather than 63. After two weeks of lost production, the government ordered the strikers to return to work; they did so but continued to campaign for the lower retirement age.

During the summer and the early autumn, a growing popular discontent expressed itself in polls. The winner was the populist right-wing Progress Party, which obtained up to 35% support. The other political parties lost adherents. The governing Norwegian Labour Party won only about 25% of those polled.

The new Labour government presented its draft budget for the coming year on October 4. Prime Minister Stoltenberg opposed the opinions of the Progress Party, declaring his intention to continue previous policies by demanding higher taxes from industry in order to strengthen the public sector in regard to its support in the areas of health, education, and housing. As predicted by political analysts, the government obtained a majority in Parliament with the support of the Socialist Left Party and the centrist coalition.

In other developments the General Assembly of the United Nations in October chose Norway to be a member of the Security Council for the following two years. In August the government opened the nation's royal palace in Oslo to the public for guided tours.

(GUDMUND SANDVIK)

OMAN

Area: 309,500 sq km (119,500 sq mi)
Population (2000 est.): 2,416,000
Capital: Muscat
Head of state and government: Sultan and Prime Minister Qabus ibn Sa'id

Oman during 2000 held the first-ever direct elections for its parliament (Majlis ash-Shura), increased the number of district representatives from 82 to 83, and doubled the turnout of voters since the previous election. In a first among Oman's fellow Gulf Cooperation Council member nations—Bahrain, Kuwait, Qatar, Saudi Arabia, and the United Arab Emirates—two women were elected.

Economically, Oman benefited immensely from the year's significantly higher international oil prices and the conclusion of lucrative contracts by which it would export substantial quantities of natural gas to India, Japan, South Korea, and Spain. Construction also progressed on the multibillion-dollar seaport and industrial zone being built at Suhar on the Gulf of Oman. The latter development was designed to strengthen the sultanate's already vital strategic importance in terms of the Strait of Hormuz, whose maritime routes Oman controlled and through which the lion's share of the oil traded on international markets was shipped.

By far the greatest breakthrough for Oman's future economic growth was its accession to the 138-member World Trade Organization. Achievement of this long-sought objective and possession of the requisite energy resources to enable it to further the country's industrialization combined to give the nation a much brighter prospect for the near future than it had experienced in quite some time.

(JOHN DUKE ANTHONY)

PAKISTAN

Area: 796,095 sq km (307,374 sq mi), excluding the 84,159-sq km Pakistani-administered portion of Jammu and Kashmir
Population (2000 est.): 141.6 million, including 4 million residents of Pakistani-administered Jammu and Kashmir and excluding 1.1 million Afghan refugees
Capital: Islamabad
Chief of state: President Mohammad Rafiq Tarar
Head of government: Chief Executive Gen. Pervaiz Musharraf

Pakistan began 2000 under a new military leader, Chief Executive Gen. Pervaiz Musharraf, who sought to revamp the country's much-abused political system and impose a new political culture that would result in greater political stability. It was the fourth attempt by a military leader in four decades to restore the rule of law. Musharraf had ousted Prime Minister Mohammad Nawaz Sharif in October 1999 in a bloodless coup d'état.

In late January Chief Justice Saeed uz Zaman was ousted from his post after he refused to take a new oath of allegiance to the military government. Following Zaman's ouster, the remaining judges on the Supreme Court bench legitimized the coup, citing the "doctrine of necessity" and claiming that extraordinary measures were needed to deal with the economic chaos left by the former Sharif administration. The court, however, imposed a three-year deadline for the military to hand over power to a civilian government.

In May, after having refused to set a timetable for his own departure, Musharraf promised to hand over power to a civilian government by late 2002. He also began putting in place what he called the "devolution of power" by trying to build a democracy based on local and municipal elections that would be out of bounds for political parties. Musharraf also announced the lowering of the minimum voting age from 21 to 18 years.

In April an antiterrorism court found Sharif guilty of having conspired to kill passengers on a commercial airline flight that had been carrying Musharraf and others from Colombo, Sri Lanka, to Karachi, Pak., by illegally preventing it from landing until it had virtually no fuel left. Instead of giving Sharif the maximum-sentence death penalty, as was widely expected, the court sentenced him to life imprisonment. The government appealed the sentence, arguing that Sharif deserved the death sentence. He was pardoned on December 10 after paying huge fines and admitting guilt under a compromise proposed by the Saudi royal family. He went into exile in Saudi Arabia.

Political violence continued unabated throughout 2000, though the number of deaths totaled just 200 during the first 10 months of the year. This was a sharp decline from the mid-1990s, when more than 1,000 people were killed each year.

Throughout the year the military government remained badly divided, and Musharraf had problems balancing the demands of the more hawkish generals who were backing him with those of some of the liberal civilians who had been supporting his government. The governors of two of the four provinces—Sindh and North-West Frontier—resigned in May and August, respectively, after having openly quarreled with Musharraf. The military leader's cabinet resembled a revolving door, with ministers arriving only to leave months or even just weeks later.

Relations with India remained frosty, as did relations with the U.S., a former close ally of Pakistan. Nonetheless, U.S. Pres. Bill Clinton visited Pakistan for half a day during his South Asian trip in March, and that in itself was viewed as a diplomatic triumph by Pakistan.

Pakistan's economy remained in a precarious state, with foreign reserves at one point tumbling to under $1 billion, just three weeks' worth of imports. Total foreign debt ballooned to some $38 billion during the year, and the trade deficit rose because of higher oil prices. In November the International Monetary Fund approved a $600 million structural loan to Pakistan that paved the way for negotiations over a $3.5 billion loan package from the IMF, the World Bank, and the Paris Club of creditor nations; also, some $1.5 billion of short-term loans that were coming due were rescheduled. With a bumper cotton crop and an improved wheat crop, Pakistan saw its gross domestic product grow 4.5% during the year. Inflation remained tame at about 4% despite the rising fuel costs. (ASSIF A. SHAMEEN)

AP/Wide World Photos

Ousted Pakistani prime minister Mohammed Nawaz Sharif waves to supporters in March as he is led by police from the Anti-Terrorism Court in Karachi.

PALAU

Area: 488 sq km (188 sq mi)
Population (2000 est.): 18,800
Provisional capital: Koror; a site on Babelthuap was designated to be the permanent capital.
Head of state and government: President Kuniwo Nakamura

Relations between Palau and Taiwan were strengthened in 2000. Taiwan opened an embassy in Palau on March 5, and Taiwan Foreign Minister Chen Chien-jen and Palau State Minister Sabias Anastacio together presided over the opening ceremony. Chen led a delegation of 60 government officials and business leaders who spent four days in Palau planning entrepreneurial enterprises. After the embassy opening Pres. Kuniwo Nakamura accepted an offer to visit Taiwan, and he subsequently held talks with Taiwanese investors in May.

Relations with Japan were also fostered. As part of the Common Agenda (a joint U.S.-Japan project addressing global issues), the Japan International Cooperation Agency spent ¥800 million (about $7.2 million) on a Palau International Coral Reef Center. The facility was expected to carry out ecological observations and to work to preserve coral reefs by examining ways to manage marine resources. In addition, Aoyama Planning Arts, Inc., obtained the support of President Nakamura for a project to link all households on the more than 200 islands constituting Palau with a communications system via a fibre-optic network. (A.R.G. GRIFFITHS)

PANAMA

Area: 75,517 sq km (29,157 sq mi)
Population (2000 est.): 2,823,000
Capital: Panama City
Head of state and government: President Mireya Moscoso

Among the objectives of the government of Panama in 2000 were the efficient management of the Panama Canal, the strengthening of national security, and the reversal of an economic slowdown.

Before control of the canal was returned to Panama on Dec. 31, 1999, many observers had expressed doubts about the Panamanian government's ability to keep party politics out of canal management. Although Pres. Mireya Moscoso either fired or forced the resignation of every major officeholder appointed by the previous administration, the Panama Canal Authority—the agency responsible for the operation of the waterway—remained largely autonomous and fulfilled its mission to run the canal in an orderly manner. Alberto Alemán Zubieta, who had served as administrator of the Panama Canal since 1994, continued to spearhead efforts to modernize the waterway.

In response to the withdrawal of U.S. troops from the isthmus, the government—with the support of the two leading opposition parties—signed a document called Fundamentals of Panamanian Security Policy. The agreement allowed, in case of external threat, for the creation of temporary special police units. Additionally, it allowed Panama to request the assistance of the UN and the Organization of American States to safeguard the Panama Canal.

On September 1 Moscoso admitted to an economic "deceleration." Gross domestic product (GDP) had increased only 3.2% in 1999, which marked the second straight year of slower growth. During the first three months of 2000, GDP grew at a 2.6% rate—an indication that the economy continued to slow. The president of the National Chamber of Commerce predicted that GDP growth would not exceed 2.5% for the entire year. Meanwhile, the unemployment rate remained in double digits. In June the government signed a letter of intent with the International Monetary Fund outlining policies Panama agreed to implement in order to win financial support from the IMF. Panama's commitments included broadening the tax base, outsourcing water company services, revamping the social security system, restructuring two state-owned banks, and freezing government employment.

At a summit meeting in Panama of 19 Latin American countries and Spain and Portugal, four people were arrested after Cuban Pres. Fidel Castro charged that a Cuban exile group was plotting to kill him. (ORLANDO J. PÉREZ)

PAPUA NEW GUINEA

Area: 462,840 sq km (178,704 sq mi)
Population (2000 est.): 4,927,000
Capital: Port Moresby
Chief of state: Queen Elizabeth II, represented by Governor-General Silas Atopare
Head of government: Prime Minister Sir Mekere Morauta

After 15 months of negotiations, the Bougainville affairs minister in the Papua New Guinea cabinet, Sir Michael Somare, agreed to present to the cabinet a radical plan to allow autonomy for Bougainville and to conduct an eventual referendum that could lead to local independence. Subsequently, however, Prime Minister Sir Mekere Morauta ruled out secession or autonomy but assured the island of special status once the Bougainville Revolutionary Army surrendered its arms. In reply the North Solomons province (Bougainville) governor, John Momis, commented that similar situations in the world had taught that no group of rebels would agree to hand in its weapons unless its objectives had been met.

In August Prime Minister Morauta pulled off something of a coup for his administration when the National Parliament voted 79–0 to amend the constitution. The Political Parties and Candidates Integrity Bill tightened controls on party registrations and was designed to stop the swapping of parties by members of Parliament once they had been elected.

Papua New Guinea continued to work hard to cement good relations with China. Foreign Minister John Kaputin held talks with Chinese Vice Pres. Hu Jintao, thanking China for its economic and technological assistance and promising to support China's one-China policy. (A.R.G. GRIFFITHS)

Torsten Blackwood/AFP Worldwide

PARAGUAY

Area: 406,752 sq km (157,048 sq mi)
Population (2000 est.): 5,496,000
Capital: Asunción
Head of state and government: President Luis Ángel González Macchi

In Paraguay the year 2000 began and ended with the country mired in a cycle of political and socioeconomic crises. On February 5 the opposition Authentic Radical Liberal Party (PLRA) opted to leave the national unity governing coalition of Pres. Luis González Macchi. The objective of the coalition was to restore stability and strengthen democracy after the 1999 assassination of Vice Pres. Luis María Argaña. As a result of the PLRA's withdrawal, several cabinet members resigned and the president lost a majority in Congress and the ability to pass much-needed legislation.

Owing to growing political uncertainty and a deteriorating socioeconomic situation, González faced several dangerous challenges that further weakened his government and Paraguayan democracy. On May 18 rebels attempted to overthrow the government. The mutineers were said to have been loyalists of retired general Lino Oviedo, a fugitive wanted in connection with the Argaña assassination. González declared a state of emergency that lasted some 30 days. More than 70 rebels were arrested, including police officers, legislators, and journalists.

The hunt for Oviedo continued until June 11, when Brazilian federal police arrested him in Foz do Iguaçu, Braz. Despite Oviedo's detention, González remained unpopular, enjoying an approval rating of only 11%. Paraguay entered another period of crisis as labour strikes and demonstrations against the government's privatization programs led to violence and a growing distrust of the political elite's ability to govern. In the meantime, Paraguayans prepared to vote in the August vice presidential elections; in an exceedingly close race, PLRA candidate Julio César Franco defeated Colorado Party candidate Felix Argaña—the son of the late vice president—by less than 1%. The PLRA's victory brought an end to the Colorado's 53-year absolute hold on power.

Paraguay's deteriorating economic situation continued to be a source of deep concern. The year's inflation rate increased to 18%. Unemployment also rose to 18%, and the country's poverty level stood at about 65% of the population. By October, Paraguay's economic situation seemed more uncertain after the removal of Federico Zayas, the well-known and internationally respected minister of economy. (FRANK O. MORA)

Autonomy for the island of Bougainville continued to dominate events in Papau New Guinea; in this photograph from 1998, members of the Bougainville Revolutionary Army arrive in Arawa for the signing of the peace treaty.

PERU

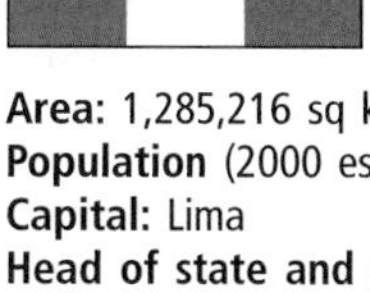

Area: 1,285,216 sq km (496,225 sq mi)
Population (2000 est.): 25,662,000
Capital: Lima
Head of state and government: President Alberto Fujimori, assisted by Prime Minister Alberto Bustamante Belaúnde and, from November 22, interim president Valentin Paniagua, assisted by Prime Minister Javier Pérez de Cuéllar

Few nations in the world underwent as tumultuous and volatile a year as did Peru in 2000. A cascade of events

Anti-Fujimori demonstrations turn violent in Lima, Peru, on October 12.
AP/Wide World Photos

threatened the very fabric of Peru's political system.

In late 1999 Alberto Fujimori, the incumbent president who had been elected to two consecutive five-year terms, announced his decision to seek a third term. The decision provoked considerable controversy, since Peru's 1993 constitution allowed a sitting president to seek immediate reelection only once. In early 2000 Fujimori forced a favourable ruling on the matter through the Constitutional Court and then began his bid for reelection.

Alejandro Toledo, an American-educated business school professor and former World Bank official, emerged as Fujimori's major opponent. During his campaign Toledo railed against Fujimori's strong-arm methods and his questionable search for a third term. On April 9, in the first round of elections, Fujimori finished on top with almost half the popular vote. There were, however, widespread allegations of voting fraud, and domestic and international pressures were sufficient to force a runoff a few weeks later. To protest the presence of fraud in the first round, Toledo announced that he would not participate in the second. The result was that Fujimori swept into office with minimal opposition; his party also won a plurality in the Congress, but not the outright majority the president sought.

When inauguration day arrived on July 28, widespread demonstrations occurred in Lima, sparked largely by outrage at Fujimori's undemocratic actions and leading to much damage to the city's downtown. Nevertheless, Fujimori took office again—but this time only briefly.

In September two scandals shook the Fujimori administration to its roots. The first involved a murky arms-smuggling scheme whereby Peruvian military officers purchased thousands of automatic weapons from Jordan and then sold them to Colombian guerrillas for a profit. The second concerned a videotape broadcast on Lima television; the tape seemed to show an opposition congressman accepting a $15,000 bribe to switch his vote to Fujimori. Both of these events implicated Vladimiro Montesinos, who had played a critical role in the Fujimori administration as head of Peru's intelligence service.

These two events persuaded Fujimori to call for new presidential and congressional elections and to disband the nation's intelligence network. Montesinos, in the meantime, first fled Peru then returned, and then fled again. At the year's end he was still missing. In November Fujimori announced from Japan that he was resigning as president and that he would not return to Peru. In his absence Valentin Paniagua was named interim president until elections could be held in April 2001. Peru's national legislature opened several investigations into charges against both Fujimori and Montesinos.

The uproar from these developments highlighted several weaknesses of Peru's political system. The nation's political parties were impotent; all potential candidates for the new elections ran on the strength of their personalities. The military was apparently in disarray; the navy and air force were reportedly against any sort of asylum or amnesty for Montesinos, while certain clusters of officers in the army (presumably those who owed their position to Montesinos) made it clear that they rigidly opposed Montesinos's arrest or trial. Nevertheless, the military showed no sign of seizing power. The U.S. as well as the Organization of American States exerted considerable pressure, first on Fujimori to restore democracy. Following his resignation, both supported Paniagua's interim government. Meanwhile, confidence in the economy weakened, as domestic and international investors showed unwillingness to invest new money, and a growing deficit meant that Peru might well have trouble in raising new international loans.

(HENRY A. DIETZ)

PHILIPPINES

Area: 300,076 sq km (115,860 sq mi)
Population (2000 est.): 76,320,000
Capital: Quezon City (designated national government centre and the location of the lower house of the legislature and some ministries); many government offices are in Manila or suburbs
Head of state and government: President Joseph Estrada

Pres. Joseph Estrada was impeached by the Philippines House of Representatives on Nov. 13, 2000, and the Senate began his trial on December 7. He was accused of bribery, corruption, betrayal of public trust, and violation of the constitution. The charges arose from accusations by Luis Singson, a provincial governor, who said that he had given Estrada $11 million in payoffs from illegal gambling and diverted tobacco taxes in return for promises of political favours. Estrada denied the charges. Vice Pres. Gloria Macapagal Arroyo joined with former presidents Corazon Aquino and Fidel Ramos in asking Estrada to resign, and nationwide demonstrations called for his resignation. Counterdemonstrations, however, revealed continued popularity for the former tough-guy movie star.

Estrada's trial capped a tumultuous year in which the Philippines struggled with poverty, rebellion, and lawlessness amid accusations of corruption, cronyism, and economic failure. Finance Minister Edgardo Espiritu resigned on January 5, criticizing what he called the government's "culture of corruption." Aprodocio Laquian, Estrada's chief of staff, said in March that the president would hold drunken parties with friends who were called advisers and issue presidential decrees, which would later have to be countermanded. Laquian was forced to resign.

Several business deals created public perceptions of governmental favouritism for Estrada's cronies. These, added to economic troubles, a stock market scandal, and guerrilla challenges, discouraged the foreign investment that was needed to help the economy grow. Estrada said in January that he would not pursue controversial constitutional changes to seek more investment by expanding foreigners' ownership rights. By September foreign investors had withdrawn $390 million from financial markets. Unemployment was high, and economic growth, at one of the lowest rates in the region, was insufficient to raise the rapidly increasing population from poverty.

Five days of typhoon rains caused a 15-m (50-ft) high mountain of garbage to collapse into a squatter community on July 11. More than 215 bodies were found in the area known as the Promised Land outside Manila, where 80,000 people earned their living by scavenging garbage.

The southern Philippines was disturbed throughout 2000 by guerrilla warfare and kidnapping. Some Muslim rebels fought for independence from the predominately Roman Catholic nation, while other Muslims seemed to be primarily bandits. In addition, the Communist New People's Army made sporadic attacks.

On April 23 a Muslim extremist group called Abu Sayyaf kidnapped 21 people, mostly Western tourists, from a Malaysian resort and took them to Jolo Island. Some journalists and Christian evangelists who went to the bandits' jungle camp to talk and pray with them were also seized. The Philippine government had ransomed earlier prisoners but refused the bandits' high demands. Libya then negotiated the release of the Westerners by September 9, reportedly for $1 million each. An American convert to Islam went to talk to the Jolo bandits on August 29 and was taken hostage. As various Abu Sayyaf bands seized more hostages, the government lost its patience, and on September 16 it sent 4,000 troops to attack the Jolo bandits. Some of the Abu Sayyaf members surrendered, but others continued to hold prisoners as they eluded troops for weeks.

A larger Islamic group, the Moro Islamic Liberation Front (MILF), continued a fight for independence that had taken an estimated 120,000 lives over three decades. After the most severe fighting between Muslim separatists and the Philippine army in 25 years, the army captured the MILF's headquarters at Camp Abubakar on Mindanao Island on July 9. Salamat Hashim, the exiled MILF leader, then called for a holy war against the government. Armed men later killed 21 Christians in a Mindanao village. (HENRY S. BRADSHER)

POLAND

Area: 313,027 sq km (120,860 sq mi)
Population (2000 est.): 38,655,000
Capital: Warsaw
Chief of state: President Aleksander Kwasniewski
Head of government: Prime Minister Jerzy Buzek

Poland experienced considerable political ferment in 2000. The two-party "Solidarity coalition" that had governed since 1997 collapsed in June, leaving a fragile and increasingly ineffectual minority government, headed by the Solidarity Electoral Action (AWS), to spend the rest of 2000 clinging to power. The AWS chairman, Marian Krzaklewski, suffered a stinging defeat in presidential elections in October, finishing third to the popular incumbent, Aleksander Kwasniewski. Although he faced 11 challengers, Kwasniewski triumphed easily in the first round of the balloting, with 53.9% of the vote. Krzaklewski finished third, with 15.6% of the vote, behind Andrzej Olechowski, a charismatic former foreign and finance minister, who won 17.3% despite running without party backing.

The infighting that caused the collapse of the ruling coalition bolstered the popularity of the main opposition party, the ex-communist Democratic Left Alliance (SLD). Buoyed by Kwasniewski's victory, the SLD was garnering about 50% support in public opinion polls in the later months of 2000. As their popularity declined, both the AWS and its erstwhile partner, the centrist Freedom Union (UW), suffered leadership crises. Krzaklewski's refusal to step down after his election defeat prompted a rebellion among the constituent parties that made up the AWS, and although Krzaklewski ultimately agreed to surrender the chairmanship at a future date, the party remained in disarray at year's end.

The UW experienced its share of turmoil, too. Having walked out of the government to protest economic reform reversals, the party lost its visibility, and its approval rating tumbled. The UW opted not to run a candidate in the presidential elections, and most of its supporters backed Olechowski. Both decisions were the work of Leszek Balcerowicz, the hard-nosed UW chairman and architect of Poland's free-market economic reforms. As disappointment with his leadership spread, Balcerowicz seized an opportunity to make a graceful exit from politics. Hanna Gronkiewicz-Waltz, the central bank president who had guided monetary policy since 1992, announced unexpectedly in October that she was stepping down to take a prestigious post at the European Bank for Reconstruction and Development. With a nod to the broad consensus that had long protected economic policy from political infighting, the president nominated Balcerowicz to take the helm at the central bank, and he was confirmed on December 22.

The AWS supported Balcerowicz's candidacy, but at a price. In return, the UW reportedly agreed to support the minority government's draft budget in March 2001, when it was expected to come to a vote. By depriving the president of a pretext to call early elections, passage of the 2001 budget would allow the AWS cabinet to serve out its full term, to September 2001. This bargain would also give the UW time to regroup under its new leader, former foreign minister Bronislaw Geremek, before fresh elections, but it was eagerly seized upon by the SLD as evidence of power-hungry maneuvering.

Although many economic decisions were hostage to similar political considerations, the Polish economy remained on a steady reform course in 2000. Growth was strong in the first half, but steep interest-rate rises, imposed to fight a current-account deficit that peaked at 8.3% of gross domestic product in March before falling back to around 7% at year's end, cut consumption and investment spending sharply. Although the growth rate was slowing as the year drew to a close, Polish GDP was expected to have risen by at least 4.5% overall in 2000. Privatization and restructuring were pushed ahead in many sectors, and investors were invited to buy their way into the power industry. The government concluded the largest privatization deal in Eastern Europe so far with the $4.3 billion sale of a 35% stake in TPSA, the former telecoms monopoly, to a consortium headed by France Télécom.

European Union membership remained the anchor of Polish foreign policy in 2000. A special parliamentary committee was formed to speed through EU-standard legislation. In its annual progress report, the European Commission hailed a "marked acceleration" in Poland's adoption of EU law and regulations. An EU summit in Nice, France, in December chose to grant Poland 27 votes—on a par with Spain—in the Council of Ministers when it joined the EU. (LOUISA VINTON)

PORTUGAL

Area: 92,365 sq km (35,662 sq mi)
Population (2000 est.): 10,005,000
Capital: Lisbon
Chief of state: President Jorge Sampaio
Head of government: Prime Minister António Guterres

Portugal's government came under pressure in 2000 as an unpopular decision in the spring to raise fuel prices by more than 10%, because of the rise in global market prices for oil, sparked popular backlash. Prime Minister António Guterres saw his popularity decline for the first time since his first electoral victory in 1995, and the government went through a series of reshuffles in an effort to maintain credibility.

Crime was a major source of discontent, and sentiment that Portugal was becoming increasingly unsafe led to the dismissal of Internal Administration Minister Fernando Gomes in September on the heels of apparent gang violence that made headlines during the summer. Opposition parties took advantage of the government's fragility to step up their efforts to trigger new elections, but Guterres's Socialist Party—one seat short of an absolute majority in the legislature—faced down a no-confidence motion and appeared likely to pass its belt-tightening 2001 budget without being forced into an early vote.

Along with the short-lived gang crime wave, which involved large groups of youths wreaking havoc on commuter train lines and robbing gasoline (petrol) stations, the country was also shocked by a gas attack on a Lisbon nightclub that panicked patrons and sparked a stampede, killing seven. The nightclub was popular with immigrants from the former colony of Angola, though investigators concluded that revenge rather than racism was behind the deadly attack. The victims included six Angolans and a Spanish tourist.

On the economic front, Portugal continued to outpace the European average for gross domestic product (GDP) growth, with the economy set to increase by more than 3.5%. Inflation, however, remained a worry, driven by falling unemployment, low interest rates, the rise in gasoline prices, and weakness of the euro. Construction of stadiums and other infrastructure for the Euro 2004 soccer championship began, and investment related to these projects was expected to add 1.5% to Portugal's GDP over the next three years.

Portugal was in the European spotlight in the first half of 2000, as it held the rotating presidency of the European Union (EU). The Portuguese presidency was praised for the informal Lisbon summit in March that formulated an Internet and e-commerce strategy for the 15-member bloc, highlighted the importance of sustainable growth and education, and made progress toward further liberalization of a number of market sectors in Europe, including telecommunications and energy. At the final EU summit in Santa Maria da Feira, near Porto, in June, the heads of state were able to hammer out a rough agreement on plans for future tax harmonization in the union.

The Portuguese national soccer team's stunning upset of England in an early game of the Euro 2000 championship and solid play throughout the series raised hopes of a cup for the underdogs, though they finally ran aground in a thrilling semifinal game against the eventual series winner, France. The defeat was softened somewhat by news that Luis Figo, a key player for the Portuguese national team, was the focus of the most expensive transfer ever in soccer history, moving from Barcelona to Real Madrid for the princely sum of $56 million.

As 2000 drew to an end, the focus of the nation turned again to the northern city of Porto, which was to be one of Europe's culture capitals, along with Rotterdam, Neth., in 2001. Infrastructure investment, which was focused on preparing the city for the related events as well as improving many urban zones, was expected to total some €212 million (about $170 million). (ERIK T. BURNS)

QATAR

Area: (including Hawar Islands, also claimed by Bahrain) 11,437 sq km (4,416 sq mi)
Population (2000 est.): 599,000
Capital: Doha
Head of state and government: Emir Sheikh Hamad ibn Khalifah ath-Thani, assisted by Prime Minister Sheikh Abdullah ibn Khalifah ath-Thani

Qatar in 2000 continued to make major inroads into the international energy industry as the world's fastest-growing exporter of natural gas. During visits to China, France, Germany, India, South Korea, Thailand, and the United Kingdom, Emir Sheikh Hamad ibn Khalifah ath-Thani concluded memo-

AFP Worldwide

Sheikh Hamad ibn Khalifah ath-Thani (right), emir of Qatar, accompanies Palestinian leader Yasir Arafat upon Arafat's arrival in Doha on November 11 to attend the Organization of the Islamic Conference summit meeting.

randums of understanding with the governments of each of those major energy-importing countries. (*See* BIOGRAPHIES.) Coupled to the assets imbedded in its prodigious and extraordinarily low-cost gas reserves, the agreements furthered Qatar's potential, in partnership with some of the world's leading corporations, to become the engine of regional economic integration in the Persian Gulf.

Qatar also played important roles in several high-profile OPEC summits that addressed the implications of spiraling international oil prices. At the summit in September, Qatar was a major force in enabling the members to achieve an agreement on a manageable price range for oil that would satisfy producers as well as consumers. The successful demarcation of the border between Qatar and Saudi Arabia was an achievement of major international significance.

(JOHN DUKE ANTHONY)

ROMANIA

Area: 237,500 sq km (91,699 sq mi)
Population (2000 est.): 22,435,000
Capital: Bucharest
Chief of state: Presidents Emil Constantinescu and, from December 21, Ion Iliescu
Head of government: Prime Ministers Mugur Isarescu and, from December 28, Adrian Nastase

The fractious coalition of centre-right and moderate left parties in office since 1996 gained a new prime minister at the end of 1999. When he took office, Mugur Isarescu, governor of the central bank since 1990, had only a few months to draw up an economic strategy for the period 2000–06 in order to prepare Romania for accession to the European Union (EU). Isarescu won praise for persuading the Social Democractic Party of Romania (PDSR), to endorse a policy committing Romania to a steady shift toward a market economy. Enjoying a runaway lead in the opinion polls, the PDSR was committed to an economic strategy drawn up in conjunction with officials from the EU, World Bank, and the International Monetary Fund (IMF) at variance with its own left-wing instincts.

A modest economic recovery after three years of recession was retarded by the most severe drought in 50 years and a consequent poor harvest, necessitating costly cereal imports. With up to 40% of the population suffering from absolute poverty, Romanians exhibited strong disillusionment with the major parties. Many now viewed them as a separate caste whose primary aim was to protect special corporate interests rather than the common good. A disenchanted Pres. Emil Constantinescu, who had failed to fulfill his reformist agenda because of obstruction from the courts, the bureaucracy, and many of his nominal supporters, announced on July 17 that he would not run for a second term.

Prime Minister Isarescu tried and failed to rally the divided centre-right when he ran as a candidate for president. On November 26, in simultaneous presidential and parliamentary elections, the PDSR triumphed. It won a near majority of seats and its leader, 71-year-old Ion Iliescu, took office for his third term as president on December 21. The most attention was paid, however, to the remarkable success of the Greater Romania Party (PRM), which reconciled the extremes of left and right and had its roots in the pre-1989 dictatorship of Nicolae Ceausescu. Corneliu Vadim Tudor, one of the most skillful demagogues in Eastern Europe, secured 30% of the vote in the presidential poll, and his party rose from nowhere to acquire 25% of parliamentary seats.

Adrian Nastase, installed as prime minister on December 28, was a 50-year-old modernizer. He signed a pact with the centre-right to oppose extremism and pass vital reforms, a rare example of cooperation between the mainstream parties. Nastase needed backing from the EU and IMF for a strategy that involved dismantling unproductive parts of the state-led economy while providing a social safety net for millions of Romanians likely to be affected by industrial closures. (TOM GALLAGHER)

RUSSIA

Area: 17,075,400 sq km (6,592,800 sq mi)
Population (2000 est.): 146,001,000
Capital: Moscow
Chief of state: President Vladimir Putin (acting until May 7)
Head of government: Prime Ministers Vladimir Putin and, from May 7 (acting until May 17), Mikhail Kasyanov

Domestic Affairs. Pres. Boris Yeltsin surprised the world on New Year's Eve 1999 by resigning six months before his official term was due to expire. Prime Minister Vladimir Putin, a former career KGB officer, was named acting president and held both posts until a presidential election at the end of March. Putin was elected in the first round of that election with 53% of the vote. International monitors gave the ballot a positive report while conceding that irregularities had taken place. Later in the year a Moscow newspaper published evidence supporting allegations of substantial vote rigging.

Following his inauguration in May, Putin appointed former finance minister Mikhail Kasyanov to head the government. Putin declared his priorities to be reestablishing a strong state, restoring law and order, and relaunching economic reform. His election was welcomed by world leaders, who expressed hopes that it would mark the beginning of a period of stability and prosperity for Russia as a whole.

Putin provided few clues as to what specific foreign and domestic policies he intended to pursue. By contrast with the drift of the late Yeltsin years, however, the new president's drive and determination were palpable. Putin's first move was to reassert central control over Russia's wayward regions and thereby turn the country into "a single economic and legal space." Under a presidential decree issued in May, Russia's 89 republics and regions were divided into seven new "federal districts." Each was to be headed by a plenipotentiary representative appointed by the president. Many of the powers that regional governors had accumulated during the Yeltsin decade were transferred to these presidential representatives. Security and law enforcement were to be key elements of their work. This was underscored by the fact that five of the seven new appointees came from the army or security services. The presidential representatives were granted ex officio membership in the Security Council, an executive body responsible directly to the president and headed by Putin's most trusted associate, Sergey Ivanov. Under Putin's leadership, this body acquired important new policy-making responsibilities.

Next, Putin relieved the governors of the right to sit in the Federation Council, the upper house of the Russian parliament. This reduced regional leaders' influence over federal policy and stripped them of their immunity from criminal prosecution. Moreover, Putin introduced legislation empowering the president to dismiss democratically elected governors and regional legislatures if they violated federal law. Putin's government rescinded tax concessions that Yeltsin had granted to some of Russia's most powerful regions and announced its intention to adjust in 2001, in the centre's favour, the division of tax revenues between the federal government and the regions.

The governors resisted, but Putin was able to push his legislation through the lower house of the parliament, the State Duma, thanks to the pro-government majority the Kremlin had commanded since the December 1999 parliamentary elections. This enabled Putin effectively to rewrite the constitution. His purpose was to assert presidential control not only over the regional barons but also over the regionally deployed officials of the federal government, who were similarly perceived as having escaped central control during the Yeltsin years.

Putin then began to implement his vow to "liquidate the oligarchs as a class," by which he meant ousting Russia's most powerful financiers and media tycoons from the corridors of power. First the tax police moved against Vladimir Gusinsky, founder of Media-Most, a private media holding that controlled the NTV independent television channel. NTV had criticized several of Putin's policies—in particular, the conduct of the military campaign in Chechnya (*see* below). Gusinsky was briefly imprisoned on charges of embezzlement; he subsequently agreed to relinquish control of NTV and left the country. Next came the turn of Boris Berezovsky, controller of Russia's most widely watched TV channel, Russian Public Television (ORT). (*See* BIOGRAPHIES.) Berezovsky claimed to have been threatened with imprisonment if he did not turn ORT over to the state.

The Kremlin denied any attempt to muzzle the press, but there was widespread concern not only over the future of NTV and ORT but also over the February disappearance, arrest, and subsequent trial (on charges of possessing a false identity document) of journalist Andrey Babitsky, whose coverage of the Chechen conflict for the U.S.-funded Radio Liberty had infuriated the Kremlin. Alarm bells rang in both Russia and the West when, in September, Putin endorsed a new information security doctrine that implied, among other things, the need to restrict access by the Russian public to foreign news media.

The federal government struggled throughout the year to assert control over the breakaway Republic of Chechnya. Allegations of human rights violations by Russian troops abounded and provoked criticism from the international community. Casualties mounted on both sides. The rebels sustained heavy losses when they were forced out of the lowland areas of the republic in the late winter, which prompted Moscow to declare that the military phase of the "antiterrorist" campaign was over. All that remained, the government claimed, was a mopping-up operation. The rebels had merely retreated to the mountains, however; from there they launched a guerrilla campaign to which Russian forces were ill-equipped to respond. In June Putin appointed Chechen Mufti Akhmed Kadyrov interim head of administration in the republic, but Moscow's failure to provide funding for postwar reconstruction prevented Kadyrov from winning the support of the local population. Nevertheless, the military campaign remained popular with the Russian population, and there was no sign that Putin was under pressure to negotiate a political settlement with the rebels.

August saw the sinking in the Barents Sea of the nuclear submarine *Kursk* with the loss of all 118 crew members aboard; the tragedy remained unexplained at year's end. The prevarication with which the Russian naval authorities and the presidential administration responded to the tragedy provoked criticism at home and abroad. Also in August a terrorist bomb attack in central Moscow killed 12 people; shortly afterward three people lost their lives when the Ostankino television tower, a Moscow landmark, was swept by fire. In a controversial move, the parliament voted in December to adopt as Russia's national anthem the music—though not the words—of the anthem of the U.S.S.R.

The Economy. Production continued to grow in 2000. Analysts began to question their original assumption that recorded growth was merely a devaluation-induced "dead cat bounce." Perhaps Russia was beginning to experience a sustainable increase in output rather than just a short-lived recovery dependent on the onetime effect of the massive August 1998 ruble devaluation combined with record-high world oil prices.

It was certainly the case that, from early 1999 to early 2000, all the main components of final demand were increasing. The growth of exports and of import-substituting production for the home market could be attributed to devaluation. After the initial shock effects of the August 1998 devaluation had worn off, however, there was also growth in household consumption, domestic investment, and government spending on goods and services—all in real (inflation-adjusted) terms. Enterprise profits grew substantially, which allowed government tax revenue to increase. Moreover, government revenue growth exceeded the requirements of debt service—hence the improvement in the federal government's budgetary balance and the scope for real growth in government spending.

Skeptics pointed out that the structural reforms that were needed in 1998 were still not under way two years later. In the absence of such reforms, the argument went, long-term growth averaging more than 2–3% a year was simply not feasible. Meanwhile, the favourable effects of devaluation were wearing off as the exchange rate stabilized around 27–29 rubles to the U.S. dollar, but Russian inflation exceeded that of Russia's trade partners; by mid-2000 there were signs that investment growth was faltering and inflation accelerating.

The inflation problem was hard for Russian policy makers to deal with. Russia's merchandise trade surplus continued to be huge; it was running at an annual rate of more than $50 billion in the first half of the year. The current account surplus was somewhat smaller but still massive; net capital flows did not offset it. Foreign exchange reserves grew, therefore, and that increased the monetary base. The inflationary pressure exerted by the growth of reserves could not be neutralized by the sale of government paper (bonds and treasury bills) because the treasury-bill market had collapsed in the 1998 financial crisis. The running of a budgetary surplus (excluding interest payments) was helping to constrain aggregate demand; nonetheless, inflation was tending to rise, and the government and the central bank could not easily contain it.

There were favourable considerations to which the more sanguine commentators could (and did) point. Most notably, the Putin administration showed signs of serious reform intentions. During the summer the parliament approved the government's proposal to institute a flat 13% income tax. The move was hailed as a first step toward reducing Russia's massive shadow economy. In June the government approved a package of reform plans. These included an action plan to the end of 2001 and a framework plan to 2010. The latter envisaged growth in gross domestic product of at least 5% a year over the following decade. The language on reforms was clearly liberal—there should be a level playing field for businesses, with government intervention reduced and barriers to competition minimized—and tax and land reform were high on the agenda. Three leading officials were serious reformers: German Gref, economy minister and the main author of the reform plan; presidential adviser Andrey Illarionov; and Finance Minister Aleksey Kudrin. Doubts centred, however, on the ability of government reformers to implement their plans. Prime Minister Kasyanov was regarded as less committed to reform; government administrative capacity was weak; corruption was pervasive; and the resistance of powerful interest groups—comprising, above all, people who had done well out of incomplete reform—would have to be overcome.

One impediment to the implementation of reform had been the power of regional governors. Most government intervention in the fate of businesses in Russia—usually propping up failing concerns—came from regional and local levels. It was above all at these levels that payment arrears and the use of barter and money surrogates had been promoted. It was also the case that effective tax reform required a separation of subnational from national tax bases, a change that could not easily be negotiated with powerful governors. Putin's assault on the powers of regional leaders was therefore expected to assist the process of reform. Even if the main motive was simply to increase Putin's own power, the president's downgrading of the governors would reduce their capacity for economic mischief.

It was less clear whether the same could be said of Putin's assault on the oligarchs. Improved tax compliance was certainly one of Russia's needs. But enforcement by various more or less forceful means had been tried from 1997 with little effect. It was also unclear whether Putin would continue the tradition of regarding some oligarchs as "more equal than others"—in short, of being in cahoots with a few financially powerful cronies. For these reasons the prospects of real progress with structural reforms remained unclear. If enough Russian businesspeople came to think that the economy would continue to grow strongly, their expectations could become self-fulfilling. In that sense it was dispiriting that capital flight showed little sign of diminishing.

Western support remained on hold. Russia's policy of defaulting on inherited Soviet-era external debt while maintaining the service of post-Soviet debt appeared to be working. In February provisional agreement was reached in the London Club with Western banks and hedge funds holding Soviet-era commercial debt; a third of that debt was to be written off and the rest upgraded into long-term Eurobonds. Progress was harder in the Paris Club, where Russia was negotiating a restructuring of Soviet-era debt to Western governments; Germany, by far the largest official creditor, opposed a write-off. There might have been progress with Paris Club debt restructuring had the International Monetary Fund given its approval to Russian economic policy. An IMF delegation visited Moscow in November, however, without reaching an agreement on structural reforms to be carried out. Meanwhile, Russia serviced the rest of its debt from its large current-account surplus, largely without new credits from the IMF or other multilateral or bilateral official sources (the exception being some World Bank disbursements of project loans). Agreement on a new deal with the IMF, providing a kind of official Western endorsement of Putin's economic policies, remained to be concluded.

Foreign Policy. Putin embarked on a busy program of foreign meetings and visits aimed at projecting Russia's interests in an assertive and energetic manner. The first half of the year saw him repairing the relations with the West that had broken down following NATO's 1999 military intervention in Yugoslavia. In February NATO Secretary-General Lord Robertson visited Moscow to put relations with the alliance back on track. This included reviving meetings of the NATO-Russia Permanent Joint Council

ITAR-TASS/AFP Worldwide

Russian Pres. Vladimir Putin (right) shakes hands with North Korea's chief of state, Kim Jong Il, at the airport in Pyongyang on July 19.

and improving cooperation within the Kosovo Force.

Putin's position was bolstered in April by the Russian parliament's ratification of the START-II nuclear arms reduction treaty just as he set out for his first foreign trip, to Minsk and London. Though the parliament also ratified the Comprehensive Test Ban Treaty, Russia remained strongly opposed to U.S. proposals to amend the Anti-Ballistic Missile Treaty in order to deploy nuclear missile defense. The Parliamentary Assembly of the Council of Europe suspended the Russian delegation's voting rights in protest against Russia's conduct of its military campaign in Chechnya.

The second half of the year saw the Putin leadership balance its contact with the West by consolidating Russia's ties with China and India as well as Soviet-era friends such as Vietnam, Mongolia, and Cuba. Overtures were also made to Japan while, in July, Putin made a landmark visit to North Korea. He returned with a proposal whereby Pyongyang would relinquish its ballistic missile development program in return for access to foreign space-rocket technology; from Moscow's standpoint this had the advantage of undermining the U.S. case for nuclear missile defense. In October Putin and the leaders of Kazakhstan, Kyrgyzstan, Tajikistan, Belarus, and Armenia signed a framework agreement for the deployment of joint forces in the face of the perceived threat of Islamic extremism in Central Asia. In December Putin traveled to Canada, where he received additional support from Prime Minister Jean Chrétein for the Russian position on defensive missile issues.

Putin pursued the reform of Russia's bloated armed forces, ordering deep cuts in both nuclear and conventional forces despite strong opposition from the military. Institutional tensions erupted in July between backers of Russia's strategic missile troops and those arguing for a shift of funding to the conventional forces.

(ELIZABETH TEAGUE)

RWANDA

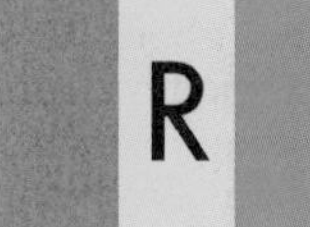

Area: 26,338 sq km (10,169 sq mi)
Population (2000 est.): 7,229,000
Capital: Kigali
Head of state and government: President Pasteur Bizimungu, in conjunction with Vice President Maj. Gen. Paul Kagame and Prime Ministers Pierre-Célestin Rwigema and, from March 8, Bernard Makuza; from March 24, President Maj. Gen. Paul Kagame (acting until April 22), assisted by Prime Minister Bernard Makuza

On March 23, 2000, Pres. Pasteur Bizimungu, a politically moderate Hutu, resigned. He had quarreled with the Tutsi-dominated ruling party, the Rwandan Patriotic Front, over several cabinet appointments. On April 22 the National Assembly confirmed Vice Pres. Maj. Gen. Paul Kagame as the new president. Some observers feared that the appointment of Kagame, a Tutsi, would weaken Rwanda's fragile ethnic power-sharing arrangement.

Rwanda during the year continued its military involvement in the Democratic Republic of the Congo. Continuing a pattern begun in 1999, Rwandan and Ugandan troops clashed around the Congolese city of Kisangani in May and June. Both countries massed troops along their common border but pulled them back after a series of high-level meetings defused but did not resolve the crisis. Rwanda and Uganda supported different rebel groups fighting against Congo Pres. Laurent Kabila. In June the UN Security Council passed a resolution demanding that both Rwanda and Uganda withdraw their forces.

Trials of those allegedly involved in the 1994 genocide continued throughout the year, both in Rwandan courts and at the UN International Criminal Tribunal for Rwanda in Arusha, Tanz. In February the Rwandan government announced that it would resume cooperation with the UN court. Rwanda severed the relationship in 1999 over the release on procedural grounds of a prominent genocide suspect. In August the UN tribunal began hearing the case of three former Rwandan media officials. They were accused of having used newspapers and radio to incite ethnic hatred. A Rwandan court acquitted Roman Catholic Bishop Augustin Misago of charges stemming from the genocide. His arrest in 1999 had strained Rwanda's relations with the Vatican. In late October former prime minister Jean Kambanda tried to revoke a guilty plea he had entered in 1998, but his motion was rejected by the UN tribunal.

In a sign of their improving relationship, Rwanda concluded a number of financial agreements with the European Union. These included grants and loans valued at nearly €160 million (about $140 million) and targeted at infrastructure and poverty-reduction programs. In October the country became eligible for preferential trade relations with the U.S. under recently enacted Africa-trade legislation.

(MATTHEW A. CENZER)

Rwandan Patriotic Army troops gather in Kigali on August 8.

Emmanuel Goujon/AFP Worldwide

SAINT KITTS AND NEVIS

Area: 269 sq km (104 sq mi)
Population (2000 est.): 38,800
Capital: Basseterre
Chief of state: Queen Elizabeth II, represented by Governor-General Cuthbert Sebastian
Head of government: Prime Minister Denzil Douglas

The St. Kitts-Nevis Labour Party (SKNLP), led by Denzil Douglas, made a clean sweep of all eight St. Kitts seats in the March 2000 general election for the National Assembly. The Nevis-based parties retained three seats—two for the Concerned Citizens Movement and one for the Nevis Reformation Party.

In St. Kitts the People's Action Movement (PAM), which had held one seat in the previous National Assembly, was eliminated from the parliament. The PAM had spent 15 years in government prior to the 1995 election, when the SKNLP was returned to power. A commission of inquiry had been looking into Finance Ministry operations during the PAM's tenure in office and found PAM administrations culpable in several respects, including having guaranteed a bank loan of $25.3 million to a private company that had proposed to establish an intra-Caribbean hydrofoil service, which unceremoniously collapsed a year after trial runs had begun.

In October PAM leader Kennedy Simmonds retired and was succeeded by former party chairman Lindsay Grant, who pledged to press the government for electoral reform.

(DAVID RENWICK)

SAINT LUCIA

Area: 617 sq km (238 sq mi)
Population (2000 est.): 157,000
Capital: Castries
Chief of state: Queen Elizabeth II, represented by Governor-General Pearlette Louisy
Head of government: Prime Minister Kenny Anthony

In March 2000 a bipartisan Constituency Boundaries Commission recommended that the number of constituencies in St. Lucia be increased from 17 to 19 before the next general election in 2002.

Following unflattering observations about St. Lucia's financial services sector from the Financial Stability Forum and the Organisation for Economic Co-operation and Development (OECD), the government moved in September to improve the country's offshore-banking image. St. Lucia requested that the International Monetary Fund make an "assessment" of the supervisory regime for offshore activities. Phillip Pierre, the minister for financial services, hoped that the IMF findings would "throw a spanner in the work of the OECD," which, he believed, was trying to "cripple the financial services sector in the Caribbean."

Vaughn Lewis, leader of the opposition United Workers' Party, resigned unexpectedly in early October. On December 31 two men attacked worshippers in a church in Castries, killing an Irish nun. They said they had been sent by God to fight corruption in the Roman Catholic Church.

(DAVID RENWICK)

SAINT VINCENT AND THE GRENADINES

Area: 389 sq km (150 sq mi)
Population (2000 est.): 113,000
Capital: Kingstown
Chief of state: Queen Elizabeth II, represented by Governor-General Sir David Jack
Head of government: Prime Ministers Sir James Fitz-Allen Mitchell and, from October 27, Arnhim Eustace

In April 2000 the House of Assembly's passage of a bill that would increase the pensions and gratuities of parliamentarians proved to be the spark that ignited an already tense political situation in St. Vincent and the Grenadines. The Organisation in Defence of Democracy (ODD)—which brought together the official opposition Unity Labour Party, trade union leaders, businessmen, and youth groups—coordinated demonstrations and protests over several days in Kingstown, causing widespread commercial disruption.

The opposition—which had been smarting ever since its loss in the June 1998 election, in which it attracted the majority of votes (55%) but won seven seats to the eight of the New Democratic Party (NDP)—used the controversial bill to vent its dissatisfaction with the NDP. As a result, an agreement was brokered by the Caribbean Community and Common Market at a meeting in Grenada between the ODD and the government of Prime Minister Sir James Fitz-Allen Mitchell, providing for an early election—in March 2001—two years before it was constitutionally mandated. Mitchell retired from the NDP presidency in August and was succeeded by Finance Minister Arnhim Eustace.

(DAVID RENWICK)

SAMOA

Area: 2,831 sq km (1,093 sq mi)
Population (2000 est.): 179,000
Capital: Apia
Chief of state: *O le Ao o le Malo* (Head of State) Malietoa Tanumafili II
Head of government: Prime Minister Tuila'epa Sa'ilele Malielegaoi

The assassination of the minister of public works in July 1999 continued to produce legal and political consequences in 2000. The two cabinet ministers who plotted the murder (and the son of one of them who actually committed the deed) were tried and found guilty, but their mandatory death sentences were commuted to life imprisonment. By-elections were held following the rulings.

The economy continued to perform strongly after recording 5.25% real growth in gross domestic product in 1999. Inflation was held at an annual rate of less than 1%; agricultural returns improved; and there was an increase to SA$100 million (about U.S. $34 million) in remittance income from Samoans living or working overseas. Owing partly to political instability in Fiji, tourism increased sharply; visitor arrivals from Europe, Australia, and New Zealand all rose by 25% over 1999. In September the government sparked controversy when, under the Money Laundering Prevention Act introduced in June, it seized $14 million that was passing through Samoan accounts.

Within the region Samoa was the strongest critic of the coup and related political development in Fiji. Samoa withdrew students from Fiji's University of the South Pacific and supported moves for the introduction of a democratic code for membership at the Pacific Islands Forum.

(BARRIE MACDONALD)

SAN MARINO

Area: 61.2 sq km (23.6 sq mi)
Population (2000 est.): 26,800
Capital: San Marino
Heads of state and government: The republic is governed by two *capitani reggenti,* or coregents, appointed every six months by a popularly elected Great and General Council.

San Marino in 2000 continued to maintain an enviable quality of life, as testified by international studies showing that it had one of the most effective medical health care systems in the world. The government wished to preserve this high quality and pursued this aim through an economic growth plan that mandated support for traditional artisan and agricultural activities as well as for high-tech investments. One of the staples of the economy was tourism, the importance of which was reflected in San Marino's formal membership in the World Tourism Organization.

Famous for its stamps and its mint, San Marino could not afford to miss the occasion of the Roman Catholic Church's Jubilee 2000 to strike a commemorative medallion that was presented to Pope John Paul II in May by the nation's ambassador to the Vatican. Special Jubilee activities were organized in May. (GREGORY O. SMITH)

SÃO TOMÉ AND PRÍNCIPE

Area: 1,001 sq km (386 sq mi)
Population (2000 est.): 144,000
Capital: São Tomé
Chief of state: President Miguel Trovoada
Head of government: Prime Minister Guilherme Posser da Costa

A cabinet reshuffle in May 2000 followed the resignation of two ministers in the cabinet of Prime Minister Guilherme Posser da Costa. Meanwhile, a legal tussle with Nigeria continued over the demarcation of boundaries off the Niger delta. It was believed that a settlement would be reached before the case was heard by the International Court of Justice, owing to São Tomé's eagerness to begin a deepwater exploration for oil, the discovery of which held out the promise of lifting this small group of islands out of poverty.

The economy remained based on cacao production. The annual per capita income was only $354, and annual gross domestic product was only $45 million; the country's debt stood at $295 million. When Pres. Miguel Trovoada met French Pres. Jacques Chirac in May, he secured a promise from Chirac that France would support a debt-relief plan from the Paris Club of creditor nations for São Tomé and Príncipe.

(CHRISTOPHER SAUNDERS)

SAUDI ARABIA

Area: 2,248,000 sq km (868,000 sq mi)
Population (2000 est.): 22,024,000
Capital: Riyadh
Head of state and government: King Fahd

Two political issues gained prominence in Saudi Arabia in 2000. The first was the formation of a family council of 18 princes to provide, among other things, a better chance for easy succession to the throne and better relations among the members of the royal family. The second important issue was that the long-standing border dispute with Yemen came to a happy end with the signing of an agreement between the two countries on June 12. Actual demarcation of the 2,500-km (1,553-mi) border was expected to start soon. In other developments Saudi-Iraqi relations witnessed a stabilization of sorts after much fluctuation. In August Iraqi Pres. Saddam Hussein branded Kuwait and Saudi Arabia "stooges for the United States and Israel," an accusation that was answered fiercely by Saudi media, which accused the Iraqi president of "transforming Iraq into a field of ruins thanks to his political wisdom." Two months later, however, Saudi Arabia did not object when Iraq was invited to the Arab summit meeting in Cairo. Additionally, Saudi Arabia asked the UN to permit it to open a border crossing between it and Iraq in order to deliver humanitarian aid to the latter. A Saudi plane en route to London was hijacked to Baghdad in mid-October; the next day Iraqi authorities returned it to Saudi Arabia with all the passengers except the two Saudi hijackers, who asked for political asylum. In November a British engineer was killed and his wife was wounded when their car exploded in Riyadh, a possible example of anti-Western sentiment.

Economically, the rising oil prices and the volume of production provided the country with its highest current account surplus since 1981. In spite of agreements by OPEC to boost production, oil prices skyrocketed to above $30 per barrel for part of the year and were expected to average $27 per barrel for the whole year, with Saudi oil production averaging about eight million barrels a day. This would wipe out the nation's current deficit and put the current surplus at no less than $22 billion–$25 billion. As in the previous year, however, and under the direct advice of Crown Prince Abdullah, the surplus was mainly going to be used not to increase spending but instead to pay off the country's foreign and domestic debts. These steps prompted Moody's Investors Service to upgrade the kingdom's financial standing. Similarly, the government did not shy away from its earlier general direction of reducing subsidies and encouraging the private sector to take a more active role in some parts of the economy. As an example, Saudi Arabia was planning a $100 billion deal with 12 leading oil companies to develop gas-fueled infrastructure. Equally important, a privatization program was about to start, and Saudia, the national airline carrier, with an annual revenue in 1999 of about $3 billion, was one of the first candidates for a partnership between the public and private sectors.

(MAHMOUD HADDAD)

SENEGAL

Area: 196,712 sq km (75,951 sq mi)
Population (2000 est.): 9,987,000
Capital: Dakar
Chief of state: Presidents Abdou Diouf and, from April 1, Abdoulaye Wade, assisted by Prime Ministers Mamadou Lamine Loum and, from April 5, Moustapha Niasse

Senegal's presidential campaign opened in January 2000 amid opposition charges that the government of Pres.

Seyllou Diallo/AFP Worldwide

Senegalese women cast their votes in the country's presidential election at a polling station in Dakar on March 19.

Abdou Diouf was preparing to manipulate the elections to its own advantage, specifically by issuing a flood of false voter registration cards. Rumours of a military coup, similar to the one that had occurred in Côte d'Ivoire on Dec. 24, 1999, swept the capital. Despite charges and countercharges, and numerous warnings of possible violence, eight candidates ran for office. The election, on February 27, took place virtually without incident. Because no candidate won more than 50% of the vote, a runoff took place on March 19 between President Diouf, head of the ruling Socialist Party, and veteran opposition leader Abdoulaye Wade (*see* BIOGRAPHIES), who was supported by a large coalition of opposition parties. To the general astonishment of the population, Wade easily defeated the incumbent. Confirming the strength of constitutional democracy in Senegal, Diouf telephoned Wade on March 20 to congratulate him on his victory and to wish him well. Wade appointed Moustapha Niasse prime minister in April. A new cabinet, which included members of seven political parties, was announced on April 3. A referendum on a new constitution was scheduled for Jan. 7, 2001.

Following talks held with the separatist Movement of Democratic Forces of Casamance (MFDC) in late January, the government lifted the bans on travel and public meetings that had been imposed upon that organization. In April the army clashed with MFDC forces near the Guinea-Bissau border; at least 18 people were killed, adding to the total of more than 1,200 deaths since the rebellion started in 1982. The border was closed for two weeks in late summer as a result of a blockade imposed by both countries.

(NANCY ELLEN LAWLER)

SEYCHELLES

Area: 455 sq km (176 sq mi)
Population (2000 est.): 81,700
Capital: Victoria
Head of state and government: President France-Albert René

Early in 2000 a high-level delegation from Libya visited the Seychelles. The two countries agreed to establish formal diplomatic relations and to exchange ambassadors. In April Air Seychelles announced the expansion of its fleet. It planned to begin leasing a Boeing 737-700 in 2001 and replace a Boeing 767-200ER with a 767-300ER. The new aircraft would fly to India, Kenya, Mauritius, South Africa, and the United Arab Emirates. The New Zealand Tourism Board (NZTB) demanded that the Seychelles Tourism Marketing Authority cease using the advertising slogan "100 percent pure"; the NZTB claimed to have used the slogan first. Although the Seychelles, which relied primarily on tourism for foreign exchange, had already spent $3 million on its international advertising campaign, it agreed to change its slogan.

In July the United States agreed to dismantle a radar facility on the island of Mahé that had been designed for satellite tracking and intelligence gathering; it had been shut down at the end of the Cold War. In September the Seychelles became the 30th nation to sign the African Union Constituent Act, which affirmed the goal of African political union.

(MATTHEW A. CENZER)

SIERRA LEONE

Area: 71,740 sq km (27,699 sq mi)
Population (2000 est.): 5,233,000 (including about 400,000 Sierra Leonean refugees temporarily residing in Guinea and other West African countries)
Capital: Freetown
Head of state and government: President Ahmad Tejan Kabbah

Late in 1999 United Nations peacekeepers arrived in Sierra Leone to monitor the implementation of the Lomé agreement. That arrangement, brokered by the UN and the Organization of African Unity, was widely criticized for granting amnesty to Revolutionary United Front (RUF) rebels accused of war crimes. Moreover, it brought RUF leader Foday Sankoh into the government as director of a commission on minerals and national reconstruction and thereby gave legal sanction to his control of the country's diamond production. The Lomé agreement was soon in tatters. RUF forces continued their brutal attacks on civilians, although their leader agreed to peace.

AP/Wide World Photos

Pro-government forces in Sierra Leone display rebel leader Foday Sankoh (right) shortly after his capture on May 17.

RUF fighters refused to disarm as required by the Lomé agreement. Several times they fired on UN forces enforcing the disarmament provision. The RUF continued to control diamond-producing areas. (*See* SIDEBAR: *Diamonds: Fuel for Conflict.*) Throughout May RUF fighters captured more than 500 UN troops. At the beginning of May, government troops and the RUF battled outside Freetown. On May 8 the first contingent of a planned 800 British troops arrived to evacuate foreign nationals. That same day protesters converged on the Freetown house of Foday Sankoh, calling on him to stop the violence. Sankoh's guards fired on the crowd, killing 19 and injuring many more. Starting on May 10 UN forces, Sierra Leone's army, and militias loyal to the government defended Freetown and pushed RUF forces away from the capital. British troops were widely credited with having helped save Freetown. On May 17 pro-government forces captured Sankoh, and the government announced its intention to try him. By the end of the month, the army and pro-government militias had advanced on rebel strongholds and captured the strategic town of Lunsar. Liberian Pres. Charles Taylor, a longtime ally of Sankoh, intervened to help secure the release of some UN hostages, while others were rescued in a series of military operations.

In mid-June most British troops withdrew, although a small force remained to train Sierra Leone's army. On August 25 a renegade rebel group, the West Side Boys, captured 12 British soldiers. Britain sent more troops to the region, including the elite Parachute Regiment, which was able to rescue some of the British hostages in a dawn raid on the rebel base. The British government pledged to continue providing training and technical advice to the army.

Late in 2000 Sierra Leone's future prospects remained unclear. The RUF continued to be operative under the leadership of Gen. Issa Sesay. Other heavily armed militias also held power in the country. In October the UN agreed to establish a war crimes tribunal for Sierra Leone and in December an offshoot of the RUF said that a precondition of "restarting" the Lomé agreement would be the release of all its political prisoners.

(MATTHEW A. CENZER)

SINGAPORE

Area: 660 sq km (255 sq mi)
Population (2000 est.): 3,278,000
Chief of state: President S.R. Nathan
Head of government: Prime Minister Goh Chok Tong

The annual summit of the Association of Southeast Asian Nations (ASEAN) was held in Singapore in November 2000. During the session Prime Minister Goh Chok Tong, who served as chairman of the summit, defended the island republic's drive to strike free-trade deals with non-ASEAN economies—especially China, Japan, and South Korea—independently of the association. Some of the ASEAN member nations that were harder hit than Singapore by the financial crisis that had struck three years earlier claimed that Singapore was out of step and looking out only for its own interests. In response, Goh pointed out that Singapore had launched a special assistance program for Indonesia and had become a donor to the Asian Development Bank's soft-loan program.

Goh seemed to solidify his hold on power during the year. When he took office in 1990, he had been widely assumed to be a transitional figure. He also operated under the psychological disadvantage of knowing that he would always be in the shadow of his popular predecessor, Lee Kuan Yew, who remained active as a senior minister. By 2000, however, Goh had become one of Southeast Asia's longest-serving elected leaders. In an interview he told reporters that he planned to stay in office at least until the next general election, which had to be held by August 2002.

Domestically, there were some signs that the government, often criticized for its authoritarian ways, was gradually loosening up. One symbolic gesture was the opening of an officially sanctioned "Speakers' Corner" in downtown Hong Lim Park. Citizens were free to talk about almost any subject without first having to obtain a police permit. As recently as 1999 Chee Soon Juan, secretary-general of the opposition Singapore Democratic Party, had been fined for making an unauthorized speech in public.

One of the more controversial moves by the government was a 13% pay increase for Singapore's civil servants. Goh's annual salary ballooned to about $1.1 million a year—more than three times that of the president of the U.S. The government justified the increase by asserting that high salaries were necessary to attract qualified people from the private sector into government service.

(TODD CROWELL)

SLOVAKIA

Area: 49,035 sq km (18,933 sq mi)
Population (2000 est.): 5,403,000
Capital: Bratislava
Chief of state: President Rudolf Schuster
Head of government: Prime Minister Mikulas Dzurinda

Slovakia continued to struggle politically and economically in the year 2000, but the country remained on its reform path. While membership negotiations with the European Union (EU) moved along relatively quickly, Slovakia's accession to the Organisation for Economic Co-operation and Development in the fall was considered the government's greatest success since taking office in October 1998.

Tensions between the four government parties heightened in mid-April when party chairman Jozef Migas and several other members of the ruling Party of the Democratic Left (SDL) supported an unsuccessful no-confidence vote in the cabinet that was called by the opposition. Although some SDL representatives condemned Migas's behaviour, he was reelected party chairman in July after dropping demands for a government reshuffle. There were conflicts at the end of the year as well within the Slovak Democratic Coalition, the largest of the government parties.

Opposition activity mounted after former prime minister Vladimir Meciar was briefly arrested on April 20 by masked police commandos in an attempt to force him to testify in several cases. Nonetheless, the opposition failed to remove Interior Minister Ladislav Pittner in a parliamentary no-confidence vote, and attendance at a series of antigovernment rallies was low. The opposition also instigated instability by calling for a referendum on early parliamentary elections; however the referendum failed when just 20% of registered voters took part in the November poll.

After Pres. Rudolf Schuster nearly died in June at a Slovak hospital during an operation on his colon, he was transported to Austria, where doctors managed to save his life. Subsequent criticism of the Slovak health care system led to the replacement the following month of Minister of Health Tibor Sagat with Roman Kovac. Defense Minister Pavol Kanis resigned in December following criticism of personnel policies at his ministry and his construction of a luxurious villa.

Political tensions also centred on national minorities as Party of the Hungarian Coalition chairman Bela Bugar several times threatened to remove his party from the ruling coalition if certain conditions were not met to strengthen the position of ethnic Hungarians. Meanwhile, the need for a solution to the Romany (Gypsy) question became increasingly urgent as Slovak Roma continued to seek asylum abroad.

The government's economic reforms started to show results during the year, and annual growth of gross domestic product was predicted at 2.1%, mainly thanks to strong exports. Nonetheless, annual inflation was expected to rise to 12.0%, while unemployment remained a significant problem, forecast at 18.6% in December. Considerable foreign investment took place during the year, most notably the sale of the eastern Slovak steel giant VSZ to U.S. Steel and Deutsche Telekom's purchase of 51% of its Slovak counterpart.

(SHARON FISHER)

SLOVENIA

Area: 20,273 sq km (7,827 sq mi)
Population (2000 est.): 1,963,000
Capital: Ljubljana
Chief of state: President Milan Kucan
Head of government: Prime Ministers Janez Drnovsek, Andrej Bajuk from May 3, and, from November 17, Janez Drnovsek

Events in Slovenia in 2000 were dominated by preparations for the regular quadrennial parliamentary elections held October 15. Two conservative parties that appealed to the same voter base, the Slovene People's Party (SLS) and the Slovene Christian Democrats (SKD), united into one at a joint congress held April 15. The new party took the name SLS+SKD Slovene People's Party. In anticipation of the unification, the SLS, which had been part of a three-party coalition government led by Prime Minister Janez Drnovsek, head of the Liberal Democracy of Slovenia, announced that it would leave the government on the day that the SLS and SKD combined. Drnovsek did not wait for this event but asked for a vote of confidence from the parliament on a plan to replace the 10 SLS members of his government with 8 independent ministers. The parliament rejected this plan, and the Drnovsek government resigned on April 8.

Maria Zarnayova/AFP Worldwide

John Goodish (right), president of U.S. Steel Kosice, unveils a new logo after the company officially took over steel giant VSZ in Kosice, Slovakia, on November 24.

The SLS+SKD and the Social Democratic Party of Slovenia (SDS, despite its name a very conservative and nationalist party) proposed that Andrej Bajuk, a recent returnee to Slovenia, head a conservative-centre government. The parliament confirmed the Bajuk government on June 7 by a 46–44 vote.

Complications soon developed. In July the parliament adopted a revised election law for the October 15 election. It reduced slightly the amount of proportional representation in the parliament in favour of more seats for candidates who won a full majority of the vote. The conservative parties, especially the SDS, strongly supported the full-majority proposal, yet the two-thirds majority required for the law to pass was provided by the SLS+SKD. Prime Minister Bajuk and his foreign minister, Lojze Peterle, so opposed this decision of their party that they resigned from the SLS+SKD and formed a party they named New Slovenia. Both remained in office, however.

The October 15 elections were won by the centre-left parties, as they gained nearly two-thirds of the 90 seats in the parliament. After several weeks of negotiations Drnovsek was able to form a coalition left-centre government consisting of his own LDS, the United List (former communist) party, SLS+SKD, the DeSUS party (whose members are primarily retirees), and the Slovene Young People's Party. Parliament approved the government on November 30, and it took office immediately. (RUDOLF M. SUSEL)

SOLOMON ISLANDS

Area: 28,370 sq km (10,954 sq mi)
Population (2000 est.): 466,000
Capital: Honiara
Chief of state: Queen Elizabeth II, represented by Governor-General John Lapli
Head of government: Prime Ministers Bartholomew Ulufa'alu and, from June 30, Manasseh Sogavare

A peace accord that ended two years of ethnic conflict in Solomon Islands was signed in October 2000. The conflict had begun when the indigenous Isatambu Freedom Movement (IFM) of Guadalcanal tried to force the expulsion of immigrants from Malaita Island.

The government became largely dysfunctional and was unable to guarantee public order, maintain services, or pay its bills; rural areas were controlled by the IFM, and the urban area was in the hands of the Malaita Eagle Force paramilitaries. An international peace-monitoring group supported local police and oversaw the surrender of weapons. In June Prime Minister Bartholomew Ulufa'alu resigned to facilitate peace negotiations and was replaced by Manasseh Sogavare, who formed a coalition government.

Political instability had a serious impact on the economy; one international fishing company suspended operations and repatriated all foreign workers, palm oil production was interrupted, and transport was disrupted. Within the government, there was conflict over whether to continue recognizing Taiwan or to establish links with Beijing. Earlier, Solomon Islands had signed a fisheries agreement with Taiwan that would allow 42 tuna vessels to work in the Solomon Islands exclusive economic zone for an annual fee of $8,000 per vessel.

(BARRIE MACDONALD)

George Gray, one of the leaders of the Isatambu Freedom Movement, was instrumental in the reaching of a peace accord in 2000 that ended two years of ethnic conflict in the Solomon Islands.

Mike Field/AFP Worldwide

SOMALIA

Area: 637,000 sq km (246,000 sq mi; including the 176,000-sq km [68,000-sq mi] area of the unilaterally declared [in 1991] and unrecognized Republic of Somaliland)
Population (2000 est.): 7,253,000 (including Somaliland); about 400,000 refugees are registered in neighbouring countries
Capital: Mogadishu; Hargeysa is the capital of Somaliland
Head of state and government: Somalia had no functioning government in 2000 until October. Designated August 27, President Abdiqassim Salad Hassan, assisted from October 8 by Prime Minister Ali Khalif Galaid

The year 2000 began with yet another failure to patch up the divisions that had torn Somalia apart for a decade. An attempt by Hussein Muhammad Aydid, Ali Mahdi Muhammad, and the three other rival faction leaders ("warlords") to set up a united administration for the former capital, Mogadishu, fell apart in February. In May, however, a more serious attempt at unification began. The first step was a reconciliation conference proposed by Pres. Ismail Omar Guelleh of Djibouti and backed by the United Nations, the Arab League, and the Organization of African Unity. Unlike the 12 previous failed peace conferences, this one was intended to bypass the warlords and consisted instead of traditional leaders, intellectuals, and senior politicians.

On May 2 the conference opened in Arta, Djibouti. While skirmishes between militias and kidnappings continued in Mogadishu, the 900 delegates adopted a charter providing for a three-year transitional government and a 245-strong transitional national assembly (TNA), with seats distributed in blocs between the four main clans, Dir, Daarood, Hawiye, and Digil-Mirifle; another bloc for an "alliance" of minority groups; and one for women representatives.

After lengthy and ferocious negotiations over the distribution of seats between rival subclans, the TNA was inaugurated, and on August 25 elected as interim president Abdiqassim Salad Hassan, a member of the powerful Hawiye-Habr Gedir subclan, who had been deputy prime minister and minister of the interior under the former dictator Muhammad Siad Barre. On October 8 he appointed as prime minister the businessman Ali Khalif Galaid.

The transitional government moved into Mogadishu in October. Ali Mahdi Muhammad was a member, but the new regime was opposed as illegitimate by Hussein Muhammad Aydid and the remaining southern factions. In a statement to the French press, Aydid said that the nomination of Galaid was a "total misunderstanding of an agreement I made with [President] Salad in Libya in September." The self-declared Republic of Somaliland in the northwest and the autonomous region of Puntland in the northeast, both of which had established a high degree of peace and economic recovery, rejected the new government and declared the delegates to it from their areas to be "traitors."

Somalia was affected by the regional drought in northeastern Africa. In May floods caused damage in the central regions, and in September, according to the UN, 750,000 people were still at risk as a result of the drought; the situation later improved, however, with a good harvest. In September the livestock exports on which Somaliland and Puntland as well as much of southern Somalia depended were endangered by six Persian Gulf nations' regional ban on imports from East African countries, following an outbreak of Rift Valley fever. In November an influx of new banknotes into the nation's currency system caused the shilling to drop to about 13,000 to the dollar, the lowest level since 1992.

(VIRGINIA LULING)

SOUTH AFRICA

Area: 1,219,090 sq km (470,693 sq mi)
Population (2000 est.): 43,421,000
Capitals (de facto): Pretoria (executive); Bloemfontein (judicial); Cape Town (legislative)
Head of state and government: President Thabo Mbeki

Domestic Affairs. During 2000 Thabo Mbeki's presidency came under criticism both abroad and at home. Opening Parliament on February 4, he announced moves to create a more investor-friendly environment, including continuation of the African National Congress (ANC) government's economic policy of privatization and deregulation, amendments to labour legislation, and the appointment of an investment council that included the chief executive officers of large international corporations. At the same time, Mbeki had harsh words for the "socially undisciplined," which included illegal strikers and tax evaders. In July at the ANC's national general council, Mbeki attacked careerism and corruption among some council members.

Mbeki identified racism as a major problem facing the country, and several conferences were held on the subject during the year. In March the South African Human Rights Commission held hearings into racism in the media. The official report on the shooting of several white soldiers by a black soldier at a military base in 1999 highlighted continued racism by whites in the armed forces.

Mbeki aroused controversy both internationally and domestically by questioning the conventional wisdom on AIDS, declaring that HIV was not its only cause and highlighting poverty as a main factor. "You cannot attribute immune deficiency solely and exclusively to a virus," he said in an interview with *Time* magazine in September. He appointed an advisory panel on AIDS that included so-called dissident scientists. The government was also criticized for its refusal to supply antiretroviral drugs to pregnant women and rape victims, though in September Mbeki made it clear that government policy was based on the thesis that HIV caused AIDS.

Local elections took place on December 5, the date delayed by an impasse between the government and traditional leaders (chiefs), supported by Mangosuthu Gatsha Buthelezi, leader of the Inkatha Freedom Party and home affairs minister, over the powers of the latter. The ANC won an estimated 59% of the vote, including the mayorships of the cities of Johannesburg and Durban.

The opposition Democratic Alliance (DA)—formed by a merger in June of the Democratic Party (DP), New National Party (NNP), and Freedom Alliance (FA)—won 22% of the vote in the local elections and the mayorship of Cape Town.

It also held 68 seats in the lower house of Parliament. Joe Seremane, chairman of the DA, had become the first black chairperson of the DP in March. Tony Leon, former DP and DA leader, in March called the ANC "the last great nationalist dinosaur, its rhetoric replete with old slogans from the ideological junkyard of the 1960s," and when the DA was formed he declared that "up until now the ANC has had a free ride." The ANC described the DA as an "alliance of hate" engaged in a last-ditch effort to perpetuate white minority rule.

Severe tensions persisted in the alliance between the Congress of South African Trade Unions (COSATU) and the ANC over economic policy. Between January and April COSATU organized demonstrations and regional one-day strikes protesting job losses, which culminated in a one-day national general strike on May 10 estimated by COSATU to involve four million workers. COSATU also claimed that the draft amendments to the labour laws (removing restrictions on working hours and the premium paid for Sunday work and making it easier to dismiss recently hired workers) were the worst attack on workers' rights since measures imposed by the apartheid regime in 1988. COSATU called on the government to abandon its economic policy and committed itself to "one general strike a quarter" from March 2001 until the labour law amendments were abandoned.

The Truth and Reconciliation Commission (TRC) continued amnesty hearings, but the government did not implement the TRC's recommendations to grant financial reparations to victims of human rights violations. At the continuing trial of Wouter Basson, the apartheid regime's chemical warfare expert, witnesses gave evidence that at least 200 sedated prisoners, some still alive, had been dumped from aircraft into the sea from a height of some 3,700 m (13,000 ft) or higher. In May the Appeal Court upheld the conviction of Allan Boesak, antiapartheid leader in the 1980s, on charges of fraud and theft, and he began serving a three-year sentence. Abe Williams, former NNP cabinet minister in the post-1994 government, was found guilty of 40 charges of fraud and theft in June and sentenced to an effective three years in prison.

Western Cape suffered during the year. The Cape peninsula was declared a disaster area in January because of widespread bush fires. There were 21 terrorist bombings in Cape Town between October 1998 and October 2000. In June the Panamanian-registered bulk carrier *Treasure* sank in Table Bay, releasing hundreds of tons of fuel oil that endangered nearby penguin colonies. Some 43,000 penguins were removed.

Foreign Affairs. The parliamentary opposition criticized President Mbeki's refusal to condemn Zimbabwe Pres. Robert Mugabe's support for the invasion of white-owned farms in his country, but the United States, the United Kingdom, and the South African Chamber of Business praised Mbeki's "quiet diplomacy." Mbeki said that such invasions would not be tolerated in South Africa but also insisted that the main issue in Zimbabwe was land reform and not violations of human rights or assaults on democracy.

The government continued to try to enforce the implementation of the 1999 Lusaka peace agreement in the Democratic Republic of the Congo. Former president Nelson Mandela was involved in mediation in the civil war in Burundi and by August had persuaded most warring factions to sign a peace plan. Ground and air crews of the South Africa's air force rescued an estimated 15,000 people trapped by floods in Mozambique in March.

The Economy. South Africa's economy appeared to pick up in the second half of 1999, growing by 3.2% in the third quarter and 3.6% in the fourth (1.2% for 1999 as a whole). It slowed again in 2000, however, to 0.8% growth in the first quarter and 1.6% in the second quarter, which necessitated a downward revision of the government forecast of 3.6% growth for the year. Observers pointed to a lack of productive foreign investment.

The budget provided R 9.9 billion (about $1.4 billion) worth of tax cuts and introduced a capital gains tax beginning in 2001. Education, health, welfare, and housing spending fell from 57% to 55.8% of noninterest spending, and military spending increased the most, by 28%. The 2000–01 budget deficit was projected at 2.6% of gross domestic product, compared with 2.4% in 1999–2000. The auditor general reported that the welfare

AP/Wide World Photos

Penguins soaked with oil that spilled from a sunken tanker near Cape Town huddle together on Dassen Island on June 30.

department had spent less than 1% of the R 204 million (about $28 million) it had received for poverty-relief programs in 1998 and that other departments had also seriously underspent.

In June 2000 foreign exchange reserves amounted to 15 weeks of imports. The government announced an intention to set annual inflation targets between 3% and 6%. The index used (called CPIX) was 6.5% in October 1999 but had risen to about 8% by July 2000. After eight interest-rate cuts in 1999, the bank rate remained steady at 14.5% for much of the year.

The black share of income rose from 29.9% in 1991 to 35.7% in 1996. During the same years, the proportion of black households in the richest 10% of the population increased from 9% to 22%, while the income of the poorest 40% of black households fell by 20%.

(MARTIN LEGASSICK)

SPAIN

Area: 505,990 sq km (195,364 sq mi)
Population (2000 est.): 40,128,000
Capital: Madrid
Chief of state: King Juan Carlos I
Head of government: Prime Minister José María Aznar López

Spain in 2000 was one of Europe's most politically stable countries. This fact served to underline the sudden and vicious return to Spanish civil life of the Basque terrorists and an uncharacteristic outbreak of ethnic intolerance.

The March 12 general elections served to ratify the right-wing administration of the Popular Party (PP), led by Prime Minister José María Aznar López. Aznar was reelected with an unexpected outright majority, defeating the leftist electoral coalition of former communists and socialists. This defeat prompted a reshuffle within the Spanish Socialist Workers' Party (PSOE); the more centrist José Luis Rodríguez Zapatero succeeded Joaquín Almunia as secretary-general.

With 52% of the vote, the PP won 183 seats (up from 156 seats) in the lower house of the parliament and therefore gained an absolute majority. The second party, the PSOE, earned 125 seats (down from 141). The second member of the leftist coalition, the United Left, earned only 8 seats (down from 21). The other seats were distributed among an array of regionalist and regional nationalist parties, particularly in Catalonia, the Basque region, and Galicia.

Unquestionably the most dramatic event of the year was the return to terrorism by Euskadi Ta Askatasuna (ETA), the Basque separatist organization, breaking a self-declared cease-fire that had held for more than one year. On January 21 Spanish Army Lieut. Col. Pedro Antonio Blanco García was murdered, and the following day nearly one million Spaniards took to Madrid's streets to protest the killing. A number of assassinations and acts of violence ensued, including the murders of a journalist and several PP and PSOE local politicians.

On August 7 four ETA members were blown up in a car loaded with guns and explosives in an industrial neighbourhood in Bilbao. One of the victims, Patxi Rementeria, was the chief of ETA's sanguinary Commando Vizcaya. The near-instinctive reaction among radical nationalists was to blame the state security forces for the bombing. In an effort to prove that this blow had not impaired its organizational capacity, ETA embarked on a dramatic crescendo of violence. A wave of vandalism and arson spread across the northern Basque provinces. On August 8 Basque business executive José María Korta was killed in Zumaya, near San Sebastián. A few hours later nine people were injured near Madrid's Chamartin train station. The spate of assassinations and other attacks increased in the ensuing months.

The deadliest episode took place on October 30, when Supreme Court Judge José Francisco Querol Lombardero, together with his driver and bodyguard, were killed in Madrid. More than 60 passersby were also wounded, including one who later died. On November 2 two

Sena Vidanagama/AFP Worldwide

Sri Lankan Pres. Chandrika Kumaratunga (right) hands over a letter of appointment to Prime Minister Ratnasiri Wickramanayake as he is sworn in for a second term at the president's residence in Colombo on October 13.

people were injured in a public garden in Barcelona, where Aznar had planned to attend an award ceremony. In most of these instances, bombs were planted in parked cars and detonated by remote control. On November 7 police arrested several suspected ETA members after two had been refused asylum in Madrid by the Cuban embassy. Ernest Lluch, health minister under the first Spanish socialist government (1982–86), was assassinated in Barcelona on November 21. This killing was timed to mark the 25th anniversary of the monarchy, which the terrorists had regarded as one of their main targets.

Aznar's military crackdown on ETA and refusal to negotiate had resulted in a number of arrests over the years, but they had apparently not deterred the organization or impaired its capacity to reinvent itself in ever more radical manifestations. ETA had repeatedly shown that it could survive the loss of senior leaders, perhaps compensating through further radicalization. ETA's leadership reportedly now included many women. Earlier random killings of police officers, members of the armed forces, and, more recently, politicians passed a new threshold when such persons as journalists and other public figures became "legitimate" targets for ETA violence. The organization carried out more than 20 assassinations during the year, the highest toll since 1992. The strength of civil society, both in the Basque country and Spain at large, was demonstrated, however, by gargantuan protest marches against terrorism, with crowds swelling up to a million strong.

Also disturbing was the upsurge of xenophobic violence culminating with anti-immigrant street riots on February 13 in the prosperous Andalusian town of El Ejido, where North African immigrants made up about 10% of the population. This was one of the most serious instances of racial violence in modern Spain, perhaps reflecting an infection of the global disease of increased intolerance of foreigners. The attacks occurred only two days after the parliament passed a bill allowing 70,000 illegal immigrants to take up residency. (DANIELE CONVERSI)

SRI LANKA

Area: 65,610 sq km (25,332 sq mi)
Population (2000 est.): 19,246,000
Capitals: Sri Jayawardenepura Kotte (legislative and judicial); Colombo (executive)
Head of state and government: President Chandrika Kumaratunga, assisted by Prime Ministers Sirimavo Bandaranaike and, from August 10, Ratnasiri Wickramanayake

Sri Lanka in 2000 completed its 17th year of civil war with no end in sight. Efforts to end the independence struggle of the Liberation Tigers of Tamil Eelam (LTTE), either through force of arms or through negotiation and constitutional reform, proved unsuccessful. At the front of the conflict in northern Sri Lanka, the army suffered a severe setback in April when its major camp at Elephant Pass fell to the rebels with heavy losses. Although military morale was badly shaken, later counteroffensives succeeded in retaking much of the lost ground. Meanwhile, following the attempted assassination of Pres. Chandrika Kumaratunga in December 1999, a series of shootings, suicide bombs, and letter bombs terrorized the southern part of the nation, killing government ministers, parliamentary candidates, innocent civilians, and often the bombers themselves.

In an attempt to placate the disaffected Tamil and Muslim communities and undercut support for the LTTE, President Kumaratunga's People's Alliance (PA) government put forward a constitutional reform bill that would have established substantially autonomous regional councils. The support of the opposition United National Party (UNP) was essential, since the government lacked the two-thirds majority needed to amend the constitution. This support was initially pledged, but after repeated protests by Buddhist clergy and other Sinhalese groups, it was withdrawn. The constitutional reform measure failed in an August parliamentary vote. A general election was then called in an effort by the PA to obtain the necessary two-thirds majority. Held in October amid considerable violence, the election weakened the PA slightly in Parliament while not greatly strengthening the UNP. President Kumaratunga was able to form a new coalition government, but it was no stronger than her previous one and left the proposed constitutional reform many votes short of approval. On October 19, as President Kumaratunga was swearing in her new cabinet, an LTTE suicide bomber shot down a helicopter gunship over Colombo. On election day Sirimavo Bandaranaike, the president's mother and until recently prime minister of Sri Lanka, died. (*See* OBITUARIES.) At year's end, the LTTE seemed more willing to negotiate with the government, but a new effort by Norway to help get talks started was blocked by the inability of the two sides to agree on preconditions.

The Sri Lankan economy grew at about 5% in 2000 despite worsening fiscal and balance of payments deficits. The prevailing insecurity discouraged private investment and forced the government to postpone its privatization program for lack of buyer interest.

(DONALD R. SNODGRASS)

SUDAN, THE

Area: 2,503,890 sq km (966,757 sq mi)
Population (2000 est.): 35,080,000
Capitals: Khartoum (executive and ministerial) and Omdurman (legislative)
Head of state and government: President and Prime Minister Lieut. Gen. Omar Hassan Ahmad al-Bashir

The three-month state of emergency declared in December 1999 by Pres. Omar Hassan al-Bashir, who believed his authority was under threat from his ally and former sponsor Hassan al-Turabi, was extended on March 12, 2000, to the end of the year. On January 24 the president had already consolidated his position by dismissing the cabinet, all state governors, and his senior advisers, and his position received a further boost in March when the Ummah Party, led by former prime minister Sadiq al-Mahdi, withdrew from the National Democratic Alliance (NDA), which was waging war on government strongholds in the east.

In April Bashir announced that there would be presidential and parliamentary elections in October, later postponed to December, and launched his own campaign for the presidency by summoning a National Congress (NC) "mobilization gathering" to take place on May 4. Turabi claimed that only he, as secretary-general of the Congress, was authorized to convene such a gathering and called for a boycott. The meeting nevertheless took place, and Bashir attacked Turabi in a speech to the delegates. Two days later the entire NC secretariat and party chiefs were suspended. The opposition subsequently decided to boycott the elections.

While the president was strengthening his position within his own circle, events in other parts of the country and relations with external bodies were not uniformly happy. Encouraged by the growth in oil exports, the government made strenuous efforts to establish a better accord with other countries, but the Canadian government was not impressed and accused the Canadian company Talisman Energy Inc. of contributing to human rights violations by its involvement in oil production in The Sudan. There was also a dispute with the UN over the government's claim that airplanes working for UN aid agencies had been transporting southern rebel leaders; this led to bombing by government forces of relief planes on the ground. In the south the heaviest fighting in several years was taking place, and the government was accused by aid agencies of using the prevention of flights carrying food to the area as a weapon of war that was threatening thousands with starvation. More promising for the nation was a request by the Organization of African Unity for the lifting of UN sanctions against it, imposed in 1996 in the interest of promoting peace and stability. In August The Sudan was restored to full membership in the International Monetary Fund. (KENNETH INGHAM)

SURINAME

Area: 163,820 sq km (63,251 sq mi)
Population (2000 est.): 431,000
Capital: Paramaribo
Head of state and government: Presidents Jules Wijdenbosch and, from August 12, Ronald Venetiaan

Jules Wijdenbosch (left), the outgoing president of Suriname, places the presidential sash onto the shoulders of the new president, Ronald Venetiaan, on August 12 in Paramaribo.

AP/Wide World Photos

The political and economic landscape in Suriname brightened with the victory of Ronald Venetiaan's New Front (NF) in the May 25, 2000, legislative elections. A critical two-thirds majority victory enabled NF members in the National Assembly to elect Venetiaan president on August 4. Venetiaan, who had served as president from 1991 to 1996, would have to deal with high inflation, a deteriorating economy, and the fallout from a succession of political crises.

A long-term and intractable problem was the powerful drug trade, which had corrupted many in business, government, and the security forces. Although some drug charges against 1980 coup leader Dési Bouterse were dismissed on appeal, a court in The Netherlands confirmed a cocaine-smuggling conviction. Bouterse, who headed the largest opposition group in the National Assembly, had not been extradited. Other challenges for Venetiaan included illegal gold and lumber extraction and two ongoing border-dispute stalemates with neighbouring Guyana. On the positive side were the expected renewal of Dutch aid, high prices for alumina (semiprocessed bauxite), and promising onshore oil fields.

Surimamese politician Henck Arron, who led the nation to independence from The Netherlands, died on December 4. (*See* OBITUARIES.)

(JOHN W. GRAHAM)

SWAZILAND

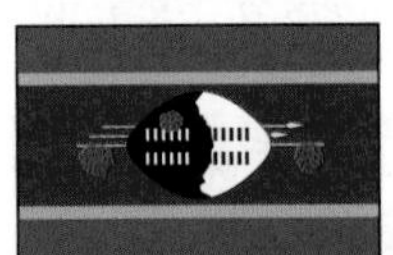

Area: 17,364 sq km (6,704 sq mi)
Population (2000 est.): 1,083,000
Capitals: Mbabane (administrative and judicial); Lozitha and Ludzidzini (royal); Lobamba (legislative)
Chief of state: King Mswati III, with much power shared by his mother, Queen Mother Ntombi Latfwala
Head of government: Prime Minister Barnabas Sibusiso Dlamini

The year 2000 began with a scandal when the speaker of the Swaziland parliament stole cow dung from the royal kraal at Ludzidzini in the course of dancing the most sacred Swazi ritual, Incwala. At that time there had been much criticism of the nation's prime minister, and his replacement was considered imminent. It became widely speculated that the speaker, Mgabhi Dlamini, would have used the cow dung as an essential ingredient in a medicinal mixture that would ensure his appointment as the next prime minister or at least would consolidate his power base in the parliament. Members of the parliament, however, had become increasingly critical and intolerant of Dlamini's inefficiency, and he was replaced as speaker.

In August during the Umhlanga (reed) dance, Swaziland's second most important national ritual, the traditional prime minister and governor of Ludzidzini, Dibanisa Mavuso, engaged in poaching and killed several impalas in excess of the legal limit. The dance always ended with a royal hunt, which was one way of controlling the wildlife population. Mavuso, however, abused tradition for his own pleasure and broke the law on wildlife conservation. He was dismissed from office but was protected from the humiliation of a court trial and a predictably certain imprisonment.

These developments underlined the difficulties facing the Swazi government. An end to this political instability was not in sight, partly because the Constitutional Review Commission completed its work after four years without drafting a constitution to direct policy in the country. A new body with expertise in writing constitutions was to be appointed to prepare a constitution ahead of the elections expected in 2003.

(ACKSON M. KANDUZA)

SWEDEN

Area: 449,964 sq km (173,732 sq mi)
Population (2000 est.): 8,864,000
Capital: Stockholm
Chief of state: King Carl XVI Gustaf
Head of government: Prime Minister Göran Persson

In 2000 a strong economy, falling unemployment, and the impact of the Internet appeared to breathe new life into the "Swedish model" of a welfare society, one that had seemed dead and buried during the deep recession of the early 1990s. With economic growth forecast at about 4%, inflation among the lowest in Europe, and the unemployment rate down to 4% of the workforce, the country bore little resemblance to the crisis-ridden state of less than 10 years ago. Talk turned from dismantling the country's system of high taxation and generous social benefits to a discussion of how these elements could be adapted to a global economy in which both capital and labour could move more freely.

Though the transformation in Sweden's economic health was helped by the general worldwide economic upturn—which boosted the strong export sector—there were also notable domestic factors, such as the state budget, which had slumped to a deficit of over 12% of gross domestic product in 1993 but now boasted a healthy surplus following some significant spending cuts. The ruling Social Democratic Labour Party (SAP), therefore, began paying back the national debt as well as introducing modest tax cuts.

Just as important was Sweden's embrace of new technology; the country had some of the world's highest levels of Internet and mobile-phone usage. The widespread understanding of the capabilities of these two technologies created a new breed of entrepreneurs, many of whom had been behind some of Europe's high-profile Internet companies. The young and flamboyant Internet entrepreneurs who had dominated the news headlines early in the year, however, struggled for survival along with many new companies after capital dried up in the summer.

Another long-term factor in Sweden's economic turnaround was telecommunications equipment manufacturer Ericsson; its extensive presence in Stockholm helped transform the capital into one of Europe's hubs of information technology (IT) research. The rapid rise of the Stockholm stock market early in the year attracted many to buying equities in IT and telecom stocks. In June more than 11% of the population bought shares in the state-owned telecom operator Telia; it was the largest privatization ever in the Nordic region. Following the stock market decline in the second half of the year, however, many Swedes sustained substantial losses.

The SAP, however, failed to capitalize on the economic boom. Opinion polls showed the party struggling to return to its postelection 36% approval level. Instead, the smaller Left Party, an SAP ally, picked up support with its program of increased public spending and opposition to Swedish membership in the European single currency.

Although a member of the European Union (EU), Sweden stayed outside the euro zone. The government promised a referendum on the issue, but public opinion was so firmly against the move that any such vote seemed distant. When Sweden assumed the rotating presidency of the EU for the first time in 2001, Prime Minister Göran Persson would have to show his enthusiasm for the EU without alienating domestic opinion; many were suspicious of EU institutions and fearful of the erosion of national sovereignty.

Persson would not be the only Swede with a difficult leadership job in 2001. The appointment in October of Sven-Göran Eriksson, the first non-English manager of the troubled England association football (soccer) team, was sure to provide sports fans in this Scandinavian country with plenty to read about. (NICHOLAS GEORGE)

SWITZERLAND

Area: 41,284 sq km (15,940 sq mi)
Population (2000 est.): 7,177,000
Capitals: Bern (administrative) and Lausanne (judicial)
Head of state and government: President Adolf Ogi (for 2000)

With its economy in good shape and a substantial budget surplus expected, Switzerland sailed through the year 2000. The nation's exports, particularly pharmaceuticals and watches, benefited from the strong dollar. While strains were experienced in some industrial sectors, average unemployment remained under 3%. Despite a sharp rise in fuel prices, long lines at filling stations, as experienced elsewhere in Europe, were unknown. Domestic spending, however, remained cautious, largely owing to increases in health insurance premiums and rents. The Swiss franc (Sw F 1= about $0.58) was once again viewed as a safe haven for money otherwise exposed to currency turbulence. The government firmly rejected a proposal by trade unions for an obligatory 36-hour workweek, instead of the existing 42 hours.

Unease over the effects of climate change was heightened by the flood catastrophe in the canton of Valais (as well as areas in nearby Italy) in mid-October. In Switzerland 15 people lost their lives, 13 of them in the mountain village of Gondo, where enormous masses of rocks and mud swept away entire houses. The Rhône River burst its banks and flooded surrounding areas, sometimes to a depth of more than two metres (six feet). Thousands had to be evacuated, and the army was called in to help. Damage estimates reached Sw F 1 billion. A nationwide appeal for funds brought an unprecedentedly generous response.

Two decisions announced by the Federal Council (the seven-member cabinet) touched off controversy. The first was a "solidarity pact" between homosexuals or lesbians, affording them certain legal rights, and the second was the "decriminalization" of the use of marijuana.

With Switzerland edging closer to European Union (EU) membership, banking secrecy came in for particular attention. As of Jan. 1, 2001, bank secrecy (which did not cover money laundering) was being eroded in regard to Americans through application of the requirement for banks to provide the names of U.S. nationals holding investments in Swiss banks. Several banks were fined for having accepted some $600 million in deposits made on behalf of the former Nigerian dictator Sani Abacha.

At the end of June, the Federal Council agreed to open procedures for a new attempt at joining the United Nations. More than half of the population, however, remained opposed to this, according to opinion polls. The first occasion had been in March 1986, when 75% of the people voted against it, despite the fact that Switzerland was a member of UN specialized agencies, several of which had their headquarters in Geneva. Membership in the EU continued to be opposed by an estimated two-thirds of the population. As agreed upon in negotiations, however, Switzerland moved ahead by allowing 40-ton trucks to travel through the country up to a limit of 300,000 crossings annually; in return, the same number of Swiss trucks would be allowed to move through EU countries. Switzerland also made plain its preference for such trucks to be transported across the country by rail.

In a September referendum 63.7% of the Swiss voters rejected a proposed 18% limit on the number of resident foreigners. This was the fifth time since 1970 that the issue had been put to a vote. Switzerland already had four national languages (German, French, Italian, Romansh), so the decision by Zürich's education department to teach English rather than French as a first foreign language beginning in 2003 encountered considerable criticism. (ALAN MCGREGOR)

SYRIA

Area: 185,180 sq km (71,498 sq mi)
Population (2000 est.): 16,306,000
Capital: Damascus
Head of state and government: Presidents Gen. Hafez al-Assad, ʽAbd al-Halim Khaddam (acting) from June 10, and, from July 17, Bashar al-Assad, assisted by Prime Ministers Mahmud az-Zuʽbi and, from March 13, Muhammad Mustafa Mero

Pres. Hafez al-Assad died unexpectedly on June 10, 2000, after having ruled Syria since November 1970. (*See* OBITUARIES.) Within hours of his death, the People's Assembly revised the country's constitution to lower the minimum age for the presidency from 40 to 34, the age of the former president's oldest surviving son, Bashar al-Assad. (*See* BIOGRAPHIES.) Meanwhile, state security forces mobilized a number of popular demonstrations in the larger cities and towns that combined expressions of grief over the former president's death with protestations of loyalty to his presumptive heir.

On June 27 the People's Assembly nominated Bashar al-Assad to be the sole candidate for election to the presidency. The balloting was carried out on July 10, with Bashar receiving 97% of the total vote. In his inaugural address on July 17, the new president reiterated the government's refusal to relinquish any part of the Golan Heights region to Israel, demanded that the United States act as an honest broker in Arab-Israeli peace talks, pledged to continue the anticorruption campaign that he had supervised over the preceding two years, and affirmed his commitment to a form of "democracy appropriate to Syria, that takes its roots from its history and respects its society." He proposed no major changes in the country's political system. Bashar was reported to have remarked to the speaker of the People's Assembly a week later, "After my father passed away, I learned the value of the organization he left behind."

AFP Worldwide

Syria's new president, Bashar al-Assad (centre), meets with King Abdullah II of Jordan (left) and King Mohammed VI of Morocco (right) at the Moroccan embassy in Cairo in October.

Three months before the transition, Prime Minister Mahmud az-Zu'bi resigned in the face of charges that he had embezzled public moneys. His successor, Muhammad Mustafa Mero, was championed by Bashar al-Assad, who told reporters that "changes are more necessary than ever in sectors such as the economy, information, education, and technology." Discreet criticism of the Ba'th regime soon began to appear in the state-run press. On July 15 an influential Damascus daily attacked a government official for claiming that poverty was nonexistent in Syria. At the end of September, 99 intellectuals, artists, and academics published an open letter to the president in a Beirut, Lebanon, newspaper, calling on him to grant citizens greater political freedom.

Negotiations with Israel remained suspended. President Assad traveled to Cairo on October 1 to discuss the future of the Arab-Israeli peace process and other regional issues. The meeting was overshadowed, however, by the fighting that erupted between Palestinians and Israelis on September 29. The president returned to Cairo for the emergency Arab summit that convened on October 21 and gave a speech that sharply condemned Israel. Meanwhile, on October 8, for the first time since 1990, a Syrian cargo plane landed in Baghdad, Iraq; it carried a delegation of senior officials, along with food and medicine.

In November President Assad signed an amnesty that set free 600 of the estimated 1,500 political prisoners in Syria. The amnesty marked the 30th anniversary of the revolution that brought Assad's late father to power.

(FRED H. LAWSON)

TAIWAN

Area: 36,185 sq km (13,971 sq mi)
Population (2000 est.): 22,186,000
Capital: Taipei
Chief of state: Presidents Lee Teng-hui and, from May 20, Chen Shui-bian
Head of government: Presidents of the Executive Yuan (Premiers) Vincent Siew, Tang Fei from May 20, and, from October 6, Chang Chun-hsiung

Domestic politics and cross-strait relations dominated the news from Taiwan in 2000. In March the island republic's second direct presidential election produced a stunning victory for the main opposition candidate, Democratic Progressive Party (DPP) nominee Chen Shui-bian. (*See* BIOGRAPHIES.) The 49-year-old former dissident won 39% of the vote, enough to narrowly defeat independent candidate James Soong, who received 37%. The ruling Kuomintang (KMT) candidate, Lien Chan, finished a distant third. Although the KMT retained control of the legislature, Chen's presidential victory terminated 50 years of uninterrupted KMT rule. Lee Teng-hui, who had crushed his DPP opponent, Peng Ming-min, in the 1996 presidential election, was unable to transfer his popularity to his would-be political heir, Lien, and was forced to resign his party leadership position. The shock of defeat prompted the KMT to initiate a thorough self-scrutiny as the party entered into opposition for the first time in its history. After his narrow electoral loss, Soong, a longtime KMT stalwart who ran as an independent only after having been denied his party's nomination, established the People First Party as a new vehicle to promote his political fortunes. As a result of Chen's victory, Taiwanese politics entered a period of flux.

The tumultuous election campaign was punctuated by harsh rhetoric from China, which threatened dire consequences if Taiwanese voters elected Chen. Chinese leaders viewed him as a dangerous advocate of Taiwanese independence. During Taiwan's first direct presidential election in 1996, China had test fired missiles off the coast of Taiwan in a crude warning to Taiwanese voters not to support pro-independence candidates. This time Beijing restricted itself to verbal warnings. Before and after his election victory, Chen downplayed his support for independence in an attempt to assuage Beijing. He said there was no need for Taiwan to declare formal independence, since it was already a de facto independent state. Spurning Chen's olive branch, Chinese leaders demanded that he explicitly endorse their narrow version of the one-China principle—something the new president refused to do. Meanwhile, the Chinese media, which avoided even mentioning Chen by name after his victory, heaped abuse on his outspoken vice president, Annette Lu, a leading feminist. Cross-strait relations remained frozen despite the new Taiwanese government's attempt to reengage Beijing in dialogue on practical issues such as trade.

In a further effort to placate Beijing and garner support for his minority government, Chen appointed retired air force general Tang Fei his premier. Tang had served the previous KMT government as minister of defense and supported Taiwan's eventual reunification with mainland China. Most of Chen's cabinet ministers, however, were members of the DPP and lacked prior experience in national-level administration. Chen's attempt at domestic political bridge building suffered a serious setback in early October when Tang, pleading ill health and exhaustion, resigned after just four months in office. His resignation was probably catalyzed by disagreement within the government over whether to complete construction of Taiwan's controversial fourth nuclear power plant, which Tang and the KMT supported but which the DPP and environmental activists opposed. Tang was replaced as premier by DPP veteran Chang Chun-hsiung. With few formal friends in the international arena, Taiwan remained dependent upon the U.S. to bolster its security. If Taiwan's international position was tenuous, domestically the peaceful transition of power from the KMT to the DPP represented a large step forward in the island's process of democratic consolidation.

Fueled by a nearly 25% surge in exports, Taiwan's economy grew at an estimated 6.5%. Unemployment was low at 3%, inflation virtually nil, and foreign currency reserves strong at $113 billion. Reacting skittishly to the election results, however, the stock market declined by 40%. Weakness in the country's vital electronics industry also clouded the economic horizon.

(STEVEN I. LEVINE)

Taiwanese president-elect Chen Shui-bian (centre) pays a visit to outgoing Pres. Lee Teng-hui (left) at Lee's home in Taipei on March 30.

AP/Wide World Photos

TAJIKISTAN

Area: 143,100 sq km (55,300 sq mi)
Population (2000 est.): 6,213,000
Capital: Dushanbe
Chief of state: President Imomali Rakhmonov
Head of government: Prime Minister Akil Akilov

Elections for the two chambers of Tajikistan's new parliament were held in February and March 2000. The party of Pres. Imomali Rakhmonov received the largest number of votes, followed by the Communist Party. The Islamic Revival Movement, one of the main opponents of the government during the 1992–97 civil war, made a surprisingly poor showing, receiving less than 10% of the vote. At the end of March, the National Reconciliation Commission, which had overseen the implementation of the peace process, was dissolved on the grounds that its work had been completed.

Although bombings and assassinations of public figures continued in Dushanbe, Tajikistan's main security concern in 2000 was Afghanistan. Uzbekistan repeatedly accused Tajikistan of harbouring Uzbek extremists who were alleged to have received training at terrorist camps in Afghanistan. Tajikistan consistently denied the charges and agreed to join Uzbekistan and other regional states in countering terrorist incursions. In July officials of the Shanghai Five (Russia, China, Kazakhstan, Kyrgyzstan, and Tajikistan) met in Dushanbe to coordinate efforts against terrorism. By the end of September, however, Tajikistan was facing a different problem with Afghanistan; thousands of refugees from the fighting in northern Afghanistan were reported to be gathering near the Tajik border. Tajik officials and international humanitarian organizations feared a large influx of refugees into Tajikistan if the Afghan Taliban succeeded in overcoming its remaining opponent, the Northern Alliance.

In April members of an illegal extremist group called Hizb-ut Tahrir were arrested in northern Tajikistan; Tajik officials asserted that the group was actually based in Uzbekistan. In August Dushanbe denied that Uzbek militants trying to enter Uzbekistan through Kyrgyzstan had passed through Tajik territory, but he later announced that Tajik border guards had stopped a group of militants trying to enter Uzbekistan directly from Tajikistan. In September Tajikistan made a formal complaint to Uzbekistan about the latter's mining of the common border.

Effects of the drought that affected much of Central Asia were especially devastating for Tajikistan's economy, still in the process of recovering from the civil war. Even before the effects of the drought were felt, the World Bank estimated that 80% of the population of Tajikistan was living in poverty. Though in July the United Nations announced that it would maintain a presence in Tajikistan to help rehabilitate the economy, most international donors were slow to respond to the Tajik government's pleas for assistance.

(BESS BROWN)

TANZANIA

Area: 945,090 sq km (364,901 sq mi)
Population (2000 est.): 35,306,000 (including about 950,000 refugees, of whom about 800,000 are from Burundi)
De facto capital: Dar es Salaam; the legislature meets in Dodoma, the capital designate
Chief of state and head of government: President Benjamin William Mkapa, assisted by Prime Minister Frederick Tulway Sumaye

The year 2000 began on a promising note for Tanzania's gold-mining industry. The first commercial gold mine, Golden Pride, had begun production in 1999, and Ashanti Goldfields Co. Ltd., owner of the Geita mine, was saved from the crisis in which it had found itself in 1999 by a debt facility agreement for $100 million signed on February 22 with Barclays Capital. Additional financial backing was provided by the South African company AngloGold Ltd., which took a 50% share in the mine, and operations at Geita were officially commissioned in August by Pres. Benjamin Mkapa. The first gold from what was expected to become East Africa's largest gold field was produced in June, three months ahead of schedule.

The right to mine two-thirds of the world's only known source of tanzanite, in the Merelani hills in the north of the country, was bought by the South African company African Gem Resources Ltd. Preliminary operations for mining tanzanite, a gemstone many times rarer than diamonds, began near the end of the year, with the government holding a 25% share in the undertaking.

Preparations for the presidential and parliamentary elections on October 29 dominated the political scene. Initially, although the main opposition parties lacked cohesion and appeared to have no dramatic policies to attract the electorate, victory for the ruling party, Chama Cha Mapinduzi (CCM), was in doubt. Critics accused the government of becoming increasingly dictatorial. Charges of extensive corruption in high places carried considerable credence, and, while President Mkapa himself was not believed to be involved, it was thought he lacked the determination to rid the country of the blight. Nationalist sentiment in Zanzibar and Pemba also appeared to threaten the islands' constitutional relationship with the mainland.

In July the selection of CCM's candidates for the October elections led to serious discontent among party members, with further accusations of bribery and even of violence in the selection process. The party's national executive committee, spurred on by President Mkapa, acted quickly to meet the criticisms. At a meeting in Dodoma in August, the committee rejected 40 of those nominated, including four cabinet ministers and some of the wealthiest candidates.

The crisis in Zanzibar over its relationship with the mainland was also in part defused when the members of the national executive committee of the CCM persuaded Zanzibar's controversial incumbent president, Salmin Amour, not to run for an unconstitutional third term. Instead, they selected as their candidate Amani Abeid Karume, son of Sheikh Abeid Amani Karume, who, along with former president Julius Nyerere, had established the United Republic of Tanzania.

In the election President Mkapa won a landslide victory over three opposition candidates, a strong endorsement of his economic reforms. In Zanzibar Karume won with 67% of the vote. Claiming that the Zanzibar election was rigged, however, many supporters of the opposition candidates joined in a boycott of the rerun of the elections in 16 of the island's 50 constituencies and of the swearing in of President Mkapa.

(KENNETH INGHAM)

THAILAND

Area: 513,115 sq km (198,115 sq mi)
Population (2000 est.): 62,423,000
Capital: Bangkok
Chief of state: King Bhumibol Adulyadej
Head of government: Prime Minister Chuan Leekpai

In Thailand autonomous administrative organizations that had been established under the country's 1997 constitution began to function in 2000, and they quickly set about curtailing corruption and abuses of power. The Election Commission, supervising the Senate polls on March 4, disqualified 78 of the 200 winners for cheating. It took five rounds of voting over four months to satisfy the commission, and the Senate did not convene until August. To prevent cheating in the polls for the House of Representatives, the Election Commission tightened the election laws. Seeking to force a House election under the old rules, opposition leader Chavalit Yongchaiyudh led colleagues in a mass resignation from the House in late June, but Prime Minister Chuan Leekpai insisted that the House would not be dissolved before the 2001 budget had been passed.

The effort to stamp out corruption in Thailand resulted in other dramatic actions during the year. Sanan Kajornprasart, the country's powerful interior minister and secretary-general of the Chuan-led Democrat Party, was forced to resign his post in March after the new National Countercorruption Commission alleged that he had intentionally understated his declared assets. The Constitutional Court found Sanan guilty and banished him from political life for five years. The National Countercorruption Commission also found evidence of undeclared shareholdings by 10 cabinet ministers. Even Chuan, who was known as the "Mr. Clean" of Thai politics, was found to have been given shares in a rural cooperative—though evidently without his knowledge.

In March a financial adviser to former Thai prime minister Chavalit Yongchaiyudh's New Aspiration Party was arrested in California as he tried to buy illicit Iraqi oil from U.S. agents posing as sellers. The following month a human trafficking case came to light when a Thai toddler—who apparently had been sold to an illegal-immigration syndicate to help holders of fake passports pass as tourist families—was taken into custody in Los Angeles.

The economy moved out of a three-year crisis, which allowed the International Monetary Fund to relax its supervisory role. Thailand's gross domestic product grew by 4–5%, exports rose, foreign investment poured in, and reserves mounted to precrisis levels. Inflation was held below 2%, and interest rates remained very low. The stock market, however, went into a long slump, and in the last quarter the nation's currency began falling sharply. Throughout the year, inland fish farmers angry over a dam project that had destroyed their livelihoods mounted noisy protests in Bangkok. By October they were joined by villagers protesting a gas pipeline and a coal-fired power station. (ROBERT WOODROW)

TOGO

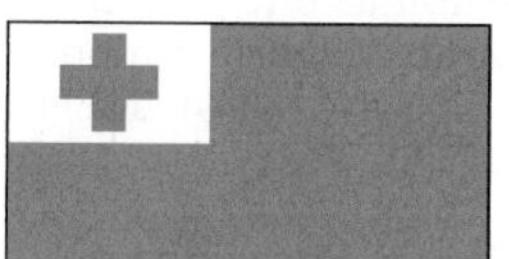

Area: 56,785 sq km (21,925 sq mi)
Population (2000 est.): 5,019,000
Capital: Lomé
Chief of state: President Gen. Gnassingbé Eyadéma
Head of government: Prime Ministers Eugene Koffi Adoboli until August 27 and, from August 31, Gabriel Agbéyomé Kodjo

The government of Togo took new action to limit press freedom on Jan. 4, 2000, by enacting an additional restrictive law. Henceforth, any insult to the head of state might incur up to six months' imprisonment and a maximum fine of $3,100. Journalists guilty of publishing what the government regarded as false information or defamation could be sentenced to three months and a $1,600 fine. Security forces prevented Togo's main opposition party, the Union of Forces of Change, from holding a protest march on January 13.

Prime Minister Eugene Adoboli lost a vote of confidence in the National Assembly on August 25 when representatives refused to accept his explanations for the government's failure to improve education, health services, water supplies, and the country's internal transport system and also to settle the question of salary arrears. Civil servants were owed up to eight months' worth of back pay. Adoboli resigned on August 27, and Pres. Gen. Gnassingbé Eyadéma appointed Gabriel Agbéyomé Kodjo, speaker of the National Assembly, to be the new prime minister.

Eyadéma was implicated in a UN report in March for violating sanctions against providing arms and fuel to Angolan rebels. Nevertheless, on September 25 the Organization of African Unity asked him to try to reconcile the conflicting political factions in Côte d'Ivoire, and on October 2 the OAU commissioned him to mediate the growing crisis in the Democratic Republic of the Congo. (NANCY ELLEN LAWLER)

TONGA

Area: 750 sq km (290 sq mi)
Population (2000 est.): 98,200
Capital: Nuku'alofa
Head of state and government: King Taufa'ahau Tupou IV, assisted by Prime Ministers of Privy Council Baron Vaea and, from January 3, Prince 'Ulukalala Lavaka Ata

In January 2000 King Taufa'ahau Tupou IV appointed as prime minister his youngest son, 'Ulukalala Lavaka Ata, rather than his oldest son, Crown Prince Tupouto'a. The latter was known to favour constitutional change, including a move away from making life appointments to cabinet and other senior political positions. The new prime minister tackled outstanding issues concerning immigration and forwarded a critical auditor general's report to the Legislative Assembly without amendment.

Tonga continued to face a severe financial challenge, with the former prime minister, Baron Vaea, acknowledging that the country's economic situation was grave and expressing concern that this could lead to increased emigration. For 2000–01 the government proposed a total budget of $75 million.

In a new departure, Tonga allowed foreign fishing vessels to operate within its Exclusive Economic Zone. It also provided encouragement for local fishing ventures by removing all duties from diesel fuel and related petroleum products.

During the year tourism, which was already showing growth, was further boosted by the effects of political instability in Fiji.

A survey of the Tonga Trench was conducted by Australian and French scientists in 2000. The scientists found 850 marine species, one-third of them not previously recorded. (BARRIE MACDONALD)

TRINIDAD AND TOBAGO

Area: 5,128 sq km (1,980 sq mi)
Population (2000 est.): 1,292,000
Capital: Port of Spain
Chief of state: President Arthur Napoleon Raymond Robinson
Head of government: Prime Minister Basdeo Panday

The nation was treated during the early months of 2000 to the rare spectacle of the chief of state, Pres. Arthur Robinson, and the head of government, Prime Minister Basdeo Panday, trading harsh words. The issues in contention were the dismissal by Panday of two senators from Tobago, Robinson's home territory before he became president; the "misrepresentation" of the state of Robinson's health by government spokesmen in parliament; and the failure of Panday to "consult" with the president on matters of state, as required by the constitution. These disagreements were eventually resolved.

In an unprecedented development, the local courts ruled against Prime Minister Panday in two cases during the year. In September Panday was found to have acted "unconstitutionally" in excluding a local media company, known to be critical of his administration, from being considered for a cellular license. The following month he was found guilty of having defamed the character of the same company's chairman, Ken Gordon, by referring to him in a public speech as a "pseudo-racist."

Prime Minister Panday's governing United National Congress (UNC) gained a narrow victory in the country's racially charged parliamentary elections in December. The UNC, supported mostly by people of East Indian descent, won 19 seats; the opposition People's National Movement (PNM), with mainly Afro-Trinidadian supporters, won 16 seats. A third party, the National Alliance for Reconstruction, gained one seat. By year's end the PNM was threatening legal challenges to two victorious UNC candidates, alleging that the candidates were citizens of other countries.

(DAVID RENWICK)

TUNISIA

Area: 164,150 sq km (63,378 sq mi)
Population (2000 est.): 9,593,000
Capital: Tunis
Chief of state: President Gen. Zine al-Abidine Ben Ali
Head of government: Prime Minister Mohamed Ghannouchi

On April 6, 2000, Tunisia's founding father, Habib Bourguiba, died at the age of 96 in his hometown of Al-Munastir, where he had been kept under house arrest ever since he was removed from power by Pres. Zine el-Abidine Ben Ali in a bloodless and legal coup in November 1987. Bourguiba's funeral, two days later, in the mausoleum he had built for himself, was attended by only four heads of state—from France, Yemen, Palestine, and Algeria—as well as by the Tunisian head of state, who was offended by the chanting of the crowds for their former leader, in implicit criticism of his regime. (*See* OBITUARIES.)

In fact, criticism of the Tunisian government's human rights record mounted despite increasingly indignant government denials. In April and May attention was focused on a hunger strike in Paris by Tunisian journalist Taoufik Ben Brik, staged because the Tunisian government had tried to revoke his passport and forbid him to travel abroad. He had been accused of publishing false information about the country when he reviewed a critical study of the Ben Ali regime and publicized the government's banning of a well-known publisher, Sihem Ben Sedrine. The government rejected claims by Amnesty International in September that there were 1,000 political prisoners in Tunisia. Nonetheless, the government retaliated against Moncef Marzouki, the spokesperson of the National Council for Liberties in Tunisia, by forcing him out of his university post after he called on Europe and the U.S. to push Tunisia to grant greater respect for human rights.

Municipal elections held at the end of May demonstrated the political dominance of the ruling party, the Democratic Constitutional Rally. That party fielded 4,150 candidates in Tunisia's 257 electoral districts, while opposition parties fielded candidates in fewer than 100 districts.

Despite poor rainfall, the economic situation continued to improve, and tourist revenues rose by 8% in the first half of the year. On March 1 Tunisia's free-trade-area agreement with the European Union came into force, and during the year Tunisia sought to improve its trading relationships with neighbouring nations and to revive the North Africa economic integration organization, the Arab Maghrib Union.

(GEORGE JOFFÉ)

Tunisian Pres. Zine al-Abidine Ben Ali was among the dignitaries in attendance at the funeral of Habib Bourguiba, Tunisia's founding father, in April. Bourguiba's mausoleum is visible in the background.

AFP Worldwide

TURKEY

Area: 779,452 sq km (300,948 sq mi)
Population (2000 est.): 65,667,000
Capital: Ankara
Chief of state: Presidents Suleyman Demirel and, from May 16, Ahmet Necdet Sezer
Head of government: Prime Minister Bulent Ecevit

The euphoria that greeted the decision in December 1999 by the Council of Ministers of the European Union (EU) to grant Turkey the status of a candidate for full membership gradually dissipated during 2000, but the three-party coalition headed by Bulent Ecevit, leader of the centre-left Democratic Left Party, pushed ahead with its program of political and economic reforms. A threat to the government's cohesion was removed when Ecevit's coalition partner, the Nationalist Action Party, agreed on January 12 to await the decision of the European Court of Human Rights before asking the Turkish Grand National Assembly to ratify the death sentence passed on the Kurdish rebel leader Abdullah Ocalan. In July the government was strengthened when Mesut Yilmaz, the leader of the third coalition party, the Motherland Party, entered the cabinet as a deputy prime minister after the Assembly had cleared him of accusations of administrative impropriety. Yilmaz was put in charge of the process of meeting the "Copenhagen criteria," the political and economic reforms required by the EU before the beginning of formal membership negotiations. The EU had earlier criticized the arrest of the mayors of the three main cities of the Kurdish-inhabited region, but the matter was resolved when the mayors were released on February 28 after a week in prison. Controversy then arose over the sentence of one year's imprisonment passed on March 10 on Necmettin Erbakan, the former leader of the banned (Islamic) Welfare Party. The sentence was confirmed on appeal, but a stay was granted until January 2001 as the government began the process of amending the law under which Erbakan was sentenced for an allegedly inflammatory public statement.

Prime Minister Ecevit failed in his attempt to give Pres. Suleyman Demirel a second term of office when a constitutional amendment to that effect was rejected by the Assembly on April 5. Ecevit then put forward Ahmet Necdet Sezer, the president of the Constitutional Court, who was supported by the leaders of all the political parties represented in the Assembly. Sezer was elected president of the republic on a third ballot on May 5 and took office on May 16. He subsequently fell out with Ecevit during the Assembly's summer recess when he vetoed two decrees, one facilitating the dismissal of public employees deemed to have been subversive and the second privatizing some government-owned banks.

The demand for a rapid purge of subversive civil servants, voiced by military commanders in the National Security Council, was intensified early in the year as a result of the discovery that some public employees had links with the Islamic terrorist organization Hezbollah, most of whose members were ethnic Kurds. Its leader, Huseyin Velioglu, was shot dead on January 17 when a safe house of the organization was raided in Istanbul. Nationwide searches revealed at least 60 bodies of people murdered by Hezbollah and buried in safe houses. As the controversy raged, President Sezer decided not to attend the Tehran summit of the Economic Cooperation Organization on June 10. Sezer made his first foreign trip as president on June 23 to the Turkish Republic of Northern Cyprus (recognized only by Turkey) and thereby stressed Turkey's support for the Turkish Cypriots. In October Sezer visited the Turkic republics of Central Asia, an area where Turkish diplomacy was active throughout the year.

The government's main efforts during the year centred on the reduction of inflation. The rise in the world price of oil and the decline in the value of the euro made it impossible to reduce consumer price inflation to 25% by the end of the year, as had been agreed upon with the International Monetary Fund (IMF). There was progress, however; consumer prices rose by 39%, as against 69% in 1999. In November a crisis of confidence hit the banking system and led to large-scale flight of capital. The situation was brought under control when the IMF granted credits in excess of $10 billion. The budget for 2001 continued the austerity policies initiated a year earlier. Nevertheless, two major projects were completed. In January the Ataturk airport in Istanbul acquired new large terminal buildings, and in September the nation's first modern subway line was opened, also in Istanbul.

(ANDREW MANGO)

TURKMENISTAN

Area: 488,100 sq km (188,500 sq mi)
Population (2000 est.): 4,885,000
Capital: Ashgabat
Head of state and government: President Saparmurad Niyazov

There was little movement in the direction of either political or economic reform in Turkmenistan during 2000. Pres. Saparmurad Niyazov retained his tight personal grip on power; he himself asserted that his main source of information, and lever of control, was the National Security Committee. Veteran Foreign Minister Boris Shikhmuradov was replaced at the end of July and then appointed a special envoy of the president with an assignment to seek a solution to the continuing conflict in Afghanistan. For the rest of the year, Turkmen foreign policy focused on Afghanistan.

"Turkmenization" of public life was intensified, with stiffened requirements on the use of the Turkmen language promulgated. Persons seeking government posts or places in institutions of higher education were required not only to demonstrate their command of Turkmen but also to undergo an investigation of their families for three generations back. Foreign languages were removed from the curriculum of most schools; according to the president,

Russian Pres. Vladimir Putin (left) meets with his Turkmeni counterpart, Saparmurad Niyazov, in Ashgabat on May 19.

AP/Wide World Photos

anyone who wished to learn a foreign language could study privately.

In April Niyazov ordered the closure of all religious schools except those operated by the state. He also put the clergy of the two registered confessions (Sunni Islam and Russian Orthodoxy) on the state payroll.

In January Nurberdy Nurmamedov, cofounder of the opposition Agzybirlik (Unity) movement, was arrested on a charge of aggravated hooliganism after a quarrel with a business partner. He was sentenced to five years in corrective labour camps and was later moved to the notorious prison in Turkmenbashi. His family and Turkmenistan's few remaining dissidents believed that the real reason for his arrest was broadcasts on the U.S.-financed Radio Liberty, in which he criticized Niyazov's policies.

Plans for construction of a trans-Caspian pipeline to ship Turkmen gas to Turkey were on hold by the end of the year. According to Western sponsors of the project, there was little hope that it would ever be realized, because there were unresolved disputes over financing and disagreement between Turkmenistan and Azerbaijan over the amount of Azerbaijani gas that could be shipped in the same pipeline.

In February Russia finalized an agreement to buy Turkmen gas in 2000 to make up for a shortfall in Russian production. Subsequent efforts by the Russians to obtain Turkmen agreement to a long-term gas deal, however, were stalled by Turkmen demands for what the Russians considered too high a price.

(BESS BROWN)

TUVALU

Area: 25.6 sq km (9.9 sq mi)
Population (2000 est.): 10,800
Capital: Government offices in Vaiaku, Fongafale islet, of Funafuti atoll
Chief of state: Queen Elizabeth II, represented by Governor-General Sir Tomasi Puapua
Head of government: Prime Ministers Ionatana Ionatana and, from December 8, Lagitupu Tuilimu (acting)

Tuvalu was admitted to the United Nations in September 2000 as the world organization's 189th member and 22 years after having achieved independence from the U.K. In his first UN address, Prime Minister Ionatana Ionatana identified issues that he believed the international community should address for the benefit of small countries: the impact of globalization on indigenous cultures (*see* ECONOMIC AFFAIRS: *Sidebar*), global climate change, and international peace and security. Also in September, Tuvalu moved from associate status to full membership in the Commonwealth of Nations, becoming the 54th member.

The assumption of a higher profile in international affairs and an increased expenditure on infrastructure and social services by the small island nation were facilitated by the receipt of financial benefits from the sale rights to the country's Internet domain name of www.tv for a return of $50 million over 10 years, a 20% share in the holding company dotTV, and a seat on its board. The first payment of $20 million was received early in the year and exceeded the usual annual government expenditure of $14 million.

Ionatana died unexpectedly in December. Prime minister since April 1999, Ionatana had enhanced Tuvalu's international profile as a small but independent nation. (BARRIE MACDONALD)

UGANDA

Area: 241,038 sq km (93,065 sq mi)
Population (2000 est.): 23,318,000
Capital: Kampala
Head of state and government: President Yoweri Museveni, assisted by Prime Minister Apolo Nsibambi

The effect of the agreement signed in Nairobi, Kenya, on Dec. 8, 1999, by the presidents of Uganda and The Sudan and aimed at ending the support each country was alleged to be giving to rebels challenging their respective governments was short-lived. Although invaders from The Sudan were the first to breach the agreement in 2000, Uganda's foreign affairs minister, Eriya Kategaya, publicly affirmed his skepticism regarding negotiations with the rebels. Critics of the government also firmly believed that a cessation of hostilities would have run counter to the aim of one of Pres. Yoweri Museveni's most active supporters, the U.S., to destabilize the Sudanese government.

The burned corpses of religious cult members lie on the floor of a church in Kanungu, Uganda, on March 20.

The government's military activities on a wider front led to the raising of a series of questions regarding the purpose of external aid, of which Uganda was a leading beneficiary, and the government's use of it. The French newspaper *La Libération* revealed in January that 55% of Uganda's military budget came as "development aid" from external donors. In May the Paris Club of creditor nations delayed debt relief because Ugandan forces had become involved in fighting with their former Rwandan allies in the Democratic Republic of the Congo, and on June 30 Amnesty International appealed to President Museveni and to Pres. Maj. Gen. Paul Kagame of Rwanda to end the atrocities by their forces in northeastern Congo.

The leading opposition parties' boycott of the referendum held on June 29 to determine whether the existing system of "no-party" government should continue contributed to the low turnout of only 47.2% of the electorate. Although the opposition claimed a moral victory because less than half the electorate had voted, the result was, in effect, a practical triumph for the government. On August 10, however, the nation's constitutional court threw out one of the two laws that validated the referendum. Museveni warned that the ruling could create a crisis in the country.

AP/Wide World Photos

When the bodies of at least 500 members of a religious cult were found on March 17 in the southwest of the county, it was thought to have been a case of mass suicide. When several more mass graves were discovered, however, it was realized that murder had been committed on a vast scale. There was speculation that the leaders of the cult, having required the members to sell their possessions and hand over their money upon joining, had carried out the killings and escaped with the proceeds after a promised apocalypse did not occur and members wanted their money returned.

In October it was reported that at least 43 people had died in northern Uganda after having contracted the Ebola virus, and that a World Health Organization team of experts had been sent to advise local authorities on how to control the outbreak. Hospitals in the area were said to be overwhelmed. By early December the number of deaths had risen to 156. (KENNETH INGHAM)

UKRAINE

Area: 603,700 sq km (233,100 sq mi)
Population (2000 est.): 49,242,000
Capital: Kiev
Chief of state: President Leonid Kuchma
Head of government: Prime Minister Viktor Yushchenko

The year 2000 began in Ukraine with a parliamentary crisis. A pro-government right-centrist majority was formed under the leadership of former president Leonid Kravchuk (United Social Democratic Party) and attempted to remove Speaker Oleksandr Tkachenko and his deputy, Adam Martynyuk. The move failed on January 21 but led to a separate session by the leftist legislators. On February 1 the new coalition chose Ivan Plyushch as speaker of the Supreme Council by a vote of 255–1. A week later the majority took over the parliament building by force, evicting Tkachenko and the leftist faction. In September Oleksandr Karpov of the Popular Democratic Party replaced Kravchuk as the leader of the right-centrist majority, but by that time the number of deputies committed to the faction had declined to 171.

The Ukrainian government anounced in mid-January its intention to hold a nationwide referendum on six propositions: the introduction of a no-confidence vote in the Supreme Council; the adoption of the constitution by referendum; the right of the president to dissolve the Supreme Council if no majority was formed within one month or if it failed to adopt a new budget within three months; the reduction of the number of deputies from 450 to 300; the formation of a second, upper, house; and the abolition of deputies' immunity from prosecution. President Kuchma subsequently accepted a decision by the Constitutional Court that declared the first two items to be unconstitutional. Despite protests from the Council of Europe, the controversial referendum was held on April 16. About 81% of the eligible voters went to the polls, and the remaining four propositions were approved by between 81% and 90% of the electorate.

In late September Kuchma dismissed Foreign Minister Borys Tarasyuk, reportedly for his failure to increase Ukrainian trade in Europe and for the lack of progress toward Ukraine's integration into European structures and associate European Union membership. Tarasyuk's successor was a former foreign minister, Anatoly Zlenko.

Ukraine's economy improved somewhat. Gross domestic product rose by 5% in the first half of the year, and industrial output (the prime factor in GDP rise) was reportedly up 11.7% in the period January–July as compared with 1999. Inflation, however, remained uncomfortably high at 25–29%, and Ukraine still owed about $2.2 billion to the International Monetary Fund. That organization admonished Ukraine's national bank for having overstated its hard currency reserves in 1997 and 1998 in order to obtain about $200 million in loans. The coal industry remained in a desperate state, and 40,000 miners went on strike in May to protest arrears in wages of almost 750 million hryvny (about $140 million) and the low rate of payment compared with other sectors of the economy. Prime Minister Viktor Yushchenko announced a Reforms for Prosperity program that anticipated an average GDP rise of 6.5% in the period 2002–04.

In June, following U.S. Pres. Bill Clinton's visit to Kiev, President Kuchma announced that the controversial Chernobyl nuclear power station would be closed by Dec. 15, 2000. The country remained desperately short of energy, however, and much time and effort were spent wrangling with Russia over the size of Ukraine's oil and gas debts.

Relations with Russia continued to be difficult. Early in the year, Russia complained about the deteriorating conditions concerning the use of the Russian language by the large Russian minority living in Ukraine. In May several Russians attacked and killed Ukrainian composer Ihor Bilozir in Lviv, allegedly for singing Ukrainian songs in a café. On May 30 some 3,000 protesters marched through the city chanting, "Down with the Russians!"

The demographic and health situations also remained grim. Ukraine's population fell further, from an estimated 49,890,000 in 1999 to some 49,242,000 in mid-2000. In August a mass poisoning occurred in Mykolayiv province, evidently the result of waste from a military facility being dumped into the soil. Several villages were evacuated after 331 people were hospitalized.

(DAVID R. MARPLES)

UNITED ARAB EMIRATES

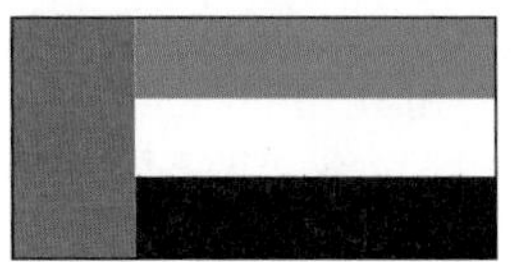

Area: 83,600 sq km (32,280 sq mi)
Population (2000 est.): 3,022,000
Capital: Abu Dhabi
Chief of state: President Sheikh Zaid ibn Sultan an-Nahayan
Head of government: Prime Minister Sheikh Maktum ibn Rashid al-Maktum

In March 2000 the United Arab Emirates (U.A.E.) signed an agreement with the American corporation Lockheed Martin to buy 80 F-16 fighter aircraft for $6.4 billion. This was the largest sale in 2000 for the U.S. of military equipment anywhere. Negotiations preceding this agreement had extended over many years. In May Russia announced that it would sell the U.A.E. $500 million worth of antiaircraft equipment.

During the year the U.A.E. moved to implement the "Dolphin" project, an agreement with neighbouring Qatar to import natural gas from Qatar's North Field. The project called for construction of a major gas pipeline from Qatar to the U.A.E. and then on to Oman, and it was expected to cost between $8 billion and $10 billion.

Since oil revenues contributed more than 25% of gross domestic product, the U.A.E. economy benefited significantly from the sharp increase in oil prices in 2000. By the year's end the economy was growing at a healthy 5.3%. Investments during the year increased oil-production capacity to three million barrels per day, but the U.A.E. complied with agreements within OPEC to produce slightly more than two million barrels per day.

(WILLIAM A. RUGH)

UNITED KINGDOM

Area: 244,101 sq km (94,248 sq mi)
Population (2000 est.): 59,714,000
Capital: London
Chief of state: Queen Elizabeth II
Head of government: Prime Minister Tony Blair

Domestic Affairs. Public confidence in the U.K.'s Labour government, headed by Prime Minister Tony Blair, was severely shaken in 2000 by a crisis that erupted suddenly in September and came close to bringing the country's economy to a standstill. A loosely knit group of farmers and truckers set out to protest the high cost of fuel. As in other countries, fuel prices in the U.K. had risen sharply following the rise in crude oil prices on the world market. In addition, fuel taxes in the U.K. were the highest in Europe. The protesters blockaded the U.K.'s oil refineries and for three days managed to prevent most gasoline and diesel supplies from reaching gas stations, industry, or public services such as hospitals. Only when it became clear that their action was having a far more drastic impact than they expected and that the support they had enjoyed from most of the public was threatening to evaporate did they suspend their blockade. They did, however, warn that they would resume it in 60 days if the government failed to tackle the cause of their complaint. On November 8, one week before the expiry of the 60 days, Gordon Brown, the chancellor of the Exchequer, announced small reductions in the duty (tax) on diesel and "clean," low-sulfur gasoline. This was enough to prevent immediate further disruptions; reductions in December in the world price of crude oil also helped to defuse the protests.

Nevertheless, in the short term, the damage to the government's reputation was severe. Labour's support fell by 10 points in two weeks—the sharpest fall recorded in the history of polls assessing the public's approval of government. Labour's standing among its traditional working-class voters fell especially sharply. For the first time since 1992, the Conservative Party regained the lead. As life began to return to normal, however, so did political allegiances, although some damage to Labour's standing persisted.

The fuel crisis was a symptom (and a sharp expression) of a wider malaise that afflicted Blair's administration. During the year opinion polls found that increasing numbers of voters thought the government was losing its way, becoming arrogant, putting presentation before substance, and failing to deliver improvements to the main public services. These claims were not made only by the government's political opponents. One of the harshest analyses was provided by Blair's own polling adviser, Philip Gould. In a private memorandum, written in May but subsequently leaked to the media, Gould warned the prime minister of "a sense that for much of the last 18 months, the Government has been drifting, growing almost monthly weaker and more diffuse."

The government's troubles were not all of its own making, and it could claim to be presiding over a successful economy, but it did seem to be paying the price for failing to think strategically. One vivid demonstration of this was provided by the House of Lords. In November 1999, as the first stage of a longer-term program to reform the Lords, most hereditary peers had been stripped of their right to attend. The government had allowed 92 to remain, most of them either Conservative or nonparty critics of the government. The effect was to ensure that Labour peers constituted only slightly over one-third of the new House of Lords. Throughout 2000 the antigovernment majority flexed its muscles more aggressively than it had ever done when the House of Lords was dominated by hereditary peers. Scarcely a week went by without the Lords' defeating the government over some aspect of its legislation. Although the government had the power to reverse these defeats by invoking its majority in the House of Commons, the procedure for doing this was slow and cumbersome. The process significantly delayed the government's program.

In Brighton, Eng., on September 26, police face protesters angry over high fuel prices.

AP/Wide World Photos

Blair faced different kinds of setbacks in other aspects of his constitutional reforms. On May 4, running as an independent, former Labour MP Ken Livingstone (*see* BIOGRAPHIES) won the election to be London's first directly elected mayor. Labour's candidate, Frank Dobson—a former health secretary in Blair's cabinet—came in a poor third, winning only 13% of the vote. (In the first count, Livingstone scored 39%, with Steven Norris, the Conservative candidate, coming in second with 27%. With no candidate winning 50%, all except the top two were eliminated and the second preferences of the eliminated candidates taken into account. Livingstone defeated Norris on the second count by 58–42%.) Labour also fared badly in separate elections on the same day to the new Greater London Assembly, winning just 30% of the party vote (almost 20 points less than its share in the 1997 general election), compared with 29% for the Conservatives, 15% for the Liberal Democrats, 11% for the Greens, and 15% for other parties.

In Wales Alun Michael resigned as first secretary on February 9, forestalling a vote of no-confidence that he looked certain to lose. Michael had been Blair's favoured candidate for the post, but he had never gained the full confidence of Labour Party members in Wales, many of whom felt that he had been imposed on them in place of their preferred candidate, Rhodri Morgan. Following Michael's resignation, Morgan was appointed unopposed. He sought to bolster Labour's position in the Welsh Assembly (where the party had 29 out of 60 seats and, therefore, did not command a majority) by seeking cooperation with the Liberal Democrats. This led to a formal coalition between the two parties, agreed to on October 5.

In Scotland, where a Labour–Liberal Democrat coalition had been in operation since the election of the country's first Parliament in May 1999, upheaval came out of the blue. First Minister Donald Dewar, often called "the father of the nation" as a tribute to his central role in bringing Scotland to devolution, died suddenly on October 11. (*See* OBITUARIES.) He was succeeded as Labour leader in Scotland, and as first minister, by Scotland's enterprise minister, Henry McLeish.

Perhaps the greatest running controversy in the U.K. during 2000 concerned the Millennium Dome, a vast circular tentlike structure 320 m (1,050 ft) in diameter—the largest enclosed space in the world. Built with money from the National Lottery, it was located in Greenwich, southeast London, next to the prime meridian line. The dome's purpose was to house a visitor attraction to celebrate different facets of British life at the start of the new millennium. It attracted only half the 12 million visitors expected, however, and needed regular injections of extra cash from the lottery to pay its bills. The decision, supported by the government, to hand over extra money diverted from other causes was widely condemned.

A fatal rail accident on October 17 had widespread repercussions. Four people were killed when an intercity express came off the rails at Hatfield, 32 km (20 mi) north of London. It quickly became clear that the track itself had been defective. Railtrack, the privately owned company that had operated the U.K.'s tracks since privatization in 1996, was criticized for putting profits before safety—a charge that the company strenuously denied. Safety checks elsewhere on the rail network uncovered other potential defects, however, and the rail system was disrupted for some weeks as low speed limits were imposed on many sections of track while the defective rails were replaced.

Some of the blame was directed at the Conservatives for the way they had privatized the rail system when they were in control of the government. A week after the Hatfield crash, the Conservatives came under fire again with the publication of the report from an official inquiry into bovine spongiform encephalopathy (BSE), widely known as "mad cow" disease. The inquiry found that some civil servants and Conservative ministers had failed to divulge the full truth in the late 1980s and early '90s about the dangers of BSE's crossing the species barrier and infecting humans. By the end of 2000, some 80 people in the U.K. had died of the human variant of BSE.

Economic Affairs. The U.K. enjoyed its eighth consecutive year of expansion as the economy grew by 3% and unemployment fell to 5%. Meanwhile, inflation remained subdued, with the underlying rate staying close to 2% throughout the year. The Bank of England raised its main "repo" interest rate early in the year in two stages from 5.5% to 6%, but the rate then remained unchanged for the rest of the year. The continuing strength of sterling continued to worry exporters, particularly manufacturers. The British currency was caught in the crossfire between a strong dollar and a weak euro; the pound lost around 10% of its value against the dollar during the year, but sterling gained further ground against the euro to end the year around 15% higher than when the euro was launched in January 1999.

In July Brown unveiled plans to raise public spending by 10% in real terms over the three years 2001–04, with the largest increases for public transport, education, and the National Health Service. In November he announced above-inflation increases for 2001 and 2002 in state retirement pensions as well as the cuts in diesel- and low-sulfur-gasoline taxes.

Public finances remained in surplus, which allowed the government to reduce the national debt. The prospects for continuing surpluses were aided by the auction in April of the third generation of mobile telephone licenses. Expected to raise around £3 billion (about $4.4 billion), they ended up raising £22.5 billion (about $32.6 billion). The success of this auction prompted a number of other countries, especially in Europe, to copy the U.K.'s example.

The continuing strength of sterling caused special problems for the U.K.'s motor industry. In March the German company Bayerische Motoren Werke AG (BMW) announced that it was selling its U.K. subsidiary, Rover Cars. Rover was eventually acquired by a newly formed consortium, Phoenix, headed by a former Rover executive. Phoenix immediately embarked on a program of rationalization and job reduction. In the second half of 2000, Rover was producing cars at only one-third the rate of just three years earlier. In May the Ford Motor Co. unveiled plans to end volume car production at its main U.K. factory, at Dagenham, in east London.

Some manufacturers with British subsidiaries—especially Japanese companies—warned that they would eventually scale back their investment in the U.K. if it remained outside the European single currency. The government, however, refused to shift from its policy of waiting until the right economic conditions materialized. In October Blair gave his clearest warning yet that this day was still some way off when he said that if a referendum was held then, he would vote against joining the euro.

Foreign Affairs. In October Blair set out his vision for Europe in a major speech in Warsaw. He criticized the European Union (EU) for losing touch with its people: "The citizens of Europe must feel that they own Europe, not that Europe owns them." He called for the EU to draw up a "charter of competences" that would set out the limits to its power and so stop it from drifting toward becoming a federal state. This way, he argued, "the EU will remain a unique combination of the intergovernmental and the supranational. Such a Europe can, in its economic and political strength, be a superpower—a superpower not a superstate."

The former dictator of Chile, Gen. Augusto Pinochet Ugarte, was finally allowed to return home on March 2. Pinochet had been arrested during a visit to the U.K. 17 months earlier after Spain requested that he be extradited on charges of having tortured Spanish citizens during his period in office. The U.K. home secretary, Jack Straw (*see* BIOGRAPHIES), decided to let him return to Chile after a team of doctors concluded that Pinochet was "at present unfit to face trial" and that "no change to that position can be expected."

Northern Ireland. Despite occasional acts of violence by small fringe groups of terrorists, the province remained at peace throughout 2000, but hopes of enduring political stability proved elusive. At the beginning of the year, the newly formed Northern Ireland Executive was in charge of powers that had been devolved to it by the British government. The executive was headed by First Minister David Trimble, the leader of the mainly Protestant Ulster Unionist Party. His deputy was Seamus Mallon from the mainly Catholic Social Democratic and Labour Party. The Executive also included members of Sinn Fein—the political arm of the Irish Republican Army (IRA)—and the Democratic Unionists.

Trimble led a divided party, many members of which felt that Sinn Fein was not fulfilling its commitment to persuade the IRA to decommission its weapons. On January 31 Gen. Sir John de Chastelain, the Canadian who had been appointed to oversee the decommissioning process, reported that the IRA had given up none of its weapons. On February 4 Trimble gave notice of his intention to resign as first minister unless the IRA had a change of heart. On February 11, to forestall the collapse of the Executive, Peter Mandelson, the U.K.'s Northern Ireland secretary, suspended all the devolved institutions.

Subsequently, Trimble said he would be willing to resume his duties as first minister without the IRA's handing in any weapons, provided that it made other arrangements to put them beyond use. This concession provoked one MP, the Rev. Martin Smyth, to challenge Trimble's leadership of the Ulster Unionists. At a special conference on March 25, Trimble defeated Smyth 57–43%.

Intensive negotiations in early May, involving the British and Irish governments, led to the IRA announcement on May 6 that it was ready to begin the process of putting its weapons beyond use "completely and verifiably." It agreed to place them in sealed dumps in the Irish Republic, where they could be examined by a team of international experts headed by Cyril Ramaphosa, a former official of South Africa's African National Congress, and Martti Ahtisaari, the former president of Finland. On this basis Trimble agreed to a restoration of the Executive. On May 27 a further special conference of his party agreed to back him by the narrow margin of 53–47%.

The Executive resumed its duties on May 30 and continued in office throughout the rest of 2000. In October Trimble defeated a further challenge to his policies from his critics within his party. This time his margin of victory was 54–46%. The issue of the permanent decommissioning of IRA arms remained unresolved, however, as the Republicans retained the power to reclaim their weapons from the arms dumps should they decide to withdraw from the peace process. (PETER KELLNER)

UNITED STATES

Area: 9,363,364 sq km (3,615,215 sq mi), including 204,446 sq km of inland water but excluding the 155,534 sq km of the Great Lakes that lie within U.S. boundaries
Population (2000 est.): 275,372,000
Capital: Washington, D.C.
Head of state and government: President Bill Clinton

The United States stormed into 2000 full of energy and confidence, its economy purring, its world leadership role unchallenged, and its two-century-old democratic experiment still vigorous. Incidence of crime, welfare dependency, and joblessness were down, and the stock market was soaring.

In February economic expansion surged through its 108th straight month, surpassing the nation's consecutive growth record set in the 1960s. A month later national capital markets hit all-time highs. A spirited battle was under way as both major political parties eagerly vied to supply the successor to Pres. Bill Clinton, whose legacy of economic prosperity and centrist-policy successes had been diminished only by personal scandal. Optimism was soaring, and the U.S. was the envy of the world in the realms of democracy, economy, cultural offerings, and military might.

By year's end, however, the national mood had markedly changed. The new tone was one of bewilderment, even creeping pessimism. The national election, far from confirming a clear new path, had ended in a puzzling stalemate capped by an unprecedented and dispiriting legal challenge. The stock market was slumping badly; consumer confidence was shaken; and economic statistics had suddenly turned ominous. The effectiveness of American world leadership was under challenge. Americans seemed badly divided, even rudderless, and commentators had difficulty pinning down a precise cause.

Politics and the Election. Ever since the end of the Cold War a decade earlier, the U.S. had struggled to find a sense of national direction. Secure in the dominance of its economy and national security apparatus, the country internally split into two relatively equal political camps. The Democratic Party favoured the government's moving more actively to assist those citizens left behind in the general prosperity, whereas the Republican Party (GOP) believed that government should step back and allow the ingenuity of the American people to produce without interference. The 2000 election, if anything, muddled the debate further—the most equivocal result in U.S. history, a near 50–50 split on virtually every level of government, with no clear call for any political party.

If any trend emerged from the national balloting, it was that the incumbent party lost. The Republican ticket of George W. Bush and Richard B. Cheney narrowly defeated Democratic challengers Albert A. Gore, Jr., and Joseph I. Lieberman. (*See* BIOGRAPHIES.) Democrats, however, narrowed their deficit in the U.S. House of Representatives for the third election in a row, leaving the Republicans with less than a 10-seat advantage. Democrats also erased the Republican lead among U.S. senators, creating a 50–50 tie in the upper chamber. It was much the same on the state level—Republicans made gains in state legislatures (where Democrats had enjoyed a slight advantage), creating a virtual tie in party control nationwide, and the GOP lost part of its sizable lead in govenorships. (*See* Special Report.)

For the first time, a presidential spouse entered elective politics. Hillary

AP/Wide World Photos

After winning election to the U.S. Senate on November 7, First Lady Hillary Rodham Clinton addresses supporters in New York City as President Clinton (background, left) and daughter, Chelsea, look on.

Rodham Clinton, though outspent by her Republican opponent, Rick Lazio, won the open U.S. Senate seat in her adopted state of New York. Only six weeks prior to the election, special counsel Robert Ray had concluded a six-year investigation of the Clintons, pointing out untruthful testimony by Hillary Clinton but concluding that there was insufficient evidence to prove indictable criminal wrongdoing. In another unusual congressional contest, a plane crash claimed the life of Missouri Gov. Mel Carnahan, Democratic challenger for the Senate seat held by John Ashcroft, only days before the election. Nonetheless, Carnahan won a narrow victory after the new governor promised to appoint Carnahan's widow, Jean, to the Senate seat.

Awaiting a signal from voters, Congress approved almost no major legislation during the year. With both parties contesting for support from the technology-driven "new economy," two bills sought by Silicon Valley were easily approved. They expanded H1-B visas for highly skilled foreign workers and settled the legality of electronic signatures for commercial transactions.

Other legislative accomplishments in a divided government were scarce. Neither Congress nor President Clinton made any serious attempt to reform Social Security or Medicare. For the third year, legislators could not establish a "patient's bill of rights" in dealing with health maintenance organizations, provide prescription-drug coverage for seniors, or enact more than nominal campaign-finance-reform legislation. Late in December, however, Clinton unveiled sweeping new rules to guard the privacy of patients' medical records; doctors and hospitals would be required to secure a patient's consent before disclosing health information to a third party. Congress also was unable to undo a June U.S. Supreme Court decision that voided state attempts to outlaw "partial-birth" abortions.

Amid charges of election-year posturing, the Republican Congress approved bills eliminating the national estate and gift tax and ending the penalty imposed on two-income married families. Both were vetoed by President Clinton, who claimed the measures disproportionately favoured the wealthy. Clinton also vetoed a measure establishing a long-sought repository for nuclear waste at Yucca Mountain, Nevada, 160 km (100 mi) northwest of Las Vegas, Nev. None of the vetoes was overridden.

The Economy. The country's historic economic expansion finally ran out of steam late in the year. The slowdown arrived abruptly, without overt warning, and economists later blamed a combination of causes, including higher oil prices, violence in the Middle East, the uncertain election, delayed effects of multiple interest-rate increases, a stock market decline, the bursting of the Internet bubble, and the simple age of the up cycle. By year's end, with economic activity slowing and consumer confidence dropping, most analysts were predicting a period of reduced growth or even an economic recession.

Fueled by world leadership in telecommunications and high tech, the U.S. economic engine actually accelerated early in the year. Effects of a widely feared year 2000 computer problem proved minimal, thanks to expensive remedial preparations. After gross domestic product (GDP) posted a robust 4.2% gain in 1999, the economy expanded by an extraordinary 5.6% in the first half of 2000. This led economists to worry anew over the potential revival of inflation, which crept steadily upward after several years in the nominal 2% range.

Under Chairman of the Board of Governors of the U.S. Federal Reserve System (Fed) Alan Greenspan (*see* BIOGRAPHIES), the inflation-fighting Fed had enacted three small interest-rate increases in 1999 and followed that with three more in early 2000, including a full 0.5% boost in May. That left interest rates 1.75% higher than in 1999, driving up costs for corporations and individuals alike. Even as those increases flowed through the system, the economy was further shocked by rapid increases in oil prices worldwide, the result of a 1999 cutback in production by OPEC cartel countries. At one point oil prices topped $35 per barrel, three times the price level in December 1998. Increased energy costs affected everyone, particularly in the Midwest, where supply and refinery problems sent gasoline prices spiraling above $2 per gallon.

The twin blows from interest and energy increases produced a marked effect on financial markets. The National Association of Securities Dealers automated quotations (Nasdaq) stock market index, heavy with high-flying technology companies and overbought dot-coms, topped out above 5000 in March and then began an erratic and prolonged descent. By year's end the average had been halved—the worst performance in Nasdaq's nearly 30-year history. (*See* ECONOMIC AFFAIRS.) The year's biggest economic story was the long-anticipated shakeout in dot-coms, companies attempting to capitalize commercially on surging use of the Internet. Dozens of once-high-flying firms exhausted their start-up funds without showing a profit during the year, and their bankruptcies or mergers contributed to the darkening mood by year's end.

By the third quarter, GDP growth was down to 2.2% and slowing. Joblessness stayed near the 30-year low rate of 3.9% established during the year, but many companies were announcing layoffs and cutbacks at year's end. Inflation rose a modest 3.5%, but it too was trending upward.

Domestic Issues. Serious crime, which had declined in the U.S. for eight consecutive years, leveled out during 2000. Incidence of eight major personal and property offenses reported to local law-enforcement authorities dropped 0.3% during the first half of the year, compared with a 9.5% decrease in 1999. Analysts noted that demographic trends spurring the decrease over the previous decade—including a reduction in the crime-prone 15–25-year-old male population—would be reversed in coming years.

Researchers funded by the federal government announced in June that they had virtually completed deciphering the entire human genetic code, well ahead of schedule. (*See* LIFE SCIENCES: *Special Report.*) A jury in Florida awarded a record $145 billion in punitive damages in a class-action suit brought against major tobacco companies by smokers afflicted with tobacco-related illnesses. Tobacco company officials warned that the verdict could prompt bankruptcies in the industry and adversely affect the 25-year, $246 billion settlement negotiated with states in 1998.

In Washington, D.C., Judge Thomas P. Jackson, who had earlier declared software giant Microsoft Corp. guilty of antitrust violations, ordered the company broken up. The decision was immediately appealed by Microsoft, which started the year as the world's most valuable enterprise. If sustained on appeal, the ruling would produce the country's largest government-mandated breakup since AT&T was restructured in 1984.

Reports of numerous deaths and injuries—eventually totaling 148 and 500, respectively—on Ford Motor Co. products, particularly the popular Explorer sports utility vehicle, prompted a historic recall of 6.5 million Firestone tires. As federal officials investigated, Ford and Firestone parent Bridgestone Corp. each blamed the other firm's manufacturing or design process for the problems. Lawmakers criticized both companies at separate House and Senate hearings. Firestone's chief executive officer made a public apology, while Ford said it would not rest until every faulty tire was replaced. By year's end, Ford had settled at least seven lawsuits and planned to settle more cases stemming from accidents involving Explorer vehicles and Firestone tires. Another major economic setback occurred when forest fires swept a dozen western states in the summer, charring more than 400,000 ha (1,000,000 ac). One particularly virulent fire, which caused an estimated $300 million damage to the federal Los Alamos (N.M.) National Laboratory alone, started as a "controlled burn" set by the U.S. Forest Service.

The booming economy and a landmark 1996 federal law helped spur a continued reduction in public-assistance rolls during the year. President Clinton noted that welfare caseloads nationwide had dropped by eight million, or 60%, during his presidency, most after passage of a bipartisan welfare-reform act just prior to the 1996 election. Apparently ending a decade-long controversy, the Food and Drug Administration (FDA) approved the U.S. sale of the European-developed "morning after" drug RU-486. The drug, also known as mifepristone, allows women to terminate a pregnancy up to several weeks following sexual contact. Republican presidential candidate George W. Bush said that he opposed the FDA move, but he stopped short of promising to reverse it.

Preliminary census results for April 2000 were released on December 28. The U.S. population swelled to 281,421,906.

Foreign Policy. No challenger emerged during the year to the U.S.'s claim as the sole world superpower. Russia, Japan, and China continued to struggle with internal economic weakness, and European attempts to consolidate were hampered by an underperforming currency and intramural political difficulties. Throughout the year the U.S. military was deployed around the world to keep the peace, and its superiority in any pitched engagement was unquestioned.

The resulting U.S. vulnerability to terrorism was underscored anew on October 12, however, when an explosives-laden rubber boat rammed a U.S. destroyer, the USS *Cole,* docked in Yemen for refueling. The resulting charge tore a major hole amidships, killing 17 American sailors and wounding 39. American investigative authorities rushed to the scene but received only desultory cooperation from sovereignty-minded Yemeni officials. U.S. forces were placed on alert worldwide, and, fearing sabotage, American authorities temporarily stopped military vessels from using Egypt's vulnerable Suez Canal.

No credible group claimed responsibility for the assault. U.S. investigators soon focused suspicion on Osama bin Laden, a Saudi dissident operating a terrorist-training organization under protection of Taliban authorities in Afghanistan. Bin Laden had reportedly planned coordinated terrorist assaults on U.S. interests worldwide on Jan. 1, 2000, including an attack on a U.S. ship visiting Yemen, but most plans had been at least temporarily thwarted.

The probe of a mysterious October 1999 EgyptAir plane crash off the coast of Nantucket, Mass., stalled as American and Egyptian investigators produced conflicting interpretations of available evidence. U.S. officials attributed the cause of the crash to a suicide by an off-duty co-pilot, Gamil al-Batouti, who was at the controls as the jumbo jet stalled and went into a fatal dive. Egyptians suggested that equipment failure prompted the disaster.

U.S. foreign-policy makers could claim a major victory when Yugoslav Pres. Slobodan Milosevic resigned on October 6. U.S.-led NATO forces conducted a major bombing campaign against the Milosevic regime in early 1999 to stop mistreatment of ethnic Albanians in Kosovo (a province of Serbia) and had maintained economic sanctions against his regime following cessation of military action. Milosevic lost an election in late September but was holding out for a runoff when Serbian citizens stormed government buildings in Belgrade, prompting an immediate change in government.

Two other peace initiatives championed by President Clinton suffered setbacks during the year. A peace plan in Ireland, which Clinton helped negotiate in 1998, stalled as the Irish Republican Army refused to decommission (surrender or destroy) its heavy weapons.

The long-running Middle East peace process, on the verge of a major breakthrough at midyear, virtually collapsed despite major efforts by Clinton and his administration. Clinton summoned Israeli Prime Minister Ehud Barak and Palestinian leader Yasir Arafat to Camp David, Maryland, on July 11–25 for intensive discussions. With Clinton shuttling between the two and exerting maximum pressure, the principals edged close to an agreement before an impasse was ultimately declared. The major sticking point was the legal status of Jerusalem, which both Arabs and Jews claimed as their capital.

In ensuing weeks the process broke down completely. Palestinian rioting began after conservative former general Ariel Sharon visited Temple Mount, technically in a neutral zone but traditionally off-limits for prominent Jewish visitors. Barak, suffering political criticism for excessive accommodation at Camp David, responded with force. As violence escalated, Israel suspended participation in the peace process, and Barak announced new national elections in 2001.

Fidel Castro, the target of U.S. economic sanctions since shortly after he took over Cuba in 1959, enjoyed propaganda victories at the U.S.'s expense. Castro mobilized Cuban public opinion to demand the return of Elián González, a six-year-old boy whose mother had died at sea while fleeing Cuba for the U.S. in late 1999. The administration announced it would comply in early January, but the boy's Miami, Fla.-based relatives sued, tying his fate up in legal wrangling for months. In April Elián's father, Juan Miguel González, traveled to the U.S. to escort his son home.

Following a legal ruling, armed agents of the Immigration and Naturalization Service stormed the Miami home of the boy's relatives in the early hours of April 22, seizing the child at gunpoint and reuniting him with his father in the Washington, D.C., area. U.S. authorities, however, prohibited the Cubans (now joined by several of Elián's Cuban classmates) from leaving until court appeals had been exhausted. Finally, on June 28, after the U.S. Supreme Court refused to issue a stay, Elián and his father returned to Havana and a highly publicized Castro welcome. Castro later in the year poked fun at election difficulties in Florida, offering to send election assistance to ensure that democracy prevailed.

(continued on page 516)

SPECIAL REPORT

The U.S. Election of 2000

by David C. Beckwith

The U.S.'s tumultuous experiment with democracy over two centuries has produced a colourful record of conflict and decision, but the presidential election of 2000 will rank near the top of any list. *Time* magazine, exaggerating only slightly, dubbed it "the wildest election in history." It produced the country's fourth president who had lost the popular vote, and the first president who owed his victory directly to a decision by the U.S. Supreme Court. As the year began, presumptive nominees Vice Pres. Al Gore and Texas Gov. George W. Bush (*see* BIOGRAPHIES) were targets of spirited primary challenges from political mavericks. Former U.S. senator Bill Bradley of New Jersey failed to wean away any of the liberal Democratic pillars backing the vice president—organized labour, minorities, and women activists. Though Bradley made a strong early effort, he lost the New Hampshire primary by a narrow 52–48% margin and never again came close to winning a state.

U.S. Sen. John McCain of Arizona was a far more serious problem for Bush, whose tightly scripted message and regal campaigning satisfied party regulars but failed to excite less-partisan voters. Bush had prepared for a challenge from the conservative wing that never materialized. Instead, the moderate McCain rolled through New Hampshire on a bus dubbed the *Straight Talk Express*, charming journalists, selling campaign finance reform, and racking up a devastating 19-point victory.

The reeling Bush forces then took off the gloves in South Carolina, employing surrogates to question war hero McCain's commitment to conservative values and party principles. The backlash from Bush's unpretty 11-point South Carolina win, however, helped carry McCain to victory the following week in Michigan, where independents and Democrats voted in large numbers. By the time the Bush campaign righted itself and ran out the clock, Bush's once-substantial advantage over Gore in funding and polls was gone.

Political scientists were unanimous that, given peace and prosperity, the incumbent vice president should win easily. Gore suffered, however, from a pedantic personal style and his association with Pres. Bill Clinton. Bush, by contrast, was widely viewed as personable and attractive, but Democrats successfully raised concerns: did he have the experience and intellectual heft to be president?

AP/Wide World Photos

Broward county canvassing board member Judge Robert Rosenberg carefully examines a disputed ballot with a magnifying glass on November 24 at the county courthouse in Fort Lauderdale, Fla.

As the parties assembled for their midsummer national conventions, both candidates were having trouble generating substantial enthusiasm. The GOP convention in Philadelphia was staged as a paean to ethnic diversity, a visual reminder of Bush's outreach to minorities and his "compassionate conservatism" campaign theme. That helped produce a double-digit poll lead for Bush. Gore countered with an energetic populist speech at the Democratic gathering in Los Angeles, his stage entrance punctuated by a long and passionate kiss with his wife, Tipper, that underlined a contrast with Clinton. Bush's lead soon disappeared, and Gore surged 10 points ahead.

In September Bush's campaign tried to scuttle appearances scheduled by the bipartisan Commission on Presidential Debates, provoking outrage from journalists weary of carefully staged campaign events. Bush was forced to reverse field, the episode seeming to confirm his lack of confidence in any matchup with the more experienced Gore. The turning point in the campaign may have been the first debate in early October. Bush delivered a competent and affable performance, exceeding expectations, while Gore repeatedly interrupted, demanded extra time, sighed audibly, and grimaced while Bush was talking. After this overbearing spectacle the polls shifted yet again, with the Republican gradually retaking a substantial lead.

Bush, however, appeared to run out of gas at the end. In the last week of the campaign, he was thrown on the defensive when news of a 1976 arrest for drunk driving surfaced, when he appeared to deny that Social Security was a government program, and when left-leaning supporters of Green Party candidate Ralph Nader (*see* BIOGRAPHIES) began to return to the Democratic fold. The result was, as one wag put it, a tie, a coin flip where the coin landed on its edge.

On election night, in a debacle for television journalism, all commercial networks declared that Gore had won

Florida. Within hours, though, they had placed Florida back in the undecided column, then awarded the state and the election to Bush, and then put the state and the election back in doubt. Bush's lead appeared to be as narrow as 400 votes out of 6.1 million cast in the state.

Exit polls showed deep splits in the electorate. Gore eventually won the national popular vote by a margin of more than 500,000. Bush won among men, 53–42%, but Gore prevailed with women, 54–43%. Despite Bush's outreach, only about 9% of African Americans sided with the Republican. Bush won virtually the entire heartland of the country, while Gore won the West Coast and most northeastern and upper Midwestern states. The overall result was close because, aided by modern polling, both candidates had successfully presented a moderate platform that appealed to the vast American centre. Nonetheless, many voters still had doubts about personal qualities; a common evaluation was that "neither man made the sale."

On November 8 both candidates immediately began flooding Florida with hundreds of lawyers and political operatives. Democrats challenged Bush's lead by starting recounts in several urban counties, claiming that inexpensive punch-card voting devices had failed to record intended Gore ballots. County officials were soon seen on television holding up ballots, eyeing "chads" with one, two, or three corners removed or searching for indentations that might reveal voter intent. Both sides replaced principle with expediency. Republicans, ordinarily states' rights advocates, eyed the Democratic Florida judiciary and began appealing to federal courts. Democrats moved to disqualify hundreds of military ballots from overseas on technicalities even as they vowed that "all votes must be counted."

Nearly 50 individual lawsuits were filed challenging aspects of the Florida election. The Florida Supreme Court (all seven members nominated by Democratic governors) twice extended the recount process, saying that protecting the right to vote was more critical than observing a legislative-set timetable. The U.S. Supreme Court (seven of nine members nominated by Republican presidents) surprised virtually all experts by stepping in and overturning both rulings. In their final decision, seven justices declared the lack of uniform standards defining voter intent amounted to a denial of equal protection of the laws. That stopped the recount and effectively decided the contest—35 days after election day.

At year's end the national economy was weakening, and polls showed that a substantial minority of citizens questioned Bush's legitimacy. Technically, Congress remained in Republican hands, but in reality it was deadlocked, divided almost evenly between the parties. The new president prepared to enter office with the weakest mandate to govern of any administration in more than a century.

David C. Beckwith is vice president of National Cable Television Association.

U.S. ELECTION 2000

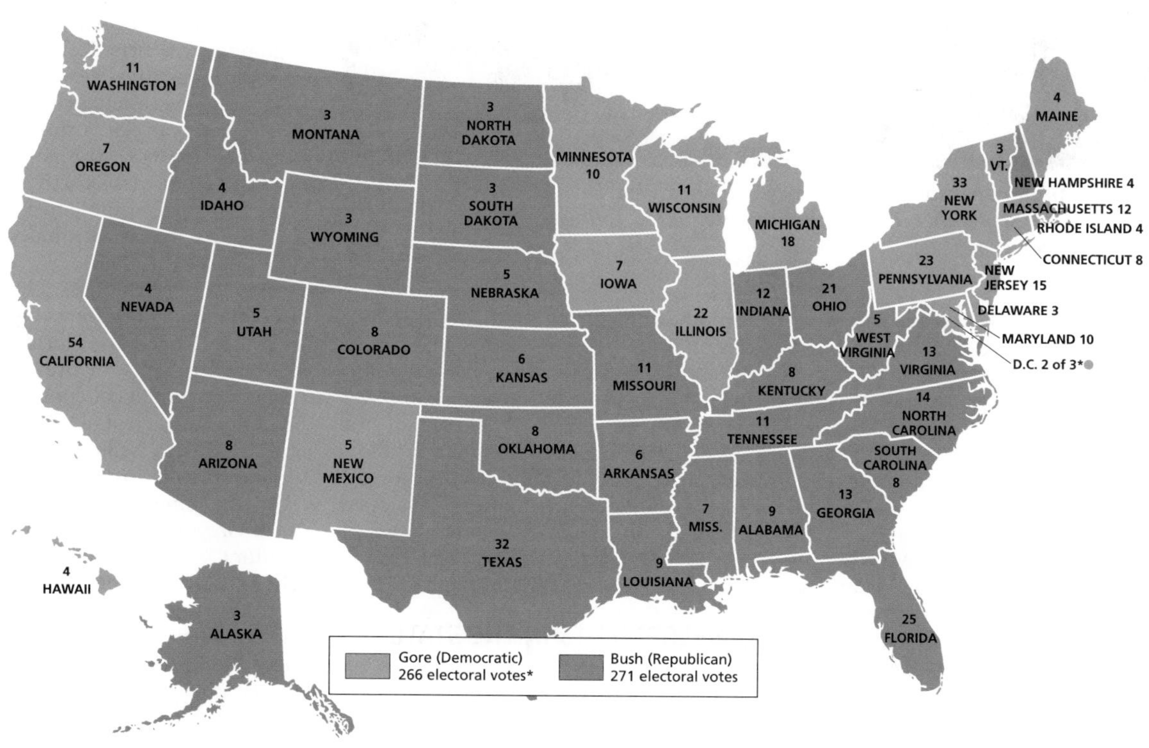

* Protesting D.C.'s lack of congressional representation, one D.C. elector cast a blank ballot.

AP/Wide World Photos

Former Los Alamos National Laboratory scientist Wen Ho Lee leaves a federal court on September 13 in Albuquerque, N.M., followed by his daughter, Alberta Lee.

(continued from page 513)

U.S. relations with China continued on an uneven path. Trade relations between the two countries were finally normalized in October, overcoming U.S. concerns over Chinese human rights problems, China's militant attitude toward Taiwan, and the exclusion of U.S. investment. China lodged vigorous objections to U.S. prosecution of Wen Ho Lee, a scientist at the Los Alamos National Laboratory accused of having sent U.S. nuclear secrets to China. After having publicly proclaimed overwhelming evidence against Lee, the U.S. abruptly allowed the Taiwan native to plead guilty to reduced charges.

The 1997 Kyoto global warming treaty, which would require the U.S. and other industrial countries to reduce greenhouse gas emissions markedly, suffered a major setback in a conference at The Hague. Complications over higher oil prices, the collapse of the Russian economy, and a plan to allow wealthy nations to buy "credits" for excessive emissions from less-developed countries prompted a near collapse of ongoing negotiations.

(DAVID C. BECKWITH)

DEVELOPMENTS IN THE STATES, 2000

As the U.S. economy continued to hum along, states enjoyed another quiet legislative year in 2000. Many state governments enacted multibillion-dollar tax cuts for a record seventh consecutive year and poured additional funding into education programs. Joblessness, dependency on welfare, and incidence of serious crime continued to fall during the year, contributing to a widespread sense among Americans of well-being and satisfaction.

There were areas of contention, however. A law recognizing homosexual "civil unions" roiled Vermont and beyond. Teachers unions dealt major blows to a drive for school vouchers in two states; Illinois Gov. George H. Ryan suspended administration of a death penalty "fraught with error"; and November elections produced controversy over voting procedures and a historic even split in partisan breakdown among state and federal legislators. Forty-six states held regular legislative sessions during the year, and 15 staged special sessions. (*See* Special Report.) Democrats won 8 of 11 gubernatorial contests, a net pickup of one. In the only election where party control changed, U.S. Rep. Robert Wise unseated West Virginia Gov. Cecil Underwood, a Republican. That narrowed the GOP advantage in governorships nationwide for 2001 to 29 Republicans, 19 Democrats, and 2 independents.

Government Structure, Powers. Nebraska voters approved, for the fourth time, term limits for their unicameral legislature. Previous measures had been invalidated by courts. Kentucky instituted annual legislative sessions, and only four states were left in which the legislature met every other year. West Virginia voters established a family court system. In North Dakota and Virginia, voters established hunting and fishing as constitutionally protected rights.

Government Relations. The extremely close national elections, highlighted by legal challenges in Florida, prompted new calls for federal oversight of traditional state and local control of balloting procedures. Each state often utilized several methods, including electronic devices, optical scanners, punch cards, lever machines, and paper ballots. In 2000 Oregon became the first state to conduct a presidential election overwhelmingly by mail. Arizona experimented with voting over the Internet in its presidential primary. Experts said there were problems with all methods and faulted existing measures for lacking consistency.

Continuing a recent trend, the U.S. Supreme Court issued yet another 5–4 ruling backing state power against federal encroachment. The court ruled that states could not be sued for violations of federal age-discrimination legislation. In another key case, however, the high court invalidated a Nebraska law prohibiting "partial-birth" abortions. A 5–4 majority found that the law "creates a significant health risk" for some women. The decision apparently doomed similar laws in 30 other states attempting to curtail second-trimester abortions.

In 1998 the U.S. Congress approved a law encouraging states to reduce their drunk-driving blood standard to 0.08% from the widely used 0.10%, without notable results. Congress, consequently, in 2000 effectively preempted state law for the 32 states that retained 0.10% or left it to the arresting officer to decide whether a motorist was inebriated, giving them two years to enact the 0.08% standard before mandating reduction of federal highway aid. Mothers Against Drunk Driving estimated that the law would result in 500 fewer highway deaths nationwide.

Congress also moved to reduce a loophole under which 20 states claimed about $2 billion in excessive Medicaid funds; the practice would be phased out over five years. Led by New York and Illinois, the states claimed to spend more than they actually did on Medicaid and received extra federal matching funds.

Finances. Buoyed by the strong national economy, states reduced taxes by a net $5.8 billion during 2000, an unprecedented seventh consecutive year of significant cuts. Fourteen state legislatures enacted new tax reductions amounting to 1% or more of state revenue, and tax increases were rare across the country. Effects of phased-in tax reductions enacted in previous fiscal years had a further impact on state balance sheets.

Ten states reduced personal income taxes, and seven states initiated or boosted the earned-income tax credit to benefit low-income workers. Sales taxes were cut in Colorado, and sales tax "holidays" or rebates were enacted in Florida, Iowa, Colorado, Maryland, and Minnesota. As oil prices spiked at midyear, Indiana Gov. Frank O'Bannon suspended the state gasoline tax, and Illinois suspended sales tax levies on gasoline. Onetime tax rebates on property or income taxes were also popular, with major programs approved in Illinois, Pennsylvania, Ohio, and Missouri.

Voters approved even more tax cuts in November balloting. After the state legislature rejected the idea, Massachusetts voters approved a $1.2 billion income tax cut, the largest in state history. During the year Washington courts invalidated a popular 1999 revenue-cutting initiative. State voters responded by approving a new rollback of state tax and fee increases that would reduce local tax payments by $1 billion. Voters in Colorado and Oregon, however, defeated broad tax-cut and spending-limit initiatives, and Arizona voters approved a sales tax increase to fund education projects.

Louisiana was the lone state with revenue problems. The legislature raised both personal income taxes and sales taxes on food and utilities. In November state voters rejected a ballot proposal to offset a proposed sales tax reduction with a larger state income tax increase.

States wrestled with tax liability arising from modern communications. Many states were losing serious revenue from lost sales taxes on Internet transactions; one estimate showed states losing $15 billion in revenue by 2003. Florida became the first state to reform overall telecommunications taxes, traditionally imposed by counties and municipalities. The new bill consolidated their imposition statewide and initiated revenue sharing with local authorities to equalize previous revenue levels.

Health and Welfare. States continued to expand oversight of health organizations during the year. Kentucky, Massachusetts, New Mexico, and Utah required health plans to cover mental illness; this brought to 31 the states mandating equal treatment for mental and physical problems. Iowa, Rhode Island, Massachusetts, and Delaware joined ten states ordering health plans to cover contraceptives. Massachusetts, Alaska, and Hawaii joined 38 states mandating coverage for diabetes.

Maine became the fourth state to reject physician-assisted suicide when voters narrowly defeated a measure to allow it. Only Oregon allowed doctors to prescribe lethal drugs to terminally ill patients. Massachusetts voters rejected a proposition for statewide universal health insurance by 2002. Colorado voters rejected a mandatory waiting period before an abortion; that left 19 states ordering a waiting period, usually 24 hours.

State welfare rolls continued to shrink during the year, which cheered backers of the 1996 federal welfare-reform law. By late 2000 welfare recipients had dropped by 49%, or 6 million individuals, in four years. All states met their federally imposed targets for putting former welfare recipients to work during the year.

Education. The nationwide drive to provide alternatives to low-performing public schools suffered major setbacks in November when voters in California and Michigan overwhelmingly defeated school voucher initiatives. A federal appeals court voided a landmark voucher program in Cleveland. Washington voters defeated a measure allowing establishment of semi-independent charter schools. Teachers unions mobilized opposition to the measures, calling them an assault on the public schools.

California voters approved a college tuition assistance plan for low-income students, the largest higher-education program since the federal GI Bill of Rights following World War II. About 30% of high-school seniors would be eligible for the $1.2 billion plan, with grants dependent on student grades.

Following positive results from a similar move in California, Arizona voters terminated bilingual education in public schools. Georgia voters ended teacher tenure. In Oregon voters turned down one measure prohibiting instruction on homosexuality and another tying teacher pay to student achievement.

Law and Justice. Guns and the death penalty were at the centre of public policy debate in states during the year, even as incidence of major property and violent crime dropped for the eighth consecutive year. Texas continued to carry out more death sentences than any other state, and Gov. George W. Bush (*see* BIOGRAPHIES) defended that record during the presidential contest. Early in 2000 Illinois Governor Ryan, also a Republican, said his state's capital punishment system was "fraught with error" following exoneration of several convicts under a death sentence; he suspended executions indefinitely.

Nationwide, states executed 85 convicts during the year, down from 98 the previous year, more than half of them in Texas and Oklahoma. South Dakota became the 13th state to ban execution of the mentally retarded.

Twenty-eight states addressed cyber crime, typically enacting laws prohibiting identity theft, outlawing the spread of computer viruses, and banning lewd proposals to minors. New Jersey joined 22 states that had established a registry of sex offenders on the Internet. More than 30 states considered legislation to regulate cell phone use in automobiles, but no major bills were approved.

Although new incidents were rare in 2000, states continued to wrestle with a wave of mass shootings in schools and public places in recent years. New York became the first state to sue gun manufacturers for making an unsafe product. Voters in Colorado and Oregon, sites of recent school shootings, required background checks for purchasers at gun shows. (*See* LAW, CRIME, AND LAW ENFORCEMENT: *Special Report.*)

Alaska voters rejected a measure to legalize marijuana, but voters in Colorado and Nevada joined six other states allowing its use as a medicine. California approved a breakthrough proposal to send nonviolent drug offenders to treatment rather than jail. Advocates predicted the measure would cut the state's prison population by 36,000, or 20%.

Environment. Numerous states struggled with adverse effects of urban sprawl, including traffic congestion, overcrowded schools, and pollution, but few dramatic steps were recorded. In an early showdown, voters in Arizona and Colorado rejected strict growth boundaries, rings around cities beyond which development would be prohibited. The measures were backed by environmentalists but opposed by real-estate concerns, construction interests, and some local officials.

California's partial deregulation of electricity in 1996—freeing power generators from regulation while retaining retail price caps—pushed several state utilities toward insolvency and created major electricity shortages. New Jersey became the first state to set targets for reducing greenhouse gases. Reasoning that lead in cathode-ray tubes posed environmental and health hazards, Massachusetts became the first state to ban computer monitors and televisions from landfills.

Gambling. South Carolina voters, a year after having rid the state of video poker machines, approved a statewide lottery, with most revenue earmarked for education. Arkansas voters rejected a proposal for a state lottery, casinos, and charity bingo. South Dakota voters rejected termination of the state's video lottery and raised the bet limit from $5 to $100 at casinos in the town of Deadwood. Massachusetts voters turned down a proposal to ban greyhound racing. With the Cold War having ended, a nuclear fallout shelter in White Sulphur Springs, W.Va., intended to protect Congress, was now surplus property. State voters, however, rejected an initiative to convert it into a casino.

Equal Rights. Vermont's legislature enacted a law recognizing "civil unions" between two persons of the same sex, embroiling the state in a political and moral conflict that was felt across the country. The measure followed a late-1999 ruling by the state Supreme Court that the state constitution prohibited discrimination against same-sex couples, a decision that some legislators said forced their hand. The new law conferred on gay and lesbian couples who chose to enter into a civil union the same rights and benefits afforded traditionally married couples, including inheritance rights and tax status.

Passage of the Vermont law produced a tumultuous election and several ramifications. Republicans won the state House for the first time in a decade, and popular Democratic Gov. Howard Dean, who signed the bill, narrowly avoided a runoff. Most observers predicted the law would survive, however. In the meantime, 8 more states joined 28 that had banned same-sex marriage since 1995, refusing to recognize unions promulgated in other states. Maine voters again turned down an initiative prohibiting discrimination against gays.

Florida's Supreme Court barred a ballot initiative prohibiting affirmative action in state employment, contracts, and college admissions; California and Washington had earlier approved similar measures. Ending a long-running controversy, South Carolina moved its Confederate flag from the Statehouse dome to a site near its Confederate Soldiers Monument. Kansas, Missouri, Tennessee, and Washington joined North Carolina and Connecticut in gathering information on traffic and criminal stops in an effort to combat "racial profiling."

Alabama voters repealed an unenforceable ban on interracial marriage, the last state to do so. Utah became the 26th state to declare English the official state language. New York gave preliminary approval to removal of 170 masculine references in the 46-page state constitution, to be replaced by gender-neutral language. Responding to complaints from Native Americans, Maine joined Minnesota and Montana in requiring that the word *squaw* be removed from public sites. Native Americans said *squaw* was demeaning because its English translation was "whore."

(DAVID C. BECKWITH)

AP/Wide World Photos

High-school students parade through the streets of Montpelier, Vt., on October 15 to demonstrate their support for civil unions for same-sex couples.

URUGUAY

Area: 176,215 sq km (68,037 sq mi)
Population (2000 est.): 3,278,000
Capital: Montevideo
Head of state and government: Presidents Julio María Sanguinetti and, from March 1, Jorge Batlle Ibáñez

In 2000 Uruguay was preoccupied with economic development and social issues, including human rights. On March 1 Jorge Batlle Ibáñez of the moderate Colorado Party, the winner of Uruguay's fourth democratic presidential election since the end of military rule in 1985, took office. He succeeded Julio María Sanguinetti, also of the Colorado Party. Batlle, a champion of neoliberal economics, called for barrier-free trade and reforms that would bring greater transparency and efficiency to the government. He retained four incumbent ministers in his 13-member cabinet—including the ministers of foreign affairs and the interior—and gave five cabinet posts to members of the Colorado's coalition partner, the Blanco Party.

On May 14 Uruguay broke with tradition by holding departmental elections separately from the presidential and legislative elections. A coalition that included the moderate Progressive Encounter and the leftist Broad Front retained power in Montevideo—the nation's capital and dominant urban centre—but 18 other more rural departments remained under the control of the Colorado and Blanco parties.

At the urging of human rights groups, a presidentially appointed commission began to investigate the fates of some 150–180 Uruguayans who had disappeared during the period 1973–85, when Uruguay's armed forces was participating in the shadowy antiterrorist campaign known as Operation Condor. In April Batlle confirmed that the missing granddaughter of renowned Argentine poet Juan Gelman was living in Uruguay and had been one of the numerous infants taken from mothers detained by Uruguayan authorities during Operation Condor; many of the infants were raised by the families of soldiers or policemen. Gelman's daughter-in-law was kidnapped in Argentina in 1976 and secretly transported to Uruguay, where she allegedly gave birth. Batlle's revelation, made only after Gelman had created a months-long storm of publicity, was the first official recognition in Uruguay of that covert policy. (STEPHEN P. DAVIS)

UZBEKISTAN

Area: 447,400 sq km (172,700 sq mi)
Population (2000 est.): 24,756,000
Capital: Tashkent
Chief of state and head of government: President Islam Karimov, assisted by Prime Minister Otkir Sultonov

During 2000 Uzbekistan's authoritarian president Islam Karimov actively sought international support against Islamic extremists whose program called for the overthrow of the secular constitution and the setting up of a radical Muslim state, much as the Taliban had done in Afghanistan. He described them as terrorists and had some success in persuading the international community to accept his interpretation. The Islamic militants, who had attempted to invade Uzbekistan in 1999, resumed their efforts in August 2000. The United States designated the Islamic Movement of Uzbekistan, the main force behind the armed attacks in neighbouring countries and in Uzbekistan itself, as a terrorist organization funded by the Saudi extremist Osama bin Laden. The U.S. provided Uzbekistan with military transport vehicles, and Russian troops joined those from Uzbekistan, Kazakhstan, and Tajikistan in antiterrorist exercises.

In balloting on January 9, Karimov was reelected president with 92% of the vote—even the rival candidate said that he had voted for him. International observers asserted that the election was neither free nor fair, while the Uzbek opposition in exile described the election as a sham. The opposition in exile also rejected Karimov's appeal at the end of January for them to return to Uzbekistan to work for the good of the country. Exiled writer-politician Muhammad Solih, one of those to whom Karimov appealed by name, noted that the president's practice of imprisoning thousands of pious Muslims merely for exercising their beliefs was the main factor in creating extremism.

On April 21 the heads of state of Uzbekistan, Tajikistan, Kazakhstan, and Kyrgyzstan met in Tashkent and agreed to pool their efforts to counter terrorism, Islamic extremism, and the drug trade. Visiting India in May, Karimov sought support against terrorism, and he repeatedly called on Russia for assurances that the country shared Uzbekistan's concern about stopping terrorism. During a visit to Tashkent in May, Russian Pres. Vladimir Putin threatened the Taliban with preemptive air strikes. The Taliban responded with a threat to attack Uzbekistan and Tajikistan and complained to the United Nations about Uzbek violations of Afghan airspace.

Uzbek television reported on August 7 that Islamic militants had launched an attack in the Surkhandarya region that borders Afghanistan. The Islamic Movement of Uzbekistan, based in Afghanistan, claimed responsibility for the incursion, which was apparently intended to set up weapons and supply depots within Uzbekistan for the future use of militant groups. Later in the summer militants assembled in northern Tajikistan apparently in order to penetrate Uzbek territory via Kyrgyzstan. (BESS BROWN)

VANUATU

Area: 12,190 sq km (4,707 sq mi)
Population (2000 est.): 199,000
Capital: Vila
Chief of state: President John Bernard Bani
Head of government: Prime Minister Barak Sopé

During 2000 the newly elected government of Barak Sopé embarked on a program to address government debts that in 1999 had stood at $70 million. A controversy arose, however, when a Thai company seeking tax-exempt status under Vanuatu law agreed to pay $5.4 million annually for five years to assist in the debt repayment.

A confrontation ensued between Parliament and Pres. John Bernard Bani over controversial legislation that would allow for greater political control over the public service; the plan was opposed by the Asian Development Bank. The Supreme Court ruled, however, that Bani could not withhold his consent. In August, Deputy Prime Minister Stanley Reginald was forced to resign after facing charges of misconduct and was replaced by James Bule, the trade minister. Attempts by the opposition to generate support for a parliamentary vote of no confidence failed, and the government retained a working majority in Parliament.

Another controversy surfaced when the fee that was charged candidates to run in provincial elections scheduled for late October was set at 100,000 vatu (about $70,000), which led some parties, considering the fees excessive, to call for a boycott of nominations. Vanuatu contributed a paramilitary force of 33 to support UN peacekeeping in East Timor and Bosnia and Herzegovina.

(BARRIE MACDONALD)

VATICAN CITY STATE

Area: 44 ha (109 ac)
Population (2000 est.): 800
Chief of state: (sovereign pontiff) Pope John Paul II
Head of administration: Secretary of State Angelo Cardinal Sodano, who heads a pontifical commission of five cardinals

Nowhere was the universality of the Roman Catholic Church's mission more evident in 2000 than in the Jubilee of Cardinals and Bishops, which brought more than 1,000 of the church's highest prelates to the city of Rome.

Pope John Paul II continued to add to his impressive record as a canonizer, including more than 100 martyrs of China among those elevated to sainthood. This embarrassed Chinese government officials, who had been known to resist the church's proselytizing efforts in their country. His beatification of Pius IX, the declaredly antimodernist pope, was also greeted with controversy in some quarters.

The greatest event of the year, certainly from the numerical standpoint, was World Youth Day, which attracted an estimated two million young people to Rome for a six-day celebration. This massive gathering was successfully accommodated, even though the visitors exceeded by three times the receptive capacity of the city. Tremendous preparation was required for this result, including the revamping of major parts of Rome.

While the Jubilee absorbed most of the pope's energies, he continued to find time to address world concerns and pressed for a settlement of the dispute over Jerusalem that would defend all the faiths involved. His concern with the Middle East was also reflected in an apostolic visit to the Holy Land. In December Israel objected to the pontiff's meeting with far-right Austrian politician Jörg Haider, who presented the pope with a Christmas tree from Carinthia. (GREGORY O. SMITH)

VENEZUELA

Area: 916,445 sq km (353,841 sq mi)
Population (2000 est.): 24,170,000
Capital: Caracas
Head of state and government: President Hugo Chávez Frías

In the July 30, 2000, presidential elections, Hugo Chávez Frías defeated Lieut. Col. Francisco Arias Cárdenas, once his closest collaborator, by a popular vote margin of 59% to 38%. The election results confirmed Chávez's appeal to the urban poor and the downwardly mobile middle class. The president's Fifth Republic Movement (MVR) and its ally, the Movement to Socialism (MAS), captured 99 of the 163 seats in Venezuela's unicameral National Assembly. Though the total number of seats won was insufficient to allow an amending of the constitution, the margin of victory allowed Chávez's supporters to pass a law that enabled him to legislate unilaterally on a broad range of political and economic matters. The MVR and MAS also captured 14 of the 23 governorships, while the Democratic Action (AD) party and Social Christians—the parties that had dominated Venezuela between 1958 and 1998—all but disappeared.

Soon after his inauguration to a six-year term, Chávez, in a gesture with huge symbolic implications, instructed his supporters in the National Assembly to authorize the interment of Gen. Isaias Medina Angarita's remains in the Panteón Nacional, the final resting place of Venezuela's most revered heroes. The

On August 31, while in Brazil to participate in the summit of South American presidents, Venezuelan Pres. Hugo Chávez Frías speaks to students at Católica University in Brasília.

Jose Varella/AFP Worldwide

then-dominant AD's 1945 overthrow of Medina, whose government was considered a military dictatorship, had long been presented as a critical landmark in the modernization and democratization of Venezuela. This resuscitation of Medina's image was another tactic to further discredit the AD. In another move to signal his new course, Chávez journeyed to the Middle East, where he urged OPEC's Arab members to unite with Venezuela against Western pressures to increase petroleum production and to lower the international price of crude oil. At the September summit of Latin American countries in Brasília, Braz., he voiced opposition to the U.S. government's initiative to help Colombia's military defeat that country's narcotic-trafficking guerrilla insurgents.

In late October Chávez played host to Cuban Pres. Fidel Castro during a five-day visit. The two toured the country, and Chávez repeatedly praised the domestic social policies of the Cuban Revolution and Castro's efforts to prevent superpower domination over Latin America. Chávez also announced that he had made a pact with Cuba similar to the Pact of San José, a 1980 agreement in which Venezuela agreed to sell petroleum at a deep discount to several Central American states.

The dramatic rise in oil prices that began in mid-1999 underpinned President Chávez's adoption of populist policies at home and advocacy in the international arena of less-developed nations' interests. During the first half of 2000, the average price for a Venezuelan "basket" of crude and refined petroleum products increased by 58.2%, and the price of a barrel of Maracaibo crude approached $26 in mid-September, when OPEC authorized an increase in production quotas. The country's share of world oil reserves stood at 7%.

Following a deep 1999 recession, Venezuela began an economic recovery in the second quarter of 2000. Inflation ran about 14%, a reduction of 6% from the 1999 rate. In October improved economic conditions led Fedepetrol—the powerful petroleum workers union—to demand and receive significant wage increases, following the threat of a production shutdown. The showdown between Chávez and the Venezuelan Confederation of Workers was taken to the polls in December. A referendum empowering Chávez to suspend all union leaders and schedule elections for their replacement was passed, though more than three-fourths of voters abstained. (DAVID J. MYERS)

VIETNAM

Area: 331,041 sq km (127,816 sq mi)
Population (2000 est.): 78,774,000
Capital: Hanoi
Chief of state: President Tran Duc Luong
Head of government: Prime Minister Phan Van Khai

On April 30, 2000, Vietnam celebrated the 25th anniversary of the end of the Vietnam War. Parades and other public festivities commemorated the event. A day before, however, the nation had lost Pham Van Dong (*see* OBITUARIES), one of its last revolutionary leaders and an architect of Vietnam's independence and reunification movements.

Throughout the year, reconciliation with the U.S. was a major theme in Vietnam. In mid-July a landmark trade agreement was reached with the U.S. Vietnam gave the U.S. access to its protected domestic economy in exchange for lower tariffs on Vietnamese goods entering American markets. Prime Minister Phan Van Khai marked the historic event with a nationwide address. For the country's more than 5,000 state-owned companies, the agreement was interpreted as the beginning of the end of substantial subsidies for the sector.

Economically, much potential remained unrealized for the nation. Partly because of the great number of deaths during the war, Vietnam had a mostly young citizenry. More than 30% of Vietnamese were under the age of 15, and 60% were 30 years old and under. Even with a literacy rate of over 90%, however, well-paying jobs remained scarce. An estimated 1.2 million Vietnamese were entering the workforce each year. All but 10% of the country's workers were on farms or in small cottage industries. Some 12 million to 15 million Vietnamese were without jobs or underemployed. Echoing movements in the rest of Asia, a burgeoning low-end Internet-related sector sputtered to life.

At the end of July, the much-awaited opening of Vietnam's first stock exchange finally occurred. The Securities Trading Centre in Ho Chi Minh City had all of two companies listed when it began operations. Even so, on opening day more than 2,000 people thronged the building to purchase shares. Given Vietnam's continuing stringent controls on financial matters and the lacklustre pace of economic growth, the development of the local market proceeded cautiously. Much remained to be done to put Vietnam on the map for international investors.

The one obviously bright spot was tourism. Some two million people visited the country during the year, 20% more than in 1999. Among the visitors were a stream of top-ranked American government officials. In March William Cohen became the first U.S. defense secretary to travel to Vietnam since the end of the war. U.S. Sen. John McCain of Arizona, a former prisoner of war and an unsuccessful presidential candidate in 2000, also made a much-publicized visit. Pres. Bill Clinton made a historic trip in November to help promote stronger cultural and business ties. He was accompanied by his wife, Hillary, on her first trip abroad since her election to the Senate.

(ALEXANDRA A. SENO)

YEMEN

Area: 555,000 sq km (214,300 sq mi)
Population (2000 est.): 17,479,000
Capital: San'a'
Chief of state: President Maj. Gen. 'Ali 'Abdallah Salih
Head of government: Prime Minister 'Abd al-Karim al-Iryani

In June 2000 Yemeni Foreign Minister 'Abd al-Qadir al-Ba Jamal and his Saudi Arabian counterpart, Saud al-Faisal, signed what Yemen called a "final and permanent treaty" concerning their common border. It was based on the Treaty of Taif of 1934, which had demarcated only a small part of the 2,500-km (1,550-mi) Yemeni-Saudi border. The two diplomats agreed to settle "in an amicable way" the undemarcated eastern end of the border, which had become the focus of tension and disagreement between Yemen and Saudi Arabia in recent years. Signed during a visit to Saudi Arabia by Pres. Maj. Gen. 'Ali 'Abdallah Salih, this new agreement was expected to result in improved relations between the two countries.

On October 12 suicide bombers in a small boat steered their craft into the side of the USS *Cole,* a U.S. destroyer in the harbour at the port of Aden. A large-scale investigation into the bombing, which killed 17 sailors and injured 39, was led by the FBI. (*See* MILITARY AFFAIRS.) (WILLIAM A. RUGH)

YUGOSLAVIA

Area: 102,173 sq km (39,449 sq mi)
Population (2000 est.): 10,662,000
Capital: Belgrade
Chief of state: Presidents Slobodan Milosevic and, from October 7, Vojislav Kostunica
Head of government: Prime Ministers Momir Bulatovic and, from November 4, Zoran Zizic

In September and October 2000, Yugoslav voters, forming a surprisingly united democratic opposition front and mounting massive public demonstrations, ended the autocratic rule of Slobodan Milosevic—a regime that had persisted for longer than a decade.

The events that led to Milosevic's overthrow surprised all parties involved. On October 5, angered by a Constitutional Court decision that had nullified the September 24 presidential election—which most believed had been won by the chief opposition candidate, Vojislav Kostunica (*see* BIOGRAPHIES)—hundreds of thousands of people converged upon Belgrade. Crowds stormed the federal parliament and took over state television. They met with little resistance from police, who often joined the demonstrators. A day later the court decision was reversed, Milosevic conceded defeat, and on October 7 Kostunica was sworn in as the new president. Opposition parties also swept to victory in federal parliamentary and municipal elections. The international community quickly recognized Kostunica's victory, and the country was promptly reinstated into the United Nations, the Organization for Security and Cooperation in Europe, and the Council of Europe after having been suspended for eight years. By year's end diplomatic relations had been reestablished with the former Yugoslav republics, the U.S., and other countries.

However great was the public astonishment and joy, discontent with the new pro-democratic leadership soon bubbled to the surface along several fault lines: a dire economic situation and severe energy crisis; continuing instability in Kosovo; new hopes for autonomy voiced by provincial leaders in Vojvodina (with a large Hungarian minority) and the Sandzak (an ethnically mixed area); debates over the future status of Montenegro, the second (with Serbia) constituent republic of Yugoslavia; and bickering between the forces that had ousted Milosevic.

Kostunica, a former law professor, had no experience in government, and the fractious coalition of 18 parties that formed his Democratic Opposition of Serbia (DOS) was difficult to hold together. Kostunica was a nationalist and frequently criticized U.S. support of nongovernmental bodies and independent media in Yugoslavia. He initially refused to cooperate with the International Criminal Tribunal for the Former Yugoslavia in The Hague in their pursuit of figures indicted as war criminals—notably Milosevic—for fear that such a move would destabilize Yugoslavia.

The drastic decline in the standard of living and economic instability continued into the post-Milosevic era. The new leadership discovered that the former regime had emptied the state coffers as well as warehouses once filled with food, fuel, and medical supplies. Inflation raged, and prices increased to such a level that staple foodstuffs, electricity, and heating were unattainable for large numbers of people. Belgrade's Institute of Economic Sciences forecast that about 30% of the population would require welfare assistance by early 2001. With no money to finance such a program, however, the state would have to rely on foreign assistance.

Meanwhile, Milosevic was still a presence on the scene; he was reelected head of the Socialist Party of Serbia on November 25. The former strongman was reportedly biding his time, convinced that the public would grow weary of Kostunica. He labeled the current leadership "traitors" and attributed his

AP/Wide World Photos

A father and his child survey the damage outside the Yugoslav parliament building in Belgrade on October 7 after demonstrators ransacked the building to protest Slobodan Milosevic's claims on the election results.

defeat as having been orchestrated by the West. He blamed the new leadership for making already difficult living conditions even worse and warned of severe economic hardships and renewed unrest to come. Milosevic's attempts to discredit the DOS failed, however. The DOS scored another victory in the December 23 elections to the Serbian parliament, taking 176 seats to the Socialists' 37.

Montenegro's ruling coalition agreed to call a referendum on the republic's status by June 2001. Milo Djukanovic, Montenegro's president, said he was convinced that Montenegro and Serbia would succeed in reaching agreement on their future relations within the Yugoslav federation.

The situation in Kosovo remained unstable. Some 42,500 members of the NATO-led Kosovo Force in the province struggled to protect Serbs, Turks, and Roma (Gypsies) from ethnic Albanians seeking revenge. All the while, organized crime activities and mutual distrust among Albanian leaders hindered efforts to rebuild the economy and civil institutions. Kosovo voters gave the majority in the communal elections to Ibrahim Rugova's Democratic League of Kosovo, and the more radical Democratic Party of Kosovo, headed by former Kosovo Liberation Army leader Hashim Thaci, finished a distant second. Because both leaders advocated Kosovo's full independence from Yugoslavia, voters viewed the election as the first step toward sovereignty. They simply opted for the less-violent methods of Rugova's party. Serbs in the province abstained from voting and by and large did not recognize the newly elected ethnic Albanians. In November ethnic Albanian militants launched an offensive into a demilitarized zone between Serbia and Kosovo in an effort to declare heavily populated Albanian districts independent of Serbia and part of Kosovo.

(MILAN ANDREJEVICH)

ZAMBIA

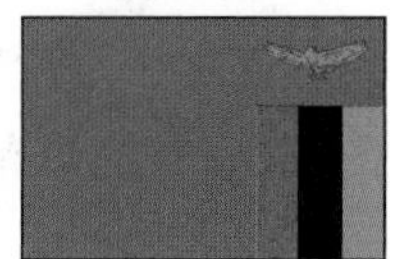

Area: 752,614 sq km (290,586 sq mi)
Population (2000 est.): 9,582,000
Capital: Lusaka
Head of state and government: President Frederick Chiluba

On March 7, 2000, Kenneth Kaunda, a former president of Zambia, announced that he would step down as leader of the United National Independence Party and retire from politics immediately. At a meeting in Ndola on May 14, the party chose Francis Nkhoma, a former member of the National Assembly and former governor of the Bank of Zambia, as its new leader and nominee for the presidency in the election to be held in 2001.

With President Chiluba scheduled to retire at the end of his second term of office in 2001, Ben Mwila, a wealthy businessman, caused considerable consternation by announcing that he would campaign to become the ruling party's candidate for the presidency. Mwila was under investigation by Zambia's auditor-general regarding the possible misuse of government funds while he was serving as minister of defense. Chiluba responded by dismissing him as minister for the environment, and he was expelled from the party. Mwila then announced in August that he had formed the Republican Party in order to pursue his presidential campaign.

After an uncertain year in 1999, the outlook for the mining industry brightened when on March 31 the government signed over the bulk of its mining assets to a consortium headed by the Anglo American Corp., while it retained a 20% share in the new company, to be known as Konkola Copper Mines. At the same ceremony, the government transferred other mines, refineries, and a smelting plant to Mopani Copper Mines PLC, a company owned by Glencore International AG of Switzerland and First Quantum Minerals Ltd. of Canada. In July the Chinese government officially commissioned the Chambishi mine, which it had bought in 1998, and offered to increase its investment in the project to $159 million over the next five years.

Foreign donors continued to demonstrate their goodwill with a European Union grant of €6.5 million (about $5.8 million) in March to assist exports of coffee, tobacco, and textiles, together with further aid to rehabilitate the Kabwe–Kapiri Mposhi road, the Livingstone airport, and Mpulungu Harbour. Japan gave $5.5 million to meet medical and housing needs but stressed that the money should be used effectively and transparently. This caution was justified because on Dec. 21, 1999, some 150 junior doctors had gone on strike as a protest against their low salaries and the lack of essential medical supplies. After the number of strikers rose to 300, the government imported doctors from Cuba but by July could no longer pay all their salaries.

(KENNETH INGHAM)

ZIMBABWE

Area: 390,757 sq km (150,872 sq mi)
Population (2000 est.): 11,343,000
Capital: Harare
Head of state and government: President Robert Mugabe

A new constitution, drafted by the government and seeking to give the president two additional six-year terms in office and also granting him the power to seize white-owned land without compensation, was firmly rejected in a ref-

Archive Photos

With her twin daughters, farmwife Pippa van Rechteren looks on as black farmworkers sing revolutionary songs outside an electric fence around her homestead north of Harare, Zimbabwe, on March 29.

erendum held on Feb. 12–13, 2000; however, only about 25% of the electorate cast its votes. Toward the end of February, men claiming to be veterans of the independence war began what proved to be a long, drawn-out campaign involving the forcible occupation of white-owned farms, the destruction of farm buildings, and physical violence against white farmers and black farm workers during which several were killed.

On March 17 the High Court ordered the squatters to quit the farms, but this led only to an increase in the violence, the attackers being convinced they had the support of the president. Protests by the British government led Pres. Robert Mugabe (*see* BIOGRAPHIES) to lay the blame on Great Britain for having reneged on its promise, given at the time of independence, to provide adequate funds to compensate white farmers for the loss of their land. Early in April Britain offered further assistance, provided the parliamentary elections to be held in June were seen to be free and fair, that the economy was restored to a firm footing, and that any further land distribution would benefit peasant farmers rather than ruling-party leaders. On April 21 President Mugabe promised that the elections would be free and fair and that the squatters would be urged to leave the farms they had occupied.

The weeks before the elections were marred by widespread violence against supporters of the opposition Movement for Democratic Change (MDC). Mugabe also imposed severe restrictions on attempts by external bodies, such as the European Union, to monitor the elections, which, he insisted, were an internal affair. In the election the MDC won 57 of the 120 contested seats and the ruling ZANU-PF 62; the government's dominance was assured, however, by the president's right to nominate an additional 30 members.

In October Mugabe announced that no action would be taken against any of those responsible for violence during the elections. Meanwhile, his campaign to seize white-owned land was intensified. In response, Pres. Thabo Mbeki of South Africa, in a reversal of his former position, announced on October 25 that this was a violation of the rule of law and had to stop. Mbeki, however, believed South Africa should continue to supply oil to Zimbabwe to prevent that nation's economy, which was in a serious state, from collapsing completely. In May the World Bank had cut off funding to Zimbabwe because of debt arrears amounting to $383 million. On August 1, after months of resistance by the government, the currency was devalued by 24%. This was followed on August 28 by a further devaluation of 3%.

Responding to an opposition motion, the speaker of the Zimbabwe House of Assembly announced on October 26 that he would appoint a committee to investigate Mugabe's suitability to continue as president. In December the Supreme Court gave Mugabe six months to develop a workable land-reform program.

(KENNETH INGHAM)

Adams, Andy. Associate Editor, *Sumo World.* Author of *Sumo; Sumo World Record Book.* •SPORTS AND GAMES: *Judo; Wrestling:* Sumo

Alder, Phillip. Syndicated Bridge Columnist. Associate Editor, *The Bridge World.* Author of *Get Smarter at Bridge.* •SPORTS AND GAMES: *Contract Bridge*

Alexander, Steve. Freelance Technology Writer. •COMPUTERS AND INFORMATION SYSTEMS

Allaby, Michael. Freelance Writer. Author of *Basics of Environmental Science* and *Facing the Future.* •THE ENVIRONMENT: *Environmental Issues; International Activities*

Allan, J.A. Professor of Geography, School of Oriental and African Studies, University of London. Author of *The Water Problem in the Middle East* and *Water and Peace in the Middle East.* •WORLD AFFAIRS: *Libya*

Anakiev, Dimitar. Freelance Writer. Author of *The Third Way.* •LITERATURE: Eastern European *(in part)*

Anam, Mahfuz. Editor, *The Daily Star,* Bangladesh. •WORLD AFFAIRS: *Bangladesh*

Andrades, Jorge Adrián. Freelance Journalist. •SPORTS AND GAMES: *Equestrian Sports:* Polo

Andrejevich, Milan. Senior Editor, *Post-Tribune* (Gary, Ind.). Adjunct Professor of Communications and History, Valparaiso University and Indiana University Northwest. Author of *The Sandžak: A Perspective of Serb-Muslim Relations.* •WORLD AFFAIRS: *Bosnia and Herzegovina; Yugoslavia*

Anthony, John Duke. President and CEO, National Council on U.S.-Arab Relations; Consultant to U.S. Department of Defense. •WORLD AFFAIRS: *Oman; Qatar*

Archibald, John J. Freelance Bowling Writer; Retired Feature Writer, St. Louis (Mo.) *Post-Dispatch.* Member of the American Bowling Congress Hall of Fame. •SPORTS AND GAMES: *Bowling:* U.S. Tenpins

Arnold, Mavis. Journalist. •WORLD AFFAIRS: *Ireland*

Aurora, Vincent. Lecturer in French and Romance Philology, Columbia University, New York City. •LITERATURE: *French:* France

Bahry, Louay. Adjunct Professor of Political Science, University of Tennessee. Author of *The Baghdad Bahn.* •WORLD AFFAIRS: *Bahrain; Iraq*

Balaban, Avraham. Professor and Chairman, Department of African and Asian Languages and Literatures, University of Florida. •LITERATURE: *Jewish:* Hebrew

Bamia, Aida A. Associate Professor of Arabic Language and Literature, University of Florida. •LITERATURE: *Arabic*

Barrett, David B. Research Professor of Missiometrics, Regent University, Virginia Beach, Va. Author of *World Christian Encyclopedia* and *Schism and Renewal in Africa.* •RELIGION: *Tables (in part)*

Beckwith, David C. Vice President, National Cable Television Association. •WORLD AFFAIRS: *United States; United States:* State and Local Affairs; *United States:* Special Report: The U.S. Election of 2000

Bernstein, Ellen. Freelance Writer and Editor, specializing in health and medicine, Chicago. •HEALTH AND DISEASE

Bird, Thomas E. The Jewish Studies Program, Queens College, City University of New York. •LITERATURE: *Jewish:* Yiddish

Bleske, Glen. Associate Professor of Journalism, California State University, Chico. •MEDIA AND PUBLISHING: *Newspapers*

Boggan, Tim. Historian, U.S.A. Table Tennis Association (USATT). Author of *Winning Table Tennis.* •SPORTS AND GAMES: *Table Tennis*

Bonds, John B. Adjunct Professor of History, The Citadel, Charleston, S.C. •SPORTS AND GAMES: *Sailing (Yachting)*

Bradley, Bill. Freelance Journalist; Publisher, *Billiard News.* •SPORTS AND GAMES: *Billiards; Bobsledding and Luge*

Bradsher, Henry S. Foreign Affairs Analyst. Author of *Afghan Communism and Soviet Intervention.* •WORLD AFFAIRS: *Philippines*

Brecher, Kenneth. Professor of Astronomy and Physics; Director, Science and Mathematics Education Center, Boston University. •MATHEMATICS AND PHYSICAL SCIENCES: *Astronomy*

Brockmann, Stephen. Associate Professor of German, Carnegie Mellon University, Pittsburgh, Pa. Author of *Literature and German Reunification.* •LITERATURE: *German*

Brokopp, John G. Specialist and Writer on equestrian racing and casino gambling; Director of Public Relations, National Jockey Club. Author of *The Get the Edge Guide to Thrifty Gambling.* •SPORTS AND GAMES: *Equestrian Sports:* Thoroughbred Racing: *United States*

Brown, Bess. Political Officer, OSCE Centre, Ashgabat, Turkmenistan. Author of *Authoritarianism in the New States of Central Asia.* •WORLD AFFAIRS: *Kazakhstan; Kyrgyzstan; Tajikistan; Turkmenistan; Uzbekistan*

Buchan, David. Diplomatic Editor, *Financial Times,* London. •WORLD AFFAIRS: *France*

Bungs, Dzintra. Consultant, Stiftung Wissenschaft und Politik, Ebenhausen, Ger. Author of *The Baltic States: Problems and Prospects of Membership of the European Union.* •WORLD AFFAIRS: *Latvia*

Burks, Ardath W. Professor Emeritus of Asian Studies, Rutgers University, New Brunswick, N.J. Author of *Japan: A Postindustrial Power.* •WORLD AFFAIRS: *Japan*

Burns, Erik T. Bureau Chief, Dow Jones Newswires, Lisbon. •WORLD AFFAIRS: *Portugal*

Cafferty, Bernard. Associate Editor, *British Chess Magazine.* Author of *The Soviet Championships.* •SPORTS AND GAMES: *Chess*

Calhoun, David R. Freelance Editor and Author. •BIOGRAPHIES *(in part)*

Campbell, Paul J. Professor of Mathematics and Computer Science, Beloit College, Beloit, Wis. Author of *For All Practical Purposes.* •MATHEMATICS AND PHYSICAL SCIENCES: *Mathematics*

Campbell, Robert. Architect and Architecture Critic. Author of *Cityscapes of Boston: An American City Through Time.* •ARCHITECTURE AND CIVIL ENGINEERING: *Architecture*

Cantwell, Bruce. Senior Consultant, My Envoy. •OBITUARIES *(in part)*

Carter, Robert W. Journalist. •SPORTS AND GAMES: *Equestrian Sports:* Show Jumping and Dressage; Steeplechasing; Thoroughbred Racing: *International*

Cenzer, Matthew A. Lecturer in History, Northwestern University, Evanston, Ill. •WORLD AFFAIRS: *Angola:* Sidebar; *Burundi; Comoros; Djibouti; Ghana; Liberia; Mauritius; Nigeria; Rwanda; Seychelles; Sierra Leone*

Chappell, Duncan. Deputy President, Federal Administrative Appeals Tribunal, Sydney, Australia. Author of *Violence at Work.* •LAW, CRIME, AND LAW ENFORCEMENT: *Crime*

Cheadle, Bruce. Journalist, Canadian Press news agency •SPORTS AND GAMES: *Curling*

Cheuse, Alan. Writing Faculty, English Department, George Mason University, Fairfax, Va.; Book Commentator, National Public Radio. Author of *The Light Possessed* and *Listening to the Page: Adventures in Reading and Writing.* •LITERATURE: *English:* United States

Christie, Bryan. Freelance Medical Writer, Edinburgh. •HEALTH AND DISEASE: *Special Report:* Socialized Medicine's Aches and Pains

Cioroslan, Dragomir. National Team Coach, U.S.A. Weightlifting, Inc. Author of *Banish Your Belly.* •SPORTS AND GAMES: *Weight Lifting*

Clark, David Draper. Managing Editor, *World Literature Today.* •LITERATURE: *English:* Other Literature in English

Clark, Janet H. •NOBEL PRIZES *(in part)*

Clarke, Douglas L. Captain, U.S. Navy (ret.); Military Analyst, Jamestown Foundation. Author of *The Missing Man: Politics and the MIA.* •MILITARY AFFAIRS

Collins, Nigel. Editor in Chief, *The Ring, KO, World Boxing,* and *Boxing 2001.* •SPORTS AND GAMES: *Boxing; Boxing:* Sidebar

Conversi, Daniele. Senior Lecturer, University of Lincolnshire, Lincoln, Eng. Author of *The Basques, the Catalans, and Spain.* •WORLD AFFAIRS: *Spain*

Cosgrave, Bronwyn. Associate Editor, *British Vogue.* Author of *Costume and Fashion: A Complete History.* •BIOGRAPHIES *(in part)*; FASHIONS

Coveney, Michael. Theatre Critic, *The Daily Mail.* Author of *The Andrew Lloyd Webber Story* and others. •PERFORMING ARTS: *Theatre:* Great Britain and Ireland

Cox, Kevin. Atlantic Correspondent, *The Globe and Mail,* Toronto. •WORLD AFFAIRS: *Canada:* Sidebar

Coyne, Patrick. Editor and Designer, *Communication Arts.* •ART, ANTIQUES, AND COLLECTIONS: *Special Report:* Design for the Third Millennium

Craine, Anthony G. Writer. •BIOGRAPHIES *(in part)*; OBITUARIES *(in part)*

Crampton, Richard J. Professor of East European History, University of Oxford, Oxford, Eng. Author of *Eastern Europe in the Twentieth Century—and After.* •WORLD AFFAIRS: *Bulgaria*

Crisp, Brian F. Associate Professor of Political Science, University of Arizona. Author of *Democratic Institutional Design.* •WORLD AFFAIRS: *Colombia*

Crow, Suzanne M. Freelance Journalist. •BIOGRAPHIES *(in part)*; WORLD AFFAIRS: *Germany*

Crowell, Todd. Senior Writer, *Asiaweek.* •WORLD AFFAIRS: *Korea, Democratic People's Republic of; Korea, Republic of; Singapore*

Curwen, Peter. Professor of Business and Management, Sheffield Hallam University, Sheffield, Eng. Author of *The U.K. Publishing Industry* and others. •MEDIA AND PUBLISHING: *Book Publishing* (international)

Cuttino, John Charles. Lyndon B. Johnson School of Public Affairs, University of Texas at Austin. •WORLD AFFAIRS: *Brazil; Brazil:* Sidebar

Dailey, Meghan. Art Historian and Critic, New York. •ART, ANTIQUES, AND COLLECTIONS: *Art Exhibitions; Painting and Sculpture*

Davis, Stephen P. Associate Editor, Encyclopædia Britannica, Inc. •BIOGRAPHIES *(in part)*; WORLD AFFAIRS: *Uruguay*

Deeb, Marius K. Professor of Middle East Studies, SAIS, Johns Hopkins University, Washington, D.C. Author of *Syria's War on Lebanon and the Peace Process 1975–2000* and others. •BIOGRAPHIES *(in part)*; WORLD AFFAIRS: *Egypt; Jordan*

de la Barre, Kenneth. Fellow, Arctic Institute of North America; Research Associate, Yukon College, Northern Research Institute. •WORLD AFFAIRS: *Arctic Regions*

Denselow, Robin. Music Writer, *The Guardian;* London Correspondent, BBC Television. Author of *When the Music's Over: The Politics of Pop.* •PERFORMING ARTS: *Music:* Popular (international)

Dietz, Henry A. Professor, Department of Government, University of Texas at Austin. Author of *Urban Poverty, Political Participation and the State: Lima 1970–1990.* •WORLD AFFAIRS: *Peru*

Dooling, Dave. Manager, NASA Microgravity Outreach, Infinity Technology, Inc. Coauthor of *Engineering Tomorrow.* •MATHEMATICS AND PHYSICAL SCIENCES: *Space Exploration*

Dowd, Siobhan. Columnist, *Literary Review* (London); *Glimmer Train* (U.S.). Author of *This Prison Where I Live* and *Roads of the Roma.* •BIOGRAPHIES *(in part)*; LITERATURE: *English:* United Kingdom

Ehringer, Gavin Forbes. Freelance Writer and Photographer; Correspondent, *People Magazine, Rocky Mountain News,* and *Western Horseman.* Coauthor of *Rodeo in America: Wranglers, Roughstock and Paydirt.* •SPORTS AND GAMES: *Introduction; Rodeo; Skiing*

El Guindi, Fadwa. Adjunct Professor of Anthropology, University of Southern California. Author of *Veil: Modesty, Privacy and Resistance.* •ANTHROPOLOGY AND ARCHAEOLOGY: *Archaeology:* Cultural

Epstein, Thomas. Adjunct Assistant Professor, Boston College. •LITERATURE: *Russian*

Fagan, Brian. Professor of Anthropology, University of California, Santa Barbara. Author of *Floods, Famines, and Emperors: El Niño and the Collapse of Civilizations.* •ANTHROPOLOGY AND ARCHAEOLOGY: *Archaeology:* Western Hemisphere

Farr, David M.L. Professor Emeritus of History, Carleton University, Ottawa. •WORLD AFFAIRS: *Canada*

Feketekuty, Geza. President, International Commercial Diplomacy Project; Distinguished Professor of Commercial Diplomacy, Monterey Institute for International Studies. • ECONOMIC AFFAIRS: Sidebar

Fendell, Robert J. Freelance Writer on automobiles and racing. Author of *The Encyclopedia of Auto Racing Greats.* •SPORTS AND GAMES: *Automobile Racing:* U.S. Auto Racing *(in part)*

Fenwick, M.J. Associate Professor of Latin American Literature, The University of Memphis. Author of *Sisters of Caliban.* •LITERATURE: *Spanish:* Latin America

Fisher, Sharon. Central European Specialist, Brussels. •WORLD AFFAIRS: *Czech Republic; Slovakia*

Flagg, Gordon. Managing Editor, *American Libraries.* •LIBRARIES AND MUSEUMS: *Libraries* (United States)

Flink, Steve. Senior Correspondent, *Tennis Week.* Author of *The Greatest Tennis Matches of the Twentieth Century.* •SPORTS AND GAMES: *Tennis*

Flores, Ramona Monette Sargan. Professor of Speech Communication and Theater Arts, University of the Philippines; Editorial Consultant, *Masks and Voices.* •MEDIA AND PUBLISHING: *Radio* (international); *Television* (international)

Follett, Christopher. Denmark Correspondent, *The Times*; Local Correspondent for Reuters News Agency, Copenhagen. Author of *Fodspor paa Cypern.* •WORLD AFFAIRS: *Denmark*

Fridovich, Irwin. James B. Duke Professor of Biochemistry, Emeritus, Duke University Medical Center, Durham, N.C. •LIFE SCIENCES: *Molecular Biology*

Fridovich-Keil, Judith L. Associate Professor, Department of Genetics, Emory University School of Medicine, Atlanta, Ga. •LIFE SCIENCES: *Special Report:* The Human Genome: The Ultimate Road Map

Fuller, Elizabeth. Editor, *Newsline,* Radio Free Europe/Radio Liberty, Prague. •WORLD AFFAIRS: *Armenia; Azerbaijan; Georgia*

Furmonavičius, Darius. Ph.D. candidate, Department of European Studies, University of Bradford, Eng. •WORLD AFFAIRS: *Lithuania*

Gallagher, Tom. Professor of European Peace Studies, University of Bradford, Eng. Author of *Outcast Europe: The Balkans 1789–1989.* •WORLD AFFAIRS: *Romania*

Ganado, Albert. Lawyer; Chairman, Malta National Archives Advisory Committee. Coauthor of *A Study in Depth of 143 Maps Representing the Great Siege of Malta of 1565* and others. •WORLD AFFAIRS: *Malta*

Garcia-Zamor, Jean-Claude. Professor of Public Administration, Florida International University. •WORLD AFFAIRS: *Haiti*

Garrod, Mark. Golf Correspondent, PA Sport, U.K. Honorary Secretary of the Association of Golf Writers. •SPORTS AND GAMES: *Golf*

Gaughan, Thomas. Library Director, Muhlenberg College, Allentown, Pa. •LIBRARIES AND MUSEUMS: *Libraries* (international)

George, Nicholas. Stockholm Correspondent, *Financial Times.* •WORLD AFFAIRS: *Sweden*

Gibbons, J. Whitfield. Professor of Ecology, Savannah River Ecology Laboratory, University of Georgia. Coauthor of *Ecoviews: Snakes, Snails and Environmental Tales.* •LIFE SCIENCES: *Zoology*

Gill, Martin J. Information and Computer Expert, F.A.O. EASTFISH; Editor, *Eurofish.* •AGRICULTURE AND FOOD SUPPLIES: *Fisheries*

Gobbie, Donn. Director of Public Relations, American Badminton League. •SPORTS AND GAMES: *Badminton*

Goldsmith, Arthur. Freelance Writer. Author of *The Camera and Its Images.* •ART, ANTIQUES, AND COLLECTIONS: *Photography*

Graham, John W. Vice Chair, Canadian Foundation for the Americas; Former Canadian Ambassador. •WORLD AFFAIRS: *Dominican Republic; Suriname*

Greskovic, Robert. Dance Critic, *The Wall Street Journal.* Author of *Ballet, 101.* •PERFORMING ARTS: *Dance:* North America

Griffiths, A.R.G. Associate Professor in History, Flinders University of South Australia. Author of *Contemporary Australia* and *Beautiful Lies.* •WORLD AFFAIRS: *Australia; Nauru; Palau; Papua New Guinea*

Guthridge, Guy G. Manager, Antarctic Information Program, U.S. National Science Foundation. •WORLD AFFAIRS: *Antarctica*

Haddad, Mahmoud. Associate Professor of History, Balamand University, Lebanon. •WORLD AFFAIRS: *Lebanon; Saudi Arabia*

Halman, Talat S. Professor and Chairman, Department of Turkish Literature, Bilkent University, Ankara, Turkey. •LITERATURE: *Turkish*

Hammer, William R. Professor and Chair, Department of Geology, Augustana College, Rock Island, Ill. Author of *Gondwana Dinosaurs from the Jurassic of Antarctica.* •LIFE SCIENCES: *Paleontology*

Hannen, Mark. National League Manager, English Basketball Association. •SPORTS AND GAMES: *Basketball:* International

Henry, Alan. Grand Prix Editor, *Autocar* (London). Motor Racing Correspondent, *The Guardian.* Author of *50 Years of World Championship Grand Prix Motor Racing.* •SPORTS AND GAMES: *Automobile Racing:* Grand Prix Racing

Hobbs, Greg. Chief Writer, *AFL Record.* •SPORTS AND GAMES: *Football:* Australian

Hoffman, Dean A. Executive Editor, *Hoof Beats.* Author of *The Hambletonian: America's Trotting Classic.* •SPORTS AND GAMES: *Equestrian Sports:* Harness Racing

Hoke, John. Publisher, *Amateur Wrestling News.* •SPORTS AND GAMES: *Wrestling*

Hollar, Sherman. Assistant Editor, Encyclopædia Britannica, Inc. •BIOGRAPHIES *(in part)*; DISASTERS; OBITUARIES *(in part)*

Homel, David. Freelance Writer; Lecturer, Concordia University, Montreal. Author of *Get on Top* and others. •LITERATURE: *French:* Canada

Hope, Thomas W. Owner, Hope Reports, Inc.; Former Film Producer. Author of *Large Screen Presentation Systems.* •PERFORMING ARTS: *Motion Pictures:* Nontheatrical Films

IEIS. International Economic Information Services. •ECONOMIC AFFAIRS: *World Economy; Stock Exchanges* (international)

Ingham, Kenneth. Emeritus Professor of History, University of Bristol, Eng. Author of *Politics in Modern Africa: The Uneven Tribal Dimension* and others. •WORLD AFFAIRS: *Angola; Congo, Democratic Republic of the (the Former Zaire); Kenya; Malawi; Mozambique; Sudan, The; Tanzania; Uganda; Zambia; Zimbabwe*

Ingram, Derek. President Emeritus, Commonwealth Journalists Association; Founding Editor, Gemini News Service. Author of *A Much-Too-Timid Commonwealth* and others. •WORLD AFFAIRS: *Commonwealth of Nations*

Ionescu, Dan. Broadcaster/Editor, Radio Free Europe/Radio Liberty. Contributor to *Transitions.* •WORLD AFFAIRS: *Moldova*

Isaacson, Lanae Hjortsvang. Editor, *Nordic Women Writers.* •LITERATURE: *Danish*

Iyob, Ruth. Associate Professor of Political Science, University of Missouri, St. Louis. •WORLD AFFAIRS: *Eritrea*

Jacobs, Charles A. President, American Anti-Slavery Group, Boston. •SOCIAL PROTECTION: *Special Report:* Slavery in the 21st Century

Jamail, Milton. Lecturer, Department of Government, University of Texas at Austin. Author of *Full Count: Inside Cuban Baseball.* •SPORTS AND GAMES: *Baseball:* Latin America

Jatar, Ana Julia. Senior Fellow and Director of The Cuba Project, Inter-American Dialogue, Washington, D.C. Author of *The Cuban Way: Capitalism, Communism and Confrontation.* •WORLD AFFAIRS: *Cuba*

Joffé, George. Senior Research Fellow, School of Oriental and African Studies, University of London. Visiting Fellow, London School of Economics and Political Science. Editor, *Perspectives on Development: The Euro-Mediterranean Partnership.* •WORLD AFFAIRS: *Algeria; Morocco; Tunisia*

Johnson, Steve. Television Critic, *Chicago Tribune.* •MEDIA AND PUBLISHING: *Radio* (U.S.); *Television* (U.S.)

Johnson, Todd M. Director, World Evangelization Research Center. Coauthor of *World Christian Encyclopedia.* •RELIGION: *Tables (in part)*

Joireman, Sandra F. Associate Professor of Political Science, St. Bonaventure University, St. Bonaventure, N.Y. Author of *Property Rights and Political Development in Ethiopia and Eritrea.* •WORLD AFFAIRS: *Ethiopia*

Jones, David G.C. Tutor, Department of Continuing Education, University of Aberystwyth, Aberystwyth, Wales. Author of *Atomic Physics.* •MATHEMATICS AND PHYSICAL SCIENCES: *Physics*

Jones, Mark P. Associate Professor of Political Science, Michigan State University. Author of *Electoral Laws and the Survival of Presidential Democracies.* •WORLD AFFAIRS: *Argentina*

Kanduza, Ackson M. Senior Lecturer and Chair, Department of History, University of Swaziland. Author of *Political Economy of Democratisation in Swaziland.* •WORLD AFFAIRS: *Swaziland*

Karimi-Hakkak, Ahmad. Professor of Persian Languages and Literature, University of Washington. Author of *Recasting Persian Poetry: Scenarios of Poetic Modernity in Iran.* •LITERATURE: *Persian*

Kazamaru, Yoshihiko. Literary Critic. •LITERATURE: *Japanese*

Kelleher, John A. Journalist and Editorial Consultant; Former Editor, *Dominion* and *Dominion Sunday Times* (Wellington). •WORLD AFFAIRS: *New Zealand*

Kelling, George H. Lieutenant Colonel, U.S. Army (ret.). Author of *Countdown to Rebellion: British Policy in Cyprus 1939–1955*. •WORLD AFFAIRS: *Cyprus*

Kellner, Peter. Journalist, *The Observer, London Evening Standard*. Author of *The New Mutualism* and others. •BIOGRAPHIES *(in part)*; WORLD AFFAIRS: *United Kingdom*

Kelly, John J., Jr. Assistant Administrator for Weather Services, National Oceanic and Atmospheric Administration. •EARTH SCIENCES: *Meteorology and Climate*

Knox, Paul. International Affairs Reporter, *The Globe and Mail*, Toronto. •WORLD AFFAIRS: *Bolivia; Ecuador*

Kovel, Ralph and Terry. Publishers. Authors of *Kovels on Antiques and Collectibles*. •ART, ANTIQUES, AND COLLECTIONS: *Antiques and Collectibles*

Krause, Stefan. Freelance Political Analyst, Brussels. •WORLD AFFAIRS: *Greece; Macedonia*

Kroll, Thomas E. Lecturer, Northwestern University, Chicago. President, Thomas Kroll Associates. Author of *Introduction to Telecommunications*. •COMPUTERS AND INFORMATION SYSTEMS: *Microelectronics; Telecommunications*

Kuptsch, Christiane. Research Officer, ISSA. •SOCIAL PROTECTION (international)

Lamb, Kevin M. Special Projects Writer, *Dayton* (Ohio) *Daily News*. Author of *Quarterbacks, Nickelbacks & Other Loose Change*. •SPORTS AND GAMES: *Football:* Canadian, U.S.

Langeneckert, Sandra. Senior Copy Editor, Encyclopædia Britannica, Inc. •BIOGRAPHIES *(in part)*

Lawler, Nancy Ellen. Professor Emeritus, Oakton Community College, Des Plaines, Ill. Author of *Soldiers of Misfortune* and others. •BIOGRAPHIES *(in part)*; WORLD AFFAIRS: *Benin; Burkina Faso; Cameroon; Central African Republic; Congo, Republic of the; Côte d'Ivoire; Gabon; Guinea; Mali; Mauritania; Niger; Senegal; Togo*

Lawson, Fred H. James Irvine Professor of Government, Mills College, Oakland, Calif. Author of *Why Syria Goes to War*. •WORLD AFFAIRS: *Syria*

Legassick, Martin. Professor of History, University of the Western Cape, Bellville, S.Af. •WORLD AFFAIRS: *South Africa*

Levine, Steven I. Mansfield Professor of Asia Pacific Studies, The Mansfield Center, University of Montana, Missoula. •WORLD AFFAIRS: *China; Taiwan*

Lindstrom, Sieg. Managing Editor, *Track & Field News*. •SPORTS AND GAMES: *Track and Field Sports (Athletics)*

Litweiler, John. Jazz Critic. Author of *The Freedom Principle: Jazz After 1958* and *Ornette Coleman: A Harmonic Life*. •BIOGRAPHIES *(in part)*; OBITUARIES *(in part)*; PERFORMING ARTS: *Music:* Jazz

Logan, Robert G. Sportswriter, *Daily Herald* (Arlington Heights, Ill.). Author of *The Bulls and Chicago: A Stormy Affair* and others. •SPORTS AND GAMES: *Basketball:* United States

Longmore, Andrew. Chief Sports Feature Writer, *The Independent*; Former Assistant Editor, *The Cricketer*. Author of *The Complete Guide to Cycling*. •BIOGRAPHIES *(in part)*; SPORTS AND GAMES: *Cricket*

Luling, Virginia. Independent Researcher, Survival International. •WORLD AFFAIRS: *Somalia*

Lundin, Immi. Freelance Journalist and Literary Critic. •LITERATURE: *Swedish*

Macdonald, Barrie. Professor of History, Massey University, Palmerston, N.Z. •WORLD AFFAIRS: *Dependent States:* Pacific; *Fiji; Kiribati; Marshall Islands; Micronesia, Federated States of; Samoa; Solomon Islands; Tonga; Tuvalu; Vanuatu*

McGregor, Alan. Freelance Journalist. •WORLD AFFAIRS: *Switzerland*

McLachlan, Keith S. Professor Emeritus, School of Oriental and African Studies, University of London. Author of *Boundaries of Modern Iran*. •WORLD AFFAIRS: *Iran*

McLellan, Joseph. Music Critic Emeritus, *The Washington Post*. •PERFORMING ARTS: *Music:* Classical

Manghnani, Murli H. Professor of Geophysics, University of Hawaii, Honolulu. •EARTH SCIENCES: *Geophysics*

Mango, Andrew. Foreign Affairs Analyst. Author of *Turkey: The Challenge of a New Role*. •WORLD AFFAIRS: *Turkey*

Marples, David R. Professor of History, University of Alberta. Author of *Belarus: A Denationalized Nation* and others. •WORLD AFFAIRS: *Belarus; Ukraine*

Matthíasson, Björn. Economist, Ministry of Finance, Iceland. •WORLD AFFAIRS: *Iceland*

Mazie, David M. Freelance Journalist. •SOCIAL PROTECTION (U.S.)

Middlebrook, Kevin J. Director, Center for U.S.-Mexican Studies, University of California, San Diego. •WORLD AFFAIRS: *Mexico*

Mora, Frank O. Associate Professor and Chair of International Studies, Rhodes College, Memphis, Tenn. •WORLD AFFAIRS: *Paraguay*

Morgan, Paul. Editor, *Rugby World*. •SPORTS AND GAMES: *Football:* Rugby Football

Morris, Jacqui M. Lecturer and Freelance Editor; Former Editor, *Oryx, The International Journal of Conservation*. •THE ENVIRONMENT: *Wildlife Conservation*

Morrison, Graham. Press Officer, British Fencing Association; Correspondent, *Daily Telegraph; Country Life*. •SPORTS AND GAMES: *Fencing*

Murray, Iain. Senior Research Analyst, Statistical Assessment Service, Washington, D.C. •LAW, CRIME, AND LAW ENFORCEMENT: *Special Report:* The U.S. Gun-Control Debate: A Critical Look

Myers, David J. Professor of Political Science, Pennsylvania State University. •WORLD AFFAIRS: *Venezuela*

Myers, Norman. Independent Scientist. •AGRICULTURE AND FOOD SUPPLIES: *Special Report:* Genetically Modified Foods: The Political Debate

Noda, Hiroki. Staff Reporter, *Jiji Press Ltd.*, Japan. •SPORTS AND GAMES: *Baseball:* Japan

O'Brien, Dan. Editor/Economist (Europe), Economist Intelligence Unit. •WORLD AFFAIRS: *Austria*

Ogden, Shepherd. Founder and President, The Cook's Garden. Author of *Straight Ahead Organic* and others. •THE ENVIRONMENT: *Gardening*

O'Leary, Christopher. Senior Writer, *Investment Dealers Digest*. •ECONOMIC AFFAIRS: *Business Overview*

Oppenheim, Lois Hecht. Professor and Chair, Political Science, University of Judaism, Los Angeles, Calif. Author of *Politics in Chile: Democracy, Authoritarianism and the Search for Development*. •WORLD AFFAIRS: *Chile*

O'Quinn, Jim. Editor in Chief, *American Theatre*. •PERFORMING ARTS: *Theatre:* U.S. and Canada

Orr, Jay. Editor and Senior Music Writer, Country.com. •PERFORMING ARTS: *Music:* Popular (U.S.)

Osborne, Keith L. Editor, *British Rowing Almanack*. Author of *Boat Racing in Britain, 1715–1975* and *One Man Went to Row*. •SPORTS AND GAMES: *Rowing*

Paarlberg, Philip L. Professor of Agricultural Economics, Purdue University, West Lafayette, Ind. •AGRICULTURE AND FOOD SUPPLIES: *Agriculture*

Paradkar, Shalaka. Assistant Editor, Britannica.com (India). •WORLD AFFAIRS: *India:* Sidebar

Parker, Ines. Freelance Writer. •WORLD AFFAIRS: *Belize*

Parsons, Neil. Professor of History, University of Botswana. Author of *King Khama, Emperor Joe, and the Great White Queen*. •WORLD AFFAIRS: *Botswana*

Pérez, Orlando J. Assistant Professor of Political Science, Central Michigan University. Editor of *Post-Invasion Panama: The Challenges of Democratization in the New World Order*. •WORLD AFFAIRS: *Panama*

Pertile, Lino. Professor of Romance Languages and Literature, Harvard University. Editor of *The Cambridge History of Italian Literature*. •LITERATURE: *Italian*

Peszek, Luan. Publications Director and Editor, *U.S.A. Gymnastics*. Author of *Gymnastics Almanac*. •SPORTS AND GAMES: *Gymnastics*

Pfeffer, Irving. Attorney. Editor of *The Financing of Small Business*. •ECONOMIC AFFAIRS: *Stock Exchanges* (North America)

Prasad, H.Y. Sharada. Vice President, Indian Council for Cultural Relations; Former Information Adviser to the Prime Minister of India. •WORLD AFFAIRS: *India*

Primorac, Max. Executive Director, Institute of World Affairs, Zagreb, Croatia. •BIOGRAPHIES *(in part)*; WORLD AFFAIRS: *Croatia*

Qian Zhongwen. Senior Research Fellow, Literature Institute, Chinese Academy of Social Sciences. •LITERATURE: *Chinese*

Rauch, Robert. Freelance Editor and Writer. •BIOGRAPHIES *(in part)*; NOBEL PRIZES *(in part)*; OBITUARIES *(in part)*

Raun, Toivo U. Professor of Central Eurasian Studies, Indiana University. Author of *Estonia and the Estonians*. •WORLD AFFAIRS: *Estonia*

Rebelo, L.S. Professor Emeritus, Department of Portuguese Studies, King's College, University of London. •LITERATURE: *Portuguese:* Portugal

Reid, Ron. Staff Writer, *Philadelphia Inquirer*. •SPORTS AND GAMES: *Ice Hockey; Ice Skating*

Renwick, David. Freelance Journalist. •WORLD AFFAIRS: *Antigua and Barbuda; Bahamas, The; Barbados; Dependent States:* Caribbean and Bermuda; *Dominica; Grenada; Guyana; Jamaica; Saint Kitts and Nevis; Saint Lucia; Saint Vincent and the Grenadines; Trinidad and Tobago*

Riggan, William. Editor, *World Literature Today*, University of Oklahoma. •LITERATURE: *Introduction*

Robinson, David. Film Critic and Historian. Author of *A History of World Cinema* and *Chaplin: His Life and Art*. •PERFORMING ARTS: *Motion Pictures*

Roby, Anne. Freelance Journalist. •WORLD AFFAIRS: *Andorra; Liechtenstein; Luxembourg; Maldives; Monaco*

Rollin, Jack. Editor, *Rothmans Football Yearbook*. Author of *World Cup 1930–1990* and others. •SPORTS AND GAMES: *Football:* Association Football (Soccer)

Rose, Leo E. Professor Emeritus of Political Science, University of California, Berkeley. •WORLD AFFAIRS: *Bhutan; Nepal*

Rosen, Jeffrey. Associate Professor of Law, George Washington University. Author of *The Unwanted Gaze: The Destruction of Privacy in America*. •COMPUTERS AND INFORMATION SYSTEMS: *Special Report:* Invasion of Privacy on the Internet

Rugh, William A. President and CEO, AMIDEAST; Former U.S. Ambassador to Yemen and the United Arab Emirates. Author of *The Arab Press*. •WORLD AFFAIRS: *United Arab Emirates; Yemen*

Rutherford, Andrew. Professor of Law and Criminal Policy, University of Southampton, Eng. Author of *Transforming Criminal Policy* and others. •LAW, CRIME, AND LAW ENFORCEMENT: *Prisons and Penology*

Sabo, Anne G. Assistant Professor of Norwegian, St. Olaf College, Northfield, Minn. •LITERATURE: *Norwegian*

Sanders, Alan J.K. Former Lecturer in Mongolian Studies, School of Oriental and African Studies, University of London. Coauthor of *Colloquial Mongolian*. •BIOGRAPHIES *(in part)*; WORLD AFFAIRS: *Mongolia*

Sandvik, Gudmund. Professor Emeritus of Legal History, Faculty of Law, University of Oslo. •WORLD AFFAIRS: *Norway*

Sarahete, Yrjö. Secretary Emeritus, Fédération Internationale des Quilleurs. •SPORTS AND GAMES: *Bowling:* World Tenpins

Saunders, Christopher. Professor of Historical Studies, University of Cape Town, S.Af. Coauthor of *South Africa: A Modern History*. •WORLD AFFAIRS: *Cape Verde; Chad; Equatorial Guinea; Gambia, The; Guinea-Bissau; Lesotho; Madagascar; Namibia; São Tomé and Príncipe*

Schmidt, Fabian. Research Analyst on Yugoslavia and Albania, Southeastern Europe Institute, Munich, Ger. •WORLD AFFAIRS: *Albania*

Schröder, Horst. Publisher, Critic, and Writer specializing in comics and popular arts, Stockholm. •PERFORMING ARTS: *Motion Pictures:* Sidebar

Schuster, Angela M.H. Senior Editor, *Archaeology*; Editor, *The Explorers Journal*. •ANTHROPOLOGY AND ARCHAEOLOGY: *Archaeology:* Eastern Hemisphere

Sego, Stephen. Freelance Journalist; Former Director, Radio Free Afghanistan. •WORLD AFFAIRS: *Afghanistan*

Seligson, Mitchell A. Daniel H. Wallace Professor of Political Science, University of Pittsburgh. Editor of *Elections and Democracy in Central America, Revisited*. •WORLD AFFAIRS: *Costa Rica*

Seno, Alexandra A. Correspondent, *Asiaweek*. •WORLD AFFAIRS: *Brunei; Cambodia; Vietnam*

Serafin, Steven R. Director, Writing Center, Hunter College, City University of New York. Editor of *The Continuum Encyclopedia of American Literature*. •NOBEL PRIZES *(in part)*

Shameen, Assif A. Senior Regional Correspondent, *Asiaweek*. •WORLD AFFAIRS: *Malaysia; Pakistan*

Shelley, Andrew. Chairman, JSM, London. Author of *Squash Rules: A Players Guide*. •SPORTS AND GAMES: *Squash*

Shepherd, Melinda C. Associate Editor, Encyclopædia Britannica, Inc. •OBITUARIES *(in part)*; SPORTS AND GAMES: *Automobile Racing:* U.S. Auto Racing *(in part)*; *Special Report:* Games of the XXVII Olympiad; WORLD AFFAIRS: *Dependent States:* Europe and the Atlantic; Indian Ocean and East Timor

Shoemaker, Alan H. Collection Manager, Riverbanks Zoological Park, Columbia, S.C. •THE ENVIRONMENT: *Zoos*

Siler, Shanda. Editorial Assistant, Encyclopædia Britannica, Inc. •BIOGRAPHIES *(in part)*; OBITUARIES *(in part)*

Simons, Paul. Freelance Journalist. Author of *The Action Plant*. •LIFE SCIENCES: *Botany*

Simpson, Jane. Freelance Writer. •PERFORMING ARTS: *Dance*: European

Sklar, Morton. Executive Director, World Organization Against Torture USA; Judge, Administrative Tribunal for OAS. Editor, *The Status of Human Rights in the United States and Torture in the U.S.* Author of *The Right to Travel* and others. •SOCIAL PROTECTION: *Human Rights*

Smentkowski, Brian. Associate Professor of Political Science, Southeast Missouri State University, Cape Girardeau, Mo. •LAW, CRIME, AND LAW ENFORCEMENT: *Court Decisions*

Smith, Gregory O. Academic Development Officer, European School of Economics. •WORLD AFFAIRS: *San Marino; Vatican City State*

Snodgrass, Donald R. Institute Fellow Emeritus, Harvard University. •WORLD AFFAIRS: *Sri Lanka*

Sparks, Karen J. Managing Editor, Encyclopædia Britannica, Inc. •OBITUARIES *(in part)*

Stern, Irwin. Lecturer in Foreign Languages, North Carolina State University. Editor of *Dictionary of Brazilian Literature*. •LITERATURE: *Portuguese:* Brazil

Summerhill, Edward. Editor, Finnish News Agency; Former Part-Time Staff Member, Reuters. •WORLD AFFAIRS: *Finland*

Sumner, David E. Associate Professor of Journalism and Head of the Magazine Program, Ball State University, Muncie, Ind. •MEDIA AND PUBLISHING: *Magazines*

Susel, Rudolph M. Editor, *American Home*. •WORLD AFFAIRS: *Slovenia*

Susser, Leslie D. Diplomatic Correspondent, *The Jerusalem Report*. Coauthor of *Shalom Friend: The Life and Legacy of Yitzhak Rabin*. •WORLD AFFAIRS: *Israel*

Swift, Richard N. Professor Emeritus of Politics, New York University. •WORLD AFFAIRS: *Multinational and Regional Organizations; United Nations*

Szczesny, Barry G. Assistant Director, Government and Public Affairs, American Association of Museums. • LIBRARIES AND MUSEUMS: *Museums* (U.S.)

Szilagyi, Zsofia. Freelance Writer. •WORLD AFFAIRS: *Hungary*

Tao, Amy R. Freelance Writer and Editor. •BIOGRAPHIES *(in part)*

Taylor, Jolanda Vanderwal. Associate Professor of Dutch and German, University of Wisconsin, Madison. •LITERATURE: *Netherlandic*; WORLD AFFAIRS: *The Netherlands*

Taylor-Robinson, Michelle M. Associate Professor of Political Science, Texas A&M University. Coauthor of *Negotiating Democracy: Transitions from Authoritarian Rule*. •WORLD AFFAIRS: *Honduras*

Teague, Elizabeth. Research Analyst, Foreign and Commonwealth Office, London. *(The opinions expressed are personal and do not necessarily represent those of the British government.)* •BIOGRAPHIES *(in part)*; WORLD AFFAIRS: *Russia*

Tesoro, José Manuel. Staff Correspondent, *Asiaweek*. •WORLD AFFAIRS: *Indonesia*

Tétreault, Mary Ann. Una Chapman Cox Distinguished Professor of International Affairs, Trinity University, San Antonio, Texas. Author of *Stories of Democracy: Politics and Society in Contemporary Kuwait* and others. •WORLD AFFAIRS: *Kuwait*

Thomas, R. Murray. Professor Emeritus of Education, University of California, Santa Barbara. Author of *Recent Theories of Human Development*. •EDUCATION

Thyagarajan, S. Deputy Editor and Hockey Correspondent, *The Hindu*. •SPORTS AND GAMES: *Field Hockey*

Tikkanen, Amy. Freelance Writer and Editor. •BIOGRAPHIES *(in part)*

Todd Middleton, Amy. Assistant Vice President, Sotheby's. •ART, ANTIQUES, AND COLLECTIONS: *Art Auctions and Sales*

Tucker, Emma. Correspondent, *Financial Times*. •WORLD AFFAIRS: *European Union*

Turner, Darrell J. Freelance Writer; Former Religion Writer, *The Journal Gazette* (Fort Wayne, Ind.). •BIOGRAPHIES *(in part)*; RELIGION

Uhlick, Lawrence R. Executive Director and General Counsel, Institute of International Bankers. •ECONOMIC AFFAIRS: *Banking*

UNHCR. The Office of the United Nations High Commissioner for Refugees. •SOCIAL PROTECTION: *Refugees and International Migration*

Utt, Roger L. Editor, *Puerta del Sol*. Former Assistant Professor of Spanish, Department of Romance Languages and Literatures, University of Chicago. •LITERATURE: *Spanish:* Spain

Verdi, Robert. Senior Writer, *New York Times Magazine* group; Contributing Columnist, *Chicago Tribune*. •SPORTS AND GAMES: *Baseball* (U.S. and Canada)

Vinton, Louisa. Editor, Economist Intelligence Unit, Vienna; Ebusinessforum.com. •WORLD AFFAIRS: *Poland*

Walker, Thomas W. Professor of Political Science, Ohio University. •WORLD AFFAIRS: *Nicaragua*

Wallenfeldt, Jeff. Senior Editor, Encyclopædia Britannica, Inc. •BIOGRAPHIES *(in part)*; PERFORMING ARTS: *Music:* Sidebar

Wanninger, Richard S. Freelance Journalist. •SPORTS AND GAMES: *Volleyball*

Watson, Rory. European Correspondent, *The Herald* (Scotland). Coauthor of *The American Express Guide to Brussels*. •WORLD AFFAIRS: *Belgium*

Wechsler, Helen J. Director, International and Ethics Programs, American Association of Museums. •LIBRARIES AND MUSEUMS: *Museums* (international)

Weil, Eric. Sports Editor, *Buenos Aires Herald*. •SPORTS AND GAMES: *Football:* Association Football (Soccer): *Latin America*

White, Martin L. Freelance Writer, Chicago. •OBITUARIES *(in part)*

Whitney, Barbara. Copy Supervisor, Encyclopædia Britannica, Inc. •BIOGRAPHIES *(in part)*; LIFE SCIENCES: Sidebar; OBITUARIES *(in part)*

Whitten, Phillip. Editor in Chief, *Swimming World*. Author of *The Complete Book of Swimming* and others. •SPORTS AND GAMES: *Swimming*

Wilkinson, John R. Sportswriter, Coventry Newspapers. •SPORTS AND GAMES: *Cycling*

Williams, Victoria C. Independent Consultant on International Affairs. •LAW, CRIME, AND LAW ENFORCEMENT: *International Law*

Wilson, Derek. Correspondent, BBC, Rome. Author of *Rome, Umbria and Tuscany*. •WORLD AFFAIRS: *Italy*

Wise, Larry. Author of *Tuning Your Compound Bow* and others. •SPORTS AND GAMES: *Archery*

Woodrow, Robert. Former Assistant Managing Editor, *Asiaweek*. •WORLD AFFAIRS: *Laos; Thailand*

Woods, Elizabeth. Writer. Author of *If Only Things Were Different (I): A Model for a Sustainable Society, Bird Salad,* and others. •LITERATURE: *English:* Canada

Woods, Michael. Science Editor, *The Toledo Blade*. •MATHEMATICS AND PHYSICAL SCIENCES: *Chemistry*; NOBEL PRIZES *(in part)*

Woodward, Ralph Lee, Jr. Neville G. Penrose Professor of Latin American Studies, Texas Christian University. Author of *Central America, a Nation Divided*. •WORLD AFFAIRS: *El Salvador; Guatemala*

Wyllie, Peter J. Emeritus Professor of Geology, California Institute of Technology, Pasadena. Author of *The Dynamic Earth* and *The Way the Earth Works*. •EARTH SCIENCES: *Geology and Geochemistry*

Zegura, Stephen L. Professor of Anthropology, University of Arizona. •ANTHROPOLOGY AND ARCHAEOLOGY: *Anthropology:* Physical

World Data

At midyear 2000 there were an estimated 6,080,141,683 people on Earth, 77,632,256 more than the year before.

CONTENTS

INTRODUCTION

Britannica World Data provides a statistical portrait of some 217 countries and dependencies of the world, at a level appropriate to the significance of each. It contains 213 country statements (the "Nations of the World" section), ranging in length from one to seven pages, and permits, in the 20 major thematic tables (the "Comparative National Statistics" [CNS] section), comparisons among these larger countries and 4 other states.

Updated annually, *Britannica World Data* is particularly intended as direct, structured support for many of Britannica's other reference works—encyclopaedias, yearbooks, atlases—at a level of detail that their editorial style or design do not permit.

Like the textual, graphic, or cartographic modes of expression of these other products, statistics possess their own inherent editorial virtues and weaknesses. Two principal goals in the creation of *Britannica World Data* were up-to-dateness and comparability, each possible to maximize separately, but not always possible to combine. If, for example, research on some subject is completed during a particular year (x), figures may be available for 100 countries for the preceding year ($x - 1$), for 140 countries for the year before that ($x - 2$), and for 180 countries for the year before that ($x - 3$).

Which year should be the basis of a thematic compilation for 217 countries so as to give the best combination of up-to-dateness and comparability? And, should $x - 1$ be adopted for the thematic table, ought up-to-dateness in the country table (for which year x is already available) be sacrificed for agreement with the thematic table? In general, the editors have opted for maximum up-to-dateness in the country statistical boxes and maximum comparability in the thematic tables.

Comparability, however, also resides in the meaning of the numbers compiled, which may differ greatly from country to country. The headnotes to the thematic tables explain many of these methodological problems; the Glossary serves the same purpose for the country statistical pages. Published data do not always provide the researcher or editor with a neat, unambiguous choice between a datum compiled on two different bases (say, railroad track length, or route length), one of which is wanted and the other not. More often a choice must be made among a variety of official, private, and external intergovernmental (UN, FAO, IMF) sources, each reporting its best data but each representing a set of problems: (1) of methodological variance from (or among) international conventions; (2) of analytical completeness (data for a single year may, successively, be projected [based on 10 months' data], preliminary [for 12 months], final, revised or adjusted, etc.); (3) of time frame, or accounting interval (data may represent a full Gregorian calendar year [preferred], a fiscal year, an Islamic or other national or religious year, a multiyear period or average [when a one-year statement would contain unrepresentative results]); (4) of continuity with previous data; and the like. Finally, published data on a particular subject may be complete and final but impossible to summarize in a simple manner. The education system of a single country may include, for example, public and private sectors; local, state, or national systems; varying grades, tracks, or forms within a single system; or opportunities for double-counting or fractional counting of a student, teacher, or institution. When no recent official data exist, or they exist, but may be suspect, the tables may show unofficial estimates, a range (of published opinion), analogous data, or no data at all.

The published basis of the information compiled is the statistical collections of Encyclopædia Britannica, Inc., some of the principal elements of which are enumerated in the Bibliography. Holdings for a given country may include any of the following: the national statistical abstract; the constitution; the most recent censuses of population; periodic or occasional reports on vital statistics, social indicators, agriculture, mining, labour, manufacturing, domestic and foreign trade, finance and banking, transportation, and communications. Further information is received in a variety of formats—telephone, letter, fax, microfilm and microfiche, and most recently, in electronic formats such as computer disks, CD-ROMs, and the Internet. So substantial had the resources of the Internet become by the previous research year that it was thought possible to add uniform resource locators (URLs) to the great majority of country pages and a number of the CNS tables (summary world sites with data on all countries still being somewhat of a rarity) so as to apprise the reader of the possibility and means to access current information on these subjects year-round.

The recommendations offered are usually to official sites (national statistical offices, general national governments, central banks, embassies, intergovernmental organizations [especially the UN Development Programme], and the like). Though often dissimilar in content, they will usually be updated year-round, expanded as opportunity permits, and lead on to related sites, such as parliamentary offices, information offices, diplomatic and consular sites, news agencies and newspapers, and, beyond, to the myriad academic, commercial, and private sites now accessible from the personal computer. While these URLs were correct and current at the time of writing, they may be subject to change.

The great majority of the social, economic, and financial data contained in this work should not be interpreted in isolation. Interpretive text of long perspective, such as that of the *Encyclopædia Britannica* itself; political, geographic, and topical maps, such as those in the *Britannica Atlas;* and recent analysis of political events and economic trends, such as that contained in the articles of the *Book of the Year,* will all help to supply analytic focus that numbers alone cannot. By the same token, study of those sources will be made more concrete by use of *Britannica World Data* to supply up-to-date geographic, demographic, and economic detail.

GLOSSARY

A number of terms that are used to classify and report data in the "Nations of the World" section require some explanation.

Those italicized terms that are used regularly in the country compilations to introduce specific categories of information (*e.g., birth rate, budget*) appear in this glossary in italic boldface type, followed by a description of the precise kind of information being offered and how it has been edited and presented.

All other terms are printed here in roman boldface type. Many terms have quite specific meanings in statistical reporting, and they are so defined here. Other terms have less specific application as they are used by different countries or organizations. Data in the country compilations based on definitions markedly different from those below will usually be footnoted.

Terms that appear in small capitals in certain definitions are themselves defined at their respective alphabetical locations.

Terms whose definitions are marked by an asterisk (*) refer to data supplied only in the larger two- to four-page country compilations.

access to services, a group of measures indicating a population's level of access to public services, including electrical power, treated public drinking water, sewage removal, and fire protection.*

activity rate, *see* participation/activity rates.

age breakdown, the distribution of a given population by age, usually reported here as percentages of total population in 15-year age brackets. When substantial numbers of persons do not know, or state, their exact age, distributions may not total 100.0%.

area, the total surface area of a country or its administrative subdivisions, including both land and inland (nontidal) water area. Land area is usually calculated from "mean low water" on a "plane table," or flat, basis.

area and population, a tabulation usually including the first-order administrative subdivisions of the country (such as the states of the United States), with capital (headquarters, or administrative seat), area, and population. When these subdivisions are especially numerous or, occasionally, nonexistent, a planning, electoral, census, or other nonadministrative scheme of regional subdivisions has been substituted.

associated state, *see* state.

atheist, in statements of religious affiliation, one who professes active opposition to religion; "nonreligious" refers to those professing only no religion, nonbelief, or doubt.

balance of payments, a financial statement for a country for a given period showing the balance among: (1) transactions in goods, services, and income between that country and the rest of the world, (2) changes in ownership or valuation of that country's monetary gold, SPECIAL DRAWING RIGHTS, and claims on and liabilities to the rest of the world, and (3) unrequited transfers and counterpart entries needed (in an accounting sense) to balance transactions and changes among any of the foregoing types of exchange that are not mutually offsetting. Detail of national law as to what constitutes a transaction, the basis of its valuation, and the size of a transaction visible to fiscal authorities all result in differences in the meaning of a particular national statement.*

balance of trade, the net value of all international goods trade of a country, usually excluding reexports (goods received only for transshipment), and the percentage that this net represents of total trade.

Balance of trade refers only to the "visible" international trade of goods as recorded by customs authorities and is thus a segment of a country's BALANCE OF PAYMENTS, which takes all visible and invisible trade with other countries into account. (Invisible trade refers to imports and exports of money, financial instruments, and services such as transport, tourism, and insurance.) A country has a favourable, or positive (+), balance of trade when the value of exports exceeds that of imports and negative (–) when imports exceed exports.

barrel (bbl), a unit of liquid measure. The barrel conventionally used for reporting crude petroleum and petroleum products is equal to 42 U.S. gallons, or 159 litres. The number of barrels of crude petroleum per metric ton, ranging typically from 6.20 to 8.13, depends upon the specific gravity of the petroleum. The world average is roughly 7.33 barrels per ton.

birth rate, the number of live births annually per 1,000 of midyear population. Birth rates for individual countries may be compared with the estimated world annual average of 25.0 births per 1,000 population between 1990 and 1995.

budget, the annual receipts and expenditures—of a central government for its activities only;

Abbreviations

Measurements

cu m	cubic metre(s)
kg	kilograms(s)
km	kilometre(s)
kW	kilowatt(s)
kW-hr	kilowatt-hour(s)
metric ton-km	metric ton-kilometre(s)
mi	mile(s)
passenger-km	passenger-kilometre(s)
passenger-mi	passenger-mile(s)
short ton-mi	short ton-mile(s)
sq km	square kilometre(s)
sq m	square metre(s)
sq mi	square mile(s)
troy oz	troy ounce(s)
yr	year(s)

Political Units and International Organizations

CACM	Central American Common Market
Caricom	Caribbean Community and Common Market
CFA	Communauté Financière Africaine
CFP	Comptoirs Françaises du Pacifique
CIS	Commonwealth of Independent States
CUSA	Customs Union of Southern Africa
E.Ger.	East Germany
EC	European Communities
EU	European Union
FAO	United Nations Food and Agriculture Organization
IMF	International Monetary Fund
OECD	Organization for Economic Cooperation and Development
OECS	Organization of Eastern Caribbean States
U.A.E.	United Arab Emirates
U.K.	United Kingdom
UNDP	United Nations Development Programme
U.S.	United States
U.S.S.R.	Union of Soviet Socialist Republics
W.Ger.	West Germany

Months

Jan.	January	Oct.	October
Feb.	February	Nov.	November
Aug.	August	Dec.	December
Sept.	September		

Miscellaneous

AIDS	Acquired Immune Deficiency Syndrome
avg.	average
c.i.f.	cost, insurance, and freight
commun.	communications
CPI	consumer price index
est.	estimate(d)
excl.	excluding
f.o.b.	free on board
GDP	gross domestic product
GNP	gross national product
govt.	government
incl.	including
mo.	month(s)
n.a.	not available (in text)
n.e.s.	not elsewhere specified
no.	number
pl.	plural
pos.	position
pub. admin.	public administration
PVC	Polyvinyl Chloride
SDR	Special Drawing Right
SITC	Standard International Trade Classification
svcs.	services
teacher tr.	teacher training
transp.	transportation
voc.	vocational
$	dollar (of any currency area)
£	pound (of any currency area)
...	not available (in tables)
—	none, less than half the smallest unit shown, or not applicable (in tables)

does not include state, provincial, or local governments or semipublic (parastatal, quasi-nongovernmental) corporations unless otherwise specified. Figures for budgets are limited to ordinary (recurrent) receipts and expenditures, wherever possible, and exclude capital expenditures—*i.e.,* funds for development and other special projects originating as foreign-aid grants or loans.

When both a recurrent and a capital budget exist for a single country, the former is the budget funded entirely from national resources (taxes, duties, excises, etc.) that would recur (be generated by economic activity) every year. It funds the most basic governmental services, those least able to suffer interruption. The capital budget is usually funded by external aid and may change its size considerably from year to year.

capital, usually, the actual seat of government and administration of a state. When more than one capital exists, each is identified by kind; when interim arrangements exist during the creation or movement of a national capital, the de facto situation is described.

Anomalous cases are annotated, such as those in which (1) the de jure designation under the country's laws differs from actual local practice (*e.g.,* Benin's designation of one capital in constitutional law, but another in actual practice), (2) international recognition does not validate a country's claim (as with the proclamation by Israel of a capital on territory not internationally recognized as part of Israel), or (3) both a state and a capital have been proclaimed on territory recognized as part of another state (as with the Turkish Republic of Northern Cyprus).

capital budget, *see* budget.

causes of death, as defined by the World Health Organization (WHO), "the disease or injury which initiated the train of morbid events leading directly to death, or the circumstances of accident or violence which produced the fatal injury." This principle, the "underlying cause of death," is the basis of the medical judgment as to cause; the statistical classification system according to which these causes are grouped and named is the *International List of Causes of Death,* the latest revision of which is the Tenth. Reporting is usually in terms of events per 100,000 population. When data on actual causes of death are unavailable, information on morbidity, or illness rate, usually given as reported cases per 100,000 of infectious diseases (notifiable to WHO as a matter of international agreement), may be substituted.

chief of state/head of government, paramount national governmental officer(s) exercising the highest executive and/or ceremonial roles of a country's government. In general usage, the chief of state is the formal head of a national state. The primary responsibilities of the chief of state may range from the purely ceremonial—convening legislatures and greeting foreign officials—to the exercise of complete national executive authority. The head of government, when this function exists separately, is the officer nominally charged (by the constitution) with the majority of actual executive powers, though they may not in practice be exercised, especially in military or single-party regimes in which effective power may reside entirely outside the executive governmental machinery provided by the constitution. A prime minister, for example, usually the actual head of government, may in practice exercise only Cabinet-level authority.

In communist countries an official identified as the chief of state may be the chairman of the policy-making organ, and the official given as the head of government the chairman of the nominal administrative/executive organ.

c.i.f. (trade valuation): *see* imports.

colony, an area annexed to, or controlled by, an independent state but not an integral part of it; a non-self-governing territory. A colony has a charter and may have a degree of self-government. A crown colony is a colony originally chartered by the British government.

commonwealth (U.K. and U.S.), a self-governing political entity that has regard to the common weal, or good; usually associated with the United Kingdom or United States. Examples include the Commonwealth of Nations (composed of independent states [from 1931 onward]), Puerto Rico since 1952, and the Northern Marianas since 1979.

communications, collectively, the means available for the public transmission of information within a country. Data are tabulated for: daily newspapers and their total circulation; radio and television as total numbers of receivers; telephone data as "main lines," or the number of subscriber lines (not receivers) having access to the public switched network; cellular telephones as number of subscribers; and facsimile machines and personal computers as number of units. For each, a rate per 1,000 persons is given.

constant prices, an adjustment to the members of a financial time series to eliminate the effect of inflation year by year. It consists of referring all data in the series to a single year so that "real" change may be seen.

constitutional monarchy, *see* monarchy.

consumer price index (CPI), also known as the retail price index, or the cost-of-living index, a series of index numbers assigned to the price of a selected "basket," or assortment, of basic consumer goods and services in a country, region, city, or type of household in order to measure changes over time in prices paid by a typical household for those goods and services. Items included in the CPI are ordinarily determined by governmental surveys of typical household expenditures and are assigned weights relative to their proportion of those expenditures. Index values are period averages unless otherwise noted.

coprincipality, *see* monarchy.

current prices, the valuation of a financial aggregate as of the year reported.

daily per capita caloric intake (supply), the calories equivalent to the known average daily supply of foodstuffs for human consumption in a given country divided by the population of the country (and the proportion of that supply provided, respectively, by vegetable and animal sources). The daily per capita caloric intake of a country may be compared with the corresponding recommended minimum daily requirement. The latter is calculated by the Food and Agriculture Organization of the United Nations from the age and sex distributions, average body weights, and environmental temperatures in a given region to determine the calories needed to sustain a person there at normal levels of activity and health. The daily per capita caloric requirement ranges from 2,200 to 2,500.

de facto population, for a given area, the population composed of those actually present at a particular time, including temporary residents and visitors (such as immigrants not yet granted permanent status, "guest" or expatriate workers, refugees, or tourists), but excluding legal residents temporarily absent.

de jure population, for a given area, the population composed only of those legally resident at a particular time, excluding temporary residents and visitors (such as "guest" or expatriate workers, refugees, or tourists), but including legal residents temporarily absent.

deadweight tonnage, the maximum weight of cargo, fuel, fresh water, stores, and persons that may safely by carried by a ship. It is customarily measured in long tons of 2,240 pounds each, equivalent to 1.016 metric tons. Deadweight tonnage is the difference between the tonnage of a fully loaded ship and the fully unloaded tonnage of that ship.

See also gross ton.

death rate, the number of deaths annually per 1,000 of midyear population. Death rates for individual countries may be compared with the estimated world annual average of 9.3 deaths per 1,000 population between 1990 and 1995.

density (of population), usually, the DE FACTO POPULATION of a country divided by its total area. Special adjustment is made for large areas of inland water, desert, or other uninhabitable areas—*e.g.,* excluding the ice cap of Greenland.

dependent state, constitutionally or statutorily organized political entity outside of and under the jurisdiction of an independent state (or a federal element of such a state) but not formally annexed to it (*see* Table).

Dependent states[1]

Australia
- Christmas Island
- Cocos (Keeling) Islands
- Norfolk Island

China
- Hong Kong
- Macau

Denmark
- Faroe Islands
- Greenland

France
- French Guiana
- French Polynesia
- Guadeloupe
- Martinique
- Mayotte
- New Caledonia
- Réunion
- Saint Pierre and Miquelon
- Wallis and Futuna

Netherlands, The
- Aruba
- Netherlands Antilles

New Zealand
- Cook Islands
- Niue
- Tokelau

United Kingdom
- Anguilla
- Bermuda
- British Virgin Islands
- Cayman Islands
- Falkland Islands
- Gibraltar
- Guernsey
- Isle of Man
- Jersey
- Montserrat
- Pitcairn Island
- Saint Helena and Dependencies
- Turks and Caicos Islands

United Nations
- East Timor

United States
- American Samoa
- Guam
- Northern Mariana Islands
- Puerto Rico
- Virgin Islands (of the U.S.)

[1]Excludes territories (1) to which Antarctic Treaty is applicable in whole or in part, (2) without permanent civilian population, (3) without internationally recognized civilian government (Western Sahara, Gaza Strip), or (4) representing unadjudicated unilateral or multilateral territorial claims.

direct taxes, taxes levied directly on firms and individuals, such as taxes on income, profits, and capital gains. The *immediate* incidence, or burden, of direct taxes is on the firms and individuals thus taxed; direct taxes on firms may, however, be passed on to consumers and other economic units in the form of higher prices for goods and services, blurring the distinction between direct and indirect taxation.

distribution of income/wealth, the portion of personal income or wealth accruing to households or individuals constituting each respective decile (tenth) or quintile (fifth) of a country's households or individuals.*

divorce rate, the number of legal, civilly recognized divorces annually per 1,000 population.

doubling time, the number of complete years required for a country to double its population at its current rate of natural increase.

earnings index, a series of index numbers comparing average wages in a collective industrial sample for a country or region with the same industries at a previous period to measure changes over time in those wages. It is most commonly reported for wages paid on a daily, weekly, or monthly basis; annual figures may represent total income or averages of these shorter periods. The scope of the earnings index varies from country to country. The index is often limited to earnings in manufacturing industries. The index for each country applies to all wage earners in a designated group and ordinarily takes into account basic wages (overtime is normally distinguished), bonuses, cost-of-living allowances, and contributions toward social security. Some countries include payments in kind. Contributions toward social security by employers are usually excluded, as are social security benefits received by wage earners.

economically active population, *see* population economically active.

education, tabulation of the principal elements of a country's educational establishment, classified as far as possible according to the country's own system of primary, secondary, and higher levels (the usual age limits for these levels being identified in parentheses), with total number of schools (physical facilities) and of teachers and students (whether full- or part-time). The student-teacher ratio is calculated whenever available data permit.

educational attainment, the distribution of the population age 25 and over with completed educations by the highest level of formal education attained or completed; it must sometimes be reported, however, for age groups still in school or for the economically active only.

emirate, *see* monarchy.

enterprise, a legal entity formed to conduct a business, which it may do from more than one establishment (place of business or service point).

ethnic/linguistic composition, ethnic, racial, or linguistic composition of a national population, reported here according to the most reliable breakdown available, whether published in official sources (such as a census) or in external analysis (when the subject is not addressed in national sources).

exchange rate, the value of one currency compared with another, or with a standardized unit of account such as the SPECIAL DRAWING RIGHT, or as mandated by local statute when one currency is "tied" by a par value to another. Rates given usually refer to free market values when the currency has no, or very limited, restrictions on its convertibility into other currencies.

exports, material goods legally leaving a country (or customs area) and subject to customs regulations. The total value and distribution by percentage of the major items (in preference to groups of goods) exported are given, together with the distribution of trade among major trading partners (usually single countries or trading blocs). Valuation of goods exported is free on board (f.o.b.) unless otherwise specified. The value of goods exported and imported f.o.b. is calculated from the cost of production and excludes the cost of transport.

external debt, public and publicly guaranteed debt with a maturity of more than one year owed to nonnationals of a country and repayable in foreign currency, goods, or services. The debt may be an obligation of a national or subnational governmental body (or an agency of either), of an autonomous public body, or of a private debtor that is guaranteed by a public entity. The debt is usually either outstanding (contracted) or disbursed (drawn).

external territory (Australia), *see* territory.

federal, consisting of first-order political subdivisions that are prior to and independent of the central government in certain functions.

federal republic, *see* republic.

federation, union of coequal, preexisting political entities that retain some degree of autonomy and (usually) right of secession within the union.

fertility rate, *see* total fertility rate.

financial aggregates, tabulation of seven-year time series, providing principal measures of the financial condition of a country, including: (1) the exchange rate of the national crurency against the U.S. dollar, the pound sterling, and the International Monetary Fund's SPECIAL DRAWING RIGHT (SDR), (2) the amount and kind of international reserves (holdings of SDRs, gold, and foreign currencies) and reserve position of the country in the IMF, and (3) principal economic rates and prices (central bank discount rate, government bond yields, and industrial stock [share] prices). For BALANCE OF PAYMENTS, the origin in terms of component balance of trade items and balance of invisibles (net) is given.*

fish catch, the live-weight equivalent of the aquatic animals (including fish, crustaceans, mollusks, etc., but excluding whales, seals, and other aquatic mammals) caught in freshwater or marine areas by national fleets and landed in domestic or foreign harbours for commercial, industrial, or subsistence purposes.

f.o.b. (trade valuation), *see* exports.

food, *see* daily per capita caloric intake.

form of government/political status, the type of administration provided for by a country's constitution—whether or not suspended by extralegal military or civil action, although such de facto administrations are identified—together with the number of members (elected, appointed, and ex officio) for each legislative house, named according to its English rendering. Dependent states (*see* Table) are classified according to the status of their political association with the administering country.

gross domestic product (GDP), the total value of the final goods and services produced by residents and nonresidents within a given country during a given accounting period, usually a year. Unless otherwise noted, the value is given in current prices of the year indicated. The *System of National Accounts* (SNA, published under the joint auspices of the UN, IMF, OECD, EC, and World Bank) provides a framework for international comparability in classifying domestic accounting aggregates and international transactions comprising "net factor income from abroad," the measure that distinguishes GDP and GNP.

gross national product (GNP), the total value of final goods and services produced both from within a given country *and* from external (foreign) transactions in a given accounting period, usually a year. Unless otherwise noted, the value is given in current prices of the year indicated. GNP is equal to GROSS DOMESTIC PRODUCT (*q.v.*) adjusted by net factor income from abroad, which is the income residents receive from abroad for factor services (labour, investment, and interest) less similar payments made to nonresidents who contribute to the domestic economy.

gross ton, volumetric unit of measure (equaling 100 cubic feet [2.83 cu m]) of the permanently enclosed volume of a ship, above and below decks available for cargo, stores, or passenger accommodation. Net, or register, tonnage exempts certain nonrevenue spaces—such as those devoted to machinery, bunkers, crew accommodations, and ballast—from the gross tonnage. *See also* deadweight tonnage.

head of government, *see* chief of state/head of government.

health, a group of measures including number of accredited physicians currently practicing or employed and their ratio to the total population; total hospital beds and their ratio; and INFANT MORTALITY RATE.

household, economically autonomous individual or group of individuals living in a single dwelling unit. A family household is one composed principally of individuals related by blood or marriage.

household income and expenditure, data for average size of a HOUSEHOLD (by number of individuals) and median household income. Sources of income and expenditures for major items of consumption are given as percentages.

In general, household income is the amount of funds, usually measured in monetary units, received by the members (generally those 14 years old and over) of a household in a given time period. The income can be derived from (1) wages or salaries, (2) nonfarm or farm SELF-EMPLOYMENT, (3) transfer payments, such as pensions, public assistance, unemployment benefits, etc., and (4) other income, including interest and dividends, rent, royalties, etc. The income of a household is expressed as a gross amount before deductions for taxes. Data on expenditure refer to consumption of personal or household goods and services; they normally exclude savings, taxes, and insurance; practice with regard to inclusion of credit purchases differs markedly.

immigration, usually, the number and origin of those immigrants admitted to a nation in a legal status that would eventually permit the granting of the right to settle permanently or to acquire citizenship.*

imports, material goods legally entering a country (or customs area) and subject to customs regulations; excludes financial movements. The total value and distribution by percentage of the major items (in preference to groups of goods) imported are given, together with the direction of trade among major trading partners (usually single countries), trading blocs (such as the European Union), or customs areas (such as Belgium-Luxembourg). The value of goods imported is given free on board (f.o.b.) unless otherwise specified; f.o.b. is defined above under EXPORTS.

The principal alternate basis for valuation of goods in international trade is that of cost, insurance, and freight (c.i.f.); its use is restricted to imports, as it comprises the principal charges needed to bring the goods to the customs house in the country of destination. Because it inflates the value of imports relative to exports, more countries have, latterly, been estimating imports on an f.o.b. basis as well.

incorporated territory (U.S.), *see* territory.

independent, of a state, autonomous and controlling both its internal and external affairs. Its date usually refers to the date from which the country was in effective control of these affairs within its present boundaries, rather than the date independence was proclaimed or the date recognized as a de jure act by the former administering power.

indirect taxes, taxes levied on sales or transfers of selected intermediate goods and services, including excises, value-added taxes, and tariffs, that are ordinarily passed on to the ultimate consumers of the goods and services. Figures given for individual countries are limited to indirect taxes levied by their respective central governments unless otherwise specified.

infant mortality rate, the number of children per 1,000 live births who die before their first birthday. Total infant mortality includes neonatal mortality, which is deaths of children within one month of birth.

invisibles (invisible trade), *see* balance of trade.

kingdom, *see* monarchy.

labour force, portion of the POPULATION ECONOMICALLY ACTIVE (PEA) comprising those most fully employed or attached to the labour market (the unemployed are considered to be "attached" in that they usually represent persons previously employed seeking to be reemployed), particularly as viewed from a short-term perspective. It normally includes those who are self-employed, employed by others (whether full-time, part-time, seasonally, or on some other less than full-time, basis), and, as noted above, the unemployed (both those previously employed and those seeking work for the first time). In the "gross domestic product and labour force" table, the majority of the labour data provided refer to population economically active, since PEA represents the longer-term view of working population and, thus, subsumes more of the marginal workers who are often missed by shorter-term surveys.

land use, distribution by classes of vegetational cover or economic use of the land area only (excluding inland water, for example, but not marshland), reported as percentages. The principal categories utilized include: (1) forest, which includes natural and planted tracts, (2) meadows and pastures, which includes land in temporary or permanent use whose principal purpose is the growing of animal fodder, (3) agricultural and under permanent cultivation, which includes temporary and permanent cropland, as well as land left fallow less than five years, but capable of being returned to production without special preparation, and (4) other, which includes built-up, wasteland, watercourses, and the like.

leisure, the principal monetary expenditures, uses, or reported preferences in the use of the individual's free time for recreation, rest, or self-improvement.*

life expectancy, the number of years a person born within a particular population group (age cohort) would be expected to live, based on actuarial calculations.

literacy, the ability to read and write a language with some degree of competence; the precise degree constituting the basis of a particular national statement is usually defined by the national census and is often tested by the census enumerator. Elsewhere, particularly where much adult literacy may be the result of literacy campaigns rather than passage through a formal educational system, definition and testing of literacy may be better standardized.

major cities, usually the five largest cities proper (national capitals are always given, regardless of size); fewer cities may be listed if there are fewer urban localities in the country. For multipage tables, 10 or more may be listed.* Populations for cities will usually refer to the city proper—*i.e.,* the legally bounded corporate entity, or the most compact, contiguous, demographically urban portion of the entity defined by the local authorities. Occasionally figures for METROPOLITAN AREAS are cited when the relevant civil entity at the core of a major agglomeration had an unrepresentatively small population.

manufacturing, mining, and construction enterprises/retail sales and service enterprises, a detailed tabulation of the principal industries in these sectors, showing for each industry the number of enterprises and employees, wages in that industry as a percentage of the general average wage, and the value of that industry's output in terms of value added or turnover.*

marriage rate, the number of legal, civilly recognized marriages annually per 1,000 population.

material well-being, a group of measures indicating the percentage of households or dwellings possessing certain goods or appliances, including automobiles, telephones, television receivers, refrigerators, air conditioners, and washing machines.*

merchant marine, the privately or publicly owned ships registered with the maritime authority of a nation (limited to those in Lloyd's of London statistical reporting of 100 or more GROSS TONS) that are employed in commerce, whether or not owned or operated by nationals of the country.

metropolitan area, a city and the region of dense, predominantly urban, settlement around the city; the population of the whole usually has strong economic and cultural affinities with the central city.

military expenditure, the apparent value of all identifiable military expenditure by the central government on hardware, personnel, pensions, research and development, etc., reported here both as a percentage of the GNP, with a comparison to the world average, and as a per capita value in U.S. dollars.

military personnel, *see* total active duty personnel.

mobility, the rate at which individuals or households change dwellings, usually measured between censuses and including international as well as domestic migration.*

monarchy, a government in which the CHIEF OF STATE holds office, usually hereditarily and for life, but sometimes electively for a term. The state may be a coprincipality, emirate, kingdom, principality, sheikhdom, or sultanate. The powers of the monarch may range from absolute (*i.e.,* the monarch both reigns and rules) through various degrees of limitation of authority to nominal, as in a constitutional monarchy, in which the titular monarch reigns but others, as elected officials, effectively rule.

monetary unit, currency of issue, or that in official use in a given country; name, spelling, and abbreviation in English according to International Monetary Fund recommendations or local practice; name of the lesser, usually decimal, monetary unit constituting the main currency; and valuation in U.S. dollars and U.K. pounds sterling, usually according to free-market or commercial rates.

See also exchange rate.

natural increase, also called natural growth, or the balance of births and deaths, the excess of births over deaths in a population; the rate of natural increase is the difference between the BIRTH RATE and the DEATH RATE of a given population. The estimated world average during 1990–95 was 15.7 per 1,000 population, or 1.57% annually. Natural increase is added to the balance of migration to calculate the total growth of that population.

net material product, *see* material product.

nonreligious, *see* atheist.

official language(s), that (or those) prescribed by the national constitution for day-to-day conduct and publication of a country's official business or, when no explicit constitutional provision exists, that of the constitution itself, the national gazette (record of legislative activity), or like official documents. Other languages may have local protection, may be permitted in parliamentary debate or legal action (such as a trial), or may be "national languages," for the protection of which special provisions have been made, but these are not deemed official. The United States, for example, does not yet formally identify English as "official," though it uses it for virtually all official purposes.

official name, the local official form(s), short or long, of a country's legal name(s) taken from the country's constitution or from other official documents. The English-language form is usually the protocol form in use by the country, the U.S. Department of State, and the United Nations.

official religion, generally, any religion prescribed or given special status or protection by the constitution or legal system of a country. Identification as such is not confined to constitutional documents utilizing the term explicitly.

organized territory (U.S.), *see* territory.

overseas department (France), *see* department.

overseas territory (France), *see* territory.

parliamentary state, *see* state.

part of a realm, a dependent Dutch political entity with some degree of self-government and having a special status above that of a colony (*e.g.,* the prerogative of rejecting for local application any law enacted by The Netherlands).

participation/activity rates, measures defining differential rates of economic activity within a population. Participation rate refers to the percentage of those employed or economically active who possess a particular characteristic (sex, age, etc.); activity rate refers to the fraction of the total population who *are* economically active.

passenger-miles, or **passenger-kilometres,** aggregate measure of passenger carriage by a specified means of transportation, equal to the number of passengers carried multiplied by the number of miles (or kilometres) each is transported. Figures given for countries are often calculated from ticket sales and ordinarily exclude passengers carried free of charge.

people's republic, *see* republic.

place of birth/national origin, if the former, numbers of native- and foreign-born population of a country by actual place of birth; if the latter, any of several classifications, including those based on origin of passport at original admission to country, on cultural heritage of family name, on self-designated (often multiple) origin of (some) ancestors, and on other systems for assigning national origin.*

political status, *see* form of government/political status.

population, the number of persons present within a country, city, or other civil entity at the date of a census of population, survey, cumulation of a civil register, or other enumeration. Unless otherwise specified, populations given are DE FACTO, referring to those actually present, rather than DE JURE, those legally resident but not necessarily present on the referent date. If a time series, noncensus year, or per capita ratio referring to a country's total population is cited, it will usually refer to midyear of the calendar year indicated.

population economically active, the total number of persons (above a set age for economic labour, usually 10–15 years) in all employment statuses—self-employed, wage- or salary-earning, part-time, seasonal, unemployed, etc. The International Labour Organisation defines the economically active as "all persons of either sex who furnish the supply of labour for the production of economic goods and services." National practices vary as regards the treatment of such groups as armed forces, inmates of institutions, persons seeking their first job, unpaid family workers, seasonal workers and persons engaged in part-time economic activities. In some countries, all or part of these groups may be included among the economically active, while in other countries the same groups may be treated as inactive. In general, however, the data on economically active population do not include students, persons occupied solely in family or household work, retired persons, persons living entirely on

their own means, and persons wholly dependent upon others.
See also labour force.

population projection, the expected population in the years 2010 and 2020, embodying the country's own projections wherever possible. Estimates of the future size of a population are usually based on assumed levels of fertility, mortality, and migration. Projections in the tables, unless otherwise specified, are medium (*i.e.,* most likely) variants, whether based on external estimates by the United Nations, World Bank, or U.S. Department of Commerce or on those of the country itself.

price and earnings indexes, tabulation comparing the change in the CONSUMER PRICE INDEX over a period of seven years with the change in the general labour force's EARNINGS INDEX for the same period.

principality, *see* monarchy.

production, the physical quantity or monetary value of the output of an industry, usually tabulated here as the most important items or groups of items (depending on the available detail) of primary (extractive) and secondary (manufactured) production, including construction. When a single consistent measure of value, such as VALUE ADDED, can be obtained, this is given, ranked by value; otherwise, and more usually, quantity of production is given.

public debt, the current outstanding debt of all periods of maturity for which the central government and its organs are obligated. Publicly guaranteed private debt is excluded. For countries that report debt under the World Bank Debtor Reporting System (DRS), figures for outstanding, long-term EXTERNAL DEBT are given.

quality of working life, a group of measures including weekly hours of work (including overtime); rates per 100,000 for job-connected injury, illness, and mortality; coverage of labour force by insurance for injury, permanent disability, and death; workdays lost to labour strikes and stoppages; and commuting patterns (length of journey to work in minutes and usual method of transportation).*

railroads, mode of transportation by self-driven or locomotive-drawn cars over fixed rails. Length-of-track figures include all mainline and spurline running track but exclude switching sidings and yard track. Route length, when given, does not compound multiple running tracks laid on the same trackbed.

recurrent budget, *see* budget.

religious affiliation, distribution of nominal religionists, whether practicing or not, as a percentage of total population. This usually assigns to children the religion of their parents.

republic, a state with elected leaders and a centralized presidential form of government, local subdivisions being subordinate to the national government. A *federal republic* (as distinguished from a unitary republic) is a republic in which power is divided between the central government and the constituent subnational administrative divisions (*e.g.,* states, provinces, or cantons) in whom the central government itself is held to originate, the division of power being defined in a written constitution and jurisdictional disputes usually being settled in a court; sovereignty usually rests with the authority that has the power to amend the constitution. A *unitary republic* (as distinguished from a federal republic) is a republic in which power originates in a central authority and is not derived from constituent subdivisions. A *people's republic,* in the dialectics of Communism, is the first stage of development toward a communist state, the second stage being a *socialist republic.* An *Islamic republic* is structured around social, ethical, legal, and religious precepts central to the Islamic faith.

retail price index, *see* consumer price index.

retail sales and service enterprises, *see* manufacturing, mining, and construction enterprises/retail sales and service enterprises.

roundwood, wood obtained from removals from forests, felled or harvested (with or without bark), in all forms.

rural, *see* urban-rural.

self-employment, work in which income derives from direct employment in one's own business, trade, or profession, as opposed to work in which salary or wages are earned from an employer.

self-governing, of a state, in control of its internal affairs in degrees ranging from control of most internal affairs (though perhaps not of public order or of internal security) to complete control of all internal affairs (*i.e.,* the state is autonomous) but having no control of external affairs or defense. In this work the term self-governing refers to the final stage in the successive stages of increasing self-government that generally precede independence.

service/trade enterprises, *see* manufacturing, mining, and construction enterprises/retail sales and service enterprises.

sex distribution, ratios, calculated as percentages, of male and female population to total population.

sheikhdom, *see* monarchy.

social deviance, a group of measures, usually reported as rates per 100,000 for principal categories of socially deviant behaviour, including specified crimes, alcoholism, drug abuse, and suicide.*

social participation, a group of measures indicative of the degree of social engagement displayed by a particular population, including rates of participation in such activities as elections, voluntary work or memberships, trade unions, and religion.*

social security, public programs designed to protect individuals and families from loss of income owing to unemployment, old age, sickness or disability, or death and to provide other services such as medical care, health and welfare programs, or income maintenance.

socialist republic, *see* republic.

sources of income, *see* household income and expenditure.

Special Drawing Right (SDR), a unit of account utilized by the International Monetary Fund (IMF) to denominate monetary reserves available under a quota system to IMF members to maintain the value of their national currency unit in international transactions.*

state, in international law, a political entity possessing the attributes of: territory, permanent civilian population, government, and the capacity to conduct relations with other states. Though the term is sometimes limited in meaning to fully independent and internationally recognized states, the more general sense of an entity possessing a *preponderance* of these characteristics is intended here. It is, thus, also a first-order civil administrative subdivision, especially of a federated union. An associated state is an autonomous state in free association with another that conducts its external affairs and defense; the association may be terminated in full independence at the instance of the autonomous state in consultation with the administering power. A *parliamentary state* is an independent state of the Commonwealth that is governed by a parliament and that may recognize the British monarch as its titular head.

structure of gross domestic product and labour force, tabulation of the principal elements of the national economy, according to standard industrial categories, together with the corresponding distribution of the labour force (when possible POPULATION ECONOMICALLY ACTIVE) that generates the GROSS DOMESTIC PRODUCT.

sultanate, *see* monarchy.

territory, a noncategorized political dependency; a first-order administrative subdivision; a dependent political entity with some degree of self-government, but with fewer rights and less autonomy than a colony because there is no charter. An *external territory* (Australia) is a territory situated outside the area of the country. An *organized territory* (U.S.) is a territory for which a system of laws and a settled government have been provided by an act of the United States Congress. An *overseas territory* (France) is an overseas subdivision of the French Republic with elected representation in the French Parliament, having individual statutes, laws, and internal organization adapted to local conditions.

ton-miles, or **ton-kilometres,** aggregate measure of freight hauled by a specified means of transportation, equal to tons of freight multiplied by the miles (or kilometres) each ton is transported. Figures are compiled from waybills (nationally) and ordinarily exclude mail, specie, passengers' baggage, the fuel and stores of the conveyance, and goods carried free.

total active duty personnel, full-time active duty military personnel (excluding militias and part-time, informal, or other paramilitary elements), with their distribution by percentages among the major services.

total fertility rate, the sum of the current age-specific birth rates for each of the child-bearing years (usually 15–49). It is the probable number of births, given present fertility data, that would occur during the lifetime of each woman should she live to the end of her child-bearing years.

tourism, service industry comprising activities connected with domestic and international travel for pleasure or recreation; confined here to international travel and reported as expenditures in U.S. dollars by tourists of all nationalities visiting a particular country and, conversely, the estimated expenditures of that country's nationals in all countries of destination.

transfer payments, *see* household income and expenditure.

transport, all mechanical methods of moving persons or goods. Data reported for national establishments include: for railroads, length of track and volume of traffic for passengers and cargo (but excluding mail, etc.); for roads, length of network and numbers of passenger cars and of commercial vehicles (*i.e.,* trucks and buses); for merchant marine, the number of vessels of more than 100 gross tons and their total deadweight tonnage; for air transport, traffic data for passengers and cargo and the number of airports with scheduled flights.

unincorporated territory (U.S.), *see* territory.

unitary republic, *see* republic.

urban-rural, social characteristic of local or national populations, defined by predominant economic activities, "urban" referring to a group of largely nonagricultural pursuits, "rural" to agriculturally oriented employment patterns. The distinction is usually based on the country's own definition of urban, which may depend only upon the size (population) of a place or upon factors like employment, administrative status, density of housing, etc.

value added, also called value added by manufacture, the gross output value of a firm or industry minus the cost of inputs—raw materials, supplies, and payments to other firms—required to produce it. Value added is the portion of the sales value or gross output value that is actually created by the firm or industry. Value added generally includes labour costs, administrative costs, and operating profits.

The Nations of the World

Afghanistan

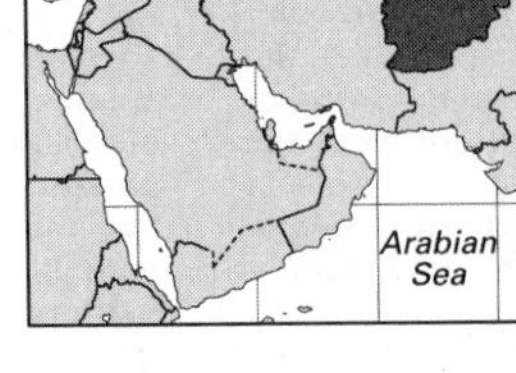

Official name[1]: Islamic Emirate of Afghanistan (Pashto and Dari [Persian] long-form names, n.a.).
Form of government: Islamic emirate.
Head of state and government: Leader of the faithful[2].
Capital: Kabul.
Official languages: Pashto; Dari (Persian).
Official religion: Islam.
Monetary unit: 1 afghani (Af) = 100 puls (puli); valuation (Oct. 6, 2000) 1 U.S.$ = Af 4,679[3]; 1 £ = Af 7,747.

Area and population[4]

Regions	area sq mi	area sq km	population 1993 estimate
Central	11,657	30,192	3,481,400
East	9,802	25,386	1,567,500
East-central	21,739	56,304	685,600
North	29,520	76,457	2,421,900
North-east	30,233	78,304	2,518,300
South	19,525	50,569	1,659,600
South-west	77,000	199,430	2,188,700
West	46,187	119,624	1,497,500
TOTAL	251,825[5]	652,225[5]	16,020,500

Demography

Population (2000): 25,889,000[6].
Density (2000): persons per sq mi 102.8, persons per sq km 39.7.
Urban-rural (1995): urban 20.0%; rural 80.0%.
Sex distribution (1997): male 51.50%; female 48.50%.
Age breakdown (1997): under 15, 43.0%; 15–29, 27.4%; 30–44, 16.2%; 45–59, 8.9%; 60–74, 3.8%; 75 and over, 0.7%.
Population projection: (2010) 33,864,000; (2020) 41,735,000.
Doubling time: 28 years.
Ethnic composition (early 1990s[6]): Pashtun 38%; Tajik 25%; Ḥazāra 19%; Uzbek 6%; Chahar Aimak, Turkmen, Balochi, and other 12%.
Religious affiliation (1997): Sunnī Muslim 84%; Shīʿī Muslim 15%; other 1%.
Major cities (1988): Kabul 700,000[7]; Kandahār (Qandahār) 225,500; Herāt 177,300; Mazār-e Sharīf 130,600; Jalālābād 55,000.

Vital statistics

Birth rate per 1,000 population (1998): 42.4 (world avg. 22.1).
Death rate per 1,000 population (1998): 17.4 (world avg. 8.9).
Natural increase rate per 1,000 population (1998): 25.0 (world avg. 13.2).
Total fertility rate (avg. births per childbearing woman; 1998): 6.0.
Life expectancy at birth (1998): male 47.3 years; female 46.3 years.

National economy

Budget (1997–98). Revenue: primarily from narcotics trade. Expenditures: more than 90% of revenue used to finance war effort.
Gross national product (1998): U.S.$6,738,000,000 (U.S.$280 per capita).

Structure of gross domestic product and labour force

	1992–93			
	in value Af '000,000[8]	% of total value	labour force	% of labour force
Agriculture	61,400	48.5	4,276,100	67.2
Manufacturing; Mining and public utilities	32,800	25.9	298,900	4.7
Construction	12,400	9.8	81,400	1.3
Transp. and commun.	5,300	4.2	139,900	2.2
Trade	12,400	9.8	420,600	6.6
Pub. admin., services	2,400	1.9	929,300	14.6
Other			214,300	3.4
TOTAL	126,700	100.0[9]	6,360,500	100.0

Public debt (external, outstanding; 1993): U.S.$5,381,000,000.
Production (metric tons except as noted). Agriculture, forestry, fishing (1999): wheat 2,834,000, rice 450,000, grapes 330,000, barley 300,000, corn (maize) 240,000, potatoes 235,000, apricots 37,500, opium poppy 4,600[10]; livestock (number of live animals) 14,300,000 sheep, 2,200,000 goats, 1,500,000 cattle, 1,160,000 asses; roundwood (1998) 8,091,000 cu m; fish catch (1997) 1,250. Mining and quarrying (1997): salt 13,000; copper (metal content) 5,000. Manufacturing (by production value in Af '000,000; 1988–89): food products 4,019; leather and fur products 2,678; textiles 1,760; printing and publishing 1,070; industrial chemicals (including fertilizers) 1,053; footwear 999. Energy production (consumption): electricity (kW-hr; 1996) 593,000,000 (703,000,000); coal (metric tons; 1996) 4,000 (4,000); petroleum products (metric tons; 1996) none (254,000); natural gas (cu m; 1996) 160,169,000 (160,169,000).
Population economically active (1994)[11]: total 5,557,000; activity rate of total population 29.4% (participation rates: female 9.0%; unemployed [1995] *c.* 8%).

Consumer price index (1990 = 100)

	1988	1989	1990	1991	1992	1993	1994
Consumer price index	64.3	83.1	100.0	266.0	420.8	563.9	676.7

Tourism: receipts (1995) U.S.$1,000,000; expenditures (1987) U.S.$1,000,000.
Land use (1994): forested 2.9%; meadows and pastures 46.0%; agricultural and under permanent cultivation 12.4%; other 38.7%.

Foreign trade[12]

Balance of trade (current prices)

	1993	1994	1995	1996	1997	1998
U.S.$'000,000	+263	–245	–193	–371	–376	–300
% of total	23.6%	54.6%	36.8%	59.8%	55.3%	50.0%

Imports (1997): U.S.$525,000,000 (1995; food 18.8%, machinery and transport equipment 15.2%, unspecified commodities 46.5%). *Major import sources* (1997): Singapore 19.2%; Japan 18.5%; China 6.9%; India 4.8%; Russia 4.0%.
Exports (1997): U.S.$149,000,000 (1995; carpets and rugs 54.3%, dried fruits and nuts 15.6%). *Major export destinations* (1997): Pakistan 20.1%; Belgium-Luxembourg 8.7%; France 7.4%; United States 6.7%; Japan 6.0%.

Transport and communications

Transport. Railroads (1997): length 16 mi (25 km). Roads (1996): total length 21,000 km (paved 13%). Vehicles (1996): passenger cars 31,000; trucks and buses 25,000. Merchant marine: none. Air transport[13]: passenger-km (1995) 276,000,000; metric ton-km cargo 38,000,000; airports (1996) 3.

Communications

Medium	date	unit	number	units per 1,000 persons
Daily newspapers	1996	circulation	113,000	5.0
Radio	1997	receivers	2,750,000	116
Television[14]	1997	receivers	270,000	11
Telephones	1998	main lines	29,000	1.2

Education and health

Educational attainment (1980). Population age 25 and over having: no formal schooling 88.5%; some primary education 6.8%; complete primary 0.3%; some secondary 1.2%; postsecondary 3.2%. *Literacy* (1995): Total population age 15 and over literate 31.5%; males 47.2%; females 15.1%.

Education (1995–96)

	schools	teachers	students	student/ teacher ratio
Primary	2,146	21,869	1,312,197	60.0
Secondary	...	19,085	512,851	26.9
Higher	...	...	12,800	...

Health: physicians (1991) 2,233 (1 per 6,701 persons); hospital beds, n.a.; infant mortality rate (1998) 143.6.
Food (1997): daily per capita caloric intake 1,745 (vegetable products 92%, animal products 8%); 72% of FAO recommended minimum requirement.

Military

Total active duty personnel (1999): no national military from 1992. *Military expenditure as percentage of GNP* (1997): n.a.; no estimates are available for the period 1987–97.

[1]Taliban gained effective control of most of the country by August 1998, but civil war continued in September 2000. [2]Title of the supreme leader of the Taliban. [3]Black market rate in April 2000: 1 U.S.$ = AF 64,000; most currency transactions are conducted with the Pakistan rupee. [4]In 1993 an administrative reorganization created 32 provinces (*wilayah*), but detailed breakdown of area and population is unavailable. [5]Detailed breakdown does not account for 6,162 sq mi (15,959 sq km), which is included in the total. [6]Including Afghan refugees estimated to number about 1.1 million in Pakistan and more than 1.2 million in Iran. [7]1993 estimate. [8]At prices of 1978–79. [9]Detail does not add to total given because of rounding. [10]Represents 75% of world production. [11]Based on settled population only. [12]Exports are f.o.b. and imports are c.i.f. [13]Ariana Afghan Airlines only. [14]Officially outlawed in 1998.

Internet resources for further information:
- **Online Center for Afghan Studies http://www.afghan-politics.org**

Albania

Official name: Republika e Shqipërisë (Republic of Albania).
Form of government: unitary multiparty republic with one legislative house (Assembly [155]).
Chief of state: President.
Head of government: Prime Minister.
Capital: Tirana (Tiranë).
Official language: Albanian.
Official religion: none.
Monetary unit: 1 lek = 100 qindars; valuation (Oct. 6, 2000) 1 U.S.$ = 148.85 leks; 1 £ = 215.32 leks.

Area and population

Provinces[1]	Capitals	area sq mi	area sq km	population 1990 estimate
Berat	Berat	396	1,027	180,489
Dibër	Peshkopi	605	1,568	153,775
Durrës	Durrës	327	848	251,029
Elbasan	Elbasan	572	1,481	248,676
Fier	Fier	454	1,175	251,115
Gjirokastër	Gjirokastër	439	1,137	67,392
Gramsh	Gramsh	268	695	44,791
Kolonjë	Ersekë	311	805	25,291
Korçë	Korçë	842	2,181	218,219
Krujë	Krujë	234	607	109,876
Kukës	Kukës	514	1,330	104,731
Lezhë	Lezhë	185	479	63,505
Librazhd	Librazhd	391	1,013	73,871
Lushnjë	Lushnjë	275	712	137,830
Mat	Burrel	397	1,028	78,754
Mirditë	Rrëshen	335	867	51,701
Përmet	Përmet	359	929	40,419
Pogradec	Pogradec	280	725	73,333
Pukë	Pukë	399	1,034	50,286
Sarandë	Sarandë	424	1,097	89,459
Shkodër	Shkodër	976	2,528	241,549
Skrapar	Çorovoda	299	775	47,605
Tepelenë	Tepelenë	315	817	51,022
Tiranë	Tirana (Tiranë)	478	1,238	374,483
Tropojë	Bajram	403	1,043	45,965
Vlorë	Vlorë	621	1,609	180,725
TOTAL		11,100[2]	28,748	3,255,891

Demography

Population (2000): 3,490,000.
Density (2000): persons per sq mi 314.4, persons per sq km 121.4.
Urban-rural (1999): urban 41.0%; rural 59.0%.
Sex distribution (1999): male 48.90%; female 51.10%.
Age breakdown (1999): under 15, 30.8%; 15–29, 26.3%; 30–44, 19.9%; 45–59, 13.0%; 60–74, 7.7%; 75 and over, 2.3%.
Population projection: (2010) 3,827,000; (2020) 4,127,000.
Doubling time: 54 years.
Ethnic composition (1989): Albanian 98.0%; Greek 1.8%; Macedonian 0.2%.
Religious affiliation (1995): Muslim 70.0%; Albanian Orthodox 7.3%; other Orthodox 4.0%; Roman Catholic 5.2%; other 13.5%.
Major cities (1991): Tirana 251,000; Durrës 86,900; Shkoder 83,700; Elbasan 83,200.

Vital statistics

Birth rate per 1,000 population (1999): 19.9 (world avg. 22.1).
Death rate per 1,000 population (1999): 6.5 (world avg. 8.9).
Natural increase rate per 1,000 population (1999): 13.4 (world avg. 13.2).
Total fertility rate (avg. births per childbearing woman; 1999): 2.4.
Marriage rate per 1,000 population (1990): 8.9.
Divorce rate per 1,000 population (1990): 0.8.
Life expectancy at birth (1999): male 68.4 years; female 74.2 years.
Major causes of death per 100,000 population: n.a.; however, principal health problems in the mid-1990s included malnutrition (especially of children).

National economy

Budget (1997). Revenue: 107,809,000,000 leks (taxes 77.6%, of which value-added tax 27.6%, import duties and export taxes 17.1%, social security contributions 16.8%, income tax 9.6%, other 6.5%; nontax revenue 22.4%). Expenditures: 165,160,000,000 leks (current expenditure 79.6%, of which interest on debt 21.2%, personnel costs 18.9%, social security 16.7%, government operations and maintenance 16.0%, other 6.8%; capital expenditure 20.4%).
Public debt (1998): U.S.$701,300,000.
Production (metric tons except as noted). Agriculture, forestry, fishing (1999): cereals 511,500; vegetables and melons 446,500 (mainly beans, peas, onions, tomatoes, cabbage, eggplants, and carrots), watermelons 220,000, potatoes 161,900; livestock (number of live animals) 1,941,000 sheep, 1,120,000 goats, 720,000 cattle, 4,000,000 poultry; roundwood (1998) 409,000 cu m; fish catch (1998) 3,200. Mining and quarrying (1999): chromium ore 79,000; copper ore 34,000. Manufacturing (1999): cement 106,000; bread 67,000; rolled steel 20,000; cheese 7,000; beer 91,000 hectolitres; wine 10,000 hectolitres. Construction (1990): 12,428 units. Energy production (consumption): electricity (kW-hr; 1999) 5,396,000,000 (5,396,000,000); coal (metric tons; 1996) 111,000 (91,000); crude petroleum (barrels; 1999) 2,368,000 (3,257,000[3]); petroleum products (metric tons; 1996) 282,000 (363,000); natural gas (cu m; 1996) 22,911,000 (22,911,000).

Gross national product (1998): U.S.$2,718,000,000 (U.S.$810 per capita).

Structure of gross domestic product and labour force

	1998 in value '000,000 leks	1998 % of total value	1995 labour force	1995 % of labour force
Agriculture	250,705	54.4	778,000	58.7
Manufacturing, mining, public utilities	55,047	12.0	95,000	7.2
Construction	58,037	12.6	21,000	1.6
Transp. and commun.	14,024	3.0	30,000	2.3
Trade }			62,000	4.7
Pub. admin., defense }	82,817	18.0	...	...
Services }			79,000	6.0
Other	—	—	260,000[4]	19.6[4]
TOTAL	460,630	100.0	1,325,000	100.0[2]

Population economically active (1998): total 1,320,000; activity rate of total population 39.4% (participation rates: ages 15–64, 69.9%; female 39.2%; unemployed 17.8%).

Price and earnings indexes (1995 = 100)

	1993	1994	1995	1996	1997	1998	1999
Consumer price index	75.7	92.8	100.0	112.7	150.1	181.1	181.8
Earnings index	...	...	...	...	...	...	...

Household income and expenditure. Average household size (1998): 3.9; annual income per rural household (1989) 80,835 leks (U.S.$ value, n.a.); sources of income: wages 53.0%, transfers from relatives abroad 21.5%, social insurance 11.4%; expenditure: n.a.
Tourism (1998): receipts U.S.$54,000,000; expenditures U.S.$5,000,000.

Foreign trade

Balance of trade (current prices)

	1993	1994	1995	1996	1997	1998	1999
U.S.$'000,000	–490	–460	–475	–678	–535	–621	–664
% of total	68.7%	62.0%	53.7%	58.2%	62.8%	60.2%	54.8%

Imports (1999): U.S.$938,000,000 (food, beverages, live animals, and tobacco 24.8%; manufactured goods 23.5%; machinery and transport equipment 19.0%; chemicals 7.6%; mineral fuels 4.7%; crude materials 4.1%). *Major import sources:* Italy 37.5%; Greece 28.1%; Germany 5.5%; Turkey 5.5%; Bulgaria 3.0%.
Exports (1999): U.S.$274,000,000 (miscellaneous manufactured articles 64.1%; manufactured goods 12.0%; crude materials 7.3%; food and beverages 6.7%). *Major export destinations:* Italy 67.3%; Greece 14.3%; Germany 6.4%; Belgium-Luxembourg 0.9%.

Transport and communications

Transport. Railroads: length (1996) 670 km; passenger-km 197,000,000; metric ton-km cargo 53,000. Roads (1996): total length 18,000 km (paved 30%). Vehicles (1996): passenger cars 67,031; trucks and buses 34,058. Merchant marine (1992): vessels (100 gross tons and over) 24; total deadweight tonnage 80,954. Air transport (1995): passenger-km 3,519,000; short ton-mi 223,000, metric ton-km 325,000; airports (1998) with scheduled flights 1.

Communications

Medium	date	unit	number	units per 1,000 persons
Daily newspapers	1996	circulation	116,000	37
Radio	1997	receivers	810,000	259
Television	1997	receivers	405,000	129
Telephones	1998	main lines	115,675	30.5
Cellular telephones	1998	subscribers	5,600	1.5
Internet	1996	users	1,000	0.3

Education and health

Educational attainment (1989). Population age 10 and over having: primary education 65.3%; secondary 29.1%; higher 5.6%. *Literacy* (1989): total population age 10 and over literate 91.8%; males 95.5%; females 88.0%.

Education (1996)

	schools	teachers	students	student/ teacher ratio
Primary (age 6–13)	1,782[5]	31,369	558,101	17.8
Secondary (age 14–17)	162[6]	4,147	71,391	17.2
Voc., teacher tr.	259[6]	2,174	18,504	8.5
Higher	10	2,348	34,257	14.6

Health (1995): physicians 4,848 (1 per 668 persons); hospital beds (1994) 10,200 (1 per 333 persons); infant mortality rate per 1,000 live births (1999) 43.1.
Food (1998): daily per capita caloric intake 2,976 (vegetable products 77%, animal products 23%); 122% of FAO recommended minimum requirement.

Military

Total active duty personnel (1996): 54,000 (army 83.3%, navy 4.6%, air force 12.1%). *Military expenditure as percentage of GNP* (1997): 1.4% (world 2.6%); per capita expenditure U.S.$19.

[1]Reorganized into 36 districts and 1 capital city (Tirana) as of 1997; detail not available. [2]Detail does not add to total given because of rounding. [3]1996. [4]Includes 171,000 undistributed unemployed. [5]1995. [6]1990.

Internet resources for further information:
- **Albanian Home Page http://albanian.com/main**

Algeria

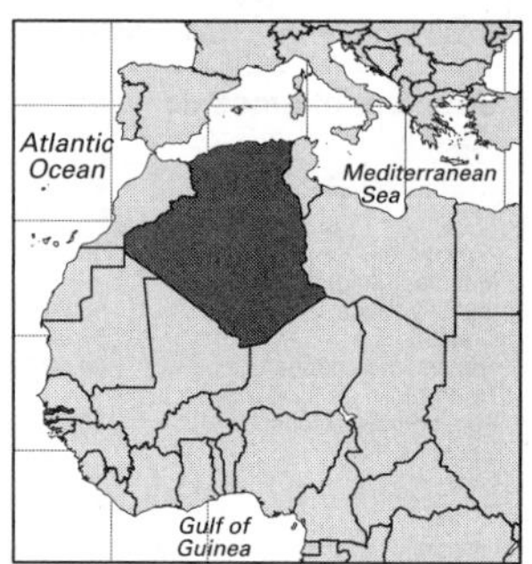

Official name: Al-Jumhūrīyah al-Jazā'irīyah ad-Dīmuqrāṭīyah ash-Sha'bīyah (Arabic) (Democratic and Popular Republic of Algeria).
Form of government: multiparty republic with two legislative bodies (Council of the Nation [144][1]; National People's Assembly [380]).
Chief of state: President.
Head of government: Prime Minister.
Capital: Algiers.
Official language: Arabic.
Official religion: Islam.
Monetary unit: 1 Algerian dinar (DA) = 100 centimes; valuation (Oct. 6, 2000) 1 U.S.$ = DA 78.40; 1 £ = DA 113.41.

Population (1998 census)

Provinces	population	Provinces	population	Provinces	population
Adrar	313,417	El-Bayadh	172,957	Ouargla	444,683
Aïn Defla	658,897	El-Oued	525,083	Oum el-Bouaghi	529,540
Aïn Temouchent	337,570	Et-Tarf	350,789	Relizane	646,175
Alger	2,423,694	Ghardaïa	311,678	Saïda	313,351
Annaba	559,898	Guelma	444,231	Sétif	1,299,116
Batna	987,475	Illizi	34,189	Sidi bel-Abbès	535,634
Béchar	232,012	Jijel	582,865	Skikda	793,146
Bejaïa	836,301	Khenchela	345,009	Souk Ahras	365,106
Biskra	568,701	Laghouat	326,862	Tamanrasset	138,704
Blida	796,616	Mascara	651,239	Tébessa	565,125
Bordj Bou Arreridj	561,471	Médéa	859,273	Tiaret	770,194
Bouira	637,042	Mila	663,578	Tindouf	27,053
Boumerdes	608,806	Mostaganem	636,884	Tipaza	507,959
Constantine	807,371	M'Sila	835,701	Tissemsilt	274,380
Djelfa	805,298	Naâma	131,846	Tizi Ouzou	1,100,297
Ech-Cheliff	874,917	Oran	1,208,171	Tlemcen	873,039
				TOTAL	29,273,343[2]

Demography

Area: 919,595 sq mi, 2,381,741 sq km.
Population (2000): 30,554,000.
Density (2000): persons per sq mi 33.2, persons per sq km 12.8.
Urban-rural (1998): urban 80.8%; rural 19.2%.
Sex distribution (1998): male 50.56%; female 49.44%.
Age breakdown (1998): under 15, 36.2%; 15–29, 30.6%; 30–44, 17.7%; 45–59, 8.9%; 60–74, 5.1%; 75 and over, 1.5%.
Population projection: (2010) 35,838,000; (2020) 41,012,000.
Doubling time: 32 years.
Ethnic composition (1992): Arab *c.* 80%; Berber *c.* 20%, of which Kabyle *c.* 13%, Shawia *c.* 6%.
Religious affiliation (1990): Muslim 99.9%, of which Sunnī 99.5%, Ibāḍīyah 0.4%; Roman Catholic 0.1%.
Major urban agglomerations (1998): Algiers (1998) 2,135,630; Oran 991,885; Constantine 689,982; Sétif 648,072; Batna 639,364.

Vital statistics

Birth rate per 1,000 population (1999): 27.0 (world avg. 22.1).
Death rate per 1,000 population (1999): 5.5 (world avg. 8.9).
Natural increase rate per 1,000 population (1999): 21.5 (world avg. 13.2).
Total fertility rate (avg. births per childbearing woman; 1999): 3.3.
Marriage rate per 1,000 population (1996): 5.6.
Life expectancy at birth (1999): male 68.1 years; female 70.5 years.
Notified cases of infectious diseases per 100,000 population (1996): measles 67.8; typhoid fever 15.2; hepatitis 11.3; dysentery 10.1; meningitis 9.4.

National economy

Budget (1997). Revenue: DA 926,600,000,000 (taxes on hydrocarbons 63.9%, value-added taxes 16.0%). Expenditures: DA 845,100,000,000 (current expenditure 69.4%, development expenditure 30.6%).
Land use (1994): forested 1.6%; meadows and pastures 13.3%; agricultural and under permanent cultivation 3.4%; other (mostly desert) 81.7%.
Production (metric tons except as noted). Agriculture, forestry, fishing (1999): wheat 1,503,000, potatoes 1,100,000, tomatoes 790,000, barley 481,000, dates 427,600, onions 400,000, olives 311,200, oranges 307,300, grapes 190,300; livestock (number of live animals) 18,000,000 sheep, 3,200,000 goats; roundwood (1997) 2,735,000 cu m; fish catch (1997) 99,332. Mining and quarrying (1999): iron ore (gross weight) 2,330,000; phosphate rock (gross weight) 1,300,000; mercury 12,000 flasks. Manufacturing (value added in U.S.$'000,000; 1995): iron and steel 634; food products 622; fabricated metal products 518; cement, bricks, and tiles 394; transport equipment 352; electrical machinery 241. Energy production (consumption): electricity (kW-hr; 1996) 20,654,000,000 (20,378,000,000); coal (metric tons; 1996) 22,000 (1,202,000); crude petroleum (barrels; 1996) 297,354,000 (165,220,000); petroleum products (metric tons; 1996) 39,628,000 (7,510,000); natural gas (cu m; 1996) 66,190,000,000 (25,981,000,000).
Household income and expenditure. Average household size (1998) 7.1; income per household: n.a.; sources of income (1997): wages and salaries 43.2%, self-employment 39.1%, transfers 17.7%; expenditure (1995): food and beverages 58.5%, transportation and communications 9.5%, clothing and footwear 13.9%, health 4.4%, other 13.7%.
Gross national product (1998): U.S.$46,389,000,000 (U.S.$1,550 per capita).

Structure of gross domestic product and labour force

	1996			
	in value DA '000,000	% of total value	labour force	% of labour force
Agriculture	277,842	12.3	881,000	12.1
Petroleum and natural gas	761,084[3]	33.8[3]		
Other mining	5,216	0.2	676,000	9.3
Manufacturing	165,875[3]	7.4[3]		
Public utilities, construction	268,873	12.0	677,000	9.3
Transp. and commun.	148,886	6.6	750,000	10.3
Trade, restaurants	352,464	15.7	615,000	8.5
Pub. admin., defense	...	...	1,479,000	20.3
Services	58,950	2.6		
Other	212,300	9.4	2,200,000[4]	30.2
TOTAL	2,251,490	100.0	7,278,000	100.0

Population economically active (1994): total 6,814,000; activity rate of population 24.8% (participation rates [1987] ages 15–64, 44.3%; female 9.2%; unemployed [1997] *c.* 28%).

Price and earnings indexes (1995 = 100)

	1992	1993	1994	1995	1996	1997	1998
Consumer price index	48.6	58.6	75.7	100.0	121.6	126.3	129.0[5]
Earnings index[6]	75.9	88.8	90.9	100.0	110.0	...	...

Public debt (external, outstanding; 1998): U.S.$28,469,000,000.
Tourism (1997): receipts from visitors U.S.$20,000,000; expenditures by nationals abroad U.S.$40,000,000.

Foreign trade[7]

Balance of trade (current prices)

	1993	1994	1995	1996	1997	1998
U.S.$'000,000	+1,453	–680	–583	+4,484	+5,206	+803
% of total	7.6%	3.5%	2.8%	19.8%	23.1%	4.1%

Imports (1996): U.S.$9,102,000,000 (food 27.5%, machinery and apparatus 15.8%, transport equipment 7.0%). *Major import sources* (1997): France 28.3%; Italy 8.7%; U.S. 8.6%; Spain 7.4%; Brazil 5.3%.
Exports (1996): U.S.$13,586,000,000 (crude and refined petroleum 61.7%, natural gas 31.7%, dates 0.5%). *Major export destinations* (1997): Italy 19.5%; U.S. 17.3%; France 14.2%; Spain 10.2%; The Netherlands 5.6%.

Transport and communications

Transport. Railroads (1997): route length 2,451 mi, 3,945 km; (1996) passenger-km 1,826,000,000; metric ton-km cargo 2,139,000,000. Roads (1995): total length 63,643 mi, 102,424 km (paved 69%). Vehicles (1996): passenger cars 725,000; trucks and buses 780,000. Air transport (1998)[8]: passenger-km 2,901,000,000; metric ton-km cargo 18,285,000; airports (1996) 28.

Communications

Medium	date	unit	number	units per 1,000 persons
Daily newspapers	1996	circulation	1,080,000	38
Radio	1997	receivers	7,100,000	253
Television	1997	receivers	3,100,000	110
Telephones	1998	main lines	1,477,000	50
Cellular telephones	1998	subscribers	18,000	0.6
Personal computers	1998	units	160,000	5.5
Internet	1998	users	2,000	0.07

Education and health

Educational attainment (1998). Percentage of economically active population age 6 and over having: no formal schooling 30.1%; primary education 29.9%; lower secondary 20.7%; upper secondary 13.4%; higher 4.3%; other 1.6%.
Literacy (1998): total population age 10 and over literate 15,314,109 (68.1%); males literate 8,650,719 (76.3%); females literate 6,663,392 (59.7%).

Education (1996–97)

	schools	teachers	students	student/ teacher ratio
Primary (age 6–11)	15,426	170,956	4,674,947	27.3
Secondary (age 12–17)	3,954[9]	151,948	2,618,242	17.2
Higher[9]	...	19,910	347,410	17.4

Health (1996): physicians 27,650 (1 per 1,015 persons); hospital beds 34,544 (1 per 812 persons); infant mortality rate per 1,000 live births (1999) 43.8.
Food (1997): daily per capita caloric intake 2,853 (vegetable products 91%, animal products 9%); 119% of FAO recommended minimum requirement.

Military

Total active duty personnel (1999): 122,000 (army 86.1%, navy 5.7%, air force 8.2%). *Military expenditure as percentage of GNP* (1997): 3.9% (world 2.6%); per capita expenditure U.S.$61.

[1]Includes 48 nonelected seats appointed by the president. [2]Sum of provincial populations; actual census total equals 29,272,343. [3]Petroleum and natural gas includes (and Manufacturing excludes) refined petroleum and manufacture of hydrocarbons. [4]Estimated number of unemployed. [5]Average of 2nd quarter and 3rd quarter. [6]Public workers only; all data based on January averages of gross income. [7]Imports c.i.f.; exports f.o.b. [8]Air Algérie. [9]1995–96.

Internet resources for further information:
- **National Office of Statistics**
http://www.ons.dz/English/indexag.htm

American Samoa

Official name: American Samoa (English); Amerika Samoa (Samoan).
Political status: unincorporated and unorganized territory of the United States[1] with two legislative houses (Senate [18]; House of Representatives [18])[2].
Chief of state: President of the United States.
Head of government: Governor.
Capital: Fagatogo[3] (legislative and judicial) and Utulei (executive).
Official languages: English; Samoan.
Official religion: none.
Monetary unit: 1 dollar (U.S.$) = 100 cents; valuation (Oct. 6, 2000) 1 U.S.$ = £0.69.

Area and population

Districts and Islands	area sq mi	area sq km	population 1990 census
Eastern District	25.0	64.7	21,175
Aunu'u Island	1.2	3.0	463
Tutuila Island	23.8	61.7	20,712
Manu'a District	21.7	56.3	1,714
Ofu Island	2.9	7.5	353
Olosega Island	2.0	5.2	225
Ta'u Island	16.8	43.6	1,136
Western District	28.0	72.5	23,868
Rose Island	—	—	—
Swains Island	1.3	3.3	16
TOTAL	76.0	196.8	46,773

Demography

Population (1999): 64,000.
Density (1999): persons per sq mi 842.1, persons per sq km 325.2.
Urban-rural (1998): urban 51.5%; rural 48.5%.
Sex distribution (1999): male 50.59%; female 49.41%.
Age breakdown (1999): under 15, 39.1%; 15–29, 24.1%; 30–44, 18.0%; 45–59, 11.4%; 60–74, 6.1%; 75 and over, 1.3%.
Population projection: (2010) 81,000; (2020) 95,000.
Doubling time: 32 years.
Ethnic composition (1990): Samoan 88.6%; Tongan 3.7%; Caucasian 1.9%; Asian 1.8%; other 4.0%.
Religious affiliation (1995): 4 major Protestant groups 60.1%; Roman Catholic 19.4%; Mormon 12.5%; other 8.0%.
Major villages (1990): Tafuna 5,174; Nu'uuli 3,893; Pago Pago 3,519 (urban agglomeration [1999] 14,000); Leone 3,013; Fagatogo 2,323[3].

Vital statistics

Birth rate per 1,000 population (1999): 26.5 (world avg. 22.1); legitimate, n.a.; illegitimate, n.a.
Death rate per 1,000 population (1999): 4.2 (world avg. 8.9).
Natural increase rate per 1,000 population (1999): 22.3 (world avg. 13.2).
Total fertility rate (avg. births per childbearing woman; 1999): 3.7.
Marriage rate per 1,000 population (1993): 6.1.
Divorce rate per 1,000 population (1993): 0.5.
Life expectancy at birth (1999): male 70.8 years; female 79.8 years.
Major causes of death per 100,000 population (1997): heart diseases 89.4; malignant neoplasms (cancers) 57.8[4]; cerebrovascular diseases 39.7; chronic obstructive pulmonary diseases 28.2; accidents 21.5; influenza and pneumonia 8.2.

National economy

Budget (1992). Revenue: U.S.$146,905,000 (U.S. government grants 73.5%; taxes 16.4%; insurance claims 3.5%; other 6.6%). Expenditures: U.S.$165,950,000 (general government 45.7%; education and culture 21.0%; health and welfare 16.0%; economic development 5.6%; public works and parks 5.1%; other 6.6%).
Tourism: receipts from visitors (1994) U.S.$10,000,000; expenditures by nationals abroad (1996) U.S.$2,000,000.
Land use (1993): forested 70%; agricultural and under permanent cultivation 15%; other 15%.
Gross national product (at current market prices; 1997): U.S.$253,000,000 (U.S.$4,300 per capita).

Structure of labour force

	1995 labour force[5]	1995 % of labour force
Agriculture, forestry, and fishing	307	2.2
Manufacturing and public utilities	4,295	31.2
Mining } Construction }	671	4.9
Transportation and communications	848	6.1
Trade	1,685	12.2
Finance	187	1.4
Public administration	2,366	17.2
Services } Other }	3,426	24.8
TOTAL	13,785	100.0

Production (metric tons except as noted). Agriculture, forestry, fishing (1999): coconuts 4,700, taros 1,500, fruits (excluding melons) 1,200, bananas 750, vegetables and melons 490; livestock (number of live animals; 1999) 10,700 pigs, 37,000 chickens; forestry, n.a.; fish catch (1998) 910, of which tunas, bonitos, and billfish 865. Mining and quarrying: n.a. Manufacturing (1994): canned tuna shipped to U.S. 211,600; other manufactures include garments, handicrafts, soap, and alcoholic beverages. Construction: n.a. Energy production (consumption): electricity (kW-hr; 1996) 130,000,000 (130,000,000); coal, none (n.a.); crude petroleum, none (n.a.); petroleum products (metric tons; 1996) none (92,000); natural gas, none (n.a.).
Population economically active (1994): total 16,822; activity rate of total population 30.5% (participation rates: ages 16–64, 51.2%; female 39.5%; unemployed 16.7%[6]).

Price index (1990 = 100)

	1990	1991	1992	1993	1994	1995	1996
Consumer price index	100.0	104.0	109.0	109.0	111.0	113.0	118.0

Public debt: n.a.
Household income and expenditure. Average household size (1995) 6.3; income per household (1995): U.S.$15,715; sources of income: n.a.; expenditure (1988): food and beverages 44.3%, housing and furnishings 23.4%, transportation and communications 14.9%, clothing and footwear 5.8%, other 11.6%.

Foreign trade[7]

Balance of trade (current prices)

	1986	1987	1988	1989	1990	1991
U.S.$'000,000	–59.6	–58.2	–33.0	–70.3	–54.3	–45.0
% of total	10.5%	9.2%	4.7%	10.3%	8.1%	6.4%

Imports (1994): U.S.$429,000,000 (petroleum and petroleum products 8.8%, food and beverages 5.2%, transport equipment 3.7%, remainder unknown). *Major import sources* (1991): United States 28.7%; Australia 5.6%; New Zealand 4.1%; Japan 3.8%; other South Pacific countries[8] 3.6%; other Asian countries[9] 3.1%.
Exports (1999): U.S.$312,800,000 (1991; tuna in airtight containers 97.4%, pet food 1.4%). *Major export destinations:* United States 100.0%.

Transport and communications

Transport. Railroads: none. Roads (1991): total length 217 mi, 350 km (paved, 43%). Vehicles (1994): passenger cars 4,672[10]; buses 199; motorcycles 27. Merchant marine (1990): vessels (100 gross tons and over) 3; total deadweight tonnage 143. Air transport (1990): incoming flights 4,426; incoming passengers 66,580; incoming cargo 706 metric tons; airports (1994) with scheduled flights 3.

Communications

Medium	date	unit	number	units per 1,000 persons
Daily newspapers	1996	circulation	5,000	85
Radio	1997	receivers	57,000	929
Television	1997	receivers	14,000	221
Telephones	1998	main lines	13,500	223
Cellular telephones	1998	subscribers	2,650	44

Education and health

Educational attainment (1995). Percentage of population age 25 and over having: no formal schooling to some secondary education 32.7%; completed secondary 61.3%; higher 6.0%. *Literacy* (1990): total population age 10 and over literate 33,993 (99.4%); males literate 17,704 (99.4%); females literate 16,589 (99.5%).

Education (1994)

	schools	teachers	students	student/ teacher ratio
Primary (age 6–14)	30	524[11]	9,637	15.0[11]
Secondary (age 14–18)	9	266[11]	3,636	14.2[11]
Vocational[11]	...	21	160	7.6
Higher[12]	1	...	1,463	...

Health (1991): physicians 26 (1 per 1,888 persons); hospital beds (1995) 140 (1 per 4.7 persons); infant mortality rate per 1,000 live births (1999) 10.5.
Food: daily per capita caloric intake, n.a.

Military

Military defense is the responsibility of the United States.

[1]American Samoans are U.S. nationals, with rights of free entry into the United States. From 1951 American Samoa has been administered by the U.S. Department of the Interior. [2]The House of Representatives includes an elected representative from Swains Island. [3]The seat of the legislature, as defined by the Constitution of American Samoa, is at Fagatogo, one of a number of villages within an urban agglomeration collectively known as Pago Pago. [4]1988–90. [5]Does not include unemployed. [6]1995. [7]Imports c.i.f.; exports f.o.b. [8]South Pacific nations not including Australia and New Zealand. [9]Asian nations not including Japan. [10]Private vehicles only. [11]1991. [12]American Samoa Community College at Mapusaga, 1990 figures.

Internet resources for further information:
- **Cape Verde Embassy (Washington, D.C.) http://www.capeverdeusembassy.org**

Andorra

Official name: Principat d'Andorra; (Principality of Andorra).
Form of government: parliamentary coprincipality with one legislative house (General Council [28]).
Chiefs of state: President of France; Bishop of Urgell, Spain.
Head of government: Head of Government.
Capital: Andorra la Vella.
Official language: Catalan.
Official religion: none[1].
Monetary unit: There is no local currency of issue; the French franc and Spanish peseta are both in circulation. 1 franc (F) = 100 centimes; 1 peseta (Pta) = 100 céntimos.
Valuation (Oct. 6, 2000)
1 U.S.$ = F 7.54, 1 £ = F 10.91;
1 U.S.$ = Ptas 191.32,
1 £ = Ptas 276.76.

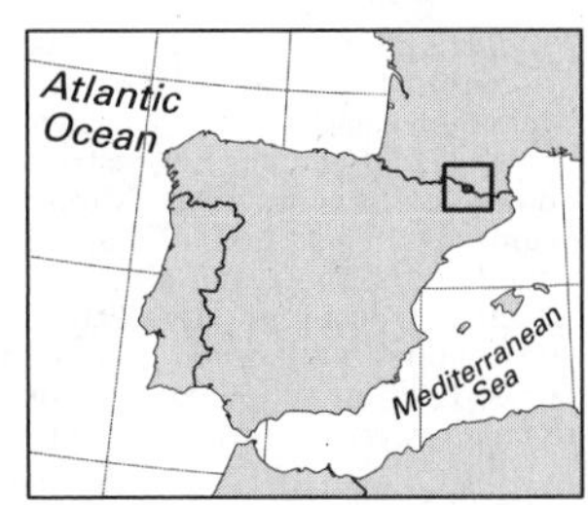

Area and population

Parishes	Capitals	area sq mi	area sq km	population 1999[2] estimate
Andorra la Vella	Andorra la Vella	49[3]	127[3]	21,513
Canillo	Canillo }	74	191	2,691
Encamp	Encamp }			10,385
La Massana	La Massana	25	65	6,092
Les Escaldes–Engordany	—	[3]	[3]	15,389
Ordino	Ordino	33	85	2,184
Sant Julià de Lòria	Sant Julià de Lòria	[3]	[3]	7,623
TOTAL		181	468	65,877

Demography

Population (2000): 66,700.
Density (2000): persons per sq mi 368.5, persons per sq km 142.5.
Urban-rural (1998): urban 95%; rural 5%.
Sex distribution (1999): male 52.36%; female 47.64%.
Age breakdown (1999): under 15, 15.2%; 15–29, 22.0%; 30–44, 29.3%; 45–59, 17.9%; 60–74, 10.6%; 75 and over, 5.0%.
Population projection: (2010) 72,000; (2020) 79,000.
Doubling time: 93 years.
Ethnic composition (by nationality; 1999): Spanish 42.8%; Andorran 21.7%; Portuguese 10.7%; French 6.7%; other nationality 6.6%; undeclared nationality 11.5%.
Religious affiliation (1995): Roman Catholic 87.1%; Protestant 0.2%; other Christian 0.5%; nonreligious/other 12.2%.
Major urban areas (1999): Andorra la Vella 21,513; Les Escaldes–Engordany 15,389; Encamp 10,385.

Vital statistics

Birth rate per 1,000 population (1998): 10.8[4] (world avg. 22.1).
Death rate per 1,000 population (1998): 3.3[4] (world avg. 8.9).
Natural increase rate per 1,000 population (1998): 7.5[4] (world avg. 13.2).
Total fertility rate (avg. births per childbearing woman; 1999): 1.3.
Marriage rate per 1,000 population (1998): 3.2.
Life expectancy at birth (1999): male 80.5 years; female 86.5 years.
Major causes of death per 100,000 population: cancers (neoplasms) 114; diseases of the circulatory system 110; diseases of the respiratory system 31; accidents and violence 26.

National economy

Budget (1997). Revenue: Ptas 50,720,000,000 (extraordinary income 45.9%, indirect taxes 41.1%, property income 7.3%). Expenditures: Ptas 50,720,000,000 (extraordinary expenditures 43.0%, current expenditures 30.8%, development expenditures 26.2%).
Public debt (1994): about U.S.$125,000,000.
Production. Agriculture (1997): tobacco 1,047 metric tons; other traditional crops include hay, potatoes, and grapes; livestock (number of live animals; 1997) 2,021 sheep[5], 1,187 cattle, 738 horses. Quarrying: small amounts of marble are quarried. Manufacturing (value of recorded exports in Ptas '000; 1997): electrical machinery and apparatus 1,397,000; motor vehicles and parts 947,000; newspapers and periodicals 743,000; clothing 632,000; toys and games 459,000; other products include furniture, cigarettes, and liqueurs. Construction (approved new building construction; 1998): 181,700 sq m. Energy production (consumption): electricity (kW-hr; 1997) 116,000,000 ([1999] 393,000,000); coal, none (n.a.); crude petroleum, none (n.a.); petroleum products, none (n.a.); natural gas, none (n.a.).
Tourism (1997): about 6,000,000 visitors; number of hotels (1996) 222.
Population economically active (1997)[6]: total 29,088; activity rate of total population 44.5% (participation rates: ages 15–64, 60.9%; female, n.a.; unemployed [1998] unofficially, none[7]).

Price and earnings indexes (1995 = 100)

	1993	1994	1995	1996	1997	1998	1999
Consumer price index[8]	91.2	95.5	100.0	103.6	105.6	107.5	110.0
Annual earnings index[9]	88.0	93.9	100.0	103.0	106.3	106.3	108.5

Gross national product (1997): U.S.$871,000,000 (U.S.$13.100 per capita)[10].

Structure of labour force[6]

	1997 labour force	1997 % of labour force
Agriculture } Mining }	199	0.7
Manufacturing	1,253	4.3
Construction	4,699	16.2
Public utilities	...	...
Transp. and commun.	...	...
Trade	5,570	19.1
Restaurants, hotels	5,470	18.8
Finance, real estate, insurance	1,276	4.4
Pub. admin., defense	3,636	12.5
Services	5,284	18.2
Other	1,701	5.8
TOTAL	29,088	100.0

Land use (1994): forested 22.0%; meadows and pastures 56.0%; agricultural and under permanent cultivation 2.0%; other 20.0%.
Household income and expenditure. n.a.

Foreign trade

Balance of trade (current prices)

	1993	1994	1995	1996	1997	1998
Ptas '000,000	–113,277	–117,876	–125,510	–129,577	–150,013	–152,777
% of total	91.1%	89.7%	91.1%	91.7%	91.4%	89.8%

Imports (1997): Ptas 157,054,000,000 (food, beverages, and tobacco 30.2%; machinery and apparatus 14.0%; chemicals and chemical products 8.7%; transport equipment 7.7%; textiles and wearing apparel 7.6%; photographic and optical goods and watches and clocks 4.5%). *Major import sources:* Spain 40.2%; France 29.2%; U.K. 5.7%; U.S. 4.9%; Germany 4.6%.
Exports (1997): Ptas 7,041,000,000 (electrical machinery and apparatus 19.8%; motor vehicles and parts 13.4%; newspapers, books, and periodicals 10.6%; clothing 9.0%; toys and games 6.5%). *Major export destinations:* Spain 47.4%; France 41.6%; Belgium 3.4%; The Netherlands 2.6%.

Transport and communications

Transport. Railroads: none; however, both French and Spanish railways stop near the border. Roads (1994): total length 167 mi, 269 km (paved 74%). Vehicles (1996): passenger cars 35,358; trucks and buses 4,238. Merchant marine: vessels (100 gross tons and over) none. Airports (1997) with scheduled flights: none.

Communications

Medium	date	unit	number	units per 1,000 persons
Daily newspapers	1996	circulation	4,000	62
Radio	1997	receivers	16,000	247
Television	1997	receivers	25,000	385
Telephones	1998	main lines	33,087	504
Cellular telephones	1998	subscribers	14,117	215
Internet	1998	users	4,500	69

Education and health

Educational attainment (mid-1980s). Percentage of population age 15 and over having: no formal schooling 5.5%; primary education 47.3%; secondary education 21.6%; postsecondary education 24.9%; unknown 0.7%. *Literacy:* resident population is virtually 100% literate.

Education (1996–97)

	schools	teachers	students	student/teacher ratio
Primary/Lower secondary (age 7–15)	12	...	5,424	...
Upper secondary	6	...	2,655	...
Higher	...	...	932[11]	...

Health: physicians (1996) 148 (1 per 434 persons); hospital beds 141 (1 per 455 persons); infant mortality rate per 1,000 live births (1998) 6.4.
Food (1995)[12]: daily per capita caloric intake 3,463 (vegetable products 67%, animal products 33%); 139% of FAO recommended minimum requirement.

Military

Total active duty personnel (1996): none. France and Spain are responsible for Andorra's external security; the police force is assisted in alternate years by either French gendarmerie or Barcelona police.

[1]Roman Catholicism enjoys special recognition in accordance with Andorran tradition. [2]January 1. [3]Andorra la Vella includes Les Escaldes–Engordany and Sant Julià de Lòria. [4]Official government figures. [5]Large herds of sheep and goats from Spain and France feed in Andorra in the summer. [6]Labour force receiving wages only; total population economically active equals 33,203. [7]The restricted size of the indigenous labour force has in the near past necessitated immigration to serve the tourist trade. [8]Consumer price index of Spain. [9]Official minimum salary as of July 1st. [10]Tourism (including winter-season sports, fairs, festivals, and income earned from low-duty imported manufactured items) and the banking system are the primary sources of GNP. [11]1997–98. [12]Composite values derived from Spanish and French food data.

Internet resources for further information:
- **Andorra National Information Centre http://www.andorra.ad/cniauk.html**
- **Department d'Estudis i d'Estadística http://www.finances.ad/estudis/indexDEE.htm**

Angola

Official name: República de Angola (Republic of Angola).
Form of government: unitary multiparty republic with one legislative house (National Assembly [220])[1].
Head of state and government: President[2].
Capital: Luanda.
Official language: Portuguese.
Official religion: none.
Monetary unit: 1 refloated kwanza[3] = 100 lwei; valuation (Oct. 6, 2000) 1 U.S.$ = refloated kwanza 12.87; 1 £ = refloated kwanza 18.62.

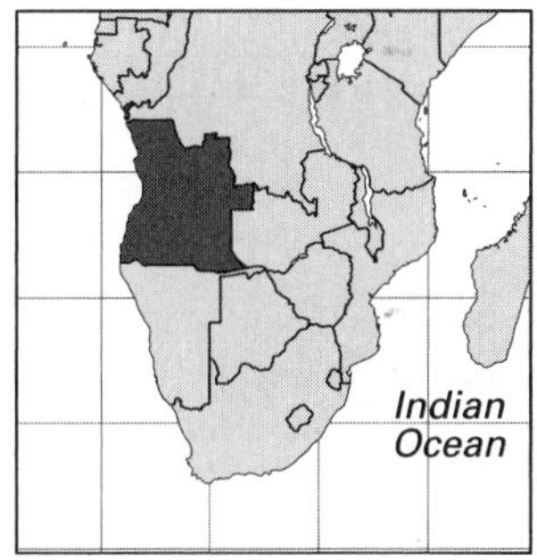

Area and population		area		population
				2000
Provinces	Capitals	sq mi	sq km	estimate
Bengo	Caxito	12,112	31,371	...
Benguela	Benguela	12,273	31,788	...
Bié	Kuito	27,148	70,314	...
Cabinda	Cabinda	2,807	7,270	...
Cunene	N'Giva	34,495	89,342	...
Huambo	Huambo	13,233	34,274	...
Huíla	Lubango	28,958	75,002	...
Kuando Kubango	Menongue	76,853	199,049	...
Kuanza Norte	N'Dalatando	9,340	24,190	...
Kuanza Sul	Sumbe	21,490	55,660	...
Luanda	Luanda	934	2,418	...
Lunda Norte	Lucapa	39,685	102,783	...
Lunda Sul	Saurimo	17,625	45,649	...
Malanje	Malanje	37,684	97,602	...
Moxico	Lwena	86,110	223,023	...
Namibe	Namibe	22,447	58,137	...
Uíge	Uíge	22,663	58,698	...
Zaire	M'Banza Kongo	15,494	40,130	...
TOTAL		481,354[4]	1,246,700	10,145,000

Demography

Population (2000): 10,145,000.
Density (2000): persons per sq mi 21.1, persons per sq km 8.1.
Urban-rural (1999): urban 33.5%; rural 66.5%.
Sex distribution (1999): male 50.61%; female 49.39%.
Age breakdown (1999): under 15, 43.2%; 15–29, 26.5%; 30–44, 16.8%; 45–59, 8.9%; 60 and over, 4.6%.
Population projection: (2010) 12,646,000; (2020) 15,750,000.
Doubling time: 32 years.
Ethnic composition (1983): Ovimbundu 37.2%; Mbundu 21.6%; Kongo 13.2%; Luimbe-Nganguela 5.4%; Nyaneka-Humbe 5.4%; Chokwe 4.2%; Luvale (Luena) 3.6%; Luchazi 2.4%; Ambo (Ovambo) 2.4%; Lunda 1.2%; Mbunda 1.2%; other 2.2%.
Religious affiliation (1995): Christian 70.1%, of which Roman Catholic 50.7%, Protestant 14.6%; traditional beliefs 29.9%.
Major cities (1999): Luanda 2,555,000; Huambo 400,000[5]; Benguela 155,000[6]; Lobito 150,000[6]; Lubango 105,000[7].

Vital statistics

Birth rate per 1,000 population (1999): 47.2 (world avg. 22.1).
Death rate per 1,000 population (1999): 25.3 (world avg. 8.9).
Natural increase rate per 1,000 population (1999): 21.9 (world avg. 13.2).
Total fertility rate (avg. births per childbearing woman; 1999): 6.6.
Life expectancy at birth (1999): male 36.9 years; female 39.3 years.
Major causes of death (percentage of total deaths; 1990): diarrheal diseases 25.8%; malaria 19.4%; cholera 7.3%; acute respiratory infections 6.8%.

National economy

Budget (1997). Revenue: NKz 637,915,000,000[3] (tax revenue 77.8%, of which income taxes 42.6%, petroleum taxes 22.6%, import duties 5.3%; other taxes 7.3%; nontax revenue 22.2%). Expenditures: NKz 598,623,000,000[3]; defense and internal security 36.3%; administration 17.7%; interest 9.9%; economic services 8.7%; education 4.9%; health 3.1%; other 19.4%).
Public debt (external, outstanding; 1998): U.S.$10,616,000,000.
Tourism: receipts (1998) U.S.$8,000,000; expenditures (1997) U.S.$70,000,000.
Household income and expenditure. Average household size (1998) 5.0; annual income per household: n.a.; sources of income: n.a.; expenditure: n.a.
Production (metric tons except as noted). Agriculture, forestry, fishing (1999): cassava 3,129,734, corn (maize) 428,045, sugarcane 340,000, bananas 290,000, oil palm fruit 250,000, sweet potatoes 182,050, millet 101,736, dry beans 67,509, pineapples 32,000, peanuts (groundnuts) 23,000, coffee 5,220; livestock (number of live animals) 3,900,000 cattle, 2,000,000 goats, 800,000 pigs, 336,000 sheep, 6,650,000 chickens; roundwood (1998) 6,472,000 cu m; fish catch (1998) 145,811. Mining and quarrying (1997): diamonds 1,212,000 carats. Manufacturing (1997): bread 150,099; wheat flour 51,957; corn flour 50,960; frozen fish 12,971; soap 10,672; pasta 2,587; leather shoes 186,000 pairs; beer 115,047 hectolitres; fabric 3,264,000 sq m. Construction (value in NKz '000,000[3]; 1986): residential 608; nonresidential 1,977. Energy production (consumption): electricity (kW-hr; 1998) 1,885,000,000 (1,885,000,000); coal, none (none); crude petroleum (barrels; 1996) 257,662,000 (12,425,000); petroleum products (metric tons; 1996) 1,300,000 (350,000); natural gas (cu m; 1996) 179,389,000 (179,389,000).
Gross national product (at current market prices; 1998): U.S.$4,578,000,000 (U.S.$380 per capita).

Structure of gross domestic product and labour force				
	1997			
	in value NKz '000,000,000[3]	% of total value	labour force	% of labour force
Agriculture	166,778	9.6	4,558,550	85.0
Mining	908,591	52.3		
Manufacturing	76,440	4.4	804,450	15.0
Construction	71,228	4.1		
Finance, Trade, Public utilities, Transp. and commun.	283,175	16.3		
Pub. admin., defense, Services	198,049	11.4		
Other	33,007[8]	1.9[8]	...	...
TOTAL	1,737,268	100.0	5,363,000	100.0

Population economically active (1997): total 5,363,000; activity rate of total population 56.1% (participation rates over age 10 [1991] 60.1%; female 38.4%).

Price and earnings indexes (1995 = 100)	1995	1996	1997	1998	1999
Consumer price index	100.0	4,245.2	13,550.1	25,327.3	97,807.0
Monthly earnings index	100.0	...	...	...	...

Land use (1995): forested 18.5%; meadows and pastures 43.3%; agricultural and under permanent cultivation 2.8%; other 35.4%.

Foreign trade

Balance of trade (current prices)	1993	1994	1995	1996	1997
U.S.$'000,000	+1,435	+1,563	+1,871	+3,055	+2,531
% of total	32.9%	35.0%	33.6%	42.8%	33.9%

Imports (1997): U.S.$2,477,000,000 (1991; current consumption goods 50.2%, capital goods 20.2%, intermediate consumption goods 18.9%, transport equipment 6.8%). *Major import sources* (1997): Portugal 20.6%; South Africa 14.1%; U.S. 13.2%; Spain 8.2%; United Kingdom 6.2%; France 5.6%; Brazil 3.8%.
Exports (1997): U.S.$5,008,000,000 (mineral fuels 90.0%, diamonds 6.9%). *Major export destinations* (1997): U.S. 63.6%; China 12.9%; Belgium 6.0%; France 3.8%; Taiwan 2.8%.

Transport and communications

Transport. Railroads (1997): route length 1,834 mi, 2,952 km; passenger-mi 203,000,000[9], passenger-km 326,000,000[9]; short ton-mi cargo 1,178,000,000[9], metric ton-km cargo 1,720,000,000[9]. Roads (1997): total length 45,128 mi, 72,626 km (paved 25%). Vehicles (1996): passenger cars 207,000; trucks and buses 25,000. Merchant marine (1992): vessels (100 gross tons and over) 113; total deadweight tonnage 123,479. Air transport (1995): passenger-mi 1,061,000,000, passenger-km 1,708,000,000; short ton-mi cargo 131,730,000, metric ton-km cargo 212,000,000; airports (1998) with scheduled flights 17.

Communications				units per 1,000
Medium	date	unit	number	persons
Daily newspapers	1996	circulation	128,000	13.1
Television	1998	receivers	1,500,000	154
Telephones	1998	main lines	72,244	7.4
Cellular telephones	1998	subscribers	9,820	1.0
Personal computers	1998	units	10,000	1.0
Internet	1998	users	2,500	0.3

Education and health

Educational attainment: n.a. *Literacy* (1998): percentage of population age 15 and over literate 41.7%; males literate 55.6%; females literate 28.5%.

Education (1991–92)	schools[10]	teachers	students	student/ teacher ratio
Primary (age 7–10)	6,308	31,062	989,443	...
Secondary (age 11–16)	5,276	5,138[11]	196,099	...
Voc., teacher tr.	...	566[11]	22,888	...
Higher	1	787	6,331	8.0

Health (1997): physicians 736 (1 per 12,985 persons); hospital beds (1990) 11,857 (1 per 845 persons); infant mortality rate per 1,000 live births (1999) 197.8.
Food (1998): daily per capita caloric intake 1,920 (vegetable products 92%, animal products 8%); 82% of FAO recommended minimum requirement.

Military

Total active duty personnel (1998): 112,500 (army 88.9%, navy 1.3%, air force 9.8%). *Military expenditure as percentage of GNP* (1997): 20.5% (world 2.6%); per capita expenditure U.S.$147.

[1]Long-term civil war resumed in September 1998 and continued in September 2000. [2]President annulled post of Prime Minister in January 1999. [3]The refloated kwanza (or [second] new kwanza), equal to 1,000 readjusted kwanza, was introduced on Jan. 1, 2000; previously, in July 1995, the readjusted kwanza, equal to 1,000 new kwanza (NKz), was introduced. [4]Detail does not add to total given because of rounding. [5]1995. [6]1983. [7]1984. [8]Import duties. [9]1988. [10]1985–86. [11]1989–90.

Internet resources for further information:
- **Official Home Page of the Republic of Angola http://www.angola.org**

Antigua and Barbuda

Official name: Antigua and Barbuda.
Form of government: constitutional monarchy with two legislative houses (Senate [17]; House of Representatives [17[1]]).
Chief of state: British Monarch represented by Governor-General.
Head of government: Prime Minister.
Capital: Saint John's.
Official language: English.
Official religion: none.
Monetary unit: 1 Eastern Caribbean dollar (EC$) = 100 cents; valuation (Oct. 6, 2000) 1 U.S.$ = EC$2.70; 1 £ = EC$3.91.

Area and population	area		population
			1991
Parishes[2]	sq mi	sq km	census
Saint George	9.3	24.1	4,473
Saint John's	28.5	73.8	35,635
Saint Mary	22.0	57.0	5,303
Saint Paul	18.5	47.9	6,117
Saint Peter	12.7	32.9	3,622
Saint Phillip	17.0	44.0	2,964
Islands[2]			
Barbuda	62.0	160.6	1,241
Redonda	0.5	1.3	[3]
TOTAL	170.5	441.6	59,355[4]

Demography

Population (2000): 71,100[5].
Density (2000): persons per sq mi 416.4, persons per sq km 160.8.
Urban-rural (1995): urban 36.5%; rural 63.5%.
Sex distribution (1991): male 48.20%; female 51.80%.
Age breakdown (1991): under 15, 30.4%; 15–29, 27.8%; 30–44, 20.5%; 45–59, 10.2%; 60–74, 7.7%; 75 and over, 3.4%.
Population projection: (2010) 75,000; (2020) 79,000.
Doubling time: 47 years.
Ethnic composition (1994): black 91.3%; mixed 3.7%; white 2.4%; Syrian/Lebanese 0.6%; Indo-Pakistani 0.4%; Amerindian 0.3%; other 1.3%.
Religious affiliation (1991): Protestant 73.7%, of which Anglican 32.1%, Moravian 12.0%, Methodist 9.1%, Seventh-day Adventist 8.8%; Roman Catholic 10.8%; Jehovah's Witness 1.2%; Rastafarian 0.8%; other religion/no religion/not stated 13.5%.
Major cities (1991): Saint John's 22,342[6].

Vital statistics

Birth rate per 1,000 population (1997): 21.6 (world avg. 22.1); (1988) legitimate 23.4%; illegitimate 76.6%.
Death rate per 1,000 population (1997): 6.4 (world avg. 8.9).
Natural increase rate per 1,000 population (1997): 15.2 (world avg. 13.2).
Total fertility rate (avg. births per childbearing woman; 1999): 1.7.
Marriage rate per 1,000 population (1995): 22.1.
Divorce rate per 1,000 population (1988): 0.2.
Life expectancy at birth (1999): male 69.1 years; female 74.0 years.
Major causes of death per 100,000 population (1993–95): diseases of the circulatory system 258.1, of which cerebrovascular disease 103.3, diseases of pulmonary circulation and other forms of heart disease 76.9; malignant neoplasms (cancers) 104.9; endocrine and metabolic disorders 73.7.

National economy

Budget (1998). Revenue: EC$362,300,000 (taxes on international transactions 35.6%, of which import duties 15.8%; consumption taxes 24.9%; nontax revenue 12.5%; corporate income taxes 7.1%). Expenditures: EC$427,300,000 (current expenditures 90.1%; development expenditures 9.9%).
Public debt (external, outstanding; end of 1998): U.S.$406,400,000.
Production (metric tons except as noted). Agriculture, forestry, fishing (1999): tropical fruit (including papayas, guavas, soursops, and oranges) 6,500, mangoes 1,300, eggplants 250, lemons and limes 220, carrots 210, "Antiguan Black" pineapples 150; livestock (number of live animals) 15,700 cattle, 12,200 sheep; roundwood, n.a.; fish catch (1997) 500. Mining and quarrying: crushed stone for local use. Manufacturing (1994): beer and malt 166,000 cases; T-shirts 179,000 units; other manufactures include cement, handicrafts, and furniture, as well as electronic components for export. Construction (1998): gross value of building applications EC$323,000,000. Energy production (consumption): electricity (kW-hr; 1997) 153,700,000 (115,300,000); coal, none (none); crude petroleum, none (none); petroleum products (metric tons; 1996) negligible (105,000); natural gas, none (none).
Population economically active (1991): total 26,753; activity rate of total population 45.1% (participation rates: ages 15–64, 69.7%; female 45.6%; unemployed [end of 1998] *c.* 5%).

Price and earnings indexes (1996 = 100)	1993	1994	1995	1996	1997	1998
Consumer price index	94.6	98.2	96.9	100.0	98.9	103.6
Annual earnings index[7]	...	...	...	100.0	100.0	106.0

Household income and expenditure. Average household size (1991) 3.2; income per household: n.a.; sources of income: n.a.; expenditure: n.a.

Gross national product (1998): U.S.$565,000,000 (U.S.$8,450 per capita).

Structure of gross domestic product and labour force	1998		1991	
	in value EC$'000,000	% of total value	labour force	% of labour force
Agriculture, fishing	56.1	3.4	1,040	3.9
Quarrying	24.3	1.5	64	0.2
Manufacturing	31.7	1.9	1,444	5.4
Construction	166.5	10.0	3,109	11.6
Public utilities	42.6	2.5	435	1.6
Transp. and commun.	289.6	17.4	2,395	9.0
Trade, restaurants, and hotels	323.7	19.4	8,524	31.9
Finance, real estate	235.7	14.1	1,454	5.4
Pub. admin., defense	247.1	14.8	2,572	9.6
Services	104.4	6.3	5,207	19.5
Other	144.5[8]	8.7[8]	509	1.9
TOTAL	1,666.2	100.0	26,753	100.0

Land use (1994): forested 11.0%; meadows and pastures 9.0%; agricultural and under permanent cultivation 18.0%; other 62.0%.
Tourism: receipts from visitors (1998) U.S.$288,300,000; expenditures by nationals abroad (1996) U.S.$26,000,000.

Foreign trade

Balance of trade (current prices)	1994	1995	1996	1997	1998
U.S.$'000,000	–263	–276	–301	–294	–321
% of total	74.8%	72.4%	80.0%	79.5%	81.6%

Imports (1998)[9]: U.S.$357,500,000 (agricultural products 11.0%, other [including petroleum products for reexport] 89%). *Major import sources* (1997): United States 26.3%; United Kingdom 10.0%; Caricom 7.8%.
Exports (1998): U.S.$36,200,000 (reexports [significantly, petroleum products reexported to neighbouring islands] 59.1%, domestic exports 40.9%). *Major export destinations* (1994)[9]: United States 40.0%; others include the United Kingdom, Canada, and Caricom.

Transport and communications

Transport. Railroad[10]. Roads (1996): total length 155 mi, 250 km (paved, n.a.). Vehicles (1995): passenger cars 13,588; trucks and buses 1,342. Merchant marine (1992): vessels (100 gross tons and over) 292; total deadweight tonnage 997,381. Air transport (1995): passenger-mi 157,000,000, passenger-km 252,000,000; (1991) short ton-mi cargo 137,000, metric ton-km cargo 200,000; airports (1996) with scheduled flights 2.

Communications				units
Medium	date	unit	number	per 1,000 persons
Daily newspapers	1996	circulation	6,000	87
Radio	1997	receivers	36,000	523
Television	1997	receivers	31,000	451
Telephones	1998	main lines	34,000	468
Cellular telephones	1996	subscribers	1,300	19

Education and health

Educational attainment (1991). Percentage of population age 25 and over having: no formal schooling 1.1%; primary education 50.5%; secondary 33.4%; higher (not university) 5.4%; university 6.2%; other/unknown 3.4%. *Literacy* (1995): percentage of total population age 15 and over literate, 90.0%.

Education (1996–97)	schools	teachers	students	student/ teacher ratio
Primary (age 5–11)	58	559	12,229	21.9
Secondary (age 12–16)	13	389	4,260	11.0
Higher[11]	1	16	46	2.9

Health (1996): physicians 75 (1 per 915 persons); hospital beds 255 (1 per 269 persons); infant mortality rate per 1,000 live births (1999) 20.7.
Food (1997): daily per capita caloric intake 2,449 (vegetable products 65%, animal products 35%); 104% of FAO recommended minimum requirement.

Military

Total active duty personnel (1997): a 150-member defense force (army 83.3%, navy 16.7%) is part of the Eastern Caribbean regional security system. Military expenditure as percentage of GNP (1998): 0.7%[9] (world average, n.a.).

[1]Directly elected seats only; attorney general and speaker may serve ex officio if they are not elected to House of Representatives. [2]Community councils on Antigua and the local government council on Barbuda are the organs of local government. [3]Uninhabited. [4]Unadjusted de jure population excluding institutionalized population; de jure population adjusted for undercount (including institutionalized population) is 63,896. [5]Includes evacuees from Montserrat. [6]Large settlements include (1991): All Saints 2,230; Liberta 1,473; Codrington 814. [7]Public sector only. [8]Net indirect taxes less imputed bank service charges. [9]Estimated percentages. [10]Mostly nonoperative privately owned tracks. [11]1994–95.

Internet resources for further information:
- **Antigua and Barbuda High Commission (London) http://www.antigua-barbuda.com**
- **Eastern Caribbean Central Bank http://www.eccb-centralbank.org**

Argentina

Official name: República Argentina (Argentina Republic).
Form of government: federal republic with two legislative houses (Senate [72]; Chamber of Deputies [257]).
Head of state and government: President[1].
Capital: Buenos Aires.
Official language: Spanish.
Official religion: Roman Catholicism.
Monetary unit: 1 peso (pl. pesos)[2] (Arg$) = 100 centavos; valuation (Oct. 6, 2000) 1 U.S.$ = Arg$1.00; 1 £ = Arg$1.45.

Area and population

Provinces	Capitals	area sq mi	area sq km	population 1999 estimate
Buenos Aires	La Plata	118,754	307,571	14,047,483
Catamarca	Catamarca	39,615	102,602	312,269
Chaco	Resistencia	38,469	99,633	940,901
Chubut	Rawson	86,752	224,686	438,236
Córdoba	Córdoba	63,831	165,321	3,059,115
Corrientes	Corrientes	34,054	88,199	909,207
Entre Ríos	Paraná	30,418	78,781	1,104,836
Formosa	Formosa	27,825	72,066	492,513
Jujuy	San Salvador de Jujuy	20,548	53,219	594,117
La Pampa	Santa Rosa	55,382	143,440	301,466
La Rioja	La Rioja	34,626	89,680	273,471
Mendoza	Mendoza	57,462	148,827	1,588,091
Misiones	Posadas	11,506	29,801	972,672
Neuquén	Neuquén	36,324	94,078	540,384
Río Negro	Viedma	78,384	203,013	606,575
Salta	Salta	60,034	155,488	1,044,973
San Juan	San Juan	34,614	89,651	574,053
San Luis	San Luis	29,633	76,748	354,959
Santa Cruz	Río Gallegos	94,187	243,943	201,642
Santa Fe	Santa Fe	51,354	133,007	3,068,765
Santiago del Estero	Santiago del Estero	52,645	136,351	720,982
Tierra del Fuego[3]	Ushuaia	8,210	21,263	109,998
Tucumán	San Miguel de Tucumán	8,697	22,524	1,278,216
Other federal entity				
Distrito Federal	Buenos Aires	77	200	3,043,431
TOTAL		1,073,400[4]	2,780,092	36,578,358[4]

Demography

Population (2000): 37,032,000[5].
Density (2000): persons per sq mi 34.5, persons per sq km 13.3.
Urban-rural (1999): urban 89.7%; rural 10.3%.
Sex distribution (1995): male 49.06%; female 50.94%.
Age breakdown (1995): under 15, 28.9%; 15–29, 24.8%; 30–44, 19.0%; 45–59, 14.1%; 60–74, 9.8%; 75 and over, 3.4%.
Population projection: (2010) 41,474,000; (2020) 45,347,000.
Ethnic composition (1986): European 85%; mestizo and Amerindian 15%.
Religious affiliation (1995): Roman Catholic 87.7%; Protestant 7.5%; Muslim 1.5%; Jewish 0.7%; other 2.6%.
Major cities (1999): Buenos Aires 2,904,192 (12,423,000[6]); Córdoba 1,275,585; Rosario 1,000,000; Mar del Plata 579,483; La Plata 556,308.

Vital statistics

Birth rate per 1,000 population (1998): 18.9 (world avg. 22.1).
Death rate per 1,000 population (1998): 7.8 (world avg. 8.9).
Natural increase rate per 1,000 population (1998): 11.1 (world avg. 13.2).
Total fertility rate (avg. births per childbearing woman; 1999): 2.6.
Life expectancy at birth (1999): male 71.4 years; female 78.4 years.
Major causes of death per 100,000 population (1995): heart disease 227.7; neoplasms (cancers) 141.6; diseases of the brain 69.2; accidents 28.0.

National economy

Budget (1996). Revenue: Arg$47,256,000,000 (current revenue 99.7%, of which tax revenue 94.6%, nontax revenue 5.3%; capital revenue 0.3%). Expenditure: Arg$49,049,000,000 (1989; social security 35.3%; economic services 16.0%; education 9.9%; defense 9.9%; debt service 7.4%).
Public debt (external, outstanding; 1998): U.S.$76,799,000,000.
Gross national product (1998): U.S.$290,261,000,000 (U.S.$8,030 per capita).

Structure of gross domestic product and labour force

	1994 in value Arg$'000,000[2]	1994 % of total value	1996 labour force	1996 % of labour force
Agriculture	13,665.7	4.8	190,300[7]	1.5[7]
Mining	4,672.7	1.7		
Manufacturing	56,443.3	20.0	1,999,600	15.9
Construction	18,858.5	6.7	1,217,400	9.7
Public utilities	4,735.5	1.7	115,700	0.9
Transp. and commun.	15,234.5	5.4	873,300	6.9
Trade, restaurants	41,132.0	14.6	2,523,800	20.0
Finance, real estate	50,267.0	17.8	1,021,800	8.1
Pub. admin., defense	71,970.8	25.6	1,010,500	8.0
Services			3,573,000	28.4
Other	4,665.0	1.7	63,500	0.5
TOTAL	281,645.0[4]	100.0	12,588,900[7]	100.0[4]

Production (metric tons except as noted). Agriculture, forestry, fishing (1997): sugarcane 19,450,000, corn (maize) 15,536,000, wheat 14,800,000, soybeans 11,000,000, sunflower seeds 5,450,000, grapes 2,500,000; livestock (number of live animals) 54,500,000 cattle, 17,300,000 sheep; roundwood (1997) 13,192,000 cu m; fish catch (1997) 1,182,725. Mining and quarrying (1997): silver 1,819,730 troy oz; gold 80,377 troy oz. Manufacturing (1997): cement 5,117,000[8]; vegetable oil 4,148,000; wheat flour 3,607,000; sugar 1,649,000; paper 1,121,000[8]; wine 13,273,000 hectolitres; beer 10,825,000 hectolitres. Energy production (consumption): electricity (kW-hr; 1995) 67,169,000,000 (69,291,000,000); coal (metric tons; 1995) 305,000 (1,677,000); crude petroleum (barrels; 1996) 275,000,000 (1995; 163,000,000); petroleum products (metric tons; 1995) 21,554,000 (20,471,000); natural gas (cu m; 1995) 17,336,000,000 (32,954,000,000).
Population economically active (1995): total 14,345,171; activity rate of total population 41.5% (participation rates; ages 15–64, 64.5%; female 36.9%; unemployed [1996] 17.0%).

Price and earning indexes (1995 = 100)[2]

	1993	1994	1995	1996	1997	1998
Consumer price index	92.9	96.7	100.0	100.2	100.7	101.6
Monthly earnings index[9]	95.2	101.7	100.0	100.7	...	...

Household size and expenditure. Average household size (1991) 3.8; expenditure (1985–86): food 38.2%, transportation 11.6%, housing 9.3%, energy 9.0%, clothing 8.0%, health 7.9%, recreation 7.5%, other 8.5%.
Tourism (1997): receipts U.S.$5,069,000,000; expenditures U.S.$2,680,000,000.

Foreign trade[10]

Balance of trade (current prices)

	1994	1995	1996	1997	1998	1999
U.S.$'000,000	–4,002	+3,005	+1,621	–2,183	–3,117	–775
% of total	11.3%	7.7%	3.5%	4.0%	5.6%	1.6%

Imports (1997): U.S.$30,377,000,000 (machinery and transport equipment 48.8%, chemical products 16.1%, manufactured products 15.0%, food products and live animals 4.0%). *Major import sources:* Brazil 22.7%; U.S. 20.0%; Italy 5.7%; Germany 5.4%; France 4.5%; Spain 4.1%; Japan 3.7%.
Exports (1997): U.S.$26,217,000,000 (food products and live animals 37.7%, machinery and transport equipment 15.0%, manufactured products 11.7%, petroleum and petroleum products 11.7%, vegetable and animal oils 8.4%, chemical products 5.9%). *Major export destinations:* Brazil 30.7%; U.S. 8.4%; Chile 7.3%; The Netherlands 3.3%; China 3.3%; Uruguay 3.1%; Italy 2.8%.

Transport and communications

Transport. Railroads (1996): length 35,753 km; passenger-km (1995) 7,996,000,000; metric ton-km cargo 8,505,500,000. Roads (1996): total length 135,630 mi, 218,276 km (paved 29%). Vehicles (1996): passenger cars 4,459,000; commercial vehicles and buses 955,000. Air transport (1997): passenger-km 6,123,890,000; metric ton-km cargo 702,888,000; airports (1997) with scheduled flights 39.

Communications

Medium	date	unit	number	units per 1,000 persons
Daily newspapers	1996	circulation	4,320,000	123
Radio	1998	receivers	21,500,000	595
Television	1997	receivers	10,309,000	289
Telephones	1997	main lines	6,824,000	191
Cellular telephones	1997	subscribers	1,997,600	56
Personal computers	1997	units	1,398,300	39
Internet	1998	users	200,000	5.5

Education and health

Educational attainment (1991). Percentage of population age 25 and over having: no formal schooling 5.7%; less than primary education 22.3%; primary 34.6%; incomplete secondary 12.5%; complete secondary 12.8%; higher 12.0%. *Literacy* (1995): percentage of total population age 15 and over literate 96.2%; males literate 96.2%; females literate 96.2%.

Education (1994–95)

	schools	teachers	students	student/ teacher ratio
Primary (age 6–12)[8]	22,636	313,764	5,044,827	16.1
Secondary (age 13–17)[11]	7,239	233,564	2,238,091	9.6
Higher	1,705	118,695	926,793	7.8

Health: physicians (1992) 88,800 (1 per 376 persons); hospital beds (1996) 115,803 (1 per 304 persons); infant mortality rate (1999) 19.1.
Food (1996): daily per capita caloric intake 3,119 (vegetable products 71%, animal products 29%); 183% of FAO recommended minimum requirement.

Military

Total active duty personnel (1998): 73,000 (army 56.2%, navy 27.4%, air force 16.4%). *Military expenditure as percentage of GNP* (1997): 1.2% (world 2.6%); per capita expenditure U.S.$104.

[1]Assisted by a ministerial coordinator who exercises general administration of the country. [2]On Jan. 1, 1992, the austral was replaced by the peso at a ratio of 10,000 to 1. [3]Area of Tierra del Fuego (province since 1991) excludes claims to British-held islands in the South Atlantic Ocean. [4]Detail does not add to total given because of rounding. [5]Includes about 2 million illegal immigrants from Bolivia and Paraguay. [6]Urban agglomeration. [7]Based on October survey; data for agriculture and mining sectors are incomplete. [8]1996. [9]Manufacturing sector only. [10]Import figures are f.o.b. in balance of trade and c.i.f. in commodities and trading partners. [11]Secondary includes vocational and teacher training.

Internet resources for further information:
- **National Institute of Statistics and Censuses http://www.indec.mecon.ar/default.htm**

Armenia

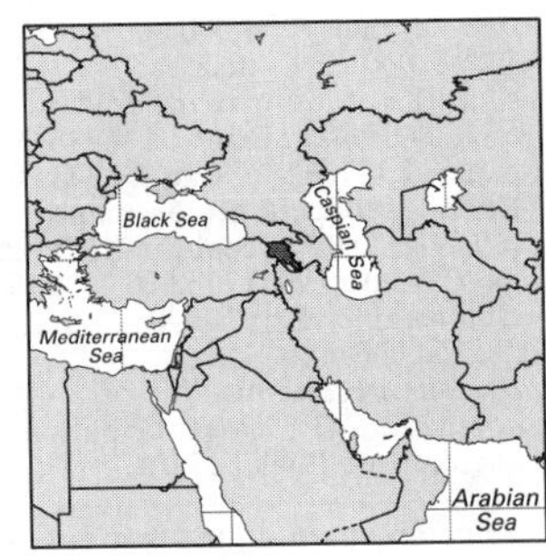

Official name: Hayastani Hanrapetut'yun (Republic of Armenia).
Form of government: unitary multiparty republic with a single legislative body (National Assembly [131]).
Head of state: President.
Head of government: Prime Minister.
Capital: Yerevan.
Official language: Armenian.
Official religion: none[1].
Monetary unit: 1 dram = 100 lumas; valuation (Oct. 6, 2000) official, 1 U.S.$ = 538.90 drams; 1 £ = 799.55 drams.

Area and population

	area		population
Regions	sq mi	sq km	2000 estimate
Aragatsotn	1,064	2,755	167,500
Ararat	812	2,104	310,800
Armavir	479	1,241	322,300
Gegharkunik	1,573	4,073	278,600
Lori	1,464	3,791	394,400
Kotayk	811	2,100	329,400
Shirak	1,034	2,679	362,300
Syunik	1,739	4,505	163,900
Vayots-Dzor	891	2,308	69,200
Tavush	1,043	2,702	156,800
Cities			
Yerevan	81	210	1,248,200
Other	493[2]	1,278[2]	
TOTAL	11,484[3]	29,743[3, 4]	3,803,400

Demography

Population (2000): 3,810,000 (de jure); *c.* 3,000,000 (de facto)[5].
Density (2000): persons per sq mi 331.8, persons per sq km 128.1.
Urban-rural (1998): urban 69.4%; rural 30.6%.
Sex distribution (1998): male 48.64%; female 51.36%.
Age breakdown (1999): under 15, 25.6%; 15–29, 23.3%; 30–44, 23.9%; 45–59, 13.5%; 60–74, 11.4%; 75 and over, 2.3%.
Population projection: (2010) 3,833,000; (2020) 3,956,000.
Doubling time: n.a.; doubling time exceeds 100 years.
Ethnic composition (1989): Armenian 93.3%; Azerbaijani 2.6%; other 4.1%.
Religious affiliation (1995): Armenian Apostolic 64.5%; other Christian 1.3%; other (mostly nonreligious) 34.2%.
Major cities (2000): Yerevan 1,248,200; Gyumri 163,000[6]; Kirovakan 76,000[6].

Vital statistics

Birth rate per 1,000 population (1999): 13.5 (world avg. 22.1); (1993) legitimate 86.0%; illegitimate 14.0%.
Death rate per 1,000 population (1999): 9.0 (world avg. 8.9).
Natural increase rate per 1,000 population (1999): 4.5 (world avg. 13.2).
Total fertility rate (avg. births per childbearing woman; 1999): 1.7.
Marriage rate per 1,000 population (1999): 3.3.
Divorce rate per 1,000 population (1999): 0.3.
Life expectancy at birth (1999): male 62.2 years; female 71.1 years.
Major causes of death per 100,000 population (1999): circulatory diseases 342.1; cancers 106.0; respiratory diseases 36.2; accidents and violence 33.2.

National economy

Budget (1996). Revenue: 116,606,000,000 drams (tax revenue 72.9%, of which value-added tax 18.4%, enterprise profits tax 14.4%, payroll tax 12.6%, grants 8.3%, income tax 7.5%, other taxes 20.0%; nontax 27.1%). Expenditures: 173,450,000,000 drams (current expenditures 74.8%, of which pensions and social welfare 18.5%, wages 10.9%, interest 10.0%, health and education 5.6%, other 29.8%; capital expenditure and net lending 24.7%).
Public debt (external, outstanding; 1997): U.S.$511,500,000.
Tourism (1997): receipts from visitors U.S.$7,000,000; expenditures by nationals abroad U.S.$41,000,000.
Land use (1994): forest 13.4%; pasture 23.1%; agriculture 20.1%; other 43.4%.
Gross national product (1998): U.S.$1,728,000,000 (U.S.$460 per capita).

Structure of net material product and labour force

	1996			
	in value '000,000 drams	% of total value	labour force	% of labour force
Agriculture	217,594	33.0	586,000	37.0
Manufacturing, mining / Public utilities	156,980	23.8	255,000	16.1
Construction	63,124	9.5	68,000	4.3
Transp. and commun.	31,023	4.7	24,000	1.5
Trade	63,262	9.6	110,200	7.0
Pub. admin., defense	—	—	28,600	1.8
Services	—	—	320,800	20.3
Other	128,327	19.4	190,900[7]	12.0[7]
TOTAL	660,310	100.0	1,583,500	100.0

Production (metric tons except as noted). Agriculture, forestry, fishing (1999): potatoes 425,200, wheat 220,000, grapes 105,900, tomatoes 145,000, barley 65,000, watermelons 60,000, apples 56,000; livestock (number of live animals) 550,000 sheep and goats, 505,000 cattle, 52,000 pigs, 2,800,000 poultry; roundwood (1998) 35,700 cu m; fish catch (1997) 3,050. Mining and quarrying (1996): copper 9,080,000; perlite 200,000; molybdenum 1,800. Manufacturing (value in '000,000 drams; 1994): machine-building and metalworking equipment 18,436; food products 13,842; chemicals 5,330; metals 5,259; construction materials 3,154; textiles 2,500; leather products 2,335. Construction (1995): 284,000 sq m. Energy production (consumption): electricity (kW-hr; 1997) 6,215,000,000 (6,215,000,000); coal (metric tons; 1996) none (5,000); crude petroleum (barrels; 1996) none (1,026,000); petroleum products (metric tons; 1996) none (358,000); natural gas (cu m; 1996) none (1,050,700).
Population economically active (1996): total 1,583,500; activity rate of total population 42.1% (participation rates: ages 16–60 75.1%; unemployed [1998] 11.0%).

Price and earnings indexes (1995 = 100)

	1993	1994	1995	1996	1997	1998
Consumer price index	1	36	100	119	135	147
Earnings index	...	...	...	...	...	...

Household income and expenditure. Average household size (1997) 4.5; income per household (1994) 47,352 drams (U.S.$153); sources of income (1994): wages and salaries 52.3%, agricultural income 7.7%, other 40.0%; expenditure (1994): goods and services 78.0%, taxes and payments to government 22.0%.

Foreign trade

Balance of trade (current prices)

	1993	1994	1995	1996	1997
U.S.$'000,000	–98.0	–178.3	–403.0	–469.2	–659.8
% of total	23.9%	29.3%	42.7%	44.7%	58.7%

Imports (1996): U.S.$759,600,000 (food products 32.4%, mineral products 28.5%, jewelry 15.2%, machinery and equipment 12.9%). *Major import sources:* former Soviet Union (FSU) 32.4%, of which Russia 14.7%, Turkmenistan 10.1%, other FSU 7.6%; non-FSU 67.6%, of which Iran 17.5%, U.S. 12.1%, Germany 2.0%, France 1.4%.
Exports (1996): U.S.$290,400,000 (jewelry 48.3%, machinery and equipment 29.7%, mineral products 9.0%). *Major export destinations:* FSU 44.1%, of which Russia 33.1%, Turkmenistan 6.0%, other FSU 5.0%; non-FSU 55.9%, of which Belgium 15.4%, Iran 13.7%, Germany 1.3%.

Transport and communications

Transport. Railroads (1998): length 516 mi, 830 km; (1996) passenger-mi 52,195,000, passenger-km 84,000,000; ton-mi cargo 218,200,000, metric ton-km cargo 351,000,000. Roads (1997): length 5,238 mi, 8,431 km (paved 100%). Vehicles (1996): passenger cars 1,300; trucks and buses 4,460. Air transport (1990): passenger-mi 3,453,000,000, passenger-km 5,556,900,000; short ton-mi cargo 34,000,000, metric ton-km cargo 49,000,000; airports (1998) 1.

Communications

Medium	date	unit	number	units per 1,000 persons
Daily newspapers	1995	circulation	80,000	23
Television	1997	receivers	820,000	216
Telephones	1998	main lines	569,000	150
Personal computers	1998	units	15,000	4.0
Internet	1998	users	4,000	1.1

Education and health

Educational attainment (1989). Percentage of population age 25 and over having: primary education or no formal schooling 7.4%; some secondary 18.6%; completed secondary and some postsecondary 57.7%; higher 13.8%. *Literacy* (1989): total population age 15 and over literate 98.8%; males literate 99.4%; females literate 98.1%.

Education (1996–97)

	schools	teachers	students	student/ teacher ratio
Primary (age 6–13)	1,402	13,620	256,475	18.8
Secondary (age 14–17)	...	57,325	365,025	6.4
Voc., teacher tr.[8]	69	...	25,200	...
Higher	14	4,065	35,517	8.7

Health (1994): physicians 13,000 (1 per 288 persons); hospital beds 30,000 (1 per 125 persons); infant mortality rate (1999) 41.1.
Food (1998): daily per capita caloric intake 2,356 (vegetable products 82%, animal products 18%); 92% of FAO recommended minimum requirement.

Military

Total active duty personnel (1998): 53,400 (army 100%). *Military expenditure as percentage of GNP* (1997): 3.5% (world 2.6%); per capita expenditure U.S.$100.

[1]The constitution provides for the right to practice the religion of one's choice. In practice, the law imposes restrictions on religious freedom. The 1991 Law on Religious Organizations establishes the separation of church and state but recognizes the Armenian Apostolic Church (the Armenian Orthodox Church) as having special status. The law requires all nonapostolic religious denominations to register with the Ministry of Justice and prohibits proselytizing. [2]Area of Lake Sevan. [3]In addition, nearly 20% of neighbouring Azerbaijan (including the 4,400-sq km geographic region of Nagorno-Karabakh [Armenian: Artsakh] has been occupied by Armenian forces since 1993. [4]Detail does not add to total given because of rounding. [5]About 1/5 of Armenia's population has left the country since 1993 because of an energy crisis. [6]1989; reduced in population by evacuation following Dec. 7, 1988, earthquake. [7]Includes 150,300 unemployed. [8]1993–94.

Internet resources for further information:
- **The Embassy of the Republic of Armenia http://www.armeniaemb.org**

Aruba

Official name: Aruba.
Political status: nonmetropolitan territory of The Netherlands with one legislative house (States of Aruba [21]).
Chief of state: Dutch Monarch represented by Governor.
Head of government: Prime Minister.
Capital: Oranjestad.
Official language: Dutch.
Official religion: none.
Monetary unit: 1 Aruban florin[1] (Af.) = 100 cents; valuation (Oct. 6, 2000) 1 U.S.$ = Af. 1.79; 1 £ = Af. 2.59.

Area and population

	area[2]		population
Census region	sq mi	sq km	1991 census
Noord/Tanki Leendert	14	37	10,056
Oranjestad East	5	13	11,266
Oranjestad West	4	10	8,779
Paradera	10	25	6,189
San Nicolas North	9	23	8,206
San Nicolas South	4	10	5,304
Santa Cruz	18	47	9,587
Savaneta	11	28	7,273
TOTAL	75	193	66,687[3, 4]

Demography

Population (2000): 96,800.
Density (2000): persons per sq mi 1,290.7, persons per sq km 501.6.
Urban-rural (1990): urban 68.4%; rural 31.6%.
Sex distribution (1999): male 49.41%; female 50.59%.
Age breakdown (1999): under 15, 22.3%; 15–29, 21.0%; 30–44, 27.8%; 45–59, 18.2%; 60–74, 8.1%; 75 and over, 2.6%.
Population projection: (2000) 102,000; (2010) 104,000.
Linguistic composition (1991): Papiamento 76.6%; English 8.9%; Spanish 7.4%; Dutch 5.4%; Portuguese 0.3%; other 1.4%[5].
Religious affiliation (1991): Christian 95.1%, of which Roman Catholic 86.2%, Protestant 7.6%, other Christian (Jehovah's Witness) 1.3%; Muslim 0.3%; Jewish 0.2%; nonreligious 2.7%; other 1.2%.
Major urban areas (1991): Oranjestad 20,045; San Nicolas 13,510.

Vital statistics

Birth rate per 1,000 population (1999): 13.6 (world avg. 22.1); (1998) legitimate 57.5%; illegitimate 42.5%.
Death rate per 1,000 population (1999): 6.1 (world avg. 8.9).
Natural increase rate per 1,000 population (1999): 6.7 (world avg. 13.2).
Total fertility rate (avg. births per childbearing woman; 1999): 1.8.
Marriage rate per 1,000 population (1998): 6.1.
Divorce rate per 1,000 population (1998): 3.6.
Life expectancy at birth (1999): male 74.8 years; female 81.7 years.
Major causes of death per 100,000 population (1998): diseases of the circulatory system 184.0, malignant neoplasms (cancers) 118.0, infectious and parasitic diseases/diseases of the respiratory system 61.7.

National economy

Budget (1999). Revenue: Af. 712,900,000 (tax revenue 85.4%, of which taxes on wages and income 32.1%, import duties 13.7%, taxes on profits 11.2%, excise taxes on gasoline 8.4%; nontax revenue 14.4%). Expenditures: Af. 736,900,000.
Production (metric tons except as noted). Agriculture, forestry, fishing: aloes are cultivated for export; small amounts of tomatoes, beans, cucumbers, gherkins, watermelons, and lettuce are grown on hydroponic farms; divi-divi pods, sour orange fruit, sorghum, and peanuts (groundnuts) are nonhydroponic crops of limited value; (livestock; number of live animals) Aruba has very few livestock; roundwood, n.a.; fish catch (1997) 205. Mining and quarrying: excavation of sand for local use. Manufacturing[6]: rum, cigarettes, aloe products, and soaps. Construction (value of residential and nonresidential buildings completed; 1992): Af. 16,900,000. Energy production (consumption): electricity (kW-hr; 1999) 738,000,000 (615,000,000); coal, none (none); crude petroleum (barrels; 1996) none (2,287,000); petroleum products (metric tons; 1996) none (238,000); natural gas, none (none).
Gross domestic product (1998): U.S.$1,728,000,000 (U.S.$18,700 per capita).

Structure of gross domestic product and labour force

	1994		1997	
	in value Af. '000,000	% of total value	labour force[7]	% of labour force[7]
Agriculture, Mining	12	0.5	198	0.4
			—	—
Manufacturing	130	5.5	2,627	5.9
Construction	156	6.5	3,395	7.6
Public utilities	77	3.2	810	1.8
Transp. and commun.	204	8.6	3,388	7.5
Trade, restaurants	636	26.7	14,240	31.8
Finance, real estate	254	10.7	4,634	10.3
Pub. admin., defense	316	13.3	4,349	9.7
Services	277	11.6	6,404	14.3
Other	319	13.4	4,795[8]	10.7[8]
TOTAL	2,381	100.0	44,840	100.0

Population economically active (1997)[7]: total 44,840; activity rate of total population 48.9% (participation rates: ages 15–64, 68.3%; female 43.8%; unemployed 7.4%).

Price and earnings indexes (1995 = 100)

	1993	1994	1995	1996	1997	1998	1999
Consumer price index	91.0	97.0	100.0	103.0	106.0	108.0	111.0
Earnings index[9]	...	92.6	100.0	103.2	106.4	108.9	...

Public debt (external, outstanding; 1998): U.S.$155,400,000.
Household income and expenditure (1999): average household size 3.6; average annual income per household: Af. 39,000 (U.S.$21,800); sources of income: n.a.; expenditure (1994)[10]: transportation and communications 20.7%, food and beverages 18.4%, clothing and footwear 11.3%, household furnishings 10.4%, housing 9.8%.
Tourism: receipts from visitors (1999) U.S.$777,700,000; expenditures by nationals abroad (1997) U.S.$130,000,000.
Land use (1998): forest, negligible; meadows and pastures, negligible, agricultural and under permanent cultivation 11.0%; other (dry savanna and built-up) 89.0%.

Foreign trade

Balance of trade (current prices)

	1994	1995	1996	1997	1998	1999
U.S.$'000,000	–311	–425	–308	–387	–347	–584
% of total	10.7%	13.6%	8.1%	10.1%	12.9%	17.1%

Imports (1999): U.S.$2,003,000,000 (petroleum [all forms] and free-zone imports 61.0%, electrical and nonelectrical machinery 8.0%, base and fabricated metals 4.3%). *Major import sources* (1999)[11]: United States 63.3%; The Netherlands 11.1%; Venezuela 3.0%; Netherlands Antilles 2.8%.
Exports (1999): U.S.$1,420,000,000 (petroleum [all forms] and free-zone exports 97.9%). *Major export destinations*[11]: United States 41.4%; Colombia 20.3%; The Netherlands 12.1%; Netherlands Antilles 8.4%.

Transport and communications

Transport. Railroads: none. Roads (1984): total length 236 mi, 380 km (paved 100%). Vehicles (1999): passenger cars 38,834; trucks and buses 990. Air transport (1998)[12]: passenger-mi 318,000,000, passenger-km 511,000,000; short ton-mi cargo, n.a., metric ton-mi cargo, n.a.; airports (1998) with scheduled flights 1.

Communications

Medium	date	unit	number	units per 1,000 persons
Daily newspapers	1996	circulation	73,000	851
Radio	1997	receivers	50,000	558
Television	1997	receivers	20,000	223
Telephones	1997	main lines	33,220	371
Cellular telephones	1998	subscribers	5,380	58

Education and health

Educational attainment (1991). Percentage of population age 25 and over having: no formal schooling or incomplete primary education 15.0%; completed primary 37.3%; completed lower secondary/vocational 28.1%; completed upper secondary/vocational 4.0%; higher vocational 5.5%; undergraduate 5.3%; graduate 1.7%; other 3.1%. *Literacy* (1990): percentage of total population age 15 and over literate 95.0%.

Education (1998–99)

	schools	teachers	students	student/ teacher ratio
Primary (age 6–12)	33	397	8,456	21.3
Secondary (age 12–17), Voc., teacher tr.	15	470	7,157	15.2
Higher	2	53	394	7.4

Health (1999): physicians (1997) 103 (1 per 870 persons); hospital beds 308 (1 per 306 persons); infant mortality rate per 1,000 live births 6.7.
Food (1997): n.a.

Military

Total active duty personnel (1999): a 45-member Dutch naval/air force contingent is stationed in Aruba and the Netherlands Antilles.

[1]The Aruban florin (Af.) is pegged to the U.S. dollar at a fixed rate of Af. 1.79 = 1 U.S.$. [2]Areas for census regions are approximate. [3]Includes 27 persons not distributed by census region. [4]Unadjusted census total; adjusted census total equals 67,423. [5]Most Arubans are racially and ethnically mixed; ethnic composition (1998): Amerindian/other 80%; other (primarily Dutch, Spanish and/or black) 20%. [6]Servicing facilities include a free zone, offshore corporate banking facilities, casino/resort complexes, a petroleum transshipment terminal, a cruise ship terminal, and ship repair and bunkering facilities. [7]Based on labour force survey of October 1. [8]Includes 3,339 unemployed. [9]Minimum wage in service and trade industries. [10]Weights of consumer price index components. [11]Excludes petroleum (all forms) and free-zone trade. [12]Air Aruba only.

Internet resources for further information:
- **Aruba Central Bureau of Statistics http://www.arubastatistics.com/toc.htm**
- **Centrale Bank van Aruba http://www.cbaruba.org**

Australia

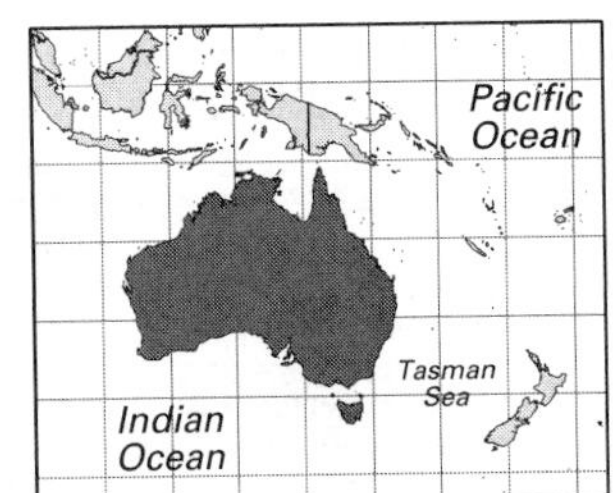

Official name: Commonwealth of Australia.
Form of government: federal parliamentary state (formally a constitutional monarchy) with two legislative houses (Senate [76]; House of Representatives [148]).
Chief of state: British Monarch represented by Governor-General.
Head of government: Prime Minister.
Capital: Canberra.
Official language: English.
Official religion: none.
Monetary unit: 1 Australian dollar ($A) = 100 cents; valuation (Oct. 6, 2000) 1 U.S.$ = $A 1.87; 1 £ = $A 2.70.

Area and population

		area		population
States	**Capitals**	sq mi	sq km	1998 estimate
New South Wales	Sydney	309,500	801,600	6,341,600
Queensland	Brisbane	666,900	1,727,200	3,456,300
South Australia	Adelaide	379,900	984,000	1,487,300
Tasmania	Hobart	26,200	67,800	471,900
Victoria	Melbourne	87,900	227,600	4,660,900
Western Australia	Perth	975,100	2,525,500	1,831,400
Territories				
Australian Capital Territory	Canberra	900	2,400	308,400
Northern Territory	Darwin	519,800	1,346,200	190,000
TOTAL		2,966,200	7,682,300	18,750,100[1]

Demography

Population (2000): 19,165,000.
Density (2000): persons per sq mi 6.5, persons per sq km 2.5.
Urban-rural (2000): urban 85.0%; rural 15.0%.
Sex distribution (1996): male 49.46%; female 50.54%.
Age breakdown (1996): under 15, 21.6%; 15–24, 14.5%; 25–44, 30.8%; 45–64, 21.0%; 65 and over, 12.1%.
Population projection: (2010) 20,925,000; (2020) 22,409,000.
Doubling time: over 100 years.
Ethnic composition (1996): white 95.2%; aboriginal 2.0%; Asian 1.3%; other 1.5%.
Religious affiliation (1996): Christian 70.9%, of which Roman Catholic 27.0%, Anglican Church of Australia 22.0%, other Protestant 21.9% (Uniting Church and Methodist 7.5%, Presbyterian 3.8%), Orthodox 2.8%, other Christian 2.4%; Muslim 1.1%; Buddhist 1.1%; Jewish 0.4%; Hindu 0.4%; no religion 16.6%; other 9.5%.
Metropolitan areas (1998): Sydney 3,986,700; Melbourne 3,371,300; Brisbane 1,574,600; Perth 1,341,900; Adelaide 1,088,400; Newcastle 473,900; Gold Coast–Tweed 379,200; Canberra-Queanbeyan 346,200; Wollongong 260,100; Hobart 195,000.
Place of birth (1998): 76.6% native-born; 23.4% foreign-born, of which Europe 10.9% (United Kingdom 6.6%[2], Italy 1.3%, Greece 0.8%, Germany 0.6%, The Netherlands 0.5%, other Europe 1.1%), Asia and Middle East 2.6%, New Zealand 1.8%, Africa, the Americas, and other 8.1%.
Mobility (1995–96). Population age 15 and over living in the same residence as in 1994: 81.6%; different residence between states, regions, and neighbourhoods 18.4%.
Households (1996). Total number of households 7,100,000. Average household size 2.6; couples only 34.1%, couples with dependent children only 40.6%, couples with nondependent children 9.0%, single parent with children 9.9%, other 6.4%.
Immigration (1996): permanent immigrants admitted 96,970, from United Kingdom and Ireland 12.8%, New Zealand 11.8%, China 7.6%, Vietnam 4.8%, Hong Kong 4.6%, India 4.4%, Philippines 3.9%, South Africa 3.2%, Bosnia and Herzegovina 3.2%, Yugoslavia 3.1%, Sri Lanka 2.2%. Refugee arrivals (1994–95): 13,600.

Vital statistics

Birth rate per 1,000 population (2000): 13.0 (world avg. 22.1); (1997) legitimate 72.0%; illegitimate 28.0%.
Death rate per 1,000 population (2000): 7.6 (world avg. 8.9).
Natural increase rate per 1,000 population (2000): 5.4 (world avg. 13.2).
Total fertility rate (avg. births per childbearing woman; 2000): 1.8.
Marriage rate per 1,000 population (1998): 5.9.
Divorce rate per 1,000 population (1998): 2.7.
Life expectancy at birth (2000): male 76.0 years; female 81.0 years.
Major causes of death per 100,000 population (1997): diseases of the circulatory system 238.2; cancers 221.2; respiratory diseases 61.9; accidents, poisoning, and violence 34.3; diabetes 15.4; suicides 14.7.

Social indicators

Educational attainment (1995). Percentage of population age 15 to 64 having: no formal schooling 0.3%; incomplete secondary education 36.3%; completed secondary 17.8%[3, 4]; postsecondary, technical, or other certificate/diploma 33.7%; university 11.9%.
Quality of working life (1996–97). Average workweek: 35.8 hours (16.8%[4] overtime). Annual rate per 100,000 workers for: accidental injury and industrial disease, 3,200[5]; death, n.a. Proportion of employed persons insured for damages or income loss resulting from: injury 100%[5]; permanent disability 100%[5]; death 100%[5]. Working days lost to industrial disputes per 1,000 employees (1996): 131. Means of transportation to work (1986): private automobile 69.4%; public transportation 10.1%; motorcycle and bicycle 3.2%; foot 6.6%; other 10.7%. Discouraged job seekers (considered by employers to be too young or too old, having language or training limitations, or no vacancies in line of work; 1996): 1.3% of labour force.

Distribution of household income (1995–96)

percentage of household income by quintile

lowest	second	third	fourth	highest
3.8%	9.1%	15.1%	23.7%	48.3%

Access to services (1976). Proportion of dwellings having access to: electricity 99.5%; bathroom 96.0%; flush toilet 92.2%; kitchen 97.9%; public sewer 73.4%.
Social participation. Eligible voters participating in last national election (1996): 95.8%; voting is compulsory. Population age 16 and over participating in voluntary work: n.a. Trade union membership in total workforce (1996): 31%.
Social deviance (1996). Offense rate per 100,000 population for: murder 3.8; sexual assault 78.7; assault 620.8; auto theft 672.2; unarmed robbery, burglary, and housebreaking 4,608.2; armed robbery 34.0. Incidence per 100,000 in general population of: alcoholism, n.a.; prisoners with drug offenses 539.5; suicide (1996) 13.1.
Material well-being (1995). Households possessing: automobile 85%; telephone 95%; refrigerator 99.7%; air conditioner 32.3%[6]; personal computers 23.0%[4]; washing machine 90.0%; central heating 3.9%[6]; swimming pool 10.1%[6].

National economy

Gross national product (1998): U.S.$387,006,000,000 (U.S.$20,640 per capita).

Structure of gross domestic product and labour force

	1995–96[7]		1996–97	
	in value $A '000,000	% of total value	labour force	% of labour force
Agriculture	15,873	3.7	437,700	4.7
Mining	18,668	4.3	81,300	0.9
Manufacturing	59,184	13.6	1,138,300	12.3
Construction	27,147	6.2	578,400	6.3
Public utilities	13,707	3.2	65,800	0.7
Transp. and commun.	40,642	9.4	548,100	6.0
Trade[8]	74,547	17.2	2,117,700	23.0
Finance, real estate	93,783	21.6	1,175,400	12.8
Pub. admin., defense	15,393	3.5	350,500	3.8
Services	67,268	15.5	1,898,800	20.6
Other	7,680[9]	1.8[9]	818,900[10]	8.9[10]
TOTAL	433,892	100.0	9,210,900	100.0

Budget (1996–97). Revenue: $A 130,160,000,000 (income tax 71.2%, of which individual 50.7%, corporate 15.1%; excise duties and sales tax 21.0%). Expenditures: $A 129,686,000,000 (social security and welfare 37.7%; health 15.0%; economic and public services 12.7%; transfers to state governments 12.9%; interest on public debt 7.5%).
Public debt (1997–98): $A 88,880,000,000.
Tourism (1998): receipts from visitors U.S.$7,335,000,000; expenditures by nationals abroad U.S.$5,388,000,000.

Manufacturing, mining, and construction enterprises (1995–96)[11]

	no. of establishments[12]	no. of employees	Turnover per person employed ($A '000)	annual turnover ($A '000,000)
Manufacturing				
Food, beverages, and tobacco	3,514	162,700	264.7	43,067
Metal products	7,522	147,700	250.0	36,918
Machinery and equipment	8,988	204,700	189.1	38,704
Chemical, petroleum, and coal products	3,009	89,500	335.8	30,058
Printing and publishing	5,265	90,800	150.6	13,675
Miscellaneous manufacturing	5,973	53,700	105.5	5,664
Wood and paper products	3,973	60,400	189.5	11,446
Nonmetallic mineral products	1,909	37,700	228.1	8,599
Textile, clothing, footwear, and leather	4,456	75,900	129.5	9,832
Mining				
Coal, oil, and gas	254	29,359	596.1	17,501
Metallic minerals	261	27,088	488.5	13,232
Nonmetallic minerals[13]	699	8,799	254.6	2,240
Construction[14]	98,100	518,200	...	34,407

Production (gross value in $A '000 except as noted). Agriculture, forestry, fishing (1996–97): livestock slaughtered 6,190,100 (cattle 3,390,100, sheep and lambs 1,038,900, poultry 1,053,300, pigs 671,100); wheat 4,878,000, wool 2,621,200, seed cotton 1,342,000, barley 1,306,100, sugarcane 1,186,400, grapes 722,600, potatoes 449,000, apples 393,800, rice 310,000, oranges 264,800, sorghum 257,000, lupins 250,000, canola 239,000, oats 227,000, bananas 217,000, tomatoes 177,000, carrots 142,000, pears 106,400, corn (maize) 80,000, peaches 60,000, tobacco 54,000, sunflower 47,000, pineapples 39,000; livestock (number of live animals; 1998) 119,600,000 sheep, 26,710,000 cattle, 2,680,000 pigs, 83,000,000 poultry; roundwood (1998) 23,059,000 cu m; fish catch (1996) 219,499 metric tons. Mining and quarrying (metric tons [tons of contained metal]; 1997): iron ore 157,100,000; bauxite 44,400,000; zinc 1,000,000; lead 531,000; copper 445,000; tin 10,158; gold 311,300 kg; diamonds 40,100,000 carats. Manufacturing (value added in U.S.$'000,000 except as noted; 1995): food products 12,239; transport equipment 5,745; printing and publishing 5,252; metal products 4,840; nonferrous metals 4,766; nonelectrical machinery 4,054. Construction (buildings completed, by value in $A '000; 1996–97): new dwellings 12,997,000; alterations and additions to dwellings 2,567,000; nonresidential 12,689,000.

Retail and service enterprises (1991–92)

	no. of estab-lishments	no. of employees	total wages and salaries ($A '000,000)	annual turnover ($A '000,000)
Retail				
Motor vehicle dealers, gasoline and tire dealers	37,305	220,661	2,572[15]	44,954
Food stores	53,166	406,299	2,461[15]	40,467[16]
Department and general stores	459	87,148	1,175[15]	10,607[16]
Clothing, fabrics, and furniture stores	21,688	91,138	965[15]	8,003[16]
Household appliances and hardware stores	14,268	75,355	629	14,429[16]
Recreational goods	...	...	...	5,879[16]
Services[5]				
Real estate agents	8,082[16]	45,956[16]	...	3,369.6[16]
Architectural services	4,409	16,204	...	945.2
Surveying services	1,175	6,964	...	481.2
Consulting engineering services	5,514[16]	30,736[16]	...	3,233.3[16]
Legal services	9,796[16]	67,494[16]	...	5,590.9[16]
Accounting services	8,389[16]	66,792[16]	...	4,939.1[16]
Computing services	9,679[16]	55,046[16]	...	8,088.3[16]
Advertising services	858	9,083	...	842.1
Market research services	174	8,064	...	251.7
Business management services	686	4,933	...	506.6

Energy production (consumption): electricity (kW-hr; 1994) 167,151,000,000 (167,151,000,000); coal (metric tons; 1994) 176,078,000 (52,678,000); crude petroleum (barrels; 1994) 159,160,000 (202,490,000); petroleum products (metric tons; 1994) 33,086,000 (33,707,000); natural gas (cu m; 1994) 25,185,000,000 (17,438,000,000).

Population economically active (1996–97): total 9,210,900; activity rate of total population 50.4% (participation rates: over age 15, 64.3%; female 43.1%; unemployed 8.6%).

Price and earnings indexes (1995 = 100)

	1992	1993	1994	1995	1996	1997	1998
Consumer price index	92.1	93.8	95.6	100.0	102.6	102.9	103.7
Weekly earnings index	90.4	92.1	95.1	100.0	104.0	108.3	112.7

Household income and expenditure (1995–96). Average household size 2.6; average annual income per household $A 31,700 (U.S.$24,200); sources of income: wages and salaries 55.5%, transfer payments 29.0%, self-employment 6.5%, other 9.0%; expenditure: food and beverages 18.4%, transportation and communications 15.5%, housing 14.2%, recreation 13.2%, household durable goods 6.6%, clothing and footwear 5.6%, health 4.5%, energy 2.8%, other 19.2%.

Financial aggregates

	1993	1994	1995	1996	1997	1998	1999[17]
Exchange rate, $A 1.00 per:							
U.S. dollar	0.68	0.73	0.74	0.79	0.74	0.63	0.66
£	0.45	0.48	0.47	0.50	0.45	0.38	0.42
SDR	0.49	0.53	0.50	0.55	0.48	0.44	0.48
International reserves (U.S.$)							
Total (excl. gold; '000,000)	11,102	11,285	11,896	14,485	16,845	15,407	15,196
SDRs ('000,000)	82	73	55	37	19	18	59
Reserve pos. in IMF ('000,000)	550	506	502	482	727	1,256	1,573
Foreign exchange ('000,000)	10,470	10,076	11,340	13,967	16,099	14,133	13,564
Gold ('000,000 fine troy oz)	7.90	7.90	7.90	7.90	2.56	2.56	2.56
% world reserves	0.9	0.9	0.9	0.9	0.3	0.3	0.3
Interest and prices							
Central bank discount (%)	5.83	5.75	5.75	5.75	...	...	...
Govt. bond yield (short-term; %)	5.63	8.19	8.42	7.53	6.00	5.02	5.53
Industrial share prices (1995 = 100)	88.8	101.4	100.0	111.6	125.4	131.2	150.4
Balance of payments (U.S.$'000,000)							
Balance of visible trade	−29	−3,277	−4,223	−635	1,849	−5,397	...
Imports, f.o.b.	42,666	50,648	57,443	61,032	63,044	61,236	...
Exports, f.o.b.	42,637	47,371	53,220	60,397	64,893	55,839	...
Balance of invisibles	−9,841	−14,139	−15,431	−15,380	−14,580	−12,087	...
Balance of payments, current account	−9,870	−17,416	−19,654	−16,015	−12,731	−17,484	...

Land use (1995): agricultural and under permanent cultivation 6.3%; other 93.7% (of which, meadows and pastures [1994] 54.2%).

Foreign trade[18]

Balance of trade (current prices)

	1994	1995	1996	1997	1998	1999[19]
$A '000,000	−3,183	−5,810	−1,424	−1,423	−7,808	−3,295
% of total	2.4%	3.9%	0.9%	0.8%	4.2%	7.5%

Imports (1997–98): $A 90,680,000,000 (machinery and transport equipment 46.2%, of which road motor vehicles 12.5%, office machines and automatic data-processing equipment 7.7%, electrical machinery 6.0%; basic manufactures 13.8%, of which textile yarn and fabrics 2.8%, iron and steel 2.6%; chemicals and related products 11.3%; mineral fuels and lubricants 4.9%; food and live animals 3.8%). *Major import sources:* U.S. 21.9%; Japan 14.0%; U.K. 6.2%; China 5.8%; Germany 5.7%.

Exports (1995–96): $A 87,766,000,000 (crude materials excluding fuels 20.4%, of which metalliferous ores and metal scrap 11.9%, textile fibres and their waste 5.8%; food and live animals 18.3%, of which cereals and cereal preparations 5.8%, meat and meat preparations 4.2%, dairy products 2.2%; mineral fuels and lubricants 17.5%, of which coal, coke, and briquettes 10.9%, petroleum, petroleum products, and natural gas 4.4%; basic manufactures 12.1%). *Major export destinations:* Japan 20.0%; U.S. 8.9%; South Korea 7.3%; New Zealand 6.5%; Taiwan 4.8%; Hong Kong 4.7%; China 4.4%; Singapore 4.2%.

Trade by commodity group (1996–97)

	imports		exports	
SITC Group	U.S.$'000,000	%	U.S.$'000,000	%
00 Food and live animals	2,277	3.7	12,366	20.5
01 Beverages and tobacco	400	0.7	577	1.0
02 Crude materials, excluding fuels	1,183	1.9	10,955	18.2
03 Mineral fuels, lubricants, and related materials	3,872	6.3	10,189	16.9
04 Animal and vegetable oils, fat, and waxes	214	0.4	187	0.3
05 Chemicals and related products, n.e.s.	6,840	11.1	2,287	3.8
06 Basic manufactures	8,414	13.7	7,817	13.0
07 Machinery and transport equipment	28,777	46.9	7,769	12.9
08 Miscellaneous manufactured articles	8,658	14.1	2,220	3.7
09 Goods not classified by kind	765	1.2	5,837	9.7
TOTAL	61,400	100.0	60,204	100.0

Direction of trade (1996–97)

	imports		exports	
	U.S.$'000,000	%	U.S.$'000,000	%
Africa	496	0.8	1,378	2.3
Asia	24,246	39.5	38,846	64.5
Japan	7,998	13.0	12,184	20.2
South America	648	1.1	730	1.2
North and Central America	15,466	25.2	4,915	8.2
United States	14,328	23.3	3,897	6.5
Europe	16,275	26.5	7,225	12.0
European Union	15,256	24.8	6,536	10.9
Russia	20	0.03	80	0.1
Other Europe	999	1.6	609	1.0
Oceania	4,117	6.7	6,317	10.5
New Zealand	2,874	4.7	4,432	7.4
Other	152	0.2	793	1.3
TOTAL	61,400	100.0	60,204	100.0

Transport and communications

Transport. Railroads (1996–97)[20]: route length (1997) 20,567 mi, 33,099 km; passenger journeys 455,850,000; short ton-mi cargo 46,697,000,000, metric ton-km cargo 68,176,000,000. Roads (1996): total length 567,300 mi, 913,000 km (paved 39%). Vehicles (1996): passenger cars 8,879,000; trucks and buses 2,129,470. Merchant marine (1994): vessels (150 gross tons and over) 90; total deadweight tonnage 3,499,527. Air transport (1998)[21]: passenger-mi 45,354,000,000, passenger-km 72,990,000,000; short ton-mi cargo 1,304,000,000, metric ton-km cargo 1,904,000,000; airports (1996) with scheduled flights 400.

Communications

Medium	date	unit	number	units per 1,000 persons
Daily newspapers	1996	circulation	5,370,000	296
Radio	1997	receivers	25,500,000	1,391
Television	1997	receivers	10,150,000	554
Telephones	1998	main lines	9,540,000	509
Cellular telephones	1998	subscribers	5,342,000	285
Personal computers	1998	units	7,700,000	411
Internet	1998	users	3,000,000	160

Education and health

Literacy (1996): total population literate, virtually 100%[22].

Education (1996)

	schools	teachers	students	student/ teacher ratio
Primary (age 6–12)	7,713	102,267	1,848,169	18.1
Secondary (age 13–17)	1,917	101,706	1,294,846	12.7
Vocational[23]	541	26,345	985,428	37.4
Higher	44[24]	26,920	634,094	23.6

Health (1996–97): physicians 47,400 (1 per 389 persons); hospital beds 80,965 (1 per 227 persons); infant mortality rate (2000) 6.0.

Food (1997): daily per capita caloric intake 3,224 (vegetable products 68%, animal products 32%); (1995) 115% of FAO recommended minimum requirement.

Military

Total active duty personnel (1998): 57,400 (army 44.3%, navy 24.9%, air force 30.8%). *Military expenditure as percentage of GNP* (1995): 2.5% (world 2.8%); per capita expenditure U.S.$465.

[1]Total includes 2,300 persons in nondelimited areas. [2]Includes both Northern Ireland and Republic of Ireland. [3]Completed highest level of secondary school available. [4]1994. [5]1992–93. [6]1983. [7]At 1989–90 prices. [8]Trade includes hotels and restaurants. [9]Less imputed bank service charges. [10]Mostly unemployed. [11]Excludes operations of single-establishment enterprises employing fewer than four persons. [12]1993–94. [13]1990–91. [14]1991–92. [15]1985–86. [16]1995–96. [17]July. [18]Exports and imports are f.o.b. in the balance of trade table. [19]Second quarter. [20]Government railways only. [21]Includes Qantas and Ansett Australia. [22]A national survey conducted in 1996 put the number of persons who had very poor literacy and numeracy skills at about 17% of the total population (age 15 to 64). [23]Includes special education. [24]1991.

Internet resources for further information:

- **Australian Bureau of Statistics http://www.abs.gov.au**

Austria

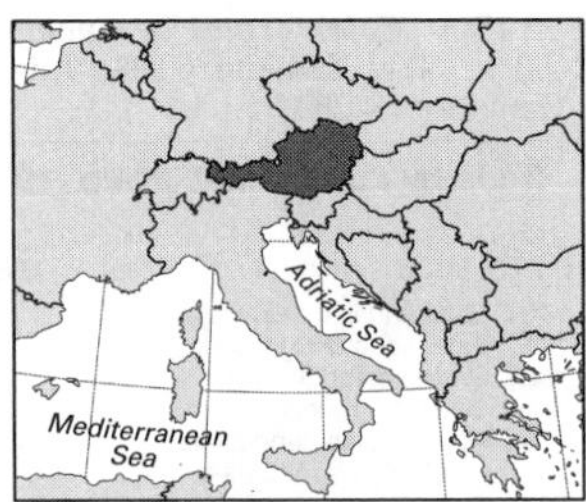

Official name: Republik Österreich (Republic of Austria).
Form of government: federal state with two legislative houses (Federal Council [64]; National Council [183]).
Chief of state: President.
Head of government: Chancellor.
Capital: Vienna.
Official language: German.
Official religion: none.
Monetary unit: 1 Austrian Schilling (S) = 100 Groschen; valuation (Oct. 6, 2000) 1 U.S.$ = S 15.82; 1 £ = S 22.89.

Area and population

		area		population
States	Capitals	sq mi	sq km	1999 estimate[1]
Burgenland	Eisenstadt	1,531	3,966	279,752
Kärnten	Klagenfurt	3,681	9,533	564,431
Niederösterreich	Sankt Pölten	7,403	19,174	1,534,001
Oberösterreich	Linz	4,626	11,980	1,372,407
Salzburg	Salzburg	2,762	7,154	513,853
Steiermark	Graz	6,327	16,388	1,204,904
Tirol	Innsbruck	4,883	12,647	661,901
Vorarlberg	Bregenz	1,004	2,601	345,272
Wien (Vienna)	—	160	415	1,609,631
TOTAL		32,378[2]	83,858	8,086,152

Demography

Population (2000): 8,091,000.
Density (2000): persons per sq mi 249.9, persons per sq km 96.5.
Urban-rural (1999): urban 64.6%; rural 35.4%
Sex distribution (1998): male 48.53%; female 51.47%.
Age breakdown (1998): under 15, 17.1%; 15–29, 19.8%; 30–44, 24.5%; 45–59, 18.8%; 60–74, 13.0%; 75 and over, 6.8%.
Population projection: (2010) 8,051,000; (2020) 8,096,000.
Doubling time: not applicable; population is stable.
Ethnic composition (national origin; 1998): Austrian 91.2%; citizens of former Yugoslavia 4.0%; Turkish 1.6%; other 3.2%.
Religious affiliation (1995): Roman Catholic 75.1%; nonreligious and atheist 8.6%; Protestant (mostly Lutheran) 5.4%; Muslim 2.1%; Eastern Orthodox 0.7%; Jewish 0.1%; other 1.9%; unknown 6.1%.
Major cities (1999[1]): Vienna 1,609,631; Graz 239,990; Linz 189,073; Salzburg 144,692; Innsbruck 110,454.

Vital statistics

Birth rate per 1,000 population (1999): 9.6 (world avg. 22.1); (1997) legitimate 70.5%; illegitimate 29.5%.
Death rate per 1,000 population (1999): 9.6 (world avg. 8.9).
Natural increase rate per 1,000 population (1999): 0.0 (world avg. 13.2).
Total fertility rate (avg. births per childbearing woman; 1998): 1.3.
Marriage rate per 1,000 population (1998): 4.8.
Divorce rate per 1,000 population (1998): 2.2.
Life expectancy at birth (1998): male 74.7 years; female 80.9 years.
Major causes of death per 100,000 population (1997): diseases of the circulatory system 533.1; malignant neoplasms (cancers) 239.2.

National economy

Budget (1996). Revenue: S 916,040,000,000 (tax revenue 90.9%, of which social security contributions 37.7%, value-added taxes 16.4%, individual income taxes 15.6%). Expenditures: S 1,009,890,000,000 (social security and welfare 41.2%; health 13.0%; education 9.2%; defense 2.6%).
National debt (end of year 1997): U.S.$120,936,000,000.
Production (metric tons except as noted). Agriculture, forestry, fishing (1998): sugar beets 2,930,000, corn (maize) 1,573,000, wheat 1,342,000, barley 1,212,000, potatoes 663,000, apples 392,000, rye 236,000, grapes 234,000, oats 203,000, rapeseed 144,000; livestock (number of live animals) 3,680,000 pigs, 2,198,000 cattle, 13,950,000 chickens; roundwood 15,325,000 cu m; fish catch (1996) 4,458. Mining and quarrying (1997): iron ore 1,794,000; magnesite 790,000; talc 142,000; high-grade graphite 12,600. Manufacturing (value added in S '000,000,000; 1995): electrical machinery and apparatus 46.7; food and beverages 46.2; nonelectrical machinery and apparatus 41.3; fabricated metals 38.9; chemicals and chemical products 38.7; transport equipment 23.3. Construction (completed in S '000,000,000; 1994): residential 31.1; nonresidential; 28.9. Energy production (consumption): electricity (kW-hr; 1998) 57,396,000 ([1995] 54,077,000,000); coal (metric tons; 1996) 1,104,000 ([1995] 5,050,000); crude petroleum (barrels; 1996) 6,799,000 ([1995] 63,053,000); petroleum products (metric tons; 1995) 7,989,000 (10,186,000); natural gas (cu m; 1996) 1,632,000,000 ([1995] 8,013,000,000).
Tourism (U.S.$'000,000; 1998): receipts U.S.$11,184; expenditures U.S.$9,511.
Population economically active (1997): total 3,884,000; activity rate of total population 48.1% (participation rates: ages 15–64 70.7%; female 42.9%; unemployed [1998] 7.2%).

Price and earnings indexes (1995 = 100)

	1994	1995	1996	1997	1998	1999	2000
Consumer price index	97.8	100.0	101.8	103.2	104.1	104.7	107.3[3]
Contractual earnings index	96.7	100.0	102.4	104.2	...	...	...

Gross national product (at current market prices; 1998): U.S.$216,697,000,000 (U.S.$26,830 per capita).

Structure of gross domestic product and labour force

	1997			
	in value S '000,000	% of total value	labour force	% of labour force
Agriculture	34,890	1.4	256,000	6.6
Mining	8,730	0.3	9,400	0.2
Manufacturing	513,630	20.4	795,500	20.5
Construction	188,550	7.5	334,900	8.6
Public utilities	70,610	2.8	38,500	1.0
Transp. and commun.	156,220	6.2	239,500	6.2
Trade, restaurants	425,990	16.9	845,700	21.8
Finance, real estate	536,500	21.3	397,000	10.2
Pub. admin., defense	284,130	11.3	} 967,800	24.9
Services	202,810	8.1		
Other	92,310[4]	3.7[4]		
TOTAL	2,514,370[2]	100.0[2]	3,884,000[2]	100.0

Household income and expenditure. Average household size (1997) 2.5; net median income per household (1993) S 291,930 (U.S.$25,110); expenditure (1994): food and beverages 16.6%, transportation and communications 15.9%, housing 15.1%, cafe and hotel expenditures 10.5%.
Land use (1994): forested 39.2%; meadows and pastures 24.3%; agricultural and under permanent cultivation 18.3%; other 18.2%.

Foreign trade[5]

Balance of trade (current prices)

	1994	1995	1996	1997	1998	1999
S '000,000,000	–116.4	–88.0	–100.6	–75.3	–67.4	–68.2
% of total	10.2%	7.1%	7.6%	5.0%	4.2%	4.0%

Imports (1997): S 790,300,000,000 (machinery and transport equipment 38.2%, of which road vehicles 11.0%, electrical machinery and apparatus 7.3%; chemicals and related products 10.6%; food products 5.6%; clothing 4.5%). *Major import sources:* Germany 41.7%; Italy 8.5%; United States 5.4%; France 4.7%; Switzerland 3.3%; The Netherlands 3.3%.
Exports (1997): S 715,000,000,000 (machinery and transport equipment 41.0%, of which road vehicles 8.6%, electrical machinery and apparatus 7.7%; chemical products 9.7%; paper and paper products 5.1%; fabricated metals 4.9%). *Major export destinations:* Germany 35.1%; Italy 8.3%; Switzerland 4.9%; Hungary 4.9%; France 4.1%; United Kingdom 4.1%.

Transport and communications

Transport. Railroads (1997)[6]: length 5,672 km; passenger-km 8,652,000,000; (1998) metric ton-km cargo 15,348,000,000. Roads (1997): total length 200,000 km (paved 100%). Vehicles (1997): passenger cars 3,782,544; trucks and buses 310,444. Air transport[7] (1998): passenger-km 11,020,000,000; metric ton-km cargo 264,656,000; airports (1996) with scheduled flights 6.

Communications

Medium	date	unit	number	units per 1,000 persons
Daily newspapers	1996	circulation	2,382,000	296
Radio	1996	receivers	6,000,000	744
Television	1997	receivers	4,000,000	496
Telephones	1998	main lines	3,999,000	495
Cellular telephones	1998	subscribers	2,030,000	251
Personal computers	1998	units	1,900,000	235
Internet	1998	users	1,100,000	136

Education and health

Educational attainment (1993). Percentage of population age 25 and over having: lower-secondary education 37.5%; vocational education ending at secondary level 44.6%; completed upper secondary 6.1%; higher vocational 5.5%; higher 6.3%. *Literacy:* virtually 100%.

Education (1997–98)

	schools	teachers	students	student/ teacher ratio
Primary/lower secondary (age 6–13)	4,539	66,466	649,075	9.8
Upper secondary/voc. (age 14–17)	700	40,305	306,691	7.6
Higher	44[8]	16,045	224,935	14.0

Health (1996): physicians 27,869[9] (1 per 289 persons); hospital beds 68,641 (1 per 117 persons); infant mortality rate per 1,000 live births (1999) 4.4.
Food (1997): daily per capita caloric intake 3,536 (vegetable products 64%, animal products 36%); 134% of FAO recommended minimum requirement.

Military

Total active duty personnel (1999): 40,500 (army 89.5%; navy, none; air force 10.5%). *Military expenditure as percentage of GNP* (1997): 0.9% (world 2.6%); per capita expenditure U.S.$222.

[1]January 1. [2]Detail does not add total given because of rounding. [3]June. [4]Value-added tax plus import duties (S 224,510,000,000) less imputed bank service charges (S 132,200,000,000) [5]Imports c.i.f., exports f.o.b. [6]Federal railways only. [7]Austrian Airlines and Lauda Air. [8]1994–95. [9]Includes 6,506 doctors in training.

Internet resources for further information:
- **Austrian Central Office of Statistics http://www.oestat.gv.at**
- **Austrian Press and Information Service (Washington, D.C.) http://www.austria.org/index.html**

Azerbaijan

Official name: Azärbayean Respsublikası (Azerbaijani Republic).
Form of government: federal multiparty republic with a single legislative body (National Assembly [125[1]]).
Head of state and government: President assisted by Prime Minister.
Capital: Baku (Azerbaijani: Bakı).
Official language: Azerbaijani.
Official religion: none.
Monetary unit: 1 manat (A.M.) = 100 gopik; valuation (Oct. 6, 2000) free rate, 1 U.S.$ = A.M. 4,537; 1 £ = A.M. 6,563.

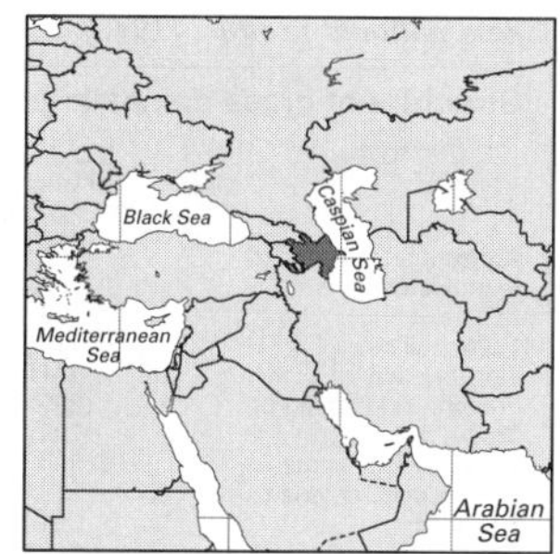

Area and population

Administative/ geographic units	Capitals	area sq mi	area sq km	population 1991 estimate
Autonomous Republic				
Naxçıvan	Naxçıvan	2,100	5,500	305,700
Geographic region				
Nagorno-Karabakh[2]	Xankändi (Stepanakert)	1,700	4,400	193,300
Capital city				
Baku (Bakı)	—	...	...	1,713,300
Others[3]	—	29,600	76,700	4,924,300
TOTAL		33,400	86,600	7,136,600

Demography

Population (2000): 8,051,000.
Density (2000): persons per sq mi 241.0, persons per sq km 93.0.
Urban-rural (1998): urban 56.6%; rural 43.4%.
Sex distribution (1999): male 49.1%; female 50.9%.
Age breakdown (1999): under 15, 32.8%; 15–29, 25.9%; 30–44, 22.3%; 45–59, 10.0%; 60–69, 5.9%; 70 and over, 3.1%.
Population projection: (2010) 8,542,000; (2020) 9,467,000.
Doubling time: 58 years.
Ethnic composition (1995): Azerbaijani 89.0%; Russian 3.0%; Lezgian 2.2%; Armenian 2.0%; other 3.8%.
Religious affiliation (1995): Muslim (mostly Shīʿī) 93.4%; Russian Orthodox 1.1%; Armenian Apostolic (Orthodox) 1.1%; other 4.4%.
Major cities (1997): Baku 1,727,200; Gäncä (formerly Kirovabad) 291,900; Sumqayıt (Sumgait) 248,500; Mingäçevir (Mingechaur) 97,200.

Vital statistics

Birth rate per 1,000 population (1999): 21.6 (world avg. 22.1); (1994) legitimate 94.8%; illegitimate 5.2%.
Death rate per 1,000 population (1999): 9.5 (world avg. 8.9).
Natural increase rate per 1,000 population (1999): 12.1 (world avg. 13.2).
Total fertility rate (avg. births per childbearing woman; 1999): 2.7.
Marriage rate per 1,000 population (1994): 6.3.
Divorce rate per 1,000 population (1994): 0.8.
Life expectancy at birth (1999): male 58.8 years; female 67.6 years.
Major causes of death per 100,000 population (1994): diseases of the circulatory system 336.3; accidents, poisoning, and violence 99.1; diseases of the respiratory system 98.6; malignant neoplasms (cancers) 67.6; diseases of the digestive system 31.7; infectious and parasitic diseases 29.0; endocrine and metabolic disorders 14.2; diseases of the nervous system 12.1.

National economy

Budget (1998). Revenue: A.M. 2,318,400,000,000 (tax revenue 93.7%, of which value-added tax 30.0%, individual income tax 17.8%, enterprise profits tax 14.1%, tax on international trade 12.6%, property tax 7.4%, excise tax 4.1%, other taxes 7.7%; nontax revenue 6.3%). Expenditures: A.M. 2,642,200,000,000 (social protection 23.3%; education 21.4%; national economy 8.6%; health 5.8%; culture 3.5%; other 37.4%).
Public debt (external, outstanding; 1998): U.S.$307,700,000.
Production (metric tons except as noted). Agriculture, forestry, fishing (1999): cereals 932,111, fruit 482,846, vegetables (except potatoes) 369,000, potatoes 334,000, cotton lint 39,000, tobacco leaves 9,000, tea 856; livestock (number of live animals) 5,502,800 sheep and goats, 1,909,800 cattle, 55,800 horses, 26,100 pigs, 13,300,000 poultry; roundwood (1993) 17,000 cu m; fish catch (1998) 4,678. Mining and quarrying (1996): iron ore 1,000,000; alunite 600,000. Manufacturing (value of production in A.M. '000,000,000; 1998): oil refinery products 2,980; electricity and gas 2,005; food products 1,972; textiles 468; chemicals 320; machine-building and metalworking equipment 249; minerals 137. Construction (1998): completed residential 532,000 sq m. Energy production (consumption): electricity (kW-hr; 1997) 16,800,000,000 (16,800,000,000); coal (metric tons; 1994) none (8,000); crude petroleum (barrels; 1997) 66,703,000 (76,672,000); petroleum products (metric tons; 1998) 7,800,000 (6,200,000); natural gas (cu m; 1998) 6,000,000,000 (6,000,000,000).
Household income and expenditure. Average household size (1997) 5.2; income per household: n.a.; sources of income (1993): wages and salaries 50.9%, agricultural income 24.0%, social benefits 10.2%; expenditure: food 61.2%, clothing 11.1%, services 3.0%.
Tourism (1998): receipts from visitors U.S.$125,000,000; expenditures by nationals abroad U.S.$170,000,000.
Gross national product (at current market prices; 1998): U.S.$3,821,000,000 (U.S.$480 per capita).

Structure of gross domestic product and labour force

	1998 in value A.M. '000,000[4]	% of total value[4]	labour force	% of labour force
Agriculture	3,472,700	21.8	835,500	22.3
Mining / Manufacturing	3,807,200	23.9	240,200	6.4
Public utilities	286,700	1.8	95,500	2.6
Construction	2,803,600	17.6	155,600	4.2
Transp. and commun.	2,198,300	13.8	168,300	4.5
Trade	971,700	6.1	704,000	18.8
Finance	270,800	1.7	11,000	0.3
Pub. admin., defense	2,118,700 (Pub. admin., Services, Other)	13.3	68,000	1.8
Services			590,500	15.8
Other			875,200[5]	23.4[5]
TOTAL	15,929,700	100.0	3,743,800	100.0[6]

Population economically active (1998): total 3,743,800, activity rate of total population 47.1% (participation rates: ages 15–59 [male], 15–54 [female] 85.9%; female 82.1%; unemployed 1.3%).

Price and earnings indexes (1995 = 100)

	1995	1996	1997	1998
Consumer price index	100.0	119.9	99.5	99.2
Monthly earnings index	...	...	...	...

Land use (1994): forest 11.0%; pasture 25.4%; agriculture 48.5%; other 15.1%.

Foreign trade[7]

Balance of trade (current prices)

	1993	1994	1995	1996	1997	1998
U.S.$'000,000	+357.6	–140.4	–122.0	–329.4	–13.0	–471
% of total	22.0%	9.9%	10.1%	20.7%	0.8%	28.0%

Imports (1998): U.S.$1,077,169,100 (machinery and equipment 40.4%, food 16.4%, metals 12.4%, chemical products 7.4%). *Major import sources:* Turkey 20.4%; Russia 18.0%; Ukraine 8.6%; U.K. 6.4%; Germany 4.3%; U.A.E. 4.2%; Iran 4.0%; U.S. 3.7%.
Exports (1998): U.S.$606,150,500,000 (petroleum products 69.1%, textile 9.2%, food 7.7%, machinery and equipment 6.0%, metals 2.2%). *Major export destinations:* Turkey 22.4%; Russia 17.4%; Georgia 12.7%; Italy 7.4%.

Transport and communications

Transport. Railroads (1998): length 2,120 km; passenger-km (1996) 550,000,000; metric ton-km cargo 4,613,000,000. Roads (1998): total length 45,870 km (paved 93.8%). Vehicles (1998): passenger cars 281,100; trucks and buses 104,300. Merchant marine (1998): vessels (100 gross tons and over) 69; total deadweight tonnage, n.a. Air transport (1995): passenger-km 1,650,000,000; metric ton-km cargo 183,000,000; airports (1998) with scheduled flights 3.

Communications

Medium	date	unit	number	units per 1,000 persons
Daily newspapers	1995	circulation	210,000	28
Television	1998	receivers	1,600,000	202
Telephones	1999	main lines	680,000	81
Cellular telephones	1999	subscribers	65,000	13.1
Internet	1998	users	950	0.1

Education and health

Educational attainment (1995). Percentage of population age 15 and over having: primary education or no formal schooling 12.1%, some secondary 9.1%; completed secondary and some postsecondary 27.5%; higher 7.6%. *Literacy* (1989): percentage of total population 15 and over literate 97.3%; males literate 98.9%; females 95.9%.

Education (1995–96)

	schools	teachers	students	student/ teacher ratio
Primary (age 6–13)	4,462	34,201	697,510	20.4
Secondary (age 14–17)	...	105,656	812,660	7.7
Voc., teacher tr.	78[8]	...	26,585	...
Higher	23[8]	18,184[8]	120,870[8]	6.6

Health (1998): physicians 28,850 (1 per 276 persons); hospital beds 71,100 (1 per 110 persons); infant mortality rate per 1,000 live births 81.6.
Food (1998): daily per capita caloric intake 2,191 (vegetable product 84%, animal products 16%); 86% of FAO recommended minimum requirements.

Military

Total active duty personnel (1998): 69,900 (army 85.3%, navy 3.1%, air force 11.6%). *Military expenditure as percentage of GNP* (1997): 1.9% (world 2.6%); per capita expenditure (1997) U.S.$29.

[1]Includes one vacant seat reserved for Nagorno-Karabakh representative. [2]Controlled by Armenian forces from mid-1993. [3]Includes 59 districts and 10 cities with limited self-government in 1999; some districts and cities have been controlled by Armenian forces from mid-1993. [4]At factor cost. [5]Includes 42,329 unemployed and 832,871 undistributed employed. [6]Detail does not add to total given because of rounding. [7]Imports c.i.f., exports f.o.b. [8]1994–95.

Internet resources for further information:
- **Statistical Committee of Azerbaijan Republic http://www.azeri.com/goscomstat**
- **Azerbaijan Republic http://www.president.az/azerbaijan/azerbaijan.htm**

Bahamas, The

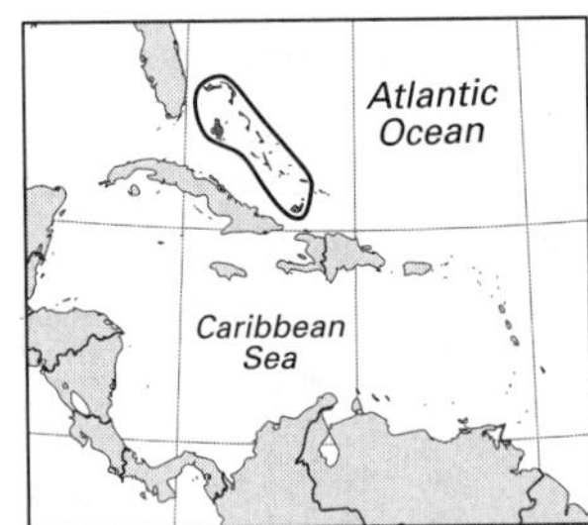

Official name: The Commonwealth of The Bahamas.
Form of government: constitutional monarchy with two legislative houses (Senate [16]; House of Assembly [40]).
Chief of state: British Monarch represented by Governor-General.
Head of government: Prime Minister.
Capital: Nassau.
Official language: English.
Official religion: none.
Monetary unit: 1 Bahamian dollar (B$) = 100 cents; valuation (Oct. 6, 2000) 1 U.S.$ = B$1.00; 1 £ = B$1.45.

Area and population

	area[1]		population
			1990
Islands and Island Groups[2]	sq mi	sq km	census
Abaco, Great and Little	649	1,681	10,034
Acklins	192	497	405
Andros	2,300	5,957	8,187
Berry Islands	12	31	628
Bimini Islands	9	23	1,639
Cat Island	150	388	1,698
Crooked and Long Cay	93	241	412
Eleuthera	187	484	7,993
Exuma, Great, and Exuma Cays	112	290	3,556
Grand Bahama	530	1,373	40,898
Harbour Island	3	8	1,219
Inagua, Great and Little	599	1,551	985
Long Island	230	596	2,954
Mayaguana	110	285	312
New Providence	80	207	172,196
Ragged Island	14	36	89
Rum Cay	30	78	53
San Salvador	63	163	465
Spanish Wells	10	26	1,372
Other uninhabited cays and rocks	9	23	—
TOTAL	5,382	13,939[3]	255,095

Demography

Population (2000): 295,000.
Density (2000)[4]: persons per sq mi 75.8, persons per sq km 29.3.
Urban-rural (1995): urban 87.5%; rural 12.5%.
Sex distribution (1995): male 48.91%; female 51.09%.
Age breakdown (1995): under 15, 31.4%; 15–29, 27.9%; 30–44, 22.5%; 45–59, 11.4%; 60–74, 5.0%; 75 and over, 1.8%.
Population projection: (2010) 315,000; (2020) 324,000.
Doubling time: 46 years.
Ethnic composition (1996): black 86.0%; white 6.0%; mixed/other 8.0%.
Religious affiliation (1995): non-Anglican Protestant 45.4% of which Baptist 17.5%; Roman Catholic 16.8%; Anglican 10.8%; other/nonreligious 27.0%.
Major cities (1990): Nassau 172,196[5]; Freeport/Lucaya 26,574; Marsh Harbour 3,611; Bailey Town 1,490; Dunmore Town (Harbour Island) 1,219.

Vital statistics

Birth rate per 1,000 population (1996): 20.7 (world avg. 22.1); (1995) legitimate 45.7%; illegitimate 54.3%.
Death rate per 1,000 population (1996): 5.4 (world avg. 8.9).
Natural increase rate per 1,000 population (1996): 15.3 (world avg. 13.2).
Total fertility rate (avg. births per childbearing woman; 1999): 2.3.
Marriage rate per 1,000 population (1996): 9.3.
Divorce rate per 1,000 population (1996): 1.4.
Life expectancy at birth (1999): male 70.9 years; female 77.6 years.
Major causes of death per 100,000 population (1995): diseases of the circulatory system 160.1; endocrine and metabolic disorders 137.4; malignant neoplasms (cancers) 85.6.[6]

National economy

Budget (1998–99). Revenue: B$730,102,000 (import taxes 45.1%, stamp taxes from imports 11.0%, business and professional licenses 7.4%, departure taxes 6.6%, fines and forfeits 6.1%). Expenditures: B$748,150,000 (education 19.7%, health 15.5%, interest on public debt 13.2%, general administration 12.8%, public order 11.1%, tourism 6.0%, defense 3.7%).
Public debt (December 1999): U.S.$1,512,000,000.
Production (value of production in B$'000 except as noted). Agriculture, forestry, fishing (1998): crayfish 54,100, poultry products 28,300, citrus and other fruit 21,300, fish 6,600, ornamental plants and flowers 6,000; roundwood (1998) 117,000 cu m. Mining and quarrying (value of export production; 1996): salt 18,100; aragonite 4,900. Manufacturing (value of export production; 1996): pharmaceuticals and other chemical products (1995) 74,200; rum 5,200. Construction (value of construction completed in B$'000,000; 1998): residential 141; nonresidential 353. Energy production (consumption): electricity (kW-hr; 1996) 1,340,000,000 (1,340,000,000); coal, none (none); crude petroleum, none (none); petroleum products (metric tons; 1996) none (555,000); natural gas, none (none).
Tourism (1997): receipts U.S.$1,416,000,000; expenditures U.S.$250,000,000.
Household income and expenditure. Average household size (1996) 3.9; income per household (1996) B$27,252 (U.S.$27,252); sources of income: n.a.; expenditure (1995)[7]: housing 32.8%, transportation and communications 14.8% food and beverages 13.8%, household furnishings 8.9%.

Gross national product (1997): U.S.$3,288,000,000 (U.S.$11,380 per capita).

Structure of gross domestic product and labour force

	1995		1996	
	in value B$'000,000	% of total value	labour force	% of labour force
Agriculture, fishing	100	3.3	6,445	4.4
Manufacturing	80	2.6	5,400	3.7
Mining	26	0.8	1,665	1.1
Public utilities	116	3.8		
Construction	71	2.3	12,045	8.2
Transp. and commun.	295	9.6	11,475	7.8
Trade, restaurants	705	23.0	38,700	26.4
Finance, real estate	599	19.5	11,125	7.6
Pub. admin., defense	210	6.8	42,295	28.8
Services	301	9.8		
Other	568[8]	18.5[8]	17,485[9]	11.9[9]
TOTAL	3,069[3]	100.0	146,635	100.0[3]

Population economically active (1996): total 146,635; activity rate of total population 51.6% (participation rates: [1994] ages 15–64, 77.8%; female 47.5%; unemployed [1998] 9.5%).

Price and earnings indexes (1995 = 100)

	1993	1994	1995	1996	1997	1998	1999
Consumer price index	96.6	98.0	100.0	101.4	101.9	103.3	104.4[10]
Annual earnings index	...	...	...	...	...	...	...

Land use (1994): forest 32.4%; pasture 0.2%; agriculture 1.0%; other 66.4%.

Foreign trade[11]

Balance of trade (current prices)

	1993	1994	1995	1996	1997	1998
B$'000,000	–792	–904	–1,067	–1,187	–1,441	–1,572
% of total	70.9%	73.0%	75.2%	76.9%	79.9%	72.4%

Imports (1996): B$1,365,000,000 (machinery and transport equipment 24.9%; food products 16.4%; petroleum for domestic use 14.1%; chemicals and chemical products 9.2%). *Major import sources*[12]: U.S. 93.8%; EC 2.3%.
Exports (1996): B$178,000,000 (domestic exports 64.3%, of which crayfish 38.9%, salt 9.8%; reexports 35.7%). *Major export destinations:* U.S. 80.1%; EC 9.0%; Canada 1.9%.

Transport and communications

Transport. Railroads: none. Roads (1995): total length 1,522 mi, 2,450 km (paved 57%). Vehicles (1996)[13]: passenger cars 89,263; trucks and buses 17,228. Merchant marine (1992): vessels (100 gross tons and over) 1,061; total deadweight tonnage 33,081,652. Air transport (1997)[14]: passenger-mi 87,000,000, passenger-km 140,000,000; short ton-mi cargo 312,000, metric ton-km cargo 455,000; airports (1997) with scheduled flights 22.

Communications

Medium	date	unit	number	units per 1,000 persons
Daily newspapers	1996	circulation	28,000	99
Radio	1997	receivers	215,000	744
Television	1997	receivers	67,000	232
Telephones	1998	main lines	105,869	367
Cellular telephones	1998	subscribers	8,072	28

Education and health

Educational attainment (1990). Percentage of population age 25 and over having: no formal schooling 3.5%; incomplete primary education 25.4%; complete primary/incomplete secondary 57.6%; complete secondary/higher 13.5%. *Literacy* (1995): total percentage age 15 and over literate 98.2%.

Education (1996–97)

	schools	teachers	students	student/ teacher ratio
Primary (age 5–10)	113	1,540	34,199	22.2
Secondary (age 11–16)[15]	...	1,352	27,970	20.7
Higher[16]	1	160	3,463	21.6

Health: physicians (1996) 419 (1 per 678 persons); hospital beds (1997) 1,119 (1 per 258 persons); infant mortality rate per 1,000 live births (1999) 18.4.
Food (1997): daily per capita caloric intake 2,499 (vegetable products 68%, animal products 32%); 103% of FAO recommended minimum requirement.

Military

Total active duty personnel (1998): 860 (paramilitary coast guard 100%). *Military expenditure as percentage of GNP* (1997): 0.9% (world 2.6%); per capita expenditure U.S.$100.

[1]Includes areas of lakes and ponds, as well as lagoons and sounds almost entirely surrounded by land; area of land only is about 3,890 sq mi (10,070 sq km). [2]For local administrative purposes, The Bahamas are divided into 25 districts comprising parts of an island, a single island, or a group of islands. [3]Detail does not add to total given because of rounding. [4]Land area only. [5]Population cited is for New Providence Island. [6]All rates include AIDS-related deaths. [7]Weights of retail price index components. [8]Includes net indirect taxes (B$503,000,000) and statistical discrepancy (B$65,000,000). [9]Includes 615 not adequately defined and 16,870 unemployed. [10]Average of 2nd and 3rd quarters. [11]Imports c.i.f.; exports f.o.b. [12]Excludes all petroleum imports. [13]New Providence and Grand Bahama only. [14]Bahamasair; scheduled traffic only. [15]Public sector only. [16]College of The Bahamas only; 1997–98.

Bahrain

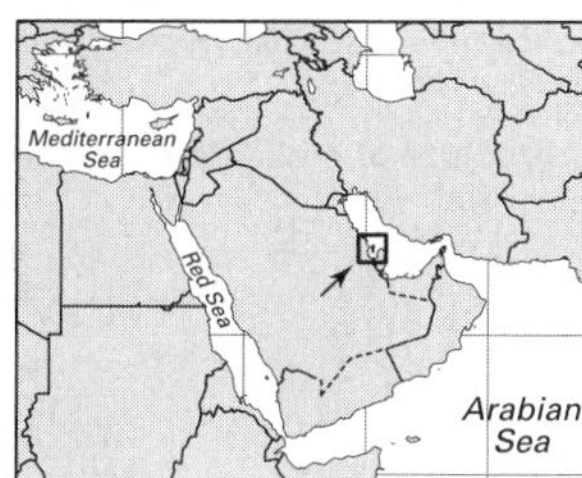

Official name: Dawlat al-Baḥrayn (State of Bahrain).
Form of government: monarchy (emirate)[1].
Chief of state: Emir.
Head of government: Prime Minister.
Capital: Manama.
Official language: Arabic.
Official religion: Islam.
Monetary unit: 1 Bahrain dinar (BD) = 1,000 fils; valuation (Oct. 6, 2000) 1 BD = U.S.$2.63 = £1.85.

Area and population

	area		population
			1991
Regions[2]	sq mi	sq km	census
Al-Gharbīyah (Western)	60.3	156.1	22,034
Al-Ḥadd	2.3	6.0	8,610
Jidd (Judd) Ḥafṣ	8.3	21.6	44,769
Al-Manāmah (Manama)	10.0	25.8	136,999
Al-Muḥarraq	6.2	16.0	74,245
Ar-Rifāʿ	112.6	291.6	49,752
Ash-Shamālīyah (Northern)	14.2	36.8	33,763
Ash-Sharqīyah (Eastern)	...	...	3,242[3]
Sitrah	11.1	28.8	36,755
Al-Wusṭā (Central)	13.6	35.2	34,304
Towns with special status			
Ḥammād	5.1	13.1	29,055
Madīnat ʿĪsā	4.8	12.4	34,509
Islands			
Ḥawār[4] and other	19.5	50.6	[2]
TOTAL	268.0	694.2[5]	508,037

Demography

Population (2000): 691,000.
Density (2000): persons per sq mi 2,578.1, persons per sq km 995.3.
Urban-rural (1995): urban 90.3%; rural 9.7%.
Sex distribution (1998): male 58.51%; female 41.49%.
Age breakdown (1998): under 15, 31.0%; 15–29, 28.4%; 30–44, 29.0%; 45–59, 8.0%; 60–74, 3.0%; 75 and over, 0.6%.
Population projection: (2010) 803,000; (2020) 900,000.
Doubling time: 41 years.
Ethnic composition (1991): Bahraini Arab 63.6%; Persian, Indian, Pakistani, and other Asians 30.3%; other Arab 3.5%; European 1.2%; other 1.4%.
Religious affiliation (1991): Muslim 81.8%, of which Shīʿī 61.3%, Sunnī 20.5%; Christian 8.5%; other 9.7%.
Major cities (1991): Manama (1992) 140,401; Ar-Rifāʿ 45,956; Al-Muḥarraq 45,337; Madīnat ʿĪsā 34,509.

Vital statistics

Birth rate per 1,000 population (1999): 21.2 (world avg. 22.1); legitimate 100%.
Death rate per 1,000 population (1999): 3.9 (world avg. 8.9).
Natural increase rate per 1,000 population (1999): 17.3 (world avg. (13.2).
Total fertility rate (avg. births per childbearing woman; 1999): 2.8.
Marriage rate per 1,000 population (1998): 5.7.
Divorce rate per 1,000 population (1998): 1.2.
Life expectancy at birth (1999): male 70.6 years; female 75.5 years.
Major causes of death per 100,000 population (1998): diseases of the circulatory system 85.9; malignant neoplasms (cancers) 37.8; diseases of the respiratory system 22.7; endocrine, nutritional, and metabolic diseases 22.7; accidents and violence 14.5; diseases of the digestive system 13.3; congenital anomalies 7.6.

National economy

Budget (1999). Revenue: BD 566,000,000 ([1995] entrepreneurial and property income 57.7%, import duties 8.4%, foreign grants 6.7%). Expenditures: BD 726,000,000 ([1995] general administration and public order 33.2%, defense 17.3%, education 13.4%, fuel and energy 9.6%, health 9.3%, transportation and communications 9.0%).
Population economically active (1991): total 226,448; activity rate of total population 44.6% (participation rates: ages 15–64, 66.1%; female 17.5%; unemployed [1997] *c.* 30%).

Price and earnings indexes (1995 = 100)

	1992	1993	1994	1995	1996	1997	1998
Consumer price index	94.1	96.5	97.3	100.0	99.8	102.0	101.6
Earnings index	...	...	...	...	...	...	...

Production (metric tons except as noted). Agriculture, forestry, fishing (1999): fruit (excluding melons) 21,800, cow's milk 14,000, dates 16,800, tomatoes 4,600, hen's eggs 2,968; livestock (number of live animals) 17,100 sheep, 16,000 goats, 13,000 cattle; fish catch (1998) 9,849. Manufacturing (barrels; 1994): gas oil 28,900,000; fuel oil 20,900,000; kerosene 10,400,000; gasoline 7,700,000; jet fuel 7,100,000; naphtha 1,860,000; propane 1,500,000; butane 1,190,000; aluminum (1998) 712,200 metric tons. Construction (permits issued; 1998): residential 6,105; nonresidential 703. Energy production (consumption): electricity (kW-hr; 1998) 5,773,000,000 (5,226,000,000); crude petroleum (barrels; 1998) 13,751,000 ([1996] 82,723,000); petroleum products (metric tons; 1996) 13,100,000 (538,000); natural gas (cu m; 1998) 10,068,000,000 (10,068,000,000).

Gross national product (1998): U.S.$4,909,000,000 (U.S.$7,640 per capita).

Structure of gross domestic product and labour force

	1998		1991	
	value in BD '000,000[6]	% of total value	labour force	% of labour force
Agriculture	21.0	0.9	5,108	2.3
Mining	316.3	13.6	3,638	1.6
Manufacturing	296.1	12.7	26,618	11.8
Construction	94.5	4.1	26,738	11.6
Public utilities	43.8	1.9	2,898	1.3
Transp. and commun.	192.7	8.3	13,789	6.1
Trade	235.0	10.1	29,961	13.2
Finance	825.7	35.5	17,256	7.6
Pub. admin., defense	433.7	18.7	83,944	37.1
Services	116.8	5.0		
Other	–250..2[7]	–10.8[7]	16,498	7.3
TOTAL	2,325.2[5]	100.0	226,448	100.0[5]

Public debt (external, outstanding; 1995): U.S.$3,200,000,000.
Household income and expenditure. Average household size (1991) 5.8; income per household: n.a.; sources of income: n.a.; expenditure (1984): food and tobacco 33.3%, housing 21.2%, household durable goods 9.8%, transportation and communications 8.5%, recreation 6.4%, clothing and footwear 5.9%, education 2.7%, health 2.3%, energy and water 2.2%.
Land use (1994): meadows and pastures 5.8%; agricultural and under permanent cultivation 2.9%; built-on and wasteland 91.3%.
Tourism (1998): receipts from visitors U.S.$366,000,000; expenditures by nationals abroad U.S.$142,000,000.

Foreign trade[8]

Balance of trade (current prices)

	1994	1995	1996	1997	1998	1999
BD '000,000	–49.3	+149.3	+160.5	+134.6	–111.3	+188.0
% of total	1.8%	5.1%	4.8%	4.3%	4.3%	6.1%

Imports (1998): BD 1,340,900,000 (machinery and transport equipment 27.6%, crude petroleum products 20.4%, food and live animals 12.8%, chemicals 11.2%). *Major import sources:* Japan 11.5%; United States 10.4%; Australia 9.7%; United Kingdom 7.4%; Saudi Arabia 7.2%; Italy 5.8%; Germany 5.7%.
Exports (1998): BD 1,229,600,000 (petroleum products 51.8%, metal and metal products 29.5%). *Major export destinations:* Saudi Arabia 8.2%; United States 6.0%; Japan 4.4%; India 2.8%; Taiwan 2.6%.

Transport and communications

Transport. Railroads: none. Roads (1998): total length 3,164 km (paved 77%). Vehicles (1997): passenger cars 149,636; trucks and buses 32,213. Merchant marine (1992): vessels (100 gross tons and over) 87; total deadweight tonnage 192,487. Air transport (1999)[9]: passenger-km 2,835,900,000; metric ton-km cargo 118,681,000; airports (1997) with scheduled flights 1.

Communications

Medium	date	unit	number	units per 1,000 persons
Daily newspapers	1996	circulation	67,000	117
Radio	1997	receivers	338,000	580
Television	1998	receivers	265,000	412
Telephones	1998	main lines	157,619	245
Cellular telephones	1998	subscribers	94,078	146
Personal computers	1998	units	60,000	93
Internet	1998	users	20,000	31

Education and health

Educational attainment (1991). Percentage of population age 25 and over having: no formal education 38.4%; primary education 26.2%; secondary 25.1%; higher 10.3%. *Literacy* (1995): percentage of population age 15 and over literate 85.2%; males literate 89.1%; females literate 79.4%.

Education (1997–98)[10]

	schools	teachers	students	student/ teacher ratio
Primary (age 6–11)	132	3,761	69,422	18.5
Secondary (age 12–17)	48	2,409	34,654	14.4
Voc., teacher tr.	7	721	7,528	10.4
Higher[11]	4[12]	655[13]	7,676[13]	11.7[13]

Health (1998): physicians 709 (1 per 907 persons); hospital beds 1,832 (1 per 351 persons); infant mortality rate per 1,000 live births (1999) 21.3.

Military

Total active duty personnel (1999): 11,000 (army 77.3%, navy 9.1%, air force 13.6%). *Military expenditure as percentage of GNP* (1997): 10.3% (world 2.6%); per capita expenditure U.S.$883.

[1]Appointed 40-member Consultative Council is an advisory body only. [2]Regions have no administrative function; the creation of four actual administrative units was begun in 1997. [3]Ash-Sharqīyah includes population of Ḥawār and other islands. [4]Also claimed by Qatar. [5]Detail does not add to total given because of rounding. [6]In purchasers' value at current prices. [7]Less imputed bank service charges. [8]Imports c.i.f. [9]One-fourth apportionment of international flights of Gulf Air (jointly administered by the governments of Bahrain, Oman, Qatar, and the United Arab Emirates). [10]Public education only. [11]Public and private education. [12]1987–88. [13]1993–94. [14]1993–94.

Internet resources for further information:

- **State of Bahrain**
http://www.bahrain.gov.bh

Bangladesh

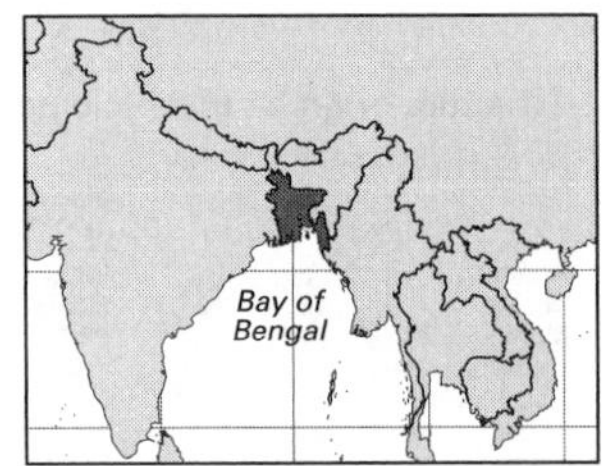

Official name: Gana Prajatantri Bangladesh (People's Republic of Bangladesh).
Form of government: unitary multiparty republic with one legislative house (Parliament [330[1]]).
Chief of state: President.
Head of government: Prime Minister.
Capital: Dhaka.
Official language: Bengali (Bangla).
Official religion: Islam.
Monetary unit: 1 Bangladesh taka (Tk) = 100 paisa; valuation (Oct. 6, 2000) 1 U.S.$ = Tk 54.10; 1 £ = Tk 78.26.

Area and population		area		population
				1991
Divisions	**Administrative centres**	sq mi	sq km	census[2]
Barisal	Barisal	5,134	13,297	7,757,334
Chittagong	Chittagong	7,906	20,476	20,823,477
Dhaka	Dhaka	12,015	31,119	33,939,848
Khulna	Khulna	8,600	22,274	13,243,054
Rajshahi	Rajshahi	13,326	34,513	27,499,727
Sylhet	Sylhet	4,863	12,596	7,149,372
Tribal region				
Chittagong Hill Tracts[3]	Rangamati	5,133	13,295	1,042,373
TOTAL		56,977	147,570	111,455,185

Demography

Population (2000): 129,194,000.
Density (2000): persons per sq mi 2,267.5, persons per sq km 875.5.
Urban-rural (1999): urban 21.0%; rural 79.0%.
Sex distribution (1996): male 51.72%; female 48.28%.
Age breakdown (1996): under 15, 42.0%; 15–29, 26.4%; 30–44, 17.8%; 45–59, 8.9%; 60–74, 3.8%; 75 and over, 1.1%.
Population projection: (2010) 150,392,000; (2020) 169,613,000.
Doubling time: 41 years.
Ethnic composition (1997): Bengali 97.7%; tribal 1.9%, of which Chakma 0.4%, Saontal 0.2%, Marma 0.1%; other 0.4%.
Religious affiliation (1991): Muslim 88.3%; Hindu 10.5%; Buddhist 0.6%; Christian 0.3%; other 0.3%.
Major cities (1991)[4]: Dhaka 6,105,160; Chittagong 2,040,663; Khulna 877,388; Rajshahi 517,136; Mymensingh 185,517[5].

Vital statistics

Birth rate per 1,000 population (1999): 25.7 (world avg. 22.1).
Death rate per 1,000 population (1999): 8.9 (world avg. 8.9).
Natural increase rate per 1,000 population (1999): 16.8 (world avg. 13.2).
Total fertility rate (avg. births per childbearing woman; 1999): 2.9.
Marriage rate per 1,000 population (1996): 10.1.
Divorce rate per 1,000 population (1981): 3.6.
Life expectancy at birth (1999): male 60.1 years; female 59.5 years.
Major causes of death (1990; percentage of recorded deaths): typhoid fever 19.8%; old age 14.8%; tetanus 10.1%; tuberculosis and other respiratory diseases 8.7%; diarrhea 6.4%; suicide, accidents, and poisoning 5.1%; high blood pressure and heart diseases 5.0%.

National economy

Budget (1997–98). Revenue: Tk 196,090,000,000 (value-added tax 38.6%; customs duties 25.0%; income taxes 9.9%; service charges 4.8%; public telephone enterprises 3.8%; interest receipts 2.8%). Expenditures: Tk 145,140,000,000 (goods and services 58.5%; transfer payments 24.1%; interest payments 13.5%).
Production (metric tons except as noted). Agriculture, forestry, fishing (1998): paddy rice 28,293,000, sugarcane 7,379,000, wheat 1,803,000, jute 1,087,000, bananas 625,000, oilseeds 591,000, pulses 508,000, mangoes 187,000, pineapples 149,000, tea 51,000; livestock (number of live animals) 33,500,000 goats, 23,400,000 cattle, 1,158,000 sheep, 854,000 buffalo, 152,875,000 chickens, 13,178,000 ducks; roundwood 32,332,000 cu m; fish catch (1996) 1,170,365. Mining and quarrying (1997): marine salt 350,000; industrial limestone 25,000. Manufacturing (value added in U.S.$'000,000; 1995): textiles 651; industrial chemicals 441; food products 331; wearing apparel 242; tobacco products 347; transport equipment 128; iron and steel 108. Construction: n.a. Energy production (consumption): electricity (kW-hr; 1996) 12,404,000,000 (12,404,000,000); coal (metric tons; 1996) none (negligible); crude petroleum (barrels; 1996) 52,000 (10,423,000); petroleum products (metric tons; 1996) 688,000 (2,049,000); natural gas (cu m; 1996) 8,278,000,000 (8,278,000,000).
Household income. Average household size (1991) 5.6; average annual income per household (1991–92) Tk 40,092 (U.S.$1,061); sources of income (1991–92): self-employment 51.6%, wages and salaries 23.1%, transfer payments 10.3%, other 15.0%; expenditure (1991–92): food and drink 66.6%, housing and rent 10.4%, energy 5.6%, clothing and footwear 4.7%, other 12.7%.
Population economically active (1995–96): total 56,014,000; activity rate of total population 46.0% (participation rates: over age 10, 64.8%; female 38.1%; unemployed 2.5%[6]).

Price and earnings indexes (1995 = 100)	1993	1994	1995	1996	1997	1998	1999
Consumer price index	87.5	92.1	100.0	104.1	109.5	118.6	126.1
Earnings index[7]	88.5	93.9	100.0	...	...	...	...

Public debt (external, outstanding; 1998): U.S.$15,804,000,000.
Gross national product (1998): U.S.$44,244,000,000 (U.S.$350 per capita).

Structure of gross domestic product and labour force	1996–97		1995–96	
	in value Tk '000,000	% of total value	labour force	% of labour force
Agriculture	418,306	29.8	34,530,000	61.7
Mining	130,111	9.3	23,000	—
Manufacturing			4,085,000	7.3
Construction	82,346	5.9	1,015,000	1.8
Public utilities	30,834	2.2	103,000	0.2
Transp. and commun.	158,040	11.3	2,308,000	4.1
Trade	125,799	9.0	6,060,000	10.8
Finance	28,084	2.0	213,000	0.4
Public admin., defense	79,048	5.6	7,677,000	13.7
Services and other	350,012	24.9		
TOTAL	1,402,580	100.0	56,014,000	100.0

Land use (1994): forest 14.6%; pasture 4.6%; agriculture 74.5%; other 6.3%.
Tourism (1998): receipts U.S.$51,000,000; expenditures U.S.$198,000,000.

Foreign trade[8]

Balance of trade (current prices)	1994	1995	1996	1997	1998	1999
Tk '000,000	–59,233	–107,720	–110,988	–99,478	–118,772	–149,493
% of total	21.7%	29.7%	28.7%	23.0%	24.8%	28.0%

Imports (1996–97): Tk 303,000,000,000 (textile yarn, fabrics, and made-up articles 24.4%; machinery and transport equipment 13.5%; chemicals 6.9%; iron and steel 6.2%; petroleum and products 5.3%). *Major import sources:* India 16.0%; Western Europe 15.0%; China 9.0%; Hong Kong 7.0%; Japan 7.0%; South Korea 6.0%; Singapore 6.0%; U.S. 3.0%.
Exports (1996–97): Tk 165,710,000,000 (ready-made garments 59.7%; fish and prawns 8.4%; jute manufactures 8.0%; hides, skins, and leather 5.4%; raw jute 3.2%; tea 0.9%). *Major export destinations:* Western Europe 49.0%; U.S. 33.0%; Japan 2.7%; Hong Kong 2.4%; Canada 2.0%.

Transport and communications

Transport. Railroads (1996–97): route length 1,681 mi, 2,706 km; passenger-mi 2,333,000,000, passenger-km 3,754,000,000; short ton-mi cargo 536,000,000, metric ton-km cargo 782,000,000. Roads (1996): total length 126,773 mi, 204,022 km (paved 12%). Vehicles (1997): passenger cars 54,784; trucks and buses 69,394. Merchant marine (1992): vessels (100 gross tons and over) 301; total deadweight tonnage 566,775. Air transport (1997)[9]: passenger-mi 2,008,734,000, passenger-km 3,232,750,000; short ton-mi cargo 338,644,000, metric ton-km cargo 494,412,000; airports with scheduled flights (1997) 8.

Communications				units per 1,000
Medium	date	unit	number	persons
Daily newspapers	1996	circulation	1,117,000	9.0
Radio	1998	receivers	8,000,000	64
Television	1998	receivers	600,000	4.8
Telephones	1998	main lines	377,964	3.0
Cellular telephones	1998	subscribers	75,000	0.6
Personal computers	1998	units	120,000	1.0
Internet	1998	users	1,200	0.01

Education and health

Educational attainment (1991). Percentage of population age 25 and over having: no formal schooling 65.4%; primary education 17.1%; secondary 13.8%; postsecondary 3.7%. *Literacy* (1995): total population age 15 and over literate 38.1%; males literate 49.4%; females literate 26.1%.

Education (1994–95)	schools	teachers	students	student/ teacher ratio
Primary (age 6–10)	62,617	248,783	16,429,000	66.0
Secondary (age 11–17)	12,553	148,878	5,531,000	37.2
Voc., teacher tr.	99	1,894	25,818	13.6
Higher	2,845	30,094	2,388,551	79.4

Health (1995): physicians 25,587 (1 per 4,759 persons); hospital beds 38,742 (1 per 3,312 persons); infant mortality rate (1999) 73.3.
Food (1997): daily per capita caloric intake 2,085 (vegetable products 97%, animal products 3%); (1995) 87% of FAO recommended minimum requirement.

Military

Total active duty personnel (1998): 121,000 (army 83.5%, navy 8.7%, air force 7.8%). *Military expenditure as percentage of GNP* (1997): 1.4% (world 2.6%); per capita expenditure U.S.$5.

[1]Includes 30 seats reserved for women. [2]Adjusted for underenumeration. [3]Autonomous region for non-Bengali tribal people was created by accord signed in December 1997 and formally established in May 1999. [4]Metropolitan population. [5]Municipal population. [6]Excluding underemployment. [7]Wage earnings in manufacturing. [8]Imports figures are f.o.b. in balance of trade. [9]Bangladesh Biman only.

Internet resources for further information:
- **Government of the People's Republic of Bangladesh http://bangladeshonline.com/gob**

Barbados

Official name: Barbados.
Form of government: constitutional monarchy with two legislative houses (Senate [21]; House of Assembly [28]).
Chief of state: British Monarch represented by Governor-General.
Head of government: Prime Minister.
Capital: Bridgetown.
Official language: English.
Official religion: none.
Monetary unit: 1 Barbados dollar (BDS$) = 100 cents; valuation (Oct. 6, 2000) 1 U.S.$ = BDS$1.99; 1 £ = BDS$2.88.

Area and population	area		population
			1990
Parishes[1]	sq mi	sq km	census
Christ Church	22	57	47,050
St. Andrew	14	36	6,346
St. George	17	44	17,905
St. James	12	31	21,001
St. John	13	34	10,206
St. Joseph	10	26	7,619
St. Lucy	14	36	9,455
St. Michael[2]	15	39	97,516
St. Peter	13	34	11,263
St. Philip	23	60	20,540
St. Thomas	13	34	11,590
TOTAL	166	430[3]	260,491

Demography

Population (2000): 267,000.
Density (2000): persons per sq mi 1,611, persons per sq km 622.
Urban-rural (1998): urban 48.9%; rural 51.1%.
Sex distribution (2000): male 48.24%; female 51.76%.
Age breakdown (2000): under 15, 22.0%; 15–29, 24.2%; 30–44, 26.1%; 45–59, 15.7%; 60–74, 7.9%; 75 and over, 4.1%.
Population projection: (2010) 273,000; (2020) 279,000.
Doubling time: n.a.; doubling time exceeds 100 years.
Ethnic composition (1990): black 92.5%; white 3.2%; mixed 2.8%; other 1.5%.
Religious affiliation (1995): Protestant 63.0%, of which Anglican 26.3%, Pentecostal 10.6%, Methodist 5.7%; Roman Catholic 4.8%; other Christian 2.0%; nonreligious/other 30.2%.
Major cities (1990): Bridgetown 6,070 (urban area 85,000); Speightstown, *c.* 3,500.

Vital statistics

Birth rate per 1,000 population (1999): 14.5 (world avg. 22.1); (1979) legitimate 26.9%; illegitimate 73.1%.
Death rate per 1,000 population (1999): 8.2 (world avg. 8.9).
Natural increase rate per 1,000 population (1999): 6.2 (world avg. 13.2).
Total fertility rate (avg. births per childbearing woman; 1999): 1.8.
Marriage rate per 1,000 population (1995): 13.5.
Divorce rate per 1,000 population (1995): 1.5.
Life expectancy at birth (1999): male 72.4 years; female 78.0 years.
Major causes of death per 100,000 population (1995): diseases of the circulatory system 369.7; malignant neoplasms (cancers) 163.6; endocrine and metabolic disorders 151.3; diseases of the respiratory system 56.3; accidents, poisonings, and violence 36.4; diseases of the digestive system 34.5; infectious and parasitic diseases 27.6; diseases of the nervous system 23.0.

National economy

Budget (1997–98). Revenue: BDS$1,458,274,000[4] (tax revenue 94.7%, of which goods and services taxes 49.5%, personal income and company taxes 29.5%, import duties 8.8%; nontax revenue 5.3%). Expenditures: BDS$1,508,869,000 (current expenditure 83.2%, of which education 18.8%, economic services 11.5%, health 10.9%, social security and welfare 8.3%).
Production (metric tons except as noted). Agriculture, forestry, fishing (1998): raw sugar 48,000, sweet potatoes 5,100, cucumbers 1,400, yams 1,320, cabbage 1,200, pumpkins 1,000, cassava 820, carrots 785, tomatoes 650, onions 480, lettuce 445; livestock (number of live animals) 41,000 sheep, 33,000 pigs, 23,000 cattle, 4,500 goats; roundwood, n.a.; fish catch (1997) 2,764. Manufacturing (value added in BDS$'000; 1995): food, beverages, and tobacco (mostly sugar, molasses, rum, beer, and cigarettes) 108,000; paper products, printing, and publishing 33,400; metal products and assembly-type goods (mostly electronic components) 28,000; textiles and wearing apparel 11,700. Construction (value added in BDS$; 1996): 151,400,000. Energy production (consumption): electricity (kW-hr; 1996) 650,000,000 (571,000,000); coal, none (none); crude petroleum (barrels; 1996) 364,000 (1,552,000); petroleum products (metric tons; 1996) 255,000 (288,000); natural gas (cu m; 1996) 29,112,000 (29,112,000).
Household income and expenditure. Average household size (1990) 3.5; income per household (1988) BDS$13,455 (U.S.$6,690); sources of income: n.a.; expenditure (1994): food 39.4%, housing 16.8%, transportation 10.5%, household operations 8.1%, alcohol and tobacco 6.4%, fuel and light 5.2%, clothing and footwear 5.0%, other 8.6%.
Population economically active (1997): total 135,800; activity rate of total population 51.3% (participation rates: ages 15 and over, 67.5%, female 62.1%, unemployed 14.5%).

Price and earnings indexes (1995 = 100)	1993	1994	1995	1996	1997	1998	1999[5]
Consumer price index	98.1	98.2	100.0	102.4	110.3	108.9	113.0
Hourly earnings index	...	...	...	...	...	...	...

Gross national product (1996): U.S.$295,131,000,000 (U.S.$8,380 per capita).

Structure of gross domestic product and labour force	1997			
	in value BDS$'000,000	% of total value	labour force	% of labour force
Agriculture, fishing	174.9	4.0	6,100	4.5
Mining	20.2[6]	0.5[6]	...	...
Manufacturing	225.8	5.2	10,700	7.8
Construction	182.9	4.2	10,200	7.5
Public utilities	127.4[6]	2.9[6]	1,500	1.1
Transp. and commun.	339.6	7.8	4,700	3.4
Trade, restaurants	1,117.6	25.6	28,200	20.7
Finance, real estate	614.3	14.1	8,100	5.9
Pub. admin., defense	611.0	14.0	46,900	34.4
Services	157.8	3.6		
Other	799.1[7]	18.3[7]	20,000[8]	14.7[8]
TOTAL	4,370.6	100.0[3]	136,400	100.0

Public debt (external, outstanding; 1998): U.S.$387,800,000.
Tourism (1998): receipts from visitors U.S.$703,000,000; expenditures by nationals abroad U.S.$82,000,000.

Foreign trade[9]

Balance of trade (current prices)	1993	1994	1995	1996	1997	1998
BDS$'000,000	–777.1	–865.6	–1,063	–1,106	–1,425	–1,510
% of total	51.0%	54.4%	52.7%	49.6%	55.7%	59.7%

Imports (1997): BDS$1,991,001,000 (retained imports 92.7%, of which capital goods 20.4%, food and beverages 15.0%, construction materials 8.2%, chemicals 5.6%, fuels 3.7%; reexported imports 7.3%). *Major import sources* (1997): U.S. 45.4%[10]; Trinidad and Tobago 9.2%; U.K. 8.1%; Canada 3.9%; Jamaica 1.2%.
Exports (1997): BDS$565,887,000 (domestic exports 74.4%, of which sugar 12.7%, chemicals 10.0%, electrical components 9.2%, rum 4.9%, margarine and lard 2.0%, clothing 1.2%; reexports 25.6%). *Major export destinations* (1997): U.K. 17.1%; U.S. 14.7%[10]; Jamaica 6.6%; Trinidad and Tobago 5.5%; St. Lucia 3.7%; Canada 3.5%; Guyana 2.8%.

Transport and communications

Transport. Railroads: none. Roads (1996): total length 1,025 mi, 1,650 km (paved 96%). Vehicles (1995): passenger cars 43,711; trucks and buses 10,583[11]. Merchant marine (1992): vessels (100 gross tons and over) 37; total deadweight tonnage 84,000. Air transport (1995): passenger arrivals 699,000, passenger departures 707,400; cargo unloaded 8,382 metric tons, cargo loaded 4,717 metric tons; airports (1997) with scheduled flights 1.

Communications Medium	date	unit	number	units per 1,000 persons
Daily newspapers	1996	circulation	53,000	199
Radio	1997	receivers	237,000	888
Television	1997	receivers	76,000	285
Telephones	1997	main lines	108,457	404
Cellular telephones	1997	subscribers	8,013	29.9
Personal computers	1995	units	15,000	57.5
Internet	1998	users	5,000	18.8

Education and health

Educational attainment (1990). Percentage of population age 25 and over having: no formal schooling 0.4%; primary education 23.7%; secondary 60.3%[12]; higher 11.2%; other 4.4%. *Literacy* (1995): total population age 15 and over literate 97.4%; males literate 98.0%; females literate 96.8%.

Education (1995–96)	schools	teachers	students	student/ teacher ratio
Primary (age 3–11)	79	994	18,513	18.6
Secondary (age 12–16)	21	1,263	21,455	17.0
Vocational[13]	8	79	996	12.6
Higher	4	544[14]	6,622	...

Health (1992): physicians 312 (1 per 842 persons); hospital beds 1,966 (1 per 134 persons); infant mortality rate per 1,000 live births (1999) 16.2.
Food (1997): daily per capita caloric intake 3,176 (vegetable products 75%, animal products 25%); 131% of FAO recommended minimum requirement.

Military

Total active duty personnel (1999): 610 (army 82.0%, navy 18.0%). *Military expenditure as percentage of GNP* (1996): 0.8% (world 2.6%); per capita expenditure U.S.$54.

[1]Parishes and city of Bridgetown have no local administrative function. [2]Includes city of Bridgetown. [3]Detail does not add to total given because of rounding. [4]Current revenue only. [5]September. [6]Mining excludes natural gas; Public utilities includes natural gas. [7]Net indirect taxes. [8]Unemployed. [9]Import figures are in c.i.f. [10]Includes Puerto Rico. [11]Includes taxis. [12]Includes composite senior. [13]1987–88. [14]1984.

Internet resources for further information:
- **Central Bank of Barbados http://www.centralbank.org.bb**

Belarus

Official name: Respublika Belarus (Republic of Belarus).
Form of government[1]: unitary multiparty republic with two legislative bodies (Council of the Republic [64]; House of Representatives [110]).
Head of state and government: President assisted by Prime Minister.
Capital: Minsk.
Official languages: Belarusian; Russian.
Official religion: none.
Monetary unit: rubel[2] (Rbl; plural rubli) valuation (Oct. 6, 2000) free rate, 1 U.S.$ = (new) Rbl 1,080; 1 £ = (new) Rbl 1,562.

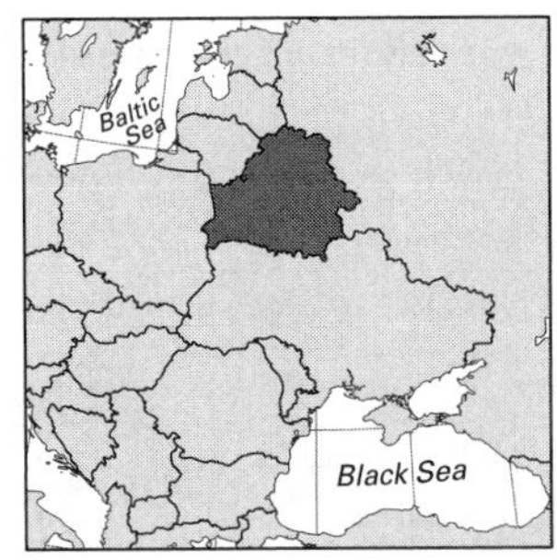

Area and population		area		population
				1998[3] estimate
Provinces	**Capitals**	sq mi	sq km	
Brest	Brest	12,700	32,800	1,501,200
Homel (Gomel)	Homel	15,600	40,400	1,576,100
Hrodno (Grodno)	Hrodno	9,700	25,000	1,191,800
Mahilyoŭ (Mogilyov)	Mahilyoŭ	11,200	29,100	1,241,300
Minsk (Mensk)	Minsk	15,500	40,200	3,283,000
Vitebsk	Vitebsk	15,500	40,100	1,410,400
TOTAL		80,200[4]	207,600[4]	10,203,800

Demography

Population (2000): 9,989,000.
Density (2000): persons per sq mi 124.6, persons per sq km 48.1.
Urban-rural (1998): urban 69.8%; rural 30.2%.
Sex distribution (1998): male 46.70%; female 53.30%.
Age breakdown (1998): under 15, 20.4%; 15–29, 21.4%; 30–44, 23.5%; 45–59, 16.3%; 60–69, 10.4%; 70 and over, 8.0%.
Population projection: (2010) 9,918,000; (2020) 9,900,000.
Doubling time: not applicable; population is declining.
Linguistic composition (1989): Belarusian 65.6%; Russian 31.9%; Ukrainian 1.3%; other 1.2%.
Religious affiliation (1995): Belarusian Orthodox 31.6%; Roman Catholic 17.7%; other (mostly nonreligious) 50.7%.
Major cities (1998): Minsk 1,717,000; Homel 513,000; Mahilyoŭ 369,000.

Vital statistics

Birth rate per 1,000 population (1998): 9.7 (world avg. 22.1); (1994) legitimate 87.9%; illegitimate 12.1%.
Death rate per 1,000 population (1998): 13.5 (world avg. 8.9).
Natural increase rate per 1,000 population (1998): –3.8 (world avg. 13.2).
Total fertility rate (avg. births per childbearing woman; 1998): 1.3.
Marriage rate per 1,000 population (1997): 6.8.
Divorce rate per 1,000 population (1997): 4.6.
Life expectancy at birth (1998): male 62.3 years; female 74.6 years.
Major causes of death per 100,000 population (1997): diseases of the circulatory system 673.9; malignant neoplasms (cancers) 191.9; accidents and violence 154.5; diseases of the respiratory system 68.7.

National economy

Budget (1997). Revenue: (old) Rbl 111,736,000,000,000 (value-added tax 30.0%, taxes on profits 14.8%, taxes on income 10.2%, excise taxes 13.1%, taxes on international trade 8.3%, other 23.6%). Expenditures: (old) Rbl 115,875,000,000,000 (education 20.1%, health 15.8%, subsidies 11.1%, capital expenditure 8.6%, Chernobyl expenditures 6.5%, transfers 5.8%, lending minus repayments 1.8%, other 30.3%[5]).
Public debt (external, outstanding; 1998): U.S.$748,000,000.
Household income and expenditure. Average household size (1998) 3.6; income per household (1995) (old) Rbl 2,400,000; sources of income (1997): wages and salaries 55.5%, business activities 20.5%, transfers 15.5%, agricultural income 1.4%; expenditure (1997): retail goods 74.9%, savings 18.6%, taxes 6.5%.
Production (metric tons except as noted). Agriculture, forestry, fishing (1999): potatoes 8,000,000, cereal 3,353,000, other vegetables 1,145,000, sugar beets 1,000,000, fruit 299,350; livestock (number of live animals) 4,515,000 cattle, 3,608,000 pigs, 233,200 horses, 182,000 sheep and goats, 40,000,000 poultry; roundwood (1998) 17,745,000 cu m; fish catch (1998) 457. Mining and quarrying (1997): potash 3,400,000; peat 3,036,000. Manufacturing (value of production in (old) Rbl '000,000; 1994): machine-building equipment 1,086,650; chemical products 659,438; food products 562,438; construction materials 142,555. Construction (1991): 5,395,000 sq m. Energy production (consumption): electricity (kW-hr; 1997) 26,057,000,000 (33,677,000,000); coal (1994) none (1,199,000); crude petroleum (barrels; 1997) 13,355,000 (86,406,000); petroleum products (1997) 9,589,000 (10,473,000); natural gas (cu m; 1997) 242,000,000 (16,402,000,000).
Population economically active (1997): 4,369,900; activity rate of total population 42.7% (participation rate: ages 16–59 [male], 16–54 [female] 81.8%; female 53.6%; unemployed [1998] 2.6%).

Price and earnings indexes (1995 = 100)	1995	1996	1997	1998
Consumer price index	100	152.7	204.5	246.1
Monthly earnings index	100	160.5	240.1	350.2

Gross national product (1998): U.S.$22,232,000 (U.S.$2,180 per capita).

Structure of gross domestic product and labour force	1997			
	in value (old) Rbl '000,000[6]	% of total value[6]	labour force	% of labour force
Agriculture	42,445	14.1	762,500	17.4
Mining / Manufacturing	111,024	36.9	1,204,300	27.6
Public utilities	8,723	2.9	197,600	4.5
Construction	21,535	7.1	311,800	7.1
Transp. and commun.	37,910	12.6	309,100	7.1
Trade	28,196	9.4	461,600	10.6
Finance / Public admin., defense / Services	31,940	10.6	915,400	20.9
Other	19,341	6.4	207,600[7]	4.8[7]
TOTAL	301,114	100.0	4,369,900	100.0

Tourism (1997): receipts U.S.$25,000,000; expenditures U.S.$114,000,000.
Land use (1994)[8]: forested 33.7%; meadows and pastures 14.1%; agricultural and under permanent cultivation 30.5%; other 21.7%.

Foreign trade

Balance of trade (current prices)	1992	1993	1994	1995	1996	1997	1998
U.S.$'000,000	+64	–569	–556	–856	–1,287	–1,388	–1,388
% of total	0.9%	12.6%	10.0%	8.3%	10.2%	8.7%	8.7%

Imports (1997): U.S.$8,689,000,000 (industrial products 96.3%, of which petroleum and gas 24.0%, machinery and metalworking 21.7%, chemical and petroleum products 16.8%, iron and steel 10.1%, food and beverages 9.6%, light industry 4.6%, wood and paper products 2.8%; agricultural products 3.7%). *Major import sources:* Russia 53.8%; Ukraine 11.1%; Germany 8.0%; Poland 2.9%; Italy 1.8%; U.S. 1.6%.
Exports (1997): U.S.$7,301,000,000 (industrial products 98.3%, of which machinery and metalworking 32.9%, chemical and petroleum products 20.9%, light industry 9.5%, petroleum and gas 8.2%, iron and steel 8.1%, food and beverages 7.5%, wood and paper products 7.1%, construction materials 2.2%; agricultural products 1.7%). *Major export destinations:* Russia 64.8%; Ukraine 5.8%; Poland 3.4%; Germany 3.0%.

Transport and communications

Transport. Railroads (1998): length 5,488 km; (1997) passenger-km 12,909,000,000; metric ton-km cargo 30,636,000,000. Roads (1998): total length 53,407 km (paved 98.6%). Vehicles (1998[3]): passenger cars 1,132,843; trucks and buses 8,867. Merchant marine (1992): vessels (100 gross tons and over) n.a.; total deadweight tonnage 18,373,000,000. Air transport (1997): passenger-km 910,000,000; metric ton-km cargo 84,000,000; airports 1.

Communications				units per 1,000
Medium	date	unit	number	persons
Daily newspapers	1997	circulation	1,437,000	140
Radio	1998	receivers	3,021,000	296
Television	1998	receivers	3,040,000	298
Telephones	1999	main lines	2,490	227
Cellular telephones	1999	subscribers	12,155	1.2
Internet	1999	users	7,500	0.7

Education and health

Educational attainment (1989). Percentage of population age 25 and over having: no formal schooling or primary education only 23.0%; some secondary 16.8%; completed secondary and some postsecondary 49.4%; higher 10.8%.

Education (1997–98)	schools	teachers	students	student/ teacher ratio
Primary (age 6–13) / Secondary (age 14–17)	4,835	145,300	1,580,000	10.9
Voc., teacher tr.	156	8,800	125,600	14.3
Higher	59	16,300	224,500	13.8

Literacy (1989): total population age 15 and over literate 7,690,000 (97.9%); males literate 3,661,000 (99.4%); females literate 4,029,000 (96.6%).
Health (1995): physicians 46,000 (1 per 224 persons); hospital beds 127,000 (1 per 81 persons); infant mortality rate per 1,000 live births (1998) 14.3.
Food (1998): daily per capita caloric intake 3,136 (vegetable products 72%, animal products 28%); 123% of FAO recommended minimum requirement.

Military

Total active duty personnel (1998): 83,000 (army 51.8%, air force and air defense 26.5%, other 21.7%). *Military expenditure as percentage of GNP* (1997): 1.7% (world 2.6%); per capita expenditure U.S.$81.

[1]Legal status of new constitution approved by referendum on Nov. 27, 1996, and legislative bodies established per this constitution are controversial. Council of the Republic contains 8 unelected seats. [2]Rubel re-denominated Jan. 1, 2000; 1,000 (old) rubli = 1 (new) rubel. [3]January 1. [4]Rounded area figures; exact area figures are 80,153 sq mi (207,595 sq km). [5]Includes expenditure arrears and statistical discrepancy. [6]At factor cost. [7]Includes 126,200 unemployed and 81,400 undistributed employed. [8]25% of Belarusian territory severely affected by radioactive fallout from Chernobyl.

Internet resources for further information:
- **Ministry of Statistics and Analysis** **http://president.gov.by/Minstat/en/main.html**
- **The Native Byelorussian WWW-server for Businessmen** **http://www.belarus.net**

Belgium

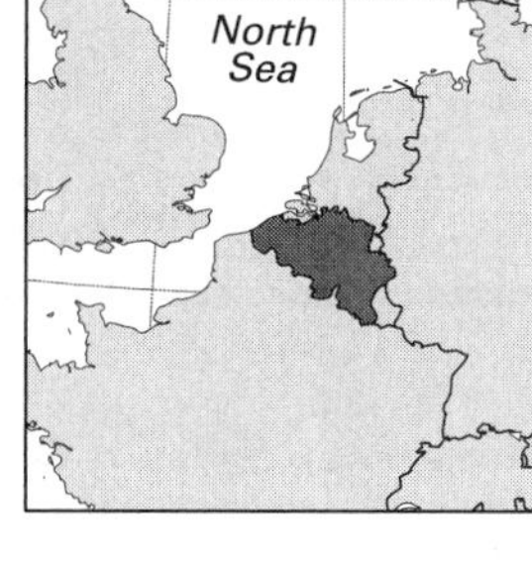

Official name: Koninkrijk België (Dutch); Royaume de Belgique (French) (Kingdom of Belgium).
Form of government: federal constitutional monarchy with a Parliament composed of two legislative chambers (Senate [71[1]]; House of Representatives [150]).
Chief of state: Monarch.
Head of government: Prime Minister.
Capital: Brussels.
Official languages: Dutch; French; German.
Official religion: none.
Monetary unit: 1 Belgian franc (BF) = 100 centimes; valuation (Oct. 6, 2000) 1 U.S.$ = BF 46.39; 1£ = BF 67.10.

Area and population

Regions[2] Provinces	Capitals	area sq mi	area sq km	population 1999[3] estimate
Brussels[4]	—	62	161	954,460
Flanders	—	5,221[5]	13,522	5,926,838
Antwerp	Antwerp	1,107	2,867	1,640,966
East Flanders	Ghent	1,151	2,982	1,359,702
Flemish Brabant[6]	Leuven	813	2,106	1,011,588
Limburg	Hasselt	935	2,422	787,491
West Flanders	Brugge	1,214	3,145	1,127,091
Wallonia	—	6,504[5]	16,844	3,332,454
Hainaut	Mons	1,462	3,786	1,280,427
Liège	Liège	1,491	3,862	1,018,259
Luxembourg	Arlon	1,714	4,440	245,140
Namur	Namur	1,415	3,666	441,205
Walloon Brabant[6]	Wavre	421	1,091	347,423
TOTAL		11,787	30,528[5]	10,213,752

Demography

Population (2000): 10,249,000.
Density (2000): persons per sq mi 869.5, persons per sq km 335.7.
Urban-rural (1996[7]): urban 96.8%; rural 3.2%.
Sex distribution (1996[7]): male 49.02%; female 50.98%.
Age breakdown (1994[3]): under 15, 18.1%; 15–29, 20.7%; 30–44, 22.7%; 45–59, 17.3%; 60–74, 15.1%; 75 and over, 6.1%.
Population projection: (2010) 10,407,000; (2020) 10,381,000.
Nationality (1992): Belgian 91.0%; Italian 2.4%; Moroccan 1.4%; French 0.9%; Turkish 0.8%; Dutch 0.6%; other 2.9%.
Religious affiliation (1995): Roman Catholic 87.9%; Muslim 2.5%; other Christian 2.4%, of which Protestant 1.0%; Jewish 0.3%; other 6.9%.
Major cities (1998[3]): Brussels 953,175[4]; Antwerp 449,745; Ghent 224,545; Charleroi 203,853; Liège 188,568.

Vital statistics

Birth rate per 1,000 population (1999): 11.1 (world avg. 22.1); (1989) legitimate 88.7%; illegitimate 11.3%.
Death rate per 1,000 population (1999): 10.2 (world avg. 8.9).
Natural increase rate per 1,000 population (1999): 0.9 (world avg. 13.2).
Total fertility rate (avg. births per childbearing woman; 1999): 1.6.
Marriage rate per 1,000 population (1997): 4.7.
Divorce rate per 1,000 population (1994): 2.2.
Life expectancy at birth (1999): male 74.3 years; female 81.1 years.
Major causes of death per 100,000 population (1992): diseases of the circulatory system 383.3; malignant neoplasms (cancers) 272.6; diseases of the respiratory system 90.6; accidents and violence 40.9.

National economy

Budget (1997). Revenue: BF 3,842,800,000,000 (income taxes 36.0%, social security contributions 33.2%, sales taxes 15.8%). Expenditures: BF 4,018,800,000,000 (current expenditures 95.3%, development expenditures 4.7%).
Public debt (1998[3]): U.S.$265,600,000,000.
Production (metric tons except as noted). Agriculture, forestry, fishing (1999[7]): sugar beets 6,150,000, potatoes 2,700,000, wheat 1,600,000, apples 447,000, barley 400,000, tomatoes 300,000; livestock (number of live animals) 7,671,000 pigs, 3,185,000 cattle, 155,000 sheep, 67,000 horses; roundwood (1998[7]) 3,765,000 cu m; fish catch (1998) 30,835. Mining and quarrying (1997): limestone 30,000,000; granite (Belgium bluestone) 2,115,000 cu m; marble 400 cu m. Manufacturing (value added in BF '000,000; 1996): metal products 468,894; food 263,382; chemicals 243,787; printing 69,991; textiles 66,524; furniture 58,115. Construction (1993): residential 33,063,000 cu m; nonresidential 42,864,000 cu m. Energy production (consumption): electricity (kW-hr; 1998) 83,244,000,000 ([1996] 80,241,000,000); coal (metric tons; 1996) negligible (11,556,000); crude petroleum (barrels; 1996) none (231,305,000); petroleum products (metric tons; 1996) 28,400,000 (17,684,000); natural gas (cu m; 1996) 2,514,000 (14,086,000,000).
Household income and expenditure. Avg. household size (1991) 2.7; sources of income (1992): wages 49.6%, transfer payments 20.7%, property income 18.8%, self-employment 10.9%; expenditure (1992): food 18.0%, housing 17.0%, transp. 13.3%, health 11.8%, durable goods 10.7%, clothing 7.7%.
Land use (1994[7]): forest 21.3%; pasture 21.0%; agriculture 24.2%; other 33.5%.
Gross national product (at current market prices; 1998): U.S.$258,968,000,000 (U.S.$25,380 per capita).

Structure of gross domestic product and labour force

	1997 in value BF '000,000	1997 % of total value	1996 labour force	1996 % of labour force
Agriculture	104,100	1.2	104,100	2.5
Mining	22,100	0.2	10,000	0.2
Manufacturing	1,846,600	21.3	754,400	18.0
Construction	424,200	4.9	254,100	6.1
Public utilities	213,000	2.5	29,400	0.7
Transp. and commun.	675,500	7.8	286,200	6.8
Trade	1,048,900	12.1	682,500	16.3
Finance	1,213,400	14.0	401,400	9.6
Pub. admin., defense	2,101,100	24.2	1,244,700	29.7
Services	633,100	7.3		
Other	393,300[8]	4.5[8]	429,300[9]	10.2[9]
TOTAL	8,675,500[5]	100.0	4,196,000[5]	100.0[5]

Population economically active (1996): total 4,196,000; activity rate 41.3% (participation rates: ages 14–64, 61.1%; female 41.6%; unemployed 9.6%).

Price and earnings indexes (1995 = 100)

	1993	1994	1995	1996	1997	1998	1999
Consumer price index	96.3	98.6	100.0	102.1	103.7	104.7	105.9
Earnings index	...	...	...	...	...	...	...

Tourism (1997): receipts U.S.$5,275,000,000; expenditures U.S.$8,275,000,000.

Foreign trade[7]

Balance of trade (current prices)

	1994	1995	1996	1997	1998	1999
BF '000,000	+453,000	+415,800	+364,000	+442,700	+562,000	+581,000
% of total	5.0%	4.2%	3.5%	3.8%	4.6%	4.4%

Imports (1997): BF 5,575,200,000,000 (machinery and transport equipment 30.0%; chemicals 15.2%; food 8.3%; mineral fuels 7.0%, of which petroleum products 5.0%; diamonds 4.1%). *Major import sources:* Germany 18.8%; The Netherlands 18.1%; France 14.4%; U.K. 9.1%.
Exports (1997): BF 6,017,900,000,000 (machinery and transport equipment 28.4%; chemicals 18.6%, of which plastics 4.5%; food 9.0%; iron and steel 5.2%; diamonds 3.7%; petroleum products 2.6%; textiles 1.7%). *Major export destinations:* Germany 19.4%; France 17.1%; The Netherlands 12.6%; U.K. 10.1%.

Transport and communications

Transport. Railroads (1997): route length 3,380 km[10]; passenger-km 6,984,000,000; metric ton-km cargo 7,465,000,000. Roads (1996): total length 143,800 km (paved 97%). Vehicles (1997): passenger cars 4,415,343; trucks and buses 449,904. Merchant marine (1992): vessels (100 gross tons and over) 232; total deadweight tonnage 218,506. Air transport (1995): passenger-km 8,619,821,000; metric ton-km cargo 756,195,000; airports (1997) 2.

Communications

Medium	date	unit	number	units per 1,000 persons
Daily newspapers	1996	circulation	1,625,000	161
Radio	1996	receivers	8,040,000	792
Television	1997	receivers	5,190,000	510
Telephones	1995	main lines	4,632,100	457
Cellular telephones	1997	subscribers	970,000	95
Personal computers	1997	units	2,390,000	235
Internet	1998	users	800,000	78.5

Education and health

Educational attainment (1981). Percentage of population age 15 and over having: less than secondary education 44.4%; lower secondary 26.5%; upper secondary 17.0%; vocational 2.9%; teacher's college 0.6%; university 3.5%.
Literacy (1995): virtually 99% literate.

Education (1996–97)

	schools	teachers	students	student/ teacher ratio
Primary (age 6–12)	4,401	72,589[11, 12]	737,823	...
Secondary (age 12–18)	1,727	110,599[13]	796,945	...
Voc., teacher tr.[13]	304	14,548[14]	155,192	...
Higher	151	10,517[14]	135,659	...

Health: physicians (1996[3]) 38,363 (1 per 264 persons); hospital beds (1994) 77,181 (1 per 131 persons); infant mortality rate (1999) 4.8.
Food (1997[7]): daily per capita caloric intake 3,619 (vegetable products 68%, animal products 32%); 137% of FAO recommended minimum requirement.

Military

Total active duty personnel (1998): 43,700 (army 64.6%, navy 5.9%, air force 26.5%, medical service 3.0%). *Military expenditure as percentage of GNP* (1997): 1.5% (world 2.6%); per capita expenditure U.S.$362.

[1]Excludes children of the monarch serving ex officio from age 18. [2]Corresponding to three language-based federal community councils: Dutch (Flanders), French (Wallonia), and bilingual (Brussels-Capital) having authority in cultural affairs; a fourth (German) community council (within Wallonia; 1999 population 70,472) lacks expression as an administrative region. [3]January 1. [4]Brussels Capital Region. [5]Detail does not add to total given because of rounding. [6]Former Brabant province divided on Jan. 1, 1995. [7]Includes Luxembourg. [8]Represents a statistical correction. [9]Includes 404,200 unemployed. [10]1996. [11]Includes preschool teachers. [12]1992–93. [13]1991–92. [14]1987–88.

Internet resources for further information:

- **Belgian Federal Government On Line http://belgium.fgov.be**
- **National Bank of Belgium http://www.nbb.be/sg/En/homee2.htm**

Belize

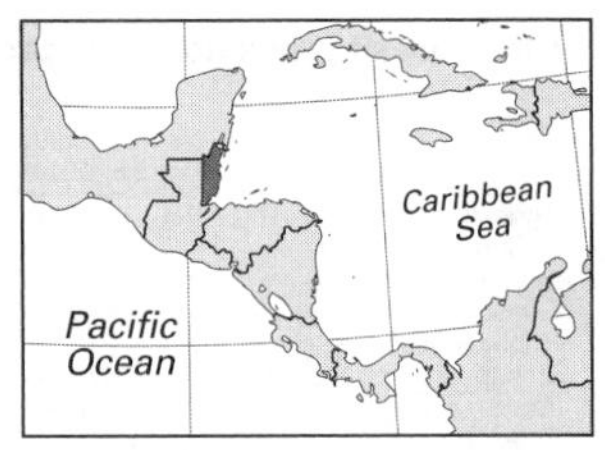

Official name: Belize.
Form of government: constitutional monarchy with two legislative houses (Senate [8[1]]; House of Representatives [29[2]]).
Chief of state: British Monarch represented by Governor-General.
Head of government: Prime Minister.
Capital: Belmopan.
Official language: English.
Official religion: none.
Monetary unit: 1 Belize dollar (BZ$) = 100 cents; valuation (Oct. 6, 2000) 1 U.S.$ = BZ$1.97[3]; 1 £ = BZ$2.85.

Area and population

		area		population
Districts	**Capitals**	sq mi	sq km	1998 estimate
Belize	Belize City	1,663	4,307	70,355
Cayo	San Ignacio	2,006	5,196	49,440
Corozal	Corozal	718	1,860	32,510
Orange Walk	Orange Walk	1,790	4,636	39,570
Stann Creek	Dangriga	986	2,554	23,965
Toledo	Punta Gorda	1,704	4,413	22,660
TOTAL		8,867[4]	22,965[4, 5]	238,500

Demography

Population (2000): 253,000.
Density (2000): persons per sq mi 28.5, persons per sq km 11.0.
Urban-rural (1998): urban 50.4%; rural 49.6%.
Sex distribution (1998): male 49.69%; female 50.31%.
Age breakdown (1998): under 15, 41.2%; 15–29, 26.5%; 30–44, 16.7%; 45–59, 8.8%; 60–74, 5.0%; 75 and over, 1.8%.
Population projection: (2010) 326,000; (2020) 401,000.
Doubling time: 28 years.
Ethnic composition (1991): mestizo (Spanish-Indian) 43.6%; Creole (predominantly black) 29.8%; Mayan Indian 11.0%; Garifuna (black-Carib Indian) 6.7%; white 3.9%; East Indian 3.5%; other or not stated 1.5%.
Religious affiliation (1991): Roman Catholic 57.7%; Protestant 34.3%, of which Anglican 7.0%, Pentecostal 6.3%, Methodist 4.2%, Seventh-day Adventist 4.1%, Mennonite 4.0%; other Christian 1.7%; other 0.3%; none or not stated 6.0%.
Major cities (1998): Belize City 55,810; Orange Walk 15,505; San Ignacio/Santa Elena 11,570; Corozal 8,085; Belmopan 7,105.

Vital statistics

Birth rate per 1,000 population (1999): 30.2 (world avg. 22.1); (1997) legitimate 40.3%; illegitimate 59.7%.
Death rate per 1,000 population (1999): 5.4 (world avg. 8.9).
Natural increase rate per 1,000 population (1999): 24.8 (world avg. 13.2).
Total fertility rate (avg. births per childbearing woman; 1999): 3.7.
Marriage rate per 1,000 population (1997): 6.6.
Divorce rate per 1,000 population (1997): 0.2.
Life expectancy at birth (1999): male 67.2 years; female 71.3 years.
Major causes of death per 100,000 population (1995): diseases of the circulatory system 119.8; accidents and violence 57.1; diseases of the respiratory system 47.8; malignant neoplasms (cancers) 38.1; infectious and parasitic diseases 23.7.

National economy

Budget (1997). Revenue: BZ$324,600,000 (tax revenue 77.4%, of which import duties 25.7%, general sales taxes 23.6%; grants 12.7%; nontax revenue 9.2%). Expenditures: BZ$362,300,000 (education 20.5%; transportation and communication 16.7%; general administration 11.4%; health 8.2%; defense 5.4%).
Tourism (1997): receipts from visitors U.S.$87,000,000; expenditures by nationals abroad U.S.$30,000,000.
Production (metric tons except as noted). Agriculture, forestry, fishing (1998): sugarcane 1,208,000, oranges 170,000, bananas 81,000, grapefruits 41,000, corn (maize) 37,000, rice 17,000, red kidney beans 5,000, coconuts 3,000; livestock (number of live animals; 1999) 58,000 cattle, 23,000 pigs, 1,400,000 chickens; roundwood (1998) 187,600 cu m; fish catch (1998) 2,620, of which shrimp 1,682, conchs 253, lobsters 251, freshwater and marine fish 111. Mining and quarrying (1997): sand and gravel 350,000; limestone 310,000. Manufacturing (1996): sugar (1997) 123,800; molasses (1997) 51,800; flour 13,000; orange concentrate 113,000 hectolitres; beer 34,000 hectolitres; grapefruit concentrate 34,000 hectolitres; cigarettes 80,000,000 units; garments 2,100,000 units. Energy production (consumption): electricity (kW-hr; 1996) 152,000,000 (177,000,000); coal, none (none); crude petroleum, none (none); petroleum products (metric tons; 1996) none (116,000); natural gas, none (none).
Household income and expenditure. Average household size (1996) 5.3; average annual income of employed head of household (1993) BZ$6,450[6] (U.S.$3,225[6]); sources of income, n.a.; expenditure (1990): food, beverages, and tobacco 34.0%, transportation 13.7%, energy and water 9.1%, housing 9.0%, clothing and footwear 8.8%, household furnishings 8.0%.
Population economically active (1998[7]): total 85,595; activity rate of total population 36.2% (participation rates: ages 14–64, 64.1%; female 34.5%; unemployed 14.3%).

Price and earnings indexes (1995 = 100)

	1993	1994	1995	1996	1997	1998	1999
Consumer price index	94.7	97.2	100.0	106.4	107.5	106.6	105.3
Monthly earnings index[8]	100.0	96.3	100.0	102.5	98.8	...	...

Public debt (external, outstanding; 1998): U.S.$282,200,000.
Gross national product (1998): U.S.$635,000,000 (U.S.$2,660 per capita).

Structure of gross domestic product and labour force

	1998		1997[7]	
	in value BZ$'000[9]	% of total value[9]	labour force	% of labour force
Agriculture, fishing, forestry	213,600	20.1	21,140	26.1
Mining	6,200	0.6	95	0.1
Manufacturing	139,800	13.1	7,980	9.9
Construction	59,600	5.6	3,835	4.7
Public utilities	35,100	3.3	985	1.2
Transp. and commun.	109,400	10.3	3,655	4.5
Trade, restaurants	199,100	18.7	15,155	18.7
Finance, real estate, insurance	143,000	13.4	2,360	2.9
Pub. admin., defense	133,600	12.6	15,140	18.7
Services	68,100	6.4		
Other	–44,200[10]	–4.2[10]	10,595[11]	13.1[11]
TOTAL	1,063,300	100.0[5]	80,940	100.0[5]

Land use (1994): forested 92.1%; meadows and pastures 2.2%; agricultural and under permanent cultivation 3.6%; other 2.1%.

Foreign trade[12]

Balance of trade (current prices)

	1993	1994	1995	1996	1997	1998
BZ$'000,000	–288.9	–217.9	–193.6	–175.7	–219.7	–257.4
% of total	34.6%	26.5%	23.0%	20.8%	23.8%	27.6%

Imports (1998): BZ$594,100,000 (machinery and transport equipment 25.6%; food and beverages 16.7%; mineral fuels and lubricants 11.1%; chemicals and chemical products 10.7%). *Major import sources:* U.S. 53.6%; Mexico 11.7%; U.K. 4.7%; Caricom 3.6%; other EU 5.3%.
Exports (1998): BZ$336,700,000 (domestic exports 90.9%, of which raw sugar 26.4%, bananas 14.6%, marine products 12.9%, citrus concentrate 12.8%, garments 11.7%; reexports 9.1%). *Major export destinations*[13]: U.S. 42.6%; U.K. 33.3%; Caricom 7.5%; other EU 11.9%.

Transport and communications

Transport. Railroads: none. Roads (1995): total length 1,398 mi, 2,250 km (paved 18%). Vehicles (1997): passenger cars 9,695; trucks and buses 11,698. Merchant marine (1992): vessels (100 gross tons and over) 32; total deadweight tonnage 45,706. Air transport (1998)[14]: passenger arrivals 199,475, passenger departures 193,620; cargo loaded 166 metric tons, cargo unloaded 1,082 metric tons. Airports (1997) with scheduled flights 9.

Communications

Medium	date	unit	number	units per 1,000 persons
Daily newspapers	1996	circulation	0	0
Radio	1997	receivers	133,000	571
Television	1997	receivers	41,000	176
Telephones	1998	main lines	31,625	138
Cellular telephones	1998	subscribers	3,438	15
Personal computers	1998	units	30,000	130
Internet	1998	users	10,000	43

Education and health

Educational attainment (1991). Percentage of population age 25 and over having: no formal schooling 13.0%; primary education 64.3%; secondary 14.9%; higher 6.6%; other 1.2%. *Literacy* (1991): total population age 14 and over literate 75,500 (70.3%).

Education (1997–98)

	schools	teachers	students	student/ teacher ratio
Primary (age 5–12)	247	2,015	53,118	26.4
Secondary (age 13–16)	30	726	11,260	15.5
Higher	12	228	2,753	12.1

Health (1998): physicians 155 (1 per 1,558 persons); hospital beds 554 (1 per 435 persons); infant mortality rate per 1,000 live births (1999) 27.0.
Food (1997): daily per capita caloric intake 2,907 (vegetable products 78%, animal products 22%); 129% of FAO recommended minimum requirement.

Military

Total active duty personnel (1999): 1,050 (army 95.2%, maritime wing 4.8%).
Military expenditure as percentage of GNP (1998): 1.4% (world, n.a.); per capita expenditure U.S.$35.

[1]Excludes president of the Senate, who may be elected by the Senate from outside its appointed membership. [2]Excludes speaker of the House of Representatives, who may be elected by the House from outside its elected membership. [3]The Belize dollar is officially pegged to the U.S. dollar. [4]Includes offshore cays totaling 266 sq mi (689 sq km). [5]Detail does not add to total given because of rounding. [6]Estimated figure for about 33,000 employed heads of household. [7]Based on April survey. [8]In manufacturing, transportation, trade, and finance. [9]At factor cost. [10]Less imputed bank service charges. [11]Includes 335 not adequately defined and 10,260 unemployed. [12]Imports c.i.f.; exports f.o.b. [13]Domestic exports only. [14]Belize international airport only.

Internet resources for further information:
- **Government of Belize http://www.belize.gov.bz**

Benin

Official name: République du Bénin (Republic of Benin).
Form of government: multiparty republic with one legislative house (National Assembly [83]).
Head of state and government: President, assisted by Prime Minister[1].
Capital[2]: Porto-Novo.
Official language: French.
Official religion: none.
Monetary unit: 1 CFA franc (CFAF) = 100 centimes; valuation (Oct. 6, 2000) 1 U.S.$ = CFAF 754.28; 1 £ = CFAF 1,091.

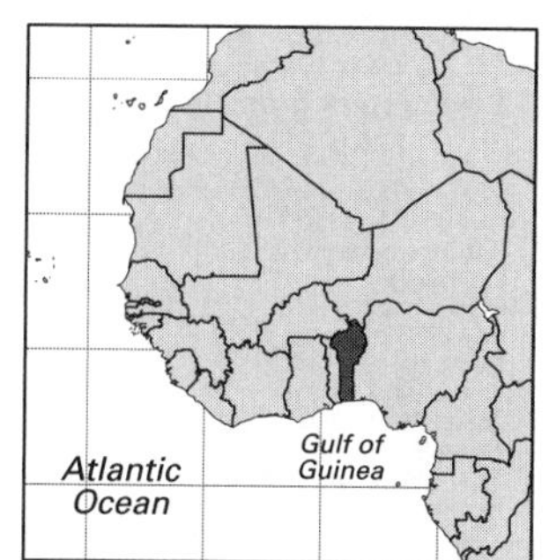

Area and population

Departments[3]	Capitals	area[4] sq mi	area[4] sq km	population 1992 census
Alibori	...	10,150	26,310	...[5]
Atacora	Natitingou	7,600	19,700	649,308[6]
Atlantique	...	1,150	2,920	1,066,373[7]
Borgou	Parakou	9,650	25,060	827,925[5]
Collines	...	5,500	14,240	...[8]
Couffo	Aplahoue	1,000	2,620	...[9]
Donga	Djougou	4,550	11,820	...[6]
Littoral	Cotonou	150	350	...[7]
Mono	Lokossa	850	2,200	676,377[9]
Ouémé	Porto-Novo	550	1,450	876,574[10]
Plateau	Ketou	1,200	3,060	...[10]
Zou	Abomey	1,950	5,030	818,998[8]
TOTAL		44,300	114,760	4,915,555

Demography

Population (2000): 6,396,000.
Density (2000): persons per sq mi 144.4, persons per sq km 55.7.
Urban-rural (1999): urban 41.5%; rural 58.5%.
Sex distribution (1999): male 49.28%; female 50.72%.
Age breakdown (1999): under 15, 47.6%; 15–29, 27.7%; 30–44, 13.8%; 45–59, 7.2%; 60–74, 3.1%; 75 and over, 0.6%.
Population projection: (2010) 8,411,000; (2020) 10,588,000.
Doubling time: 30 years.
Ethnic composition (1992): Fon 39.7%; Yoruba (Nago) 12.1%; Adjara 11.1%; Bariba 8.6%; Aizo 8.6%; Somba (Otomary) 6.6%; Fulani 5.6%; other 7.7%.
Religious affiliation (1992): Christian 35.4%, of which Roman Catholic 25.9%, Protestant 9.5%; traditional beliefs, including voodoo 35.0%; Muslim 20.6%; other 9.0%.
Major cities (1994): Cotonou 750,000; Porto-Novo 200,000; Djougou 132,000; Abomey-Calavi 125,565[11]; Parakou 120,000.

Vital statistics

Birth rate per 1,000 population (1999): 45.4 (world avg. 22.1).
Death rate per 1,000 population (1999): 12.4 (world avg. 8.9).
Natural increase rate per 1,000 population (1999): 33.0 (world avg. 13.2).
Total fertility rate (avg. births per childbearing woman; 1999): 6.4.
Life expectancy at birth (1999): male 52.0 years; female 56.2 years.

National economy

Budget (1998). Revenue: CFAF 255,100,000,000 (tax revenue 71.5%; grants 17.3%; nonfiscal receipts 11.2%). Expenditures: CFAF 233,400,000,000 (current expenditures 64.5%, of which debt service 12.7%; development expenditure 34.3%).
Production (metric tons except as noted). Agriculture, forestry, fishing (1999): cassava 2,377,339, yams 1,770,973, corn (maize) 822,739, seed cotton 436,240, sorghum 153,782, tomatoes 149,427, oil palm fruit 135,000, peanuts (groundnuts) 121,263, dry beans 94,342, karité nuts (shea nuts) 15,000; livestock (number of live animals; 1999) 1,345,000 cattle, 1,087,000 goats, 634,000 sheep, 470,000 pigs, 29,000,000 chickens; roundwood (1998) 5,994,000 cu m; fish catch (1997) 43,771. Manufacturing (1998): cement 380,000[12]; cotton fibre 175,000; meat 70,000; wheat flour 12,500; palm oil 11,000. Energy production (consumption): electricity (kW-hr; 1996) 6,000,000 (269,432,000); coal, none (none); crude petroleum (barrels; 1996) 652,000 (negligible); petroleum products (metric tons; 1996) none (149,000); natural gas, none (none).
Public debt (external, outstanding; 1998): U.S.$1,469,000,000.
Gross national product (1998): U.S.$2,252,000,000 (U.S.$380 per capita).

Structure of gross domestic product and labour force

	1997 in value CFAF '000,000,000	1997 % of total value	1992 labour force[13]	1992 % of labour force[13]
Agriculture	477.3	41.0	1,147,746	55.0
Mining	4.8	0.4	661	0.0
Manufacturing	102.4	8.8	160,406	7.7
Public utilities	10.0	0.9	1,176	0.1
Construction	54.6	4.7	51,655	2.5
Transp. and communications	88.2	7.6	52,837	2.5
Trade } Finance }	222.6	19.1	432,501	20.7
			3,106	0.1
Pub. admin., defense	86.5	7.4 }	164,544	7.9
Services	117.5	10.1 }		
Other	—	—	70,814	3.4
TOTAL	1,163.9	100.0	2,085,446	100.0[14]

Population economically active (1997): total 2,608,000; activity rate of total population 44.2% (participation rates: ages 15–64, 84.3%; female 48.3%; unemployed, n.a.).

Price and earnings indexes (1995 = 100)

	1992	1993	1994	1995	1996	1997	1998
Consumer price index	62.8	63.1	87.4	100.0	104.9	108.6	114.8
Hourly earnings index	...	...	...	...	...	...	...

Household income and expenditure. Average household size (1992) 5.9; income per household (1983) U.S.$240; sources of income; self-employement 73.7%, wages and salaries 26.3%; expenditure: n.a.
Land use (1995): agricultural and under permanent cultivation 17.0%; other 83.0% (of which [1994] forested 30.7%, meadows and pastures 4.0%).
Tourism (1998): receipts from visitors U.S.$33,000,000; expenditures by nationals abroad U.S.$7,000,000.

Foreign trade

Balance of trade (current prices)

	1992	1993	1994	1995	1996	1997
CFAF '000,000,000	–50.1	–56.1	–36.5	–76.0	–64.2	–69.7
% of total	33.7%	22.5%	9.6%	15.8%	12.9%	13.1%

Imports (1997): CFAF 300,800,000,000 (cotton yarn and fabric 20.2%; machinery and transport equipment 16.2%; rice 7.4%; iron and steel 4.5%). *Major import sources* (1995): France 27.1%; United Kingdom 9.6%; China 9.3%; Thailand 9.1%; Hong Kong 8.8%; The Netherlands 5.6%; United States 4.8%; Germany 4.3%.
Exports (1997): CFAF 231,100,000,000 (cotton yarn 51.6%, reexport 38.5%, cotton seed 2.8%, crude petroleum 2.2%). *Major export destinations* (1997): Brazil 18.0%; Portugal 11.0%; Morocco 10.0%; India 6.5%; Libya 6.0%; Italy 4.5%; United States 4.5%.

Transport and communications

Transport. Railroads (1997): length 359 mi, 578 km; passenger-mi 75,683,000, passenger-km 121,800,000; short ton-mi cargo 193,495,000, metric ton-km cargo 311,400,000. Roads (1996): total length 4,217 mi, 6,787 km (paved 20.0%). Vehicles (1996): passenger cars 37,772; trucks and buses 8,058. Merchant marine (1992): vessels (100 gross tons and over) 12; total deadweight tonnage 210. Air transport (1998)[15]: passenger-mi 160,477,000, passenger-km 258,263,000; short ton-mi cargo 8,404,000, metric ton-km cargo 13,524,000; airports (1998) with scheduled flights 1.

Communications

Medium	date	unit	number	units per 1,000 persons
Daily newspapers	1996	circulation	12,000	2
Radio	1996	receivers	620,000	110
Television	1997	receivers	60,000	10.4
Telephones	1998	main lines	38,354	6.1
Cellular telephones	1998	subscribers	6,286	1.0
Internet	1998	users	2,000	0.3

Education and health

Educational attainment (1992). Percentage of population age 25 and over having: no formal schooling 78.5%; primary education 10.8%; some secondary 8.2%; secondary 1.2%; postsecondary 1.3%. *Literacy* (1995): total percentage of population age 15 and over literate 37.0%; males literate 48.7%; females literate 25.8%.

Education (1996–97)

	schools	teachers	students	student/ teacher ratio
Primary	3,072	13,957	779,329	55.8
Secondary	145[16]	5,352	146,135	27.3
Voc., teacher tr.[16]	14	283	4,873	17.2
Higher	1[16]	962	14,085	14.6

Health: physicians (1993) 363 (1 per 14,216 persons); hospital beds (1993) 1,235 (1 per 4,182 persons); infant mortality rate (1999) 97.8.
Food (1998): daily per capita caloric intake 2,571 (vegetable products 96%, animal products 4%); 112% of FAO recommended minimum requirement.

Military

Total active duty personnel (1999): 4,800 (army 93.8%, navy 3.1%, air force 3.1%). *Military expenditure as percentage of GNP* (1997): 1.3% (world 2.6%); per capita expenditure U.S.$5.

[1]Office of Prime Minister vacant from May 1998. [2]Porto-Novo, the official capital established under the constitution, is the seat of the legislature, but the president and most government ministers reside in Cotonou. [3]Administrative structure announced in 1997. [4]Estimated figures. [5]Borgou includes Alibori. [6]Atacora includes Donga. [7]Atlantique includes Littoral. [8]Zou includes Collines. [9]Mono includes Couffo. [10]Ouémé includes Plateau. [11]1992. [12]1996. [13]Age 10 years and over. [14]Detail does not add to total given because of rounding. [15]Represents 1/11 of the traffic of Air Afrique, which is operated by 11 West African states. [16]1993–94.

Internet resources for further information:
- **Découvrez la République du Bénin http://planben.intnet.bj**

Bermuda

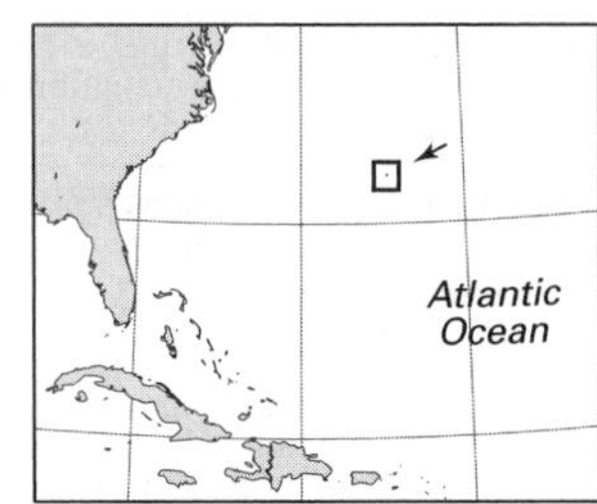

Official name: Bermuda.
Political status: colony (United Kingdom) with two legislative houses (Senate [11]; House of Assembly [40]).
Chief of state: British Monarch, represented by Governor.
Head of government: Premier.
Capital: Hamilton.
Official language: English.
Official religion: none.
Monetary unit: 1 Bermuda dollar (Bd$) = 100 cents; valuation (Oct. 6, 2000) 1 U.S.$ = Bd$1.00[1]; 1 £ = Bd$1.45.

Area and population	area		population
			1991
Municipalities	sq mi	sq km	census
Hamilton	0.3	0.8	1,100
St. George	0.5	1.3	1,648
Parishes			
Devonshire	2.0	5.1	7,371
Hamilton	2.0	5.1	4,680
Paget	2.1	5.3	4,877
Pembroke[2]	1.8	4.6	10,407
St. George's[3, 4]	3.5	8.0	2,975
Sandys	2.1	5.4	6,437
Smith's	1.8	4.7	5,261
Southampton	2.2	5.6	5,804
Warwick	2.0	5.1	7,900
TOTAL	20.5[5, 6]	53.1[5, 6]	58,460[7]

Demography

Population (2000): 63,000.
Density (2000): persons per sq mi 3,073, persons per sq km 1,186.
Urban-rural (1998): urban 100.0%; rural, none.
Sex distribution (1997): male 48.61%; female 51.39%.
Age breakdown (1991): under 15, 19.5%; 15–29, 24.0%; 30–44, 26.8%; 45–59, 16.3%; 60 and over, 13.4%.
Population projection: (2010) 67,000; (2020) 69,000.
Doubling time: 99 years.
Ethnic composition (1991): black 57.8%; white 36.2%; other 6.0%.
Religious affiliation (1991): Protestant 66.9%, of which Anglican 27.5%, Methodist 13.9%, Seventh Day Adventist 6.3%; Roman Catholic 14.9%; nonreligious 10.2%; other 8.0%.
Major cities (1991): St. George 1,648; Hamilton 1,100.

Vital statistics

Birth rate per 1,000 population (1996): 13.9 (world avg. 22.1); legitimate 57.7%; illegitimate 42.3%.
Death rate per 1,000 population (1996): 6.9 (world avg. 8.9).
Natural increase rate per 1,000 population (1996): 7.0 (world avg. 13.2).
Total fertility rate (avg. births per childbearing woman; 1999): 1.8.
Marriage rate per 1,000 population (1996): 15.4.
Divorce rate per 1,000 population (1996): 3.7.
Life expectancy at birth (1999): male 74.8 years; female 78.7 years.
Major causes of death per 100,000 population (1993): diseases of the circulatory system 318.6; malignant neoplasms (cancers) 212.4; infectious and parasitic diseases 61.4; accidents and violence 39.8.

National economy

Budget (1999). Revenue: Bd$562,200,000 (customs duty 31.3%; payroll tax 27.0%; fees, sales, recoveries, and other miscellaneous receipts 15.0%; tax on international companies 6.3%). Expenditures: Bd$545,700,000 (current expenditure 91.4%, of which public debt 2.3%; development expenditure 8.6%).
Public debt (external, outstanding; 1998): n.a.
Production (value in Bd$'000 except as noted). Agriculture, forestry, fishing (1996): vegetables 3,000, milk 2,060, fruits 800, eggs 450, honey 181; livestock (number of live animals; 1999) 900 horses, 600 cattle, 45,000 chickens; roundwood, n.a.; fish catch (metric tons; 1998) 457, of which crustaceans and mollusks 38. Mining and quarrying: crushed stone for local use. Manufacturing: industries include pharmaceuticals, cosmetics, electronics, fish processing, handicrafts, and small boat building[8]. Construction: residential 19,100; nonresidential 118,600. Energy production (consumption): electricity (kW-hr; 1996) 525,000,000 (525,000,000); coal, none (none); crude petroleum, none (none); petroleum products (metric tons; 1996) none (151,000); natural gas, none (none).
Land use (1988): forested 20.0%; meadows and pastures 0.9%; agricultural and under permanent cultivation 3.1%; built-on, wasteland, and other 76.0%.
Tourism: receipts from visitors (1997) U.S.$478,000,000; expenditures by nationals abroad (1993) U.S.$140,000,000.
Population economically active (1991): total 35,222; activity rate of total population 60.2%[7] (participation rates: ages 15–64, 80.9%[7]; female 47.1%[7]; unemployed [1995] 1.5%).

Price and earnings indexes (1995 = 100)							
	1993	1994	1995	1996	1997	1998	1999
Consumer price index	95.4	97.5	100.0	102.5	104.6	106.7	109.3
Weekly earnings index[9]	93.5	97.1	100.0	103.0	...	...	...

Gross national product (1997): U.S.$2,128,000,000 (U.S.$34,470 per capita).

Structure of gross domestic product and labour force	1995–96		1997[10]	
	in value U.S.$'000	% of total value	labour force[11]	% of labour force
Agriculture, fishing	...	...	400	1.1
Quarrying	...	...	106	0.3
Manufacturing	...	...	889	2.5
Construction	...	...	2,043	5.8
Public utilities	...	...	522	1.5
Transp. and commun.	...	...	2,220	6.3
Trade, restaurants	...	...	10,914	30.9
Finance, real estate	...	...	5,240	14.8
Pub. admin., defense	...	...	4,608	13.1
Services	...	...	5,687	16.1
Other[12]	...	...	2,667	7.6
TOTAL	2,024,000	100.0	35,296	100.0

Household income and expenditure (1993). Average household size 2.5; average annual income per household Bd$65,676 (U.S.$65,676); sources of income: wages and salaries 65.3%, imputed income from owner occupancy 10.6%, self-employment 9.0%, net rental income 4.8%, pensions 3.3%, interest 3.3%; dividends 2.1%, other 1.7%; expenditure: housing 27.7%, household furnishings 16.6%, food and nonalcoholic beverages 14.6%, health care 7.6%, transportation 7.3%, foreign travel 6.0%, clothing and footwear 4.9%, recreation 4.8%, education 3.8%, energy 3.3%, alcohol and tobacco 2.2%, other 1.2%.

Foreign trade

Balance of trade (current prices)						
	1993	1994	1995	1996	1997	1998
Bd$'000,000	–495	–514	–496	–514	–554	–564
% of total	86.4%	87.4%	82.1%	82.4%	81.0%	80.3%

Imports (1997): Bd$631,900,000 (machinery and transport equipment 23.8%; food and beverages 19.1%; chemicals and chemical products 7.8%; mineral fuels 7.2%; clothing 7.0%). *Major import sources:* United States 76.0%; Canada 5.5%; United Kingdom 4.9%; France 1.2%.
Exports (1993): Bd$35,272,000 (reexports 99.99%, of which drugs and medicine 71.12%; Bermuda-originated exports 0.01%). *Major export destinations* (1995): United States 49.8%; United Kingdom 6.2%; nonspecified 44.0%.

Transport and communications

Transport. Railroads: none. Roads (1997): total length 140 mi, 225 km (paved 100%)[13]. Vehicles (1996): passenger cars 21,220; trucks and buses 4,007. Merchant marine (1990): vessels (100 gross tons and over) 105; total deadweight tonnage 7,800,242. Air transport (1996): passenger arrivals 519,772, passenger departures 516,759; cargo unloaded 5,909 metric tons, cargo loaded 727 metric tons; airports (1998) with scheduled flights 1.

Communications				units
Medium	date	unit	number	per 1,000 persons
Daily newspapers	1996	circulation	17,000	277
Radio	1997	receivers	82,000	1,328
Television	1997	receivers	66,000	1,069
Telephones	1998	main lines	53,730	865
Cellular telephones	1998	subscribers	12,572	202

Education and health

Educational attainment (1991). Percentage of total population age 25 and over having: no formal schooling 0.5%; incomplete or complete primary 18.2%; incomplete or complete secondary 62.9%; higher 18.4%. *Literacy* (1997): total population age 15 and over literate, 98%.

Education (1996–97)	schools	teachers	students	student/ teacher ratio
Primary (age 5–11)	26	478	5,883	12.3
Secondary (age 12–16)	...	355	3,726	10.5
Higher	1	...	543	...

Health (1996): physicians 96 (1 per 639 persons); hospital beds 251[14] (1 per 244 persons); infant mortality rate per 1,000 live births 3.6.
Food (1997): daily per capita caloric intake 3,025 (vegetable products 73%, animal products 27%); 120% of FAO recommended minimum requirement.

Military

Total active duty personnel (1997): 700; part-time defense force assists police and is drawn from Bermudian conscripts.

[1]The Bermuda dollar is at par with the U.S. dollar. [2]Excludes the area and population of the city of Hamilton. [3]Excludes the area and population of the town of St. George. [4]Includes the 2.0 sq mi (5.2 sq km) area of the former U.S. military base closed in 1995. [5]Includes 0.4 sq mi (1.1 sq km) of uninhabited islands. [6]Detail (including areas cited in footnote 5) does not add to total given because of rounding. [7]Excludes 12,624 short-term visitors, 2,889 on-base military personnel, and 864 institutionalized persons. [8]The economy of Bermuda is overwhelmingly based on service industries such as tourism, insurance companies, offshore financial centres, e-commerce companies, and ship repair facilities. [9]Service industry. [10]August. [11]Employed only; excludes family workers. [12]Extra-territorial organizations and bodies. [13]Excludes 138 mi (222 km) of paved private roads. [14]Excludes beds in geriatric, rehabilitation, and hospice units.

Internet resources for further information:
- **The Bermuda Chamber of Commerce http://www.bermudacommerce.com**

Bhutan

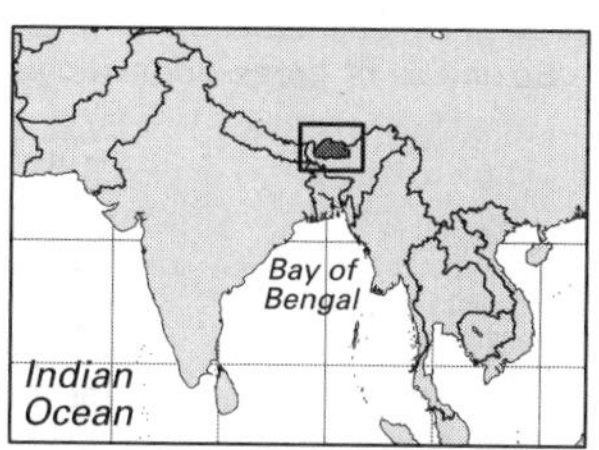

Official name: Druk-Yul (Kingdom of Bhutan).
Form of government: constitutional[1] monarchy with one legislative house (National Assembly [150[2]]).
Chief of state: Monarch[1].
Head of government: Chairman of Council of Ministers[1].
Capital: Thimphu.
Official language: Dzongkha (a Tibetan dialect).
Official religion: Mahāyāna Buddhism.
Monetary unit: 1 ngultrum[3] (Nu) = 100 chetrum; valuation (Oct. 6, 2000) 1 U.S.$ = Nu 46.11; 1 £ = Nu 66.70.

Area and population

Districts	Capitals	area sq mi	area sq km	population 1998 estimate
Bumthang	Jakar	1,150	2,990	...
Chhukha	Chhukha	...	...	...
Chirang	Damphu	310	800	...
Dagana	Dagana	540	1,400	...
Gaylegphug	Gaylegphug	1,020	2,640	...
Ha	Ha	830	2,140	...
Lhuntshi	Lhuntshi	1,120	2,910	...
Mongar	Mongar	710	1,830	...
Paro	Paro	580	1,500	...
Pema Gatsel	Pema Gatsel	150	380	...
Punakha	Punakha	2,330	6,040	...
Samchi	Samchi	830	2,140	...
Samdrup Jongkhar	Samdrup Jongkhar	900	2,340	...
Shemgang	Shemgang	980	2,540	...
Tashigang	Tashigang	1,640	4,260	...
Thimphu	Thimphu	630	1,620	...
Tongsa	Tongsa	570	1,470	...
Wangdi Phodrang	Wangdi Phodrang	1,160	3,000	...
TOTAL		18,150[4, 5]	47,000[4, 5]	633,000[6]

Demography

Population (2000): 667,000[6].
Density (2000): persons per sq mi 36.7, persons per sq km 14.2.
Urban-rural (1999): urban 7.0%; rural 93.0%.
Sex distribution (1988): male 50.97%; female 49.03%.
Age breakdown (1988): under 15, 40.3%; 15–29, 26.4%; 30–44, 16.5%; 45–59, 10.5%; 60–74, 5.2%; 75 and over, 1.1%.
Population projection: (2010) 840,000; (2020) 1,031,000.
Doubling time: 25 years.
Ethnic composition (1993): Bhutiā (Ngalops) 50.0%; Nepalese (Gurung) 35.0%; Sharchops 15.0%.
Religious affiliation (1998): Buddhist 75.0%; Hindu 25.0%.
Major cities (1993): Thimphu 30,340; Phuntsholing 10,000[7].

Vital statistics

Birth rate per 1,000 population (1999): 36.9 (world avg. 22.1).
Death rate per 1,000 population (1999): 9.4 (world avg. 8.9).
Natural increase rate per 1,000 population (1999): 27.5 (world avg. 13.2).
Total fertility rate (avg. births per childbearing woman; 1999): 5.4.
Marital status of population 15 years and over (1985): married 71.2%; single 19.7%; widowed 7.5%; divorced 1.6%.
Divorce rate per 1,000 population: n.a.
Life expectancy at birth (1999): male 60.0 years; female 63.0 years.
Major causes of death (percentage distribution; 1989): respiratory tract infections 19.5%; diarrhea/dysentery 15.2%; skin infections 12.2%; parasitic worm infestations 10.0%; malaria 9.4%.

National economy

Budget (1998–99). Revenue: Nu 6,844,000,000 (internal revenue 45.2%, grants from UN and other international agencies 21.6%, grants from government of India 33.2%). Expenditures: Nu 6,999,000,000 (capital expenditures 59.3%, current expenditures 40.7%).
Public debt (external, outstanding; 1998): U.S.$119,600,000.
Production (metric tons except as noted). Agriculture, forestry, fishing (1999): oranges 58,000, rice 50,000, corn (maize) 39,000, potatoes 34,100, sugarcane 12,800, green peppers and chilies 8,500, millet 7,000, apples 5,500, wheat 5,000, barley 4,000, pulses 1,600; livestock (number of live animals) 435,000 cattle, 74,900 pigs, 58,500 sheep, 42,100 goats, 29,900 horses; roundwood (1998) 1,702,000 cu m; fish catch (1997) 330. Mining and quarrying (1997): limestone 270,000; dolomite 250,000; gypsum 50,000. Manufacturing (value in Nu '000,000; 1994): chemical products 419.0; cement 255.1; wood board products 230.6; distillery products 178.3; processed fruits 103.0. Construction (number of buildings completed; 1977–78): residential 10; nonresidential (guest house) 1. Energy production (consumption): electricity (kW-hr; 1996) 1,737,000,000 (261,000,000); coal (metric tons; 1996) 2,000 (23,000); crude petroleum, none (n.a.); petroleum products (metric tons; 1996) none (39,000); natural gas, none (n.a.).
Household income and expenditure. Average household size (1980) 5.4[6]; income per household: n.a.; sources of income: n.a.; expenditure (1979): food 72.3%, clothing 21.2%, energy 3.7%, household durable goods 0.7%, personal effects and other 2.1%.
Gross national product (at current market prices; 1998): U.S.$354,000,000 (U.S.$470 per capita).

Structure of gross domestic product and labour force

	1997 in value Nu '000,000	1997 % of total value	1984 labour force	1984 % of labour force
Agriculture	5,288	38.4	303,000[8]	87.2
Mining	310	2.2		
Manufacturing	1,742	12.7		
Construction	1,206	8.8		
Trade	1,014	7.4		
Public utilities	1,732	12.6	3,000[8]	0.9
Transportation and communications	1,018	7.4		
Finance	495	3.6		
Pub. admin., defense / Services	1,363	9.9	12,000[8] / 30,000[8]	3.4 / 8.5[9]
Other	–417[10]	–3.0[10]	...	...
TOTAL	13,751	100.0	348,000	100.0

Population economically active (1984)[6]: total 348,000; activity rate of total population 53.4% (participation rates: ages 15–64, 94.8%; female 55.0%; unemployed 6.5%).

Price and earnings indexes (1995 = 100)

	1991	1992	1993	1994	1995	1996	1997
Consumer price index	66.1	76.8	85.4	91.3	100.0	108.8	115.9
Earnings index	...	...	...	...	...	...	...

Land use (1994): forested 66.0%; meadows and pastures 5.8%; agricultural and under permanent cultivation 2.8%; other 25.4%.
Tourism (1997): receipts from visitors U.S.$6,000,000; expenditures by nationals abroad, n.a.

Foreign trade[11]

Balance of trade (current prices)

	1993	1994	1995	1996	1997
Nu '000,000	–754.9	–793.7	–292.8	–971.4	–703.9
% of total	15.9%	16.0%	4.2%	12.0%	7.6%

Imports (1997): Nu 4,978,000,000 ([12]petroleum products 4.6%, rice 4.6%, vegetable fats and oils 3.0%, steel products 2.4%, wheat 2.0%, industrial machinery 1.7%). *Major import source* (1997–98): India 70.5%.
Exports (1997): Nu 4,274,100,000 ([12]electricity 21.0%, calcium carbide 15.0%, particle board 8.0%, cement 7.1%). *Major export destination* (1997–98): India 94.5%.

Transport and communications

Transport. Railroads: none. Roads (1996): total length 1,998 mi, 3,285 km (paved 61%). Vehicles (1988): passenger cars 2,590; trucks and buses 1,367. Merchant marine: none. Air transport (1996): passenger-mi 29,000,000, passenger-km 46,000,000; metric ton-km cargo, n.a.; airports (1997) with scheduled flights 1.

Communications

Medium	date	unit	number	units per 1,000 persons
Radio	1997	receivers	37,000	19
Television	1997	receivers	11,000	5.5
Telephones	1998	main lines	10,437	16
Personal computers	1998	units	2,500	3.9
Internet	...	users	...	...

Education and health

Educational attainment: n.a. *Literacy* (1995 est.): total population age 15 and over literate 42.2%; males literate 56.2%; females literate 28.1%

Education (1994)

	schools	teachers	students	student/ teacher ratio
Primary (age 7–11)	235[13]	1,611	60,089	37.3
Secondary (age 12–16)	31[14]	544	7,299	13.4
Voc., teacher tr.	8[14]	95	1,822[14]	12.2[14]
Higher	2[14]	57[14]	2,055	9.1[14]

Health: physicians (1994) 100 (1 per 8,000 persons); hospital beds 970 (1 per 825 persons); infant mortality rate per 1,000 live births (1999) 60.
Food (1975–77): daily per capita caloric intake 2,058 (vegetable products 98%, animal products 2%); 89% of FAO recommended minimum requirement.

Military

Total active duty personnel (1993): about 7,000 (army 100%).

[1]There is no formal constitution, but a form of constitutional monarchy is in place; reforms in July 1998 curtailed the powers of the monarchy and increased the powers of the Council of Ministers. [2]Includes 45 nonelective seats occupied by representatives of the King and religious groups. [3]Indian currency is also accepted legal tender; the ngultrum is at par with the Indian rupee. [4]2,700 sq mi (7,000 sq km) are not included in the district area totals. [5]Includes Chhukha area. [6]Excludes nearly 100,000 Bhutanese of Nepalese origin declared stateless by the Bhutanese government in late 1990. [7]1982. [8]Derived value. [9]Includes 6.5% with no occupation. [10]Imputed bank service charges. [11]Import figures are c.i.f. in balance of trade, commodities, and trading partners. [12]1996. [13]1993. [14]1990.

Internet resources for further information:

- **The Library of Congress Country Studies: Bhutan http://lcweb2.loc.gov/frd/cs/bttoc.html**

Bolivia

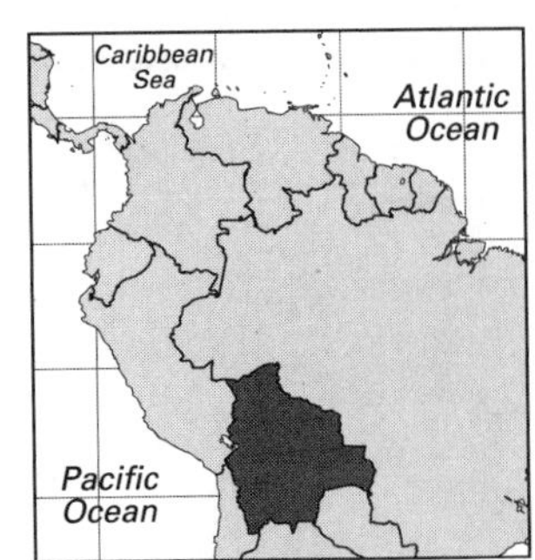

Official name: República de Bolivia (Republic of Bolivia).
Form of government: unitary multiparty republic with two legislative houses (Chamber of Senators [27]; Chamber of Deputies [130]).
Head of state and government: President.
Capitals: La Paz (administrative); Sucre (judicial).
Official languages: Spanish, Aymara, Quechua.
Official religion: Roman Catholicism.
Monetary unit: 1 boliviano (Bs) = 100 centavos; valuation (Oct. 6, 2000) 1 U.S.$ = Bs 6.26; 1 £ = Bs 9.06.

Area and population

Departments	Capitals	area sq mi	area sq km	population 2000[1] estimate
Beni	Trinidad	82,458	213,564	366,047
Chuquisaca	Sucre	19,893	51,524	589,948
Cochabamba	Cochabamba	21,479	55,631	1,524,724
La Paz	La Paz	51,732	133,985	2,406,377
Oruro	Oruro	20,690	53,588	393,991
Pando	Cobija	24,644	63,827	57,316
Potosí	Potosí	45,644	118,218	774,696
Santa Cruz	Santa Cruz	143,098	370,621	1,812,522
Tarija	Tarija	14,526	37,623	403,079
TOTAL		424,164	1,098,581	8,328,700

Demography

Population (2000): 8,329,000.
Density (2000): persons per sq mi 19.6, persons per sq km 7.6.
Urban-rural (2000): urban 63.7%; rural 36.3%.
Sex distribution (2000): male 49.99%; female 50.01%.
Age breakdown (1995): under 15, 40.6%; 15–29, 27.5%; 30–44, 16.3%; 45–59, 9.6%; 60–74, 5.0%; 75 and over, 1.0%.
Population projection: (2010) 10,229,000; (2020) 12,193,000.
Doubling time: 34 years.
Ethnic composition (1996): Indian 55.0%; mestizo 30.0%; white 15.0%.
Religious affiliation (1995): Roman Catholic 88.5%; Protestant 9.0%; other 2.5%.
Major cities (2000): Santa Cruz 1,016,137; La Paz 1,000,899; Cochabamba 607,129; El Alto 568,919; Oruro 232,311; Sucre 192,238.

Vital statistics

Birth rate per 1,000 population (2000): 31.9 (world avg. 22.1).
Death rate per 1,000 population (2000): 8.6 (world avg. 8.9).
Natural increase rate per 1,000 population (2000): 23.3 (world avg. 13.2).
Total fertility rate (avg. births per childbearing woman; 1999): 3.8.
Marriage rate per 1,000 population (1980): 4.8.
Life expectancy at birth (1999): male 60.8 years; female 65.9 years.
Major causes of death (percentage of total registered deaths; 1980–81): infectious and parasitic diseases 23.9%; diseases of the circulatory system 19.5%; diseases of the respiratory system 14.0%; accidents, homicides, and violence 9.8%; diseases of the digestive system 8.6%.

National economy

Budget (1998). Revenue: Bs 11,698,500,000 (tax revenue 78.9%, of which indirect taxes 49.0%, taxes on petroleum and petroleum products 18.8%; nontax revenue 8.9%). Expenditures: Bs 13,681,300,000 (current expenditure 78.8%, of which wages and salaries 31.3%, transfers 21.9%; capital expenditure 21.2%).
Production (metric tons except as noted). Agriculture, forestry, fishing (1999): sugarcane 4,160,000, soybeans 762,000, potatoes 783,000, bananas and plantains 767,000, corn (maize) 613,000, cassava 400,000, rice 189,000, sorghum 148,000, wheat 140,000; livestock (number of live animals) 8,575,000 sheep, 6,556,000 cattle, 2,715,000 pigs, 1,500,000 goats, 631,000 asses, 322,000 horses; roundwood (1998) 1,989,000 cu m; fish catch (1998) 6,055. Mining and quarrying (metric tons of pure metal; 1998): zinc 150,709; lead 13,848; tin 10,542; silver 402; gold 14.4. Manufacturing (value added in U.S.$'000; 1994): petroleum products 375; food products 169; beverages 99; nonmetal mineral products 36; textiles 23; printing and publishing 19; nonferrous metals 18. Construction (1985)[2]: residential dwellings 226. Energy production (consumption): electricity (kW-hr; 1998) 3,771,000,000 (3,252,000,000); coal, none (none); crude petroleum (barrels; 1998) 12,628,000 (10,382,000); petroleum products (metric tons; 1996) 1,325,000 (1,480,000); natural gas (cu m; 1998) 3,106,000,000 (1,511,000,000).
Population economically active (1997): total 3,645,165; activity rate of total population 46.6% (participation rates: ages 15–64, 72.1%; female 43.7%; unemployed 2.1%).

Price and earnings indexes (1995 = 100)

	1994	1995	1996	1997	1998	1999
Consumer price index	90.8	100.0	112.4	117.7	126.8	129.5
Monthly earnings index[3]	92.7	100.0	108.8	117.1	146.3	...

Gross national product (at current market prices; 1998): U.S.$8,013,000,000 (U.S.$1,010 per capita).
Tourism (1998): receipts U.S.$174,000,000; expenditures U.S.$172,000,000.

Structure of gross domestic product and labour force

	1999 in value Bs '000[4]	1999 % of total value[4]	1997 labour force[5]	1997 % of labour force[5]
Agriculture	3,105,038	14.1	1,541,859	42.3
Mining	1,998,841	9.1	63,871	1.7
Manufacturing	3,649,645	16.6	393,451	10.8
Construction	824,155	3.7	187,015	5.1
Public utilities	452,631	2.1	11,029	0.3
Transp. and commun.	2,383,850	10.9	170,531	4.7
Trade	1,866,818	8.5	632,415	17.3
Finance	2,235,150	10.2	78,842	2.2
Pub. admin., defense	1,954,104	8.9	490,728 (Pub. admin., defense and Services)	13.5
Services	1,658,209	7.6		
Other	1,820,911[6]	8.3[6]	75,424[7]	2.1[7]
TOTAL	21,949,352	100.0	3,645,165	100.0

Public debt (external, outstanding; 1998): U.S.$4,307,000,000.
Household income and expenditure. Average household size (1997): 4.4; average annual income per household: n.a.; sources of income: n.a.; expenditure (1988): food 35.5%, transportation and communications 17.7%, housing 14.8%, household durable goods 7.3%, clothing and footwear 5.1%, beverages and tobacco 4.5%, recreation 2.7%, health 2.1%, education 0.3%.
Land use (1994): forested 53.5%; meadows and pastures 24.4%; agricultural and under permanent cultivation 2.2%; other 19.9%.

Foreign trade[8]

Balance of trade (current prices)

	1994	1995	1996	1997	1998	1999
U.S.$'000,000	–89.3	–162.5	–313.4	–531.6	–721.0	–42.9
% of total	4.1%	6.9%	12.1%	18.6%	24.6%	2.0%

Imports (1998): U.S.$1,983,000,000 (raw materials 42.2%, of which raw materials for industry 32.8%; capital goods 40.0%, of which transportation equipment 23.1%, capital goods for industry 15.9%; consumer goods 18.2%, of which nondurable consumer goods 9.3%, durable consumer goods 8.9%; other 0.4%). *Major import sources:* U.S. 26.3%; Japan 20.0%; Brazil 10.3%; Argentina 10.0%; Chile 6.0%; Peru 3.7%; France 1.1%.
Exports (1998): U.S.$1,104,900,000 (zinc 14.1%; soybeans 13.6%; gold 10.1%; silver 6.6%; oils 5.8%; natural gas 5.1%; tin 5.1%; timber 4.6%). *Major export destinations:* U.S. 18.4%; U.K. 17.8%; Peru 11.9%; Argentina 10.9%; Chile 2.9%; Brazil 2.4%; Germany 1.9%.

Transport and communications

Transport. Railroads (1997): route length 2,187 mi, 3,519 km; passenger-mi 84,900,000, passenger-km 136,700,000; short ton-mi cargo 358,900,000, metric ton-km cargo 524,200,000. Roads (1996): total length 30,696 mi, 49,400 km (paved 6%[9]). Vehicles (1996): passenger cars 223,829; trucks and buses 138,536. Merchant marine (1992): vessels (100 gross tons and over) 1; total deadweight tonnage 15,765. Air transport (1998)[10]: passenger-mi 1,222,-606,000, passenger-km 1,967,597,000; short ton-mi cargo 28,743,000, metric ton-km cargo 41,964,000; airports (1997) with scheduled flights 14.

Communications

Medium	date	unit	number	units per 1,000 persons
Daily newspapers	1996	circulation	420,000	55
Radio	1997	receivers	5,250,000	675
Television	1998	receivers	930,000	117
Telephones	1997	main lines	535,000	69
Cellular telephones	1998	subscribers	218,000	27
Personal computers	1998	units	60,000	7.5
Internet	1998	users	17,000	2.1

Education and health

Educational attainment (1992). Percentage of population age 25 and over having: no formal schooling 23.3%; some primary 20.3%; primary education 21.7%; some secondary 9.0%; secondary 6.5%; some higher 5.0%; higher 4.8%; not specified 9.4%. *Literacy* (1995): total population age 15 and over literate 82.3%; males literate 92.1%; females literate 79.4%.

Education (1990–91)

	schools[11]	teachers	students	student/teacher ratio
Primary (age 6–13)	9,758	51,763	1,278,775	24.7
Secondary (age 14–17)	724	12,434 (Secondary and Voc., teacher tr.)	219,232	17.6
Voc., teacher tr.	47			
Higher[12]	10	4,261	109,503	25.7

Health (1994): physicians 1,976 (1 per 3,663 persons); hospital beds 7,203 (1 per 1,005 persons); infant mortality rate per 1,000 live births (1999) 62.0.
Food (1997): daily per capita caloric intake 2,214 (vegetable products 81%, animal products 19%); 93% of FAO recommended minimum requirement.

Military

Total active duty personnel (1999): 32,500 (army 76.9%, navy 13.8%, air force 9.2%). *Military expenditure as percentage of GNP* (1997): 1.9% (world 2.6%); per capita expenditure U.S.$20.

[1]January 1. [2]National government sponsored only. [3]December. [4]In 1990 prices. [5]Population 10 years of age and over. [6]Net import duties. [7]Unemployed. [8]Import figures are f.o.b. in balance of trade and c.i.f. for commodities and trading partners. [9]1995. [10]LAB airlines only. [11]1986–87. [12]1991–92.

Internet resources for further information:

- **Instituto Nacional de Estadística http://www.ine.gov.bo**
- **UNDP Bolivia http://guf.pnud.bo/bolbrief.htm**

Bosnia and Herzegovina[1]

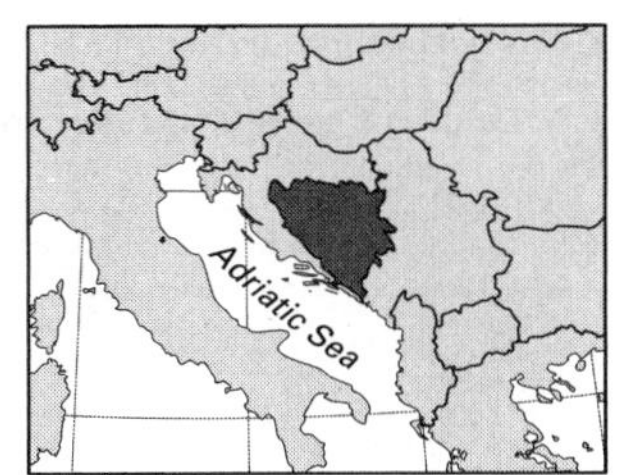

Official name: Bosna i Hercegovina (Bosnia and Herzegovina).
Form of government: federal multiparty republic with bicameral legislature (House of Peoples [15[2]]; House of Representatives [42]).
Chiefs of state: Tripartite presidency.
Head of government: Prime Minister (Chairman of the Council of Ministers).
Capital: Sarajevo.
Official language: Bosnian.
Official religion: none.
Monetary unit: 1 marka[3, 4] (KM) = 100 pfenning; valuation (Oct. 6, 2000) 1 U.S.$ = KM 2.25; 1 £ = KM 3.25.

Area and population

		area		population
Autonomous Regions	Principal city	sq mi	sq km	1991 estimate[5]
Cantons				
Federation of Bosnia and Herzegovina	Sarajevo	10,068	26,076	2,742,000
Central Bosnia	Travnik	1,240[6]	3,200[6]	305,000
Goražde	Goražde	170[6]	440[6]	78,000
Neretva	Mostar	1,680[6]	4,360[6]	253,000
Posavina	Orašje	90[6]	240[6]	61,000
Sarajevo	Sarajevo	460[6]	1,190[6]	526,000
Tuzla-Podrinje	Tuzla	1,120[6]	2,890[6]	555,000
Una-Sava	Bihać	1,690[6]	4,390[6]	358,000
Western Bosnia	Livno	1,910[6]	4,930[6]	117,000
Western Herzegovina	Ljubuški	450[6]	1,160[6]	60,000
Zenica-Doboj	Zenica	1,270[6]	3,300[6]	429,000
Republika Srpska	Banja Luka	9,673	25,053	1,628,000
TOTAL		19,741	51,129	4,370,000

Demography

Population (2000)[7]: 3,836,000.
Density (2000)[7]: persons per sq mi 194.3, persons per sq km 75.0.
Urban-rural (1999): urban 42.5%; rural 57.5%.
Sex distribution (1995): male 49.46%; female 50.54%.
Age breakdown (1995): under 15, 21.9%; 15–29, 23.5%; 30–44, 26.3%; 45–59, 15.7%; 60–74, 10.6%; 75 and over, 2.0%.
Population projection: (2010) 4,103,000; (2020) 4,182,000.
Ethnic composition (1999): Bosniac 44.0%; Serb 31.0%; Croat 17.0%; other 8.0%.
Religious affiliation (1999): Sunnī Muslim 43.0%; Serbian Orthodox 30.0%; Roman Catholic 18.0%; other (mostly nonreligious) 9.0%.
Major cities (1991): Sarajevo (1997) 360,000; Banja Luka (1997) 160,000; Zenica 96,027; Tuzla 83,770; Mostar 75,865.

Vital statistics

Birth rate per 1,000 population (1999): 13.2 (world avg. 22.1); (1993) legitimate 92.6%; illegitimate 7.4%.
Death rate per 1,000 population (1999): 8.7 (world avg. 8.9).
Natural increase rate per 1,000 population (1999): 4.5 (world avg. 13.2).
Total fertility rate (avg. births per childbearing woman; 1999): 1.7.
Marriage rate per 1,000 population (1991): 6.0.
Divorce rate per 1,000 population (1991): 0.3.
Life expectancy at birth (1999): male 66.9 years; female 73.0 years.
Major causes of death per 100,000 population (1989): circulatory diseases 344.1; malignant neoplasms (cancers) 122.6; accidents, violence, and poisoning 47.1; digestive system diseases 29.2; respiratory diseases 29.0.

National economy

Budget (1998). Revenue: KM 3,148,000,000 (tax revenue 64.6%, of which taxes on goods and services 37.8%, customs duties 12.9%; nontax revenue 35.4%). Expenditures: KM 3,657,000,000 (social funds 24.9%; district, canton, or municipal expenditures 22.7%; disability benefits 10.2%; defense 10.1%).
Public debt (external, outstanding; 1998): U.S.$2,981,000,000.
Gross domestic product (1998): U.S.$3,899,000,000 (U.S.$1,110 per capita).
Tourism (1996): receipts from visitors U.S.$16,000,000; expenditures by nationals abroad, n.a.

Structure of gross domestic product and labour force

	1998		1990	
	in value U.S.$'000,000	% of total value	labour force[8]	% of labour force[9]
Agriculture	624	16.0	39,053	3.8
Manufacturing, mining	874	22.4	496,190	48.3
Construction	222	5.7	74,861	7.3
Public utilities	82	2.1	22,345	2.2
Transp. and commun.	308	7.9	68,798	6.7
Trade, restaurants	667	17.1	130,914	12.8
Finance, real estate	218	5.6	38,686	3.8
Pub. admin., defense	335	8.6	} 155,411	} 15.1
Services } Other	569	14.6		
TOTAL	3,899	100.0	1,026,258	100.0

Production (metric tons except as noted). Agriculture, forestry, fishing (1999): potatoes 380,000, wheat 188,000, corn (maize) 160,000, cabbages 80,000, oats 51,000, plums 25,000, tobacco 4,300; livestock (number of live animals) 350,000 cattle, 285,000 sheep; roundwood (1998) 40,000 cu m; fish catch (1997) 2,550. Mining (1996): iron ore (gross weight) 100,000; bauxite 75,000; kaolin 3,000; barite (concentrate) 2,000. Manufacturing (1996): cement 150,000; crude steel 115,000; pig iron 100,000. Energy production (consumption): electricity (kW-hr; 1996) 2,203,000,000 (2,408,000,000); coal (metric tons; 1996) 1,640,000 (1,640,000); petroleum products (metric tons; 1996) none (516,000); natural gas (cu m; 1996) none (252,000,000).
Population economically active (1991): total 992,000; activity rate of total population 22.7% (participation rates: ages 15–64, 35.6%; female [1990] 37.7%; unemployed [1999] 40–45%).
Land use (1994): forested 53.1%; meadows and pastures 23.5%; agricultural and under permanent cultivation 15.7%; other 7.7%.

Price and earnings indexes (1995 = 100)

	1994	1995	1996	1997	1998	1999
Retail price index[9]	104.5	100.0	75.5	83.7	87.9	87.6
Monthly earnings index	...	...	...	...	...	...

Household income and expenditure. Average household size (1991) 3.4; income per household (1990) Din 72,850[10] (U.S.$6,437); sources of income (1990): wages 53.2%, transfers 18.2%, self-employment 12.0%, other 16.6%; expenditure (1988): food 41.3%, clothing 8.3%, fuel and lighting 7.8%, housing 7.8%, transportation 6.0%, beverages and tobacco 5.7%.

Foreign trade[10]

Balance of trade (current prices)

	1994	1995	1996	1997	1998	1999
U.S.$'000,000	–739	–930	+336	–1,758	–1,709	–1,415
% of total	91.1%	75.4%	100.0%	60.4%	51.1%	42.1%

Imports (1998)[10]: U.S.$2,526,000,000. *Major import sources:* Croatia 28%; Germany 15%; Slovenia 14%; Italy 12%; Hungary 6%.
Exports (1998)[10]: U.S.$817,000,000. *Major export destinations:* Croatia 29%; Italy 22%; Germany 19%; Slovenia 8%; Austria 4%.

Transport and communications

Transport. Railroads (1999)[11]: length 1,031 km; passenger-km 31,100,000; metric ton-km cargo 92,800,000. Roads (1996): total length 21,846 km (paved 52%). Vehicles (1996): passenger cars 96,182; trucks and buses 10,919. Air transport (1998)[12]: passenger-km 40,390,000; metric ton-km 430,000. Airports (1997) with scheduled flights 1.

Communications

Medium	date	unit	number	units per 1,000 persons
Daily newspapers	1995	circulation	520,000	155
Radio	1997	receivers	940,000	282
Television	1997	receivers	...	...
Telephones	1997	main lines	333,000	100
Cellular telephones	1997	subscribers	25,181	7.6

Education and health

Educational attainment: n.a. *Literacy:* n.a.

Education (1990–91)

	schools	teachers	students	student/ teacher ratio
Primary (age 7–14)	2,205	23,369	539,875	23.1
Secondary (age 15–18)	238	9,030	172,063	19.1
Higher	44	2,802	37,541	13.4

Health: physicians (1998) 5,000[10] (1 per 700 persons); hospital beds (1996) 15,586 (1 per 208 persons); infant mortality rate (1999) 26.4.
Food: daily per capita caloric intake 2,801 (vegetable products 91%, animal products 9%); 110% of FAO recommended minimum requirement.

Military

Total active duty personnel (1999): n.a.; about 31,000 troops of the NATO-commanded Stabilization Force are stationed in Bosnia and Herzegovina to assure implementation of the Dayton accords. *Military expenditure as percentage of GNP* (1997): 5.9% (world 2.6%); per capita expenditure U.S.$78.

[1]Government structure provided for by Dayton accords and constitutions of 1993 and 1994 is being implemented in stages since formal signing of peace accord on Dec. 14, 1995. [2]All seats are nonelective. [3]An interim currency, the marka (or "convertible mark"; KM), was introduced on June 22, 1998, to replace another interim currency, the Bosnian dinar (BD), at a rate of 1 KM to 100 BD. [4]The KM is pegged to the German Mark (DM) at a rate of 1 KM to 1 DM. [5]Unofficial estimates based on 1991 census. [6]Areas of cantons are approximated figures. [7]Excludes more than 300,000 refugees in adjacent countries and Western Europe. [8]Excludes 28,000 workers in the private sector. [9]Federation of Bosnia and Herzegovina only. [10]Estimated figures. [11]1991–95 war destroyed much infrastructure; limited service resumed in 1998. [12]Air Bosna only.

Internet resources for further information:
- **Central Bank of Bosnia and Herzegovina http://www.cbbh.gov.ba**
- **Embassy of Bosnia and Herzegovina (Washington, D.C.) http://www.bosnianembassy.org**
- **Office of the High Representative in Bosnia and Herzegovina http://www.ohr.int**

Botswana

Official name: Republic of Botswana.
Form of government: multiparty republic with one legislative body[1] (National Assembly [46[2]]).
Head of state and government: President.
Capital: Gaborone.
Official language: English[3].
Official religion: none.
Monetary unit: 1 pula (P) = 100 thebe; valuation (Oct. 6, 2000) 1 U.S.$ = P 5.26; 1 £ = P 7.61.

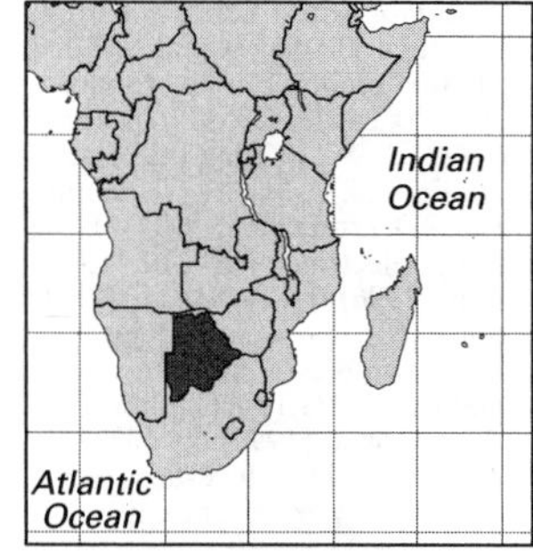

Area and population

Districts	Capitals	area sq mi	area sq km	population 1997 estimate
Barolong	...	773	2,003	19,837
Central	Serowe	57,039	147,730	457,349
Ghanzi	Ghanzi	45,525	117,910	27,099
Kgalagadi	Tsabong	41,290	106,940	34,537
Kgatleng	Mochudi	3,073	7,960	63,712
Kweneng	Molepolole	13,857	35,890	189,672
Ngwaketse	Kanye	10,219	26,467	143,370
North East	Masunga	1,977	5,120	47,312
North West				
Chobe	Kasane	8,031	20,800	16,845
Ngamiland	Maun	33,359	86,400	104,090[4]
Okavango	Orapa	8,776	22,730	[4]
South East	Ramotswa	687	1,780	54,091
Towns[5]				
Francistown	—	31	79	88,195
Gaborone	—	65	169	183,487
Jwaneng	—	39	100	14,866
Lobatse	—	16	42	29,872
Orapa	—	7	17	10,244
Selebi-Pikwe	—	19	50	45,651
Sowa	—	61	159	3,154
TOTAL		224,607[6]	581,730	1,533,383

Demography

Population (2000): 1,576,000.
Density (2000): persons per sq mi 7.0, persons per sq km 2.7.
Urban-rural (1999): urban 29.4%; rural 70.6%.
Sex distribution (2000): male 48.58%; female 51.42%.
Age breakdown (2000): under 15, 40.6%; 15–29, 30.8%; 30–44, 15.0%; 45–59, 7.7%; 60–74, 4.3%; 75 and over, 1.6%.
Population projection: (2010) 1,502,000; (2020) 1,318,000.
Doubling time: 93 years.
Ethnic composition (1983): Tswana 75.5%; Shona 12.4%; San (Bushman) 3.4%; Khoikhoin (Hottentot) 2.5%; Ndebele 1.3%; other 4.9%.
Religious affiliation (1997): traditional beliefs 55.0%; African Christian 27.5%; Protestant 13.5%; Roman Catholic 4.0%.
Major cities (1997): Gaborone 183,487; Francistown 88,195; Selebi-Pikwe 45,651; Molepolole 36,931; Kanye 31,354.

Vital statistics

Birth rate per 1,000 population (2000): 29.6 (world avg. 22.1); (1986) legitimate 28.8%[7]; illegitimate 71.2%[7].
Death rate per 1,000 population (2000): 22.1 (world avg. 8.9).
Natural increase rate per 1,000 population (2000): 7.5 (world avg. 13.2).
Total fertility rate (avg. births per childbearing woman; 2000): 3.8.
Marriage rate per 1,000 population (1987): 1.6.
Life expectancy at birth (1993): male 59.5 years; female 65.6 years.

National economy

Budget (1997–98). Revenue: P 8,468,900,000 (mineral royalties 57.7%, customs and excise taxes 14.0%, property income 13.2%, non-mineral income tax 6.4%). Expenditures: P 7,616,400,000 (education 24.2%, defense 8.4%, health 5.1%, interest 1.3%).
Population economically active (1995): total 439,933; activity rate of total population 29.9% (participation rates: ages 15–64, 59.6%[8]; female 35.5%, unemployed 21.5%).

Price and earnings indexes (1995 = 100)

	1993	1994	1995	1996	1997	1998	1999
Consumer price index	81.9	90.5	100.0	110.1	119.6	127.6	136.6
Monthly earnings index	89.2	93.5	100.0	...	...	...	...

Public debt (external, outstanding; 1998): U.S.$508,200,000.
Tourism (1998): receipts U.S.$175,000,000; expenditures U.S.$126,000,000.
Production (metric tons except as noted). Agriculture, forestry, fishing (1999): cereals 19,800 (of which sorghum 13,000, corn [maize] 5,000, millet 1,300), pulses 16,000, vegetables and melons 15,000, tubers 12,000, fruits 9,500; livestock (number of live animals) 2,380,000 cattle, 1,835,000 goats, 250,000 sheep, 237,500 mules and asses, 33,000 horses; roundwood (1998) 1,066,000 cu m; fish catch (1998) 2,000. Mining and quarrying (1998): nickel 19,432; copper 15,593; cobalt 352; diamonds 19,773,000 carats. Manufacturing (value adder in P '000,000; 1994): food products 164.3; wearing apparel 78.9; paper and paper products 28.0; industrial chemicals 18.7; wood products 17.5. Construction (value added in P '000,000; 1995–96): 877,900. Energy production (consumption): electricity (kW-hr; 1993) 970,000,000 (970,000,000); coal (metric tons; 1992) 901,452 (n.a.); crude petroleum, none (n.a.).

Gross national product (1998): U.S.$4,795,000,000 (U.S.$3,070 per capita).

Structure of gross domestic product and labour force

	1996–97 in value P '000,000	1996–97 % of total value	1995 labour force	1995 % of labour force
Agriculture	617,200	3.4	53,779	12.2
Mining	6,486,800	36.0	15,133	3.4
Manufacturing	853,300	4.7	29,530	6.7
Construction	988,000	5.5	41,025	9.3
Public utilities	314,400	1.7	2,805	0.6
Transp. and commun.	621,700	3.4	7,715	1.8
Trade[9]	3,016,800	16.7	54,156	12.3
Finance	1,885,900	10.5	4,096	0.9
Pub. admin., defense	2,998,000	16.6	102,564	23.3
Services	695,100	3.9	14,948	3.4
Other	–462,100[10]	–2.5[10]	114,182[11]	26.0[11]
TOTAL	18,015,100	100.0[6]	439,933	100.0[6]

Household income and expenditure (1991). Average household size 4.8; average annual income per household (1985–86) P 3,910 (U.S.$2,080); sources of income (1987): wages and salaries 73.3%, self-employment 15.9%, transfers 10.8%; expenditure: food 39.4%, household durable goods 14.0%, rent and services 13.3%, transportation 13.1%, clothing 5.6%, health 2.3%.
Land use (1994): forest 46.8%; pasture 45.2%; agriculture 0.7%; other 7.3%.

Foreign trade[12]

Balance of trade (current prices)

	1993	1994	1995	1996	1997	1998
P '000,000	668.4	1,216.3	1,623.6	2,398.9	2,140.7	217.7
% of total	8.4%	14.0%	15.6%	17.3%	11.5%	1.1%

Imports (1997): P 8,255,800,000 (machinery and transport equipment 37.6%, of which transport equipment 20.0%; food, beverages, and tobacco 13.1%; metal and metal products 10.7%; chemical and rubber products 9.1%). *Major import sources:* Customs Union of Southern Africa (CUSA) 72.4%; South Korea 9.5%; Zimbabwe 4.5%; U.K. 2.0%; U.S. 1.1%.
Exports (1997): P 10,390,700,000 (diamonds 73.8%; vehicles and parts 11.4%; copper-nickel matte 4.6%; textiles 2.4%; meat products 2.2%). *Major export destinations*: U.K. 56.2%; CUSA 14.3%; Zimbabwe 3.7%; U.S. 1.0%.

Transport and communications

Transport. Railroads (1996–97): length 603 mi[13], 971 km[13]; passenger-km 96,000,000; metric ton-km cargo 795,000. Roads (1996): total length 11,388 mi, 18,327 km (paved 25%). Vehicles (1996): passenger cars 30,517; trucks and buses 59,710. Merchant marine: none. Air transport (1998)[14]: passenger-km 56,835,000; metric ton-km cargo 211,000; airports (1998) 7.

Communications

Medium	date	unit	number	units per 1,000 persons
Daily newspapers	1996	circulation	40,000	27
Radio	1997	receivers	237,000	154
Television	1998	receivers	30,000	20
Telephones	1998	main lines	102,000	65
Personal computers	1998	units	40,000	25
Internet	1998	users	10,000	6.5

Education and health

Educational attainment (1993). Percentage of population age 25 and over having: no formal schooling 34.7%; primary education 44.1%; some secondary 19.8%; postsecondary 1.4%. *Literacy* (2000): total population over age 15 literate 934,200 (77.2%); males literate 449,200 (74.4%); females literate 485,000 (79.8%).

Education (1997)

	schools	teachers	students	student/ teacher ratio
Primary (age 6–13)	714	11,454	322,268	28.1
Secondary (age 14–18)	274	6,772	116,076	17.1
Voc., teacher tr.	53	2,889	11,482	4.0
Higher	1	507[15]	8,007	10.0[15]

Health (1994): physicians 339 (1 per 4,395 persons); hospital beds (1993) 3,299 (1 per 434 persons); infant mortality rate 39.0.
Food (1998): daily per capita caloric intake 2,159 (vegetable products 82%, animal products 18%); 93% of FAO recommended minimum requirement.

Military

Total active duty personnel (1999): 9,000 (army 94.4%, navy, none [land locked], air force 5.6%). *Military expenditure as percentage of GNP* (1997): 5.1% (world 2.6%); per capita expenditure U.S.$168.

[1]In addition, the House of Chiefs, a 15-member body consisting of chiefs, subchiefs, and associated members, serves in an advisory capacity to the government. [2]Including four specially elected members and two nonelective seats. [3]Tswana is the national language. [4]Ngamiland includes Okavango. [5]Areas are included with respective district totals; population figures are not included with district totals. [6]Detail does not add to total given because of rounding. [7]Registered births only. [8]1991. [9]Includes hotels. [10]Imputed bank service charge. [11]Includes 94,528 unemployed. [12]Import figures are f.o.b. in balance of trade and c.i.f. in commodities and trading partners. [13]1995. [14]Air Botswana only. [15]1994.

Internet resources for further information:
- **Bank of Botswana http://www.bankofbotswana.bw**
- **Republic of Botswana: The Government of Botswana Web Site http://www.gov.bw/home.html**

Brazil

Official name: República Federativa do Brasil (Federative Republic of Brazil).
Form of government: multiparty federal republic with 2 legislative houses (Federal Senate [81]; Chamber of Deputies [513]).
Chief of state and government: President.
Capital: Brasília.
Official language: Portuguese.
Official religion: none.
Monetary unit: 1 real[1] = 100 centavos; valuation (Oct. 6, 2000) 1 U.S.$ = 1.85 reais; 1 £ = 2.68 reais.

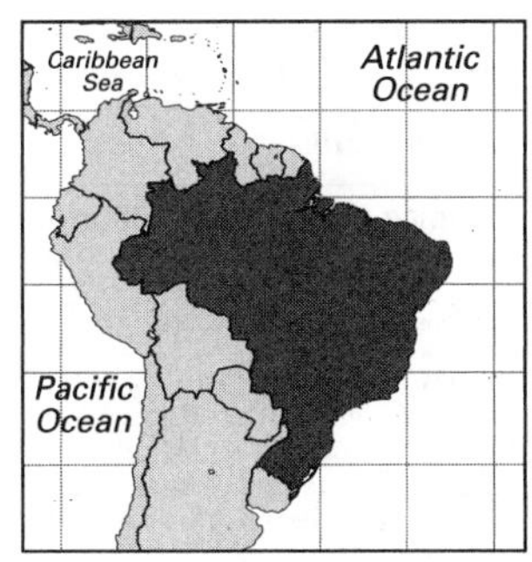

Area and population

States	Capitals	area sq mi	area sq km	population 1996 census
Acre	Rio Branco	59,132	153,150	483,593
Alagoas	Maceió	10,785	27,933	2,633,251
Amapá	Macapá	55,388	143,454	379,459
Amazonas	Manaus	609,200	1,577,820	2,389,279
Bahia	Salvador	219,034	567,295	12,541,675
Ceará	Fortaleza	56,505	146,348	6,809,290
Espírito Santo	Vitória	17,836	46,194	2,802,707
Goiás	Goiânia	131,772	341,289	4,514,967
Maranhão	São Luís	128,713	333,366	5,222,183
Mato Grosso	Cuiabá	350,120	906,807	2,235,832
Mato Grosso do Sul	Campo Grande	138,286	358,159	1,927,834
Minas Gerais	Belo Horizonte	227,176	588,384	16,672,613
Pará	Belém	483,850	1,253,165	5,510,849
Paraíba	João Pessoa	21,848	56,585	3,305,616
Paraná	Curitiba	77,108	199,709	9,003,804
Pernambuco	Recife	38,200	98,938	7,399,071
Piauí	Teresina	97,444	252,379	2,673,085
Rio de Janeiro	Rio de Janeiro	16,954	43,910	13,406,308
Rio Grande do Norte	Natal	20,582	53,307	2,558,660
Rio Grande do Sul	Porto Alegre	108,905	282,062	9,634,688
Rondônia	Porto Velho	92,090	238,513	1,229,306
Roraima	Boa Vista	86,918	225,116	247,131
Santa Catarina	Florianópolis	36,851	95,443	4,875,244
São Paulo	São Paulo	96,066	248,809	34,119,110
Sergipe	Aracaju	8,514	22,050	1,624,020
Tocantins	Palmas	107,499	278,421	1,048,642
Federal District				
Distrito Federal	Brasília	2,248	5,822	1,821,946
Disputed areas[2]		1,149	2,977	—
TOTAL		3,300,171[3, 4]	8,547,404[3, 4]	157,070,163

Demography

Population (2000): 166,113,000.
Density (2000): persons per sq mi 50.3, persons per sq km 19.4.
Urban-rural (1996): urban 78.4%; rural 21.6%.
Sex distribution (1996): male 49.30%; female 50.70%.
Age breakdown (1996): under 15, 31.5%; 15–29, 28.0%; 30–44, 20.7%; 45–59, 11.6%; 60–74, 6.0%; 75 and over, 1.9%; unknown 0.3%.
Population projection: (2010) 187,862,000; (2020) 207,697,000.
Doubling time: 67 years.
Racial composition (1995)[5]: white 54.4%; mulatto and mestizo 40.1%; black and black/Amerindian 4.9%; Asian 0.5%, Amerindian 0.1%.
Religious affiliation (1995): Catholic 74.3%[6], of which Roman Catholic 72.3%[6]; Protestant 23.2%, of which Pentecostal 19.1%; other Christian 0.9%; other 1.6%.
Major cities[7] *and metropolitan areas* (1996): São Paulo 9,839,436 (16,583,234); Rio de Janeiro 5,551,538 (10,192,097); Salvador 2,211,539 (2,709,084); Belo Horizonte 2,091,448 (3,803,249); Fortaleza 1,965,513 (2,582,820); Brasília 1,692,248 (1,821,946); Curitiba 1,476,253 (2,425,361); Recife 1,346,045 (3,087,967); Porto Alegre 1,288,879 (3,246,869); Manaus 1,157,357; Belém 1,144,312 (1,485,569); Goiânia 1,004,098 (1,435,025); Guarulhos 972,384[8]; Campinas 908,906 (1,537,533).

Other principal cities[7] **(1996)**

	population		population		population
Campo Grande	600,069	Natal	656,037	São Gonçalo	833,379[10]
Contagem	492,350[9]	Niterói	450,364[10]	São Jose dos Campos	486,467
Duque de Caxias	715,089[10]	Nova Iguaçu	826,188[10]	São Luis	780,823
Feira de Santana	450,487	Osasco	622,912[8]	Teresina	655,473
Jaboatão	529,966[11]	Ribeirão Preto	456,252	Uberlândia	438,986
João Pessoa	549,363	Santo André	625,564[8]		
Maceió	723,230	São Bernardo do Campo	660,396[8]		

Families (1996). Average family size 3.9; 1–2 persons 25.2%, 3 persons 20.3%, 4 persons 22.2%, 5–6 persons 23.3%, 7 or more persons 9.0%.
Domestic migration. Percent of population moving to different *município* between 1991 and 1996: 7.6%.
Emigration: Emigration for economic opportunity accelerated in the 1980s. By 1995 it was officially estimated that 1–2.5 million Brazilians lived outside of Brazil. Emigrants' most popular destinations in order of preference are the United States, Japan, and the United Kingdom.

Vital statistics

Birth rate per 1,000 population (1999): 19.5 (world avg. 22.1).
Death rate per 1,000 population (1999): 9.1 (world avg. 8.9).
Natural increase rate per 1,000 population (1999): 10.4 (world avg. 13.2).
Total fertility rate (avg. births per childbearing woman; 1999): 2.2.
Marriage rate per 1,000 population (1995): 4.7.
Divorce rate per 1,000 population (1995): 0.6.
Life expectancy at birth (1999): male 58.6 years; female 68.2 years.
Major causes of death per 100,000 population (1995)[12]: diseases of the circulatory system 213; accidents, murder, and violence 100; malignant neoplasms (cancers) 86; diseases of the respiratory system 72; endocrine, metabolic, and nutritional disorders 43; infectious and parasitic diseases 34; birth trauma and other conditions originating in the perinatal period 33; diseases of the digestive system 33; ill-defined conditions 126.

Social indicators

Educational attainment (1996). Percentage of population age 25 and over having: no formal schooling or less than one year of primary education 17.7%; lower primary only 19.1%; upper primary 30.7%; complete primary to some secondary 11.6%; complete secondary to some higher 13.9%; complete higher 6.2%; unknown 0.8%.

Distribution of income (1995)[13]

percentage of national income by decile/quintile

1	2	3	4	5	6	7	8	9	10 (highest)
0.8	1.7	—5.7—		—9.9—		—17.7—		16.3	47.9

Quality of working life. Annual estimated rate per 100,000 insured workers (1990) for: on-the-job injury 2,032; industrial illness 17; death 4. Proportion of labour force participating in national social insurance system (1990): 50.1%. Proportion of formally employed population receiving minimum wage (1993): 25.0%.
Access to services (1995)[5]. Proportion of households having access to: electricity 91.7%, of which urban households having access 98.6%, rural households having access 62.9%; safe public (piped) water supply 71.3%, of which urban households having access 85.4%, rural households having access 11.6%; public (piped) sewage system 39.5%, of which urban household having access 48.2%, rural households having access 3.2%; no sewage disposal 11.4%, of which urban households having no disposal 3.5%, rural households having no disposal 40.9%.
Social participation. Voting is mandatory for national elections. Trade union membership in total workforce (1991): 16,748,155. Practicing Roman Catholic population in total affiliated Roman Catholic population (1990): 25%.
Social deviance. Annual murder rate per 100,000 population (1996): Brazil 23, Rio de Janeiro only 69, São Paulo only 55.
Leisure. Favourite leisure activities include: playing soccer, dancing, rehearsing all year in neighbourhood samba groups for celebrations of Carnival, and competing in water sports, volleyball, and basketball.
Material well-being (1995)[5]. Households possessing: telephone 22.3%, of which urban 26.7%, rural 3.5%; colour television receiver 60.9%, of which urban 69.8%, rural 23.3%; refrigerator 74.8%, of which urban 83.4%, rural 38.7%; washing machine (1996) 30.4%, of which urban 35.3%, rural 9.3%.

National economy

Gross national product (1998): U.S.$767,568,000,000 (U.S.$4,630 per capita).

Structure of gross domestic product and labour force

	1995 in value R$ '000,000[1, 14]	1995 % of total value	1997 labour force[5, 15]	1997 % of labour force
Agriculture	68,290	12.2	16,770,700	22.3
Mining	5,867	1.0	774,300	1.0
Public utilities	14,198	2.5		
Manufacturing	123,821	22.0	8,507,000	11.3
Construction	45,124	8.0	4,583,500	6.1
Transportation and communications	30,702	5.5	2,759,000	3.7
Trade	38,037	6.8	9,222,800[16]	12.3[16]
Finance, real estate	42,824	7.6	...	...
Pub. admin., defense	70,154	12.5	25,436,300[17]	33.8[17]
Services	162,097	28.9		
Other	–39,333[18]	–7.0[18]	7,159,700[19]	9.5[19]
TOTAL	561,781	100.0	75,213,300	100.0

Budget. Revenue (1995): R$320,178,000,000 (development receipts 62.6%, of which credits 58.4%; current receipts 37.4%, of which social contributions 19.3% [including social security 9.2%], taxes 13.3%). Expenditures: R$320,178,000,000 (administration and planning 59.5%; social welfare 13.9%; regional development 6.0%; health and sanitation 4.9%; agriculture 3.1%; education 2.7%; defense and public order 2.6%).
Public debt (external, outstanding; 1998): U.S.$98,959,000,000.
Production ('000 metric tons except as noted). Agriculture, forestry, fishing (1998): sugarcane 338,348, soybeans 31,357, corn (maize) 29,297, oranges 22,987, cassava 19,809, rice 7,796, bananas 5,551, tomatoes 2,692, potatoes 2,634, wheat 2,222, dry beans 2,184, papayas 1,700, coffee 1,690, pineapples 1,607, cashew apples 1,450, seed cotton 1,219, onions 835, apples 787, tangerines 749[20], grapes 738, apples 653, sweet potatoes 650, coconuts 649, sorghum 611, tobacco 510, mangoes 456, lemons and limes 455, cacao beans 282, maté 247, peanuts (groundnuts) 186, sisal 126, palm oil (1996) 76, garlic 55, natural rubber 54, cashews 45, Brazil nuts 25; livestock (number of live animals) 161,000,000 cattle, 31,427,000 pigs, (1996) 18,300,000 sheep, 6,400,000 horses; roundwood (1998) 220,313,000 cu m, of which fuelwood 114,052,000 cu m, sawlogs and veneer logs 47,779,000 cu m, pulpwood 30,701,000 cu m; fish catch (1996) 850, of which freshwater fishes 212. Mining and quarrying (value of export production in U.S.$'000,000; 1996): iron ore 2,668; semifinished copper 165; ferroniobium 153; bauxite 115; granite 97; semifinished tin 68; kaolin (clay) 65; manganese 55; asbestos 35; gemstones (1994) 27; gold production for both domestic use and export 1,833,000 troy oz; Brazil is also a world-leading producer of high-quality grade quartz and

tantalum. Manufacturing (value added in U.S.$'000,000; 1994): food products 19,450; transport equipment 16,050; paints, soaps, drugs, and medicines 15,600; electrical machinery 12,350; nonelectrical machinery 11,600; industrial chemicals 11,000; iron and steel 8,800; textiles 7,100; fabricated metals 6,000; cement, bricks, and tiles 5,700; paper and paper products 5,250. Construction (authorized[21]; 1987): residential 20,090,000 sq m; nonresidential 8,180,000 sq m.

Land use (1994): forested 57.7%; meadows and pastures 21.9%; agricultural and under permanent cultivation 6.0%; other 14.4%.

Manufacturing enterprises (1994)

	no. of enterprises	number of labourers	wages of labourers as a % of avg. of all mfg. wages	value added in producer's prices (in CR$'000,000,0001)[22]
Chemical products (incl. pharmaceuticals)	2,538	327,600	183.4	1,351
Food products	4,805	539,200	69.3	1,040
Nonelectrical machinery	1,937	264,700	132.8	994
Fabricated metals, iron and steel, and nonferrous metals	2,273	378,500	133.1	923
Transport equipment	777	303,400	173.9	784
Electrical machinery	1,248	211,000	152.6	591
Textiles	1,367	250,400	68.3	379
Nonmetallic mineral products	1,656	145,400	95.6	369
Paper and paper products	740	113,100	119.9	296
Clothing and footwear	2,231	397,700	51.5	272
Publishing and printing	851	107,300	125.7	226
Plastics	792	113,600	83.7	193
Beverages	481	74,000	92.2	178
Rubber products	430	57,400	117.7	91
Wood and wood products (excl. furniture)	832	81,200	50.8	91
Furniture	776	78,900	54.3	86

Population economically active (1996)[5, 15]: total 74,138,441; activity rate of total population 48.7% (participation rates: ages 15–59, 73.2%; female 40.4%; unemployed [May 1999] officially 8%).

Price and earnings indexes (1995 = 100)

	1994	1995	1996	1997	1998	1999	2000[23]
Consumer price index	60.2	100.0	115.8	123.8	127.7	133.9	141.5
Monthly earnings index[24]	73.9	100.0	120.0	130.0	141.7	...	...

Tourism (1998): receipts U.S.$3,678,000,000; expenditures U.S.$5,731,000,000.

Retail trade enterprises (1993)

	no. of enterprises	total no. of employees	annual wage as a % of all trade wages	annual values of sales in Cr$'000,000,0001
Vehicles, new and used; parts	5,239	241,299	133.8	1,939
General merchandise stores (including food products)	3,260	328,303	93.0	1,432
Gas stations	11,302	139,348	94.5	942
Clothing, footwear, and apparel	4,654	189,980	90.2	479
Electronics, furniture, kitchenware, and antiques	2,476	101,439	100.1	446
Metal products, lumber, glass, and construction materials	6,192	126,136	85.7	395
Food, beverages, and tobacco	3,423	64,432	73.2	246
Pharmaceutical and cosmetic products	1,816	55,069	94.4	241
Agricultural and industrial equipment and machinery	1,980	43,171	115.3	189

Households. Average household size (1997) 3.8.

Family income and expenditure (1993). Average family size 3.7[5]; annual income per family Cr$608,364 (U.S.$2,178[5, 25]); sources of income (1987–88)[26]: wages and salaries 62.4%, self-employed 14.7%, transfers 10.9%, other 12.0%; expenditure (1995–96)[27]: housing, energy, and household furnishings 28.8%, food and beverages 23.4%, transportation and communications 13.8%, health care 9.2%, education and recreation 8.4%.

Financial aggregates[28]

	1995	1996	1997	1998	1999	2000[23]
Exchange rate, reais[1] per:						
U.S. dollar	.973	1.039	1.116	1.209	1.789	1.800
£	1.508	1.506	1.846	2.011	2.892	2.722
SDR	1.446	1.495	1.506	1.702	2.455	2.407
International reserves (U.S.$)						
Total (excl. gold; '000,000)	49,708	58,323	50,827	42,580	34,796	27,145
SDRs ('000,000)	1	1	1	2	10	29
Reserve pos. in IMF ('000,000)	—	—	—	—	—	—
Foreign exchange ('000,000)	49,707	58,322	50,826	42,578	34,786	27,116
Gold ('000,000 fine troy oz.)	4.58	3.69	3.03	4.60	3.17	1.72
% world reserves	0.50	0.41	0.34	0.48	0.44	0.18
Interest and prices						
Central bank discount (%)	...	25.34	45.09	39.41	21.37	20.40
Govt. bond yield (%)	...	...	...	...	...	...
Industrial share prices	...	...	...	...	...	...
Balance of payments (U.S.$'000,000)						
Balance of visible trade	–3,157	–5,453	–8,372	–6,603	–1,207	...
Imports, f.o.b.	49,663	53,304	61,358	57,739	49,219	...
Exports, f.o.b.	46,506	47,851	52,986	51,136	48,012	...
Balance of invisibles	–14,979	–17,795	–23,839	–27,226	–23,866	...
Balance of payments current account	–18,136	–23,248	–30,491	–33,829	–25,073	...

Energy production (consumption): electricity (kW-hr; 1996) 289,812,000,000 ([1997] 274,272,000,000); coal (metric tons; 1996) 4,805,000 (17,294,000); crude petroleum (barrels; 1997) 305,518,000 ([1996] 485,343,000); petroleum products (metric tons; 1996) 57,378,000 (66,388,000); natural gas (cu m; 1997) 9,567,000,000 ([1996] 4,936,000,000); carburant alcohol (barrels; 1997) 76,650,000 (76,650,000).

Foreign trade

Balance of trade (current prices)

	1994	1995	1996	1997	1998	1999
U.S.$'000,000	+10,861	–3,157	–5,453	–8,372	–6,603	–1,207
% of total	14.0%	3.3%	5.4%	7.3%	6.1%	1.2%

Imports (1997): U.S.$61,358,000,000 (machinery and apparatus 32.2%, chemicals and chemical products 14.5%, mineral fuels 10.1%, motor vehicles 8.8%, food products 5.4%). *Major import sources:* United States 23.3%; Argentina 13.2%; Germany 8.3%; Japan 5.9%; Italy 5.6%; France 2.7%; Canada 2.4%; United Kingdom 2.4%; South Korea 2.2%; China 1.9%.

Exports (1997): U.S.$52,986,000,000 (transportation equipment and components 12.8%, fabricated metal products 11.4%, soybeans 10.8%, chemicals and chemical products 7.2%, nonelectrical machinery and apparatus 6.4%, coffee 5.8%, iron ore and other ores 5.8%, paper and cellulose 3.8%, electrical and electronic equipment 3.4%, sugar 3.3%). *Major export destinations:* United States 17.5%; Argentina 13.5%; The Netherlands 7.4%; Japan 5.7%; Germany 4.8%; Italy 3.2%; Belgium 2.8%; Paraguay 2.6%; United Kingdom 2.3%; Chile 2.2%.

Transport and communications

Transport. Railroads: route length (1995) 18,578 mi, 29,899 km; passenger-mi 9,009,000,000, passenger-km 14,498,000,000; short ton-mi cargo 93,455,-000,000, metric ton-km cargo 136,442,000,000. Roads (1996): total length 1,230,000 mi, 1,980,000 km (paved 9%). Vehicles (1995): passenger cars 12,000,000; trucks and buses 3,160,689. Air transport (1998)[29]: passenger-mi 27,550,000,000, passenger-km 44,338,000,000; short ton-mi cargo 1,105,-000,000, metric ton-km cargo 1,614,000,000; airports (1995) with scheduled flights 139.

Communications

Medium	date	unit	number	units per 1,000 persons
Daily newspapers	1996	circulation	6,472,000	41
Radio	1997	receivers	71,000,000	446
Television	1997	receivers	36,500,000	229
Telephones	1998	main lines	19,987,000	124
Cellular telephones	1998	subscribers	7,761,000	48
Personal computers	1998	units	5,000,000	31
Internet	1998	users	2,500,000	15

Education and health

Literacy (1995)[30]: total population age 15 and over literate 91,100,000 (83.3%); males literate 45,200,000 (83.3%); females literate 45,900,000 (83.2%).

Education (1996)

	schools	teachers	students	student/teacher ratio
Primary (age 7–14)	195,767	1,388,247	33,131,270	23.9
Secondary (age 15–17)	15,213	326,827	5,739,077	17.6
Higher[31]	851	141,482	1,661,034	11.7

Health: physicians (1997) 205,828 (1 per 774 persons); hospital beds (1996) 501,876 (1 per 313 persons); infant mortality rate per 1,000 live births (1999) 39.3.

Food (1997): daily per capita caloric intake 2,974 (vegetable products 80%, animal products 20%); 124% of FAO recommended minimum requirement.

Military

Total active duty personnel (1999): 291,000 (army 64.9%, navy 17.9%, air force 17.2%). *Military expenditure as percentage of GNP* (1997): 1.8% (world 2.6%); per capita expenditure U.S.$89.

[1]The real (R$) replaced the cruzeiro real (CR$) on July 1, 1994, at a rate of 2,750 cruzeiros reais to 1 real (a rate par to the U.S.$ on that date). Previously, the cruzeiro real replaced the cruzeiro (Cr$) at a rate of 1,000 cruzeiros to 1 cruzeiro real on Aug. 2, 1993; the cruzeiro replaced the new cruzado (NCz$) at a rate of 1 to 1 on March 16, 1990; and the new cruzado replaced the (old) cruzado (Cz$) at a rate of 1,000 (old) to 1 new on Jan. 15, 1989. [2]Area in dispute between Ceará and Piauí. [3]Detail does not add to total given because of rounding. [4]Land area excluding inland water is 3,265,076 sq mi (8,456,508 sq km). [5]Excludes rural population of Acre, Amapá, Amazonas, Pará, Rondônia, and Roraima. [6]Includes syncretic Afro-Catholic cults having Spiritist beliefs and rituals. [7]Populations are for *municípios,* which may include adjacent urban or rural districts. [8]Within São Paulo metropolitan area. [9]Within Belo Horizonte metropolitan area. [10]Within Rio de Janeiro metropolitan area. [11]Within Recife metropolitan area. [12]Projected rates based on about 74% of total deaths. [13]As of 1992, 33,000,000 Brazilians lived in extreme poverty (more than half of whom lived in the nine states of the north-east). [14]At factor cost. [15]Excludes members of armed forces in barracks. [16]Excludes restaurants and hotels. [17]Includes restaurants and hotels. [18]Less imputed bank service charges. [19]Includes finance and real estate, not adequately defined, and unemployed. [20]Includes mandarin oranges, satsuma oranges, and clementines. [21]Urban construction only for 74 cities. [22]1993. [23]June. [24]Minimum wages. [25]Based on end-of-year exchange rate. [26]Based on 10,408,833 families in Brazil's nine largest metropolitan regions. [27]Based on survey of 11 metropolitan areas only. [28]End-of-period figures. [29]TAM, Transbrasil, VARIG, and VASP airlines only. [30]In the late 1990s, functional literacy was 30.5% of total population over age 15. [31]1994.

Internet resources for further information:

- **IBGE: Instituto Brasileiro de Geografia e Estatística**
  http://www.ibge.gov.br
- **Central Bank of Brazil: Economic Data**
  http://www.bcb.gov.br/defaulti.htm

Brunei

Official name: Negara Brunei Darussalam (State of Brunei, Abode of Peace).
Form of government: monarchy (sultanate)[1].
Head of state and government: Sultan.
Capital: Bandar Seri Begawan.
Official language: Malay[2].
Official religion: Islam.
Monetary unit: 1 Brunei dollar (B$) = 100 cents; valuation (Oct. 6, 2000) 1 U.S.$ = B$1.75; 1 £ = B$2.53.

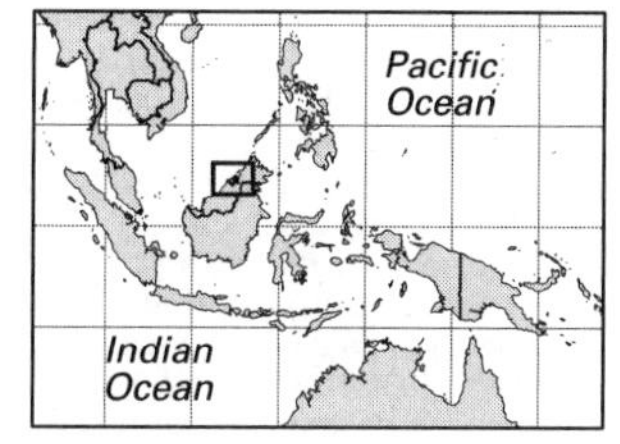

Area and population

Districts	Capitals	area sq mi	area sq km	population 1998 estimate
Belait	Kuala Belait	1,052	2,724	65,300
Brunei and Muara	Bandar Seri Begawan	220	571	213,800
Temburong	Bangar	504	1,304	9,300
Tutong	Tutong	450	1,166	35,200
TOTAL		2,226	5,765	323,600

Demography

Population (2000): 336,000.
Density (2000): persons per sq mi 150.9, persons per sq km 58.3.
Urban-rural (1999): urban 72.0%; rural 28.0%.
Sex distribution (1998): male 53.06%; female 46.94%.
Age breakdown (1996): under 15, 32.9%; 15–29, 27.5%; 30–44, 25.5%; 45–59, 9.4%; 60 and over, 4.7%.
Population projection: (2010) 408,000; (2020) 475,000.
Doubling time: 39 years.
Ethnic composition (1999): Malay 67.6%; Chinese 14.9%; other indigenous 5.9%; Indian and other 11.6%.
Religious affiliation (1991): Muslim 67.2%; Buddhist 12.8%; Christian 10.0%; other religions and nonreligious 10.0%.
Major cities (1991): Bandar Seri Begawan 45,867[3]; Kuala Belait 21,163; Seria 21,082; Tutong 13,049.

Vital statistics

Birth rate per 1,000 population (1999): 21.1 (world avg. 22.1); (1982) legitimate 99.6%; illegitimate 0.4%.
Death rate per 1,000 population (1999): 3.1 (world avg. 8.9).
Natural increase rate per 1,000 population (1999): 18.0 (world avg. 13.2).
Total fertility rate (avg. births per childbearing woman; 1999): 2.7.
Marriage rate per 1,000 population (1995): 6.1.
Divorce rate per 1,000 population (1992): 1.1.
Life expectancy at birth (1999): male 74.0 years; female 78.0 years.
Major causes of death per 100,000 population (1994): cardiovascular disease 51.8; malignant neoplasms (cancers) 41.8; accidents, poisoning, and violence 20.0; pneumonia 12.3; congenital anomalies 7.3.

National economy

Budget (1998). Revenue: B$2,775,000,000 (tax revenue 54.6%, of which corporate income tax 47.3%, import duty 7.2%; nontax revenue 45.4%, of which property income 33.8%, commercial receipts 10.9%). Expenditures: B$4,295,000,000 (current expenditure 65.5%; capital expenditure 34.5%).
Public debt (exernal, outstanding): none.
Tourism (1995): receipts from visitors U.S.$40,000,000; expenditures by nationals abroad U.S.$1,000,000.
Production (metric tons except as noted). Agriculture, forestry, fishing (1999): vegetables and melons 8,700, fruits (excluding melons) 5,225, cassava 1,500, pineapples 700, rice 290; livestock (number of live animals) 6,000 buffalo, 4,500 pigs, 3,302 goats, 1,924 cattle, 4,929,000 chickens; roundwood (1998) 296,000 cu m; fish catch (1997) 4,677. Mining and quarrying: other than petroleum and natural gas, none except sand and gravel for construction. Manufacturing (1998): gasoline 187,600; distillate fuel oils 147,800; kerosene 76,500. Construction (value in B$'000,000; 1989): residential 26.2; nonresidential 5.1. Energy production (consumption): electricity (kW-hr; 1996) 1,575,000,000 (1,575,000,000); coal, none (none); crude petroleum (barrels; 1996) 60,000,000 (900,000); petroleum products (metric tons; 1996) 851,000 (909,000); natural gas (cu m; 1996) 9,218,000,000 (1,269,000,000).
Population economically active (1991): total 111,955; activity rate of total population 43.0% (participation rates: ages 15–64, 67.6%; female 32.9%; unemployed 4.7%).

Price and earnings indexes (1995 = 100)

	1991	1992	1993	1994	1995	1996	1997
Consumer price index	87.2	88.3	92.2	94.3	100.0	101.8	103.7
Earnings index	...	...	...	...	...	...	...

Household income and expenditure. Average household size (1991) 5.8; income per household: n.a.; sources of income: n.a.; expenditure (1990): food 38.7%, transportation and communications 19.9%, housing 18.6%, clothing 6.4%, other 16.4%.
Gross national product (at current market prices; 1998): U.S.$7,209,000,000 (U.S.$22,278 per capita).

Structure of gross domestic product and labour force

	1998 in value B$'000,000	1998 % of total value	1991 labour force	1991 % of labour force
Agriculture	231	2.8	2,162	1.9
Mining, Manufacturing	2,975	36.7	9,397	8.4
Construction	539	6.7	14,145	12.6
Public utilities	88	1.1	2,223	2.0
Transportation and communications	351	4.3	5,392	4.8
Trade	780	9.6	15,404	13.8
Finance	520	6.4	5,807	5.2
Services	2,847	35.1	52,121	46.6
Other	–220	–2.7	5,304[4]	4.7[4]
TOTAL	8,111	100.0	111,955	100.0

Land use (1994): forested 85.4%; meadows and pastures 1.1%; agricultural and under permanent cultivation 1.3%; other 12.2%.

Foreign trade[5]

Balance of trade (current prices)

	1992	1993	1994	1995	1996	1997
B$'000,000	+1,497.4	+577.5	+530.0	+338.0	+153.2	+819.0
% of total	23.7%	8.6%	8.8%	5.2%	2.1%	11.5%

Imports (1997): B$3,154,000,000 (machinery and transport equipment 39.0%, manufactured goods 25.5%, miscellaneous manufactured articles 11.6%, food and live animals 11.1%, chemicals 6.4%, crude materials 3.4%, beverages and tobacco 1.9%). *Major import sources:* ASEAN 45.5%, of which Singapore 25.6%, Malaysia 13.6%; EEC 17.9%; Japan 11.2%; United States 10.0%.
Exports (1997): B$3,973,000,000 (natural gas 46.8%, crude petroleum 41.5%, petroleum products 2.8%). *Major export destinations:* Japan 53.1%; ASEAN 20.9%, of which Thailand 11.2%, Singapore 6.6%; South Korea 18.1%; Taiwan 2.7%.

Transport and communications

Transport. Railroads[6]: length 12 mi, 19 km. Roads (1996): total length 1,064 mi, 1,712 km (paved 75%). Vehicles (1997): passenger cars 91,047; trucks and buses 15,918. Merchant marine (1992): vessels (100 gross tons and over) 51; total deadweight tonnage 349,718. Marine transport (1998): cargo loaded 25,900,000 metric tons, cargo unloaded 1,195,200 metric tons. Air transport (1998): passenger-mi 1,742,000,000, passenger-km 2,803,000,000; short ton-mi cargo 75,020,000, metric ton-km cargo 109,527,000; airports (1996) with scheduled flights 1.

Communications

Medium	date	unit	number	units per 1,000 persons
Daily newspapers	1996	circulation	21,000	69
Radio	1997	receivers	93,000	302
Television	1997	receivers	77,000	250
Telephones	1996	main lines	78,794	258
Cellular telephones	1996	subscribers	43,524	143
Personal computers	1995	units	8,000	27
Internet	1998	users	10,000	32

Education and health

Educational attainment (1991). Percentage of population age 25 and over having: no formal schooling 17.0%; primary education 43.3%; secondary 26.3%; postsecondary and higher 12.9%; not stated 0.5%. *Literacy* (1995): percentage of total population age 15 and over literate 89.1%; males literate 93.2%; females literate 84.6%.

Education (1998)

	schools	teachers	students	student/ teacher ratio
Primary (age 5–11)[7]	184	3,858	58,548	15.2
Secondary (age 12–20)	38	2,636	30,956	11.7
Voc., teacher tr.	9	516	2,553	4.9
Higher	4	370	2,080	5.6

Health (1996): physicians 281 (1 per 1,086 persons); hospital beds 961 (1 per 317 persons); infant mortality rate per 1,000 live births (1999) 9.0.
Food (1998): daily per capita caloric intake 2,851 (vegetable products 78%, animal products 22%); 127% of FAO recommended minimum requirement.

Military

Total active duty personnel (1999): 5,000[8] (army 78.0%, navy 14.0%, air force 8.0%). *Military expenditure as percentage of GNP* (1997): 4.6% (world 2.6%); per capita expenditure U.S.$1,190.

[1]A nonelective 21-member body advises the sultan on legislative matters. [2]All official documents that must be published by law in Malay are, however, also required to be issued in an official English version as well. [3]1988 metropolitan area population estimate. [4]Mostly unemployed. [5]Import data is c.i.f. [6]Privately owned. [7]Includes preprimary. [8]All services form part of the army.

Internet resources for further information:
- **Brunei Darussalam http://www.brunet.bn**

Bulgaria

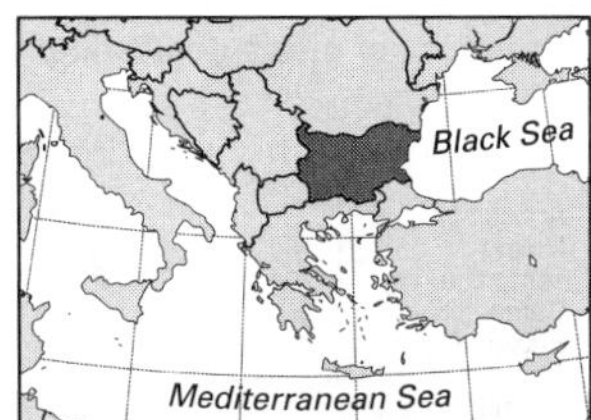

Official name: Republika Bŭlgaria (Republic of Bulgaria).
Form of government: unitary multiparty republic with one legislative body (National Assembly [240]).
Chief of state: President.
Head of government: Prime Minister.
Capital: Sofia.
Official language: Bulgarian.
Official religion: none[1].
Monetary unit: 1 lev (Lw; leva)[2] = 100 stotinki; valuation (Oct. 6, 2000) 1 U.S.$ = 2.25 (new) leva; 1 £ = 3.24 (new) leva.

Area and population		area		population
Regions[3]	Capitals	sq mi	sq km	1999[4] estimate
Burgas	Burgas	5,685	14,724	829,627
Khaskovo	Khaskovo	5,338	13,824	882,051
Lovech	Lovech	5,849	15,150	960,082
Montana	Mikhaylovgrad	4,095	10,607	593,546
Plovdiv	Plovdiv	5,245	13,585	1,194,044
Ruse	Ruse	4,187	10,843	741,759
Sofiya	Sofia (Sofiya)	7,344	19,021	942,037
Varna	Varna	4,606	11,929	887,517
City Commune				
Sofiya	Sofia (Sofiya)	506	1,311	1,199,708
TOTAL		42,855	110,994	8,230,371

Demography

Population (2000): 8,172,000.
Density (2000): persons per sq mi 190.7, persons per sq km 73.6.
Urban-rural (1999): urban 68.0%; rural 32.0%.
Sex distribution (1999): male 48.77%; female 51.23%.
Age breakdown (1999): under 15, 16.2%; 15–29, 22.0%; 30–44, 20.3%; 45–59, 19.8%; 60–74, 16.3%; 75 and over, 5.4%.
Population projection: (2010) 7,344,000; (2020) 6,631,000.
Ethnic composition (1992): Bulgarian 83.2%; Turkish 9.4%; Gypsy 3.6%; other 1.3%.
Religious affiliation (1995): Bulgarian Orthodox 36.5%, Protestant 1.4%, Roman Catholic 0.8%; Sunnī Muslim 13.1%; other/nonreligious 47.8%.
Major cities (1998): Sofia 1,122,302; Plovdiv 342,584; Varna 299,801.

Vital statistics

Birth rate per 1,000 population (1998): 7.9 (world avg. 22.1).
Death rate per 1,000 population (1998): 14.3 (world avg. 8.9).
Natural increase rate per 1,000 population (1998): –6.4 (world avg. 13.2).
Total fertility rate (avg. births per childbearing woman; 1999): 1.2.
Life expectancy at birth (1999): male 68.7 years; female 76.0 years.
Major causes of death per 100,000 population (1998): diseases of the circulatory system 954.4; malignant neoplasms (cancers) 192.9; diseases of the respiratory system 67.6; accidents, poisoning, and violence 60.7.

National economy

Budget (1998). Revenue: 8,913,064,200,000 (old) leva (tax revenue 79.4%, of which social insurance 22.9%, value-added tax 20.6%, income tax 11.5%, profit tax 9.6%, excises 7.6%, customs and duties 5.0%, other 2.2%; nontax revenue 20.0%; other 0.6%). Expenditures: 8,689,188,600,000 (old) leva (social insurance 27.1%; administration 16.3%; wages 12.9%; interest on debt 11.0%; capital expenditure 10.9%; defense 10.8%; education 10.2%).
Public debt (external, outstanding; 1998): U.S.$7,781,000,000.
Gross national product (1998): U.S.$10,085,000,000 (U.S.$2,220 per capita).

Structure of gross domestic product and labour force	1997			
	in value '000,000 (old) leva	% of total value	labour force	% of labour force
Agriculture, forestry, and fishing	3,987,312	23.3	800,353	22.3
Manufacturing, mining	3,457,569	20.2	812,941	22.7
Construction	422,179	2.5	139,002	3.8
Transp. and commun.	1,124,858	6.6	228,231	6.4
Trade	1,468,148	8.6	382,505	10.7
Public utilities, housing	603,460	3.5	88,764	2.5
Finance	2,793,211	16.3	49,608	1.4
Pub. admin., defense	555,899	3.3	78,899	2.2
Services	824,866	4.8	488,097	13.6
Other	1,866,231[5]	10.9[5]	513,400[6]	14.3[6]
TOTAL	17,103,433	100.0	3,581,800	100.0[7]

Production (metric tons except as noted). Agriculture, forestry, fishing (1999): wheat 3,000,000, corn (maize) 1,100,000, sunflower seeds 700,000, grapes 636,000, barley 500,000; livestock (number of live animals) 2,774,000 sheep, 1,721,000 pigs, 1,048,000 goats, 671,000 cattle; roundwood (1998) 3,041,000 cu m; fish catch (1998) 10,756. Mining and quarrying (1997): iron ore 895,000; lead 72,975; zinc 72,755; manganese 55,600; silver 23,790 kg. Manufacturing (value of production in '000,000 (old) leva; 1997): food, beverages, and tobacco 2,834,413; chemical and oil processing 1,633,583; machine and metalworking 1,460,220; metallurgy 890,614; electronic and electrical equipment 524,383. Construction (1998): residential 421,241 sq m; nonresidential 162,357. Energy production (consumption): electricity (kW-hr; 1998) 42,803,000,000 (42,803,000,000); coal (metric tons; 1998) 31,248,000 (34,200,000); crude petroleum (barrels; 1998) 232,360 (50,979,000); petroleum products (metric tons; 1996) 5,810,000 (4,361,000); natural gas (cu m; 1996) 44,000,000 (6,197,000,000).
Household income and expenditure. Average household size (1998) 3.0; income per household (1998) 4,569 (new) leva (U.S.$2,595); sources of income (1998): wages and salaries 37.7%, self-employment in agriculture 19.5%, transfer payments 16.3%; expenditure (1998): food 49.0%, housing and energy 10.4%, transportation 6.2%, clothing 5.9%, health 3.6%, household durable goods 3.0%, education and culture 2.5%, other 22.4%.
Land use (1995): forested 30.2%; meadows and pastures 16.2%; agricultural and under permanent cultivation 38.0%; other 15.6%.
Population economically active (1997): total 3,581,800; activity rate of total population 51.9% (participation rates: age 16–59 [male], 16–54 [female] 57.3%; female 47.6%; unemployed 13.7%).

Price and earnings indexes (1995 = 100)	1992	1993	1994	1995	1996	1997	1998
Consumer price index	18.2	31.5	61.7	100.0	223.0	2,636.6	3,224.3
Monthly earnings index	28.6	44.5	68.4	100.0	174.4	1,864.4	...

Tourism (1998): receipts from visitors U.S.$966,000,000; expenditures by nationals abroad U.S.$519,000,000.

Foreign trade[8]

Balance of trade (current prices)	1994	1995	1996	1997	1998	1999
'000,000 (new) leva	–10.8	–20.3	–32.3	+12.9	–1,195	–2,740
% of total	2.4%	2.8%	1.8%	0.0%	7.3%	15.9%

Imports (1997): 8,268,462,200 (new) leva (petroleum and natural gas 28.7%; machine-building and metalworking equipment 13.9%; chemical products 9.9%; electrical and electronic equipment 6.6%; food, beverages, and tobacco 6.3%; textiles and knitwear 4.5%). *Major import sources:* Russia 28.0%; Germany 11.8%; Italy 7.2%; Greece 4.2%; U.S. 3.7%; Ukraine 3.7%; France 3.2%.
Exports (1997): 8,281,386,500 (new) leva (chemicals and plastics 22.3%; food, beverages, and tobacco 13.5%; machine-building and metalworking equipment 9.6%; clothing and footwear 7.1%). *Major export destinations:* Italy 11.7%; Germany 9.5%; Turkey 9.0%; Greece 8.2%; Russia 7.9%.

Transport and communications

Transport. Railroads (1998): track length 6,470 km; (1997) passenger-km 5,866,000,000; metric ton-km cargo 7,444,000,000. Roads (1998): length 37,320 km (paved 92%). Vehicles (1998): cars 1,730,506; trucks and buses 251,382. Merchant marine (1998): vessels (100 gross tons and over) 107; deadweight tonnage (1995) 391,000. Air transport (1997): passenger-mi 1,258,742,000, passenger-km 2,025,752,000; short ton-mi cargo 18,872,000, metric ton-km cargo 30,371,000; airports (1997) with scheduled flights 3.

Communications Medium	date	unit	number	units per 1,000 persons
Daily newspapers	1998	circulation	2,145,000	254
Television	1998	receivers	3,310,000	394
Telephones	1998	main lines	2,742,000	328.9
Cellular telephones	1998	subscribers	127,000	11.2
Personal computers	1996	units	250,000	29.9
Internet	1998	users	10,300	0.9

Education and health

Educational attainment (1992). Percentage of population age 25 and over having: no formal schooling 4.7%; incomplete primary education 12.5%; primary 31.9%; secondary 35.7%; higher 15.0%. *Literacy* (1995): total population age 15 and over literate 98.0%; males literate 98.8%; females literate 97.4%.

Education (1997–98)	schools	teachers	students	student/ teacher ratio
Primary (age 6–14) / Secondary (age 15–17)	3,258	69,850	940,794	13.5
Voc., teacher tr.	545	18,563	196,351	10.6
Higher	86	22,382	266,747	11.9

Health (1998): physicians 28,823 (1 per 285 persons); hospital beds 85,408 (1 per 97 persons); infant mortality rate per 1,000 live births 12.8.
Food (1998): daily per capita caloric intake 2,740 (vegetable products 75%, animal products 25%); 110% of FAO recommended minimum requirement.

Military

Total active duty personnel (1999): 80,760 (army 70.8%, navy 6.5%, air force 22.7%). *Military expenditure as percentage of GNP* (1997): 3.0% (world 2.6%); per capita expenditure U.S.$114.

[1]Bulgaria has no official religion; the 1991 constitution, however, refers to Eastern Orthodoxy as the "traditional" religion. [2]The lev was re-denominated as of July 5, 1999; as of this date 1,000 (old) leva = 1 (new) lev. [3]Administratively reorganized into 28 regions as of 1999; detailed breakdown is not available. [4]Beginning of the year. [5]Indirect taxes less bank service charges. [6]Includes 22,000 undistributable employed and 491,400 unemployed. [7]Detail does not add to total given because of rounding. [8]Imports c.i.f.; exports f.o.b.

Internet resources for further information:

- **National Statistical Institute of the Republic of Bulgaria http://www.acad.bg/BulRTD/nsi/index.htm**

Burkina Faso

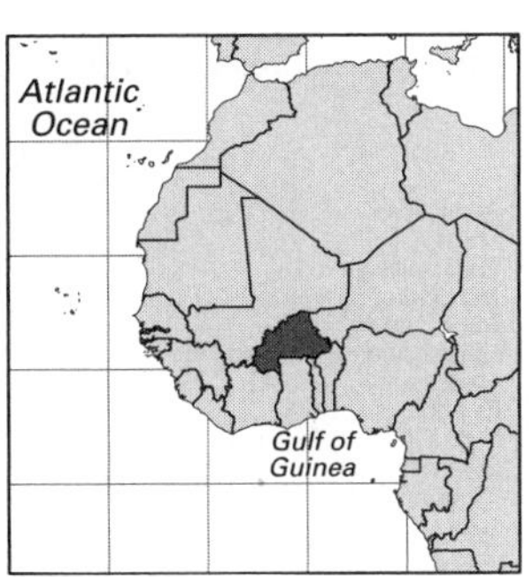

Official name: Burkina Faso (Burkina Faso).
Form of government: multiparty republic with one advisory body (Chamber of Representatives [178[1]]) and one legislative body (National Assembly [111]).
Chief of state: President.
Head of government: Prime Minister.
Capital: Ouagadougou.
Official language: French.
Official religion: none.
Monetary unit: 1 CFA franc (CFAF) = 100 centimes; valuation (Oct. 6, 2000) 1 U.S.$ = CFAF 754.28; 1 £ = CFAF 1,091.

Area and population[2]

Territorial collectivities	Capitals	area sq mi	area sq km	population 1991 estimate
Bam	Kongoussi	1,551	4,017	173,516
Bazéga	Kombissiri	2,051	5,313	352,104
Bougouriba	Diébougou	2,736	7,087	242,986
Boulgou	Tenkodogo	3,488	9,033	465,845
Boulkiemde	Koudougou	1,598	4,138	393,900
Comoé	Banfora	7,102	18,393	296,083
Ganzourgou	Zorgho	1,578	4,087	223,555
Gnagna	Bogandé	3,320	8,600	272,203
Gourma	Fada N'Gourma	10,275	26,613	350,336
Houé	Bobo-Dioulasso	6,438	16,672	724,803
Kadiogo	Ouagadougou	451	1,169	652,377
Kénédougou	Orodara	3,207	8,307	162,010
Kossi	Nouna	5,088	13,177	389,360
Kouritenga	Koupéla	628	1,627	227,060
Mouhoun	Dédougou	4,032	10,442	329,115
Nahouri	Pô	1,484	3,843	119,144
Namentenga	Boulsa	2,994	7,755	214,564
Oubritenga	Ziniaré	1,812	4,693	328,682
Oudalan	Gorom Gorom	3,879	10,046	123,495
Passoré	Yako	1,575	4,078	232,278
Poni	Gaoua	4,000	10,361	258,647
Sanguie	Réo	1,994	5,165	234,079
Sanmatenga	Kaya	3,557	9,213	404,563
Sèno	Dori	5,202	13,473	269,892
Sissili	Léo	5,303	13,736	297,598
Soum	Djibo	5,154	13,350	217,972
Sourou	Tougan	3,663	9,487	313,355
Tapoa	Diapaga	5,707	14,780	187,785
Yatenga	Ouahigouya	4,746	12,292	558,318
Zoundwéogo	Manga	1,333	3,453	175,166
TOTAL		105,946	274,400	9,190,791

Demography

Population (2000): 11,946,000.
Density (2000): persons per sq mi 112.8, persons per sq km 43.5.
Urban-rural (1999): urban 17.0%; rural 83.0%.
Sex distribution (1999): male 48.70%; female 51.30%.
Age breakdown (1999): under 15, 47.7%; 15–29, 27.3%; 30–44, 13.0%; 45–59, 7.4%; 60–74, 3.8%; 75 and over, 0.8%.
Population projection: (2010) 15,424,000; (2020) 19,402,000.
Ethnic composition (1983): Mossi 47.9%; Mande 8.8%; Fulani 8.3%; Lobi 6.9%; Bobo 6.8%; Senufo 5.3%; Grosi 5.1%; Gurma 4.8%; Tuareg 3.3%.
Religious affiliation (1994): Muslim 50%; traditional beliefs 40%; Christian (mostly Roman Catholic) 10%.
Major cities (1993): Ouagadougou 690,000; Bobo-Dioulasso 300,000; Koudougou 105,000; Ouahigouya 38,902[3]; Banfora 35,319[3].

Vital statistics

Birth rate per 1,000 population (1999): 45.7 (world avg. 22.1).
Death rate per 1,000 population (1999): 17.2 (world avg. 8.9).
Natural increase rate per 1,000 population (1999): 28.5 (world avg. 13.2).
Total fertility rate (avg. births per childbearing woman; 1999): 6.5.
Life expectancy at birth (1999): male 46.5 years; female 47.3 years.

National economy

Budget (1999). Revenue: CFAF 238,100,000,000 (tax revenue 93.4%, of which sales tax 43.3%, import duties 25.3%, personal income taxes 22.6%, other 2.2%; nontax revenue 6.6%). Expenditures: CFAF 246,900,000,000 (wages and salaries 27.5%; investment 27.3%; health and education 22.4%; transfers 17.3%; debt service 5.5%).
Public debt (external, outstanding; 1998): U.S.$1,229,000,000.
Production (metric tons except as noted). Agriculture, forestry, fishing (1999): sorghum 1,178,400, millet 945,000, corn (maize) 468,900, sugarcane 400,000, peanuts (groundnuts) 281,400, seed cotton 280,000, rice 94,200, pulses 22,000, sweet potatoes 17,300, sesame 12,600, cassava 2,000; livestock (number of live animals) 7,950,000 goats, 6,350,000 sheep, 4,550,000 cattle, 21,000,000 chickens; roundwood (1998) 10,794,000 cu m; fish catch (1998) 8,335. Mining and quarrying (1999): gold 869 kg[4]; silver 120 kg. Manufacturing (1999): sugar 29,905; flour 21,454; edible oils 11,850; soap 9,910; beer 387,000 hectolitres; soft drinks 155,000 hectolitres; printed fabric 1,462,000 sq m; bicycles 24,079 units; mopeds 17,364 units; cigarettes 60,000,000 packets. Construction (value added in CFAF; 1995): 62,400,000,000. Energy production (consumption): electricity (kW-hr; 1998) 267,000,000 (267,000,000); crude petroleum, none (n.a.); petroleum products (metric tons; 1996) none (315,000).
Gross national product (1998): U.S.$2,575,000,000 (U.S.$240 per capita).

Structure of gross domestic product and labour force

	1999 in value CFAF '000,000	1999 % of total value	1991 labour force	1991 % of labour force
Agriculture	469,000	29.5	4,293,784	91.8
Mining }	325,400	20.5	2,590	0.1
Manufacturing }			51,694	1.1
Construction	85,200	5.4	11,016	0.2
Public utilities	13,800	0.9	3,844	0.1
Transp. and commun.	65,000	4.1	15,041	0.3
Trade	189,200	11.9	120,314	2.6
Finance	...	...	2,075	—
Pub. admin., defense } Services }	352,400	22.2	111,556	2.4
Other	88,600[5]	5.6[5]	67,279[6]	1.4[6]
TOTAL	1,588,600	100.0[7]	4,679,193	100.0

Population economically active (1991): total 4,679,193; activity rate 50.9% (participation rates: over age [1988] 10, 78.1%; female 48.7%; unemployed 1.1%).

Price and earnings indexes (1995 = 100)

	1993	1994	1995	1996	1997	1998	1999
Consumer price index	74.4	93.1	100.0	106.2	108.6	114.2	112.9
Earnings index	...	...	...	...	...	...	...

Household income and expenditure. Average household size (1985) 6.2; average annual income per household CFAF 303,000 (U.S.$640); sources of income: n.a.; expenditure (1985)[8]: food 38.7%, transportation 18.6%, electricity and fuel 13.7%, beverages 9.0%, health 5.2%, housing 5.1%.
Tourism: receipts (1998) U.S.$42,000,000; expenditures (1994) U.S.$23,000,000.
Land use (1994): forest 50.5%; pasture 21.9%; agriculture 13.0%; other 14.6%.

Foreign trade

Balance of trade (current prices)

	1994	1995	1996	1997	1998	1999
CFAF '000,000	–114.4	–163.9	–227.2	–204.6	–231.4	–212.1
% of total	30.0%	34.4%	41.5%	38.0%	49.1%	40.4%

Imports (1999): CFAF 368,700,000,000 (capital equipment 36.8%, petroleum products 16.9%, food products 12.3%, raw materials 9.5%). *Major import sources* (1998): France 29.8%; Côte d'Ivoire 17.4%; Japan 5.4%; United States 3.6%; Italy 3.3%; The Netherlands 3.0%; Germany 2.9%.
Exports (1999): CFAF 156,600,000,000 (raw cotton 53.4%, live animals 10.1%, hides and skins 7.5%, gold 5.9%). *Major export destinations* (1998): France 23.1%; Belgium 10.8%; Côte d'Ivoire 9.8%; Singapore 3.6%; Mali 1.7%.

Transport and communications

Transport. Railroads (1995)[9]: route length 386 mi, 622 km; passenger-km 202,000,000; metric ton-km cargo 45,000,000. Roads (1996): total length 7,519 mi, 12,100 km (paved 16%). Vehicles (1996): passenger cars 38,220; trucks and buses 17,980. Merchant marine: none. Air transport (1993): passenger-km 217,154,000; metric ton-km cargo 34,204,000; airports (1998) 2.

Communications

Medium	date	unit	number	units per 1,000 persons
Daily newspapers	1996	circulation	14,000	1.3
Radio	1997	receivers	370,000	34.0
Television	1997	receivers	100,000	9.1
Telephones	1998	main lines	41,218	3.6
Cellular telephones	1998	subscribers	2,730	0.2
Personal computers	1998	units	10,000	0.9
Internet	1998	users	1,000	0.1

Education and health

Educational attainment (1985). Percentage of population age 10 and over having: no formal schooling 86.1%; some primary 7.3%; general secondary 2.2%; specialized secondary and postsecondary 3.8%; other 0.6%. *Literacy* (1995): percentage of total population age 15 and over literate 23.0%; males literate 31.2%; females literate 13.1%.

Education (1995–96)

	schools	teachers	students	student/ teacher ratio
Primary	3,568	14,037	702,204	50.0
Secondary	252	4,162	137,257	33.0
Vocational	41	731	9,539	13.0
Higher	9	632	9,531	15.1

Health (1991): physicians 341 (1 per 27,158 persons); hospital beds 5,041 (1 per 1,837 persons); infant mortality rate (1999) 110.3.
Food (1998): daily per capita caloric intake 2,149 (vegetable products 95%, animal products 5%); 91% of FAO recommended minimum requirement.

Military

Total active duty personnel (1998): 5,600 (army 96.6%, air force 3.4%). *Military expenditure as percentage of GNP* (1997): 2.8% (world 2.6%); per capita expenditure U.S.$6.

[1]All seats are appointed or indirectly elected. [2]In 1997 the number of territorial collectivities was increased from 30 to 45; detailed breakdown is not available. [3]1985. [4]Officially marketed gold only; does not include substantial illegal production. [5]Includes indirect taxes less imputed bank service charges and subsidies. [6]Includes 49,819 unemployed. [7]Detail does not add to total given because of rounding. [8]Weights of consumer price index components; Ouagadougou only. [9]Passenger-km and metric ton-km cargo figures are based on traffic between Abidjan, Côte d'Ivoire, and Ouagadougou.

Burundi

Official name: Republika y'u Burundi (Rundi); République du Burundi (French) (Republic of Burundi).
Form of government: transitional regime[1] with one legislative house (Transitional National Assembly [121[1]]).
Head of state and government: President assisted by two Vice Presidents[2].
Capital: Bujumbura.
Official languages: Rundi; French.
Official religion: none.
Monetary unit: 1 Burundi franc (FBu) = 100 centimes; valuation (Oct. 6, 2000) 1 U.S.$ = FBu 802.60; 1 £ = FBu 1,161.

Area and population

		area		population
Provinces	Capitals	sq mi	sq km	1990 census
Bubanza	Bubanza	420	1,089	222,953
Bujumbura	Bujumbura	509	1,319	608,931
Bururi	Bururi	952	2,465	385,490
Cankuzo	Cankuzo	759	1,965	142,707
Cibitoke	Cibitoke	631	1,636	279,843
Gitega	Gitega	764	1,979	565,174
Karuzi	Karuzi	563	1,457	287,905
Kayanza	Kayanza	476	1,233	443,116
Kirundo	Kirundo	658	1,703	401,103
Makamba	Makamba	757	1,960	223,799
Muramvya	Muramvya	593	1,535	441,653
Muyinga	Muyinga	709	1,836	373,382
Ngozi	Ngozi	569	1,474	482,246
Rutana	Rutana	756	1,959	195,834
Ruyigi	Ruyigi	903	2,339	238,567
TOTAL LAND AREA		10,019	25,949	
INLAND WATER		721	1,867	
TOTAL		10,740	27,816	5,292,793[3]

Demography

Population (2000): 6,055,000.
Density (2000): persons per sq mi 563.8, persons per sq km 217.7.
Urban-rural (1999): urban 8.6%; rural 91.4%.
Sex distribution (1999): male 49.51%; female 50.49%.
Age breakdown (1999): under 15, 47.5%; 15–29, 26.1%; 30–44, 15.0%; 45–59, 7.1%; 60–74, 3.3%; 75 and over, 1.0%.
Population projection: (2010) 7,669,000; (2020) 9,553,000.
Doubling time: 29 years.
Ethnic composition (1995): Rundi 98.0%, of which Hutu 82.5%, Tutsi 14.5%; Twa Pygmy 1.0%; other 2.0%.
Religious affiliation (1990): Roman Catholic 65.1%; Protestant 13.8%; Muslim 1.6%; nonreligious 18.6%; traditional beliefs 0.3%; other 0.6%.
Major cities (1990): Bujumbura (1994) 300,000; Gitega 101,827; Bururi 15,816; Ngozi 14,511; Cibitoke 8,280.

Vital statistics

Birth rate per 1,000 population (1999): 40.8 (world avg. 22.1).
Death rate per 1,000 population (1999): 16.6 (world avg. 8.9).
Natural increase rate per 1,000 population (1999): 24.2 (world avg. 13.2).
Total fertility rate (avg. births per childbearing woman; 1999): 6.3.
Life expectancy at birth (1999): male 45.5 years; female 47.2 years.
Major causes of death: n.a.; however, major health problems include malaria, influenza, diarrheal diseases, measles, and AIDS.

National economy

Budget (1999). Revenue: FBu 70,400,000,000 (tax revenue 92.9%, of which taxes on goods and services 39.3%, taxes on international trade 23.3%, income tax 13.8%, corporate tax 13.1%, administrative receipts 3.4%; nontax revenue 7.1%). Expenditures: FBu 99,000,000,000 (wages and salaries 29.1%, goods and services 28.0%, subsidies and transfers 8.5%, public debt 6.1%).
Tourism (1998): receipts from visitors U.S.$1,000,000; expenditures by nationals abroad U.S.$12,000,000.
Production (metric tons except as noted). Agriculture, forestry, fishing (1999): bananas 1,511,270, sweet potatoes 734,172, cassavas 617,483, dry beans 227,428, sugarcane 175,000, corn (maize) 128,706, yams and taros 102,861, sorghum 59,992, rice 58,630, coffee 30,000, potatoes 24,393, millet 10,105, peanuts (groundnuts) 9,883, wheat 7,085; livestock (number of live animals) 593,657 goats, 329,000 cattle, 165,000 sheep, 61,000 pigs, 4,400,000 chickens; roundwood (1998) 1,799,000 cu m; fish catch (1998) 32,039. Mining and quarrying (1995): peat 8,000; kaolin clay 5,000; gold 10 kg. Manufacturing (1998): beer 1,036,321 hectolitres; carbonated beverages 60,390 hectolitres; cottonseed oil 133,600 litres; cigarettes 316,820,000 units; blankets 174,407 units; footwear 74,890 pairs[4]. Construction: n.a. Energy production (consumption): electricity (kW-hr; 1998): 107,081,000 (112,209,000); coal, none (n.a.); crude petroleum, none (n.a.); petroleum products (metric tons; 1998) none (60,667); natural gas, none (n.a.); peat (metric tons; 1995) 8,000 (8,000).
Land use (1994): forested 12.7%; meadows and pastures 38.6%; agricultural and under permanent cultivation 45.9%; other 2.8%.
Gross national product (1998): U.S.$911,000,000 (U.S.$140 per capita).

Structure of gross domestic product and labour force

	1999		1990	
	in value FBu '000,000	% of total value	labour force	% of labour force
Agriculture	183,000	46.3	2,574,443	93.1
Mining	2,900	0.7	1,419	—
Public utilities			1,672	0.1
Manufacturing	26,400	6.7	33,867	1.2
Construction	18,400	4.7	19,737	0.7
Transp. and communications	14,200	3.6	8,504	0.3
Trade	14,800	3.7	25,822	0.9
Finance	...	...	2,005	0.1
Pub. admin., defense	72,500	18.4	85,191	3.1
Services	9,600	2.4		
Other	53,100[5]	13.4[5]	13,270	0.5
TOTAL	394,900	100.0[3]	2,765,945[3]	100.0

Public debt (external, outstanding; 1998): U.S.$1,079,000,000.
Population economically active (1997): total 3,475,000; activity rate of total population 63.1% (participation rates (1991): ages 15–64, 91.4%; female 48.9%; unemployed, n.a.).

Price and earnings indexes (1995 = 100)

	1993	1994	1995	1996	1997	1998	1999
Consumer price index	73.0	83.8	100.0	126.4	165.8	186.5	192.8
Earnings index	...	...	...	...	...	...	...

Household income and expenditure. Average household size (1998) 5.0; income per household: n.a.; sources of income: n.a.; expenditure[6]: (1990) food 59.6%, clothing and footwear 11.1%, furniture and household goods 6.0%, energy and water 5.8%, housing 4.4%, other 13.1%.

Foreign trade

Balance of trade (current prices)

	1993	1994	1995	1996	1997	1998
FBu '000,000	–34,683	–26,434	–24,018	–26,039	–12,482	–26,700
% of total	53.6%	30.6%	31.1%	53.6%	16.9%	31.8%

Imports (1998): FBu 55,300,000,000 (1994; machinery and transport equipment 21.3%, food and food products 17.9%, petroleum products 8.2%, pharmaceutical products 6.4%). *Major import sources* (1997): Belgium-Luxembourg 23.2%; France 21.0%; Zambia 8.2%; The Netherlands 7.5%; Germany 6.4%; Japan 5.2%; United States 1.2%; Kenya 1.2%.
Exports (1998): FBu 28,600,000,000 (coffee 79.7%, tea 17.1%, animal hides and skins 0.2%). *Major export destinations* (1997): United Kingdom 25.2%; Germany 21.4%; Belgium-Luxembourg 10.0%; France 8.1%; United States 0.9%; Rwanda 0.4%.

Transport and communications

Transport. Railroads: none. Roads (1996): total length 8,997 mi, 14,480 km (paved 7%). Vehicles (1996): passenger cars 19,200; trucks and other vehicles 18,240. Air transport (1998)[7]: passenger arrivals 12,113, departures 11,725; cargo loaded 1,490 metric tons, unloaded 9,329 metric tons; airports (1998) 1.

Communications

Medium	date	unit	number	units per 1,000 persons
Daily newspapers	1996	circulation	20,000	3.2
Radio	1997	receivers	440,000	69
Television	1997	receivers	25,000	3.9
Telephones	1998	main lines	18,500	2.9
Cellular telephones	1998	subscribers	620	0.1
Internet	1998	users	150	0.03

Education and health

Educational attainment: n.a. *Literacy* (1995): percentage of total population age 15 and over literate 35.3%; males literate 49.7%; females literate 22.5%.

Education (1996)

	schools	teachers	students	student/ teacher ratio
Primary (age 6–11)	1,418[8]	10,400[8]	453,746	...
Secondary (age 12–18)	113[9]	2,562[8]	56,887	...
Vocational and teacher training	...	...	5,712	...
Higher	8[9]	556[8]	4,379	...

Health (1996): physicians 329 (1 per 16,507 persons); hospital beds 3,560 (1 per 1,526 persons); infant mortality rate per 1,000 live births (1999) 72.3.
Food (1998): daily per capita caloric intake 1,578 (vegetable products 97%, animal products 3%); 75% of FAO recommended minimum requirement.

Military

Total active duty personnel (1999): 40,000 (army 100%). *Military expenditure as percentage of GNP* (1997): 6.1% (world 2.6%); per capita expenditure U.S.$11.

[1]Transitional government following military coup of July 1996 still in place as of October 2000. [2]Per Transitional Constitutional Act of June 6, 1998. [3]Detail does not add to total given because of rounding. [4]1994. [5]Indirect taxes less subsidies. [6]Weights of consumer price index components. [7]Figures for Bujumbura airport only. [8]1992–93. [9]1990–91.

Cambodia

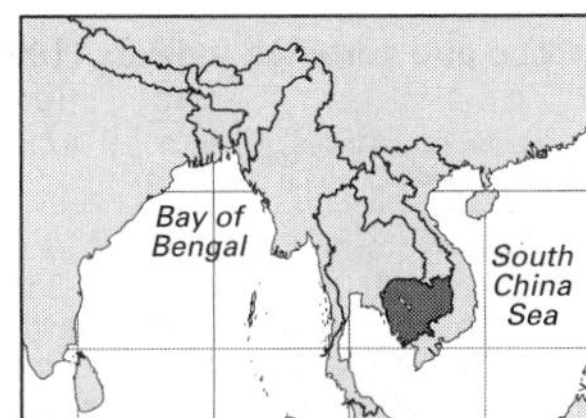

Official name: Preah Reach Ana Pak Kampuchea (Kingdom of Cambodia).
Form of government: constitutional monarchy with two legislative houses (Senate [61[1]]; National Assembly [122]).
Chief of state: King.
Head of government: Prime minister[2].
Capital: Phnom Penh.
Official language: Khmer.
Official religion: Buddhism.
Monetary unit: 1 riel = 100 sen; valuation (Oct. 6, 2000) 1 U.S.$ = 3,825 riels; 1 £ = 5,533 riels.

Area and population		area		population
				1998
Provinces	Capitals	sq mi	sq km	census
Banteay Mean Chey	...	2,579	6,679	577,772
Bat Dambang	Bat Dambang	4,518	11,702	793,129
Kampong Cham	Kampong Cham	3,783	9,799	1,608,914
Kampong Chhnang	Kampong Chhnang	2,132	5,521	417,693
Kampong Spueu	Kampong Spueu	2,709	7,017	598,882
Kampong Thum	Kampong Thum	5,334	13,814	569,060
Kampot	Kampot	1,881	4,873	528,405
Kandal	...	1,378	3,568	1,075,125
Kaoh Kong	Kaoh Kong	4,309	11,160	132,106
Kracheh	Kracheh	4,283	11,094	263,175
Krong Kaeb	...	130	336	28,660
Krong Pailin	...	310	803	22,906
Krong Preah Sihanouk	...	335	868	155,690
Mondol Kiri	Senmonorom	5,517	14,288	32,407
Otdar Mean Cheay	...	2,378	6,158	68,279
Phnom Penh	...	112	290	999,804
Pousat	Pousat	4,900	12,692	360,445
Preah Vihear	Phum Tbeng Mean Cheay	5,324	13,788	119,261
Prey Veaeng	Prey Veaeng	1,885	4,883	946,042
Rotanak Kiri	Lumphat	4,163	10,782	94,243
Siem Reab	Siem Reab	3,976	10,299	696,164
Stueng Traeng	Stueng Traeng	4,283	11,092	81,074
Svay Rieng	Svay Rieng	1,145	2,966	478,252
Takaev	Takaev	1,376	3,563	790,168
TOTAL LAND AREA		68,740	178,035	
INLAND WATER		1,158	3,000	
TOTAL		69,898	181,035	11,437,656

Demography

Population (2000): 12,371,000.
Density (2000)[3]: persons per sq mi 180.0, persons per sq km 69.5.
Urban-rural (1998): urban 20.9%; rural 79.1%.
Sex distribution (1998): male 48.19%; female 51.81%.
Age breakdown (1998): under 15, 42.8%; 15–29, 26.1%; 30–44, 17.3%; 45–59, 8.6%; 60–74, 4.2%; 75 and over, 1.0%.
Population projection: (2010) 16,345,000; (2020) 20,012,000.
Doubling time: 29 years.
Ethnic composition (1994): Khmer 88.6%; Vietnamese 5.5%; Chinese 3.1%; Cham 2.3%; other (Thai, Lao, and Kola) 0.5%.
Religious affiliation (1994): Buddhist 95%; Muslim 2%; other 3%.
Major cities (1987): Phnom Penh 920,000[4]; Batdambang 45,000; Kampong Cham 33,000; Pursat 16,000; Kampong Chhnang 15,000.

Vital statistics

Birth rate per 1,000 population (1999): 34.9 (world avg. 22.1).
Death rate per 1,000 population (1999): 11.3 (world avg. 8.9).
Natural increase rate per 1,000 population (1999): 23.6 (world avg. 13.2).
Total fertility rate (avg. births per childbearing woman; 1999): 4.9.
Life expectancy at birth (1999): male 53 years; female 60 years.
Major causes of death per 100,000 population: n.a.; however, major health problems include tuberculosis, malaria, and pneumonia. Violence, acts of war, and military ordnance (especially unexploded mines) remain hazards.

National economy

Budget (1999). Revenue: 1,224,000,000,000 riels (taxes on international trade 36.0%; indirect taxes 27.1%, of which value-added taxes 13.7%; nontax revenue 28.2%). Expenditures: 1,485,000,000,000 riels (current expenditure 74.4%, of which civil administration 36.1%, defense and security 30.7%; development expenditure 25.6%).
Public debt (external, outstanding; 1997): U.S.$2,031,000,000.
Production (metric tons except as noted). Agriculture, forestry, fishing (1999): rice 3,800,000, bananas 145,000, sugarcane 138,000, roots and tubers 111,000 (of which cassava 67,500, sweet potatoes 25,000), oranges 63,000, corn (maize) 50,000, rubber 40,000, mangoes 33,000, soybeans 27,700, tobacco leaves 10,000; livestock (number of live animals; 1999) 2,821,000 cattle, 2,438,000 pigs, 694,000 buffalo, 16,498,000 chickens and ducks; roundwood (1998) 8,008,000 cu m; fish catch (1997) 114,600. Mining and quarrying (1995): legal mining is confined to fertilizers, salt, and construction materials. Manufacturing (value added in '000,000 riels; 1995): glass and glass products 42,659; cigarettes 1,064.5; wearing apparel 37,567; rubber products 30,114; processed meat, fish, fruits, and vegetables 24,521; sawmilling and planing of wood 18,099; tobacco products 10,163. Construction: n.a. Energy production (consumption): electricity (kW-hr; 1996) 201,000,000 (201,000,000); petroleum products (metric tons; 1996) none (163,000).
Household income and expenditure. Average household size (1998) 5.2.

Gross domestic product (1998): U.S.$2,945,000,000 (U.S.$260 per capita).

Structure of gross domestic product and labour force	1998		1996	
	in value '000,000,000 riels	% of total value	labour force	% of labour force
Agriculture	5,443	50.6	3,732,000	72.6
Mining	33	0.3	1,406,000	27.4
Manufacturing	665	6.2		
Construction	794	7.4		
Public utilities	95	0.9		
Transp. and commun.	445	4.1		
Trade	1,530	14.3		
Public admin., defense	344	3.2		
Services Other	1,401	13.0		
TOTAL	10,750	100.0	5,138,000	100.0

Population economically active (1996): total 4,904,294; activity rate of total population 47.4% (participation rates: ages 15 and over, 78.9%; female 52.7%).

Price and earnings indexes (1995 = 100)	1993	1994	1995	1996	1997	1998	1999
Consumer price index	113.7	99.0	100.0	110.1	113.6	130.3	135.6
Earnings index	...	...	...	...	...	...	...

Tourism (1997): receipts U.S.$143,000,000; expenditures U.S.$12,000,000.
Land use (1994): forested 69.1%; meadows and pastures 8.5%; agricultural and under permanent cultivation 21.7%; other 0.7%.

Foreign trade[5]

Balance of trade (current prices)	1993	1994	1995	1996	1997	1998
U.S.$'000,000	−188	−275	−425	−459	−268	−228
% of total	24.9%	22.9%	21.0%	26.1%	13.3%	10.2%

Imports (1998): U.S.$1,334,000,000 (cigarettes 11.2%; petroleum products 10.4%; motorcycles 2.8%; clothing 1.6%). *Major import sources* (1996): Singapore 34.2%; Thailand 23.9%; Vietnam 7.3%.
Exports (1998): U.S.$999,000,000 (reexports 39.6%; garments 39.0%; sawn timber and logs 17.8%, rubber 2.5%). *Major export destinations* (1996): Thailand 13.0%; Singapore 13.0%; India 9.3%.

Transport and communications

Transport. Railroads (1995): length (1999) 403 mi, 649 km; passenger-km 38,443,600; metric ton-km 7,797,600. Roads (1997): total length 22,226 mi, 35,769 km (paved 8%). Vehicles (1997): passenger cars 52,919; trucks and buses 13,574. Merchant marine (1992): vessels (100 gross tons and over) 3; total deadweight tonnage 3,839. Air transport (1977): passenger-mi 26,098,800, passenger-km 42,000,000; short ton-mi cargo 274,000, metric ton-km cargo 400,000; airports (1997) with scheduled flights 8.

Communications Medium	date	unit	number	units per 1,000 persons
Daily newspapers	1996	circulation	17,000	1.7
Radio	1997	receivers	1,340,000	128
Television	1997	receivers	94,000	9.0
Telephones	1998	main lines	20,044	1.9
Cellular telephones	1998	subscribers	61,345	5.7
Personal computers	1997	units	9,000	0.9
Internet	1997	users	700	0.1

Education and health

Educational attainment (1998). Percentage of population age 25 and over having: no formal schooling 2.1%; some primary education 56.6%; primary 24.7%; some secondary 11.8%; secondary and above 4.8%. *Literacy* (1998): percentage of total population age 15 and over literate 67.3%; males literate 79.5%; females literate 57.0%.

Education (1997–98)	schools	teachers	students	student/ teacher ratio
Primary (age 6–10)	5,026	43,282	2,011,772	46.5
Secondary (age 11–16)	440[6]	16,820	302,951	18.0
Voc., teacher tr.	65[6]	2,315	9,983	4.3
Higher	9[6]	1,001	8,901	8.9

Health: physicians (1994) 1,200 (1 per 7,900 persons); hospital beds (1994) 12,098[7] (1 per 791 persons); infant mortality rate (1999) 81.
Food (1998): daily per capita caloric intake 2,078 (vegetable products 92%, animal products 8%); 94% of FAO recommended minimum requirement.

Military

Total active duty personnel (1999)[8]: 149,000 (army 66.4%, navy 2.0%, air force 1.4%, provincial 30.2%). *Military expenditure as percentage of GNP* (1997): 4.1% (world 2.6%); per capita expenditure U.S.$11.

[1]Includes 2 nonelected seats. [2]A single prime minister was head of government from November 1998 per the king's forced moral persuasion. [3]Based on land area. [4]1994 estimate. [5]Trade balance statistics indicate imports are f.o.b. [6]1992–93. [7]Public hospitals only. [8]Figures include provincial and exclude paramilitary forces.

Internet resources for further information:
- **Cambodian Information Center http://www.cambodia.org**
- **National Institute of Statistics http://www.nis.gov.lch**

Cameroon

Official name: République du Cameroun (French); Republic of Cameroon (English).
Form of government: unitary multiparty republic with one legislative house (National Assembly [180]).
Chief of state: President.
Head of government: Prime Minister.
Capital: Yaoundé.
Official languages: French; English.
Official religion: none.
Monetary unit: 1 CFA franc (CFAF) = 100 centimes; valuation (Oct. 6, 2000) 1 U.S.$ = CFAF 754.28; 1 £ = CFAF 1,091.

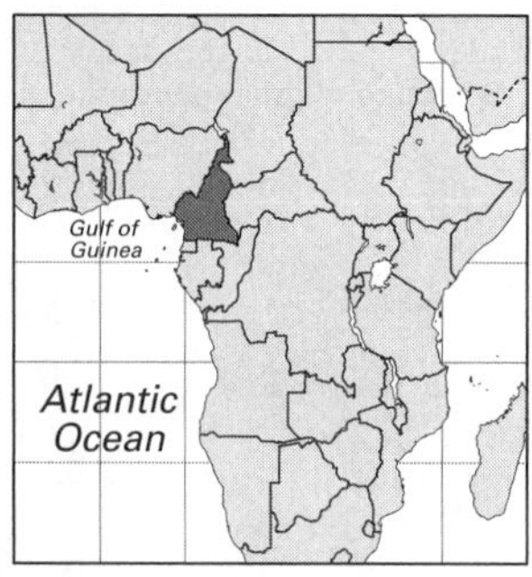

Area and population

Regions	Capitals	area sq mi	area sq km	population 1987 census
Adamoua	Ngaoundéré	24,591	63,691	495,200
Centre	Yaoundé	26,613	68,926	1,651,600
Est	Bertoua	42,089	109,011	517,200
Extrême-Nord	Maroua	13,223	34,246	1,855,700
Littoral	Douala	7,814	20,239	1,354,800
Nord	Garoua	25,319	65,576	832,200
Nord-Ouest	Bamenda	6,877	17,810	1,237,400
Ouest	Bafoussam	5,356	13,872	1,339,800
Sud	Ebolowa	18,189	47,110	373,800
Sud-Ouest	Buea	9,448	24,471	838,000
LAND AREA		179,519	464,952	
INLAND WATER		4,051	10,492	
TOTAL		183,569[1]	475,442[1]	10,495,700

Demography

Population (2000): 15,422,000.
Density (2000)[2]: persons per sq mi 84.0; persons per sq km 32.4.
Urban-rural (1999): urban 48.1%; rural 51.9%.
Sex distribution (1999): male 50.20%; female 49.80%.
Age breakdown (1999): under 15, 42.9%; 15–29, 27.7%; 30–44, 15.6%; 45–59, 8.7%; 60–74, 4.1%; 75 and over, 1.0%.
Population projection: (2010) 19,202,000; (2020) 22,869,000.
Doubling time: 28 years.
Ethnic composition (1983): Fang 19.6%; Bamileke and Bamum 18.5%; Duala, Luanda, and Basa 14.7%; Fulani 9.6%; Tikar 7.4%; Mandara 5.7%; Maka 4.9%; Chamba 2.4%; Mbum 1.3%; Hausa 1.2%; French 0.2%; other 14.5%.
Religious affiliation (1990): Roman Catholic 34.7%; animist 26.0%; Muslim 21.8%; Protestant 17.5%.
Major cities (1992): Douala 1,200,000; Yaoundé 800,000; Garoua 160,000; Maroua 140,000; Bafoussam 120,000.

Vital statistics

Birth rate per 1,000 population (1999): 36.9 (world avg. 22.1).
Death rate per 1,000 population (1999): 11.8 (world avg. 8.9).
Natural increase rate per 1,000 population (1999): 25.1 (world avg. 13.2).
Total fertility rate (avg. births per childbearing woman; 1999): 4.9.
Life expectancy at birth (1999): male 54.3 years; female 55.9 years.
Major causes of death per 100,000 population: n.a.; however, major health problems include measles, malaria, tuberculosis of respiratory system, anemias, meningitis, and intestinal obstruction and hernia.

National economy

Budget (1998–99). Revenue: CFAF 838,000,000,000 (taxes on goods and services 40.5%; income tax 20.8%; customs duties 16.5%; oil revenue 15.9%). Expenditures: CFAF 1,023,000,000,000 (current expenditure 80.9%, of which debt services 27.6%, wages and salaries 26.9%, goods and services 16.3%, transfers 9.8%; capital expenditure 19.1%).
Public debt (external, outstanding; 1998): U.S.$8,096,000,000.
Gross national product (1998): U.S.$8,736,000,000 (U.S.$610 per capita).

Structure of gross domestic product and labour force

	1998–99 in value CFAF '000,000,000	1998–99 % of total value	1985 labour force	1985 % of labour force
Agriculture	1,789	33.1	2,900,871	74.0
Mining	243	4.5	1,793	0.1
Manufacturing	703	13.0	174,498	4.5
Construction	157	2.9	66,684	1.7
Public utilities	119	2.2	3,522	0.1
Transp. and commun.			51,688	1.3
Trade			154,014	3.9
Finance	2,395	44.3	8,009	0.2
Services			292,922	7.5
Public admin., defense				
Other	...	...	263,634	6.7
TOTAL	5,406	100.0	3,917,635	100.0

Household income and expenditure. Average household size (1998) 5.7; average annual income per household (1983)[3] U.S.$420; sources of income: n.a.; expenditure (1993)[3]: food 49.1%, housing 18.0%, transportation and communications 13.0%, health 8.6%, clothing 7.6%, recreation 2.4%.
Population economically active (1991): total 4,740,000; activity rate of total population 40.0% (participation rates [1985]: ages 15–69, 66.3%; female 38.5%; unemployed, n.a.).

Price and earnings indexes (1995 = 100)

	1993	1994	1995	1996	1997	1998
Consumer price index	65.0	87.8	100.0	104.7	105.8	105.9
Earnings index	...	...	...	...	...	...

Production (metric tons except as noted). Agriculture, forestry, fishing (1999): cassava 1,500,000, sugarcane 1,350,000, plantains 1,000,000, bananas 990,000, corn (maize) 600,000, sorghum 500,000, vegetables and melons 430,000, sweet potatoes 220,000, seed cotton 190,000, palm oil 150,000, cacao 150,000, yams 130,000, peanuts (groundnuts) 100,000, millet 71,000, rice 65,000, coffee 61,500, natural rubber 54,000, palm kernels 52,000; livestock (number of live animals) 5,900,000 cattle, 3,880,000 sheep, 3,850,000 goats, 1,430,000 pigs; roundwood (1998) 15,172,000 cu m; fish catch (1998) 97,000. Mining and quarrying (1996): pozzolana 100,000; aluminum 82,000; limestone 50,000; tin ore and concentrate 1. Manufacturing (value added in CFAF '000,000; 1994): beverages 49,314; wood and wood products 42,756; rubber and plastic products 38,928; food products 30,030; iron and steel products 29,424; textiles 20,113; refined petroleum products 17,888; industrial chemicals 8,559; pottery, china, and earthenware 6,773; paper products 3,652. Construction (1983): residential 230,400 sq m; nonresidential 51,100 sq m. Energy production (consumption): electricity (kW-hr; 1996) 2,753,000,000 (2,753,000,000); coal (metric tons; 1996) 1,000 (1,000); crude petroleum (barrels; 1996) 42,770,000 (6,856,000); petroleum products (metric tons; 1996) 1,040,000 (1,107,000); natural gas, none (n.a.).
Land use (1994): forested 77.1%; meadows and pastures 4.3%; agricultural and under permanent cultivation 15.1%; other 3.5%.
Tourism (1995): receipts U.S.$36,000,000; expenditures U.S.$105,000,000.

Foreign trade

Balance of trade (current prices)

	1994	1995	1996	1997	1998	1999
CFAF '000,000,000	+223.7	+398.8	+277.5	+290.6	+209.4	+112.4
% of total	15.7%	24.4%	18.1%	15.6%	10.7%	6.0%

Imports (1998–99): CFAF 881,500,000,000 (semifinished goods 15.9%; industrial equipment 13.3%; food and beverages 11.3%; minerals 10.6%; transport equipment 10.3%; unrecorded trade 6.1%). *Major import sources:* France 25.6%; Germany 6.4%; U.S. 5.7%; Japan 5.0%; Belgium-Luxembourg 4.8%; Italy 4.3%; The Netherlands 2.6%; United Kingdom 2.6%.
Exports (1998–99): CFAF 993,900,000,000 (crude petroleum 31.6%; lumber 12.1%; coffee 7.5%; cocoa 7.4%; aluminum 5.0%; cotton 4.7%). *Major export destinations:* Italy 22.4%; France 12.6%; Spain 9.4%; The Netherlands 9.4%; Portugal 3.3%; Germany 1.9%.

Transport and communications

Transport. Railroads (1997): route length 625 mi, 1,006 km; (1995) passenger-mi 197,000,000, passenger-km 317,000,000; short ton-mi cargo 556,000,000, metric ton-km cargo 812,000,000. Roads (1997): total length 30,074 mi, 48,400 km (paved 8%). Vehicles (1997): passenger cars 98,000; trucks and buses 64,350. Merchant marine (1992): vessels (100 gross tons and over) 47; total deadweight tonnage 39,797. Air transport (1996): passenger-mi 347,970,000, passenger-km 560,000,000; short ton-mi cargo 56,540,000, metric ton-km cargo 91,000,000; airports (1998) with scheduled flights 5.

Communications

Medium	date	unit	number	units per 1,000 persons
Daily newspapers	1996	circulation	91,000	6.7
Radio	1997	receivers	2,270,000	163
Television	1998	receivers	480,000	33.5
Telephones	1997	main lines	75,200	5.4
Cellular telephones	1997	subscribers	4,200	0.3
Personal computers	1998	units	30,000	2.1
Internet	1998	users	2,000	0.1

Education and health

Educational attainment (1976). Percentage of population age 15 and over having: no schooling 51.1%; primary education 41.7%; some postprimary 0.2%; secondary 5.7%; some postsecondary 0.3%; higher 0.2%; other 0.8%. *Literacy* (1995): percentage of total population age 15 and over literate 63.4%; males literate 75.0%; females literate 52.1%.

Education (1994–95)

	schools	teachers	students	student/ teacher ratio
Primary (age 6–14)	6,801	40,970	1,896,722	46.3
Secondary (age 15–24)	388[4]	14,917	459,068	30.8
Vocational	220[4]	5,885	91,779	15.6
Higher[5]	5[4]	1,086	33,177	30.5

Health: physicians (1996) 1,031 (1 per 13,510 persons); hospital beds (1988) 29,285 (1 per 371 persons); infant mortality rate (1999) 72.2.
Food (1998): daily per capita caloric intake 2,209 (vegetable products 94%, animal products 6%); 95% of FAO recommended minimum requirement.

Military

Total active duty personnel (1999): 13,100 (army 87.8%, navy 9.9%, air force 2.3%). *Military expenditure as percentage of GNP* (1997): 3.0% (world 2.6%); per capita expenditure U.S.$16.

[1]Detail does not add to total given because of rounding. [2]Based on land area. [3]Weights of consumer price index components. [4]1986–87. [5]1990–91.

Internet resources for further information:
- **Investir en Zone Franc http://www.izf.net/izf/Index.htm**

Canada

Official name: Canada.
Form of government: federal multiparty parliamentary state with two legislative houses (Senate [105]; House of Commons [301]).
Chief of state: Queen of Canada (British Monarch).
Representative of chief of state: Governor-General.
Head of government: Prime Minister.
Capital: Ottawa.
Official languages: English; French.
Official religion: none.
Monetary unit: 1 Canadian dollar (Can$) = 100 cents; valuation (Oct. 6, 2000) 1 U.S.$ = Can$1.50; 1 £ = Can$2.17.

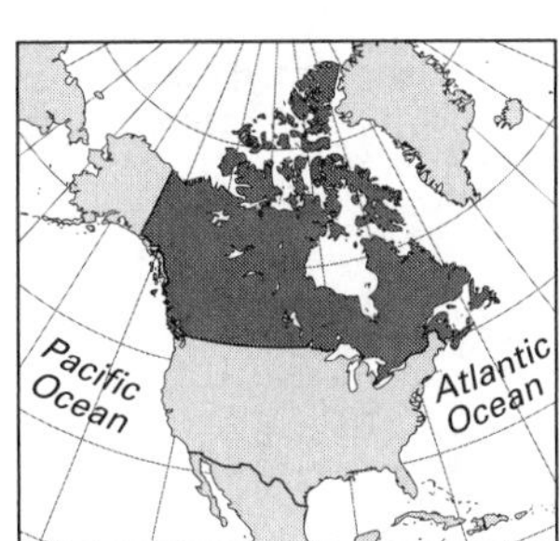

Area and population

Provinces	Capitals	area sq mi	area sq km	population 1999 estimate
Alberta	Edmonton	255,287	661,190	2,968,992
British Columbia	Victoria	365,948	947,800	4,029,253
Manitoba	Winnipeg	250,947	649,950	1,143,391
New Brunswick	Fredericton	28,355	73,440	754,741
Newfoundland	St. John's	156,649	405,720	541,164
Nova Scotia	Halifax	21,425	55,490	940,825
Ontario	Toronto	412,581	1,068,580	11,560,899
Prince Edward Island	Charlottetown	2,185	5,660	137,796
Quebec	Quebec	594,860	1,540,680	7,363,262
Saskatchewan	Regina	251,866	652,330	1,028,137
Territories				
Northwest Territories	Yellowknife	1,322,910[1]	3,426,320[1]	41,668
Nunavut[2]	Iqaluit	[1]	[1]	27,146
Yukon Territory	Whitehorse	186,661	483,450	30,688
TOTAL		3,849,674	9,970,610	30,567,962

Demography

Population (2000): 30,770,000.
Density (2000)[3]: persons per sq mi 8.6, persons per sq km 3.3.
Urban-rural (1996): urban 77.9%; rural 22.1%.
Sex distribution (1999): male 49.53%; female 50.47%.
Age breakdown (1997): under 15, 19.8%; 15–29, 20.7%; 30–44, 25.5%; 45–59, 17.7%; 60–74, 11.0%; 75 and over, 5.3%.
Population projection: (2010) 33,142,000; (2020) 35,199,000.
Doubling time: not applicable; doubling time exceeds 100 years.
Ethnic origin (1991): French 22.8%; British 20.8%; German 3.4%; Italian 2.8%; Chinese 2.2%; Amerindian and Inuktitut (Eskimo) 1.7%; Ukrainian 1.5%; Dutch 1.3%; multiple origin and other 43.5%[4].
Religious affiliation (1991): Roman Catholic 45.7%; Protestant 36.2% (including Anglican 8.1%); Eastern Orthodox 1.4%; Jewish 1.2%; Muslim 0.9%; Buddhist 0.6%; Hindu 0.6%; nonreligious 12.5%; other 0.9%.
Major metropolitan areas (1996): Toronto 4,263,757; Montreal 3,326,510; Vancouver 1,831,665; Ottawa-Hull 1,010,498; Edmonton 862,597; Calgary 821,628; Quebec 671,889; Winnipeg 667,209; Hamilton 624,360; London 398,616.

Other metropolitan areas (1996)

	population		population		population
Chicoutimi-Jonquière	160,454	Regina	193,652	Sherbrooke	147,384
Halifax	332,518	St. Catharines–Niagara	372,406	Sudbury	160,488
Kitchener	382,940	St. John's	174,051	Trois Rivières	139,956
Oshawa	268,773	Saskatoon	219,056	Victoria	304,287
				Windsor	278,685

Place of birth (1996): 83.4% native-born; 16.6% foreign-born, of which United Kingdom 2.2%, other European 4.2%, Asian countries 5.2%, United States 0.8%, other 4.2%.
Mobility (1991). Population living in the same residence as in 1986: 53.3%; different residence, same municipality 23.2%; same province, different municipality 15.9%; different province 3.9%; different country 3.7%.
Households (1997). Total number of households 11,580,000. Average household size 2.5; 1 person 25.2%, 2 persons 33.0%, 3 persons 16.7%, 4 persons 16.3%, 5 or more persons 8.8%. Family households (1995): 7,879,700 (70.1%), nonfamily 3,363,300 (29.1%, of which 1 person 83.3%).
Immigration (1994): permanent immigrants admitted 223,875, from Hong Kong 19.7%, Philippines 8.5%, India 7.7%, China 5.6%, Taiwan 3.3%, Sri Lanka 3.0%, United States 2.8%, Vietnam 2.8%, United Kingdom 2.7%; refugee arrivals 19,089.

Vital statistics

Birth rate per 1,000 population (1998): 11.4 (world avg. 22.1); (1985) legitimate 83.8%; illegitimate 16.2%.
Death rate per 1,000 population (1998): 7.2 (world avg. 8.9).
Natural increase rate per 1,000 population (1998): 4.2 (world avg. 13.2).
Total fertility rate (avg. births per childbearing woman; 1999): 1.7.
Marriage rate per 1,000 population (1996): 5.4.
Divorce rate per 1,000 population (1995): 2.7.
Life expectancy at birth (1996): male 74.9 years; female 81.2 years.
Major causes of death per 100,000 population (1995): diseases of the circulatory system 267.2; malignant neoplasms (cancers) 195.3; diseases of the respiratory system 63.8; accidents and violence 45.8 (including suicide 13.4).

Social indicators

Educational attainment (1996). Percentage of population age 15 and over having: no formal schooling or not known 4.2%; at least primary education 12.3%; some secondary 19.6%; completed secondary 19.8%; postsecondary 30.5%; university graduates 13.6%.

Distribution of income (1991)

percentage of national income by quintile

1	2	3	4	5 (highest)
5.3%	13.6%	19.7%	25.9%	35.5%

Quality of working life (1997). Average workweek: 31.3 hours. Annual rate per 100,000 workers for (1996): injury, accident, or industrial illness 3,320[5]; death 4.6. Average days lost to labour stoppages per 1,000 employee-workdays (1997): 0.9. Average duration of journey to work (1983): 23 minutes[6] (automobile 72.8%, public transportation 17.3%, other 9.9%). Rate per 1,000 workers of discouraged (unemployed no longer seeking work; 1983): 10.5.
Access to services (1990). Proportion of households having access to: electricity 100.0%; public water supply 99.8%; public sewage collection 99.3%.
Social participation. Eligible voters participating in last national election (June 1997): 67.0%. Population over 18 years of age participating in voluntary work (1987): 27.0%. Union membership in total workforce (1992): 29.7%. Practicing religious population in total affiliated population (1996): 92.5%.
Social deviance (1996). Offense rate per 100,000 population for: violent crime 990, of which assault 8.8[7], sexual assault 111.0[7], homicide 1.9; property crime 5,211, of which auto theft 601, burglary 1,325.
Leisure (1992). Favourite leisure activities (hours weekly): television 15.3; social time 12.7; reading 3.5; sports and entertainment 0.9.
Material well-being (1995). Households possessing: automobile 74.5%, of which two or more 21.7%; telephone 98.5%; radio 98.9%; colour television 98.5%; refrigerator 99.7%; central air conditioner 24.6%[8]; cable television 73.4%; video recorder 82.1%; microwave oven 83.4%.

National economy

Gross national product (1998): U.S.$580,872,000,000 (U.S.$19,170 per capita).

Structure of gross domestic product and labour force

	1998 in value Can$'000,000[9]	% of total value	labour force	% of labour force
Agriculture	17,823	2.5	551,000	3.5
Mining	27,502	3.8	169,000	1.1
Manufacturing	128,850	17.9	2,254,000	14.4
Construction	40,242	5.6	767,000	4.9
Public utilities	24,445	3.4	138,000	0.9
Transp. and commun.	56,968	7.9	929,000	5.9
Trade	86,064	11.9	2,423,000	15.5
Finance	117,976	16.4	789,000	5.0
Pub. admin., defense	44,610	6.2	795,000	5.1
Services	176,523	24.5	5,513,000	35.3
Other	—	—	1,305,000[10]	8.3[10]
TOTAL	721,003[11]	100.0[12]	15,632,000[12]	100.0[12]

Budget (1996–97). Revenue: Can$153,769,000,000 (individual income taxes 44.5%, value-added tax 19.0%, corporate income tax 11.0%, import duties 1.7%). Expenditures: Can$167,294,000,000 (social services 28.9%, public debt interest 27.0%, defense and social protection 10.2%, education 2.4%, health 0.7%).
National debt (1996): Can$569,691,000,000.
Tourism (1997): receipts U.S.$8,763,000,000; expenditures U.S.$11,268,000,000.

Manufacturing, mining, and construction enterprises (1993)

	no. of estab-lishments	no. of employees	weekly wages as a % of avg. of all mfg. wages	annual value added (Can$'000,000)
Manufacturing				
Food and beverages	3,202	216,000	100.7	20,110
Transport equipment	1,224	187,000	144.3	19,430
Chemicals and related products	1,396	97,000	142.0	12,860
Machinery	4,000	129,000	125.0	9,130
Electrical and electronic products	1,176	104,000	133.6	8,520
Printing, publishing, and related products	4,655	125,000	111.1	8,500
Paper and related products	651	101,000	152.1	7,890
Wood	2,201	100,000	109.3	7,880
Primary metals	417	85,000	155.2	7,790
Metal fabricating	3,287	106,000	113.6	6,290
Rubber and plastic	1,394	85,000	112.3	5,900
Textiles	1,057	60,000	88.4	3,600
Nonmetallic mineral products	1,519	44,000	125.4	3,440
Wearing apparel	1,923	85,000	67.4	3,220
Petroleum and coal products	170	16,000	189.5	2,560
Furniture and fixtures	1,965	50,000	91.5	2,310
Tobacco products industries	17	5,000	184.5	1,220
Mining[5]	1,232	113,000	...	29,650
Construction[13]	...	800,000	121.7	28,182

Production (metric tons except as noted). Agriculture, forestry, fishing (1999): wheat 25,007,000, barley 12,691,000, rapeseed 8,285,000, corn (maize) 7,900,000, potatoes 4,260,000, oats 3,538,000, soybeans 2,640,000, vegetables 2,142,000 (of which tomatoes 535,000, carrots 325,000, onions 161,000, cabbage 135,000), dry peas 2,070,000, linseed 1,106,000, sugar beets 1,000,000, apples 510,000; livestock (number of live animals) 12,981,000 cattle, 12,403,000 pigs, 656,000 sheep, 508,000 horses; roundwood (1998) 185,859,000 cu m; fish catch (1997) 1,030,523. Mining and quarrying (1997): iron ore 37,284,000; zinc 1,017,081; copper 646,477; nickel 180,584; lead 170,380; uranium 11,416; molybdenum 7,540; silver 1,213 kg; gold 169.1 kg. Manufacturing (value-added in Can$'000,000[9]; 1996): transportation equipment 16,181.7; electrical products 12,570.7; food 10,556.6; chemical products 8,159.1; paper products 7,755.9; metal products 6,467.8; wood products 5,371.4; printing and publishing 4,288.8; rubber and plastic products 3,890.4; machinery 3,797.0; wearing apparel 2,079.0; textile 2,008.3; furniture 1,774.7. Construction (value-added in Can$'000,000[9]; 1996): residential 6,683.8; nonresidential 20,001.7.

Service enterprises (1988)

	no. of enterprises	no. of employees[14]	weekly wages as a % of all wages	annual sales (Can$'000,000)
Retail trade				
Motor vehicle dealers	...	79,800	...	35,917
Food stores	...	213,400	...	35,187
Service stations	...	63,700	...	14,612
Department stores	...	[15]	...	13,271
Clothing stores	...	50,200	...	7,486
Pharmacies	...	52,400	...	7,459
Furniture and appliance stores	...	62,100	...	4,447
Automotive stores	...	31,500	...	3,767
General merchandise	...	231,700[15]	...	3,109
Sporting goods	...	...	...	2,669
General stores	...	[15]	...	2,415
Hardware stores	...	17,300	...	1,824
Shoe stores	...	18,400	...	1,599
Jewelry stores	...	14,000	...	1,215
Variety stores	...	45,100	...	1,057

Energy production (consumption): electricity (kW-hr; 1994) 554,186,000,000 (510,272,000,000); coal (metric tons; 1994) 72,824,000 (52,229,000); crude petroleum (barrels; 1994) 638,633,000 (507,557,000); petroleum products (metric tons; 1994) 87,161,000 (77,264,000); natural gas (cu m; 1994) 148,129,000,000 (78,223,000,000).

Population economically active (1998): total 15,632,000; activity rate of total population 51.0% (participation rates: ages 15–64, 75.4%; female 45.4%; unemployed 8.3%).

Price and earnings indexes (1995 = 100)

	1993	1994	1995	1996	1997	1998	1999
Consumer price index	97.7	97.9	100.0	101.6	103.2	104.2	106.0
Hourly earnings index[16]	97.7	98.6	100.0	103.2	104.1	106.3	106.5

Household income and expenditure (1995). Average household size 2.6; average annual income per family (1994) Can$54,153 (U.S.$39,655); sources of income (1995): wages and salaries 57.0%, transfer payments 20.7%, property and entrepreneurial income 13.7%, profits 8.6%; expenditure (1992): housing 24.7%[17], food 15.5%, transportation and communications 15.3%, household durable goods 9.1%, recreation 8.4%, clothing 5.1%, health 4.3%, education 3.0%.

Financial aggregates

	1993	1994	1995	1996	1997	1998
Exchange rate, Can$ per:						
U.S. dollar	1.29	1.36	1.37	1.36	1.38	1.48
£	1.94	2.09	2.17	2.13	2.27	2.46
SDR	1.82	2.05	2.03	1.97	1.93	2.16
International reserves (U.S.$)						
Total (excl. gold; '000,000)	12,481	12,286	15,049	20,422	17,823	23,308
SDRs ('000,000)	1,062	1,148	1,177	1,168	1,126	1,098
Reserve pos. in IMF ('000,000)	948	919	1,243	1,226	1,575	2,299
Foreign exchange ('000,000)	10,471	10,219	12,629	18,028	15,122	19,991
Gold ('000,000 fine troy oz)	6.05	3.89	3.41	3.09	3.09	2.49
% world reserves	0.65	0.43	0.38	0.34	0.35	0.26
Interest and prices						
Central bank discount (%)	4.11	7.43	5.79	3.25	4.50	5.25
Govt. bond yield (%)	7.85	8.63	8.28	7.50	6.42	5.47
Industrial share prices (1995 = 100)	88.1	96.6	100.0	118.8	145.7	152.4
Balance of payments (U.S.$'000,000)						
Balance of visible trade,	7,612	12,202	22,341	30,062	17,135	12,625
of which:						
Imports, f.o.b.	−136,418	−151,290	−167,513	−175,737	−200,485	−204,614
Exports, f.o.b.	144,030	163,492	189,854	205,799	217,620	217,238
Balance of invisibles	−31,481	−29,590	−31,034	−27,254	−27,439	−23,838
Balance of payments, current account	−23,869	−17,388	−8,693	−2,808	−10,304	−11,213

Land use (1994): forested 53.6%; meadows and pastures 3.0%; agricultural and under permanent cultivation 4.9%; built-on, wasteland, and other 38.5%.

Foreign trade

Balance of trade (current prices)

	1993	1994	1995	1996	1997	1998	1999
Can$'000,000,000	+12.1	+19.3	+38.7	+42.2	+25.5	+19.8	+35.1
% of total	3.4%	4.5%	7.9%	8.3%	4.5%	3.2%	5.2%

Imports (1997): Can$276,846,000,000 (machinery and transport equipment 54.8%, of which motor vehicles 21.9%; chemical products 7.0%; food 5.6%; petroleum and energy products 3.8%; forestry products 0.8%). *Major import sources:* U.S. 67.6%; Japan 4.6%; Mexico 2.6%; U.K. 2.4%; China 2.3%; Germany 2.0%; France 1.9%; Taiwan 1.3%; Italy 1.1%; South Korea 1.0%.

Exports (1997): Can$301,101,000,000 (machinery and transport equipment 45.8%, of which motor vehicles 23.3%; mineral fuels 8.9%, of which crude petroleum 3.3%; food 8.2%, of which wheat 1.7%; lumber 5.6%; newsprint and paper products 3.9%; wood pulp 2.1%). *Major export destinations:* U.S. 82.2%; Japan 3.8%; U.K. 1.3%; South Korea 1.0%; Germany 0.9%; China 0.8%.

Trade by commodities (1996)

SITC Group	imports U.S.$'000,000	imports %	exports U.S.$'000,000	exports %
00 Food and live animals	8,621.7	5.0	12,663.3	6.3
01 Beverages and tobacco	816.9	0.5	985.6	0.5
02 Crude materials, excluding fuels	5,548.4	3.2	21,638.6	10.7
03 Mineral fuels, lubricants, and related materials	7,502.7	4.4	20,513.9	10.2
04 Animal and vegetable oils, fats, and waxes	...	...	...	...
05 Chemicals and related products, n.e.s.	14,005.8	8.2	11,119.4	5.5
06 Basic manufactures	21,588.0	12.6	32,789.0	16.3
07 Machinery and transport equipment	87,181.5	51.0	78,636.8	39.0
08 Miscellaneous manufactured articles	18,860.7	11.0	11,209.0	5.6
09 Goods not classified by kind	6,615.7	3.9	11,442.8	5.7
TOTAL	171,007.2[18]	100.0[18]	201,573.7[18]	100.0[18]

Direction of trade (1997)

	imports U.S.$'000,000	imports %	exports U.S.$'000,000	exports %
Africa	1,521	0.8	1,417	0.7
Asia	26,072	13.3[12]	17,271	8.1
China	5,438	2.8	2,752	1.3
Japan	9,018	4.6	7,250	3.4
Taiwan	2,498	1.3	1,126	0.5
Other	9,118	4.7	6,143	2.9
Americas	140,529	71.9[12]	181,712	85.3
United States	131,948	67.5	177,317	83.2
Mexico	4,968	2.5	916	0.4
Other Americas	3,595	1.8	3,479	1.6
Europe	19,997	10.2	11,192	5.2
EU	19,321	9.9	10,551	5.0
Other Europe	676	0.3	641	0.3
Oceania	1,121	0.6	1,138	0.5
TOTAL	195,463[18, 19]	100.0[18, 19]	213,020[18]	100.0[18]

Transport and communications

Transport. Railroads (1996): length 65,403 km; passenger-km 1,519,000,000; metric ton-km cargo 282,489,000,000. Roads (1995): total length 1,021,000 km (paved 35%). Vehicles (1996): passenger cars 13,217,336; trucks and buses 3,643,652. Merchant marine (1993): vessels (100 gross tons and over) 1,049; total deadweight tonnage 1,910,000. Air transport (1996): passenger-km 80,071,826,000; metric ton-km cargo 1,780,980,000; airports (1997) with scheduled flights 269.

Communications

Medium	date	unit	number	units per 1,000 persons
Daily newspapers	1996	circulation	4,718,000	159
Radio	1997	receivers	32,300,000	1,077
Television	1997	receivers	21,443,000	708
Telephones	1998	main lines	19,206,000	635
Cellular telephones	1998	subscribers	5,320,000	176
Personal computers	1998	units	10,000,000	331
Internet	1998	users	7,500,000	248

Education and health

Literacy (1986): total population age 15 and over literate 18,745,000 (96.6%); males literate (1975) 8,003,000 (95.6%); females literate (1975) 8,182,000 (95.7%).

Education (1995–96)

	schools[20]	teachers	students	student/teacher ratio
Primary (age 6–14) / Secondary (age 14–18)	16,465	296,027	5,440,334	18.4
Postsecondary and higher	265	64,100[21]	1,394,489[22]	14.4[21]

Health: physicians (1995) *c.* 55,000 (1 per 538 persons); hospital beds (1993) 163,399 (1 per 177 persons); infant mortality rate (1997) 5.5.

Food (1997): daily per capita caloric intake 3,119 (vegetable products 73%, animal products 27%); 117% of FAO recommended minimum requirement.

Military

Total active duty personnel (1999): 60,600 (army 34.5%, navy 14.8%, air force 24.8%, not identified by service 25.9%). *Military expenditure as percentage of GNP* (1997): 1.3% (world 2.6%); per capita expenditure U.S.$257.

[1]Area for Northwestern Territories includes Nunavut. [2]Nunavut came into existence on April 1, 1999. [3]Based on land area of 3,558,096 sq mi (9,215,430 sq km). [4]Includes 4.0% who are of both French and British origin. [5]1990. [6]Urban areas. [7]1991. [8]1989. [9]At prices of 1992. [10]Unemployed. [11]GDP at current values in 1998 is Can$892,000,000,000. [12]Detail does not add to total given because of rounding. [13]1988. [14]1984. [15]Department and General stores included with General merchandise. [16]Manufacturing only. [17]Includes energy and utilities. [18]Detail does not add to total because of discrepancies in estimates. [19]Total for imports includes U.S$3,299,000,000 (1.7% of total imports; mostly special transactions) not distributable by region. [20]1996–97. [21]1993–94. [22]Includes 431,740 part-time students.

Internet resources for further information:

- **Statistics Canada http://www.statcan.ca**

Cape Verde

Official name: República de Cabo Verde (Republic of Cape Verde).
Form of government: multiparty republic with one legislative house (National Assembly [72]).
Chief of state: President.
Head of government: Prime Minister.
Capital: Praia.
Official language: Portuguese.
Official religion: none.
Monetary unit: 1 escudo (C.V.Esc.)[1] = 100 centavos; valuation (Oct. 6, 2000) 1 U.S.$ = C.V.Esc. 129.48; 1 £ = C.V.Esc. 187.30.

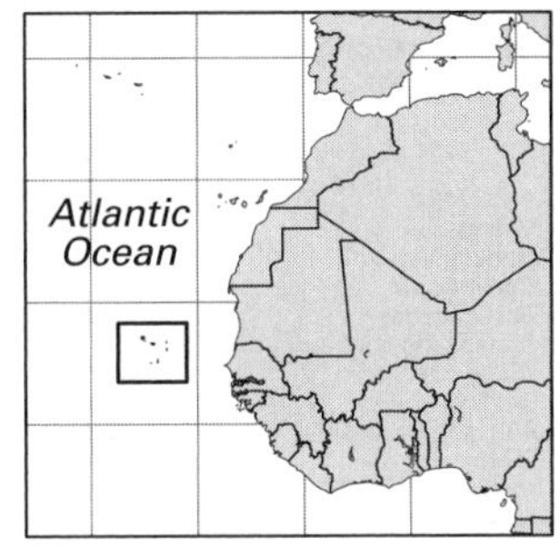

Area and population

Island Groups / Islands/Counties[2] / Counties	Capitals	area sq mi	area sq km	population 1990 census
Leeward Islands		696[3]	1,803	221,537
Brava	Nova Sintra	26	67	6,975
Fogo				
Mosteiros[4]	…	184	476	33,902
São Filipe	São Filipe			
Maio	Porto Inglês	104	269	4,969
Santiago		383	991	175,691
Praia	Praia	153	396	82,802
Santa Catarina	Assomada	94	243	41,584
Santa Cruz	Pedra Badejo	58	149	25,892
São Domingos[4]		…	…	…
Tarrafal	Tarrafal	78	203	25,413
Windward Islands		861[3]	2,230	119,954
Boa Vista	Sal Rei	239	620	3,452
Sal	Santa Maria	83	216	7,715
Santo Antão		300	779	43,845
Paúl	Pombas	21	54	8,121
Porto Novo	Porto Novo	215	558	14,873
Ribeira Grande	Ponta do Sol	64	167	20,851
São Nicolau	Ribeira Brava	150	388	13,665
São Vicente[5]	Mindelo	88	227	51,277
TOTAL		1,557	4,033	341,491

Demography

Population (2000): 401,000.
Density (2000): persons per sq mi 257.5, persons per sq km 99.4.
Urban-rural (1990): urban 29.7%; rural 70.3%.
Sex distribution (1999): male 48.09%; female 51.91%.
Age breakdown (1999): under 15, 44.2%; 15–29, 24.5%; 30–44, 16.9%; 45–59, 5.6%; 60 and over, 8.8%.
Population projection: (2010) 431,000; (2020) 448,000.
Doubling time: 30 years.
Ethnic composition (1986): mixed 71.0%; black 28.0%; white 1.0%.
Religious affiliation (1995): Roman Catholic 95.9%; Protestant and other 4.1%.
Major cities (1995): Praia 68,000; Mindelo 47,109[6]; São Filipe 5,616[6].

Vital statistics

Birth rate per 1,000 population (1999): 30.8 (world avg. 22.1); (1989) legitimate 28.9%; illegitimate 71.1%.
Death rate per 1,000 population (1999): 7.6 (world avg. 8.9).
Natural increase rate per 1,000 population (1999): 23.2 (world avg. 13.2).
Total fertility rate (avg. births per childbearing woman; 1999): 4.3.
Marriage rate per 1,000 population (1990): 4.5.
Divorce rate per 1,000 population: n.a.
Life expectancy at birth (1999): male 65.4 years; female 72.0 years.
Major causes of death per 100,000 population (1987): enteritis and other diarrheal diseases 97.4; heart disease 77.9; malignant neoplasms (cancers) 47.9; pneumonia 46.4; accidents, poisoning, and violence 44.0.

National economy

Budget (1998). Revenue: C.V.Esc. 11,656,000,000 (tax revenue 72.1%, of which taxes on international trade 42.1%, income taxes 26.3%, other taxes 3.7%; nontax revenue 27.9%). Expenditures: C.V.Esc. 19,037,000,000 (current expenditure 56.3%, of which wages and salaries 25.7%, transfers 14.0%, public debt 9.9%, goods and services 1.8%; capital expenditure 43.7%).
Public debt (external, outstanding; 1998): U.S.$257,300,000.
Tourism (1998): receipts from visitors U.S.$20,000,000; expenditures by nationals abroad U.S.$24,000,000.
Production (metric tons except as noted). Agriculture, forestry, fishing (1999): sugarcane 12,500, corn (maize) 10,000, bananas 6,000, coconuts 5,000, vegetables (including melons) 4,800, fruits (except melons) 4,500, sweet potatoes 3,800, cassava 3,000, potatoes 2,000; livestock (number of live animals) 636,000 pigs, 112,000 goats, 22,000 cattle, 9,000 sheep; roundwood, n.a.; fish catch (1998) 9,999. Mining and quarrying (1992): salt 4,000. Manufacturing (1998): flour 25,916; bread 5,628[7]; paint 628[8]; canned tuna 337[7]; cigarettes 43[8]; beer 4,324,560 litres; soft drinks 922,714[8] litres. Construction (1982): residential C.V.Esc. 365,800,000; nonresidential C.V.Esc. 1,700,000. Energy production (consumption): electricity (kW-hr; 1998) 100,764,000,000 (80,039,000,000); coal, none (none); crude petroleum, none (none); petroleum products (metric tons; 1998) none (98,392); natural gas, none (none).
Gross national product (1998): U.S.$499,000,000 (U.S.$1,200 per capita).

Structure of gross domestic product and labour force

	1998 in value C.V.Esc. '000,000	1998 % of total value	1990 labour force	1990 % of labour force
Agriculture	5,960	12.2	29,876	24.7
Manufacturing			5,520	4.6
Public utilities	4,992	10.3	883	0.7
Mining			410	0.3
Construction	4,304	8.8	22,722	18.9
Transp. and commun.	8,575	17.6	6,138	5.1
Trade	9,240	19.0	12,747	10.6
Finance	5,704	11.7	821	0.7
Pub. admin., defense	6,577	13.5	17,358	14.4
Services	3,315	6.8		
Other	…	…	24,090	20.0
TOTAL	48,667	100.0[3]	120,565	100.0

Population economically active (1997): total 160,000; activity rate of total population 41.2% (participation rates (1990): ages 15–64, 64.3%; female 39.0%; unemployed (1990), 25.8%).

Price and earnings indexes (1995 = 100)

	1993	1994	1995	1996	1997	1998	1999
Consumer price index	89.0	92.0	100.0	106.0	115.0	120.0	126.0
Monthly earnings index	85.8	87.9	100.0	…	…		…

Land use (1994): forest 0.2%; pasture 6.2%; agriculture 11.2%; other 82.4%.
Household income and expenditure. Average household size (1990) 5.1; income per household: n.a.; sources of income: n.a.; expenditure (1988): food 51.1%, housing, fuel, and power 13.5%, beverages and tobacco 11.8%, transportation and communications 8.8%, household durable goods 6.9%, other 7.9%.

Foreign trade

Balance of trade (current prices)

	1993	1994	1995	1996	1997	1998
U.S.$'000,000	–170.3	–171.2	–208.4	–176.1	–171.0	–176.2
% of total	81.3%	80.9%	80.6%	74.8%	68.0%	76.2%

Imports (1999): C.V.Esc. 19,999,000,000 (food 39.0%, machinery and apparatus 19.4%, nonmetallic mineral products 9.7%, metal products 8.2%, transport equipment 7.8%). *Major import sources* (1998): Portugal 49.9%; The Netherlands 11.8%; U.S. 3.1%; Spain 2.7%.
Exports (1998): C.V.Esc. 2,702,000,000 (shoes 22.5%; clothing 7.1%; fish and fish preparations 6.7%; reexports 62.1%). *Major export destinations* (1998): Portugal 89.3%; Spain 7.9%.

Transport and communications

Transport. Railroads: none. Roads (1996): total length 680 mi, 1,095 km (paved 78%). Vehicles (1996): passenger cars 3,280; trucks and buses 820. Merchant marine (1992): vessels (100 gross tons and over) 42: total deadweight tonnage 30,921. Air transport (1994)[9]: passenger-mi 106,000,000, passenger-km 171,000,000; short ton-mi cargo 13,156,000, metric ton-km cargo 19,207,000; airports (1997) with scheduled flights 9.

Communications

Medium	date	unit	number	units per 1,000 persons
Radio	1997	receivers	71,000	179.0
Television	1997	receivers	2,000	5.1
Telephones	1998	main lines	39,985	98.0
Cellular telephones	1998	subscribers	1,020	2.6
Personal computers	1998	units	…	…
Internet	1998	users	2,000	5.1

Education and health

Educational attainment (1990). Percentage of population age 25 and over having: no formal schooling 47.9%; primary 40.9%; incomplete secondary 3.9%; complete secondary 1.4%; higher 1.5%; unknown 4.4%. *Literacy* (1995): total population age 15 and over literate 71.6%; males literate 81.4%; females literate 63.8%.

Education (1993–94)

	schools	teachers	students	student/ teacher ratio
Primary (age 7–12)	370[10]	2,657	78,173	29.4
Secondary (age 13–17)	16[11]	438	11,808	27.0
Voc., teacher tr.	3[11]	94[12]	2,289	…
Higher	…	…	…	…

Health (1996): physicians 66 (1 per 5,818 persons); hospital beds (1987) 625 (1 per 550 persons); infant mortality rate per 1,000 live births (1999) 55.6.
Food (1998): daily per capita caloric intake 3,099 (vegetable products 85%, animal products 15%); 132% of FAO recommended minimum requirement.

Military

Total active duty personnel (1999): 1,100 (army 90.9%, air force 9.1%). *Military expenditure as percentage of GNP* (1997): 0.9% (world 2.6%); per capita expenditure U.S.$10.

[1]Fixed par value rate, announced March 13, 1998, between the Cape Verde escudo and Portuguese escudo became effective Jan. 1, 1999. [2]Island/county areas are coterminous except Fogo, Santiago, and Santo Antão islands. [3]Detail does not add to total given because of rounding. [4]Created after the 1990 census; adjusted areas and populations not available. [5]Includes Santa Luzia Island, which is uninhabited. [6]1990. [7]1995. [8]1996. [9]TACV airline only. [10]1991. [11]1986–87. [12]Vocational teachers only.

Central African Republic

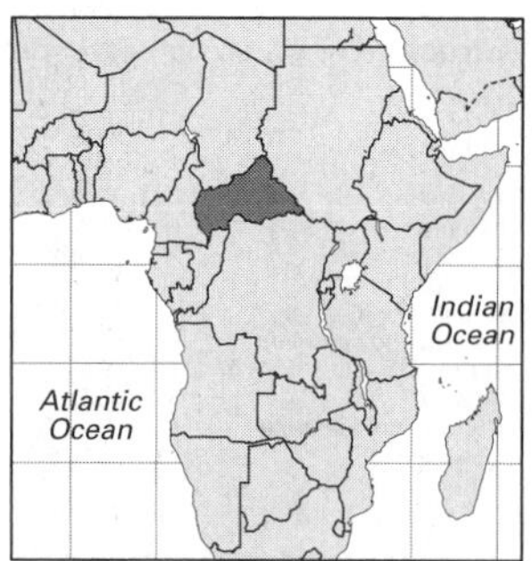

Official name: République Centrafricaine (Central African Republic).
Form of government: multiparty republic with one legislative body (National Assembly [109[1]]).
Chief of state: President.
Head of government: Prime Minister.
Capital: Bangui.
Official languages: French; Sango.
Official religion: none.
Monetary unit: 1 CFA franc (CFAF) = 100 centimes; valuation (Oct. 6, 2000) 1 U.S.$ = CFAF 754.28; 1 £ = CFAF 1,091.

Area and population

		area		population
Prefectures	Capitals	sq mi	sq km	1988 census
Bamingui-Bangoran	Ndélé	22,471	58,200	28,643
Basse-Kotto	Mobaye	6,797	17,604	194,750
Haut-Mbomou	Obo	21,440	55,530	27,113
Haute-Kotto	Bria	33,456	86,650	58,838
Kemo	Sibut	6,642	17,204	82,884
Lobaye	Mbaïki	7,427	19,235	169,554
Mambéré-Kadéï	Berbérati	11,661	30,203	230,364
Mbomou	Bangassou	23,610	61,150	119,252
Nana-Gribizi	Kaga-Bandoro	7,721	19,996	95,497
Nana-Mambéré	Bouar	10,270	26,600	191,970
Ombella-M'poko	Boali	12,292	31,835	180,857
Ouaka	Bambari	19,266	49,900	208,332
Ouham	Bossangoa	19,402	50,250	262,950
Ouham-Pendé	Bozoum	12,394	32,100	287,653
Sangha-Mbaéré	Nola	7,495	19,412	65,961
Vakaga	Birao	17,954	46,500	32,118
Autonomous commune				
Bangui	Bangui	26	67	451,690
TOTAL		240,324	622,436	2,688,426

Demography

Population (2000): 3,513,000.
Density (2000): persons per sq mi 14.6, persons per sq km 5.6.
Urban-rural (1999): urban 40.7%; rural 59.3%.
Sex distribution (1999): male 49.43%; female 50.57%.
Age breakdown (1999): under 15, 43.6%; 15–29, 27.7%; 30–44, 15.0%; 45–59, 8.2%; 60–74, 4.2%; 75 and over, 1.3%.
Population projection: (2010) 4,135,000; (2020) 4,672,000.
Doubling time: 35 years.
Ethnolinguistic composition (1988): Baya (Gbaya) 23.7%; Banda 23.4%; Mandjia 14.7%; Ngbaka 7.6%; Sara 6.5%; Mbum 6.3%; Kare 2.4%; French 0.1%; other 15.3%.
Religious affiliation (1995): Christian 42.7%, of which Protestant 25.6% (Baptist 19.6%, other Protestant 5.9%), Roman Catholic 16.9%, other Christian 0.2%; traditional beliefs 24.0%; Muslim 15.0%; other 18.3%.
Major cities (1994): Bangui 524,000; Berbérati 47,000; Bouar 43,000; Bambari 41,000; Carnot 41,000; Bossangoa 33,000.

Vital statistics

Birth rate per 1,000 population (1999): 38.0 (world avg. 22.1).
Death rate per 1,000 population (1999): 18.3 (world avg. 8.9).
Natural increase rate per 1,000 population (1999): 19.7 (world avg. 13.2).
Total fertility rate (avg. births per childbearing woman; 1999): 5.0.
Life expectancy at birth (1999): male 45.4 years; female 49.1 years.

National economy

Budget (1997). Revenue: CFAF 45,000,000,000 (taxes 94.2%, of which international trade tax 38.0%, indirect domestic tax 36.7%, other 19.5%; nontax receipts 5.8%). Expenditures: CFAF 82,900,000,000 (current expenditure 63.0%, of which wages 32.1%; capital expenditure 37.0%).
Public debt (external, outstanding; 1998): U.S.$829,800,000.
Production (metric tons except as noted). Agriculture, forestry, fishing (1999): cassava 559,000, yams 360,000, bananas 115,000, peanuts (groundnuts) 110,000, taro 100,000, corn (maize) 95,000, sugarcane 90,000, plantains 82,000, seed cotton 36,000, sesame seeds 36,000, pulses 29,000, sorghum 29,000, oranges 22,000, paddy rice 21,000, millet 12,000, coffee 12,000; livestock (number of live animals) 2,992,100 cattle, 2,350,000 goats, 622,000 pigs, 20,600 sheep, 3,900,000 chickens; roundwood (1998) 3,518,000 cu m; fish catch (1998) 13,000. Mining and quarrying (1997): gold 29 kg, diamonds 486,800 carats[2]. Manufacturing (value added in U.S.$'000; 1994): food, beverages, and tobacco 19,000; chemical products 3,000; wood products 2,000; textiles, wearing apparel, and leather products 1,000; transport equipment 1,000. Construction (1992)[3]: residential 10,052 sq m; nonresidential 82,411 sq m. Energy production (consumption): electricity (kW-hr; 1996) 104,000,000 (104,000,000); coal, none (none); crude petroleum, none (none); petroleum products (metric tons; 1996) none (92,000); natural gas, none (none).
Household income and expenditure. Average household size (1998) 5.9; average annual income per household (1988) CFAF 91,985 (U.S.$435); sources of income: n.a.; expenditure (1991)[4]: food 70.5%, clothing 8.5%, other manufactured products 7.6%, energy 7.3%, services (including transportation and communications, recreation, and health) 6.1%.
Gross national product (1998): U.S.$1,053,000,000 (U.S.$300 per capita).

Structure of gross domestic product and labour force

	1997		1988	
	in value CFAF '000,000	% of total value	labour force	% of labour force
Agriculture	303,700	51.1	1,113,900	80.4
Mining	21,600	3.6	15,400	1.1
Manufacturing	48,000	8.0	22,400	1.6
Construction	26,600	4.5	7,000	0.5
Public utilities	4,800	0.8	1,500	0.1
Transp. and commun.	14,700	2.5	1,500	0.1
Trade	79,900	13.4	118,000	8.5
Services	29,600	5.0	15,600	1.1
Pub. admin., defense	32,000	5.4	91,700	6.6
Other	33,700[5]	5.7[5]	—	—
TOTAL	594,600	100.0	1,387,000	100.0

Population economically active (1988): total 1,186,972; activity rate of total population 48.2% (participation rates: ages 15–64, 78.3%; female 46.8%; unemployed 7.5%).

Price and earnings indexes (1995 = 100)

	1992	1993	1994	1995	1996	1997	1998
Consumer price index[3]	69.4	67.4	83.9	100.0	103.7	105.4	103.4
Earnings index	...	...	...	100.0	...	...	...

Land use (1994): forest 75.0%; meadows 4.8%; agriculture 3.2%; other 17.0%.
Tourism (1997): receipts U.S.$5,000,000; expenditures U.S.$39,000,000.

Foreign trade

Balance of trade (current prices)

	1992	1993	1994	1995	1996	1997
CFAF '000,000,000	−10.1	−4.5	+6.6	−1.6	+2.8	+5.3
% of total	15.2%	6.7%	4.1%	0.9%	1.9%	3.0%

Imports (1997): CFAF 84,400,000,000 (1992; food products 22.2%, transportation equipment 16.6%, chemical products 13.7%, energy products 11.0%). *Major import sources:* France 30.5%; Côte d'Ivoire 18.0%; Cameroon 10.8%; Germany 3.6%; Belgium-Luxembourg 3.6%; United States 2.4%.
Exports (1997): CFAF 89,700,000,000 (diamonds 38.7%, wood 25.4%, cotton 16.1%, coffee 10.3%). *Major export destinations:* Belgium-Luxembourg 36.2%; Côte d'Ivoire 5.2%; Spain 4.4%; France 3.0%; Democratic Republic of the Congo 1.8%; Republic of the Congo 1.1%.

Transport and communications

Transport. Railroads: none. Roads (1996): total length 14,900 mi, 24,000 km (paved 2%). Vehicles (1995): passenger cars 9,500; trucks and buses 7,000. Merchant marine: vessels (100 gross tons and over) none. Air transport (1996)[6]: passenger-mi 139,644,000, passenger-km 224,736,000; short ton-mi cargo 11,247,000, metric ton-km cargo 16,420,000; airports[7] (1998) 1.

Communications

Medium	date	unit	number	units per 1,000 persons
Daily newspapers	1996	circulation	6,000	1.8
Radio	1997	receivers	283,000	83.0
Television	1997	receivers	18,000	5.3
Telephones	1998	main lines	9,563	2.8
Cellular telephones	1998	subscribers	710	0.2
Internet	1999	users	...	...

Education and health

Educational attainment (1988). Percentage of population age 10 and over having: no formal schooling 59.3%; primary education 29.6%; lower secondary 7.5%; upper secondary 2.3%; higher 1.3%. *Literacy* (1995): total population age 15 and over literate 60.0%; males literate 68.5%; females literate 52.4%.

Education (1991–92)

	schools	teachers	students	student/ teacher ratio
Primary (age 6–11)	930[8]	4,004[8]	277,961	...
Secondary (age 12–18)	46[8]	845[8]	42,263	...
Vocational	[9]	[9]	1,477	...
Higher[10]	1	139	2,923	21.0

Health (1992): physicians 157 (1 per 18,660 persons); hospital beds (1991) 4,258 (1 per 672 persons); infant mortality rate (1999) 103.4.
Food (1998): daily per capita caloric intake 2,056 (vegetable products 91%, animal products 9%); 91% of FAO recommended minimum requirement.

Military

Total active duty personnel (1999): 2,650[11] (army 94.3%; navy, none; air force 5.7%). *Military expenditure as percentage of GNP* (1997): 3.9% (world 2.6%); per capita expenditure U.S.$12.

[1]Number increased as of November–December 1998 elections. [2]An unknown but substantial amount is believed to be smuggled out of the country annually. [3]Bangui only. [4]Weights of consumer price index components. [5]Indirect taxes and customs duties. [6]Represents 1/11 of the traffic of Air Afrique, which is operated by 11 West African states. [7]International air service only. [8]1990–91. [9]Included with secondary. [10]University of Bangui only. [11]Excludes 2,300 gendarmerie, who are part of the armed forces.

Internet resources for further information:
- **Central African Republic http://www.africa.co.uk/country/cenafrep.htm**

Chad

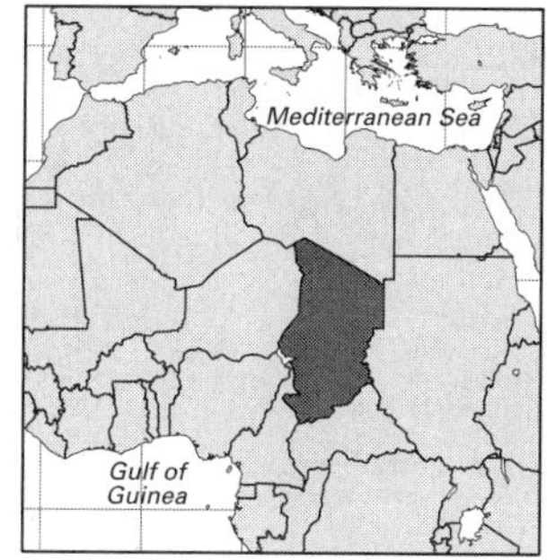

Official name: Jumhūrīyah Tshad (Arabic); République du Tchad (French) (Republic of Chad).
Form of government: unitary republic with one legislative body (National Assembly [125]).
Chief of state: President.
Head of government: Prime Minister.
Capital: N'Djamena.
Official languages: Arabic; French.
Official religion: none.
Monetary unit: 1 CFA franc (CFAF) = 100 centimes; valuation (Oct. 6, 2000) 1 U.S.$ = CFAF 754; 1 £ = CFAF 1,091.

Area and population

Préfectures	Capitals	area sq mi	area sq km	population 1993 census
Batha	Ati	34,285	88,800	288,458
Biltine	Biltine	18,090	46,850	184,807
Borkou-Ennedi-Tibesti	Faya Largeau	231,795	600,350	73,185
Chari-Baguirmi	N'Djamena	32,010	82,910	1,251,906
Guéra	Mongo	22,760	58,950	306,253
Kanem	Mao	44,215	114,520	279,927
Lac	Bol	8,620	22,320	252,932
Logone Occidental	Moundou	3,357	8,695	455,489
Logone Oriental	Doba	10,825	28,035	441,064
Mayo-Kebbi	Bongor	11,625	30,105	825,158
Moyen-Chari	Sarh	17,445	45,180	738,595
Ouaddaï	Abéché	29,436	76,240	543,900
Salamat	Am Timan	24,325	63,000	184,403
Tandjilé	Laï	6,965	18,045	453,854
TOTAL		495,755[1]	1,284,000	6,279,931

Demography

Population (2000): 8,425,000.
Density (2000): persons per sq mi 17.0, persons per sq km 6.6.
Urban-rural (1999): urban 23.4%; rural 76.6%.
Sex distribution (1998): male 49.42%; female 50.58%.
Age breakdown (1999): under 15, 47.6%; 15–29, 26.0%; 30–44, 14.2%; 45–59, 7.7%; 60–74, 3.7%; 75 and over, 0.8%.
Population projection: (2010) 11,616,000; (2020) 15,772,000.
Doubling time: 27 years.
Ethnolinguistic composition (1993): Sara 27.7%; Sudanic Arab 12.3%; Mayo-Kebbi peoples 11.5%; Kanem-Bornu peoples 9.0%; Ouaddaï peoples 8.7%; Hadjeray (Hadjaraï) 6.7%; Tangale (Tandjilé) peoples 6.5%; Gorane peoples 6.3%; Fitri-Batha peoples 4.7%; Fulani (Peul) 2.4%; other 4.2%.
Religious affiliation (1993): Muslim 53.9%; Christian 34.7%, of which Roman Catholic 20.3%, Protestant 14.4%; traditional beliefs 7.4%; other 4.0%.
Major cities (1993): N'Djamena 530,965; Moundou 282,103; Bongor 196,713; Sarh 193,753; Abéché 187,936; Doba 185,461.

Vital statistics

Birth rate per 1,000 population (1999): 43.1 (world avg. 22.1).
Death rate per 1,000 population (1999): 16.6 (world avg. 8.9).
Natural increase rate per 1,000 population (1999): 26.5 (world avg. 13.2).
Total fertility rate (avg. births per childbearing woman; 1999): 5.7.
Life expectancy at birth (1999): male 46.1 years; female 51.1 years.

National economy

Budget (1998). Revenue: CFAF 127,100,000,000 (tax revenue 54.9%, of which taxes on international trade 21.6%, income tax 18.3%, taxes on goods and services 11.3%, other taxes 3.7%; nontax revenue 5.1%; grants 40.0%). Expenditures: CFAF 153,800,000,000 (current expenditure 49.0%, of which government salaries 20.5%, materials and supply 10.7%, defense 6.2%, debt service 5.8%, transfer payments 5.6%, other 0.2%; capital expenditure 51.0%).
Public debt (external, outstanding; 1998): U.S.$1,005,000,000.
Tourism: receipts from visitors (1994) U.S.$12,000,000; expenditures by nationals abroad U.S.$26,000,000.
Production (metric tons except as noted). Agriculture, forestry, fishing (1999): sorghum 636,900, peanuts (groundnuts) 471,150, millet 365,600, cassava 275,000, seed cotton 261,272, yams 240,000, corn (maize) 172,100, rice 100,000; livestock (number of live animals) 5,582,092 cattle, 4,968,256 goats, 2,431,555 sheep, 700,000 camels, 4,800,000 chickens; roundwood (1998) 1,919,000 cu m; fish catch (1998) 84,000. Mining and quarrying (1997): aggregate (gravel) 170,000; limited commercial production of natron (10,000) and salt; artisanal gold production. Manufacturing (1998): cotton fibre 61,700[2]; refined sugar 29,000; soap 2,958[2]; woven cotton fabrics 1,100,000 metres; edible oil 160,000 hectolitres; beer 135,000 hectolitres; cigarettes 43,000,000 packs; bicycles 3,444 units[2]. Energy production (consumption): electricity (kW-hr; 1998) 74,878,000 (56,489,000); coal, none (none); crude petroleum, none (none); petroleum products (metric tons; 1998) none (47,057); natural gas, none (none).
Household income and expenditure (1993). Average household size 5.0; average annual income per household CFAF 96,806 (U.S.$458); sources of income (1995–96; urban) informal-sector employment and entrepreneurship[3] 36.7%, transfers 24.8%, wages 23.6%, ownership of real estate 8.6%; expenditure (1983)[4]: food 45.3%, health 11.9%, energy 5.8%, clothing 3.3%.
Population economically active (1997): total 3,433,000; activity rate of total population 47.9% (participation rates: over age 15, 72.3%; female 44.5%; unemployed [1993] 0.6%).

Price and earnings indexes (1995 = 100)

	1993	1994	1995	1996	1997	1998	1999
Consumer price index	65.3	91.7	100.0	112.4	118.7	133.1	124.1
Earnings index	...	...	...	...	...	...	...

Gross national product (1998): U.S.$1,658,000,000 (U.S.$230 per capita).

Structure of gross domestic product and labour force

	1998 in value CFAF '000,000	1998 % of total value	1993 labour force	1993 % of labour force
Agriculture	376,700	38.3	1,903,492	83.0
Manufacturing	117,800	12.0	33,670	1.5
Construction	15,400	1.6	10,885	0.5
Mining }	5,400	0.5	756	—
Public utilities }			2,026	0.1
Transp. and commun. }	239,900	24.4	13,252	0.6
Trade and finance }			179,169	7.8
Pub. admin., defense	104,700	10.6	61,875	2.7
Services	92,100	9.4	79,167	3.4
Other	32,200[5]	3.3[5]	9,311	0.4
TOTAL	984,200	100.0[1]	2,293,603	100.0

Land use (1994): forested 25.7%; meadows and pastures 35.7%; agricultural and under permanent cultivation 2.6%; other 36.0%.

Foreign trade

Balance of trade (current prices)

	1994	1995	1996	1997	1998
CFAF '000,000,000	–38.0	–17.3	–34.9	–42.3	–29.7
% of total	20.2%	6.6%	13.4%	14.7%	9.3%

Imports (1998): CFAF 175,000,000,000 (1983; petroleum products 16.8%; cereal products 16.8%; pharmaceutical products and chemicals 11.5%; machinery and transport equipment 8.5%, of which transport equipment 7.3%; electrical equipment 5.7%; textiles 2.9%; raw and refined sugar 2.3%). *Major import sources* (1997[6]): France 41.3%; Nigeria 10.1%; Cameroon 7.2%; India 5.8%; Belgium-Luxembourg 5.1%; Italy 4.3%; Portugal 2.9%.
Exports (1998): CFAF 145,300,000,000 (cotton lint 59.3%; other 40.7%). *Major export destinations* (1997[6]): Portugal 29.9%; Germany 14.2%; Thailand 7.5%; Costa Rica 6.0%; Hong Kong 4.8%; Taiwan 4.8%; France 3.7%.

Transport and communications

Transport. Railroads: none. Roads (1996): total length 33,400 km (paved 1%). Vehicles (1996): passenger cars 10,560; trucks and buses 14,550. Air transport (1996)[7]: passenger-km 233,000,000; metric ton-km cargo 37,000,000; airports (1998) with scheduled flights 1.

Communications

Medium	date	unit	number	units per 1,000 persons
Daily newspapers	1997	circulation	2,000	0.2
Radio	1997	receivers	1,310,000	205.9
Television	1998	receivers	12,000	1.8
Telephones	1999	main lines	8,631	1.2
Internet	1999	users	335	0.03

Education and health

Educational attainment (1993). Percentage of economically active population age 15 and over having: no formal schooling 81.1%; Qur'ānic education 4.2%; primary education 11.2%; secondary education 2.7%; higher education 0.3%; professional education 0.5%. *Literacy* (1995): percentage of total population age 15 and over literate 48.1%; males literate 62.1%; females literate 34.7%.

Education (1995–96)

	schools	teachers	students	student/ teacher ratio
Primary (age 6–12)	2,660	9,395	591,493	63.0
Secondary (age 13–19)	153	2,468	90,100	36.5
Voc., teacher tr.	18	216	2,926	13.5
Higher[8]	8	288	3,446	12.0

Health (1993): physicians 217 (1 per 27,765 persons); hospital beds 3,962 (1 per 1,521 persons); infant mortality rate per 1,000 live births (1999) 115.
Food (1998): daily per capita caloric intake 2,171 (vegetable products 95%, animal products 5%); 96% of FAO recommended minimum requirement.

Military

Total active duty personnel (1999): 30,350[9] (army 82.4%; navy, none; air force 1.2%; paramilitary 16.4%). *Military expenditure as percentage of GNP* (1997): 2.7% (world 2.6%); per capita expenditure U.S.$6.

[1]Detail does not add to total given because of rounding. [2]1996. [3]Not reported to fiscal authorities. [4]Capital city only. [5]VAT and import taxes. [6]Based on direction of trade data (analysis of reports of trading partners, rather than country's own customs data). [7]One-eleventh portion of total traffic of Air Afrique, which is operated by 11 West African states. [8]Universities and equivalent institutions only. [9]Excludes 900 French troops.

Internet resources for further information:
- **CIA World Factbook—Chad http://www.odci.gov/cia/publications/factbook/geos/cd.html**
- **Chad—A Country Study http://lcweb2.loc.gov/frd/cs/tdtoc.html**
- **Inestir en Zone Franc http://www.izf.net/izf/Index.htm**

Chile

Official name: República de Chile (Republic of Chile).
Form of government: multiparty republic with two legislative houses (Senate [48[1]]; Chamber of Deputies [120]).
Head of state and government: President.
Capital: Santiago[2].
Official language: Spanish.
Official religion: none.
Monetary unit: 1 peso (Ch$) = 100 centavos; valuation (Oct. 6, 2000) 1 U.S.$ = Ch$560.65; 1 £ = Ch$811.01.

Area and population[3]

Regions	Capitals	area sq mi	area sq km	population 1999 estimate
Aisén del General Carlos Ibáñez del Campo	Coihaique	42,095	109,025	93,600
Antofagasta	Antofagasta	48,820	126,444	462,300
Araucanía	Temuco	12,300	31,858	865,000
Atacama	Copiapó	29,179	75,573	269,100
Bío-Bío	Concepción	14,258	36,929	1,815,800
Coquimbo	La Serena	15,697	40,656	569,800
Libertador General Bernardo O'Higgins	Rancagua	6,319	16,365	778,800
Los Lagos	Puerto Montt	25,868	66,997	1,050,600
Magallanes y la Antártica Chilena	Punta Arenas	50,979	132,034	156,500
Maule	Talca	11,700	30,302	906,900
Santiago, Región Metropolitana de	Santiago	5,926	15,349	6,013,200
Tarapacá	Iquique	22,663	58,698	392,600
Valparaíso	Valparaíso	6,331	16,396	1,543,600
TOTAL		292,135[4]	756,626[4]	14,917,800

Demography

Population (2000): 15,211,000.
Density (2000): persons per sq mi 52.1, persons per sq km 20.1.
Urban-rural (1999): urban 85.4%; rural 14.6%.
Sex distribution (1999): male 49.55%; female 50.45%.
Age breakdown (1999): under 15, 27.9%; 15–29, 24.6%; 30–44, 22.5%; 45–59, 14.7%; 60–74, 7.7%; 75 and over, 2.6%.
Population projection: (2010) 17,010,000; (2020) 18,774,000.
Doubling time: 58 years.
Ethnic composition (1992): European and mestizo 89.7%; Araucanian (Mapuche) 9.6%; Aymara 0.5%; Rapa Nui Polynesian 0.2%.
Religious affiliation (1992): Roman Catholic 76.7%; Protestant 13.2%; atheist and nonreligious 5.8%; other 4.3%.
Major cities (1999): Greater Santiago 4,640,635; Concepción 362,589; Viña del Mar 330,736; Valparaíso 283,489; Talcahuano 269,265; Temuco 253,451.

Vital statistics

Birth rate per 1,000 population (1999): 17.7 (world avg. 22.1).
Death rate per 1,000 population (1999): 5.5 (world avg. 8.9).
Natural increase rate per 1,000 population (1999): 11.7 (world avg. 13.2).
Total fertility rate (avg. births per childbearing woman; 1999): 2.2.
Life expectancy at birth (1999): male 72.2 years; female 79.0 years.
Major causes of death per 100,000 population (1994): diseases of the circulatory system 149.5; malignant neoplasms (cancers) 111.9; accidents and adverse effects 64.3; diseases of the respiratory system 61.2.

National economy

Budget (1999). Revenue: Ch$7,580,300,000,000 (income from taxes 85.3%, nontax revenue 14.7%). Expenditures: Ch$8,392,800,000,000 (social security and welfare 29.1%, transfers 24.3%, wages 19.6%, capital expenditure 16.6%, economic affairs and services 8.3%).
Public debt (external, outstanding; 1998): U.S.$4,986,000,000.
Population economically active (1999): total 5,822,700; activity rate of total population 38.6% (participation rates [1995]: ages 15–64, 58.6%; female 32.4%; unemployed [1999] 9.7%).

Price and earnings indexes (1995 = 100)

	1993	1994	1995	1996	1997	1998	1999
Consumer price index	83.0	92.0	100.0	107.0	114.0	120.0	124
Monthly earnings index	84.4	88.7	100.0	114.4	124.7	...	...

Production (metric tons except as noted). Agriculture, forestry, fishing (1999): sugar beets 3,100,000, grapes 1,575,000, tomatoes 1,243,000, wheat 1,196,600, apples 1,165,000, corn (maize) 624,000, potatoes 994,694, onions (dry) 262,000, oats 201,000, barley 81,000, rice 61,000; livestock (number of live animals) 4,116,000 sheep, 4,134,000 cattle, 2,221,000 pigs; roundwood (1998) 31,670,000 cu m; fish catch (1998) 3,265,300. Mining (1998): iron 8,277,000; copper 3,843,000; zinc 26,000; molybdenum 25,000; silver 1,300,000 kg; gold 43,253 kg. Manufacturing (value added in Ch$'000,000; 1997): food products 3,810,200; metal and metal products 2,631,900; petroleum and petroleum products 1,100,200; paper and paper products 964,900; beverages 807,400; nonmetallic mineral products 593,000. Construction (1994): residential 7,049,369 sq m; nonresidential 2,875,935 sq m. Energy production (consumption): electricity (kW-hr; 1996) 31,278,000,000 (31,278,000,000); coal (metric tons; 1996) 1,119,000 (3,558,000); crude petroleum (barrels; 1996) 3,364,000 (61,498,000); petroleum products (metric tons; 1996) 8,608,000 (10,373,000); natural gas (cu m; 1996) 2,056,000,000 (1,983,000,000).
Gross national product (1998): U.S.$73,935,000,000 (U.S.$4,990 per capita).

Structure of gross domestic product and labour force

	1999 in value Ch$'000,000[5]	1999 % of total value	1995 labour force	1995 % of labour force
Agriculture	586,000	7.3	809,700	15.4
Mining	801,900	10.0	93,200	1.8
Manufacturing	1,177,500	14.7	861,500	16.3
Construction	374,000	4.7	410,700	7.8
Public utilities	189,500	2.4	28,100	0.5
Transp. and commun.	735,800	9.2	400,500	7.6
Trade	1,375,000	17.1	974,100	18.5
Finance	1,079,800	13.5	340,100	6.4
Pub. admin., defense; Services	1,707,700	21.2	1,322,800	25.1
Other	–6,500[6]	–0.1[6]	33,500[7]	0.6[7]
TOTAL	8,020,700	100.0	5,274,200	100.0

Household income and expenditure. Average household size (1998) 4.6; average annual income per household (1994) Ch$5,981,706 at November prices (U.S.$12,552); sources of income (1990): wages and salaries 75.1%, transfer payments 12.0%, other 12.9%; expenditure (1989): food 27.9%, clothing 22.5%, housing 15.2%, transportation 6.4%.
Tourism (1998): receipts U.S.$1,062,000,000; expenditures U.S.$906,000,000.

Foreign trade

Balance of trade (current prices)

	1994	1995	1996	1997	1998	1999
U.S.$'000,000	+660	+1,384	–1,147	–1,343	–2,483	+479
% of total	2.9%	4.5%	3.6%	3.8%	7.7%	1.6%

Imports (1999): U.S.$15,137,000,000 (intermediate goods 59.5%; capital goods 21.8%; consumer goods 18.7%). *Major import sources:* U.S. 20.8%; Argentina 13.9%; Brazil 6.7%; Japan 4.4%; Germany 4.3%; France 2.9%.
Exports (1999): U.S.$15,616,000,000 (mining products 44.4%, of which copper 37.7%; industrial products 38.5%; foodstuffs 17.1%). *Major export destinations:* U.S. 19.4%; Japan 14.3%; United Kingdom 6.8%; Argentina 4.6%; Brazil 4.3%; Germany 3.5%; Taiwan 3.2%.

Transport and communications

Transport. Railroads (1997): length 4,084 mi, 6,572 km; passenger-km 814,543,000; metric ton-km cargo 2,329,246,000[8]. Roads (1996): total length 49,590 mi, 79,800 km (paved 14%). Vehicles (1996): passenger cars 1,017,052; trucks and buses 573,177. Air transport (1996): passenger-km 6,787,000,000; metric ton-km cargo 1,419,000,000; airports (1998) with scheduled flights 23.

Communications

Medium	date	unit	number	units per 1,000 persons
Daily newspapers	1996	circulation	1,410,000	98
Radio	1997	receivers	5,180,000	354
Television	1998	receivers	3,500,000	236
Telephones	1998	main lines	2,753,000	186
Cellular telephones	1998	subscribers	964,250	65
Personal computers	1998	units	714,000	48.2
Internet	1998	users	250,000	16.9

Education and health

Educational attainment (1992). Percentage of population age 25 and over having: no formal schooling 5.7%; primary education 44.2%; secondary 42.2%; higher 7.9%. *Literacy* (1995): total population age 15 and over literate 95.2%; males 95.4%; females 95.0%.

Education (1995)

	schools	teachers	students	student/teacher ratio
Primary (age 6–13)	8,702	80,155	2,149,501	26.8
Secondary (age 14–17)[9]	2,956[10]	51,042	679,165	13.3
Higher	201[10]	18,084[11]	367,094	...

Health (1998): physicians 17,645 (1 per 840 persons); hospital beds (1997) 31,000 (1 per 472 persons); infant mortality rate per 1,000 live births (1999) 9.9.
Food (1998): daily per capita caloric intake 2,844 (vegetable products 78%, animal products 22%); 117% of FAO recommended minimum requirement.

Military

Total active duty personnel (1999): 93,000 (army 54.8%, navy 31.2%, air force 14.0%). *Military expenditure as percentage of GNP* (1997): 3.9% (world 2.6%); per capita expenditure U.S.$196.

[1]Includes 10 nonelective seats. [2]Legislative bodies meet in Valparaíso. [3]Excludes the 480,000-sq mi (1,250,000-sq km) section of Antarctica claimed by Chile (and administered as part of Magallanes y la Antártica Chilean region) and "inland" (actually tidal) water areas. The 1992 census population of Chilean-claimed Antarctica was 126. [4]Includes 205 sq mi (530 sq km) of waters, known as Laguna del Desierto, lost in a border dispute with Argentina, resolved on Oct. 21, 1994. [5]In constant prices of 1986. [6]Less imputed bank service charges. [7]Includes unemployed not previously employed. [8]1994. [9]Includes vocational. [10]1988. [11]Universities only.

Internet resources for further information:
- **Gobierno de Chile**
  http://www.gobiernodechile.cl

China

Official name: Chung-hua Jen-min Kung-ho-kuo (People's Republic of China).
Form of government: single-party people's republic with one legislative house (National People's Congress [2,984]).
Chief of state: President.
Head of government: Premier.
Capital: Peking (Beijing).
Official language: Mandarin Chinese.
Official religion: none.
Monetary unit: 1 Renminbi (yuan) (Y) = 10 jiao = 100 fen; valuation (Oct. 6, 2000) 1 U.S.$ = Y 8.28; 1 £ = Y 11.98.

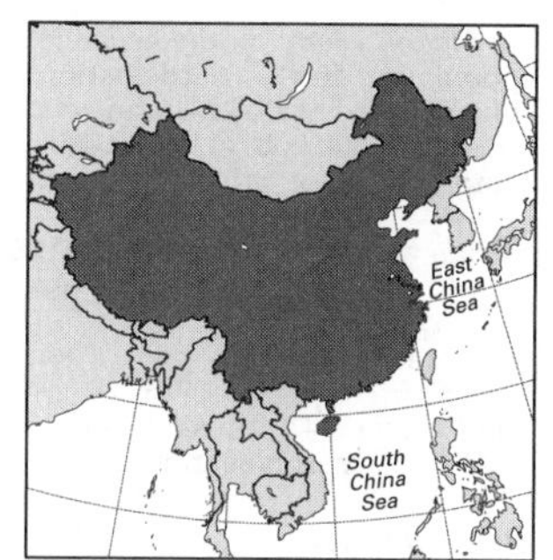

Area and population[1, 2]

Provinces	Capitals	area sq mi	area sq km	population 1999 estimate
Anhwei (Anhui)	Ho-fei (Hefei)	54,000	139,900	62,370,000
Chekiang (Zhejiang)	Hang-chou (Hangzhou)	39,300	101,800	44,750,000
Fukien (Fujian)	Fu-chou (Fuzhou)	47,500	123,100	33,160,000
Hainan (Hainan)	Hai-k'ou (Haikou)	13,200	34,300	7,620,000
Heilungkiang (Heilongjiang)	Harbin	179,000	463,600	37,920,000
Honan (Henan)	Cheng-chou (Zhengzhou)	64,500	167,000	93,870,000
Hopeh (Hebei)	Shih-chia-chuang (Shijiazhuang)	78,200	202,700	66,140,000
Hunan (Hunan)	Ch'ang-sha (Changsha)	81,300	210,500	65,320,000
Hupeh (Hubei)	Wu-han (Wuhan)	72,400	187,500	59,380,000
Kansu (Gansu)	Lan-chou (Lanzhou)	141,500	366,500	25,430,000
Kiangsi (Jiangxi)	Nan-ch'ang (Nanchang)	63,600	164,800	42,310,000
Kiangsu (Jiangsu)	Nanking (Nanjing)	39,600	102,600	72,130,000
Kirin (Jilin)	Ch'ang-ch'un (Changchun)	72,200	187,000	26,580,000
Kwangtung (Guangdong)	Canton (Guangzhou)	76,100	197,100	72,700,000
Kweichow (Guizhou)	Kuei-yang (Guiyang)	67,200	174,000	37,100,000
Liaoning (Liaoning)	Shen-yang (Shenyang)	58,300	151,000	41,710,000
Shansi (Shanxi)	T'ai-yüan (Taiyuan)	60,700	157,100	32,040,000
Shantung (Shandong)	Chi-nan (Jinan)	59,200	153,300	88,830,000
Shensi (Shaanxi)	Sian (Xi'an)	75,600	195,800	36,180,000
Szechwan (Sichuan)	Ch'eng-tu (Chengdu)	210,800	546,000	85,500,000
Tsinghai (Qinghai)	Hsi-ning (Xining)	278,400	721,000	5,100,000
Yunnan (Yunnan)	K'un-ming (Kunming)	168,400	436,200	41,920,000
Autonomous regions				
Inner Mongolia (Nei Monggol)	Hu-ho-hao-t'e (Hohhot)	454,600	1,177,500	23,620,000
Kwangsi Chuang (Guangxi Zhuang)	Nan-ning (Nanning)	85,100	220,400	47,130,000
Ningsia Hui (Ningxia Hui)	Yin-ch'uan (Yinchuan)	25,600	66,400	5,430,000
Sinkiang Uighur (Xinjiang Uygur)	Wu-lu-mu-c'hi (Urumqi)	635,900	1,646,900	17,740,000
Tibet (Xizang)	Lhasa	471,700	1,221,600	2,560,000
Municipalities				
Chungking (Chongqing)	—	8,900	23,000	30,750,000
Peking (Beijing)	—	6,500	16,800	12,570,000
Shanghai (Shanghai)	—	2,400	6,200	14,740,000
Tientsin (Tianjin)	—	4,400	11,300	9,590,000
TOTAL		3,696,100[3]	9,572,900[3]	1,259,090,000[4]

Demography

Population (2000): 1,265,207,000.
Density (2000): persons per sq mi 342.3, persons per sq km 132.2.
Urban-rural (2000): urban 32.0%; rural 68.0%.
Sex distribution (1999): male 50.98%; female 49.02%.
Age breakdown (1998): under 15, 24.3%; 15–29, 24.6%; 30–44, 24.8%; 45–59, 15.2%; 60–74, 8.8%; 75 and over, 2.3%.
Population projection: (2010) 1,362,769,000; (2020) 1,438,287,000.
Doubling time: 82 years.
Ethnic composition (1990): Han (Chinese) 91.96%; Chuang 1.37%; Manchu 0.87%; Hui 0.76%; Miao 0.65%; Uighur 0.64%; Yi 0.58%; Tuchia 0.50%; Mongolian 0.42%; Tibetan 0.41%; Puyi 0.23%; Tung 0.22%; Yao 0.18%; Korean 0.17%; Pai 0.14%; Hani 0.11%; Kazakh 0.10%; Tai 0.09%; Li 0.09%; other 0.51%.
Religious affiliation (1980): nonreligious 51.9%; Chinese folk-religionist 20.1%; atheist 12.0%; Buddhist 8.5%; Christian 6.0%; Muslim 1.4%; other 0.1%.
Major cities (1990): Shanghai 7,496,509; Peking 5,769,607; Tientsin 4,574,689; Shen-yang 3,603,712; Wu-han 3,284,229; Canton 2,914,281; Harbin 2,443,398; Chungking (Chongqing) 2,266,772; Nanking 2,090,204; Sian 1,959,044; Talien (Dalian) 1,723,302; Ch'eng-tu 1,713,255; Ch'ang-ch'un 1,679,270; T'ai-yüan 1,533,884; Tsinan 1,480,915; Ch'ing-tao (Qingdao) 1,459,195; An-shan (Anshan) 1,203,986; Fu-shun 1,202,388; Lan-chou 1,194,640; Cheng-chou 1,159,679; Tzu-po (Zibo) 1,138,074; K'un-ming 1,127,411.
Households (1996). Average rural household size 4.4; urban household size 3.2. Family households (1990): 277,390,000 (99.4%); collective 1,671,000 (0.6%).

Vital statistics

Birth rate per 1,000 population (2000): 15.4 (world avg. 22.1).
Death rate per 1,000 population (2000): 7.0 (world avg. 8.9).
Natural increase rate per 1,000 population (2000): 8.4 (world avg. 13.2).
Total fertility rate (avg. births per childbearing woman; 2000): 1.8.
Marriage rate per 1,000 population (1996): 7.6.
Divorce rate per 1,000 population (1996): 0.9.
Life expectancy at birth (2000): male 69.0 years; female 73.0 years.
Major causes of death per 100,000 population (1996)[5]: perinatal causes 199.8; malignant neoplasms (cancers) 172.3; diseases of the circulatory system 132.4; diseases of the respiratory system 68.6; accidents, violence, and poisoning 26.5; digestive diseases 25.5.

Social indicators

Educational attainment (1990). Percentage of population age 25 and over having: no schooling 29.3%; incomplete primary 34.3%; completed primary 34.4%; postsecondary 2.0%.

Distribution of urban household income (1996)

avg. per capita income by quintile (avg. Y 4,845)

first quintile	second quintile	third quintile	fourth quintile	fifth quintile
Y 2,801	Y 3,780	Y 4,580	Y 5,599	Y 8,039

Quality of working life (1991). Average workweek: 48 hours. Annual rate per 100,000 workers for: injury or accident, n.a.; industrial illness, n.a.; death, n.a. Funds for pensions and social welfare relief (1996): Y 181,780,000,000. Average days lost to labour stoppages per 1,000 workdays: n.a. Average duration of journey to work: n.a. Method of transport: n.a. Rate per 1,000 workers of discouraged (unemployed no longer seeking work): n.a.
Access to services. Proportion of communes having access to electricity (1979) 87.1%. Percentage of urban population with: safe public water supply (1996) 95.0%; public sewage collection, n.a.; public fire protection, n.a.
Social participation. Eligible voters participating in last national election: n.a. Population participating in voluntary work: n.a. Trade union membership in total labour force (1996): 14.7%. Practicing religious population in total affiliated population: n.a.
Social deviance. Annual reported arrest rate per 100,000 population (1986) for: property violation 20.7; infringing personal rights 7.2; disruption of social administration 3.3; endangering public security 1.0[6].
Leisure. Favourite leisure activities: n.a.
Material well-being (1996). Urban families possessing (number per family): bicycles 1.9; televisions 1.2; washing machines 0.9; refrigerators 0.7; sewing machines 0.6; cameras 0.3. Rural families possessing (number per family): bicycles 1.4; televisions 0.9; sewing machines 0.6; washing machines 0.2.

National economy

Gross national product (at current market prices; 1998): U.S.$923,560,000,000 (U.S.$750 per capita).

Structure of gross national product and labour force

	1997 in value Y '000,000,000	1997 % of total value	1996 labour force ('000)	1996 % of labour force
Agriculture	1,396.88	18.7	329,100	47.2
Mining }	3,175.23	42.5	10,310	1.5
Manufacturing }			97,630	14.0
Construction	501.80	6.7	34,080	4.9
Public utilities	...	...	2,730	0.4
Transp. and commun.	452.55	6.0	20,130	2.9
Trade	628.15	8.4	45,110	6.5
Finance	...	...	3,760	0.5
Pub. admin.	...	...	10,930	1.6
Services	1,322.63	17.7	29,010	4.2
Other	...	...	113,860[7]	16.3[7]
TOTAL	7,477.24	100.0	696,650	100.0

Budget (1996). Revenue: Y 433,370,000,000 (taxes on goods and services 58.5%; grants 13.9%; funds collected for income taxes 10.4%; nontax revenue 8.8%; import duties 7.0%). Expenditures: Y 540,650,000,000 (defense 13.2%; general public services 7.2%; agriculture 4.6%; industry 2.8%; public order 2.2%; education 2.1%; utilities 2.0%; other economic affair expenditures 14.1%; nonfunctional expenditures 50.4%).
Public debt (external, outstanding; 1998): U.S.$99,424,000,000.
Tourism: receipts from visitors (1998) U.S.$12,602,000,000; expenditures by nationals abroad U.S.$9,205,000,000.

Retail and catering enterprises (1996)

	no. of enterprises	no. of employees	annual wage as a % of all wages	annual gross output value (Y '000,000)
Retail trade	13,963,162	31,892,181	...	...
Food, beverage, and tobacco	5,177,416	10,738,924	...	241,350
Articles for daily use	3,242,769	8,614,944	...	88,470
Textile goods, garments, shoes, and hats	2,018,136	4,030,888	...	125,250
Sundry goods for daily use	799,486	1,670,984	...	...
Hardwares, electrical appliances, and chemicals	583,466	1,828,788	...	...
Medicines and medical appliances	123,534	405,424	...	57,980
Books and newspapers	140,856	365,424	...	23,110
Other	1,877,499	4,236,805	...	...
Catering trade	2,587,730	7,753,108	...	...
Restaurants	1,181,732	4,321,824	...	...
Fast-food eateries	397,561	1,049,829	...	...
Other	1,008,437	2,381,455	...	...

Production (metric tons except as noted). Agriculture, forestry, fishing (1998): grains—rice 193,079,000, corn (maize) 124,338,000, wheat 110,000,000, sorghum 5,057,000, barley 3,800,000, millet 3,001,000; oilseeds—soybeans 13,913,000, peanuts (groundnuts) 11,970,000, rapeseed 8,300,000, sunflower seeds 1,400,000; fruits and nuts—watermelons 25,300,000, apples 19,490,000, pears 7,396,000, cantaloupes 6,379,000, oranges 2,258,000; other—sweet potatoes 104,208,000, sugarcane 87,542,000, potatoes 44,447,000, cabbage 16,905,000, tomatoes 16,369,000, sugar beets 14,470,000, cucumbers 14,262,000, seed cotton 13,503,000, onions 10,040,000, eggplants 10,026,000, garlic 5,690,000, tobacco leaves 2,374,000, tea 689,000; livestock (number of live animals) 482,967,000 pigs, 137,723,000 goats, 118,152,000 sheep, 96,195,000 cattle, 20,818,000 water buffalo, 9,667,000 asses, 8,855,000 horses, 3,118,000,000 chickens, 512,000,000 ducks; roundwood 305,266,000 cu m; fish catch (1997) 15,722,344. Mining and quarrying (1997): metal concentrates—zinc 1,400,000, copper 1,020,000, lead 650,000, antimony 101,000, tin 61,000, tungsten 24,000; metal ores—iron ore 249,000,000, bauxite 8,000,000, manganese ore 7,000,000, silver 1,300, gold 175; nonmetals—salt 29,280,000, gypsum 7,300,000, soda ash 7,030,000, barite 3,500,000, fluorspar 2,400,000, magnesite 2,400,000, talc 2,350,000, asbestos 250,000. Manufacturing (1997): cement 492,600,000; rolled steel 94,900,000; chemical fertilizer 29,111,000; paper and paperboard 21,660,000; sulfuric acid 19,462,000; sugar 6,800,000; cotton yarn 5,312,000; cotton fabrics 20,370,000,000 m; cigarettes 34,020,000 cases; colour television sets 26,430,000 units; household washing machines 12,571,000 units; household refrigerators 9,861,000 units; motor vehicles 1,625,000 units. Construction (1996): residential 1,221,880,000 sq m; nonresidential 406,380,000 sq m. Distribution of industrial production (percentage of total value of output by sector; 1978 [1996]): state-operated enterprises 80.6% (28.5%); collectives 19.2% (39.4%); privately operated enterprises 0.2% (32.1%). Retail sales (percentage of total sales by sector; 1978 [1996]): state-operated enterprises 90.5% (27.3%); collectives 7.4% (18.4%); privately operated enterprises 2.1% (54.3%).

Manufacturing and mining enterprises (1996)

	no. of enterprises	no. of employees[8]	annual wages as a % of avg. of all wages[9]	annual gross output value (Y '000,000)
Manufacturing				
Machinery, transport equipment, and metal manufactures,	23,032	21,560	96.7	880,886
of which,				
Metal products	2,641	1,810,000	...	23,593
Industrial equipment	8,875	7,020,000	...	183,951
Transport equipment	4,303	3,540,000	...	187,581
Electronic goods	1,579	1,630,000	...	70,046
Measuring equipment	1,179	820,000	...	14,738
Textiles	4,031	6,340,000	95.5	161,949
Garments	1,177	1,680,000	...	11,359
Foodstuffs,	18,191	4,710,000	87.5	383,264
of which,				
Food processing	14,520	3,170,000	...	196,393
Beverages	3,367	1,210,000	...	70,368
Tobacco manufactures	304	330,000	...	116,503
Chemicals,	10,707	8,140,000	92.1	537,768
of which,				
Pharmaceuticals	2,044	1,020,000	...	53,749
Plastics	1,667	1,050,000	...	15,167
Secondary forest products (including paper and stationery)	3,664	2,310,000	96.1	51,238
Primary forest products	877	1,140,000	114.3	16,750
Mining				
Nonferrous and ferrous metals	1,163	810,000	107.6	22,711
Crude petroleum	71	1,250,000	...	149,525
Coal	2,011	5,050,000	119.8	105,946

Energy production (consumption): electricity (kW-hr; 1994) 928,083,000,000 (926,037,000,000); coal (metric tons; 1994) 1,239,902,000 (1,231,928,000); crude petroleum (barrels; 1994) 1,069,320,000 (1,024,375,000); petroleum products (metric tons; 1994) 106,629,000 (114,972,000); natural gas (cu m; 1994) 17,540,000,000 (17,540,000,000).

Financial aggregates[10]

	1992	1993	1994	1995	1996	1997	1998
Exchange rate, Y per:							
U.S. dollar	5.75	5.80	8.45	8.32	8.30	8.28	8.28
£	8.70	8.59	13.18	12.90	12.95	13.58	13.74
SDR	7.91	7.97	12.33	12.36	11.93	11.17	11.66
International reserves (U.S.$)							
Total (excl. gold; '000,000)	20,620	22,387	52,914	75,377	107,039	142,762	149,188
SDRs ('000,000)	419	484	539	582	614	602	676
Reserve pos. in IMF ('000,000)	758	704	755	1,216	1,396	2,270	3,553
Foreign exchange	19,443	21,199	51,620	73,579	105,029	139,890	144,959
Gold ('000,000 fine troy oz)	12.7	12.7	12.7	12.7	12.7	12.7	12.7
% world reserves	1.4	1.4	1.4	1.4	1.4	1.4	1.4
Interest and prices							
Central bank discount (%)	7.20	10.08	10.08	10.44	9.00	8.55	4.59
Govt. bond yield (%)	...	...	...	...	...	...	...
Industrial share prices	...	...	...	...	...	...	...
Balance of payments (U.S.$'000,000)							
Balance of visible trade,	+5,183	−10,654	+7,290	+18,050	+19,535	+46,222	+46,613
of which:							
Imports, f.o.b.	−64,385	−86,313	−95,271	−110,060	−131,542	−136,448	−136,914
Exports, f.o.b.	69,568	75,659	102,561	128,110	151,077	182,670	183,527
Balance of invisibles	+1,218	−955	−382	−16,432	−12,292	−16,504	−17,288
Balance of payments, current account	+6,401	−11,609	+6,908	+1,618	+7,243	+29,718	+29,325

Household income and expenditure. Average household size (1996) 3.7; rural household 4.4, urban household 3.2. Average annual income per household Y 13,459; rural household Y 12,406, urban household Y 15,503. Sources of income: rural household (1996)—income from household businesses 79.6%, wages 16.1%, other 4.3%; urban household (1996)—wages 80.5%, business income 5.9%, other 13.6%. Expenditure (1996): rural household—food 56.3%, housing 13.9%, cultural activities 8.4%, clothing 7.2%, household materials 5.4%, health 3.7%, transportation 3.0%; urban household—food 48.6%, clothing 13.5%, cultural activities 9.6%, household materials 7.6%, housing 7.7%, transportation 5.8%, health 3.7%.

Population economically active (1996): total 696,650,000; activity rate of total population 56.9% (participation rates: over ages 15, 75.9%; female 49.7%[11]; unemployed 9.8%). Urban workforce by sector 1978 (1996): state enterprises 74,500,000 (112,440,000); collectives 20,000,000 (30,160,000); self-employment or privately run enterprises 150,000 (5,555,000).

Price and earnings indexes (1995 = 100)

	1992	1993	1994	1995	1996	1997	1998
Consumer price index	58.8	68.8	85.6	100.0	108.3	111.3	110.5
Annual earnings index[12]	126.7	157.5	212.1	257.0	290.2	...	...

Land use (1994): forested 14.0%; meadows and pastures 42.9%; agricultural and under permanent cultivation 10.3%; other 32.8%.

Foreign trade[13]

Balance of trade (current prices)

	1993	1994	1995	1996	1997	1998
U.S.$'000,000	−10,654	+7,290	+18,050	+19,535	+46,222	+46,613
% of total	6.6%	3.7%	7.6%	6.9%	14.5%	14.5%

Imports (1997): U.S.$142,361,000,000 (machinery and transport equipment 37.1%; products of textile industries, rubber and metal products 22.6%; chemical and related products 13.6%; inedible raw materials 8.4%; mineral fuel and lubricants 7.2%; food and live animals 3.0%). *Major import sources* (1996): Japan 21.0%; Taiwan 11.7%; United States 11.6%; South Korea 9.0%; Hong Kong 5.6%; Germany 5.3%; Russia 3.7%; Singapore 2.6%; Australia 2.5%; Italy 2.3%; France 1.6%.

Exports (1997): U.S.$182,696,000,000 (machinery and transport equipment 23.9%; products of textile industries, rubber and metal products 18.8%; food and live animals 6.1%; chemicals and allied products 5.6%; mineral fuels and lubricants 3.8%; inedible raw materials 2.3%). *Major export destinations* (1996): Hong Kong 21.8%; Japan 20.4%; United States 17.7%; South Korea 5.0%; Germany 3.9%; Singapore 2.5%; The Netherlands 2.3%; Taiwan 1.9%.

Transport and communications

Transport. Railroads (1996): length 47,672 mi, 76,721 km; passenger-mi 206,629,000,000, passenger-km 332,537,000,000; short ton-mi cargo 888,403,000,000, metric ton-km cargo 1,297,046,000,000. Roads (1996): total length 736,814 mi, 1,185,789 km (paved 80%). Vehicles (1996): passenger cars 4,880,200; trucks and buses 5,750,300. Merchant marine (1992): vessels (100 gross tons and over) 2,390: total deadweight tonnage 20,657,996. Air transport (1996): passenger-mi 46,469,000,000, passenger-km 74,784,000,000; short ton-mi cargo 1,708,000,000, metric ton-km cargo 2,493,000,000; airports (1996) with scheduled flights 113.

Communications

Medium	date	unit	number	units per 1,000 persons
Daily newspapers	1994	circulation	27,790,000	23
Radio	1997	receivers	417,000,000	335
Television	1997	receivers	400,000,000	321
Telephones	1998	main lines	87,421,000	70
Cellular telephones	1998	subscribers	23,863,000	19
Personal computers	1998	units	11,200,000	8.9
Internet	1998	users	2,100,000	1.7

Education and health

Literacy (1995): total population age 15 and over literate 81.5%; males literate 89.9%; females literate 72.7%.

Education (1997)

	schools	teachers	students	student/teacher ratio
Primary (age 7–13)	628,840	5,794,000	139,954,000	24.2
Secondary (age 13–17)	78,642	3,587,000	60,179,000	16.8
Secondary specialized	4,143	276,000	4,654,000	16.9
Higher	1,020	405,000	3,174,000	7.8

Health (1997): physicians 1,985,000 (1 per 620 persons); hospital beds 2,903,000 (1 per 424 persons); infant mortality rate per 1,000 live births (2000) 39.0.

Food (1997): daily per capita caloric intake 2,897 (vegetable products 82%, animal products 18%); (1995) 116% of FAO recommended minimum requirement.

Military

Total active duty personnel (1998): 2,820,000 (army 74.1%, navy 9.2%, air force 16.7%). *Military expenditure as percentage of GNP* (1995): 2.3% (world 2.8%); per capita expenditure U.S.$53.

[1]Names of the provinces, autonomous regions, and municipalities are stated in conventional form, followed by Pinyin transliteration; names of capitals are stated in conventional form or Wade-Giles transliteration, followed by Pinyin transliteration. [2]Data for Taiwan, Quemoy and Matsu (parts of Fukien province occupied by Taiwan); Hong Kong (which reverted to China from British administration on July 1, 1997) and Macau (which reverted to China from Portuguese administration on Dec. 20, 1999) are excluded. [3]Includes 4,600 sq mi (11,900 sq km) not shown separately. [4]Total includes servicemen not assigned to any political division and discrepancies between provincial and national estimates. [5]Based on urban sample population. [6]Excludes arrests for anti-Communist activities. [7]Includes unemployed. [8]In state-owned and collective-owned industries only. [9]1979. [10]Exchange rates and international reserves are period average figures. [11]1987. [12]Average annual wage in industrial establishments in urban areas. [13]Imports and exports f.o.b.

Internet resource for further information:

- **Embassy of The People's Republic of China http://www.china-embassy.org**
- **China Statistical Information Net http://www.stats.gov.cn/english/index.html**

Colombia

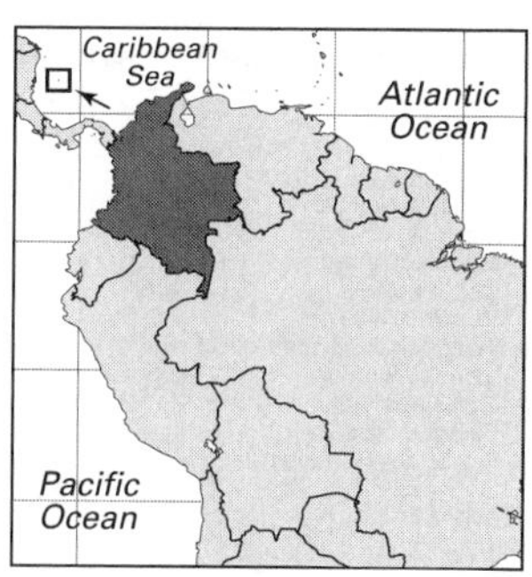

Official name: República de Colombia (Republic of Colombia).
Form of government: unitary, multiparty republic with two legislative houses (Senate [102]; House of Representatives [163[1]]).
Head of state and government: President.
Capital: Santafé de Bogotá, D.C.
Official language: Spanish.
Official religion: none.
Monetary unit: 1 peso (Col$) = 100 centavos; valuation (Oct. 6, 2000) 1 U.S.$ = Col$2,193; 1 £ = Col$3,172.

Area and population

		area		population
Departments	**Capitals**	sq mi	sq km	1997 estimate
Antioquia	Medellín	24,445	63,912	5,243,906
Atlántico	Barranquilla	1,308	3,388	1,984,910
Bolívar	Cartagena	10,030	25,978	1,843,630
Boyacá	Tunja	8,953	23,189	1,351,829
Caldas	Manizales	3,046	7,888	1,084,081
Caquetá	Florencia	34,349	88,965	396,537
Cauca	Popayán	11,316	29,308	1,197,874
Cesar	Valledupar	8,844	22,905	873,044
Chocó	Quibdó	17,965	46,530	409,599
Córdoba	Montería	9,660	25,020	1,353,922
Cundinamarca	Santafé de Bogotá, D.C.	8,735	22,623	1,975,564
Huila	Neiva	7,680	19,890	894,109
La Guajira	Riohacha	8,049	20,848	459,326
Magdalena	Santa Marta	8,953	23,188	1,218,836
Meta	Villavicencio	33,064	85,635	659,825
Nariño	Pasto	12,845	33,268	1,558,045
Norte de Santander	Cúcuta	8,362	21,658	1,252,867
Orinoquía-Amazonía[2]	...	186,519	483,083	1,002,599
Quindío	Armenia	712	1,845	535,711
Risaralda	Pereira	1,598	4,140	905,780
San Andrés y Providencia	San Andrés	17	44	65,700
Santander	Bucaramanga	11,790	30,537	1,911,830
Sucre	Sincelejo	4,215	10,917	749,152
Tolima	Ibagué	9,097	23,562	1,310,963
Valle	Cali	8,548	22,140	3,970,302
Capital District				
Santafé de Bogotá, D.C.		613[3]	1,587[3]	6,004,782
TOTAL		440,762[3]	1,141,568[3]	40,214,723

Demography

Population (2000): 42,299,000[4].
Density (2000): persons per sq mi 96.0, persons per sq km 37.1.
Urban-rural (1999): urban 73.5%; rural 26.5%.
Sex distribution (1999): male 49.16%; female 50.84%.
Age breakdown (1999): under 15, 32.5%; 15–29, 26.9%; 30–44, 22.4%; 45–59, 11.3%; 60–74, 5.5%; 75 and over, 1.4%.
Population projection: (2010) 49,690,000; (2020) 56,569,000.
Ethnic composition (1985): mestizo 58.0%; white 20.0%; mulatto 14.0%; black 4.0%; mixed black-Indian 3.0%; Amerindian 1.0%.
Religious affiliation (1995): Roman Catholic 91.9%; other 8.1%.
Major cities (1999): Santafé de Bogotá, D.C., 6,276,428; Cali 2,110,571; Medellín 1,957,928; Barranquilla 1,226,292; Bucaramanga 520,874.

Vital statistics

Birth rate per 1,000 population (1999): 23.4 (world avg. 22.1).
Death rate per 1,000 population (1999): 5.8 (world avg. 8.9).
Natural increase rate per 1,000 population (1998): 16.0 (world avg. 13.2).
Total fertility rate (avg. births per childbearing woman; 1999): 2.7.
Life expectancy at birth (1999): male 66.1 years; female 74.0 years.
Major causes of death per 100,000 population (1994): accidents, violence, and suicides 114.5, of which homicide with firearms 73.1; malignant neoplasms (cancers) 58.3; ischemic heart disease 50.4; infectious and parasitic diseases 13.7.

National economy

Budget (1998). Revenue: Col$16,706,000,000,000 (tax revenue 70.8%, nontax revenue 25.6%, transfers 3.6%). Expenditures: Col$21,526,000,000,000 (current expenditure 77.0%, of which wages 23.9%, interest 12.2%, goods and services 10.9%; capital expenditure 23.0%).
Public debt (external, outstanding; 1998): U.S.$16,930,000,000.
Land use (1994): forest 22.0%; pasture 18.2%; agriculture 5.7%; other 54.1%.
Tourism (1998): receipts U.S.$939,000,000; expenditures U.S.$1,124,000,000.
Production (metric tons except as noted). Agriculture, forestry, fishing (1999): sugarcane 36,900,000, plantains 2,789,000, potatoes 2,705,413, rice 2,059,374, cassava 1,956,051, bananas 1,570,000, corn 974,583, coffee 648,000; livestock (number of live animals) 25,614,200 cattle, 2,195,600 sheep, 2,764,000 pigs; roundwood (1998) 18,618,000 cu m; fish catch (1998) 167,464. Mining and quarrying (1997): iron ore 631,500; salt 560,300; gold 521,800 troy oz; silver 109,500 troy oz; emeralds 6,305,903 carats[5]. Manufacturing (value added in Col$'000,000; 1996): processed food 9,362,300; beverages 2,485,900; textiles 2,107,300; machinery and electrical apparatus 2,049,000; transport equipment 1,632,700; paper products 1,581,700. Energy production (consumption): electricity (kW-hr; 1996) 44,605,000,000 (44,769,000,000); coal (metric tons; 1996) 30,065,000 (4,919,000); petroleum (barrels; 1996) 237,395,000 (113,211,000); petroleum products (metric tons; 1996) 13,310,000 (10,913,000); natural gas (cu m; 1996) 5,674,035,000 (5,674,035,000).
Gross national product (1998): U.S.$100,667,000,000 (U.S.$2,470 per capita).

Structure of gross domestic product and labour force

	1998		1980	
	in value Col$'000,000	% of total value	labour force	% of labour force
Agriculture	10,330,739	13.7	2,412,413	28.5
Mining	3,213,148	4.3	49,740	0.6
Manufacturing	10,809,494	14.4	1,136,735	13.4
Construction	3,778,973	5.0	242,191	2.9
Public utilities	6	6	44,233	0.5
Transp. and commun.	6,007,799	8.0	352,623	4.2
Trade	8,790,382	11.7	1,261,633	14.9
Finance	6	6	278,210	3.2
Pub. admin., defense	6,783,180	9.0	1,998,460	23.6
Services	6	6		
Other	25,471,697[6]	33.9[6]	690,762[7]	8.2[7]
TOTAL	75,185,412	100.0	8,467,000	100.0

Population economically active (1998): total 6,550,679[8]; activity rate 47.4% (participation rates: ages 15–69, 67.7%; female 45.1%; unemployed 19.7%).

Price and earnings indexes (1995 = 100)

	1993	1994	1995	1996	1997	1998	1999
Consumer price index	66.8	82.7	100.0	120.2	142.5	172.0	191.3
Monthly earnings index	...	...	100.0	119.5	144.6	171.4	198.8

Household income and expenditure. Average household size (1998) 5.3; sources of income (1992): wages 45.1%, self-employment 35.4%, transfer payments 14.2%; expenditure (1992): food 34.2%, transportation 18.5%, housing 7.8%, health care 6.4%, household durable goods 5.7%, clothing 4.5%.

Foreign trade[9]

Balance of trade (current prices)

	1994	1995	1996	1997	1998	1999
U.S.$'000,000	–2,620.8	–2,795.7	–2,206.7	–2,886.5	–3,272.0	–1,586.3
% of total	13.5%	12.1%	9.4%	11.1%	12.6%	7.4%

Imports (1998): U.S.$14,634,000,000 (1997; machinery and transport equipment 41.2%, chemicals 21.0%, vegetable products 7.7%, metals 5.1%, food and tobacco 4.4%, paper and paper products 3.4%). *Major import sources* (1997): U.S. 41.5%; Venezuela 10.0%; Germany 5.0%; Japan 4.3%.
Exports (1998): U.S.$11,362,000,000 (1997; petroleum products 23.5%, coffee 19.6%, chemicals 9.4%, coal 7.7%, food and tobacco 5.9%, textiles and apparel 5.5%). *Major export destinations* (1997): U.S. 37.8%; Venezuela 8.9%; Germany 6.3%; Ecuador 4.7%; Peru 4.7%; Japan 3.1%.

Transport and communications

Transport. Railroads (1997): route length 2,000 mi, 3,230 km; passenger-mi 9,646,000[10], passenger-km 15,524,000[10]; metric ton-km cargo 736,247,000. Roads (1997): total length 71,800 mi, 115,564 km (paved 12%). Vehicles (1996): cars 762,000; trucks 672,000. Air transport (1997): passenger-km 5,991,000,000; metric ton-km cargo 836,000,000; airports (1998) 43.

Communications

Medium	date	unit	number	units per 1,000 persons
Daily newspapers	1996	circulation	1,800,000[11]	46[11]
Radio	1997	receivers	21,000,000	524
Television	1998	receivers	8,000,000	203
Telephones	1998	main lines	6,367,000	161
Cellular telephones	1998	subscribers	1,800,000	46
Personal computers	1998	units	1,024,000	26
Internet	1998	users	350,000	8.9

Education and health

Educational attainment (1985). Percentage of population age 25 and over having: no schooling 15.3%; primary education 50.1%; secondary 25.4%; higher 6.8%; not stated 2.4%. *Literacy* (1995): population age 15 and over literate 91.3%; males literate 91.2%; females literate 91.4%.

Education (1996)

	schools	teachers	students	student/ teacher ratio
Primary (6–10)	48,933	193,911	4,916,934	25.4
Secondary (11–16)	7,895	165,976	2,323,653	14.0
Higher	266	75,568	673,353	8.9

Health: physicians (1997) 40,355 (1 per 1,102 persons); hospital beds 40,043 (1 per 1,000 persons); infant mortality rate (1999) 25.6.
Food (1998): daily per capita caloric intake 2,559 (vegetable products 82%, animal products 18%); 110% of FAO recommended minimum requirement.

Military

Total active duty personnel (1999): 144,000 (army 84.0%, navy 10.4%, air force 5.6%). *Military expenditure as percentage of GNP* (1997): 3.7% (world 2.6%); per capita expenditure U.S.$91.

[1]Two seats are occupied by representatives from indigenous communities. [2]Geographic designation for eight political entities in eastern Colombia elevated to departmental status in the early 1990s. [3]Detail does not add to total given because of rounding. [4]De jure figure; about 2,000,000 Colombians left the country between 1997 and 2000 because of the violence and high unemployment. [5]1995. [6]Services include public utilities and finance. [7]Includes unemployed. [8]The data relate to Bogota, Barranquilla, Medellín, Cali, Bucaramanga, Manizales, and Pasto. [9]Import figures are f.o.b. in balance of trade and c.i.f. in commodities and trading partners. [10]1992. [11]Circulation for 26 newspapers only.

Internet resources for further information:

- **National Administration Department of Statistics http://www.dane.gov.co**

Comoros[1]

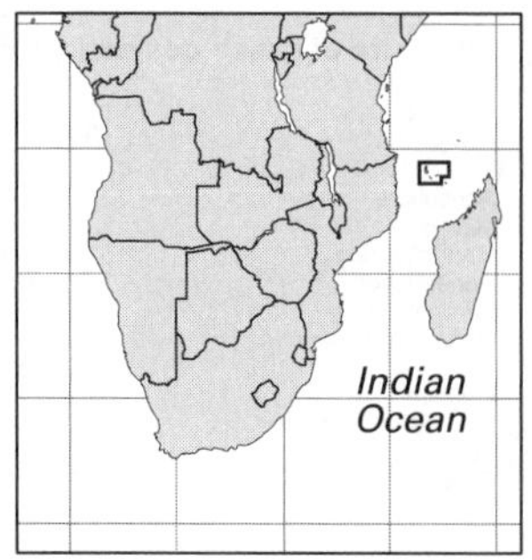

Official name: Jumhurīyat al-Qumur al-Ittihādīyah al-Islāmīyah (Arabic); République Fédérale Islamique des Comores (French) (Federal Islamic Republic of the Comoros)[2].
Form of government: transitional military regime[3].
Head of state and government: Head of State assisted by Prime Minister.
Capital: Moroni.
Official languages: Comorian; Arabic; French.
Official religion: Islam.
Monetary unit: 1 Comorian franc (CF) = 100 centimes; valuation (Oct. 6, 2000) 1 U.S.$ = CF 570.56; 1 £ = CF 825.38.

Area and population

Islands	Capitals	area sq mi	area sq km	population 2000 estimate
Mwali (Mohéli)	Fomboni	112	290	28,600
Nzwani (Anjouan)[4]	Mutsamudu	164	424	219,500
Ngazidja (Grande-Comore)	Moroni	443	1,148	261,100
TOTAL		719	1,862	509,200[5]

Demography

Population (2000): 578,000[6].
Density (2000): persons per sq mi 803.9, persons per sq km 310.4.
Urban-rural (1995): urban 24.1%; rural 75.9%.
Sex distribution (1991): male 49.49%; female 50.51%.
Age breakdown (1995)[7]: under 15, 44.9%; 15–29, 28.5%; 30–44, 14.5%; 45–59, 7.7%; 60–74, 3.6%; 75 and over, 0.8%.
Population projection[6]: (2010) 773,000; (2020) 1,000,000.
Doubling time: 23 years.
Ethnic composition (1995): nearly all Comorian (a mixture of Bantu, Arab, Malay, and Malagasy peoples).
Religious affiliation (1995): Sunnī Muslim 99.3%; other 0.7%.
Major cities (1995): Moroni 34,168; Mutsamudu (1991) 20,000; Domoni (1990) 8,000; Fomboni (1990) 5,600.

Vital statistics

Birth rate per 1,000 population (1999): 40.2 (world avg. 22.1).
Death rate per 1,000 population (1999): 9.8 (world avg. 8.9).
Natural increase rate per 1,000 population (1999) 30.4 (world avg. 13.2).
Total fertility rate (avg. births per childbearing woman; 1999): 5.4.
Marriage rate per 1,000 population: n.a.[8]
Divorce rate per 1,000 population: n.a.
Life expectancy at birth (1999): male 57.5 years; female 61.8 years.
Major causes of death per 100,000 population: n.a.; however, major diseases include malaria (afflicts 80–90% of the adult population), tuberculosis, leprosy, and kwashiorkor (a nutritional deficiency disease).

National economy

Budget (1998). Revenue: CF 14,066,000,000 (tax revenue 64.0%, grants 29.4%, nontax revenue 6.6%). Expenditures: CF 16,307,000,000 (current expenditures 85.4%, development expenditures 14.6%).
Production (metric tons except as noted). Agriculture, forestry, fishing (1997): coconuts 60,000[7], bananas 60,000[9], cassava 50,700, taro 8,500, corn (maize) 3,800, rice 2,900, cloves 2,000[9], vanilla 180[9], ylang-ylang essence 67[9], other export crops grown in small quantities include coffee, cinnamon, and tuberoses; livestock (number of live animals; 1998) 40,000 goats, 40,000 cattle; roundwood, n.a.; fish catch (1997) 12,500. Mining and quarrying: sand, gravel, and crushed stone from coral mining for local construction. Manufacturing: products of small-scale industries include processed vanilla and ylang-ylang, cement, handicrafts, soaps, soft drinks, woodwork, and clothing. Construction: n.a. Energy production (consumption): electricity (kW-hr; 1996) 30,900,000 (21,400,000); coal, none (none); crude petroleum, none (none); petroleum products (metric tons; 1996) none (22,000); natural gas, none (none).
Population economically active (1991): total 215,000; activity rate of total population 44.4% (participation rates: ages 10 years and over, 57.8%; female 40.0%; unemployed [1998] 30%).

Price and earnings indexes (1995 = 100)

	1993	1994	1995	1996	1997	1998
Consumer price index	74.5	93.4	100.0	102.4	104.0	108.2
Monthly earnings index[10]	73.0	88.3	100.0	...	...	...

Tourism (1997): receipts from visitors U.S.$26,100,000; expenditures by nationals abroad U.S.$4,600,000.
Public debt (external, outstanding; 1998): U.S.$188,100,000.
Household income and expenditure. Average household size (1995) 6.3[11]; average annual income per household (1995) CF 188,985 (U.S.$505)[11]; sources of income: n.a.; expenditure (1993)[12]: food and beverages 67.3%, clothing and footwear 11.6%, tobacco and cigarettes 4.1%, energy 3.8%.
Gross national product (at current market prices; 1998): U.S.$197,000,000 (U.S.$370 per capita).

Structure of gross domestic product and labour force

	1997 in value CF '000,000	1997 % of total value	1980 labour force[13]	1980 % of labour force
Agriculture, fishing	32,743	38.7	53,063	53.3
Mining	...	...	62	0.1
Manufacturing	4,513	5.3	3,946	4.0
Construction	5,231	6.2	3,267	3.3
Public utilities	1,105	1.3	129	0.1
Transportation and communications	3,305	3.9	2,118	2.1
Trade, restaurants, hotels	23,630	27.9	1,873	1.9
Finance, insurance	3,224	3.8	237	0.2
Public admin., defense	12,538	14.8	2,435	2.5
Services	415	0.5	4,646	4.7
Other	–1,994[14]	–2.4[14]	27,687[15]	27.8[15]
TOTAL	84,710	100.0	99,463	100.0

Land use (1994)[7]: forested 17.9%; meadows and pastures 6.7%; agricultural and under permanent cultivation 44.9%; other 30.5%.

Foreign trade[16]

Balance of trade (current prices)

	1993	1994	1995	1996	1997
CF '000,000,000	–10.6	–17.2	–19.2	–22.2	–23.6
% of total	46.2%	64.8%	69.4%	82.0%	81.8%

Imports (1997): CF 26,270,300,000 (rice 15.0%, petroleum products 11.0%, meat and fish 9.6%, cement 7.9%, vehicles 7.4%, iron and steel 3.8%). *Major import sources:* France 34.6%; South Africa 11.1%; Pakistan 9.8%; Kenya 6.7%.
Exports (1997): CF 2,630,600,000 (vanilla 42.6%, ylang-ylang 27.2%, cloves 13.7%). *Major export destinations:* France 42.4%; United States 16.9%; Germany 12.0%; Mayotte and Madagascar 11.0%.

Transport and communications

Transport. Railroads: none. Roads (1996): total length 559 mi, 900 km (paved [1995] 76%). Vehicles (1996): passenger cars 9,100; trucks and buses 4,950. Merchant marine (1992): vessels (100 gross tons and over) 6; total deadweight tonnage 3,579. Air transport (1996): passenger-mi 1,900,000, passenger-km 3,000,000; short ton-mi cargo, n.a., metric ton-mi cargo, n.a.; airports (1997) with scheduled flights 2.

Communications

Medium	date	unit	number	units per 1,000 persons
Daily newspapers	1997	circulation	0	0
Radio	1997	receivers	90,000	170
Television	1997	receivers	1,000	1.8
Telephones	1998	main lines	6,226	11

Education and health

Educational attainment (1980). Percentage of population age 25 and over having: no formal schooling 56.7%; Qur'anic school education 8.3%; primary 3.6%; secondary 2.0%; higher 0.2%; not specified 29.2%. *Literacy* (1995)[7]: total population age 15 and over literate 192,000 (57.0%); males literate 108,000 (64.0%); females literate 84,000 (50.0%).

Education (1995–96)

	schools	teachers	students	student/ teacher ratio
Primary (age 7–12)	327	1,508	78,527	52.1
Secondary (age 13–19)	...	591	21,192	35.9
Higher	...	...	348	...

Health (1995): physicians 64[17] (1 per 7,800[17] persons); hospital beds 1,450[17] (1 per 342[17] persons); infant mortality rate per 1,000 live births (1999) 88.8.
Food (1997): daily per capita caloric intake 1,858 (vegetable products 94%, animal products 6%); 79% of FAO recommended minimum requirement.

Military

Total active duty personnel (1997): 1,500. *Military expenditure as percentage of GNP:* n.a.

[1]Excludes Mayotte, an overseas possession of France, unless otherwise indicated. [2]Long-form name change to the Union of the Comoro Islands is pending from May 1999. [3]Constitutional charter was promulgated on May 5, 1999, by colonel leading coup. [4]Secession from the Comoros from October 1997 was not internationally recognized as of November 2000. [5]De facto figure. Nearly 100,000 Comorians reside abroad, of which 37% are in France proper, 30% are in Madagascar, 20% are in East Africa, 10% are in Mayotte, and 3% are in Réunion. [6]De jure figure(s). [7]Includes Mayotte. [8]In the early 1990s, 20% of adult men had more than one wife. [9]1998. [10]July average for government employees only. [11]Based on sample survey of 2,004 households on all three islands. [12]Weights of consumer price index components for Moroni. [13]The wage labour force was very small in 1995; total of less than 7,000 including government employees, and less than 2,000 excluding them. [14]Less imputed bank service charge. [15]Not adequately defined. [16]Imports c.i.f.; exports f.o.b. [17]Estimated figure.

Internet resources for further information:

- **Comoro Islands (unofficial)**
  http://www.ksu.edu/sasw/comoros/comoros.html

Congo, Democratic Republic of the

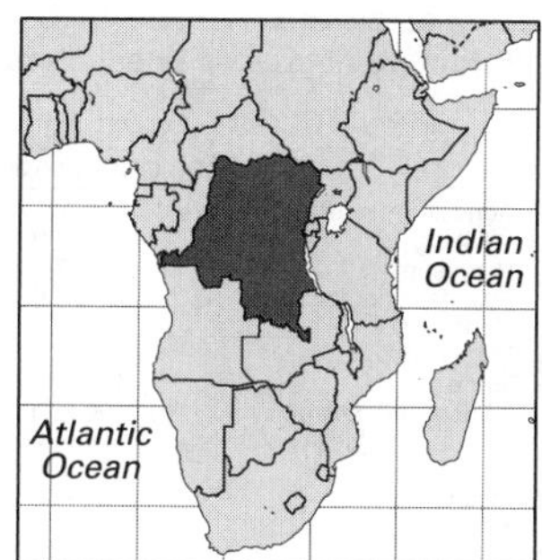

Official name: République Democratique du Congo (Democratic Republic of the Congo).
Form of government: transitional military regime[1] with one legislative body (Assembly[2] [300 nonelected seats]).
Chief of state: President.
Capitals: Kinshasa (executive and judicial[2, 3]); Lubumbashi (legislative[2]).
Official languages: French; English.
Official religion: none.
Monetary unit: Congolese franc (FC)[4]; valuation (Oct. 6, 2000) 1 U.S.$ = FC 4.50; 1 £ = FC 6.51.

Area and population

		area		population
Provinces	Capitals	sq mi	sq km	1994 estimate
Bandundu	Bandundu	114,154	295,658	4,907,000
Bas-Congo	Matadi	20,819	53,920	2,578,000
Equateur	Mbandaka	155,712	403,292	4,789,000
Kasai-Occidental	Kananga	59,746	154,742	3,117,000
Kasai-Oriental	Mbuji-Mayi	65,754	170,302	3,778,000
Katanga	Lubumbashi	191,845	496,877	5,602,000
Maniema	Kindu	51,062	132,250	1,048,000[5]
Nord-Kivu	Goma	22,967	59,483	3,546,000[5]
Orientale	Kisangani	194,302	503,239	5,432,000
Sud-Kivu	Bukavu	25,147	65,130	3,093,000[3]
City				
Kinshasa	—	3,848	9,965	4,655,000
TOTAL		905,354[6]	2,344,858	42,545,000

Demography

Population (2000): 51,965,000.
Density (2000): persons per sq mi 57.4, persons per sq km 22.2.
Urban-rural (1999): urban 29.9%; rural 70.1%.
Sex distribution (1999): male 49.42%; female 50.58%.
Age breakdown (1999): under 15, 48.3%; 15–29, 26.8%; 30–44, 13.8%; 45–59, 7.1%; 60–74, 3.3%; 75 and over, 0.7%.
Population projection: (2010) 69,846,000; (2020) 92,376,000.
Doubling time: 23 years.
Ethnic composition (1983): Luba 18.0%; Kongo 16.1%; Mongo 13.5%; Rwanda 10.3%; Azande 6.1%; Bangi and Ngale 5.8%; Rundi 3.8%; Teke 2.7%; Boa 2.3%; Chokwe 1.8%; Lugbara 1.6%; Banda 1.4%; other 16.6%.
Religious affiliation (1995): Roman Catholic 41.0%; Protestant 32.0%; indigenous Christian 13.4%, of which Kimbanguist 13.0%; other Christian 0.8%; Muslim 1.4%; traditional beliefs and other 11.4%.
Major cities (1994): Kinshasa 4,655,313; Lubumbashi 851,381; Mbuji-Mayi 806,475; Kolwezi 417,800; Kisangani 417,517; Kananga 393,030.

Vital statistics

Birth rate per 1,000 population (1999): 46.4 (world avg. 22.1).
Death rate per 1,000 population (1999): 15.0 (world avg. 8.9).
Natural increase rate per 1,000 population (1999): 31.4 (world avg. 13.2).
Total fertility rate (avg. births per childbearing woman; 1999): 6.5.
Life expectancy at birth (1999): male 47.3 years; female 51.7 years.

National economy

Budget (1996). Revenue: U.S.$374,000,000 (customs duties and taxes on international trade 33.4%; taxes on mining production 11.2%; other revenues 55.3%). Expenditures: U.S.$1,163,000,000 (debt service 71.5%, of which external 62.7%, domestic 8.8%; wages and salaries 6.4%; foreign-financed capital expenditure 5.2%).
Public debt (external, outstanding; 1998): U.S.$8,949,000,000.
Tourism (1997): receipts U.S.$9,000,000; expenditures U.S.$7,000,000.
Production (metric tons except as noted). Agriculture, forestry, fishing (1999): cassava 17,100,000, plantains 1,970,000, sugarcane 1,750,000, corn (maize) 1,220,000, oil palm fruit 950,000, peanuts (groundnuts) 414,000, rice 365,000, bananas 319,000, yams 282,000, sweet potatoes 265,000, mangoes 215,000, papayas 208,000, pineapples 205,000, oranges 200,000, dry beans 140,000, coffee 45,000, seed cotton 27,000, natural rubber 9,000; livestock (number of live animals) 4,600,000 goats, 1,180,000 pigs, 950,000 cattle, 950,000 sheep, 22,000,000 chickens; roundwood (1998) 49,534,000 cu m; fish catch (1997) 162,061. Mining and quarrying (1998): copper (metal content) 34,994; cobalt (metal content) 3,914; zinc (metal content) 1,234; gold 134 kg; diamonds 24,463,000 carats. Manufacturing (1995): iron and steel 965,000; cement 194,000; sugar 82,461; soap 46,773; tires 50,000 units; printed fabrics 15,728,000 sq m; matches 3,305,000 packs; shoes 1,600,000 pairs; beer 1,781,000 hectolitres; soft drinks 807,000 hectolitres. Energy production (consumption): electricity (kW-hr; 1996) 5,408,000,000 (5,408,000,000); coal (metric tons; 1996) 95,000 (140,000); crude petroleum (barrels; 1996) 8,403,000 (505,000); petroleum products (metric tons; 1996) 48,000 (459,000); natural gas, none (none).
Household income and expenditure. Average household size (1998) 2.3; average annual income per household (1982) Z 1,200[4] (U.S.$209); sources of income: n.a.; expenditure (1985): food 61.7%, housing and energy 11.5%, clothing and footwear 9.7%, transportation 5.9%, furniture and utensils 4.9%.

Gross national product (1998): U.S.$5,433,000,000 (U.S.$110 per capita).

Structure of gross domestic product and labour force

	1995		1991	
	in value Z '000,000[4]	% of total value	labour force	% of labour force
Agriculture	21,248,000	58.0	9,021,000	65.1
Mining	1,591,000	4.3		
Manufacturing	2,365,000	6.5		
Construction	845,000	2.3	2,200,000	15.9
Public utilities	604,000	1.6		
Transp. and commun.	1,023,000	2.8		
Trade	6,114,000	16.7		
Pub. admin., defense	483,000	1.3		
Finance and services	2,038,000	5.6	2,627,000	19.0
Other	313,000	0.9		
TOTAL	36,622,000[6]	100.0	13,848,000	100.0

Population economically active (1997): total 19,618,000; activity rate 42.0% (participation rates: [1987]: over age 10, 57.4%; female 43.5%).

Price and earnings indexes (1995 = 100)

	1993	1994	1995	1996	1997
Consumer price index	0.1	15.6	100.0	758.8	2,090.7
Earnings index	...	...	...	...	...

Land use (1994): forested 76.7%; meadows and pastures 6.6%; agricultural and under permanent cultivation 3.5%; other 13.2%.

Foreign trade[7]

Balance of trade (current prices)

	1993	1994	1995	1996	1997	1998
U.S.$'000,000	+477	+643	+581	+708	+771	+781
% of total	26.3%	33.8%	25.0%	27.8%	28.2%	32.3%

Imports (1998): U.S.$819,000,000 (non-oil 94.0%; oil 6.0%). *Major import sources*[8] (1997): South Africa 21.3%; Belgium-Luxembourg 14.2%; Nigeria 6.0%; Zambia 4.8%; China 4.7%; The Netherlands 4.6%; France 4.2%; U.S. 4.1%; Germany 3.0%; Italy 2.3%.
Exports (1998): U.S.$1,600,000,000 (1995; diamonds 17.2%, crude petroleum 11.4%, coffee 8.8%, copper 7.9%). *Major export destinations*[8] (1997): Belgium-Luxembourg 42.7%; U.S. 22.3%; South Africa 8.0%; Italy 3.9%.

Transport and communications

Transport. Railroads (1996)[9]: length 5,138 km; passenger-km 29,000,000[10]; metric ton-km cargo 176,000,000[10]. Roads (1996): total length 154,027 km (paved 2%). Vehicles (1996): passenger cars 787,000; trucks and buses 60,000. Air transport (1996): passenger-km 279,000,000; metric ton-km cargo 42,000,000; airports (1997) with scheduled flights 22.

Communications

Medium	date	unit	number	units per 1,000 persons
Daily newspapers	1996	circulation	124,000	2.7
Radio	1997	receivers	18,030,000	376.0
Television	1997	receivers	6,478,000	135.0
Telephones	1998	main lines	22,000	0.4
Cellular telephones	1998	subscribers	8,900	0.2
Internet	1998	users	...	...

Education and health

Educational attainment: n.a. *Literacy* (1995): percentage of total population age 15 and over literate 77.3%; males literate 86.6%; females literate 67.7%.

Education (1994–95)

	schools	teachers	students	student/ teacher ratio
Primary (age 6–11)	14,885	121,054	5,417,506	44.8
Secondary (age 12–17)	4,276[11]	59,325[11]	640,298[12]	22.6[11]
Voc., teacher tr.	[11]	[11]	701,148[12]	[11]
Higher	...	3,873[13]	93,266	15.9[13]

Health: physicians (1990) 2,469 (1 per 15,584 persons); hospital beds (1986) 68,508 (1 per 487 persons); infant mortality rate (1999) 99.5.
Food (1998): daily per capita caloric intake 1,701 (vegetable products 97%, animal products 3%); 77% of FAO recommended minimum requirement.

Military

Total active duty personnel (1999): 55,900 (army 99.4%, navy 0.6%; about 13,500 foreign forces support the government, and about 9,000 foreign forces oppose the government. *Military expenditure as percentage of GNP* (1997): 5.0% (world 2.6%); per capita expenditure U.S.$5.

[1]The civil war begun in August 1998 was halted by cease-fire in September 1999 and resumed in November 1999. [2]From August 2000. [3]Kisangani to become the judicial capital when the civil war ends per July 2000 announcement. [4]The new zaïre (NZ) replaced the (old) zaïre (Z) at a rate of 3,000,000 (old) zaïres to 1 NZ on Oct. 22, 1993; the Congolese franc (FC) replaced the new zaïre (NZ) at a rate of FC 1 to NZ 100,000 on July 1, 1998. Both zaïres ceased to be legal tender on June 30, 1999. [5]Estimated to account for division of former Kivu province. [6]Detail does not add to total given because of rounding. [7]Imports c.i.f.; exports f.o.b. [8]DOT (Direction of Trade) valuation; the valuation as the sum of all known trading partners, by external analysis, rather than as the reported sum of the country's own trade data. [9]Traffic statistics are for services operated by the Zaire National Railways (SNCZ), which controls more than 90% of the country's total rail facility. [10]1994. [11]Secondary includes Voc., teacher tr. [12]1993–94. [13]1989.

Internet resource for further information:

- **Zaire—A Country Study http://lcweb2.loc.gov/frd/cs/zrtoc.html**

Congo, Republic of the

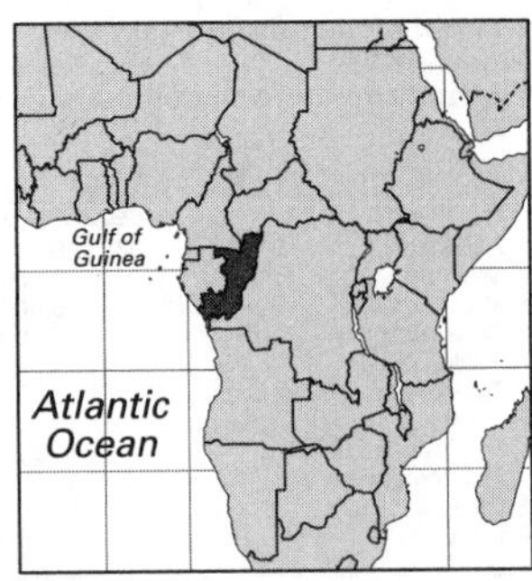

Official name: République du Congo (Republic of the Congo).
Form of government: transitional[1] regime with one legislative house (National Transitional Council [75]).
Chief of state and government: President.
Capital: Brazzaville.
Official language: French[2].
Official religion: none.
Monetary unit: 1 CFA franc (CFAF) = 100 centimes; valuation (Oct. 6, 2000) 1 U.S.$ = CFAF 754.28; 1 £ = CFAF 1,091.

Area and population

Regions	Capitals	area sq mi	area sq km	population 1992 estimate
Bouenza	Madingou	4,733	12,258	177,357
Cuvette Est	Owando	28,900	74,850	151,839
Cuvette Ouest	Ewo			
Kouilou	Pointe-Noire	5,270	13,650	89,296
Lékoumou	Sibiti	8,089	20,950	74,420
Likouala	impfondo	25,500	66,044	70,675
Niari	Loubomo	10,007	25,918	120,077
Plateaux	Djambala	14,826	38,400	119,722
Pool	Kinkala	13,110	33,955	182,671
Sangha	Ouesso	21,542	55,795	35,961
Communes				
Brazzaville	—	39	100	937,579
Loubomo	—	7	18	83,605
Mossendjo	—	2	5	16,405
Nkayi	—	3	8	42,465
Ouesso	—	2	5	16,171
Pointe-Noire	—	17	44	576,206
TOTAL		132,047	342,000	2,694,449

Demography

Population (2000): 2,831,000.
Density (2000): persons per sq mi 21.4, persons per sq km 8.3.
Urban-rural (1999): urban 61.8%; rural 38.2%.
Sex distribution (1999): male 49.17%; female 50.83%.
Age breakdown (1999): under 15, 42.5%; 15–29, 28.8%; 30–44, 16.0%; 45–59, 7.6%; 60–74, 4.1%; 75 and over, 1.0%.
Population projection: (2010) 3,491,000; (2020) 4,209,000.
Doubling time: 30 years.
Ethnic composition (1983): Kongo 51.5%; Teke 17.3%; Mboshi 11.5%; Mbete 4.9%; Punu 3.0%; Sango 2.7%; Maka 1.8%; Pygmy 1.5%; other 5.8%.
Religious affiliation (1995): Roman Catholic 40.9%; traditional beliefs 32.9%; Protestant 24.2%; Muslim 2.0%.
Major cities (1992): Brazzaville 937,579; Pointe-Noire 576,206; Loubomo 83,605; Nkayi 42,465; Mossendjo 16,405.

Vital statistics

Birth rate per 1,000 population (1999): 39.0 (world avg. 22.1).
Death rate per 1,000 population (1999): 16.3 (world avg. 8.9).
Natural increase rate per 1,000 population (1999): 22.7 (world avg. 13.2).
Total fertility rate (avg. births per childbearing woman; 1999): 5.1.
Life expectancy at birth (1999): male 44.9 years; female 50.4 years.
Major causes of morbidity and mortality in the 1990s included malaria, acute respiratory infections, diarrhea, trauma, helminthiasis, and sexually transmitted diseases.

National economy

Budget (1997). Revenue: CFAF 399,600,000,000 (1996; petroleum revenue 59.6%; nonpetroleum receipts 40.4%). Expenditures: CFAF 515,800,000,000 (debt service 34.1%; goods and services 29.5%; salaries 20.2%; transfers and subsidies 5.3%).
Public debt (external, outstanding; 1998): U.S.$4,250,000,000.
Production (metric tons except as noted). Agriculture, forestry, fishing (1999): cassava 800,000, sugarcane 455,000, oil palm fruit 90,000, plantains 78,000, bananas 52,000, sweet potatoes 25,000, peanuts (groundnuts) 25,000, avocados 25,000, yams 13,500, pineapples 13,000, cacao beans 2,000, coffee 1,400, rubber 1,000; livestock (number of live animals) 285,000 goats, 115,000 sheep, 75,000 cattle, 45,000 pigs; roundwood (1998) 4,314,000 cu m; fish catch (1998) 40,000. Mining and quarrying (1997): artisanal extraction of gold only. Manufacturing (1995): residual fuel oil 258,000; cement 100,000; distillate fuel oils 90,000; aviation gas 53,000; gasoline 49,000; kerosene 48,000; refined sugar 21,000; wheat flour 16,000; dried, cured, or salted fish 4,000[3]; cigarettes 655,000,000 cartons[4]; mechanical cultivators 294,404 units[3]; beer 507,000 hectolitres[4]; soft drinks 220,000 hectolitres[4]; cotton textiles 1,800,000 m[5]; veneer sheets 35,000 cu m[5]; footwear 300,000 pairs[6]. Energy production (consumption): electricity (kW-hr; 1996) 438,000,000 (553,000,000); crude petroleum (barrels; 1996) 77,837,000 (11,882,000); petroleum products (metric tons; 1996) 534,000 (507,000); natural gas (cu m; 1996) 3,357,000 (3,357,000).
Household income and expenditure. Average household size (1984) 5.2; income per household: n.a.; sources of income: n.a.; expenditure (1977)[7, 8]: food, beverages, and tobacco 62.0%, housing 10.1%, transportation and recreation 8.6%, clothing and footwear 6.9%, fuel, energy, and water 5.7%, health and medical care 3.8%.
Gross national product (1998): U.S.$1,899,000,000 (U.S.$680 per capita).

Structure of gross domestic product and labour force

	1996 in value CFAF '000,000[9]	1996 % of total value	1991 labour force	1991 % of labour force
Agriculture, forestry, fishing	119,600	9.7	471,000	59.1
Petroleum	500,700	40.6	101,000	12.7
Manufacturing, mining	94,300	7.6		
Construction	18,000	1.5		
Public utilities	15,800	1.3	225,000	28.2
Trade	137,700	11.2		
Transp. and commun.	90,800	7.4		
Pub. admin., defense	124,000	10.0		
Services	80,200	6.5		
Other	53,600	4.3	—	—
TOTAL	1,234,700	100.0[10]	797,000	100.0

Population economically active (1997): total 1,110,000; activity rate of total population 42.0% (participation rates [1984]: ages 15–64, 54.0%; female [1997] 43.4%; unemployed[11] [1984] 2.3%).

Price and earnings indexes (1995 = 100)

	1993	1994	1995	1996
Consumer price index[7]	55.0	82.4	100	99.8
Earnings index	...	...	...	...

Land use (1994): forested 58.3%; meadows and pastures 29.3%; agricultural and under permanent cultivation 0.5%; other 11.9%.
Tourism (1997): receipts U.S.$10,000,000; expenditures U.S.$64,000,000.

Foreign trade

Balance of trade (current prices)

	1992	1993	1994	1995	1996	1997
CFAF '000,000,000	+214.8	+168.6	+192.2	+260.8	+100.0	+448.8
% of total	52.5%	38.6%	22.0%	28.7%	6.7%	29.9%

Imports (1997): CFAF 524,900,000,000 (1991; machinery and transport equipment 38.0%, basic manufactures 27.4%, food and live animals 11.2%, chemicals and chemical products 8.4%, mineral fuels 3.2%, beverages and tobacco 2.3%). *Major import sources:* France 23.3%; U.S. 9.2%; Belgium 7.6%; U.K. 6.9%; Italy 5.6%; China 5.6%; The Netherlands 4.4%; Hong Kong 4.1%.
Exports (1997): CFAF 973,700,000,000 (1995; petroleum and petroleum products 84.6%, wood and wood products 8.4%, other 7.0%). *Major export destinations:* U.S. 19.3%; Taiwan 16.0%; Belgium 11.5%; Germany 7.5%; Italy 4.9%.

Transport and communications

Transport. Railroads: (1997) length 894 km; (1995) passenger-km 302,000,000; metric ton-km cargo 267,000,000. Roads (1996): total length 12,800 km (paved 10%). Vehicles (1996): passenger cars 37,240; trucks and buses 15,520. Air transport (1998)[12]: passenger-km 258,272,000; metric ton-km cargo 13,524,000; airports (1998) with scheduled flights 10.

Communications

Medium	date	unit	number	units per 1,000 persons
Daily newspapers	1995	circulation	20,000	7.8
Radio	1997	receivers	341,000	126
Television	1997	receivers	33,000	12
Telephones	1998	main lines	22,000	7.9
Cellular telephones	1998	subscribers	3,390	1.2
Internet	1998	users	...	...

Education and health

Educational attainment (1984). Percentage of population age 25 and over having: no formal schooling 58.7%; primary education 21.4%; secondary education 16.9%; postsecondary 3.0%. *Literacy* (1995): total population age 15 and over literate 80.7%; males literate 87.5%; females literate 74.4%.

Education (1996–97)

	schools	teachers	students	student/ teacher ratio
Primary (age 6–13)	1,612	6,926	489,546	70.7
Secondary (age 14–18)	238[13]	5,466	190,409	34.8
Voc., teacher tr.	60[13]	1,746	23,606	13.5
Higher[14]	12	1,341	16,602	12.4

Health: physicians (1995) 632 (1 per 4,083 persons); hospital beds (1989) 4,817 (1 per 446 persons); infant mortality rate per 1,000 live births (1999) 103.2.
Food (1998): daily per capita caloric intake 2,241 (vegetable products 93%, animal products 7%); 101% of FAO recommended minimum requirement.

Military

Total active duty personnel (1999): 10,000 (army 80.0%, navy 8.0%, air force 12.0%). *Military expenditure as percentage of GNP* (1997): 4.1% (world 2.6%); per capita expenditure U.S.$28.

[1]From February 1998 through October 2000. [2]"Functional" national languages are Lingala and Monokutuba. [3]1992. [4]1994. [5]1993. [6]1990. [7]European households only; Brazzaville. [8]Cost-of-living components. [9]At current factor cost. [10]Detail does not add to total given because of rounding. [11]Previously employed only. [12]Represents 1/11 of the traffic of Air Afrique, which is operated by 11 African states. [13]1989. [14]1995.

Costa Rica

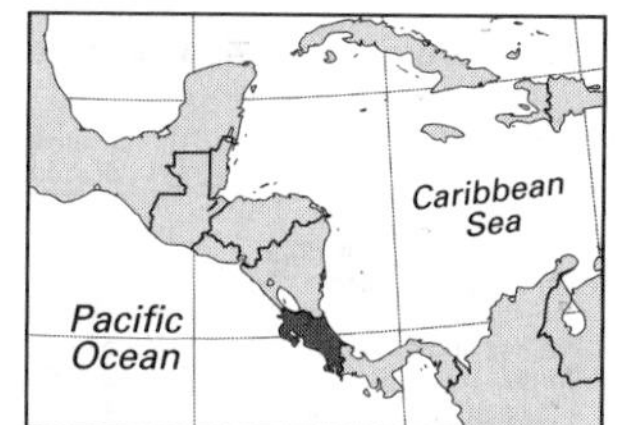

Official name: República de Costa Rica (Republic of Costa Rica).
Form of government: unitary multiparty republic with one legislative house (Legislative Assembly [57]).
Head of state and government: President.
Capital: San José.
Official language: Spanish.
Official religion: Roman Catholicism.
Monetary unit: 1 Costa Rican colón (₡) = 100 céntimos; valuation (Oct. 6, 2000) 1 U.S.$ = ₡313.23; 1 £ = ₡453.10.

Area and population

		area		population
Provinces	Capitals	sq mi	sq km	1999[1] estimate
Alajuela	Alajuela	3,766	9,753	638,173
Cartago	Cartago	1,207	3,125	398,687
Guanacaste	Liberia	3,915	10,141	279,264
Heredia	Heredia	1,026	2,657	286,112
Limón	Limón	3,548	9,188	275,819
Puntarenas	Puntarenas	4,354	11,277	396,149
San José	San José	1,915	4,959	1,284,493
TOTAL		19,730[2]	51,100	3,558,697

Demography

Population (2000): 3,644,000.
Density (2000): persons per sq mi 184.7, persons per sq km 71.3.
Urban-rural (1997): urban 49.3%; rural 50.7%.
Sex distribution (1999): male 50.46%; female 49.54%.
Age breakdown (1997): under 15, 33.6%; 15–29, 26.7%; 30–44, 21.6%; 45–59, 11.0%; 60–74, 5.5%; 75 and over, 1.6%.
Population projection: (2010) 4,238,000; (2020) 4,765,000.
Doubling time: 40 years.
Ethnic composition (1993): white 87.0%; mestizo 7.0%; black/mulatto 3.0%; East Asian (mostly Chinese) 2.0%; Amerindian 1.0%.
Religious affiliation (1995): Roman Catholic 86.0%; Protestant 9.3%, of which Pentecostal 4.9%; other Christian 2.4%; other 2.3%.
Major cities/metropolitan areas (1999/1998): San José 339,128[3] (1,015,203); Limón 60,398[4]; Alajuela 52,395[4] (177,812); San Isidro de El General 44,369[4]; Cartago 33,069[5] (111,080); Heredia 30,584[4] (95,017).

Vital statistics

Birth rate per 1,000 population (1998): 21.8 (world avg. 22.1); legitimate 50.3%; illegitimate 49.7%.
Death rate per 1,000 population (1998): 4.2 (world avg. 8.9).
Natural increase rate per 1,000 population (1998): 17.6 (world avg. 13.2).
Total fertility rate (avg. births per childbearing woman; 1998): 2.6.
Marriage rate per 1,000 population (1997): 6.5.
Divorce rate per 1,000 population (1995): 1.4.
Life expectancy at birth (1999): male 73.1 years; female 78.2 years.
Major causes of death per 100,000 population (1994): diseases of the circulatory system 126.6, of which ischemic heart disease 59.8; malignant neoplasms (cancers) 80.0; diseases of the respiratory system 40.6; accidents 36.1.

National economy

Budget (1998). Revenue: ₡459,700,000,000 (general sales tax 38.3%, selective taxes on goods and services 21.6%, income and profit taxes 19.3%, import duties 11.0%). Expenditures: ₡562,300,000,000 (current expenditures 91.3%, development expenditures 8.7%).
Public debt (external, outstanding; 1998): U.S.$3,047,000,000.
Gross national product (1998): U.S.$9,771,000,000 (U.S.$2,770 per capita).

Structure of gross domestic product and labour force

	1998			
	in value ₡'000,000,000	% of total value	labour force	% of labour force
Agriculture, forestry, fishing	410	15.2	261,584	19.0
Mining	505	18.7	1,595	0.1
Manufacturing			203,501	14.8
Construction	67	2.5	81,176	5.9
Public utilities	82	3.0	13,103	1.0
Transp. and commun.	170	6.3	73,272	5.3
Trade, restaurants	554	20.5	251,735	18.3
Finance, real estate	312	11.6	70,119	5.1
Public administration	367	13.6	333,685	24.2
Services	229	8.5		
Other	—	—	86,770[6]	6.3[6]
TOTAL	2,696	100.0[2]	1,376,540	100.0

Production (metric tons except as noted). Agriculture, forestry, fishing (1999): sugarcane 3,950,000, bananas 2,101,000, oil palm fruit 440,000, pineapples 400,000, oranges 283,200, rice 262,200, coffee 147,000, cassava 119,500, potatoes 91,700, plantains 90,000, other products include other tropical fruits, cut flowers, and ornamental plants grown for export; livestock (number of live animals) 1,617,000 cattle, 290,000 pigs, 17,000,000 chickens; roundwood (1998) 5,311,000 cu m; fish catch (1997) 33,613, of which shrimp 5,717. Mining and quarrying (1997): limestone 1,500,000; gold 17,700 troy oz. Manufacturing (value added in ₡'000,000; 1996): food products 90,498; beverages 43,101; fertilizers and pesticides 18,360; plastic products 12,196; radio, television, and communications equipment 10,955; paper and paper products 10,589; wearing apparel 9,519. Construction (completed; 1997): 1,760,000 sq m. Energy production (consumption): electricity (kW-hr; 1996) 4,853,000,000 (4,997,000,000); coal, none (none); crude petroleum (barrels; 1996) none (4,523,000); petroleum products (metric tons; 1996) 597,000 (1,387,000); natural gas, none (none).
Population economically active (1998): total 1,376,540; activity rate of total population 41.2% (participation rates: ages 12–59, 59.3%; female 32.6%; unemployed 5.6%).

Price and earnings indexes (1995 = 100)

	1993	1994	1995	1996	1997	1998	1999
Consumer price index	71.5	81.2	100.0	117.5	133.1	148.6	162.9[7]
Monthly earnings index[8]	70.3	81.6	100.0	115.1	132.7	155.0	...

Tourism (1997): receipts U.S.$719,000,000; expenditures U.S.$358,000,000.
Household income and expenditure. Average household size (1997) 4.1; average annual household income (1997) ₡1,468,597 (U.S.$6,314); sources of income (1987–88): wages and salaries 61.0%, self-employment 22.6%, transfers 9.6%; expenditure (1987–88): food and beverages 39.1%, housing and energy 12.1%, transportation 11.6%, household furnishings 10.9%.
Land use (1994): forested 30.8%; meadows and pastures 45.8%; agricultural and under permanent cultivation 10.4%; other 13.0%.

Foreign trade[9]

Balance of trade (current prices)[10]

	1994	1995	1996	1997	1998
U.S.$'000,000	–1,715	–1,590	–1,617	–2,009	–3,208
% of total	29.0%	23.8%	22.6%	25.3%	34.5%

Imports (1998)[10]: U.S.$6,255,000,000 (raw materials for industry 50.6%, capital goods for industry 14.9%, nondurable consumer goods 11.9%, durable consumer goods 8.6%). *Major import sources*[11]: U.S. 38.8%; Japan 7.6%; Mexico 6.9%; Venezuela 3.8%; Guatemala 3.1%.
Exports (1998): U.S.$3,047,000,000 (bananas 21.8%, coffee 13.3%, processed food and tobacco products 9.3%, fish and shrimp 7.6%, machinery and metal products 6.0%, tropical fruit 5.5%). *Major export destinations*[12]: U.S. 42%; United Kingdom 7%; Germany 7%; The Netherlands 6%; Guatemala 5%.

Transport and communications

Transport. Railroads[13]. Roads (1997): total length 22,119 mi, 35,597 km (paved 17%). Vehicles (1997): passenger cars 294,083; trucks and buses 163,428. Merchant marine (1992): vessels (100 gross tons and over) 24; total deadweight tonnage 8,368. Air transport (1998)[14]: passenger-mi 2,167,000,000, passenger-km 3,487,000,000; short-ton mi cargo 61,904,000, metric ton-km cargo 90,378,000; airports (1996) 14.

Communications

Medium	date	unit	number	units per 1,000 persons
Daily newspapers	1996	circulation	320,000	94
Radio	1997	receivers	980,000	283
Television	1997	receivers	525,000	152
Telephones	1998	main lines	659,996	187
Cellular telephones	1998	subscribers	108,770	31
Personal computers	1998	units	150,000	43
Internet (est.)	1998	users	100,000	28

Education and health

Educational attainment (1996): Percentage of population age 5 and over having: no formal schooling 11.7%; incomplete pirmary education 28.5%; complete primary 25.8%; incomplete secondary 16.0%; complete secondary 9.0%; higher 8.5%; other/unknown 0.5%. *Literacy* (1995): total population age 15 and over literate 2,118,000 (94.8%); males literate 1,054,000 (94.7%); females literate 1,064,000 (95.0%).

Education (1998)

	schools	teachers	students	student/ teacher ratio
Primary (age 7–12)	3,711	19,235	529,637	27.5
Secondary (age 13–17)	353[15]	10,943	202,415	18.5
Higher	40[15]	...	83,106[15]	...

Health (1997): physicians 5,500 (1 per 630 persons); hospital beds 5,953 (1 per 582 persons); infant mortality rate per 1,000 live births (1998) 12.6.
Food (1997): daily per capita caloric intake 2,649 (vegetable products 82%, animal products 18%); 118% of FAO recommended minimum requirement.

Military

Paramilitary expenditure as percentage of GNP (1997): 0.6% (world 2.6%); per capita expenditure U.S.$17. The army was officially abolished in 1948. Paramilitary (police) forces had 8,400 members in 1999.

[1]January 1. [2]Detail does not add to total given because of rounding. [3]Population of San José canton. [4]District population. [5]Population of two districts. [6]Includes 10,235 not adequately defined and 76,535 unemployed. [7]June. [8]Data for July average of each year. [9]Imports c.i.f.; exports f.o.b. [10]Includes goods imported for reassembly. [11]Excludes goods imported for reassembly. [12]Estimated figures. [13]Rail service was suspended in June 1995 because of a lack of funds and was resumed (in part) from October 1998. [14]Lacsa (Costa Rican Airlines) only. [15]1997.

Internet resources for further information:
- **Central Bank of Costa Rica: Economic Indicators http://websiec.bccr.fi.cr/indicadores/indice.web**
- **Government of Costa Rica http://www.casapres.go.cr**

Côte d'Ivoire

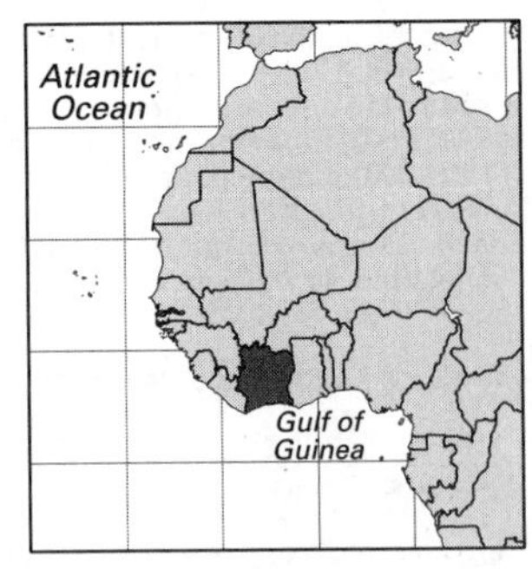

Official name: République de Côte d'Ivoire (Republic of Côte d'Ivoire [Ivory Coast][1]).
Form of government: transitional regime[2].
Chief of state and government: President assisted by Prime Minister[2].
Capital: Abidjan (de facto; legislative).
Capital designate: Yamoussoukro (de jure; administrative).
Official language: French.
Official religion: none.
Monetary unit: 1 CFA franc (CFAF) = 100 centimes; valuation (Oct. 6, 2000) 1 U.S.$ = CFAF 754.28; 1 £ = CFAF 1,091.

Area and population (1988 census)[3]

Department	area sq km	population	Department	area sq km	population
Abengourou	5,200	216,058	Guiglo	11,220	170,321
Abidjan	8,550	2,485,847	Issia	3,590	195,663
Aboisso	6,250	225,895	Katiola	9,420	130,635
Adzopé	5,230	237,870	Korhogo	12,500	390,229
Agboville	3,850	203,493	Lakota	2,730	116,771
Agnibilékrou	1,700	84,349	Man	4,990	294,724
Bangolo	2,060	79,979	Mankono	10,660	123,362
Béoumi	2,820	90,327	M'bahiakro	5,460	102,531
Biankouma	4,950	98,236	Odiénné	20,600	169,764
Bondoukou	10,040	174,251	Oumé	2,400	141,268
Bongouanou	5,570	224,958	Sakassou	1,880	59,362
Bouaflé	3,980	165,822	San-Pédro	6,900	170,669
Bouaké	4,700	450,594	Sassandra	5,190	108,090
Bouna	21,470	135,813	Séguéla	11,240	121,235
Boundiali	7,895	127,847	Sinfra	1,690	121,903
Dabakala	9,670	81,820	Soubré	8,270	310,790
Daloa	5,450	359,753	Tabou	5,440	58,147
Danané	4,600	222,839	Tanda	6,490	204,070
Daoukro	3,610	86,494	Tengréla	2,200	54,847
Dimbokro	4,920	141,968	Tiassalé	3,370	133,708
Divo	7,920	387,106	Touba	8,720	107,886
Duékoué	2,930	102,168	Toumodi	2,780	80,802
Ferkessedougou	17,728	172,893	Vavoua	6,160	168,292
Gagnoa	4,500	276,217	Yamoussoukro	6,160	281,442
Grand-Lahou	2,280	52,559	Zuénoula	2,830	114,027
			TOTAL	320,763[4]	10,815,694

Demography

Population (2000): 15,981,000.
Density (2000): persons per sq mi 128.4, persons per sq km 49.6.
Urban-rural (1998): urban 45.3%; rural 54.7%.
Sex distribution (1998): male 50.94%; female 49.06%.
Age breakdown (1999): under 15, 46.6%; 15–29, 27.6%; 30–44, 14.6%; 45–59, 7.6%; 60–64, 3.0%; 65 and over, 0.6%.
Population projection: (2010) 20,003,000; (2020) 23,748,000.
Ethnolinguistic composition (1988)[5]: Akan 41.8%; Voltaic 16.3%; Malinke 15.9%; Kru 14.6%; Southern Mande 10.7%; other 0.7%.
Religious affiliation (1988): Muslim 38.7%; Catholic 20.8%; animist 17.0%; atheist 13.4%; Protestant 5.3%, excluding Harrism (1.4%); other 3.4%.
Major cities (1995): Abidjan (1996) 2,500,000; Bouaké 330,000; Daloa 123,000; Yamoussoukro 110,000.

Vital statistics

Birth rate per 1,000 population (1999): 41.8 (world avg. 22.1).
Death rate per 1,000 population (1999): 16.2 (world avg. 8.9).
Natural increase rate per 1,000 population (1999): 25.6 (world avg. 13.2).
Total fertility rate (avg. births per childbearing woman; 1999): 5.9.
Life expectancy at birth (1999): male 44.5 years; female 47.7 years.

National economy

Budget (1997). Revenue: CFAF 1,372,100,000,000 (tax revenue 81.1%, of which import taxes and duties 22.7%, export taxes 12.6%, taxes on profits 10.7%, income tax 7.1%; nontax revenue 15.7%; grants 3.2%). Expenditures: CFAF 1,191,300,000,000 (wages and salaries 34.3%, capital expenditure 31.3%, debt service 25.5%; other 8.9%).
Public debt (external, outstanding; 1998): U.S.$10,800,000,000.
Production (metric tons except as noted). Agriculture, forestry, fishing (1999): yams 2,923,175, cassava 1,672,599, plantains 1,405,441, sugarcane 1,155,000, paddy rice 1,161,518, cacao beans 1,153,000, corn (maize) 571,018, coffee 365,000, cotton seed 270,000, palm oil 250,200, bananas 241,017, coconuts 193,000, rubber 118,860; livestock (number of live animals) 1,370,000 sheep, 1,330,000 cattle, 1,070,000 goats, 275,000 pigs, 29,000,000 chickens; roundwood (1998) 13,283,000 cu m; fish catch (1997) 67,617. Mining and quarrying (1997): gold 4,000 kg; diamonds 84,300 carats. Manufacturing (value added in CFAF '000,000,000; 1993): meat products 717, chemicals 357, cocoa and chocolate 275, leather products 275, fabricated metal products 191. Energy production (consumption): electricity (kW-hr; 1996) 3,221,000,000 (2,309,000,000); crude petroleum (barrels; 1996) 9,258,000 (31,446,000); petroleum products (metric tons; 1996) 2,192,000 (2,161,000).
Household income and expenditure. Average household size (1998) 8.0; expenditure (1992–93)[6]: food 48.0%, transportation 12.2%, clothing 10.1%, energy and water 8.5%, housing 7.8%, household equipment 3.4%.
Gross national product (1998): U.S.$10,190,000,000 (U.S.$700 per capita).

Structure of gross domestic product and labour force

	1996 in value CFAF '000,000,000	1996 % of total value	1994 labour force	1994 % of labour force
Agriculture	1,531.7	28.0	2,886,000	51.1
Manufacturing, mining, and public utilities	954.5	17.4	650,000	11.5
Construction	156.3	2.9		
Transp. and commun.	514.4	9.4	2,112,000	37.4
Trade	929.5	17.0		
Public admin., defense	438.3	8.0		
Services	693.1	12.7		
Other (customs receipts)	255.8	4.7		
TOTAL	5,473.6	100.0[7]	5,648,000	100.0

Population economically active (1997): total 5,684,000; activity rate of total population 37.7% (participation rates: [1994] over ages 10, 64.3%; female 33.0%).

Price and earnings indexes (1995 = 100)

	1992	1993	1994	1995	1996	1997	1998
Consumer price index	67.9	69.4	87.5	100.0	102.5	108.2	113.3
Minimum earnings index	90.9	90.9	90.9	100.0	102.7	108.3	...

Tourism (1997): receipts U.S.$88,000,000; expenditures U.S.$282,000,000.

Foreign trade

Balance of trade (current prices)

	1994	1995	1996	1997	1998	1999
CFAF '000,000,000	+700	+681	+777	+777	+810	+830
% of total	28.2%	21.7%	21.6%	19.5%	19.9%	19.2%

Imports (1997): CFAF 1,602,000,000,000 (food and food products 19.4%, machinery and transport equipment 18.6%, crude and refined petroleum 18.5%, plastics 4.6%, iron and steel products 4.4%). *Major import sources* (1995): France 32.0%; Nigeria 19.6%; U.S. 5.9%; Ghana 4.0%; Germany 3.9%; Italy 3.8%.
Exports (1997): CFAF 2,379,000,000,000 (cocoa beans and products 33.5%, petroleum products 16.8%, coffee and coffee products 7.3%, wood and wood products 7.0%, fish products 5.3%, cotton and cotton cloth 3.0%). *Major export destinations:* France 17.3%; The Netherlands 13.2%; United States 7.5%; Italy 5.3%; Mali 4.9%; Germany 4.8%.

Transport and communications

Transport. Railroads (1995): route length 639 km; passenger-km 129,000,000; metric ton-km cargo 58,000,000. Roads (1996): total length 50,400 km (paved 9.7%). Vehicles (1996): passenger cars 293,000; trucks and buses 163,000. Air transport (1996): passenger-km 307,000,000; metric ton-km cargo 44,000,000; airports (1998) 5.

Communications

Medium	date	unit	number	units per 1,000 persons
Daily newspapers	1996	circulation	231,000	17
Radio	1998	receivers	1,600,000	97
Television	1998	receivers	937,000	66
Telephones	1999	main lines	170,000	12
Cellular telephones	1999	subscribers	91,212	6.4
Personal computers	1999	units	65,000	5.9
Internet	1999	users	10,000	0.7

Education and health

Educational attainment (1988). Percentage of population age 6 and over having: no formal schooling 60.0%; Koranic school 3.6%; primary education 24.8%; secondary 10.7%; higher 0.9%. *Literacy* (1995): percentage of population age 15 and over literate 40.1%; males 49.9%; females 30.0%.

Education (1995–96)

	schools	teachers	students	student/ teacher ratio
Primary (age 7–12)	7,401	40,529	1,662,285	41.0
Secondary (age 13–19)	147	15,959	489,740	30.7
Vocational[8]	...	1,424	11,037	7.8
Higher[8]	...	1,657	43,147	26.0

Health: physicians (1996) 1,318 (1 per 11,111 persons); hospital beds (1993) 7,928 (1 per 1,698 persons); infant mortality rate (1999) 94.2.
Food (1998): daily per capita caloric intake 2,695 (vegetable products 96%, animal products 4%); 117% of FAO recommended minimum requirement.

Military

Total active duty personnel (1999): 8,400[9] (army 81.0%, navy 10.7%, air force 8.3%). *Military expenditure as percentage of GNP* (1997): 1.1% (world avg. 2.6%); per capita expenditure U.S.$7.

[1]Since 1986, Côte d'Ivoire has requested that the French form of the country's name be used as the official protocol version in all languages. [2]As of November 2000. [3]As of late 1998 Côte d'Ivoire had 58 departments within 16 regions. [4]Total area per more recent survey is 322,463 sq km; breakdown of that area by department is not available. [5]"Ivoirian" nationals only, representing about 60% of the de facto population in 1999. [6]Weights of consumer price index components for a worker's family living in the capital city. [7]Detail does not add to total given because of rounding. [8]1994–95. [9]Excludes 570 French troops.

Internet resources for further information:
- **Côte d'Ivoire—A Country Study http://lcweb2.loc.gov/frd/cs/citoc.html**

Croatia

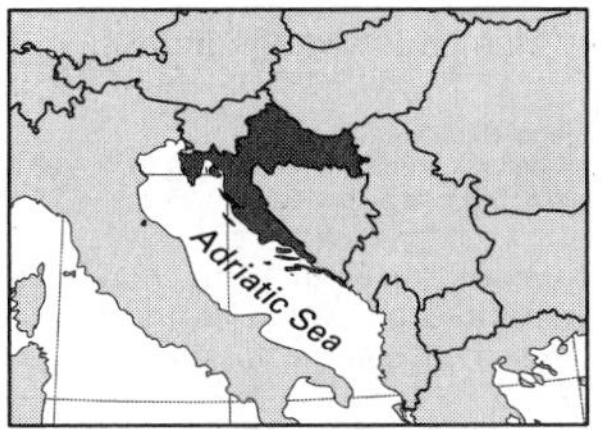

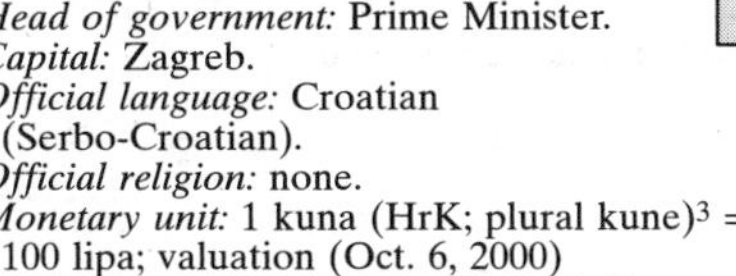

Official name: Republika Hrvatska (Republic of Croatia).
Form of government: multiparty republic with a two-chambered legislature (House of Counties [68[1]]; House of Representatives [152[2]]).
Head of state: President.
Head of government: Prime Minister.
Capital: Zagreb.
Official language: Croatian (Serbo-Croatian).
Official religion: none.
Monetary unit: 1 kuna (HrK; plural kune)[3] = 100 lipa; valuation (Oct. 6, 2000) 1 U.S.$ = HrK 8.62; 1 £ = HrK 12.47.

Area and population[4]

Counties	area sq km	population 1991 census	Counties	area sq km	population 1991 census
Bjelovar-Bilogora	2,638	144,042	Šibenik-Knin	2,994	152,477
Dubrovnik-Neretva	1,782	126,329	Sisak-Moslavina	4,448	251,023
Istria	2,813	204,346	Slavonski Brod-Posavina	2,027	174,998
Karlovac	3,622	184,577	Split-Dalmatia	4,524	474,019
Koprivnica-Križevci	1,734	129,397	Varaždin	1,260	187,853
Krapina-Zagorje	1,230	148,779	Virovitica-Podravina	2,021	104,625
Lika-Senj	5,350	85,135	Vukovar-Srijem	2,448	231,241
Medimurje	730	119,866	Zadar	3,643	214,777
Osijek-Baranja	4,149	367,193	Zagreb	3,078	283,298
Požega-Slavonia	1,821	99,334	**City**		
Primorje-Gorski kotar	3,590	323,130	Zagreb	640	777,826
			TOTAL	56,542	4,784,265

Demography

Population (2000): 4,282,000.
Density (2000): persons per sq mi 196.1, persons per sq km 75.7.
Urban-rural (1995): urban 56.9%; rural 43.1%.
Sex distribution (1995): male 48.34%; female 51.66%.
Age breakdown (1995): under 15, 18.9%; 15–29, 20.5%; 30–44, 22.7%; 45–59, 18.8%; 60–74, 15.3%; 75 and over, 3.8%.
Population projection: (2010) 4,505,000; (2020) 4,560,000.
Ethnic composition (1991): Croat 78.1%; Serb 12.1%; Muslims 0.9%; Hungarians 0.5%; Slovene 0.5%; other 7.9%.
Religious affiliation (1997): Roman Catholic 72.1%; Eastern Orthodox 14.1%; Muslim 1.3%; other 12.5%.
Major cities (1991): Zagreb 777,826[4]; Split 200,459; Rijeka 167,964; Osijek 129,792; Zadar 76,343.

Vital statistics

Birth rate per 1,000 population (1997): 12.1 (world avg. 22.1); legitimate 92.7%; illegitimate 7.3%.
Death rate per 1,000 population (1997): 11.4 (world avg. 8.9).
Natural increase rate per 1,000 population (1997): 0.7 (world avg. 13.2).
Total fertility rate (avg. births per childbearing woman; 1999): 1.9.
Marriage rate per 1,000 population (1997): 5.3.
Divorce rate per 1,000 population (1997): 0.8.
Life expectancy at birth (1999): male 69.5 years; female 77.1 years.
Major causes of death per 100,000 population (1996): diseases of the circulatory system 547.4; cancers 227.2; accidents, violence, and poisoning 70.7; diseases of the digestive system 52.1; diseases of the respiratory system 41.4.

National economy

Budget (1999). Revenue: HrK 67,907,000,000 (sales tax 34.1%, social security contributions 32.2%, excise taxes 9.5%). Expenditures: HrK 70,358,000,000 (social security and welfare 37.8%, health 14.0%, defense 7.7%, education 7.4%).
Population economically active (1991): total 2,040,000; activity rate 42.6% (participation rates: ages 15–64, 61.1%; female 42.8%; unemployed 11.2%).
Public debt (external, outstanding; 1998): U.S.$4,910,000,000.

Price and earnings indexes (1995 = 100)

	1994	1995	1996	1997	1998	1999	2000
Consumer price index	96.2	100.0	104.3	108.6	115.6	119.9	123.7[5]
Annual earnings index	69	100	112	131	147	168[6]	...

Production (metric tons except as noted). Agriculture, forestry, fishing (1999): corn (maize) 2,135,000, sugar beets 1,114,000, potatoes 729,000, wheat 558,000, grapes 394,000, barley 125,000, soybeans 116,000, sunflower seed 72,400, plums 38,000; livestock (number of live animals) 1,362,000 pigs, 489,000 sheep, 439,000 cattle; roundwood (1998) 3,398,000 cu m; fish catch (1997) 19,885. Mining and quarrying (1998): gypsum 100,000; ferrochromium 15,000. Manufacturing (value added in U.S.$'000,000; 1996): food products 895; transport equipment 425; electrical machinery 362; textiles 285; wearing apparel 260. Construction (value in HrK '000,000; 1997): residential 3,404; nonresidential 9,434. Energy production (consumption): electricity (kW-hr; 1998) 10,356,000,000 ([1996] 12,878,000,000); hard coal (metric tons; 1998) 48,000 ([1996] 117,000); lignite (metric tons; 1996) 2,000 (149,000); crude petroleum (barrels; 1998) 8,532,000 ([1996] 38,248,000); petroleum products (metric tons; 1996) 4,500,000 (3,393,000); natural gas (cu m; 1998) 1,566,000,000 ([1996] 2,584,000,000).

Gross national product (1998): U.S.$20,786,000,000 (U.S.$4,620 per capita).

Structure of gross domestic product and labour force

	1998 in value HrK '000,000[3]	1998 % of total value	1991 labour force	1991 % of labour force
Agriculture	9,840	6.6	265,000	13.0
Mining	616	0.4	613,000	30.0
Manufacturing	32,881	22.2		
Construction	7,807	5.3	98,000	4.8
Public utilities	4,439	3.0	32,700	1.6
Transp. and commun.	10,608	7.2	120,000	5.9
Trade	16,672	11.2	163,000	8.0
Finance, real estate	17,639	11.9	60,400	3.0
Pub. admin., defense	11,878	8.0	315,000	15.4
Services	13,108[7]	8.8[7]	80,700	4.0
Other	22,803[8]	15.4[8]	292,200[9]	14.3[9]
TOTAL	148,291	100.0	2,040,000	100.0

Household income and expenditure. Average household size (1991) 3.1; income per household (1990) Din 165,813[3] (U.S.$14,650); sources (1990): self-employment 40.8%, wages 40.2%, transfers 12.1%, other 6.9%; expenditure (1988): food 34.2%, transportation 9.3%, clothing 8.6%, housing 8.3%, energy 7.6%, drink and tobacco 5.1%, durable goods 4.5%, health care 4.3%.
Land use (1994): forest 37.1%; pasture 19.3%; agriculture 21.6%; other 22.0%.

Foreign trade

Balance of trade (current prices)

	1993	1994	1995	1996	1997	1998
U.S.$'000,000	–742	–1,172	–3,268	–3,690	–5,224	–3,842
% of total	8.7%	11.3%	26.1%	28.9%	38.3%	29.7%

Imports (1998): U.S.$8,383,000,000 (machinery and transport equipment 35.2%; chemicals and chemical products 11.7%; food and live animals 8.1%; mineral fuels and lubricants 7.1%). *Major import sources:* Germany 19.2%; Italy 17.9%; Slovenia 8.6%; Austria 7.3%; France 4.8%.
Exports (1998): U.S.$4,541,000,000 (machinery and transport equipment 30.4%; clothing 12.2%; chemical and chemical products 12.7%; food 8.4%; mineral fuels and lubricants 5.8%). *Major export destinations:* Italy 17.7%; Germany 16.9%; Bosnia and Herzegovina 14.4%; Slovenia 9.5%; Austria 5.4%.

Transport and communications

Transport. Railroads (1997): length 2,726 km; passenger-km 981,000,000; metric ton-km cargo 1,876,000,000. Roads (1997): total length 27,840 km (paved 82%). Vehicles (1997): passenger cars 932,278; trucks and buses 114,505. Merchant marine (1994): cargo ships 155. Air transport (1997): passenger-km 546,000,000; metric ton-km cargo 2,997,000; airports (1997) 4.

Communications

Medium	date	unit	number	units per 1,000 persons
Daily newspapers	1996	circulation	515,000	110
Radio	1997	receivers	1,510,000	324
Television	1997	receivers	1,220,000	262
Telephones	1998	main lines	1,558,000	365
Cellular telephones	1998	subscribers	182,500	43.0
Personal computers	1998	units	500,000	117
Internet	1998	users	200,000	47.0

Education and health

Educational attainment (1991). Percentage of population age 15 and over having: no schooling or unknown 10.1%; less than full primary education 21.2%; primary 23.4%; secondary 36.0%; postsecondary and higher 9.3%. *Literacy* (1995): population age 15 and over literate 98.3%; males 99.4%; females 97.3%.

Education (1997–98)

	schools	teachers	students	student/ teacher ratio
Primary (age 7–14)	2,127	26,199	423,165	16.2
Secondary (age 15–18)	577	16,942	199,863	11.8
Voc., teacher tr.	2	72	848	11.8
Higher	67	6,181	89,173	14.4

Health (1997): physicians 9,315 (1 per 501 persons); hospital beds 27,472 (1 per 170 persons); infant mortality rate per 1,000 live births (1997) 8.2.
Food (1997): daily per capita caloric intake 2,445 (vegetable products 81%, animal products 19%); 96% of FAO recommended minimum requirement.

Military

Total active duty personnel (1999): 61,000 (army 86.9%, navy 4.9%, air force and air defense 8.2%). *Military expenditure as percentage of GNP* (1997): 6.3% (world 2.6%).

[1]Includes 5 nonelective seats. [2]Includes six seats representing Croatians abroad. [3]On Jan. 1, 1990, the Yugoslav new dinar (Din), equal to 10,000 Yugoslav old dinars (Din), was introduced. On Dec. 23, 1991, the Croatian dinar (HrD) was introduced at parity with the Yugoslav new dinar, which it replaced as Croatia's official currency. On May 30, 1994, the kuna (HrK), equal to 1,000 Croatian dinars, was introduced. [4]As of 1998 administrative reorganization. [5]January. [6]Average of 2nd and 3rd quarters. [7]Includes not adequately defined. [8]Import and turnover taxes less imputed bank service charges. [9]Includes unemployed and private sector.

Internet resources for further information:
- **Croatian Bureau of Statistics http://www.dzs.hr/Eng/Default2.htm**
- **Ministry of Foreign Affairs http://www.mvp.hr**

Cuba

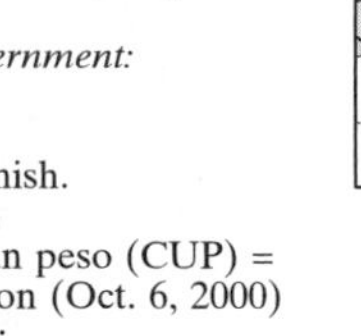

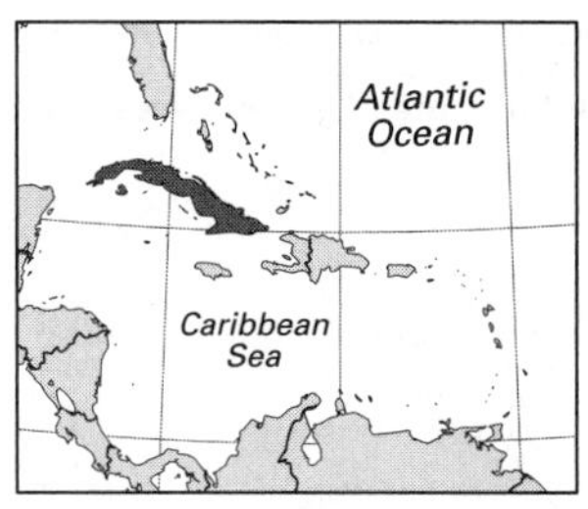

Official name: República de Cuba (Republic of Cuba).
Form of government: unitary socialist republic with one legislative house (National Assembly of the People's Power [601]).
Head of state and government: President.
Capital: Havana.
Official language: Spanish.
Official religion: none.
Monetary unit: 1 Cuban peso (CUP) = 100 centavos; valuation (Oct. 6, 2000) 1 U.S.$ = 21.00 CUP; 1 £ = 30.38 CUP.

Area and population

Provinces	Capitals	area sq mi	area sq km	population 1998[1] estimate
Camagüey	Camagüey	6,174	15,990	780,762
Ciego de Avila	Ciego de Avila	2,668	6,910	403,134
Cienfuegos	Cienfuegos	1,613	4,178	391,666
Ciudad de la Habana[2]	—	281	727	2,198,392
Granma	Bayamo	3,232	8,372	824,897
Guantánamo	Guantánamo	2,388	6,186	508,864
Holguín	Holguín	3,591	9,301	1,020,660
La Habana[3]	Havana	2,213	5,731	693,889
Las Tunas	Las Tunas	2,544	6,589	523,810
Matanzas	Matanzas	4,625	11,978	654,516
Pinar del Río	Pinar del Río	4,218	10,925	729,330
Sancti Spíritus	Sancti Spíritus	2,604	6,744	457,921
Santiago de Cuba	Santiago de Cuba	2,382	6,170	1,023,293
Villa Clara	Santa Clara	3,345	8,662	832,356
Special municipality				
Isla de la Juventud	Nueva Gerona	926	2,398	78,818
TOTAL		42,804	110,861	11,122,308

Demography

Population (2000): 11,148,000.
Density (2000): persons per sq mi 260.4, persons per sq km 100.6.
Urban-rural (1999): urban 75.2%; rural 24.8%.
Sex distribution (1999): male 51.98%; female 48.02%.
Age breakdown (1999): under 15, 21.7%; 15–29, 23.4%; 30–44, 25.6%; 45–59, 16.0%; 60–74, 9.0%; 75 and over, 4.3%.
Population projection: (2010) 11,526,000; (2020) 11,799,000.
Ethnic composition (1994): mixed 51.0%; white 37.0%; black 11.0%; other 1.0%.
Religious affiliation (1995): Roman Catholic 39.5%; Protestant 2.4%; other Christian 0.2%; other (mostly Santéria) 57.9%.
Major cities (1993): Havana 2,175,995; Santiago de Cuba 440,084; Camagüey 293,961; Holguín 242,085; Guantánamo 207,796.

Vital statistics

Birth rate per 1,000 population (1998): 13.6 (world avg. 22.1).
Death rate per 1,000 population (1998): 7.0 (world avg. 8.9).
Natural increase rate per 1,000 population (1998): 6.6 (world avg. 13.2).
Total fertility rate (avg. births per childbearing woman; 1999): 1.6.
Marriage rate per 1,000 population (1992): 17.7.
Divorce rate per 1,000 population (1993): 6.0.
Life expectancy at birth (1999): male 73.6 years; female 78.5 years.
Major causes of death per 100,000 population (1998): heart disease 142.6; malignant neoplasms (cancers) 111.0; cerebrovascular disease 52.9; accidents 39.0; influenza and pneumonia 31.3; diseases of the blood vessels 21.9.

National economy

Budget (1999). Revenue: CUP 13,575,000,000. Expenditures: CUP 14,270,000,000 (education and health 26.5%; investment 11.9%; other 61.6%).
Public debt (external, outstanding; 1999): U.S.$11,078,000,000.
Production (metric tons except as noted). Agriculture, forestry, fishing (1999): sugarcane 35,000,000, rice 420,000, oranges and tangerines 406,500, potatoes 330,000, grapefruit 300,000, plantains 275,000, cassava 190,000, tomatoes 180,000, corn (maize) 130,000, bananas 115,000; livestock (number of live animals) 4,650,000 cattle, 2,400,000 pigs, 13,500,000 chickens; roundwood (1998) 2,756,000 cu m; fish catch (1998) 62,154. Mining and quarrying (1998): nickel 67,700; chromite 30,000. Manufacturing (value added in U.S.$'000,000; 1990): tobacco products 2,629; food products 1,033; beverages 358; chemical products 354; transport equipment 225; nonelectrical machinery 176. Construction (gross value of construction in CUP '000,000; 1989): residential 227; nonresidential 872. Energy production (consumption): electricity (kW-hr; 1996) 13,236,000,000 (13,236,000,000); coal (metric tons; 1996) none (163,000); crude petroleum (barrels; 1996) 9,377,000 (9,899,000); petroleum products (metric tons; 1996) 4,767,000 (8,240,000); natural gas (cu m; 1996) 43,002,000 (43,002,000).
Household income and expenditure. Average household size (1998) 3.4; average annual income per household (1982) CUP 3,680 (U.S.$4,330); sources of income (1982): wages and salaries 57.3%, bonuses and other payments 42.7%; personal consumption (1989): food 26.7%, other retail purchases 60.5%, transportation services 5.4%, energy 2.7%, value of self-produced and consumed food 1.5%, household repairs 1.3%, other 1.9%.
Population economically active (1988): total 4,570,236; activity rate of total population 43.7% (participation rates: over age 15, 56.9%; female [1998] 37.0%; unemployed [1998] 6.0%).

Price and earnings indexes (1985 = 100)

	1983	1984	1985	1986	1987	1988	1989
Implicit consumer price deflator index	94.9	98.0	100.0	101.4	102.8	103.1	...
Monthly earnings index[4]	95.9	99.0	100.0	100.1	98.1	99.6	100.0

Tourism: receipts from visitors (1998) U.S.$1,571,000,000; expenditures by nationals abroad (1990) U.S.$48,000,000.
Gross domestic product (1999): U.S.$18,600,000,000 (U.S.$1,700 per capita).

Structure of gross domestic product and labour force

	1994 in value[5] CUP '000,000	1994 % of total value	1989 labour force[4]	1989 % of labour force
Agriculture	879.4	6.8	721,100	20.4
Mining	97.5	0.8		
Manufacturing	3,340.6	26.0	767,500	21.8
Public utilities	350.0	2.7		
Construction	383.9	3.0	344,300	9.8
Transp. and commun.	708.7	5.5	235,900	6.7
Finance, insurance	492.4	3.8	21,700	0.6
Trade	2,935.2	22.8	395,300	11.2
Public administration	—	—	151,700	4.3
Services	3,680.6	28.6	835,700	23.7
Other	—	—	53,400	1.5
TOTAL	12,868.3	100.0	3,526,600	100.0

Land use (1994): forested 23.7%; meadows and pastures 27.0%; agricultural and under permanent cultivation 30.7%; other 18.6%.

Foreign trade[6]

Balance of trade (current prices)

	1994	1995	1996	1997	1998	1999
U.S.$'000,000	−797	−1,166	−1,179	−1,200	−1,300	−1,800
% of total	24.4%	28.3%	24.4%	25.2%	25.5%	39.1%

Imports (1999): U.S.$3,200,000,000 (1992; mineral fuels and lubricants 39.4%, food and live animals 25.4%, machinery and transport equipment 15.8%, chemicals 6.9%, basic manufactures 6.6%, inedible crude materials 3.2%). *Major import sources:* Spain 22.4%; France 10.6%; Canada 9.8%; Italy 7.9%; China 5.2%; Argentina 2.9%; Russia 2.9%.
Exports (1999): U.S.$1,400,000,000 (1992; sugar 63.4%, minerals and concentrates 10.6%, fish products 5.9%, raw tobacco and tobacco products 4.6%, citrus and other agricultural products 3.4%). *Major export destinations* (1998): Russia 22.0%; Canada 13.4%; The Netherlands 13.4%; Spain 7.2%; China 5.4%.

Transport and communications

Transport. Railroads (1999): length 2,987 mi, 4,807 km; (1994) passenger-km 2,347,000,000; metric ton-km cargo 645,000,000. Roads (1997): total length 37,815 mi, 60,858 km (paved 49%). Vehicles (1997): passenger cars 172,574; trucks and buses 185,495. Air transport (1997): passenger-km 3,543,176,000; metric ton-km cargo 56,239,000; airports with scheduled flights (1998) 14.

Communications

Medium	date	unit	number	units per 1,000 persons
Daily newspapers	1996	circulation	1,300,000	118
Radio	1997	receivers	3,900,000	352
Television	1998	receivers	2,660,000	239
Telephones	1998	main lines	388,000	35
Cellular telephones	1998	subscribers	4,056	0.4
Internet	1998	users	25,000	2.2

Education and health

Educational attainment (1981). Percentage of population age 25 and over having: no formal schooling or some primary education 39.6%; completed primary 26.6%; secondary 29.6%; higher 4.2%. *Literacy* (1995): total population age 15 and over literate 95.7%; males 96.2%; females 95.3%.

Education (1996–97)

	schools	teachers	students	student/ teacher ratio
Primary (age 6–11)	9,864	78,625	1,028,880	13.0
Secondary (age 12–17)	2,175[7]	71,025	778,028	11.0
Voc., teacher tr.	618[7]	27,267[8]	244,253[8]	9.0[8]
Higher	35[7]	22,967[8]	104,595	...

Health (1998): physicians 63,554 (1 per 175 persons); hospital beds 80,684 (1 per 123 persons); infant mortality rate per 1,000 live births (1999) 6.4.
Food (1998): daily per capita caloric intake 2,473 (vegetable products 88%, animal products 12%); 107% of FAO recommended minimum requirement.

Military

Total active duty personnel (1999): 60,000 (army 75.0%, navy 8.3%, air force 16.7%). *Military expenditure as percentage of GDP* (1997): 2.3% (world 2.6%); per capita expenditure: U.S.$65.

[1]July 1. [2]Province coextensive with the city of Havana. [3]Province bordering the city of Havana on the east, south, and west. [4]State sector only; excludes military and unemployed. [5]At constant 1981 prices. [6]Imports c.i.f.; exports f.o.b. [7]1989–90. [8]1995–96.

Internet resources for further information:

- **CubaNet http://www.cubanet.org**
- **República de Cuba: Ministerio de Salud Pública http://www3.itu.int/missions/Cuba/ANUARIO98/Portada.htm**
- **Cuba: the Web Site of the Government of the Republic of Cuba http://cubagov.cu**

Cyprus

Island of Cyprus

Area: 3,572 sq mi, 9,251 sq km.
Population (2000): 865,000[1].

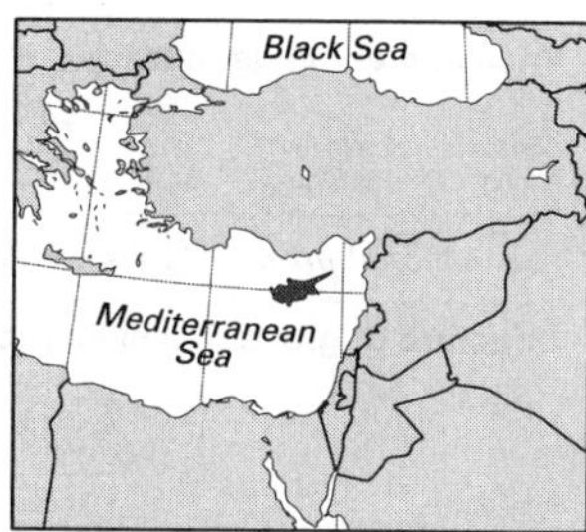

Two de facto states currently exist on the island of Cyprus: the Republic of Cyprus (ROC), predominantly Greek in character, occupying the southern two-thirds of the island, which is the original and still the internationally recognized de jure government of the whole island; and the Turkish Republic of Northern Cyprus (TRNC), proclaimed unilaterally Nov. 15, 1983, on territory originally secured for the Turkish Cypriot population by the July 20, 1974, intervention of Turkey. Only Turkey recognizes the TRNC, and the two ethnic communities have failed to reestablish a single state. Provision of separate data below does not imply recognition of either state's claims but is necessitated by the continuing lack of unified data.

Republic of Cyprus

Official name: Kipriakí Dimokratía (Greek); Kıbrıs Cumhuriyeti (Turkish) (Republic of Cyprus).
Form of government: unitary multiparty republic with a unicameral legislature (House of Representatives [80[2]]).
Head of state and government: President.
Capital: Lefkosia (Nicosia).
Official languages: Greek; Turkish.
Monetary unit: 1 Cyprus pound (£C) = 100 cents; valuation (Oct. 6, 2000) 1 £C = U.S.$1.52 = £1.05.

Demography

Area[3]: 2,276 sq mi, 5,896 sq km.
Population (2000): 673,000[4].
Urban-rural (1998[5]): urban 68.9%; rural 31.1%.
Age breakdown (1998[5]): under 15, 24.2%; 15–29, 21.5%; 30–44, 22.3%; 45–59, 16.8%; 60–74, 10.5%; 75 and over, 4.7%.
Ethnic composition (1992): Greek Cypriot 95.1%; British 0.8%; other 4.1%.
Religious affiliation (1995): Orthodox 96.3%, of which Greek Orthodox 93.4%, Armenian Apostolic 2.9%; Roman Catholic 1.5%; other 2.2%.
Urban areas (1998[5]): Lefkosia 194,100[6]; Limassol 152,900; Larnaca 68,000.

Vital statistics

Birth rate per 1,000 population (1998): 13.4 (world avg. 22.1).
Death rate per 1,000 population (1998): 8.2 (world avg. 8.9).
Natural increase rate per 1,000 population (1998): 5.2 (world avg. 13.2).
Life expectancy at birth (1997): male 75.0 years; female 80.0 years.

National economy

Budget (1998). Revenue: £C 1,473,900,000 (income taxes 19.7%, value-added taxes 15.3%, social security contributions 14.9%). Expenditures: £C 1,731,-500,000 (current expenditures 89.7%, development expenditures 10.3%).
Tourism (1998): receipts U.S.$1,718,000,000; expenditures U.S.$410,000,000.
Household expenditure (1994): food and beverages 23.0%, transportation and communications 14.5%, expenditures in cafes and hotels 14.5%.
Gross national product (at current market prices; 1998): U.S.$8,983,000,000 (U.S.$11,920 per capita).

Structure of gross domestic product and labour force

	1998			
	in value £C '000,000	% of total value	labour force	% of labour force
Agriculture, fishing	204.6	4.4	29,000	9.3
Mining	13.0	0.3	600	0.2
Manufacturing	508.0	10.9	40,200	13.0
Construction	357.0	7.7	24,500	7.9
Public utilities	99.9	2.1	1,600	0.5
Transportation and communications	393.3	8.5	19,600	6.3
Trade	911.2	19.6	77,800	25.0
Finance, insurance	890.2	19.1	24,600	7.9
Pub. admin., defense	635.6	13.7	71,100	22.9
Services	400.9	8.6		
Other	236.4	5.1	21,800[7]	7.0[7]
TOTAL	4,650.1	100.0	310,800	100.0

Production. Agriculture (in '000 metric tons; 1997): grapes 101.0, potatoes 81.5, oranges 50.5, grapefruit 47.0, tomatoes 34.0, lemons 23.0. Manufacturing (value added in £C '000,000; 1996): food 84.7; cement, bricks, and tiles 48.2; wearing apparel 38.0; beverages 37.4; fabricated metal products 34.8. Energy production: electricity (kW-hr; 1997) 2,712,000,000.

Foreign trade[8]

Imports (1998): £C 1,904,700,000 (consumer goods 34.2%; transport equipment 12.9%; capital goods 11.2%; mineral fuels 6.6%). *Major import sources:* U.S. 12.5%; U.K. 11.3%; Italy 9.4%; Germany 8.5%; Greece 8.2%.
Exports (1998): £C 551,134,000 (reexports 55.6%[9]; domestic exports 38.7%, of which clothing 5.3%, chemicals 5.2%; ships' stores 5.7%). *Major export destinations:* U.K. 14.6%; Russia 10.3%, Greece 9.8%; Lebanon 5.5%; United Arab Emirates 4.9%.

Transport and communications

Transport. Roads (1997): total length 10,654 km (paved 58%). Vehicles (1997): cars 234,976; trucks and buses 108,452. Merchant marine (1992): vessels 1,416; deadweight tonnage 36,198,083. Air transport (1998)[10]: passenger-km 2,711,000,000; metric ton-km cargo 38,158,000; airports (1996) 2.

Communications

Medium	date	unit	number	units per 1,000 persons
Daily newspapers[11]	1996	circulation	84,000	111
Radio[11]	1997	receivers	310,000	406
Television[11]	1997	receivers	248,000	325
Telephones	1998	main lines	404,710	601
Cellular telephones	1998	subscribers	116,429	173
Internet	1998	users	30,000	45

Education and health

Educational attainment (1992). Percentage of population age 25 and over having: no formal schooling 5.1%; higher education 17.0%. *Literacy* (1992): population age 15 and over literate 95.2%; male 97.8%; female 92.8%.

Education (1996–97)

	schools	teachers	students	student/ teacher ratio
Primary (age 6–11)	376	4,159	64,761	15.6
Secondary (age 12–17) Vocational	125	5,757	61,266	10.6
Higher	35	812	9,982	12.3

Health (1997): physicians 1,725 (1 per 379 persons); hospital beds 3,113 (1 per 210 persons); infant mortality rate per 1,000 live births (1998) 7.0.

Internet resources for further information:

- **Central Bank of Cyprus http://www.centralbank.gov.cy**
- **Rep. of Cyprus Statistical Service http://www.pio.gov.cy/dsr**

Turkish Republic of Northern Cyprus

Official name: Kuzey Kıbrıs Türk Cumhuriyeti (Turkish) (Turkish Republic of Northern Cyprus).
Capital: Lefkoşa (Nicosia).
Official language: Turkish.
Monetary unit: 1 Turkish lira (LT) = 100 kurush; valuation (Oct. 6, 2000) 1 U.S.$ = LT 671,175; 1 £ = LT 970,922.
Population (2000): 192,000[1] (Lefkoşa 36,834[12]; Gazimağusa 23,295[12]).
Ethnic composition (1996): Turkish Cypriot/Turkish 96.4%; other 3.6%.

Structure of gross domestic product and labour force

	1998		1995	
	in value LT '000,000,000	% of total value	labour force	% of labour force
Agriculture and fishing	18,076	7.9	17,383	22.6
Mining and manufacturing	17,203	7.5	8,348	10.8
Construction	10,132	4.4	9,584	12.4
Public utilities	10,836	4.7		
Transportation and communications	22,713	9.9	6,510	8.5
Trade, restaurants	36,624	16.0	8,367	10.9
Pub. admin.	49,486	21.6	16,589	21.5
Finance, real estate	25,077	10.9	9,673	12.6
Services	20,514	8.9		
Other	18,823[13]	8.2[13]	567[14]	0.7[14]
TOTAL	229,484	100.0	77,021	100.0

Budget (1998). Revenue: U.S.$406,200,000 (aid from Turkey 33.3%, direct taxes 25.2%, indirect taxes 19.8%, loans 7.3%). Expenditures: U.S.$406,200,000 (investments 13.6%, defense 10.4%, other 76.0%).
Imports (1998): U.S.$390,100,000 (transport equipment 18.6%, prepared foodstuffs 12.3%). *Major import sources:* Turkey 59.3%; U.K. 12.8%.
Exports (1998): U.S.$53,400,000 (ready-made garments 40.2%, citrus fruits 24.0%). *Major export destinations:* Turkey 50.7%; U.K. 30.9%.

Education (1998–99)

	schools	teachers	students	student/ teacher ratio
Primary (age 7–11)	91	1,093	16,773	15.3
Secondary (age 12–17)	30	1,256	13,981	11.1
Vocational	10	363	1,890	5.2
Higher	8	884	21,912	24.8

Health (1998): physicians 451 (1 per 416 persons); hospital beds 1,002 (1 per 187 persons); infant mortality rate per 1,000 live births 5.8.

Internet resources for further information:

- **Turkish Republic of Northern Cyprus http://www.cypnet.com/.ncyprus/root.html**

[1]Includes 70,000 "settlers" from Turkey and 33,000 Turkish military in the TRNC; excludes 3,200 British military in the Sovereign Base Areas (SBA) in the ROC and 1,300 UN peacekeeping forces. [2]Twenty-four seats reserved for Turkish Cypriots are not occupied. [3]Area includes 99 sq mi (256 sq km) of British military SBA and *c.* 107 sq mi (*c.* 278 sq km) of the UN Buffer Zone. [4]Excludes British and UN military forces. [5]January 1. [6]ROC only. [7]Includes 10,400 unemployed. [8]Imports c.i.f.; exports f.o.b. [9]Mainly cigarettes, vehicles, and consumer electronics. [10]Cyprus Airways. [11]Island of Cyprus. [12]1996 census. [13]Import duties. [14]Unemployed.

Czech Republic

Official name: Česká Republika.
Form of government: unitary multiparty republic with two legislative houses (Senate [81]; Chamber of Deputies [200]).
Chief of state: President.
Head of government: Prime Minister.
Capital: Prague.
Official language: Czech.
Official religion: none.
Monetary unit: 1 koruna (Kč) = 100 halura; valuation (Oct. 6, 2000) 1 U.S.$ = 40.98 Kč
1 £ = 59.28 Kč

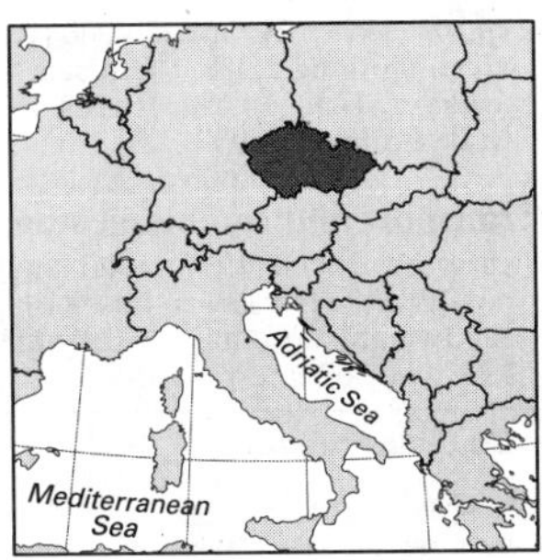

Area and population

Geographic Regions[1]	Principal cities	area sq mi	area sq km	population 1999[2] estimate
Central Bohemia	Prague	4,253	11,014	1,108,465
East Bohemia	Hradec Králové	4,340	11,240	1,233,215
North Bohemia	Ustí nad Labem	3,011	7,799	1,180,325
North Moravia	Ostrava	4,273	11,068	1,964,888
South Bohemia	České Budějovice	4,381	11,346	700,685
South Moravia	Brno	5,802	15,028	2,051,389
West Bohemia	Plzeň	4,199	10,875	857,384
Capital city				
Prague	—	192	496	1,193,270
TOTAL		30,450[3]	78,866	10,289,621

Demography

Population (2000): 10,273,000.
Density (2000): persons per sq mi 337.4, persons per sq km 130.3.
Urban-rural (1999): urban 74.6%; rural 25.4%.
Sex distribution (1998): male 48.64%; female 51.36%.
Age breakdown (1998): under 15, 17.4%; 15–29, 23.5%; 30–44, 20.5%; 45–59, 20.6%; 60–74, 13.0%; 75 and over, 5.0%.
Population projection: (2010) 10,157,000; (2020) 9,891,000.
Doubling time: not applicable; population is declining.
Ethnic composition (1991): Czech 81.2%; Moravian 13.2%; Slovak 3.1%; Polish 0.6%; German 0.5%; Silesian 0.4%; Gypsy 0.3%; Hungarian 0.2%; Ukrainian 0.1%; other 0.4%.
Religious affiliation (1991): Roman Catholic 39.0%; Protestant 4.3%, of which Czechoslovak Brethren Reformed 2.0%, Czechoslovak Hussite 1.7%; other Christian 0.6%; nonreligious/other 39.9%; not stated 16.2%.
Major cities (1998): Prague 1,200,455; Brno 385,866; Ostrava 323,177; Plzeň 169,391; Olomouc 103,890.

Vital statistics

Birth rate per 1,000 population (1999): 9.0 (world avg. 22.1); (1997) legitimate 82.2%; illegitimate 17.8%.
Death rate per 1,000 population (1999): 10.9 (world avg. 8.9).
Natural increase rate per 1,000 population (1999): –1.9 (world avg. 13.2).
Total fertility rate (avg. births per childbearing woman; 1999): 1.2.
Marriage rate per 1,000 population (1997): 5.6.
Divorce rate per 1,000 population (1997): 3.2.
Life expectancy at birth (1999): male 70.8 years; female 78.0 years.
Major causes of death per 100,000 population (1997): diseases of the circulatory system 614.7; malignant neoplasms (cancers) 271.8; accidents, poisoning, and violence 76.2; diseases of the respiratory system 41.9; diseases of the digestive system 39.1; diseases of the genitourinary system 13.2.

National economy

Budget (1997). Revenue: Kč 508,951,000,000 (taxes 56.5%, of which value-added tax 23.1%, excise tax 12.6%, corporate tax 8.2%, personal income tax 6.5%, other taxes 6.1%; social security 37.5%; other revenue 6.0%). Expenditures: Kč 524,668,000,000 (current expenditures 85.6%, of which social security 39.2%, education 11.3%, defense and security 8.2%, capital expenditures 7.5%, transfers to local budgets 6.9%).
Public debt (external, outstanding; 1998): U.S.$12,901,000,000.
Production (metric tons except as noted). Agriculture, forestry, fishing (1999): cereals 6,900,275 (of which wheat 3,955,750, barley 2,227,000, corn [maize] 210,000, rye 206,000), sugar beets 2,580,000, potatoes 1,580,000; livestock (number of live animals) 4,001,000 pigs, 1,657,000 cattle, 27,846,000 chickens; roundwood (1998) 8,447,000 cu m; fish catch (1997) 20,013. Mining and quarrying (1996): limestone 13,100; kaolin 3,320. Manufacturing (value added in U.S.$'000,000; 1995): food products 1,244; nonelectrical machinery 1,152; nonferrous metals 851; iron and steel 813; transport equipment 800; electrical machinery 551. Energy production (consumption): electricity (kW-hr; 1996) 60,977,000,000 (60,974,000,000); coal and lignite (metric tons; 1998) 67,536,000 ([1996] 67,216,000); crude petroleum (barrels; 1996) 1,031,000 (55,833,000); petroleum products (metric tons; 1996) 5,845,000 (6,130,000); natural gas (cu m; 1998) 304,000,000 ([1996] 8,990,000,000).
Household income and expenditure. Average household size (1996) 2.9; income per household (1996) Kč 243,043 (U.S.$8,942); sources of income (1996[3]): wages and salaries 66.7%, transfer payments 27.6%, other 5.7%; expenditure (1996): food and beverages 25.6%, housing and utilities 11.3%, household durable goods 7.3%, clothing and footwear 7.2%, other 48.6%.
Population economically active (1997): total 5,469,500; activity rate of total population 53.0% (participation rates: ages 15–59 [male], 15–54 [female] 77.8%; female 44.0%; [1998] unemployed 6.1%).

Price and earnings indexes (1995 = 100)

	1994	1995	1996	1997	1998	1999
Consumer price index	91.7	100.0	108.8	118.0	130.6	133.4
Annual earnings index	84.4	100.0	118.4	130.8	143.1	155.1

Gross national product (1998): U.S.$53,034,000,000 (U.S.$5,150 per capita).

Structure of gross domestic product and labour force

	1995 in value Kč '000,000	1995 % of total value	1997 labour force	1997 % of labour force
Agriculture	60,500	5.0	284,000	5.2
Mining and manufacturing	340,000	28.1	1,471,900	26.9
Construction	71,600	5.9	470,600	8.6
Public utilities	63,700	5.3	94,900	1.7
Transportation and communications	72,600	6.0	384,700	7.0
Trade	133,700	11.0	822,500	15.0
Finance	116,100	9.6	345,500	6.3
Pub. admin., defense	118,100	9.7	317,500	5.8
Services	183,900	15.2	743,200	13.6
Other	51,800	4.3	534,700[4]	9.8[4]
TOTAL	1,212,000	100.0[3]	5,469,500	100.0[3]

Tourism (1998): receipts from visitors U.S.$3,719,000,000; expenditures by nationals abroad U.S.$1,869,000,000.
Land use (1994): forested 33.3%; meadows and pastures 11.3%; agricultural and under permanent cultivation 43.0%; other 12.4%.

Foreign trade

Balance of trade (current prices)

	1994	1995	1996	1997	1998	1999
Kč '000,000	–35,146	–95,733	–240,148	–139,688	–76,319	–68,124
% of total	3.6%	7.7%	18.0%	8.8%	4.3%	3.5%

Imports (1997): Kč 862,144,000,000 (machinery and transport equipment 38.0%, manufactured goods 19.3%, chemicals 12.2%, fuels and lubricants 8.6%). *Major import sources:* Germany 31.9%; Slovakia 8.4%; Russia 6.8%; Austria 6.1%; Italy 5.5%; Poland 3.2%.
Exports (1997): Kč 722,456,000,000 (machinery and transport equipment 37.7%, manufactured goods 26.8%, miscellaneous manufactured articles 13.7%, chemicals 8.8%, inedible crude materials, except fuel 4.0%, mineral fuels and lubricants 3.8%). *Major export destinations:* Germany 35.7%; Slovakia 12.9%; Austria 6.4%; Poland 5.7%; Italy 3.7%; Russia 3.4%.

Transport and communications

Transport. Railroads (1997): length 9,430 km; passenger-km 7,710,000,000; metric ton-km cargo 22,406,000,000. Roads (1997): total length 125,905 km (paved 44.1%). Vehicles (1997): passenger cars 3,547,745; trucks and buses 402,353. Merchant marine (1993): vessels (oceangoing) 18; total deadweight tonnage 514,126. Air transport (1997): passenger-km 3,522,649,000; metric ton-km 27,233,000; airports (1997) with scheduled flights 2.

Communications

Medium	date	unit	number	units per 1,000 persons
Daily newspapers	1996	circulation	2,620,000	254
Television	1997	receivers	4,600,000	446
Telephones	1997	main lines	3,280,000	318
Cellular telephones	1997	subscribers	526,000	51.1
Personal computers	1997	units	850,000	82.5
Internet	1998	users	400,000	38.9

Education and health

Educational attainment (1991). Percentage of adult population having: no schooling and incomplete primary 31.7%; complete secondary 58.6%; higher 8.5%. *Literacy* (1990): total population age 15 and over literate 8,170,442 (100%); males literate 3,914,080 (100%); females literate 4,256,362 (100%).

Education (1997–98)

	schools	teachers	students	student/ teacher ratio
Primary (age 6–14)	4,132	65,259	1,092,476	16.7
Secondary (age 15–18)	364	10,419	125,885	12.1
Voc., teacher tr.	756	14,989	173,850	11.6
Higher	23	13,216	165,754	12.5

Health (1997): physicians 39,831 (1 per 259 persons); hospital beds 70,457 (1 per 146 persons; (1997) infant mortality rate per 1,000 live births 5.9.
Food (1997): daily per capita caloric intake 3,244 (vegetable products 75%, animal products 25%); 131% of FAO recommended minimum requirement.

Military

Total active duty personnel (1998): 40,300 (army 62.8%, air force 37.2%). *Military expenditure as percentage of GNP* (1997): 1.9% (world 2.6%); per capita expenditure: U.S.$193.

[1]Elections for new administrative breakdown of 14 regions (including the city of Prague) took place in November 2000. [2]January 1. [3]Detail does not add to total given because of rounding. [4]Includes 204,000 employed with second job, 188,300 people with disabilities, and 16,400 nondistributable.

Internet resources for further information:
- **Czech Statistical Office http://www.czso.cz**

Denmark

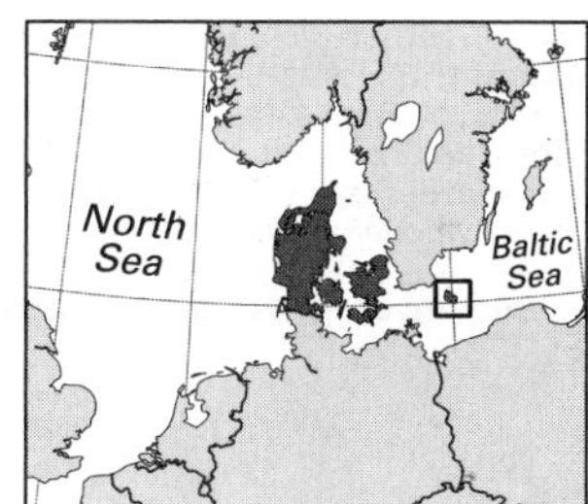

Official name: Kongeriget Danmark (Kingdom of Denmark).
Form of government: parliamentary state and constitutional monarchy with one legislative house (Folketing [179]).
Chief of state: Danish Monarch.
Head of government: Prime Minister.
Capital: Copenhagen.
Official language: Danish.
Official religion: Evangelical Lutheran.
Monetary unit: 1 Danish krone (Dkr; plural kroner) = 100 øre; valuation (Oct. 6, 2000) 1 U.S.$ = Dkr 8.57; 1 £ = Dkr 12.39.

Area and population[1]

		area		population
Counties	**Capitals**	sq mi	sq km	1997[2] estimate
Århus	Århus	1,761	4,561	628,725
Bornholm	Rønne	227	588	45,018
Frederiksborg	Hillerød	520	1,347	356,854
Fyn	Odense	1,346	3,486	471,422
København	—	203	526	609,123
Nordjylland	Ålborg	2,383	6,173	492,155
Ribe	Ribe	1,209	3,132	223,335
Ringkøbing	Ringkøbing	1,874	4,854	271,483
Roskilde	Roskilde	344	891	226,683
Sønderjylland	Åbenrå	1,521	3,939	253,639
Storstrøm	Nykøbing Falster	1,312	3,398	257,776
Vejle	Vejle	1,157	2,997	342,597
Vestsjælland	Sorø	1,152	2,984	290,793
Viborg	Viborg	1,592	4,122	232,630
Municipalities				
Copenhagen (København)	—	34	88	483,658
Frederiksberg	—	3	9	89,230
TOTAL		16,639[3]	43,096[3]	5,275,121

Demography

Population (2000): 5,339,000.
Density (2000): persons per sq mi 320.9, persons per sq km 123.9.
Urban-rural (1999): urban 85.0%; rural 15.0%.
Sex distribution (1999[2]): male 49.41%; female 50.59%.
Age breakdown (1999[2]): under 15, 18.2%; 15–29, 19.2%; 30–44, 22.4%; 45–59, 20.5%; 60–74, 12.6%; 75 and over, 7.1%.
Population projection: (2010) 5,513,000; (2020) 5,676,000.
Doubling time: not applicable; population is stable.
Ethnic composition (1998[2])[4]: Danish 95.3%; Asian 1.7%, of which Turkish 0.7%; residents of former Yugoslavia 0.6%; other Scandinavian 0.6%; African 0.4%; other 1.4%.
Religious affiliation (1995): Evangelical Lutheran 87.0%; other Christian 1.7%; Muslim 1.5%; other/nonreligious 9.8%.
Major urban areas (1998): Greater Copenhagen 1,379,413; Århus 487,969; Odense 145,296; Ålborg 119,157; Frederiksberg 89,230[5, 6].

Vital statistics

Birth rate per 1,000 population (1999): 12.3 (world avg. 22.1); (1995) legitimate 53.5%; illegitimate 46.5%.
Death rate per 1,000 population (1999): 11.0 (world avg. 8.9).
Natural increase rate per 1,000 population (1999): 1.3 (world avg. 13.2).
Total fertility rate (avg. births per childbearing woman; 1999): 1.7.
Marriage rate per 1,000 population (1997): 6.5.
Divorce rate per 1,000 population (1997): 2.4.
Life expectancy at birth (1999): male 74.0 years; female 79.1 years.
Major causes of death per 100,000 population (1995): malignant neoplasms (cancers) 296.6; ischemic heart disease 242.3; cerebrovascular disease 105.9.

National economy

Budget (1997)[7]. Revenue: Dkr 612,077,000,000 (direct taxes 52.2%, indirect taxes 30.7%). Expenditures: Dkr 626,536,000,000 (social security assistance 31.8%, education 12.2%, welfare services 10.1%, health 8.4%, defense 2.8%).
National debt (end of year; 1996): Dkr 664,128,000,000.
Tourism (1998): receipts U.S.$3,211,000,000; expenditures U.S.$4,462,000,000.
Population economically active (1997): total 2,863,330; activity rate of total population 54.5% (participation rates: ages 15–64 [1996] 79.1%; female 46.1%; unemployed [1997] 6.8%).

Price and earnings indexes (1995 = 100)

	1993	1994	1995	1996	1997	1998	1999
Consumer price index	96.0	98.0	100.0	102.1	104.4	106.3	108.9
Hourly earnings index	92.7	96.7	100.0	...	...	...	...

Household income and expenditure. Average household size (1997) 2.2; income per household (1988) Dkr 199,354 (U.S.$29,613); expenditure (1993): housing 22.9%, food and beverages 17.9%, transportation and communications 15.5%, recreation 8.3%, household furnishings 6.1%, energy 6.1%.
Production (in Dkr '000,000 except as noted). Agriculture, forestry, fishing (value added; 1996): pork 17,574, milk 11,322, beef 3,125, wheat 3,091, barley 2,498, flowers and plants 2,622, mink furs 1,676; roundwood (1997) 2,135,000 cu m; fish catch (1997) 1,826,852 metric tons. Mining and quarrying (1994): sand and gravel 24,829,000 cu m; chalk 3,522,000 cu m. Manufacturing (value added; 1994): food products 38,325, of which meat 11,170; nonelectrical machinery and apparatus 23,331; chemicals and chemical products 18,504; electrical machinery and apparatus 14,428; printing and publishing 9,649; fabricated metals 9,479. Construction (completed; 1995): residential 1,375,000 sq m; nonresidential 3,573,000 sq m. Energy production (consumption): electricity (kW-hr; 1999) 38,604,000,000 ([1996] 39,582,000,000); coal (metric tons; 1996) none (10,948,000); crude petroleum (barrels; 1999) 112,843,000 ([1996] 80,374,000); petroleum products (metric tons; 1996) 10,426,000 (7,730,000); natural gas (cu m) 7,540,000,000 ([1996] 4,185,000,000).
Gross national product (1998): U.S.$175,160,000,000 (U.S.$33,040 per capita).

Structure of gross domestic product and labour force

	1996		1997	
	in value Dkr '000,000[8]	% of total value[8]	labour force	% of labour force
Agriculture, fishing	35,741	4.1	120,100	4.2
Mining	9,959	1.2		
Manufacturing	169,138	19.6	475,200	16.6
Construction	50,210	5.8	157,500	5.5
Public utilities	17,082	2.0	18,700	0.7
Transp. and commun.	78,141	9.1	178,900	6.3
Trade, restaurants	113,965	13.2	477,900	16.7
Finance, real estate	162,799	18.9	296,300	10.3
Pub. admin., defense	193,419	22.4	931,700	32.5
Services	56,461	6.5		
Other	–24,251[9]	–2.8[9]	207,300[10]	7.2[10]
TOTAL	862,666[3]	100.0	2,863,300[3]	100.0

Land use (1994): forested 10.5%; meadows and pastures 7.5%; agricultural and under permanent cultivation 55.9%; other 26.1%.

Foreign trade[11]

Balance of trade (current prices)

	1994	1995	1996	1997	1998	1999
Dkr '000,000	+41,596	+26,171	+32,889	+24,353	+13,776	+30,911
% of total	8.6%	4.9%	6.0%	4.0%	2.2%	4.8%

Imports (1997): Dkr 293,522,100,000 (machinery and apparatus 22.7, chemicals and chemical products 10.7%, food and live animals 10.3%, transport equipment and parts 7.9%). *Major import sources:* Germany 21.5%; Sweden 12.7%; The Netherlands 7.8%; U.K. 7.5%; Norway 5.3%; France 5.3[12].
Exports (1997): Dkr 321,185,400,000 (machinery and apparatus 23.3%, food and live animals 22.0%, pharmaceuticals 4.9%, mineral fuels and lubricants 4.7%, furniture 4.0%). *Major export destinations:* Germany 21.2%; Sweden 11.3%; U.K. 9.7%; Norway 6.2%; France 5.2%[12].

Transport and communications

Transport. Railroads (1998): route length 2,743 km; passenger-km 4,988,000,000[13]; metric ton-km cargo 1,619,000,000[13]. Roads (1998): total length 71,437 km (paved 100%). Vehicles (1998): passenger cars 1,782,369; trucks and buses 349,734. Air transport (1996)[14]: passenger-km 5,376,000,000; metric ton-km cargo 170,768,000; airports (1996) with scheduled flights 13.

Communications

Medium	date	unit	number	units per 1,000 persons
Daily newspapers	1996	circulation	1,628,000	309
Radio	1997	receivers	6,020,000	1,145
Television	1997	receivers	3,000,000	569
Telephones	1998	main lines	3,496,000	659
Cellular telephones	1998	subscribers	1,931,000	364
Personal computers	1998	units	2,000,000	377
Internet	1998	users	1,000,000	189

Education and health

Educational attainment (1996). Percentage of population age 25–69 having: completed lower secondary or not stated 39.4%; completed upper secondary or vocational 40.5%; advanced vocational 6.1%; undergraduate 9.1%; graduate 4.9%. *Literacy:* virtually 100%.

Education (1995–96)

	schools	teachers	students	student/ teacher ratio
Primary/lower secondary (age 7–15)	2,522	58,500[15]	606,488	10.4[15]
Upper secondary (age 16–18)	151	11,000[15]	73,436	6.8[15]
Vocational	242	12,000[15]	171,664	13.6[15]
Higher	167	8,000[15]	160,675	19.5[15]

Health (1996): physicians (1994) 14,497 (1 per 358 persons); hospital beds 24,966 (1 per 210 persons); (1999) infant mortality rate per 1,000 live births 5.1.
Food (1997): daily per capita caloric intake 3,407 (vegetable products 63%, animal products 37%); 127% of FAO recommended minimum requirement.

Military

Total active duty personnel (1998): 32,100 (army 71.3%, navy 11.5%, air force 17.1%). *Military expenditure as percentage of GNP* (1997): 1.8% (world 2.6%); per capita expenditure U.S.$529.

[1]Excludes the Faroe Islands and Greenland. [2]January 1. [3]Detail does not add to total given because of rounding. [4]Based on nationality. [5]Within Greater Copenhagen. [6]1997. [7]Includes both central and local governments. [8]At factor cost. [9]Imputed bank service charges. [10]Includes 13,300 not adequately defined and 194,000 unemployed. [11]Imports c.i.f., exports f.o.b. [12]Includes Monaco. [13]1997. [14]Danish share of Scandinavian Airlines System (scheduled air service only) and Maersk Air. [15]1993–94.

Internet resources for further information:
- **Statistics Denmark http://www2.dst.dk/internet/startuk.htm**

Djibouti

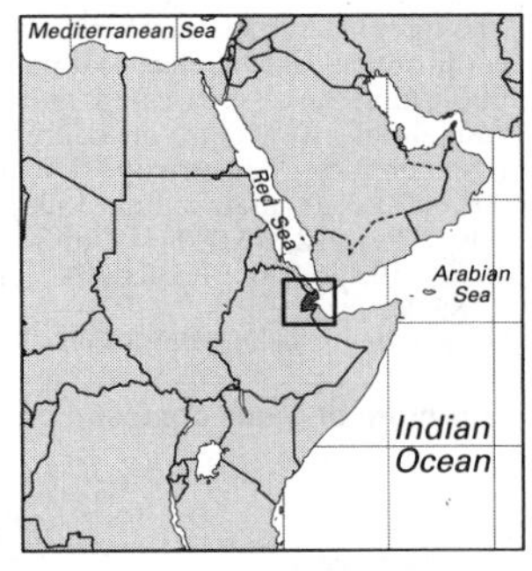

Official name: Jumhūrīyah Jībūtī (Arabic); République de Djibouti (French) (Republic of Djibouti).
Form of government: multiparty republic with one legislative house (National Assembly [65]).
Head of state and government: President.
Capital: Djibouti.
Official languages: Arabic; French.
Official religion: none.
Monetary unit: 1 Djibouti franc (DF) = 100 centimes; valuation (Oct. 6, 2000) 1 U.S.$ = DF 173.90; 1 £ = DF 251.41.

Area and population

		area[1]		population
Districts	Capitals	sq mi	sq km	1982 estimate
ʿAlī Sabīḥ (Ali-Sabieh)	ʿAlī Sabīḥ	925	2,400	15,000
Dikhil	Dikhil	2,775	7,200	30,000
Djibouti	Djibouti	225	600	200,000
Obock	Obock	2,200	5,700	15,000
Tadjoura (Tadjourah)	Tadjoura	2,825	7,300	30,000
TOTAL		8,950	23,200	335,000[2]

Demography

Population (2000): 451,000.
Density (2000): persons per sq mi 50.4, persons per sq km 19.4.
Urban-rural (1999): urban 83.1%; rural 16.9%.
Sex distribution (1999): male 51.66%; female 48.34%.
Age breakdown (1999): under 15, 47.5%; 15–29, 28.9%; 30–44, 13.1%; 45–59, 5.2%; 60–74, 4.7%; 75 and over, 0.6%.
Population projection: (2010) 579,000; (2020) 729,000.
Doubling time: 27 years.
Ethnic composition (1983): Somali 61.7%, of which Issa 33.4%, Gadaboursi 15.0%, Issaq 13.3%; Afar 20.0%; Arab (mostly Yemeni) 6.0%; European 4.0%; other (refugees) 8.3%.
Religious affiliation (1995): Sunnī Muslim 97.2%; Christian 2.8%, of which Roman Catholic 2.2%, Orthodox 0.5%, Protestant 0.1%.
Major city and towns (1989): Djibouti 383,000[3]; ʿAlī Sabīḥ 4,000; Tadjoura 3,500; Dikhil 3,000.

Vital statistics

Birth rate per 1,000 population (1999): 41.2 (world avg. 22.1).
Death rate per 1,000 population (1999): 15.1 (world avg. 8.9).
Natural increase rate per 1,000 population (1999): 26.1 (world avg. 13.2).
Total fertility rate (avg. births per childbearing woman; 1999): 5.9.
Marriage rate per 1,000 population (1982): 6.7.
Divorce rate per 1,000 population (1982): 1.9.
Life expectancy at birth (1999): male 48.7 years; female 52.3 years.
Major causes of death (percentage of total deaths [infants and children to age 10, district of Djibouti only]; 1984): diarrhea and acute dehydration 16.0%; malnutrition 16.0%; poisoning 11.0%; tuberculosis 6.0%; acute respiratory disease 6.0%; malaria 6.0%; anemia 6.0%; heart disease 2.0%; kidney disease 1.0%; other ailments 19.0%; no diagnosis 11.0%.

National economy

Budget (1998)[4]. Revenue: DF 23,154,000,000 (tax revenue 87.5%, of which domestic consumption taxes 27.1%, wages and salary tax 13.7%, surcharge on khat 8.9%, income and profit tax 6.1%; nontax revenue 12.5%). Expenditures: DF 30,427,000,000 (current expenditures 80.0%, of which general administration 26.7%, defense and mobilization 20.0%, education 8.7%, health 5.4%; capital expenditures 20.0%).
Tourism (1995): receipts from visitors U.S.$4,000,000; expenditures by nationals abroad U.S.$4,000,000.
Production (metric tons except as noted). Agriculture, forestry, fishing (1999): vegetables and melons 22,390, of which tomatoes 1,000, eggplant 45; livestock (number of live animals) 511,000 goats, 463,000 sheep, 269,000 cattle, 66,000 camels, 8,500 asses; roundwood, n.a.; fish catch (1998) 350. Mining and quarrying: mineral production limited to locally used construction materials and evaporated salt. Manufacturing (1999): structural detail, n.a.; main products include furniture, nonalcoholic beverages, meat and hides, light electromechanical goods, and mineral water. Construction (1989): 53,900 sq m. Energy production (consumption): electricity (kW-hr; 1996) 185,000,000 (185,000,000); firewood and charcoal, n.a. (n.a.); coal, none (n.a.); crude petroleum, none (n.a.); petroleum products (metric tons; 1996) none (119,000); natural gas, none (n.a.); geothermal, wind, and solar resources are substantial but largely undeveloped.
Population economically active (1991): total 282,000; activity rate of total population 61.5% (participation rates: over age 10, 70.4%; female 40.8%; unemployed [1987] *c.* 40–50%).

Price and earnings indexes (1990 = 100)

	1990	1991	1992	1993	1994	1995	1996
Consumer price index[5]	100.0	106.8	110.4	115.3	122.8	128.8	134.2
Earnings index	...	...	...	...	...	...	....

Household income and expenditure. Average household size (1985)[6] 7.2; income per household: n.a.; sources of income (1976): wages and salaries 51.6%, self-employment 36.0%, transfer payments 10.5%, other 1.9%; expenditure (expatriate households; 1984): food 50.3%, energy 13.1%, recreation 10.4%, housing 6.4%, clothing 1.7%, personal effects 1.4%, health care 1.0%, household goods 0.3%, other 15.4%.
Public debt (external, outstanding; 1998): U.S.$263,800,000.
Gross national product (1996): U.S.$485,000,000 (U.S.$790 per capita).

Structure of gross domestic product and labour force

	1998		1991	
	in value DF '000,000	% of total value	labour force	% of labour force
Agriculture	2,917	3.2	212,000	75.2
Mining	—	—		
Manufacturing	4,239	4.6	31,000	11.0
Construction	6,971	7.6		
Public utilities	4,850	5.3		
Transp. and commun.	15,824	17.4	39,000	13.8
Trade	14,481	15.9		
Finance	8,772	9.6		
Pub. admin., defense	18,469	20.3		
Services	4,340	4.8		
Other	10,335	11.3	...	...
TOTAL	91,198	100.0	282,000	100.0

Land use (1994): forested 0.9%; meadows and pastures 56.1%; agricultural and under permanent cultivation[7]; built-on, wasteland, and other 43.0%.

Foreign trade

Balance of trade (current prices)

	1993	1994	1995	1996	1997	1998
U.S.$'000,000	−183.9	−180.7	−169.2	−161.1	−161.4	−179.7
% of total	56.4%	61.6%	69.0%	67.0%	65.3%	60.3%

Imports (1998): U.S.$238,800,000 (food, beverages, khat, and tobacco 53.2%; petroleum products 12.4%; machinery and electric appliances 10.9%; base metals and base metal products 4.9%; chemical products 4.6%; transport equipment 4.3%; clothing and footwear 3.7%). *Major import sources:* France 12.5%; Ethiopia 12.0%; Italy 9.2%; U.K. 6.2%; Saudi Arabia 5.7%; Japan 4.2%.
Exports (1998): U.S.$59,100,000,000 (1992; unspecified special transactions 60.0%; live animals [including camels] 21.3%; basic manufactures 5.2%; crude materials 4.5%). *Major export destinations:* Somalia 53.0%; Yemen 22.5%; Ethiopia 5.0%; Saudi Arabia 0.7%.

Transport and communications

Transport. Railroads (1997): length (1989) 66 mi, 106 km; passenger-mi 361,000,000, passenger-km 762,000,000; short ton-mile cargo 144,000,000, metric ton-km cargo 232,000,000. Roads (1996): total length 1,796 mi, 2,890 km (paved 13%). Vehicles (1996): passenger cars 9,200; trucks and buses 2,040. Merchant marine (1992): vessels (100 gross tons and over) 10; total deadweight tonnage 4,090. Air transport (1997): passengers handled 107,369; metric tons of freight handled 7,290; airports (1998) with scheduled flights 1.

Communications

Medium	date	unit	number	units per 1,000 persons
Daily newspapers	1995	circulation	500	0.8
Radio	1997	receivers	52,000	84
Television	1997	receivers	28,000	45
Telephones	1998	main lines	7,932	12.7
Cellular telephones	1998	subscribers	220	0.3
Internet	1998	users	400	0.9

Education and health

Educational attainment: n.a. *Literacy* (1995): percentage of population age 15 and over literate 46.2%; males literate 60.3%; females literate 32.7%.

Education (1996–97)

	schools	teachers	students	student/ teacher ratio
Primary (age 6–11)	81[8]	1,005[8]	33,960	...
Secondary (age 12–18) / Voc., teacher tr.	26[9]	628[8]	11,628	...
Higher	1[9]	13[9]	130[8]	...

Health (1996): physicians 60 (1 per 7,100 persons); hospital beds[10] (1989) 1,383 (1 per 369 persons); infant mortality rate per 1,000 live births (1999) 105.2.
Food (1998): daily per capita caloric intake 2,074 (vegetable products 90%, animal products 10%); 89% of FAO recommended minimum requirement.

Military

Total active duty personnel (1999): 9,600[11] (army 83.3%, navy 2.1%, air force 2.1%, paramilitary 12.5%). *Military expenditure as percentage of GNP* (1997): 4.1% (world 2.6%); per capita expenditure U.S.$47.

[1]Original figures are those given in sq km; sq mi equivalent is rounded to appropriate level of generality. [2]Includes 45,000 persons not distributed by district. [3]1995 estimate. [4]Preliminary. [5]Based on expatriates' expenditures. [6]City of Djibouti only. [7]In 1988–89 only 1,005 acres (407 hectares) of land were cultivated. [8]1995–96. [9]1991. [10]Public health facilities only. [11]Excludes 2,600 French troops.

Dominica

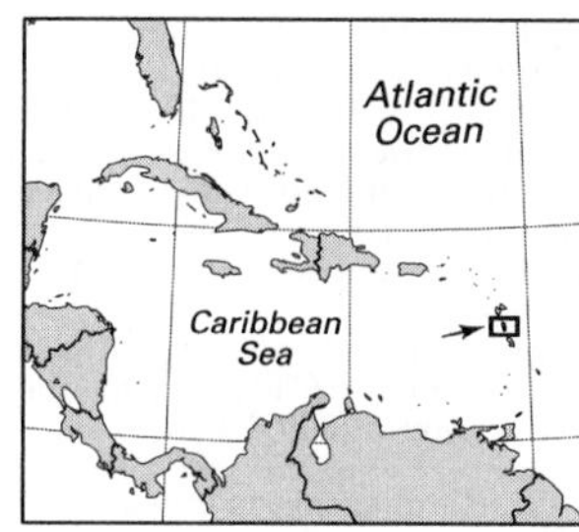

Official name: Commonwealth of Dominica.
Form of government: multiparty republic with one legislative house (House of Assembly [32[1]]).
Chief of state: President.
Head of government: Prime Minister.
Capital: Roseau.
Official language: English.
Official religion: none.
Monetary unit: 1 East Caribbean dollar (EC$) = 100 cents; valuation (Oct. 6, 2000) 1 U.S.$ = EC$2.70; 1 £ = EC$3.91.

Area and population

Parishes	area sq mi	area sq km	population 1991 census
St. Andrew	69.3	179.6	11,106
St. David	49.0	126.8	6,977
St. George	20.7	53.5	20,365
St. John	22.5	58.5	4,990
St. Joseph	46.4	120.1	6,183
St. Luke	4.3	11.1	1,552
St. Mark	3.8	9.9	1,943
St. Patrick	32.6	84.4	8,929
St. Paul	26.0	67.4	7,495
St. Peter	10.7	27.7	1,643
TOTAL	285.3[2]	739.0[2]	71,183[3]

Demography

Population (2000): 76,300.
Density (2000): persons per sq mi 267.1; persons per sq km 103.1.
Urban-rural (1998): urban 70%; rural 30%.
Sex distribution (1991): male 49.78%; female 50.22%.
Age breakdown (1991): under 15, 33.3%; 15–29, 28.3%; 30–44, 16.3%; 45–59, 9.7%; 60 and over, 11.8%; unknown, 0.6%.
Population projection: (2010) 79,000; (2020) 81,000.
Doubling time: 62 years.
Ethnic composition (1991): black 89.1%; mixed race 7.2%; Amerindian/Carib 2.4%; white 0.4%; other 0.7%; not stated 0.2%.
Religious affiliation (1991): Roman Catholic 70.1%; six largest Protestant groups 17.2%, of which Seventh-day Adventist 4.6%, Pentecostal 4.3%, Methodist 4.2%; other 8.9%; nonreligious 2.9%; unknown 0.9%.
Major towns (1991): Roseau 15,853; Portsmouth 3,621; Marigot 2,919; Atkinson 2,518; Mahaut 2,372.

Vital statistics

Birth rate per 1,000 population (1999): 18.7 (world avg. 22.1); (1991) legitimate 24.1%; illegitimate 75.9%.
Death rate per 1,000 population (1999): 7.4 (world avg. 8.9).
Natural increase rate per 1,000 population (1999): 11.3 (world avg. 13.2).
Total fertility rate (avg. births per childbearing woman; 1999): 2.1.
Marriage rate per 1,000 population (1996): 3.1.
Divorce rate per 1,000 population (1996): 0.7.
Life expectancy at birth (1999): male 70.3 years; female 76.1 years.
Major causes of death per 100,000 population (1994): diseases of the circulatory system 237.8, of which hypertensive disease 93.8, diseases of pulmonary circulation and other forms of heart disease 72.0; malignant neoplasms (cancers) 125.0; endocrine and metabolic disorders 59.8; infectious and parasitic diseases 46.2; diseases of the respiratory system 38.0.

National economy

Budget (1998–99). Revenue: EC$232,700,000 (tax revenue 73.9%, of which consumption taxes on imports 26.9%, income taxes 20.9%; nontax revenue 14.7%; grants 9.2%). Expenditures: EC$260,300,000 (current expenditures 77.1%; development expenditures 22.9%).
Public debt (external, outstanding; 1998): U.S.$90,900,000.
Land use (1994): forested 66.0%; meadows and pastures 3.0%; agricultural and under permanent cultivation 23.0%; other 8.0%.
Tourism: receipts from visitors (1998) U.S.$42,800,000; expenditures by nationals abroad (1996) U.S.$7,000,000.
Gross national product (at current market prices; 1998): U.S.$230,000,000 (U.S.$3,150 per capita).

Structure of gross domestic product and labour force

	1998 in value EC$'000,000[4]	1998 % of total value[4]	1991 labour force[5]	1991 % of labour force[5]
Agriculture	121.2	20.3	7,344	30.8
Mining	5.3	0.9	65	0.3
Manufacturing	52.5	8.8	1,947	8.2
Construction	46.7	7.8	2,819	11.8
Public utilities	29.9	5.0	304	1.3
Transportation and communications	100.5	16.8	1,202	5.0
Trade, hotels, restaurants	83.2	13.9	3,658	15.4
Finance, real estate	83.9	14.0	810	3.4
Services }	120.8	20.2	3,446	14.5
Pub. admin., defense }			1,520	6.4
Other	–45.5[6]	–7.6[6]	699	2.9
TOTAL	598.4[7]	100.0[7]	23,814	100.0

Population economically active (1991): total 26,364; activity rate of total population 38.0% (participation rates: ages 15–64, 62.4%; female 34.5%; unemployed [1994] 23%).

Price and earnings indexes (1995 = 100)

	1993	1994	1995	1996	1997	1998	1999
Consumer price index	98.7	98.7	100.0	101.7	104.2	105.2	106.2[8]
Earnings index	...	...	...	...	...	...	...

Household income and expenditure. Average household size (1991) 3.6; income per household: n.a.; sources of income: n.a.; expenditure (1984)[9]: food and nonalcoholic beverages 43.1%, housing and utilities 16.1%, transportation 11.6%, clothing and footwear 6.5%, household furnishings 6.0%.
Production (metric tons except as noted). Agriculture, forestry, fishing (1998): bananas 28,640[10], root crops 23,168 (of which dasheens 11,903, yams 7,560, tanias 3,534), plantains 22,236, grapefruit 19,100, coconuts 8,906, oranges 7,230, limes 3,560, mangoes 1,700, pepper 340, bay oil 12; livestock (number of live animals: 1999) 13,400 cattle, 9,700 goats, 7,600 sheep; roundwood, n.a.; fish catch (1997) 855 metric tons. Mining and quarrying: pumice, limestone, and sand and gravel are quarried primarily for local consumption. Manufacturing (value of production in EC$'000; 1998): toilet soap 21,816; laundry soap 16,467; crude coconut oil 1,848; toothpaste 1,662 metric tons; other products include fruit juices, beer, garments, bottled spring water, and cardboard boxes. Energy production (consumption): electricity (kW-hr; 1996) 37,000,000 (37,000,000); coal, none (none); crude petroleum, none (none); petroleum products (metric tons; 1996) none (26,000); natural gas, none (none).

Foreign trade[11]

Balance of trade (current prices)

	1993	1994	1995	1996	1997	1998
EC$'000,000	–121.3	–132.8	–194.9	–222.4	–224.2	–196.8
% of total	31.5%	34.3%	44.4%	43.4%	44.7%	36.6%

Imports (1997): EC$363,200,000 ([12]food, beverages, and tobacco products 22%; machinery 16%; mineral fuels 7%; transport equipment 7%). *Major import sources:* U.S. 38.3%; Trinidad and Tobago 13.9%; U.K. 10.4%; Japan 4.4%; Barbados 3.8%.
Exports (1997): EC$139,000,000 (manufactured exports 50.5%, of which coconut-based laundry and toilet soaps 32.1%; agricultural exports 44.7%, of which bananas 30.1%; reexports 1.9%). *Major export destinations:* U.K. 32.8%; Jamaica 22.3%; Antigua and Barbuda 6.1%; Guadeloupe 5.9%; Barbados 5.6%.

Transport and communications

Transport. Railroads: none. Roads (1996): total length 485 mi, 780 km (paved 50%). Vehicles (1994): passenger cars 6,581; trucks and buses 2,825. Merchant marine (1992): vessels (100 gross tons and over) 7; total deadweight tonnage 3,153. Air transport: (1991) passenger arrivals 43,312, passenger departures, n.a.; (1997) cargo unloaded 575 metric tons, cargo loaded 363 metric tons; airports (1996) with scheduled flights 2.

Communications

Medium	date	unit	number	units per 1,000 persons
Radio	1997	receivers	46,000	608
Television	1997	receivers	6,000	79
Telephones	1996	main lines	18,737	250
Cellular telephones	1998	subscribers	650	8.6

Education and health

Educational attainment (1991). Percentage of population age 25 and over having: no formal schooling 4.2%; primary education 78.4%; secondary 11.0%; higher vocational 2.3%; university 2.8%; other/unknown 1.3%. *Literacy* (1994): total population age 15 and over literate, *c.* 44,000 (90.0%).

Education (1997–98)

	schools	teachers	students	student/teacher ratio
Primary	63	587	13,636	23.2
Secondary	15	293	5,455	18.6
Higher[13]	2	34	484	14.2

Health (1998): physicians 38 (1 per 2,007 persons); hospital beds 262 (1 per 291 persons); infant mortality rate per 1,000 live births (1999) 17.7.
Food (1997): daily per capita caloric intake 3,059 (vegetable products 78%, animal products 22%); 126% of FAO recommended minimum requirement.

Military

Total active duty personnel (1997): none[14].

[1]Includes 22 seats that are elective (including speaker if elected from outside of the House of Assembly) and 10 seats that are nonelective (including 9 appointees of the president and the attorney general serving ex officio). [2]Area breakdown by parish is based on 1961 survey. Total area of Dominica per more recent survey is 290 sq mi (750 sq km). [3]Includes institutionalized population of 1,717. [4]At current factor cost. [5]Employed persons only. [6]Less imputed banking service charge. [7]Detail does not add to total given because of rounding. [8]Average of 2nd and 3rd quarters. [9]Weights of consumer price index components. [10]Export production only. [11]Imports c.i.f.; exports f.o.b. [12]Estimated figures. [13]1992–93. [14]300-member police force includes a coast guard unit.

Internet resources for further information:
- **Eastern Caribbean Central Bank**
  http://www.eccb-centralbank.org

Dominican Republic

Official name: República Dominicana (Dominican Republic).
Form of government: multiparty republic with two legislative houses (Senate [30]; Chamber of Deputies [149]).
Head of state and government: President.
Capital: Santo Domingo.
Official language: Spanish.
Official religion: none[1].
Monetary unit: 1 Dominican peso (RD$) = 100 centavos; valuation (Oct. 6, 2000) 1 U.S.$ = RD$16.00; 1 £ = RD$23.14.

Area and population

Provinces	area sq km	population 1993 census	Provinces	area sq km	population 1993 census
Azua	2,532	199,684	Monte Cristi	1,925	95,705
Baoruco	1,283	105,206	Monte Plata	2,633	167,148
Barahona	1,739	64,835	Pedernales	2,077	18,054
Dajabón	1,021	68,606	Peravia	1,648	201,851
Duarte	1,605	281,879	Puerto Plata	1,857	261,485
Elías Piña	1,424	64,641	Salcedo	440	101,810
El Seíbo	1,786	96,770	Samaná	854	75,253
Espaillat	838	202,376	San Cristóbal	1,265	420,820
Hato Mayor	1,329	80,074	San Juan	3,571	252,637
Independencia	2,008	39,541	San Pedro de Macorís	1,255	212,368
La Altagracia	3,010	115,685	Sánchez Ramírez	1,196	163,166
La Romana	654	166,550	Santiago	2,836	710,803
La Vega	2,286	344,721	Santiago Rodríguez	1,112	62,144
María Trinidad Sánchez	1,271	124,957	Santo Domingo[2]	1,401	2,193,046
Monseñor Nouel	992	149,318	Valverde	823	152,257
			TOTAL	48,671[3]	7,293,390

Demography

Population (2000): 8,443,000.
Density (2000): persons per sq mi 449.3, persons per sq km 173.5.
Urban-rural (1993): urban 56.1%; rural 43.9%.
Sex distribution (1993): male 48.69%; female 51.31%.
Age breakdown (1995): under 15, 35.1%; 15–29, 29.0%; 30–44, 19.8%; 45–59, 9.9%; 60–74, 4.9%; 75 and over, 1.3%.
Population projection: (2010) 9,884,000; (2020) 11,378,000.
Doubling time: 34 years.
Ethnic composition (1993): mixed 73%; white 16%; black 11%.
Religious affiliation (1995): Roman Catholic 81.8%; Protestant 6.4%; other Christian 0.6%; other 11.2%.
Major urban centres (1993): Santo Domingo 1,609,966[4]; Santiago 365,463; La Romana 140,204; San Pedro de Macorís 124,735; San Francisco de Macorís 108,485.

Vital statistics

Birth rate per 1,000 population (1999): 25.6 (world avg. 22.1).
Death rate per 1,000 population (1999): 4.8 (world avg. 8.9).
Natural increase rate per 1,000 population (1999): 20.8 (world avg. 13.2).
Total fertility rate (avg. births per childbearing woman; 1999): 3.0.
Marriage rate per 1,000 population (1994): 2.0.
Life expectancy at birth (1999): male 70.9 years; female 75.1 years.
Major causes of death per 100,000 population (1985)[5]: diseases of the circulatory system 165; infectious diseases 85; malignant neoplasms (cancers) 45.

National economy

Budget (1998). Revenue: RD$38,566,000,000 (tax revenue 93.8%, of which taxes on goods and services 47.7%, import duties 27.0%, income taxes 17.9%; nontax revenue 5.3%). Expenditures: RD$41,179,000,000 (current expenditure 72.2%; development expenditure 27.8%).
Public debt (external, outstanding; 1998): U.S.$3,530,000,000.
Gross national product (1998): U.S.$14,629,000,000 (U.S.$1,770 per capita).

Structure of gross domestic product and labour force

	1998		1997	
	in value RD$'000,000	% of total value	labour force	% of labour force
Agriculture	28,171	11.6	529,000	16.7
Mining	4,722	2.0	8,400	0.3
Manufacturing	40,215	16.6	483,300	15.3
Construction	29,307	12.1	153,600	4.9
Public utilities	5,105	2.1	20,300	0.6
Transp. and commun.	28,061	11.6	202,700	6.4
Trade, restaurants	48,063	19.9	647,600	20.5
Finance, real estate	21,172	8.8	34,000	1.1
Pub. admin., defense	18,839	7.8	125,400	4.0
Services }	18,255	7.5	447,500	14.2
Other }			503,700[6]	16.0[6]
TOTAL	241,910	100.0	3,155,500	100.0

Production (metric tons except as noted). Agriculture, forestry, fishing (1998): sugarcane 5,097,000, rice 475,000, bananas 359,000, plantains 341,000, cacao beans 59,000, coffee 57,000, pulses 56,000; livestock (number of live animals) 2,528,000 cattle, 960,000 pigs, 38,000,000 chickens; roundwood (1997) 982,300 cu m; fish catch (1997) 14,536. Mining (1998): nickel (metal content) 25,200; gold 40,700 troy oz. Manufacturing (1998)[7]: cement 1,872,000; refined sugar 105,000; beer 2,990,000 hectolitres; rum 420,000 hectolitres. Energy production (consumption): electricity (kW-hr; 1998) 7,928,000,000 (4,594,000,000); coal (metric tons; 1996) none (128,000); crude petroleum (barrels; 1996) none (17,035,000); petroleum products (metric tons; 1996) 2,147,000 (3,671,000); natural gas, none (none).
Tourism: receipts (1998) U.S.$2,142,000,000; expenditures (1996) U.S.$242,000,000.
Population economically active (1993): total 2,556,225; activity rate of total population 35.0% (participation rates: ages 15–64, 54.3%; female 24.9%; unemployed [1999] 13.8%).

Price and earnings indexes (1995 = 100)

	1993	1994	1995	1996	1997	1998	1999
Consumer price index	82.1	88.9	100.0	105.4	114.1	119.3	125.3[8]
Annual earnings index[9]	83.3	83.3	100.0	100.0	120.0	120.0	...

Household income and expenditure. Average household size (1993) 3.9; average income: n.a.; sources of income: n.a.; expenditure (1980–85): food and beverages 46.0%, housing 10.0%, household goods 8.0%.
Land use (1994): forested 12.4%; meadows and pastures 43.4%; agricultural and under permanent cultivation 30.6%; other 13.6%.

Foreign trade[10]

Balance of trade (current prices)

	1993	1994	1995	1996	1997	1998
U.S.$'000,000	–2,193	–2,256	–2,292	–2,635	–3,175	–4,008
% of total	64.6%	60.5%	56.8%	58.2%	61.0%	69.3%

Imports (1998): U.S.$4,897,000,000[11] (capital goods 22.1%; consumer durables 13.2%; crude petroleum and petroleum products 11.0%). *Major import sources* (1997)[12]: U.S. 56%; Venezuela 23%; Mexico 9%; Japan 4%.
Exports (1998): U.S.$889,000,000[13] (ships' stores 15.8%; ferronickel 15.0%; cacao and cocoa 13.6%; raw sugar 13.2%; raw coffee 7.2%). *Major export destinations* (1997): U.S. 53.9%; Belgium 11.9%; Puerto Rico 7.0%.

Transport and communications

Transport. Railroads (1997)[14]: route length 1,083 mi, 1,743 km. Roads (1996): total length 7,829 mi, 12,600 km (paved 49%). Vehicles (1996): passenger cars 224,000; trucks and buses 151,550. Air transport (1997)[15]: passenger-mi 9,823,000, passenger-km, 15,808,000; short ton-mi cargo 7,962,000, metric ton-km cargo 11,624,000: airports (1997) 7.

Communications

Medium	date	unit	number	units per 1,000 persons
Daily newspapers	1996	circulation	416,000	53
Radio	1997	receivers	1,440,000	179
Television	1997	receivers	770,000	96
Telephones	1998	main lines	763,928	94
Cellular telephones	1998	subscribers	255,912	31

Education and health

Educational attainment. n.a. *Literacy* (1995): total population age 15 and over literate, *c.* 4,164,000 (82.1%); males literate, *c.* 2,118,000 (82.0%); females literate, *c.* 2,046,000 (82.2%).

Education (1994–95)

	schools	teachers	students	student/ teacher ratio
Primary (age 6–13)	4,001	42,135	1,462,722	34.7
Secondary (age 14–17)	...	10,757	240,441	22.4
Voc. teacher tr.	...	1,297	22,795	17.6
Higher[16]	...	9,041	176,995	19.6

Health: physicians (1997) 17,460 (1 per 460 persons); hospital beds (1996) 11,921 (1 per 662 persons); infant mortality rate per 1,000 live births (1999) 37.5.
Food (1997): daily per capita caloric intake 2,288 (vegetable products 85%, animal products 15%); 101% of FAO recommended minimum.

Military

Total active duty personnel (1999): 24,500 (army 61.2%, navy 16.3%, air force 22.5%). *Military expenditure as percentage of GNP* (1997): 1.1% (world 2.6%); per capita expenditure U.S.$21.

[1]Roman Catholicism is the state religion per concordat with Vatican City. [2]National district. [3]Mainland total 48,512 sq km and offshore islands total 159 sq km. [4]Urban population of national district. [5]Projected rates based on about 60% of total deaths. [6]Unemployed. [7]Excludes free-zone sector for reexport (mostly ready-made garments) employing (1998) 195,000. [8]June. [9]Minimum wage for medium-sized businesses in private sector. [10]Excludes free zones. [11]Excludes 1998 imports of free zones equaling U.S.$2,701,000,000. [12]Estimated figures. [13]Excludes 1998 reexports of free zones equaling U.S.$4,100,000,000. [14]Most track is privately owned and serves the sugar industry only. [15]Aerochago and Dominair airlines. [16]1996–97.

Internet resources for further information:
- **Banco Central de la Republica Dominicana**
  http://www.bancentral.gov.do
- **Oficina Nacional de Estadística**
  http://www.estadistica.gov.do

Ecuador

Official name: República del Ecuador (Republic of Ecuador).
Form of government: unitary multiparty republic with one legislative house (National Congress [121]).
Head of state and government: President.
Capital: Quito.
Official language: Spanish[1].
Official religion: none.
Monetary unit[2]: 1 dollar (U.S.$); valuation (Oct. 6, 2000) 1 U.S.$ = £ 0.69; 1 £ = U.S.$1.45.

Area and population

Regions / Provinces	Capitals	area sq mi	area sq km	population 2000 estimate
Amazonica				
Morona-Santiago	Macas	13,100	33,930	143,000
Napo[3]	Tena	9,918	25,690	162,000
Pastaza	Puyo	11,496	29,774	62,000
Sucumbíos	Nueva Loja	7,076	18,327	145,000
Zamora-Chinchipe	Zamora	8,923	23,111	103,000
Costa				
El Oro	Machala	2,259	5,850	560,000
Esmeraldas	Esmeraldas	5,884	15,239	434,000
Guayas	Guayaquil	7,916	20,503	3,421,000
Los Ríos	Babahoyo	2,770	7,175	663,000
Manabí	Portoviejo	7,289	18,879	1,268,000
Insular				
Galápagos	Puerto Baquerizo Moreno	3,093	8,010	17,000
Sierra				
Azuay	Cuenca	3,137	8,125	627,000
Bolívar	Guaranda	1,521	3,940	184,000
Cañar	Azogues	1,205	3,122	217,000
Carchi	Tulcán	1,392	3,605	167,000
Chimborazo	Riobamba	2,536	6,569	425,000
Cotopaxi	Latacunga	2,344	6,072	303,000
Imbabura	Ibarra	1,760	4,559	330,000
Loja	Loja	4,257	11,026	429,000
Pichincha	Quito	4,987	12,915	2,466,000
Tungurahua	Ambato	1,288	3,335	447,000
TOTAL		105,037[4, 5]	272,045[5]	12,646,000[6]

Demography

Population (2000): 12,646,000.
Density (2000): persons per sq mi 120.4, persons per sq km 46.5.
Urban-rural (1998): urban 61.0%; rural 39.0%.
Sex distribution (1998): male 50.23%; female 49.77%.
Age breakdown (1997): under 15, 35.4%; 15–29, 29.1%; 30–59, 28.9%; 60 and over, 6.6%.
Population projection: (2010) 14,899,000; (2020) 16,904,000.
Ethnic composition (1989): Amerindian 40.0%; mestizo 40.0%; white 15.0%; black 5.0%.
Religious affiliation (1995): Roman Catholic 93.4%; other 6.6%.
Major cities (2000): Guayaquil 2,118,000; Quito 1,616,000; Cuenca 278,000; Machala 217,000; Portoviejo 181,000; Ambato 174,000.

Vital statistics

Birth rate per 1,000 population (1999): 22.3[7] (world avg. 22.1).
Death rate per 1,000 population (1999): 5.1[7] (world avg. 8.9).
Natural increase rate per 1,000 population (1999): 11.4[7] (world avg. 13.2).
Total fertility rate (avg. births per childbearing woman; 1999): 2.6.
Marriage rate per 1,000 population (1997): 5.6[6].
Life expectancy at birth (1999): male 69.5 years; female 74.9 years.
Major causes of death per 100,000 population (1995): circulatory diseases 55.1; accidents, poisoning, and violence 29.2; pneumonia 27.2; diabetes mellitus 15.4; neoplasms (cancers) 12.7; parasitic diseases 12.2.

National economy

Budget (1996). Revenue: S/. 10,233,300,000,000 (petroleum revenue 45.9%, indirect taxes 30.9%, direct taxes 11.1%). Expenditures: S/. 11,836,700,000,000 (administration 40.8%, debt service 20.7%, subsidies 7.4%).
Public debt (external, outstanding; 1998): U.S.$12,589,000,000.
Production (metric tons except as noted). Agriculture, forestry, fishing (1999): sugarcane 6,800,000, bananas 4,563,000, rice 1,043,000, corn (maize) 688,000; livestock (live animals) 5,534,000 cattle, 2,892,000 pigs, 2,182,000 sheep, 64,736,000 chickens; roundwood (1998) 11,340,000 cu m; fish catch (1997) 688,297. Mining and quarrying (1994): limestone 1,900,000; gold 7,000 kg. Manufacturing (value added in S/. '000,000; 1996): chemical products 2,364,091; food products 1,779,894; nonmetallic mineral products 453,148; textiles 305,369. Construction (in S/.; 1992)[8]: residential 93,166,704,000; nonresidential 58,102,274,000. Energy production (consumption): electricity (kW-hr; 1996) 9,260,000,000 (9,260,000,000); crude petroleum (barrels; 1996) 137,203,000 (58,373,000); petroleum products (metric tons; 1996) 7,130,000 (5,726,000); natural gas (cu m; 1996) 534,000,000 (534,000,000).
Household income and expenditure. Average household size (1990) 4.1; average annual income per household (1995) S/. 9,825,610 (U.S.$3,830); sources of income (1995): self-employment 70.9%, wages 16.0%, transfer payments 6.7%, other 6.4%; expenditure (1995): food and tobacco 37.9%, transportation and communications 15.0%, clothing 9.2%, household furnishings 6.5%.
Population economically active (1997): total 3,373,810; activity rate of total population 44.9% (participation rates: ages 15 and over, 64.2%; female 39.1%.

Price and earnings indexes (1995 = 100)

	1993	1994	1995	1996	1997	1998	1999
Consumer price index	63.9	81.4	100.0	124.4	162.5	221.1	336.7
Hourly earnings index[9]	46.8	69.2	100.0	135.8	...	...	...

Gross national product (1998): U.S.$18,450,000,000 (U.S.$1,520 per capita).

Structure of gross domestic product and labour force

	1998 in value S/. '000,000[10]	1998 % of total value[10]	1997 labour force	1997 % of labour force
Agriculture	39,342	17.3	520,970	15.4
Mining	30,788	13.5	11,240	0.3
Manufacturing	35,239	15.5	475,280	14.1
Construction	5,837	2.6	185,130	5.5
Public utilities	3,176	1.4	10,230	0.3
Transp. and commun.	14,236	6.2	175,580	5.2
Trade	30,784	13.5	870,900	25.8
Finance	8,083	3.6	138,550	4.1
Pub. admin., defense	15,508	6.8	983,140	29.1
Services	43,166	18.9		
Other	1,519[11]	0.7[11]	2,790[12]	0.1[12]
TOTAL	227,678	100.0	3,373,810	100.0[4]

Tourism (1998): receipts U.S.$291,000,000; expenditures U.S.$241,000,000.

Foreign trade[13]

Balance of trade (current prices)

	1994	1995	1996	1997	1998	1999
U.S.$'000,000	+508.0	+532.4	+1,510.5	+709.5	–809.8	+1,714.1
% of total	7.3%	6.6%	18.3%	7.3%	8.8%	23.8%

Imports (1997): U.S.$4,510,600,000 (machines and transport equipment 35.6%, industrial supplies 34.9%, consumer goods 14.1%, food and live animals 7.6%, mineral fuels 7.6%). *Major import sources:* U.S. 30.5%; Colombia 10.6%; Venezuela 6.7%; Japan 5.8%; Germany 4.2%; Spain 3.6%.
Exports (1997): U.S.$5,214,100,000 (food and live animals 56.6%, of which bananas 25.4%, crustaceans 16.8%; crude petroleum 26.9%). *Major export destinations:* U.S. 38.2%; Colombia 6.8%; Italy 5.2%; Chile 4.6%.

Transport and communications

Transport. Railroads (1995): route length 966 km; passenger-km 47,000,000; metric ton-km cargo 2,592,000. Roads (1997): total length 43,197 km (paved 19%). Vehicles (1996): passenger cars 464,902; trucks and buses 52,630. Air transport (1998): passenger-km 923,822,000; metric ton-km cargo 116,378,000.

Communications

Medium	date	unit	number	units per 1,000 persons
Daily newspapers	1996	circulation	820,000	70
Radio	1997	receivers	4,150,000	348
Television	1997	receivers	1,550,000	130
Telephones	1998	main lines	990,842	81
Cellular telephones	1998	subscribers	242,812	20
Personal computers	1998	units	225,000	18
Internet	1998	users	15,000	1.2

Education and health

Educational attainment (1990). Percentage of population age 25 and over having: no formal schooling 2.2%; incomplete primary 54.3%; primary 28.0%; postsecondary 15.5%. *Literacy* (1995): total population age 15 and over literate 90.1%; males 92.0%; females 88.2%.

Education (1996–97)

	schools	teachers	students	student/ teacher ratio
Primary (age 4–12)	17,367	74,601	1,888,172	25.3
Secondary (age 12–18) / Vocational	2,207[14]	62,630[15]	813,557[15]	13.0[15]
Higher	21[14]	12,856[16]	206,541[16]	16.1[16]

Health (1997): physicians 20,243 (1 per 590 persons); hospital beds 18,510 (1 per 645 persons); infant mortality rate (1999) 30.7.
Food (1997): daily per capita caloric intake 2,679 (vegetable products 82%, animal products 18%); 117% of FAO recommended minimum requirement.

Military

Total active duty personnel (1999): 57,100 (army 87.6%, navy 7.2%, air force 5.2%). *Military expenditure as percentage of GNP* (1997): 4.0% (world 2.6%); per capita expenditure U.S.$62.

[1]Quechua and Shuar are also official languages for the indigenous peoples. [2]The United States dollar became the principal national currency from March 2000 and was formally adopted as the national currency on Sept. 9, 2000; the pegged value of the Sucre (S/.), the former national currency, to the U.S. dollar from March 2000 was S/. 25,000 = 1 U.S.$. [3]Includes Orellana province (pop. 70,000) created in 1998. [4]Detail does not add to total given because of rounding. [5]Includes 884 sq mi (2,289 sq km) in nondelimited areas. [6]Total includes 73,000 persons in nondelimited areas. [7]Excluding nomadic Indian tribes. [8]Authorized construction in Cuenca, Guayaquil, and Quito only. [9]General minimum wage; index used is 1990 = 100. [10]At constant 1975 prices. [11]Minus imputed bank services plus gross import duties. [12]Activities not adequately defined. [13]Import figures are f.o.b. in balance of trade and c.i.f. for commodities and trading partners. [14]1986–87. [15]1992–93. [16]1990–91.

Internet resources for further information:

- **Instituto Nacional de Estadistica y Censos (in Spanish) http://www4.inec.gov.ec**
- **Banco Central del Ecuador http://www.bce.fin.ec**

Egypt

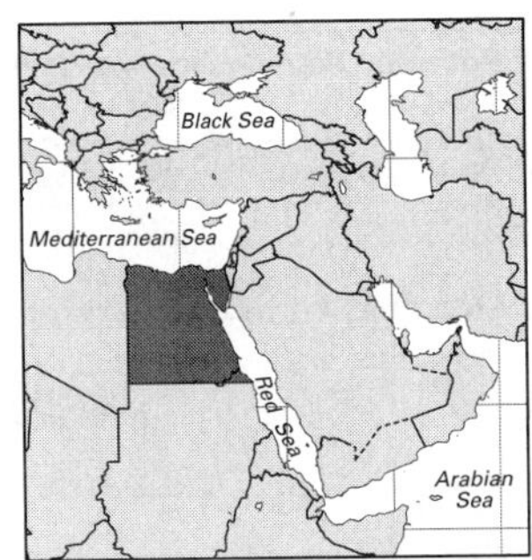

Official name: Jumhūrīyah Miṣr al-ʿArabīyah (Arab Republic of Egypt).
Form of government: republic with one legislative house (People's Assembly [454[1]]).
Chief of state: President.
Head of government: Prime Minister.
Capital: Cairo.
Official language: Arabic.
Official religion: Islam.
Monetary unit: 1 Egyptian pound (£E) = 100 piastres; valuation (Oct. 6, 2000) 1 U.S.$ = £E 3.66; 1 £ = £E 5.30.

Area and population

Regions / Governorates	Capitals	area sq mi	area sq km	population 1996 census
Frontier				
Al-Baḥr al-Aḥmar	Al-Ghurdaqah	78,643	203,685	155,695
Janūb Sīnāʾ	Aṭ-Ṭūr	12,796	33,140	54,495
Maṭrūḥ	Marsā Maṭrūḥ	81,897	212,112	211,866
Shamāl Sīnāʾ	Al-ʿArīsh	10,646	27,574	252,750
Al-Wādī al-Jadīd	Al-Khārijah	145,369	376,505	141,737
Lower Egypt				
Al-Buḥayrah	Damanhūr	3,911	10,130	3,981,209
Ad-Daqahlīyah	Al-Manṣūrah	1,340	3,471	4,223,655
Dumyāṭ	Dumyāṭ	227	589	914,614
Al-Gharbīyah	Ṭanṭā	750	1,942	3,404,827
Al-Ismāʿīlīyah (Ismailia)	—	557	1,442	715,009
Kafr ash-Shaykh	Kafr ash-Shaykh	1,327	3,437	2,222,920
Al-Minūfīyah	Shibīn al-Kawm	592	1,532	2,758,499
Al-Qalyūbīyah	Banhā	387	1,001	3,302,860
Ash-Sharqīyah	Az-Zaqāzīq	1,614	4,180	4,287,848
Upper Egypt				
Aswān	Aswān	262	679	973,671
Asyūṭ	Asyūṭ	600	1,553	2,802,185
Banī Suwayf	Banī Suwayf	510	1,322	1,860,180
Al-Fayyūm	Al-Fayyūm	705	1,827	1,989,881
Al-Jīzah	Al-Jīzah	32,878	85,153	4,779,865
Al-Minyā	Al-Minyā	873	2,262	3,308,875
Qinā	Qinā	715[2]	1,851[2]	2,441,420
Sawhāj	Sawhāj	597	1,547	3,125,000
Urban				
Būr Saʿīd (Port Said)	—	28	72	469,533
Al-Iskandarīyah (Alexandria)	—	1,034	2,679	3,328,196
Al-Qāhirah (Cairo)	—	83	214	6,789,497
Al-Uqṣur (Luxor)	—	...[2]	...[2]	360,503
As-Suways (Suez)	—	6,888	17,840	417,610
TOTAL		385,229	997,739	59,274,400[3]

Demography

Population (2000): 65,871,000.
Density (2000): persons per sq mi 171.0, persons per sq km 66.0.
Urban-rural (1996): urban 43.0%; rural 57.0%.
Sex distribution (2000): male 50.50%; female 49.50%.
Age breakdown (2000): under 15, 35.1%; 15–29, 28.5%; 30–44, 19.0%; 45–59, 11.3%; 60–74, 5.0%; 75 and over, 1.0%.
Population projection: (2010) 76,905,000; (2020) 87,086,000.
Doubling time: 40 years.
Ethnic composition (1986): Egyptian 99.9%; other 0.1%.
Religious affiliation (1990): Sunnī Muslim *c.* 90%; Christian *c.* 10%[4].
Major cities ('000; 1996): Cairo 6,789 (10,345[5]); Alexandria 3,328; Al-Jīzah 2,222; Shubrā al-Khaymah 871; Port Said 470; Suez 418.

Vital statistics

Birth rate per 1,000 population (2000): 25.4 (world avg. 22.1).
Death rate per 1,000 population (2000): 7.8 (world avg. 8.9).
Natural increase rate per 1,000 population (2000): 17.6 (world avg. 13.2).
Total fertility rate (avg. births per childbearing woman; 2000): 3.2.
Life expectancy at birth (2000): male 61.3 years; female 65.5 years.

National economy

Budget (1997–98). Revenue: £E 69,084,000,000 (income and profits taxes 22.7%, sales taxes 18.3%, customs duties 17.8%, oil revenue 7.0%, Suez Canal fees 4.2%). Expenditures: £E 71,703,000,000 (wages and pensions 31.0%, public debt interest 21.5%).
Public debt (external, outstanding; 1998): U.S.$27,670,000,000.
Population economically active (1995): total 17,725,900; activity rate 29.9% (participation rates: ages 15–64, 49.8%; female 22.0%; unemployed 13.5%).

Price and earnings indexes (1995 = 100)

	1992	1993	1994	1995	1996	1997	1998
Consumer price index	71.3	79.9	86.4	100.0	108.3	112.8	114.4
Annual earnings index	72.7	86.4	93.2	100.0	...	...	...

Production ('000; metric tons except as noted). Agriculture, forestry, fishing (1999): sugarcane 14,500, wheat 6,347, rice 5,900, tomatoes 5,900, corn (maize) 5,500, potatoes 2,000, oranges 1,525, watermelons 1,500; livestock ('000; number of live animals) 4,400 sheep, 3,300 goats, 3,180 buffalo, 3,180 cattle, 87,000 chickens; roundwood (1998) 2,764,000 cu m; fish catch (1996) 310. Mining and quarrying (1996–97): kaolin 258,725; quartz 90,393; feldspar 53,783. Manufacturing (1995–96): cement 17,200; nitrate fertilizers 7,354; sugar 1,131; cotton yarn 275; refrigerators 373,000 units[6]; automobiles 6,800 units[6]. Construction (1992–93): urban residential units 123,098. Energy production (consumption): electricity ('000,000 kW-hr; 1995) 48,864 (48,864); coal ('000 metric tons; 1995) n.a. (1,544); crude petroleum ('000 barrels; 1995) 323,110 (192,284); petroleum products ('000 metric tons; 1995) 26,996 (17,684); natural gas ('000,000 cu m; 1995) 13,568 (13,568).
Gross national product (1998): U.S.$79,185,000,000 (U.S.$1,290 per capita).

Structure of gross domestic product and labour force

	1995–96[7] in value £E '000,000	1995–96[7] % of total value	1995 labour force	1995 % of labour force
Agriculture	24,470	16.0	5,215,600	29.4
Mining (petroleum)	41,335	26.9	40,700	0.2
Manufacturing			2,183,500	12.3
Construction	7,898	5.1	967,600	5.5
Public utilities	3,190	2.1	166,800	0.9
Transp. and commun.	16,116[8]	10.5[8]	907,600	5.1
Trade	28,545[9]	18.6[9]	1,587,700	9.0
Finance	8,832	5.8	282,700	1.6
Pub. admin., defense, services	11,150	7.3	3,990,800	22.5
Other	11,833	7.7	2,382,900[10]	13.5[10]
TOTAL	153,369	100.0	17,725,900	100.0

Household income and expenditure. Average household size (1986) 4.9; expenditure (1986–87)[11]: food 55.7%, clothing 10.9%, housing 10.5%.
Tourism (1998): receipts U.S.$2,564,000,000; expenditures U.S.$1,153,000,000.

Foreign trade[12]

Balance of trade (current prices)

	1992	1993	1994	1995	1996	1997
U.S.$'000,000	–5,242	–5,959	–6,271	–8,314	–9,505	–9,293
% of total	46.2%	56.9%	49.2%	54.6%	57.3%	54.2%

Imports (1995–96): U.S.$13,826,400,000 (machinery and transport equipment 29.7%; foodstuffs 20.9%; iron and steel products 9.5%; chemical products 3.9%). *Major import sources:* U.S. 18.9%; Germany 9.6%; Italy 7.6%.
Exports (1995–96): U.S.$4,592,800,000 (petroleum and petroleum products 48.5%; cotton yarn, textiles, and clothing 12.5%; basic metals and manufactures 5.4%). *Major export destinations:* Italy 18.6%; U.S. 11.1%.

Transport and communications

Transport. Railroads (1998): length 4,810 km; passenger-km 47,992,000,000[13]; metric ton-km cargo 2,336,000,000[13]. Roads (1996): length 64,000 km (paved 78%). Vehicles (1996): passenger cars 1,354,000; trucks and buses 496,000. Inland water (1998): Suez Canal, number of transits 13,472; metric ton cargo 386,099,000. Air transport (1998): passenger-km 8,040,000,000; metric ton-km cargo 213,168,000; airports (1997) 11.

Communications

Medium	date	unit	number	units per 1,000 persons
Daily newspapers	1996	circulation	2,400,000	38.0
Radio	1997	receivers	20,500,000	330
Television	1996	receivers	7,700,000	127
Telephones	1998	main lines	3,972,000	63
Cellular telephones	1998	subscribers	90,786	1.4
Personal computers	1998	units	600,000	9.5
Internet	1998	users	100,000	1.6

Education and health

Literacy (1995): total population age 15 and over literate 51.4%; males 63.6%; females 38.8%.

Education (1997–98)[14]

	schools	teachers	students	student/teacher ratio
Primary (age 6–11)[15]	18,522	310,116	7,499,303	24.1
Secondary (age 12–17)[15]	7,307[13]	259,618	4,835,938	18.6
Vocational	1,351[13]	138,277	1,912,040	13.8
Teacher training	56[13]	750	9,576	12.8
Higher	12[16]	38,828[13]	850,051	...

Health: physicians (1996) 129,000 (1 per 472 persons); hospital beds (1994) 113,020 (1 per 515 persons); infant mortality rate (2000) 62.3.
Food (1997): daily per capita caloric intake 3,287 (vegetable products 93%, animal products 7%); 130% of FAO recommended minimum requirement.

Military

Total active duty personnel (1997): 450,000 (army 71.1%, navy 4.4%, air force [including air defense] 24.5%). *Military expenditure as percentage of GNP* (1997): 2.8% (world 2.6%); per capita expenditure U.S.$3.4.

[1]Includes 10 nonelective seats. [2]The area of Al-Uqṣur (Luxor) is included with Qinā governorate. [3]Excludes 2,180,000 Egyptians abroad. [4]According to the 1986 census, the Christian population of Egypt was 5.9% of the total; this figure is considered by some external authorities to understate the Christian population by as much as 60%. [5]1999 urban agglomeration. [6]1992–93. [7]At 1991–92 constant prices. [8]Transportation includes earnings from traffic on the Suez Canal. [9]Trade includes restaurants and hotels. [10]Unemployed and those seeking work for the first time. [11]Weight of consumer price components; urban households only. [12]Import figures are c.i.f.; export figures are f.o.b. [13]1993–94. [14]1996–97. [15]Data exclude 1,770 primary and 1,449 secondary schools in the Al-Azhar education system. [16]Universities only.

Internet resources for further information:
- **Egypt State Information Service http://www.sis.gov.eg**
- **Ministry of Economy http://www.economy.gov.eg**

El Salvador

Official name: República de El Salvador (Republic of El Salvador).
Form of government: republic with one legislative house (Legislative Assembly [84]).
Chief of state and government: President.
Capital: San Salvador.
Official language: Spanish.
Official religion: none[1].
Monetary unit: 1 colón (₡) = 100 centavos; valuation (Oct. 6, 2000) 1 U.S.$ = ₡8.74; 1 £ = ₡12.65.

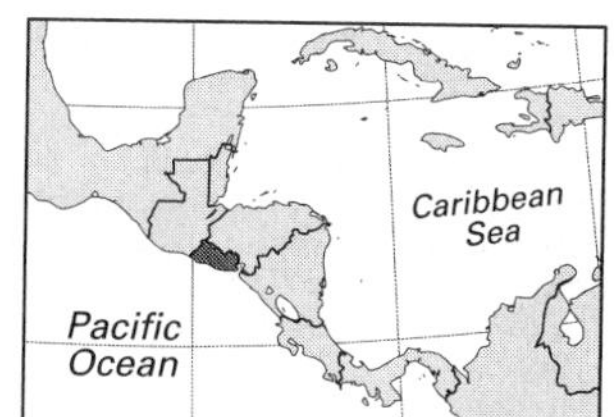

Area and population		area		population
				1992
Departments	Capitals	sq mi	sq km	census
Ahuachapán	Ahuachapán	479	1,240	261,188
Cabañas	Sensuntepeque	426	1,104	138,426
Chalatenango	Chalatenango	779	2,017	177,320
Cuscatlán	Cojutepeque	292	756	178,502
La Libertad	Nueva San Salvador	638	1,653	513,866
La Paz	Zacatecoluca	473	1,224	245,915
La Unión	La Unión	801	2,074	255,565
Morazán	San Francisco	559	1,447	160,146
San Miguel	San Miguel	802	2,077	403,411
San Salvador	San Salvador	342	886	1,512,125
San Vicente	San Vicente	457	1,184	143,003
Santa Ana	Santa Ana	781	2,023	458,587
Sonsonate	Sonsonate	473	1,225	360,183
Usulután	Usulután	822	2,130	310,362
TOTAL		8,124	21,041[2]	5,118,599

Demography

Population (2000): 6,123,000.
Density (2000): persons per sq mi 753.7, persons per sq km 291.0.
Urban-rural (1998): urban 46.0%; rural 54.0%.
Sex distribution (1998): male 49.04%; female 50.96%.
Age breakdown (1995): under 15, 37.4%; 15–29, 30.4%; 30–44, 15.8%; 45–59, 9.5%; 60–74, 5.4%; 75 and over 1.5%.
Population projection: (2010) 7,293,000; (2020) 8,494,000.
Doubling time: 30 years.
Ethnic composition (1993): mestizo (white and Indian) 89.0%; Amerindian 10.0%; white 1.0%.
Religious affiliation (1995): Roman Catholic 78.2%; Protestant 17.1%, of which Pentecostal 13.3%; other Christian 1.9%; other 2.8%.
Major urban areas (1992): San Salvador 415,346 (metro area 1,522,126); Soyapango 261,122[3]; Santa Ana 139,389; Mejicanos 131,972[3]; San Miguel 127,696.

Vital statistics

Birth rate per 1,000 population (1999): 29.4 (world avg. 22.1); (1994) legitimate 29.4%; illegitimate 70.6%.
Death rate per 1,000 population (1999): 6.4 (world avg. 8.9).
Natural increase rate per 1,000 population (1999): 23.0 (world avg. 13.2).
Total fertility rate (avg. births per childbearing woman; 1999): 3.4.
Marriage rate per 1,000 population (1994): 5.1.
Divorce rate per 1,000 population (1994): 0.5.
Life expectancy at birth (1999): male 65.8 years; female 73.2 years.
Major causes of death per 100,000 population (1994)[4]: diseases of the circulatory system 124; violence 73; accidents 62; malignant neoplasms (cancers) 52; infectious and parasitic diseases 42; ill-defined conditions 129.

National economy

Budget. Revenue (1997): ₡11,345,000,000 (sales taxes 50.2%, corporate taxes 14.7%, individual income taxes 11.7%, import duties 11.2%). Expenditures: ₡12,027,000,000 (education 19.6%, police 16.3%, general public services 13.6%, transportation and communications 12.4%, health 10.3%, defense 7.1%).
Public debt (external, outstanding; 1998): U.S.$2,443,000,000.
Production (metric tons except as noted). Agriculture, forestry, fishing (1999): sugarcane 5,500,000, corn (maize) 683,500, sorghum 181,500, coffee 143,800, dry beans 71,700, bananas 70,000, rice 60,400, yautia 53,000, tobacco 1,100; livestock (number of live animals) 1,141,000 cattle, 335,000 pigs; roundwood (1998) 5,129,000 cu m; fish catch (1997) 10,987, of which crustaceans 3,920. Mining and quarrying (1997): limestone 3,000,000 metric tons. Manufacturing (value added in ₡'000,000; 1996): food products 1,426; wearing apparel 1,009; soaps, cleansers, and cosmetics 932; refined petroleum 865; beverages 756; textiles 589; nonmetallic mineral products 453. Construction (buildings completed; 1993): residential 650,000 sq m; nonresidential 296,000 sq m. Energy production (consumption): electricity (kW-hr; 1998) 3,762,000,000 (3,184,000,000); coal, none (none); crude petroleum (barrels; 1996) none (5,358,000); petroleum products (metric tons; 1996) 698,000 (1,348,000); natural gas, none (none).
Household income and expenditure. Average household size (1992–93): 4.8; average income per household (1992–93): ₡22,930 (U.S.$2,562); expenditure (1990–91)[5]: food and beverages 37.0%, housing 12.1%, transportation and communications 10.2%, clothing and footwear 6.7%.
Population economically active (1995): total 2,136,400; activity rate of total population 39.1% (participation rates: ages 15–64, 62.9%; female 37.1%; unemployed [1998] 7.5%).

Price and earnings indexes (1995 = 100)	1994	1995	1996	1997	1998	1999	2000[6]
Consumer price index	90.9	100.0	109.8	114.7	117.6	118.2	118.7
Monthly earnings index[7]	91.4	100.0	108.5	116.7	121.9	...	...

Gross national product (at current market prices; 1998): U.S.$11,207,000,000 (U.S.$1,850 per capita).

Structure of gross domestic product and labour force	1998		1997	
	in value ₡'000,000	% of total value	labour force	% of labour force
Agriculture	12,532	12.1	547,100	24.3
Mining	417	0.4	1,700	0.1
Manufacturing	22,591	21.8	334,100	14.8
Construction	4,389	4.2	138,700	6.1
Public utilities	1,681	1.6	15,200	0.7
Transportation and communications	8,304	8.0	96,700	4.3
Trade	19,850	19.1	445,100	19.7
Finance, real estate	12,191	11.7	30,300	1.3
Public admin., defense	7,116	6.9	467,100	20.7
Services	14,795	14.2		
Other			180,000[8]	8.0[8]
TOTAL	103,864[2]	100.0	2,256,000	100.0

Tourism (1997): receipts U.S.$75,000,000; expenditures U.S.$75,000,000.
Land use (1994): forested 5.0%; meadows and pastures 29.5%; agricultural and under permanent cultivation 35.2%; other 30.3%.

Foreign trade[9]

Balance of trade (current prices)	1993	1994	1995	1996	1997	1998
U.S.$'000,000	−1,180.5	−1,448.9	−1,855.3	−1,646.5	−1,607.6	−1,849.6
% of total	44.6%	47.1%	48.2%	44.6%	37.5%	42.3%

Imports (1997): U.S.$2,961,500,000 (chemicals and chemical products 17.0%, food and beverages 13.6%, nonelectrical machinery and equipment 12.8%, mineral fuels 11.4%). *Major import sources:* U.S. 41.4%; Guatemala 10.9%; Mexico 7.9%; Costa Rica 3.9%; Germany 3.2%.
Exports (1997): U.S.$1,353,900,000 (coffee 38.1%, paper and paper products 4.8%, pharmaceuticals 3.9%, raw sugar 3.9%, refined petroleum products 3.3%). *Major export destinations:* Guatemala 19.5%; U.S. 19.2%; Germany 17.5%; Honduras 10.0%; Costa Rica 8.2%.

Transport and communications

Transport. Railroads (1997): route length 562 km[10]; (1996) passenger-km 4,800,000; (1996) metric ton-km cargo 17,300,000. Roads (1997): total length 10,029 km (paved 20%). Vehicles (1997): passenger cars 177,488; trucks and buses 184,859. Air transport: (1996) passenger-km 2,181,000,000; (1995) metric ton-km cargo 16,006,000; airports (1997) with scheduled flights 1.

Communications				units
Medium	date	unit	number	per 1,000 persons
Daily newspapers	1996	circulation	278,000	49
Radio	1997	receivers	2,750,000	475
Television	1997	receivers	4,000,000	692
Telephones	1998	main lines	482,566	82
Cellular telephones	1998	subscribers	106,114	18
Internet	1998	users	30,000	5.1

Education and health

Educational attainment (1992): Percentage of population over age 25 having: no formal schooling 34.7%; incomplete primary education 37.6%; complete primary[11] 10.8%; secondary 9.4%; higher technical 2.4%; incomplete undergraduate 1.1%; complete undergraduate 2.9%; other/unknown 1.1%.
Literacy (1992): total population age 15 and over literate 2,326,800 (74.1%); males literate 1,141,007 (77.4%); females literate 1,185,793 (71.3%).

Education (1996)	schools	teachers	students	student/ teacher ratio
Primary (age 7–15)	5,025	34,496	1,130,900	32.8
Secondary (age 16–18)	...	9,255	143,588	15.5
Higher	...	5,919	112,266	19.0

Health: physicians (1997) 6,177 (1 per 936 persons); hospital beds (1996) 9,571 (1 per 593 persons); infant mortality rate per 1,000 live births (1999) 30.2.
Food (1997): daily per capita caloric intake 2,562 (vegetable products 88%, animal products 12%); 112% of FAO recommended minimum requirement.

Military

Total active duty personnel (1999): 24,600 (army 90.7%, navy 2.8%, air force 6.5%). *Military expenditure as percentage of GNP* (1997): 0.9% (world 2.6%); per capita expenditure U.S.$17.

[1]Roman Catholicism, although not official, enjoys special recognition in the constitution. [2]Detail does not add to total given because of rounding. [3]Within San Salvador metropolitan area. [4]Projected rates based on about 77% of total deaths. [5]536,628 urban households only. [6]January. [7]Private sector only. [8]Unemployed. [9]Imports c.i.f., exports f.o.b. [10]283 km are operational in 1997. [11]Education completed through ninth grade.

Internet resources for further information:
- **Banco Central de Reserva de El Salvador http://www.bcr.gob.sv**

Equatorial Guinea

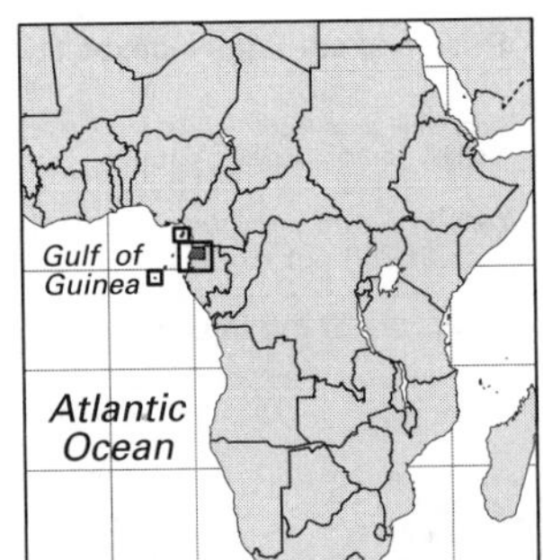

Official name: República de Guinea Ecuatorial (Republic of Equatorial Guinea).
Form of government: republic with one legislative house (House of Representatives of the People [80]).
Chief of state: President.
Head of government: Prime Minister.
Capital: Malabo.
Capital designate: Bata[1].
Official languages: Spanish; French.
Official religion: none.
Monetary unit: 1 CFA franc (CFAF) = 100 centimes; valuation (Oct. 6, 2000) 1 U.S.$ = CFAF 754.28; 1 £ = CFAF 1,091.

Area and population

Regions / Provinces	Capitals	area sq mi	area sq km	population 1987 estimate
Insular		785[2]	2,034	70,280
Annobón	Palé	7	17	2,360
Bioko Norte	Malabo	300	776	56,600
Bioko Sur	Luba	479	1,241	11,320
Continental		10,045[2]	26,017	259,950
Centro-Sur	Evinayong	3,834	9,931	55,970
Kie-Ntem	Ebebiyin	1,522	3,943	74,050
Litoral[3]	Bata	2,573	6,665	75,640
Wele-Nzas	Mongomo	2,115	5,478	54,290
TOTAL		10,831[2]	28,051	330,230

Demography

Population (2000): 474,000.
Density (2000): persons per sq mi 43.8, persons per sq km 16.9.
Urban-rural (1998): urban 45.7%; rural 54.3%.
Sex distribution (1998): male 49.30%; female 50.70%.
Age breakdown (1999): under 15, 42.8%; 15–29, 26.8%; 30–44, 15.7%; 45–59, 8.8%; 60–74, 4.9%; 75 and over, 1.0%.
Population projection: (2010) 604,000; (2020) 755,000.
Doubling time: 27 years.
Ethnic composition (1995): Fang 82.9%; Bubi 9.6%; other 7.5%.
Religious affiliation (1995): Roman Catholic 93.1%; other 6.9%.
Major cities (1983): Malabo 30,418; Bata 24,308; Ela-Nguema 6,179; Campo Yaunde 5,199; Los Angeles 4,079.

Vital statistics

Birth rate per 1,000 population (1999): 38.5 (world avg. 22.1); legitimate, n.a.; illegitimate, n.a.
Death rate per 1,000 population (1999): 13.0 (world avg. 8.9).
Natural increase rate per 1,000 population (1999): 25.5 (world avg. 13.2).
Total fertility rate (avg. births per childbearing woman; 1999): 5.0.
Marriage rate per 1,000 population: n.a.
Divorce rate per 1,000 population: n.a.
Life expectancy at birth (1999): male 52.0 years; female 56.8 years.
Major causes of death per 100,000 population: n.a.; however, major diseases include malaria (about 24% of total mortality), respiratory infections (12% of mortality), cholera, leprosy, trypanosomiasis (sleeping sickness), and waterborne (especially gastrointestinal) diseases.

National economy

Budget (1996). Revenue: CFAF 24,637,000,000 (domestic revenue 95.1%, of which oil revenue 46.9%, tax revenue 36.8%, nontax revenue 11.4%; foreign grants 4.9%). Expenditures: CFAF 32,955,000,000 (current expenditure 60.6%, of which goods and services 23.8%, salaries 17.3%, interest on debt 15.6%, transfers 3.9%; capital expenditure 9.7%).
Public debt (external, outstanding; 1997): U.S.$208,600,000.
Gross national product (at current market prices; 1998): U.S.$478,000,000 (U.S.$1,110 per capita).

Structure of gross domestic product and labour force

	1998 in value CFAF '000,000	1998 % of total value	1983 labour force	1983 % of labour force
Agriculture, fishing	40,480	15.0	59,390	57.9
Forestry	17,719	6.6		
Crude petroleum	164,969	61.3	1,616	1.6
Manufacturing	1,007	0.4		
Construction	7,752	2.9	1,929	1.9
Public utilities	3,368	1.3	224	0.2
Transportation and communications	2,100	0.8	1,752	1.7
Trade	9,625	3.6	3,059	3.0
Finance, real estate	2,135	0.8	409	0.4
Pub. admin., defense	12,723	4.7	8,377	8.2
Services	4,959	1.8		
Other	2,427[4]	0.9[4]	25,809	25.2
TOTAL	269,266[2]	100.0[2]	102,565	100.0[2]

Production (metric tons except as noted). Agriculture, forestry, fishing (1999): roots and tubers 84,000 (of which cassava 49,000, sweet potatoes 35,000), bananas 15,000, coconuts 8,000, coffee 6,300, palm oil 5,000, cacao beans 5,000, palm kernels 3,000; livestock (number of live animals) 36,000 sheep, 8,100 goats, 5,300 pigs, 4,800 cattle; roundwood (1998) 811,000 cu m; fish catch (1997) 6,090. Mining and quarrying: details, n.a.; however, in addition to quarrying for construction materials, unexploited deposits of iron ore, lead, zinc, manganese, and molybdenum are present. Manufacturing (1998): sawn timber 21,500 cu m; processed timber 3,900 cu m. Construction: n.a. Energy production (consumption): electricity (kW-hr; 1996) 20,000,000 (20,000,000); coal, none (none); crude petroleum (barrels; 1998) 30,295,000 ([1996] 37,000); petroleum products (metric tons; 1996) none (42,000); natural gas, none (none).
Population economically active (1997): total 177,000; activity rate of total population 40.0% (participation rates: ages 15–64, 74.7%; female 35.4%; unemployed [1983] 24.2%).

Price and earnings indexes (1995 = 100)

	1990	1991	1992	1993	1994	1995	1996
Consumer price index	56.4	58.2	61.3	64.1	88.6	100	105.2
Earnings index	...	...	...	...	...	...	...

Household income and expenditure. Average household size (1980) 4.5; income per household: n.a.; sources of income (1988): wages and salaries 57.0%, business income 42.0%, other 1.0%; expenditure (1988): food and beverages 62.0%, clothing and footwear 10.0%; medical care 6.0%.
Tourism: tourism is a government priority but remains undeveloped.
Land use (1994): forested 65.2%; meadows and pastures 3.7%; agricultural and under permanent cultivation 8.2%; built-on, wasteland, and other 22.9%.

Foreign trade

Balance of trade (current prices)

	1992	1993	1994	1995	1996	1997
CFAF '000,000,000	−8.9	−5.5	−6.0	−14.6	−106.3	−66.8
% of total	22.5%	12.2%	7.7%	13.9%	33.5%	10.3%

Imports (1996): CFAF 211,429,000,000 (petroleum sector 78.8%; other 21.2%). *Major import sources:* United States 23.4%; Spain 18.6%; France 15.3%; Cameroon 12.5%; The Netherlands 4.4%; Italy 3.2%.
Exports (1996): CFAF 105,083,000,000 (petroleum 67.7%; wood 25.8%; cocoa 2.9%). *Major export destinations:* United States 65.6%; Spain 8.6%; China 7.1%; Japan 6.6%; Portugal 2.5%; France 2.5%.

Transport and communications

Transport. Railroads: none. Roads (1996): total length 1,740 mi, 2,800 km (paved 13%). Vehicles (1994): passenger cars 6,500; trucks and buses 4,000. Merchant marine (1992): vessels (100 gross tons and over) 3; total deadweight tonnage 6,699. Air transport (1996): passenger-mi 4,000,000, passenger-km 7,000,000; short ton-mi cargo 700,000, metric ton-km cargo 1,000,000; airports (1998) with scheduled flights 1.

Communications

Medium	date	unit	number	units per 1,000 persons
Daily newspapers	1996	circulation	2,000	4.9
Radio	1997	receivers	180,000	428
Television	1997	receivers	4,000	9.8
Telephones	1998	main lines	5,580	12.9
Cellular telephones	1999	units	297	0.7
Internet	1998	users	...	...

Education and health

Educational attainment (1983). Percentage of population age 15 and over having: no schooling 35.4%; some primary education 46.6%; primary 13.0%; secondary 2.3%; postsecondary 1.1%; not specified 1.6%. *Literacy* (1995): percentage of total population age 15 and over literate 77.8%; males literate 89.3%; females literate 67.4%.

Education (1993–94)

	schools	teachers	students	student/ teacher ratio
Primary (age 6–11)	781	1,381	75,751	54.9
Secondary (age 12–17)	...	466	14,511	31.1
Voc., teacher tr.	...	122	2,105	17.3
Higher	...	58	578	10.0

Health: physicians (1996) 106 (1 per 4,065 persons); hospital beds (1990) 992 (1 per 350 persons); infant mortality rate per 1,000 live births (1999) 91.2.
Food: daily per capita caloric intake, n.a.

Military

Total active duty personnel (1999): 1,320 (army 83.3%, navy 9.1%, air force 7.6%). *Military expenditure as percentage of GNP* (1996): 1.5% (world 2.6%); per capita expenditure U.S.$6.

[1]Government offices and ministries are moving to Bata in stages between 2000 and 2003. [2]Detail does not add to total given because of rounding. [3]Includes three islets in Corisco Bay. [4]Import duties.

Internet resources for further information:
- **Investir en Zone Franc**
  http://www.izf.net/izf/Index.htm

Eritrea

Official name: State of Eritrea.
Form of government: transitional regime with one interim legislative body (Transitional National Assembly [150][1]).
Head of state and government: President.
Capital: Asmara.
Official language: none.
Official religion: none.
Monetary unit: nakfa[2] = 100 cents; valuation (Oct. 6, 2000) 1 U.S.$ = Nfa 9.50; 1 £ = Nfa 13.74.

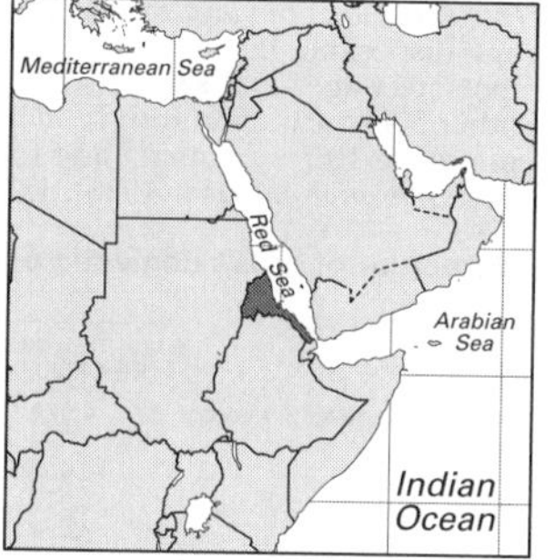

Area and population

Regions[4]	Capitals	area[3] sq mi	area[3] sq km	population 1997 estimate
Debub-Keih-Bahri	Asseb (Aseb)	10,660	27,600	...
Semien-Keih-Bahri	Massawa (Mitsiwa)	10,730	27,800	...
Anseba	Keren	8,960	23,200	...
Gash-Barka	Barentu	12,820	33,200	...
Debub	Mendefera	3,090	8,000	...
Maekel	Asmara (Asmera)	500	1,300	...
TOTAL		46,770[5]	121,100	3,590,000

Demography

Population (2000): 4,136,000.
Density (2000): persons per sq mi 88.4, persons per sq km 34.2.
Urban-rural (1992): urban 16.3%; rural 83.7%.
Sex distribution (1999): male 49.89%; female 50.11%.
Age breakdown (1999): under 15, 42.9%; 15–29, 29.1%; 30–44, 13.8%; 45–59, 9.1%; 60–74, 4.1%; 75 and over, 1.0%.
Population projection: (2010) 5,709,000; (2020) 7,399,000.
Doubling time: 23 years.
Linguistic composition (1976): Tigrinya 49.0%; Tigré 31.7%; Afar 4.3%; Hedareb 3.9%; Bilen 3.1%; Saho 3.0%; Kunama 2.7%; Nara 2.1%; Rashaida 0.3%.
Religious affiliation (1995): Muslim 69.3%; Christian 30.7% (almost all Eritrean Orthodox).
Major cities (1992): Asmara 400,000; Asseb 50,000; Keren 40,000; Massawa 40,000; Mendefera 14,833[6].

Vital statistics

Birth rate per 1,000 population (1999): 42.5 (world avg. 22.1).
Death rate per 1,000 population (1999): 12.5 (world avg. 8.9).
Natural increase rate per 1,000 population (1999): 30.0 (world avg. 13.2).
Total fertility rate (avg. births per childbearing woman; 1999): 5.9.
Marriage rate per 1,000 population (1992): 6.8.
Divorce rate per 1,000 population: n.a.
Life expectancy at birth (1999): male 53.0 years; female 57.8 years.
Major causes of death per 100,000 population: n.a.; morbidity (principal causes of illness) arises mainly in malaria and other infectious diseases, parasitic infections, malnutrition, diarrheal diseases, and dysenteries.

National economy

Budget (1997). Revenue: Nfa 1,967,400,000 (taxes 48.8%, of which direct taxes 22.8%, import duties 15.2%, indirect taxes 10.8%; nontax revenue 51.2%). Expenditures: Nfa 2,588,800,000 (current expenditure 55.8%, of which wages and salaries 27.3%, materials 20.1%; capital 44.2%).
Public debt (external, outstanding; 1998): U.S.$144,100,000.
Production (metric tons except as noted). Agriculture, forestry, fishing (1999): cereals 270,000, sorghum 150,000, roots and tubers 125,000, barley 40,000, millet 30,000, pulses 30,000, vegetables and melons 28,000, wheat 15,000, corn (maize) 15,000, sesame seeds 4,200, dry beans 3,000, peanuts (groundnuts) 1,800, chickpeas 1,000; livestock (number of live animals) 1,530,000 sheep, 1,400,000 goats, 1,320,000 cattle, 69,000 camels; fish catch (1996) 3,272, of which artisanal fisheries 818. Mining and quarrying (1995): salt 305,120; marble and granite are quarried, as are sand and aggregate (gravel) for construction; deposits of copper, zinc, mica, gold, iron, manganese, nickel, and lead exist but remain unexploited. Manufacturing (gross value in Nfa '000; 1997): food production 203,700; beverages 159,600; leather products and shoes 69,400; textile products 62,800; chemical products 59,700; metal products 44,300; nonmetallic products 28,500; tobacco and matches 16,600; paper and printing products 11,300. Construction (1997): Nfa 270,794,000. Energy production: energy resources include hydroelectricity, fossil fuels, geothermal power, coal, biogas, solar power, and wind; commercial electricity production for 1997 was 179,192,000 kW-hr.
Household income and expenditure. Average household size (1998) 4.7; average annual income per household: n.a.; sources of income: n.a.; expenditure: n.a.
Persons economically active: n.a.

Price and earnings indexes (December 1992 = 100)

	1991	1992	1993	1994	1995
Consumer price index[7]	91.9	100.0	119.2	127.4	141.3
Earnings index	...	...	...	...	...

Gross national product (at current market prices; 1998): U.S.$781,000,000 (U.S.$200 per capita).

Structure of gross domestic product and labour force

	1997 in value Br '000,000	1997 % of total value	1992 labour force	1992 % of labour force
Agriculture	390.3	8.3	647	2.6
Manufacturing	656.0	13.9	11,894	48.3
Mining	4.5	0.1	292	1.2
Public utilities	65.1	1.4	2,284	9.3
Construction	515.4	10.9	298	1.2
Transp. and commun.	488.9	10.4	3,126	12.7
Trade	1,134.1	24.1	597	2.4
Finance	189.4	4.0	382	1.6
Pub. admin., defense	706.8	15.0	} 5,001	} 20.3
Services	50.8	1.1		
Other	511.6[8]	10.8[8]		
TOTAL	4,712.9	100.0	24,621[5]	100.0[5]

Tourism (1997): receipts from visitors U.S.$90,000,000.
Land use (1994): forested 7.3%; agricultural and under permanent cultivation 5.1%; meadows and pastures 69.0%; other (predominantly barren land) 18.6%.

Foreign trade[9]

Balance of trade (current prices)

	1993	1994	1995	1996	1997
U.S.$'000,000	–239.0	–331.4	–323.2	–418.5	–436.4
% of total	58.1%	72.0%	66.7%	68.7%	80.4%

Imports (1997): U.S.$489,500,000 (machinery and transport equipment 37.8%, manufactured goods 22.2%, food products 19.6%, chemical products 6.0%, raw materials 2.2%, animal and vegetable oil 1.9%, petroleum and petroleum products 1.7%). *Major import sources:* Saudi Arabia 15.7%[10]; Italy 13.7%; United Arab Emirates 13.1%; Ethiopia 9.0%; Germany 5.5%; United Kingdom 4.6%; Japan 4.1%; United States 3.1%; The Netherlands 1.7%; The Sudan 0.7%.
Exports (1997): U.S.$53,100,000 (raw materials 34.5%, food products 21.7%, manufactured goods 17.1%, machinery and transport equipment 2.9%, beverages and tobacco 2.4%, chemical products 2.2%). *Major export destinations:* Ethiopia 63.5%; The Sudan 16.6%; Italy 4.9%; Saudi Arabia 1.9%; Germany 0.6%; United Kingdom 0.5%.

Transport and communications

Transport. Railroads (1998): a 190-mi (306-km) rail line that formerly connected Massawa and Agordat is currently under reconstruction. A 43-mi (70-km) section of the Asmara–Massawa line was opened. A 24-mi (38-km) section between Amatere and Demas townships was reopened on Jan. 4, 1997. Roads (1996): total length 2,491 mi, 4,010 km (paved 22%). Vehicles (1996): automobiles 5,940, trucks and buses, n.a. Merchant marine: vessels (100 gross tons and over) n.a. Air transport (1993)[11]: passenger arrivals 47,645[12], passenger departures 42,548[12]; short ton cargo handled 25,907[13], metric ton cargo handled 28,557[13]; airports (1997) with scheduled flights 2.

Communications

Medium	date	unit	number	units per 1,000 persons
Radio	1995	receivers	310,000	89.6
Television	1998	receivers	50,000	13.0
Telephones	1998	main lines	23,967	6.2
Internet	1998	users	300	0.1

Education and health

Literacy (1993): total population literate *c.* 20%.

Education (1996–97)

	schools	teachers	students	student/ teacher ratio
Primary (age 7–12)	549	5,476	240,737	44.0
Secondary (age 13–18)	86[14]	1,959	88,054	44.9
Voc., teacher tr.	4[14]	112	1,145	10.2
Higher[15]	1	198	3,096	15.6

Health (1993): physicians 69 (1 per 36,000 persons); hospital beds (1986–87): 2,449 (1 per 1,100 persons); infant mortality rate per 1,000 live births (1999) 78.2.
Food (1998): daily per capita caloric intake 1,744 (vegetable 94.9%, animal products 5.1%); 75% of FAO recommended minimum requirement.

Military

Total active duty personnel (1999): estimated strength of Eritrean armed forces (predominantly former guerrillas) is between 180,000 and 200,000. As of Sept. 15, 2000, the United Nations had authorized the deployment of a 4,200 member peacekeeping force to be stationed along the Eritrea–Ethiopian border.

[1]New constitution adopted on May 23, 1997; scheduled election date for permanent legislature is December 2001. [2]The nakfa was introduced in July 1997 as the new national currency; the Ethiopian birr (Br) will eventually be phased out. [3]Approximate figures. The published total area is 46,774 sq mi (121,144 sq km); water area is 7,776 sq mi (20,140 sq km). [4]On May 20, 1995, a resolution was approved dividing the country into six administrative regions. [5]Detail does not add to total given because of rounding. [6]1989. [7]Asmara only; year-end. [8]Including indirect taxes less subsidies. [9]Imports c.i.f. [10]Saudi Arabia is a transshipment point; not all goods included here are of Saudi Arabian origin. [11]Asmara airport only. [12]January to June only. [13]1987–88. [14]1992–93. [15]1997–98.

Estonia

Official name: Eesti Vabariik (Republic of Estonia).
Form of government: unitary multiparty republic with a single legislative body (Riigikogu[1] [101]).
Chief of state: President.
Head of government: Prime Minister.
Capital: Tallinn.
Official language: Estonian.
Official religion: none.
Monetary unit: 1 kroon (EEK) = 100 sents; valuation (Oct. 6, 2000) 1 U.S.$ = EEK 17.99; 1 £ = EEK 26.03.

Area and population

Counties	Capitals	area sq mi	area sq km	population 1999[2] estimate
Harju	Tallinn	1,672	4,332	535,131
Hiiu	Kärdla	395	1,023	11,798
Ida-Viru	Jõhvi	1,299	3,364	195,460
Järva	Paide	1,013	2,623	43,144
Jõgeva	Jõgeva	1,005	2,604	41,377
Lääne	Haapsalu	920	2,383	31,850
Lääne-Viru	Rakvere	1,338	3,465	75,819
Pärnu	Pärnu	1,856	4,806	100,100
Põlva	Põlva	836	2,165	35,610
Rapla	Rapla	1,151	2,980	40,137
Saare	Kuressaare	1,128	2,922	40,111
Tartu	Tartu	1,156	2,993	151,010
Valga	Valga	789	2,044	38,668
Viljandi	Viljandi	1,321	3,422	62,336
Võru	Võru	890	2,305	43,029
TOTAL		16,769[3, 4, 5]	43,431[3, 4, 5]	1,445,580

Demography

Population (2000): 1,435,000.
Density (2000)[3]: persons per sq mi 85.6, persons per sq km 33.0.
Urban-rural (1999): urban 69.1%; rural 30.9%.
Sex distribution (1997): male 46.53%; female 53.47%.
Age breakdown (1999): under 15, 18.6%; 15–29, 21.9%; 30–44, 21.4%; 45–59, 18.2%; 60–74, 14.8%; 75 and over, 5.1%.
Population projection: (2010) 1,375,000; (2020) 1,335,000.
Ethnic composition (1999): Estonian 65.2%; Russian 28.1%; Ukrainian 2.5%; Belarusian 1.5%; Finnish 0.9%; other 1.8%.
Religious affiliation (1995): Christian 38.1%, of which Estonian Orthodox 19.6%, Evangelical Lutheran 13.7%; other (mostly nonreligious) 61.9%.
Major cities (1999[2]): Tallinn 411,594; Tartu 100,577; Narva 73,831; Kohtla-Järve 66,542; Pärnu 51,357.

Vital statistics

Birth rate per 1,000 population (1998): 8.5 (world avg. 22.1); legitimate 47.8%; illegitimate 52.2%.
Death rate per 1,000 population (1998): 13.4 (world avg. 8.9).
Natural increase rate per 1,000 population (1998): –4.9 (world avg. 13.2).
Total fertility rate (avg. births per childbearing woman; 1998): 1.2.
Marriage rate per 1,000 population (1998): 3.7.
Divorce rate per 1,000 population (1998): 3.1.
Life expectancy at birth (1998): male 64.4 years; female 75.5 years.
Major causes of death per 100,000 population (1998): diseases of the circulatory system 732.8; malignant neoplasms (cancers) 235.1; accidents, violence and homicide 162.2; diseases of the digestive system 44.4.

National economy

Budget (1998). Revenue: EEK 24,130,000,000 (social security contributions 32.9%, value-added taxes 26.6%, excise taxes 11.6%, personal income taxes 11.4%). Expenditures: EEK 24,103,000,000 (social security and welfare 30.6%, health 16.4%, education 8.6%, police 7.3%, defense 4.0%).
Public debt (external, outstanding; 1998): U.S.$231,300,000.
Production (metric tons except as noted). Agriculture, forestry, fishing (1999): potatoes 340,000, barley 198,000, wheat 135,000, oats 85,000, rye 44,000, rapeseed 30,000; livestock (number of live animals) 326,400 pigs, 307,500 cattle; roundwood (1998) 6,061,000 cu m; (1997) fish catch 123,873. Mining and quarrying (1998): oil shale 10,913,000; peat 333,500. Manufacturing (value of production in EEK '000,000; 1996): meat and meat products 2,888; dairy products 2,260; products of wood (excluding furniture) 2,054; beverages 1,566; fish and fish products 1,492; furniture 1,483; textiles 1,471. Construction (value of construction in EEK '000,000; 1997): residential 641; nonresidential 4,376. Energy production (consumption): electricity (kW-hr; 1998) 8,521,000,000 (5,579,000,000); hard coal (metric tons; 1996) none (97,000); lignite (metric tons; 1996) 14,700,000 (16,000,000); crude petroleum, none (n.a.); petroleum products (metric tons; 1996) 344,000 (1,200,000); natural gas (cu m; 1996) none (689,000,000).
Population economically active (1997): total 707,800[6]; activity rate of total population 48.4% (participation rates: ages 15–64, 71.3%; female 47.9%; unemployed [June 1997–May 1998] 9.9%).

Price and earnings indexes (1995 = 100)

	1994	1995	1996	1997	1998	1999
Consumer price index	77.7	100.0	123.1	136.1	147.2	152.1
Annual earnings index	71.9	100.0	126.7	151.6	174.0	...

Household income and expenditure (1998). Average household size 2.3; average disposable income per household EEK 53,049 (U.S.$3,769); sources of income: wages and salaries 63.8%, transfers 24.1%, self-employment 6.2%, other 5.9%; expenditure[7]: food and beverages 35.5%, housing 14.6%, transportation 10.7%, clothing and footwear 9.0%.
Gross national product (1998): U.S.$4,878,000,000 (U.S.$3,360 per capita).

Structure of gross domestic product and labour force

	1998 in value EEK '000,000	1998 % of total value	1997 labour force[8, 9]	1997 % of labour force[8, 9]
Agriculture, fishing, forestry	4,079	5.6	60,800	8.5
Mining	763	1.0	7,600	1.1
Manufacturing	10,038	13.7	144,100	20.1
Public utilities	2,517	3.4	17,600	2.5
Construction	3,999	5.5	47,400	6.6
Trade, restaurants	12,818	17.5	105,200	14.7
Transp. and commun.	8,900	12.2	59,400	8.3
Finance, real estate	9,519	13.0	42,600	5.9
Pub. admin., defense	2,853	3.9	34,300	4.8
Services	5,909	8.1	95,800	13.3
Other	11,821[10]	16.1[10]	103,200[11]	14.4[11]
TOTAL	73,213[12]	100.0	717,800[12]	100.0[12]

Tourism (1997): receipts U.S.$465,000,000; expenditures U.S.$118,000,000.
Land use (1994): forest 44.7%; pasture 7.2%; agriculture 32.2%; other 15.9%.

Foreign trade[13]

Balance of trade (current prices)

	1993	1994	1995	1996	1997	1998
EEK '000,000	–1,195	–4,557	–8,046	–13,861	–20,925	–21,812
% of total	5.3%	11.9%	16.0%	21.7%	20.4%	19.3%

Imports (1998): EEK 67,364,000,000 (electrical and nonelectrical machinery 25.5%, foodstuffs 16.9%, transportation equipment 9.3%). *Major import sources:* Finland 22.6%; Russia 11.1%; Germany 10.8%; Sweden 9.0%.
Exports (1998): EEK 45,552,000,000 (electrical and nonelectrical machinery 19.7%, foodstuffs 15.9%, wood and wood products 12.7%, textiles and clothing 11.5%). *Major export destinations:* Finland 18.7%; Sweden 16.7%; Russia 13.4%; Latvia 9.4%; Germany 5.5%.

Transport and communications

Transport. Railroads (1998): route length 1,018 km; passenger-km 236,000,000; metric ton-km cargo 6,079,000,000. Roads (1998): total length 16,430 km (paved 51%). Vehicles (1998): passenger cars 451,000; trucks and buses 86,900. Air transport (1998)[14]: passenger-km 166,742,000; metric ton-km cargo 901,000; airports (1997) 1.

Communications

Medium	date	unit	number	units per 1,000 persons
Daily newspapers	1996	circulation	255,000	174
Radio	1997	receivers	1,010,000	693
Television	1997	receivers	605,000	415
Telephones	1998	main lines	499,000	344
Cellular telephones	1998	subscribers	247,000	170
Personal computers	1998	units	50,000	34
Internet	1998	users	150,000	103

Education and health

Educational attainment (1989). Percentage of persons age 25 and over having: no formal schooling 2.2%; primary education 39.0%; secondary 45.1%; higher 13.7%.

Education (1995–96)

	schools	teachers	students	student/ teacher ratio
Primary (age 7–12)	727	...	125,718	...
Secondary (age 13–17)	...	9,299	95,342	10.3
Vocational	...	1,793	16,870	9.4
Higher[15]	37	...	40,621	...

Health (1998): physicians 4,471 (1 per 324 persons); hospital beds 10,509 (1 per 138 persons); infant mortality rate per 1,000 live births 9.3.
Food (1997): daily per capita caloric intake 2,849 (vegetable products 72%, animal products 28%); 111% of FAO recommended minimum requirement.

Military

Total active duty personnel (1999): 4,800 (army 90.0%, navy 7.1%, air force 2.9%). *Military expenditure as a percentage of GNP* (1997): 1.5% (world 2.6%); per capita expenditure U.S.$76.

[1]Official legislation bans translation of parliament's name. [2]January 1. [3]Area used by Estonian government to calculate population densities. [4]Total area including the Estonian portion of Lake Peipus (590 sq mi [1,529 sq km]), Lake Võrtsjärv, and Muuga harbour is 17,462 sq mi (45,227 sq km). [5]Total includes 1,596 sq mi (4,133 sq km) of Baltic Sea islands. [6]First quarter average. [7]For a two-adult household with one child. [8]Ages 15–69 only. [9]Annual average. [10]Includes net taxes (EEK 8,406,000,000) less imputed bank service charges (EEK 1,000,000,000). [11]Includes 33,800 not adequately defined and 69,400 unemployed. [12]Detail does not add to total given because of rounding. [13]Imports c.i.f.; exports f.o.b. [14]Estonian Air. [15]1998–99.

Internet resource for further information:
- **Estonian Ministry of Economic Affairs http://www.mineco.ee/english**
- **Statistical Office of Estonia http://www.stat.ee/wwwstat/eng_stat**

Ethiopia

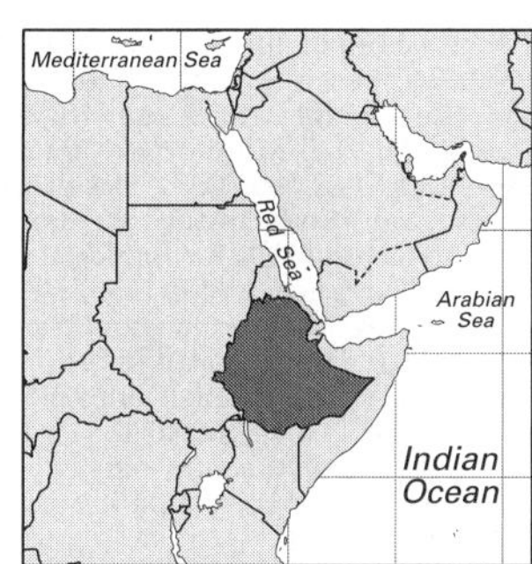

Official name: Federal Democratic Republic of Ethiopia.
Form of government: federal republic[1] with two legislative houses (Federal Council [108]; Council of People's Representatives [546]).
Chief of state: President.
Head of government: Prime Minister.
Capital: Addis Ababa.
Official language: none[2].
Official religion: none.
Monetary unit: 1 birr (Br) = 100 cents; valuation (Oct. 6, 2000) 1 U.S.$ = Br 8.20; 1 £ = Br 11.86.

Area and population

Regional states	Capitals	area sq mi	area sq km	population 1994 census
Afar	Aysaita	...	...	1,106,383
Amhara	Bahir Dar	66,000	170,000	13,834,297
Benishangul/ Gumuz	Asosa	20,000	51,000	460,459
Gambella	Gambella	9,758	25,274	181,862
Harari	Harar	131	340	131,139
Oromiya	Addis Ababa	136,560	353,690	18,732,525
Somali	Jijiga	116,000	300,000	3,439,860[3]
Southern Nations, Nationalities and Peoples'	Awasa	44,000	114,000	10,377,028
Tigray	Mekele	31,000	80,000	3,136,267
Cities				
Addis Ababa	...	208	540	2,300,000
Dire Dawa	...	500	1,300	251,864
TOTAL		437,794	1,133,882	...

Demography

Population (2000): 64,117,000.
Density (2000): persons per sq mi 146.5, persons per sq km 56.5.
Urban-rural (1999): urban 17.2%; rural 82.8%.
Sex distribution (1999): male 50.19%; female 49.81%.
Age breakdown (1999): under 15, 46.7%; 15–29, 26.5%; 30–44, 14.3%; 45–59, 8.0%; 60–74, 3.7%; 75 and over, 0.8%.
Population projection: (2010) 82,312,000; (2020) 103,163,000.
Ethnolinguistic composition (1994): Galla (Oromo) 31.8%; Amharic 29.3%; Somali 6.2%; Tigrinya 5.9%; Walaita 4.6%; Gurage 4.2%; Sidamo 3.4%; Afar 1.9%; Hadya-Libide 1.7%; other 11.0%.
Religious affiliation (1994): Ethiopian Orthodox 50.3%; Muslim 32.9%; Protestant 10.1%; traditional beliefs 4.8%; Roman Catholic 0.6%; other 1.3%.
Major cities (1994): Addis Ababa 2,112,737; Dire Dawa 164,851; Harar 131,139; Nazret 127,842; Gonder 112,249.

Vital statistics

Birth rate per 1,000 population (1999): 45.3 (world avg. 22.1).
Death rate per 1,000 population (1999): 17.5 (world avg. 8.9).
Natural increase rate per 1,000 population (1999): 27.8 (world avg 13.2).
Total fertility rate (avg. births per childbearing woman; 1999): 7.1.
Life expectancy at birth (1999): male 44.7 years; female 46.3 years.
Major causes of death (1987–88)[4, 5]: infectious and parasitic diseases 33.1%; respiratory diseases 15.7%; digestive system diseases 10.7%.

National economy

Budget (1997–98). Revenue: Br 9,686,000,000 (taxes 54.4%, of which import duties 21.0%, income and profit tax 17.1%, sales tax 12.2%, export duties 1.9%; nontax revenue 29.2%; grants 13.1%; privatization receipts 3.3%). Expenditures: Br 7,140,000,000 (general services 45.2%, of which defense 29.3%; social services 24.1%, of which education 15.8%, public health 5.6%; debt payment 12.3%).
Public debt (external, outstanding; 1998): U.S.$9,618,000,000.
Tourism (1998): receipts U.S.$11,000,000; expenditures U.S.$46,000,000.
Gross national product (1998): U.S.$6,169,000,000 (U.S.$100 per capita).

Structure of gross domestic product and labour force[4]

	1997–98 in value Br '000,000[7]	1997–98 % of total value	1995[6] labour force	1995[6] % of labour force
Agriculture	6,687.0	45.7	21,605,317	88.6
Manufacturing, mining	1,055.8	7.2	401,535	1.6
Construction	412.1	2.8	61,232	0.3
Public utilities	223.1	1.5	17,066	0.1
Transp. and commun.	907.8	6.2	103,154	0.4
Trade	1,263.3	8.7	935,937	3.8
Finance	999.2	6.8	19,451	0.1
Pub. admin., defense	1,848.3	12.7		
Services	1,234.4	8.4	1,252,224	5.1
Other	—	—		
TOTAL	14,631.0	100.0	24,395,916	100.0

Production (metric tons except as noted). Agriculture, forestry, fishing (1999): corn (maize) 2,840,000, sugarcane 2,200,000, sorghum 1,340,000, wheat 1,150,000, barley 970,000, millet 381,486, potatoes 370,000, yams 267,000, coffee 232,020, seed cotton 45,500; livestock (number of live animals) 35,095,230 cattle, 22,000,000 sheep, 16,950,000 goats, 8,580,000 horses, mules, and asses, 1,050,000 camels; roundwood (1998) 50,148,000 cu m; fish catch (1998) 14,000. Mining and quarrying (1995): cement 400,000; limestone 200,000; salt 165,000; gold 4,500 kg; platinum 48 troy oz. Manufacturing (gross value in Br '000; 1997): food 1,351,200; beverages 876,408; textiles 593,341; leather and shoes 483,364; cigarettes 240,371; paper and paper products 126,316; chemicals 29,688. Construction (authorized; 1987–88)[4, 8]: residential 260,251 sq m; nonresidential 63,346 sq m, of which commercial 16,994 sq m. Energy production (consumption)[4]: electricity (kW-hr; 1996) 1,675,000,000 (1,675,000,000); coal, none (n.a.); crude petroleum (barrels; 1996) n.a. (5,549,000); petroleum products (metric tons; 1996) 612,000 (861,000); natural gas, n.a. (n.a.).
Land use (1994): forest 13.3%; pasture 20.0%; agriculture 11.0%; other 55.7%.
Population economically active (1997): total 26,408,000; activity rate of total population 44.8% (participation rates [1995]: ages 15–64, 72.2%; female [1997] 41.0%; unemployed [1994] 62.9%).

Price index (1995 = 100)

	1993	1994	1995	1996	1997	1998	1999
Consumer price index	84.5	90.9	100.0	94.6	91.4	98.9	110.0

Household income and expenditure. Average household size (1998) 5.0; income per household (1981–82)[4] Br 1,728 (U.S.$835); sources of income (1981–82): self-employment 79.5%, wages and salaries 0.2%, other 20.3%; expenditure (1988)[4]: food 66.7%, fuel and power 15.9%, clothing and footwear 6.8%, health care 3.1%, education 2.5%, household goods 2.1%.

Foreign trade

Balance of trade (current prices)

	1993	1994	1995	1996	1997	1998
U.S.$'000,000	–507.1	–553.7	–713.7	–384.7	–430.5	–473.9
% of total	56.0%	42.7%	45.8%	27.0%	26.8%	29.4%

Imports (1997–98): Br 7,615,100,000 (consumer goods 24.9%, semifinished goods 17.2%, petroleum products 16.2%, transport equipment 13.2%, food and live animals 13.9%, machinery 13.1%, raw materials 2.1%). *Major import sources:* Japan 10.5%; Germany 9.8%; Saudi Arabia 9.7%; Italy 9.5%; U.K. 6.0%; India 5.7%; U.S. 4.7%.
Exports (1997–98): Br 3,966,000,000 (coffee 69.8%, hides 8.4%, pulses 2.5%, petroleum products 0.2%). *Major export destinations:* Germany 24.8%; Japan 12.2%; Saudi Arabia 9.9%; Italy 6.8%; U.S. 6.8%; Belgium 4.4%; France 3.6%.

Transport and communications

Transport. Railroads (1996–97)[9]: length 782 km; passenger-km 157,000,000; metric ton-km cargo 106,000,000. Roads (1996): total length 19,500 km (paved 15%). Vehicles (1997): passenger cars 52,012; trucks and buses 39,936. Air transport (1997)[10]: passenger-km 1,915,000,000; metric ton-km cargo 328,000,000; airports (1997) 31.

Communications

Medium	date	unit	number	units per 1,000 persons
Daily newspapers	1997	circulation	86,000	1.5
Radio	1997	receivers	11,750,000	202
Television	1998	receivers	340,000	5.7
Telephones	1998	main lines	164,140	2.8
Internet	1998	users	6,000	0.1

Education and health

Educational attainment: n.a. *Literacy* (1995): total population age 15 and over literate 35.5%; males 45.5%; females 25.3%.

Education (1994–95)

	schools	teachers	students	student/ teacher ratio
Primary (age 7–12)	9,276	83,113	2,722,192	32.8
Secondary (age 13–18)	1,209[11]	22,779	747,142	32.8
Voc., teacher tr.	...	826	9,103	11.0
Higher	11[12]	1,937	32,671	16.9

Health: physicians (1988)[4] 1,466 (1 per 30,195 persons); hospital beds (1986–87)[4] 11,745 (1 per 3,873 persons); infant mortality rate (1999) 102.8.
Food (1998): daily per capita caloric intake 1,805 (vegetable products 94%, animal products 6%); 77% of FAO recommended minimum.

Military

Total active duty personnel (1999): 375,500 (army 93.3%, air force 6.7%); 4,200 UN troops authorized from mid-September 2000 for Ethiopian-Eritrean border area not in place as of mid-November 2000. *Military expenditure as percentage of GNP* (1997): 1.9% (world 2.6%); per capita expenditure U.S.$2.

[1]Federal republic formally established on Aug. 22, 1995. [2]Amharic is the "working" language of the Federal Democratic Republic of Ethiopia. [3]1997 enumeration. [4]Includes Eritrea. [5]Percentage of illnesses in a sample population of hospital outpatients. [6]For age 10 and up. [7]At 1980–81 factor cost. [8]Addis Ababa only. [9]Includes 62 mi (100 km) of the Chemin de Fer Djibouti-Ethiopiën (CDE) in Djibouti; excludes 190 mi (306 km) of Northern Ethiopia Railway, not in use since 1978. [10]Ethiopian Airlines only. [11]1985–86. [12]1983–84.

Internet resources for further information:
- **Ethiopian Embassy (Washington, D.C.) http://www.ethiopianembassy.org**

Faroe Islands[1]

Official name: Føroyar (Faroese); Færøerne (Danish) (Faroe Islands).
Political status: self-governing region of the Danish realm[2] with a single legislative body (Lagting [32]).
Chief of state: Danish Monarch represented by High Commissioner.
Head of home government: Prime Minister
Capital: Tórshavn (Thorshavn).
Official languages: Faroese; Danish.
Official religion: Evangelical Lutheran.
Monetary unit: 1 Danish krone[3] (Dkr) = 100 øre; valuation (Oct. 6, 2000) 1 U.S.$ = Dkr 8.57; 1£ = Dkr 12.39.

Area and population

Districts	Capitals	area sq mi	area sq km	population 1998 estimate
Klaksvík	...	[4]	[4]	5,012
Nordhara Eysturoy (Østerø Nordre)	...	[5]	[5]	1,540
Nordhoy (Norderøernes)	...	93[4]	241[4]	682
Sandoy (Sandø)	...	48	125	1,480
Streymoy (Strømø)	...	151[6]	392[6]	3,995
Sudhuroy (Suderø)	...	65	167	5,026
Sydhra Eysturoy (Østerø Søndre)	...	110[5]	286[5]	8,304
Tórshavn (Thorshavn)	...	[6]	[6]	16,126
Vágar (Vágø)	...	73	188	2,636
TOTAL		540	1,399	44,801

Demography

Population (2000): 45,600.
Density (2000): persons per sq mi 84.4, persons per sq km 32.6.
Urban-rural (2000): urban[6] 36.3%; rural 63.7%.
Sex distribution (2000): male 51.76%; female 48.24%.
Age breakdown (2000): under 15, 23.0%; 15–29, 21.1%; 30–44, 19.5%; 45–59, 18.4%; 60–74, 11.5%; 75 and over, 6.5%.
Population projection: (2000) 48,300; (2010) 50,800.
Ethnic composition: n.a.
Religious affiliation (1995): Evangelical Lutheran Church of Denmark 80.8%; Plymouth Brethren 10.1%; Roman Catholic 0.2%; other (mostly nonreligious) 8.9%.
Major towns (1998): Tórshavn 14,542; Klaksvík 4,583; Runavík 2,383; Tvøroyri 1,795; Argja 1,584.

Vital statistics

Birth rate per 1,000 population (1999): 13.6 (world avg. 22.1); (1998) legitimate 62.0%; illegitimate 38.0%.
Death rate per 1,000 population (1999): 8.8 (world avg. 8.9).
Natural increase rate per 1,000 population (1999): 4.8 (world avg. 13.2).
Total fertility rate (avg. births per childbearing woman; 2000): 2.3.
Marriage rate per 1,000 population (1998): 4.7.
Divorce rate per 1,000 population (1994): 0.8.
Life expectancy at birth (2000): male 74.2 years; female 79.9 years.
Major causes of death per 100,000 population (1992): diseases of the circulatory system 354.5, of which ischemic heart disease 222.1, cerebrovascular disease 81.2; malignant neoplasms (cancers) 192.2; diseases of the respiratory system 59.8, of which pneumonia 36.3, bronchitis, emphysema, and asthma 17.1; suicides 8.5; automobile accidents 4.3.

National economy

Budget (1999). Revenue: Dkr 3,104,530,000 (income taxes 33.8%; customs and excise duties 32.4%; transfers from the Danish government 30.4%). Expenditures: Dkr 3,105,530,000 (health and social welfare 43.3%; education 16.6%; debt service 7.7%; agriculture, fishing, and commerce 7.5%; administration 6.0%).
Public debt (external; 1999): U.S.$51,000,000.
Gross national product (at current market prices; 1997): U.S.$890,000,000 (U.S.$20,220 per capita).

Structure of gross domestic product and labour force

	1999		1977	
	in value Dkr '000,000	% of total value	labour force	% of labour force
Agriculture	53	0.8	282	1.6
Fishing	1,344	20.5	3,032	17.2
Mining	18	0.3	3,854	21.9
Manufacturing	744	11.4		
Construction	321	4.9	1,952	11.1
Public utilities	150	2.3	[7]	[7]
Transp. and commun.	552	8.4	1,944	11.1
Trade, hotels	768	11.7	2,237[7]	12.7[7]
Finance and real estate	1,145	17.5	[7]	[7]
Pub. admin., defense	1,556	23.8	2,927	16.6
Services	234	3.6	796	4.5
Other	–340[8]	–5.2[8]	561[9]	3.2[9]
TOTAL	6,546[10]	100.0	17,585	100.0[10]

Production (metric tons except as noted). Agriculture, forestry, fishing (2000): potatoes 1,500, other vegetables, grass, hay, and silage are produced; livestock (number of live animals) 68,100 sheep, 2,000 cattle; fish catch (1999) 358,013 (of which blue whiting 105,106, mackeral 56,476, saithe 34,423, cod 33,725, capelin 24,275, prawns, shrimps, and other crustaceans 20,916, haddock 19,697). Mining and quarrying: negligible[11]. Manufacturing (value added in Dkr '000,000; 1999): processed fish 393; all other manufacturing 351; important products include handicrafts and woolen textiles and clothing. Construction (1993): completed dwellings 41. Energy production (consumption): electricity (kW-hr; 1997) 181,000,000 (181,000,000); coal, none (none); crude petroleum, none (none); petroleum products (metric tons; 1996) none (206,000); natural gas, none (none).
Tourism (1987): receipts from visitors U.S.$10,000,000; expenditures by nationals abroad U.S.$42,600,000.
Population economically active (1997): total 26,500; activity rate of total population *c.* 60% (participation rates: age 14–64, n.a.; female *c.* 46%; unemployed *c.* 10%).

Price and earnings indexes (1995 = 100)

	1995	1996	1997	1998	1999	2000
Consumer price index	100.0	102.6	106.0	109.6	114.6	119.6
Hourly wage index	100.0	100.0	101.5	102.5	104.4	109.3

Household income and expenditure. Average household size (1977) 3.7; average annual income per household: n.a.; sources of income[12]: self-employment 11.7%, wages and salaries 88.3%; expenditure (1980): food and beverages 40.9%, fuel and energy 18.9%, housing 17.5%, clothing and footwear 11.3%, other 11.4%.
Land use (1994): forested, none; meadows and pastures, none; agricultural and under permanent cultivation 2.1%; other 97.9%.

Foreign trade

Balance of trade (current prices)

	1994	1995	1996	1997	1998	1999
Dkr '000,000	+523	+260	+270	+198	+331	–24
% of total	14.4%	6.8%	5.9%	4.0%	6.0%	0.4%

Imports (1999): Dkr 3,276,000,000 (goods for household consumption 25.7%; machinery and transport equipment 16.1%; petroleum products 8.1%). *Major import sources:* Denmark 27.8%; Norway 26.1%; Germany 7.2%; United Kingdom 5.9%; Sweden 4.5%.
Exports (1999): Dkr 3,252,154,000 (fish for human consumption 90.3%, of which frozen fish 29.9%, fresh chilled fish 15.3%, dried, salted, and smoked fish 13.8%; ships 4.3%). *Major export destinations*: Denmark 32.1%; United Kingdom 21.2%; France 9.4%; Spain 6.7%; Germany 6.7%; United States 4.6%.

Transport and communications

Transport. Railroads: none. Roads (1998): total length 285 mi, 458 km (paved, n.a.). Vehicles (1998): passenger cars 17,819; trucks and buses 3,121. Merchant marine (1998): vessels (20 gross tons and over) 232; total gross tonnage 77,435. Air transport (1998): airports with scheduled flights 1.

Communications

Medium	date	unit	number	units per 1,000 persons
Daily newspapers	1996	circulation	6,000	136
Radio	1997	receivers	26,000	582
Television	1996	receivers	14,000	298
Telephones	1998	main lines	24,000	544
Cellular telephones	1998	subscribers	6,500	147
Internet	1998	users	5,000	113

Education and health

Education (1997–98)

	schools	teachers	students	student/ teacher ratio
Primary (first 7 grades)	68	...	5,037	...
Secondary			2,750	...
Voc., teacher tr.	11	...	2,195[13]	...
Higher[14]	1	18	70[15]	...

Health (1998): physicians 83 (1 per 537 persons); hospital beds 277 (1 per 161 persons); infant mortality rate per 1,000 live births (1998) 9.5.
Food (1979–81): daily per capita caloric intake 3,195 (vegetable products 68%, animal products 32%); 120% of FAO recommended minimum requirement.

Military

Defense responsibility lies with Denmark.

[1]English-language alternative spelling is Faeroe Islands. [2]Referendum for possible future independence is planned for 2001. [3]The local currency, the Faroese króna (Fkr), is equivalent to the Danish krone. Banknotes used are Faroese or Danish; coins are Danish. [4]Nordhoy contains Klaksvík. [5]Sydhra Eysturoy contains Nordhara Eysturoy. [6]Streymoy contains Tórshavn. [7]Trade, hotels includes Public utilities and Finance and real estate. [8]Imputed bank service charges. [9]Not adequately defined. [10]Detail does not add to total given because of rounding. [11]The maritime boundary demarcation agreement between the Shetland Islands (U.K.) and the Faroes in May 1999 allowed for the exploration of deep-sea petroleum. [12]Percentages refer to principal sources of income of economically active population. [13]1996–97. [14]University of the Faroe Islands. [15]Full-time students only.

Internet resources for further information:

- **Statistics Faroe Islands http://www.hagstova.Fo/Welcome_uk.html**
- **Governmental Bank: Information Memorandum on the Faroe Islands http://www.landsbank.fo**

Fiji

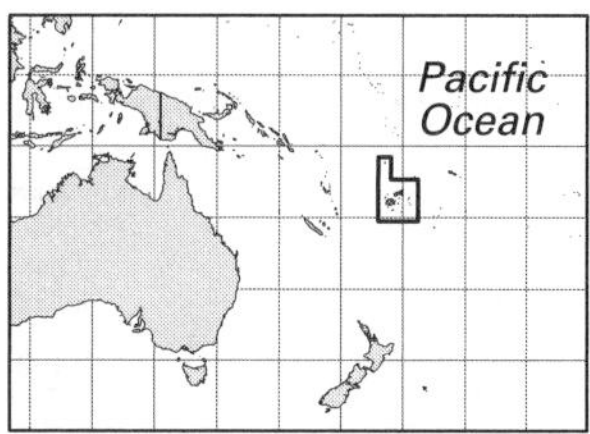

Official name: Republic of the Fiji Islands.
Form of government[1]: interim regime.
Chief of state: President.
Head of government: Prime Minister.
Capital: Suva.
Official language: [2].
Official religion: none
Monetary unit: 1 Fiji dollar (F$) = 100 cents; valuation (Oct. 6, 2000) 1 U.S.$ = F$2.25; 1 £ = F$3.25.

Area and population

Divisions Provinces	Capitals	area sq mi	area sq km	population 1996 census
Central	Suva			
Naitasiri	—	643	1,666	126,641
Namosi	—	220	570	5,742
Rewa	—	105	272	101,547
Serua	—	320	830	15,461
Tailevu	—	369	955	48,216
Eastern	Levuka			
Kadavu	—	185	478	9,535
Lau	—	188	487	12,211
Lomaiviti	—	159	411	16,214
Rotuma	—	18	46	2,810
Northern	Labasa			
Bua	—	532	1,379	14,988
Cakaudrove	—	1,087	2,816	44,321
Macuata	—	774	2,004	80,207
Western	Lautoka			
Ba	—	1,017	2,634	212,197
Nadroga-Navosa	—	921	2,385	54,083
Ra	—	518	1,341	30,904
TOTAL	—	7,055[3]	18,272[3]	775,077

Demography

Population (2000): 819,000.
Density (2000): persons per sq mi 116.1, persons per sq km 44.8.
Urban-rural (1996): urban 46.4%; rural 53.6%.
Sex distribution (2000): male 50.25%; female 49.75%.
Age breakdown (2000): under 15, 33.4%; 15–29, 28.3%; 30–44, 20.3%; 45–59, 12.1%; 60–74, 5.2%; 75 and over, 0.7%.
Population projection: (2010) 942,000; (2020) 1,072,000.
Doubling time: 39 years.
Ethnic composition (1996): Fijian 50.8%; Indian 43.7%[4]; other 5.5%.
Religious affiliation (1986): Christian 52.9%; Hindu 38.1%; Muslim 7.8%; Sikh 0.7%; other 0.5%.
Major cities (1996; "urban centres"): Suva 167,421; Lautoka 42,917; Nadi 30,791; Labasa 24,187; Nausori 21,645.

Vital statistics

Birth rate per 1,000 population (1999): 23.7 (world avg. 22.1); (1978) legitimate 82.7%; illegitimate 17.3%.
Death rate per 1,000 population (1999): 5.8 (world avg. 8.9).
Natural increase rate per 1,000 population (1999): 17.9 (world avg. 13.2).
Total fertility rate (avg. births per childbearing woman; 1999): 2.9.
Life expectancy at birth (1999): male 65.2 years; female 70.1 years.
Major causes of death per 100,000 population (1987): diseases of the circulatory system 153.4; malignant neoplasms (cancers) 35.5; accidents, poisoning, and violence 32.2; diseases of the respiratory system 31.7.

National economy

Budget (1998). Revenue: F$848,646,000 (income taxes, estate taxes, and gift duties 58.4%; customs duties and port dues 27.0%; fees, royalties, and sales 5.5%). Expenditures: F$1,029,456,000 (departmental expenditure 61.1%; public-debt charges 35.8%; pensions and gratuities 3.1%).
Production (metric tons except as noted). Agriculture, forestry, fishing (1999): sugarcane 4,398,000, coconuts 209,000, cassava 27,000, taro 26,000, paddy rice 18,000, sweet potatoes 7,400, bananas 6,400, yams 3,400, tomatoes 2,800, pineapples 2,500; livestock (number of live animals) 345,000 cattle, 235,000 goats, 112,000 pigs; roundwood (1998) 594,000 cu m; fish catch (1998) 28,212. Mining and quarrying (1995): gold 3,477 kg; silver 1,572 kg. Manufacturing (U.S.$'000,000; 1994): food products 84; wearing apparel 28; wood and wood products 16; beverages 15; chemical products 13. Construction (1995): residential 97,000 sq m; nonresidential 64,000 sq m. Energy production (consumption): electricity (kW-hr; 1996) 545,000,000 (545,000,000); coal (metric tons; 1996) none (22,000); crude petroleum, none (n.a.); petroleum products (metric tons; 1996) none (219,000); natural gas, none (n.a.).
Tourism (1998): receipts from visitors U.S.$266,000,000; expenditures by nationals abroad U.S.$51,000,000.
Land use (1994): forested 64.9%; agricultural and under permanent cultivation 14.2%; meadows and pastures 9.5%; other 11.4%.
Population economically active (1986): total 241,160; activity rate of total population 33.7% (participation rates: ages 15–64, 56.0%; female 21.2%; unemployed [1990] 6.4%).

Price and earnings indexes (1995 = 100)

	1993	1994	1995	1996	1997	1998	1999
Consumer price index	97.3	97.9	100.0	103.1	106.5	112.6	114.8
Earnings index	…	…	…	…	…	…	…

Gross national product (1998): U.S.$1,748,000,000 (U.S.$2,210 per capita).

Structure of gross domestic product and labour force

	1997 in value F$'000[5]	1997 % of total value[5]	1986 labour force	1986 % of labour force
Agriculture	323,600	17.3	106,305	44.1
Mining	62,722	3.4	1,345	0.5
Manufacturing	267,452	14.3	18,106	7.5
Construction	82,306	4.4	11,786	4.9
Public utilities	78,967	4.2	2,154	0.9
Transp. and commun.	245,294	13.1	13,151	5.4
Trade	310,196	16.6	26,010	10.8
Finance	249,115	13.3	6,016	2.5
Pub. admin., defense; Services	364,640	19.5	36,619	15.2
Other	–115,828[6]	–6.1[6]	19,668[7]	8.2[7]
TOTAL	1,868,464	100.0	241,160	100.0

Public debt (external, outstanding; 1998): U.S.$140,000,000.
Household income and expenditure. Average household size (1986) 5.7; income per household (1980) F$2,837 (U.S.$3,546); sources of income (1973): wages and salaries 81.5%, self-employment 9.1%, other 9.4%; expenditure (1991[8]): food, beverages, and tobacco 41.5%, housing and energy 21.4%, transportation and communications 12.9%, household durable goods 6.5%.

Foreign trade

Balance of trade (current prices)

	1993	1994	1995	1996	1997	1998
F$'000,000	–521.42	–409.36	–454.45	–225.26	–334.16	–204.8
% of total	30.7%	20.4%	22.9%	10.9%	16.8%	9.2%

Imports (1997): F$1,392,664,000 (durable manufactures 27.6%; machinery and transport equipment 20.6%; food, beverages, and tobacco 14.8%; petroleum products 14.1%; miscellaneous manufactured consumer articles 12.4%; chemicals 7.8%). *Major import sources:* Australia 45.2%; New Zealand 15.4%; Japan 6.9%; United States 5.2%; Singapore 4.2%; China 2.9%; Taiwan 2.4%; Hong Kong 2.2%; Thailand 1.9%; United Kingdom 1.8%.
Exports (1997)[9]: F$714,621,000 (sugar 24.4%; clothing 23.5%; gold 8.7%; fish 5.3%; timber 3.5%; molasses 1.8%; coconut oil 0.8%). *Major export destinations*[10]: Australia 40.5%; United Kingdom 21.4%; Japan 13.4%; United States 10.2%; New Zealand 6.3%; Malaysia 2.4%.

Transport and communications

Transport. Railroads (1995)[11]: length 370 mi, 595 km. Roads (1995): total length 3,200 mi, 5,100 km (paved 20%). Vehicles (1995): passenger cars 49,712; trucks and buses 33,928. Merchant marine (1992): vessels (100 gross tons and over) 64; total deadweight tonnage 60,444. Air transport (1996)[12]: passenger-km 1,194,652,000; metric ton-km cargo 75,367,000; airports(1997) with scheduled flights 13.

Communications

Medium	date	unit	number	units per 1,000 persons
Daily newspapers	1996	circulation	40,000	51
Radio	1997	receivers	500,000	636
Television	1998	receivers	80,000	100
Telephones	1998	main lines	76,933	97
Cellular telephones	1998	subscribers	8,000	10
Internet	1998	users	5,000	6.3

Education and health

Educational attainment (1986). Percentage of population age 25 and over having: no formal schooling 28.3%; primary only 19.1%; some secondary 44.1%; secondary 4.1%; postsecondary 3.3%; other 1.1%. *Literacy* (1995): total population age 15 and over literate 91.6%; males literate 93.8%; females literate 89.3%.

Education (1997)

	schools	teachers	students	student/ teacher ratio
Primary (age 5–15)	693[13]	5,011	142,781	28.5
Secondary (age 16–19)	142[13]	3,519	70,098	19.9
Voc., teacher tr.[13]	45	625	7,283	11.6
Higher[14]	5[15]	277	7,908	28.5

Health (1997): physicians 409 (1 per 1,913 persons); hospital beds 1,805 (1 per 433 persons); infant mortality rate per 1,000 live births (1999) 14.9.
Food (1998): daily per capita caloric intake 2,852 (vegetable products 82%, animals products 18%); 125% of FAO recommended minimum requirement.

Military

Total active duty personnel (1999): 3,500 (army 91.4%, navy 8.6%, air force, none). *Military expenditure as percentage of GNP* (1997): 2.4% (world 2.6%); per capita expenditure U.S.$61.

[1]The constitution was suspended in mid-May 2000. An interim government was announced in July 2000 to serve until July 2003. [2]English, Fijian, and Hindustani (Fijian Hindī) have equal status per 1998 constitution. [3]Detail does not add to total given because of rounding. [4]The emigration of Indian population after the coup in 1987 has resulted in the reemergence of a Fijian majority. [5]Constant 1989 prices. [6]Less imputed bank service charges. [7]Not stated and unemployed. [8]Weights of consumer price index components based on 3,000 urban households. [9]Excludes reexports valued at F$138,906,000. [10]Based on exports of local products only. [11]Owned by the Fiji Sugar Corporation. [12]Air Pacific only. [13]1992. [14]1991. [15]1983.

Internet resources for further information:
- **Fiji Islands Statistics Bureau http://www.statsfiji.gov.fj**
- **Fiji Government Online http://www.fiji.gov.fj/core/home/html**

Finland

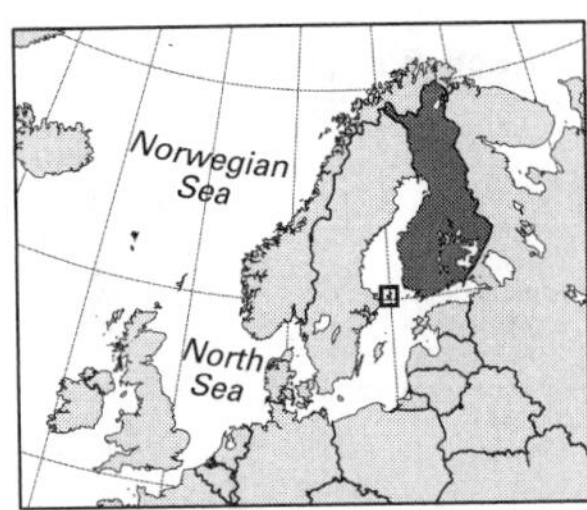

Official name: Suomen Tasavalta (Finnish); Republiken Finland (Swedish) (Republic of Finland).
Form of government: multiparty republic with one legislative house (Parliament [200[1]]).
Chief of state: President.
Head of government: Prime Minister.
Capital: Helsinki.
Official languages: none[2].
Official religion: none[3].
Monetary unit: 1 markka (Fmk) = 100 penniä, valuation (Oct. 6, 2000) 1 U.S.$ = Fmk 6.84; 1 £ = Fmk 9.89.

Area and population

		area		population
				2000
Provinces	Capitals	sq mi	sq km	estimate[4]
Åland (Ahvenamaa)	Mariehamn (Maarianhamina)	599	1,552	25,706
Eastern Finland	Mikkeli	23,444	60,720	595,113
Lapland	Rovaniemi	38,203	98,946	194,352
Oulu	Oulu	23,773	61,572	453,469
Southern Finland	Hämeenlinna	13,273	34,378	2,068,259
Western Finland	Turku	31,265	80,976	1,834,403
TOTAL		130,559[5, 6]	338,145[5, 6]	5,171,302

Demography

Population (2000): 5,178,000.
Density (2000)[7]: persons per sq mi 44.0, persons per sq km 17.0.
Urban-rural (2000): urban 60.4%; rural 39.6%[8].
Sex distribution (2000): male 48.79%; female 51.21%.
Age breakdown (2000): under 15, 18.2%; 15–29, 18.7%; 30–44, 21.8%; 45–59, 21.5%; 60–74, 13.4%; 75 and over, 6.4%.
Population projection: (2010) 5,239,000; (2020) 5,246,000.
Doubling time: not applicable; population is stable.
Linguistic composition (2000): Finnish 92.5%; Swedish 5.7%; other 1.8%.
Religious affiliation (2000): Evangelical Lutheran 85.2%; Finnish (Greek) Orthodox 1.1%; nonreligious 12.6%; other 1.1%.
Major cities (2000): Helsinki 551,123 (metro area 945,725); Espoo 209,667[9]; Tampere 193,174; Vantaa 176,386[9]; Turku 172,107; Oulu 117,670.

Vital statistics

Birth rate per 1,000 population (1999): 11.2 (world avg. 22.1); (1998) legitimate 62.8%; illegitimate 37.2%.
Death rate per 1,000 population (1999): 9.6 (world avg. 8.9).
Natural increase rate per 1,000 population (1999): 1.6 (world avg. 13.2).
Total fertility rate (avg. births per childbearing woman; 1998): 1.7.
Marriage rate per 1,000 population (1998): 4.7.
Divorce rate per 1,000 population (1998): 2.7.
Life expectancy at birth (1998): male 73.5 years; female 80.8 years.
Major causes of death per 100,000 population (1996): ischemic heart diseases 253.1; malignant neoplasms (cancers) 201.2; cerebrovascular diseases 103.3; diseases of the respiratory system 82.2; accidents 80.5.

National economy

Budget (1998). Revenue: Fmk 186,885,000,000 (income and property taxes 27.9%, value-added taxes 25.0%, excise duties 13.8%, loans 8.6%). Expenditures: Fmk 186,883,000,000 (social security and health 23.4%, state debt 13.7%, education 12.7%, agriculture 5.7%, defense 5.4%).
National debt (December 1997): U.S.$77,360,000,000.
Tourism (in U.S.$'000,000; 1998): receipts 1,631; expenditures 2,063.
Production (metric tons except as noted). Agriculture, forestry, fishing (1997): silage 5,630,000, barley 2,003,000, sugar beets 1,355,000, oats 1,243,000, potatoes 754,000, wheat 464,000; livestock (number of live animals; 1998) 1,467,000 pigs, 1,145,000 cattle, 203,000 reindeer; roundwood (1998) 51,281,000 cu m; fish catch (1996) 184,288. Mining and quarrying (1997): chromite (gross weight) 611,000; gold 4,800 kilograms. Manufacturing (value added in Fmk '000,000; 1995): wood pulp, paper, and paperboard 27,414; nonelectrical machinery 19,213; electrical machinery 13,129; food products 10,159; printing and publishing 7,391; iron and steel 6,214; industrial and basic chemicals 5,362. Construction (completed; 1997): residential 9,250,000 cu m; nonresidential 22,190,000 cu m. Energy production (consumption): electricity (kW-hr; 1998) 67,092,000,000 ([1997] 71,352,000,000); coal (metric tons; 1996) none (7,704,000); crude petroleum (barrels; 1996) none (71,746,000); petroleum products (metric tons; 1996) 11,861,000 (10,355,000); natural gas (cu m; 1996) none (3,582,000,000).
Population economically active (1996): total 2,531,000; activity rate of total population 49.4% (participation rates: ages 15–64, 73.8%; female 47.1%; unemployed [1999] 10.2%).

Price and earnings indexes (1995 = 100)

	1994	1995	1996	1997	1998	1999	2000
Consumer price index	99.0	100.0	100.6	101.8	103.2	104.4	108.3[10]
Annual earnings index	95.5	100.0	103.9	106.0	...	...	...

Household income and expenditure (1996). Average household size 2.2; disposable income per household Fmk 132,900 (U.S.$28,930); sources of disposable income: wages and salaries 74.9%, self-employment 8.3%, transfer payments 4.4%, other 12.4%; expenditure (1996): housing and energy 27.9%, transportation and communications 21.2%, food and beverages 16.5%.

Gross national product (1998): U.S.$125,091,000,000 (U.S.$24,280 per capita).

Structure of gross domestic product and labour force

	1997		1996	
	in value Fmk '000,000	% of total value	labour force	% of labour force
Agriculture, fishing	7,844	1.4	165,000	6.5
Forestry	13,826	2.6		
Mining	1,968	0.4	5,000	0.2
Manufacturing	142,162	26.4	490,000	19.3
Public utilities	13,934	2.6	25,000	1.0
Construction	34,374	6.4	161,000	6.4
Transp. and commun.	47,846	8.9	176,000	6.9
Trade, restaurants	59,524	11.1	364,000	14.4
Finance, real estate	106,634	19.8	265,000	10.5
Pub. admin., defense	99,006	18.4	154,000	6.1
Services	14,790	2.7	633,000	25.0
Other	–3,815	–0.7	93,000[11]	3.7[11]
TOTAL	538,093	100.0	2,531,000	100.0

Land use (1994): forested 76.1%; meadows and pastures 0.4%; agricultural and under permanent cultivation 8.5%; other 15.0%.

Foreign trade[12]

Balance of trade (current prices)

	1994	1995	1996	1997	1998	1999
Fmk '000,000	+33,552	+49,952	+42,170	+51,845	+56,918	...
% of total	12.2%	16.9%	13.6%	13.9%	14.2%	13.9%

Imports (1997): Fmk 160,995,000,000 (nonelectrical machinery and apparatus 15.3%; electrical machinery and apparatus 14.5%; mineral fuels 9.6%; automobiles 7.6%). *Major import sources:* Germany 14.5%; Sweden 12.1%; U.K. 7.8%; Russia 7.8%; U.S. 7.3%; Japan 5.3%; France 4.8%.
Exports (1997): Fmk 212,840,000,000 (paper and paper products 20.6%; electrical machinery and apparatus 17.9%; nonelectrical machinery and apparatus 14.2%; wood products and furniture 6.5%). *Major export destinations:* Germany 11.0%; U.K. 10.0%; Sweden 9.8%; Russia 7.3%; U.S. 6.9%; France 4.2%; The Netherlands 4.1%.

Transport and communications

Transport. Railroads: route length (1997) 5,886 km; passenger-km 3,376,000,000; metric ton-km cargo 9,856,000,000. Roads (1997): total length[13] 77,796 km (paved 64%). Vehicles (1997): passenger cars 1,948,126; trucks and buses 275,394. Air transport (1998)[14]: passenger-km 10,714,000,000; metric ton-km cargo 208,936,000; airports (1996) 24.

Communications

Medium	date	unit	number	units per 1,000 persons
Daily newspapers	1996	circulation	2,332,000	455
Radio	1997	receivers	7,700,000	1,498
Television	1997	receivers	3,200,000	623
Telephones	1998	main lines	2,855,000	554
Cellular telephones	1998	subscribers	2,947,000	572
Personal computers	1998	units	1,800,000	349
Internet	1998	users	1,473,000	286

Education and health

Educational attainment (end of 1996). Percentage of population age 25 and over having: incomplete upper-secondary education 42.7%; complete upper secondary or vocational 42.5%; higher 14.8%. *Literacy:* virtually 100%.

Education (1997–98)

	schools	teachers	students	student/ teacher ratio
Primary/Lower Secondary (age 7–15)	4,319	...	592,375	...
Upper Secondary (age 16–18)	457	...	138,356	...
Voc. (incl. higher)	421	21,245[15]	242,000	9.5[15]
Higher	37	7,790[15]	206,100	16.4[15]

Health (1997): physicians 15,192[16] (1 per 338 persons); hospital beds (1995) 46,362[17] (1 per 110 persons); infant mortality rate per 1,000 live births (1998) 4.2.
Food (1997): daily per capita caloric intake 3,100 (vegetable products 61%, animal products 39%); 114% of FAO recommended minimum requirement.

Military

Total active duty personnel (1998): 31,700 (army 75.7%, navy 15.8%, air force 8.5%). *Military expenditure as percentage of GNP* (1997): 1.7% (world 2.6%); per capita expenditure U.S.$381.

[1]Includes one representative from Åland not taking part in the 1999 general elections. [2]Finnish and Swedish were official languages until mid-1995 and national languages thereafter. [3]The Evangelical Lutheran and Finnish (Greek) Orthodox churches have special recognition. [4]January 1. [5]Detail does not add to total given because of rounding. [6]Total includes land area of 117,580 sq mi (304,529 sq km) and inland water area of 12,979 sq mi (33,616 sq km). [7]Based on land area only. [8]Includes semi-urban (16.5% of total). [9]Within Helsinki metro area. [10]July. [11]Includes 83,000 unemployed persons not previously employed and 10,000 not adequately defined. [12]Imports c.i.f., exports f.o.b. [13]Excludes Åland Islands. [14]Finnair only. [15]1994–95. [16]Registered professionals of working age. [17]Excludes beds in hospitals operated by specialized institutions.

Internet resources for further information:
- **Embassy of Finland (Washington, D.C.) http://www.finland.org/facts.html**
- **Statistics Finland http://www.stat.fi/index_en.html**

France

Official name: République Française (French Republic).
Form of government: republic with two legislative houses (Parliament; Senate [321], National Assembly [577]).
Chief of state: President.
Head of government: Prime Minister.
Capital: Paris.
Official language: French.
Official religion: none.
Monetary unit: 1 franc (F) = 100 centimes; valuation (Oct. 6, 2000) 1 U.S.$ = F 7.54; 1 £ = F 10.91.

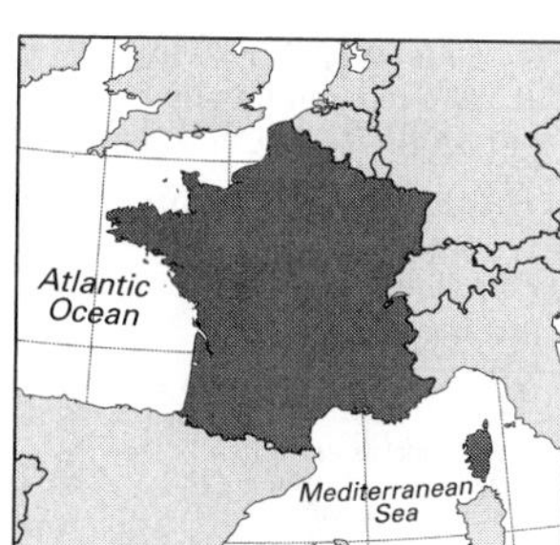

Area and population

Regions / Departments	Capitals	area sq mi	area sq km	population 1999 census
Alsace				
Bas-Rhin	Strasbourg	1,836	4,755	1,026,120
Haut-Rhin	Colmar	1,361	3,525	708,025
Aquitaine				
Dordogne	Périgueux	3,498	9,060	388,293
Gironde	Bordeaux	3,861	10,000	1,287,334
Landes	Mont-de-Marsan	3,569	9,243	327,334
Lot-et-Garonne	Agen	2,070	5,361	305,380
Pyrénées-Atlantiques	Pau	2,952	7,645	600,018
Auvergne				
Allier	Moulins	2,834	7,340	344,721
Cantal	Aurillac	2,211	5,726	150,778
Haute-Loire	Le Puy	1,922	4,977	209,113
Puy-de-Dôme	Clermont-Ferrand	3,077	7,970	604,266
Basse-Normandie				
Calvados	Caen	2,142	5,548	648,385
Manche	Saint-Lô	2,293	5,938	481,471
Orne	Alençon	2,356	6,103	292,337
Bourgogne				
Côte-d'Or	Dijon	3,383	8,763	506,755
Nièvre	Nevers	2,632	6,817	225,198
Saône-et-Loire	Mâcon	3,311	8,575	544,893
Yonne	Auxerre	2,868	7,427	333,221
Bretagne				
Côtes-d'Armor	Saint-Brieuc	2,656	6,878	542,373
Finistère	Quimper	2,600	6,733	852,418
Ille-et-Vilaine	Rennes	2,616	6,775	867,533
Morbihan	Vannes	2,634	6,823	643,873
Centre				
Cher	Bourges	2,793	7,235	314,428
Eure-et-Loir	Chartres	2,270	5,880	407,665
Indre	Châteauroux	2,622	6,791	231,139
Indre-et-Loire	Tours	2,366	6,127	554,003
Loir-et-Cher	Blois	2,449	6,343	314,968
Loiret	Orléans	2,616	6,775	618,126
Champagne-Ardenne				
Ardemmes	Charleville-Mézières	2,019	5,229	290,130
Aube	Troyes	2,318	6,004	292,131
Haute-Marne	Chaumont	2,398	6,211	194,873
Marne	Châlons-sur-Marne	3,151	8,162	565,229
Corse[1] (Corsica)				
Corse-du-Sud	Ajaccio	1,550	4,014	118,593
Haute-Corse	Bastia	1,802	4,666	141,603
Franche-Comté				
Doubs	Besançon	2,021	5,234	499,062
Haute-Saône	Vesoul	2,070	5,360	229,732
Jura	Lons-le-Saunier	1,930	4,999	250,857
Territoire de Belfort	Belfort	235	609	137,408
Haute-Normandie				
Eure	Évreux	2,332	6,040	541,054
Seine-Maritime	Rouen	2,424	6,278	1,239,138
Île-de-France				
Essonne	Évry	696	1,804	1,134,238
Hauts-de-Seine	Nanterre	68	176	1,428,881
Paris	Paris	40	105	2,125,246
Seine-et-Marne	Melun	2,284	5,915	1,193,767
Seine-Saint-Denis	Bobigny	91	236	1,382,861
Val-de-Marne	Créteil	95	245	1,227,250
Val-d'Oise	Pontoise	481	1,246	1,105,464
Yvelines	Versailles	882	2,284	1,354,304
Languedoc-Roussillon				
Aude	Carcassonne	2,370	6,139	309,770
Gard	Nîmes	2,260	5,853	623,125
Hérault	Montpellier	2,356	6,101	896,441
Lozère	Mende	1,995	5,167	73,509
Pyrénées-Orientales	Perpignan	1,589	4,116	392,803
Limousin				
Corrèze	Tulle	2,261	5,857	232,576
Creuse	Guéret	2,149	5,565	124,470
Haute-Vienne	Limoges	2,131	5,520	353,893
Lorraine				
Meurthe-et-Moselle	Nancy	2,024	5,241	713,779
Meuse	Bar-le-Duc	2,400	6,216	192,198
Moselle	Metz	2,400	6,216	1,023,447
Vosges	Épinal	2,268	5,874	380,952
Midi-Pyrénées				
Ariège	Foix	1,888	4,890	137,205
Aveyron	Rodez	3,373	8,736	263,808
Gers	Auch	2,416	6,257	172,335
Haute-Garonne	Toulouse	2,436	6,309	1,046,338
Haute-Pyrénées	Tarbes	1,724	4,464	222,368
Lot	Cahors	2,014	5,217	160,197
Tarn	Albi	2,223	5,758	343,402
Tarn-et-Garonne	Montauban	1,435	3,718	206,034
Nord-Pas-de-Calais				
Nord	Lille	2,217	5,742	2,555,020
Pas-de-Calais	Arras	2,576	6,671	1,441,568
Pays de la Loire				
Loire-Atlantique	Nantes	2,631	6,815	1,134,266
Maine-et Loire	Angers	2,767	7,166	732,942
Mayenne	Laval	1,998	5,175	285,338
Sarthe	Le Mans	2,396	6,206	529,851
Vendée	La Roche-sur-Yon	2,595	6,720	539,664
Picardie				
Aisne	Laon	2,845	7,369	535,842
Oise	Beauvais	2,263	5,860	766,441
Somme	Amiens	2,382	6,170	555,551
Poitou-Charentes				
Charente	Angoulême	2,300	5,956	339,628
Charente-Maritime	La Rochelle	2,650	6,864	557,024
Deux-Sèvres	Niort	2,316	5,999	344,392
Vienne	Poitiers	2,699	6,990	399,024
Provence-Alpes–Côte d'Azur				
Alpes-de-Haute-Provence	Digne	2,674	6,925	139,561
Alpes-Maritimes	Nice	1,660	4,299	1,011,326
Bouches-du-Rhône	Marseille	1,964	5,087	1,835,719
Hautes-Alpes	Gap	2,142	5,549	121,419
Var	Toulon	2,306	5,973	898,441
Vaucluse	Avignon	1,377	3,567	499,685
Rhône-Alpes				
Ain	Bourg-en-Bresse	2,225	5,762	515,270
Ardèche	Privas	2,135	5,529	286,023
Drôme	Valence	2,521	6,530	437,778
Haute-Savoie	Annecy	1,694	4,388	631,679
Isère	Grenoble	2,869	7,431	1,094,006
Loire	Saint-Étienne	1,846	4,781	728,524
Rhône	Lyon	1,254	3,249	1,578,869
Savoie	Chambéry	2,327	6,028	373,258
TOTAL		210,026	543,965	60,186,184

Demography

Population (2000): 58,835,000.
Density (2000): persons per sq mi 280.1, persons per sq km 108.2.
Urban-rural (1999): urban 75.4%; rural 24.6%.
Sex distribution (1999): male 48.75%; female 51.25%.
Age breakdown (1998[2]): under 15, 19.0%; 15–29, 20.7%; 30–44, 22.1%; 45–59, 17.8%; 60–74, 13.6%; 75 and over, 6.8%.
Population projection: (2010) 60,591,000; (2020) 61,365,000.
Doubling time: not applicable; doubling time exceeds 100 years.
Ethnolinguistic composition (1990): French (mother tongue) 93.6%, of which fully or substantially bilingual in Occitan 2.7%, German (mostly Alsatian) 2.6%, Breton 1.0%, Catalan 0.4%; Arabic 2.5%; other 3.9%.
Religious affiliation (1997): Roman Catholic 76.3%; Muslim 5.5%; Protestants 2.4%; other 15.8%.
Major cities (1990): Paris 2,152,423 (metropolitan area 9,060,257); Marseille 800,550 (1,231,082); Lyon 415,487 (1,262,223); Toulouse 358,658 (608,430); Nice 342,439 (475,507); Strasbourg 252,338 (338,483); Nantes 244,995 (492,255); Bordeaux 210,336 (685,456); Montpellier 207,996 (236,788).
National origin (1990): French 93.6%, of which Martiniquais 0.2%, Guadeloupian 0.2%, Réunionese 0.2%; Portuguese 1.1%; Algerian 1.1%; Moroccan 1.0%; Italian 0.4%; Spanish 0.4%; Turkish 0.3%; other 2.1%.
Mobility (1990). Population living in same residence as in 1982: 51.4%; same region 89.0%; different region 8.8%; different country 2.2%.
Households (1993). Average household size 2.6; 1 person 27.7%, 2 persons 32.0%, 3 persons 17.4%, 4 persons 14.7%, 5 persons or more 8.2%. Family households (1990): 14,118,940 (72.1%); nonfamily 5,471,460 (27.9%, of which 1-person 24.6%).
Immigration (1994): immigrants admitted 64,102 (Algeria 13.6%, Morocco 12.3%, Turkey 7.3%, Tunisia 3.4%, Sri Lanka 2.7%, Lebanon 1.3%).

Vital statistics

Birth rate per 1,000 population (1998): 12.6 (world avg. 22.1); (1994) legitimate 63.9%; illegitimate 36.1%.
Death rate per 1,000 population (1998): 9.2 (world avg. 8.9).
Natural increase rate per 1,000 population (1998): 3.4 (world avg. 13.2).
Total fertility rate (avg. births per childbearing woman; 1997): 1.7.
Marriage rate per 1,000 population (1998): 4.8.
Divorce rate per 1,000 population (1996): 2.0.
Life expectancy at birth (1997): male 74.6 years; female 82.3 years.
Major causes of death per 100,000 population (1997): heart disease and other circulatory diseases 291.6; malignant neoplasms (cancers) 252.2; accidents and violence 74.4; respiratory diseases 74.4; digestive tract diseases 44.8.

Social indicators

Educational attainment (1990). Percentage of population age 25 and over having: primary 22.1%; lower secondary 7.8%; higher secondary and vocational 29.4%; postsecondary 11.6%; undeclared attainment 29.1%.

Distribution of income (1984)

percentage of household income by quintile				
1	2	3	4	5 (highest)
7.1%	12.3%	17.1%	23.2%	40.3%

Quality of working life. Average workweek (1994): 38.9 hours. Annual rate per 100,000 workers for: injury or accident 5,322 (deaths 0.8%); accidents in transit to work 708 (deaths 68.3); industrial illness 16.6[3]; death 4.8[3]. Average days lost to labour stoppages per 1,000 workers (1994): 21.0. Average length of journey to work (1990): 8.7 mi (14 km).
Access to services (1992). Proportion of dwellings having: central heating 86.0%; piped water 97.0%; indoor plumbing 95.8%.
Social participation. Eligible voters participating in last (May and June 1997) national election: *c.* 78%. Population over 15 years of age participating in voluntary associations: 28.0%.

Social deviance. Offense rate per 100,000 population (1995) for: murder 0.7, rape 12.6, other assault 328.8; theft (including burglary and housebreaking) 6,304.4. Incidence per 100,000 in general population of: alcoholism, n.a. (deaths related to alcoholism; 1991) 5.0; suicide (1993) 21.1.
Leisure (1987–88). Participation rate for favourite leisure activities: watching television 82%; reading magazines 79%; listening to radio 75%; entertaining relatives 64%; visiting relatives 61%; attending fairs/expositions 56%.
Material well-being (1994). Households possessing: automobile 79.5%; colour television 92.4%; VCR 52.8%; refrigerator 99.0%, washing machine 89.4%.

National economy

Gross national product (1998): U.S.$1,465,399,000,000 (U.S.$24,210 per capita).

Structure of gross domestic product and labour force

	1995			
	in value F '000,000	% of total value	labour force	% of labour force
Agriculture	183,444	2.6	1,026,000	4.1
Mining	57,507	0.8	118,900	0.5
Manufacturing	1,542,442	21.8	3,992,700	15.8
Construction	342,836	4.8	1,466,600	5.8
Public utilities	178,069	2.5	162,900	0.6
Transp. and commun.	433,518	6.1	1,272,800	5.0
Trade[4]	1,012,441	14.3	3,482,000	13.8
Finance	320,501	4.5	601,900	2.4
Pub. admin., defense	1,323,570	18.7	6,248,100	24.7
Services	1,290,922	18.2	3,953,800	15.7
Other	403,238[5]	5.7[5]	2,934,600[6]	11.6[6]
TOTAL	7,088,488	100.0	25,260,300	100.0

Budget (1996). Revenue: F 1,552,100,000,000 (value-added taxes 49.1%; direct taxes 38.2%; customs taxes 10.2%). Expenditure: F 1,541,300,000,000 (education 22.5%, defense 15.6%, debt service 14.7%, social welfare 10.8%).

Manufacturing enterprises (1995)

	no. of enterprises[7]	no. of employees	annual salaries as a % of avg. of all salaries[7]	annual value added (F '000,000)
Food products	55,197	545,900	87	208,065
Transport equipment	4,293	508,700	108	167,357
Electrical machinery	15,620	433,600	118	156,221
Iron and steel	27,847	403,800	96	131,376
Mechanical equipment	32,134	390,300	104	127,637
Petroleum refineries	180	46,200	174	117,041
Printing, publishing	30,359	231,900	125	83,083
Textiles and wearing apparel	29,701	281,500	78	63,633
Rubber products	5,875	204,200	94	57,758
Chemical products	1,442	102,100	128	51,146
Paper and paper products	1,916	101,500	102	38,585
Metal products	442	43,700	103	28,115
Glass products	1,536	52,400	104	16,638
Footwear	4,236	55,400	75	12,970

Production (metric tons except as noted). Agriculture, forestry, fishing (1999): wheat 37,086,000, sugar beets 31,422,000, corn (maize) 14,869,000, barley 9,584,000, grapes 6,800,000, potatoes 6,500,000, rapeseed 4,459,000, dry peas 3,200,000, sunflower seeds 2,040,000, apples 1,954,000, tomatoes 864,000, carrots 670,000, green peas 550,000, oats 550,000, lettuce 490,000, cauliflower 470,000, peaches 468,000, string beans 380,000, onions 330,000, sorghum 305,000; livestock (number of live animals) 20,214,000 cattle, 16,190,000 pigs, 10,240,000 sheep, 1,199,000 goats; roundwood (1998) 35,586,000 cu m; fish catch (1997) 829,845. Mining and quarrying (1997): potash 700,000; iron ore 500,000; bauxite 130,800[8]; uranium 580; gold 144,678 troy oz; silver 64,301 troy oz. Manufacturing (1995): cement 19,896,000; crude steel 18,132,000; pig iron 12,876,000; paper products 8,700,000; rubber products 619,400, of which tires 59,268,000 units; aluminum 586,000; automobiles 3,200,000 units. Construction (dwelling units completed; 1993) 299,000.

Retail trade enterprises (1995[1])

	no. of enterprises	no. of employees	weekly wages as a % of all wages	annual turnover (F '000,000)
Large food stores	4,373	385,402	...	617,222
Clothing stores	51,873	195,535	...	126,504
Pharmacies	22,301	126,508	...	121,980
Small food stores	64,565	163,474	...	110,928
butcher shops	21,548	59,962	...	36,732
Furniture stores	7,179	53,080	...	54,390
Electrical and electronics stores	10,990	55,560	...	43,995
Department stores	736	35,074	...	27,741
Publishing and paper	15,083	40,375	...	24,591
Gas, coal, and other energy products	6,042	25,375	...	19,204

Energy production (consumption)[9]: electricity (kW-hr; 1994) 475,622,000,000 (412,454,000,000); coal (metric tons; 1994) 8,039,000 (21,809,900); crude petroleum (barrels; 1994) 20,297,000 (562,907,000); petroleum products (metric tons; 1994) 69,078,000 (66,994,000); natural gas (cu m; 1994) 2,517,200,000 (33,449,900,000).
Population economically active (1995): total 25,260,300; activity rate of total population 43.4% (participation rates: ages 15–64, 67.6%[10]; female 45.0%; unemployed 11.7%).

Price and earnings indexes (1995 = 100)

	1993	1994	1995	1996	1997	1998	1999
Consumer price index	96.6	98.3	100.0	102.0	103.2	103.9	104.5
Earnings index	96.3	99.2	100.0	101.9	104.7	107.6	110.0

Household income and expenditure (1995). Average household size 2.6; average annual income per household F 302,560 (U.S.$60,610); sources of income: wages and salaries 70.0%, self-employment 24.4%, social security 5.6%, expenditure (1997): housing 22.5%, food 17.9%, transportation 16.3%, health 10.3%, recreation and education 7.4%, clothing 5.2%.
Tourism (1998): receipts U.S.$29,931,000,000; expenditures U.S.$17,791,000,000.
Public debt (1998): F 5,030,000,000,000 (U.S.$853,000,000,000).

Financial aggregates

	1993	1994	1995	1996	1997	1998
Exchange rate, F per:						
U.S. dollar	5.90	5.35	4.90	5.24	5.99	5.62
£	8.73	8.35	7.60	8.90	9.90	9.35
SDR	8.10	7.80	7.28	7.53	8.08	7.92
International reserves (U.S.$)						
Total (excl. gold; '000,000)	22,649	26,257	26,853	26,796	30,927	44,312
SDRs ('000,000)	331	362	955	981	971	1,107
Reserve pos. in IMF ('000,000)	2,310	2,375	2,756	2,695	2,859	4,452
Foreign exchange	20,008	23,520	23,142	23,120	27,097	38,753
Gold ('000,000 fine troy oz)	81.85	81.85	81.85	81.85	81.89	102.37
% world reserves	8.7	8.7	9.1	9.0	9.2	10.6
Interest and prices						
Central bank discount (%)	9.50	9.50	...	...	...	...
Govt. bond yield (%)	6.91	8.52	7.59	6.39	5.63	4.69
Industrial share prices (1995 = 100)	109.8	109.7	100.0	113.0	148.3	200.1
Balance of payments (U.S.$'000,000)						
Balance of visible trade	8,418	7,868	11,175	15,099	28,170	26,170
Imports, f.o.b.	187,873	215,593	259,225	258,963	256,130	275,530
Exports, f.o.b.	196,291	223,461	270,400	274,062	284,200	301,700
Balance of invisibles	3,503	263	5,268	5,412	11,300	13,990
Balance of payments, current account	11,921	8,128	16,443	20,511	39,470	40,160

Land use (1994): forest 27.3%; pasture 19.3%; agriculture 35.4%; other 18.0%.

Foreign trade

Balance of trade (current prices)

	1993	1994	1995	1996	1997	1998
F '000,000,000	+89.5	+50.7	+62.7	+85.7	+170.4	+160.1
% of total	3.9%	2.0%	2.2%	3.0%	5.3%	4.6%

Imports (1995): F 1,380,400,000,000 (machinery and transport equipment 38.5%, of which transport equipment 14.6%; agricultural products 11.0%; chemicals 8.4%; fuels 6.9%). *Major import sources:* Germany 18.3%; Italy 9.9%, U.K. 9.5%; Belgium-Luxembourg 8.8%; Spain 6.1%; U.S. 6.1%.
Exports (1995): F 1,428,800,000,000 (machinery and transport equipment 42.6%, of which transport equipment 19.5%; agricultural products 15.1%; chemical products 8.4%; plastics 3.2%). *Major export destinations:* Germany 17.7%; Italy 9.5%; Belgium-Luxembourg 8.6%; U.K. 7.6%; U.S. 7.4%.

Transport and communications

Transport. Railroads (1995): route length 31,940 km; passenger-km 55,470,000,000; metric ton-km cargo 47,400,000,000. Roads (1995): total length 812,700 km (paved [1985] 92%). Vehicles (1995): passenger cars 25,100,000; trucks and buses 5,005,000. Merchant marine (1992): vessels (100 gross tons and over) 729; total deadweight tonnage 4,981,027. Air transport (1996): passenger-km 78,073,000,000; metric ton-km cargo 11,300,000,000[10]; airports (1996) with scheduled flights 61.

Communications

Medium	date	unit	number	units per 1,000 persons
Daily newspapers	1996	circulation	12,725,000	218
Radio	1997	receivers	55,300,000	946
Television	1998	receivers	36,000,000	603
Telephones	1998	main lines	34,000,000	570
Cellular telephones	1998	subscribers	11,210,000	188
Personal computers	1998	units	12,400,000	208
Internet	1998	users	3,500,000	58.7

Education and health

Literacy (1980): total population literate 41,112,000 (98.8%); males literate 19,933,000 (98.9%); females literate 21,179,000 (98.7%).

Education (1996–97)

	schools	teachers	students	student/teacher ratio
Primary (age 6–10)	41,000[11]	211,192	4,004,704	19.0
Secondary (age 11–18) } Voc., teacher tr.	11,212[11]	483,493	4,333,690 } 1,646,377	12.4
Higher	1,062[12]	141,410	2,062,495	14.6

Health: physicians (1995) 169,554 (1 per 343 persons); hospital beds 679,731 (1 per 86 persons); infant mortality rate (1998) 4.8.
Food (1997): daily per capita caloric intake 3,518 (vegetable products 62%, animal products 38%); 139% of FAO recommended minimum requirement.

Military

Total active duty personnel (1999): 317,300 (army 56.2%, navy 19.7%, air force 24.1%). *Military expenditure as percentage of GNP* (1997): 3.0% (world 2.6%); per capita expenditure U.S.$708.

[1]In May 1992 Corse was granted local autonomy (with its own directly elected assembly), changing its regional status to "territorial collective." [2]January 1. [3]1989. [4]Includes hotels. [5]Imputed rents and imputed bank service charges. [6]Unemployed. [7]1991. [8]1995. [9]All energy statistics include Monaco. [10]1994. [11]1995–96. [12]1988–89.

Internet resources for further information:
- **INSEE http://www.insee.fr/fr/home**
- **City Population http://www.citypopulation.de**

French Guiana

Official name: Département de la Guyane française (Department of French Guiana).
Political status: overseas department of France with two legislative houses (General Council [19]; Regional Council [31]).
Chief of state: President of France.
Heads of government: Prefect (for France); President of the General Council (for French Guiana); President of the Regional Council (for French Guiana).
Capital: Cayenne.
Official language: French.
Official religion: none.
Monetary unit: 1 French franc (F) = 100 centimes; valuation (Oct. 6, 2000) 1 U.S.$ = F 7.54; 1 £ = F 10.91.

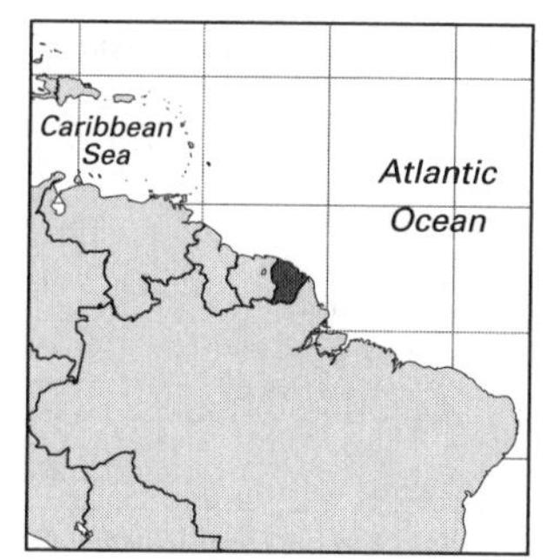

Area and population

Arrondissements	Capitals	area sq mi	area sq km	population 1999 census
Cayenne	Cayenne	17,590	45,559	119,660
Saint-Laurent-du-Maroni	Saint-Laurent-du-Maroni	15,809	40,945	37,553
TOTAL		33,399	86,504	157,213

Demography

Population (2000): 165,700.
Density (2000): persons per sq mi 5.0, persons per sq km 1.9.
Urban-rural (1999): urban 77.6%; rural 22.4%.
Sex distribution (2000): male 53.01%; female 46.99%.
Age breakdown (2000): under 15, 30.6%; 15–29, 22.6%; 30–44, 22.8%; 45–59, 15.8%; 60–74, 6.2%; 75 and over, 2.0%.
Population projection: (2010) 204,000; (2020) 233,000.
Doubling time: 40 years.
Ethnic composition (by nationality; 1990): Guianese 70.4%; Surinamese 11.6%, Haitian 7.8%, Brazilian 5.9%; other (other West Indian, Hmong, other South Americans) 4.3%[1].
Religious affiliation (1995): Roman Catholic 82.1%; other 17.9%.
Major cities (1999)[2]: Cayenne 50,594 (urban agglomeration 84,181); Saint-Laurent-du-Maroni 19,211; Kourou 19,107; Matoury18,032[3]; Rémire-Montjoly15,555[3].

Vital statistics

Birth rate per 1,000 population (2000): 22.4 (world avg. 22.1); (1993) legitimate 20.0%; illegitimate 80.0%.
Death rate per 1,000 population (2000): 4.7 (world avg. 8.9).
Natural increase rate per 1,000 population (2000): 17.7 (world avg. 13.2).
Total fertility rate (avg. births per childbearing woman; 2000): 3.2.
Marriage rate per 1,000 population (1993): 5.0.
Divorce rate per 1,000 population (1993): 0.4.
Life expectancy at birth (2000): male 75.0 years; female 81.9 years.
Major causes of death per 100,000 population (1991): violence and suicide 96.6; diseases of the circulatory system 94.2; malignant neoplasms (cancers) 55.0; infectious and parasitic diseases 52.4; diseases of the respiratory system 20.8.

National economy

Budget (1995). Revenue: F 945,000,000 (current receipts 78.2%, of which taxes 50.8%, revenue from French central government 22.5%; development receipts 21.8%). Expenditures: F 945,000,000 (current expenditures 78.2%; capital expenditures 21.8%).
Production (metric tons except as noted). Agriculture, forestry, fishing (2000): rice 31,000, cassava 10,400, sugarcane 5,300, cabbages 4,800, taro 4,100, bananas 3,900, tomatoes 3,100, cucumbers 2,800, plantains 2,600, lemons and limes 1,300; livestock (number of live animals) 10,500 pigs, 9,000 cattle; roundwood (1998) 118,000 cu m; fish catch (1998) 7,709. Mining and quarrying: gold (1997) 96,500 troy oz.; stone, sand, and gravel (1994) 1,034 metric tons. Manufacturing (1998): pork 1,245; chicken meat 461; finished wood products 3,172 cu m[4]; rum 2,728 hectolitres; other products include leather goods, clothing, rosewood essence, yogurt, and beer. Number of satellites launched from the European Space Agency, Kourou (1999): 10[5]. Construction (authorized, 1996): residential 169,400 sq m; nonresidential authorized 85,900 sq m. Energy production (consumption): electricity (kW-hr; 1998) 566,000,000 ([1996] 455,000,000); coal, none (none); crude petroleum, none (none); petroleum products (metric tons; 1996) none (285,000); natural gas, none (none).
Public debt (external, outstanding; 1997): n.a.
Household income and expenditure. Average household size (1999) 3.3; income per household (1980) F 75,762 (U.S.$16,776); sources of income (1989): wages and salaries 64.4%, industrial and commercial profits 15.4%, pensions and rents 18.0%, other 2.2%; expenditure (1994)[6]: food and beverages 28.7%, housing 11.7%, energy 9.0%, clothing and footwear 6.4%, health 2.7%, other 41.5%.
Land use (1994): forested 90.6%; meadows and pastures 0.1%; agricultural and under permanent cultivation 0.2%; other 9.1%.
Gross national product (at current market prices; 1997): U.S.$1,430,000,000 (U.S.$9,410 per capita).

Structure of gross domestic product and labour force

	1992 in value F '000,000	1992 % of total value	1990 labour force	1990 % of labour force
Agriculture, forestry, fishing	578	7.2	4,177	8.7
Mining	726	9.1	250	0.5
Manufacturing			2,477	5.1
Construction	868	10.9	4,440	9.2
Public utilities	47	0.6	403	0.8
Finance, real estate	1,185	14.8	408	0.8
Transp. and commun.	921	11.5	1,867	3.8
Trade	961	12.0	3,152	6.5
Pub. admin., defense	1,856	23.3	12,068	25.0
Services	909	11.4	7,352	15.2
Other	–75	–0.9	11,722[7]	24.3[7]
TOTAL	7,976[8]	100.0[8]	48,306	100.0[8]

Population economically active (1998): total 61,100; activity rate of total population 39.0% (participation rates (1990): ages 15–64, 67.3%; female 38.2%; unemployed [1998] 21.4%).

Price and earnings indexes (December 1990 = 100)[9]

	1993	1994	1995	1996	1997	1998
Consumer price index	106.8	108.9	110.1	111.2	112.2	112.5
Monthly earnings index[10]	106.9	109.4	112.3	112.3	114.5	127.8

Tourism (1996): number of tourist arrivals 63,300.

Foreign trade

Balance of trade (current prices)

	1993	1994	1995[11]	1996[11]	1997	1998
F '000,000	–2,740	–2,919	–2,983	–2,878	–2,913	–2,852
% of total	70.0%	63.8%	68.9%	64.4%	61.4%	70.9%

Imports (1998): F 3,449,000,000 (food products 21.3%; unspecified 78.7%). *Major import sources* (1997): France 51.6%; United States 14.3%; Trinidad and Tobago 6.0%.
Exports (1996): F 856,000,000 (gold 21.5%; shrimp 20.5%; parts for air and space vehicles 14.6%; rice 7.0%). *Major export destinations* (1997): France 61.5%; Switzerland 6.6%; United States 2.2%.

Transport and communications

Transport. Railroads: none. Roads (1996): total length 774 mi, 1,245 km (paved, n.a.). Vehicles (1993): passenger cars 29,100; trucks and buses 10,600. Merchant marine: n.a. Air transport (1998): passenger arrivals 204,078, passenger departures 199,637; cargo unloaded 4,083 metric tons, cargo loaded 2,483 metric tons; airports (1998) with scheduled flights 1.

Communications

Medium	date	unit	number	units per 1,000 persons
Daily newspapers	1996	circulation	2,000	7.0
Radio	1997	receivers	104,000	650
Television	1996	receivers	27,000	180
Telephones	1998	main lines	46,000	277

Education and health

Educational attainment (1990). Percentage of population age 25 and over having: incomplete primary education or no declaration 61.7%; completed primary 5.3%; some secondary 15.9%; completed secondary 8.2%; some higher 4.9%; completed higher 4.0%. *Literacy* (1982): total population age 16 and over literate 38,964 (82.0%); males literate 21,021 (82.5%); females literate 17,943 (81.3%).

Education (1994–95)

	schools	teachers	students	student/teacher ratio
Primary (age 6–11)	131	1,267	27,700[12]	19.2
Secondary (age 12–18)	28	968	17,100[12]	14.3
Higher[13]	1	...	239	...

Health: physicians (1998) 223 (1 per 684 persons); hospital beds (1996) 730 (1 per 196 persons); infant mortality rate per 1,000 live births (2000) 14.0.
Food (1992): daily per capita caloric intake 2,900 (vegetable products 70%, animal products 30%); 128% of FAO recommended minimum requirement.

Military

Total active duty personnel (1999): 2,200[14].

[1]Racial composition (1993): black 58%; Amerindian 5%; other 37%. [2]Commune population. [3]Within Cayenne urban agglomeration. [4]1996. [5]In 1991 the European Space Agency accounted for 28.7% of GDP, 28.2% of employed labour force, and 70.9% of imports. [6]Weights of consumer price index components. [7]Unemployed. [8]Detail does not add to the total given because of rounding. [9]Indexes based on end-of-year figures. [10]Based on minimum-level wage in public administration. [11]Excludes December. [12]1996–97. [13]Université des Antilles et de la Guyane, Cayenne campus: 1997–98. [14]Includes French Foreign Legion troops assigned to guard the Kourou Space Centre.

French Polynesia

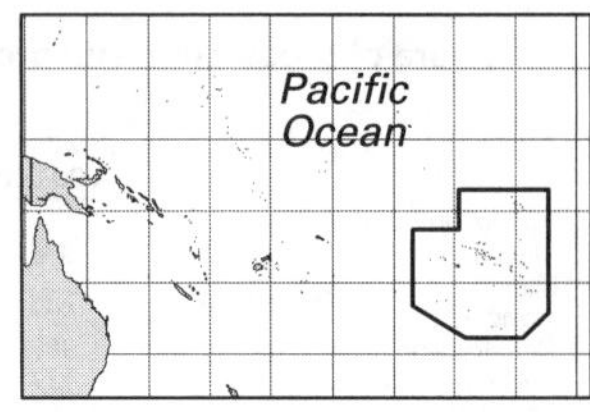

Official name: Territoire de la Polynésie française (French); Polynesia Farani (Tahitian) (Territory of French Polynesia).
Political status: overseas territory (France) with one legislative house (Territorial Assembly [41]).
Chief of state: President of France.
Head of government: High Commissioner (for France); President of the Council of Ministers (for French Polynesia).
Capital: Papeete.
Official languages: French; Tahitian.
Official religion: none.
Monetary unit: 1 Franc de la Comptoirs française du pacifique (CFPF) = 100 centimes; valuation (Oct. 6, 2000) 1 U.S.$ = CFPF 136.84; 1 £ = CFPF 197.95.

Area and population		area		population
				1996
Circumscriptions	Capitals	sq mi	sq km	census
Îles Australes	Mataura	57	148	6,563
Îles Marquises	Talohae	405	1,049	8,064
Îles sous le Vent	Uturoa	156	404	26,838
Îles Tuamotu et Gambler	Papeete	280	726	15,370
Îles du Vent	Papeete	461	1,194	162,686
TOTAL		1,544[1]	4,000[1]	219,521

Demography

Population (2000): 234,000.
Density (2000)[2]: persons per sq mi 172.2, persons per sq km 66.5.
Urban-rural (1999): urban 57.0%; rural 43.0%.
Sex distribution (1996): male 51.92%; female 48.08%.
Age breakdown (1996): under 15, 33.6%; 15–29, 27.2%; 30–44, 21.8%; 45–59, 11.3%; 60–74, 5.1%; 75 and over, 1.0%.
Population projection: (2010) 269,000; (2020) 309,000.
Doubling time: 39 years.
Ethnic composition (1996): Polynesian and part-Polynesian 82.8%; European (mostly French) 11.9%; Asian (mostly Chinese) 4.7%; other 0.6%.
Religious affiliation (1995): Protestant 50.2%, of which Evangelical Church of French Polynesia (Presbyterian) 46.1%; Roman Catholic 39.5%; other Christian 9.9%, of which Mormon 5.9%; other 0.4%.
Major cities (1996)[3]: Faaa 25,888[4]; Papeete 25,553 (urban agglomeration [1999] 121,000); Punaauia 19,524[4]; Pirae 13,974[4]; Mahina 11,640[4].

Vital statistics

Birth rate per 1,000 population (1999): 22.8 (world avg. 22.1); (1996) legitimate 35.4%; illegitimate 64.6%.
Death rate per 1,000 population (1999): 4.7 (world avg. 8.9).
Natural increase rate per 1,000 population (1999): 18.1 (world avg. 13.2).
Total fertility rate (avg. births per childbearing woman; 1999): 2.8.
Marriage rate per 1,000 population (1996): 5.7.
Life expectancy at birth (1999): male 70.0 years; female 75.0 years.
Major causes of death per 100,000 population (1994–95): diseases of the circulatory system 123; malignant neoplasms (cancers) 104; accidents, suicide, and violence 52; respiratory diseases 47; diseases of the digestive system 17.

National economy

Budget (1998). Revenue: CFPF 85,671,000,000 (indirect taxes 60.3%, direct taxes and nontax revenue 39.7%). Expenditures: CFPF 114,143,000,000 (current expenditure 72.5%; capital expenses 27.5%).
Tourism (1998): number of visitors 189,000; receipts from visitors U.S.$354,000,000; number of hotel rooms 3,021; occupancy percentage 59.0%; expenditures by nationals abroad, n.a.
Public debt (external, outstanding; 1995): U.S.$863,000,000[5].
Production (metric tons except as noted). Agriculture, forestry, fishing (1999): coconuts 85,000, copra (1998) 11,000, cassava 5,500, potatoes 5,000, pineapples 3,500, sugarcane 2,800, watermelon 1,100, tomatoes 900, cucumbers 700, bananas 650; livestock (number of live animals) 33,000 pigs, 6,500 cattle, 16,000 goats; roundwood, n.a.; fish catch (1998) 11,406; export production of black pearls (1998) 6,050 kg. Mining and quarrying: estimated annual production of phosphates range from 1,000,000 to 1,200,000 tons. Manufacturing (1999): coconut oil 6,386; other manufactures include *monoï* oil (primarily refined coconut and sandalwood oils), beer, printed cloth, and sandals. Construction (buildings completed; 1994): 102,305 sq m. Energy production (consumption): electricity (kW-hr; 1996) 360,000,000 (360,000,000); coal, none (none); crude petroleum, none (none); petroleum products (metric tons; 1996) none (183,000); natural gas, none (none).
Household income and expenditure (1986). Average household size (1996) 4.3; average annual income per household CFPF 2,153,112 (U.S.$17,831); sources of income (1993): salaries 61.9%, self-employment 21.5%, transfer payments 16.6%; expenditure: food and beverages 32.1%, household furnishings 12.3%, transportation 12.2%, energy 8.1%, recreation and education 6.9%, clothing 6.3%.
Gross domestic product (at current market prices; 1998): U.S.$4,052,500,000 (U.S.$18,068 per capita).

Structure of gross domestic product and labour force	1993		1996	
	in value CFPF '000,000	% of total value	labour force	% of labour force
Agriculture	12,872	3.9	10,888	12.5
Manufacturing[6]	22,034	6.7	6,424	7.4
Construction	18,735	5.7	4,777	5.5
Public utilities	6,917	2.1	459	0.5
Transp. and commun.	...	...	3,788	4.4
Trade	...	...	9,357	10.7
Finance, real estate	...	...	1,865	2.1
Pub. admin., defense	94,557	28.7	13,475	15.5
Services[7]	174,151	52.9	23,514	27.0
Other	—	—	12,574[8]	14.4[8]
TOTAL	329,266	100.0	87,121	100.0

Population economically active (1996): total 87,121; activity rate of total population 39.7% (participation rates: ages 14 and over, 68.3%; female 38.7%; unemployed 13.2%).

Price and earnings indexes (1990 = 100)[9]	1990	1991	1992	1993	1994	1995	1996
Consumer price index	100.0	100.6	102.4	103.9	105.6	106.8	108.0
Monthly earnings index	100.0	102.2	104.4	106.6	...	...	...

Land use (1998): forested and other 81.4%; meadows and pastures 5.5%; agricultural and under permanent cultivation 13.1%.

Foreign trade[10]

Balance of trade (current prices)	1994	1995	1996	1997	1998	1999
CFPF '000,000	–65,539	–73,835	–71,118	–82,819	–99,800	–81,654
% of total	59.5%	67.8%	60.3%	71.5%	75.1%	65.7%

Imports (1997): CFPF 99,300,000,000 (machinery and appliances 16.3%, food products 6.8%, pharmaceutical products 3.1%, metal manufactures 2.6%). *Major import sources* (1996): France 43.9%; United States 13.7%; Australia 7.0%; New Zealand 6.6%; Japan 3.5%; Italy 3.3%; Germany 3.1%.
Exports (1997): CFPF 16,481,000,000 (black cultured pearls 61.6%, coconut oil 1.6%, mother-of-pearl 1.4%, vanilla 0.5%[11]). *Major export destinations* (1996): Japan 40.6%; France 28.7%; United States 8.7%; New Caledonia 2.9%.

Transport and communications

Transport. Railroads: none. Roads (1996): total length 549 mi, 884 km (paved 44%). Motor vehicles (1993): passenger cars 37,000; trucks and buses 15,300. Merchant marine (1992): vessels (100 gross tons and over) 41; total deadweight tonnage 16,547. Air transport (1998): passengers carried 1,219,907; freight handled 9,542 metric tons; airports (1994) with scheduled flights 17.

Communications				units
Medium	date	unit	number	per 1,000 persons
Daily newspapers	1996	circulation	24,000	110
Radio	1997	receivers	128,000	574
Television	1997	receivers	40,000	179
Telephones	1998	main lines	53,089	232
Cellular telephones	1998	subscribers	11,060	48
Personal computers	1995	units	20,000	1.2
Internet	1998	users	3,000	13

Education and health

Educational attainment (1996). Percentage of population age 15 and over having: no formal schooling 4.9%; primary education 37.4%; secondary 49.0%; higher 8.7%. *Literacy* (1983): total population age 15 and over literate 98,314 (95.0%); males literate 51,910 (94.9%); females literate 46,404 (95.0%).

Education (1996–97)	schools	teachers	students	student/ teacher ratio
Primary (age 6–10)	170	2,811	29,415	10.5
Secondary (age 11–17)	32[12]	1,897	28,438	15.0
Vocational[13]	[14]	316	3,730	11.8
Higher[15]	4	70	701	10.0

Health (1996): physicians 384 (1 per 175 persons); hospital beds 981 (1 per 447 persons); infant mortality rate per 1,000 live births (1999) 11.0.
Food (1998): daily per capita caloric intake 2,924 (vegetable products 72%, animal products 28%); 128% of FAO recommended minimum requirement.

Military

Total active duty personnel (1999): 2,000 French military personnel. *Military expenditure as percentage of GNP:* n.a.

[1]Approximate total area including inland water; total land area is 1,359 sq mi (3,521 sq km). [2]Based on land area. [3]Populations cited are for communes. [4]Part of Papeete urban agglomeration. [5]Includes long-term private debt not guaranteed by the government. [6]Includes mining. [7]Includes finance, real estate, trade, and transportation and communications. [8]Includes not adequately defined and unemployed. [9]All end-of-year. [10]Imports c.i.f.; exports f.o.b. [11]Remaining exports are primarily professional goods including military and aeronautical equipment and parts. [12]1989–90. [13]1991–92. [14]Included with secondary schools. [15]1988–89.

Internet resources for further information:
- **Polynésie francaise**
  http://www.ciral.ulaval.ca./alx/amlxmonde/pacifique/polfr.htm
  http://www.outre-mer.gouv.fr/domtom/polynesie/index.htm

Gabon

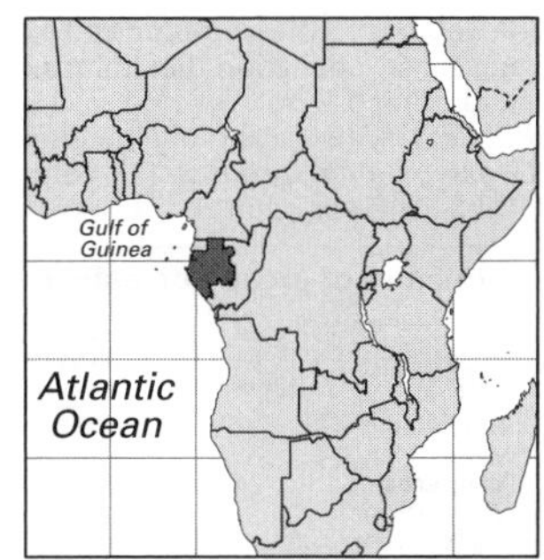

Official name: République Gabonaise (Gabonese Republic).
Form of government: unitary multiparty republic with a Parliament comprising two legislative houses (Senate [91]; National Assembly [120]).
Chief of state: President.
Head of government: Prime Minister.
Capital: Libreville.
Official language: French.
Official religion: none.
Monetary unit: 1 CFA franc (CFAF) = 100 centimes; valuation (Oct. 6, 2000) 1 U.S.$ = CFAF 754.28; 1 £ = CFAF 1,091.

Area and population

		area		population
Provinces	**Capitals**	sq mi	sq km	1993 census[1]
Estuaire	Libreville	8,008	20,740	463,187
Haut-Ogooué	Franceville	14,111	36,547	104,301
Moyen-Ogooué	Lambaréné	7,156	18,535	42,316
Ngounié	Mouila	14,575	37,750	77,781
Nyanga	Tchibanga	8,218	21,285	39,430
Ogooué-Ivindo	Makokou	17,790	46,075	48,862
Ogooué-Lolo	Koulamoutou	9,799	25,380	43,915
Ogooué-Maritime	Port-Gentil	8,838	22,890	97,913
Woleu-Ntem	Oyem	14,851	38,465	97,271
TOTAL		103,347[2]	267,667	1,014,976

Demography

Population (2000): 1,208,000.
Density (2000): persons per sq mi 11.7, persons per sq km 4.5.
Urban-rural (1998): urban 46.9%; rural 53.1%.
Sex distribution (1998): male 49.44%; female 50.56%.
Age breakdown (1999): under 15, 33.3%; 15–29, 25.7%; 30–44, 15.3%; 45–59, 16.2%; 60–74, 8.0%; 75 and over, 1.4%.
Population projection: (2010) 1,309,000; (2020) 1,386,000.
Doubling time: 47 years.
Ethnic composition (1983): Fang 35.5%; Punu, Sira, and Nzebi 16.9%; Mpongwe 15.1%; Mbete 14.2%; other 18.3%.
Religious affiliation (1995): Christian 79.9%, of which Roman Catholic 50.1%, Protestant 18.0%; traditional beliefs 19.1%; Muslim 1.0%.
Major cities (1993); Libreville 362,386; Port-Gentil 80,841; Franceville 30,246; Oyem 22,669; Moanda 21,921.

Vital statistics

Birth rate per 1,000 population (1999): 27.9 (world avg. 22.1).
Death rate per 1,000 population (1999): 13.1 (world avg. 8.9).
Natural increase rate per 1,000 population (1999): 14.8 (world avg. 13.2).
Total fertility rate (avg. births per childbearing woman; 1999): 3.8.
Life expectancy at birth (1999): male 54.0 years; females 60.1 years.
Major causes of death per 100,000 population: n.a.; however, in the 1990s major causes of morbidity and mortality included malaria, shigellosis (infection with dysentery), tetanus, cardiovascular diseases, trypanosomiasis, and tuberculosis.

National economy

Budget (1997). Revenue: CFAF 914,700,000,000 (oil revenues 62.4%; taxes on international trade 18.8%; customs duties 10.7%; other revenues 8.1%). Expenditures: CFAF 756,100,000,000 (current expenditure 71.5%, of which wages and salaries 25.0%, service on public debt 23.5%; capital expenditure 28.5%).
Public debt (external, outstanding; 1998): U.S.$3,833,000,000.
Tourism (1995): receipts from visitors U.S.$7,000,000; expenditures by nationals abroad U.S.$173,000,000.
Production (metric tons except as noted). Agriculture, forestry, fishing (1999): roots and tubers 436,300 (of which cassava 225,000, yams 150,000, taro 58,500), plantains 280,000, sugarcane 175,000, corn (maize) 31,000, peanuts (groundnuts) 17,000, bananas 11,500, natural rubber 11,000, palm oil 3,000, cacao beans 700; livestock (number of live animals) 212,000 pigs, 195,000 sheep, 90,000 goats, 35,000 cattle, 3,100,000 chickens; roundwood (1998) 5,332,000 cu m; fish catch (1997) 44,772. Mining and quarrying (1997): manganese ore 1,995,500; uranium ore 516,000. Manufacturing (1995): fuel oil 295,000; diesel and gas oil 274,000; cement 130,000; kerosene 88,000; wheat flour 27,000; refined sugar 15,000; beer 816,419 hectolitres; soft drinks 415,613 hectolitres; plywood 52,500,000 cu m; textiles are also significant. Energy production (consumption): electricity (kW-hr) 1,076,000,000 (917,000,000); crude petroleum (barrels; 1997) 135,873,000 ([1996] 6,120,000); petroleum products (metric tons; 1997) 676,300 (549,500); natural gas (cu m; 1996) 826,000,000 (826,000,000).
Population economically active (1997): total 542,000; activity rate of total population 45.5% (participation rates [1985]: ages 15–64, 68.2%; female 44.5%; unemployed [1996] 20%).
Household income and expenditure. Average household size (1998) 6.1; income per household: n.a.; sources of income (1983): private sector 73.4%, public sector 26.6%; expenditure (1969)[3]: food and tobacco 54.7%, clothing and footwear 17.5%, housing 13.0%, recreation 6.6%, transportation and communications 6.3%, health care 1.9%.

Price and earnings indexes (1995 = 100)

	1995	1996	1997	1998
Consumer price index	100.0	100.7	104.1	108.4
Earnings index	100.0	103.6	102.5	101.2

Land use (1994): forested 77.2%; meadows and pastures 18.2%; agricultural and under permanent cultivation 1.8%; other 2.8%.
Gross national product (1998): U.S.$4,922,000,000 (U.S.$4,170 per capita).

Structure of gross domestic product and labour force

	1997		1993	
	in value CFAF '000,000	% of total value	labour force	% of labour force
Agriculture, forestry, fishing	224,500	7.4	156,000[4]	41.6
Mining	1,306,100	43.3		
Manufacturing	167,100	5.5	43,000[4]	11.5
Construction	116,300	3.9		
Public utilities	36,400	1.2		
Transp. and commun.	143,400	4.8		
Trade	245,800	8.2	115,000[4]	30.7
Finance	13,000	0.4		
Services	345,400	11.5		
Pub. admin., defense	267,100	8.9	61,000[4]	16.2
Other	148,600[5]	4.9[5]	...	...
TOTAL	3,013,700	100.0	376,000[2]	100.0

Foreign trade

Balance of trade (current prices)

	1992	1993	1994	1995	1996	1997
CFAF '000,000	+362,800	+419,400	+882,000	+870,800	+1,095,800	+1,198,200
% of total	43.6%	46.7%	50.6%	49.3%	52.5%	50.9%

Imports (1997): CFAF 578,100,000,000 (machinery and mechanical equipment 26.4%, food and agricultural products 23.1%, consumer products 15.5%, transport equipment 11.5%, metals 6.2%). *Major import sources:* France 39.1%; Belgium 9.7%; U.S. 8.1%; U.K. 4.3%; Japan 4.0%.
Exports (1997): CFAF 1,776,300,000,000 (crude petroleum and petroleum products 77.1%, wood 14.5%, manganese ore and concentrate 5.0%, uranium ore and concentrate 0.7%). *Major export destinations:* U.S. 68.2%; France 8.1%; other EU 4.4%; Japan 3.2%; Africa 1.6%.

Transport and communications

Transport. Railroads (1998): route length 506 mi, 814 km; passenger-km 85,000,000[6]; metric ton-km cargo carried 503,000,000[7]. Roads (1996): total length 4,760 mi, 7,670 km (paved 8.2%). Vehicles (1997): passenger cars 24,750; trucks and buses 16,490. Merchant marine (1992): vessels (100 gross tons and over) 29; total deadweight tonnage 30,186. Air transport (1996): passenger-mi 452,000,000, passenger-km 728,000,000; short ton-mi cargo 62,100,000, metric ton-km cargo 100,000,000; airports (1997) with scheduled flights 17.

Communications

Medium	date	unit	number	units per 1,000 persons
Daily newspapers	1997	circulation	33,000	30.0
Radio	1997	receivers	195,000	16.1
Television	1997	receivers	150,000	12.6
Telephones	1998	main lines	37,253	32.7
Cellular telephones	1998	subscribers	9,500	3.3
Personal computers	1998	units	8,500	7.0
Internet	1999	users	2,000	1.7

Education and health

Educational attainment of economically active population (1993): none, or incomplete primary 37.7%; complete primary 32.1%; complete secondary 16.4%; postsecondary certificate or degree 13.8%. *Literacy* (1995): total population age 15 and over literate 63.2%; males literate 73.7%; females literate 53.3%.

Education (1995–96)

	schools	teachers	students	student/ teacher ratio
Primary	1,147	4,944	250,606	50.7
Secondary	88	2,683	72,888	27.2
Voc., teacher tr.	11	411	7,664	18.6
Higher[8, 9]	2	299	3,000	10.0

Health: physicians (1989) 448 (1 per 2,377 persons); hospital beds (1988) 5,329 (1 per 199 persons); infant mortality rate per 1,000 live births (1998) 83.1.
Food (1998): daily per capita caloric intake 2,560 (vegetable products 87%, animal products 13%), 109% of FAO recommended minimum requirement.

Military

Total active duty personnel (1999): 4,700 (army 68.1%, navy 10.6%, air force 21.3%), excluding 700 French troops. *Military expenditure as percentage of GNP* (1997): 2.0% (world 2.6%); per capita expenditure U.S.$76.

[1]De jure; excludes nonnationals numbering 100,000 to 150,000 (mainly West African) prior to their large-scale expulsion in February 1995. [2]Detail does not add to total given because of rounding. [3]Libreville only. [4]Derived values. [5]Import duties. [6]1996. [7]1995. [8]Universities only. [9]1991–92.

Internet resources for further information:
- **Gabon: The Country Fact Book**
http://www.gabon-net.com/english/facts.html

Gambia, The

Official name: The Republic of the Gambia.
Form of government: multiparty republic[1] with one legislative house (National Assembly [49])[2].
Head of state and government: President[1].
Capital: Banjul.
Official language: English.
Official religion: none.
Monetary unit: 1 dalasi (D) = 100 butut; valuation (Oct. 6, 2000) 1 U.S.$ = D 13.92; 1 £ = D 20.14.

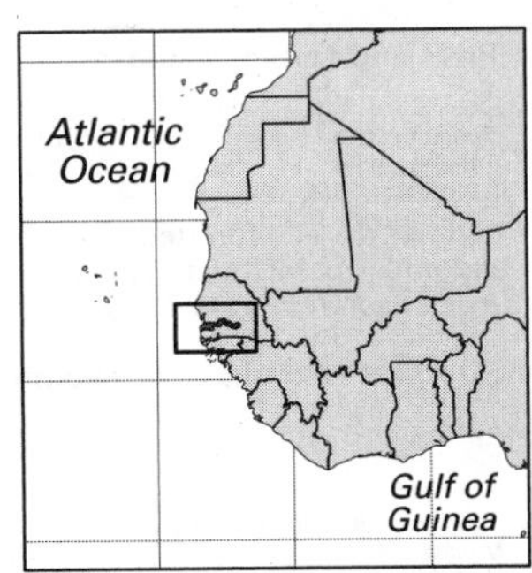

Area and population

Divisions	Capitals	area sq mi	area sq km	population 1993 census[3]
Kombo St. Mary[4, 5]	Kanifing	29	76	228,214
Lower River	Mansakonko	625	1,618	65,146
MacCarthy Island	Kuntaur/Georgetown	1,117	2,894	156,021
North Bank	Kerewan	871	2,256	156,462
Upper River	Basse	799	2,069	155,059
Western	Brikama	681	1,764	234,917
City				
Banjul[5]	—	5	12	42,326
TOTAL		4,127[6]	10,689[6]	1,038,145

Demography

Population (2000): 1,367,000.
Density (2000)[7]: persons per sq mi 331.2, persons per sq km 127.9.
Urban-rural (1999): urban 36.8%; rural 63.2%.
Sex distribution (1999): male 49.98%; female 50.02%.
Age breakdown (1999): under 15, 45.4%; 15–29, 26.1%; 30–44, 15.6%; 45–59, 8.6%; 60–74, 3.5%; 75 and over, 0.8%.
Population projection: (2010) 1,833,000; (2020) 2,365,000.
Doubling time: 24 years.
Ethnic composition (1993): Malinke 34.1%; Fulani 16.2%; Wolof 12.6%; Diola 9.2%; Soninke 7.7%; other 20.2%.
Religious affiliation (1993): Muslim 95.0%; Christian 4.0%; traditional beliefs and other 1.0%.
Major cities/urban areas (1986): Serekunda 102,600[4]; Banjul 42,326 (Greater Banjul 270,540[5, 8]); Brikama 24,300; Bakau 23,600[4]; Farafenni 10,168[9].

Vital statistics

Birth rate per 1,000 population (1999): 42.8 (world avg. 22.1); legitimate, n.a.; illegitimate, n.a.
Death rate per 1,000 population (1999): 13.5 (world avg. 8.9).
Natural increase rate per 1,000 population (1999): 29.3 (world avg. 13.2).
Total fertility rate (avg. births per childbearing woman; 1999): 5.8.
Marriage rate per 1,000 population: n.a.
Divorce rate per 1,000 population: n.a.
Life expectancy at birth (1998): male 50.9 years; female 54.7 years.
Major causes of death per 100,000 population: n.a.; however, major infectious diseases include malaria, gastroenteritis and dysentery, pneumonia and bronchitis, measles, schistosomiasis, and whooping cough.

National economy

Budget (1999). Revenue: D 944,500,000 (tax revenue 81.9%, of which import duties and excises 29.0%, income taxes 19.4%, sales tax 6.9%; nontax revenue 11.1%; grants 7.0%). Expenditures: D 1,118,200,000 (wages and salaries 26.9%; interest payments 22.2%; goods and services 16.9%; education and culture 13.1%; health 7.9%; defense 3.6%).
Production (metric tons except as noted). Agriculture, forestry, fishing (1999): peanuts (groundnuts) 123,000, millet 83,000, paddy rice 31,700, corn (maize) 20,400, sorghum 18,000, cassava 6,000, seed cotton 4,740, pulses (mostly beans) 4,000, palm oil 3,000, palm kernels 2,000; livestock (number of live animals) 360,000 cattle, 265,000 goats, 190,000 sheep; roundwood (1998) 661,000 cu m; fish catch (1998) 29,002, of which Atlantic Ocean 26,702, inland water 2,300. Mining and quarrying: sand and gravel are excavated for local use. Manufacturing (value of production in D '000; 1982): processed food, including peanut and palm-kernel oil 62,878; beverage 10,546; textiles 3,253; chemicals and related products 1,031; nonmetals 922; printing and publishing 358; leather 150. Construction: n.a. Energy production (consumption): electricity (kW-hr; 1998) 122,187,000 (122,187,000); coal, none (none); crude petroleum, none (none); petroleum products (metric tons; 1998) none (44,000); natural gas, none (none).
Population economically active (1998); total 575,140; activity rate of total population 47.3% (participation rates: [1983] ages 15–64, 78.2%; female 46.3%; unemployed, n.a.).

Price and earnings indexes (1995 = 100)

	1993	1994	1995	1996	1997	1998	1999
Consumer price index	91.9	93.5	100.0	101.1	103.9	105.1	108.1
Earnings index	...	...	...	...	...	...	...

Tourism (1998): receipts from visitors U.S.$32,000,000; expenditures by nationals abroad U.S.$16,000,000.
Household income and expenditure. Average household size (1998) 9.4; income per household: n.a.; sources of income: n.a.; expenditure (1991)[10]: food and beverages 58.0%, clothing and footwear 17.5%, energy and water 5.4%, housing 5.1%, education, health, transportation and communications, recreation, and other 14.0%.
Public debt (external, outstanding; 1998): U.S.$451,300,000.
Gross national product (at current market prices; 1998): U.S.$408,000,000 (U.S.$340 per capita).

Structure of gross domestic product and labour force

	1999 in value D '000,000	1999 % of total value	1983 labour force	1983 % of labour force
Agriculture	1,466.5	29.6	239,940	73.7
Mining	11	11	66	0.0
Manufacturing	234.6	4.7	8,144	2.5
Construction	236.2[11]	4.8[11]	4,373	1.3
Public utilities	82.0	1.7	1,233	0.4
Transp. and commun.	717.6	14.5	8,014	2.5
Trade	735.0	14.8	16,551	5.1
Finance	299.8	6.0	4,577	1.4
Public administration	421.6	8.5	8,295	2.5
Services	204.4	4.1	9,381	2.9
Other	557.9[12]	11.3[12]	25,049[13]	7.7[13]
TOTAL	4,955.6	100.0	325,623	100.0

Land use (1994): forested 10.0%; meadows and pastures 19.0%; agricultural and under permanent cultivation 17.2%; built-on area, wasteland, and other 53.8%.

Foreign trade[14]

Balance of trade (current prices)

	1994	1995	1996	1997	1998	1999
D '000,000	–1,695.0	–1,586.0	–2,318.5	–1,624.0	–2,319.4	–2,106.2
% of total	71.5%	83.6%	84.7%	84.4%	80.2%	96.3%

Imports (1999): D 2,186,820,000 (food 32.9%; basic manufactures 23.9%; machinery and transport equipment 20.7%; mineral fuels and lubricants 7.2%; chemicals and related products 7.3%; vegetable oils 3.0%). *Major import sources:* China 17.2%; Hong Kong 10.6%; U.K. 8.7%; The Netherlands 7.3%; Senegal 5.2%; France 4.7%; Côte d'Ivoire 4.3%; Thailand 1.0%.
Exports (1999): D 80,600,000 (domestic exports 13.3%, of which groundnuts 8.3%, fish products 2.2%; reexports 86.7%). *Major export destinations:* Belgium-Luxembourg 61.0%; Japan 19.4%; U.K. 6.8%; Spain 1.8%.

Transport and communications

Transport. Railroads: none. Roads (1996): total length 1,678 mi, 2,700 km (paved 35%). Vehicles (1996): passenger cars 8,640; trucks and buses 9,000. Merchant marine (1992): vessels (100 gross tons and over) 11; total deadweight tonnage 2,029. Air transport (1994): passenger-mi 31,100,000, passenger-km 50,000,000; cargo 3,107,000 short ton-mi, metric ton-km 5,000,000; airports (1997) with scheduled flights 1.

Communications

Medium	date	unit	number	units per 1,000 persons
Daily newspapers	1996	circulation	2,000	1.7
Radio	1997	receivers	196,000	165
Television	1997	receivers	4,000	3.6
Telephones	1998	main lines	25,609	20.6
Cellular telephones	1998	subscribers	5,048	4.1
Internet	1998	users	2,500	2.0

Education and health

Educational attainment (1973). Percentage of population age 20 and over having: no formal schooling 90.8%; primary education 6.2%; secondary 2.6%; higher 0.4%. *Literacy* (1995): total population age 15 and over literate 38.6%; males literate 52.8%; females literate 24.9%.

Education (1998–99)

	schools	teachers	students	student/ teacher ratio
Primary (age 8–14)	331	4,572	150,403	32.9
Secondary (age 15–21)[15]	85	1,936	46,769	24.2
Postsecondary	4	155[16]	1,082[16]	7.0

Health: physicians (1997) 43 (1 per 28,791 persons); hospital beds (1994) 780 (1 per 1,428 persons); infant mortality rate per 1,000 live births (1999) 80.8.
Food (1998): daily per capita caloric intake 2,559 (vegetable products 95%, animal products 5%); 107% of FAO recommended minimum requirement.

Military

Total active duty personnel (1999): 875. *Military expenditure as percentage of GNP* (1997): 3.7% (world 2.6%); per capita expenditure U.S.$12.

[1]Established by new constitution effective Jan. 16, 1997. Presidential elections of September 1996 did not meet international standards. [2]Includes 4 nonelective seats. [3]Preliminary. [4]Kombo St. Mary includes the urban areas of Serekunda and Bakau. [5]Kombo St. Mary and Banjul city make up Greater Banjul. [6]Includes inland water area of 2,077 sq km (802 sq mi). [7]Based on land area only. [8]1993. [9]1983. [10]Low-income population in Banjul and Kombo St. Mary only; weights of consumer price index components. [11]Construction includes mining. [12]Indirect taxes. [13]Not adequately defined. [14]Imports c.i.f. in balance of trade and f.o.b. in commodities and trading partners. [15]Includes teacher training and vocational. [16]1994.

Internet resources for further information:

- **Official WWW Site of The Republic of The Gambia http://www.Gambia.com**

Georgia

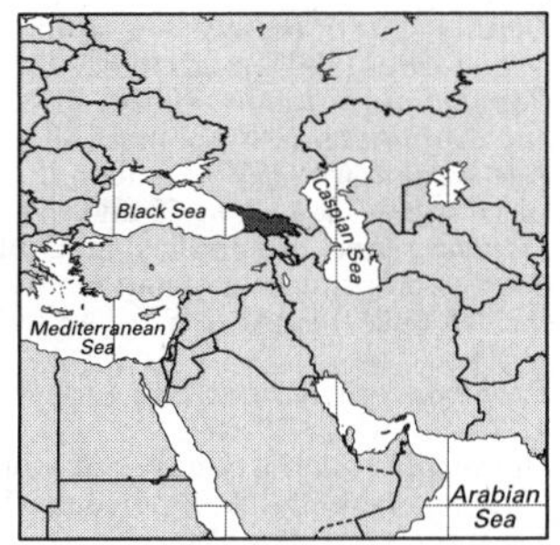

Official name: Sak'art'velo (Georgia).
Form of government: unitary multiparty republic with a single legislative body (Parliament [235]).
Head of state and government: President, assisted by Minister of State.
Capital: T'bilisi.
Official language: Georgian.
Official religion: none[1].
Monetary unit: 1 Georgian lari[2] = 100 tetri; valuation (Oct. 6, 2000) 1 U.S.$ = 1.96 lari; 1 £ = 2.84 lari.

Area and population

		area		population
Autonomous republics	Capitals	sq mi	sq km	1993[3] estimate
Abkhazia[4]	Sokhumi (Sukhumi)	3,359	8,700	516,600
Ajaria (Achara)	Bat'umi	1,120	2,900	386,700
Districts				
Guria	Ozurget'i	785	2,033	160,800
Imereti	K'ut'aisi	2,500	6,475	788,900
Kakheti	T'elavi	4,367	11,311	464,000
Kvemo Kartli	Rust'avi	2,344	6,072	601,500
Mts'khet'a-Mtianeti	Mts'khet'a	2,620	6,786	43,800
Ragha-Lechkhumi & Kvemo Svaneti	Ambrolauri	1,927	4,990	45,400
Samegrelo & Zemo Svaneti	Zugdidi	2,873	7,440	418,100
Samtskhe-Javakheti	Akhalts'ikhe	2,476	6,413	198,800
Shida Kartli[5]	Gori	2,212	5,729	485,900
City				
T'bilisi	...	...	...	1,271,800
TOTAL		26,911[6]	69,700[6]	5,405,400[7]

Demography

Population (2000): 5,020,000.
Density (2000): persons per sq mi 187.1, persons per sq km 72.2.
Urban-rural (1996): urban 55.2%; rural 44.8%.
Sex distribution (1995): male 47.71%; female 52.29%.
Age breakdown (1995): under 15, 23.8%; 15–29, 22.0%; 30–44, 22.3%; 45–59, 15.6%; 60–74, 12.7%; 75 and over, 3.6%.
Population projection: (2010) 4,815,000; (2020) 4,785,000.
*Ethnic composition (*1989): Georgian 70.1%; Armenian 8.1%; Russian 6.3%; Azerbaijani 5.7%; Ossetian 3.0%; Greek 1.9%; Abkhazian 1.8%; other 3.1%.
Religious affiliation (1995): Christian 46.2%, of which Georgian Orthodox 36.7%, Armenian Apostolic 5.6%, Russian Orthodox 2.7%, other Christian 1.2%; Sunni Muslim 11.0%; other (mostly nonreligious) 42.8%.
Major cities (1997): T'bilisi [1998] 1,398,968; K'ut'aisi 240,000; Rust'avi 158,000; Bat'umi 137,100; Zugdidi 105,000[8].

Vital statistics

Birth rate per 1,000 population (1999): 11.1 (world avg. 22.1).
Death rate per 1,000 population (1999): 14.3 (world avg. 8.9).
Natural increase rate per 1,000 population (1999): –3.2 (world avg. 13.2).
Total fertility rate (avg. births per childbearing woman; 1999): 1.4.
Marriage rate per 1,000 population (1996): 3.7.
Life expectancy at birth (1999): male 61.1 years; female 68.3 years.
Major causes of death per 100,000 population (1995): diseases of the circulatory system 569.6; malignant neoplasms (cancers) 63.4; accidents, poisoning, and violence 44.7; diseases of the digestive system 30.3.

National economy

Budget (1998). Revenue: 726,200,000 lari[2] (tax revenue 65.6%, of which value-added tax 34.9%, excise tax 14.9%; extrabudgetary revenue 21.7%; nontax revenue 8.0%; grants 4.7%). Expenditures: 938,800,000 lari[2] (current expenditure 89.5%; development expenditure 5.9%; net lending 4.6%).
Public debt (external, outstanding; 1998): U.S.$1,311,000,000.
Population economically active (1993): total 1,920,000[9]; activity rate of total population 35.7% (participation rates: ages 16–59 [male], 16–54 [female] 58.1%; female [1996] 46.0%; unemployed [1997] 6.4%[10]).

Price and earnings indexes (1995 = 100)

	1993	1994	1995	1996	1997	1998	1999
Consumer price index	0.24	38.0	100.0	139.4	149.3	154.6	183.9[11]
Monthly earnings index[12]	0.18	39.5	100.0	231.4	361.8	...	...

Production (metric tons except as noted). Agriculture, forestry, fishing (1999): corn (maize) 486,000, potatoes 433,000, tomatoes 310,000, wheat 243,500, grapes 230,000, apples 110,000, tea 60,000, sunflower seed 43,000; livestock (number of live animals) 1,051,000 cattle, 550,000 sheep; roundwood, n.a.; fish catch (1997) 6,933. Mining and quarrying (1996): manganese ore 97,000. Manufacturing (1995)[13]: steel 88,000; cigarettes 1,900,000,000 units; wine 412,000 hectolitres; beer 67,000 hectolitres. Energy production (consumption): electricity (kW-hr; 1996) 7,195,000,000 (7,315,000,000); coal (metric tons; 1996) 20,000 (230,000); crude petroleum (barrels; 1996) 938,000 (938,000); petroleum products (metric tons; 1996) 22,000 (104,000); natural gas (cu m; 1996) 2,896,000 (917,831,000).
Gross national product (at current market prices; 1998): U.S.$5,281,000,000 (U.S.$970 per capita).

Structure of net material product and labour force

	1997		1995	
	in value '000,000 lari[2, 14]	% of total value	labour force[15]	% of labour force
Agriculture	1,917	28.2	516,000	29.6
Mining, Manufacturing, Public utilities	653	9.6	264,000	15.2
Construction	326	4.8	90,000	5.2
Transp. and commun.	673	9.9	52,000	3.0
Trade, restaurants	1,496	22.0	257,000	14.8
Finance, real estate	...	...	10,000	0.6
Pub. admin., defense	...	...	35,000	2.0
Services	...	...	516,000	29.6
Other	25.5	1,733		
TOTAL	6,798	100.0	1,740,000	100.0

Household income and expenditure (1993). Average household size 4.0; income per household: n.a.; sources of income: wages and salaries 34.5%, benefits 21.9%, agricultural income 21.6%, other 22.0%; expenditure: taxes 42.5%, retail goods 32.3%, savings 16.4%, transportation 4.2%.

Foreign trade[16]

Balance of trade (current prices)

	1993	1994	1995	1996	1997	1998
U.S.$'000,000	–448	–365	–337	–519	–657	–475
% of total	32.9%	32.4%	31.8%	56.5%	59.4%	64.1%

Imports (1996): U.S.$718,400,000 (mineral fuels 37.0%; cereal preparations 16.7%; machinery and transport equipment 9.2%; sugar and sugar products 5.0%). *Major import sources* (1997): Russia 13.4%; Azerbaijan 12.4%; Turkey 12.3%; United States 7.5%; Ukraine 6.0%.
Exports (1996): U.S.$199,400,000 (fabricated metals 19.1%; tea and spices 9.6%; beverages 8.1%; iron and steel 6.1%; fruits and nuts 5.6%). *Major export destinations* (1997): Russia 29.8%; Turkey 13.1%; Azerbaijan 10.9%; Armenia 8.2%; Switzerland 6.0%.

Transport and communications

Transport. Railroads (1997): 1,546 km; (1995) passenger-km 371,000,000; (1993) metric ton-km cargo 1,750,000,000. Roads (1996): 20,700 km (paved 93%). Vehicles (1996): passenger cars 427,000; trucks and buses 41,510. Air transport (1997)[17]: passenger-km 127,077,000; metric ton-km cargo 840,000; airports (1997) with scheduled flights 1.

Communications

Medium	date	unit	number	units per 1,000 persons
Daily newspapers	1996	circulation	0	—
Radio	1997	receivers	3,020,000	586
Television	1997	receivers	2,570,000	499
Telephones	1998	main lines	628,770	123
Cellular telephones	1998	subscribers	60,000	12
Internet	1998	users	5,000	1.0

Education and health

Education (1996–97)

	schools	teachers	students	student/ teacher ratio
Primary (age 6–9)	3,201	16,542	293,325	17.7
Secondary (age 10–16)	3,139[18]	55,817	424,465	7.6
Voc., teacher tr.	...	2,146	19,593	9.1
Higher	23	25,549	163,345	6.4

Food (1997): daily per capita caloric intake 2,614 (vegetable products 88%, animal products 12%); 102% of FAO recommended minimum requirement.
Health (1997): physicians 21,846 (1 per 236 persons); hospital beds 24,500 (1 per 210 persons); infant mortality rate per 1,000 live births (1999) 52.0.

Military

Total active duty personnel (1999): 26,300 (army 47.9%, air force 9.1%, navy 2.9%, centrally controlled units/other 40.1%). About 5,000 Russian troops remained in Georgia in mid-1999. *Military expenditure as percentage of GNP* (1997): 1.4% (world 2.6%); per capita expenditure U.S.$31.

[1]Special recognition is given to the Georgian Orthodox Church. [2]The Georgian lari, introduced Sept. 25, 1995, replaced the Georgian coupon, at a rate of 1,000,000 coupons to 1 lari; the Georgian lari became the sole legal tender as of Oct. 2, 1995. The Georgian coupon had been introduced April 5, 1993, at par with the Russian ruble. [3]January 1. [4]Abkhazia adopted a constitution declaring it an independent state on Nov. 26, 1994; on Feb. 9, 1995, it was granted wider autonomy within Georgia; attainment of full national autonomy remains in dispute. [5]The northern half of Shida Kartli is roughly equivalent to South Ossetia. In March 1997 the separatist region of South Ossetia was given autonomous region status by the Georgian government, but its final status was unresolved in May 2000. [6]Detail does not add to total given because of rounding. [7]Excludes population of 23,200 with unknown distribution by autonomous republic or district. [8]Includes internally displaced persons from Abkhazia. [9]Excludes informal sector. [10]Registered only. [11]Average of 2nd and 3rd quarters. [12]Government employees only. [13]Excludes Abkhazia and South Ossetia. [14]Includes official estimates for informal sector. [15]Employed persons in formal sector only. [16]Imports c.i.f.; exports f.o.b. [17]Orbi Georgian Airways. [18]1995–96.

Internet resources for further information:

- **Embassy of Georgia in the United States of America**
  http://www.georgiaemb.org
- **Social-Economic Situation in Georgia**
  http://www.parliament.ge/GENERAL/stat/emain.htm

Germany

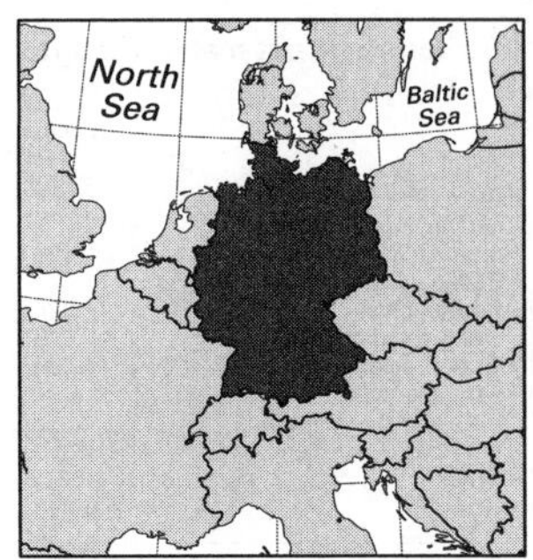

Official name: Bundesrepublik Deutschland (Federal Republic of Germany).
Form of government: federal multiparty republic with two legislative houses (Federal Council [69]; Federal Diet [669]).
Chief of state: President.
Head of government: Chancellor.
Capital: Berlin, some ministries remain in Bonn.
Official language: German.
Official religion: none.
Monetary unit: 1 Deutsche Mark (DM) = 100 Pfennige; valuation (Oct. 6, 2000) 1 U.S.$ = DM 1.83; 1 £ = DM 3.03.

Area and population

States Administrative districts	Capitals	area sq mi	area sq km	population 1997 estimate
Baden-Württemberg	Stuttgart	13,804	35,752	10,392,600[1]
Freiburg	Freiburg	3,613	9,357	2,104,200
Karlsruhe	Karlsruhe	2,671	6,919	2,659,900
Stuttgart	Stuttgart	4,076	10,558	3,888,600
Tübingen	Tübingen	3,443	8,918	1,740,000
Bayern	Munich	27,240	70,551[1]	12,056,700
Mittelfranken	Ansbach	2,798	7,246	1,675,900
Niederbayern	Landshut	3,988	10,330	1,155,500
Oberbayern	Munich	6,768	17,530	3,992,700
Oberfranken	Bayreuth	2,792	7,230	1,113,700
Oberpfalz	Regensburg	3,741	9,690	1,062,300
Schwaben	Augsburg	3,859	9,994	1,730,900
Unterfranken	Würzburg	3,294	8,532	1,325,700
Berlin	—	344	891	3,446,600
Brandenburg	Potsdam	11,381	29,476	2,561,700
Bremen	Bremen	156	404	676,200
Hamburg	Hamburg	292	755	1,706,800
Hessen	Wiesbaden	8,152	21,114[1]	6,031,300[1]
Darmstadt	Darmstadt	2,874	7,445	3,697,300
Giessen	Giessen	2,078	5,381	1,060,700
Kassel	Kassel	3,200	8,289	1,273,200
Mecklenburg-Vorpommern	Schwerin	8,946	23,170	1,815,800
Niedersachsen	Hannover	18,383	47,612[1]	7,832,300
Braunschweig	Braunschweig	3,126	8,097	1,675,900
Hannover	Hannover	3,493	9,046	2,149,800
Lüneburg	Lüneburg	5,986	15,505	1,622,500
Weser-Ems	Oldenburg	5,778	14,965	2,384,100
Nordrhein-Westfalen	Düsseldorf	13,158	34,078[1]	17,962,200[1]
Arnsberg	Arnsberg	3,090	8,002	3,824,800
Detmold	Detmold	2,517	6,518	2,032,500
Düsseldorf	Düsseldorf	2,042	5,289	5,288,200
Köln	Köln	2,844	7,365	4,226,100
Münster	Münster	2,665	6,903	2,590,500
Rheinland-Pfalz	Mainz	7,662[1]	19,846[1]	4,009,800
Koblenz	Koblenz	3,117	8,072	1,503,500
Rheinhessen-Pfalz	Mainz	2,646	6,852	1,997,900
Trier	Trier	1,901	4,923	508,400
Saarland	Saarbrücken	992	2,570	1,082,700
Sachsen	Dresden	7,109	18,413	4,537,600[1]
Chemnitz	—	2,354	6,097	1,677,500
Dresden	—	3,062	7,930	1,753,500
Leipzig	—	1,693	4,836	1,106,700
Sachsen-Anhalt	Magdeburg	7,895[1]	20,447[1]	2,714,700
Dessau	Dessau	1,652	4,280	568,300
Halle	Halle/Saale	1,710	4,430	899,400
Magdeburg	Magdeburg	4,532	11,738	1,247,000
Schleswig-Holstein	Kiel	6,089	15,770	2,749,600
Thüringen	Erfurt	6,244	16,171	2,484,900
TOTAL		137,846[1]	357,021[1]	82,061,200[1]

Demography

Population (2000): 82,225,000.
Major cities (1996): Berlin 3,467,300; Hamburg 1,708,500; Munich 1,232,800; Cologne 964,400; Frankfurt am Main 648,400; Essen 612,300; Dortmund 597,900; Stuttgart 585,400; Düsseldorf 570,800; Bremen 548,900; Duisburg 533,900; Hannover 522,700; Nürnberg 492,000.

Other principal cities (1996)

	population		population		population
Aachen	247,800	Heilbronn	121,600	Neuss	148,900
Augsburg	258,800	Herne	179,200	Oberhausen	224,400
Bergisch Gladbach	105,700	Hildesheim	106,100	Offenbach am Main	116,600
Bielefeld	323,700	Ingolstadt	112,500	Oldenburg	152,100
Bochum	339,300	Jena	100,900	Osnabrück	167,700
Bonn	298,600	Kaiserslautern	101,900	Paderborn	134,600
Bottrop	121,500	Karlsruhe	276,100	Pforzheim	118,800
Braunschweig	252,300	Kassel	201,400	Potsdam	135,900
Bremerhaven	129,800	Kiel	244,100	Recklingshausen	126,900
Chemnitz	263,300	Koblenz	109,300	Regensburg	125,400
Cottbus	122,400	Krefeld	248,600	Remscheld	121,800
Darmstadt	138,700	Leipzig	465,200	Reutlingen	108,900
Dresden	466,600	Leverkusen	162,300	Rostock	224,000
Erfurt	210,000	Lübeck	216,100	Saarbrücken	185,700
Erlangen	101,100	Ludwigshafen		Salzgitter	117,400
Freiburg		am Rhein	167,000	Schwerin	113,300
im Breisgau	199,600	Magdeburg	255,500	Siegen	111,100
Fürth	108,700	Mainz	183,700	Solingen	165,400
Gelsenkirchen	289,800	Mannheim	311,700	Ulm	116,100
Gera	122,500	Moers	106,900	Wiesbaden	267,100
Göttingen	126,300	Mönchenglad-		Witten	104,500
Hagen	211,300	bach	266,800	Wolfsburg	125,800
Halle an der Saale	280,100	Mülheim		Wuppertal	380,700
Hamm	182,800	an der Ruhr	176,100	Würzburg	127,000
Heidelberg	138,700	Münster	265,000	Zwickau	101,900

Density (2000): persons per sq mi 596.5, persons per sq km 230.3.
Urban-rural (1997[2]): urban 82.4%; rural 17.6%.
Population projection: (2010) 81,154,000; (2020) 77,984,000.
Sex distribution (1997[2]): male 48.72%; female 51.28%.
Age breakdown (1997[2]): under 15, 15.0%; 15–29, 18.3%; 30–44, 24.4%; 45–59, 19.6%; 60–74, 15.3%; 75 and over, 7.4%.
Doubling time: not applicable; doubling time exceeds 100 years.
Ethnic composition (by nationality; 1998[2]): German 91.3%; Turkish 2.6%, of which (1990) Kurdish *c.* 0.5%; Italian 0.7%; Greek 0.4%; Polish 0.3%; other 4.7%.
Religious affiliation: (1995) Lutheran 40.8%, Roman Catholic 33.9%, Muslim 2.1%, other 23.2%.
Households (1997). Number of households 37,457,000; average household size 2.2; 1 person 35.4%, 2 persons 32.6%, 3 persons 15.3%, 4 persons 12.1%, 5 or more persons 4.6%.

Vital statistics

Birth rate per 1,000 population (1997): 9.9 (world avg. 22.1); legitimate 82.0%; illegitimate 18.0%.
Death rate per 1,000 population (1996): 10.5 (world avg. 8.9).
Natural increase rate per 1,000 population (1996): –0.6 (world avg. 13.2).
Total fertility rate (avg. births per childbearing woman; 1997): 1.4.
Marriage rate per 1,000 population (1997): 5.1.
Divorce rate per 1,000 population (1997): 2.3.
Life expectancy at birth (1995–97): male 74.1 years; female 80.2 years.
Major causes of death per 100,000 population (1996): diseases of the circulatory system 520.0; malignant neoplasms (cancers) 259.9, of which bronchial, lung, and tracheal 44.9; diseases of the respiratory system 65.7, of which pneumonia 21.2, chronic bronchitis 13.2; suicide 14.9.

Social indicators

Educational attainment (1996). Percentage of population age 25 and over having: primary and lower secondary 54.5%; intermediate secondary 16.3%; vocational secondary 9.3%; post-secondary and higher (all levels) 18.3%.
Quality of working life. Average workweek (1996): 39.2 hours. Annual rate per 100,000 workers (1993) for: injuries or accidents at work 4,808; deaths, including commuting accidents, 6.7. Proportion of labour force insured for damages of income loss resulting from: injury, virtually 100%; permanent disability, virtually 100%; death, virtually 100%. Average days lost to labour stoppages per 1,000 workers (1996): 4.1.

Distribution of income (1993)[3]

percentage of household income by quintile				
1	2	3	4	5 (highest)
6.5	1.8	17.3	27.2	37.2

Access to services. Proportion of dwellings (1996) having: electricity, virtually 100%; piped water supply, virtually 100%; flush sewage disposal (1993) 98.4%; public fire protection, virtually 100%.
Social participation. Eligible voters participating in last (September 1998) national election *c.* 81%. Trade union membership in total workforce (1994): *c.* 27%. Practicing religious population (1994): 5% of Protestants and 25% of Roman Catholics "regularly" attend religious services.
Social deviance (1996). Offense rate per 100,000 population for: murder and manslaughter 4.9; sexual abuse 33.1, of which rape and forcible sexual assault 9.7, child molestation 9.4; robbery 71.3; assault and battery 129.2; theft 693.4. Incidence per 100,000 in general population (late 1970s) of: alcoholism 2,500–3,000; drug and substance abuse 650; suicide (1996) 14.9.
Material well-being (1997; median income)[3]. Households possessing: automobile 95.8%; telephone 99.7%; colour television receiver 96.9%; refrigerator 79.3%; washing machine 97.9%; home freezer 73.8%; personal computer 54.2%; video recorder 83.8%.

Recreational and leisure activities[3]

(Monthly household expenditures, 1997; median income)

Activity	DM	percentage
Vacations	203	24.0
Expenditures for motor vehicles	119	14.0
Sporting and camping equipment and sporting events	121	14.3
Televisions, radios, and their fees	91	10.7
Books, newspapers, and magazines	66	7.8
Gardening and pets	54	6.4
Games and toys	38	4.5
Visits to theatre and cinema	23	2.7
Photographic and moviemaking equipment and film	21	2.5
Tools	8	0.9
Other activities	103	12.2
TOTAL	847	100.0

National economy

Budget (1997). Revenue: DM 1,787,720,000,000 (taxes 83.6%). Expenditures: DM 1,876,383,000,000 (pensions and other social security payments 34.1%, purchase of current goods and services 22.3%, personnel costs 20.8%).
Total national debt (1998): DM 718,440,000,000.
Production (value of production in DM except as noted; 1996–97). Agriculture, forestry, fishing: cereal grains 6,819,000,000, fruits 3,455,000,000, flowers and ornamental plants 3,140,000,000, sugar beets 2,549,000,000, grapes for wine 2,322,000,000, vegetables 2,204,000,000, potatoes 1,559,000,000, tree nurseries 2,040,000,000, oilseed crops 765,000,000; livestock (number of live animals; 1999) 26,299,000 pigs, 14,943,000 cattle, 2,298,000 sheep, 102,731,000,000 chickens; roundwood (1998) 36,441,000 cu m; fish catch (metric tons; 1996) 298,017. Mining and quarrying (metric tons; 1997): potash 35,900,000.

Manufacturing (value added at factor cost in DM '000,000; 1996): capital equipment 252,226, of which machinery 90,213, transport equipment 80,418; electrical equipment 57,269; chemicals (including pharmaceuticals) 60,842; food and beverages 39,184; plastics and other synthetic products 27,853; glass and ceramic products 22,730; furniture and other wood products 16,651; paper products 12,948; textiles 8,636; clothing 5,467. Construction (newly completed buildings, sq m; 1996): residential 43,937,000; nonresidential 43,593,000.

Manufacturing, mining, and construction enterprises (1996)

	no. of enter-prises[4]	no. of employees	wages as a % of avg. of all wages[3, 5]	annual gross production value (DM '000,000)
Manufacturing	38,770	6,402,000	100.0	2,077,699
of which				
Road and motor vehicles	799	742,000	112.6	303,801
Machinery (nonelectric)	5,742	1,012,000	99.6	254,366
Chemical	1,289	532,000	102.7	220,367
Food and beverages	4,380	537,000	90.0	219,025
Machinery and appliances (electric)	2,445	703,000	106.0	210,357
Petroleum and natural gas	53	23,000	124.1	123,801
Rubber and plastic products	2,569	345,000	...	86,006
Glass and ceramics	3,393	267,000	...	70,439
Textiles	1,268	138,000	81.8	31,429
Wood and wood products	1,996	123,000	83.8	30,423
Mining and quarrying	787	169,000	105.3	29,094
Construction	24,848	1,403,000	100.0	249,327

Energy production (consumption): electricity (kW-hr; 1994) 528,221,000,000 (530,558,000,000); hard coal (metric tons; 1994) 57,623,000 (66,255,000); lignite (metric tons; 1994) 207,077,000 (209,308,000); crude petroleum (barrels; 1994) 21,535,000 (793,500,000); petroleum products (metric tons; 1994) 99,578,000 (113,839,000); natural gas (cu m; 1994) 20,904,000,000 (92,770,000,000).

Gross national product (at current market prices; 1998): U.S.$2,179,802,000,000 (U.S.$26,505 per capita).

Structure of gross domestic product and labour force

	1997			
	in value DM '000,000	% of total value	labour force	% of labour force
Agriculture	39,930	1.1	903,000	2.2
Public utilities, mining	87,610	2.4	426,000	1.1
Manufacturing	865,390	23.8	8,121,000	20.2
Construction	208,000	5.7	2,723,000	6.7
Transportation and communications	186,250	5.1	1,856,000	4.6
Trade	320,370	8.8	4,664,000	11.6
Finance, real estate	508,000	14.0	1,172,000	2.9
Services	829,380	22.8	9,865,000	24.5
Pub. admin., defense	493,110	13.5	3,197,000	7.9
Other	103,760	2.8	7,353,000[6]	18.2[6]
TOTAL	3,641,800	100.0	40,280,000	100.0[1]

Population economically active (1997): total 40,280,000; activity rate of total population 49.0% (participation rates: ages 15–64, 70.5%; female 43.1%; unemployed 10.7%).

Price and earnings indexes (1995 = 100)

	1993	1994	1995	1996	1997	1998	1999
Consumer price index	95.6	98.2	100.0	101.5	103.3	104.3	104.9
Hourly earnings index	...	...	...	...	...	...	...

Household income and expenditure. Average annual income per household (1997[3]) DM 84,624 (U.S.$48,090); sources of take-home income: wages 77.6%, self-employment 12.0%, transfer payments 10.4%; expenditure: rent 24.5%, food and beverages 21.0%, transportation 17.1%, entertainment, education, and leisure 11.9%, household operations, durables, and maintenance 7.1%, clothing and footwear 6.2%.

Tourism (1998): receipts U.S.$16,429,000,000; expenditures U.S.$46,939,000,000.

Financial aggregates[7]

	1992	1993	1994	1995	1996	1997	1998
Exchange rate, DM per:							
U.S. dollar	1.6140	1.7263	1.5488	1.4335	1.5548	1.7341	1.7597
£	2.4404	2.1988	2.4207	2.2219	2.6285	2.8399	2.9148
SDR	2.2193	2.3712	2.2610	2.1309	2.2357	2.4180	2.3556
International reserves (U.S.$)							
Total (excl. gold; '000,000)	90,967	77,640	77,363	85,005	83,178	77,587	74,024
SDRs ('000,000)	841	962	1,114	2,001	1,907	1,788	1,868
Reserve pos. in IMF ('000,000)	4,239	3,951	4,030	5,210	5,468	5,946	8,023
Foreign exchange	85,877	72,727	72,219	77,794	75,083	69,853	64,133
Gold ('000,000 fine troy oz)	95.18	95.18	95.18	95.18	95.18	95.18	118.98
% world reserves	10.24	10.43	10.46	10.48	10.52	10.69	12.31
Interest and prices							
Central bank discount (%)	8.3	4.8	4.5	3.0	2.5	2.5	2.5
Govt. bond yield (%)	8.0	6.3	6.7	6.5	5.6	5.1	4.4
Industrial share prices (1995 = 100)[8]	84.5	90.6	102.7	100.0	114.1	156.3	200.0
Balance of payments (U.S.$'000,000,000)							
Balance of visible trade	28.72	41.75	51.68	66.12	71.21	71.75	79.04
Imports, f.o.b.	401.51	340.73	378.59	457.10	488.22	439.3	460.95
Exports, f.o.b.	430.23	382.49	430.27	523.22	519.44	511.08	539.99
Balance of invisibles	−47.34	−55.06	−71.86	−87.67	−84.99	−74.52	−82.48
Balance of payments, current account	−19.14	−13.87	−20.94	−22.56	−13.78	−2.77	−3.44

Service enterprises (1991)

	no. of enter-prises	no. of employees	weekly wages as a % of all wages	annual turnover (DM '000,000)
Gas	151	37,000	...	42,228
Water	183	40,000	...	3,443
Electrical power	462	296,000	...	147,076
Transport				
air	133	57,390	...	20,270
buses	6,054	192,869	...	12,586
rail	1	416,199	...	14,697
shipping	1,449	9,076	...	...
Communications				
press	2,452	240,075	...	31,096
film[9]	615	3,000	...	836
Postal services	17,616[10]	652,573	...	68,346
Hotels and restaurants	135,141	652,251	...	60,257
Wholesale trade	36,605[10]	1,214,000	...	1,015,984
Retail trade	152,629	2,241,000	...	605,755

Land use (1994): forest 30.6%; pasture 15.1%; agriculture 19.9%; other 34.4%.

Foreign trade

Balance of trade (current prices)

	1994	1995	1996	1997	1998	1999[11]
DM '000,000,000	+88.73	+103.40	+117.35	+137.35	+148.66	+76.90
% of total	6.8%	7.4%	8.0%	8.4%	8.4%	8.2%

Imports (1997): DM 755,864,700,000 (machinery and transport equipment 34.2%, of which road transport equipment 9.9%, electrical machinery other than office equipment 6.9%, office equipment and computers 4.7%; chemicals and chemical products 8.8%, of which organic chemical products 2.1%, unfabricated plastics 1.6%; food and beverages 7.4%, of which fruits and vegetables 2.5%, coffee, tea, and cocoa 1.1%, meat and meat products 1.0%; mineral fuels 7.6%, of which crude petroleum and petroleum products 5.2%, natural gas 1.9%; clothing 5.2%; iron and steel 2.5%; furniture 1.4%). *Major import sources:* France 10.5%; The Netherlands 8.5%; Italy 7.8%; U.S. 7.7%; U.K. 7.0%; Belgium 6.2%; Japan 4.9%; Switzerland 3.9%; Austria 3.7%.

Exports (1997): DM 886,776,200,000 (machinery and transport equipment 49.6%, of which road transport equipment 16.6%, electrical machinery other than office equipment 7.9%, office equipment 2.4%; chemicals and chemical products 13.2%, of which organic chemical products 2.5%, unfabricated plastics 2.3%). *Major export destinations:* France 10.6%; U.S. 8.6%; U.K. 8.4%; Italy 7.3%; The Netherlands 7.0%; Belgium-Luxembourg 5.8%; Austria 5.2%; Switzerland 4.5%; Spain 3.7%; Japan 2.3%; Sweden 2.3%.

Transport and communications

Transport. Railroads (1997): length 54,188 mi[12], 87,207 km[12]; passengers carried 1,735,000,000; passenger-mi 39,780,000,000, passenger-km 64,020,000,000; short ton-mi cargo 49,797,000,000, metric ton-km cargo 72,703,000,000. Roads (1997): total length 143,584 mi, 231,076 km (paved 99%). Vehicles (1998[2]): passenger cars 41,326,900; trucks and buses 2,428,300. Merchant marine (1995): vessels (100 gross tons and over) 1,476; total deadweight tonnage 5,721,000. Air transport (1997): passengers carried 34,584,000; passenger-mi 46,743,881,000, passenger-km 75,227,128,000; short ton-mi cargo 4,223,897,000, metric ton-km cargo 6,166,783,000; airports (1997) 35.

Communications

Medium	date	unit	number	units per 1,000 persons
Daily newspapers	1996	circulation	25,500,000	311
Radio	1997	receivers	77,800,000	948
Television	1998	receivers	47,950,000	584
Telephones	1998	main lines	46,530,000	567
Cellular telephones	1998	subscribers	13,925,000	170
Personal computers	1998	units	25,000,000	305
Internet	1998	users	7,500,000	91.4

Education and health

Health (1997): physicians 282,737 (1 per 290 persons); dentists 62,024 (1 per 1,323 persons); hospital beds (1996) 593,743 (1 per 138 persons); infant mortality rate per 1,000 live births (1996) 5.0.

Education (1995–96)

	schools	teachers	students	student/ teacher ratio
Primary (age 6–10)	17,910	199,623	3,634,342	18.2
Secondary (age 10–19)	17,711	402,472	5,822,242	14.5
Voc., teacher tr.	9,245	107,548	2,435,753	22.6
Higher	335	152,401	1,838,456	12.1

Food (1997): daily per capita caloric intake 3,382 (vegetable products 69%, animal products 31%); 127% of FAO recommended minimum requirement.

Military

Total active duty personnel (1999): 332,800 (army 68.6%, navy 8.4%, air force 23.0%). *Military expenditure as percentage of GNP* (1997): 1.6% (world 2.6%); per capita expenditure U.S.$401.

[1]Detail does not add to total given because of rounding. [2]January 1. [3]Former West Germany only. [4]Establishments with 20 or more workers only. [5]1994. [6]Includes 4,308,000 unemployed. [7]End-of-period figures unless footnoted otherwise. [8]Period averages. [9]1984. [10]1990. [11]In billions of Euros (1 Euro = 1.96 DM). [12]1996.

Internet resources for further information:

- **Federal Statistical Office of Germany http://www.statistik-bund.de/e_home.htm**

Ghana

Official name: Republic of Ghana.
Form of government: unitary multiparty republic with one legislative house (House of Parliament [200]).
Head of state and government: President.
Capital: Accra.
Official language: English.
Official religion: none.
Monetary unit: 1 cedi (₵) = 100 pesewas; valuation (Oct. 6, 2000) 1 U.S.$ = ₵7,200; 1 £ = ₵10,416.

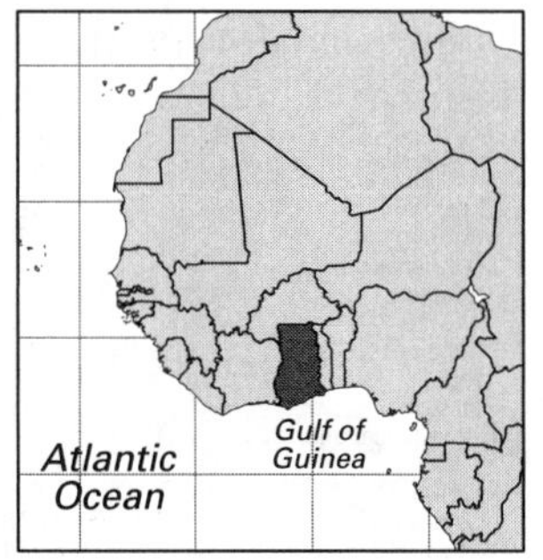

Area and population

Regions[2]	Capitals	area sq mi	area sq km	population 1991[1] estimate
Ashanti	Kumasi	9,417	24,389	2,485,766
Brong-Ahafo	Sunyani	15,273	39,557	1,432,971
Central	Cape Coast	3,794	9,826	1,359,861
Eastern	Koforidua	7,461	19,323	2,003,235
Greater Accra	Accra	1,253	3,245	1,696,170
Northern	Tamale	27,175	70,384	1,389,105
Upper East	Bolgatanga	3,414	8,842	921,196
Upper West	Wa	7,134	18,476	526,398
Volta	Ho	7,942	20,570	1,432,971
Western	Sekondi-Takoradi	9,236	23,921	1,374,483
TOTAL		92,098[3]	238,533	14,622,156

Demography

Population (2000): 19,534,000.
Density (2000): persons per sq mi 212.1, persons per sq km 81.9.
Urban-rural (1999): urban 37.8%; rural 62.2%.
Sex distribution (1999): male 49.77%; female 50.23%.
Age breakdown (2000): under 15, 41.9%; 15–29, 27.7%; 30–44, 17.4%; 45–59, 7.8%; 60–74, 4.2%; 75 and over, 1.0%.
Population projection: (2010) 22,650,000; (2020) 25,263,000.
Doubling time: 36 years.
Ethnolinguistic composition (1983): Akan 52.4%; Mossi 15.8%; Ewe 11.9%; Ga-Adangme 7.8%; Gurma 3.3%; Yoruba 1.3%; other 7.5%.
Religious affiliation (1991–92): Christian 64.1%, of which African Christian 29.3%, Protestant 20.1%, Roman Catholic 14.7%; traditional beliefs 17.6%; Muslim 14.4%; other 3.9%.
Major cities (1988[1]): Accra 949,100; Kumasi 385,200; Tamale 151,100; Tema 110,000; Sekondi-Takoradi 103,600.

Vital statistics

Birth rate per 1,000 population (2000): 29.8 (world avg. 22.1); legitimate, n.a.; illegitimate, n.a.
Death rate per 1,000 population (2000): 10.2 (world avg. 8.9).
Natural increase rate per 1,000 population (2000): 19.6 (world avg. 13.2).
Total fertility rate (avg. births per childbearing woman; 2000): 4.0.
Life expectancy at birth (2000): male 56.1 years; females 58.8 years.
Major causes of death per 100,000 population: n.a.; however, principal infectious diseases as a percentage of outpatients (1989): malaria 43.8%, respiratory infections (including tuberculosis) 8.0%, diarrheal diseases 6.7%, intestinal worms 3.1%.

National economy

Budget (1996). Revenue: ₵1,997,600,000,000 (excise and value-added taxes 36.7%, of which petroleum tax 14.5%; import-export duties 27.3%; income taxes 21.7%; nontax revenue 14.4%). Expenditures (1995): ₵1,697,-893,000,000 (1994; education 22.3%; debt service 20.1%; health 6.9%; transportation and communications 5.3%; social security and welfare 3.6%; defense 2.9%).
Public debt (external, outstanding; 1998): U.S.$5,570,000,000.
Production (metric tons except as noted). Agriculture, forestry, fishing (2000): roots and tubers 12,893,000 (of which cassava 7,845,000, yams 3,249,000, taro 1,707,000), cereals 1,686,000 (of which corn [maize] 1,014,000, sorghum 302,000, rice 210,000, millet 160,000), bananas and plantains 2,061,000, cacao 409,000, coconuts 310,000, oranges 270,000, tomatoes 216,000, peanuts (groundnuts) 212,000, sugarcane 147,000, palm kernels 34,000, lemons and limes 30,000, pulses 20,000; livestock (number of live animals) 2,739,000 goats, 2,516,000 sheep, 1,273,000 cattle, 352,000 pigs, 17,467,000 chickens; roundwood (1998) 21,905,000 cu m; fish catch (1998) 442,692. Mining and quarrying (1998): manganese ore 384,173; bauxite 341,121; gold 113,054 kg; diamonds 805,742 carats. Manufacturing (value added in ₵; 1993): tobacco 71,474,700,000; footwear 60,350,600,000; chemical products 40,347,600,000; beverages 36,167,000,000; metal products 35,121,700,000; petroleum products 32,143,500,000; textiles 18,278,600,000; machinery and transport equipment 9,525,700,000. Construction (value added in ₵; 1994) 171,129,000,000. Energy production (consumption): electricity (kW-hr; 1996) 6,631,000,000 (6,405,000,000); coal (metric tons; 1998) none (3,000); crude petroleum (barrels; 1998) none (7,315,000); petroleum products (metric tons; 1998) 926,000 (1,077,000); natural gas, none (n.a.).
Tourism (1997): receipts U.S.$266,000,000; expenditures U.S.$23,000,000.
Household income and expenditure. Average household size (1984) 4.9; average annual income per household (1978) ₵9,600 (U.S.$[4]); sources of income: n.a.; expenditure (1978): food 57.4%, clothing 14.3%, housing 11.5%, transportation and communications 3.3%, health care 1.3%.
Gross national product (1998): U.S.$7,269,000,000 (U.S.$390 per capita).

Structure of gross domestic product and labour force

	1996 in value ₵'000,000	1996 % of total value	1984 labour force	1984 % of labour force
Agriculture	4,895,000	46.0	3,310,967	59.4
Mining	190,000	1.8	26,828	0.5
Manufacturing	964,000	9.1	588,418	10.5
Construction	376,000	3.5	64,686	1.2
Public utilities	215,000	2.0	15,437	0.3
Transp. and commun.	431,000	4.0	122,806	2.2
Trade[5]	2,176,000	20.5	792,147	14.2
Finance	404,000	3.8	27,475	0.5
Pub. admin., defense	957,000	9.0	97,548	1.7
Services			376,168	6.7
Other	26,000[6]	0.2[6]	157,624[7]	2.8[7]
TOTAL	10,633,000[3]	100.0[3]	5,580,104	100.0

Population economically active (1984): total 5,580,104; activity rate of total population 45.4% (participation rates: over age 15, 82.5%; female 51.2%; unemployed 2.8%).

Price and earnings indexes (1995 = 100)

	1993	1994	1995	1996	1997	1998	1999
Consumer price index	50.2	62.7	100.0	146.6	187.4	214.8	241.5
Monthly earnings index	...	...	...	...	...	...	...

Land use (1994): forest 42.2%; pasture 36.9%; agriculture 19.0%; other 1.9%.

Foreign trade

Balance of trade (current prices)

	1994	1995	1996	1997	1998	1999
U.S.$'000,000	–353.1	–256.6	–366.0	–638.3	–805.7	–1,111.5
% of total	12.6%	4.6%	10.4%	17.6%	16.2%	20.8%

Imports (1994): U.S.$1,579,900,000 (1987; machinery 28.1%; mineral fuels 14.0%; chemicals 12.0%; food 5.2%). *Major import sources:* Germany 13.7%; U.K. 12.1%; U.S. 11.7%; France 5.4%; Italy 4.8%.
Exports (1994): U.S.$1,226,800,000 (gold 44.7%; food 26.3%, of which cocoa 26.1%; logs and sawn timber 13.5%; electricity 4.6%; diamonds 1.7%). *Major export destinations*: U.K. 15.5%; Italy 7.9%; Japan 6.7%; U.S. 6.6%; Germany 5.5%; France 4.0%.

Transport and communications

Transport. Railroads (1993): route length 592 mi, 953 km; passenger-mi 731,400,000, passenger-km 1,177,000,000; short ton-mi cargo 93,906,000, metric ton-km cargo 137,100,000. Roads (1996): total length 24,000 mi, 38,700 km (paved 40%). Vehicles (1996): passenger cars 90,000; trucks and buses 45,000. Merchant marine (1992): vessels (100 gross tons and over) 155; total deadweight tonnage 130,977. Air transport (1996)[8]: passenger-mi 407,073,000, passenger-km 655,122,000; short ton-mi cargo 20,239,000, metric ton-km cargo 29,549,000; airports (1996) with scheduled flights 1.

Communications

Medium	date	unit	number	units per 1,000 persons
Daily newspapers	1996	circulation	250,000	14
Radio	1997	receivers	4,400,000	236
Television	1998	receivers	1,900,000	99
Telephones	1998	main lines	144,000	7.5
Cellular telephones	1997	subscribers	22,000	1.2
Personal computers	1998	units	40,000	2.1
Internet	1998	users	6,000	0.3

Education and health

Educational attainment (1984). Percentage of population age 25 and over having: no formal schooling 60.4%; primary education 7.1%; middle school 25.4%; secondary 3.5%; vocational and other postsecondary 2.9%; higher 0.6%. *Literacy* (2000): total population age 15 and over literate 8,070,000 (70.2%); males literate 4,520,000 (79.8%); females literate 3,550,000 (61.2%).

Education (1991–92)

	schools	teachers	students	student/ teacher ratio
Primary (6–12)	11,056	66,068	1,796,490	27.2
Secondary (13–20)	5,540	43,367	816,578	18.8
Voc., teacher tr.[9]	957	422	13,232	31.4
Higher[9]	16	700	9,274	13.2

Health: physicians (1994) 735 (1 per 22,970 persons); hospital beds (1994) 26,455 (1 per 638 persons); infant mortality rate per 1,000 live births (2000) 57.
Food (1998): daily per capita caloric intake 2,568 (vegetable products 97%, animal products 3%): 112% of FAO minimum recommended requirement.

Military

Total active duty personnel (1999): 7,000 (army 71.4%, navy 14.3%, air force 14.3%). *Military expenditure as percentage of GNP* (1997): 0.7% (world 2.8%); per capita expenditure U.S.$3.

[1]January 1. [2]Government administration has been decentralized to the local level of 103 district assemblies, 4 municipal assemblies, and 3 metropolitan assemblies. [3]Detail does not add to total given because of rounding. [4]Unofficial 1978 exchange rate (7.5 to 9.9 times the official rate) does not permit meaningful conversion into other currencies. [5]Trade includes hotels. [6]Import duties and statistical adjustments less imputed bank service charges. [7]Unemployed only. [8]Ghana Airways only. [9]1989–90.

Internet resources for further information:
- **Ghana Fact Sheet http://www.macroint.com/dhs**

Greece

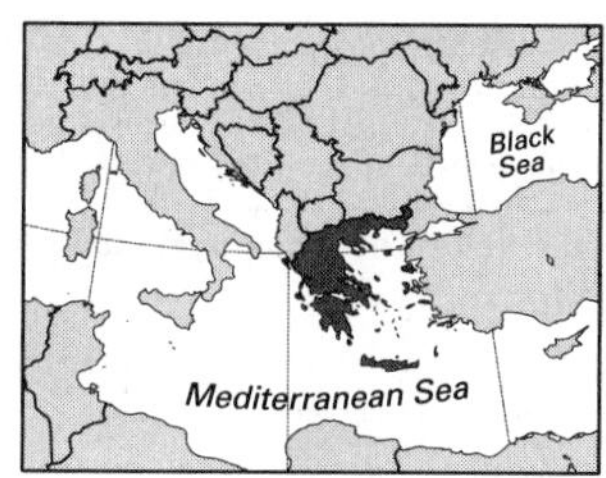

Official name: Ellinikí Dhimokratía (Hellenic Republic).
Form of government: unitary multiparty republic with one legislative house (Greek Chamber of Deputies [300]).
Chief of state: President.
Head of government: Prime Minister.
Capital: Athens.
Official language: Greek.
Official religion: Eastern Orthodox.
Monetary unit: 1 drachma (Dr) = 100 lepta; valuation (Oct. 6, 2000) 1 U.S.$ = Dr 390.28; 1 £ = Dr 564.56.

Area and population

Geographic Regions[1]		area sq mi	area sq km	population 1991 census
Anatolikí Makedhonía kaí Thráki	(Eastern Macedonia and Thrace)	5,466	14,157	570,496
Attikí	(Attica)	1,470	3,808	3,523,407
Dhytikí Ellás	(Western Greece)	4,382	11,350	707,687
Dhytikí Makedhonía	(Western Macedonia)	3,649	9,451	293,015
Iónioi Nísoi	(Ionian Islands)	891	2,307	193,734
Ípiros	(Epirus)	3,553	9,203	339,728
Kedrikí Makedhonía[2]	(Central Macedonia)	7,393	19,147	1,710,513
Kríti	(Crete)	3,218	8,336	540,054
Nótion Aiyaíon	(Southern Aegean)	2,041	5,286	257,481
Pelopónnisos	(Peloponnesos)	5,981	15,490	607,428
Stereá Ellás	(Central Greece)	6,004	15,549	582,280
Thessalía	(Thessaly)	5,420	14,037	734,846
Vóreion Aiyaíon	(Northern Aegean)	1,481	3,836	199,231
TOTAL		50,949	131,957	10,259,900

Demography

Population (2000): 10,562,000.
Density (2000): persons per sq mi 207.3, persons per sq km 80.0.
Urban-rural (1996): urban 65.7%; rural 34.3%.
Sex distribution (1996): male 49.23%; female 50.77%.
Age breakdown (1996): under 15, 16.4%; 15–29, 22.4%; 30–44, 21.1%; 45–59, 18.1%; 60–74, 15.8%; 75 and over, 6.2%.
Population projection: (2010) 10,718,000; (2020) 10,596,000.
Doubling time: not applicable; doubling time exceeds 100 years.
Ethnic composition (1995[3]): Greek 98.5%; Turkish 0.9%; other 0.6%.
Religious affiliation (1995): Christian 95.2%, of which Eastern Orthodox 94.0, Roman Catholic 0.5%; Muslim 1.3%; other 3.5%.
Major cities (1991): Athens 772,072; Thessaloníki 383,967; Piraeus (Piraiévs) 182,671; Pátrai 152,570; Peristérion 137,288.

Vital statistics

Birth rate per 1,000 population (1999): 9.4 (world avg. 22.1); (1996) legitimate 96.7%; illegitimate 3.3%.
Death rate per 1,000 population (1999): 9.5 (world avg. 8.9).
Natural increase rate per 1,000 population (1999): –0.1 (world avg. 13.2).
Total fertility rate (avg. births per childbearing woman; 1999): 1.3.
Marriage rate per 1,000 population (1998): 5.3.
Divorce rate per 1,000 population (1997): 0.8.
Life expectancy at birth (1999): male 75.7 years; female 81.1 years.
Major causes of death per 100,000 population (1996): diseases of the circulatory system 492.4, of which cerebrovascular disease 172.8, ischemic heart disease 124.9; malignant neoplasms (cancers) 213.4; respiratory disease 54.9; accidents and violent death 42.8, of which suicide 3.4.

National economy

Budget (1997). Revenue: Dr 15,295,250,000,000[4] (indirect and excise taxes 31.6%, direct taxes 18.1%, European Community 4.9%). Expenditures: Dr 15,295,250,000,000 (1994; health and social insurance 5.5%, defense 4.0%, education and culture 3.4%, police and justice systems 1.5%).
Public debt (1997): U.S.$18,331,000,000.
Tourism (1998): receipts U.S.$5,182,000,000; expenditures U.S.$1,756,000,000.
Production (metric tons except as noted). Agriculture, forestry, fishing (1999): sugar beets 2,350,000, olives 2,068,000, tomatoes 2,060,000, wheat 1,900,000, corn (maize) 1,816,000, grapes 1,200,000, oranges 900,000, watermelons 650,000, peaches and nectarines 600,000, apples 358,000, barley 320,000, cabbages 210,000, rice 209,000, lemons and limes 190,000; livestock (number of live animals) 8,756,000 sheep, 5,700,000 goats, 875,000 pigs, 585,000 cattle, 28,000,000 chickens; roundwood (1998) 495,000 cu m; fish catch (1997) 163,714. Mining and quarrying (1997): bauxite 1,875,000; nickel 17,600[5]. Manufacturing (value added in Dr '000,000; 1995): food, beverages, and tobacco 694,431; chemicals 402,133; textiles 257,555; paper and printing 208,696; transport equipment 148,767; clothing and footwear 137,524. Construction (value of completed buildings in Dr; 1995): residential 3,612,900,000; nonresidential 26,498,200,000. Energy production (consumption): electricity (kW-hr; 1996) 47,079,000,000 (48,429,000,000); coal (metric tons; 1996) 59,781,000 (62,894,000); crude petroleum (barrels; 1996) 3,144,000 (128,379,000); petroleum products (metric tons; 1996) 18,572,000 (15,174,000); natural gas (cu m; 1996) 53,868,000 (57,430,000).
Household income and expenditure. Average household size (1993–94) 2.9; income per household Dr 3,900,000 (U.S.$15,660); sources of income (1994): property and entrepreneurial income 54.5%, wages and salaries 27.9%, transfer payments 17.6%; expenditure: food 35.7%, transportation 14.7%, clothing and footwear 13.0%, housing 8.6%, education 6.5%, other 21.5%.
Gross national product (1998): U.S.$123,394,000,000 (U.S.$11,740 per capita).

Structure of gross domestic product and labour force

	1997 in value Dr '000,000[6]	% of total value[6]	labour force	% of labour force
Agriculture	2,466,100	8.6	765,000	17.8
Mining	192,000	0.7	17,300	0.4
Manufacturing	3,885,400	13.5	558,700	13.0
Construction	2,194,300	7.6	249,000	5.8
Public utilities	590,600	2.0	40,700	1.0
Transp. and commun.	1,925,400	6.7	246,700	5.7
Trade	4,227,900	14.7	872,500	20.3
Finance	1,298,800	4.5	257,000	6.0
Pub. admin., defense	4,894,300	17.0	847,300	19.7
Services	3,987,700	13.8		
Other	3,172,500[7]	11.0[7]	440,400[8]	10.2[8]
TOTAL	28,835,000	100.0[9]	4,294,400[9]	100.0[9]

Population economically active (1997): total 4,248,500; activity rate of total population 40.9% (participation rates: ages 15–64[10], 61.5%; female 39.2%; unemployed 10.2%).

Price and earnings indexes (1995 = 100)

	1993	1994	1995	1996	1997	1998	1999
Consumer price index	82.8	91.8	100.0	108.2	114.7	119.6	122.8
Hourly earnings index	78.1	88.3	100.0	108.6	118.3	123.9	...

Land use (1994): forest 20.3%; pasture 40.7%; agriculture 27.2%; other 11.8%.

Foreign trade[11]

Balance of trade (current prices)

	1992	1993	1994	1995	1996	1997
Dr '000,000,000	–2,561.5	–3,117.4	–2,931.0	–3,471.0	–4,311.8	–5,235.2
% of total	40.5%	44.6%	39.2%	40.6%	48.6%	52.6%

Imports (1996): Dr 6,905,019,000,000 (machinery and transport equipment 30.0%; chemical products 12.4%; food 11.9%, of which meat products 3.0%, dairy products 2.1%; crude petroleum 8.7%). *Major import sources:* Italy 16.7%; Germany 14.4%; France 8.0%; U.K. 6.7%; The Netherlands 6.3%; U.S. 3.3%.
Exports (1996): Dr 2,855,837,000,000 (food 16.7%; machinery and transport equipment 8.2%; petroleum 8.2%; textiles 4.3%; tobacco 4.3%). *Major export destinations:* Germany 18.3%; Italy 13.4%; U.K. 6.0%; France 4.9%.

Transport and communications

Transport. Railroads (1995): route length 2,474 km; passenger-km 1,513,000,000; metric ton-km cargo 306,000,000. Roads (1994): total length 38,265 km (paved 94%). Vehicles (1996): passenger cars 2,339,421; trucks and buses 939,923. Merchant marine (1996): vessels (100 gross tons and over) 2,013; total deadweight tonnage 27,935,000. Air transport (1996): passenger-km 8,533,169,000; metric ton-km cargo 118,738,000; airports (1997) 36.

Communications

Medium	date	unit	number	units per 1,000 persons
Daily newspapers	1996	circulation	1,600,000	153
Radio	1997	receivers	5,020,000	478
Television	1997	receivers	2,540,000	242
Telephones	1998	main lines	5,536,000	526
Cellular telephones	1998	subscribers	2,057,000	196
Personal computers	1998	units	550,000	52
Internet	1998	users	350,000	33

Education and health

Educational attainment (1991). Percentage of population age 25 and over having: no formal schooling (illiterate) 6.8%; some primary education 10.6%; completed primary 39.7%; lower secondary 10.8%; higher secondary 20.6%; some postsecondary 4.9%; a degree from institution of higher education 6.6%. *Literacy* (1991): total population age 15 and over literate 7,870,000 (95.2%); males literate 3,900,000 (97.7%); females literate 3,970,000 (93.0%).

Education (1993–94)

	schools	teachers	students	student/ teacher ratio
Primary (age 6–12)	7,254	44,981	731,500	16.3
Secondary (age 12–18)	2,972	53,956	704,127	13.1
Voc., teacher tr.	682	12,877	160,951	12.5
Higher	18	9,402	107,968	11.5

Health (1997): physicians 43,030 (1 per 244 persons); hospital beds 52,474 (1 per 200 persons); infant mortality rate per 1,000 live births (1999) 6.7.
Food (1997): daily per capita caloric intake 3,649 (vegetable products 78%, animal products 22%); 136% of FAO recommended minimum requirement.

Military

Total active duty personnel (1998): 168,500 (army 68.8%, navy 11.6%, air force 19.6%). *Military expenditure as percentage of GNP* (1997): 4.6% (world 2.6%); per capita expenditure U.S.$527.

[1]Actual administration is divided between 52 departments and one autonomous self-governing monastic region (Mount Athos). [2]Includes Mount Athos (Ávion Óros). [3]Greek government states there are no ethnic divisions in Greece. [4]Deficit financing includes Dr 3,418,000,000,000 of domestic borrowing and Dr 1,734,000,000,000 from foreign loans. [5]Metal content of ore. [6]At factor cost. [7]Income from ownership of buildings and statistical discrepancies. [8]Unemployed. [9]Detail does not add to total given because of rounding. [10]1996. [11]Imports c.i.f.; exports f.o.b.

Internet resources for further information:
- **Greek Indexer http://www.gr-indexer.gr**

Greenland

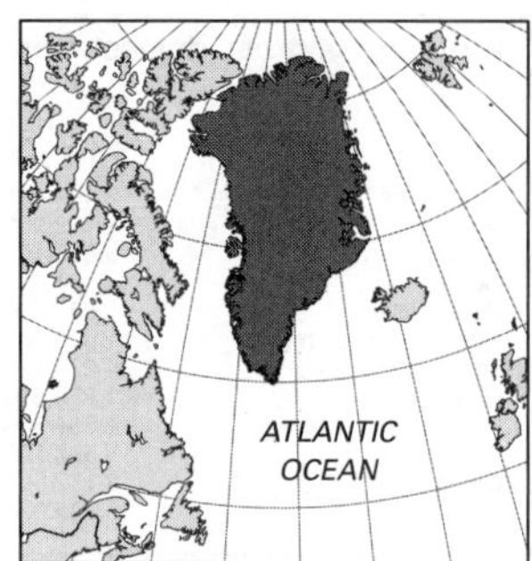

Official name: Kalaallit Nunaat (Greenlandic); Grønland (Danish) (Greenland).
Political status: integral part of the Danish realm with one legislative house (Parliament [31]).
Chief of state: Danish Monarch.
Heads of government: High Commissioner (for Denmark); Prime Minister (for Greenland).
Capital: Nuuk (Godthåb).
Official languages: Greenlandic; Danish.
Official religion: Evangelical Lutheran (Lutheran Church of Greenland).
Monetary unit: 1 Danish krone (Dkr) = 100 øre; valuation (Oct. 6, 2000) 1 U.S.$ = Dkr 8.59; 1 £ = Dkr 12.39.

Area and population

Counties / Communes	area sq mi	area sq km	population 1999 estimate[1]
Avanersuaq (Nordgrønland)	41,200	106,700	
Qaanaaq (Thule)	...	...	857
Kitaa (Vestgrønland)	46,000	119,100	
Aasiaat (Egedesminde)	...	...	3,460
Ilulissat (Jakobshavn)	...	...	4,629
Ivittuut (Ivigtut)	...	...	171
Kangaatsiaq (Kangâtsiaq)	...	...	1,495
Maniitsoq (Sukkertoppen)	...	...	3,791
Nanortalik	...	...	2,577
Narsaq (Narssaq)	...	...	2,081
Nuuk (Godthåb)	...	...	13,566
Paamiut (Frederikshåb)	...	...	2,110
Qaqortoq (Julianehåb)	...	...	3,481
Qasigiannguit (Christianshåb)	...	...	1,569
Qeqertarsuaq (Godhavn)	...	...	1,056
Sisimiut (Holsteinsborg)	...	...	5,385
Upernavik	...	...	2,883
Uummannaq (Umanaq)	...	...	2,785
Tunu (Østgrønland)	44,700	115,900	
Ittoqqortoormiit (Scoresbysund)	...	...	558
Tasiilaq (Ammassalik)	...	...	2,913
TOTAL (ICE-FREE)	131,900	341,700	56,087[2]
PERMANENT ICE[3]	708,100	1,833,900	
TOTAL	840,000	2,175,600	

Demography

Population (2000): 56,200.
Density[3] (2000): persons per sq mi 0.43, persons per sq km 0.16.
Urban-rural (1999): urban (town) 81.2%; rural (settlement) 18.8%.
Sex distribution (1999): male 53.38%; female 46.62%.
Age breakdown (1999): under 15, 27.4%; 15–29, 19.6%; 30–44, 29.3%; 45–59, 15.9%; 60–69, 5.3%; 70 and over, 2.5%.
Population projection: (2010) 57,100; (2020) 58,000.
Doubling time: 64 years.
Ethnic composition (by place of birth; 1999): born in Greenland 87.9%; born elsewhere 12.1%.
Religious affiliation (1995): Protestant 67.2%, of which Evangelical Lutheran 64.8%, Pentecostal 1.4%; other Christian 0.6%; other/nonreligious 32.2%.
Major towns (1999[1]): Nuuk (Godthåb) 13,566; Sisimiut (Holsteinsborg) 5,385; Ilulissat (Jakobshavn) 4,629; Maniitsoq (Sukkertoppen) 3,791; Qaqortog (Julianehåb) 3,481.

Vital statistics

Birth rate per 1,000 population (1997): 19.6 (world avg. 22.1); (1993) legitimate 29.2%; illegitimate 70.8%.
Death rate per 1,000 population (1997): 8.7 (world avg. 8.9).
Natural increase rate per 1,000 population (1997): 10.9 (world avg. 13.2).
Total fertility rate (avg. births per childbearing woman; 1997): 2.6.
Marriage rate per 1,000 population (1993): 7.1.
Divorce rate per 1,000 population (1993): 2.7.
Life expectancy at birth (1999): male 62.9 years; female 68.5 years.
Major causes of death per 100,000 population (1995): diseases of the circulatory system 214.4, of which cerebrovascular disease 68.8, ischemic heart disease 64.9; malignant neoplasms (cancers) 198.7; suicides 90.5; accidents 80.6.

National economy

Budget (1998). Revenue: Dkr 4,304,000,000 (block grant from Danish government 59.8%; taxes and royalties for Greenland treasury 13.5%; import duties 11.3%; EEC fishery license fees 6.4%; other 6.6%). Expenditures (1997): Dkr 5,987,442,000 (current expenditure 93.3%, of which wages and salaries 35.9%, social welfare 22.3%, culture and education 15.3%, health 10.7%, defense 5.5%; capital [development] expenditure 6.7%).
Public debt (external, outstanding; 1995): U.S.$243,000,000.
Tourism (1997): number of overnight visitors 181,043.
Production (metric tons except as noted). Fishing, animal products: fish catch (1998) 372,974 (by local boats 128,630, of which shrimp 73,581, halibut 29,965, cod 11,776; by foreign boats 123,748); livestock (number of live animals; 1999) 22,000 sheep, 4,800 reindeer; animal products (value of external sales in Dkr '000; 1998) sealskins 31,044, polar bear skins 579. Mining[4]: none. Manufacturing: principally handicrafts and fish processing. Construction: residential (1992[1]) 18,624 sq m; nonresidential (1985) 12,300 sq m. Energy production (consumption): electricity (kW-hr; 1998) 205,700,000 (158,300,000); coal, none (none); crude petroleum, none (84[5]); petroleum products (metric tons; 1991) none (214,000); natural gas, none (none).
Gross national product (1997): U.S.$1,142,000,000 (U.S.$20,381 per capita).

Structure of gross domestic product[5] and labour force

	1998 in value Dkr '000,000	1998 % of total value	2000 labour force	2000 % of labour force
Fishing, hunting, and sheep farming	...	...	...	...
Mining	...	...	...	...
Manufacturing	...	...	...	...
Construction	...	...	...	...
Transp. and commun.	...	...	...	...
Trade, restaurants	...	...	...	...
Public utilities	...	...	...	...
Public administration	...	...	...	...
Private services	...	...	...	...
Other	...	...	...	...
TOTAL	7,719	100.0	31,518[1]	100.0

Population economically active (2000[1]): total 31,518; activity rate of total population 56.2% (participation rates: ages 15–60, 86.6%; female [1987] 43.4%; unemployed [1999] 10.0%).

Price and earnings indexes (January 1995 = 100)[6]

	1995	1996	1997	1998	1999
Consumer price index	100	100.7	101.6	102.1	103.0
Monthly earnings index	100	102.4	103.5	103.0	102.9

Household income and expenditure. Average household size (1998): 2.6; income per person (1997): Dkr 144,700 (U.S.$17,700); sources of income: n.a.; expenditure (1994): food, beverages, and tobacco 41.6%, housing and energy 22.4%, transportation and communications 10.2%, recreation 6.4%.
Land use (1994): forested 0.03%; meadows and pastures 0.69%; agricultural and under permanent cultivation, none; other (principally ice cap) 99.28%.

Foreign trade

Balance of trade (current prices)

	1995	1996	1997	1998	1999
DKr '000,000	–625	–784	–857	–947	–859
% of total	7.3%	16.8%	19.5%	21.8%	18.2%

Imports (1999): Dkr 2,789,000 (1998; machinery and transport equipment 26.1%; special transactions not elsewhere specified 16.8%; manufactured goods 14.9%; food and live animals 12.1%; miscellaneous manufactured articles 11.4%; petroleum and petroleum products 9.3%; beverages and tobacco 4.0%). *Major import sources* (1998): Denmark 65.2%; Norway 12.0%; U.S. 3.0%; Japan 2.9%; Germany 2.3%; Sweden 1.8%.
Exports (1999): Dkr 1,930,000 (1998; fish and fish products 91.7%, of which shrimp 69.0%, other goods 31.0%). *Major export destinations* (1998): Denmark 84.3%; U.K. 3.5%; Japan 3.4%; U.S. 2.1%; Norway 1.6%.

Transport and communications

Transport. Railroads: none. Roads (1998): total length 93 mi, 150 km (paved 60%). Vehicles (1998): passenger cars 2,242; trucks and buses 1,474. Merchant marine (1992): vessels (100 gross tons and over) 82; total deadweight tonnage, 54,169. Air transport (1998)[7]: passenger-mi 103,769,000, passenger-km 167,000,000; short ton-mi cargo 232,000[8], metric ton-km cargo 339,000; airports (1998) with scheduled flights 18.

Communications

Medium	date	unit	number	units per 1,000 persons
Daily newspapers	1996	circulation	1,000	18
Radio	1997	receivers	27,000	482
Television	1997	receivers	22,000	393
Telephones	1998	main lines	24,968	446
Cellular telephones	1998	subscribers	8,899	159

Education and health

Educational attainment (1970). Percent of adult population ages 14 through 39 having: primary education 61.7%; secondary 25.9%. *Literacy* (1999): total population age 15 and over literate: virtually 100%.

Education (1998–99)

	schools	teachers	students	student/ teacher ratio
Primary (age 6–15)	88	975	9,341	9.6
Secondary (age 15–19)	3	...	1,746	5.9
Voc., teacher tr.[9]	8	110	650	
Higher[9]	2	35	200	5.7

Health (1998): physicians 84 (1 per 668 persons); hospital beds (1993) 465 (1 per 125 persons); infant mortality rate per 1,000 live births 25.4.

Military

Total active duty personnel. Denmark is responsible for Greenland's defense. Greenlanders are not liable for military service.

[1]January 1. [2]Includes 714 people not distributed by county. [3]Area of permanent ice not distributable by county; population density calculated with reference to ice-free area only. [4]Greenland's only mine closed in 1990. [5]1994. [6]All figures denote January. [7]Greenlandair only. [8]1985. [9]1986–87.

Grenada

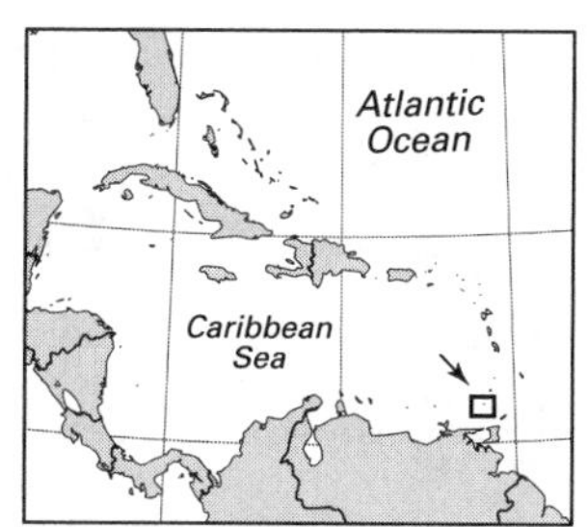

Official name: Grenada.
Form of government: constitutional monarchy with two legislative houses (Senate [13]; House of Representatives [15[1]]).
Chief of state: British Monarch represented by Governor-General.
Head of government: Prime Minister.
Capital: St. George's.
Official language: English.
Official religion: none.
Monetary unit: 1 East Caribbean dollar (EC$) = 100 cents; valuation (Oct. 6, 2000) 1 U.S.$ = EC$2.70; 1 £ = EC$3.90.

Area and population

		area		population
Local Councils	**Principal towns**	sq mi	sq km	1991 census
Carriacou	Hillsborough	10	26	5,726
Petite Martinique	...	3	8	
St. Andrew	Grenville	38	99	24,135
St. David	...	17	44	11,011
St. George	...	25[2]	65[2]	27,373
St. John	Gouyave	14	35	8,752
St. Mark	Victoria	10	25	3,861
St. Patrick	Sauteurs	16	42	10,118
Town				
St. George's	—	2	2	4,621
TOTAL		133	344	95,597

Demography

Population (2000): 102,000.
Density (2000): persons per sq mi 766.9, persons per sq km 296.5.
Urban-rural (1999)[3]: urban 37.4%; rural 62.6%.
Sex distribution (1991): male 49.20%; female 50.80%.
Age breakdown (1991): under 15, 38.4%; 15–29, 25.8%; 30–44, 16.1%; 45–59, 8.9%; 60–74, 7.6%; 75 and over, 3.2%.
Population projection: (2010) 110,000; (2020) 119,000.
Doubling time: 32 years.
Ethnic composition (1991): black 84.9%; mixed 11.0%; Indo-Pakistani 3.0%; white 0.7%; other 0.4%.
Religious affiliation (1995): Roman Catholic 57.8%; Protestant 37.6%, of which Anglican 14.4%, Pentecostal 8.3%, Seventh-day Adventist 7.0%; other 4.6%, of which Rastafarian *c.* 3.0%.
Major localities (1991): St. George's 4,621; Gouyave 3,000[4]; Grenville 2,000[4].

Vital statistics

Birth rate per 1,000 population (1999): 27.6 (world avg. 22.1); (1987) legitimate 18.1%; illegitimate 81.9%.
Death rate per 1,000 population (1999): 5.2 (world avg. 8.9).
Natural increase rate per 1,000 population (1999): 22.4 (world avg. 13.2).
Total fertility rate (avg. births per childbearing woman; 1999): 3.6.
Marriage rate per 1,000 population (1991): 4.3.
Divorce rate per 1,000 population (1991): 0.8.
Life expectancy at birth (1999): male 62.7 years; female 66.3 years.
Major causes of death per 100,000 population (1987): diseases of the circulatory system 264.3; malignant neoplasms (cancers) 82.8; endocrine and metabolic diseases 57.3; diseases of the respiratory system 45.6; diseases of the digestive system 38.2; ill-defined conditions 209.1.

National economy

Budget (1998). Revenue: EC$229,000,000 (current revenue 90.0%, of which tax on international trade 52.3%, general sales taxes 17.8%, income taxes 9.6%; grants from abroad 10.0%). Expenditures: EC$281,700,000 (current expenditure 73.7%, of which wages 37.2%, transfers 16.1%, debt 11.6%; capital expenditure 26.3%).
Public debt (external, outstanding; 1998): U.S.$113,000,000.
Tourism (1998): receipts from visitors U.S.$59,000,000; expenditures by nationals abroad U.S.$5,000,000.
Gross national product (at current market prices; 1998): U.S.$313,000,000 (U.S.$3,250 per capita).

Structure of gross domestic product and labour force

	1997		1991	
	in value EC$'000,000[5]	% of total value[5]	labour force[6]	% of labour force[6]
Agriculture	53.8	9.5	4,223	17.1
Quarrying	3.1	0.5	126	0.5
Manufacturing	39.9	7.0	1,881	7.6
Construction	41.7	7.3	3,168	12.9
Public utilities	28.7	5.1	350	1.4
Transportation and communications	139.1	24.5	1,614	6.5
Trade, restaurants	113.6	20.0	5,149	20.9
Finance, real estate	77.4	13.6	866	3.5
Pub. admin., defense	93.6	16.5	1,738	7.1
Services	15.7	2.8	3,372	13.7
Other	–38.7[7]	–6.8[7]	2,163	8.8
TOTAL	567.9	100.0	24,650	100.0

Production (metric tons except as noted). Agriculture, forestry, fishing (1999): coconuts 6,800, sugarcane 6,600, bananas 4,400, roots and tubers 3,000, nutmeg, 2,500, grapefruit 2,000, mangoes 1,800, avocados 1,700, cacao 1,100, oranges 900, other crops include cotton, limes, cinnamon, cloves, and pimiento; livestock (number of live animals) 13,000 sheep, 7,000 goats, 5,300 pigs; roundwood, n.a.; fish catch (1998) 1,713. Mining and quarrying: excavation of gravel for local use. Manufacturing (value of production in EC$'000; 1997): wheat flour 13,390; soft drinks 9,798; beer 7,072; animal feed 5,852; rum 5,497; toilet paper 4,237; malt 4,192; stout 3,835; cigarettes 1,053. Construction: n.a. Energy production (consumption): electricity (kW-hr; 1996) 95,000,000 (95,000,000); coal, none (none); crude petroleum, none (none); petroleum products (metric tons; 1996) none (55,000); natural gas, none (none).
Household income and expenditure. Average household size (1991) 3.7; income per household (1988) EC$7,097 (U.S.$2,629); sources of income: n.a.; expenditure (1987): food, beverages, and tobacco 40.7%, household furnishings and operations 13.7%, housing 11.9%, transportation 9.1%, personal effects and medical care 8.6%.
Population economically active (1988): total 38,920; activity rate of total population 39.9% (participation rate: ages 15–65, 72.7%; female 48.6%; unemployed [1997] 17.0%).

Price and earnings indexes (1995 = 100)

	1992	1993	1994	1995	1996	1997	1998
Consumer price index	92.0	94.6	98.2	100.0	102.0	103.0	104.2
Annual earnings index[8]	85.9	89.7	95.1	100.0	...	...	...

Land use (1994): forested 9.0%; meadows and pastures 3.0%; agricultural and under permanent cultivation 35.0%; other 53.0%.

Foreign trade[9]

Balance of trade (current prices)

	1993	1994	1995	1996	1997
U.S.$'000,000	–122.5	–94.8	–106.3	–126.4	–140.7
% of total	74.0%	65.8%	63.0%	75.0%	73.1%

Imports (1997): U.S.$166,600,000 (machinery and transport equipment 25.8%; food 21.6%; basic manufactures 18.6%; chemicals and chemical products 7.4%). *Major import sources:* Trinidad and Tobago 40.4%; United States 24.6%; United Kingdom 7.1%; Barbados 3.8%; Japan 3.8%; St. Vincent and the Grenadines 1.6%.
Exports (1997): U.S.$25,900,000 (domestic exports 91.5%, of which nutmeg 26.3%, fish 14.3%, cocoa beans 7.3%, clothing 4.6%; reexports 8.5%). *Major export destinations:* Germany 46.9%; United States 12.2%; St. Lucia 6.1%; Trinidad and Tobago 6.1%.

Transport and communications

Transport. Railroads: none. Roads (1996): total length 646 mi, 1,040 km (paved 61%). Vehicles (1991)[10]: passenger cars 4,739; trucks and buses 3,068. Merchant marine (1992): vessels (100 gross tons and over) 3; total deadweight tonnage 484. Air transport (1997)[11]: passengers 322,000; cargo 2,300 metric tons; airports (1998) with scheduled flights 2.

Communications

Medium	date	unit	number	units per 1,000 persons
Radio	1997	receivers	57,000	615
Television	1997	receivers	33,000	353
Telephones	1999	main lines	27,484	298
Cellular telephones	1999	subscribers	1,410	15

Education and health

Educational attainment (1991). Percentage of population age 25 and over having: no formal schooling 1.8%; primary education 74.9%; secondary 15.5%; higher 4.7%, of which university 2.8%; other/unknown 3.1%. *Literacy* (1995): total population age 15 and over literate 50,000 (85.0%).

Education (1996–97)

	schools	teachers	students	student/ teacher ratio
Primary (age 5–11)[12]	58	879	23,449	26.7
Secondary (age 12–6)[12]	19[13]	381[13]	7,367	19.3
Vocational	...	...	...	...
Higher[13, 14]	1	66	651	9.9

Health (1997): physicians 80 (1 per 1,236 persons); hospital beds 340 (1 per 290 persons); infant mortality rate per 1,000 live births (1999) 11.1.
Food (1998): daily per capita caloric intake 2,681 (vegetable products 77%, animal products 23%); 111% of FAO recommended minimum requirement.

Military

Total active duty personnel (1997)[15]: *Military expenditure as percentage of GNP:* n.a.; per capita expenditure, n.a.

[1]Excludes the speaker, who may be elected from outside its elected membership. [2]St. George local council includes St. George's town. [3]Urban defined as St. George's town and St. George local council. [4]1987. [5]At factor cost. [6]Employed persons only. [7]Less imputed bank service charges. [8]Private sector only. [9]Imports c.i.f.; exports f.o.b. [10]Registered vehicles only. [11]Point Salines airport. [12]Excludes private schools. [13]1994–95. [14]Excludes Grenada Teachers' College. [15]The 730-member police force includes an 80-member paramilitary unit and a 30-member coast guard unit.

Guadeloupe

Official name: Département de la Guadeloupe (Department of Guadeloupe).
Political status: overseas department (France[1]) with two legislative houses (General Council [43]; Regional Council [41]).
Chief of state: President of France.
Heads of government: Commissioner of the Republic (for France); President of the General Council (for Guadeloupe); President of the Regional Council (for Guadeloupe).
Capital: Basse-Terre.
Official language: French.
Official religion: none.
Monetary unit: 1 French franc (F) = 100 centimes; valuation (Oct. 6, 2000) 1 U.S.$ = F 7.54; 1 £ = F 10.91.

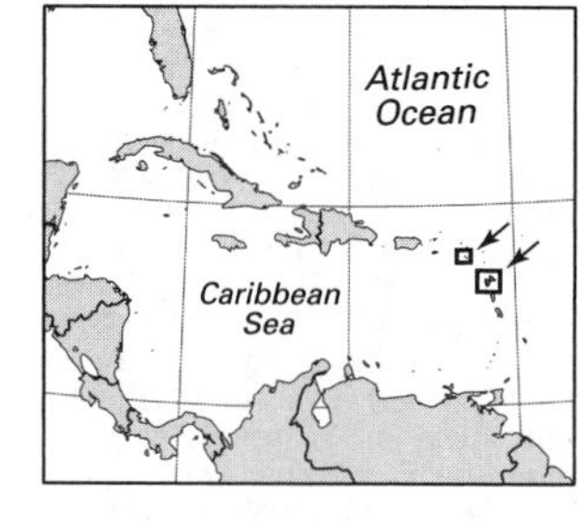

Area and population

		area		population
Arrondissements	**Capitals**	sq mi	sq km	1999 census
Basse-Terre[2]	Basse-Terre	330	855	175,691
Pointe-à-Pitre[3]	Pointe-à-Pitre	299	775	210,875
Saint-Martin-Saint-Barthélemy[4]	Marigot	28	74	35,930
TOTAL		687[5, 6]	1,780[5, 6]	422,496

Demography

Population (2000): 428,000.
Density (2000): persons per sq mi 650.4, persons per sq km 251.0.
Urban-rural (1999)[7]: urban 99.6%; rural 0.4%.
Sex distribution (1999): male 48.89%; female 51.11%.
Age breakdown (1995): under 15, 26.1%; 15–29, 27.5%; 30–44, 22.3%; 45–59, 13.1%; 60–74, 7.7%; 75 and over, 3.3%.
Population projection: (2010) 470,000; (2020) 502,000.
Doubling time: 118 years.
Ethnic composition (1991): Creole (mulatto) 77.0%; black 10.0%; Guadeloupe mestizo (French-East Asian) 10.0%; white 2.0%; other 1.0%
Religious affiliation (1995): Roman Catholic 81.1%; Jehovah's Witness 4.8%; Protestant 4.7%; other 9.4%.
Major communes (1999): Les Abymes 63,054; Saint-Martin 29,078; Le Gosier 25,360; Baie-Mahault 23,389; Pointe-à-Pitre 20,948; Le Moule 20,827.

Vital statistics

Birth rate per 1,000 population (1997): 18.2 (world avg. 22.1); legitimate 37.0%; illegitimate 63.0%.
Death rate per 1,000 population (1997): 5.9 (world avg. 8.9).
Natural increase rate per 1,000 population (1997): 12.3 (world avg. 13.2).
Total fertility rate (avg. births per childbearing woman; 1997): 2.3.
Marriage rate per 1,000 population (1997): 4.7.
Divorce rate per 1,000 population (1997): 1.3.
Life expectancy at birth (1997): male 73.3 years; female 80.1 years.
Major causes of death per 100,000 population (1996): diseases of the circulatory system 183.7; malignant neoplasms (cancers) 134.8; accidents, violence, and poisoning 68.1; diseases of the respiratory system 32.1; diseases of the digestive system 31.4; endocrine and metabolic diseases 26.2; infectious and parasitic diseases 23.8.

National economy

Budget (1998). Revenue: F 4,227,000,000 (tax revenues 69.0%, of which direct taxes 42.5%, value-added taxes 25.1%; advances, loans, and transfers 26.8%). Expenditures: F 7,874,000,000 (current expenditures 70.6%, capital [development] expenditures 10.6%; advances and loans 18.8%).
Public debt (external, outstanding; 1990[8]): U.S.$58,000,000.
Tourism (1998): receipts from visitors U.S.$466,000,000; expenditures, n.a.
Production (metric tons except as noted). Agriculture, forestry, fishing (1999): sugarcane 499,980, bananas 141,140, yams 9,030, pineapples 6,900, plantains 5,870, sweet potatoes 3,410, melons 3,240, tomatoes 3,080, lettuce 3,030, cucumbers and gherkins 2,620; livestock (number of live animals) 80,410 cattle, 63,000 goats, 15,000 pigs; roundwood (1998) 15,000 cu m; fish catch (1998) 9,084. Mining and quarrying (1993): pumice 210,000. Manufacturing (1996): cement 282,571; raw sugar 48,896; rum 66,483 hectolitres; other products include clothing, wooden furniture and posts, and metalware. Construction (buildings authorized; 1992): residential 358,474 sq m; nonresidential 160,084 sq m. Energy production (consumption): electricity (kW-hr; 1996) 1,098,000,000 (987,600,000); coal, none (none); crude petroleum, none (none); petroleum products (metric tons; 1996) none (456,000); natural gas, none (none).
Population economically active (1998): total 182,200; activity rate of total population 41.8% (participation rates: ages [1995] 15–64, 73.2%; female 46.8%; unemployed 30.7%).

Price and earnings indexes (1995 = 100)[9]

	1990	1991	1992	1993	1994	1995	1996[10]
Consumer price index	87.5	89.2	91.4	93.3	96.9	100.0	99.3
Monthly earnings index[11]	92.0	93.8	96.3	96.6	98.0	100.0	100.8

Gross national product (1995): U.S.$3,877,000,000 (U.S.$9,145 per capita).

Structure of gross domestic product and labour force

	1995		1998	
	in value F '000,000	% of total value	labour force	% of labour force
Agriculture	1,080.7	4.1	8,200	4.5
Mining, manufacturing	1,744.9	6.6	7,900	4.3
Construction	1,880.1	7.2	13,000	7.1
Public utilities	...	...	...	...
Transp. and commun.	2,156.2	8.2	4,200	2.3
Trade[12]	6,121.6	23.4	20,700	11.4
Finance, real estate	1,043.2	4.0	3,500	1.9
Pub. admin., defense	9,926.7	37.9	43,400	23.8
Services	3,210.2	12.2	24,400	13.4
Other	–957.4[13]	–3.6[13]	56,900[14]	31.2[14]
TOTAL	26,206.2	100.0	182,200	100.0[6]

Household income and expenditure. Average household size (1990) 3.4; income per household (1988) F 105,400 (U.S.$17,700); sources of income (1988): wages and salaries 78.9%, self-employment 12.7%, transfer payments 8.4%; expenditure (1994–95): housing 26.2%, food and beverages 21.4%, transportation and communications 14.1%, household durables 6.0%, culture and leisure 4.2%.
Land use (1994): forest 39.1%; pasture 14.2%; agriculture 16.0%; other 30.7%.

Foreign trade

Balance of trade (current prices)

	1993	1994	1995	1996	1997	1998
F '000,000	–7,309	–7,693	–8,655	–9,635	–9,274	–9,996
% of total	83.2%	82.0%	84.3%	83.6%	86.3%	88.2%

Imports (1998): F 10,663,000,000 (consumer goods 23.7%, food and agriculture products 21.1%, machinery and equipment 19.7%, transport vehicles and parts 12.3%). *Major import sources:* France 63.4%; Germany 4.4%; Italy 3.5%; Martinique 3.4%; U.S. 2.9%; Japan 1.9%.
Exports (1998): F 667,000,000 (1995; bananas 25.4%, sugar 11.4%, rum 4.4%, melons 2.9%). *Major export destinations:* France 68.5%; Martinique 9.4%; Italy 4.8%; Belgium-Luxembourg 3.3%; French Guiana 3.0%.

Transport and communications

Transport. Railroads: none. Roads (1998): total length 1,988 mi, 3,415 km (paved [1986] 80%). Vehicles (1993); passenger cars 101,600; trucks and buses 37,500. Merchant marine (1992): vessels (100 gross tons and over) 20; deadweight tonnage 4,430. Air transport (1998): passenger arrivals and departures 1,807,100; cargo handled 16,496 metric tons, cargo unloaded 5,493 metric tons; airports (1997) with scheduled flights 7.

Communications

Medium	date	unit	number	units per 1,000 persons
Daily newspapers	1995	circulation	35,000	81
Radio	1997	receivers	113,000	258
Television	1998	receivers	116,000	269
Telephones	1998	main lines	197,000	445
Personal computers	1998	units	...	...
Internet	1998	users	...	...

Education and health

Educational attainment (1990). Percentage of population age 25 and over having: incomplete primary, or no declaration 59.8%; primary education 14.5%; secondary 19.0%; higher 6.7%. *Literacy* (1982): total population age 15 and over literate 225,400 (90.1%); males literate 108,700 (89.7%); females literate 116,700 (90.5%).

Education (1998–99)

	schools	teachers	students	student/ teacher ratio
Primary (age 6–10)	348	2,936	40,042	13.6
Secondary (age 11–17) / Vocational	85	3,392	51,491	15.2
Higher[15]	1	...	10,919	...

Health (1998): physicians 760 (1 per 550 persons); hospital beds 2,796 (1 per 149 persons); infant mortality rate per 1,000 live births (1997) 8.2.
Food (1995): daily per capita caloric intake 2,732 (vegetable products 75%, animal products 25%); 129% of FAO recommended minimum requirement.

Military

Total active duty personnel (1994): 535 French troops.

[1]Guadeloupe elects 4 deputies and 2 senators to French parliament. [2]Comprises Basse-Terre 327 sq mi (848 sq km), pop. 172,693, and Îles des Saintes 5 sq mi (13 sq km), pop. 2,998. [3]Comprises Grande-Terre 228 sq mi (590 sq km), pop 196,767; Marie-Galante 61 sq mi (158 sq km), pop. 12,488; La Désirade 8 sq mi (20 sq km), pop. 1,620; and the uninhabited Îles de la Petite-Terre. [4]Comprises the French part of Saint-Martin 20 sq mi (54 sq km), pop. 29,079; Saint-Barthélemy 8 sq mi (21 sq km), pop. 6,852; and the small, uninhabited island of Tintamarre. [5]Total area includes 29 sq mi (75 sq km) not allocated by arrondissement. [6]Detail does not add to total given because of rounding. [7]Urban defined as locality with 2,000 or more inhabitants. [8]Includes external long-term private debt not guaranteed by the government. [9]Base and indexes are end of year unless footnoted. [10]March. [11]Based on minimum-level wage of public employees. [12]Includes hotels. [13]Less imputed bank service charges. [14]Includes 55,900 unemployed. [15]University of Antilles-French Guiana, Guadeloupe campus.

Internet resources for further information:
- **Guadeloupe: Présentation générale (in French) http://www.outre-mer.gouv.fr/domtom/guadeloupe**

Guam

Official name: Teritorion Guam (Chamorro); Territory of Guam (English).
Political status: self-governing, organized, unincorporated territory of the United States with one legislative house (Guam Legislature [15]).
Chief of state: President of the United States.
Head of government: Governor.
Capital: Agana (Hagåtña).
Official languages: Chamorro; English.
Official religion: none.
Monetary unit: 1 United States dollar (U.S.$) = 100 cents; valuation (Oct. 6, 2000) 1 U.S.$ = £0.69.

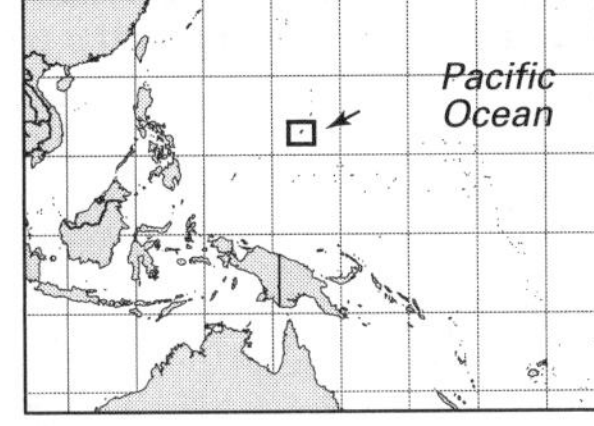

Area and population

Election Districts	area sq mi	area sq km	population[1] 1994 estimate
Agana	1	3	1,248
Agana Heights	1	3	3,995
Agat	11	29	5,434
Asan	6	16	2,268
Barrigada	9	23	9,692
Chalan Pago-Ordot	6	16	4,876
Dededo	30	78	34,761
Inarajan	19	49	2,705
Mangilao	10	26	11,485
Merizo	6	16	1,908
Mongmong-Toto-Maite	2	5	6,404
Piti	7	18	2,717
Santa Rita	16	42	12,275
Sinajana	1	3	2,912
Talofofo	17	44	2,531
Tamuning	6	16	18,267
Umatac	6	16	983
Yigo	35	91	15,572
Yona	20	52	5,848
TOTAL	209[2]	541[2, 3]	145,881

Demography

Population (2000): 155,000.
Density (2000)[2]: persons per sq mi 714.3, persons per sq km 276.3.
Urban-rural (1999): urban 39.0%; rural 61.0%.
Sex distribution (1990): male 53.99%; female 46.01%.
Age breakdown (1990): under 15, 29.8%; 15–29, 29.9%; 30–44, 22.4%; 45–59, 11.2%; 60–74, 5.2%; 75 and over, 1.5%.
Population projection: (2010) 184,000; (2020) 211,000.
Doubling time: 37 years.
Ethnic composition (1990): Pacific Islander 42.4%, of which Chamorro 37.5%; Asian 29.5%, of which Filipino 22.6%, Korean 3.0%; white 14.4%; mixed 9.7%; black 2.4%; other 1.6%.
Religious affiliation (1995): Roman Catholic 74.7%; Protestant 12.8%; other Christian 2.4%; other 10.1%.
Major populated places (1990): Tamuning 9,534; Apra Harbor 7,956; Mangilao 5,608; Andersen Air Force Base 5,531; Agana (Hagåtña) 1,139.

Vital statistics

Birth rate per 1,000 population (1999): 23.7 (world avg. 22.1); (1997) legitimate 50.1%; illegitimate 49.9%.
Death rate per 1,000 population (1999): 4.5 (world avg. 8.9).
Natural increase rate per 1,000 population (1999): 19.2 (world avg. 13.2).
Total fertility rate (avg. births per childbearing woman; 1999): 3.3.
Marriage rate per 1,000 population (1997): 9.5.
Divorce rate per 1,000 population (1995): 4.3.
Life expectancy at birth (1999): male 73.0 years; female 78.0 years.
Major causes of death per 100,000 population (1996): heart diseases 134.5; malignant neoplasms (cancers) 73.8; accidents, poisonings, and violence 35.2; diabetes mellitus 28.3; pneumonia 9.7; liver diseases 9.7.

National economy

Budget (1997–98). Revenue: U.S.$738,100,000 (local taxes 68.7%, federal contributions 25.5%, interest 2.2%, licenses, fees, and permits 1.7%). Expenditures: U.S.$501,900,000 (current expenditures 80.2%, debt service 10.6%, capital expenditures 8.6%).
Public debt (external, outstanding): n.a.
Tourism (1997): receipts from visitors U.S.$1,450,000,000.
Land use (1998): forested 14.6%; meadows and pastures 14.5%; agricultural and under permanent cultivation 21.8%; other 49.1%.
Production. Agriculture, forestry, fishing (value of production in U.S.$'000; 1996): eggplant 625, long beans 592, bananas 418, cucumbers 348, watermelons 232, papayas 101; livestock (number of live animals) 205,000 poultry, 4,000 pigs, 610 goats; fish catch (metric tons; 1998) 253, value of aquaculture production (1996) U.S.$1,442,000. Mining and quarrying: sand and gravel. Manufacturing (value of sales in U.S.$'000; 1997): printing and publishing 40,307,000; food processing 24,333,000; stone, clay, and glass products 16,914; fabricated metal products 4,367. Construction (gross value of building and construction permits in U.S.$; 1998): residential 125,207,000; nonresidential 196,681,000. Energy production (consumption): electricity (kW-hr; 1996) 825,000,000 (825,000,000); petroleum products (metric tons; 1996) none (1,329,000).
Gross domestic product (1998): U.S.$3,302,700,000 (U.S.$20,660 per capita).

Structure of gross domestic product and labour force

	1995 in value U.S.$'000,000	1995 % of total value	1999 labour force[4]	1999 % of labour force
Agriculture	5	5	300	0.5
Manufacturing	5	5	1,880	3.0
Construction	379.0	12.5	6,490	10.2
Trade	622.9	20.6	13,690	21.6
Transp. and commun.	5	5	5,230	8.3
Finance	5	5	2,720	4.3
Pub. admin. (local)	513.3	16.9	19,760	31.2
Pub. admin., defense (federal)	452.7	14.9		
Services	486.9	16.1	13,280	21.0
Other	575.4[5]	19.0[5]	—	—
TOTAL	3,030.2	100.0	63,350	100.0[3]

Population economically active (1997): total 71,400; activity rate of total population 45.7% (participation rates: over age 16 [1994] 69.3%[6]; female [1994] 43.3%[6]; unemployed [June 1999] 15.2%).

Price and earnings indexes (1996 = 100)

	1996	1997	1998	1999
Consumer price index	100.0	101.6	101.2	100.9
Hourly earnings index	...	...	...	...

Household income and expenditure. Average household size (1998) 3.9[7]; average annual income per household (1998) U.S.$47,374[7]; sources of income: n.a.; expenditure (1978): housing 28.6%, food 24.1%, transportation 18.0%, clothing 10.6%, entertainment 5.1%, medical care 4.7%.

Foreign trade

Balance of trade (current prices)

	1991	1992	1993	1994	1995	1996
U.S.$'000,000	–358	–384	–355	–528	–584	–600
% of total	74.3%	74.4%	70.3%	86.3%	88.0%	88.2%

Imports (1998–99[8]): U.S.$205,800,000 (food products 34.2%; leather products including footwear 15.8%; motor vehicles and parts 14.3%; construction materials 6.4%; clothing 5.0%). *Major import sources:* n.a.
Exports (1999): U.S.$75,700,000 (food products 54.7%, of which fish 53.8%; petroleum and natural gas products 20.0%; tobacco products 6.7%). *Major export destinations:* Japan 53.9%; Federated States of Micronesia 18.6%; Palau 6.3%; Hong Kong 2.0%.

Transport and communications

Transport. Railroads: none. Roads (1999): total length 550 mi, 885 km (paved 76%). Vehicles (1995): passenger cars 79,800; trucks and buses 34,700. Merchant marine (1992): vessels (100 gross tons and over) 5, total deadweight tonnage 50; surface cargo loaded, unloaded, or transshipped (1998) 2,053,000 metric tons. Air transport (1998): passenger arrivals 1,375,000; passenger departures 1,378,000; cargo loaded and unloaded (1997) 35,295 metric tons; airports (1999) with scheduled flights 1.

Communications

Medium	date	unit	number	units per 1,000 persons
Daily newspapers	1996	circulation	28,000	178
Radio	1997	receivers	221,000	1,400
Television	1997	receivers	106,000	668
Telephones	1997	main lines	71,136	453
Cellular telephones	1997	subscribers	5,673	36

Education and health

Educational attainment (1995). Percentage of population age 25 and over having: no formal schooling to some secondary education 26.9%; completed secondary 55.4%; completed higher 17.7%. *Literacy* (1990): total population age 15 and over literate 99.0%; males literate 99.0%; females literate 99.0%.

Education (1996)

	schools	teachers	students	student/ teacher ratio
Primary (age 5–10)	24	1,091	18,896	17.3
Secondary (age 11–18) / Vocational	6	943	18,068	19.2
Higher	5	...	3,383	...

Health (1999): physicians 130[9] (1 per 1,169 persons); hospital beds 192[10] (1 per 792 persons); infant mortality rate per 1,000 live births 10.0.

Military

Total active duty U.S. personnel (1999): 3,890 (army, 1.0%; navy 47.6%; air force 51.4%).

[1]Includes active-duty military personnel, U.S. Department of Defense employees, their dependents, and Guamanian nationals. [2]Total area per most recent survey including area designated as inland water equals 217 sq mi (561 sq km). [3]Detail does not add to total given because of rounding. [4]Employed persons only. [5]Other includes Agriculture, Manufacturing, Transportation and communications, and Finance. [6]Excludes nonimmigrant aliens and civilians living on military reservations. [7]Excludes U.S. military and dependents. [8]Fiscal year November 1998–October 1999. [9]Members of Guam Medical Society only. [10]Guam Memorial Hospital only.

Internet resources for further information:
- **The Official Guam U.S.A. Website http://ns.gov.gu**
- **Government of Guam: Economic Overview http://www.admin.gov.gu/commerce/economy.htm**

Guatemala

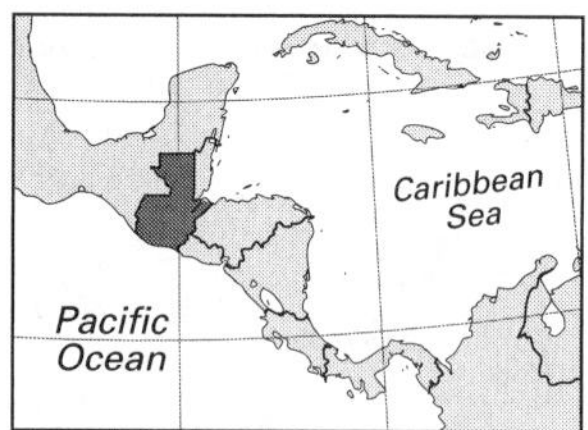

Official name: República de Guatemala (Republic of Guatemala).
Form of government: republic with one legislative house (Congress of the Republic [113]).
Head of state and government: President.
Capital: Guatemala City.
Official language: Spanish.
Official religion: none
Monetary unit: 1 quetzal (Q) = 100 centavos; valuation (Oct. 6, 2000) 1 U.S.$ = Q 7.84; 1 £ = Q 11.33.

Area and population

Departments	Capitals	area sq mi	area sq km	population 2000 estimate[1]
Alta Verapaz	Cobán	3,354	8,686	814,300
Baja Verapaz	Salamá	1,206	3,124	203,430
Chimaltenango	Chimaltenango	764	1,979	427,602
Chiquimula	Chiquimula	917	2,376	313,150
El Progreso	Guastatoya (Progreso)	742	1,922	143,197
Escuintla	Escuintla	1,693	4,384	483,768
Guatemala	Guatemala City	821	2,126	2,578,526
Huehuetenango	Huehuetenango	2,857	7,400	879,987
Izabal	Puerto Barrios	3,490	9,038	333,956
Jalapa	Jalapa	797	2,063	270,055
Jutiapa	Jutiapa	1,243	3,219	385,909
Petén	Flores	13,843	35,854	333,389
Quetzaltenango	Quetzaltenango	753	1,951	678,251
Quiché	Santa Cruz del Quiché	3,235	8,378	588,831
Retalhuleu	Retalhuleu	717	1,856	241,921
Sacatepéquez	Antigua Guatemala	180	465	259,265
San Marcos	San Marcos	1,464	3,791	844,486
Santa Rosa	Cuilapa	1,141	2,955	319,814
Sololá	Sololá	410	1,061	307,791
Suchitepéquez	Mazatenango	969	2,510	403,609
Totonicapán	Totonicapán	410	1,061	361,303
Zacapa	Zacapa	1,039	2,690	212,794
TOTAL		42,042[2]	108,889	11,385,334

Demography

Population (2000): 11,385,000.
Density (2000): persons per sq mi 270.8, persons per sq km 104.6.
Urban-rural (2000): urban 39.4%; rural 60.6%.
Sex distribution (1998): male 50.44%; female 49.56%.
Age breakdown (1998): under 15, 44.2%; 15–29, 28.0%; 30–44, 14.6%; 45–59, 7.9%; 60–74, 4.3%; 75 and over, 1.0%.
Population projection: (2010) 14,631,000; (2020) 18,123,000.
Doubling time: 24 years.
Ethnic composition (1994): Amerindian 42.8%; non-Amerindian 57.2%.
Religious affiliation (1995): Roman Catholic 75.9%, of which Catholic/traditional syncretist 25.0%; Protestant 21.8%; other Christian 1.3%; other 1.0%.
Major cities (1995): Guatemala City 1,167,495; Mixco 436,668; Villa Nueva 165,567; Chinautla 61,335; Amatitlan 40,229.

Vital statistics

Birth rate per 1,000 population (1999): 35.6 (world avg. 22.6).
Death rate per 1,000 population (1999): 6.8 (world avg. 8.9).
Natural increase rate per 1,000 population (1999): 28.8 (world avg. 13.7).
Total fertility rate (avg. births per childbearing woman; 1999): 4.7.
Marriage rate per 1,000 population (1995): 4.6.
Divorce rate per 1,000 population (1995): 0.05.
Life expectancy at birth (1999): male 63.8 years; female 69.2 years.
Major causes of death per 100,000 population (1988): infectious and parasitic diseases 121.6; diseases of the respiratory system 110.8; perinatal causes 58.7; malnutrition 50.2; dehydration 18.5.

National economy

Budget (1998). Revenue: Q 11,997,000,000 (tax revenue 90.3%, nontax revenue 8.9%). Expenditures: Q 14,828,000,000 (current expenditures 61.7%, of which disbursements for wages and salaries 25.3%, transfer payments 18.0%; capital expenditures 38.3%).
Public debt (external, outstanding; 1998): U.S.$2,990,000,000.
Tourism (1998): receipts U.S.$394,000,000; expenditures U.S.$157,000,000.
Production (metric tons except as noted). Agriculture, forestry, fishing (1999): sugarcane 15,459,000, corn (maize) 1,109,000 bananas 733,000, oil palm fruit 340,000, coffee 200,000, tomatoes 149,000; livestock (number of live animals) 2,300,000 cattle, 825,000 pigs, 24,000,000 chickens; roundwood (1998) 12,995,000 cu m; fish catch (1998) 10,847. Mining and quarrying (1997): gypsum 30,000; iron ore 3,300; antimony ore 880. Manufacturing (value added in Q '000,000; 1998[3]): food and beverage products 298; clothing and textiles 119; machinery and metal products 55. Construction (value of buildings authorized in Q '000,000; 1991)[4]: residential 170.2; nonresidential 127.5. Energy production (consumption): electricity (kW-hr; 1996) 3,500,000,000 (3,500,000,000); crude petroleum (barrels; 1996) 5,256,000 (5,198,000); petroleum products (metric tons; 1996) 687,000 (1,990,000).
Household income and expenditure. Average household size (1994) 5.2; income per household (1989) Q 4,306 (U.S.$1,529); sources of income: n.a.; expenditure (1981): food 64.4%, housing and energy 16.0%, transportation and communications 7.0%, household furnishings 5.0%, clothing 3.1%.
Gross national product (1998): U.S.$17,759,000,000 (U.S.$1,640 per capita).

Structure of gross domestic product and labour force

	1998 in value Q '000,000[3]	1998 % of total value	1995 labour force	1995 % of labour force
Agriculture	1,103	23.4	1,798,227	58.1
Mining	30	0.6	3,095	0.1
Manufacturing	640	13.6	420,928	13.6
Construction	113	2.4	126,898	4.1
Public utilities	162	3.4	9,285	0.3
Transp. and commun.	426	9.0	77,377	2.5
Trade	1,162	24.6	225,940	7.3
Finance, real estate	461	9.8 }		
Pub. admin., defense	356	7.5 }	371,407	12.0
Services	269	5.7 }		
Other	—	—	61,901[5]	2.0[5]
TOTAL	4,722	100.0	3,095,058	100.0

Population economically active (1996): total 3,183,173; activity rate of total population 29.1% (participation rates [1994] ages 15–64, 51.0%; female 19.5%; unemployed [1995] 1.4%[6]).

Price and earnings indexes (1995 = 100)

	1993	1994	1995	1996	1997	1998	1999
Consumer price index	83.2	92.2	100.0	111.1	121.3	129.8	136.1
Annual earnings index[7]	70.0	82.4	100.0	121.8	136.7	151.0	...

Land use (1998): forested and nonarable land 58.4%; meadows and pastures 24.0%; agricultural and under permanent cultivation 17.6%.

Foreign trade[8]

Balance of trade (current prices)

	1994	1995	1996	1997	1998	1999
U.S.$'000,000	–755.3	–692.0	–849.7	–1,198.7	–1,582.9	–1,613.0
% of total	19.9%	13.8%	17.3%	20.4%	23.5%	25.2%

Imports (1998): U.S.$4,650,900,000 (intermediate goods 34.9%, consumer goods 29.5%, capital goods 26.3%, lubricants and fuels 6.1%, construction materials 3.2%). *Major import sources:* United States 41.5%; Mexico 10.4%; Japan 4.5%; Venezuela 3.3%; Germany 2.8%.
Exports (1998): U.S.$2,846,700,000 (coffee 20.4%, sugar 11.0%, bananas 6.2%, petroleum 2.0%). *Major export destinations:* United States 32.2%; Germany 4.3%; Mexico 4.1%; Japan 2.2%.

Transport and communications

Transport. Railroads (1996): route length 884 km; passenger-km (1995) 16,580,000; metric ton-km cargo 85,615,000. Roads (1996): total length 13,100 km (paved 28%). Vehicles (1996): passenger cars 102,000; trucks and buses 97,000. Air transport (1995)[9]: passenger-km 500,000,000; metric ton-km cargo 70,000,000; airports (1996) 2.

Communications

Medium	date	unit	number	units per 1,000 persons
Daily newspapers	1996	circulation	338,000	33
Radio	1997	receivers	835,000	79
Television	1997	receivers	640,000	61
Telephones	1998	main lines	517,000	48
Cellular telephones	1998	subscribers	111,445	10
Personal computers	1998	units	90,000	8.3
Internet	1998	users	50,000	4.6

Education and health

Educational attainment (1994). Percentage of population age 25 and over having: no formal schooling 45.2%; incomplete primary education 20.8%; complete primary 18.0%; some secondary 4.8%; secondary 7.2%; higher 4.0%. *Literacy* (1995): total population age 15 and over literate 55.6%; males literate 62.5%; females literate 48.6%.

Education (1996)

	schools	teachers	students	student/ teacher ratio
Primary (age 7–12)	12,409	43,403	1,510,811	34.8
Secondary (age 13–18)	1,274[10] }	22,624	375,528	16.6
Voc., teacher tr.	626[10] }			
Higher	5[11]	4,346[11]	80,228[12]	16.0[11]

Health (1988): physicians (1997) 9,812 (1 per 1,072 persons); hospital beds (1995) 10,974 (1 per 909 persons); infant mortality rate (1999) 46.2.
Food (1998): daily per capita caloric intake 2,159 (vegetable products 90%, animal products 10%); 99% of FAO recommended minimum requirement.

Military

Total active duty personnel (1999): 31,400 (army 93.0%, navy 4.8%, air force 2.2%). *Military expenditure as percentage of GNP* (1996): 1.4% (world 2.6%); per capita expenditure U.S.$23.

[1]Adjusted for underenumeration in 1994 census. [2]Detail does not add to total given because of rounding. [3]At prices of 1958. [4]Private construction in Guatemala City metropolitan area only. [5]Persons in activities not adequately defined. [6]Registered unemployed; majority of economically active population is estimated to be underemployed. [7]Based on employees entitled to social security. [8]Import figures are f.o.b. in balance of trade and c.i.f. for commodities and trading partners. [9]Aviateca Airlines only. [10]1991. [11]1989. [12]1995.

Internet resources for further information:

- **Banco de Guatemala (Spanish only) http://www.banguat.gob.gt**
- **Instituto Nacional de Estadistica http://www.ine.gob.gt**

Guernsey[1]

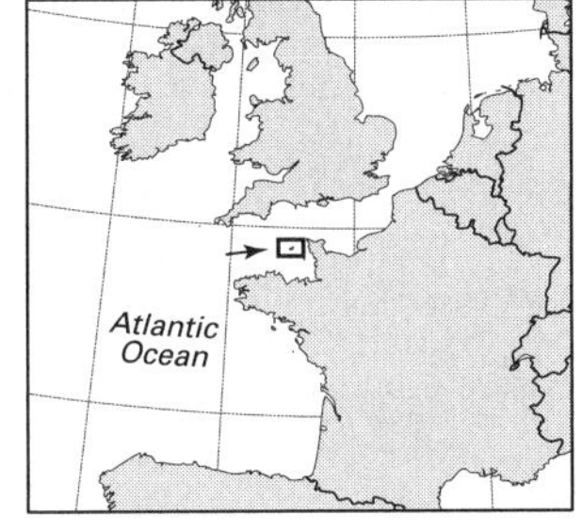

Official name: Bailiwick of Guernsey.
Political status: Crown dependency (United Kingdom) with one legislative house (States of Deliberation [57[2, 3, 4]]).
Chief of state: British Monarch represented by Lieutenant Governor.
Head of government: [5].
Capital: St. Peter Port.
Official language: English.
Official religion: n.a..
Monetary unit: 1 Guernsey pound[6] = 100 pence; valuation (Oct. 6, 2000) 1 Guernsey pound = U.S.$1.45.

Area and population	area		population
	sq mi	sq km	1996 census
Parishes of Guernsey	24.3	63.0	58,581
Castel	3.9	10.1	8,922
Forest	1.6	4.1	1,423
St. Andrew	1.7	4.5	2,342
St. Martin	2.8	7.3	6,082
St. Peter Port	2.6	6.6	16,194
St. Peter	2.4	6.2	2,151
St. Sampson	2.3	6.0	8,540
St. Saviour	2.4	6.3	2,469
Torteval	1.2	3.1	954
Vale	3.4	8.8	9,504
Dependencies of Guernsey	5.9	15.1	2,797
Alderney	3.1	7.9	2,147[7]
Brechou	0.1	0.3	0
Herm	0.5	1.3	97
Jethou	0.1	0.2	3
Lihou	0.1	0.2	0
Little Sark	0.4	1.0	550
Sark (Great Sark)	1.6	4.2	
TOTAL	30.2	78.1	61,378

Demography

Population (2000): 64,100.
Density (2000): persons per sq mi 2,121.9, persons per sq km 820.7.
Sex distribution (1996): male 48.13%; female 51.87%.
Age breakdown (1996): under 15, 17.6%; 15–29, 20.6%; 30–44, 22.3%; 45–59, 19.0%; 60–74, 13.2%; 75 and over, 7.3%.
Population projection: (2010) 66,000; (2020) 67,000.
Doubling time: n.a.; doubling time exceeds 100 years.
Population by place of birth (1996): Guernsey 65.5%, United Kingdom 27.2%, Portugal 1.9%, Jersey 0.7%, Ireland 0.7%, Alderney 0.3%, Sark 0.1%, other 3.6%.
Religious affiliation (*c.* 1990): Anglican 65.2%; other 34.8%.
Major cities (1996)[8]: St. Peter Port 16,194; Vale 9,504; Castel 8,922; St. Sampson 8,540; St. Martin 6,082.

Vital statistics

Birth rate per 1,000 population (1999): 10.5 (world avg. 22.1).
Death rate per 1,000 population (1999): 8.2 (world avg. 8.9).
Natural increase rate per 1,000 population (1999): 2.3 (world avg. 13.2).
Total fertility rate (avg. births per childbearing woman; 1999): 1.3.
Marriage rate per 1,000 population (1995): 6.0.
Divorce rate per 1,000 population (1993): 2.5.
Life expectancy at birth (1999): male 76.5 years; female 82.6 years.
Major causes of death per 100,000 population (1993): diseases of the circulatory system 423.5; malignant neoplasms (cancers) 288.0; diseases of the respiratory system 133.8; endocrine and metabolic disorders 25.4; accidents, poisoning, and violence 22.0; diseases of the digestive system 11.8.

National economy

Budget (1999). Revenue: £306,991,000 (income tax 79.7%; custom duties and excise taxes 5.7%; document duties 2.7%; corporation taxes 2.1%; automobile taxes 1.9%). Expenditures: £244,418,000 (welfare 31.1%; health 26.2%; education 15.9%; administrative services 6.7%; law and order 4.9%; community services 4.1%).
Public debt: n.a.
Gross national product (at current market prices; 1999): U.S.$1,902,230,000 (U.S.$29,810 per capita).

Structure of gross domestic product and labour force	1999		1996	
	in value £'000	% of total value	labour force	% of labour force
Horticulture, fishing	25,596	2.2	1,893	6.2
Mining	—		—	—
Manufacturing	38,812	3.4	2,084	6.8
Construction	59,623	5.2	2,676	8.7
Public utilities	9	9	447	1.5
Transp. and commun.	10	10	1,260	4.1
Finance, real estate[11]	706,483[9]	61.7[9]	5,928	19.3
Pub. admin., defense	302,010[10]	26.4[10]	1,908	6.2
Services			14,252	46.4
Other	12,998	1.1	245	0.8
TOTAL	1,145,522	100.0	30,693	100.0

Production (metric tons except as noted). Agriculture, forestry, fishing (1999): tomatoes 2,449[12], flowers 1,153,857 boxes, of which roses 287,915 boxes, freesia 184,467 boxes, carnations 161,273 boxes; livestock (number of live animals) 3,262 cattle; roundwood n.a.; fish catch (1997)[13]: 4,368, of which crustaceans 2,934 (sea spiders and crabs 2,713), molluscs 743 (abalones, winkles, and conch 438), marine fish 691. Mining and quarrying: n.a. Manufacturing: milk 98,830 hectolitres. Construction: n.a. Energy production (consumption): electricity, n.a. (273,013,000).
Household income and expenditure (1999). Average household size (1996) 2.6; expenditure: housing 21.6%, food 12.7%, household goods and services 11.2%, recreation services 9.2%, transportation 8.5%, clothing and footwear 5.6%, personal goods 4.9%, energy 4.1%.
Population economically active (1999): total 31,153; activity rate of total population 48.8% (participation rates: ages 15–64, n.a.; female n.a.; unemployed n.a.).

Retail price and earnings indexes (1994 = 100)	1994	1995	1996	1997	1998	1999	2000
Consumer price index[14]	100.0	103.0	105.5	108.8	113.2	115.7	120.1
Earnings index	...	...	...	...	...	...	...

Tourism (1996): receipts £176,000,000.

Foreign trade

Imports (1997): principal imports petrol and oils. *Major import sources* (1997): mostly United Kingdom.
Exports (1999): £525,718,000 (mostly flowers and tomatoes). *Major export destinations* (1999): mostly United Kingdom.

Transport and communications

Transport. Railroads: n.a. Vehicles (1999): passenger cars 36,460; trucks and buses 7,247. Air transport: (1997) passenger arrivals 870,869; (1996) freight loaded and unloaded 7,616 metric tons; airports (1999) with scheduled flights 2[15].

Communications Medium	date	unit	number	units per 1,000 persons
Daily newspapers	1998	circulation	15,784	260
Telephones	1998	main lines	48,102	776
Cellular telephones	1998	subscribers	11,841	191
Facsimile machines	1995	units	700	11.7

Education and health

Educational attainment: n.a. *Literacy* (1993): percentage of total population age 15 and over literate 100.0%; males literate 100.0%; females literate 100.0%.

Education (1993)	schools	teachers	students	student/ teacher ratio
Primary (age 5–10)	22[16]	236	4,697	19.9
Secondary (age 11–16)	8[16]	276	3,642	13.2
Higher[17]	1	...	215[18]	...

Health (1999): physicians 93 (1 per 654 persons); hospital beds, n.a.; infant mortality rate per 1,000 live births (1999) 5.2.
Food (1998[19]): daily per capita caloric intake 3,257 (vegetable products 68%, animal products 32%); 129% of FAO recommended minimum requirement.

Military

Total active duty personnel[20]: n.a.

[1]Data excludes Alderney and Sark unless otherwise noted. [2]Elected only; excludes those serving ex-officio. [3]Headed by the Bailiff. [4]Alderney and Sark have their own parliaments. The States of Alderney has an elected president and 12 people's deputies. The Chief Please of Sark consists of 40 *tenants* or landowners and 12 people's deputies. [5]The government of Guernsey is conducted by committees appointed by the States of Deliberation. [6]Equivalent in value to pound sterling (£). [7]Based on 1996 estimate. [8]Parishes. [9]Utilities and trade included in Finance, real estate. [10]Transportation is included in Public administration, defense and Services. [11]Mostly from 79 banks (located offshore) and 581 insurance companies (352 offshore and 217 domestic). [12]1998. [13]Includes Jersey. [14]March. [15]Includes one airport on Alderney. [16]1992. [17]1996–97. [18]Full students. [19]Data for the United Kingdom. [20]The United Kingdom is responsible for defense.

Internet resources for further information:
- **The States of Guernsey http://www.gov.gg**

Guinea

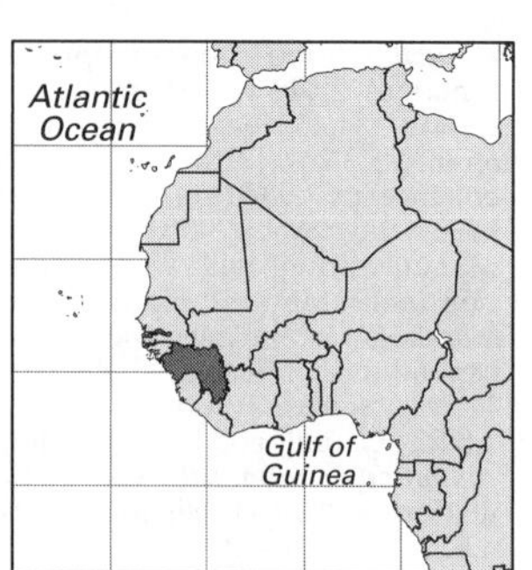

Official name: République de Guinée (Republic of Guinea).
Form of government: unitary multiparty republic with one legislative house (National Assembly [114 seats]).
Head of state and government: President assisted by extraconstitutional Prime Minister[1].
Capital: Conakry.
Official language: French.
Official religion: none.
Monetary unit: 1 Guinean franc (GF) = 100 cauris; valuation (Oct. 6, 2000) 1 U.S.$ = GF 1,750; 1 £ = GF 2,532.

Area and population

Regions[1]	Capitals	area sq mi	area sq km	population 1983 census
Beyla	Beyla	6,738	17,452	161,347
Boffa	Boffa	1,932	5,003	141,719
Boké	Boké	3,881	10,053	225,207
Conakry	Conakry	119	308	705,280
Coyah (Dubréka)	Coyah	2,153	5,576	134,190
Dabola	Dabola	2,317	6,000	97,986
Dalaba	Dalaba	1,313	3,400	132,802
Dinguiraye	Dinguiraye	4,247	11,000	133,502
Faranah	Faranah	4,788	12,400	142,923
Forécariah	Forécariah	1,647	4,265	116,464
Fria	Fria	840	2,175	70,413
Gaoual	Gaoual	4,440	11,500	135,657
Guéckédou	Guéckédou	1,605	4,157	204,757
Kankan	Kankan	7,104	18,400	229,861
Kérouané	Kérouané	3,070	7,950	106,872
Kindia	Kindia	3,409	8,828	216,052
Kissidougou	Kissidougou	3,425	8,872	183,236
Koubia	Koubia	571	1,480	98,053
Koundara	Koundara	2,124	5,500	94,216
Kouroussa	Kouroussa	4,647	12,035	136,926
Labé	Labé	973	2,520	253,214
Lélouma	Lélouma	830	2,150	138,467
Lola	Lola	1,629	4,219	106,654
Macenta	Macenta	3,363	8,710	193,109
Mali	Mali	3,398	8,800	210,889
Mamou	Mamou	2,378	6,160	190,525
Mandiana	Mandiana	5,000	12,950	136,317
Nzérékoré	Nzérékoré	1,460	3,781	216,355
Pita	Pita	1,544	4,000	227,912
Siguiri	Siguiri	7,626	19,750	209,164
Télimélé	Télimélé	3,119	8,080	243,256
Tougué	Tougué	2,394	6,200	113,272
Yomou	Yomou	843	2,183	74,417
TOTAL		94,926[2]	245,857	5,781,014

Demography

Population (2000): 7,466,000.
Density (2000): persons per sq mi 78.7, persons per sq km 30.4.
Urban-rural (1998): urban 31.3%; rural 68.7%.
Sex distribution (1998): male 50.28%; female 49.72%.
Age breakdown (1999): under 15, 43.6%; 15–29, 26.9%; 30–44, 16.0%; 45–59, 9.0%; 60–74, 3.9%; 75 and over, 0.6%.
Population projection: (2010) 9,281,000; (2020) 11,440,000.
Doubling time: 29 years.
Ethnic composition (1990): Fulani 40.3%; Malinke 25.8%; Susu 11.0%; Kissi 6.5%; Kpelle 4.8%; other 11.6%.
Religious affiliation (1983): Muslim 86.9%; traditional beliefs 4.6%; Christian 4.3%; other 4.2%.
Major cities (1983): Conakry (1993) 1,090,610; Kankan 55,010; Nzérékoré 44,598; Kindia 39,121; Kissidougou 30,724.

Vital statistics

Birth rate per 1,000 population (1999): 40.6 (world avg. 22.1).
Death rate per 1,000 population (1999): 17.3 (world avg. 8.9).
Natural increase rate per 1,000 population (1999): 23.3 (world avg. 13.2).
Total fertility rate (avg. births per childbearing woman; 1999): 5.5.
Life expectancy at birth (1999): male 44.0 years; female 49.1 years.

National economy

Budget (1998). Revenue: GF 624,500,000,000 (current revenues 79.5%, of which indirect taxes 34.8%, mining sector 20.2%, tax on trade 11.5%, direct taxes 7.7%, nontax revenue 5.3%; foreign aid 20.5%). Expenditures: GF 655,600,000,000 (wages and salaries 27.6%, goods and services 13.6%, interest 9.8%, transfers 8.1%; capital spending 38.2%).
Production (metric tons except as noted). Agriculture, forestry, fishing (1999): roots and tubers 1,064,888 (of which cassava 811,869, sweet potatoes 134,940, yams 88,635), fruits 996,078 (of which plantains 429,000, bananas 150,000, pineapples 71,858), paddy rice 750,000, vegetables and melons 420,000, sugarcane 220,000, peanuts (groundnuts) 173,682, corn (maize) 88,690; livestock (number of live animals) 2,368,000 cattle, 864,000 goats, 687,000 sheep, 54,000 pigs, 8,900,000 chickens; roundwood (1998) 8,650,000 cu m; fish catch (1997) 102,589. Mining and quarrying (1996): bauxite 15,888,600; alumina 564,237; gold 7,863 kg[3]. Manufacturing (value of production in GF '000; 1985): corrugated and sheet iron 571,081; plastics 462,242; tobacco products 375,154; cement 326,138; printed matter 216,511. Energy production (consumption): electricity (kW-hr; 1996) 541,000,000 (541,000,000); petroleum products (metric tons; 1996) none (356,000).

Gross national product (1998): U.S.$3,777,000,000 (U.S.$530 per capita).

Structure of gross domestic product and labour force

	1998 in value GF '000,000,000[4]	1998 % of total value	1983 labour force	1983 % of labour force
Agriculture, forestry, fishing	824.8	20.6	1,423,615	78.2
Mining	630.3	15.7	12,241	0.7
Manufacturing	153.9	3.8	11,215	0.6
Construction	350.6	8.7	9,115	0.5
Public utilities	20.8	0.5	3,205	0.2
Transp. and commun.	243.6	6.1	29,496	1.6
Trade, finance	1,116.8	27.8	40,865	2.0
Pub. admin., defense; Services	166.1	4.1	137,600	7.5
Other	505.8[5]	12.6[5]	155,679	8.5
TOTAL	4,012.7	100.0[2]	1,823,031	100.0

Public debt (external, outstanding; 1998): U.S.$3,126,000,000.
Population economically active (1997): total 3,321,000; activity rate of total population 44.8% (participation rates [1983]: ages 15–64, 63.5%; female 47.3%; unemployed, n.a.).

Price and earnings indexes (1995 = 100)

	1994	1995	1996	1997	1998
Consumer price index	94.7	100.0	102.9	104.9	110.3
Annual salary index	...	...	...	...	...

Household income and expenditure. Average household size (1997): 4.1; average annual income per capita (1984) GS 7,660 (U.S.$305); expenditure (1985): food 61.5%, health 11.2%, clothing 7.9%, housing 7.3%.
Tourism (1998): receipts U.S.$1,000,000; expenditures U.S.$27,000,000.
Land use (1994): forest 27.3%; pasture 43.5%; agriculture 3.3%; other 25.9%.

Foreign trade

Balance of trade (current prices)

	1993	1994	1995	1996	1997	1998
U.S.$'000,000	–21.6	–169.7	–39.0	+111.2	+117.6	+137.4
% of total	1.9%	14.1%	3.2%	9.6%	10.3%	10.7%

Imports (1997): U.S.$571,800,000 (capital goods 52.4%, consumer products 18.0%, food 17.1%, petroleum 12.5%). *Major import sources:* France 24.8%; U.S. 9.8%; Belgium 7.9%; Côte d'Ivoire 6.6%; China 5.6%.
Exports (1998): U.S.$709,200,000 (bauxite 45.7%, gold 17.7%, alumina 14.1%, diamonds 7.2%, fish 5.4%, coffee 3.3%). *Major export destinations*: U.S. 16.4%; Hong Kong 14.7%; Belgium 13.7%; Spain 12.4%; Ireland 12.2%.

Transport and communications

Transport. Railroads (1998): route length 662 km; (latest) passenger-km 41,500,000; metric ton-km cargo 7,300,000. Roads (1997): total length 30,500 km (paved 16.5%). Vehicles (1996): passenger cars 14,100; trucks and buses 21,000. Air transport (1995): passenger-km 52,000,000; metric ton-km cargo 5,000,000; airports (1998) 1.

Communications

Medium	date	unit	number	units per 1,000 persons
Daily newspapers	1988	circulation	13,000	2.0
Radio	1998	receivers	325,000	43
Television	1998	receivers	312,000	43
Telephones	1999	main lines	36,780	4.8
Cellular telephones	1999	subscribers	21,567	2.8
Personal computers	1998	units	25,000	3.2
Internet	1999	users	500	0.06

Education and health

Educational attainment of those age 6 and over having attended school (1983): primary 55.2%; secondary 32.7%; vocational 3.4%; higher 8.7%. *Literacy* (1995): percentage of total population age 15 and over literate 35.9%; males 49.9%; females 21.9%.

Education (1997–98)

	schools	teachers	students	student/teacher ratio
Primary (age 7–12)	3,723	13,883	674,732	48.6
Secondary (age 13–18)	239	4,958	143,245	28.9
Voc., teacher tr.[6]	55	1,268	8,569	6.8
Higher[7, 8]	2	947	8,151	8.6

Health: physicians (1991) 920 (1 per 6,840 persons); hospital beds (1988) 3,382 (1 per 1,652 persons); infant mortality rate (1998) 126.3.
Food (1998): daily per capita caloric intake 2,315 (vegetable products 97%, animal products 3%); 100% of FAO recommended minimum requirement.

Military

Total active duty personnel (1998): 9,700 (army 87.6%, navy 4.1%, air force 8.2%). *Military expenditure as percentage of GNP* (1997): 1.5% (world 2.6%); per capita expenditure U.S.$7.

[1]Regions represent second-level administration; Guinea is divided into 7 provinces and 1 city (Conakry) at the first level of administration. [2]Detail does not add to total given because of rounding. [3]1995 reported figure to government of artisanal production; excludes artisanal production smuggled out of country. [4]1994 prices. [5]Includes services and indirect taxes. [6]1995–96. [7]1996–97. [8]Universities only.

Internet resources for further information:
- **Welcome to Guinea http://www.guinee.net**

Guinea-Bissau

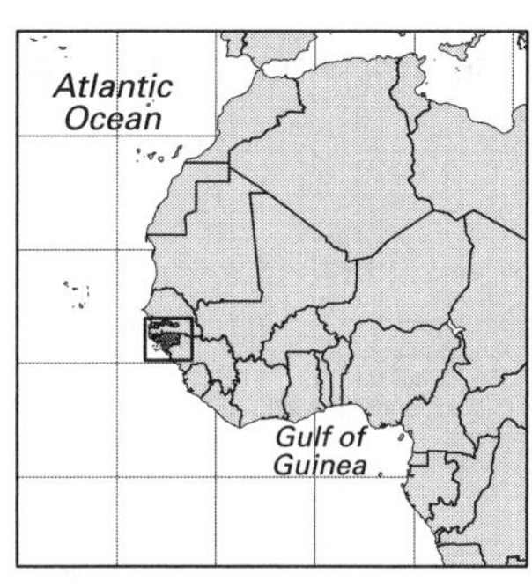

Official name: Républica da Guiné-Bissau (Republic of Guinea-Bissau).
Form of government: transitional regime with one legislative house (National People's Assembly [102]).
Chief of state: President.
Head of government: Prime Minister.
Capital: Bissau.
Official language: Portuguese.
Official religion: none.
Monetary unit: 1 CFA franc[1] (CFAF) = 100 centimes; valuation (Oct. 6, 2000) 1 U.S.$ = CFAF 754.28; 1 £ = CFAF 1,091.

Area and population

Regions	Chief towns	area sq mi	area sq km	population 1991 census
Bafatá	Bafatá	2,309	5,981	143,377
Biombo	Quinhámel	324	840	60,420
Bolama	Bolama	1,013	2,624	26,691
Cacheu	Cacheu	1,998	5,175	146,980
Gabú	Gabú	3,533	9,150	134,971
Oio	Bissorã	2,086	5,403	156,084
Quinara	Fulacunda	1,212	3,138	44,793
Tombali	Catió	1,443	3,736	72,441
Autonomous Sector				
Bissau	—	30	78	197,610
TOTAL		13,948[2]	36,125[2]	983,367

Demography

Population (2000): 1,286,000.
Density (2000)[3]: persons per sq mi 118.4, persons per sq km 45.7.
Urban-rural (1996): urban 22.0%; rural 78.0%.
Sex distribution (1997): male 48.52%; female 51.48%.
Age breakdown (1997): under 15, 42.7%; 15–29, 28.1%; 30–44, 15.4%; 45–59, 9.2%; 60–74, 3.8%; 75 and over, 0.8%.
Population projection: (2010) 1,614,000; (2020) 1,998,000.
Doubling time: 29 years.
Ethnic composition (1995): Balante 30%; Fulani 20%; Mandyako 14%; Malinke 13%; Pepel 7%; nonindigenous Cape Verdean mulatto 2%; other 14%.
Religious affiliation (1991): Muslim 46%; traditional beliefs 36%; Christian 15%, of which Roman Catholic 13%; nonreligious 3%.
Major cities (1979): Bissau 233,000[4]; Bafatá 13,429; Gabú 7,803; Mansôa 5,390; Catió 5,179.

Vital statistics

Birth rate per 1,000 population (1999): 39.9 (world avg. 22.1).
Death rate per 1,000 population (1999): 15.9 (world avg. 8.9).
Natural increase rate per 1,000 population (1999): 24.0 (world avg. 13.2).
Total fertility rate (avg. births per childbearing woman; 1999): 5.3.
Marriage rate per 1,000 population (1981): 0.1.
Divorce rate per 1,000 population: n.a.
Life expectancy at birth (1999): male 46.4 years; female 50.9 years.
Major causes of death per 100,000 population: n.a.; however, major diseases include tuberculosis of the respiratory system, whooping cough, typhoid fever, cholera, bacillary dysentery and amebiasis, malaria, pneumonia, and meningococcal infections; malnutrition is widespread.

National economy

Budget (1998). Revenue: CFAF 10,500,000,000 (foreign grants 37.1%; taxes on international trade 21.6%, of which import duties 12.9%; nontax revenues 19.8%, of which fishing licenses 7.3%; taxes on goods and services 10.7%; income taxes 8.2%). Expenditures: CFAF 30,200,000,000 (current expenditures 75.2%, of which scheduled external interest payments 27.0%; capital expenditures 24.8%).
Production (metric tons except as noted). Agriculture, forestry, fishing (1999): rice 130,000, oil palm fruit 80,000, roots and tubers 77,500, coconuts 44,000, cashew nuts 38,000, plantains 36,000, millet 30,000, peanuts (groundnuts) 18,000; livestock (number of live animals) 520,000 cattle, 340,000 pigs, 315,000 goats, 280,000 sheep, 850,000 chickens; roundwood (1998) 589,000 cu m; fish catch (1997) 7,250, of which marine fish 5,664, crustaceans and molluscs 1,336. Mining and quarrying: extraction of construction materials only. Manufacturing (1997): processed wood 21,400; fresh pork 9,720; wood products 7,000; dried and smoked fish 6,600; vegetable oils 4,100; fresh beef 3,850; soap 3,000; animal hides 1,277[5]; distilled liquor 13,000 hectolitres[4]. Energy production (consumption): electricity (kW-hr; 1998) 40,100,000 ([1996] 43,000,000); coal, none (none); crude petroleum, none (none); petroleum products (metric tons; 1996) none (75,000); natural gas, none (none).
Population economically active (1992): total 471,000; activity rate of total population 46.9% (participation rates [1991]: over age 10, 67.1%; female 40.5%; unemployed, n.a.).

Price and earnings indexes (1995 = 100)

	1994	1995	1996	1997	1998	1999[6]
Consumer price index	68.8	100.0	150.7	224.7	239.4	236.7
Monthly earnings index	...	...	...	...	...	...

Public debt (external, outstanding; 1998): U.S.$873,100,000.
Gross national product (at current market prices; 1998): U.S.$184,000,000 (U.S.$160 per capita).

Structure of gross domestic product and labour force

	1998 in value CFAF '000,000	1998 % of total value	1994 labour force	1994 % of labour force
Agriculture	74,831	61.7	365,000	77.2
Mining, Manufacturing, Public utilities	11,134	9.2	21,000	4.5
Construction	4,071	3.4		
Transportation and communications	2,333	1.9		
Trade	23,624	19.5	87,000	18.3
Finance, services	897	0.7		
Pub. admin., defense	3,067	2.5		
Other	1,357[7]	1.1[7]		
TOTAL	121,313[8]	100.0	473,000	100.0

Tourism: n.a.
Land use (1994): forested 38.1%; meadows and pastures 38.4%; agricultural and under permanent cultivation 12.1%; other 11.4%.
Household income and expenditure. Average household size (1996) 6.9; income per household: n.a; sources of income: n.a.; expenditure: n.a.

Foreign trade[9]

Balance of trade (current prices)

	1994	1995	1996	1997	1998	1999
CFAF '000,000	–15,950	–24,680	–24,210	–23,500	–21,400	–28,000
% of total	32.5%	50.1%	52.3%	29.3%	40.4%	31.6%

Imports (1997): CFAF 51,800,000,000 (foodstuffs 35.1%, of which rice 25.1%; transport equipment 14.1%; fuel and lubricants 10.7%; construction materials 9.6%). *Major import sources* (1998): The Netherlands 38.8%; Portugal 27.8%; China 24.8%.
Exports (1997): CFAF 28,300,000,000 (cashews 94.0%; sawn wood 1.6%; shrimp 0.8%; logs 0.8%). *Major export destinations* (1995): India 87.8%; Portugal 10.2%; France 1.0%; Spain 0.8%.

Transport and communications

Transport. Railroads: none. Roads (1996): total length 2,734 mi, 4,400 km (paved 10%). Vehicles (1996): passenger cars 7,120; trucks and buses 5,640. Merchant marine (1992): vessels (100 gross tons and over) 19; total deadweight tonnage 1,846. Air transport (1996): passenger-mi 6,200,000, passenger-km 10,000,000; short ton-mi cargo, n.a., metric ton-km cargo, n.a., airports (1997) with scheduled flights 2.

Communications

Medium	date	unit	number	units per 1,000 persons
Daily newspapers	1996	circulation	6,000	5.1
Radio	1997	receivers	49,000	41
Television	1997	receivers	0	0
Telephones	1998	main lines	8,079	6.6
Internet	1998	users	300	0.2

Education and health

Educational attainment (1979). Percentage of population age 7 and over having: no formal schooling or knowledge of reading and writing 90.4%; primary education 7.9%; secondary 1.0%; technical 0.5%; higher 0.2%. *Literacy* (1995): total population age 15 and over literate 54.9%; males literate 68.0%; females literate 42.5%.

Education (1994–95)

	schools	teachers	students	student/teacher ratio
Primary (age 7–13)	...	...	100,369	...
Secondary (age 13–18)	...	...	7,000[10]	...

Health: physicians (1991) 184 (1 per 5,556 persons); hospital beds (1993) 1,300 (1 per 834 persons); infant mortality rate per 1,000 live births (1999) 114.1.
Food (1997): daily per capita caloric intake 2,430 (vegetable products 93%, animal products 7%); 105% of FAO recommended minimum requirement.

Military

Total active duty personnel (1999): 7,250[11] (army 93.8%, navy 4.8%, air force 1.4%). *Military expenditure as percentage of GNP* (1997): 3.2% (world 2.6%); per capita expenditure U.S.$7.

[1]The CFA franc replaced the Guinea-Bissau peso in May 1997. [2]Includes water area of about 3,089 sq mi (8,000 sq km). [3]Based on land area of 10,859 sq mi (28,125 sq km). [4]1995. [5]1993. [6]Average of 2nd and 3rd quarters. [7]Indirect taxes. [8]Detail does not add to total given because of rounding. [9]Imports c.i.f.; exports f.o.b. [10]1993–94. [11]Excludes 2,000 paramilitary (gendarmes).

Internet resources for further information:

- **Investir en Zone Franc http://www.izf.net/izf/Index.htm**

Guyana

Official name: Co-operative Republic of Guyana.
Form of government: unitary multiparty republic with one legislative house (National Assembly [65[1]]).
Head of state and government: President.
Capital: Georgetown.
Official language: English.
Official religion: none.
Monetary unit: 1 Guyana dollar (G$) = 100 cents; valuation (Oct. 6, 2000) 1 U.S.$ = G$180.50; 1 £ = G$261.10.

Area and population

Administrative Regions		Capitals	area sq mi	area sq km	population 1986 estimate
Region 1	(Barima–Waini)	Mabaruma	7,853	20,339	18,516
Region 2	(Pomeroon–Supenaam)	Anna Regina	2,392	6,195	41,966
Region 3	(Essequibo Islands–West Demerara)	Vreed en Hoop	1,450	3,755	102,760
Region 4	(Demerara–Mahaica)	Paradise	862	2,233	310,758
Region 5	(Mahaica–Berbice)	Fort Wellington	1,610	4,170	55,556
Region 6	(East Berbice–Corentyne)	New Amsterdam	13,998	36,255	148,967
Region 7	(Cuyuni–Mazaruni)	Bartica	18,229	47,213	17,941
Region 8	(Potaro–Siparuni)	Mahdia	7,742	20,052	5,672
Region 9	(Upper Takutu–Upper Essequibo)	Lethem	22,313	57,790	15,338
Region 10	(Upper Demerara–Berbice)	Linden	6,595	17,081	38,598
TOTAL			83,044[2]	215,083[2]	756,072

Demography

Population (2000): 792,000.
Density (2000)[3]: persons per sq mi 10.4, persons per sq km 4.0.
Urban-rural (1998): urban 37.1%; rural 62.9%.
Sex distribution (1995): male 49.46%; female 50.54%.
Age breakdown (1995): under 15, 32.2%; 15–29, 30.1%; 30–44, 22.2%; 45–59, 9.5%; 60–74, 4.8%; 75 and over, 1.2%.
Population projection: (2010) 827,000; (2020) 856,000.
Doubling time: 71 years.
Ethnic composition (1992–93): East Indian 49.4%; black (African Negro and Bush Negro) 35.6%; mixed 7.1%; Amerindian 6.8%; Portuguese 0.7%; Chinese 0.4%.
Religious affiliation (1995): Christian 40.9%, of which Protestant 27.5% (including Anglican 8.6%), Roman Catholic 11.5%, Ethiopian Orthodox 1.1%; Hindu 34.0%; Muslim 9.0%; other 16.1%.
Major cities (1992): Georgetown (1995) 254,000; Linden 27,200; New Amsterdam 17,700.

Vital statistics

Birth rate per 1,000 population (1999): 18.1 (world avg. 22.1).
Death rate per 1,000 population (1999): 8.2 (world avg. 8.9).
Natural increase rate per 1,000 population (1999): 9.9 (world avg. 13.2).
Total fertility rate (avg. births per childbearing woman; 1999): 2.1.
Life expectancy at birth (1999): male 61.3 years; female 67.6 years.
Major causes of death per 100,000 population (1994)[4]: diseases of the circulatory system 274.3, of which cerebrovascular disease 99.2, ischemic heart diseases 75.2, diseases of pulmonary circulation and other forms of heart disease 57.9%; accidents and violence 76.1; endocrine and metabolic disorders 58.9; diseases of the respiratory system 50.1.

National economy

Budget (1999): Revenue: G$36,544,000,000 (tax revenue 91.6%, of which consumption taxes 32.0%, income taxes on companies 22.2%, personal income taxes 15.5%, import duties 11.4%; nontax revenue 8.2%). Expenditures: G$41,983,000,000 (current expenditure 71.2%, of which debt charges 13.8%; development expenditure 28.8%).
Production (metric tons except as noted). Agriculture, forestry, fishing (1999): rice 365,469, raw sugar 321,438, coconuts 56,449, cassava (manioc) 25,957, plantains 14,000, bananas 11,177, pineapples 7,000; livestock (number of live animals) 220,000 cattle, 130,000 sheep, 11,600,000 chickens; roundwood 442,000 cu m; fish catch (1997) 57,409, of which shrimps and prawns 19,060. Mining and quarrying (1999): bauxite 2,359,272; gold 414,905 troy oz; diamonds (1998) 34,385 carats. Manufacturing (1999): flour 35,290; rum 137,800 hectolitres; beer and stout 129,200 hectolitres; soft drinks 3,975,000 cases; pharmaceuticals 7,600,000 tablets; garments 2,900,000 units. Construction: n.a. Energy production (consumption): electricity (kW-hr; 1998) 431,300,000 ([1996] 255,000,000); coal, none (none); crude petroleum, none (none); petroleum products (metric tons; 1996) none (311,000); natural gas, none (none).
Population economically active (1992–93); total 278,000; activity rate of total population 38.8% (participation rates: ages 15–64, 61.8%; female 34.1%; unemployed [1998] *c.* 12%).

Price and earnings indexes (1995 = 100)

	1994	1995	1996	1997	1998	1999
Consumer price index[5]	89.8	100.0	106.6	109.9	115.0	123.6
Earnings index	...	...	...	...	...	...

Gross national product (at current market prices; 1998): U.S.$661,000,000 (U.S.$780 per capita).

Structure of gross domestic product and labour force

	1999 in value G$'000,000	1999 % of total value	1980 labour force	1980 % of labour force
Sugar	16,142[6]	13.4[6]		
Other agriculture	17,543[7]	14.5[7]	50,316	20.4
Fishing, forestry	8,851	7.3		
Mining	13,923	11.5	9,669	3.9
Manufacturing	3,681[8, 9]	3.1[8, 9]	28,980	11.8
Construction	4,771	4.0	7,024	2.8
Public utilities	[9]	[9]	2,850	1.2
Transp. and commun.	7,138	5.9	9,412	3.8
Trade	4,268	3.5	15,231	6.2
Finance, real estate	7,235	6.0	2,944	1.2
Pub. admin., defense	16,976	14.1	29,948	12.1
Services	1,570	1.3	29,295	11.9
Other	18,570[10]	15.4[10]	61,002[11]	24.7[11]
TOTAL	120,668	100.0	246,671	100.0

Public debt (external, outstanding; 1998): U.S.$1,369,000,000.
Household income and expenditure. Average household size (1997) 4.5.
Tourism (1997) receipts from visitors U.S.$39,000,000; expenditures by nationals abroad U.S.$22,000,000.
Land use (1994): forested 83.8%; meadows and pastures 6.3%; agricultural and under permanent cultivation 2.5%; other 7.4%.

Foreign trade[12]

Balance of trade (current prices)

	1994	1995	1996	1997	1998	1999
U.S.$'000,000	–42.9	–40.8	–20.2	–34.2	–54.2	–25.2
% of total	4.4%	4.0%	1.7%	2.8%	4.7%	2.3%

Imports (1999): U.S.$550,200,000 (consumer goods 35.2%; capital goods 29.6%; fuels and lubricants 13.1%). *Major import sources* (1998)[13]: U.S. 28%; Trinidad and Tobago 21%; Netherlands Antilles 14%; U.K. 7%; Japan 3%.
Exports (1999): U.S.$525,000,000 (domestic exports 96.1%, of which sugar 25.9%, gold 20.7%; bauxite 14.7%, rice 13.5%, timber 7.1%; reexports 3.9%). *Major export destinations* (1998)[13]: U.S. 24%; Canada 23%; U.K. 19%; Netherlands Antilles 10%.

Transport and communications

Transport. Railroads: [14]. Roads (1996): total length 4,952 mi, 7,970 km (paved 7%). Vehicles (1995): passenger cars 24,000; trucks and buses 9,000. Air transport (1996)[15]: passenger-mi 154,000,000, passenger-km 248,000,000; short ton-mi cargo 2,300,000, metric ton-km cargo 3,300,000; airports (1996) with scheduled flights 1[16].

Communications

Medium	date	unit	number	units per 1,000 persons
Daily newspapers	1996	circulation	42,000	54
Radio	1997	receivers	420,000	539
Television	1997	receivers	46,000	59
Telephones	1998	main lines	59,910	77
Cellular telephones	1998	subscribers	1,454	1.9
Personal computers	1998	units	20,000	26
Internet	1998	users	2,000	2.6

Education and health

Educational attainment (1980). Percentage of population age 25 and over having: no formal schooling 8.1%; primary education 72.8%; secondary 17.3%; higher 1.8%. *Literacy* (1995): total population age 15 and over literate, *c.* 511,000 (98.1%); males literate, *c.* 254,000 (98.6%); females literate, *c.* 257,000 (97.5%).

Education (1996–97)

	schools	teachers	students	student/ teacher ratio
Primary (age 6–11)	420	3,461	102,000	29.5
Secondary (age 12–17)	...	2,150[17]	62,043	29.5[17]
Higher	...	612[17]	8,965	12.5[17]

Health: physicians (1997) 153 (1 per 5,090 persons); hospital beds (1996) 3,242 (1 per 240 persons); infant mortality rate per 1,000 live births (1999) 39.8.
Food (1998): daily per capita caloric intake 2,476 (vegetable products 85%, animal products 15%); 109% of FAO recommended minimum requirement.

Military

Total active duty personnel (1999): 1,600 (army 87.5%, navy 6.3%, air force 6.2%) *Military expenditure as percentage of GNP* (1997): 1.1% (world 2.6%); per capita expenditure U.S.$10.

[1]Includes 12 indirectly elected seats. [2]Includes inland water area equaling *c.* 7,000 sq mi (*c.* 18,000 sq km). [3]Based on land area only. [4]Projected rates based on about 78% of total deaths. [5]Weights of consumer price index components for Georgetown only. [6]Includes sugar manufacturing. [7]Includes rice manufacturing. [8]Excludes sugar and rice manufacturing. [9]Manufacturing includes Public utilities. [10]Indirect taxes less subsidies. [11]Represents "not stated." [12]Imports c.i.f.; exports f.o.b. [13]Estimated figures. [14]No public railways. [15]Scheduled traffic only. [16]International only; domestic air service is provided on a charter basis. [17]1995–96.

Internet resources for further information:
- **Guyana News and Information http://www.guyana.org**

Haiti

Official name: Repiblik Dayti (Haitian Creole); République d'Haïti (French) (Republic of Haiti).
Form of government: multiparty republic with two legislative houses (Senate [27[1]]; Chamber of Deputies [82[1]]).
Chief of state: President.
Head of government: Prime Minister.
Capital: Port-au-Prince.
Official languages: Haitian Creole; French.
Official religion: none[2].
Monetary unit: 1 gourde (G) = 100 centimes; valuation (Oct. 6, 2000) 1 U.S.$ = G 22.50; 1 £ = G 32.55.

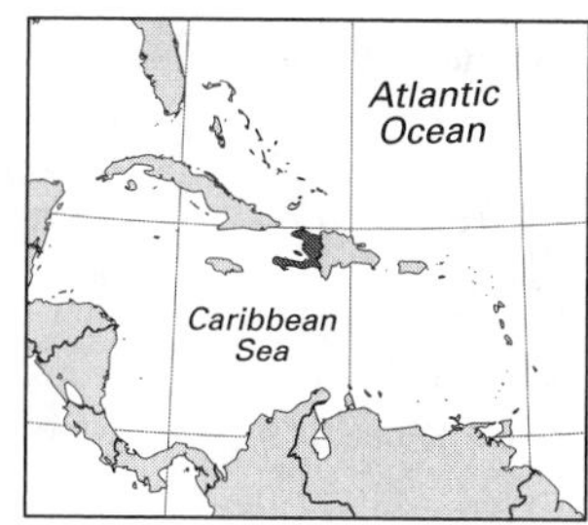

Area and population

Departements	Capitals	area sq mi	area sq km	population 1997 estimate
Artibonite	Gonaïves	1,924	4,984	1,052,834
Centre	Hinche	1,419	3,675	508,199
Grand'Anse	Jérémie	1,278	3,310	660,420
Nord	Cap-Haïtien	813	2,106	785,687
Nord-Est	Fort-Liberté	697	1,805	255,601
Nord-Ouest	Port-de-Paix	840	2,176	439,984
Ouest	Port-au-Prince	1,864	4,827	2,651,115
Sud	Les Cayes	1,079	2,794	671,112
Sud-Est	Jacmel	781	2,023	466,810
TOTAL		10,695	27,700	7,491,762[3]

Demography

Population (2000): 6,868,000[4].
Density (2000): persons per sq mi 642.2, persons per sq km 247.9.
Urban-rural (1999): urban 35.1%; rural 64.9%.
Sex distribution (1998)[5]: male 48.91%; female 51.09%.
Age breakdown (1998)[5]: under 15, 40.2%; 15–29, 27.2%; 30–44, 17.1%; 45–59, 9.6%; 60–74, 4.7%; 75 and over, 1.2%.
Population projection[4]: (2010) 7,950,000; (2020) 9,072,000.
Doubling time: 41 years.
Ethnic composition (1998): black/mulatto 99.0%; other 1.0%.
Religious affiliation (1995): Roman Catholic 68.5%[6]; Protestant 24.1%, of which Baptist 5.9%, Pentecostal 5.3%, Seventh-day Adventist 4.6%; other 7.4%.
Major cities (1997): Port-au-Prince 917,112 (metropolitan area 1,556,588); Carrefour 306,074[7]; Delmas 257,247[7]; Cap-Haïtien 107,026; Pétionville 76,155[7].

Vital statistics

Birth rate per 1,000 population (1999): 32.2 (world avg. 22.1).
Death rate per 1,000 population (1999): 15.3 (world avg. 8.9).
Natural increase rate per 1,000 population (1999): 16.9 (world avg. 13.2).
Total fertility rate (avg. births per childbearing woman; 1999): 4.6.
Life expectancy at birth (1999): male 47.3 years; female 50.9 years.
Major causes of death per 100,000 population (1982)[8]: infectious and parasitic diseases 46.0; diseases of the circulatory system 11.9; diseases associated with malnutrition 8.5; ill-defined conditions 115.2.

National economy

Budget (1998)[9]. Revenue: G 5,371,000,000 (general sales tax 26.4%; customs duties 20.1%; excises 15.9%; taxes on income and profits 11.7%). Expenditures: G 6,036,000,000 (current expenditure 80.0%, of which interest on public debt 7.2%; development expenditure 20.0%).
Public debt (external, outstanding; 1998): U.S.$980,000,000.
Production (metric tons except as noted). Agriculture, forestry, fishing (1999): sugarcane 1,000,100, cassava (manioc) 325,000, plantains 290,000, bananas 290,000, mangoes 225,000, corn (maize) 215,000, yams 195,000, sweet potatoes 172,000, rice 102,000, sorghum 96,000, avocados 45,000, coffee 28,000, sisal 5,700, cacao 4,500; livestock (number of live animals) 1,618,000 goats, 1,300,000 cattle, 800,000 pigs, 490,000 horses; roundwood (1998) 6,397,000 cu m; fish catch (1997) 5,630. Mining and quarrying: small amounts of limestone, calcareous clay, salt, and marble. Manufacturing (1995–96): cement 84,000[10]; essential oils (mostly amyris, neroli, and vetiver) 227[10]; cigarettes 837,900,000 units; malt liquor 13,800,000 bottles; beer 4,200,000 bottles; articles assembled for reexport (gross export value in U.S.$'000,000; 1997–98) 211.2, of which garments 199.3, travel goods and handbags 2.8, sports equipment and toys 2.3. Energy production (consumption): electricity (kW-hr; 1996) 633,000,000 (633,000,000); coal (metric tons) none (none); crude petroleum, none (none); petroleum products (metric tons; 1996) none (341,000); natural gas, none (none).
Land use (1994): forested 5.1%; meadows and pastures 18.0%; agricultural and under permanent cultivation 33.0%; other 43.9%.
Population economically active (1996): total 3,209,000; activity rate of total population 49.3% (participation rates: ages 15–64 [1990] 64.8%; female 43.0%; unemployed unofficially about 60%).

Price and earnings indexes (1995 = 100)

	1994	1995	1996	1997	1998	1999	2000[11]
Consumer price index	78.4	100.0	120.6	145.4	160.8	174.8	186.3
Daily earnings index[12]	41.7	100.0	100.0	100.0	100.0	...	...

Household income and expenditure. Average household size (1982) 4.4; average annual income of urban wage earners (1984): G 1,545 (U.S.$309); expenditure (1986–87)[13]: food, beverages, and tobacco 51.1%, household furnishings 9.2%, clothing and footwear 8.7%, transportation 7.6%.
Gross national product (1998): U.S.$3,163,000,000 (U.S.$410 per capita).

Structure of gross domestic product and labour force

	1997–98[14] in value G '000,000[15]	1997–98[14] % of total value	1990 labour force	1990 % of labour force
Agriculture, forestry	1,403	30.2	1,535,444	57.3
Mining	10	0.2	24,012	0.9
Manufacturing	330	7.1	151,387	5.6
Construction	562	12.1	28,001	1.0
Public utilities	42	0.9	2,577	0.1
Transp. and commun.	98	2.1	20,691	0.8
Trade, restaurants	622	13.4	352,970	13.2
Finance, real estate	366	7.9	5,057	0.2
Services	216	4.6	155,347	5.8
Pub. admin., defense	829	17.8		
Other	174[16]	3.7[16]	403,654[17]	15.1[17]
TOTAL	4,652	100.0	2,679,140	100.0

Tourism: receipts from visitors (1997) U.S.$57,000,000; expenditures by nationals abroad (1996) U.S.$37,000,000.

Foreign trade[14, 18, 19]

Balance of trade (current prices)

	1993–94	1994–95	1995–96	1996–97	1997–98	1998–99
U.S.$'000,000	–75.5	–344.1	–540.2	–511.1	–527.2	–769.5
% of total	25.9%	55.6%	64.6%	56.7%	48.1%	67.9%

Imports (1997–98): U.S.$811,500,000 ([20]food and live animals 27%, machinery and transport equipment 16%, petroleum and derivatives 9%, animal and vegetable oils 7%). *Major import sources* (1998)[20]: United States 60%; Japan 4%; Dominican Republic 4%; France 3%; Colombia 3%.
Exports (1997–98): U.S.$284,300,000 ([20]reexports [mostly clothing] 74%, handicrafts [includes wood carvings, paintings, and woven sisal products] 7%, coffee 7%). *Major export destinations* (1998)[20]: United States 88%; Belgium 3%, France 3%.

Transport and communications

Transport. Railroad (1998) none. Roads (1996): total length 2,585 mi, 4,160 km (paved 24%). Vehicles (1996): passenger cars 32,000; trucks and buses 21,000. Air transport (1994)[21]: passenger arrivals 167,882, passenger departures 177,072; cargo unloaded 11,967 metric tons, cargo loaded 10,087 metric tons; airports (1997) with scheduled flights 2.

Communications

Medium	date	unit	number	units per 1,000 persons
Daily newspapers	1996	circulation	20,000	3.1
Radio	1997	receivers	415,000	63
Television	1997	receivers	38,000	5.8
Telephones	1997	main lines	60,000	9.1

Education and health

Educational attainment (1986–87). Percentage of population age 25 and over having: no formal schooling 59.5%; primary education 30.5%; secondary 8.6%; vocational and teacher training 0.7%; higher 0.7%. *Literacy* (1995): total population age 15 and over literate 1,930,000 (45.0%); males literate 992,000 (48.0%); females literate 938,000 (42.2%).

Education (1994–95)

	schools	teachers	students	student/ teacher ratio
Primary (age 6–12)	10,071	30,205	1,110,398	36.8
Secondary (age 13–18) / Voc., teacher tr.	1,038	...	195,418	...
Higher[22, 23]	2	817	12,204	14.9

Health: physicians (1993–94) 641[24] (1 per 9,846 persons); hospital beds (1996) 5,241 (1 per 1,242 persons); infant mortality rate per 1,000 live births (1999) 98.9.
Food (1998): daily per capita caloric intake 1,876 (vegetable products 94%, animal products 6%); 83% of FAO recommended minimum requirement.

Military

Total active duty personnel: [25].

[1]Statutory membership; membership of Senate in October 2000 was 19. [2]Roman Catholicism has special recognition. [3]Official population projection based on 1982 census. [4]De facto estimate(s). [5]Based on de jure population. [6]About 80% of all Roman Catholics also practice voodoo. [7]Within Port-au-Prince metropolitan area. [8]Public health facilities only. [9]Excludes G 3,700,000,000 in foreign grants. [10]1992–93. [11]February. [12]Standard minimum wage rate. [13]Based on nationwide sample survey of 3,120 households. [14]For fiscal year ending September 30. [15]At prices of 1975–76. [16]Indirect taxes including import duties. [17]Includes 63,975 not adequately defined and 339,679 officially unemployed. [18]Includes reexports. [19]Import figures c.i.f., export figures f.o.b. [20]Estimated percentages. [21]Port-au-Prince Airport only. [22]Port-au-Prince universities only. [23]1997–98. [24]Public health services only. [25]The Haitian army was disbanded in 1995. A UN force provided security between April 1995 and December 1997 and supervised the creation of a 5,300-member (1999) national police force.

Internet resources for further information:

- **Embassy of Haiti (Washington, D.C.) (mostly French language) http://www.haiti.org**

Honduras

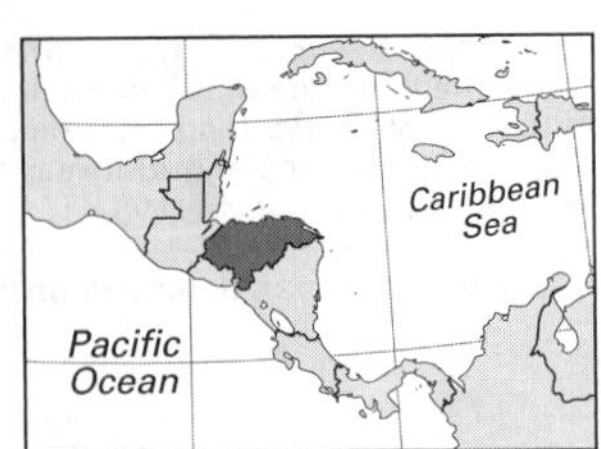

Official name: República de Honduras (Republic of Honduras).
Form of government: multiparty republic with one legislative house (National Assembly [128]).
Head of state and government: President.
Capital: Tegucigalpa[1].
Official language: Spanish.
Official religion: none.
Monetary unit: 1 Honduran lempira (L) = 100 centavos; valuation (Oct. 6, 2000) 1 U.S.$ = L 14.92; 1 £ = L 21.58.

Area and population

		area		population
Departments	Administrative centres	sq mi	sq km	1991 estimate
Atlántida	La Ceiba	1,641	4,251	255,000
Choluteca	Choluteca	1,626	4,211	309,000
Colón	Trujillo	3,427	8,875	164,000
Comayagua	Comayagua	2,006	5,196	257,000
Copán	Santa Rosa de Copán	1,237	3,203	226,000
Cortés	San Pedro Sula	1,527	3,954	706,000
El Paraíso	Yuscarán	2,787	7,218	277,000
Francisco Morazán	Tegucigalpa	3,068	7,946	878,000
Gracias a Dios	Puerto Lempira	6,421	16,630	37,000
Intibucá	La Esperanza	1,186	3,072	130,000
Islas de la Bahía	Roatán	100	261	24,000
La Paz	La Paz	900	2,331	112,000
Lempira	Gracias	1,656	4,290	180,000
Ocotepeque	Nueva Ocotepeque	649	1,680	77,000
Olancho	Juticalpa	9,402	24,351	309,000
Santa Bárbara	Santa Bárbara	1,975	5,115	291,000
Valle	Nacaome	604	1,565	121,000
Yoro	Yoro	3,065	7,939	355,000
TOTAL		43,277[2]	112,088[2]	4,708,000

Demography

Population (2000): 6,490,000.
Density (2000)[3]: persons per sq mi 149.4, persons per sq km 57.7.
Urban-rural (1999): urban 45.8%; rural 54.2%.
Sex distribution (1998): male 50.36%; female 49.64%.
Age breakdown (1998): under 15, 42.6%; 15–29, 28.4%; 30–44, 16.2%; 45–59, 7.8%; 60–74, 3.9%; 75 and over, 1.1%.
Population projection: (2010) 7,979,000; (2020) 9,166,000.
Doubling time: 29 years.
Ethnic composition (1987): mestizo 89.9%; Amerindian 6.7%; black (including Black Carib) 2.1%; white 1.3%.
Religious affiliation (1995): Roman Catholic 86.7%; Protestant 10.4%, of which Pentecostal 5.7%; other 2.9%.
Major cities (1999): Tegucigalpa 988,400[4]; San Pedro Sula 452,100; El Progreso 104,100; La Ceiba 103,400; Choluteca 92,400.

Vital statistics

Birth rate per 1,000 population (1999): 31.0 (world avg. 22.1).
Death rate per 1,000 population (1999): 7.1 (world avg. 8.9).
Natural increase rate per 1,000 population (1999): 23.9 (world avg. 13.2).
Total fertility rate (avg. births per childbearing woman; 1999): 4.0.
Marriage rate per 1,000 population (1983): 4.9.
Divorce rate per 1,000 population (1983): 0.4.
Life expectancy at birth (1999): male 63.2 years; female 66.3 years.
Major causes of death per 100,000 population (1983): diseases of the circulatory system 48.4; infectious and parasitic diseases 46.6; accidents and violence 42.2; diseases of the respiratory system 26.3.

National economy

Budget (1998). Revenue: L 13,197,000,000 (current revenue 99.8%, of which indirect taxes 65.1%, direct taxes 25.6%, nontax revenue 6.9%, transfers 2.2%). Expenditures: L 11,367,000,000 (current expenditure 72.6%; capital expenditure 27.4%).
Public debt (external, outstanding; 1998): U.S.$3,946,000,000.
Production (metric tons except as noted). Agriculture, forestry, fishing (1999): sugarcane 4,286,000, bananas 861,000, oil palm fruit 522,000, corn (maize) 478,000, plantains 250,000, coffee 164,000, oranges 79,000, cantaloupes 78,000, sorghum 71,000, pineapples 70,000; livestock (number of live animals) 2,061,000 cattle, 700,000 pigs, 18,000,0000 chickens; roundwood (1998) 7,176,000 cu m; fish catch (1998) 14,881. Mining and quarrying (1997): gypsum 28,000; salt 25,000; zinc 25,500; lead 3,400; gold 150 kilograms. Manufacturing (value added in L '000,000; 1996): food products 1,937.3; wearing apparel 1,266.4; beverages 699.6; nonmetallic mineral products 503.6; wood products 325.7; consumer chemicals 319.7. Construction (value of private construction in L '000,000; 1999)[5]: residential 813.8; nonresidential 890.7. Energy production (consumption): electricity (kW-hr; 1996) 2,815,000,000 (2,819,000,000); coal, none (none); crude petroleum (barrels; 1992) none (3,064,000); petroleum products (metric tons; 1996) none (1,157,000).
Household income and expenditure. Average household size (1988) 5.4; income per household: n.a.; sources of income (1985): wages and salaries 58.8%, transfer payments 1.8%, other 39.4%; expenditure (1986): food 44.4%, utilities and housing 22.4%, clothing and footwear 9.0%, household furnishings 8.3%, health care 7.0%, transportation 3.0%, other 5.9%.
Land use (1998): forested and other 67.9%; meadows and pastures 13.8%; agricultural and under permanent cultivation 18.3%.
Gross national product (1998): U.S.$4,564,000,000 (U.S.$740 per capita).

Structure of gross domestic product and labour force

	1999			
	in value L '000,000[6]	% of total value	labour force	% of labour force
Agriculture	10,635	16.2	834,900	39.2
Mining	1,325	2.0	4,200	0.2
Manufacturing	12,916	19.6	249,000	11.7
Construction	3,516	5.4	158,300	7.4
Public utilities	3,208	4.9	20,100	0.9
Transp. and commun.	3,423	5.2	58,600	2.7
Trade	8,365	12.7	240,400	11.3
Finance, real estate	10,950	16.7	48,400	2.3
Public admin., defense	4,153	6.3	517,400	24.3
Services	7,261	11.0		
TOTAL	65,752	100.0	2,131,300	100.0

Population economically active (1999): total 2,131,300; activity rate of total population 33.4% (participation rates: over age 15 [1998] 61.2%; female [1998] 34.6%; unemployed [1998] 4.3%).

Price and earnings indexes (1995 = 100)

	1993	1994	1995	1996	1997	1998	1999
Consumer price index	63.5	77.2	100.0	123.8	148.8	169.2	188.9
Daily earnings index[7]	...	84.4	100.0	119.3	158.0	184.9	...

Tourism (1998): receipts U.S.$164,000,000; expenditures U.S.$61,000,000.

Foreign trade[8]

Balance of trade (current prices)

	1994	1995	1996	1997	1998	1999
U.S.$'000,000	−382	−273	−341	−505	−683	−1,254
% of total	15.8%	9.5%	10.7%	14.1%	17.1%	32.5%

Imports (1999): U.S.$2,727,800,000 (machinery and electrical equipment 20.8%, industrial chemicals 13.0%, transport equipment 12.1%, food products 10.3%, mineral fuels and lubricants 9.4%). *Major import sources:* United States 47.1%; Guatemala 7.4%; Mexico 4.8%; Japan 4.7%; Costa Rica 2.5%; The Netherlands 1.4%.
Exports (1999): U.S.$1,303,900,000 (coffee 20.5%, shrimp and lobsters 15.5%, melons 3.7%, lead and zinc 3.4%). *Major export destinations:* United States 35.4%; Germany 7.5%; El Salvador 6.4%; Guatemala 5.8%; Nicaragua 4.8%; Belgium 4.2%.

Transport and communications

Transport. Railroads (1989): length (1999) 614 mi, 988 km; passenger-km 7,700,000; metric ton-km cargo 30,200,000. Roads (1999): total length 9,073 mi, 14,602 km (paved 18%). Vehicles (1995): passenger cars 81,439; trucks and buses 170,006. Merchant marine (1992): vessels (100 gross tons and over) 966; total deadweight tonnage 1,437,321. Air transport (1995): passenger-mi 212,000,000, passenger-km 341,000,000; short ton-mi cargo 23,000,000, metric ton-km cargo 33,000,000; airports (1996) with scheduled flights 8.

Communications

Medium	date	unit	number	units per 1,000 persons
Daily newspapers	1996	circulation	320,000	55
Radio	1997	receivers	2,450,000	410
Television	1997	receivers	570,000	95
Telephones	1998	main lines	249,737	40
Cellular telephones	1998	subscribers	34,896	5.6
Personal computers	1998	units	50,000	8.0
Internet	1998	users	18,000	2.9

Education and health

Educational attainment (1988). Percentage of population age 10 and over having: no formal schooling 33.4%; primary education 50.1%; secondary education 13.4%; higher 3.1%. *Literacy* (1995): total population age 15 and over literate 72.7%; males literate 72.6%; females literate 72.7%.

Education (1999)

	schools	teachers	students	student/ teacher ratio
Primary (age 7–13)	8,768	33,431	1,099,714	32.9
Secondary (age 14–19) / Voc., teacher tr.	661[9]	14,539	187,561	12.9
Higher	8[9]	3,600	52,139	14.5

Health: physicians (1993) 3,803 (1 per 1,358 persons); hospital beds (1999) 5,720 (1 per 1,098 persons); infant mortality rate (1999) 40.8.
Food (1998): daily per capita caloric intake 2,343 (vegetable products 85%, animal products 15%); 104% of FAO recommended minimum.

Military

Total active duty personnel (1999): 8,300 (army 66.3%, navy 12.0%, air force 21.7%). *Military expenditure as percentage of GNP* (1995): 1.3% (world 2.7%); per capita expenditure U.S.$9.

[1]Tegucigalpa and adjacent city of Comayagüela jointly form the capital according to the constitution. [2]The 1993 area is 43,433 sq mi (112,492 sq km); breakdown by department is not available. [3]Based on the revised area. [4]Population cited is for Central District (Tegucigalpa and Comayagüela). [5]Tegucigalpa, San Pedro Sula, and 10 other urban centres. [6]At factor cost. [7]Official minimum wages in all sectors. [8]Import figures are f.o.b. in balance of trade and c.i.f. for commodities and trading partners. [9]1995.

Internet resources for further information:
- **Banco Central de Honduras http://www.bch.hn/frames.htm**

Hong Kong

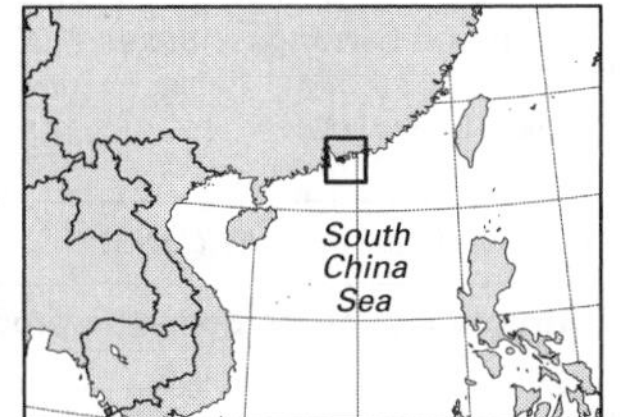

Official name: Xianggang Tebie Xingzhengqu (Chinese); Hong Kong Special Administrative Region (English).
Political status: special administrative region[1] (People's Republic of China) with one legislative house (Legislative Council [60[2]]).
Head of state and government: Chief Executive.
Capital: None[3].
Official languages: Chinese; English.
Official religion: none.
Monetary unit: 1 Hong Kong dollar (HK$) = 100 cents; valuation (Oct. 6, 2000) 1 U.S.$ = HK$7.80; 1 £ = HK$11.28.

Area and population

Area	area sq mi	area sq km	population 1996 census
Hong Kong Island	30.9	80.1	1,312,637
Kowloon and New Kowloon	18.0	46.5	1,987,996
New Territories	372.7	965.3	2,906,733
Marine	—	—	10,190
TOTAL	421.6	1,091.9	6,217,556

Demography

Population (2000): 6,782,000.
Density (2000): persons per sq mi 16,086.6, persons per sq km 6,211.3.
Urban-rural (1999): urban 100.0%.
Sex distribution (2000): male 48.69%; female 51.31%.
Age breakdown (2000): under 15, 17.1%; 15–29, 20.8%; 30–44, 29.0%; 45–59, 18.1%; 60–74, 10.6%; 75 and over, 4.4%.
Population projection: (2010) 7,588,000; (2020) 8,489,000.
Doubling time: not applicable; doubling time exceeds 100 years.
Linguistic composition (1991)[4]: Chinese 96.8%, of which Cantonese 88.7%; English 2.2%; other 1.0%.
Religious affiliation (1997): predominantly Buddhist and Taoist; however, there are about 260,000 Protestants (1994), 254,100 Roman Catholics, 50,000 Muslims, and 12,000 Hindus.

Vital statistics

Birth rate per 1,000 population (1999): 7.5 (world avg. 22.1); (1985) legitimate 94.5%; illegitimate 5.5%.
Death rate per 1,000 population (1999): 4.8 (world avg. 8.9).
Natural increase rate per 1,000 population (1999): 2.7 (world avg. 13.2).
Total fertility rate (avg. births per childbearing woman; 1999): 1.3.
Marriage rate per 1,000 population (1999): 4.6.
Life expectancy at birth (1998): male 76.9 years; female 82.3 years.
Major causes of death per 100,000 population (1998): malignant neoplasms (cancers) 160.5; diseases of the circulatory system 126.7; diseases of the respiratory system 99.6; accidents and poisoning 29.3; diseases of the digestive system 21.2; diseases of the genitourinary system 19.6.

National economy

Budget (1997–98). Revenue: HK$275,220,000,000 (earning and profit taxes 33.3%; capital revenue 27.9%; indirect taxes 23.7%, of which entertainment and stamp duties 10.8%, duties 3.1%). Expenditures: HK$194,360,000,000 (education 16.9%; health 14.4%; housing 12.7%; law and order 12.2%; social welfare 11.2%; transportation and public works 11.1%; culture and recreation 6.7%).
Gross domestic product (1998): U.S.$166,021,000,000 (U.S.$24,830 per capita).

Structure of gross domestic product and labour force

	1997			
	in value HK$'000,000	% of total value	labour force	% of labour force
Agriculture	1,464	0.1		
Mining	273	—	443,900	13.9
Manufacturing	82,156	6.1		
Construction	73,139	5.4	306,200	9.5
Public utilities	29,220	2.2	[5]	[5]
Transp. and commun.	116,551	8.7	346,400	10.8
Trade	328,258	24.5	952,200	29.6
Finance, insurance, and real estate	333,338	24.9	399,500	12.4
Pub. admin., defense, and services	218,423	16.3	666,500	20.7
Other	158,362[6]	11.8[6]	101,300[5, 7]	3.1[5, 7]
TOTAL	1,341,184	100.0	3,216,000	100.0

Tourism (1997): receipts from visitors U.S.$9,242,000,000.
Production (metric tons except as noted). Agriculture, forestry, fishing (1996): vegetables 76,000, fruits and nuts 5,230, field crops 660, milk 439, eggs 30,600,000 units; livestock (number of live animals) 288,000 pigs[8], 270 cattle, 3,290,000 chickens; roundwood 206,000 cu m; fish catch 175,130. Manufacturing (value added in HK$; 1996): publishing and printed materials 11,452,000,000; wearing apparel 11,004,000,000; textiles 9,470,000,000; electrical and electronic products 7,815,000,000; machinery and equipment 5,792,000,000; office equipment 4,565,000,000; basic metals and fabricated metal products 4,484,000,000. Construction (1998)[9]: residential 875,000 sq m; nonresidential 1,652,000 sq m. Energy production (consumption): electricity (kW-hr; 1995) 27,916,000,000 (33,979,000,000); coal (metric tons; 1995) none (9,109,000); petroleum products (metric tons; 1995) none (3,387,000).
Population economically active (1998): total 3,358,600; activity rate of total population 50.2% (participation rates: over age 15, 62.0%; female 48.5%; unemployed 4.7%).

Price and earnings indexes (1995 = 100)

	1993	1994	1995	1996	1997	1998	1999
Consumer price index	84.3	97.3	100.0	106.3	112.5	115.7	111.1
Daily earnings index[10]	83.0	89.5	100.0	104.5	...	...	...

Household income and expenditure. Average household size (1998) 3.3; monthly income per household (1996) HK$17,500 (U.S.$2,300); sources of income: n.a.; expenditure (1994–95): food 29.5%, housing 28.8%, transportation and vehicles 7.8%, clothing and footwear 6.7%, durable goods 5.5%.
Land use (1995): forested 20.1%; agricultural and under permanent cultivation 5.8%; fishponds 1.5%; built-on, scrublands, and other 72.6%.

Foreign trade[11]

Balance of trade (current prices)

	1994	1995	1996	1997	1998	1999
HK$'000,000	–80,695	–146,994	–137,664	–159,141	–81,443	–43,718
% of total	3.3%	5.2%	4.7%	5.8%	2.9%	1.6%

Imports (1998): HK$1,429,092,000,000 (machinery and transport equipment 39.4%, manufactured goods 18.5%, chemicals and other related products 6.4%, food and beverages 4.9%, mineral fuels and lubricants 1.7%). *Major import sources:* China 36.0%; Japan 11.1%; U.S. 6.6%; Taiwan 6.4%; South Korea 4.3%; Singapore 3.8%.
Exports (1998): HK$188,454,000,000[12] (clothing accessories and apparel 39.7%, electrical machinery 14.2%, textile fabrics 5.7%, watches and clocks 4.7%, office and automatic data-processing machines 3.5%, telecommunications equipment 3.3%, jewelry 2.5%, printed materials 2.2%, articles of artificial resins and plastics 0.9%). *Major export destinations:* China 29.8%; U.S. 29.1%; U.K. 5.3%; Germany 5.2%; Taiwan 3.5%; Japan 3.4%.

Transport and communications

Transport. Railroads (1995): route length 21 mi, 34 km; passenger-mi 2,231,000,000, passenger-km 3,591,000,000; short ton-mi cargo 68,000,000[13], metric ton-km cargo 99,000,000[13]. Roads (1998): total length 1,158 mi, 1,865 km (paved 100%). Vehicles (1998): passenger cars 318,000; trucks and buses 134,000. Air transport (1998): passenger arrivals 10,283,998, passenger departures 10,208,910; airports (1997) with scheduled flights 1.

Communications

Medium	date	unit	number	units per 1,000 persons
Daily newspapers	1996	circulation	5,000,000	792
Radio	1998	receivers	3,700,000	553
Television	1998	receivers	1,749,000	262
Telephones	1998	main lines	3,708,000	554
Cellular telephones	1995	subscribers	798,400	129
Personal computers	1995	units	720,000	116
Internet	1998	users	1,000,000	150

Education and health

Educational attainment (1996). Percentage of population age 15 and over having: no formal schooling 9.5%; primary education 22.6%; secondary 46.6%; matriculation 6.1%; nondegree higher 4.8%; higher degree 10.4%.
Literacy (1995): total population age 15 and over literate 92.2%; males literate 96.0%; females literate 88.2%.

Education (1997–98)

	schools	teachers	students	student/teacher ratio
Primary (age 6–11)	847	19,710[14]	461,911	23.7[14]
Secondary (age 12–18)	503	22,777[14]	458,118	21.2[14]
Vocational	9	2,488[15]	63,351	18.5[15]
Higher	21	1,422[15]	91,835	32.4[15]

Health (1997): physicians 9,289[16] (1 per 686 persons); hospital beds 30,896 (1 per 210 persons); infant mortality rate per 1,000 live births (1998) 3.2.
Food (1997): daily per capita caloric intake 3,206 (vegetable products 68%, animal products 32%); 140% of FAO recommended minimum requirement.

Military

Total active duty personnel [17].

[1]On July 1, 1997, Hong Kong reverted to China as a special administrative region in which the existing socioeconomic system would remain unchanged for a period of 50 years. [2]24 seats are directly elected by ordinary voters; the remaining 36 seats are elected/appointed by special interest groups and a committee. [3]Victoria, for some time, had been regarded as the capital because it had been the seat of the British administration of the Crown Colony. [4]Excludes about 59,000 Vietnamese refugees, about 1% of the population. [5]Other includes Public utilities. [6]Indirect taxes less subsidies. [7]Includes 71,300 unemployed. [8]Excludes local pigs not slaughtered in abattoirs. [9]Usable floor area only. [10]September. [11]Imports are c.i.f., exports f.o.b. [12]Excludes reexports valued at HK$1,159,195,000,000. [13]1994. [14]1995–96. [15]1987–88. [16]Registered personnel; all may not be present and working in the country. [17]British forces completed their final withdrawal on June 30, 1997. On July 1, 1997, the recently passed Garrison Law took effect, allowing for an unarmed garrison to be established in Hong Kong and used only at the governor's request.

Internet resources for further information:
- **Census and Statistics Department http://www.info.gov.hk/censtatd**

Hungary

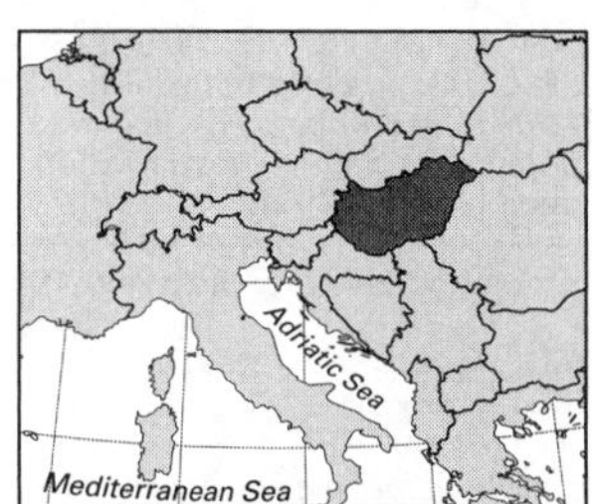

Official name: Magyar Köztársaság (Republic of Hungary).
Form of government: unitary multiparty republic with one legislative house (National Assembly [386[1]]).
Chief of state: President.
Head of government: Prime Minister.
Capital: Budapest.
Official language: Hungarian.
Official religion: none.
Monetary unit: 1 forint (Ft) = 100 filler; valuation (Oct. 6, 2000) 1 U.S.$ = Ft 301.86; 1 £ = Ft 436.66.

Area and population

Counties	Capitals	area sq mi	area sq km	population 1998[2] estimate
Bács-Kiskun	Kecskemét	3,251	8,420	537,000
Baranya	Pécs	1,710	4,430	405,000
Békés	Bekéscsaba	2,174	5,631	398,000
Borsod-Abaúj-Zemplén	Miskolc	2,798	7,247	739,000
Csongrád	Szeged	1,646	4,263	422,000
Fejér	Székesfehérvár	1,688	4,373	427,000
Győr-Moson-Sopron	Győr	1,568	4,062	425,000
Hajdú-Bihar	Debrecen	2,398	6,211	546,000
Heves	Eger	1,404	3,637	326,000
Jász-Nagykun-Szolnok	Szolnok	2,165	5,607	417,000
Komárom-Esztergom	Tatabánya	869	2,251	310,000
Nógrád	Salgótarján	982	2,544	219,000
Pest	Budapest[3]	2,468	6,393	1,005,000
Somogy	Kaposvár	2,331	6,036	334,000
Szabolcs-Szatmár-Bereg	Nyíregyháza	2,292	5,937	572,000
Tolna	Szekszárd	1,430	3,703	247,000
Vas	Szombathely	1,288	3,337	269,000
Veszprém	Veszprém	1,791	4,639	376,000
Zala	Zalaegerszeg	1,461	3,784	298,000
Capital City				
Budapest[3]		203	525	1,863,000
TOTAL		35,919[4]	93,030	10,135,000

Demography

Population (2000): 10,022,000.
Density (2000): persons per sq mi 279.0, persons per sq km 107.7.
Urban-rural (1998): urban 63.0%; rural 37.0%.
Sex distribution (1998): male 47.78%; female 52.22%.
Age breakdown (1998): under 15, 17.5%; 15–29, 22.8%; 30–44, 20.8%; 45–59, 19.4%; 60–74, 14.1%; 75 and over, 5.4%.
Population projection: (2010) 9,718,000; (2020) 9,375,000.
Ethnic composition (1993): Hungarian 92%; Gypsy 3%; German 1%; Slovak 1%; Jewish 1%; Southern Slav 1%; other 1%.
Religious affiliation (1995): Christian 89.1%, of which Roman Catholic 63.1%, Protestant 25.5% (of which Reformed 19.8%, Lutheran 4.5%); Jewish 0.8%; other 10.1%.
Major cities (1998[2]): Budapest 1,863,000; Debrecen 207,000; Miskolc 176,000.

Vital statistics

Birth rate per 1,000 population (1999): 9.4 (world avg. 22.1); (1996) legitimate 77.6%; illegitimate 22.4%.
Death rate per 1,000 population (1999): 14.2 (world avg. 8.9).
Natural increase rate per 1,000 population (1999): –4.8 (world avg. 13.2).
Total fertility rate (avg. births per childbearing woman; 1999): 1.3.
Marriage rate per 1,000 population (1998): 4.5.
Life expectancy at birth (1999): male 66.7 years; female 75.7 years.
Major causes of death per 100,000 population (1997): diseases of the circulatory system 687.4; malignant neoplasms (cancers) 321.0.

National economy

Budget (1997). Revenue: Ft 3,207,300,000,000 (social security contributions 28.6%, value-added tax 21.0%, income tax 18.4%, nontax revenue 12.5%). Expenditures: Ft 3,644,200,000,000 (social security and welfare 30.8%, interest payments 22.8%, health 6.4%, education 2.5%, defense 1.8%).
Production (metric tons except as noted). Agriculture, forestry, fishing (1998): corn (maize) 6,500,000, wheat 4,974,000, sugar beets 3,200,000, barley 1,336,000, sunflower seed 706,000, grapes 669,000, apples 500,000; livestock (number of live animals) 4,931,000 pigs, 871,000 cattle; roundwood 3,601,000 cu m; fish catch (1996) 22,866. Mining and quarrying (1997): bauxite 743,000. Manufacturing (value of production in Ft '000,000; 1997): food and beverages 1,079,000; chemicals and chemical products 504,000; motor vehicles 435,000; refined petroleum products 347,000; base metals 307,000; computers 302,000. Energy production (consumption): electricity (kW-hr; 1998) 36,960,000,000 ([1997] 37,545,000,000); coal (metric tons; 1998) 14,496,000 ([1997] 16,242,000); crude petroleum (barrels; 1998) 8,416,000 ([1997] 50,717,000); petroleum products (metric tons; 1995) 6,262,000 (6,455,000); natural gas (cu m; 1998) 4,178,000,000 ([1997] 12,200,000,000).
Land use (1994): forested 19.1%; meadows and pastures 12.4%; agricultural and under permanent cultivation 53.9%; other 14.6%.
Public debt (external, outstanding; 1998): U.S.$15,941,000,000.
Population economically active (1998): total 4,211,000; activity rate of total population 41.5% (participation rates: ages [1997] 15–59, 61.5%; female [1997] 44.2%; unemployed [April 1998–March 1999] 7.5%).

Price and earnings indexes (1995 = 100)

	1993	1994	1995	1996	1997	1998	1999
Consumer price index	65.6	77.9	100.0	123.6	146.2	167.1	184.3
Monthly earnings index	69.9	87.2	100.0	120.4	...	...	...

Gross national product (1998): U.S.$45,660,000,000 (U.S.$4,510 per capita).

Structure of gross domestic product and labour force

	1997			
	in value Ft '000,000[5]	% of total value[5]	labour force[6]	% of labour force[6]
Agriculture, forestry	441,800	5.2	287,900	7.2
Mining	34,400	0.4	27,200	0.7
Manufacturing	1,811,400	21.2	864,100	21.6
Construction	350,300	4.1	219,200	5.5
Public utilities	287,800	3.4	97,400	2.4
Transp. and commun.	727,600	8.5	310,000	7.8
Trade, restaurants	1,001,800	11.7	617,700	15.5
Finance, real estate	1,482,100	17.4	229,600	5.7
Public administration, defense	1,198,400	14.0	293,800	7.4
Services	221,100	2.6	699,500	17.5
Other	984,700[7]	11.5[7]	348,800[8]	8.7[8]
TOTAL	8,541,400	100.0	3,995,100[4]	100.0

Household income and expenditure. Average household size (1998) 2.5; income per household[9] (1995) Ft 1,117,239 (U.S.$8,011); sources of income (1996): wages 49.0%, transfers 17.4%, mixed income/other 33.6%; expenditure (1996): food 33.1%; housing and energy 23.7%; transportation and communications 12.4%; culture and recreation 6.4%.

Foreign trade

Balance of trade (current prices)

	1993	1994	1995	1996	1997	1998	1999
Ft '000,000,000	–317.7	–362.8	–284.8	–447.1	–394.4	–567.3	–707.1
% of total	16.2%	13.8%	8.3%	10.3%	5.2%	5.4%	5.6%

Imports (1997): Ft 3,961,100,000,000 (nonelectrical machinery and apparatus 19.6%, electrical machinery and apparatus 15.6%, mineral fuels 9.6%, road vehicles 5.4%). *Major import sources:* Germany 27.0%; Austria 10.6%; Russia 9.2%; Italy 7.3%; France 4.4%.
Exports (1997): Ft 3,566,800,000,000 (food 11.7%, office machines and computers 8.9%, power generating machinery 8.0%, clothing 5.9%, road vehicles and parts 5.7%). *Major export destinations:* Germany 37.3%; Austria 11.4%; Italy 6.1%; Russia 5.1%; France 3.8%.

Transport and communications

Transport. Railroads (1996): 13,161 km; passenger-km (1998) 8,884,000,000; metric ton-km cargo (1997) 8,183,000,000. Roads (1997): total length 188,203 km (paved 43%). Vehicles (1997): passenger cars 2,297,115; trucks and buses 333,858. Air transport (1998)[10]: passenger-km 2,510,000,000; metric ton-km cargo 37,011,000; airports (1997) with scheduled flights 1.

Communications

Medium	date	unit	number	units per 1,000 persons
Daily newspapers	1996	circulation	1,895,000	186
Radio	1997	receivers	7,000,000	689
Television	1997	receivers	4,450,000	438
Telephones	1998	main lines	3,219,000	316
Cellular telephones	1997	subscribers	707,000	70
Personal computers	1997	units	500,000	49
Internet	1998	users	300,000	30

Education and health

Educational attainment (1990). Population age 25 and over having: no formal schooling 1.3%; primary education 57.9%; secondary 30.7%; higher 10.1%.
Literacy (1995): population age 15 and over literate 8,304,000 (99.2%).

Education (1997–98)

	schools	teachers	students	student/ teacher ratio
Primary (age 6–13)	3,750	82,904	964,000	11.6
Secondary (age 14–17)	989	30,280	368,600	12.2
Higher	90	19,853	152,900	7.7

Health (1998): physicians 36,170 (1 per 279 persons); hospital beds 83,400 (1 per 121 persons); infant mortality rate per 1,000 live births 9.7.
Food (1997): daily per capita caloric intake 3,313 (vegetable products 68%, animal products 32%); 126% of FAO recommended minimum requirement.

Military

Total active duty personnel (1998): 34,900[11] (army 67.0%, air force 33.0%). *Military expenditure as percentage of GNP* (1997): 1.9% (world 2.6%); per capita expenditures U.S.$129.

[1]Excludes 13 seats set aside for ethnic minorities. [2]January 1. [3]Budapest acts as the capital of Pest county even though it is administratively not part of Pest county. [4]Detail does not add to total given because of rounding. [5]At purchaser's prices. [6]Excludes persons on child care leave. [7]Represents net taxes on commodities less imputed bank service charge. [8]Unemployed. [9]Adjusted disposable income including government transfers. [10]Malév airlines only. [11]Excludes paramilitary border guards.

Internet resources for further information:

- **Embassy of the Republic of Hungary http://www.hungaryemb.org**
- **Hungarian Central Statistical Office http://www.ksh.hu/eng/index.html**

Iceland

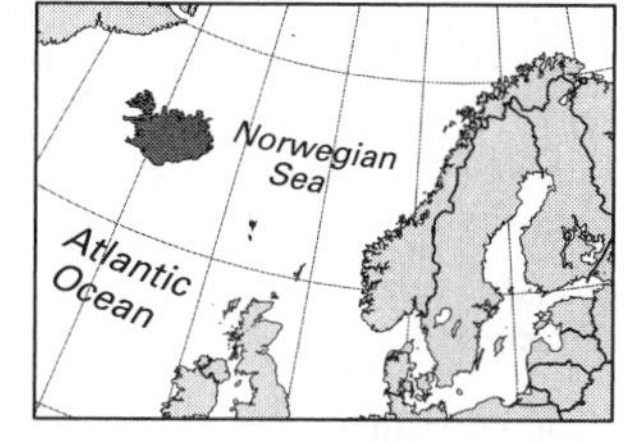

Official name: Lýdhveldidh Ísland (Republic of Iceland).
Form of government: unitary multiparty republic with one legislative house (Althing [63]).
Chief of state: President.
Head of government: Prime Minister.
Capital: Reykjavík.
Official language: Icelandic.
Official religion: Evangelical Lutheran.
Monetary unit: 1 króna (ISK) = 100 aurar; valuation (Oct. 6, 2000) 1 U.S.$ = ISK 83.82; 1 £ = ISK 121.25.

Area and population

Constituencies[2]	Principal centres	area sq mi	area sq km	population 1999[1] estimate
Austurland	Egilsstadhir	8,491	21,991	12,117
Nordhurland eystra	Akureyri	8,636	22,368	26,357
Nordhurland vestra	Saudhárkrókur	5,055	13,093	9,464
Reykjanes	...	765[3]	1,982[3]	77,805
Reykjavík	Reykjavík	3	3	109,763
Sudhurland	Selfoss	9,735	25,214	20,839
Vestfirdhir	Ísafjördhur	3,657	9,470	8,318
Vesturland	Borgarnes	3,360	8,701	14,054
TOTAL		39,699	102,819	278,717

Demography

Population (2000): 280,000.
Density (2000)[4]: persons per sq mi 30.4, persons per sq km 11.8.
Urban-rural (1998): urban 92.0%; rural 8.0%.
Sex distribution (1999): male 50.06%; female 49.94%.
Age breakdown (1998): under 15, 23.5%; 15–29, 22.9%; 30–44, 22.6%; 45–59, 15.8%; 60–74, 10.2%; 75 and over, 5.0%.
Population projection: (2010) 306,000; (2020) 335,000.
Doubling time: 81 years.
Ethnic composition (1998)[5]: Icelandic 95.0%; Danish 0.8%; Swedish 0.6%; persons born in the United States 0.5%; Poland 0.4%; German 0.3%; other 2.4%.
Religious affiliation (1999): Protestant 93.0%, of which Evangelical Lutheran 88.7%, other Lutheran 3.8%; Roman Catholic 1.7%; other and not specified 5.3%.
Major cities (1999): Reykjavík 109,152 (urban area 171,515); Kópavogur 22,587[6]; Hafnarfjördhur 19,150[6]; Akureyri 15,143; Gardhabær 7,928[6].

Vital statistics

Birth rate per 1,000 population (1998): 15.3 (world avg. 22.1); (1998) legitimate 36.0%; illegitimate 64.0%.
Death rate per 1,000 population (1998): 6.7 (world avg. 8.9).
Natural increase rate per 1,000 population (1998): 8.6 (world avg. 13.2).
Total fertility rate (avg. births per childbearing woman; 1998): 2.0.
Marriage rate per 1,000 population (1998): 5.6.
Divorce rate per 1,000 population (1998): 1.8.
Life expectancy at birth (1998): male 76.8 years; female 81.1 years.
Major causes of death per 100,000 population (1994): diseases of the circulatory system 300.4, of which ischemic heart diseases 175.6, cerebrovascular disease 69.2; malignant neoplasms (cancers) 166.5; diseases of the respiratory system 80.1.

National economy

Budget (1997). Revenue: ISK 193,567,000,000 (indirect taxes 49.1%, of which value-added taxes 26.0%; direct taxes 44.4%; nontax revenue 6.5%). Expenditures: ISK 197,804,000,000 (health and welfare 39.6%; education 14.3%; general administration 8.7%; communications 7.5%; cultural affairs 6.2%; agriculture 4.0%).
Production (metric tons except as noted). Agriculture, forestry, fishing (1999): potatoes 9,000, silage 1,612,500 cu m, hay 722,800 cu m; livestock (number of live animals) 490,500 sheep, 77,300 horses, 74,500 cattle; fish catch (value in ISK '000,000; 1999) cod 21,548, shrimp 7,583, redfish 4,922, haddock 4,348, herring 2,883, Greenland halibut 1,882. Mining and quarrying (1998): diatomite 27,100. Manufacturing (value added in ISK '000,000; 1993): preserved and processed fish 17,534; printing and publishing 5,020; fabricated metal products 3,996; meat 2,569; wood furniture 2,275. Construction (completed; 1997): residential 581,000 cu m; nonresidential 1,299,000 cu m. Energy production (consumption): electricity (kW-hr; 1998) 5,131,000,000 ([1996] 5,131,000,000); coal (metric tons; 1996) none (66,000); crude petroleum, none (none); petroleum products (metric tons; 1996) none (623,000); natural gas, none (none).
Land use (1994): forested 1.2%; meadows and pastures 22.7%; agricultural and under permanent cultivation 0.1%; other 76.0%.
Population economically active (1998): total 152,100; activity rate of total population 55.5% (participation rates: ages 16–74, 79.5%; female 46.8%; unemployed 2.7%).

Price and earnings indexes (1995 = 100)

	1993	1994	1995	1996	1997	1998	1999
Consumer price index	96.9	98.4	100.0	102.3	104.1	105.9	109.3
Hourly earnings index	96.3	96.8	100.0	...	...	...	...

Tourism (1998): receipts U.S.$207,000,000; expenditures U.S.$396,000,000.
Gross national product (1998): U.S.$7,626,000,000 (U.S.$27,830 per capita).

Structure of gross domestic product and labour force

	1996 in value ISK '000,000[7]	1996 % of total value[7]	1998 labour force	1998 % of labour force
Agriculture	8,883	1.8	6,500	4.3
Fishing	38,285	7.9	6,200	4.1
Fish processing	17,718	3.6	7,400	4.9
Manufacturing	47,928	9.9	17,400	11.4
Construction	25,976	5.3	10,900	7.2
Public utilities	16,431	3.4	1,500	1.0
Transp. and commun.	33,265	6.8	10,800	7.1
Trade, restaurants	53,310	10.9	25,000	16.5
Finance, real estate	78,215	16.1	14,200	9.4
Public administration	53,188	11.0	7,000	4.6
Health, education, other services	21,917	4.5	40,900	27.0
Other	91,338[8]	18.8[8]	3,788[9]	2.5[9]
TOTAL	486,454	100.0	151,688[10]	100.0

Public debt (1999): U.S.$2,636,200,000.
Household income and expenditure. Average household size (1990)[11] 3.6; annual income per household (1995)[11] ISK 1,976,066 (U.S.$30,546); sources of income (1995): wages and salaries 74.1%, pension 10.5%, self-employment 2.7%, other 12.7%; expenditure (1995): food and beverages 24.0%, transportation and communications 20.8%, recreation and education 13.9%, household furnishings and equipment 8.3%, clothing and footwear 8.0%, energy 4.3%, health 4.0%.

Foreign trade[12]

Balance of trade (current prices)

	1994	1995	1996	1997	1998	1999
ISK '000,000	+10,113	+2,993	−10,304	−12,014	−39,516	−36,189
% of total	4.7%	1.3%	3.9%	4.4%	12.6%	11.1%

Imports (1999): ISK 182,321,500,000 (nonelectrical machinery and apparatus 11.2%; road vehicles 11.0%; food products 8.9%; chemicals 8.0%; electrical machinery and apparatus 6.3%; crude petroleum and petroleum products 5.2%). *Major import sources:* Germany 11.8%; U.S. 10.9%; Norway 10.4%; U.K. 9.2%; Denmark 8.1%; Sweden 6.2%; Japan 5.5%.
Exports (1999): ISK 144,928,100,000 (marine products 61.2%, of which frozen fish 36.3%, salted fish 15.0%; lobster and shrimp 8.3%; aluminum 15.6%; transportation equipment 4.5%). *Major export destinations:* U.K. 19.6%; U.S. 14.7%; Germany 13.1%; The Netherlands 6.0%; France 5.2%; Spain 5.2%.

Transport and communications

Transport. Railroads: none. Roads (1996): total length 7,691 mi, 12,378 km (paved 25%). Vehicles (1999): passenger cars 151,409; trucks and buses 19,428. Merchant marine (1992): vessels (100 gross tons and over) 394; total deadweight tonnage 114,851. Air transport (1999)[13]: passenger-mi 2,272,749,000, passenger-km 3,657,642,000; short ton-mi cargo 50,966,000, metric ton-km cargo 74,409,000; airports (1996) with scheduled flights 24.

Communications

Medium	date	unit	number	units per 1,000 persons
Daily newspapers	1996	circulation	145,000	535
Radio	1997	receivers	260,000	950
Television	1998	receivers	100,000	365
Telephones	1998	main lines	178,428	651
Cellular telephones	1998	subscribers	91,468	333
Personal computers	1998	units	90,000	328
Internet	1998	users	100,000	365

Education and health

Educational attainment: n.a. *Literacy:* virtually 100%.

Education (1998–99)

	schools[14]	teachers	students	student/teacher ratio
Primary/lower secondary (age 7–15)	205	3,518	42,421	12.1
Upper Secondary (age 16–19)	35	1,483	18,097	12.2
Higher	14	508[14]	8,158	15.7[14]

Health: physicians (1997) 884 (1 per 307 persons); hospital beds (1993) 2,798[15] (1 per 95 persons); infant mortality rate (1999) 3.6.
Food (1998): daily per capita caloric intake 3,222 (vegetable products 59%, animal products 41%); 121% of FAO recommended minimum requirement.

Military

Total active duty personnel (1999): 120 coast guard personnel; NATO-sponsored U.S.-manned Iceland Defense Force (1999): 1,640. *Military expenditure as percentage of GNP* (1997): none (world average 2.6%).

[1]December 1. [2]Constituencies are electoral districts. Actual local administration is based on towns or rural districts. [3]Reykjanes includes Reykjavík. [4]Population density calculated with reference to 9,191 sq mi (23,805 sq km) area free of glaciers, lava fields, and lakes. [5]By country of birth. [6]Within Reykjavík urban area. [7]Breakdown by sector is estimated. [8]Indirect taxes, statistical discrepancy, and production of private nonprofit institution less imputed bank service charges and subsidies. [9]Unemployed. [10]Detail does not add to total given because of rounding. [11]Based on sample survey. [12]Imports c.i.f.; exports f.o.b. [13]Icelandair only. [14]1996–97. [15]Excludes nursing wards in old-age homes.

Internet resources for further information:
- **Statistics Iceland http://www.statice.is**
- **The Icelandic Government (some Icelandic only) http://brunnur.stjr.is/interpro/stjr/stjr.nsf/pages/english-index**
- **Embassy of Iceland (Washington, D.C.) http://www.iceland.org**

India

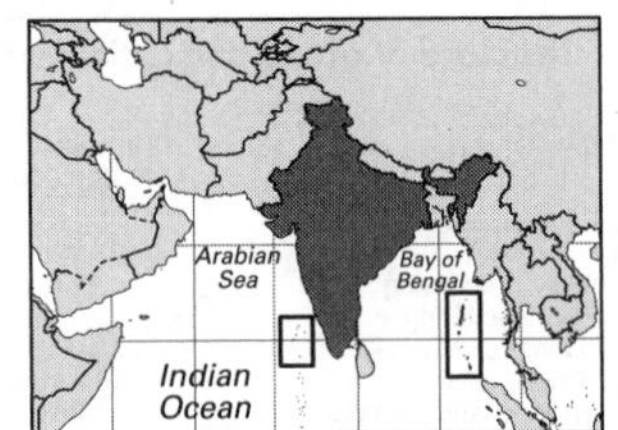

Official name: Bharat (Hindi); Republic of India (English).
Form of government: multiparty federal republic with two legislative houses (Council of States [245[1]], House of the People [545[2]]).
Chief of state: President.
Head of government: Prime Minister.
Capital: New Delhi.
Official languages: Hindi; English.
Official religion: none.
Monetary unit: 1 Indian rupee (Re, plural Rs) = 100 paise; valuation (Oct. 6, 2000) 1 U.S.$ = Rs 46.11; 1 £ = Rs 66.70.

Area and population

States[3]	Capitals	area sq mi	area sq km	population 1994 estimate
Andhra Pradesh	Hyderabad	106,195	275,045	71,800,000
Arunachal Pradesh	Itanagar	32,333	83,743	965,000
Assam	Dispur	30,285	78,438	24,200,000
Bihar[3]	Patna	67,134	173,877	93,080,000
Goa	Panaji	1,429	3,702	1,235,000
Gujarat	Gandhinagar	75,685	196,024	44,235,000
Haryana	Chandigarh	17,070	44,212	17,925,000
Himachal Pradesh	Shimla	21,495	55,673	5,530,000
Jammu and Kashmir	Srinagar	38,830	100,569	8,435,000
Karnataka	Bangalore	74,051	191,791	48,150,000
Kerala	Trivandrum	15,005	38,863	30,555,000
Madhya Pradesh[3]	Bhopal	171,215	443,446	71,950,000
Maharashtra	Mumbai (Bombay)	118,809	307,713	85,565,000
Manipur	Imphal	8,621	22,327	2,010,000
Meghalaya	Shillong	8,660	22,429	1,960,000
Mizoram	Aizawl	8,140	21,081	775,000
Nagaland	Kohima	6,401	16,579	1,410,000
Orissa	Bhubaneshwar	60,119	155,707	33,795,000
Punjab	Chandigarh	19,445	50,362	21,695,000
Rajasthan	Jaipur	132,140	342,239	48,040,000
Sikkim	Gangtok	2,740	7,096	444,000
Tamil Nadu	Chennai (Madras)	50,216	130,058	58,840,000
Tripura	Agartala	4,049	10,486	3,065,000
Uttar Pradesh[3]	Lucknow	113,673	294,411	150,695,000
West Bengal	Kolkata (Calcutta)	34,267	88,752	73,600,000
Union Territories				
Andaman and Nicobar Islands	Port Blair	3,185	8,249	322,000
Chandigarh	Chandigarh	44	114	725,000
Dadra and Nagar Haveli	Silvassa	190	491	153,000
Daman and Diu	Daman	43	112	111,000
Lakshadweep	Kavaratti	12	32	56,000
Pondicherry	Pondicherry	190	492	894,000
National Capital Territory				
Delhi	Delhi	572	1,483	10,865,000
TOTAL		1,222,243[4]	3,165,596[4]	913,070,000[5]

Demography

Population (2000): 1,014,004,000.
Density (2000)[4]: persons per sq mi 829.6, persons per sq km 320.3.
Urban-rural (1999): urban 28.1%; rural 71.9%.
Sex distribution (1995): male 51.66%; female 48.34%.
Age breakdown (1995): under 15, 35.4%; 15–29, 27.0%; 30–44, 19.2%; 45–59, 11.2%; 60–74, 5.9%; 75 and over, 1.3%.
Population projection: (2010) 1,168,000,000; (2020) 1,312,000,000.
Doubling time: 40 years.
Linguistic composition (1991)[6]: Hindi 27.58% (including associated languages and dialects, 39.85%); Bengali 8.22%; Telugu 7.80%; Marathi 7.38%; Tamil 6.26%; Urdu 5.13%; Gujarati 4.81%; Kannada 3.87%; Malayalam 3.59%; Oriya 3.32%; Punjabi 2.76%; Assamese 1.55%; Bhili/Bhilodi 0.66%; Santhali 0.62%; Kashmiri 0.47%[7]; Gondi 0.25%; Sindhi 0.25%; Nepali 0.25%; Konkani 0.21%; Tulu 0.18%; Kurukh 0.17%; Manipuri 0.15%; Bodo 0.14%; Khandeshi 0.12%; other 3.26%. Hindi (66.00%) and English (19.00%) are also spoken as lingua francas (second languages).
Major cities (1991): (*urban agglomerations;* 1995) Greater Mumbai (Greater Bombay) 9,925,891 (15,093,000); Delhi 7,206,704 (9,882,000); Kolkata (Calcutta) 4,399,819 (11,673,000); Chennai (Madras) 3,841,396 (5,906,000); Bangalore 3,302,296 (4,749,000); Hyderabad 3,145,939 (5,343,000); Ahmadabad 2,954,526 (3,688,000); Kanpur 1,879,420 (2,356,000); Nagpur 1,624,752 (1,847,000); Lucknow 1,619,115 (2,029,000); Pune 1,566,651 (2,940,000); New Delhi[8] 301,297.

Other principal cities (1991)

	population		population		population
Agra	891,790	Indore	1,091,674	Rajkot	612,458
Allahabad	806,486	Jabalpur	764,586	Ranchi	599,306
Amritsar	708,835	Jaipur	1,458,183	Sholapur (Solapur)	604,215
Aurangabad	573,272	Jalandhar (Jullundur)	509,510	Srinagar	850,000[12]
Bareilly	590,661	Jodhpur	666,279	Surat	1,505,872
Bhopal	1,062,771	Kalyan[10]	1,014,557	Thane (Thana)[10]	803,389
Chandigarh	510,565	Kota	537,371	Trivandrum	699,872
Cochin (Kochi)	582,588	Ludhiana	1,042,740	Vadodara (Baroda)	1,061,598
Coimbatore	816,321	Madurai	940,989	Varanasi (Benares)	932,399
Faridabad	617,717	Meerut	753,778	Vijayawada	701,827
Guwahati	584,342	Mysore	606,755	Vishakhapatnam	752,037
Gwalior	690,765	Nashik (Nasik)	656,925		
Howrah (Haora)[9]	950,435	Patna	917,243		
Hubli-Dharwad	648,298	Pimpri-Chinchwad[11]	517,083		

Religious affiliation (1995): Hindu 81.3%; Muslim 12.0%, of which Sunnī 9.0%, Shīʿī 3.0%; Christian 2.3%, of which Protestant 1.1%, Roman Catholic 1.0%; Sikh 1.9%; Buddhist 0.8%; Jain 0.4%; Zoroastrian 0.01%; other 1.3%.
Households (1991)[13]. Total households 151,032,898. Average household size 5.6; 1–2 persons 12.1%, 3–5 persons 44.4%, 6–8 persons 30.5%, 9 or more persons 13.0%. Average number of rooms per household 2.2; 1 room 40.5%, 2 rooms 30.6%, 3 rooms 13.8%, 4 rooms 7.1%, 5 rooms 3.2%, 6 or more rooms 3.9%, unspecified number of rooms 0.9%. Average number of persons per room 2.6.

Vital statistics

Birth rate per 1,000 population (1998)[14]: 26.4 (world avg. 22.1).
Death rate per 1,000 population (1998)[14]: 9.0 (world avg. 8.9).
Natural increase rate per 1,000 population (1998)[14]: 17.4 (world avg. 13.2).
Total fertility rate (avg. births per childbearing woman; 1999): 3.2.
Marital status of male (female) population age 6 and over (1992–93): single 48.3% (37.1%); married 47.5% (55.2%); widowed 3.6% (7.2%); divorced or separated 0.6% (0.5%).
Life expectancy at birth (1999): male 61.5 years; female 62.7 years.
Major causes of death per 100,000 population (1987)[15]: diseases of the circulatory system 227; infectious and parasitic diseases 215; diseases of the respiratory system 108; certain conditions originating in the perinatal period 108; accidents, homicide, and other violence 102; diseases of the digestive system 48; diseases of the nervous system 43; malignant neoplasms (cancers) 41; endocrine, metabolic, and nutritional disorders 30; diseases of the blood and blood-forming organs 25; ill-defined conditions 129.

Social indicators

Educational attainment (1991)[13, 16]. Percentage of population age 25 and over having: no formal schooling 57.5%; incomplete primary education 28.0%; complete primary or some secondary 7.2%; complete secondary or higher 7.3%.

Distribution of expenditure (1994)

percentage of household expenditure by decile/quintile

1	2	3	4	5	6	7	8	9	10 (highest)
4.1	5.1	—13.0—		—16.8—		—21.7—		14.3	25.0

Quality of working life. Average workweek (1989): 42 hours[17]. Rate of fatal (nonfatal) injuries per 100,000 industrial workers (1989) 17 (3,625)[17]. Employees covered under Employee's State Insurance Scheme (1991) 6,070,000; number of beneficiaries 26,749,000[17]. Agricultural workers in servitude to creditors (early 1990s) 10–20%.
Access to services (1991). Percentage of total (urban, rural) households having access to: electricity for lighting purposes 42.4% (75.8%, 30.5%); attached toilet or nearby latrine 23.7% (63.9%, 9.5%). Source of drinking water: piped water 32.3%, well 32.2%, hand pump or tube well 30.0%, river or canal 2.0%, public tank 1.3%, other 2.2%.
Social participation. Eligible voters participating in September/October 1999 national election: 59.6%. Trade union membership (1998): *c.* 16,000,000.
Social deviance (1990)[18]. Offense rate per 100,000 population for: murder 4.1; dacoity (gang robbery) 1.3; theft and housebreaking 56.6; riots 12.0. Rate of suicide per 100,000 population (1991): 9.0.
Material well-being (1994). Households possessing: black and white television receivers 18.8%, colour television receivers 6.3%, videocassette recorders 1.3%, refrigerators 6.9%, washing machines 2.3%.

National economy

Gross national product (1998): U.S.$427,407,000,000 (U.S.$440 per capita).

Structure of gross domestic product and labour force

	1996–97 in value Rs '000,000,000	1996–97 % of total value	1993–94 labour force	1993–94 % of labour force
Agriculture, forestry	3,101	27.0	240,700,000	64.7
Mining	205	1.8	2,600,000	0.7
Manufacturing	2,226	19.4	39,100,000	10.5
Construction	685	6.0	11,900,000	3.2
Public utilities	329	2.9	1,500,000	0.4
Transp. and commun.	886	7.7	10,400,000	2.8
Trade, restaurants	1,676	14.6	27,500,000	7.4
Finance, real estate	1,080	9.4	} 38,300,000	10.3
Pub. admin., defense	606	5.3		
Services	696	6.1		
TOTAL	11,492[5]	100.0[5]	372,000,000	100.0

Budget (1998–99). Revenue: Rs 2,953,800,000,000 (tax revenue 48.1%, of which excise taxes 18.9%, customs duties 16.3%, corporation taxes 9.0%; nontax revenue 35.7%, of which economic services 20.2%, interest receipts 9.5%; other sources of revenue 16.2%). Expenditures: Rs 2,953,800,000,000 (interest payments and debt servicing 25.4%; transportation 11.5%; defense 10.8%; grants to state governments 9.3%; communications 6.9%; agriculture 5.3%; social services 5.0%).
Public debt (external, outstanding; 1998): U.S.$85,207,000,000.
Production (in '000 metric tons except as noted). Agriculture, forestry, fishing (1998): sugarcane 265,000; cereals 219,444 (of which rice 122,244, wheat 66,000, millet 10,500, corn [maize] 10,000, sorghum 9,000); fruits 38,684 (of which mangoes 12,000, bananas 10,200, oranges 2,000, apples 1,300, pineapples 1,100, lemons and limes 1,000); oilseeds 31,015 (of which peanuts [groundnuts] 8,300, soybeans 6,100, rapeseed 4,935, sunflower seeds 1,500, castor beans 900, sesame 650); pulses 14,237 (of which chickpeas 5,754, dry beans 3,600, pigeon peas 2,450), coconuts 10,000, seed cotton 7,720, eggplants 6,000, jute 1,500, tea 870, tobacco 635, natural rubber 542, garlic 451, cashews 430, betel 300, coffee 228, ginger 180, pepper 55; livestock (num-

ber of live animals; 1998) 209,489,000 cattle, 120,560,000 goats, 91,784,000 water buffalo, 56,472,000 sheep, 16,005,000 pigs, 1,030,000 camels; roundwood (1998) 306,455,000 cu m, of which fuelwood 281,425,000 cu m, industrial roundwood 25,030,000; fish catch (metric tons; 1996) 5,260,000, of which marine fish 2,420,000, freshwater fish 2,336,000, crustaceans 411,000, cephalopods 86,000. Mining and quarrying (1997–98): limestone 108,144; iron ore 46,000[19]; bauxite 5,904; manganese 643[19]; chromium 421[19]; zinc 176[19]; copper 54[19]; lead 43[19]; gold 84,900 troy oz; diamonds 30,700 carats. Manufacturing (in '000 metric tons except as noted; 1997–98): cement 82,872; finished steel 14,302; refined sugar 13,248; nitrogenous fertilizers 10,464; paper and paperboard 4,296; soda ash 1,567; jute textiles 1,400; aluminum 549; polyester fibre 336; bicycles 9,766,000 units; motorcycles and scooters 3,046,000 units; power-driven pumps 692,000 units; passenger cars and jeeps 468,900 units; passenger buses and trucks 265,800 units; cotton cloth (excluding hosiery) 14,704,000,000 sq m; other important manufactured products include drugs and pharmaceuticals, computer software, gold jewelry, and silk goods.

Manufacturing enterprises (1994–95)[20]

	no. of factories	no. of persons engaged	avg. wages as a % of avg. of all wages	annual value added (Rs '000,000)[21]
Chemicals and chemical products,	8,252	672,100	147.1	161,876
of which fertilizers/pesticides	645	101,400	213.6	39,159
drugs and medicine	2,173	181,500	150.3	34,518
synthetic fibres	308	65,800	209.3	29,889
paints, soaps, and cosmetics	1,793	95,800	126.1	20,358
Textiles	15,220	1,394,800	85.1	104,124
Food products,	21,127	1,205,800	61.7	90,757
of which refined sugar	1,261	327,100	95.1	36,881
Iron and steel	3,379	452,200	154.5	82,988
Electrical machinery/apparatus,	5,385	417,700	142.7	79,981
of which industrial machinery	2,031	167,700	166.5	30,766
communications equipment/TVs	1,336	133,300	131.1	28,898
Transport equipment,	5,922	747,400	138.7	73,278
of which motor vehicles	3,614	351,400	153.5	43,522
Nonelectrical machinery/apparatus	8,521	477,100	135.2	64,585
Refined petroleum	143	30,500	245.6	41,328
Bricks, cement, plaster products	9,377	365,300	75.6	32,564
Nonferrous basic metals	2,994	179,100	108.8	24,742
Wearing apparel	3,292	244,300	54.0	24,110
Fabricated metal products	7,287	244,100	100.8	22,159
Paper and paper products	2,504	161,400	101.5	18,390

Energy production (consumption): electricity (kW-hr; 1999) 473,214,000,000 ([1996] 433,914,000,000); coal (metric tons; 1999) 292,356,000 ([1996] 319,233,000); crude petroleum (barrels; 1999) 247,426,000 ([1996] 492,646,000); petroleum products (metric tons; 1996) 47,648,000 (67,219,000); natural gas (cu m; 1999) 20,006,000,000 ([1996] 27,113,000,000).

Financial aggregates[22]

	1994	1995	1996	1997	1998	1999	2000
Exchange rate, Rs per:							
U.S. dollar	31.38	35.18	35.93	39.28	42.48	43.49	44.58[23]
£	49.03	54.53	61.01	64.96	70.67	70.30	66.64[23]
SDR	45.81	52.30	51.67	53.00	59.81	59.69	58.85[23]
International reserves (U.S.$)							
Total (excl. gold; '000,000)	19,698	17,922	20,170	24,688	27,341	32,667	35,039[23]
SDRs ('000,000)	2	139	122	77	83	4	2[23]
Reserve pos. in IMF ('000,000)	310	316	306	287	300	671	645[23]
Foreign exchange ('000,000)	19,386	17,467	19,742	24,324	26,958	31,992	34,392[23]
Gold ('000,000 fine troy oz)	11.800	12.780	12.781	12.740	11.487	11.502	11.502[23]
% world reserves	1.3	1.4	1.4	1.4	1.2	1.2	1.2[23]
Interest and prices							
Central bank discount (%)	12.0	12.0	12.0	9.0	9.0	8.0	7.0[23]
Advance (prime) rate (%)	14.8	15.5	16.0	13.8	13.5	12.5	11.8[23]
Industrial share prices (1995 = 100)[24]	119.3	100.0	91.3	84.5	76.8	78.4[25]	...
Balance of payments (U.S.$'000,000)							
Balance of visible trade	–4,150	–6,718	–10,052	–10,028	–10,752	–8,028	...
Imports, f.o.b.	29,673	37,957	43,789	45,730	44,828	45,556	...
Exports, f.o.b.	25,523	31,239	33,737	35,702	34,076	37,528	...
Balance of invisibles	+2,474	+1,155	+4,096	+7,063	+3,849	+5,244	...
Balance of payments, current account	–1,676	–5,563	–5,956	–2,965	–6,903	–2,784	...

Land use (1994): forested 23.0%; meadows and pastures 3.8%; agricultural and under permanent cultivation 57.1%; other 16.1%.

Population economically active (1993–94): total 372,000,000; activity rate of total population *c.* 41% (participation rates: n.a.; female 32.5%; unemployed[26]).

Price and earnings indexes (1995 = 100)

	1994	1995	1996	1997	1998	1999	2000[27]
Consumer price index	90.7	100.0	109.0	116.8	132.2	138.4	143.0
Earnings index	...	...	...	...	...	...	...

Household income and expenditure. Average household size (1991)[13] 5.6; sources of income (1984–85): salaries and wages 42.2%, self-employed 39.7%, interest 8.6%, profits and dividends 6.0%, rent 3.5%; expenditure (1994–95): food 51.1%, transportation and communications 12.5%, clothing and footwear 10.4%, housing 5.4%, energy 3.9%, education and recreation 3.4%.

Service enterprises (net value added in Rs '000,000; 1994–95): wholesale and retail trade 1,076,210; transport and storage 547,590; community and social services 509,910; construction 489,590; finance 322,560; real estate and business services 234,890[28]; electricity, gas, and steam 205,880.

Tourism: receipts from visitors (1998) U.S.$2,935,000,000; expenditures by nationals abroad U.S.$1,713,000,000.

Foreign trade[29, 30]

Balance of trade (current prices)

	1992–93	1993–94	1994–95	1995–96	1996–97	1997–98
Rs '000,000	–96,870	–33,500	–72,970	–163,250	–200,030	–252,680
% of total	8.3%	2.3%	4.2%	7.1%	7.8%	9.5%

Imports (1997–98): Rs 1,515,540,000,000 (mineral fuels and lubricants 20.2%; nonelectrical machinery 8.7%; precious and semiprecious stones 7.7%; chemicals 7.3%; electronic goods 4.9%). *Major import sources:* U.S. 8.9%; Switzerland 6.3%; Saudi Arabia 6.2%; Germany 6.1%; Belgium 6.0%; Kuwait 5.7%; U.K. 5.7%; Japan 5.2%; United Arab Emirates 4.3%.

Exports (1997–98): Rs 1,262,860,000,000 (cut and polished diamonds and jewelry 15.1%; chemicals and chemical products 13.2%; machinery, transport equipment, metal products, and iron and steel 12.3%; ready-made garments 11.1%; cotton yarn, fabrics, and thread 9.6%; marine products 3.4%; leather and leather manufactures 2.7%). *Major export destinations:* U.S. 19.5%; U.K. 6.0%; Hong Kong 5.6%; Japan 5.5%; Germany 5.5%; United Arab Emirates 4.7%; Belgium 3.5%; Italy 3.2%; Russia 2.9%; The Netherlands 2.3%.

Transport and communications

Transport. Railroads (1995–96): route length 39,093 mi, 62,915 km; (1997–98) passenger-mi 230,250,000,000, passenger-km 370,560,000,000; (1997–98) short ton-mi cargo 194,609,000,000, metric ton-km cargo 284,124,000,000. Roads (1996): total length 2,062,727 mi, 3,319,644 km (paved 46%). Vehicles (1996): passenger cars 4,189,000; trucks and buses 2,234,000. Air transport (1997–98): passenger-mi 14,511,000,000, passenger-km 23,354,000,000; short ton-mi cargo 330,244,000, metric ton-km cargo 482,148,000; airports (1996) with scheduled flights 66.

Communications

Medium	date	unit	number	units per 1,000 persons
Daily newspapers	1993	circulation	18,800,000	21
Radio	1997	receivers	116,000,000	120
Television	1997	receivers	63,000,000	65
Telephones	1998	main lines	21,594,000	22
Cellular telephones	1998	subscribers	1,195,000	1.2
Personal computers	1998	units	2,700,000	2.8
Internet	1998	users	500,000	0.5

Education and health

Literacy (1995): total population age 15 and over literate 315,600,000 (52.0%); males literate 205,100,000 (65.5%); females literate 110,500,000 (37.7%).

Education (1996–97)

	schools	teachers	students	student/teacher ratio
Primary (age 6–10)	598,354	1,789,733	110,393,406	61.7
Secondary (age 11–17)	249,899	2,122,325	58,926,623	27.8
Higher	25,045	615,880	6,412,716	10.4

Health (1992): physicians 410,875 (1 per 2,173 persons); hospital beds 642,103 (1 per 1,357 persons); infant mortality rate (1998) 72.0[14].

Food (1997): daily per capita caloric intake 2,496 (vegetable products 93%, animal products 7%); 113% of FAO recommended minimum requirement.

Military

Total active duty personnel (1998): 1,175,000 (army 83.4%, navy 4.7%, air force 11.9%); personnel in paramilitary forces for border security 185,000. *Military expenditure as percentage of GNP* (1997): 2.8% (world 2.6%); per capita expenditure U.S.$11.

[1]Council of States can have a maximum of 250 members; a maximum of 12 of these members may be nominated by the president. [2]Includes 2 nonelective seats. [3]Three new states were created in November 2000. Chattisgarh was created from part of Madhya Pradesh, has an area of 56,510 sq mi (146,361 sq km), and a (1991) population of 17,620,00; Jharkhand was created from part of Bihar, has an area of 28,832 sq mi (74,677 sq km), and a (1991) population of 21,840,000; Uttaranchal was created from part of Uttar Pradesh, has an area of 24,385 sq mi (63,157 sq km), and a (1991) population of 7,050,000. [4]Excludes 46,976 sq mi (121,667 sq km) of territory claimed by India as part of Jammu and Kashmir but occupied by Pakistan or China; inland water constitutes 9.0% of total area of India (including all of Indian-claimed Jammu and Kashmir). [5]Detail does not add to total given because of rounding. [6]Mother tongue unless otherwise noted. [7]1981. [8]Within Delhi urban agglomeration. [9]Within Calcutta urban agglomeration. [10]Within Greater Mumbai urban agglomeration. [11]Within Pune urban agglomeration. [12]1990 estimate. [13]Excludes Jammu and Kashmir. [14]Based on a sample registration scheme. [15]Projected rates based on about 3.5% of total deaths (317,392 registered deaths out of an estimated total of nearly 9,000,000 deaths). [16]No formal schooling (1991): males 43.3%, females 72.8%; complete secondary or higher education (1991): males 10.6%, females 3.7%. [17]Data apply to the workers employed in the "organized sector" only (28.3 million in 1996–97, of which 19.6 million are employed in the public sector and 8.7 million are employed in the private sector); few legal protections exist for the more than 350 million workers in the "unorganized sector." [18]Crimes reported to National Crime Records Bureau by police authorities of state governments. [19]Approximate metal content of ore. [20]Establishments with at least 10 workers on any workday and all establishments employing 20 or more workers. [21]In factor values. [22]End-of-period unless otherwise noted. [23]May. [24]Period average. [25]Average of first quarter. [26]Average number of registered unemployed in December 1997 was 39,100,000. [27]April. [28]1993–94. [29]Imports c.i.f.; exports f.o.b. [30]Fiscal year beginning April 1.

Internet resources for further information:

- **India Image: Directory of Government Web Sites http://www.nic.in**
- **Census of India http://www.censusindia.net**
- **Press Information Bureau (Government of India) http://pib.nic.in**

Indonesia

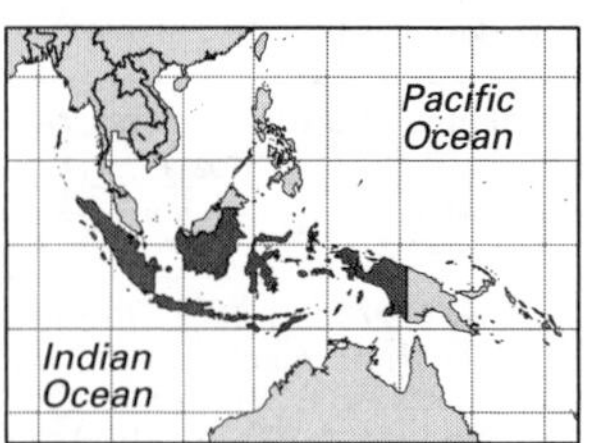

Official name: Republik Indonesia (Republic of Indonesia).
Form of government: unitary multiparty republic with two legislative houses (People's Consultative Assembly [700[1]]; House of People's Representatives [500[2]]).
Head of state and government: President.
Capital: Jakarta.
Official language: Indonesian (Bahasa Indonesia).
Official religion: monotheism.
Monetary unit: 1 Indonesian rupiah (Rp) = 100 sen; valuation (Oct. 6, 2000) 1 U.S.$ = Rp 8,800; 1 £ = Rp 12,730.

Area and population

Island(s) / Provinces	area (sq km)	population ('000) 1995 estimate
Bali and the Lesser Sunda Islands[3]	73,135	10,140
Bali	5,633	2,902
East Nusa Tenggara	47,349	3,583
West Nusa Tenggara	20,153	3,655
Celebes (Sulawesi)[4]	191,800	13,772
Central Sulawesi	63,689	1,948
North Sulawesi	27,488	2,652
Southeast Sulawesi	38,140	1,594
South Sulawesi	62,483	7,578
Java[4]	127,499	114,988
Central Java	32,549	29,688
East Java	47,923	33,886
Jakarta[5]	664	9,160
West Java	43,177	39,337
Yogyakarta[6]	3,186	2,917
Kalimantan[4, 7]	547,891	10,520
Central Kalimantan	153,564	1,637
East Kalimantan	210,985	2,331
South Kalimantan	36,535	2,900
West Kalimantan	146,807	3,652
Maluku (Moluccas)	77,871	2,095
Maluku	...	...
North Maluku[8]	...	...
Papua[4, 9]	421,981	1,956
Central Papua[10]	...	...
East Papua[10]	...	...
West Papua[10]	...	...
Sumatra[4]	482,393	40,969
Aceh[6]	55,390	3,860
Bengkulu	19,789	1,415
Jambi	53,436	2,383
Lampung	35,385	6,680
North Sumatra	71,680	11,145
Riau	94,561	3,925
South Sumatra	109,254	7,233
West Sumatra	42,898	4,328
TOTAL	1,922,570[3]	194,440[3]

Demography

Population (2000): 209,342,000.
Density (2000)[3]: persons per sq mi 282.0, persons per sq km 108.9.
Urban-rural (1999): urban 39.0%; rural 61.0%.
Sex distribution (1995): male 49.77%; female 50.23%.
Age breakdown (1995): under 15, 35.6%; 15–29, 27.5%; 30–44, 19.6%; 45–59, 10.8%; 60–74, 5.4%; 75 and over, 1.1%.
Population projection: (2010) 237,973,000; (2020) 261,802,000.
Ethnolinguistic composition (1990): Javanese 39.4%; Sundanese 15.8%; Indonesian (Malay) 12.1%; Madurese 4.3%; Minang 2.4%; other 26.0%.
Religious affiliation (1990): Muslim 87.2%; Christian 9.6%, of which Roman Catholic 3.6%; Hindu 1.8%; Buddhist 1.0%; other 0.4%.
Major cities (1995): Jakarta (1996) 9,341,000; Surabaya (1996) 2,743,000; Bandung (1996) 2,429,000; Medan 1,909,700; Palembang 1,283,100; Tangerang 1,144,500; Semarang 1,097,800; Ujung Pandang 1,029,900; Malang 716,400; Bandar Lampung 598,900.

Vital statistics

Birth rate per 1,000 population (1999): 23.0 (world avg. 22.1).
Death rate per 1,000 population (1999): 6.3 (world avg. 8.9).
Natural increase rate per 1,000 population (1999): 16.7 (world avg. 13.2).
Total fertility rate (avg. births per childbearing woman; 1999): 2.7.
Marriage rate per 1,000 population (1996–97): 7.5[11].
Life expectancy at birth (1999): male 65.3 years; female 70.1 years.
Major causes of death (percent distribution, 1986): infectious and parasitic diseases 43.5%; diseases of the respiratory system 21.9%; cardiovascular diseases 9.7%; diseases of the nervous system 6.0%.

National economy

Budget (1998–99). Revenue: RP 134,302,000,000,000 (oil and gas revenues 37.0%, value-added tax 21.5%, income tax 18.8%, nontax revenue 8.7%, excise taxes 5.8%). Expenditures: RP 215,590,000,000,000 (transfers 33.1%, national development 31.5%, administrative 18.9%, debt repayment 14.4%).
Public debt (external, outstanding; 1999): U.S.$66,944,000,000.
Production (metric tons except as noted). Agriculture, forestry, fishing (1998): rice 48,472,000, sugarcane 27,500,000, palm fruit oil 26,800,000, cassava 14,728,000, corn (maize) 10,059,000, natural rubber 1,564,000; livestock (number of live animals) 15,198,000 goats, 12,239,000 cattle, 8,151,000 sheep, 3,145,000 buffalo; roundwood 202,989,000 cu m; fish catch (1997) 4,790,000. Mining and quarrying (1998): copper concentrate 2,640,000; nickel ore 1,642,000; bauxite 513,000; gold 118,246 kg. Manufacturing (value added in RP '000,000,000; 1996)[12]: textiles 9,611.8; transport equipment 9,330.6; tobacco products 8,839.9; iron and steel 8,703.1; food products 7,862.5; electrical machinery 6,766.2. Energy production (consumption): electricity (kW-hr; 1996) 73,794,000,000 (73,794,000,000); coal (metric tons; 1999) 70,704,000 ([1996] 15,796,000); crude petroleum (barrels; 1999) 500,642,000 ([1996] 311,201,000); petroleum products (metric tons; 1996) 43,307,000 (40,759,000); natural gas (cu m; 1998) 84,348,000,000 ([1996] 38,885,000,000).
Gross national product (1998): U.S.$130,600,000,000 (U.S.$640 per capita).

Structure of gross domestic product and labour force

	1998		1997	
	in value Rp '000,000,000	% of total value	labour force[13]	% of labour force[13]
Agriculture	186,482	18.9	35,849,000	41.2
Mining	127,217	12.9	897,000	1.0
Manufacturing	259,563	26.2	11,215,000	12.9
Construction	53,841	5.4	4,200,000	4.8
Public utilities	11,531	1.2	233,000	0.3
Transp. and commun.	53,640	5.4	4,138,000	4.8
Trade	147,478	14.9	17,221,000	19.8
Finance, real estate	81,470	8.2	657,000	0.7
Pub. admin., defense	37,250	3.8	12,637,000	14.5
Services	31,101	3.1		
Other	...	...	3,000	—
TOTAL	989,573	100.0	87,050,000	100.0

Population economically active: total (1997): 87,050,000; activity rate 43.2% (participation rates: over age 10, 57.1%; unemployed 4.7%).

Price and earnings indexes (1995 = 100)

	1993	1994	1995	1996	1997	1998	1999
Consumer price index	84.2	91.4	100.0	108.0	115.2	181.7	218.9
Earnings index[14]	64.3	83.9	100.0	105.4	116.1	...	...

Household income and expenditure. Average household size (1995) 4.3.
Tourism (1998): receipts U.S.$4,045,000,000; expenditures U.S.$2,102,000,000.

Foreign trade[15]

Balance of trade (current prices)

	1992	1993	1994	1995	1996	1997
U.S.$'000,000	+4,937	+8,872	+11,496	+8,883	+5,285	+9,456
% of total	9.2%	13.4%	16.8%	10.8%	5.6%	9.3%

Imports (1997): U.S.$41,679,800,000 (machinery and transport equipment 42.2%, basic manufactures 15.6%, chemicals 14.2%, mineral fuels 9.7%, crude materials 7.1%). *Major import sources:* Japan 19.8%; U.S. 13.1%; Singapore 8.2%; Germany 6.3%.
Exports (1997): U.S.$53,443,600,000 (crude petroleum 10.3%, natural gas 9.1%, plywood 8.6%, garments 5.4%, processed rubber 3.7%). *Major export destinations:* Japan 23.4%; U.S. 13.4%; Singapore 10.2%; Netherlands 3.4%.

Transport and communications

Transport. Railroads (1997): route length 6,458 km; passenger-km 16,392,000,000; metric ton-km cargo 8,208,000,000. Roads (1997): length 342,700 km (paved 54%). Vehicles (1997): passenger cars 2,639,523; trucks and buses 2,159,799. Air transport (1997): passenger-km 25,340,000,000; metric ton-km cargo 735,700,000; airports (1996) 81.

Communications

Medium	date	unit	number	units per 1,000 persons
Daily newspapers	1996	circulation	4,665,000	23
Radio	1998	receivers	26,000,000	128
Television	1997	receivers	26,778,000	134
Telephones	1998	main lines	5,571,600	27
Cellular telephones	1998	subscribers	1,065,820	5.3
Personal computers	1998	units	1,700,000	8.4
Internet	1998	users	300,000	1.5

Education and health

Educational attainment (1990). Percentage of population age 25 and over having: no schooling 34.6%; less than complete primary 28.2%; primary 23.3%; secondary 12.5%; higher 1.4%. *Literacy* (1995 est.): total population age 15 and over literate 83.8%; males literate 89.6%; females literate 78.0%.

Education (1996–97)

	schools	teachers	students	student/ teacher ratio
Primary (age 7–12)	150,595	1,165,786	25,755,083	22.1
Secondary (age 13–18)	28,609	645,270	10,255,524	15.9
Voc., teacher tr.	3,400	109,127	1,628,100	14.9
Higher	1,370	158,357	2,350,971	14.8

Health (1996): physicians 31,435 (1 per 6,259 persons); hospital beds 120,083 (1 per 1,639 persons); infant mortality rate (1999) 43.7.
Food (1997): daily per capita caloric intake 2,886 (vegetable products 95%, animal products 5%); (1995) 126% of FAO recommended minimum.

Military

Total active duty personnel (1998): 299,000 (army 78.6%, navy 14.4%, air force 7.0%). *Military expenditure as percentage of GNP* (1997): 2.3% (world 2.6%); per capita expenditure U.S.$24.

[1]Includes the 500 members of the House of People's Representatives plus 200 other appointees. [2]Includes 38 nonelective seats reserved for the military. [3]Excludes area and population of East Timor; the UN assumed formal control of East Timor on Oct. 26, 1999. [4]Includes area and population of nearby islands. [5]Formally a metropolitan district. [6]Formally a special autonomous district. [7]Kalimantan is the name of the Indonesian part of the island of Borneo. [8]New province created in 1999. [9]Also known as West Papua; known as Irian Jaya before 2000. [10]Unofficial names of provinces created in 2000. [11]Muslim population only. [12]Medium and large manufacturing establishments only. [13]Employed people only. [14]Based on minimum monthly wages. [15]Imports and exports are f.o.b. in balance of trade.

Internet resources for further information:
- **Central Bureau of Statistics http://www.bps.go.id**

Iran

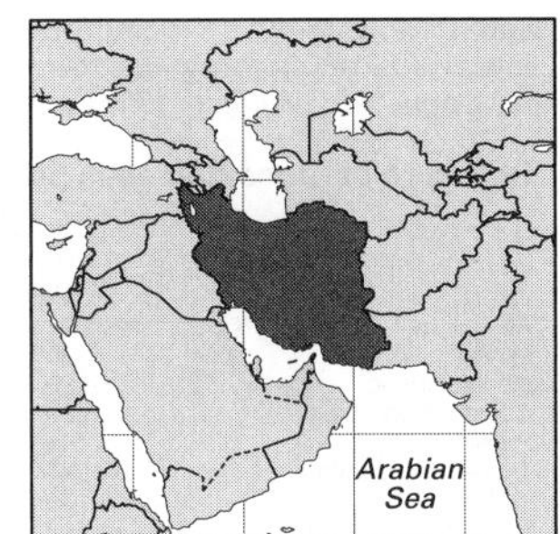

Official name: Jomhūrī-ye Eslamī-ye Irān (Islamic Republic of Iran).
Form of government: unitary Islamic republic with one legislative house (Islamic Consultative Assembly [290]).
Supreme political/religious authority: Leader[1].
Head of state and government: President.
Capital: Tehrān.
Official language: Farsī (Persian).
Official religion: Islam.
Monetary unit: 1 rial (Rls); valuation (Oct. 6, 2000) 1 U.S.$ = Rls 1,748[2]; 1 £ = Rls 2,528[2].

Area and population

Provinces	area sq km	1996 census population	Provinces	area sq km	1996 census population
Ardabīl	17,881	1,168,000	Khūzestān	63,238	3,747,000
Āzārbāyjān-e Gharbī	39,487	2,496,000	Kohkīlūyeh va Būyer Aḥmadī	15,563	544,000
Āzārbāyjān-e Sharqī	47,830	3,326,000	Kordestān	29,151	1,346,000
Būshehr	23,191	744,000	Lorestān	28,392	1,584,000
Chahār Maḥāll va Bakhtīārī	16,201	761,000	Markazi	29,406	1,229,000
Eṣfahān	107,027	3,923,000	Māzandarān	43,525[3]	4,028,000[3]
Fārs	122,416	3,817,000	Qazvīn	[4]	[4]
Gilan	14,106	2,242,000	Qom	11,237	853,000
Golestān	[3]	[3]	Semnān	96,816	501,000
Hamadān	19,547	1,678,000	Sīstān va Balūchestān	178,431	1,723,000
Hormozgān	71,193	1,062,000	Tehrān	31,952	11,176,000
Ilām	20,151	488,000	Yazd	73,467	751,000
Kermān	181,814	2,004,000	Zanjān	24,312[4]	1,037,000[4]
Kermānshāhān	24,741	1,779,000	TOTAL	1,633,841	60,055,000
Khorāsān	302,766	6,048,000			

Demography

Population (2000): 62,704,000[5, 6].
Density (2000): persons per sq mi 99.4, persons per sq km 38.4.
Urban-rural (1996): urban 61.3%; rural 38.7%.
Sex distribution (1996): male 50.81%; female 49.19%.
Age breakdown (1996): under 15, 39.5%; 15–29, 28.4%; 30–44, 17.2%; 45–59, 8.2%; 60–74, 5.5%; 75 and over, 1.2%.
Population projection: (2010) 70,494,000; (2020) 80,482,000.
Doubling time: 50 years.
Ethnic composition (1995): Persian 51%; Azerbaijani 24%; Gīlaki/Mazāndarānī 8%; Kurd 7%; Arab 3%; Lurī 2%; Balochi 2%; other 3%.
Religious affiliation (1996): Muslim 99.6% (Shīʿī 93.9%, Sunnī 5.7%); Christian 0.13%; Zoroastrian 0.05%; Jewish 0.02%; other 0.25%.
Major cities (1996): Tehrān 6,758,845; Mashhad 1,887,405; Eṣfahān 1,266,072; Tabriz 1,191,043; Shīrāz 1,053,025; Karaj 940,968; Ahvāz 804,980.

Vital statistics

Birth rate per 1,000 population (1999): 19.4 (world avg. 22.1).
Death rate per 1,000 population (1999): 5.5 (world avg. 8.9).
Natural increase rate per 1,000 population (1999): 13.9 (world avg. 13.2).
Total fertility rate (avg. births per childbearing woman; 1999): 2.4.
Life expectancy at birth (1999): male 68.1 years; female 70.7 years.
Major causes of death per 100,000 population (1990)[7]: diseases of the circulatory system 304; accidents and violence 108; malignant neoplasms (cancers) 61; diseases of the respiratory system 48; infectious diseases 34.

National economy

Budget (1998–99). Revenue: Rls 53,762,000,000,000 (taxes 34.8%, of which corporate 14.7%, import duties 8.2%; petroleum and natural gas revenue 30.9%; other 34.3%). Expenditures: Rls 71,474,000,000,000 (current expenditure 75.3%; development expenditure 24.7%).
Public debt (external, outstanding; 1999): U.S.$7,679,000,000.
Tourism (1997): receipts U.S.$327,000,000; expenditures U.S.$253,000,000.
Gross national product (1998): U.S.$102,242,000,000 (U.S.$1,650 per capita).

Structure of gross domestic product and labour force

	1997–98		1996	
	in value Rls '000,000,000[8]	% of total value[8]	labour force	% of labour force
Agriculture, forestry	55,455	19.8	3,357,263	21.0
Petroleum, natural gas	31,525	11.2	119,884	0.7
Other mining	1,616	0.6		
Manufacturing	44,317	15.8	2,551,962	15.9
Construction	11,364	4.1	1,650,481	10.3
Public utilities	6,480	2.3	150,631	0.9
Transp. and commun.	21,108	7.5	972,792	6.1
Trade, restaurants	47,387	16.9	1,927,067	12.0
Finance, real estate	29,414	10.5	301,962	1.9
Pub. admin., defense	33,045	11.8	1,618,100	10.1
Services			1,664,402	10.4
Other	–1,325[9]	–0.5[9]	1,712,028[10]	10.7[10]
TOTAL	280,386	100.0	16,026,572	100.0

Production (metric tons except as noted). Agriculture, forestry, fishing (1998): wheat 12,000,000, sugar beets 4,754,000, citrus fruits 3,639,000, potatoes 3,300,000, tomatoes 2,700,000, rice 2,600,000, barley 2,300,000, grapes 2,200,000, apples 2,000,000, onions 1,540,000, corn (maize) 1,000,000, dates 900,000, pulses 559,000, seed cotton 486,000, nuts 341,000 (of which pistachios 130,000); livestock (number of live animals) 53,000,000 sheep, 8,600,000 cattle; roundwood (1998) 7,099,000 cu m; fish catch (1997) 349,921. Mining and quarrying (1997): copper ore 14,200,000; iron ore 12,750,000; gypsum 8,900,000; lead-zinc ore 1,850,000; chromite 835,000. Manufacturing (value added in U.S.$'000,000; 1995): iron and steel 1,393; food products 1,170; textiles 989; transport equipment 763; electrical machinery 716; bricks, tiles, and cement 703. Energy production (consumption): electricity (kW-hr; 1997–98) 97,744,000,000 ([1995] 81,330,000,000); coal (metric tons; 1997) 1,750,000 (1,320,000); crude petroleum (barrels; 1997–98) 1,322,000,000 ([1995] 347,700,000); petroleum products (metric tons; 1995) 47,736,000 (49,207,000); natural gas (cu m; 1997–98) 47,600,000,000 (47,600,000,000).
Population economically active (1996): total 16,026,572; activity rate 26.7% (participation rates: ages 15–64 [1991] 46.8%; female 12.7%).

Price and earnings indexes (1990–91 = 100)

	1993–94	1994–95	1995–96	1996–97	1997–98	1998–99
Consumer price index	184.5	245.2	361.7	457.2	528.5	620.7
Daily earnings index[11]	161.4	200.4	278.2	372.1	438.8	...

Household income and expenditure. Average household size (1996): 4.8; income per urban household (1988) Rls 1,339,970 (U.S.$19,536); sources of urban income (1988): wages 37.4%, self-employment 30.5%, other 32.1%; expenditure (1990–91): food, beverages, and tobacco 42.6%[12], housing and energy 24.9%, clothing 11.8%, household furnishings 6.4%.
Land use (1994): forest 7.0%; pasture 26.9%; agriculture 11.1%; other 55.0%.

Foreign trade

Balance of trade (current prices)

	1993–94	1994–95	1995–96	1996–97	1997–98	1998–99
U.S.$'000,000	–1,207	+7,633	+5,586	+7,910	+4,258	–896
% of total	3.2%	24.4%	17.9%	21.5%	13.1%	3.3%

Imports (1996–97): U.S.$14,467,000,000 (nonelectrical machinery 15.4%, iron and steel 13.6%, grains and derivatives 12.4%, electrical machinery 7.8%, transportation equipment 4.6%). *Major import sources:* Germany 13.9%; Belgium 6.1%; Japan 5.8%; Switzerland 5.4%; Argentina 5.3%.
Exports (1996–97): U.S.$22,377,000,000 (petroleum and natural gas 86.1%, carpets 2.9%, pistachios 2.1%). *Major export destinations:* U.K. 17.5%; Japan 17.0%; Italy 8.1%; South Korea 7.7%; Greece 5.0%.

Transport and communications

Transport. Railroads (1996): route length 3,703 mi, 5,960 km; passenger-km 7,044,000,000; metric ton-km cargo 13,638,000,000. Roads (1996): length 100,700 mi, 162,000 km (paved 50%). Vehicles (1996): passenger cars 1,793,000; trucks and buses 692,000. Air transport (1998)[13]: passenger-km 6,093,000,000; metric ton-km cargo 97,653,000; airports (1996) with scheduled flights 19.

Communications

Medium	date	unit	number	units per 1,000 persons
Daily newspapers	1996	circulation	1,651,000	28
Radio	1997	receivers	17,000,000	280
Television	1997	receivers	4,610,000	76
Telephones	1998	main lines	7,355,000	120
Cellular telephones	1998	subscribers	389,974	6.4
Personal computers	1996	units	2,000,000	33
Internet	1998	users	100,000	1.6

Education and health

Educational attainment (1986). Percentage of population age 25 and over having: no formal schooling 12.8%; secondary education 38.0%; higher 7.8%.
Literacy (1994): total population age 15 and over literate 25,300,000 (72.1%); males literate 14,200,000 (78.4%); females literate 11,100,000 (65.8%).

Education (1996–97)

	schools	teachers	students	student/ teacher ratio
Primary (age 7–11)	63,101	298,755	9,238,393	30.9
Secondary (age 12–18)[14]	...	228,869	7,284,611	31.8
Voc., teacher tr.[14]	...	20,418	368,218	18.0
Higher[15]	...	40,477	579,070	14.3

Health (1996–97): physicians 50,770 (1 per 1,182 persons); hospital beds 98,549 (1 per 609 persons); infant mortality rate (1998) 31.3.
Food (1997): daily per capita caloric intake 2,836 (vegetable products 90%, animal products 10%); 118% of FAO recommended minimum requirement.

Military

Total active duty personnel (1998): 543,000 (revolutionary guard corps 23.0%, army 64.5%, navy 3.8%, air force 8.7%). *Military expenditure as percentage of GNP* (1997): 3.0% (world 2.6%); per capita expenditure U.S.$78.

[1]Not required to be a supreme theological authority. [2]Official floating rate. [3]Golestān province was created in December 1997 from part of Māzandarān province. [4]Zanjān province includes Qazvīn province (created January 1997). [5]De jure estimate. [6]Excludes more than 1,200,000 Afghan refugees and 500,000 Iraqi refugees. [7]Projected rates based on about 20% of total deaths. [8]At factor cost. [9]Less imputed bank service charge. [10]Includes 1,455,000 unemployed. [11]Construction sector only. [12]Includes café and hotel expenditures. [13]Iran Air. [14]1994–95. [15]Excludes private universities.

Internet resources for further information:

- **Embassy of the Islamic Republic of Iran (London)**
  http://www.iran-embassy.org.uk

Iraq

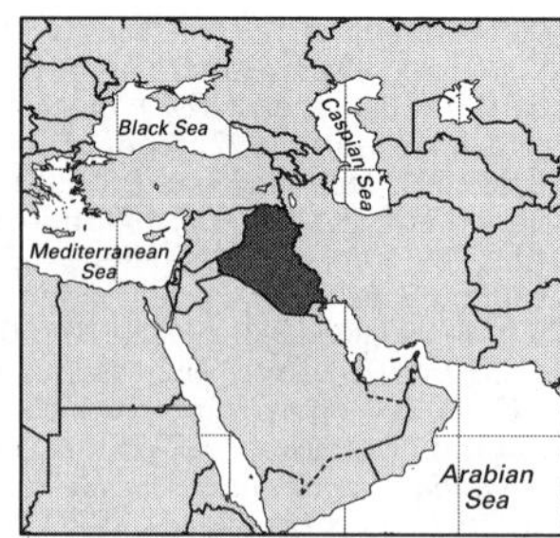

Official name: Al-Jumhūrīyah al-ʿIrāqīyah (Republic of Iraq).
Form of government: unitary multiparty[1] republic with one legislative house (National Assembly [220[2]]).
Head of state and government: President.
Capital: Baghdad.
Official language: Arabic[3].
Official religion: Islam.
Monetary unit: 1 Iraqi dinar (ID) = 20 dirhams = 1,000 fils; valuation (Oct. 6, 2000) 1 ID = U.S.$3.12 = £2.17.

Area and population

Governorates	Capitals	area[4] sq mi	area[4] sq km	population 1991 estimate
Al-Anbār	Ar-Ramādī	53,208	137,808	865,500
Bābil	Al-Ḥillah	2,163	5,603	1,221,100
Baghdād	Baghdad	1,572	4,071	3,910,900
Al-Baṣrah[4]	Basra	7,363	19,070	1,168,800
Dhī Qār	An-Nāṣirīyah	4,981	12,900	1,030,900
Diyālā	Baʿqūbah	6,828	17,685	1,037,600
Karbalāʾ	Karbalāʾ	1,944	5,034	567,600
Maysān	Al-ʿAmārah	6,205	16,072	524,200
Al-Muthannā	As-Samāwah	19,977	51,740	350,000
An-Najaf	An-Najaf	11,129	28,824	666,400
Nīnawā	Mosul	14,410	37,323	1,618,700
Al-Qādisiyah	Ad-Dīwānīyah	3,148	8,153	595,600
Ṣalāḥ ad-Dīn	Tikrīt	9,407	24,363	772,200
At-Taʾmīm	Karkūk (Kirkūk)	3,737	9,679	605,900
Wāsiṭ	Al-kūt	6,623	17,153	605,700
Kurdish Autonomous Region[5]				
Dahūk	Dahūk	2,530	6,553	309,300
Irbīl	Irbīl	5,820	15,074	928,400
As-Sulaymānīyah	As-Sulaymānīyah	6,573	17,023	1,124,200
LAND AREA		167,618	434,128	
OTHER[6]		357	924	
TOTAL		167,975	435,052	17,903,000

Demography

Population (2000): 22,676,000.
Density (2000): persons per sq mi 135.0, persons per sq km 52.1.
Urban-rural (1999): urban 76.4%; rural 23.6%.
Sex distribution (1999): male 50.86%; female 49.14%.
Age breakdown (2000): under 15, 42.1%; 15–29, 30.4%; 30–44, 15.6%; 45–59, 7.4%; 60–74, 3.5%; 75 and over, 1.0%.
Population projection: (2010) 29,672,000; (2020) 36,908,000.
Doubling time: 25 years.
Ethnic composition (1983): Arab 77.1%; Kurd 19.0%; Azerbaijani 1.7%; Assyrian 0.8%; other 1.4%.
Religious affiliation (1994): Shīʿī Muslim 62.5%; Sunnī Muslim 34.5%; Christian (primarily Chaldean rite and Syrian rite Roman Catholic and Nestorian) 2.7%; other (primarily Yazīdī syncretist) 0.3%.
Major cities (1987): Baghdad (1995; urban agglomeration) 4,478,000; Mosul 664,221; Irbīl 485,968; Karkūk (Kirkūk) 418,624; Al-Baṣrah 406,296.

Vital statistics

Birth rate per 1,000 population (2000): 35.0 (world avg. 22.1).
Death rate per 1,000 population (2000): 6.4 (world avg. 8.9).
Natural increase rate per 1,000 population (2000): 28.6 (world avg. 13.2).
Total fertility rate (avg. births per childbearing woman; 2000): 4.9.
Marriage rate per 1,000 population (1992): 7.8.
Life expectancy at birth (2000): male 65.4 years; female 67.6 years.
Major causes of death. Prior to the Gulf War (1990) the leading causes (in descending order) were: circulatory diseases, injury and poisoning, cancer, and congenital anomalies; since 1990, additional mortality has been attributed to deprivation of medical care and malnutrition consequent upon the imposition of UN sanctions, especially among children and other vulnerable populations.

National economy

Budget (1992). Revenue: ID 13,935,000,000. Expenditures: ID 13,935,000,000. Details of more recent budgets are not available.
Production (metric tons except as noted). Agriculture, forestry, fishing (2000): dates 540,000, wheat 384,000, watermelons 380,000, tomatoes 300,000, oranges 270,000, grapes 270,000, barley 226,000, cantaloupes 195,000, potatoes 150,000, rice 130,000, cucumbers 125,000; livestock (number of live animals) 6,100,000 sheep, 1,150,000 cattle; roundwood (1998) 177,000 cu m; fish catch (1998) 22,574. Mining and quarrying (1995): sulfur 475,000; phosphate rock 440,000. Manufacturing (value added in U.S.$'000,000; 1994): refined petroleum 127; bricks, tiles, and cement 100; industrial chemicals 79; food products 59; metal products 28. Construction (authorized; 1991): residential 4,558,000 sq m; nonresidential 410,000 sq m. Energy production (consumption): electricity (kW-hr; 1996) 29,660,000,000 (29,660,000,000); coal, none (none); crude petroleum (barrels; 1996) 269,267,000 (208,671,000); petroleum products (metric tons; 1996) 23,375,000 (22,305,000); natural gas (cu m; 1996) 3,240,000,000 (3,240,000,000).
Household income and expenditure (1988). Average household size 8.9; sources of income: self-employment 33.9%, wages and salaries 23.9%, transfers 23.0%, rent 18.6%; expenditure: food and beverages 50.2%, housing and energy 19.9%, clothing and footwear 10.6%.
Gross domestic product (1996): U.S.$11,500,000,000 (U.S.$540 per capita).

Structure of gross domestic product and labour force

	1992		1988	
	in value ID '000,000[7]	% of total value	labour force	% of labour force
Agriculture	20,844	35.1	477,264	11.6
Mining	230	0.4	60,701	1.5
Manufacturing	5,620	9.5	337,293	8.2
Construction	2,259	3.8	460,788	11.2
Public utilities	181	0.3	41,200	1.0
Transp. and commun.	5,947	10.0	266,233	6.4
Trade	15,190	25.6	281,877	6.8
Finance, real estate	4,692	7.9	41,532	1.0
Pub. admin., defense, and services	7,209	12.2	2,160,406	52.3
Other	–2,824	–4.8		
TOTAL	59,348	100.0	4,127,294	100.0

Public debt (external, outstanding; 1994): U.S.$20,000,000,000.
Population economically active (1988): total 4,127,294; activity rate of total population 24.7% (participation rates: ages 15–64, 45.3%; female 12.0%).

Price index (1995 = 100)

	1990	1991	1992	1993	1994	1995	1996
Consumer price index	0.2	0.6	1.7[8]	5.2[8]	20[8]	100[8]	550[8]

Tourism (1995): receipts U.S.$13,000,000; expenditures, n.a.
Land use (1994): forest 0.4%; pasture 9.1%; agriculture 13.1%; other 77.4%.

Foreign trade[9, 10]

Balance of trade (current prices)[8]

	1990	1991	1992	1993	1994	1995
U.S.$'000,000	+5,587	–1,633	–2,199	–1,956	–1,518	–2,081
% of total	36.6%	66.3%	73.3%	68.8%	66.5%	71.3%

Imports (1995): U.S.$2,500,000,000[8] (agricultural products 42.7%, of which cereals 9.9%; unspecified 57.3%). *Major import sources*[11]: Jordan 49.0%; Turkey 17.0%; Hungary 15.0%; Switzerland 8.0%.
Exports (1995): U.S.$419,000,000[8] (mostly crude petroleum and petroleum products). *Major export destinations:* Jordan 98.0%.

Transport and communications

Transport. Railroads (1997): route length 2,032 km[12]; passenger-km 1,169,000,000; metric ton-km cargo 956,000,000. Roads (1996): total length 47,400 km (paved 86%). Vehicles (1995): passenger cars 672,000; trucks and buses 368,000. Air transport: [13].

Communications

Medium	date	unit	number	units per 1,000 persons
Daily newspapers	1996	circulation	407,000	20
Radio	1997	receivers	4,850,000	229
Television	1996	receivers	1,700,000	82
Telephones	1998	main lines	675,000	31

Education and health

Educational attainment (1987). Percentage of population age 10 and over having: no formal schooling 52.8%; primary education 21.5%; secondary 11.6%; higher 4.1%; unknown 10.0%. *Literacy* (1995): total population age 15 and over literate 58.0%; males 70.7%; females 45.0%.

Education (1995–96)

	schools	teachers	students	student/ teacher ratio
Primary (age 6–11)	8,145	145,455	2,903,923	20.0
Secondary (age 12–17)	2,635[14]	52,393	1,037,482	19.8
Voc., teacher tr.	310[14]	9,903	122,939	12.4
Higher[14]	12	11,847	201,984	17.0

Health (1993): physicians 8,787 (1 per 2,181 persons); hospital beds 27,202 (1 per 704 persons); infant mortality rate per 1,000 live births (2000) 62.5.
Food (1998): daily per capita caloric intake 2,419 (vegetable products 96%, animal products 4%); 100% of FAO recommended minimum requirement.

Military

Total active duty personnel (1999): 429,000 (army 91.3%, navy 0.5%, air force 8.2%). *Military expenditure as percentage of GDP* (1997): 4.9% (world 2.6%); per capita expenditure U.S.$59.

[1]Multipartyism is officially authorized, but political power is in fact concentrated in a single-party apparatus. [2]Elective seats as of March 2000 elections; 30 additional seats allotted to the Kurdish Autonomous Region were filled by presidential appointment. [3]Kurdish is official in the Kurdish Autonomous Region only. [4]Includes territory ceded to Kuwait as of Jan. 15, 1993. [5]De facto self-government between 1992 and 1996. [6]Territorial water at the mouth of the Shaṭṭ al-ʿArab. [7]At factor cost. [8]Estimated figure(s). [9]Imports c.i.f.; exports f.o.b. [10]UN-imposed trade sanctions in place from August 1990 through October 1997. [11]Based on estimated imports equaling U.S.$608,000,000. [12]1995. [13]No scheduled air service since June 1992. [14]1994–95.

Internet resources for further information:
- **Permanent Mission of Iraq to the United Nations (official site) http://www.undp.org/missions/iraq**
- **Iraq Foundation (unofficial) http://www.iraqfoundation.org**

Ireland

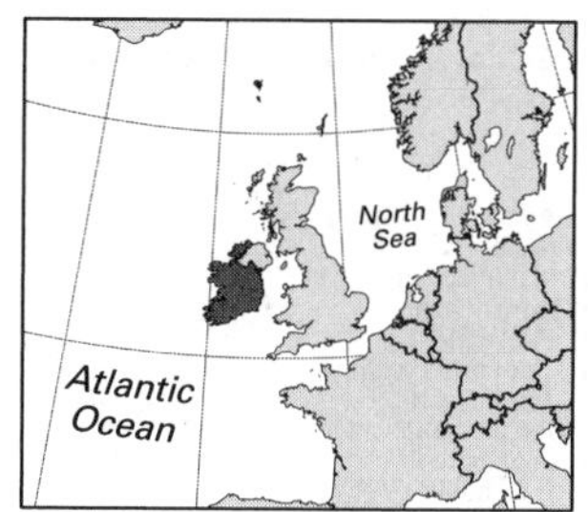

Official name: Éire (Irish); Ireland[1] (English).
Form of government: unitary multiparty republic with two legislative houses (Senate [60[2]]; House of Representatives [166]).
Chief of state: President.
Head of government: Prime Minister.
Capital: Dublin.
Official languages: Irish; English.
Official religion: none.
Monetary unit: 1 Irish pound (£Ir) = 100 new pence; valuation (Oct. 6, 2000) 1 £Ir = U.S.$1.11 = £0.76.

Area and population

Provinces Counties	area sq km	population 1996 census	Provinces Counties	area sq km	population 1996 census
Connacht	17,122	433,000	Munster	24,127	1,033,000
Galway[3]	5,940	189,000	Clare	3,188	94,000
Leitrim	1,525	25,000	Cork[3]	7,460	420,000
Mayo	5,398	111,000	Kerry	4,701	126,000
Roscommon	2,463	52,000	Limerick[3]	2,686	165,000
Sligo	1,796	56,000	Tipperary North Riding	1,996	58,000
Leinster	19,633	1,922,000[4]	Tipperary South Riding	2,258	75,000
Carlow	896	42,000	Waterford[3]	1,838	95,000
Dublin[3, 5]	922	1,057,000	Ulster (part of)	8,012	234,000[4]
Kildare	1,694	135,000	Cavan	1,891	53,000
Kilkenny	2,062	75,000	Donegal	4,830	129,000
Laoighis	1,719	53,000	Monaghan	1,291	51,000
Longford	1,044	30,000	TOTAL LAND AREA	68,895[4]	
Louth	823	92,000	INLAND WATER	1,390	
Meath	2,336	109,000	TOTAL	70,285[6]	3,622,000
Offaly	1,998	59,000			
Westmeath	1,763	63,000			
Wexford	2,351	104,000			
Wicklow	2,025	102,000			

Demography

Population (2000): 3,783,000.
Density (2000): persons per sq mi 135.0, persons per sq km 52.1.
Urban-rural (1996): urban 58.0%; rural 42.0%.
Sex distribution (1996): male 49.64%; female 50.36%.
Age breakdown (1996): under 15, 23.7%; 15–24, 17.5%, 25–44, 28.0%; 45–59, 15.6%; 60–74, 12.3%; 75 and over, 2.9%.
Population projection: (2010) 4,161,000; (2020) 4,372,000.
Religious affiliation (1991): Roman Catholic 91.6%; Church of Ireland (Anglican) 2.5%; Presbyterian 0.4%; other 5.5%.
Major cities (1996)[7]: Dublin 481,000; Cork 127,000; Galway 57,000; Limerick 52,000; Waterford 43,000.

Vital statistics

Birth rate per 1,000 population (1999): 14.4 (world avg. 22.1).
Death rate per 1,000 population (1999): 8.2 (world avg. 8.9).
Natural increase rate per 1,000 population (1999): 6.2 (world avg. 13.2).
Total fertility rate (avg. births per childbearing woman; 1999): 1.9.
Life expectancy at birth (1999): male 73.9 years; female 79.5 years.
Major causes of death per 100,000 population (1998): heart and circulatory diseases 364.4, of which ischemic heart diseases 199.3; malignant neoplasms (cancers) 206.9; respiratory disease 131.8, of which pneumonia 62.0.

National economy

Budget (1998). Revenue: £Ir 15,497,000,000 (income taxes 35.6%, value-added tax 25.9%, excise taxes 17.2%). Expenditures: £Ir 15,196,000,000 (social welfare 31.4%, health 19.0%, debt service 17.3%, education 15.4%).
Public debt (1996): U.S.$47,876,000,000.
Gross national product (1998): U.S.$69,322,000,000 (U.S.$18,710 per capita).

Structure of gross domestic product and labour force

	1998		1996	
	in value £Ir '000,000[8]	% of total value[8]	labour force	% of labour force
Agriculture	2,790	5.3	136,000	9.2
Mining	20,692	39.7	5,000	0.3
Manufacturing			246,000	16.7
Construction			86,000	5.8
Public utilities			14,000	0.9
Transp. and commun.	8,776	16.8	80,000	5.4
Trade			273,000[9]	18.5[9]
Pub. admin., defense	2,184	4.2	76,000	5.2
Services	17,741	34.0	369,000	25.0
Finance			[9]	[9]
Other			191,000[10]	13.0[10]
TOTAL	52,183	100.0	1,650,000	100.0

Tourism (1997): receipts U.S.$3,189,000,000; expenditures U.S.$2,223,000,000.
Production (metric tons except as noted). Agriculture, forestry, fishing (1998): sugar beets 1,400,000, barley 1,073,000, wheat 673,000, potatoes 482,000, oats 119,000, milk (1995) 51,900,000 hectolitres; livestock (number of live animals)[11] 8,373,000 sheep, 7,795,000 cattle, 1,819,000 pigs; roundwood (1997) 2,180,000 cu m; fish catch (1996) 332,316. Mining and quarrying (1997): gypsum 477,000; zinc ore 194,800[12]; lead ore 45,000[12]. Manufacturing (value added in £Ir '000,000; 1995): office equipment and computers 2,163; basic chemicals 2,112; reproduction of recorded media 1,531; pharmaceuticals 884; alcoholic beverages 735. Construction (1998): residential 6,098,000 sq m; nonresidential 4,122,000 sq m. Energy production (consumption): electricity (kW-hr; 1995) 17,878,000,000 (17,863,000,000); coal (metric tons; 1995) 1,000 (2,441,000); crude petroleum (barrels; 1995) none (16,000,000); petroleum products (metric tons; 1995) 2,180,000 (4,976,000,000); natural gas (cu m; 1995) 2,500,000,000 (2,629,000,000).
Population economically active (1996): total 1,475,000; activity rate 40.7% (participation rates: ages 15–64, 59.2%[13]; unemployed 11.9%[14]).

Price and earnings indexes (1995 = 100)

	1993	1994	1995	1996	1997	1998	1999
Consumer price index	95.3	97.5	100.0	101.7	103.2	105.7	107.4
Weekly earnings index	95.1	97.8	100.0	102.5	105.4	110.2	...

Household income and expenditure. Average household size (1997) 3.1; income per household (1994–95): £Ir 16,224 (U.S.$25,100); expenditure (1996)[15]: food and beverages 35.4%, transportation 13.9%, rent/household goods 11.6%.

Foreign trade[16]

Balance of trade (current prices)

	1993	1994	1995	1996	1997	1998	1999[17]
£Ir '000,000	+4,945	+5,470	+7,206	+7,978	+9,454	+13,939	+22,845
% of total	14.2%	13.7%	14.9%	15.1%	15.4%	18.2%	20.9%

Imports (1996): £Ir 22,468,200,000 (machinery and transport equipment 42.0%, chemicals 12.3%, manufactured goods 10.8%, food 6.9%, petroleum and petroleum products 3.7%, crude materials [inedible] 1.8%, beverages and tobacco 1.0%). *Major import sources:* U.K. 31.9%; U.S. 15.4%; Germany 6.8%; Japan 5.4%; Singapore 4.4%; France 3.9%; The Netherlands 3.0%.
Exports (1996): £Ir 30,294,300,000 (machinery and transport equipment 34.7%, chemical products 22.2%, food 13.7%, manufactured goods 4.5%). *Major export destinations:* U.K. 21.9%; Germany 12.9%; U.S. 9.3%; France 8.2%.

Transport and communications

Transport. Railroads (1996): route length 1,947 km; passenger-km 1,295,000,000; metric ton-km cargo 570,000,000. Roads (1996): length 92,500 km (paved 94%). Vehicles (1996): passenger cars 1,057,383; trucks and buses 161,355. Air transport (1998)[18]: passenger-km 6,466,383,000; metric ton-km cargo 129,648,000; airports (1996) 9.

Communications

Medium	date	unit	number	units per 1,000 persons
Daily newspapers	1996	circulation	543,000	150
Radio	1998	receivers	2,150,000	580
Television	1996	receivers	1,653,000	457
Telephones	1997	main lines	1,500,000	409
Cellular telephones	1997	subscribers	533,000	146
Personal computers	1997	units	880,000	240
Internet	1998	users	300,000	81

Education and health

Educational attainment (1991). Percentage of population age 15 and over having: primary education or no schooling 33.7%; secondary 42.7%; some postsecondary 12.6%; university or like institution 11.0%.

Education (1995–96)

	schools	teachers	students	student/ teacher ratio
Primary (age 6–11)[19]	3,201	21,052	478,692	22.7
Secondary (age 12–18)	445	12,736	223,605	17.6
Voc., teacher tr.	323	8,166	146,648	18.0
Higher	30	4,873	93,980	19.3

Health: physicians (1998) 8,114 (1 per 457 persons); hospital beds (1995) 11,953[20] (1 per 301 persons); infant mortality rate (1999) 5.7.
Food (1997): daily per capita caloric intake 3,565 (vegetable products 68%, animal products 32%); 142% of FAO recommended minimum requirement.

Military

Total active duty personnel (1998): 11,500 (army 80.8%, navy 9.6%, air force 9.6%). *Military expenditure as percentage of GNP* (1997): 1.2% (world 2.6%); per capita expenditure U.S.$203.

[1]As provided by the constitution; the 1948 Republic of Ireland Act provides precedent for this longer formulation of the official name but, per official sources, "has not changed the usage *Ireland* as the name of the state in the English language." [2]Includes 11 nonelective seats. [3]Includes separately administered county boroughs with same name. [4]Detail does not add to total given because of rounding. [5]Includes the three counties of Dun Laoghaire–Rathdown, Fingal, and South Dublin (established Jan. 1, 1994) with respective 1996 census populations of 190,000, 167,700, and 218,700. [6]Area per more recent survey is 70,273 sq km. [7]Population of Ireland's five administrative county boroughs. [8]At factor cost. [9]Trade includes Finance. [10]Unemployed. [11]June. [12]Metal content of ores. [13]1988. [14]April. [15]November. [16]Imports c.i.f.; exports f.o.b. [17]For Euros. [18]Aer Lingus only. [19]National schools only. [20]Acute-care public hospitals only.

Internet resources for further information:
- **Central Statistics Office (Ireland) http://www.cso.ie**

Isle of Man

Official name: Isle of Man[1].
Political status: crown dependency (United Kingdom) with two legislative bodies[2] (Legislative Council [11[3]]; House of Keys [24]).
Chief of state: British Monarch represented by Lieutenant-Governor.
Head of government: Chief Minister assisted by the Council of Ministers.
Capital: Douglas.
Official language: English.
Official religion: none.
Monetary unit: 1 Manx pound[4] = 100 new pence; valuation (Oct. 6, 2000) 1 Manx pound = U.S.$1.45.

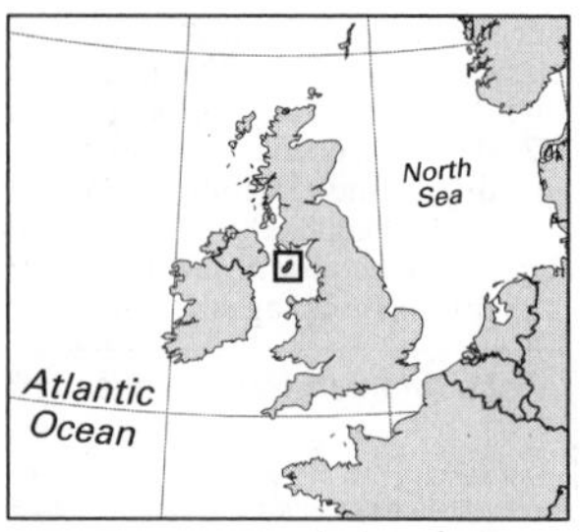

Area and population

	area sq km	population 1996 census		area sq km	population 1996 census
Towns			**Parishes** (cont.)		
Castletown	0.4	2,958	Ballaugh	24.6	812
Douglas	6.7	23,487	Braddan	45.1	2,527
Peel	1.3	3,819	Bride	23.5	405
Ramsey	1.2	6,874	German	46.1	1,038
			Jurby	19.1	624
Villages			Lezayre	65.3	1,047
Laxey	[5]	1,433	Lonan	38.1[5]	1,292
Onchan	26.4	8,656	Malew	51.7	2,140
Port Erin	2.6	3,218	Marown	26.6	1,564
Port St. Mary	1.4	1,874	Maughold	36.2	858
			Michael	35.5	1,261
Parishes			Patrick	42.9	1,198
Andreas	31.9	1,144	Rushen	26.2	1,441
Arbory	18.1	1,622	Santon	17.2	422
			TOTAL	588.1	71,714

Demography

Population (2000): 73,100.
Density (2000): persons per sq mi 322.0, persons per sq km 124.3.
Urban-rural (1999): urban 76.3%; rural 23.7%.
Sex distribution (1996): male 48.52%; female 51.48%.
Age breakdown (1996): under 15, 17.6%; 15–29, 19.0%; 30–44, 20.6%; 45–59, 19.5%; 60–74, 14.4%; 75 and over, 8.9%.
Population projection: (2010) 77,000; (2020) 80,000.
Population by place of birth (1996): Isle of Man 49.9%; United Kingdom 44.1%, of which England 37.5%, Scotland 3.3%, Northern Ireland 2.1%; Ireland 2.4%.
Religious affiliation (1980): Christian 93.0%, of which Anglican 62.0%, non-Anglican Protestant (mostly Methodist) 20.0%, Roman Catholic 10.0%; other/nonreligious 7.0%.
Major cities (1996): Douglas 23,487; Onchan 8,656; Ramsey 6,874; Peel 3,819; Port Erin 3,218.

Vital statistics

Birth rate per 1,000 population (1999): 12.3 (world avg. 22.1); (1998) legitimate 65.5%; illegitimate 34.5%.
Death rate per 1,000 population (1999): 13.5 (world avg. 8.9).
Natural increase rate per 1,000 population (1999): –1.2 (world avg. 13.2).
Total fertility rate (avg. births per childbearing woman; 1999): 1.6.
Marriage rate per 1,000 population (1998): 6.0.
Divorce rate per 1,000 population (1996): 4.0.
Life expectancy at birth (1999): male 73.9 years; female 80.8 years.
Major causes of death per 100,000 population (1998): diseases of the circulatory system 504.3, of which ischemic heart diseases 247.3, cerebrovascular disease 96.7; neoplasms (cancers) 298.4; diseases of the respiratory system 225.2.

National economy

Budget (1997–98). Revenue: £265,716,000 (customs duties and excise taxes 51.7%; income taxes 43.7%, of which resident 34.6%, nonresident 9.1%; interest on investments 4.2%). Expenditures: £240,140,000 (health and social security 42.2%; education 19.2%; transportation 6.4%; home affairs 6.3%; tourism and recreation 5.4%).
Public debt n.a.
Production. Agriculture, forestry, fishing (1998): main crops include hay, oats, barley, wheat, and orchard crops; livestock (number of live animals) 173,900 sheep, 34,000 cattle, 6,600 pigs; roundwood n.a.; fish catch (value of catch in £ sterling; 1997): scallops 1,666,000; whitefish 244,000; herring 138,000. Mining and quarrying: sand and gravel. Manufacturing (value added in U.S.$; 1996–97): electrical and nonelectrical machinery/apparatus, textiles, other 103,700,000; food and beverages 18,600,000. Energy production (consumption): electricity (kW-hr; 1997–98) n.a. (275,400,000); crude petroleum, none (n.a.); petroleum products, n.a. (n.a.); natural gas, none (n.a.).
Household income and expenditure. Average household size (1996) 2.4; income per household (1981–82)[6, 7]: £7,479 (U.S.$13,721); sources of income (1981–82)[6, 7]: wages and salaries 64.1%, transfer payments 16.9%, interest and dividends 11.2%, self-employment 6.6%; expenditure (1981–82)[6, 7]: food and beverages 31.0%, transportation 14.9%, energy 11.0%, housing 7.9%, clothing and footwear 7.0%.
Gross domestic product (at current market prices; 1997–98): U.S.$1,319,000,000 (U.S.$18,270 per capita).

Structure of gross domestic product and labour force

	1997–98		1996	
	in value £ '000[8]	% of total value	labour force	% of labour force
Agriculture, fishing	10,726	1.5	938	2.7
Mining; Manufacturing	80,981	11.2	3,562	10.2
Construction	44,587	6.2	3,372	9.7
Public utilities	15,062	2.1	462	1.3
Transp. and commun.	63,198	8.8	2,688	7.7
Trade, hotels	69,109	9.6	4,457	12.8
Finance, real estate, insurance	320,414	44.5[9]	5,941	17.1
Pub. admin., defense	40,850	5.7	2,147	6.2
Services	167,826	23.3[9]	10,005	28.7
Other	–93,071	–12.9	1,239[10]	3.6[10]
TOTAL	719,682	100.0	34,811	100.0

Population economically active (1996): total 34,811; activity rate of total population 48.5% (participation rates: ages 16 and over 59.8%; female 44.0%; unemployed 3.5%).

Price and earnings indexes (1995 = 100)

	1993	1994	1995	1996	1997	1998
Retail price index	94.6	97.2	100.0	102.9	105.2	108.3
Weekly earnings index[11]	92.7	95.0	100.0	102.9	110.0	115.0

Tourism: receipts, n.a.; expenditures by nationals abroad, n.a.
Land use: n.a.

Foreign trade

Imports (1998): n.a. *Major import sources* (1998): mostly the United Kingdom.
Exports (1998): traditional exports include scallops, herring, beef, lambs, and tweeds. *Major export destinations* (1998): mostly the United Kingdom.

Transport and communications

Transport. Railroads (1998): route length 32 mi, 52 km[12]. Roads (1998): total length, more than 500 mi, more than 805 km (paved, n.a.). Vehicles (1998): passenger cars 40,168; trucks and buses, n.a. Merchant marine (1999): vessels (100 gross tons and over) 219; total deadweight tonnage, n.a. Air transport (1998)[13]: passenger-mi 526,161,000, passenger-km 846,775,000; short ton-mi cargo 115,000, metric ton-km cargo 168,000; airports (1999) with scheduled flights 1.

Communications

Medium	date	unit	number	units per 1,000 persons
Daily newspapers	1997	circulation	—[14]	—
Television	1997	receivers	27,000	375
Telephones	1996	main lines	46,000	641

Education and health

Educational attainment: n.a. *Literacy:* n.a.

Education (1998–99)

	schools	teachers	students	student/ teacher ratio
Primary (age 5–10)	33	...	6,210	...
Secondary (age 11–16)	5	...	4,732	...
Higher[15]	1	...	1,128[16]	...

Health (1998): physicians 117 (1 per 619 persons); hospital beds 505 (1 per 143 persons); infant mortality rate per 1,000 live births (1996–98 avg.) 2.3.
Food (1998)[17]: daily per capita caloric intake 3,257 (vegetable products 68%, animal products 32%); 129% of FAO recommended minimum requirement.

Military

Total active duty personnel: [18].

[1]Ellan Vannin in Manx Gaelic. [2]Collective name is Tynwald. [3]Includes 3 nonelected seats. [4]Equivalent in value to pound sterling (£). [5]Lonan includes Laxey. [6]Fiscal year ending March 31st. [7]Based on survey of 259 households; "high income" and "pensioner" households are excluded. [8]At factor cost. [9]Most GDP in 1999 was derived from 66 banks (most of which are "offshore"), 77 investment businesses, and 193 insurance companies. [10]Includes 5 not adequately defined and 1,234 unemployed. [11]June only. [12]Length of three tourist (novel) railways operating in summer. [13]Manx Airlines. [14]Isle of Man has 2 weekly newspapers and 1 biweekly newspaper. [15]1997–98. [16]Includes enrollees at Isle of Man College and students abroad. [17]Data for United Kingdom. [18]The United Kingdom is responsible for defense.

Internet resources for further information:
- **Isle of Man Government**
  http://www.gov.im

Israel

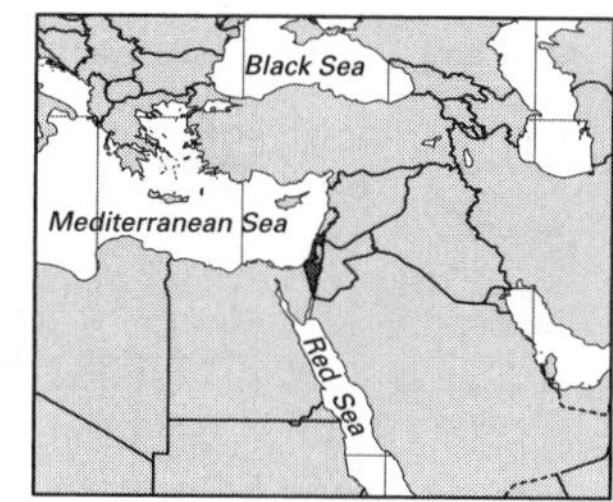

Official name: Medinat Yisra'el (Hebrew); Isrā'īl (Arabic) (State of Israel).
Form of government: multiparty republic with one legislative house (Knesset [120]).
Chief of state: President.
Head of government: Prime Minister.
Capital: Jerusalem is the proclaimed capital of Israel and the actual seat of government, but recognition of its status as capital by the international community has largely been withheld pending final settlement of territorial and other issues through peace talks between Israel and the Arab parties concerned.
Official languages: Hebrew; Arabic.
Official religion: none.
Monetary unit: 1 New (Israeli) sheqel (NIS) = 100 agorot; valuation (Oct. 6, 2000) 1 U.S.$ = NIS 4.06; 1 £ = NIS 5.86.

Area and population

		area[1]		population
Districts	Capitals	sq mi	sq km	1999[2] estimate
Central (Ha Merkaz)	Ramla	493	1,276	1,358,200
Haifa (Ḥefa)	Haifa	333	863	788,600
Jerusalem (Yerushalayim)	Jerusalem	225	582	717,000
Northern (Ha Ẕafon)	Tiberias	1,275	3,302	1,026,700
Southern (Ha Darom)	Beersheba	5,494	14,231	840,000
Tel Aviv	Tel Aviv–Yafo	66	171	1,138,700
TOTAL		7,886	20,425	5,869,200[3]

Demography

Population (2000): 6,107,000.
Density (2000)[3]: persons per sq mi 778.4, persons per sq km 300.5.
Urban-rural (1999[2]): urban 91.4%; rural 8.6%.
Sex distribution (1999): male 49.72%; female 50.28%.
Age breakdown (1999): under 15, 27.9%; 15–29, 25.1%; 30–44, 19.5%; 45–59, 14.4%; 60–74, 8.7%; 75 and over, 4.4%.
Population projection: (2010) 6,946,000; (2020) 7,647,000.
Ethnic composition (1999): Jewish 79.2%; Arab and other 20.8%.
Religious affiliation (1999): Jewish 79.2%; Muslim (mostly Sunnī) 14.9%; Christian 2.1%; Druze 1.6%; other 2.2%.
Major cities (1999[2]): Jerusalem 633,700; Tel Aviv–Yafo 348,100; Haifa 265,700; Rishon LeẔiyyon 188,200; Ḥolon 163,100; Petah Tiqwa 159,400.

Vital statistics

Birth rate per 1,000 population (1999): 19.5 (world avg. 22.1); (1994)[4] legitimate 98.2%; illegitimate 1.8%.
Death rate per 1,000 population (1999): 6.2 (world avg. 8.9).
Natural increase rate per 1,000 population (1999): 13.3 (world avg. 13.2).
Total fertility rate (avg. births per childbearing woman; 1999): 2.7.
Marriage rate per 1,000 population (1998): 6.7.
Divorce rate per 1,000 population (1998): 1.6.
Life expectancy at birth (1999): male 76.4 years; female 80.5 years.
Major causes of death per 100,000 population (1995): diseases of the circulatory system 271.6; malignant neoplasms (cancers) 145.2; diseases of the respiratory system 26.5; accidents 24.0.

National economy

Budget (1999). Revenue: NIS 178,023,000,000 (tax revenue 74.4%, of which income tax and property tax 35.5%, value-added tax 26.3%, sales tax and fuel tax 4.3%; nontax revenue 18.7%; grants 6.9%). Expenditures: NIS 178,023,000,000 (current expenditure 90.8%; of which transfers 37.1% interest on loans 13.4%; defense 11.6%; capital expenditure 5.2%; reserve 4.0%).
Public debt (1996): U.S.$26,215,000,000.
Gross national product (1998): U.S.$96,483,000,000 (U.S.$16,180 per capita).

Structure of gross domestic product and labour force

	1998			
	in value NIS '000,000[5]	% of total value[5]	labour force	% of labour force
Agriculture	9,727	2.8	49,000	2.2
Manufacturing, mining	81,293	23.4	392,000	17.4
Construction	36,130	10.4	132,000	5.9
Public utilities	7,295	2.1	20,000	0.9
Transp. and commun.	40,994	11.8	123,000	5.5
Trade	} 171,965	} 49.5	349,000	15.4
Finance			288,000[6]	12.8[6]
Public and community services			667,000[7]	29.6[7]
Services			32,000[8]	1.4[8]
Other			219,600[9]	8.9[9]
TOTAL	347,404	100.0	2,271,600	100.0

Production (metric tons except as noted). Agriculture, forestry, fishing (1999): tomatoes 463,000, oranges 385,000, grapefruit 335,000, potatoes 333,800, watermelons 333,400, seed cotton 133,981, cucumbers 115,480, apples 102,000, corn (maize) 91,400, wheat 80,000; livestock (number of live animals) 300,000 cattle, 340,000 sheep, 163,000 pigs, 73,000 goats, 25,340,000 chickens; roundwood (1998) 124,000 cu m; fish catch (1997) 23,300. Mining and quarrying (1996): phosphate rock 2,450,000, potash 2,500,000. Manufacturing (1996): cement 6,723,000; polyethylene 144,147[10]; sulfuric acid 130,000[10]; paper 114,403; cardboard 113,278; chlorine 34,630; wine 12,733,000 litres[10]. Construction (1998): residential 7,265,000 sq m; nonresidential 3,530,000 sq m. Energy production (consumption): electricity (kW-hr; 1998) 37,934,000 (32,649,000); coal (metric tons; 1996) none (7,808,000); crude petroleum (barrels; 1996) 29,000 (77,000,000); petroleum products (metric tons; 1996) 9,963,000 (9,579,000); natural gas (cu m; 1996) 13,143,000 (13,143,000).
Population economically active (1998)[11]: total 2,271,600; activity rate 39.6% (participation rates: over ages 15, 53.6%; female 46.3%; unemployed 8.6%).

Price and earnings indexes (1995 = 100)

	1993	1994	1995	1996	1997	1998	1999
Consumer price index	80.9	90.9	100.0	111.3	121.3	127.9	134.5
Daily earnings index	78.8	87.1	100.0	113.9	130.8	143.9	155.4

Household income and expenditure (1998). Average household size 3.6; monthly income per household[12] (1995) NIS 6,125 (U.S.$2,034); sources of income (1993)[12]: salaries and wages 63.4%, allowances and assistance 18.9%, self-employment 14.6%, other 3.1%; expenditure (1998): housing 23.7%, food, beverages, and tobacco 21.1%, household durable goods 8.2%, clothing, footwear, and personal goods 4.5%, energy 4.2%, transportation 3.1%.
Tourism (1998): receipts U.S.$2,657,000,000; expenditures U.S.$2,376,000,000.

Foreign trade[13]

Balance of trade (current prices)

	1994	1995	1996	1997	1998	1999
U.S.$'000,000	–8,353	–10,533	–11,075	–8,191	–6,056	–7,366
% of total	19.8%	21.7%	21.2%	15.4%	11.5%	12.5%

Imports (1998): U.S.$27,469,000,000 (investment goods 16.8%; consumer goods 14.3%; diamonds 14.2%; fuel and lubricants 6.7%). *Major import sources:* U.S. 19.9%; Belgium 10.5%; Germany 9.0%; U.K. 7.6%; Italy 6.8%.
Exports (1998): U.S.$23,302,800,000 (1997; machinery and transport equipment 31.0%; diamonds 25.3%; chemicals 12.2%; apparel 4.4%; rubber and plastics 3.9%; food, beverages, and tobacco 2.3%). *Major export destinations:* U.S. 35.4%; U.K. 5.7%; Germany 4.8%; Belgium 4.7%; Hong Kong 3.4%; Japan 3.2%.

Transport and communications

Transport. Railroads (1997): route length 610 km; passenger-km 346,000,000, metric ton-km cargo 992,000,000. Roads (1998): total length 15,464 km (paved 100%). Vehicles (1998): passenger cars 1,273,000; trucks and buses 294,100. Air transport (1998)[14]: passenger-km 12,146,000,000; metric ton-km cargo 1,117,335,000; airports (1998) with scheduled flights 7.

Communications

Medium	date	unit	number	units per 1,000 persons
Daily newspapers	1997	circulation	1,650,000	288
Radio	1997	receivers	3,070,000	524
Television	1997	receivers	1,690,000	288
Telephones	1998	main lines	2,819,000	471
Cellular telephones	1998	subscribers	2,147,000	358
Personal computers	1998	units	1,300,000	217
Internet	1998	users	450,000	75

Education and health

Educational attainment (1991). Percentage of population age 25 and over having: no formal schooling 6.7%; primary 22.5%; secondary 39.6%; postsecondary, vocational, and higher 31.2%. *Literacy* (1995): total population age 15 and over literate 95.6%; males literate 97.7%; females literate 93.6%.

Education (1997–98)

	schools	teachers	students	student/ teacher ratio
Primary (age 6–13)	1,651	57,738	532,070	9.2
Secondary (age 14–17)[15]	653	62,054	414,405	6.7
Vocational, teacher tr.	338	17,141[16]	106,393	...
Higher	7	9,546	181,038	19.0

Health (1998): physicians (1997) 21,100 (1 per 269 persons); hospital beds 36,400 (1 per 156 persons); infant mortality rate (1999) 8.1.
Food (1998): daily per capita caloric intake 3,466 (vegetable products 81%, animal products 19%); 135% of FAO recommended minimum.

Military

Total active duty personnel (1999): 173,500 (army 75.0%, navy 3.7%, air force 21.3%). *Military expenditure as percentage of GNP* (1997): 9.7% (world 2.6%); per capita expenditure U.S.$1,698.

[1]Excluding West Bank (2,278 sq mi [5,900 sq km]), Gaza Strip (140 sq mi [363 sq km]), Golan Heights (454 sq mi [1,176 sq km]), East Jerusalem (27 sq mi [70 sq km]), Sea of Galilee (63 sq mi [164 sq km]), and the Dead Sea (120 sq mi [310 sq km]). [2]January 1. [3]Includes population of Golan Heights and East Jerusalem and excludes Jewish population of the West Bank and Gaza Strip (169,400). [4]Jewish population only. [5]1997 prices. [6]Finance includes other business activities. [7]Public and community services includes education, health, social, and personal services. [8]Services includes private households with domestic personnel. [9]Includes 202,000 unemployed. [10]1993. [11]Civilian labour force. [12]Urban population only. [13]Import figures are c.i.f. in balance of trade; import and export figures are net gross for commodities and trading partners. [14]El Al only. [15]Includes intermediate schools. [16]1992–93.

Internet resources for further information:
- **Central Bureau of Statistics (Israel) http://www.cbs.gov.il**

Italy

Official name: Repubblica Italiana (Italian Republic).
Form of government: republic with two legislative houses (Senate [326[1]]; Chamber of Deputies [630]).
Chief of state: President.
Head of government: Prime Minister.
Capital: Rome.
Official language: Italian.
Official religion: none.
Monetary unit: 1 lira (Lit, plural lire) = 100 centesimi; valuation (Oct. 6, 2000) 1 U.S.$ = Lit 2,226; 1 £ = Lit 3,221.

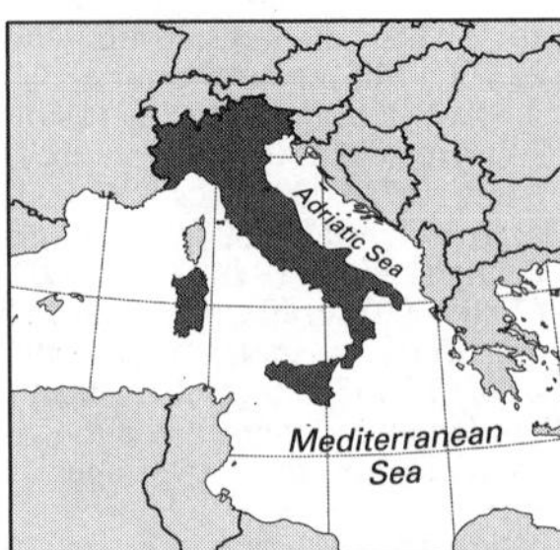

Area and population

Regions / Provinces[3]	Capitals	area sq mi	area sq km	population 1996[2] estimate[4]
Abruzzi	L'Aquila	4,168	10,794	1,270,591
Chieti	Chieti	999	2,587	388,276
L'Aquila	L'Aquila	1,944	5,034	303,879
Pescara	Pescara	473	1,225	292,202
Teramo	Teramo	752	1,948	286,234
Basilicata	Potenza	3,858	9,992	609,238
Matera	Matera	1,331	3,447	208,154
Potenza	Potenza	2,527	6,545	401,084
Calabria	Catanzaro	5,823	15,080	2,075,842
Catanzaro	Catanzaro	924	2,392	384,496
Cosenza	Cosenza	2,568	6,650	753,815
Crotone	Crotone	662	1,716	179,336
Reggio di Calabria	Reggio di Calabria	1,229	3,183	579,009
Vibo Valentia	Vibo Valentia	440	1,139	179,186
Campania	Naples	5,249	13,595	5,762,518
Avellino	Avellino	1,078	2,792	441,675
Benevento	Benevento	800	2,071	295,803
Caserta	Caserta	1,019	2,639	840,737
Napoli	Naples	452	1,171	3,098,397
Salerno	Salerno	1,900	4,922	1,085,906
Emilia-Romagna	Bologna	8,542	22,123	3,924,456
Bologna	Bologna	1,429	3,702	905,838
Ferrara	Ferrara	1,016	2,632	355,341
Forlì-Cesena	Forlì	969	2,510	350,158
Modena	Modena	1,039	2,690	609,723
Parma	Parma	1,332	3,449	392,018
Piacenza	Piacenza	1,000	2,589	266,363
Ravenna	Ravenna	718	1,859	349,992
Reggio nell'Emilia	Reggio nell'Emilia	885	2,292	429,865
Rimini	Rimini	154	400	265,158
Friuli-Venezia Giulia	Trieste	3,029	7,845	1,188,897
Gorizia	Gorizia	180	467	138,041
Pordenone	Pordenone	878	2,273	276,010
Trieste	Trieste	82	212	254,746
Udine	Udine	1,889	4,893	520,100
Lazio	Rome	6,642	17,203	5,202,098
Frosinone	Frosinone	1,251	3,239	489,923
Latina	Latina	869	2,251	497,632
Rieti	Rieti	1,061	2,749	150,305
Roma	Rome	2,066	5,352	3,774,987
Viterbo	Viterbo	1,395	3,612	289,251
Liguria	Genoa	2,092	5,418	1,658,513
Genova	Genoa	709	1,836	933,127
Imperia	Imperia	446	1,155	216,996
La Spezia	La Spezia	341	882	225,285
Savona	Savona	596	1,545	283,105
Lombardia	Milan	9,211	23,857	8,924,870
Bergamo	Bergamo	1,051	2,722	936,667
Brescia	Brescia	1,846	4,782	1,065,172
Como	Como	497	1,288	531,160
Cremona	Cremona	684	1,771	330,946
Lecco	Lecco	315	816	302,575
Lodi	Lodi	302	783	190,196
Mantova	Mantova	903	2,339	368,725
Milano	Milan	765	1,980	3,720,534
Pavia	Pavia	1,145	2,965	494,640
Sondrio	Sondrio	1,240	3,212	177,079
Varese	Varese	463	1,199	807,176
Marche	Ancona	3,743	9,693	1,443,172
Ancona	Ancona	749	1,940	440,239
Ascoli Piceno	Ascoli Piceno	806	2,087	365,826
Macerata	Macerata	1,071	2,774	298,295
Pesaro e Urbino	Pesaro	1,117	2,892	338,812
Molise	Campobasso	1,713	4,438	331,446
Campobasso	Campobasso	1,123	2,909	239,227
Isernia	Isernia	590	1,529	92,219
Piemonte	Turin	9,807[5]	25,399	4,288,866
Alessandria	Alessandria	1,375	3,560	433,300
Asti	Asti	583	1,511	209,798
Biella	Biella	352	913	190,728
Cuneo	Cuneo	2,665	6,903	551,373
Novara	Novara	530	1,373	339,375
Torino	Turin	2,637	6,830	2,220,724
Verbano-Cusio-Ossola	Verbania	858	2,221	161,248
Vercelli	Vercelli	806	2,088	182,320
Puglia	Bari	7,470	19,348	4,082,953
Bari	Bari	1,980	5,129	1,560,347
Brindisi	Brindisi	710	1,838	413,334
Foggia	Foggia	2,774	7,185	699,214
Lecce	Lecce	1,065	2,759	817,524
Taranto	Taranto	941	2,437	592,534
Sardegna	Cagliari	9,301	24,090	1,660,701
Cagliari	Cagliari	2,662	6,895	769,993
Nuoro	Nuoro	2,720	7,044	272,985
Oristano	Oristano	1,016	2,631	158,131
Sassari	Sassari	2,903	7,520	459,592
Sicilia (Sicily)	Palermo	9,926	25,709	5,094,735
Agrigento	Agrigento	1,175	3,042	475,669
Caltanissetta	Caltanissetta	822	2,128	282,999
Catania	Catania	1,371	3,552	1,088,323
Enna	Enna	989	2,562	186,145
Messina	Messina	1,254	3,248	683,315
Palermo	Palermo	1,927	4,992	1,240,252
Ragusa	Ragusa	623	1,614	297,378
Siracusa	Siracusa	814	2,109	406,566
Trapani	Trapani	951	2,462	434,088
Toscana	Florence	8,877	22,992[5]	3,523,238
Arezzo	Arezzo	1,248	3,232	316,735
Firenze	Florence	1,365	3,536	952,908
Grosseto	Grosseto	1,739	4,504	216,713
Livorno	Livorno	468	1,213	336,759
Lucca	Lucca	684	1,773	375,591
Massa-Carrara	Massa-Carrara	447	1,157	201,242
Pisa	Pisa	945	2,448	384,550
Pistoia	Pistoia	373	965	265,995
Prato	Prato	133	344	221,528
Siena	Siena	1,475	3,821	251,217
Trentino-Alto Adige	Bolzano	5,258	13,618	913,169
Bolzano-Bozen	Bolzano	2,857	7,400	451,563
Trento	Trento	2,401	6,218	461,606
Umbria	Perugia	3,265	8,456	825,910
Perugia	Perugia	2,446	6,334	602,276
Terni	Terni	819	2,122	223,634
Valle d'Aosta	Aosta	1,259	3,262	118,723
Veneto	Venice	7,090	18,364	4,433,060
Belluno	Belluno	1,420	3,678	211,996
Padova	Padova	827	2,142	835,029
Rovigo	Rovigo	691	1,789	245,314
Treviso	Treviso	956	2,477	757,864
Venezia	Venice	950	2,460	817,597
Verona	Verona	1,195	3,096	801,363
Vicenza	Vicenza	1,051	2,722	763,897
TOTAL		116,324[6]	301,277[6]	57,332,996

Demography

Population (2000): 57,723,000.
Density (2000): persons per sq mi 496.2, persons per sq km 191.6.
Urban-rural (1999): urban 66.9%; rural 33.1%.
Sex distribution (1999): male 48.53%; female 51.47%.
Age breakdown (1996[2]): under 15, 14.9%; 15–29, 21.9%; 30–44, 21.7%; 45–59, 19.0%; 60–74, 15.8%; 75 and over, 6.7%.
Population projection: (2010) 57,498,000; (2020) 55,626,000.
Doubling time: not applicable; population stable.
Ethnolinguistic composition (1983): Italian 94.1%; Sardinian 2.7%; Rhaetian 1.3%; other 1.9%.
Religious affiliation (1996): Roman Catholic 81.7%; nonreligious 13.6%; Muslim 1.2%; other 3.5%.
Major cities (2000[2, 4]): Rome 2,643,581; Milan 1,300,977; Naples 1,002,619; Turin 903,703; Palermo 683,794; Genoa 636,104; Bologna 381,161; Florence 376,682; Catania 337,862; Bari 331,848; Venice 277,305.
National origin (1991): Italian 99.3%; foreign-born 0.7%, of which European 0.3%, African 0.2%, Asian 0.1%, other 0.1%.
Mobility (1991). Population living in the same commune as in 1986: 93.3%; another commune, same province 3.4%; different province 2.5%; abroad 0.8%.
Households. Average household size (1991) 2.7; composition of households: 1 person 19.5%, 2 persons 21.9%, 3 persons 25.2%, 4 persons 21.4%, 5 or more persons 12.0%. Family households (1991): 15,538,335 (73.8%); nonfamily 5,527,105 (26.2%), of which one-person 19.5%.
Immigration (1995): immigrants 96,710, from Europe 32.7%, of which EC countries 23.9%; Africa 15.9%; Western Hemisphere 15.5%; Asia 11.1%.

Vital statistics

Birth rate per 1,000 population (1999): 9.2 (world avg. 22.1); (1996) legitimate 91.7%; illegitimate 8.3%.
Death rate per 1,000 population (1999): 9.9 (world avg. 8.9).
Natural increase rate per 1,000 population (1999): –0.7 (world avg. 13.2).
Total fertility rate (avg. births per childbearing woman; 1999): 1.2.
Marriage rate per 1,000 population (1997): 4.7.
Divorce rate per 1,000 population (1994): 0.5.
Life expectancy at birth (1999): male 75.7 years; female 82.3 years.
Major causes of death per 100,000 population (1995): diseases of the circulatory system 424.3; malignant neoplasms 258.2; diseases of the respiratory system 59.1; diseases of the digestive system 52.2; accidents and violence 38.8.

Social indicators

Educational attainment (1995). Percentage of labour force age 15 and over having: basic literacy or primary education 40.4%; secondary 30.5%; post-secondary technical training 5.1%; some college 19.2%; college degree 4.3%.
Quality of working life. Average workweek (1995): 37.0 hours. Annual rate per 100,000 workers (1996) for: injury or accident 3,208; death 7.5. Percentage of labour force insured for damages or income loss (1992) resulting from: injury 100%; permanent disability 100%; death 100%. Number of working days lost to labour stoppages per 1,000 workers (1996): 97. Average duration of journey to work: n.a. Rate per 1,000 workers of discouraged (unemployed no longer seeking work; 1990): 1.1.
Material well-being. Rate per 1,000 of population possessing (1995): telephone 434; automobile 550; television 436.
Social participation. Eligible voters participating in last national election (April 21, 1996): 91.0%. Trade union membership in total workforce (1990): c. 28%.
Social deviance (1997). Offense rate per 100,000 population for: murder 2.6; rape 57.2; assault 210.4[7]; theft, including burglary and housebreaking 2,715; suicide 6.3[8].
Access to services (1991). Nearly 100% of dwellings have access to electricity, a safe water supply, and toilet facilities.

Leisure (1992). Favourite leisure activities (as percentage of household spending on culture): sporting events 17.8%; cinema 16.3%; theatre 14.0%.

National economy

Gross national product (1998): U.S.$1,157,001,000,000 (U.S.$20,090 per capita).

Structure of gross domestic product and labour force

	1997			
	in value (Lit '000,000,000)	% of total value	labour force	% of labour force
Agriculture	51,332	2.6	1,731,300	7.8
Mining	9	9	9	9
Manufacturing	500,096[9]	25.6[9]	4,671,300[9]	21.0[9]
Construction	94,887	4.9	1,564,100	7.0
Public utilities	9	9	9	9
Transp. and commun.	126,692	6.5	1,385,400	6.2
Trade	358,361	18.4	4,882,400	22.0
Finance	91,166	4.7	424,100	1.9
Pub. admin., defense	257,221	13.2	4,251,900	19.2
Services	253,331	13.0	3,292,600	14.8
Other	217,594[10]	11.1[10]	11	11
TOTAL	1,950,680	100.0	22,203,100	100.0[5]

Budget (1995). Revenue: Lit 472,066,000,000,000 (income taxes 41.0%, of which individual 35.1%, corporate 5.9%; value-added and excise taxes 30.6%). Expenditures: Lit 696,860,000,000,000 (debt service 27.5%; social security 18.4%; education 9.1%; transportation 4.7%; defense 2.8%).
Public debt (1998[12]): U.S.$1,319,000,000,000.
Tourism (1998): receipts U.S.$29,866,000,000; expenditures U.S.$17,653,000,000.

Manufacturing, mining, and construction enterprises (1995)

	no. of enterprises	no. of employees[13]	hourly wages as a % of avg. of all wages	annual value added (Lit '000,000,000)
Manufacturing				
Metal products	5,780	360,979	...	36,249
Machinery (nonelectrical)	4,503	379,027	...	35,221
Industrial chemicals	1,206	180,836	...	27,505
Electrical machinery	2,962	303,439	...	26,306
Food products	2,549	224,025	...	22,878
Transport equipment	1,122	275,077	...	22,642
Printing, publishing[14]	2,086	148,757	...	16,150
Pottery, ceramics, and glass	2,128	149,586	...	14,361
Textiles[15]	3,514	215,387	...	14,335
Rubber and plastic products	1,836	123,119	...	12,711
Wearing apparel	2,436	114,059	...	7,279
Paper and paper products[14]	...	...	...	...
Petroleum and gas	108	22,566	...	4,221
Mining and quarrying	340	20,013	...	5,991
Construction	6,228	1,564,100	...	94,887

Production (metric tons except as noted). Agriculture, forestry, fishing (1999): sugar beets 12,521,000, grapes 9,208,000, corn (maize) 9,031,000, wheat 7,840,000, tomatoes 5,369,000, olives 2,679,000, potatoes 2,224,000, apples 2,115,000, oranges 1,921,000, peaches and nectarines 1,428,000, rice 1,400,000, soybeans 1,231,000, barley 1,200,000; livestock (number of live animals) 10,770,000 sheep, 8,225,000 pigs, 7,150,000 cattle, 130,000,000 chickens; roundwood (1998) 4,367,000 cu m; fish catch (1996) 609,768. Mining and quarrying (1997): rock salt 3,507,000; feldspar 2,200,000; barite 26,300; lead 17,600; zinc 15,400. Manufacturing (1996): cement 33,714,914[7]; crude steel 24,284,900; pig iron 10,324,300; glass 3,981,047[7]; textiles 2,340,600; sulfuric acid 2,214,000; wine 60,000,000 hectolitres; beer 10,616,173 hectolitres[7]; olive oil 6,290,000 hectolitres[15]; 6,995,818 washing machines[7]; 5,908,224 refrigerators[7]; 3,063,999 motorized road vehicles, of which 1,562,865 automobiles, 984,016 motorcycles, 258,529 trucks and buses; 2,779,827 colour televisions[7]. Construction (1996): residential 65,945,764 cu m; commercial 81,430,355 cu m.

Service enterprises (1997)

	no. of enterprises[16]	no. of employees	hourly wage as a % of all wages	annual value added (Lit '000,000,000)
Public utilities	327	257,000[7]	...	102,495[7]
Transportation / Communications	3,230	1,385,400	...	126,692
Finance	...	424,000	...	91,166
Wholesale and retail trade	8,115	4,882,400	...	358,361
Pub. admin., services	...	4,251,900	...	257,221

Energy production (consumption): electricity (kW-hr; 1994) 231,783,000,000 (269,382,000,000); coal (metric tons; 1994) 267,000 (16,672,000); crude petroleum (barrels; 1994) 33,422,000 (582,644,000); petroleum products (metric tons; 1994) 83,049,000 (89,500,000); natural gas (cu m; 1994) 20,209,000,000 (48,326,000,000).
Population economically active (1997): total 22,203,100; activity rate of total population 38.6% (participation rates: ages 15–64, 57.7%[8] female 34.6%[8]; unemployed 12.6%).

Price and earnings indexes (1995 = 100)

	1994	1995	1996	1997	1998	1999
Consumer price index	95.0	100.0	104.0	106.1	108.2	110.0
Earnings index	97.0	100.0	103.2	106.9	109.9	112.4

Household income and expenditure (1995). Average household size 2.7; average annual income per household (1984) Lit 19,692,000 (U.S.$11,208); sources of income (1994): salaries and wages 40.2%, property income and self-employment 37.9%, transfer payments 21.9%; expenditure (1994): food and beverages 21.7%, housing 19.5%, transportation and communications 16.8%, recreation and education 6.4%.

Financial aggregates

	1993	1994	1995	1996	1997	1998
Exchange rate, Lit per:						
U.S. dollar	1,573.7	1,612.4	1,628.9	1,530.6	1,759.2	1,653.1
£	2,363.7	2,469.6	2,571.2	2,690.8	2,909.4	2,749.9
SDR	2,340.5	2,379.2	2,355.7	2,200.9	2,373.6	2,327.6
International reserves (U.S.$)						
Total (excl. gold; '000,000)	27,545	32,265	34,905	45,948	55,739	29,888
SDRs ('000,000)	241	125	53[14]	29	67	111
Reserve pos. in IMF ('000,000)	2,164	2,033	1,963	1,855	2,241	4,330
Foreign exchange ('000,000)	25,140	30,107	32,942	44,064	54,431	25,447
Gold ('000,000 fine troy oz)	66.67	66.67	66.67	66.67	66.67	83.36
% world reserves	7.3	7.3	7.3	7.3	7.5	8.6
Interest and prices						
Central bank discount (%)	8.00	7.50	9.00	7.50	5.50	3.00
Govt. bond yield (%)	11.21	10.57	11.98	8.93	6.47	4.55
Industrial share prices (1990 = 100)	83.5	104.1	95.4	96.0	137.7	220.5
Balance of payments (U.S.$'000,000)						
Balance of visible trade	32,825	35,497	44,082	60,822	39,877	35,361
Imports, f.o.b.	−136,328	−154,308	−187,254	−190,021	−200,527	−206,941
Exports, f.o.b.	169,153	189,805	231,336	250,843	240,404	242,572
Balance of invisibles	−21,763	−19,875	−18,378	−20,823	−7,474	−15,363
Balance of payments, current account	11,062	15,622	25,704	−39,999	32,403	19,998

Land use (1994): forest 23.0%; pasture 15.4%; agriculture 37.9%; other 23.7%.

Foreign trade

Balance of trade (current prices)

	1993	1994	1995	1996	1997	1998
Lit '000,000,000	50,789	50,957	65,841	67,775	51,609	45,972
% of total	10.6%	9.1%	9.6%	9.6%	6.8%	5.8%

Imports (1997): Lit 354,455,700,000,000 (machinery and transport equipment 33.8%, of which transport equipment 12.6%, chemicals 13.8%; metal 10.9%; food 7.6%; textiles 5.4%; plastics 2.2%). *Major import sources:* Germany 18.0%; France 13.2%; U.K. 6.7%; The Netherlands 6.2%; U.S. 5.0%; Spain 4.8%; Belgium-Luxembourg 4.7%.
Exports (1997): Lit 405,731,600,000,000 (machinery and transport equipment 40.8%, of which transport equipment 10.3%, electrical machinery 9.6%, textiles and wearing apparel 11.4%; chemicals 8.2%; plastics 3.4%). *Major export destinations:* Germany 16.4%; France 12.2%; U.S. 7.9%; U.K. 7.2%; Spain 5.2%.

Transport and communications

Transport. Railroads (1997): length 19,527 km; passenger-km 69,675,000,000; metric ton-km cargo 25,447,000,000. Roads (1995): total length 314,360 km (paved 100%). Vehicles (1995): passenger cars 31,700,000; trucks and buses 5,127,000. Merchant marine (1995): vessels (100 gross tons and over) 1,355; total deadweight tonnage 6,905,313. Air transport (1996): passenger-km 29,471,000,000; metric ton-km cargo 1,219,000,000; airports (1997) 34.

Communications

Medium	date	unit	number	units per 1,000 persons
Daily newspapers	1996	circulation	5,985,000	105
Radio	1997	receivers	50,500,000	880
Television	1998	receivers	28,000,000	488
Telephones	1998	main lines	25,986,000	453
Cellular telephones	1998	subscribers	20,489,000	357
Personal computers	1998	units	10,000,000	174
Internet	1998	users	3,000,000	52.2

Education and health

Literacy (1995): total population age 15 and over literate 48,100,000 (98.1%); males literate 23,800,000 (98.6%); females literate 24,300,000 (97.6%).

Education (1997–98)

	schools	teachers	students	student/ teacher ratio
Primary (age 6–10)	19,418	289,055[17]	2,816,161	9.8[17]
Secondary (age 11–18)	8,829	214,861[17]	1,806,613	8.9[17]
Voc., teacher tr.	7,848	313,001[17]	2,628,377	8.5[17]
Higher[18, 19]	48	58,874	1,601,873	27.2

Health (1994): physicians (1993) 207,319 (1 per 193 persons); hospital beds 355,739 (1 per 161 persons); infant mortality rate (1997) 5.5.
Food (1997): daily per capita caloric intake 3,507 (vegetable products 74%, animal products 26%); 139% of FAO recommended minimum requirement.

Military

Total active duty personnel (1999): 265,500 (army 62.4%, navy 14.3%, air force 23.3%). *Military expenditure as percentage of GNP* (1997): 2.0% (world 2.6%); per capita expenditure U.S.$395.

[1]Includes 11 nonelective seats. [2]January 1. [3]Six provinces were created in 1992. [4]Resident population only. [5]Detail does not add to total given because of rounding. [6]The total area for Italy, per 1998 survey, is 301,337 sq km (116,347 sq mi). [7]1995. [8]1996. [9]Manufacturing includes Mining and Public utilities. [10]Other includes indirect import charges and building rental less imputed bank service charges. [11]The 2,804,000 unemployed are not calculated separately. [12]Includes domestic and foreign public debt. [13]Total number of persons engaged. [14]Printing, publishing includes Paper and paper products. [15]1993. [16]Enterprises with 20 or more persons engaged. [17]1995–96. [18]Universities only. [19]1994–95.

Internet resources for further information:
- **National Statistical Institute http://www.istat.it/homeing.html**

Jamaica

Official name: Jamaica.
Form of government: constitutional monarchy with two legislative houses (Senate [21]; House of Representatives [60]).
Chief of state: British Monarch represented by Governor-General.
Head of government: Prime Minister.
Capital: Kingston.
Official language: English.
Monetary unit: 1 Jamaica dollar (J$) = 100 cents; valuation (Oct. 6, 2000) 1 U.S.$ = J$44.00; 1 £ = J$63.65.

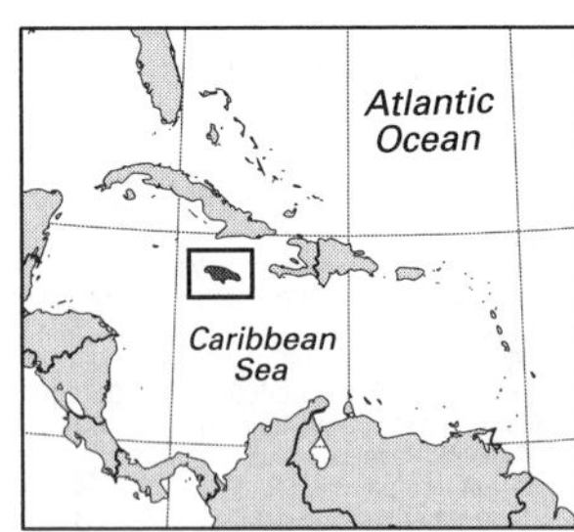

Area and population

Parishes	Capitals	area sq mi	area sq km	population 1999[1] estimate
Clarendon	May Pen	462	1,196	227,100
Hanover	Lucea	174	450	67,900
Kingston	[2]	8	22	[3]
Manchester	Mandeville	321	830	183,000
Portland	Port Antonio	314	814	79,400
Saint Andrew	[2]	166	431	707,400
Saint Ann	Saint Ann's Bay	468	1,213	162,000
Saint Catherine	Spanish Town	460	1,192	409,500
Saint Elizabeth	Black River	468	1,212	148,900
Saint James	Montego Bay	230	595	176,100
Saint Mary	Port Maria	236	611	112,900
Saint Thomas	Morant Bay	287	743	91,400
Trelawny	Falmouth	338	875	72,700
Westmoreland	Savanna-la-Mar	312	807	137,900
TOTAL		4,244	10,991	2,576,200

Demography

Population (2000): 2,619,000.
Density (2000): persons per sq mi 617.1, persons per sq km 238.3.
Urban-rural (1998): urban 55.1%; rural 44.9%.
Sex distribution (1998): male 49.85%; female 50.15%.
Age breakdown (1998): under 15, 31.5%; 15–29, 27.5%; 30–44, 20.9%; 45–59, 10.4%; 60–74, 6.6%; 75 and over, 3.1%.
Population projection: (2010) 2,815,000; (2020) 3,087,000.
Doubling time: 41 years.
Ethnic composition (1982): black 74.7%; mixed black 12.8%; East Indian 1.3%; other 11.2%, of which not stated 9.5%.
Religious affiliation (1995): Protestant 39.0%, of which Pentecostal 10.5%, Seventh-day Adventist 6.1%, Baptist 5.3%; Roman Catholic 10.4%; Anglican 3.7%; other (including nonreligious) 46.9%[4].
Major cities (1991): Kingston 103,771[5] (metropolitan area 587,798); Spanish Town 92,383; Portmore 90,138; Montego Bay 83,446; May Pen 46,785.

Vital statistics

Birth rate per 1,000 population (1998): 23.1 (world avg. 22.1).
Death rate per 1,000 population (1998): 6.2 (world avg. 8.9).
Natural increase rate per 1,000 population (1998): 16.9 (world avg. 13.2).
Total fertility rate (avg. births per childbearing woman; 1997): 2.8.
Marriage rate per 1,000 population (1996): 7.4.
Life expectancy at birth (1999): male 73.1 years; female 77.0 years.
Major causes of death per 100,000 population (1991): diseases of the circulatory system 189.4; malignant neoplasms (cancers) 84.1; endocrine and metabolic disorders 51.3; diseases of the respiratory system 30.1.

National economy

Budget (1998–99). Revenue J$74,096,000,000 (tax revenue 90.4%, of which income taxes 34.9%, consumption taxes 28.3%, custom duties 9.6%; nontax revenue 9.6%). Expenditures: J$93,267,000,000 (current expenditure 91.5%, of which debt interest 37.4%).
Public debt (external, outstanding; 1998): U.S.$3,079,000,000.
Production (metric tons except as noted). Agriculture, forestry, fishing (1999): sugarcane 2,400,000, yams 198,400, vegetables and melons 183,701, citrus fruits 154,000, bananas 130,000, coconuts 115,000, pumpkins, squash, and gourds 42,000, plantains 33,500, sweet potatoes 27,000, cabbages 23,000, carrots 22,000, tomatoes 18,000; livestock (number of live animals) 440,000 goats, 400,000 cattle, 180,000 pigs; roundwood (1998) 342,700 cu m; fish catch (1998) 6,720. Mining and quarrying (1998): bauxite 4,034,600; alumina 3,440,000; gypsum 154,500. Manufacturing (value added in constant 1991–95 prices, J$'000,000; 1995): machinery and equipment 593.6; food processing 580.3; petroleum products 351.3; rubber and plastic products 324.1; textiles and clothing 257.0; tobacco and tobacco products 255.2; metal and nonmetallic products 223.6. Construction (1995): residential units completed 7,067[6]; factory space completed 6,989 sq m[7]. Energy production (consumption): electricity (kW-hr; 1996) 6,038,000,000 (6,038,000,000); coal, none (none); crude petroleum (barrels; 1996) none (7,828,000); petroleum products (metric tons; 1996) 1,055,000 (3,135,000); natural gas, none (none).
Population economically active (October 1999): total 1,115,600; activity rate of total population 43.1% (participation rates: ages 14 and over 64.1%; female 44.7%; unemployed 16.0%).

Price and earnings indexes (1995 = 100)

	1993	1994	1995	1996	1997	1998	1999
Consumer price index	61.7	83.4	100.0	126.4	138.6	150.6	165.3
Earnings index	...	...	...	...	...	...	...

Gross national product (1998): U.S.$4,481,000,000 (U.S.$1,740 per capita).

Structure of gross domestic product and labour force

	1998 in value J$'000,000	% of total value	labour force	% of labour force
Agriculture	18,534.7	7.9	203,775	18.0
Mining	11,340.8	4.9	5,575	0.5
Manufacturing	35,014.2	15.1	84,100	7.4
Construction	26,320.4	11.4	79,700	7.1
Public utilities	5,323.2	2.3	6,450	0.6
Transp. and commun.	27,389.5	11.8	54,925	4.9
Trade	57,967.0	25.0	205,375	18.2
Pub. admin., defense	29,327.0	12.7		
Finance, real estate	30,089.4	13.0	312,275	27.7
Services	7,067.7	3.0		
Other	–16,595.2[8]	–7.1[8]	176,225[9]	15.6[9]
TOTAL	231,778.7	100.0	1,128,600[10]	100.0

Household income and expenditure. Average household size (1991) 4.2; average annual income per household (1988) J$8,356 (U.S.$1,525); sources of income (1989): wages and salaries 66.1%, self-employment 19.3%, transfers 14.6%; expenditure (1988)[11]: food and beverages 55.6%, housing 7.9%, fuel and other household supplies 7.4%, health care 7.0%, transportation 6.4%.
Tourism (1998): receipts U.S.$1,197,000,000; expenditures U.S.$198,000,000.

Foreign trade

Balance of trade (current prices)

	1993	1994	1995	1996	1997	1998	1999
U.S.$'000,000	–815.1	–551.2	–829.3	–994.2	–1,120.8	–1,101.9	–1,654.8
% of total	34.9%	28.7%	18.7%	23.5%	24.8%	25.7%	40.1%

Imports (1999): U.S.$2,892,761,000 (raw materials 50.5%, of which fuels 10.8%; consumer goods 33.2%, of which food 9.4%; capital goods 16.3%, of which machinery and apparatus 7.6%). *Major import sources* (1997): U.S. 48.1%; Trinidad and Tobago 7.8%; Japan 6.9%; France 5.0%; U.K. 3.7%; Canada 3.0%; Mexico 2.6%.
Exports (1999): U.S.$1,237,982,000 (crude materials 55.7%; food 19.1%; beverages and tobacco 4.8%; chemicals 3.6%; machinery and transport equipment 2.2%; manufactured goods 0.7%). *Major export destinations:* U.S. 33.4%; Canada 14.1%; U.K. 13.4%; The Netherlands 10.2%; Norway 5.8%; Japan 2.3%.

Transport and communications

Transport. Railroads (1991): route length 129 mi; 208 km; passenger-mi 12,127,000[7], passenger-km 19,516,000[7]; short ton-mi cargo 1,700,000, metric ton-km cargo 2,482,000. Roads (1996): total length 11,800 mi, 19,000 km (paved 71%). Vehicles (1997–98): passenger cars 156,751; trucks and buses 61,482. Air transport (1999)[12]: passenger-mi 1,037,565,000, passenger-km 1,669,803,000; short ton-mi cargo 20,186,000, metric ton-km cargo 29,471,000; airports (1997) with scheduled flights 4.

Communications

Medium	date	unit	number	units per 1,000 persons
Daily newspapers	1996	circulation	158,000	63
Radio	1997	receivers	1,215,000	483
Television	1998	receivers	480,000	187
Telephones	1997	main lines	419,362	165
Cellular telephones	1996	subscribers	54,640	22
Personal computers	1998	units	100,000	39
Internet	1998	users	50,000	20

Education and health

Educational attainment (1982). Percentage of population age 25 and over having: no formal schooling 3.2%; some primary education 79.8%; some secondary 15.0%; complete secondary and higher 2.0%. *Literacy* (2000): total population age 15 and over literate 88%; males literate 83%; females literate 91%.

Education (1994–95)

	schools	teachers	students	student/ teacher ratio
Primary (age 6–11)[13]	788[14]	11,283	319,298	28.3
Secondary (age 12–16)	126	8,377	207,035	24.7
Voc., teacher tr.	18	950	15,898	16.7
Higher	15[15]	1,047[16]	24,200	17.9[16]

Health (1995): physicians 417[17] (1 per 6,043 persons); hospital beds (1993) 5,023 (1 per 492 persons); infant mortality rate (1998) 14.5.
Food (1998): daily per capita caloric intake 2,711 (vegetable products 83%, animal products 17%); 121% of FAO recommended minimum requirement.

Military

Total active duty personnel (1999): 2,830 (army 88.3%; coast guard 6.7%; air force 5.0%). *Military expenditure as percentage of GNP* (1997): 0.9% (world 2.6%); per capita expenditure U.S.$20.

[1]January 1. [2]The parishes of Kingston and Saint Andrew are jointly administered from the Half Way Tree section of Saint Andrew. [3]Kingston included with Saint Andrew. [4]Includes *c.* 0.7% Rastafarian. [5]City of Kingston is coextensive with Kingston parish. [6]51% public sector. [7]1990. [8]Less imputed service charges. [9]Includes 186,700 unemployed. [10]Detail does not add to total given because of rounding. [11]Weights of consumer price index components. [12]Air Jamaica only. [13]Includes lower-secondary students at all-age schools. [14]1991–92. [15]1988–89. [16]1987–88. [17]Public health only.

Internet resources for further information:
- **Statistics Institute of Jamaica http://www.statinja.com**

Japan

Official name: Nihon (Japan).
Form of government: constitutional monarchy with a national Diet consisting of two legislative houses (House of Councillors [252]; House of Representatives [480]).
Chief of state: Emperor.
Head of government: Prime Minister.
Capital: Tokyo.
Official language: Japanese.
Official religion: none.
Monetary unit: 1 yen (¥) = 100 sen; valuation (Oct. 6, 2000) 1 U.S.$ = ¥108.76; 1 £ = ¥157.33.

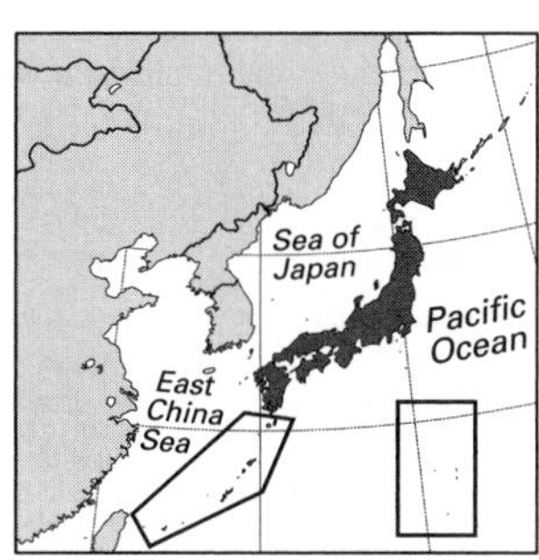

Area and population

Regions / Prefectures	Capitals	area sq mi	area sq km	population 1999[1] estimate
Chūbu				
Aichi	Nagoya	1,984	5,139	7,007,775
Fukui	Fukui	1,619	4,192	830,550
Gifu	Gifu	4,091	10,596	2,117,661
Ishikawa	Kanazawa	1,621	4,198	1,185,592
Nagano	Nagano	5,245	13,585	2,223,124
Niigata	Niigata	4,857	12,579	2,489,782
Shizuoka	Shizuoka	3,001	7,773	3,776,318
Toyama	Toyama	1,642	4,252	1,125,354
Yamanashi	Kōfu	1,723	4,463	893,090
Chūgoku				
Hiroshima	Hiroshima	3,269	8,467	2,883,178
Okayama	Okayama	2,738	7,092	1,959,159
Shimane	Matsue	2,559[2]	6,629[2]	763,716
Tottori	Tottori	1,349[2]	3,494[2]	614,091
Yamaguchi	Yamaguchi	2,358	6,107	1,538,134
Hokkaidō				
Hokkaidō (Territory)	Sapporo	32,247	83,520	5,694,913
Kantō				
Chiba	Chiba	1,989	5,151	5,920,437
Gumma	Maebashi	2,454	6,356	2,029,569
Ibaraki	Mito	2,353	6,094	3,002,449
Kanagawa	Yokohama	928	2,403	8,443,277
Saitama	Urawa	1,467	3,799	6,929,091
Tochigi	Utsunomiya	2,476	6,414	2,011,849
Kinki				
Hyōgo	Kōbe	3,236	8,381	5,483,627
Mie	Tsu	2,231	5,778	1,864,388
Nara	Nara	1,425	3,692	1,449,184
Shiga	Ōtsu	1,551	4,016	1,333,106
Wakayama	Wakayama	1,824	4,725	1,074,078
Kyūshū				
Fukuoka	Fukuoka	1,916	4,963	4,999,811
Kagoshima	Kagoshima	3,539	9,167	1,788,311
Kumamoto	Kumamoto	2,860	7,408	1,864,675
Miyazaki	Miyazaki	2,986	7,735	1,175,600
Nagasaki	Nagasaki	1,588	4,113	1,524,666
Ōita	Ōita	2,447	6,338	1,225,847
Saga	Saga	942	2,440	883,624
Ryukyu				
Okinawa	Naha	871	2,255	1,311,608
Shikoku				
Ehime	Matsuyama	2,190	5,672	1,496,917
Kagawa	Takamatsu	727	1,883	1,029,464
Kōchi	Kōchi	2,744	7,107	810,279
Tokushima	Tokushima	1,601	4,146	829,529
Tohoku				
Akita	Akita	4,484[3]	11,613[3]	1,196,166
Aomori	Aomori	3,714[3]	9,619[3]	1,475,439
Fukushima	Fukushima	5,322	13,784	2,135,216
Iwate	Morioka	5,898	15,277	1,414,100
Miyagi	Sendai	2,815	7,292	2,360,193
Yamagata	Yamagata	3,601	9,327	1,250,370
Metropolis				
Tōkyō[4]	Tokyo	836	2,166	11,837,408
Urban prefectures				
Kyōto[5]	Kyōto	1,781	4,613	2,632,630
Ōsaka[5]	Ōsaka	722	1,869	8,800,979
TOTAL		145,883[6, 7]	377,835[6, 7]	126,686,324

Demography

Population (2000): 126,920,000.
Density (2000): persons per sq mi 870.0, persons per sq km 335.9.
Urban-rural (1995): urban 77.6%; rural 22.4%.
Sex distribution (1999[8]): male 48.9%; female 51.1%.
Age breakdown (1999[8]): under 15, 14.8%; 15–29, 20.9%; 30–44, 19.3%; 45–59, 22.2%; 60–74, 16.0%; 75 and over, 6.8%.
Population projection: (2010) 127,926,000; (2020) 124,249,000.
Doubling time: not applicable; doubling time exceeds 100 years.
Composition by nationality (1997[9]): Japanese 99.1%; Korean 0.5%; Chinese 0.2%; other 0.2%.
Place of birth (1995): 99.3% native-born; 0.7% foreign-born (mainly Korean).
Immigration (1998[9]): permanent immigrants/registered aliens admitted 1,482,707, from North and South Korea 43.5%, Taiwan, Hong Kong, and China 17.0%, Brazil 15.7%, Philippines 6.3%, United States 2.9%, Peru 2.7%, Thailand 1.4%, United Kingdom 1.0%, Indonesia 0.8%, Vietnam 0.8%, Canada 0.6%, Iran 0.5%, India 0.5%, other 6.3%.
Major cities (1995): Tokyo 11,771,819; Yokohama 3,307,408; Ōsaka 2,602,352; Nagoya 2,152,258; Sapporo 1,756,968; Kyōto 1,463,601; Kōbe 1,423,830; Fukuoka 1,284,741; Kawasaki 1,202,811; Hiroshima 1,108,868; Kita-Kyūshū 1,019,522.

Other principal cities (1995)

	population		population		population
Akashi	287,613	Kakogawa	260,588	Okayama	616,056
Akita	312,035	Kanazawa	453,977	Okazaki	322,615
Amagasaki	488,574	Kashiwa	317,752	Ōmiya	433,768
Aomori	294,165	Kasugai	277,579	Ōtsu	276,331
Asahikawa	360,569	Kawagoe	323,345	Sagamihara	570,594
Chiba	856,882	Kawaguchi	448,801	Sakai	802,965
Fujisawa	368,636	Kōchi	322,077	Sendai	971,263
Fukui	255,601	Koriyama	324,831	Shimonoseki	259,791
Fukushima	285,745	Koshigaya	298,285	Shizuoka	474,089
Fukuyama	374,510	Kumamoto	650,322	Suita	342,794
Funabashi	540,814	Kurashiki	422,824	Takamatsu	330,997
Gifu	407,145	Machida	360,418	Takatsuki	362,259
Hachiōji	503,320	Maebashi	284,780	Tokorozawa	320,448
Hakodate	298,868	Matsudo	461,489	Tokushima	268,712
Hamamatsu	561,568	Matsuyama	460,870	Toyama	325,303
Higashi-Ōsaka	517,228	Miyazaki	300,054	Toyohashi	352,913
Himeji	470,986	Morioka	286,478	Toyonaka	398,912
Hirakata	400,130	Nagano	358,512	Toyota	341,038
Hiratsuka	253,818	Nagasaki	438,724	Urawa	453,300
Ibaraki	258,237	Naha	301,928	Utsunomiya	435,446
Ichihara	277,080	Nara	359,234	Wakayama	393,951
Ichikawa	440,527	Neyagawa	258,440	Yamagata	254,485
Ichinomiya	267,359	Niigata	494,785	Yao	276,658
Iwaki	360,497	Nishinomiya	390,388	Yokkaichi	285,777
Kagoshima	546,294	Ōita	426,981	Yokosuka	432,202

Religious affiliation (1995): Shintō and related religions 93.1%[10]; Buddhism 69.6%; Christian 1.2%; other 8.1%.
Households (1995). Total households 43,899,923; average household size 2.8; composition of households 1 person 25.6%, 2 persons 23.0%, 3 persons 18.5%, 4 persons 18.8%, 5 persons 8.0%, 6 or more persons 6.1%. Family households 32,533,000 (74.1%); nonfamily 11,366,900 (25.9%), of which 1 person 11,239,400 (25.6%).

Type of household (1993)

Total number of occupied dwelling units: 40,835,000

	number of dwellings	percentage of total
by kind of dwelling		
exclusively for living	38,457,000	94.3
mixed use	168,000	0.4
combined with nondwelling	2,149,000	5.3
detached house	24,141,000	59.2
apartment building	14,267,000	35.0
tenement (substandard or overcrowded building)	2,163,000	5.3
other	203,000	0.5
by legal tenure of householder		
owned	24,453,000	59.9
rented	15,721,000	38.9
other	599,000	1.5
by kind of amenities		
flush toilet	30,524,000	74.7
bathroom	38,196,000	93.5
by year of construction		
prior to 1945	2,146,000	5.4
1945–70	9,700,000	24.3
1971–80	12,548,000	31.5
1981–87	9,258,000	23.2
1988–93	6,224,000	15.6

Mobility (October 1990). Population living in same residence as in October 1985, 74.7%; different residence, same town 9.5%; same prefecture 7.9%; different prefecture 7.6%; different country 0.3%.

Vital statistics

Birth rate per 1,000 population (1998): 10.8 (world avg. 22.5); (1985) legitimate 99.0%; illegitimate 1.0%.
Death rate per 1,000 population (1998): 6.4 (world avg. 8.9).
Natural increase rate per 1,000 population (1998): 4.4 (world avg. 13.2).
Total fertility rate (avg. births per childbearing woman; 1997): 1.4.
Marriage rate per 1,000 population (1996): 6.3; average age at first marriage men 28.5 years, women 26.4 years.
Divorce rate per 1,000 population (1996): 1.6.
Life expectancy at birth (1997): male 77.2 years; female 83.8 years.
Major causes of death per 100,000 population (1996): circulatory diseases 223.4, of which cerebrovascular disease 112.6; malignant neoplasms (cancers) 217.5; pneumonia and bronchitis 64.9; accidents and adverse effects 49.2, of which suicide 17.8; nephritis, nephrotic syndrome, and nephrosis 13.0; cirrhosis of the liver 13.2; diabetes mellitus 10.3.

Social indicators

Educational attainment (1990). Percentage of population age 25 years and over having: primary education 34.3%; secondary 44.5%; postsecondary 21.2%.

Distribution of income (1997)

percentage of average household income by quintile

1	2	3	4	5 (highest)
11.1	15.2	18.8	23.2	31.7

Quality of working life. Average workweek (1996): 39.1 hours. Annual rate of industrial deaths per 100,000 workers (1996): 2.6. Proportion of labour force insured for damages or income loss resulting from injury, permanent disability, and death (1991): 50.1%. Average man-days lost to labour stoppages per 1,000,000 workdays (1997): 6.2. Average duration of journey to work (1988)[11]: 26.8 minutes (1983; 26.7% private automobile. 67.4% public transportation, 5.5% taxi, 0.4% other). Rate per 1,000 workers of discouraged (unemployed no longer seeking work: 1997): 89.4.

Access to services (1989). Proportion of households having access to: gas supply 64.6%; safe public water supply 94.0%; public sewage collection 89.4%.

Social participation. Eligible voters participating in last national election (October 1996): 59.6%. Population 15 years and over participating in social-service activities on a voluntary basis (1991): 26.3%. Trade union membership in total workforce (1996): 18.7%.

Social deviance (1996). Offense rate per 100,000 population for: homicide 1.0; rape 1.2; robbery 2.0; larceny and theft 1,262.9. Incidence in general population of: alcoholism, n.a.; drug and substance abuse, n.a. Rate of suicide per 100,000 population: 17.8.

Leisure/use of personal time

Discretionary daily activities (1996)
(Population age 10 years and over)

	weekly average hrs./min.
Total discretionary daily time	6:12
of which	
Hobbies and amusements	0:36
Sports	0:13
Learning (except schoolwork)	0:12
Social activities	0:04
Associations	0:27
Radio, television, newspapers, and magazines	2:59
Rest and relaxation	1:15
Other activities	0:20

Major leisure activities (1996)
(Population age 15 years and over)

	percentage of participation		
	male	female	total
Sports	81.7	70.5	76.1
Light gymnastics	25.9	30.6	28.3
Swimming	24.6	20.9	22.8
Bowling	33.7	24.6	29.2
Learning (except schoolwork)	30.7	30.6	30.6
Travel (1991)			
Domestic	72.7	68.3	70.4
Foreign	10.4	7.6	9.0

Material well-being (1994). Households possessing: automobile 79.7%; telephone, virtually 100%; colour television receiver 99.3%; refrigerator 98.9%; air conditioner 72.3%; washing machine 99.4%; vacuum cleaner 98.7%; videocassette recorder 82.8%; camera 86.8%; microwave oven 84.3%; compact disc player 53.8%.

National economy

Gross national product (at current market prices; 1998): U.S.$4,089,140,000,000 (U.S.$32,350 per capita).

Structure of gross domestic product and labour force

	1996		1997	
	in value ¥'000,000,000	% of total value	labour force	% of labour force
Agriculture, fishing	9,308	1.9	3,500,000	5.2
Mining	1,073	0.2	70,000	0.1
Manufacturing	121,554	24.3	14,420,000	21.3
Construction	52,768	10.6	6,850,000	10.1
Public utilities	14,130	2.8	360,000	0.5
Transportation and communications	33,289	6.7	4,120,000	6.1
Trade	60,691	12.1	14,750,000	21.8
Finance	89,696	17.9	2,530,000	3.7
Pub. admin., defense	39,749	8.0	2,150,000	3.2
Services	98,610	19.7	16,480,000	24.3
Other	–21,006[12]	–4.2[12]	2,540,000[13]	3.7[13]
TOTAL	499,861[7]	100.0	67,770,000	100.0

Budget (1998). Revenue: ¥58,522,000,000,000 (income tax 28.0%; corporation tax 26.1%; value-added tax 18.5%; liquor and tobacco tax 5.3%; fuel taxes 4.5%; stamp duties 3.1%; customs duties 1.6%). Expenditures: ¥77,669,000,000,000 (debt service 22.2%; social security 19.1%; public works 11.6%; culture, education, and science 8.2%; national defense 6.4%; pensions 2.0%).

Public debt (1998): U.S.$2,412,200,000,000 (¥278,847,900,000,000).

Population economically active (1997): total 67,770,000; activity rate of total population 53.8% (participation rates: age 15 and over, 63.7%; female 42.9%; unemployed 3.2%).

Price and earnings indexes (1995 = 100)

	1993	1994	1995	1996	1997	1998	1999
Consumer price index	99.4	100.1	100.0	100.1	101.8	102.5	102.2
Monthly earnings index	95.7	97.9	100.0	101.9	103.4	103.1	103.6

Household income and expenditure (1997). Average household size 2.8; average annual income per household ¥6,989,400 (U.S.$56,614); sources of income (1994): wages and salaries 59.0%, transfer payments 20.5%, self-employment 12.8%, other 7.3%; expenditure (1997): food 22.3%, transportation and communications 11.6%, recreation 9.6%, housing 6.7%, clothing and footwear 5.7%, fuel, light, and water charges 5.7%, education 5.4%, furniture and household utensils 3.5%, medical care 2.9%.

Tourism (1997): receipts from visitors U.S.$4,326,000,000; expenditures by nationals abroad U.S.$33,041,000,000.

Land use (1994): forested 66.4%; meadows and pastures 1.8%; agricultural and under permanent cultivation 11.7%; other 20.1%.

Manufacturing and mining enterprises (1996)

	no. of establishments	avg. no. of persons engaged	annual wages as a % of avg. of all mfg. wages	annual value added (¥'000,000,000)
Electrical machinery	29,826	1,703,000	102.7	20,165
Transport equipment	13,787	909,000	123.9	13,398
Nonelectrical machinery	40,499	1,089,000	116.6	12,769
Food, beverages, and tobacco	45,737	1,248,000	71.3	12,353
Chemical products	5,224	389,000	135.3	11,902
Fabricated metal products	45,358	797,000	98.4	8,110
Printing and publishing	25,763	534,000	119.5	6,903
Ceramic, stone, and clay	18,851	418,000	99.9	5,005
Iron and steel	5,544	285,000	142.2	4,921
Plastic products	18,912	440,000	89.8	4,246
Paper and paper products	10,207	264,000	100.6	3,280
Apparel products	30,753	555,000	50.8	2,292
Nonferrous metal products	3,569	158,000	120.0	2,092
Textiles	14,969	248,000	80.7	1,739
Precision instruments	5,686	188,000	97.8	1,738
Furniture and fixtures	14,690	206,000	85.6	1,591
Rubber products	4,680	148,000	103.1	1,567
Lumber and wood products	15,463	207,000	78.3	1,533
Petroleum and coal products	1,105	33,000	160.2	1,110
Leather products	4,645	60,000	67.2	368
Mining and quarrying	616	11,686	108.0	98

Energy production (consumption): electricity (kW-hr; 1994) 964,328,000,000 (964,382,000,000); coal (metric tons; 1994) 6,949,000 (123,099,000); crude petroleum (barrels; 1994) 3,958,000 (1,647,000,000); petroleum products (metric tons; 1994) 185,612,000, of which (by volume) diesel 32.8%, heavy fuel oil 25.5%, gasoline 19.8%, kerosene and jet fuel 15.0% (193,545,000); natural gas (cu m; 1994) 2,276,600,000 (61,101,700,000). Composition of energy supply by source (1994): crude oil and petroleum products 55.8%, coal 17.2%, natural gas 11.3%, nuclear power 11.9%, hydroelectric power 3.0%, other 0.8%. Domestic energy demand by end use (1994): mining and manufacturing 42.6%, residential and commercial 25.9%, transportation 24.1%, other 7.4%.

Financial aggregates

	1993	1994	1995	1996	1997	1998	1999[14]
Exchange rate[15], ¥ per:							
U.S. dollar	111.85	99.74	102.30	116.00	129.95	115.60	115.20
£	172.27	157.59	158.56	196.97	214.11	192.30	186.51
SDR	153.63	145.61	152.86	166.80	175.34	162.77	157.16
International reserves (U.S.$)							
Total (excl. gold; '000,000)	98,524	125,860	183,250	216,648	219,648	215,471	259,537
SDRs ('000,000)	1,543	2,083	2,707	2,648	2,638	2,663	2,552
Reserve pos. in IMF ('000,000)	8,261	8,100	8,100	6,671	9,144	9,593	7,307
Foreign exchange ('000,000)	88,720	115,146	172,443	207,335	207,866	203,215	249,678
Gold ('000,000 fine troy oz)	24.23	24.23	24.23	24.23	24.23	24.23	24.23
% world reserves	2.6	2.6	2.7	2.7	2.7	2.5	2.6
Interest and prices							
Central bank discount (%)[15]	1.75	1.75	0.50	0.50	0.50	0.50	0.50
Govt. bond yield (%)	3.69	3.71	2.27	2.23	1.69	1.10	1.03[16]
Industrial share prices (1995 = 100)	110.4	115.8	100.0	116.3	101.1	85.4	99.8[17]
Balance of payments (U.S.$'000,000,000)							
Balance of visible trade	141.6	145.9	132.1	83.56	101.60	122.39	...
Imports, f.o.b.	209.7	238.2	297.2	316.72	307.64	251.66	...
Exports, f.o.b.	351.3	384.2	429.3	400.28	409.24	374.04	...
Balance of invisibles	–10.1	–16.7	–20.9	–17.68	–7.25	–1.69	...
Balance of payments, current account	131.5	129.2	111.2	65.88	94.35	120.70	...

Retail and wholesale trade and services (1994)

	no. of establishments	avg. no. of employees	annual sales (¥'000,000,000)
Retail trade	1,499,948	7,384,143	143,325
Food and beverages	569,403	2,740,000	43,021
Grocery	65,174	715,000	16,986
Liquors	92,436	278,000	5,966
General merchandise	4,839	494,000	20,391
Department stores	2,267	478,000	19,976
Motor vehicles and bicycles	89,345	569,000	17,539
Apparel and accessories	225,714	789,000	14,269
Gasoline service stations	72,177	441,000	11,818
Furniture and home furnishings	144,368	563,000	11,557
Books and stationery	72,007	679,000	5,158
Wholesale trade	429,302	4,581,000	514,317
Machinery and equipment	97,691	1,165,000	110,808
General machinery except electrical	41,618	425,000	30,991
Motor vehicles and parts	17,942	225,000	29,308
General merchandise	1,159	61,000	91,717
Farm, livestock, and fishery products	42,537	445,000	56,954
Food and beverages	53,687	573,000	47,381
Minerals and metals	19,809	242,000	47,281
Building materials	50,152	406,000	32,641
Textiles, apparel, and accessories	40,970	407,000	30,461
Chemicals	17,011	172,000	21,486
Drugs and toilet goods	19,710	288,000	21,048

Production (metric tons except as noted). Agriculture, forestry, fishing (1998): rice 11,200,000, sugar beets 3,685,000, potatoes 3,400,000, cabbages 2,700,000, sugarcane 1,430,000, onions 1,240,000, sweet potatoes 1,130,000, apples 900,000, cucumbers 800,000, tomatoes 800,000, carrots 720,000, watermelons 620,000, wheat 569,000, lettuce 540,000, eggplants 490,000, cantaloupes 430,000, pears 428,000, spinach 340,000, grapes 251,000, pumpkins 230,000, yams 210,000, strawberries 200,000, barley 193,000, peaches 176,000, soybeans 145,000, oranges 131,000, cauliflower 130,000, tea 91,000, green beans 76,000, tobacco 68,000, green peas 40,000; livestock (number of live animals) 9,800,000 pigs, 4,700,000 cattle, 30,000 horses, 28,500 goats, 16,300 sheep, 306,000,000 chickens; roundwood (1998) 21,545,000 cu m; fish catch (1996) 5,974,000, of which mackerel 1,350,000, sardines 773,000, squid 663,000, Alaska pollack 331,000, crabs 48,000. Mining and quarrying (1997): limestone 201,380,000; silica stone 18,124,000; dolomite 4,015,000; pyrophyllite 620,000; zinc 71,569; lead 5,227; copper 932; tungsten 578[18]; silver 87,210 kg; gold 8,170 kg. Manufacturing (1997): crude steel 104,545,000; steel products 96,982,000; cement 91,938,000; pig iron 78,519,000; sulfuric acid 6,828,000; plastic products 6,448,000; fertilizers 5,884,000; spun yarn 507,475; newsprint 3,192,300; synthetic fabrics 2,046,600,000 sq m; cotton fabrics 917,000,000 sq m; finished products (in number of units) 541,070,000 watches and clocks, 30,350,000[19] air conditioners, 20,171,000[20] electronic desk calculators, 12,725,000[19] videocassette recorders, 9,394,000 cameras, 9,218,000[19] computers, 8,898,000 video cameras, 8,494,000 passenger cars, 6,672,000 colour television receivers, 6,595,000 facsimile machines, 5,975,000 bicycles, 5,369,000 electric refrigerators, 4,818,000 automatic washing machines, 3,624,000 microwave ovens, 2,676,000 motorcycles, 1,903,000[19] photocopy machines. Construction (value in ¥'000,000; 1996): residential 44,240,000; nonresidential 28,800,000.

Foreign trade

Balance of trade (current prices)

	1994	1995	1996	1997	1998	1999
¥'000,000,000	+12,419	+9,998	+6,737	+9,982	+13,991	+12,279
% of total	18.1%	13.7%	8.1%	10.9%	16.0%	14.8%

Imports (1997): ¥40,956,000,000,000 (machinery and transport equipment 28.0%, food products 13.6%, petroleum and petroleum products 10.3%, chemicals and chemical products 6.9%, textiles 6.6%). *Major import sources:* United States 22.3%; China 12.4%; Indonesia 4.3%; Australia 4.3%; South Korea 4.3%; Taiwan 3.7%; Germany 3.7%; United Arab Emirates 3.6%; Saudi Arabia 3.5%; Malaysia 3.4%.

Exports (1997): ¥50,938,000,000,000 (electrical machinery 23.6%, motor vehicles 14.0%, chemicals 7.1%, scientific and optical equipment 4.8%, iron and steel products 3.8%, textiles and allied products 2.0%). *Major export destinations:* United States 27.8%; Taiwan 6.5%; Hong Kong 6.5%; South Korea 6.2%; China 5.3%; Singapore 4.8%; Germany 4.3%; Thailand 3.5%; Malaysia 3.4%; United Kingdom 3.3%.

Trade by commodity group (1996)

	imports		exports	
SITC group	U.S.$'000,000	%	U.S.$'000,000	%
00 Food and live animals; 01 Beverages and tobacco	50,584	14.5	1,558	0.4
02 Crude materials, excluding fuels	31,612[21]	9.1[21]	3,033[21]	0.7[21]
03 Mineral fuels, lubricants, and related materials	60,931	17.4	2,197	0.5
04 Animal and vegetable oils, fats, and waxes	[21]	[21]	[21]	[21]
05 Chemicals and related products, n.e.s.	22,570	6.5	27,922	6.8
06 Basic manufactures	38,049	10.9	45,733	11.1
07 Machinery and transport equipment	85,058	24.4	285,090	69.4
08 Miscellaneous manufactured articles	53,215	15.2	34,562	8.4
09 Goods not classified by kind	7,167	2.0	10,852	2.6
TOTAL	349,186	100.0	410,947	100.0[7]

Direction of trade (1997)

	imports		exports	
	U.S.$'000,000	%	U.S.$'000,000	%
Africa	5,097	1.5	5,375	1.3
Asia	163,802	48.4	187,875	44.6
South America	8,971	2.6	7,503	1.8
North America and Central America	88,110	26.0[7]	136,847	32.5
United States	75,975	22.4	118,383	28.1
other North and Central Am.	12,135	3.5	18,464	4.4
Europe	55,323	16.3[7]	73,848[7]	17.5
EU	45,266	13.4	65,728	15.6
Russia	3,988	1.2	1,009	0.2
other Europe	6,069	1.8	7,114	1.7
Oceania	17,341	5.1	9,618	2.3
TOTAL	338,646[7]	100.0[7]	421,067[7]	100.0

Transport and communications

Transport. Railroads (1996): length 16,937 mi, 27,258 km; rolling stock—locomotives 1,787[22], passenger cars 25,973[22], freight cars 12,688[22]; passengers carried 22,598,000,000[23]; passenger-mi 249,888,000,000, passenger-km 402,156,000,000; short ton-mi cargo 17,102,000,000, metric ton-km cargo 24,968,000,000. Roads (1996): total length 713,333 mi, 1,148,000 km (paved 73%). Vehicles (1997): passenger cars 48,684,000; trucks 19,402,000; buses 240,000. Merchant marine (1997): vessels (100 gross tons and over) 6,756; total deadweight tonnage 17,582,000. Air transport (1996): passengers carried 96,495,000; passenger-mi 79,512,400,000, passenger-km 127,963,000,000; short ton-mi cargo 4,641,000,000, metric ton-km cargo 6,776,000,000; airports (1996) with scheduled flights 73.

Distribution of traffic (1996)

	cargo carried ('000,000 tons)	% of national total	passengers carried ('000,000)	% of national total
Road	6,177	90.8	61,543	72.9
Rail (intercity)	74	1.1	22,593	26.8
Urban transport (1995)	—	—	24,041	...
road	—	—	10,701	...
rail	—	—	13,340	...
Inland water	547	8.0	148	0.2
Air	1	0.0	82	0.1
TOTAL	6,799	100.0[7]	84,366[23]	100.0[23]

Communications

Medium	date	unit	number	units per 1,000 persons
Daily newspapers	1996	circulation	72,705,000	578
Radio	1997	receivers	120,500,000	955
Television	1997	receivers	86,500,000	686
Telephones	1998	main lines	63,580,000	503
Cellular telephones	1998	subscribers	47,285,000	374
Personal computers	1998	units	30,000,000	237
Internet	1998	users	16,740,000	132

Radio and television broadcasting (1994): total radio stations 1,340, of which commercial 481; total television stations 14,625, of which commercial 7,736. Commercial broadcasting hours (by percentage of programs; 1994): reports—radio 13.0%, television 21.0%; education—radio 3.4%, television 12.0%; culture—radio 14.9%, television 24.7%; entertainment—radio 67.6%, television 40.0%. Advertisements (daily average; 1994): radio 148, television 295.

Other communications media (1996)

	titles
Print	
Books (new)	60,462
of which	
Social sciences	12,607
Fiction	11,680
Arts	8,358
Engineering	5,479
Natural sciences	4,533
History	3,824
Philosophy	2,794
Magazines/journals	4,178
Weekly	112
Monthly	2,848
Cinema	
Feature films	610
Domestic	289
Foreign	321

	traffic ('000)
Electronic	
Telegram	40,368
Domestic	40,198
International	170
Fax service	1,015[24]
Post	
Mail	25,385,000
Domestic	24,971,000
International	414,000
Parcels	392,300
Domestic	386,000
International	6,300

Education and health

Literacy: total population age 15 and over literate, virtually 100%.

Education (1997)

	schools	teachers	students	student/teacher ratio
Primary (age 6–11)	24,376	420,901	7,855,387	18.7
Secondary (age 12–17)	16,753	546,337	8,852,840	16.2
Higher	1,243	166,051	3,136,834	18.9

Health (1996): physicians 240,908 (1 per 522 persons); dentists 85,518 (1 per 1,471 persons); nurses 928,896 (1 per 136 persons); pharmacists 194,300 (1 per 648 persons); midwives 23,615 (1 per 5,330 persons); hospital beds 1,664,629 (1 per 74 persons), of which general 75.9%, mental 21.7%, tuberculosis 1.9%, other 0.5%; infant mortality rate per 1,000 live births (1998) 3.6.

Food (1995): daily per capita caloric intake 2,932 (vegetable products 80%, animal products 20%); 125% of FAO recommended minimum.

Military

Total active duty personnel (1999): 236,300[25] (army 61.7%, navy 18.5%, air force 19.1%). *Military expenditure as percentage of GNP* (1997): 1.0% (world 2.6%); per capita expenditure U.S.$325.

[1]October 1. [2]Excludes Lake Naka (38 sq mi [98 sq km]), which is part of both Shimane and Tottori prefectures. [3]Excludes Lake Towada (23 sq mi [60 sq km]), which is part of both Akita and Aomori prefectures. [4]Part of Kantō geographic region. [5]Part of Kinki geographic region. [6]1987 survey (includes Lake Naka and Lake Towada); total area per 1996 survey equals 145,884 sq mi (377,837 sq km). [7]Detail does not add to total given because of rounding. [8]August 1. [9]January 1. [10]Many Japanese practice both Shintōism and Buddhism. [11]Applies to passengers carried within metropolitan areas only. [12]Import duties and statistical discrepancy less imputed bank service charge. [13]Includes 2,200,000 unemployed. [14]July. [15]End of period. [16]May. [17]June. [18]1992. [19]1996. [20]1994. [21]Crude materials includes Animal and vegetable oils, fats, and waxes. [22]1995. [23]Totals do not include Urban transport. [24]Number of subscribers. [25]Includes 1,400 personnel not allocated to specific branch.

Internet resources for further information:

- **Bank of Japan http://www.boj.or.jp/en/index.htm**
- **Economic Planning Agency of Japan http://www.epa.go.jp/e-e/menu.html**
- **Statistics Bureau and Statistics Center (Japan) http://www.stat.go.jp/english/1.htm**

Jersey

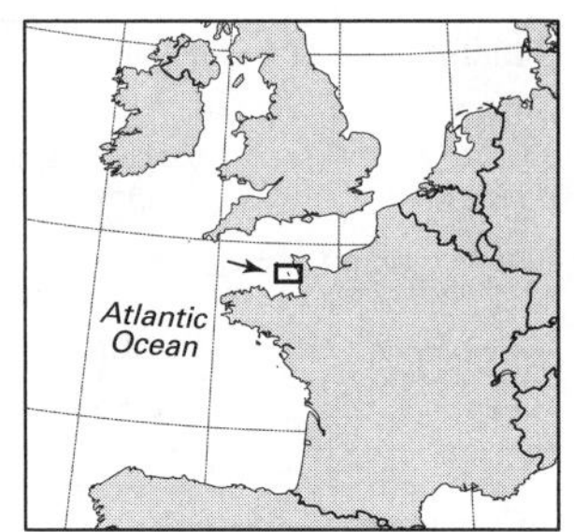

Official name: Bailiwick of Jersey.
Political status: Crown dependency (United Kingdom) with one legislative house (States of Jersey [57][1]).
Chief of state: British Monarch represented by Lieutenant Governor.
Head of government: [2].
Capital: Saint Helier.
Official language: English[3].
Official religion: none.
Monetary unit: 1 Jersey pound (£J) = 100 pence; valuation (Oct. 6, 2000) 1 Jersey pound = U.S.$1.45; at par with the British pound.

Area and population	area		population
			1996
Parishes	sq mi	sq km	census
Grouville	3.0	7.8	4,658
St. Brelade	4.9	12.8	9,560
St. Clement	1.6	4.2	7,986
St. Helier	3.3	8.6	27,523
St. John	3.4	8.7	2,520
St. Lawrence	3.7	9.5	4,773
St. Martin	3.8	9.9	3,423
St. Mary	2.5	6.5	1,475
St. Ouen	5.8	15.0	3,685
St. Peter	4.5	11.6	4,228
St. Saviour	3.6	9.3	12,680
Trinity	4.7	12.3	2,639
TOTAL	44.9	116.2	85,150

Demography

Population (2000): 88,900.
Density (2000): persons per sq mi 1,975.6, persons per sq km 766.4.
Sex distribution (1996): male 48.61%; female 51.39%.
Age breakdown (1996): under 15, 16.6%; 15–29, 20.8%; 30–44, 25.2%; 45–59, 18.7%; 60–74, 12.2%; 75 and over, 6.5%.
Population projection: (2010) 91,900; (2020) 93,100.
Population by place of birth (1996): Jersey 52.7%; United Kingdom, Guernsey, or Isle of Man 34.5%; Portugal 5.4%; Ireland 2.6%; France 1.1%; other European Union 1.1%; other 2.6%.
Religious affiliation (1981): Anglican 61.5%; Roman Catholic 23.1%; other (mostly Protestant) 15.4%.
Major cities (1996)[4]: St. Helier 27,523, St. Saviour 12,680, St. Brelade 9,560.

Vital statistics

Birth rate per 1,000 population (1999): 11.9 (world avg. 22.1).
Death rate per 1,000 population (1999): 9.1 (world avg. 8.9).
Natural increase rate per 1,000 population (1999): 2.8 (world avg. 13.2).
Total fertility rate (avg. births per childbearing woman; 1999): 1.5.
Marriage rate per 1,000 population (1996): n.a.
Divorce rate per 1,000 population (1996): n.a.
Life expectancy at birth (1999): male 76.1 years; female 81.9 years.
Major causes of death per 100,000 population: n.a.

National economy

Budget (2000). Revenue: £388,389,000 (corporate income tax 43.0%, individual income tax 26.9%, self-employment tax 11.6%, spirits and tobacco tax 6.0%, international business 5.4%, tax on fuel 3.0%). Expenditures: £300,030,000 (current expenditure 79.2%, of which health 27.8%, education 21.3%, social security 20.5%; capital expenditure 20.8%).
Public debt: none.
Production. Agriculture, forestry, fishing: fruits and vegetables, mostly potatoes and greenhouse tomatoes; greenhouse flowers are important export crops; livestock (number of live animals; 1999) 7,315 cattle, of which about 4,500 dairy cattle; roundwood, none; fish catch (1997)[5]: 4,368, of which crustaceans 2,934 (including sea spiders and crabs 2,713); mollusks 743 (including abalones, winkles, and conch 438); marine fish 691. Mining and quarrying: n.a. Manufacturing: light industry, mainly electrical goods, textiles and clothing; dairy products (including 179 hectolitres of milk in 1999). Construction: n.a. Energy production (consumption): electricity (kW-hr; 1995) 266,000,000 (467,000,000); crude petroleum, none (n.a.); petroleum products, n.a. (n.a.); natural gas, none (n.a.).
Gross national product (at current market prices; 1995): U.S.$2,670,000,000 (U.S.$30,940 per capita).

Structure of gross domestic product and labour force	1996			
	in value[6] £J'000,000	% of total value	labour force	% of labour force
Agriculture, fishing	74	5.0	2,162	4.6
Mining	...	...	193	0.4
Manufacturing	30	2.0	1,727	3.7
Construction	...	...	4,187	8.9
Public utilities	...	...	619	1.3
Transp. and commun.	...	...	2,602	5.5
Trade, hotels, restaurants	354[7]	24.0[7]	10,961	23.3
Finance, real estate[8]	811	55.0	11,604	24.7
Pub. admin., defense	...	...	2,140	4.6
Services	...	...	9,248	19.7
Other	206[9]	14.0[9]	1,549[10]	3.3[10]
TOTAL	1,475	100.0	46,992	100.0

Household income and expenditure. Average household size (1996) 2.4; income per household: n.a.; sources of income: n.a.; expenditure (1998–99)[11]: housing 20.1%, recreation 16.5%, transportation 12.8%, household furnishings 11.6%, food 11.5%, alcoholic beverages 6.0%, clothing and footwear 5.5%.
Population economically active (1996): total 46,992; activity rate of total population 55.2% (participation rates: ages 15–64, n.a.; female 44.6%; unemployed 3.3%).

Price index (1995 = 100)[12]	1995	1996	1997	1998	1999	2000
Consumer price index	100.0	103.6	107.2	111.7	115.6	120.2

Tourism (1996): receipts U.S.$429,000,000; expenditures by nationals abroad, n.a.; number of visitors for at least one night 670,000.
Land use (1997): land under cultivation 56.8%, other 43.2%.

Foreign trade

Imports: [13]. *Major import sources* (1999): mostly the United Kingdom.
Exports: [13]; agricultural exports (1996): £45,400,000 (potatoes 61.2%, greenhouse tomatoes 17.2%, zucchini 6.4%, greenhouse carnations and narcissus 6.0%). *Major export destinations:* mostly the United Kingdom.

Transport and communications

Transport. Railroads: none. Roads (1995): total length 346 mi, 557 km (paved 100%). Vehicles (1995): passenger cars 58,491; trucks and buses 9,109. Air transport (1999)[14]: passenger-mi 553,291,000, passenger-km 890,438,000; short ton-mi cargo 632,000, metric ton-km cargo 923,000; airports (1999) with scheduled flights 1.

Communications				units
Medium	date	unit	number	per 1,000 persons
Daily newspapers	1997	circulation	25,542	299
Telephones	1998	main lines	68,721	781
Cellular telephones	1998	subscribers	18,255	208
Internet	1996	users	1,000	12

Education and health

Educational attainment: n.a. *Literacy* (1996): total population age 15 and over literate 71,033 (100.0%).

Education (1996)	schools	teachers	students	student/ teacher ratio
Primary (age 5–10)	32	313[15]	6,906	...
Secondary (age 11–16)	14	373[15]	4,924	...
Voc., teacher tr.	...	...	...	...
Higher	1	...	1,298	...

Health (1995): physicians 95 (1 per 895 persons); hospital beds 651 (1 per 130 persons); infant mortality rate per 1,000 live births (1997–99) 5.9.
Food (1998): daily per capita caloric intake, n.a.

Military

Total active duty personnel (1999): none; defense is the responsibility of the U.K.

[1]53 elected members include 12 senators popularly elected for six-year terms, 12 constables popularly elected triennially, and 29 deputies also popularly elected triennially; 4 nonelected members include the bailiff, the dean of Jersey, the attorney general, and the solicitor general. [2]Executive committees appointed by the States of Jersey (alternately called States Assembly). [3]Until the 1960s French was an official language of Jersey and is still used by the court and legal professions; Jerriais, a Norman-French dialect, is spoken by a small number of residents. [4]Population of parishes. [5]Includes Guernsey. [6]Calculation based on percentage distribution. [7]Represents tourism-related businesses. [8]Jersey is an international finance centre with 79 banks in 1998 and over 33,000 registered companies; of more than U.S.$160,000,000,000 deposited in the island, 62 percent is in foreign (not £J or £) currency. [9]Represents investment income from abroad received by residents. [10]Unemployed seeking work. [11]Weights of retail price index components. [12]June. [13]Customs ceased recording imports and exports as of 1980. [14]Jersey European Airways. [15]1990.

Internet resources for further information:
- **An Introduction to Jersey**
  http://www.adwebjersey.co.uk/states.html
- **This is Jersey**
  http://www.thisisjersey.com

Jordan

Official name: Al-Mamlakah al-Urdunnīyah al-Hāshimīyah (Al-Urdun) (Hashemite Kingdom of Jordan).
Form of government: constitutional monarchy with two legislative houses (Senate [40[1]]; House of Representatives [80]).
Head of state and government: King assisted by Prime Minister.
Capital: Amman.
Official language: Arabic.
Official religion: Islam.
Monetary unit: 1 Jordan dinar (JD) = 1,000 fils; valuation (Oct. 6, 2000) JD 1.00 = U.S.$1.41 = £0.97.

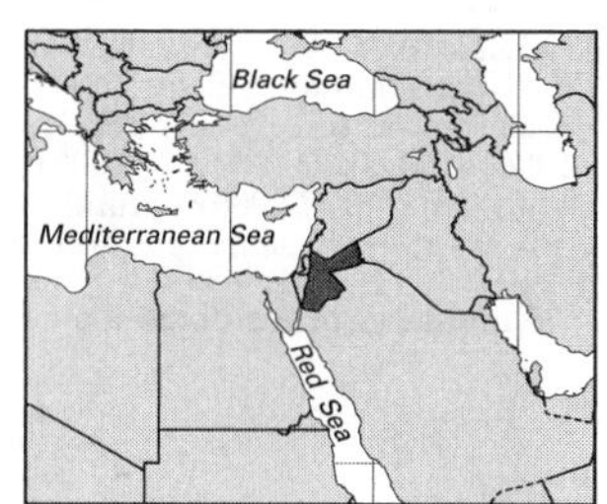

Area and population

Governorates	Capitals	area sq mi	area sq km	population 1999 estimate[2]
ʿAjlūn	ʿAjlun	159	412	105,500
ʿAmman	Amman	3,178	8,231	1,809,800
Al-ʿAqabah	Al-ʿAqabah	2,542	6,583	95,400
Al-Balqāʾ	Aṣ-Ṣalt	415	1,076	312,200
Irbid	Irbid	626	1,621	848,300
Jarash	Jarash	155	402	139,800
Al-Karak	Al-Karak	1,242	3,217	191,400
Maʿān	Maʿān	12,804	33,163	92,700
Mādabā	Mādabā	775	2,008	121,300
Al-Mafraq	Al-Mafraq	10,207	26,435	219,000
Aṭ-Ṭafīlah	Aṭ-Ṭafīlah	816	2,114	72,500
Az-Zarqāʾ	Az-Zarqāʾ	1,575	4,080	747,900
TOTAL		34,495[3]	89,342	4,755,800

Demography

Population (2000): 4,982,000.
Density (2000): persons per sq mi 144.4, persons per sq km 55.8.
Urban-rural (1999): urban 73.6%; rural 26.4%.
Sex distribution (1999): male 52.23%; female 47.77%.
Age breakdown (2000): under 15, 37.9%; 15–29, 30.9%; 30–44, 18.3%; 45–59, 7.8%; 60–74, 4.2%; 75 and over, 0.9%.
Population projection: (2010) 6,486,000; (2020) 7,920,000.
Doubling time: 30 years.
Ethnic composition (1995): Arab 98%, of which Palestinian *c.* 50%; Circassian 1%; Armenian 1%.
Religious affiliation (1995): Sunnī Muslim 96.5%; Christian 3.5%.
Major cities (1994): Amman 963,490; Az-Zarqāʾ 344,524; Irbid 208,201; Aṣ-Ṣalt 187,014; Ar-Ruṣayfah 131,130; Al-Mafraq 109,841.

Vital statistics

Birth rate per 1,000 population (2000): 26.2 (world avg. 22.1).
Death rate per 1,000 population (2000): 2.6 (world avg. 8.9).
Natural increase rate per 1,000 population (2000): 23.6 (world avg. 13.2).
Total fertility rate (avg. births per childbearing woman; 2000): 3.4.
Life expectancy at birth (2000): male 74.9 years; female 79.9 years.
Major causes of death per 100,000 population: n.a.

National economy

Budget (1998 est.). Revenue: JD 1,688,000,000 (taxes 50.8%, of which sales tax 20.7%, custom duties 17.1%, income and profits taxes 8.3%; nontax 37.1%, of which licenses and fees 11.4%; external aid 12.0%). Expenditures: JD 2,047,000,000 (current 81.9%, of which defense 24.1%, interest expense 11.7%, wages and salaries 17.2%; capital construction 18.1%).
Public debt (external, outstanding; 1998): U.S.$7,056,000,000.
Production (metric tons except as noted). Agriculture, forestry, fishing (1999): tomatoes 305,100, watermelons 97,400, potatoes 92,600, cucumbers 73,900, bananas 72,500, olives 55,000, lemons and limes 41,600, apples 34,200, pumpkins and squash 31,400, cabbages 28,400; livestock (number of live animals) 2,000,000 sheep, 795,000 goats, 65,000 cattle, 18,000 camels; roundwood (1998) 3,000 cu m; fish catch (1998) 470. Mining and quarrying (1998): phosphate ore 5,925,000; potash 1,527,000. Manufacturing (value added in JD '000; 1997): chemicals 130,276; nonmetallic mineral products, pottery, and china 114,897; tobacco 96,380; food products 80,994; refined petroleum 60,028; plastic products 25,627. Construction (permits issued; 1998): residential 3,427,600 sq m; nonresidential 669,600. Energy production (consumption): electricity (kW-hr; 1996) 6,058,000,000 (6,058,000,000); crude petroleum (barrels: 1996) 14,400 (23,790,000); petroleum products (metric tons; 1996) 3,102,000 (3,932,000).
Land use (1994): forest 0.8%; pasture 8.9%; agriculture 4.6%; other 85.7%.
Tourism (1998): receipts U.S.$853,000,000; expenditures U.S.$451,000,000.
Population economically active (1993): total 859,300: activity rate of total population 22.2% (participation rates: over age 15, 43.6%; female 14.0%; unemployed [1996] 13.0%).

Price and earnings indexes (1995 = 100)

	1993	1994	1995	1996	1997	1998	1999
Consumer price index	94.4	97.7	100.0	106.5	109.7	114.6	115.3
Daily earnings index	...	...	...	...	...	...	...

Gross national product (1998): U.S.$5,252,000,000 (U.S.$1,150 per capita).

Structure of gross domestic product and labour force

	1997 in value JD '000,000	1997 % of total value	1993 labour force	1993 % of labour force
Agriculture	151.1	3.1	54,995	6.4
Mining	202.4	4.1	91,086	10.6
Manufacturing	840.1	17.0		
Construction	224.2	4.5	60,151	7.0
Public utilities	117.8	2.4	6,015	0.7
Transp. and commun.	672.9	13.6	57,573	6.7
Trade[4]	546.0	11.0	129,754	15.1
Finance	804.3	16.3	24,920	2.9
Pub. admin., defense	890.9	18.0	434,806	50.6
Services[5]	216.5	4.4		
Other	279.6[6]	5.6[6]		
TOTAL	4,945.8	100.0	859,300	100.0

Household income and expenditure. Average household size (1995) 6.1; income per household (1995) JD 4,010 (U.S.$5,725); sources of income (1995): wages and salaries 51.4%, rent and property income 23.8%, transfer payments 13.7%, self-employment 11.1%; expenditure (1992): food and beverages 40.6%, housing and energy 26.9%, transportation 11.2%, clothing and footwear 8.2%, education 3.5%, health care 2.2%.

Foreign trade

Balance of trade (current prices)

	1994	1995	1996	1997	1998	1999
JD '000,000	–1,367.4	–1,349.3	–1,851.0	–1,609.0	–1,436.5	–1,336.4
% of total	40.7%	35.2%	41.8%	38.2%	36.0%	34.0%

Imports (1998): JD 2,719,900,000 (machinery and transport equipment 28.5%; food and live animals 19.6%; chemicals and chemical products 12.7%; mineral fuels 9.4%; iron and steel 4.0%). *Major import sources:* Germany 9.8%; United States 9.5%; Iraq 8.8%; Japan 5.8%; United Kingdom 5.1%; Italy 4.9%.
Exports (1998): JD 1,275,600,000 (domestic goods 81.9%, of which chemicals and chemical products 25.3%, phosphate fertilizers 11.0%, potash 8.7%, fruits, vegetables, and nuts 8.3%, machinery and transport equipment 3.5%; reexports 18.1%). *Major export destinations*[7]: India 11.2%; Iraq 10.3%; Saudi Arabia 9.9%; Lebanon 2.9%; Kuwait 2.6%.

Transport and communications

Transport. Railroads (1995): route length 677 km; passenger traffic was negligible; metric ton-km cargo 1,336,000,000[8]. Roads (1998): total length 7,133 km (paved 100%). Vehicles (1996): passenger cars 213,874; trucks and buses 79,153. Merchant marine (1995): vessels (1,000 gross tons and over) 1; total deadweight tonnage 15,794. Air transport (1998)[9]: passenger-km 4,064,737,000; metric ton-km cargo 219,219,000; airports (1997) 2.

Communications

Medium	date	unit	number	units per 1,000 persons
Daily newspapers	1996	circulation	250,000	57
Radio	1997	receivers	1,660,000	395
Television	1998	receivers	520,000	85
Telephones	1998	main lines	511,000	83
Cellular telephones	1998	subscribers	70,000	12
Personal computers	1998	units	77,000	12
Internet	1998	users	61,000	10

Education and health

Educational attainment (2000). Percentage of population age 25 and over having: no formal schooling 16.7%; primary education 49.2%; secondary 16.7%; postsecondary and vocational 9.5%; higher 8.2%. *Literacy* (2000): percentage of population age 15 and over literate 88.8%; males literate 94.9%; females literate 84.4%.

Education (1995–96)

	schools	teachers	students	student/ teacher ratio
Primary (age 6–14)	2,531	51,721	1,074,877	20.8
Secondary (age 15–17)	741[10]	8,615	143,014	16.6
Voc., teacher tr.	54[10]	2,306	33,109	14.4
Higher	55[11]	4,821[12]	99,020[12]	20.5

Health (1998): physicians 7,480 (1 per 625 persons); hospital beds 8,565 (1 per 546 persons); infant mortality rate per 1,000 live births (1998) 33.2.
Food (1998): daily per capita caloric intake 2,791 (vegetable products 88%, animal products 12%); 113% of FAO recommended minimum requirement.

Military

Total active duty personnel (1999): 104,000 (army 86.5%, navy 0.5%, air force 13.0%). *Military expenditure as percentage of GDP* (1997): 9.0% (world 2.6%); per capita expenditure U.S.$145.

[1]Appointed by king. [2]January 1. [3]Detail does not add to total given because of rounding. [4]Includes hotels. [5]Includes domestic help employed in households. [6]Imputed bank service charges. [7]Domestic exports only. [8]For Aqaba Railway Corporation only. [9]Royal Jordanian airlines only. [10]1993–94. [11]1988–89. [12]Includes community colleges.

Internet resources for further information:
- **Dept. of Statistics http://www.dos.gov.jo**
- **Jordan National Information System http://www.nic.gov.jo**

Kazakhstan

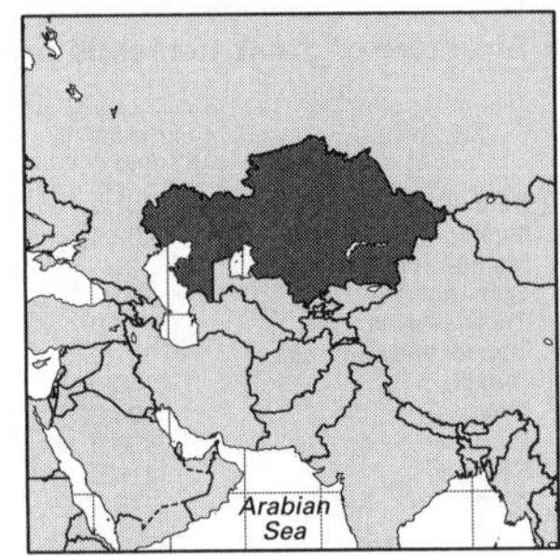

Official name: Qazaqstan Respūblīkasy (Republic of Kazakhstan).
Form of government: unitary republic with a Parliament consisting of two chambers (Senate [39[1]] and Assembly [77]).
Head of state and government: President assisted by Prime Minister.
Capital: Astana[2].
Official language: Kazakh[3].
Official religion: none.
Monetary unit[4]: 1 tenge (T) = 100 tiyn; valuation (Oct. 6, 2000) free rate, 1 U.S.$ = 142.51 tenge; 1 £ = 206.15 tenge.

Area and population		area		population
Provinces	Capitals	sq mi	sq km	1995 estimate
Almaty (Alma-Ata)	Almaty (Alma-Ata)	86,500[5]	224,200[5]	1,684,600
Aqmola[6, 7]	Astana[2]	35,500	92,000	845,700
Aqtöbe	Aqtöbe	116,050	300,600	752,800
Atyraū	Atyraū	45,800	118,600	459,600
Batys Qazaqstan	Oral	58,400	151,300	669,800
Mangghystaū	Aqtaū	63,950	165,600	324,400
Ongtüstik Qazaqstan	Shymkent	45,300	117,300	1,987,800
Pavlodar	Pavlodar	48,200	124,800	943,600
Qaraghandy	Qaraghandy	165,250	428,000	1,754,500
Qostanay[6]	Qostanay	44,000	113,900	1,055,300
Qyzylorda	Qyzylorda	87,250[8]	226,000[8]	606,100
Shyghys Qazaqstan	Shyghys Qazaqstan	109,400	283,300	1,750,500
Soltüstik Qazaqstan	Petropavl	47,500	123,200	1,257,900
Torghay[6]	*Arqalyq*	*43,150*	*111,800*	*305,900*
Zhambyl	Zhambyl (Aullye-Ata)	55,700	144,300	1,039,600
Cities				
Almaty (Alma-Ata)	—	5	5	1,172,400
Astana[7]	—	...	...	...
Bayqongyr (Leninsk)	—	8	8	68,600
TOTAL		1,052,100[9]	2,724,900	16,679,100

Demography

Population (2000): 14,913,000.
Density (2000): persons per sq mi 14.2, persons per sq km 5.5.
Urban-rural (1997): urban 57.0%; rural 43.0%.
Sex distribution (1997): male 48.61%; female 51.39%.
Age breakdown (1997): under 15, 29.3%; 15–29, 25.4%; 30–44, 22.2%; 45–59, 12.9%; 60 and over, 10.2%.
Population projection: (2010) 15,397,000; (2020) 16,525,000.
Ethnic composition (1995)[10]: Kazakh 46.0%; Russian 34.7%; Ukrainian 4.9%; German 3.1%; Uzbek 2.3%; Tatar 1.9%; other 7.1%.
Religious affiliation (1995): Muslim (mostly Sunnī) 47.0%; Russian Orthodox 8.2%; Protestant 2.1%; other (mostly nonreligious) 42.7%.
Major cities (1997): Almaty (Alma-Ata) 1,064,300; Qaraghandy (Karaganda) 452,700; Shymkent (Chimkent) 393,400; Pavlodar 326,500.

Vital statistics

Birth rate per 1,000 population (1997): 14.7 (world avg. 22.6); (1994) legitimate 86.6%; illegitimate 13.4%.
Death rate per 1,000 population (1997): 10.1 (world avg. 8.9).
Natural increase rate per 1,000 population (1997): 4.6 (world avg. 13.7).
Total fertility rate (avg. births per childbearing woman; 1997): 1.9.
Marriage rate per 1,000 population (1996): 6.4.
Divorce rate per 1,000 population (1996): 2.5.
Life expectancy at birth (1999): male 63.0 years; female 73.0 years.
Major causes of death per 100,000 population (1996): diseases of the circulatory system 436.2; malignant neoplasms (cancers) 133.0; accidents, poisoning, and violence 101.1; diseases of the respiratory system 71.0.

National economy

Budget (1998). Revenue: 262,916,000,000 tenge (taxes on goods and services 32.6%, social security contributions 23.4%, income, profits, and capital gains taxes 8.5%, taxes on international trade 3.7%, payroll taxes 3.2%). Expenditures: 318,252,000,000 tenge (social security and welfare 38.1%, general public services 7.9%, health 7.7%, public order 7.3%, defense 5.1%).
Public debt (external, outstanding; 1998): U.S.$3,040,000,000.
Population economically active (1995): total 6,976,000; activity rate of total population 41.8% (participation rates: ages 16–59 [male], 16–54 [female] 80.1%; female [1994] 48.0%; unemployed 2.3%).

Price and earnings indexes (1995 = 100)							
	1993	1994	1995	1996	1997	1998	1999
Consumer price index	1.8	36.2	100.0	139.3	163.5	175.2	189.6
Monthly earnings index	2.7	36.1	100.0	142.9	178.5	202.3	229.5

Production (metric tons except as noted). Agriculture, forestry, fishing (1999): wheat 11,242,000, barley 2,265,000, potatoes 1,695,000, oats 194,000, sugar beets 294,000; livestock (number of live animals) 9,556,000 sheep and goats, 3,958,000 cattle, 986,000 horses, 892,000 pigs; roundwood (1998) 315,000 cu m; fish catch (1997) 41,367. Mining and quarrying (1998): titanium 12,000,000; magnesium 9,000,000; iron ore 8,693,000; nickel 6,000,000; bauxite 3,400,000; chromite 1,600,000. Manufacturing (value of production in '000,000 tenge; 1996): food products 107,397; nonferrous metallurgy 89,052; ferrous metallurgy 81,026; machinery 52,168; chemical products 28,974; construction materials 23,239. Construction (1994): residential 2,300,000 sq m. Energy production (consumption): electricity (kW-hr; 1996) 58,657,000,000 (65,502,000,000); coal (metric tons; 1996) 76,597,000 (55,852,000); crude petroleum (barrels; 1996) 150,000,000 (63,000,000); petroleum products (metric tons; 1996) 10,894,000 (10,627,000); natural gas (cu m; 1996) 7,107,000,000 (10,609,000,000).
Gross national product (1998): U.S.$20,856,000,000 (U.S.$1,340 per capita).

Structure of gross domestic product and labour force	1998		1995	
	in value '000,000 tenge	% of total value	labour force	% of labour force
Agriculture	147,385	8.4	1,442,000	20.7
Manufacturing, mining, public utilities	383,614	21.9	1,372,000	19.7
Construction	77,652	4.4	364,000	5.2
Transp. and commun.	192,944	11.0	507,000	7.3
Trade	303,133	17.4	1,035,000	14.8
Finance			334,000	4.8
Pub. admin., defense / Services (Finance, Pub. admin., defense, Services)	642,992	36.8		
Pub. admin., defense / Services			1,664,000	23.9
Other	...	...	258,000[11]	3.7[11]
TOTAL	1,747,720	100.0[9]	6,976,000	100.0[9]

Household income and expenditure. Average household size (1989) 4.0; income per household: n.a.; sources of income (1994): salaries and wages 67.7%, social benefits 16.9%, agricultural income 5.8%, other 9.6%; expenditure (1994): retail goods 60.6%, taxes 16.8, services 11.7%, other 10.9%.

Foreign trade[12]

Balance of trade (current prices)						
	1993	1994	1995	1996	1997	1998
U.S.$'000,000	–414	–920	+114.1	–335.0	–276.4	–750.1
% of total	4.2%	12.3%	1.1%	2.6%	2.0%	6.0%

Imports (1998): U.S.$6,574,700,000 (electrical equipment and mechanical tools 18.3%, vehicles 5.9%, nonfood consumer goods 5.4%, foodstuffs 3.7%, petroleum products 2.8%). *Major import sources:* Russia 39.4%; Germany 8.6%; U.S. 6.3%; U.K. 5.0%; Uzbekistan 2.3%.
Exports (1998): U.S.$5,773,800,000 (oil and gas condensate 28.6%, rolled ferrous metal 8.9%, refined copper 8.8%, coal 5.6%, grain 5.1%). *Major export destinations:* Russia 28.9%; U.K. 9.0%; China 7.2%; Switzerland 6.1%.

Transport and communications

Transport. Railroads: (1999) route length 13,500 km; (1998) passenger-km 13,000,000,000; metric ton-km cargo 107,500,000,000. Roads (1997): total length 125,796 km (paved 83%). Vehicles (1997): passenger cars 973,323; trucks and buses 361,920. Air transport (1995): passenger-km 2,429,000,000; metric ton-km cargo 237,000,000; airports (1997) with scheduled flights 20.

Communications				
Medium	date	unit	number	units per 1,000 persons
Radio	1997	receivers	6,470,000	395
Television	1997	receivers	3,880,000	237
Telephones	1998	main lines	1,775,000	109
Cellular telephones	1998	subscribers	29,700	1.8
Personal computers	...	units	...	...
Internet	1998	users	20,000	1.2

Education and health

Educational attainment (1989). Population age 25 and over having: primary education or no formal schooling 16.2%; some secondary 19.8%; completed secondary and some postsecondary 54.1%; higher 9.9%. *Literacy* (1989): population age 15 and over literate 97.5%; males 99.1%; females 96.1%.

Education (1996–97)	schools	teachers	students	student/ teacher ratio
Primary (age 7–13)	8,611[13]	262,000[13]	1,342,035	11.7[13]
Secondary (age 14–17)	...	...	1,743,623	...
Voc., teacher tr.	3,504[14]	...	177,679	...
Higher	69[14]	...	260,043[13]	...

Health (1997): physicians 55,800 (1 per 287 persons); hospital beds 136,000 (1 per 115 persons); infant mortality rate per 1,000 live births (1999) 33.

Military

Total active duty personnel (1999): 65,800 (army 71.1%, air force 28.9%). *Military expenditure as percentage of GNP* (1997): 1.3% (world avg. 2.6%); per capita expenditure U.S.$41.

[1]Includes 7 nonelective seats. [2]City of Akmola (Kazakh: Aqmola; new capital replacing Almaty) was renamed Astana on May 6, 1998. [3]Russian commands equal status with Kazakh at state-owned organizations and bodies of local government per a law effective July 16, 1997. [4]On Nov. 25, 1993, the Kazakh tenge became the sole legal tender. [5]Area of Almaty city included with Almaty province. [6]Torghay province was abolished April 23, 1997; its area and population were divided between Aqmola and Qostanay provinces, but adjusted figures are not yet available. [7]Aqmola province includes Astana city. [8]Area of Bayqongyr city included with Qyzylorda province. [9]Detail does not add to total given because of rounding. [10]Kazakh and Russian percents for 1998 equaled 52 and 31, respectively. [11]Includes 139,600 undistributed unemployed and 118,400 undistributed employed. [12]Imports and exports are f.o.b. in balance of trade. [13]1995–96. [14]1994–95.

Internet resources for further information:
- **Kazakstan Human Development Report 1995 http://www.undp.org/rbec/nhdr/kazakstan**
- **Agency on Statistics of Kazakhstan http://www.kazstat.asdc.kz**

Kenya

Official name: Jamhuri ya Kenya (Swahili); Republic of Kenya (English).
Form of government: unitary multiparty republic with one legislative house (National Assembly [224[1]]).
Head of state and government: President.
Capital: Nairobi.
Official languages: Swahili; English.
Official religion: none.
Monetary unit: 1 Kenya shilling[2] (K Sh) = 100 cents; valuation (Oct. 6, 2000) 1 U.S.$ = K Sh 79.02; 1 £ = K Sh 114.31.

Area and population

Provinces	Provincial headquarters	area sq mi	area sq km	population 1993 estimate
Central	Nyeri	5,087	13,176	3,626,000
Coast	Mombasa	32,279	83,603	2,155,000
Eastern	Embu	61,734	159,891	4,334,000
North Eastern	Garissa	48,997	126,902	408,000
Nyanza	Kisumu	6,240	16,162	4,041,000
Rift Valley	Nakuru	67,131	173,868	5,690,000
Western	Kakamega	3,228	8,360	3,035,000
Special area				
Nairobi	—	264	684	1,678,000
TOTAL		224,961[3]	582,646	24,967,000

Demography

Population (2000): 30,340,000.
Density (2000): persons per sq mi 134.9, persons per sq km 52.1.
Urban-rural (1999): urban 32.2%; rural 67.8%.
Sex distribution (1999): male 50.15%; female 49.85%.
Age breakdown (1999): under 15, 43.6%; 15–29, 31.2%; 30–44, 14.1%; 45–59, 7.0%; 60–74, 3.3%; 75 and over, 0.8%.
Population projection: (2010) 33,068,000; (2020) 34,001,000.
Doubling time: 39 years.
Ethnic composition (1989): Kikuyu 17.7%; Luhya 12.4%; Luo 10.6%; Kalenjin 9.8%; Kamba 9.8%; other 39.7%.
Religious affiliation (1995): Christian 63.7%, of which Protestant 28.2%, Roman Catholic 19.5%, other Christian (mostly African Indigenous, Anglican, Eastern Orthodox) 16.0%; Muslim 6.0%; other 30.3%.
Major cities (1989): Nairobi 1,504,900[4]; Mombasa 465,000; Kisumu 185,100; Nakuru 162,800; Eldoret 104,900; Nueri 88,600.

Vital statistics

Birth rate per 1,000 population (1999): 31.8 (world avg. 22.1).
Death rate per 1,000 population (1999): 13.9 (world avg. 8.9).
Natural increase rate per 1,000 population (1999): 17.9 (world avg. 13.2).
Total fertility rate (avg. births per childbearing woman; 1999): 4.0.
Life expectancy at birth (1998): male 47.6 years; female 49.3 years.
Major causes of death per 100,000 population: n.a.; however, major infectious diseases include AIDS, malaria, gastroenteritis, venereal diseases, diarrhea and dysentery, trachoma, amebiasis, and schistosomiasis.

National economy

Budget (1996–97). Revenue: K Sh 155,032,000,000 (tax revenue 83.4%, nontax revenue 12.9%, grants 3.7%). Expenditures: K Sh 168,403,000,000 (1995–96; recurrent expenditure 80.7%, of which interest on debt 24.3%, administration 21.9%, education 19.3%, defense 5.9%, health 5.8%; development expenditure 19.3%).
Production (metric tons except as noted). Agriculture, forestry, fishing (1999): sugarcane 5,200,000, corn (maize) 2,100,000, cassava 920,000, sweet potatoes 720,000, plantains 380,000, potatoes 350,000, pineapples 290,000, pulses 240,000, tea 220,000, bananas 220,000, wheat 135,000, sorghum 130,000, coffee 66,000, coconuts 65,000, barley 50,000, millet 50,000, tomatoes 31,000, sisal 26,000, seed cotton 15,000, tobacco 10,000, cotton seeds 8,000, cashew nuts 8,000, sunflower seeds 5,500; livestock (number of live animals) 13,392,000 cattle, 7,600,000 goats, 5,800,000 sheep; roundwood (1998) 29,337,000 cu m; fish catch (1998) 172,592, of which freshwater fish 95.0%. Mining and quarrying (1995): soda ash 218,450; fluorite 80,230; salt 71,400. Manufacturing (value added in K£'000[2]; 1994): food products 639,000; machinery and transport equipment 233,000; beverages and tobacco 190,000; chemical products 168,000; metal products 125,000; paper and paper products 87,000; plastic products 65,000; clothing and footwear 55,000. Construction (1990): residential 411,000 sq m; nonresidential 182,000 sq m. Energy production (consumption): electricity (kW-hr; 1996) 3,745,000,000 (3,920,000,000); coal (metric tons; 1996) none (100,000); crude petroleum (barrels; 1996) none (13,487,000); petroleum products (metric tons; 1996) 1,722,000 (2,016,000).
Public debt (external, outstanding; 1998): U.S.$5,629,000,000.
Household income and expenditure. Average household size (1998): 3.4; average annual income per household: n.a.; sources of income: n.a.; expenditure (1980): food 46.5%, housing 10.0%, furniture and utensils 9.4%, transportation 8.4%, clothing and footwear 7.7%, energy 2.6%, health 2.2%.
Tourism (1998): receipts from visitors U.S.$233,000,000; expenditures by nationals abroad U.S.$147,000,000.
Population economically active (1997): total 14,592,000; activity rate of total population 50.0% (participation rates [1985]: ages 15–64, 76.2%; female [1997] 46.1%; unemployed, n.a.).

Price and earnings indexes (1995 = 100)

	1993	1994	1995	1996	1997	1998	1999
Consumer price index	76.9	99.2	100.0	108.8	121.9	129.0	132.4
Earnings index	...	...	...	...	...	...	...

Gross national product (1998): U.S.$10,201,000,000 (U.S.$350 per capita).

Structure of gross domestic product and labour force

	1996 in value K Sh '000,000	1996 % of total value	1995 labour force[5]	1995 % of labour force[6]
Agriculture	130,471	30.0	294,000	18.9
Mining	741	0.2	5,000	0.3
Manufacturing	45,645	10.5	205,000	13.1
Construction	20,012	4.6	76,000	4.9
Public utilities	5,515	1.3	23,000	1.5
Transp. and commun.	34,277	7.9	79,000	5.1
Trade	82,895	19.0	135,000	8.7
Finance	79,055	18.1	78,000	5.0
Pub. admin., defense; Services	36,869	8.5	663,000	42.6
Other	—	—	—	—
TOTAL	435,480	100.0[3]	1,558,000	100.0

Land use (1994): forest 29.5%; pasture 37.4%; agriculture 8.0%; other 25.1%.

Foreign trade[6]

Balance of trade (current prices)

	1993	1994	1995	1996	1997	1998
K Sh '000,000	–23,209	–27,938	–57,884	–50,260	–70,714	–71,780
% of total	13.0%	13.8%	22.9%	17.5%	22.8%	22.8%

Imports (1997): U.S.$3,294,000,000 (machinery and transport equipment 28.9%, manufactured goods 22.0%, mineral fuels 15.6%, chemical products 14.5%, food and beverages 12.4%). *Major import sources:* Middle East 15.8%; United Kingdom 10.7%; United States 7.9%; Japan 7.4%; India 7.5%; South Africa 7.4%; Germany 6.0%; Italy 5.2%; United States 3.6%; Saudi Arabia 2.0%.
Exports (1997): U.S.$2,105,000,000 (tea 20.5%, coffee [not roasted] 14.3%, petroleum products 7.8%, horticulture 7.3%, fruits and vegetables 3.1%, cement 2.1%, soda ash 1.1%, hides and skins 0.6%). *Major export destinations:* Uganda 15.1%; Tanzania 12.9%; United Kingdom 11.4%; Germany 6.8%; The Netherlands 4.8%; United States 3.0%.

Transport and communications

Transport. Railroads (1996): route length 1,885 mi, 3,034 km; passenger-mi 239,000,000; passenger-km 385,000,000; short ton-mi cargo 813,000,000, metric ton-km cargo 1,309,000,000. Roads (1996): total length 39,600 mi, 63,800 km (paved 14%). Vehicles (1996): passenger cars 278,000; trucks and buses 81,200. Merchant marine (1992): vessels (100 gross tons and over) 29; total deadweight tonnage 11,649. Air transport (1996): passenger-mi 1,062,000,000, passenger-km 1,709,000,000; short ton-mi cargo 126,100,000, metric ton-km cargo 203,000,000; airports (1997) with scheduled flights 11.

Communications

Medium	date	unit	number	units per 1,000 persons
Daily newspapers	1996	circulation	263,000[7]	9.4[7]
Radio	1997	receivers	3,070,000	107
Television	1998	receivers	640,000	21.9
Telephones	1998	main lines	288,251	9.9
Cellular telephones	1998	subscribers	6,819	0.2
Personal computers	1998	units	100,000	3.4
Internet	1998	users	15,000	0.5

Education and health

Educational attainment (1979). Percentage of population age 25 and over having: no formal schooling 58.6%; primary education 32.2%; some secondary 7.9%; complete secondary and higher 1.3%. *Literacy* (1995): total population over age 15 literate 77.3%; males literate 85.6%; females literate 69.1%.

Education (1993)

	schools	teachers	students	student/ teacher ratio
Primary (age 5–11)	15,906	181,975	5,544,998	30.5
Secondary (age 12–17)	2,878	41,484	632,388	15.2
Voc., teacher tr.	62	...	29,593[8]	...
Higher	14	4,392[8, 9]	88,180[8]	8.1[8, 9]

Health (1994): physicians 4,558 (1 per 5,999 persons); hospital beds 37,271 (1 per 734 persons); infant mortality rate per 1,000 live births (1999): 69.6.
Food (1998): daily per capita caloric intake 1,968 (vegetable products 88%, animal products 12%); 86% of FAO recommended minimum requirement.

Military

Total active duty personnel (1999): 24,200 (army 84.7%, navy 5.0%, air force 10.3%). *Military expenditure as percentage of GNP* (1997): 7.2% (world 2.6%); per capita expenditure U.S.$7.

[1]Includes 14 nonelective seats. [2]Kenya pound (K£) as a unit of account equals 20 K Sh. [3]Detail does not add to total given because of rounding. [4]1999. [5]Employed persons only. [6]Import figures are c.i.f. [7]Circulation for four newspapers only. [8]1993. [9]Universities only.

Internet resources for further information:
- **Central Bank of Kenya http://www.africaonline.co.ke/cbk**

Kiribati

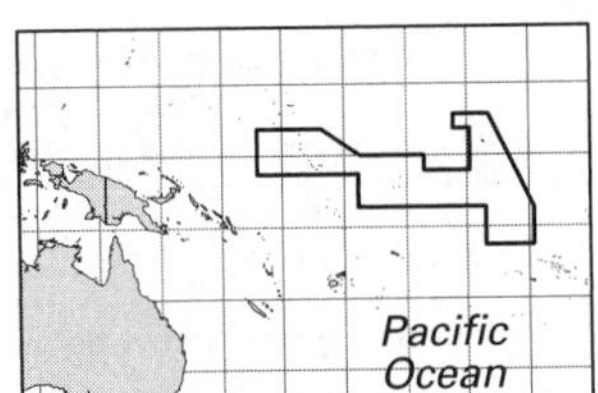

Official name: Republic of Kiribati.
Form of government: unitary republic with a unicameral legislature (House of Assembly [42[1]]).
Head of state and government: President.
Capital: Bairiki, on Tarawa Atoll.
Official language: English.
Official religion: none.
Monetary unit: 1 Australian Dollar ($A) = 100 cents; valuation (Oct. 6, 2000) 1 U.S.$ = $A 1.87; 1 £ = $A 2.70.

Area and population

Island Groups / Islands	Capitals	area[2] sq mi	area[2] sq km	population 1995 census
Gilberts Group	Bairiki Islet	110	286[3]	71,757
Abaiang	Tuarabu	7	18	6,020
Abemama	Kariatebike	11	27	3,442
Aranuka	Takaeang	5	12	1,015
Arorae	Roreti	3	9	1,248
Banaba	Anteeren	2	6	339
Beru	Taubukinberu	7	18	2,784
Butaritari	Butaritari	5	13	3,909
Kuria	Tabontebike	6	16	971
Maiana	Tebangetua	6	17	2,184
Makin	Makin	3	8	1,830
Marakei	Rawannawi	5	14	2,724
Nikunau	Rungata	7	19	2,009
Nonouti	Teuabu	8	20	3,042
Onotoa	Buariki	6	16	1,918
Tabiteuea North	Utiroa	10	26	3,383
Tabiteuea South	Buariki	5	12	1,404
Tamana	Bakaka	2	5	1,181
Tarawa North	Abaokoro	6	15	4,004
Tarawa South	Bairiki	6	16	28,350
Line Group	Kiritimati	192	496	5,818
Northern		167	432	5,818
Kiritimati (Christmas)	London	150	388	3,225
Tabuaeran (Fanning)	Paelau	13	34	1,615
Teraina (Washington)	Washington	4	10	978
Southern (Caroline [Millennium], Flint, Malden, Starbuck, Vostok)		25	64	—
Phoenix Group (Birnie, Enderbury, Kanton [Canton], McKean, Manra [Sydney], Nikumaroro [Gardner], Orona [Hull], Rawaki [Phoenix])	Kanton	11	29	83
TOTAL		313	811	77,658

Demography

Population (2000): 92,000.
Density (2000)[4]: persons per sq mi 328.5, persons per sq km 126.7.
Urban-rural (1998): urban 37.0%; rural 63.0%.
Sex distribution (1995): male 49.55%; female 50.45%.
Age breakdown (1995): under 15, 41.2%; 15–29, 25.8%; 30–44, 18.3%; 45–59, 9.3%; 60–74, 4.4%; 75 and over, 1.0%.
Population projection: (2010) 115,000; (2020) 142,000.
Doubling time: 29 years.
Ethnic composition (1995): I-Kiribati 97.7%; mixed (part I-Kiribati and other) 1.5%; Tuvaluan 0.3%; European 0.2%; other 0.3%.
Religious affiliation (1995): Roman Catholic 54.3%; Kiribati Protestant (Congregational) 37.9%; Bahā'ī 2.6%; other Protestant 2.5%; other Christian (Mormon) 1.7%; other/nonreligious 1.0%.
Major cities (1999): Tarawa (urban area) 32,000.

Vital statistics

Birth rate per 1,000 population (1999): 32.9 (world avg. 22.1); legitimate, n.a.; illegitimate, n.a.
Death rate per 1,000 population (1999): 9.2 (world avg. 8.9).
Natural increase rate per 1,000 population (1999): 23.7 (world avg. 13.2).
Total fertility rate (avg. births per childbearing woman; 1999): 4.4.
Marriage rate per 1,000 population (1988): 5.2.
Life expectancy at birth (1999): male 56.5 years; female 62.4 years.
Major causes of death per 100,000 population (1993): senility without mention of psychosis 61.2; stroke 39.1; diarrhea 37.8; hepatitis 32.5; diabetes mellitus 28.6; malnutrition 23.4; meningitis 18.2.

National economy

Budget (1997). Revenue: $A 79,100,000 (nontax revenue 46.6%, tax revenue 20.4%, grants 33.0%). Expenditures: $A 79,100,000 (current expenditure 66.3%, of which wages 25.4%; capital expenditure 33.7%).
Public debt (external, outstanding; 1993): U.S.$18,000,000.
Tourism (1998): receipts from visitors U.S.$1,400,000; expenditures by nationals abroad (1996) U.S.$4,000,000.
Production (metric tons except as noted). Agriculture, forestry, fishing (1999): coconuts 85,000, roots and tubers 6,500 (of which taro 1,600), vegetables and melons 5,000, bananas 4,700, tropical fruit 1,150; livestock (number of live animals) 9,500 pigs, 300,000 chickens; fish catch (1997) 23,000. Mining and quarrying: none. Manufacturing (1996): processed copra 9,321; other important products are processed fish, baked goods, clothing, and handicrafts. Energy production (consumption): electricity (kW-hr; 1996) 7,000,000 (7,000,000); coal, none (n.a.); crude petroleum, none (n.a.); petroleum products (metric tons; 1996) none (7,000).
Gross national product (1998): U.S.$101,000,000 (U.S.$1,170 per capita).

Structure of gross domestic product and labour force

	1996 in value[5] $A '000	1996 % of total[5] value	1990 labour force	1990 % of labour force
Agriculture, fishing	4,832	12.4	23,137[6]	71.0[6]
Mining	—	—	—	—
Manufacturing	344	0.9	622	1.9
Construction	1,024	2.6	339	1.0
Public utilities	947	2.4	301	0.9
Transp. and commun.	4,822	12.4	921	2.8
Trade	7,238	18.5	1,341	4.1
Finance	2,215	5.7	441	1.4
Pub. admin., defense	12,780	32.8	2,123	6.5
Services	1,346	3.4	2.286	7.0
Other	3,470[7]	8.9[7]	1,099[8]	3.4[8]
TOTAL	39,018	100.0	32,610	100.0

Population economically active (1995): total 38,407; activity rate of total population 49.5% (participation rates: over age 15, 84.0%; female 47.8%; unemployed 0.2%).

Price and earnings indexes (1990 = 100)

	1990	1991	1992	1993	1994	1995	1996
Consumer price index	100.0	103.7	109.2	115.6	123.0	127.4	126.7
Earnings index	...	...	...	...	...	...	...

Household income and expenditure. Average household size (1995) 6.5; income per household: n.a.; sources of income (1978): wages 69.7%, self-employment 21.4%, transfer payments 6.0%, other 2.9%; expenditure (1982): food 50.0%, tobacco and alcohol 14.0%, clothing 8.0%, transportation 8.0%, housing, energy, and household operation 7.5%.
Land use (1994): forest 2.7%; agricultural and under permanent cultivation 50.7%; other 46.6%.

Foreign trade

Balance of trade[9] (current prices)

	1992	1993	1994	1995	1996
$A '000	–44,882	–36,443	–29,303	–38,826	–40,382
% of total	88.8%	80.7%	68.1%	69.0%	73.1%

Imports (1996): $A 47,829,000 (food and live animals 33.4%; machinery and transport equipment 18.1%; basic manufactures 14.6%; mineral fuels 10.3%; beverages and tobacco 6.7%; chemicals 6.6%; crude materials 2.1%). *Major import sources:* Australia 46.1%; Fiji 18.7%; Japan 8.6%; New Zealand 8.4%; China 5.9%; United States 3.3%.
Exports (1996): $A 7,447,000 (domestic exports 91.7%, of which copra 62.8%, pet fish 11.6%, fish and fish preparations 4.0%, seaweed 3.6%; reexports 8.3%). *Major export destinations* (1994): Japan 32.9%; United States 17.1%; Hong Kong 12.9%; Bangladesh 8.6%; Germany 8.6%; Malaysia 7.1%.

Transport and communications

Transport. Roads (1996): total length 416 mi, 670 km (paved 5%). Vehicles (1988): passenger cars 222; trucks and buses 115. Merchant marine (1992): vessels (100 gross tons and over) 7; total deadweight tonnage 2,685. Air transport (1996): passenger-mi 4,350,000, passenger-km 7,000,000; short ton-mi cargo 621,000, metric ton-km cargo 1,000,000; airports 9.

Communications

Medium	date	unit	number	units per 1,000 persons
Radio	1997	receivers	17,000	212
Television	1997	receivers	1,000	15
Telephones	1999	main lines	2,802	34
Internet	1998	users	...	...

Education and health

Educational attainment (1995). Percentage of population age 25 and over having: no schooling 7.8%; primary education 68.5%; secondary or higher 23.7%.
Literacy (1995): population age 15 and over literate 90%.

Education (1997)

	schools	teachers	students	student/ teacher ratio
Primary (age 6–13)	86	727	17,594	24.2
Secondary (age 14–18)	9[10]	215	4,403	20.5
Voc., teacher tr.	11	23	333	14.5
Higher[11]	—	—	—	—

Health: physicians (1993) 10 (1 per 7,687 persons); hospital beds (1990) 283 (1 per 253 persons); infant mortality rate per 1,000 live births (1999) 56.8.
Food (1998): daily per capita caloric intake 2,977 (vegetable products 89%, animal products 11%); 130% of FAO recommended minimum requirement.

[1]Includes two nonelective members. [2]Includes uninhabited islands. [3]Detail does not add to total given because of rounding. [4]Based on inhabited island areas (280 sq mi, [726 sq km]) only. [5]1991 constant prices. [6]Includes 20,568 persons engaged in "village work" (subsistence agriculture or fishing). [7]Indirect taxes less subsidies and imputed bank service charge. [8]Includes 900 unemployed. [9]Exports do not include reexports. [10]Includes vocational. [11]54 students overseas in 1993.

Korea, North

Official name: Chosŏn Minjujuŭi In'min Konghwaguk (Democratic People's Republic of Korea).
Form of government: unitary single-party republic with one legislative house (Supreme People's Assembly [687]).
Chief of state: Chairman of the National Defense Commission[1].
Head of state and government: Premier.
Capital: P'yŏngyang.
Official language: Korean.
Official religion: none.
Monetary unit: 1 won = 100 chŏn; valuation (Oct. 6, 2000) 1 U.S.$ = 46.98 won; 1 £ = 67.95 won.

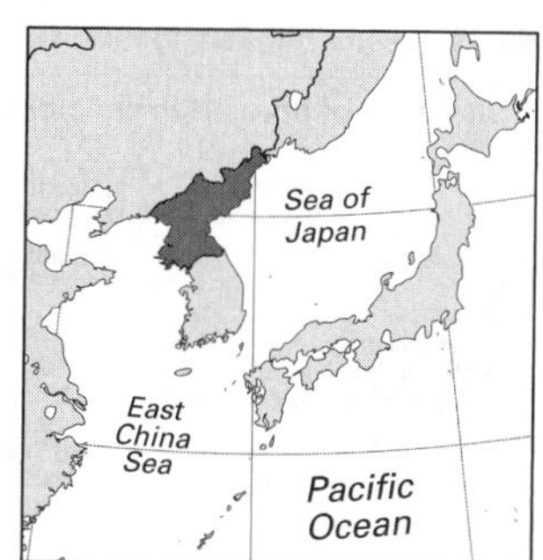

Area and population

Provinces	Capitals	area sq mi	area sq km	population[2] 1987 estimate
Chagang-do	Kanggye	6,551	16,968	1,156,000
Kangwŏn-do	Wŏnsan	4,306	11,152	1,227,000
North Hamgyŏng (Hamgyŏng-pukto)	Ch'ŏngjin	6,784	17,570	2,003,000
North Hwanghae (Hwanghae-pukto)	Sariwŏn	3,091	8,007	1,409,000
North Pyŏngan (P'yŏngan-pukto)	Sinŭiju	4,707[3]	12,191[3]	2,380,000
South Hamgyŏng (Hamgyŏng-namdo)	Hamhŭng	7,324	18,970	2,547,000
South Hwanghae (Hwanghae-namdo)	Haeju	3,090	8,002	1,914,000
South Pyŏngan (P'yŏngan-namdo)	P'yŏngsan	4,470	11,577	2,653,000
Yanggang-do	Hyesan	5,528	14,317	628,000
Special cities				
Kaesŏng	—	485	1,255	331,000
Namp'o	—	291	753	715,000
P'yŏngyang	—	772	2,000	2,355,000
Special district				
Hyangsan-chigu	—	[3]	[3]	28,000
TOTAL		47,399	122,762	19,346,000

Demography

Population (2000): 21,688,000.
Density (2000): persons per sq mi 457.6, persons per sq km 176.7.
Urban-rural (1998): urban 62.2%; rural 37.8%.
Sex distribution (1999): male 48.42%; female 51.58%.
Age breakdown (1999): under 15, 25.6%; 15–29, 25.3%; 30–44, 24.2%; 45–59, 14.5%; 60–74, 8.7%; 75 and over, 1.7%.
Population projection: (2010) 23,753,000; (2020) 25,143,000.
Ethnic composition (1989): Korean 99.8%; Chinese 0.2%.
Religious affiliation (1980): atheist or nonreligious 68.3%; traditional beliefs 15.6%; Ch'ŏndogyo 13.9%; Buddhist 1.7%; Christian 0.5%.
Major cities (1993): P'yŏngyang 2,500,000[4, 5]; Namp'o 731,448; Hamhŭng 709,000; Ch'ŏngjin 582,480; Kaesŏng 334,433; Sinŭiju 326,011.

Vital statistics

Birth rate per 1,000 population (1995–2000): 18.3 (world avg. 22.1).
Death rate per 1,000 population (1995–2000): 15.8 (world avg. 8.9).
Natural increase rate per 1,000 population (1995–2000): 2.5 (world avg. 13.2).
Total fertility rate (avg. births per childbearing woman; 1995–2000): 2.0.
Marriage rate per 1,000 population (1987): 9.3.
Divorce rate per 1,000 population (1987): 0.2.
Life expectancy at birth (1995–2000): male 50.8 years; female 57.4 years.
Major causes of death per 100,000 population (1986); diseases of the circulatory system 224.9; malignant neoplasms (cancers) 69.0; diseases of the digestive system 51.6; diseases of the respiratory system 46.7; injuries and poisoning 38.2; infectious and parasitic diseases 19.4.

National economy

Budget (1998). Revenue: 20,015,000,000 won (turnover tax and profits from state enterprises). Expenditures: 19,790,000,000 won (1994; national economy 67.8%, social and cultural affairs 19.0%, defense 11.6%).
Population economically active (1997)[6]: total 11,898,000; activity rate of total population 55.8% (participation rates [1988–93]: ages 15–64, 49.5%; female 46.0%; unemployed, n.a.).
Production (metric tons except as noted). Agriculture, forestry, fishing (1999): rice 2,343,000, potatoes 1,400,000, corn (maize) 1,235,000, cabbages 600,000, apples 630,000, soybeans 340,000, wheat 188,700, pears 120,000, sweet potatoes 106,000, barley 105,720, peaches and nectarines 100,000, watermelons 100,000, cucumbers and gherkins 60,000, tomatoes 60,000, tobacco leaves 60,000, millet 10,000, oats 10,000; livestock (number of live animals) 2,970,000 pigs, 1,900,000 goats, 565,000 cattle, 185,000 sheep, 10,371,000 chickens; roundwood (1998) 4,800,000 cu m; fish catch (1997): 236,462. Mining and quarrying (1996): iron ore (metal content) 5,100,000; magnesite (metal content) 1,600,000; phosphate rock 520,000; sulfur 250,000; zinc 900,000; lead (metal content) 40,000; fluorspar 40,000; graphite 40,000; copper 16,000; silver 50; gold 5,000 kg. Manufacturing (1996): cement 17,000,000; crude steel 8,100,000; pig iron 6,600,000; coke 3,500,000; steel semimanufactures 2,700,000[7]; chemical fertilizers 2,500,000[7]; meat 259,200[5]; gasoline 8,600,000 barrels; textile fabrics 350,000,000 sq m[7]. Construction: n.a. Energy production (consumption): electricity (kW-hr; 1996) 35,000,000 (35,000,000); coal (metric tons; 1996) 30,451,000 (75,757,000); crude petroleum (barrels; 1996) none (15,800,000); petroleum products (metric tons; 1996) 2,785,000 (4,258,000).

Household income and expenditure. Average household size (1987) 4.8; average annual income per household (1980) 3,677 won (U.S.$4,275); sources of income: n.a.; expenditure (1984)[8]: food 46.5%, clothing 29.9%, furniture 3.8%, energy 3.3%, housing 0.6%.
Public debt (external, outstanding; 1996): U.S.$12,000,000,000.
Gross national product (1997): U.S.$17,700,000,000 (U.S.$740 per capita).

Structure of gross domestic product and labour force

	1997 in value U.S.$'000,000	% of total value	labour force	% of labour force
Agriculture	...	...	3,853,000	32.4
Mining and manufacturing	...	...	} 8,045,000	} 67.6
Construction	...	...		
Public utilities	...	...		
Transp. and commun.	...	...		
Trade	...	...		
Finance	...	...		
Pub. admin., defense	...	...		
Services	...	...		
Other	...	...		
TOTAL	21,800	100.0	11,898,000	100.0

Land use (1994): forested 61.2%; meadows and pastures 0.4%; agricultural and under permanent cultivation 16.6%; other 21.8%.

Foreign trade[9]

Balance of trade (current prices)

	1991	1992	1993	1994	1995	1996
U.S.$'000,000	–764.7	–600.0	–600.0	–429.5	–880.0	–1,040
% of total	35.6%	18.8%	22.7%	20.4%	42.7%	36.3%

Imports (1996): U.S.$1,950,000,000 (crude petroleum, coal and coke, industrial machinery and transport equipment [including trucks], industrial chemicals, textile yarn and fabrics, and grain are among the major imports). *Major import sources* (1995): China 30.0%; Japan 15.8%; Austria 9.3%; Ukraine 5.9%.
Exports (1996): U.S.$912,000,000 (minerals [including lead, magnesite, zinc], metallurgical products [iron and steel, nonferrous metals], cement, agricultural products [including fish, grain, fruit and vegetables, tobacco], and manufactured goods [textile fabrics, clothing] are among the major exports). *Major export destinations* (1995): Japan 31.4%; Austria 17.3%; India 6.9%.

Transport and communications

Transport. Railroads (1998): length 8,533 km. Roads (1997): total length 14,526 mi, 23,377 km (paved 8%). Vehicles (1990): passenger cars 248,000. Merchant marine (1992): vessels (100 gross tons and over) 100; total deadweight tonnage 951,222. Air transport (1995): passenger-mi 128,600,000, passenger-km 207,000,000; short ton-mi cargo 13,670,000, metric ton-km cargo 22,000,000; airports (1998) with scheduled flights 1.

Communications

Medium	date	unit	number	units per 1,000 persons
Daily newspapers	1996	circulation	4,500,000	199
Radio	1997	receivers	3,360,000	146
Television	1997	receivers	1,200,000	52
Telephones	1995	main lines	1,104,000	47

Education and health

Educational attainment (1987–88). Percentage of population age 16 and over having attended or graduated from postsecondary-level school: 13.7%.
Literacy (1997): 95%.

Education (1988)

	schools	teachers	students	student/ teacher ratio
Primary (age 6–9)	4,810[10]	59,000	1,543,000	26.2
Secondary (age 10–15)[10]	4,840	111,000	2,468,000	22.2
Voc., teacher tr.	473[11]	...	220,000[10]	...
Higher	46	23,000	325,000	14.1

Health (1993): physicians 61,200 (1 per 370 persons); hospital beds (1989) 290,590 (1 per 74 persons); infant mortality rate (1995–2000) 82.6.
Food (1997): daily per capita caloric intake 1,899 (vegetable products 94%, animal products 6%); 81% of FAO recommended minimum requirement.

Military

Total active duty personnel (1998): 1,083,000 (army 87.8%, navy 4.2%, air force 8.0%). *Military expenditure as percentage of GNP* (1997): 27.5% (world 2.6%); per capita expenditure U.S.$282.

[1]Position in effect from Sept. 5, 1998. It is defined as an enhanced military post with revised constitutional powers. [2]Civilian population only; UN cites a 1993 census total of 21,123,376, but details are not available. [3]North P'yŏngan includes special district of Hyangsan-chigu. [4]1996 estimate. [5]Urban agglomeration for 1999 equals 3,136,000. [6]The Democratic People's Republic of Korea categorizes economically active as including students in higher education, retirees, and heads of households, as well as those in the civilian labour force. [7]1994. [8]Workers and clerical workers only. [9]Imports are f.o.b. [10]1987. [11]1986.

Internet resources for further information:
- **Korean News http://www.kcna.co.jp**
- **United States Department of Energy http://www.eia.doe.gov/emeu/cabs/nkorea.html**

Korea, South

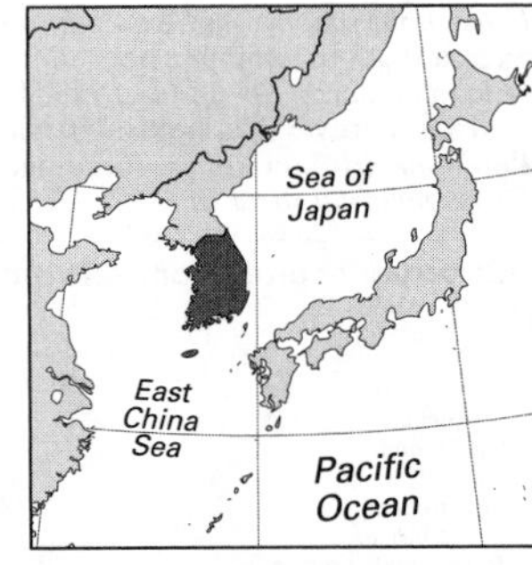

Official name: Taehan Min'guk (Republic of Korea).
Form of government: unitary multiparty republic with one legislative house (National Assembly [273]).
Head of state and government: President, assisted by Prime Minister.
Capital: Seoul.
Official language: Korean.
Official religion: none.
Monetary unit: 1 won (W) = 100 chon; valuation (Oct. 6, 2000) 1 U.S.$ = W 1,118; 1 £ = W 1,617.

Area and population

		area		population
				1995
Provinces	**Capitals**	sq mi	sq km	census
Cheju	Cheju	713	1,846	505,442
Kangwŏn	Ch'unch'ŏn'	6,384	16,536	1,466,794
Kyŏnggi	Suwŏn	3,913	10,136	7,649,914
North Chŏlla	Chŏnju	3,107	8,047	1,902,205
North Ch'ungch'ŏng	Ch'ŏngju	2,870	7,433	1,396,481
North Kyŏngsang	Taegu	7,344	19,021	2,676,344
South Chŏlla	Kwangju	4,616	11,956	2,066,865
South Ch'ungch'ŏng	Taejŏn	3,317	8,590	1,767,105
South Kyŏngsang	Masan	4,059	10,512	3,845,569[1]
Metropolitan cities				
Inch'ŏn	Inch'ŏn	370	958	2,307,618
Kwangju	Kwangju	193	501	1,257,504
Pusan	Pusan	290	751	3,813,814
Sŏul (Seoul)	Seoul	234	605	10,229,262
Taegu	Taegu	342	885	2,449,139
Taejŏn	Taejŏn	208	540	1,272,143
Ulsan	Ulsan	408	1,056	1
TOTAL		38,368	99,373	44,606,199

Demography

Population (2000): 47,275,000.
Density (2000): persons per sq mi 1,232.1, persons per sq km 475.7.
Urban-rural (1999): urban 85.0%; rural 15.0%.
Sex distribution (1997): male 50.38%; female 49.62%.
Age breakdown (1997): under 15, 22.4%; 15–29, 27.3%; 30–44, 25.9%; 45–59, 14.5%; 60–74, 7.9%; 75 and over, 2.0%.
Population projection: (2010) 50,886,000; (2020) 52,759,000.
Doubling time: 83 years.
Ethnic composition (1990): Korean 99.9%; other 0.1%.
Religious affiliation (1995): religious 50.7%, of which Buddhist 23.2%, Protestant 19.7%, Roman Catholic 6.6%, Confucian 0.5%, Wonbulgyo 0.2%, Ch'ŏndogyo 0.1%, other 0.4%; nonreligious 49.3%.
Major cities (1995): Seoul 10,229,262; Pusan 3,813,814; Taegu 2,449,139; Inch'ŏn 2,307,618; Taejŏn 1,272,143.

Vital statistics

Birth rate per 1,000 population (1999): 15.3 (world avg. 22.1).
Death rate per 1,000 population (1999): 5.8 (world avg. 8.9).
Natural increase rate per 1,000 population (1999): 9.5 (world avg. 13.2).
Total fertility rate (avg. births per childbearing woman; 1999): 1.7.
Marriage rate per 1,000 population (1997): 6.8.
Divorce rate per 1,000 population (1997): 1.6.
Life expectancy at birth (1999): male 70.5 years; female 78.4 years.
Major causes of death per 100,000 population (1997): diseases of the circulatory system 121.5; malignant neoplasms (cancers) 115.4; accidents, poisoning, and violence 70.6; diseases of the digestive system 34.4.

National economy

Budget (1997). Revenue: W 91,979,000,000,000 (taxes on goods and services 33.3%, income taxes 26.4%, nontax revenue 13.4%, social security contributions 9.2%, taxes on international trade 6.3%). Expenditures: W 79,004,000,000,000 (education 20.5%, defense 16.7%, social security and welfare 10.8%, transportation and communications 10.4%, agriculture 8.0%, public order 6.1%, general public services 5.1%).
Production (metric tons except as noted). Agriculture, forestry, fishing (1998): rice 7,312,000, cabbages 2,895,000, dry onions 872,000, apples 652,000, tangerines 649,000; livestock (number of live animals) 6,700,000 pigs, 3,279,000 cattle, 88,000,000 chickens; roundwood 1,461,000 cu m; fish catch (1997) 2,204,047. Mining and quarrying (1997): copper ore 225,000; iron ore 166,000; zinc concentrate 8,992. Manufacturing (1997): cement 60,317,000; pig iron 22,712,000; newsprint 1,409,728; polyvinyl chloride resin 1,087,479; woolen fabrics 13,981,000 sq m; colour television receivers 16,407,000 units; passenger cars 2,313,000 units. Construction (permits authorized; 1998): residential 31,154,000 sq m; nonresidential 19,810,000 sq m. Energy production (consumption): electricity (kW-hr; 1999) 239,328,000,000 ([1996] 227,554,000,000); coal (metric tons; 1999) 4,140,000 ([1996] 50,277,000); crude petroleum (barrels; 1996) none (721,829,000); petroleum products (metric tons; 1996) 83,721,000 (74,869,000); natural gas (cu m; 1996) none (12,814,000,000).
Household income and expenditure (1998)[2]. Average household size 3.6; income per household W 47,224,000 (U.S.$33,697); sources of income: wages 60.5%, other 39.5%; expenditure: food and beverages 27.6%, education and recreation 15.3%, transportation and communications 14.6%, utilities 5.4%, clothing and footwear 5.4%, health care 4.4%, household durable goods 3.9%, housing 3.5%, other 19.9%.

Gross national product (1998): U.S.$398,825,000,000 (U.S.$8,600 per capita).

Structure of gross domestic product and labour force

	1998			
	in value W '000,000,000[3]	% of total value	labour force	% of labour force
Agriculture	23,650.5	5.9	2,424,000	11.3
Mining	1,356.7	0.3	20,000	0.1
Manufacturing	117,013.7	29.4	3,884,000	18.2
Construction	41,964.7	10.5	1,577,000	7.4
Public utilities	9,763.3	2.5		
Transp. and commun.	31,592.0	7.9		
Trade	48,490.1	12.2	12,022,000	56.2
Finance	76,634.1	19.2		
Pub. admin., defense	29,041.7	7.3		
Services	27,280.3	6.9		
Other	–8,474.5[4]	–2.1[4]	1,463,000[5]	6.8[5]
TOTAL	398,312.6	100.0	21,390,000	100.0

Public debt (external, outstanding; 1999): U.S.$57,956,000,000.
Population economically active (1998): total 21,390,000; activity rate 46.1% (participation rates: ages 15 and over, 60.7%; female [1997] 40.9%; unemployed 6.8%).

Price and earnings indexes (1995 = 100)

	1993	1994	1995	1996	1997	1998	1999
Consumer price index	90.1	95.7	100.0	104.9	109.6	117.8	118.8
Monthly earnings index	78.8	91.0	100.0	112.2	118.0	114.4	131.2

Tourism (1998): receipts from visitors U.S.$5,890,000,000; expenditures by nationals abroad U.S.$2,069,000,000.

Foreign trade[6]

Balance of trade (current prices)

	1993	1994	1995	1996	1997	1998
U.S.$'000,000	–1,564	–6,335	–10,061	–20,624	–8,452	+39,031
% of total	0.9%	3.2%	3.9%	7.4%	3.0%	17.3%

Imports (1998): U.S.$93,281,800,000 (machinery and transport equipment 36.7%, mineral fuels and lubricants 19.5%, manufactured consumer goods 13.6%, chemicals 8.5%, inedible crude materials 7.4%). *Major import sources:* U.S. 21.8%; Japan 18.1%; China 7.0%; Australia 5.0%; Saudi Arabia 4.7%; Germany 3.6%.
Exports (1998): U.S.$132,313,100,000 (machinery and transport equipment 39.7%, manufactured consumer goods 24.6%, chemicals 6.8%, mineral fuels 3.5%). *Major export destinations:* U.S. 17.2%; Japan 9.2%; China 9.0%; Hong Kong 7.0%; Taiwan 3.9%; Switzerland 3.7%; United Kingdom 3.2%.

Transport and communications

Transport. Railroads (1997): length 6,580 km; passenger-km 30,073,000,000; metric ton-km cargo 12,710,000,000. Roads (1997): total length 84,968 km (paved 74%). Vehicles (1997): passenger cars 7,586,474; trucks and buses 2,826,953. Air transport (1997): passenger-km 59,376,000,000; metric ton-km cargo 7,955,352,000; airports (1996) with scheduled flights 14.

Communications

Medium	date	unit	number	units per 1,000 persons
Daily newspapers	1995	circulation	17,700,000	394
Radio	1997	receivers	47,500,000	1,033
Television	1997	receivers	15,900,000	346
Telephones	1998	main lines	20,089,000	433
Cellular telephones	1998	subscribers	14,019,000	302
Personal computers	1998	units	7,282,000	157
Internet	1998	users	3,103,000	67

Education and health

Educational attainment (1995). Percentage of population age 25 and over having: no formal schooling 8.5%; primary education or less 17.7%; some secondary and secondary 53.1%; postsecondary 20.6%. *Literacy* (1995): total population age 15 and over literate 98.0%; males 99.3%; females 96.7%.

Education (1998)

	schools	teachers	students	student/ teacher ratio
Primary (age 6–13)	14,661	166,842	4,368,473	26.2
Secondary (age 14–19)	3,885	157,696	3,410,862	21.6
Vocational	797	44,577	937,218	21.0
Higher	994	51,964	2,480,138	47.7

Health (1997): physicians 62,609 (1 per 735 persons); hospital beds 220,427 (1 per 209 persons); infant mortality rate per 1,000 live births (1999) 10.0.
Food (1997): daily per capita caloric intake 3,155 (vegetable products 84%, animal products 16%); (1995) 139% of FAO recommended minimum.

Military

Total active duty personnel (1998): 672,000 (army 83.3%, navy 8.9%, air force 7.8%). *Military expenditure as percentage of GNP* (1997): 3.4% (world 2.6%); per capita expenditure U.S.$326.

[1]Kyongsang-namdo includes Ulsan-si. [2]Excludes farm households. [3]At 1995 constant prices. [4]Import duties less imputed bank service charges. [5]Unemployed. [6]Imports c.i.f.; exports f.o.b.

Internet resources for further information:
- **National Statistical Office http://www.nso.go.kr**

Kuwait

Official name: Dawlat al-Kuwayt (State of Kuwait).
Form of government: constitutional monarchy with one legislative body (National Assembly [65[1]]).
Head of state and government: Emir[2].
Capital: Kuwait City.
Official language: Arabic.
Official religion: Islam.
Monetary unit: 1 Kuwaiti dinar (KD) = 1,000 fils; valuation[3] (Oct. 6, 2000) 1 KD = U.S.$3.22 = £2.27.

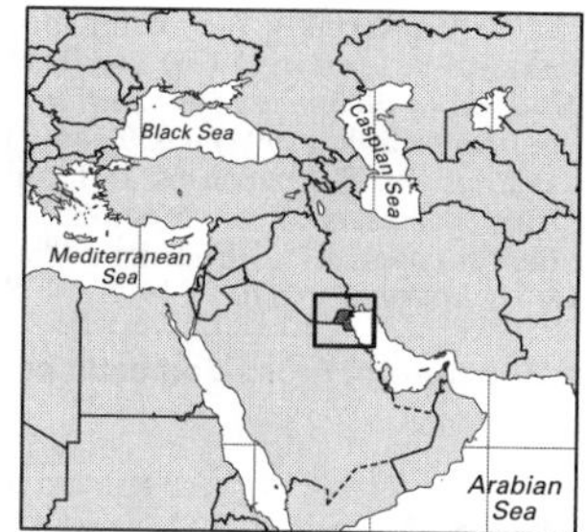

Area and population[4]

Governorates	Capitals	area sq mi	area sq km	population[5] 1997 estimate
Al-Aḥmadī	Al-Aḥmadī	1,984	5,138	303,769
Al-Farwānīyah	Al-Farwānīyah	...	...	483,501
Al-Jahrā'	Al-Jahrā'	4,372	11,324	244,552
Capital	Kuwait City	38	98	296,327
Ḥawallī	Ḥawallī	138	358	481,121
Islands[6]	—	347	900	...
TOTAL		6,880[7]	17,818	1,809,270[5]

Demography

Population (2000): 1,984,000.
Density (2000): persons per sq mi 288.4, persons per sq km 111.3.
Urban-rural (1995): urban 97.0%; rural 3.0%.
Sex distribution (1997): male 61.08%; female 38.92%.
Age breakdown (1997): under 15, 25.8%; 15–29, 26.8%; 30–44, 34.1%; 45–59, 10.7%; 60 and over, 2.6%.
Population projection: (2010) 2,803,000; (2020) 3,761,000.
Doubling time: 39 years.
Ethnolinguistic composition (1995): Arabic 78%; other 22%.
Religious affiliation (1995): Muslim 85%, of which Sunnī 45%, Shīʿī 30%; other Muslim 10%; other (mostly Christian and Hindu) 15.0%.
Major cities (1995): As-Sālimīyah 130,215; Qalīb ash-Shuyūkh 102,178; Ḥawallī 82,238; Abraq Khīṭān 63,628; Kuwait City 28,859.

Vital statistics

Birth rate per 1,000 population (1999): 22.8 (world avg. 22.1).
Death rate per 1,000 population (1999): 2.4 (world avg. 8.9).
Natural increase rate per 1,000 population (1999): 20.4 (world avg. 13.2).
Total fertility rate (avg. births per childbearing woman; 1999): 3.4.
Marriage rate per 1,000 population (1995): 10.2.
Divorce rate per 1,000 population (1995): 3.3.
Life expectancy at birth (1999): male 75.2 years; female 76.6 years.
Major causes of death per 100,000 population (1995): circulatory diseases 87.5; accidents, poisoning, and violence 35.8; cancers 24.9; respiratory diseases 12.3; congenital anomalies 11.3; endocrine, nutritional, and metabolic diseases 8.2; infectious and parasitic diseases 6.7; genitourinary diseases 6.0.

National economy

Budget[8] (1998–99). Revenue: KD 2,443,500,000 (oil revenue 77.5%). Expenditures: KD 4,362,000,000 (salaries 30.4%, transfers 22.5%, construction projects and land acquisitions 10.0%, goods and services 7.3%, others 29.8%).
Public debt: n.a.
Tourism (1998): receipts from visitors U.S.$207,000,000; expenditures by nationals abroad U.S.$2,517,000,000.
Gross national product (1996): U.S.$35,901,000,000 (U.S.$20,470 per capita).

Structure of gross domestic product and labour force

	1998 in value KD '000,000	1998 % of total value	1996 labour force[9]	1996 % of labour force[9]
Agriculture	37.0	0.5	23,400	1.9
Mining (oil sector)	2,370.4	30.9	8,600	0.7
Manufacturing	914.7	11.9	83,600	6.8
Construction	247.4	3.2	136,500	11.1
Public utilities	−1.1	0.0	8,600	0.7
Transp. and commun.	464.3	6.1	44,300	3.6
Trade[10]	747.8	9.7	206,600	16.8
Finance and business services	1,103.1	14.4	43,100	3.5
Pub. admin., defense / Services	2,026.2	26.4	597,800	48.6
Other	−238.6[11]	−3.1[11]	77,500	6.3
TOTAL	7,671.2	100.0	1,230,000	100.0

Production (metric tons except as noted). Agriculture, forestry, fishing (1998): tomatoes 38,857, cucumber and gherkins 32,608, eggplants 28,629, onions 3,758, garlic 494; livestock (number of live animals) 421,053 sheep, 129,754 goats, 18,481 cattle, 8,600 camels; fish catch (1997) 7,826. Mining and quarrying (1996): sulfur 576,000; lime 35,000. Manufacturing (value added in KD '000,000; 1995): refined petroleum products 2,010; food products 143; clothing and apparel 125; fabricated metal products 120; industrial chemicals 102; nonelectrical machinery 71. Construction (floor area of new construction; 1995): residential 2,018,600 sq m; nonresidential 141,200 sq m. Energy production (consumption): electricity (kW-hr; 1998) 29,988,000,000 ([1996] 25,925,000,000); coal, none (none): crude petroleum (barrels; 1999) 795,000,000 ([1996] 283,000,000); petroleum products (metric tons; 1996) 36,572,000 (6,478,000); natural gas (cu m; 1996) 9,098,000,000 (9,098,000,000).

Population economically active (1995): total 746,408; activity rate of total population 47.4% (participation rates: ages 15–59, 70.7%; female 26.1%; unemployed 0.7%).

Price and earnings indexes (1995 = 100)

	1992	1993	1994	1995	1996	1997	1998
Consumer price index	94.6	95.0	97.4	100.0	103.6	104.2	104.4
Earnings index	...	...	...	...	...	...	...

Household income and expenditure. Average household size (1995) 3.9; annual income per household (1973)[12] KD 4,246 (U.S.$12,907); sources of income (1986): wages and salaries 53.8%, self-employment 20.8%, other 25.4; expenditure (1992): food, beverages, and tobacco 37.0%, housing and energy 18.7%, transportation 15.3%, household appliances and services 11.1%, clothing and footwear 10.0%, education and health 2.5%.
Land use (1994): forest 0.1%; pasture 7.7%; agriculture 0.3%; other 91.9%.

Foreign trade[13]

Balance of trade (current prices)

	1993	1994	1995	1996	1997	1998
U.S.$'000,000	+3,323	+4,668	+5,579	+6,997	+6,534	+1,900
% of total	19.3%	26.1%	27.8%	30.6%	29.7%	11.0%

Imports (1998): KD 2,626,150,000 (machinery and transport equipment 41.2%, manufactured goods 18.3%, miscellaneous manufactured articles 13.7%, food and live animals 13.6%, chemical products 7.8%, inedible crude materials except fuel 1.8%). *Major import sources:* U.S. 15.4%; Japan 13.6%; Germany 7.0%; Saudi Arabia 6.2%; U.K. 5.8%; Italy 5.8%; France 3.7%; India 3.5%.
Exports (1998)[14]: KD 2,911,600,000 (crude petroleum and petroleum products 97.9%). *Major export destinations:* Singapore 12.0%; Saudi Arabia 11.7%; U.A.E. 9.3%; India 7.1%; Egypt 5.1%; China 4.8%; Belgium-Luxembourg 4.7%; Pakistan 4.1%.

Transport and communications

Transport. Railroads: none. Roads (1996): total length 2,765 mi, 4,450 km (paved 81%). Vehicles (1996): passenger cars 538,000; trucks and buses 155,000. Merchant marine (1992): vessels (100 gross tons and over) 209; total deadweight tonnage 3,188,526. Air transport (1997): passenger-mi 3,728,000,000, passenger-km 6,000,000,000; short ton-mi cargo 255,202,000, metric ton-km cargo 372,588,000; airports (1997) with scheduled flights 1.

Communications

Medium	date	unit	number	units per 1,000 persons
Daily newspapers	1996	circulation	635,000	377
Radio	1997	receivers	1,175,000	678
Television	1997	receivers	875,000	505
Telephones	1998	main lines	427,000	229
Cellular telephones	1998	subscribers	250,000	134
Personal computers	1998	units	190,000	102
Internet	1998	users	60,000	32

Education and health

Educational attainment (1988). Percentage of population age 25 and over having: no formal schooling 44.8%; primary education 8.6%; some secondary 15.1%; complete secondary 15.1%; higher 16.4%. *Literacy* (1995): total population age 15 and over literate 79.3%; males literate 82.3%; females literate 76.0%.

Education (1997–98)

	schools	teachers	students	student/ teacher ratio
Primary (age 6–9)	286	10,798	142,308	13.2
Secondary (age 10–17)	409[15]	20,867	222,079	10.6
Voc., teacher tr.	36[15]	320	2,214	6.9
Higher	1[16]	1,691[17]	29,509[17]	17.5[17]

Health (1996): physicians 3,255 (1 per 619 persons); hospital beds 4,425[18] (1 per 456 persons); infant mortality rate per 1,000 live births (1999) 11.9.
Food (1997): daily per capita caloric intake 3,096 (vegetable products 76%, animal products 24%); (1995) 131% of FAO recommended minimum requirement.

Military

Total active duty personnel (1997): 15,300 (army [including central staff] 71.9%, navy 11.8%, air force 16.3%). *Military expenditure as percentage of GNP* (1997): 7.5% (world 2.6%); per capita expenditure U.S.$1,525.

[1]Fifty elected seats in National Assembly may include Cabinet ministers; Cabinet ministers not elected to National Assembly serve ex officio. [2]Assisted by prime minister. [3]Composite rate; pegged rate to a basket of currencies. [4]Area of governorates reflects situation prior to Amiri Decree No. 156 of 1988, which established Al-Farwānīyah governorate; but population figures account for the reorganization. [5]Estimates based on census taken on April 23, 1995. [6]Bubian Island 333 sq mi (863 sq km) and Warba Island 14 sq mi (37 sq km). [7]Detail does not add to total given because of rounding. [8]Approved budget. [9]Size of labour force and subtotal figures derived from percentages. [10]Trade includes restaurants and hotels. [11]Includes import duties and imputed bank service charges. [12]Kuwaiti households only. [13]Imports and exports are f.o.b. in the balance of trade table. [14]Total exports and reexports include oil and non-oil, but breakdown by destination is derived from non-oil exports. [15]1995–96. [16]1994–95. [17]1996–97. [18]Public hospitals only.

Internet resources for further information:

- **Central Bank of Kuwait http://www.cbk.gov.kw**
- **Kuwait Information Office (Washington, D.C.) http://www.kuwait-info.org**
- **Ministry of Planning http://www.mop.gov.kw/indexe.htm**

Kyrgyzstan

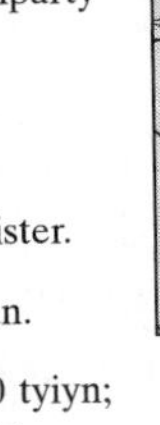

Official name: Respublika Kirgizstan (Kyrgyz); Kyrgyz Respublikasy (Russian); (Kyrgyz Republic).
Form of government: unitary multiparty republic with two legislative houses (Assembly of People's Representatives [45]; Legislative Assembly [60]).
Head of state and government: President assisted by Prime Minister.
Capital: Bishkek.
Official languages: Kyrgyz; Russian.
Official religion: none.
Monetary unit: 1 som (K.S.) = 100 tyiyn; valuation (Oct. 6, 2000) 1 U.S.$ = K.S. 48.12; 1 £ = K.S. 69.60.

Area and population

		area		population
Provinces	**Capitals**	sq mi	sq km	1993[1] estimate
Chüy (Chu)	Kara-Balta	7,200	18,700	774,000
Jalal-Abad (Dzhalal-Abad)	Jalal-Abad (Dzhalal-Abad)	15,200	39,500	812,800
Naryn	Naryn	18,300	47,300	267,900
Osh	Osh	14,700	38,100	1,360,900
Talas	Talas	4,400	11,400	203,000
Ysyk-Köl (Issyk-Kul)	Ysyk-Köl (Issyk-Kul)	16,800	43,500	429,300
City				
Bishkek (Frunze)	—	...	...	634,100
TOTAL		76,600[2]	198,500[2]	4,482,000

Demography

Population (2000): 4,895,000.
Density (2000): persons per sq mi 63.4, persons per sq km 24.5.
Urban-rural (1999): urban 40.0%; rural 60.0%.
Sex distribution (1997): male 49.37%; female 50.63%.
Age breakdown (1997): under 15, 37.3%; 15–29, 26.3%; 30–44, 19.5%; 45–59, 8.8%; 60–74, 6.5%; 75 and over, 1.6%.
Population projection: (2010) 5,687,000; (2020) 6,627,000.
Doubling time: 40 years.
Ethnic composition (1996): Kyrgyz 59.7%; Russian 16.2%[1]; Uzbek 14.1%; Ukrainian 1.7%; Tatar 1.2%; Kazakh 0.9%; other 6.2%.
Religious affiliation (1997): Muslim (mostly Sunnī) 70.0%; Russian Orthodox 5.7%; other 24.3%.
Major cities (1996): Bishkek (Frunze) 585,800; Osh 220,500; Jalal-Abad 74,200[3]; Tokmok 71,200[3]; Kara-Köl 64,300[3].

Vital statistics

Birth rate per 1,000 population (1999): 24.8 (world avg. 22.6); (1994) legitimate 83.2%; illegitimate 16.8%.
Death rate per 1,000 population (1999): 7.2 (world avg. 8.9).
Natural increase rate per 1,000 population (1999): 17.6 (world avg. 13.7).
Total fertility rate (avg. births per childbearing woman; 1999): 3.1.
Marriage rate per 1,000 population (1995): 6.0.
Divorce rate per 1,000 population (1995): 1.3.
Life expectancy at birth (1999): male 64.0 years; female 72.0 years.
Major causes of death per 100,000 population (1996): diseases of the circulatory system 278.5; diseases of the respiratory system 75.0; malignant neoplasms (cancers) 25.7; accidents, poisoning, and violence 21.4; infectious and parasitic diseases 12.6; diseases of the digestive system 9.8.

National economy

Budget (1998). Revenue: K.S. 6,090,700,000 (tax revenue 79.9%, of which taxes on goods and services 54.2%, taxes on income and profits 14.6%, taxes on international trade 6.2%; nontax revenue 18.7%). Expenditures: K.S. 7,531,600,000 (education 22.3%; social security 13.0%; general public services 13.5%; health 12.8%; economic development 11.2%; defense 6.5%).
Public debt (external, outstanding; 1998): U.S.$909,200,000.
Land use (1994): forest 3.7%; pasture 45.4%; agriculture 7.2%; other 43.7%.
Population economically active (1995): total 1,692,000; activity rate of total population 37.2% (1993; participation rates: ages 16–59 [male], 16–54 [female] 81.1%; female 49.0%; (1996) unemployed 4.3%).

Price and earnings indexes (1995 = 100)

	1993	1994	1995	1996	1997	1998	1999
Consumer price index	...	...	100.0	131.9	162.9	179.9	244.5
Monthly earnings index	22.8	63.4	100.0	133.3	184.7	228.3	...

Production (metric tons except as noted). Agriculture, forestry, fishing (1999): grain 1,630,000, potatoes 957,000, vegetables (other than potatoes) and melons 485,000, fruit (excluding melons) 109,000, seed cotton 87,000; livestock (number of live animals) 3,570,000 sheep and goats, 825,000 cattle, 320,000 horses, 80,000 pigs; roundwood (1998) 42,400 cu m; fish catch (1997) 300. Mining and quarrying (1998): antimony 1,297; mercury 630; uranium 450; gold 21 kg. Manufacturing (value of production in '000,000 som; 1994): textiles 1,112; processed foods 729; ferrous and nonferrous metals 678; machinery and metalwork 650; construction materials 258; footwear and leather goods 89. Construction (1992): residential 1,232,000 sq m. Energy production (consumption): electricity (kW-hr; 1996) 13,480,000,000 (11,400,000,000); coal (metric tons; 1996) 410,000 (1,018,000); crude petroleum (barrels; 1996) 600,000 (500,000); petroleum products (metric tons; 1996) 3,000 (566,000); natural gas (cu m; 1996) 26,000,000 (1,053,000,000).
Household income and expenditure (1990). Average household size 4.7; income per household (1994) 4,359 som (U.S.$325.30); sources of income: wages and salaries 49.7%, pensions and stipends 11.1%, income from sale of agricultural products 3.5%, other 35.7%; expenditure: food and clothing 48.0%, health care 13.1%, housing 5.9%, cultural affairs 5.2%, appliances 4.4%.
Gross national product (1998): U.S.$1,771,000,000 (U.S.$380 per capita).

Structure of gross domestic product and labour force

	1998		1997	
	in value K.S. '000,000	% of total value	labour force	% of labour force
Agriculture	12,324.2	36.0	815,600	48.3
Mining, Manufacturing	5,559.2	16.3	171,600	10.2
Public utilities	812.8	2.4	...	...
Construction	1,537.3	4.5	57,000	3.4
Transp. and commun.	1,535.0	4.5	79,200	4.7
Trade	4,501.8	13.2	172,400	10.2
Finance	410.1	1.2	14,300	0.8
Public admin., defense	1,035.5	3.0	60,300	3.6
Services	3,492.5	10.2	269,700	16.0
Other	2,973.0	8.7	49,200	2.9
TOTAL	34,181.4	100.0	1,689,300	100.0[4]

Tourism (1997): receipts from visitors, U.S.$7,000,000; expenditures by nationals abroad, U.S.$4,000,000.

Foreign trade[5]

Balance of trade (current prices)

	1993	1994	1995	1996	1997	1998
U.S.$'000,000	–107.1	–86.1	–122.1	–251.7	–15.3	–220.6
% of total	13.6%	11.2%	13.0%	19.2%	1.2%	17.1%

Imports (1997): U.S.$709,300,000 (oil and gas 24.8%, machine-building equipment 21.7%, chemical products 13.5%, food products 11.7%, light industrial products 6.8%). *Major import sources:* Russian Federation 26.9%; Uzbekistan 18.1%; Kazakhstan 9.8%; Turkey 6.2%; United States 5.6%.
Exports (1997): U.S.$603,800,000 (metals 36.3%, electricity 13.8%, food products 13.2%, machinery 10.2%, light industrial products 10.0%, construction materials 4.4%). *Major export destinations:* Switzerland 26.9%; Uzbekistan 16.8%; Russian Federation 16.4%; Kazakhstan 14.4%; China 5.2%.

Transport and communications

Transport. Railroads (1999): length 424 km; (1995) passenger-km 30,000,000; metric ton-km cargo 403,000,000. Roads (1996): total length 18,500 km (paved 91%). Vehicles (1996): passenger cars 146,000; trucks and buses, n.a. Air transport (1996): passenger-km 4,408,000,000; metric ton-km cargo 65,199,000; airports (1997) with scheduled flights 2.

Communications

Medium	date	unit	number	units per 1,000 persons
Daily newspapers	1996	circulation	67,000	15
Radio	1997	receivers	520,000	113
Television	1997	receivers	210,000	45
Telephones	1998	main lines	355,000	76
Cellular phones	1998	subscribers	1,350	0.3
Personal computers	...	units	...	...
Internet	1998	users	2,512	0.5

Education and health

Educational attainment (1989). Percentage of population age 19 and over having: primary education 4.7%; some secondary 20.9%; completed secondary 44.4%; some postsecondary 19.3%; higher 10.7%. *Literacy* (1989): total population age 15 and over literate 4,130,562 (97.0%); males literate 2,048,536 (98.6%); females literate 2,082,026 (95.5%).

Education (1995–96)

	schools	teachers	students	student/ teacher ratio
Primary (age 6–13)	1,885	24,086	473,077	19.7
Secondary (age 14–17)	1,474[6]	38,915	498,849	12.8
Voc., teacher tr.	53[6]	3,371	32,005	9.5
Higher	23[6]	3,691	49,744	13.5

Health (1997): physicians 15,100 (1 per 307 persons); hospital beds 40,700 (1 per 114 persons); infant mortality rate per 1,000 live births (1999) 39.
Food (1998): daily per capita caloric intake 2,535 (vegetable products 78%, animal products 22%); 99% of FAO recommended minimum requirement.

Military

Total active duty personnel (1999): 9,200 (army 73.9%, air force 26.1%). *Military expenditure as percentage of GNP* (1997): 1.6% (world 2.6%); per capita expenditure U.S.$35.

[1]Russian population declined between 1989 and 1998 from 21.0% to 14.6%. [2]Total area per more recent survey is 77,200 sq mi (199,900 sq km). [3]1991. [4]Detail does not add to total given because of rounding. [5]Imports and exports in balance of trade are f.o.b. [6]1993–94.

Internet resources for further information:

- **National Statistical Committee of the Kyrgyz Republic http://nsc.bishkek.su/Eng/Home/Start.html**
- **Embassy of the Kyrgyz Republic http://www.kyrgyzstan.org**

Laos

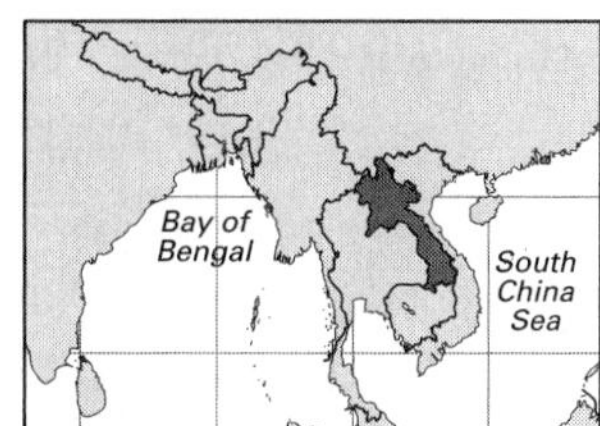

Official name: Sathalanalat Paxathipatai Paxaxôn Lao (Lao People's Democratic Republic).
Form of government: unitary single-party people's republic with one legislative house (National Assembly[1] [99]).
Chief of state: President.
Head of government: Prime Minister.
Capital: Vientiane (Viangchan).
Official language: Lao.
Official religion: none.
Monetary unit: 1 kip (KN) = 100 at; valuation (Oct. 6, 2000) managed floating rate, 1 U.S.$ = KN 7,565; 1 £ = KN 10,944.

Area and population

Provinces	Capitals	area sq mi	area sq km	population 1995 estimate
Attapu	Attapu	3,985	10,320	87,700
Bokèo	Houayxay	2,392	6,196	114,900
Bolikhamxai	Pakxan	5,739	14,863	164,900
Champasak	Pakxé	5,952	15,415	503,300
Houaphan	Xam Nua	6,371	16,500	247,300
Khammouan	Thakhek	6,299	16,315	275,400
Louangnamtha	Louangnamtha	3,600	9,325	115,200
Louangphrabang	Louangphrabang	6,515	16,875	367,200
Oudomxay	Xay	5,934	15,370	211,300
Phôngsali	Phôngsali	6,282	16,270	153,400
Salavan	Salavan	4,128	10,691	258,300
Savannakhét	Savannakhét	8,407	21,774	674,900
Special Region	...	2,743	7,105	54,200
Viangchan	Muang Phôn-Hông	6,149	15,927	286,800
Xaignabouli	Xaignabouli	6,328	16,389	293,300
Xékong	Thong	2,959	7,665	64,200
Xiangkhoang	Phônsavan	6,131	15,880	201,200
Municipalities				
Viangchan	Vientiane (Viangchan)	1,514	3,920	531,800
TOTAL		91,429[2]	236,800	4,605,300

Demography

Population (2000): 5,497,000.
Density (2000): persons per sq mi 60.1, persons per sq km 23.2.
Urban-rural (1999): urban 23.0%; rural 77.0%.
Sex distribution (1996): male 49.42%; female 50.58%.
Age breakdown (1996): under 15, 44.2%; 15–29, 25.4%; 30–44, 16.0%; 45–59, 8.7%; 60–74, 4.5%; 75 and over, 1.2%.
Population projection: (2010) 6,993,000; (2020) 8,637,000.
Doubling time: 27 years.
Ethnic composition (2000): Lao-Lum (Lao) 53.0%; Lao-Theung (Mon-Khmer) 23.0%; Lao-Tai (Tai) 13.0%; Lao-Soung (Miao [Hmong] and Man [Yao]) 10.0%; other (ethnic Chinese or Vietnamese) 1.0%.
Religious affiliation (1980): Buddhist 57.8%; tribal religionist 33.6%; Christian 1.8%, of which Roman Catholic 0.8%, Protestant 0.2%; Muslim 1.0%; atheist 1.0%; Chinese folk religionist 0.9%; none 3.8%; other 0.1%.
Major cities (1985): Vientiane (Viangchan) 178,203; Savannakhét 96,652; Louangphrabang 68,399; Pakxé 47,323.

Vital statistics

Birth rate per 1,000 population (1999): 38.8 (world avg. 22.6).
Death rate per 1,000 population (1999): 13.0 (world avg. 8.9).
Natural increase rate per 1,000 population (1999): 25.8 (world avg. 13.7).
Total fertility rate (avg. births per childbearing woman; 1999): 5.6.
Marriage rate per 1,000 population: n.a.
Divorce rate per 1,000 population: n.a.
Life expectancy at birth (1999): male 53.0 years; female 55.0 years.
Major causes of death per 100,000 population (incomplete, 1990): malaria 7.6; pneumonia 3.0; meningitis 1.5; diarrhea 1.2; tuberculosis 0.8.

National economy

Budget (1998–99). Revenue: KN 1,312,100,000,000 (taxes 52.3%, foreign grants 37.0%, nontax revenue 10.7%). Expenditures: KN 1,685,100,000,000 (current expenditure 31.8%, capital expenditure 68.2%).
Public debt (external, outstanding; 1998): U.S.$2,373,000,000.
Tourism (1997): receipts from visitors U.S.$73,000,000; expenditures by nationals abroad U.S.$21,000,000.
Population economically active (1989): total 1,888,000; activity rate of total population 49.0% (participation rates [1985]: ages 15–64, 84.2%; female 45.3%; unemployed [1994] 2.6%).

Price and earnings indexes (1995 = 100)

	1993	1994	1995	1996	1997	1998	1999
Consumer price index	78.3	83.6	100.0	113.0	144.1	275.2	628.7
Earnings index	...	...	....	...	...	...	...

Production (metric tons except as noted). Agriculture, forestry, fishing (1999): rice 2,103,000, sugarcane 174,000, corn (maize) 96,000, sweet potatoes 81,000, cassava 70,000, pineapples 34,000, melons 33,000, potatoes 33,000, oranges 28,000, seed cotton 26,000, bananas 22,000, coffee 18,000; livestock (number of live animals) 1,937,000 pigs, 1,497,000 cattle, 1,286,000 water buffalo, 200,000 goats, 28,000 horses, 13,882,000 chickens; roundwood (1998) 4,591,000 cu m; fish catch (1997) 40,000. Mining and quarrying (1997): gypsum 145,000; rock salt 18,000; tin (metal content) 618. Manufacturing (1998): plastic products 3,225; tobacco 1,000; detergent 912; nails 624; clothing 23,000,000 pieces; cigarettes 55,000,000 packs; beer 332,000 hectolitres; soft drinks 125,000 hectolitres. Construction: n.a. Energy production (consumption): electricity (kW-hr; 1996) 1,294,000,000 (517,000,000); coal (metric tons; 1996) 1,000 (1,000); crude petroleum, n.a. (n.a.); petroleum products (metric tons; 1996) none (107,000); natural gas, n.a. (n.a.).
Gross national product (1998): U.S.$1,583,000,000 (U.S.$320 per capita).

Structure of gross domestic product and labour force

	1998 in value KN '000,000[3]	1998 % of total value	1989 labour force	1989 % of labour force
Agriculture	517,100	52.1	1,359,000	72.0
Manufacturing	164,500	16.6		
Mining	4,100	0.4		
Construction	26,700	2.7		
Public utilities	20,500	2.1		
Transp. and commun.	56,800	5.7	58,533	8.1
Trade	119,900	12.1		
Finance	29,800	3.0		
Pub. admin., defense / Services	43,100	4.3		
Other	10,400	1.0		
TOTAL	992,900	100.0	1,888,000	100.0

Household income and expenditure. Average household size (1985) 6.0%; average annual income per household KN 3,710 (U.S.$371); sources of income: n.a.; expenditure: n.a.
Land use (1994): forested 54.4%; meadows and pastures 3.5%; agricultural and under permanent cultivation 3.9%; other 38.2%.

Foreign trade[4]

Balance of trade (current prices)

	1994	1995	1996	1997	1998	1999
U.S.$'000,000	–263.7	–239.3	–366.8	–347.0	–183.3	–214.0
% of total	30.5%	25.6%	36.2%	32.6%	19.9%	25.6%

Imports (1998): U.S.$552,800,000 (consumption goods 42.3%; investment goods 41.0%, of which construction and electrical equipment 14.7%, motor vehicles 7.1%; materials for garment assembly 12.1%). *Major import sources* (1997): Thailand 52.0%; Vietnam 3.9%; Japan 1.6%; Hong Kong 1.5%; China 0.8%.
Exports (1998): U.S.$369,500,000 (wood products 34.3%; garments 20.8%; electricity 18.0%; coffee 14.3%). *Major export destinations* (1997): Vietnam 42.7%; Thailand 22.1%; France 6.3%; Belgium 5.6%; Germany 5.1%.

Transport and communications

Transport. Railroads: none. Roads (1996): total length 13,870 mi, 22,321 km (paved [1995] 14%). Vehicles (1996): passenger cars 16,320; trucks and buses 4,200. Merchant marine (1992): vessels (100 gross tons and over) 1; total deadweight tonnage 1,469. Air transport (1995): passenger-mi 29,000,000, passenger-km 48,000,000; short ton-mi cargo 3,000,000, metric ton-km cargo 5,000,000; airports (1996) with scheduled flights 11.

Communications

Medium	date	unit	number	units per 1,000 persons
Daily newspapers	1996	circulation	18,000	3.7
Radio	1997	receivers	730,000	145
Television	1997	receivers	52,000	10
Telephones	1998	main lines	28,472	5.5
Cellular telephones	1998	subscribers	6,453	1.2
Personal computers	1996	units	5,000	1.1
Internet	...	users	...	...

Education and health

Educational attainment (1985). Percentage of population age 6 and over having: no schooling 49.3%; primary 41.2%; secondary 9.1%; higher 0.4%. *Literacy* (1995): total population age 15 and over literate 56.6%; males literate 69.4%; females literate 44.4%.

Education (1996–97)

	schools	teachers	students	student/ teacher ratio
Primary (age 6–10)	7,896	25,831	786,335	30.4
Secondary (age 11–16)	750[5]	10,717	180,160	16.8
Voc., teacher tr.	139[6]	1,600[7]	9,400[7]	5.9[7]
Higher	9[5]	1,369	12,732	9.3

Health: physicians (1995) 3,100 (1 per 1,563 persons); hospital beds (1990) 10,364 (1 per 402 persons); infant mortality rate (1999) 90.
Food (1998): daily per capita caloric intake 2,175 (vegetable products 94%, animal products 6%); 98% of FAO recommended minimum requirement.

Military

Total active duty personnel (1999): 29,100 (army 85.9%, navy 2.1%, air force 12.0%). *Military expenditure as percentage of GNP* (1997): 3.4% (world 2.6%); per capita expenditure U.S.$12.

[1]Formerly known as the Supreme People's Assembly. [2]Detail does not add to total given because of rounding. [3]At constant 1990 prices. [4]Import figures are c.i.f. in balance of trade and commodities. [5]1989–90. [6]1988–89. [7]1995–96.

Internet resources for further information:
- **Discovering Laos http://www.laoembassy.com/discover/index.htm**

Latvia

Official name: Latvijas Republika (Republic of Latvia).
Form of government: unitary multiparty republic with a single legislative body (Parliament, or Saeima [100]).
Chief of state: President.
Head of government: Prime Minister.
Capital: Riga.
Official language: Latvian.
Official religion: none.
Monetary unit: 1 lats (Ls; plural lati) = 100 santimi; valuation (Oct. 6, 2000) 1 U.S.$ = 0.62 lats; 1 £ = 0.90 lats.

Area and population

Cities	area sq km	population 1999 estimate[1]	Districts	area sq km	population 1999 estimate[1]
Daugavpils	72	115,450	Jelgava	1,604	34,797
Jelgava	60	70,931	Krāslava	2,285	37,529
Jūrmala	100	58,865	Kuldīga	2,502	38,113
Liepāja	60	95,427	Liepāja	3,594	49,682
Rēzekne	17	40,557	Limbaži	2,602	40,558
Riga	307	796,732	Ludza	2,569	38,231
Ventspils	46	46,501	Madona	3,346	47,423
			Ogre	1,840	63,611
Districts			Preiļi	2,041	41,418
Aizkraukle	2,565	42,189	Rēzekne	2,655	41,485
Alūksne	2,243	27,031	Rīga (Riga)	3,059	146,121
Balvi	2,386	31,036	Saldus	2,182	38,737
Bauska	1,882	51,464	Talsi	2,751	49,261
Cēsis	3,067	61,247	Tukums	2,447	55,044
Daugavpils	2,525	44,053	Valka	2,437	34,932
Dobele	1,633	40,784	Valmiera	2,365	60,174
Gulbene	1,877	28,998	Ventspils	2,472	13,968
Jēkabpils	2,998	57,096	TOTAL	64,589	2,439,445[2]

Demography

Population (2000): 2,369,000[2].
Density (2000): persons per sq mi 95.0, persons per sq km 36.7.
Urban-rural (1999[1]): urban 69.0%; rural 31.0%.
Sex distribution (1999[1]): male 46.32%; female 53.68%.
Age breakdown (1998[1]): under 15, 18.5%; 15–29, 21.0%; 30–44, 22.0%; 45–59, 18.2%; 60–74, 15.2%; 75 and over, 5.1%.
Population projection: (2010) 2,219,000; (2020) 2,119,000.
Ethnic composition (1999[1]): Latvian 55.7%; Russian 32.3%; Belarusian 3.9%; Ukrainian 2.9%; Polish 2.2%; Lithuanian 1.3%; other 1.7%.
Religious affiliation (1995): Christian 39.6%, of which Protestant 16.7% (of which Lutheran 14.6%), Roman Catholic 14.9%, Orthodox 8.0%; Jewish 0.6%; other (mostly nonreligious) 59.8%.
Major cities (1999[1]): Riga 796,732; Daugavpils 115,450; Liepāja 95,427; Jelgava 70,931; Jūrmala 58,865.

Vital statistics

Birth rate per 1,000 population (1998): 7.5 (world avg. 22.1); legitimate 62.9%; illegitimate 37.1%.
Death rate per 1,000 population (1998): 14.0 (world avg. 8.9).
Natural increase rate per 1,000 population (1998): –6.5 (world avg. 13.2).
Total fertility rate (avg. births per childbearing woman; 1998): 1.1.
Marriage rate per 1,000 population (1998): 3.9.
Divorce rate per 1,000 population (1998): 2.5.
Life expectancy at birth (1998): male 64.1 years; female 75.5 years.
Major causes of death per 100,000 population (1998): diseases of the circulatory system 775.6; malignant neoplasms (cancers) 231.8; accidents, poisoning, and violence 161.8; diseases of the digestive system 42.2.

National economy

Budget (1998). Revenue: Ls 1,577,400,000 (social security contributions 27.1%, value-added taxes 20.1%, personal income taxes 13.9%, excises 10.7%, nontax revenue 10.1%). Expenditures: Ls 1,572,300,000 (social security and welfare 34.4%, education 15.7%, health 9.4%, police 5.8%, defense 2.4%).
Production (metric tons except as noted). Agriculture, forestry, fishing (1999): grasses for forage and silage 13,800,000, hay 1,355,000, potatoes 795,500, sugar beets 451,500, wheat 351,900, barley 232,600, rye 88,700; livestock (number of live animals) 403,400 pigs, 375,700 cattle; roundwood (1998) 10,030,000 cu m; fish catch (1997) 106,027. Mining and quarrying (1998): peat 171,700; gypsum 119,100. Manufacturing (value added in Ls '000,000; 1996): alcoholic beverages 58.7; fish processing 32.8; dairy products 26.9; bakery products 26.4; sawn wood 23.3; wearing apparel 20.5; veneer/plywood 20.5. Energy production (consumption): electricity (kW-hr; 1998) 5,797,000,000 (5,133,000,000); coal (1996) none (293,000); crude petroleum, none (none); petroleum products (1996) none (2,079,000); natural gas (cu m; 1996) none (938,000,000).
Household income and expenditure. Average household size (1996) 2.7; annual disposable income per household (1996) Ls 1,659 (U.S.$3,011); sources of income (1998): wages and salaries 55.8%, pensions and transfers 25.7%, self-employment 9.5%; expenditure (1998): food, beverages, and tobacco 46.4%, housing and energy 16.6%, transportation and communications 9.8%, clothing and footwear 6.9%.
Public debt (external, outstanding; 1998): U.S.$413,300,000.
Gross national product (1998): U.S.$5,917,000,000 (U.S.$2,420 per capita).

Structure of gross domestic product and labour force

	1998			
	in value Ls '000,000	% of total value	labour force[3]	% of labour force[3]
Agriculture, forestry	155.0	4.1	184,000	15.2
Mining and quarrying	5.0	0.1	2,000	0.2
Manufacturing	662.9	17.6	171,000	14.1
Construction	169.2	4.5	63,000	5.2
Public utilities	127.4	3.4	19,000	1.6
Transp. and commun.	464.5	12.3	90,000	7.4
Trade	606.1	16.1	191,000	15.7
Finance, real estate	298.4	7.9	62,000	5.1
Pub. admin., defense	329.5	8.7	64,000	5.3
Services	461.4	12.2	197,000	16.2
Other	494.1[4]	13.1[4]	169,500[5]	14.0[5]
TOTAL	3,773.5	100.0	1,212,500	100.0

Population economically active (1997): total 1,186,100; activity rate of total population 48.2% (participation rates: ages 15–64, 70.2%; female 48.1%; unemployed [1998] 7.6%).

Price and earnings indexes (1995 = 100)

	1994	1995	1996	1997	1998	1999	2000[6]
Consumer price index	80.0	100.0	117.6	127.5	133.4	136.6	140.7
Annual earnings index	80.6	100.0	114.9	139.7	148.9	107.5	...

Land use (1994): forested 44.4%; meadows and pastures 12.4; agricultural and under permanent cultivation 27.0%; other 16.2%.

Foreign trade[7]

Balance of trade (current prices)

	1994	1995	1996	1997	1998	1999
Ls '000,000	–142	–235	–428	–541	–727	–644
% of total	11.4%	14.6%	21.2%	21.8%	25.4%	25.4%

Imports (1998): Ls 1,881,000,000 (machinery and equipment 20.5%, chemicals and chemical products 11.1%, mineral fuels 10.5%, transport vehicles 10.4%, base and fabricated metals 8.4%). *Major import sources:* Germany 16.8%; Russia 11.8%; Finland 9.5%; Sweden 7.2%; Estonia 6.6%.
Exports (1998): Ls 1,069,000,000 (wood and paper products 33.5%, textiles and clothing 16.1%, food and beverages 9.8%, base and fabricated metals 9.8%). *Major export destinations:* Germany 15.6%; U.K. 13.5%; Russia 12.1%; Sweden 10.3%; Lithuania 7.4%.

Transport and communications

Transport. Railroads (1998): length 2,413 km; passenger-km (1998) 1,059,000,000; metric-km cargo (1998) 12,995,000,000. Roads (1997): total length 55,942 km (paved 38%). Vehicles (1997): passenger cars 431,816; trucks and buses 95,329. Air transport (1998): passenger-km 298,000,000; metric ton-km cargo 9,000,000; airports with scheduled flights (1996) 1.

Communications

Medium	date	unit	number	units per 1,000 persons
Daily newspapers	1996	circulation	616,000	247
Radio	1997	receivers	1,760,000	713
Television	1997	receivers	1,220,000	494
Telephones	1998	main lines	741,358	303
Cellular telephones	1998	subscribers	167,460	68
Internet	1998	users	100,000	41

Education and health

Educational attainment (1989). Percentage of population age 25 and over having: no formal schooling 0.6%; incomplete primary education 18.5%; complete primary 21.2%; secondary 46.3%; higher 13.4%. *Literacy* (1995): percentage of total population age 15 and over literate 99.6%.

Education (1996–97)

	schools	teachers	students	student/ teacher ratio
Primary	1,074	10,883[8]	146,653	13.5[8]
Secondary	...	24,112	196,148	8.1
Vocational	...	5,740	43,170	7.5
Higher	28	4,486	56,187	12.5

Health (1998): physicians 6,900 (1 per 355 persons); hospital beds 23,165 (1 per 106 persons); infant mortality rate per 1,000 live births (1998) 15.0.
Food (1996): daily per capita caloric intake 2,919 (vegetable products 73%, animal products 27%); 114% of FAO recommended minimum requirement.

Military

Total active duty personnel (1999): 3,600[9] (army 70.9%, navy 23.3%, air force 5.8%). *Military expenditure as percentage of GNP* (1997): 0.9% (world 2.6%); per capita expenditure U.S.$39.

[1]January 1. [2]March 2000 preliminary census figure equals 2,375,339. [3]Annual average official estimate. [4]Indirect taxes less subsidies. [5]Represents nonworking job seekers, of which 91,800 (7.6%) are registered unemployed. [6]February. [7]Imports are f.o.b. in balance of trade and c.i.f. for commodities and trading partners. [8]Full-time teachers only. [9]Excludes 3,500 border guards classified as paramilitary.

Internet resources for further information:
- **Bank of Latvia http://www.bank.lv**
- **Central Statistical Bureau of Latvia http://www.csb.lv**

Lebanon

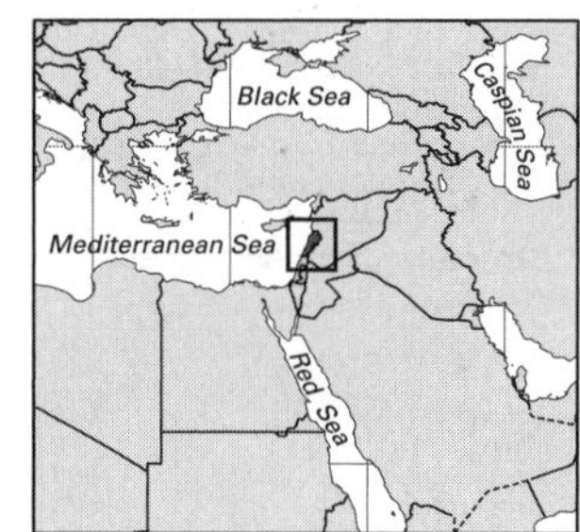

Official name: Al-Jumhūrīyah al-Lubnānīyah (Lebanese Republic).
Form of government: unitary multiparty republic with one legislative house (National Assembly [128])[1].
Chief of state: President.
Head of government: Prime Minister.
Capital: Beirut.
Official language: Arabic.
Official religion: none.
Monetary unit: 1 Lebanese pound (£L) = 100 piastres; valuation (Oct. 6, 2000) 1 U.S.$ = £L 1,514; 1 £ = £L 2,191.

Area and population

Governorates	Capitals	area sq mi	area sq km	population 1996 estimate
Bayrūt	Beirut (Bayrūt)	7	18	407,403
Al-Biqā'	Zaḥlah	1,653	4,280	399,890
Jabal Lubnān	B'abdā	753	1,950	1,145,458
Al-Janūb	Sidon (Ṣaydā)	772[2]	2,001[2]	283,056
An-Nabaṭīyah	An-Nabaṭīyah	[2]	[2]	205,412
Ash-Shamāl	Tripoli (Ṭarābulus)	765	1,981	670,609
TOTAL		4,016[3]	10,400[3]	3,111,828

Demography

Population (2000): 3,578,000.
Density (2000): persons per sq mi 890.9, persons per sq km 344.0.
Urban-rural (1999): urban 89.4%; rural 10.6%.
Sex distribution (1999): male 48.42%; female 51.58%.
Age breakdown (1999): under 15, 28.4%; 15–29, 33.9%; 30–44, 18.1%; 45–59, 10.2%; 60–74, 7.2%; 75 and over, 2.2%.
Population projection: (2010) 4,056,000; (2020) 4,417,000.
Doubling time: 50 years.
Ethnic composition (1996): Arab *c.* 93%, of which Lebanese *c.* 84%, Palestinian *c.* 9%; Armenian *c.* 6%; Kurd and other *c.* 1%.
Religious affiliation (1995): Muslim 55.3%, of which Shī'ī 34.0%, Sunnī 21.3%; Christian 37.6%, of which Catholic 25.1% (Maronite 19.0%, Greek Catholic or Melchite 4.6%), Orthodox 11.7% (Greek Orthodox 6.0%, Armenian Apostolic 5.2%), Protestant 0.5%; Druze 7.1%.
Major cities (1994)[4]: Beirut 1,100,000; Tripoli 240,000; Sidon (Ṣaydā) 150,000; Jūniyah 100,000; Zaḥlah 100,000; Tyre 80,000.

Vital statistics

Birth rate per 1,000 population (1999): 20.5 (world avg. 22.1).
Death rate per 1,000 population (1999): 6.5 (world avg. 8.9).
Natural increase rate per 1,000 population (1999): 14.0 (world avg. 13.2).
Total fertility rate (avg. births per childbearing woman; 1999): 2.1.
Life expectancy at birth (1999): male 68.6 years; female 73.4 years.
Major causes of death: n.a.

National economy

Budget (1996). Revenue: £L 4,022,000,000,000 (indirect taxes 46.7%, of which customs revenues 44.7%; direct taxes 14.3%, of which income tax 8.7%, property tax 3.1%; real estate fees 6.8%; miscellaneous taxes and fees 32.2%). Expenditures: £L 6,458,000,000,000 (current expenditures 86.0%, of which debt service 40.3%, salaries and wages 34.7%; capital expenditures 14.0%).
Production (metric tons except as noted). Agriculture, forestry, fishing (1999): tomatoes 325,000, sugar beets 290,000, potatoes 250,000, grapes 245,000, cucumbers and gherkins 180,000, oranges 154,500, apples 118,000, lemons and limes 110,500, olives 90,000, onions 80,000; livestock (number of live animals) 460,000 goats, 355,000 sheep, 82,000 cattle, 62,000 pigs, 31,000,000 chickens; roundwood (1998) 407,000 cu m; fish catch (1998) 3,520. Mining and quarrying (1996): lime 16,000; salt 4,000; gypsum 2,000. Manufacturing (1998): cement 3,316,000; paper 42,000; olive oil 7,000. Construction (1998): 9,817,000 sq m[5]. Energy production (consumption): electricity (kW-hr; 1998) 7,662,000,000 (9,010,000,000); coal, n.a. (none); crude petroleum (barrels; 1998) none (1,358,000); petroleum products (metric tons; 1998) none (3,204,000).
Land use (1994): forested 7.8%; meadows and pastures 1.0%; agricultural and under permanent cultivation 29.9%; wasteland and other areas 61.3%.
Gross national product (1998): U.S.$14,975,000,000 (U.S.$3,560 per capita).

Structure of gross domestic product and labour force

	1995 in value U.S.$'000,000	% of total value	labour force	% of labour force
Agriculture	380	4.0	143,900	14.0
Mining	—	—		
Manufacturing	1,235	13.0	277,600	27.0
Construction	950	10.0		
Public utilities / Transp. and commun.	2,375[6]	25.0[6]		
Trade	2,660	28.0	606,500	59.0
Finance / Real estate and business services / Services	1,900	20.0		
Pub. admin., defense	[6]	[6]		
TOTAL	9,500	100.0	1,028,000	100.0

Population economically active (1995): total 1,028,000; activity rate of total population 25.4% (participation rates: over age 15 [1988] 44%; female *c.* 30%; unemployed n.a.).

Price and earnings indexes (1990 = 100)

	1991	1992	1993	1994	1995	1996	1997
Consumer price index	151.5	333.3	430.3	466.0	494.0	438.1	447.1
Wages index[7]	104.2	85.4	78.3	118.5	134.7	...	...

Public debt (external, outstanding; 1998): U.S.$3,980,000,000.
Household income and expenditure. Average household size (1998) 4.4; average annual income per household (1994) £L 2,400,000 (U.S.$1,430); sources of income (1974): wages 27.9%, transfers 3.0%, other 69.1%; expenditure (1966)[8]: food 42.8%, housing 16.8%, clothing 8.6%, health care 7.2%.
Tourism (1996): receipts from visitors U.S.$715,000,000.

Foreign trade[9]

Balance of trade (current prices)

	1994	1995	1996	1997	1998	1999
U.S.$'000,000	–4,798	–5,770	–6,643	–6,880	–6,408	–5,530
% of total	76.4%	74.5%	76.4%	84.1%	82.9%	80.3%

Imports (1998): £L 10,718,900,000,000 (1995; machinery and transport equipment 27.0%, metals and metal products 9.8%, mineral products 8.8%, processed food 7.8%, chemicals 6.7%). *Major import sources* (1997): Italy 13.2%; France 9.5%; U.S. 9.2%; Germany 8.7%; Switzerland 6.6%.
Exports (1998): £L 1,086,400,000,000 (pharmaceuticals and detergents 15.2%, food and beverages 15.1%, machinery and transport equipment 10.2%, paper products 8.9%, aluminum products 6.1%, metals and metal products 4.3%, gold products 2.6%). *Major export destinations*[10] (1997): Saudi Arabia 15.0%; U.A.E. 9.0%; France 7.1%; U.S. 6.0%; Syria 5.9%; Jordan 3.9%.

Transport and communications

Transport. Railroads (1998)[11]: length 222 km. Roads (1996): total length 6,350 km (paved 95%). Vehicles (1996): passenger cars 1,217,000; trucks and buses 86,640. Merchant marine (1992): vessels (100 gross tons and over) 163; total deadweight tonnage 438,165. Air transport (1996)[12]: passenger-km 1,889,000,000; metric ton-km cargo 46,274,000; airports (1998) 1.

Communications

Medium	date	unit	number	units per 1,000 persons
Daily newspapers	1995	circulation	435,000	141
Radio	1997	receivers	2,850,000	907
Television	1998	receivers	1,120,000	351
Telephones	1998	main lines	620,000	194
Cellular telephones	1998	subscribers	500,000	157
Personal computers	1998	units	125,000	39
Internet	1998	users	100,000	31

Education and health

Educational attainment: n.a. *Literacy* (1995): total population age 15 and over literate 1,829,000 (92.4%); males literate 94.7%; females literate 90.3%.

Education (1996–97)

	schools	teachers	students	student/ teacher ratio
Primary (age 5–9)	2,160	22,810[13]	382,309	...
Secondary (age 10–16)	1,405[13]	21,344[13]	292,002	...
Voc., teacher tr.	275[14]	7,745	55,848	7.2
Higher	20	10,444	81,588	7.8

Health (1997): physicians 7,203 (1 per 476 persons); hospital beds (1995) 11,596 (1 per 319 persons); infant mortality rate per 1,000 live births (1999) 30.4.
Food (1998): daily per capita caloric intake 3,270 (vegetable products 86%, animal products 14%); 132% of FAO recommended minimum.

Military

Total active duty personnel (1999): Lebanese national armed forces 67,900 (army 95.7%, navy 2.5%, air force 1.8%). External regular military forces include: UN peacekeeping force in Lebanon 4,496; Syrian army 22,000. *Military expenditure as percentage of GDP* (1997): 3.0% (world 2.6%); per capita expenditure: U.S.$135.

[1]The current legislature was elected between August and September 2000; one-half of its membership is Christian and one-half Muslim/Druze. [2]Al-Janūb includes An-Nabaṭīyah. [3]Includes water area of 66 sq mi (170 sq km) not distributed by governorate. [4]Urban agglomeration. [5]Permits authorized. [6]Public utilities and transportation and communications includes public administration and defense. [7]Based on minimum wage, in real terms. [8]Weights based on consumer price index components. For capital city only. [9]Imports are f.o.b. in balance of trade and c.i.f. in commodities and trading partners. [10]Domestic exports only; reexports not included. [11]Apart from a 14-mi (23-km) section delivering oil from the Zahrani refinery to a thermal power station serving Beirut, no passenger or general cargo track is currently in use. [12]MEA-Airliban international flights only [13]1981–82. [14]1994–95.

Internet resources for further information:

- **Central Administration for Statistics http://www.cas.gov.lb/english/index.html**
- **U.S. Embassy of Lebanon http://www.embofleb.org**
- **Bank of Lebanon http://www.bdl.gov.lb**

Lesotho

Official name: Lesotho (Sotho); Kingdom of Lesotho (English).
Form of government[1]*:* multiparty republic with 2 legislative houses (Senate [33]; National Assembly [80]).
Chief of state: King.
Head of government: Prime Minister.
Capital: Maseru.
Official languages: Sotho; English.
Official religion: Christianity.
Monetary unit: 1 loti (plural maloti [M]) = 100 lisente; valuation (Oct. 6, 2000) 1 U.S.$ = M 7.29; 1 £ = M 10.54.

Area and population

		area		population
Districts	Capitals	sq mi	sq km	1995 estimate[2]
Berea	Teyateyaneng	858	2,222	206,200
Butha-Buthe	Butha-Buthe	682	1,767	135,400
Leribe	Hlotse	1,092	2,828	349,500
Mafeteng	Mafeteng	818	2,119	259,000
Maseru	Maseru	1,652	4,279	400,200
Mohale's Hoek	Mohale's Hoek	1,363	3,530	231,300
Mokhotlong	Mokhotlong	1,573	4,075	100,300
Qacha's Nek	Qacha's Nek	907	2,349	86,800
Quthing	Quthing	1,126	2,916	151,900
Thaba-Tseka	Thaba-Tseka	1,649	4,270	136,200
TOTAL		11,720	30,355	2,056,800

Demography

Population (2000): 2,143,000[3].
Density (2000)[3]: persons per sq mi 182.8, persons per sq km 70.6.
Urban-rural (1992): urban 20.9%; rural 79.1%.
Sex distribution (1995): male 49.23%; female 50.77%.
Age breakdown (1995): under 15, 41.3%; 15–29, 27.0%; 30–44, 16.0%; 45–59, 9.1%; 60–74, 5.0%; 75 and over, 1.6%.
Population projection[3]: (2010) 2,339,000; (2020) 2,382,000.
Doubling time: 39 years.
Ethnic composition (1986): Sotho 85.0%; Zulu 15.0%.
Religious affiliation (1995): Christian 70.1%, of which Roman Catholic 39.0%, Protestant (mostly Presbyterian) 14.1%, African Christian 11.4%; other (mostly traditional beliefs) 29.9%.
Major urban centres (1986): Maseru (1996) 160,100; Maputsoe 20,000; Teyateyaneng 14,251; Mafeteng 12,667; Hlotse 9,595.

Vital statistics

Birth rate per 1,000 population (1999): 31.3 (world avg. 22.1); legitimate, n.a; illegitimate, n.a.
Death rate per 1,000 population (1999): 13.2 (world avg. 8.9).
Natural increase rate per 1,000 population (1999): 18.1 (world avg. 13.2).
Total fertility rate (avg. births per childbearing woman; 1999): 4.0.
Marriage rate per 1,000 population: n.a.
Divorce rate per 1,000 population: n.a.
Life expectancy at birth (1999): male 51.4 years; female 54.7 years.
Major causes of death per 100,000 population: n.a.; however, major diseases include typhoid fever and infectious and parasitic diseases.

National economy

Budget (1999–2000). Revenue: M 2,580,700,000 (customs receipts 45.8%, grants and nontax revenue 28.8%, income tax 13.5%, sales tax 10.2%). Expenditures: M 2,913,500,000 (personal emoluments 41.9%, capital expenditure 32.4%, subsidies and transfers 13.0%, interest payments 12.7%).
Production (metric tons except as noted). Agriculture, forestry, fishing (1999): corn (maize) 125,000, roots and tubers 85,000, sorghum 33,000, vegetables 19,000, wheat 15,000, fruit 14,000, dry beans 9,300, dry peas 3,000; livestock (number of live animals) 720,000 sheep, 560,000 goats, 510,000 cattle, 152,000 asses, 98,000 horses, 63,000 pigs, 1,700,000 chickens; roundwood (1998) 1,594,000 cu m; fish catch (1998) 30. Mining and quarrying (1998): diamonds 2,398 carats. Manufacturing (value added in U.S.$'000,000; 1995): food products 58; beverages 38; textiles 14; chemical products 9; metal products 4; wearing apparel 4. Construction (permits issued in M '000,000; 1999): residential 3.76; nonresidential 65.10. Energy production (consumption): electricity (kW-hr; 1988) 1,000,000 (n.a.); coal, none (n.a); petroleum, none (n.a.); natural gas, none (n.a.).
Public debt (external, outstanding; 1998): U.S.$660,600,000.
Tourism (1998): receipts from visitors U.S.$18,000,000; expenditures by nationals abroad U.S.$12,000,000.
Population economically active (1993): total 617,871; activity rate of total population 45.1% (participation rates: ages 15–64 [1986] 79.8%; female 23.7%; unemployed [1992] 35.0%).

Price and earnings indexes (1995 = 100)

	1993	1994	1995	1996	1997	1998	1999
Consumer price index	84.6	91.5	100.0	109.3	...	...	135.2
Annual earnings index[4]	79.5	86.6	100.0	114.2	126.1	146.9	165.4

Household income and expenditure. Average household size (1986) 4.8; average annual income per household (1986–87) M 2,832 (U.S.$1,297); sources of income (1986–87): transfer payments 44.7%, self-employment 27.8%, wages and salaries 22.4%, other 5.1%; expenditure (1989): food 48.0%, clothing 16.4%, household durable goods 11.9%, housing and energy 10.1%, transportation 4.7%.
Gross national product (at current market prices; 1998): U.S.$1,167,000,000 (U.S.$570 per capita).

Structure of gross domestic product and labour force

	1998		1986	
	in value M '000,000[5]	% of total value[5]	labour force	% of labour force
Agriculture	645.7	16.9	474,171	66.2
Mining	2.6	0.1	6,446	0.9
Manufacturing	508.5	13.3	19,339	2.7
Construction	573.9	15.1	31,516	4.4
Public utilities	168.5	4.4	1,433	0.2
Transp. and commun.	131.0	3.4	5,014	0.7
Trade	352.9	9.3	22,204	3.1
Finance	330.4	8.7	3,581	0.5
Pub. admin., defense	661.8	17.4	17,907	2.5
Services	41.5	1.1	126,780	17.7
Other	390.9[6]	10.3[6]	7,879	1.1
TOTAL	3,807.7	100.0	716,270[7]	100.0[7]

Land use (1998): meadows and pastures 65.9%; agricultural and under permanent cultivation 10.7%; other 23.4%.

Foreign trade[8]

Balance of trade (current prices)

	1993	1994	1995	1996	1997	1998
U.S.$'000,000	–734.1	–666.7	–825.2	–811.7	–828.3	–672.6
% of total	73.3%	69.9%	72.1%	68.5%	67.9%	63.5%

Imports (1998): M 5,199,800,000 (1990; manufactured goods [excluding chemicals, machinery, and transport equipment] 42.5%; food and live animals 19.1%; machinery and transport equipment 15.3%; petroleum products 8.6%). *Major import sources:* Customs Union of Southern Africa 88.7%; Asia 7.2%; Europe 2.3%, of which European Economic Community 2.0%; the Americas 1.3%.
Exports (1998): M 1,109,600,000 (manufactured goods 71.6%; machinery and transport equipment 15.1%; food and live animals 4.0%; beverages and tobacco 3.5%; crude materials 1.8%). *Major export destinations:* Customs Union of Southern Africa 65.5%; the Americas 33.6%; Europe 0.5%.

Transport and communications

Transport. Railroads (1999): length 1.6 mi, 2.6 km. Roads (1996): total length 3,079 mi, 4,955 km (paved 18%). Vehicles (1996): passenger cars 12,610; trucks and buses 25,000. Merchant marine: vessels (100 gross tons and over) none. Air transport (1996): passenger-mi 3,900,000, passenger-km 6,200,000; short ton-mi cargo 395,000, metric ton-km cargo 577,000; airports (1997).

Communications

Medium	date	unit	number	units per 1,000 persons
Daily newspapers	1996	circulation	15,000	7.6
Radio	1997	receivers	104,000	52
Television	1997	receivers	54,000	27
Telephones	1998	main lines	20,100	9.7
Cellular telephones	1998	subscribers	9,831	4.8
Personal computers	...	units	...	...
Internet	...	users	...	...

Education and health

Educational attainment (1986–87). Percentage of population age 10 and over having: no formal education 22.9%; primary 52.8%; secondary 23.2%; higher 0.6%. *Literacy* (1995): total population age 15 and over literate 849,700 (71.3%); males literate 468,000 (81.1%); females literate 381,700 (62.3%).

Education (1996–97)

	schools	teachers	students	student/ teacher ratio
Primary (age 6–12)	1,249	7,898	374,628	47.4
Secondary (age 13–17)	187[9]	2,817	67,454	23.9
Vocational	9[9]	61	678	11.1
Higher	1[9]	574	4,614	8.0

Health: physicians (1995) 105 (1 per 18,527 persons); hospital beds (1992) 2,400 (1 per 765 persons); infant mortality rate per 1,000 live births (1999) 77.6.
Food (1998): daily per capita caloric intake 2,210 (vegetable products 95%, animal products 5%); 97% of FAO recommended minimum requirement.

Military

Total active duty personnel (1999): 2,000[10]. *Military expenditure as percentage of GNP* (1997): 2.5% (world 2.6%); per capita expenditure U.S.$16.

[1]The Interim Political Authority, which was mandated to make Lesotho more democratic, postponed national elections until mid-2001 at the earliest. [2]De jure population. [3]Excludes absentee miners working in South Africa. [4]Based on average annual wages, including overtime, of mine workers. [5]At 1995 prices. [6]Indirect taxes less imputed bank service charges. [7]Approximately 117,600 persons (*c.* 40% of Lesotho's adult male labour force) were employed as mine workers in South Africa in 1993; by May 2000 this figure had declined to 54,000. [8]Import figures are f.o.b. in balance of trade and c.i.f. in commodities and trading partners. [9]1993–94. [10]Royal Lesotho Defence Force.

Internet resources for further information:
- **Central Bank of Lesotho http://www.centralbank.org.ls**

Liberia

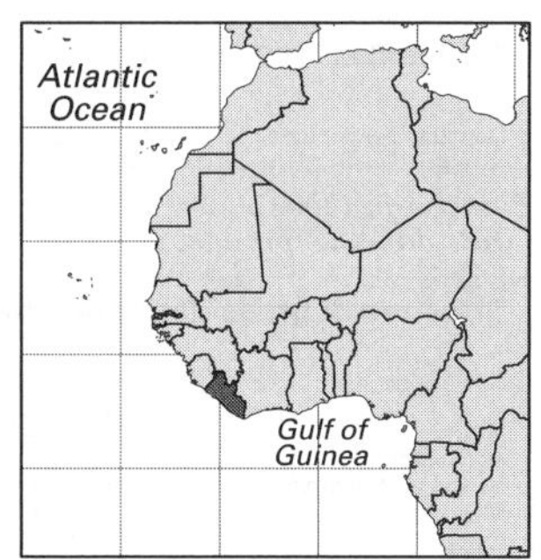

Official name: Republic of Liberia.
Form of government: multiparty republic with two legislative houses (Senate [26]; House of Representatives [64]).
Head of state and government: President.
Capital: Monrovia.
Official language: English.
Official religion: none.
Monetary unit: 1 Liberian dollar (L$) = 100 cents; valuation (Oct. 6, 2000) 1 U.S.$ = L$1.00[1]; 1 £ = L$1.45.

Area and population

Counties	Capitals	area sq mi	area sq km	population 1986 estimate
Bomi	Tubmanburg	755	1,955	67,300
Bong	Gbarnga	3,127	8,099	268,100
Grand Bassa	Buchanan	3,382	8,759	166,900
Grand Cape Mount	Robertsport	2,250	5,827	83,900
Grand Gedeh	Zwedru	6,575[2]	17,029[2]	109,000[2]
Grand Kru	Barclayville	[3]	[3]	[3]
Lofa	Voinjama	7,475	19,360	261,000
Margibi	Kakata	1,260	3,263	104,000
Maryland	Harper	2,066[3]	5,351[3]	137,700[3]
Montserrado	Bensonville	1,058	2,740	582,400
Nimba	Sanniquellie	4,650	12,043	325,700
River Gee	...	[2]	[2]	[2]
Rivercess	Rivercess City	1,693	4,385	39,900
Sinoe	Greenville	3,959	10,254	65,400
TOTAL		38,250[4]	99,067[4, 5]	2,221,300[6]

Demography

Population (2000): 3,164,000.
Density (2000): persons per sq mi 83.8, persons per sq km 32.4.
Urban-rural (1999): urban 44.2%; rural 55.8%.
Sex distribution (1999): male 49.32%; female 50.68%.
Age breakdown (1999): under 15, 43.1%; 15–29, 26.8%; 30–44, 15.3%; 45–59, 9.5%; 60–74, 4.1%; 75 and over, 1.2%.
Population projection: (2010) 4,073,000; (2020) 5,294,000.
Doubling time: 23 years.
Ethnic composition (1984): Kpelle 19.4%; Bassa 13.9%; Grebo 9.0%; Gio 7.8%; Kru 7.3%; Mano 7.1%; other 35.5%.
Religious affiliation (1995): traditional beliefs 63.0%; Christian 21.0%, of which Protestant 13.5%, African Christian 5.1%, Roman Catholic 2.4%; Muslim 16.0%.
Major cities (1999): Monrovia 479,000; Harbel 60,000[7]; Gbarnga 30,000[8]; Buchanan 25,000[7]; Yekepa 16,000[7].

Vital statistics

Birth rate per 1,000 population (1999): 47.8 (world avg. 22.1).
Death rate per 1,000 population (1999): 16.9 (world avg. 8.9).
Natural increase rate per 1,000 population (1999): 30.9 (world avg. 13.2).
Total fertility rate (avg. births per childbearing woman; 1999): 6.5.
Marriage rate per 1,000 population: n.a.
Divorce rate per 1,000 population: n.a.
Life expectancy at birth (1999): male 49.2 years; female 52.1 years.
Major causes of death per 100,000 population: n.a.; however, major health problems include complications during pregnancy, malaria, pneumonia, anemia, malnutrition, measles, and AIDS. Violence and acts of war were major causes of both morbidity and mortality from 1990 onward.

National economy

Budget (1999). Revenue: U.S.$65,500,000,000 (tax revenue 92.2%, of which import duties and consular fees 29.9%, maritime revenue 23.2%, income and profit taxes 22.4%, sales tax 15.9%, property taxes 0.5%). Expenditures: U.S.$67,500,000,000 (current expenditure 85.2%, of which goods and services 49.3%, wages 21.6%, subsidies and transfers 8.8%, interest on debt 5.2%; development expenditure 8.3%; other 6.5%).
Tourism: receipts from visitors (1986) U.S.$6,000,000; expenditures by nationals abroad, n.a.
Population economically active (1997): total 1,183,000; activity rate 51.4% (participation rates: ages 10–64 [1994] 64.0%; female 39.5%; unemployed [1996] 95%).

Price and earnings indexes (1990 = 100)

	1989	1990	1991	1992	1993	1994	1995
Consumer price index	79.8	100.0	110.0	121.0	133.1	146.4	161.0
Earnings index	...	...	...	...	...	...	...

Production (metric tons except as noted). Agriculture, forestry, fishing (1999): cassava 313,000, sugarcane 250,000, rice 210,000, oil palm fruit 152,000, bananas 90,000, plantains 35,000, natural rubber 35,000, yams 20,000, coffee 3,000, cacao beans 500; livestock (number of live animals) 220,000 goats, 210,000 sheep, 120,000 pigs, 36,000 cattle, 3,500,000 chickens; roundwood (1998) 3,021,000 cu m; fish catch (1998) 10,830. Mining and quarrying (1998): diamonds 7,719 carats[9]; gold 72 kg[9]. Manufacturing (1996): palm oil 45,000; cement 8,300[10]; cigarettes 22,000,000 units[11]; soft drinks 171,000 hectolitres[12]; beer 158,000 hectolitres[12]. Construction: n.a. Energy production (consumption): electricity (kW-hr; 1996) 488,000,000 (488,000,000); coal, none (none); crude petroleum, none (none); petroleum products (metric tons; 1994) none (106,000); natural gas, none (none).
Public debt (external, outstanding; 1998): U.S.$1,092,000,000.
Household income and expenditure. Average household size (1983) 4.3; income per household: n.a.; sources of income: n.a.; expenditure: n.a.
Gross national product (1996): U.S.$1,174,000,000 (U.S.$490 per capita).

Structure of gross domestic product and labour force

	1999 in value U.S.$'000,000	1999 % of total value	1994 labour force	1994 % of labour force
Agriculture	337.7	75.3	676,000	68.1
Mining	9.8	2.2		
Manufacturing	21.4	4.8		
Construction	6.9	1.5		
Public utilities	2.3	0.5	77,000	7.7
Transp. and commun.	21.6	4.8		
Trade	17.0	3.8		
Finance	13.3	3.0		
Pub. admin., defense	11.2	2.5		
Services	10.3	2.3	240,000	24.2
Other	–3.2[13]	–0.7[13]		
TOTAL	448.3	100.0	993,000	100.0

Land use (1994): forested 47.8%; meadows and pastures 20.8%; agricultural and under permanent cultivation 3.8%; other 27.6%.

Foreign trade

Balance of trade (current prices)

	1994	1995	1996	1997	1998	1999
U.S.$'000,000	–5,393	–4,829	–2,718	–217.9	–118.5	–111.8
% of total	81.7%	71.7%	54.5%	81.1%	58.1%	50.1%

Imports (1999): U.S.$167,500,000 (food and live animals 31.9%, machinery and transport equipment 21.7%, petroleum and petroleum products 10.4%, basic manufactures 10.2%, chemicals 7.9%, beverages and tobacco 4.2%). *Major import sources* (1998): South Korea 26.8%; Italy 21.7%; Japan 16.9%; France 13.4%; Croatia 5.7%; Singapore 4.8%.
Exports (1999): U.S.$55,700,000 (rubber 56.9%, logs and timber 39.1%, cocoa 2.0%, coffee 1.8%). *Major export destinations* (1999): United States 54.3%; France 24.3%; Singapore 5.2%; Belgium 4.4%; Italy 3.3%; Malaysia 2.4%.

Transport and communications

Transport. Railroads (1998): route length 304 mi, 490 km; short ton-mi cargo 534,000,000, metric ton-km cargo 860,000,000. Roads (1996): total length 6,600 mi, 10,600 km (paved 6%). Vehicles (1996): passenger cars 9,400; trucks and buses 25,000. Merchant marine (1992): vessels (100 gross tons and over) 1,672; total deadweight tonnage 97,373,965. Air transport (1992): passenger-mi 4,300,000, passenger-km 7,000,000; short ton-mi cargo 68,000, metric ton-km cargo 100,000; airports (1998) with scheduled flights 1.

Communications

Medium	date	unit	number	units per 1,000 persons
Daily newspapers	1996	circulation	35,000	16
Radio	1997	receivers	790,000	329
Television	1997	receivers	70,000	29
Telephones	1996	main lines	6,371	2.2

Education and health

Educational attainment, n.a. *Literacy* (1995): total population age 15 and over literate 705,000 (38.3%); males literate 523,000 (53.9%); females literate 182,000 (22.4%).

Education (1980)

	schools	teachers	students	student/ teacher ratio
Primary (age 6–12)	1,651	9,099	167,000[10]	...
Secondary (age 13–18)	419	1,129	51,666	45.8
Voc., teacher tr.	6	63	2,322	36.9
Higher	3	...	5,716[10]	...

Health: physicians (1992) 257 (1 per 8,333 persons); hospital beds, n.a.; infant mortality rate (1999) 136.9.
Food (1998): daily per capita caloric intake 1,979 (vegetable products 97%, animal products 3%); 88% of FAO recommended minimum requirement.

Military

Total active duty personnel: About 14,000 in all armed forces as of 1998. West African (ECOMOG) peacekeepers withdrew in January 1999 and the civil war resumed in remote locales as of April 1999. *Military expenditure as percentage of GNP:* n.a.

[1]Par value rate to U.S.$ ineffective from January 1998; the independent free market exchange rate was roughly L$41 = U.S.$1 in July 2000. [2]Figures for River Gee (created June 2000) included with Grand Gedeh. [3]Figures for Grand Kru included in Maryland. [4]Total area per more recent survey is 37,743 sq mi (97,754 sq km). [5]Detail does not add to total given because of rounding. [6]Includes 10,000 persons not allocated by county. [7]1985. [8]1986. [9]Export figure. [10]1993. [11]1992. [12]1988. [13]Import duties less imputed bank service charges.

Internet resources for further information:
- **Liberian Daily News Bulletin (link) http://www.africanews.org/west/liberia**

Libya

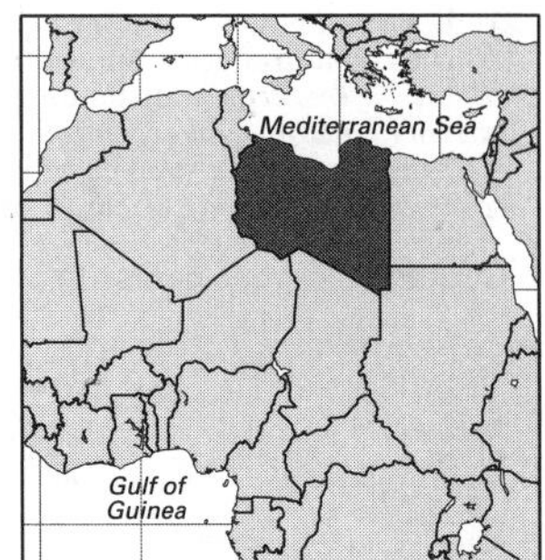

Official name: Al-Jamāhīrīyah al-ʿArabīyah al-Lībīyah ash-Shaʿbīyah al-Ishtirākīyah (Socialist People's Libyan Arab Jamahiriya).
Form of government: socialist state with one policy-making body (General People's Congress [760]).
Chief of state: Muammar al-Qaddafi (de facto)[1]; Secretary of General People's Congress (de jure).
Head of government: Secretary of the General People's Committee (prime minister).
Capital: Tripoli[2].
Official language: Arabic.
Official religion: Islam.
Monetary unit: 1 Libyan dinar (LD) = 1,000 dirhams; valuation[3] (Nov. 15, 2000) 1 U.S.$ = LD 1.73; 1 £ = LD 2.59.

Area and population

Administrative regions[4]	Capitals	area sq mi	area sq km	population 1988 estimate
Banghāzī	Banghāzī	5,800	15,000	512,200
Al-Jabal al-Akhḍar	Al-Bayḍā'	14,300	37,000	308,300
Al-Jabal al-Gharbī	Gharyān	33,600	87,000	204,300
Khalīj Surt	Surt	145,200	376,000	382,100
Al-Kufrah	Al-Kufrah	186,900	484,000	23,800
Margib	Al-Khums	11,200	29,000	408,900
Marzūq	Marzūq	135,100	350,000	45,200
Nikāt al-Khums	Zuwārah	39,000	101,000	196,000
Sabhā	Sabhā	31,700	82,000	121,700
Ṭarābulus	Tripolic (Ṭarābulus)	1,200	3,000	1,083,100
Ṭubruq	Ṭubruq	32,400	84,000	110,900
Wādī al-Ḥa'iṭ	Awbārī	40,500	105,000	49,600
Az-Zāwiyah	Az-Zāwiyah	1,500	4,000	326,500
TOTAL		678,400	1,757,000	3,772,600

Demography

Population (2000): 5,115,000.
Density (2000): persons per sq mi 7.5, persons per sq km 2.9.
Urban-rural (1999): urban 87.3%; rural 12.7%.
Sex distribution (1999): male 51.47%; female 48.53%.
Age breakdown (1999): under 15, 36.5%; 15–29, 32.3%; 30–44, 17.7%; 45–59, 7.8%; 60–74, 4.5%; 75 and over, 1.2%.
Population projection: (2010) 6,447,000; (2020) 7,740,000.
Doubling time: 29 years.
Ethnic composition (1995): Libyan Arab 78%; Berber 1%; other 21% (mostly Egyptians, Sudanese, and Chadians).
Religious affiliation (1995): Sunnī Muslim 97.0%; other 3.0%.
Major cities (1995): Tripoli 1,140,000; Banghāzī 650,000; Miṣrātah 280,000; Surt 150,000; Az-Zāwiyah (1988) 89,338.

Vital statistics

Birth rate per 1,000 population (1999): 27.6 (world avg. 22.1).
Death rate per 1,000 population (1999): 3.5 (world avg. 8.9).
Natural increase rate per 1,000 population (1999): 24.1 (world avg. 13.2).
Total fertility rate (avg. births per childbearing woman; 1999): 3.8.
Marriage rate per 1,000 population (1991): 5.1[5].
Divorce rate per 1,000 population (1988): 0.6[5].
Life expectancy at birth (1999): male 73.1 years; female 77.4 years.
Major causes of death per 100,000 population: n.a.; however, the main causes of hospital mortality in 1987 were injuries and poisoning 15.5%, diseases of the circulatory system 11.6%, conditions originating in the perinatal period 11.4%, diseases of the respiratory system 7.0%, neoplasms (cancers) 4.4%.

National economy

Budget (1998). Revenue: LD 5,311,000,000 (oil revenues 68.4%, other 31.6%). Expenditures: LD 5,311,000,000 (1990–91; current expenditures 55.7%, of which municipalities 39.4%, education and scientific research 4.3%, health 2.7%; capital expenditures 44.3%, of which agriculture and land reclamation 13.6%, industry 5.3%).
Production (metric tons except as noted). Agriculture, forestry, fishing (1998): tomatoes 250,000, potatoes 230,000, olives 200,000, onions 190,000, watermelons 180,000, barley 135,000, wheat 30,000; livestock (number of live animals; 1998) 3,700,000 sheep, 1,300,000 goats, 155,000 cattle, 103,000 camels, 24,000,000 chickens; roundwood (1998) 651,000 cu m; fish catch (1998) 33,594. Mining and quarrying (1997): lime 280,000; gypsum 180,000; salt 32,000. Manufacturing (value of production in '000,000 LD; 1996): base metals 212, electrical equipment 208, petrochemicals 175, food products 79, cement and other building materials 68. Energy production (consumption): electricity (kW-hr; 1996) 18,300,000,000 (18,300,000,000); coal (metric tons; 1996) none (5,000); crude petroleum (barrels; 1999) 481,380,000 ([1996] 112,725,000); petroleum products (metric tons; 1996) 14,070,000 (7,863,000); natural gas (cu m; 1996) 6,392,000,000 (5,192,000,000).
Land use (1994): forested 0.5%; meadows and pastures 7.6%; agricultural and under permanent cultivation 1.2%; desert and built-up areas 90.7%.
Population economically active (1996): total 1,224,000; activity rate of total population 26.1% (participation rates [1993]: ages 10 and over, 35.2%; female 9.8%; unemployed [1999] 30.0%).

Price index (1995 = 100)

	1989	1990	1991	1992	1993	1994	1995
Consumer price index	33.9	38.4	42.9	49.3	59.2	76.9	100.0

Public debt (2000): n.a.[6]
Gross domestic product (1998): U.S.$32,662,500,000 (U.S.$6,700 per capita).

Structure of gross domestic product and labour force

	1996 in value LD '000,000	% of total value	labour force	% of labour force
Agriculture	782.5	6.6	219,500	17.0
Mining and quarrying	3,036.5	25.8	31,000	2.5
Manufacturing	1,107.0	9.4	128,500	10.5
Construction	797.0	6.8	171,000	14.0
Public utilities	240.5	2.0	35,500	2.9
Transp. and commun.	1,025.5	8.7	104,000	8.5
Trade	1,345.5	11.4	73,000	6.0
Finance, insurance	739.5	6.3	22,000	1.8
Pub. admin., defense	2,247.5	19.1	439,500	35.9
Services	461.0	3.9		
TOTAL	11,782.5	100.0	1,224,000	100.0

Household income and expenditure. Average household size (1980) 5.1; income per household: n.a.; sources of income: n.a.; expenditure (1977): food 37.2%, housing and energy 32.2%, transportation 9.4%, education and recreation 8.5%, clothing 6.9%, health care 3.3%.
Tourism (1998): receipts U.S.$18,000,000; expenditures U.S.$143,000,000.

Foreign trade[7]

Balance of trade (current prices)[8]

	1994	1995	1996	1997	1998	1999
U.S.$'000,000	+1,026	+2,781	+2,519	+2,716	+471	+2,974
% of total	6.5%	18.2%	15.1%	15.9%	3.9%	25.7%

Imports (1997)[9]: U.S.$5,593,000,000 (machinery 25.9%; food products 20.0%; road vehicles 10.1%; chemical products 7.5%). *Major import sources:* Italy 15.8%; Germany 12.8%; Japan 8.1%; U.K. 7.8%; France 6.2%.
Exports (1997): U.S.$9,029,000,000 (crude petroleum 76.4%; refined petroleum 16.5%; iron and steel 1.5%). *Major export destinations:* Italy 36.2%; Germany 15.0%; Spain 9.1%; Turkey 5.6%; Austria 5.2%.

Transport and communications

Transport. Railroads: none. Roads (1996): total length 81,600 km (paved 57%). Vehicles (1996): passenger cars 809,514; trucks and buses 357,528. Merchant marine (1992): vessels (100 gross tons and over) 150; total deadweight tonnage 1,223,589. Air transport (1997): passenger-km 377,000,000; metric ton-km cargo, n.a.; airports with scheduled flights: n.a.

Communications

Medium	date	unit	number	units per 1,000 persons
Daily newspapers	1996	circulation	71,000	14
Radio	1997	receivers	1,350,000	259
Television	1996	receivers	680,000	122
Telephones	1998	main lines	500,000	91
Cellular telephones	1998	subscribers	20,000	4.1

Education and health

Educational attainment (1984). Percentage of population age 25 and over having: no formal schooling (illiterate) 59.7%; incomplete primary education 15.4%; complete primary 8.5%; some secondary 5.2%; secondary 8.5%; higher 2.7%. *Literacy* (1995): percentage of total population age 15 and over literate 76.2%; males literate 87.9%; females literate 63.0%.

Education (1995–96)

	schools	teachers	students	student/ teacher ratio
Primary (age 6–12)	2,733[10]	122,020	1,333,679	10.9
Secondary (age 13–18)	...	17,668	189,202[11]	...
Voc., teacher tr.	480	...	147,689[12]	...
Higher	13	...	126,348	...

Health: physicians (1997) 6,092 (1 per 781 persons); hospital beds (1998) 18,100[13] (1 per 312 persons); infant mortality rate (1999) 31.4.
Food (1998): daily per capita caloric intake 3,267 (vegetable products 89%, animal products 11%); 138% of FAO recommended minimum requirement.

Military

Total active duty personnel (1999): 65,000 (army 53.8%, navy 12.3%, air force 33.9%). *Military expenditure as percentage of GNP* (1995): 6.1% (world 2.7%); per capita expenditure U.S.$389.

[1]No formal titled office exists. [2]Policy-making body (General People's Congress) may meet in Surt or Tripoli. [3]Commercial exchange rate. [4]Libya is divided into 26 administrative regions as of 1998; area and population breakdown is not available. [5]Registered events; incomplete to some degree. [6]Libya had no foreign debt in 2000. [7]Imports f.o.b. in balance of trade and c.i.f. in commodities and trading partners. [8]Per IMF *International Financial Statistics* (November 2000). [9]Per UN *International Trade Statistics Yearbook* (1998). [10]1994–95. [11]1992–93. [12]1993–94. [13]Includes beds in clinics.

Internet resources for further information:
- **CIA World Factbook—Libya**
  http://www.odci.gov/cia/publications/factbook/geos/ly.html

Liechtenstein

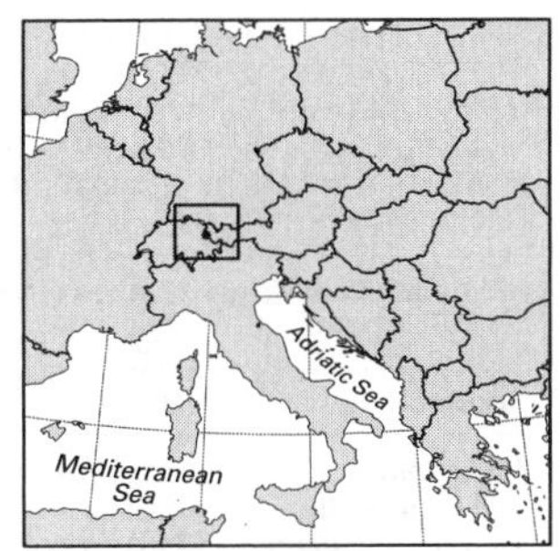

Official name: Fürstentum Liechtenstein (Principality of Liechtenstein).
Form of government: constitutional monarchy with one legislative house (Diet [25]).
Chief of state: Prince.
Head of government: Prime Minister.
Capital: Vaduz.
Official language: German.
Official religion: none.
Monetary unit: 1 Swiss franc (Sw F) = 100 centimes; valuation (Oct. 6, 2000) 1 U.S.$ = Sw F 1.75; 1 £ = Sw F 2.53.

Area and population

Regions / Communes	area sq mi	area sq km	population 1999[1] estimate
Oberland	48.3	125.2	21,509
Balzers	7.6	19.6	4,118
Planken	2.0	5.3	347
Schaan	10.3	26.8	5,262
Triesen	10.2	26.4	4,168
Triesenberg	11.5	29.8	2,508
Vaduz	6.7	17.3	5,106
Unterland	13.4[2]	34.8	10,506
Eschen	4.0	10.3	3,571
Gamprin	2.4	6.1	1,173
Mauren	2.9	7.5	3,114
Ruggell	2.9	7.4	1,693
Schellenberg	1.4	3.5	955
TOTAL	61.8[2]	160.0	32,015

Demography

Population (2000): 32,600.
Density (2000): persons per sq mi 527.5, persons per sq km 203.8.
Urban-rural: n.a.
Sex distribution (1998[1]): male 48.55%; female 51.45%.
Age breakdown (1998[1]): under 15, 18.7%; 15–29, 22.3%; 30–44, 25.4%; 45–59, 19.4%; 60–74, 9.7%; 75 and over, 4.5%.
Population projection: (2010) 36,400; (2020) 40,600.
Doubling time: n.a.; doubling time exceeds 100 years.
Ethnic composition (1999[1]): Liechtensteiner 65.2%; Swiss 12.1%; Austrian 6.3%; German 3.4%; Italian 2.8%; other 10.2%.
Religious affiliation (1997[1]): Roman Catholic 80.0%; Protestant 7.5%; Muslim 3.3%; Eastern Orthodox 0.7%; atheist 0.6%; other 7.9%.
Major cities (1998[1]): Schaan 5,096; Vaduz 4,975.

Vital statistics

Birth rate per 1,000 population (1999): 12.1 (world avg. 22.1); (1997) legitimate 86.0%; illegitimate 14.0%.
Death rate per 1,000 population (1999): 6.8 (world avg. 8.9).
Natural increase rate per 1,000 population (1999): 5.3 (world avg. 13.2).
Total fertility rate (avg. births per childbearing woman; 1999): 1.5.
Marriage rate per 1,000 population (1998): 13.2.
Divorce rate per 1,000 population (1994): 1.4.
Life expectancy at birth (1999): male 74.7 years; female 82.2 years.
Major causes of death per 100,000 population (1997): diseases of the circulatory system 290.4; malignant neoplasms (cancers) 165.5; old age 59.3; accidents, poisonings, and acts of violence 49.9; diseases of the respiratory system 28.1.

National economy

Budget (1998). Revenue: Sw F 665,200,000 (taxes and interest 74.0%, customs duties and repayments 15.6%, investment income 8.6%, real estate capital-gains taxes and death and estate taxes 1.8%). Expenditures: Sw F 570,900,000 (financial affairs 31.5%, social welfare 17.3%, education 16.0%, transportation 12.3%, general administration 8.9%, public safety 5.0%, health 4.8%).
Public debt: none.
Tourism (1998): 123,252 tourist overnight stays; receipts from visitors, n.a.; expenditures by nationals abroad, n.a.
Population economically active (1999[1]): total 15,855; activity rate of total population 49.5% (participation rates: ages 15–64, 69.8%; female 40.3%; unemployed 2.0%).

Price and earnings indexes (1995 = 100)

	1993	1994	1995	1996	1997	1998	1999
Consumer price index	97.4	98.2	100.0	100.8	101.3	101.4	102.2
Earnings index	...	...	...	...	...	...	...

Household income and expenditure. Average household size (1990) 2.7; income per household: n.a.; sources of earned income (1987): wages and salaries 92.9%, self-employment 7.1%; expenditure (1990)[3]: rent 20.9%, food 17.7%, transportation 11.0%, education and self-improvement 9.7%, clothing 7.0%, health 4.7%.
Production (metric tons except as noted). Agriculture, forestry, fishing (1987): silo corn (maize) 27,880, potatoes 1,040, wheat 460, barley 416, grapes (1996) 150; livestock (number of live animals; 1999) 6,000 cattle, 3,000 pigs, 2,900 sheep; commercial timber (1998) 19,527 cu m; fish catch, n.a. Mining and quarrying: n.a. Manufacturing (1997): processed milk 13,304; milk for whipped cream 262; yogurt 82; cheese 3; wine (1993) 635.2 hectolitres; small-scale precision manufacturing includes optical lenses, electron microscopes, electronic equipment, and high-vacuum pumps; metal manufacturing, construction machinery, and ceramics are also important. Construction (1997): residential 344,515 cu m; nonresidential 282,145 cu m. Energy production (consumption): electricity (kW-hr; 1997) 75,842,000 (263,372,000); coal (metric tons; 1996) none (24); petroleum products (metric tons; 1995) none (49,291); natural gas (cu m; 1994) none (19,350,000).
Gross domestic product (1996): U.S.$714,000,000 (U.S.$23,000 per capita).

Structure of gross domestic product and labour force

	1996 in value U.S.$	1996 % of total value	1999[1] labour force	1999[1] % of labour force
Agriculture	...	...	303	1.9
Manufacturing	...	...	4,429	27.9
Construction	...	...	1,426	9.0
Public utilities	...	...	160	1.0
Transportation and communications	...	...	537	3.4
Trade, public accommodation	...	...	2,270	14.3
Finance, insurance, real estate	...	...	1,223	7.7
Pub. admin., defense	...	...	1,155	7.3
Services	...	...	4,352	27.4
Other	...	...	...	...
TOTAL	714,000,000	100.0	15,855[4]	100.0[2]

Land use (latest): forested 34.8%; meadows and pastures 15.7%; agricultural and under permanent cultivation 24.3%; other 25.2%.

Foreign trade

Balance of trade (current prices)

	1992	1993	1994	1995	1996	1997
Sw F '000,000	+947.1	+1,024.2	+1,043.3	+1,078.0	+1,165.3	+1,515.0
% of total	30.6%	33.8%	33.1%	33.5%	34.0%	39.1%

Imports (1997): Sw F 1,179,318,000 (machinery and transport equipment 35.2%; other finished goods 23.6%; metal products 12.5%; limestone, cement, and other building materials 12.4%; unrefined and semifabricated metal 5.7%; chemical products 5.2%). *Major import sources:* n.a.
Exports (1997): Sw F 2,694,357,000 (machinery and transport equipment 49.2%; metal products 15.1%; other finished goods 12.7%; limestone, cement, and other building materials 9.8%; chemical products 7.7%; food and beverages 4.2%). *Major export destinations* (1998): European Economic Community countries 49.5%; Switzerland 12.7%; other 37.8%.

Transport and communications

Transport. Railroads (1998): length 11.5 mi, 18.5 km; passenger and cargo traffic, n.a. Roads (1997): total length 201 mi, 323 km. Vehicles (1999): passenger cars 21,150; trucks and buses (1997) 2,684. Merchant marine: none. Air transport: none.

Communications

Medium	date	unit	number	units per 1,000 persons
Daily newspapers	1996	circulation	19,000	602
Radio	1997	receivers	21,000	658
Television	1997	receivers	12,000	364
Telephones	1998	main lines	19,762	618

Education and health

Educational attainment (1990). Percentage of population not of preschool age or in compulsory education having: no formal schooling 0.3%; primary and lower secondary education 39.3%; higher secondary and vocational 47.6%; some postsecondary 7.4%; university 4.2%; other and unknown 1.1%.
Literacy: virtually 100%.

Education (1998–99)

	schools	teachers	students	student/teacher ratio
Primary (age 7–12)	14	151	2,048	13.6
Secondary (age 13–19)	9	162	1,859	11.5
Vocational[5]	2	309	2,307	7.5

Health: physicians (1997) 41 (1 per 764 persons); hospital beds 108 (1 per 288 persons); infant mortality rate per 1,000 live births (1999).
Food (1998)[6]: daily per capita caloric intake 3,531 (vegetable products 65%, animal products 35%); 134% of FAO recommended minimum requirement.

Military

Total active duty personnel: none. *Military expenditure as percentage of GNP:* none.

[1]January 1. [2]Detail does not add to total given because of rounding. [3]Household expenditures are taken from a 1986 Swiss sample survey; a similarity of consumption patterns is assumed. [4]Employed only; excludes 7,940 foreign employees. [5]1997–98. [6]Figures are derived from statistics for Switzerland and Austria.

Lithuania

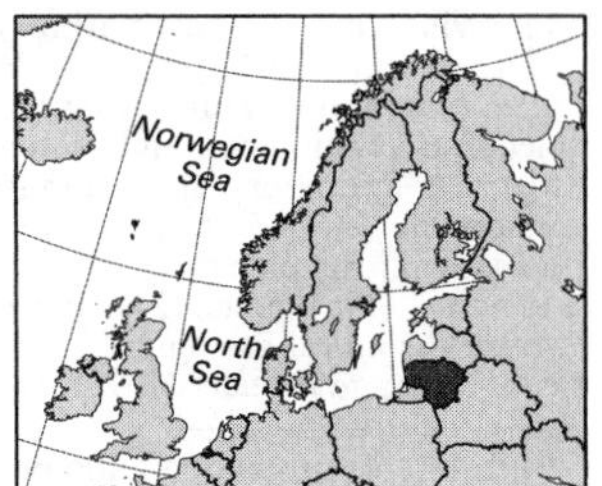

Official name: Lietuvos Respublika (Republic of Lithuania).
Form of government: unitary multiparty republic with a single legislative body, the Seimas (141).
Head of state: President.
Head of government: Prime Minister.
Capital: Vilnius.
Official language: Lithuanian.
Official religion: none.
Monetary unit: 1 litas (LTL) = 100 centai; valuation (Oct. 6, 2000) 1 U.S.$ = LTL 4.00[1]; 1 £ = LTL 5.79.

Area and population

Provinces	Capitals	area sq mi	area sq km	population 2000 estimate[2]
Alytus	Alytus	2,095	5,425	202,184
Kaunas	Kaunas	3,154	8,170	753,531
Klaipėda	Klaipėda	2,219	5,746	415,591
Marijampolė	Marijampolė	1,723	4,463	198,248
Panevėžys	Panevėžys	3,043	7,881	320,826
Šiauliai	Šiauliai	3,379	8,751	400,898
Tauragė	Tauragė	1,496	3,874	129,832
Telšiai	Telšiai	1,598	4,139	182,839
Utena	Utena	2,780	7,201	200,094
Vilnius	Vilnius	3,726	9,650	894,493
TOTAL		25,212[3]	65,300	3,698,536

Demography

Population (2000): 3,697,000.
Density (2000): persons per sq mi 146.6, persons per sq km 56.6.
Urban-rural (2000)[2]: urban 68.2%; rural 31.8%.
Sex distribution (1999)[2]: male 47.16%; female 52.84%.
Age breakdown (1999)[2]: under 15, 20.3%; 15–29, 21.9%; 30–44, 22.7%; 45–59, 16.9%; 60–74, 13.6%; 75 and over, 4.6%.
Population projection: (2010) 3,635,000; (2020) 3,631,000.
Ethnic composition (1997): Lithuanian 81.6%; Russian 8.2%; Polish 6.9%; Belarusian 1.5%; Ukrainian 1.0%; other 0.8%.
Religious affiliation (1995): Roman Catholic 72.2%; Russian Orthodox 2.5%; Protestant 1.3%; other (mostly nonreligious) 24.0%.
Major cities (2000)[2]: Vilnius 577,969; Kaunas 412,614; Klaipėda 202,484; Šiauliai 146,570; Panevėžys 133,696; Alytus 77,526.

Vital statistics

Birth rate per 1,000 population (1998): 10.0 (world avg. 22.1); legitimate 82.0%; illegitimate 18.0%.
Death rate per 1,000 population (1998): 11.0 (world avg. 8.9).
Natural increase rate per 1,000 population (1998): –1.0 (world avg. 13.2).
Total fertility rate (avg. births per childbearing woman; 1998): 1.4.
Marriage rate per 1,000 population (1998): 5.0.
Divorce rate per 1,000 population (1998): 3.2.
Life expectancy at birth (1998): male 66.5 years; female 76.9 years.
Major causes of death per 100,000 population (1997): diseases of the circulatory system 613.9; malignant neoplasms (cancers) 199.7; accidents, injury, homicide 146.9.

National economy

Budget (1998). Revenue: LTL 9,378,000,000 (value-added tax 38.5%, individual income tax 25.8%, excise taxes 14.3%, nontax revenue 7.5%). Expenditures: LTL 9,916,000,000 (education 27.7%, police 12.3%, social security and welfare 10.0%, health 6.6%, defense 4.5%).
Gross national product (1998): U.S.$9,411,000,000 (U.S.$2,540 per capita).

Structure of gross national product and labour force

	1998 in value LTL '000,000	% of total value	labour force[4]	% of labour force
Agriculture, forestry	3,881	9.1	356,000	20.1
Mining	9,051	21.2	3,100	0.2
Manufacturing			286,900	16.2
Construction	3,043	7.1	118,200	6.7
Public utilities	...	...	40,600	2.3
Transp. and commun.	3,666	8.6	96,900	5.5
Trade	6,796	15.9	265,400	15.0
Finance, real estate	4,181	9.8	58,600	3.3
Pub. admin., defense	2,568	6.0	69,100	3.9
Services	5,148	12.0	361,300	20.4
Other	4,433[5]	10.4[5]	113,700[6]	6.4[6]
TOTAL	42,768[3]	100.0[3]	1,769,800	100.0

Production (metric tons except as noted). Agriculture, forestry, fishing (1999): hay 2,621,000, potatoes 1,699,000, sugar beets 890,000, wheat 837,300, barley 835,000, cabbages 200,000, apples 100,000, oats 75,000, rapeseed 71,900; livestock (number of live animals) 1,168,000 pigs, 928,000 cattle; roundwood (1998) 4,879,000 cu m; fish catch (1997) 19,837. Mining and quarrying: limestone (1995) 3,000,000; peat (1997) 295,000. Manufacturing (value of production in LTL '000,000; 1997): food and beverages 5,785; refined petroleum products 3,488; wearing apparel 1,378; textiles 1,312; chemicals and chemical products 1,222; wood and wood products (excluding furniture) 902. Energy production (consumption): electricity (kW-hr; 1998) 17,988,000,000 ([1996] 11,630,000,000); coal (metric tons; 1996) none (338,000); crude petroleum (barrels; 1996) 1,136,000 (27,583,000); petroleum products (metric tons; 1996) 3,974,000 (2,993,000); natural gas (cu m; 1996) none (2,327,000,000).
Public debt (external outstanding; 1998): U.S.$1,215,800,000.
Population economically active (1997)[7]: total 1,819,800; activity rate of total population 49.1% (participation rates: ages 14–64, 71.1%; female 47.3%; unemployed [1998] 6.4%).

Price and earnings indexes (1995 = 100)

	1993	1994	1995	1996	1997	1998	1999
Consumer price index	41.6	71.6	100.0	124.6	135.7	142.5	143.6
Annual earnings index	36.6	69.7	100.0	136.0	169.4	201.8	214.0

Household income and expenditure. Average household size (1997) 2.9; average annual household disposable income (1997): LTL 12,914 (U.S.$3,228); sources of income (1998): wages and salaries 52.7%, transfers 21.3%, self-employment 14.8%, other 11.2%; expenditure (1998): food, beverages, and expenditures in cafes/hotels 54.6%, housing and energy 12.4%, transportation and communications 8.6%, clothing and footwear 8.0%.
Land use (1994): forested 30.4%; meadows and pastures 7.6%; agricultural and under permanent cultivation 53.9%; other 8.1%.
Tourism (1997): receipts from visitors U.S.$360,000,000; expenditures by nationals abroad U.S.$277,000,000.

Foreign trade[8]

Balance of trade (current prices)

	1993	1994	1995	1996	1997	1998
LTL '000,000	–1,091	–1,278	–3,774	–4,815	–7,136	–8,332
% of total	5.9%	7.3%	14.8%	12.7%	18.8%	21.9%

Imports (1998): LTL 23,174,000,000 (machinery/apparatus 18.4%, mineral fuels 14.3%, motor vehicles 11.4%, chemicals and chemical products 9.2%, textiles and clothing 8.8%). *Major import sources:* Russia 21.1%; Germany 18.2%; Poland 5.5%; Italy 4.4%; Denmark 3.8%.
Exports (1998): LTL 14,842,000,000 (mineral fuels 18.6%, textiles and clothing 18.6%, food products 12.3%, machinery/apparatus 10.8%, chemicals and chemical products 9.6%). *Major export destinations:* Russia 16.5%; Germany 13.1%; Latvia 11.1%; Belarus 8.9%; Ukraine 7.8%.

Transport and communications

Transport. Railroads (1998): route length 1,241 mi, 1,997 km; passenger-mi 444,000,000, passenger-km 715,000,000; short ton-mi cargo 5,661,000,000, metric ton-km cargo 8,265,000,000. Roads (1998): total length 44,350 mi, 71,375 km (paved 91%). Vehicles (1998): passenger cars 980,910; trucks and buses 105,022. Air transport (1998)[9]: passenger-mi 190,503,000, passenger-km 306,585,000; short ton-mi cargo 1,781,000, metric ton-km cargo 2,600,000; airports with scheduled flights (1996) 3.

Communications

Medium	date	unit	number	units per 1,000 persons
Daily newspapers	1996	circulation	344,000	93
Radio	1997	receivers	1,900,000	513
Television	1997	receivers	1,700,000	459
Telephones	1998	main lines	1,109,800	300
Cellular telephones	1998	subscribers	267,615	72
Personal computers	1998	units	200,000	54
Internet	1998	users	80,000	22

Education and health

Educational attainment (1989). Percentage of population age 25 and over having: no schooling 9.1%; incomplete and complete primary education 21.3%; incomplete and complete secondary 57.0%; postsecondary 12.6%. *Literacy* (1995): total population age 15 and over literate 99.2%.

Education (1996–97)

	schools	teachers	students	student/ teacher ratio
Primary (7–10)[10]	...	14,095	225,071	16.0
Secondary (11–18)[10]	...	32,172	325,480	10.1
Voc., teacher tr.[11]	104	5,078	56,400	11.1
Higher	...	13,136	83,645	6.4

Health (1998): physicians 14,622 (1 per 253 persons); hospital beds 35,612 (1 per 104 persons); infant mortality rate per 1,000 live births 9.3.
Food (1998): daily per capita caloric intake 3,104 (vegetable products 78%, animal products 22%); 121% of FAO recommended minimum requirement.

Military

Total active duty personnel (1999): 10,130[12] (army 77.4%, navy 13.0%, air force 9.6%). *Military expenditure as percentage of GNP* (1997): 0.8% (world 2.6%); per capita expenditure U.S.$34.

[1]Pegged value to U.S.$ since April 1994. [2]January 1. [3]Detail does not add to total given because of rounding. [4]Annual average. [5]Taxes less imputed bank service charges and subsidies. [6]Unemployed. [7]As of September. [8]Imports c.i.f.; exports f.o.b. [9]Lithuanian and Lietuva airlines. [10]Excludes special education. [11]1998–99. [12]Excludes 3,900 paramilitary in border police or coast guard.

Internet resources for further information:

- **Lithuanian Department of Statistics http://www.std.lt**

Luxembourg

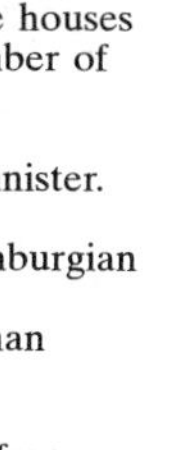

Official name: Groussherzogtum Lëtzebuerg (Luxemburgian); Grand-Duché de Luxembourg (French); Grossherzogtum Luxemburg (German) (Grand Duchy of Luxembourg).
Form of government: constitutional monarchy with two legislative houses (Council of State [21][1]; Chamber of Deputies [60]).
Chief of state: Grand Duke.
Head of government: Prime Minister.
Capital: Luxembourg.
Official language: none: Luxemburgian (national); French (used for most official purposes); German (lingua franca).
Official religion: none.
Monetary unit: 1 Luxembourg franc (Lux F) = 100 centimes; valuation (Oct. 6, 2000) 1 U.S.$ = Lux F 46.39; 1 £ = Lux F 67.10.

Area and population

Districts / Cantons	area sq mi	area sq km	population 1995[2] estimate
Diekirch	447	1,157	60,900
Clervaux	128	332	11,300
Diekirch	92	239	24,600
Redange	103	267	12,000
Vianden	21	54	2,900
Wiltz	102	265	10,100
Grevenmacher	203	525	46,700
Echternach	72	186	13,000
Grevenmacher	82	211	19,400
Remich	49	128	14,300
Luxembourg	349	904	298,000
Capellen	77	199	34,200
Esch	94	243	122,700
Luxembourg (Ville et Campagne)	92	238	120,500
Mersch	86	224	20,600
TOTAL	999	2,586	406,600[3]

Demography

Population (2000): 439,000.
Density (2000): persons per sq mi 439.4, persons per sq km 169.8.
Urban-rural (1999): urban 91.1%; rural 8.9%.
Sex distribution (1996[2]): male 49.08%; female 50.92%.
Age breakdown (1996): under 15, 18.5%; 15–29, 19.6%; 30–44, 24.8%; 45–59, 18.0%; 60–74, 13.5%; 75 and over, 5.6%.
Population projection: (2010) 493,000; (2020) 542,000.
Doubling time: not applicable; population stable.
Ethnic composition (nationality; 1999[2]): Luxemburger 64.4%; Portuguese 13.0%; Italian 4.7%; French 4.1%; Belgian 3.2%; German 2.4%; English 1.1%; other 7.1%.
Religious affiliation (1996): Roman Catholic 95.1%; other 4.9%.
Major cities (1997[2]): Luxembourg 78,300; Esch-sur-Alzette 24,600; Differdange 16,500; Dudelange 16,200; Petage 13,200.

Vital statistics

Birth rate per 1,000 population (1999): 13.0 (world avg. 22.1); (1998) legitimate 82.5%; illegitimate 17.5%.
Death rate per 1,000 population (1999): 8.8 (world avg. 8.9).
Natural increase rate per 1,000 population (1999): 4.2 (world avg. 13.2).
Total fertility rate (avg. births per childbearing woman; 1999): 1.7.
Marriage rate per 1,000 population (1997): 4.8.
Divorce rate per 1,000 population (1997): 2.4.
Life expectancy at birth (1999): male 73.7 years; female 80.2 years.
Major causes of death per 100,000 population (1997): circulatory diseases 371.7, of which ischemic heart disease and myocardial infarction 118.8, cerebrovascular disease 104.5; malignant neoplasms (cancers) 281.4.

National economy

Budget (1998). Revenue: Lux F 170,310,600,000 (income and excise taxes 58.2%, customs taxes 13.4%). Expenditures: Lux F 170,413,400,000 (social security 21.3%, education 11.7%, transportation 8.2%, administration 6.5%, defense 2.7%, debt service 0.9%).
Public debt (1997): U.S.$668,420,000.
Tourism (1997): receipts from visitors U.S.$297,000,000.
Production (metric tons except as noted). Agriculture, forestry, fishing (1997): barley 68,460, wheat 57,100, rye 26,800, potatoes 22,600, oats 13,250, sugar beets 8,600, apples 3,920; livestock (number of live animals) 212,335 cattle, 77,149 pigs; roundwood (1994) 411,600 cu m. Mining and quarrying (1987): sand and gravel 956,810; gypsum 420,000; crushed stone 344,841. Manufacturing (1994): steel 3,073,268; pig iron 1,926,890; milk 261,600; beef and pork 23,120; wine 179,998 hectolitres. Construction (1997): residential 440,840 sq m; nonresidential 93,100 sq m. Energy production (consumption): electricity (kW-hr; 1996) 1,307,000,000 (6,211,000,000); coal (metric tons; 1996) none (242,000); crude petroleum, none (none); petroleum products (metric tons; 1996) none (1,584,000); natural gas (cu m; 1996) none (729,000,000).
Gross national product (1998): U.S.$19,293,000,000 (U.S.$45,100 per capita).

Structure of gross domestic product and labour force

	1995 in value Lux F '000,000	1995 % of total value	1997 labour force	1997 % of labour force
Agriculture	5,174	1.1	5,700	2.5
Mining	4	4	4	4
Manufacturing	78,920[4]	17.4[4]	32,300[4]	14.3[4]
Construction	35,875	7.9	24,500	10.8
Public utilities	8,099	1.8	1,800	0.8
Transp. and commun.	27,505	6.1	17,400	7.7
Trade	65,419	14.4	44,800	19.8
Finance	91,929	20.2	20,100	8.9
Pub. admin., defense	63,644	14.0	27,400	12.1
Services	142,200	31.3	52,500	23.2
Other	–64,572[5]	–14.2[5]	...	...
TOTAL	454,193	100.0	226,500	100.0[3]

Population economically active (1997): total 226,500; activity rate of total population 53.8% (participation rates: ages 15–64, 51.4%; female 38.2%; unemployed 3.5%).

Price and earnings indexes (1995 = 100)

	1993	1994	1995	1996	1997	1998	1999
Consumer price index	96.0	98.1	100.0	96.9	98.3	100.1	...
Hourly earnings index	91.2	95.4	100.0	...	...	...	...

Household income and expenditure. Average household size (1991) 2.6; income per household (1992) Lux F 1,438,000 (U.S.$44,700); sources of income (1992): wages and salaries 67.1%, transfer payments 28.1%; self-employment 4.8%, expenditure (1994): food, beverages, and tobacco 19.7%, housing 17.3%, transportation and communications 16.2%, household goods and furniture 9.9%, clothing and footwear 8.2%, health 7.9%.
Land use (1992): forested 34.2%; meadows and pastures 25.6%; agricultural and under permanent cultivation 23.2%; other 17.0%.

Foreign trade

Balance of trade (current prices)

	1993	1994	1995	1996	1997	1998
Lux F '000,000	–62,300	–61,500	–62,400	–71,100	–82,800	–82,200
% of total	13.3%	12.3%	12.0%	13.9%	14.4%	8.0%

Imports (1997): Lux F 334,588,000,000 (machinery and transport equipment 48.7%; mineral products 9.1%; chemicals 7.8%; food 5.0%). *Major import sources:* Belgium 37.7%; Germany 28.1%; France 11.9%; U.S. 5.8%; The Netherlands 3.8%; Italy 2.4%.
Exports (1997): Lux F 250,266,000,000 (machinery and transport equipment 57.3%; plastics and rubber products 12.9%; textiles 5.7%; chemicals 5.7; food 3.4%). *Major export destinations:* Germany 26.5%; France 19.5%; Belgium 13.3%; U.K. 6.7%; Italy 5.4%; The Netherlands 5.0%; U.S. 3.5%.

Transport and communications

Transport. Railroads (1997): route length 170 mi, 274 km; passenger-mi 169,166,000, passenger-km 272,246,000; short ton-mi cargo 419,835,000, metric ton-km cargo 612,949,000. Roads (1996[2]): total length 3,206 mi, 5,160 km (paved 99%). Vehicles (1998[2]): passenger cars 244,129; trucks and buses 27,283. Merchant marine (1992): vessels (100 gross tons and over) 54; total deadweight tonnage 2,603,611. Air transport (1997): passenger arrivals 715,719, departures 720,690; airports (1997) with scheduled flights 1.

Communications

Medium	date	unit	number	units per 1,000 persons
Daily newspapers	1996	circulation	135,000	325
Radio	1997	receivers	285,000	677
Television	1997	receivers	163,000	387
Telephones	1998	main lines	293,083	687
Cellular telephones	1998	subscribers	130,500	306
Personal computers	1998	units	310,000	726
Internet	1998	users	50,000	117

Education and health

Educational attainment: n.a. *Literacy* (1995): virtually 100% literate.

Education (1997–98)

	schools	teachers	students	student/ teacher ratio
Primary (age 6–11)[6]	...	1,882	28,862	15.3
Secondary (age 12–18)	...	1,686[7]	9,463[8]	5.3[7]
Voc., teacher tr.	...	2,904[7, 9]	19,020	5.7[7, 9]
Higher[7]	1	200	1,100	5.5

Health (1996[2]): physicians 908 (1 per 454 persons); hospital beds (1995[2]) 4,443 (1 per 92 persons); infant mortality rate per 1,000 live births (1999) 4.7.
Food (1995): daily per capita caloric intake 3,530 (vegetable products 68%, animal products 32%); 134% of FAO recommended minimum.

Military

Total active duty personnel (1998): 811 (army 100.0%). *Military expenditure as percentage of GNP* (1997): 0.8% (world 2.6%); per capita expenditure U.S.$318.

[1]Has limited legislative authority. [2]January 1. [3]Detail does not add to total given because of rounding. [4]Manufacturing includes mining. [5]Imputed bank service charges. [6]Public schools only. [7]1994–95. [8]1996–97. [9]Vocational schools only.

Internet resources for further information:
- **STATEC: Luxembourg in Figures http://statec.gouvernement.lu**

Macau[1]

Official name: Aomen Tebie Xingzhengqu (Chinese); Regiño Administrativa Especial de Macau (Portuguese) (Macau Special Administrative Region).
Political status: special administrative region (China) with one legislative house (Legislative Council [23[2]]).
Head of state and government: Chief Executive.
Capital: Macau.
Official languages: Chinese; Portuguese.
Official religion: none.
Monetary unit: 1 pataca[3] (MOP) = 100 avos; valuation (Oct. 6, 2000) 1 U.S.$ = MOP 8.03; 1 £ = MOP 11.61.

Area and population

Geographical areas	area sq mi	area sq km	population 1991 census
Islands	5.3	13.8	10,148
Coloane	2.9	7.6	3,111
Taipa	2.4	6.2	7,037
Macau	3.0	7.8	326,460
Marine	—	—	2,856
TOTAL	8.3[4]	21.6[4]	339,464

Demography

Population (2000): 440,000.
Density (2000): persons per sq mi 48,352, persons per sq km 18,644.
Urban-rural (1999): urban, virtually 100%[5].
Sex distribution (1998): male 47.55%; female 52.45%.
Age breakdown (1998): under 15, 24.0%; 15–29, 23.0%; 30–44, 29.4%; 45–59, 13.8%; 60–74, 6.7%; 75 and over, 3.1%.
Population projection: (2010) 521,000; (2020) 608,000.
Doubling time: 87 years.
Nationality (1991): Chinese 68.2%; Portuguese 27.9%; English 1.8%; other 2.1%.
Religious affiliation (1998): nonreligious 60.8%; Buddhist 16.7%; other 22.5%.
Major city (1991): Macau 326,460.

Vital statistics

Birth rate per 1,000 population (1999): 12.6 (world avg. 22.1); legitimate, n.a.; illegitimate, n.a.
Death rate per 1,000 population (1999): 4.6 (world avg. 8.9).
Natural increase rate per 1,000 population (1999): 8.0 (world avg. 13.2).
Total fertility rate (avg. births per childbearing woman; 1999): 1.4.
Marriage rate per 1,000 population (1998): 3.4.
Divorce rate per 1,000 population (1998): 0.6.
Life expectancy at birth (1999): male 75.0 years; female 80.0 years.
Major causes of death per 100,000 population (1998): diseases of the circulatory system 117.1; malignant neoplasms (cancers) 77.8; diseases of the respiratory system 39.3; accidents, poisoning, and violence 23.9; diseases of the genitourinary system 11.4; diseases of the digestive system 11.1; infectious and parasitic diseases 10.0; endocrine and metabolic disorders 3.9; obstetric and perinatal disorders 3.3.

National economy

Budget (1998). Revenue: 14,831,099,000 patacas (recurrent receipts 69.1%, autonomous agency receipts 21.4%, capital receipts 2.2%). Expenditures: 14,831,099,000 patacas (recurrent payments 61.1%, autonomous agency expenditures 21.4%, capital payments 17.5%).
Tourism (1997): receipts from visitors U.S.$2,947,000,000; expenditures by nationals abroad U.S.$153,000,000.
Land use (1992): built-on area, wasteland, and other 100.0%.
Gross domestic product (at current market prices; 1998): U.S.$6,826,000,000 (U.S.$15,850 per capita).

Structure of labour force

	1998 labour force	1998 % of labour force
Agriculture	300	0.1
Mining	100	—
Manufacturing	41,500	19.7
Construction	11,800	5.6
Public utilities	1,400	0.7
Transportation and communications	13,700	6.5
Trade	54,600	25.9
Finance	13,600	6.5
Public administration } Services }	64,000	30.4
Other	9,700	4.6
TOTAL	210,700	100.0

Production (metric tons except as noted). Agriculture, forestry, fishing (1999): eggs 650; livestock (number of live animals) 500,000 chickens; fish catch (1997) 1,500. Quarrying (value added in '000,000 patacas; 1997): 13. Manufacturing (value added in '000,000 patacas; 1997): wearing apparel 2,161; textiles 607; electrical appliances 131; printing and publishing 97; nonmetallic mineral products 92; food products 83; footwear 53. Construction (1998): residential 742,955 sq m; nonresidential 226,237 sq m. Energy production (consumption): electricity (kW-hr; 1996) 1,620,000,000 (1,794,000,000); coal (metric tons) none (none); crude petroleum (barrels) none (none); petroleum products (metric tons; 1996) none (459,000); natural gas, none (none).
Public debt (long-term, external; 1995): U.S.$506,000,000.
Population economically active (1998): total 210,700; activity rate of total population 48.9% (participation rates: age 15–64, 70.2%; female 44.8%; unemployed 4.6%).

Price and earnings indexes (1995 = 100)

	1992	1993	1994	1995	1996	1997	1998
Consumer price index[6]	...	...	...	100.0	99.4	102.8	103.0
Earnings index	...	...	...	...	...	...	...

Household income and expenditure. Average household size (1991) 3.5; income per household: n.a.; sources of income: n.a.; expenditure (1987–88): food 38.3%, housing 19.7%, education, health, and other services 12.1%, transportation 7.4%, clothing and footwear 6.8%, energy 4.0%, household durable goods 3.7%, other goods 8.0%.

Foreign trade[7]

Balance of trade (current prices)

	1993	1994	1995	1996	1997	1998
'000,000 patacas	–1,902	–2,071	–354	–32	+526	+1,487
% of total	6.3%	6.5%	1.1%	0.1%	1.6%	4.6%

Imports (1998): 15,596,446,000 patacas (raw materials 54.1%, capital goods 14.2%, foodstuffs 9.3%, fuels and lubricants 6.3%). *Major import sources:* China 32.7%; Hong Kong 23.7%; European Economic Community 10.5%; Taiwan 9.9%; Japan 7.8%; United States 4.7%.
Exports (1998): 17,083,616,000 patacas (garments 76.4%, textiles 4.5%, machinery and mechanical appliances 3.5%, textile yarn and thread 3.1%, footwear 2.2%). *Major export destinations:* United States 47.7%; European Economic Community 30.5%; Hong Kong 7.6%; China 6.8%; Taiwan 1.5%; Japan 0.7%.

Transport and communications

Transport. Railroads: none. Roads (1996): total length 31 mi, 50 km (paved 100%). Vehicles (1998): passenger cars 45,184; trucks and buses 6,578. Merchant marine (1990): vessels 6; total gross tonnage 3,512. Air transport: none.

Communications

Medium	date	unit	number	units per 1,000 persons
Daily newspapers	1996	circulation	200,000	455
Radio	1997	receivers	160,000	356
Television	1997	receivers	49,000	109
Telephones	1998	main lines	173,893	404
Cellular telephones	1998	subscribers	75,476	175
Personal computers	1995	units	40,000	94
Internet	1998	users	30,000	70

Education and health

Educational attainment (1991). Population age 25 and over having: no formal schooling 13.1%; incomplete primary education 16.0%; completed primary 19.9%; some secondary 45.1%; post-secondary 5.9%. *Literacy* (1995): percentage of population age 15 and over literate 91.7%; males literate 95.6%; females literate 88.2%.

Education (1997–98)

	schools	teachers	students	student/ teacher ratio
Primary (age 6–11)	81	1,744	47,235	27.1
Secondary (age 12–18)	47	1,577	28,280	17.9
Teacher tr.	2	47	699	14.9
Higher	7	818	7,682	9.4

Health (1998): physicians 369 (1 per 1,167 persons); hospital beds 1,086 (1 per 396 persons); infant mortality rate per 1,000 live births (1999) 10.
Food (1998): daily per capita caloric intake 2,471 (vegetable products 76%, animal products 24%); 108% of FAO recommended minimum requirement.

Military

Total active duty personnel (1999): The Portuguese garrison has been replaced by People's Liberation Army units, which are now responsible for Macau's defense and security.

[1]Macau reverted to Chinese sovereignty on Dec. 20, 1999. [2]After Oct. 15, 2001, the Legislative Council shall be composed of 27 members. [3]The pataca free-floats with the Hong Kong dollar and has a parity of 1.03 patacas = HK$1.00; the Chinese renminbi and Hong Kong dollar are both acceptable in Macau. [4]Landfill in late 1990s increased total area to 9.1 sq mi (23.6 sq km). [5]About 1% of Macau's population live on sampans and other vessels. [6]Excluding rent; base year is July 1995–June 1996. [7]Import figures are c.i.f.

Internet resources for further information:

- **Government of Macau Special Administrative Region, P.R.C. http://www.macau.gov.mo**

Macedonia

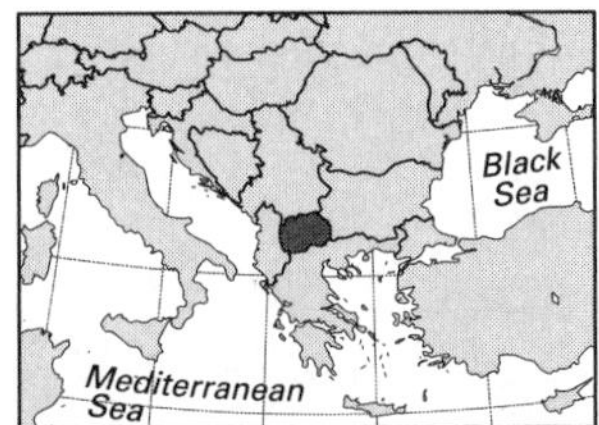

Official name[1]: Republika Makedonija (Republic of Macedonia).
Form of government: unitary multiparty republic with a unicameral legislative (Assembly [120]).
Head of state: President.
Head of government: Prime Minister.
Capital: Skopje.
Official language: Macedonian.
Official religion: none.
Monetary unit: denar; valuation (Oct. 6, 2000) 1 U.S.$ = 65.40 denar; 1 £ = 94.60 denar.

Area and population (1994 census)

Administrative districts[2]	area sq km	population	Administrative districts[2]	area sq km	population
Berovo	806	19,737	Negotino	734	23,094
Bitola	1,798	106,012	Ohrid	1,069	60,841
Brod	924	10,912	Prilep	1,675	93,248
Debar	274	26,449	Probištip	326	16,373
Delčevo	589	25,052	Radoviš	735	30,378
Demir Hisar	443	10,321	Resen	739	17,467
Gevgelija	757	34,767	Skopje[3]	1,818	541,280
Gostivar	1,341	108,189	Štip	815	50,531
Kavadarci	1,132	41,801	Struga	507	62,305
Kičevo	854	53,044	Strumica	952	89,759
Kočani	570	48,105	Sveti Nikole	649	21,391
Kratovo	376	10,855	Tetovo	1,080	174,748
Kriva Palanka	720	25,112	Titov Veles	1,536	65,523
Kruševo	239	11,981	Valandovo	331	12,049
Kumanovo	1,212	126,543	Vinica	432	19,010
			TOTAL	25,713[4]	1,936,877

Demography

Population (2000): 2,041,000.
Density (2000): persons per sq mi 205.6, persons per sq km 79.4.
Urban-rural (1994): urban 59.8%; rural 40.2%.
Sex distribution (1998): male 50.05%; female 49.95%.
Age breakdown (1998): under 15, 23.3%; 15–29, 24.0%; 30–44, 22.2%; 45–59, 16.4%; 60–64, 4.6%; 65 and over, 9.5%.
Population projection: (2010) 2,115,000; (2020) 2,170,000.
Ethnic composition (1994): Macedonian 66.5%; Albanian 22.9%; Turkish 4.0%; Gypsy 2.0%; Serb 2.0%; other 2.6%.
Religious affiliation (1995): Serbian (Macedonian) Orthodox 54.2%; Sunnī Muslim 30.0%; other 15.8%.
Major cities (1994): Skopje 440,577; Bitola 75,386; Prilep 67,371; Kumanovo 66,237; Tetovo 50,376.

Vital statistics

Birth rate per 1,000 population (1998): 14.6 (world avg. 22.1); legitimate 90.5%; illegitimate 9.5%.
Death rate per 1,000 population (1998): 8.4 (world avg. 8.9).
Natural increase rate per 1,000 population (1998): 6.2 (world avg. 13.2).
Total fertility rate (avg. births per childbearing woman; 1995): 2.0.
Marriage rate per 1,000 population (1998): 7.0.
Life expectancy at birth (1996–98): male 70.4 years; female 74.7 years.
Major causes of death per 100,000 population (1997): diseases of the circulatory system 462.8; malignant neoplasms 138.3; diseases of the respiratory system 39.5; accidents, violence, and poisoning 32.4; diseases of the digestive system 15.9.

National economy

Budget (1996). Revenue: 64,184,000,000 denar (social security contributions 38.1%, income and profits tax 17.1%, excise taxes 16.3%, sales tax 11.3%, import duties 10.4%). Expenditure: 63,970,000,000 denar (1995; pensions 24.1%, wages and salaries 22.7%, health 13.3%).
Tourism (1998): receipts from visitors U.S.$15,000,000; expenditures by nationals abroad U.S.$30,000,000.
Production (metric tons except as noted). Agriculture, forestry, fishing (1999): wheat 378,000, grapes 244,000, corn (maize) 200,000, potatoes 180,000; livestock (number of live animals) 1,550,000 sheep, 290,000 cattle, 60,000 pigs, 3,340,000 chickens; roundwood (1998) 720,000 cu m; fish catch (1997) 1,388 (all freshwater). Mining and quarrying (1998[5]): lead 17,000; copper 8,000; zinc 3,500; iron 1,000; refined silver 20,000 kg. Manufacturing (1998): cement 461,195; steel sheets 276,464; detergents 21,990; wool yarn 3,252; refrigerators 4,007 units; freezers 3,488 units; leather footwear 1,382,000 pairs; cotton fabric 13,700,000 sq m; cigarettes 7,009,000 units. Construction (value in '000,000 denars; 1998) residential 331; nonresidential 834). Energy production (consumption): electricity (kW-hr; 1996) 6,489,000,000 (6,489,000,000); coal (metric tons; 1996) 7,195,000 (7,330,000); crude petroleum (barrels; 1996) none (6,047,000); petroleum products (metric tons; 1996) 770,000 (1,383,000); natural gas (cu m; 1993) none (269,100,000).
Population economically active (1998): total 823,800; activity rate 41.1% (participation rates: ages 15–64, 61.2%; female 38.5%; unemployed 34.5%).

Price and earnings indexes (1995 = 100)

	1994	1995	1996	1997	1998	1999
Consumer price index	85.9	100.0	102.7	103.8	104.4	103.0
Earnings index[6]	90.6	100.0	102.8	...	...	...

Gross national product (1998): U.S.$2,584,000,000 (U.S.$1,290 per capita).

Structure of gross domestic product and labour force

	1997		1998	
	in value '000,000 denar	% of total value	labour force	% of labour force
Agriculture	20,764	11.2	94,800	11.5
Mining and manufacturing	38,351	20.7	173,800	21.1
Construction	10,131	5.5	...	...
Public utilities	4,904	2.6	...	...
Transp. and commun.	11,301	6.1	...	...
Trade	20,104	10.9	55,400	6.7
Finance	10,157	5.5	...	...
Pub. admin., defense	32,271	17.4	72,700	8.8
Services	7,268	3.9	35,600	4.3
Other	29,730[7]	16.1[7]	391,500[8]	47.5[8]
TOTAL	184,982[9]	100.0[9]	823,800	100.0[9]

External debt (1998): U.S.$1,944,000,000.
Land use (1994): forested 38.9%; meadows and pastures 24.7%; agricultural and under permanent cultivation 25.7%; other 10.7%.
Household income and expenditure (1994). Average household size 3.8; income per household Din 49,635 (U.S.$1,223); sources of income: wages and salaries 59.9%, transfers payments 17.0%, transfers from abroad 13.4%, other 9.7%; expenditure: food 42.2%, fuel and lighting 7.5%, clothing and footwear 7.4%, transportation and communications 7.2%, drink and tobacco 7.0%, health care 4.7%, education and entertainment 3.2%.

Foreign trade

Balance of trade (current prices)

	1994	1995	1996	1997	1998
U.S.$'000,000	–397.8	–514.9	–316.5	–387.6	–604.0
% of total	15.5%	17.6%	11.0%	13.9%	18.7%

Imports (1998): U.S.$1,310,697,000 (machinery and transport equipment 19.1%, manufactured products 14.5%, food products 13.4%, chemical products 10.6%, petroleum products 8.5%). *Major import sources:* Germany 13.3%; Yugoslavia 12.8%; Slovenia 7.8%; Ukraine 6.2%; Italy 5.7%; United States 5.3%.
Exports (1998): U.S.$1,914,663,000 (manufactured products 34.2%, machinery and transport equipment 7.5%, food products 5.0%, chemical products 5.0%, raw materials 4.3%). *Major export destinations:* Germany 21.4%; Yugoslavia 18.3%; United States 13.3%; Italy 7.0%; Greece 6.4%.

Transport and communications

Transport. Railroads (1998): length 575 mi, 925 km; passenger-mi 93,200,000, passenger-km 150,000,000; short ton-mi cargo 279,000,000, metric ton-km cargo 408,000,000. Roads (1998): length 7,154 mi, 11,513 km (paved 63%). Vehicles (1998): passenger cars 288,678; trucks and buses 24,745. Merchant marine: n.a. Air transport (1998): passenger-mi 553,460,000, passenger-km 890,710,000; short ton-mile cargo transported 239,200,000, metric tons cargo transported 163,840,000; airports (1997) with scheduled flights 2.

Communications

Medium	date	unit	number	units per 1,000 persons
Daily newspapers	1996	circulation	41,000	20
Radio	1997	receivers	410,000	204
Television	1998	receivers	500,000	249
Telephones	1998	main lines	457,000	228
Internet	1998	users	20,000	10

Education and health

Educational attainment (1981). Percentage of population age 15 and over having: less than full primary education 45.3%; primary 28.1%; secondary 21.2%; postsecondary and higher 5.1%; unknown 0.3%. *Literacy* (1981): total population age 10 and over literate 1,365,000 (89.1%); males literate 729,000 (94.2%); females literate 636,000 (83.8%).

Education (1997–98)

	schools	teachers	students	student/teacher ratio
Primary (age 7–14)	1,043	13,376	256,275	19.2
Secondary (age 15–18)	93	5,226	84,059	16.1
Higher[10]	30	1,385	36,141	26.1

Health (1998): physicians 4,508 (1 per 445 persons); hospital beds 10,333 (1 per 194 persons); infant mortality rate per 1,000 live births 16.3.

Military

Total active duty personnel (1999): 15,700 (army 95.5%, air force 4.5%). *Military expenditure as percentage of GNP* (1997): 2.5% (world 2.6%); per capita expenditure U.S.$42.

[1]Member of the United Nations under the name The Former Yugoslav Republic of Macedonia. [2]Local government reorganized September 1996 from 34 administrative districts into 123 municipalities. [3]The city of Skopje comprised five administrative districts. [4]Total includes 280 sq km of inland water not distributed by district. [5]Contained metal. [6]Based on nominal net wages per worker. [7]Includes import duties, customs imputed rents, and statistical discrepancy. [8]Includes 284,064 unemployed. [9]Detail does not add to total given because of rounding. [10]1998–99.

Internet resources for further information:
- **Secretariat of Information http://www.sinf.gov.mk**
- **National Bank of the Republic of Macedonia http://www.nbrm.gov.mk**

Madagascar

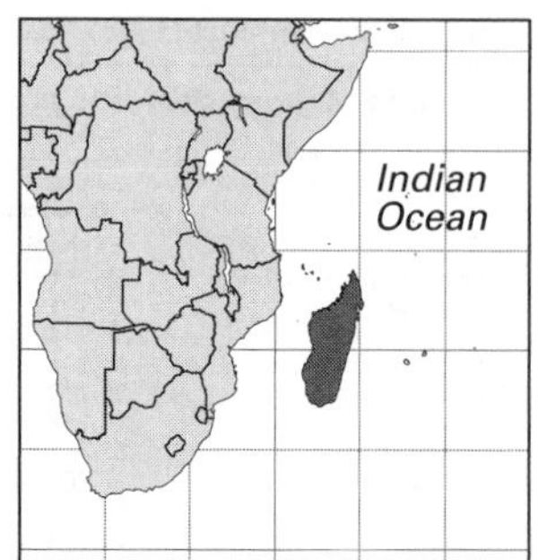

Official name: Repoblikan'i Madagasikara (Malagasy); République de Madagascar (French) (Republic of Madagascar).
Form of government: federal[1] multiparty republic with one legislative house (National Assembly [150]).
Heads of state and government: President assisted by Prime Minister.
Capital: Antananarivo.
Official languages: [2].
Official religion: none.
Monetary unit: 1 Malagasy franc (FMG) = 100 centimes; valuation (Oct. 6, 2000) 1 U.S.$ = FMG 6,697; 1 £ = FMG 9,688.

Area and population

		area		population
				1993
Autonomous provinces[1]	**Capitals**	sq mi	sq km	census
Antananarivo	Antananarivo	22,503	58,283	3,483,236
Antsirañana	Antsirañana	16,620	43,046	942,410
Fianarantsoa	Fianarantsoa	39,526	102,373	2,671,150
Mahajanga	Mahajanga	57,924	150,023	1,330,612
Toamasina	Toamasina	27,765	71,911	1,935,330
Toliary	Toliary	62,319	161,405	1,729,419
TOTAL		226,658	587,041	12,092,157

Demography

Population (2000): 15,506,000.
Density (2000): persons per sq mi 68.4, persons per sq km 26.4.
Urban-rural (1999): urban 29.0%; rural 71.0%.
Sex distribution (2000): male 49.70%; female 50.30%.
Age breakdown (2000): under 15, 45.0%; 15–29, 26.5%; 30–44, 15.8%; 45–59, 7.9%; 60–74, 3.8%; 75 and over, 1.0%.
Population projection: (2010) 20,993,000; (2020) 28,405,000.
Doubling time: 25 years.
Ethnic composition (1983): Malagasy 98.9%, of which Merina 26.6%, Betsimisaraka 14.9%, Betsileo 11.7%, Tsimihety 7.4%, Sakalava 6.4%, Antandroy 5.3%; Comorian 0.3%; Indian and Pakistani 0.2%; French 0.2%; Chinese 0.1%; other 0.3%.
Religious affiliation (1997): traditional beliefs 52.0%; Christian 41.0%, of which Roman Catholic 21.3%, Protestant 19.7%; Muslim 7.0%.
Major cities (1993): Antananarivo 1,103,304; Toamasina 137,782; Antsirabe 126,062; Fianarantsoa 109,248; Mahajanga 106,780.

Vital statistics

Birth rate per 1,000 population (2000): 43.2 (world avg. 22.1).
Death rate per 1,000 population (2000): 13.0 (world avg. 8.9).
Natural increase rate per 1,000 population (2000): 30.2 (world avg. 13.2).
Total fertility rate (avg. births per childbearing woman; 2000): 5.9.
Life expectancy at birth (2000): male 52.3 years; female 56.8 years.
Major causes of death per 100,000 population: n.a.; however, major causes of death in the early 1990s included maternal and perinatal diseases, malaria, infectious and parasitic diseases, malnutrition, diarrhea, and respiratory diseases.

National economy

Budget (1998). Revenue: FMG 2,875,000,000,000 (taxes 71.9%, of which duties on trade 41.0%, value-added tax 17.4%, income tax 12.4%; grants and nontax receipts 28.1%). Expenditures: FMG 3,702,000,000,000 (current expenditure 56.4%, of which debt service 12.6%, general administration 12.3%, defense 7.8%, education 7.0%, health 3.4%, agriculture 1.3%; capital expenditure 43.6%).
Production (metric tons except as noted). Agriculture, forestry, fishing (1999): paddy rice 2,637,000, cassava 2,435,000, sugarcane 2,180,000, sweet potatoes 520,000, potatoes 285,000, bananas 265,000, mangoes 206,000, corn (maize) 181,000, taro 160,000, oranges 85,000, coconuts 85,000, dry beans 81,800, coffee 65,000, pineapples 52,000, peanuts (groundnuts) 34,000, seed cotton 32,500; livestock (number of live animals) 10,353,000 cattle, 1,700,000 pigs, 1,410,000 goats, 790,000 sheep, 17,500,000 chickens; roundwood (1998) 9,517,000 cu m; fish catch (1998) 114,394. Mining and quarrying (1998): chromite ore 119,000; marine salt 30,000; graphite 14,300; mica 431; gold 200 kg[3]; in addition, a wide variety of semiprecious stones and gemstones are produced. Manufacturing (1997): cotton cloth 11,572,000 sq m, refined sugar 82,343 metric tons, cement 44,102 metric tons, soap 15,000, cigarettes 3,159 metric tons, beer 457,914 hectolitres, fuel oil 211,522 cu m, gas oil 125,317 cu m, kerosene 72,148 cu m, gasoline 96,573 cu m, shoes 831,000 pairs. Construction (1986)[4]: residential 19,700 sq m; nonresidential 5,700 sq m. Energy production (consumption): electricity (kW-hr; 1996) 683,000,000 (683,000,000); coal (metric tons; 1996) none (14,000); crude petroleum (barrels; 1996) none (1,530,000); petroleum products (metric tons; 1996) 191,000 (358,000); natural gas, none (n.a.).
Household income and expenditure. Average household size (1993) 4.6[5]; average annual income per household: n.a.; sources of income (1975)[5]: wages and salaries 58.8%, self-employment 14.1%, other 27.1%; expenditure (1983)[4, 6]: food 60.4%, fuel and light 9.1%, clothing and footwear 8.6%, household goods and utensils 2.4%.
Gross national product (1998): U.S.$3,741,000,000 (U.S.$260 per capita).

Structure of gross domestic product and labour force

	1994		1993	
	in value FMG '000,000[7]	% of total value[7]	labour force	% of labour force
Agriculture	1,819,339	33.1	5,100,000	86.2
Manufacturing	597,024	10.9	86,000	1.5
Mining	16,087	0.3		
Construction	64,224	1.2	46,000	0.8
Public utilities	106,654	1.9		
Transp. and commun.	954,436	17.4	42,000	0.7
Trade	600,464	10.9	149,000	2.5
Finance	80,293	1.5		
Services	924,244	16.8	243,000	4.1
Pub. admin., defense	334,735	6.0	208,000	3.5
Other	...	...	40,000	0.7
TOTAL	5,497,500	100.0	5,914,000	100.0

Population economically active (1993): total 5,914,000; activity rate of total population 48.9% (participation rates [1995]: over age 10, 59.4%; female 38.4%; unemployed, n.a.).

Price and earnings indexes (1995 = 100)

	1993	1994	1995	1996	1997	1998	1999
Consumer price index	48.3	67.1	100.0	119.8	125.1	132.9	146.1
Annual earnings index[8]	55.2	71.4	100.0	...	...	...	...

Public debt (external, outstanding; 1998): U.S.$4,107,000,000.
Land use (1994): forest 39.9%; pasture 41.3%; agriculture 5.3%; other 13.5%.
Tourism (1998): receipts from visitors U.S.$91,000,000; expenditures by nationals abroad U.S.$119,000,000.

Foreign trade

Balance of trade

	1993	1994	1995	1996	1997	1998
FMG '000,000,000	–396.7	–161.9	–764.5	–840.4	–1,253.1	–1,480.3
% of total	28.4%	6.1%	19.6%	25.7%	35.5%	36.1%

Imports (1997): FMG 2,917,600,000,000 (crude petroleum 13.6%, food 9.8%, motor vehicles 9.6%, petroleum products 6.8%, medicine and pharmaceuticals 4.2%). *Major import sources* (1997): France 23.0%; South Africa 9.6%; Iran 8.8%; Japan 6.1%; Germany 4.3%.
Exports (1997): FMG 1,414,300,000,000 (shrimp 24.7%; coffee 11.8%; cotton fabrics 6.3%; cloves and clove oil 4.4%; vanilla 3.5%). *Major export destinations* (1997): France 45.2%; Japan 9.0%; Germany 4.9%; U.S. 3.8%; Italy 3.0%.

Transport and communications

Transport. Railroads: route length (1993) 680 mi, 1,095 km; (1991) passenger-mi 152,000,000, passenger-km 245,000,000; short ton-mi cargo 90,000,000, metric ton-km cargo 132,000,000. Roads (1996): total length 30,967 mi, 49,837 km (paved 17%). Vehicles (1996): passenger cars 62,000; trucks and buses 16,460. Air transport (1998): passenger-mi 519,000,000, passenger-km 836,000,000; short ton-mi cargo 20,230,000, metric ton-km cargo 29,533,000; airports (1994) with scheduled flights 44.

Communications

Medium	date	unit	number	units per 1,000 persons
Daily newspapers	1996	circulation	66,000	4.6
Radio	1997	receivers	3,050,000	209
Television	1998	receivers	340,000	22.0
Telephones	1998	main lines	47,193	3.1
Internet	1998	users	3,000	0.2

Education and health

Educational attainment: n.a. *Literacy* (1995): percentage of total population age 15 and over literate 45.7%; males literate 59.8%; females literate 32.0%.

Education (1995–96)

	schools	teachers	students	student/ teacher ratio
Primary (age 6–13)	13,325	44,145	1,638,187	37.1
Secondary (age 14–18)	1,142[9]	16,795	302,036	18.0
Voc., teacher tr.	61[10]	1,150	8,479	7.3
Higher	5[9]	921	18,458	20.0

Health: physicians (1996) 1,470 (1 per 9,351 persons); hospital beds (1989) 10,900 (1 per 1,029 persons); infant mortality rate (2000) 87.0.
Food (1998): daily per capita caloric intake 2,001 (vegetable products 90%, animal products 10%); 89% of FAO recommended minimum requirement.

Military

Total active duty personnel (1997): 21,000 (army 95.2%, navy 2.4%, air force 2.4%). *Military expenditure as percentage of GNP* (1997): 1.5% (world 2.6%); per capita expenditure U.S.$4.

[1]Each of the six autonomous provinces is adopting its own statutory laws per article 2 of the 1998 constitution. [2]The 1998 constitution identifies Malagasy as the "national" language, although neither Malagasy nor French, the languages of the two official texts of the constitution, is itself "official." [3]1994. [4]Antananarivo only. [5]Malagasy households only. [6]Weights of consumer price index components; excludes housing. [7]At factor cost. [8]Average salary, all public employees, including military. [9]1988–89. [10]1987–88.

Internet resources for further information:

- **Mission of Madagascar to the United Nations (Geneva; French, summary only in English) http://www3.itu.ch/MISSIONS/Madagascar**

Malawi

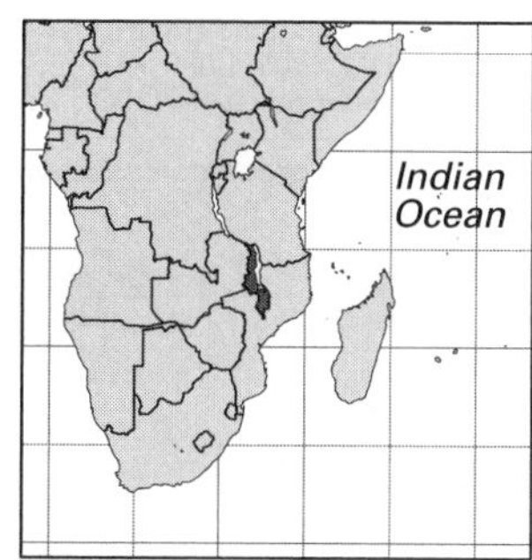

Official name: Republic of Malawi.
Form of government: multiparty republic with one legislative house (National Assembly [192]).
Head of state and government: President.
Capital: [1].
Official language: none.
Official religion: none.
Monetary unit: 1 Malawi kwacha (MK) = 100 tambala; valuation (Oct. 6, 2000) 1 U.S.$ = MK 76.50; 1 £ = MK 110.66.

Area and population

Regions / Districts	Capitals	area sq mi	area sq km	population 1998[2] census
Central	Lilongwe	13,742	35,592	4,041,636
Dedza	Dedza	1,399	3,624	483,136
Dowa	Dowa	1,174	3,041	409,087
Kasungu	Kasungu	3,042	7,878	476,018
Lilongwe	Lilongwe	2,378	6,159	1,337,777
Mchinji	Mchinji	1,296	3,356	318,759
Nkhotakota	Nkhotakota	1,644	4,259	230,361
Ntcheu	Ntcheu	1,322	3,424	370,988
Ntchisi	Ntchisi	639	1,655	167,353
Salima	Salima	848	2,196	248,157
Northern	Mzuzu	10,398	26,931	1,229,360
Chitipa	Chitipa	1,656	4,288	125,619
Karonga	Karonga	1,295	3,355	194,275
Mzimba	Mzimba	4,027	10,430	610,058
Nkhata Bay	Nkhata Bay	1,579	4,089	171,134
Rumphi	Rumphi	1,841	4,769	128,274
Southern	Blantyre	12,260	31,753	4,567,490
Balaka	Balaka	847	2,193	252,046
Blantyre	Blantyre	777	2,012	782,226
Chikwawa	Chikwawa	1,836	4,755	342,664
Chiradzulu	Chiradzulu	296	767	235,123
Machinga	Machinga	1,456	3,771	366,196
Mangochi	Mangochi	2,422	6,273	599,935
Mulanje	Mulanje	794	2,056	428,079
Mwanza	Mwanza	886	2,295	136,910
Nsanje	Nsanje	750	1,942	194,481
Phalombe	Phalombe	538	1,394	231,448
Thyolo	Thyolo	662	1,715	457,954
Zomba	Zomba	996	2,580	540,428
TOTAL LAND AREA		36,400	94,276	
INLAND WATER		9,347	24,208	
TOTAL		45,747	118,484	9,838,486

Demography

Population (2000): 10,386,000.
Density (2000)[3]: persons per sq mi 285.3, persons per sq km 110.2.
Urban-rural (1987): urban 10.7%; rural 89.3%.
Sex distribution (1998): male 48.89%; female 51.11%.
Age breakdown (1987): under 15, 46.0%; 15–29, 25.4%; 30–44, 14.5%; 45–59, 8.1%; 60 and over, 6.0%.
Population projection: (2010) 11,621,000; (2020) 12,318,000.
Ethnic composition (1983): Maravi (including Nyanja, Chewa, Tonga, and Tumbuka) 58.3%; Lomwe 18.4%; Yao 13.2%; Ngoni 6.7%; other 3.4%.
Religious affiliation (1995): Christian 50.3%, of which Protestant 20.5%, Roman Catholic 18.0%; Muslim 20.0%; traditional beliefs 10.0%; other 19.7%.
Major cities (1998): Blantyre 478,155; Lilongwe 435,964; Mzuzu 87,030.

Vital statistics

Birth rate per 1,000 population (1999): 39.2 (world avg. 22.1).
Death rate per 1,000 population (1999): 22.3 (world avg. 8.9).
Natural increase rate per 1,000 population (1999): 16.9 (world avg. 13.2).
Total fertility rate (avg. births per childbearing woman; 1999): 5.5
Life expectancy at birth (1999): male 37.3 years; female 38.4 years.
Major causes of death per 100,000 population (1986)[4]: infectious and parasitic diseases 711, of which malaria 270, diarrheal diseases 148, measles 128; malnutrition 267; diseases of the respiratory system 265.

National economy

Budget (1997–98). Revenue: MK 8,366,200,000 (tax revenue 96.7%, of which income tax 40.3%, sales tax 35.1%; nontax revenue 3.3%). Expenditures: MK 12,785,600,000 (administration 17.3%, education 16.5%, health 7.0%).
Public debt (external, outstanding; 1998): U.S.$2,310,000,000.
Production (metric tons except as noted). Agriculture (1999): corn (maize) 2,480,000, sugarcane 1,900,000, potatoes 385,000, plantains 205,000, cassava 200,000, tobacco 113,000, peanuts (groundnuts) 100,000, bananas 95,000; livestock (number of live animals) 1,260,000 goats, 750,000 cattle, 230,000 pigs, 110,000 sheep; roundwood (1998) 9,692,000 cu m; fish catch (1998) 41,111. Mining and quarrying (1998): limestone 171,900; gemstone 934 kg. Manufacturing (value added in MK '000; 1986): chemicals 30,805; textiles 19,630; food products 11,988; beverages 11,988; tobacco 9,480. Construction (value in MK; 1994): 41,700,000[5]. Energy production (consumption): electricity (kW-hr; 1996) 874,000,000 (874,000,000); coal (metric tons; 1996) none (17,000); petroleum products (metric tons; 1996) none (199,000).
Tourism: receipts (1998) U.S.$15,000,000; expenditures (1994) U.S.$15,000,000.
Land use (1994): forested 39.3%; meadows and pastures 19.6%; agricultural and under permanent cultivation 18.1%; other 23.0%.
Population economically active (1987): total 3,457,753; activity rate 43.3% (participation rates: age 15–64, 84.6%; female 51.5%; unemployed 5.4%).

Price and earnings indexes (1995 = 100)

	1993	1994	1995	1996	1997	1998	1999
Consumer price index	40.5	54.5	100.0	137.6	150.2	194.9	282.4
Earnings index	...	...	...	...	...	...	...

Gross national product (1998): U.S.$2,168,000,000 (U.S.$210 per capita).

Structure of gross domestic product and labour force

	1998 in value MK '000,000[6]	1998 % of total value[6]	1987 labour force	1987 % of labour force
Agriculture	4,582.8	36.3	2,967,933	85.8
Mining	111.9	0.9	7,164	0.2
Manufacturing	1,659.1	13.1	97,776	2.8
Construction	228.3	1.8	46,875	1.4
Public utilities	170.5	1.3	8,833	0.2
Transp. and commun.	531.0	4.2	24,863	0.7
Trade	3,117.1	24.7	94,445	2.7
Finance	1,088.5	8.6	5,590	0.3
Public administration	1,220.9	9.6	147,039	4.3
Services	262.0	2.1		
Other	–332.5[7]	–2.6[7]	57,235	1.6
TOTAL	12,639.6	100.0	3,457,753	100.0

Household income and expenditure (1979–80). Average household size (1997–98) 4.3; income per household MK 1,934 (U.S.$2,419); sources of income: wages 83.3%, household enterprise 6.0%; expenditure (1990)[8]: food 55.5%, clothing and footwear 11.7%, housing 9.6%, household goods 8.4%.

Foreign trade[9]

Balance of trade (current prices)

	1993	1994	1995	1996	1997	1998
MK '000,000	–29.0	+247.3	+1,840	+1,632	+1,118	+4,764
% of total	1.0%	4.6%	17.4%	12.5%	6.8%	16.7%

Imports (1995): MK 7,254,949,000 (1990; transport equipment 9.2%, petroleum products 8.3%, clothing 3.8%, pharmaceutical products 2.2%). *Major import sources:* South Africa 44.4%; Germany 4.5%; U.K. 4.3%; United States 3.7%.
Exports (1995): MK 6,192,563,000 (tobacco 63.2%, tea 6.7%, sugar 6.5%, cotton 0.9%). *Major export destinations:* South Africa 16.2%; Germany 14.7%; Japan 11.1%; U.S. 10.9%; Mozambique 7.6%.

Transport and communications

Transport. Railroads (1995–96): route length 495 mi, 797 km; passenger-km 18,048,000; metric ton-km cargo 43,431,000. Roads (1997): total length 10,222 mi, 16,451 km (paved 19%). Vehicles (1996): passenger cars 27,000; trucks and buses 29,700. Air transport (1995)[10]: passenger-km 110,000,000; metric ton-km cargo 14,000,000; airports (1997) 5.

Communications

Medium	date	unit	number	units per 1,000 persons
Daily newspapers	1996	circulation	22,000[11]	2.3[11]
Radio	1997	receivers	2,600,000	258
Telephones	1998	main lines	37,371	3.7
Cellular telephones	1998	subscribers	10,500	1.0
Personal computers	1998	units	8,000	0.8
Internet	1998	users	2,000	0.2

Education and health

Educational attainment (1987). Percentage of population age 25 and over having: no formal education 55.0%; primary education 39.8%; secondary and higher 5.2%. *Literacy* (1995): total population age 15 and over literate 56.4%; males literate 71.9%; females literate 41.8%.

Education (1995–96)

	schools	teachers	students	student/ teacher ratio
Primary (age 6–13)	3,706	49,138	2,887,107	58.8
Secondary (age 14–18)	94[12]	2,948	139,386	47.3
Teacher tr., voc.	13[12]	224	2,525	11.3
Higher	6[13]	531	5,561	10.5

Health: physicians (1989) 186 (1 per 47,634 persons); hospital beds (1987) 12,617 (1 per 627 persons); infant mortality rate (1999) 123.4.
Food (1998): daily per capita caloric intake 2,226 (vegetable products 98%, animal products 2%); 96% of FAO recommended minimum requirement.

Military

Total active duty personnel (1999): 5,000 (army 100%; navy, none; air force, none). *Military expenditure as percentage of GNP* (1997): 1.0% (world 2.6%); per capita expenditure U.S.$3.

[1]A capital is not designated in the 1994 constitution. Current government operations are divided between Lilongwe (ministerial, financial, and legislative) and Blantyre (executive and judicial). [2]Preliminary. [3]Based on land area. [4]Estimates based on reported inpatient deaths in hospitals, constituting an estimated 8% of total deaths. [5]Cities of Blantyre, Lilongwe, and Mzuzu only. [6]At constant prices of 1994. [7]Less imputed bank service charges. [8]Weights of consumer price index components, cities of Blantyre and Lilongwe only. [9]Import figures are f.o.b. in balance of trade and c.i.f. in commodities and trading partners. Reexports included in balance of trade, excluded from commodities and trading partners. [10]Air Malawi only. [11]Circulation for one newspaper only. [12]1989–90. [13]Universities only.

Internet resources for further information:

- **National Statistical Office of Malawi**
  http://www.nso.malawi.net

Malaysia

Official name: Malaysia.
Form of government: federal constitutional monarchy with two legislative houses (Senate [70[1]]; House of Representatives [193]).
Chief of state: Yang di-Pertuan Agong (Paramount Ruler).
Head of government: Prime Minister.
Capital: Kuala Lumpur[2].
Official language: Malay.
Official religion: Islam.
Monetary unit: 1 ringgit, or Malaysian dollar (RM) = 100 cents; valuation[3] (Oct. 6, 2000) 1 U.S.$ = RM 3.80; 1 £ = RM 5.50.

Area and population		area		population
Regions				1991
States	**Capitals**	sq mi	sq km	census
East Malaysia				
Sabah	Kota Kinabalu	28,425	73,620	1,734,685
Sarawak	Kuching	48,050	124,449	1,642,771
West Malaysia				
Johor	Johor Baharu	7,331	18,986	2,069,740
Kedah	Alor Setar	3,639	9,426	1,302,241
Kelantan	Kota Baharu	5,761	14,920	1,181,315
Melaka	Melaka	637	1,651	506,321
Negeri Sembilan	Seremban	2,565	6,643	692,897
Pahang	Kuantan	13,886	35,965	1,045,003
Perak	Ipoh	8,110	21,005	1,877,471
Perlis	Kangar	307	795	183,824
Pulau Pinang	George Town	398	1,030	1,064,166
Selangor	Shah Alam	3,071	7,955	2,297,159
Terengganu	Kuala Terengganu	5,002	12,955	766,244
Federal Territories				
Kuala Lumpur	—	94	243	1,145,342
Labuan	—	35	92	54,241
TOTAL		127,311	329,735	17,563,420

Demography

Population (2000): 23,260,000.
Density (2000): persons per sq mi 182.7, persons per sq km 70.5.
Urban-rural (2000): urban 57.0%; rural 43.0%.
Sex distribution (1999): male 51.22%; female 48.78%.
Age breakdown (1999): under 15, 33.5%; 15–29, 28.2%; 30–44, 21.0%; 45–59, 11.3%; 60–74, 4.9%, 75 and over, 1.1%.
Population projection: (2010) 27,903,000; (2020) 32,809,000.
Doubling time: 35 years.
Ethnic composition (1999): Malay and other indigenous 57.9%; Chinese 24.7%; Indian 7.0%; other nonindigenous 3.2%; noncitizen 7.2%.
Religious affiliation (1980): Muslim 52.9%; Buddhist 17.3%; Chinese folk religionist 11.6%; Hindu 7.0%; Christian 6.4%; other 4.8%.
Major cities (1991): Kuala Lumpur 1,145,342; Ipoh 382,853; Johor Baharu 328,436; Melaka 296,897; Petaling Jaya 254,350.

Vital statistics

Birth rate per 1,000 population (1999): 24.4 (world avg. 22.1).
Death rate per 1,000 population (1999): 4.4 (world avg. 8.9).
Natural increase rate per 1,000 population (1999): 20.0 (world avg. 13.2).
Total fertility rate (avg. births per childbearing woman; 1999): 3.1.
Life expectancy at birth (1999): male 71.0 years; female 75.0 years.
Major causes of death per 100,000 population (1996): diseases of the circulatory system 37.2; malignant neoplasms 19.8; infectious and parasitic diseases 15.2; accidents, homicide, and other violence 13.2; respiratory diseases 8.7%.

National economy

Budget (1998). Revenue: RM 68,058,000,000 (income tax 41.3%, taxes on goods and services 21.6%, nontax revenue 18.4%, taxes on international trade 11.0%). Expenditures: RM 42,766,000,000 (education 24.3%, defense and internal security 14.6%, general administration 11.1%, health 8.2%, trade and industry 3.3%, agriculture 2.8%).
Tourism (1998): receipts from visitors U.S.$2,456,000,000; expenditures by nationals abroad (1997) U.S.$2,478,000,000.
Population economically active (1997): total 8,569,200; activity rate 39.6% (participation rates: ages 15–64, 64.0%; female 34.0%; unemployed 2.2%).

Price index (1995 = 100)	1992	1993	1994	1995	1996	1997	1998
Consumer price index	88.4	91.6	95.0	100.0	103.5	106.2	111.8

Production (metric tons except as noted). Agriculture, forestry, fishing (1998): palm oil 8,315,000, rice 1,940,000, sugarcane 1,600,000, rubber 971,100, bananas 530,000, pineapples 143,000; livestock (number of live animals) 3,148,000 pigs, 693,000 cattle, 115,000,000 chickens; roundwood 46,031,000 cu m; fish catch (1997) 1,172,922. Mining and quarrying (1997): iron ore 269,087; bauxite 279,066; copper concentrates 80,675; tin concentrates 5,070. Manufacturing (1997): cement 12,668,000; refined sugar 1,155,000; wheat flour 720,000; plywood 4,513,000 cu m; radio receivers 33,491,000 units; automotive tires 13,716,000 units. Construction (completed; 1986)[4]: residential 8,809,100 sq m; nonresidential 959,900 sq m. Energy production (consumption): electricity (kW-hr; 1994) 39,975,000,000 (40,027,000,000); coal (metric tons; 1994) 174,000 (1,876,000); crude petroleum (barrels; 1994) 237,742,000 (100,021,000); petroleum products (metric tons; 1994) 11,406,000 (17,007,000); natural gas (cu m; 1994) 24,411,000,000 (13,166,000,000).
Gross national product (1998): U.S.$81,311,000,000 (U.S.$3,670 per capita).

Structure of gross domestic product and labour force	1997			
	in value RM '000,000[5]	% of total value	labour force	% of labour force
Agriculture	16,804	12.0	1,481,200	17.3
Mining	9,475	6.7	38,500	0.4
Manufacturing	50,270	35.7	2,002,500	23.4
Construction	6,732	4.8	793,200	9.3
Public utilities	3,543	2.5	50,900	0.6
Transp. and commun.	10,530	7.5	423,300	4.9
Trade	17,289	12.3	1,577,900	18.4
Finance	16,239	11.5	447,200	5.2
Pub. admin., defense / Services	15,535	11.1	1,754,500	20.5
Other	–5,733[6]	–4.1[6]	...	...
TOTAL	140,684	100.0	8,569,200	100.0

Public debt (external, outstanding; 1998): U.S.$18,158,000,000.
Household income and expenditure. Average household size (1991) 4.9; annual income per household (1995) RM 24,080 (U.S.$9,620); sources of income: n.a.; expenditure (1983): food 28.7%, transportation 20.9%, recreation and education 11.0%, housing 10.2%, household durable goods 7.7%.

Foreign trade[7]

Balance of trade (current prices)	1990	1991	1992	1993	1994	1995
RM '000,000	+7,947	+3,165	+11,446	+15,095	+12,628	+8,794
% of total	5.3%	1.7%	5.9%	6.6%	4.3%	2.4%

Imports (1996): RM 197,280,000,000 (machinery and transport equipment 60.1%, basic manufactures 13.4%, chemicals 6.8%, food 4.9%, mineral fuels 2.6%). *Major import sources:* Japan 24.5%; U.S. 15.4%; Singapore 13.4%; South Korea 5.2%; Taiwan 5.0%; Australia 2.8%.
Exports (1996): RM 197,026,000,000 (machinery and transport equipment 55.3%, basic manufactures 9.3%, mineral fuels 8.1%, animal and vegetable oils 6.0%, inedible crude materials 5.5%, chemicals 3.2%). *Major export destinations:* Singapore 20.4%; U.S. 18.2%; Japan 13.4%; Hong Kong 5.9%; Taiwan 4.1%; U.K. 3.4%; South Korea 3.0%.

Transport and communications

Transport. Railroads (1996): track length (1995) 1,791 km; passenger-km 1,396,000,000[8]; metric ton-km cargo 1,417,000,000[8]. Roads (1996): total length 94,500 km (paved 75%). Vehicles (1997): passenger cars 3,333,423; trucks and buses 618,066. Air transport (1997): passenger-km 28,704,000,000; metric ton-km cargo 1,428,528,000; airports (1997) 39.

Communications				units
Medium	date	unit	number	per 1,000 persons
Daily newspapers	1996	circulation	3,345,000	163
Radio	1997	receivers	9,100,000	434
Television	1997	receivers	3,600,000	172
Telephones	1998	main lines	4,384,000	202
Cellular telephones	1998	subscribers	2,200,000	101
Personal computers	1998	units	1,300,000	60
Internet	1998	users	800,000	37

Education and health

Educational attainment (1996). Percentage of population age 25 and over having: no formal schooling 16.7%; primary education 33.7%; secondary 42.8%; higher 6.8%. *Literacy* (1995): total population age 15 and over literate 83.5%; males literate 89.1%; females literate 78.1%.

Education (1997)	schools	teachers	students	student/ teacher ratio
Primary (age 7–12)	7,084	150,681	2,871,000	19.1
Secondary (age 13–19)	1,460	91,659	1,768,000	19.3
Voc., teacher tr.	78	3,007	27,000	9.0
Higher	51	15,684[9]	230,000[9]	14.7[9]

Health (1997): physicians 14,248 (1 per 1,521 persons); hospital beds 42,821 (1 per 506 persons); infant mortality rate per 1,000 live births (2000) 11.0.
Food (1997): daily per capita caloric intake 2,977 (vegetable products 81%, animal products 19%); (1995) 126% of FAO recommended minimum.

Military

Total active duty personnel (1998): 110,000 (army 77.2%, navy 11.4%, air force 11.4%). *Military expenditure as percentage of GDP* (1995): 3.0% (world 2.6%); per capita expenditure U.S.$122.

[1]Includes 40 appointees of the Paramount Ruler; the remaining 30 are indirectly elected at different times. [2]The transfer to the new federal administrative centre at Putrajaya will occur between 1999 and 2005. [3]Pegged to the U.S. dollar at RM 3.80 = 1 U.S.$ on Oct. 6, 2000. [4]Results of the Central Bank Survey of four major towns: Kuala Lumpur, Shah Alam, Kelang, and Seberang Prai. [5]At constant prices of 1978. [6]Net bank service charges. [7]Import figures are f.o.b. in balance of trade. [8]Peninsular Malaysia and Singapore. [9]1996.

Internet resources for further information:
- **Department of Statistics http://www.statistics.gov.my**
- **Malaysian Information Services (English) http://penerangan.gov.my**

Maldives

Official name: Divehi Jumhuriyya (Republic of Maldives).
Form of government: republic with one legislative house (Majlis[1] [42[2, 3]]).
Head of state and government: President.
Capital: Male.
Official language: Divehi.
Official religion: Islam.
Monetary unit: 1 Maldivian rufiyaa (Rf) = 100 laari; valuation (Oct. 6, 2000) 1 U.S.$ = Rf 11.70; 1 £ = Rf 16.92.

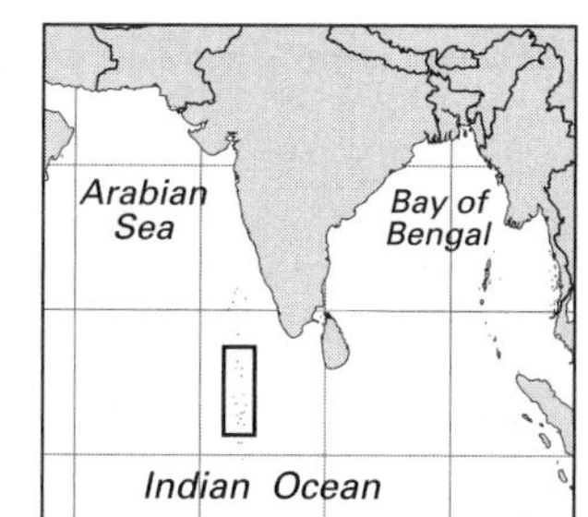

Area and population[4]

Administrative atolls	Capitals	area sq mi	area sq km	population 1995 census[5]
North Thiladhunmathi (Haa-Alifu)	Dhidhdhoo	...	...	13,657
South Thiladhunmathi (Haa-Dhaalu)	Nolhivaranfaru	...	...	14,769
North Miladhunmadulu (Shaviyani)	Farukolhu-funadhoo	...	...	10,462
South Miladhunmadulu (Noonu)	Manadhoo	...	...	10,096
North Maalhosmadulu (Raa)	Ugoofaaru	...	...	12,528
South Maalhosmadulu (Baa)	Eydhafushi	...	...	8,727
Faadhippolhu (Lhaviyani)	Naifaru	...	...	8,847
Male (Kaafu)	Thulusdhoo	...	...	11,650
Ari Atoll Uthuru Gofi (Alifu)	Rasdhoo	...	...	5,340
Ari Atoll Dhekunu Gofi (Alifu)	Mahibadhoo	...	...	6,404
Felidhu Atoll (Vaavu)	Felidhoo	...	...	1,779
Mulakatholhu (Meemu)	Muli	...	...	4,810
North Nilandhe Atoll (Faafu)	Magoodhoo	...	...	3,167
South Nilandhe Atoll (Dhaalu)	Kudahuvadhoo	...	...	4,825
Kolhumadulu (Thaa)	Veymandoo	...	...	9,651
Hadhdhunmathi (Laamu)	Hithadhoo	...	...	10,192
North Huvadhu Atoll (Gaafu-Alifu)	Viligili	...	...	8,164
South Huvadhu Atoll (Gaafu-Dhaalu)	Thinadhoo	...	...	11,984
Foammulah (Gnyaviyani)	Foahmulah	...	...	6,971
Addu Atoll (Seenu)	Hithadhoo	...	...	17,648
Capital island				
Male (Maale)		...	...	62,973
TOTAL		115	298	244,644

Demography

Population (2000): 285,000.
Density (2000): persons per sq mi 2,478, persons per sq km 956.4.
Urban-rural (1999): urban 28.0%; rural 72.0%.
Sex distribution (1997): male 51.17%; female 48.83%.
Age breakdown (1997): under 15, 44.8%; 15–29, 27.7%; 30–44, 15.0%; 45–59, 7.3%; 60–74, 4.4%; 75 and over, 0.8%.
Population projection: (2010) 364,000; (2020) 465,000.
Doubling time: 25 years.
Ethnic composition: the majority is principally of Sinhalese and Dravidian extraction; Arab, African, and Negrito influences are also present.
Religious affiliation: virtually 100% Sunnī Muslim.
Major cities (1995): Male 62,973.

Vital statistics

Birth rate per 1,000 population (1999): 34.5 (world avg. 22.1).
Death rate per 1,000 population (1999): 6.9 (world avg. 8.9).
Natural increase rate per 1,000 population (1999): 27.6 (world avg. 13.2).
Total fertility rate (avg. births per childbearing woman; 1999): 5.2.
Marriage rate per 1,000 population (1996): 9.6.
Divorce rate per 1,000 population (1996): 2.8.
Life expectancy at birth (1999): male 66.5 years; female 70.2 years.
Major causes of death per 100,000 population (1988): rheumatic fever 106.0; ischemic heart diseases 65.0; bronchitis, emphysema, and asthma 61.0; tetanus 23.5; tuberculosis 13.0; accidents and suicide 10.0.

National economy

Budget (1998). Revenue: Rf 1,941,400,000 (taxation 45.9%, nontax revenue 45.8%, foreign aid 8.2%). Expenditures: Rf 2,216,300,000 (general public services 40.7%, education 19.0%, housing 10.5%, health 10.0%, transportation and communications 9.5%).
Public debt (external, outstanding; 1998): U.S.$169,700,000.
Production (metric tons except as noted). Agriculture, forestry, fishing (1999): vegetables and melons 25,300, coconuts 13,000, fruits (excluding melons) 8,850, roots and tubers (including cassava, sweet potatoes, and yams) 7,010; fish catch (1997) 107,676. Mining and quarrying: coral for construction materials. Manufacturing: details, n.a.; however, major industries include boat building and repairing, coir yarn and mat weaving, coconut and fish processing, lacquerwork, garment manufacturing, and handicrafts. Energy production (consumption): electricity (kW-hr; 1996) 63,000,000 (63,000,000); petroleum products (metric tons; 1996) none (97,000).
Tourism (1997): receipts from visitors U.S.$286,000,000; expenditures by nationals abroad U.S.$38,000,000.
Population economically active (1995): total 67,476; activity rate of total population 27.6% (participation rates: ages 15–64, 62.6%; female 27.1%; unemployed [1995] 0.9%).

Price index (1995 = 100)

	1992	1993	1994	1995	1996	1997	1998
Consumer price index	76.3	91.7	94.8	100.0	106.3	114.3	112.7

Household income and expenditure (1990). Average household size 7.2; annual income per household Rf 2,616 (U.S.$274), sources of income: n.a.; expenditure (1981)[6]: food and beverages 61.8%, housing equipment 17.0%, clothing 8.0%, recreation and education 5.9%, transportation 2.6%, health 2.5%, rent 1.6%.
Gross national product (1998): U.S.$296,000,000 (U.S.$1,130 per capita).

Structure of gross domestic product and labour force

	1997 in value Rf '000[7]	1997 % of total value	1990 labour force	1990 % of labour force
Agriculture[8]	262,200	17.0	14,117	25.0
Mining	24,200	1.6	496	0.9
Manufacturing	90,400	5.9	8,441	15.0
Public utilities			445	0.8
Construction	171,500	11.1	3,151	5.6
Transp. and commun.	110,700	7.2	5,321	9.4
Trade	302,800	19.7	8,884	15.7
Finance	454,500	29.6	1,058	1.9
Public administration, defense	121,200	7.9	11,848	21.0
Services				
Other	...	...	2,674	4.7
TOTAL	1,537,500	100.0	56,435	100.0

Land use (1994): forested 3.3%; meadows and pastures 3.3%; agricultural and under permanent cultivation 10.0%; built-on, wasteland, and other 83.4%.

Foreign trade[9]

Balance of trade (current prices)

	1994	1995	1996	1997	1998	1999
U.S.$'000,000	–149.2	–186.1	–206.3	–233.8	–235.3	–290.4
% of total	61.9%	65.3%	63.5%	61.5%	60.7%	69.5%

Imports (1996): Rf 3,551,289,000 (machinery and transport equipment 27.9%, basic manufactures 23.7%, food and live animals 21.4%, petroleum products 9.1%). *Major import sources:* Singapore 32.0%; India 12.0%; Malaysia 8.5%; Sri Lanka 7.6%; United Kingdom 3.6%; Japan 3.5%.
Exports (1996): Rf 699,190,000 (canned fish 28.0%, yellowfin tuna 20.5%, apparel and clothing 17.4%, dried skipjack tuna 11.0%). *Major export destinations:* United Kingdom 21.7%; Sri Lanka 18.3%; United States 10.2%; Germany 10.8%; Japan 10.6%; Thailand 9.5%.

Transport and communications

Transport. Railroads: none. Roads: total length, n.a. Vehicles (1997): passenger cars 1,716; trucks and buses 586. Merchant marine (1992): vessels (100 gross tons and over) 44; total deadweight tonnage 78,994. Air transport (1995): passengers carried 159,000; passenger-km 71,000,000; airports (1997) with scheduled flights 5.

Communications

Medium	date	unit	number	units per 1,000 persons
Daily newspapers	1996	circulation	5,000	19
Radio	1997	receivers	34,000	129
Television	1997	receivers	7,000	28
Telephones	1998	main lines	19,985	73
Cellular telephones	1998	subscribers	1,600	5.8
Personal computers	1995	units	3,000	12
Internet	1998	users	1,500	5.4

Education and health

Educational attainment (1990). Percentage of population age 15 and over having: no standard passed 25.6%; primary standard 37.2%; middle standard 25.9%; secondary standard 6.3%; preuniversity 3.4%; higher 0.4%; not stated 1.2%. *Literacy* (1995): total population age 15 and over literate 93.2%; males literate 93.0%; females literate 93.3%.

Education (1998)

	schools	teachers	students	student/teacher ratio
Primary (age 6–11)	228	1,992	48,895	24.5
Secondary (age 11–18)	9[10]	291[10]	15,933[11]	12.3[10]
Voc., teacher tr.	10[10]	52[10]	452[11]	8.9[10]
Higher	—	—	—	—

Health (1996): physicians 99 (1 per 1,995 persons); hospital beds 318 (1 per 806 persons); infant mortality rate per 1,000 live births (1999) 47.
Food (1998): daily per capita caloric intake 2,451 (vegetable products 81%, animal products 19%); 111% of FAO recommended minimum requirement.

Military

Total active duty personnel: Maldives maintains a single security force numbering about 700–1,000; it performs both army and police functions.

[1]Also known or translated as People's Majlis, Citizens' Council, or Citizens' Assembly. [2]Excludes nonelective seats. [3]The new constitution went into effect Jan. 1, 1998. [4]Maldives is divided into 20 administrative districts corresponding to atoll groups; arrangement shown here is from north to south. Total area excludes 34,634 sq mi (89,702 sq km) of tidal waters. [5]Preliminary results. [6]Weights of consumer price index components. [7]At 1985 prices. [8]Primarily fishing. [9]Import figures are f.o.b. in balance of trade and c.i.f. for commodities and trading partners. [10]1986. [11]1992.

Internet resources for further information:
- **Governments on the WWW: Maldives http://www.gksoft.com/govt/en/mv.html**

Mali

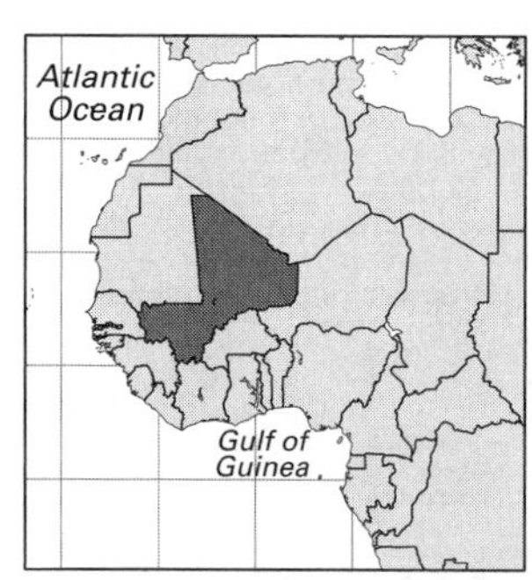

Official name: République du Mali (Republic of Mali).
Form of government: multiparty republic with one legislative house (National Assembly [147])[1].
Chief of state: President.
Head of government: Prime Minister.
Capital: Bamako.
Official language: French.
Official religion: none.
Monetary unit: 1 CFA franc (CFAF) = 100 centimes; valuation (Oct. 6, 2000) 1 U.S.$ = CFAF 754.28; 1 £ = CFAF 1,091.

Area and population

		area		population
				1995
Regions	Capitals	sq mi	sq km	estimate
Gao	Gao	65,858	170,572	408,000[2]
Kayes	Kayes	46,233	119,743	1,245,000
Kidal	Kidal	58,467	151,430	[2]
Koulikoro	Koulikoro	37,007	95,848	1,462,000
Mopti	Mopti	30,509	79,017	1,423,000
Ségou	Ségou	25,028	64,821	1,579,000
Sikasso	Sikasso	27,135	70,280	1,521,000
Tombouctou	Timbuktu (Tombouctou)	191,743	496,611	462,000
District				
Bamako	Bamako	97	252	913,000
TOTAL		482,077	1,248,574	9,013,000

Demography

Population (2000): 10,686,000.
Density (2000): persons per sq mi 22.2, persons per sq km 8.6.
Urban-rural (1998): urban 28.7%; rural 71.3%.
Sex distribution (1997): male 49.3%; female 50.7%.
Age breakdown (1999): under 15, 47.2%; 15–29, 26.6%; 30–44, 13.2%; 45–59, 8.0%; 60–74, 4.1%; 75 and over, 0.9%.
Population projection: (2010) 14,349,000; (2020) 18,984,000.
Doubling time: 24 years.
Linguistic composition (1987): Bambara-Malinké-Dyula (-Dioula) 50.3%; Fulani (Peulh-Foulfoulbe) 10.7%; Dogon-Kado 6.9%; Songhaï-Djerma 6.3%; Soninké-Marka 6.3%; Tamashek-Bella (Berber) 4.2%; Minianka 3.9%; Senufo 2.4%; Bwa- (Bobo-) Dafing 2.3%; Bozo-Somono 2.0%; other 4.7%.
Religious affiliation (1995): Muslim 90%; traditional beliefs 9%; Christian 1%.
Major cities (1987): Bamako 800,000[3]; Ségou 88,877; Mopti 73,979; Sikasso 73,050; Gao 54,874.

Vital statistics

Birth rate per 1,000 population (1999): 49.6 (world avg. 22.1).
Death rate per 1,000 population (1999): 19.5 (world avg. 8.9).
Natural increase rate per 1,000 population (1999): 30.1 (world avg. 13.2).
Total fertility rate (avg. births per childbearing woman; 1999): 6.9.
Life expectancy at birth (1999): male 45.2 years; female 47.5 years.
Major causes of death per 100,000 population: n.a.; morbidity ([notified cases of illness] by cause as a percentage of all reported infectious disease; 1985): malaria 62.1%; measles 10.3%; amebiasis 10.3%; syphilis and gonococcal infections 6.0%; influenza 4.9%.

National economy

Budget (1998). Revenue: CFAF 320,100,000,000 (tax revenue 71.1%, grants 23.2%, nontax revenue 5.7%). Expenditures: CFAF 365,300,000,000 (current expenditure 46.2%, of which wages and salaries 16.2%, interest on public debt 4.2%; capital expenditure 53.8%).
Public debt (external, outstanding; 1998): U.S.$2,827,000,000.
Tourism (1998): receipts from visitors U.S.$50,000,000; expenditures by nationals abroad U.S.$29,000,000.
Population economically active (1997): total 5,042,000; activity rate of total population 51.5% (participation rates (1987): ages 15–64, 67.4%; female 46.3%; unemployed 0.8%).

Price and earnings indexes (1995 = 100)

	1992	1993	1994	1995	1996	1997	1998
Consumer price index	71.8	71.6	88.2	100.0	106.8	106.4	110.7
Hourly earnings index	...	...	...	100.0	...	...	...

Production (metric tons except as noted). Agriculture, forestry, fishing (1999): millet 641,088, rice 589,048, sorghum 559,260, seed cotton 522,903, corn (maize) 341,490, sugarcane 302,982, peanuts (groundnuts) 144,330, sweet potatoes 15,820; livestock (number of live animals) 14,500,000 goats and sheep, 6,058,000 cattle, 652,000 asses, 292,000 camels, 136,000 horses, 65,000 pigs; roundwood (1998) 6,436,900 cu m; fish catch (1997) 99,610. Mining and quarrying (1997): limestone 20,000; phosphate 3,000; iron oxide 708; gypsum 500; gold 8,400 kg; silver 150 kg. Manufacturing (1996): sugar 25,000; cement 21,000; soap 10,097[4]; soft drinks 68,609 hectolitres[4]; beer 41,690 hectolitres[4]; shoes 111,000 pairs[4]; cigarettes 114,928 cartons[4]. Construction: n.a. Energy production (consumption): electricity (kW-hr; 1996) 335,000,000 (335,000,000); coal, none (n.a.); crude petroleum, none (n.a.); petroleum products (metric tons; 1996) none (154,000); natural gas, none (n.a.).
Gross national product (1998): U.S.$2,646,000,000 (U.S.$250 per capita).

Structure of gross domestic product and labour force

	1998		1987	
	in value CFAF '000,000	% of total value	labour force	% of labour force
Agriculture	384,600	44.0	2,802,722	82.2
Mining	48,200	5.5	1,524	—
Manufacturing	79,800	9.1	186,243	5.5
Construction	46,500	5.3	13,065	0.4
Public utilities	39,900	4.6	3,157	0.1
Transp. and commun.			6,174	0.2
Trade	138,200	15.8	158,892	4.7
Finance			320	—
Pub. admin., defense	38,300	4.4	158,704	4.6
Services	58,900	6.7	...	...
Other	40,500[5]	4.6[5]	78,470	2.3
TOTAL	874,900	100.0	3,409,271	100.0

Household income and expenditure. Average household size (1997) 5.0; average annual income per household: n.a.; sources of income: n.a.; expenditure (1986–87)[6]: food 54.6%, clothing 14.2%, transportation and communications 11.9%, housing and energy 8.7%, household durable goods 4.2%.
Land use (1994): forested 5.7%; meadows and pastures 24.6%; forest 9.7%; agricultural and under permanent cultivation 2.1%; other 63.6%.

Foreign trade[7]

Balance of trade (current prices)

	1992	1993	1994	1995	1996	1997
CFAF '000,000,000	−94.6	−93.0	−162.5	−154.4	−173.3	−110.5
% of total	33.0%	32.1%	30.3%	25.9%	28.2%	14.4%

Imports (1997): CFAF 438,200,000,000 (machinery, appliances, and transport equipment 29.5%; food products 14.5%; petroleum products 13.9%; construction products 10.7%; chemicals 8.9%). *Major import sources:* Côte d'Ivoire 19.8%; France 17.7%; United Kingdom 3.9%; Belgium-Luxembourg 3.0%; Germany 2.0%; Spain 1.6%; China 1.4%.
Exports (1997): CFAF 327,700,000,000 (raw cotton and cotton products 49.2%; gold 35.8%; live animals 9.4%). *Major export destinations:* China 9.5%; Belgium-Luxembourg 4.3%; Spain 2.7%; France 1.7%; Côte d'Ivoire 1.5%; Germany 1.0%.

Transport and communications

Transport. Railroads (1995): route length 398 mi, 641 km; passenger-mi 577,600,000, passenger-km 929,600,000; short ton-mi cargo 337,280,000, metric ton-km cargo 542,800,000. Roads (1996): total length 9,383 mi, 15,100 km (paved 12%). Vehicles (1996): passenger cars 26,190; trucks and buses 18,240. Merchant marine: vessels (100 gross tons and over) none. Air transport (1996)[8]: passenger-mi 139,808,000, passenger-km 225,000,000; short ton-mi cargo 23,000,000, metric ton-km cargo 37,000,000; airports (1998) with scheduled flights 9.

Communications

Medium	date	unit	number	units per 1,000 persons
Daily newspapers	1997	circulation	45,000	4.6
Radio	1997	receivers	1,600,000	163
Television	1998	receivers	120,000	11
Telephones	1999	main lines	26,758	2.5
Cellular phones	1999	subscribers	4,473	0.4
Internet	1999	users	1,000	0.1

Education and health

Educational attainment (1987). Percentage of population age 6 and over having: no formal schooling 86.0%; primary education 12.5%; secondary 1.2%; postsecondary and higher 0.3%. *Literacy* (1995): Percentage of total population age 15 and over literate 1,760,000 (31.0%); males literate 1,084,000 (39.4%); females literate 676,000 (23.1%).

Education (1997–98)

	schools	teachers	students	student/ teacher ratio
Primary (age 6–14)	2,511	10,853	862,875	79.5
Secondary (age 15–17)	307[9]	4,549[10]	166,372	...
Vocational	...	21,737	7,200	3.0
Higher	7	796[11]	13,847	17.4

Health: physicians (1993) 483 (1 per 18,376 persons); hospital beds (1987) 3,430 (1 per 2,253 persons); infant mortality rate per 1,000 live births (1999) 125.1.
Food (1998): daily per capita caloric intake 2,118 (vegetable products 90%, animal products 10%); 90% of FAO recommended minimum requirement.

Military

Total active duty personnel (1998): 7,350 (army 93.9%, navy 0.7%, air force 5.4%). *Military expenditure as percentage of GNP* (1997): 1.7% (world 2.6%); per capita expenditure U.S.$4.

[1]Multiparty legislative elections held in March 1997 were annulled by the constitutional court; new elections were held in July and August. [2]Kidal region was created in May 1991 from the northern half of Gao region as a concession to Tuareg separatists. Separate data not available. [3]1995 estimate. [4]1995. [5]Import taxes. [6]Weights of consumer price index components. [7]Imports are in c.i.f. [8]Represents 1/11 of the traffic of Air Afrique, which is operated by 11 West African states. [9]1991–92. [10]1995–96. [11]1996–97.

Internet resources for further information:

- **Embassy of Mali (Washington, D.C.)**
  http://www.maliembassy-usa.org

Malta

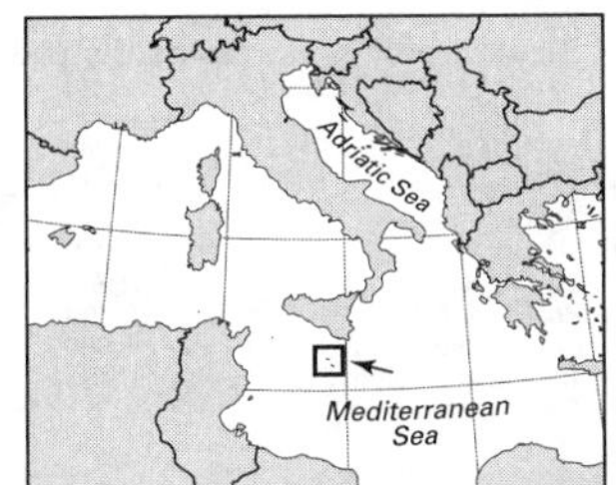

Official name: Repubblikka ta' Malta (Maltese); Republic of Malta (English).
Form of government: unitary multiparty republic with one legislative house (House of Representatives [65[1]]).
Chief of state: President.
Head of government: Prime Minister.
Capital: Valletta.
Official languages: Maltese; English.
Official religion: Roman Catholicism.
Monetary unit: 1 Maltese lira (Lm) = 100 cents = 1,000 mils; valuation[2] (Oct. 6, 2000) 1 U.S.$ = Lm 0.46; 1 £ = Lm 0.66.

Area and population

	area		population
			1999[3]
Census regions[4]	sq mi	sq km	census
Gozo and Comino	27	70	29,180
Inner Harbour	6	15	87,413
Northern	30	78	45,043
Outer Harbour	12	32	113,119
South Eastern	20	53	51,484
Western	27	69	52,279
TOTAL	122	316[5]	378,518

Demography

Population (2000): 382,000.
Density (2000): persons per sq mi 3,131, persons per sq km 1,209.
Urban-rural (1996): urban 89.7%; rural 10.3%.
Sex distribution (1999[3]): male 49.58%; female 50.42%.
Age breakdown (1999[3]): under 15, 20.8%; 15–29, 21.6%; 30–44, 21.2%; 45–59, 19.8%; 60–74, 11.9%; 75 and over, 4.7%.
Population projection: (2010) 410,000; (2020) 451,000.
Ethnic composition (by nationality; 1995): Maltese 95.3%; British 1.6%; other 3.1%.
Religious affiliation (1996): Roman Catholic 93.4%; other 6.6%.
Major cities (1999[3]): Birkirkara 21,350; Qormi 17,881; Sliema 12,308; Hamrun 11,014; Valletta 7,100.

Vital statistics

Birth rate per 1,000 population (1998): 11.9 (world avg. 22.1); legitimate 91.8%; illegitimate 8.2%.
Death rate per 1,000 population (1998): 9.1 (world avg. 8.9).
Natural increase rate per 1,000 population (1998): 2.8 (world avg. 13.2).
Total fertility rate (avg. births per childbearing woman; 1995): 1.8.
Marriage rate per 1,000 population (1998): 6.3.
Divorce rate per 1,000 population: n.a.
Life expectancy at birth (1998): male 74.4 years; female 80.1 years.
Major causes of death per 100,000 population (1998): diseases of the circulatory system 353.1; malignant neoplasms 191.2; diseases of the respiratory system 79.7; endocrine and metabolic diseases of the blood 33.1; accidents, poisoning, and violence 26.5; diseases of the digestive system 23.6.

National economy

Budget (1999). Revenue: Lm 637,852,000 (direct taxes 42.7%; indirect taxes 32.6%; nontax revenue 23.1%; foreign grants 1.5%). Expenditures: Lm 690,965,000 (recurrent expenditures 84.6%, of which social security 27.2%[6], education 10.4%[6], health 10.0%[6], debt service 4.9%[6], defense 4.2%[6]; capital expenditure 15.4%).
Public debt (1998): U.S.$2,224,400,000.
Production (metric tons except where noted). Agriculture, forestry, fishing (1999): vegetables 58,850 (of which tomatoes 32,800, cabbage 3,500, melons 2,600, garlic 2,000, onions 1,200), potatoes 32,000, grapes 10,000, barley 2,000; livestock (number of live animals; 1999) 69,000 pigs, 21,000 cattle, 16,000 sheep, 9,050 goats; fish catch 979,432. Quarrying (value of production in Lm; 1996): 6,898,000. Manufacturing (value of sales in Lm; 1994–95): machinery and transport equipment 402,993,000; food 103,733,000; textiles and wearing apparel 80,813,000; paper and printing 40,610,000; chemicals 35,151,000. Construction (buildings completed; 1996): residential 3,360[7]; nonresidential 1,859. Energy production (consumption): electricity (kW-hr; 1996) 1,514,000,000 (1,514,000,000); coal (metric tons; 1996) none (310,000); crude petroleum, none (n.a.); petroleum products (metric tons; 1996) none (342,000).
Population economically active (1998): total 144,824; activity rate of total population 38.4% (participation rates: ages 15–64 [1985] 45.9%; female 27.6%; unemployed 5.1%).

Price and earnings indexes (1995 = 100)

	1993	1994	1995	1996	1997	1998	1999
Consumer price index	92.4	96.2	100.0	102.5	105.7	108.2	110.5
Average weekly earnings	92.8	96.8	100.0	104.3	...	...	...

Household income and expenditure. Average household size (1985) 3.3; average annual income per household (1982) Lm 4,736 (U.S.$11,399); sources of income (1993): wages and salaries 63.8%, professional and unincorporated enterprises 19.3%, rents, dividends, and interest 16.9%; expenditure (1993): food and beverages 27.9%, transportation and communications 15.7%, household furnishings and operations 9.5%, recreation, entertainment, and education 7.2%, clothing and footwear 6.9%, housing 5.5%, health 3.3%, tobacco 2.6%.

Tourism (1998): receipts from visitors U.S.$661,000,000; expenditures by nationals abroad U.S.$193,000,000.
Gross domestic product (1998): U.S.$3,807,000,000 (U.S.$10,100 per capita).

Structure of gross domestic product and labour force

	1998			
	in value Lm '000	% of total value	labour force	% of labour force
Agriculture	32,605	2.7	2,522	1.7
Manufacturing	271,334	22.7	33,924	23.4
Mining Construction	36,073	3.0	5,440	3.8
Public utilities	8	8	2,004	1.4
Transp. and commun.	75,819	6.3	10,199	7.0
Trade	136,096	11.4	24,256[9]	16.7[9]
Finance	96,941	8.1	5,370	3.7
Pub. admin., defense	279,887[8]	23.4[8]	32,151	22.2
Services	134,308	11.2	16,630	11.5
Other	134,869	11.3	12,328[10]	8.5[10]
TOTAL	1,197,932	100.0[5]	144,824	100.0[5]

Land use (1994): agricultural and under permanent cultivation 40.6%; other (infertile clay soil with underlying limestone) 59.4%.

Foreign trade[11]

Balance of trade (current prices)

	1993	1994	1995	1996	1997	1998	1999
Lm '000,000	–312.6	–326.4	–362.8	–383.7	–352.5	–335.1	–348.6
% of total	23.2%	21.6%	21.2%	23.5%	21.8%	19.2%	18.0%

Imports (1998): Lm 1,034,994,000 (machinery and transport equipment 50.3%, manufactured and semimanufactured goods 24.8%, food 9.3%, chemicals 7.7%, mineral fuels 3.8%). *Major import sources:* Italy 19.3%; France 17.8%; U.K. 12.4%; Germany 10.5%; U.S. 8.9%.
Exports (1998): Lm 703,442,000 (machinery and transport equipment 64.6%, manufactured 27.7%, food and live animals 2.0%). *Major export destinations:* France 20.5%; U.S. 18.0%; Singapore 14.3%; Germany 12.8%; U.K. 7.8%; Italy 4.7%.

Transport and communications

Transport. Railroads: none. Roads (1997): total length 1,219 mi, 1,961 km (paved 94%). Vehicles (1998): passenger cars 185,247; trucks and buses 49,520. Merchant marine (1992): vessels (100 gross tons and over) 889; total deadweight tonnage 17,073,207. Air transport (1998): passenger-mi 1,172,982,000, passenger-km 1,887,736,000; short ton-mi cargo 7,689,800; metric ton-km cargo 11,227,000; airports (1999) with scheduled flights 1.

Communications

Medium	date	unit	number	units per 1,000 persons
Daily newspapers	1996	circulation	54,000	145
Radio	1997	receivers	255,000	680
Television	1998	receivers	200,000	530
Telephones	1998	main lines	191,500	499
Cellular telephones	1998	subscribers	22,500	59
Facsimile machines	1996	units	6,000	16
Personal computers	1998	units	100,000	260

Education and health

Educational attainment (1967). Percentage of economically active population having: no formal schooling 10.8%; primary education 60.4%; lower secondary 3.4%; upper secondary 17.6%; technical secondary 3.9%; post-secondary and higher 3.9%. *Literacy* (2000): total population age 15 and over literate 279,000 (92.1%); males literate 138,000 (91.4%); females literate 141,000 (92.8%).

Education (1995–96)

	schools	teachers	students	student/ teacher ratio
Primary (age 5–10)	111	1,990	35,479	17.8
Secondary (age 11–17)	59	2,679	29,907	20.9
Voc., teacher tr.	22	541	4,539	8.4
Higher[12]	1	470	5,805	12.3

Health (1996): physicians 925 (1 per 403 persons); hospital beds 2,140 (1 per 174 persons); infant mortality rate per 1,000 live births (1998) 5.3.
Food (1998): daily per capita caloric intake 3,382 (vegetable products 73%, animal products 27%); 135% of FAO recommended minimum requirement.

Military

Total active duty personnel (1999): 1,900 (army 100%). *Military expenditure as percentage of GNP* (1997): 0.9% (world 2.6%); per capita expenditure U.S.$81.

[1]As of September 1998 elections. [2]The Maltese lira is tied to the currencies of several principal trading partners. [3]January 1. [4]Data are reported according to census regions as of January 1993 rather than the 67 new "local administrative districts" (local councils) created between 1993 and 1998. [5]Detail does not add to total given because of rounding. [6]1997. [7]Dwellings completed. [8]Pub. admin., defense includes Public utilities. [9]Includes hotels and catering. [10]Includes 7,437 unemployed. [11]Import figures are f.o.b. in balance of trade and c.i.f. for commodities and trading partners. [12]1994–95.

Internet resources for further information:

- **Central Office of Statistics http://www.magnet.mt/info/general.html**

Marshall Islands

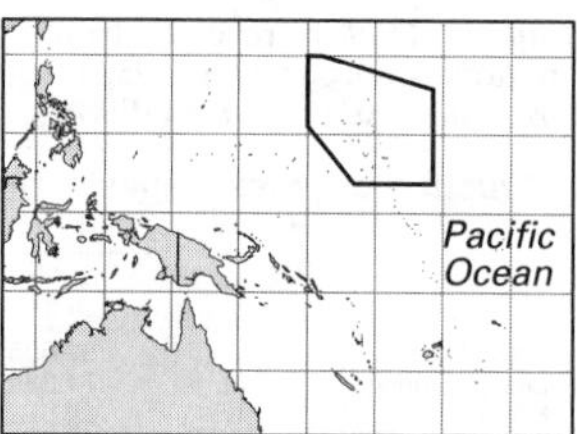

Official name: Majōl (Marshallese); Republic of the Marshall Islands (English).
Form of government: unitary republic with two legislative houses (Council of Iroij [12][1]; Nitijela [33]).
Head of state and government: President.
Capital: Majuro.
Official languages: Marshallese (Kajin-Majōl); English.
Official religion: none.
Monetary unit: 1 U.S. dollar (U.S.$) = 100 cents; valuation (Oct. 6, 2000) 1 £ = U.S.$1.45.

Area and population

Atolls/Islands	area sq mi	area sq km	population 1999 census[2]
Ailinglaplap	5.67	14.68	1,959
Ailuk	2.07	5.36	...
Arno	5.00	12.95	2,069
Aur	2.17	5.62	...
Bikini	2.32	6.01	...
Ebon	2.22	5.75	902
Enewetak	2.26	5.85	...
Jabat	0.22	0.57	...
Jaluit	4.38	11.34	1,609
Kili	0.36	0.93	...
Kwajalein	6.33	16.39	10,902
Lae	0.56	1.45	...
Lib	0.36	0.93	...
Likiep	3.96	10.26	...
Majuro	3.75	9.71	23,676
Maloelap	3.75	9.71	...
Mejit	0.72	1.86	...
Mili	6.15	15.93	1,032
Namorik	1.07	2.77	...
Namu	2.42	6.27	903
Rongelap	3.07	7.95	...
Ujae	0.72	1.86	...
Ujelang	0.67	1.74	...
Utrik	0.94	2.43	...
Wotho	1.67	4.32	...
Wotje	3.16	8.18	866
Other atolls	4.10	10.62	...
TOTAL	70.07	181.48[3]	50,840

Demography

Population (2000): 51,600.
Density (2000): persons per sq mi 737.1, persons per sq km 285.1.
Urban-rural (1999): urban 71.0%; rural 29.0%.
Sex distribution (2000): male 42.45%; female 57.55%.
Age breakdown (1997): under 15, 50.2%; 15–29, 26.0%; 30–44, 13.9%; 45–59, 6.5%; 60–74, 2.6%; 75 and over, 0.8%.
Population projection: (2010) 60,000; (2020) 69,000.
Doubling time: 18 years.
Ethnic composition (nationality; 1988): Marshallese 96.9%; other Pacific islanders 1.7%; Filipino 0.5%; all other 0.9%.
Religious affiliation (1995): Protestant 62.8%; Roman Catholic 7.1%; Mormon 3.1%; Jehovah's Witness 1.0%; other (mostly nonreligious) 26.0%.
Major cities (1999): Majuro 23,676; Ebeye (1988) 8,324.

Vital statistics

Birth rate per 1,000 population (2000): 45.2 (world avg. 22.1).
Death rate per 1,000 population (2000): 6.4 (world avg. 8.9).
Natural increase rate per 1,000 population (2000): 38.8 (world avg. 13.2).
Total fertility rate (avg. births per childbearing woman; 2000): 6.6.
Life expectancy at birth (2000): male 63.7 years; female 67.4 years.
Major causes of death per 100,000 population (1990–93)[4]: infectious and parasitic diseases 169.9; circulatory diseases 155.1; respiratory diseases 105.1; malignant neoplasms (cancers) 68.4; digestive diseases 63.3; accidents, injuries, and violence 36.7.

National economy

Budget (1997–98). Revenue: U.S.$61,400,000 (U.S. government grants 59.7%, income tax 12.7%, import tax 10.7%, value-added and excise taxes 4.4%, fishing rights 2.9%, fees and charges 2.1%). Expenditures: U.S.$50,900,000 (wages and salaries 33.4%, goods and services 32.4%, capital expenditures 14.3%, interest payments 10.8%, subsidies 7.1%).
Production (metric tons except as noted). Agriculture, forestry, fishing (1997): coconuts 140,000, copra 18,000, cassava 12,000, sweet potatoes 3,000, bananas 2,000; livestock (number of live animals) 32,000 pigs, 14,000 cattle; roundwood, n.a.; fish catch (1998) 400. Mining and quarrying: high-grade phosphate mining on Ailinglaplap Atoll, quarrying of sand and aggregate for local construction only. Manufacturing (1995): copra 7,728 coconut oil and processed (chilled or frozen) fish are important products; the manufacture of handicrafts and personal items (clothing, mats, boats, etc.) by individuals is also significant. Construction (1994): value added U.S.$9,300,000. Energy production (consumption): electricity (kW-hr; 1994) 57,891,000 (57,891,000); coal, none (n.a.); gasoline, oil, and lubricants (barrels; 1988)[5] n.a. (84,588).
Public debt (external, outstanding; 1996–97): U.S.$124,900,000.
Gross national product (at current market prices; 1998): U.S.$96,000,000 (U.S.$1,540 per capita).

Structure of gross domestic product and labour force

	1996–97 in value U.S.$'000	1996–97 % of total value	1988 labour force	1988 % of labour force
Agriculture	14,400	14.8	2,150	18.7
Mining	300	0.3	2	—
Manufacturing	2,200	2.3	945	8.2
Public utilities	2,400	2.5	82	0.7
Construction	6,600	6.8	1,076	9.4
Transp. and commun.	6,400	6.6	537	4.7
Trade, restaurants, hotels	17,300	17.8	1,394	12.1
Finance, insurance, real estate	14,700	15.2	833	7.3
Public administration	12,100	12.5	3,035	26.4
Services	17,200	17.7		
Other	3,400[6]	3.5[6]	1,434[7]	12.5[7]
TOTAL	97,000	100.0	11,488	100.0

Land use (1989)[8]: forested 22.5%; meadows and pastures 13.5%; agricultural and under permanent cultivation 33.1%; other 30.9%.
Household income and expenditure. Average household size (1988) 8.7; income per household (1979) U.S.$3,366; sources of income: n.a.; expenditure (1982): food 57.7%, housing 15.6%, clothing 12.0%, personal effects and other 14.7%.
Population economically active (1988): total 11,488; activity rate of total population 26.5% (participation rates: over age 14, 54.1%; female 30.1%; unemployed 12.5%).

Price and earnings indexes (1995 = 100)

	1993	1994	1995	1996	1997
Consumer price index	87.4	92.4	100.0	109.6	114.9
Earnings index	...	...	...	...	...

Tourism (1998): receipts from visitors U.S.$3,000,000; expenditures by nationals abroad, n.a.

Foreign trade[9]

Balance of trade (current prices)

	1992	1993	1994	1995	1996	1997
U.S.$'000,000	–52.6	–53.4	–48.2	–52.0	–53.6	–48.3
% of total	74.1%	77.7%	52.1%	53.0%	58.6%	65.6%

Imports (1997): U.S.$60,995,000 (mineral fuels and lubricants 23.4%, food, beverages, and tobacco 22.8%, machinery and transport equipment 9.5%, manufactured goods 7.4%, chemical products 6.6%). *Major import sources:* U.S. 47.2%; Guam 4.8%; Australia 4.0%; Singapore 3.4%; Japan 3.3%.
Exports (1997): U.S.$12,665,000 (chilled fish 78.2%, frozen fish 10.7%, crude coconut oil 9.6%). *Major export destinations:* U.S. *c.* 80.0%; other *c.* 20.0%.

Transport and communications

Transport. Vehicles (1995): passenger cars 1,374; trucks and buses 262. Merchant marine (1992): vessels (100 gross tons and over) 35; total deadweight tonnage 4,182,356. Air transport (1996): passenger-km 28,000,000; metric ton-km cargo 5,000; airports (1997) with scheduled flights 25.

Communications

Medium	date	unit	number	units per 1,000 persons
Telephones	1997	main lines	3,500	44.2

Education and health

Educational attainment (1988). Percentage of population age 25 and over having: no grade completed 5.1%; elementary education 43.2%; secondary 39.7%; higher 11.4%; not stated 0.6%. *Literacy* (latest): total population age 15 and over literate 19,377 (91.2%); males literate 9,993 (92.4%); females literate 9,384 (90.0%).

Education (1994–95)

	schools	teachers	students	student/ teacher ratio
Primary (age 6–14)	103	669	13,355	20.0
Secondary (age 15–18)	12	144	2,400	16.7
Voc., teacher tr.	...	...	...	...
Higher	...	...	...	...

Health (1997): physicians 34 (1 per 1,785 persons); hospital beds 129 (1 per 470 persons); infant mortality rate per 1,000 live births (2000) 41.

Military

Under the 1984 Compact of Free Association, the United States provides for the defense of the Republic of the Marshall Islands.

[1]Council of Iroij is an advisory body only. [2]Partial breakdown of final census results. [3]Detail does not add to total given because of rounding. [4]Registered deaths only. [5]Import only. [6]Import duties less imputed bank service charges. [7]Includes 1,432 unemployed. [8]Data are for the former Trust Territory of the Pacific Islands. [9]Imports in balance of trade table is c.i.f.

Internet resources for further information:
- **RMI Online, Internet Guide to the Republic of the Marshall Islands http://www.rmiembassyus.org**

Martinique

Official name: Département de la Martinique (Department of Martinique).
Political status: overseas department (France) with two legislative houses (General Council [45]; Regional Council [41]).
Chief of state: President of France.
Heads of government: Prefect (for France); President of the General Council (for Martinique); President of the Regional Council (for Martinique).
Capital: Fort-de-France.
Official language: French.
Official religion: none.
Monetary unit: 1 French franc (F) = 100 centimes; valuation (Oct. 6, 2000) 1 U.S.$ = F 7.54; 1 £ = F 10.91.

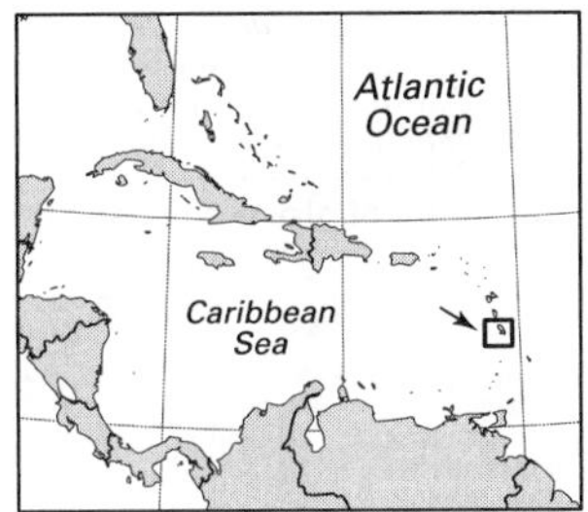

Area and population

Arrondissements	Capitals	area sq mi	area sq km	population 1999 census
Fort-de-France	Fort-de-France	66	171	166,139
Le Marin	Le Marin	158	409	106,818
La Trinité	La Trinité	131	338	85,006
Saint-Pierre	Saint-Pierre	81	210	23,464
TOTAL		436	1,128	381,427

Demography

Population (2000): 385,000.
Density (2000): persons per sq mi 883.0, persons per sq km 341.3.
Urban-rural (1999): urban 94.6%; rural 5.4%.
Sex distribution (1999): male 49.34%; female 50.66%.
Age breakdown (1999): under 15, 23.1%; 15–29, 25.2%; 30–44, 25.1%; 45–59, 13.2%; 60–74, 9.0%; 75 and over, 4.4%.
Population projection: (2010) 415,000; (2020) 436,000.
Doubling time: 70 years.
Ethnic composition (1983): mulatto 93.7%; French (metropolitan and Martinique white) 2.6%; East Indian 1.7%; other 2.0%.
Religious affiliation (1995): Roman Catholic 86.5%; Protestant 8.0% (mostly Seventh-day Adventist); Jehovah's Witness 1.6%; other 3.9%, including Hindu, syncretist, and nonreligious.
Major communes (1999): Fort-de-France 94,049; Le Lamentin 35,460; Le Robert 21,201; Schoelcher 20,845; Sainte-Marie 20,058.

Vital statistics

Birth rate per 1,000 population (1999): 16.4 (world avg. 22.1); (1992) legitimate 34.1%; illegitimate 65.9%.
Death rate per 1,000 population (1999): 6.4 (world avg. 8.9).
Natural increase rate per 1,000 population (1999): 10.0 (world avg. 13.2).
Total fertility rate (avg. births per childbearing woman; 1999): 1.8.
Marriage rate per 1,000 population (1997): 4.1.
Divorce rate per 1,000 population (1996): 1.1.
Life expectancy at birth (1999): male 78.9 years; female 77.2 years.
Major causes of death per 100,000 population (1996): diseases of the circulatory system 206.8; malignant neoplasms (cancers) 150.3; accidents, poisoning, and violence 47.2; diseases of the respiratory system 36.3; endocrine and metabolic disorders 27.8; diseases of the digestive system 27.2.

National economy

Budget (1994). Revenue: F 1,816,000,000 (general receipts from French central government and local administrative bodies 45.0%; tax receipts 34.0%, of which indirect taxes 19.5%, direct taxes 14.5%). Expenditures: F 1,816,000,000 (health and social assistance 42.0%; wages and salaries 16.7%; other administrative services 7.2%; debt amortization 5.0%).
Public debt (1994): U.S.$186,700,000.
Production (metric tons except as noted). Agriculture, forestry, fishing (1999): bananas 321,454, sugarcane 188,827, pineapples 20,200, plantains 13,000, roots and tubers 11,750, lettuce 7,800, yams 4,700, tomatoes 4,300, cucumbers and gherkins 3,200, melons 2,900, coconuts 1,137, sweet potatoes 970; livestock (number of live animals) 42,000 sheep, 33,000 pigs, 30,000 cattle, 21,800 goats; roundwood (1998) 12,000 cu m; fish catch (1998) 5,500. Mining and quarrying (1996): pumice 130,000; sand and gravel for local construction. Manufacturing (1998): cement 225,000; processed pineapples 20,210; sugar 6,543; rum 68,716 hectolitres; other products include clothing, fabricated metals, and yawls and sails. Construction (buildings authorized; 1994): residential permits 6,893; nonresidential 113,279 sq m. Energy production (consumption): electricity (kW-hr; 1996) 906,000,000 (906,000,000); coal, none (none); crude petroleum (barrels; 1996) none (5,827,000); petroleum products (metric tons; 1996) 738,000 (566,000); natural gas, none (none).
Household income and expenditure. Average household size (1997) 3.0; income per household (1989) F 147,150 (U.S.$24,525); sources of income (1989): wages and salaries 80%, other 20%; expenditure (1993): food and beverages 32.1%, transportation and communications 20.7%, housing and energy 10.6%, household durable goods 9.4%, clothing and footwear 8.0%, education and recreation 5.4%, health care 5.2%, other 8.6%.
Tourism (1997): receipts from visitors U.S.$400,000,000; expenditures by nationals abroad, n.a.

Gross domestic product (1997): U.S.$4,271,000,000 (U.S.$11,325 per capita).

Structure of gross domestic product and labour force

	1992 in value F '000,000	1992 % of total value	1990 labour force	1990 % of labour force
Agriculture, fishing	1,106.3	5.0	8,445	5.1
Mining, manufacturing	1,770.6	8.0	9,706	5.9
Construction	1,145.3	5.2	9,298	5.6
Public utilities	483.6	2.2		
Transp. and commun.	1,427.6	6.5	6,673	4.0
Trade, restaurants, hotels	4,022.1	18.2	13,965	8.5
Finance, real estate, insurance	2,590.1	11.7	26,489	16.1
Pub. admin., defense	5,416.0	24.5	35,541	21.6
Services	3,906.9	17.7		
Other	224.9[1]	1.0[1]	54,760[2]	33.2[2]
TOTAL	22,093.4	100.0	164,877	100.0

Population economically active (1998): total 165,900; activity rate of total population 41.6% (participation rates: ages 15–64, 71.2%; [1997] female 32.6%; unemployed [1998] 28.2%).

Price and earnings indexes (1990 = 100)

	1992	1993	1994	1995	1996	1997	1998
Consumer price index[3]	108.4	109.6	114.0	115.9	118.1	119.2	120.6
Monthly earnings index[4]	105.7	107.5	109.1	111.3	112.3	116.8	...

Land use (1994): forested 45.3%; meadows and pastures 13.2%; agricultural and under permanent cultivation 17.0%; other 24.5%.

Foreign trade[5]

Balance of trade (current prices)

	1993	1994	1995	1996	1997	1998
F '000,000	–7,744	–7,877	–8,604	–8,987	–8,676	–8,305
% of total	78.0%	76.4%	78.2%	80.5%	78.6%	71.0%

Imports (1998): F 9,997,000,000 (1996; consumer goods 23.9%, goods for intermediate consumption [inputs to the manufacturing process changed or destroyed in the final product] 15.9%, automobiles 15.0%, professional equipment 15.2%, energy products 8.3%). *Major import sources* (1996): France 62.3%; Italy 4.1%; Venezuela 3.8%; Germany 3.3%; United States 3.0%; U.K. 2.0%; Guadeloupe 0.9%.
Exports (1998): F 1,692,000,000 (1996; bananas 36.9%, refined petroleum 19.9%, rum 11.3%, yachts and boats 7.1%). *Major export destinations* (1996): France 51.7%; Guadeloupe 21.0%; U.K. 7.2%; French Guiana 3.8%.

Transport and communications

Transport. Railroads: none. Roads (1994): total length 1,299 mi, 2,091 km (paved [1988] 75%). Vehicles (1993): passenger cars 108,300; trucks and buses 32,200. Merchant marine (1992): vessels (100 gross tons and over) 6; total deadweight tonnage 1,121. Air transport (1997): passenger arrivals and departures 1,552,000; cargo handled 14,400 metric tons; airports (1998) with scheduled flights 1.

Communications

Medium	date	unit	number	units per 1,000 persons
Daily newspapers	1996	circulation	30,000	78
Radio	1997	receivers	82,000	213
Television	1997	receivers	66,000	171
Telephones	1999	main lines	172,192	443
Cellular telephones	1999	subscribers	55,000	141
Internet	1999	users	...	...

Education and health

Educational attainment (1990). Percentage of population age 25 and over having: incomplete primary, or no declaration 54.3%; primary education 18.0%; secondary 20.0%; higher 7.7%. *Literacy* (1982): total population age 15 and over literate 206,807 (92.5%); males literate 97,538 (91.8%); females literate 109,269 (93.2%).

Education (1997)

	schools	teachers	students	student/ teacher ratio
Primary (age 6–11)	273	2,603	55,569	21.3
Secondary (age 12–18)[6]	76	2,888	36,605	12.7
Vocational[6]	...	896	11,101	12.4
Higher	1	99[7]	3,079	45.3[7]

Health (1998): physicians 780 (1 per 487 persons); hospital beds 2,907 (1 per 131 persons); infant mortality rate per 1,000 live births (1999) 8.2.
Food (1998): daily per capita caloric intake 2,865 (vegetable products 75%, animal products 25%); 118% of FAO recommended minimum requirement.

Military

Total active duty personnel (1998): 2,200 French troops.

[1]Import duties, value-added tax less imputed bank service charge. [2]Unemployed. [3]Figures are end-of-year unless otherwise footnoted. [4]Based on minimum-level wage of public employees. [5]Imports c.i.f.; exports f.o.b. [6]1995–96. [7]1993–94.

Mauritania

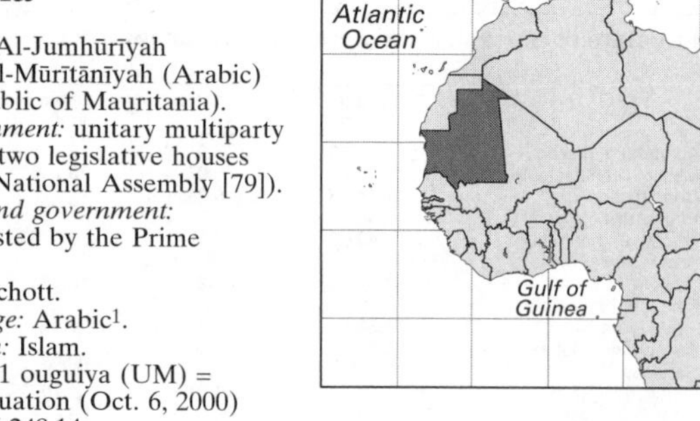

Official name: Al-Jumhūrīyah al-Islāmīyah al-Mūrītānīyah (Arabic) (Islamic Republic of Mauritania).
Form of government: unitary multiparty republic with two legislative houses (Senate [56]; National Assembly [79]).
Head of state and government: President assisted by the Prime Minister.
Capital: Nouakchott.
Official language: Arabic[1].
Official religion: Islam.
Monetary unit: 1 ouguiya (UM) = 5 khoums; valuation (Oct. 6, 2000) 1 U.S.$ = UM 248.14; 1 £ = UM 358.95.

Area and population

Regions	Capitals	area sq mi	area sq km	population 1996 estimate
El-'Açâba	Kiffa	14,100	36,600	200,640
Adrar	Atar	83,100	215,300	89,425
Brakna	Aleg	13,000	33,800	225,531
Dakhlet Nouadhibou	Nouadhibou	8,600	22,300	97,639
Gorgol	Kaédi	5,300	13,600	211,565
Guidimaka	Sélibaby	4,000	10,300	141,350
Hodh ech-Chargui	Néma	70,600	182,700	261,203
Hodh el-Gharbi	'Ayoûn el-'Atroûs	20,600	53,400	194,103
Inchiri	Akjoujt	18,100	46,800	13,718
Tagant	Tidjikdja	36,800	95,200	76,908
Tiris Zemmour	Zouérate	97,600	252,900	42,617
Trarza	Rosso	26,200	67,800	206,801
Capital District				
Nouakchott	Nouakchott	400	1,000	608,228
TOTAL		398,000[2]	1,030,700	2,369,728

Demography

Population (2000): 2,668,000.
Density (2000): persons per sq mi 6.7, persons per sq km 2.6.
Urban-rural (1999): urban 56.5%; rural 43.5%.
Sex distribution (1998): male 49.58%; female 50.42%.
Age breakdown (1995): under 15, 44.4%; 15–29, 26.7%; 30–44, 15.7%; 45–59, 8.1%; 60–74, 4.2%; 75 and over, 0.9%.
Population projection: (2010) 3,561,000; (2020) 4,671,000.
Doubling time: 24 years.
Ethnic composition (1993)[3]: Moor 70% (of which about 40% "black" Moor [Ḥarāṭīn, or African Sudanic] and about 30% "white" Moor [Bidan, or Arab-Berber]); other black African 30% (mostly Wolof, Tukulor, Soninke, and Fulani).
Religious affiliation (1994): Sunnī Muslim 99.5%; Roman Catholic 0.2%; other 0.3%.
Major cities (1992): Nouakchott 881,000[4]; Nouadhibou 72,305; Kaédi 35,241; Kiffa 29,292[5]; Rosso 27,783[5].

Vital statistics

Birth rate per 1,000 population (1999): 43.7 (world avg. 22.1).
Death rate per 1,000 population (1999): 14.3 (world avg. 8.9).
Natural increase rate per 1,000 population (1999): 29.4 (world avg. 13.2).
Total fertility rate (avg. births per childbearing woman; 1999): 6.4.
Life expectancy at birth (1999): male 48.3 years; female 52.4 years.

National economy

Budget (1997). Revenue: UM 44,800,000,000 (tax revenue 58.3%, of which taxes on goods and services 26.5%; import taxes 12.1%, income taxes 9.6%; nontax revenue 39.9%, of which fishing royalties and penalties 32.3%). Expenditures: UM 32,110,000,000 (wages and salaries 24.9%; interest on public debt 15.3%; defense 11.4%).
Land use (1994): forested 4.3%; meadows and pastures 38.3%; agricultural and under permanent cultivation 0.2%; desert 57.2%.
Production (metric tons except as noted). Agriculture, forestry, fishing (1999): rice 101,900, sorghum 74,800, dates 22,000, cow peas 22,000, pulses 12,000, millet 10,400; livestock (number of live animals) 6,200,000 sheep, 4,133,000 goats, 1,395,000 cattle, 1,185,000 camels; roundwood (1998) 15,000 cu m; fish catch (metric tons; 1997) 82,000, of which octopuses 23,500[6]. Mining and quarrying (gross weight; 1997): iron ore 11,700,000; gypsum 12,500. Manufacturing (1996): cow's milk 91,000[7]; goat's milk 77,000[7]; meat 58,200, of which fresh mutton and lamb 24,600, fresh beef and veal 10,200; hides and skins 4,600; cement, tiles, and bricks 5.9[8]; fabricated metal products 5.4[8]; paper and paper products 2.1[8]. Energy production (consumption): electricity (kW-hr; 1996) 153,000,000 (153,000,000); coal (metric tons; 1996) none (6,000); crude petroleum (barrels; 1996) none (6,927,000); petroleum products (metric tons; 1996) 840,000 (927,000); natural gas, none (none).
Population economically active (1994): total 687,000; activity rate of total population 31.3% (participation rates: over age 10 [1991] 45.5%; female 22.9%).

Price and earnings indexes (1995 = 100)

	1991	1992	1993	1994	1995	1996	1997
Consumer price index[9]	74.9	82.4	90.1	93.9	100.0	104.7	109.5
Monthly earnings index[10]	...	...	96.0	98.0	100.0	102.0	104.1

Household income and expenditure. Average household size (1996): 5.3; expenditure (1990): food and beverages 73.1%, clothing and footwear 8.1%, energy and water 7.7%, transportation and communications 2.0%.
Gross national product (1998): U.S.$1,033,000,000 (U.S.$410 per capita).

Structure of gross domestic product and labour force

	1997 in value UM '000,000	1997 % of total value	1988 labour force	1988 % of labour force
Agriculture, livestock	37,117	22.2	225,238	38.5
Mining	16,075	9.6	6,322	1.1
Manufacturing	16,447	9.9	5,630	1.0
Public utilities }	14,344	8.6	1,326	0.2
Construction }			12,291	2.1
Transp. and commun.	12,627	7.6	8,378	1.4
Trade and finance	25,511	15.3	73,451	12.5
Services	11,270	6.8 }	86,807	14.8
Pub. admin., defense	16,852	10.1 }		
Other	16,688[11]	10.0[11]	166,366[12]	28.4[12]
TOTAL	166,930[2]	100.0[2]	585,809	100.0

Public debt (external, outstanding; 1998): U.S.$2,214,000,000.
Tourism (1997): receipts U.S.$11,000,000; expenditures U.S.$24,000,000.

Foreign trade

Balance of trade (current prices)

	1993	1994	1995	1996	1997	1998
U.S.$'000,000	+2.6	+47.4	+183.8	+133.9	+1.6	+40.0
% of total	0.3%	6.3%	23.9%	16.2%	0.2%	5.9%

Imports (1997): U.S.$403,400,000 (imports for National Industrial and Mining Company 20.2%; petroleum products 13.6%; investment including food aid 10.0%; equipment and machinery 6.5%). *Major import sources:* France 25.5%; Spain 7.5%, Germany 6.7%, Belgium-Luxembourg 6.4%, Thailand 5.1%.
Exports (1997): U.S.$405,000,000 (iron ore 52.4%; fish 47.6%, of which cephalopods 28.3%). *Major export destinations:* Japan 23.3%; Italy 16.7%; France 13.9%; Spain 8.3%; Belgium-Luxembourg 7.1%.

Transport and communications

Transport. Railroads (1998): route length 437 mi, 704 km; passenger-km, negligible; (1997) metric ton-km cargo 2,340,000,000. Roads (1996): total length 4,760 mi, 7,660 km (paved 11%). Vehicles (1996): passenger cars 18,810; trucks and buses 10,450. Air transport (1998)[13]: passenger-km 258,263,000; metric ton-km cargo 13,524,000; airports (1997) with scheduled flights 9.

Communications

Medium	date	unit	number	units per 1,000 persons
Daily newspapers	1996	circulation	1,000	0.4
Radio	1997	receivers	360,000	147
Television	1997	receivers	62,000	25
Telephones	1998	main lines	14,746	5.9
Personal computers	1998	units	13,800	5.5
Internet	1998	users	1,000	0.4

Education and health

Educational attainment (1988). Percentage of population age 25 and over having: no formal schooling 60.8%; primary and incomplete secondary 34.1%; secondary 3.8%; higher 1.3%. *Literacy* (1995): percentage of total population age 15 and over literate 37.7%; males literate 49.6%; females literate 26.3%.

Education (1995–96)

	schools	teachers	students	student/teacher ratio
Primary (age 6–11)[14]	2,392	6,225	312,671	50.2
Secondary (age 12–17)	...	1,865	49,221	26.4
Voc., teacher tr.[15]	...	202	2,544	12.6
Higher	...	270	8,496	31.5

Health: physicians (1994) *c.* 200 (1 per 11,085 persons); hospital beds (1988) 1,556 (1 per 1,217 persons); infant mortality rate per 1,000 live births (1999) 79.6.
Food (1998): daily per capita caloric intake 2,640 (vegetable products 83%, animal products 17%); 114% of FAO recommended minimum requirement.

Military

Total active duty personnel (1999): 15,650 (army 95.8%, navy 3.2%, air force 1.0%). *Military expenditure as percentage of GNP* (1997): 2.3% (world 2.6%); per capita expenditure U.S.$10.

[1]The 1991 constitution names Arabic as the official language and the following as national languages: Arabic, Fulani, Soninke, and Wolof. [2]Detail does not add to total given because of rounding. [3]Estimated figures; 1988 census data for ethnicity/race not released by the government. [4]Urban agglomeration; 1999. [5]1988. [6]Fish catch (1996) including foreign fishing vessels equals 564,200 metric tons. [7]1994. [8]1993 value added of production in U.S.$'000,000. [9]Nouakchott only. [10]Civil servants only. [11]Indirect taxes. [12]Mostly unemployed. [13]Data represent 1/11 of the total scheduled traffic of Air Afrique. [14]1996–97. [15]Excludes health-related programs.

Internet resources for further information:
- **Mauritania Government Official Site http://www.mauritania.mr**

Mauritius

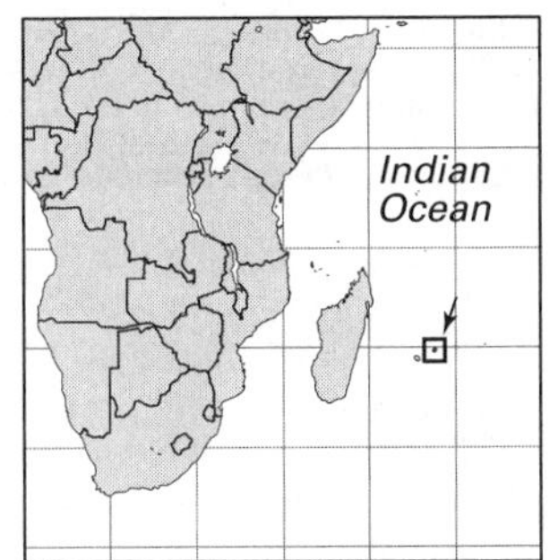

Official name: Republic of Mauritius.
Form of government: republic with one legislative house (National Assembly [70[1]]).
Chief of state: President.
Head of government: Prime Minister.
Capital: Port Louis.
Official language: English.
Official religion: none.
Monetary unit: 1 Mauritian rupee (Mau Re; plural Mau Rs) = 100 cents; valuation (Oct. 6, 2000) 1 U.S.$ = Mau Rs 26.60; 1 £ = Mau Rs 38.48.

Area and population

Islands Districts/Dependencies	Administrative Centres	area sq mi	area sq km	population 1998 estimate
Mauritius		720	1,865	1,124,500
Black River	Tamarin	100	259	52,600
Flacq	Centre de Flacq	115	298	122,900
Grand Port	Mahébourg	100	260	105,900
Moka	Moka	89	231	73,500
Pamplemousses	Pamplemousses	69	179	115,400
Plaines Wilhems	Rose Hill	78	203	354,300
Port Louis	Port Louis	17	43	137,500
Rivière du Rempart	Poudre d'Or	57	148	97,000
Savanne	Souillac	95	245	65,400
Mauritian dependencies				
Agalega[2]; Cargados Carajos Shoals (Saint Brandon)[2]	...	27	71	[3]
Rodrigues[4]	...	40	104	35,200
TOTAL		788[5]	2,040[5]	1,159,700

Demography

Population (2000): 1,184,000.
Density (2000): persons per sq mi 1,502.5, persons per sq km 580.4.
Urban-rural (1999): urban 41.1%; rural 58.9%.
Sex distribution (1999): male 49.98%; female 50.02%.
Age breakdown (1999): under 15, 25.9%; 15–29, 25.9%; 30–44, 24.9%; 45–59, 14.5%; 60–74, 6.9%; 75 and over, 1.9%.
Population projection: (2010) 1,281,000; (2020) 1,364,000.
Doubling time: 58 years.
Ethnic composition (1992): Indo-Pakistani 68.0%; Creole (mixed Caucasian, Indo-Pakistani, and African) 27.0%; Chinese 3.0%; white 2.0%.
Religious affiliation (1990): Hindu 50.6%; Roman Catholic 27.2%; Muslim 16.3%; Protestant 5.2%; Buddhist 0.3%; other 0.4%.
Major cities (1995): Port Louis 145,584; Beau Bassin-Rose Hill 98,014; Vacoas-Phoenix 95,600; Curepipe 77,765; Quatre Bornes 74,636.

Vital statistics

Birth rate per 1,000 population (1999): 16.9[6] (world avg. 22.1).
Death rate per 1,000 population (1999): 6.9[6] (world avg. 8.9).
Natural increase rate per 1,000 population (1999): 10.0[6] (world avg. 13.2).
Total fertility rate (avg. births per childbearing woman; 1999): 2.0[6].
Marriage rate per 1,000 population (1998): 9.4[6].
Divorce rate per 1,000 population (1997): 0.8[6].
Life expectancy at birth (1999): male 66.7 years; female 74.5 years.
Major causes of death per 100,000 population (1998): diseases of the circulatory system 331.0; malignant neoplasms (cancers) 65.0; diseases of the respiratory system 63.0; homicide, suicide, and accidents 44.0.

National economy

Budget (1997–98). Revenue: Mau Rs 18,501,000,000 (tax revenue 84.8%, of which import duties 33.3%, taxes on goods and services 32.5%, income tax 13.0%; nontax revenue 14.0%; grants 1.2%). Expenditures: Mau Rs 21,872,000,000 (social security 19.4%, government services 18.8%, education 16.0%, interest on debt 16.0%, economic services 11.4%, health 8.1%).
Tourism (1998): receipts from visitors U.S.$485,000,000; expenditures by nationals abroad U.S.$177,000,000.
Public debt (external, outstanding; 1998): U.S.$1,152,000,000.
Gross national product (1998): U.S.$4,329,000,000 (U.S.$3,730 per capita).

Structure of gross domestic product and labour force

	1998 in value Mau Rs '000,000	% of total value	labour force[7, 8]	% of labour force[7, 8]
Agriculture	7,150	7.5	30,400	10.4
Mining	135	0.1	200	0.1
Manufacturing	20,650	21.6	111,200	38.0
Construction	4,940	5.2	8,900	3.0
Public utilities	1,900	2.0	3,200	1.1
Transp. and commun.	9,315	9.7	15,100	5.1
Trade	14,795	15.4	27,800	9.5
Finance	13,585	14.2	13,700	4.7
Pub. admin., defense	8,900	9.3	61,800	21.1
Services	4,860	5.1	17,900	6.1
Other	9,520[9]	9.9[9]	2,600	0.9
TOTAL	95,750	100.0	292,800[8]	100.0[8]

Production (metric tons except as noted). Agriculture, forestry, fishing (1999): sugarcane 3,500,000, vegetables 23,000, potatoes 15,000, roots and tubers 11,750, tomatoes 11,000, bananas 9,400, onions 6,750, cabbages 6,300, pineapples 1,500, peanuts (groundnuts) 600; livestock (number of live animals) 93,000 goats, 27,000 cattle, 20,000 pigs, 7,200 sheep; roundwood (1998) 14,760 cu m; fish catch (1998) 13,734. Manufacturing (value added in Mau Rs '000; 1994): apparel 5,065,000; beverages and tobacco 1,995,800; food products 1,580,400; metal and metal products 882,900; textile yarn and fabrics 676,400; chemical products 505,600. Construction (1998): residential 1,204,000 sq m; nonresidential 276,000 sq m. Energy production (consumption): electricity (kW-hr; 1998) 1,364,800 (1,364,800); coal (metric tons; 1998) none (86,300); petroleum products (metric tons; 1998) none (576,000).
Population economically active (1998): total 507,000; activity rate of total population 43.8% (participation rates: ages 12 and over, 55.6%; female 37.1%; unemployed 5.7%).

Price and earnings indexes (1995 = 100)

	1992	1993	1994	1995	1996	1997	1998
Consumer price index	79.5	87.9	94.3	100.0	106.6	113.8	121.6
Earnings index	...	...	...	100.0	...	...	...

Household income and expenditure. Average household size (1998) 5.6; income per household (1997) Mau Rs 10,179 (U.S.$1,700); sources of income (1990): salaries and wages 48.4%, entrepreneurial income 41.2%, transfer payments 10.4%; expenditure: food, beverages, and tobacco 40.4%, transportation 14.8%, housing 13.3%, clothing and footwear 8.1%, recreation, entertainment, education, and cultural services 6.2%, utilities 4.6%, health 3.5%.
Land use (1994): forested 21.7%; meadows and pastures 3.4%; agricultural and under permanent cultivation 52.2%; other 22.7%.

Foreign trade

Balance of trade (current prices)

	1993	1994	1995	1996	1997	1998
Mau Rs '000,000	–7,327	–10,451	–7,607	–9,501	–6,381	–10,177
% of total	13.7%	17.8%	12.4%	13.1%	7.5%	11.4%

Imports (1998): Mau Rs 49,811,000,000 (manufactured goods classified chiefly by material 34.6%, machinery and transport equipment 22.8%, food 13.8%, chemicals 7.8%, mineral fuels and lubricants 6.3%, inedible crude materials excluding fuels 3.9%, animal and vegetable oils and fats 1.3%). *Major import sources:* France 11.1%; South Africa 10.5%; India 9.3%; Taiwan 5.2%; United Kingdom 5.2%; Japan 5.1%; Hong Kong 5.0%; Germany 4.1%; Italy 3.7%; Australia 3.4%; Malaysia 2.9%.
Exports (1998): Mau Rs 39,634,000,000 (clothing 55.9%, sugar 21.3%, yarn 3.7%, chemicals 0.5%, other 18.6%). *Major export destinations:* United Kingdom 32.3%; France 17.1%; United States 16.3%; Germany 5.3%; Italy 3.5%.

Transport and communications

Transport. Railroads: none. Roads (1998): total length 1,184 mi, 1,905 km (paved 93%). Vehicles (1998): passenger cars 46,300; trucks and buses 12,100. Air transport (1998)[10]: passenger-km 3,858,695; metric ton-km cargo 819,432,000; airports (1998) with scheduled flights 1.

Communications

Medium	date	unit	number	units per 1,000 persons
Daily newspapers	1996	circulation	85,000	76
Radio	1997	receivers	420,000	371
Television	1997	receivers	218,700	189
Telephones	1998	main lines	245,367	214
Cellular telephones	1998	subscribers	60,462	53
Personal computers	1998	units	90,000	78
Internet	1998	users	12,500	11

Education and health

Educational attainment (1990). Percentage of population age 25 and over having: no formal education 18.3%; incomplete primary 42.6%; primary 6.1%; incomplete secondary 18.0%; secondary 13.1%; higher 1.9%. *Literacy* (1995): percentage of total population age 15 and over literate 82.9%; males literate 87.1%; females literate 78.8%.

Education (1998)

	schools	teachers	students	student/ teacher ratio
Primary (age 5–12)	285	5,065	130,505	25.7
Secondary (age 12–20)	133	4,820	94,364	19.6
Voc., teacher tr.	13	1,170[11]	5,496	...
Higher	3	461	6,429	13.9

Health (1998): physicians 1,033 (1 per 1,123 persons); hospital beds 3,826 (1 per 303 persons); infant mortality rate per 1,000 live births (1999) 18.4[6].
Food (1998): daily per capita caloric intake 2,944 (vegetable products 87%, animal products 13%); 130% of FAO recommended minimum requirement.

Military

Total active duty personnel: none; however, a special 1,300-person paramilitary force ensures internal security. *Military expenditure as percentage of GNP* (1997): 0.3% (world 2.6%); per capita expenditure U.S.$10.

[1]Includes 8 "bonus" seats allocated to minor parties. [2]Administered directly from Port Louis. [3]Included in total population. [4]Administered by resident commissioner assisted by local council. [5]Detail does not add to total given because of rounding. [6]Excludes Agalega and Cargados Carajos Shoals. [7]Employed persons in large establishments only. [8]Total labour force equals 507,000 and includes 223,000 employees of small businesses or self-employed and 29,000 unemployed. [9]Indirect taxes less imputed bank service charges. [10]Air Mauritius only. [11]1997.

Internet resources for further information:
- **Central Statistical Office http://ncb.intnet.mu/cso.htm**

Mayotte

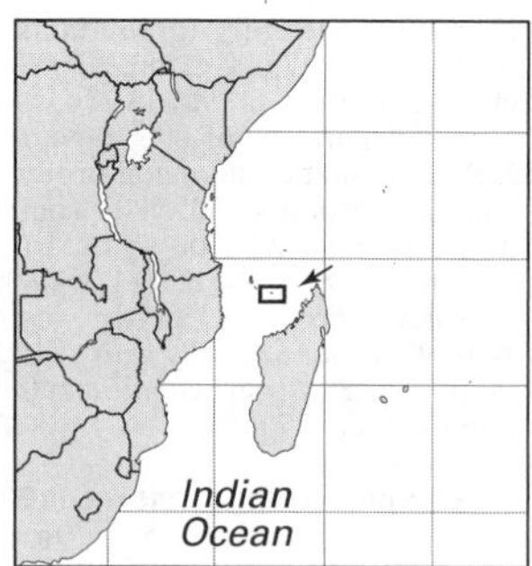

Official name: Collectivité Departementale de Mayotte (Departmental Collectivity of Mayotte)[1].
Political status: overseas dependency of France[2] with one legislative house (General Council [19]).
Chief of state: President of France.
Head of government: Prefect (for France); President of the General Council (for Mayotte).
Capitals: Dzaoudzi (French administrative); Mamoudzou (local administrative)[3].
Official language: French.
Official religion: none.
Monetary unit: 1 French (metropolitan) franc (F) = 100 centimes; valuation (Oct. 6, 2000) 1 U.S.$ = F 7.54; 1 £ = F 10.91.

Area and population

Islands / Communes	Capitals	area sq mi	area sq km	population 1997 census
Grande Terre				
Acoua	Acoua	4.9	12.6	4,446
Bandraboua	Bandraboua	12.5	32.4	6,406
Bandrele	Bandrele	14.1	36.5	4,958
Boueni	Boueni	5.4	14.1	4,673
Chiconi	Chiconi	3.2	8.3	6,042
Chirongui	Chirongui	10.9	28.3	5,144
Dembeni	Dembeni	15.0	38.8	5,554
Kani-Keli	Kani-Keli	7.9	20.5	4,155
Koungou	Koungou	11.0	28.4	10,165
Mamoudzou	Mamoudzou	16.2	41.9	32,733
M'tsangamouji	M'tsangamouji	8.4	21.8	5,098
M'tzamboro	M'tzamboro	5.3	13.7	6,335
Ouangani	Ouangani	7.3	19.0	4,838
Sada	Sada	4.3	11.2	7,434
Tsingoni	Tsingoni	13.4	34.8	5,507
Petite Terre				
Dzaoudzi-Labattoir	Dzaoudzi	2.6	6.7	10,792
Pamandzi	Pamandzi	1.7	4.3	7,040
TOTAL		144.1	373.2[4]	131,320

Demography

Population (2000): 156,000.
Density (2000): persons per sq mi 1,075.9, persons per sq km 416.0.
Urban-rural (1985): urban 59.7%; rural 40.3%.
Sex distribution (1997): male 50.68%; female 49.32%.
Age breakdown (1997): under 15, 44.3%; 15–29, 29.9%; 30–44, 15.6%; 45–59, 6.6%; 60–74, 2.7%; 75 and over, 0.9%.
Population projection: (2010) 231,000; (2020) 312,000.
Doubling time: 19 years.
Place of birth (1997): Mayotte 73.6%[5]; nearby islands of the Comoros 19.9%[5]; metropolitan France 2.8%; other 3.7%.
Religious affiliation (1997): Sunnī Muslim 96.8%; Christian, principally Roman Catholic, 3.1%; other 0.1%.
Major towns (1997[6]): Mamoudzou 32,733; Dzaoudzi 10,792; Koungou 10,165.

Vital statistics

Birth rate per 1,000 population (1999): 46.1 (world avg. 22.1).
Death rate per 1,000 population (1999): 9.4 (world avg. 8.9).
Natural increase rate per 1,000 population (1999): 36.7 (world avg. 13.2).
Total fertility rate (avg. births per childbearing woman; 1999): 6.4.
Marriage rate per 1,000 population: n.a.; *marital status of adult population* (1997): monogamous marriage 48.5%, polygamous marriage 6.9%, other 44.6%.
Divorce rate per 1,000 population: 16.2.
Life expectancy at birth (1999): male 57.0; female 61.1.
Morbidity (number of reported cases of infectious diseases; 1985): malaria 73; syphilis 63; gonorrhea 61; tuberculosis 14; typhoid 14; leprosy 12.

National economy

Budget (1993). Revenue: F 551,700,000 (current revenue 68.8%, of which subsidies 40.0%, indirect taxes 16.8%, direct taxes 4.9%; development revenue 31.2%, of which loans 11.6%, subsidies 7.9%). Expenditures: F 551,700,000 (current expenditure 68.8%, development expenditure 31.2%).
Public debt: n.a.
Production (metric tons except as noted). Agriculture, forestry, fishing (1997): bananas 30,200, cassava 10,000, cinnamon 27,533 kg, ylang-ylang 14,300 kg, vanilla 4,417 kg; livestock (number of live animals; 1997) 25,000 goats, 17,000 cattle, 2,000 sheep; roundwood, n.a.; fish catch (1998) 1,570. Mining and quarrying: negligible. Manufacturing: mostly processing of agricultural products and materials used in housing construction (including siding and roofing materials, joinery, and latticework). Construction (public works authorized in F '000; 1999): residential 128,991; nonresidential 119,294. Energy production (consumption): electricity (kW-hr; 1999) 68,387,000 (68,387,000); coal, none (none); crude petroleum, none (none); petroleum products, none (n.a.); natural gas, none (none).
Household income and expenditure. Average household size (1997) 4.6; income per household: n.a.; sources of income: n.a.; expenditure (1991)[7]: food 42.2%, clothing and footwear 31.5%, household furnishings 8.8%, energy and water 6.8%, transportation 5.1%.
Gross national product (1998): U.S.$486,409,000 (U.S.$3,704 per capita).

Structure of gross domestic product and labour force

	1997 in value U.S.$'000	% of total value	labour force	% of labour force
Agriculture, forestry, and fishing	...	...	4,824	11.2
Mining	...	...	80	0.2
Manufacturing	...	...	1,083	2.5
Construction	...	...	3,840	9.0
Public utilities	...	...	399	0.9
Transp. and commun.	...	...	1,563	3.6
Trade	...	...	3,057	7.1
Finance, insurance, real estate	...	...	647	1.5
Pub. admin., defense	...	...	4,526	10.6
Services	...	...	5,074	11.8
Other	...	...	17,803[8]	41.5[8]
TOTAL	154,900	100.0	42,896	100.0[4]

Population economically active (1997): total 42,896; activity rate of total population 32.7% (participation rates: ages 15–64, 58.6%; female 43.4%; unemployed 41.5%).

Price and earnings indexes (1995 = 100)

	1995	1996	1997	1998	1999
Consumer price index	100.0	105.3	108.9	111.1	112.2
Monthly earnings index[9]	100.0	106.3	109.5	112.2	113.4

Land use (1987): meadows 35.0%; agricultural 29.0%; other 36.0%.
Tourism (number of visitors; 1997): 9,500.

Foreign trade

Balance of trade (current prices)

	1994	1995	1996	1997	1998	1999
F '000,000	...	...	–520.8	–620.4	–660.0	–615.7
% of total	...	...	92.9%	96.0%	95.7%	96.0%

Imports (1999): F 628,266,000 (1997; food products 23.8%; machinery 20.4%; transport equipment 10.4%; metals and metal products 10.3%; chemical products 7.7%). *Major import sources* (1997): France 66.0%; South Africa 14.0%; Asia 11.0%.
Exports (1999): F 12,540,000 (1997; domestic exports 37.2%, of which ylang-ylang 27.9%, vanilla 3.5%; reexports 62.8%). *Major export destinations* (1997): France 80.0%; Comoros 15.0%.

Transport and communications

Transport. Railroads: none. Roads (1997): total length 145 mi, 233 km (paved 77%). Vehicles (1997): 6,553. Merchant marine: n.a. Air transport (1997): passenger arrivals and departures 75,077; cargo unloaded and loaded 1,119 metric tons; airports (1998) with scheduled flights 1.

Communications

Medium	date	unit	number	units per 1,000 persons
Daily newspapers[10]	1998	circulation	...	...
Radio	1996	receivers	50,000	427
Television	1996	receivers	3,500	31
Telephones	1998	main lines	12,200	95
Cellular telephones	1998	subscribers	...	...
Personal computers	1998	units	...	...

Education and health

Educational attainment (1991). Percentage of population age 25 and over having: no formal education 72.8%; primary 14.2%; lower secondary 7.5%; higher secondary 3.2%; higher 2.3%. *Literacy* (1997): total population age 15 and over literate 63,053 (86.1%).

Education (1992–93)

	schools	teachers	students	student/teacher ratio
Primary (age 6–11)	88[11]	555	25,805[12]	38.9
Secondary (age 12–18)	8[12]	246	6,190[12]	16.2
Voc., teacher tr.	2[11]	17[11]	839	23.1[11]
Higher	—	—	—	—

Health: physicians (1997) 57 (1 per 2,304 persons); hospital beds 186 (1 per 706 persons); infant mortality rate per 1,000 live births (1999) 73.2.
Food: daily per capita caloric intake, n.a.

Military

Total active duty personnel (1999): 2,850 French troops are assigned to Mayotte and Réunion.

[1]The extraconstitutional status of departmental collectivity (between an overseas department and an overseas territory) was approved by the residents of Mayotte in mid-2000. [2]Final status of Mayotte has not yet been determined; it is claimed by Comoros as an integral part of that country. [3]Representatives of the French government in Mayotte continue to occupy offices in the original capital of Dzaoudzi. Local administrative (General Council) offices are in Mamoudzou. [4]Detail does not add to total given because of rounding. [5]Nearly all ethnic Comorian (a mixture of Bantu, Arab, and Malagasy peoples). [6]Population of communes. [7]Weights of consumer price index components. [8]Unemployed. [9]Based on minimum-level wage of public employees. [10]One weekly newspaper has a total circulation of 15,000. [11]1989–90. [12]1997.

Mexico

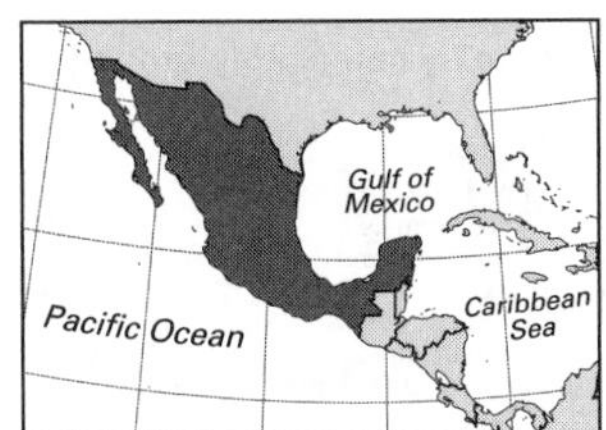

Official name: Estados Unidos Mexicanos (United Mexican States).
Form of government: federal republic with two legislative houses (Senate [128]; Chamber of Deputies [500]).
Head of state and government: President.
Capital: Mexico City.
Official language: Spanish.
Official religion: none.
Monetary unit: 1 Mexican peso[1] (Mex$) = 100 centavos; valuation (Oct. 6, 2000) 1 U.S.$ = Mex$9.46; 1 £ = Mex$13.68.

Area and population

		area		population
States	Capitals	sq mi	sq km	2000 census[2]
Aguascalientes	Aguascalientes	2,112	5,471	943,506
Baja California Norte	Mexicali	26,997	69,921	2,487,700
Baja California Sur	La Paz	28,369	73,475	423,516
Campeche	Campeche	19,619	50,812	689,656
Chiapas	Tuxtla Gutiérrez	28,653	74,211	3,920,515
Chihuahua	Chihuahua	94,571	244,938	3,047,867
Coahuila	Saltillo	57,908	149,982	2,295,808
Colima	Colima	2,004	5,191	540,679
Durango	Durango	47,560	123,181	1,445,922
Guanajuato	Guanajuato	11,773	30,491	4,656,761
Guerrero	Chilpancingo	24,819	64,281	3,075,083
Hidalgo	Pachuca	8,036	20,813	2,231,392
Jalisco	Guadalajara	31,211	80,836	6,321,278
México	Toluca	8,245	21,355	13,083,359
Michoacán	Morelia	23,138	59,928	3,979,177
Morelos	Cuernavaca	1,911	4,950	1,552,878
Nayarit	Tepic	10,417	26,979	919,739
Nuevo León	Monterrey	25,067	64,924	3,826,240
Oaxaca	Oaxaca	36,275	93,952	3,432,180
Puebla	Puebla	13,090	33,902	5,070,346
Querétaro	Querétaro	4,420	11,449	1,402,010
Quintana Roo	Chetumal	19,387	50,212	873,804
San Luis Potosi	San Luis Potosi	24,351	63,068	2,296,363
Sinaloa	Culiacán	22,521	58,328	2,534,835
Sonora	Hermosillo	70,291	182,052	2,213,370
Tabasco	Villahermosa	9,756	25,267	1,889,367
Tamaulipas	Ciudad victoria	30,650	79,384	2,747,114
Tlaxcala	Tlaxcala	1,551	4,016	961,912
Veracruz	Xalapa (Jalapa)	27,683	71,699	6,901,111
Yucatán	Mérida	14,827	38,402	1,655,707
Zacatecas	Zacatecas	28,283	73,252	1,351,207
Federal District				
Distrito Federal	—	571	1,479	8,591,309
TOTAL		756,066	1,958,201	97,361,711

Demography

Population (2000): 98,881,000[3].
Density (2000): persons per sq mi 130.8, persons per sq km 50.5.
Urban-rural (1990): urban 71.3%; rural 28.7%.
Sex distribution (1997): male 48.75%; female 51.25%.
Age breakdown (1997): under 15, 34.9%; 15–29, 28.8%; 30–44, 18.6%; 45–59, 10.3%; 60 and over, 7.4%.
Population projection: (2010) 112,891,000[3]; (2020) 124,976,000[3].
Doubling time: 30 years.
Ethnic composition (1990): mestizo 60.0%; Amerindian 30.0%; Caucasian 9.0%; other 1.0%.
Religious affiliation (1995): Roman Catholic 90.4%; Protestant (including Evangelical) 3.8%; other 5.8%.
Major cities (1990): Mexico City 9,815,795; Guadalajara 1,650,042; Ciudad Netzahualcóyotl 1,255,456; Monterrey 1,068,996; Puebla 1,007,170; Juarez 789,522; León 758,279; Tijuana 698,752; Mérida 523,422; Chihuahua 516,153.
Place of birth (1990): 93.1% native-born; 6.9% foreign-born and unknown.
Mobility (1990). Population 5 years and older living in the same state as in 1985: 94.3%; different state 4.9%; unspecified 0.8%.
Households. Total households (1995) 19,403,409; distribution by size (1995): 1 person 5.7%, 2 persons 10.9%, 3 persons 15.8%, 4 persons 20.1%, 5 persons 17.7%, 6 persons 11.6%, 7 or more persons 18.2%. Family households (1990): 17,064,507 (98.4%); nonfamily 1,039,738 (1.3%); unspecified 256,554 (0.3%).
Immigration (1987): permanent immigrants admitted 72,649.
Emigration (1996): legal immigrants into the United States 163,600.

Vital statistics

Birth rate per 1,000 population (1998): 27.8 (world avg. 22.1); (1983) legitimate 72.5%; illegitimate 27.5%.
Death rate per 1,000 population (1998): 4.6 (world avg. 8.9).
Natural increase rate per 1,000 population (1998): 23.2 (world avg. 13.2).
Total fertility rate (avg. births per childbearing woman; 1998): 2.8.
Marriage rate per 1,000 population (1994): 7.2.
Divorce rate per 1,000 population (1995): 0.4.
Life expectancy at birth (1998): male 68.6 years; female 74.8 years.
Major causes of death per 100,000 population (1998): diseases of the circulatory system 104.1; malignant neoplasms (cancers) 57.6; diseases of the digestive system 43.5; diseases of the respiratory system 43.3; conditions originating in the perinatal period 20.7.

Social indicators

Access to services (1995). Proportion of dwellings having: electricity 93.2%; piped water supply 85.6%; drained sewage 74.7%.
Educational attainment (1992). Population age 15 and over having: no primary education 14.1%; some primary 22.3%; completed primary 20.7%; incomplete secondary 10.4%; complete secondary 24.2%; higher 8.3%.

Distribution of income (1994)

percentage of household income by quintile

1	2	3	4	5 (highest)
4.8	8.6	12.8	19.5	54.3

Quality of working life. Average workweek (1997): 44.8 hours[4]. Annual rate (1992) per 100,000 insured workers for: temporary disability 6,426; indemnification for permanent injury 239; death 18. Labour stoppages (1997): 39, involving 9,375 workers. Average duration of journey to work: n.a. Method of transport: n.a. Rate per 1,000 workers of discouraged (unemployed no longer seeking work): n.a.
Social participation. Eligible voters participating in last national election (1991): *c.* 60%. Population participating in voluntary work: n.a. Trade union membership in total workforce: n.a. Practicing religious population in total affiliated population: national average of weekly attendance (1993) 11%; (1970) weekly attendance 10% of urban dwellers, 25% of rural dwellers; yearly attendance 55% of urban dwellers, 73% of rural dwellers.
Social deviance (1991). Criminal cases tried by local authorities per 100,000 population for: murder 60.3; rape 22.4; other assault 301.0; theft 703.8. Incidence per 100,000 in general population of: alcoholism, n.a.; drug and substance abuse, n.a.[5]; suicide (1994) 2.47.
Leisure (1985). Favourite leisure activities (average daily paid attendance): cinema 582,416; sporting events 31,518; live theatre 16,400; museums and archaeological sites 12,169; bullfights 3,049.
Material well-being (1985). Households possessing: radio 96%; television 73%; washing machine 33%; automobile 29%; telephone 27%; refrigerator 23%.

National economy

Gross national product (1998): U.S.$368,059,000,000 (U.S.$3,840 per capita).

Structure of gross domestic product and labour force

	1997			
	in value Mex$'000,000[1]	% of total value	labour force[6]	% of labour force[6]
Agriculture	169,234.4	5.3	9,020,000	23.5
Mining	38,077.1	1.2	107,000	0.3
Manufacturing	633,552.4	19.9	6,294,000	16.4
Construction	123,239.8	3.9	1,764,000	4.6
Public utilities	33,280.2	1.0	189,000	0.5
Transp. and commun.	318,155.7	10.0	1,524,000	4.0
Trade	644,262.7	20.2	7,881,000	20.5
Finance	435,471.0	13.7	1,483,000	3.9
Pub. admin., defense } Services }	602,677.8	18.9	8,883,000	23.2
Other	189,490.2[7]	5.9[7]	1,201,000[8]	3.1[8]
TOTAL	3,187,441.3	100.0	38,345,000[9]	100.0

Budget (1996). Revenue: Mex$384,466,000,000[1] (income tax 26.6%, sales tax 18.8%). Expenditures: Mex$387,810,000,000[1] (education 24.5%, social security and welfare 19.3%, interest on public debt 18.6%).
Public debt (external, outstanding; 1998); U.S.$87,996,000,000.
Tourism (1998): receipts from visitors U.S.$7,897,000,000; expenditures by nationals abroad U.S.$4,268,000,000.

Manufacturing, mining, and construction enterprises (1993)

	no. of enterprises	no. of employees ('000)	yearly wages as a % of avg. of all wages[10]	value added (Mex$'000,000[1, 10])
Manufacturing	266,033	3,174.4	97.5	20,950,900
Metal products	46,667[11]	955.6[11]	114.2[11]	6,605,300[11]
Chemicals	7,321	371.2	152.3	4,228,000
Food, beverages, and tobacco	91,894	679.3	86.4	3,378,700
Textiles and apparel	44,071	530.6	80.0	2,414,800
Iron and steel	401	57.4	128.2	1,332,400
Nonmetallic mineral products	24,397	181.8	98.6	1,177,700
Paper and printing	15,022	193.2	100.0	1,127,900
Wood and wood products	31,549	162.6	62.8	497,000
Nonelectrical machinery and transport equipment	[11]	[11]	...[11]	[11]
Electrical machinery	[11]	[11]	...[11]	[11]
Other manufactures	4,711	42.7	...	189,200
Mining	2,845	95.6	161.0	1,643,800
Construction	5,308[10]	342.4[10]	62.1	1,414,800

Production (metric tons except as noted). Agriculture, forestry, fishing (1998): sugarcane 48,895,000, corn (maize) 18,476,000, sorghum 6,455,000, oranges 3,329,000, wheat 3,232,000, tomatoes 2,283,000, bananas 1,557,000, mangoes 1,504,000, dry beans 1,244,000, lemons and limes 1,211,000, avocados 813,000, cottonseed 659,000, watermelons 500,000, papayas 498,000, barley 496,000, rice 483,000, grapes 414,000, pineapples 350,000, coffee (green) 306,000, cauliflower 210,000, carrots 207,000; livestock (number of live animals) 30,500,000 cattle, 14,994,000 pigs, 9,381,000 goats, 8,000,000 ducks, 6,250,000 horses, 5,990,000 sheep, 3,300,000 turkeys, 3,270,000 mules, 3,250,000 asses, 408,800,000 chickens; roundwood 21,996,000 cu m; fish catch 1,233,292. Mining and quarrying (1997): salt 8,508,000, iron 6,128,000, gypsum 4,236,000, silica 1,549,000, sulfur 917,361, dolomite 908,773, phosphate 707,239, fluorite 492,960, zinc 383,388, copper 343,262, barite 240,033, manganese 192,311, lead 178,690, silver 2,536,397 kg, gold 26,062 kg. Manufacturing (gross value of production in Mex$'000[1]; 1994): machinery and equipment 82,169,495; food, beverages, and tobacco products 64,399,498; chemical products 50,455,651;

metal products 25,363,292; mineral products 17,074,973; paper and paper products 9,209,617; textiles 8,555,146. Construction (gross value of new construction, in Mex$'000,000[1]; 1985): residential 154,835; nonresidential 168,096.

Trade and service enterprises (1993)

	no. of establish-ments	no. of employees	yearly wage as a % of avg. of all wages[12]	annual income (Mex$'000,000[1])
Trade	1,208,779	2,969,786	...	565,728,373
Wholesale	68,919	631,802	...	249,597,035
Retail	1,139,860	2,337,984	...	316,131,338
Boutiques (excluding food products)	422,299	922,890	...	108,507,889
Food and tobacco speciality stores	671,050	991,911	...	65,305,180
Automobile, tire, and auto parts dealers	32,138	152,821	...	47,888,576
Small supermarkets and grocery stores	8,719	168,752	...	48,769,283
Gasoline stations	3,042	35,340	...	32,517,091
Other	2,612	66,270	...	13,143,319
Services	711,843	2,766,750	85.2	200,001,682
Professional services	130,475	652,148	77.9	53,533,318
Food and beverage services	677	11,258	...	1,012,369
Transp. and travel agencies	9,967	62,767	133.4	11,858,406
Lodging	9,913	151,445	...	8,960,922
Automotive repair	112,293	252,950	...	7,263,560
Educational services (private)	20,622	247,086	134.3	10,815,238
Medical and social assistance	79,748	203,348	206.4	7,497,794
Amusement services (cinemas and theatres)	4,855	65,608	148.9	9,845,129
Recreation	20,973	65,936	...	3,065,672
Other repair	72,129	104,478	...	2,625,370
Commercial and professional organizations	1,946	11,946	77.9	264,770
Other	248,245	937,780	49.9	83,259,134

Energy production (consumption): electricity (kW-hr; 1996) 162,526,000,000 (162,625,000,000); coal (metric tons; 1996) 10,372,000 (11,725,000); crude petroleum (barrels; 1996) 1,034,000,000 (487,000,000); petroleum products (metric tons; 1996) 77,790,000 (85,279,000); natural gas (cu m; 1996) 28,464,000,000 (30,850,000,000).

Population economically active (1997): total 38,344,650; activity rate of total population 40.7% (participation rates: ages 15–64, 63.1%; female 34.5%; unemployed 2.7%[6]).

Price and earnings indexes (1995 = 100)

	1993	1994	1995	1996	1997	1998	1999
Consumer price Index	69.3	74.1	100.0	134.4	162.1	187.9	219.1
Monthly earnings index	85.7	90.9	100.0	...	156.6	...	...

Household income and expenditure. Average household size (1995) 4.7; income per household (1989) Mex$3,461[1] (U.S.$1,384); sources of income (1992): wages and salaries 61.5%, property and entrepreneurship 29.1%, transfer payments 7.8%, other 1.6%; expenditure (1992): food, beverages, and tobacco 36.9%, housing (includes household furnishings) 25.2%, transportation and communications 10.1%, clothing and footwear 8.5%, recreation and entertainment 5.5%, health and medical services 3.5%.

Financial aggregates[1, 13]

	1993	1994	1995	1996	1997	1998	1999 (7 mos.)
Exchange rate, Mex$ per:							
U.S. dollar	3.116	3.375	6.419	7.599	7.919	9.136	9.367
£	4.680	5.164	10.132	11.867	12.969	15.133	14.742
SDR	4.266	7.774	11.361	11.289	10.906	13.890	12.800
International reserves (U.S.$)							
Total (excl. gold; '000,000)	25,110	6,278	16,847	19,433	28,797	31,799	32,060
SDRs ('000,000)	223	177	1,597	257	661	337	857
Reserve pos. in IMF ('000,000)	—	—	—	—	—	—	—
Foreign exchange	24,886	6,101	15,250	19,176	28,136	31,461	31,203
Gold ('000,000 fine troy oz)	0.48	0.43	0.51	0.26	0.19	0.22	0.21
% world reserves	0.05	0.05	0.06	0.03	0.02	0.03	0.02
Interest and prices							
Treasury bill rate	15.03	14.10	48.44	31.39	19.80	24.76	20.54
Balance of payments (U.S.$'000,000)							
Balance of visible trade,	−13,481	−18,464	+7,089	+6,531	+623	−7,743	...
of which:							
Imports, f.o.b.	−65,366	−79,347	−72,454	−89,469	−109,808	−125,243	...
Exports, f.o.b.	51,885	60,882	79,543	96,000	110,431	117,500	...
Balance of invisibles	−9,919	−11,198	−8,665	−8,454	−8,077	−8,044	...
Balance of payments, current account	−23,400	−29,662	−1,576	−1,923	−7,454	−15,787	...

Land use (1994): forest 25.5%; pasture 39.0%; agriculture 13.0%; other 22.5%.

Foreign trade

Balance of trade (current prices)

	1994	1995	1996	1997	1998	1999
U.S.$'000,000	−13,481	−18,464	+6,531	+623	−7,742	−5,361
% of total	11.5%	13.2%	3.5%	0.3%	3.2%	1.9%

Imports (1998): U.S.$125,373,100,000 (intermediate goods 77.3%; capital goods 13.8%; consumer goods 8.9%). *Major import sources:* U.S. 74.8%; Japan 3.9%; Germany 3.6%; Canada 1.8%; Italy 1.2%; China 1.1%.

Exports (1998): U.S.$117,459,600,000 (manufacturing goods 90.7%; crude petroleum 6.1%; agricultural goods 3.7%). *Major export destinations:* U.S. 85.6%; Canada 2.0%; Japan 1.0%; Spain 0.9%; Germany 0.7%; U.K. 0.6%.

Trade by commodity group (1995)

	imports		exports	
SITC group	U.S.$'000,000	%	U.S.$'000,000	%
00 Food and live animals	3,225	4.4	5,434	6.8
01 Beverages and tobacco	144	0.2	585	0.7
02 Crude materials, excluding fuels	3,213	4.4	2,007	2.5
03 Mineral fuels, lubricants, and related materials	1,585	2.1	8,186	10.3
04 Animal and vegetable oils, fats, and waxes	581	0.8	—	—
05 Chemicals and related products, n.e.s.	6,899	9.3	3,876	4.9
06 Basic manufactures	12,377	16.7	8,982	11.3
07 Machinery and transport equipment	31,693	42.8	41,634	52.4
08 Miscellaneous manufactured articles	9,318	12.6	8,507	10.7
09 Goods not classified by kind	4,958	6.7	218	0.3
TOTAL[14]	73,993	100.0	79,489[9]	100.0[9]

Direction of trade (1997)

	imports		exports	
	U.S.$'000,000	%	U.S.$'000,000	%
Western Hemisphere	86,770	79.0	103,280	93.5
United States	82,182	74.8	94,531	85.6
Latin America and the Caribbean	2,620	2.4	6,592	6.0
Canada	1,968	1.8	2,157	1.9
Europe	10,940	10.0	4,486	4.1
EU	9,901	9.0	4,020	3.6
EFTA	615	0.6	358	0.3
Russia	—	—	—	—
Other Europe	424	0.4	108	0.2
Asia	11,148	10.2	2,228	2.0
Japan	4,334	3.9	1,156	1.0
Africa	264	0.2	107	0.1
Other	686	0.6	330	0.3
TOTAL	109,808	100.0	110,431	100.0

Transport and communications

Transport. Railroads (1995): route length (1997) 16,543 mi, 26,623 km; passenger-mi 1,118,000,000, passenger-km 1,800,000,000; short ton-mi cargo 28,578,000,000, metric ton-km cargo 41,723,000,000. Roads (1997): total length 199,824 mi, 321,586 km (paved 37%[15]). Vehicles (1996): passenger cars 8,607,000; trucks and buses 4,426,000. Merchant marine (1992): vessels (100 gross tons and over) 635; total deadweight tonnage 1,495,311. Air transport (1996): passenger-mi 14,864,396,000, passenger-km 23,921,973,000; short ton-mi cargo 1,778,544,000, metric ton-km cargo 2,596,631; airports (1997) 83.

Communications

Medium	date	unit	number	units per 1,000 persons
Daily newspapers	1996	circulation	9,030,000	97
Radio	1997	receivers	31,000,000	329
Television	1998	receivers	25,000,000	261
Telephones	1998	main lines	9,927,000	103
Cellular telephones	1998	subscribers	3,349,000	35
Personal computers	1998	units	4,500,000	47
Internet	1998	users	1,350,000	14

Education and health

Literacy (1995): total population age 15 and over literate 89.6%; males literate 91.8%; females literate 87.4%.

Education (1996–97)

	schools	teachers	students	student/ teacher ratio
Primary (age 6–12)	95,855	524,927	14,651,000	27.9
Secondary (age 12–18)	24,402	275,331	4,809,000	17.5
Voc., teacher tr.	6,610	63,674	883,000	13.9
Higher	9,562	316,404	3,834,000	12.1

Health: physicians (1994) 146,021 (1 per 613 persons); hospital beds 107,288 (1 per 864 persons); infant mortality rate per 1,000 live births (1998) 25.8.

Food (1997): daily per capita caloric intake 3,097 (vegetable products 83%, animal products 17%); 133% of FAO recommended minimum requirement.

Military

Total active duty personnel (1999): 178,770 (army 72.7%, navy 20.7%, air force 6.6%). *Military expenditure as percentage of GNP* (1997): 1.1% (world 2.6%); per capita expenditure U.S.$44.

[1]The Mexican new peso, equivalent to 1,000 old Mexican pesos, was introduced on Jan. 1, 1993. On Jan. 1, 1996, the name of the currency was changed to Mexican peso. [2]Preliminary. [3]Population estimate not based on 2000 preliminary census results. [4]Manufacturing only. [5]Through 1982, cannabis remained the most abused drug. [6]2nd quarter. [7]Imputed bank service charge. [8]Includes 1,054,000 unemployed persons. [9]Detail does not add to total given because of rounding. [10]1988. [11]Metal products includes Nonelectrical machinery and transport equipment and Electrical machinery. [12]1984. [13]Exchange rates and treasury bill rates are expressed in period averages; international reserves are expressed in end-of-period rates. [14]Totals include adjustments of unspecified nature. [15]1996.

Internet resources for further information:

- **National Institute of Statistics, Geography, and Informatics http://www.inegi.gob.mx/difusion/ingles/portadai.html**

Micronesia

Official name: Federated States of Micronesia.
Political status: federal republic in free association with the United States with one legislative house (Congress [14])[1].
Head of state and government: President.
Capital: Palikir, on Pohnpei.
Official language: none.
Official religion: none.
Monetary unit: 1 U.S. dollar (U.S.$) = 100 cents; valuation (Oct. 6, 2000) 1 £ = U.S.$1.45.

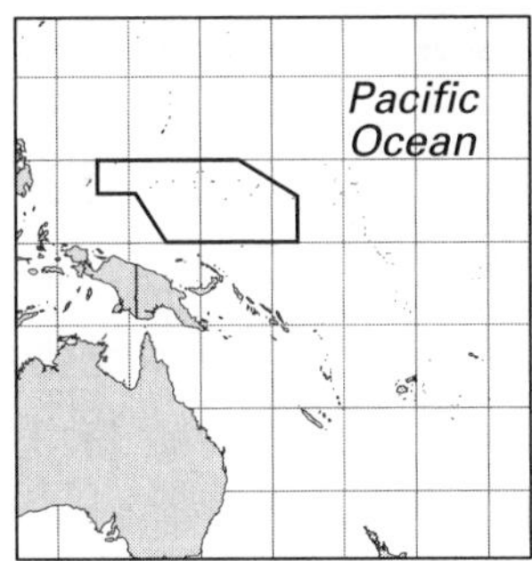

Area and population

States / Major Islands	area sq mi	area sq km	population 1994 census
Chuuk(Truk)	49.1	127.2	53,319
Weno (Moen) Islands	7.0	18.1	16,121
Kosrae	42.3	109.6	7,317
Kosrae Island	42.3	109.6	7,317
Pohnpei	133.3	345.2	33,692
Pohnpei Island	129.0	334.1	31,540
Yap	45.9	118.9	11,178
Yap Island	38.7	100.2	6,919
TOTAL	270.8[2]	701.4[2]	105,506

Demography

Population (2000): 118,000.
Density (2000): persons per sq mi 435.7, persons per sq km 168.2.
Urban-rural (1999): urban 29.3%; rural 70.7%.
Sex distribution (2000): male 51.26%; female 48.74%.
Age breakdown (1999): under 15, 40.6%; 15–29, 28.4%; 30–44, 16.5%; 45–59, 9.1%; 60 and over, 5.4%.
Population projection: (2010) 141,000; (2020) 143,000.
Doubling time: 33 years.
Ethnic composition (1994): Chuukese 46.7%; Pohnpeian 24.3%; Kosraean 6.8%; Yapese 5.4%; Mortlockese 4.9%; Filipino 0.8%; other 11.1%.
Religious affiliation (1996): Christianity is the predominant religious tradition; Catholic 52.9%, Protestant 47.1%; the Kosraeans, Pohnpeians, and Trukese are mostly Protestant and the Yapese mostly Roman Catholic.
Major cities (1994): Weno (Moen) 16,121; Tol 4,816; Kolonia 6,660.

Vital statistics

Birth rate per 1,000 population (2000): 27.1 (world avg. 22.1); legitimate, n.a.; illegitimate, n.a.
Death rate per 1,000 population (2000): 6.0 (world avg. 8.9).
Natural increase rate per 1,000 population (2000): 21.1 (world avg. 13.2).
Total fertility rate (avg. births per childbearing woman; 2000): 3.8.
Marriage rate per 1,000 population: n.a.
Divorce rate per 1,000 population: n.a.
Life expectancy at birth (2000): male 66.7 years; female 70.6 years.
Major causes of death per 100,000 population (1997)[3]: diseases of the cerebrovascular system 90.3; endocrine and metabolic diseases 64.4; homicide, suicide, and accidents 55.4; diseases of the respiratory system 42.0; malignant neoplasms (cancers) 34.0; infectious and parasitic diseases 26.8 (with especially high morbidity rates for tuberculosis and leprosy).

National economy

Budget (1997–98). Revenue: U.S.$152,300,000 (external grants 60.0%; tax revenue 15.1%; fishing rights fees 13.4%). Expenditures: U.S.$154,700,000 (current expenditures 79.6%, of which government services 71.4%, transfer payments 4.7%, debt services 3.4%; capital expenditure 20.4%).
Public debt (external, outstanding; 1994–95): U.S.$119,500,000.
Population economically active (1994): total 27,573; activity rate of total population 26.3% (participation rates: ages 15–64, 43.6%; female 33.8%; unemployed 15.3%).

Price and earnings indexes (1995 = 100)

	1990	1991	1992	1993	1994	1995
Price index	79.9	83.1	87.2	92.5	96.2	100.0
Annual wage index[4]	...	...	86.4	94.5	95.2	100.0

Production (metric tons except as noted). Agriculture, forestry, fishing: n.a.; however, Micronesia's major crops include coconuts (which provide annually more than 4,000 tons of copra), breadfruit, cassava, sweet potatoes, peppers, and a variety of tropical fruits (including bananas); livestock comprises mostly pigs and poultry; fish catch (1998) 15,393, of which skipjack tuna 15,000, yellowfin tuna 5,000. Mining and quarrying: quarrying of sand and aggregate for local construction only. Manufacturing: n.a.; however, copra and coconut oil, traditionally important products, are being displaced by garment production; the manufacture of handicrafts and personal items (clothing, mats, boats, etc.) by individuals is also important. Construction: n.a. Energy production (consumption): electricity (kW-hr; 1997) 100,333,000 (100,333,000); coal, none (n.a.); crude petroleum, none (n.a.); petroleum products (metric tons; 1992) none (77,000); natural gas, none (n.a.).

Household income and expenditure. Average household size (1994) 6.8; annual income per household (1994) U.S.$8,645; sources of income (1994): wages and salaries 51.8%, operating surplus 23.0%, social security 2.1%; expenditure (1985): food and beverages 73.5%.
Land use (1984)[5]: forested 22.5%; meadows and pastures 13.5%; agricultural and under permanent cultivation 33.5%; other 30.5%.
Gross national product (at current market prices; 1998): U.S.$204,000,000 (U.S.$1,800 per capita).

Structure of gross domestic product and labour force

	1996 in value U.S.$'000,000	1996 % of total value	1994 labour force	1994 % of labour force
Agriculture and fishing[6]	34.7	19.1	7,375	26.7
Mining	0.7	0.4	42	0.2
Manufacturing	2.6	1.4	656	2.4
Construction	1.9	1.0	1,171	4.2
Public utilities	2.0	1.1	279	1.0
Transp. and commun.	8.5	4.7	727	2.6
Finance	4.2	2.3	632	2.3
Services	3.1	1.7	2,125	7.7
Trade[7]	43.6	24.0	2,258	8.2
Public administration	80.4	44.3	8,092	29.3
Other			4,216[8]	15.2[8]
TOTAL	181.6[2]	100.0	27,573	100.0[2]

Tourism (1998): expenditures U.S.$4,383,000; number of visitors 16,283.

Foreign trade

Balance of trade (current prices)

	1992	1993	1994	1995	1996
U.S.$'000,000	–109.1	–93.7	–75.5	–59.1	–52.0
% of total	66.0%	41.4%	43.5%	48.0%	44.1%

Imports (1998): U.S.$82,486,915 (1997; food, beverages, and tobacco 41.9%; manufactured goods 32.0%; machinery and transport equipment 28.4%; petroleum products 11.2%; chemicals 4.4%). *Major import sources* (1997): United States (including Guam) 72.5%; Japan 13.5%; Australia 6.6%.
Exports (1998): U.S.$8,037,207 (1997; marine products 89.2%; agricultural products 4.4%, of which bananas 3.2%, copra 1.2%). *Major export destinations* (1992): Japan 80.0%; United States 9.3%; Guam 8.3%; South Pacific Region 2.4%.

Transport and communications

Transport. Railroads: none. Roads (1990): total length 140 mi, 226 km (paved 17%). Vehicles (1998): passenger cars 2,044; trucks and buses 354. Merchant marine (1997[9]): vessels (100 gross tons and over) 19; deadweight tonnage 9,200. Air transport: n.a.; airports (1997) with scheduled flights 4.

Communications

Medium	date	unit	number	units per 1,000 persons
Radio	1996	receivers	70,000	667
Television	1996	receivers	2,000	21
Telephones	1998	main lines	9,100	80
Internet	1995	users	1,000	10

Education and health

Educational attainment (1998). Percentage of population age 25 and over having: no formal schooling 4.4%; primary education 46.0%; some secondary 18.3%; secondary 12.9%; some college 14.7%; bachelors degree 2.9%; higher 0.8%. *Literacy* (1994): total population age 10 and over literate 69,779 (93.9%); males literate 35,688 (94.7%); females literate 34,091 (93.0%).

Education (1997–98)

	schools	teachers	students	student/ teacher ratio
Elementary (age 6–12)	171	1,486	25,915	18.6
Secondary (age 13–18)	24	418	6,809	16.2
College	1	71	1,884	26.5

Health (1998): physicians 68 (1 per 1,677 persons); hospital beds (1997) 260 (1 per 447 persons); infant mortality rate per 1,000 live births (2000) 33.5.
Food: daily per capita caloric intake, n.a.

Military

External security is provided by the United States.

[1]On Nov. 3, 1986, the United States unilaterally terminated the UN trusteeship it held over the Federated States of Micronesia (FSM), thus formally initiating their free-association political status. On Dec. 22, 1990, the United Nations Security Council joined the Trusteeship Council, which had endorsed the termination of the trusteeship in May 1986. [2]Detail does not add to total given because of rounding. [3]Based on registered deaths only. [4]Public sector only. [5]Includes all areas formerly constituting the U.S. Trust Territory of the Pacific Islands. [6]Includes subsistence farming and fishing. [7]Includes hotels. [8]Un-employed. [9]January 1.

Internet resources for further information:
- **General Information on The FSM http://fsmgov.org**

Moldova

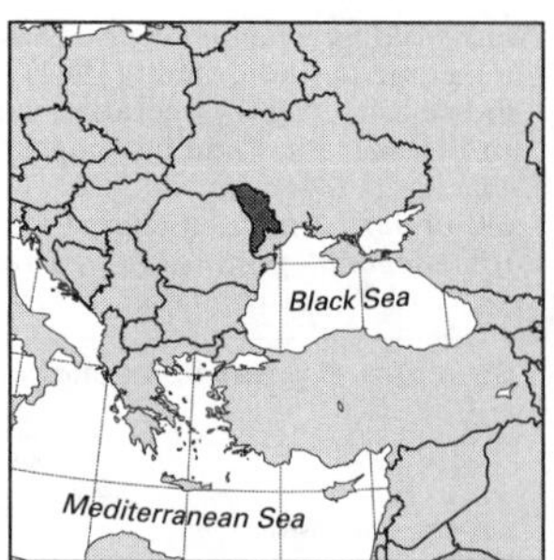

Official name: Republica Moldova (Republic of Moldova).
Form of government: unitary parliamentary republic[1] with a single legislative body (Parliament [101]).
Head of state: President.
Head of government: Prime Minister.
Capital: Chişinău.
Official language: Romanian[2].
Official religion: none.
Monetary unit: 1 Moldovan leu (plural lei) = 100 bani; valuation (Oct. 6, 2000) free rate, 1 U.S.$ = 12.27 Moldovan lei; 1 £ = 17.75 Moldovan lei.

Area and population

Administrative subdivisions[3, 4]

Cities	area sq km	population 1993	Rural districts	area sq km	population 1993
Bălţi	...	159,420	Drochia	780	80,828
Cahul	...	43,259	Dubăsari	670	53,962
Chişinău	160	735,229	Edineţ	860	90,948
Dubăsari	...	24,243	Făleşti	1,070	95,025
Orhei	...	37,887	Floreşti	830	76,987
Râbniţa	...	61,824	Glodeni	760	65,781
Soroca	...	41,461	Grigoriopol	820	52,326
Tighina (Bendery)	...	137,423	Hânceşti	1,350	118,255
Tiraspol	...	203,865	Ialoveni	930	87,749
Ungheni	...	38,462	Leova	720	51,987
			Nisporeni	760	81,626
Rural districts			Ocniţa	660	63,073
Anenil Noi	830	77,468	Orhei	1,100	95,523
Basarabeasca	660	43,765	Râbniţa	850	32,793
Brinceni	810	83,340	Rezina	670	55,494
Cahul	800	44,489	Rişcani	1,000	83,456
Cainari	...	42,755	Sângerei	1,020	91,684
Călăraş	760	84,442	Slobozia	960	113,823
Camenca	820	59,356	Şoldăneşti	560	46,696
Cantemir	860	61,126	Soroca	870	58,097
Căuşeni	1,120	72,999	Ştefan-Vodă	1,030	76,702
Ciadâr-Lunga	720	68,698	Străşeni	760	96,107
Cimişlia	1,170	61,089	Taraclia	620	45,912
Comrat	840	71,273	Teleneşti	860	76,886
Criuleni	850	91,783	Ungheni	1,070	79,525
Donduşeni	890	66,483	Vulcăneşti	930	62,193
			TOTAL	33,700[5]	4,345,577

Demography

Population (2000): 4,298,000[6].
Density (2000): persons per sq mi 330.2, persons per sq km 127.5.
Urban-rural (1999): urban 54.4%; rural 45.6%.
Sex distribution (1999): male 47.85%; female 52.15%.
Age breakdown (2000): under 15, 23.2%; 15–29, 24.9%; 30–44, 21.4%; 45–59, 16.3%; 60–74, 11.0%; 75 and over, 3.2%.
Population projection: (2010) 4,403,000; (2020) 4,604,000.
Doubling time: not applicable; doubling time exceeds 100 years.
Ethnic composition (1989): Moldovan 62.0%; Russian 23.1%; Ukrainian 8.5%; Gagauz 3.2%; Bulgarian 1.6%; other 1.6%.
Religious affiliation (1995): Orthodox 46.0%, of which Romanian Orthodox 35.0%, Russian Orthodox 9.5%; other Christian 3.5%; Jewish 0.9%; other 49.6%.
Major cities (1993): Chişinău 657,775; Tiraspol 184,852; Bălţi 156,081.

Vital statistics

Birth rate per 1,000 population (2000): 12.9 (world avg. 22.1); (1995) legitimate 87.7%; illegitimate 12.3%.
Death rate per 1,000 population (2000): 12.6 (world avg. 8.9).
Natural increase rate per 1,000 population (2000): 0.3 (world avg. 13.2).
Total fertility rate (avg. births per childbearing woman; 2000): 1.6.
Marriage rate per 1,000 population(1994): 7.8.
Life expectancy at birth (2000): male 59.9 years; female 69.2 years.
Major causes of death per 100,000 population (1994): circulatory diseases 500.7; cancers 136.1; accidents and violence 113.3; digestive system diseases 110.4.

National economy

Budget (1997). Revenue: 3,473,000,000 lei (value-added tax 23.8%, excise taxes 12.4%, personal income tax 7.4%, profits tax 6.2%, duties and customs taxes 3.3%). Expenditures: 2,354,000,000,000 lei (current expenditures 94.5%, of which education 20.4%, health care 12.5%, interest payments 9.1%; capital expenditure 5.5%).
Public debt (external, outstanding; 1998): U.S.$808,000,000.
Land use (1994): forest 10.6%; pasture 10.9%; agriculture 75.9%; other 2.6%.
Production (metric tons except as noted). Agriculture, forestry, fishing (2000): sugar beets 1,800,000, corn (maize) 900,000, wheat 770,000, grapes 350,000, potatoes 342,000, apples 215,000; livestock (number of live animals) 974,000 sheep, 705,000 pigs, 416,000 cattle; roundwood (1998) 406,000 cu m; fish catch (1998) 491. Mining and quarrying (1995): sand and gravel 376,000; gypsum 13,600. Manufacturing ('000,000 lei; 1995): food 1,446,824; machinery 383,153; construction materials 164,198; textiles 57,283. Construction (1994): 127,200,000 lei. Energy production (consumption): electricity (kW-hr; 1996): 6,122,000,000 (7,728,000,000); coal (metric tons; 1996) none (1,124,000,000); crude petroleum (barrels; 1990) none (51,625,000); petroleum products (metric tons; 1996) none (915,000); natural gas (cu m; 1996) none (2,611,000,000).
Gross national product (at current market prices; 1998): U.S.$1,652,000,000 (U.S.$380 per capita).

Structure of gross domestic product and labour force

	1997		1994	
	in value '000,000 lei	% of total value	labour force	% of labour force
Agriculture	2,248	26.0	767,000	45.1
Manufacturing, mining	1,992	23.0	232,000	13.7
Public utilities	163	1.9	39,000	2.2
Construction	349	4.0	91,000	5.4
Transp. and commun.	293	3.4	73,000	4.3
Trade[7]	652	7.5	107,000	6.3
Finance	341	3.9	20,000	1.2
Pub. admin., defense	1,043	12.0	32,000	1.9
Services	440	5.1	305,000	18.0
Other	1,134[8]	13.1[8]	33,000	1.9
TOTAL	8,655	100.0[9]	1,699,000	100.0

Population economically active (1994): total (1995) 1,693,000; activity rate of total population 44.8% (participation rates: ages 16–59 [male], 16–54 [female] 85.2%; female 53.0%; unemployed 1.4%).

Price and earnings indexes (1995 = 100)

	1993	1994	1995	1996	1997	1998	1999
Consumer price index	...	89.2	100.0	120.9	130.6	139.2	203.2
Earnings index	144.7	78.7	100.0	...	...	...	...

Household income and expenditure. Average household size (1989) 3.4; income per household: n.a.; sources of income (1994): wages and salaries 41.2%, social benefits 15.3%, agricultural income 10.4%, other 33.1%; expenditure (1995): food and drink 49.1%, clothing 9.7%, health 4.1%.

Foreign trade

Balance of trade (current prices)

	1993	1994	1995	1996	1997	1998
U.S.$'000,000	–180	–54	–32	–274	–348	–388
% of total	16.6%	4.2%	2.1%	14.5%	16.4%	23.2%

Imports (1996): 4,967,200,000 lei (mineral products 36.8%, machinery 14.5%, agricultural goods 10.8%, chemical products 6.6%, textiles 5.1%). *Major import sources:* Ukraine 27.5%; Russia 27.3%; Romania 6.7%.
Exports (1996): 3,691,200,000 lei (food and agricultural goods 72.8%, textile products 6.2%, machinery 5.3%, metals and metal products 1.7%). *Major export destinations:* Russia 53.6%; Romania 9.4%; Ukraine 5.9%.

Transport and communications

Transport. Railroads (1997): length 2,710 km; passenger-km 949,300,000; metric ton-km cargo 3,133,600,000[10]. Roads (1995): total length 12,259 km (paved 87.2%). Vehicles (1996): passenger cars 166,757; trucks and buses 67,638. Air transport (1994): passenger-km 225,000; metric ton-km cargo 1,000,000; airports (1997) 1.

Communications

Medium	date	unit	number	units per 1,000 persons
Daily newspapers	1996	circulation	261,000	59
Radio	1997	receivers	3,220,000	736
Television	1998	receivers	1,300,000	297
Telephones	1998	main lines	657,000	150
Personal computers	1998	units	28,000	6.4
Internet	1998	users	11,000	2.5

Education and health

Educational attainment (1989). Percentage of population age 15 and over having: no formal schooling or some primary education 24.5%; some secondary 20.4%; secondary 46.4%; higher 8.7%. *Literacy* (2000): total population age 15 and over literate 98.9%; males 99.6%; females 98.3%.

Education (1996–97)

	schools	teachers	students	student/ teacher ratio
Primary (age 7–13)	1,700[11]	14,097	320,725	22.8
Secondary (age 14–17)		28,615[12]	419,256	...
Voc., teacher tr.	64[11]	...	26,105	...
Higher	20[11]	8,814	93,759	10.6

Health (1995): physicians 17,200 (1 per 250 persons); hospital beds 53,000 (1 per 82 persons); infant mortality rate per 1,000 live births (2000) 43.3.
Food (1998): daily per capita caloric intake 2,763 (vegetable products 85%, animal products 15%); 107.9% of FAO recommended minimum requirement.

Military

Total active duty personnel (1999): 10,650 (army 90.1%, air force 9.9%). *Military expenditure as percentage of GNP* (1997): 1.0% (world 2.6%); per capita expenditure U.S.$14.

[1]Moldova is officially a parliamentary republic from Oct. 27, 2000. [2]Officially designated Moldovan per constitution. [3]Area and population figures include the Gagauz autonomous region (1,800 sq km; pop. *c.* 200,000). [4]Moldova (including the Transdniestrian republic) is divided into 40 *rayons*, 4 cities, and the Gagauz A.R. as of the administrative reorganization of the late 1990s. [5]Total includes approximately 320 sq km (125 sq mi) not distributed by administrative subdivision. [6]Approximately 500,000 Moldovans work in western Europe. [7]Includes hotels. [8]Import and production taxes less subsidies. [9]Detail does not add to total given because of rounding. [10]1995. [11]1995–96. [12]Secondary includes Voc., teacher tr.

Internet resources for further information:
- **Moldova.Net http://www.moldova.net**

Monaco

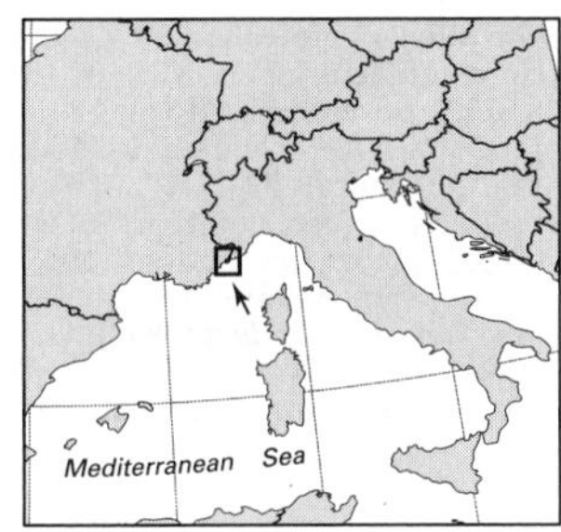

Official name: Principauté de Monaco (Principality of Monaco).
Form of government: constitutional monarchy with one legislative body (National Council [18]).
Chief of state: Prince.
Head of government[1]: Minister of State assisted by the Council of Government.
Capital: [2].
Official language: French.
Official religion: Roman Catholicism.
Monetary unit: 1 French franc (F) = 100 centimes; valuation (Oct. 6, 2000) 1 U.S.$ = F 7.54; 1 £ = F 10.91[3].

Area and population

		area		population
Quarters[2]	Capitals	sq mi	sq km	1990 census
Fontvieille	—	0.13	0.33	1,961
La Condamine	—	0.23	0.61	12,158
Monaco-Ville	—	0.07	0.19	1,151
Monte-Carlo	—	0.32	0.82	14,702
TOTAL		0.75	1.95	29,972

Demography

Population (2000): 31,700.
Density (2000): persons per sq mi 42,267, persons per sq km 16,256.
Urban-rural (2000): urban 100%; rural 0%.
Sex distribution (1999): male 47.56%; female 52.44%.
Age breakdown (1999): under 15, 14.9%; 15–29, 14.1%; 30–44, 21.4%; 45–59, 21.2%; 60–74, 17.4%; 75 and over, 11.0%.
Population projection: (2000) 33,000; (2010) 34,000.
Doubling time: not applicable.
National composition (1990): French 40.2%; Monégasque 16.9%; Italian 16.7%; British 4.5%; Belgian 2.4%; other 19.3%.
Religious affiliation (1995): Christian 85.3%, of which Roman Catholic 80.9%, Protestant 4.0%; Jewish 3.1%; nonreligious and other 11.6%.

Vital statistics

Birth rate per 1,000 population (1999): 10.2 (world avg. 22.1).
Death rate per 1,000 population (1999): 13.2 (world avg. 8.9).
Natural increase rate per 1,000 population (1999): –3.0 (world avg. 13.2).
Total fertility rate (avg. births per childbearing woman; 1999): 1.8.
Marriage rate per 1,000 population (1997): 6.0.
Divorce rate per 1,000 population (1997): 2.5.
Life expectancy at birth (1996): male 74.7 years; female 82.9 years.
Major causes of death per 100,000 population: n.a.; however, principal causes are those of a developed country with an older population.

National economy

Budget (1997). Revenue: F 3,225,658,000 (value-added taxes 50.0%).[4] Expenditures: F 3,139,854,000.
Public debt: n.a.
Production. Agriculture, forestry, fishing: some horticulture and greenhouse cultivation; no agriculture as such. Mining and quarrying: none. Manufacturing: in the 1990s, principal manufactures included chemicals, cosmetics, perfumery, and pharmaceuticals; light electronics and precision instruments; paper and card manufactures; fabricated plastics; and clothing. Construction: n.a. Energy production (consumption): electricity (kW-hr; 1997) 403,000,000 (imported from France); coal, none (n.a.); crude petroleum, none (n.a.); natural gas, none (n.a.).
Gross domestic product (1994): U.S.$765,000,000[5] (U.S.$24,460 per capita).

Distribution of value of sales and labour force

	1992		1990	
	in value F '000,000	% of total value	labour force[6]	% of labour force[6]
Agriculture	...	...	41	0.3
Manufacturing	3,650	11.3	3,754	29.8
Construction / Public utilities	7	7	122	1.0
Hotels, restaurants	1,140	3.5	1,445	11.5
Transportation and communications	...	...	3,491 (Transportation and communications, Finance, real estate, Services)	27.8
Finance, real estate	3,780[7]	11.6[7]		
Services	23,870	73.6		
Pub. admin., defense	...	...	2,828	22.5
Other	—	—	893[8]	7.1[8]
TOTAL	32,440	100.0	12,574	100.0

Population economically active (1990): total 12,574 (42.0%); female participation in labour force 5,002 (39.8%); ages 17–64, 63.6%; unemployed (1996) 3.0%.

Price and earnings indexes (1990 = 100)

	1991	1992	1993	1994	1995	1996	1997
Consumer price index[9]	103.2	105.7	107.9	109.7	111.6	113.9	115.2
Hourly earnings index	...	...	...	...	...	...	...

Household income and expenditure. Average household size (1998) 2.2; average annual income per household: n.a.; sources of income: n.a.; expenditure: n.a.
Tourism (1997): 2,257 hotel rooms (1996); 781,907 overnight stays; 258,604 visitors.
Land use (2000): forested 0%; meadows and pastures 0%; agricultural and under permanent cultivation 0%; built-up and other 100%.

Foreign trade

Monaco participates in a customs union (since 1963) with France; separate figures are not available.

Transport and communications

Transport. Railroads (1997): length 1.1 mi, 1.7 km; passengers 2,171,100; cargo 3,357 tons. Roads (1997): total length 31 mi, 50 km (paved 100%). Vehicles (1997): passenger cars 21,120; trucks and buses 2,770. Merchant marine (1997): vessels (100 gross tons and over) 9; total deadweight tonnage (1989) 4,959. Air transport (1999): traffic, not applicable; airports with scheduled flights: none[10].

Communications

Medium	date	unit	number	units per 1,000 persons
Daily newspapers	1995	circulation	8,000	250
Radio	1995	receivers	33,000	990
Television	1995	receivers	24,000	721
Telephones	1999	main lines	33,000	990
Cellular telephones	1999	subscribers	12,000	360
Personal computers	1998	units	...	...
Internet	1998	users	...	...

Education and health

Education (1996–97)

	schools	teachers	students	student/ teacher ratio
Primary (age 6–10)	8	127	1,917	15.1
Secondary (age 11–17)	6	192	2,416	12.6
Vocational	4	89	532	6.0
Higher	1	...	112	...

Literacy: virtually 100%.
Health (1997): physicians 188 (1 per 170 persons); hospital beds 555 (1 per 58 persons); infant mortality rate per 1,000 live births (1999) 6.0.
Food: daily per capita caloric intake, n.a.; assuming consumption patterns similar to France (1998) 3,541 (vegetable products 62%, animal products 38%), 141% of FAO recommended minimum requirement.

Military

Defense responsibility lies with France according to the terms of the Versailles Treaty of 1919.

[1]Under the authority of the prince. [2]The principality is a single administrative unit, and no separate area within it is distinguished as capital. [3]Monégasque coins of equal value to French coins also circulate. [4]The main sources of revenue in 1997 were financial activities (about 50%) and tourism (about 25%); receipts from gambling had declined to about 4%. [5]UN estimate. [6]Officially economically active per 1990 census; the employed labour force in 1998 (including many foreign workers) was 32,697. [7]Finance, real estate includes Construction and Public utilities. [8]Includes not adequately defined. [9]The index is for France, which is united with Monaco in a customs and monetary union. [10]Fixed-wing service is provided at Nice, France; helicopter service is available at Fontvieille; passengers carried (1997) 131,038.

Internet resources for further information:

- **Welcome to Monaco (official guide)**
  http://www.monaco.mc/monaco/index.html

Mongolia

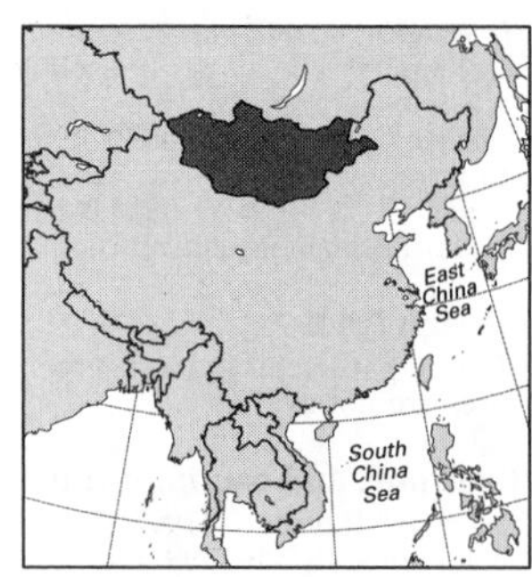

Official name: Mongol Uls (Mongolia).
Form of government: unitary multiparty republic with one legislative house (State Great Hural [76]).
Chief of state: President.
Head of government: Prime Minister.
Capital: Ulaanbaatar (Ulan Bator).
Official language: Khalkha Mongolian.
Official religion: none.
Monetary unit: 1 tugrik (Tug) = 100 möngö; valuation (Oct. 6, 2000) 1 U.S.$ = Tug 1,086; 1 £ = Tug 1,571.

Area and population

		area		population
				1998[1]
Provinces	**Capitals**	sq mi	sq km	estimate
Arhangay	Tsetserleg	21,400	55,300	103,700
Bayan-Ölgiy	Ölgiy	17,600	45,700	96,200
Bayanhongor	Bayanhongor	44,800	116,000	91,600
Bulgan	Bulgan	18,800	48,700	66,100
Darhan-Uul	Darhan	1,270	3,280	94,200
Dornod	Choybalsan	47,700	123,600	84,300
Dornogovĭ	Saynshand	42,300	109,500	49,900
Dundgovĭ	Manalgovi	28,800	74,700	54,400
Dzavhan	Uliastay	31,900	82,500	105,000
Govĭ-Altay	Altay	54,600	141,400	74,900
Govĭ-Sümber	Choyr	2,140	5,540	13,100
Hentiy	Öndörhaan	31,000	80,300	77,700
Hovd	Hovd	29,400	76,100	93,000
Hövsgöl	Mörön	38,800	100,600	123,600
Ömnögovĭ	Dalandzadgad	63,900	165,400	46,200
Orhon	Erdenet	320	840	72,500
Övörhangay	Arvayheer	24,300	62,900	116,900
Selenge	Sühbaatar	15,900	41,200	107,000
Sühbaatar	Baruun-Urt	31,800	82,300	59,700
Töv	Dzüünmod	28,600	74,000	113,700
Uvs	Ulaangom	26,900	69,600	100,500
Autonomous municipality				
Ulaanbaatar	—	1,800	4,700	668,800
TOTAL		603,930[2]	1,564,160	2,413,000

Demography

Population (2000): 2,399,000.
Density (2000): persons per sq mi 4.0, persons per sq km 1.5.
Urban-rural (1999): urban 63.0%; rural 37.0%.
Sex distribution (1999): male 49.60%; female 50.40%.
Age breakdown (1999): under 15, 34.6%; 15–29, 30.6%; 30–44, 20.8%; 45–59, 8.3%; 60–69, 3.3%; 70 and over, 2.4%.
Population projection: (2010) 2,787,000; (2020) 3,174,000.
Doubling time: 44 years.
Ethnic composition (1989): Khalkha Mongol 78.8%; Kazakh 5.9%; Dörbed Mongol 2.7%; Bayad 1.9%; Buryat Mongol 1.7%; Dariganga Mongol 1.4%; other 7.6%.
Religious affiliation (1995): Tantric Buddhist (Lamaism) 96.0%; Muslim 4.0%.
Major cities (1999): Ulaanbaatar (Ulan Bator) 691,000; Darhan 72,600; Erdenet 65,700; Choybalsan 38,500; Ölgiy 23,700.

Vital statistics

Birth rate per 1,000 population (1999): 22.4 (world avg. 22.1).
Death rate per 1,000 population (1999): 6.4 (world avg. 8.9).
Natural increase rate per 1,000 population (1999): 16.0 (world avg. 13.2).
Total fertility rate (avg. births per childbearing woman; 1999): 2.5.
Marriage rate per 1,000 population (1999): 9.7.
Divorce rate per 1,000 population (1999): 0.7.
Life expectancy at birth (1999): male 65.0 years; female 68.0 years.
Major causes of death per 100,000 population: n.a.; however, in the early 1990s, major causes of mortality included diseases of the cardiovascular system, diseases of the respiratory system, and diseases of the cerebrovascular system.

National economy

Budget (1999). Revenue: Tug 243,504,400,000 (taxes 67.9%, of which sales tax 27.0%, social security contribution 15.3%, special taxes 10.2%, income taxes 8.5%, custom duties 3.7%; nontax revenue 19.4%). Expenditures: Tug 334,455,400,000 (transfers to provincial governments 11.2%; capital investment 8.8%; wages 7.5%; defense 5.8%; general social services 5.6%).
Public debt (external; 1998): U.S.$633,600,000.
Tourism (1998): receipts U.S.$33,000,000; expenditures U.S.$45,000,000.
Population economically active (1998): total 840,877; activity rate of total population 36.7% (participation rates: ages 15 and over 59.2%; female 48.0%; unemployed 5.7%).

Price and earnings indexes (1995 = 100)

	1993	1994	1995	1996	1997	1998	1999
Consumer price index	34.0	63.8	100.0	149.3	203.9	223.0	239.9
Monthly earnings index	...	59.7	100.0	146.4	185.4	234.4	...

Production (metric tons except as noted). Agriculture, forestry, fishing (1999): wheat 171,520, potatoes 63,765, vegetables and melons 46,524; livestock (number of live animals) 14,694,000 sheep, 11,062,000 goats, 3,726,000 cattle, 3,059,000 horses, 356,500 camels, 21,000 pigs; roundwood (1998) 631,000 cu m; fish catch (1997) 181. Mining and quarrying (1998): fluorspar 612,000; copper 358,400; molybdenum 4,240; gold 9,531 kg. Manufacturing (value added by manufacturing in Tug '000,000; 1996): food products 10,261.3; textiles 6,522.8; beverages 3,316.6; clothing and apparel 2,782.6; nonmetallic mineral products 1,708.8; leather and footwear 1,374.1; wood products 847.0; printing 834.2; chemicals 724.9. Construction (1994): residential 120,400 sq m. Energy production (consumption): electricity (kW-hr; 1996) 2,580,000,000 (2,975,000,000); coal (metric tons; 1996) 5,111,000 (4,928,000); petroleum products (metric tons; 1996) none (544,000).
Gross national product (1998): U.S.$995,000,000 (U.S.$380 per capita).

Structure of gross domestic product and labour force

	1998			
	in value Tug '000,000[3]	% of total value	labour force	% of labour force
Agriculture	74,200	37.2	394,100	45.9
Manufacturing and mining	64,700	32.5	97,900	11.4
Construction	3,500	1.8	27,500	3.2
Transp. and commun.	8,800	4.4	33,400	3.9
Trade	29,600	14.8	...	...
Services[4]	18,600	9.3	239,700	27.9
Other	...	...	66,700[5]	7.8[5]
TOTAL	199,400	100.0	859,300	100.0[2]

Household income and expenditure (1999): Average household size 4.4; monthly income per household Tug 67,426 (U.S.$66); sources of income: wages and salaries 36.4%, transfer payments 11.7%, self-employment 41.2%[6], other 10.7%; expenditure: food 41.1%, housing 11.4%, clothing 9.7%, education 7.5%, transportation and communications 7.1%, healthcare 3.6%.
Land use (1998): forest and other 24.4%; pasture 74.8%; agriculture 0.8%.

Foreign trade[7]

Balance of trade (current prices)

	1994	1995	1996	1997	1998	1999
U.S.$'000,000	+97.7	+58.0	−26.6	−16.8	−158.1	−246.9
% of total	15.9%	6.5%	3.0%	1.8%	18.6%	13.9%

Imports (1998): U.S.$582,400,000 (capital equipment 33.5%, energy 15.7%, food 13.9%, consumer goods 12.6%, raw materials and spare parts 10.8%). *Major import sources:* Russia 29.9%; Japan 11.8%; China 11.6%; South Korea 7.5%; United States 7.2%; France 5.3%; Germany 5.1%.
Exports (1998): U.S.$462,300,000 (mineral products 59.0%, textile and cashmere products 13.5%, wool, hides, and leather goods 5.5%). *Major export destinations:* China 29.3%; Switzerland 20.4%; Russia 11.8%; South Korea 9.6%; United States 8.5%.

Transport and communications

Transport. Railroads (1999): length 1,815 km; passenger-km 559,800,000; metric ton-km cargo 1,942,000. Roads (1996): total length 50,000 km (paved 3%). Vehicles (1999): passenger cars 39,921; trucks and buses 31,061. Air transport (1996): passenger-km 525,000,000; metric ton-km cargo 48,000,000; airports (1997) with scheduled flights 1.

Communications

Medium	date	unit	number	units per 1,000 persons
Daily newspapers	1996	circulation	68,000	27
Radio	1997	receivers	360,000	142
Television	1997	receivers	118,000	47
Telephones	1998	main lines	96,004	38
Cellular telephones	1998	subscribers	5,300	2.1
Personal computers	1997	units	13,000	5.4
Internet	1997	users	1,200	0.5

Education and health

Educational attainment (1989). Percentage of population age 10 and over having: primary education 33.7%; some secondary 31.9%; complete secondary 16.9%; vocational secondary 9.4%; some higher and complete higher 8.1%. *Literacy* (1995): percentage of total population age 15 and over literate 82.9%; males literate 88.6%; females literate 77.2%.

Education (1996–97)

	schools	teachers	students	student/ teacher ratio
Primary (age 6–12)	308	7,587	234,193	30.9
Secondary (age 13–16)	337	12,503	184,100	14.7
Vocational (age 16–18)	38	668	11,308	16.9
Higher	86	4,491	44,088	9.8

Health (1999): physicians 6,162 (1 per 384 persons) hospital beds 17,877 (1 per 132 persons); infant mortality rate per 1,000 live births (1999) 49.
Food (1998): daily per capita caloric intake 2,010 (vegetable products 59%, animal products 41%); 83% of FAO recommended minimum requirement.

Military

Total active duty personnel (1999): 9,100 (army 82.4%, air force 17.6%). *Military expenditure as percentage of GNP* (1997): 1.9% (world 2.6%); per capita expenditure U.S.$8.

[1]January. [2]Detail does not add to total given because of rounding. [3]At constant prices of 1993. [4]Services includes finance, public administration, and defense. [5]Includes unemployed and foreign workers. [6]Includes income from agricultural cooperatives. [7]Import value in balance of trade table is c.i.f.

Internet resources for further information:
- **Mongolia Online http://www.mol.mn**
- **Cyber Mongolia http://www.mongol.net**
- **National Statistics Office of Mongolia http://statis.pmis.gov.mn**

Morocco

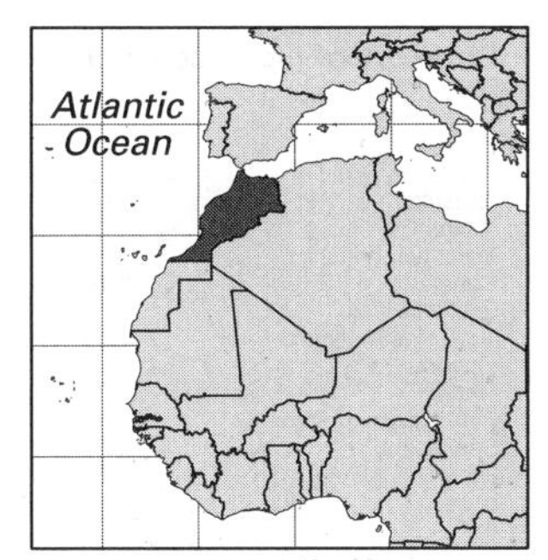

Official name: Al-Mamlakah al-Maghribīyah (Kingdom of Morocco).
Form of government: constitutional monarchy with two legislative houses (House of Councillors [270]; House of Representatives [325]).
Chief of state and head of government: King assisted by Prime Minister.
Capital: Rabat.
Official language: Arabic.
Official religion: Islam.
Monetary unit: 1 Moroccan dirham (DH) = 100 Moroccan francs; valuation (Oct. 6, 2000) 1 U.S.$ = DH 10.98; 1 £ = DH 15.88.

Population (1994 census)[1]

Regions	Principal urban centres	Population
Oued Eddahab-Lagouira	Dakhla	36,751
Laâyoune-Bojador-Sakia El-Hamra	Laâyoune	175,669
Guelmim-Es Semara	Guelmim	386,075
Sous-Massa-Draâ	Agadir-Idda ou Tanane	2,622,947[2]
Gharb-Chrarda-Béni Hsen	Kénitra	1,625,082
Chaouia-Ouardigha	Settat	1,554,241
Marrakech-Tensift-El Haouz	Marrakech-Ménara	2,724,204
Oriental	Oujda-Angad	1,768,691
Grand Casablanca	Casablanca-Anfa	3,094,203
Rabat-Salé-Zemmour-Zaër	Rabat	1,985,602
Doukkala-Abda	Safi	1,793,458
Tadla-Azilal	Béni Mellal	1,324,662
Meknès-Tafilalt	Meknès-El Menzeh	1,903,790
Fès-Boulemane	Fès Jedid-Dar Dbibegh	1,322,473
Taza-Al Hoceïma-Taounate	Al-Hoceïma	1,719,837
Tangier-Tetouan	Tangier-Assilah	2,036,032
TOTAL		26,073,717

Demography

Area[1]: 274,461 sq mi, 710,850 sq km.
Population (2000)[1]: 29,067,000.
Density (1999)[1]: persons per sq mi 105.9, persons per sq km 40.9.
Urban-rural (1999): urban 52.7%; rural 47.3%.
Sex distribution (1999): male 49.89%; female 50.11%.
Age breakdown (1999): under 15, 35.7%; 15–29, 28.9%; 30–44, 18.9%; 45–59, 9.2%; 60–74, 5.3%; 75 and over, 2.0%.
Population projection[1]: (2010) 34,078,000; (2020) 38,885,000.
Doubling time: 39 years.
Ethnolinguistic composition (1995): Arabic 65%; Berber 33%; other 2%.
Religious affiliation (1995): Muslim (mostly Sunnī) 99.8%; Christian 0.1%; other (mostly Jewish) 0.1%.
Major urban areas (1994): Casablanca 2,940,623; Rabat-Salé 1,385,872; Fès 774,574; Marrakech 745,541; Oujda 678,778; Agadir 550,200.

Vital statistics

Birth rate per 1,000 population (1999): 25.3 (world avg. 22.1).
Death rate per 1,000 population (1999): 6.1 (world avg. 8.9).
Natural increase rate per 1,000 population (1999): 19.2 (world avg. 13.2).
Total fertility rate (avg. birth per childbearing woman; 1999): 3.2.
Life expectancy at birth (1999): male 66.6 years; female 71.1 years.
Major causes of death (1989)[3]: childhood diseases 22.9%; circulatory diseases 15.4%; accidents 7.3%; infectious and parasitic diseases 6.3%; cancers 5.6%.

National economy

Budget. Revenue (1997): DH 79,747,000,000 (taxes on income and profits 25.2%; value-added tax 22.7%; excise taxes 17.9%; international trade 15.0%; stamp tax 4.4%). Expenditures (1997): DH 86,058,000,000 (current expenditure 78.7%, of which wages 39.7%, debt payment 20.1%; capital expenditure 21.3%).
Public debt (external, outstanding; 1998): U.S.$19,325,000,000.
Tourism (1998): receipts U.S.$1,449,000,000; expenditures U.S.$316,000,000.
Production (metric tons except as noted). Agriculture, forestry, fishing (1999): sugar beets 3,223,400, wheat 2,153,540, barley 1,473,980, sugarcane 1,372,900, potatoes 1,140,780, oranges 873,500, tomatoes 857,410; livestock (number of live animals) 16,576,400 sheep, 5,114,400 goats, 2,559,800 cattle, 979,800 asses, 150,000 horses, 100,000 chickens, 36,000 camels; roundwood (1998) 1,746,000 cu m; fish catch (1997) 625,000. Mining and quarrying (1996): phosphate rock 20,792,000; barite 283,000; zinc 152,000; lead 108,000; copper 38,000; silver 199. Manufacturing (value added in DH '000,000; 1996): food 39,280; chemical products 13,508; textiles 12,392. Construction (authorized, urban areas; 1994): residential 7,069,557 sq m; nonresidential 998,424 sq m. Energy production (consumption): electricity (kW-hr; 1996) 12,178,000,000 (13,228,000,000); coal (metric tons; 1996) 504,000 (2,649,000); crude petroleum (barrels; 1996) 30,400 (45,600,000); petroleum products (metric tons; 1996) 5,112,000 (5,888,000); natural gas (cu m; 1996) 20,399,000 (20,399,000).
Population economically active (1998): total 5,137,539; activity rate 34.4% (participation rates: over age 15, 48.1%; female 23.8%; unemployed 19.0%).

Price index (1995 = 100)

	1993	1994	1995	1996	1997	1998	1999
Consumer price index	89.6	94.2	100.0	103.0	103.9	106.9	107.6
Earnings index	...	...	...	...	...	...	...

Gross national product (1998): U.S.$34,421,000,000 (U.S.$1,240 per capita).

Structure of gross domestic product and labour force

	1996		1993	
	in value DH '000,000	% of total value	labour force	% of labour force
Agriculture	65,478	20.4	2,906,000	34.0
Mining	5,539	1.7		
Manufacturing	54,384	16.9	2,650,000	31.0
Construction	13,515	4.2		
Public utilities	24,568	7.7		
Transp. and commun.	18,152	5.7		
Trade	35,755	11.1		
Finance	...	...	2,991,000	35.0
Pub. admin., defense	39,350	12.3		
Services	39,724	12.4		
Other	24,454	7.6		
TOTAL	320,919	100.0	8,547,000	100.0

Household income and expenditure. Average household size (1998) 5.7; expenditure (1994)[4]: food 45.2%, housing 12.5%, transportation 7.6%.

Foreign trade

Balance of trade (current prices)

	1994	1995	1996	1997	1998	1999
DH '000,000	–23,353	–19,981	–17,830	–16,398	–21,306	–23,294
% of total	24.1%	14.5%	12.9%	10.9%	13.3%	13.9%

Imports (1999): DH 95,577,000,000 (1996; capital goods 23.5%; food, beverages, and tobacco 17.1%; energy products 17.0%; consumer goods 14.6%). *Major import sources* (1996): France 20.8%; Spain 8.8%; U.S. 7.4%; Germany 6.1%.
Exports (1999): DH 72,283,000,000 (1996; food 31.6%; consumer goods 23.0%; minerals 11.0%). *Major export destinations* (1996): France 28.3%; Spain 9.9%; Japan 6.9%; India 6.3%; Italy 6.3%.

Transport and communications

Transport. Railroads (1996): route length 1,768 km; passenger-km 1,776,000,000; metric ton-km cargo 4,757,000,000. Roads (1996): total length 57,810 km (paved 52%). Vehicles (1996): passenger cars 1,018,146; trucks and buses 278,075. Air transport (1996): passenger-km 4,489,000,000[5]; metric ton-km cargo 380,000,000; airports (1998) 11.

Communications

Medium	date	unit	number	units per 1,000 persons
Daily newspapers	1996	circulation	704,000	27
Radio	1997	receivers	6,640,000	247
Television	1997	receivers	3,100,000	115
Telephones	1999	main lines	1,515,000	55
Cellular telephones	1999	subscribers	116,645	4.2
Personal computers	1999	units	200,000	7.1
Internet	1999	users	40,000	1.4

Education and health

Educational attainment (1982). Percentage of population age 25 and over having: no formal education 47.8%; some primary education 47.8%; some secondary 3.8%; higher 0.6%. *Literacy* (1995): total population over age 15 literate 43.7%; males literate 56.6%; females literate 31.0%.

Education (1996–97)

	schools	teachers	students	student/ teacher ratio
Primary (age 7–12)	5,806	114,406	3,160,907	27.6
Secondary (age 13–17)	451[6]	84,202	1,345,589	16.0
Vocational[7]	562[8]	...	96,460	...
Higher	13[9]	13,155	31,743	11.0

Health (1994): physicians 8,838 (1 per 2,923 persons); hospital beds 26,407 (1 per 978 persons); infant mortality rate (1999) 51.6.
Food (1998): daily per capita caloric intake 3,165 (vegetable products 93%, animal products 7%); 131% of FAO recommended minimum requirement.

Military

Total active duty personnel (1999): 196,300 (army 89.1%, navy 4.0%, air force 6.9%). *Military expenditure as percentage of GDP* (1997): 4.3% (world 2.6%); per capita expenditure U.S.$49.

[1]Includes Western Sahara, annexure of Morocco whose unresolved political status (from 1991) will be decided by a UN-sponsored referendum unscheduled in October 2000; Western Sahara area: 97,344 sq mi, 252,120 sq km; Western Sahara population (2000 est.) 245,000. [2]Difference between national total and sum of all other region totals, which were known. [3]Registered deaths of urban population only. [4]Weights of consumer price index components. [5]Royal Air Maroc only. [6]1994–95. [7]Excludes teacher training. [8]1991–92. [9]Universities only.

Internet resources for further information:
- **Moroccan Ministry of Communication http://www.mincom.gov.ma**
- **Moroccan Ministry of Economic Forecasting http://www.mpep.gov.ma**

Mozambique

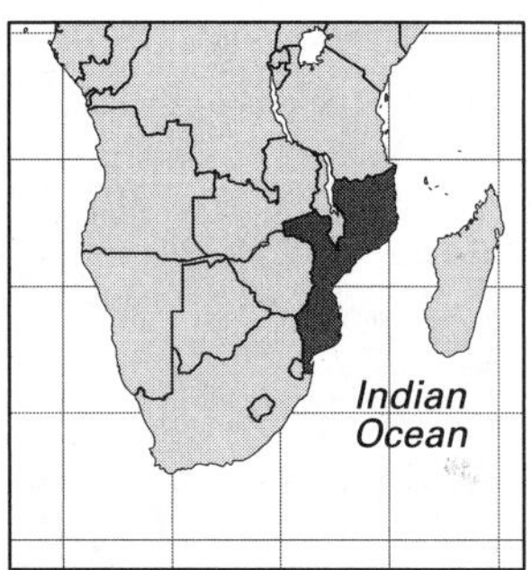

Official name: República de Moçambique (Republic of Mozambique).
Form of government: multiparty republic[1] with a single legislative house (Assembly of the Republic [250]).
Head of state and government: President assisted by the Prime Minister.
Capital: Maputo.
Official language: Portuguese.
Official religion: none.
Monetary unit: 1 metical (Mt; plural meticais) = 100 centavos; valuation (Oct. 6, 2000) 1 U.S.$ = Mt 16,100; 1 £ = Mt 23,290.

Area and population

Provinces	Capitals	area sq mi	area sq km	population 1997 census
Cabo Delgado	Pemba	31,902	82,625	1,287,814
Gaza	Xai-Xai	29,231	75,709	1,062,380
Inhambane	Inhambane	26,492	68,615	1,123,079
Manica	Chimoio	23,807	61,661	974,208
Maputo	Maputo	9,944	25,756	806,179
Nampula	Nampula	31,508	81,606	2,975,747
Niassa	Lichinga	49,828	129,055	756,287
Sofala	Beira	26,262	68,018	1,289,390
Tete	Tete	38,890	100,724	1,144,604
Zambézia	Quelimane	40,544	105,008	2,891,809
City				
Maputo	—	232	602	966,837
TOTAL LAND AREA		308,642[2]	799,379	
INLAND WATER		5,019	13,000	
TOTAL		313,661	812,379	15,278,334

Demography

Population (2000): 19,105,000[3].
Density (2000)[4]: persons per sq mi 61.9, persons per sq km 23.9.
Urban-rural (1999): urban 38.9%; rural 61.1%.
Sex distribution (1999): male 49.39%; female 50.61%.
Age breakdown (2000): under 15, 42.9%; 15–29, 29.1%, 30–44, 15.1%; 45–59, 8.5%; 60–74, 3.7%; 75 and over, 0.7%.
Population projection: (2010) 20,504,000[3]; (2020) 20,626,000[3].
Linguistic composition (1997): Makua 26.3%; Tsonga 11.4%; Lomwe 7.6%; Sena 7.0%; Portuguese 6.5%; Chuaba 6.3%; other Bantu languages 33.0%; other 1.9%.
Religious affiliation (1995): traditional beliefs 47.0%; Muslim 28.2%; Christian 24.8%, of which Roman Catholic 11.6%, Protestant 9.2%.
Major cities (1997): Maputo 966,837; Matola 424,662; Beira 397,368; Nampula 303,346.

Vital statistics

Birth rate per 1,000 population (2000): 38.0 (world avg. 22.1).
Death rate per 1,000 population (2000): 23.3 (world avg. 8.9).
Natural increase rate per 1,000 population (2000): 14.7 (world avg. 13.2).
Total fertility rate (avg. births per childbearing woman; 2000): 4.9.
Marriage rate per 1,000 population (1974): 0.7.
Divorce rate per 1,000 population (1973): 0.01.
Life expectancy at birth (1995): male 46.8 years; female 49.5 years.

National economy

Budget (1997). Revenue: Mt 4,522,000,000 (1995; sales tax 47.8%, customs taxes 24.0%, individual income tax 16.6%). Expenditures: Mt 8,196,000,000 (current expenditure 52.2%, of which goods and services 23.6%, administrative salaries 22.3%, defense and security 19.4%; capital expenditure 47.8%).
Public debt (external, outstanding; 1998): U.S.$5,651,000,000.
Production (metric tons except as noted). Agriculture, forestry, fishing (2000): cassava 4,643,000, corn (maize) 1,109,000, sugarcane 440,000, coconuts 300,000, sorghum 252,000, rice 158,000, peanuts (groundnuts) 100,000, bananas 59,000; livestock (number of live animals) 1,320,000 cattle, 392,000 goats, 180,000 pigs, 125,000 sheep, 28,000,000 chickens; roundwood (1998) 17,977,000 cu m; fish catch (1998) 36,775. Mining and quarrying (1994): marine salt 40,000; bauxite 9,620; copper 133[5, 6]; garnet 3,000 kg; gemstones 6,865 carats. Manufacturing (value in Mt '000,000; 1995): food processing 696,611; beverages and tobacco 395,871; textiles 207,378; nonmetallic mineral products 140,193; wood and cork products 134,951; chemical products 116,335; rubber products 87,827; clothing 82,123; machinery and transport equipment 72,507. Construction (value in Mt; 1994) 157,700,000. Energy production (consumption): electricity (kW-hr; 1996) 568,000,000 (1,168,000,000); coal, none (none); crude petroleum, none (none[7]); petroleum products (metric tons; 1994) none[7] (251,000); natural gas, none (none).
Population economically active (1980): total 5,671,290; activity rate 48.6% (participation rates: over age 15, 87.3%; female 52.4%; unemployed 1.7%).

Price and earnings indexes (1995 = 100)

	1993	1994	1995	1996	1997	1998	1999
Consumer price index	39.7	64.8	100.0	146.9	156.3	157.1	160.3
Monthly earning index[8]	42.3	70.2	100.0	143.6	...	...	...

Gross national product (1998): U.S.$3,478,000,000 (U.S.$210 per capita).

Structure of gross domestic product and labour force

	1995 in value Mt '000,000	1995 % of total value	1980 labour force	1980 % of labour force
Agriculture	5,018,000	25.5	4,754,831	83.8
Mining }	3,395,000[9]	17.2[9]	73,425	1.3
Manufacturing }			273,369	4.8
Construction	2,405,000	12.2	42,121	0.7
Public utilities	[10]	[10]	[10]	[10]
Transp. and commun.	2,454,000	12.5	77,025	1.4
Finance	...	...	...	...
Trade	2,049,000	10.4	112,244	2.0
Pub. admin., defense	1,657,000	8.4 }	243,449[10]	4.3[10]
Services	2,191,000[10]	11.1[10] }		
Other	514,000	2.6	94,826[11]	1.7[11]
TOTAL	19,685,000[2, 12]	100.0[2]	5,671,290	100.0

Household income and expenditure. Average family size (1992–93) 6.7[13]; income per household: n.a.; source of income (1992–93)[13]: wages and salaries 51.6%, self-employment 12.5%, barter 11.5%, private farming 7.7%; expenditure (1992–93)[13]: food, beverages, and tobacco 74.6%; housing and energy 11.7%; transportation and communications 4.7%; clothing and footwear 3.7%; education and recreation 1.4%; health 0.8%.
Land use (1994): forested 22.1%; meadows and pastures 56.1%; agricultural and under permanent cultivation 4.0%; other 17.8%.

Foreign trade[14]

Balance of trade (current prices)

	1994	1995	1996	1997	1998	1999
Mt '000,000,000	–2,300	–4,954	–6,224	–6,090	–6,793	–11,430
% of total	54.0%	61.2%	55.4%	53.8%	55.0%	62.5%

Imports (1996): U.S.$782,640,000 (machinery and transport equipment 32.3%, food and beverages 18.3%, basic manufactures 17.4%, petroleum products 9.6%). *Major import sources:* South Africa 34.5%; European Union 27.1%; Portugal 6.3%; U.S. 4.2%; Japan 4.0%; Zimbabwe 3.9%.
Exports (1996): U.S.$226,090,000 (food and beverages 66.4%, of which shell fish 38.1%; machinery and transport equipment 11.5%, cotton 5.7%, sugar and honey 5.7%). *Major export destinations:* European Union 34.7%; South Africa 19.4%; India 11.8%; U.S. 11.4%; Japan 7.6%.

Transport and communications

Transport. Railroads (1995): route length 1,940 mi, 3,123 km; passenger-mi 194,000,000, passenger-km 312,000,000; short ton-mi cargo 612,000,000, metric ton-km cargo 893,000,000. Roads (1996): total length 18,890 mi, 30,400 km (paved 18.8%). Vehicles (1995): passengers cars 84,000; trucks and buses 26,800. Air transport (1996): passenger-mi 161,511,000, passenger-km 259,927,000; short ton-mi cargo 3,709,000, metric ton-km cargo 5,415,000; airports (1997) with scheduled flights 7.

Communications

Medium	date	unit	number	units per 1,000 persons
Daily newspapers	1996	circulation	49,000	2.7
Radio	1997	receivers	730,000	40
Television	1998	receivers	95,000	5.0
Telephones	1998	main lines	75,000	4.0
Cellular telephones	1998	subscribers	6,700	0.4
Personal computers	1998	units	40,000	2.1
Internet	1998	users	3,500	0.2

Education and health

Literacy (2000): percentage of total population age 15 and over literate 43.8%; males literate 59.9%; females literate 28.4%.

Education (1995)

	schools	teachers	students	student/teacher ratio
Primary (age 5–19)	4,167	24,575	1,415,428	57.6
Secondary (age 10–16)[15]	239[16]	4,376	165,868	37.9
Voc., teacher tr.	31[16]	1,239	19,313	15.6
Higher	3[16]	715	6,639	9.2

Health: physicians (1996) 120[17] (1 per 124,697 persons); hospital beds (1997) 12,630 (1 per 1,210 persons); infant mortality rate per 1,000 live births (2000) 139.9.
Food (1998): daily per capita caloric intake 1,911 (vegetable products 97%, animal products 3%); 82% of FAO recommended minimum requirement.

Military

Total active duty personnel (1999): 5,100–6,100[18]. *Military expenditure as percentage of GNP* (1997): 2.8% (world 2.6%); per capita expenditure U.S.$4.

[1]Mozambique adopted a new multiparty constitution that became effective on Nov. 30, 1990, but was amended on Oct. 29, 1996, to create autonomous local governments. The first multiparty elections took place on Oct. 27–29, 1994. [2]Detail does not add to total given because of rounding. [3]Estimate from UN time series not adjusted for 1997 census. [4]Based on land area. [5]1990. [6]Metal content only. [7]Internal disorder and a lack of foreign exchange have brought importation of crude petroleum and the production of refined petroleum products practically to a halt. [8]Agricultural workers only. [9]Manufacturing includes fishing. [10]Services includes Public utilities. [11]Unemployed. [12]Reported as gross output. [13]City of Maputo only. [14]Import figures are c.i.f. [15]Includes the two stages of secondary education and the upper-level primary stage. [16]1994. [17]Government personnel only. [18]Estimate; approximately 80% are in the army.

Internet resources for further information:
- **Mozambique http://www.hmnet.com/africa/mozambique/mozambique.html**
- **Mozambique Country Profile http://www.mbendi.co.za/cymzcy.htm**

Myanmar (Burma)

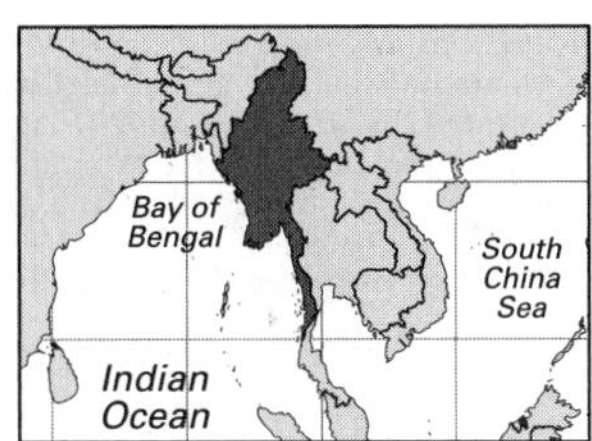

Official name: Pyidaungzu Myanma Naingngandaw (Union of Myanmar).
Form of government: military regime.
Head of state and government: Chairman of the State Peace and Development Council.
Capital: Yangôn (Rangoon).
Official language: Burmese.
Official religion: none.
Monetary unit: 1 Myanmar kyat (K) = 100 pyas; valuation[1] (Oct. 6, 2000) 1 U.S.$ = K 6.25; 1 £ = K 9.04.

Area and population

Divisions	Capitals	area sq mi	area sq km	population 1994 estimate
Irrawaddy (Ayeyarwady)	Bassein (Pathein)	13,567	35,138	6,107,000
Magwe (Magway)	Magwe (Magway)	17,305	44,820	4,067,000
Mandalay	Mandalay	14,295	37,024	5,823,000
Pegu (Bago)	Pegu (Bago)	15,214	39,404	4,607,000
Sagaing	Sagaing	36,535	94,625	4,889,000
Tenasserim (Tanintharyi)	Tavoy (Dawei)	16,735	43,343	1,187,000
Yangôn	Yangôn (Rangoon)	3,927	10,171	5,037,000
States				
Chin	Hakha	13,907	36,019	438,000
Kachin	Myitkyinā	34,379	89,041	1,135,000
Karen	Pa-an (Hpa-an)	11,731	30,383	1,323,000
Kayah	Loi-kaw	4,530	11,733	228,000
Mon	Moulmein (Mawlamyine)	4,748	12,297	2,183,000
Rakhine (Arakan)	Sittwe (Akyab)	14,200	36,778	2,482,000
Shan	Taunggyi	60,155	155,801	4,416,000
TOTAL		261,228	676,577	43,922,000

Demography

Population (2000): 41,735,000.
Density (2000): persons per sq mi 159.8, persons per sq km 61.7.
Urban-rural (1999): urban 27.0%; rural 73.0%.
Sex distribution (1997): male 49.65%; female 50.35%.
Age breakdown (1997): under 15, 33.3%; 15–29, 27.7%, 30–44, 19.8%; 45–59, 11.5%; 60 and over, 7.7%.
Population projection: (2010) 43,674,000; (2020) 44,775,000.
Doubling time: 57 years.
Ethnic composition (1983): Burman 69.0%; Shan 8.5%; Karen 6.2%; Rakhine 4.5%; Mon 2.4%; Chin 2.2%; Kachin 1.4%; other 5.8%.
Religious affiliation (1983): Buddhist 89.1%; Christian 4.9%; Muslim 3.8%; other 2.2%.
Major cities (1983): Yangôn (Rangoon) 2,513,023; Mandalay 532,949; Moulmein (Mawlamyine) 219,961; Pegu (Bago) 150,528; Bassein (Pathein) 144,096.

Vital statistics

Birth rate per 1,000 population (1999): 20.8 (world avg. 22.1).
Death rate per 1,000 population (1999): 9.1 (world avg. 8.9).
Natural increase rate per 1,000 population (1999): 11.7 (world avg. 13.2).
Total fertility rate (avg. births per childbearing woman; 1997): 2.7.
Marriage rate per 1,000 population: n.a.
Divorce rate per 1,000 population: n.a.
Life expectancy at birth (1999): male 59.0 years; female 63.0 years.
Major causes of death per 100,000 population (1994): infectious and parasitic diseases 27.7; circulatory diseases 17.4; respiratory diseases 15.1; malignant neoplasms (cancers) 7.6; malnutrition 3.2.

National economy

Budget (1998–99). Revenue: K 80,400,000,000 (nontax revenue 55.6%; revenue from taxes 43.7%, of which taxes on goods and services 17.4%, taxes on income 15.3%; foreign grants 0.7%). Expenditures: K 72,100,000,000 (defense 34.0%; agriculture and forestry 13.3%; interest payments 12.5%; education 11.1%; public works and housing 8.7%; general services 6.8%).
Public debt (external, outstanding; 1998): U.S.$5,071,000,000.
Tourism: receipts from visitors (1997) U.S.$34,000,000; expenditures by nationals abroad (1992) U.S.$16,000,000.
Production (metric tons except as noted). Agriculture, forestry, fishing (1999): rice 17,075,000, sugarcane 5,429,000, pulses 1,895,000, peanuts (groundnuts) 562,000, plantains 423,000, corn (maize) 303,000, sesame seeds 210,000, seed cotton 158,000; livestock (number of live animals) 10,740,000 cattle, 6,100,000 ducks, 3,715,000 pigs, 2,391,000 buffalo, 1,732,000 sheep and goats, 39,529,000 chickens; roundwood (1998) 22,430,000 cu m; fish catch (1997) 917,666. Mining and quarrying (1997–98): gypsum 40,642; copper concentrates 14,634; refined lead 1,585; tin concentrates 154; refined silver 9,381 kilograms. Manufacturing (1996): cement 513,000; fresh meat 116,000; fertilizers 66,000; refined sugar 43,000; cheese 29,000; butter 10,100; plywood 24,000 cu m; cigarettes 1,727,000,000 units; clay bricks 60,900,000 units. Construction (units; 1987–88)[2]: residential 1,193; nonresidential 1,483. Energy production (consumption): electricity (kW-hr; 1996) 4,256,000,000 (4,256,000,000); coal (metric tons; 1996) 72,000 (78,000); crude petroleum (barrels; 1996) 2,800,000 (5,300,000); petroleum products (metric tons; 1996) 679,000 (1,227,000); natural gas (cu m; 1996) 1,576,000,000 (1,576,000,000).
Household income and expenditure. Average household size (1994) 5.6; average annual income per household: n.a.; sources of income: n.a.; expenditure (1994)[3]: food and beverages 67.1%, fuel and lighting 6.6%, transportation 4.0%, charitable contributions 3.1%, medical care 3.1%.
Gross national product (1996): U.S.$119,334,000,000 (U.S.$2,610 per capita).

Structure of gross domestic product and labour force

	1997–98 in value K '000,000	% of total value	labour force[4]	% of labour force[4]
Agriculture	659,596	59.5	12,093,000	65.9
Mining	5,547	0.5	121,000	0.7
Manufacturing	78,801	7.1	1,666,000	9.1
Construction	26,494	2.4	400,000	2.2
Public utilities	1,558	0.1	26,000	0.1
Transp. and commun.	43,727	3.9	495,000	2.7
Trade	257,613	23.2	1,781,000	9.7
Finance	3,014	0.3	1,485,000	8.1
Public admin., services	13,293	1.2		
Other	19,911	1.8	270,000	1.5
TOTAL	1,109,554	100.0	18,337,000	100.0

Population economically active (1997–98): total 19,743,000; activity rate of total population 42.5% (participation rates: ages 15–64 [1983] 64.2%; female [1987–88] 35.3%; unemployed 6.2%).

Price and earnings indexes (1995 = 100)

	1993	1994	1995	1996	1997	1998	1999
Consumer price index	64.4	79.9	100.0	116.3	150.8	228.5	270.5
Monthly earning index	...	...	...	...	...	...	...

Land use (1994): forested 49.3%; meadows and pastures 0.5%; agricultural and under permanent cultivation 15.3%; other 34.9%.

Foreign trade[5]

Balance of trade (current prices)

	1994	1995	1996	1997	1998	1999
K '000,000	–509.2	–2,738.4	–3,612.5	–7,320.1	–10,183.5	–7,390.4
% of total	5.1%	22.1%	29.0%	40.3%	43.0%	34.3%

Imports (1997–98): K 12,735,900,000 (machinery and transport equipment 28.6%, intermediate raw materials 19.9%, basic manufactures 15.8%, capital construction materials 12.3%, consumer durable goods 4.3%). *Major import sources:* Singapore 31.1%; Japan 15.3%; Thailand 9.8%; China 9.4%; Malaysia 7.0%; South Korea 5.5%; Indonesia 4.8%.
Exports (1997–98): K 5,415,800,000 (pulses and beans 22.3%, teak 11.1%, fish and fish products 4.6%, hardwood 2.5%, rubber 2.1%). *Major export destinations:* India 22.6%; Singapore 13.2%; Thailand 11.9%; China 10.6%; Hong Kong 5.8%; Japan 3.8%; United States 3.5%.

Transport and communications

Transport. Railroads (1998): route length (1999–2000) 3,955 km; passenger-km 3,948,000,000; metric ton-km cargo 984,000,000. Roads (1996): total length 28,200 km (paved 12%). Vehicles (1996): passenger cars 27,000; trucks and buses 42,000. Air transport (1995–96): passenger-km 438,000,000; metric ton-km cargo 3,212,000; airports (1996) 19.

Communications

Medium	date	unit	number	units per 1,000 persons
Daily newspapers	1996	circulation	449,000	10
Radio	1997	receivers	4,200,000	96
Television	1997	receivers	260,000	5.9
Telephones	1998	main lines	229,320	5.2
Cellular telephones	1998	subscribers	8,516	0.2
Personal computers	...	units	...	...
Internet	...	users	...	...

Education and health

Educational attainment (1983). Percentage of population age 25 and over having: no formal schooling 55.8%; primary education 39.4%; secondary 4.6%; religious 0.1%; postsecondary 0.1%. *Literacy* (1995): total population age 15 and over literate 83.1%; males literate 88.7%; females literate 77.7%.

Education (1997–98)

	schools	teachers	students	student/ teacher ratio
Primary (age 5–9)	35,877	167,134	5,145,400	30.8
Secondary (age 10–15)	2,091	56,955	1,545,600	27.1
Voc., teacher tr.[6]	103	2,462	25,374	10.3
Higher	923	17,089	385,300	22.5

Health (1995–96): physicians 12,950 (1 per 3,114 persons); hospital beds 28,732 (1 per 1,404 persons); infant mortality rate per 1,000 live births (1997) 71.
Food (1998): daily per capita caloric intake 2,832 (vegetable products 96%, animal products 4%); 131% of FAO recommended minimum requirement.

Military

Total active duty personnel (1999): 429,000 (army 95.6%, navy 2.3%, air force 2.1%). *Military expenditure as percentage of GNP* (1996): 7.6% (world 2.6%); per capita expenditure U.S.$87.

[1]Pegged rate to the Special Drawing Right of the International Monetary Fund. [2]Construction Corporation activity only. [3]Yangôn only. [4]Employed only. [5]Import figures are c.i.f. in balance of trade and in commodities and trading partners. [6]1994–95.

Internet resources for further information:
- **Myanmar Home Page http://www.myanmar.com/e-index.html**

Namibia

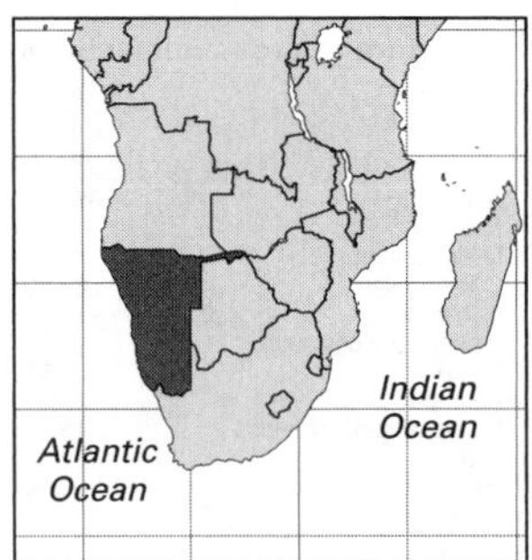

Official name: Republic of Namibia.
Form of government: republic with two legislative houses (National Council[1] [26]; National Assembly [72[2]]).
Head of state and government: President.
Capital: Windhoek.
Official language: English.
Official religion: none.
Monetary unit: 1 Namibian dollar (N$) = 100 cents; valuation (Oct. 6, 2000) 1 U.S.$ = N$7.29; 1 £ = N$10.54.

Area and population[3]

Regions	Chief towns	area sq mi	area sq km	population 1992 estimate
Erongo[3]	Omaruru	24,602	63,719	98,500
Hardap	Mariental	42,428	109,888	80,000
Karas	Keetmanshoop	62,288	161,324	73,000
Khomas	Windhoek	14,210	36,804	161,000
Kunene	Opuwo	55,697	144,254	58,500
Liambezi	Katima Mulilo	7,541	19,532	92,000
Ohangwena	Oshikango	4,086	10,582	178,000
Okavango	Rundu	16,763	43,417	136,000
Omaheke	Gobabis	32,715	84,731	55,600
Omusati	Ongandjera	5,265	13,637	158,000
Oshana	Oshakati	2,042	5,290	159,000
Oshikoto	Tsumeb	10,273	26,607	176,000
Otjozondjupa	Grootfontein	40,667	105,327	85,000
Other		2	6	1,000
TOTAL		318,580[4]	825,118	1,511,600

Demography

Population (2000): 1,771,000.
Density (2000): persons per sq mi 5.6, persons per sq km 2.1.
Urban-rural (1999): urban 39.8%; rural 60.2%.
Sex distribution (1999): male 49.85%; female 50.15%.
Age breakdown (1999): under 15, 43.2%; 15–29, 28.6%, 30–44, 15.1%; 45–59, 7.7%; 60–74, 4.0%; 75 and over, 1.4%.
Population projection: (2010) 1,908,000; (2020) 1,956,000.
Doubling time: 40 years.
Ethnic composition (1991): Ovambo 50.7%; Nama 12.5%; Kavango 9.7%; Herero 8.0%; San (Bushman) 1.9%; Tswana 0.4%; other 16.8%.
Religious affiliation (1995): Protestant (mostly Lutheran) 57.0%; Roman Catholic 16.6%; African Christian 7.0%; other 19.4%.
Major cities (1990): Windhoek 125,000; Swakopmund 15,500; Rundu 15,000; Rehoboth 15,000; Keetmanshoop 14,000.

Vital statistics

Birth rate per 1,000 population (1999): 35.7 (world avg. 22.1).
Death rate per 1,000 population (1999): 18.3 (world avg. 8.9).
Natural increase rate per 1,000 population (1999): 17.4 (world avg. 13.2).
Total fertility rate (avg. births per childbearing woman; 1999): 4.9.
Life expectancy at birth (1999): male 45.8 years; female 42.5 years.
Major causes of death per 100,000 population: n.a.; however, in the early 1990s, tuberculosis had become a serious problem (especially in the southern regions); AIDS cases, while few, were increasing exponentially.

National economy

Budget (1999–2000). Revenue: N$7,128,400,000 (customs taxes 31.4%, general sales tax 28.2%, individual income taxes 17.9%, nontax revenues 8.9%, mining taxes 3.1%). Expenditures: N$8,009,400,000 (1996–97; education 23.2%, health and welfare 10.3%, transportation 6.1%, defense 5.8%, social security 5.4%).
Tourism (1998): receipts from visitors U.S.$288,000,000; expenditures by nationals abroad U.S.$88,000,000.
Public debt (1997): U.S.$697,000,000.
Production (metric tons except as noted). Agriculture, forestry, fishing (1999): roots and tubers 260,000, cereals 71,100,000 (of which millet 46,300, corn [maize] 18,300, sorghum 3,300, wheat 3,000), fruits 10,000, vegetables and melons 10,000, pulses 8,000; livestock (number of live animals) 2,100,000 sheep, 2,000,000 cattle, 1,700,000 goats; fish catch (1998) 352,188. Mining and quarrying (1998): diamonds 1,440,000 carats (mostly gem quality); zinc 78,617; copper 8,014; uranium 3,257; silver 740,000 troy oz; gold 60,500 troy oz. Manufacturing: n.a.; products include cut gems (primarily diamonds), fur products (karakul), processed foods (fish, meats, and dairy products), textiles, carved wood products, refined metals (copper and lead). Construction (value of buildings completed in N$'000,000; 1994): residential 347.7; nonresidential 160.4. Energy production (consumption): electricity (kW-hr; 1992) 1,714,000,000 (1,714,000,000); coal, none (n.a.); crude petroleum, none (n.a.).
Population economically active: total (1991) 493,580; activity rate of total population, 34.9% (participation rates: ages 15–64, 61.3%; female 43.5%; unemployed 20.1%).

Price and earnings indexes (1995 = 100)

	1994	1995	1996	1997	1998	1999
Consumer price index	90.9	100.0	108.0	117.5	124.8	135.5
Earnings index	…	…	…	…	…	…

Household income and expenditure. Average household size (1991) 5.2; average annual income per household (1980) R 3,223 (U.S.$4,143); sources of income (1992): wages and salaries 69.0%, income from property 25.6%, transfer payments 5.4%; expenditure: n.a.
Gross national product (1998): U.S.$3,217,000,000 (U.S.$1,940 per capita).

Structure of gross domestic product and labour force

	1998 in value N$'000,000	1998 % of total value	1991 labour force[5]	1991 % of labour force
Agriculture	1,804	10.7	189,929	38.5
Mining	1,876	11.2	14,686	3.0
Manufacturing	2,414	14.3	22,884	4.6
Construction	323	1.9	18,638	3.8
Public utilities	353	2.1	2,974	0.6
Transp. and commun.	613	3.6	9,322	1.9
Trade[6]	1,476	8.8	37,820	7.7
Finance	1,480	8.8	8,547	1.7
Services	507	3.0	89,541	18.1
Public administration and defense	3,999	23.8		
Other[7]	1,981	11.8	99,239[8]	20.1[8]
TOTAL	16,826	100.0	493,580	100.0

Land use (1994): forested 15.2%; meadows and pastures 46.2%; agricultural and under permanent cultivation 0.8%; other 37.8%.

Foreign trade

Balance of trade (current prices)

	1991	1992	1993	1994	1995	1996
U.S.$'000,000	+102	+79	+122	+165	–98	–25
% of total	4.3%	3.0%	5.0%	6.6%	3.5%	0.9%

Imports (1994): N$4,467,700,000 (machinery and transport equipment 27.1%, of which transport equipment 16.2%; food and live animals 22.3%; minerals and fuels 11.4%; chemical products 8.1%). *Major import sources* (1993): South Africa 87.0%[9]; Germany 3.0%; France 2.0%; Japan 2.0%.
Exports (1994): N$4,692,000,000 (minerals 50.1%, of which diamonds 31.4%; food and live animals 47.0%, of which fish and fish products 28.6%, cattle and meat products 12.6%; karakul pelts 0.2%). *Major export destinations* (1993): U.K. 34.0%; South Africa 27.0%; Japan 10.0%; Spain 6.0%.

Transport and communications

Transport. Railroads: length (1995) 1,480 mi, 2,382 km; passenger-km 34,700,000; metric ton-km 1,077,000,000. Roads (1996): total length 25,130 mi, 65,220 km (paved 7.7%). Vehicles (1996): passenger cars 74,875; trucks and buses 66,500[10]. Merchant marine (1992): vessels (100 gross tons and over) 30; total deadweight tonnage 5,874. Air transport (1996)[11]: passenger-km 756,000,000; metric ton-km cargo 23,000,000; airports (1997) with scheduled flights 11.

Communications

Medium	date	unit	number	units per 1,000 persons
Daily newspapers	1996	circulation	30,000	19
Radio	1997	receivers	232,000	143
Television	1998	receivers	63,000	38
Telephones	1998	main lines	114,000	69
Cellular telephones	1998	subscribers	20,000	12
Personal computers	1998	units	40,000	24
Internet	1998	users	5,000	6.0

Education and health

Educational attainment (1991). Percentage of population age 25 and over having: no formal schooling 35.1%; primary education 31.9%; secondary 28.5%; higher 4.5%. *Literacy* (2000): total population age 15 and over literate 830,200 (82.1%); males literate 416,000 (82.9%); females literate 414,200 (81.2%).

Education (1994)

	schools	teachers	students	student/ teacher ratio
Primary (age 6–12)	933	10,912[12]	366,666	32.0[12]
Secondary (age 13–19)	114	2,534[13]	101,838	29.3[13]
Voc., teacher tr.	17	140[14]	1,503	11.9[14]
Higher	7	213[15]	6,523	11.8[15]

Health: physicians (1992) 324 (1 per 4,594 persons); hospital beds (1989) 6,997 (1 per 216 persons); infant mortality rate per 1,000 live births (1999) 69.6.
Food (1998): daily per capita caloric intake 2,096 (vegetable products 90%, animal products 10%); 92% of FAO recommended minimum requirement.

Military

Total active duty personnel (1999): 9,000 (army 98.9%, navy 1.1%[16]). *Military expenditure as percentage of GNP* (1997): 2.7% (world 2.6%); per capita expenditure U.S.$57.

[1]Mostly an advisory body. [2]72 elected and up to 6 appointed members. [3]Includes the 434 sq mi (1,124 sq km) district of Walvis Bay (1992 population estimate, 23,000) that was jointly administered with South Africa from November 1992 to March 1994. [4]Detail does not add to total given because of rounding. [5]Includes more than 140,000 nonwage (informal) workers. [6]Includes hotels. [7]Includes import duties and excise taxes. [8]Unemployed. [9]Includes goods from other countries shipped via South Africa. [10]1995. [11]Namib Air only. [12]1992. [13]1990. [14]1989. [15]1991. [16]Coast Guard for fishery protection.

Internet resources for further information:
- **Namibia Fact Sheet http://www.emulateme.com/namibia.htm**

Nauru

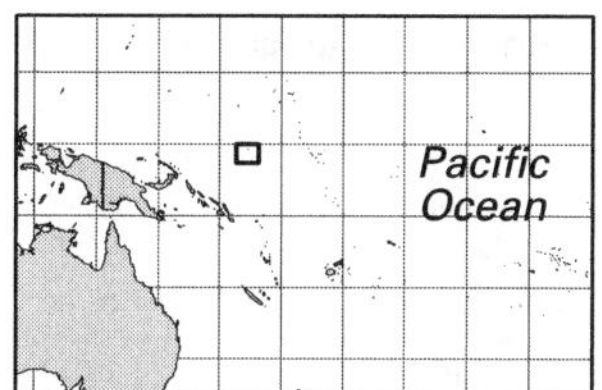

Official name: Naoero (Republic of Nauru).
Form of government: republic with one legislative house (Parliament [18]).
Head of state and government: President.
Capital: [1].
Official language: none.
Official religion: none.
Monetary unit: 1 Australian dollar ($A) = 100 cents; valuation (Oct. 6, 2000) 1 U.S.$ = $A 1.87; 1 £ = $A 2.70.

Area and population

Districts	area sq mi	area sq km	population 1992 census[2]
Aiwo	0.4	1.1	1,072
Anabar	0.6	1.5	320
Anetan	0.4	1.0	427
Anibare	1.2	3.1	165
Baitsi	0.5	1.2	450
Boe	0.2	0.5	750
Buada	1.0	2.6	661
Denigomodu	0.3	0.9	2,548
Ewa	0.5	1.2	355
Ijuw	0.4	1.1	206
Meneng	1.2	3.1	1,269
Nibok	0.6	1.6	577
Uaboe	0.3	0.8	447
Yaren	0.6	1.5	672
TOTAL	8.2	21.2	9,919

Demography

Population (2000): 11,800.
Density (2000): persons per sq mi 1,439, persons per sq km 557.
Urban-rural (1999): urban 100%; rural 0%.
Sex distribution (1999): male 50.50%; female 49.50%.
Age breakdown (1999): under 15, 41.6%; 15–29, 25.5%; 30–44, 19.7%; 45–59, 10.0%; 60–74, 2.9%; 75 and over 0.3%.
Population projection: (2000) 14,300; (2010) 16,700.
Doubling time: 33 years.
Ethnic composition (1992): Nauruan 68.9%; other Pacific Islander 23.7%, of which Kiribati 12.8%, Tuvaluan 8.7%; Asian 5.9%, of which Filipino 2.5%, Chinese 2.3%; other 1.5%.
Religious affiliation (1995): Protestant 53.5%, of which Congregational 35.3%, Pentecostal 4.8%; Roman Catholic 27.5%; other 19.0%.
Major cities: none; population of Yaren district (1996) 700.

Vital statistics

Birth rate per 1,000 population (1999): 28.3 (world avg. 22.1); legitimate, n.a.; illegitimate, n.a.
Death rate per 1,000 population (1999): 7.5 (world avg. 8.9).
Natural increase rate per 1,000 population (1999): 20.8 (world avg. 13.2).
Total fertility rate (avg. births per childbearing woman; 1999): 3.8.
Marriage rate per 1,000 population (1995): 5.3.
Divorce rate per 1,000 population: n.a.
Life expectancy at birth (1999): male 57.0 years; female 64.1 years.
Major causes of death per 100,000 population: n.a.[3]

National economy

Budget (1999). Revenue: $A 38,700,000[4]. Expenditures: $A 37,200,000.
Public debt (external, outstanding; beginning of 1996): *c.* U.S.$150,000,000.
Tourism: receipts from visitors (1999) virtually none; expenditures by nationals abroad, n.a.
Gross national product (at current market prices; 1997): U.S.$128,000,000 (U.S.$11,538 per capita).

Distribution of gross domestic product and labour force

	1995 in value U.S.$'000,000	1995 % of total value	1997 labour force[5, 6, 7]	1997 % of labour force
Agriculture	...	...	...	...
Mining (phosphate)	...	...	528	24.7
Manufacturing	...	...	...	...
Construction	...	...	...	...
Public utilities	...	...	...	...
Transportation and communications	...	...	...	...
Hotels	...	...	137	6.4
Finance	...	...	33	1.6
Services	...	...	...	...
Pub. admin.	...	...	1,238	58.0
Other	...	...	198	9.3
TOTAL	368	100.0	2,134	100.0

Production (metric tons except as noted). Agriculture, forestry, fishing (1999): coconuts 1,600, vegetables 450, tropical fruit (including mangoes) 275; almonds, figs, and pandanus are also cultivated, but most foodstuffs and beverages (including water) are imported; livestock (number of live animals) 3,000 pigs; roundwood, none; fish catch 500. Mining and quarrying (1998): phosphate rock (gross weight) 500,000. Manufacturing: none; virtually all consumer manufactures are imported. Construction: n.a. Energy production (consumption): electricity (kW-hr; 1996) 32,000,000 (32,000,000); coal, none (n.a.); crude petroleum, none (n.a.); petroleum products (metric tons; 1996) none (45,000); natural gas, none (n.a.).
Population economically active (1992): 2,453[6, 8]; activity rate of total population 35.9% (participation rates: over age 15, n.a.; female, n.a.; unemployed, 18.2%).
Price and earnings indexes: [9].
Household income and expenditure. Average household size (1992) 10.0[6]; income per household: n.a.; sources of income: n.a.; expenditure: n.a.
Land use (1995): forested, nil; meadows and pastures, nil; agricultural and under permanent cultivation *c.* 10%[10]; other *c.* 90%[11].

Foreign trade

Balance of trade (current prices)

	1990	1991	1992	1993	1994	1995
U.S.$'000,000	+50	+12	+15	+21	+20	+20
% of total	61.0%	22.2%	27.8%	34.4%	33.3%	33.3%

Imports (1995): U.S.$20,000,000 (agricultural products 20.5%, of which food 14.5%; remainder 79.5%). *Major import sources:* Australia more than 50%; United Kingdom *c.* 10%; New Zealand *c.* 10%.
Exports (1995): U.S.$40,000,000 (phosphate, virtually 100%). *Major export destinations:* New Zealand *c.* 50%; Australia *c.* 25%.

Transport and communications

Transport. Railroads (1997): length 3 mi, 5 km; passenger traffic, n.a.; metric ton-km cargo, n.a. Roads (1996): total length 19 mi, 30 km (paved 79%). Vehicles (1989): passenger cars, trucks, and buses 1,448. Merchant marine (1992): vessels 2, total deadweight tonnage 5,791. Air transport (1996): passenger-mi 151,000,000, passenger-km 243,000,000; short ton-mi cargo 15,000,000, metric ton-km cargo 24,000,000; airports (1999) with scheduled flights 1.

Communications

Medium	date	unit	number	units per 1,000 persons
Daily newspapers	1999	circulation	—	—
Radio	1997	receivers	7,000	609
Television	1997	receivers	500	48
Telephones	1999	main lines	1,700	149
Cellular telephones	1999	subscribers	850	75
Personal computers	1998	units	...	...
Internet	1998	users	...	...

Education and health

Educational attainment (1992).[6] Percentage of population age 5 and over having primary education or less 77.4%; secondary education 12.9%; higher 4.1%; not stated 5.6%. *Literacy* (1995): total population age 15 and over literate 99%.

Education (1997)[6]

	schools	teachers	students	student/ teacher ratio
Primary (age 6–13) / Secondary (age 14–17)	3	64	1,379	21.5
Vocational	3	53	1,113	21.0
Higher	—	—	—	—

Health: physicians (1995) 17 (1 per 637 persons); hospital beds (1990) 207 (1 per 46 persons); infant mortality rate per 1,000 live births (1999) 11.1.
Food (1998)[12]: daily per capita caloric intake 3,011 (vegetable products 70%, animal products 30%); 128% of FAO recommended minimum requirement.

Military

Total active duty personnel (1999): Nauru does not have any military establishment. The defense is assured by Australia, but no formal agreement exists.

[1]Government offices are located in Yaren district. [2]Preliminary. [3]Morbidity is often associated with dietary and social problems (particularly obesity and alcoholism). In 1989, 32% of adult Nauruans were diagnosed with diabetes mellitus. [4]Largely from phosphate exports. [5]Employed only. [6]Nauruan only. [7]Most non-Nauruans are phosphate industry contract workers. [8]Excludes activity not stated. [9]Minimum wage remained constant between November 1992 and the end of 1997. [10]Cultivatable coastal strip. [11]Phosphate-extracted interior wasteland. [12]Data for Oceania.

Nepal

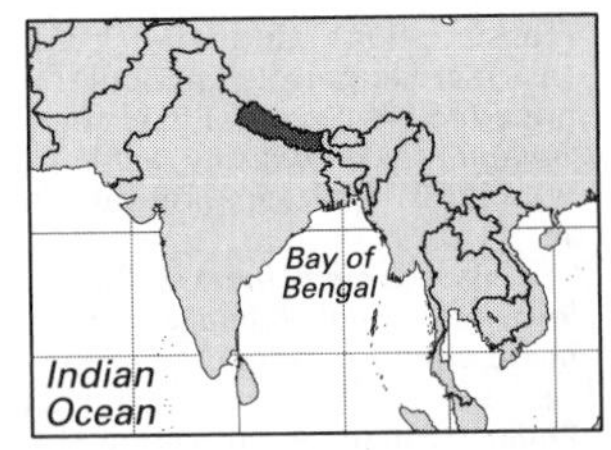

Official name: Nepāl Adhirājya (Kingdom of Nepal).
Form of government: constitutional monarchy with a bicameral parliament consisting of two legislative houses (National Council [60[1]]; House of Representatives [205]).
Chief of state: King.
Head of government: Prime Minister.
Capital: Kāthmāndu.
Official language: Nepālī.
Official religion: Hinduism.
Monetary unit: 1 Nepalese rupee (NRs) = 100 paisa (pice); valuation (Oct. 6, 2000) 1 U.S.$ = NRs 73.65; 1 £ = NRs 106.54.

Area and population		area		population
				1991
Development regions		sq mi	sq km	census
Zones	**Capitals**			
Eastern	Dhankūtā	10,987	28,456	4,446,749
Koshī	Dharān	3,733	9,669	1,728,247
Mechī	Ilam	3,165	8,196	1,118,210
Sāgarmāthā	Rājbiraj	4,089	10,591	1,600,292
Central	Kāthmāndu	10,583	27,410	6,183,955
Bāgmatī	Bhaktapur	3,640	9,428	2,250,805
Janakpur	Sindhulimādī	3,733	9,669	2,061,816
Nārāyanī	Hetaudā	3,210	8,313	1,871,334
Western	Pokharā	11,351	29,398	3,770,678
Dhawalāgiri	Bagluri	3,146	8,148	490,877
Gandakī	Chāme	4,740	12,275	1,266,128
Lumbinī	Butawal	3,465	8,975	2,013,673
Mid-western	Surkhet	16,362	42,378	2,410,414
Bherī	Nepālganj	4,071	10,545	1,103,043
Karnālī	Mānma	8,244	21,351	260,529
Rāptī	Tulsipur	4,047	10,482	1,046,842
Far-western	Dipāyal	7,544	19,539	1,679,301
Mahākālī	Dadeldhurā	2,698	6,989	664,952
Setī	Silgadhī	4,846	12,550	1,014,349
TOTAL		56,827	147,181	18,491,097

Demography

Population (2000): 24,702,000.
Density (2000): persons per sq mi 434.7, persons per sq km 167.8.
Urban-rural (1999): urban 11.0%; rural 89.0%.
Sex distribution (1997): male 50.20%; female 49.80%.
Age breakdown (1996): under 15, 43.1%; 15–29, 26.0%; 30–44, 16.0%; 45–59, 9.4%; 60–74, 4.6%; 75 and over, 0.9%.
Population projection: (2010) 30,758,000; (2020) 36,925,000.
Doubling time: 29 years.
Ethnic composition (1991): Nepalese 53.2%; Bihārī (including Maithilī and Bhojpurī) 18.4%; Tharu 4.8%; Tamang 4.7%; Newār 3.4%; Magar 2.2%; Abadhi 1.7%; other 11.6%.
Religious affiliation (1991): Hindu 86.5%; Buddhist 7.8%; Muslim 3.5%; Christian 0.2%; other 2.0%.
Major cities (1993 est.): Kāthmāndu 535,000; Lalitpur 190,000; Birātnagar 132,000; Bhaktapur 130,000.

Vital statistics

Birth rate per 1,000 population (1999): 33.8 (world avg. 22.1).
Death rate per 1,000 population (1999): 10.1 (world avg. 8.9).
Natural increase rate per 1,000 population (1999): 23.7 (world avg. 13.2).
Total fertility rate (avg. births per childbearing woman; 1999): 4.4.
Life expectancy at birth (1999): male 58.0 years; female 58.0 years.
Major causes of death per 100,000 population: n.a.; however, the leading causes of mortality are infectious and parasitic diseases, diseases of the respiratory system, and diseases of the nervous system.

National economy

Budget (1999). Revenue: NRs 40,698,000,000 (taxes on goods and services 29.2%, taxes on international trade 23.9%, foreign grants 14.5%, income taxes 14.2%, state property revenues 8.4%, administrative fees 5.5%). Expenditures: NRs 58,391,000,000 (education 13.6%, transport and communications 11.4%, fuel and energy 9.0%, health 6.5%, agriculture 5.5%, housing 4.7%, defense 4.5%, public order 4.3%, general public services 3.7%).
Public debt (external, outstanding; 1998): U.S.$2,591,000,000.
Land use (1994): forested 42.0%; meadows and pastures 14.6%; agricultural and under permanent cultivation 17.2%; other 26.2%.
Tourism (1998): receipts from visitors U.S.$153,000,000; expenditures by nationals abroad U.S.$78,000,000.
Production (metric tons except as noted). Agriculture, forestry, fishing (1999): rice 3,710,000, sugarcane 1,972,000, corn (maize) 1,346,000, potatoes 1,091,000, wheat 1,086,000, millet 291,000, pulses 213,000; livestock (number of live animals) 7,030,698 cattle, 6,204,616 goats, 3,470,600 buffalo, 855,159 sheep, 825,132 pigs; roundwood (1998) 21,474,000 cu m; fish catch (1997) 23,206. Mining and quarrying (1997): limestone 369,000; salt 7,000; talc 6,800. Manufacturing (value added in U.S.$'000,000; 1995): textiles 78; food products 74; wearing apparel 54; tobacco products 41; nonmetal mineral products 35. Construction: n.a. Energy production (consumption): electricity (kW-hr; 1996) 1,218,000,000 (1,243,000,000); coal (metric tons; 1996) none (50,000); petroleum products (metric tons; 1996) none (427,000).
Gross national product (1998): U.S.$4,889,000,000 (U.S.$210 per capita).

Structure of gross domestic product and labour force	1998–99		1991	
	in value NRs '000,000[2]	% of total value[2]	labour force	% of labour force
Agriculture	129,600	37.6	5,961,788	81.2
Mining	1,800	0.5	2,367	—
Manufacturing	31,800	9.2	150,051	2.0
Construction	33,500	9.7	35,658	0.5
Public utilities	5,300	1.5	11,734	0.2
Transp. and commun.	26,800	7.8	50,808	0.7
Trade	38,700	11.2	256,012	3.5
Finance	35,100	10.2	20,847	0.3
Services	29,900	8.7	752,019	10.3
Other	12,400[3]	3.6[3]	98,302	1.3
TOTAL	344,900	100.0	7,339,586	100.0

Population economically active (1991): total 7,339,586; activity rate of total population 39.7% (participation rates: ages 10 years and over, 57.0%; female 45.5%; unemployed [1996] 4.9%).

Price and earnings indexes (1995 = 100)	1993	1994	1995	1996	1997	1998	1999
Consumer price index	85.8	92.9	100.0	109.2	113.6	125.0	135.1
Monthly earnings index[4]	...	...	100.0	100.0	100.0	110.1	...

Household income and expenditure (1984–85). Average household size (1991) 5.6; income per household NRs 14,796 (U.S.$853); sources of income: self-employment 63.4%, wages and salaries 25.1%, rent 7.5%, other 4.0%; expenditure: food and beverages 61.2%, housing 17.3%, clothing 11.7%, health care 3.7%, education and recreation 2.9%, transportation and communications 1.2%, other 2.0%.

Foreign trade[5]

Balance of trade (current prices)	1994	1995	1996	1997	1998	1999
U.S.$'000,000	–790.2	–960.9	–1,106.0	–1,278.1	–757.1	–880.7
% of total	51.7%	57.9%	58.7%	60.7%	44.0%	38.3%

Imports (1996–97): NRs 96,006,000,000 (basic manufactured goods 47.6%; machinery and transport equipment 14.7%; chemicals 8.8%; mineral fuels and lubricants 7.5%; food and live animals, chiefly for food 6.6%; crude materials except fuels 5.5%). *Major import sources:* India 23.3%; Hong Kong 14.3%; Singapore 13.0%; Japan 11.2%; China 6.4%; New Zealand 5.1%.
Exports (1996–97): NRs 22,481,000,000 (basic manufactures 48.7%; miscellaneous manufactures 29.2%; food and live animals, chiefly for food 12.6%; chemicals and drugs 5.9%; crude materials except fuels 2.6%). *Major export destinations:* U.S. 34.4%; India 9.5%; Bangladesh 1.4%; China 0.9%.

Transport and communications

Transport. Railroads (1995–96): route length (1999) 59 km; passengers carried 1,379,000; freight handled 5,320 metric tons. Roads (1997): total length 7,700 km (paved 42%). Vehicles (1997–98): passenger cars 47,541; trucks and buses 29,371. Air transport (1995): passenger-km 856,000,000; metric ton-km cargo 93,000,000; airports (1996) with scheduled flights 24.

Communications				units
Medium	date	unit	number	per 1,000 persons
Daily newspapers	1996	circulation	250,000	11
Radio	1997	receivers	840,000	38
Television	1997	receivers	130,000	5.8
Telephones	1998	main lines	202,363	8.9
Personal computers	1998	units	50,000	2.2
Internet	1998	users	15,000	0.7

Education and health

Educational attainment (1981). Percentage of population age 25 and over having: no formal schooling 41.2%; primary education 29.4%; secondary 22.7%; higher 6.8%. *Literacy* (1995): total population age 15 and over literate 27.5%; males literate 40.9%; females literate 14.0%.

Education (1996)	schools	teachers	students	student/ teacher ratio
Primary (age 6–10)	22,218	89,378	3,447,607	38.6
Secondary (age 11–15) } Vocational }	7,582[6]	36,127	1,121,335	31.0
Higher	3[7]	4,925[8]	105,694	22.4[8]

Health (1996): physicians 872 (1 per 25,745 persons); hospital beds 3,604 (1 per 6,229 persons); infant mortality rate per 1,000 live births (1999) 79.
Food (1998): daily per capita caloric intake 2,170 (vegetable products 93%, animal products 7%); 99% of FAO recommended minimum requirement.

Military

Total active duty personnel (1999): 46,000 (army 99.5%, air force 0.5%). *Military expenditure as percentage of GNP* (1997): 0.8% (world 2.6%); per capita expenditure U.S.$2.

[1]Includes 10 members nominated by the king. [2]Estimate. [3]Includes indirect taxes. [4]Minimum monthly wage rates for unskilled industrial workers in Kāthmāndu, Birgunj, and Biratnagar; 1994–95 = 100. [5]Import figures are f.o.b. in balance of trade and c.i.f. for commodities and trading partners. [6]1995. [7]1993. [8]1991.

Internet resources for further information:
- **Nepal Home Page http://www.info-nepal.com**

Netherlands, The

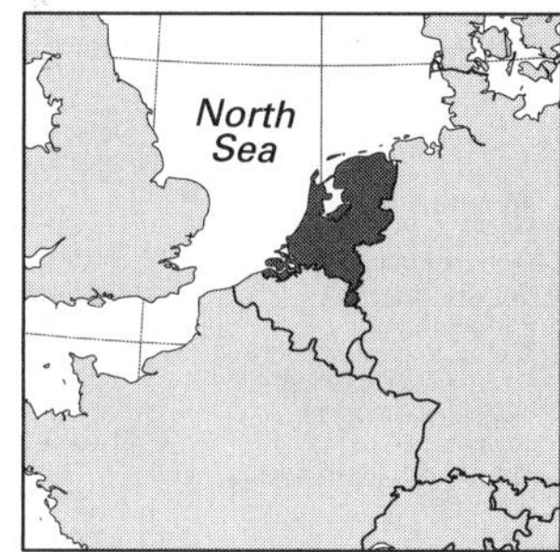

Official name: Koninkrijk der Nederlanden (Kingdom of The Netherlands).
Form of government: constitutional monarchy with a parliament (States General) comprising two legislative houses (First Chamber [75]; Second Chamber [150]).
Chief of state: Monarch.
Head of government: Prime Minister.
Seat of government: The Hague.
Capital: Amsterdam.
Official language: Dutch.
Official religion: none.
Monetary unit: 1 Netherlands guilder (f.) = 100 cents; valuation (Oct. 6, 2000) 1 U.S.$ = f. 2.53; 1 £ = f. 3.66.

Area and population

Provinces	Capitals	area sq mi	area sq km	population 1999[1] estimate
Drenthe	Assen	1,024	2,652	467,100
Flevoland	Lelystad	551	1,426	306,500
Friesland	Leeuwarden	1,298	3,361	621,200
Gelderland	Arnhem	1,929	4,995	1,906,800
Groningen	Groningen	905	2,344	560,000
Limburg	Maastricht	837	2,167	1,139,300
Noord-Brabant	's-Hertogenbosch	1,907	4,938	2,337,700
Noord-Holland	Haarlem	1,027	2,660	2,503,200
Overijssel	Zwolle	1,288	3,337	1,070,400
Utrecht	Utrecht	524	1,356	1,098,700
Zeeland	Middelburg	692	1,792	370,600
Zuid-Holland	The Hague	1,104	2,860	3,378,800
TOTAL LAND AREA		13,085[2]	33,889[2]	
INLAND WATER		2,949	7,637	
TOTAL		16,033[2]	41,526[2]	15,760,200[2]

Demography

Population (2000): 15,896,000.
Density (2000)[3]: persons per sq mi 991.5, persons per sq km 382.8.
Urban-rural (1997[1]): urban 91.9%; rural 8.1%.
Sex distribution (1999[1]): male 49.45%; female 50.55%.
Age breakdown (1999[1]): under 15, 18.5%; 15–29, 19.8%; 30–44, 24.1%; 45–59, 19.5%; 60–74, 12.1%; 75 and over, 6.0%.
Population projection: (2010) 16,638,000; (2020) 17,089,000.
Doubling time: not applicable; vital rates and net migration in near balance.
Ethnic composition (by place of origin [including 2nd generation]; 1999[1]): Netherlander 88.0%; Turkish 1.8%; Surinamese 1.7%; Moroccan 1.5%; Indonesian 1.4%; Netherlands Antillean/Aruban 0.5%; other 5.1%.
Religious affiliation (1997[1]): Roman Catholic 32.0%; Dutch Reformed Church 15.0%; Calvinist 8.0%; Muslim 4.3%; Hindu 0.5%; other 2.2%; no religion 38.0%.
Major urban agglomerations (1999[1]): Amsterdam 1,121,303; Rotterdam 1,089,979; The Hague 701,211; Utrecht 559,054; Eindhoven 412,707.

Vital statistics

Birth rate per 1,000 population (1999): 12.7 (world avg. 22.1); (1996) legitimate 82.9%; illegitimate 17.1%.
Death rate per 1,000 population (1999): 8.9 (world avg. 8.9).
Natural increase rate per 1,000 population (1999): 3.8 (world avg. 13.2).
Total fertility rate (avg. births per childbearing woman; 1999): 1.6.
Marriage rate per 1,000 population (1999): 5.5.
Life expectancy at birth (1998): male 75.2 years; female 80.7 years.
Major causes of death per 100,000 population (1996): malignant neoplasms (cancers) 243.4, of which lung cancer 55.7; ischemic heart diseases 135.7; pneumonia 38.0; accidents, poisoning, and violence 33.4.

National economy

Budget (1997). Revenue: f. 324,360,000,000 (social security taxes 41.1%; income and corporate taxes 24.8%; value-added and excise taxes 22.7%; property taxes 3.0%). Expenditures: f. 337,620,000,000 (social security and welfare 37.4%; health 14.8%; education 10.0%; interest payments 9.1%; defense 3.9%; transportation 3.5%).
Public debt (1998): U.S.$217,464,000,000.
Tourism (1998): receipts U.S.$6,788,000,000; expenditures U.S.$10,975,000,000.
Production (metric tons except as noted). Agriculture, forestry, fishing (1999): potatoes 7,704,000, sugar beets 5,800,000, wheat 1,000,000, onions 650,000, tomatoes 510,000, cucumbers 485,000, apples 470,000, barley 240,000; livestock (number of live animals; 1999) 13,418,000 pigs, 4,184,000 cattle, 1,465,000 sheep; roundwood (1998) 884,000 cu m; fish catch (1996) 521,377. Manufacturing (value added in f. '000,000; 1995): chemicals 17,075; foodstuffs 15,446; machinery and transport equipment 10,495; electrical machinery 9,081; publishing 7,489. Construction (buildings completed by value in f. '000,000; 1996): residential 14,232; nonresidential 10,699. Energy production (consumption): electricity (kW-hr; 1995) 80,832,000,000 (92,225,000,000); coal (metric tons; 1995) none (14,660,000); crude petroleum (barrels; 1995) 18,647,000 (410,846,000); petroleum products (metric tons; 1995) 61,479,000 (30,305,000); natural gas (cu m; 1995) 88,861,000,000 (50,057,000,000).
Household income and expenditure (1994). Average household size (1999) 2.3; income per household f. 59,739 (U.S.$32,824); sources of income: wages 81.6%, profits 12.8%, property income 5.6%; expenditure: rent 26.2%; food, beverages, and tobacco 18.0%; education and recreation 16.2%; transportation and communications 13.4%; clothing and footwear 7.1%; household furnishings and appliances 6.6%; health care 5.7%; other 6.8%.
Gross national product (1998): U.S.$389,055,000,000 (U.S.$24,780 per capita).

Structure of gross domestic product and labour force

	1996 in value f. '000,000	1996 % of total value	1997 labour force	1997 % of labour force
Agriculture	19,866	3.0	259,000	3.4
Mining	17,754	2.7	13,000	0.2
Manufacturing	103,708	15.5	1,103,000	14.5
Construction	33,444	5.0	448,000	5.9
Public utilities	11,166	1.7	42,000	0.6
Transp. and commun.	48,972	7.3	423,000	5.6
Trade	93,245	14.0	1,462,000	19.2
Finance	4	4	1,014,000	13.3
Pub. admin., defense	4	4	529,000	6.9
Services	293,778[4]	44.0[4]	1,740,000	22.8
Other	45,707[5]	6.8[5]	583,000[6]	7.7[6]
TOTAL	667,640	100.0	7,616,000	100.0[2]

Population economically active (1997): total 7,616,000; activity rate of total population 48.9% (participation rates: ages 15–64, 72.1%; female 42.4%; unemployed 5.5%).

Price and earnings indexes (1995 = 100)

	1993	1994	1995	1996	1997	1998	1999
Consumer price index	95.4	98.1	100.0	102.1	104.3	106.3	108.6
Hourly earnings index	97.1	98.9	100.0	101.7	104.7	108.0	...

Land use (1994): forested 10.3%; meadows and pastures 31.0%; agricultural and under permanent cultivation 28.0%; other 30.7%.

Foreign trade

Balance of trade (current prices)

	1993	1994	1995	1996	1997	1998	1999
f. '000,000	+26,706	+25,767	+31,155	+28,361	+32,732	+28,696	+26,292
% of total	5.5%	4.8%	5.2%	4.4%	4.5%	3.8%	3.3%

Imports (1996): f. 304,559,000,000 (machinery and transport equipment 34.4%, chemicals and chemical products 11.5%, food 10.3%). *Major import sources:* Germany 20.4%; Belgium-Luxembourg 10.3%; U.K. 8.9%; U.S. 8.4%; France 6.8%.
Exports (1996): f. 332,920,000,000 (machinery and transport equipment 28.5%, food 15.3%, chemicals and chemical products 15.2%, petroleum, petroleum products, and gas 8.3%). *Major export destinations:* Germany 25.9%; Belgium-Luxembourg 12.0%; France 9.9%; U.K. 8.4%.

Transport and communications

Transport. Railroads (1996): length 2,795 km; passenger-km 14,091,000,000; metric ton-km cargo 3,123,000,000. Roads (1996): total length 124,530 km (paved 91%). Vehicles (1996): passenger cars 5,740,000; trucks and buses 681,000. Merchant marine (1993): vessels (100 gross tons and over) 399; total deadweight tonnage 2,874,000. Air transport (1998): passenger-km 57,279,000,000; metric ton-km cargo 3,862,752,000; airports (1996) 6.

Communications

Medium	date	unit	number	units per 1,000 persons
Daily newspapers	1996	circulation	4,753,000	306
Radio	1998	receivers	12,000,000	764
Television	1997	receivers	8,500,000	545
Telephones	1998	main lines	9,337,000	595
Cellular telephones	1998	subscribers	3,351,000	213
Personal computers	1998	units	5,000,000	318
Internet	1998	users	1,600,000	102

Education and health

Educational attainment (1995). Percentage of population ages 15–64 having: primary education 14.9%; secondary 65.7%; higher 19.4%. *Literacy:* virtually 100% literate.

Education (1995–96)

	schools	teachers[7]	students	student/ teacher ratio[7]
Primary (age 6–12)	7,411	99,031	1,477,000	15.7
Secondary (age 12–18)	1,124	89,370	868,000	7.7
Voc., teacher tr.	218	18,613	519,000	28.0
Higher	20	...	408,000	10.2

Health (1995[1]): physicians 37,493 (1 per 412 persons); hospital beds 85,579 (1 per 181 persons); infant mortality rate per 1,000 live births (1999) 5.0.
Food (1997): daily per capita caloric intake 3,284 (vegetable products 65%, animal products 35%); 122% of FAO recommended minimum requirement.

Military

Total active duty personnel (1998): 57,180 (army 47.2%, navy 24.1%, air force 21.0%, other[8] 7.7%). *Military expenditure as percentage of GNP* (1997): 1.9% (world 2.6%); per capita expenditure U.S.$438.

[1]January 1. [2]Detail does not add to total given because of rounding. [3]Based on land area only. [4]Services includes Finance and Pub. admin., defense. [5]Imputed value added tax less subsidies and bank service charges. [6]Includes 422,000 unemployed. [7]1990–91. [8]Includes 3,600 military police and 800 interservice personnel.

Internet resources for further information:
- **Statistics Netherlands http://www.cbs.nl/en/index.htm**

Netherlands Antilles

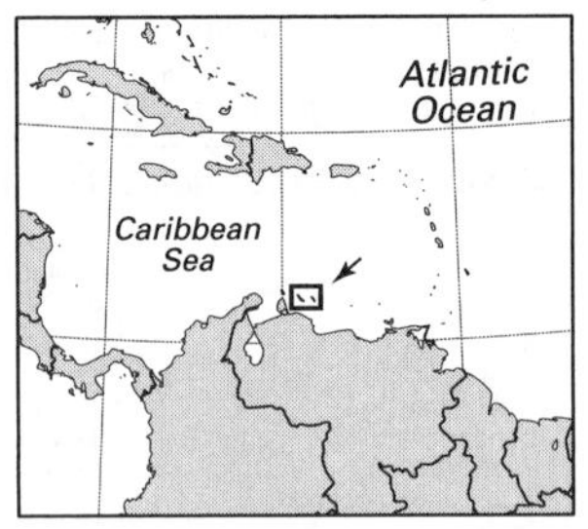

Official name: Nederlandse Antillen (Netherlands Antilles).
Political status: nonmetropolitan territory of The Netherlands with one legislative house (States of the Netherlands Antilles [22])[1].
Chief of state: Dutch Monarch represented by Governor.
Head of government: Prime Minister.
Capital: Willemstad.
Official language: Dutch.
Official religion: none.
Monetary unit: 1 Netherlands Antillean guilder (NA f.) = 100 cents; valuation (Oct. 6, 2000) 1 U.S.$ = NA f. 1.78; 1 £ = NA f. 2.57.

Area and population

		area		population
Island councils	Capitals	sq mi	sq km	1998[2] estimate
Leeward Islands				
Bonaire	Kralendijk	111	288	14,539
Curaçao	Willemstad	171	444	153,664
Windward Islands				
Saba	The Bottom	5	13	1,531
Sint Eustatius, or Statia	Oranjestad	8	21	2,237
Sint Maarten[3] (Dutch part only)	Philipsburg	13	34	38,876
TOTAL		308	800	210,847

Demography

Population (2000): 221,000.
Density (2000): persons per sq mi 717.5, persons per sq km 276.3.
Urban-rural (1998): urban 69.5%; rural 30.5%.
Sex distribution (1992): male 47.87%; female 52.13%.
Age breakdown (1992): under 15, 26.0%; 15–29, 23.9%; 30–44, 25.5%; 45–59, 14.3%; 60–74, 7.3%; 75 and over, 3.0%.
Population projection: (2010) 240,000; (2020) 256,000.
Doubling time: 63 years.
Ethnic composition (1995): black/other 85%; other (mostly Carib Amerindian, white, and East Asian) 15%.
Religious affiliation (1992): Roman Catholic 73.9%; Protestant 10.4%, of which Methodist 3.0%, Seventh-day Adventist 2.2%; Jehovah's Witness 1.5%; Jewish 0.3%; Muslim 0.2%; nonreligious 6.3%; other 8.9%.
Major cities: Willemstad (urban area; 1999) 123,000; Philipsburg (1981) 6,000.

Vital statistics

Birth rate per 1,000 population (1997): 17.0 (world avg. 22.1); (1988)[4] legitimate 51.6%; illegitimate 48.4%.
Death rate per 1,000 population (1997): 5.9 (world avg. 8.9).
Natural increase rate per 1,000 population (1997): 11.1 (world avg. 13.2).
Total fertility rate (avg. births per childbearing woman; 1999): 2.1.
Marriage rate per 1,000 population (1997): 6.6.
Divorce rate per 1,000 population (1997): 2.9.
Life expectancy at birth (1999): male 72.3 years; female 76.7 years.
Major causes of death per 100,000 population (1993): infectious and parasitic diseases/diseases of the respiratory system 209.0; diseases of the circulatory system 180.2; malignant neoplasms (cancers) 117.7; endocrine and metabolic diseases 46.5; accidents 39.7.

National economy

Budget (1999). Revenue: NA f. 498,300,000 (tax revenue 83.2%, of which import duties 28.0%, sales tax 20.4%, excise on gasoline 18.8%; nontax revenue 15.3%). Expenditures: NA f. 626,200,000 (current expenditures 91.9%; development expenditures 8.1%).
Production (metric tons except as noted). Agriculture, forestry, fishing: [5]; livestock (number of live animals; 1999) 13,000 goats, 7,300 sheep, 2,600 asses, 135,000 chickens; roundwood, n.a.; fish catch (1997) 1,105. Mining and quarrying (1997): salt 432,225, sulfur by-product 27,600. Manufacturing (1996): residual fuel oil 5,013,000; gas-diesel oils 2,218,000; other manufactures include electronic parts, cigarettes, textiles, rum, and Curaçao liqueur. Construction (number of buildings completed; 1997)[6]: residential 621; nonresidential 480. Energy production (consumption): electricity (kW-hr; 1996) 1,482,000,000 (1,482,000,000); coal, none (none); crude petroleum (barrels; 1996) none (93,334,000); petroleum products (metric tons; 1996) 9,952,000 (851,000); natural gas, none (none).
Land use (1998): forested, negligible; meadows and pastures, negligible; agricultural and under permanent cultivation 10.0%; other (dry savanna) 90.0%.
Tourism (1999): receipts from visitors U.S.$762,000,000; expenditures by nationals abroad U.S.$383,000,000.
Household income and expenditure. Average household size (1981) 3.7; income per household: n.a.; sources of income: n.a.; expenditure (1996)[6, 7]: housing 26.5%, transportation and communications 19.9%, food 14.7%, household furnishings 8.8%, recreation and education 8.2%, clothing and footwear 7.5%.
Gross national product (at current market prices; 1995): U.S.$2,455,000,000 (U.S.$11,980 per capita).

Structure of gross domestic product and labour force

	1995		1992	
	in value NA f. '000,000	% of total value	labour force	% of labour force
Agriculture, Mining	31.8	0.7	788	0.9
Manufacturing	281.8	6.6	6,935	7.9
Construction	282.5	6.6	6,474	7.4
Public utilities	165.2	3.9	1,241	1.4
Transp. and commun.[8]	557.0	13.1	4,984	5.7
Trade, hotels, restaurants	1,065.0	25.1	20,832	23.7
Finance, real estate, insurance	944.1	22.2	8,190	9.3
Pub. admin., defense	771.9	18.2	24,674	28.1
Services[9]	370.3	8.7		
Other	–219.1[10]	–5.2[10]	13,638[11]	15.5[11]
TOTAL	4,250.5	100.0[12]	87,756	100.0[12]

Population economically active (1992): total 87,756; activity rate of total population 46.3% (participation rates: ages 15–64, 68.6%; female 45.1%; unemployed [1998] 16.7%).

Price index (1996 = 100)

	1993	1994	1995	1996	1997	1998	1999
Consumer price index	92.3	93.9	96.5	100.0	103.3	104.4	104.0[13]
Monthly earnings index[14]	...	...	...	100.0	100.0	100.0	...

Public debt (external, outstanding; 1999): U.S.$294,600,000.

Foreign trade

Balance of trade (current prices)

	1994	1995	1996	1997	1998	1999
NA. f '000,000	–1,770	–1,939	–2,003	–1,998	–1,815	–1,905
% of total	67.0%	71.3%	70.8%	67.6%	62.6%	60.4%

Imports (1999): NA f. 2,375,000,000 (nonpetroleum domestic imports 71.3%, crude petroleum and petroleum products 14.8%, imports of Curaçao free zone 13.9%). *Major import sources* (1998)[15]: Venezuela 37%; United States 22%; Mexico 7%; The Netherlands 5%; Italy 5%.
Exports (1999): NA f. 470,000,000 (reexports of Curaçao free zone 59.1%, nonpetroleum domestic exports 37.5%, petroleum products 3.4%). *Major export destinations* (1998)[15]: United States 23%; Guatemala 10%; The Bahamas 6%; Guyana 6%; Chile 4%.

Transport and communications

Transport. Railroads: none. Roads (1992): total length 367 mi, 590 km (paved, 51%). Vehicles (1996): passenger cars 75,105; trucks and buses 17,753. Air transport (1998)[16]: passenger arrivals and departures 959,000; freight loaded and unloaded 11,100 metric tons; airports (1995) with scheduled flights 6.

Communications

Medium	date	unit	number	units per 1,000 persons
Daily newspapers	1996	circulation	70,000	341
Radio	1997	receivers	217,000	1,039
Television	1997	receivers	69,000	330
Telephones	1996	main lines	93,295	462
Cellular telephones	1998	subscribers	16,000	75

Education and health

Educational attainment (1992). Percentage of employed population having: no formal schooling or some primary education 21.5%; completed primary 50.8%; completed vocational or secondary 24.3%; completed higher 3.4%.
Literacy (1995): total population age 15 and over literate 194,900 (96.6%); males literate 93,300 (96.6%); females literate 101,600 (96.6%).

Education (1997–98)

	schools	teachers	students	student/ teacher ratio
Primary (age 6–12)	85[17]	1,111	24,061	21.7
Secondary (age 12–17)	21	...	8,372	...
Voc., teacher tr.	33	...	8,254	...
Higher	1	97	686	7.1

Health (1997): physicians 339 (1 per 616 persons); hospital beds 1,466 (1 per 142 persons); infant mortality rate per 1,000 live births (1999) 12.2.
Food (1998): daily per capita caloric intake 2,659 (vegetable products 64%, animal products 36%); 110% of FAO recommended minimum requirement.

Military

Total active duty personnel (1999): a 45-member Dutch naval/air force contingent is stationed in the Netherlands Antilles and Aruba.

[1]The Netherlands Antilles included Aruba before Jan. 1, 1986. [2]January 1. [3]In June 2000 the voters of Sint Maarten approved by referendum to withdraw from the Netherlands Antilles. [4]Excludes Sint Eustatius. [5]Mostly tomatoes, beans, cucumbers, gherkins, melons, and lettuce grown on hydroponic farms; aloes grown for export, divi-divi pods, and sour orange fruit are nonhydroponic crops. [6]Curaçao only. [7]Weights of consumer price index components. [8]Includes ship repair and transshipment and storage of cargo. [9]Includes extraterritorial organizations and bodies. [10]Less imputed bank service charges. [11]Includes 13,434 unemployed. [12]Detail does not add to total given because of rounding. [13]Average of 2nd and 3rd quarters. [14]Minimum wages only. [15]Estimated figures. [16]Curaçao airport only. [17]1996–97.

Internet resources for further information:
- **Central Bank of the Netherlands Antilles http://www.centralbank.an**
- **Statistics of the Netherlands Antilles http://www.gov.an/cbs**

New Caledonia

Official name: Nouvelle-Calédonie (New Caledonia)[1].
Political status: overseas country[1] (France) with one legislative house (Congress[2] [54]).
Chief of state: President of France represented by High Commissioner.
Head of government: President.
Capital: Nouméa.
Official language[3].
Official religion: none.
Monetary unit: 1 franc of the Comptoirs français du Pacifique (CFPF) = 100 centimes; valuation (Oct. 6, 2000) 1 U.S.$ = CFPF 136.84; 1 £ = CFPF 197.95.

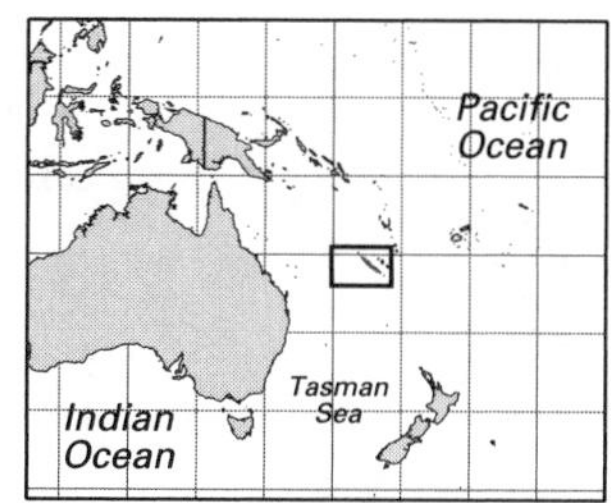

Area and population

Provinces Island(s)	Capitals	area sq mi	area sq km	population 1996 census
Loyauté (Loyalty)	Wé	765	1,981	20,877
Maré		248	642	6,896
Lifou		466	1,207	10,007
Ouvéa		51	132	3,974
Nord (Northern)	Koné	3,305	8,561	41,413
Belep		27	70	923
New Caledonia (part)		3,278	8,491	40,490
Sud (Southern)	Nouméa	3,102	8,033	134,546
New Caledonia (part)		3,043	7,881	132,875
Pins		59	152	1,671
TOTAL		7,172	18,575	196,836

Demography

Population (2000): 211,000.
Density (2000): persons per sq mi 29.4, persons per sq km 11.4.
Urban-rural (1999): urban 75.7%; rural 24.3%.
Sex distribution (1996): male 51.23%; female 48.77%.
Age breakdown (1996): under 15, 30.7%; 15–29, 27.2%; 30–44, 21.3%; 45–59, 13.3%; 60–74, 5.9%; 75 and over, 1.6%.
Population projection: (2010) 246,000; (2020) 279,000.
Doubling time: 46 years.
Ethnic composition (1996): Melanesian 45.3%, of which local (Kanak) 44.1%, Vanuatuan 1.2%; European 34.1%; Wallisian or Futunan 9.0%; Indonesian 2.6%; Tahitian 2.6%; Vietnamese 1.4%; other 5.0%.
Religious affiliation (1995): Roman Catholic 61.3%; Protestant 14.5%, of which Presbyterian 12.3%; Muslim 4.0%; other Christian 2.3%; other 17.9%.
Major cities (1996): Nouméa 76,293 (urban agglomeration 118,823); Mont-Dore 20,780[4]; Dumbéa 13,888[4].

Vital statistics

Birth rate per 1,000 population (1999): 20.8 (world avg. 22.1); (1996) legitimate 36.4%; illegitimate 63.6%.
Death rate per 1,000 population (1999): 5.3 (world avg. 8.9).
Natural increase rate per 1,000 population (1999): 15.5 (world avg. 13.2).
Total fertility rate (avg. births per childbearing woman; 1999): 2.5.
Marriage rate per 1,000 population (1999): 4.5.
Divorce rate per 1,000 population (1996): 0.8.
Life expectancy at birth (1999): male 69.8 years; female 75.8 years.
Major causes of death per 100,000 population (1996): diseases of the circulatory system 124.2; malignant neoplasms (cancers) 110.6; accidents, poisonings, and violence 63.9; diseases of the respiratory system 60.3.

National economy

Budget (1999). Revenue: CFPF 77,477,000,000 (indirect taxes 49.7%, direct taxes 30.9%, French government subsidies 8.6%, tobacco excises 6.3%). Expenditures: CFPF 74,218,000,000 (current expenditure 93.4%, development expenditure 6.6%).
Production (metric tons except as noted). Agriculture, forestry, fishing (1999): roots and tubers 21,100, of which yams 11,000, sweet potatoes 3,000; coconuts 16,000; vegetables 3,785; fruit 3,021; cereals 1,870, of which maize (corn) 1,650; livestock (number of live animals) 120,000 cattle, 38,000 pigs, 390,000 chickens; roundwood (1998) 4,800 cu m; fish catch (1997) 3,421, of which shrimp 1,107, sea urchins and echinoderms 505. Mining and quarrying (metric tons; 1999): nickel ore 6,562,000, of which nickel content (1997) 110,000; cobalt (1997) 800. Manufacturing (metric tons; 1999): cement 92,714; ferronickel (metal content) 45,289; nickel matte (metal content) 11,353; other manufactures include beer, copra cake, and soap. Energy production (consumption): electricity (kW-hr; 1996) 1,476,000,000 (1,476,000,000); coal (metric tons; 1996) none (168,000); crude petroleum, none (none); petroleum products (metric tons; 1996) none (409,000); natural gas, none (none).
Tourism: receipts from visitors (1996) U.S.$109,000,000; expenditures by nationals abroad, n.a.
Population economically active (1996): total 80,589; activity rate of total population 40.9% (participation rates: over age 14, 57.3%; female 39.7%; unemployed 18.6%).

Price and earnings indexes (1995 = 100)[6]

	1993	1994	1995	1996	1997	1998	1999
Consumer price index	96.5	98.4	100.0	101.7	103.7	104.0	104.1
Earnings index[7]	96.6	98.4	100.0	101.2	...	...	...

Land use (1994): forested 38.7%; meadows and pastures 11.8%; agricultural and under permanent cultivation 0.7%; other 48.8%.
Gross national product (at current market prices; 1997): U.S.$2,140,000,000 (U.S.$10,660 per capita).

Structure of gross domestic product and labour force

	1997 in value CFPF '000,000	1997 % of total value	1996 labour force	1996 % of labour force
Agriculture	6,439	1.9	4,663	5.8
Mining	13,307	3.8	4,408[8]	5.5[8]
Manufacturing	38,766	11.1	3,072[9]	3.8[9]
Construction	17,447	5.0	6,890	8.5
Public utilities	5,370	1.5	697	0.8
Transp. and commun.	23,415	6.7	2,968	3.7
Trade	80,054	22.9	8,375	10.4
Finance }	76,543	21.9	5,550	6.9
Services }			17,218	21.4
Pub. admin., defense	87,919	25.2	10,536	13.1
Other	—	—	16,212[10]	20.1[10]
TOTAL	349,260	100.0	80,589	100.0

Public debt (external, outstanding; 1995): U.S.$1,033,000,000.[5]
Household income and expenditure (1991). Average household size (1996) 3.8; average annual income per household CFPF 3,361,233 (U.S.$32,879)[11]; sources of income: wages and salaries 68.2%, transfer payments 13.7%, other 18.1%; expenditure: food and beverages 25.9%, housing 20.4%, transportation and communications 16.1%, recreation 4.8%.

Foreign trade[12]

Balance of trade (current prices)

	1994	1995	1996	1997	1998	1999
CFPF '000,000	–45,601	–35,714	–41,616	–40,949	–58,910	–68,125
% of total	35.3%	25.9%	28.8%	26.2%	42.0%	43.2%

Imports (1999): CFPF 112,888,000,000 (machinery and apparatus 20.0%, food 16.2%, transportation equipment 15.6%, mineral fuels 9.4%, chemicals and chemical products 7.8%). *Major import sources* (1998): France 52.2%; Australia 13.9%; New Zealand 5.3%; Singapore 4.2%; Japan 3.4%.
Exports (1999): CFPF 44,763,000,000 (ferronickel 54.8%, nickel ore 18.8%, nickel matte 13.9%, shrimp 4.2%). *Major export destinations:* Japan 32.2%; France 22.1%; Taiwan 8.4%; South Korea 7.6%; Australia 7.1%.

Transport and communications

Transport. Railroads: none. Roads (1996): total length 3,582 mi, 5,764 km (paved [1993] 52%). Vehicles: passenger cars (1996) 56,700; trucks and buses (1993) 21,200. Air transport (1999)[13]: passenger arrivals 171,887, passenger departures 170,815; (1998) freight unloaded 3,530 metric tons, freight loaded 1,371 metric tons; airports (1999) with scheduled flights 11.

Communications

Medium	date	unit	number	units per 1,000 persons
Daily newspapers	1996	circulation	24,000	121
Radio	1997	receivers	107,000	533
Television	1997	receivers	52,000	259
Telephones	1998	main lines	49,259	241
Cellular telephones	1998	subscribers	13,040	64
Internet	1996	users	500	2.5

Education and health

Educational attainment (1996). Percentage of population age 14 and over having: no formal schooling 5.7%; primary education 28.9%; lower secondary 30.2%; upper secondary 24.6%; higher 10.5%. *Literacy:* n.a.

Education (1996)

	schools	teachers	students	student/ teacher ratio
Primary (age 6–10)	279	1,622	22,942	14.1
Secondary (age 11–17) }	46	2,021	20,360	13.0
Vocational }	14		5,916	
Higher	4	79	1,749	22.1

Health (1996): physicians 362 (1 per 549 persons); hospital beds 898 (1 per 221 persons); infant mortality rate per 1,000 live births (1999) 6.3.
Food (1998): daily per capita caloric intake 2,812 (vegetable products 74%, animal products 26%); 123% of FAO recommended minimum requirement.

Military

Total active duty personnel (1999): 2,300 French troops. *Military expenditure as percentage of GNP:* n.a.

[1]The Nouméa Accord granting New Caledonia limited autonomy (with likely independence by 2013) was formally signed on May 5, 1998, approved by referendum in New Caledonia in November 1998, and passed by both houses of the French Parliament by February 1999. [2]Operates in association with 3 provincial assemblies. [3]Kanak languages and French have special recognition per Nouméa Accord. [4]Within Nouméa urban agglomeration. [5]Includes long-term private debt not guaranteed by the government. [6]All figures are end-of-year. [7]Based on minimum hourly wage. [8]Includes metallurgy. [9]Excludes metallurgy. [10]Includes 1,194 military conscripts and 15,018 unemployed. [11]Includes both monetary (92%) and nonmonetary income (8%). [12]Imports c.i.f.; exports f.o.b. [13]La Tontouta international airport only.

Internet resources for further information:
- **Overseas Departments and Territories of France http://www.outre-mer.gouv.fr/domtom**

New Zealand

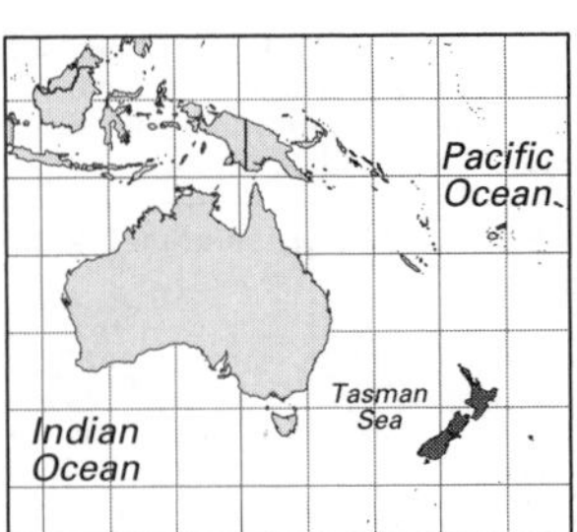

Official name: New Zealand (English); Aotearoa (Māori).
Form of government: constitutional monarchy with one legislative house (House of Representatives [120[1]]).
Chief of state: British Monarch, represented by Governor-General.
Head of government: Prime Minister.
Capital: Wellington.
Official languages: English; Māori.
Official religion: none.
Monetary unit: 1 New Zealand dollar ($NZ) = 100 cents; valuation (Oct. 6, 2000) 1 U.S.$ = $NZ 2.48; 1 £ = $NZ 3.59.

Area and population	area		population
Islands / Regional Councils	sq mi	sq km	1998 estimate
North Island	44,702	115,777	2,866,300[2]
Auckland	...	...	1,159,400
Bay of Plenty	...	...	238,300
Gisborne[3]	...	...	46,700
Hawkes Bay	...	...	146,200
Manawatu-Wanganui	...	...	231,700
Northland	...	...	143,400
Taranaki	...	...	106,700
Waikato	...	...	365,200
Wellington	...	...	428,700
South Island	58,384	151,215	925,000
Canterbury	...	...	487,400
Marlborough[3]	...	...	39,700
Nelson[3]	...	...	41,400
Otago	...	...	188,300
Southland	...	...	95,700
Tasman[3]	...	...	39,600
West Coast	...	...	32,900
Offshore islands	1,368	3,542	700[4]
TOTAL	104,454	270,534	3,792,000

Demography

Population (2000): 3,835,000.
Density (2000): persons per sq mi 36.7, persons per sq km 14.2.
Urban-rural (1996): urban 85.0%; rural 15.0%.
Sex distribution (1999): male 49.26%; female 50.74%.
Age breakdown (1996): under 15, 23.0%; 15–29, 22.7%; 30–44, 23.1%; 45–59, 15.9%; 60–74, 10.6%; 75 and over, 4.7%.
Population projection: (2010) 4,245,000; (2020) 4,564,000.
Ethnic composition (1996)[5]: European 88.6%; Māori 15.1%; other Polynesian 5.8%; Asian 5.0%; other 0.5%.
Religious affiliation (1996): Christian 60.8%, of which Protestant 39.4% (including Anglican 17.5%), Roman Catholic 13.1%; nonreligious 24.7%; other religions/not specified 14.5%.
Major cities (1997): Auckland 372,600; Christchurch 320,500; Manukau 271,100; North Shore 182,300; Wellington 164,600.

Vital statistics

Birth rate per 1,000 population (1998): 14.6 (world avg. 22.1); (1996) legitimate 58.0%; illegitimate 42.0%.
Death rate per 1,000 population (1998): 6.9 (world avg. 8.9).
Natural increase rate per 1,000 population (1998): 7.7 (world avg. 13.2).
Total fertility rate (avg. births per childbearing woman; 1999): 1.9.
Life expectancy at birth (1999): male 74.8 years; female 80.8 years.
Major causes of death per 100,000 population (1995): diseases of the circulatory system 317.8, of which ischemic heart disease 183.1; malignant neoplasms (cancers) 202.9; diseases of the respiratory system 82.5.

National economy

Budget (1996–97). Revenue: $NZ 34,778,000,000 (income taxes 58.9%, taxes on goods and services 22.2%, nontax revenue 7.5%). Expenditures: $NZ 32,953,000,000 (social services 38.3%, health 17.1%, education 16.2%).
Tourism (1998): receipts U.S.$1,726,000,000; expenditures U.S.$1,405,000,000.
Production (metric tons except as noted). Agriculture, forestry, fishing (1998): apples 500,500, barley 340,000, wheat 265,000, corn (maize) 176,000; livestock (number of live animals) 47,595,000 sheep, 8,772,000 cattle, 340,000 pigs; roundwood (1998) 16,531,000 cu m; fish catch (1996) 612,223. Mining and quarrying (1996): limestone 3,438,343; iron ore and sand concentrate 2,333,715; silver 29,300 kg; gold 11,600 kg. Manufacturing (1996–97): wood pulp 1,405,300; chemical fertilizers 1,365,000; yarn 21,302; beer 343,457,000 litres; footwear 2,840,000 pairs[6]; carpets 9,980,000 sq m. Energy production (consumption): electricity (kW-hr; 1995) 34,375,000,000 (34,375,000,000); coal (metric tons; 1995) 3,517,000 (2,667,000); crude petroleum (barrels; 1996) 13,000,000 ([1995] 35,000,000); petroleum products (metric tons; 1995) 4,587,000 (4,500,000); natural gas (cu m; 1995) 4,763,000,000 (4,209,000,000).
Population economically active (1999[7]): total 1,876,000; activity rate 49.4% (participation rates: over age 15, 65.4%; female 45.1%; unemployed 7.2%).

Price and earnings indexes (1995 = 100)	1993	1994	1995	1996	1997	1998	1999
Consumer price index	94.1	96.4	100.0	102.3	103.5	104.8	104.7
Weekly earnings index	94.4	97.0	100.0	...	...	...	...

Gross national product (1998): U.S.$55,356,000,000 (U.S.$14,600 per capita).

Structure of gross domestic product and labour force	1996–97		1997[7]	
	in value $NZ '000,000[8]	% of total value	labour force	% of labour force
Agriculture	4,652	5.4	149,900	8.3
Mining[9]	2,357	2.7	4,500	0.2
Manufacturing	15,907	18.4	285,200	15.8
Construction	3,296	3.8	111,200	6.2
Public utilities	2,290	2.6	11,700	0.6
Transp. and commun.	9,449	10.9	101,600	5.6
Trade	12,646	14.6	355,200	19.7
Finance	18,785	21.7	205,400	11.4
Pub. admin., defense	9,228	10.6	458,600	25.4
Services	5,463	6.3		
Other	2,617	3.0	122,700[10]	6.8[10]
TOTAL	86,690	100.0	1,806,000	100.0

Household income and expenditure. Average household size (1996) 2.8; annual income per household[11] (1996–97) $NZ 59,444 (U.S.$40,143); sources of income (1998): wages and salaries 65.8%, transfer payments 15.2%, self-employment 9.8%, other 9.2%; expenditure (1996–97): housing 20.2%, transportation 18.2%, food 16.4%, household goods 13.7%, clothing 3.8%.
Land use (1994): forest 27.9%; pasture 50.4%; agriculture 14.2%; other 7.5%.

Foreign trade[12]

Balance of trade (current prices)	1993	1994	1995	1996	1997	1998
$NZ '000,000	+3,120.0	+2,028.0	+1,068.9	+1,162.0	+902.0	+812.0
% of total	8.7%	5.2%	2.6%	2.8%	2.2%	1.8%

Imports (1998–99): $NZ 23,742,000,000 (machinery 24.7%; transport equipment 15.3%; textiles and textile products 5.7%; mineral fuels 5.7%; plastics 4.2%). *Major import sources:* Australia 22.0%; U.S. 18.5%; Japan 12.0%; China 5.1%; U.K. 4.8%; Germany 4.5%.
Exports (1998–99): $NZ 22,554,000,000 (food 39.4%; metals and metal products 6.4%; wood and wood products 6.2%; machinery 4.6%; wool 3.5%). *Major export destinations:* Australia 21.2%; U.S. 13.4%; Japan 12.7%; U.K. 5.9%; South Korea 3.7%; China 2.8%.

Transport and communications

Transport. Railroads (1997): route length 4,100 km; passenger journeys 11,576,000; metric ton-km cargo (1998) 3,624,000,000. Roads (1997): total length 91,996 km (paved 61%). Vehicles (1998–99): passenger cars 1,831,118; trucks and buses (1996) 351,494. Merchant marine (1992): vessels (100 gross tons and over) 139; total deadweight tonnage 279,805. Air transport[13] (1998): passenger-km 17,946,000,000; metric ton-km cargo 821,000,000; airports (1997) 36.

Communications Medium	date	unit	number	units per 1,000 persons
Daily newspapers	1996	circulation	804,000	216
Radio	1996	receivers	3,700,000	996
Television	1996	receivers	1,845,000	497
Telephones	1998	main lines	1,868,000	492
Cellular telephones	1998	subscribers	790,000	208
Personal computers	1998	units	1,100,000	290
Internet	1998	users	600,000	158

Education and health

Educational attainment (1991). Percentage of population age 25 and over having: primary and some secondary education 54.9%; secondary 31.1%; higher 6.9%; not specified 6.1%[6]. *Literacy:* virtually 100.0%.

Education (1997)	schools	teachers	students	student/ teacher ratio
Primary (age 5–12)[14]	2,394	24,644	468,139	19.0
Secondary (age 13–17)	338	15,117	229,961	15.2
Voc., teacher tr.	29	5,416	106,654	19.7
Higher[15]	7	4,867	106,486	21.9

Health (1998): physicians (1997) 12,399 (1 per 318 persons); hospital beds 23,454 (1 per 164 persons); infant mortality rate per 1,000 live births 5.5.
Food (1997): daily per capita caloric intake 3,395 (vegetable products 62%, animal products 28%); 129% of FAO recommended minimum requirement.

Military

Total active duty personnel (1998): 9,550 (army 46.1%, air force 31.9%, navy 22.0%. *Military expenditure as percentage of GNP* (1997): 1.3% (world 2.6%); per capita expenditure U.S.$204.

[1]Includes six elected seats allocated to Māoris. [2]Includes negligible population on Kermadec islands. [3]Reorganized as a unitary authority that is administered by a district council with regional powers. [4]Includes an estimated population of 700 people on Chatham and Campbell islands. [5]Percentages add up to more than 100.0 as people specified more than one ethnic group on the 1996 census form. [6]1994–95. [7]March. [8]Constant 1992 prices. [9]Includes fishing and forestry. [10]Includes 116,000 unemployed. [11]Disposable income. [12]Import figures are f.o.b. in balance of trade and c.i.f. in commodities and trading partners. [13]Air New Zealand only. [14]Includes 101 composite schools that provide both primary and secondary education. [15]Universities only.

Internet resources for further information:
- **Statistics New Zealand Te Tari Tatau http://www.stats.govt.nz/statsweb.nsf**
- **The Press On-Line New Zealand News http://www.press.co.nz**

Nicaragua

Official name: República de Nicaragua (Republic of Nicaragua).
Form of government: unitary multiparty republic with one legislative house (National Assembly [93[1]]).
Head of state and government: President.
Capital: Managua.
Official language: Spanish.
Official religion: none.
Monetary unit: 1 córdoba oro (C$)[2] = 100 centavos; valuation (Oct. 6, 2000) 1 U.S.$ = C$12.67; 1 £ = C$18.33.

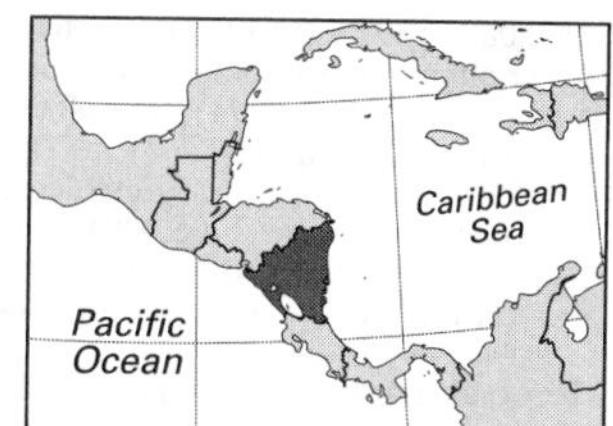

Area and population

Departments	Capitals	area[3] sq mi	area[3] sq km	population 1995 census
Boaco	Boaco	1,639	4,244	136,949
Carazo	Jinotepe	405	1,050	149,407
Chinandega	Chinandega	1,902	4,926	350,212
Chontales	Juigalpa	2,463	6,378	144,635
Estelí	Estelí	902	2,335	174,894
Granada	Granada	359	929	155,683
Jinotega	Jinotega	3,766	9,755	257,933
León	León	1,972	5,107	336,894
Madriz	Somoto	619	1,602	107,567
Managua	Managua	1,418	3,672	1,093,760
Masaya	Masaya	228	590	241,354
Matagalpa	Matagalpa	3,291	8,523	383,776
Nueva Segovia	Ocotal	1,206	3,123	148,492
Río San Juan	San Carlos	2,885	7,473	70,143
Rivas	Rivas	832	2,155	140,432
Autonomous regions				
North Atlantic	Puerto Cabezas	12,417	32,159	192,716
South Atlantic[4]	Bluefields	10,582	27,407	272,252
TOTAL LAND AREA		46,884[5]	121,428	
INLAND WATER		4,009	10,384	
TOTAL		50,893	131,812	4,357,099

Demography

Population (2000): 5,070,000.
Density (2000)[6]: persons per sq mi 108.1, persons per sq km 41.8.
Urban-rural (1995): urban 54.4%; rural 45.6%.
Sex distribution (1995): male 49.28%; female 50.72%.
Age breakdown (1995): under 15, 45.1%; 15–29, 27.4%; 30–44, 15.1%; 45–59, 7.3%; 60–74, 3.7%; 75 and over, 1.4%.
Population projection: (2010) 6,529,000; (2020) 7,997,000.
Doubling time: 29 years.
Ethnic composition (1997): mestizo (Spanish/Indian) 69.0%; white 17.0%; black 9.0%; Amerindian 5.0%.
Religious affiliation (1995): Roman Catholic 72.9%; Protestant 16.7%, of which Evangelical 15.1%, Moravian 1.5%; nonreligious 8.5%; other 1.9%.
Major cities (1995): Managua 864,201; León 123,865; Chinandega 97,387; Masaya 88,971; Granada 71,783; Estelí 71,550.

Vital statistics

Birth rate per 1,000 population (1999): 29.1 (world avg. 22.1).
Death rate per 1,000 population (1999): 5.0 (world avg. 8.9).
Natural increase rate per 1,000 population (1999): 24.1 (world avg. 13.2).
Total fertility rate (avg. births per childbearing woman; 1999): 3.4.
Life expectancy at birth (1999): male 66.5 years; female 70.4 years.
Major causes of death per 100,000 population (1994)[7]: diseases of the circulatory system 126; accidents, injuries, and violence 77; infectious and parasitic diseases 55; conditions originating in the perinatal period 53; diseases of the respiratory system 51.

National economy

Budget (1998). Revenue: C$6,581,000,000 (tax revenue 85.7%, of which import duties 23.0%, excise taxes on petroleum products 16.7%, general sales taxes 14.2%, income taxes 12.3%; grants 10.3%). Expenditures: C$7,037,000,000 (current expenditure 67.2%; development expenditure 31.6%).
Public debt (external, outstanding; 1998): U.S.$5,212,000,000.
Production (metric tons except as noted). Agriculture, forestry, fishing (1999): sugarcane 3,748,000, corn (maize) 302,000, rice 137,000, dry beans 94,000, sorghum 83,000, oranges 71,000, bananas 69,000, coffee 65,000, manioc (cassava) 51,000, soybeans 31,500; livestock (number of live animals) 1,693,000 cattle, 400,000 pigs; roundwood (1998) 4,198,000 cu m; fish catch (1997) 16,130, of which shrimp 6,437. Mining and quarrying (1997): gold 109,000 troy oz. Manufacturing (value added in C$'000,000; 1998[8]): food 1,816; beverages 1,245; cement, bricks, tiles 381; refined petroleum 209; tobacco products 202. Energy production (consumption): electricity (kW-hr; 1998) 2,084,000,000 (1,392,000,000); coal, none (none); crude petroleum (barrels; 1996) none (4,479,000); petroleum products (metric tons; 1996) 593,000 (882,000); natural gas, none (none).
Tourism (1997): receipts from visitors U.S.$74,000,000; expenditures by nationals abroad U.S.$65,000,000.
Land use (1994): forested 26.3%; meadows and pastures 45.3%; agricultural and under permanent cultivation 10.5%; other 17.9%.
Population economically active (1995): total 1,447,847; activity rate of total population 33.2% (participation rates: 15–64, 59.5%; female 29.5%; unemployed [1998] 13.2%).

Price and earnings indexes (1995 = 100)

	1993	1994	1995	1996	1997	1998	1999
Consumer price index	84	90	100	112	122	138	153
Monthly earnings index	92	98	100	106	119	...	...

Gross national product (1998): U.S.$1,756,000,000 (U.S.$370 per capita).

Structure of gross domestic product and labour force

	1997 in value C$'000,000	1997 % of total value	1995 labour force	1995 % of labour force
Agriculture, forestry	6,439	33.8	484,153	33.4
Mining	174	0.9	4,117	0.3
Manufacturing	2,980	15.6	107,919	7.5
Construction	746	3.9	45,362	3.1
Public utilities	230	1.2	6,022	0.4
Transp. and commun.	652	3.4	40,119	2.8
Trade, restaurants	4,587	24.1	205,982	14.2
Finance, real estate	999	5.2	7,143	0.5
Pub. admin., defense	1,218	6.4	233,322	16.1
Services	1,044	5.5		
Other	—	—	313,708[9]	21.7[9]
TOTAL	19,069	100.0	1,447,847	100.0

Household income and expenditure. Average household size (1995) 5.8.

Foreign trade[10]

Balance of trade (current prices)

	1994	1995	1996	1997	1998	1999
U.S.$'000,000	–433.5	–263.8	–362.5	–703.3	–810.5	–1,139.4
% of total	38.2%	20.0%	21.3%	36.0%	41.4%	51.2%

Imports (1999): U.S.$1,845,700,000 (capital goods 32.2%, nondurable consumer goods 23.9%, mineral fuels 8.7%). *Major import sources:* U.S. 34.5%; Costa Rica 11.4%; Guatemala 7.3%; Panama 6.9%.
Exports (1999): U.S.$543,800,000 (coffee 24.9%, manufactured products 19.9%, crustaceans 15.4%, beef 7.7%, raw sugar 5.6%, gold 5.6%). *Major export destinations:* U.S. 37.7%; El Salvador 12.5%; Germany 9.8%; Honduras 6.5%; Costa Rica 5.1%.

Transport and communications

Transport. Railroads:[11]. Roads (1996): total length 18,000 km (paved 10%). Vehicles (1996): passenger cars 73,000; trucks and buses 61,650. Air transport (1995)[12]: passenger-km 78,985,000; metric ton-km cargo 8,985,000; airports (1997) with scheduled flights 10.

Communications

Medium	date	unit	number	units per 1,000 persons
Daily newspapers	1996	circulation	135,000	30
Radio	1997	receivers	1,240,000	265
Television	1997	receivers	320,000	68
Telephones	1998	main lines	140,000	29
Cellular telephones	1998	subscribers	20,000	4.2
Personal computers	1998	units	35,000	7.3
Internet	1998	users	15,000	3.1

Education and health

Educational attainment (1995). Percentage of population age 25 and over having: no formal schooling 30.6%, no formal schooling (literate) 3.9%, primary education 39.2%, secondary 17.0%, technical 3.1%, incomplete undergraduate 2.2%; complete undergraduate 4.0%. *Literacy* (1995): total population age 15 and over literate 1,769,000 (74.0%); males literate 853,000 (74.4%); females literate 916,000 (73.6%).

Education (1997)

	schools	teachers	students	student/ teacher ratio
Primary (age 7–12)	7,224[13]	21,020[14]	783,002[13]	36.3[14]
Secondary (age 13–18)	451[15]	5,990[16]	220,670[16]	36.8[16]
Higher	10[15]	3,840	48,758	12.7

Health: physicians (1997) 3,725 (1 per 1,255 persons); hospital beds (1996) 6,666 (1 per 674 persons); infant mortality rate (1999) 35.9.
Food (1998): daily per capita caloric intake 2,208 (vegetable products 92%, animal products 8%); 98% of FAO recommended minimum requirement.

Military

Total active duty personnel (1999): 16,000 (army 87.5%, navy 5.0%, air force 7.5%). *Military expenditure as percentage of GNP* (1997): 1.5% (world 2.6%); per capita expenditure U.S.$6.

[1]Includes three unsuccessful 1996 presidential candidates meeting special conditions. [2]The córdoba oro (gold cordoba), introduced in August 1990, circulated simultaneously with the new córdoba until April 30, 1991, when the new córdoba ceased to be legal tender; on April 30, 1 córdoba oro equaled 5,000,000 new córdobas. [3]Lakes and lagoons are excluded from the areas of departments and autonomous regions. [4]A new department, Zelaya Central, was to be created in mid-2000 from part of South Atlantic Autonomous Region. [5]Detail does not add to total given because of rounding. [6]Based on land area. [7]Projected rates based on about 55% of total deaths. [8]At prices of 1980. [9]Includes 68,925 not adequately defined and 244,783 unemployed. [10]Imports f.o.b. in balance of trade and c.i.f. in commodities and trading partners. [11]Railroad service ended in January 1994. [12]Nica only. [13]1998. [14]1996. [15]1994. [16]1995.

Internet resources for further information:
- **Banco Central de Nicaragua http://www.bcn.gob.ni**

Niger

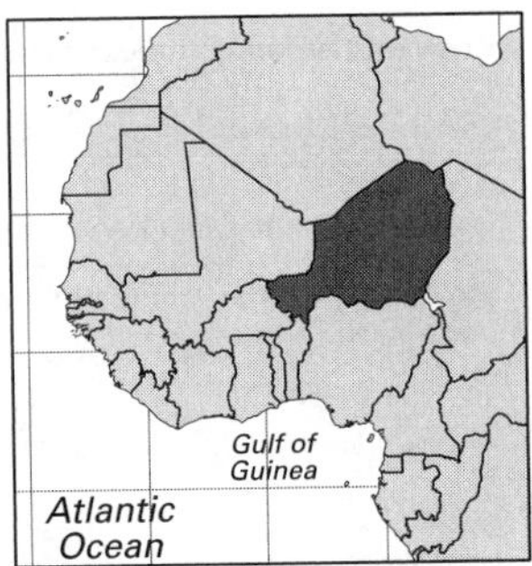

Official name: République du Niger (Republic of Niger).
Form of government: multiparty republic[1] with one legislative house (National Assembly [83]).
Head of state and government: President, assisted by Prime Minister.
Capital: Niamey.
Official language: French.
Official religion: none.
Monetary unit: 1 CFA franc (CFAF) = 100 centimes; valuation (Oct. 6, 2000) 1 U.S.$ = CFAF 754.28; 1 £ = CFAF 1,091.

Area and population

		area[2]		population
Departments	Capitals	sq mi	sq km	1990 estimate
Agadez	Agadez	244,869	634,209	189,000
Diffa	Diffa	54,138	140,216	227,000
Dosso	Dosso	11,970	31,002	982,000
Maradi	Maradi	14,896	38,581	1,415,000
Tahoua	Tahoua	41,188	106,677	1,373,000
Tillabéri	Tillabéri	34,863[3]	90,293[3]	1,818,000[3]
Zinder	Zinder	56,151	145,430	1,467,000
City				
Niamey	Niamey	[3]	[3]	[3]
TOTAL		458,075	1,186,408	7,471,000

Demography

Population (2000): 10,076,000.
Density (2000)[2]: persons per sq mi 20.6, persons per sq km 8.0.
Urban-rural (1999): urban 20.1%; rural 79.9%.
Sex distribution (1995): male 49.40%; female 50.60%.
Age breakdown (1995): under 15, 48.4%; 15–29, 25.7%; 30–44, 14.4%; 45–59, 7.5%; 60–74, 3.4%; 75 and over, 0.6%.
Population projection: (2010) 13,140,000; (2020) 16,800,000.
Doubling time: 25 years.
Ethnic composition (1988): Hausa 53.0%; Zerma- (Djerma-) Songhai 21.2%; Tuareg 10.4%; Fulani (Peul) 9.8%; Kanuri-Nanga 4.4%; Teda 0.4%; Arab 0.3%; Gurma 0.3%; other 0.2%.
Religious affiliation (1995): Muslim, primarily Sunnī, 88.7%; traditional beliefs 11.0%; Christian 0.3%.
Major cities (1988): Niamey 391,876 (urban agglomeration [1999] 731,000); Zinder 119,827; Maradi 110,005; Tahoua 49,948; Agadez 32,272.

Vital statistics

Birth rate per 1,000 population (1999): 52.1 (world avg. 22.1).
Death rate per 1,000 population (1999): 23.6 (world avg. 8.9).
Natural increase rate per 1,000 population (1999): 28.5 (world avg. 13.2).
Total fertility rate (avg. births per childbearing woman; 1999): 7.2.
Marriage rate per 1,000 population: n.a.
Divorce rate per 1,000 population: n.a.
Life expectancy at birth (1999): male 41.1 years; female 40.8 years.
Major causes of death: n.a.; however, among selected major causes of infectious disease registered at medical facilities were malaria, measles, diarrhea, meningitis, pneumonia, diphtheria, tetanus, viral hepatitis, and poliomyelitis; malnutrition and shortages of trained medical personnel are widespread.

National economy

Budget (1998). Revenue: CFAF 164,400,000,000 (taxes 59.3%, external aid and gifts 34.1%, nontax revenue 6.6%). Expenditures: CFAF 188,000,000,000 (current expenditures 69.2%, development expenditures 30.8%).
Public debt (external, outstanding; 1998): U.S.$1,449,000,000.
Tourism: receipts from visitors (1999) U.S.$21,000,000; expenditures by nationals abroad (1997) U.S.$24,000,000.
Gross national product (1998): U.S.$2,023,000,000 (U.S.$200 per capita).

Structure of gross domestic product and labour force

	1998		1988	
	in value CFAF '000,000	% of total value	labour force[4]	% of labour force
Agriculture	488,900	40.5	1,764,049	76.2
Mining	49,100	4.1	5,295	0.2
Manufacturing	78,100	6.5	65,793	2.8
Construction	24,700	2.0	13,742	0.6
Public utilities	23,400	1.9	1,778	0.1
Transp. and commun.	64,700	5.4	14,764	0.6
Trade and finance	201,200	16.6	210,354	9.1
Pub. admin., defense	96,600	8.0	59,271	2.6
Services	140,800	11.7	63,991	2.8
Other	40,600[5]	3.4[5]	116,657	5.0
TOTAL	1,208,100	100.0[6]	2,315,694	100.0

Production (metric tons except as noted). Agriculture, forestry, fishing (1999): millet 2,253,000, cowpeas 641,000, sorghum 481,000, cassava (manioc) 230,000, onions 180,000, peanuts (groundnuts) 108,100, rice 73,000, tomatoes 65,000, tobacco leaf 930; livestock (number of live animals) 6,469,000 goats, 4,312,000 sheep, 2,174,000 cattle, 530,000 asses, 404,000 camels, 94,000 horses; roundwood (1998) 6,460,000 cu m; fish catch (1997) 6,341. Mining and quarrying (1998): salt (1997) 3,000; uranium 3,516. Manufacturing (value added in CFAF '000,000; 1997): traditional-sector handicrafts 56,200; food 1,320; soaps and other chemical products 1,249; construction materials 836. Construction (value added in CFAF; 1994): 16,100,000,000. Energy production (consumption): electricity (kW-hr; 1996) 177,000,000 (373,000,000); coal (metric tons; 1996) 173,000 (173,000); crude petroleum, none (none); petroleum products (metric tons; 1996) none (205,000); natural gas, none (none).
Population economically active (1988)[4]: total 2,315,694; activity rate of total population 31.9% (participation rates: ages 15–64, 55.2%; female 20.4%).

Price and earnings indexes (1995 = 100)

	1994	1995	1996	1997	1998	1999	2000
Consumer price index	90.4	100.0	105.3	108.4	113.3	110.7	109.7[7]
Annual earnings index	...	...	...	...	...	...	...

Household income and expenditure. Average household size (1998) 6.3; income per household: n.a.; expenditure (1987): food and beverages 43.1%, housing 22.8%, clothing 10.0%.
Land use (1994): forested 2.0%; meadows and pastures 8.2%; agricultural and under permanent cultivation 2.9%; other (largely desert) 86.9%.

Foreign trade

Balance of trade (current prices)

	1993	1994	1995	1996	1997	1998
CFAF '000,000	–3,600	–20,000	–5,500	–13,400	–15,600	–21,100
% of total	2.2%	7.7%	1.9%	3.9%	4.7%	5.7%

Imports (1998): CFAF 196,700,000,000 (consumer goods 74.0%, of which food products 24.1%, petroleum products 7.0%; intermediate and capital goods 26.0%). *Major import sources*[8]: France 17%; Côte d'Ivoire 9%; Belgium 5%; Germany 4%; unspecified countries/special categories 37%.
Exports (1998): CFAF 175,600,000,000 (uranium 43.6%; livestock [mostly live cattle, sheep, and goats] 13.8%; cowpeas 7.1%). *Major export destinations*[8]: France 52%; South Korea 34%; United Kingdom 4%.

Transport and communications

Transport. Railroads: none. Roads (1996): total length 6,276 mi, 10,100 km (paved 8%). Vehicles (1996): passenger cars 38,220, trucks and buses 15,200. Air transport (1998)[9]: passenger-mi 160,477,000, passenger-km 258,263,000; short ton-mi cargo 9,263,000, metric ton-km cargo 13,524,000; airports (1996) with scheduled flights 6.

Communications

Medium	date	unit	number	units per 1,000 persons
Daily newspapers	1996	circulation	2,000	0.2
Radio	1997	receivers	680,000	73
Television	1997	receivers	125,000	13
Telephones	1998	main lines	18,114	1.9
Cellular telephones	1998	subscribers	1,349	0.1
Personal computers	1998	units	3,000	0.3
Internet	1998	users	300	0.03

Education and health

Educational attainment (1988). Percentage of population age 25 and over having: no formal schooling 85.0%; Koranic education 11.2%; primary education 2.5%; secondary 1.1%; higher 0.2%. *Literacy* (1995): total population age 15 and over literate 641,000 (13.6%); males literate 482,000 (20.9%); females literate 159,000 (6.6%).

Education (1997–98)

	schools	teachers	students	student/ teacher ratio
Primary (age 7–12)	3,175	11,545	482,065	41.8
Secondary (age 13–19)[10]	...	3,579	97,675	27.3
Voc., teacher tr.[10]	...	215	2,145	10.0
Higher[11]	2	355	5,569	15.7

Health: physicians (1993) 237 (1 per 35,141 persons); hospital beds (1987) *c.* 3,500 (1 per 2,000 persons); infant mortality rate per 1,000 live births (1999) 126.2.
Food (1998): daily per capita caloric intake 1,966 (vegetable products 94%, animal products 6%); 84% of FAO recommended minimum requirement.

Military

Total active duty personnel (1999): 5,300 (army 98.1%, air force 1.9%). *Military expenditure as percentage of GNP* (1997): 1.1% (world 2.6%); per capita expenditure U.S.$2.

[1]From January 2000 based on November 1999 elections; transitional military regime in power between April 1999 and January 2000. [2]The departmental areas and total shown are obsolete. The total area, according to more recent official estimates, is 489,000 sq mi (1,267,000 sq km); but subtotals distributing this total among the departments remain unpublished. [3]Tillabéri includes Niamey. [4]Excluding nomadic population. [5]Import taxes and duties. [6]Detail does not add to total given because of rounding. [7]February. [8]Estimated figures. [9]Represents 1/11 of the traffic of Air Afrique, which is operated by 11 West African states. [10]1996–97. [11]Université de Niamey and École Nationale d'Administration du Niger only.

Internet resources for further information:
- **United Nations Development Program for Niger**
http://www.intnet.ne/pnud_fr.html

Nigeria

Official name: Federal Republic of Nigeria.
Form of government: federal republic with two legislative bodies (Senate [109]; House of Representatives [360])[1].
Head of state and government: President.
Capital: Abuja (Federal Capital Territory)[2, 3].
Official language: English.
Official religion: none.
Monetary unit: 1 Nigerian naira (₦) = 100 kobo; valuation (Oct. 6, 2000) 1 U.S.$ = ₦108.35; 1 £ = ₦156.73.

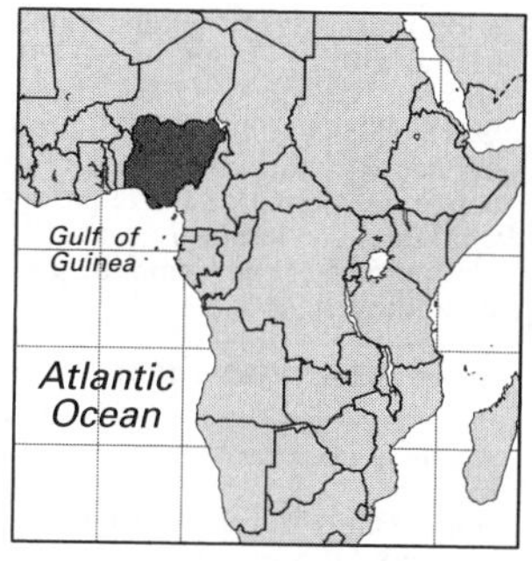

Area and population

States[4]	area sq km[2]	population 1995 estimate
Abia	6,320[5]	2,569,362[5]
Adamawa	36,917	2,374,892
Akwa Ibom	7,081	2,638,413
Anambra	4,844	3,094,783
Bauchi	64,605[6]	4,801,569[6]
Bayelsa	[7]	[7]
Benue	34,059	3,108,754
Borno	70,898	2,903,238
Cross River	20,156	2,085,926
Delta	17,698	2,873,711
Ebonyi	[5]	[5]
Edo	17,802	2,414,919
Ekiti	[8]	[8]
Enugu	12,831[5]	3,534,633[5]
Gombe	[6]	[6]
Imo	5,530	2,779,028
Jigawa	23,154	3,164,134
Kaduna	46,053	4,438,007
Kano	20,131	6,297,165
Katsina	24,192	4,336,363
Kebbi	36,800	2,305,768
Kogi	29,833	2,346,936
Kwara	36,825	1,751,464
Lagos	3,345	6,357,253
Niger	76,363	2,775,526
Nassarawa	[9]	[9]
Ogun	16,762	2,614,747
Ondo	20,959[8]	4,343,230[8]
Osun	9,251	2,463,185
Oyo	28,454	3,900,803
Plateau	58,030[9]	3,671,498[9]
Rivers	21,850[7]	4,454,337[7]
Sokoto	65,735[10]	4,911,118[10]
Taraba	54,473	1,655,443
Yobe	45,502	1,578,172
Zamfara	[10]	[10]
Federal Capital Territory		
Abuja	7,315	423,391
TOTAL	923,768	98,967,768

Demography

Population (2000): 123,338,000.
Density (2000): persons per sq mi 345.8, persons per sq km 133.5.
Urban-rural (1996): urban 40.1%; rural 59.9%.
Sex distribution (1996): male 49.57%; female 50.43%.
Age breakdown (1995): under 15, 45.6%; 15–29, 25.7%; 30–44, 15.7%; 45–59, 8.5%; 60–74, 3.8%; 75 and over, 0.7%.
Population projection: (2010) 155,588,000; (2020) 187,437,000.
Doubling time: 26 years.
Ethnic composition (1983): Hausa 21.3%; Yoruba 21.3%; Igbo (Ibo) 18.0%; Fulani 11.2%; Ibibio 5.6%; Kanuri 4.2%; Edo 3.4%; Tiv 2.2%; Ijaw 1.8%; Bura 1.7%; Nupe 1.2%; other 8.1%.
Religious affiliation (1995): Muslim 43.0%; Christian 35.3%, of which Protestant 20.0%, Roman Catholic 8.2%; African indigenous 19.0%; other 2.7%.
Major cities (1992): Lagos 1,347,000; Ibadan 1,295,000; Kano 699,900; Ogbomosho 660,600; Oshogbo 441,600; Ilorin 430,600.

Vital statistics

Birth rate per 1,000 population (1999): 40.6 (world avg. 22.1).
Death rate per 1,000 population (1999): 13.6 (world avg. 8.9).
Natural increase rate per 1,000 population (1999): 27.0 (world avg. 13.2).
Total fertility rate (avg. births per childbearing woman; 1999): 5.7.
Life expectancy at birth (1999): male 51.7 years; female 52.1 years.

National economy

Budget (1997). Revenue: ₦384,603,000,000 (petroleum royalties and rents 36.3%; import duties, excise taxes, and fees 24.4%; personal income tax 13.3%; company income tax 10.1%). Expenditures: ₦312,322,000,000 (recurrent expenditure 48.0%, of which debt service 15.6%, education 4.2%, health 1.5%, transportation and communications 0.7%; capital expenditure 52.0%).
Public debt (external, outstanding; 1999): U.S.$23,455,000,000.
Production (metric tons except as noted). Agriculture, forestry, fishing (1999): cassava 32,695,000, yams 24,768,000, sorghum 7,103,000, millet 5,956,000, corn (maize) 5,127,000, taro 3,823,000, rice 3,275,000, peanuts (groundnuts) 2,534,000, cow peas 2,055,000, plantains 1,560,000, sweet potatoes 1,560,000, tomatoes 801,000; livestock (number of live animals) 24,500,000 goats, 19,610,000 cattle, 14,000,000 sheep, 7,600,000 pigs; roundwood (1998) 117,387,000 cu m; fish catch (1997) 383,417. Mining and quarrying (1998): limestone 3,660,000; marble 22,460; lead and zinc 682[11]. Manufacturing (value added in ₦'000,000; 1995): food and beverages 25,415; textiles 16,193; chemical products 11,181; machinery and transport equipment 5,639; paper products 2,828. Construction: n.a. Energy production (consumption): electricity (kW-hr; 1996) 14,820,000,000 (14,820,000,000); coal (metric tons; 1996) 50,000 (50,000); crude petroleum (barrels; 1999) 702,767,000 ([1996] 46,853,000); petroleum products (metric tons; 1996) 5,520,000 (6,155,000); natural gas (cu m; 1996) 4,477,000,000 (4,477,000,000).
Tourism (1998): receipts U.S.$142,000,000; expenditures U.S.$1,567,000,000.
Household income and expenditure. Avg. household size (1995) 4.7; annual income per household (1992–93) ₦15,000 (U.S.$760): sources of income (1979): self-employment 49.4%, wages 30.2%, interest 5.4%, rent 4.7%, transfer payments 4.3%; expenditures (1979): food 53.0%, fuel and light 11.4%, clothing 6.0%, transportation 4.7%, household goods 3.8%, other 21.1%.

Gross national product (1998): U.S.$36,373,000,000 (U.S.$300 per capita).

Structure of gross domestic product and labour force

	1997		1986	
	in value ₦'000,000	% of total value	labour force	% of labour force
Agriculture	1,023,833	32.7	13,259,000	43.1
Mining[12]	1,296,866	41.4	6,800	0.1
Manufacturing	149,248	4.8	1,263,700	4.1
Construction	17,964	0.6	545,600	1.8
Public utilities	2,070	0.1	130,400	0.4
Transp. and commun.	73,917	2.4	1,111,900	3.6
Trade[13]	419,462	13.4	7,417,400	24.1
Finance	103,929	3.3	120,100	0.4
Pub. admin., defense	21,361	0.7	} 4,902,100	} 15.9
Services	20,594	0.6		
Other	...	...	2,008,500[14]	6.5[14]
TOTAL	3,129,243[15]	100.0	30,765,500	100.0

Population economically active (1993–94): total 29,000,000; activity rate 31.0% (participation rates: ages 15–59, 64.4%; female 44.0%; unemployed [1992] 4.0%).

Price and earnings indexes (1995 = 100)

	1993	1994	1995	1996	1997	1998	1999
Consumer price index	36.9	57.9	100.0	129.3	139.9	154.3	164.6
Earnings index	...	...	...	...	...	...	...

Land use (1994): forest 15.7%; pasture 43.9%; agriculture 35.9%; other 4.5%.

Foreign trade

Balance of trade (current prices)

	1992	1993	1994	1995	1996	1997
₦'000,000	+76,298	+69,145	+76,677	+91,796	+746,996	+395,946
% of total	22.8%	18.8%	22.8%	6.5%	39.9%	19.0%

Imports (1995): ₦111,728,000,000 (machinery and transport equipment 42.0%; manufactured goods [mostly iron and steel products, textiles, and paper products] 24.0%; chemicals 17.0%; food 8.4%). *Major import sources* (1992): Germany 18.9%; U.K. 17.8%; Belgium-Luxembourg 9.5%; U.S. 9.2%; France 7.4%.
Exports (1995): ₦220,408,900,000 (crude petroleum 94.8%; cocoa beans 0.7%; rubber 0.3%; other exports include cocoa products, textiles, and cashew nuts). *Major export destinations:* U.S. 40.1%; France 8.5%; Italy 4.6%; U.K. 0.6%.

Transport and communications

Transport. Railroads (1993): length[16] 3,505 km; passenger-km 555,000,000; metric ton-km cargo 2,185,000. Roads (1996): total length 62,598 km (paved 19%). Vehicles (1995): passenger cars 663,000; trucks and buses 68,300. Merchant marine (1992): vessels (100 gross tons and over) 271; total deadweight tonnage 733,329. Air transport[17] (1995): passenger-km 819,160,000; metric ton-km cargo 1,904,000; airports (1996) 12.

Communications

Medium	date	unit	number	units per 1,000 persons
Daily newspapers	1996	circulation	2,500,000	24
Radio	1996	receivers	20,500,000	197
Television	1997	receivers	6,500,000	61
Telephones	1998	main lines	407,000	3.5
Cellular telephones	1998	subscribers	20,000	0.2
Personal computers	1998	units	650,000	5.6
Internet	1997	users	4,000	0.03

Education and health

Literacy (2000): total population age 15 and over literate 40,700,000 (64.1%); males literate 22,600,000 (62.3%); females literate 18,100,000 (56.2%).

Education (1994–95)

	schools	teachers	students	student/teacher ratio
Primary (age 6–12)	38,649	435,210	16,191,000	37.2
Secondary (age 12–17)	6,074	152,596	4,451,000	29.2
Voc., teacher tr.	376[18]	15,738[19]	391,583[19]	24.9[19]
Higher	31	12,103	228,000	18.8

Health (1995): physicians 27,230 (1 per 3,707 persons); hospital beds 68,350 (1 per 1,477 persons); infant mortality rate (1999) 74.9.
Food (1997): daily per capita caloric intake 2,735 (vegetable products 96%, animal products 4%); 116% of FAO recommended minimum requirement.

Military

Total active duty personnel (1998): 77,000 (army 80.5%, navy 7.2%, air force 12.3%). *Military expenditure as percentage of GNP* (1997): 1.4% (world 2.6%); per capita expenditure U.S.$17.

[1]Civilian government elected in May 1999. [2]Statutory transfer of capital from Lagos to Abuja took place in December 1991. [3]Judiciary and some ministries remain in Lagos, the former capital. [4]In October 1996 six new states were created: Bayelsa, Ebonyi, Ekiti, Gombe, Nassarawa, and Zamfara. [5]Ebonyi is included partly in Abia and partly in Enugu. [6]Bauchi includes Gombe. [7]Rivers includes Bayelsa. [8]Ondo includes Ekiti. [9]Plateau includes Nassarawa. [10]Sokoto includes Zamfara. [11]Metal content. [12]Includes ₦1,294,160,000,000 (41.3%) from petroleum and natural gas. [13]Includes hotels. [14]Includes 1,263,000 unemployed. [15]Detail does not add to total given because of rounding. [16]1995. [17]Nigeria Airways only. [18]1987–88. [19]1988–89.

Northern Mariana Islands

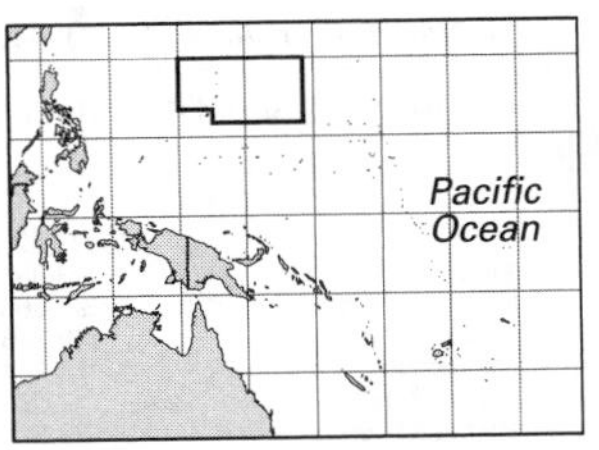

Official name: Commonwealth of the Northern Mariana Islands.
Political status: self-governing commonwealth in association with the United States[1], having two legislative houses (Senate [9]; House of Representatives [18]).
Chief of state: President of the United States[2].
Head of government: Governor.
Capital: Capital Hill, Saipan.
Official languages[3]: Chamorro, Carolinian, and English.
Official religion: none.
Monetary unit: 1 dollar (U.S.$) = 100 cents; valuation (Oct. 6, 2000) 1£ = U.S.$1.45.

Area and population

		area		population
				1995
Municipal councils	Seats	sq mi	sq km	census
Northern Islands[4]	...	55.3	143.2	8
Rota (island)[5]	Songsong	32.8	85.0	3,509
Saipan (island)	Chalan Kanoa	46.5	120.4	52,698
Tinian and Aguijan[5]	San Jose	41.9	108.5	2,631
TOTAL		176.5[6]	457.1[6]	58,846[7]

Demography

Population (2000): 71,900.
Density (2000): persons per sq mi 407.9, persons per sq km 157.5.
Urban-rural (1999): urban 55.0%; rural 45.0%.
Sex distribution (1995): male 49.75%; female 50.25%.
Age breakdown (1995): under 15, 24.3%; 15–29, 31.7%; 30–44, 31.6%; 45–59, 9.7%; 60–74, 2.2%; 75 and over, 0.5%.
Population projection: (2010) 99,000; (2020) 123,000.
Doubling time: 38 years.
Ethnic composition (1995[8]): Filipino 33.1%; Chamorro 24.1%; Chinese 11.5%; Carolinian 10.1%; other Asian 7.6%; Micronesian 7.1%; white 3.0%; other 3.5%.
Religious affiliation (1995[9]): Roman Catholic 59.6%; Protestant 18.7%; other Christian 1.4%; other 20.3%.
Major villages (1995[10]): Garapan 6,634; San Antonio 6,256; Chalan Kanoa 6,229; Capital Hill 2,698; San Jose (on Tinian) 1,896; Songsong (on Rota) 1,339.

Vital statistics

Birth rate per 1,000 population (1999[11]): 21.1 (world avg. 22.1); (1992) legitimate, 51.2%; illegitimate, 48.8%.
Death rate per 1,000 population (1999[11]): 2.4 (world avg. 8.9).
Natural increase rate per 1,000 population (1999[11]): 18.7 (world avg. 13.2).
Total fertility rate (avg. births per childbearing woman; 1999[11]): 1.8.
Marriage rate per 1,000 population (1989): 28.5.
Divorce rate per 1,000 population (1986): 2.9.
Life expectancy at birth (1999[11]): male 72.0 years; female 78.4 years.
Major causes of death per 100,000 population (1994–96 avg.): diseases of the circulatory system 53.3, of which cerebrovascular disease 25.8, ischemic heart diseases 21.8; malignant neoplasms (cancers) 33.3; accidents 29.8; diabetes mellitus 10.9.

National economy

Budget (1994–95). Revenue: U.S.$217,100,000 (local revenue 87.7%, grants from U.S. Office of Insular Affairs for capital improvements 12.3%). Expenditures: U.S.$190,400,000 (general government 46.1%, education 19.6%, health and social welfare 18.4%, public safety 6.6%).
Tourism (1998): receipts from visitors, U.S.$394,000,000; expenditures by nationals abroad, n.a.
Land use (1990): forested, n.a.; meadows and pastures 3.7%; agricultural and under permanent cultivation 4.0%; other 92.3%.
Gross national product (1999): U.S.$664,600,000 (U.S.$9,600 per capita).

Structure of labour force

	1995	
	labour force	% of labour force
Agriculture, forestry, and fishing	419	1.2
Mining and quarrying	...	...
Manufacturing	7,770	22.8
Public utilities	...	...
Construction	3,627	10.7
Transp. and commun.	2,540	7.5
Trade	5,980	17.6
Finance, insurance, and real estate	723	2.1
Pub. admin., defense	2,552	7.5
Services	10,429	30.6
Other	...	...
TOTAL	34,040	100.0

Production (metric tons except as noted). Agriculture, forestry, fishing (1989): melons 165, cucumbers 83, bananas 46, betelnuts 38, Chinese cabbage 33, coconuts 30, eggplant 23; livestock (number of live animals) 4,513 cattle, 1,260 pigs, 482 goats, 9,580 chickens; roundwood, n.a.; fish catch (1998) 235. Mining and quarrying: negligible amount of quarrying for building material. Manufacturing (value of sales in U.S.$'000,000; 1997): garments 700; stone, glass, or ceramic products 21; food products 6. Construction (new permits in U.S.$'000,000; 1998): 63.3. Energy production (consumption): electricity (kW-hr) n.a.[12]; coal, none (none); crude petroleum, none (none); petroleum products, none (none); natural gas, none (none).
Population economically active (1995): total 37,393; activity rate of total population 63.5% (participation rates: ages 16 and over, 85.3%; female 48.1%; unemployed 7.1%).

Price index (1990 = 100)

	1992	1993	1994	1995	1996	1997
Consumer price index	116.9	122.0	125.4	127.7	131.5	132.9

Public debt (external, outstanding; 1995): U.S.$27,000,000.
Household income and expenditure. Average household size (1995) 4.0; average income per household (1995) U.S.$30,296; sources of income: n.a.; expenditure: n.a.

Foreign trade

Balance of trade (current prices)

	1986	1987	1988	1989	1990	1991
U.S.$'000,000	–33[13]	–93[13]	–208[13]	–162	–138	–129
% of total	57.4%[13]	79.1%[13]	89.4%[13]	34.7%	25.3%	19.7%

Imports (1991): U.S.$392,250,000 (machinery and transport equipment 22.2%, petroleum and petroleum products 20.9%, special transactions not elsewhere specified 14.8%, food 13.9%, manufactured goods 11.7%, manufactured articles 8.8%, beverages and tobacco 5.4%). *Major import sources:* United States 18.2%, Japan 16.6%, other Asian countries 10.3%, Australia 3.4%, unspecified countries 51.5%.
Exports (1999): U.S.$1,049,000,000 (clothing and accessories 99.9%). *Major export destinations:* nearly all to the United States.

Transport and communications

Transport. Railroads: none. Roads (1998): total length *c.* 225 mi, *c.* 360 km (paved, nearly 100%). Vehicles (1993): passenger cars 12,000; trucks and buses 6,300. Merchant marine (1992): vessels (100 gross tons and over) 2; total deadweight tonnage 856. Air transport (1993[14]): aircraft landings 21,555; boarding passengers 590,857; airports (1999) with scheduled flights 2[15].

Communications

Medium	date	unit	number	units per 1,000 persons
Radio	1999	receivers	10,500	152
Television	1999	receivers	4,100	59
Telephones	1997	main lines	20,000	313
Cellular telephones	1995	subscribers	1,200	21
Personal computers	...	units	...	...
Internet	...	users	...	...

Education and health

Educational attainment (1995). Percentage of population age 25 and over having: no formal schooling 0.7%; primary education, 5.5%; some secondary 13.5%; completed secondary 38.8%; some postsecondary 23.3%; completed undergraduate 18.2%. *Literacy* (1990): total population age 10 and over literate 35,490 (98.8%); males literate 18,790 (99.0%); females literate 16,700 (98.6%).

Education (1996–97)

	schools	teachers	students	student/ teacher ratio
Primary (age 6–11)	16[16]	597	6,952	18.4
Secondary (age 12–17)	9[16]		4,003	
Vocational	—	—	—	—
Higher[17]	1	...	845	...

Health: physicians (1986): 23 (1 per 1,326 persons); hospital beds (1998): 74 (1 per 899 persons); infant mortality rate per 1,000 live births (1999): 5.9[11].
Food: n.a.

Military

The United States is responsible for military defense; headquarters of the U.S. Pacific Command are in Hawaii.

[1]Persons born in the Northern Marianas are U.S. citizens. [2]Residents elect a nonvoting representative to U.S. Congress. [3]In 1990, 90.5 percent of residents five years old and over spoke English, although 95.2 percent of residents spoke a language other than English at home, of which Chamorro 29.9 percent and Carolinian 4.8 percent. [4]Comprises the islands of Agrihan, Pagan, and Alamagan, as well as nine other uninhabited islands: Farallon de Pajaros (Uracas), Maug (East, West, and North islands), Asuncion, Guguan, Serigan, Anatahan, and Farallon de Medinilla. [5]Comprises Tinian island and the uninhabited island of Aguijan, which is 2.7 square miles in area. [6]Area measured at high tide; at low tide, total dry land area is 184.0 square miles (476.6 square km). [7]Includes 27,478 U.S. citizens and 31,368 aliens working primarily in the garment industry. [8]Includes aliens. [9]Unofficial estimate. [10]All villages are unincorporated census designated places. [11]U.S. Census Bureau estimate. [12]The installed electrical capacity in 1992 was 114,020 kilowatts. [13]Estimate. [14]Saipan International Airport only. [15]International flights are regularly scheduled at Saipan and at Rota; Tinian has nonscheduled domestic service. Additional domestic airports mainly handle charter flights. [16]1993–94. [17]Northern Marianas College; 1995–96.

Norway

Official name: Kongeriket Norge (Kingdom of Norway).
Form of government: constitutional monarchy with one legislative house (Parliament [165]).
Chief of state: King.
Head of government: Prime Minister.
Capital: Oslo.
Official language: Norwegian.
Official religion: Evangelical Lutheran.
Monetary unit: 1 Norwegian krone (NKr) = 100 øre; valuation (Oct. 6, 2000) 1 U.S.$ = NKr 9.23; 1 £ = NKr 13.35.

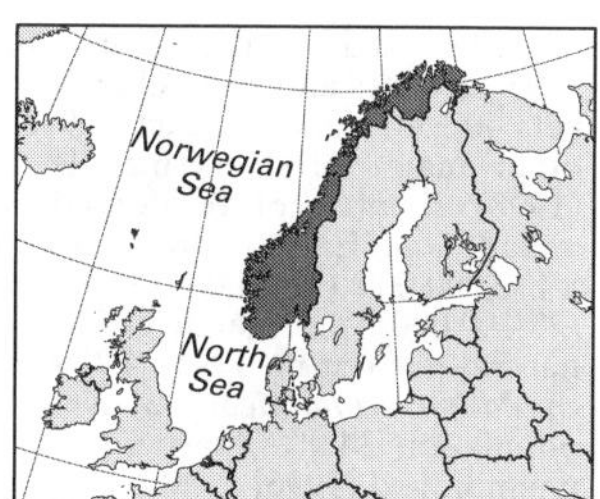

Area and population

Counties	Capitals	area[1] sq mi	area[1] sq km	population 1999[2] estimate
Akershus	—	1,898	4,917	460,564
Aust-Agder	Arendal	3,557	9,212	101,487
Buskerud	Drammen	5,763	14,927	235,018
Finnmark	Vadsø	18,779	48,637	74,061
Hedmark	Hamar	10,575	27,388	186,321
Hordaland	Bergen	6,036	15,634	431,882
Møre og Romsdal	Molde	5,832	15,104	242,538
Nordland	Bodø	14,798	38,327	238,547
Nord-Trøndelag	Steinkjer	8,647	22,396	126,797
Oppland	Lillehammer	9,726	25,191	182,239
Oslo	Oslo	175	454	502,867
Østfold	Moss	1,615	4,183	246,018
Rogaland	Stavanger	3,529	9,141	369,059
Sogn og Fjordane	Leikanger	7,189	18,620	107,648
Sør-Trøndelag	Trondheim	7,271	18,838	260,855
Telemark	Skien	5,913	15,315	164,523
Troms	Tromsø	10,032	25,984	150,200
Vest-Agder	Kristiansand	2,811	7,281	153,998
Vestfold	Tønsberg	856	2,216	210,707
TOTAL		125,004[3]	323,758[3]	4,445,329

Demography

Population (2000): 4,487,000.
Density (2000): persons per sq mi 35.9, persons per sq km 13.6.
Urban-rural (1990): urban 75.0%; rural 25.0%.
Sex distribution (1999[2]): male 49.48%; female 50.52%.
Age breakdown (1999[2]): under 20, 25.8%; 20–29, 14.0%; 30–49, 28.9%; 50–69, 19.6%; 70–79, 7.4%; 80 and over, 4.2%.
Population projection: (2010) 4,656,000; (2020) 4,824,000.
Ethnic composition (by country of citizenship; 1999[2]): Norway 96.3%; Sweden 0.5%; Denmark 0.4%; Bosnia and Herzegovina 0.3%; United Kingdom 0.3%; United States 0.2%; Pakistan 0.2%; Germany 0.1%; Yugoslavia 0.1%; Iraq 0.1%; Somalia 0.1%; Iran 0.1%; other 1.4%.
Major cities (1999)[5]: Oslo 502,867; Bergen 227,276; Trondheim 147,187.

Vital statistics

Birth rate per 1,000 population (1998): 13.2 (world avg. 22.1); (1998) legitimate 51.0%; illegitimate 49.0%.
Death rate per 1,000 population (1998): 10.0 (world avg. 8.9).
Natural increase rate per 1,000 population (1998): 3.2 (world avg. 13.2).
Total fertility rate (avg. births per childbearing woman; 1998): 1.8.
Marriage rate per 1,000 population (1997): 5.4.
Divorce rate per 1,000 population (1997): 2.3.
Life expectancy at birth (1998): male 75.5 years; female 81.3 years.
Major causes of death per 100,000 population (1995): malignant neoplasms (cancers) 249.6; ischemic heart disease 221.3; cerebrovascular disease 114.4.

National economy

Budget (1996). Revenue: NKr 523,628,000,000 (value-added taxes 31.0%, social security taxes 18.7%, taxes on interest and dividends 7.9%). Expenditures: NKr 463,394,000,000 (social security and welfare 36.7%, health 14.2%, education 13.4%, debt service 5.8%).
Land use (1994): forested 27.2%; meadows and pastures 0.4%; agricultural and under permanent cultivation 2.9%; built-up and other 69.5%.
Production (metric tons except as noted). Agriculture, forestry, fishing (1998): barley 640,000, potatoes 470,000, oats 378,000, wheat 371,000; livestock (number of live animals) 2,450,000 sheep, 1,018,000 cattle, 770,000 pigs; roundwood (1998) 8,556,000 cu m; fish catch (1997) 2,844,206, of which herring 916,940, cod 400,839, saithe 183,583, capelin 155,731. Mining and quarrying (1997)[6]: iron ore 710,000, ilmenite-titanium 557,000, copper 28,100, zinc 5,700. Manufacturing (value added in NKr '000,000; 1994): machinery and equipment 37,194; paper and paper products 19,748; food products 17,375; wood products 8,133; chemical products 6,851. Construction (1996): residential 2,907,000 sq m; nonresidential 3,545,000 sq m. Energy production (consumption): electricity (kW-hr; 1995) 123,136,000,000 (116,774,000,000); coal (metric tons; 1995) 292,000 (1,019,000); crude petroleum (barrels; 1996) 1,126,000,000 ([1995] 93,000,000); petroleum products (metric tons; 1995) 12,435,000 (6,648,000); natural gas (cu m; 1995) 27,663,000,000 (3,865,000,000).
Household income and expenditure. Average household size (1994) 2.3; consumption expenditure per household (1996) NKr 311,430 (U.S.$48,285); expenditure (1994): housing 25.3%, transportation 20.1%, food 13.9%, recreation and education 11.0%, household furniture and equipment 8.4%, clothing and footwear 6.5%.
Gross national product (1998): U.S.$152,049,000,000 (U.S.$34,310 per capita).

Structure of gross domestic product and labour force

	1997 in value NKr '000,000	% of total value	labour force	% of labour force
Agriculture	21,661	2.0	104,000	4.6
Mining	2,052	0.2	25,000	1.1
Crude petroleum and natural gas	161,280	14.9	...	...
Manufacturing	120,638	11.1	331,000	14.6
Construction	40,893	3.8	136,000	6.0
Public utilities	23,384	2.1	21,000	0.9
Transp. and commun.	99,575	9.2	164,000	7.2
Trade	111,474[7]	10.3[7]	399,000	17.6
Finance	168,704	15.5	215,000	9.5
Pub. admin., defense	166,813	15.4	793,000	35.0
Services	54,181	5.0		
Other	114,134	10.5	77,525[8]	3.5[8]
TOTAL	1,084,788[3]	100.0	2,265,525	100.0

Population economically active (1997): total 2,265,525; activity rate of total population 51.4% (participation rates: ages 16–64 [1996] 79.1%; female 46.0%; unemployed 4.9%).

Price and earnings indexes (1995 = 100)

	1993	1994	1995	1996	1997	1998	1999
Consumer price index	96.3	97.6	100.0	101.3	103.9	106.2	108.7
Hourly earnings index	93.9	96.6	100.0	104.2	108.4[9]	...	...

Public debt (1997): U.S.$33,763,000,000.
Tourism (1997): receipts from visitors U.S.$2,216,000,000.

Foreign trade[10]

Balance of trade (current prices)

	1994	1995	1996	1997	1998	1999
NKr '000,000	+51,736	+57,256	+90,410	+90,189	+25,998	+84,886
% of total	11.9%	12.1%	16.4%	15.1%	4.5%	13.8%

Imports (1997): NKr 252,232,000,000 (machinery and transport equipment 39.1%, of which road vehicles 9.3%, ships 5.3%; metals and metal products 9.4%, of which iron and steel 4.2%; food products 5.2%, of which fruits and vegetables 1.3%; petroleum products 2.4%). *Major import sources:* Sweden 15.7%; Germany 13.5%; U.K. 9.4%; Denmark 7.0%.
Exports (1997): NKr 342,421,000,000 (petroleum products 44.1%; machinery and transport equipment 11.5%; metals and metal products 11.1%; food products 7.6%, of which fish 6.8%). *Major export destinations:* U.K. 19.3%; The Netherlands 11.4%; Germany 10.9%; Sweden 8.8%.

Transport and communications

Transport. Railroads (1997): route length 4,021 km; passenger-km 2,561,000,000; metric ton-km cargo 2,399,000,000. Roads (1998): total length 91,254 km (paved 74%). Vehicles (1997): passenger cars 1,758,001; trucks and buses 435,427. Merchant marine (1995): vessels (100 gross tons and over) 1,597; total deadweight tonnage 20,834,000. Air transport (1997): passenger-km 9,927,331,000; metric ton-km cargo 1,128,093,000; airports (1996) 50.

Communications

Medium	date	unit	number	units per 1,000 persons
Daily newspapers	1996	circulation	2,578,000	588
Radio	1996	receivers	4,000,000	913
Television	1997	receivers	2,550,000	579
Telephones	1997	main lines	2,325,010	527
Cellular telephones	1997	subscribers	1,676,763	380
Personal computers	1997	units	1,589,000	360
Internet	1998	users	1,000,000	226

Education and health

Educational attainment (1996). Percentage of population age 16 and over having: primary and lower secondary education 33.5%; higher secondary 46.3%; higher 20.2%. *Literacy* (1995): virtually 100% literate.

Education (1995–96)

	schools	teachers	students	student/ teacher ratio
Primary (age 7–12)	3,314	37,966	479,249	12.6
Secondary (age 13–18) and vocational	546	20,849	177,868	8.5
Higher	60[11]	12,055	194,133	16.1

Health (1996): physicians 15,368 (1 per 285 persons); hospital beds 21,754 (1 per 201 persons); infant mortality rate per 1,000 live births (1998) 4.0.
Food (1997): daily per capita caloric intake 3,357 (vegetable products 67%, animal products 33%); 125% of FAO recommended minimum requirement.

Military

Total active duty personnel (1998): 28,000 (army 54.3%, navy 21.8%, air force 23.9%). *Military expenditure as percentage of GNP* (1995): 2.7% (world avg. 2.8%); per capita expenditure U.S.$804.

[1]Excludes Svalbard and Jan Mayen (24,360 sq mi [63,080 sq km]). [2]January 1. [3]Detail does not add to total given because of rounding. [4]Includes the Norwegian population of Svalbard and Jan Mayen, registered as residents in municipalities on the mainland. [5]Population of municipalities. [6]Metal content of ore. [7]Includes hotels. [8]Includes 73,525 unemployed. [9]2nd quarter. [10]Imports c.i.f. in balance of trade. [11]The number of colleges is lower than in recent years because of reorganization.

Internet resources for further information:
- **Statistics Norway http://www.ssb.no/www-open/english**

Oman

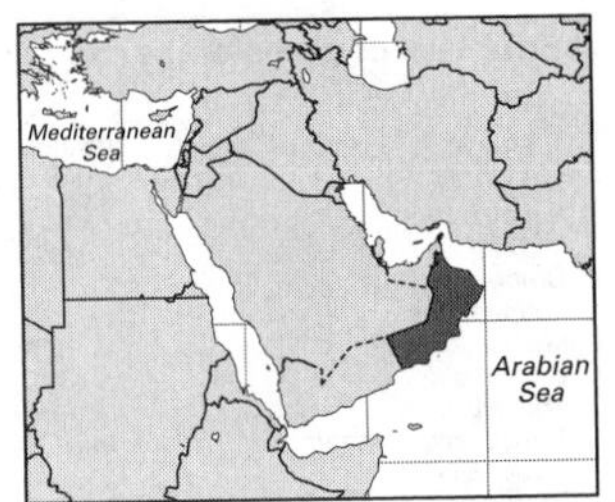

Official name: Salṭanat ʿUmān (Sultanate of Oman).
Form of government: monarchy with two advisory bodies (Council of State [41[1]]; Consultative Council [82[2]]).
Head of state and government: Sultan.
Capital: Muscat[3].
Official language: Arabic.
Official religion: Islam.
Monetary unit: 1 rial Omani (RO) = 1,000 baizas; valuation (Oct. 6, 2000) 1 RO = U.S.$2.63 = £1.78.

Area and population		area[4]		population
				1998
Regions	Capitals	sq mi	sq km	estimate
Al-Bāṭinah	Ar-Rustāq; Ṣuḥār	4,850	12,500	640,600
Ad-Dākhilīyah	Nizwā; Samā'il	12,300	31,900	260,728
Ash-Sharqīyah	Ibrā; Ṣūr	14,200	36,800	293,098
Al-Wusṭa	Haymā'	30,750	79,700	19,356
Aẓ-Ẓāhirah	Al-Buraymī; ʿIbrī	17,000	44,000	205,389
Governorates				
Masqaṭ	Muscat (Masqaṭ)	1,350	3,500	621,719
Musandam	Khaṣab	700	1,800	32,541
Ẓufār (Dhofar)	Salālah	38,350	99,300	214,211
TOTAL		119,500	309,500	2,287,642

Demography

Population (2000): 2,416,000.
Density (2000): persons per sq mi 20.2, persons per sq km 7.8.
Urban-rural (1999): urban 82.7%; rural 17.3%.
Sex distribution (1998): male 58.3%; female 41.7%.
Age breakdown (1998): under 15, 36.8%; 15–29, 29.7%; 30–44, 22.1%; 45–59, 7.9%; 60 and over, 3.5%.
Population projection: (2010) 3,359,000; (2020) 4,461,000.
Doubling time: 21 years.
Ethnic composition (1993): Omani Arab 73.5%; Indian 13.3%; Bangladeshi 4.3%; Pakistani (mostly Balochī) 3.1%; Egyptian 1.6%; other 4.2%.
Religious affiliation (1993): Muslim 87.7%, of which Ibāḍiyah Muslim *c.* 75% (principal minorities are Sunnī Muslim and Shīʿī Muslim); Hindu 7.4%; Christian 3.9%; Buddhist 0.5%; other 0.5%.
Major cities (1993): As-Sīb 155,000[5]; Salālah 116,000; Bawshar 107,500[5]; Ṣuḥār 84,300; ʿIbrī 76,000; Muscat 40,900 (urban agglomeration [1999] 887,000).

Vital statistics

Birth rate per 1,000 population (1999): 38.0 (world avg. 22.1).
Death rate per 1,000 population (1999): 4.2 (world avg. 8.9).
Natural increase rate per 1,000 population (1999): 33.8 (world avg. 13.2).
Total fertility rate (avg. births per childbearing woman; 1999): 6.1.
Life expectancy at birth (1999): male 69.4 years; female 73.7 years.
Major causes of death per 100,000 population: n.a.; however, the main causes of hospital deaths in 1995 were diseases of the circulatory system 34.1%, infectious diseases 11.1%, malignant neoplasms (cancers) 9.4%, perinatal problems 7.2%, diseases of the respiratory system 6.3%.

National economy

Budget (1999). Revenue: RO 2,091,000,000 (oil revenue 72.1%; other 27.9%). Expenditures: RO 2,440,000,000 (current expenditure 77.9%, of which civil ministries 42.1%, defense 27.6%, interest paid on loans 4.9%; capital development projects and subsidies 22.1%).
Public debt (external, outstanding; 1998): U.S.$2,228,000,000.
Gross national product (1998): U.S.$13,135,000,000 (U.S.$5,950 per capita).

Structure of gross domestic product and labour force	1999			
	in value RO '000,000	% of total value	labour force	% of labour force
Agriculture[6]	156.8	2.6	54,053	9.4
Mining	2,335.7	38.9	4,779	0.8
Manufacturing	258.0	4.3	66,418	11.6
Construction	160.3	2.7	112,195	19.6
Public utilities	67.9	1.1	1,054	0.2
Transp. and commun.	446.2	7.4	3,868	0.7
Trade	810.7[7]	13.5[7]	154,219	26.9
Finance	702.2[8]	11.7[8]	5,951	1.0
Pub. admin., defense	677.6	11.3	99,025	17.3
Services	509.7[9]	8.5[9]	72,180	12.6
Other	–113.8[10]	–1.9[10]	—	—
TOTAL	6,011.3	100.0[11]	573,742[12]	100.0[11]

Tourism (1995): receipts U.S.$92,000,000; expenditures U.S.$47,000,000.
Household income and expenditure. Average household size (1998) 6.9; income per household: n.a.; sources of income: n.a.; expenditure (1990): housing and utilities 27.8%, food, beverage, and tobacco 26.4%, transportation 19.8%, clothing and shoes 7.8%, household goods and furniture 6.1%, education, health services, entertainment, and other 12.1%.
Production (metric tons except as noted). Agriculture, forestry, fishing (1999): vegetables and melons 164,000 (of which watermelons 32,000), dates 135,000, bananas 28,000, mangoes 12,000, onions 9,400, potatoes 5,700, papayas 2,900, tobacco leaf 2,450, wheat 1,400; livestock (number of live animals) 728,000 goats, 160,000 sheep, 148,000 cattle, 97,000 camels, 3,200,000 chickens; fish catch (1998) 106,164. Mining and quarrying (1998): copper 24,360; silver 4,692 kg; gold 569 kg. Manufacturing (value of production in RO '000,000; 1993): textiles and apparel 78,200; food and beverages 72,930; chemical products 40,950; wood products 5,950; metal products 4,200; paper products 360; other major products include refined petroleum products. Construction (1998): number of residential permits 5,372; nonresidential permits 448; mixed 263. Energy production (consumption): electricity (kW-hr; 1998) 8,172,000,000 (7,784,000,000); crude petroleum (barrels; 1998) 328,300,000 (27,100,000); petroleum products (metric tons; 1996) 3,770,000 (1,656,000); natural gas (cu m; 1996) 4,723,300,000 (4,723,300,000).
Population economically active (1993)[13]: total 704,798; activity rate of total population 34.9% (participation rates: over age 15, 60.9%; female 9.7%; unemployed [1996] *c.* 20%).

Price and earnings indexes (1995 = 100)	1993	1994	1995	1996	1997	1998	1999
Consumer price index	102.1	101.3	100.0	100.3	100.0	99.5	100.6
Earnings index	...	...	...	...	...	...	...

Land use (1994): meadows and pastures 4.7%; agricultural and under permanent cultivation 0.3%; other (mostly desert and developed area) 95.0%.

Foreign trade[14]

Balance of trade (current prices)	1994	1995	1996	1997	1998	1999
RO '000,000	+627	+700	+1,064	+1,001	–66.6	+977.9
% of total	17.2%	17.6%	23.2%	20.6%	1.5%	21.4%

Imports (1999): RO 1,797,100,000 (machinery and transport equipment 41.4%, basic manufactured goods 17.0%, food and live animals 13.9%, beverages and tobacco 7.8%, miscellaneous manufactured articles 7.1%). *Major import sources:* United Arab Emirates 28.1%; Japan 15.2%; United Kingdom 6.8%; United States 6.4%; Germany 4.0%; India 3.5%; France 3.5%; Saudi Arabia 3.4%.
Exports (1999): RO 2,775,000,000 (domestic exports 83.6%, of which petroleum 76.4%, manufactured goods 2.9% [of which copper and copper products 0.8%], food and live animals 2.5%, mineral fuels 0.9%; re-exports 16.4%, of which machinery and transport equipment 11.3%). *Major export destinations*[15]: United Arab Emirates 42.0%; Iran 7.0%; Saudi Arabia 6.8%; Yemen 5.3%; United States 5.1%; United Kingdom 4.6%; Tanzania 4.5%.

Transport and communications

Transport. Railroads: none. Roads (1998): total length 20,518 mi, 33,020 km (paved 24%). Vehicles: automobiles (1996) 211,000; trucks and buses 97,020. Merchant marine (1992): vessels (100 gross tons and over) 26; total deadweight tonnage 11,727. Air transport (1997)[16]: passenger-mi 821,200,000, passenger-km 1,321,600,000; short ton-mi cargo 16,805,000; metric ton-km cargo 27,045,000; airports (1997) with scheduled flights 6.

Communications				units
Medium	date	unit	number	per 1,000 persons
Daily newspapers	1996	circulation	63,000	28
Radio	1997	receivers	1,400,000	607
Television	1998	receivers	1,400,000	588
Telephones	1998	main lines	219,956	92
Cellular telephones	1998	subscribers	103,032	43
Personal computers	1998	units	50,000	21
Internet	1998	users	20,000	8.3

Education and health

Educational attainment (1993). Percentage of population age 15 and over having: no formal schooling (illiterate) 41.2%; no formal schooling (literate) 14.9%; primary 18.9%; secondary 21.1%; higher technical 2.0%; higher undergraduate 1.5%; higher graduate 0.1%; other 0.3%. *Literacy* (1995): percentage of total population age 15 and over literate 64.0%; males literate 74.6%; females literate 50.7%.

Education (1998–99)	schools	teachers	students	student/ teacher ratio
Primary (age 6–14)	397	12,421	315,557	25.4
Secondary (age 15–17)[17]	685	12,862	229,031	17.8
Voc., teacher tr.	10	954	9,936	10.4
Higher[18]	1	695	6,605	9.5

Health (1998): physicians 2,099 (1 per 1,090 persons); hospital beds 4,443 (1 per 515 persons); infant mortality rate per 1,000 live births (1999) 24.2.

Military

Total active duty personnel (1999): 43,500 (army 72.4%, navy 9.7%, air force 9.4%); foreign troops 3,700. *Military expenditure as percentage of GDP* (1997): 26.1% (world 2.6%); per capita expenditure U.S.$795.

[1]All seats are nonelected. [2]Filled by 114,000 appointed voters. [3]Most ministries have moved to suburbs. [4]Approximate; no comprehensive survey of surface area has ever been carried out in Oman. [5]Within Muscat urban agglomeration. [6]Agriculture includes fishing. [7]Trade includes restaurants and hotels. [8]Finance includes business services and real estate. [9]Services include education and health. [10]Includes import taxes less bank service charges. [11]Detail does not add to total given because of rounding. [12]Employed only; includes 474,717 expatriate workers in private sector and 99,025 government employees, of which 68.1% are Omani. [13]Non-Omani workers constituted 61.3% of the labour force in 1993. [14]Imports c.i.f.; exports f.o.b. [15]Non-oil exports only; includes reexports. [16]Oman airline and one-fourth apportionment of international flights of Gulf Air. [17]Includes preparatory. [18]University only.

Internet resources for further information:
- **Ministry of Information http://www.omanet.com**

Pakistan

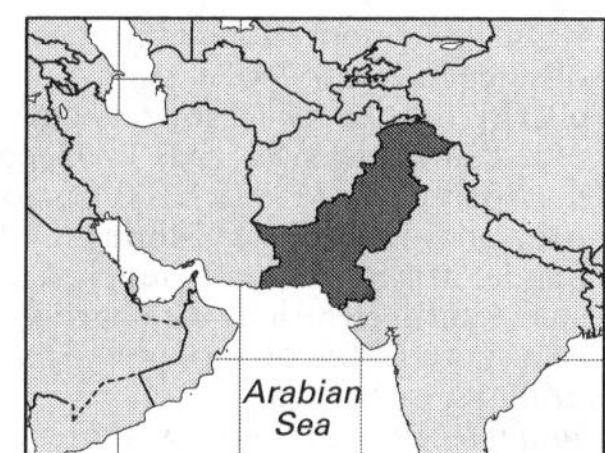

Official name: Islam-i Jamhuriya-e Pakistan (Islamic Republic of Pakistan).
Form of government: interim military regime.
Chief of state and government: Chief Executive, assisted by the National Security Council[1].
Capital: Islamabad.
Official language: Urdu.
Official religion: Islam.
Monetary unit: 1 Pakistan rupee (PRs) = 100 paisa, valuation (Oct. 6, 2000) 1 U.S.$ = PRs 59.45; 1 £ = PRs 86.00.

Area and population		area[2]		population
				1998
Provinces	**Capitals**	sq mi	sq km	census[3]
Balochistan	Quetta	134,051	347,190	6,511,000
North-West Frontier	Peshawar	28,773	74,521	17,555,000
Punjab	Lahore	79,284	205,344	72,585,000
Sindh	Karachi	54,407	140,914	29,991,000
Federally Administered Tribal Areas	...	10,509	27,220	3,138,000
Federal Capital Area				
Islamabad	...	350	906	799,000
TOTAL		307,374	796,095	130,579,000

Demography

Population (2000)[3]: 141,553,775.
Density (2000): persons per sq mi 460.5, persons per sq km 177.8.
Urban-rural (1998)[3, 4]: urban 33.3%; rural 66.7%.
Sex distribution (1998)[3, 4]: male 51.95%; female 48.05%.
Age breakdown (1998)[3, 4]: under 15, 43.2%; 15–29, 26.9%; 30–44, 15.6%; 45–59, 8.8%; 60–74, 4.3%; 75 and over, 1.2%.
Population projection[3]: (2010) 171,373,000; (2020) 199,744,808.
Doubling time: 30 years.
Linguistic composition (1981): Punjabi 48.2%; Pashto 13.1%; Sindhi 11.8%; Saraiki 9.8%; Urdu 7.6%; other 9.5%.
Religious affiliation (1993): Muslim 95.0%[5]; Christian 2.0%; Hindu 1.8%; others (including Ahmadiyah) 1.2%.
Major cities (1998): Karachi 9,269,000; Lahore 5,063,000; Faisalabad 1,977,000; Rawalpindi 1,406,000; Multan 1,182,000; Islamabad 525,000.

Vital statistics

Birth rate per 1,000 population (1999): 33.1 (world avg. 22.1).
Death rate per 1,000 population (1999): 9.8 (world avg. 8.9).
Natural increase rate per 1,000 population (1999): 23.3 (world avg. 13.2).
Total fertility rate (avg. births per childbearing woman; 1999): 4.7.
Life expectancy at birth (1999): male 59.9 years; female 61.5 years.
Major cause of death (percentage of total deaths; 1987): malaria 18.2%; childhood diseases 12.1%; diseases of digestive system 9.8%; diseases of respiratory system 9.2%; infection of intestinal tract 7.7%.

National economy

Budget (1997–98). Revenue: PRs 450,212,000,000 (nontax receipts 22.7%, income taxes 22.3%, customs duties 19.3%, excise taxes 14.4%, surcharges 6.7%). Expenditures: PRs 461,906,000,000 (public-debt service 53.7%, defense 29.0%, grants and subsidies 5.9%, general administration 4.4%).
Public debt (external, outstanding; 1998): U.S.$26,061,000,000.
Production (metric tons except as noted). Agriculture, forestry, fishing (1998): sugarcane 53,104,000, wheat 17,868,000, rice 7,011,000, seed cotton 4,486,000, potatoes 1,426,000, corn (maize) 1,260,000, chickpeas 767,000, rapeseed 275,000; livestock (number of live animals) 48,575,000 goats, 32,383,000 sheep, 21,213,000 buffalo, 18,000,000 cattle, 200,000,000 chickens; roundwood 30,908,000 cu m; fish catch (1997) 575,137. Mining and quarrying (1996–97): limestone 9,720,000; rock salt 1,024,000; gypsum 561,000; silica sand 180,000; chromite 30,000. Manufacturing (1995–96): cement 9,571,000; chemical fertilizers 4,165,000, of which urea 3,257,000; refined sugar 2,470,000; cotton yarn 1,465,000; vegetable products 717,000; industrial chemicals 397,000; jute textiles 70,600; cotton textiles 327,000,000 sq m; cigarettes 44,701,000,000 units; motor-vehicle tires 1,003,000 units; bicycles 545,000 units; sewing machines 82,800 units. Energy production (consumption): electricity (kW-hr; 1997–98) 59,088,000,000 ([1996] 56,946,000,000); coal (metric tons; 1997–98) 3,144,000 ([1996] 4,718,000); crude petroleum (barrels; 1997–98) 20,520,000 ([1996] 49,609,000); petroleum products (metric tons; 1996) 5,890,000 (15,842,000); natural gas (cu m; 1997–98) 19,809,000,000 ([1996] 17,894,000).
Household income and expenditure (1988). Average household size 6.3; income per household PRs 25,572 (U.S.$1,420); sources of income: self-employment 56.0%, wages and salaries 22.0%, other 22.0%; expenditure: food 47.0%, housing 12.0%, clothing and footwear 8.0%, other 33.0%.
Population economically active (1996–97): total 37,150,000; activity rate of total population 27.5% (participation rates: ages 15–64, 41.3%; female [1994–95] 12.8%; unemployed 5.4%).

Price index (1995 = 100)	1993	1994	1995	1996	1997	1998	1999
Consumer price index	79.2	89.0	100.0	110.4	122.9	130.6	136.0

Gross national product (1998): U.S.$61,451,000,000 (U.S.$470 per capita).

Structure of gross domestic product and labour force	1997–98		1996–97	
	in value PRs '000,000	% of total value	labour force	% of labour force
Agriculture	659,965	23.9	16,450,000	44.3
Mining	12,831	0.5	3,690,000	9.9
Manufacturing	426,662	15.4		
Construction	87,898	3.2	2,530,000	6.8
Public utilities	97,090	3.5	290,000	0.8
Transp. and commun.	258,943	9.4	1,780,000	4.8
Trade	402,032	14.6	5,100,000	13.7
Finance	183,369	6.6	5,310,000	14.3
Pub. admin., defense	190,046	6.9		
Services	214,444	7.8		
Other	226,245	8.2	2,000,000[6]	5.4[6]
TOTAL	2,759,525	100.0	37,150,000	100.0

Tourism (1997): receipts U.S.$117,000,000; expenditures U.S.$364,000,000.
Land use (1994): forest 4.5%; pasture 6.5%; agriculture 27.7%; other 61.3%.

Foreign trade[7]

Balance of trade (current prices)	1994	1995	1996	1997	1998	1999
U.S.$'000,000	–1,531.6	–3,495.6	–2,856.3	–2,869.8	–820.4	...
% of total	9.4%	17.9%	13.3%	14.0%	4.6%	10.0%

Imports (1996–97): U.S.$11,894,200,000 (petroleum products 19.0%, power-generating machinery 8.4%, specialized machinery 5.5%, organic chemicals 5.4%, fixed vegetable oil and fats 5.3%, general industrial machinery 4.1%, wheat 4.0%, iron and steel manufactures 3.9%). *Major import sources:* U.S. 12.0%; Japan 8.7%; Kuwait 6.9%; Saudi Arabia 6.0%; United Arab Emirates 5.7%; Germany 5.6%; U.K. 5.0%; Malaysia 4.7%; China 4.6%.
Exports (1996–97): U.S.$8,320,300,000 (textile fabrics 54.2%, ready-made garments 21.4%, rice 5.6%, leather goods 3.0%, cotton fibres and waste 0.9%). *Major export destinations:* U.S. 17.8%; Hong Kong 9.3%; Germany 7.5%; U.K. 7.2%; Japan 5.8%; United Arab Emirates 4.7%; Netherlands 3.3%; Italy 2.9%.

Transport and communications

Transport. Railroads (1996–97): route length 8,775 km; passenger-km 20,476,000,000; metric ton-km cargo 5,229,000,000. Roads (1997): total length 142,874 mi, 229,934 km (paved 58%). Vehicles (1997): passenger cars 665,102; trucks and buses 291,683. Merchant marine (1992): vessels (100 gross tons and over) 73; total deadweight tonnage 513,823. Air transport (1998): passenger-km 10,972,000,000; metric ton-km cargo 402,396,000; airports (1997) 35.

Communications				units
Medium	date	unit	number	per 1,000 persons
Daily newspapers	1995	circulation	2,800,000	21
Radio	1997	receivers	13,500,000	102
Television	1997	receivers	3,100,000	23
Telephones	1998	main lines	2,757,000	20
Cellular telephones	1998	subscribers	202,000	1.5
Personal computers	1998	units	561,000	4.1
Internet	1998	users	61,900	0.5

Education and health

Educational attainment (1990). Percentage of population age 25 and over having: no formal schooling 73.8%; some primary education 9.7%; secondary 14.0%; postsecondary 2.5%. *Literacy* (1995): total population age 15 and over literate 37.8%; males literate 50.0%; females literate 24.4%.

Education (1997–98)	schools	teachers	students	student/ teacher ratio
Primary (age 5–9)	158,511	346,000	16,642,000	48.1
Secondary (age 10–14)	25,913	259,200	5,545,000	21.4
Voc., teacher tr.	673	7,500	95,000	12.7
Higher	984	34,100	1,053,000	30.9

Health (1997): physicians 78,470 (1 per 1,724 persons); hospital beds 89,929 (1 per 1,504 persons); infant mortality rate per 1,000 live births (1999) 84.6.
Food (1997): daily per capita caloric intake 2,476 (vegetable products 85%, animal products 15%); (1995) 107% of FAO recommended minimum.

Military

Total active duty personnel (1998): 587,000 (army 88.6%, navy 3.7%, air force 7.7%). *Military expenditure as percentage of GNP* (1997): 5.7% (world 2.6%); per capita expenditure U.S.$26.

[1]Military leader (from October 1999) given three years to restore democracy per ruling announced by Pakistani Supreme Court in May 2000. [2]Excludes 32,494 sq mi (84,159 sq km) area of Pakistani-administered Jammu and Kashmir (comprising both Azad Kashmir [AK] and the Northern Areas [NA]). [3]Excludes Afghan refugees (2000; 1,100,000) and the population of AK and NA (2000; *c.* 4,000,000). [4]Excludes Federally Administered Tribal Areas. [5]Mostly Sunni, with Shīʿī comprising about 20% of total population. [6]Mostly unemployed. [7]Import figures are c.i.f.

Internet resources for further information:

- **Government of Pakistan: http://www.pak.gov.pk**

Palau

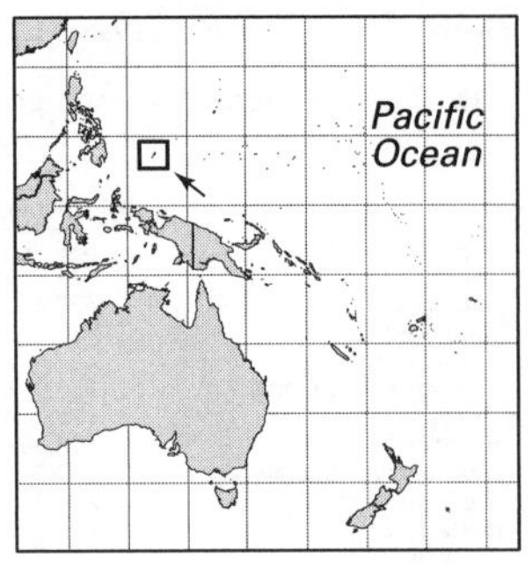

Official name: Belu'u er a Belau (Palauan); Republic of Palau (English).
Form of government: unitary republic with a national congress composed of two legislative houses (Senate [14]; House of Delegates [16]).
Head of state and government: President.
Capital: Koror[1].
Official languages[2]: Palauan; English.
Official religion: none.
Monetary unit: 1 U.S. dollar (U.S.$) = 100 cents; valuation (Oct. 6, 2000) 1 £ = U.S.$1.45.

Area and population

	area		population
States	sq mi	sq km	1995 census
Aimeliik	20	52	419
Airai	17	44	1,481
Angaur	3	8	193
Hatobohel	1	3	51
Kayangel	1	3	124
Koror	7	18	12,299
Melekeok	11	28	261
Ngaraard	14	36	421
Ngarchelong	4	10	253
Ngardmau	18	47	162
Ngatpang	18	47	221
Ngchesar	16	41	228
Ngeremlengui	25	65	281
Ngiwal	10	26	176
Peleliu	5	13	575
Sonsorol	1	3	80
Other			
Rock Islands	18	47	—
TOTAL	188[3]	488[3]	17,225

Demography

Population (2000): 18,800.
Density (2000): persons per sq mi 100.0, persons per sq km 38.5.
Urban-rural (1990): urban 59.6%; rural 40.4%.
Sex distribution (1999): male 53.49%; female 46.51%.
Age breakdown (1999): under 15, 27.1%; 15–29, 24.1%; 30–44, 27.8%; 45–59, 14.0%; 60–74, 5.0%; 75 and over 2.0%.
Population projection: (2010) 21,600; (2020) 23,500.
Doubling time: 39 years.
Ethnic composition (1997): Palauan 74.5%; Filipino 16.0%; Chinese 3.2%; other Micronesian and other 6.3%.
Religious affiliation (1995): Roman Catholic 38.4%; Protestant 24.7%; Modekne 26.5%; other 10.4%.
Major cities (1995): Koror 12,000.

Vital statistics

Birth rate per 1,000 population (1999): 20.1 (world avg. 22.1).
Death rate per 1,000 population (1999): 7.5 (world avg. 8.9).
Natural increase rate per 1,000 population (1999): 12.6 (world avg. 13.2).
Total fertility rate (avg. births per childbearing woman; 1999): 2.5.
Marriage rate per 1,000 population: n.a.
Divorce rate per 1,000 population: n.a.
Life expectancy at birth (1999): male 65.2 years; female 71.5 years.
Major causes of death per 100,000 population (1993): diseases of the circulatory system 192.9; malignant and benign neoplasms (cancers) 136.9; accidents, poisoning, and violence 112.0; diseases of the respiratory system 43.6; infectious and parasitic diseases 43.6.

National economy

Budget (1999). Revenue: U.S.$59,102,000 (grants from the U.S. 40.5%, tax revenue 39.0%, nontax revenue 20.5%). Expenditures: U.S.$69,900,000 (current expenditure 86.0%, of which wages and salaries 38.9%; capital expenditure 14.0%).
Gross national product (at current market prices; 1997)[4]: U.S.$159,800,000 (U.S.$8,806 per capita).

Structure of gross domestic product and labour force

	1998		1995	
	in value U.S.$'000	% of total value	labour force	% of labour force
Agriculture, fisheries	6,135	4.8	724	8.7
Mining	145	0.1		
Manufacturing	1,016	0.8	1,165[5]	14.0[5]
Public utilities	–427	–0.3	[6]	[6]
Construction	10,006	7.7	[5]	[5]
Transportation and communications	20,649	16.0	435[6]	5.2[6]
Trade	34,671	26.8	1,448	17.3
Finance	15,802	12.2	122	1.5
Public administration, defense	28,879	22.3	2,292	27.5
Services	9,214	7.1	1,573	18.8
Other	3,161[7]	2.4[7]	584[8]	7.0[8]
TOTAL	129,251	100.0[3]	8,368	100.0

Production (metric tons except as noted). Agriculture, forestry, fishing (value of sales in U.S.$; 1993): eggs 262,701, fruit and vegetables 126,325, betel nuts 60,376, root crops (taro, cassava, sweet potatoes) 43,718; livestock (number of live animals; 1984) pigs 1,343, cows 82, goats 52, poultry 9,500; roundwood, n.a.; fish catch (1997) 1,500 (major species are parrot fish, snapper, unicorn fish, and rabbitfish). Mining and quarrying: n.a. Manufacturing: includes handicrafts and small items. Construction: n.a. Energy production (consumption): electricity (kW-hr; 1996) 208,000,000 (208,000,000); coal, none (n.a.); crude petroleum, none (n.a.); petroleum products, none (80,000); natural gas, none (n.a.).
Public debt (external, outstanding; 1998): U.S.$1,433,000.
Tourism (1999): receipts from visitors U.S.$68,200,000.
Population economically active (1995): total 8,368; activity rate of total population 48.6% (participation rates: over age 15, 69.0%; female 39.6%; unemployed 7.0%.
Land use: n.a.
Household income and expenditure. Average household size (1997) 4.9; income per household (1989) U.S.$8,882; sources of income (1989): wages 63.7%, social security 12.0%, self-employment 7.4%, retirement 5.5%, interest, dividend, or net rental 4.3%, remittance 4.1%, public assistance 1.0%, other 2.0%; expenditure (1997): food 42.2%, beverages and tobacco 14.8%, entertainment 13.1%, transportation 6.4%, clothing 5.7%, household goods 2.7%, other 15.1%.

Foreign trade[9]

Imports (1998): U.S.$63,222,000 (1997; machinery and transport equipment 27.8%; food, beverages, and tobacco 27.1%; manufactured articles 27.1%; mineral fuels 13.2%; chemicals and related products 4.5%). *Major import sources:* United States 44.1%; Guam 19.3%; Japan 14.8%; Singapore 14.3%; Taiwan 5.4%; China 2.6%; Hong Kong 1.9%.
Exports (1998): U.S.$11,095,000 (1984; food and agricultural raw materials 69.1%; manufactured goods 30.9%). *Major export destinations* (1984): Japan 58.8%; United States 8.0%.

Transport and communications

Transport. Railroads: none. Roads (1993): total length 40 mi, 64 km (paved 59%). Vehicles (1994): passenger cars and trucks 4,271. Merchant marine (1991): vessels (100 gross tons and over) 4; total deadweight tonnage, n.a. Air transport (1993): passenger arrivals 50,366, passenger departures 49,376; airports (1997) with scheduled flights 1.

Communications

Medium	date	unit	number	units per 1,000 persons
Radio	1997	receivers	12,000	663.0
Television	1997	receivers	11,000	606.0
Telephones	1994	main lines	2,615	160.0

Education and health

Educational attainment (1997). Percentage of population age 25 and over having: no formal schooling 0.1%; some primary education 4.4%; completed primary 5.7%; some secondary 16.3%; completed secondary 41.0%; some postsecondary 13.0%; higher 19.5%. *Literacy* (1997): total population age 15 and over literate 99.9%.

Education (1997)

	schools[10]	teachers[10]	students	student/ teacher ratio
Primary (age 6–13)	26	289	1,450	...
Secondary (age 14–18)	6	[11]	490	...
Higher[12]	1	...	130	...

Health (1990): physicians[13] 10 (1 per 1,518 persons); hospital beds 70 (1 per 200 persons); infant mortality rate per 1,000 live births (1999) 17.7.
Food: daily per capita caloric intake, n.a.

Military

The United States is responsible for the external security of Palau, as specified in the Compact of Free Association of Oct. 1, 1994.

[1]A site on Babelthuap is to be the eventual permanent capital. [2]Sonsorolese-Tobian is also, according to official sources, considered an official language. [3]Detail does not add to total given because of rounding. [4]Gross national product comprises U.S. government spending only. [5]Manufacturing includes Construction. [6]Transportation and communications includes Public utilities. [7]Includes import duties and imputed bank service charge. [8]Unemployed. [9]Export and import figures are f.o.b. [10]1987. [11]Included with primary. [12]Palau Community College. [13]Government-employed health personnel only.

Internet resources for further information:
- **Republic of Palau Economic Report (Bank of Hawaii) http://www.boh.com/econ/index.asp**
- **Palau Visitors Authority http://www.visit-palau.com**

Panama

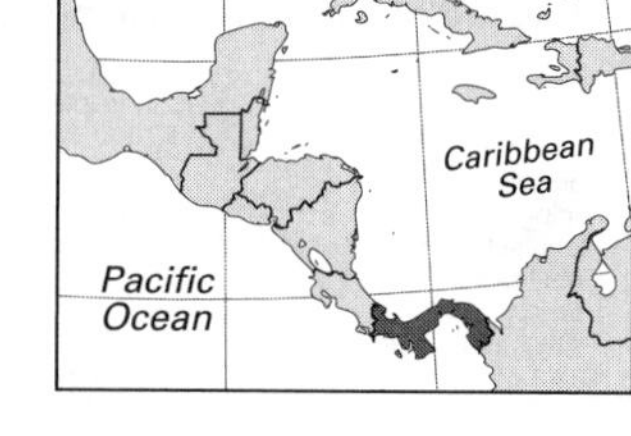

Official name: República de Panamá (Republic of Panama).
Form of government: multiparty republic with one legislative house (Legislative Assembly [71]).
Head of state and government: President assisted by Vice Presidents.
Capital: Panama City.
Official language: Spanish.
Official religion: none.
Monetary unit: 1 balboa (B) = 100 cents; valuation (Oct. 6, 2000) 1 U.S.$ = B 1.00; 1 £ = B 1.45.

Area and population

		area		population
Provinces	Capitals	sq mi	sq km	2000 preliminary census
Bocas del Toro	Bocas del Toro	3,376[1]	8,745[1]	88,983
Chiriquí	David	3,341[1]	8,653[1]	363,624
Coclé	Penonomé	1,902	4,927	200,541
Colón	Colón	1,888	4,890	200,808
Darién	La Palma	4,823[2]	12,491[2]	39,782
Herrera	Chitré	904	2,341	102,018
Los Santos	Las Tablas	1,470	3,806	83,120
Panamá	Panama City	3,789[3]	9,814[3]	1,375,116
Veraguas	Santiago	4,339[1]	11,239[1]	207,136
Indigenous districts				
Emberá	...	1,614[2]	4,180[2]	8,182
Ngöbe Buglé	...	[1]	[1]	110,619
Kuna de Madungandí	...	800[3]	2,073[3]	3,304
Kuna Yala (San Blas)	El Porvenir	910	2,357	32,411
TOTAL		29,157[4]	75,517[4]	2,815,644

Demography

Population (2000): 2,823,000.
Density (2000): persons per sq mi 96.8, persons per sq km 37.4.
Urban-rural (1999): urban 56.0%; rural 44.0%.
Sex distribution (2000): male 50.46%; female 49.54%.
Age breakdown (1995): under 15, 33.4%; 15–29, 28.4%; 30–44, 19.7%; 45–59, 11.0%; 60–74, 5.6%; 75 and over, 1.9%.
Population projection: (2010) 3,150,000; (2020) 3,443,000.
Doubling time: 47 years.
Ethnic composition (1992): mestizo 64.0%; black and mulatto 14.0%; white 10.0%; Amerindian 8.0%; Asian 4.0%.
Religious affiliation (1995): Roman Catholic 80.2%; Protestant 15.0%, of which Pentecostal 8.4%; other Christian 1.6%; other 3.2%.
Major cities (2000): Panama City 463,093 (urban agglomeration [1999] 1,141,000); San Miguelito 291,769[5]; Tocumen 81,250[6]; David 76,481; Arraiján 63,753[6].

Vital statistics

Birth rate per 1,000 population (1999): 20.1 (world avg. 22.1).
Death rate per 1,000 population (1999): 5.0 (world avg. 8.9).
Natural increase rate per 1,000 population (1999): 15.1 (world avg. 13.2).
Total fertility rate (avg. births per childbearing woman; 1999): 2.4.
Marriage rate per 1,000 population (1997): 4.1[7].
Divorce rate per 1,000 population (1997): 0.7[7].
Life expectancy at birth (1999): male 72.5 years; female 78.0 years.
Major causes of death per 100,000 population (1997): diseases of the circulatory system 122.1; malignant neoplasms (cancers) 64.4; accidents 37.1; diseases of the respiratory system 25.4; infectious and parasitic diseases 21.2.

National economy

Budget (1997). Revenue: B 2,266,300,000 (tax revenue 70.3%, of which income taxes 20.2%, social security contributions 19.1%; nontax revenue 26.8%, of which entrepreneurial and property income 15.4%). Expenditures: B 2,341,300,000 (social security and welfare 20.5%; health 18.7%; education 18.3%; economic affairs 8.0%; defense 5.0%).
Public debt (external, outstanding; 1998): U.S.$5,413,000,000.
Production (metric tons except as noted). Agriculture, forestry, fishing (1999): sugarcane 2,050,000, bananas 650,000, rice 232,000, plantains 115,000, corn (maize) 89,800, yams 36,900, oranges 27,000, coffee 10,400, tobacco 2,200; livestock (number of live animals; 1999) 1,400,000 cattle, 252,000 pigs, 165,000 horses; roundwood (1998) 1,098,300 cu m; fish catch (value of production in B '000,000; 1998): fish 63, shrimps 40. Mining and quarrying (1997): limestone 326,000; gold 38,600 troy oz. Manufacturing (value of production in B '000,000; 1998): food products 1,203, of which meat 341, dairy products 144; refined petroleum 299; beverages 176; cement, bricks, and tiles 154. Energy production (consumption): electricity (kW-hr; 1998) 4,183,000,000 (3,416,000,000); coal (metric tons; 1996) none (56,000); crude petroleum (barrels; 1996) none (12,615,000); petroleum products (metric tons; 1996) 1,171,000 (1,497,000); natural gas (cu m; 1996) none (60,736,000).
Tourism (1998): receipts from visitors U.S.$378,800,000; expenditures by nationals abroad U.S.$176,200,000.
Household income and expenditure. Average household size (2000) 4.2; average annual income per household (1990) B 5,450 (U.S.$5,450); expenditure (1983–84)[8]: food and beverages 34.9%, transportation and communications 15.1%, housing and energy 12.6%, education and recreation 11.7%.
Population economically active (1998)[7]: total 1,083,580; activity rate of total population 42.2%[9] (participation rates: ages 15–69 [1997] 64.3%, female [1997] 35.6%, unemployed 13.6%).

Price and earnings indexes (1995 = 100)

	1994	1995	1996	1997	1998	1999	2000
Consumer price index	99.0	100.0	101.3	102.5	103.2	104.5	105.9[10]
Monthly earnings index	...	...	...	...	...	...	...

Gross national product (1998): U.S.$8,275,000,000 (U.S.$2,990 per capita).

Structure of gross domestic product and labour force

	1998			
	in value B '000,000[11]	% of total value	labour force[7]	% of labour force
Agriculture, fishing	545.1	7.9	171,560	15.8
Mining	17.0	0.2	934	0.1
Manufacturing	673.4	9.7	106,076	9.8
Construction	279.4	4.0	80,680	7.4
Public utilities	293.8	4.2	9,827	0.9
Transp. and commun.	901.1	13.0	69,176	6.4
Trade, restaurants	1,410.3	20.3	244,108	22.5
Finance, real estate	1,746.8	25.2	66,264	6.1
Pub. admin.	711.3	10.3	72,696	6.7
Services	397.0	5.7	224,118	20.7
Other	–42.3[12]	–0.6[12]	38,141	3.5
TOTAL	6,932.9	100.0[4]	1,083,580	100.0[4]

Land use (1994): forested 43.8%; meadows and pastures 19.8%; agricultural and under permanent cultivation 8.9%; other 27.5%.

Foreign trade[13, 14]

Balance of trade (current prices)

	1994	1995	1996	1997	1998	1999
B '000,000	–1,862	–1,958	–2,215	–2,358	–2,693	–2,695
% of total	63.3%	62.9%	66.2%	64.5%	65.6%	62.1%

Imports (1998): B 3,398,000,000 (machinery and apparatus 22.9%, transport equipment 15.1%, mineral fuels 10.3%, chemicals and chemical products 9.6%). *Major import sources:* U.S. 39.7%; Colón Free Zone 12.8%; Japan 9.0%; Mexico 4.8%; Ecuador 3.2%.
Exports (1998): B 705,000,000 (bananas 19.7%, shrimps 19.4%, fish 7.9%, sugar 3.6%, clothing 3.6%). *Major export destinations:* U.S. 40.0%; Sweden 7.2%; Costa Rica 6.6%; Spain 5.4%; Belgium 4.3%.

Transport and communications

Transport. Railroads (1997): route length 220 mi, 354 km. Roads (1997): total length 7,022 mi, 11,301 km (paved 33%). Vehicles: passenger cars (1996) 203,760; trucks and buses 74,637. Panama Canal traffic (1997–98): ocean-going transits 13,158; cargo 189,865,000 metric tons. Air transport (1998)[15]: passenger-km 1,373,000,000; metric ton-km cargo 21,778,000; airports (1996) 10.

Communications

Medium	date	unit	number	units per 1,000 persons
Daily newspapers	1996	circulation	166,000	63
Radio	1997	receivers	815,000	306
Television	1997	receivers	510,000	191
Telephones	1998	main lines	418,756	154
Cellular telephones	1998	subscribers	80,000	29
Personal computers	1998	units	75,000	28
Internet	1998	users	30,000	11

Education and health

Educational attainment (1990). Percentage of population age 25 and over having: no formal schooling 11.6%; primary 41.6%; secondary 28.7%; undergraduate 12.4%; graduate 0.7%; other/unknown 5.0%. *Literacy* (1995): total population age 15 and over literate 1,590,000 (90.8%).

Education (1997)

	schools	teachers	students	student/teacher ratio
Primary (age 6–11)	2,866	15,058	377,898	25.1
Secondary (age 12–17) Voc., teacher tr.	417	12,450	223,155	17.9
Higher	14	6,409	95,341	14.9

Health (1998): physicians 3,518 (1 per 772 persons); hospital beds 7,287 (1 per 373 persons); infant mortality rate per 1,000 live births (1999) 21.6.
Food (1998): daily per capita caloric intake 2,476 (vegetable products 78%, animal products 22%); 107% of FAO recommended minimum requirement.

Military

Total active duty personnel (1999): 11,000-member national police force. *Military expenditure as percentage of GNP* (1997): 1.4% (world avg. 2.6%); per capita expenditure U.S.$43.

[1]The 2,700 sq mi- (7,000 sq km-) Ngöbe Buglé indigenous district (*comarca*) was created in 1996 from parts of Bocas del Toro, Chiriquí, and Veraguas provinces. [2]Areas are unofficial. [3]Kuna de Madungandí indigenous district (*comarca*) was created in 1996 from part of Panamá province. [4]Detail does not add to total given because of rounding. [5]District adjacent to Panama City within Panama City urban agglomeration. [6]Within Panama City urban agglomeration. [7]Excludes indigenous population. [8]Panama City only. [9]Estimated figure. [10]April. [11]At prices of 1982. [12]Imputed finance service charges less import duties. [13]Imports c.i.f.; exports f.o.b. [14]Excludes Colón Free Zone (1998 imports f.o.b. B 5,319,000,000; 1998 reexports f.o.b. B 5,969,000,000, of which machinery and apparatus 28.4%, textiles and clothing 21.3%). [15]COPA only.

Internet resources for further information:
- **Dirección de Estadistica y Censo http://www.contraloria.gob.pa/direcciones/estycenso/index.htm**

Papua New Guinea

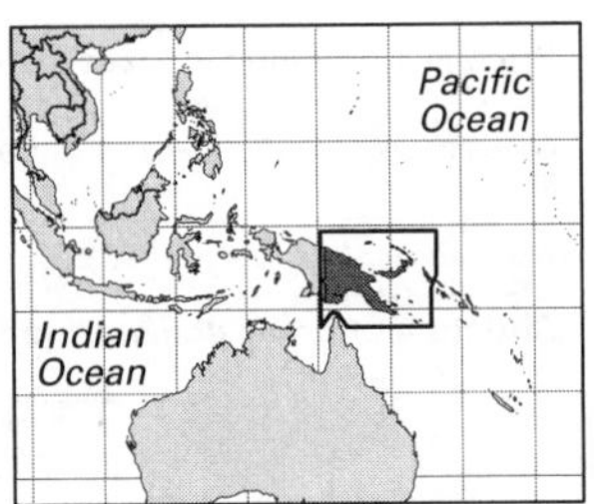

Official name: Independent State of Papua New Guinea.
Form of government: constitutional monarchy with one legislative house (National Parliament [109]).
Chief of state: British Monarch represented by Governor-General.
Head of government: Prime Minister.
Capital: Port Moresby.
Official language: English[1].
Official religion: none.
Monetary unit: 1 Papua New Guinea kina (K) = 100 toea; valuation (Oct. 6, 2000) 1 U.S.$ = K 2.80; 1 £ = K 4.05.

Area and population

Provinces	Administrative centres	area sq mi	area sq km	population 1990 census[2]
Bougainville[3]	Arawa (Buka)	3,600	9,300	[3]
Central	Port Moresby (Central)	11,400	29,500	140,584
East New Britain	Rabaul	6,000	15,500	184,408
East Sepik	Wewak	16,550	42,800	248,308
Eastern Highlands	Goroka	4,300	11,200	299,619
Enga	Wabag	4,950	12,800	238,357
Gulf	Kerema	13,300	34,500	68,060
Madang	Madang	11,200	29,000	270,299
Manus	Lorengau	800	2,100	32,830
Milne Bay	Alotau (Samarai)	5,400	14,000	157,288
Morobe	Lae	13,300	34,500	363,535
National Capital District	Port Moresby	100	240	193,242
New Ireland	Kavieng	3,700	9,600	87,194
Oro (Northern)	Popondetta	8,800	22,800	96,762
Sandaun (West Sepik)	Vanimo	14,000	36,300	135,185
Simbu (Chimbu)	Kundiawa	2,350	6,100	183,801
Southern Highlands	Mendi	9,200	23,800	302,724
West New Britain	Kimbe	8,100	21,000	127,547
Western	Daru	38,350	99,300	108,705
Western Highlands	Mount Hagen	3,300	8,500	291,090
TOTAL		178,704[4]	462,840	3,529,538[5]

Demography

Population (2000): 4,927,000.
Density (2000): persons per sq mi 27.6, persons per sq km 10.6.
Urban-rural (2000): urban 15.0%; rural 85.0%.
Sex distribution (2000): male 51.30%; female 48.70%.
Age breakdown (2000): under 15, 38.8%; 15–29, 28.7%; 30–44, 17.1%; 45–59, 9.7%; 60–74, 4.7%; 75 and over, 1.0%.
Population projection: (2010) 6,171,000; (2020) 7,400,000.
Ethnic composition (1983): New Guinea Papuan 84.0%; New Guinea Melanesian 15.0%; other 1.0%.
Religious affiliation (1990): non-Anglican Protestant 64.3%, of which Evangelical Lutheran 23.2%, Uniting Church 12.7%, Seventh-day Adventist 8.1%, Pentecostal 7.1%; Roman Catholic 28.3%; Anglican 3.9%; other (mostly animists) 3.5%.
Major cities (1990)[2]: Port Moresby 193,242; Lae 80,655; Madang 27,057; Wewak 23,224; Goroka 17,855.

Vital statistics

Birth rate per 1,000 population (2000): 32.7 (world avg. 22.1).
Death rate per 1,000 population (2000): 8.0 (world avg. 8.9).
Natural increase rate per 1,000 population (2000): 24.7 (world avg. 13.2).
Total fertility rate (avg. births per childbearing woman; 2000): 4.4.
Life expectancy at birth (2000): male 61.1 years; female 65.3 years.
Major causes of death per 100,000 population (1993): acute respiratory infections 34.6; pneumonia 27.8; meningitis 7.6; conditions originating from perinatal period 6.2; malaria 3.8.

National economy

Budget (1999). Revenue: K 2,485,000,000 (direct taxes 41.7%, indirect taxes 29.2%, foreign grants 18.6%, nontax revenue 10.5%). Expenditures: K 2,630,000,000 (current expenditure 67.2%, of which transfer to provincial governments 19.0%, interest payments 15.2%; development expenditure 32.8%).
Public debt (external, outstanding; 1998): U.S.$1,410,000,000.
Production (metric tons except as noted). Agriculture, forestry, fishing (1999): coconuts 734,000, bananas 680,000, sweet potatoes 460,000, sugarcane 400,000, palm oil 299,000, yams 200,000, taro 160,000, cassava 112,000, coffee 66,000, palm kernels 63,000, cacao 40,000, pineapples 10,500, tea 7,260; livestock (number of live animals) 1,500,000 pigs, 86,000 cattle, 3,600,000 chickens; roundwood (1998) 8,772,000 cu m; fish catch (1998) 67,640. Mining and quarrying (1996): copper 186,715; silver 59,037 kg; gold 51,573 kg. Manufacturing (value added, in K; 1985): food, beverages, and tobacco 162,558,000; metals, metal products, machinery, and equipment 47,493,000; wood products 29,807,000. Construction (value in K; 1994)[6]: total 95,600,000. Energy production (consumption): electricity (kW-hr; 1996) 1,790,000,000 (1,790,000,000); coal (metric tons; 1996) none (1,000); crude petroleum (barrels; 1996) 546,000 (7,500); natural gas (cu m; 1996) 83,300,000 (83,300,000); petroleum products (metric tons; 1996) 50,000 (727,000).
Land use (1997): forested 92.3%; agricultural and under permanent cultivation 1.5%; meadows and pastures 0.2%; other 6.0%.
Gross national product (at current market prices; 1998): U.S.$4,104,000,000 (U.S.$890 per capita).

Structure of gross domestic product and labour force

	1998[7] in value K '000,000	1998[7] % of total value	1980 labour force[8]	1980 % of labour force[8]
Agriculture	1,885	24.4	564,500	77.0
Mining	2,007	26.0	4,300	0.6
Manufacturing	693	9.0	14,000	1.9
Construction	458	5.9	21,600	2.9
Public utilities	104	1.3	2,800	0.4
Transp. and commun.	409	5.3	17,400	2.4
Trade	93	9.0	25,100	3.4
Finance	87	1.1	4,500	0.6
Pub. admin., defense Services	971	12.6	77,100	10.5
Other	407	5.4	1,500	0.2
TOTAL	7,714	100.0	732,800	100.0[4]

Population economically active (1980)[8]: total 732,800; activity rate 24.6% (participation rates: over age 10, 35.2%; female 39.8%; unemployed 12.8%[9]).

Price and earnings indexes (1995 = 100)

	1993	1994	1995	1996	1997	1998	1999
Consumer price index	82.9	85.3	100.0	111.6	116.0	131.8	151.5
Weekly earnings index	100.0	100.0	100.0	...	...	...	...

Tourism (1996): receipts U.S.$68,000,000; expenditures U.S.$77,000,000.

Foreign trade[10]

Balance of trade (current prices)

	1994	1995	1996	1997	1998	1999
K '000,000	+1,326.0	+1,780.0	+1,318.0	+928.4	+1,356.1	+2,173.1
% of total	33.2%	35.5%	24.8%	17.9%	24.2%	28.5%

Imports (1997): K 2,827,000,000 (1990; machinery and transport equipment 38.7%; basic manufactures 20.4%; food and live animals 17.9%; chemicals 7.5%; mineral fuels, lubricants, and related materials 2.7%). *Major import sources* (1997): Australia 51.2%; U.S. 13.6%; Singapore 7.6%; Japan 7.3%; New Zealand 3.8%; Hong Kong 2.4%; U.K. 0.7%.
Exports (1997): K 3,141,000,000 (1998; gold 33.0%; crude oil 21.0%; copper 13.1%; coffee 7.7%; palm oil 7.5%; cocoa beans 2.3%). *Major export destinations* (1997): Australia 40.6%; Japan 13.1%; U.K. 9.4%; U.S. 8.7%; Germany 7.2%.

Transport and communications

Transport. Railroads: none. Roads (1986): total length 19,736 km (paved 6%). Vehicles (1994): passenger cars 13,000; trucks and buses 32,000. Air transport (1993): passenger-km 738,366,000; metric ton-km cargo 82,369,000; airports (1996) with scheduled flights 129.

Communications

Medium	date	unit	number	units per 1,000 persons
Daily newspapers	1996	circulation	65,000	15
Radio	1997	receivers	410,000	91
Television	1995	receivers	100,000	23
Telephones	1996	main lines	47,000	11
Facsimile machines	1995	units	800	0.2
Internet	1996	users	50,000	12

Education and health

Educational attainment (1990). Percentage of population age 25 and over having: no formal schooling 82.6%; some primary education 8.2%; completed primary 5.0%; some secondary 4.2%. *Literacy* (1995 est.): total population age 15 and over literate 72.2%; males literate 81.0%; females literate 62.7%.

Education (1995)

	schools	teachers	students	student/ teacher ratio
Primary (age 7–12)	2,790	13,652	525,995	38.5
Secondary (age 13–16)	135[11]	2,415[12]	68,818	24.1[12]
Voc., teacher tr.	117[11]	878[12]	9,941	12.9[12]
Higher	2[11]	902[13]	13,663	7.1[13]

Health: physicians (1998) 342 (1 per 13,708 persons); hospital beds (1989) 15,335 (1 per 234 persons); infant mortality rate (2000) 59.9.
Food (1998): daily per capita caloric intake 2,158 (vegetable products 89%, animal products 11%); 95% of FAO minimum.

Military

Total active duty personnel (1997): 4,300 (army 88.4%, navy 9.3%, air force 2.3%). *Military expenditure as percentage of GNP* (1997): 1.3% (world 2.6%); per capita expenditure U.S.$14.

[1]The national languages are English, Tok Pisin (English Creole), and Motu. [2]Preliminary results. [3]An agreement in principle to establish an autonomous provincial government was reached in 2000; population data unavailable because of civil insurrection. [4]Detail does not add to total given because of rounding. [5]Excludes an estimated population of 160,000 in the North Solomons (Bougainville area), 4,500 people in remote areas, and an estimated foreign population of about 20,000–30,000. [6]Construction starts. [7]International Monetary Fund estimate. [8]Citizens of Papua New Guinea over age 10 involved in "money-raising activities" only. [9]1997; in six urban centres. [10]Import figures are f.o.b. in balance of trade and c.i.f. for commodities and trading partners. [11]1990. [12]1992. [13]1986.

Internet resources for further information:

- **Prime Minister's Office of Papua New Guinea http://www.pm.gov.pg/pmsoffice/PMsoffice.nsf**

Paraguay

Official name: República del Paraguay (Spanish); Tetã Paraguáype (Guaraní)(Republic of Paraguay).
Form of government: multiparty republic with two legislative houses (Senate [46[1]]; Chamber of Deputies [80]).
Head of state and government: President.
Capital: Asunción.
Official languages: Spanish; Guaraní.
Official religion: none[2].
Monetary unit: 1 Paraguayan Guaraní (₲) = 100 céntimos; valuation (Oct. 6, 2000) 1 U.S.$ = ₲3,500; 1 £ = ₲5,063.

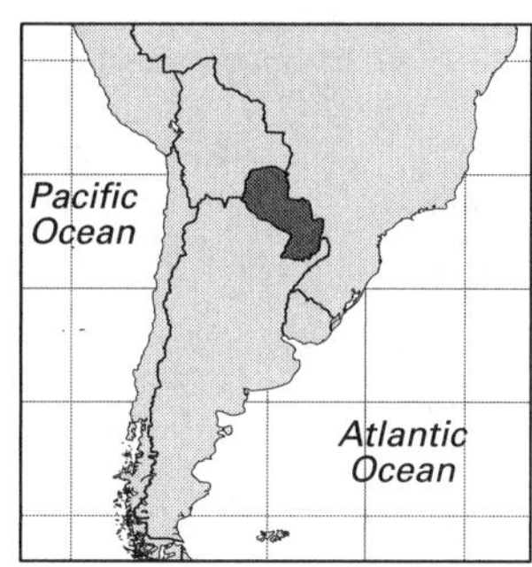

Area and population		area		population
Regions				1997
Departments	Capitals	sq mi	sq km	estimate
Occidental		95,338	246,925	126,214
Alto Paraguay	Fuerte Olimpo	31,795	82,349	13,831
Boquerón	Filadelfia	35,393	91,669	35,238
Presidente Hayes	Pozo Colorado	28,150	72,907	77,145
Oriental		61,710	159,827	4,959,111
Alto Paraná	Ciudad del Este	5,751	14,895	595,276
Amambay	Pedro Juan Caballero	4,994	12,933	127,011
Asunción[3]	—	45	117	550,060
Caaguazú	Coronel Oviedo	4,430	11,474	442,161
Caazapá	Caazapá	3,666	9,496	141,559
Canindiyú	Salto del Guairá	5,663	14,667	133,075
Central	Asunción	952	2,465	1,174,212
Concepción	Concepción	6,970	18,051	185,496
Cordillera	Caacupé	1,910	4,948	215,663
Guairá	Villarrica	1,485	3,846	173,668
Itapúa	Encarnación	6,380	16,525	454,757
Misiones	San Juan Bautista	3,690	9,556	98,607
Ñeembucú	Pilar	4,690	12,147	86,965
Paraguarí	Paraguarí	3,361	8,705	247,675
San Pedro	San Pedro	7,723	20,002	332,926
TOTAL		157,048	406,752	5,085,325

Demography

Population (2000): 5,496,000.
Density (2000): persons per sq mi 35.0, persons per sq km 13.5.
Urban-rural (1997): urban 52.8%; rural 47.2%.
Sex distribution (1999): male 50.21%; female 49.79%.
Age breakdown (1999): under 15, 39.3%; 15–29, 26.2%; 30–44, 17.9%; 45–59, 9.9%; 60–74, 5.1%; 75 and over, 1.6%.
Population projection: (2010) 6,980,000; (2020) 8,470,000.
Ethnic composition (1997): mixed (white/Amerindian) *c.* 95%; Amerindian *c.* 2%; other *c.* 3%.
Religious affiliation (1995): Roman Catholic 88.5%; Protestant 5.0%; other 6.5%.
Major cities (1992): Asunción 500,938; Ciudad del Este 133,881; San Lorenzo 133,395; Lambaré 99,572; Fernando de la Mora 95,072.

Vital statistics

Birth rate per 1,000 population (1999): 31.6 (world avg. 22.1).
Death rate per 1,000 population (1999): 4.9 (world avg. 8.9).
Natural increase rate per 1,000 population (1999): 26.7 (world avg. 13.2).
Total fertility rate (avg. births per childbearing woman; 1999): 4.2.
Marriage rate per 1,000 population (1992): 3.9[4].
Life expectancy at birth (1999): male 71.0 years; female 76.0 years.
Major causes of death per 100,000 population (1994)[5]: diseases of the circulatory system 163.0; malignant neoplasms (cancers) 53.0; accidents 48.0; diseases of the respiratory system 31.0; infectious and parasitic diseases 29.0.

National economy

Budget (1999): Revenue: ₲4,011,200,000,000 (tax revenue 69.4%, of which taxes on goods and services 39.0%, income tax 13.4%, customs duties 10.3%, social security 6.7%; nontax revenue including grants 30.6%). Expenditures: ₲4,605,800,000,000 (current expenditure 75.6%, of which wages 42.6%, transfers 21.9%, goods and services 4.5%, interest on debt 4.1%; capital expenditure 24.4%).
Public debt (external, outstanding; 1998): U.S.$1,593,000,000.
Population economically active (1996): total 1,747,488; activity rate 35.3% (participation rates [1992]: ages 12 and over, 51.0%; female 23.8%; unemployed [1998] 7.2%).

Price index (1995 = 100)	1993	1994	1995	1996	1997	1998	1999
Consumer price index	73.1	88.2	100.0	109.8	117.5	131.0	139.9

Production (metric tons except as noted). Agriculture, forestry, fishing (1999): cassava 3,500,000, soybeans 3,303,500, sugarcane 2,872,270, corn (maize) 817,000, oranges 230,632, seed cotton 202,283, lint cotton 120,000, sweet potatoes 79,365, bananas 69,968; livestock (number of live animals) 9,863,000 cattle, 2,500,000 pigs, 15,000,000 chickens; roundwood (1998) 8,097,000 cu m; fish catch (1998) 26,000. Mining and quarrying (1997): limestone 600,000; kaolin 66,700; gypsum 4,500. Manufacturing (value added in constant prices of 1982, ₲'000,000; 1998): food products 59,100; wood products and furniture 23,500; handicrafts 10,300; printing and publishing 9,200; leather and hides 7,000; textiles 6,600; nonmetal products 6,600; petroleum products 3,800. Energy production (consumption): electricity (kW-hr; 1996) 48,200,000,000 (7,938,000,000); crude petroleum (barrels; 1996) none (1,143,000); petroleum products (metric tons; 1996) 157,000 (1,084,000).
Gross national product (1998): U.S.$9,172,000,000 (U.S.$1,760 per capita).

Structure of gross domestic product and labour force	1998		1996	
	in value ₲'000,000,000	% of total value	labour force	% of labour force
Agriculture	7,037.2	28.3	559,042	32.0
Mining	119.6	0.5	2,568	0.1
Manufacturing	3,385.3	13.6	181,983	10.4
Construction	1,291.7	5.2	142,678	8.2
Public utilities	1,498.9	6.0	13,150	0.8
Transp. and commun.	1,216.0	4.9	55,972	3.2
Trade, Finance	5,772.8	23.2	224,210	12.8
Pub. admin., defense	1,454.3	5.9	330,697	18.9
Services, Other	3,077.9	12.4	237,188[6]	13.6[6]
TOTAL	24,853.7	100.0	1,747,488	100.0

Household income and expenditure. Average household size (1998) 4.7; sources of income (1989): wages and salaries 33.9%, transfer payments 2.5%.
Tourism (1998): receipts U.S.$595,000,000; expenditures U.S.$142,000,000.

Foreign trade[7]

Balance of trade (current prices)	1994	1995	1996	1997	1998	1999
U.S.$'000,000	–1,323.6	–1,887.6	–1,807.0	–1,868.5	–1,866.4	–1,456.7
% of total	44.8%	50.5%	46.4%	46.2%	45.9%	41.8%

Imports (1998): U.S.$2,470,800,000 (machinery and transport equipment 30.6%, of which transport equipment 8.1%; food, beverages, and tobacco 23.7%; fuels and lubricants 7.6%; chemicals and pharmaceuticals 5.4%). *Major import sources:* Brazil 32.2%; U.S. 20.2%; Argentina 15.6%; Hong Kong 6.9%; Japan 2.7%.
Exports (1998): U.S.$1,014,100,000 (soybean flour 43.4%; cotton fibres 9.1%; timber 6.9%; vegetable oil 7.5%, of which processed meats 6.7%; soybean oil 6.0%; hides and skins 3.8%). *Major export destinations:* Brazil 28.1%; Argentina 25.7%; The Netherlands 15.3%; Japan 4.8%; Chile 4.7%; U.S. 2.7%; Italy 2.0%.

Transport and communications

Transport. Railroads (1998): route length 441 km; passenger-km 3,000,000; metric ton-km cargo 5,500,000. Roads (1997): total length 29,500 km (paved 10%). Vehicles (1996): passenger cars 71,000; trucks 50,000. Air transport (1997): passenger-km 215,000,000; metric ton-km cargo 19,000,000; airports (1998) 5.

Communications				units
Medium	date	unit	number	per 1,000 persons
Daily newspapers	1996	circulation	213,000	43
Radio	1997	receivers	925,000	182
Television	1997	receivers	515,000	101
Telephones	1998	main lines	288,540	55
Cellular telephones	1998	subscribers	215,350	41
Internet	1998	users	10,000	0.2

Education and health

Educational attainment (1992). Percentage of population age 15 and over having: no formal schooling 7.0%; primary education 61.2%; secondary 23.2%; higher 6.6%; not stated 2.0%. *Literacy* (1995): percentage of total population age 15 and over literate 92.1%; males literate 93%; female literate 90.6%.

Education (1996)	schools	teachers	students	student/ teacher ratio
Primary (age 7–12)	5,928	41,713	895,777	21.5
Secondary (age 13–18)[8]	1,454	17,668	293,651	16.6
Higher	2	742[9]	42,302	...

Health (1995): physicians 3,730 (1 per 1,294 persons); hospital beds 6,759 (1 per 714 persons); infant mortality rate per 1,000 live births (1999) 32.3.
Food (1998): daily per capita caloric intake 2,600 (vegetable products 77%, animals products 23%); 113% of FAO recommended minimum requirement.

Military

Total active duty personnel (1999): 20,200 (army 73.8%, navy 17.8%, air force 8.4%). *Military expenditure as percentage of GNP* (1997): 1.3% (world 2.6%), per capita expenditure U.S.$25.

[1]Includes one nonelective seat. Former president Juan Carlos Wasmosy became senator-for-life in August 1998. [2]Roman Catholicism, although not official, enjoys special recognition in the 1992 constitution. [3]Asunción is the capital city, not a department. [4]Civil Registry records only. [5]Reporting areas only (constituting about 75 percent of the total population). [6]Includes 171,312 unemployed. [7]Imports are f.o.b. [8]Includes vocational and teacher training. [9]1993–94.

Internet resources for further information:
- **Banco Central del Paraguay**
http://www.bcp.gov.py
- **Dirección General Estadística, Encuestas y Censos**
http://www.dgeec.gov.py/index.htm

Peru

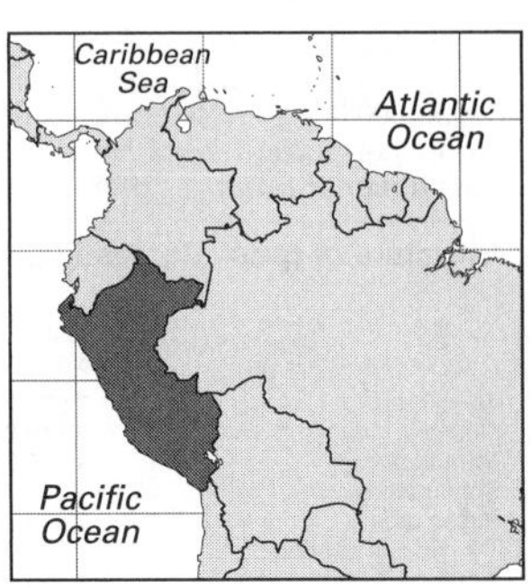

Official name: República del Perú (Spanish) (Republic of Peru).
Form of government[1]: unitary multiparty republic with one legislative house (Congress [120]).
Head of state and government: President, assisted by Prime Minister.
Capital: Lima.
Official languages: Spanish; Quechua; Aymara.
Official religion: Roman Catholicism.
Monetary unit[2]: 1 nuevo sol (S/.) = 100 céntimos; valuation (Oct. 6, 2000) 1 U.S.$ = S/. 3.50; 1 £ = S/. 5.06.

Area and population

		area		population
Regions[3]	Capitals	sq mi	sq km	2000 estimate
Andres Avelino Cáceres	...	40,707	105,430	2,215,087
Arequipa	...	24,458	63,345	1,072,958
Chavín	...	15,686	40,627	1,067,282
Grau	...	15,661	40,562	1,739,611
Inca	...	66,696	172,741	1,667,892
José Carlos Mariátegui	...	40,081	103,809	1,623,960
La Libertad	...	9,873	25,570	1,465,970
Loreto	...	142,414	368,852	880,471
Los Libertadores-Wari	...	34,340	88,939	1,600,132
Nor Oriental del Marañón	...	33,486	86,728	2,911,053
San Martín	...	19,789	51,253	743,668
Ucayali	...	39,541	102,411	424,410
Department				
Lima	...	13,437	34,802	7,475,495
Constitutional Province				
Callao	Callao	57	147	773,701
TOTAL		496,225[4]	1,285,216	25,661,690

Demography

Population (2000): 25,662,000.
Density (2000) persons per sq mi 51.7, persons per sq km 20.0.
Urban-rural (2000): urban 72.3%; rural 27.7%.
Sex distribution (2000): male 49.59%; female 50.41%.
Age breakdown (2000): under 15, 33.4%; 15–29, 29.1%; 30–44, 19.3%; 45–59, 10.9%; 60–74, 5.7%; 75 and over, 1.6%.
Population projection: (2010) 29,885,000; (2020) 33,757,000.
Ethnic composition (1981): Quechua 47.1%; mestizo 32.0%; white 12.0%; Aymara 5.4%; other Amerindian 1.7%; other 1.8%.
Religious affiliation (1995) Roman Catholic 88.8%; Protestant 6.7%; other Christian 1.5%; other 3.0%.
Major cities (1993): metropolitan Lima 5,706,127; Arequipa 619,156; Callao 615,046; Trujillo 509,312; Chiclayo 411,536.

Vital statistics

Birth rate per 1,000 population (1999): 26.1 (world avg. 22.6); (1977) legitimate 57.8%; illegitimate 42.2%.
Death rate per 1,000 population (1999): 5.7 (world avg. 8.9).
Natural increase rate per 1,000 population (1999): 20.4 (world avg. 13.7).
Total fertility rate (avg. births per childbearing woman; 1999): 3.2.
Marriage rate per 1,000 population (1993): 4.1[5].
Life expectancy at birth (1999): male 68.1 years; female 72.8 years.
Major causes of death per 100,000 population (1989): diseases of the circulatory system 115.3; respiratory diseases 100.2; infectious diseases 84.5; malignant neoplasms 72.9; accidents, poisoning, and violence 53.6.

National economy

Budget (1998). Revenue: S/. 25,980,000,000 (taxes on goods and services 54.3%; income taxes 22.6%; import duties 9.5%; nontax revenue 7.0%; payroll tax 4.9%). Expenditures: S/. 27,389,000,000 (current expenditure 69.5%, of which wages and salaries 36.6%, transfer payments 15.7%; capital expenditure 19.4%; interest payments 11.1%).
Public debt (external, outstanding; 1998): U.S.$20,803,000,000.
Tourism (1998): receipts U.S.$913,000,000; expenditures U.S.$466,000,000.
Production (metric tons except as noted). Agriculture, forestry, fishing (1999): sugarcane 6,900,000, potatoes 3,050,000, rice 1,947,000, plantains 1,344,000, corn (maize) 1,058,000, cassava 862,000; livestock (number of live animals) 13,700,000 sheep, 4,898,000 cattle, 2,784,000 pigs, 2,068,000 goats, 79,917,000 chickens; roundwood (1998) 9,157,000 cu m; fish catch (1998) 4,338,437. Mining and quarrying (1998): iron ore 3,224,000; zinc 725,000; copper 356,000; lead 228,000; silver 1,832. Manufacturing (value in S/. '000,000[6]; 1996): processed foods 275.1; base metal products 188.6; textiles and leather products 129.5; industrial chemicals 112.3; wood products 80.0. Construction (value in S/. '000,000[6]; 1996): residential 32.1; nonresidential 26.8. Energy production (consumption): electricity (kW-hr; 1996) 20,038,000,000 (20,038,000,000); coal (metric tons; 1996) 58,000 (302,000); crude petroleum (barrels; 1996) 44,000,000 (52,000,000); petroleum products (metric tons; 1996) 6,956,000 (6,078,000); natural gas (cu m; 1996) 208,000,000 (208,000,000).
Household income and expenditure. Average household size (1993) 5.1; income per household (1988) I/. 1,086,620[2] (U.S.$2,173); sources of income (1991): business income 67.1%, wages 23.3%, transfers 7.6%, other 2.0%; expenditure (1990): food 29.4%, recreation and education 13.2%, household durables 10.1%, clothing and footwear 8.5%, transportation 7.5%, health 7.0%.
Gross national product (1998): U.S.$60,491,000,000 (U.S.$2,440 per capita).

Structure of gross domestic product and labour force

	1998		1992	
	in value S/. [6]	% of total value	labour force	% of labour force
Agriculture	643,100	13.2	2,658,000	33.0
Mining	533,400	10.9	198,000	2.4
Manufacturing	1,029,300	21.1	840,000	10.4
Construction	473,400	9.7	300,000	3.7
Public utilities	...	...	25,000	0.3
Transp. and commun.	...	...	355,000	4.4
Trade	...	...	1,297,000	16.1
Finance	...	...	192,000	2.4
Services	2,195,700[7]	45.1[7]	2,199,000[8]	27.3[8]
TOTAL	4,874,900	100.0	8,064,000	100.0

Population economically active (1998): total 7,407,280; activity rate of total population 45.7% (participation rates: over age 15, 66.9%; female 43.8%; unemployed 7.7%).

Price and earnings indexes (1995 = 100)

	1993	1994	1995	1996	1997	1998	1999
Consumer price index	72.8	90.0	100.0	111.5	121.1	129.9	134.4
Monthly earnings index[9]	69.4	98.5	100.0	106.8	114.8	...	...

Land use (1998): forest and other 75.7%; pasture 21.1%; agricultural 3.2%.

Foreign trade[10]

Balance of trade (current prices)

	1994	1995	1996	1997	1998	1999
U.S.$'000,000	−1,095.2	−2,111.6	−1,996.5	−1,738.3	−2,477.2	−612.2
% of total	10.8%	15.9%	14.5%	11.3%	17.8%	4.8%

Imports (1998): U.S.$8,200,000,000 (raw and intermediate materials 41.3%, machinery 24.9%, consumer goods 23.0%, transport equipment 6.7%). *Major import sources:* U.S. 32.5%; Colombia 7.4%; Germany 5.6%; Venezuela 4.3%.
Exports (1998): U.S.$5,722,900,000 (gold 16.2%, copper and copper products 13.6%, zinc products 7.8%, fish meal fodder 6.8%, coffee 5.0%, petroleum and derivatives 3.9%, lead products 3.7%, silver 2.3%, tin 2.1%). *Major export destinations:* U.S. 32.3%; Japan 8.7%; United Kingdom 4.8%; Switzerland 4.2%; Spain 4.1%; Venezuela 3.9%; South Korea 3.4%.

Transport and communications

Transport. Railroads (1996): route length 1,992 km; passenger-km 171,091,000; metric ton-km cargo 850,329,000. Roads (1996): total length 73,766 km (paved 12%). Vehicles (1996): passenger cars 557,042; trucks and buses 359,374. Air transport (1996): passenger-km 2,634,000,000; metric ton-km cargo 251,000,000; airports (1996) 27.

Communications

Medium	date	unit	number	units per 1,000 persons
Daily newspapers	1996	circulation	2,000,000	84
Radio	1997	receivers	6,650,000	273
Television	1997	receivers	3,060,000	126
Telephones	1998	main lines	1,555,100	63
Cellular telephones	1998	subscribers	743,000	30
Personal computers	1998	units	450,000	18
Internet	1998	users	200,000	8.1

Education and health

Educational attainment (1993). Percentage of population age 15 and over having: no formal schooling 12.3%; less than primary education 0.3%; primary 31.5%; secondary 35.5%; higher 20.4%. *Literacy* (1995): total population age 15 and over literate 88.0%; males 93.5%; females 82.7%.

Education (1997)

	schools	teachers	students	student/ teacher ratio
Primary (age 6–11)	33,017	153,951	4,163,180	27.0
Secondary (age 12–16)	8,452[11]	106,614	1,969,501	18.5
Voc., teacher tr.[11]	2,531	12,392	256,763	20.7
Higher	994[11]	45,443	657,586	14.5

Health: physicians (1996) 24,708 (1 per 969 persons); hospital beds (1994) 42,979 (1 per 538 persons); infant mortality rate per 1,000 live births (1999) 39.
Food (1998): daily per capita caloric intake 2,420 (vegetable products 86%, animal products 14%); 103% of FAO recommended minimum requirement.

Military

Total active duty personnel (1999): 115,000 (army 65.2%, navy 21.7%, air force 13.1%). *Military expenditure as percentage of GNP* (1997): 2.1% (world 2.6%); per capita expenditure U.S.$55.

[1]The constitution promulgated in December 1993 replaced the 1980 constitution. [2]The nuevo sol was introduced in January 1991 replacing the inti (abbrev.: I/.). [3]The regional administrative structure established in 1987 has been made functional only very slowly because of financing problems. [4]Detail does not add to total given because of rounding. [5]Excludes Indian jungle population; based on incomplete information. [6]At 1979 prices. [7]Includes public utilities, transportation and communications, trade, finance, and public administration. [8]Includes public administration and other. [9]Estimate for Lima metropolitan area only; private sector nominal wages. [10]Imports and exports in balance of trade is f.o.b. [11]1996.

Internet resources for further information:
- **Instituto Nacional de Estadística e Informática (Spanish) http://www.inei.gob.pe**

Philippines

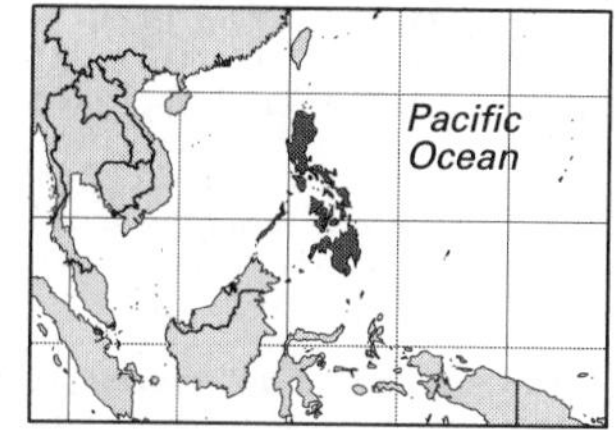

Official name: Republika ng Pilipinas (Pilipino); Republic of the Philippines (English).
Form of government: unitary republic with two legislative houses (Senate [24]; House of Representatives [260[1]]).
Chief of state and head of government: President.
Capital: Quezon City/Manila[2].
Official languages: Pilipino; English.
Official religion: none.
Monetary unit: 1 Philippine peso (₱) = 100 centavos; valuation (Oct. 6, 2000) 1 U.S.$ = ₱ 46.30; 1 £ = ₱ 66.98.

Area and population

Regions	area sq mi	area sq km	population 2000 census[3]
Bicol	6,808	17,633	4,629,000
Cagayan Valley	10,362	26,838	2,756,000
Caraga	7,277	18,847	2,076,000
Central Luzon	7,039	18,231	7,797,000
Central Mindanao	5,549	14,373	2,494,000
Central Visayas	5,773	14,951	5,404,000
Eastern Visayas	8,275	21,432	3,589,000
Ilocos	4,958	12,840	4,174,000
National Capital	246	636	10,492,000
Nothern Mindanao	5,418	14,033	2,738,000
Southern Mindanao	10,479	27,141	5,125,000
Southern Tagalog	18,117	46,924	11,320,000
Western Mindanao	6,194	16,042	3,045,000
Western Visayas	7,808	20,223	6,147,000
Autonomous Regions			
Cordillera	7,063	18,294	1,352,000
Muslim Mindanao	4,493	11,638	2,191,000
TOTAL	115,860[4]	300,076	75,329,000

Demography

Population (2000): 76,320,000.
Density (2000): persons per sq mi 658.7, persons per sq km 254.3.
Urban-rural (2000): urban 59.0%; rural 41.0%.
Sex distribution (2000): male 50.37%; female 49.63%.
Age breakdown (2000): under 15, 36.2%; 15–29, 28.1%; 30–44, 19.0%; 45–59, 10.7%; 60–74, 4.8%; 75 and over, 1.2%.
Population projection: (2010) 91,868,000; (2020) 105,507,000.
Doubling time: 32 years.
Ethnic composition (by mother tongue of households; 1995): Pilipino (Tagalog) 29.3%; Cebuano 23.3%; Ilocano 9.3%; Hiligaynon Ilongo 9.1%; Bicol 5.7%; Waray 3.8%; Pampango 3.0%; Pangasinan 1.8%; other 14.7%.
Religious affiliation (1996): Roman Catholic 82.9%; Protestant 5.4%; Muslim 4.6%; Aglipayan (Philippine Independent Church) 2.6%; other 4.5%.
Major cities (2000)[3]: Quezon City 2,160,000; Manila 1,673,000; Caloocan 1,233,000; Davao 1,147,000; Cebu 662,000; Zamboanga 600,000.

Vital statistics

Birth rate per 1,000 population (2000): 27.1 (world avg. 22.1); (1982) legitimate 93.9%; illegitimate 6.1%.
Death rate per 1,000 population (2000): 5.6 (world avg. 8.9).
Natural increase rate per 1,000 population (2000): 21.5 (world avg. 13.2).
Total fertility rate (avg. births per childbearing woman; 2000); 3.4.
Life expectancy at birth (2000): male 67.0 years; female 71.0 years.
Major causes of death per 100,000 population (1993): heart disease 69.1; vascular diseases 55.8; pneumonia 53.1; malignant neoplasms (cancers) 37.9; tuberculosis 36.7; accidents 20.1.

National economy

Budget (1997). Revenue: ₱ 470,105,000,000 (income taxes 34.9%, taxes on goods and services 28.4%, international duties 20.2%, nontax revenues 12.3%). Expenditures: ₱ 467,319,000,000 (education 20.4%, debt service 16.7%, transportation and communications 13.6%, general public services 9.8%).
Production (metric tons except as noted). Agriculture, forestry, fishing (1998): sugarcane 27,000,000, coconuts 10,492,780, rice 8,554,824, corn (maize) 3,823,184, bananas 3,549,950, pineapples 1,495,120; livestock (number of live animals) 10,210,000 pigs, 6,500,000 goats, 3,004,000 buffalo, 136,887,000 chickens; roundwood 41,548,000 cu m; fish catch (1996) 2,269,231. Mining and quarrying (1997): coal 1,045,551; nickel ore 567,616; copper concentrate 187,639; gold 32,500 kg; silver 20,664 kg. Manufacturing (gross value added in ₱ '000,000; 1997)[5]: food products 220,200; electrical machinery 45,600; chemicals 44,200; petroleum and coal products 42,800. Construction (private, authorized; 1997): residential ₱ 31,748,899,000; nonresidential ₱ 78,321,014,000. Energy production (consumption): electricity (kW-hr; 1994) 26,425,000,000 (26,425,000,000); coal (metric tons; 1994) 1,733,000 (2,503,000); crude petroleum (barrels; 1994) 2,186,000 (90,808,000); petroleum products (metric tons; 1994) 11,350,000 (12,559,000).
Household income and expenditure (1997). Average household size (1995) 5.1; income per family ₱ 123,881 (U.S.$3,150); sources of income: wages 45.2%, business profits 39.0%, self-employment 9.1%, transfers 6.7%; expenditure: food, beverage, and tobacco 46.0%, housing 15.4%, transportation 5.6%, fuel and power 5.3%, clothing 3.3%.
Gross national product (1998): U.S.$78,938,000,000 (U.S.$1,050 per capita).

Structure of gross domestic product and labour force

	1997 in value ₱ '000,000	1997 % of total value	1998 labour force	1998 % of labour force
Agriculture	487,000	19.9	11,035,000	36.5
Mining	16,000	0.6	115,000	0.4
Manufacturing	538,000	21.9	2,704,000	9.0
Construction	159,000	6.5	1,612,000	5.3
Public utilities	65,000	2.6	135,000	0.4
Transp. and commun.	119,000	4.9	1,821,000	6.0
Trade	317,000	12.9	4,235,000	14.0
Finances	282,000	11.5	665,000	2.2
Services	470,000	19.2	5,367,000	17.8
Others	–1,000[6]	—	2,550,000[7]	8.4[7]
TOTAL	2,452,000	100.0	30,239,000	100.0

Public debt (external, outstanding; 1998): U.S.$28,189,000,000.
Population economically active (1995): total 28,382,000; activity rate 40.4% (participation rates: ages 15–64, 65.6%; female 37.4%; unemployed [1998] 8.4%).

Price and earnings indexes (1995 = 100)

	1992	1993	1994	1995	1996	1997	1998
Consumer price index	79.9	85.4	92.6	100.0	109.0	115.5	126.7
Daily earnings index[8]	81.4	82.3	100.0	100.0	113.8	127.6	...

Tourism (1998): receipts U.S.$2,413,000,000; expenditures U.S.$1,950,000,000.

Foreign trade[9]

Balance of trade (current prices)

	1993	1994	1995	1996	1997	1998
₱ '000,000	–176,298	–212,086	–229,214	–299,998	–316,285	–69,991
% of total	22.5%	23.2%	20.3%	21.9%	17.5%	3.0%

Imports (1997): U.S.$35,660,239,000 (power generating and specialized machinery 10.7%, telecommunications equipment and electrical machinery 10.3%, mineral fuels and lubricants 8.6%, chemicals 7.8%, transport equipment 7.2%). *Major import sources:* Japan 20.8%; United States 20.0%; South Korea 6.1%; Singapore 6.1%; Taiwan 5.1%; Hong Kong 4.3%.
Exports (1997): U.S.$25,227,701,000 (electronics 42.3%, garments 9.3%, coconut oil 2.7%, ignition wiring sets 2.1%, woodcraft and furniture 1.8%, gold 1.1%). *Major export destinations:* United States 34.9%; Japan 16.6%; The Netherlands 6.6%; Singapore 6.4%; Hong Kong 4.6%.

Transport and communications

Transport. Railroads (1997): route length 897 km; passenger-km 171,600,000; metric ton-km cargo (1996) 1,476,000. Roads (1997): total length 161,313 km (paved 18%). Vehicles (1997); passenger cars 743,299; trucks and buses 244,065. Air transport (1997)[10]: passenger-km 16,872,000,000; metric ton-km cargo 471,915,000; airports (1996) with scheduled flights 21.

Communications

Medium	date	unit	number	units per 1,000 persons
Daily newspapers	1996	circulation	5,700,000	82
Radio	1997	receivers	11,500,000	161
Television	1997	receivers	3,700,000	52
Telephones	1998	main lines	2,700,000	37
Cellular telephones	1998	subscribers	1,733,652	24
Personal computers	1998	units	1,100,000	15
Internet	1998	users	150,000	2.1

Education and health

Education attainment (1995). Percentage of population age 15 and over having: no schooling 3.7%; elementary education 35.8%; secondary 38.4%; postsecondary 21.9%; not stated 0.2%. *Literacy* (1995): total population age 15 and over literate 94.6%; males literate 95.0%; females literate 94.3%.

Education (1996–97)

	schools	teachers	students	student/ teacher ratio
Primary (age 7–12)	37,645	341,183	11,902,501	34.9
Secondary (age 13–16) / Voc., teacher tr.	6,369	154,705	4,888,246	31.6
Higher[11]	1,286	66,876	2,017,972	30.2

Health: physicians (1993) 78,445 (1 per 849 persons); hospital beds (1996) 81,789 (1 per 855 persons); infant mortality rate per 1,000 live births (2000) 33.0.
Food (1997): daily per capita caloric intake 2,366 (vegetable products 85%, animal products 15%); (1995) 106% of FAO recommended minimum.

Military

Total active duty personnel (1998): 117,800 (army 63.2%, navy 22.0%, air force 14.8%). *Military expenditure as percentage of GNP* (1995): 1.5% (world 2.8%); per capita expenditure U.S.$17.

[1]Includes 38 vacant seats. [2]And other Manila suburbs of the National Capital Region. [3]Preliminary. [4]Detail does not add to total given because of rounding. [5]Manufacturing firms with 10 or more workers. [6]Statistical discrepancy. [7]Mostly unemployed. [8]Minimum wages in nonagricultural activities in the National Capital Region. [9]Import figures are f.o.b. in balance of trade and c.i.f. for commodities and trading partners. [10]Philippines Airlines only. [11]1995–96.

Internet resources for further information:
- **National Statistics Office http://www.census.gov.ph**
- **Government Website http://www.neda.gov.ph/LINKS/gov_site.htm**

Poland

Official name: Rzeczpospolita Polska (Republic of Poland).
Form of government: unitary multiparty republic with two legislative houses (Senate [100]; Diet [460]).
Chief of state: President.
Head of government: Prime Minister.
Capital: Warsaw.
Official language: Polish.
Official religion: none[1].
Monetary unit: 1 zloty (Zł)[2] = 100 groszy; valuation (Oct. 6, 2000) 1 U.S.$ = Zł 4.56; 1 £ = Zł 6.59.

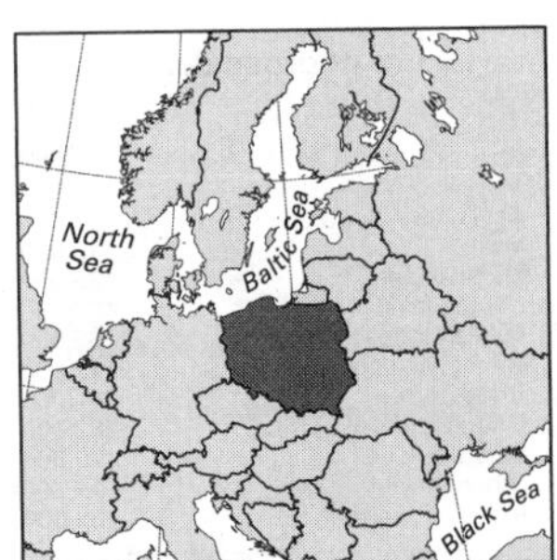

Area and population[3]

Provinces	Capitals	area sq mi	area sq km	population 1999 estimate
Dolnośląskie	Wrocław	7,701	19,946	2,979,700
Kujawsko-pomorskie	Bydgoszcz/Torun	6,969	18,051	2,100,300
Lubelskie	Lublin	9,697	25,115	2,237,200
Lubuskie	Gorzow/Zielona Gora	5,400	13,985	1,023,000
Łódzkie	Łódź	7,036	18,223	2,657,600
Małopolskie	Kraków	5,885	15,242	3,218,600
Mazowieckie	Warsaw (Warszawa)	13,790	35,715	5,064,900
Opolskie	Opole	3,634	9,412	1,088,700
Podkarpackie	Rzeszów	6,907	17,890	2,123,800
Podlaskie	Białystok	7,791	20,180	1,222,900
Pomorskie	Gdańsk	7,032	18,212	2,188,800
Śląskie	Katowice	4,752	12,309	4,874,700
Świętokrzyskie	Kielce	4,468	11,571	1,324,000
Warmińsko-Mazurskie	Olsztyn	9,344	24,202	1,464,400
Wielkopolskie	Poznań	11,561	29,942	3,353,000
Zachodniopomorskie	Szczecin	8,893	23,032	1,732,000
TOTAL		120,860	313,027	38,653,600

Demography

Population (2000): 38,655,000.
Density (2000): persons per sq mi 319.8, persons per sq km 123.5.
Urban-rural (1999): urban 61.9; rural 38.1%.
Sex distribution (1998): male 48.61%; female 51.39%.
Age breakdown (1998): under 15, 20.6%; 15–29, 23.3%; 30–44, 22.2%; 45–59, 17.5%; 60–74, 12.2%; 75 and over, 4.2%.
Population projection: (2010) 38,764,000; (2020) 39,003,000.
Ethnic composition (1995): Polish 97.6%; Ukrainian 0.6%; other 1.8%.
Religious affiliation (1995): Roman Catholic 90.7%; Orthodox and other 9.3%.
Major cities (1999[4]): Warsaw 1,618,468; Łódź 806,728; Kraków 740,666; Wrocław 637,877; Poznań 578,235; Gdańsk 458,988.

Vital statistics

Birth rate per 1,000 population (1999): 9.9 (world avg. 22.1); (1985) legitimate 95.0%; illegitimate 5.0%.
Death rate per 1,000 population (1999): 9.9 (world avg. 8.9).
Natural increase rate per 1,000 population (1999): 0.0 (world avg. 13.2).
Total fertility rate (avg. births per childbearing woman; 1999): 1.4.
Marriage rate per 1,000 population (1997): 5.3.
Divorce rate per 1,000 population (1997): 1.1.
Life expectancy at birth (1999): male 68.9 years; female 77.4 years.
Major causes of death per 100,000 population (1995): diseases of the circulatory system 504.6; malignant neoplasms (cancers) 202.4; accidents, poisoning, and violence 74.6; diabetes mellitus 13.0; infectious and parasitic diseases 6.4.

National economy

Budget (1997). Revenue: Zł 119,772,100,000 (income tax 36.7%, value-added tax 30.8%, excise tax 14.9%). Expenditures: Zł 125,674,900,000 (social security 16.9%, finance 15.4%, health 15.0%, welfare 8.7%, education 5.2%).
Public debt (external, outstanding; 1997): U.S.$35,136,000,000.
Gross national product (1998): U.S.$151,285,000,000 (U.S.$3,910 per capita).

Structure of gross domestic product and labour force

	1997 in value Zł '000,000	% of total value	labour force	% of labour force
Agriculture	22,770.6	4.9	3,117,000	18.2
Mining and manufacturing	106,952.2	22.8	3,843,000	22.5
Public utilities	14,072.7	3.0		
Construction	32,767.1	7.0	1,003,000	5.9
Transp. and commun.	26,611.2	5.7	936,000	5.5
Trade	90,709.9	19.3	2,202,000	12.9
Finance	45,730.3	9.7	752,000	4.4
Public administration	22,122.7	4.7	782,000	4.6
Services	33,670.9	7.2	2,545,000	14.9
Other	73,964.5[5]	15.7[5]	1,923,000[6]	11.2[6]
TOTAL	469,372.1	100.0	17,103,000	100.0[7]

Production (metric tons except at noted). Agriculture, forestry, fishing (1995): (value of production in Zł '000,000) potatoes 6,606, wheat 3,055, rye 1,421, sugar beets 1,075; livestock (number of live animals; 1998) 19,168,000 pigs, 6,955,000 cattle; roundwood (1998) 14,349,000 cu m; fish catch (1996) 451,346. Mining and quarrying (1997): sulfur 2,043,000; copper ore (metal content) 414,800; silver (recoverable metal content) 1,038. Manufacturing (value of production in Zł '000,000; 1995): food and beverages 52,558; machinery and transport equipment 33,372; chemicals 16,360. Construction (1995): 61,000 units, of which residential 31,100. Energy production (consumption): electricity ('000,000 kW-hr; 1999) 140,868 ([1996] 136,666); hard coal ('000 metric tons; 1999) 111,444 ([1996] 109,355); lignite ('000 metric tons; 1999) 60,840 ([1996] 63,864); crude petroleum (barrels; 1996) 2,400,000 (107,000,000); petroleum products (metric tons; 1996) 13,691,000 (16,305,000); natural gas (cu m; 1999) 4,741,000,000 ([1996] 14,160,000,000).
Population economically active (1995): total 17,004,000; activity rate of total population 44.0% (participation rates: over age 15, 66.9%; female 45.9%; unemployed [1996] 14.3%).

Price and earnings indexes (1995 = 100)

	1993	1994	1995	1996	1997	1998	1999
Consumer price index	59.2	78.9	100.0	120.2	139.3	155.6	167.0
Monthly earnings index	53.7	70.7	100.0	126.3	151.6	174.2	189.9

Household income and expenditure (1995). Average household size (1997) 2.9; average annual income Zł 8,431 (U.S.$2,990); sources of income: wages 55.7%, social security benefits 32.5% (of which pensions 26.6%), self-employment 6.9%, other 4.9%; expenditure: food 39.7%, housing 20.6%, clothing 7.0%.
Tourism (1998): receipts U.S.$7,946,000,000; expenditures U.S.$4,430,000,000.
Land use (1994): forest 28.8%; meadow 13.3%; agricultural and under permanent cultivation 47.0%; other 10.9%.

Foreign trade

Balance of trade (current prices)

	1993	1994	1995	1996	1997	1998
Zł '000,000	–8,262	–9,826	–14,987	–34,412	–54,418	–67,443
% of total	13.8%	11.1%	11.9%	20.7%	24.4%	26.2%

Imports (1997): Zł 138,897,800,000 (machinery and transport equipment 36.0%, manufactured goods 19.6%, chemicals 13.8%, miscellaneous manufactured articles 9.4%, mineral fuels and lubricants 8.7%, food 6.8%). *Major import sources:* Germany 24.1%; Italy 10.0%; Russia 6.3%; U.K. 5.5%.
Exports (1997): Zł 84,479,600,000 (manufactured goods 26.5%, miscellaneous manufactured articles 21.7%, machinery and transport equipment 21.6%, food 11.9%, chemicals 7.9%, mineral fuels and lubricants 6.6%). *Major export destinations:* Germany 32.9%; Russia 8.4%; Italy 5.9%.

Transport and communications

Transport. Railroads (1996): length 23,986 km; passenger-km 26,635,000,000; metric ton-km cargo 69,116,000,000. Roads (1997): total length 377,048 km (paved 66%). Vehicles (1997): passenger cars 8,533,449; trucks and buses 1,594,797. Merchant marine (1992): vessels (100 gross tons and over) 644; total deadweight tonnage 4,314,308. Air transport (1997): passenger-km 4,930,000,000; metric ton-km cargo 116,000,000; airports (1997) 8.

Communications

Medium	date	unit	number	units per 1,000 persons
Daily newspapers	1996	circulation	4,351,000	113.0
Radio	1997	receivers	20,200,000	522.6
Television	1998	receivers	16,000,000	414.0
Telephones	1998	main lines	8,812,000	227.9
Cellular telephones	1998	subscribers	1,928,000	49.9
Personal computers	1998	units	1,700,000	44.0
Internet	1998	users	1,581,000	40.9

Education and health

Educational attainment (1988). Percentage of population age 15 and over having: no formal schooling or less that full primary education 6.4%; primary 38.8%; secondary 48.3%; higher 6.5%. *Literacy* (1995): 99.8%.

Education (1997–98)

	schools	teachers	students	student/teacher ratio
Primary (age 7–14)	19,299	322,600	4,896,400	15.2
Secondary (age 15–18)	1,847	39,200	757,700	19.3
Voc., teacher tr.	9,320	89,900	1,750,700	19.5
Higher	246	73,300	1,091,800	14.9

Health (1996): physicians 88,523 (1 per 436 persons); hospital beds 243,036 (1 per 159 persons); infant mortality rate per 1,000 live births (1999) 8.9.
Food (1997): daily per capita caloric intake 3,366 (vegetable products 74%, animal products 26%); 128% of FAO recommended minimum.

Military

Total active duty personnel (1998): 240,650 (army 70%, navy 7%, air force 23%). *Military expenditure as percentage of GNP* (1997): 2.3% (world 2.6%); per capita expenditure U.S.$145.

[1]The 1997 Constitution of Poland specifies freedom of religion; the 1997 concordat with Vatican City (signed unilaterally by the Polish prime minister in May 1997), however, provides special recognition to Roman Catholicism. [2]On Jan. 1, 1995, the złoty was redenominated at a rate of 10,000 old złoty to 1 new złoty. [3]In July 1998 a bill was signed into law that reorganized Poland into 16 new provinces. [4]January 1. [5]Includes import duties and value-added tax. [6]Unemployed. [7]Detail does not add to total given because of rounding.

Internet resources for further information:

- **Polish Official Statistics http://www.stat.gov.pl/english/index.htm**
- **Polish World http://www.polishworld.com**

Portugal

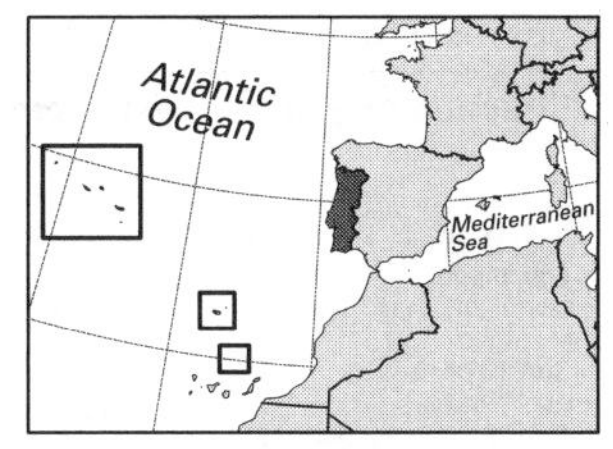

Official name: República Portuguesa (Portuguese Republic).
Form of government: republic with one legislative house (Assembly of the Republic [230]).
Chief of state: President.
Head of government: Prime Minister.
Capital: Lisbon.
Official language: Portuguese.
Official religion: none.
Monetary unit: 1 escudo (Esc) = 100 centavos; valuation (Oct. 6, 2000) 1 U.S.$ = Esc 230.53; 1 £ = Esc 333.48.

Area and population

		area		population
Continental Portugal				1993[1]
Districts	**Capitals**	sq mi	sq km	estimate
Aveiro	Aveiro	1,081	2,800	658,400
Beja	Beja	3,947	10,223	166,500
Braga	Braga	1,041	2,695	754,700
Bragança	Bragança	2,547	6,597	154,700
Castelo Branco	Castelo Branco	2,555	6,616	211,800
Coimbra	Coimbra	1,533	3,971	425,400
Évora	Évora	2,856	7,396	172,400
Faro	Faro	1,925	4,986	342,000
Guarda	Guarda	2,139	5,540	185,400
Leiria	Leiria	1,354	3,508	426,200
Lisboa	Lisbon (Lisboa)	1,065	2,758	2,048,000
Portalegre	Portalegre	2,341	6,064	132,400
Porto	Porto	904	2,341	1,652,000
Santarém	Santarém	2,590	6,707	441,900
Setúbal	Setúbal	1,955	5,064	716,200
Viana do Castelo	Viana do Castelo	853	2,210	248,300
Vila Real	Vila Real	1,662	4,305	233,100
Viseu	Viseu	1,934	5,009	398,800
Azores (Açores) Autonomous Region	Ponta Delgada	868	2,247	237,800
Madeira Autonomous Region	Funchal	306	794	253,800
TOTAL		35,456[2, 3]	91,831[2, 3]	9,859,600[4]

Demography

Population (2000): 10,005,000.
Density (2000): persons per sq mi 280.6, persons per sq km 108.3.
Urban-rural (1996): urban 36.0%; rural 64.0%.
Sex distribution (1996): male 48.16%; female 51.84%.
Age breakdown (1995): under 15, 18.9%; 15–29, 23.6%; 30–44, 21.6%; 45–59, 16.6%; 60–74, 13.9%; 75 and over, 5.4%.
Population projection: (2010) 10,175,000; (2020) 10,348,000.
Nationality (1996): Portuguese 98.2%; Cape Verdean 0.4%; other 1.4%.
Religious affiliation (1995): Christian 94.8%, of which Roman Catholic 92.2%, Protestant 1.5%, other Christian (Jehovah's Witness 0.7%; Mormon 0.4%) 1.1%; Muslim 0.1%; other and nonreligious 5.1%.
Major cities (1991): Lisbon 677,790 (urban agglomeration [1999] 3,754,000); Porto 310,637; Amadora 124,337; Funchal 109,957; Coimbra 96,142.

Vital statistics

Birth rate per 1,000 population (1999): 11.5 (world avg. 22.1).
Death rate per 1,000 population (1999): 10.3 (world avg. 8.9).
Natural increase rate per 1,000 population (1999): 1.2 (world avg. 13.2).
Total fertility rate (avg. births per childbearing woman; 1999): 1.5.
Life expectancy at birth (1999): male 72.0 years; females 79.2 years.
Major causes of death per 100,000 population (1996): circulatory diseases 450.1; malignant neoplasms (cancers) 209.6; respiratory diseases 86.3.

National economy

Budget (1995). Revenue: Esc 6,110,600,000,000 (import duties and excise taxes 36.7%, social security taxes 290.0%, income and inheritance taxes 24.2%). Expenditures: Esc 6,332,900,000,000 (1988; education 12.4%, health 9.8%, defense 6.6%, administration 5.3%, public works 2.8%).
Public debt (1996): U.S.$40,504,000,000.
Production (metric tons except as noted). Agriculture, forestry, fishing (1999): potatoes 1,150,000, tomatoes 1,100,000, corn (maize) 765,000, grapes 550,000, sugar beets 420,000, wheat 360,000, olives 280,000, oranges 230,000, apples 170,000, pears 160,000, rice 155,000, cabbages 140,000, carrots 100,000, cork (1992) 91,870[5]; livestock (number of live animals) 6,300,000 sheep, 2,341,000 pigs, 1,267,000 cattle; roundwood (1998) 8,428,000 cu m; fish catch (1997) 229,108. Mining and quarrying (1997): salt 597,772; copper 111,017; tin 6,459; tungsten 1,790. Manufacturing (value added in Esc '000,000; 1995): petroleum refining 424,700; machinery and transport equipment 412,300; food and beverages 312,800; wearing apparel and footwear 303,000; textiles 262,100; printing and publishing 133,700; tobacco 130,000. Energy production (consumption): electricity (kW-hr; 1998) 33,144,000,000 ([1996] 34,651,000,000); coal (metric tons; 1996) negligible (5,471,000); crude petroleum (barrels; 1996) none (86,157,000); petroleum products (metric tons; 1996) 10,716,000 (10,666,000).
Tourism (1997): receipts U.S.$4,277,000,000; expenditures U.S.$2,164,000,000.
Household income and expenditure. Average household size (1991) 3.1; income per household: n.a.; sources of income (1994–95): wages and salaries 45.8%, property and entrepreneurial income 32.4%, transfer payments 21.5%; expenditure (1994–95): food 23.9%, housing 20.6%, transportation and communications 18.9%, clothing and footwear 6.3%, health 4.6%, other 25.7%.
Gross national product (1998): U.S.$106,391,000,000 (U.S.$10,670 per capita).

Structure of gross domestic product and labour force

	1993		1997	
	in value Esc '000,000	% of total value	labour force	% of labour force
Agriculture	489,476	3.7	616,900	12.7
Mining	113,243	0.8	15,800	0.3
Manufacturing	3,417,963	25.8	954,500	19.6
Construction	699,267	5.3	411,500	8.4
Public utilities	551,164	4.2	37,200	0.8
Trade[6]	2,474,801	18.6	856,300	17.6
Finance	1,246,248	9.4	337,600	6.9
Transp. and commun.	825,319	6.2	179,300	3.7
Services	2,477,083	18.7	191,300	3.9
Pub. admin., defense	976,901	7.4	824,200	16.9
Other	...	...	445,200[7]	9.1[7]
TOTAL	13,271,465	100.0[4]	4,870,100[4]	100.0[3]

Population economically active (1997): total 4,870,100; activity rate of total population 49.3% (participation rates: ages 15–64, 68.5%; female 45.2%; unemployed 6.6%).

Price and earnings indexes (1995 = 100)

	1993	1994	1995	1996	1997	1998	1999
Consumer price index	91.5	96.0	100.0	103.1	105.3	108.3	110.8
Annual earnings index	...	...	...	...	...	...	...

Land use (1994): forest 35.9%; pasture 10.9%; agriculture 31.5%; other 21.7%.

Foreign trade

Balance of trade (current prices)

	1994	1995	1996	1997	1998	1999
Esc '000,000	–1,538.7	–1,526.9	–1,631.2	–1,944.6	–2,453.8	–2,763.9
% of total	20.5%	17.9%	17.7%	18.8%	21.6%	23.5%

Imports (1996): Esc 5,427,132,000,000 (machinery and transport equipment 37.5%, of which road vehicles and parts 14.8%; chemicals and chemical products 10.4%; food products 9.2%; textiles 8.0%; food and live animals 6.4%; mineral fuels 5.8%). *Major import sources:* Spain 22.5%; Germany 15.5%; France 11.1%; Italy 8.3%; U.K. 6.7%; The Netherlands 4.4%.
Exports (1996): Esc 3,795,868,000,000 (textiles and wearing apparel 35.0%; machinery and transport equipment 33.0%, of which transport equipment 16.4%; footwear 8.0%; cork and wood products 4.4%; chemicals and chemical products 4.3%). *Major export destinations:* Germany 19.0%; Spain 14.8%; France 14.6%; U.K. 11.1%; The Netherlands 5.0%; U.S. 4.7%.

Transport and communications

Transport. Railroads (1996): route length 3,072 km; passenger-km 4,503,199,000; metric ton-km cargo 2,177,618,000. Roads (1996): total length 68,732 km (paved 88%). Vehicles (1997): passenger cars 2,865,000; trucks and buses 219,696[8]. Merchant marine (1992): vessels (100 gross tons and over) 332; total deadweight tonnage 1,129,382. Air transport (1996): passenger-km 7,977,817,000; metric ton-km cargo 209,674,000; airports (1997) 16.

Communications

Medium	date	unit	number	units per 1,000 persons
Daily newspapers	1996	circulation	744,000	75
Radio	1996	receivers	3,000,000	306
Television	1997	receivers	5,200,000	523
Telephones	1998	main lines	4,117,000	413
Cellular telephones	1998	subscribers	3,076,000	309
Personal computers	1998	units	810,000	81
Internet	1998	users	600,000	60

Education and health

Educational attainment (1991). Percentage of population age 25 and over having: no formal schooling 16.1%; some primary education 61.5%; some secondary 10.6%; postsecondary 3.5%. *Literacy* (2000): total population age 15 and over literate 92.2%; males 94.8%; females 90.0%.

Education (1993–94)

	schools	teachers	students	student/ teacher ratio
Primary (age 5–11)	12,069	73,221	910,650	12.4
Secondary (age 12–19)	663	69,095[9]	749,838	11.3[9]
Vocational	214	[9]	28,627	[9]
Higher[10]	273	30,998[11]	236,537	6.9[11]

Health (1996): physicians 29,902 (1 per 332 persons); hospital beds 39,210 (1 per 253 persons); infant mortality rate per 1,000 live births (1999) 6.2.
Food (1997): daily per capita caloric intake 3,667 (vegetable products 73%, animal products 27%); 149% of FAO recommended minimum requirement.

Military

Total active duty personnel (1998): 53,600 (army 46.3%, navy 31.4%, air force 13.6%, paramilitary national guard 8.7%). *Military expenditure as percentage of GNP* (1997): 2.4% (world 2.6%); per capita expenditure U.S.$240.

[1]January 1. [2]Does not include 117 sq mi (304 sq km) of water areas comprising the Tagus and Sado estuaries and the Aveiro Lagoon. [3]Total area per more recent survey (including estuaries and Aveiro Lagoon) is 35,662 sq mi (92,365 sq km). [4]Detail does not add to total given because of rounding. [5]1992. [6]Includes hotels. [7]Includes 324,100 unemployed. [8]1994. [9]Secondary includes Vocational. [10]Includes teacher colleges. [11]1992–93.

Internet resources for further information:
- **Instituto Nacional de Estatística http://www.ine.pt**

Puerto Rico

Official name: Estado Libre Asociado de Puerto Rico; Commonwealth of Puerto Rico.
Political status: self-governing commonwealth in association with the United States, having two legislative houses (Senate [27[1]]; House of Representatives [51[1]]).
Chief of state: President of the United States.
Head of government: Governor.
Capital: San Juan.
Official languages: Spanish; English.
Monetary unit: 1 U.S. dollar (U.S.$) = 100 cents; valuation (Oct. 6, 2000) 1 £ = U.S.$1.45.

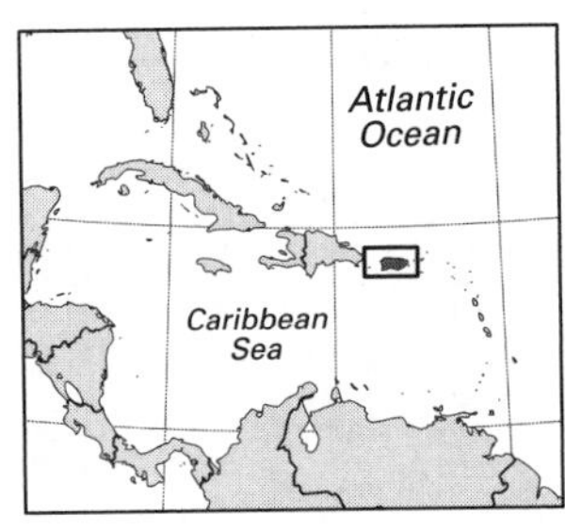

Population (1999 estimate)

Municipio	population	Municipio	population	Municipio	population
Adjuntas	19,644	Fajardo	38,605	Naguabo	25,382
Aguada	40,010	Florida	9,107	Naranjito	29,272
Aguadilla	67,050	Guánica	21,630	Orocovis	25,155
Agunas Buenas	31,841	Guayama	44,066	Patillas	21,904
Aibonito	27,993	Guayanilla	28,538	Peñuelas	27,199
Añasco	28,556	Guaynabo	104,936	Ponce	193,640
Arecibo	102,294	Gurabo	34,006	Quebradillas	26,093
Arroyo	20,153	Hatillo	40,897	Rincón	14,317
Barceloneta	27,524	Hormigueros	17,070	Río Grande	51,267
Barranquitas	29,031	Humacao	60,036	Sabana Grande	24,917
Bayamón	236,688	Isabela	43,118	Salinas	30,597
Cabo Rojo	49,368	Jayuya	16,891	San Germán	38,814
Caguas	145,193	Juana Díaz	52,461	San Juan	439,604
Camuy	33,235	Juncos	43,591	San Lorenzo	38,444
Canóvanas	51,925	Lajas	27,797	San Sebastián	43,854
Carolina	192,088	Lares	33,016	Santa Isabel	20,155
Cataño	32,365	Las Marías	9,887	Toa Alta	61,579
Cayey	51,117	Las Piedras	32,137	Toa Baja	94,837
Ceiba	18,946	Loíza	28,070	Trujillo Alto	78,442
Ciales	20,997	Luquillo	18,877	Utuado	35,475
Cidra	50,019	Manatí	42,079	Vega Alta	37,553
Coamo	37,330	Maricao	6,130	Vaga Baja	62,329
Comerío	20,583	Maunabo	13,874	Vieques	9,584
Corozal	36,804	Mayagüez	100,463	Villalba	24,713
Culebra	1,771	Moca	38,424	Yabucoa	41,743
Dorado	35,104	Morovis	34,014	Yauco	45,289
				TOTAL	3,889,507

Demography

Area: 3,515 sq mi, 9,104 sq km.
Population (2000): 3,916,000.
Density (1999): persons per sq mi 1,114.1, persons per sq km 430.1.
Urban-rural (1990): urban 74.9%; rural 25.1%.
Sex distribution (1999): male 48.26%; female 51.74%.
Age breakdown (1999): under 15, 24.2%; 15–29, 25.6%; 30–44, 20.4%; 45–59, 15.8%; 60–74, 9.4%; 75 and over, 4.6%.
Population projection: (2010) 4,088,000; (2020) 4,196,000.
Doubling time: 90 years.
Linguistic composition (1990): Spanish 51.3%; Spanish-English 46.9%; English 0.5%; other 1.3%.
Religious affiliation (1995): Roman Catholic 64.8%; Protestant 28.7%; other 6.5%.
Major urban agglomerations (1998): San Juan 2,004,054; Ponce 366,273; Caguas 315,921; Mayagüez 258,283; Arecibo 176,814.

Vital statistics

Birth rate per 1,000 population (1999): 15.1 (world avg. 22.1).
Death rate per 1,000 population (1999): 7.3 (world avg. 8.9).
Natural increase rate per 1,000 population (1999): 7.8 (world avg. 13.2).
Total fertility rate (avg. births per childbearing woman; 1999): 1.9.
Marriage rate per 1,000 population (1996): 8.7.
Life expectancy at birth (1999): male 70.9 years; female 80.0 years.
Major causes of death per 100,000 population (1993): heart disease 142.6; cancers 95.4; diabetes 55.1; cerebrovascular disease 38.0; pneumonia and influenza 29.2.

National economy

Budget. Revenue (1997–98): U.S.$8,784,000,000 (tax revenue 68.3%, of which income taxes 45.5%, excise taxes 15.5%, intergovernment transfers 31.7%). Expenditures (1997–98): U.S.$6,263,000,000 (welfare 25.6%, education 20.3%, debt service 9.0%, public safety and protection 8.7%, health 3.5%).
Public debt (outstanding; 1998): U.S.$19,782,000,000.
Tourism (1998): receipts U.S.$2,233,000,000; expenditures U.S.$874,000,000.
Production (in metric tons except as noted). Agriculture, forestry, fishing (1999): sugarcane 307,358; plantains 76,140; bananas 38,215; pineapples 19,204; mangoes 17,245; oranges 16,057; pumpkins, squash, and gourds 16,329; coffee 11,567; livestock (number of live animals) 388,307 cattle, 174,748 pigs; roundwood, n.a.; fish catch (1997) 2,744 metric tons. Mining (value of production in U.S.$'000; 1993): stone 50. Manufacturing (value added in U.S.$'000,000; 1997): chemicals, pharmaceuticals, and allied products 21,393; food 3,532; machinery and metal products 2,940; petroleum products 849; clothing 679. Energy production (consumption): electricity (kW-hr; 1996) 19,029,000,000 (19,029,000,000); coal (metric tons; 1996) none (170,000); crude petroleum (barrels; 1996) none (43,980,000); petroleum products (metric tons; 1996) 5,877,000 (6,743,000); natural gas, none (none).

Gross national product (1997): U.S.$25,380,000,000 (U.S.$7,010 per capita).

Structure of gross domestic product and labour force

	1997–98		1997	
	in value U.S.$'000,000	% of total value	labour force	% of labour force
Agriculture	402.2	0.7	31,000	2.4
Manufacturing	23,015.6	42.8	162,000	12.5
Mining	1,323.3	2.5	1,000	0.1
Construction			64,000	4.9
Public utilities	4,068.9	7.6	15,000	1.1
Transp. and commun.			44,000	3.4
Trade	6,989.7	13.0	228,000	17.6
Finance, real estate	6,898.4	12.8	37,000	2.9
Pub. admin., defense	5,246.0	9.7	261,000	20.1
Services	5,758.0	10.7	285,000	22.0
Other	123.3[2]	0.2[2]	170,000[3]	13.1[3]
TOTAL	53,825.4	100.0	1,298,000	100.0[4]

Population economically active (1997): total 1,298,000; activity rate 34.1% (participation rates: ages 16 and over, 48.0%; female 39.5%; unemployed 13.1%).

Price and earnings indexes (1995 = 100)

	1991	1992	1993	1994	1995	1996	1997
Consumer price index	88.4	90.8	93.5	96.1	100.0	118.0	122.8
Hourly earnings index[5]	...	...	...	...	...	...	...

Household income and expenditure (1997). Average family size 3.5; income per family U.S.$29,783; sources of income: wages and salaries 57.0%, transfers 31.9%, self-employment 6.2%, rent 4.9%; expenditure: food and beverages 20.2%, health care 15.2%, transportation 13.6%, household furnishings 13.2%, housing and energy 11.7%, recreation 8.0%.

Foreign trade

Balance of trade (current prices)

	1993	1994	1995	1996	1997	1998
U.S.$'000,000	+3,405	+5,098	+4,995	+3,884	+2,559	+6,107
% of total	9.4%	13.3%	11.7%	9.2%	5.6%	10.1%

Imports (1997–98): U.S.$27,308,700,000 (chemicals [all forms] 26.8%, electrical machinery 11.8%, food 10.2%, transport equipment 9.6%, petroleum and petroleum products 7.2%, nonelectrical machinery 6.8%, professional and scientific instruments 4.2%, clothing and textiles 4.2%). *Major import sources* (1995–96): U.S. 62.5%; Japan 6.4%; Dominican Republic 4.0%; U.K. 2.9%.
Exports (1997–98): U.S.$33,416,400,000 (chemicals and chemical products 43.6%, nonelectrical machinery 13.2%, food 12.1%, electrical machinery 7.7%). *Major export destinations:* U.S. 88.5%; other 11.5%.

Transport and communications

Transport. Railroads (1988)[6]: length 59 mi, 96 km. Roads (1996): total length 8,948 mi, 14,400 km (paved 100%). Vehicles (1996): passenger cars 878,000; trucks and buses 190,000. Merchant marine: n.a. Air transport (1998): passenger arrivals and departures 9,285,000; cargo loaded and unloaded 275,500 metric tons[7]; airports (1998) with scheduled flights 7.

Communications

Medium	date	unit	number	units per 1,000 persons
Daily newspapers	1996	circulation	475,000	127
Radio	1997	receivers	2,700,000	714
Television	1998	receivers	1,250,000	278
Telephones	1997	main lines	1,322,000	324
Cellular telephones	1998	subscribers	580,000	150
Internet	1998	users	100,000	25.9

Education and health

Educational attainment (1990). Percentage of population age 25 and over having: primary education 26.8%; some secondary 23.5%; complete secondary 21.0%; higher 28.7%. *Literacy* (1995): total population age 15 and over literate 92.8%; males literate 92.7%; females literate 92.8%.

Education (1985–86)

	schools	teachers	students	student/ teacher ratio
Primary (age 5–12)	1,542	18,359	427,582	23.3
Secondary (age 13–18)	395	13,612	334,661	24.6
Voc., teacher tr.	52	...	149,191	...
Higher	45	9,045	156,818	17.3

Health: physicians (1992) 6,269 (1 per 575 persons); hospital beds (1993–94) 9,598 (1 per 381 persons); infant mortality rate (1998) 10.5.

Military

Total active duty personnel (1992): 3,518 U.S. personnel.

[1]Number of members per constitution. Excludes additional seats allotted to either the Senate or House of Representatives to meet 1/3 total representation requirements for minority parties per constitution. [2]Statistical discrepancy. [3]Unemployed. [4]Detail does not add to total given because of rounding. [5]Manufacturing sector only. [6]Privately owned railway for sugarcane transport only. [7]Handled by the Luis Muñoz Marín International Airport only.

Qatar

Official name: Dawlat Qaṭar (State of Qatar).
Form of government: monarchy (emirate)[1]; Islamic law is the basis of legislation in the state.
Heads of state and government: Emir assisted by Prime Minister.
Capital: Doha.
Official language: Arabic.
Official religion: Islam.
Monetary unit: 1 riyal (QR) = 100 dirhams; valuation (Oct. 6, 2000) 1 U.S.$ = QR 3.64; 1 £ = QR 5.27.

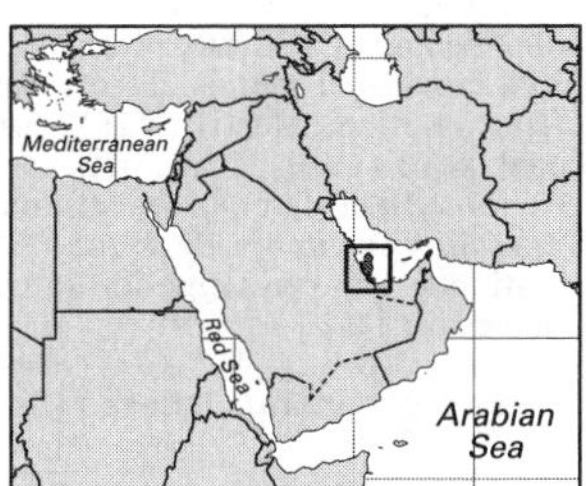

Area and population

Municipalities	Capitals	area sq mi	area sq km	population 1992 estimate
Ad-Dawḥah (Doha)	—	51	132	313,639
Al-Ghuwayrīyah	Al-Ghuwayrīyah	241	622	2,349
Jarayān al-Bāṭinah	Jarayān al-Bāṭinah	1,434	3,715	3,932
Al-Jumaylīyah	Al-Jumaylīyah	990[2]	2,565[2]	10,414
Al-Khawr	Al-Khawr	385	996	12,982
Ar-Rayyān	Ar-Rayyān	343	889	132,785
Ash-Shamāl	Madinat ash-Shamāl	348	901	6,323
Umm Ṣalāl	Umm Ṣalāl Muḥammad	190	493	16,110
Al-Wakrah	Al-Wakrah	430	1,114	34,185
TOTAL		4,416[3]	11,437[3]	532,719

Demography

Population (2000): 599,000.
Density (2000): persons per sq mi 135.6; persons per sq km 52.4.
Urban-rural (1999): urban 92.3%; rural 7.7%.
Sex distribution (1999): male 66.0%; female 34.0%.
Age breakdown (1999): under 15, 26.8%; 15–29, 22.2%; 30–44, 28.2%; 45–59, 18.5%; 60–74, 3.9%; 75 and over, 0.4%.
Population projection: (2010) 692,000; (2020) 761,000.
Doubling time: 53 years.
Ethnic composition (1995): Arab 40%; other (mostly Pakistanis, Indians, and Iranians) 60%.
Religious affiliation (1995): Muslim (mostly Sunnī) 95%; other 5%.
Major cities (1993): Doha 339,471; Ar-Rayyān 143,046; Al-Wakrah 30,976; Umm Salal 16,785.

Vital statistics

Birth rate per 1,000 population (1999): 16.3 (world avg. 22.1).
Death rate per 1,000 population (1999): 4.1 (world avg. 8.9).
Natural increase rate per 1,000 population (1999): 12.2 (world avg. 13.2).
Total fertility rate (avg. births per childbearing woman; 1999): 3.3.
Marriage rate per 1,000 population (1994): 2.8.
Divorce rate per 1,000 population (1994): 1.0.
Life expectancy at birth (1999): male 69.7 years; female 74.6 years.
Major causes of death per 100,000 population (1992): diseases of the circulatory system 56.9; injuries and poisoning 36.0; neoplasms (including benign neoplasms) 21.4; certain conditions originating in the perinatal period 11.1; diseases of the respiratory system 7.5; endocrine, metabolic, and nutritional diseases and immunity disorders 7.3; diseases of the digestive system 3.4; signs, symptoms, and ill-defined conditions 10.9.

National economy

Budget (1998–99). Revenue: QR 12,219,000,000 (crude oil about 90%). Expenditures: QR 15,404,000,000 (current expenditure 89.5%, of which wages and salaries 36.0%; capital expenditure 10.5%).
Production (metric tons except as noted). Agriculture, forestry, fishing (1999): dates 23,000, tomatoes 11,500, pumpkin and squash 8,000, dry onions 4,980, barley 4,800, melons 3,450, watermelons 1,950; livestock (number of live animals; 1999) 207,000 sheep, 177,000 goats, 47,800 camels, 14,000 cattle; roundwood, n.a.; fish catch (1998) 5,279. Mining and quarrying (1996): limestone 900,000; sulfur 61,000; gypsum, sand and gravel, and clay are also produced. Manufacturing (value added in QR '000,000; 1994): refined petroleum 919; chemical products 887; iron and steel 319; pottery, china, and earthenware 219; textiles and apparel 193; food, beverages, and tobacco 99; metal products 89; wood products and furniture 79. Construction (1992): residential 12,420 units; nonresidential 1,416 units. Energy production (consumption): electricity (kW-hr; 1996) 6,340,000,000 (6,340,000,000); coal, none (n.a.); crude petroleum (barrels; 1999) 224,910,000 ([1996] 22,425,000); petroleum products (metric tons; 1996) 5,430,000 (745,000); natural gas (cu m; 1996) 13,700,000,000 (13,700,000,000).
Tourism (1994): receipts and expenditures, n.a.; total number of tourists staying in hotels 241,000.
Land use (1994): meadows and pastures 4.5%; agricultural and under permanent cultivation 0.7%; built-up, desert, and other 94.7%.
Population economically active (1997): total 280,122; activity rate of total population 49.2% (participation rates: ages 15–64 [1988], 80.8%; female 13.5%; unemployed, n.a.).

Price and earnings indexes (1995 = 100)

	1993	1994	1995	1996	1997	1998
Consumer price index	95.9	97.1	100.0	107.4	110.4	113.3
Earnings index	...	...	...	...	...	...

Gross national product (1998): U.S.$6,473,000,000 (U.S.$11,600 per capita).

Structure of gross domestic product and labour force

	1997 in value QR '000,000	1997 % of total value	1988 labour force	1988 % of labour force
Agriculture	292	0.9	4,544	1.6
Oil sector	12,750	38.1	7,657	2.6
Manufacturing	2,505	7.5	10,627	3.6
Construction	2,270	6.8	64,213	21.9
Public utilities	435	1.3	3,672	1.3
Transportation	1,265	3.8	11,877	4.1
Trade	2,557	7.6	34,246	11.7
Finance	3,510	10.5	6,172	2.1
Pub. admin., defense; Services; Other	7,880	23.5	149,560	51.1
TOTAL	33,464	100.0	292,568	100.0

Household income and expenditure. Average household size (1998) 7.0; income per household: n.a.; sources of income (1988): wages and salaries 80.8%, rents and royalties 10.6%, self-employment 5.6%, other 3.0%; expenditure (1993): food 28.7%, transportation 19.3%, housing 12.4%, clothing 10.6%, education 7.6%, health 1.2%.

Foreign trade

Balance of trade (current prices)[4]

	1993	1994	1995	1996	1997	1998
QR '000,000	+5,154	+4,729	+1,940	+4,546	+3,143	+1,307
% of total	29.6%	27.9%	8.1%	19.5%	12.6%	5.1%

Imports (1998): QR 13,407,000,000 (1994; machinery and transport equipment 39.7%, manufactured goods 21.8%, food and live animals 13.2%, chemicals and chemical products 7.0%, raw materials 3.4%). *Major import sources* (1996): United Kingdom 11.9%; United States 11.1%; Italy 10.8%; Japan 9.3%; France 8.2%; Germany 7.6%; Saudi Arabia 6.0%; UAE 4.5%.
Exports (1998): QR 14,714,000,000 (1994; mineral fuels and lubricants 81.2%, chemicals and chemical products 10.4%, manufactured goods 5.9%). *Major export destinations* (1998): Japan 51.6%; South Korea 10.0%; Singapore 8.9%; Thailand 4.1%; United Arab Emirates 2.3%; India 1.4%.

Transport and communications

Transport. Railroads: none. Roads (1996): total length 764 mi, 1,230 km (paved 90%). Vehicles (1996): passenger cars 126,000; trucks and buses 64,000. Merchant marine (1992): vessels (100 gross tons and over) 65; total deadweight tonnage 635,580. Air transport (1998)[5]: passenger-mi 1,372,000,000, passenger-km 2,207,971,000; short ton-mi cargo 54,700,000, metric ton-km cargo 88,007,000; airports (1998) with scheduled flights 1.

Communications

Medium	date	unit	number	units per 1,000 persons
Daily newspapers	1995	circulation	90,000	161
Radio	1997	receivers	250,000	432
Television	1998	receivers	490,000	846
Telephones	1998	main lines	150,508	260
Cellular telephones	1998	subscribers	65,786	11.4
Personal computers	1998	units	70,000	120.9
Internet	1998	users	20,000	34.5

Education and health

Educational attainment (1986). Percentage of population age 25 and over having: no formal education 53.3%, of which illiterate 24.3%; primary 9.8%; preparatory (lower secondary) 10.1%; secondary 13.3%; postsecondary 13.3%; other 0.2%. *Literacy* (1995): total population age 15 and over literate 460,000 (79.4%); males literate 298,000 (79.2%); females literate 122,000 (79.9%).

Education (1995–96)[6]

	schools	teachers	students	student/ teacher ratio
Primary (age 6–11)	174	5,864	53,631	9.1
Secondary (age 12–17)	123	3,738	37,924	10.1
Vocational[7]	3	120	670	5.6
Higher	1	643	8,475	13.2

Health: physicians (1996) 703 (1 per 793 persons); hospital beds (1994) 1,118 (1 per 509 persons); infant mortality rate per 1,000 live births (1999) 23.0.
Food: daily per capita caloric intake, n.a.

Military

Total active duty personnel (1999): 11,800 (army 72.0%, navy 15.3%, air force 12.7%). *Military expenditure as percentage of GNP* (1996): 10.5% (world 2.6%); per capita expenditure U.S.$1,540.

[1]Provisional constitution of 1970 provided limited constitutional forms but has not been fully implemented. [2]Includes area of unpopulated Hawar Islands (also claimed by Bahrain). [3]Includes approximately 4 sq mi (10 sq km) of area not distributed by municipalities. [4]Balance based on f.o.b. valuation of imports. [5]Qatar Airways. [6]Public schools only; available detail for private schools (1991–92) included 17,728 primary students, 1,695 secondary students, and 1,465 teachers. [7]1994–95.

Internet resources for further information:
- **Qatar Ministry of Foreign Affairs http://www.mofa.gov.qa**

Réunion

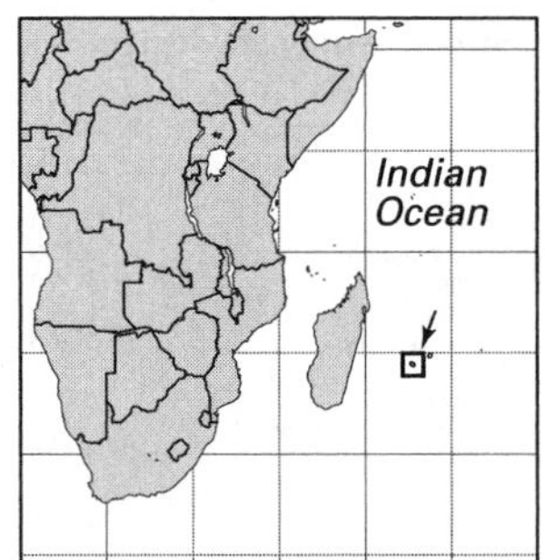

Official name: Département de la Réunion (Department of Réunion)[1].
Political status: overseas department (France) with two legislative houses (General Council [47]; Regional Council [45]).
Chief of state: President of France.
Heads of government: Prefect (for France); President of General Council (for Réunion); President of Regional Council (for Réunion).
Capital: Saint-Denis.
Official language: French.
Official religion: none.
Monetary unit: 1 French franc (F) = 100 centimes; valuation (Oct. 6, 2000) 1 U.S.$ = F 7.54; 1 £ = F 10.91.

Area and population

		area		population
				1999
Arrondissements	**Capitals**	sq mi	sq km	census
Saint-Benoît	Saint-Benoît	285	737	101,804
Saint-Denis	Saint-Denis	163	421	236,599
Saint-Paul	Saint-Paul	180	467	138,551
Saint-Pierre	Saint-Pierre	341	883	229,346
TOTAL		968[2, 3]	2,507[2, 3]	706,300

Demography

Population (2000): 727,000.
Density (2000): persons per sq mi 751.0, persons per sq km 290.0.
Urban-rural (1999): urban 71.6%; rural 28.4%[4].
Sex distribution (1997): male 48.88%; female 51.12%.
Age breakdown (1997): under 15, 29.3%; 15–29, 26.5%; 30–44, 22.5%; 45–59, 12.6%; 60–74, 6.9%; 75 and over, 2.2%.
Population projection: (2010) 829,000; (2020) 932,000.
Doubling time: 50 years.
Ethnic composition (1983): mixed race 63.5%; South Asian/predominantly South Asian 28.2%; Chinese 2.2%; white 1.9%; East African 1.1%; other 3.1%.
Religious affiliation (1995): Roman Catholic 89.4%; Pentecostal 2.7%; other Christian 1.8%; other (mostly Muslim) 6.1%.
Major cities (1999): Saint-Denis 131,557 (agglomeration 158,139); Saint-Pierre 60,323 (agglomeration 129,238).

Vital statistics

Birth rate per 1,000 population (1998): 19.3 (world avg. 22.1); (1997) legitimate 41.5%; illegitimate 58.5%.
Death rate per 1,000 population (1998): 5.4 (world avg. 8.9).
Natural increase rate per 1,000 population (1998): 13.9 (world avg. 13.2).
Total fertility rate (avg. births per childbearing woman; 1997): 2.2.
Marriage rate per 1,000 population (1998): 4.8.
Divorce rate per 1,000 population (1997): 1.3.
Life expectancy at birth (1998): male 70.2 years; female 78.5 years.
Major causes of death per 100,000 population (1996): diseases of the circulatory system 170.7; malignant neoplasms (cancers) 98.0; accidents, suicide, and violence 53.0; diseases of the respiratory system 48.5.

National economy

Budget (1998). Revenue: F 4,624,000,000 (receipts from the French central government and local administrative bodies 52.7%, tax receipts 20.2%, loans 8.9%). Expenditures: F 4,300,000,000 (current expenditures 68.7%, development expenditures 31.3%).
Public debt (external, outstanding): n.a.
Tourism (1998): receipts U.S.$265,000,000; expenditures, n.a.
Gross national product (at current market prices; 1997): U.S.$5,680,000,000 (U.S.$8,264 per capita).

Structure of gross domestic product and labour force

	1995		1994	
	in value F '000,000	% of total value	labour force	% of labour force
Agriculture, fishing	1,392	3.6	12,015	5.0
Manufacturing, mining	3,101	8.0	9,854	4.1
Construction }	1,761	4.5	16,711	7.0
Public utilities }			...	...
Transp. and commun.	1,753	4.5	5,495	2.3
Trade, restaurants	6,140	15.8	22,587	9.4
Finance, real estate, business services	9,823	25.4	11,148	4.7
Pub. admin., defense }	16,524	42.7	23,678	9.9
Services }			50,986	21.3
Other	–1,760[5]	–4.5[5]	86,905[6]	36.3[6]
TOTAL	38,734	100.0	239,379	100.0

Production (metric tons except as noted). Agriculture, forestry, fishing (1999): sugarcane 1,800,000, corn (maize) 17,000, cabbages 14,000, pineapples 13,000, tomatoes 11,500, bananas 10,000, pimento 430, ginger 95, vanilla 30, tobacco 20, geranium essence (1998) 6.3; livestock (number of live animals) 89,000 pigs, 38,000 goats, 27,000 cattle; roundwood (1998) 36,100 cu m; fish catch (1998) 6,453. Mining and quarrying: gravel and sand for local use. Manufacturing (value added in F '000,000; 1997): food and beverages 1,019, of which meat and milk products 268; construction materials (mostly cement) 394; fabricated metals 258; printing and publishing 192. Energy production (consumption): electricity (kW-hr; 1998) 1,431,000,000 ([1996] 1,132,000,000); coal, none (none); crude petroleum, none (none); petroleum products (metric tons; 1996) none (509,000); natural gas, none (none).
Population economically active (1998): total 288,760; activity rate of total population 41.2% (participation rates: ages 15–64, 57.5%; female 44.3%; unemployed 41.1%).

Price and earnings indexes (December 1997 = 100)[7]

	1993	1994	1995	1996	1997	1998	1999
Consumer price index	92.4	94.8	96.7	98.6	100.0	101.0	102.1
Monthly earnings index[8]	...	96.5	98.9	98.9	100.0	101.4	102.8

Household income and expenditure. Average household size (1999) 3.3; average annual income per household (1997) F 136,800 (U.S.$23,438); sources of income (1997): wages and salaries and self-employment 41.8%, transfer payments 41.3%, other 16.9%; expenditure (1994–95): food and beverages 22.0%, transportation and communications 19.0%, housing and energy 10.0%, household furnishings 8.0%, recreation 6.0%.
Land use (1994): forested 35.2%; meadows and pastures 4.8%; agricultural and under permanent cultivation 19.6%; other 40.4%.

Foreign trade

Balance of trade (current prices)

	1994	1995	1996	1997	1998	1999
F '000,000	–12,116	–12,458	–13,180	–13,011	–14,095	–12,937
% of total	86.4%	85.7%	86.0%	83.9%	85.3%	85.3%

Imports (1998): F 15,310,000,000 (food and agricultural products 17.1%, transport equipment 14.7%, machinery and apparatus 13.4%, clothing and footwear 6.8%). *Major import sources:* France 66.0%; EC 14.0%.
Exports (1998): F 1,215,000,000 (sugar 58.9%, machinery, apparatus, and transport equipment 17.5%, rum 2.5%, lobster 1.7%). *Major export destinations:* France 70.0%; EC 9.0%; Madagascar 4.5%; Mauritius 2.3%.

Transport and communications

Transport. Railroads:[9]. Roads (1994): total length 1,711 mi, 2,754 km (paved [1991] 79%). Vehicles (1999)[10]: passenger cars 190,300; trucks and buses 44,300. Air transport (1998): passenger arrivals 677,487, passenger departures 674,651; cargo unloaded 15,060 metric tons, cargo loaded 7,270 metric tons; airports (1999) with scheduled flights 2.

Communications

Medium	date	unit	number	units per 1,000 persons
Daily newspapers	1996	circulation	83,000	123
Radio	1997	receivers	173,000	252
Television	1997	receivers	127,000	185
Telephones	1998	main lines	242,664	347
Cellular telephones	1998	subscribers	50,300	72

Education and health

Educational attainment (1986–87). Percentage of population age 25 and over having: no formal schooling 18.8%; primary education 44.3%; lower secondary 21.6%; upper secondary 11.0%; higher 4.3%. *Literacy* (1996): total population age 16–66 literate 373,487 (91.3%); males literate 179,154 (89.9%); females literate 194,333 (92.7%).

Education (1997–98)

	schools	teachers	students	student/ teacher ratio
Primary (age 6–10)	351	...	76,364	...
Secondary (age 11–17)	111	...	96,811	...
Higher[11]	1	286	9,103	31.8

Health (1999[10]): physicians 1,346 (1 per 525 persons); hospital beds (1998[10]) 2,734 (1 per 254 persons); infant mortality rate per 1,000 live births (1997) 6.4%.
Food (1995): daily per capita caloric intake 3,308 (vegetable products 79%, animals products 21%); 146% of FAO recommended minimum requirement.

Military

Total active duty personnel (1999): 3,700 French troops[12].

[1]In October 2000 the French National Assembly amended the law for overseas departments and split Réunion into two departments (North Réunion and South Réunion) as of Jan. 1, 2001. [2]Detail does not add to total given because of rounding. [3]Indian Ocean islets administered by France from Réunion are excluded from total. Areas of these islets, which have no permanent population, are: Îles Glorieuses 1.9 sq mi (5.0 sq km), Île Juan de Nova 1.7 sq mi (4.4 sq km), Île Tromelin 0.4 sq mi (1.0 sq km), Bassas da India 0.1 sq mi (0.2 sq km), Île Europa 7.8 sq mi (20.2 sq km). [4]Includes semi-urban. [5]Less imputed bank service charges. [6]Includes 2,621 not adequately defined and 84,284 unemployed. [7]Indexes refer to December. [8]Minimum salary in public administration. [9]No public railways; railways in use are for sugar industry. [10]January 1. [11]University only. [12]Includes troops stationed on Mayotte.

Internet resources for further information:
- **INSEE: Réunion**
  http://www.insee.fr/fr/insee_regions/reunion/home/home_page.asp
- **Ministère de l'Outre-mer (Paris)**
  http://www.outre-mer.gouv.fr/domtom/reunion/index.htm

Romania

Official name: România (Romania).
Form of government: unitary republic with two legislative houses (Senate [143]; Assembly of Deputies [343[1]]).
Chief of state: President.
Head of government: Prime Minister.
Capital: Bucharest.
Official language: Romanian.
Official religion: none.
Monetary unit: 1 Romanian leu (plural lei) = 100 bani; valuation (Oct. 6, 2000) 1 U.S.$ = 24,358 lei; 1 £ = 35,236 lei.

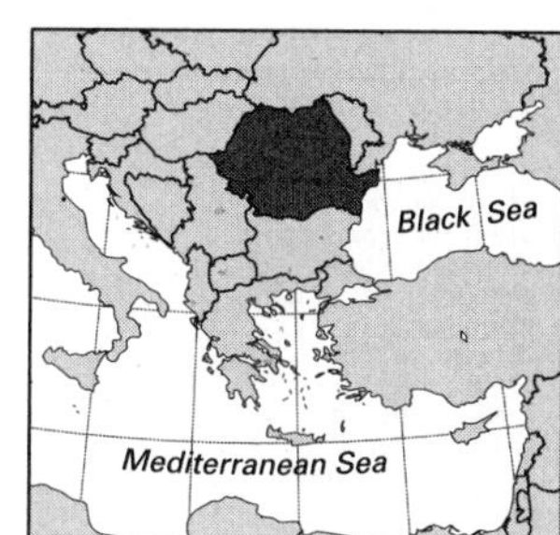

Area and population

Counties	Capitals	area sq mi	area sq km	population 1997 estimate
Alba	Alba Iulia	2,406	6,231	402,097
Arad	Arad	2,954	7,652	476,988
Arges	Pitești	2,626	6,801	676,005
Bacău	Bacău	2,551	6,606	746,131
Bihor	Oradea	2,909	7,535	625,596
Bistrița-Năsăud	Bistrița	2,048	5,305	326,539
Botoșani	Botoșani	1,917	4,965	460,115
Brăila	Brăila	1,824	4,724	388,891
Brașov	Brașov	2,066	5,351	636,434
Buzău	Buzău	2,344	6,072	508,492
Călărași	Călărași	1,959	5,074	332,884
Caraș-Severin	Reșița	3,283	8,503	360,773
Cluj	Cluj-Napoca	2,568	6,650	724,355
Constanța	Constanța	2,724	7,055	746,686
Covasna	Sfântu Gheorghe	1,431	3,705	231,491
Dâmbovița	Târgoviște	1,558	4,036	553,986
Dolj	Craiova	2,862	7,413	749,311
Galați	Galați	1,709	4,425	641,647
Giurgiu	Giurgiu	1,356	3,511	298,795
Gorj	Târgu Jiu	2,178	5,641	397,714
Harghita	Miercurea-Ciuc	2,552	6,610	343,330
Hunedoara	Deva	2,709	7,016	543,109
Ialomița	Slobozia	1,718	4,449	304,740
Iași	Iași	2,112	5,469	823,735
Maramureș	Baia Mare	2,400	6,215	533,672
Mehedinți	Drobeta-Turnu Severin	1,892	4,900	325,344
Mureș	Târgu Mureș	2,585	6,696	602,626
Neamț	Piatra Neamț	2,274	5,890	583,141
Olt	Slatina	2,126	5,507	513,961
Prahova	Ploiești	1,812	4,694	864,159
Sălaj	Zalău	1,486	3,850	259,304
Satu Mare	Satu Mare	1,701	4,405	392,054
Sibiu	Sibiu	2,093	5,422	444,701
Suceava	Suceava	3,303	8,555	711,568
Teleorman	Alexandria	2,224	5,760	466,010
Timiș	Timișoara	3,356	8,692	692,870
Tulcea	Tulcea	3,255	8,430	265,778
Vâlcea	Râmnicu Vâlcea	2,203	5,705	433,356
Vaslui	Vaslui	2,045	5,297	460,840
Vrancea	Focșani	1,878	4,863	391,762
Municipality				
Bucharest	Bucharest	703	1,820	2,304,934
TOTAL		91,699[2]	237,500	22,545,924

Demography

Population (2000): 22,435,000.
Density (2000): persons per sq mi 244.6, persons per sq km 94.5.
Urban-rural (1999): urban 57.7%; rural 42.3%.
Sex distribution (1999): male 49.11%; female 50.89%.
Age breakdown (1999): under 15, 18.8%; 15–29, 24.4%; 30–44, 20.8%; 45–59, 17.4%; 60–74, 14.3%; 75 and over, 4.3%.
Population projection: (2010) 21,930,000; (2020) 21,267,000.
Ethnic composition (1992): Romanian 90.7%; Hungarian 7.2%; other 2.1%.
Religious affiliation (1992): Romanian Orthodox 86.8%; Protestant 5.5%; Roman Catholic 5.1%; Greek Orthodox 1.0%; Muslim 0.2%; other 1.4%.
Major cities (1997): Bucharest 2,027,512; Iași 348,399; Constanța 344,876; Timișoara 334,098; Cluj-Napoca 332,792; Galați 331,360.

Vital statistics

Birth rate per 1,000 population (1999): 10.7 (world avg. 22.1).
Death rate per 1,000 population (1999): 12.3 (world avg. 8.9).
Natural increase rate per 1,000 population (1999): –1.6 (world avg. 13.2).
Total fertility rate (avg. births per childbearing woman; 1999): 1.4.
Marriage rate per 1,000 population (1995): 6.8.
Divorce rate per 1,000 population (1995): 1.5.
Life expectancy at birth (1999): male 65.8 years; female 73.8 years.
Major causes of death per 100,000 population (1998): circulatory disease 738.6; cancers 173.4; diseases of the digestive system 71.6; respiratory disease 71.0.

National economy

Budget ('000,000,000,000 lei; 1996). Revenue: 76.7 (social security 23.0%, personal income tax 18.2%, value-added tax 15.2%). Expenditures: 85.6 (social security 28.2%, debt service 10.0%, education 9.6%, health 7.5%).
Tourism (1998): receipts U.S.$260,000,000; expenditures U.S.$451,000,000.
Production (metric tons). Agriculture (2000): wheat 4,320,000, corn (maize) 4,200,000, potatoes 3,650,000, sugar beets 1,500,000, grapes 1,250,000; livestock (number of live animals) 7,972,000 sheep, 5,951,000 pigs, 3,154,000 cattle; roundwood (1998) 11,515,000 cu m; fish catch (1998) 9,020. Mining (1995): iron 184,000; bauxite 174,000; zinc 35,000; copper 24,000. Manufacturing (value-added in '000,000,000,000 lei; 1996): food products 5.8; beverages 3.0; iron and steel 1.6; glass products 1.5; textiles 1.4; motor vehicles 1.3; electrical machinery 0.9. Construction (1995): 9,300 dwelling units. Energy production (consumption): electricity (kW-hr; 1996) 61,350,000,000 (62,157,000,000); coal (metric tons; 1996) 41,869,000 (45,477,000); crude petroleum (barrels; 1996) 70,558,000 (100,440,000); petroleum products (metric tons; 1996) 10,956,000 (10,933,000); natural gas (cu m; 1996) 14,460,000,000 (20,401,000,000).
Public debt (external, outstanding; 1998): U.S.$6,962,000,000.
Gross national product (1998): U.S.$30,596,000,000 (U.S.$1,360 per capita).

Structure of gross domestic product and labour force

	1998 in value '000,000,000 lei	% of total value	labour force	% of labour force
Agriculture	20,662.0	19.1	4,342,200	37.5
Industry[3]	37,054.4	34.2	2,750,600	23.8
Construction	7,468.8	6.9	433,500	3.7
Transp. and commun.	9,374.3	8.6	529,400	4.6
Trade	10,907.5	10.1	1,068,000	9.2
Finance	} 18,011.1	} 16.6	81,800	0.7
Pub. admin. / Services			} 1,639,500	14.2
Other	4,912.8	4.5	732,400[4]	6.3[4]
TOTAL	108,390.5[2]	100.0	11,577,300[2]	100.0

Population economically active (1998): total 11,577,300; activity rate 51.4% (participation rates: ages 15–64, 67.2%[5]; female 42.8%; unemployed 6.3%).

Price and earnings indexes (1995 = 100)

	1993	1994	1995	1996	1997	1998	1999
Consumer price index	31.9	75.6	100.0	138.8	353.7	562.7	820.4
Annual earnings index	28.3	64.9	100.0	149.0	295.0	502.9	719.6

Household income and expenditure. Average household size (1992) 3.1; income per household (1989) 73,500 lei (U.S.$4,940); sources of income (1982): wages 62.6%; expenditure (1989): food 51.1%; housing 16.4%.

Foreign trade

Balance of trade (current prices)

	1994	1995	1996	1997	1998	1999
U.S.$'000,000	–411.1	–1,576.7	–2,470.5	–1,980.3	–403.3	–1,087.4
% of total	3.2%	9.1%	13.2%	10.5%	9.4%	6.0%

Imports (1996): 10,368,000,000,000 lei (mineral fuels 25.4%, machinery and transport equipment 24.1%, textiles 12.0%, chemicals 8.4%). *Major import sources:* Germany 16.5%; Italy 15.6%; Russia 13.1%; France 4.8%.
Exports (1996): 10,272,827,000,000 lei (textiles 20.8%, mineral products 9.2%, chemicals 9.0%, machinery 8.0%, footwear 6.1%). *Major export destinations:* Germany 18.2%; Italy 16.6%; France 5.6%; U.K. 2.9%; U.S. 2.2%.

Transport and communications

Transport. Railroads (1997): length 11,365 km[6]; passenger-km 15,794,000,000; metric ton-km cargo 24,789,000,000. Roads (1996): length 153,358 km (paved 51%). Vehicles (1997): cars 2,605,565; trucks and buses 427,579. Merchant marine (1992): vessels (100 gross tons and over) 439; total deadweight tonnage 4,845,539. Air transport (1998): passenger-km 1,712,300,000; metric ton-km cargo 12,110,000; airports (1997) 8.

Communications

Medium	date	unit	number	units per 1,000 persons
Daily newspapers	1996	circulation	6,800,000	297
Radio	1997	receivers	7,200,000	319
Television	1998	receivers	5,400,000	240
Telephones	1998	main lines	3,649,000	162
Personal computers	1998	units	230,000	10
Internet	1998	users	200,000	8.7

Education and health

Educational attainment (1992). Percentage of population age 25 and over having: no schooling 5.4%; some primary education 24.4%; some secondary 63.2%; postsecondary 6.9%. *Literacy* (2000): total population age 15 and over literate 98.2%; males 99.1%; females 97.3%.

Education (1996–97)

	schools	teachers	students	student/ teacher ratio
Primary (age 6–9)	13,978	175,426	2,546,231	14.5
Secondary (age 10–17)	1,295	64,485	792,788	12.3
Voc., teacher tr.	1,692	10,942	351,900	32.2
Higher	102	23,447	354,488	15.1

Health: physicians (1994) 47,990 (1 per 474 persons); hospital beds (1992) 174,900 (1 per 130 persons); infant mortality rate (1999) 20.3.
Food (1998): daily per capita caloric intake 3,263 (vegetable products 78%, animal products 22%); 132% of FAO recommended minimum requirement.

Military

Total active duty personnel (1999): 207,000 (army 51.2%, navy 10.0%, air force 21.0%, other 17.8%). *Military expenditure as percentage of GNP* (1997): 2.4% (world 2.6%); per capita expenditure U.S.$102.

[1]Includes 15 nonelective seats. [2]Detail does not add to total given because of rounding. [3]Mining, manufacturing, and public utilities. [4]Unemployed. [5]1992. [6]1994.

Internet resources for further information:
- **Embassy of Romania (Washington, D.C.) http://www.roembus.org**

Russia

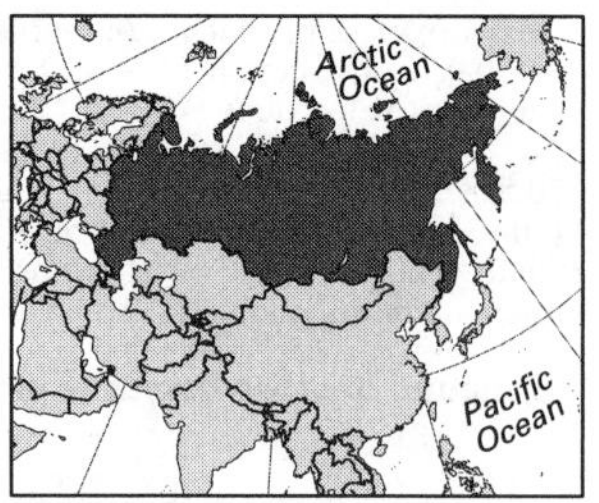

Official name: Rossiyskaya Federatsiya (Russian Federation).
Form of government: federal multiparty republic with a bicameral legislative body (Federal Assembly comprising a Federation Council [178] and a State Duma [450]).
Head of state: President.
Head of government: Prime Minister.
Capital: Moscow.
Official language: Russian.
Official religion: none.
Monetary unit: 1 ruble[1] (Rub) = 100 kopecks; valuation (Oct. 6, 2000) market rate, 1 U.S.$ = Rub 27.95; 1 £ = Rub 40.43.

Area and population

		area		population
Federal Districts	Capitals	sq mi	sq km	1996[2] estimate
Central	Moscow	252,000	652,800	37,763,000
Belgorod (region)		10,500	27,100	1,469,000
Bryansk (region)		13,500	34,900	1,480,000
Ivanovo (region)		9,200	23,900	1,266,000
Kaluga (region)		11,500	29,900	1,097,000
Kostroma (region)		23,200	60,100	806,000
Kursk (region)		11,500	29,800	1,347,000
Lipetsk (region)		9,300	24,100	1,250,000
Moscow (city)		[3]	[3]	8,664,000
Moskva (Moscow; region)		18,200[3]	47,000[3]	6,597,000
Oryol (region)		9,500	24,700	914,000
Ryazan (region)		15,300	39,600	1,325,000
Smolensk (region)		19,200	49,800	1,172,000
Tambov (region)		13,200	34,300	1,310,000
Tula (region)		9,900	25,700	1,815,000
Tver (region)		32,500	84,100	1,651,000
Vladimir (region)		11,200	29,000	1,645,000
Voronezh (region)		20,200	52,400	2,504,000
Yaroslavl (region)		14,100	36,400	1,451,000
Far Eastern	Khabarovsk	2,400,000	6,215,900	7,505,000
Amur (region)		140,400	363,700	1,038,000
Chukot (autonomous district)		284,800[4]	737,700[4]	91,000[4]
Kamchatka (region)		182,400	472,300	411,000
Khabarovsk (territory)		304,500	788,600	1,571,000
Koryak (autonomous district)		*116,400*[4]	*301,500*[4]	*33,000*[4]
Magadan (region)		178,100	461,400	258,000
Primorye (territory)		64,100	165,900	2,255,000
Sakha (republic)		1,198,200	3,103,200	1,023,000
Sakhalin (region)		33,600	87,100	648,000
Yevreyskaya (autonomous region)		13,900	36,000	210,000
North Caucasus	Rostov-na-Donu	227,300	589,200	21,790,000
Adygeya (republic)		2,900	7,600	450,000
Astrakhan (region)		17,000	44,100	1,029,000
Chechnia (republic)[5]		[6]	[6]	[6]
Dagestan (republic)		19,400	50,300	2,098,000
Ingushetiya (republic)		7,400[6]	19,300[6]	1,165,000[6]
Kabardino-Balkariya (republic)		4,800	12,500	790,000
Kalmykiya (republic)		29,400	76,100	319,000
Karachayevo-Cherkesiya (republic)		5,400	14,100	436,000
Krasnodar (territory)		29,300	76,000	5,044,000
Rostov (region)		38,900	100,800	4,425,000
Severnaya Osetiya–Alania (republic)		3,100	8,000	663,000
Stavropol (territory)		25,700	66,500	2,667,000
Volgograd (region)		44,000	113,900	2,704,000
Northwest	St. Petersburg	648,000	1,677,900	14,873,000
Archangelsk (region)		226,800	587,400	1,521,000
Kaliningrad (region)		5,800	15,100	932,000
Kareliya (republic)		66,600	172,400	785,000
Komi (republic)		160,600	415,900	1,185,000
Leningrad (region)		33,200[7]	85,900[7]	1,676,000
Murmansk (region)		55,900	144,900	1,048,000
Nenets (autonomous district)		*68,100*[4]	*176,400*[4]	*48,000*[4]
Novgorod (region)		21,400	55,300	743,000
Pskov (region)		21,400	55,300	832,000
St. Petersburg (city)		[7]	[7]	4,801,000
Vologda (region)		56,300	145,700	1,350,000
Siberia	Novosibirsk	1,974,800	5,114,800	21,102,000
Agin Buryat (autonomous district)		*7,300*[4]	*19,000*[4]	*79,000*[4]
Altay (republic)		35,700	92,600	202,000
Altay (territory)		65,300	169,100	2,690,000
Buryatiya (republic)		135,600	351,300	1,053,000
Chita (region)		166,600	431,500	1,295,000
Evenk (autonomous district)		*296,400*[4]	*767,600*[4]	*20,000*[4]
Irkutsk (region)		296,500	767,900	2,795,000
Kemerovo (region)		36,900	95,500	3,063,000
Khakasiya (republic)		23,900	61,900	586,000
Krasnoyarsk (territory)		903,400	2,339,700	3,106,000
Novosibirsk (region)		68,800	178,200	2,749,000
Omsk (region)		53,900	139,700	2,176,000
Taymyr (autonomous district)		*332,900*[4]	*862,100*[4]	*47,000*[4]
Tomsk (region)		122,400	316,900	1,078,000
Tuva (republic)		65,800	170,500	309,000
Ust-Ordyn Buryat		*8,600*[4]	*22,400*[4]	*143,000*[4]
Urals	Yekaterinburg	690,600	1,788,900	12,657,000
Chelyabinsk (region)		33,900	87,900	3,689,000
Khanty-Mansi (autonomous district)		*202,000*[4]	*523,100*[4]	*1,331,000*[4]
Kurgan (region)		27,400	71,000	1,112,000
Sverdlovsk (region)		75,200	194,800	4,686,000
Tyumen (region)		554,100	1,435,200	3,170,000
Yamalo-Nenets (autonomous district)		*289,700*[4]	*750,300*[4]	*488,000*[4]
Volga	Nizhny Novgorod	400,100	1,035,900	32,286,000
Bashkortostan (republic)		55,400	143,600	4,097,000
Chuvashiya (republic)		7,100	18,300	1,361,000
Kirov (region)		46,600	120,800	1,634,000

Area and population (continued)

Komi-Permyak (autonomous district)	*12,700*[4]	*32,900*[4]	*157,000*[4]
Mari-El (republic)	9,000	23,200	766,000
Mordoviya (republic)	10,100	26,200	956,000
Nizhny Novgorod (region)	28,900	74,800	3,727,000
Orenburg (region)	47,900	124,000	2,229,000
Penza (region)	16,700	43,200	1,562,000
Perm (region)	62,000	160,600	3,009,000
Samara (region)	20,700	53,600	3,312,000
Saratov (region)	38,700	100,200	2,739,000
Tatarstan (republic)	26,300	68,000	3,760,000
Udmurtia (republic)	16,300	42,100	1,639,000
Ulyanovsk (region)	14,400	37,300	1,495,000
TOTAL	6,592,800	17,075,400	147,976,000

Demography

Population (2000): 146,001,000.
Density (2000): persons per sq mi 22.1, persons per sq km 8.6.
Urban-rural (1999): urban 73.0%; rural 27.0%.
Sex distribution (1999): male 46.76%; female 53.24%.
Age breakdown (1999): under 15, 18.8%; 15–29, 22.2%; 30–44, 23.4%; 45–59, 17.3%; 60–74, 14.2%; 75 and over, 4.1%.
Population projection: (2010) 142,328,000; (2020) 138,978,000.
Ethnic composition (1997): Russian 86.6%; Tatar 3.2%; Ukrainian 1.3%; Chuvash 0.9%; Bashkir 0.7%; Chechen 0.6%; Mordovian 0.5%; Belorussian 0.3%; other 5.9%.
Religious affiliation (1995): Russian Orthodox 16.3%; Muslim 10.0%; Protestant 0.9%; Jewish 0.4%; other (mostly nonreligious) 72.4%.
Major cities (1997): Moscow 8,405,000; St. Petersburg 4,216,000; Nizhny Novgorod 1,371,000; Novosibirsk 1,367,000; Yekaterinburg 1,275,000; Samara 1,170,000; Omsk 1,158,000; Chelyabinsk 1,085,000; Kazan 1,084,000; Ufa 1,082,000; Perm 1,025,000; Rostov-na-Donu 1,023,000.

Other principal cities (1997)

	population		population		population
Astrakhan	490,000	Krasnoyarsk	874,000	Simbirsk (Ulyanovsk)	679,000
Barnaul	591,000	Naberezhnye Chelny	522,000	Tolyatti	712,000
Irkutsk	591,000	Novokuznetsk	566,000	Tula	525,000
Izhevsk	654,000	Orenburg	531,000	Vladivostok	623,000
Kemerovo	500,000	Penza	534,000	Volgograd	1,005,000
Khabarovsk	615,000	Ryazan	535,000	Voronezh	910,000
Krasnodar	650,000	Saratov	892,000	Yaroslavl	625,000

Mobility (1989). Population living in the same residence as in 1988: 78.8%; different residence, same oblast 11.5%; different republic 9.7%.
Households (1998). Total family households 52,407,000; average household size 2.8[8]; 2 persons 26.2%; 3 persons 22.6%; 4 persons 20.5%; 5 persons or more 11.5%. Population in family households (1989): 128,787,000 (87.0%), nonfamily population 19,254,000 (13.0%).

Vital statistics

Birth rate per 1,000 population (1999): 9.0 (world avg. 22.1); (1994) legitimate 80.4%; illegitimate 19.6%.
Death rate per 1,000 population (1999): 13.8 (world avg. 8.9).
Natural increase rate per 1,000 population (1999): –4.8 (world avg. 13.2).
Total fertility rate (avg. births per childbearing woman; 1999): 1.3.
Marriage rate per 1,000 population (1998): 5.8.
Divorce rate per 1,000 population (1998): 3.4.
Life expectancy at birth (1999): male 61.8 years; female 72.7 years.
Major causes of death per 100,000 population (1998): circulatory diseases 749; malignant neoplasms (cancers) 203; accidents, poisoning, and violence 185, of which suicide 35, murder 23; respiratory diseases 57; digestive diseases 38; infectious and parasitic diseases 19.

Social indicators

Educational attainment (1998). Percentage of population age 16 and over having: primary or no formal education 11.2%; some secondary 25.3%; secondary and some postsecondary 40.9%; higher and postgraduate 22.6%.
Quality of working life (1998). Average workweek: 40 hours. Annual rate per 100,000 workers of: injury or accident 530; industrial illness 18.2; death 14.2. Proportion of labour force insured for damages or income loss resulting from: injury 100%; permanent disability 100%; death 100%. Average days lost to labour stoppages per 1,000 workdays (1992): 1.1.
Access to services (1990). Proportion of dwellings having access to: electricity, virtually 100%; safe public water supply 94%; public sewage collection 92%; central heating 92%; bathroom 87%; gas 72%; hot water 79%.
Social participation. Eligible voters participating in last national election (2000): 64.2%. Trade union membership in total workforce (1989): 100%. Practicing religious population in total affiliated population (1991): 32%.
Social deviance. Offense rate per 100,000 population (1998) for: murder 20.2; rape 6.1; serious injury 30.8; larceny-theft 862.1. Incidence per 100,000 population (1992) of: alcoholism 1,727.5; substance abuse 25.1; suicide 26.5.
Material well-being (1998). Durable goods possessed per 100 family households: automobile 35; radio receiver 101; television receiver 116; refrigerator or freezer 94; washing machine 81; camera 37; motorcycle 23; bicycle 53.

National economy

Budget (1998). Revenue: Rub 657,100,000,000,000 (tax revenue 82.8%, of which value-added tax 23.8%, profit tax 14.7%, individual income tax 10.8%, excise tax 10.3%; nontax revenue 17.2%). Expenditures: Rub 753,000,000,000,000 (social and cultural 31.7%; interest on foreign debt 14.2%; defense 7.5%; law enforcement 5.7%; administrative 4.0%).
Public debt (external, outstanding: 1998): U.S.$164,000,000,000.
Gross national product (1998): U.S.$331,776,000,000 (U.S.$2,260 per capita.)

Structure of gross domestic product and labour force

	1998			
	in value Rub '000,000	% of total value	labour force	% of labour force
Agriculture	161,100,000	6.0	8,282,000	11.4
Mining / Manufacturing / Public utilities	781,335,000	29.1	14,150,000	19.5
Construction	193,320,000	7.2	5,410,000	7.5
Transp. and commun.	308,775,000	11.5	5,043,000	7.0
Trade	545,055,000	20.3	8,900,000	12.3
Finance	340,995,000	12.7	760,000	1.0
Services	206,745,000	7.7	16,761,000	23.1
Pub. admin., defense	147,675,000	5.5	2,570,000	3.5
Other	...	...	10,642,200[9]	14.7[9]
TOTAL	2,685,000,000	100.0	72,518,200	100.0

Production (metric tons except as noted). Agriculture, forestry, fishing (1999): potatoes 31,200,000, wheat 30,960,000, vegetables (other than potatoes) 15,400,000, sugar beets 15,200,000, barley 10,600,000, oats 4,800,000, rye 4,780,000, sunflower seeds 4,200,000, corn (maize) 1,070,000, millet 924,000, peas 680,000, buckwheat 578,000, rice 444,000; livestock (number of live animals) 28,634,000 cattle, 17,300,000 pigs; 13,650,000 sheep; roundwood (1998) 115,600,000 cu m; fish catch (1998) 4,661,853. Mining and quarrying (1997): nickel 260,000,000; chrome ore 151,000,000; iron ore 70,800,000; tin 7,500,000; molybdenum 8,500,000; antimony 6,000,000; gold 3,955,000 troy oz. Manufacturing (1996): crude steel 49,253,000; pig iron 37,079,000; rolled steel 39,000,000[10]; cement 27,792,000; mineral fertilizers 9,076,000; sulfuric acid 5,764,000; cellulose 4,193,000[10]; synthetic resins and plastics 1,794,000[10]; cardboard 1,298,000[10]; caustic soda 871,000; detergents 296,000[10]; synthetic fibres 216,000[10]; cotton fabrics 1,120,000,000 sq m; silk fabrics 148,981,000 sq m; linen fabrics 111,700,000 sq m; wool fabrics 66,900,000 sq m; cigarettes 112,379,000,000 units; watches 7,563,000 units; television receivers 324,000 units; refrigerators 966,000 units; passenger cars 868,000 units; washing machines 762,000 units; vacuum cleaners 691,000 units; tape recorders 671,000[10] units; bicycles 348,000 units; cameras 217,000 units; sewing machines 43,000 units; motorcycles 41,000 units; video recorders 20,900[10] units; leather footwear 36,764,000 pairs; vodka and liquors 12,200,000[10] hectolitres; champagne 8,200,000[10] hectolitres; grape wine 1,460,000[10] hectolitres; beer 208,000 hectolitres; brandy 171,400[10] hectolitres. Construction (1998): residential 30,700,000 sq m; nonresidential (1995) 26,400,000 sq m.

Manufacturing, mining, and construction enterprises (1995)

	no. of enterprises	no. of employees	monthly wages as a % of avg. of all wages[11]	value added (Rub '000,000,000)
Manufacturing				
Machinery and metal products	48,905	4,842,000	98.2	27,234
Fuel and energy	1,758	1,554,000	133.3	44,211
Metallurgy	2,158	1,248,000	124.3	26,437
Chemicals	23,027	2,432,000	94.1	17,934
Light industry	23,007	1,368,000	80.0	2,931
Food	14,713	1,514,000	100.1	12,886
Other industries	19,073	2,085,000	...	4,685
Building materials	8,359	994,000	108.2	3,761

Energy production (consumption): electricity (kW-hr; 1999) 827,200,000,000 ([1996] 827,700,000,000); hard coal (metric tons; 1996) 166,500,000 (161,020,000); lignite (metric tons; 1996) 93,600,000 (86,091,000); crude petroleum (barrels; 1998) 2,175,000,000 ([1996] 1,315,000,000); petroleum products (metric tons; 1996) 157,884,000 (105,168,000); natural gas (cu m; 1998) 434,095,000,000 ([1996] 323,175,000,000); peat (metric tons; 1995) 4,401,000 (3,683,000); oil shale (metric tons; 1994) 2,000,000 (1993; 3,300,000).

Population economically active (1998): total 72,572,000; activity rate of total population 49.5% (participation rates: ages 15–64, 73.2%; female 47.1%; unemployed [1999] 13.3%).

Price and earnings indexes (1990 = 100)

	1991	1992	1993	1994	1995	1996
Consumer price index	192.7	2,800	27,900	112,100	221,300	269,500
Monthly earnings index	180.9	1,978	19,361	71,494	101,700	264,000

Household income and expenditure. Average household size (1998) 2.8; income per household: Rub 32,447 (U.S.$1,297); sources of income (1998): wages 40.5%, pensions and stipends 13.3%, income from entrepreneurial activities 16.5%, property income 5.6%; other 24.1%[12]; expenditure (1998): food 51.4%, taxes and other financial payments 13.9%, clothing 13.0%, furniture and household appliances 7.0%, transportation 2.2%.

Land use (1994): forest 44.9%; pasture 5.2%; agriculture 7.7%; other 42.2%.

Tourism (1997): receipts U.S.$6,900,000,000; expenditures U.S.$10,113,000,000.

Foreign trade[13]

Balance of trade (current prices; non-CIS)

	1993	1994	1995	1996	1997	1998
U.S.$'000,000	+11,491	+17,024	+20,151	+19,771	+14,713	+15,164
% of total	14.9%	14.4%	14.2%	12.6%	9.1%	11.4%

Imports (1998): U.S.$56,800,000,000 (machinery and transport equipment 23.9%, food 17.5%, chemicals 10.3%, ferrous and nonferrous metals 4.6%, wood and wood products 2.6%, fuels and lubricants 2.5%, textiles and clothing 2.2%). *Major import sources:* Germany 11.9%; Belarus 11.1%; Ukraine 7.0%; U.S. 6.3%; Kazakhstan 4.9%; Italy 4.6%; Finland 3.5%; Poland 3.1%; France 2.8%.

Exports (1998): U.S.$74,800,000,000 (fuels and lubricants 36.4%, ferrous and nonferrous metals 19.3%, machinery and transport equipment 9.2%, chemicals 7.3%, precious metals 5.4%, forestry products 4.5%). *Major export destinations:* Ukraine 8.3%; Germany 8.2%; Belarus 7.1%; U.S. 6.2%; China 4.8%; The Netherlands 4.7%; Italy 4.4%; Kazakhstan 3.3%.

Trade by commodity group (1996)

	imports		exports	
SITC group	U.S.$'000,000	%	U.S.$'000,000	%
00 Food and live animals	11,028	24.3	1,654	1.9
02 Raw materials. excl. fuels	5,614	12.4	20,843	24.7
03 Mineral fuels, lubricants	1,703	3.6	38,365	45.5
05 Chemicals	6,140	13.5	6,899	8.2
65 Textile yarn, fabrics	894	2.0	555	0.7
07 Machinery and transport equip.	11,859	26.1	7,477	8.8
08 Misc. manufactured articles	8,200	18.1	8,594	10.2
TOTAL	45,438	100.0	84,387	100.0

Direction of trade (1997)

	imports		exports	
	U.S.$'000,000	%	U.S.$'000,000	%
Africa	488	0.9	753	0.9
Asia	5,211	10.0	11,845	14.1
Japan	985	1.9	2,935	3.5
South America	941	1.8	291	0.3
North and Central America	4,942	9.5	6,334	7.5
United States	4,061	7.8	4,951	5.9
Europe	40,218	77.2	64,861	77.1
EU	19,578	37.6	27,998	33.3
EFTA	938	1.8	3,937	4.7
other Europe	19,702	37.8	32,926	39.1
Oceania	326	0.6	32	0.1
TOTAL	52,129[14]	100.0	84,154[14]	100.0

Transport and communications

Transport. Railroads (1998): length 151,000 km; passenger-km 152,300,000,000; metric ton-km cargo 1,020,000,000. Roads (1997): total length 570,719 km (paved 79%). Vehicles (1997): passenger cars 17,631,600; trucks and buses 4,905,900. Air transport (1998): passenger-km 56,500,000,000; metric ton-km cargo 2,000,000,000; airports (1998) 75.

Distribution of traffic (1995)

	cargo carried ('000,000 tons)	% of national total	passengers carried ('000,000)	% of national total
Intercity transport			26,549	56.2
Road	1,441	41.7	22,817	48.3
Rail	1,028	29.7	1,833	3.9
Sea and river	203	5.9	32	0.1
Air	1	...	34	0.1
Pipeline	783	22.7	—	—
Urban transport			20,684	43.8
Road	—	—	86	0.2
Rail	—	—	20,598	43.6
TOTAL	3,456	100.0	47,233	100.0

Communications

Medium	date	unit	number	units per 1,000 persons
Daily newspapers	1996	circulation	15,517,000	105
Radio	1997	receivers	61,500,000	417
Television	1997	receivers	51,300,000	389
Telephones	1999	main lines	29,031,000	469
Cellular telephones	1999	subscribers	747,160	5.1
Personal computers	1999	units	6,000,000	40.7
Internet	1999	users	1,000,000	6.8

Education and health

Health (1998): physicians 682,000 (1 per 215 persons); hospital beds 1,731,000 (1 per 85 persons); infant mortality rate per 1,000 live births (1998) 21.1.

Education (1998–99)

	schools	teachers	students	student/teacher ratio
Primary (age 6–13) / Secondary (age 14–17)	69,613	1,811,000	21,966,900	12.1
Voc., teacher tr.	3,590	...	1,676,000	...
Higher	913	282,400	3,597,900	12.7

Food (1998): daily per capita caloric intake 2,835 (vegetable products 76%; animal products 24%); 111% of FAO recommended minimum.

Military

Total active duty personnel (1998): 1,004,100[15] (army 34.6%, navy 17.1%, air force 18.4%, other 29.9%). *Military expenditure as percentage of GNP* (1997): 5.8% (world 2.6%); per capita expenditure U.S.$283.

[1]On Jan. 1, 1998, a (new) ruble was introduced; 1 (new) ruble is equivalent to 1,000 (old) rubles, data given in (old) rubles. [2]January. [3]Moskva (Moscow; region) includes Moscow (city). [4]With the exception of the Chukot autonomous district, which has formally separated from Magadan region, all autonomous districts are administratively part of another region, republic, or territory, within which their area and population are included. [5]The final status of Chechnia was unresolved in November 2000. [6]Ingushetiya's area and population include Chechnia. [7]Leningrad (region), St. Petersburg (city). [8]1994. [9]Includes 8,876,200 unemployed. [10]1995. [11]1990. [12]Includes hidden salaries. [13]Imports c.i.f. [14]Detail does not add to total given because of rounding. [15]Includes 200,000 military personnel not included elsewhere.

Internet resources for further information:

- **Russian Statistical Agency http://www.gks.ru/eng/default.asp**
- **Permanent Mission of the Russian Federation to the United Nations http://www.un.int/russia**

Rwanda

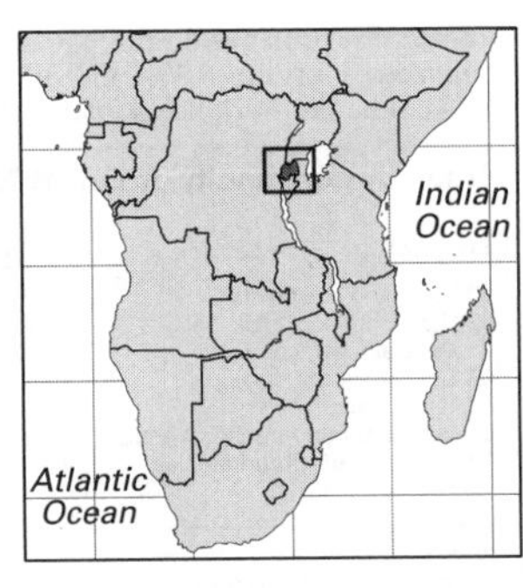

Official name: Repubulika y'u Rwanda (Rwanda); République Rwandaise (French); Republic of Rwanda (English).
Form of government: transitional regime[1] with one legislative body (Transitional National Assembly [74]).
Head of state and government: President assisted by Prime Minister.
Capital: Kigali.
Official languages: Rwanda; French; English.
Official religion: none.
Monetary unit: 1 Rwanda franc (RF); valuation (Oct. 6, 2000) 1 U.S.$ = RF 359.03; 1 £ = RF 519.35.

Area and population

Prefectures	Capitals	area sq mi	area sq km	population 1991 census
Butare	Butare	709	1,837	766,839
Byumba[2]	Byumba	1,838	4,761	783,350
Cyangugu	Cyangugu	712	1,845	515,129
Gikongoro	Gikongoro	794	2,057	464,585
Gisenyi	Gisenyi	791	2,050	734,697
Gitarama	Gitarama	845	2,189	851,516
Kibungo[2]	Kibungo	1,562	4,046	655,368
Kibuye	Kibuye	658	1,705	470,747
Kigali	Kigali (city)	1,159	3,002	918,869
Kigali (city)	—	45	116	237,782
Nyagatare[2]	...	...	...	...
Ruhengeri	Ruhengeri	642	1,663	766,112
TOTAL LAND AREA		9,757[3]	25,271	
TOTAL		10,169	26,338	7,164,994

Demography

Population (2000): 7,229,000.
Density (2000): persons per sq mi 710.9, persons per sq km 274.5.
Urban-rural (1999): urban 6.0%; rural 94.0%.
Sex distribution (1999): male 49.57%; female 50.43%.
Age breakdown (1999): under 15, 43.5%; 15–29, 29.8%; 30–44, 15.1%; 45–59, 7.2%; 60–74, 3.5%; 75 and over, 0.9%.
Population projection: (2010) 7,876,000; (2020) 8,027,000.
Doubling time: 47 years.
Ethnic composition (1996): Hutu 80.0%; Tutsi 19.0%; Twa 1.0%.
Religious affiliation (1996): Roman Catholic 65.0%; Protestant 9.0%; Muslim 1.0%; indigenous beliefs and other 25.0%.
Major cities (1991): Kigali 237,782; Ruhengeri 29,578[4]; Butare 28,645[4]; Gisenyi 21,918[4].

Vital statistics

Birth rate per 1,000 population (1999): 35.7 (world avg. 22.1); (1978) legitimate 94.9%; illegitimate 5.1%.
Death rate per 1,000 population (1999): 21.1 (world avg. 8.9).
Natural increase rate per 1,000 population (1999): 14.6 (world avg. 13.2).
Total fertility rate (avg. births per childbearing woman; 1999): 5.3.
Marriage rate per 1,000 population (1984)[5]: 2.5.
Life expectancy at birth (1999): male 38.6 years; female 40.1 years.
Major causes of death per 100,000 population: n.a.; however, principal causes in 1999 were malaria, bronchopneumonia, diarrhea, AIDS, pulmonary diseases, cerebrospinal meningitis, kwashiorkor, and road accidents.

National economy

Budget (1998). Revenue: RF 99,000,000,000 (grants 33.3%, taxes on goods and services 28.9%, import and export duties 16.0%, income tax 3.4%). Expenditures: RF 117,400,000,000 (capital expenditures 35.9%, wages 24.6%, goods and services 21.7%, transfers 7.9%, debt payment 4.9%).
Production (metric tons except as noted). Agriculture, forestry, fishing (1999): plantains 2,897,433, sweet potatoes 862,562, cassava 316,934, potatoes 175,889, sorghum 107,566, corn [maize] 54,912, coffee 18,800; livestock (number of live animals) 725,541 cattle, 634,046 goats, 290,000 sheep, 159,625 pigs; roundwood (1998) 3,000,000 cu m; fish catch (1998) 6,641. Mining and quarrying (1997): cassiterite (tin ore) 330; wolframite (tungsten ore) 188; gold 17 kg. Manufacturing (1997): cement 58,929; lye soap 6,966; beer 650,000 hectolitres; nonalcoholic beverages 363,000 hectolitres; textiles 5,298,000 metres. Energy production (consumption): electricity (kW-hr; 1998) 153,630,000 (186,080,000); petroleum products (metric tons; 1998) none (95,500); natural gas (cu m; 1996) 179,389 (179,389).
Population economically active (1991): total 3,649,000; activity rate of total population 50.2% (participation rates: ages 14–74 [1989] 46.3%; female 53.5%; unemployed, n.a.).

Price and earnings indexes (1995 = 100)

	1993	1994	1995	1996	1997	1998	1999
Consumer price index	50.3	...	100.0	107.4	120.3	127.8	124.7
Earnings index	100.0	100.0	100.0	120.0	...	...	...

Public debt (external, outstanding; 1998): U.S.$1,120,000,000.
Tourism: receipts (1993) U.S.$2,000,000; expenditures (1992) U.S.$17,000,000.
Land use (1994): forested 10.1%; meadows and pastures 28.4%; agricultural and under permanent cultivation 47.4%; other 14.1%.

Gross national product (1998): U.S.$1,864,000,000 (U.S.$230 per capita).

Structure of gross domestic product and labour force

	1998 in value RF '000,000	1998 % of total value	1989 labour force	1989 % of labour force
Agriculture	278,600	44.1	2,832,557	90.1
Mining	400	0.1	4,691	0.2
Manufacturing	79,700	12.6	45,089	1.4
Construction	41,500	6.6	38,237	1.2
Public utilities	3,000	0.5	2,562	0.1
Transp. and commun.	26,100	4.1	7,333	0.2
Trade	66,900	10.6	80,026	2.6
Pub. admin., defense	41,700	6.6	123,147	3.9
Services	94,200	14.9		
Other	—	—	9,414	0.3
TOTAL	632,100	100.0[3]	3,143,056	100.0

Household income and expenditure. Average household size (1991) 4.7; average annual income per household (1983) RF 122,870 (U.S.$1,300); sources of income (1977): self-employment 71.0%, salaries and wages 16.5%, transfers 9.5%; expenditure (1982): food 44.2%, housing 13.2%, clothing and footwear 11.4%, transportation 10.3%, household equipment 8.4%.

Foreign trade

Balance of trade (current prices)

	1993	1994	1995	1996	1997	1998
U.S.$'000,000	−200.1	−335.2	−143.7	−151.3	−184.5	−193.3
% of total	59.7%	83.9%	58.8%	55.0%	52.5%	60.8%

Imports (1998): U.S.$255,700,000 (intermediate goods 26.8%, capital goods 23.7%, food 19.3%, energy products 13.6%). *Major import sources* (1998): Kenya 25.8%; U.S. 8.4%; Belgium 5.9%; France 5.2%; Germany 3.8%; The Netherlands 3.1%; Italy 2.8%; U.K. 1.7%; Democratic Republic of the Congo 1.7%.
Exports (1998): U.S.$62,400,000 (coffee 42.8%, tea 36.7%, hides and skins 3.5%). *Major export destinations* (1998): Belgium 47.6%; Germany 25.4%; U.S. 6.3%; Italy 6.3%.

Transport and communications

Transport. Railroads: none. Roads (1996): total length 9,528 mi, 14,900 km (paved 9%). Vehicles (1995): passenger cars 13,000; trucks 17,100. Air transport: (1994) passenger-mi 1,243,000, passenger-km 2,000,000; (1991) metric ton cargo loaded 2,674, metric ton cargo unloaded 4,794; airports (1998) with scheduled flights 2.

Communications

Medium	date	unit	number	units per 1,000 persons
Daily newspapers	1995	circulation	500	0.1
Radio	1997	receivers	601,000	101
Telephones	1998	main lines	10,825	1.6
Internet	1998	users	...	...

Education and health

Educational attainment (1978). Percentage of population age 25 and over having: no formal schooling 76.9%; some primary education 16.8%; complete primary education 4.0%; some secondary and complete secondary education 2.0%; some postsecondary vocational and higher education 0.3%. *Literacy* (1995): percentage of total population age 15 and over literate 67.0%; males literate 73.7%; females literate 60.6%.

Education (1991–92)

	schools	teachers	students	student/ teacher ratio
Primary (age 7–15)	1,710	18,937	1,104,902	58.3
Secondary (age 16–19)[6]	...	3,413	94,586	27.7
Higher[7]	3[8]	646	3,389	5.2

Health: physicians (1992) 150 (1 per 50,000 persons); hospital beds (1990) 12,152 (1 per 588 persons); infant mortality rate (1999) 120.1.
Food (1998): daily per capita caloric intake 2,035 (vegetable products 96%, animal products 4%); 88% of FAO recommended minimum requirement.

Military

Total active duty personnel (1999): 40,000 (army 100%). *Military expenditure as percentage of GNP* (1997): 4.4% (world 2.6%); per capita expenditure U.S.$10.

[1]Five-year transitional period from November 1994 was extended to July 2003 in June 1999. [2]Nyagatare prefecture created in mid-1990s from parts of Byumba and Kibungo prefectures. [3]Detail does not add to total given because of rounding. [4]De jure population only. [5]Excludes marriages not registered in court. [6]Includes vocational and teacher training. [7]1989–90. [8]1985.

Internet resources for further information:
- **CIA World Factbook—Rwanda http://www.odci.gov/cia/publications/factbook/geos/rw.htm**

Saint Kitts and Nevis

Official name: Federation of Saint Kitts and Nevis[1].
Form of government: constitutional monarchy with one legislative house (National Assembly [15[2]]).
Chief of state: British Monarch represented by Governor-General.
Head of government: Prime Minister.
Capital: Basseterre.
Official language: English.
Official religion: none.
Monetary unit: 1 Eastern Caribbean dollar (EC$) = 100 cents; valuation (Oct. 6, 2000) 1 U.S.$ = EC$2.70; 1 £ = EC$3.90.

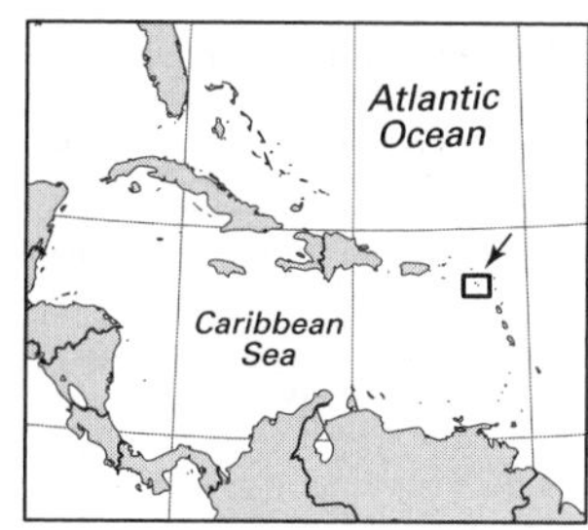

Area and population

Islands	Capitals	area sq mi	area sq km	population 1995 estimate
Nevis[3]	Charlestown	36.0	93.2	8,010
St. Kitts	Basseterre	68.0	176.2	35,340
TOTAL		104.0	269.4	43,350

Demography

Population (2000): 38,800.
Density (2000): persons per sq mi 373.1, persons per sq km 144.0.
Urban-rural (1998): urban 33.3%; rural 66.7%.
Sex distribution (1999): male 49.41%; female 50.59%.
Age breakdown (1999): under 15, 30.8%; 15–29, 25.0%; 30–44, 22.1%; 45–59, 10.5%; 60–74, 7.2%; 75 and over, 4.4%.
Population projection: (2010) 40,300; (2020) 44,500.
Doubling time: 73 years.
Ethnic composition (1991): black 94.9%; mixed/white/Indo-Pakistani 5.1%.
Religious affiliation (1995): Protestant 84.6%, of which Anglican 25.2%, Methodist 25.2%, Pentecostal 8.4%, Moravian 7.6%; Roman Catholic 6.7%; other 8.7%.
Major towns (1994): Basseterre 12,605; Charlestown 1,411.

Vital statistics

Birth rate per 1,000 population (1999): 19.5 (world avg. 22.1); (1983) legitimate 19.2%; illegitimate 80.8%.
Death rate per 1,000 population (1999): 10.0 (world avg. 8.9).
Natural increase rate per 1,000 population (1999): 9.5 (world avg. 13.2).
Total fertility rate (avg. births per childbearing woman; 1999): 2.5.
Marriage rate per 1,000 population: n.a.
Divorce rate per 1,000 population: n.a.
Life expectancy at birth (1999): male 66.8 years; female 72.5 years.
Major causes of death per 100,000 population (1985): diseases of the circulatory system 443.2, of which cerebrovascular disease 220.5, diseases of pulmonary circulation and other heart disease 122.7; malignant neoplasms (cancers) 95.5.

National economy

Budget (1996). Revenue: EC$208,300,000 (tax revenue 68.9% of which taxes on international transactions 37.4%, income taxes 15.7%, consumption taxes 14.4%; nontax revenue 26.7%). Expenditures: EC$231,700,000 (current expenditure 85.9%; development expenditure 14.1%).
Production (metric tons except as noted). Agriculture, forestry, fishing (1999): sugarcane 196,784, tropical fruit 1,300, coconuts 1,000, roots and tubers 700, potatoes 211, pulses 210, cabbages 175, sweet potatoes 170, tomatoes 120, onions 75; sea island cotton is grown on Nevis; livestock (number of live animals) 14,500 goats, 8,000 sheep, 3,600 cattle, 3,000 pigs; roundwood, n.a.; fish catch (1997) 161. Mining and quarrying: excavation of sand for local use. Manufacturing (1996): raw sugar 20,249; molasses 6,000[4]; carbonated beverages 47,000 hectolitres[5]; beer 17,200 hectolitres[5]; other manufactures include electronic components, garments, footwear, and batik. Construction (value added; 1994): EC$57,000,000. Energy production (consumption): electricity (kW-hr; 1996) 82,000,000 (82,000,000); coal, none (none); crude petroleum, none (none); petroleum products (metric tons; 1996) none (33,000); natural gas, none (none).
Gross national product (1998): U.S.$253,000,000 (U.S.$6,190 per capita).

Structure of gross domestic product and labour force

	1995 in value EC$'000,000	1995 % of total value	1994 labour force[6]	1994 % of labour force[6]
Sugarcane	13.4	2.0	1,525[7]	9.2[7]
Other agriculture, forestry, fisheries	18.0	2.7	914	5.5
Mining	1.9	0.3	29	0.2
Manufacturing	59.7	8.9	1,290[8]	7.8[8]
Construction	67.0	10.0	1,745	10.5
Public utilities	9.3	1.4	416	2.5
Transportation and communications	87.4	13.1	534	3.2
Trade, restaurants	131.2	19.6	3,367	20.3
Finance, real estate	87.7	13.1	3,708[9]	22.3[9]
Pub. admin., defense	101.9	15.3	2,738	16.5
Services	24.1	3.6	[9]	[9]
Other	66.1[10]	9.9[10]	342	2.1
TOTAL	667.7	100.0[11]	16,608	100.0[11]

Household income and expenditure. Average household size (1980) 3.7; average annual income per wage earner (1994) EC$9,940 (U.S.$3,681); sources of income: n.a.; expenditure (1978)[12]: food, beverages, and tobacco 55.6%, household furnishings 9.4%, housing 7.6%, clothing and footwear 7.5%, fuel and light 6.6%, transportation 4.3%, other 9.0%.
Public debt (external, outstanding; 1997): U.S.$59,900,000.
Population economically active (1980): total 17,125; activity rate of total population 39.5% (participation rates: ages 15–64, 69.5%; female 41.0%; unemployed [1997] 4.5%).

Price and earnings indexes (1995 = 100)

	1991	1992	1993	1994	1995	1996
Consumer price index	90.6	93.2	94.9	97.4	100.0	102.5
Earnings index	...	...	...	...	...	....

Land use (1994): forested 17%; meadows and pastures 3%; agricultural and under permanent cultivation 39%; other 41%.
Tourism (1997): receipts from visitors U.S.$72,000,000; expenditures by nationals abroad U.S.$6,000,000.

Foreign trade

Balance of trade (current prices)

	1993	1994	1995	1996	1997
EC$'000,000	–177	–211	–217	–242	–291.2
% of total	46.2%	53.3%	52.4%	55.8%	57.0%

Imports (1997): EC$401,100,000 (machinery and transport equipment 30.3%, basic and miscellaneous manufactures 20.6%, food 16.1%, chemicals and chemical products 8.2%). *Major import sources:* United States 45.5%; Caricom countries 13.4%, of which Trinidad and Tobago 9.8%; United Kingdom 9.7%.
Exports (1997): EC$109,900,000 (food 56,0%, machinery and transport equipment [mostly electronic goods] 31.7%). *Major export destinations* (1997): United States 55.0%; United Kingdom 32.6%; Caricom countries 2.9%.

Transport and communications

Transport. Railroads (1995)[12]: length 22 mi, 36 km. Roads (1996): total length 199 mi, 320 km (paved 43%). Vehicles (1991): passenger cars 3,700; trucks and buses 2,200. Merchant marine (1992): vessels (100 gross tons and over) 1; total deadweight tonnage 550. Air transport: passenger arrivals (1992) 123,195[13]; passenger departures, n.a.; cargo handled, n.a.; airports (1998) with scheduled flights 2.

Communications

Medium	date	unit	number	units per 1,000 persons
Radio	1997	receivers	28,000	701
Television	1997	receivers	10,000	264
Telephones	1998	main lines	17,181	418
Cellular telephones	1998	units	205	5

Education and health

Educational attainment (1980). Percentage of population age 25 and over having: no formal schooling 1.1%; primary education 29.6%; secondary 67.2%; higher 2.1%. *Literacy* (1990): total population age 15 and over literate 25,500 (90.0%); males literate 13,100 (90.0%); females literate 12,400 (90.0%).

Education (1997–98)

	schools	teachers	students	student/ teacher ratio
Primary (age 5–12)	23	320	5,928	18.5
Secondary (age 13–17)	9	341	4,548	13.3
Higher[14]	1	51	394	7.7

Health (1998): physicians 50 (1 per 815 persons); hospital beds 244 (1 per 167 persons); infant mortality rate per 1,000 live births (1999): 18.7.
Food (1998): daily per capita caloric intake 2,766 (vegetable products 75%, animal products 25%); 114% of FAO recommended minimum requirement.

Military

Total active duty personnel: in July 1997 the National Assembly approved a bill creating a 50-member army.

[1]Both Saint Christopher and Nevis and the Federation of Saint Christopher and Nevis are officially acceptable, variant, short- and long-form names of the country. [2]Includes 4 nonelective seats. [3]Nevis has full internal self-government. The Nevis legislature is subordinate to the National Assembly only with regard to external affairs and defense. [4]1994. [5]1991. [6]Employed persons only. [7]Includes sugar manufacturing. [8]Excludes sugar manufacturing. [9]Finance, real estate includes Services. [10]Net of indirect taxes less imputed service charge. [11]Detail does not add to total given because of rounding. [12]Light railway serving the sugar industry on Saint Kitts. [13]Saint Kitts airport only. [14]1992–93.

Internet resources for further information:

- **Official web site of the Government of St. Kitts & Nevis http://www.stkittsnevis.net**

Saint Lucia

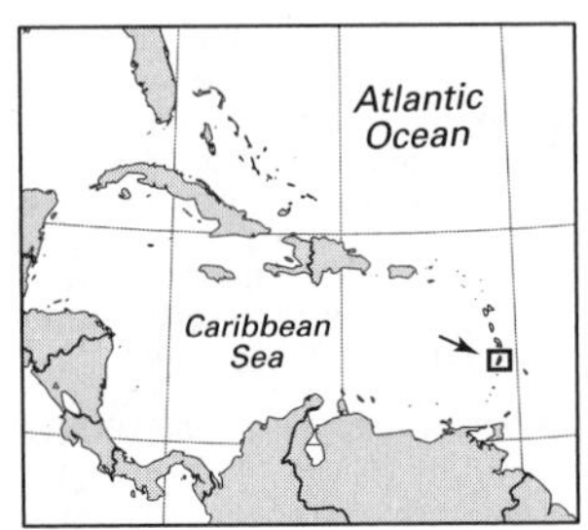

Official name: Saint Lucia.
Form of government: constitutional monarchy with a Parliament consisting of two legislative chambers (Senate [11]; House of Assembly [17[1]]).
Chief of state: British Monarch represented by Governor-General.
Head of government: Prime Minister.
Capital: Castries.
Official language: English.
Official religion: none.
Monetary unit: 1 Eastern Caribbean dollar (EC$) = 100 cents; valuation (Oct. 6, 2000) 1 U.S.$ = EC$2.70; 1 £ = EC$3.90.

Area and population

Districts	Capitals	area sq mi	area sq km	population 1997 estimate
Anse-la-Raye	Anse-la-Raye	18	47	5,963
Canaries	Canaries			1,828
Castries	Castries	31	79	59,788
Choiseul	Choiseul	12	31	7,092
Dennery	Dennery	27	70	12,405
Gros Islet	Gros Islet	39	101	14,082
Laborie	Laborie	15	38	8,488
Micoud	Micoud	30	78	16,895
Soufrière	Soufrière	19	51	8,809
Vieux Fort	Vieux Fort	17	44	14,271
TOTAL		238[2]	617[2]	149,621

Demography

Population (2000): 157,000.
Density (2000): persons per sq mi 659.7, persons per sq km 254.5.
Urban-rural (1998): urban 37.3%; rural 62.7%.
Sex distribution (1997): male 48.34%; female 51.66%.
Age breakdown (1999): under 15, 33.5%; 15–29, 30.9%; 30–44, 20.4%; 45–59, 8.0%; 60–74, 4.9%; 75 and over, 2.3%.
Population projection: (2010) 178,000; (2020) 200,000.
Doubling time: 41 years.
Ethnic composition (1990): black 90.5%; mixed 5.5%; East Indian 3.2%; white 0.8%.
Religious affiliation (1995): Roman Catholic 79.2%; Protestant 19.4%, of which Pentecostal 5.4%, Seventh-day Adventist 5.2%; other 1.4%.
Major city (1997): Castries city proper 2,249 (urban area 13,938).

Vital statistics

Birth rate per 1,000 population (1999): 22.8 (world avg. 22.1); legitimate (1998) 14.2%; illegitimate 85.8%.
Death rate per 1,000 population (1999): 5.5 (world avg. 8.9).
Natural increase rate per 1,000 population (1999): 17.3 (world avg. 13.2).
Total fertility rate (avg. births per childbearing woman; 1999): 2.5.
Marriage rate per 1,000 population (1997): 3.1.
Divorce rate per 1,000 population (1997): 0.2.
Life expectancy at birth (1999): male 68.5 years; female 75.9 years.
Major causes of death per 100,000 population (1996): diseases of the circulatory system 282.9; malignant neoplasms (cancers) 74.1; diseases of the respiratory system 41.5; infectious and parasitic diseases 37.4; endocrine and metabolic disorders 19.0; ill-defined conditions 63.2.

National economy

Budget (1998–99). Revenue: EC$469,900,000 (current revenue 86.9%, of which consumption duties on imported goods 24.4%; taxes on income and profits 21.9%; import duties 14.7%; nontax revenue 9.2%; grants 3.9%). Expenditures: EC$496,600,000 (current expenditures 69.4%; development expenditures and net lending 30.6%).
Public debt (external, outstanding; 1998): U.S.$153,600,000.
Tourism (1997): receipts from visitors U.S.$282,000,000; expenditures by nationals abroad (1996) U.S.$29,000,000.
Production (metric tons except as noted). Agriculture, forestry, fishing (1999): bananas 80,000, mangoes 27,000, coconuts 12,000, yams 3,800, tropical fruit 2,750, grapefruit 1,393, plantains 1,296, cassava 980, vegetables 950, oranges 705; livestock (number of live animals; 1999) 14,750 pigs, 12,500 sheep, 12,450 cattle, 9,800 goats; roundwood, n.a.; fish catch (1998) 1,462. Mining and quarrying: excavation of sand for local construction and pumice. Manufacturing (value of production in EC$'000; 1998): alcoholic beverages and tobacco 31,120; paper products and cardboard boxes 28,747; electrical and electronic components 16,245; food 9,535; garments 6,563; textile 3,999; refined coconut oil 2,330; copra 1,330. Construction (buildings approved; 1994): residential 61,400 sq m; nonresidential 41,350 sq m. Energy production (consumption): electricity (kW-hr; 1998) 235,881,000 (213,000,000); coal, none (none); crude petroleum, none (none); petroleum products (metric tons; 1998) none (25,000); natural gas, none (none).
Household income and expenditure. Average household size (1991) 4.0; income per household: n.a.; sources of income: n.a.; expenditure (1982)[3]: food 46.8%, housing 13.5%, clothing and footwear 6.5%, transportation and communications 6.3%, household furnishings 5.8%, other 21.1%.
Population economically active (1998): total 73,660; activity rate of total population 49.2% (participation rates: ages 15–64, 79.1%; female 44.4%; unemployed 22.2%).

Price and earnings indexes (1995 = 100)

	1992	1993	1994	1995	1996	1997	1998
Consumer price index	91.0	92.0	94.5	100.0	101.0	101.0	103.7
Earnings index[4]	...	...	...	...	...	...	...

Gross national product (at current market prices; 1998): U.S.$556,000,000 (U.S.$3,660 per capita).

Structure of gross domestic product and labour force

	1998 in value EC$'000,000[4]	% of total value[4]	labour force[5]	% of labour force
Agriculture	114	8.1	17,310	23.5
Mining	7	0.5	221	0.3
Manufacturing	83	5.9	6,850	9.3
Construction	103	7.3	5,893	8.0
Public utilities	73	5.2	1,105	1.5
Transportation and communications	253	18.0	4,788	6.5
Trade, restaurants	374	26.6	19,225	26.1
Finance, real estate	305	21.7	3,168	4.3
Pub. admin., defense	206	14.7	9,797	13.3
Services	51	3.6	1,252	1.7
Other	–165[6]	–11.7[6]	4,051	5.5
TOTAL	1,404	100.0[7]	73,660	100.0

Land use (1994): forested 13%; meadows and pastures 5%; agricultural and under permanent cultivation 30%; other 52%.

Foreign trade

Balance of trade (current prices)

	1994	1995	1996	1997	1998
U.S.$'000,000	–165.7	–155.2	–177.6	–209.1	–201.1
% of total	45.3%	40.5%	47.3%	56.2%	56.2%

Imports (1998): U.S.$279,600,000 (food 21.7%; machinery and transportation equipment 21.1%; manufactured goods 19.0%; chemicals and chemical products 8.6%; crude petroleum and petroleum products 8.5%). *Major import sources:* United States 40.0%; Caricom countries 21.2%, of which Trinidad and Tobago 11.5%; United Kingdom 9.2%; Japan 4.4%; Canada 2.8%.
Exports (1998): U.S.$78,500,000 (bananas 50.5%; clothing 7.5%; primarily paper and paperboard 5.9%; beer 5.0%). *Major export destinations:* United Kingdom 60.0%; United States 21%; Caricom countries 16.3%.

Transport and communications

Transport. Railroads: none. Roads (1997): total length 750 mi, 1,210 km (paved 5%). Vehicles (1997): passenger cars 14,783; trucks and buses 1,020. Merchant marine (1992): vessels (100 gross tons and over) 7; total deadweight tonnage 2,070. Air transport (1994)[8]: passenger arrivals 573,000, passenger departures 581,000; cargo unloaded 2,002 metric tons, cargo loaded 3,918 metric tons; airports (1998) with scheduled flights 2.

Communications

Medium	date	unit	number	units per 1,000 persons
Radio	1997	receivers	100,000	668
Television	1997	receivers	40,000	267
Telephones	1999	main lines	40,373	266
Cellular telephones	1999	subscribers	1,900	12.5

Education and health

Educational attainment (1980). Percentage of population age 25 and over having: no formal schooling 17.5%; primary education 74.4%; secondary 6.8%; higher 1.3%. *Literacy* (1995): about 82%.

Education (1997–98)

	schools	teachers	students	student/ teacher ratio
Primary (age 5–11)	84	1,160	30,536	26.3
Secondary (age 12–16)	17	620	11,405	18.4
Vocational[9]	1	34	806	23.7
Higher[9]	1	389	870	2.4

Health (1997): physicians 81 (1 per 1,847 persons); hospital beds 527 (1 per 284 persons); infant mortality rate per 1,000 live births (1999) 16.1.
Food (1998): daily per capita caloric intake 2,842 (vegetable products 75%, animal products 25%); 117% of FAO recommended minimum requirement.

Military

Total active duty personnel (1994): [10].

[1]Represents elected seats only. Attorney general and speaker serve ex officio. [2]Total includes the uninhabited 30 sq mi (78 sq km) Central Forest Reserve. [3]Castries area only. [4]At factor cost in current prices. [5]Based on the percentage given. [6]Less imputed bank service charges. [7]Detail does not add to total given because of rounding. [8]Combined data for both Castries and Vieux Fort airports. [9]1992–93. [10]The more than 500-member police force includes a specially trained paramilitary unit and a coast guard unit.

Internet resources for further information:
- **Saint Lucian Government Statistics Department http://www.stats.gov.lc**

Saint Vincent and the Grenadines

Official name: Saint Vincent and the Grenadines.
Form of government: constitutional monarchy with one legislative house (House of Assembly [21[1]]).
Chief of state: British Monarch represented by Governor-General.
Head of government: Prime Minister.
Capital: Kingstown.
Official language: English.
Official religion: none.
Monetary unit: 1 Eastern Caribbean dollar (EC$) = 100 cents; valuation (Oct. 6, 2000) 1 U.S.$ = EC$2.70; 1 £ = EC$3.90.

Area and population

Census Divisions[2]	area sq mi	area sq km	population 1997 estimate
Island of Saint Vincent			
Barrouallie	14.2	36.8	5,430
Bridgetown	7.2	18.6	7,865
Calliaqua	11.8	30.6	21,189
Chateaubelair	30.9	80.0	6,313
Colonarie	13.4	34.7	8,240
Georgetown	22.2	57.5	7,627
Kingstown (city)	1.9	4.9	16,151
Kingstown (suburbs)	6.4	16.6	11,233
Layou	11.1	28.7	6,259
Marriaqua	9.4	24.3	9,256
Sandy Bay	5.3	13.7	2,917
Saint Vincent Grenadines			
Northern Grenadines	9.0	23.3	5,759
Southern Grenadines	7.5	19.4	2,985
TOTAL	150.3	389.3[3]	111,224

Demography

Population (2000): 113,000.
Density (2000): persons per sq mi 751.8, persons per sq km 290.3.
Urban-rural (1997)[4]: urban 24.6%; rural 75.4%.
Sex distribution (1999): male 50.50%; female 49.50%.
Age breakdown (1999): under 15, 31.3%; 15–29, 31.2%; 30–44, 19.6%; 45–59, 9.4%; 60–74, 5.9%; 75 and over, 2.6%.
Population projection: (2010) 119,000; (2020) 125,000.
Doubling time: 54 years.
Ethnic composition (1995): black 82.0%; mixed 13.9%; other 4.1%.
Religious affiliation (1995): Protestant 57.0%, of which Anglican 17.9%, Pentecostal 14.9%, Methodist 10.5%; Roman Catholic 10.7%; other/nonreligious 32.3%.
Major city (1997): Kingstown 16,151.

Vital statistics

Birth rate per 1,000 population (1999): 19.0 (world avg. 22.1); legitimate, n.a.; illegitimate, n.a.
Death rate per 1,000 population (1999): 6.3 (world avg. 8.9).
Natural increase rate per 1,000 population (1999): 12.7 (world avg. 13.2).
Total fertility rate (avg. births per childbearing woman; 1999): 2.2.
Marriage rate per 1,000 population (1997): 4.6.
Divorce rate per 1,000 population (1997) : 0.8.
Life expectancy at birth (1999): male 70.3 years; female 73.7 years.
Major causes of death per 100,000 population (1997): diseases of the circulatory system 228.4, of which ischemic heart disease 94.4, cerebrovascular diseases 70.1; malignant neoplasms (cancers) 90.0; endocrine and metabolic disorders 56.6; diseases of the respiratory system 42.2; infectious and parasitic diseases 36.8.

National economy

Budget (1998). Revenue: EC$285,200,000 (current revenue 73.8%, of which income tax 25.1%, consumption duties on imports 23.3%, taxes on goods and services 9.3%, import duties 7.9%, other 8.2%; grants 14.5%; nontax revenue 9.5%; capital revenue 2.2%). Expenditures: EC$303,100,000 (current expenditure 65.9%, of which wages 36.2%, transfers 11.4%; development expenditure 34.1%).
Tourism (1998): receipts from visitors U.S.$74,800,000; expenditures by nationals abroad (1996) U.S.$6,000,000.
Production (metric tons except as noted). Agriculture, forestry, fishing (1999): bananas 43,000, coconuts 23,600, roots and tubers 9,000, eddoes and dasheens[5] 4,247[6], corn (maize) 2,000, sweet potatoes 1,500, mangoes 1,400, yams 1,200, oranges 960, lemons and limes 870, ginger 892[6], arrowroot starch 177[6], nutmegs 105[6], soursops, guavas, and papayas are also important; livestock (number of live animals) 13,000 sheep, 9,400 pigs, 6,200 cattle; roundwood, n.a.; fish catch (1998) 835. Mining and quarrying: sand and gravel for local use. Manufacturing (export value of manufactures in U.S.$'000,000; 1995): packaged flour 8.7; packaged rice 6.4; other goods (mostly garments, sporting goods, and electronic goods) 8.1. Construction (gross floor area planned; 1997): 530,500 sq m. Energy production (consumption): electricity (kW-hr; 1998) 82,773,000 (82,773,000); coal, none (none); crude petroleum, none (none); petroleum products (metric tons; 1996) none (41,000); natural gas, none (none).

Gross national product (1998): U.S.$290,000,000 (U.S.$2,560 per capita).

Structure of gross domestic product and labour force

	1998 in value EC$'000,000	1998 % of total value	1991 labour force	1991 % of labour force
Agriculture, forestry, fishing	78.3	9.2	8,377	20.1
Mining	2.3	0.3	98	0.2
Manufacturing	49.5	5.8	2,822	6.8
Construction	101.9	11.9	3,535	8.5
Public utilities	40.6	4.7	586	1.4
Transp. and commun.	148.4	17.4	2,279	5.5
Trade, restaurants	128.6	15.1	6,544	15.7
Finance, real estate	71.6	8.4	1,418	3.4
Pub. admin., defense	129.6	15.2	7,696	18.5
Services	12.9	1.5		
Other	90.5[7]	10.6[7]	8,327[8]	20.0[8]
TOTAL	854.2	100.0[3]	41,682	100.0[3]

Public debt (external, outstanding; 1998): U.S.$101,400,000.
Population economically active (1991): total 41,682; activity rate of total population 39.1% (participation rates: ages 15–64, 67.5%; female 35.9%; unemployed [1996] more than 30%).

Price and earnings indexes (1995 = 100)

	1993	1994	1995	1996	1997	1998	1999
Consumer price index	97.3	98.3	100.0	104.4	104.9	107.1	108.2
Daily earnings index[9]	100.0	100.0	100.0	...	...	...	...

Household income and expenditure. Average household size (1991) 3.9; income per household (1988) EC$4,579 (U.S.$1,696); sources of income: n.a.; expenditure (1975–76); food and beverages 59.8%, clothing 7.7%, household furnishings 6.6%, housing 6.3%, energy 6.2%, other 13.4%.
Land use (1994): forested 36%; meadows and pastures 5%; agricultural and under permanent cultivation 28%; other 31%.

Foreign trade

Balance of trade (current prices)

	1992	1993	1994	1995	1996	1997	1998
U.S.$'000,000	–37.9	–62.3	–66.5	–57.4	–74.3	–104.1	–119.5
% of total	19.3%	36.0%	40.5%	31.7%	41.4%	52.4%	54.6%

Imports (1998): U.S.$169,100,000 (basic manufactures 33.7%; food products 23.1%; machinery and transport equipment 22.2%; chemical products 9.7%; fuels 5.6%). *Major import sources:* United States 39.4%; Caricom countries 24.5%, of which Trinidad and Tobago 16.8%; United Kingdom 12.5%; other 6.8%.
Exports (1998): U.S.$49,600,000 (domestic exports 94.1%, of which bananas 41.5%, packaged flour 13.9%, packaged rice 12.9%, eddoes and dasheens[5] 3.8%; reexports 5.9%). *Major export destinations:* Caricom countries 49.1%, of which Trinidad and Tobago 11.0%, St. Lucia 10.4%; United Kingdom 42.2%; United States 5.2%; other 3.5%.

Transport and communications

Transport. Railroads: none. Roads (1996): total length 646 mi, 1,040 km (paved 31%). Vehicles (1997): passenger cars 6,089; trucks and buses 3,670. Merchant marine (1997): vessels (100 gross tons and over) 946; total deadweight tonnage 1,253,000. Air transport (1997): passenger arrivals 125,400; passenger departures 130,166; airports (1998) with scheduled flights 5.

Communications

Medium	date	unit	number	units per 1,000 persons
Radio	1995	receivers	65,000	591
Television	1995	receivers	17,700	161
Telephones	1999	main lines	21,045	188
Cellular telephones	1999	subscribers	750	6.7
Internet	1998	users	...	...

Education and health

Educational attainment (1980). Percentage of population age 25 and over having: no formal schooling 2.4%; primary education 88.0%; secondary 8.2%; higher 1.4%. *Literacy* (1991): total population age 15 and over literate 64,000 (96.0%).

Education (1997–98)

	schools	teachers	students	student/ teacher ratio
Primary (age 5–11)	60	1,007	21,347	21.2
Secondary (age 12–18)	21	379	7,775	20.5
Voc., teacher tr.[10]	3	49[11]	415	...

Health (1998): physicians 59 (1 per 1,883 persons); hospital beds 209 (1 per 531 persons); infant mortality rate per 1,000 live births (1999) 17.7.
Food (1998): daily per capita caloric intake 2,554 (vegetable products 82%, animal products 18%); 106% of FAO recommended minimum requirement.

Military

Total active duty personnel (1992): 634-member police force includes a coast guard and paramilitary unit.

[1]Includes 6 nonelective seats; excludes speaker who may be elected from within or from outside of the House of Assembly membership. [2]For statistical purposes and the election of legislative representatives only. [3]Detail does not add to total given because of rounding. [4]Urban defined as Kingstown and suburbs. [5]Varieties of taro roots. [6]1997. [7]Net of indirect taxes less imputed bank service charges. [8]Unemployed. [9]Minimum wage in private sector. [10]1996–97. [11]1993–94.

Samoa[1]

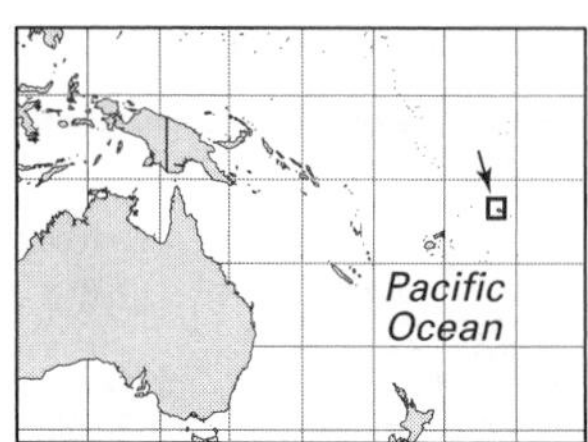

Official name: Malo Sa'oloto Tuto'atasi o Samoa (Samoan); Independent State of Samoa (English).
Form of government: constitutional monarchy[2] with one legislative house (Legislative Assembly [49]).
Chief of state: Head of State.
Head of government: Prime Minister.
Capital: Apia.
Official languages: Samoan; English.
Official religion: none.
Monetary unit: 1 tala (SA$[3], plural tala) = 100 sene; valuation (Oct. 6, 2000) 1 U.S.$ = SA$3.46; 1 £ = SA$5.01.

Area and population

Islands / Political Districts	area sq mi	area sq km	population 1991 census
Savaii	659	1,707	45,050
Fa'aseleleaga			...
Gaga'emauga			...
Gaga'ifomauga			...
Palauli			...
Satupa'itea			...
Vaisigano			...
Upolu	432	1,119	116,248
A'ana			...
Aiga-i-le-Tai			...
Atua			...
Tuamasaga			...
Vaa-o-Fonoti			...
TOTAL	1,093[4]	2,831[4]	161,298

Demography

Population (2000): 179,000.
Density (2000): persons per sq mi 163.8, persons per sq km 63.2.
Urban-rural (1999): urban 21.0%; rural 79.0%.
Sex distribution (1991): male 52.45%; female 47.55%.
Age breakdown (1991): under 15, 40.6%; 15–29, 29.9%; 30–44, 14.6%; 45–59, 8.8%; 60–74, 5.0%; 75 and over, 1.1%.
Population projection: (2010) 176,000; (2020) 178,000.
Doubling time: 30 years.
Ethnic composition (1997): Samoan (Polynesian) 92.6%; Euronesian (European and Polynesian) 7.0%; European 0.4%.
Religious affiliation (1995): Mormon 25.8%; Congregational 24.6%; Roman Catholic 21.3%; Methodist 12.2%; Pentecostal 8.0%; Seventh-day Adventist 3.9%; other Christian 1.7%; other 2.5%.
Major city (1999): Apia 38,000.

Vital statistics

Birth rate per 1,000 population (1999): 28.1 (world avg. 22.1); (1978) legitimate 43.5%; illegitimate 56.5%.
Death rate per 1,000 population (1999): 4.9 (world avg. 8.9).
Natural increase rate per 1,000 population (1999): 23.2 (world avg. 13.2).
Total fertility rate (avg. births per childbearing woman; 1999): 4.0.
Marriage rate per 1,000 population (1992)[5]: 5.0.
Divorce rate per 1,000 population (1989)[5]: 0.2.
Life expectancy at birth (1999): male 70.0 years; female 74.0 years.
Major causes of death (percent distribution; 1992)[5]: congestive heart failure 14.0%; malignant neoplasms (cancers) 11.0%; cerebrovascular diseases 8.0%; injury and poisoning 8.0%; pneumonia 6.0%; septicemia 6.0%; diabetes mellitus 4.0%; intestinal infectious diseases 2.0%.

National economy

Budget (1998–99). Revenue: WS$276,900,000 (tax revenue 56.1%; grants 30.7%; nontax revenue 13.2%). Expenditures: WS$279,400,000 (current expenditure 61.9%; development expenditure 32.3%; net lending 5.8%).
Public debt (external, outstanding; 1998): U.S.$154,300,000.
Production (metric tons except as noted). Agriculture, forestry, fishing (1999): coconuts 130,000, taro 36,900, bananas 10,000, papayas 10,000, pineapples 5,700, mangoes 4,900, avocados 1,700, cacao beans 400; livestock (number of live animals) 178,800 pigs, 26,000 cattle, 350,000 chickens; roundwood (1998) 131,000 cu m; fish catch (1997) 4,590. Mining and quarrying: n.a. Manufacturing (in WS$'000; 1990): beer 8,708; cigarettes 6,551; coconut cream 5,576; sawn wood 3,662; coconut oil 3,442; corned meat 2,905; soap 1,487; paints 1,457. Construction (permits issued in WS$; 1995): residential 7,749,000; commercial, industrial, and other 30,867,000. Energy production (consumption): electricity (kW-hr; 1996) 65,000,000 (65,000,000); coal, none (n.a.); crude petroleum, none (n.a.); petroleum products (metric tons; 1996) none (43,000).
Household income and expenditure. Average household size (1981) 5.1; income per household (1972) WS$1,518 (U.S.$2,200); sources of income (1972): wages 49.4%, self-employment 22.8%, remittances, gifts, and other assistance 18.0%, land rent 8.7%, other 1.1%; expenditure (1987)[6]: food 58.8%, transportation 9.0%, housing and furnishings 5.1%, fuel and lighting 5.0%, clothing 4.2%, other goods and services 1.9%, other 16.0%.
Tourism (1998): receipts from visitors U.S.$38,000,000; expenditures by nationals abroad U.S.$4,000,000.
Gross national product (1998): U.S.$181,000,000 (U.S.$1,070 per capita).

Structure of gross domestic product and labour force

	1997 in value WS$'000	1997 % of total value	1986 labour force	1986 % of labour force
Agriculture	102,700	17.2	29,023	63.6
Mining	...	...	1,587	3.5
Manufacturing	112,400	18.9		
Construction	32,000	5.4	62	0.1
Public utilities	14,800	2.5	855	1.9
Transp. and commun.	65,800	11.0	1,491	3.3
Trade	101,900	17.1	1,710	3.7
Finance	43,300	7.3	842	1.8
Pub. admin., defense	54,600	9.2	9,436	20.7
Services	67,600	11.4		
Other	...	...	629	1.4
TOTAL	595,100	100.0	45,635	100.0

Population economically active (1994): total 47,207; activity rate of total population 28.7% (participation rates: ages 15–64 [1981] 48.6%; female [1991] 32.0%).

Price and earnings indexes (1995 = 100)

	1992	1993	1994	1995	1996	1997	1998
Consumer price index	90.3	91.9	103.0	100.0	105.4	112.6	115.1
Earnings index	...	...	...	...	...	...	...

Land use (1994): forested 47.3%; meadows and pastures 0.4%; agricultural and under permanent cultivation 43.1%; other 9.2%.

Foreign trade[7]

Balance of trade (current prices)

	1994	1995	1996	1997	1998	1999
WS$'000	−197,226	−213,494	−222,258	−208,846	−242,409	−285,070
% of total	91.5%	83.0%	81.7%	73.0%	73.7%	69.8%

Imports (1997): WS$247,377,000 ([1996]; food 33.9%, industrial supplies 26.4%, machinery 16.9%, petroleum products 11.8%, consumer goods 11.0%). *Major import sources:* New Zealand 37.9%; Australia 20.7%; United States 15.6%; Fiji 15.0%; Japan 4.5%; Hong Kong 0.9%; Singapore 0.5%.
Exports (1997): WS$38,531,000 (fresh fish 33.0%, copra 21.1%, coconut oil 18.1%, coconut cream 12.8%, beer 4.3%, kava 4.0%, copra meal 1.5%). *Major export destinations:* New Zealand 48.1%; American Samoa 15.3%; Australia 9.2%; United States 3.3%; Germany 2.9%.

Transport and communications

Transport. Railroads: none. Roads (1996): total length 491 mi, 790 km (paved 42%). Vehicles (1995): passenger cars 1,068; trucks and buses 1,169. Merchant marine (1997): vessels (100 gross tons and over) 7; total deadweight tonnage 6,501. Air transport (1996): passenger-km 265,000,000; metric ton-km cargo 26,000,000; airports (1997) with scheduled flights 3.

Communications

Medium	date	unit	number	units per 1,000 persons
Radio	1997	receivers	178,000	1,035
Television	1997	receivers	11,000	61
Telephones	1998	main lines	8,480	49
Cellular telephones	1998	subscribers	3,000	17
Personal computers	1998	units	900	5.2
Internet	1998	users	400	2.3

Education and health

Educational attainment (1981). Percentage of population age 25 and over having: some primary education 16.5%; complete primary 24.5%; some secondary 52.1%; complete secondary 3.1%; higher 2.0%; unknown 1.8%.
Literacy (1981): virtually 100%.

Education (1996)

	schools	teachers	students	student/ teacher ratio
Primary (age 5–11)	155[8]	1,479	35,378	23.9
Secondary (age 12–18)	38[9]	665	12,672	19.1
Voc., teacher tr.	4[10]	37[11]	228[11]	6.2[11]
Higher[10]	6	25	271	10.8

Health: physicians (1996) 62 (1 per 2,919 persons); hospital beds (1991) 863 (1 per 255 persons); infant mortality rate per 1,000 live births (1999) 22.
Food (1992): daily per capita caloric intake 2,828 (vegetable products 74%, animal products 26%); 124% of FAO recommended minimum requirement.

Military

No military forces are maintained; New Zealand is responsible for defense.

[1]In July 1997 the short-form name of the country was officially changed from Western Samoa to Samoa. [2]According to the constitution, the current Head of State, paramount chief HH Malietoa Tanumafili II, will hold office for life. Upon his death, the monarchy will functionally cease, and future Heads of State will be elected by the Legislative Assembly. [3]Symbol of the monetary unit changed from WS$ to SA$ as of July 1997. [4]Total includes 2 sq mi (5 sq km) of uninhabited islands. [5]Registered only. [6]Consumer price index components. [7]Import figures are c.i.f. in balance of trade and in commodities and trading partners. [8]1995. [9]1982. [10]1983. [11]1986–87.

Internet resources for further information:

- **Trading with New Zealand: Samoa**
  http://www.tradenz.govt.nz/intelligence/profiles/samoa.html

San Marino

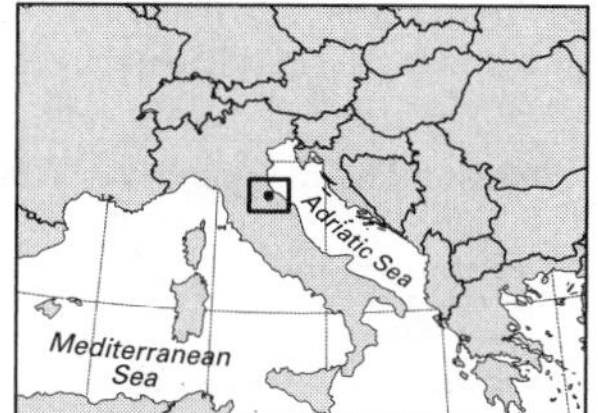

Official name: Serenissima Repubblica di San Marino (Most Serene Republic of San Marino).
Form of government: unitary multiparty republic with one legislative house (Great and General Council [60]).
Head of state and government: Captains-Regent (2).
Capital: San Marino.
Official language: Italian.
Official religion: none.
Monetary unit: 1 Italian lira (Lit; plural lire) = 100 centesimi; valuation (Oct. 6, 2000) 1 U.S.$ = Lit 2,226; 1 £ = Lit 3,221.

Area and population

		area		population
Castles	Capitals	sq mi	sq km	1997[1] estimate
Acquaviva	Acquaviva	1.88	4.86	1,264
Borgo Maggiore	Borgo	3.48	9.01	5,358
Chiesanuova	Chiesanuova	2.11	5.46	866
Città	San Marino	2.74	7.09	4,350
Domagnano	Domagnano	2.56	6.62	2,207
Faetano	Faetano	2.99	7.75	870
Fiorentino	Fiorentino	2.53	6.56	1,798
Montegiardino	Montegiardino	1.28	3.31	717
Serravalle/Dogano	Serravalle	4.07	10.53	8,085
TOTAL		23.63[2]	61.19	25,515

Demography

Population (2000): 26,800.
Density (2000): persons per sq mi 1,134.2, persons per sq km 438.0.
Urban-rural (1999): urban 96.2%; rural 3.8%.
Sex distribution (2000): male 48.34%; female 51.66%.
Age breakdown (2000): under 15, 15.7%; 15–29, 18.8%; 30–44, 25.5%; 45–59, 18.8%; 60–74, 14.0%; 75 and over, 7.2%.
Population projection: (2010) 31,100; (2020) 36,200.
Doubling time: not applicable; natural population growth is negligible.
Ethnic composition (1997[1]): Sammarinesi 83.1%; Italian 12.0%; other 4.8%.
Religious affiliation (1995): Roman Catholic 89.2%; Jehovah's Witness 1.2%; other 9.6%.
Major cities (1997[1]): Serravalle/Dogano 4,802; Borgo Maggiore 2,394; San Marino 2,294; Murata 1,549; Domagnano 1,048.

Vital statistics

Birth rate per 1,000 population (2000): 10.9 (world avg. 22.1); (1985) legitimate 95.2%; illegitimate 4.8%.
Death rate per 1,000 population (2000): 7.6 (world avg. 8.9).
Natural increase rate per 1,000 population (2000): 3.3 (world avg. 13.2).
Total fertility rate (avg. births per childbearing woman; 2000): 1.3.
Marriage rate per 1,000 population (1992–96): 8.1.
Divorce rate per 1,000 population (1991–95): 1.0.
Life expectancy at birth (2000): male 77.6 years; female 85.0 years.
Major causes of death per 100,000 population (1994–98): disease of the circulatory system 338.3; malignant neoplasms (cancers) 224.5; accidents, violence, and suicide 60.9; diseases of the respiratory system 9.5.

National economy

Budget (1995). Revenue: Lit 374,900,000,000 (indirect taxes 44.9%; direct taxes 28.9%; social security 17.8%). Expenditures: Lit 377,300,000,000 (current expenditures 46.8%, of which social security 39.9%, wages and salaries 30.8%; capital expenditures 6.7%; other 46.5%).
Public debt: n.a.
Tourism: number of tourist arrivals (1996) 3,345,381; receipts from visitors (1994) U.S.$252,500,000; expenditures by nationals abroad, n.a.
Population economically active (1999): total 19,347; activity rate of total population 73.2% (participation rates: ages 15–64, 88.4%; female 41.2%; unemployed 4.4%).

Price and earnings indexes (1990 = 100)

	1989	1990	1991	1992	1993	1994	1995
Consumer price index	94.0	100.0	108.0	115.7	121.9	128.0	134.3
Earnings index	...	...	...	...	...	...	...

Household income and expenditure. Total number of households (1997[1]) 10,093; average household size 2.5; income per household: n.a.; sources of income: n.a.; expenditure (1991)[3]: food, beverages, and tobacco 22.1%, housing, fuel, and electrical energy 20.9%, transportation and communications 17.6%, clothing and footwear 8.0%, furniture, appliances, and goods and services for the home 7.2%, education 7.1%, health and sanitary services 2.6%, other goods and services 14.5%.
Production (metric tons except as noted). Agriculture, forestry, fishing[4]: wheat *c.* 4,400, grapes *c.* 700, barley *c.* 500; livestock (number of live animals; 1998) 831 cattle, 748 pigs. Manufacturing (1998): processed meats 324,073 kg, of which beef 226,570 kg, pork 87,764 kg, veal 7,803 kg; cheese 61,563 kg; butter 12,658 kg; milk 1,167,620 litres; yogurt 5,131 litres; other major products include electrical appliances, musical instruments, printing ink, paint, cosmetics, furniture, floor tiles, gold and silver jewelry, clothing, and postage stamps. Construction (new units completed; 1998): residential 69; nonresidential 165. Energy production (consumption): all electrical power is imported via electrical grid from Italy (consumption, n.a.); coal, none (n.a.); crude petroleum, none (n.a.); petroleum products, none (n.a.); natural gas, none (n.a.).
Gross national product (at current market prices; 1994): U.S.$408,000,000 (U.S.$16,900 per capita).

Structure of labour force (1999)

	labour force	% of labour force
Agriculture	254	1.3
Manufacturing	5,962	30.8
Construction and public utilities	1,608	8.3
Transportation and communications	396	2.1
Trade	3,508	18.1
Finance and insurance	533	2.8
Services	2,021	10.4
Public administration and defense	4,211	21.8
Other	854[5]	4.4[5]
TOTAL	19,347	100.0

Land use (1985): agricultural and under permanent cultivation 74%; meadows and pastures 22%; forested, built-on, wasteland, and other 4%.

Foreign trade

Balance of trade: n.a. San Marino and Italy form a single customs area; separate figures for San Marino are not available.
Imports: manufactured goods of all kinds, oil, and gold. *Major import source:* Italy.
Exports: wine, wheat, woolen goods, furniture, wood, ceramics, building stone, dairy products, meat, and postage stamps. *Major export destination:* Italy.

Transport and communications

Transport. Railroads: none (nearest rail terminal is at Rimini, Italy, 17 mi [27 km] northeast). Roads (1998): total length 156 mi, 252 km. Vehicles (1998): passenger cars 25,571; trucks and buses 4,013[6]. Merchant marine: vessels (100 gross tons and over) none. Air transport: airports with scheduled flights, none; there is, however, a heliport that provides passenger and cargo service between San Marino and Rimini, Italy, during the summer months.

Communications

Medium	date	unit	number	units per 1,000 persons
Daily newspapers	1996	circulation	2,000	72
Radio	1997	receivers	16,000	610
Television	1998	receivers	9,000	358
Telephones	1998	main lines	19,000	773
Cellular telephones	1998	subscribers	5,000	196

Education and health

Educational attainment (1997[1]). Percentage of population age 14 and over having: basic literacy[7] or primary education 35.6%; secondary 30.7%; some postsecondary 27.9%; higher degree 5.8%. *Literacy* (1997[1]): total population age 15 and over literate 21,885 (99.1%); males literate 10,546 (99.4%); females literate 11,339 (98.8%).

Education (1997–98)

	schools	teachers	students	student/ teacher ratio
Primary (age 6–10)	14	196	1,227	6.3
Secondary (age 11–18)	4	151	1,083	7.2
Voc., teacher tr.	...	44[8]	428[9]	6.2[8]
Higher	1	...	...	...

Health (1998): physicians 84 (1 per 310 persons); hospital beds 152 (1 per 172 persons); infant mortality rate per 1,000 live births (2000) 6.3.
Food (1995)[10]: daily per capita caloric intake 3,608 (vegetable products 74%, animal products 26%); 143% of FAO recommended minimum requirement.

Military

Total active duty personnel (1999): none[11]. *Military expenditure as percentage of national budget* (1992): 1.0% (world 3.6%); per capita expenditure (1987) U.S.$155.

[1]January 1. [2]Detail does not add to total given because of rounding. [3]Weighting coefficients for component expenditures are those of the 1991 official Italian consumer price index for the North-Central region of Italy. [4]Early 1980s. [5]Unemployed. [6]1996. [7]Includes 0.9 percent illiterate population. [8]1993–94. [9]1995–96. [10]Figures are for Italy. [11]Defense is provided by a public security force of about 50; all fit males ages 16–55 constitute a militia.

Internet resources for further information:
- **San Marino http://www.emulateme.com/sanmarino.htm**

São Tomé and Príncipe

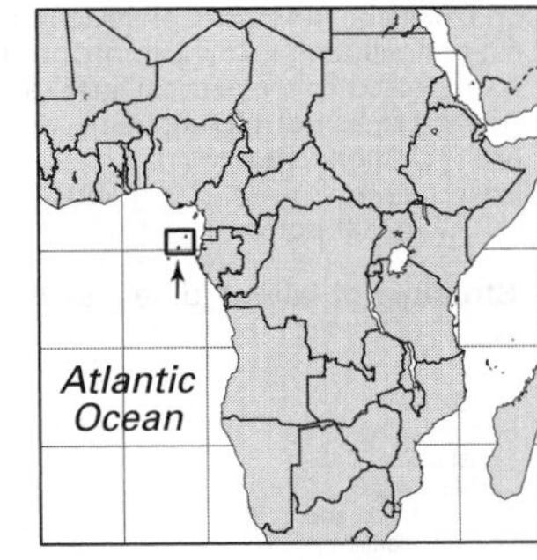

Official name: República democrática de São Tomé e Príncipe (Democratic Republic of São Tomé and Príncipe).
Form of government: Multiparty republic with one legislative house (National Assembly [55]).
Chief of state: President.
Head of government: Prime Minister.
Capital: São Tomé.
Official language: Portuguese.
Official religion: none.
Monetary unit: 1 dobra (Db) = 100 cêntimos; valuation (Oct. 6, 2000) 1 U.S.$ = Db 2,390; 1 £ = Db 3,457.

Area and population		area		population
Islands	**Capitals**	sq mi	sq km	1991 census[1]
Districts				
São Tomé		332	859	114,507
Agua Grande	São Tomé	7	17	43,420
Cantagalo	Santana	46	119	11,421
Caué	São João Angolares	103	267	5,541
Lemba	Neves	88	229	9,448
Lobata	Guadalupe	41	105	13,101
Mé-Zóchi	Trindade	47	122	31,576
Autonomous Island		55	142	5,639
Príncipe	Santo António	55	142	5,639
TOTAL		386	1,001	120,146

Demography

Population (2000): 144,000.
Density (2000): persons per sq km 373.1, persons per sq km 143.9.
Urban-rural (1999): urban 46.0%; rural 54.0%.
Sex distribution (1999): male 49.26%, female 50.74%.
Age breakdown (1999): under 15, 47.6%; 15–29, 27.3%; 30–44, 12.5%; 45–59, 6.4%; 60–74, 4.8%; 75 and over, 1.4%.
Population projection: (2010) 177,000; (2020) 218,000.
Doubling time: 20 years.
Ethnolinguistic composition: mestiços, angolares (descendants of Angolan slaves), forros (descendants of freed slaves), serviçais (alien contract labourers), and tongas (children of serviçais) speak Portuguese; non-Portuguese-speaking Europeans speak French and Spanish.
Religious affiliation (1995): Roman Catholic, about 89.5%; remainder mostly Protestant, predominantly Seventh-day Adventist and an indigenous Evangelical Church.
Major cities (1991): São Tomé 43,420; Trindade 11,388[2]; Santana 6,190[2]; Neves 5,919[2]; Santo Amaro 5,878[2].

Vital statistics

Birth rate per 1,000 population (1999): 43.2 (world avg. 22.1); (1977) legitimate 9.8%; illegitimate 90.2%.
Death rate per 1,000 population (1999): 8.0 (world avg. 8.9).
Natural increase rate per 1,000 population (1999): 35.2 (world avg. 13.2).
Total fertility rate (avg. births per childbearing woman; 1999): 6.1.
Marriage rate per 1,000 population: n.a.
Divorce rate per 1,000 population: n.a.
Life expectancy at birth (1998): male 63.5 years; females 66.3 years.
Major causes of death per 100,000 population (1987): malaria 160.6; direct obstetric causes 76.7; pneumonia 74.0; influenza 61.5; anemias 47.3; hypertensive disease 32.1.

National economy

Budget (1997). Revenue: Db 55,528,000,000 (grants 43.7%; taxes 38.2%, of which import taxes 8.5%, sales taxes 7.5%, export taxes 3.4%; nontax revenue 18.1%). Expenditures: Db 140,174,000,000 (capital 60.3%; recurrent expenditure 39.7%, of which debt service 15.9%, personnel costs 8.4%, transfers 6.3%, goods and services 5.0%, defense 1.2%).
Public debt (external, outstanding; 1998): U.S.$233,400,000.
Tourism (1997): receipts from visitors U.S.$2,000,000; expenditures by nationals abroad U.S.$1,000,000.
Production (metric tons except as noted). Agriculture, forestry, fishing (1999): coconuts 28,000, taro 23,060, bananas 18,000, vegetables 6,100, cassava 4,840, cacao 4,197, fruits (other than melon) 2,100, corn (maize) 1,487, yams 1,200, coffee 58; livestock (number of live animals) 4,750 goats, 4,000 cattle, 2,550 sheep, 2,100 pigs; roundwood (1998) 9,000 cu m; fish catch (1998) 3,305, principally marine fish and shellfish. Mining and quarrying: some quarrying to support local construction industry. Manufacturing (value in Db; 1995): beer 880,000; clothing 679,000; lumber 369,000; bakery products 350,000; palm oil 228,000; soap 133,000; ceramics 87,000. Construction (1972): buildings authorized 44 (5,561 sq m, of which residential 3,698, mixed residential-commercial 1,361, commercial 502). Energy production (consumption): electricity (kW-hr; 1996) 15,000,000 (15,000,000); coal, none (n.a.); crude petroleum, none (n.a.); petroleum products (metric tons; 1996) none (25,000); natural gas, none (n.a.).
Household income and expenditure. Average household size (1981): 4.0; income per household: n.a.; sources of income: n.a.; expenditure (1995)[3]: food 71.9%, housing and energy 10.2%, transportation and communications 6.4%, clothing and other items 5.3%, household durable goods 2.8%, education and health 1.7%.

Population economically active (1994): total 51,789; activity rate of total population 40.8% (participation rates [1981] ages 15–64, 61.1%; female [1991] 32.4%; unemployed [1994] 29.0%).

Price and earnings indexes (1995 = 100)					
	1993	1994	1995	1996	1997
Consumer price index	57.5	72.9	100.0	137.6	231.4
Earnings index	...	...	...	...	...

Gross national product (1998): U.S.$38,000,000 (U.S.$270 per capita).

Structure of gross domestic product and labour force	1997		1994	
	in value Db '000,000	% of total value	labour force	% of labour force
Agriculture	46,682	23.3	14,022	27.1
Mining	...	...	...	...
Manufacturing / Public utilities	7,875	4.0	2,327	4.5
Construction	29,469	14.7	3,365	6.5
Transp. and commun.	37,508	18.8	2,829	5.5
Trade			5,184	10.0
Finance	15,134	7.6	194	0.3
Pub. admin., defense	44,669	22.3	4,023	7.8
Services	18,664	9.3	...	...
Other	...	...	19,845[4]	38.3[4]
TOTAL	200,001	100.0	51,789	100.0

Land use (1994): meadows and pastures 1.3%; agricultural and under permanent cultivation 54.0%; forest, built-on, wasteland, and other 44.7%.

Foreign trade

Balance of trade (current prices)						
	1992	1993	1994	1995	1996	1997
U.S.$'000,000	–17.2	–20.4	–18.5	–18.3	–14.9	–13.9
% of total	62.1%	66.2%	61.3%	64.2%	60.3%	56.7%

Imports (1997): U.S.$19,200,000 (capital goods 29.2%, food and other agricultural products 19.8%, petroleum products 19.8%). *Major import sources:* Portugal 26.3%; France 17.9%; Angola 6.7%; Belgium 5.8%; Japan 3.3%; Germany 1.6%; Gabon 0.8%; Italy 0.4%.
Exports (1997): U.S.$5,300,000 (cocoa 86.8%). *Major export destinations:* The Netherlands 50.9%; Germany 5.7%; Portugal 5.7%.

Transport and communications

Transport. Railroads: none. Roads (1996): total length 199 mi, 320 km (paved 68%). Vehicles (1996): passenger cars 4,040; trucks and buses 1,540. Merchant marine (1992): vessels (100 gross tons and over) 4; total deadweight tonnage 2,277. Air transport (1997): passenger-mi 6,000,000, passenger-km 9,000,000; short ton-mi cargo 700,000, short ton-km cargo 1,000,000; airports (1998) 2.

Communications				
Medium	date	unit	number	units per 1,000 persons
Radio	1997	receivers	38,000	272
Television	1997	receivers	23,000	163
Telephones	1998	main lines	3,122	22
Facsimile machines	1995	units	200	1.5

Education and health

Educational attainment (1981). Percentage of population age 25 and over having: no formal schooling 56.6%; incomplete primary education 18.0%; primary 19.2%; incomplete secondary 4.6%; complete secondary 1.3%; postsecondary 0.3%. *Literacy* (1981): total population age 15 and over literate 28,114 (54.2%); males literate 17,689 (70.2%); females literate 10,425 (39.1%).

Education (1997)	schools	teachers	students	student/ teacher ratio
Primary (age 6–13)	69	638	21,760	34.1
Secondary (age 14–18)[5]	10	415	12,280	29.6
Voc., teacher tr.	...	...	...	...
Higher	...	...	...	...

Health: physicians (1996) 61 (1 per 2,147 persons); hospital beds (1983) 640 (1 per 158 persons); infant mortality rate per 1,000 live births (1999) 52.0.
Food (1998): daily per capita caloric intake 2,201 (vegetable products 96%, animal products 4%); 94% of FAO recommended minimum requirement.

Military

Total active duty personnel: a police force of about 900 men from 1992. *Military expenditure as percentage of GNP* (1997): 0.9% (world 2.6%); per capita expenditure U.S.$2.

[1]Preliminary. [2]1981. [3]Weights based on CPI components. [4]Includes 15,000 unemployed. [5]Includes vocational.

Internet resources for further information:
- **São Tomé e Príncipe Homepage (unofficial) http://www.stome.com**

Saudi Arabia

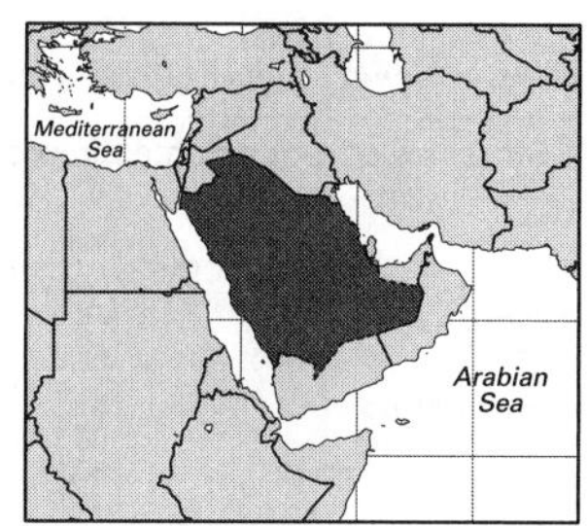

Official name: Al-Mamlakah al-ʿArabīyah as-Saʿūdīyah (Kingdom of Saudi Arabia).
Form of government: monarchy[1].
Head of state and government: King.
Capital: Riyadh.
Official language: Arabic.
Official religion: Islam.
Monetary unit: 1 Saudi riyal (SRls) = 100 halalah; valuation (Oct. 6, 2000) 1 U.S.$ = SRls 3.75; 1 £ = SRls 5.42.

Area and population

Geographic Regions / Administrative Regions[3]	Capitals	area[2] sq mi	area[2] sq km	population 1985 estimate
Al-Gharbīyah (Western)		—	—	3,043,189
Al-Bāḥah	Al-Bāḥah	6,000	15,000	...
Al-Madīnah al-Munawwarah	Medina (Al-Madīnah)	67,000	173,000	...
Makkah al-Mukarramah	Mecca (Makkah)	63,000	164,000	...
Al-Janūbīyah (Southern)		—	—	625,017
ʿAsīr	Abha	31,000	81,000	...
Jīzān	Jīzān	7,000	17,000	...
Najrān	Najrān	46,000	119,000	...
Ash-Shamālīyah (Northern)		—	—	679,476
Al-Ḥudūd ash-Shamālīyah (Northern Borders)	ʿArʿar	46,000	120,000	...
Al-Jawf	Sakākah	54,000	139,000	...
Tabūk	Tabūk	42,000	108,000	...
Ash-Sharqīyah (Eastern)		—	—	3,030,765
Ash-Sharqīyah (Eastern)	Ad-Dammām	274,000	710,000	...
Al-Wūsṭā (Central)		—	—	3,632,092
Ḥāʾil	Ḥāʾil	48,000	125,000	...
Al-Qaṣīm	Buraydah	25,000	65,000	...
Ar-Riyāḍ	Riyadh (Ar-Riyāḍ)	159,000	412,000	...
TOTAL		868,000	2,248,000	11,010,539[4]

Demography

Population (2000): 22,024,000.
Density (2000)[2]: persons per sq mi 25.4, persons per sq km 9.8.
Urban-rural (2000): urban 83.0%; rural 17.0%.
Sex distribution (2000): male 55.33%; female 44.67%.
Age breakdown (2000): under 15, 42.6%; 15–29, 22.8%; 30–44, 17.9%; 45–59, 12.1%; 60–74, 3.9%; 75 and over, 0.7%.
Population projection: (2010) 30,546,000; (2020) 41,880,000.
Doubling time: 22 years.
Ethnic composition by nationality (1995): Saudi *c.* 66%; foreigners *c.* 34%, of which South Asians *c.* 14%, Egyptians *c.* 7%.
Religious affiliation (1992): Sunnī Muslim 93.3%; Shīʿī Muslim 3.3%; Christian 3.0%; other 0.4%.
Major cities (1991): Riyadh (Ar-Riyāḍ) 1,800,000; Jiddah 1,500,000; Mecca (Makkah) 630,000; Aṭ-Ṭāʾif 410,000; Medina 400,000.

Vital statistics

Birth rate per 1,000 population (2000): 37.5 (world avg. 22.1).
Death rate per 1,000 population (2000): 6.0 (world avg. 8.9).
Natural increase rate per 1,000 population (2000): 31.5 (world avg. 13.2).
Total fertility rate (avg. births per childbearing woman; 2000): 6.3.
Life expectancy at birth (2000): male 66.1 years; female 69.5 years.
Major causes of death per 100,000 population: n.a.

National economy

Budget (1998). Revenue: SRls 178,000,000,000 (oil revenues 78.5%). Expenditures: SRls 196,000,000,000 (defense and security 39.9%, human resource development 23.2%, public administration, municipal transfers, and subsidies 20.1%, health and social development 8.4%).
Public debt: n.a.
Production (metric tons except as noted). Agriculture, forestry, fishing (1999): wheat 1,800,000; alfalfa 1,400,000; dates 600,000; tomatoes 465,000; watermelons 460,000; barley 400,000; potatoes 250,000; sorghum 220,000; dry onions 210,000; grapes 130,000; cantaloupes 130,000; livestock (number of live animals) 8,042,000 sheep, 4,400,000 goats, 425,000 camels; fish catch (1997) 54,015. Mining and quarrying (1995): gypsum (1994) 337,573; gold 8,080 kg. Manufacturing (value added in U.S.$'000,000; 1995): industrial chemicals 3,014; cement, glass, and other nonmetal mineral products 943; refined petroleum 830; iron and steel 561; metal products 589; food, beverages, and tobacco 493; plastic products 221. Energy production (consumption): electricity (kW-hr; 1996) 104,118,000,000 (104,118,000,000); coal, none (none); crude petroleum (barrels; 1999) 2,673,000,000 ([1996] 635,000,000); petroleum products (metric tons; 1996) 97,311,000 (45,396,000); natural gas (cu m; 1998) 36,285,000,000 ([1996] 41,339,000,000).
Land use (1994): forested 0.8%; meadows and pastures 55.8%; agricultural and under permanent cultivation 1.8%; built-on, waste, and other 41.6%.
Population economically active (1994): total 5,614,000; activity rate of total population 32.2% (participation rates [1988] ages 15–64, 59.1%, female 3.5%; unemployed [1997] *c.* 25%).

Price and earnings indexes (1995 = 100)

	1993	1994	1995	1996	1997	1998	1999
Consumer price index	94.8	95.4	100.0	101.2	101.3	100.7	99.3
Earnings index	...	...	...	...	...	...	...

Gross national product (1998): U.S.$143,361,000,000 (U.S.$6,910 per capita).

Structure of gross domestic product and labour force

	1997		1990	
	in value[5] SRls '000,000	% of total value	labour force	% of labour force
Agriculture	33,127	6.1	569,200	9.9
Mining	203,550	37.2	3,500	0.1
Oil sector			46,800	0.8
Manufacturing	52,238	9.5	374,900	6.5
Construction	46,314	8.5	944,100	16.4
Public utilities	898	0.2	126,900	2.2
Transp. and commun.	32,610	6.0	262,300	4.5
Trade	35,114	6.4	898,300	15.6
Finance	28,990[6]	5.3[6]	99,000	1.7
Pub. admin., defense	97,232	17.8	624,800	10.8
Services	14,352	2.6	1,822,000	31.6
Other	2,987[7]	0.5		
TOTAL	547,412	100.0[8]	5,771,800	100.0[8]

Household income and expenditure. Average household size (1992) 6.1; income per household: n.a.; sources of income: n.a.; expenditure (1988)[9]: food 37%, housing 21%, transportation and communications 15%, clothing 8%, household furnishings 7%, education and entertainment 2%.
Tourism (in U.S.$'000,000): receipts (1997) 1,420; expenditures, n.a.

Foreign trade[10]

Balance of trade (current prices)

	1993	1994	1995	1996	1997	1998
U.S.$'000,000	+16,522	+21,289	+24,683	+24,359	+34,611	+12,237
% of total	24.2%	33.3%	32.6%	28.3%	39.4%	18.2%

Imports (1997): SRls 106,763,000,000 (machinery and appliances 19.9%, transport equipment 15.7%, base metals and articles 9.1%, chemicals and chemical products 8.2%, vegetables 7.4%, textiles and clothing 6.6%, live animals and animal products 4.6%). *Major import sources:* U.S. 21.9%; U.K. 10.7%; Japan 6.6%; Switzerland 5.8%; Germany 5.0%; Italy 4.6%.
Exports (1997): SRls 223,516,000,000[11] (crude petroleum 70.4%; refined petroleum products and petrochemicals 21.7%). *Major export destinations*[12]: U.S. 17.5%; Japan 15.0%; S. Korea 10.5%; Singapore 6.0%; The Netherlands 4.3%; France 4.0%.

Transport and communications

Transport. Railroads (1995): route length 1,390 km; (1993–94) passenger-km 139,000,000; (1993–94) metric ton-km cargo 816,000,000. Roads (1996): total length 162,000 km (paved 42.7%). Vehicles (1996): passenger cars 1,744,000; trucks and buses 1,192,000. Merchant marine (1992): vessels (100 gross tons and over) 301; total deadweight tonnage 1,381,651. Air transport (1995)[13]: passenger-km 18,820,000,000; metric ton-km cargo 951,500,000; airports (1997) with scheduled flights 25.

Communications

Medium	date	unit	number	units per 1,000 persons
Daily newspapers	1996	circulation	1,105,000	59
Radio	1997	receivers	6,250,000	313
Television	1996	receivers	4,900,000	252
Telephones	1998	main lines	2,878,000	140
Cellular telephones	1998	subscribers	627,321	30
Personal computers	1998	units	1,000,000	48
Internet	1998	users	20,000	1.0

Education and health

Educational attainment (1986). Percentage of population age 25 and over having: no formal schooling 31.8%; primary, secondary, or higher education 68.2%. *Literacy* (1995): percentage of population age 15 and over literate 62.8%; males literate 71.5%; females literate 50.2%.

Education (1996–97)

	schools	teachers	students	student/teacher ratio
Primary (age 6–12)	11,506	175,458	2,256,185	12.9
Secondary (age 13–18)	6,346[14]	115,907	1,500,072	12.9
Voc., teacher tr.	293[14, 15]	3,974	42,917	10.8
Higher	77[14]	15,868	273,992	17.3

Health (1995): physicians 30,306 (1 per 590 persons); hospital beds 41,916 (1 per 427 persons); infant mortality rate per 1,000 live births (2000) 52.9.
Food (1997): daily per capita caloric intake 2,783 (vegetable products 81%, animal products 19%); 115% of FAO recommended minimum requirement.

Military

Total active duty personnel (1998): 105,500 (army 66.4%, navy 12.8%, air force 20.9%). *Military expenditure as percentage of GDP* (1997): 14.5% (world 2.6%); per capita expenditure U.S.$1,050.

[1]Assisted by the Consultative Council consisting of 90 appointed members. [2]Estimated; not adjusted to reflect June 2000 Saudi Arabia boundary agreement with Yemen. [3]13 administrative regions created September 1993. [4]Preliminary 1992 census total 16,929,294; detail, n.a. [5]In producers' values at current prices. [6]Finance includes real estate and business services. [7]Other equals import duties less imputed bank services charge. [8]Detail does not add to total given because of rounding. [9]Urban middle-income households only. [10]Import figures are f.o.b. in balance of trade and c.i.f. in commodities and trading partners. [11]Includes reexports. [12]1996. [13]Domestic and international operation of Saudi Arabian Airlines. [14]1994–95. [15]Includes intermediate colleges.

Internet resources for further information:

- **Ministry of Information http://www.saudinf.com**

Senegal

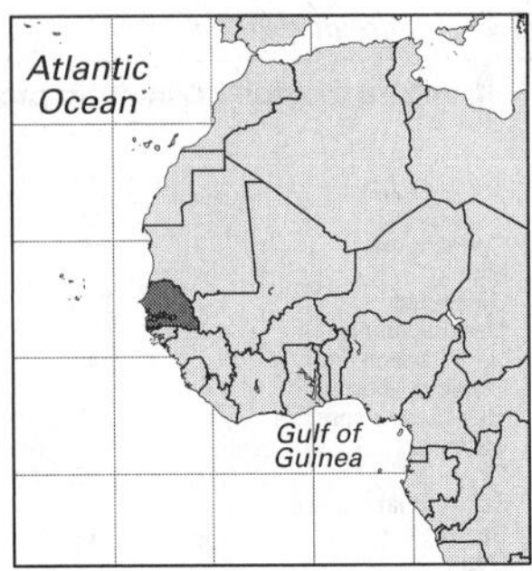

Official name: République du Sénégal (Republic of Senegal).
Form of government: multiparty republic with two legislative houses (Senate [60[1, 2]]; National Assembly [140]).
Head of state and government: President assisted by Prime Minister.
Capital: Dakar.
Official language: French.
Official religion: none.
Monetary unit: 1 CFA franc (CFAF) = 100 centimes; valuation (Oct. 6, 2000) 1 U.S.$ = CFAF 754.28; 1 £ = CFAF 1,019.

Area and population

Regions	Capitals	area sq mi	area sq km	population 1994 estimate
Dakar	Dakar	212	550	1,869,000
Diourbel	Diourbel	1,683	4,359	750,000
Fatick	Fatick	3,064	7,935	569,000
Kaolack	Kaolack	6,181	16,010	948,000
Kolda	Kolda	8,112	21,011	689,000
Louga	Louga	11,270	29,188	525,000
Saint-Louis	Saint-Louis	17,034	44,117	749,000
Tambacounda	Tambacounda	23,012	59,602	449,000
Thiès	Thiès	2,549	6,601	1,115,000
Ziguinchor	Ziguinchor	2,834	7,339	467,000
TOTAL		75,951	196,712	8,127,000[3]

Demography

Population (2000): 9,987,000.
Density (2000): persons per sq mi 131.5, persons per sq km 50.8.
Urban-rural (1999): urban 46.3%; rural 53.7%.
Sex distribution (1999): male 49.87%; female 50.13%.
Age breakdown (2000): under 15, 44.6%; 15–29, 27.5%; 30–44, 15.6%; 45–59, 7.7%; 60–74, 3.7%; 75 and over, 0.9%.
Population projection: (2010) 13,221,000; (2020) 16,855,000.
Doubling time: 24 years.
Ethnic composition (1988): Wolof 48.1%; Serer 12.6%; Peul (Fulani) and Tukulor 21.7%; Diola 5.0%; Malinke (Mandingo) 3.7%; other 8.9%.
Religious affiliation (1988): Sunnī Muslim 92.0%; traditional beliefs and other 6.0%; Christian (predominantly Roman Catholic) 2.0%.
Major cities (1994): Dakar 785,071 (urban agglomeration 1,869,323[4]); Thiès 216,381; Kaolack 193,115; Ziguinchor 161,680; Rufisque 138,837[5]; Saint-Louis 132,444.

Vital statistics

Birth rate per 1,000 population (2000): 37.9 (world avg. 22.1).
Death rate per 1,000 population (2000): 8.6 (world avg. 8.9).
Natural increase rate per 1,000 population (2000): 29.3 (world avg. 13.2).
Total fertility rate (avg. births per childbearing woman; 2000): 5.2.
Marriage rate per 1,000 population: n.a.[6]
Divorce rate per 1,000 population: n.a.
Life expectancy at birth (2000): male 60.6 years; female 63.8 years.
Major causes of death (percentage of officially confirmed deaths from infectious diseases only; 1988): malaria 44.8%; tetanus 17.8%; meningitis 15.3%; tuberculosis of respiratory system 10.4%.

National economy

Budget (1997). Revenue: CFAF 432,200,000,000 (value-added taxes 30.3%, individual income tax 12.4%, taxes on petroleum products 9.1%, corporate income tax 6.7%). Expenditures: CFAF 432,200,000,000 (current expenditures 73.5%, of which education 19.0%, defense 9.3%, health 3.7%; development expenditure 26.5%).
Production (metric tons except as noted). Agriculture, forestry, fishing (2000): sugarcane 887,000, peanuts (groundnuts) 828,000, millet 506,000, watermelons 260,000, paddy rice 240,000, sorghum 147,000, mangoes 75,000, corn (maize) 66,000, oil palm fruit 64,000, onions 61,000, cassava 42,000; livestock (number of live animals) 4,300,000 sheep, 3,595,000 goats, 2,960,000 cattle, 510,000 horses; roundwood (1998) 4,934,000 cu m; fish catch (1998) 425,766. Mining and quarrying (1996): phosphate 1,376,000; salt 87,600[7]. Manufacturing (1996): tobacco 1,425,000; phosphates 1,384,000; cement 811,000; peanut oil 91,200; vegetable oil 84,200; sugar 68,400; soap 46,300. Construction (authorized; 1993)[5]: residential 357,000 sq m; nonresidential 235,000 sq m. Energy production (consumption): electricity (kW-hr; 1998) 1,160,000,000 (1,160,000,000); coal, none (none); crude petroleum (barrels; 1998) none (6,392,000); petroleum products (metric tons; 1998) 852,000 (895,000); natural gas, none (none).
Population economically active (1991): total 2,739,476; activity rate of total population 36.1% (participation rates [1988]: ages 15–60, 53.1%; female 25.6%; unemployed [1992] 24.4%).

Price and earnings indexes (1995 = 100)

	1993	1994	1995	1996	1997	1998	1999
Consumer price index[8]	70.1	92.7	100.0	102.8	104.6	105.8	106.6
Hourly earnings index	...	...	...	...	...	...	...

Household income and expenditure. Average household size (1991) 8.7; average annual income per household: n.a.; sources of income: n.a.; expenditure (early 1980s): food 49%, clothing and footwear 11%, housing 7%, education 6%.

Public debt (external, outstanding; 1998): U.S.$3,274,000,000.
Gross national product (1998): U.S.$4,683,000,000 (U.S.$520 per capita).

Structure of gross domestic product and labour force

	1997 in value CFAF '000,000,000	1997 % of total value	1991 labour force	1991 % of labour force
Agriculture	476.9	18.3	1,789,467	65.3
Mining }	406.5	15.6	1,998	0.1
Manufacturing }			161,124	5.9
Public utilities	51.3	2.0	...	...
Construction	126.5	4.8	60,935	2.2
Transp. and commun.	286.7	11.0	58,081	2.1
Trade[9]	649.5	24.9	378,241	13.8
Finance	...	...	4,623	0.2
Services	416.4	16.0	...	...
Pub. admin., defense	193.2	7.4	268,721	9.8
Other	—	—	16,286	0.6
TOTAL	2,607.0	100.0	2,739,476	100.0

Tourism (1997): receipts U.S.$153,000,000; expenditures U.S.$53,000,000.
Land use (1994): forested 39.5%; meadows and pastures 29.6%; agricultural and under permanent cultivation 12.2%; other 18.7%.

Foreign trade[10]

Balance of trade (current prices)

	1993	1994	1995	1996	1997	1998	1999
CFAF '000,000,000	–151.8	–215.7	–219.8	–143.9	–154.7	–258.9	–300.3
% of total	29.6%	21.4%	20.3%	12.5%	12.5%	18.5%	19.9%

Imports (1998): CFAF 793,000,000,000 (1995: agricultural products 34.5%, of which rice 7.1%, fixed vegetable oils 5.2%; capital goods 15.0%[11]; refined petroleum 11.0%[11]). *Major import sources:* France 35.8%; United States 5.9%; Germany 5.2%; Spain 4.6%; Nigeria 4.4%.
Exports (1998): CFAF 575,700,000,000 (1995[11]: fish and crustaceans 28.0%; chemical products 12.0%; peanut [groundnut] oil 11.0%; phosphates 3.0%). *Major export destinations:* France 9.8%; Mali 8.5%; Mauritania 3.9%; Cameroon 1.6%.

Transport and communications

Transport. Railroads: (1995) route length 761 mi, 1,225 km; (1993) passenger-mi 128,000,000, passenger-km 206,000,000; short ton-mi cargo 476,000,000, metric ton-km cargo 695,000,000. Roads (1996): total length 9,060 mi, 14,700 km (paved 29%). Vehicles (1996): passenger cars 85,488, trucks and buses 36,962. Merchant marine (1992): vessels (100 gross tons and over) 183; total deadweight tonnage 27,473. Air transport (1996)[12]: passenger-mi 139,644,000, passenger-km 224,736,000; short ton-mi cargo 11,247,000, metric ton-km cargo 16,420,000; airports (1996) with scheduled flights 7.

Communications

Medium	date	unit	number	units per 1,000 persons
Daily newspapers	1996	circulation	45,000	5.3
Radio	1997	receivers	1,240,000	141
Television	1998	receivers	370,000	41
Telephones	1998	main lines	140,000	16
Cellular telephones	1998	subscribers	22,000	2.4
Personal computers	1998	units	120,000	13
Internet	1998	users	7,500	0.8

Education and health

Educational attainment (1988). Percentage of population age 6–34 having: no formal schooling 62.6%; primary education 25.7%; secondary 8.4%; higher 0.8%; other 2.5%. *Literacy* (1995): percentage of total population age 15 and over literate 1,960,000 (37.3%); males literate 1,220,000 (47.2%); females literate 740,000 (27.6%).

Education (1996–97)

	schools	teachers	students	student/ teacher ratio
Primary (age 6–12)	3,530	16,567	954,758	57.6
Secondary (age 13–18)	359[13]	6,219	206,934	33.3
Vocational	19[13]	182[13]	4,624	40.1[13]
Higher[13, 14]	2	784	16,733	21.3

Health (1992): physicians 520 (1 per 14,825 persons); hospital beds 7,408 (1 per 1,041 persons); infant mortality rate per 1,000 live births (2000): 58.1.
Food (1998): daily per capita caloric intake 2,277 (vegetable products 91%, animal products 9%); 95.7% of FAO recommended minimum requirement.

Military

Total active duty personnel (1999): 13,400[15] (army 90.9%, navy 5.5%, air force 3.6%). *Military expenditure as percentage of GNP* (1997): 1.6% (world 2.6%); per capita expenditure U.S.$7.

[1]Includes 12 nonelected seats. [2]New legislative chamber established January 1999. [3]Detail does not add to total given because of rounding. [4]Urbanized area of Pikine (1994 population estimate 855,287) is within Dakar urban agglomeration. [5]Within Dakar urban agglomeration. [6]In 1996 about half of all women lived in polygymous unions. [7]1994. [8]Capital region only. [9]Includes hotels. [10]Imports f.o.b.; exports c.i.f. [11]Estimated figure(s). [12]Represents 1/11 of total international scheduled traffic of Air Afrique (government-supported airline of 11 West African countries). [13]1992–93. [14]Universities only; 1994–95. [15]Excludes 1,200 French troops.

Internet resources for further information:
- **République du Sénégal (French language only) http://www.primature.sn**

Seychelles

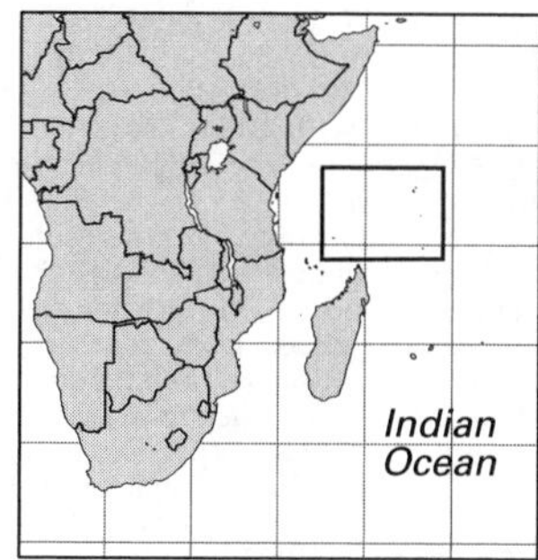

Official name: Repiblik Sesel (Creole); Republic of Seychelles (English); République des Seychelles (French).
Form of government: multiparty republic with one legislative house (National Assembly [34]).
Head of state and government: President.
Capital: Victoria.
Official languages: none[1].
Official religion: none.
Monetary unit: 1 Seychelles rupee (SR) = 100 cents; valuation (Oct. 6, 2000) 1 U.S.$ = SR 5.85; 1 £ = SR 8.46.

Area and population

Island Groups	Capital	area sq mi	area sq km	population 1994 census
Central (Granitic) group				
La Digue and satellites	—	6	15	1,990
Mahé and satellites	Victoria	59	153	66,134
Praslin and satellites	—	15	40	5,722
Silhouette	—	8	20	485
Other islands	—	2	4	0
Outer (Coralline) islands	—	86	223	0
TOTAL		176	455	74,331

Demography

Population (2000): 81,700.
Density (2000): persons per sq mi 462.4, persons per sq km 179.6.
Urban-rural (1999): urban 63.0%; rural 37.0%.
Sex distribution (1999): male 48.32%; female 51.68%.
Age breakdown (1999): under 15, 29.3%; 15–29, 30.1%; 30–44, 23.7%; 45–59, 8.5%; 60–74, 5.8%; 75 and over, 2.6%.
Population projection: (2010) 85,500; (2020) 89,100.
Doubling time: 58 years.
Ethnic composition (1983): Seychellois Creole (mixture of Asian, African, and European) 89.1%; Indian 4.7%; Malagasy 3.1%; Chinese 1.6%; English 1.5%.
Religious affiliation (1996): Roman Catholic 86.6%; other Christian (mostly Anglican) 9.3%; Hindu 1.3%; other 2.8%.
Major city (1999): Victoria 28,000.

Vital statistics

Birth rate per 1,000 population (1999): 18.2 (world avg. 22.1); (1998) legitimate 24.7%; illegitimate 75.3%.
Death rate per 1,000 population (1999): 7.0 (world avg. 8.9).
Natural increase rate per 1,000 population (1999): 11.2 (world avg. 13.2).
Total fertility rate (avg. births per childbearing woman; 1999): 1.9.
Marriage rate per 1,000 population (1998): 4.5.
Divorce rate per 1,000 population (1998): 1.0.
Life expectancy at birth (1999): male 64.5 years; female 75.8 years.
Major causes of death per 100,000 population (1998): diseases of the circulatory system 238.4, of which cerebrovascular disease 74.0; malignant neoplasms (cancers) 105.3; accidents 57.0; diseases of the respiratory system 52.0; diseases of the digestive system 51.9; infectious and parasitic diseases 36.8.

National economy

Budget (1999). Revenue: SR 1,399,600,000 (1997; customs taxes and duties 42.3%, transfers from Social Security Fund 17.4%, administrative fees 11.2%, income tax 10.5%, business taxes 6.1%, fees and fines 1.3%, grants 0.2%). Expenditures: SR 1,754,000,000 (1997; wages and salaries 27.4%, capital expenditure 17.5%, transfers 17.2%, debt service 16.5%, defense 3.3%).
Tourism: receipts from visitors (1998) U.S.$111,000,000; expenditures by nationals abroad (1997) U.S.$30,000,000.
Land use (1994): forested 11.1%; agricultural and under permanent cultivation 15.6%; built-on, wasteland, and other 73.3%.
Gross national product (1998): U.S.$505,000,000 (U.S.$6,420 per capita).

Structure of gross domestic product and labour force

	1997 in value SR '000,000	% of total value	labour force[2]	% of labour force
Agriculture	109.8	4.1	1,759	6.2
Mining, manufacturing	355.7	13.1	3,553[3]	12.6[3]
Construction	218.5	8.1	2,521	8.9
Public utilities	57.6	2.1	[3]	[3]
Trade	248.0	9.2	2,360	8.3
Transportation and communications	823.8	30.4	3,121	11.0
Finance	286.0	10.6	1,518	5.4
Pub. admin., defense	371.0	13.7	2,595	9.2
Services	65.1	2.4	9,871	34.9
Other	171.9[4]	6.3[4]	999	3.5
TOTAL	2,707.4	100.0	28,297	100.0

Production (metric tons except as noted). Agriculture, forestry, fishing (1999): coconuts 3,200, bananas 1,950, cinnamon 650, tea 260; livestock (number of live animals) 18,200 pigs, 5,150 goats, 1,400 cattle, 540,000 chickens; fish catch (1999) 4,418, of which (1998) jack 30.2%, snapper 18.3%, capitaine 8.3%, mackerel 4.8%. Mining and quarrying (1998): guano 5,000. Manufacturing (1999): canned tuna 33,234; soft drinks 105,610 hectolitres; beer and stout 67,680 hectolitres; fruit juices 22,530 hectolitres; cigarettes 60,300,000 units. Energy production (consumption): electricity (kW-hr; 1999) 172,400,000 (172,400,000); coal, none (n.a.); crude petroleum, none (n.a.); petroleum products (metric tons; 1996) none (55,000); natural gas, none (n.a.).
Population economically active (1999): total 30,786; activity rate of total population 38.3% (participation rates: ages 15–64 [1989] 74.3%; female [1989] 42.5%; unemployed 11.5%).

Price and earnings indexes (1995 = 100)

	1993	1994	1995	1996	1997	1998	1999
Consumer price index	98.5	100.3	100.0	98.9	99.5	102.1	108.6
Monthly earnings index	95.7	96.0	100.0	...	...	...	...

Public debt (external, outstanding; 1998): U.S.$145,100,000.
Household income and expenditure. Average household size (1994) 4.3; average annual income per household (1978) SR 18,480 (U.S.$2,658); sources of income: wages and salaries 77.2%, self-employment 3.8%, transfer payments 3.2%; expenditure (1991–92): food and beverages 47.6%, housing 15.1%, clothing and footwear 8.6%, transportation 8.0%, energy and water 7.4%, recreation 6.7%, household and personal goods 6.6%.

Foreign trade

Balance of trade (current prices)

	1994	1995	1996	1997	1998	1999
SR '000,000	–786.7	–855.7	–1,188.7	–1,131.4	–1,140.1	–1,544.3
% of total	60.6%	62.8%	46.1%	49.4%	49.6%	50.0%

Imports (1999): SR 2,316,200,000 (manufactured goods 30.8%, machinery and transport equipment 29.5%, food, beverages, and tobacco 22.2%, mineral fuels [including petroleum], lubricants, and related materials 9.9%, chemicals 6.0%). *Major import sources* (1997): South Africa 14.5%; United Kingdom 11.8%; Bahrain 11.2%; Singapore 11.2%; France 9.6%; Italy 4.7%; Japan 3.1%; India 2.6%; The Netherlands 2.5%.
Exports (1999): SR 771,900,000[5] (canned tuna 70.2%, petroleum products 21.9%[6], other fish, including dried shark fins 1.9%, frozen prawns 1.0%, cinnamon bark 0.3%). *Major export destinations* (1997)[7]: France 29.2%; Germany 27.3%; Italy 24.0%; Japan 7.0%; South Africa 4.0%; United Kingdom 3.7%.

Transport and communications

Transport. Railroads: none. Roads (1999): total length 263 mi, 424 km (paved 87%). Vehicles (1997): passenger cars 7,120; trucks and buses 1,980. Merchant marine (1992): vessels (100 gross tons and over) 9; total deadweight tonnage 3,337. Air transport (1999): passenger arrivals 155,000, passenger departures 156,000; metric ton cargo unloaded 4,526, metric ton cargo loaded 1,960; airports (1998) with scheduled flights 2.

Communications

Medium	date	unit	number	units per 1,000 persons
Daily newspapers	1996	circulation	3,000	46
Radio	1997	receivers	42,000	560
Television	1998	receivers	12,000	149
Telephones	1999	main lines	16,635	207
Cellular telephones	1999	subscribers	16,316	203
Internet	1998	users	2,000	25

Education and health

Educational attainment (1994). Percentage of population age 12 and over having: primary education 37.0%; some secondary 16.8%; complete secondary 19.0%; vocational 15.2%; postsecondary 3.0%; not stated 9.0%. *Literacy* (1994): total population age 12 and over literate 49,136 (87.5%); males literate 24,086 (86.3%); females literate 25,050 (88.6%).

Education (2000)

	schools	teachers	students	student/ teacher ratio
Primary (age 6–15)	25	708	10,026	14.2
Secondary (age 16–18)	13	535	7,742	14.5
Voc., teacher tr.	1[8]	134	1,818	13.6

Health (1999): physicians 104 (1 per 773 persons); hospital beds 445 (1 per 181 persons); infant mortality rate per 1,000 live births (1999) 18.2.
Food (1998): daily per capita caloric intake 2,462 (vegetable products 81%, animal products 19%); 106% of FAO recommended minimum requirement.

Military

Total active duty personnel (1999): 450[9]. *Military expenditure as percentage of GNP* (1997): 3.8% (world 2.6%); per capita expenditure U.S.$194.

[1]Creole, English, and French are all national languages per 1993 constitution. [2]Excludes unemployed, self-employed, and domestic workers. [3]Mining, manufacturing includes Public utilities. [4]Import duties less bank service charges. [5]Includes SR 194,200,000 of reexports. [6]Items reexported. [7]Domestic exports only. [8]1994. [9]All services form part of the army.

Internet resources for further information:
- **Seychelles in Figures http://www.seychelles.net/hendrick**

Sierra Leone

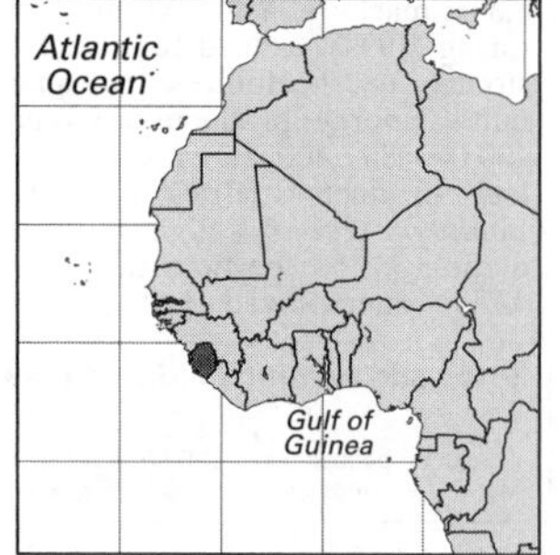

Official name: Republic of Sierra Leone.
Form of government: republic with one legislative body (Parliament [80[1]])[2].
Head of state and government: President.
Capital: Freetown.
Official language: English.
Official religion: none.
Monetary unit: 1 leone (Le) = 100 cents; valuation (Oct. 6, 2000) 1 U.S.$ = Le 2,039; 1 £ = Le 2,950.

Area and population

Provinces / Districts	Capitals	area sq mi	area sq km	population 1985 census[3]
Eastern Province	Kenema	6,005	15,553	960,551
Kailahun	Kailahun	1,490	3,859	233,839
Kenema	Kenema	2,337	6,053	337,055
Kono	Sefadu	2,178	5,641	389,657
Northern Province	Makeni	13,875	35,936	1,259,641
Bombali	Makeni	3,083	7,985	317,729
Kambia	Kambia	1,200	3,108	186,231
Koinaduga	Kabala	4,680	12,121	183,286
Port Loko	Port Loko	2,208	5,719	329,344
Tonkolili	Magburaka	2,704	7,003	243,051
Southern Province	Bo	7,604	19,694	741,377
Bo	Bo	2,015	5,219	268,671
Bonthe (incl. Sherbro)	Bonthe	1,339	3,468	105,007
Moyamba	Moyamba	2,665	6,902	250,514
Pujehun	Pujehun	1,585	4,105	117,185
Western Area[4]	Freetown	215	557	554,243
TOTAL		27,699	71,740	3,515,812

Demography

Population (2000): 5,233,000[5].
Density (2000): persons per sq mi 188.9, persons per sq km 72.9.
Urban-rural (1999): urban 36.0%; rural 64.0%.
Sex distribution (1999): male 48.47%; female 51.53%.
Age breakdown (1999): under 15, 44.7%; 15–29, 26.2%; 30–44, 14.6%; 45–59, 9.3%; 60–74, 4.4%; 75 and over, 0.8%.
Population projection: (2010) 6,930,000; (2020) 8,820,000.
Doubling time: 27 years.
Ethnic composition (1983): Mende 34.6%; Temne 31.7%; Limba 8.4%; Kono 5.2%; Bullom-Sherbro 3.7%; Fulani 3.7%; Kuranko 3.5%; Yalunka 3.5%; Kissi 2.3%; other 3.4%.
Religious affiliation (1993): Muslim 60.0%; traditional 30.0%; Christian 10.0%.
Major cities (1985): Freetown 469,776; Koidu–New Sembehun 80,000; Bo 26,000; Kenema 13,000; Makeni 12,000.

Vital statistics

Birth rate per 1,000 population (1999): 46.2 (world avg. 22.1).
Death rate per 1,000 population (1999): 19.9 (world avg. 8.9).
Natural increase rate per 1,000 population (1999): 26.3 (world avg. 13.2).
Total fertility rate (avg. births per childbearing woman; 1999): 6.1.
Life expectancy at birth (1999): male 42.1 years; female 47.8 years.
Major causes of death per 100,000 population: n.a.; however, the major diseases are malaria, tuberculosis, leprosy, measles, tetanus, and diarrhea.

National economy

Budget (1996–97). Revenue: Le 85,708,000,000 (customs duties 47.4%; excise taxes 25.4%; corporate income tax 9.5%; personal income tax 7.3%). Expenditures: Le 143,293,000,000 (recurrent expenditures 75.6%, of which transfers 24.4%, wages and salaries 19.8%, goods and services 18.9%, debt service 12.5%; capital expenditures 24.4%).
Gross national product (1998): U.S.$703,000,000 (U.S.$140 per capita).

Structure of gross domestic product and labour force

	1994–95 in value Le '000,000	1994–95 % of total value	1997 labour force	1997 % of labour force
Agriculture	275,327.5	38.8	1,052,000	63.8
Mining	119,229.2	16.8	297,000	18.0
Manufacturing	61,475.3	8.6		
Construction	15,788.2	2.2		
Public utilities	2,816.8	0.4	300,000	18.2
Transp. and commun.	61,267.5	8.6		
Trade[6]	98,270.1	13.8		
Finance	14,732.2	2.1		
Pub. admin., defense	19,844.9	2.8		
Services	12,308.9	1.7		
Other	29,329.7[7]	4.2[7]		
TOTAL	710,389.3[8]	100.0	1,649,000	100.0

Production (metric tons except as noted). Agriculture, forestry, fishing (1999): rice 247,235, cassava 239,597, oil palm fruit 163,000, pulses 40,000, peanuts (groundnuts) 29,010, plantains 26,000, tomatoes 25,000, sugarcane 21,000, sweet potatoes 20,000, coffee 17,350, sorghum 17,200, cacao beans 10,920, mangoes 6,500, millet 4,725; livestock (number of live animals) 400,000 cattle, 350,000 sheep, 190,000 goats, 52,000 pigs; roundwood (1998) 3,315,000 cu m; fish catch (1998) 52,700. Mining and quarrying (1997)[9]: bauxite (1994) 735,000; rutile and ilmenite (titanium ores) (1994) 184,000; diamonds 104,000 carats; gold 322 troy oz. Manufacturing (value added in Le '000,000; 1993): food 36,117; chemicals 10,560; earthenware 1,844; printing and publishing 1,171; metal products 1,073; furniture 647. Construction (value added in Le; 1994–95): 15,788,200,000. Energy production (consumption): electricity (kW-hr; 1996) 241,000,000 (241,000,000); crude petroleum (barrels; 1996) none (1,657,000); petroleum products (metric tons; 1996) 173,000 (128,000).
Household income and expenditure. Average household size (1998) 6.3; average annual income per household (1984): U.S.$320; sources of income (1984): self-employment 61.6%, wages and salaries 27.9%, other 10.5%; expenditure (1989): food 66.2%, clothing 9.9%, housing 5.8%, transportation 4.4%, household goods 4.0%, recreation and education 3.8%, health 3.5%.
Public debt (external, outstanding; 1998): U.S.$944,000,000.
Population economically active (1996): total 1,610,000; activity rate of total population 34.8% (participation rates [1991]: ages 10–64, 53.3%; female 32.4%; unemployed [registered; 1992] 10.6%).

Price index (1995 = 100)

	1993	1994	1995	1996	1997	1998	1999
Consumer price index	63.9	79.4	100.0	123.1	141.5	191.8	257.2

Tourism (1996): receipts U.S.$10,000,000; expenditures U.S.$2,000,000.
Land use (1994): forest 28.5%; pasture 30.7%; agriculture 7.5%; other 33.3%.

Foreign trade[10]

Balance of trade (current prices)

	1994	1995	1996	1997	1998	1999
Le '000,000	–20,742	–84,480	–150,622	–64,598	–137,744	–142,509
% of total	13.3%	70.1%	63.6%	67.7%	86.8%	86.3%

Imports (1999): Le 153,856,000,000 (1995–96; food and live animals 51.6%; fuels and lubricants 11.6%; chemicals 10.2%; machinery and transport equipment 8.9%; beverages and tobacco 2.7%; crude minerals 2.5%). *Major import sources* (1998): U.K. 20.0%; U.S. 13.0%; Belgium 7.5%; Italy 6.5%; Nigeria 5.5%; South Africa 4.5%.
Exports (1999): Le 11,347,000,000 (1995–96; mineral exports 56.4%, of which diamonds 50.6%, rutile [titanium ore] 5.7%; cocoa 5.0%; coffee 3.7%; reexports 4.8%). *Major export destinations* (1999): Belgium 40.8%; United States 7.5%; Spain 6.1%; U.K. 4.1%.

Transport and communications

Transport. Railroads (1995): length 52 mi, 84 km. Roads (1996): total length 7,270 mi, 11,700 km (paved 11%). Vehicles (1996): passenger cars 17,640; trucks and buses 10,890. Air transport (1996): passenger-mi 15,000,000, passenger-km 24,000,000; short ton-mi cargo 1,400,000, metric ton-km cargo 2,000,000; airports (1998) with scheduled flights 1.

Communications

Medium	date	unit	number	units per 1,000 persons
Daily newspapers	1996	circulation	20,000	4.7
Radio	1997	receivers	1,121,000	253
Television	1998	receivers	60,000	13
Telephones	1998	main lines	17,000	3.8
Internet	1998	users	5,000	1.1

Education and health

Educational attainment (1985). Percentage of population age 5 and over having: no formal schooling 64.1%; primary education 18.7%; secondary 9.7%; higher 1.5%. *Literacy* (1995): total population age 15 and over literate 791,000 (31.4%); males literate 555,000 (45.4%); females 236,000 (18.2%).

Education (1992–93)

	schools	teachers	students	student/teacher ratio
Primary (age 5–11)	1,643	10,595	267,425	25.2
Secondary (age 12–18)	167	4,313	70,900	16.4
Voc., teacher tr.	44	709	7,756	10.9
Higher[11]	2	257	2,571	10.0

Health: physicians (1996) 339 (1 per 13,696 persons); hospital beds (1988) 4,025 (1 per 980 persons); infant mortality rate per 1,000 live births (1999) 150.8.
Food (1998): daily per capita caloric intake 2,045 (vegetable products 97%, animal products 3%); 89% of FAO recommended minimum requirement.

Military

Total active duty personnel (1999): 3,000 (army *c.* 93%, navy *c.* 7%, air force, none)[12]. *Military expenditure as percentage of GNP* (1997): 5.9% (world 2.6%); per capita expenditure U.S.$10.

[1]Includes 12 paramount chiefs elected to represent each of the provincial districts. [2]Peace accord signed in July 1999 ending nine years of civil war was inactive in December 2000. [3]Preliminary figures exclude adjustment for underenumeration; adjusted total is 3,760,000. [4]Not officially a province; the administration of the Western Area is split among Greater Freetown (the city and its suburbs) and other administrative bodies. [5]Includes about 400,000 Sierra Leonean refugees in neighbouring countries (mostly Guinea). [6]Includes hotels. [7]Import duties less imputed bank service charges. [8]Detail does not add to total given because of rounding. [9]All mining and quarrying production was suspended or greatly reduced after 1994 because of the civil war. [10]Import c.i.f.; exports f.o.b. [11]1990–91. [12]UN troops authorized from October 1999 numbered 12,500 in October 2000; 2,000 British troops arrived in Sierra Leone in May 2000 and remained there in December 2000.

Internet resources for further information:
- **Sierra Leone http://www.Sierra-Leone.org**
- **The Commonwealth OnLine: Sierra Leone http://www.tcol.co.uk/sierra/index.htm**

Singapore

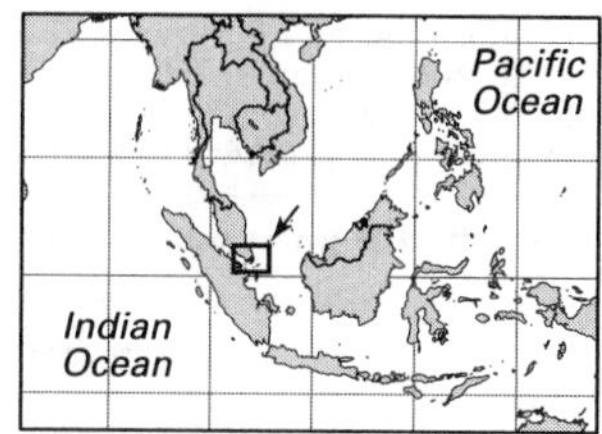

Official name: Hsin-chia-p'o Kung-ho-kuo (Mandarin Chinese); Republik Singapura (Malay); Singapore Kudiyarasu (Tamil); Republic of Singapore (English).
Form of government: unitary multiparty republic with one legislative house (Parliament [93[1]]).
Chief of state: President.
Head of state government: Prime Minister.
Capital: Singapore.
Official languages: Chinese; Malay; Tamil; English.
Official religion: none.
Monetary unit: 1 Singapore dollar (S$) = 100 cents; valuation (Oct. 6, 2000) 1 U.S.$ = S$1.75; 1 £ = S$2.53.

Population (1990 census)

Census division[2]	population	Census division[2]	population	Census division[2]	population
Alexandra	27,245	Henderson	18,445	Nee Soon East	58,651
Aljunied	51,669	Hong Kah Central	48,379	Nee Soon South	49,771
Ang Mo Kio	35,814	Hong Kah North	33,265	Pasir Panjang	35,824
Ayer Rajah	44,977	Hong Kah South	37,900	Paya Lebar	41,903
Bedok	22,032	Hougang	36,774	Potong Pasir	32,992
Boon Lay	39,249	Jalan Besar	28,298	Punggol	68,270
Boon Teck	22,652	Jalan Kayu	34,907	Queenstown	19,676
Braddell Heights	47,738	Joo Chiat	35,777	Radin Mas	35,730
Brickworks	10,593	Jurong	74,696	Sembawang	28,039
Bukit Batok	44,918	Kaki Bukit	32,782	Serangoon Gardens	44,702
Bukit Gombak	46,149	Kallang	34,178	Siglap	36,022
Bukit Merah	18,666	Kampong Chai Chee	33,928	Tampines East	41,474
Bukit Panjang	95,827	Kampong Glam	29,481	Tampines North	73,634
Bukit Timah	47,056	Kampong Kembangan	33,510	Tampines West	38,833
Buona Vista	23,873	Kampong Ubi	40,682	Tanah Merah	32,314
Cairnhill	48,445	Kebun Baru	36,878	Tanglin	43,544
Changi	50,003	Kim Keat	28,538	Tanjong Paper	29,217
Changkat	41,995	Kim Seng	23,683	Teck Ghee	26,622
Cheng San	27,821	Kolam Ayer	22,420	Telok Blangah	29,157
Chong Boon	32,174	Kreta Ayer	29,631	Thomson	71,345
Chong Pang	38,613	Kuo Chuan	26,968	Tiong Bahru	27,468
Chua Chu Kang	43,465	Leng Kee	28,886	Toa Payoh	22,811
Clementi	37,635	Macpherson	23,764	Ulu Pandan	42,923
Eunos	52,976	Marine Parade	31,003	West Coast	46,052
Fengshan	27,285	Moulmein	33,872	Whampoa	18,285
Geylang Serai	36,800	Mountbatten	23,891	Yio Chu Kang	28,589
Geyang West	34,560	Nee Soon Central	47,032	Yuhua	32,733
				TOTAL	3,016,379

Demography

Area: 254.8 sq mi, 659.9 sq km.
Population (2000)[3]: 3,278,000.
Density (2000): persons per sq mi 12,865, persons per sq km 4,967.
Urban-rural: urban 100.0%.
Sex distribution (2000): male 49.96%; female 50.04%.
Age breakdown (2000): under 15, 21.5%; 15–34, 30.1%; 35–54, 33.9%; 55–74, 12.1%; 75 and over, 2.4%.
Population projection: (2010) 3,949,000; (2020) 4,758,000.
Doubling time: 82 years.
Ethnic composition (2000): Chinese 76.8%; Malay 13.9%; Indian 7.9%.
Religious affiliation (1995)[4]: Buddhist 31.9%; Taoist 22.0%; Muslim 14.9%; Christian 12.9%; Hindu 3.3%; traditional beliefs 0.5%; nonreligious 14.5%.

Vital statistics

Birth rate per 1,000 population (1999): 13.4 (world avg. 22.1).
Death rate per 1,000 population (1999): 4.8 (world avg. 8.9).
Natural increase rate per 1,000 population (1999): 8.6 (world avg. 13.2).
Total fertility rate (avg. births per childbearing woman; 1998): 1.5.
Marriage rate per 1,000 population (1998): 6.0.
Divorce rate per 1,000 population (1998): 7.7[5].
Life expectancy at birth (2000): male 75.0 years; female 80.0 years.
Major causes of death per 100,000 population (1995): diseases of the circulatory system 160.3; malignant neoplasms (cancers) 112.4; diseases of the respiratory system 84.0; accidents, poisoning, and violence 32.1.

National economy

Budget (1998). Revenue: S$28,213,000,000 (income tax 34.7%, nontax revenue 21.5%, assets taxes 6.6%, goods and services tax 6.0%, customs and excise duties 5.7%). Expenditures: S$24,793,000,000 (security 34.3%, education 19.0%, communications 8.3%, trade and industry 7.7%, housing 6.6%).
Production (metric tons except as noted). Agriculture, forestry, fishing (1998): vegetables and fruits 4,811; livestock (number of live animals) 2,000,000 chickens; fish catch 7,730. Mining and quarrying (value of output in S$; 1994): granite 75,800,000. Manufacturing (value added in S$'000,000; 1996): electronic products 16,982.1; chemical products 3,326.5; machinery and equipment 2,623.3; transport equipment 2,216.1; fabricated metal products 2,121.1; petroleum products 2,038.3. Construction (starts; 1998): residential 4,919,000 sq m; nonresidential 2,403,000 sq m. Energy production (consumption): electricity (kW-hr; 1994) 20,676,000,000 (20,585,000,000); crude petroleum (barrels; 1994) none (408,800,000); petroleum products (metric tons; 1994) 47,760,000 (18,989,000).
Household income and expenditure. Average household size (1990) 4.2; income per household (1993) S$45,948 (U.S.$28,437); sources of income (1987–88): wages 81.2%, self-employment 16.8%, transfer payments and other 2.0%; expenditure (1992–93): food 30.0%, housing costs and furnishings 23.4%, transportation and communications 15.8%, recreation and education 9.0%, clothing and footwear 6.1%, health 2.8%, others 12.9%.
Gross national product (1998): U.S.$95,453,000,000 (U.S.$30,170 per capita).

Structure of gross domestic product and labour force

	1998		1996	
	in value S$'000,000[6]	% of total value[6]	labour force[7]	% of labour force[7]
Agriculture	173.7	0.1	3,700	0.2
Quarrying	16.2	...		
Manufacturing	28,397.7	23.5	406,300	23.2
Construction	11,040.0	9.1	115,000	6.6
Public utilities	2,170.9	1.8	7,200	0.4
Transp. and commun.	16,828.0	13.9	195,300	11.2
Trade	22,519.6	18.6	405,900	23.2
Finance	34,326.1	28.3	246,000	14.1
Services	13,060.2	10.8	367,700	21.0
Other	–7,420.9[8]	–6.1[8]	1,000[9]	0.1[9]
TOTAL	121,111.5	100.0	1,748,100	100.0

Population economically active (1998): total 1,931,800; activity rate of total population 50.0% (participation rates: ages 15 and over, 63.9%; [1995] female 38.7%; unemployed 3.2%).

Price and earnings indexes (1995 = 100)

	1992	1993	1994	1995	1996	1997	1998
Consumer price index	93.2	95.4	98.3	100.0	101.4	103.4	103.1
Monthly earnings index	81.3	86.4	94.0	100.0	105.8	111.8	114.9

Tourism (1998): receipts U.S.$5,162,000,000; expenditures U.S.$2,676,000,000.

Foreign trade[10]

Balance of trade (current prices)

	1991	1992	1993	1994	1995	1996
S$'000,000	–5,770	–7,490	–10,338	–216	+1,178	+1,631
% of total	2.7%	3.5%	4.1%	0.1%	0.4%	0.5%

Imports (1998): S$169,863,500,000 (office machines 13.2%, crude petroleum 5.0%, telecommunications apparatus 4.8%, electric power machinery 4.1%, scientific instruments 3.3%, petroleum products 3.0%, industrial machinery 2.6%). *Major import sources:* U.S. 18.4%; Japan 16.7%; Malaysia 15.5%; China 4.8%; Thailand 4.8%, Taiwan 3.8%; Germany 3.4%.
Exports (1998): S$183,763,300,000 (office machines 27.9%, telecommunications apparatus 6.1%, petroleum products 5.7%, optical instruments 2.5%, electrical circuit apparatus 2.1%, industrial machinery 1.7%, clothing 1.3%). *Major export destinations:* U.S. 19.9%; Malaysia 15.2%; Hong Kong 8.4%; Japan 6.6%; Taiwan 4.3%; Thailand 3.8%; China 3.7%.

Transport and communications

Transport. Railroads (1997): length 83 km. Roads (1997): total length 3,017 km (paved 97%). Vehicles (1998): passenger cars 395,226; trucks and buses 152,480. Air transport (1997): passenger-km 55,096,000,000; metric ton-km cargo 4,760,000,000; airports (1999) 1.

Communications

Medium	date	unit	number	units per 1,000 persons
Daily newspapers	1996	circulation	1,095,000	324
Radio	1997	receivers	2,550,000	744
Television	1997	receivers	1,330,000	388
Telephones	1998	main lines	1,778,000	562
Cellular telephones	1998	subscribers	1,095,300	346
Personal computers	1998	units	1,450,000	458
Internet	1998	users	750,000	237

Education and health

Educational attainment (1995). Percentage of population age 25 and over having: no schooling 14.3%; primary education 27.7%; secondary 50.4%; postsecondary 7.6%. *Literacy* (1990): total population age 10 and over literate 89.1%; males literate 95.1%; females literate 83.0%.

Education (1996)

	schools	teachers	students	student/teacher ratio
Primary (age 6–11)	198	10,618	269,668	25.4
Secondary (age 12–18)	174	10,354	207,719	20.1
Voc., teacher tr.	11	1,212	8,233	6.8
Higher	7	6,689	92,140	13.8

Health (1998): physicians 5,148 (1 per 615 persons); hospital beds 11,389 (1 per 278 persons); infant mortality rate per 1,000 live births (2000) 5.0.
Food (1988–90): daily per capita caloric intake 3,121 (vegetable products 76%, animal products 24%); 136% of FAO recommended minimum requirement.

Military

Total active duty personnel (1998): 72,500 (army 69.0%, navy 12.4%, air force 18.6%). *Military expenditure as percentage of GNP* (1997): 4.0% (world [1995] 2.8%); per capita expenditure U.S.$1,321.

[1]Includes 10 nonelective seats. [2]The census divisions have no administrative function. [3]De jure population. [4]De jure population aged 10 years and over. [5]Includes annulments. [6]At prices of 1990. [7]Employed only. [8]Imputed bank service charges. [9]Activities not adequately defined. [10]Import figures are f.o.b. in balance of trade.

Internet resources for further information:
- **Statistics Singapore http://www.singstat.gov.sg**

Slovakia

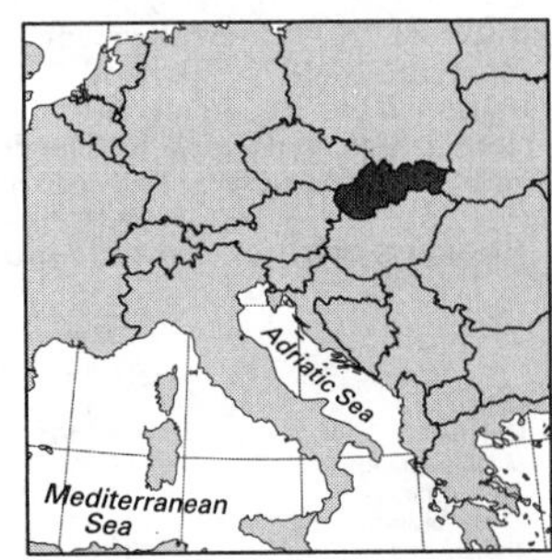

Official name: Slovenská Republika (Slovak Republic).
Form of government: unitary multiparty republic with one legislative house (National Council [150]).
Chief of state: President.
Head of government: Prime Minister.
Capital: Bratislava.
Official language: Slovak.
Official religion: none.
Monetary unit: 1 Slovak koruna (Sk) = 100 halura; valuation (Oct. 6, 2000) 1 U.S.$ = Sk 50.58; 1 £ = Sk 73.01.

Area and population

Regions[1]	Capitals	area sq mi	area sq km	population 1998[2] estimate
Banská Bystrica	Banská Bystrica	3,651	9,455	663,845
Bratislava	Bratislava	793	2,053	618,673
Košice	Košice	2,607	6,753	761,116
Nitra	Nitra	2,449	6,343	717,241
Prešov	Prešov	3,472	8,993	777,301
Trenčín	Trenčín	1,738	4,501	610,349
Trnava	Trnava	1,602	4,148	549,621
Žilina	Žilina	2,621	6,788	689,504
TOTAL		18,933	49,035[3]	5,387,650

Demography

Population (2000): 5,403,000.
Density (2000): persons per sq mi 285.4, persons per sq km 110.2.
Urban-rural (1998): urban 60.2%; rural 39.8%.
Sex distribution (1999): male 48.62%; female 51.38%.
Age breakdown (1999): under 15, 20.1%; 15–29, 24.8%; 30–44, 21.9%; 45–59, 17.8%; 60–74, 11.1%; 75 and over, 4.3%.
Population projection: (2010) 5,480,000; (2020) 5,559,000.
Doubling time: not applicable; population growth is negligible.
Ethnic composition (1998): Slovak 85.7%; Hungarian 10.6%; Gypsy 1.6%; Czech 1.1%; Ruthenian 0.3%; Ukrainian 0.3%; German 0.1%; other 0.3%.
Religious affiliation (1991): Roman Catholic 60.3%; nonreligious and atheist 9.7%; Protestant 7.9%, of which Slovak Evangelical 6.2%, Reformed Christian 1.6%; Greek Catholic 3.4%; Eastern Orthodox 0.7%; other 18.0%.
Major cities (1998[2]): Bratislava 451,395; Košice 242,170; Prešov 93,461.

Vital statistics

Birth rate per 1,000 population (1999): 10.4 (world avg. 22.1); (1996) legitimate 86.0%; illegitimate 14.0%.
Death rate per 1,000 population (1999): 9.7 (world avg. 8.9).
Natural increase rate per 1,000 population (1999): 0.7 (world avg. 13.2).
Total fertility rate (avg. births per childbearing woman; 1999): 1.3.
Marriage rate per 1,000 population (1999): 5.1.
Divorce rate per 1,000 population (1999): 1.8.
Life expectancy at birth (1999): male 69.4 years; female 77.6 years.
Major causes of death per 100,000 population (1997): diseases of the circulatory system 529; malignant neoplasms (cancers) 209; diseases of the respiratory system 70; diseases of the digestive system 41.

National economy

Budget (1998). Revenue: Sk 304,100,000,000 (tax revenue 87.5%, of which social security contribution 33.0%, value-added tax 18.2%, income tax 14.0%; nontax revenue 12.5%). Expenditures: Sk 340,200,000,000 (current expenditure 86.1%, of which social welfare 31.6%, wages 16.6%, health 13.1%, debt service 5.1%; investment 13.9%).
Public debt (external, outstanding; 1997): U.S.$4,658,000,000.
Production (metric tons except as noted). Agriculture, forestry, fishing (1999): cereals 2,874,700 (of which wheat 1,206,700, corn [maize] 779,286, barley 760,500, rye 74,200); livestock (number of live animals) 1,592,599 pigs, 704,792 cattle, 326,199 sheep; roundwood (1998) 5,532,000 cu m; fish catch (1998) 2,531. Mining and quarrying (1997): iron ore 1,056,000; copper ore 670,000. Manufacturing (1997): crude steel 3,484,000; pig iron 3,172,000; cement 3,136,000; plastic and resins 405,270; flour 328,000; nitrogenous fertilizers 226,102; cotton yarn 9,384; beer 5,577,000 hectolitres; refrigerators and freezers 30,092 units. Construction (1997): residential 281,298 dwellings. Energy production (consumption): electricity (kW-hr; 1998) 25,465,000,000 (21,020,000,000); coal (metric tons; 1996) 3,829,000 (7,142,000); crude petroleum (barrels; 1997) 462,800 (38,497,000); petroleum products (metric tons; 1996) 3,930,000 (2,134,000); natural gas (cu m; 1997) 284,000,000 (5,743,400,000).
Population economically active (1999): total 2,662,000; activity rate of total population 47.6% (participation rates [1997]: ages 15–64, 76.8%; female 67.3%; unemployed [1999] 17.1%).

Price and earnings indexes (1995 = 100)

	1993	1994	1995	1996	1997	1998	1999
Consumer price index	80.2	91.0	100.0	105.8	112.3	119.8	132.5
Annual earnings index	74.8	87.5	100.0	110.2	110.2	122.4	146.9

Household income and expenditure. Average household size (1997) 3.2; income per household (1997) Sk 74,052 (U.S.$2,194); sources of income (1997): wages and salaries 54.4%, transfer payments 20.4%, other 25.2%; expenditure (1997): food and beverages 22.3%, deposits 12.4%, clothing and footwear 7.9%, transportation 7.3%, social insurance 7.0%, housing 6.8%, income tax 5.7%, recreation 5.6%, household durable goods 4.4%, other 20.6%.
Gross national product (1998): U.S.$19,941,000,000 (U.S.$3,700 per capita).

Structure of gross domestic product and labour force

	1999 in value Sk '000,000	1999 % of total value	1998 labour force	1998 % of labour force
Agriculture	33,200	4.3	183,253	8.9
Mining and manufacturing	185,600	23.8	553,877	26.9
Construction	31,300	4.0	154,427	7.5
Public utilities	30,000	3.8	55,594	2.7
Transp. and commun.	68,200	8.8	152,368	7.4
Trade	168,600	21.6	350,034	17.0
Finance	[4]	[4]	172,958	8.4
Pub. admin., defense	94,300	12.1	}	
Services	128,000[4]	16.4[4]	436,513	21.2
Other	40,000[5]	5.1[5]	}	
TOTAL	779,300[3]	100.0[3]	2,059,024[6]	100.0[6]

Land use (1994): forested 40.6%; meadows and pastures 17.0%; agricultural and under permanent cultivation 32.9%; other 9.5%.

Foreign trade

Balance of trade (current prices)

	1995	1996	1997	1998	1999
U.S.$'000,000	−228	−2,293	−2,081	−2,353	−1,104
% of total	1.3%	11.5%	9.7%	9.9%	5.1%

Imports (1999): U.S.$11,301,000,000 (1998; machinery and transport equipment 40.0%; semimanufactured products 18.1%; petroleum and petroleum products 10.9%; chemical products 10.7%; manufactured products 10.0%). *Major import sources:* Germany 26.2%; Czech Republic 16.7%; Italy 7.1%; Russian Federation 12.0%; Austria 4.8%; France 3.9%; Poland 2.8%.
Exports (1999): U.S.$10,197,000,000 (machinery and transport equipment 39.5%; manufactured goods 27.3%; fuels 15.3%; chemical products 7.9%; food, beverages, and tobacco 5.0%). *Major export destinations:* Germany 27.7%; Czech Republic 18.1%; Italy 8.8%; Austria 8.1%; Poland 5.3%; Hungary 4.5%.

Transport and communications

Transport. Railroads (1997): length 3,673 km; passenger-km 3,057,000,000; metric ton-km cargo 12,373,000,000. Roads (1997): total length 17,627 km (paved, n.a.). Vehicles (1997): passenger cars 1,135,914; trucks and buses 100,254. Merchant marine: n.a. Air transport (1997): passenger-km 231,396,000; metric ton-km cargo 729,000; airports (1998) with scheduled flights 2.

Communications

Medium	date	unit	number	units per 1,000 persons
Daily newspapers	1996	circulation	989,000	184
Television	1997	receivers	1,397,400	259
Telephones	1998	main lines	1,539,000	286
Cellular telephones	1998	subscribers	465,364	8.7
Internet	1998	users	500,000	93

Education and health

Educational attainment (1991). Percentage of adult population having: incomplete primary education 0.7%; primary and incomplete secondary 37.9%; complete secondary 50.9%; higher 9.5%; unknown 1.0%. *Literacy* (1997): total population age 15 and over literate 4,253,972 (100%); males literate 2,042,437 (100%); females literate 2,211,535 (100%).

Education (1997–98)

	schools	teachers	students	student/ teacher ratio
Primary (age 6–14)	2,482	39,535	645,941	16.3
Secondary (age 15–18)	198	5,849	80,116	13.7
Voc., teacher tr.	365	10,104	116,681	11.5
Higher	18	8,544	83,942	9.8

Health (1997): physicians 17,940 (1 per 300 persons); hospital beds 61,288 (1 per 88 persons); infant mortality rate per 1,000 live births (1999) 8.3.
Food (1998): daily per capita caloric intake 2,953 (vegetable products 72%, animal products 28%); 121% of FAO recommended minimum requirement.

Military

Total active duty personnel (1999): 44,880 (army 73.3%, air force 26.7%). *Military expenditure as percentage of GNP* (1997): 2.1% (world 2.6%); per capita expenditure U.S.$167.

[1]Based on administrative reorganization effective from July 1996. [2]January 1. [3]Detail does not add to total given because of rounding. [4]Services include finance. [5]Bank service charges and indirect taxes. [6]Excluding 407,000 unemployed and women on regular and additional maternity leave and including employees with a second job.

Internet resources for further information:
- **Statistical Office of the Slovak Republic http://www.statistics.sk**
- **Embassy of the Slovak Republic (Washington, D.C.) http://www.slovakemb.com**

Slovenia

Official name: Republika Slovenija (Republic of Slovenia).
Form of government: unitary multiparty republic with two legislative houses (National Council [40]; National Assembly [90]).
Head of state: President.
Head of government: Prime Minister.
Capital: Ljubljana.
Official language[1]: Slovene.
Official religion: none.
Monetary unit: 1 Slovene tolar (SIT; plural tolarji) = 100 stotin; valuation (Oct. 6, 2000) 1 U.S.$ = 241.6 tolarji; 1 £ = 348.70 tolarji.

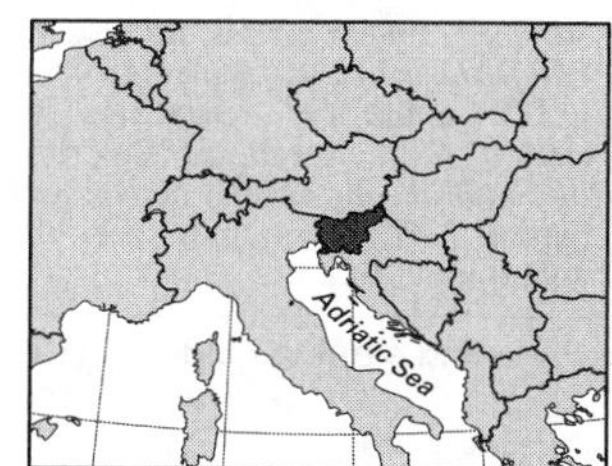

Area and population

Statistical regions[2]	Principal cities	area sq mi	area sq km	population 1998 estimate
Dolenjska	Novo mesto	653	1,690	105,926
Gorenjska	Kranj	825	2,137	195,580
Goriška	Nova Gorica	898	2,325	119,967
Koroška	Ravne na Koroškem	401	1,041	73,961
Notranjsko-kraška	Postojna	562	1,456	50,163
Obalno Kraško	Koper	403	1,044	102,565
Osrednjeslovenska	Ljubljana	1,367	3,540	517,022
Podravska	Maribor	838	2,170	319,617
Pomurska	Murska Sobota	516	1,337	125,441
Savinjska	Celje	920	2,384	255,541
Spodnjeposavska	Krško	342	885	70,187
Zasavska	Trbovlje	102	264	46,633
TOTAL		7,827	20,273	1,982,603

Demography

Population (2000): 1,963,000.
Density (2000): persons per sq mi 250.8, persons per sq km 96.8.
Urban-rural (1999): urban 50.3%; rural 49.7%.
Sex distribution (1998): male 48.78%; female 51.22%.
Age breakdown (1998): under 15, 17.0%; 15–29, 22.1%; 30–44, 23.8%; 45–59, 18.7%; 60–74, 13.8%; 75 and over, 4.6%.
Population projection: (2010) 2,005,000; (2020) 2,019,000.
Ethnic composition (1991): Slovene 87.8%; Croat 2.8%; Serb 2.4%; Bosnian Muslim 1.4%; Hungarian (Magyar) 0.4%; other 5.2%.
Religious affiliation (1995): Christian 86.2%, of which Roman Catholic 82.7%, Orthodox 2.0%, Protestant 1.3%; Muslim 1.0%; other 12.8%.
Major cities (1997): Ljubljana 274,377; Maribor 132,058; Kranj 51,983; Novo mesto 51,608; Celje 49,776.

Vital statistics

Birth rate per 1,000 population (1998): 9.0 (world avg. 22.1); (1997) legitimate 70.2%; illegitimate 29.8%.
Death rate per 1,000 population (1998): 9.6 (world avg. 8.9).
Natural increase rate per 1,000 population (1998): –0.6 (world avg. 13.2).
Total fertility rate (avg. births per childbearing woman; 1999): 1.3.
Marriage rate per 1,000 population (1997): 3.8.
Divorce rate per 1,000 population (1997): 1.0.
Life expectancy at birth (1999): male 70.7 years; female 78.7 years.
Major causes of death per 100,000 population (1997): circulatory diseases 381.1; cancers 243.9; accidents, homicides, and suicides 88.6; respiratory diseases 81.0; digestive diseases 55.2.

National economy

Budget (1998). Revenue: SIT 1,489,671,000,000 (taxes 54.5%, of which value-added taxes 29.7%, individual income taxes 17.4%; social security contributions 34.4%; nontax revenue 10.2%). Expenditures: SIT 1,507,944,000,000 (pension fund 28.6%; social services [excluding pension fund] 16.0%; health care 14.7%; interest payments 2.7%).
Public debt (external, outstanding; 1997): U.S.$2,067,000,000.
Production (metric tons except as noted). Agriculture, forestry, fishing (1998): potatoes 495,000, corn (maize) 355,000, sugar beets 289,000, wheat 191,000, grapes 128,000; livestock (number of live animals) 578,000 pigs, 446,000 cattle; roundwood (1998) 2,209,000 cu m; fish catch (1997) 2,345. Mining and quarrying (1997): ferrosilicon 10,000; kaolin 10,000. Manufacturing (value added in U.S.$'000,000; 1995): food products 762; electrical machinery 534; iron and steel 509; industrial chemicals 438; paper and paper products 406; furniture 323; nonelectrical machinery 322. Energy production (consumption): electricity (kW-hr; 1997) 12,349,000,000 (9,971,000,000); coal (metric tons; 1997) 4,953,000 (5,456,000); crude petroleum (barrels; 1997) 10,000 ([1995] 2,917,000); petroleum products (metric tons; 1995) 488,000 (2,256,000); natural gas (cu m; 1995) 16,709,000 (800,279,000).
Land use (1994): forest 53.2%; pasture 24.8%; agricultural 11.6%; other 10.4%.
Household income and expenditure. Average household size (1994) 3.1; income per household (1996) SIT 2,105,727 (U.S.$15,556); sources of income (1996): wages 53.4%, transfers 23.8%, self-employment 10.0%, other 12.8%; expenditure (1996): food 25.7%, transportation 18.3%, household furnishings and operation 11.2%, clothing and footwear 8.5%, recreation 6.0%, energy 6.0%, housing 4.6%.
Gross national product (1998): U.S.$19,385,000,000 (U.S.$9,780 per capita).

Structure of gross domestic product and labour force

	1997 in value SIT '000,000	% of total value	labour force	% of labour force
Agriculture, forestry	108,184	3.7	108,000	11.2
Mining	33,908	1.2	7,000	0.7
Manufacturing	706,266	24.3	290,000	30.1
Construction	143,158	4.9	55,000	5.7
Public utilities	73,492	2.5	13,000	1.3
Transp. and commun.	204,827	7.0	51,000	5.3
Trade, restaurants	371,607	12.8	145,000	15.0
Finance, real estate	400,488	13.8	61,000	6.3
Pub. admin., defense	149,612	5.1	36,000	3.7
Services	369,519	12.7	130,000	13.5
Other	346,214[3]	11.9[3]	69,000[4]	7.2[4]
TOTAL	2,907,277[5]	100.0[5]	967,000[5]	100.0

Population economically active (1997): total 967,000; activity rate 48.6% (participation rates: ages 15–64, 67.9%; female 46.4%; unemployed [May 1998–April 1999] 7.7%).

Price and earnings indexes (1995 = 100)

	1994	1995	1996	1997	1998	1999	2000[6]
Consumer price index	88.8	100.0	109.7	119.7	129.9	138.5	150.7
Monthly earnings index	84.3	100.0	114.8	127.9	140.1	153.2	165.9

Tourism (1998): receipts U.S.$1,117,000,000; expenditures U.S.$575,000,000.

Foreign trade[7]

Balance of trade (current prices)

	1994	1995	1996	1997	1998	1999
U.S.$'000,000	–476	–1,176	–1,111	–997	–1,062	–1,348
% of total	3.4%	6.6%	6.3%	5.6%	5.5%	7.3%

Imports (1998): U.S.$10,110,000,000 (machinery and transport equipment 36.4%, chemicals and chemical products 10.6%, food 5.7%, mineral fuels 5.6%). *Major import sources:* Germany 20.7%; Italy 16.8%; France 12.4%; Austria 7.9%; Croatia 4.3%.
Exports (1998): U.S.$9,048,000,000 (machinery and transport equipment 36.7%, chemicals and chemical products 10.4%, food 2.6%, mineral fuels 1.9%). *Major export destinations:* Germany 28.4%; Italy 13.9%; Croatia 9.0%; France 8.3%; Austria 6.9%.

Transport and communications

Transport. Railroads (1997): length 746 mi, 1,201 km; passenger-km 616,-000,000; metric ton-km cargo 2,852,000,000. Roads (1997): total length 9,158 mi, 14,851 km (paved 82%). Vehicles (1997): passenger cars 764,789; trucks and buses 59,450. Air transport (1997): passenger-mi 421,000,000, passenger-km 677,000,000; short ton-mi cargo 2,447,000, metric ton-km cargo 3,572,000; airports (1996) 1.

Communications

Medium	date	unit	number	units per 1,000 persons
Daily newspapers	1996	circulation	397,000	199
Radio	1997	receivers	630,000	317
Television	1997	receivers	700,000	352
Telephones	1998	main lines	757,000	382
Cellular telephones	1998	subscribers	161,606	82
Personal computers	1998	units	500,000	252
Internet	1998	users	200,000	101

Education and health

Educational attainment (1991). Percentage of population age 25 and over having: no formal schooling 0.7%; incomplete and complete primary education 45.1%; incomplete and complete secondary 42.4%; higher 10.4%; unknown 1.4%. *Literacy* (1991): virtually 100%.

Education (1996–97)

	schools	teachers	students	student/ teacher ratio
Primary (age 7–14)	824	15,443	200,437	13.0
Secondary (age 15–18)	223	10,809	115,570	10.7
Higher	...	3,846	50,667	13.2

Health (1998): physicians 4,520 (1 per 439 persons); hospital beds (1997) 11,233 (1 per 177 persons); infant mortality rate per 1,000 live births 5.2.

Military

Total active duty personnel (1998): 9,550 (army 100%). *Military expenditure as percentage of GNP* (1997): 5.2% (world 2.6%); per capita expenditure U.S.$614.

[1]Hungarian and Italian are official in autochthonous Hungarian and Italian communities. [2]Actual first-order administration is based on 147 municipalities. [3]Corrections less imputed bank service charges. [4]Unemployed. [5]Detail does not add to total given because of rounding. [6]May. [7]Imports c.i.f.; exports f.o.b.

Internet resources for further information:

- **Statistical Office of the Republic of Slovenia http://www.sigov.si/zrs/eng/index.html**
- **Bank of Slovenia http://www.bsi.si**

Solomon Islands

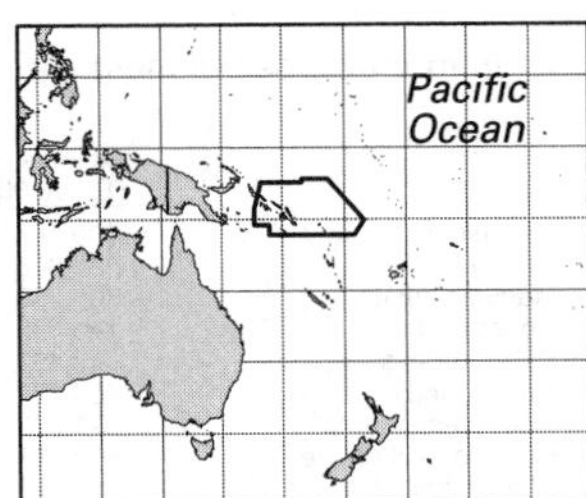

Official name: Solomon Islands.
Form of government: constitutional monarchy with one legislative house (National Parliament [50]).
Chief of state: British Monarch represented by Governor-General.
Head of government: Prime Minister.
Capital: Honiara.
Official language: English.
Official religion: none.
Monetary unit: 1 Solomon Islands dollar (SI$) = 100 cents; valuation (Oct. 6, 2000) 1 U.S.$ = SI$5.16; 1 £ = SI$7.46.

Area and population

Provinces	Capitals	area sq mi	area sq km	population 1997 estimate
Central Islands	Tulagi	237	615	30,071[1]
Choiseul	Taro	1,481	3,837	[2]
Guadalcanal	Honiara	2,060	5,336	61,243
Isabel	Buala	1,597	4,136	22,653
Makira	Kira Kira	1,231	3,188	29,110
Malaita	Auki	1,631	4,225	105,882
Rennell and Bellona	Tigoa	259	671	[1]
Temotu	Santa Cruz	334	865	21,159
Western	Gizo	2,114	5,475	95,193[2]
Capital Territory				
Honiara	—	8	22	45,610
TOTAL		10,954[3]	28,370	410,921

Demography

Population (2000): 466,000.
Density (2000): persons per sq mi 42.5, persons per sq km 16.4.
Urban-rural (1999): urban 19.0%; rural 81.0%.
Sex distribution (1996): male 51.65%; female 48.35%.
Age breakdown (1996): under 15, 43.7%; 15–29, 28.7%; 30–44, 15.2%; 45–59, 8.1%; 60–74, 3.6%; 75 and over, 0.7%.
Population projection: (2010) 610,000; (2020) 748,000.
Doubling time: 23 years.
Ethnic composition (1986): Melanesian 94.2%; Polynesian 3.7%; other Pacific Islander 1.4%; European 0.4%; Asian 0.2%; other 0.1%.
Religious affiliation (1986): Christian 96.6%, of which Protestant 75.7% (including Church of Melanesia [Anglican] 33.9%), Roman Catholic 19.2%; traditional beliefs 2.1%; other 1.3%.
Major cities (1986)[4]: Honiara 43,643[5]; Gizo 3,727; Auki 3,262; Kira Kira 2,585; Buala 1,913.

Vital statistics

Birth rate per 1,000 population (1999): 34.6 (world avg. 22.1).
Death rate per 1,000 population (1999): 3.9 (world avg. 8.9).
Natural increase rate per 1,000 population (1999): 30.7 (world avg. 13.2).
Total fertility rate (avg. births per childbearing woman; 1999): 4.7.
Marriage rate per 1,000 population: n.a.
Divorce rate per 1,000 population: n.a.
Life expectancy at birth (1999): male 70.0 years; female 74.0 years.
Major causes of death per 100,000 population (1990): respiratory diseases 22.4; diarrheal diseases 13.6; malaria 10.0.

National economy

Budget (1998). Revenue: SI$557,800,000 (foreign grants 33.0%, taxes on foreign trade 25.8%, income taxes 19.5%, taxes on goods and services 13.1%, nontax revenue 8.6%). Expenditures: SI$558,700,000 (capital expenditure 35.9%, administrative 28.6%, wages and salaries 27.2%, interest payments 8.3%).
Tourism: receipts from visitors (1998) U.S.$13,000,000; expenditures by nationals abroad U.S.$6,000,000.
Land use (1994): forested 87.5%; meadows and pastures 1.4%; agricultural and under permanent cultivation 2.0%; other 9.1%.
Gross national product (at current market prices; 1998): U.S.$315,000,000 (U.S.$760 per capita).

Structure of gross domestic product and labour force

	1996 in value SI$ '000[6]	1996 % of total value	1993 labour force[7]	1993 % of labour force
Agriculture	107,400	32.9	8,106	27.4
Mining	200	0.1	2,844	9.6
Manufacturing	11,300	3.5		
Construction	19,600	6.0	977	3.3
Public utilities	5,100	1.6	245	0.8
Transportation and communications	18,500	5.7	1,723	5.8
Trade	28,900	8.8	3,390	11.5
Finance	13,500	4.1	1,144	3.9
Pub. admin., defense	68,100	20.8	4,303	14.6
Services			6,845	23.1
Other	54,300	16.6	...	...
TOTAL	326,900	100.0[3]	29,577	100.0

Household income and expenditure. Average household size (1996) 5.8; average annual income per household[8] (1983) SI$1,010 (U.S.$1,160); sources of income (1983): wages and salaries 74.1%, self-employment, remittances, gifts, and other assistance 25.9%; expenditure (1992)[9]: food 46.8%, housing 11.0%, household operations 10.9%, transportation 9.9%, recreation and health 7.9%, clothing 5.7%, drinks and tobacco 5.0%.
Population economically active (1993): total 29,577[7]; activity rate of total population 8.3% (participation rates: ages 15–60 [1986] 98.6%; female 22.6%; unemployed n.a.).

Price and earnings indexes (1995 = 100)

	1993	1994	1995	1996	1997	1998	1999
Consumer price index	80.5	91.2	100.0	111.8	120.8	135.7	146.9
Annual earnings index[7]	142.8	...	...	...	...	...	...

Production (metric tons except as noted). Agriculture, forestry, fishing (1999): coconuts 240,000, palm oil fruit 140,000, sweet potatoes 73,000, taro 32,000, yams 24,500, vegetables and melons 6,850, cacao beans 3,454; livestock (number of live animals) 58,000 pigs, 10,000 cattle, 185,000 chickens; roundwood (1998) 872,000 cu m; fish catch (1997) 53,442. Mining and quarrying (1998): gold 33,300 troy oz. Manufacturing (1997): palm oil 30,100, copra 23,500, coconut oil 3,900, cocoa 2,200, (1996) sawnwood 12,000 cu m. Construction (gross value in SI$ in Honiara; 1994): residential 9,508,000; nonresidential 11,151,000. Energy production (consumption): electricity (kW-hr; 1996) 32,000,000 (32,000,000); coal none (n.a.); petroleum products (metric tons; 1996) none (52,000); natural gas, none (n.a.).
Public debt (external, outstanding; 1998): U.S.$108,300,000.

Foreign trade[10]

Balance of trade (current prices)

	1993	1994	1995	1996	1997	1998
U.S.$'000,000	−7.81	−0.06	+13.77	+10.96	−28.08	−18.07
% of total	2.9%	0.0%	4.3%	3.5%	8.2%	6.0%

Imports (1996): SI$536,870,000 (machinery and transport equipment 30.3%, basic manufactured goods 22.2%, food and live animals 15.1%, mineral fuels and lubricants 11.3%). *Major import sources:* Australia 44.1%; Japan 12.5%; Singapore 7.0%; United States 2.1%; Thailand 1.8%; United Kingdom 1.6%.
Exports (1996): SI$656,300,000 (timber products 60.6%, fish products 18.3%, palm oil products 10.9%, copra 4.1%, cacao beans 2.2%). *Major export destinations:* Japan 40.1%; South Korea 19.4%; United Kingdom 18.4%; Thailand 3.8%; Australia 2.3%; Singapore 2.2%.

Transport and communications

Transport. Railroads: none. Roads (1996): total length 1,360 km (paved 2.5%). Vehicles (1993): passenger cars 2,052; trucks and buses 2,574. Merchant marine (1992): vessels (100 gross tons and over) 33; total deadweight tonnage 4,985. Air transport (1999): passenger-km 47,278,000; metric ton-km cargo 1,250,000; airports (1997) with scheduled flights 21.

Communications

Medium	date	unit	number	units per 1,000 persons
Radio	1997	receivers	57,000	141
Television	1997	receivers	3,000	6.2
Telephones	1998	main lines	7,885	20
Cellular telephones	1998	subscribers	702	1.7
Personal computers	...	units	...	...
Internet	1998	users	2,000	4.8

Education and health

Educational attainment (1986)[11]. Percentage of population age 25 and over having: no schooling 44.4%; primary education 46.2%; secondary 6.8%; higher 2.6%. *Literacy* (1976): total population age 15 and over literate 55,500 (54.1%); males 33,600 (62.4%); females 21,900 (44.9%).

Education (1994)

	schools	teachers	students	student/ teacher ratio
Primary (age 7–12)	520	2,510	73,120	29.1
Secondary (age 13–18)	23	618	7,981	12.9
Voc., teacher tr.[12]	1	...	...	...
Higher[12]	1	...	...	...

Health (1997): physicians 31 (1 per 13,258 persons); hospital beds 210 (1 per 1,957 persons); infant mortality rate per 1,000 live births (1999) 22.
Food (1998): daily per capita caloric intake 2,130 (vegetable products 92%, animal products 8%); 93% of FAO recommended minimum requirement.

Military

Total active duty personnel: no military forces are maintained, but a police force of 475 provides internal security.

[1]Central Islands includes Rennell and Bellona. [2]Western includes Choiseul. [3]Detail does not add to total given because of rounding. [4]Ward populations. [5]1996. [6]At 1985 factor cost. [7]Persons employed in the monetary sector only; 1990 = 100. [8]Public-service earnings. [9]Retail price index components. [10]Import figures are f.o.b. [11]Indigenous population only. [12]Vocational and teacher training are carried out at the College of Higher Education.

Internet resources for further information:
- **Solomon Islands Home Page http://www.solomons.com**

Somalia[1]

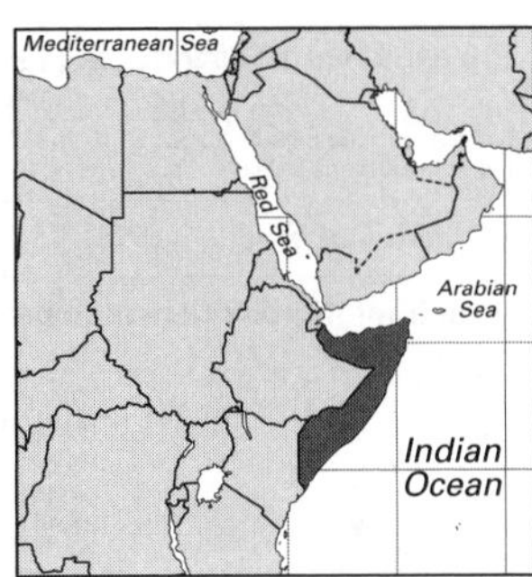

Official name: Soomaaliya (Somali)(Somalia).
Form of government: transitional regime[2] with one legislative body (Transitional National Assembly [245[3]]).
Head of state and government: President assisted by Prime Minister.
Capital: Mogadishu[4].
Official languages: Somali; Arabic.
Official religion: Islam.
Monetary unit: 1 Somali shilling (So.Sh.) = 100 cents; valuation (Oct. 6, 2000)
1 U.S.$ = So.Sh. 2,620[5];
1 £ = So.Sh. 3,790.

Area and population

Regions	Capitals	area sq mi	area sq km	population 1980 estimate
Bakool	Xuddur	10,000	27,000	148,700
Banaadir	Mogadishu (Muqdisho)	400	1,000	520,100
Bari	Boosaaso	27,000	70,000	222,300
Bay	Baydhabo	15,000	39,000	451,000
Galguduud	Dhuusamarreeb	17,000	43,000	255,900
Gedo	Garbahaarrey	12,000	32,000	235,000
Hiiraan	Beledweyne	13,000	34,000	219,300
Jubbada Dhexe	Bu'aale	9,000	23,000	147,800
Jubbada Hoose	Kismaayo	24,000	61,000	272,400
Mudug	Gaalkacyo	27,000	70,000	311,200
Nugaal	Garoowe	19,000	50,000	112,200
Sanaag	Ceerigaabo	21,000	54,000	216,500
Shabeellaha Dhexe	Jawhar	8,000	22,000	352,000
Shabeellaha Hoose	Marka	10,000	25,000	570,700
Togdheer	Burao	16,000	41,000	383,900
Woqooyi Galbeed	Hargeysa	17,000	45,000	655,000
TOTAL		246,000[6]	637,000	5,074,000

Demography

Population (2000): 7,253,000.
Density (2000): persons per sq mi 29.5, persons per sq km 11.4.
Urban-rural (1999): urban 27.1%; rural 72.9%.
Sex distribution (1999): male 50.20%; female 49.80%.
Age breakdown (1999): under 15, 44.2%; 15–29, 27.2%; 30–44, 17.7%; 45–59, 6.5%; 60–74, 3.5%; 75 and over, 0.9%.
Population projection: (2010) 9,922,000; (2020) 13,023,000.
Doubling time: 23 years.
Ethnic composition (1983): Somali 98.3%[7]; Arab 1.2%; Bantu 0.4%; other 0.1%.
Religious affiliation (1995): Sunnī Muslim 99.9%; other 0.1%.
Major cities (1990): Mogadishu 1,162,000[8]; Hargeysa 90,000; Kismaayo 90,000; Berbera 70,000; Marka 62,000.

Vital statistics

Birth rate per 1,000 population (1999): 48.2 (world avg. 22.1).
Death rate per 1,000 population (1999): 18.7 (world avg. 8.9).
Natural increase rate per 1,000 population (1999): 29.5 (world avg. 13.2).
Total fertility rate (avg. births per childbearing woman; 1999): 7.3.
Life expectancy at birth (1999): male 44.7 years; female 47.9 years.

National economy

Budget (1991). Revenue: So.Sh. 151,453,000,000 (domestic revenue sources, principally indirect taxes and import duties 60.4%; external grants and transfers 39.6%). Expenditures: So.Sh. 141,141,000,000 (general services 46.9%; economic and social services 31.2%; debt service 7.0%).
Public debt (external, outstanding; 1998): U.S.$1,886,000,000.
Production (metric tons except as noted). Agriculture, forestry, fishing (1999): fruits (excluding melons) 210,000, sugarcane 210,000, corn (maize) 150,000, bananas 55,000, cassava 65,000, sorghum 55,000, sesame seed 22,000, beans 14,000, dates 10,000, seed cotton 4,550, other forest products include khat, frankincense, and myrrh; livestock (number of live animals) 13,000,000 sheep, 12,000,000 goats, 6,000,000 camels, 5,000,000 cattle; roundwood (1998) 7,955,000 cu m; fish catch (1998) 16,000. Mining and quarrying (1992): salt 2,000 metric tons. Manufacturing (value added in So.Sh. '000,000; 1988): food 794; cigarettes and matches 562; hides and skins 420; paper and printing 328; plastics 320; chemicals 202; beverages 144. Construction (value added in So.Sh.; 1991): 51,100,000,000. Energy production (consumption): electricity (kW-hr; 1998) 265,000,000 (246,000,000); coal, none (n.a.); crude petroleum (barrels; 1991) n.a. (806,000); petroleum products (metric tons; 1991) none (59,000); natural gas, none (n.a.).
Household income and expenditure. Average household size (1980) 4.9; income per household: n.a.; sources of income: n.a.; expenditure (1983)[9]: food and tobacco 62.3%, housing 15.3%, clothing 5.6%, energy 4.3%, other 12.5%.
Population economically active (1991): total 3,215,000; activity rate of total population 40.9% (participation rates [1987] over age 10, 63.1%; female 48.7%; unemployed n.a.).

Price and earnings indexes (1990 = 100)

	1989	1990	1991	1992	1993	1994	1995
Consumer price index[10]	100.0	240.0	372.2	507.4	630.7	749.8	872.1
Earnings index	...	...	...	...	...	...	...

Gross national product (1996): U.S.$706,000,000 (U.S.$110 per capita).

Structure of gross domestic product and labour force

	1991 in value So.Sh. '000,000	% of total value	labour force	% of labour force
Agriculture	867,500	64.5	2,275,000	70.8
Mining	2,700	0.2		
Manufacturing	59,200	4.4	336,000	10.4
Construction	51,100	3.8		
Public utilities	9,400	0.7		
Transp. and commun.	80,700	6.0		
Trade	125,000	9.3		
Finance	45,700	3.4	604,000	18.8
Pub. admin., defense	80,700	6.0		
Services	30,900	2.3		
Other	–8,100	–0.6		
TOTAL	1,344,900[6]	100.0	3,215,000	100.0

Tourism: receipts from visitors (1986) U.S.$8,000,000; expenditures by nationals abroad (1983) U.S.$13,000,000.
Land use (1994): forest 25.5%; pasture 68.6%; agriculture 1.6%; other 4.3%.

Foreign trade[11]

Balance of trade (current prices)

	1993	1994	1995	1996	1997	1998
U.S.$'000,000	–146	–133	–48	–95	–112	–140
% of total	38.4%	32.8%	14.2%	21.0%	25.8%	27.2%

Imports (1998): U.S.$327,000,000 (1995; agricultural products 38.0%, of which raw sugar 16.1%, rice 7.8%, wheat 5.0%; unspecified 62.0%). *Major import sources* (1997): Djibouti 20%; Kenya 11%; Belarus 11%; India 10%; Saudi Arabia 9%; Brazil 9%.
Exports (1998): U.S.$187,000,000 (1995; agricultural products 51.4%, of which live sheep and goats 40.0%, bananas 6.9%, live camels and cattle 4.3%; other 48.6%). *Major export destinations* (1997): Saudi Arabia 57%; United Arab Emirates 15%; Italy 12%; Yemen 8%.

Transport and communications

Transport. Railroads: none. Roads (1996): total length 13,700 mi, 22,100 km (paved 12%). Vehicles (1996): passenger cars 1,020; trucks and buses 6,440. Merchant marine (1992): vessels (100 gross tons and over) 28; total deadweight tonnage 18,496. Air transport (1991): passenger-mi 81,000,000, passenger-km 131,000,000; short ton-mi cargo 3,000,000, metric ton-km cargo 5,000,000; airports (1998) with scheduled flights 1.

Communications

Medium	date	unit	number	units per 1,000 persons
Daily newspapers	1996	circulation	10,000	1.2
Radio	1997	receivers	470,000	53
Television	1997	receivers	135,000	15
Telephones	1998	main lines	15,000	1.5

Education and health

Educational attainment: n.a. *Literacy* (1995): percentage of total population age 15 and over literate 24%; males literate 36%; females literate 14%.

Education (1989–90)

	schools	teachers	students	student/ teacher ratio
Primary (age 6–14)	1,125	8,208	377,000	20.9
Secondary (age 15–18)	82	2,109	44,000	20.3
Voc., teacher tr.	21	498	10,400	9.7
Higher	1	549	4,640	...

Health: physicians (1997) 265 (1 per 25,034 persons); hospital beds (1985) 5,536 (1 per 1,130 persons); infant mortality rate (1999) 125.8.
Food (1998): daily per capita caloric intake 1,531 (vegetable products 60%, animal products 40%); 66% of FAO recommended minimum requirement.

Military

Total active duty personnel: clan warfare between 1991 and mid-2000. *Military expenditure as percentage of GNP* (1990): 0.9% (world 4.3%); per capita expenditure U.S.$1.

[1]Proclamation of a "Republic of Somaliland" by the Somali National Movement in May 1991 on territory corresponding to the former British Somaliland (which unified with the former Italian Trust Territory of Somalia to form Somalia in 1960) had received no international recognition by November 2000. This entity represented about a quarter of Somalia's territory. [2]From August 2000. [3]Includes 44 seats allotted to each of 4 major clans, 24 seats allotted to minor clans and tribes, 25 seats allotted to women, and 20 nominees of president. [4]Baidoa was pending interim capital from July 2000. [5]In June 1999 about 10,000 So.Sh. equaled 1 U.S.$ on the black market. [6]Detail does not add to total given because of rounding. [7]The Somali are divided into six major clans, of which four are predominantly pastoral (representing *c.* 70% of the population) and two are predominantly agricultural (representing *c.* 20% of the population); the remainder are urban dwellers with less clan identification. [8]1999. [9]Mogadishu only. [10]Reported inflation rate. [11]Imports c.i.f.; exports f.o.b.

Internet resources for further information:
- **Somalia Web Page**
  http://www.abyssiniacybergateway.net/somalia
- **CIA World Factbook: Somalia**
  http://www.odci.gov/cia/publications/factbook/index.html

South Africa

Official name: Republic of South Africa (English).
Form of government: multiparty republic with two legislative houses (National Council of Provinces [90]; National Assembly [400]).
Head of state and government: President.
Capitals (de facto): Pretoria[1] (executive); Bloemfontein (judicial); Cape Town (legislative).
Official languages: [2].
Official religion: none.
Monetary unit: 1 rand (R) = 100 cents; valuation (Oct. 6, 2000) 1 U.S.$ = R 7.29; 1 £ = R 10.54.

Area and population

		area		population
Provinces	Capitals	sq mi	sq km	1996 census[3]
Eastern Cape	Bisho	65,475	169,580	6,302,525
Free State	Bloemfontein	49,993	129,480	2,633,504
Gauteng	Johannesburg	6,568	17,010	7,348,423
KwaZulu-Natal	Pietermaritzburg	35,560	92,100	8,417,021
Mpumalanga	Nelspruit	30,691	79,490	2,800,711
Northern Cape	Kimberley	139,703	361,830	840,321
Northern Province	Pietersburg	47,842	123,910	4,929,368
North West	Mafikeng/Mmabatho	44,911	116,320	3,354,825
Western Cape	Cape Town	49,950	129,370	3,956,875
TOTAL		470,693	1,219,090	40,583,573

Demography

Population (2000): 43,421,000.
Density (2000): persons per sq mi 92.2, persons per sq km 35.6.
Urban-rural (1996): urban 53.7%; rural 46.3%.
Sex distribution (1996): male 47.98%; female 52.02%.
Age breakdown (1996): under 15, 33.9%; 15–29, 28.6%; 30–44, 19.4%; 45–59, 9.9%; 60–74, 5.3%; 75 and over, 1.7%; unknown, 1.2%.
Population projection[3]: (2010) 41,108,000; (2020) 36,744,000.
Doubling time: 79 years.
Ethnic composition (1995): black 76.3%, of which Zulu *c.* 22.0%, Xhosa *c.* 18.0%, Pedi *c.* 9.0%, Sotho *c.* 7.0%, Tswana *c.* 7.0%, Tsonga *c.* 3.5%, Swazi *c.* 3.0%; white 12.7%; Coloured 8.5%; Asian 2.5%.
Religious affiliation (1991)[4]: Christian 66.4%, of which Protestant 36.6%, black independent churches 22.2%, Roman Catholic 7.6%; Hindu 1.3%; Muslim 1.1%; nonreligious 1.2%; other/traditional beliefs 30.0%.
Major cities (1991)[5]: Cape Town 2,350,157; Johannesburg[1] 1,916,063[6]; Durban[1] 1,137,378; Pretoria[1] 1,080,187; Port Elizabeth[1] 853,204.

Vital statistics

Birth rate per 1,000 population (1999): 22.2 (world avg. 22.1).
Death rate per 1,000 population (1999): 13.5 (world avg. 8.9).
Natural increase rate per 1,000 population (1999): 8.7 (world avg. 13.2).
Marriage rate per 1,000 population (1996): 3.6.
Total fertility rate (avg. births per childbearing woman; 1999): 2.6.
Life expectancy at birth (1999): male 51.9 years; female 54.2 years.
Major causes of death per 100,000 population (1993–94): accidents and violence 221.9; diseases of the circulatory system 102.3; infectious and parasitic diseases 51.8; ill-defined conditions 424.0.

National economy

Budget (1997–98). Revenue: R 163,000,000,000 (personal income taxes 39.9%, value-added taxes 24.6%, company income taxes 13.7%). Expenditures: R 190,200,000,000 (education 21.1%, interest on public debt 20.2%, health 10.6%, police and prisons 9.9%, defense 5.6%).
Public debt (external, outstanding; 1999): U.S.$10,627,000,000.
Production (in R '000,000 except as noted). Agriculture, forestry, fishing (in value of production; 1996): corn (maize) 5,995, poultry 4,659, beef 2,899, sugarcane 2,207, temperate fruits 1,976, wheat 1,929, milk 1,802, vegetables 1,688, citrus fruits 1,377, grapes 1,214, potatoes 971, sheep and goat meat 970; roundwood (1998) 25,332,000 cu m; fish catch (1997) 509,390 metric tons. Mining and quarrying (in value of sales; 1996): gold 26,482; rough diamonds 16,431[7]; coal 14,910; platinum-group metals 7,638; iron ore 1,692; copper 1,489; nickel 983. Manufacturing (in U.S.$'000,000 value added; 1995): food products 3,028; iron and steel 2,700; transport equipment 2,334; metal products 1,825; nonelectrical machinery 1,819; beverages 1,660; refined petroleum 1,457. Energy production (consumption): electricity (kW-hr; 1999) 203,532,000,000 ([1998] 187,517,000,000); coal (metric tons; 1999) 220,320,000 ([1996] 136,903,000[8]); crude petroleum (barrels; 1996) 3,650,000 (158,511,000[8]); petroleum products (metric tons; 1996) 19,174,000[8] (16,857,000[8]); natural gas (cu m; 1996): 1,840,000,000[8] (1,840,000,000[8]).
Tourism (1998): receipts U.S.$2,738,000,000; expenditures U.S.$1,842,000,000.
Household income and expenditure. Average household size (1996) 4.5; average annual disposable income per household (1996)[9] R 47,600 (U.S.$11,070); expenditure (1998): food, beverages, and tobacco 31.3%; transportation 14.3%; housing 9.3%; household furnishings and operation 8.9%.
Population economically active (1995): total 14,356,000; activity rate of total population 35.1% (participation rates: over age 15, *c.* 53%; female 43.6%; unemployed [1997] *c.* 25%).

Price and earnings indexes (1995 = 100)

	1994	1995	1996	1997	1998	1999	2000[10]
Consumer price index	92.1	100.0	107.4	116.5	124.6	130.5	139.2
Monthly earnings index	...	...	...	...	...	...	...

Gross national product (1998): U.S.$136,868,000,000 (U.S.$3,310 per capita).

Structure of gross domestic product and labour force

	1998		1995	
	in value R '000,000	% of total value	labour force	% of labour force
Agriculture	26,620	4.0	1,295,000	9.0
Mining	44,462	6.6	471,000	3.3
Manufacturing	127,461	18.9	1,526,000	10.6
Construction	20,741	3.1	483,000	3.4
Public utilities	21,123	3.1	95,000	0.7
Transp. and commun.	63,489	9.4	520,000	3.6
Trade	89,342	13.3	1,769,000	12.3
Finance, real estate	124,120	18.4	654,000	4.6
Pub. admin., defense	116,522	17.3	3,137,000	21.9
Services	19,394	2.9		
Other	19,879	3.0	4,405,000[11]	30.7[11]
TOTAL	673,153	100.0	14,356,000[12]	100.0[12]

Land use (1994): forest 6.7%; pasture 66.7%; agriculture 10.8%; other 15.8%.

Foreign trade

Balance of trade (current prices)

	1994	1995	1996	1997	1998	1999
R '000,000	+15,862	+2,783	+11,547	+13,202	+2,192	+16,091
% of total	9.3%	1.4%	4.6%	4.8%	0.8%	5.2%

Imports (1995): R 98,614,000,000 (machinery and apparatus 31.9%, chemicals and chemical products 12.5%, motor vehicles 11.6%). *Major import sources* (1997): Germany 13.5%; U.S. 12.4%; U.K. 11.2%; Japan 7.4%; Iran 5.4%.
Exports (1995): R 101,397,000,000 (gold 19.9%, base metals and metal products 15.4%, gem diamonds 9.8%, food 7.4%). *Major export destinations* (1997): U.K. 12.0%; U.S. 5.5%; Japan 4.9%; Germany 4.0%; unspecified 24.2%.

Transport and communications

Transport. Railroads: route length (1997) 20,319 km[13]; passenger-km (1992–93) 895,000,000[13]; metric ton-km cargo (1994–95) 95,260,000,000. Roads (1995): length 331,265 km (paved 41%). Vehicles (1996): passenger cars 4,004,000; trucks and buses 1,664,000. Air transport (1998)[14]: passenger-km 15,855,000,000; metric ton-km cargo 294,809,000; airport (1996) 24.

Communications

Medium	date	unit	number	units per 1,000 persons
Daily newspapers	1996	circulation	1,288,000	31
Radio	1997	receivers	13,750,000	324
Television	1997	receivers	5,200,000	122
Telephones	1998	main lines	5,075,000	118
Cellular telephones	1998	subscribers	2,500,000	58
Personal computers	1998	units	2,100,000	49
Internet	1998	users	1,266,000	30

Education and health

Educational attainment (1994). Percentage of population age 25 and over having: no formal schooling 14.5%; primary/incomplete secondary 61.6%; secondary/incomplete higher 20.4%; complete higher 3.1%; other/unknown 0.4%. *Literacy* (1995): total population age 15 and over literate: 81.8%.

Education (1996)

	schools	teachers	students	student/ teacher ratio
Primary (age 6–12)	20,863	224,896	8,159,530	36.3
Secondary (age 13–17)	...	128,611	3,749,449	29.2
Higher[15]	...	27,099	617,897	22.8

Health: physicians (1996) 23,855 (1 per 1,742 persons); hospital beds 135,694 (1 per 306 persons); infant mortality rate per 1,000 live births (1999) 57.1.
Food (1997): daily per capita caloric intake 2,990 (vegetable products 86%, animal products 14%); 122% of FAO recommended minimum.

Military

Total active duty personnel (1998): 82,400 (army 71.1%, navy 6.7%, air force 13.2%, intraservice medical service 9.0%). *Military expenditure as percentage of GNP* (1997): 1.8% (world 2.6%); per capita expenditure U.S.$55.

[1]Name change pending October 2000; new name may apply to differently demarcated area. [2]Afrikaans; English; Ndebele; Pedi (North Sotho); Sotho (South Sotho); Swazi; Tsonga; Tswana (West Sotho); Venda; Xhosa; Zulu. [3]Adjusted final figure. [4]Excludes formerly nominally independent Transkei, Venda, Bophuthatswana, and Ciskei (TVBC). [5]Population of urban areas. [6]The 1991 population of the Witwatersrand (including East Rand [1,379,000], Far East Rand [701,000], and West Rand [870,000] urban areas) is 4,866,000. [7]1995. [8]Includes Botswana, Lesotho, Namibia, and Swaziland. [9]Estimated figures. [10]July. [11]Includes 201,000 not adequately defined and 4,204,000 unemployed. [12]Detail does not add to total given because of rounding. [13]Excludes suburban lines. [14]SAA only. [15]1994.

Internet resources for further information:
- **South African Reserve Bank http://www.resbank.co.za**
- **Statistics South Africa http://www.statssa.gov.za**

Spain

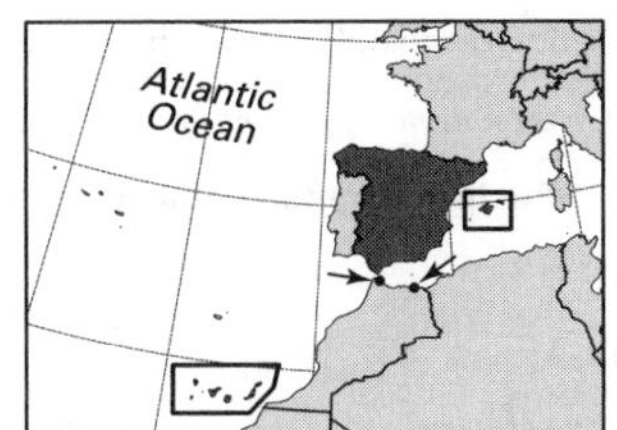

Official name: Reino de España (Kingdom of Spain).
Form of government: constitutional monarchy with two legislative houses (Senate [259[1]]; Congress of Deputies [350]).
Chief of state: King.
Head of government: Prime Minister.
Capital: Madrid.
Official languages: Castilian Spanish[2].
Official religion: none.
Monetary unit: 1 peseta (Pta) = 100 céntimos; valuation (Oct. 6, 2000) 1 U.S.$ = Ptas 191.32; 1 £ = Ptas 276.76.

Area and population

		area		population
Autonomous communities	Capitals	sq mi	sq km	1998[3] estimate
Andalucía	Seville	33,822	87,599	7,236,459
Aragón	Zaragoza	18,425	47,720	1,183,234
Asturias	Oviedo	4,094	10,604	1,081,834
Baleares (Balearic Islands)	Palma de Mallorca	1,927	4,992	796,483
Canarias (Canary Islands)	Santa Cruz de Tenerife	2,875	7,447	1,630,015
Cantabria	Santander	2,504	5,321	527,137
Castilla-La Mancha	Toledo	30,680	79,461	1,716,152
Castilla y León	Valladolid	36,380	94,224	2,484,603
Cataluña	Barcelona	12,399	32,113	6,147,610
Ceuta	—	8	20	72,117
Extremadura	Mérida	16,075	41,634	1,069,419
Galicia	Santiago de Compostela	11,419	29,575	2,724,544
La Rioja	Logroño	1,948	5,045	263,644
Madrid	Madrid	3,100	8,028	5,091,336
Melilla	—	5	12	60,108
Murcia	Murcia	4,368	11,314	1,115,068
Navarra	Pamplona	4,012	10,391	530,819
País Vasco (Basque Country)	Vitoria (Gasteiz)	2,793	7,234	2,098,628
Valencia	Valencia	8,979	23,255	4,023,441
TOTAL		195,364[4, 5]	505,990[5]	39,852,651

Demography

Population (2000): 40,128,000.
Density (2000): persons per sq mi 205.4, persons per sq km 79.3.
Urban-rural (1990): urban 78.4%; rural 21.6%.
Sex distribution (2000)[6]: male 48.87%; female 51.13%.
Age breakdown (2000)[6]: under 15, 15.0%; 15–29, 22.8%; 30–44, 23.1%; 45–59, 17.5%; 60–74, 14.4%; 75 and over, 7.2%.
Population projection: (2010) 40,289,000; (2020) 39,362,000.
Ethnolinguistic composition (1991): Spanish 74.4%; Catalan 16.9%; Galician 6.4%; Basque 1.6%; other 0.7%.
Religious affiliation (1995): Roman Catholic 66.7%; Muslim 1.2%; Protestant 0.8%; other 31.3%.
Major cities (1998)[3, 7]: Madrid 2,881,506; Barcelona 1,505,581; Valencia 739,412; Seville 701,927; Zaragoza 603,367.

Vital statistics

Birth rate per 1,000 population (1998): 9.2 (world avg. 22.1).
Death rate per 1,000 population (1998): 9.1 (world avg. 8.9).
Natural increase rate per 1,000 population (1998): 0.1 (world avg. 13.2).
Total fertility rate (avg. births per childbearing woman; 1998): 1.1.
Life expectancy at birth (1998): male 74.8 years; female 82.1 years.
Major causes of death per 100,000 population (1996): circulatory diseases 339.9; malignant neoplasms (cancers) 227.2; respiratory diseases 88.4.

National economy

Budget (1998). Revenue: Ptas 17,242,300,000,000 (direct taxes 46.2%; indirect taxes 40.0%, of which value-added tax on products 25.4%; other taxes on production 13.4%). Expenditures: Ptas 18,729,900,000,000 (health 19.1%; public debt 17.0%; education 6.1%; pensions 4.9%; defense 4.8%).
Tourism (1997): receipts U.S.$26,651,000,000; expenditures U.S.$4,467,000,000.
Gross national product (1998): U.S.$555,244,000,000 (U.S.$14,100 per capita).

Structure of gross domestic product and labour force

	1997			
	in value Ptas '000,000	% of total value	labour force	% of labour force
Agriculture	2,446,900	3.1	1,316,600	8.2
Mining			70,000	0.4
Manufacturing	18,425,900	23.7	2,720,500	16.9
Public utilities			86,200	0.5
Construction	5,889,900	7.6	1,545,000	9.6
Transp. and commun.	...	...	815,100	5.1
Trade			3,337,000	20.7
Finance	46,271,300	59.5	1,265,300	7.8
Services			3,465,600	21.5
Pub. admin., defense				
Other	4,752,200[8]	6.1[8]	1,499,200[9]	9.3[9]
TOTAL	77,786,100[4]	100.0	16,121,000[4]	100.0

Production (metric tons except as noted). Agriculture, forestry, fishing (1998): barley 10,902,000, sugar beets 8,918,000, wheat 5,347,000, grapes 4,842,000, corn (maize) 4,154,000, olives 3,564,000, tomatoes 3,554,000, potatoes 3,184,000, oranges 2,402,000; livestock (number of live animals) 24,542,000 sheep, 19,346,000 pigs, 5,884,000 cattle, 2,895,000 goats; roundwood (1998) 16,021,000 cu m; fish catch (1996) 1,326,000. Mining and quarrying (metal content in metric tons; 1997): zinc 147,000; iron ore 58,000[10]; lead 23,000. Manufacturing (value added in U.S.$'000; 1994): machinery and transport equipment 20,322,000; food products 11,072,000; chemical products 8,618,000; publishing products 6,082,000; wood products 3,208,000. Construction (1997): dwellings 370,487. Energy production (consumption): electricity (kW-hr; 1995) 166,380,000,000 (170,866,000,000); coal (metric tons; 1995) 28,403,000 (42,640,000); crude petroleum (barrels; 1995) 6,000,000 (415,000,000); petroleum products (metric tons; 1995) 47,064,000 (42,327,000); natural gas (cu m; 1995) 178,000,000 (8,879,000,000).
Public debt (1998): Ptas 47,019,100,000,000 (U.S.$314,719,000,000).
Population economically active (1997): total 16,121,000; activity rate of total population 41.0% (participation rates: ages [1995] 16–64, 60.7%, female 38.3%; unemployed 22.9%).

Price and earnings indexes (1995 = 100)

	1993	1994	1995	1996	1997	1998	1999
Consumer price index	91.2	95.5	100.0	103.6	105.6	107.5	109.8
Monthly earnings index	91.3	95.4	100.0	105.3	109.6	...	115.5

Household income and expenditure. Average household size (1991) 3.4; income per household (1996) Ptas 2,964,843 (U.S.$23,408); expenditure (1995): housing 26.0%, food 24.0%, transportation 12.8%, clothing and footwear 7.4%, household goods and services 6.1%.

Foreign trade[11]

Balance of trade (current prices)

	1993	1994	1995	1996	1997	1998
Ptas '000,000	–2,376.4	–2,559.7	–2,767.1	–2,504.5	–2,699.1	–3,547.1
% of total	13.2%	11.6%	10.8%	8.8%	8.1%	9.8%

Imports (1997): Ptas 17,966,455,000,000 (machinery 12.0%; energy products 9.0%, of which crude petroleum 8.9%; transportation equipment 9.0%; agricultural products 7.0%). *Major import sources:* France 17.4%; Germany 14.8%; Italy 9.4%; U.K. 8.1%; Japan 2.8%.
Exports (1997): Ptas 15,267,643,000,000 (transport equipment 19.2%; agricultural products 15.1%; machinery 8.0%). *Major export destinations:* France 18.3%; Germany 13.4%; Italy 9.8%; U.K. 8.1%.

Transport and communications

Transport. Railroads (1996)[12]: route length 13,280 km; passenger-km 15,605,000,000; metric ton-km cargo 9,794,000,000. Roads (1997): length 346,548 km (paved 99%). Vehicles (1997): cars 15,297,366; trucks and buses 3,256,009. Air transport (1997): passenger-km 51,649,279,000; metric ton-km cargo 5,257,000; airports (1997) with scheduled flights 25.

Communications

Medium	date	unit	number	units per 1,000 persons
Daily newspapers	1996	circulation	3,931,000	99
Radio	1998	receivers	12,000,000	332
Television	1997	receivers	19,900,000	500
Telephones	1997	main lines	15,854,000	398
Cellular telephones	1997	subscribers	4,338,000	109
Personal computers	1997	units	4,800,000	121
Internet	1998	users	1,733,000	43

Education and health

Educational attainment (1997). Percentage of economically active population age 16 and over having: no formal schooling 6.4%[13]; primary 26.6%; secondary 58.9%; higher 8.1%.

Education (1995–96)

	schools	teachers	students	student/ teacher ratio
Primary (age 6–11)	16,540[14]	162,112	2,799,960	17.3
Secondary (age 12–18)[15]	25,775[16]	270,866	4,117,052	15.2
Higher	1,415[16]	89,093	1,591,863	17.9

Health (1995): physicians 162,650 (1 per 241 persons); hospital beds (1991) 168,514 (1 per 234 persons); infant mortality rate (1998) 5.2.
Food (1997): daily per capita caloric intake 3,310 (vegetable products 74%, animal products 26%); 135% of FAO recommended minimum requirement.

Military

Total active duty personnel (1998): 193,950 (army 65.5%, navy 19.0%, air force 15.5%). *Military expenditure as percentage of GNP* (1995): 1.6% (world 2.8%); per capita expenditure U.S.$221.

[1]At the March 2000 elections, 208 seats were directly elected and 51 indirectly elected by the parliaments of the autonomous communities. [2]The constitution states that "Castilian is the Spanish official language of the State," but that "all other Spanish languages will also be official in the corresponding Autonomous Communities." [3]De jure population for January 1. [4]Detail does not add to total given because of rounding. [5]Includes other enclaves (*plazas de soberanía*). [6]Estimate based on 1991 census. [7]For municipios, which may contain rural population. [8]Import taxes and value-added tax on products. [9]Includes 799,500 unemployed persons not previously employed. [10]The decrease in iron ore production is due to the lack of mining at Minas de Alquife (Granda). [11]Imports in c.i.f., exports f.o.b. [12]Spanish National Railways (RENFE) only. [13]Includes illiterate. [14]1993–94. [15]Includes vocational. [16]1992–93.

Internet resources for further information:
- **"Sí Spain" (Embassy of Spain, Ottawa, Canada) http://www.docuweb.ca/SiSpain**
- **National Institute of Statistics http://www.ine.es**

Sri Lanka

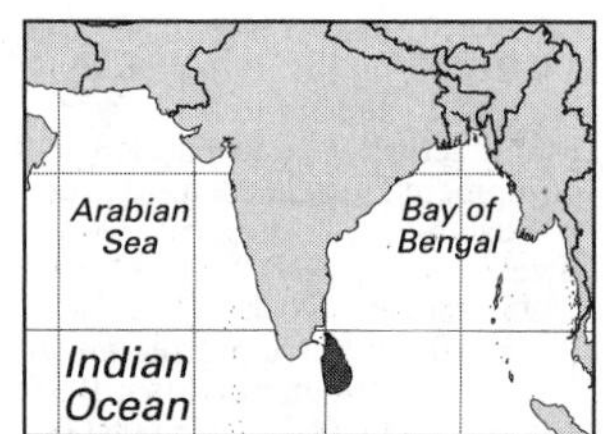

Official name: Śri Lanka Prajatantrika Samajavadi Janarajaya (Sinhala); Ilangai Jananayaka Socialisa Kudiarasu (Tamil) (Democratic Socialist Republic of Sri Lanka).
Form of government: unitary multiparty republic with one legislative house (Parliament [225]).
Head of state and government: President assisted by Prime Minister.
Capitals: Colombo (executive); Sri Jayewardenepura Kotte (Colombo suburb; legislative and judicial).
Official languages: Sinhala; Tamil.
Official religion: none.
Monetary unit: 1 Sri Lanka rupee (SL Rs) = 100 cents; valuation (Oct. 6, 2000) 1 U.S.$ = SL Rs 79.15; 1 £ = SL Rs 114.50.

Area and population

		area		population
Districts	**Capitals**	sq mi	sq km	1994 estimate
Amparai	Amparai	1,705	4,415	512,000
Anuradhapura	Anuradhapura	2,772	7,179	750,000
Badulla	Badulla	1,104	2,861	735,000
Batticaloa	Batticaloa	1,102	2,854	443,000
Colombo	Colombo	270	699	2,062,000
Galle	Galle	638	1,652	983,000
Gampaha	Gampaha	536	1,387	1,568,000
Hambantota	Hambantota	1,007	2,609	537,000
Jaffna	Jaffna	396	1,025	896,000
Kalutara	Kalutara	617	1,598	969,000
Kandy	Kandy	749	1,940	1,286,000
Kegalle	Kegalle	654	1,693	763,000
Kilinochchi	Kilinochchi	494	1,279	110,000
Kurunegala	Kurunegala	1,859	4,816	1,481,000
Mannar	Mannar	771	1,996	140,000
Matale	Matale	770	1,993	434,000
Matara	Matara	495	1,283	810,000
Monaragala	Monaragala	2,177	5,639	367,000
Mullaitivu	Mullaitivu	1,010	2,617	98,000
Nuwara Eliya	Nuwara Eliya	672	1,741	541,000
Polonnaruwa	Polonnaruwa	1,271	3,293	336,000
Puttalam	Puttalam	1,186	3,072	626,000
Ratnapura	Ratnapura	1,264	3,275	972,000
Trincomalee	Trincomalee	1,053	2,727	327,000
Vavuniya	Vavuniya	759	1,967	119,000
TOTAL		25,332	65,610	17,865,000

Demography

Population (2000): 19,246,000.
Density (2000): persons per sq mi 759.8, persons per sq km 293.3.
Urban-rural (1999): urban 23.0%; rural 77.0%.
Sex distribution (1996): male 50.97%; female 49.03%.
Age breakdown (1995): under 15, 35.2%; 15–29, 29.7%; 30–44, 17.9%; 45–59, 10.6%; 60–74, 5.2%; 75 and over, 1.4%.
Population projection: (2010) 20,832,000; (2020) 22,120,000.
Doubling time: 66 years.
Ethnic composition (1991)[1]: Sinhalese 82.7%; Tamil 8.9%; Sri Lankan Moor 7.7%; other 0.7%.
Religious affiliation (1981): Buddhist 69.3%; Hindu 15.5%; Christian 7.6%; Muslim 7.5%; other 0.1%.
Major cities (1997): Colombo 800,982; Dehiwala–Mount Lavinia 220,780; Moratuwa 213,000; Kandy 150,532; Jaffna 145,600.

Vital statistics

Birth rate per 1,000 population (1999): 17.2 (world avg. 22.1); (1986) legitimate 96.3%; illegitimate 3.7%.
Death rate per 1,000 population (1999): 6.4 (world avg. 8.9).
Natural increase rate per 1,000 population (1999): 10.8 (world avg. 13.2).
Total fertility rate (avg. births per childbearing woman; 1999): 2.0.
Marriage rate per 1,000 population (1993): 8.5.
Life expectancy at birth (1999): male 69.1 years; female 74.1 years.
Major causes of death per 100,000 population (1989): diseases of the circulatory system 47.8; violence and poisoning 38.6; malignant neoplasms 26.7.

National economy

Budget (1999). Revenue: SL Rs 148,206,000,000 (sales and turnover tax 27.5%, import duties 19.4%, excise taxes 14.8%, income taxes 11.6%, nontax revenue 10.5%). Expenditures: SL Rs 212,984,000,000 (current expenditure 79.7%, development expenditure 20.3%).
Public debt (external, outstanding; 1999): U.S.$7,649,000,000.
Tourism (1998): receipts U.S.$231,000,000; expenditures U.S.$202,000,000.
Production (metric tons except as noted). Agriculture, forestry, fishing (1998): rice 2,692,335, coconuts 1,999,000, sugarcane 946,247, plantains 590,000; livestock (number of live animals) 1,599,000 cattle, 720,700 buffalo, 519,300 goats; roundwood 10,479,700 cu m; fish catch (1997) 240,000. Mining and quarrying (1997); quartz stone 9,350,000; limestone 901,000; titanium concentrate 21,940; gemstones U.S.$62,500,000. Manufacturing (value added, in U.S.$'000,000; 1995): food, beverages, and tobacco 601; textiles and apparel 391; petrochemicals 116. Construction (units completed; 1993): residential 1,128; nonresidential 96. Energy production (consumption): electricity (kW-hr; 1997) 5,148,000,000 ([1996] 4,366,000,000); coal (metric tons, 1996) none (negligible); crude petroleum (barrels; 1996) none (15,063,000); petroleum products (metric tons; 1996) 1,908,000 (2,188,000).
Gross national product (1998): U.S.$15,176,000,000 (U.S.$810 per capita).

Structure of gross domestic product and labour force

	1997		1996	
	in value SL Rs '000,000	% of total value	labour force[1]	% of labour force[1]
Agriculture	175,774	21.9	1,962,670	31.5
Mining	16,587	2.1	68,660	1.1
Manufacturing	131,876	16.4	838,030	13.4
Construction	56,434	7.0	320,880	5.1
Public utilities	} 423,027	} 52.6	24,520	0.4
Transp. and commun.			259,480	4.2
Trade			705,140	11.3
Finance			118,020	1.9
Pub. admin., defense			} 1,083,130	} 17.4
Services				
Other			857,583[2]	13.7[2]
TOTAL	803,698	100.0	6,238,113	100.0

Population economically active: total (1997) 6,213,086; activity rate 40.2% (participation rates: ages 15 and over, 55.2%; female 32.4%; unemployed 10.2%[1]).

Price and earnings indexes (1995 = 100)

	1993	1994	1995	1996	1997	1998	1999
Consumer price index	85.6	92.9	100.0	115.9	127.0	138.9	145.4
Average wage index[3]	96.7	98.9	100.0	109.3	117.0	132.1	...

Household income and expenditure (1992). Average household size (1994) 4.6[1]; income per household SL Rs 116,100 (U.S.$2,600); sources of income: wages 48.5%, property income and self-employment 41.8%, transfers 9.7%; expenditure: food 58.6%, transportation 16.0%, clothing 8.4%.

Foreign trade

Balance of trade (current prices)

	1994	1995	1996	1997	1998	1999
SL Rs '000,000	–77,022	–77,084	–74,275	–41,449	–63,164	–91,443
% of total	19.5%	16.5%	14.1%	7.0%	9.4%	12.4%

Imports (1998): SL Rs 369,013,000,000 (textile products 25.9%, machinery and mechanical appliances 16.7%, vegetable products 6.4%, chemical products 6.1%). *Major import sources*[4]: India 9.9%; Japan 8.5%; Singapore 5.1%.
Exports (1998): SL Rs 305,849,000,000 (clothing and accessories 49.0%[4], tea 16.3%, gems 4.5%[4], natural rubber 1.7%[4]). *Major export destinations*[4]: U.S. 35.9%; U.K. 11.3%; Germany 5.0%; Japan 5.0%.

Transport and communications

Transport. Railroads (1996): route length 1,463 km; passenger-km 3,241,000,000; metric ton-km cargo 107,500,000. Roads (1996): total length 99,200 km (paved 40%). Vehicles (1996): passenger cars 107,000; trucks and buses 150,160. Air transport (1997): passenger-km 4,248,000,000; metric ton-km cargo 182,472,000; airports (1996) 1.

Communications

Medium	date	unit	number	units per 1,000 persons
Daily newspapers	1996	circulation	530,000	29
Radio	1996	receivers	3,846,000	210
Television	1997	receivers	1,685,000	91
Telephones	1998	main lines	523,529	28
Cellular telephones	1998	subscribers	174,202	9.3
Personal computers	1997	units	76,000	4.1
Internet	1998	users	20,000	1.1

Education and health

Educational attainment (1981). Percentage of population age 25 and over having: no schooling 15.5%; less than complete primary education 12.1%; complete primary 52.3%; postprimary 14.7%; secondary 3.0%; higher 1.1%; unspecified 1.3%. *Literacy* (1995): percentage of population age 15 and over literate 90.2%; males literate 93.4%; females literate 87.2%.

Education (1995)

	schools	teachers	students	student/ teacher ratio
Primary (age 5–10)	9,657	70,537	1,962,498	27.8
Secondary (age 11–17)	5,771[5]	103,572	2,314,054	22.3
Voc., teacher tr.[6]	23	437	8,908	20.4
Higher	8[6]	2,636[5]	63,660	24.2

Health (1999): physicians 6,938 (1 per 2,740 persons); hospital beds (1997) 52,298 (1 per 355 persons); infant mortality rate per 1,000 live births 17.0.
Food (1997): daily per capita caloric intake 2,302 (vegetable products 94%, animal products 6%); (1995) 102% of FAO recommended minimum.

Military

Total active duty personnel (1998): 112,500 (army 82.2%, navy 8.9%, air force 8.9%). *Military expenditure as percentage of GNP* (1997): 5.1% (world 2.6%); per capita expenditure U.S.$41.

[1]Excludes the Northern and Eastern provinces where Tamils are in the majority. [2]Mainly unemployed. [3]Agricultural minimum rates. [4]1997. [5]1992. [6]1991.

Internet resources for further information:
- **Central Bank of Sri Lanka http://www.lanka.net/centralbank**
- **Statistics http://www.lk/statistics.html**

Sudan, The

Official name: Jumhūrīyat as-Sūdān (Republic of the Sudan).
Form of government: Islamic military regime[1].
Head of state and government: President.
Capitals: Khartoum (executive); Omdurman (legislative).
Official language: Arabic[2].
Official religion: [3].
Monetary unit: 1 Sudanese dinar (Sd)[4]; valuation (Oct. 6, 2000) 1 U.S.$ = Sd 258.70; 1 £ = Sd 374.22.

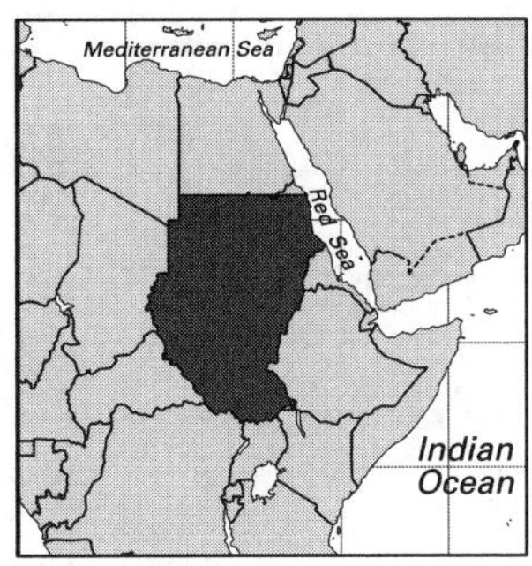

Area and population

		area		population
States[5]	Capitals	sq mi	sq km	1983 census
Aʿālī an-Nīl (Upper Nile)	Malakāl	92,198	238,792	1,599,605
Baḥr al-Ghazāl (Bahr el-Ghazal)	Wāw	77,566	200,894	2,265,510
Dārfūr (Darfur)	al-Fāshir	194,404	508,684	3,093,699
al-Istiwāʾīyah (Equatoria)	Juba	76,436	197,969	1,406,181
al-Kharṭūm (Khartoum)	Khartoum	10,874	28,165	1,802,299
Kurdufān (Kordofan)	al-Ubayyiḍ	146,817	380,255	3,093,294
ash-Shamālīyah (Northern)	ad-Dāmir	183,800	476,040	1,083,024
ash-Sharqīyah (Eastern)	Kassalā	128,987	334,074	2,208,209
al-Wusṭā (Central)	Wad Madanī	53,675	139,017	4,012,543
TOTAL		966,757[6]	2,503,890[6]	20,564,364[7]

Demography

Population (2000): 35,080,000.
Density (2000): persons per sq mi 36.3, persons per sq km 14.0.
Urban-rural (1999): urban 35.2%; rural 64.8%.
Sex distribution (1998): male 50.14%; female 49.86%.
Age breakdown (1995): under 15, 43.9%; 15–29, 27.0%; 30–44, 15.6%; 45–59, 8.8%; 60–74, 3.9%; 75 and over, 0.8%.
Population projection: (2000) 45,485,000; (2010) 56,162,000.
Doubling time: 24 years.
Ethnic composition (1983): Sudanese Arab 49.1%; Dinka 11.5%; Nuba 8.1%; Beja 6.4%, Nuer 4.9%; Azande 2.7%; Bari 2.5%; Fur 2.1%; other 12.7%.
Religious affiliation (1992): Sunnī Muslim *c.* 72%; traditional beliefs *c.* 17%; Christian *c.* 11%, of which Roman Catholic *c.* 7%.
Major cities (1993): Omdurman 1,267,077; Khartoum 924,505; Khartoum North 879,105; Port Sudan 305,385; Kassalā 234,270; Nyala 228,778.

Vital statistics

Birth rate per 1,000 population (1999): 39.2 (world avg. 22.1).
Death rate per 1,000 population (1999): 10.5 (world avg. 8.9).
Natural increase rate per 1,000 population (1999): 28.7 (world avg. 13.2).
Total fertility rate (avg. births per childbearing woman; 1999): 5.6.
Life expectancy at birth (1999): male 55.1 years; female 57.2 years.
Major causes of death per 100,000 population: n.a.

National economy

Budget (1999–2000). Revenue: Sd 206,700,000,000[4] (import duties 26.0%, non-tax revenue 25.8%, excise duties 11.9%, taxes on business profits 11.1%). Expenditures: Sd 227,200,000,000[4] (current expenditure 85.8%, development expenditure 14.2%).
Public debt (external, outstanding; 1998): U.S.$9,226,000,000.
Tourism (1998): receipts U.S.$8,000,000; expenditures U.S.$30,000,000.
Production (metric tons except as noted). Agriculture, forestry, fishing (1999): sugarcane 5,950,000, sorghum 3,045,000, peanuts (groundnuts) 980,000, millet 499,000, sesame seeds 220,000, seed cotton 205,000, dates 175,500, tea 170,000, wheat 168,000, gum arabic 28,000[8]; livestock (number of live animals) 42,500,000 sheep, 37,500,000 goats, 35,000,000 cattle, 3,150,000 camels; roundwood (1998) 9,486,000 cu m; fish catch (1997) 48,072. Mining and quarrying (1997): salt 50,000; gold 161,000 troy oz. Manufacturing (1999): raw sugar 622,000; flour 532,000; cement 267,000; vegetable oils 100,000; cattle-hides and horsehides 34,700[9]; shoes 48,000,000 pairs. Construction: n.a. Energy production (consumption): electricity (kW-hr; 1999) 2,243,000,000 (1,317,000,000); coal, none (none); crude petroleum (barrels; 1996) none (7,616,000); petroleum products (metric tons; 1996) 878,000 (1,039,000); natural gas, none (none).
Gross national product (1998): U.S.$8,224,000,000 (U.S.$290 per capita).

Structure of gross domestic product and labour force

	1999		1983	
	in value Sd '000,000,000[10]	% of total value	labour force[11]	% of labour force[11]
Agriculture	1,040	42.6	4,028,705	63.5
Mining	21	0.9	6,534	0.1
Manufacturing	217	8.9	266,693	4.2
Construction	157	6.4	139,282	2.2
Public utilities	19	0.8	43,728	0.7
Transportation and communications	142	5.8	215,474	3.4
Trade, hotels	492	20.1	314,676	5.0
Finance				
Services	354	14.5	550,409	8.7
Pub. admin., defense				
Other	—	—	777,480[12]	12.2[12]
TOTAL	2,442	100.0	6,342,981	100.0

Population economically active (1993): total 8,866,000; activity rate of total population 32.3% (participation rates: ages 15–64 [1983] 57.4%; female 22.3%; unemployed *c.* 30.0%).

Price and earnings indexes (1995 = 100)

	1994	1995	1996	1997	1998	1999	2000
Consumer price index	59.4	100.0	232.8	341.5	399.9	463.8	488.1[13]
Earnings index	...	...	...	...	...	...	...

Household income and expenditure. Average household size: n.a.; income per household: n.a.[14]; expenditure (1983): food and beverages 63.6%, housing 11.5%, household goods 5.5%, clothing and footwear 5.3%.
Land use (1994): forested 18.1%; meadows and pastures 46.3%; agricultural and under permanent cultivation 5.5%; desert and other 30.1%.

Foreign trade[15]

Balance of trade (current prices)

	1994	1995	1996	1997	1998	1999
U.S.$'000,000	–676	–663	–927	–985	–1,329	–632
% of total	41.0%	37.4%	42.8%	45.2%	52.7%	28.8%

Imports (1999): U.S.$1,412,000,000 (machinery and equipment 25.4%; foodstuffs 19.5%, of which wheat and wheat flour 8.7%; petroleum products 13.0%; transport equipment 9.3%). *Major import sources:* Saudi Arabia 11.8%; France 8.6%; Italy 6.3%; U.A.E. 5.5%; Germany 5.4%; U.K. 5.1%.
Exports (1999): U.S.$780,000,000 (crude petroleum 35.4%; sesame seeds 16.3%; sheep and lambs 13.0%; gold 7.1%; cotton 5.8%). *Major export destinations:* Saudi Arabia 18.1%; Japan 15.7%; U.K. 9.2%; South Korea 7.9%; Italy 7.1%.

Transport and communications

Transport. Railroads: route length (1998) 4,595 km; (1995–96) passenger-km 161,000,000; (1995–96) metric ton-km cargo 1,965,000,000. Roads (1996): total length 11,900 km (paved 36%). Vehicles (1996): passenger cars 285,000; trucks and buses 53,000. Air transport (1998)[16]: passenger-km 530,671,000; metric ton-km cargo 20,293,000; airports (1997) with scheduled flights 3.

Communications

Medium	date	unit	number	units per 1,000 persons
Daily newspapers	1996	circulation	737,000	24
Radio	1997	receivers	7,550,000	235
Television	1997	receivers	2,380,000	74
Telephones	1998	main lines	162,225	4.9
Cellular telephones	1998	subscribers	8,600	0.3
Personal computers	1998	units	55,000	1.7
Internet	1998	users	500	0.02

Education and health

Educational attainment (1983). Percentage of population age 25 and over having: no formal schooling 76.7%; complete secondary 2.0%; higher 0.8%. *Literacy* (1995): total population age 15 and over literate 8,720,000 (50.8%); males 5,460,000 (63.5%); females 3,260,000 (38.3%).

Education (1996–97)

	schools	teachers	students	student/teacher ratio
Primary (age 7–12)	11,158	102,987	3,000,048	29.1
Secondary (age 13–18)	...	15,504	405,583	26.2
Vocational	...	761	26,421	34.7
Higher[17]	6	1,417	52,260	36.9

Health: physicians (1994) 2,736 (1 per 10,900 persons); hospital beds (1986) 18,571 (1 per 1,222 persons); infant mortality rate (1999) 71.8.
Food (1998): daily per capita caloric intake 2,444 (vegetable products 80%, animal products 20%); 104% of FAO recommended minimum.

Military

Total active duty personnel (1999): 94,700 (army 95.0%, navy 1.8%, air force 3.2%). *Military expenditure as percentage of GNP* (1997): 4.6% (world 2.6%); per capita expenditure U.S.$13.

[1]A state of emergency (along with dissolution of parliament) imposed Dec. 12, 1999, was extended through November 2000. [2]English has been designated the "principal" language in southern Sudan. [3]Islamic law and custom are sources of national law per suspended 1998 constitution. [4]The Sudanese dinar (Sd), introduced May 1992 at a value equal to 10 Sudanese pounds (LSd), officially replaced the Sudanese pound on March 1, 1999. [5]Local administrative reorganization into 26 new states was announced in February 1994 and confirmed in June 1998; area and population breakdown was not available in 2000. [6]Including *c.* 50,000 sq mi (130,000 sq km) of inland water area. [7]Preliminary unadjusted 1993 census figure was 24,940,683, including an estimated 3,850,000 in the southern Sudan. [8]1998–99. [9]1996. [10]At factor cost. [11]Excludes nomads, the homeless, and institutionalized persons. [12]Includes 592,759 unemployed not previously employed. [13]April. [14]Average annual income of paid worker (1992) U.S.$216. [15]Imports c.i.f.; exports f.o.b. [16]Sudan Airways only. [17]Universities only.

Internet resources for further information:

- **The Sudan Page (unofficial)** **http://www.sudan.net**

Suriname

Official name: Republiek Suriname (Republic of Suriname).
Form of government: multiparty republic with one legislative house (National Assembly [51]).
Head of state and government: President.
Capital: Paramaribo.
Official language: Dutch.
Official religion: none.
Monetary unit: 1 Suriname guilder (Sf) = 100 cents; valuation (Oct. 6, 2000) 1 U.S.$ = Sf 809.50; 1 £ = Sf 1,171.

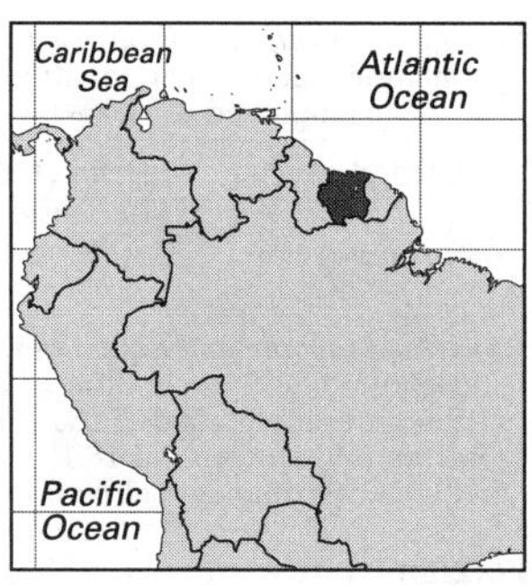

Area and population		area		population
				1992
Districts	**Capitals**	sq mi	sq km	estimate
Brokopondo	Brokopondo	2,843	7,364	7,554
Commewijne	Nieuw Amsterdam	908	2,353	22,822
Coronie	Totness	1,507	3,902	3,151
Marowijne	Albina	1,786	4,627	18,339
Nickerie	Nieuw Nickerie	2,067	5,353	37,200
Para	Onverwacht	2,082	5,393	13,693
Saramacca	Groningen	1,404	3,636	12,320
Sipaliwini	...	50,412	130,566	26,458
Wanica	Lelydorp	171	443	69,114
Town district				
Paramaribo	Paramaribo	71	183	240,000
TOTAL		63,251[1]	163,820[1]	465,651

Demography

Population (2000): 431,000.
Density (2000): persons per sq mi 6.8, persons per sq km 2.6.
Urban-rural (1998): urban 51.0%; rural 49.0%.
Sex distribution (1999): male 50.74%; female 49.26%.
Age breakdown (1999): under 15, 32.5%; 15–29, 27.6%; 30–44, 22.1%; 45–59, 9.7%; 60–74, 6.4%; 75 and over, 1.7%.
Population projection: (2010) 450,000; (2020) 457,000.
Doubling time: 44 years.
Ethnic composition (1999): Indo-Pakistani 37.0%; Suriname Creole 31.0%; Javanese 15.0%; Bush Negro 10.0%; Amerindian 2.5%; Chinese 2.0%; white 1.0%; other 1.5%.
Religious affiliation (1995): Hindu 27.4%; Roman Catholic 21.0%; Muslim 19.6%; Protestant (mostly Moravian) 16.4%; other 15.6%.
Major cities (1980): Paramaribo 289,000[2]; Nieuw Nickerie 6,078; Meerzorg 5,355; Marienburg 3,633.

Vital statistics

Birth rate per 1,000 population (1999): 21.7 (world avg. 22.1).
Death rate per 1,000 population (1999): 5.7 (world avg. 8.9).
Natural increase rate per 1,000 population (1999): 16.0 (world avg. 13.2).
Total fertility rate (avg. births per childbearing woman; 1999): 2.5.
Marriage rate per 1,000 population (1991): 4.9.
Divorce rate per 1,000 population (1991): 2.5.
Life expectancy at birth (1999): male 68.4 years; female 73.2 years.
Major causes of death per 100,000 population (1992): noncommunicable diseases 769.0; external and other causes 608.1; communicable and perinatal diseases 232.8; ill-defined diseases 279.0.

National economy

Budget (1996). Revenue: Sf 90,874,600,000 (direct taxes 42.2%; indirect taxes 32.2%; bauxite levy 25.0%; other 0.6%). Expenditures: Sf 96,957,700,000 (current expenditures 99.6%, of which wages and salaries 28.5%, transfers 13.7%, debt service 1.7%; capital expenditures 0.4%).
Production (metric tons except as noted). Agriculture, forestry, fishing (1999): rice 180,400, sugarcane 90,000, bananas 55,000, plantains 13,000, oranges 12,000, coconuts 9,400, cassava 4,000, cucumbers 3,220, watermelons 2,700, tomatoes 1,625, cabbage 990, grapefruit 940; livestock (number of live animals) 102,000 cattle, 25,000 pigs, 10,600 sheep, 10,000 goats, 2,200,000 chickens; roundwood (1998) 183,000 cu m; fish catch (1997) 13,000. Mining and quarrying (1997): bauxite 3,877,000; gold 6,993 troy oz. Manufacturing (value of production at factor cost in Sf; 1993): food products 992,000,000; beverages 558,000,000; tobacco 369,000,000; chemical products 291,000,000; pottery and earthenware 258,000,000; wood products 180,000,000. Construction (value of building authorized; 1985): residential Sf 46,500,000; nonresidential Sf 8,100,000. Energy production (consumption): electricity (kW-hr; 1996) 1,621,000,000 (1,621,000,000); hard coal (metric tons) none (n.a.); crude petroleum (barrels; 1996) 1,519,000 (1,227,000); petroleum products (metric tons; 1996) none (478,000); natural gas, none (none).
Household income and expenditure. Average household size (1998) 4.8; income per household: n.a.; sources of income (1975): wages and salaries 74.6%, transfer payments 3.2%, other 22.2%; expenditure (1968–69): food and beverages 40.0%, household furnishings 12.3%, clothing and footwear 11.0%, transportation and communications 9.5%, recreation and education 8.4%, energy 6.9%, housing 4.4%, other 7.5%.
Land use (1994): forested 96.2%; meadows and pastures 0.1%; agricultural and under permanent cultivation 0.4%; other 3.3%.
Gross national product (at current market prices; 1998): U.S.$684,000,000 (U.S.$1,660 per capita).

Structure of gross domestic product and labour force	1996		1994	
	in value Sf '000,000[3]	% of total value[3]	labour force	% of labour force
Agriculture, forestry	104.4	7.0	19,940[4]	20.3[4]
Mining	190.8	12.9	3,181	3.2
Manufacturing	148.9	10.1	4,432	4.5
Construction	47.3	3.2	1,656	1.7
Public utilities	126.7	8.6	1,288	1.3
Transp. and commun.	139.3	9.4	2,112	2.1
Trade[5]	123.9	8.4	4,383	4.5
Finance, real estate	551.3	37.2	1,954	2.0
Pub. admin., defense	289.0	19.5	38,552	39.2
Services	7.4	0.5	2,010	2.0
Other	–248.0[6]	–16.7[6]	18,732[7]	19.1[7]
TOTAL	1,481.0	100.0[8]	98,240	100.0[8]

Public debt (external, outstanding; 1996): U.S.$216,500,000.
Population economically active (1994): total 98,240; activity rate of total population 24.3% (participation rates[9, 10]: ages 15–64, 56.0%; female 37.5%; unemployed [1996] 10.7%).

Price and earnings indexes (1995 = 100)	1991	1992	1993	1994	1995	1996	1997
Consumer price index	1.8	2.6	6.4	29.8	100.0	99.3	106.4
Earnings index	...	...	...	...	...	...	...

Tourism (1997): receipts from visitors U.S.$43,000,000; expenditures by nationals abroad U.S.$3,000,000[11].

Foreign trade

Balance of trade (current prices)	1991	1992	1993	1994	1995	1996
U.S.$'000,000	–117.9	–110.8	–77.2	–99.3	+38.3	+18.8
% of total	11.3%	10.2%	8.0%	20.4%	4.6%	2.2%

Imports (1995): Sf 258,916,700,000 (raw materials 36.4%, investment goods 25.2%, fuels and lubricants 11.1%, food and live animals 9.7%, cars and motorcycles 3.8%). *Major import sources:* U.S. 42.1%; The Netherlands 19.8%; Trinidad and Tobago 7.4%; Netherlands Antilles 2.6%; Japan 2.1%.
Exports (1995): Sf 211,020,600,000 (1994; alumina 63.6%, shrimp and fish 9.7%, rice 9.6%, aluminum 9.3%, petroleum 3.0%, bananas 2.9%). *Major export destinations:* The Netherlands 27.9%; Norway 24.9%; U.S. 22.3%; Japan 6.1%; Brazil 5.2%.

Transport and communications

Transport. Railroads (1997)[12]: length 187 mi, 301 km; passengers, not applicable; cargo, n.a. Roads (1996): total length 2,815 mi, 4,530 km (paved 26%). Vehicles (1996): passenger cars 46,408; trucks and buses 19,255. Merchant marine (1992): vessels (100 gross tons and over) 24; total deadweight tonnage 15,721. Air transport (1996): passenger-mi 548,885,000, passenger-km 883,347,000; short ton-mi cargo 65,865,000, metric ton-km cargo 106,000,000; airports (1998) with scheduled flights 1.

Communications				units
Medium	date	unit	number	per 1,000 persons
Daily newspapers	1996	circulation	50,000	122
Radio	1997	receivers	300,000	728
Television	1997	receivers	63,000	153
Telephones	1999	main lines	67,308	163
Cellular telephones	1999	subscribers	6,007	14.5
Internet	1999	users	7,236	17.5

Education and health

Educational attainment: n.a. *Literacy* (1995): total population age 15 and over literate 271,000 (93.0%); males literate 137,000 (95.1%); females literate 134,000 (91.0%).

Education (1995–96)	schools	teachers	students	student/ teacher ratio
Primary (age 6–11)	304	3,611	75,585	20.9
Secondary (age 12–18)	104	2,286	31,918	13.9
Teacher training	1	...	1,462	...
Higher	1	155	1,335	8.6

Health: physicians (1998) 166 (1 per 2,518 persons); hospital beds (1998) 1,449 (1 per 288 persons); infant mortality rate per 1,000 live births (1999) 26.0.
Food (1998): daily per capita caloric intake 2,633 (vegetable products 86%, animal products 14%); 117% of FAO recommended minimum requirement.

Military

Total active duty personnel (1998): 1,800[13] (army 77.8%, navy 13.3%, air force 8.9%). *Military expenditure as percentage of GNP* (1997): 1.2% (world 2.6%); per capita expenditure U.S.$43.

[1]Area excludes 6,809 sq mi (17,635 sq km) of territory disputed with Guyana. [2]1997. [3]At factor cost; 1980 prices. [4]Derived value. [5]Includes hotels. [6]Indirect taxes less subsidies and imputed bank service charges. [7]Includes 11,300 unemployed. [8]Detail does not add to total given because of rounding. [9]Districts of Wanica and Paramaribo only. [10]1992. [11]1995. [12]There are no public railways operating in Suriname. [13]All services are part of the army.

Internet resources for further information:
- **Suriname Home Page http://www.sesrtcic.org/dir-sur/surhome.htm**

Swaziland

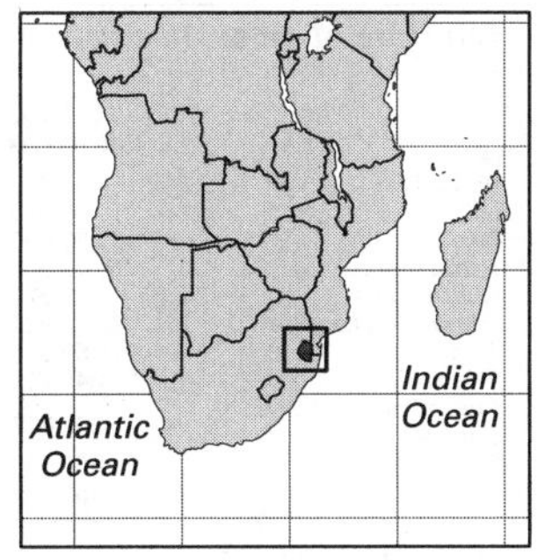

Official name: Umbuso weSwatini (Swazi); Kingdom of Swaziland (English).
Form of government[1]: monarchy with two legislative houses (Senate [30[2]]; House of Assembly [65[3]]).
Head of state and government: King, assisted by Prime Minister.
Capitals: Mbabane (administrative and judicial); Lozitha and Ludzidzini (royal); Lobamba (legislative).
Official languages: Swazi; English.
Official religion: none.
Monetary unit: 1 lilangeni[4] (plural emalangeni [E]) = 100 cents; valuation (Oct. 6, 2000) 1 U.S.$ = E 7.29; 1 £ = E 10.54.

Area and population

Districts	Capitals	area sq mi	area sq km	population 1997 census
Hhohho	Mbabane	1,378	3,569	269,826
Lubombo	Siteki	2,296	5,947	201,696
Manzini	Manzini	1,571	4,068	292,100
Shiselweni	Nhlangano	1,459	3,780	217,100
TOTAL		6,704	17,364	980,722[5]

Demography

Population (2000): 1,083,000.
Density (2000): persons per sq mi 161.6, persons per sq km 62.4.
Urban-rural (1997): urban 22.6%; rural 77.4%.
Sex distribution (1997): male 48.28%; female 51.72%.
Age breakdown (1997): under 15, 42.5%; 15–29, 29.2%; 30–44, 15.5%; 45–59, 7.8%; 60–74, 3.3%; 75 and over, 1.2%; unknown 0.5%.
Population projection: (2010) 1,216,000; (2020) 1,296,000.
Doubling time: 32 years.
Ethnic composition (1983): Swazi 84.3%; Zulu 9.9%; Tsonga 2.5%; Indian 0.8%; Pakistani 0.8%; Portuguese 0.2%; other 1.5%.
Religious affiliation (1995): Christian 66.7%, of which African indigenous 44.7%, Protestant 14.8%, Roman Catholic 5.3%; other (mostly traditional beliefs) 33.3%.
Major cities (1986): Manzini 52,000; Mbabane 38,290; Nhlangano 4,107; Piggs Peak 3,223; Siteki 2,271.

Vital statistics

Birth rate per 1,000 population (1999): 41.1 (world avg. 22.1).
Death rate per 1,000 population (1999): 19.3 (world avg. 8.9).
Natural increase rate per 1,000 population (1999): 21.8 (world avg. 13.2).
Total fertility rate (avg. births per childbearing woman; 1999): 5.9.
Life expectancy at birth (1999): male 40.8 years; female 43.3 years.
Major causes of death (1992)[6]: accidents and injuries 15.8%; infectious intestinal diseases 13.3%; tuberculosis 10.3%; malnutrition 6.2%; respiratory diseases 5.3%; circulatory diseases 5.0%; digestive diseases 4.6%.

National economy

Budget (1999–2000). Revenue: E 2,436,400,000 (receipts from Customs Union of Southern Africa 50.1%; tax on income and profits 25.8%; sales tax 12.0%; foreign-aid grants 3.5%; property income 2.1%; fees, services, and fines 1.1%). Expenditures: E 2,630,700,000 (recurrent expenditure 78.2%, of which general administration 28.0%, education 17.3%, economic services 11.2%, justice and police 8.0%, health 6.5%, defense 4.8%).
Gross national product (1998): U.S.$1,384,000,000 (U.S.$1,400 per capita).

Structure of gross domestic product and labour force

	1999 in value E '000	1999 % of total value	1986 labour force	1986 % of labour force
Agriculture	904,900	11.7	30,197	18.8
Mining	51,400	0.7	5,245	3.3
Manufacturing	2,148,700	27.7	14,742	9.2
Construction	278,800	3.6	7,661	4.8
Public utilities	117,700	1.5	1,315	0.8
Transp. and commun.	290,600	3.7	7,526	4.7
Trade	530,500	6.8	12,348	7.7
Finance	333,300	4.3	1,931	1.2
Pub. admin., defense	1,158,100	15.0	32,309	20.1
Services	82,100	1.1		
Other	1,849,700[7]	23.9[7]	47,081[8]	29.4[8]
TOTAL	7,746,000[9]	100.0	160,355	100.0

Population economically active (1986): total 160,355; activity rate of total population 23.5% (participation rates: ages 15 and over, 44.1%; female 34.2%; unemployed 27.0%).

Price and earnings indexes (1995 = 100)

	1993	1994	1995	1996	1997	1998	1999
Consumer price index	78.3	89.1	100.0	106.4	114.0	123.3	130.8
Weekly earnings index[10]	...	...	100.0	100.0	95.7	95.7	98.3

Public debt (external, outstanding; 1998): U.S.$222,500,000.
Production (metric tons except as noted). Agriculture, forestry, fishing (1999): sugarcane 3,700,000, corn (maize) 113,000, oranges 31,200, grapefruit and pomelo 25,400, seed cotton 16,200, roots and tubers 8,300 (of which potatoes 6,000, sweet potatoes 2,300), pineapples 8,000, dry beans 5,000, peanuts (groundnuts) 4,600; livestock (number of live animals) 652,000 cattle, 438,000 goats, 31,000 pigs, 26,000 sheep, 980,000 chickens; roundwood (1998) 1,494,000 cu m; fish catch (1998) 60. Mining and quarrying (1999): asbestos 22,912; diamonds 64,000 carats[11]. Manufacturing (value added in U.S.$'000; 1994): food and beverages 244,000, of which beverage processing 153,000; paper and paper products 35,000; textiles 19,000; printing and publishing products 18,000; clothing 7,000; metal and metal products 7,000. Construction (value in E; 1996)[12]: residential 34,100,000; nonresidential 17,500,000. Energy production (consumption): electricity (kW-hr; 1991) 387,000,000 (815,000,000); coal (metric tons; 1999) 426,299 (1989; 28,454); crude petroleum, n.a. (n.a.).
Household income and expenditure. Average household size (1986) 5.7; annual income per household (1985) E 332 (U.S.$151); sources of income (1985): wages and salaries 44.4%, self-employment 22.2%, transfers 12.2%, other 21.2%; expenditure (1985): food and beverages 33.5%, rent and fuel 13.4%, household durable goods 12.8%, transportation and communications 8.8%, clothing and footwear 6.0%, recreation 3.3%.
Tourism (1997): receipts U.S.$37,000,000; expenditures U.S.$44,000,000.

Foreign trade

Balance of trade (current prices)

	1995	1996	1997	1998	1999
U.S.$'000,000	−197	−204	−127	−100	−130
% of total	10.2%	10.7%	6.2%	4.9%	6.6%

Imports (1998): U.S.$1,068,000,000 (machinery and transport equipment 26.2%; manufactured items 17.0%; foodstuffs 15.8%; chemicals 13.9%; minerals, fuels, and lubricants 11.8%). *Major import sources* (1997–98): South Africa 82.9%; U.K. 1.7%; U.S. 0.9%; Zimbabwe 0.2%; Spain 0.2%.
Exports (1998): U.S.$921,000,000 (sugar 11.0%; wood and wood products 8.1%; refrigerators 7.5%; cotton yarn 2.3%; paper and paper products 2.0%; canned fruits 1.4%; citrus fruits 1.3%; asbestos 1.0%). *Major export destinations* (1997): South Africa 74.0%; Italy 8.7%; Mozambique 5.2%; U.S. 2.4%; U.K. 2.1%; Zimbabwe 1.7%.

Transport and communications

Transport. Railroads (1995)[13]: length 187 mi, 301 km; passenger-mi 752,000,000[14], passenger-km 1,210,000,000[14]; short ton-mi cargo 1,993,000,000[15], metric ton-km cargo 2,910,000,000[15]. Roads (1996): total length 2,367 mi, 3,810 km (paved 29%). Vehicles (1997): passenger cars 31,882; trucks and buses 32,772. Air transport (1995)[16]: passenger-mi 30,710,000, passenger-km 49,423,000; short ton-mi cargo 87,000, metric ton-km cargo 127,000; airports (1997) with scheduled flights 1.

Communications

Medium	date	unit	number	units per 1,000 persons
Daily newspapers	1996	circulation	24,000	24.3
Radio	1997	receivers	155,000	153
Television	1998	receivers	108,000	104
Telephones	1998	main lines	28,999	28.0
Cellular telephones	1998	subscribers	4,700	4.5
Personal computers	1998	units	278	0.3
Internet	1998	users	1,000	1.0

Education and health

Educational attainment (1986). Percentage of population age 25 and over having: no formal schooling 42.1%; some primary education 23.9%; complete primary 10.5%; some secondary 19.2%; complete secondary and higher 4.3%.
Literacy (1995): total population age 15 and over literate 76.7%; males literate 78.0%; females literate 75.6%.

Education (1997)

	schools	teachers	students	student/ teacher ratio
Primary (age 6–13)	529	6,094	205,829	33.8
Secondary (age 14–18)	175	3,067	58,197	19.0
Voc., teacher tr.[17]	5	228	2,958	13.0
Higher	1	190[17]	2,132	9.1[17]

Health: physicians (1996) 148 (1 per 6,663 persons); hospital beds (1984) 1,608 (1 per 396 persons); infant mortality rate per 1,000 live births (1999) 108.3.
Food (1997): daily per capita caloric intake 2,503 (vegetable products 87%, animal products 13%); 108% of FAO recommended minimum requirement.

Military

Total active duty personnel (1983): 2,657. *Military expenditure as percentage of GNP* (1997): 2.7% (world 2.6%); per capita expenditure U.S.$34.

[1]The Constitutional Review Committee announced by the King in July 1996 continued to prepare a new draft constitution in mid-1999. [2]Includes 20 nonelective seats. [3]Includes 10 nonelective seats. [4]The lilangeni is at par with the South African rand. [5]Includes residents abroad. [6]Percentage of deaths of known cause at government, mission, and private hospitals. [7]Includes indirect taxes less imputed bank service charges and subsidies. [8]Includes 43,925 unemployed. [9]Detail does not add to total given because of rounding. [10]Manufacturing sector only. [11]1994. [12]Urban areas under the jurisdiction of the Manzini and Mbabane town councils only. [13]Swaziland's only passenger train service was terminated in May 2000. [14]1988. [15]1991. [16]Royal Swazi National Airways only; international flights only. [17]1993–94.

Internet resources for further information:
- **Central Bank of Swaziland http://www.centralbank.sz**
- **Swaziland on the Internet http://www.realnet.co.sz**

Sweden

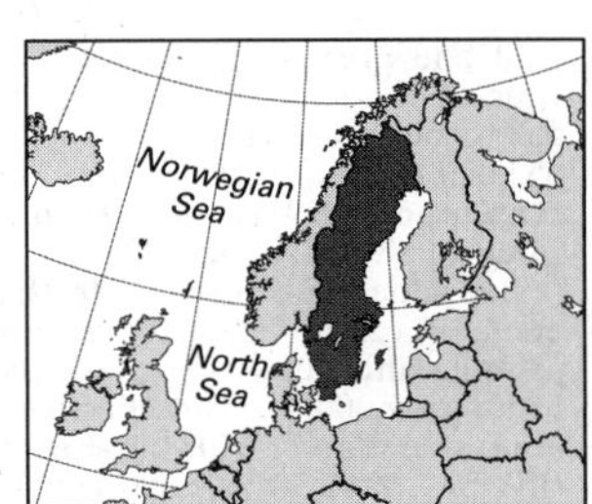

Official name: Konungariket Sverige (Kingdom of Sweden).
Form of government: constitutional monarchy and parliamentary state with one legislative house (Parliament [349]).
Chief of state: King.
Head of government: Prime Minister.
Capital: Stockholm.
Official language: Swedish.
Official religion: none[1].
Monetary unit: 1 Swedish krona (SKr) = 100 ore; valuation (Oct. 6, 2000) 1 U.S.$ = SKr 9.81; 1 £ = SKr 14.20.

Area and population

Counties	Capitals	area sq mi	area sq km	population 1999[2] estimate
Blekinge	Karlskrona	1,136	2,941	151,414
Dalarna	Falun	10,885	28,193	282,898
Gävleborg	Gävle	7,024	18,192	282,226
Gotland	Visby	1,212	3,140	57,643
Halland	Halmstad	2,106	5,454	272,539
Jämtland	Östersund	19,090	49,443	131,766
Jönköping	Jönköping	4,044	10,475	328,059
Kalmar	Kalmar	4,313	11,171	238,104
Kronoberg	Växjö	3,266	8,458	178,078
Norrbotten	Luleå	38,190	98,911	260,473
Örebro	Örebro	3,288	8,517	274,584
Östergötland	Linköping	4,078	10,562	412,411
Skåne	Malmo	4,258	11,027	1,120,426
Södermanland	Nyköping	2,341	6,062	256,269
Stockholm	Stockholm	2,506	6,490	1,783,440
Uppsala	Uppsala	2,698	6,989	291,413
Värmland	Karlstad	6,790	17,586	278,313
Västerbotten	Umeå	21,390	55,401	257,803
Västernorrland	Härnösand	8,370	21,678	251,884
Västmanland	Västerås	2,433	6,302	257,661
Västra Götaland	Göteborg	9,244	23,942	1,486,918
TOTAL LAND AREA		158,663[3]	410,934	
INLAND WATER		15,071	39,035	
TOTAL		173,734	449,969	8,854,322

Demography

Population (2000): 8,864,000.
Density (2000)[4]: persons per sq mi 55.9, persons per sq km 21.6.
Urban-rural (1999): urban 83.3%; rural 16.7%.
Sex distribution (1999): male 49.57%; female 50.43%.
Age breakdown (1997[2]): under 15, 18.8%; 15–29, 19.0%; 30–44, 20.6%; 45–59, 19.6%; 60–74, 13.4%; 75 and over, 8.6%.
Population projection: (2010) 8,873,000; (2020) 8,920,000.
Ethnic composition (1997[2]): Swedish 89.3%; Finnish 2.3%; Yugoslavian 0.8%; Iranian 0.6%; Bosnian 0.5%; other 6.5%.
Religious affiliation (1997[2]): Church of Sweden 86.1% (nominally; about 30% nonpracticing); Roman Catholic 2.0%; Pentecostal 1.1%; other 12.6%.
Major cities (1999): Stockholm 736,113; Göteborg 459,593; Malmö 254,904; Uppsala 187,302; Linköping 131,948.

Vital statistics

Birth rate per 1,000 population (1999): 10.1 (world avg. 22.1); (1997) legitimate 46.1%; illegitimate 53.9%.
Death rate per 1,000 population (1999): 10.6 (world avg. 8.9).
Natural increase rate per 1,000 population (1999): –0.5 (world avg. 13.2).
Total fertility rate (avg. births per childbearing woman; 1999): 1.5.
Marriage rate per 1,000 population (1997): 3.6.
Divorce rate per 1,000 population (1997): 2.4.
Life expectancy at birth (1999): male 76.9 years; female 82.2 years.
Major causes of death per 100,000 population (1996): heart disease 404.4; malignant neoplasms (cancers) 234.8; cerebrovascular disease 114.4.

National economy

Budget (1997). Revenue: SKr 648,928,000,000 (value-added and excise taxes 35.2%, social security 29.8%, income and capital gains taxes 16.9%, property taxes 3.6%). Expenditures: SKr 655,156,000,000 (health and social affairs 25.1%, debt service 15.0%, defense 6.2%, education 5.2%).
Public debt (1999[2]): U.S.$76,235,000,000.
Production (metric tons except as noted). Agriculture, forestry, fishing (1998): sugar beets 2,500,000, wheat 2,287,000, barley 1,706,000, potatoes 1,263,000, oats 1,149,000; livestock (number of live animals) 2,309,000 pigs, 1,706,000 cattle, 407,000 sheep; roundwood (1998) 60,224,000 cu m; fish catch (1996) 412,153. Mining and quarrying (1997): iron ore 21,893,000; copper 315,000; zinc 284,000. Manufacturing (value added, in SKr '000,000; 1994): machinery and transport equipment 119,630; paper products 42,503; food 24,145; wood products 12,359; textiles and wearing apparel 3,767. Construction (dwellings completed; 1995): 12,678. Energy production (consumption): electricity (kW-hr; 1994) 142,889,000,000 (143,150,000,000); coal (metric tons; 1994) none (3,305,000); crude petroleum (barrels; 1994) 36,200 (128,773,000); petroleum products (metric tons; 1994) 16,616,000 (13,961,000); natural gas (cu m; 1994) none (763,223,000).
Tourism (1998): receipts U.S.$4,189,000,000; expenditures U.S.$7,723,000,000.
Land use (1994): forest 68.0%; pasture 1.4%; agriculture 6.8%; other 23.8%.
Gross national product (1998): U.S.$226,454,000 (U.S.$25,580 per capita).

Structure of gross domestic product and labour force

	1995 in value SKr '000,000	1995 % of total value	1996 labour force	1996 % of labour force
Agriculture	34,770	2.4	115,000	2.7
Mining	4,525	0.3	} 809,000	} 18.8
Manufacturing	352,301	24.3		
Public utilities	42,283	2.9		
Construction	77,575	5.3	225,000	5.2
Transp. and commun.	94,824	6.5	} 762,000	} 17.7
Trade	169,339	11.6		
Finance	343,791	23.6	433,000	10.0
Pub. admin., defense } Services	392,817	27.0	1,616,000	37.5
Other	–58,806[5]	–4.0[5]	349,000[6]	8.1[6]
TOTAL	1,453,419	100.0[3]	4,310,000[3]	100.0

Population economically active (1996): total 4,310,000; activity rate of total population 48.7% (participation rates: ages 16–64, 77.8%; female 48.1%; unemployed 8.0%).

Price and earnings indexes (1995 = 100)

	1993	1994	1995	1996	1997	1998	1999
Consumer price index	95.0	98.0	100.0	100.0	101.0	101.0	101.1
Hourly earnings index	95.7	97.9	100.0	101.9	103.4	103.1	...

Household income and expenditure. Average household size (1994) 2.1[7]; median income per household SKr 396,100 (U.S.$51,330); sources of income (1992): wages and salaries 58.9%, transfer payments 25.8%, self-employment 15.3%; expenditure (1995): housing and energy 29.6%, food 20.9%, transportation 16.1%, education and recreation 9.2%.

Foreign trade

Balance of trade (current prices)

	1994	1995	1996	1997	1998	1999
SKr '000,000	82,735	82,735	120,000	131,600	129,700	135,100
% of total	9.6%	8.1%	11.8%	11.6%	10.7%	10.7%

Imports (1996): SKr 447,600,000,000 (machinery and transport equipment 40.4%; chemicals 10.4%; food 6.6%). *Major import sources:* Germany 18.8%; U.K. 10.2%; Norway 7.8%; Denmark 7.5%; U.S. 5.8%.
Exports (1996): SKr 567,300,000,000 (machinery and transport equipment 47.4%, of which electrical machinery 17.2%; paper products 9.1%; chemicals 8.7%; iron and steel products 5.5%). *Major export destinations:* Germany 11.7%; U.K. 9.6%; Norway 8.4%; U.S. 8.3%; Denmark 6.3%.

Transport and communications

Transport. Railroads (1996): length 6,756 mi, 10,874 km; passenger-km 6,348,000,000; metric ton-km cargo 18,840,000,000. Roads (1998[2]): total length 121,807 mi, 196,030 km (paved 72%[8]). Vehicles (1997[2]): passenger cars 3,655,000; trucks and buses 339,000. Merchant marine (1997[2]): vessels (100 gross tons and over) 450; total deadweight tonnage 2,948,000. Air transport (1997): passenger-km 14,247,396,000; metric ton-km cargo 293,455,000; airports (1996) 48.

Communications

Medium	date	unit	number	units per 1,000 persons
Daily newspapers	1996	circulation	3,933,000	446
Radio	1997	receivers	8,250,000	932
Television	1998	receivers	4,700,000	531
Telephones	1998	main lines	5,965,000	674
Cellular telephones	1998	subscribers	4,108,000	464
Personal computers	1998	units	3,200,000	361
Internet	1998	users	3,500,000	395

Education and health

Educational attainment (1997[2]). Percentage of population age 16–64 having: primary education 27.8%; lower secondary education 31.2%; higher secondary 15.7%; some postsecondary 25.3%. *Literacy* (1997): virtually 100%.

Education (1996–97)

	schools	teachers	students	student/ teacher ratio
Primary (age 7–12)	4,936	81,000	958,972	11.8
Secondary (age 13–18)	641	28,305	310,000	11.0
Higher[9]	...	29,487	268,448	9.1

Health (1997): physicians 23,000 (1 per 384 persons); hospital beds 38,139 (1 per 232 persons); infant mortality rate per 1,000 live births (1999) 3.4.
Food (1997): daily per capita caloric intake 3,194 (vegetable 66%, animal 34%).

Military

Total active duty personnel (1999): 53,100 (army 66.1%, navy 17.3%, air force 16.6%). *Military expenditure as percentage of GNP* (1997): 2.5% (world 2.6%); per capita expenditure U.S.$626.

[1]As of January 1, 2000, Lutheran Church ceased being the official religion. [2]January 1. [3]Detail does not add to total given because of rounding. [4]Density based on land area only. [5]Includes statistical discrepancies less imputed bank service charges. [6]Includes 347,000 unemployed. [7]1990. [8]1996. [9]1994–95.

Internet resources for further information:
- **Statistics Sweden http://www.scb.se/scbeng/svsiffror/svsiffroreng.htm**

Switzerland

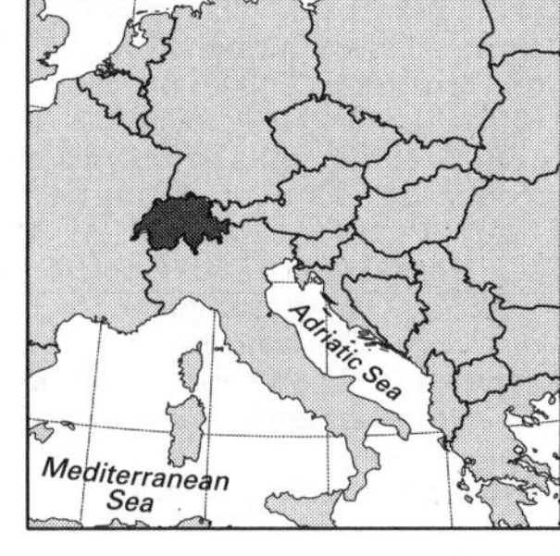

Official name: Confédération Suisse (French); Schweizerische Eidgenossenschaft (German); Confederazione Svizzera (Italian) (Swiss Confederation)[1].
Form of government: federal state with two legislative houses (Council of States [46]; National Council [200]).
Head of state and government: President of the Federal Council.
Capitals: Bern (administrative); Lausanne (judicial).
Official languages: French; German; Italian; Romansh (locally).
Official religion: none.
Monetary unit: 1 Swiss Franc (Sw F) = 100 centimes; valuation (Oct. 6, 2000) 1 U.S.$ = Sw F 1.75; 1 £ = Sw F 2.53.

Area and population

		area		population
Cantons	Capitals	sq mi	sq km	1999[2] estimate
Aargau	Aarau	542	1,404	536,462
Appenzell Ausser-Rhoden[3]	Herisau	94	243	53,816
Appenzell Inner-Rhoden[3]	Appenzell	66	172	14,873
Basel-Landschaft[3]	Liestal	200	518	256,761
Basel-Stadt[3]	Basel	14	37	190,505
Bern	Bern	2,301	5,959	941,144
Fribourg	Fribourg	645	1,671	232,086
Genève	Geneva	109	282	398,910
Glarus	Glarus	264	685	38,698
Graubünden	Chur	2,743	7,105	186,118
Jura	Delémont	324	838	68,995
Luzern	Luzern	576	1,493	343,254
Neuchâtel	Neuchâtel	310	803	165,594
Nidwalden[3]	Stans	107	276	37,320
Obwalden[3]	Sarnen	190	491	31,989
Sankt Gallen	Sankt Gallen	782	2,026	444,891
Schaffhausen	Schaffhausen	115	298	73,725
Schwyz	Schwyz	351	908	126,479
Solothurn	Solothurn	305	791	243,450
Thurgau	Frauenfeld	383	991	226,479
Ticino	Bellinzona	1,086	2,812	306,179
Uri	Altdorf	416	1,077	35,612
Valais	Sion	2,017	5,224	274,458
Vaud	Lausanne	1,240	3,212	611,613
Zug	Zug	92	239	96,517
Zürich	Zürich	668	1,729	1,187,609
TOTAL		15,940	41,284	7,123,537[4]

Demography

Population (2000): 7,177,000.
Density (2000): persons per sq mi 450.3, persons per sq km 173.8.
Urban-rural (1999): urban 67.5%; rural 32.5%.
Sex distribution (1999): male 48.83%; female 51.17%.
Age breakdown (1999): under 15, 17.5%; 15–29, 18.5%; 30–44, 24.3%; 45–59, 19.6%; 60–74, 13.0%; 75 and over, 7.1%.
Population projection: (2010) 7,299,000; (2020) 7,309,000.
Linguistic composition (1990): German 63.6%; French 19.2%; Italian 7.6%; Spanish 1.7%; Portuguese 1.4%; Romansh 0.6%; other 5.9%.
Religious affiliation (1990): Roman Catholic 46.2%; Protestant 40.0%; Muslim 2.2%; Orthodox Christian 1.0%; Jewish 0.3%; other 10.3%.
Major urban agglomerations (1999[2]): Zürich 935,118; Geneva 452,248; Basel 402,387; Bern 317,367; Lausanne 286,106; Luzern 180,427.

Vital statistics

Birth rate per 1,000 population (1999): 10.3 (world avg. 22.1); (1998) legitimate 91.2%; illegitimate 8.8%.
Death rate per 1,000 population (1999): 8.3 (world avg. 8.9).
Natural increase rate per 1,000 population (1999): 2.0 (world avg. 13.2).
Total fertility rate (avg. births per childbearing woman; 1998): 1.5.
Marriage rate per 1,000 population (1998): 5.4.
Life expectancy at birth (1997–98): male 76.5 years; female 82.5 years.
Major causes of death per 100,000 population (1996): heart disease 226.4, of which ischemic 145.9, other 80.5; malignant neoplasms (cancers) 222.7.

National economy

Budget (1996)[5]. Revenue: Sw F 91,911,000,000 (social security contributions 46.2%, turnover taxes 13.1%, income taxes 13.0%). Expenditures: Sw F 96,095,000,000 (social security and welfare 52.0%, health 15.6%, economic affairs 11.7%, defense 5.8%, education 2.6%).
National debt (end of year; 1999): Sw F 102,254,000,000.
Tourism (1998): receipts from visitors U.S.$7,815,000,000; expenditures by nationals abroad U.S.$7,094,000,000.
Production (metric tons except as noted). Agriculture, forestry, fishing (1998): cow's milk 3,905,000, sugar beets 1,125,000, wheat 616,000, potatoes 602,000, apples 365,000, barley 327,000, grapes 151,000; livestock (number of live animals) 1,637,000 cattle, 1,486,000 pigs; roundwood 4,500,000 cu m; fish catch (1997) 1,859. Mining (1997): salt 400,000. Manufacturing (value added in U.S.$'000,000; 1995): electrical machinery 10,752; chemicals and chemical products 10,372; nonelectrical machinery 10,269; food products 6,472. Energy production (consumption): electricity (kW-hr; 1999) 66,696,000,000 ([1996] 56,117,000,000); coal (metric tons; 1996) none (183,000); crude petroleum (barrels; 1996) none (38,534,000); petroleum products (metric tons; 1996) 5,103,000 (11,738,000); natural gas (cu m; 1996) negligible (2,902,000,000).
Gross national product (1998): U.S.$284,119,000,000 (U.S.$39,980 per capita).

Structure of gross domestic product and labour force

	1994		1997	
	in value SwF '000,000	% of total value	labour force	% of labour force
Agriculture	9,230	2.6	176,000	4.4
Manufacturing	80,997	23.0	693,000	17.4
Mining	...	...	6,000	0.2
Public utilities	7,741	2.2	24,000	0.6
Construction	24,749	7.0	296,000	7.4
Transp. and commun.	22,173	6.3	248,000	6.2
Trade	61,092	17.3	880,000	22.0
Finance, insurance[6]	84,744	24.0	553,000	13.9
Pub. admin., defense	45,647	12.9	152,000	3.8
Services	27,769	7.9	775,000	19.4
Other	–11,218[7]	–3.2[7]	188,000[8]	4.7[8]
TOTAL	352,924	100.0	3,991,000[9]	100.0

Population economically active (1996)[10]: total 3,925,000; activity rate of total population 55.4% (participation rates: ages 15–64, 79.3%; female 43.6%; unemployed [April 1999–March 2000] 2.5%).

Price and earnings indexes (1995 = 100)

	1994	1995	1996	1997	1998	1999[10]	2000
Consumer price index	98.2	100.0	100.8	101.3	101.4	102.2	103.8[11]
Annual earnings index	98.7	100.0	101.2	101.7	...	...	...

Household income and expenditure (1997). Average household size 2.0; average disposable income per household Sw F 69,635 (U.S.$47,981); sources of income (1995): wages 62.5%, transfer payments 18.1%; expenditure (1997): housing and energy 23.6%, food 16.3%, health care 12.8%, transportation 10.7%.
Land use (1994): forested 31.6%; meadows and pastures 29.0%; agricultural and under permanent cultivation 11.0%; other 28.4%.

Foreign trade[12]

Balance of trade (current prices)

	1994	1995	1996	1997	1998	1999
Sw F '000,000	+3,219	+1,753	+1,925	+330	+2,247	+1,030
% of total	1.7%	0.9%	1.0%	0.1%	1.0%	0.5%

Imports (1997): Sw F 110,087,000,000 (machinery and electronics 21.0%, chemical products 15.3%, vehicles 10.3%, food products 8.1%). *Major import sources:* Germany 30.2%; France 11.0%; Italy 9.8%; U.S. 7.9%; U.K. 6.5%.
Exports (1997): Sw F 110,417,000,000 (industrial machinery 18.2%, pharmaceuticals 15.2%, fabricated and base metals 8.2%, watches 7.5%, electrical machinery and electronics 7.3%). *Major export destinations:* Germany 22.4%; U.S. 10.3%; France 9.0%; Italy 7.5%; U.K. 5.8%.

Transport and communications

Transport. Railroads: length (1996) 3,132 mi, 5,041 km; passenger-km 11,630,000,000[13]; metric ton-km cargo 7,382,000,000[13]. Roads (1997): total length 44,147 mi, 71,048 km. Vehicles (1997): passenger cars 3,323,421; trucks and buses 279,347. Air transport (1998)[14]: passenger-km 28,044,000,000; metric ton-km cargo 1,895,000,000; airports (1996) with scheduled flights 5.

Communications

Medium	date	unit	number	units per 1,000 persons
Daily newspapers	1996	circulation	2,383,000	337
Radio	1997	receivers	7,100,000	1,002
Television	1997	receivers	3,310,000	467
Telephones	1998	main lines	4,803,000	676
Cellular telephones	1998	subscribers	1,672,000	235
Personal computers	1998	units	3,000,000	422
Internet	1998	users	1,000,000	141

Education and health

Educational attainment (1997). Percentage of resident Swiss and resident alien population age 25–64 having: lower secondary education or less 20%; vocational 50%; upper secondary 7%; higher technical 13%; university 10%.
Health (1996): physicians 12,711[15] (1 per 556 persons); hospital beds 47,020 (1 per 150 persons); infant mortality rate per 1,000 live births (1999) 3.4.
Food (1997): daily per capita caloric intake 3,223 (vegetable products 65%, animal products 35%); 120% of FAO recommended minimum.

Military

Total active duty personnel (1998): 3,300[16]. *Military expenditure as percentage of GNP* (1997): 1.4% (world 2.6%); per capita expenditure U.S.$545.

[1]Short-form name in Romansh is Svizzra. [2]January 1. [3]Demicanton; functions as a full canton. [4]Includes 1,383,645 resident aliens. [5]Consolidated central government. [6]Includes consulting services. [7]Import duties less imputed bank charges. [8]Unemployed. [9]Labour force includes 936,000 foreign workers. [10]Excludes armed forces and seasonal workers. [11]June. [12]Imports c.i.f.; exports f.o.b. [13]Swiss Federal Railways only. [14]Swissair only. [15]Hospital-based physicians with private practice. [16]Excludes 390,000 reservists.

Internet resources for further information:
- **Embassy of Switzerland (Washington, D.C.) http://www.swissemb.org**
- **Swiss Federal Statistical Office http://www.statistik.admin.ch/eindex.htm**

Syria

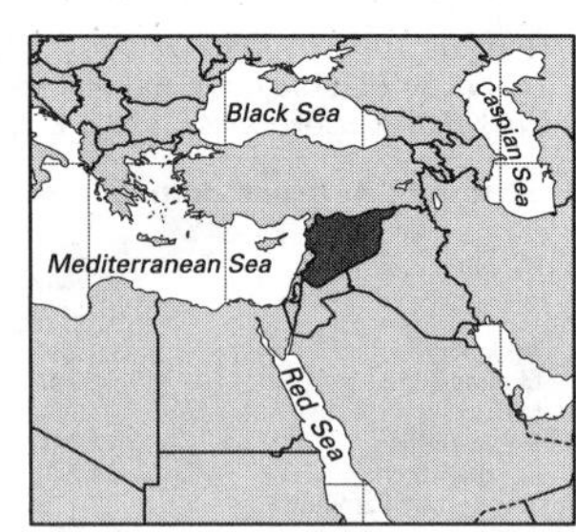

Official name: Al-Jumhūrīyah al-ʿArabīyah as-Sūrīyah (Syrian Arab Republic).
Form of government: unitary multiparty[1] republic with one legislative house (People's Council [250]).
Head of state and government: President.
Capital: Damascus.
Official language: Arabic.
Official religion: none[2].
Monetary unit: 1 Syrian pound (LS) = 100 piastres; valuation[3] (Oct. 6, 2000) 1 U.S.$ = LS 52.50; 1 £ = LS 75.94.

Area and population

Governorates	Capitals	area sq mi	area sq km	population 1995 estimate
Darʿā	Darʿā	1,440	3,730	623,000
Dayr az-Zawr	Dayr az-Zawr	12,765	33,060	722,000
Dimashq	Damascus	6,962	18,032	1,730,000
Ḥalab	Aleppo	7,143	18,500	3,035,000
Ḥamāh	Ḥamāh	3,430	8,883	1,120,000
Al-Ḥasakah	Al-Ḥasakah	9,009	23,334	1,050,000
Ḥimṣ	Homs	16,302	42,223	1,247,000
Idlib	Idlib	2,354	6,097	922,000
Al-Lādhiqīyah	Latakia	887	2,297	766,000
Al-Qunayṭirah	Al-Qunayṭirah	719[4]	1,861[4]	50,000
Ar-Raqqah	Ar-Raqqah	7,574	19,616	566,000
As-Suwaydāʾ	As-Suwaydāʾ	2,143	5,550	270,000
Ṭarṭūs	Ṭarṭūs	730	1,892	596,000
Municipality				
Damascus	—	41	105	1,489,000
TOTAL		71,498[4]	185,180[4]	14,186,000

Demography

Population (2000): 16,306,000.
Density (2000): persons per sq mi 228.1, persons per sq km 88.1.
Urban-rural (1999): urban 54.0%; rural 46.0%.
Sex distribution (1999): male 51.24%; female 48.76%.
Age breakdown (1999): under 15, 41.4%; 15–29, 30.4%; 30–44, 16.3%; 45–59, 7.2%; 60–74, 3.8%; 75 and over, 0.9%.
Population projection: (2010) 20,606,000; (2020) 24,676,000.
Doubling time: 27 years.
Ethnic composition (1992): Arab 90.0%; Kurdish 9.0%; other 1.0%.
Religious affiliation (1992): Muslim 86.0%, of which Sunnī 74.0%, ʿAlawite (Shīʿī) 12.0%; Christian 5.5%; Druze 3.0%; other 5.5%.
Major cities (1994): Aleppo 1,591,400; Damascus 1,549,932; Homs 644,204; Latakia 306,535; Ḥamāh 229,000.

Vital statistics

Birth rate per 1,000 population (1999): 31.4 (world avg. 22.1).
Death rate per 1,000 population (1999): 5.4 (world avg. 8.9).
Natural increase rate per 1,000 population (1999): 26.0 (world avg. 13.2).
Total fertility rate (avg. births per childbearing woman; 1999): 4.1.
Marriage rate per 1,000 population (1995)[5]: 8.4.
Life expectancy at birth (1999): male 67.1 years; female 69.3 years.
Major causes of death per 100,000 population (1989): n.a.; however, the leading causes of mortality among the total population were diseases of the circulatory system 39.6%, injuries and poisoning 9.1%, diseases of the nervous system 7.4%, diseases of the respiratory system 7.4%.

National economy

Budget (1998). Revenue: LS 237,300,000,000 (1995; current revenues 81.3%, capital [development] revenues 18.7%). Expenditures: LS 237,300,000,000 (1995; current expenditures 54.3%, capital [development] expenditures 45.7%).
Public debt (external, outstanding; 1998): U.S.$16,328,000,000.
Gross national product (1998): U.S.$15,532,000,000 (U.S.$1,020 per capita).

Structure of gross domestic product and labour force

	1997[6] in value LS '000,000	1997[6] % of total value	1991 labour force	1991 % of labour force
Agriculture	188,673	25.9	916,952	26.3
Mining	168,154[7]	23.1[7]	6,651	0.2
Manufacturing			456,162	13.1
Construction	29,916	4.1	340,779	9.8
Public utilities	7	7	8,422	0.2
Transp. and commun.	90,396	12.4	166,965	4.8
Trade	145,082	19.9	378,250	10.9
Finance	30,869	4.2	24,651	0.7
Pub. admin.	60,056	8.2	951,104	27.3
Services	15,648	2.1		
Other	...	...	235,432[8]	6.8[8]
TOTAL	728,794	100.0[9]	3,485,368	100.0[9]

Production (metric tons except as noted). Agriculture, forestry, fishing (1999): wheat 2,690,815, sugar beets 950,000, seed cotton 835,000, grapes 451,000, barley 424,489, olives 400,570, oranges 274,896, apples 272,850, tomatoes 250,000, potatoes 250,000, eggplants 128,000; livestock (number of live animals) 15,000,000 sheep, 1,200,000 goats, 905,000 cattle; roundwood (1998) 50,000 cu m; fish catch (1998) 7,097. Mining and quarrying (1997): phosphate rock 2,471,000; gypsum 246,000; salt 119,000; marble blocks 18,000,000 cu m. Manufacturing (1997): cement 4,838,000; refined sugar 176,000; cottonseed cake 127,000; olive oil 126,000; glass and pottery products 64,000; vegetable oil 43,000; tobacco 10,000; television receivers 128,200 units; refrigerators 48,400 units. Construction (1993): residential 628,000 sq m; nonresidential 209,000 sq m. Energy production (consumption): electricity (kW-hr; 1997) 18,259,000,000 (18,259,000,000); crude petroleum (barrels; 1996) 189,426,000 (84,083,000); petroleum products (metric tons; 1996) 11,580,000 (10,287,000); natural gas (cu m; 1996) 2,614,000,000 (2,614,000,000).
Population economically active (1991); total 3,845,368; activity rate of total population 27.8% (participation rates: ages 15 and over, 49.0%; female 10.2%; unemployed 6.1%).

Price and earnings indexes (1995 = 100)

	1993	1994	1995	1996	1997	1998	1999
Consumer price index	80.3	92.6	100.0	108.2	110.8	110.2	107.3
Earnings index	...	...	...	...	...	...	...

Average household size (1998): 4.9; income per household: n.a.; sources of income: n.a.; expenditure (1987)[10]: food 58.8%, rent, fuel, and light 16.0%, clothing 7.5%, household goods 5.8%, transportation 2.4%, education and recreation 2.1%.
Tourism (1998): receipts U.S.$1,190,000,000; expenditures U.S.$580,000,000.
Land use (1994): steppe and pasture 45.2%; cultivable 30.1%; forested 2.6%; other 22.1%.

Foreign trade[11]

Balance of trade (current prices)

	1994	1995	1996	1997	1998	1999
LS '000,000	–21,550	–12,860	–15,500	–1,250	–11,280	–4,130
% of total	21.3%	13.8%	14.7%	1.4%	14.8%	5.0%

Imports (1997): LS 45,210,700,000 (machinery and transport equipment 22.8%, food and beverages 17.1%, basic metals and manufactures 14.8%, chemicals and chemical products 9.6%, textiles 9.4%, resins 6.8%). *Major import sources:* Germany 8.1%; Italy 7.2%; United States 6.4%; Turkey 5.3%; France 4.0%; Japan 3.7%; Romania 3.6%; China 3.6%; Belgium 3.4%.
Exports (1997): LS 43,952,800,000 (crude petroleum and petroleum products 55.5%, fresh vegetables and fruits 7.6%, textiles and fabrics 7.3%, raw cotton 6.3%, live animals and meat 1.3%). *Major export destinations:* Italy 24.5%; France 19.7%; Turkey 10.0%; Lebanon 8.4%; Spain 5.6%; Saudi Arabia 5.4%; Russia 2.6%.

Transport and communications

Transport. Railroads (1997): route length 2,425 km; passenger-km 292,000,000; metric ton-km cargo 1,364,000,000. Roads (1997): total length 41,451 km (paved 23%). Vehicles (1996): passenger cars 139,592; trucks and buses 281,930. Air transport (1997): passenger-km 1,205,271,000; metric ton-km cargo 15,621,000; airports (1998) with scheduled flights 5.

Communications

Medium	date	unit	number	units per 1,000 persons
Daily newspapers	1996	circulation	287,000	20
Radio	1997	receivers	4,150,000	278
Television	1998	receivers	1,060,000	69.1
Telephones	1998	main lines	1,463,000	95.4
Facsimile machines	1998	units	22,000	1.4
Personal computers	1998	units	200,000	13.0
Internet	1998	users	10,000	0.7

Education and health

Educational attainment (1984). Percentage of population age 10 and over having: no schooling 20.1%; knowledge of reading and writing 26.3%; primary education 29.3%; secondary 18.4%; certificate 3.3%; higher 2.7%. *Literacy* (1995): percentage of population age 15 and over literate 74.4%; males literate 88.3%; females literate 60.4%.

Education (1996–97)

	schools	teachers	students	student/ teacher ratio
Primary (age 6–11)	10,783	114,689	2,690,205	23.5
Secondary (age 12–18)	2,526[12]	52,182	865,042	16.6
Voc., teacher tr.	292[12]	12,479	92,622	7.4
Higher[13]	4[12]	4,773	215,734	...

Health (1998): physicians 22,293 (1 per 694 persons); hospital beds (1995) 17,623 (1 per 832 persons); infant mortality rate per 1,000 live births (1999) 36.1.
Food (1998): daily per capita caloric intake 3,378 (vegetable products 88%, animal products 12%); 136% of FAO recommended minimum requirement.

Military

Total active duty personnel (1999): 316,000 (army 68.0%, navy 1.9%, air force 30.1%). *Military expenditure as percentage of GNP* (1997): 5.6% (world 2.6%); per capita expenditure U.S.$211.

[1]Parties ideologically compatible with the Baʿth Party. [2]Islam is required to be the religion of the head of state and is the basis of the legal system. [3]Definition of rate unknown; Syria had five different exchange rates in February 2000. [4]Includes territory in the Golan Heights recognized internationally as part of Syria. [5]Syrian Arabs only. [6]In purchasers' values. [7]Manufacturing and Mining includes Public utilities. [8]Unemployed. [9]Detail does not add to total given because of rounding. [10]Weights of consumer price index components for Damascus only. [11]Import figures are c.i.f. [12]1994–95. [13]University-level institutions only.

Taiwan

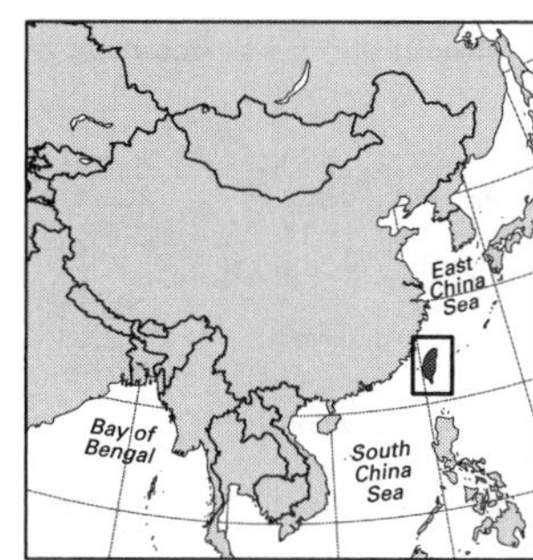

Official name: Chung-hua Min-kuo (Republic of China).
Form of government: multiparty republic with a Legislature (Legislative Yuan [225])[1].
Chief of state: President.
Head of government: Premier.
Capital: Taipei.
Official language: Mandarin Chinese.
Official religion: none.
Monetary unit: 1 New Taiwan dollar (NT$) = 100 cents; valuation (Oct. 6, 2000) 1 U.S.$ = NT$31.30; 1 £ = NT$45.27.

Area and population

Taiwan area Counties	area sq km	population 1999[2] estimate	Municipalities	area sq km	population 1999[2] estimate
Chang-hua	1,074	1,302,416	Chia-i	60	263,171
Chia-i	1,902	565,038	Chi-lung	133	382,718
Hsin-chu	1,428	429,294	Hsin-chu	104	357,609
Hua-lien	4,629	356,440	Kao-hsiung	154	1,465,423
I-lan	2,137	465,095	T'ai-chung	163	922,762
Kao-hsiung	2,793	1,227,673	T'ai-nan	176	723,249
Miao-li	1,820	559,555	Taipei	272	2,640,285
Nan-t'ou	4,106	545,756			
P'eng-hu	127	89,181	**non-Taiwan area Counties**		
P'ing-tung	2,776	910,011	Kinmen (Quemoy) }		
T'ai-chung	2,051	1,471,751	Lienchiang (Matsu) }	179	57,639[3]
T'ai-nan	2,016	1,100,871			
T'ai-pei	2,052	3,472,501			
T'ai-tung	3,515	249,158	TOTAL	36,179[4]	21,966,182
T'ao-yüan	1,221	1,660,709			
Yün-lin	1,291	747,877			

Demography

Population (2000)[5]: 22,186,000.
Density (2000)[5]: persons per sq mi 1,588.2, persons per sq km 613.2.
Urban-rural (1991)[6]: urban 74.7%; rural 25.3%.
Sex distribution (1998)[6]: male 51.27%; female 48.73%.
Age breakdown (1999): under 15, 21.4%; 15–29, 25.8%; 30–44, 25.6%; 45–59, 15.4%; 60–74, 8.9%; 75 and over, 2.9%.
Population projection: (2010) 24,144,000; (2020) 26,275,000.
Ethnic composition (1997): Han Chinese, Chinese mainland minorities, and others 98.2%; indigenous tribal peoples 1.8%, of which Ami 0.6%.
Religious affiliation (1997)[7, 8]: Buddhism 22.4%; Taoism 20.7%; I-kuan Tao 4.3%; Protestant 1.6%; Roman Catholic 1.4%; other Christian 0.3%; Muslim 0.2%; Bahāʾī 0.1%; other 49.0%.
Major cities (1999): Taipei 2,640,285; Kao-hsiung 1,465,423; T'ai-chung 922,762; T'ai-nan 723,249; Chung-ho (1998) 388,174; Chi-lung 382,718.

Vital statistics

Birth rate per 1,000 population (1999): 12.9 (world avg. 22.1).
Death rate per 1,000 population (1999): 5.7 (world avg. 8.9).
Natural increase rate per 1,000 population (1999): 7.2 (world avg. 13.2).
Total fertility rate (avg. births per childbearing woman; 1999): 1.8.
Life expectancy at birth (1999): male 73.4 years; female 79.1 years.
Major causes of death per 100,000 population (1998)[6]: malignant neoplasms 133.4; cerebrovascular diseases 57.9; heart disease 50.3; accidents and suicide 50.0; diabetes 34.3; liver diseases 22.5; pneumonia 20.3; kidney diseases 15.7.

National economy

Budget (1997[9]). Revenue: NT$2,074,064,000,000 (income taxes 17.0%, business tax 10.8%, land tax 8.4%, commodity tax 7.1%, customs duties 5.0%). Expenditures: NT$2,066,751,000,000 (administration and defense 26.0%, education 18.2%).
Population economically active (1990): total 10,236,324; activity rate 50.5% (participation rates: ages 15–64, 72.5%; female 38.5%; unemployed [1998] 2.7%).

Price and earnings indexes (1995 = 100)

	1993	1994	1995	1996	1997	1998	1999
Consumer price index	92.6	96.4	100.0	103.1	104.0	105.7	105.9
Monthly earnings index[10]	88.9	94.8	100.0	104.2	108.9	112.0	115.8

Production (metric tons except as noted). Agriculture, forestry, fishing (1997): sugarcane 3,902,000, rice 1,663,000, citrus fruits 494,680, corn (maize) 337,617, pineapples 300,686, sweet potatoes 208,000, bananas 204,735; livestock (number of live animals) 7,966,887 pigs, 315,216 goats, 166,393 cattle; timber 32,778 cu m; fish catch 909,218. Mining and quarrying (1990): silver 3,926 kg. Manufacturing (1998): cement 19,651,000; steel ingots 17,150,000; paperboard 4,067,000; fertilizers 1,808,476; polyester filament 1,614,849; polyvinyl chloride plastics 1,157,963; telephones 7,736,597 units; televisions 988,430 units. Construction (1995): total residential and nonresidential 46,221,000 sq m. Energy production (consumption): electricity (kW-hr; 1998) 155,450,000,000 ([1996] 111,140,000,000); coal (metric tons; 1996) 147,500 (29,983,000); crude petroleum (barrels; 1996) 335,000 (226,387,000); natural gas (cu m; 1996) 870,000,000 (4,500,000,000).
Tourism (1998): receipts from visitors U.S.$3,372,000,000; expenditures by nationals abroad U.S.$5,050,000,000.

Gross national product (1998): U.S.$297,953,000,000 (U.S.$13,900 per capita).

Structure of gross domestic product and labour force[6]

	1998 in value NT$'000,000	% of total value	labour force[11]	% of labour force[11]
Agriculture	251,454	2.8	822,000	8.6
Mining	43,690	0.5	12,000	0.1
Manufacturing	2,359,676	27.0	2,611,000	27.3
Construction	368,222	4.2	865,000	9.1
Public utilities	203,089	2.3	35,000	0.4
Transp. and commun.	616,351	7.0	477,000	5.0
Trade	1,483,727	17.0	2,047,000	21.4
Finance	2,022,751	23.1	645,000	6.8
Pub. admin., defense	896,700	10.3 }		
Services	783,704	9.0 }	1,776,000	18.6
Other	–282,430[12]	–3.2[12]	257,000[13]	2.7[13]
TOTAL	8,746,934	100.0	9,547,000	100.0

Household income and expenditure (1995). Average household size (1998) 3.4; income per household (1998) NT$1,248,254 (U.S.$38,746); expenditure: food 25.5%, education and recreation 18.4%, rent, fuel, and power 17.2%, transportation 10.5%, health care 8.1%, clothing 4.7%, furniture 2.9%.

Foreign trade

Balance of trade (current prices)

	1994	1995	1996	1997	1998	1999
NT$'000,000	+194,400	+206,700	+361,500	+205,500	+189,700	+341,000
% of total	4.1%	3.6%	6.0%	3.0%	2.6%	4.6%

Imports (1998): NT$3,503,569,000,000 (electronic machinery 17.3%, nonelectrical machinery 11.5%, chemicals 9.5%, metals and metal products 9.1%, transportation equipment 5.3%). *Major import sources:* Japan 25.8%; U.S. 18.8%; South Korea 5.4%; Germany 4.9%; Malaysia 3.5%; Singapore 3.1%.
Exports (1998): NT$3,693,269,000,000 (machinery and electric 50.0%, textile products 13.2%, plastic articles 6.2%, transportation equipment 4.7%). *Major export destinations:* U.S. 26.6%; Hong Kong 22.4%; Japan 8.4%; Germany 3.7%; Singapore 2.9%.

Transport and communications

Transport. Railroads (1998): track length 3,879 km; passenger-km 9,793,000,000; metric ton-km cargo 1,404,000,000. Roads (1997): total length 20,189 km (paved 89%[14]). Vehicles (1998): passenger cars 4,536,600; trucks and buses 834,200. Air transport (1998): passenger-km 39,218,000,000; metric ton-km cargo 4,129,300,000; airports (1996) 13.

Communications

Medium	date	unit	number	units per 1,000 persons
Radio	1996	receivers	8,620,000	402
Television	1997	receivers	7,100,000	327
Telephones	1998	main lines	11,500,000	527
Cellular telephones	1998	subscribers	4,727,000	216
Personal computers	1998	units	3,478,000	159
Internet	1998	users	3,011,000	138

Education and health

Educational attainment (1997). Percentage of population age 25 and over having: no formal schooling 7.9%; less than complete primary education 6.3%; primary 22.3%; incomplete secondary 25.7%; secondary 21.7%; some college 9.6%; higher 6.5%. *Literacy* (1995): population age 15 and over literate 15,930,382 (94.7%); males 8,445,588 (98.1%); females 7,484,794 (91.2%).

Education (1997–98)

	schools	teachers	students	student/ teacher ratio
Primary (age 6–12)	2,540	92,104	1,905,690	20.7
Secondary (age 13–18)	947	79,001	1,365,683	17.3
Vocational	204	20,410	509,065	24.9
Higher	139	38,806	856,186	22.1

Health (1998): physicians 27,168 (1 per 807 persons); hospital beds 124,564 (1 per 176 persons); infant mortality rate per 1,000 live births (1999) 7.2.

Military

Total active duty personnel (1998): 376,000 (army 63.8%, navy 18.1%, air force 18.1%). *Military expenditure as percentage of GNP* (1997): 4.6% (world 2.6%); per capita expenditure U.S.$606.

[1]The National Assembly became a nonstanding body with limited specialized authority per April 2000 amendment; the Legislature is the formal lawmaking body. [2]March. [3]Population breakdown as of July 1, 2000: Kinmen (Quemoy) 51,395; Lienchiang (Matsu) 6,608. [4]Total area per more recent survey is 36,185 sq km. [5]Includes Quemoy and Matsu groups. [6]For Taiwan area only, excluding Quemoy and Matsu groups. [7]Formal subscribers to religious beliefs. [8]Almost all Taiwanese adults engage in religious practices stemming from one or a combination of traditional folk religions. [9]General government. [10]In manufacturing. [11]Civilian employed persons only. [12]Import duties less imputed bank service charge. [13]Unemployed. [14]1996.

Internet resources for further information:
- **The Republic of China Yearbook 1998 http://www.gio.gov.tw/info/yb97/html/content.htm**
- **Directorate-General of Budget, Accounting and Statistics (Taiwan) http://www.dgbasey.gov.tw/english/dgbas_e0.htm**
- **National Statistics of Taiwan, the Republic of China http://www.stat.gov.tw**

Tajikistan

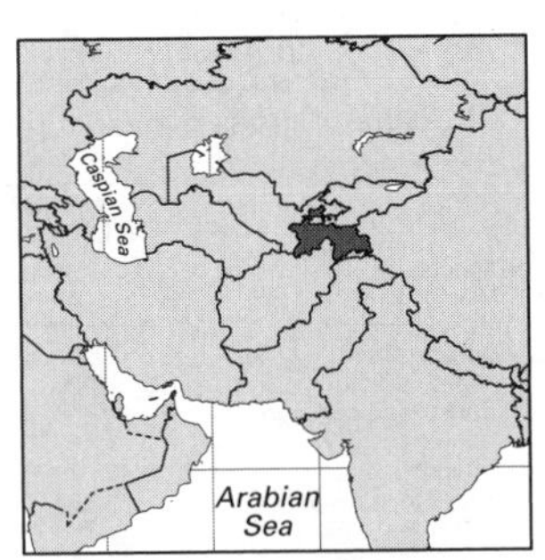

Official name: Jumhurii Tojikiston (Republic of Tajikistan).
Form of government: parliamentary republic with two legislative houses (National Assembly [33[1]]; Assembly of Representatives [63]).
Chief of state: President.
Head of government: Prime Minister.
Capital: Dushanbe.
Official language: Tajik (Tojik).
Official religion: none.
Monetary unit: 1 Tajik ruble[2]; valuation (Oct. 6, 2000) 1 U.S.$ = 2,296 Tajik rubles; 1 £ = 3,321 Tajik rubles.

Area and population		area		population
				1991
Oblasts	Capitals	sq mi	sq km	estimate
Khujand	Khujand	10,100	26,100	1,635,900
Khatlon (Qŭrghonteppa)	Qŭrghonteppa	9,500	24,600	1,781,600
Autonomous oblast				
Kŭhistoni Badakhshon (Gorno-Badakhshan)	Khorugh	24,600	63,700	167,100
City				
Dushanbe	—	100	300	591,900
Other[3]	—	11,000	28,400	1,181,800
TOTAL		55,300	143,100	5,358,300

Demography

Population (2000): 6,312,000.
Density (2000): persons per sq mi 114.1, persons per sq km 44.1.
Urban-rural (1999): urban 33.0%; rural 67.0%.
Sex distribution (1996): male 51.22%; female 48.78%.
Age breakdown (1993): under 15, 43.8%; 15–29, 26.8%; 30–44, 16.1%; 45–59, 7.2%; 60–74, 4.8%; 75 and over, 1.3%.
Population projection: (2010) 7,847,000; (2020) 9,784,000.
Doubling time: 29 years.
Ethnic composition (1991): Tajik 62.2%; Uzbek 23.1%; Russian 9.7%; Tatar 1.4%; Kyrgyz 1.3%; Ukrainian 0.7%; German 0.3%; other 1.3%.
Religious affiliation (1995): Sunnī Muslim 80.0%; Shīʿī Muslim 5.0%; Russian Orthodox 1.5%; Jewish 0.1%; other (mostly nonreligious) 13.4%.
Major cities (1991): Dushanbe 591,900; Khujand (formerly Leninabad) 164,500; Kŭlob 79,300; Qŭrghonteppa 58,400; Urateppa 47,700.

Vital statistics

Birth rate per 1,000 population (1999): 34.0 (world avg. 22.1); (1994) legitimate 90.8%; illegitimate 9.2%.
Death rate per 1,000 population (1999): 8.6 (world avg. 8.9).
Natural increase rate per 1,000 population (1999): 25.4 (world avg. 13.2).
Total fertility rate (avg. births per childbearing woman; 1999): 4.4.
Marriage rate per 1,000 population (1994): 6.8.
Divorce rate per 1,000 population (1994): 0.8.
Life expectancy at birth (1999): male 61.2 years; female 67.6 years.
Major causes of death per 100,000 population (1993): diseases of the circulatory system 225.5; violence, poisoning, and accidents 184.0; diseases of the respiratory system 160.6; infectious and parasitic diseases 129.9; malignant neoplasms (cancers) 42.3; diseases of the digestive system 20.9.

National economy

Budget (1998). Revenue: 115,144,000,000 Tajik rubles (tax revenue 96.6%, of which taxes on aluminum and cotton 35.6%, income and profit taxes 18.4%, value-added tax 17.2%, customs duties 10.7%; nontax revenue 3.4%). Expenditures: 153,797,000,000 Tajik rubles (national economy 26.2%, education 14.4%, defense 8.8%, law enforcement 8.3%, health 7.6%, state bodies and administration 5.7%).
Production (metric tons except as noted). Agriculture, forestry, fishing (1999): vegetables and melons 526,300, grain 521,000, milk 302,000, potatoes 136,000; livestock (number of live animals) 2,247,000 sheep and goats, 911,500 cattle, 2,000 pigs, 600,000 poultry; roundwood, n.a.; fish catch (1997) 285. Mining and quarrying (1998): aluminum 195,630; lead 3,500[4]; gold 3.2. Manufacturing (value of production in '000,000 Tajik rubles; 1996): ferrous and nonferrous metals 80,333; textiles 35,023; grain mill products 23,526; bakery products 16,908; basic chemicals 7,586; jewelry 3,552; processed fruits and vegetables 2,339. Energy production (consumption): electricity (kW-hr; 1996) 15,000,000,000 (15,320,000,000); coal (metric tons; 1996) 20,000 (120,000); crude petroleum (barrels; 1996) 146,600 (146,600); petroleum products (metric tons; 1996) n.a. (1,116,000); natural gas (cu m; 1996) 54,000,000 (1,276,000).
Public debt (external, outstanding; 1998): U.S.$706,900,000.
Tourism: receipts from visitors, n.a.; expenditures by nationals abroad, n.a.
Population economically active (1998): total 1,855,000; activity rate of total population 30.4% (participation rates: ages 16–59 [male], 16–54 [female] 60.3%; female [1996] 46.5%; unemployed 3.0%).

Price and earnings indexes (1995 = 100)	1993	1994	1995	1996	1997	1998
Consumer price index	5.4	18.4	100.0	298.0	511.0	...
Monthly earnings index	22.1	47.7	100.0	383.7	680.6	1,175.1

Gross national product (1998): U.S.$2,256,000,000 (U.S.$370 per capita).

Structure of gross domestic product and labour force	1998			
	in value '000,000 Tajik rubles	% of total value	labour force	% of labour force
Agriculture	202,897	19.8	1,167,000	62.9
Mining / Manufacturing	185,144	18.1	149,000	8.0
Public utilities	...	...	...	...
Construction	18,751	1.8	52,000	2.8
Transp. and commun.	9,932	1.0	52,000	2.8
Trade	166,881	16.3	63,000	3.4
Finance	...	...	...	...
Public administration, defense	...	...	20,000	1.1
Services	225,036	21.9	281,000	15.1
Other	216,570[5]	21.1	71,000[6]	3.8[6]
TOTAL	1,025,211	100.0	1,855,000	100.0[7]

Household income and expenditure. Average household size (1989) 6.1; (1995) income per household: 18,744 Tajik rubles (U.S.$114); sources of income (1995): wages and salaries 34.5%, self-employment 34.0%, borrowing 2.4%, pension 2.0%, other 27.1%, expenditure: food 81.5%, clothing 10.2%, transport 2.5%, fuel 2.1%, other 3.7%.
Land use (1994): forest 3.8%; pasture 24.8%; agriculture 6.0%; other 65.4%.

Foreign trade[8]

Balance of trade (current prices)	1993	1994	1995	1996	1997	1998
U.S.$'000,000	–183	–127	–59	–16	–63	–145
% of total	16.7%	10.2%	3.6%	1.0%	4.1%	11.0%

Imports (1998): U.S.$731,000,000 (electricity 16.0%, petroleum products and natural gas 15.6%, alumina 15.0%, grain and flour 5.6%). *Major import sources* (1996): Uzbekistan 29.8%; Switzerland 14.9%; United Kingdom 11.7%; Russia 11.1%; Kazakhstan 7.8%; Turkmenistan 3.9%; Ukraine 2.9%.
Exports (1998): U.S.$586,000,000 (aluminum 39.9%, cotton fibre 19.1%; electricity 17.6%). *Major export destinations* (1996): The Netherlands 28.3%; Uzbekistan 24.8%; Switzerland 10.8%; Russia 10.2%; Kazakhstan 3.2%.

Transport and communications

Transport. Railroads (1995): length 294.5 mi, 474.0 km; passenger-mi 77,000,000, passenger-km 124,000,000; short ton-mi cargo 1,449,000,000, metric ton-km cargo 2,115,000,000. Roads (1996): total length 8,500 mi, 13,700 km (paved 83%). Vehicles (1996): passenger cars 680,000; trucks and buses, 8,190. Merchant marine: vessels (100 gross tons and over) n.a.; total deadweight tonnage, n.a. Air transport (1995): passenger-mi 1,386,000,000, passenger-km 2,231,000,000; short ton-mi cargo 140,000,000, metric ton-km cargo 205,000,000; airports (1997) with scheduled flights 1.

Communications				units
Medium	date	unit	number	per 1,000 persons
Daily newspapers	1996	circulation	120,000	21
Radio	1997	receivers	850,000	143
Television	1997	receivers	20,000,000	3.3
Telephones	1998	main lines	221,324	37
Cellular phones	1998	subscribers	420	0.1
Personal computers	...	units	...	...
Internet	...	users	...	...

Education and health

Educational attainment (1989). Percentage of population age 25 and over having: primary education or no formal schooling 16.3%; some secondary 21.1%; completed secondary and some postsecondary 55.1%; higher 7.5%. *Literacy* (1995): percentage of total population age 15 and over literate 98.7%; males literate 99.3%; females literate 98.1%.

Education (1996–97)	schools	teachers	students	student/ teacher ratio
Primary (age 6–13)	3,432	27,172	638,674	23.5
Secondary (age 14–17)[9]	...	112,532	688,150	6.1
Voc., teacher tr.	...	...	29,482[10]	...
Higher	...	...	76,613	...

Health (1996): physicians 12,456 (1 per 475 persons); hospital beds 43,400 (1 per 136 persons); infant mortality rate per 1,000 live births (1999) 114.8.
Food: daily per capita caloric intake (1998) 2,176 (vegetable products 94%, animal products 6%); 85% of FAO recommended minimum requirement.

Military

Total active duty personnel (1999): 7,000 (army 100%); more than 14,000 Russian troops remained in Tajikistan in late 1999. *Military expenditure as percentage of GNP* (1997): 1.7% (world 2.6%); per capita expenditure U.S.$19.

[1]Eight members are appointed by the President. [2]A new currency, the samani (equal to 1,000 Tajik rubles), was introduced on Oct. 30, 2000. [3]No oblast-level administration. [4]1996. [5]Includes 111,441,000,000 rubles in undistributed GDP and 105,129,000,000 rubles in indirect taxes. [6]Mostly unemployed. [7]Detail does not add to total given because of rounding. [8]Import total in balance of trade is c.i.f. [9]Excludes special education. [10]1994–95.

Internet resources for further information:
- **Tajikistan Resource Page**
http://www.soros.org/tajik/tajktxtf.html
- **Interactive Central Asia Resource Project: Tajikistan**
http://ns1.rockbridge.net/personal/bichel/tajik.htp

Tanzania

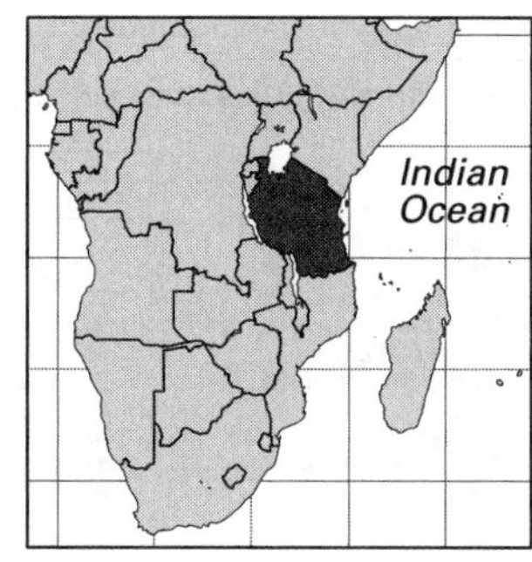

Official name: Jamhuri ya Muungano wa Tanzania (Swahili); United Republic of Tanzania (English).
Form of government: unitary multiparty republic with one legislative house (National Assembly [275[1]]).
Head of state and government: President.
Seat of government: Dar es Salaam (Capital designate, Dodoma)[2].
Official languages: Swahili; English.
Official religion: none.
Monetary unit: 1 Tanzania shilling (T Sh) = 100 cents; valuation (Oct. 6, 2000) 1 U.S.$ = T Sh 796; 1 £ = T Sh 1,151.

Area and population

Administrative Regions	area sq km	population 1995 estimate
Mainland Tanzania (Tanganyika)		
Arusha	82,306	1,640,399
Dar es Salaam	1,393	1,651,534
Dodoma	41,311	1,502,344
Iringa	56,864	1,467,144
Kagera	28,388	1,652,991
Kigoma	37,037	1,043,491
Kilimanjaro	13,309	1,345,523
Lindi	66,046	784,658
Mara	19,566	1,178,340
Mbeya	60,350	1,791,522
Morogoro	70,799	1,525,577
Mtwara	16,707	1,079,495
Mwanza	19,592	2,280,206
Pwani (Coast)	32,407	774,297
Rukwa	68,635	843,424
Ruvuma	63,498	950,649
Shinyanga	50,781	2,151,539
Singida	49,341	960,947
Tabora	76,151	1,257,650
Tanga	26,808	1,590,381
Autonomous Territory		
Zanzibar and Pemba[3]		
Pemba	906	322,466
Zanzibar	1,554	456,934
TOTAL LAND AREA	883,749	
INLAND WATER	59,050	
TOTAL	942,799[4]	28,251,511

Demography

Population (2000): 35,306,000.
Density (1999)[5]: persons per sq mi 96.8, persons per sq km 37.4.
Urban-rural (1999): urban 31.7%; rural 68.3%.
Sex distribution (1999): male 49.67%; female 50.33%.
Age breakdown (1999): under 15, 45.0%; 15–29, 28.7%; 30–44, 14.1%; 45–59, 7.7%; 60–74, 3.6%; 75 and over, 0.9%.
Population projection: (2010) 44,957,000; (2020) 54,774,000.
Doubling time: 25 years.
Ethnolinguistic composition (1987): Nyamwezi and Sukuma 21.1%; Swahili 8.8%; Hehet and Bena 6.9%; Haya 5.9%; Makonde 5.9%; Nyakyusa 5.4%; Chagga 4.9%; other 41.1%.
Religious affiliation (1997): Christian *c.* 44%; Muslim *c.* 37%; animist *c.* 19%.

Vital statistics

Birth rate per 1,000 population (1999): 40.6 (world avg. 22.1).
Death rate per 1,000 population (1999): 12.8 (world avg. 8.9).
Natural increase rate per 1,000 population (1999): 27.8 (world avg. 13.2).
Total fertility rate (avg. births per childbearing woman; 1999): 5.6.
Life expectancy at birth (1999): male 51.6 years; female 53.5 years.
Major causes of death per 100,000 population: n.a.; however, the major diseases include malaria, bilharziasis, tuberculosis, and sleeping sickness.

National economy

Budget (1998–99). Revenue: T Sh 689,470,000,000 (import duties 31.7%, sales and excise tax 23.7%, income tax 23.6%). Expenditures: T Sh 898,800,000,000 (wages 24.5%, interest payments on debt 12.9%).
Public debt (external, outstanding; 1998): U.S.$6,404,000,000.
Tourism (1998): receipts from visitors U.S.$570,000,000; expenditures by nationals abroad U.S.$493,000,000.
Gross national product (1998)[6]: U.S.$7,154,000,000 (U.S.$220 per capita).

Structure of gross domestic product and labour force

	1999		1991	
	in value T Sh '000,000	% of total value	labour force	% of labour force
Agriculture	2,611,946	40.1	10,540,000	80.3
Mining	88,516	1.4		
Manufacturing	432,843	6.6	614,000	4.7
Construction	303,092	4.6		
Public utilities	92,647	1.4		
Transp. and commun.	288,699	4.4		
Trade	734,298	11.3		
Finance	830,380	12.7	1,969,000	15.0
Pub. admin., defense	471,424	7.2		
Services	156,184	2.4		
Other	514,321[7]	7.9[7]	...	...
TOTAL	6,524,350	100.0	13,123,000	100.0

Production (metric tons except as noted). Agriculture (1999): cassava 7,181,500, corn (maize) 2,457,745, sugarcane 1,354,999, bananas 751,601, plantains 752,000, rice 676,000, sorghum 561,030, sweet potatoes 500,000, coconuts 400,000, millet 194,372; livestock (number of live animals) 14,350,000 cattle, 9,900,000 goats, 4,150,000 sheep, 28,000,000 chickens; roundwood (1998) 39,022,000 cu m; fish catch (1998) 348,000. Mining and quarrying (1994): gemstones (including emeralds, sapphires, and rubies) 33,000 kg; gold 3,370 kg; diamonds 15,700 carats. Manufacturing (1999): cement 833,000; petroleum products 287,000; sugar 153,000; iron sheets 23,000; rolled steel 9,500; beer 1,239,000 hectolitres; cigarettes 3,400,000,000 units; textiles 49,800,000 sq m. Energy production (consumption): electricity (kW-hr; 1996) 1,737,000,000 (1,737,000,000); coal (metric tons; 1995) 5,000 (5,000); crude petroleum (barrels; 1996) none (4,317,000); petroleum products (metric tons; 1996) 583,000 (656,000).
Population economically active (1994): total 13,852,000; activity rate 48.0% (participation rates [1991]: over age 10, 87.8%; female 40.0%).

Price index (1995 = 100)

	1993	1994	1995	1996	1997	1998	1999
Consumer price index	58.5	77.9	100.0	121.0	140.4	158.4	170.9

Household income and expenditure. Average household size (1998) 5.4; income per household: n.a.; sources of income: n.a.; expenditure (1994): food 64.2%, clothing 9.9%, housing 8.3%, energy 7.6%, transportation 4.1%.
Land use (1995): forested 37.0%; meadows and pastures 39.6%; agricultural and under permanent cultivation 4.2%; other 19.2%.

Foreign trade

Balance of trade (current prices)

	1994	1995	1996	1997	1998	1999
T Sh '000,000	–385,977	–433,525	–363,605	–379,905	–517,779	–809,445
% of total	42.1%	35.7%	29.2%	30.2%	36.6%	49.6%

Imports (1999): U.S.$1,630,600,000 (consumer goods 33.9%, machinery 20.9%, transport equipment 18.2%, food 10.8%). *Major import sources:* Japan 10.9%; U.K. 7.8%; U.S. 6.0%; Kenya 5.8%; India 5.6%.
Exports (1999): U.S.$541,000,000 (cashew nuts 18.3%, coffee 14.2%, minerals 13.2%, tobacco 8.0%, cotton 5.2%, tea 4.5%). *Major export destinations:* India 19.5%; U.K. 17.0%; Japan 8.0%; The Netherlands 5.7%; Singapore 4.5%; Germany 4.0%; Kenya 3.8%; U.S. 3.3%.

Transport and communications

Transport. Railroads (1997): length 3,569 km; passenger-journeys 694,000,000[8]; metric ton-km cargo 1,354,000,000[8]. Roads (1996): length 88,200 km (paved 4.2%). Vehicles (1996): passenger cars 23,760; trucks and buses 115,700. Merchant marine (1992): vessels (100 gross tons and over) 43; deadweight tonnage 48,465. Air transport (1995)[9]: passenger-km 184,383,000; metric ton-km 2,904,000; airports (1998) with scheduled flights 11.

Communications

Medium	date	unit	number	units per 1,000 persons
Daily newspapers	1996	circulation	120,000	3.9
Radio	1997	receivers	8,800,000	280
Television	1997	receivers	103,000	3.3
Telephones	1998	main lines	121,769	3.8
Cellular telephones	1998	subscribers	37,940	1.2
Personal computers	1998	units	55,000	1.7
Internet	1998	users	3,000	0.2

Education and health

Educational attainment (1978). Percentage of population age 10 and over having: no schooling 48.6%; some primary education 40.7%; completed primary 8.7%; secondary and higher 1.9%. *Literacy* (1995): percentage of population age 15 and over literate 67.8%; males 79.4%; females 56.8%.

Education (1996)[10]

	schools	teachers	students	student/ teacher ratio
Primary (age 7–13)	10,927	108,874	3,942,888	36.2
Secondary (age 14–19)	491[11]	11,659	199,093	17.1
Teacher training	40[11]	1,062	12,571	11.8
Higher	...	1,650	12,776	7.7

Health (1993): physicians 1,365 (1 per 20,511 persons); hospital beds 26,820 (1 per 1,000 persons); infant mortality rate (1999) 82.5.
Food (1998): daily per capita caloric intake 1,999 (vegetable products 93%, animal products 7%); 81% of FAO recommended minimum requirement.

Military

Total active duty personnel (1999): 34,000 (army 88.2%, navy 2.9%, air force 8.9%). *Military expenditure as percentage of GNP* (1997): 1.3% (world 2.6%); per capita expenditure U.S.$3.

[1]Includes 5 indirectly elected seats from Zanzibar and Pemba and 37 indirectly elected seats for women and the attorney general serving ex officio. [2]The movement of the capital from Dar es Salaam to Dodoma began in the early 1980s and was scheduled to be completed by 1992; as of 1999 only the prime minister's office and legislature were located in Dodoma. [3]Has local internal government structure; Zanzibar has 3 administrative regions, Pemba has 2. [4]A recent survey indicates a total area of 364,901 sq mi (945,090 sq km). [5]Based on the total area of 364,901 sq mi. [6]Mainland Tanzania only. [7]Includes bank service charge. [8]Tanzanian Railways only; 1995. [9]Air Tanzania only. [10]Excludes Zanzibar and Pemba. [11]1994.

Internet resources for further information:
- **Bank of Tanzania http://www.bot-tz.org**

Thailand

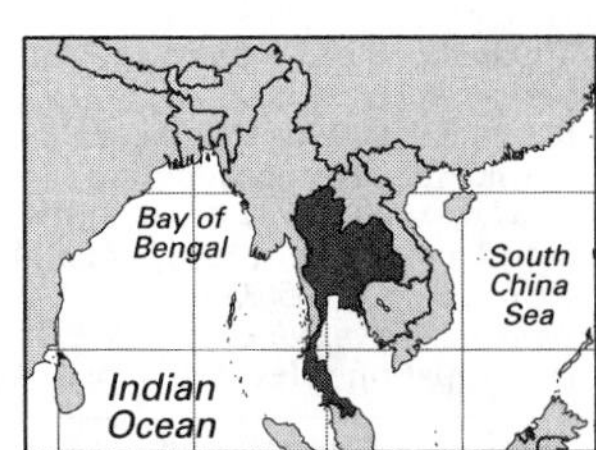

Official name: Muang Thai, or Prathet Thai (Kingdom of Thailand).
Form of government: constitutional monarchy with two legislative houses (Senate [200]; House of Representatives [393]).
Chief of state: King.
Head of government: Prime Minister.
Capital: Bangkok.
Official language: Thai.
Official religion: Buddhism.
Monetary unit: 1 Thai baht (B) = 100 stangs; valuation (Oct. 6, 2000) 1 U.S.$ = B 42.48; 1 £ = B 61.46.

Area and population

	area		population
Regions[1]	sq mi	sq km	1997 estimate[2]
Bangkok Metropolis	2,995	7,758	9,114,852
Central	6,407	16,594	2,941,524
Eastern	14,094	36,503	4,064,872
Northeastern	65,195	168,854	21,095,841
Northern	65,500	169,644	12,091,337
Southern	27,303	70,715	7,944,865
Western	16,621	43,047	3,562,936
TOTAL	198,115	513,115	60,816,227

Demography

Population (2000): 62,423,000.
Density (2000): persons per sq mi 315.1, persons per sq km 121.7.
Urban-rural (2000): urban 31.0%; rural 69.0%.
Sex distribution (1999): male 49.86%; female 50.14%.
Age breakdown (1999): under 15, 26.0%; 15–29, 27.7%; 30–44, 23.3%; 45–59, 14.1%; 60–74, 7.2%; 75 and over, 1.7%.
Population projection: (2010) 67,581,000; (2020) 70,860,000.
Doubling time: 67 years.
Ethnic composition (1983): Thai 79.5%, of which Siamese 52.6%, Lao 26.9%; Chinese 12.1%; Malay 3.7%; Khmer 2.7%; other 2.0%.
Religious affiliation (1996): Buddhist 92.6%; Muslim 5.3%; Christian 1.3%; other 0.8%.
Major cities (1991)[3]: Bangkok 5,620,591; Nonthaburi 264,201; Nakhon Ratchasima 202,503; Chiang Mai 161,541; Khon Kaen 131,478.

Vital statistics

Birth rate per 1,000 population (2000): 16.3 (world avg. 22.1).
Death rate per 1,000 population (2000): 5.9 (world avg. 8.9).
Natural increase rate per 1,000 population (2000): 10.4 (world avg. 13.2).
Total fertility rate (avg. births per childbearing woman; 2000): 1.8.
Marriage rate per 1,000 population (1997): 6.5.
Divorce rate per 1,000 population (1997): 1.0.
Life expectancy at birth (2000): male 71.0 years; female 76.0 years.
Major causes of death per 100,000 population (1996): diseases of the heart 79.1; accidents, homicide, and poisonings 78.4; malignant neoplasms (cancers) 51.4; hypertension and cerebrovascular disease 16.1; pneumonia and other lung diseases 12.8; diseases of the liver and the pancreas 12.6.

National economy

Budget (1997). Revenue: B 870,421,000,000 (taxes on goods and services 42.4%; income taxes 31.7%; taxes on international trade 12.1%). Expenditures: B 901,716,000,000 (education 21.6%; transportation and communications 15.9%; defense 11.6%; agriculture 9.2%; health 8.6%; housing 5.7%; public order and safety 5.6%).
Production (metric tons except as noted). Agriculture, forestry, fishing (1996): sugarcane 46,024,900, rice 23,240,178, cassava 15,958,500, corn (maize) 4,986,420, natural rubber 2,162,411, pineapples 1,734,030, bananas 1,700,000, soybean 370,954, tobacco 74,250; livestock (number of live animals) 7,000,000 cattle, 4,815,000 pigs, 4,000,000 buffalo, 165,000,000 chickens; roundwood 39,561,000 cu m; fish catch (1996) 3,647,900. Mining and quarrying (1997): limestone 58,796,000; gypsum 8,558,000; kaolin clay 367,000; zinc ore 91,132; lead ore 12,438; fluorite 7,826; tin concentrates 756. Manufacturing (1995): cement 33,445,000; refined sugar 5,201,800; synthetic fibre 540,800; galvanized iron sheet 370,000; tin plate 250,500; jute products 76,000. Construction (1990): residential 16,343,000 sq m; nonresidential 13,449,000 sq m. Energy production (consumption): electricity (kW-hr; 1994) 74,452,000,000 (75,278,000,000); coal (metric tons; 1994) 17,095,000 (17,198,000); crude petroleum (barrels; 1994) 9,583,000 (137,883,000); petroleum products (metric tons; 1994) 21,291,000 (28,850,000); natural gas (cu m; 1994) 9,513,000,000 (9,513,000,000).
Tourism (1998): receipts from visitors U.S.$5,934,000,000; expenditures by nationals abroad U.S.$1,448,000,000.
Land use (1994): forested 29.0%; meadows and pastures 1.6%; agricultural and under permanent cultivation 40.0%; other 29.4%.
Population economically active (1997): total 32,000,100; activity rate of total population 53.0% (participation rates: over age 13, 69.1%; female 43.9%; unemployed 2.3%).

Price and earnings indexes (1995 = 100)

	1992	1993	1994	1995	1996	1997	1998
Consumer price index	87.1	90.0	94.5	100.0	105.8	111.8	120.8
Monthly earnings index	86.5	93.2	87.3	100.0	...	...	...

Gross national product (1998): U.S.$131,916,000,000 (U.S.$2,160 per capita).

Structure of gross domestic product and labour force

	1996		1995	
	in value B '000,000	% of total value	labour force[3]	% of labour force[3]
Agriculture	507,339	11.0	12,973,900	40.5
Mining	62,290	1.4	58,100	0.2
Manufacturing	1,305,772	28.4	4,996,400	15.6
Construction	340,959	7.4	2,983,500	9.3
Public utilities	106,550	2.3	174,400	0.6
Transp. and commun.	337,333	7.3	1,098,500	3.4
Trade	712,498	15.5	4,602,600	14.4
Finance	457,555	10.0		
Pub. admin., defense	167,857	3.7	4,399,800	13.8
Services	600,135	13.0		
Other	...	...	712,900[4]	2.2[4]
TOTAL	4,598,288	100.0	32,000,100	100.0

Public debt (external, outstanding; 1998): U.S.$28,113,000,000.
Household income and expenditure (1996). Average household size 3.7; average annual income per household B 129,348 (U.S.$5,104); sources of income (1994): wages and salaries 41.2%, self-employment 30.2%, transfer payments 7.1%, other 21.5%; expenditure: food, tobacco, and beverages 30.2%, housing 19.1%, entertainment and recreation 15.1%, transportation and communications 15.0%, clothing 14.2%, medical and personal care 8.8%.

Foreign trade[5]

Balance of trade (current prices)

	1990	1991	1992	1993	1994	1995
U.S.$'000,000	–6,750	–5,990	–4,161	–4,297	–3,726	–7,968
% of total	12.9%	9.6%	6.1%	5.6%	4.0%	6.7%

Imports (1997): B 1,924,958,000,000 (1996; power generating equipment 19.4%, electrical machinery 18.7%, mineral fuels and lubricants 8.6%, road vehicles 7.0%, iron and steel 6.0%, plastics 3.2%, organic chemicals 3.0%). *Major import sources:* Japan 25.6%; U.S. 13.9%; Singapore 5.0%; Malaysia 4.8%; Germany 4.7%; Taiwan 4.6%; China 3.6%; South Korea 3.5%.
Exports (1997): B 1,811,763,000,000 (1996; electrical machinery 18.1%, power generating equipment 16.8%, garments 6.0%, rubber products 5.8%, live fish 4.5%, precious jewelry 4.0%, cereals 3.7%). *Major export destinations:* U.S. 19.6%; Japan 15.0%; Singapore 11.0%; Hong Kong 5.9%; Malaysia 4.3%; U.K. 3.7%; The Netherlands 3.2%; China 3.1%.

Transport and communications

Transport. Railroads (1997[6]): route length 4,041 km; passenger-km 11,804,000,000; metric ton-km cargo (1996) 3,384,000,000. Roads (1996): total length 64,600 km (paved 98%). Vehicles (1999): passenger cars 1,661,000; trucks and buses 2,855,000. Air transport (1998): passenger-km 34,339,507,000; metric ton-km cargo 1,522,198,000; airports (1996) 25.

Communications

Medium	date	unit	number	units per 1,000 persons
Daily newspapers	1996	circulation	3,800,000	64
Radio	1997	receivers	13,959,000	234
Television	1997	receivers	15,190,000	254
Telephones	1998	main lines	5,038,000	84
Cellular telephones	1998	subscribers	1,957,000	32
Personal computers	1998	units	1,300,000	22
Internet	1998	users	200,000	3.3

Education and health

Educational attainment (1990). Percentage of population age 25 and over having: no formal schooling 11.8%; primary education 71.3%; secondary 9.5%; postsecondary 6.6%; unknown 0.8%. *Literacy* (1995): total population age 15 and over literate 93.8%; males literate 96.0%; females literate 91.6%.

Education (1995–96)

	schools	teachers	students	student/ teacher ratio
Primary (age 7–12)	34,001	445,542[7]	5,961,855	19.3[7]
Secondary (age 13–18)	2,318[7]	107,025[7]	3,144,482	19.8[7]
Voc., teacher tr.	679[7]	40,116[7]	649,808	19.8[7]
Higher	102[7]	38,423	1,220,481	31.8

Health (1996): physicians 17,335 (1 per 3,461 persons); hospital beds 128,879 (1 per 466 persons); infant mortality rate (2000) 22.0.
Food (1997): daily per capita caloric intake 2,360 (vegetable products 88%, animal products 12%); (1995) 103% of FAO recommended minimum requirement.

Military

Total active duty personnel (1998): 306,000 (army 62.1%, navy 23.9%, air force 14.0%). *Military expenditure as percentage of GNP* (1995): 2.5% (world 2.8%); per capita expenditure U.S.$68.

[1]Actual local administration is based on 76 provinces. [2]Based on registration records. [3]February; economically active persons 13 years and over. [4]Mostly unemployed. [5]Import figures are f.o.b. in balance of trade and c.i.f. for commodities and trading partners. [6]Traffic data refer to fiscal year ending September 30. [7]1993.

Internet resources for further information:
- **Thailand-WWW Virtual Library http://www.nectec.or.th/WWW-VL-Thailand.html**
- **National Statistical Office Thailand http://www.nso.go.th/eng/index.htm**

Togo

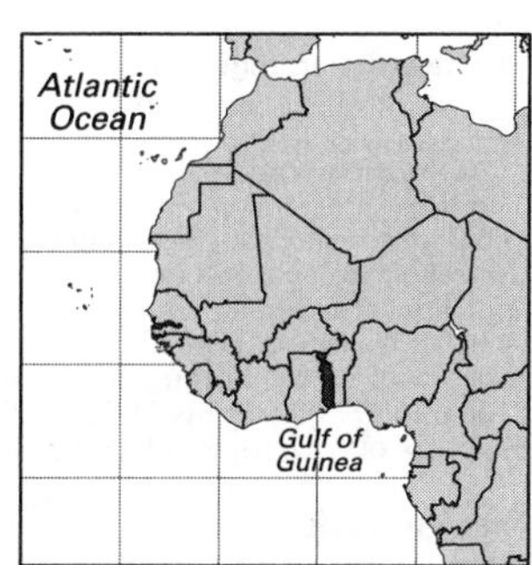

Official name: République Togolaise (Togolese Republic).
Form of government: multiparty republic[1] with one legislative body (National Assembly [81]).
Chief of state: President[1].
Head of government: Prime Minister.
Capital: Lomé.
Official language: French.
Official religion: none.
Monetary unit: 1 CFA franc (CFAF) = 100 centimes; valuation (Oct. 6, 2000) 1 U.S.$ = CFAF 754.28; 1 £ = CFAF 1,091.

Area and population

Regions / Prefectures	Capitals	area sq mi	area sq km	population 1989 estimate
Centrale	Sokodé			339,000
Sotouboua	Sotouboua	2,892	7,491	162,500
Tchamba	Tchamba	1,214	3,143	54,500
Tchaoudjo	Sokodé	984	2,549	122,000
De la Kara	Kara			531,500
Assoli	Bafilo	362	938	41,000
Bassar	Bassar	2,444	6,330	152,000
Binah	Pagouda	180	465	61,000
Doufelgou	Niamtougou	432	1,120	75,000
Kéran	Kandé	419	1,085	49,500
Kozah	Kara	653	1,692	153,000
Des Plateaux	Atakpamé			810,500
Amou	Amlamé	773	2,003	98,500
Haho	Notsé	1,406	3,641	139,000
Kloto	Kpalimé	1,072	2,777	233,500
Ogou	Atakpamé	2,349	6,083	204,000
Wawa	Badou	954	2,471	135,500
Des Savanes	Dapaong			410,500
Oti	Sansanné-Mango	1,453	3,762	98,500
Tône	Dapaong	1,869	4,840	312,000
Maritime	Lomé			1,300,000[2]
Golfe	Lomé	133	345	560,000
Lacs	Aného	275	713	172,500
Vo	Vogan	290	750	125,000
Yoto	Tabligbo	483	1,250	187,000
Zio	Tsévié	1,288	3,337	255,000
TOTAL		21,925	56,785	3,391,500

Demography

Population (2000): 5,019,000.
Density (2000): persons per sq mi 228.9, persons per sq km 88.4.
Urban-rural (1998): urban 32.2%; rural 67.8%.
Sex distribution (1999): male 49.18%; female 50.82%.
Age breakdown (1999): under 15, 46.6%; 15–29, 27.5%; 30–44, 14.6%; 45–59, 7.5%; 60–74, 3.2%; 75 and over, 0.6%.
Population projection: (2010) 6,245,000; (2020) 7,197,000.
Doubling time: 25 years.
Ethnic composition (1981): Ewe-Adja 43.1%; Tem-Kabre 26.7%; Gurma 16.1%; Kebu-Akposo 3.8%; Ana-Ife (Yoruba) 3.2%; non-African 0.3%; other 6.8%.
Religious affiliation (1993): traditional beliefs 50%; Christian 35%, of which Roman Catholic 23%; Muslim 15%.
Major cities (1983): Lomé 366,476; Sokodé 48,098[2]; Kpalimé 27,669[2].

Vital statistics

Birth rate per 1,000 population (1999): 38.9 (world avg. 22.1).
Death rate per 1,000 population (1999): 11.1 (world avg. 8.9).
Natural increase rate per 1,000 population (1999): 27.8 (world avg. 13.2).
Total fertility rate (avg. births per childbearing woman; 1999): 5.7.
Life expectancy at birth (1999): male 53.1 years; female 57.1 years.
Morbidity (reported cases of illness; 1989): malaria 730,162; injury and trauma 218,949; diarrheal diseases 153,074; diseases of the respiratory system 90,061.

National economy

Budget (1998). Revenue: CFAF 142,400,000,000 (tax revenue 81.0%, of which taxes on international trade 40.3%, public enterprise taxes 10.0%, sales tax 9.6%; grants 10.4%; nontax revenue 8.6%). Expenditures: CFAF 187,500,000,000 (current expenditure 70.9%, of which wages 31.4%, materials and supplies 20.2%; transfers 14.0%; other 5.4%; debt service 9.6%).
Public debt (external, outstanding; 1997): U.S.$1,207,000,000.
Production (metric tons except as noted). Agriculture, forestry, fishing (1997): yams 696,147, cassava 579,381, corn (maize) 350,484, vegetables 150,000, sorghum 136,558, oil palm fruit 115,000, rice 86,663, millet 40,693, peanuts (groundnuts) 27,157, bananas 16,100, coffee 14,000, coconuts 14,000, pulses 6,000; livestock (number of live animals) 1,110,000 goats, 850,000 pigs, 740,000 sheep, 222,800 cattle, 7,500,000 chickens; roundwood (1998) 1,182,000 cu m; fish catch (1997) 14,290. Mining and quarrying (1996): phosphate rock 2,700,000; limestone is quarried for cement manufacture. Manufacturing (value added in CFAF '000,000; 1998): food products, beverages, and tobacco manufactures 41,400; metallic goods 12,000; nonmetallic manufactures 8,500; textiles, clothing, and leather 4,900; wood products 4,700; paper, printing, and publishing 4,600; chemicals 3,600. Construction (value added in CFAF; 1995): 19,958,000,000. Energy production (consumption): electricity (kW-hr; 1997) 34,700,000 (282,200,000); petroleum products (metric tons; 1998) none (231,000).
Gross national product (1998): U.S.$1,453,000,000 (U.S.$330 per capita).

Structure of gross domestic product and labour force

	1998 in value CFAF '000,000,000	1998 % of total value	1994 labour force	1994 % of labour force
Agriculture	375.1	42.1	1,041,000	67.7
Mining	52.0	5.8		
Manufacturing	81.3	9.1	177,000	11.5
Construction	27.2	3.1		
Public utilities	27.5	3.1		
Transp. and commun.	47.3	5.3		
Trade and finance	151.1	17.0	318,000	20.7
Pub. admin., defense	62.1	7.0		
Services	67.0	7.5		
TOTAL	890.6	100.0	1,538,000[3]	100.0[3]

Population economically active (1994): total 1,538,000; activity rate of total population 33.8% (participation rates over age 10, 50.7%; female 35.6%; unemployed 16–18%).

Price and earnings indexes (1995 = 100)

	1993	1994	1995	1996	1997	1998
Consumer price index	61.7	85.9	100.0	104.7	113.3	114.0
Hourly earnings index	...	...	...	...	...	...

Household income and expenditure. Average household size (1998) 6.0; average annual income per household (1980) CFAF 102,000 (U.S.$452); sources of income: n.a.; expenditure (1987): food and beverages 45.9%, household durable goods 13.9%, clothing 11.4%, housing 5.9%, services 20.5%.
Land use (1994): forested 16.5%; meadows and pastures 3.7%; agricultural and under permanent cultivation 44.7%; other 35.1%.
Tourism: receipts (1995) U.S.$13,000,000; expenditures (1994) U.S.$18,000,000.

Foreign trade

Balance of trade (current prices)

	1994	1995	1996	1997	1998
CFAF '000,000	+7,800	+2,500	–21,300	–17,700	–18,600
% of total	3.2%	0.7%	5.2%	3.4%	3.7%

Imports (1998): CFAF 263,400,000,000 (consumer goods 55.8%; capital equipment 18.8%; intermediate goods 18.0%; petroleum products 7.4%). *Major import sources* (1998): Ghana 21%; France 12.7%; China 12.0%; Nigeria 2.1%; Japan 1.8%.
Exports (1998): CFAF 244,800,000,000 (domestic exports 80.4%, of which cotton 24.5%, phosphates 22.0%, coffee 9.1%, cocoa 4.3%; reexports 19.6%). *Major export destinations* (1998): Canada 12.1%; Bolivia 9.5%; Nigeria 7.4%; France 3.8%; Ghana 3.1%.

Transport and communications

Transport. Railroads (1996): route length 395 km; (1996) passenger-km 16,500,000; metric ton-km cargo 49,000,000. Roads (1996): total length 7,520 km (paved 32%). Vehicles (1996): passenger cars 79,200; trucks and buses 34,240. Merchant marine (1992): vessels (100 gross tons and over) 8; total deadweight tonnage 20,633. Air transport (1996)[4]: passenger-km 224,736,000; metric ton-km cargo 16,420,000; airports (1998) 2.

Communications

Medium	date	unit	number	units per 1,000 persons
Daily newspapers	1996	circulation	15,000	3.6
Radio	1998	receivers	720,000	167
Television	1998	receivers	80,000	18.5
Telephones	1999	main lines	31,395	7.1
Cellular telephones	1999	subscribers	7,500	1.7
Personal computers	1998	units	25,000	5.8
Internet	1999	users	75,000	17.0

Education and health

Educational attainment (1981). Percentage of population age 25 and over having: no formal schooling 76.5%; primary education 13.5%; secondary 8.7%; higher 1.3%. *Literacy* (1995): total population age 15 and over literate 51.7%; males 67.0%; females 37.0%.

Education (1996–97)

	schools	teachers	students	student/ teacher ratio
Primary (age 6–11)	3,283[5]	18,535	859,574	46.4
Secondary (age 12–18)	314[6]	4,736[5]	169,178	...
Vocational	18[7]	653	9,076	13.9
Higher[8]	1	443	11,639	26.3

Health: physicians (1995) 320 (1 per 13,158 persons); hospital beds (1990) 5,307 (1 per 694 persons); infant mortality rate (1999) 72.6.
Food (1998): daily per capita caloric intake 2,513 (vegetable products 96%, animal products 4%); 109% of FAO recommended minimum requirement.

Military

Total active duty personnel (1999): 6,950 (army 93.5%, navy 2.9%, air force 3.6%). *Military expenditure as percentage of GNP* (1997): 2.0% (world 2.6%); per capita expenditure U.S.$6.

[1]Personal military-supported rule from 1967 continues under constitution approved by referendum in September 1992. [2]1981. [3]Detail does not add to total given because of rounding. [4]Represents 1/11 of the traffic of Air Afrique, which is operated by 11 West African states. [5]1995–96. [6]1990. [7]1987. [8]University only.

Internet resources for further information:
- **President of the Republic http://www.republicoftogo.com**

Tonga

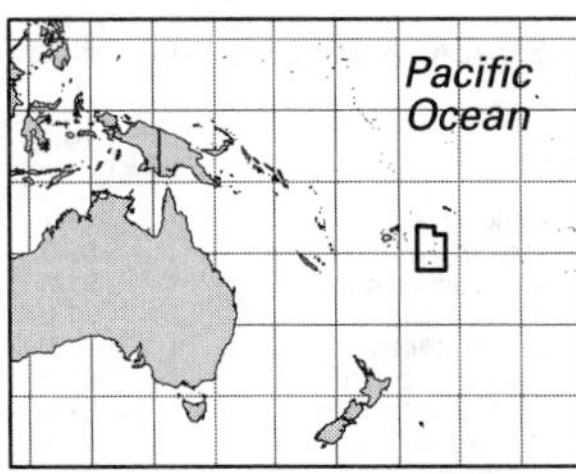

Official name: Pule'anga Fakatu'i 'o Tonga (Tongan); Kingdom of Tonga (English).
Form of government: constitutional monarchy with one legislative house (Legislative Assembly [30[1]]).
Head of state and government: King assisted by Privy Council.
Capital: Nuku'alofa.
Official languages: Tongan; English.
Official religion: none.
Monetary unit: 1 pa'anga[2] (T$) = 100 seniti; valuation (Oct. 6, 2000) 1 U.S.$ = T$1.87; 1 £ = T$2.70.

Area and population		area		population
				1996
Divisions	Capitals	sq mi	sq km	census
'Eua[3]	'Ohonua	33.7	87.4	4,934
Ha'apai[4]	Pangai	42.5	110.0	8,138
Niuas[5]	Hihifo	27.7	71.7	2,018
Tongatapu[3]	Nuku'alofa	100.6	260.5	66,979
Vava'u[4]	Neiafu	46.0	119.2	15,715
TOTAL LAND AREA		278.1[6]	720.3[6]	
INLAND WATER		11.4	29.6	
TOTAL		289.5	749.9	97,784

Demography

Population (2000): 100,000.
Density (2000)[7]: persons per sq mi 359.6, persons per sq km 138.8.
Urban-rural (1999): urban 45.0%; rural 55.0%.
Sex distribution (1996): male 50.74%; female 49.26%.
Age breakdown (1996): under 15, 39.1%; 15–29, 28.0%; 30–44, 15.1%; 45–59, 10.0%; 60–74, 6.0%; 75 and over, 1.8%.
Population projection: (2010) 104,000; (2020) 108,000.
Doubling time: 35 years.
Ethnic composition (1996): Tongan and part Tongan 98.2%; other 1.8%.
Religious affiliation (1998): Free Wesleyan 41.2%; Roman Catholic 15.8%; Mormon 13.6%; other (mostly other Protestant) 29.4%.
Major cities (1986): Nuku'alofa (1996) 22,400[8]; Neiafu 3,879; Haveluloto 3,070.

Vital statistics

Birth rate per 1,000 population (1999): 25.9 (world avg. 22.1).
Death rate per 1,000 population (1999): 6.0 (world avg. 8.9).
Natural increase rate per 1,000 population (1999): 19.9 (world avg. 13.2).
Total fertility rate (avg. births per childbearing woman; 1999): 3.6.
Marriage rate per 1,000 population (1992): 8.2.
Divorce rate per 1,000 population (1992): 1.1.
Life expectancy at birth (1999): male 67.7 years; female 72.2 years.
Major causes of death per 100,000 population (1993)[9]: circulatory diseases 58.1; nervous system diseases 51.0; senility 27.6; diabetes mellitus 17.3.

National economy

Budget (1997–98). Revenue: T$63,000,000 (foreign-trade taxes 47.9%, government services revenue 20.0%, direct taxes 13.8%, indirect taxes 11.6%, interest and rent 3.5%). Expenditures[10]: T$63,000,000 (education 18.4%, general administration 13.8%, health 13.2%, law and order 12.5%, public works and communications 9.2%, agriculture 6.2%).
Production (metric tons except as noted). Agriculture, forestry, fishing (1999): yams 31,000, cassava 28,000, taro 27,200, coconuts 24,500, fruits 12,500, vegetables 7,308, sweet potatoes 5,137; livestock (number of live animals) 80,853 pigs, 13,939 goats, 11,400 horses, 9,318 cattle, 266,000 chickens; roundwood (1998) 4,600 cu m; fish catch (1997) 2,739. Mining and quarrying (1982): coral 150,000; sand 25,000. Manufacturing (output in T$'000,000; 1996): food products and beverages 8,203; paper products 1,055; chemical products 964; metal products 889; textile and wearing apparel 742; nonmetallic products 715. Construction (value in T$; 1984): residential 9,552,300; nonresidential 11,377,100. Energy production (consumption): electricity (kW-hr; 1996) 34,000,000 (34,000,000); petroleum (barrels) none (none); petroleum products (metric tons; 1996) n.a. (38,000).
Gross national product (1998): U.S.$173,000,000 (U.S.$1,750 per capita).

Structure of gross domestic product and labour force	1997–98		1990	
	in value T$'000,000	% of total value	labour force	% of labour force
Agriculture	74.9	32.1	11,682	36.5
Mining	0.7	0.3	4,665	14.6
Manufacturing	7.6	3.3		
Construction	10.5	4.5	1,257	3.9
Public utilities	3.7	1.6	408	1.3
Transp. and commun.	17.1	7.3	1,821	5.7
Trade	25.6	11.0	2,597	8.1
Finance	24.3	10.4	1,188	3.7
Pub. admin., defense	30.9	13.2	7,052	22.0
Services	11.4	4.9		
Other	26.5	11.4	1,343	4.2
TOTAL	233.2	100.0	32,013	100.0

Population economically active (1996–97): total 33,908; activity rate 34.7% (participation rates: ages 15 and over 57.0%; female 36.0%; unemployed 13.3%).

Price and earnings indexes (1995 = 100)	1993	1994	1995	1996	1997	1998	1999
Consumer price index	97.6	98.6	100.0	103.0	105.2	108.6	113.5
Quarterly earnings index	...	...	...	...	...	...	...

Public debt (external, outstanding; 1998): U.S.$64,100,000.
Household income and expenditure. Average household size (1996) 6.0; income per household: n.a.; sources of income: n.a.; expenditure (1991–92)[11]: food 43.2%, transportation 15.5%, household 14.2%, housing 6.4%, tobacco and beverages 5.4%, clothing and footwear 4.2%.
Tourism (1998): receipts U.S.$12,000,000; expenditures (1997) U.S.$3,000,000.
Land use (1994): forest 11.1%; pasture 5.6%; agriculture 66.7%; other 16.6%.

Foreign trade[12]

Balance of trade (current prices)	1994	1995	1996	1997	1998	1999
T$'000,000	–72.8	–79.6	–75.5	–79.3	–90.8	–96.4
% of total	66.5%	68.3%	69.9%	75.6%	79.6%	70.7%

Imports (1998–99): T$104,900,000 (food and live animals 31.8%, basic manufactures 17.4%, machinery and transport equipment 17.0%, mineral fuels 11.8%, chemicals 7.8%). *Major import sources:* New Zealand 35.0%; Australia 28.6%; U.S. 13.1%; Fiji 8.6%; Japan 4.9%.
Exports (1998–99): T$12,000,000 (squash 35.8%, fish 24.2%, vanilla beans 6.7%, root crops 2.5%). *Major export destinations:* Japan 40.8%; U.S. 17.5%; New Zealand 14.2%; Fiji 5.8%; Australia 3.3%.

Transport and communications

Transport. Railroads: none. Roads (1996): total length 680 km (paved 27%). Vehicles (1996): passenger cars 1,140, commercial vehicles 780. Merchant marine (1992): vessels (100 gross tons and over) 15; total deadweight tonnage 13,740. Air transport (1996): passenger-km 11,000,000; metric ton-km cargo 1,000,000; airports (1996) with scheduled flights 6.

Communications Medium	date	unit	number	units per 1,000 persons
Daily newspapers	1996	circulation	7,000	72
Radio	1997	receivers	61,000	619
Television	1997	receivers	2,000	21
Telephones	1996	main lines	7,780	79
Cellular telephones	1996	subscribers	302	3.1

Education and health

Educational attainment (1986). Percentage of population age 25 and over having: complete primary 38.3%; lower secondary 30.3%; secondary 23.4%; postsecondary 4.9%; higher 1.0%; not stated 2.1%. *Literacy* (1976): total population age 15 and over literate 46,456 (92.8%); males 23,372 (92.9%); females 23,084 (92.8%).

Education (1994)	schools	teachers	students	student/ teacher ratio
Primary (age 6–11)	115	701	16,540	23.6
Secondary (age 12–18)	38	809	15,702	19.4
Voc., teacher tr.	9	67	824	12.3
Higher[13]	1	19	226	11.9

Health: physicians (1997) 43 (1 per 2,279 persons); hospital beds (1992) 307 (1 per 320 persons); infant mortality rate per 1,000 live births (1999) 37.9.
Food (1992): daily per capita caloric intake 2,946 (vegetable products 82%, animal products 18%); 129% of FAO recommended minimum requirement.

Military

Total active duty personnel (1996): 125-member naval force; an air force was created in 1996. *Military expenditure as percentage of GNP* (1989): 4.9% (world 4.9%); per capita expenditure U.S.$21.

[1]Includes 12 nonelective seats and 9 nobles elected by the 33 hereditary nobles of Tonga. [2]The pa'anga was pegged at par to the Australian dollar through Feb. 8, 1991, but beginning Feb. 11, 1991, it was linked to a weighted basket of foreign currencies. [3]'Eua and Tongatapu together comprise Tongatapu island group. [4]Also the name of an island group. [5]Also known as Niuatoputapu island group. [6]Total includes 27.6 sq mi (71.5 sq km) of uninhabited islands. [7]Based on land area. [8]Population of urban agglomeration (1999) is 37,000. [9]Reported inpatient deaths at all hospitals. [10]Excludes amortization of public debt and sinking funds. [11]Current weight of consumer price index components. [12]Import data used in computing balance of trade is c.i.f. [13]1992.

Internet resources for further information:

- **Tonga Page http://user.cs.tu-berlin.de/~minibbjd/tonga/index.html**

Trinidad and Tobago

Official name: Republic of Trinidad and Tobago.
Form of government: multiparty republic with two legislative houses (Senate [31]; House of Representatives [36[1]]).
Chief of state: President.
Head of government: Prime Minister.
Capital: Port of Spain.
Official language: English.
Official religion: none.
Monetary unit: 1 Trinidad and Tobago dollar (TT$) = 100 cents; valuation (Oct. 6, 2000) 1 U.S.$ = TT$6.24; 1 £ = TT$9.03.

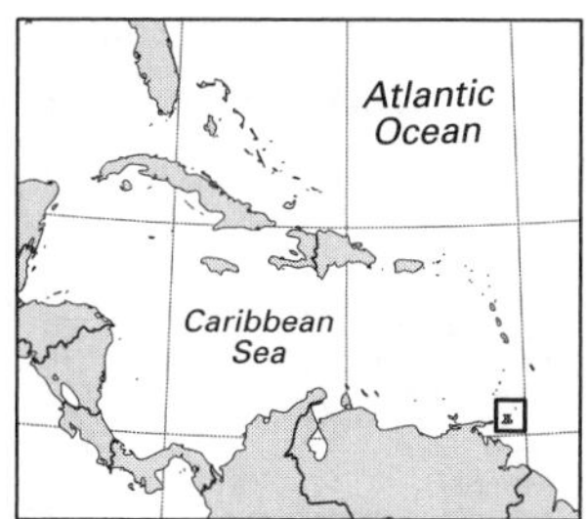

Area and population

		area		population
Counties[2]	Capitals	sq mi	sq km	1990 census
Caroni	Chaguanas	191.0	494.7	120,508
Nariva/Mayaro	Rio Claro	349.0	903.9	36,781
St. Andrew/St. David	Sangre Grande	360.0	932.4	62,944
St. George	Tunapuna	354.0	916.9	445,620
St. Patrick	Siparia	252.0	652.7	120,129
Victoria	Princes Town	315.0	815.9	210,833
Cities				
Port of Spain	—	4.0	10.4	50,878
San Fernando	—	3.0	7.8	30,092
Boroughs				
Arima	—	4.0	10.4	29,695
Chaguanas	—	23.0	59.6	56,601
Point Fortin	—	9.0	23.3	20,025
Unitary State				
Tobago	Scarborough	116.0	300.4	50,282
TOTAL		1,980.1[3]	5,128.4	1,234,388

Demography

Population (2000): 1,292,000.
Density (2000): persons per sq mi 652.5, persons per sq km 251.9.
Urban-rural (1999): urban 73.6%; rural 26.4%.
Sex distribution (1998): male 49.81%; female 50.19%.
Age breakdown (1995): under 15, 30.3%; 15–29, 26.6%; 30–44, 22.0%; 45–59, 12.3%; 60–74, 6.5%; 75 and over, 2.3%.
Population projection: (2010) 1,353,000; (2020) 1,418,000.
Ethnic composition (1990): East Indian 40.3%; black 39.6%; mixed 18.4%; white 0.6%; Chinese 0.4%; other/not stated 0.7%.
Religious affiliation (1990): six largest Protestant bodies 29.7%; Roman Catholic 29.4%; Hindu 23.7%; Muslim 5.9%; other 11.3%.
Major cities (1990): Chaguanas 56,601; Port of Spain 43,396[4]; San Fernando 30,115[5]; Arima 29,483[5]; Point Fortin 20,025; Scarborough 4,000.

Vital statistics

Birth rate per 1,000 population (1997): 14.5 (world avg. 22.1).
Death rate per 1,000 population (1997): 7.2 (world avg. 8.9).
Natural increase rate per 1,000 population (1997): 7.3 (world avg. 13.2).
Total fertility rate (avg. births per childbearing woman; 1999): 1.9.
Marriage rate per 1,000 population (1996): 5.6.
Divorce rate per 1,000 population (1996): 1.2.
Life expectancy at birth (1999): male 65.1 years; female 70.2 years.
Major causes of death per 100,000 population (1994): diseases of the circulatory system 286.4; malignant neoplasms (cancers) 94.3; endocrine and metabolic disorders 90.0; accidents, violence, and homicide 52.8.

National economy

Budget (1999). Revenue: TT$9,789,000,000 (company taxes 21.2%, of which petroleum sector 9.2%; individual income taxes 20.3%; value-added taxes 17.0%; nontax revenues 8.3%). Expenditures: TT$11,076,000,000 (current expenditures 95.6%; development expenditures 4.4%).
Tourism (1998): receipts from visitors U.S.$201,000,000; expenditures by nationals abroad U.S.$67,000,000.
Production (metric tons except as noted). Agriculture, forestry, fishing (1999): sugarcane 1,200,000, coconuts 22,000, oranges 15,000, rice 7,037, pigeon peas 3,180, cocoa 1,270, coffee 367; livestock (number of live animals) 59,000 goats, 8,500,000 chickens; roundwood (1998) 60,000 cu m; fish catch (1997) 15,012. Mining and quarrying (1999): natural asphalt 12,600. Manufacturing (1999): anhydrous ammonia and urea (nitrogenous fertilizers) 3,946,800; methanol 2,149,800; steel billets 723,900; cement 688,400; steel wire rods 638,200; refined sugar 43,600; beer and stout 418,800 hectolitres[4]; rum 78,000 hectolitres[4]. Energy production (consumption): electricity (kW-hr; 1997) 4,848,000,000 ([1996] 4,541,000,000); coal, none (none); crude petroleum (barrels; 1999) 35,903,000 ([1996] 39,840,000); petroleum products (metric tons; 1996) 5,454,000 (1,448,000); natural gas (cu m; 1997) 8,136,000,000 ([1996] 7,509,000,000).
Public debt (external, outstanding; 1998): U.S.$1,476,000,000.
Household income and expenditure. Average household size (1998) 3.8; average income per household (1988) TT$21,760 (U.S.$5,661); expenditure (1993): food, beverages, and tobacco 25.5%, housing 21.6%, transportation 15.2%, household furnishings 14.3%, clothing and footwear 10.4%.
Gross national product (at current market prices; 1998): U.S.$5,811,000,000 (U.S.$4,520 per capita).

Structure of gross domestic product and labour force

	1999		1998	
	in value TT$'000,000	% of total value	labour force	% of labour force
Agriculture	891	2.2	41,300	7.4
Petroleum, natural gas, quarrying	8,834[6]	21.5	21,700[7]	3.9
Manufacturing[6]	3,333[7]	8.1	59,800[6]	10.7
Construction	4,232	10.3	83,500	14.9
Public utilities	849	2.1	6,900	1.2
Transp. and commun.	3,827	9.3	38,100	6.8
Trade	6,944	16.9	98,600	17.6
Finance, real estate	5,706	13.9	43,100	7.7
Pub. admin., defense	3,918	9.5	165,400	29.6
Services	2,605	6.3		
Other	–95[8]	–0.2[8]	400	0.1
TOTAL	41,044[3]	100.0[3]	558,700[3]	100.0[3]

Population economically active (1998): total 558,700; activity rate of total population 43.6% (participation rates: [1995] ages 15–64, 65.4%; female 38.3%; unemployed [1999] 13.1%).

Price and earnings indexes (1995 = 100)

	1993	1994	1995	1996	1997	1998	1999
Consumer price index	87.4	95.1	100.0	103.4	107.2	113.2	117.0
Weekly earnings index[9]	95.5	93.6	100.0	102.5	109.5	114.9	...

Land use (1994): forested 45.8%; meadows and pastures 2.1%; agricultural and under permanent cultivation 23.8%; other 28.3%.

Foreign trade[10]

Balance of trade (current prices)

	1994	1995	1996	1997	1998	1999
TT$'000,000	+4,354	+3,938	+1,488	–2,818	–4,666	+398
% of total	24.5%	16.2%	5.5%	8.1%	14.1%	1.1%

Imports (1998): TT$18,887,000,000 (machinery and apparatus 30.8%, fuels 12.2%, food 7.3%, transport equipment 6.2%). *Major import sources* (1999): United States 39.8%; Venezuela 11.9%; Japan 5.1%; Canada 4.9%; United Kingdom 4.7%.
Exports (1998): TT$14,221,000,000 (refined petroleum 29.6%, crude petroleum 10.6%, anhydrous ammonia 10.6%, iron and steel 8.8%, reexports 7.1%, methanol 6.3%). *Major export destinations* (1999): United States 39.3%; Caricom 26.1%, of which Jamaica 8.7%, Barbados 5.3%; EC 5.7%.

Transport and communications

Transport. Railroads: none. Roads (1995): total length 8,320 km (paved 51%). Vehicles (1996): passenger cars 122,000; trucks and buses 24,000. Air transport (1996): passenger-km 2,658,000,000; metric ton-km cargo 265,000,000; airports (1996) with scheduled flights 2.

Communications

Medium	date	unit	number	units per 1,000 persons
Daily newspapers	1996	circulation	156,000	123
Radio	1997	receivers	680,000	535
Television	1997	receivers	425,000	334
Telephones	1998	main lines	264,000	206
Cellular telephones	1998	subscribers	26,287	20
Personal computers	1998	units	60,000	47
Internet	1998	users	20,000	16

Education and health

Educational attainment (1990). Percentage of population age 25 and over having: no formal schooling 4.5%; primary education 56.4%; secondary 32.1%; higher 3.4%; other/not stated 3.6%. *Literacy* (1995): total population age 15 and over literate 886,000 (97.9%).

Education (1996–97)

	schools	teachers	students	student/ teacher ratio
Primary (age 5–11)	476	7,311	181,030	24.8
Secondary (age 12–16)	...	5,070	104,349	20.6
Higher[11]	1	510	6,641	13.0

Health: physicians (1997) 1,074 (1 per 1,183 persons); hospital beds (1996) 6,622 (1 per 191 persons); infant mortality rate (1997) 17.1.
Food (1998): daily per capita caloric intake 2,711 (vegetable products 85%, animal products 15%); 112% of FAO recommended minimum requirement.

Military

Total active duty personnel (1999): 2,700 (army 74.1%, coast guard 25.9%). *Military expenditure as percentage of GNP* (1997): 1.5% (world 2.6%); per capita expenditure U.S.$65.

[1]Excludes speaker, who may be elected from outside the House of Representatives. [2]Counties administratively reorganized into nine regions in 1992. [3]Detail does not add to total given because of rounding. [4]1996. [5]1991. [6]Includes refined petroleum and petrochemicals. [7]Excludes refined petroleum and petrochemicals. [8]Net of value-added taxes less imputed bank service charges. [9]Manufacturing only. [10]Imports c.i.f.; exports f.o.b. [11]1998–99; University of the West Indies, St. Augustine campus only.

Internet resources for further information:
- **Central Bank of Trinidad and Tobago http://www.central-bank.org.tt**

Tunisia

Official name: Al-Jumhūrīyah at-Tūnisīyah (Republic of Tunisia).
Form of government: multiparty republic with one legislative house (Chamber of Deputies [182]).
Chief of state: President.
Head of government: Prime Minister.
Capital: Tunis.
Official language: Arabic.
Official religion: Islam.
Monetary unit: 1 dinar (D) = 1,000 millimes; valuation (Oct. 6, 2000) 1 U.S.$ = D 1.44; 1 £ = D 2.09.

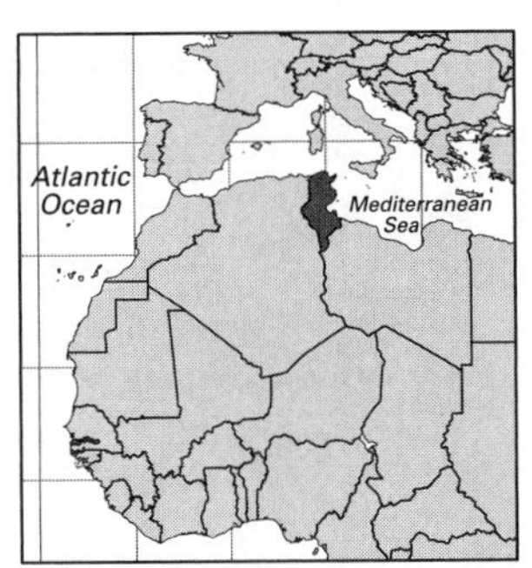

Area and population

		area		population
Governorates	Capitals	sq mi	sq km	1994 census[1]
Al-Ariānah	Al-Ariānah	602	1,558	568,818
Bājah	Bājah	1,374	3,558	305,457
Banzart	Bizerte (Banzart)	1,423	3,685	484,250
Bin 'Arūs	Bin 'Arūs	294	761	371,724
Jundūbah	Jundūbah	1,198	3,102	403,768
Al-Kāf	Al-Kāf	1,917	4,965	272,277
Madanīn	Madanīn	3,316	8,588	385,596
Al-Mahdīyah	Al-Mahdīyah	1,145	2,966	334,084
Al-Munastīr	Al-Munastīr	393	1,019	363,436
Nābul	Nābul	1,076	2,788	579,864
Qābis	Qābis	2,770	7,175	310,272
Qafṣah	Qafṣah	3,471	8,990	307,662
Al-Qaṣrayn	Al-Qaṣrayn	3,114	8,066	387,244
Al-Qayrawān	Al-Qayrawān	2,591	6,712	530,725
Qibilī	Qibilī	8,527	22,084	131,564
Ṣafāqis	Ṣafāqis	2,913	7,545	732,865
Sīdī Bū Zayd	Sīdī Bū Zayd	2,700	6,994	378,052
Siliānah	Siliānah	1,788	4,631	245,727
Sūsah	Sūsah	1,012	2,621	435,075
Taṭāuīn	Taṭāuīn	15,015	38,889	135,184
Tawzar	Tawzar	1,822	4,719	89,038
Tūnis	Tunis (Tūnis)	134	346	890,092
Zaghwān	Zaghwān	1,069	2,768	142,937
TOTAL		63,378[2]	164,150[2]	8,785,711

Demography

Population (2000): 9,593,000.
Density (2000): persons per sq mi 151.4, persons per sq km 58.4.
Urban-rural (1994): urban 61.0%; rural 39.0%.
Sex distribution (1994): male 50.53%; female 49.47%.
Age breakdown (1994): under 15, 34.8%; 15–29, 28.5%; 30–44, 18.8%; 45–59, 9.6%; 60–74, 6.4%; 75 and over, 1.9%.
Population projection: (2010) 10,661,000; (2020) 11,641,000.
Doubling time: 54 years.
Ethnic composition (1983): Arab 98.2%; Berber 1.2%; French 0.2%; Italian 0.1%; other 0.3%.
Religious affiliation (1995): Sunnī Muslim 99.5%; Christian 0.3%; other 0.2%.
Major cities (commune; 1994): Tunis 674,100; Ṣafāqis 230,900; Aryānah 152,700; Ettadhamen 149,200; Sūsah 125,000.

Vital statistics

Birth rate per 1,000 population (1999): 18.1 (world avg. 22.1).
Death rate per 1,000 population (1999): 5.0 (world avg. 8.9).
Natural increase rate per 1,000 population (1999): 13.1 (world avg. 13.2).
Total fertility rate (avg. births per childbearing woman; 1999): 2.1.
Marriage rate per 1,000 population (1995): 6.0.
Life expectancy at birth (1999): male 71.9 years; female 75.1 years.
Major causes of death per 100,000 population: n.a.; however, of approximately 12,000 deaths[3] for which a cause was reported in 1992, complications of pregnancy and childbirth represented 31.6%, circulatory diseases 22.4%, accidents and poisoning 14.9%, respiratory diseases 7.2%.

National economy

Budget (1998). Revenue: D 6,579,000,000 (tax revenue 89.4%, of which goods and services 37.0%, social security 16.9%, income tax 15.6%, import duties 11.3%; nontax revenue 10.6%). Expenditures: D 7,115,000,000 (economic services 23.3%; education 19.6%; social security 15.1%; public order 8.0%; health 7.1%; social welfare 7.1%; defense 6.0%; housing 6.0%).
Public debt (external, outstanding; 1998): U.S.$9,727,000,000.
Production (metric tons except as noted). Agriculture, forestry, fishing (1999): wheat 1,400,000, olives 950,000, tomatoes 863,500, barley 410,000, potatoes 297,700, watermelons 290,000, grapes 110,000, sugar beets 89,400; livestock (number of live animals) 6,600,000 sheep, 1,300,000 goats, 780,000 cattle; roundwood (1998) 3,200,000 cu m; fish catch (1998) 89,273. Mining and quarrying (1996): phosphate rock 6,400,000; iron ore 130,000; zinc 32,000. Manufacturing (1996): cement 4,560,000; phosphoric acid 1,063,000; flour 679,000; semolina 597,000; lime 464,000; crude steel 187,000; sugar 91,000. Energy production (consumption): electricity (kW-hr; 1998) 7,937,000 (1996; 7,851,000); coal (metric tons; 1996) 2,000 (2,000); crude petroleum (barrels; 1998) 30,656,000 (1996; 7,097,000); petroleum products (metric tons; 1996) 1,844,000 (3,106,000); natural gas (cu m; 1996) 6,348,500,000 (1,951,900,000).
Household income and expenditure. Average household size (1998) 4.9; income per household: n.a.; sources of income: n.a.; expenditure (1985): food and beverages 39.0%, household durable goods 11.2%, housing 10.7%, transportation 9.0%, recreation 7.1%, clothing and footwear 6.0%, energy 5.1%, health care 3.0%, education 1.8%, other 7.1%.

Gross national product (1998): U.S.$19,193,000,000 (U.S.$2,060 per capita).

Structure of gross domestic product and labour force

	1998		1994	
	in value D '000,000	% of total value	labour force	% of labour force
Agriculture	2,829	12.4	501,000	21.6
Mining	219	1.0	36,800	1.6
Public utilities	1,060	4.7		
Manufacturing	4,146	18.2	455,700	19.6
Construction	1,037	4.6	305,800	13.2
Transp. and commun.	1,770	7.9	[4]	[4]
Trade	5,509	24.2	315,600	13.6
Finance	3,201			
Pub. admin., defense		14.1	667,100[4]	28.7[4]
Services				
Other	2,953[5]	13.0[5]	38,600	1.7
TOTAL	22,724	100.0[6]	2,320,600	100.0

Population economically active (1997): total 3,502,000; activity rate of total population 37.9% (participation rates [1989]: ages 15–64, 42.2%; female [1997] 30.9%; unemployed [1996] 15.0%).

Price and earnings indexes (1995 = 100)

	1993	1994	1995	1996	1997	1998	1999
Consumer price index	89.9	94.1	100.0	103.7	107.5	110.9	113.9
Hourly earnings index	...	...	...	...	...	...	...

Land use (1994): forested 4.3%; meadows and pastures 20.0%; agricultural and under permanent cultivation 31.9%; other 43.8%.
Tourism (1998): receipts U.S.$1,557,000,000; expenditures U.S.$168,000,000.

Foreign trade[7]

Balance of trade (current prices)

	1994	1995	1996	1997	1998	1999
D '000,000	–1,950.7	–2,291.2	–2,126.9	–2,608.1	–2,944.5	–3,103.6
% of total	17.2%	18.1%	16.5%	17.5%	18.4%	18.2%

Imports (1998): D 9,476,100,000 (consumer products 35.3%, raw materials 28.6%, machinery and electrical equipment 23.0%, food products 8.3%, energy 4.8%). *Major import sources:* France 27.1%; Italy 19.9%; Germany 12.0%.
Exports (1998): D 6,531,600,000 (clothing and accessories 50.3%, machinery and electrical products 16.0%, phosphate products 13.5%, energy 6.4%). *Major export destinations:* France 27.0%; Germany 15.4%; Belgium 6.1%; Libya 3.9%.

Transport and communications

Transport. Railroads (1997): route length 2,158 km; (1996) passenger-km 988,000,000; metric ton-km cargo 2,329,000,000. Roads (1996): total length 23,100 km (paved 79%). Vehicles (1996): passenger cars 269,000; trucks and buses 312,000. Air transport (1999)[8]: passenger-km 2,761,878,000; metric ton-km cargo 19,236,000; airports (1998) 5.

Communications

Medium	date	unit	number	units per 1,000 persons
Daily newspapers	1996	circulation	280,000	31
Radio	1997	receivers	2,060,000	224
Television	1998	receivers	970,000	103.9
Telephones	1998	main lines	752,180	80.6
Cellular telephones	1998	subscribers	38,973	4.2
Personal computers	1998	units	138,000	14.8
Internet	1998	users	10,000	1.1

Education and health

Educational attainment (1989). Percentage of population age 25 and over having: no formal schooling 54.9%; primary 26.9%; secondary 14.3%; higher 3.4%; unspecified 0.5%. *Literacy* (1995): total population age 15 and over literate 66.7%; males literate 78.6%; females literate 54.6%.

Education (1996–97)

	schools	teachers	students	student/ teacher ratio
Primary (age 6–11)	4,428	60,101	1,450,916	24.1
Secondary (age 12–18)	712[9]	45,411	882,730	19.4
Teacher tr. [10, 11]	...	237	3,839	16.2
Higher[14]	...	6,641	121,787	18.3

Health (1997): physicians 6,464 (1 per 1,570 persons); hospital beds (1994) 15,759 (1 per 556 persons); infant mortality rate (1999) 31.4.
Food (1998): daily per capita caloric intake 3,008 (vegetable products 91%, animal products 9%); 133% of FAO recommended minimum requirement.

Military

Total active duty personnel (1999): 35,000 (army 77.1%, navy 12.9%, air force 10.0%). *Military expenditure as percentage of GNP* (1997): 2.0% (world 2.6%); per capita expenditure U.S.$39.

[1]Preliminary. [2]Total includes 3,714 sq mi (9,620 sq km) of territory that is not distributed by governorate. [3]Recorded deaths from urban areas only, including complete figures for Tunis. [4]Services includes transportation and communications. [5]Indirect taxes less subsidies. [6]Detail does not add to total given because of rounding. [7]Imports c.i.f. [8]Tunis Air only. [9]1994–95. [10]1987–88. [11]Teacher training only.

Internet resources for further information:
- **Tunisia Online http://www.tunisiaonline.com**
- **National Statistics Institute (French only) http://www.ins.nat.tn**

Turkey

Official name: Türkiye Cumhuriyeti (Republic of Turkey).
Form of government: multiparty republic with one legislative house (Turkish Grand National Assembly [550]).
Chief of state: President.
Head of government: Prime Minister.
Capital: Ankara.
Official language: Turkish.
Official religion: none.
Monetary unit: 1 Turkish lira (LT) = 100 kurush; valuation (Oct. 6, 2000) 1 U.S.$ = LT 671,175; 1 £ = LT 970,922.

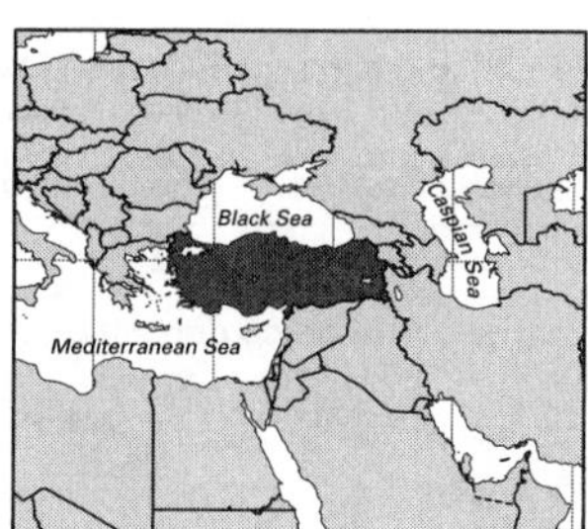

Area and population

Geographic regions[1]	area sq mi	area sq km	population 1997 estimate
Akdeniz kıyısı (Mediterranean Coast)	22,933	59,395	6,266,958
Batı Anadolu (West Anatolia)	29,742	77,031	4,074,955
Doğu Anadolu (East Anatolia)	68,074	180,180	7,351,461
Güneydoğu Anadolu (Southeast Anatolia)	15,347	35,880	3,205,251
İç Anadolu (Central Anatolia)	91,254	236,347	14,049,774
Karadeniz kıyısı (Black Sea Coast)	31,388	81,295	6,816,009
Marmara ve Ege kıyıları (Marmara and Aegean coasts)	33,035	85,560	13,677,750[2]
Trakya (Thrace)	9,175	23,764	7,168,094[2]
TOTAL	300,948	779,452	62,610,252

Demography

Population (2000): 65,667,000.
Density (2000): persons per sq mi 218.2, persons per sq km 84.2.
Urban-rural (1997): urban 64.7%; rural 35.3%.
Sex distribution (1997): male 50.54%; female 49.46%.
Age breakdown (1995): under 15, 31.1%; 15–29, 29.7%; 30–44, 20.1%; 45–59, 11.1%; 60–74, 6.6%; 75 and over, 1.4%.
Population projection: (2010) 73,322,000; (2020) 79,679,000.
Doubling time: 47 years.
Ethnic composition (1994): Turks (including Turkmen) 80–88%; Kurds 10–20%; Arabs 1.5%; others 0.3%.
Religious affiliation (1994): Sunnī Muslim *c.* 80.0%; Shīʿī Muslim *c.* 19.8%, of which nonorthodox Alevi *c.* 14.0%; Christian *c.* 0.2%.
Major cities (1996): Istanbul 8,023,329; Ankara 2,890,025; İzmir 2,073,669; Adana 1,099,154; Bursa 1,057,016; Gaziantep 758,438; Konya 600,062.

Vital statistics

Birth rate per 1,000 population (1999): 19.3 (world avg. 22.1).
Death rate per 1,000 population (1999): 6.0 (world avg. 8.9).
Natural increase rate per 1,000 population (1999): 13.3 (world avg. 13.2).
Total fertility rate (avg. births per childbearing woman; 1999): 2.2.
Marriage rate per 1,000 population (1996): 7.8.
Divorce rate per 1,000 population (1996): 0.5.
Life expectancy at birth (1999): male 68.4 years; female 73.1 years.
Major causes of death per 100,000 population (1995)[3]: diseases of the circulatory system 322; malignant neoplasms (cancers) 71; accidents and violence 32; infectious and parasitic diseases 20; ill-defined conditions 129.

National economy

Budget (1998). Revenue: LT 11,888,000,000,000,000 (indirect taxes 41.5%, direct taxes 36.2%, nontax revenue 20.8%). Expenditures: LT 15,585,000,000,000,000 (interest payments 39.6%, personnel 24.8%, investments 6.4%).
Tourism (1998): receipts from visitors U.S.$7,809,000,000; expenditures by nationals abroad U.S.$1,754,000,000.
Production (in '000 metric tons except as noted). Agriculture, forestry, fishing (1998): wheat 21,000, sugar beets 20,000, barley 9,000, tomatoes 6,600, potatoes 5,315, grapes 3,650, apples 2,500, seed cotton 2,093, corn (maize) 2,300, olives 1,550, cottonseed 1,423, sunflower seeds 860, oranges 830, lentils 586, hazelnuts 580, apricots 538, pears 415, tobacco 262, figs 260, sultana raisins 250, tea 120, garlic 106, honey 63[4], attar of roses 800 kg[5]; livestock (number of live animals) 30,238,000 sheep, 11,185,000 cattle, 615,000[4] angora goats; roundwood (1998) 16,080,000 cu m; fish catch (1997) 454,810. Mining (1998): chromite 2,080[6]; boron 1,769[6]; bauxite 462; copper ore (metal content) 34.2. Manufacturing (1995)[7]: refined petroleum 4,583; food products 3,944; textiles 3,907; transport equipment 3,048; iron and steel 2,453; paints, soaps, and pharmaceuticals 2,301. Energy production (consumption): electricity (kW-hr; 1998) 110,832,000,000 ([1997] 80,862,000,000); hard coal (metric tons; 1998) 2,136,000 ([1995] 8,548,000); lignite (metric tons; 1998) 62,481,000 ([1995] 52,343,000); crude petroleum (barrels; 1998) 23,052,000 ([1995] 190,306,000); petroleum products (metric tons; 1995) 24,101,000 (25,057,000); natural gas (cu m; 1995) 168,600,000 (6,222,000,000).
Land use (1994): forested 26.2%; meadows and pastures 16.1%; agricultural and under permanent cultivation 36.1%; other 21.6%.
Household income and expenditure (1994). Average household size 4.5; income per household LT 165,089,000 (U.S.$5,576); expenditure: food, tobacco, and café expenditures 38.5%, housing 22.8%, clothing 9.0%.
Population economically active (1997)[8]: total 22,359,000; activity rate of total population 35.8% (participation rates: ages 15–64, 53.1%; female 26.8%; unemployed [1998] 6.2%).

Price and earnings indexes (1995 = 100)

	1993	1994	1995	1996	1997	1998	1999
Consumer price index	25.8	53.2	100.0	180.3	335.0	618.5	1,019.7
Annual earnings index[9]	...	52.5	100.0	190.4	376.8	650.3	...

Gross national product (1998): U.S.$200,530,000,000 (U.S.$3,160 per capita).

Structure of gross domestic product and labour force

	1998 in value LT '000,000,000,000[10]	1998 % of total value	1997 labour force[8]	1997 % of labour force[8]
Agriculture	8,158	17.6	8,220,000	36.8
Mining	455	1.0	176,000	0.8
Manufacturing	7,434	16.0	3,602,000	16.1
Construction	2,670	5.8	1,323,000	5.9
Public utilities	1,207	2.6	111,000	0.5
Transp. and commun.	6,975	15.1	926,000	4.1
Trade	8,549	18.4	2,916,000	13.1
Finance, real estate	4,289	9.3	516,000	2.3
Pub. admin., defense	4,782	10.3	3,024,000	13.5
Services	1,792	3.9		
Other	—	—	1,545,000[11]	6.9[11]
TOTAL	46,311	100.0	22,359,000	100.0

Public debt (external, outstanding; 1998): U.S.$49,932,000,000.

Foreign trade[12]

Balance of trade (current prices)

	1994	1995	1996	1997	1998	1999
U.S.$'000,000	–5,164	–14,073	–20,403	–22,298	–18,947	–14,104
% of total	12.5%	24.5%	30.5%	29.8%	26.0%	21.0%

Imports (1997): U.S.$48,559,000,000 (nonelectrical machinery 18.9%; transport equipment 11.7%; chemicals and chemical products 10.3%; mineral fuels 7.9%; electrical and electronic equipment 7.9%). *Major import sources:* Germany 16.5%; Italy 9.2%; U.S. 8.9%; France 6.1%; U.K. 5.7%.
Exports (1997): U.S.$26,261,000,000 (textiles and clothing 37.0%; iron and steel 7.6%; electrical and electronic machinery 5.5%; edible fruits 5.0%). *Major export destinations:* Germany 20.0%; Russia 7.8%; U.S. 7.7%; U.K. 5.8%; Italy 5.3%.

Transport and communications

Transport. Railroads (1997): length 5,348 mi, 8,607 km; (1998) passenger-km 6,252,000,000; (1998) metric ton-km cargo 8,532,000,000. Roads (1997): total length 237,610 mi, 382,397 km (paved 25%). Vehicles (1997): passenger cars 3,767,162; trucks and buses 985,320. Air transport (1998)[13]: passenger-km 13,033,000,000; metric ton-km cargo 243,259,000; airports (1996) 26.

Communications

Medium	date	unit	number	units per 1,000 persons
Daily newspapers	1996	circulation	6,845,000	111
Radio	1997	receivers	11,300,000	181
Television	1997	receivers	18,000,000	288
Telephones	1998	main lines	16,960,000	265
Cellular telephones	1998	subscribers	3,506,000	55
Personal computers	1998	units	1,550,000	24
Internet	1998	users	450,000	7.0

Education and health

Educational attainment (1993). Percentage of population age 25 and over having: no formal schooling 30.5%; incomplete primary education 6.6%; complete primary 40.4%; incomplete secondary 3.1%; complete secondary or higher 19.1%; unknown 0.3%. *Literacy* (1995): total population age 15 and over literate 33,605,000 (82.3%); males literate 19,191,000 (91.7%); females literate 14,414,000 (72.4%).

Education (1996–97)

	schools	teachers	students	student/ teacher ratio
Primary (age 6–10)	47,313	217,131	6,389,060	29.4
Secondary (age 11–16)	11,144	139,497	3,427,715	24.6
Voc., teacher tr.	4,046	72,537	1,333,177	18.4
Higher	817[14]	50,313	1,434,033	28.5

Health: physicians (1996) 70,947[15] (1 per 867 persons); hospital beds (1997) 144,984 (1 per 431 persons); infant mortality rate (1999) 50.7.
Food (1997): daily per capita caloric intake 3,525 (vegetable products 89%, animal products 11%); 140% of FAO recommended minimum requirement.

Military

Total active duty personnel (1997): 639,000 (army 82.2%, navy 8.0%, air force 9.8%). *Military expenditure as percentage of GNP* (1997): 4.0% (world 2.6%); per capita expenditure U.S.$124.

[1]Administratively divided into 80 provinces as of 1998. [2]Estimated figures. [3]Projected rates based on about 42% of total deaths. [4]1997. [5]1993. [6]1995. [7]Value added in U.S.$'000,000. [8]Civilian population only. [9]Istanbul wage earners only. [10]At factor cost. [11]Unemployed. [12]Imports c.i.f.; exports f.o.b. [13]Turkish Airlines only. [14]1995–96. [15]Includes assistant doctors.

Internet resources for further information:
- **Ministry of Foreign Affairs http://www.mfa.gov.tr**
- **Republic of Turkey http://www.turkey.org**
- **State Institute of Statistics http://www.die.gov.tr**

Turkmenistan

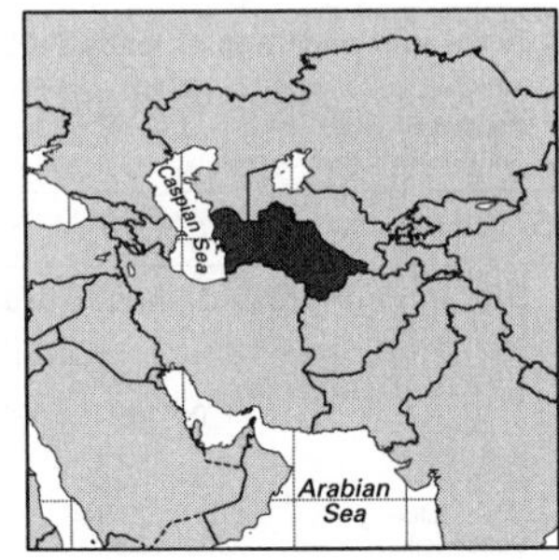

Official name: Türkmenistan (Turkmenistan).
Form of government: unitary republic with one legislative body (Majlis [Parliament; 50]).
Head of state and government: President assisted by the People's Council[1].
Capital: Ashgabat (formerly Ashkhabad).
Official language: Turkmen.
Official religion: none.
Monetary unit: manat; valuation (Oct. 6, 2000) 1 U.S.$ = 5,200 manat; 1 £ = 7,522 manat.

Area and population

		area		population
Provinces	**Capitals**	sq mi	sq km	1996 estimate
Ahal	Ashgabat	37,500	97,100	677,700
Balkan	Nebitdag	53,500	138,600	389,700
Dashhowuz	Dashhowuz	28,100	72,700	956,500
Lebap	Turkmenabad (Chärjew)	36,000	93,200	947,700
Mary	Mary	33,400	86,400	1,046,700
City				
Ashgabat	—	...	...	548,500
TOTAL		188,500[2]	488,100[2]	4,566,800

Demography

Population (2000): 4,885,000.
Density (2000): persons per sq mi 25.9, persons per sq km 10.0.
Urban-rural (1999): urban 45.0%; rural 55.0%.
Sex distribution (1996): male 49.59%; female 50.41%.
Age breakdown (1995): under 15, 40.4%; 15–29, 27.6%; 30–44, 18.7%; 45–59, 7.5%; 60–74, 4.7%; 75 and over, 1.1%.
Population projection: (2010) 5,878,000; (2020) 7,046,000.
Doubling time: 34 years.
Ethnic composition (1997): Turkmen 77.0%; Uzbek 9.2%; Russian 6.7%; Kazakh 2.0%; Tatar 0.8%; other 4.3%.
Religious affiliation (1995): Muslim (mostly Sunnī) 87.0%; Russian Orthodox 2.4%; other (mostly nonreligious) 10.6%.
Major cities (1997): Ashgabat 540,600; Turkmenabad (Chärjew) 189,200; Dashhowuz 141,800; Mary 101,000; Nebitdag 87,800.

Vital statistics

Birth rate per 1,000 population (1999): 27.6 (world avg. 22.1); (1998) legitimate 96.2%; illegitimate 3.8%.
Death rate per 1,000 population (1999): 7.0 (world avg. 8.9).
Natural increase rate per 1,000 population (1999): 20.6 (world avg. 13.2).
Total fertility rate (avg. births per childbearing woman; 1999): 3.5.
Marriage rate per 1,000 population (1994): 8.7.
Divorce rate per 1,000 population (1994): 1.5.
Life expectancy at birth (1999): male 62.0 years; female 69.0 years.
Major causes of death per 100,000 population (1994): diseases of the circulatory system 337.1; diseases of the respiratory system 150.3; infectious and parasitic diseases 75.7; accidents, poisoning, and violence 60.1; malignant neoplasms (cancers) 56.8; diseases of the digestive system 31.1.

National economy

Budget (1999). Revenue: 3,693,100,000,000 manat (value-added tax 25.6%, pension and social security fund 22.5%, repayments of scheduled gas 13.0%, excise tax 10.2%, personal income tax 6.1%). Expenditures: 3,894,300,000,000 manat (education 26.9%, pension and social security 15.6%, defense and security 14.9%, health 14.1%, agriculture 5.7%).
Public debt (external, outstanding; 1998): U.S.$1,731,000,000.
Production (metric tons except as noted). Agriculture, forestry, fishing (1999): cereals 1,567,200, seed cotton 1,300,000, vegetables and melons 336,400, fruit excluding melons 193,600; livestock (number of live animals) 6,025,000 sheep and goats, 880,000 cattle, 48,000 pigs, 4,250,000 poultry; roundwood (1990) 4,000,000 cu m; fish catch (1997) 8,828. Mining and quarrying (1996): gypsum 169,577, sodium sulphate 30,820, sulfur 8,112. Manufacturing (value of production in '000,000 manat; 1994): ferrous and nonferrous metals 278; machinery and metalworks 223; food products 129; chemical products 90; construction materials 52; wood products 31. Construction (1994): 1,700,000 sq m. Energy production (consumption): electricity (kW-hr; 1996) 10,100,000,000 (7,300,000,000); coal (metric tons; 1996) none (100,000); crude petroleum (barrels; 1996) 28,000,000 (29,000,000); petroleum products (metric tons; 1996) 2,223,000 (2,266,000); natural gas (cu m; 1996) 33,991,000,000 (10,803,000,000).
Household income and expenditure. Average household size (1998) 5.0; income per household: n.a.); sources of income (1996): wages and salaries 70.6%, pensions and grants 20.9%, self-employment 2.3%[3], nonwage income of workers 1.1%; expenditure (1996): goods 26.8%, services 13.5%, taxes and other payments 9.4%.
Land use (1994): forested 8.2%; meadows and pastures 61.6%; agricultural and under permanent cultivation 3.0%; other 27.2%.
Population economically active (1996): total 1,680,000; activity rate of total population 36.8% (participation rates [1995]: ages 16–59 [male] 16–54 [female] 81.0%; female 41.0%; unemployed 3.0%[4]).

Price and earnings indexes (1994 = 100)[5]

	1994	1995	1996	1997	1998
Consumer price index	100	1,362	7,431	27,502	32,122
Monthly earnings index	100	739	6,334	11,282	16,163

Gross national product (1997): U.S.$2,987,000,000 (U.S.$640 per capita).

Structure of gross domestic product and labour force

	1998		1996	
	in value '000,000 manat	% of total value	labour force	% of labour force
Agriculture	3,256,000	24.6	746,000	44.4
Mining, Manufacturing, Public utilities	3,862,000	29.2	165,000	9.8
Construction	1,582,000	11.9	155,000	9.2
Transp. and commun.	1,372,000	10.4	83,000	4.9
Trade	687,000	5.2	106,700	6.4
Finance	...	...	8,000	0.5
Public administration, defense	...	...	25,000	1.5
Services	1,678,000	12.7	347,000	20.7
Other	804,000	6.1	44,000	2.6
TOTAL	13,241,000	100.0[2]	1,680,000[2]	100.0

Tourism (1998): receipts from visitors U.S.$192,000,000.

Foreign trade[6]

Balance of trade (current prices)

	1994	1995	1996	1997	1998
U.S.$'000,000	+485	+536	+329	−231	−523
% of total	12.5%	15.4%	10.8%	13.0%	30.0%

Imports (1998): U.S.$1,137,100,000 (machinery and equipment 39.1%, food products 8.0%, chemicals 5.1%, medicines 1.8%). *Major import sources:* Ukraine 16.1%; Turkey 13.1%; Russia 11.6%; Germany 6.9%; U.S. 6.4%; Uzbekistan 5.2%; Armenia 3.0%.
Exports (1998): U.S.$614,100,000 (natural gas and oil products 54.6%, cotton 22.0%, electricity 5.2%). *Major export destinations:* Iran 24.1%; Turkey 18.3%; Azerbaijan 6.9%; U.K. 4.9%; Russia 4.7%; Tajikistan 4.5%.

Transport and communications

Transport. Railroads (1996): length 1,317 mi, 2,120 km; passenger-km 2,104,000,000, metric ton-km cargo 6,779,000,000. Roads (1996): total length 13,700 km (paved 83%). Vehicles (1995): passenger cars 220,000; trucks and buses, 58,200. Air transport (1996): passenger-km 1,562,000,000; metric ton-km cargo 143,000,000; airports (1997) with scheduled flights 1.

Communications

Medium	date	unit	number	units per 1,000 persons
Radio	1997	receivers	1,225,000	289
Television	1997	receivers	820,000	194
Telephones	1998	main lines	354,000	82
Cellular phones	1998	subscribers	3,000	0.7
Personal computers	...	units	...	...
Internet	...	users	...	...

Education and health

Educational attainment (1989). Percentage of population age 25 and over having: primary education or no formal schooling 13.6%; some secondary 21.3%; completed secondary and some postsecondary 56.8%; higher 8.3%. *Literacy* (1989): total population age 15 and over literate 3,453,000 (97.7%); males literate 1,714,000 (98.8%); females literate 1,739,000 (96.6%).

Education (1994–95)

	schools	teachers	students	student/ teacher ratio
Primary (age 6–13), Secondary (age 14–17)	1,900	72,900	940,600	12.9
Voc., teacher tr.	78	...	26,000	...
Higher	15	...	29,435[7]	...

Health (1995): physicians 13,500 (1 per 330 persons); hospital beds 46,000 (1 per 97 persons); (1999) infant mortality rate per 1,000 live births 53.
Food (1998): daily per capita caloric intake 2,684 (vegetable products 81%, animal products 19%); 105% of FAO recommended minimum requirement.

Military

Total active duty personnel (1999): 18,000 (army 83.3%; air force 16.7%). *Military expenditure as percentage of GNP* (1997): 4.6% (world 2.6%); per capita expenditure U.S.$71.

[1]The People's Council is the ultimate representative organ of governmental supervision and is composed of the president, membership of the Majlis, elected members, and a variety of ex officio members of national, provincial, and local government. [2]Detail does not add to total given because of rounding. [3]Mainly agricultural income. [4]Every Turkmen citizen is guaranteed employment, so that unemployment does not officially exist. However, the 1995 Household Survey indicates an unemployment rate of about 3 percent of the labour force (defined as those actively seeking employment but not employed as a proportion of the labour force). [5]December. [6]Import data in balance of trade is c.i.f. [7]1995–96.

Internet resources for further information:
- **Turkmenistan Human Development Under Transition 1997 http://www.undp.org/rbec/pubs/nhdr97/summary/turkmenistan.htm**
- **Embassy of Turkmenistan http://www.turkmenistanembassy.org**

Tuvalu

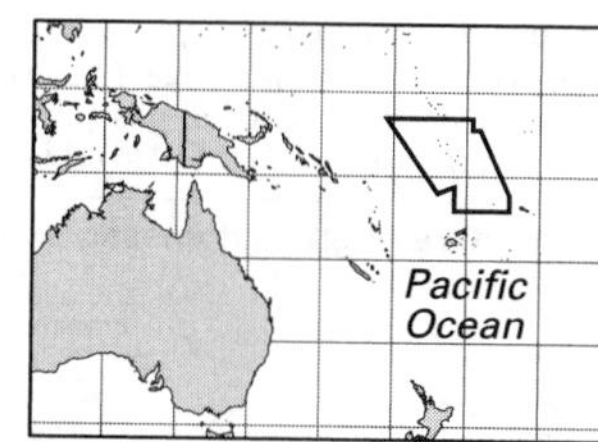

Official name: Tuvalu.
Form of government: constitutional monarchy with one legislative house (Parliament [12]).
Chief of state: British Monarch, represented by Governor-General.
Head of government: Prime Minister.
Capital: government offices are at Vaiaku, Fongafale islet, of Funafuti atoll.
Official language: none.
Official religion: none.
Monetary units[1]: 1 Tuvalu dollar = 1 Australian dollar ($T = $A) = 100 Tuvalu and Australian cents; valuation (Oct. 6, 2000) 1 U.S.$ = $A 1.87; 1 £ = $A 2.70.

Area and population

	area		population
Islands[2]	sq mi	sq km	1991 census
Funafuti	1.08	2.79	3,172
Nanumaga	1.07	2.78	717
Nanumea	1.49	3.87	901
Niulakita	0.16	0.42	74
Niutao	0.98	2.53	889
Nui	1.09	2.83	661
Nukufetau	1.15	2.99	831
Nukulaelae	0.70	1.82	359
Vaitupu	2.16	5.60	1,280
TOTAL	9.90[3, 4]	25.63	8,884[5]

Demography

Population (2000): 10,800.
Density (2000): persons per sq mi 1,090.9, persons per sq km 421.4.
Urban-rural (1999): urban 51.0%; rural 49.0%.
Sex distribution (1997): male 48.59%; female 51.41%.
Age breakdown (1997): under 15, 35.7%; 15–29, 23.2%; 30–44, 23.4%; 45–59, 10.5%; 60–74, 6.1%; 75 and over, 1.1%.
Population projection: (2010) 12,600; (2020) 14,800.
Doubling time: 50 years.
Ethnic composition (1979): Tuvaluan (Polynesian) 91.2%; mixed (Polynesian/Micronesian/other) 7.2%; European 1.0%; other 0.6%.
Religious affiliation (1995): Church of Tuvalu (Congregational) 85.4%; Seventh-day Adventist 3.6%; Roman Catholic 1.4%; Jehovah's Witness 1.1%; Bahā'ī 1.0%; other 7.5%.
Major locality (1995): Fongafale, on Funafuti atoll, 4,000.

Vital statistics

Birth rate per 1,000 population (1998): 22.6 (world avg. 22.6); (1989) legitimate 82.2%; illegitimate 17.8%.
Death rate per 1,000 population (1998): 8.6 (world avg. 8.9).
Natural increase rate per 1,000 population (1998): 14.0 (world avg. 13.7).
Total fertility rate (avg. births per childbearing woman; 1998): 3.1.
Marriage rate per 1,000 population: n.a.
Divorce rate per 1,000 population: n.a.
Life expectancy at birth (1998): male 62.7 years; female 65.1 years.
Major causes of death per 100,000 population (1985): diseases of the digestive system 170.0; diseases of the circulatory system 150.0; diseases of the respiratory system 120.0; diseases of the nervous system 120.0; malignant neoplasms (cancers) 70.0; infectious and parasitic diseases 40.0; endocrine and metabolic disorders 20.0; ill-defined conditions 430.0; in 1992 the leading causes of death included liver diseases, meningitis, tuberculosis, and still and perinatal deaths; other health problems included acute respiratory infections, diarrhea, filariasis, conjunctivitis, fish poisoning, diabetes, rheumatism, and hypertension.

National economy

Budget (1996). Revenue: $A 7,905,000 (nontax revenues 67.2%; taxes 32.8%). Expenditures: $A 8,203,000 (1987; capital [development] expenditures 68.9%, of which marine transport 20.7%, education 13.0%, fisheries 5.6%, health 3.1%; current expenditures 31.1%).
Public debt (external; 1993): U.S.$6,000,000.
Gross national product (at current market prices; 1996): U.S.$7,000,000 (U.S.$650 per capita).

Structure of gross domestic product and labour force

	1995		1991	
	in value[6] $A	% of total value	labour force	% of labour force
Agriculture, fishing, forestry	3,152,000	22.2	4,020	68.0
Mining	317,000	2.2	—	—
Manufacturing[7]	452,000	3.2	60	1.0
Construction	1,963,000	13.9	240	4.0
Public utilities	345,000	2.4	—	—
Transp. and commun.	599,000	4.2	60	1.0
Trade, hotels, and restaurants	2,043,000	14.4	240	4.0
Finance	1,390,000	9.8	—	—
Pub. admin., defense; Services	3,922,000	27.7	1,290	22.0
TOTAL	14,183,000	100.0	5,910	100.0

Production (metric tons except as noted). Agriculture[8], forestry, fishing (1999): coconuts 1,800, bananas 180, hens' eggs 12, other agricultural products include breadfruit, pulaka (taro), pandanus fruit, sweet potatoes, and pawpaws; livestock (number of live animals) 27,000 chickens, 12,600 pigs, 7,000 ducks; forestry, n.a.; fish catch (1998) 400. Mining and quarrying[9]: n.a. Manufacturing (1988): copra 90; handicrafts and baked goods are also important. Construction: n.a.; however, the main areas of construction activity are roadworks, coastal protection, government facilities, and water-related infrastructure projects. Energy production (consumption): electricity (kW-hr; 1992) 1,300,000 (1,300,000); coal, none (none); crude petroleum, none (n.a.); petroleum products, none (n.a.); natural gas, none (none).
Tourism (1998): receipts from visitors U.S.$200,000; expenditures by nationals abroad, n.a.
Population economically active (1991): total 5,910; activity rate of total population 65.3% (participation rates: ages 15–64, 85.5%; female [1979] 51.3%; unemployed [1979] 4.0%).

Price and earnings indexes (1990 = 100)

	1992	1993	1994	1995	1996	1997	1998
Consumer price index	100.1	102.3	103.7	109.0	109.8	111.5	112.4
Earnings index	...	...	...	...	...	...	...

Household income and expenditure. Average household size (1979) 6.4; average annual income per household $A 2,575 (U.S.$2,044); sources of income (1987): agriculture and other 45.0%, cash economy only 38.0%, overseas remittances 17.0%; expenditure (1992)[10]: food 45.5%, housing and household operations 11.5%, transportation 10.5%, alcohol and tobacco 10.5%, clothing 7.5%, other 14.5%.
Land use (1987): agricultural and under permanent cultivation 73.6%[11]; scrub 16.1%; other 10.3%.

Foreign trade[12]

Balance of trade (current prices)

	1993	1994	1995	1996	1997	1998
$A '000	–9,344	–10,513	–6,373	–5,638	–7,771	–11,341
% of total	91.8%	93.0%	94.4%	88.6%	91.2%	98.8%

Imports (1998): $A 11,408,000 (1989; food 29.3%, manufactured goods 28.2%, petroleum and petroleum products 12.8%, machinery and transport equipment 12.2%, chemicals 7.1%, beverages and tobacco 3.9%). *Major import sources* (1995): Fiji 65.8%; Australia 17.1%; New Zealand 3.9%; United Kingdom 3.3%; United States 2.0%; Germany 1.3%; The Netherlands 1.3%.
Exports (1998): $A 67,000 (1989; clothing and footwear 29.5%, copra 21.5%, fruits and vegetables 8.0%). *Major export destinations* (1995): South Africa 63.6%; Colombia 9.1%; Belgium-Luxembourg 9.1%.

Transport and communications

Transport. Railroads: none. Roads (1996): total length 8 km (paved, none). Vehicles[13]: n.a. Merchant marine (1992): vessels (100 gross tons and over) 6; total deadweight tonnage 16,005. Air transport (1977): passenger arrivals (Funafuti) 1,443; cargo, n.a.; airports (1997) with scheduled flights 1.

Communications

Medium	date	unit	number	units per 1,000 persons
Radio	1996	receivers	4,000	400
Television	1996	receivers	100	13
Telephones	1994	main lines	113	11.5

Education and health

Educational attainment (1991). Percentage of population age 25 and over having: no formal schooling 0.8%; primary education 71.4%; secondary 16.2%; higher 7.0%. *Literacy* (1990): total population literate in Tuvaluan 8,593 (95.0%); literacy in English estimated at 45.0%.

Education (1991)

	schools	teachers[14]	students	student/ teacher ratio
Primary (age 5–11)	11	72	1,906[15]	...
Secondary (age 12–18)	1	21	314	...
Vocational	1	10	58	...
Higher	—	—	—	—

Health (1999): physicians 8 (1 per 1,375 persons); hospital beds (1990) 30 (1 per 302 persons); infant mortality rate per 1,000 live births (1998): 26.2.

Military

Total active duty personnel: none; Tuvalu relies on Australian-trained volunteers from Fiji and Papua New Guinea.

[1]The value of the Tuvalu dollar is pegged to the value of the Australian dollar, which is also legal currency in Tuvalu. [2]Local government councils have been established on all islands except Niulakita. [3]Another survey puts the area at 9.4 sq mi (24.4 sq km). [4]Detail does not add to total given because of rounding. [5]De facto population. [6]At 1988 factor cost. [7]Including cottage industry. [8]Because of poor soil quality, only limited subsistence agriculture is possible on the islands. [9]Research into the mineral potential of Tuvalu's maritime exclusive economic zone (289,500 sq mi [750,000 sq km] of the Pacific Ocean) is currently being conducted by the South Pacific Geo-Science Commission. [10]Weights of consumer price index components. [11]Capable of supporting coconut palms, pandanus, and breadfruit. [12]Imports are c.i.f. [13]There are several cars, tractors, trailers, and light trucks on Funafuti; a few motorcycles are in use on most islands. [14]1990. [15]1994.

Internet resources for further information:
- **Tuvalu http://www.emulateme.com/tuvalu.htm**

Uganda

Official name: Republic of Uganda.
Form of government: nonparty republic with one legislative house (Parliament [280[1]])[2].
Head of state and government: President.
Capital: Kampala.
Official language: English.
Official religion: none.
Monetary unit: 1 Uganda shilling (U Sh) = 100 cents; valuation (Oct. 6, 2000) 1 U.S.$ = U Sh 1,825; 1 £ = U Sh 2,640.

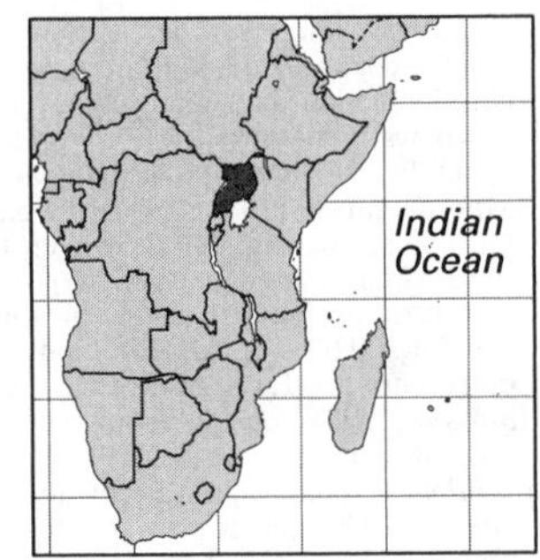

Area and population (1991 census)

Regions[3] Districts	area sq km	population	Regions[3] Districts	area sq km	population
Central			Arua	7,830	624,600
Kalangala	5,716	16,400	Gulu	11,735	338,700
Kampala	238	773,500	Kitgum	16,136	350,300
Kiboga	3,774	140,800	Kotido	13,208	190,700
Luwero	9,198	449,200	Lira	7,251	498,300
Masaka	10,611	831,300	Moroto	14,113	171,500
Mpigi	6,222	915,400	Moyo	5,006	178,500
Mubende	6,536	497,500	Nebbi	2,891	315,900
Mukono	14,242	816,200	Western		
Rakai	4,973	382,000	Bundibugyo	2,338	116,000
Eastern			Bushenyi	5,396	734,800
Iganga	13,113	944,000	Hoima	5,492	197,800
Jinja	734	284,900	Kabale	1,827	412,800
Kamuli	4,348	480,700	Kabarole	8,361	741,400
Kapchorwa	1,738	116,300	Kasese	3,205	343,000
Kumi	2,861	237,000	Kibaale	4,718	219,300
Mbale	2,546	706,600	Kisoro	662	184,900
Pallisa	1,919	356,000	Masindi	9,326	253,500
Soroti	10,060	430,900	Mbarara	10,839	929,600
Tororo	2,634	554,000	Ntungamo	...	...
Northern			Rukungiri	2,753	388,000
Apac	6,488	460,700	TOTAL	241,038[4]	16,582,700[5, 6]

Demography

Population (2000): 23,318,000.
Density (2000): persons per sq mi 250.6, persons per sq km 96.7.
Urban-rural (1999): urban 13.8%; rural 86.2%.
Sex distribution (1999): male 49.96%; female 50.04%.
Age breakdown (1999): under 15, 51.1%; 15–29, 26.1%; 30–44, 13.6%; 45–59, 5.7%; 60–74, 2.9%; 75 and over, 0.6%.
Population projection: (2010) 31,395,000; (2020) 42,005,000.
Doubling time: 22 years.
Ethnolinguistic composition (1991): Ganda 18.1%; Nkole 10.7%; Kiga 8.4%; Soga 8.2%; Lango 5.9%; Lugbara 4.7%; Gisu 4.5%; Acholi 4.4%.
Religious affiliation (1995): Christian 66%, of which Roman Catholic 33%, Protestant 33% (of which mostly Anglican); traditional beliefs 18%; Muslim 16%.
Major cities (1991): Kampala 1,154,000[7]; Jinja 61,000; Mbale 53,600; Masaka 49,100; Gulu 42,800; Entebbe 41,600.

Vital statistics

Birth rate per 1,000 population (1999): 48.6 (world avg. 22.1).
Death rate per 1,000 population (1999): 18.9 (world avg. 8.9).
Natural increase rate per 1,000 population (1999): 29.7 (world avg. 13.2).
Total fertility rate (avg. births per childbearing woman; 1999): 7.0.
Life expectancy at birth (1999): male 41.9 years; female 43.2 years.

National economy

Budget (1997–98). Revenue: U Sh 1,193,100,000,000 (taxes 62.7%, of which customs duties 25.5%, sales taxes 20.2%, income taxes 10.5%; grants 33.3%). Expenditures: U Sh 1,239,900,000,000 (current expenditures 58.7%, of which wages and salaries 20.6%, education 16.6%, security 11.0%, health 4.3%; capital expenditures 41.3%).
Public debt (external, outstanding; 1998): U.S.$3,402,000,000.
Tourism (1997): receipts from visitors U.S.$135,000,000; expenditures by nationals abroad U.S.$137,000,000.
Land use (1994): forest 31.5%; pasture 9.1%; agriculture 34.0%; other 25.4%.
Population economically active (1991): total 8,365,000; activity rate of total population 49.6% (participation rates: ages 15–64, 78.9%[8]; female 35.2%).

Price and earnings indexes (1995 = 100)

	1993	1994	1995	1996	1997	1998	1999
Consumer price index	84.0	92.0	100.0	107.0	115.0	115.0	122.0
Earnings index	...	...	...	...	...	...	...

Production (metric tons except as noted). Agriculture, forestry, fishing (1999): plantains 9,400,000, cassava 3,400,000, sweet potatoes 2,520,000, sugarcane 1,600,000, corn (maize) 780,000, millet 638,000, sorghum 454,000, potatoes 449,000, coffee 198,000, peanuts (groundnuts) 183,000, rice 96,000; livestock (number of live animals) 5,700,000 cattle, 3,650,000 goats, 1,970,000 sheep, 960,000 pigs, 23,000,000 chickens; roundwood (1998) 15,649,000 cu m; fish catch (1998) 220,626. Mining and quarrying (1997): gold 3,000 kg. Manufacturing (1998): cement 278,800; sugar 93,000; soap 36,100; metal products 22,400; meat 3,706; footwear 995,000 pairs; beer 552,000 hectolitres. Energy production (consumption): electricity (kW-hr; 1998) 1,282,800,000 (872,000,000); coal (metric tons) none (none); crude petroleum (barrels) none (none); petroleum products (metric tons; 1996) none (319,000); natural gas (cu m) none (none).
Gross national product (1998): U.S.$6,566,000,000 (U.S.$310 per capita).

Structure of gross domestic product and labour force

	1998–99		1991	
	in value U Sh '000,000	% of total value	labour force	% of labour force
Agriculture	3,489,000	40.3	6,724,000	80.4
Mining	49,000	0.6	478,000	5.7
Manufacturing	690,000	8.0		
Construction	565,000	6.5		
Public utilities	108,000	1.2		
Transp. and commun.	335,000	3.9	1,163,000	13.9
Trade	1,091,000	12.6		
Finance Pub. admin., defense	1,279,000	14.8		
Services	281,000	3.2		
Other	778,000	9.0	...	...
TOTAL	8,665,000	100.0[5]	8,365,000	100.0

Household income and expenditure (1998). Average household size 4.7; income per household: n.a.; sources of income (1992–93)[8, 9]: wages and self-employment 86.4%; transfers 11.7%; rent 1.9%; expenditure (1992–93)[8]: food and beverages 64.0%; rent, energy, and services 18.3%; education 5.0%; health 4.2%.

Foreign trade[10]

Balance of trade (current prices)

	1994	1995	1996	1997	1998
U Sh '000,000,000	–456.5	–578.2	–633.8	–831.1	–952.7
% of total	36.7%	39.3%	34.1%	41.1%	50.1%

Imports (1997–98): U.S.$1,411,100,000 (1996; machinery and transport equipment 33.8%, basic manufactures 22.0%, chemicals 15.9%, food and live animals 7.3%). *Major import sources* (1996): Kenya 21.5%; U.K. 14.2%; Japan 9.1%; United Arab Emirates 6.1%; Germany 4.2%; U.S. 3.1%.
Exports (1997–98): U.S.$458,400,000 (unroasted coffee 58.7%, tea 7.6%, fish 6.1%, cotton 2.5%). *Major export destinations* (1996): U.K. 20.8%; Belgium-Luxembourg 12.3%; Spain 9.1%; U.S. 8.1%; France 6.4%; Germany 4.3%.

Transport and communications

Transport. Railroads (1998): route length 1,241 km; passenger-km (1996) 27,000,000; metric ton-km cargo (1996) 236,000,000. Roads (1996): total length 26,800 km (paved 7.7%). Vehicles (1996): passenger cars 35,361; trucks and buses 48,430. Merchant marine (1992): vessels (100 gross tons and over) 2; total deadweight tonnage 8,600[11]. Air transport (1997): passenger-km 52,117,000; metric ton-km cargo 5,000,000; airports (1998) 1.

Communications

Medium	date	unit	number	units per 1,000 persons
Daily newspapers	1997	circulation	40,000	2.1
Radio	1997	receivers	2,600,000	130
Television	1998	receivers	580,000	28.0
Telephones	1998	main lines	56,919	2.8
Cellular telephones	1998	subscribers	30,000	1.5
Personal computers	1998	units	40,000	2.0
Internet	1998	users	15,000	0.7

Education and health

Educational attainment (1991). Percentage of population age 25 and over having: no formal schooling or less than one full year 46.9%; primary education 42.1%; secondary 10.5%; higher 0.5%. *Literacy* (1995): population age 15 and over literate 6,732,000 (61.8%); males literate 3,948,000 (73.7%); females literate 2,784,000 (50.2%).

Education (1995)

	schools	teachers	students	student/ teacher ratio
Primary (age 5–11)[12]	8,531	76,134	2,636,409	34.6
Secondary (age 12–15)[12]	...	14,447	255,158	17.7
Voc., teacher tr.[12]	...	1,788	36,063	20.2
Higher	...	2,006	29,343	14.6

Health (1993): physicians 840 (1 per 22,399 persons); hospital beds (1989) 20,136 (1 per 817 persons); infant mortality rate (1999) 95.2.
Food (1998): daily per capita caloric intake 2,216 (vegetable products 94%, animal products 6%); 95% of FAO recommended minimum requirement.

Military

Total active duty personnel (1999): 30,000–40,000[13]. *Military expenditure as percentage of GNP* (1997): 4.2% (world 2.6%); per capita U.S.$12.

[1]62 of 276 elected seats are allocated to special interest groups; all government ministers not elected to the National Assembly (4 in 2000) serve ex officio. [2]New constitution promulgated on Oct. 8, 1995. [3]Regions are geographic areas with no administrative function. [4]Includes water area of 43,989 sq km; Uganda's portion of Lake Victoria comprises 30,960 sq km. [5]Detail does not add to total given because of rounding. [6]Preliminary figure; final census total equals 16,671,705. [7]1998. [8]Based on first nationally representative household survey. [9]Highest quartile only. [10]Imports c.i.f.; exports f.o.b. [11]1988. [12]Public sector only. [13]Breakdown by branch of service is unavailable.

Internet resources for further information:
- **Uganda Online National Information Center (unofficial web site) http://www.nic.ug**

Ukraine

Official name: Ukrayina (Ukraine).
Form of government: unitary multiparty republic with a single legislative body (Supreme Council [450]).
Head of state: President.
Head of government: Prime Minister.
Capital: Kiev (Kyyiv).
Official language: Ukrainian.
Official religion: none.
Monetary unit: hryvnia (pl. hryvny)[1]; (Oct. 6, 2000) free rate, 1 U.S.$ = 5.46 hryvny; 1 £ = 7.90 hryvny.

Area and population

Autonomous republic	area sq km	population 1998 estimate
Crimea (Krym)	27,000[2]	2,157,700
Cities		
Kiev	[3]	2,629,300
Sevastopol	[2]	397,300
Provinces		
Cherkasy	20,900	1,478,700
Chernihiv	31,900	1,318,500
Chernivtsi	8,100	938,500
Dnipropetrovsk	31,900	3,775,400
Donetsk	26,500	5,064,400
Ivano-Frankivsk	13,900	1,463,600
Kharkiv	31,400	3,024,400
Kherson	28,500	1,246,800
Khmelnytsky	20,600	1,485,700
Kirovohrad	24,600	1,197,800

Provinces	area sq km	population 1998 estimate
Kyyiv (Kiev)	28,900[3]	1,864,000
Luhansk	26,700	2,706,400
Lviv	21,800	2,739,600
Mykolayiv	24,600	1,322,500
Odessa	33,300	2,547,800
Poltava	28,800	1,708,300
Rivne	20,100	1,192,200
Sumy	23,800	1,369,800
Ternopil	13,800	1,168,400
Vinnytsya	26,500	1,847,100
Volyn	20,200	1,067,900
Zakarpatska	12,800	1,288,200
Zaporizhzhya	27,200	2,042,500
Zhytomyr	29,900	1,457,100
TOTAL	603,700	50,499,900

Demography

Population (2000): 49,242,000.
Density (2000): persons per sq mi 211.2, persons per sq km 81.6.
Urban-rural (1999): urban 67.9%; rural 32.1%.
Sex distribution (1999): male 46.30%; female 53.70%.
Age breakdown (1999): under 15, 18.4%; 15–29, 21.7%; 30–44, 21.8%; 45–59, 17.7%; 60–74, 15.6%; 75 and over, 4.8%.
Population projection: (2010) 46,277,000; (2020) 44,443,000.
Ethnic composition (1998): Ukrainian 64.7%; Russian 32.8%; Jewish 0.7%; Moldovan 0.6%; Tatar 0.4%; Belarusian 0.3%; other 0.5%.
Religious affiliation (1995): Ukrainian Orthodox (Russian patriarchy) 19.5%; Ukrainian Orthodox (Kiev patriarchy) 9.7%; Ukrainian Catholic (Uniate) 7.0%; Protestant 3.6%; other Orthodox 1.6%; Roman Catholic 1.2%; Jewish 0.9%; other (mostly nonreligious) 56.5%.
Major cities (1998): Kiev 2,629,300; Kharkiv 1,521,400; Dnipropetrovsk 1,122,400; Donetsk 1,065,400; Odessa 1,027,400.

Vital statistics

Birth rate per 1,000 population (1999): 9.2 (world avg. 22.1); (1993) legitimate 87.0%; illegitimate 13.0%.
Death rate per 1,000 population (1999): 16.4 (world avg. 8.9).
Total fertility rate (avg. births per childbearing woman; 1999): 1.3.
Natural increase rate per 1,000 population (1999): –7.2 (world avg. 13.2).
Life expectancy at birth (1999): male 60.2 years; female 71.9 years.
Major causes of death per 100,000 population (1995): circulatory diseases 874.0; neoplasms (cancers) 199.0; accidents 160.0; respiratory diseases 89.0.

National economy

Budget (1998). Revenue: 36,892,000,000 hryvny (tax revenue 95.5%, of which taxes on goods and services 31.5%, payroll tax 29.3%, income tax 26.3%, property tax 3.0%, excise tax 2.6%, other 2.8%; nontax revenue 4.5%). Expenditures: 39,714,000,000 hryvny (social security 36.3%; national economy 15.1%; education 11.3%; health 9.1%; defense 3.4%).
Public debt (external; 1998): U.S.$8,606,000,000.
Production (metric tons except as noted). Agriculture, forestry, fishing (1999): potatoes 15,405,100, sugar beets 13,890,000, wheat 13,476,200, barley 6,382,100, corn (maize) 1,732,500, rye 908,000, oats 759,300; livestock (number of live animals) 11,722,000 cattle, 10,083,000 pigs, 2,026,000 sheep and goats; roundwood (1998) 10,052,000 cu m; fish catch (1998) 462,308. Mining and quarrying (1998): iron ore 50,700,000; manganese 2,226,000; uranium 500,000. Manufacturing (value in '000 hryvny; 1998): ferrous metals 19,000,000; machinery 13,000,000; processed foods 12,000,000; fuels 10,000,000; chemicals 5,000,000. Energy production (consumption): electricity (kW-hr; 1997) 176,700,000,000 (175,646,000,000); hard coal (metric tons; 1999) 81,648,000 ([1996] 79,500,000); lignite (metric tons; 1999) 1,188,000 ([1996] 4,300,000); crude petroleum (barrels; 1997) 30,053,000 (89,443,000); petroleum products (1996) 11,759,000 (16,168,000); natural gas (cu m; 1998) 17,920,000,000 (17,920,000,000).
Population economically active (1997): total 22,598,000; activity rate of total population 44.6% (participation rates: ages 16–59 [male] 15–64 [female] 79.7%; female [1994] 51.0%; unemployed [1998] 3.7%[4]).

Price and earnings indexes (December 1996 = 100)[5]

	1994	1995	1996	1997	1998
Consumer price index	25.4	71.6	100.0	110.1	132.1
Monthly earnings index	...	...	100.0	108.9	115.0

Gross national product (1998): U.S.$49,207,000,000 (U.S.$980 per capita).

Structure of gross domestic product and labour force

	1998		1997	
	in value '000,000 hryvny	% of total value	labour force	% of labour force
Agriculture	12,000	11.4	4,903,000	21.7
Mining, Manufacturing, Public utilities	26,000	24.8	4,822,000	21.3
Construction	5,000	4.8	1,194,000	5.3
Transp. and commun.	14,000	13.3	1,308,000	5.8
Trade	8,000	7.6	1,522,000	6.7
Finance, Pub. admin., defense, Services	26,000	24.8	3,440,000	15.2
Other	14,000[6]	13.3[6]	5,409,000[7]	23.9[7]
TOTAL	105,000	100.0	22,598,000	100.0[8]

Tourism (1997): receipts U.S.$135,000,000, expenditures U.S.$137,000,000.
Household income and expenditure (1996). Average household size (1998) 3.0; income per household (1996) 4,968 hryvny[1]; sources of income (1995); wages and salaries 66.4%, sales of agricultural products 9.3%, subsidies 6.9%, pensions 6.5%, remuneration from abroad 5.3%; expenditures (1995): food and beverages 43.1%, consumer goods 27.5%, services 7.2%, housing 6.7%, taxes 6.2%.

Foreign trade

Balance of trade (current prices)

	1994	1995	1996	1997	1998	1999
U.S.$'000,000	–2,575	–2,702	–4,296	–4,205	–2,584	–482
% of total	8.5%	8.7%	12.1%	12.0%	8.6%	1.9%

Imports (1998): U.S.$16,283,000,000 (1997; fuel and energy products 33.9%; machinery 18.8%; chemicals 11.0%; food 4.6%; industrial products 3.8%; ferrous and nonferrous metals 3.4%; wood and wood products 2.5%). *Major import sources* (1997): Russia 39.9%; Germany 6.7%; Turkmenistan 5.0%; U.S. 3.3%; Poland 2.8%; Italy 2.0%; Belarus 2.0%.
Exports (1998): U.S.$13,699,000,000 (1997; ferrous metals 38.3%; machinery 12.8%; chemicals 13.1%; food 11.7%; fuels 7.4%; industrial products 4.2%). *Major export destinations* (1997): Russia 24.7%; China 7.0%; Belarus 5.4%; Turkey 4.2%; Germany 3.7%; Italy 2.6%.

Transport and communications

Transport. Railroads (1998): length 22,564 km; passenger-km 54,500,000,000; metric ton-km cargo (1997) 160,419,000,000. Roads (1997): total length 172,378 km (paved 95%). Vehicles (1997): passenger cars 4,885,691. Air transport (1998): passenger-km 1,972,134,000; metric ton-km cargo (1996) 44,205,000; airports (1998) with scheduled flights 12.

Communications

Medium	date	unit	number	units per 1,000 persons
Daily newspapers	1996	circulation	2,780,000	54
Radio	1997	receivers	45,050,000	382
Television	1997	receivers	18,050,000	353
Telephones	1999	main lines	9,698,000	190
Cellular telephones	1999	subscribers	115,500	2.3
Personal computers	1999	units	700,000	14
Internet	1999	users	150,000	2.9

Education and health

Educational attainment (1989). Percentage of population age 15 and over having: some primary education 6.8%; completed primary 13.8%; some secondary 18.4%; completed secondary 31.1%; some postsecondary 19.5%; higher 10.4%. *Literacy* (1989): percentage of total population age 15 and over literate 98.4%; males literate 99.5%; females literate 97.4%.

Education (1995–96)

	schools	teachers	students	student/ teacher ratio
Primary (age 6–13), Secondary (age 14–17)	21,900	576,000[9]	7,007,000	...
Voc., teacher tr.	782	...	618,000	...
Higher	255	...	922,800	...

Health (1998): physicians 150,382 (1 per 334 persons); hospital beds 508,030 (1 per 99 persons); infant mortality rate per 1,000 live births (1999) 21.7.
Food (1998): daily per capita caloric intake 2,878 (vegetable products 79%, animal products 21%); 112% of FAO recommended minimum requirement.

Military

Total active duty personnel (1998): 311,400 (army 49.7%, air force 32.1%, navy 4.2%, other 14.0%). *Military expenditure as percentage of GNP* (1997) 3.7% (world 2.6%); per capita expenditure U.S.$85.

[1]On Sept. 2, 1996, the karbovanets, a transitional currency, was replaced by the hryvnia at a 100,000-to-1 ratio. [2]Crimea includes area of Sevastopol. [3]Kyyiv includes area of Kiev (city). [4]Official figure. [5]All indexes are for December only. [6]Less imputed bank service charges, net indirect taxes, and taxes on production. [7]Includes 2,646,000 self-employed and 2,763,000 unemployed. [8]Detail does not add to total given because of rounding. [9]1994–95.

Internet resources for further information:

- **National Bank of Ukraine**
  http://www.bank.gov.ua/ENGL/DEFAULT.htm

United Arab Emirates

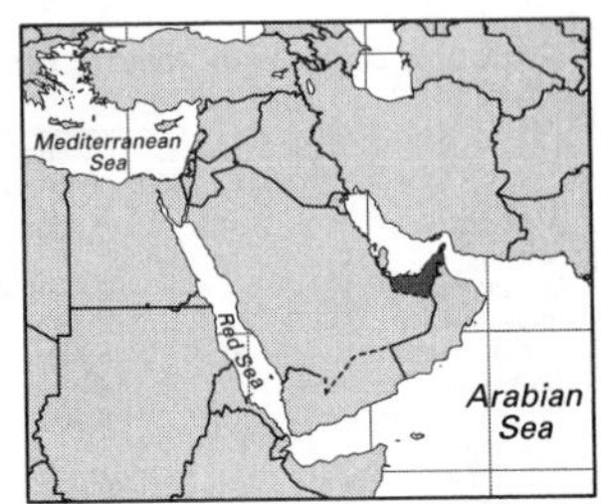

Official name: Al-Imārāt al-ʿArabīyah al-Muttaḥidah (United Arab Emirates).
Form of government: federation of seven emirates with one appointive advisory body (Federal National Council [40[1]]).
Chief of state: President.
Head of government: Prime Minister.
Capital: Abu Dhabi.
Official language: Arabic.
Official religion: Islam.
Monetary unit: 1 U.A.E. dirham (Dh) = 100 fils; valuation (Oct. 6, 2000) 1 U.S.$ = Dh 3.67; 1 £ = Dh 5.31.

Area and population

Emirates	Capitals	area sq mi	area sq km	population 1999 estimate
Abu Dhabi (Abū Ẓaby)	Abu Dhabi	28,210[2]	73,060[2]	1,127,000
ʿAjmān (Ajman)	ʿAjmān	100	260	161,000
Dubayy (Dubai)	Dubayy	1,510	3,900	858,000
Al-Fujayrah (Fujairah)	Al-Fujayrah	500	1,300	92,000
Ra's al-Khaymah (Ras al-Khaimah)	Ra's al-Khaymah	660	1,700	165,000
Ash-Shāriqah (Sharjah)	Ash-Shāriqah	1,000	2,600	491,000
Umm al-Qaywayn (Umm al-Qaiwain)	Umm al-Qaywayn	300	780	44,000
TOTAL		32,280	83,600	2,938,000

Demography

Population (2000): 3,022,000.
Density (2000): persons per sq mi 93.6, persons per sq km 36.1.
Urban-rural (1998): urban 85.1%; rural 14.9%.
Sex distribution (1999): male 67.22%; female 32.78%.
Age breakdown (1999): under 15, 26.2%; 15–29, 29.2%; 30–44, 33.3%; 45–59, 9.6%; 60–74, 1.4%; 75 and over, 0.3%.
Population projection: (2010) 3,751,000; (2020) 4,257,000.
Doubling time: 50 years.
Ethnic composition (1993): expatriates of Bangladesh, India, Pakistan, and Sri Lanka 45.0%; Arabs 25.0%, of which non-UAE Arabs (primarily Egyptians) 13.0%, UAE Arabs 12.0%; Iranians 17.0%; other Asians and Africans 8.0%; Europeans and North Americans 5.0%.
Religious affiliation (1995): Muslim 96.0% (Sunnī 80.0%, Shīʿī 16.0%); other (mostly Christian and Hindu) 4.0%.
Major cities (1995): Dubayy 669,181; Abu Dhabi 398,695; Ash-Shāriqah 320,095; Al-ʿAyn 225,970; ʿAjmān 114,395; Ra's al-Khaymah 77,550.

Vital statistics

Birth rate per 1,000 population (1999): 18.0 (world avg. 22.1).
Death rate per 1,000 population (1999): 3.6 (world avg. 8.9).
Natural increase rate per 1,000 population (1999): 14.4 (world avg. 13.2).
Total fertility rate (avg. births per childbearing woman; 1999): 3.6.
Marriage rate per 1,000 population (1995): 2.7.
Divorce rate per 1,000 population (1995): 0.9.
Life expectancy at birth (1999): male 71.4 years; female 76.3 years.
Major causes of death per 100,000 population (1998): cardiovascular diseases 44.1; accidents and poisoning 31.1; malignant neoplasms (cancers) 15.3; congenital anomalies 9.4.

National economy

Budget (1998). Revenue: Dh 19,895,000,000 (emirate contributions 70.1%; enterprise profits, fees, and charges 29.9%). Expenditures: Dh 21,393,000,000 (current expenditures 90.7%, of which interior and defense 40.9%, education and health 22.5%; development 6.3%; loans and equity 3.0%).
Gross domestic product (1998): U.S.$48,673,000,000 (U.S.$17,870 per capita).

Structure of gross domestic product and labour force

	1998 in value Dh '000,000[3]	1998 % of total value[3]	1997 labour force	1997 % of labour force
Agriculture	5,834	3.4	99,500	7.6
Crude petroleum production	36,951	21.7	20,500	1.6
Mining and quarrying	635	0.4	3,600	0.3
Manufacturing	20,190	11.9	155,000	11.8
Construction	16,243	9.6	250,600	19.0
Public utilities	4,140	2.4	23,000	1.8
Transp. and commun.	12,310	7.2	95,800	7.3
Trade	23,820	14.0	209,200	15.9
Finance, real estate	29,240	17.2	52,800	4.0
Pub. admin., defense	19,700	11.6	142,800	10.9
Services	4,847	2.5	245,200	18.7
Other	−3,844[4]	−2.3[4]	15,500	1.2
TOTAL	170,066	100.0	1,313,500	100.0[5]

Public debt: n.a.
Tourism (1996): total number of tourist arrivals 1,768,000.
Production (metric tons except as noted). Agriculture, forestry, fishing (1999): tomatoes 745,000, dates 295,000, cantaloupes and watermelons 65,000, cabbages 31,200, pumpkins and squash 31,000, eggplants 24,500, lemons and limes 21,000, cucumbers and gherkins 16,000, mangoes 10,500; livestock (number of live animals) 1,050,000 goats, 440,000 sheep, 195,000 camels, 85,000 cattle, 14,500,000 chickens; fish catch (1997) 114,000. Mining and quarrying (1996): sulfur 259,000; gypsum 90,000; chromite 56,000; lime 50,000. Manufacturing (value of production in Dh '000,000; 1993): chemical products 13,086; fabricated metal products 2,234; food, beverages, and tobacco 2,122; nonmetallic mineral products 2,025; basic metal manufactures 1,992; textiles, clothing, and leather products 1,135. Energy production (consumption): electricity (kW-hr; 1996) 19,250,000,000 (19,250,000,000); crude petroleum (barrels; 1996) 777,000,000 (77,268,000); petroleum products (metric tons; 1996) 17,485,000 (7,765,000); natural gas (cu m; 1997) 31,000,000,000 (29,509,000,000[6]).
Population economically active (1997): total 1,313,500; activity rate of total population 50.9% (participation rates [1995]: over age 15, 55.4%; female 19.4%; unemployment 1.8%).

Price and earnings indexes (1995 = 100)

	1991	1992	1993	1994	1995	1996	1997
Consumer price index[7]	81.5	86.9	91.3	95.8	100.0	103.2	106.7
Annual earnings index	...	...	104.1	101.1	100.0	103.0	102.7

Household income and expenditure. Average household size (1998) 5.3; income per household: n.a.; sources of income: n.a.; expenditure (1991): rent, fuel, and light 23.9%, food 22.7%, transportation and communications 14.1%, durable household goods 11.6%, education, recreation, and entertainment 8.6%.
Land use (1994): forested, virtually none; meadows and pastures 2.4%; agricultural and under permanent cultivation 0.5%; built-on, wasteland, and other 97.1%.

Foreign trade

Balance of trade (current prices)

	1992	1993	1994	1995	1996	1997
Dh '000,000,000	+16.6	+21.1	+16.5	+22.6	+29.5	+30.4
% of total	10.1%	12.0%	8.8%	11.0%	12.7%	12.2%

Imports (1997): Dh 109,100,000,000 (machinery and transport equipment 38.4%, basic manufactures 24.8%, food and live animals 9.7%, chemicals 6.1%, crude minerals 1.6%, mineral fuels 1.4%). *Major import sources:* Japan 10.2%; United States 9.4%; United Kingdom 8.7%; China 8.0%; Germany 6.9%; India 5.8%; Italy 5.2%; South Korea 5.1%.
Exports (1997): Dh 139,500,000,000 (crude petroleum 37.6%, natural gas 7.1%, refined petroleum products 4.8%). *Major export destinations:* Japan 36.2%; India 6.6%; Singapore 6.4%; South Korea 6.1%; Iran 3.7%; Oman 3.7%.

Transport and communications

Transport. Railroads: none. Roads (1996): total length 3,004 mi, 4,835 km (paved 100%). Vehicles (1996): passenger cars 201,000; trucks and buses 56,950. Merchant marine (1992): vessels (100 gross tons and over) 276; total deadweight tonnage 1,491,728. Air transport (1998)[8]: passenger-mi 9,714,000,000, passenger-km 15,633,000,000; short ton-mi cargo 1,646,000,000, metric ton-km cargo 2,403,000,000; airports (1998) with scheduled flights 6.

Communications

Medium	date	unit	number	units per 1,000 persons
Daily newspapers	1996	circulation	384,000	170
Radio	1997	receivers	820,000	355
Television	1997	receivers	700,000	260
Telephones	1999	main lines	915,223	389
Cellular telephones	1999	subscribers	493,278	210
Personal computers	1999	units	250,000	106
Internet	1999	users	200,000	85

Education and health

Educational attainment (1995). Percentage of population age 10 and over having: no formal schooling 47.6%; primary education 27.8%; secondary 16.0%, higher 8.6%. *Literacy* (1995): total population age 15 and over literate 79.2%; males literate 78.9%; females literate 79.8%.

Education (1996–97)

	schools	teachers	students	student/teacher ratio
Primary (age 6–11) } Secondary (age 12–18) }	512[9]	16,148	259,509	16.1
		12,388[10]	178,839	12.0[10]
Vocational	9[11]	249	1,925	7.7
Higher	4	510[12]	17,950	19.2[12]

Health (1994): physicians 4,095 (1 per 545 persons); hospital beds 6,193 (1 per 360 persons); infant mortality rate per 1,000 live births (1998) 8.7.
Food (1998): daily per capita caloric intake 3,372 (vegetable products 75%, animal products 25%); 139% of FAO recommended minimum requirement.

Military

Total active duty personnel (1998): 64,500 (army 91.5%, navy 2.3%, air force 6.2%). *Military expenditure as percentage of GDP* (1997): 6.9% (world 2.6%); per capita expenditure U.S.$1,004.

[1]All appointed seats. [2]Approximate, based on reported total and on reported partial areas for smaller emirates. [3]At factor cost. [4]Imputed bank service charges. [5]Detail does not add to total given because of rounding. [6]1996. [7]Abu Dhabi only. [8]Emirates Air and one-fourth apportionment of Gulf Air. [9]1991–92. [10]1994–95. [11]1990–91. [12]1992–93.

Internet resources for further information:
- **U.A.E. Home Page http://www.emirates.org**

United Kingdom

Official name: United Kingdom of Great Britain and Northern Ireland.
Form of government: constitutional monarchy with two legislative houses (House of Lords [699[1]]; House of Commons [659]).
Chief of state: Sovereign.
Head of government: Prime Minister.
Capital: London.
Official language: English.
Official religion: Churches of England and Scotland "established" (protected by the state, but not "official") in their respective countries; no established church in Northern Ireland or Wales.
Monetary unit: 1 pound sterling (£) = 100 new pence; valuation (Oct. 6, 2000) 1 £ = U.S.$1.45; 1 U.S.$ = £0.69.

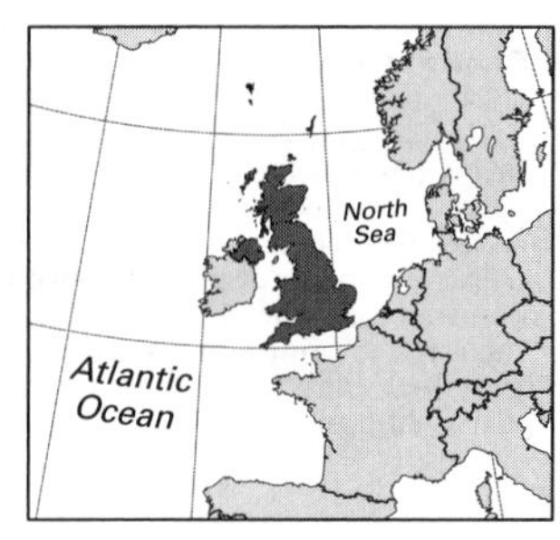

Population (1998 estimate)

Countries[2]	population		population		population
England	49,493,300	Peterborough	156,000	**Unitary Districts**	
Counties		Plymouth	253,000	Aberdeen City	213,100
Bedfordshire	373,300	Poole	141,500	Aberdeenshire	226,300
Buckinghamshire	478,700	Portsmouth	188,800	Angus	110,100
Cambridgeshire	563,800	Reading	147,800	Argyll and Bute	90,000
Cheshire	672,400	Redcar and		City of Edinburgh	450,200
Cornwall	490,400	Cleveland	138,300	Clackmannanshire	48,600
Cumbria	492,900	Rutland	35,700	Dumfries and	
Derbyshire	734,300	Slough	111,700	Galloway	147,300
Devon	692,400	Southampton	216,000	Dundee City	146,700
Dorset	387,300	South		East Ayrshire	121,300
Durham	506,400	Gloucestershire	241,000	East Dumbarton-	
East Sussex	491,300	Southend	176,000	shire	109,600
Essex	1,294,700	Stockton-on-Tees	181,000	East Lothian	89,600
Gloucestershire	557,300	Stoke-on-Trent	251,500	East Renfrewshire	88,000
Hampshire	1,238,000	Swindon	179,700	Falkirk	144,100
Hertfordshire	1,033,600	Telford and		Fife	348,900
Isle of Wight[3]	127,000	Wrenkin	149,800	Glasgow City	619,700
Kent	1,332,000	Thurrock	135,000	Highland	208,300
Lancashire	1,136,300	Torbay	123,000	Inverclyde	85,400
Leicestershire	598,700	Warrington	190,200	Midlothian	80,900
Lincolnshire	623,100	West Berkshire	144,200	Moray	85,900
Norfolk	790,300	Windsor and		North Ayrshire	139,700
North Yorkshire	565,000	Maidenhead	140,500	North Lanarkshire	326,700
Northamptonshire	615,800	Wokingham	145,300	Orkney Islands	19,600
Northumberland	309,600	York	177,400	Perth and Kinross	133,000
Nottinghamshire	744,800	**Metropolitan**		Renfrewshire	177,800
Oxfordshire	616,700	**Counties/Greater**		Scottish Borders	106,300
Shropshire	280,400	**London**		Shetland Islands	22,900
Somerset	489,300	Greater London[4]	7,187,300	South Ayrshire	114,400
Staffordshire	809,700	Greater		South Lanarkshire	306,900
Suffolk	671,100	Manchester	2,577,400	Stirling	83,100
Surrey	1,060,500	Merseyside	1,409,400	West Dumbarton-	
Warwickshire	506,700	South Yorkshire	1,304,100	shire	94,900
West Sussex	751,800	Tyne and Wear	1,115,800	Western Isles	27,900
Wiltshire	425,800	West Midlands	2,628,200	West Lothian	153,100
Worcestershire	538,200	West Yorkshire	2,113,300	Northern Ireland	1,663,200
Unitary Councils		Wales	2,933,500	**Districts**	
Bath and		**Unitary Districts**		Antrim	47,500
NE Somerset	167,300	Anglesey	65,400	Ards	67,800
Blackburn with		Blaenau Gwent	72,000	Armagh	53,200
Darwen	140,000	Bridgend	131,400	Ballymena	58,200
Blackpool	150,500	Caerphilly	169,600	Ballymoney	24,900
Bournemouth	162,400	Cardiff	320,900	Banbridge	37,700
Bracknell Forest	110,700	Carmarthenshire	169,000	Belfast	297,200
Brighton and		Ceredigion	70,700	Carrickfergus	35,700
Hove	255,800	Conway	111,900	Castlereagh	64,500
Bristol	402,300	Denbighshire	90,500	Coleraine	54,700
Darlington	101,400	Flintshire	147,000	Cookstown	31,800
Derby	235,800	Gwynedd	117,500	Craigavon	79,100
East Riding of		Merthyr Tydfil	57,000	Derry	104,700
Yorkshire	312,800	Monmouthshire	86,300	Down	61,200
Halton	121,700	Neath and		Dungannon	47,100
Hartlepool	91,900	Port Talbot	138,800	Fermanagh	55,500
Herefordshire	167,900	Newport	139,200	Larne	30,300
Kingston upon		Pembrokeshire	113,700	Limvady	30,800
Hull	261,800	Powys	126,000	Lisburn	106,600
Leicester	294,300	Rhondda, Cynon,		Magherafelt	37,900
Luton	183,300	Taff	240,400	Moyle	15,000
Medway	242,600	Swansea	229,500	Newry and Mourne	84,900
Middlesborough	145,100	Torfaen	90,200	Newtownabbey	79,600
Milton Keynes	203,200	The Vale of		North Down	73,500
NE Lincolnshire	156,200	Glamorgan	121,300	Omagh	47,000
North Lincolnshire	152,300	Wrexham	125,200	Strabane	36,800
North Somerset	188,700	Scotland	5,120,300	TOTAL	59,210,300
Nottingham City	286,800				

Demography

Population (2000): 59,714,000.
Area: 94,248 sq mi; 244,101 sq km, of which England 50,351 sq mi, 130,410 sq km; Wales 8,015 sq mi, 20,758 sq km; Scotland 30,421 sq mi, 78,789 sq km; Northern Ireland (figures represent remainder) 5,461 sq mi, 14,144 sq km.
Density (2000): persons per sq mi 633.6, persons per sq km 244.6.
Urban-rural (1999): urban 88.2%; rural 10.8%.
Sex distribution (1999): male 49.08%; female 50.92%.
Age breakdown (1997): under 15, 19.3%; 15–29, 19.9%; 30–44, 22.3%; 45–59, 18.1%; 60–74, 13.2%; 75 and over, 7.2%.
Population projection: (2010) 61,589,000; (2020) 61,589,000.
Ethnic composition (1992–94)[5]: white 93.7%; Asian Indian 1.8%; Pakistani 1.4%; black 1.4%; other and not stated 1.6%.
Religious affiliation (1995): Christian 65.9%, of which Protestant 53.4% (Anglican 43.5%, Presbyterian 4.5%, Methodist 2.2%), Roman Catholic 9.8%, Orthodox 1.0%, other Christian 1.7%; Muslim 2.6%; Hindu 0.6%; Sikh 0.5%; Jewish 0.5%; other/nonreligious 29.9%.
Major cities (1996): Greater London 7,074,300; Birmingham 1,020,600; Leeds 726,900; Glasgow 616,400; Sheffield 530,400; Bradford 483,400; Liverpool 468,000; Edinburgh 448,900; Manchester 430,800; Bristol 399,600; Kirklees 388,800; Wirral 329,200.
Place of birth (1991): U.K. 93.2% (52,721,000); foreign-born 6.8%, of which India 1.5%, Ireland 1.1%, Caribbean 0.9%, Pakistan 0.9%, other 2.2%.
Mobility (1991)[5]. Population living in the same residence as 1990: 90.1%; different residence, same country (of Great Britain) 8.1%; different residence, different country of Great Britain 1.2%; from outside Great Britain 0.6%.
Households (1994)[5]. Average household size 2.4; 1 person 27%, 2 persons 34%, 3 persons 16%, 4 persons 15%, 5 persons 6%, 6 or more persons 2%. Family household: 16,900,000 (72.0%), nonfamily 6,600,000 (28.0%, of which 1-person 12.0%).
Immigration (1996): permanent residents 272,000, from Australia 5.5%, United States 5.2%, Bangladesh, India, and Sri Lanka 2.9%, New Zealand 2.6%, Pakistan 2.6%, South Africa 1.5%, Canada 1.1%, other 78.6%, of which EU 12.1%.

Vital statistics

Birth rate per 1,000 population (1999): 11.9 (world avg. 22.1); (1997) legitimate 63.2%; illegitimate 36.8%.
Death rate per 1,000 population (1999): 10.4 (world avg. 8.9).
Natural increase rate per 1,000 population (1999): 1.5 (world avg. 13.2).
Total fertility rate (avg. births per childbearing woman; 1999): 1.7.
Marriage rate per 1,000 population (1996): 5.4.
Divorce rate per 1,000 population (1996)[5]: 2.7.
Life expectancy at birth (1996): male 74.4 years; female 79.7 years.
Major causes of death per 100,000 population (1997): diseases of the circulatory system 442.1, of which ischemic heart disease 237.6, cerebrovascular disease 112.4; malignant neoplasms (cancers) 261.2; diseases of the respiratory system 165.8, of which pneumonia 106.6; diseases of the digestive system 39.5; diseases of the endocrine system 13.8, of which diabetes mellitus 11.0; diseases of the genitourinary system 12.5; suicide 7.0.

Social indicators

Educational attainment (1981). Percentage of population age 25 and over having: primary or secondary education only 89.7%; some postsecondary 4.8%; bachelor's or equivalent degree 4.9%; higher university degree 0.6%.

Distribution of disposable income (1996–97)

percentage of household income by quintile

1	2	3	4	5 (highest)
7.9	10.6	12.4	26.6	42.5

Quality of working life (1998). Average workweek (hours): male 41.0, female 34.8. Annual rate per 100,000 workers for (1996): injury or accident 553.6; death 1.0. Proportion of labour force (employed persons) insured for damages or income loss resulting from: injury 100%; permanent disability 100%; death 100%. Average days lost to labour stoppages per 1,000 employee workdays 1997: 0.04. Principal means of transport to work (1991; London only): public transportation 81%, private automobile 15%, motor or pedal cycle 2%, other 2%.
Access to services (1991)[5]. Proportion of households having access to: bath or shower 98.7%; toilet 99.8%; central heating 81.1%.
Social participation. Eligible voters participating in last national election (May 1997): 71.3%. Population age 16 and over participating in voluntary work (1987)[5]: 22%. Trade union membership in total workforce (1996) 28.6%.
Social deviance (1997)[5]. Offense rate per 100,000 population for: theft and handling stolen goods 4,123.8; burglary 1,933.5; violence against the person 477.7; fraud and forgery 256.0; robbery 120.2; sexual offense 63.2.
Leisure (1994). Favourite leisure activities (hours weekly): watching television 17.1; listening to radio 10.3; reading 8.8, of which books 3.8, newspapers 3.3; gardening 2.1.
Material well-being (1997). Households possessing: automobile 69.8%, telephone 94.1%, television receiver 98.3% (colour 95%)[6], refrigerator 98.5%, central heating 88.6%, washing machine 90.6%, video recorder 84.1%.

National economy

Budget (1997–98). Revenue: £287,026,000,000 (income tax 41.0%, customs and excise taxes 31.3%, social security contributions 17.2%). Expenditures: £289,621,000,000 (1996–97; social security 24.9%, health 11.0%, debt interest 7.2%, defense 7.2%).
Gross national product (1998): U.S.$1,264,262,000,000 (U.S.$21,410 per capita).

Structure of gross domestic product and labour force

	1998			
	in value £'000,000	% of total value	labour force	% of labour force
Agriculture	10,970	1.3	272,000	1.0
Mining[7]	14,340	1.7	302,000	1.1
Manufacturing	166,210	19.7	4,076,000	14.2
Construction	44,720	5.3	1,003,000	3.5
Public utilities	18,560	2.2	142,000	0.5
Transp. and commun.	71,720	8.5	1,389,000	4.8
Trade[8]	127,400	15.1	4,037,000	14.0
Finance	232,870	27.6	1,064,000	3.7
Pub. admin., defense	145,960	17.3	5,828,000	20.3
Services	43,870	5.2	5,124,000	17.8
Other	–32,895[9]	–3.9[9]	5,476,000[10]	19.1[10]
TOTAL	843,725	100.0	28,713,000	100.0

Total national debt (March 31, 1997): £404,283,000,000.
Land use (1994): forested 10.4%; meadows and pastures 45.9%; agricultural and under permanent cultivation 24.8%; other 18.9%.
Tourism (1998): receipts U.S.$20,978,000,000; expenditures U.S.$32,267,000,000.
Production (metric tons except as noted). Agriculture, forestry, fishing (1999): wheat 14,655,000, sugar beets 10,002,000, potatoes 7,000,000, barley 6,730,000, rapeseed 1,764,000, carrots 618,000, oats 600,000, green peas 417,000; livestock (number of live animals) 44,471,000 sheep, 11,339,000 cattle, 7,720,000 pigs; roundwood (1998) 7,403,000 cu m; fish catch (1997) 1,017,159. Mining and quarrying (1997): limestone 102,800,000; tin and lead 5,600. Manufacturing (value added in £'000,000; 1996): electrical and optical equipment 18,270; food and beverages 17,622; paper, printing, and publishing 16,214; chemicals and chemical products 15,819; metals and metal products 15,199; transport equipment 13,914; machinery and equipment 12,196; textiles and leather products 7,186. Construction (value in £; 1995)[5]: residential 7,135,000,000; nonresidential 13,877,000,000.

Financial aggregates

	1992	1993	1994	1995	1996	1997	1998
Exchange rate							
U.S. dollar per £	1.76	1.50	1.53	1.58	1.56	1.64	1.66
SDRs per £	1.10	1.08	1.07	1.04	1.18	1.22	1.81
International reserves (U.S.$)							
Total (excl. gold; '000,000,000)	36.64	36.78	41.01	42.02	39.90	32.32	32.21
SDRs ('000,000,000)	0.54	0.29	0.49	0.41	0.34	0.47	0.47
Reserve pos. in IMF ('000,000,000)	2.01	1.86	1.99	2.42	2.43	2.97	4.38
Foreign exchange ('000,000,000)	34.09	34.63	38.53	39.18	37.12	28.88	27.36
Gold ('000,000 fine troy oz)	18.61	18.45	18.44	18.43	18.43	18.42	23.00
% world reserves	2.0	2.0	2.0	2.0	2.0	2.1	2.4
Interest and prices							
Central bank discount (%)	...	...	...	...	...	...	...
Govt. bond yield (%) long term	9.12	7.87	8.05	8.26	8.10	7.09	5.45
Industrial share prices (1995 = 100)	77.9	89.4	96.1	100.0	113.3	128.3	150.5
Balance of payments (U.S.$'000,000)							
Balance of visible trade,	–24,618	–20,570	–16,127	–18,266	–18,870	–20,540	–34,020
Imports, f.o.b.	212,058	201,802	222,263	259,154	278,400	–299,810	–305,800
Exports, f.o.b.	187,440	181,232	206,136	240,888	259,530	279,270	271,780
Balance of invisibles	3,904	4,179	13,736	7,697	19,110	12,620	33,870
Balance of payments, current account	–20,714	–16,391	–2,391	–10,569	240	–7,920	–150

Manufacturing, mining, and construction enterprises (1993)

	no. of enter-prises	no. of employees	annual wages as a % of avg. of all wages	annual value added (£'000,000)
Manufacturing				
Food, beverages, and tobacco	9,463	554,700	...	16,559
Paper and paper products; printing and publishing	26,825	430,400	...	13,438
Electrical and data-processing equipment	13,902	512,800	...	13,209
Transport equipment	3,704	414,200	...	12,815
Chemical engineering	3,809	270,200	...	12,538
Machinery and equipment	11,636	387,500	...	9,391
Rubber and plastics	5,103	228,500	...	5,679
Metal manufacturing	3,524	144,400	...	4,197
Textiles	7,256	171,800	...	3,498
Clothing and footwear	8,119	211,800	...	2,716
Mineral-oil processing	148	13,100	...	1,618
Wood and wood products	7,767	73,600	...	1,292
Mining				
Extraction of coal, mineral oil, and natural gas	358	80,000[11]	...	10,261
Extraction of minerals other than fuels	921	30,200	...	1,090
Construction	199,363	1,016,000[11]	...	19,274

Retail trade enterprises (1992)

	no. of enter-prises	no. of employees	weekly wage as a % of all wages	annual turnover (£'000,000)[12]
Food and grocery, of which	60,119	854,000	...	51,462
large grocery	71	579,000	...	40,837
other grocery	18,557	95,000	...	4,086
meats	12,149	58,000	...	2,523
Household goods, of which	45,532	299,000	...	20,881
electrical and musical goods	10,887	87,000	...	7,270
furniture	11,927	60,000	...	4,575
Drink, confectionery, and tobacco, of which	46,671	254,000	...	13,810
tobacco and confectionery	41,502	215,000	...	10,880
Clothing and footwear, of which	24,923	264,000	...	12,428
women's, girls', and infants' wear	13,624	102,000	...	4,771
footwear	3,098	67,000	...	2,589
men's and boys' wear	3,751	37,000	...	2,063
Pharmaceuticals	7,560	87,000	...	5,231

Energy production (consumption): electricity (kW-hr; 1994) 325,383,000,000 (342,270,000,000); coal (metric tons; 1994) 47,717,000 (80,582,000); crude petroleum (barrels; 1994) 888,454,000 (629,354,000); petroleum products (metric tons; 1994) 86,184,000 (75,021,000); natural gas (cu m; 1994) 76,680,000,000 (79,391,000,000).
Population economically active (1998): total 28,713,000, activity rate of total population 48.5% (participation rates: ages 16–64, 68.0%; female 44.7%; unemployed 6.2%).

Price and earnings indexes (1995 = 100)

	1993	1994	1995	1996	1997	1998	1999
Consumer price index	94.4	96.7	100.0	102.4	105.7	109.3	111.0
Monthly earnings index	93.1	96.7	100.0	103.5	108.0	113.5	119.0

Household income and expenditure (1996–97). Average household size 2.4; average annual disposable income per household £18,494 (U.S.$31,400); sources of income: wages and salaries 66.6%, social security benefits 13.1%, income from self-employment 7.8%, dividends and interest 6.9%; expenditure: food and beverages 17.0%, transport and vehicles 16.6%, housing 15.6%, household goods 8.2%, clothing 6.1%, energy 3.8%.

Foreign trade

Balance of trade (current prices)

	1994	1995	1996	1997	1998	1999
£'000,000	–14,534	–14,702	–16,549	–15,540	–25,466	–29,765
% of total	5.2%	4.6%	4.7%	4.3%	7.2%	8.2%

Imports (1997): £189,079,000,000 (machinery and transport equipment 43.8%, of which electrical equipment 19.7%, road vehicles 11.8%; chemicals 9.5%, of which organic chemicals 2.4%, plastics 2.3%; food 7.4%; clothing and footwear 4.7%; petroleum and petroleum products 2.8%; textiles 2.7%; paper and paperboard 2.5%). *Major import sources:* Germany 13.7%; U.S. 13.2%; France 9.5%; The Netherlands 6.6%; Ireland 4.9%; Belgium-Luxembourg 4.5%; Italy 4.3%; Spain 3.6%; Sweden 2.4%.
Exports (1997): £172,908,000,000 (machinery and transport equipment 45.9%, of which electrical equipment 19.9%, road vehicles 8.6%; chemicals 12.6%, of which organic chemicals 2.9%; petroleum and petroleum products 5.5%; professional and scientific 4.1%; food 3.8%; iron and steel products 2.1%). *Major export destinations:* U.S. 12.1%; Germany 11.9%; France 9.5%; The Netherlands 8.0%; Ireland 5.4%; Belgium-Luxembourg 4.8%; Italy 4.7%; Spain 3.9%; Sweden 2.6%; Japan 2.4%; Switzerland 1.7%.

Transport and communications

Transport. Railroads (1995–96)[13]: length 23,518 mi[14], 37,849 km[14]; passenger-mi 18,154,000,000, passenger-km 29,216,000,000; ton-mi cargo 2,026,000,000, metric ton-km cargo 2,916,000,000[15]. Roads (1997): total length 228,042 mi, 369,867 km (paved 100%). Vehicles (1997)[5]: passenger cars 21,681,000, trucks and buses 2,317,000. Merchant marine (1992): vessels (over 100 gross tons) 1,631; total deadweight tonnage 4,355,063. Air transport (1996): passenger-mi 77,575,900,000, passenger-km 124,846,500,000; short ton-mi cargo 2,662,600,000, metric ton-km cargo 3,831,900,000; airports (1997) 57.

Communications

Medium	date	unit	number	units per 1,000 persons
Daily newspapers	1996	circulation	19,332,000	332
Radio	1997	receivers	84,500,000	1,443
Television	1998	receivers	38,000,000	644
Telephones	1998	main lines	32,829,000	557
Cellular telephones	1998	subscribers	14,874,000	252
Personal computers	1998	units	15,500,000	263
Internet	1998	users	8,000,000	136

Education and health

Literacy (1990): total population literate, virtually 100%[16].

Education (1994–95)[17]

	schools	teachers	students	student/ teacher ratio
Primary (age 5–10)	32,385	231,659	4,906,439	21.2
Secondary (age 11–19)		228,187	3,779,262	16.6
Voc., teacher tr.	...	...	586,000[18]	...
Higher[19]	70	c. 48,000	c. 810,000	c. 17.0

Health (1993)[5]: physicians 92,474 (1 per 629 persons); hospital beds 283,814 (1 per 205 persons); infant mortality rate (1999) 5.8.
Food (1997): daily per capita caloric intake 3,276 (vegetable products 69%, animal products 31%); 130% of FAO recommended minimum requirement.

Military

Total active duty personnel (1999): 212,400 (army 53.4%, navy 20.6%, air force 26.0%). *Military expenditure as percentage of GNP* (1997): 2.7% (world 2.6%); per capita expenditure U.S.$600.

[1]All but 92 of the more than 600 hereditary peers lost their right to vote on Nov. 11, 1999. [2]The reorganization of first-order administrative units was completed in 1999; England's former 46 counties (including 7 metropolitan counties) reorganized into 35 counties, 45 unitary districts, 6 metropolitan counties, and Greater London; Wales's former 8 counties reorganized into 22 unitary districts; Scotland's former 9 regions and 3 island councils organized into 32 unitary districts; Northern Ireland remained. [3]Only unitary district with county status. [4]Has administrative authority from July 2000. [5]Great Britain only. [6]1992. [7]Includes petroleum extraction. [8]Includes hotels. [9]Plus rent; less imputed bank service charges. [10]Includes 1,766,000 unemployed and 3,499,000 self-employed not distributed by sector and 211,000 military personnel. [11]1992. [12]Includes value-added taxes. [13]British Rail only. [14]1990. [15]Much of British Rail's freight business was sold during 1996. [16]A survey in 1986–87, however, put the number of functional illiterates at 9–12% of the adult population. [17]Public sector only. [18]1992–93. [19]Universities only.

Internet resources for further information:
- **Office for National Statistics http://www.statistics.gov.uk**

United States

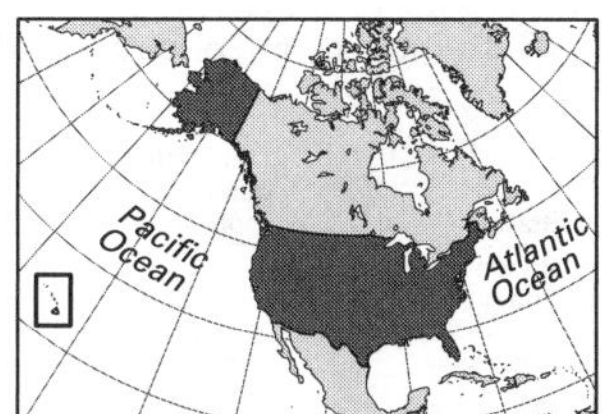

Official name: United States of America.
Form of government: federal republic with two legislative houses (Senate [100]; House of Representatives [435[1]]).
Head of state and government: President.
Capital: Washington, D.C.
Official language: none.
Official religion: none.
Monetary unit: 1 dollar (U.S.$) = 100 cents; valuation (Oct. 6, 2000) 1 U.S.$ = £0.69; 1 £ = U.S.$1.45.

Area and population

States	Capitals	area sq mi	area sq km	population 2000 census (prelim.)
Alabama	Montgomery	51,718	133,950	4,447,100
Alaska	Juneau	587,875	1,522,595	626,932
Arizona	Phoenix	114,006	295,275	5,130,632
Arkansas	Little Rock	53,182	137,741	2,673,400
California	Sacramento	158,647	410,895	33,871,648
Colorado	Denver	104,100	269,619	4,301,261
Connecticut	Hartford	5,006	12,966	3,405,565
Delaware	Dover	2,026	5,247	783,600
Florida	Tallahassee	58,680	151,981	15,982,378
Georgia	Atlanta	58,930	152,629	8,186,453
Hawaii	Honolulu	6,459	16,729	1,211,537
Idaho	Boise	83,574	216,456	1,293,953
Illinois	Springfield	57,918	150,008	12,419,293
Indiana	Indianapolis	36,420	94,328	6,080,485
Iowa	Des Moines	56,276	145,755	2,926,324
Kansas	Topeka	82,282	213,110	2,688,418
Kentucky	Frankfort	40,411	104,664	4,041,769
Louisiana	Baton Rouge	47,719	123,592	4,468,976
Maine	Augusta	33,128	85,801	1,274,923
Maryland	Annapolis	10,455	27,078	5,296,486
Massachusetts	Boston	8,262	21,399	6,349,097
Michigan	Lansing	96,705	250,466	9,938,444
Minnesota	St. Paul	86,943	225,182	4,919,479
Mississippi	Jackson	47,695	123,530	2,844,658
Missouri	Jefferson City	69,709	180,546	5,595,211
Montana	Helena	147,046	380,849	902,195
Nebraska	Lincoln	77,359	200,360	1,711,263
Nevada	Carson City	110,567	286,368	1,998,257
New Hampshire	Concord	9,283	24,043	1,235,786
New Jersey	Trenton	7,790	20,176	8,414,350
New Mexico	Santa Fe	121,598	314,939	1,819,046
New York	Albany	53,013	137,304	18,976,457
North Carolina	Raleigh	52,672	136,420	8,049,313
North Dakota	Bismarck	70,704	183,123	642,200
Ohio	Columbus	44,828	116,104	11,353,140
Oklahoma	Oklahoma City	69,903	181,049	3,450,654
Oregon	Salem	97,052	251,364	3,421,399
Pennsylvania	Harrisburg	45,759	118,516	12,281,054
Rhode Island	Providence	1,213	3,142	1,048,319
South Carolina	Columbia	31,117	80,593	4,012,012
South Dakota	Pierre	77,121	199,743	754,844
Tennessee	Nashville	42,145	109,155	5,689,283
Texas	Austin	266,873	691,201	20,851,820
Utah	Salt Lake City	84,904	219,901	2,233,169
Vermont	Montpelier	9,615	24,903	608,827
Virginia	Richmond	40,598	105,149	7,078,515
Washington	Olympia	68,126	176,446	5,894,121
West Virginia	Charleston	24,232	62,761	1,808,344
Wisconsin	Madison	65,500	169,645	5,363,675
Wyoming	Cheyenne	97,819	253,351	493,782
District				
District of Columbia	—	68	176	572,059
TOTAL		3,675,031[2]	9,518,323[2]	281,421,906

Demography

Population (2000): 275,372,000[3].
Density (2000)[3]: persons per sq mi 74.3, persons per sq km 28.7.
Urban-rural (1996): urban 76.4%; rural 23.6%.
Sex distribution (1996): male 48.93%; female 51.07%.
Age breakdown (1996): under 15, 21.8%; 15–29, 20.8%; 30–44, 24.4%; 45–59, 16.5%; 60–74, 10.8%; 75 and over, 5.7%.
Population projection: (2010) 299,911,000; (2020) 324,958,000.
Doubling time: not applicable; doubling time exceeds 100 years.
Population by race and Hispanic[4] origin (1996): non-Hispanic white 73.1%; non-Hispanic black 12.0%; Hispanic 10.7%; Asian and Pacific Islander 3.5%; American Indian and Eskimo 0.7%.
Religious affiliation (1995): Christian 85.3%, of which Protestant 57.9%, Roman Catholic 21.0%, other Christian 6.4%; Jewish 2.1%; Muslim 1.9%; nonreligious 8.7%; other 2.0%.
Mobility (1996). Population living in the same residence as in 1995: 84.0%; different residence, same county 10.0%; different county, same state 3.0%; different state 3.0%; moved from abroad 1.0%.
Households (1998). Total households 102,528,000 (married-couple families 54,317,000 [53.0%]). Average household size (1998) 2.6; 1 person 25.6%, 2 persons 32.2%, 3 persons 16.9%, 4 persons 15.0%, 5 or more persons 10.2%. Family households: 70,880,000 (69.1%); nonfamily 31,648,000 (30.9%), of which 1-person 83.2%.
Immigration (1996[5]): permanent immigrants admitted 915,900, from Mexico 17.9%, Philippines 6.1%, India 4.9%, Vietnam 4.6%, China 4.6%, Dominican Republic 4.3%, Cuba 2.9%, Ukraine 2.3%, Russia 2.2%, Jamaica 2.1%, South Korea 2.0%, Poland 1.7%. Refugee arrivals (1997[5]): 112,158.

Components of population change (1990–98)

States	Net change in population	Annual percentage change	Births	Deaths	Net migration
Alabama	312,000	0.9	507,000	343,000	148,000
Alaska	64,000	1.4	89,000	20,000	–5,000
Arizona	1,003,000	3.1	592,000	278,000	689,000
Arkansas	188,000	1.0	293,000	217,000	112,000
California	2,881,000	1.2	4,709,000	1,811,000	–17,000
Colorado	676,000	2.4	453,000	198,000	421,000
Connecticut	–13,000	–0.5	380,000	239,000	–154,000
Delaware	77,000	1.4	87,000	51,000	41,000
Florida	1,978,000	1.8	1,585,000	1,209,000	1,602,000
Georgia	1,164,000	2.1	930,000	464,000	698,000
Hawaii	85,000	0.9	156,000	59,000	–12,000
Idaho	222,000	2.5	147,000	69,000	144,000
Illinois	615,000	0.7	1,553,000	865,000	–73,000
Indiana	355,000	0.8	694,000	429,000	90,000
Iowa	86,000	0.4	312,000	228,000	2,000
Kansas	151,000	0.7	309,000	191,000	33,000
Kentucky	250,000	0.8	439,000	302,000	113,000
Louisiana	147,000	0.4	563,000	321,000	–95,000
Maine	16,000	0.2	124,000	95,000	–13,000
Maryland	354,000	0.9	615,000	333,000	72,000
Massachusetts	131,000	0.3	697,000	452,000	–114,000
Michigan	522,000	0.7	1,154,000	676,000	44,000
Minnesota	350,000	1.0	538,000	300,000	112,000
Mississippi	177,000	0.8	346,000	218,000	49,000
Missouri	322,000	0.8	621,000	436,000	137,000
Montana	81,000	1.2	93,000	61,000	49,000
Nebraska	84,000	0.7	194,000	124,000	14,000
Nevada	545,000	4.8	198,000	95,000	442,000
New Hampshire	76,000	0.8	128,000	74,000	22,000
New Jersey	367,000	0.6	965,000	596,000	–2,000
New Mexico	222,000	1.7	227,000	98,000	93,000
New York	185,000	0.1	2,286,000	1,369,000	–732,000
North Carolina	914,000	1.6	854,000	517,000	577,000
North Dakota	–1,000	0.0	71,000	48,000	–24,000
Ohio	362,000	0.4	1,302,000	850,000	–90,000
Oklahoma	201,000	0.8	388,000	264,000	77,000
Oregon	440,000	1.8	353,000	225,000	312,000
Pennsylvania	119,000	0.1	1,292,000	1,037,000	–136,000
Rhode Island	–15,000	–0.2	113,000	79,000	–49,000
South Carolina	350,000	1.2	444,000	265,000	171,000
South Dakota	42,000	0.7	88,000	56,000	10,000
Tennessee	553,000	1.4	609,000	409,000	353,000
Texas	2,773,000	1.9	2,680,000	1,107,000	1,200,000
Utah	377,000	2.5	323,000	86,000	140,000
Vermont	28,000	0.6	61,000	40,000	7,000
Virginia	602,000	1.2	778,000	422,000	246,000
Washington	823,000	2.0	649,000	329,000	503,000
West Virginia	18,000	0.1	176,000	165,000	7,000
Wisconsin	332,000	0.8	571,000	365,000	126,000
Wyoming	27,000	0.7	54,000	29,000	2,000
District					
District of Columbia	–84,000	–1.8	80,000	54,000	–110,000
TOTAL/RATE	21,534,000	8.7	32,870,000	18,568,000	7,232,000

Major cities (1999): New York 7,428,162; Los Angeles 3,633,591; Chicago 2,799,050; Houston 1,845,967; Philadelphia 1,417,601; San Diego 1,238,974; Phoenix 1,211,466; San Antonio 1,147,213; Dallas 1,076,214; Detroit 965,084.

Other principal cities (1999)

	population		population		population
Akron	211,822	Honolulu	395,327	Pittsburgh	336,882
Albuquerque	420,578	Indianapolis	738,907	Portland (Ore.)	503,637
Anaheim	300,650	Jacksonville	695,877	Raleigh	261,205
Anchorage	257,808	Jersey City	230,458	Riverside	265,721
Arlington (Tex.)	311,962	Kansas City (Mo.)	437,764	Rochester	214,470
Atlanta	401,726	Las Vegas	418,658	Sacramento	406,899
Austin	587,873	Lexington (Ky.)	243,785	St. Louis	333,960
Bakersfield	222,352	Lincoln	215,928	St. Paul	256,213
Baltimore	632,681	Long Beach	435,027	St. Petersburg	234,647
Baton Rouge	210,667	Louisville	253,128	San Francisco	746,777
Birmingham	249,459	Madison	210,674	San Jose	867,675
Boston	555,249	Memphis	606,109	Santa Ana	309,290
Buffalo	295,619	Mesa (Ariz.)	368,811	Seattle	537,150
Charlotte	520,829	Miami	369,253	Stockton	245,020
Cincinnati	330,914	Milwaukee	572,424	Tampa	290,973
Cleveland	501,662	Minneapolis	353,395	Toledo	307,946
Colorado Springs	350,199	Nashville	506,385	Tucson	466,591
Columbus	671,247	New Orleans	460,913	Tulsa	381,579
Corpus Christi	281,774	Newark	263,087	Virginia Beach	433,461
Denver	499,775	Norfolk	225,875	Washington, D.C.	519,000
El Paso	612,770	Oakland	365,210	Wichita	335,562
Fort Worth	502,369	Oklahoma City	475,322		
Fresno	404,141	Omaha	386,742		

Place of birth (1990): native-born 227,078,000 (91.3%); foreign-born 21,632,000 (8.7%), of which Mexico 4,447,000, Germany (East and West) 1,163,000, Philippines 998,000, Canada 871,000, United Kingdom 765,000, Cuba 751,000, South Korea 663,000, Italy 640,000, Vietnam 556,000, China 543,000, India 463,000, Japan 422,000, Poland 397,000, U.S.S.R. 337,000.

Vital statistics

Birth rate per 1,000 population (1999): 14.3 (world avg. 22.1); (1994) legitimate 67.4%; illegitimate 32.6%.
Death rate per 1,000 population (1999): 8.7 (world avg. 8.9).
Natural increase rate per 1,000 population (1999): 5.6 (world avg. 13.2).
Total fertility rate (avg. births per childbearing woman; 1999): 2.0.
Marriage rate per 1,000 population (1997): 8.9; median age at first marriage (1991): men 26.3 years, women 24.1 years.
Divorce rate per 1,000 population (1997): 4.3.
Life expectancy at birth (1997): white male 73.8 years, black and other male 68.9[6] years; white female 79.9 years, black and other female 76.1[6] years.

Vital statistics (1995)

States	Live births	Birth rate per 1,000 population	Death rate per 1,000 population	Infant mortality rate per 1,000 live births	Abortion rate per 1,000 live births	Life expectancy
Alabama	60,300	14.2	10.0	9.8	248.8	73.6
Alaska	10,200	17.0	4.2	7.7	196.1	...
Arizona	72,500	17.2	8.4	7.5	248.3	76.1
Arkansas	35,200	14.2	10.8	8.8	170.5	74.3
California	552,000	17.5	7.1	6.3	434.8	75.9
Colorado	54,300	14.5	6.7	6.5	294.7	77.0
Connecticut	44,300	13.5	9.0	7.2	383.7	76.9
Delaware	10,300	14.3	8.8	7.5	582.5	74.8
Florida	188,700	13.3	10.8	7.5	466.3	75.8
Georgia	112,300	15.6	8.1	9.4	329.5	73.6
Hawaii	18,600	15.7	6.4	5.8	430.1	78.2
Idaho	18,000	15.5	7.3	6.1	111.1	76.9
Illinois	185,800	15.7	9.2	9.4	366.0	74.9
Indiana	82,800	14.3	9.2	8.4	169.1	75.4
Iowa	36,800	13.0	9.9	8.2	163.0	77.3
Kansas	37,200	14.5	9.3	7.0	268.8	76.8
Kentucky	52,400	13.6	9.6	7.6	152.7	74.4
Louisiana	65,600	15.1	9.1	9.8	228.7	73.0
Maine	13,900	11.2	9.5	6.5	215.8	73.1
Maryland	72,400	14.4	8.3	8.9	428.2	76.4
Massachusetts	81,600	13.4	9.1	5.2	502.5	74.8
Michigan	134,600	14.1	8.8	8.3	364.0	75.0
Minnesota	63,300	13.7	8.1	6.7	237.0	77.8
Mississippi	41,300	15.3	10.0	10.5	72.6	73.0
Missouri	73,000	13.7	10.2	7.4	150.7	75.3
Montana	11,100	12.8	8.9	7.0	270.3	76.2
Nebraska	23,200	14.2	9.3	7.4	172.4	76.9
Nevada	25,000	16.4	8.2	5.7	640.0	74.2
New Hampshire	14,700	12.8	8.0	5.5	204.1	76.7
New Jersey	114,800	14.5	9.3	6.6	531.4	75.4
New Mexico	26,900	16.0	7.4	6.2	185.9	75.7
New York	271,400	15.0	9.3	7.7	648.5	74.7
North Carolina	101,600	14.1	9.0	9.2	344.5	74.5
North Dakota	8,500	13.2	9.3	7.2	117.6	77.6
Ohio	154,100	13.8	9.5	8.7	266.1	75.3
Oklahoma	45,700	13.9	10.0	8.3	196.9	75.1
Oregon	42,800	13.6	9.0	6.1	373.8	76.4
Pennsylvania	151,800	12.6	10.6	7.8	270.1	75.4
Rhode Island	12,800	12.9	9.8	7.2	468.8	76.5
South Carolina	50,900	13.9	9.1	9.6	216.1	73.5
South Dakota	10,500	14.4	9.5	9.5	95.2	76.9
Tennessee	73,200	13.9	9.8	9.3	245.9	74.3
Texas	322,800	17.2	7.4	6.5	275.7	75.1
Utah	39,600	20.3	5.6	5.4	101.0	77.7
Vermont	6,800	11.6	8.5	6.0	294.1	76.5
Virginia	92,600	14.0	8.0	7.8	334.8	75.2
Washington	77,200	14.2	7.5	5.9	323.8	76.8
West Virginia	21,200	11.6	11.1	7.9	141.5	74.3
Wisconsin	67,500	13.2	8.8	7.3	192.6	76.9
Wyoming	6,300	13.0	7.7	7.7	...	76.2
District						
District of Columbia	9,000	16.3	12.4	16.2	2,333.3	68.0
TOTAL/RATE	3,899,400	14.8	8.8	7.6	349.8	75.8

Major causes of death per 100,000 population (1997[7]): cardiovascular diseases 353.9, of which ischemic heart disease 177.3, cerebrovascular diseases 60.0, atherosclerosis 10.0; malignant neoplasms (cancers) 202.4; diseases of the respiratory system 72.0, of which pneumonia 31.2; accidents and adverse effects 34.1, of which motor-vehicle accidents 16.5; diabetes mellitus 23.3; suicide 11.5; AIDS 10.6; chronic liver disease and cirrhosis 9.3.

Death rates by major causes (1996)

States	Total rate of death per 100,000 population	Circulatory diseases	Cancer	Pulmonary diseases	Suicide and homicide	Other
Alabama	1,002.3	382.8	222.4	40.7	24.0	332.4
Alaska	425.4	108.4	106.4	18.6	26.7	165.3
Arizona	826.4	284.3	187.9	48.1	26.5	279.6
Arkansas	1,057.2	423.0	237.5	44.5	22.4	329.8
California	700.9	265.9	160.2	35.8	20.3	218.7
Colorado	672.9	216.5	147.9	43.3	23.8	241.4
Connecticut	902.8	362.9	218.2	37.0	14.2	270.5
Delaware	897.2	325.6	232.9	38.5	21.3	278.9
Florida	1,065.6	414.0	261.8	53.5	23.3	313.0
Georgia	799.0	296.1	169.1	34.4	21.8	277.6
Hawaii	671.4	258.7	157.2	20.2	14.2	221.1
Idaho	732.7	258.2	167.1	40.1	19.1	248.2
Illinois	895.6	352.5	209.2	36.8	19.7	277.4
Indiana	906.9	355.5	214.0	44.6	19.4	259.7
Iowa	976.2	401.7	227.7	47.2	11.3	308.2
Kansas	929.3	354.4	207.8	44.0	18.6	279.9
Kentucky	959.7	373.2	232.4	50.1	18.6	303.7
Louisiana	909.9	329.6	214.1	33.1	30.5	279.3
Maine	944.3	343.6	237.4	53.0	13.8	333.5
Maryland	827.3	287.7	200.4	34.7	21.8	254.1
Massachusetts	908.2	331.5	229.0	40.1	8.0	324.5
Michigan	871.6	352.0	204.1	38.4	20.0	271.3
Minnesota	798.3	280.4	189.9	36.1	10.5	259.3
Mississippi	982.4	414.1	212.0	37.1	25.2	282.8
Missouri	1,006.0	410.5	223.2	46.7	22.9	324.8
Montana	876.4	306.1	201.1	61.9	24.0	283.1
Nebraska	937.2	371.8	201.3	47.4	11.4	307.5
Nevada	822.4	290.7	199.1	55.5	33.7	237.2
New Hampshire	808.2	310.0	205.3	42.4	11.8	214.7
New Jersey	916.4	352.6	229.3	35.2	7.3	361.4
New Mexico	728.4	232.2	159.9	38.1	29.5	218.8
New York	904.0	390.4	209.8	33.6	14.8	257.7
North Carolina	905.3	344.1	207.5	41.1	21.6	282.2
North Dakota	934.1	370.6	216.3	43.4	12.0	281.4
Ohio	941.6	366.8	226.7	45.9	9.4	303.6
Oklahoma	1,003.3	416.1	215.9	47.4	22.2	301.7
Oregon	902.5	321.2	209.5	51.2	20.9	299.7
Pennsylvania	1,072.3	434.0	253.1	44.9	17.7	322.6

Death rates by major causes (1996) (continued)

States	Total rate of death per 100,000 population	Circulatory diseases	Cancer	Pulmonary diseases	Suicide and homicide	Other
Rhode Island	964.0	388.8	254.1	41.4	8.4	271.3
South Carolina	920.7	350.1	206.0	39.4	23.6	301.6
South Dakota	828.0	365.9	210.4	40.1	18.9	192.7
Tennessee	966.8	380.7	218.4	43.2	23.1	301.4
Texas	731.7	273.3	167.3	33.3	19.9	237.9
Utah	555.5	186.5	105.2	23.0	14.3	226.5
Vermont	827.3	307.1	205.0	41.3	11.2	262.7
Virginia	801.5	298.6	190.4	33.9	20.4	258.2
Washington	763.7	275.0	181.9	40.0	18.7	248.1
West Virginia	1,118.4	453.2	255.9	80.2	20.1	309.0
Wisconsin	874.9	346.6	203.2	38.8	11.6	274.7
Wyoming	748.2	252.1	180.5	50.9	18.3	246.4
District						
District of Columbia	1,219.4	365.6	254.0	29.8	59.8	510.2
U.S. RATE	872.5	336.7	203.4	40.0	29.5	262.9

Morbidity rates of infectious diseases per 100,000 population (1997): chlamydia 196.8; gonorrhea 121.4; chicken pox 35.0; AIDS 21.8; syphilis 17.6; salmonellosis 15.6; shigellosis 8.6; hepatitis A (infectious) 11.2; tuberculosis 7.4; lyme disease 4.8; hepatitis B (serum) 3.9; pertussis 2.5.

Leading cause of death by age group (1996)

	Number of deaths			Total death rate (per 100,000 population)	Percentage of all deaths
	Total	Male	Female		
All ages[8]	2,314,690	1,163,569	1,151,121	872.5	100.0
1 to 4 years	5,948	3,349	2,599	38.3	0.26
Accidents	638	1,290	857	13.8	0.03
Malignant neoplasms	424	246	178	2.7	0.02
Homicide	420	214	206	2.7	0.02
Circulatory diseases	217	111	106	1.4	0.01
HIV infection	147	74	77	0.9	0.01
5 to 14 years	8,330	5,003	3,327	21.7	0.36
Accidents	3,433	2,183	1,250	8.9	0.15
Malignant neoplasms	1,023	582	446	2.7	0.04
Homicide	514	311	203	1.3	0.02
Circulatory diseases	499	181	153	1.3	0.02
Suicide	302	225	77	0.8	0.01
15 to 24 years	32,433	24,313	8,130	89.6	1.40
Accidents	13,809	10,273	3,536	38.1	0.6
Homicide	6,548	5,655	893	18.1	0.28
Suicide	4,358	3,724	634	12.0	0.19
Malignant neoplasms	1,632	955	677	4.5	0.07
Circulatory diseases	1,373	843	530	3.9	0.06
25 to 44 years	147,180	100,374	46,806	175.7	6.36
Accidents	27,092	20,273	6,819	32.3	1.17
Malignant neoplasms	21,894	9,996	11,898	26.1	0.95
HIV infection	21,865	17,505	4,180	25.9	0.94
Circulatory diseases	20,009	13,561	6,448	23.9	0.86
Suicide	12,602	10,148	4,802	15.0	0.54
45 to 64 years	378,054	232,041	146,013	703.6	16.33
Malignant neoplasms	131,455	69,965	61,490	244.7	5.68
Circulatory diseases	130,684	86,974	43,710	243.2	5.65
Accidents	16,717	11,826	4,891	31.1	0.72
Diabetes mellitus	12,887	6,802	5,885	23.6	0.56
Liver disease and cirrhosis	10,743	7,708	3,035	20.0	0.46
65 and over	1,713,725	782,151	931,574	5,061.1	74.04
Circulatory diseases	844,157	374,051	470,106	2,493.0	36.47
Malignant neoplasms	382,988	200,096	182,892	1,131.1	16.55
Pneumonia and influenza	74,979	32,721	42,258	221.4	3.24
Diabetes mellitus	46,376	19,244	27,132	137.0	2.00
Accidents	30,830	15,197	15,633	91.0	1.33

Incidence of chronic health conditions per 1,000 population (1994): chronic sinusitus 133.9; arthritis 128.3; deformities or orthopedic impairments 119.2; hypertension 108.3; hay fever 100.3; hearing impairment 85.9; heart conditions 85.5; asthma 55.9; chronic bronchitis 53.8; migraine 43.2.

Social indicators

Educational attainment (1996). Percentage of population age 25 and over having: some primary 9.3%; incomplete secondary 16.5%; secondary 35.1%; some postsecondary 25.5%; 4-year higher degree or more 13.6%. Number of earned degrees (1995): bachelor's degree 1,192,000; master's degree 405,000; doctor's degree 43,000; first-professional degrees (in fields such as medicine, theology, and law) 77,000.

Distribution of income (1995)

percentage of disposable household income by quintile

1	2	3	4	5 (highest)
4.8	10.4	16.0	23.0	46.5

Quality of working life (1996). Average workweek: 39.2 hours. Annual rate per 100,000 workers for (1995): injury or accident 2,720; death 4.0. Proportion of labour force insured for damages or income loss resulting from: injury, permanent disability, and death (1988) 56.6%. Average days per 1,000 workdays lost to labour stoppages (1996): 1.6. Average duration of journey to work (1990): 22.4 minutes (private automobile 94.7%, of which drive alone 80.0%, carpool 14.7%; take public transportation 5.3%). Rate per 1,000 employed workers of discouraged workers (unemployed no longer seeking work; 1992): 6.9.

Access to services (1995). Proportion of occupied dwellings having access to: electricity, virtually 100.0%; safe public water supply 99.4% (12.6% from wells); public sewage collection 77.0%; septic tanks 22.8%.
Social participation. Eligible voters participating in last presidential election (2000): 51.2%. Population age 18 and over participating in voluntary work (1995): 48.8%. Trade-union membership in total workforce (1996): 14.5%. Practicing religious population in total affiliated population (church attendance; 1987) once a week 47%; once in six months 67%; once a year 74%.
Social deviance (1997). Offense rate per 100,000 population for: murder 6.8; rape 35.9; robbery 186.0; aggravated assault 382.0; motor-vehicle theft 506.0; burglary and housebreaking 920.0; larceny-theft 2,887; drug-abuse violation 434.2 (1995); drunkenness 200.2 (1995). Drug and substance users (population age 26 and over; 1994): alcohol 41.2%; tobacco (cigarettes) 33.5%; marijuana 16.0%; cocaine 0.4%; analgesics 1.3%; tranquilizers 0.2%; stimulants 0.4%; hallucinogens 1.2%; heroin, n.a. Rate per 100,000 population of suicide (1997): 11.5.

Crime rates per 100,000 population in metropolitan areas[9] (1999)

		violent crime			
	total	murder	rape	robbery	assault
Atlanta	2,794	35.6	79.9	1,014	1,665
Baltimore[10]	2,420	43.4	66.7	1,199	1,111
Boston	1,308	5.6	60.7	444	797
Chicago	...	22.9	...	731	1,172
Dallas	1,434	17.7	61.6	591	764
Detroit	2,277	43.0	81.8	811	1,342
Houston	1,166	13.1	40.5	452	660
Los Angeles	1,290	11.7	35.4	397	845
Miami	2,129	17.1	30.6	833	1,248
Minneapolis	1,399	13.3	128	593	665
New York	1,063	9.0	22.9	486	545
Pittsburgh	904	14.5	41.0	469	379
St. Louis	2,279	38.9	43.1	836	1,361
San Francisco	878	8.6	25.8	465	378
Washington, D.C.	1,628	46.4	47.8	644	889

		property crime		
	total	burglary	larceny	auto theft
Atlanta	11,015	2,134	7,058	1,824
Baltimore[10]	8,363	1,772	5,363	1,227
Boston	5,009	615	3,176	1,218
Chicago	6,198	1,083	3,988	1,126
Dallas	8,317	1,824	4,834	1,659
Detroit	8,246	1,894	3,579	2,774
Houston	5,973	1,340	3,579	1,053
Los Angeles	3,320	592	2,049	679
Miami	8,717	1,985	5,182	1,550
Minneapolis	7,299	1,574	4,631	1,094
New York	2,969	545	1,890	534
Pittsburgh	5,404	925	3,531	949
St. Louis	12,007	2,352	7,665	1,990
San Francisco	4,923	740	3,383	800
Washington, D.C.	6,434	976	4,176	1,282

Leisure (1992). Favourite leisure activities (percentage of total population age 18 and over that undertook activity at least once in the previous year): movie 59.0%, amusement park 50.0%, sports event 37.0%, live theatre 31.0%, art museum 27.0%; reading literature 54.0%, playing sports 39.0%.
Material well-being (1995). Occupied dwellings with householder possessing: automobile 84.9%[11]; telephone 93.9%; radio receiver 99.0%; television receiver 98.3%; air conditioner 68.4%[12]; washing machine 77.1%[12]; videocassette recorder 81.0%; cable television 63.4%.
Recreational expenditures (1995): U.S.$401,700,000,000 (television and radio receivers, computers, and video equipment 23.2%; sports supplies 10.9%; nondurable toys and sports equipment 10.6%; golfing, bowling, and other participatory activities 9.2%; magazines and newspapers 6.3%; books and maps 5.2%; spectator amusements 5.0%, of which theatre and opera 2.2%, movies 1.4%, spectator sports 1.3%; flowers, seeds, and potted plants 3.5%).

National economy

Budget (1999). Revenue: U.S.$1,827,300,000,000 (individual income tax 48.1%, social-insurance taxes and contributions 33.5%, corporation income tax 10.1%, other 8.3%). Expenditures: U.S.$1,704,500,000,000 (social security and medicare 34.0%, defense 16.2%, income security 13.9%, interest on debt 13.5%, health 8.3%, other 14.1%).
Total national debt (1999): U.S.$5,606,500,000,000.

Manufacturing, mining, and construction enterprises (1995)

	no. of enterprises[13]	no. of employees	hourly wages as a % of all wages	value added (U.S.$'000,000)
Manufacturing				
Chemical and related products	12,109	839,000	135.2	196,906
Food and related products	20,624	1,525,000	104.0	180,975
Electric and electronic machinery	15,962	1,534,000	101.1	173,920
Machinery, except electrical	52,135	1,926,000	114.9	172,945
Transportation equipment	10,500	1,523,000	144.7	172,926
Printing and publishing	...	1,534,000	...	125,936
Fabricated metal products	36,105	1,465,000	105.3	102,672
Instruments and related products	10,326	809,000	111.2	92,534
Paper and related products	6,342	630,000	125.5	79,836
Rubber and plastic products	14,515	1,018,000	95.8	73,023
Primary metals	6,771	688,000	127.8	69,594
Stone, clay, and glass products	16,166	503,000	108.4	42,424
Lumber and wood	33,982	741,000	88.9	40,937
Apparel and related products	22,872	950,100	66.3	39,519
Textile-mill products	6,412	606,800	81.8	32,705
Petroleum and coal products	2,254	110,000	167.5	31,580
Furniture and fixtures	11,613	514,000	85.6	26,238
Tobacco products	138	31,300	191.6	24,715
Leather and leather products	2,193	86,000	69.7	4,126
Miscellaneous manufacturing industries	16,544	397,000	87.2	25,672

Manufacturing, mining, and construction enterprises (1995) (continued)

	no. of enterprises[13]	no. of employees	hourly wages as a % of all wages	value added (U.S.$'000,000)
Mining				
Oil and gas extraction	20,891[14]	320,700	127.9	79,700[14]
Coal mining	3,060[14]	105,300	159.9	17,283[14]
Nonmetallic, except fuels	5,804[14]	109,900	117.3	9,619[14]
Metal mining	1,023[14]	52,100	145.5	7,180[14]
Construction				
Special trade contractors	367,800[14]	3,383,500	134.6	122,422[14]
Heavy construction contractors	37,300[14]	814,200	129.5	49,066[14]
General contractors and operative builders	168,200[14]	1,251,100	123.4	63,743[14]

Gross national product (1999): U.S.$9,288,200,000,000 (U.S.$34,030 per capita).

Structure of gross domestic product and labour force

	1998			
	in value U.S.$'000,000,000	% of total value	labour force[15]	% of labour force[15]
Agriculture	125.2	1.4	3,378,000	2.4
Mining	105.9	1.2	620,000	0.4
Manufacturing	1,432.8	16.4	20,733,000	15.0
Construction	373.2	4.3	8,518,000	6.2
Public utilities	216.6	2.5	9,307,000 (Public utilities and Transp. and commun.)	6.8
Transp. and commun.	542.5	6.2		
Trade[16]	1,395.7	15.9	27,203,000	19.8
Finance	1,674.2	19.1	8,605,000	6.2
Public administration, defense	1,100.1	12.6	5,887,000	4.3
Services	1,841.3	21.0	47,212,000	34.3
Other	−47.6	−0.5	6,210,000[17]	4.5[17]
TOTAL	8,759.9	100.0[18]	137,673,000	100.0[18]

Gross domestic product and national income

(in U.S.$'000,000,000)

	1995	1996	1997	1998	1999
Gross domestic product	7,245.8	7,576.1	8,110.9	8,511.0	9,299.2
By type of expenditure					
Personal consumption expenditures	4,924.3	5,151.4	5,493.7	5,807.9	6,268.7
Durable goods	606.4	632.1	673.0	724.7	761.3
Nondurable goods	1,486.1	1,545.1	1,600.6	1,662.4	1,845.5
Services	2,831.6	2,974.3	3,220.1	3,420.8	3,661.9
Gross private domestic investment	1,066.3	1,117.0	1,256.0	1,367.1	1,650.1
Fixed investment	1,028.2	1,101.5	1,188.6	1,307.8	1,606.8
Changes in business inventories	33.7	15.4	67.4	59.3	43.3
Net exports of goods and services	−114.2	−98.7	−93.4	−151.2	−254.0
Exports	774.8	855.2	965.4	959.0	990.2
Imports	888.9	953.9	1,058.8	1,110.2	1,224.2
Government purchases of goods and services	1,260.7	1,406.4	1,454.6	1,487.1	1,634.4
Federal	472.7	523.1	520.2	520.6	568.6
State and local	788.8	886.8	934.4	966.5	1,003.8
By major type of product					
Goods output	2,697.4	2,799.8	2,978.5	3,104.0	3,510.2
Durable goods	1,179.8	1,232.3	1,343.8	1,416.2	1,687.3
Nondurable goods	1,517.6	1,567.5	1,634.8	1,687.8	1,831.9
Services	3,920.8	4,105.2	4,414.1	4,641.0	4,934.6
Structures	627.6	671.1	718.3	765.9	854.3
National income (incl. capital consumption adjustment)	5,799.2	6,164.2	6,646.5	6,994.7	7,469.7
By type of income					
Compensation of employees	4,209.1	4,448.5	4,687.2	4,981.0	5,299.8
Proprietors' income	478.3	527.7	551.2	577.2	663.5
Rental income of persons	122.2	150.2	158.2	162.6	143.4
Corporate profits	588.6	670.2	817.9	824.6	856.0
Net interest	401.0	403.3	432.0	449.3	507.1
By industry division (excl. capital consumption adjustment)					
Agriculture, forestry, fishing	94.0	114.1	106.0	104.2	109.2
Mining and construction	301.2	325.9	357.6	381.1	433.1
Manufacturing	1,026.3	1,069.1	1,150.0	1,168.7	1,193.3
Durable	597.1	628.6	659.4	684.2	704.6
Nondurable	429.3	440.5	491.6	484.4	488.7
Transportation	189.4	196.5	208.0	216.2	236.9
Communications	136.6	148.5	139.3	149.3	161.9
Public utilities	125.0	126.5	133.6	135.3	135.9
Wholesale and retail trade	805.6	857.8	927.4	989.2	1,077.0
Finance, insurance, real estate	991.9	1,037.0	1,192.0	1,273.5	1,366.9
Services	1,335.9	1,441.1	1,513.6	1,624.9	1,782.9
Government and government enterprise	820.3	843.1	877.5	906.3	953.2
Other	−7.0	−8.9	−8.0	−20.4	−11.0

Business activity (1996): number of businesses 23,241,000 (sole proprietorships 73.0%, active corporations 19.9%, active partnerships 7.1%), of which services 10,088,000, wholesaling and retailing 4,461,000; business receipts $16,775,000,000,000 (active corporations 88.8%, sole proprietorships 5.0%, active partnerships 6.2%), of which wholesaling and retailing U.S.$4,856,000,000,000, services U.S.$1,945,000,000,000; net profit U.S.$1,128,000,000,000 (active corporations 71.4%, sole proprietorships 15.7%, partnerships 12.9%), of which services U.S.$190,000,000,000, wholesaling and retailing U.S.$95,000,000,000. New business starts and business failures (1995): total number of new business starts 168,158; total failures 71,194, of which commercial service 21,850, retail trade 12,952; failure rate per 10,000 concerns 90.0; current liabilities of failed concerns U.S.$37,507,000,000; average liability U.S.$526,830. Business expenditures for new plant and equipment (1995): total U.S.$594,465,000,000, of which trade, services, and communications U.S.$244,829,000,000, manufacturing businesses U.S.$172,308,000,000 (durable goods 53.0%, nondurable goods 47.0%), public utilities U.S.$42,816,000,000, transportation U.S.$37,021,000,000, mining and construction U.S.$35,985,000.

Components of gross domestic product (1996)

States	Gross state product (U.S.$'000,000,000)	Personal income (U.S.$'000,000,000)	Disposable personal income (U.S.$'000,000,000)	Per capita disposable personal income (U.S.$)
Alabama	99.2	86.0	76.3	18,334
Alaska	24.2	14.9	13.0	21,707
Arizona	111.5	94.6	83.2	19,345
Arkansas	56.4	47.5	41.9	17,304
California	962.7	808.2	696.4	22,674
Colorado	116.2	98.2	82.4	22,751
Connecticut	124.0	111.7	92.2	29,598
Delaware	28.3	20.1	17.2	24,430
Florida	360.5	348.9	308.0	21,894
Georgia	216.0	168.9	147.1	20,620
Hawaii	36.3	30.1	26.5	22,531
Idaho	27.9	23.6	20.5	17,687
Illinois	370.8	318.1	274.1	23,855
Indiana	155.8	131.9	114.6	20,166
Iowa	76.3	63.6	55.1	20,014
Kansas	68.0	59.7	52.0	20,879
Kentucky	95.4	76.8	66.9	17,918
Louisiana	121.1	85.6	76.9	18,384
Maine	28.9	26.1	22.9	19,256
Maryland	143.2	140.0	128.0	24,386
Massachusetts	208.6	181.4	150.9	25,990
Michigan	263.3	239.3	209.0	21,794
Minnesota	141.6	119.5	101.1	22,205
Mississippi	56.4	47.6	43.5	16,532
Missouri	145.1	123.3	108.0	20,706
Montana	18.5	16.9	15.0	17,465
Nebraska	47.2	37.9	32.9	20,503
Nevada	53.7	41.7	35.8	22,742
New Hampshire	34.1	31.1	27.4	24,438
New Jersey	278.4	250.2	212.0	27,422
New Mexico	42.7	32.2	28.9	17,327
New York	613.3	529.9	450.4	25,713
North Carolina	204.2	162.6	141.1	20,099
North Dakota	15.7	13.2	11.7	17,837
Ohio	304.4	262.2	228.9	21,093
Oklahoma	72.8	64.5	57.2	18,006
Oregon	87.0	73.9	63.4	20,517
Pennsylvania	328.5	299.2	261.5	22,434
Rhode Island	25.6	24.3	21.1	22,297
South Carolina	89.5	74.0	65.5	18,147
South Dakota	20.3	15.3	13.9	19,195
Tennessee	140.8	116.9	105.0	20,390
Texas	551.8	426.2	375.2	20,868
Utah	50.4	39.1	33.7	17,370
Vermont	14.6	13.2	11.7	20,401
Virginia	197.8	168.4	144.4	22,388
Washington	159.6	139.5	122.1	23,154
West Virginia	37.2	33.2	29.8	16,803
Wisconsin	139.2	120.4	103.3	20,634
Wyoming	16.8	10.4	9.1	19,801
District				
District of Columbia	51.2	18.4	15.7	30,372
TOTAL/AVERAGE	7,633.0	6,480.4	5,624.3	21,908

Retail and wholesale trade and services (1996)

	no. of establishments[14]	no. of employees[19]	hourly wage as a % of all wages[19]	annual sales or receipts (U.S.$'000,000)
Retail trade	1,564,200	20,988,000	66.9	2,445,300
Automotive dealers	198,400	2,228,300	91.4	592,900
Food stores	182,500	3,376,600	70.5	423,300
General merchandise group stores	36,700	2,466,200	65.8	312,800
Eating and drinking places	449,100	7,432,500	46.6[20]	236,500
Gasoline service stations	99,300	647,100	60.5	155,000
Building materials, hardware, garden supply, and mobile home dealers	69,900	888,800	79.4	134,500
Furniture, home furnishings, equipment stores	114,500	937,900	88.4	133,500
Apparel and accessory stores	142,400	1,085,700	65.4	113,700
Drugstores and proprietary stores	45,700	607,800	77.5	90,700
Liquor stores	29,500	112,200	...	22,800
Wholesale trade	495,500[21]	6,367,000	107.7	2,420,700
Durable goods	313,500[21]	3,693,000	111.5	1,245,800
Professional and commercial equipment	46,800[21]	768,700	133.5	231,400
Motor vehicles, automotive equipment	47,300[21]	498,000	98.1	211,100
Machinery, equipment, and supplies	73,900[21]	774,300	112.5	187,300
Electrical goods	39,300[21]	477,400	116.2	173,800
Metals and minerals, except petroleum	11,200[21]	140,300	110.5	98,400
Lumber and other construction materials	19,500[21]	242,700	102.5	85,800
Hardware, plumbing, heating equipment and supplies	24,700[21]	290,600	105.8	70,500
Furniture and home furnishings	16,500[21]	149,600	97.7	43,600
Miscellaneous durable goods	34,300[21]	327,200	88.5	143,900
Nondurable goods	182,000[21]	2,674,000	102.3	1,174,900
Groceries and related products	42,900[21]	890,700	105.4	315,400
Petroleum and petroleum products	16,100[21]	166,400	96.6	177,800
Farm-products raw materials	11,600[21]	109,000	78.1	130,200
Drugs, drug proprietaries, and druggists' sundries	6,100[21]	197,100	128.2	102,900
Paper and paper products	19,700[21]	262,700	106.7	82,700
Apparel and accessories	19,600[21]	212,700	100.4	75,500
Beer, wine, and distilled alcoholic beverages	5,300[21]	155,900	116.3	56,400
Chemicals and allied products	14,200[21]	140,100	116.4	53,500
Miscellaneous nondurable goods	43,700[21]	539,800	84.5	180,500

Retail and wholesale trade and services (1996) (continued)

	no. of establishments[14]	no. of employees[19]	hourly wage as a % of all wages[19]	annual sales or receipts (U.S.$'000,000)
Services	2,342,300	33,106,000	98.4	1,826,200[19]
Health	476,200	9,280,900	108.0	382,600[19]
Business, except computer services	273,500	6,628,100	92.9	272,100[19]
Computer and data-processing services	66,800	1,043,300	154.0	152,200[19]
Legal services	161,600	946,200	140.0	114,400[19]
Automotive repair, services, garages	178,400	1,031,200	86.4	98,300[19]
Management and public relations	61,300	813,200	125.5	89,700[19]
Hotels and motels	53,500	1,724,400	68.1	86,300[19]
Amusement and recreation	90,800	1,720,600	73.2	77,400[19]
Engineering services	42,600	579,000	154,7	76,600[19]
Personal services	201,800	1,115,000	65.6	69,900[19]
Motion pictures	42,700	601,700	121.8	58,100[19]

Daily consumption of water (1995)

(in gallons)

States	Total consumption ('000,000,000)	Per capita	Irrigation	Public consumption	Industrial processes	Thermo-electric
Alabama	6,967	1,670	139	875	753	5,200
Alaska	318	350	1	90	197	30
Arizona	6,775	1,620	5,670	846	197	62
Arkansas	8,326	3,540	5,940	419	187	1,780
California	45,072	1,130	28,900	5,740	802	9,630
Colorado	13,738	3,590	12,700	732	191	115
Connecticut	4,427	389	28	448	11	3,940
Delaware	1,483	1,050	48	101	64	1,270
Florida	18,079	509	3,470	2,360	649	11,600
Georgia	5,718	799	722	1,250	676	3,070
Hawaii	1,860	853	652	218	20	970
Idaho	13,330	13,000	13,000	254	76	...
Illinois	19,757	1,680	180	1,950	527	17,100
Indiana	9,000	1,570	116	784	2,410	5,690
Iowa	2,888	1,070	39	418	301	2,130
Kansas	5,101	2,040	3,380	384	77	1,260
Kentucky	4,358	1,150	12	521	375	3,450
Louisiana	9,506	2,270	769	677	2,580	5,480
Maine	314	178	27	135	16	136
Maryland	7,655	289	57	907	331	6,360
Massachusetts	5,499	189	82	759	88	4,570
Michigan	11,997	1,260	227	1,490	1,910	8,370
Minnesota	3,258	736	157	573	438	2,090
Mississippi	2,786	1,140	1,740	377	294	375
Missouri	6,937	1,320	567	757	63	5,550
Montana	8,813	10,200	8,550	161	80	22
Nebraska	10,403	6,440	7,550	328	175	2,350
Nevada	2,241	1,480	1,640	479	95	27
New Hampshire	1,296	388	6	130	50	1,110
New Jersey	6,091	269	125	1,120	486	4,360
New Mexico	3,451	2,080	2,990	337	69	55
New York	16,591	567	30	3,140	321	13,100
North Carolina	8,983	1,070	239	939	385	7,420
North Dakota	1,038	1,750	117	85	17	819
Ohio	10,427	944	27	1,560	650	8,190
Oklahoma	1,870	543	864	597	285	124
Oregon	7,130	2,520	6,170	572	379	9
Pennsylvania	9,606	802	16	1,730	1,930	5,930
Rhode Island	406	138	2	121	7	275
South Carolina	6,180	1,690	53	614	703	4,810
South Dakota	403	631	269	97	32	5
Tennessee	10,023	1,920	24	831	868	8,300
Texas	29,290	1,300	9,450	3,420	2,920	13,500
Utah	4,337	2,200	3,530	506	253	48
Vermont	534	967	4	66	12	452
Virginia	8,183	826	30	911	622	6,620
Washington	8,798	1,620	6,470	1,300	652	376
West Virginia	4,557	2,530	...	217	1,330	3,010
Wisconsin	7,134	1,420	169	692	453	5,820
Wyoming	7,028	14,700	6,590	100	118	220
District						
District of Columbia	10	18	...	...	1	10
TOTAL/AVERAGE	389,972	1,280	133,538	43,118	26,126	187,190

Production. Agriculture, forestry, fishing (value of production/catch in U.S.$'000,000 except as noted; 1999): corn (maize) 17,950, soybeans 12,451, wheat 5,904, cotton lint 3,836, grapes 2,943, potatoes 2,783, tobacco 2,329, oranges 1,807, apples 1,679, rice 1,257, sugar beets 1,181[22], strawberries 1,118[22], sugarcane 1,061, peanuts (groundnuts) 992, sorghum 971, head lettuce 971, tomatoes 820, mushrooms 709, almonds 677, onions 654, carrots 642, dry beans 588, cottonseed 562, barley 553, bell peppers 466, peaches 464, sweet corn 458, broccoli 455, cantaloupes 393, sunflower seeds 354, grapefruit 339, avocados 332, pears 297, pecans 274, watermelons 268, lemons 260, green beans 255; livestock (number of live animals; 1999) 98,500,000 cattle, 62,206,000 pigs, 7,235,000 sheep, 6,000,000 horses, 1,400,000,000 chickens; roundwood (1998) 420,458,000 cu m; fish and shellfish catch (1997) 3,467, of which fish 1,722 (including salmon 270, Alaska pollack 243), shellfish 1,744 (including shrimp 544, crabs 429). Mining (metal content in metric tons except as noted; 1996): iron 39,342,000; copper 1,910,000; zinc 620,000; lead 430,000; molybdenum 57,000; vanadium 2,700; mercury 550; silver 1,800,000 kg; gold 325,000 kg; helium 101,000,000 cu m. Quarrying (metric tons; 1996): crushed stone 1,300,000,000; sand and gravel 992,000,000; cement 75,000,000; clay 44,000,000; phosphate rock 43,000,000; common salt 40,000,000; gypsum 17,000,000; lime 18,900,000. Manufacturing (1996): motor vehicles 329,155; industrial machinery 135,393; electronic components 127,996; computers and office equipment 103,270; meat products 102,103; aircraft 83,394; commercial printing 67,842; medical instruments 47,406; cigarettes 28,987; household furniture 25,426; photographic equipment 22,297; household appliances 22,157; missiles and space vehicles 17,928; ships and boats 15,634; toys and sporting goods 14,748; audio and video equipment 11,266. Construction (completed; 1996): private U.S.$427,776,000,000, of which residential U.S.$246,899,000,000, nonresidential U.S.$140,692,000,000; public U.S.$141,132,000,000.

Energy production (consumption): electricity (kW-hr; 1994) 3,268,250,000,000 (3,312,888,000,000); coal (metric tons; 1994) 937,580,000 (843,873,000); crude petroleum (barrels; 1994) 2,464,000,000 (5,024,000,000); petroleum products (metric tons; 1994) 704,201,000 (737,681,000); natural gas (cu m; 1994) 530,014,000,000 (592,209,000,000). Domestic production of energy by source (1994): coal 31.2%, natural gas 27.6%, crude petroleum 19.9%, other[23] 21.3%.

Energy consumption by sector

('000,000,000,000 Btu)

States	Total	Residential	Commercial	Industrial	Trans-portation	Per capita ('000,000 Btu)
Alabama	1,975.1	353.2	182.6	991.3	448.0	457.3
Alaska	696.8	49.5	66.7	419.2	161.4	1,143.6
Arizona	1,114.9	251.6	238.2	226.8	398.3	244.7
Arkansas	1,012.9	195.3	119.4	430.2	268.0	401.5
California	7,697.1	1,340.4	1,193.5	2,289.7	2,873.5	238.5
Colorado	1,133.5	255.0	240.2	302.4	335.9	291.2
Connecticut	824.5	254.7	189.9	164.4	215.5	252.2
Delaware	273.2	57.3	42.8	106.0	67.1	373.4
Florida	3,579.4	1,002.7	761.1	582.0	1,233.6	244.3
Georgia	2,634.5	561.8	391.9	835.7	845.1	351.9
Hawaii	241.9	21.5	23.8	76.3	120.3	203.9
Idaho	491.1	91.1	82.9	202.0	115.1	405.8
Illinois	3,897.4	986.5	722.4	1,356.5	832.0	327.6
Indiana	2,663.7	503.5	301.9	1,242.7	615.6	454.2
Iowa	1,090.7	240.5	156.3	417.5	276.4	382.4
Kansas	1,060.0	210.9	183.3	389.3	276.5	408.5
Kentucky	1,776.8	327.7	199.6	848.0	401.5	454.6
Louisiana	3,994.9	326.6	222.0	2,617.3	829.0	918.0
Maine	538.4	102.1	57.8	271.9	106.6	433.5
Maryland	1,349.2	387.6	322.3	277.7	361.6	264.8
Massachusetts	1,533.5	426.4	371.3	312.9	422.9	250.7
Michigan	3,249.2	795.9	577.8	1,099.5	776.0	332.4
Minnesota	1,688.9	377.8	227.5	635.6	448.0	360.4
Mississippi	1,098.4	205.3	117.5	432.4	343.2	402.3
Missouri	1,744.8	459.4	337.1	374.8	573.5	323.0
Montana	395.1	70.4	55.6	167.6	101.5	449.6
Nebraska	604.4	140.5	123.2	160.1	180.6	364.8
Nevada	575.3	108.9	88.8	198.1	179.5	343.2
New Hampshire	302.2	83.9	55.6	78.9	83.8	257.7
New Jersey	2,574.8	565.3	520.4	655.0	834.1	319.8
New Mexico	595.2	87.5	101.8	217.5	188.4	344.1
New York	4,129.6	1,104.7	1,118.9	949.8	956.2	227.7
North Carolina	2,416.5	583.1	414.1	773.3	646.0	325.4
North Dakota	351.9	61.7	46.5	168.2	75.5	549.1
Ohio	4,115.7	930.8	649.2	1,640.5	895.2	367.9
Oklahoma	1,405.6	273.1	196.2	550.3	386.0	423.8
Oregon	1,108.1	234.9	180.0	386.3	306.9	341.8
Pennsylvania	3,927.3	935.8	607.8	1,477.9	905.8	326.7
Rhode Island	235.9	72.1	52.2	52.4	59.2	238.9
South Carolina	1,426.8	291.5	191.0	614.1	330.2	379.4
South Dakota	244.8	61.8	41.1	61.5	80.4	331.6
Tennessee	2,067.8	475.3	139.4	905.1	548.0	385.2
Texas	11,278.2	1,310.2	1,080.4	6,542.3	2,345.3	580.2
Utah	674.4	120.0	106.5	254.2	193.7	327.5
Vermont	162.5	46.1	27.3	36.7	52.4	275.7
Virginia	2,115.3	518.7	451.9	532.5	612.2	314.1
Washington	1,835.3	435.5	321.2	757.8	320.8	380.6
West Virginia	803.4	150.9	97.2	391.1	164.2	442.5
Wisconsin	1,791.6	403.6	278.9	708.8	400.3	346.0
Wyoming	423.1	41.0	44.5	235.3	102.3	882.1
District						
Dist. of Columbia	177.4	38.3	110.0	3.2	25.9	335.4
TOTAL/AVERAGE	93,398.5	18,930.0	14,429.2	35,420.3	24,619.0	349.0

Energy consumption by source (1994): petroleum and petroleum products 38.8%, natural gas 24.0%, coal 22.0%, other[23] 15.2%; by end use: industrial 38.0%, residential and commercial 35.0%, transportation 26.5%.

Energy consumption by source

('000,000,000,000 Btu)

States	Petroleum	Natural gas	Coal	Hydroelectric power	Nuclear electric power
Alabama	562.5	336.3	887.5	114.6	315.6
Alaska	224.0	443.6	11.2	13.1	...
Arizona	427.4	121.7	343.2	98.0	306.4
Arkansas	309.7	277.7	260.2	28.9	141.9
California	3,341.9	1,865.1	53.9	487.6	362.2
Colorado	412.2	314.7	340.3	17.6	...
Connecticut	412.5	131.5	24.4	15.7	66.1
Delaware	139.0	55.9	50.8	0.0	...
Florida	1,629.6	510.7	694.5	2.2	270.6
Georgia	1,017.1	392.2	725.6	51.6	317.9
Hawaii	221.4	2.8	3.6	1.1	...
Idaho	159.4	69.0	7.3	138.9	...
Illinois	1,272.8	1,140.6	906.9	1.1	741.2
Indiana	859.2	579.8	1,372.1	4.6	...
Iowa	371.3	274.3	380.5	9.7	41.7
Kansas	379.7	362.0	338.6	0.1	87.2
Kentucky	599.1	248.0	951.8	36.2	...
Louisiana	1,612.2	1,737.7	205.6	10.0	167.5
Maine	253.2	5.8	5.9	76.3	53.8
Maryland	518.2	198.1	292.2	25.4	128.5
Massachusetts	690.7	367.5	113.1	16.8	56.6
Michigan	998.4	1,026.7	789.3	26.2	285.0
Minnesota	638.6	375.1	345.5	92.9	128.5
Mississippi	424.0	277.4	128.1	0.0	98.0
Missouri	721.1	297.5	629.7	12.8	94.4
Montana	175.3	63.2	135.7	143.0	...
Nebraska	235.6	133.8	179.0	16.6	100.5
Nevada	216.1	127.6	169.5	22.4	...
New Hampshire	156.6	19.4	36.2	29.2	104.6
New Jersey	1,228.0	624.6	62.4	0.0	117.1
New Mexico	209.4	228.2	279.2	2.2	...
New York	1,569.3	1,159.9	294.3	343.3	374.2

Energy consumption by source (continued)

('000,000,000,000 Btu)

States	Petroleum	Natural gas	Coal	Hydroelectric power	Nuclear electric power
North Carolina	885.1	220.8	687.0	66.2	358.2
North Dakota	119.8	51.5	404.1	40.8	...
Ohio	1,236.6	972.0	1,448.8	4.1	147.9
Oklahoma	469.6	580.2	349.9	21.5	...
Oregon	363.9	175.3	20.3	491.3	...
Pennsylvania	1,329.3	752.7	1,432.3	23.2	729.5
Rhode Island	97.3	87.7	0.1	9.4	...
South Carolina	445.1	154.1	352.5	23.6	462.9
South Dakota	116.7	37.4	33.2	82.5	...
Tennessee	690.9	289.3	648.6	111.6	243.5
Texas	5,166.4	4,123.0	1,475.4	9.9	379.9
Utah	251.6	167.8	355.0	10.8	...
Vermont	85.2	7.4	...	41.0	40.4
Virginia	792.9	248.4	378.8	6.2	279.2
Washington	842.1	247.5	90.9	1,045.5	59.4
West Virginia	257.6	164.5	898.3	14.8	...
Wisconsin	550.0	408.0	452.8	29.3	107.5
Wyoming	145.5	107.6	473.0	12.7	...
District					
District of Columbia	35.4	34.2	0.6	0.0	...
TOTAL	35,886.2	22,598.1	20,519.6	3,881.3	7,167.6

Household income[24] level by selected characteristics (1997)

Characteristics	Number of households ('000)	Number ('000) Under $15,000	$15,000–$34,999	$35,000–$74,999	$75,000 and over	Median income ($)
Total/Average	102,528	19,622	28,830	35,229	18,847	37,005
Age of householder						
15 to 24 years	5,435	1,736	2,175	1,270	254	22,583
25 to 34 years	19,033	2,937	5,630	7,882	2,584	38,174
35 to 44 years	23,943	2,867	5,702	9,899	5,475	46,359
45 to 54 years	19,547	2,194	4,044	7,490	5,818	51,875
55 to 64 years	13,072	2,311	7,294	4,468	3,044	41,356
65 years and over	21,497	7,575	8,031	4,219	1,671	20,761
Size of household						
One person	26,327	10,863	9,141	5,082	1,241	18,762
Two persons	32,965	4,204	10,354	12,108	6,299	39,343
Three persons	17,331	2,068	4,047	7,080	4,136	47,115
Four persons	15,358	1,324	2,973	6,629	4,432	53,165
Five persons	7,048	336	1,448	2,968	1,906	50,407
Six persons	2,232	253	535	914	530	46,465
Seven or more persons	1,276	184	330	447	305	42,343
Educational attainment of householder						
Total[25]	97,093	17,886	26,656	33,958	18,594	38,190
Less than 9th grade	7,369	3,567	2,507	1,065	231	15,541
Some high school	9,686	3,723	3,382	2,138	443	19,851
High school graduate	30,739	5,911	9,974	11,446	3,409	33,779
Some college, no degree	17,225	2,514	5,020	6,654	3,038	40,015
Associate degree	7,263	806	1,840	3,099	1,518	45,258
Bachelor's degree	16,098	985	2,880	6,601	5,633	59,048
Master's degree	5,735	276	785	2,130	2,544	68,115
Professional degree	1,693	56	146	474	1,017	92,228
Doctorate degree	1,285	48	123	353	762	87,232

Household income and expenditure. Average household size (1997) 2.6; average (median) annual income per household U.S.$37,005, of which average white household U.S.$35,766, average Hispanic[4] household U.S.$22,860, average black household U.S.$22,393; sources of income: wages and salaries 55.8%, transfer payments 16.5%, self-employment 7.9%, other 19.8%; expenditure: transportation 18.6%, housing 18.4%, food 14.0%, fuel and utilities 6.8%, household furnishings 5.9%, recreation 5.5%, health 5.4%, wearing apparel 5.3%, education 1.5%, other 18.6%.

Financial aggregates

	1993	1994	1995	1996	1997	1998	1999
Exchange rate, U.S.$ per:							
£[26]	1.50	1.53	1.58	1.56	1.65	1.66	1.62
SDR[26]	1.40	1.43	1.52	1.45	1.38	1.36	1.37
International reserves (U.S.$)[27]							
Total (excl. gold; '000,000,000)	62.35	63.28	74.78	64.04	58.91	70.71	60.50
SDRs ('000,000,000)	9.02	10.04	11.04	10.31	10.03	10.60	10.35
Reserve pos. in IMF ('000,000,000)	11.80	12.03	14.65	15.43	18.07	24.11	17.97
Foreign exchange ('000,000,000)	41.53	41.22	49.10	38.29	30.81	36.00	32.18
Gold ('000,000 fine troy oz)	261.79	261.73	261.70	261.66	261.61	261.78	261.67
% world reserves	28.67	28.70	29.00	28.86	29.52	27.09	27.13
Interest and prices							
Central bank discount (%)[27]	3.00	4.75	5.25	5.00	5.00	4.50	5.00
Govt. bond yield (%)[26]	4.44	6.26	6.26	6.44	6.35	5.26	5.49
Industrial share prices[26] (1995 = 100)	80.6	84.1	100.0	123.5	159.3	198.7	251.3
Balance of payments (U.S.$'000,000,000)							
Balance of visible trade	−112.74	−164.33	−158.78	−189.25	−181.87	−231.10	−343.26
Imports, f.o.b.	−580.51	−668.87	−743.52	−803.23	−870.57	−913.60	−1,029.92
Exports, f.o.b.	467.77	504.54	584.71	613.98	688.70	682.50	686.66
Balance of invisibles	3.49	162.83	10.55	40.52	52.58	87.25	5.86
Balance of payments, current account	−109.25	−1.50	−148.23	−148.73	−129.29	−143.85	−337.4

Average employee earnings

	average hourly earnings in U.S.$		average weekly earnings in U.S.$	
	July 1998	July 1999	July 1998	July 1999
Manufacturing				
Durable goods	13.77	14.38	571.46	598.21
Lumber and wood products	11.17	11.51	460.20	474.21
Furniture and fixtures	10.91	11.25	439.67	452.25
Stone, clay, and glass products	13.59	14.01	595.24	612.24
Primary metal industries	15.56	16.04	670.64	699.34
Fabricated metal products	12.88	13.46	535.81	558.59
Machinery, except electrical	14.43	15.06	610.39	628.00
Electrical and electronic equipment	13.13	13.49	533.08	550.39
Transportation equipment	16.86	17.94	691.26	755.27
Instruments and related products	13.78	14.26	560.85	584.66
Miscellaneous manufacturing	10.85	11.30	425.32	442.96
Nondurable goods	12.81	13.22	520.09	536.73
Food and kindred products	11.80	12.15	490.88	507.87
Tobacco manufactures	20.59	21.22	809.19	855.17
Textile mill products	10.36	10.71	418.54	434.83
Apparel and other textile products	8.48	8.83	312.91	325.83
Paper and allied products	15.64	16.07	674.08	691.01
Printing and publishing	13.44	13.80	512.06	524.40
Chemicals and allied products	17.19	17.48	734.01	744.65
Petroleum and coal products	20.83	21.37	933.18	931.73
Rubber and miscellaneous plastics products	11.91	12.36	489.50	506.76
Leather and leather products	9.14	9.56	337.27	350.85
Nonmanufacturing				
Metal mining	18.21	18.23	819.45	833.11
Coal mining	18.95	19.51	811.06	852.59
Oil and gas extraction	16.61	17.03	712.57	740.81
Nonmetallic minerals, except fuels	14.85	15.16	709.83	717.07
Construction	16.66	17.23	669.73	687.48
Transportation and public utilities	15.27	15.73	606.22	613.47
Wholesale trade	14.04	14.54	537.73	558.34
Retail trade	8.69	9.02	258.96	268.80
Finance, insurance, and real estate	13.94	14.53	503.23	524.53
Hotels, motels, and tourist courts	8.73	9.01	280.23	284.72
Health services	13.69	14.20	453.14	467.18
Legal services	18.05	19.00	628.14	663.10
Miscellaneous services	17.79	18.16	610.20	631.97

Median household income[24]

(in constant 1997 U.S.$)

States	1987	1990	1995	1996	1997
Alabama	27,881	28,682	27,372	30,997	31,939
Alaska	46,953	48,258	50,503	53,990	47,944
Arizona	37,792	35,887	32,503	32,363	32,740
Arkansas	26,600	27,981	27,186	27,745	26,162
California	42,592	40,880	38,976	39,703	39,694
Colorado	37,407	37,740	42,870	41,890	43,233
Connecticut	46,429	47,732	42,382	43,085	43,985
Delaware	41,317	37,827	36,784	40,211	43,033
Florida	34,599	32,769	31,326	31,344	32,455
Georgia	37,743	33,845	35,911	33,242	36,663
Hawaii	49,481	47,795	45,129	42,730	40,934
Idaho	29,324	31,075	34,413	35,505	33,404
Illinois	38,266	39,962	40,094	40,462	41,283
Indiana	31,816	33,068	35,159	35,953	38,889
Iowa	31,351	33,510	37,407	33,971	33,783
Kansas	36,145	36,738	31,954	33,333	36,471
Kentucky	29,208	30,430	31,394	33,157	33,452
Louisiana	30,163	27,513	29,434	30,956	33,260
Maine	33,343	33,726	35,658	35,492	32,772
Maryland	49,407	47,717	43,222	45,002	46,685
Massachusetts	45,552	44,511	40,624	40,400	40,023
Michigan	39,139	36,763	38,362	40,125	38,742
Minnesota	39,676	38,639	39,949	41,932	42,564
Mississippi	26,156	24,779	27,948	27,289	28,499
Missouri	33,513	33,564	36,676	35,051	36,553
Montana	28,927	28,705	29,232	29,342	29,212
Nebraska	32,874	33,748	34,679	34,794	34,692
Nevada	37,975	39,324	38,002	39,424	38,854
New Hampshire	45,689	50,109	41,253	40,311	40,998
New Jersey	48,377	47,565	46,259	48,557	48,021
New Mexico	29,328	30,748	27,372	25,662	30,086
New York	37,277	38,794	34,783	36,222	35,798
North Carolina	32,157	32,332	33,679	36,418	35,840
North Dakota	31,897	31,024	30,635	32,192	31,661
Ohio	36,413	36,856	36,798	34,852	36,134
Oklahoma	30,646	29,944	27,709	28,067	31,351
Oregon	35,375	35,957	38,307	36,306	37,247
Pennsylvania	35,920	35,618	36,359	35,700	37,517
Rhode Island	39,972	39,257	37,238	37,835	34,797
South Carolina	35,391	35,287	30,616	35,460	34,262
South Dakota	29,883	30,173	31,150	30,203	29,694
Tennessee	29,923	27,743	30,557	31,496	30,636
Texas	34,927	34,664	33,742	33,831	35,075
Utah	37,482	37,014	38,419	37,888	42,775
Vermont	35,908	38,188	35,622	33,100	35,053
Virginia	42,380	43,070	38,147	40,111	42,957
Washington	38,598	39,434	37,458	37,518	44,562
West Virginia	24,311	27,184	26,202	25,826	27,488
Wisconsin	37,255	37,713	43,132	40,919	39,595
Wyoming	38,981	36,177	33,205	31,663	33,423
District					
District of Columbia	38,790	33,637	32,382	32,699	31,860
U.S. AVERAGE	36,714	36,770	35,887	36,306	37,005

Average annual expenditure of "consumer units" (households, plus individuals sharing households or budgets; 1995): total U.S.$32,277, of which housing U.S.$10,465, transportation U.S.$6,016, food U.S.$4,505, pensions and social security U.S.$2,593, health care U.S.$1,732, clothing U.S.$1,704, other U.S.$5,262.

Selected household characteristics (1996). Total number of households 99,627,000, of which (by race) white 84.8%, black 11.6%, other 3.6%; in central cities 31.4%[14], in suburbs 46.3%[14], outside metropolitan areas 22.3%[14]; (by tenure[14]) owned 64,045,000 (64.7%), rented 34,946,000 (35.3%); family households 69,594,000, of which married couple 76.9%, female head with own children[28] under age 18, 11.0%, female head without own children[28] under 18, 7.0%; nonfamily households 30,033,000, of which female living alone 48.6%, male living alone 34.2%, other 17.2%.

Population economically active (1998): total 137,673,000[15]; activity rate of total population 50.9% (participation rates: ages 15–64, 77.4%; female 46.2%; unemployed 4.5%).

Price and earnings indexes (1995 = 100)

	1993	1994	1995	1996	1997	1998	1999
Consumer price index	94.8	97.3	100.0	102.9	105.3	107.0	109.3
Hourly earnings index[29]	95.0	97.5	100.0	103.3	106.4	109.1	...

Tourism (1997): receipts from visitors U.S.$94,163,000,000; expenditures by nationals abroad U.S.$69,455,000,000; number of foreign visitors 47,754,000 (15,127,000 from Canada, 8,433,000 from Mexico, 10,390,000 from Europe); number of nationals traveling abroad 52,735,000 (17,700,000 to Mexico, 13,401,000 to Canada).

Land use (1994): forested 32.3%; meadows and pastures 26.1%; agricultural and under permanent cultivation 20.5%; other 21.0%.

Foreign trade

Balance of trade (current prices)

	1994	1995	1996	1997	1998	1999
U.S.$'000,000,000	–151.3	–158.8	–189.2	–181.9	–231.1	–343.3
% of total	12.9%	12.0%	13.4%	–11.7%	14.5%	20.0%

Imports (1997): U.S.$870,670,700,000 (machinery and transport equipment 44.9%, of which motor vehicles and parts 16.3%; wearing apparel 5.8%; chemicals and chemical products 5.6%; petroleum and petroleum products 4.7%; food and live animals 2.6%). *Major import sources:* Canada 19.3%; Japan 14.0%; Mexico 9.9%; China 7.2%; Germany 5.0%; United Kingdom 3.8%; Taiwan 3.7%; South Korea 2.7%; Singapore 2.3%; France 2.3%; Italy 2.2%; Malaysia 2.1%; Thailand 1.4%; Hong Kong 1.2%; Brazil 1.1%.

Exports (1997): U.S.$689,182,400,000 (machinery and transport equipment 46.4%, of which motor vehicles and parts 15.7%; chemicals and related products 9.4%; scientific and precision equipment 5.4%; food and live animals 4.5%). *Major export destinations:* Canada 22.0%; Japan 9.5%; Mexico 10.4%; United Kingdom 5.3%; South Korea 3.6%; Germany 3.5%; Taiwan 3.0%; The Netherlands 2.9%; Singapore 2.6%; France 2.3%; Hong Kong 2.2%; Belgium 1.9%.

Trade by commodity group (1996)

	imports		exports	
SITC Group	U.S.$'000,000	%	U.S.$'000,000	%
00 Food and live animals	31,114[30]	3.8[30]	45,774	7.3
01 Beverages and tobacco	7,031	0.9	8,025	1.3
02 Crude materials, excluding fuels	22,871	2.8	32,253	5.2
03 Mineral fuels, lubricants, and related materials	77,126	9.4	12,512	2.0
04 Animal and vegetable oils, fat, and waxes	[30]	[30]	1,743	0.3
05 Chemicals and related products, n.e.s.	45,799	5.6	61,202	9.8
06 Basic manufactures	98,861	12.1	57,025	9.2
07 Machinery and transport equipment	368,994	45.1	305,749	49.1
08 Miscellaneous manufactured articles	136,598	16.7	67,820	10.9
09 Goods not classified by kind	29,580	3.6	30,682	4.9
TOTAL	817,627[31]	100.0	622,784[31]	100.0

Direction of trade (1997)

	imports		exports	
	U.S.$'000,000	%	U.S.$'000,000	%
Africa	21,165	2.4	11,380	1.6
South Africa	2,616	0.3	3,000	0.4
Other Africa	18,549	2.1	8,380	1.2
Americas	315,761	35.1[18]	284,533	41.4[18]
Canada	171,440	19.1	150,134	21.8
Caribbean countries and Central America	18,581	2.1	19,319	2.8
Mexico	87,167	9.7	71,738	10.4
South America	38,573	4.3	43,342	6.3
Asia	366,350	40.8[18]	213,862	31.1[18]
China	65,832	7.3	12,805	1.9
Japan	124,266	13.8	65,673	9.6
Other Asia	176,252	19.6	135,384	19.7
Europe	194,189	21.6	168,320	24.5
EU	162,628	18.1	140,825	20.5
Russia	4,524	0.5	3,289	0.5
Other Europe	27,037	3.0	24,206	3.5
Oceania	6,927	0.8[18]	14,313	2.1
Australia	4,911	0.5	12,041	1.8
Other Oceania	2,016	0.2	2,272	0.3
TOTAL	898,661[31]	100.0[31]	687,581[31]	100.0[31]

Transport and communications

Transport. Railroads (1997): length[14] 137,900 mi, 222,000 km; passenger-mi 14,000,000,000, passenger-km 22,500,000,000; short ton-mi cargo 1,421,000,000,000, metric ton-km cargo 2,075,000,000. Roads (1997): total length 3,944,597 mi, 6,348,226 km (paved 91.0%). Vehicles (1997): passenger cars 129,749,000; trucks and buses 78,005,000. Merchant marine (1996): vessels (1,000 gross tons and over) 509; total deadweight tonnage 18,585,000. Air transport (1995): passenger-mi 540,400,000,000, passenger-km 869,700,000,000; short ton-mi cargo 14,568,400,000, metric ton-km cargo 21,269,500,000; localities (1996) with scheduled flights 834[32]. Certified route passenger/cargo air carriers (1992) 77; operating revenue (U.S.$'000,000; 1991) 74,942, of which domestic 56,119, international 18,823; operating expenses 76,669, of which domestic 56,596, international 20,073.

Intercity passenger and freight traffic by mode of transportation (1993)

	cargo traffic ('000,000,000 ton-mi)	% of nat'l total	passenger traffic ('000,000,000 passenger-mi)	% of nat'l total
Rail	1,183	38.1	14	0.7
Road	871	28.0	1,718	81.7
Inland water	467	15.1	—	—
Air	12	0.4	370	17.6
Petroleum pipeline	572	18.4	—	—
TOTAL	3,105	100.0	2,102	100.0

Communications

Medium	date	unit	number	units per 1,000 persons
Daily newspapers	1996	circulation	57,100,000	215
Radio	1997	receivers	575,000,000	2,116
Television	1998	receivers	231,000,000	849
Telephones	1998	main lines	179,822,000	661
Cellular telephones	1998	subscribers	85,018,000	312
Personal computers	1998	units	124,000,000	456
Internet	1998	users	60,000,000	220

Other communications media (1996)

	titles
Print	
Books (new)	46,898
of which	
Agriculture	443
Art	1,511
Biography	2,238
Business	1,266
Education	1,215
Fiction	3,919
General works	2,061
History	2,466
Home economics	1,027
Juvenile	4,291
Language	592
Law	764
Literature	2,412
Medicine	2,866
Music	322
Philosophy, psychology	1,749
Poetry, drama	1,119
Religion	2,725
Science	2,576
Sociology, economics	8,180
Sports, recreation	1,198
Technology	1,572
Travel	386
Periodicals[10]	3,731
of which	
Agriculture	153
Business and economics	262
Chemistry and physics	170
Children's periodicals	78
Education	203
Engineering	265
Fine and applied arts	145
General interest	181
History	151
Home economics	90
Industrial arts	106
Journalism and commun.	90
Labour and industrial relations	70
Law	273
Library and information sciences	118
Literature and language	158
Mathematics and science	238
Medicine	182
Philosophy and religion	130
Physical education and recreation	151
Political science	136
Psychology	138
Sociology and anthropology	149
Zoology	94
Cinema[19]	
Feature films	419

	traffic
Cellular telephones	
Number of subscribers	44,043,000

	(pieces of mail)
Post	
Mail	182,661,000,000
Domestic	181,662,000,000
International	999,000,000

Education and health

Literacy: studies in the late 1980s indicated that adult "functional" literacy may not exceed 85%.

Education (1995–96)

	schools	teachers	students	student/teacher ratio
Primary (age 5–13)[33]	85,393[34]	1,784,000	33,410,000	18.7
Secondary and vocational (age 14–17)		1,187,000	17,390,000	14.6
Higher, including teacher-training colleges	5,758[35]	833,000	14,210,000	17.1

Food (1997): daily per capita caloric intake 3,699 (vegetable products 73%, animal products 27%); 140% of FAO recommended minimum requirement. Per capita consumption of major food groups (kilograms annually; 1995): milk 255.7; fresh fruits 123.2; cereal products 114.5; fresh vegetables 110.4; red meat 74.8; sweeteners 69.3; potatoes 58.7; poultry products 43.8; fats and oils 30.8; fish and shellfish 21.8.

Health (1995): doctors of medicine 720,300[36] (1 per 365 persons), of which office-based practice 427,300 (including specialties in internal medicine 17.0%, general and family practice 14.0%, pediatrics 7.9%, obstetrics and gynecology 6.8%, general surgery 5.6%, psychiatry 5.4%, anesthesiology 5.6%, orthopedics 4.0%, ophthalmology 4.3%); doctors of osteopathy 35,700; nurses 2,116,000 (1 per 124 persons); dentists 190,000 (1 per 1,385 persons); hospital beds 1,081,000 (1 per 243 persons), of which nonfederal 92.9% (community hospitals 80.8%, psychiatric 10.2%, long-term general and special 1.8%), federal 7.1%; infant mortality rate per 1,000 live births (1997) 7.1.

Physicians and nurses (1997)[37]

States	Physicians Total	Physicians Rate per 100,000 population	Nurses Total	Nurses Rate per 100,000 population
Alabama	8,399	194	33,200	768
Alaska	975	160	6,700	1,099
Arizona	9,094	200	34,600	760
Arkansas	4,622	185	18,500	733
California	78,502	244	178,500	555
Colorado	9,099	234	31,300	796
Connecticut	11,236	344	33,000	1,010
Delaware	1,688	230	8,000	1,088
Florida	34,100	232	123,700	843
Georgia	15,292	204	54,700	730
Hawaii	3,001	252	9,100	763
Idaho	1,817	150	7,200	596
Illinois	30,373	253	107,200	894
Indiana	11,238	192	47,600	812
Iowa	4,885	171	29,900	1,048
Kansas	5,246	202	22,300	857
Kentucky	8,018	205	31,500	806
Louisiana	10,364	239	33,600	772
Maine	2,663	214	13,300	1,071
Maryland	18,469	362	43,400	852
Massachusetts	24,597	402	72,900	1,192
Michigan	21,329	218	81,100	829
Minnesota	11,590	247	48,200	1,028
Mississippi	4,273	156	20,600	754
Missouri	12,175	225	52,300	967
Montana	1,655	188	7,300	831
Nebraska	3,530	213	15,100	911
Nevada	2,837	169	10,400	620
New Hampshire	2,694	230	11,100	947
New Jersey	23,101	287	66,500	825
New Mexico	3,595	209	12,000	696
New York	68,107	375	169,500	934
North Carolina	16,688	225	65,500	881
North Dakota	1,401	219	7,200	1,123
Ohio	25,688	230	103,000	920
Oklahoma	5,514	166	19,900	599
Oregon	7,152	221	27,500	848
Pennsylvania	33,849	282	129,800	1,081
Rhode Island	3,199	324	11,400	1,155
South Carolina	7,609	201	29,200	771
South Dakota	1,309	177	7,500	1,017
Tennessee	12,983	242	47,300	881
Texas	37,987	196	127,100	656
Utah	4,060	197	13,300	644
Vermont	1,698	288	5,200	883
Virginia	15,708	233	55,600	825
Washington	12,859	229	44,000	784
West Virginia	3,806	210	15,400	848
Wisconsin	11,630	224	46,400	892
Wyoming	801	167	4,400	917
District				
District of Columbia	3,722	702	8,600	1,623
TOTAL/AVERAGE	656,197	245	2,203,000	823

Military

Total active duty personnel (1998): 1,401,600 (army 34.2%, navy 27.2%, air force 26.4%, marines 12.2%). *Military expenditure as percentage of GNP* (1995): 3.8% (world 2.8%); per capita expenditure U.S.$1,056. *Military aid* (1993): total $4,143,000,000 (Middle East 76.2%, of which Israel 43.4%, Egypt 31.4%; Europe 20.8%, of which Turkey 10.9%; Latin America 1.8%).

[1]Excludes 5 delegates having only committee voting rights. [2]Total area per most recent official survey equals 3,675,267 sq mi (9,518,898 sq km). [3]Includes military personnel residing overseas. [4]Persons of Hispanic origin may be of any race. [5]Fiscal year ending Sept. 30, 1996. [6]1996. [7]Data for 12-month period ending February 28. [8]Includes deaths with age not known. [9]Estimated crimes include unreported crimes. [10]1997. [11]1988. [12]1993. [13]1987. [14]1994. [15]Excludes military personnel overseas. [16]Includes hotels. [17]Unemployed. [18]Detail does not add to total given because of rounding. [19]1995. [20]Excludes tips. [21]1992. [22]1998. [23]Includes hydroelectric, nuclear, and geothermal power. [24]Gross income from all sources, including transfer payments to individuals. [25]Householder 25 years old or older. [26]Period average. [27]End-of-year. [28]"Own children" includes adopted children and stepchildren. [29]Manufacturing sector only. [30]Animal and vegetable oils included in Food and live animals. [31]Detail does not add to total given because of statistical discrepancies in the data. [32]Includes 292 localities in Alaska. [33]Primary includes kindergarten. [34]1993–94. [35]1992–93. [36]646,000 professionally active. [37]Nonfederal physicians and nurses only.

Internet resources for further information:

- **U.S. Census Bureau http://www.census.gov**
- **1996 Statistical Abstract http://www.census.gov/prod/2/gen/96statab/96statab.html**

Uruguay

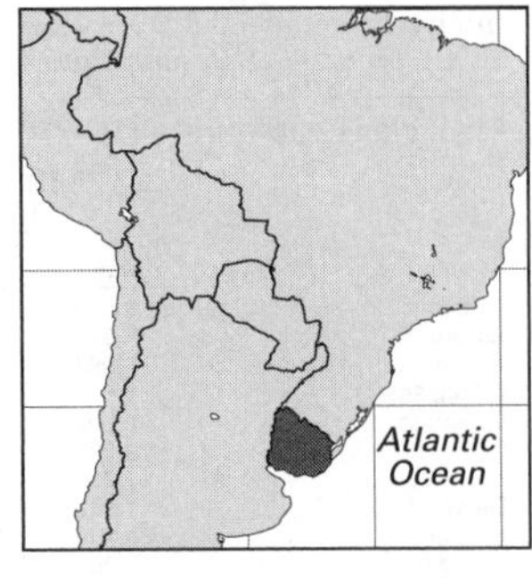

Official name: República Oriental del Uruguay (Oriental Republic of Uruguay).
Form of government: republic with two legislative houses (Senate [31][1]; Chamber of Representatives [99]).
Head of state and government: President.
Capital: Montevideo.
Official language: Spanish.
Official religion: none.
Monetary unit: 1 peso uruguayo[2] = 100 centesimos; valuation (Oct. 6, 2000) 1 U.S.$ = Ur$12.38;
1 £ = Ur$17.92.

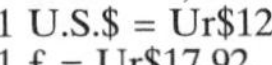

Area and population		area		population
Departments	**Capitals**	sq mi	sq km	1996 census
Artigas	Artigas	4,065	11,928	75,786
Canelones	Canelones	1,751	4,536	410,524
Cerro Largo	Melo	5,270	13,648	81,218
Colonia	Colonia del Sacramento	2,358	6,106	117,380
Durazno	Durazno	4,495	11,643	56,986
Flores	Trinidad	1,986	5,144	25,348
Florida	Florida	4,022	10,417	68,257
Lavalleja	Minas	3,867	10,016	60,618
Maldonado	Maldonado	1,851	4,793	113,884
Montevideo	Montevideo	205	530	1,378,705
Paysandú	Paysandú	5,375	13,922	107,706
Río Negro	Fray Bentos	3,584	9,282	48,730
Rivera	Rivera	3,618	9,370	97,959
Rocha	Rocha	4,074	10,551	71,492
Salto	Salto	5,468	14,163	115,244
San José	San José de Mayo	1,927	4,992	91,874
Soriano	Mercedes	3,478	9,008	83,741
Tacuarembó	Tacuarembó	5,961	15,438	84,078
Treinta y Tres	Treinta y Tres	3,679	9,529	49,846
TOTAL LAND AREA		67,574	175,016	
INLAND WATER		463	1,199	
TOTAL		68,037	176,215	3,139,376

Demography

Population (2000): 3,278,000.
Density (2000): persons per sq mi 48.2, persons per sq km 18.6.
Urban-rural (1996): urban 88.7%; rural 11.3%.
Sex distribution (2000): male 48.51%; female 51.49%.
Age breakdown (2000): under 15, 24.8%; 15–29, 23.4%; 30–44, 19.4%; 45–59, 15.3%; 60–74, 11.9%; 75 and over, 5.2%.
Population projection: (2010) 3,540,000; (2020) 3,794,000.
Ethnic composition (1990): white (mostly Spanish, Italian, or mixed Spanish-Italian) 86.0%; mestizo 8.0%; mulatto or black 6.0%.
Religious affiliation (1997): Roman Catholic 78.5%[3]; Protestant 4.5%; other Christian 3.5%; Jewish 0.9%; other 12.6%.
Major cities (1985): Montevideo (1996) 1,378,707; Salto 80,823; Paysandú 76,191; Las Piedras 58,288; Rivera 57,316.

Vital statistics

Birth rate per 1,000 population (1999): 16.8 (world avg. 22.6).
Death rate per 1,000 population (1999): 8.8 (world avg. 8.9).
Total fertility rate (avg. births per childbearing woman; 1999): 2.3.
Marriage rate per 1,000 population (1996): 5.6.
Divorce rate per 1,000 population (1996): 2.1.
Life expectancy at birth (1999): male 72.7 years; female 79.2 years.
Major causes of death per 100,000 population (1990): diseases of the circulatory system 378.4; malignant neoplasms 222.8; respiratory diseases 76.3.

National economy

Budget (1998). Revenue: Ur$70,664,000,000 (taxes on goods and services 39.4%, social security contributions 28.6%, income taxes 12.6%, nontax revenue 7.1%, receipts from foreign trade 3.7%). Expenditures: Ur$72,673,000,000 (social security and welfare 61.4%, general public services 7.4%, education 7.0%, health 5.8%, interest payments 4.7%).
Public debt (external, outstanding; 1998): U.S.$5,142,000,000.
Production (metric tons except as noted). Agriculture, forestry, fishing (1999): rice 1,328,000, wheat 377,000, maize 243,000, oranges 186,000, sugarcane 185,000, sunflower seed 161,000; livestock (number of live animals) 15,500,000 sheep, 10,700,000 cattle; roundwood (1998) 6,163,000 cu m; fish catch (1998) 140,609. Mining and quarrying (1997): hydraulic cement 770,000; gypsum 183,000. Manufacturing (value added in U.S.$'000,000; 1995): food products 1,012; beverages 426; chemical products 402; textiles 281; tobacco products 211. Construction (approvals; 1994): residential 301,666 sq m; nonresidential 177,752 sq m. Energy production (consumption): electricity (kW-hr; 1996) 6,666,000,000 (6,538,000,000); crude petroleum, none (13,942,000); petroleum products (metric tons; 1996) 1,821,000 (1,626,000).
Land use (1998): forested and other 15.2%; meadows and pastures 77.3%; agricultural and under permanent cultivation 7.5%.
Household income and expenditure. Avg. household size (1985) 3.3; avg. annual income per household (1985) NUr$266,261[2] (U.S.$2,625); sources of income[4]: wages 53.5%, self-employment 17.0%, transfer payments and other 29.5%; expenditure (1982–83)[5]: food 39.9%, housing 17.6%, transportation and communications 10.4%, health care 9.3%, clothing 7.0%.
Gross national product (1998): U.S.$19,960,000,000 (U.S.$6,070 per capita).

Structure of gross domestic product and labour force	1998		1993	
	in value Ur$'000	% of total value	labour force	% of labour force
Agriculture	18,511,900	8.5	47,700	3.8
Mining	569,800	0.3	2,100	0.2
Manufacturing	38,748,000	17.8	254,300	20.2
Construction	10,621,000	4.9	86,400	6.9
Public utilities	9,990,500	4.6	16,900	1.3
Transp. and commun.	15,871,100	7.3	67,900	5.4
Trade	25,725,000	11.8	231,300	18.3
Finance	58,364,300	26.7	68,400	5.4
Pub. admin., defense	22,148,900	10.1	455,800	36.1
Services	25,876,000	11.8		
Other	–8,282,000[6]	–3.8[6]	30,200[7]	2.4[7]
TOTAL	218,144,500	100.0	1,261,000	100.0

Population economically active (1998): total 1,239,400[8]; activity rate 47.0% (participation rates: ages 14 and over, 60.4%; female 44.0%).

Price and earnings indexes (1995 = 100)	1993	1994	1995	1996	1997	1998	1999
Consumer price index	48.6	70.3	100.0	128.3	153.8	170.4	180.0
Monthly earnings index[8]	49.6	72.4	100.0	115.1	138.2	155.9	167.3

Tourism (1998): receipts U.S.$695,000,000; expenditures U.S.$265,000,000.

Foreign trade[9]

Balance of trade (current prices)	1994	1995	1996	1997	1998	1999
U.S.$'000,000	–706.0	–563.0	–686.9	–704.4	–772.1	–868.4
% of total	15.5%	11.6%	12.3%	11.2%	12.0%	15.9%

Imports (1999): U.S.$3,356,770,000 (machinery and appliances 22.2%; chemical products 14.6%; mineral products 11.6%; transport equipment 9.1%; processed foods 7.1%; synthetic plastics, resins, and rubber 7.0%; metal products 4.8%). *Major import sources* (1998): Argentina 22.0%; Brazil 20.8%; United States 12.1%; France 4.7%; Italy 4.6%; Spain 3.7%.
Exports (1999): U.S.$2,236,848,000 (live animals and live-animal products 30.1%; vegetable products 15.8%; textiles and textile products 11.8%; hides and skins 9.8%; processed foods 5.4%). *Major export destinations* (1998): Brazil 33.8%; Argentina 18.5%; United States 5.7%; Germany 4.0%.

Transport and communications

Transport. Railroads (1996): route length 2,073 km; metric ton-km cargo 180,000,000. Roads (1997): length 8,683 km[10] (paved 30%). Vehicles (1997): passenger cars 516,889; trucks and buses 50,264. Air transport (1996): passenger-km 640,000,000; metric ton-km cargo 62,000,000; airports (1997) 1.

Communications				units
Medium	date	unit	number	per 1,000 persons
Daily newspapers	1996	circulation	950,000	293
Radio	1997	receivers	1,970,000	603
Television	1997	receivers	782,000	239
Telephones	1998	main lines	823,501	250
Cellular telephones	1998	subscribers	196,000	60
Personal computers	1998	units	300,000	91
Internet	1998	users	230,000	70

Education and health

Educational attainment (1996). Percentage of population age 25 and over having: no formal schooling 3.4%; primary education 53.6%; secondary 31.7%; higher 10.1%; unknown 1.2%. *Literacy* (1995 est.): population age 15 and over literate 97.3%; males 96.9%; females 97.7%.

Education (1997)	schools	teachers	students	student/ teacher ratio
Primary (age 6–11)	2,410	16,721	348,195	20.8
Secondary (age 12–17)	413	19,104	192,399	10.1
Vocational	101	...	58,246	...
Higher	2	9,907[11]	79,691[11]	8.0[11]

Health (1999): physicians 12,357 (1 per 263 persons); hospital beds 6,651 (1 per 488 persons); infant mortality rate (1999) 13.5.
Food (1998): daily per capita caloric intake 2,866 (vegetable products 65%, animal products 35%); 107% of FAO recommended minimum requirement.

Military

Total active duty personnel (1999): 25,600 (army 68.8%, navy 19.5%, air force 11.7%). *Military expenditure as percentage of GNP* (1997): 1.4% (world 2.6%); per capita expenditure U.S.$88.

[1]Includes the vice president, who serves as ex officio presiding officer. [2]The peso uruguayo (Uruguayan peso [Ur$]) replaced the new Uruguayan peso (Nur$) on March 1, 1993. [3]About 30–40% of Roman Catholics are estimated to be nonreligious. [4]Salaried employees only. [5]Weights of consumer price index components in Montevideo. [6]Includes indirect taxes less imputed bank service charges. [7]Includes unemployed not previously employed. [8]From urban areas only. [9]Import figures are f.o.b. in balance of trade. [10]Excludes streets under local control. [11]1996.

Internet resources for further information:

- **Instituto Nacional de Estadistica—Uruguay**
http://www.ine.gub.uy/principal.htm
- **Uruguay: Datos Estadisticos**
http://www.rau.edu.uy/uruguay/generalidades/Uy.estad.htm

Uzbekistan

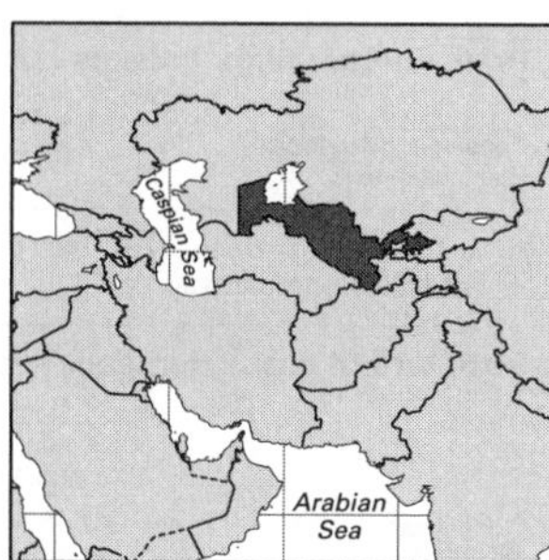

Official name: Ŭzbekiston Respublikasi (Republic of Uzbekistan).
Form of government: multiparty republic with a single legislative body (Supreme Assembly [250]).
Heads of state and government: President assisted by Prime Minister.
Capital: Tashkent (Toshkent).
Official language: Uzbek.
Official religion: none.
Monetary unit: sum (plural sumy); valuation (Oct. 6, 2000) 1 U.S.$ = 775 sumy; 1 £ = 1,121 sumy.

Area and population

		area		population
Autonomous Republic	Administrative centres	sq mi	sq km	1993 estimate
Qoraqalpoghiston	Nuqus	63,700	164,900	1,343,000
Provinces				
Andijon	Andijon	1,600	4,200	1,899,000
Bukhoro	Bukhara (Bukhoro)	15,200	39,400	1,262,000
Farghona	Fergana (Farghona)	2,700	7,100	2,338,000
Jizzakh	Jizzakh	7,900	20,500	831,000
Khorazm	Urganch	2,400	6,300	1,135,000
Namangan	Namangan	3,100	7,900	1,652,000
Nawoiy	Nawoiy	42,800	110,800	715,000
Qashqadaryo	Qarshi	11,000	28,400	1,812,000
Samarqand	Samarkand (Samarqand)	6,300	16,400	2,322,000
Sirdaryo	Guliston	2,000	5,100	600,000
Surkhondaryo	Termiz	8,000	20,800	1,437,000
Tashkent (Toshkent)	Tashkent (Toshkent)	6,000[1]	15,600[1]	2,236,000
City				
Tashkent (Toshkent)	—	[1]	[1]	2,121,000
TOTAL		172,700	447,400	21,703,000

Demography

Population (2000): 24,756,000.
Density (2000): persons per sq mi 143.3, persons per sq km 55.3.
Urban-rural (1999): urban 37.1%; rural 62.9%.
Sex distribution (1999): male 49.55%; female 50.45%.
Age breakdown (1999): under 15, 37.9%; 15–29, 27.7%; 30–44, 19.4%; 45–59, 8.1%; 60–74, 5.5%; 75 and over, 1.4%.
Population projection: (2010) 29,280,000; (2020) 34,465,000.
Doubling time: 39 years.
Ethnic composition (1998): Uzbek 75.8%; Russian 6.0%; Tajik 4.8%; Kazakh 4.1%; Tatar 1.6%; other 7.7%.
Religious affiliation (1995): Muslim (mostly Sunnī) 88.0%; Russian Orthodox 1.0%; Jewish 0.2%; other (mostly nonreligious) 10.8%.
Major cities (1996): Tashkent 2,137,000[2]; Samarkand 362,400; Namangan 362,300; Andijon 319,900; Bukhara 238,200.

Vital statistics

Birth rate per 1,000 population (1999): 26.3 (world avg. 22.1); (1994) legitimate 96.5%; illegitimate 3.5%.
Death rate per 1,000 population (1999): 7.9 (world avg. 8.9).
Natural increase rate per 1,000 population (1999): 18.4 (world avg. 13.2).
Total fertility rate (avg. births per childbearing woman; 1999): 3.1.
Marriage rate per 1,000 population (1994): 7.9.
Divorce rate per 1,000 population (1994): 1.1.
Life expectancy at birth (1999): male 60.3 years; female 67.7 years.
Major causes of death per 100,000 population (1993): diseases of the circulatory system 303.6; diseases of the respiratory system 115.0; accidents, poisoning, and violence 50.0; cancers 48.7; infectious and parasitic diseases 38.4; diseases of the digestive system 31.8; diseases of the nervous system 10.3; endocrine and metabolic disorders 10.3.

National economy

Budget (1998). Revenue: 440,140,000,000 sumy (taxes on income and profits 31.5%, value-added tax 30.2%, excise taxes 18.9%, property and land taxes 12.5%, other 6.9%). Expenditures: 488,297,000,000 sumy (social and cultural affairs 34.2%, investments 19.4%, national economy 11.2%, transfers 9.2%, administration 2.3%, interest on debt 2.0%, other 21.7%).
Household income and expenditure (1995). Average household size (1998) 5.5; income per household 35,165 sumy (U.S.$1,040); sources of income: wages and salaries 63.0%, subsidies, grants, and nonwage income 34.9%, other 2.1%; expenditure: food and beverages 71%, clothing and footwear 14%, recreation 6%, household durables 4%, housing 3%.
Public debt (external, outstanding; 1998): U.S.$2,485,000,000.
Production (metric tons except as noted). Agriculture, forestry, fishing (1999): seed cotton 3,680,000, vegetables 2,800,000, fruit (except grapes) and berries 1,350,000, grapes 650,000, potatoes 649,600, rice 541,000, barley 109,000; livestock (number of live animals) 8,000,000 sheep, 5,225,200 cattle, 697,900 goats, 208,000 pigs, 13,935,000 chickens; roundwood (1990) 15,000 cu m; fish catch (1998) 2,798. Mining and quarrying (1998): copper 89,930; zinc 38,000; uranium 2,000; gold 85. Manufacturing (metric tons except as noted; 1998): cement 3,358,000; cotton fibre 1,138,000; mineral fertilizer 897,000; steel 360,000; ferrous metal products 322,000; television sets 192,468 units; passenger cars 54,456; video recorders 50,096 units; refrigerators 16,000 units; tractors 3,000 units. Construction (1992): residential 7,000,000,000 sq m. Energy production (consumption): electricity (kW-hr; 1998) 46,056,000,000 (46,100,000,000); coal (metric tons; 1998) 2,952,000 (2,792,000); crude petroleum (barrels; 1998) 59,400,000 (57,870,000); petroleum products (metric tons; 1998) 8,104,000 (6,934,000); natural gas (cu m; 1998) 51,245,000,000 (44,246,000,000).
Gross national product (1998): U.S.$22,900,000,000 (U.S.$950 per capita).

Structure of gross domestic product and labour force

	1999			
	in value '000,000 sumy	% of total value	labour force[3]	% of labour force[3]
Agriculture	521,627	26.9	3,091,000	35.0
Manufacturing and mining	283,425	14.6	1,126,000	12.8
Construction	149,803	7.7	578,000	6.5
Transp. and commun.	120,125	6.2	379,000	4.3
Trade	169,344	8.7	716,000	8.1
Finance, Pub. admin., defense, Services	399,882	20.6	2,003,000	22.7
Other	297,903[4]	15.3[4]	938,000[5]	10.6[5]
TOTAL	1,942,109	100.0	8,831,000[6]	100.0

Population economically active (1999): total 8,831,000; activity rate of total population 36.4% (participation rates: ages 16–59 [male], 16–54 [female] 70.4%; female [1994] 43.0%; unemployed 0.6%[7]).

Price and earnings indexes (1995 = 100)

	1994	1995	1996	1997	1998
Consumer price index	44.4	100	...	...	...
Monthly earnings index	28.5	100	202.4	345.5	506.0

Tourism (1997): receipts U.S.$19,000,000.
Land use (1994): forested 2.9%; meadows and pastures 46.5%; agricultural and under permanent cultivation 10.1%; other 40.5%.

Foreign trade

Balance of trade (current prices)

	1993	1994	1995	1996	1997	1998
U.S.$'000,000	–378	+214	+237	–706	–72	+171
% of total	6.2%	3.8%	3.5%	9.1%	1.0%	3.0%

Imports (1998): U.S.$2,717,000,000 (machinery and metalworking products 49.6%, food products 20.9%, other 29.5%). *Major import sources:* Western Europe 30.6%; Russia 20.5%; Asia 14.2%; Kazakhstan 5.2%; Ukraine 3.2%.
Exports (1998): U.S.$2,888,000,000 (cotton fibre 41.5%, energy 22.7%, gold 6.0%, other 29.8%). *Major export destinations:* Western Europe 33.7%; Russia 22.6%; Asia 11.6%; Ukraine 5.4%; Kazakhstan 5.4%; Tajikistan 2.9%; Turkmenistan 2.5%.

Transport and communications

Transport. Railroads (1997): length 3,655 km; (1995) passenger-km 2,500,-000,000; (1995) metric ton-km cargo 16,907,000,000. Roads (1997): total length 84,400 km (paved 87%). Vehicles (1994): passenger cars 865,300; buses 14,500. Air transport (1996): passenger-km 3,460,000,000; metric ton-km cargo 321,000,000; airports (1998) with scheduled flights 9.

Communications

Medium	date	unit	number	units per 1,000 persons
Daily newspapers	1996	circulation	75,000	3.3
Television	1998	receivers	6,600,000	274
Telephones	1999	main lines	1,537,000	65
Cellular telephones	1999	subscribers	26,826	1.1
Internet	1999	users	10,000	0.4

Education and health

Educational attainment (1989). Percentage of population age 25 and over having: primary education or no formal schooling 13.3%; some secondary 19.8%; completed secondary and some postsecondary 57.7%; higher 9.2%. *Literacy* (1997): percentage of total population age 15 and over literate 99.0%.

Education (1995–96)

	schools	teachers	students	student/ teacher ratio
Primary (age 6–13), Secondary (age 14–17)	9,300	413,000	5,090,000	12.3
Voc., teacher tr.[8]	248	22,164[9]	240,100	...
Higher[8]	55	...	272,300	...

Health (1995): physicians 76,000 (1 per 302 persons); hospital beds 192,000 (1 per 120 persons); infant mortality rate per 1,000 live births (1999) 71.6.
Food (1998): daily per capita caloric intake 2,564 (vegetable products 83%, animal products 17%); 100% of FAO recommended minimum requirement.

Military

Total active duty personnel (1999): 74,000 (army 67.6%, air force 5.4%, other 27.0%). *Military expenditure as percentage of GNP* (1996): 2.5% (world 2.6%); per capita expenditure U.S.$62.

[1]Tashkent province includes Tashkent City. [2]1998 estimate. [3]August. [4]Includes value-added taxes: excise taxes plus net import taxes minus subsidies. [5]Includes 882,600 persons on forced leave and 55,400 unemployed. [6]Detail does not add to total given because of rounding. [7]Official unemployment rate. [8]1998. [9]1992–93.

Internet resources for further information:
- **Welcome to Uzbekistan http://www.gov.uz**
- **Republic of Uzbekistan http://www.uzbekistan.org**

Vanuatu

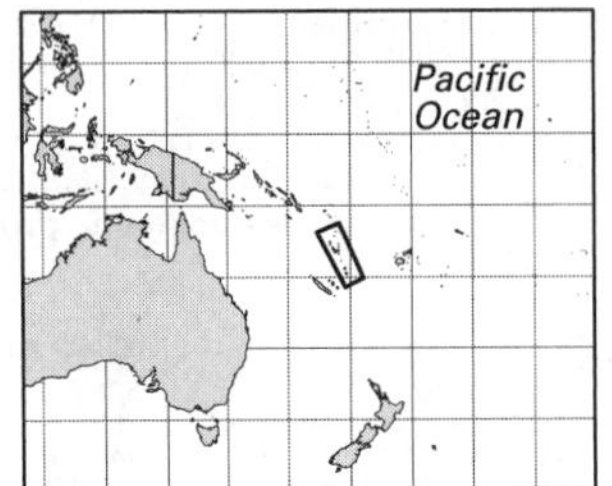

Official name: Ripablik blong Vanuatu (Bislama); République de Vanuatu (French); Republic of Vanuatu (English).
Form of government: republic with a single legislative house (Parliament [52]).
Chief of state: President.
Head of government: Prime Minister.
Capital: Vila.
Official languages: Bislama; French; English.
Official religion: none.
Monetary unit: vatu (VT); valuation (Oct. 6, 2000) 1 U.S.$ = VT 142.93; 1 £ = VT 206.76.

Area and population

		area		population
				1989
Provinces	Capitals	sq mi	sq km	census
Malampa	...	1,073	2,779	28,185
Penama	...	463	1,198	22,299
Sanma	...	1,640	4,248	25,581
Shefa	...	562	1,455	38,471
Tafea	...	628	1,627	22,423
Torba	...	341	882	5,985
TOTAL		4,707	12,190[1]	142,944[2]

Demography

Population (2000): 199,000.
Density (2000): persons per sq mi 42.3, persons per sq km 16.3.
Urban-rural (1999): urban 21.5%; rural 78.5%.
Sex distribution (1999): male 51.36%; female 48.64%.
Age breakdown (1999): under 15, 37.8%; 15–29, 29.4%; 30–44, 18.2%; 45–59, 9.7%; 60–74, 4.0%; 75 and over, 0.9%.
Population projection: (2010) 232,000; (2020) 263,000.
Doubling time: 27 years.
Ethnic composition (1989): Ni-Vanuatu 97.9%; European 1.0%; other Pacific Islanders 0.4%; other 0.7%.
Religious affiliation (1989): Christian 77.2%, of which Presbyterian 35.8%, Roman Catholic 14.5%, Anglican 14.0%, Seventh-day Adventist 8.2%; Custom 4.6%; nonreligious 1.7%; unknown 4.0%; other 12.5%.
Major towns (1999): Vila (Port-Vila) 30,139; Luganville 11,360.

Vital statistics

Birth rate per 1,000 population (1999): 31.7 (world avg. 22.1).
Death rate per 1,000 population (1999): 5.9 (world avg. 8.9).
Natural increase rate per 1,000 population (1999): 25.8 (world avg. 13.2).
Total fertility rate (avg. births per childbearing woman; 1999): 4.2.
Marriage rate per 1,000 population (1985): *c.* 7.4.
Divorce rate per 1,000 population (1985): less than 0.7.
Life expectancy at birth (1999): male 66.0 years; female 70.0 years.
Major causes of death per 100,000 population (1994)[3]: diseases of the circulatory system 39.0; diseases of the respiratory system 30.4; malignant neoplasms (cancers) 29.2; infectious and parasitic diseases 25.0; diseases of the digestive system 9.7.

National economy

Budget (1998). Revenue: VT 8,536,000,000 (taxes on international trade 33.0%; taxes on goods and services 32.0%; foreign grants 20.9%; nontax revenue 10.2%). Expenditures: VT 12,611,000,000 (current expenditure 58.0%, of which general public services 17.2%, education 13.2%, public order and safety 8.4%, health 6.6%, economic affairs and services 5.8%; capital expenditure 42.0%).
Household income and expenditure (1985)[4]. Average household size (1989) 5.1; income per household U.S.$11,299; sources of income: wages and salaries 59.0%, self-employment 33.7%; expenditure (1990)[4, 5]: food and nonalcoholic beverages 30.5%, housing 20.7%, transportation 13.2%, health and recreation 12.3%, tobacco and alcohol 10.4%.
Production (metric tons except as noted). Agriculture, forestry, fishing (1999): coconuts 339,000, roots and tubers 65,000, bananas 12,500, vegetables and melons 9,800, peanuts (groundnuts) 1,750, cacao beans 1,500, corn (maize) 700; livestock (number of live animals) 151,000 cattle, 62,000 pigs, 12,000 goats, 320,000 chickens; roundwood (1998) 63,200 cu m; fish catch (1997) 2,589. Mining and quarrying: small quantities of coral-reef limestone, crushed stone, sand, and gravel. Manufacturing (value added in VT '000,000; 1995): food, beverages, and tobacco 645; wood products 423; fabricated metal products 377; paper products 125; chemical, rubber, plastic, and nonmetallic products 84; textiles, clothing, and leather 54. Construction (approvals in Vila and Luganville; 1992): residential 20,386 sq m; nonresidential 19,876 sq m. Energy production (consumption): electricity (kW-hr; 1996) 30,000,000 (30,000,000); coal, none (none); crude petroleum, none (none); petroleum products (metric tons; 1996) none (20,000); natural gas, none (none).
Land use (1994): forested 75.0%; meadows and pastures 2.0%; agricultural 11.8%; other 11.2%.
Population economically active (1989): total 66,957; activity rate of total population 47.0% (participation rates: ages 15–64, 85.0%; female 46.3%; unemployed 0.5%).

Price and earnings indexes (1995 = 100)

	1993	1994	1995	1996	1997	1998
Consumer price index	95.6	97.8	100.0	100.9	103.8	107.2
Earnings index	...	...	...	...	...	...

Gross national product (at current market prices; 1998): U.S.$231,000,000 (U.S.$1,260 per capita).

Structure of gross domestic product and labour force

	1997		1989	
	in value VT '000,000	% of total value	labour force	% of labour force
Agriculture	7,193	24.7	49,811	74.4
Mining	...	...	1	—
Manufacturing	1,442	5.0	891	1.3
Construction	1,613	5.5	1,302	1.9
Public utilities	500	1.7	109	0.2
Transportation and communications	2,138	7.3	1,031	1.5
Trade	9,551	32.7	2,713	4.1
Finance	2,042	7.0	646	1.0
Pub. admin., defense	3,362	11.5	7,892 }	11.8
Services	1,883	6.5		
Other	–548[6]	–1.9[6]	2,561	3.8
TOTAL	29,176	100.0	66,957	100.0

Public debt (external, outstanding; 1998): U.S.$54,200,000.
Tourism (1998): receipts from visitors U.S.$52,000,000; expenditures by nationals abroad U.S.$8,000,000.

Foreign trade[7]

Balance of trade (current prices)

	1994	1995	1996	1997	1998	1999
VT '000,000	–7,493	–7,486	–7,520	–6,801	–6,934	–6,187
% of total	56.3%	54.1%	52.7%	45.4%	44.5%	39.9%

Imports (1997): VT 10,888,000,000 (machinery and transport equipment 25.7%, food and live animals 19.7%, basic manufactures 15.2%, mineral fuels 10.6%, chemical products 6.2%, beverages and tobacco 3.6%). *Major import sources:* Australia 42.1%; France 13.5%; New Zealand 12.2%; Japan 7.3%; Fiji 6.0%.
Exports (1997): VT 4,087,000,000 (copra 49.0%, timber 12.3%, beef 10.2%, cacao beans 5.9%). *Major export destinations*[8]: European Union 45.9%; Bangladesh 12.6%; Japan 10.4%; New Caledonia 4.5%; Australia 2.3%.

Transport and communications

Transport. Railroads: none. Roads (1996): total length 665 mi, 1,070 km (paved 24%). Vehicles (1996): passenger cars 4,000; trucks and buses 2,600. Merchant marine (1992): vessels (100 gross tons and over) 280; total deadweight tonnage 3,259,594. Air transport (1999): passenger-mi 110,800,000, passenger-km 178,316,000; short ton-mi cargo 1,318,000, metric ton-km 1,924,000; airports (1996) with scheduled flights 29.

Communications

Medium	date	unit	number	units per 1,000 persons
Radio	1997	receivers	62,000	350
Television	1997	receivers	2,000	14
Telephones	1996	main lines	4,500	26
Cellular telephones	1995	subscribers	100	0.6
Personal computers	...	units	...	...
Internet	...	users	...	...

Education and health

Educational attainment (1989). Percentage of population age 6 and over having: no formal schooling or less than one year 22.3%; some primary education 52.6%; lower-level secondary 18.3%; upper-level secondary and higher 4.8%; not stated 2.0%. *Literacy* (1979): total population age 15 and over literate 32,120 (52.9%); males 18,550 (57.3%); females 13,570 (47.8%).

Education (1992)

	schools	teachers	students	student/ teacher ratio
Primary (age 6–11)[9]	272	852	26,267	30.8
Secondary (age 11–18)	27	220	4,269	19.4
Voc., teacher tr.	...	50[10]	444	...
Higher	1[11]	13[12]	124[13]	...

Health (1997): physicians 21 (1 per 8,524 persons); hospital beds 573 (1 per 312 persons); infant mortality rate per 1,000 live births (1999) 37.
Food (1998): daily per capita caloric intake 2,737 (vegetable products 86%, animal products 14%); 120% of FAO recommended minimum requirement.

Military

Total active duty personnel: Vanuatu has a paramilitary force of about 300.

[1]Detail does not add to total given because of rounding. [2]1999 census total equals 193,219. [3]Deaths reported to the Ministry of Health only. [4]Vila and Luganville only. [5]Weights of consumer price index components. [6]Imputed bank service charges. [7]Imports c.i.f.; exports f.o.b. [8]Destination of domestic exports only. [9]Excludes independent private schools. [10]1981. [11]1989. [12]1983. [13]1991.

Internet resources for further information:

- **Vanuatu Online**
  http://www.vanuatu.net.vu/VanuatuOnlineDirectory.html

Venezuela

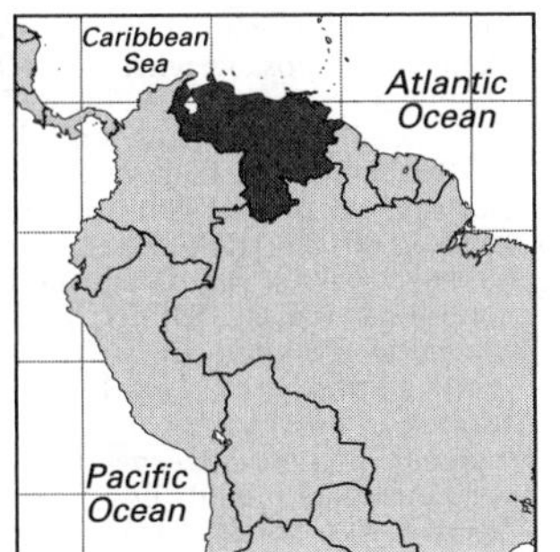

Official name[1]: República Bolivariana de Venezuela (Bolivarian Republic of Venezuela).
Form of government[1]: federal multiparty republic with a unicameral legislature (National Assembly [165]).
Head of state and government: President.
Capital: Caracas.
Official language: Spanish.
Official religion: none.
Monetary unit: 1 bolívar (B, plural Bs) = 100 céntimos; valuation (Oct. 6, 2000) 1 U.S.$ = Bs 691.26; 1 £ = Bs 999.94.

Area and population

States	Capitals	area sq mi	area sq km	population 1997 estimate
Amazonas	Puerto Ayacucho	67,900	175,750	96,976
Anzoátegui	Barcelona	16,700	43,300	1,077,435
Apure	San Fernando de Apure	29,500	76,500	415,051
Aragua	Maracay	2,708	7,014	1,399,987
Barinas	Barinas	13,600	35,200	545,013
Bolívar	Ciudad Bolívar	91,900	238,000	1,207,527
Carabobo	Valencia	1,795	4,650	1,935,461
Cojedes	San Carlos	5,700	14,800	241,365
Delta Amacuro	Tucupita	15,500	40,200	123,491
Falcón	Coro	9,600	24,800	719,458
Guárico	San Juan de Los Morros	25,091	64,986	605,878
Lara	Barquisimeto	7,600	19,800	1,491,940
Mérida	Mérida	4,400	11,300	706,870
Miranda	Los Teques	3,070	7,950	2,424,862
Monagas	Maturín	11,200	28,900	573,967
Nueva Esparta	La Asunción	440	1,150	349,139
Portuguesa	Guanare	5,900	15,200	764,284
Sucre	Cumaná	4,600	11,800	799,935
Táchira	San Cristóbal	4,300	11,100	981,607
Trujillo	Trujillo	2,900	7,400	573,537
Yaracuy	San Felipe	2,700	7,100	487,441
Zulia	Maracaibo	24,400	63,100	2,974,233
Other federal entities				
Dependencias Federales	—	50	120	...
Distrito Federal[2]	Caracas	745	1,930	2,281,695
TOTAL		352,144[3, 4]	912,050[3]	22,777,152

Demography

Population (2000): 24,170,000.
Density (2000): persons per sq mi 63.3, persons per sq km 26.4.
Urban-rural (1997): urban 86.1%; rural 13.9%.
Sex distribution (1997): male 50.35%; female 49.65%.
Age breakdown (1997): under 15, 35.4%; 15–29, 27.6%; 30–44, 19.9%; 45–59, 10.8%; 60–74, 5.0%; 75 and over, 1.3%.
Population projection: (2010) 28,716,000; (2020) 32,911,000.
Ethnic composition (1993): mestizo 67%; white 21%; black 10%; Indian 2%.
Religious affiliation (1996): Roman Catholic 92.7%; other 7.3%.
Major cities (1992): Caracas 1,964,846; Maracaibo (1990) 1,249,670; Valencia 1,034,033; Barquisimeto 692,599; Ciudad Guayana 523,578.

Vital statistics

Birth rate per 1,000 population (1999): 22.3 (world avg. 22.1); (1974) legitimate 47.0%; illegitimate 53.0%.
Death rate per 1,000 population (1999): 4.9 (world avg. 8.9).
Natural increase rate per 1,000 population (1999): 17.4 (world avg. 13.2).
Total fertility rate (avg. births per childbearing woman; 1999): 2.6.
Marriage rate per 1,000 population (1997): 3.8.
Divorce rate per 1,000 population (1997): 0.9.
Life expectancy at birth (1999): male 70.0 years; female 76.2 years.
Major causes of death per 100,000 population (1996): heart diseases 102.9; cancers 59.0; accidents 35.8; cardiovascular diseases 33.0.

National economy

Budget (1998). Revenue: Bs 9,017,475,000,000 (tax revenues 73.6%; nontax revenues 26.4%, of which oil revenues 24.9%). Expenditures: Bs 10,460,235,000,000 (subsidies 43.7%, goods and services 23.9%; capital expenditure 18.9%; debt service 11.8%).
Public debt (external, outstanding; 1998): U.S.$26,692,000,000.
Tourism (1998): receipts U.S.$961,000,000; expenditures U.S.$2,451,000,000.
Production (metric tons except as noted). Agriculture, forestry, fishing (1999): sugarcane 6,850,000, corn (maize) 1,024,000, bananas 1,000,394, rice 670,000, plantains 578,000, cassava 588,000, sorghum 402,000, potatoes 352,000; livestock (number of live animals) 15,992,400 cattle, 4,500,000 pigs, 4,000,000 goats, 110,000,000 chickens; roundwood (1998) 2,038,000 cu m; fish catch (1998) 506,177. Mining and quarrying (1998): iron ore 19,305,000; bauxite 4,633,000; gold 14,046 kg; diamonds (1997) 401,068 carats. Manufacturing (value added in 1984 Bs '000,000; 1997): ferrous and nonferrous metals 16,355; food products 13,277; chemicals 10,004; beverages 9,480; clothing, textiles, leather, and shoes 8,311; metal products 6,413; clay, glass, and nonmetallic mineral products 6,195; rubber and plastic products 4,798. Energy production (consumption): electricity (kW-hr; 1996) 74,968,000,000 (74,817,000,000); coal (metric tons; 1996) 3,486,000 (328,000); crude petroleum (barrels; 1996) 1,005,526,000 (370,722,000); petroleum products (metric tons; 1996) 54,847,000 (23,096,000); natural gas (cu m; 1996) 39,411,000,000 (39,411,000,000).
Gross national product (1998): U.S.$82,096,000,000 (U.S.$3,530 per capita).

Structure of gross domestic product and labour force

	1998 in value Bs '000,000	1998 % of total value	1997 labour force	1997 % of labour force
Agriculture	2,394,000	5.0	792,482	8.3
Petroleum and natural gas, Mining	5,846,000	12.1	93,846	1.0
Manufacturing	7,728,000	16.0	1,211,413	12.7
Construction	3,190,000	6.6	745,094	7.8
Public utilities	942,000	2.0	71,399	0.8
Transp. and commun.	4,773,000	9.9	551,947	5.8
Trade	8,490,000	17.6	2,061,940	21.7
Finance	7,577,000	15.7	460,837	4.8
Pub. admin., defense	2,857,000	5.9	2,482,055	26.1
Services	4,398,000	9.1		
Other	...	...	1,036,112[5]	10.9[5]
TOTAL	48,195,000	100.0[4]	9,507,125	100.0[4]

Population economically active (1997): total 9,507,125; activity rate 41.7% (participation rates: over age 15, 64.6%; female 35.9%; unemployed 10.6%).

Price index (1995 = 100)

	1993	1994	1995	1996	1997	1998	1999
Consumer price index	38.9	62.5	100.0	199.9	299.9	407.2	503.2

Household income and expenditure. Average household size (1990) 5.1; average annual income per household (1981) Bs 42,492 (U.S.$9,899); expenditure (1995): food 40.6%, housing 13.8%, transportation and communications 8.6%, clothing 5.3%, health 3.1%, education and recreation 2.9%.
Land use (1998): forest and other 75.3%; pasture 20.7%; agriculture 4.0%.

Foreign trade[6]

Balance of trade (current prices)

	1994	1995	1996	1997	1998	1999
Bs '000,000	+1,159,400	+1,407.7	+5,996.8	+3,858.3	+1,642.2	+4,388.5
% of total	32.7%	27.2%	44.3%	23.1%	9.6%	21.7%

Imports (1998)[7]: U.S.$7,794,000,000 (processed industrial supplies 28.0%, machinery 22.1%, transport equipment 22.1%, manufactured consumer goods 17.8%, construction materials 5.4%). *Major import sources:* U.S. 46.0%; Andean Pact countries 7.0%; Japan 5.0%; Germany 4.1%; Italy 3.9%.
Exports (1998): U.S.$17,534,000,000 (crude petroleum and petroleum products 69.8%, basic and precious metals 6.6%). *Major export destinations:* U.S. 48.5%; Andean Pact countries 11.1%; Canada 2.1%; United Kingdom 2.0%.

Transport and communications

Transport. Railroads (1996): length (1994) 627 km; passenger-km 149,905; metric ton-km cargo 54,474,000. Roads (1997): total length 95,664 km (paved 36%). Vehicles (1997): passenger cars 1,505,000; trucks and buses 542,000. Merchant marine (1992): vessels (over 100 gross tons) 271; total deadweight tonnage 1,355,419. Air transport (1996): passenger-km 5,800,000,000; metric ton-km cargo 639,000,000; airports (1997) with scheduled flights 20.

Communications

Medium	date	unit	number	units per 1,000 persons
Daily newspapers	1996	circulation	4,600,000	206
Radio	1997	receivers	10,750,000	472
Television	1997	receivers	4,100,000	180
Telephones	1998	main lines	2,712,000	117
Cellular telephones	1998	subscribers	2,015,000	87
Personal computers	1998	units	1,000,000	43
Internet	1998	users	350,000	15

Education and health

Educational attainment (1993). Percentage of population age 25 and over having: no formal schooling 8.0%; primary education or less 43.7%; some secondary and secondary 38.3%; postsecondary 10.0%. *Literacy* (1995 est.): total population age 15 and over literate 91.1%; males 91.8%; females 90.3%.

Education (1996–97)

	schools	teachers	students	student/ teacher ratio
Primary (age 7–12)	14,601	202,195	4,262,221	21.1
Secondary (age 13–17)[8]	2,177	39,601	377,984	9.5
Higher	99[9]	43,833[9]	717,192	12.6[10]

Health (1997): physicians 28,341 (1 per 804 persons); hospital beds 38,924 (1 per 585 persons); infant mortality rate (1999) 26.5.
Food (1998): daily per capita caloric intake 2,358 (vegetable products 84%, animal products 16%); 95% of FAO recommended minimum.

Military

Total active duty personnel (1999): 79,000 (army 72.1%, navy 19.0%, air force 8.9%). *Military expenditure as percentage of GNP* (1997): 2.2% (world 2.6%); per capita expenditure U.S.$82.

[1]Based on the new constitution, which was approved by referendum on Dec. 15, 1999. [2]Includes state of Vargas, created in November 1998. [3]Area per more recent survey is 353,841 sq mi (916,445 sq km). [4]Detail does not add to total given because of rounding. [5]Mostly unemployed. [6]Imports and exports are f.o.b. in balance of trade. [7]Data is for first six months of 1998. [8]Includes vocational and teacher training. [9]1990–91. [10]1991–92.

Internet resources for further information:
- **Central Office of Statistics and Informatics http://www.ocei.gov.ve**
- **Embassy of the Republic of Venezuela http://www.embassy.org/embassies/ve.html**

Vietnam

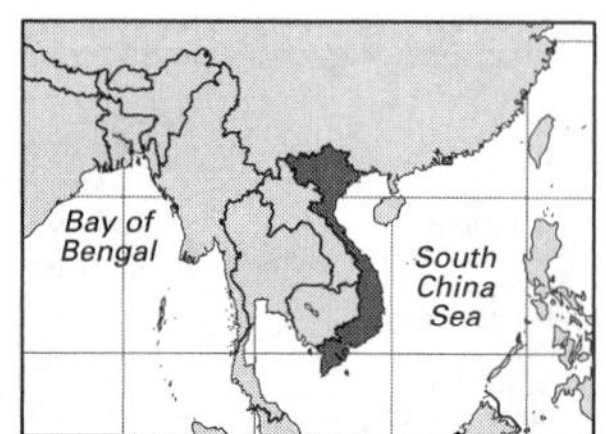

Official name: Cong Hoa Xa Hoi Chu Nghia Viet Nam (Socialist Republic of Vietnam).
Form of government: socialist republic with one legislative house (National Assembly [450]).
Head of state: President.
Head of government: Prime Minister.
Capital: Hanoi.
Official language: Vietnamese.
Official religion: none.
Monetary unit: 1 dong (D) = 10 hao = 100 xu; valuation (Oct. 6, 2000) 1 U.S.$ = D 14,260; 1 £ = D 20,629.

Area and population

		area		population
Geographic Regions[1]	**Principal cities**	sq mi	sq km	1993 estimate
Central Highlands	Da Lat	21,455	55,569	2,903,500
North Central Coast	Hue	19,763	51,187	9,516,900
Northeastern South Region	Ho Chi Minh City	9,066	23,481	8,692,900
North Mountains and Midlands	Thai Nguyen	39,749	102,949	12,109,300
Mekong River Delta	Long Xuyen	15,280	39,575	15,531,600
Red River Delta	Hanoi	4,810	12,457	13,808,800
South Central Coast	Da Nang	17,692	45,823	7,374,700
TOTAL		127,816[2]	331,041	70,982,500[3]

Demography

Population (2000): 78,774,000.
Density (2000): persons per sq mi 616.3, persons per sq km 238.0.
Urban-rural (1999): urban 19.6%; rural 80.4%.
Sex distribution (1997): male 49.03%; female 50.97%.
Age breakdown (1997): under 15, 35.5%; 15–29, 28.3%; 30–44, 20.2%; 45–59, 8.5%; 60–74, 5.8%; 75 and over, 1.7%.
Population projection: (2010) 90,192,000; (2020) 100,985,000.
Doubling time: 45 years.
Ethnic composition (1989): Vietnamese 87.1%; Tho (Tay) 1.8%; Chinese (Hoa) 1.5%; Tai 1.5%; Khmer 1.4%; Muong 1.4%; Nung 1.1%; other 4.2%.
Religious affiliation (1995): Buddhist 66.7%; Christian 8.7%, of which Roman Catholic 7.7%, Protestant 1.0%; Cao Dai (a New-Religionist group) 3.5%; Hoa Hao (a New-Religionist group) 2.1%; other 19.0%.
Major cities (1992): Ho Chi Minh City 4,549,000[4]; Hanoi 2,154,900[5]; Haiphong 783,133; Da Nang 382,674; Buon Ma Thuot 282,095; Nha Trang 221,331; Hue 219,149; Can Tho 215,587.

Vital statistics

Birth rate per 1,000 population (1999): 22.0 (world avg. 22.1).
Death rate per 1,000 population (1999): 6.3 (world avg. 8.9).
Natural increase rate per 1,000 population (1999): 15.7 (world avg. 13.2).
Total fertility rate (avg. births per childbearing woman; 1999): 2.6.
Marriage rate per 1,000 population: n.a.
Divorce rate per 1,000 population: n.a.
Life expectancy at birth (1999): male 66.5 years; female 71.5 years.
Major causes of death per 100,000 population: n.a.

National economy

Budget (1996). Revenue: D 62,387,000,000,000 (tax revenue 85.4%, of which taxes on trade 24.2%, turnover taxes 16.1%, taxes on profits 15.4%; nontax revenues 12.1%; grants 2.5%). Expenditures: D 62,889,000,000,000 (current expenditures 75.8%, of which social services 32.6%; capital expenditures 24.2%).
Public debt (external, outstanding; 1998): U.S.$19,775,000,000.
Gross national product (1998): U.S.$26,535,000,000 (U.S.$350 per capita).

Structure of gross domestic product and labour force

	1997			
	in value D '000,000,000[6]	% of total value	labour force	% of labour force
Agriculture, forestry, fishing	22,400	13.3	25,400,000	68.5
Public utilities	5,700	3.4	200,000	0.5
Mining	15,000	8.9	200,000	0.5
Manufacturing	42,500	25.2	3,300,000	8.9
Construction	18,500	11.0	1,000,000	2.7
Transp. and commun.	7,300	4.3	900,000	2.4
Trade and restaurants	29,800	17.7	3,200,000	8.6
Finance, insurance	8,900	5.3	700,000	1.9
Pub. admin., services	9,300	5.5	2,200,000	5.9
Other	9,100	5.4		
TOTAL	168,500	100.0	37,000,000[2]	100.0[2]

Tourism (1995): receipts from visitors U.S.$86,000,000; expenditures by nationals abroad, n.a.
Production (metric tons except as noted). Agriculture, forestry, fishing (1998): rice 29,142,000, sugarcane 13,843,000, cassava 1,783,000, corn (maize) 1,612,000, sweet potatoes 1,517,000, bananas 1,315,000, coconuts 1,271,000, coffee 409,000, groundnuts (peanuts) 386,000, oranges 379,000, natural rubber 226,000, pineapples 196,000, pimento 74,000, tea 51,000; livestock (number of live animals) 50,000,000 ducks, 18,132,000 pigs, 3,984,000 cattle, 2,951,000 buffalo; roundwood (1998) 35,910,000 cu m, of which fuelwood 31,412,000 cu m, industrial roundwood 4,498,000 cu m; fish catch (1997) 1,066,000, of which marine fish 670,000. Mining and quarrying (1997): phosphate rock (gross weight) 490,000; tin (metal content) 4,700; gold 10,000 kg. Manufacturing (1997): cement 7,475,000; raw sugar 589,000[6]; crude steel 330,000; phosphate fertilizers 137,000; beer 5,330,000[7] hectolitres; garments 145,000,000 units[8]; bicycles 56,000 units. Energy production (consumption): electricity (kW-hr; 1996) 16,320,000,000 (16,320,000,000); coal (metric tons; 1997) 7,600,000 ([1996] 5,551,000); crude petroleum (barrels; 1997) 60,000,000 ([1996] 283,300); petroleum products (metric tons; 1996) 38,000 (5,483,000); natural gas (cu m; 1996): 7,700,000 (7,700,000).
Population economically active (1989): total 30,521,019; activity rate 47.4% (participation rates: ages 15–64, 79.9%; female 51.7%; unemployed [1997] 10.3%).
Household income and expenditure. Average household size (1989) 4.8; income per household (1990)[9] D 577,008 (U.S.$93); sources of income: n.a.; expenditure (1990): food 62.4%, clothing 5.0%, household goods 4.6%, education 2.9%, housing 2.5%.
Land use (1994): forested 29.6%; meadows and pastures 1.0%; agricultural and under permanent cultivation 21.5%; other 47.9%.

Foreign trade[10]

Balance of trade (current prices)

	1992	1993	1994	1995	1996	1997
U.S.$'000,000	–109	–939	–1,772	–2,706	–3,888	–2,371
% of total	1.8%	13.6%	17.9%	19.9%	21.1%	11.8%

Imports (1996): U.S.$11,144,000,000 (machinery and transport equipment 30.5%, basic manufactures 21.4%, chemicals and chemical products 16.3%, mineral fuels 11.1%). *Major import sources* (1997): Singapore 12.9%; South Korea 12.5%; Taiwan 10.1%; Japan 9.9%; China 8.4%.
Exports (1996): U.S.$7,256,000,000 (crude petroleum 18.3%, garments 15.7%, rice 11.7%, fish and fish products 8.9%, footwear 7.2%, coffee 4.6%). *Major export destinations* (1997): Japan 22.7%; Germany 8.3%; Singapore 5.7%; France 5.0%; Australia 4.9%.

Price and earnings indexes (January 1997 = 100)

	1997	1998	1999
Consumer price index	100.0	104.2	113.7
Earnings index	...	...	...

Transport and communications

Transport. Railroads (1996): route length 1,648 mi, 2,652 km; (1998) passenger-mi 1,668,000,000, passenger-km 2,685,000,000; (1998) short ton-mile cargo 1,007,000,000, metric ton-km cargo 1,470,000,000. Roads (1996): total length 58,000 mi, 93,300 km (paved 25%). Vehicles (1994): passenger cars, trucks, and buses 200,000. Air transport (1997)[11]: passenger-mi 2,352,000,000, passenger-km 3,785,000,000; short ton-mile cargo 70,949,000, metric ton-km cargo 103,584,000; airports (1997) with scheduled flights 12.

Communications

Medium	date	unit	number	units per 1,000 persons
Daily newspapers	1996	circulation	300,000	4.1
Radio	1997	receivers	8,200,000	109
Television	1997	receivers	3,570,000	47
Telephones	1998	main lines	2,000,000	26
Cellular telephones	1998	subscribers	187,000	2.4
Personal computers	1998	units	500,000	6.5
Internet	1998	users	10,000	0.1

Education and health

Educational attainment (1989). Percentage of population age 25 and over having: no formal education (illiterate) 16.6%; incomplete and complete primary 69.8%; incomplete and complete secondary 10.6%; higher 2.6%; unknown 0.4%. *Literacy* (1995): percentage of population age 15 and over literate 91.1%; males 94.8%; females 87.8%.

Education (1997–98)

	schools	teachers	students	student/ teacher ratio
Primary (age 7–12)	...	324,431	10,431,337	32.2
Secondary (age 13–18)	...	226,491	6,642,350	29.3
Vocational[12]	...	9,336	172,400	18.5
Higher	109[13]	23,522[12]	509,300[12]	21.7[12]

Health (1997): physicians 32,900 (1 per 2,283 persons); hospital beds 197,900 (1 per 380 persons); infant mortality rate per 1,000 live births (1999) 32.2.
Food (1997): daily per capita caloric intake 2,484 (vegetable products 91%, animal products 9%); 115% of FAO recommended minimum requirement.

Military

Total active duty personnel (1998): 484,000 (army 85.1%, navy 8.7%, air force 6.2%). *Military expenditure as percentage of GNP* (1997): 2.8% (world 2.6%); per capita expenditure U.S.$45.

[1]Seven geographic regions are divided into 60 provinces as of the administrative reorganization of 1997. [2]Detail does not add to total given because of rounding. [3]Total includes 1,044,800 persons not distributed in geographic and region estimates. [4]1999. [5]1993. [6]At prices of 1992. [7]1996. [8]1995. [9]Wage workers and government officials only. [10]Imports c.i.f.; exports f.o.b. [11]Vietnam Airlines only. [12]1996–97. [13]1995–96.

Internet resources for further information:
- **Ministry of Foreign Affairs http://www.mofa.gov.vn**

Virgin Islands (U.S.)

Official name: Virgin Islands of the United States.
Political status: organized unincorporated territory of the United States with one legislative house (Senate [15]).
Chief of state: President of the United States.
Head of government: Governor.
Capital: Charlotte Amalie.
Official language: English.
Official religion: none.
Monetary unit: 1 U.S. dollar (U.S.$) = 100 cents; valuation (Oct. 6, 2000) 1 £ = U.S.$1.45.

Area and population		area		population
				1995
Islands[1]	**Principal Towns**	sq mi	sq km	estimate
St. Croix	Christiansted	84	218	51,389
St. John	—	20	52	4,030
St. Thomas	Charlotte Amalie	32	83	54,259
TOTAL		136	353	109,678

Demography

Population (2000): 121,000.
Density (2000): persons per sq mi 889.1, persons per sq km 345.4.
Urban-rural (1998): urban 45.7%; rural 54.3%.
Sex distribution (1999): male 47.06%; female 52.94%.
Age breakdown (1999): under 15, 28.2%; 15–29, 22.3%; 30–44, 18.2%; 45–59, 19.0%; 60–74, 9.3%; 75 and over, 3.0%.
Population projection: (2010) 133,000; (2020) 144,000.
Doubling time: 65 years.
Ethnic composition (1995)[2]: black 76.7%[3]; white 10.4%[3]; other 12.9%[3].
Religious affiliation (1993): Baptist 42.0%; Roman Catholic 34.0%; Episcopalian 17.0%; other 7.0%.
Major towns (1990): Charlotte Amalie 12,331; Christiansted 2,555; Frederiksted 1,064.

Vital statistics

Birth rate per 1,000 population (1999): 16.1 (world avg. 22.1); (1998) legitimate 30.2%; illegitimate 69.8%[4].
Death rate per 1,000 population (1999): 5.3 (world avg. 8.9).
Natural increase rate per 1,000 population (1999): 10.8 (world avg. 13.2).
Total fertility rate (avg. births per childbearing woman; 1999): 2.3.
Marriage rate per 1,000 population (1993): 35.1.
Divorce rate per 1,000 population (1993): 4.5.
Life expectancy at birth (1999): male 70.2 years; female 73.6 years.
Major causes of death per 100,000 population (1997): diseases of the heart 111.3; malignant neoplasms (cancers) 103.9; cerebrovascular diseases 44.5; diabetes mellitus 32.3; accidents 31.4; homicide 27.1.

National economy

Budget. Revenue (1993–94): U.S.$332,300,000 (1988; personal income tax 39.9%, gross receipts tax 19.5%, corporate income tax 10.6%, property tax 7.6%, excise tax 4.2%). Expenditures (1993–94): U.S.$422,200,000 (1991; education 28.8%, health 20.0%, executive branch 10.5%, public safety 5.7%, public works 5.5%, College of the Virgin Islands 3.6%).
Production. Agriculture, forestry, fishing (value of sales in U.S.$'000; 1998): milk 1,263, livestock and livestock products 655 (of which cattle and calves 439, hogs and pigs 46), ornamental plants and other nursery products 364, vegetables 329 (notably tomatoes and cucumbers), fruits and nuts 185 (notably mangoes, bananas, and avocados), poultry 21; livestock (number of live animals) 3,636 cattle, 3,074 sheep, 2,944 goats, 1,436 hogs and pigs, 3,538 chickens; roundwood, n.a.; fish catch (1998) 910 metric tons. Mining and quarrying: sand and crushed stone for local use. Manufacturing (U.S.$'000[5]; 1997): food and food products 31,949; stone, clay, and glass products 21,897; print and publishing 21,127; transportation equipment 4,920; fabricated metal products 3,352. Construction: n.a. Energy production (consumption): electricity (kW-hr; 1996) 1,075,000,000 (1,075,000,000); coal (metric tons; 1996) none (250,000); crude petroleum (barrels; 1996) none (119,528,000); petroleum products (metric tons; 1996) 15,096,000 (2,284,000); natural gas, none (none).
Tourism (1998): receipts from visitors U.S.$921,000,000; number of hotel rooms (1995) 5,148; occupancy percentage 61.3%[6]; expenditures by nationals abroad, n.a.
Household income and expenditure. Average household size (1990) 3.1; average annual income per household (1989) U.S.$29,953; sources of income (1984): wages and salaries 65.7%, transfer payments 13.0%, interest, dividends, and rent 12.7%, self-employment 2.6%; expenditure n.a.
Population economically active (1995)[7]: total 47,810; activity rate of total population 46.6%[8] (participation rates: ages 16–64, 72.5%[8]; female 47.8%[8]; unemployed 5.3%).

Price and earnings indexes (1995 = 100)	1994	1995	1996	1997	1998	1999
Consumer price index[9]	97.3	100.0	102.9	105.3	107.0	109.3
Annual earnings index	...	...	...	...	...	...

Gross national product (at current market prices; 1997): U.S.$2,666,000,000 (U.S.$18,287 per capita).

Structure of gross domestic product and labour force	1989		1995	
	in value U.S.$'000,000	% of total value	labour force[10]	% of labour force
Agriculture, fishing	...	...	3,110	6.5
Mining	...	...	11	11
Manufacturing	...	...	2,370[12]	5.0[12]
Construction	...	...	1,140[11]	2.4[11]
Public utilities	...	...	12	12
Transp. and commun.	...	...	2,560	5.4
Trade, hotels, restaurants	...	...	9,740	20.4
Finance, insurance, real estate	...	...	1,830	3.8
Pub. admin., defense	...	...	13,770	28.8
Services	...	...	10,490	21.9
Other	...	...	2,800[13]	5.8[13]
TOTAL	1,344[14]	100.0	47,810	100.0

Public debt (1999): U.S.$1,200,000,000.
Land use (1994): forested 5.9%; meadows and pastures 26.5%; agricultural and under permanent cultivation 20.6%; other 47.0%.

Foreign trade

Balance of trade (current prices)	1982	1983	1984	1985	1986	1987
U.S.$'000,000	–300.2	–1,019.5	–786.4	–383.5	–523.8	–1,175
% of total	2.9%	12.2%	9.0%	5.4%	11.0%	21.1%

Imports (1995): U.S.$3,200,300,000[15]. *Major import sources:* United States 32.6%; other countries 67.4%.
Exports (1995): U.S.$3,026,300,000[16]. *Major export destinations:* United States 92.7%; other countries 7.3%.

Transport and communications

Transport. Railroads: none. Roads (1996): total length 532 mi, 856 km (paved, n.a.). Vehicles (1993): passenger cars 51,000; trucks and buses 13,300. Merchant marine (1992): vessels (100 gross tons and over) 1. Shipping (1988): cruise ship arrivals 1,228; passenger arrivals 1,062,010. Air transport (1989)[17]: passenger arrivals and departures 1,897,000; cargo loaded and unloaded 4,600 metric tons; airports (1999) with scheduled flights 2.

Communications				units
Medium	date	unit	number	per 1,000 persons
Daily newspapers	1996	circulation	42,000	364
Radio	1996	receivers	107,000	927
Television	1996	receivers	67,000	580
Telephones	1998	main lines	64,851	548
Cellular telephones	1992	subscribers	2,000	18

Education and health

Educational attainment (1990). Percentage of population age 25 and over having: incomplete primary education 4.0%; completed lower secondary 19.2%; incomplete upper secondary 20.3%; completed upper secondary 25.2%; incomplete undergraduate 16.2%; completed undergraduate 9.3%; graduate degrees 5.8%. *Literacy:* n.a.

Education (1992–93)[18]	schools	teachers	students	student/ teacher ratio
Primary (age 5–12)	62	790	14,544	18.4
Secondary (age 12–18)	...	541[19]	12,502	17.1[19]
Higher	1	266	2,924	11.0

Health (1989): physicians 130 (1 per 780 persons); hospital beds 252 (1 per 402 persons); infant mortality rate per 1,000 live births (1999) 9.9.
Food: daily per capita caloric intake, n.a.

Military

Total active duty personnel: no domestic military force is maintained; the United States is responsible for defense and external security.

[1]May be administered by officials assigned by the governor. [2]Includes an overall Hispanic population of 17.4%. [3]Includes Hispanic population. [4]Percentage of legitimate births may be an underestimation due to the common practice of consensual marriage. [5]Figures are for sales and receipts. [6]1993. [7]Excludes armed forces. [8]1990. [9]U.S. mainland. [10]Employed labour force as of September 30; excludes armed forces. [11]Construction includes mining. [12]Manufacturing includes public utilities. [13]Includes 2,740 unemployed. [14]Tourism accounts for more than 70% of gross domestic product. [15]Breakdown of 1992 imports from U.S. only, totaling U.S.$1,768,000,000: crude petroleum 60.7%, food and beverages 4.5%, iron and steel (all forms) 4.5%, fuel oils 3.2%. [16]Breakdown of 1999 exports to U.S. only, totaling U.S.$2,971,899,000: petroleum products 90.4%, chemicals and chemical products 2.4%, antibiotics 0.4%, alcoholic beverages 0.3%. [17]St. Croix and St. Thomas airports. [18]Public schools only. [19]1990–91.

Yemen

Official name: Al-Jumhūrīyah al-Yamanīyah (Republic of Yemen).
Form of government: multiparty republic with one legislative house (House of Representatives [301]).
Head of state: President[1].
Head of government: Prime Minister.
Capital: Ṣanʿāʾ.
Official language: Arabic.
Official religion: Islam.
Monetary unit: 1 Yemeni Rial (YRls) = 100 fils; valuation (Oct. 6, 2000): 1 U.S.$ = YRls 162.40; 1 £ = YRls 234.92.

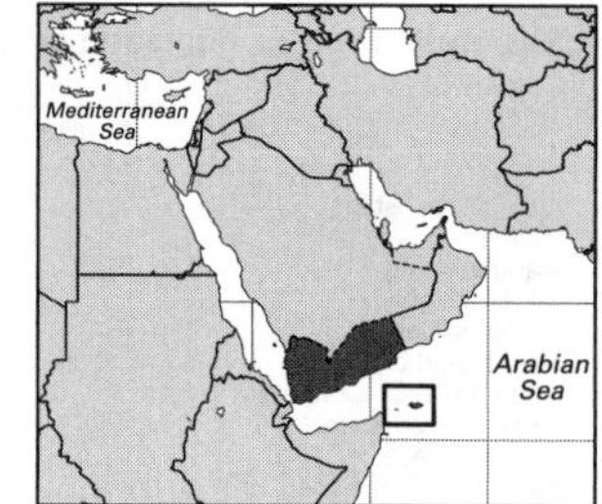

Area and population

Governorates	Capitals	area sq mi	area sq km	population 1994 census
Northern Yemen				
Al-Bayḍāʾ	Al-Bayḍāʾ	4,310	11,170	509,265
Dhamār	Dhamār	3,430	8,870	1,050,346
Ḥajjah	Ḥajjah	3,700	9,590	1,262,590
Al-Ḥudaydah	Al-Ḥudaydah	5,240	13,580	1,749,944
Ibb	Ibb	2,480	6,430	1,959,313
Al-Jawf	Al-Jawf	...	...	157,096
Al-Maḥwīt	Al-Maḥwīt	830	2,160	403,465
Maʾrib	Maʾrib	15,400	39,890	167,388
Ṣaʿdah	Ṣaʿdah	4,950	12,810	486,059
Ṣanʿāʾ	Ṣanʿāʾ	7,840	20,310	1,910,286
Taʿizz	Taʿizz	4,020	10,420	2,205,947
Southern Yemen				
Abyān	Zinjibār	8,297	21,489	414,543
ʿAdan	Aden	2,695	6,980	562,162
Ḥaḍramawt	Al-Mukallā	59,991	155,376	870,025
Laḥij	Laḥij	4,928	12,766	634,652
Al-Mahrah	Al-Ghayḍah	25,618	66,350	112,512
Shabwah	ʿAtāq	28,536	73,908	377,080
TOTAL		182,278[2, 3]	472,099[2]	14,832,673

Demography

Population (2000): 17,479,000.
Density (2000)[4]: persons per sq mi 81.6, persons per sq km 31.5.
Urban-rural (1998): urban 36.1%; rural 63.9%.
Sex distribution (1999): male 51.02%; female 48.98%.
Age breakdown (1999): under 15, 47.8%; 15–29, 27.2%; 30–44, 13.4%; 45–59, 7.0%; 60–74, 3.4%; 75 and over, 1.2%.
Population projection: (2010) 24,637,000; (2020) 34,195,000.
Doubling time: 21 years.
Ethnic composition (1999): predominantly Arab.
Religious affiliation (1995): Muslim 99.9%, of which Sunnī *c.* 60%, Shīʿī *c.* 40%; other 0.1%.
Major cities (1994): Ṣanʿāʾ 954,400; Aden 398,300; Taʿizz 317,600; Al-Ḥudaydah 298,500; Al-Mukallā 122,400.

Vital statistics

Birth rate per 1,000 population (1999): 43.5 (world avg. 22.1).
Death rate per 1,000 population (1999): 10.2 (world avg. 8.9).
Natural increase rate per 1,000 population (1999): 33.3 (world avg. 13.2).
Total fertility rate (avg. births per childbearing woman; 1999): 7.1.
Life expectancy at birth (1999): male 57.3 years; female 61.2 years.
Major causes of death per 100,000 population: n.a.; however, infant, child, and maternal mortality were very high (130, 190, and 100 per 1,000 live births, respectively).

National economy

Budget (1997). Revenue: YRls 281,667,000,000 (1995; current revenue 75.7%, of which state property revenue 26.9%, international trade 18.4%, taxes on income and profits 15.6%; development revenue 19.7%; loans and grants 4.7%). Expenditures: YRls 290,571,000,000 (1995; defense 25.2%; education 17.6%; public order and safety 8.1%; health 4.7%).
Production (metric tons except as noted). Agriculture, forestry, fishing (1999): sorghum 320,891, tomatoes 247,899, potatoes 200,363, grapes 159,534, oranges 154,317, wheat 144,366, bananas 87,663, onions 76,595, millet 65,916, papayas 63,142; livestock (number of live animals) 4,595,112 sheep, 4,150,228 goats, 1,288,753 cattle, 500,000 asses, 182,936 camels, 27,300,000 chickens; roundwood (1998) 324,000 cu m; fish catch (1998) 110,000. Mining and quarrying (1996): gypsum 103,000; salt 86,000. Manufacturing (value of production in YRls '000,000; 1996): food, beverages, and tobacco 43,927; chemicals and chemical products 42,369; nonmetallic mineral products 8,571; paper products 8,562; basic metal industries 3,040; clothing, textiles, and leather 1,693; wood products 392. Construction: n.a. Energy production (consumption): electricity (kW-hr; 1996) 2,334,000,000 (2,334,000,000); coal, none (n.a.); crude petroleum (barrels; 1996) 128,315,000 (40,559,000); petroleum products (metric tons; 1996) 3,494,000 (3,304,000).
Population economically active (1996): total 4,945,000; activity rate of total population 30.0% (participation rates [1994]: age 15 and over, 45.8%; female 18.2%; unemployed [1995] 30%).

Price index (1995 = 100)

	1992	1993	1994	1995	1996	1997	1998
Consumer price index	33.0	44.0	64.0	100.0	130.0	137.0	148.0

Gross national product (1998): U.S.$4,630,000,000 (U.S.$280 per capita).

Structure of gross domestic product and labour force

	1996 in value Y Rls '000,000[5]	1996 % of total value	1986 labour force	1986 % of labour force
Agriculture	132,945	23.9	1,151,348	56.3
Mining	91,941	16.6	11,771	0.6
Manufacturing	56,778	10.2	94,913	4.6
Public utilities	11,488	2.1	160,952	7.9
Construction	20,647	3.7	32,852	1.6
Transp. and commun.	39,254	7.1	107,611	5.3
Trade	79,724	14.4	248,979	12.2
Finance, real estate	31,306	5.6	8,757	0.4
Pub. admin., defense	79,218	14.3	226,054	11.1
Services	12,515	2.2	...	...
Other	–475[6]	–0.1[6]	...	...
TOTAL	555,341	100.0	2,043,237	100.0

Household income and expenditure. Average household size (1997) 7.0.
Tourism (1997): receipts U.S.$69,000,000; expenditures U.S.$81,000,000.
Public debt (external, outstanding; 1998): U.S.$4,900,000,000.
Land use (1994): forest 3.8%; pasture 30.4%; agriculture 2.9%; other 62.9%.

Foreign trade[7]

Balance of trade

	1993	1994	1995	1996	1997	1998
U.S.$'000,000	–2,212.5	–1,154.5	+242.8	+634.6	+490.2	–700.5
% of total	64.4%	31.2%	7.3%	13.5%	10.9%	18.9%

Imports (1995): U.S.$1,537,800,000 (machinery and transport equipment 23.1%, basic manufactured goods 23.0%, food and live animals 22.1%, chemical products 8.2%, mineral fuels 7.9%, beverages and tobacco 2.1%). *Major import sources* (1997): U.A.E. 9.0%; Saudi Arabia 8.0%; U.S. 7.0%; France 6.0%; Brazil 5.0%.
Exports (1995): U.S.$1,780,600,000 (mineral fuels 95.3%, food and live animals 2.5%, crude minerals 1.2%). *Major export destinations* (1997): China 31.0%; South Korea 19.0%; Taiwan 17.0%; Thailand 5.0%; Brazil 5.0%; Japan 5.0%.

Transport and communications

Transport. Railroads: none. Roads (1996): total length 64,725 km (paved 8.1%). Vehicles (1995): passenger cars 229,084; trucks and buses 282,615. Air transport (1994): passenger-km 1,183,000,000; metric ton-km cargo 119,000,000; airports (1998) with scheduled flights 12.

Communications

Medium	date	unit	number	units per 1,000 persons
Daily newspapers	1996	circulation	230,000	15
Radio	1997	receivers	1,050,000	64
Television	1997	receivers	470,000	29
Telephones	1999	main lines	249,515	14.8
Cellular telephones	1999	subscribers	18,000	1.1
Internet	1999	users	4,000	0.4

Education and health

Educational attainment (1986)[8]. Percentage of population age 10 and over having: no formal schooling 74.2%; reading and writing ability 19.8%; primary education 4.0%; secondary education 0.6%; higher 0.6%; not specified 0.8%. *Literacy* (1994): percentage of total population age 15 and over literate 43.2%; males literate 68.6%; females literate 23.1%.

Education (1994–95)

	schools	teachers	students	student/ teacher ratio
Primary (age 7–12)	11,013[9]	78,646[10]	2,493,017[10]	31.7[10]
Secondary (age 13–18)[10]	1,224	11,130	232,506	20.9
Voc., teacher tr.[10]	125	369	15,074	40.9
Higher[10]	2	1,991	90,826	45.6

Health (1998): physicians 3,883 (1 per 4,211 persons); hospital beds 9,143 (1 per 1,788 persons); infant mortality rate per 1,000 live births (1999) 72.2.
Food (1998): daily per capita caloric intake 2,087 (vegetable products 93%, animal products 7%); 86% of FAO recommended minimum requirement.

Military

Total active duty personnel (1998): 66,300 (army 92.0%, navy 2.7%, air force 5.3%). *Military expenditure as percentage of GNP* (1997): 8.1% (world 2.6%); per capita expenditure U.S.$26.

[1]Presidential Council assisting the President was abolished by a constitutional amendment of September 1994. [2]An agreement to resolve the long-undemarcated north-eastern boundary with Saudi Arabia (which increased Yemen's total area to roughly 214,300 sq mi [555,000 sq km]) was signed in June 2000. [3]Detail does not add to total given because of rounding. [4]Based on the higher total area estimate of 214,300 sq mi (555,000 sq km). [5]In purchasers' value at current prices. [6]Includes import duties of 18.5 million Yemeni Rials less imputed bank service charges. [7]Imports are c.i.f. [8]Yemen Arab Republic only. [9]1993–94. [10]Public schools only, which comprise the vast majority of schools in Yemen.

Internet resources for further information:
- **The Yemen Times http://www.yementimes.com**
- **Yemen Info Homepage http://www.yemeninfo.gov.ye**

Yugoslavia

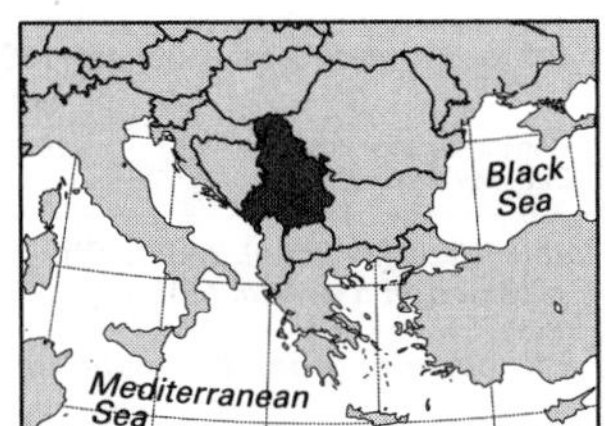

Official name: Savezna Republika Jugoslavija (Federal Republic of Yugoslavia).
Form of government: federal multiparty republic with two legislative houses (Chamber of Republics [40]; Chamber of Citizens [138]).
Chief of state: Federal President.
Head of government: Prime Minister.
Capital: Belgrade.
Official language: Serbian (Serbo-Croatian).
Official religion[1]: none.
Monetary unit[2]: 1 Yugoslav new dinar (second) = 100 paras; valuation (Oct. 6, 2000) 1 U.S.$ = 12.18 Yugoslav new dinars; 1 £ = 17.61 Yugoslav new dinars.

Area and population

Republics	Capitals	area sq mi	area sq km	population 1997 estimate
Montenegro	Podgorica	5,333	13,812	631,164
Serbia	Belgrade	21,609	55,968	5,762,954
Autonomous province[3]				
Vojvodina	Novi Sad	8,304	21,506	1,954,432
Geographical region				
Kosovo (Kosova)[4, 5]	Priština	4,203	10,887	2,227,742
TOTAL		39,449	102,173	10,576,292

Demography

Population (2000): 10,662,000.
Density (2000): persons per sq mi 270.3, persons per sq km 104.4.
Urban-rural (1999): urban 52.0%; rural 48.0%.
Sex distribution (1999): male 49.53%; female 50.47%.
Age breakdown (1991): under 15, 22.8%; 15–29, 21.6%; 30–44, 21.7%; 45–59, 17.1%; 60–74, 12.2%; 75 and over, 3.5%; unknown, 1.1%.
Population projection: (2010) 10,667,000; (2020) 10,561,000.
Ethnic composition (1991): Serb 62.6%; Albanian 16.5%; Montenegrin 5.0%; multi-ethnic 3.4%; Hungarian 3.3%; Sandzak and Bosniak Muslim 3.2%; Romany (Gypsy) 1.4%; Croat 1.1%; other 3.5%.
Religious affiliation (1995): Serbian Orthodox 62.6%; Muslim 19.0%; Roman Catholic 5.8%; other, mostly nonreligious 12.6%.
Major cities (2000): Belgrade 1,194,878; Novi Sad 182,778; Niš 182,583; Priština 186,611; Kragujevac 154,489; Podgorica 130,875.

Vital statistics

Birth rate per 1,000 population (1997): 12.4 (world avg. 22.1).
Death rate per 1,000 population (1997): 10.6 (world avg. 8.9).
Natural increase rate per 1,000 population (1997): 1.8 (world avg. 13.2).
Total fertility rate (avg. births per childbearing woman; 1997): 1.7.
Marriage rate per 1,000 population (1997): 5.3.
Life expectancy at birth (1995): male 69.9 years; female 74.7 years.
Major causes of death per 100,000 population (1997): diseases of the circulatory system 585.0; malignant neoplasms (cancers) 169.0; accidents, violence, and poisoning 45.0; diseases of the respiratory system 39.0.

National economy

Budget (1998). Revenue: 44,200,696,000 Yugoslav new dinars (turnover tax 30.3%, social security tax 22.1%, income tax 20.6%). Expenditure: 44,200,696,000 Yugoslav new dinars (government 20.8%, health 20.0%, education 12.2%, other 47.0%).
Production (metric tons except as noted). Agriculture, forestry, fishing (1999): corn (maize) 6,100,000, sugar beets 2,318,000, wheat 2,167,000, potatoes 991,000, sunflower seeds 460,000, plums 460,000, watermelons 285,000; livestock (number of live animals) 4,372,000 pigs, 2,392,000 sheep, 1,831,000 cattle, 24,322,000 poultry; roundwood 1,320,000 cu m; fish catch 6,845. Mining and quarrying (1998): copper ore 19,939,000; lead-zinc ore 1,249,000; magnesite 81,000; aluminum and ingots 61,000; salt 19,305; asbestos ore 19,000; refined silver 34,000 kg. Manufacturing (1998): wheat flour 830,000; crude steel 949,000; pig iron 826,000; sulfuric acid 211,000; nitric acid 185,000; electrolytic copper 94,000; refined lead 24,000; welded pipes 43,000; rolled copper 27,055; medicines 22,871. Construction (residential units constructed; 1998): 14,768. Energy production (consumption): electricity (kW-hr; 1998) 40,651,000,000 (40,651,000,000); coal (metric tons; 1998) 44,072,000 (44,072,000); crude petroleum (barrels; 1998) 6,773,000 (6,047,000[6]); petroleum products (metric tons; 1998) 763,000 (1,383,000[6]); natural gas (cu m; 1998) 731,000,000 (2,935,400,000[6]).
Land use (1994): forested 17.3%; meadows and pastures 20.7%; agricultural and under permanent cultivation 40.0%; other 22.0%.
Population economically active (1998): total 4,508,900; activity rate 42.6% (1998; participation rates: over age 15, 58.3%; female [1995] 43.7%; [1999] unemployed 19.8%).

Price and earnings indexes (1996 = 100)

	1994	1995	1996	1997	1998
Consumer price index	30.2	51.2	100.0	121.6	173.3
Annual earnings index	...	...	100.0	147.1	108.0

Tourism (1997): receipts from visitors U.S.$41,000,000; expenditures, n.a.
Household income and expenditure. Average household size (1998) 3.2; income per household (1998) 34,582 Yugoslav new dinars (U.S.$3,400); sources of income (1998): wages and salaries 50.3%, pensions 14.8%, self-employment 9.2%, other 25.7%; expenditure (1998): food 52.8%, fuel and light 10.4%, beverages and tobacco 7.3%, clothing and footwear 6.7%, health 5.0%, transportation and communications 4.9%, education 2.1%, housing 1.1%, other 9.1%.
Gross national product (1998): U.S.$13,742,000,000 (U.S.$1,289 per capita).

Structure of gross material product and labour force

	1997 in value '000,000 Yugoslav new dinars	1997 % of total value	1998 labour force	1998 % of labour force
Agriculture	19,679.5	21.8	102,700	2.3
Mining; Manufacturing	30,790.3	34.1	835,800	18.5
Construction	5,809.4	6.4	126,900	2.8
Public utilities	239.8	0.3	55,000	1.2
Transp. and commun.	9,671.4	10.7	142,800	3.2
Trade	15,085.4	16.7	293,800	6.5
Finance	...	...	...	...
Pub. admin., defense; Services	9,098.8	10.1	615,900	13.7
Other	—	—	2,336,000[7]	51.8[7]
TOTAL	90,374.6	100.0[8]	4,508,900	100.0

Foreign trade

Balance of trade (current prices)

	1995	1996	1997	1998
Din '000,000	–2,193	–10,442	–12,225	–18,470
% of total	29.5%	34.2%	28.5%	26.0%

Imports (1998): Din 44,805,000,000 (manufactured goods 20.8%, machinery and transport equipment 18.4%, chemicals 16.9%, mineral fuels and lubricants 15.0%, food and live animals 8.2%). *Major import sources:* Germany 12.5%; Italy 10.9%; Russia 10.7%; Macedonia 5.2%.
Exports (1998): Din 26,335,000,000 (manufactured goods 38.5%, machinery and transport equipment 14.2%, chemicals 13.4%, food 8.3%). *Major export destinations:* Italy 11.6%; Macedonia 10.8%; Germany 8.9%; Russia 8.6%; Switzerland 5.3%; Greece 4.0%; U.K. 3.6%; Hungary 2.9%.

Transport and communications

Transport. Railroads (1998): length 4,069 km; (1998) passenger-km 1,744,000,000; metric ton-km cargo 2,432,000,000. Roads (1998): total length 50,497 km (paved 60%). Vehicles (1994): passenger cars 1,400,000; trucks and buses 132,000. Merchant marine (1998): cargo vessels 22. Air transport (1996): passenger-mi 649,950,000, passenger-km 1,046,000,000; short ton-mi cargo 3,594,000,000, metric ton-km cargo 5,784,000,000; airports (1998) 5.

Communications

Medium	date	unit	number	units per 1,000 persons
Daily newspapers	1995	circulation	1,363,000	256
Radio	1997	receivers	1,384,000	131
Television	1997	receivers	2,692,000	254
Telephones	1999	main lines	2,319,000	218
Cellular telephones	1999	subscribers	240,000	22.6
Personal computers	1999	units	220,000	40
Internet	1999	users	100,000	9.4

Education and health

Educational attainment (1991). Percentage of population age 15 and over having: less than full primary education 33.5%; primary 25.0%; secondary 32.2%; postsecondary and higher 9.3%. *Literacy* (1991): total population age 10 and over literate 93.0%; males literate 97.2%; females literate 88.9%.

Education (1998–99)

	schools	teachers	students	student/teacher ratio
Primary (age 7–14)	4,431	52,294	864,199	16.5
Secondary (age 15–18)	561	27,766	367,587	13.2
Higher	83	10,998	147,981	13.5

Health (1997): physicians 22,498 (1 per 471 persons); hospital beds 58,576 (1 per 181 persons); infant mortality rate per 1,000 live births (1997) 14.3.
Food (1998): daily per capita caloric intake 2,963 (vegetable products 64%, animal products 36%); 117% of FAO recommended minimum.

Military

Total active duty personnel (1998)[9]: 108,700 (army 78.2%, air force 15.4%, navy 6.6%). *Military expenditure as percentage of government expenditure* (1991): 3.9% (world 4.0%); per capita expenditure U.S.$167.

[1]Government gives "preferential treatment" to the Serbian Orthodox Church according to the U.S. Department of State, *Country Reports on Human Rights Practices for 1996.* [2]Montenegro adopted the Deutsche Mark as its legal tender in mid-November 2000. [3]Vojvodina is administratively part of the Republic of Serbia. [4]Region under interim UN administration from mid-1999. [5]Kosovo adopted the Deutsche Mark as its official currency in September 1999. [6]1996. [7]Includes 1,069,600 unemployed. [8]Detail does not add to total given because of rounding. [9]42,500 troops from over 30 NATO and non-NATO countries were deployed in Kosovo by September 2000.

Internet resources for further information:
- **Federal Statistical Office of Yugoslavia http://www.szs.sv.gov.yu/homee.htm**
- **Federal Republic of Yugoslavia Official Web Site http://www.gov.yu**

Zambia

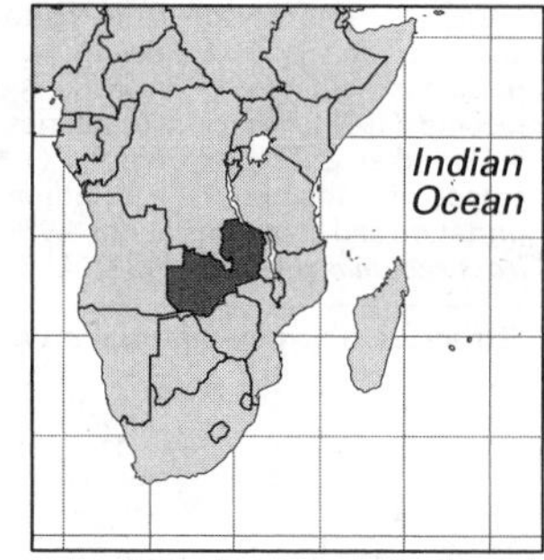

Official name: Republic of Zambia.
Form of government: multiparty republic with one legislative house (National Assembly [156[1]]).
Head of state and government: President.
Capital: Lusaka.
Official language: English.
Official religion: none[2].
Monetary unit: 1 Zambian kwacha (K) = 100 ngwee; valuation (Oct. 6, 2000) 1 U.S.$ = K 3,445; 1 £ = K 4,984.

Area and population		area		population
				1990
Provinces	Capitals	sq mi	sq km	census
Central	Kabwe	36,446	94,395	725,611
Copperbelt	Ndola	12,096	31,328	1,579,542
Eastern	Chipata	26,682	69,106	973,818
Luapula	Mansa	19,524	50,567	526,705
Lusaka	Lusaka	8,454	21,896	1,207,980
North-Western	Solwezi	48,582	125,827	383,146
Northern	Kasama	57,076	147,826	867,795
Southern	Livingstone	32,928	85,283	946,353
Western	Mongu	48,798	126,386	607,497
TOTAL		290,586	752,614	7,818,447

Demography

Population (2000): 9,582,000.
Density (2000): persons per sq mi 32.9, persons per sq km 12.7.
Urban-rural (1998): urban 43.9%; rural 56.1%.
Sex distribution (1999): male 49.68%; female 50.32%.
Age breakdown (1999): under 15, 47.9%; 15–29, 30.3%; 30–44, 12.4%; 45–59, 5.6%; 60–74, 3.1%; 75 and over, 0.7%.
Population projection: (2010) 11,482,000; (2020) 13,365,000.
Doubling time: 37 years.
Ethnolinguistic composition (1990): Bemba peoples 39.7%; Maravi (Nyanja) peoples 20.1%; Tonga peoples 14.8%; North-Western peoples 8.8%; Barotze peoples 7.5%; Tumbuka peoples 3.7%; Mambwe peoples 3.4%; other 2.0%.
Religious affiliation (1995): Christian 47.8%, of which Protestant 22.9%, Roman Catholic 16.9%, African Christian 5.6%; traditional beliefs 27.0%; Muslim 1.0%; other 24.2%.
Major cities (1990): Lusaka 982,362 (metro. area, 1,400,000[3]); Ndola 376,311; Kitwe 348,571; Mufulira 175,025.

Vital statistics

Birth rate per 1,000 population (1999): 42.4 (world avg. 22.1); legitimate, n.a.; however, marriage is both early and universal, suggesting that legitimate births are a relatively high proportion of all births.
Death rate per 1,000 population (1999): 22.1 (world avg. 8.9).
Natural increase rate per 1,000 population (1999): 20.3 (world avg. 13.2).
Total fertility rate (avg. births per childbearing woman; 1999): 5.7.
Life expectancy at birth (1999): male 37.1 years; female 37.5 years.
Major causes of death per 100,000 population: n.a.

National economy

Budget (1998). Revenue: K 1,529,054,000,000 (tax revenue 71.5%, of which income tax 24.9%, excise taxes 13.8%, value-added tax 13.1%, company income tax 5.9%; grants 26.0%; nontax revenue 2.5%). Expenditures: K 1,943,165,000,000 (current expenditures 65.0%, of which debt service 21.7%, education 7.7%, transfers 7.7%, health 5.7%, defense 1.4%; capital expenditures 35.0%).
Production (metric tons except as noted). Agriculture, forestry, fishing (1999): sugarcane 1,600,000, corn (maize) 855,868, cassava 850,000, fruits and vegetables 378,500 (of which onions 26,000, tomatoes 24,000, oranges 3,400), millet 69,617, wheat 89,743, sweet potatoes 52,000, peanuts (groundnuts) 50,965, soybeans 26,695, sorghum 25,493, seed cotton 23,000, sunflower seeds 6,748, tobacco 3,100; livestock (number of live animals) 2,373,000 cattle, 1,069,000 goats, 324,000 pigs, 120,000 sheep, 28,000,000 chickens; roundwood (1998) 8,042,000 cu m; fish catch (1997) 65,902. Mining and quarrying (1998): copper (metal content) 355,000; cobalt (metal content) 4,016; silver 6,684 kg; gold 307 kg[4]. Manufacturing (value added in K '000,000; 1994): food products 39,765.1; beverages 36,596.5; chemicals and pharmaceuticals 32,141.5; textiles 15,358.5; tobacco 14,060.2; iron and steel, nonferrous metals, and fabricated metal products 13,874.6. Construction (value added in K; 1995): 45,663,000,000. Energy production (consumption): electricity (kW-hr; 1996) 7,795,000,000 (6,315,000,000); coal (metric tons; 1996) 350,000 (345,000); crude petroleum (barrels; 1996) none (4,178,000); petroleum products (metric tons; 1996) 515,000 (453,000); natural gas, none (n.a.).
Household income and expenditure. Average household size (1997) 5.0; average annual income per household (1981) K 1,041 (U.S.$908); sources of income (1981): wages and salaries 94.0%, other 6.0%; expenditure (1977): food 37.7%, housing 11.0%, clothing 8.3%, transportation 4.3%, education 2.1%, health 1.0%.
Tourism (1997): receipts U.S.$75,000,000; expenditures, n.a.
Population economically active (1996): total 3,454,000; activity rate of total population 38.2% (participation rates [1991]: over age 10, 52.6%; female 29.6%; unemployed 17.4%[5]).

Price and earnings indexes (1995 = 100)	1991	1992	1993	1994	1995	1996	1997
Consumer price index	6.2	16.8	48.5	74.5	100.0	146.3	182.6
Earnings index	...	...	...	...	...	...	...

Public debt (external, outstanding; 1997): U.S.$5,233,000,000.
Gross national product (1998): U.S.$3,234,000,000 (U.S.$330 per capita).

Structure of gross domestic product and labour force	1998		1990	
	in value K '000,000	% of total value	labour force	% of labour force
Agriculture	1,080,000	17.3	1,872,000	68.9
Mining	378,000	6.1	56,800	2.1
Manufacturing	713,000	11.4	50,900	1.9
Construction	316,000	5.1	29,100	1.1
Public utilities	241,000	3.9	8,900	0.3
Transp. and commun.	362,000	5.8	25,600	0.9
Trade	1,201,000	19.2	30,700	1.1
Finance	1,014,000	16.2	24,200	0.9
Pub. admin., defense / Services	560,000	9.0	111,600	4.1
Other	376,000[6]	6.0[6]	506,100	18.6
TOTAL	6,241,000	100.0	2,716,000[7]	100.0[7]

Land use (1994): forest 43.0%; pasture 40.4%; agriculture 7.1%; other 9.5%.

Foreign trade

Balance of trade (current prices)	1994	1995	1996	1997	1998
U.S.$'000,000	+63	−8	−62	−27	−148
% of total	3.0%	0.3%	3.0%	1.1%	7.8%

Imports (1998): U.S.$1,022,000,000 (1988; machinery and transport equipment 38.3%; basic manufactures 19.8%; chemicals 16.9%; mineral fuels, lubricants, and electricity 12.3%; food 3.8%). *Major import sources* (1997): South Africa 48.4%; United Kingdom 8.1%; Zimbabwe 7.3%; Saudi Arabia 6.2%.
Exports (1998): U.S.$873,600,000 (copper 49.3%; cobalt 17.7%; nonmetal exports 33.0%). *Major export destinations* (1997): Japan 10.9%; Saudi Arabia 9.9%; Thailand 8.7%; India 8.0%; France 6.7%; United Kingdom 6.0%; Zimbabwe 5.0%; U.S. 4.5%.

Transport and communications

Transport. Railroads (1997)[8]: length 787 mi, 1,266 km; passenger-mi 166,000,000, passenger-km 267,000,000; short ton-mi cargo 316,000,000, metric ton-km cargo 462,000,000. Roads (1997): total length 24,170 mi, 38,898 km (paved 18%). Vehicles (1995): passenger cars 157,000; trucks and buses 81,000. Merchant marine: vessels (100 gross tons and over) none. Air transport (1996)[9]: passenger arrivals and departures 284,000; metric ton cargo unloaded and loaded 8,800; airports (1998) with scheduled flights 4.

Communications Medium	date	unit	number	units per 1,000 persons
Daily newspapers	1996	circulation	114,000	14
Radio	1997	receivers	1,030,000	120
Television	1997	receivers	660,000	77.8
Telephones	1999	main lines	77,700	8.8
Cellular telephones	1999	subscribers	5,161	0.6
Internet	1999	users	3,000	0.3

Education and health

Educational attainment (1993)[10]. Percentage of population age 14 and over having: no formal schooling 18.6%; some primary education 54.8%; some secondary 25.1%; higher 1.5%. *Literacy* (1995): population age 15 and over literate 3,890,000 (78.2%); males literate 2,060,000 (85.6%); females literate 1,830,000 (71.3%).

Education (1996)	schools	teachers	students	student/ teacher ratio
Primary (age 7–13)	3,907	38,528[11]	1,670,000	...
Secondary (age 14–18)	246	5,786[12]	255,000	...
Voc., teacher tr.	26[13]	846[13]	7,982[14]	...
Higher	2	640	4,470	7.0

Health: physicians (1993) 786 (1 per 10,917 persons); hospital beds (1989) 22,461 (1 per 349 persons); infant mortality rate per 1,000 live births (1999) 93.7.
Food (1998): daily per capita caloric intake 1,970 (vegetable products 95%, animal products 5%); 84% of FAO recommended minimum requirement.

Military

Total active duty personnel (1999): 21,600 (army 92.6%; navy, none; air force 7.4%). *Military expenditure as percentage of GNP* (1997): 1.1% (world 2.6%); per capita expenditure U.S.$4.

[1]Includes 5 nonelective seats. [2]Zambia was declared a Christian nation according to the preamble of a constitutional amendment in 1996. [3]1996 estimate; urban agglomeration. [4]In 1997 legal and illegal exports of emeralds were estimated to equal U.S.$20,000,000 (about 20% of world total). [5]1987. [6]Less imputed bank service charge. [7]Detail does not add to total given because of rounding. [8]Excludes Tanzania-Zambia Railway Authority (TAZARA) data. [9]Lusaka airport only. [10]Based on a sample survey of 35,502 persons. [11]1995. [12]1988. [13]1989. [14]1990.

Internet resources for further information:
• **Zambian National WWW Server (Zamnet) http://www.zamnet.zm**

Zimbabwe

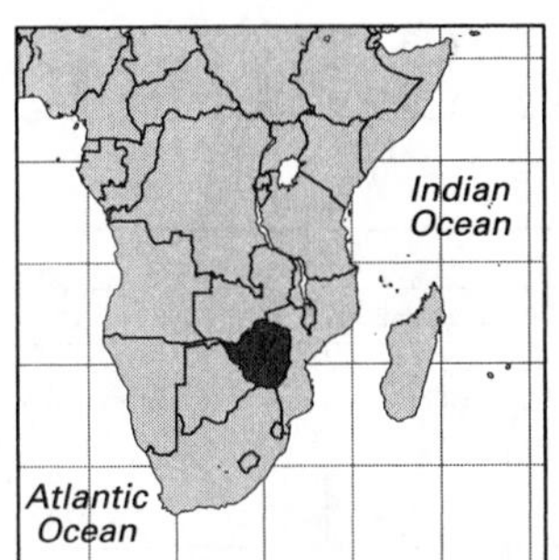

Official name: Republic of Zimbabwe.
Form of government: multiparty republic with one legislative house (House of Assembly [150[1]]).
Head of state and government: President.
Capital: Harare.
Official language: English.
Official religion: none.
Monetary unit: 1 Zimbabwe dollar (Z$) = 100 cents; valuation (Oct. 6, 2000) 1 U.S.$ = Z$53.10; 1 £ = Z$76.81.

Area and population

Provinces	Capitals	area sq mi	area sq km	population 1992 census[2]
Bulawayo	—	185	479	620,936
Harare	—	337	872	1,478,810
Manicaland	Mutare	14,077	36,459	1,537,676
Mashonaland Central	Bindura	10,945	28,347	857,318
Mashonaland East	Marondera	12,444	32,230	1,033,336
Mashonaland West	Chinhoyi	22,178	57,441	1,116,928
Masvingo	Masvingo	21,840	56,566	1,221,845
Matabeleland North	...	28,967	75,025	640,957
Matabeleland South	Gwanda	20,916	54,172	591,747
Midlands	Gweru	18,983	49,166	1,302,214
TOTAL		150,872	390,757	10,401,767

Demography

Population (2000): 11,343,000.
Density (2000): persons per sq mi 75.2, persons per sq km 29.0.
Urban-rural (1998): urban 33.9%; rural 66.1%.
Sex distribution (1999): male 50.43%; female 49.57%.
Age breakdown (1999): under 15, 40.7%; 15–29, 32.1%; 30–44, 14.9%; 45–59, 7.1%; 60–74, 4.0%; 75 and over, 1.2%.
Population projection: (2010) 11,057,000; (2020) 9,997,000.
Doubling time: not applicable; doubling time exceeds 100 years.
Ethnolinguistic composition (1982): African 97.6%, of which Shona-speaking Bantu 70.8%, Ndebele-speaking Bantu 15.8%; European 2.0%; Asian 0.1%; other 0.3%.
Religious affiliation (1995): Christian 45.4%, of which Protestant (including Anglican) 23.5%, African indigenous 13.5%, Roman Catholic 7.0%; animist 40.5%; other 14.1%.
Major cities (1992): Harare 1,184,169; Bulawayo 620,936; Chitungwiza 274,035; Mutare 131,808; Gweru 124,735.

Vital statistics

Birth rate per 1,000 population (1999): 25.4 (world avg. 22.1).
Death rate per 1,000 population (1999): 21.3 (world avg. 8.9).
Natural increase rate per 1,000 population (1999): 4.1 (world avg. 13.2).
Total fertility rate (avg. births per childbearing woman; 1999): 3.4.
Life expectancy at birth (1999): male 40.3 years; female 37.4 years.
Major causes of death per 100,000 population (1990): infectious and parasitic diseases 64.7; accidents and poisoning 44.4; diseases of the circulatory system 40.9; diseases of the respiratory system 39.5; malignant neoplasms (cancers) 28.4; diseases of the digestive system 12.1; diseases of the nervous system 9.4; endocrine and metabolic disorders 4.9.

National economy

Budget (1997–98). Revenue: Z$57,596,000,000 (tax revenue 93.0%, of which income tax 48.0%, sales tax 20.4%, customs duties 17.3%, excise tax 4.2%; nontax revenue 7.0%). Expenditures: Z$70,332,000,000 (recurrent expenditures 92.1%, of which goods and services 48.5%, interest payments 25.0%, transfer payments 18.4%).
Population economically active (1992): total 3,600,000; activity rate of total population 34.6% (participation rates: over age 15, 63.4%; female 39.8%; unemployed 7.2%[3]).

Price and earnings indexes (1995 = 100)

	1992	1993	1994	1995	1996	1997	1998
Consumer price index	52.3	66.7	81.6	100.0	121.4	144.2	190.1
Earnings index	...	...	...	...	...	...	...

Production (metric tons except as noted). Agriculture, forestry, fishing (1999): sugarcane 4,657,000, corn (maize) 1,520,000, wheat 320,000, seed cotton 268,000, tobacco 193,000, cassava 170,000, vegetables (including melons) 122,000, peanuts (groundnuts) 113,000, soybeans 107,000, sorghum 85,000, bananas 82,000, oranges 72,000, millet 53,000; livestock (number of live animals) 5,500,000 cattle, 2,770,000 goats, 525,000 sheep, 272,000 pigs, 15,000,000 chickens; roundwood (1998) 8,378,000 cu m; fish catch (1998) 16,386 metric tons. Mining and quarrying (value of production in Z$; 1997): gold 3,076,800,000; nickel 944,500,000; asbestos 927,900,000; coal 817,100,000; chrome 263,500,000; copper 162,300,000. Manufacturing (value in Z$; 1994): foodstuffs 6,746,300,000; metals and metal products 5,662,700,000; chemicals and petroleum products 3,314,800,000; beverages and tobacco 3,208,400,000; textiles 2,607,700,000; clothing and footwear 1,732,200,000; paper, printing, and publishing 1,553,700,000; transport equipment 1,454,400,000; wood and furniture 1,136,500,000; nonmetallic mineral products 1,076,600,000; other manufactured goods 323,300,000. Construction (Z$; 1996): residential 1,045,301,000; commercial 182,000,000; industrial 76,021,000. Energy production (consumption): electricity (kW-hr; 1996) 7,819,000,000 (10,991,000,000); coal (metric tons; 1996) 5,247,000 (5,242,000); crude petroleum, none (none); petroleum products (metric tons; 1996) none (1,375,000).
Public debt (external, outstanding; 1998): U.S.$3,341,000,000.
Household income and expenditure. Average household size (1992) 4.8; income per household Z$1,689 (U.S.$2,628); sources of income: n.a.; expenditure (1990[4]): food, beverages, and tobacco 39.1%, housing 18.7%, clothing and footwear 9.8%, transportation 8.4%, education 7.6%, household durable goods 7.2%, health 2.8%, recreation 2.0%, other 4.4%.
Gross national product (1998): U.S.$7,214,000,000 (U.S.$620 per capita).

Structure of gross domestic product and labour force

	1996 in value Z$'000,000[5]	1996 % of total value[5]	1995 labour force[6]	1995 % of labour force[6]
Agriculture	15,283	20.0	334,000	26.9
Mining	3,846	5.0	59,000	4.7
Manufacturing	14,668	19.2	185,900	15.0
Construction	1,943	2.5	71,800	5.8
Public utilities	2,409	3.2	9,500	0.8
Transp. and commun.	4,200	5.5	50,900	4.1
Trade	15,630	20.5	100,600	8.2
Finance	7,896	10.4	21,100	1.7
Pub. admin., defense	3,324	4.4	406,800	32.8
Services	5,472	7.2		
Other	1,572[7]	2.1[7]	...	...
TOTAL	76,243	100.0	1,239,600	100.0

Tourism (1997): receipts U.S.$230,000,000; expenditures U.S.$120,000,000.

Foreign trade

Balance of trade (current prices)

	1993	1994	1995	1996	1997	1998
U.S.$'000,000	+98	+169	+89	+249	+230	+79
% of total	3.1%	4.5%	2.0%	5.2%	4.5%	2.0%

Imports (1998): U.S.$1,968,000,000 (1996; machinery and transport equipment 38.7%, of which transport equipment 9.1%; manufactured goods 16.7%, of which textiles 2.6%, paper and paperboard 1.8%; fuels 10.4%, of which petroleum 9.7%). *Major import sources* (1996): South Africa 38.3%; U.K. 7.9%; Japan 5.1%; U.S. 5.0%; Germany 4.9%; France 3.1%; Italy 2.5%; The Netherlands 1.8%.
Exports (1998)[8]: U.S.$2,047,000,000 (1996; domestic exports 86.8%, of which tobacco 30.5%, gold sales 12.3%, ferroalloys 6.7%, nickel metal 3.2%, cotton 2.7%, asbestos 2.6%, cut flowers 1.4%, corn [maize] 1.2%). *Major export destinations* (1996): U.K. 10.1%; South Africa 9.6%; Germany 7.9%; U.S. 6.7%; Japan 5.1%; Zambia 4.3%; Italy 4.3%; Botswana 4.0%; The Netherlands 3.8%.

Transport and communications

Transport. Railroads (1998): route length 2,759 km; passenger-km 408,223,000; metric ton-km cargo 4,603,000. Roads (1996): total length 18,338 km (paved 47%). Vehicles (1996): passenger cars 323,000; trucks and buses 32,000. Air transport (1999)[9]: passenger-km 874,998,000; metric ton-km cargo 35,062,000; airports (1997) with scheduled flights 7.

Communications

Medium	date	unit	number	units per 1,000 persons
Daily newspapers	1996	circulation	209,000	19
Radio	1997	receivers	1,140,000	102
Television	1997	receivers	370,000	33
Telephones	1997	main lines	212,000	19
Personal computers	1998	units	130,000	12
Internet	1998	users	10,000	0.9

Education and health

Educational attainment (1992). Percentage of population age 25 and over having: no formal schooling 22.3%; primary 54.3%; secondary 13.1%; higher 3.4%. *Literacy* (1995): percentage of total population age 15 and over literate 85.1%; males literate 90.4%; females literate 79.9%.

Education (1998)

	schools	teachers	students	student/ teacher ratio
Primary (age 7–13)	4,706	64,538	2,507,098	38.8
Secondary (age 14–19)	1,530	30,482	847,296	27.8
Voc., teacher tr.[10]	25	1,479	27,431	18.5
Higher[11]	28[10]	3,581	46,492	13.0

Health: physicians (1996) 1,603 (1 per 6,904 persons); hospital beds (1996) 22,975 (1 per 501 persons); infant mortality rate (1999) 61.4.
Food (1998): daily per capita caloric intake 2,153 (vegetable products 92%, animal products 8%); 90% of FAO recommended minimum requirement.

Military

Total active duty personnel (1999): 39,000 (army 89.7%, air force 10.3%). *Military expenditure as percentage of GNP* (1997): 3.8% (world 2.6%); per capita expenditure U.S.$29.

[1]Includes 30 nonelective seats. [2]Preliminary results. [3]Does not take into consideration seasonal unemployment of communal workers; 1986–87. [4]Based on consumer price index. [5]At factor cost. [6]Wage-earning workers only. [7]Less imputed bank service charges. [8]Excludes gold sales and reexports. [9]Air Zimbabwe only. [10]1992. [11]Includes postsecondary vocational and teacher training at the higher level.

Internet resources for further information:
- **Reserve Bank of Zimbabwe http://www.rbz.co.zw**

Comparative National Statistics

World and regional summaries

region/bloc	area and population, 1998						gross national product, 1998						labour force, 1990		
	area		population			population projection, 2020	total ('000,000 U.S.$)	% agricul-ture	% industry	% ser-vices	growth rate, 1990–98	GNP per capita (U.S.$)	total ('000)	% male	% female
	square miles	square kilometres	total	per sq mi	per sq km										
World	52,433,280	135,801,650	6,048,469,000	115.4	44.5	7,493,272,000	28,108,910	4	32	64	1.7	4,980	2,353,806	63.8	36.2
Africa	11,717,440	30,348,170	800,810,000	68.3	26.4	1,166,571,000	533,070	17	34	49	0.3	700	242,784	65.6	34.4
Central Africa	2,552,970	6,612,160	94,127,000	36.9	14.2	158,008,000	28,800	33	34	34	–4.3	320	26,428	64.7	35.3
East Africa	2,473,690	6,406,680	246,854,000	99.8	38.5	361,082,000	62,640	30	19	51	0.7	270	85,082	58.8	41.2
North Africa	3,287,830	8,515,370	175,280,000	53.3	20.6	242,507,000	216,950	15	37	48	1.1	1,340	40,016	84.6	15.4
Southern Africa	1,032,300	2,673,660	49,994,000	48.4	18.7	43,696,000	147,440	4	39	57	–0.0	3,100	14,532	64.3	35.7
West Africa	2,370,650	6,140,300	234,555,000	98.9	38.2	361,278,000	77,240	32	32	36	0.6	340	76,726	63.8	36.2
Americas	16,245,580	42,075,810	819,044,000	50.4	19.5	1,018,191,000	10,433,890	3	29	68	2.0	12,990	293,723	66.5	33.5
Anglo-America[3]	8,301,330	21,500,350	306,268,000	36.9	14.2	360,291,000	8,487,190	2	27	71	2.0	28,220	135,438	58.7	41.3
Canada	3,849,670	9,970,610	30,770,000	8.0	3.1	35,199,000	580,870	2	31	67	1.1	19,170	13,360	60.2	39.8
United States	3,615,220	9,363,360	275,372,000	76.2	29.4	324,958,000	7,902,980	2	27	71	2.1	29,240	122,005	58.6	41.4
Latin America	7,944,250	20,575,460	512,776,000	64.5	24.9	657,900,000	1,946,700	8	34	58	1.9	3,870	158,285	73.1	26.9
Caribbean	90,720	234,910	36,738,000	405.0	156.4	43,760,000	91,160	6	34	60	0.4	2,470	13,813	66.9	33.1
Central America	202,240	523,820	35,531,000	175.7	67.8	51,200,000	53,980	16	22	61	2.1	1,570	9,520	78.5	21.5
Mexico	756,070	1,958,200	98,881,000	130.8	50.5	124,976,000	368,060	5	27	68	0.6	3,840	30,487	72.9	27.1
South America	6,895,220	17,858,530	341,626,000	49.5	19.1	437,964,000	1,433,500	8	37	55	2.4	4,270	104,465	73.6	26.4
Andean Group	2,112,170	5,470,500	128,317,000	60.8	23.5	171,108,000	343,660	9	38	53	2.4	2,780	34,715	75.6	24.4
Brazil	3,300,170	8,547,400	166,113,000	50.3	19.4	207,697,000	767,570	8	36	56	1.7	4,630	55,026	72.6	27.4
Other South America	1,482,880	3,840,630	47,196,000	31.8	12.3	59,159,000	322,270	8	36	56	4.0	7,000	14,724	72.4	27.6
Asia	12,313,840	31,892,470	3,669,732,000	298.0	115.1	4,546,500,000	7,083,410	8	37	55	2.9	2,160	1,464,452	64.5	35.5
Eastern Asia	4,546,020	11,774,190	1,492,897,000	328.4	126.8	1,678,984,000	5,856,040	5	39	57	2.7	4,030	775,590	57.4	42.6
China	3,696,100	9,572,900	1,265,207,000	342.3	132.2	1,438,287,000	923,560	18	49	33	9.6	750	669,693	56.7	43.3
Japan	145,880	377,840	126,920,000	870.0	335.9	124,249,000	4,089,140	2	37	61	1.3	32,350	62,202	62.1	37.9
South Korea	38,330	99,270	47,275,000	1,233.4	476.2	52,759,000	398,830	5	44	51	4.9	8,600	18,664	66.2	33.8
Other Eastern Asia	665,710	1,724,180	53,495,000	80.4	31.0	63,689,000	444,510	2	27	71	3.8	8,940	25,031	58.8	41.2
South Asia	1,938,850	5,021,590	1,355,541,000	699.1	269.9	1,783,351,000	559,470	25	29	46	3.8	430	411,136	77.4	22.6
India	1,222,240	3,165,600	1,014,004,000	829.6	320.3	1,311,747,000	427,410	25	30	45	4.3	440	322,944	74.8	25.2
Pakistan	307,370	796,100	141,554,000	460.5	177.8	199,745,000	61,450	25	25	50	1.5	470	33,698	87.5	12.5
Other South Asia	409,240	1,059,890	199,983,000	488.7	188.7	271,859,000	70,610	26	28	46	3.0	370	54,494	86.2	13.8
Southeast Asia	1,742,100	4,512,010	514,221,000	295.2	114.0	651,759,000	612,200	16	37	47	3.8	1,210	189,297	63.0	37.0
ASEAN	1,313,900	3,420,980	453,733,000	345.3	133.3	577,196,000	551,970	12	39	49	4.2	1,250	164,976	63.2	36.8
Non-ASEAN	428,200	1,109,030	60,488,000	141.3	54.5	74,563,000	60,230	58	11	31	0.2	940	24,321	62.2	37.8
Southwest Asia	4,086,870	10,584,680	307,073,000	75.1	29.0	432,406,000	780,630	11	35	54	0.2	2,640	88,429	69.4	30.6
Central Asia	1,545,790	4,003,400	55,761,000	36.1	13.9	74,447,000	50,780	21	29	50	–6.0	920	20,728	54.8	45.2
Gulf Cooperation Council	1,031,350	2,671,050	30,736,000	29.8	11.5	56,020,000	253,330	4	47	49	–0.8	8,850	6,511	91.7	8.3
Iran	630,830	1,633,840	62,704,000	99.4	38.4	80,482,000	102,240	20	36	44	1.8	1,650	15,253	82.0	18.0
Other Southwest Asia	878,900	2,276,390	157,872,000	179.6	69.4	221,457,000	374,280	13	27	60	1.7	2,490	45,936	68.7	31.3
Europe	8,868,840	22,970,380	728,110,000	82.1	31.7	723,799,000	9,592,600	3	30	67	0.8	13,150	340,666	57.1	42.9
Eastern Europe	7,437,260	19,262,550	338,311,000	45.5	17.6	324,397,000	803,550	9	36	55	–4.1	2,360	171,080	50.6	49.4
Russia	6,592,800	17,075,400	146,001,000	22.1	8.6	138,978,000	331,780	9	42	49	–7.2	2,260	72,286	47.6	52.4
Ukraine	233,100	603,700	49,242,000	211.2	81.6	44,443,000	49,210	11	30	59	–11.4	980	25,401	48.0	52.0
Other Eastern Europe	611,360	1,583,450	143,068,000	234.0	90.4	140,976,000	422,560	8	33	59	1.0	2,940	73,393	54.4	45.6
Western Europe	1,431,580	3,707,830	389,799,000	272.3	105.1	399,402,000	8,789,050	2	29	68	1.4	22,590	169,586	63.6	36.4
European Union (EU)	1,249,710	3,236,760	377,013,000	301.7	116.5	385,969,000	8,331,470	2	29	68	1.4	22,130	163,771	63.6	36.4
France	210,030	543,970	58,835,000	280.1	108.2	61,365,000	1,465,400	2	26	72	1.2	24,210	25,404	60.1	39.9
Germany	137,850	357,020	82,207,000	596.4	230.3	84,897,000	2,179,800	1	30	69	0.9	26,570	38,981	60.7	39.3
Italy	116,350	301,340	57,723,000	496.1	191.6	55,626,000	1,157,000	3	31	66	1.0	20,090	23,339	68.1	31.9
Spain	195,360	505,990	40,128,000	205.4	79.3	39,362,000	555,240	4	32	64	1.7	14,100	14,456	75.5	24.5
United Kingdom	94,250	244,110	59,714,000	633.6	244.6	63,453,000	1,264,260	2	31	67	2.0	21,410	27,766	61.4	38.6
Other EU	495,870	1,284,330	78,406,000	158.1	61.0	81,266,000	1,709,770	4	29	68	1.8	21,950	33,825	63.4	36.6
Non-EU	181,870	471,070	12,786,000	70.3	27.1	13,433,000	457,580	3	29	68	1.1	36,230	5,815	61.9	38.1
Oceania	3,287,580	8,514,820	30,773,000	9.4	3.6	38,211,000	461,310	4	26	70	2.5	15,440	12,181	63.0	37.0
Australia	2,969,910	7,692,030	19,165,000	6.5	2.5	22,409,000	387,010	3	26	71	2.8	20,640	7,963	61.9	38.1
Pacific Ocean Islands	317,670	822,790	11,608,000	36.5	14.1	15,802,000	74,300	8	24	68	1.1	6,670	4,218	65.0	35.0

[1]Refers only to the outstanding long-term external public and publicly guaranteed debt of the 137 countries that report under the World Bank's Debtor Reporting System (DRS). [2]World total includes

Africa

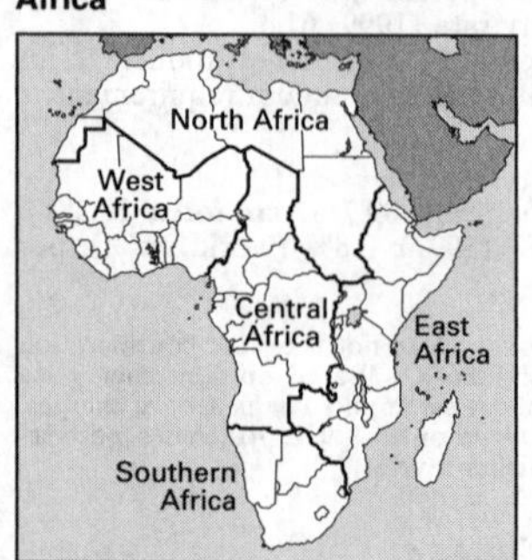

Americas

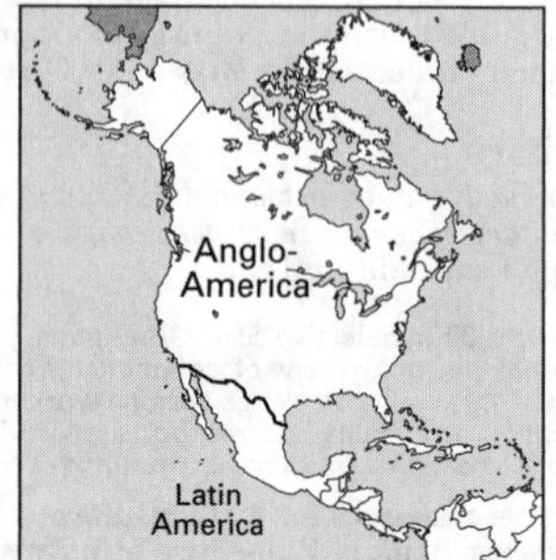

Asia

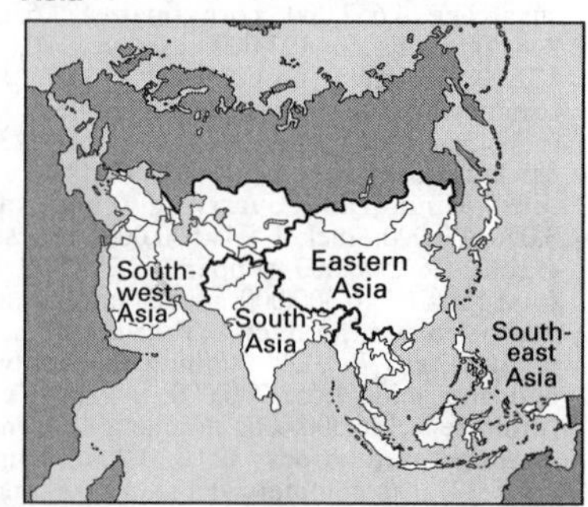

economic indicators							social indicators									region/bloc
pop. per 1,000 ha of arable land, 1998	electricity consumption (kW-hr per capita), 1996	trade ('000,000 U.S.$), 1998			debt ('000,000 U.S.$), 1998[1]		life expectancy (years), 2000		health			food (% FAO recommended minimum), 1998	literacy (%) (latest)		
		imports (c.i.f.)	exports (f.o.b.)	balance	total	% of GNP	male	female	pop. per doctor (latest)	infant mortality per 1,000 births, 2000	pop. having safe water (%); (1989–98)		male	female	
4,270	2,345	5,670,613	5,474,996[2]	−195,617[2]	1,448,868	24.2	64.7	68.9	730	53.6	76	118	83.7	71.0	World
4,300	507	140,047	126,853	−13,194	256,537	51.6	51.1	53.2	2,560	86.9	57	104	65.9	45.5	Africa
4,100	126	7,828	6,994	−834	38,029	132.1	46.9	50.4	12,890	107.8	44	83	77.7	56.4	Central Africa
5,590	142	18,172	16,013	−2,159	51,760	86.7	45.0	46.5	13,620	95.4	44	84	65.4	44.1	East Africa
4,100	693	56,196	52,715	−3,481	94,417	50.4	63.2	66.8	890	57.7	82	125	64.8	40.1	North Africa
2,990	3,888	29,439	25,891	−3,548	12,018	8.3	49.6	50.8	1,610	63.0	70	116	81.6	80.0	Southern Africa
3,940	128	28,412	25,240	−3,172	60,313	78.1	50.3	51.5	6,260	86.6	52	113	58.4	37.5	West Africa
2,240	6,200	1,528,175	1,425,746	−102,429	391,495	20.8	68.6	75.2	520	25.4	83	128	91.3	89.9	Americas
1,350	13,421	1,165,588	1,104,705	−60,883	—	—	74.4	80.2	370	6.7	91	140	96.1	95.7	Anglo-America[3]
660	17,455	219,150	198,530	−20,620	—	—	76.0	83.0	540	5.1	100	119	96.6	96.6	Canada
1,530	12,980	944,644	904,575	−40,069	—	—	74.2	79.9	360	6.8	90	142	95.7	95.3	United States
3,720	1,737	362,587	321,041	−41,546	391,495	20.8	65.2	72.2	690	32.6	78	119	87.8	85.6	Latin America
6,390	1,610	28,950	25,256	−3,694	9,997	31.2	67.6	72.4	380	43.5	77	102	83.8	83.0	Caribbean
4,930	629	23,202	34,805	+11,603	23,333	43.2	66.9	72.2	950	35.8	76	105	73.6	68.1	Central America
3,800	1,754	137,709	104,240	−33,469	87,996	23.9	68.5	74.7	810	26.2	85	135	91.8	87.4	Mexico
3,450	1,861	172,726	156,740	−15,986	270,169	18.9	63.8	71.5	710	33.0	76	117	88.4	87.0	South America
8,900	1,575	68,680	60,121	−8,559	86,307	25.1	67.9	74.3	830	31.3	79	106	92.6	88.7	Andean Group
3,040	2,026	63,314	59,053	−4,261	98,959	12.9	58.5	67.6	770	38.0	76	122	83.3	83.2	Brazil
1,580	2,009	40,732	37,556	−3,166	84,903	26.5	71.4	78.1	410	20.7	71	129	96.0	95.7	Other South America
7,200	1,140	1,378,224	1,283,051	−95,173	568,520	20.3	65.8	69.0	970	50.9	75	117	81.2	63.7	Asia
10,930	1,775	807,833	749,452	−58,381	158,014	11.9	70.3	74.6	610	26.5	71	125	91.4	77.0	Eastern Asia
10,010	891	140,385	154,843	+14,458	99,424	10.8	69.6	73.3	620	28.9	67	126	89.9	72.7	China
27,880	8,074	281,243	254,114	−27,129	—	—	77.5	84.1	530	3.9	97	123	100.0	100.0	Japan
27,180	5,022	93,282	81,259	−12,023	57,956	14.5	70.8	78.5	740	7.9	93	131	99.3	96.7	South Korea
13,400	4,270	292,923	259,236	−33,687	634	63.7	71.2	76.9	500	18.4	96	107	95.9	91.4	Other Eastern Asia
6,520	402	68,420	61,099	−7,321	137,601	24.8	61.3	62.4	2,100	70.3	80	108	62.4	35.5	South Asia
6,080	459	43,458	38,604	−4,854	85,207	19.9	61.9	63.1	1,920	64.9	81	112	65.5	37.7	India
6,920	407	9,308	8,873	−435	26,061	42.4	60.3	61.9	1,840	82.5	79	106	50.0	24.4	Pakistan
9,710	104	15,654	13,622	−2,032	26,333	40.6	59.1	59.1	5,080	84.6	78	89	53.5	30.9	Other South Asia
8,050	613	283,858	269,222	−14,636	170,725	33.5	64.5	69.5	3,120	40.3	70	120	91.8	83.3	Southeast Asia
9,200	689	279,776	265,148	−14,628	161,179	35.9	65.8	71.1	3,100	35.4	72	120	92.6	84.9	ASEAN
4,170	81	4,082	4,074	−8	9,546	15.8	53.5	56.7	3,240	75.7	53	121	86.0	71.6	Non-ASEAN
3,010	2,105	218,113	203,278	−14,835	102,180	24.4	65.8	70.3	610	52.3	79	116	86.7	72.4	Southwest Asia
1,430	2,675	11,237	10,253	−984	8,872	17.5	59.2	67.7	330	77.1	85	98	98.8	96.1	Central Asia
7,610	6,472	94,584	85,454	−9,130	2,228	16.1	67.7	71.1	620	46.2	95	122	73.8	55.8	Gulf Cooperation Council
3,640	1,180	13,107	11,983	−1,124	7,679	7.5	68.3	71.1	1,200	30.0	95	117	78.4	65.8	Iran
3,810	1,545	99,185	95,588	−3,597	83,401	33.1	66.6	70.9	690	51.8	65	122	87.8	68.1	Other Southwest Asia
2,480	5,603	2,539,663	2,499,599	−40,064	230,386	29.4	70.0	77.9	300	10.8	99	125	99.0	97.5	Europe
1,570	4,419	247,515	240,899	−6,616	230,386	29.4	64.1	73.9	290	18.1	95	116	99.1	96.6	Eastern Europe
1,170	5,588	42,476	52,731	+10,255	119,314	36.0	62.0	72.7	240	20.3	...	111	99.5	96.8	Russia
1,530	3,482	14,676	14,204	−472	8,606	17.5	60.4	71.9	330	21.7	97	112	99.5	97.4	Ukraine
2,470	3,550	190,363	173,964	−16,399	102,466	25.4	67.5	75.9	370	15.1	94	122	98.7	96.1	Other Eastern Europe
5,040	6,660	2,292,148	2,258,700	−33,448	—	—	75.0	81.5	300	5.1	100	134	98.9	98.2	Western Europe
4,960	6,433	2,168,432	2,121,340	−47,092	—	—	74.9	81.5	290	5.1	100	134	98.8	98.1	European Union (EU)
3,180	7,518	285,520	307,195	+21,675	—	—	74.9	82.9	330	4.5	100	141	98.9	98.7	France
6,910	6,582	463,263	474,552	+11,289	—	—	74.3	80.8	290	4.8	100	128	100.0	100.0	Germany
6,960	4,870	215,911	209,376	−6,535	—	—	75.9	82.4	180	5.9	100	143	97.8	96.4	Italy
2,790	4,384	130,073	132,526	+2,453	—	—	75.3	82.5	240	5.0	99	136	98.1	95.1	Spain
9,450	6,232	309,790	319,251	+9,461	—	—	75.0	80.5	720	5.6	100	129	100.0	100.0	United Kingdom
4,720	7,815	763,875	678,440	−85,435	—	—	74.8	80.9	320	4.9	100	132	97.9	97.2	Other EU
9,170	13,533	123,716	137,360	+13,644	—	—	76.3	82.3	480	4.4	100	123	99.9	99.9	Non-EU
540	7,735	84,504	75,492	−9,012	1,931	28.6	73.2	78.8	480	24.0	86	117	96.3	94.0	Oceania
350	9,820	66,843	59,534	−7,309	—	—	76.9	82.7	400	5.0	95	120	99.5	99.5	Australia
5,530	4,009	17,661	15,958	−1,703	1,931	28.6	67.0	72.2	770	40.3	68	111	89.8	82.7	Pacific Ocean Islands

U.S.$64,255,000,000 undistributable by region. [3]Anglo-America includes Canada, the United States, Greenland, Bermuda, and St. Pierre and Miquelon.

Europe

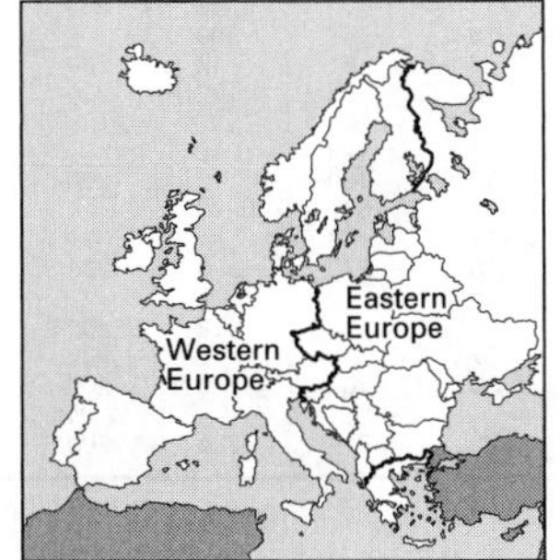

Eastern Europe

Oceania

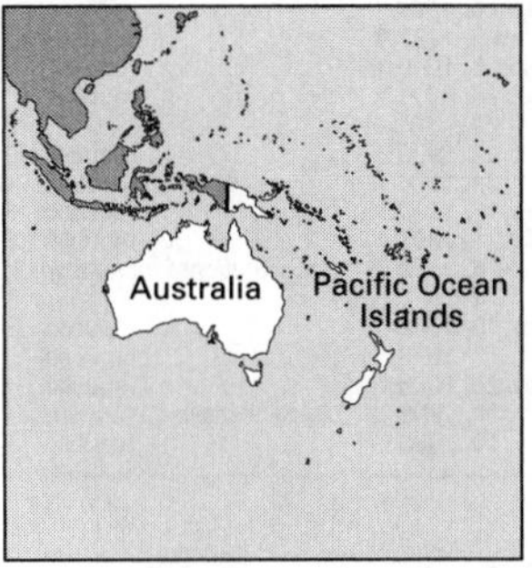

Government and international organizations

This table summarizes principal facts about the governments of the countries of the world, their branches and organs, the topmost layers of local government constituting each country's chief administrative subdivisions, and the participation of their central governments in the principal intergovernmental organizations of the world.

In this table "date of independence" may refer to a variety of circumstances. In the case of the newest countries, those that attained full independence after World War II, the date given is usually just what is implied by the heading—the date when the country, within its present borders, attained full sovereignty over both its internal and external affairs. In the case of longer established countries, the choice of a single date may be somewhat more complicated, and grounds for the use of several different dates often exist. The reader should refer to appropriate Britannica articles on national histories and relevant historical acts. In cases of territorial annexation or dissolution, the date given here refers either to the final act of union of a state composed of smaller entities or to the final act of separation from a larger whole (*e.g.,* the separation of Bangladesh from Pakistan in 1971).

The date of the current, or last, constitution is in some ways a less complicated question, but governments sometimes do not, upon taking power, either adhere to existing constitutional forms or trouble to terminate the previous document and legitimize themselves by the installation of new constitutional forms. Often, however, the desire to legitimize extraconstitutional political activity by associating it with existing forms of long precedent leads to partial or incomplete modification, suspension, or abrogation of a constitution, so that the actual day-to-day conduct of government may be largely unrelated to the provisions of a constitution still theoretically in force. When a date in this column is given in italics, it refers to a document that has been suspended, abolished by extraconstitutional action, or modified extensively.

The characterizations adopted under "type of government" represent a compromise between the forms provided for by the national constitution and the more pragmatic language that a political scientist might adopt to describe these same systems. For an explanation of the application of these terms in the Britannica World Data, *see* the Glossary at page 533.

The positions denoted by the terms "chief of state" and "head of government" are usually those identified with those functions by the constitution. The duties of the chief of state may range from largely ceremonial responsibilities, with little or no authority over the day-to-day conduct of government, to complete executive authority as the effective head of government. In certain countries, an official of a political party or a revolutionary figure outside the constitutional structure may exercise the powers of both positions.

Membership in the legislative house(s) of each country as given here includes all elected or appointed members, as well as ex officio members (those who by virtue of some other office or title are members of the body), whether voting or nonvoting. The legislature of a country with a unicameral system is shown as the upper house in this table.

The number of administrative subdivisions for each country is listed down to the second level. A single country may, depending on its size, complexity, and historical antecedents, have as many as five levels of administrative subordination or it may have none at all. Each level of subordination may have several kinds of subdivisions.

Government and international organizations

country	date of independence[a]	date of current or last constitution[b]	type of government	executive branch[c]		legislative branch[d]		admin. subdivisions		seaward claims	
				chief of state	head of government	upper house (members)	lower house (members)	first-order (number)	second-order (number)	territorial (nautical miles)	fishing/economic (nautical miles)
Afghanistan	Aug. 19, 1919	—	Islamic emirate	——leader of the faithful[1]——		...	...	...	...	—	—
Albania	Nov. 28, 1912	Nov. 28, 1998	republic	president	prime minister	155	—	37	309	12	[2]
Algeria	July 5, 1962	Dec. 7, 1996[3]	republic	president	prime minister	144	380	48	553	12	[4]
American Samoa	—	July 1, 1967	territory (U.S.)	U.S. president	governor	18	21	3	14	12	200
Andorra	Dec. 6, 1288	May 4, 1993	parl. coprincipality	[6]	head of govt.	28	—	7	...	—	—
Angola	Nov. 11, 1975	Aug. 27, 1992	republic	——president[7]——		220[8]	—	18	163	20	200
Antigua and Barbuda	Nov. 1, 1981	Nov. 1, 1981	constitutional monarchy	British monarch	prime minister	17[9]	17	30	—	12[10]	200[10]
Argentina	July 9, 1816	Aug. 24, 1994[11]	federal republic	——president[12]——		72	257	24	503	12	200
Armenia	Sept. 23, 1991	July 5, 1995[13]	republic	president	prime minister	131	—	11	...	—	—
Aruba	—	Jan. 1, 1986	overseas territory (Neth.)	Dutch monarch	[14]	21	—	...	...	12	200
Australia	Jan. 1, 1901	July 9, 1900	federal parl. state[16]	British monarch	prime minister	76	148	8	*c.* 900	12	200
Austria	Oct. 30, 1918	Oct. 1, 1920	federal state	president	chancellor	64	183	9	98	—	—
Azerbaijan	Aug. 30, 1991	Nov. 12, 1995[13]	federal republic	——president[17]——		124[18]	—	2	71	...	...
Bahamas, The	July 10, 1973	July 10, 1973	constitutional monarchy	British monarch	prime minister	16	40	—	25	12	200
Bahrain	Aug. 15, 1971	June 1973	monarchy (emirate)	emir	prime minister	40[20]	...	...	—	12	[21]
Bangladesh	March 26, 1971	Dec. 16, 1972	republic	president	prime minister	330	—	7	64	12	200
Barbados	Nov. 30, 1966	Nov. 30, 1966	constitutional monarchy	British monarch	prime minister	21	28	—	—	12	200
Belarus	Aug. 25, 1991	Nov. 27, 1996[22]	republic	——president[17]——		64[22]	110[22]	6	118	—	—
Belgium	Oct. 4, 1830	Feb. 17, 1994	fed. const. monarchy	monarch	prime minister	71[23]	150	[24]	589	12	[21]
Belize	Sept. 21, 1981	Sept. 21, 1981	constitutional monarchy	British monarch	prime minister	8	29	[25]	...	12[26]	200
Benin	Aug. 1, 1960	Dec. 2, 1990	republic	——president——		83	—	12	77	200	200
Bermuda	—	June 8, 1968	dependent territory (U.K.)	British monarch	[27]	11	40	11	—	12	200
Bhutan	March 24, 1910	—	[28]	monarch	chairman CM	150	—	20	...	—	—
Bolivia	Aug. 6, 1825	Feb. 2, 1967	republic	——president——		27	130	9	112	—	—
Bosnia and Herzegovina	March 1, 1992	Dec. 14, 1995[29]	federal republic	[30]	chairman CM	15	42	2	10[31]	...	...
Botswana	Sept. 30, 1966	Sept. 30, 1966	republic	——president——		15[20]	46	19	...	—	—
Brazil	Sept. 7, 1822	Oct. 5, 1988	federal republic	——president——		81	513	27	5,656	12	200
Brunei	Jan. 1, 1984	*Sept. 29, 1959*	monarchy (sultanate)	——sultan——		21[20]	—	4	...	12	200
Bulgaria	Oct. 5, 1908	July 12, 1991	republic	president	prime minister	240	—	28	...	12	200
Burkina Faso	Aug. 5, 1960	June 11, 1991	republic	president	prime minister	178[20]	111	45	...	—	—
Burundi	July 1, 1962	June 6, 1998[32]	republic[33]	——president[34]——		121	—	15	122	—	—
Cambodia	Nov. 9, 1953	March 4, 1999[35]	constitutional monarchy	king	prime minister	61	122	24	180	12	200
Cameroon	Jan. 1, 1960	Jan. 18, 1996	republic	president	prime minister	180	—	10	56	50	[2]
Canada	July 1, 1867	April 17, 1982	federal parl. state[16]	Canadian GG[36]	prime minister	105	301	12	...	12	200
Cape Verde	July 5, 1975	Sept. 25,1992	republic	president	prime minister	72	—	16	...	12[10]	200[10]
Central African Republic	Aug. 13, 1960	Jan. 14, 1995	republic	president	prime minister	109	—	17	69	—	—
Chad	Aug. 11, 1960	April 14, 1996	republic	president	prime minister	125	—	14	53	—	—
Chile	Sept. 18, 1810	March 11, 1981	republic	——president——		48	120	13	51	12	200
China	1523 BC	Dec. 4, 1982	people's republic	president	premier SC	2,979	—	31	332	12	[2]
Colombia	July 20, 1810	July 5, 1991	republic	——president——		102	163	33	1,011	12	200
Comoros	July 6, 1975	May 5, 1999[37]	republic[33]	——head of state[17]——		—	—	...	...	12[10]	200[10]
Congo, Dem. Rep. of the	June 30, 1960	*April 9, 1994*	republic[33]	——president——		300	—	11	...	12	200
Congo, Rep. of the	Aug. 15, 1960	Nov. 3, 1997[38]	republic[33]	——president——		75	...	16	47	200	[2]
Costa Rica	Sept. 15, 1821	Nov. 9, 1949	republic	——president——		57	—	7	81	12	200
Côte d'Ivoire	Aug. 7, 1960	July 23, 2000[13]	republic	——president[17]——		175	—	16	58	12	200
Croatia	June 25, 1991	Dec. 22, 1990	republic	president	prime minister	68	152	21	123	12	...
Cuba	May 20, 1902	Feb. 24, 1976	socialist republic	——president——		601	—	15	169	12	200
Cyprus[40]	Aug. 16, 1960	Aug. 16, 1960	republic	——president——		56[41]	—	...	647	12	[2]
Czech Republic	Jan. 1, 1993	Jan. 1, 1993	republic	president	prime minister	81	200	14	76	—	—
Denmark	*c.* 800	June 5, 1953	constitutional monarchy	monarch	prime minister	179	—	16	275	3	200
Djibouti	June 27, 1977	Sept. 15, 1992	republic	——president——		65	—	5	...	12	200
Dominica	Nov. 3, 1978	Nov. 3, 1978	republic	president	prime minister	32	—	37	—	12	200
Dominican Republic	Feb. 27, 1844	Nov. 28, 1966[42]	republic	——president——		30	149	30	160	6	200
East Timor	—	Oct. 26, 1999	UN transitional admin.	——UN administrator[43]——		—	—	...	...	...	...
Ecuador	May 24, 1822	Aug. 10, 1998	republic	——president——		121	—	22	214	200	200

Finally, in the second half of the table are listed the memberships each country maintains in the principal international intergovernmental organizations of the world. This part of the table may also be utilized to provide a complete membership list for each of these organizations as of Dec. 1, 2000.

Notes for the column headings

a. The date may also be either that of the organization of the present form of government or the inception of the present administrative structure (federation, confederation, union, etc.).
b. Constitutions whose dates are in italic type had been wholly or substantially suspended or abolished as of late 2000.
c. For abbreviations used in this column see the list on the facing page.
d. When a legislative body has been adjourned or otherwise suspended, figures in parentheses indicate the number of members in the legislative body as provided for in constitution or law.
e. States contributing funds to or receiving aid from UNICEF in 1997.
f. 15 nations with judicial representation in ICJ in 2000.
g. Palestine (Liberation Organization) also a member.

International organizations, conventions

ACP	African, Caribbean, and Pacific (Lomé IV) convention
ADB	Asian Development Bank
APEC	Asia-Pacific Economic Cooperation Council
CARICOM	Caribbean Community and Common Market
EU	The European Union
ECOWAS	Economic Community of West African States
FAO	Food and Agriculture Org.
FZ	The Franc Zone
GCC	Gulf Cooperation Council
I-ADB	Inter-American Development Bank
IAEA	International Atomic Energy Agency
IBRD	International Bank for Reconstruction and Development
ICAO	International Civil Aviation Org.
ICJ	International Court of Justice
IDA	International Development Association
IDB	Islamic Development Bank
IFC	International Finance Corporation
ILO	International Labour Org.
IMF	International Monetary Fund
IMO	International Maritime Org.
ITU	International Telecommunication Union
LAS	League of Arab States
OAS	Organization of American States
OAU	Organization of African Unity
OPEC	Organization of Petroleum Exporting Countries
SPC	South Pacific Commission
UNCTAD	United Nations Conference on Trade and Development
UNESCO	United Nations Educational Scientific and Cultural Org.
UNICEF	United Nations Children's Fund
UNIDO	United Nations Industrial Development Org.
UPU	Universal Postal Union
WHO	World Health Org.
WIPO	World Intellectual Property Org.
WMO	World Meteorological Org.
WTO	World Trade Org.

Abbreviations used in the executive-branch column

CM	Council of Ministers
EC	Executive Council
FC	Federal Council
GG	Governor-General
GPC	General People's Committee
NDC	National Defense Commission
NSC	National Security Council
PC	People's Council
PNA	Palestine National Authority
SC	State Council
SPDC	State Peace and Development Council

membership in international organizations																																					country
United Nations (date of admission)	UN organs★ and affiliated intergovernmental organizations																				Commonwealth of Nations	regional multipurpose						economic										
	UNCTAD★	UNICEF★e	ICJ★f	FAO	IAEA	IBRD	ICAO	IDA	IFC	ILO	IMF	IMO	ITU	UNESCO	UNIDO	UPU	WHO	WIPO	WMO	WTO		EU	GCC	LASg	OAS	OAU	SPC	ACP	ADB	APEC	CARICOM	ECOWAS	FZ	I-ADB	IDBg	OPEC	
1946	•	•		•	•	•	•	•	•	•	•		•	•	•	•	•		•										•						•		Afghanistan
1955	•	•		•	•	•	•	•	•	•	•	•	•	•	•	•	•	•	•	•															•		Albania
1962	•	•	•	•	•	•	•	•	•	•	•	•	•	•	•	•	•	•	•	5				•		•									•	•	Algeria
—																•											•										American Samoa
1993	•												•	•			•	•	•	5																	Andorra
1976	•	•		•	•	•	•	•	•	•	•	•	•	•	•	•	•	•	•	•						•		•									Angola
1981	•	•		•		•	•		•	•	•	•	•	•		•	•	•	•	•	•				•			•			•						Antigua and Barbuda
1945	•	•		•	•	•	•	•	•	•	•	•	•	•	•	•	•	•	•	•					•									•			Argentina
1992	•	•		•	•	•	•	•	•	•	•		•	•	•	•	•	•	•	5																	Armenia
—														15		•			•																		Aruba
1945	•	•		•	•	•	•	•	•	•	•	•	•	•	•	•	•	•	•	•	•						•		•	•							Australia
1955	•	•		•	•	•	•	•	•	•	•	•	•	•	•	•	•	•	•	•		•							•					•			Austria
1992	•	•		•		•	•	•	•	•	•	•	•	•	•	•	•	•	•	19															•		Azerbaijan
1973	•	•		•		•	•		•	•	•	•	•	•	•	•	•	•	•	5	•				•			•			•			•			Bahamas, The
1971	•	•		•		•	•		•	•	•	•	•	•	•	•	•	•	•	•			•	•											•		Bahrain
1974	•	•		•	•	•	•	•	•	•	•	•	•	•	•	•	•	•	•	•	•								•						•		Bangladesh
1966	•	•		•		•	•		•	•	•	•	•	•	•	•	•	•	•	•	•				•			•			•			•			Barbados
1945	•	•			•	•	•		•	•	•		•	•	•	•	•	•	•	5																	Belarus
1945	•	•		•	•	•	•	•	•	•	•	•	•	•	•	•	•	•	•	•		•							•					•			Belgium
1981	•	•		•		•	•	•	•	•	•	•	•	•	•	•	•		•	•	•				•			•			•			•			Belize
1960	•	•		•	•	•	•	•	•	•	•	•	•	•	•	•	•	•	•	•						•		•				•	•		•		Benin
—																•			•																		Bermuda
1971	•	•		•		•	•	•			•		•	•	•	•	•	•		5									•								Bhutan
1945	•	•		•	•	•	•	•	•	•	•	•	•	•	•	•	•	•	•	•					•									•			Bolivia
1992	•	•		•	•	•	•		•	•	•	•	•	•	•	•	•	•	•	19																	Bosnia and Herzegovina
1966	•	•		•		•	•	•	•	•	•		•	•	•	•	•	•	•	•	•					•		•									Botswana
1945	•	•	•	•	•	•	•	•	•	•	•	•	•	•	•	•	•	•	•	•					•									•			Brazil
1984	•					•	•				•	•	•			•	•	•	•	•	•									•					•		Brunei
1955	•	•		•	•	•	•	•	•	•	•	•	•	•	•	•	•	•	•	•																	Bulgaria
1960	•	•		•	•	•	•	•	•	•	•		•	•	•	•	•	•	•	•						•		•				•	•		•		Burkina Faso
1962	•	•		•		•	•	•	•	•	•		•	•	•	•	•	•	•	•						•		•									Burundi
1955	•	•		•	•	•	•	•	•	•	•	•	•	•	•	•	•	•	•	5									•								Cambodia
1960	•	•		•	•	•	•	•	•	•	•	•	•	•	•	•	•	•	•	•	•					•		•					•		•		Cameroon
1945	•	•		•	•	•	•	•	•	•	•	•	•	•		•	•	•	•	•	•				•				•	•				•			Canada
1975	•	•		•		•	•	•	•	•	•	•	•	•	•	•	•	•	•	5						•		•				•					Cape Verde
1960	•	•		•		•	•	•	•	•	•		•	•	•	•	•	•	•	•						•		•					•				Central African Republic
1960	•	•		•		•	•	•	•	•	•		•	•	•	•	•	•	•	•						•		•					•		•		Chad
1945	•	•		•	•	•	•	•	•	•	•	•	•	•	•	•	•	•	•	•					•					•				•			Chile
1945	•	•	•	•	•	•	•	•	•	•	•	•	•	•	•	•	•	•	•	5								•	•	•							China
1945	•	•		•	•	•	•	•	•	•	•	•	•	•	•	•	•	•	•	•					•									•			Colombia
1975	•	•		•		•	•	•	•	•	•		•	•	•	•	•		•					•		•		•					•		•		Comoros
1960	•	•		•	•	•	•	•	•	•	•	•	•	•	•	•	•	•	•	•						•		•									Congo, Dem. Rep. of the
1960	•	•		•		•	•	•	•	•	•	•	•	•	•	•	•	•	•	•						•		•					•				Congo, Rep. of the
1945	•	•		•	•	•	•	•	•	•	•	•	•	•	•	•	•	•	•	•					•									•			Costa Rica
1960	•	•		•	•	•	•	•	•	•	•	•	•	•	•	•	•	•	•	•						•		•				•	•				Côte d'Ivoire
1992	•	•		•	•	•	•	•	•	•	•	•	•	•	•	•	•	•	•	•														•			Croatia
1945	•	•		•	•		•			•		•	•	•	•	•	•	•	•	•					39												Cuba
1960	•	•		•	•	•	•	•	•	•	•	•	•	•	•	•	•	•	•	•	•																Cyprus[40]
1993	•	•		•	•	•	•	•	•	•	•	•	•	•	•	•	•	•	•	•																	Czech Republic
1945	•	•		•	•	•	•	•	•	•	•	•	•	•	•	•	•	•	•	•		•							•					•			Denmark
1977	•	•		•		•	•	•	•	•	•	•	•	•	•	•	•		•	•				•		•		•							•		Djibouti
1978	•	•		•		•		•	•	•	•	•	•	•	•	•	•	•	•	•	•				•			•			•						Dominica
1945	•	•		•	•	•	•	•	•	•	•	•	•	•	•	•	•		•	•					•			•						•			Dominican Republic
—																																					East Timor
1945	•	•		•	•	•	•	•	•	•	•	•	•	•	•	•	•	•	•	•					•									•			Ecuador

Government and international organizations (continued)

country	date of independence[a]	date of current or last constitution[b]	type of government	executive branch[c]: chief of state	executive branch[c]: head of government	legislative branch[d]: upper house (members)	legislative branch[d]: lower house (members)	admin. subdivisions: first-order (number)	admin. subdivisions: second-order (number)	seaward claims: territorial (nautical miles)	seaward claims: fishing/economic (nautical miles)
Egypt	Feb. 28, 1922	Sept. 11, 1971	republic	president	prime minister	454	—	27	186	12[44]	200[44]
El Salvador	Jan. 30, 1841	Dec. 20, 1983	republic	—president—		84	—	14	262	200	200
Equatorial Guinea	Oct. 12, 1968	Nov. 16, 1991[13]	republic	president	prime minister	80	—	7	18	12	200
Eritrea	May 24, 1993	May 23, 1997[45]	republic[33]	—president—		150	—	6	...	...	...
Estonia	Feb. 24, 1918	July 3, 1992	republic	president	prime minister	101	—	15	46	12	...
Ethiopia	c. 1000 BC	Aug. 22, 1995[46]	federal republic	president	prime minister	108	546	11	57	—	—
Faroe Islands	—	April 1, 1948	part of Danish realm	Danish monarch	[47]	32	—	9	48	3	200
Fiji	Oct. 10, 1970	*July 27, 1998*	interim authority	president	prime minister	(32)	(71)	...	...	12[10]	200[10]
Finland	Dec. 6, 1917	July 17, 1919[48]	republic	president	prime minister	200	—	6	20	12[49]	12
France	August 843	Oct. 4, 1958	republic	president	prime minister	321	577	22	96	12	200
French Guiana	—	Feb. 28, 1983	overseas dept. (Fr.)	French president	[50]	19	31	2	22	12	200
French Polynesia	—	Sept. 6, 1984	overseas territory (Fr.)	French president	[51]	41	—	5	48	12	200
Gabon	Aug. 17, 1960	March 26, 1991	republic	president	prime minister	91	120	9	37	12	200
Gambia, The	Feb. 18, 1965	Jan. 16, 1997	republic	—president—		49	—	7	45	12	200
Gaza Strip	—	May 4, 1994[52]	interim authority	—chairman PNA—		89	—	5	...	...	...
Georgia	April 9, 1991	Oct. 17, 1995	republic	—president[53]—		235	—	12	74	...	...
Germany	May 5, 1955	May 23, 1949	federal republic	president	chancellor	69	669	16	32	12[44]	200
Ghana	March 6, 1957	Jan. 7, 1993	republic	—president—		200	—	10	110	12	200
Greece	Feb. 3, 1830	June 11, 1975	republic	president	prime minister	300	—	53	448	6/10	[2]
Greenland	—	May 1, 1979	part of Danish realm	Danish monarch	[47]	31	—	18	...	3	200
Grenada	Feb. 7, 1974	Feb. 7, 1974	constitutional monarchy	British monarch	prime minister	13	15	9	...	12	200
Guadeloupe	—	Feb. 28, 1983	overseas dept. (Fr.)	French president	[50]	42	43	3	34	12	200
Guam	—	Aug. 1, 1950	territory (U.S.)	U.S. president	governor	15	—	...	—	12	...
Guatemala	Sept. 15, 1821	Jan. 14, 1986	republic	—president—		113	—	22	313	12	200
Guernsey	—	Jan. 1, 1949[48]	crown dependency (U.K.)	British monarch[54]	[55]	59	—	2	10	...	...
Guinea	Oct. 2, 1958	Dec. 23, 1990[38]	republic	—president[56]—		114	—	8	34	12	200
Guinea-Bissau	Sept. 10, 1974	May 11, 1991	republic[33]	president	prime minister	102	—	9	37	12	200
Guyana	May 26, 1966	Oct. 6, 1980	cooperative republic	—president—		65	—	10	71	12	200
Haiti	Jan. 1, 1804	March 29, 1987	republic	president	prime minister	27	82	9	41	12	200
Honduras	Nov. 5, 1838	Jan. 20, 1982	republic	—president—		128	—	18	297	12	200
Hong Kong	—	July 1, 1997	[57]	—chief executive EC—		60	—	18	...	12	[2]
Hungary	Nov. 16, 1918	Oct. 18, 1989[38]	republic	president	prime minister	386[58]	—	20	195	—	—
Iceland	June 17, 1944	June 17, 1944	republic	president	prime minister	63	—	165	—	12	200
India	Aug. 15, 1947	Jan. 26, 1950	federal republic	president	prime minister	245	545	35	...	12	200
Indonesia	Aug. 17, 1945	Aug. 17, 1945	republic	—president—		700	500	29	...	12[10]	200[10]
Iran	Oct. 7, 1906	Dec. 2–3, 1979	Islamic republic	—president[59]—		290	—	28	282	12	50[60]
Iraq	Oct. 3, 1932	Sept. 22, 1968[61]	republic	—president—		250	—	18	96	12	[2]
Ireland	Dec. 6, 1921	Dec. 29, 1937	republic	president	prime minister	60	166	34	86	12	200
Isle of Man	—	1961[48]	crown dependency (U.K.)	British monarch[54]	chief minister	11	24	24	—	12[62]	...
Israel	May 14, 1948	June 1950[48]	republic	president	prime minister	120	—	6	15	12	[2]
Italy	March 17, 1861	Jan. 1, 1948	republic	president	prime minister	326	630	20	102	12	[2]
Jamaica	Aug. 6, 1962	Aug. 6, 1962	constitutional monarchy	British monarch	prime minister	21	60	13	—	12	200
Japan	c. 660 BC	May 3, 1947	constitutional monarchy	emperor	prime minister	252	480	47	3,233	12[63]	200
Jersey	—	Jan. 1, 1949[48]	crown dependency (U.K.)	British monarch[54]	[64]	58	—	12	—	3	...
Jordan	May 25, 1946	Jan. 8, 1952	constitutional monarchy	—king[17]—		40	80	12	...	3	[2]
Kazakhstan	Dec. 16, 1991	Sept. 6, 1995	republic	—president[17]—		39	77	17	...	—	—
Kenya	Dec. 12, 1963	Dec. 12, 1963	republic	—president—		224	—	8	...	12	200
Kiribati	July 12, 1979	July 12, 1979	republic	—president—		42	—	3	6	12[10]	200[10]
Korea, North	Sept. 9, 1948	Sept. 5, 1998[65]	socialist republic	chairman NDC	premier	687	—	13	172	12	200
Korea, South	Aug. 15, 1948	Feb. 25, 1988	republic	—president[17]—		273	—	16	195	12[66]	12
Kuwait	June 19, 1961	Nov. 16, 1962	const. mon. (emirate)	—emir[17]—		50[67]	—	5	—	12	[2]
Kyrgyzstan	Aug. 31, 1991	May 5, 1993	republic	—president[17]—		45	60	7	89	—	—
Laos	Oct. 23, 1953	Aug. 15, 1991	republic	president	prime minister	99	—	18	114	—	—
Latvia	Nov. 18, 1918	Nov. 7, 1922	republic	president	prime minister	100	—	33	70	12	...
Lebanon	Nov. 26, 1941	Sept. 21, 1990	republic	president	prime minister	128	—	6	c. 700	12	[2]
Lesotho	Oct. 4, 1966	April 2, 1993	constitutional monarchy	king	prime minister	33[20]	80	10	...	—	—
Liberia	July 26, 1847	Aug. 20, 1995[68]	republic	—president—		26	64	14	...	200	[2]
Libya	Dec. 24, 1951	March 2, 1977	socialist state[69]	leader[70]	sec. GPC	760	—	26	...	12[71]	[2]
Liechtenstein	July 12, 1806	Oct. 5, 1921	constitutional monarchy	prince	head of govt.	25	—	11	...	—	—
Lithuania	Feb. 16, 1918	Nov. 6, 1992	republic	president	prime minister	141	—	10	56	12	...
Luxembourg	May 10, 1867	Oct. 17, 1868	constitutional monarchy	grand duke	prime minister	21[20]	60	3	12	—	—
Macau	—	Dec. 20, 1999	[53]	—chief executive EC—		23	—	...	...	6	12
Macedonia	Nov. 17, 1991	Nov. 17, 1991	republic	president	prime minister	120	—	123	...	—	—
Madagascar	June 26, 1960	April 8, 1998	federal republic	—president[17]—		150	—	6	113	12	200
Malawi	July 6, 1964	May 18, 1994	republic	—president—		192	—	3	26	—	—
Malaysia	Aug. 31, 1957	Aug. 31, 1957	fed. const. monarchy	paramount ruler	prime minister	70	193	15	132	12	200
Maldives	July 26, 1965	Jan. 1, 1998	republic	—president—		42[67]	—	21	...	12[10]	[44]
Mali	Sept. 22, 1960	Feb. 25, 1992	republic	president	prime minister	147	—	9	701	—	—
Malta	Sept. 21, 1964	Dec. 13, 1974	republic	president	prime minister	65	—	1	67	12	25
Marshall Islands	Dec. 22, 1990	May 1, 1979	republic	—president—		12[20]	33	...	—	12[10]	200
Martinique	—	Feb. 28, 1983	overseas dept. (Fr.)	French president	[50]	45	41	4	34	12	200
Mauritania	Nov. 28, 1960	July 21, 1991	republic	—president[17]—		56	79	13	53	12	200
Mauritius	March 12, 1968	March 12, 1992	republic	president	prime minister	70	—	11	130	12	200
Mayotte	—	Dec. 24, 1976	dept. collectivity (Fr.)	French president	[72]	19	—	17	—	12	200
Mexico	Sept. 16, 1810	Feb. 5, 1917	federal republic	—president—		128	500	32	2,435	12	200
Micronesia	Dec. 22, 1990	Jan. 1, 1981	federal republic	—president—		14	—	4	...	12	200
Moldova	Aug. 27, 1991	Aug. 27, 1994	parliamentary republic[73]	president	prime minister	101	—	2	45	—	—
Monaco	Feb. 2, 1861	Dec. 17, 1962	constitutional monarchy	prince	min. of state[74]	18	—	1	—	12	[2]
Mongolia	March 13, 1921	Feb. 12, 1992	republic	president	prime minister	76	—	22	342	—	—
Morocco	March 2, 1956	Oct. 7, 1996	constitutional monarchy	—king[17]—		270	325	16[75]	69[75]	12	200
Mozambique	June 25, 1975	Nov. 30, 1990	republic	—president—		250	—	11	112	12	200
Myanmar (Burma)	Jan. 4, 1948	*Jan. 4, 1974*	republic	—chairman SPDC—		(492)	—	14	58	12	200
Namibia	March 21, 1990	March 21, 1990	republic	—president—		26	72[67]	13	—	12	200
Nauru	Jan. 31, 1968	Jan. 31, 1968	republic	—president—		18	—	1	—	12	200
Nepal	Nov. 13, 1769	Nov. 9, 1990	constitutional monarchy	king	prime minister	60	205	14	75	—	—

membership in international organizations: United Nations (date of admission)	UNCTAD*	UNICEF*e	ICJ*f	FAO	IAEA	IBRD	ICAO	IDA	IFC	ILO	IMF	IMO	ITU	UNESCO	UNIDO	UPU	WHO	WIPO	WMO	WTO	Commonwealth of Nations	EU	GCC	LAS[g]	OAS	OAU	SPC	ACP	ADB	APEC	CARICOM	ECOWAS	FZ	I-ADB	IDB[g]	OPEC	country
	UN organs* and affiliated intergovernmental organizations																				Commonwealth	regional multipurpose						economic									
1945	●	●		●	●	●	●	●	●	●	●	●	●	●	●	●	●	●	●	●				●		●									●		Egypt
1945	●	●		●	●	●	●	●	●	●	●	●	●	●	●	●	●	●	●	●					●									●			El Salvador
1968	●	●		●		●	●	●	●	●	●	●	●	●	●	●	●	●								●		●					●				Equatorial Guinea
1993	●	●		●		●	●	●	●	●	●	●	●	●	●	●	●	●	●							●											Eritrea
1991	●	●		●	●	●	●		●	●	●	●	●	●	●	●	●	●	●	●																	Estonia
1945	●	●		●	●	●	●	●	●	●	●	●	●	●	●	●	●		●	●						●		●									Ethiopia
—																●																					Faroe Islands
1970	●	●		●		●	●	●	●	●	●	●	●	●	●	●	●	●	●	●	●						●	●	●								Fiji
1955	●	●		●	●	●	●	●	●	●	●	●	●	●	●	●	●	●	●	●		●							●					●			Finland
1945	●	●	●	●	●	●	●	●	●	●	●	●	●	●	●	●	●	●	●	●		●					●		●				●	●			France
—																●																	●				French Guiana
—																●			●								●						●				French Polynesia
1960	●	●		●	●	●	●	●	●	●	●	●	●	●	●	●	●	●	●	●						●		●					●		●		Gabon
1965	●	●		●		●	●	●	●	●	●	●	●	●	●	●	●	●	●	●	●					●		●				●			●		Gambia, The
—		●														●																					Gaza Strip
1992	●	●		●	●	●	●	●	●	●	●	●	●	●	●	●	●		●	●																	Georgia
1973	●	●	●	●	●	●	●	●	●	●	●	●	●	●	●	●	●	●	●	●		●							●					●			Germany
1957	●	●		●	●	●	●	●	●	●	●	●	●	●	●	●	●	●	●	●	●					●		●				●					Ghana
1945	●	●		●	●	●	●	●	●	●	●	●	●	●	●	●	●	●	●	●		●															Greece
—																●																					Greenland
1974	●	●		●		●	●	●	●	●	●		●	●	●	●	●	●		●	●				●			●			●						Grenada
—																●																	●				Guadeloupe
—																●											●										Guam
1945	●	●		●	●	●	●	●	●	●	●	●	●	●	●	●	●	●	●	●					●									●			Guatemala
—																●																					Guernsey
1958	●	●		●		●	●	●	●	●	●	●	●	●	●	●	●	●	●	●						●		●				●			●		Guinea
1974	●	●		●		●	●	●	●	●	●	●	●	●	●	●	●	●	●	●						●		●				●	●		●		Guinea-Bissau
1966	●	●		●		●	●	●	●	●	●	●	●	●	●	●	●	●	●	●	●				●			●			●			●			Guyana
1945	●	●		●	●	●	●	●	●	●	●	●	●	●	●	●	●	●	●	●					●			●			●			●			Haiti
1945	●	●		●	●	●	●	●	●	●	●	●	●	●	●	●	●	●	●	●					●									●			Honduras
—		●										15				●			●	●									●	●							Hong Kong
1955	●	●	●	●	●	●	●	●	●	●	●	●	●	●	●	●	●	●	●	●																	Hungary
1946	●	●		●	●	●	●	●	●	●	●	●	●	●		●	●	●	●	●																	Iceland
1945	●	●		●	●	●	●	●	●	●	●	●	●	●	●	●	●	●	●	●	●								●								India
1950	●	●		●	●	●	●	●	●	●	●	●	●	●	●	●	●	●	●	●									●	●					●	●	Indonesia
1945	●	●		●	●	●	●	●	●	●	●	●	●	●	●	●	●		●																●	●	Iran
1945	●	●		●	●	●	●	●	●	●	●	●	●	●	●	●	●	●	●					●											●	●	Iraq
1955	●	●		●	●	●	●	●	●	●	●	●	●	●	●	●	●	●	●	●		●															Ireland
—																●																					Isle of Man
1949	●	●		●	●	●	●	●	●	●	●	●	●	●	●	●	●	●	●	●														●			Israel
1955	●	●		●	●	●	●	●	●	●	●	●	●	●	●	●	●	●	●	●		●							●					●			Italy
1962	●	●		●	●	●	●	●	●	●	●	●	●	●	●	●	●	●	●	●	●				●			●			●			●			Jamaica
1956	●	●	●	●	●	●	●	●	●	●	●	●	●	●	●	●	●	●	●	●									●	●				●			Japan
—																●																					Jersey
1955	●	●	●	●	●	●	●	●	●	●	●	●	●	●	●	●	●	●	●	●				●											●		Jordan
1992	●	●			●	●	●	●	●	●	●	●	●	●	●	●	●	●	●	19									●						●		Kazakhstan
1963	●	●		●	●	●	●	●	●	●	●	●	●	●	●	●	●	●	●	●	●					●		●									Kenya
1999		●			●	●	●	●	●		●		●	●		●	●				●						●	●	●								Kiribati
1991	●	●		●			●					●	●	●	●	●	●	●	●																		Korea, North
1991	●	●		●	●	●	●	●	●	●	●	●	●	●	●	●	●	●	●	●									●	●							Korea, South
1963	●	●		●	●	●	●	●	●	●	●	●	●	●	●	●	●	●	●	●			●	●											●	●	Kuwait
1992	●	●		●		●	●	●	●	●	●		●	●	●	●	●	●	●	●									●						●		Kyrgyzstan
1955	●	●		●		●	●	●	●	●	●		●	●	●	●	●	●	●	19									●								Laos
1991	●	●		●	●	●	●	●	●	●	●	●	●	●		●	●	●	●	●																	Latvia
1945	●	●		●	●	●	●	●	●	●	●	●	●	●	●	●	●	●	●	19				●											●		Lebanon
1966	●	●		●		●	●	●	●	●	●		●	●	●	●	●	●	●	●	●					●		●									Lesotho
1945	●	●		●	●	●	●	●	●	●	●	●	●	●	●	●	●	●	●							●		●				●					Liberia
1955	●	●		●	●	●	●	●	●	●	●	●	●	●	●	●	●	●	●					●		●									●	●	Libya
1990	●				●								●			●	●	●		●																	Liechtenstein
1991	●	●		●	●	●	●		●	●	●	●	●	●	●	●	●	●	●	19																	Lithuania
1945	●	●		●	●	●	●	●	●	●	●	●	●	●	●	●	●	●	●	●		●															Luxembourg
—				●								15		15		●			●	●																	Macau
1993	●	●		●	●	●	●	●	●	●	●	●	●	●	●	●	●	●	●	19																	Macedonia
1960	●	●	●	●	●	●	●	●	●	●	●	●	●	●	●	●	●	●	●	●						●		●									Madagascar
1964	●	●		●		●	●	●	●	●	●	●	●	●	●	●	●	●	●	●	●					●		●									Malawi
1957	●	●		●	●	●	●	●	●	●	●	●	●	●	●	●	●	●	●	●	●								●	●					●		Malaysia
1965	●	●		●		●	●	●	●		●	●	●	●	●	●	●		●	●	●								●						●		Maldives
1960	●	●		●	●	●	●	●	●	●	●		●	●	●	●	●	●	●	●						●		●				●	●		●		Mali
1964	●	●		●	●	●	●			●	●	●	●	●	●	●	●	●	●	●	●																Malta
1991	●	●		●	●	●	●	●	●		●	●	●			●	●										●		●								Marshall Islands
—																●																	●				Martinique
1961	●	●		●		●	●	●	●	●	●	●	●	●	●	●	●	●	●	●				●		●		●				●			●		Mauritania
1968	●	●		●	●	●	●	●	●	●	●	●	●	●	●	●	●	●	●	●	●					●		●									Mauritius
—																●																	●				Mayotte
1945	●	●		●	●	●	●	●	●	●	●	●	●	●	●	●	●	●	●	●					●					●				●			Mexico
1991	●	●				●	●	●	●		●		●	●		●	●		●								●		●								Micronesia
1992	●	●		●	●	●	●	●	●	●	●		●	●	●	●	●	●	●	5																	Moldova
1993	●	●			●		●					●	●	●		●	●	●																			Monaco
1961	●	●		●	●	●	●	●	●	●	●	●	●	●	●	●	●	●	●	●									●								Mongolia
1956	●	●		●	●	●	●	●	●	●	●	●	●	●	●	●	●	●	●	●				●											●		Morocco
1975	●	●		●		●	●	●	●	●	●	●	●	●	●	●	●	●	●	●	●					●		●							●		Mozambique
1948	●	●		●	●	●	●	●	●	●	●	●	●	●	●	●	●	●	●	●									●								Myanmar (Burma)
1990	●	●		●	●	●	●	5	●	●	●	●	●	●	●	●	●	●	●	●	●					●		●									Namibia
1999							●						●	●		●	●				●						●		●								Nauru
1955	●	●		●		●	●	●	●	●	●	●	●	●	●	●	●	●	●	5									●								Nepal

Government and international organizations (continued)

country	date of independence[a]	date of current or last constitution[b]	type of government	executive branch[c]		legislative branch[d]		admin. subdivisions		seaward claims	
				chief of state	head of government	upper house (members)	lower house (members)	first-order (number)	second-order (number)	territorial (nautical miles)	fishing/economic (nautical miles)
Netherlands, The	March 30, 1814	Feb. 17, 1983	constitutional monarchy	monarch	prime minister	75	150	12	538	12	200
Netherlands Antilles	—	Dec. 29, 1954	overseas territory (Neth.)	Dutch monarch	[14]	22	—	5	—	12	200
New Caledonia	—	February 1999	overseas country (Fr.)	French president[76]	president	54	—	3	33	12	200
New Zealand	Sept. 26, 1907	June 30, 1852[48]	constitutional monarchy	British monarch	prime minister	120	—	12	74	12	200
Nicaragua	April 30, 1838	Jan. 9, 1987	republic	—president—		93	—	17	151	200	200
Niger	Aug. 3, 1960	Aug. 9, 1999[38]	republic	—president[17]—		83	—	8	35	—	—
Nigeria	Oct. 1, 1960	May 5, 1999	federal republic	—president—		109	360	37	990	30	200
Northern Mariana Is.	—	Jan. 9, 1978	commonwealth (U.S.)	U.S. president	governor	9	18	4	—	12	200
Norway	June 7, 1905	May 17, 1814	constitutional monarchy	king	prime minister	165	—	19	435	4	200
Oman	Dec. 20, 1951	Nov. 6, 1996[77]	monarchy (sultanate)	—sultan—		[78]	—	8	60	12	200
Pakistan	Aug. 14, 1947	*Aug. 14, 1973*	republic	—chief executive NSC—		(87)	(217)	16[79]	...	12	200
Palau	Oct. 1, 1994	Jan. 1, 1981	republic	—president—		14	16	16	—	3	200
Panama	Nov. 3, 1903	May 20, 1983[35]	republic	—president[80]—		71	—	13	75	200	[2]
Papua New Guinea	Sept. 16, 1975	Sept. 16, 1975	constitutional monarchy	British monarch	prime minister	109	—	20	267	12[10]	200[10]
Paraguay	May 14, 1811	June 22, 1992	republic	—president—		46	80	18	217	—	—
Peru	July 28, 1821	Dec. 29, 1993	republic	—president[17]—		120	—	14/28[81]	194	200	200
Philippines	July 4, 1946	Feb. 11, 1987	republic	—president—		24	260[82]	16	92	...	200[10]
Poland	Nov. 10, 1918	Oct. 17, 1997	republic	president	prime minister	100	460	16	308	12	[83]
Portugal	*c.* 1140	April 25, 1976	republic	president	prime minister	230	—	20	308	12	200
Puerto Rico	—	July 25, 1952	commonwealth (U.S.)	U.S. president	governor	27[84]	51[84]	78	...	12	200
Qatar	Sept. 3, 1971	July 1970[61]	monarchy	—emir[17]—		35[20]	—	9	—	12	[85]
Réunion	—	Feb. 28, 1983	overseas dept. (Fr.)	French president	[50]	47	45	4	24	12	200
Romania	May 21, 1877	Dec. 13, 1991	republic	president	prime minister	143	343	41	2.687	12[44]	200[44]
Russia	Dec. 8, 1991	Dec. 24, 1993	federal republic	president	prime minister	178	450	7	89	12	...
Rwanda	July 1, 1962	May 5, 1995[86]	republic[33]	—president[17]—		74	—	12	155	—	—
St. Kitts and Nevis	Sept. 19, 1983	Sept. 19, 1983	constitutional monarchy	British monarch	prime minister	15	—	1	—	12	200
St. Lucia	Feb. 22, 1979	Feb. 22, 1979	constitutional monarchy	British monarch	prime minister	11	17[9]	10	—	12	200
St. Vincent	Oct. 27, 1979	Oct. 27, 1979	constitutional monarchy	British monarch	prime minister	21	—	6	—	12	200
Samoa	Jan. 1, 1962	Oct. 28, 1960	[87]	head of state	prime minister	49	—	11	—	12	200
San Marino	855	Oct. 8, 1600	republic	—captains-regent (2)—		60	—	9	—	—	—
São Tomé and Príncipe	July 12, 1975	Sept. 10, 1990	republic	president	prime minister	55	—	1	6	12[10]	200[10]
Saudi Arabia	Sept. 23, 1932	[88]	monarchy	—king—		90[20]	—	13	103	12	[2]
Senegal	Aug. 20, 1960	March 7, 1963	republic	—president[17]—		60	140	10	30	12[44]	200[44]
Seychelles	June 29, 1976	June 21, 1993	republic	—president—		34	—	...	...	12	200
Sierra Leone	April 27, 1961	Oct. 1, 1991	republic	—president—		80	—	4	12	200	[2]
Singapore	Aug. 9, 1965	June 3, 1959[48]	republic	president	prime minister	93	—	—	—	3	12
Slovakia	Jan. 1, 1993	Jan. 1, 1993	republic	president	prime minister	150	—	8	79	—	—
Slovenia	June 25, 1991	Dec. 23, 1991	republic	president	prime minister	40	90	201	—	...	...
Solomon Islands	July 7, 1978	July 7, 1978	constitutional monarchy	British monarch	prime minister	50	—	10	...	12[10]	200[10]
Somalia	July 1, 1960	July 1, 1960	republic[33]	—president[17]—		245	—	2	...	200	200
South Africa	May 31, 1910	June 30, 1997	republic	—president—		90	400	9	360	12	200
Spain	1492	Dec. 29, 1978	constitutional monarchy	king	prime minister	259	350	19	50	12	200[89]
Sri Lanka	Feb. 4, 1948	Sept. 7, 1978	republic	—president—		225	—	...	...	12	200
Sudan, The	Jan. 1, 1956	*June 30, 1998*[90]	Islamic military regime	—president—		(400)	—	26	66	12	[2]
Suriname	Nov. 25, 1975	Nov. 25, 1987	republic	—president—		51	—	10	...	12	200
Swaziland	Sept. 6, 1968	*Sept. 6, 1968*	monarchy	—king[17]—		30[20]	65[20]	4	55	—	—
Sweden	before 836	Jan. 1, 1975	constitutional monarchy	king	prime minister	349	—	21	289	12	[21]
Switzerland	Sept. 22, 1499	Jan. 1, 2000	federal state	—president FC—		46	200	26	2,929	—	—
Syria	April 17, 1946	March14, 1973	republic	—president—		250	—	14	47	35	[2]
Taiwan	Oct. 25, 1945	Dec. 25, 1947[48]	republic	president	premier	225	—	2	25	24	200
Tajikistan	Sept. 9, 1991	Nov. 6, 1994	republic	president	prime minister	33	63	5	...	—	—
Tanzania	Dec. 9, 1961	April 25, 1977	republic	—president—		275	—	1	25	12	200
Thailand	1350	Oct. 11, 1997	constitutional monarchy	king	prime minister	200	393	76	794	12	200
Togo	April 27, 1960	Sept. 27, 1992[13]	republic	president	prime minister	81	—	5	21	30	200
Tonga	June 4, 1970	Nov. 4, 1875	constitutional monarchy[91]	—monarch[92]—		30	—	2	23	12	200
Trinidad and Tobago	Aug. 31, 1962	July 27, 1976	republic	president	prime minister	31	36	15	...	12[10]	200[10]
Tunisia	March 20, 1956	June 1, 1959	republic	president	prime minister	182	—	23	257	12	[2]
Turkey	Oct. 29, 1923	Nov. 7, 1982	republic	president	prime minister	550	—	80	829	12[93]	[21]
Turkmenistan	Oct. 27, 1991	May 18, 1992	republic	—president PC—		50	—	6	...	—	—
Tuvalu	Oct. 1, 1978	Oct. 1, 1986	constitutional monarchy	British monarch	prime minister	12	—	8	—	12[10]	200[10]
Uganda	Oct. 9, 1962	Oct. 8, 1995	republic	—president[17]—		280	—	39	...	—	—
Ukraine	Aug. 24, 1991	June 28, 1996	republic	president	prime minister	450	—	27	485	12	200
United Arab Emirates	Dec. 2, 1971	Dec. 2, 1971	federation of emirates	president	prime minister	40[20]	—	7	—	12	200
United Kingdom	Dec. 6, 1921	[95]	constitutional monarchy	monarch	prime minister	699	659	...	...	12[62]	200
United States	July 4, 1776	March 4, 1789	federal republic	—president—		100	435	51	3,043	12	200
Uruguay	Aug. 25, 1828	Feb. 15, 1967	republic	—president—		31	99	19	...	200	200
Uzbekistan	Aug. 31, 1991	Dec. 8, 1992	republic	—president[17]—		250	—	14	162	...	...
Vanuatu	July 30, 1980	July 30, 1980	republic	president	prime minister	52	—	6	...	12[10]	200[10]
Venezuela	July 5, 1811	Dec. 20, 1999	federal republic	—president—		165	—	25	332	12	200
Vietnam	Sept. 2, 1945	April 15, 1992	socialist republic	president	prime minister	450	—	60	479	12	200
Virgin Islands (U.S.)	—	July 22, 1954	territory (U.S.)	U.S. president	governor	15	—	...	...	12	200
West Bank	—	May 4, 1994[52]	interim authority	—chairman PNA—		89	—	11	...	—	—
Western Sahara	—	—	annexure of Morocco	—	—	—	—	...	...	12	200
Yemen	December 1918	Sept. 29, 1994[97]	republic	president	prime minister	301	—	17	...	12	200
Yugoslavia	Dec. 1, 1918	April 27, 1992	federal republic	federal president	prime minister	40	138	2	25[98]	...	...
Zambia	Oct. 24, 1964	May 28, 1996[3]	republic	—president—		156	—	9	57	—	—
Zimbabwe	April 18, 1980	April 18, 1980	republic	—president—		150	—	10	80	—	—

[1]Title of the Supreme Leader of the Taliban. [2]Territorial sea claim. [3]Date president signed new constitution. [4]Varies between 32 and 52 nautical miles. [5]Pending. [6]President of France and Bishop of Urgell, Spain. [7]President annulled post of prime minister in January 1999. [8]Includes 70 UNITA members expelled September 1998. [9]Excludes possible ex officio members. [10]Measured from claimed archipelagic baselines. [11]Promulgation date of significant amendments to July 9, 1853, constitution. [12]Assisted by the ministerial coordinator. [13]Date of referendum approving new constitution. [14]Executive responsibilities divided between (for The Netherlands) the governor and (locally) the prime minister. [15]Associate member. [16]Formally a constitutional monarchy. [17]Assisted by the prime minister. [18]Excludes one vacant seat reserved for Nagorno-Karabakh representative. [19]Observer status. [20]Body with limited or no legislative authority. [21]Defined by the equidistant line. [22]Legal status is controversial. [23]Excludes children of the monarch serving ex officio from age 18. [24]10 provincial councils; 5 region/community councils. [25]6 districts; 8 town boards. [26]3 nautical miles from the mouth of the Sarstoon River (southern boundary with Guatemala) to Ranguana Caye. [27]Executive responsibilities divided between (for the U.K.) the governor and (locally) the premier of the Cabinet. [28]Resembles a constitutional monarchy without a formal constitution. [29]Date of international treaty confirming the existence of a single state. [30]Tripartite presidency. [31]Excludes Republika Srpska. [32]Promulgation of transitional constitutional act. [33]Transitional government. [34]Assisted by vice presidents. [35]Date significant amendments adopted. [36]Governor-general can exercise all the powers of the reigning monarch of the Commonwealth. [37]Date of interim constitutional charter. [38]Transitional constitution. [39]Suspended membership. [40]Republic of Cyprus only. [41]Occupied seats only. [42]Date UN assumed formal transitional administration. [43]Assisted by Chairman of National Consultative Council from July 2000. [44]Zone defined by geographic coordinates. [45]Date new constitution approved by constituent assembly. [46]Date new republic was formally established. [47]Executive responsibilities divided between (for Denmark) the high commissioner and (locally) the prime minister. [48]Evolving body of constitutional law. [49]3 nautical miles in the Gulf of Finland. [50]Executive responsibilities divided among (for France) the prefect and (locally) the president of the General Council and the president of the Regional Council. [51]Executive responsibilities divided between (for France) the high commissioner and (locally) the president of the territorial government. [52]Date of agreement

membership in international organizations																																					country
United Nations (date of admission)	UN organs★ and affiliated intergovernmental organizations																			Commonwealth of Nations	regional multipurpose						economic										
	UNCTAD★	UNICEF★e	ICJ★f	FAO	IAEA	IBRD	ICAO	IDA	IFC	ILO	IMF	IMO	ITU	UNESCO	UNIDO	UPU	WHO	WIPO	WMO	WTO		EU	GCC	LASg	OAS	OAU	SPC	ACP	ADB	APEC	CARICOM	ECOWAS	FZ	I-ADB	IDBg	OPEC	
1945	•	•	•	•	•	•	•	•	•	•	•	•	•	•	•	•	•	•	•	•		•							•					•			Netherlands, The
—														15		•			•	•																	Netherlands Antilles
—																•			•	•							•						•				New Caledonia
1945	•	•		•	•	•	•	•	•	•	•	•	•	•	•	•	•	•	•	•	•						•		•	•							New Zealand
1945	•	•		•	•	•	•	•	•	•	•	•	•	•	•	•	•	•	•	•					•									•			Nicaragua
1960	•	•		•	•	•	•	•	•	•	•		•	•	•	•	•	•	•	•						•		•				•	•		•		Niger
1960	•	•		•	•	•	•	•	•	•	•	•	•	•	•	•	•	•	•	•	•					•		•				•				•	Nigeria
—																•											•										Northern Mariana Is.
1945	•	•		•	•	•	•	•	•	•	•	•	•	•	•	•	•	•	•	•									•					•			Norway
1971	•	•		•		•	•	•	•	•	•	•	•	•	•	•	•	•	•	•			•	•											•		Oman
1947	•	•		•	•	•	•	•	•	•	•	•	•	•	•	•	•	•	•	•	39								•						•		Pakistan
1994		•		•		•	•		•		•			•		•	•										•										Palau
1945	•	•		•	•	•	•	•	•	•	•	•	•	•	•	•	•	•	•	•					•									•			Panama
1975	•	•		•		•	•	•	•	•	•	•	•	•	•	•	•	•	•	•	•						•	•	•	•							Papua New Guinea
1945	•	•		•	•	•	•	•	•	•	•	•	•	•	•	•	•	•	•	•					•									•			Paraguay
1945	•	•		•	•	•	•	•	•	•	•	•	•	•	•	•	•	•	•	•					•					•				•			Peru
1945	•	•		•	•	•	•	•	•	•	•	•	•	•	•	•	•	•	•	•									•	•							Philippines
1945	•	•		•	•	•	•	•	•	•	•	•	•	•	•	•	•	•	•	•																	Poland
1955	•	•		•	•	•	•	•	•	•	•	•	•	•	•	•	•	•	•	•		•												•			Portugal
—				15												•	15																				Puerto Rico
1971	•	•		•	•	•	•			•	•	•	•	•	•	•	•	•	•	•			•	•											•	•	Qatar
—																•																	•				Réunion
1955	•	•		•	•	•	•	•	•	•	•	•	•	•	•	•	•	•	•	•																	Romania
1991	•	•	•		•	•	•	•	•	•	•	•	•	•	•	•	•	•	•	5										•							Russia
1962	•	•		•		•	•	•	•	•	•		•	•	•	•	•	•	•	•						•		•									Rwanda
1983	•	•		•		•		•	•	•	•			•	•	•	•	•		•	•				•			•			•						St. Kitts and Nevis
1979	•	•		•		•	•	•	•	•	•	•	•	•	•	•	•	•	•	•	•				•			•			•						St. Lucia
1980	•	•		•		•	•	•		•	•	•	•	•	•	•	•	•		•	•				•			•			•						St. Vincent
1976	•	•		•		•	•	•	•		•	•	•	•		•	•		•	19	•						•	•	•								Samoa
1992	•	•		•			•			•	•		•	•		•	•	•	•																		San Marino
1975	•	•		•		•	•	•		•	•	•	•	•	•	•	•	•	•							•		•									São Tomé and Príncipe
1945	•	•		•	•	•	•	•	•	•	•	•	•	•	•	•	•	•	•	5			•	•											•	•	Saudi Arabia
1960	•	•		•	•	•	•	•	•	•	•	•	•	•	•	•	•	•	•	•						•		•				•	•		•		Senegal
1976	•	•		•		•	•		•	•	•	•	•	•	•	•	•		•	5	•					•		•									Seychelles
1961	•	•	•	•	•	•	•	•	•	•	•	•	•	•	•	•	•	•	•	•	•					•		•				•			•		Sierra Leone
1965	•	•			•	•	•		•	•	•	•	•			•	•	•	•	•	•								•	•							Singapore
1993	•	•		•	•	•	•	•	•	•	•	•	•	•	•	•	•	•	•	•																	Slovakia
1992	•	•		•	•	•	•	•	•	•	•	•	•	•	•	•	•	•	•	•														•			Slovenia
1978	•	•		•		•	•	•	•	•	•	•	•	•		•	•		•	•	•						•	•	•								Solomon Islands
1960	•	•		•		•	•	•	•	•	•	•	•	•	•	•	•	•	•					•		•		•							•		Somalia
1945	•	•		•	•	•	•	•	•	•	•	•	•	•	•	•	•	•	•	•	•					•											South Africa
1955	•	•		•	•	•	•	•	•	•	•	•	•	•	•	•	•	•	•	•		•							•					•			Spain
1955	•	•		•	•	•	•	•	•	•	•	•	•	•	•	•	•	•	•	•	•								•								Sri Lanka
1956	•	•		•	•	•	•	•	•	•	39	•	•	•	•	•	•	•	•	19				•		•		•							•		Sudan, The
1975	•	•		•		•	•			•	•	•	•	•	•	•	•	•	•	•					•			•			•			•			Suriname
1968	•	•		•		•	•	•	•	•	•		•	•	•	•	•	•	•	•	•					•		•									Swaziland
1946	•	•		•	•	•	•	•	•	•	•	•	•	•	•	•	•	•	•	•		•							•					•			Sweden
—	•	•		•	•	•	•	•	•	•	•	•	•	•	•	•	•	•	•	•									•					•			Switzerland
1945	•	•		•	•	•	•	•	•	•	•	•	•	•	•	•	•		•					•											•		Syria
—																				5									•	•							Taiwan
1992	•	•		•		•	•	•	•	•	•	•	•	•	•	•	•	•	•																•		Tajikistan
1961	•	•		•	•	•	•	•	•	•	•	•	•	•	•	•	•	•	•	•	•					•		•									Tanzania
1946	•	•		•	•	•	•	•	•	•	•	•	•	•	•	•	•	•	•	•									•	•							Thailand
1960	•	•		•		•	•	•	•	•	•	•	•	•	•	•	•	•	•	•						•		•				•	•				Togo
1999	•	•		•		•	•	•	•		•		•	•	•	•	•			19	•						•	•	•								Tonga
1962	•	•		•		•	•	•	•	•	•	•	•	•	•	•	•	•	•	•	•				•			•			•			•			Trinidad and Tobago
1956	•	•		•	•	•	•	•	•	•	•	•	•	•	•	•	•	•	•	•				•		•									•		Tunisia
1945	•	•		•	•	•	•	•	•	•	•	•	•	•	•	•	•	•	•	•									•						•		Turkey
1992	•	•		•		•	•	5	•	•	•	•	•	•	•	•	•	•	•																•		Turkmenistan
2000		•											•	•	•	•	•				•94						•	•	•								Tuvalu
1962	•	•		•	•	•	•	•	•	•	•		•	•	•	•	•	•	•	•	•					•		•							•		Uganda
1945	•	•			•	•	•	5	•	•	•	•	•	•	•	•	•	•	•	5																	Ukraine
1971	•	•		•	•	•	•	•	•	•	•	•	•	•	•	•	•	•	•	•			•	•											•	•	United Arab Emirates
1945	•	•	•	•	•	•	•	•	•	•	•	•	•	•	•	•	•	•	•	•	•	•					•		•					•			United Kingdom
1945	•	•	•	•	•	•	•	•	•	•	•	•	•		•	•	•	•	•	•					•		•		•	•				•			United States
1945	•	•		•	•	•	•		•	•	•	•	•	•	•	•	•	•	•	•					•									•			Uruguay
1992	•	•			•	•	•	•	•	•	•		•	•	•	•	•	•	•	19									•								Uzbekistan
1981	•	•		•		•	•	•	•		•	•	•	•	•	•	•		•	19	•						•	•	•								Vanuatu
1945	•	•	•	•	•	•	•		•	•	•	•	•	•	•	•	•	•	•	•					•									•		•	Venezuela
1977	•	•		•	•	•	•	•	•	•	•	•	•	•	•	•	•	•	•	5									•	•							Vietnam
—																•															•						Virgin Islands (U.S.)
—		•																																			West Bank
—																										96											Western Sahara
1947	•	•		•	•	•	•	•	•	•	•	•	•	•	•	•	•	•	•	19				•											•		Yemen
1945	•	•		•	•	5	•	5	5	•		•	•	•	•	•	•	•	•																		Yugoslavia
1964	•	•		•	•	•	•	•	•	•	•		•	•	•	•	•	•	•	•	•					•		•									Zambia
1980	•	•		•	•	•	•	•	•	•	•		•	•	•	•	•	•	•	•	•					•		•									Zimbabwe

providing for Palestinian self-rule. [53]Assisted by the minister of state. [54]Represented by the lieutenant governor. [55]Executive committees appointed by the States of Deliberation. [56]Assisted by extraconstitutional prime minister. [57]Special administrative region (China). [58]Excludes 13 seats set aside for ethnic minorities. [59]Shares coexecutive authority with spiritual leader. [60]Sea of Oman only; median line boundaries in Persian Gulf. [61]Provisional constitution. [62]Median line between the Isle of Man and the United Kingdom. [63]3 nautical miles in 5 straits. [64]Executive committees appointed by the States Assembly. [65]Essentially 1992 constitution with new preamble. [66]3 nautical miles in Korea Strait. [67]Elected seats only. [68]Date of peace accord. [69]Formally a *jamahiriya*, translated as "the masses of people"; in fact, a military dictatorship. [70]De facto chief of state. [71]Based on Gulf of Sidra closing line (32° 30′ N), in part. [72]Executive responsibilities divided between (for France) the prefect and (locally) the president of the General Council. [73]From Oct. 27, 2000. [74]Under prince's authority. [75]Includes Western Sahara annexure. [76]Represented by High Commissioner. [77]Basic law promulgated by sultan. [78]Has 2 consultative bodies with advisory authority only. [79]Includes federally administered tribal areas, excludes Jammu and Kashmir. [80]Assisted by vice presidents. [81]Two concomitant administrative systems. [82]Includes vacant seats. [83]Defined by international treaties. [84]Excludes additional seats for both houses of the legislature to meet 1/3 total representation requirements for minority parties per constitution. [85]Limits of continental shelf or median boundaries. [86]Date constitution adopted by transitional legislature. [87]Mixed political system approximating a constitutional monarchy. [88]Royal decrees from March 1, 1992, created first written rules of governance. [89]Atlantic Ocean only. [90]A state of emergency existed in The Sudan from December 1999 through November 2000. [91]In practice resembles a system of monarchical absolutism. [92]Assisted by Privy Council. [93]Black Sea and Mediterranean Sea; 6 nautical miles in Aegean Sea. [94]Special member. [95]Based on evolving body of statutes and common law. [96]Membership held by the Sahrawi Arab Democratic Republic. [97]Effective date of significant amendments. [98]Serbia only excluding Kosovo.

Area and population

This table provides the area and population for each of the countries of the world and for all but the smallest political dependencies having a permanent civilian population. The data represent the latest published and unpublished data for both the surveyed area of the countries and their populations, the latter both as of a single year (2000) to provide the best comparability and as of the most recent census to provide the fullest comparison of certain demographic measures that are not always available between successive national censuses. The 2000 midyear estimates represent a combination of national, United Nations (UN) or other international organizations, and *Encyclopædia Britannica* estimates so as to give the best fit to available published series, to take account of unpublished information received via Internet, facsimile, or correspondence, and to incorporate the results of very recent censuses for which published analyses are not yet available.

One principal point to bear in mind when studying these statistics is that all of them, whatever degree of precision may be implied by the exactness of the numbers, are estimates—all of varying, and some of suspect, accuracy—even when they *contain* a very full enumeration. The United States—which has a long tradition both of census taking and of the use of the most sophisticated analytical tools in processing the data—is unable to determine within 2.1% (the estimated 1990 undercount) its total population nationally. And that is an *average* underenumeration. In states and larger cities, where enumeration of particular populations, both legal and illegal, is most difficult, the accuracy of the enumerated count may be off as much as 4% at a state level and as much as 10% for a single city. The high accuracy attained by census operations in China may approach 0.25% of rigorously maintained civil population registers. Other national census operations not so based, however, are inherently less accurate. For example, Ethiopia's first-ever census in 1984 resulted in figures that were 30% or more above prevailing estimates; Nigeria's 1991 census corrected decades of miscounts and was well below prevailing estimates. An undercount of 2–8% is more typical, but even census operations offering results of 30% or more above or below prevailing estimates can still represent well-founded benchmarks from which future planning may proceed. The editors have tried to take account of the range of variation and accuracy in published data, but it is difficult to establish a value for many sources of inaccuracy unless some country or agency has made a conscientious effort to establish both the relative accuracy (precision) of its estimate and the absolute magnitude of the quantity it is trying to measure—for example, the number of people in Cambodia who died at the hands of the Khmer Rouge. If a figure of 2,000,000 is adopted, what is its accuracy: ± 1%, 10%, 50%? Are the original data documentary or evidentiary, complete or incomplete, analytically biased or unbiased, in good agreement with other published data?

Many similar problems exist and in endless variations: What is the extent of southern European immigration to western Europe in search of jobs? How many refugees from Afghanistan, Liberia, Rwanda, or Burundi are there in surrounding countries? How many undocumented aliens are there in the United States? How many Palestinians are there in the Middle East (they are politically inconvenient to enumerate everywhere)? How many Amerindians exist (remain, preserving their original language and a mode of life unassimilated by the larger national culture) in the countries of South America? How many people have died or emigrated as a result of the civil violence in Central America?

Area and population

country	area			population (latest estimate)					population (latest census)				
	square miles	square kilometres	rank	total midyear 2000	rank	density per sq mi	density per sq km	% annual growth rate 1995–2000	census year	total	male (%)	female (%)	urban (%)
Afghanistan	251,825	652,225	41	25,889,000	38	102.8	39.7	3.8	1979	13,051,358[1]	51.4	48.6	15.1
Albania	11,100	28,748	142	3,490,000	128	314.4	121.1	1.5	1989	3,182,417	51.5	48.5	35.7
Algeria	919,595	2,381,741	11	30,554,000	35	33.2	12.8	2.2	1998	29,276,767	50.4	49.6	48.6[2]
American Samoa	77	199	206	65,400	205	849.4	328.6	2.8	1990	46,773	51.4	48.6	33.4
Andorra	181	468	194	66,700	204	368.5	142.5	0.8	1992[3]	61,599	53.1	46.9	62.5[4]
Angola	481,354	1,246,700	24	10,145,000	74	21.1	8.1	2.0	1970	5,673,046	52.1	47.9	14.2
Antigua and Barbuda	171	442	196	71,000	203	416.4	160.8	1.0	1991	63,896	48.2	51.8	36.2
Argentina	1,073,400	2,780,092	8	37,032,000	31	34.5	13.3	1.3	1991	32,615,528	48.9	51.1	88.4
Armenia	11,484	29,743	141	3,810,000	122	331.8	128.1	0.3	1989	3,287,677	49.3	50.7	67.8
Aruba	75	193	207	96,800	196	1,290.7	501.6	3.4	1991	66,687	49.2	50.8	...
Australia	2,969,910	7,692,030	6	19,165,000	52	6.5	2.5	1.2	1996	17,892,423	49.5	50.5	85.3[5]
Austria	32,378	83,858	115	8,091,000	87	249.9	96.5	0.1	1991	7,795,786	48.2	51.8	64.5
Azerbaijan	33,400	86,600	113	8,051,000	88	241.0	93.0	0.9	1999	7,953,000	48.2	51.8	53.8[6]
Bahamas, The	5,382	13,939	159	295,000	175	54.8	21.2	1.2	1990	255,095	49.0	51.0	64.3
Bahrain	268	694	187	691,000	160	2,578.4	995.4	3.7	1991	508,037	57.9	42.1	88.4
Bangladesh	56,977	147,570	93	129,194,000	8	2,267.5	875.5	1.6	1991	111,455,185	51.4	48.6	20.2
Barbados	166	430	197	267,000	178	1,608.4	620.9	0.2	1990[7]	257,083	47.7	52.3	37.9[8]
Belarus	80,153	207,595	85	9,989,000	78	124.6	48.1	–0.6	1989	10,199,709	46.9	53.1	65.5
Belgium	11,787	30,528	139	10,249,000	73	869.5	335.7	0.2	1991	9,978,681	48.9	51.1	96.6[9]
Belize	8,867	22,965	150	253,000	179	28.5	11.0	3.2	2000	240,204	50.5	49.5	47.5[5]
Benin	44,300	114,760	101	6,396,000	96	144.4	55.7	3.2	1992	4,915,555	48.6	51.4	35.7
Bermuda	21	54	213	63,000	207	3,000.0	1,166.7	0.7	1991[7]	58,460	48.5	51.5	100.0
Bhutan	18,150	47,000	131	667,000	161	36.7	14.2	2.8	...	...	51.6[10]	48.4[10]	7.0[10]
Bolivia	424,164	1,098,581	28	8,329,000	85	19.6	7.6	2.4	1992	6,420,792	49.4	50.6	57.5
Bosnia and Herzegovina	19,741	51,129	127	3,836,000	120	194.3	75.0	2.7	1991	4,377,033	49.9	50.1	39.6
Botswana	224,607	581,730	47	1,576,000	146	7.0	2.7	1.4	1991	1,326,796	47.8	52.2	23.9
Brazil	3,300,171	8,547,404	5	166,113,000	5	50.3	19.4	1.4	1991	146,825,475	49.4	50.6	75.6
Brunei	2,226	5,765	168	336,000	174	150.9	58.3	2.5	1991	260,482	52.8	47.2	66.6
Bulgaria	42,855	110,994	103	8,172,000	86	190.7	73.6	–0.6	1992	8,487,317	49.1	50.9	67.2
Burkina Faso	105,946	274,400	73	11,946,000	64	112.8	43.5	2.8	1996	10,312,609	48.2	51.8	15.0[10]
Burundi	10,740	27,816	145	6,055,000	100	563.8	217.7	2.2	1990[7]	5,292,793	48.6	51.4	6.3
Cambodia	69,898	181,035	89	12,371,000	63	177.0	68.3	2.7	1998	11,437,656	48.2	51.8	22.0[12]
Cameroon	183,569	475,442	53	15,422,000	59	84.0	32.4	2.6	1987	10,516,232	49.0	51.0	38.3
Canada	3,849,674	9,970,610	2	30,770,000	34	8.0	3.1	0.9	1996	28,846,761	49.1	50.9	77.9
Cape Verde	1,557	4,033	170	401,000	171	257.5	99.4	1.2	1990	341,491	47.3	52.7	44.1
Central African Republic	240,324	622,436	43	3,513,000	127	14.6	5.6	1.9	1988	2,688,426	49.1	50.9	36.5
Chad	495,755	1,284,000	21	8,425,000	84	17.0	6.6	3.4	1993	6,279,931	47.9	52.1	21.4
Chile	292,135	756,626	38	15,211,000	60	52.1	20.1	1.4	1992	13,348,401	49.1	50.9	83.5
China	3,696,100	9,572,900	3	1,265,207,000	1	342.3	132.3	1.0	1990	1,133,682,501	51.6	48.4	26.4
Colombia	440,762	1,141,568	26	42,299,000	27	96.0	37.1	1.9	1993	33,109,840	49.2	50.8	70.3[8]
Comoros	719	1,862	176	578,000	163	803.9	310.4	3.1	1991	446,817	49.5	50.5	28.5
Congo, Dem. Rep. of the	905,354	2,344,858	12	51,965,000	23	57.4	22.2	2.6	1984	29,671,407	49.2	50.8	29.1[13]
Congo, Rep. of the	132,047	342,000	63	2,831,000	133	21.4	8.3	2.4	1984[7]	1,909,248	48.7	51.3	52.0
Costa Rica	19,730	51,100	128	3,644,000	125	184.7	71.3	1.8	1984	2,416,809	50.0	50.0	43.9
Côte d'Ivoire	124,504	322,463	68	15,981,000	56	128.4	49.6	2.3	1988	10,815,694	51.1	48.9	39.0
Croatia	21,831	56,542	126	4,282,000	117	196.1	75.7	–0.8	1991	4,784,265	48.5	51.5	54.3
Cuba	42,804	110,861	104	11,149,000	67	260.4	100.6	0.3	1993	10,904,466	50.3	49.7	74.4
Cyprus[14]	3,572	9,251	165	865,000	156	242.2	93.5	1.0	1992[7, 15]	615,013	49.8	50.2	67.7
Czech Republic	30,450	78,866	117	10,273,000	72	337.4	130.3	–0.1	1991	10,302,215	48.5	51.5	75.2
Denmark	16,639	43,096	133	5,339,000	104	320.9	123.9	0.4	1999[3]	5,313,577	49.4	50.6	85.0
Djibouti	8,950	23,200	149	451,000	166	50.4	19.4	1.4	1983	273,974	51.9	48.1	82.8[13]
Dominica	290	750	184	76,300	200	263.1	101.7	0.5	1991	71,183	49.8	50.2	...
Dominican Republic	18,792	48,671	130	8,443,000	83	449.3	173.5	1.7	1993	7,293,390	48.7	51.3	56.1
East Timor	5,641	14,609	158	885,000	155	156.9	60.6	1.7	1990	747,750	51.7	48.3	7.8
Ecuador	105,037	272,045	74	12,646,000	62	120.4	46.5	2.0	1990	9,648,189	49.7	50.3	55.4

Still, much information is accurate, well founded, and updated regularly. The sources of these data are censuses; national population registers (cumulated periodically); registration of migration, births, deaths, and so on; sample surveys to establish demographic conditions; and the like.

The statistics provided for area and population by country are ranked, and the population densities based on those values are also provided. The population densities, for purposes of comparison within this table, are calculated on the bases of the 2000 midyear population estimate as shown and of total area of the country. Elsewhere in individual country presentations the reader may find densities calculated on more specific population figures and more specialized area bases: land area for Finland (because of its many lakes) or ice-free area for Greenland (most of which is ice cap). The data in this section conclude with the estimated average annual growth rate for the country (including both natural growth and net migration) during the five-year period, 1995–2000.

In the section containing census data, information supplied includes the census total (usually de facto, the population actually present, rather than de jure, the population legally resident, who might be anywhere); the male-female breakdown; the proportion that is urban (according to the country's own definition); and finally an analysis of the age structure of the population by 15-year age groups. This last analysis may be particularly useful in distinguishing the type of population being recorded—young, fast-growing nations show a high proportion of people under 30 (most countries in sub-Saharan Africa and the Middle East have nearly one-half of their population under 15 years), while other nations (for example Sweden, which suffered no age-group losses in World War II) exhibit quite uniform proportions.

Finally, a section is provided giving the population of each country at 10-year intervals from 1950 to 2020. The data for years past represent the best available analysis of the published data by the country itself, by the demographers of the UN, or by the editors of Britannica. The projections for 2010 and 2020 similarly represent the best fit of available data through the 1990s with projected population structure and growth rates during the next two decades. The evidence of the last 30 years with respect to similar estimates published about 1970, however, shows how cloudy is the glass through which these numbers are read. In 1970 no respectable Western analyst would have imagined proposing that mainland China could achieve the degree of birth control that it apparently has since then (as evidenced by the results of 1982 and 1990 censuses); on the other hand, even the Chinese admit that their methods have been somewhat Draconian and that they have already seen some backlash in terms of higher birth rates among those who have so far postponed larger families. How much is "some" by 2010? Compound that problem with all the social, economic, political, and biological factors that can affect 217 countries' populations, and the difficulty facing the prospective compiler of such projections may be appreciated.

Specific data about the vital rates affecting the data in this table may be found in great detail in both the country statistical boxes in "The Nations of the World" section and in the *Vital statistics, marriage, family* table, beginning at page 802.

Percentages in this table for male and female population will always total 100.0, but percentages by age group may not, for reasons such as nonresponse on census forms, "don't know" responses (which are common in countries with poor birth registration systems), and the like.

age distribution (%)						population (by decade, '000s)								country
0–14	15–29	30–44	45–59	60–74	75 and over	1950	1960	1970	1980	1990	2000	2010 projection	2020 projection	
44.5	26.9	15.8	8.6	3.6	0.6	8,150	9,829	12,431	14,985	14,750	25,889	33,864	41,735	Afghanistan
33.0	28.9	18.5	11.7	5.9	1.9	1,227	1,623	2,157	2,671	3,258	3,490	3,827	4,127	Albania
38.8[2]	29.2[2]	17.5[2]	8.5[2]	4.8[2]	1.2[2]	8,956	10,800	14,330	18,666	24,698	30,554	35,838	41,012	Algeria
38.1	29.0	18.1	9.4	4.3	1.1	19	20	27	32	47	65	81	95	American Samoa
16.3	27.7	27.2	15.1	9.9	3.8	6	8	19	33	53	67	72	78	Andorra
41.7	23.2	17.0	7.4	3.8	1.0	4,118	4,797	5,606	6,741	8,056	10,145	12,646	15,750	Angola
30.4	27.8	20.5	10.2	7.7	3.4	45	55	66	69	64	71	75	79	Antigua and Barbuda
30.6	23.3	19.3	13.9	9.6	3.3	17,150	20,616	23,962	28,094	32,527	37,032	41,474	45,347	Argentina
30.3	25.7	20.8	13.6	6.4	3.2	1,354	1,867	2,520	3,067	3,545	3,810	3,833	3,956	Armenia
24.4	22.0	27.0	16.1	7.2	3.0	51	57	61	60	64	97	102	104	Aruba
22.1[5]	24.2[5]	23.4[5]	15.0[5]	11.1[5]	4.4[5]	8,219	10,315	12,552	14,741	17,065	19,165	20,925	22,409	Australia
17.4	23.7	21.6	17.2	13.4	6.7	6,935	7,048	7,447	7,549	7,718	8,091	8,051	8,096	Austria
32.8[6]	29.7[6]	16.8[6]	12.8[6]	5.7[6]	2.2[6]	2,896	3,895	5,172	6,165	7,166	8,051	8,542	9,467	Azerbaijan
32.2	30.8	19.7	10.6	5.0	1.8	79	110	170	210	257	295	315	324	Bahamas, The
31.7	28.4	28.2	8.0	3.1	0.6	110	149	210	334	503	691	803	900	Bahrain
41.5	25.2	16.2	8.1	4.3	1.1	45,646	54,622	67,403	88,077	109,897	129,194	150,392	169,613	Bangladesh
24.1	27.1	22.1	11.4	9.9	5.4	209	232	235	249	261	267	273	279	Barbados
23.0	22.4	20.6	18.0	11.5	4.5	7,745	8,190	9,040	9,650	10,190	9,989	9,918	9,900	Belarus
18.2	21.8	22.5	16.9	14.1	6.6	8,639	9,153	9,690	9,859	9,967	10,249	10,407	10,381	Belgium
43.9[5]	27.9[5]	14.9[5]	7.2[5]	4.4[5]	1.6[5]	68	90	120	146	189	253	326	401	Belize
48.6	24.2	14.5	6.6	4.1	1.9	1,673	2,055	2,620	3,444	4,656	6,396	8,411	10,558	Benin
19.5	24.0	26.8	16.4	—13.3—		37	43	53	55	59	63	67	69	Bermuda
40.2[10]	26.0[10]	17.4[10]	10.1[10]	5.2[10]	1.1[10]	...	...	...	...	519	667	823	1,001	Bhutan
41.2	26.2	16.8	8.9	—6.5—		2,714	3,351	4,212	5,355	6,573	8,329	10,229	12,193	Bolivia
23.5[9]	26.3[9]	22.6[9]	16.9[9]	8.9[9]	2.7[9]	2,662	3,240	3,703	4,092	4,424	3,826	4,103	4,182	Bosnia and Herzegovina
42.8	27.3	14.3	7.3	4.1	2.2	430	497	584	903	1,304	1,576	1,502	1,318	Botswana
34.7	28.1	19.3	10.6	5.7	1.6	53,444	72,594	95,847	118,617	143,581	166,113	187,862	207,697	Brazil
34.5	29.3	24.2	7.9	—4.1—		45	83	128	185	258	336	408	475	Brunei
20.5	19.2	—39.8—		—20.5—		7,251	7,867	8,490	8,862	8,718	8,172	7,344	6,631	Bulgaria
47.9[11]	26.8[11]	12.9[11]	7.6[11]	3.9[11]	0.9[11]	4,376	4,866	5,626	6,939	9,037	11,946	15,424	19,402	Burkina Faso
46.4	25.3	15.4	7.0	4.0	1.7	2,363	2,812	3,513	4,138	5,285	6,055	7,669	9,553	Burundi
42.8	26.1	17.2	8.5	4.3	1.1	4,163	5,364	6,996	6,499	8,965	12,371	16,345	20,012	Cambodia
46.4	24.5	14.6	8.7	4.1	1.6	4,888	5,609	6,727	8,747	11,761	15,422	19,202	22,869	Cameroon
19.9	20.9	25.7	17.2	11.1	5.2	13,737	17,909	21,324	24,561	27,634	30,770	33,142	35.199	Canada
45.0	27.3	11.4	8.0	5.5	2.9	146	197	269	296	349	401	431	448	Cape Verde
43.2	27.5	15.0	9.2	4.1	0.8	1,260	1,467	1,827	2,244	2,803	3,513	4,135	4,672	Central African Republic
48.1	24.6	14.7	7.2	4.2	1.3	2,608	3,042	3,728	4,535	6,018	8,425	11,616	15,772	Chad
29.4	27.3	21.2	12.2	7.2	2.5	6,082	7,608	9,496	11,147	13,100	15,211	17,010	18,774	Chile
27.7	31.0	20.7	12.1	6.9	1.7	556,613	667,070	818,316	981,242	1,133,683	1,265,207	1,362,769	1,438,287	China
34.5	28.5	20.1	10.0	5.3	1.6	12,568	16,857	22,561	28,447	34,970	42,299	49,690	56,569	Colombia
47.6[9]	27.0[9]	13.1[9]	7.7[9]	3.5[9]	1.0[9]	148	183	236	334	429	578	773	1,000	Comoros
47.3[13]	25.9[13]	14.1[13]	8.1[13]	3.8[13]	0.8[13]	13,569	16,462	21,395	28,129	37,991	51,965	69,846	92,377	Congo, Dem. Rep. of the
44.7	27.2	13.3	9.1	4.6	0.7	768	931	1,183	1,620	2,218	2,831	3,491	4,209	Congo, Rep. of the
37.9	31.5	15.8	9.2	4.4	1.2	862	1,236	1,731	2,246	2,994	3,644	4,238	4,765	Costa Rica
46.8	27.3	15.0	7.5	2.8	0.6	2,860	3,565	5,427	8,261	11,919	15,981	20,003	23,748	Côte d'Ivoire
19.4	20.7	22.7	18.3	12.9	4.5	3,837	4,036	4,205	4,383	4,508	4,282	4,505	4,560	Croatia
22.3	29.4	21.3	14.8	8.4	3.9	5,850	7,028	8,572	9,780	10,603	11,148	11,526	11,799	Cuba
25.4	22.0	22.3	15.4	10.2	4.7	494	573	615	631	757	865	956	1,056	Cyprus[14]
21.0	21.8	22.6	16.8	12.7	5.1	8,925	9,539	9,830	10,292	10,298	10,273	10,157	9,891	Czech Republic
18.2	19.2	22.4	20.5	12.6	7.1	4,271	4,581	4,929	5,123	5,141	5,339	5,513	5,676	Denmark
39.4	32.9	16.9	7.4	2.8	0.6	60	78	158	279	370	451	579	729	Djibouti
33.3	28.3	16.3	9.7	—11.8—		51	60	70	75	72	76	79	81	Dominica
36.5[16]	29.5[16]	18.4[16]	9.6[16]	4.8[16]	1.2[16]	2,353	3,231	4,423	5,697	7,098	8,443	9,884	11,378	Dominican Republic
...	...	...	...	...	...	433	501	605	581	740	885	1,015	1,139	East Timor
38.8	28.5	17.3	9.0	4.7	1.7	3,307	4,421	5,958	8,123	10,264	12,646	14,899	16,904	Ecuador

Area and population (continued)

country	area			population (latest estimate)					population (latest census)				
	square miles	square kilo-metres	rank	total midyear 2000	rank	density per sq mi	density per sq km	% annual growth rate 1995–2000	census year	total	male (%)	female (%)	urban (%)
Egypt	385,229	997,739	30	65,871,000	15	171.0	66.0	2.0	1996	59,312,914	51.2	48.8	42.6
El Salvador	8,124	21,041	151	6,123,000	98	753.7	291.0	1.9	1992	5,118,599	48.6	51.4	50.4
Equatorial Guinea	10,831	28,051	144	474,000	164	43.8	16.9	2.5	1983	300,060	48.8	51.2	28.2
Eritrea	46,774	121,144	99	4,136,000	118	88.4	34.1	3.6	1984	2,703,998	49.9	50.1	15.1
Estonia	17,462	45,227	132	1,435,000	147	82.2	31.7	–0.7	2000	1,370,500	46.1	53.9	71.6[6]
Ethiopia	437,794	1,133,882	27	64,117,000	17	146.5	56.5	2.8	1994	53,477,265	50.3	49.7	9.9[17]
Faroe Islands	540	1,399	178	45,500	210	84.3	32.5	0.9	1999	45,409	51.8	48.2	...
Fiji	7,055	18,272	155	819,000	157	116.1	44.8	1.3	1996	775,077	50.8	49.2	46.4
Finland	130,559	338,145	64	5,178,000	106	39.7	15.3	0.3	1990	4,998,478	48.5	51.5	79.7
France	210,026	543,965	49	58,835,000	21	280.1	108.2	0.3	1999	58,518,748	48.7[18]	51.3[18]	74.0[18]
French Guiana	33,399	86,504	114	165,000	186	4.9	1.9	3.6	1999	157,274	52.1[18]	47.9[18]	79.4[18]
French Polynesia	1,544	4,000	171	233,000	181	150.9	58.3	1.5	1996	219,521	51.9	48.1	55.0[19]
Gabon	103,347	267,667	76	1,208,000	151	11.7	4.5	1.2	1993	1,011,710	49.3	50.7	73.2
Gambia, The	4,127	10,689	163	1,367,000	148	331.2	127.9	3.4	1993	1,038,145	50.1	49.9	36.7
Gaza Strip	140	363	200	1,147,000	153	8,129.9	3,159.8	5.5	1995[3, 20]	1,054,000	50.9	49.1	...
Georgia	26,911	69,700	121	5,020,000	108	186.5	72.0	–1.0	1989	5,443,359	47.2	52.8	55.7
Germany	137,847	357,021	62	82,207,000	12	596.4	230.3	0.1	1987[21]	61,077,042	48.0	52.0	85.3[8]
Ghana	92,098	238,533	81	19,534,000	50	212.1	81.9	2.1	1984	12,296,081	49.3	50.7	32.0
Greece	50,949	131,957	96	10,562,000	70	207.3	80.0	0.2	1991	10,264,156	49.3	50.7	58.9
Greenland	836,330	2,166,086	14	56,200	208	0.1	0.0	0.2	1999[3]	56,087	53.4	46.6	81.2
Grenada	133	344	202	102,000	194	766.9	296.5	0.9	1991	95,597	48.8	51.2	33.5
Guadeloupe	658	1,705	177	428,000	170	650.5	251.0	1.0	1999	422,496	48.9[18]	51.1[18]	48.4[18]
Guam	217	561	191	155,000	189	714.3	276.3	1.5	1990	133,152	53.3	46.7	38.2
Guatemala	42,042	108,889	105	11,385,000	65	270.8	104.6	2.7	1994	8,331,874	49.3	50.7	35.0
Guernsey	30	78	211	64,100	206	2,136.7	821.8	0.4	1996[22]	58,681	48.1	51.9	...
Guinea	94,926	245,857	78	7,466,000	89	78.7	30.4	0.9	1996	7,165,750	48.8	51.2	26.0
Guinea-Bissau	13,948	36,125	137	1,286,000	150	92.2	35.6	2.4	1991	983,367	48.4	51.6	20.3[9]
Guyana	83,044	215,083	84	792,000	158	9.5	3.7	0.5	1991	701,704	49.2	50.8	35.4[13]
Haiti	10,695	27,700	146	6,868,000	93	642.2	247.9	1.3	1982	5,053,792	48.5	51.5	20.6
Honduras	43,433	112,492	102	6,490,000	95	149.4	57.7	3.3	1988	4,376,839	49.6	50.4	39.4
Hong Kong	422	1,092	180	6,782,000	94	16,086.3	6,211.2	2.0	1996[7]	6,217,556	50.0	50.0	100.0
Hungary	35,919	93,030	110	10,022,000	76	279.0	107.7	–0.4	1990	10,375,323	48.1	51.9	61.8
Iceland	39,699	102,819	106	280,000	177	7.1	2.7	0.9	1996[3]	269,735	50.1	49.9	91.9
India	1,222,243	3,165,596	7	1,014,004,000	2	829.6	320.2	1.7	1991	846,302,688	51.9	48.1	25.7
Indonesia	742,308	1,922,570	16	209,342,000	4	282.0	108.9	1.6	1990	178,631,196	49.9	50.1	30.9
Iran	630,830	1,633,841	18	62,704,000	18	99.4	38.4	1.2	1996	60,055,488	50.8	49.2	61.3
Iraq	167,975	435,052	58	22,676,000	45	135.0	52.1	3.0	1997	22,017,983	49.7	50.3	74.5[13]
Ireland	27,133	70,273	120	3,783,000	123	139.4	53.8	1.0	1996	3,626,087	49.6	50.4	57.0
Isle of Man	227	588	190	73,100	201	321.9	124.3	0.5	1996[7]	71,714	48.5	51.5	74.7
Israel[23, 24]	7,886	20,425	152	6,107,000	99	774.4	299.0	2.5	1995[7, 25]	5,548,523	49.3	50.7	86.9[26]
Italy	116,347	301,337	71	57,723,000	22	496.1	191.6	0.1	1991	57,103,833	48.6	51.4	67.1[27]
Jamaica	4,244	10,991	162	2,619,000	136	617.1	238.3	1.0	1991	2,374,193	49.0	51.0	50.4
Japan	145,884	377,837	61	126,920,000	9	870.0	335.9	0.2	1995	125,570,246	49.0	51.0	78.1[13]
Jersey	45	116	210	88,900	198	1,975.6	766.4	0.6	1996	85,150	48.6	51.4	...
Jordan[28]	34,489	89,326	112	4,982,000	110	144.5	55.8	3.4	1994	4,095,579	52.2	47.8	78.6
Kazakhstan	1,052,090	2,724,900	9	14,913,000	61	14.2	5.5	–1.1	1999	15,049,100	48.5[6]	51.5[6]	57.2[6]
Kenya	224,961	582,646	46	30,340,000	36	134.9	52.1	2.1	1999	28,679,000	49.4	50.6	23.6[8]
Kiribati	313	811	182	92,000	197	293.9	113.4	2.5	1995	77,658	49.5	50.5	36.5
Korea, North	47,399	122,762	98	21,688,000	49	457.6	176.7	0.1	1993	21,213,378	48.7	51.3	58.9
Korea, South	38,368	99,373	108	47,275,000	25	1,232.1	475.7	0.9	1995[7]	44,608,726	50.2	49.8	81.0[13]
Kuwait	6,880	17,818	156	1,984,000	143	288.4	111.3	3.3	1995	1,575,983	58.0	42.0	97.0[13]
Kyrgyzstan	77,200	199,900	86	4,895,000	112	63.4	24.5	1.5	1989	4,290,442	48.9	51.1	38.2
Laos	91,429	236,800	83	5,497,000	101	60.1	23.2	2.6	1995	4,581,258	49.5	50.5	20.7[13]
Latvia	24,938	64,589	124	2,415,000	138	96.8	37.4	–0.8	1989	2,680,029	46.6	53.4	71.1
Lebanon	4,016	10,400	164	3,578,000	126	890.9	344.0	1.4	1970	2,126,325	50.8	49.2	60.1
Lesotho	11,720	30,355	140	2,143,000	141	182.8	70.6	2.0	1986[7]	1,577,536	48.2	51.8	16.0
Liberia	37,743	97,754	109	3,164,000	131	83.8	32.4	9.8	1984	2,101,628	50.6	49.4	38.8
Libya	678,400	1,757,000	17	5,115,000	107	7.5	2.9	1.9	1995[7]	4,404,986	50.8	49.2	85.3[13]
Liechtenstein	62	160	209	32,600	212	527.5	203.8	1.1	1980	25,215	49.6	50.4	...
Lithuania	25,212	65,300	123	3,697,000	124	146.6	56.6	–0.1	1989	3,689,779	47.4	52.6	68.0
Luxembourg	999	2,586	173	439,000	168	439.4	169.8	1.4	1991	384,634	49.0	51.0	85.9[9]
Macau	9.1	23.6	215	440,000	167	48,351.6	18,644.1	1.5	1991	339,464	48.5	51.5	97.0
Macedonia	9,928	25,713	148	2.041,000	142	205.6	79.4	0.6	1994	1,945,932	50.4	49.6	58.7
Madagascar	226,658	587,041	45	15,506,000	58	68.4	26.4	3.1	1993[7]	12,092,157	49.5	50.5	26.4[13]
Malawi	45,747	118,484	100	10,386,000	71	227.0	87.7	1.7	1987	7,988,507	48.4	51.6	10.7
Malaysia	127,311	329,735	66	23,260,000	44	182.7	70.5	2.4	1991	17,566,982	50.5	49.5	50.6
Maldives	115	298	204	285,000	176	2,478.3	956.4	2.7	1995	244,814	50.9	49.1	25.5
Mali	482,077	1,248,574	23	10,686,000	68	22.2	8.6	3.1	1987	7,696,348	48.9	51.1	22.0
Malta	122	316	203	382,000	173	3,139.7	1,208.9	0.6	1995	378,132	49.4	50.6	85.3[29]
Marshall Islands	70	181	208	51,600	209	737.1	285.1	1.5	1999	50,840	51.1[19]	48.9[19]	64.5[19]
Martinique	436	1,128	179	385,000	172	883.0	341.3	0.7	1999	381,427	48.4[18]	51.6[18]	80.5[18]
Mauritania	398,000	1,030,700	29	2,668,000	135	6.7	2.6	2.6	1988	1,864,236	49.5	50.5	39.1
Mauritius	788	2,040	175	1,184,000	152	1,502.5	580.4	1.1	1990	1,056,827	49.9	50.1	39.3
Mayotte	145	375	199	156,000	188	1,075.9	416.0	5.3	1997	131,320	50.7	49.3	59.7[29]
Mexico	756,066	1,958,201	15	98,881,000	11	130.8	50.5	1.6	2000	97,361,711	48.6	51.4	71.3
Micronesia	271	701	186	118,000	192	435.7	168.2	1.9	1994	105,506	51.1	48.9	19.4[30]
Moldova	13,000	33,700	138	4,298,000	116	330.6	127.5	–0.2	1989	4,337,592	47.5	52.5	46.9
Monaco	0.75	1.95	217	31,700	213	42,266.7	16,256.4	0.5	1990	29,972	47.5	52.5	100.0
Mongolia	603,909	1,564,116	19	2,399,000	139	4.0	1.5	1.4	2000	2,382,500	49.6	50.4	58.6
Morocco	177,117	458,730	55	28,822,000	37	162.7	62.8	1.9	1994	25,821,571	49.7	50.3	51.7
Mozambique	313,661	812,379	35	19,105,000	53	60.9	23.5	2.0	1997	16,099,246	47.9	52.1	28.6
Myanmar (Burma)	261,228	676,577	40	41,735,000	28	159.8	61.7	0.8	1983	35,307,913	49.6	50.4	24.0
Namibia	318,580	825,118	34	1,771,000	145	5.6	2.1	2.0	1991	1,401,711	48.6	51.4	32.8
Nauru	8.2	21.2	216	11,800	216	1,439.0	556.6	2.2	1992	9,919	51.2	48.8	100.0
Nepal	56,827	147,181	94	24,702,000	41	434.7	167.8	2.4	1991	18,491,097	49.9	50.1	9.6

age distribution (%)						population (by decade, '000s)								country
0–14	15–29	30–44	45–59	60–74	75 and over	1950	1960	1970	1980	1990	2000	2010 projection	2020 projection	
37.7	27.6	18.6	10.4	5.0	0.7	20,461	26,085	33,329	40,546	53,051	65,871	76,905	87,068	Egypt
38.7	28.7	16.0	9.2	5.4	1.9	1,940	2,582	3,604	4,566	5,100	6,123	7,293	8,494	El Salvador
41.7	25.1	15.7	11.2	5.3	1.0	211	244	270	256	368	474	604	755	Equatorial Guinea
46.1	23.0	15.9	8.9	4.4	1.6	1,403	1,612	2,153	2,555	2,945	4,136	5,709	7,399	Eritrea
17.7[10]	22.1[10]	21.4[10]	18.4[10]	15.0[10]	5.4[10]	1,101	1,216	1,365	1,473	1,571	1,435	1,375	1,335	Estonia
46.6[17]	22.7[17]	15.6[17]	8.9[17]	4.5[17]	1.7[17]	20,175	24,252	29,673	36,413	48,335	64,117	82,312	103,163	Ethiopia
23.8	19.4	21.0	18.2	11.3	1.8	31	35	39	44	48	45	48	51	Faroe Islands
35.4	27.4	20.7	11.4	4.2	0.9	289	394	520	634	738	819	942	1,072	Fiji
19.3	20.5	24.6	17.1	12.9	5.7	4,009	4,430	4,606	4,800	4,986	5,178	5,239	5,246	Finland
19.1[18]	22.6[18]	22.8[18]	15.6[18]	12.8[18]	7.1[18]	41,736	45,684	50,770	53,880	56,697	58,835	60,591	61,365	France
33.4[18]	27.3[18]	23.2[18]	10.2[18]	4.4[18]	1.5[18]	27	33	49	68	116	165	204	233	French Guiana
33.6[11]	27.2[11]	21.8[11]	11.3[11]	5.1[11]	1.0[11]	62	84	109	151	197	233	269	309	French Polynesia
33.8[16]	23.7[16]	17.0[16]	17.4[16]	6.9[16]	1.2[16]	416	446	514	806	1,069	1,208	1,309	1,386	Gabon
43.8	27.7	15.1	6.8	3.5	1.4	305	391	502	676	962	1,367	1,833	2,365	Gambia, The
50.3	25.8	13.1	6.2	3.7	0.9	...	...	370	456	630	1,147	1,872	2,623	Gaza Strip
24.8	24.1	19.2	17.5	10.8	3.6	3,516	4,147	4,694	5,048	5,457	5,020	4,815	4,785	Georgia
14.6	24.0	20.1	20.6	13.6	7.2	68,373	72,673	77,772	78,289	79,433	82,207	84,013	84,897	Germany
45.0	26.4	14.6	8.1	4.1	1.8	5,297	6,958	8,789	10,998	15,360	19,534	22,650	25,223	Ghana
19.3	22.2	20.3	18.3	14.1	5.9	7,566	8,327	8,793	9,643	10,161	10,562	10,718	10,596	Greece
27.4	19.6	29.3	15.9	— 7.8 —		23	33	41	50	56	56	57	58	Greenland
42.5[9]	30.4[9]	12.9[9]	6.6[9]	5.5[9]	2.1[9]	76	90	95	89	95	102	110	119	Grenada
24.9[18]	29.5[18]	21.4[18]	12.5[18]	8.3[18]	3.4[18]	206	265	320	327	388	428	470	502	Guadeloupe
30.0	30.0	22.6	10.8	5.5	1.1	60	67	86	107	134	155	184	211	Guam
44.0	26.1	15.8	8.3	— 5.8 —		2,969	3,963	5,243	6,820	8,749	11,385	14,631	18,123	Guatemala
17.6	20.6	22.3	19.0	13.2	7.3	44	45	51	53	63	64	66	67	Guernsey
44.1[11]	26.5[11]	15.9[11]	9.0[11]	3.9[11]	0.6[11]	2,586	3,019	3,587	4,320	5,936	7,466	9,281	11,440	Guinea
43.9[9]	26.5[9]	16.1[9]	8.8[9]	3.7[9]	1.0[9]	573	617	620	789	996	1,286	1,614	1,998	Guinea-Bissau
35.4[9]	31.5[9]	17.8[9]	9.0[9]	4.8[9]	1.5[9]	428	560	714	759	759	792	827	856	Guyana
39.2	26.9	15.6	10.0	5.4	2.9	3,097	3,723	4,605	5,056	6,028	6,868	7,950	9,072	Haiti
46.8	25.8	14.4	7.9	3.8	1.4	1,390	1,873	2,553	3,316	4,681	6,490	7,979	9,166	Honduras
18.5	22.6	29.5	15.1	10.7	3.6	1,974	3,074	3,942	5,063	5,705	6,872	7,588	8,489	Hong Kong
21.3	19.4	22.5	17.9	13.4	5.6	9,338	9,984	10,337	10,693	10,365	10,022	9,718	9,375	Hungary
24.0	22.9	22.8	15.2	10.2	4.9	143	176	204	228	255	280	306	335	Iceland
37.3	26.6	18.3	10.6	5.5	1.3	369,880	445,857	555,042	690,462	850,558	1,014,004	1,168,205	1,311,747	India
36.6	28.3	18.1	10.6	5.2	1.1	75,449	92,701	119,467	146,449	178,302	209,342	237,973	261,802	Indonesia
44.3	26.6	15.1	8.2	4.8	0.8	16,913	21,554	28,359	38,783	54,134	62,704	70,494	80,482	Iran
43.8[2]	30.2[2]	14.5[2]	6.9[2]	3.6[2]	1.0[2]	5,163	6,822	9,413	13,233	18,135	22,676	29,672	36,908	Iraq
26.7	24.1	20.2	13.8	10.6	4.6	2,969	2,834	2,954	3,421	3,506	3,783	4,161	4,372	Ireland
17.3[5]	20.7[5]	20.4[5]	17.0[5]	15.3[5]	9.2[5]	55	49	52	64	69	73	77	80	Isle of Man
28.9[13]	25.2[13]	20.0[13]	12.9[13]	9.0[13]	4.0[13]	...	2,114	2,958	3,862	4,613	6,107	6,946	7,647	Israel[23, 24]
15.9	23.7	20.9	18.4	14.4	6.7	47,104	50,200	53,822	56,434	56,749	57,723	57,498	55,626	Italy
34.4	30.6	16.6	9.0	— 9.4 —		1,403	1,629	1,891	2,133	2,369	2,619	2,815	3,087	Jamaica
15.9	21.5	19.7	22.0	15.0	5.9	83,200	93,419	103,720	116,807	123,478	126,920	127,626	124,249	Japan
15.5[5]	24.9[5]	23.5[5]	17.0[5]	11.9[5]	6.8[5]	57	63	71	76	84	89	92	93	Jersey
42.2	31.4	13.8	8.1	— 4.5 —		1,095	1,384	1,795	2,183	3,306	4,982	6,486	7,920	Jordan[28]
31.9[6]	26.3[6]	19.4[6]	13.2[6]	6.9[6]	2.3[6]	6,693	9,982	13,106	14,994	16,708	14,913	15,397	16,525	Kazakhstan
47.8[6]	27.6[6]	13.1[6]	6.6[6]	3.4[6]	1.5[6]	6,121	8,157	11,272	16,685	23,767	30,340	33,068	34,001	Kenya
41.2	25.8	18.3	9.3	4.4	1.0	33	41	49	58	71	92	115	143	Kiribati
29.5[16]	31.9[16]	21.3[16]	11.0[16]	5.0[16]	1.2[16]	9,471	10,392	13,912	17,114	20,019	21,688	23,753	25,143	Korea, North
23.0	27.6	25.7	14.5	7.4	1.9	21,147	25,142	32,976	38,124	42,869	47,275	50,886	52,759	Korea, South
40.4[13]	25.7[13]	22.5[13]	8.6[13]	2.2[13]	0.6[13]	145	292	748	1,358	2,141	1,984	2,803	3,761	Kuwait
37.5	27.0	16.3	10.9	6.2	2.1	1,740	2,173	2,965	3,631	4,395	4,895	5,687	6,627	Kyrgyzstan
45.4[13]	26.5[13]	14.9[13]	8.1[13]	4.2[13]	1.0[13]	1,886	2,309	2,845	3,293	4,210	5,497	6,993	8,637	Laos
21.4	21.7	20.3	19.2	12.0	5.3	1,949	2,129	2,374	2,544	2,671	2,415	2,261	2,160	Latvia
42.6	23.8	16.7	9.1	— 7.7 —		1,364	1,786	2,383	3,086	3,147	3,578	4,056	4,417	Lebanon
40.7	25.1	16.6	10.7	5.6	1.3	726	859	1,067	1,344	1,732	2,143	2,339	2,382	Lesotho
43.2	28.2	14.7	7.7	4.4	1.8	824	1,055	1,397	1,892	2,190	3,164	4,073	5,294	Liberia
45.4[13]	26.4[13]	14.7[13]	9.1[13]	3.7[13]	0.6[13]	961	1,338	1,999	3,065	4,140	5,115	6,447	7,740	Libya
23.0	26.5	24.1	14.1	9.2	3.1	14	16	21	26	29	33	36	41	Liechtenstein
22.6	23.8	20.0	17.9	10.9	4.8	2,567	2,779	3,148	3,439	3,722	3,697	3,635	3,631	Lithuania
17.3	21.5	23.8	17.5	12.8	7.1	296	314	339	364	382	439	493	542	Luxembourg
24.1	27.2	29.4	9.6	7.3	2.3	188	169	221	243	332	440	521	608	Macau
24.8	24.1	22.3	15.8	10.6	2.4	1,225	1,366	1,574	1,792	1,893	2,041	2,115	2,171	Macedonia
45.1[16]	26.8[16]	15.1[16]	7.7[16]	4.3[16]	1.0[16]	4,620	5,482	6,766	8,677	11,522	15,506	20,993	28,405	Madagascar
46.1	25.4	14.5	8.0	— 6.0 —		2,817	3,450	4,489	6,129	9,219	10,386	11,621	12,318	Malawi
36.7	27.6	20.0	9.9	4.6	1.2	6,187	7,908	10,466	13,764	17,857	23,260	27,903	32,809	Malaysia
46.4	26.2	14.3	7.7	4.3	0.9	82	106	128	155	215	285	364	465	Maldives
46.1	23.9	15.0	8.9	4.9	1.2	3,688	4,486	5,525	6,731	8,228	10,686	14,349	18,984	Mali
21.9	20.9	22.5	18.8	11.6	4.3	308	329	326	324	354	382	410	451	Malta
51.0[19]	24.5[19]	14.6[19]	5.5[19]	3.6[19]	0.8[19]	11	15	22	31	45	52	60	69	Marshall Islands
23.1[18]	28.9[18]	20.5[18]	13.5[18]	9.7[18]	4.3[18]	222	252	287	326	360	385	415	436	Martinique
44.1	26.6	15.0	8.1	4.7	1.4	960	1,057	1,227	1,550	1,984	2,668	3,561	4,671	Mauritania
29.7	28.9	22.3	10.9	6.6	1.6	479	662	829	966	1,059	1,184	1,281	1,364	Mauritius
43.5	29.9	15.6	6.6	2.7	1.7	17	25	35	52	89	156	231	312	Mayotte
38.3	29.4	16.6	8.9	4.5	1.7	27,737	36,945	50,596	67,570	83,226	98,881	112,891	124,976	Mexico
46.4[30]	26.8[30]	12.6[30]	8.5[30]	4.5[30]	1.1[30]	30	40	57	77	101	118	141	143	Micronesia
27.9	22.9	21.0	15.6	9.7	2.9	2,341	3,004	3,595	4,002	4,365	4,298	4,403	4,604	Moldova
12.3	16.7	21.2	20.4	17.9	10.8	18	21	24	27	30	32	33	34	Monaco
41.9[6]	29.2[6]	14.6[6]	8.5[6]	— 5.8[6] —		747	931	1,248	1,663	2,086	2,399	2,787	3,174	Mongolia
37.0[4]	29.6[4]	17.3[4]	9.2[4]	5.4[4]	1.5[4]	8,953	11,640	15,126	19,177	23,837	28,822	33,777	38,527	Morocco
43.5[2]	28.6[2]	15.1[2]	8.5[2]	3.6[2]	0.7[2]	6,250	7,472	9,304	12,103	14,276	19,105	20,504	20,626	Mozambique
38.6	28.7	15.5	10.9	5.2	1.1	19,488	22,836	27,386	33,281	38,519	41,735	43,674	44,775	Myanmar (Burma)
41.7	28.8	14.7	7.8	— 6.9 —		464	591	765	975	1,409	1,771	1,908	1,956	Namibia
41.8	25.0	20.7	8.2	— 2.8 —		3	4	7	8	10	12	14	17	Nauru
42.3	25.7	16.7	9.7	4.7	0.9	8,989	10,305	11,919	15,016	19,325	24,702	30,758	36,925	Nepal

Area and population (continued)

country	area			population (latest estimate)					population (latest census)				
	square miles	square kilo-metres	rank	total midyear 2000	rank	density		% annual growth rate 1995–2000	census year	total	male (%)	female (%)	urban (%)
						per sq mi	per sq km						
Netherlands, The	16,033	41,526	134	15,896,000	57	991.5	382.8	0.6	1999[3]	15,654,200	49.4	50.6	94.2
Netherlands Antilles	308	800	183	210,000	183	681.8	262.5	0.8	1992	189,474	47.9	52.1	...
New Caledonia	7,172	18,575	154	211,000	182	29.4	11.4	1.7	1996	196,836	51.2	48.8	59.4[6]
New Zealand	104,454	270,534	75	3,835,000	121	36.7	14.2	0.9	1996	3,681,546	49.1	50.9	85.0
Nicaragua	50,893	131,812	97	4,813,000	114	94.6	36.5	2.4	1995	4,357,099	49.3	50.7	54.4
Niger	489,000	1,267,000	22	10,076,000	75	20.6	8.0	2.8	1988[5]	7,228,552	49.5	50.5	15.3
Nigeria	356,669	923,768	32	123,338,000	10	345.8	133.5	2.8	1991	88,514,501	50.3	49.7	35.0[8]
Northern Mariana Islands	184	477	193	71,900	202	390.8	150.7	4.3	1990	43,345	52.6	47.4	28.0
Norway	125,004	323,758	67	4,487,000	115	35.9	13.9	0.6	1990	4,247,546	49.4	50.6	72.0
Oman	119,500	309,500	70	2,416,000	137	20.2	7.8	2.5	1993	2,018,074	58.4	41.6	71.7
Pakistan[31]	307,374	796,095	36	141,554,000	7	460.5	177.8	2.3	1998	130,579,571	52.0	48.0	33.3
Palau	188	488	192	18,800	215	100.0	38.5	2.0	1995	17,255	53.5	46.5	69.4[18]
Panama	29,157	75,517	118	2,823,000	134	96.8	37.4	1.9	1990	2,329,329	50.6	49.4	53.7
Papua New Guinea	178,704	462,840	54	4,927,000	111	27.6	10.6	2.5	1990[32]	3,607,954	52.7	47.3	15.2
Paraguay	157,048	406,752	59	5,496,000	102	35.0	13.5	2.6	1992	4,123,550	50.2	49.8	50.5
Peru	496,225	1,285,216	20	25,662,000	39	51.7	20.0	1.7	1993	22,639,443	49.7	50.3	70.1
Philippines	115,860	300,076	72	76,320,000	14	658.7	254.3	2.2	2000	75,329,000	50.4[33]	49.6[33]	48.6[18]
Poland	120,860	313,027	69	38,655,000	30	319.8	123.5	0.0	1988	37,878,641	48.7	51.3	61.2
Portugal	35,662	92,365	111	10,005,000	77	280.6	108.3	0.2	1991	9,862,540	48.2	51.8	48.2
Puerto Rico	3,515	9,104	166	3,916,000	119	1,114.1	430.1	1.0	1990	3,522,037	48.4	51.6	71.2
Qatar	4,416	11,437	161	599,000	162	135.6	52.4	1.8	1997	522,023	65.6	34.4	88.0[34]
Réunion	968	2,507	174	727,000	159	751.0	290.0	1.9	1999	709,468	19.2[18]	50.8[18]	73.4[18]
Romania	91,699	237,500	82	22,435,000	46	244.7	94.5	–0.2	1992	22,760,449	49.1	50.9	54.4
Russia	6,592,800	17,075,400	1	146,001,000	6	22.1	8.6	–0.3	1989	147,400,537	46.9	53.1	73.6
Rwanda	10,169	26,338	147	7,229,000	91	710.9	274.5	5.0	1991	7,164,994	48.7	51.3	5.4
St. Kitts and Nevis	104	269	205	38,800	211	373.1	144.0	–0.5	1991	40,618	49.1	50.9	48.9[8]
St. Lucia	238	617	189	157,000	187	659.7	254.5	1.5	1991	133,308	48.5	51.5	44.1[8]
St. Vincent and the Grenadines	150	389	198	113,000	193	751.8	290.3	0.5	1991	106,499	49.9	50.1	24.6
Samoa	1,093	2,831	172	179,000	185	163.8	63.2	–0.2	1991	161,298	52.5	47.5	21.2
San Marino	24	61	212	26,800	214	1,134.2	438.0	1.5	1976	19,149	50.4	49.6	90.1[9]
São Tomé and Príncipe	386	1,001	181	144,000	190	373.1	143.9	2.2	1991	117,504	49.4	50.6	44.1[27]
Saudi Arabia	868,000	2,248,000	13	22,024,000	48	25.4	9.8	3.4	1992	16,929,294	55.9	44.1	77.3[8]
Senegal	75,951	196,712	87	9,987,000	79	131.5	50.8	3.1	1988	6,928,405	48.7	51.3	38.6
Seychelles	176	455	195	81,700	199	464.2	179.6	1.7	1994	74,205	49.9	50.1	35.5[35]
Sierra Leone	27,699	71,740	119	5,233,000	105	188.9	72.9	3.0	1985	3,517,530	49.6	50.4	31.8
Singapore	255	660	188	3,278,000	130	12,865.0	4,967.4	1.9	2000[7]	3,263,209	50.0	50.0	100.0
Slovakia	18,933	49,035	129	5,403,000	103	285.4	110.2	0.1	1991	5,268,935	48.9	51.1	56.8
Slovenia	7,827	20,273	153	1,963,000	144	250.8	96.8	–0.2	1991	1,974,839	48.5	51.5	48.9
Solomon Islands	10,954	28,370	143	466,000	165	42.5	16.4	3.3	1986	285,176	51.9	48.1	15.7
Somalia	246,000	637,000	42	7,253,000	90	29.5	11.4	2.9	1975	4,089,203	50.1	49.9	25.4
South Africa	470,693	1,219,090	25	43,421,000	26	92.2	35.6	0.9	1996	40,583,573	48.1	51.9	53.7
Spain	195,364	505,990	51	40,128,000	29	205.4	79.3	0.3	1991	38,999,181	49.1	50.9	75.3
Sri Lanka	25,332	65,610	122	19,246,000	51	759.8	293.3	1.2	1981	14,848,364	50.8	49.2	21.5
Sudan, The	966,757	2,503,890	10	35,080,000	33	36.3	14.0	2.8	1993	24,940,683	50.2	49.8	31.3[13]
Suriname	63,251	163,820	92	431,000	169	6.8	2.6	0.8	1980	354,860	49.5	50.5	49.1[13]
Swaziland	6,704	17,364	157	1,083,000	154	161.5	62.4	2.5	1997	929,718	47.3	52.7	23.1
Sweden	173,734	449,969	56	8,864,000	82	51.0	19.7	0.1	1996[3]	8,837,496	49.4	50.6	83.9
Switzerland	15,940	41,284	135	7,177,000	92	450.3	173.8	0.4	1990[36]	6,873,687	49.3	50.7	68.9
Syria	71,498	185,180	88	16,306,000	55	228.1	88.1	2.6	1994	13,782,315	51.1	48.9	52.2[13]
Taiwan	13,971	36,985	136	22,186,000	47	1,588.0	613.1	0.8	1990[7]	20,393,628	52.1	47.9	74.5
Tajikistan	55,300	143,100	95	6,312,000	97	114.1	44.1	1.6	1989	5,108,576	49.7	50.3	32.6
Tanzania	364,901	945,090	31	35,306,000	32	96.8	37.4	2.5	1988	23,174,336	48.9	51.1	18.5
Thailand	198,115	513,115	50	62,423,000	19	315.1	121.7	1.0	2000	60,606,947	49.2	50.8	31.1
Togo	21,925	56,785	125	5,019,000	109	228.9	88.4	3.6	1981	2,719,567	48.7	51.3	15.2
Tonga	290	750	185	100,000	195	345.4	133.4	0.6	1996[7]	97,784	50.7	49.3	30.7[37]
Trinidad and Tobago	1,980	5,128	169	1,292,000	149	652.5	251.9	0.5	1990	1,234,388	50.1	49.9	64.8
Tunisia	63,378	164,150	91	9,593,000	80	151.4	58.4	1.3	1994	8,785,711	50.6	49.4	61.0
Turkey	300,948	779,452	37	65,667,000	16	218.2	84.2	1.4	1990	56,473,035	50.7	49.3	59.0
Turkmenistan	188,500	488,100	52	4,885,000	113	25.9	10.0	1.8	1995	4,483,251	49.6	50.4	46.0
Tuvalu	9.9	25.6	214	10,800	217	1,090.9	421.4	1.5	1991	9,043	48.4	51.6	42.5
Uganda	93,065	241,038	80	23,318,000	43	250.6	96.7	2.8	1991	16,671,705	49.1	50.9	11.3
Ukraine	233,100	603,700	44	49,242,000	24	211.2	81.6	–0.9	1989	51,706,746	46.3	53.7	66.9
United Arab Emirates	32,280	83,600	116	3,022,000	132	93.6	36.1	4.9	1995	2,411,041	66.6	33.4	77.3
United Kingdom	94,248	244,101	79	59,714,000	20	633.6	244.6	0.4	1991[7]	56,467,000	48.4	51.6	89.1[8]
United States	3,615,215	9,363,364	4	275,372,000	3	76.2	29.4	0.9	1990[38]	248,709,873	48.7	51.3	75.2
Uruguay	68,037	176,215	90	3,278,000	129	48.2	18.6	0.9	1996	3,151,662	48.4	51.6	89.3
Uzbekistan	172,700	447,400	57	24,756,000	40	143.3	55.3	1.7	1989	19,905,158	49.3	50.7	40.7
Vanuatu	4,707	12,190	160	199,000	184	42.3	16.3	3.1	1999	193,219	51.6[6]	48.4[6]	21.5
Venezuela	353,841	916,445	33	24,170,000	42	68.3	26.4	2.0	1990	19,405,429	49.7	50.3	84.0
Vietnam	127,816	331,041	65	78,774,000	13	616.3	238.0	1.6	1999	76,324,753	49.2	50.8	20.1[6]
Virgin Islands (U.S.)	136	352	201	121,000	191	889.7	343.8	1.2	1990	101,809	48.3	51.7	37.2
West Bank[39]	2,270	5,900	167	2,184,000	140	962.1	370.2	7.1	1995[3, 20]	1,707,000	51.2	48.8	...
Western Sahara	97,344	252,120	77	245,000	180	2.5	1.0	2.4	1994	252,146	...	...	90.7
Yemen	214,300	555,000	48	17,479,000	54	81.6	31.5	3.3	1994	14,587,807	51.2	48.8	23.5
Yugoslavia	39,449	102,173	107	10,662,000	69	270.3	104.4	0.0	1991	10,394,026	49.6	50.4	53.2[8]
Zambia	290,586	752,614	39	9,582,000	81	33.0	12.7	1.9	1990	7,818,447	49.2	50.8	42.0
Zimbabwe	150,872	390,757	60	11,343,000	66	75.2	29.0	0.7	1992	10,412,548	48.8	51.2	30.6

[1]Settled population only. [2]1997 estimate. [3]Civil register; not a census. [4]1994 estimate. [5]1991 census. [6]1989 census. [7]Data are for de jure population. [8]1990 estimate. [9]1991 estimate. [10]2000 estimate. [11]1996 estimate. [12]1998 estimate. [13]1995 estimate. [14]Except census, data are for the island of Cyprus. [15]Republic of Cyprus only. [16]1993 estimate. [17]1984 census. [18]1990 census. [19]1988 census. [20]Projections from 1995 demographic survey. [21]Former West Germany only. [22]Data exclude Alderney (population 2,297) and Sark (population 604). [23]Area figures exclude the West Bank, East Jerusalem, Gaza Strip, and Golan Heights. [24]Population figures include Golan Heights and East Jerusalem and exclude Israelis in the West Bank and Gaza Strip.

age distribution (%)						population (by decade, '000s)								country
0–14	15–29	30–44	45–59	60–74	75 and over	1950	1960	1970	1980	1990	2000	2010 projection	2020 projection	
18.5	19.8	24.1	19.5	12.1	6.0	10,027	11,417	12,958	14,150	14,952	15,896	16,638	17,089	Netherlands, The
26.0	23.9	25.5	14.3	7.3	3.0	112	136	163	174	188	210	228	242	Netherlands Antilles
32.6[6]	28.6[6]	19.8[6]	12.1[6]	5.4[6]	1.6[6]	59	79	110	140	171	211	246	278	New Caledonia
23.2[5]	24.6[5]	22.4[5]	14.4[5]	10.9[5]	4.5[5]	1,909	2,377	2,820	3,144	3,363	3,835	4,245	4,564	New Zealand
45.1	27.5	15.0	7.2	3.7	1.4	1,098	1,493	2,053	2,804	3,643	4,813	5,839	6,808	Nicaragua
48.7	24.8	14.6	6.8	3.6	1.5	2,482	3,168	4,182	5,629	7,627	10,076	13,140	16,800	Niger
47.9[8]	21.9[8]	14.3[8]	9.0[8]	5.2[8]	1.6[8]	31,797	39,914	51,099	69,593	92,483	123,338	155,588	187,437	Nigeria
23.8	33.5	30.7	9.1	2.3	0.5	6	9	10	17	44	72	99	123	Northern Mariana Islands
18.8	22.9	22.1	15.1	13.9	7.2	3,265	3,581	3,877	4,086	4,241	4,487	4,656	4,824	Norway
41.0	25.5	21.9	7.8	2.9	0.9	489	499	779	1,060	1,625	2,416	3,359	4,461	Oman
43.2	26.9	15.6	8.8	4.3	1.2	39,448	50,387	65,706	85,219	113,975	141,554	171,373	199,744	Pakistan[31]
30.3[18]	27.8[18]	22.8[18]	10.5[18]	6.4[18]	2.2[18]	7	9	12	13	15	19	22	23	Palau
34.8	29.2	18.2	10.2	5.5	2.0	893	1,148	1,531	1,950	2,335	2,823	3,150	3,443	Panama
41.9	28.5	16.6	8.7	—3.2—		1,412	1,747	2,288	2,991	3,825	4,927	6,171	7,400	Papua New Guinea
40.1	27.6	18.7	8.3	4.2	1.1	1,351	1,774	2,351	3,136	4,219	5,496	6,980	8,470	Paraguay
37.0	28.6	17.7	9.8	—7.0—		7,632	9,931	13,193	17,324	21,569	25,662	29,885	33,757	Peru
39.6[18]	28.7[18]	17.3[18]	9.2[18]	4.2[18]	1.1[18]	20,988	27,561	36,850	48,286	60,937	76,320	91,868	105,507	Philippines
25.4	21.2	23.3	15.5	10.4	4.2	24,824	29,561	32,526	35,578	38,057	38,655	38,764	39,003	Poland
20.0	23.7	20.2	17.1	13.7	5.3	8,405	8,826	9,040	9,766	9,896	10,005	10,175	10,348	Portugal
27.2	25.1	20.4	14.1	9.2	4.0	2,218	2,360	2,721	3,210	3,537	3,916	4,088	4,196	Puerto Rico
29.7[2]	30.7[2]	31.0[2]	7.0[2]	1.4[2]	0.2[2]	47	59	151	229	485	599	692	761	Qatar
29.5[18]	29.8[18]	20.3[18]	11.7[18]	6.5[18]	2.1[18]	244	338	447	507	601	727	829	932	Réunion
22.4	22.9	20.8	17.1	—16.8—		16,311	18,403	20,253	22,201	23,207	22,435	21,930	21,267	Romania
23.1	22.0	21.9	17.6	11.2	4.2	101,937	119,632	130,425	139,045	148,082	146,001	142,328	138,978	Russia
45.6	28.6	12.4	8.4	3.9	0.9	2,439	3,032	3,769	5,139	6,962	7,229	7,876	8,027	Rwanda
36.9[9]	31.8[9]	14.5[9]	6.0[9]	6.9[9]	3.8[9]	49	51	46	44	41	39	40	44	St. Kitts and Nevis
36.8	29.4	16.3	8.7	6.3	2.5	79	86	101	122	134	157	178	200	St. Lucia
37.2	29.5	16.1	8.3	6.4	2.5	67	80	86	99	105	113	119	125	St. Vincent and the Grenadines
40.5	30.0	14.6	8.7	—6.0—		82	111	143	155	170	179	176	178	Samoa
24.4	23.0	19.9	17.4	11.4	3.9	13	15	19	21	23	27	31	36	San Marino
46.9	26.2	12.2	8.0	—6.7—		60	64	74	94	117	144	177	218	São Tomé and Príncipe
42.1[27]	22.8[27]	21.6[27]	9.9[27]	3.0[27]	0.6[27]	3,860	4,718	6,109	9,949	15,847	22,024	30,546	41,880	Saudi Arabia
47.5	26.1	13.6	7.8	—5.0—		2,654	3,270	4,318	5,640	7,360	9,987	13,221	16,855	Senegal
33.6[35]	30.3[35]	15.3[35]	10.7[35]	7.1[35]	2.9[35]	34	42	54	63	70	82	85	89	Seychelles
43.9[34]	25.6[34]	15.7[34]	9.6[34]	4.5[34]	0.7[34]	2,087	2,396	2,789	3,327	4,227	5,233	6,930	8,820	Sierra Leone
21.5	21.2	28.4	18.2	8.2	2.5	1,022	1,639	2,075	2,282	2,705	3,278	3,949	4,758	Singapore
25.0	22.7	22.8	14.6	10.7	4.2	3,463	3,994	4,528	4,984	5,298	5,403	5,480	5,559	Slovakia
20.0	22.4	23.7	17.4	11.9	4.6	1,467	1,580	1,727	1,901	1,998	1,963	2,005	2,019	Slovenia
47.3	25.7	13.9	8.1	—4.9—		107	126	163	232	335	466	610	748	Solomon Islands
45.6	24.9	15.5	7.4	—5.4—		2,438	2,956	3,667	5,791	6,675	7,253	9,922	13,023	Somalia
33.9	28.6	19.4	9.8	5.3	1.8	13,596	17,417	22,739	29,252	38,176	43,421	41,108	36,744	South Africa
19.4	24.9	20.0	16.5	13.6	5.6	27,868	30,303	33,779	37,636	38,798	40,128	40,289	39,362	Spain
35.3	29.6	17.9	10.6	5.2	1.4	7,678	9,889	12,514	14,747	16,993	19,246	20,832	22,120	Sri Lanka
43.0	27.0	16.4	9.3	3.7	0.6	8,051	10,589	13,788	19,064	26,627	35,080	45,485	56,162	Sudan, The
39.3	29.5	13.8	10.0	4.5	2.8	208	285	373	355	395	431	450	457	Suriname
44.3	28.6	14.4	7.7	3.4	1.6	277	352	455	606	852	1,083	1,216	1,296	Swaziland
18.8	19.3	20.4	19.4	13.6	8.4	7,041	7,498	8,081	8,310	8,559	8,864	8,873	8,920	Sweden
16.8	22.8	23.2	18.0	12.5	6.7	4,715	5,429	6,270	6,362	6,712	7,177	7,299	7,308	Switzerland
47.3[4]	27.8[4]	13.8[4]	6.7[4]	3.7[4]	0.8[4]	3,495	4,533	6,258	8,774	12,436	16,306	20,606	24,676	Syria
27.1	27.8	23.1	12.3	7.9	1.8	7,619	10,668	14,583	17,705	20,279	22,186	24,144	26,275	Taiwan
42.9	28.1	13.8	9.0	4.6	1.6	1,532	2,083	2,942	3,968	5,303	6,312	7,847	9,784	Tajikistan
45.8	26.7	13.5	7.8	4.5	1.7	7,935	10,260	13,842	18,939	26,244	35,306	44,957	54,774	Tanzania
28.8[18]	30.4[18]	21.2[18]	12.3[18]	5.7[18]	1.6[18]	20,010	26,392	35,037	46,538	56,096	62,423	67,581	70,860	Thailand
49.8	24.8	13.1	6.8	3.3	2.0	1,172	1,456	1,964	2,596	3,691	5,019	6,245	7,179	Togo
40.6[37]	29.0[37]	13.8[37]	10.1[37]	5.0[37]	1.4[37]	50	65	80	92	96	100	104	108	Tonga
33.5	27.2	19.9	10.7	6.4	2.3	668	828	941	1,082	1,227	1,292	1,353	1,418	Trinidad and Tobago
34.8	28.5	18.8	9.6	6.4	1.9	3,517	4,149	5,099	6,443	8,207	9,593	10,661	11,641	Tunisia
35.0	28.6	18.4	10.9	5.6	1.6	21,122	28,217	35,758	45,121	56,085	65,667	73,322	79,679	Turkey
40.5[6]	28.8[6]	15.5[6]	9.1[6]	4.7[6]	1.4[6]	1,211	1,594	2,189	2,860	3,668	4,885	5,878	7,046	Turkmenistan
34.6	24.0	20.7	11.3	—9.2—		5	5	6	8	9	11	13	15	Tuvalu
47.3	27.7	13.1	6.9	3.7	1.3	5,522	7,262	9,728	12,298	17,186	23,318	31,395	42,005	Uganda
21.5	21.0	20.6	18.5	10.7	7.7	36,906	42,783	47,317	50,034	51,892	49,242	46,277	44,443	Ukraine
26.3	29.2	33.2	9.6	1.4	0.3	70	90	223	1,042	1,844	3,002	3,751	4,257	United Arab Emirates
19.1	21.9	21.2	16.7	14.1	7.0	50,290	52,372	55,632	56,330	57,561	59,714	61,589	63,453	United Kingdom
21.5	23.4	23.9	14.4	11.5	5.3	152,271	180,671	204,879	227,726	249,973	275,372	299,911	324,958	United States
25.1	22.9	19.6	15.1	12.2	5.1	2,194	2,531	2,824	2,914	3,041	3,278	3,540	3,794	Uruguay
40.8	28.4	15.0	9.3	4.7	1.8	6,314	8,559	11,973	15,977	20,515	24,756	29,280	34,465	Uzbekistan
45.5[6]	26.6[6]	15.2[6]	8.4[6]	3.7[6]	0.6[6]	52	66	85	117	147	199	232	263	Vanuatu
38.3	28.1	18.6	9.3	4.5	1.2	5,094	7,579	10,721	15,091	19,502	24,170	28,716	32,911	Venezuela
39.0[6]	28.7[6]	16.0[6]	9.1[6]	5.6[6]	1.6[6]	25,348	31,656	42,577	53,661	66,338	78,744	90,192	100,985	Vietnam
28.9	23.7	22.0	16.0	7.3	2.2	27	32	63	100	104	121	133	144	Virgin Islands (U.S.)
44.6	28.4	14.0	7.4	4.4	1.2	...	...	608	733	1,011	2,184	3,227	4,128	West Bank[39]
...	...	...	...	...	...	14	32	76	126	191	245	301	357	Western Sahara
47.6[4]	28.7[4]	11.9[4]	7.4[4]	3.6[4]	0.7[4]	4,461	5,483	6,628	8,527	12,023	17,479	24,637	34,195	Yemen
22.8	21.6	21.7	17.1	12.2	3.5	7,106	7,932	8,681	9,515	9,766	10,662	10,667	10,561	Yugoslavia
47.3	28.2	12.9	7.3	3.5	0.7	2,553	3,254	4,252	5,700	7,851	9,582	11,482	13,365	Zambia
45.1	28.3	14.0	7.2	3.9	1.2	2,853	4,011	5,515	7,170	10,103	11,343	11,057	9,997	Zimbabwe

[25]Includes East Jerusalem and Israelis in the West Bank, Gaza Strip, and Golan Heights. [26]1983 census. [27]1992 estimate. [28]Excludes the West Bank. [29]1985 census. [30]1980 census. [31]Excludes Afghan refugees (1997; 1.2 million) and the area (32,494 sq mi [84,159 sq km]) and population (1997; 3.9 million) of Pakistani-occupied Jammu and Kashmir. [32]Excludes an estimated 155,000 persons in North Solomons province and five remote census districts. [33]1995 census. [34]1985 estimate. [35]1987 census. [36]Includes resident aliens; excludes seasonal workers. [37]1986 census. [38]Excludes 515,000 armed forces overseas. [39]Excludes East Jerusalem.

Major cities and national capitals

The following table lists the principal cities or municipalities (those exceeding 100,000 in population [75,000 for 11 of the largest countries]) of the countries of the world, together with figures for each national capital (indicated by a ★), regardless of size.

Most of the populations given refer to a so-called city proper, that is, a legally defined, incorporated, or chartered area defined by administrative boundaries and by national or state law. Some data, however, refer to the municipality, or commune, similar to the medieval city-state in that the city is governed together with its immediately adjoining, economically dependent areas, whether urban or rural in nature. Some countries define no other demographic or legal entities within such communes or municipalities, but many identify a centre, seat, head (*cabecera*), or locality that corresponds to the most densely populated, compact, contiguous core of the municipality. Because the amount of work involved in carefully defining these "centres" may be considerable, the necessary resources usually exist only at the time of a national census (generally 5 or 10 years apart). Between censuses, therefore, it may be possible only to track the growth of the municipality as a whole. Thus, in order to provide the most up-to-date data for cities in this table, figures referring to municipalities or communes may be given (identified by the abbreviation "MU"), even though the country itself may define a smaller, more closely knit city proper. Specific identification of municipalities is provided in this table *only* when the country also publishes data for a more narrowly defined city proper; it is *not* provided when the sole published figure is the municipality, whether or not this is the proper local administrative term for the entity.

Problems also exist in the identification of cities in terms of named legal entities. There is, for example, a single municipality (*commune*) named Brussel (Brussels) at the centre of the Brussels agglomeration in Belgium; the *commune* numbers only about 136,000 population, while the agglomeration, which is understood by most people to constitute the city, numbers nearly a million. Both are shown so as to apprise the reader of the existence of a problem.

For certain countries, more than one form of the name of the city is given, usually to permit recognition of recent place name changes or of *forms* of the place name likely to be encountered in press stories if the title of the city's entry in the *Encyclopædia Britannica* is spelled according to a different romanization or spelling policy.

Chinese names for China are usually given in their Pinyin spelling, the official Chinese system encountered in official documents and maps. For Taiwan, the Wade-Giles spelling of place names is used.

Sources for this data were usually the national census and statistical abstracts of the countries concerned, supplemented by Internet sources.

Internet sources for further information

- City Population: http://www.citypopulation.de/cities.html

Major cities and national capitals

country city	population
Afghanistan (early 1990s est.)	
Herāt	186,800
★ Kābul	700,000[1]
Kandahār (Qandahār)	237,500
Mazār-e Sharīf	127,800
Albania (1999 est.)	
★ Tiranë	279,000
Algeria (1998)	
★ Algiers	1,519,570
Annaba	348,554
Batna	242,514
Béchar	131,010
Bejaïa	147,076
Biskra (Beskra)	170,956
Blida (el-Boulaida)	226,512
Bordj Bou Arreridj	128,535
Constantine (Qacentina)	462,187
Djelfa	154,265
Ech-Cheliff (el-Asnam)	179,768
El-Eulma	105,130
El-Wad	104,801
Ghardaïa	110,724
Ghilizane	104,285
Guelma	108,734
Jijel	106,003
Khenchela	106,082
Médéa	123,535
Mostaganem	124,399
Oran (Wahran)	692,516
Saïda	110,865
Sétif (Stif)	211,859
Sidi bel Abbès	180,260
Skikda	152,335
Souq Ahras	115,882
Tébessa (Tbessa)	153,246
Tihert	145,332
Tlemcen (Tilimsen)	155,162
Touggourt	113,625
Wargla (Ouargla)	129,402
American Samoa (1990)	
★ Fagatogo (legislative and judicial)	2,323[2]
★ Utulei (executive)	930[2]
Andorra (1999 est.)	
★ Andorra la Vella	21,513
Angola (1999 est.)	
Huambo	400,000[3]
★ Luanda	2,555,000
Antigua and Barbuda (1991)	
★ Saint John's	22,342
Argentina (1999 est.)	
Almirante Brown	550,000
Avellaneda	342,193
Bahía Blanca	281,161
Belén de Escobar	192,992
Berazategui	296,759
★ Buenos Aires	2,904,192
Caseros	341,398
Catamarca	140,000
Comodoro Rivadavia	144,074
Concordia	131,716
Córdoba	1,275,585
Corrientes	325,628
Esteban Echeverría	234,188
Florencio Valera	331,358
Formosa	197,057
General San Martín	409,879
General Sarmiento	209,450
Godoy Cruz	205,955
Hurlingham	165,986
Ituzaingo	154,437
José Carlos Paz	219,624
La Matanza (San Justo)	1,241,264
La Plata	556,308
La Rioja	138,074
Lanús	470,000
Las Heras	183,511
Lomas de Zamora	609,621
Mar del Plata	579,483
Mendoza	119,681
Mercedes	100,876
Merlo	430,213
Moreno	398,023
Morón	340,645
Neuquén	327,374
Paraná	256,602
Pilar	166,587
Posadas	250,000
Quilmes	550,069
Resistencia	280,000
Río Cuarto	150,000
Rosario	1,000,000
Salta	457,223
San Carlos de Bariloche	105,093
San Fernando	146,896
San Isidro	296,935
San Juan	120,000
San Luis	146,855
San Miguel	246,503
San Miguel de Tucumán	519,252
San Nicolás de los Arroyos	132,909
San Rafael	111,066
San Salvador de Jujuy	226,961
Santa Fe	400,000
Santiago del Estero	202,876
Tigre	299,376
Trelew	101,425
Vicente López	279,464
Villa Krause	100,000
Villa Nueva	224,116
Armenia (1995 est.)	
Gyumri (Kumayri; Leninakan)	120,000[4]
★ Yerevan	1,248,700
Aruba (1996 est.)	
★ Oranjestad	21,000
Australia (1998 est.)	
Adelaide UC[5]	978,100[6]
Adelaide	12,922
Charles Sturt	103,012
Marion	77,547
Onkaparinga	146,367
Port Adelaide Enfield	101,225
Salisbury	112,344
Tea Tree Gully	96,972
Brisbane UC[5]	1,291,117[6]
Brisbane	848,741
Ipswich	132,232
Logan	165,924
Canberra-Queanbeyan UC[5]	322,723[6]
Canberra	306,000
Melbourne UC[5]	2,865,329[6]
Banyule	119,486
Bayside	88,449
Boroondara	157,208
Brimbank	158,032
Casey	160,845
Dandenong	132,091
Darebin	129,005
Frankston	111,081
Glen Eira	122,535
Hobsons Bay	80,825
Hume	126,350
Kingston	132,895
Knox	141,016
Manningham	112,503
Maroondah	97,321
Melbourne	44,619
Monash	161,996
Moonee Valley	111,898
Moreland	137,258
Port Philip	78,680
Stonnington	90,546
Whitehorse	145,611
Whittlesea	111,040
Wyndham	80,931
Perth UC[5]	1,096,829[6]
Gosnells	79,372
Melville	95,854
Perth	5,957
Stirling	175,569
Wanneroo	154,641
Sydney UC[5]	3,276,207[6]
Bankstown	167,839
Blacktown	248,525
Blue Mountains	75,855
Campbelltown	149,489
Canterbury	140,435
Fairfield	190,920
Gosford	155,144
Holroyd	86,280
Liverpool	137,066
Parramatta	144,366
Penrith	171,420
Randwick	125,359
Rockdale	90,372
Ryde	97,598
South Sydney	83,752
Sydney	24,883
Other cities	
Ballarat	80,330
Bendigo	86,451
Cairns	118,834
Geelong	186,307
Gold Coast	380,270
Lake Macquarie	180,826
Newcastle	139,171
Shoalhaven	81,253
Toowoomba	86,968
Townsville	87,235
Wollongong	185,397
Austria (1999 est.)	
Graz	239,990
Innsbruck	110,454
Linz	190,136
Salzburg	144,692
★ Vienna	1,609,631
Azerbaijan (1997 est.)	
★ Baku (Baky)	1,727,200
Gäncä (Gyandzha)	291,900
Sumqayit (Sumgait)	248,500
Bahamas, The (1990)	
★ Nassau	172,196[7]
Bahrain (1995 est.)	
★ Al-Manāmah	148,000
Bangladesh (1991)	
Barisal	188,000
Bogra	130,000
Brahmanbaria	125,000
Chittagong	1,599,000
Comilla	156,000
★ Dhaka (Dacca)	3,839,000
Dinajpur	138,000
Gazipur	104,000
Jamalpur	111,000
Jessore	154,000
Khulna	731,000
Mymensingh	202,000
Naogaon	110,000
Narayanganj	296,000
Narsinghdi	106,000
Nawabganj (Nowabgonj)	141,000
Pabna	112,000
Rajshahi	318,000
Rangpur	207,000
Saidpur	105,000
Savar	115,000
Sirajganj	108,000
Sylhet	109,000
Tangail	114,000
Tongi	181,000
Barbados (1990)	
★ Bridgetown	6,070
Belarus (1998 est.)	
Baranovichi (Baranavichy)	173,000
Bobruysk (Babrujsk)	227,000
Borisov (Barysau)	153,000
Brest (Bierascie)	297,000
Gomel (Homiel)	513,000
Grodno (Horadnia)	306,000
Lida	100,000
★ Minsk	1,717,000
Mogilyov (Mahilou)	369,000
Mozyr (Mazyr)	109,000
Orsha (Vorsha)	138,000
Pinsk	132,000
Soligorsk	102,000
Vitebsk (Viciebsk)	364,000
Belgium (1997 est.)	
Antwerp	453,030
Brugge (Bruges)	115,500
★ Brussels	133,845
agglomeration	948,122[8]
Charleroi	204,899
Ghent	225,469
Liège (Luik)	189,510
Namur	105,243
Schaerbeek	104,042
Belize (1998 est.)	
★ Belmopan	7,105
Benin (1992)	
★ Cotonou (official)	533,212
Djougou	132,192
Parakou	106,708
★ Porto-Novo (de facto)	177,660
Bermuda (1995 est.)	
★ Hamilton	1,100
Bhutan (1993 est.)	
★ Thimphu	30,340
Bolivia (2000 est.)	
Cochabamba	607,129
El Alto	568,919
★ La Paz (administrative)	1,000,899
Oruro	232,311
Potosí	147,351
Quillacollo	132,579
Santa Cruz	1,016,137
★ Sucre (judicial)	192,238
Tarija	135,679
Bosnia and Herzegovina (1997 est.)	
Banja Luka	160,000
★ Sarajevo	360,000
Botswana (1995 est.)	
★ Gaborone	182,000
Brazil (1996)	
Alagoinhas	103,578
Almirante Tamandaré	80,058
Alvorada	161,885
Americana	167,790
Ananindeua	95,630
Anápolis	244,670
Angra dos Reis	85,074
Aparecida de Goiânia	265,868
Apucarana	93,595
Aracaju	428,194
Araçatuba	157,773
Araguaina	98,546
Araguari	88,435
Arapiraca	138,243
Araraquara	160,248
Araras	89,344
Assis	78,948
Atibaia	84,751
Bagé	94,695
Barbacena	88,336
Barra do Piraí	80,893
Barra Mansa	162,495
Barreiras	87,455
Barretos	95,689
Barueri	177,256
Bauru	287,530
Bayeux	83,958
Belém	851,705
Belford Roxo	399,319

country city	population
Belo Horizonte	2,080,068
Betim	236,483
Birigui	81,563
Blumenau	198,862
Boa Vista	150,442
Botucatu	95,215
Bragança Paulista	98,678
★ Brasília	1,692,248
Cabo (de Santo Agostinho)	125,055
Cabo Frio	101,886
Cachoeirinha	95,844
Cachoeiro de Itapemirim	127,450
Camaçari	128,937
Camaragibe	111,119
Campina Grande	326,016
Campinas	872,652
Campo Grande	592,007
Campos	333,604
Canoas	284,059
Carapicuíba	327,882
Cariacica	290,291
Caruaru	199,209
Cascavel	205,392
Castanhal	106,665
Catanduva	98,942
Caucaia	188,739
Caxias	90,369
Caxias do Sul	293,725
Chapecó	113,988
Colatina	81,577
Colombo	145,988
Conselheiro Lafaiete	88,193
Contagem	453,884
Coronel Fabriciano	91,425
Corumbá	76,302
Cotia	126,956
Crato	77,899
Criciúma	143,229
Cubatão	96,693
Cuiabá	426,903
Curitiba	1,476,253
Diadema	323,116
Divinópolis	164,600
Dourados	139,695
Duque de Caxias	710,624
Embu	195,628
Esteio	75,159
Eunápolis	75,769
Feira de Santana	393,943
Ferraz	120,749
Florianópolis	250,657
Fortaleza	1,965,513
Foz do Iguaçu	228,326
Franca	261,327
Francisco Morato	105,881
Franco de Rocha	92,831
Garanhuns	96,443
Goiânia	997,500
Governador Valadares	220,839
Gravataí	190,127
Guaíba	84,022
Guarapuava	132,857
Guaratinguetá	92,107
Guarujá	226,357
Guarulhos	953,210
Hortolândia	115,720
Ibirité	123,632
Ilhéus	172,627
Imperatriz	215,218
Indaiatuba	119,346
Ipatinga	194,371
Itabira	80,938
Itaboraí	169,873
Itabuna	177,944
Itaguaí	108,680
Itajaí	129,241
Itapecerica da Serra	109,088
Itapetininga	99,886
Itapevi	133,523
Itaquaquecetuba	228,344
Itu	112,006
Ituiutaba	81,213
Jaboatão	457,664
Jacareí	158,180
Jandira	75,352
Jaú	97,088
Jequié	134,910
Ji-Paraná	80,783
João Pessoa	549,363
Joinville	372,691
Juàzeiro	133,117
Juàzeiro do Norte	180,142
Juiz de Fora	419,226
Jundiaí	276,547
Lages	138,669
Limeira	196,577
Linhares	91,930
Londrina	400,292
Luziânia	232,866
Macaé	110,034
Macapá	209,663
Maceió	667,827
Magé	171,420
Manaus	1,150,193
Marabá	123,378
Maracanaú	159,493
Marília	170,746
Maringá	260,955
Mauá	342,909
Mogi Guaçu	104,988
Moji das Cruzes	279,945
Montes Claros	253,082
Mossoró	190,045
Muriaé	76,933
Natal	656,037
Nilópolis	155,272
Niterói	450,364
Nossa Senhora de Socorro	105,057
Nova Friburgo	146,779
Nova Iguaçu	823,054
Novo Hamburgo	211,377
Olinda	349,380
Osasco	622,912
Ourinhos	81,977
Palhoça	78,610
Palmas	82,535
Paranaguá	108,032
Parnaíba	112,586
Parnamirim	78,337
Passo Fundo	150,205
Passos	82,080
Patos	82,309
Patos de Minas	99,414
Paulista	229,515
Paulo Afonso	80,273
Pelotas	282,713
Petrolina	142,432
Petrópolis	263,369
Pindamonhangaba	106,897
Pinhais	82,787
Piracicaba	290,935
Poá	83,945
Poços de Caldas	117,094
Ponta Grossa	244,298
Porto Alegre	1,255,054
Porto Velho	238,314
Pouso Alegre	83,648
Praia Grande	150,388
Presidente Prudente	162,339
Queimados	108,522
Recife	1,346,045
Resende	84,394
Ribeirão das Neves	151,829
Ribeirão Pires	97,550
Ribeirão Preto	454,124
Rio Branco	201,347
Rio Claro	148,628
Rio de Janeiro	5,551,538
Rio Grande	171,420
Rio Verde	90,598
Rondonópolis	129,894
Sabará	80,751
Salto	86,928
Salvador	2,209,464
Santa Bárbara d'Oeste	158,122
Santa Cruz do Sul	83,389
Santa Luzia	141,380
Santa Maria	214,065
Santa Rita	85,605
Santana do Livramento	79,467
Santarém	180,189
Santo André	624,820
Santo Antônio do Descoberto	98,235
Santos	410,496
São Bernardo do Campo	641,390
São Caetano do Sul	139,825
São Carlos	164,103
São Gonçalo	833,379
São João de Meriti	434,323
São José	137,659
São José do Rio Prêto	304,893
São José dos Campos	462,429
São José dos Pinhais	151,209
São Leopoldo	178,549
São Lourenço da Mata	78,776
São Luís	762,172
São Paulo	9,391,112
São Vicente	279,346
Sapucaia do Sul	113,333
Serra	268,712
Sertãozinho	83,509
Sete Lagoas	163,292
Sobral	115,883
Sorocaba	428,153
Sumaré	166,909
Susano (Suzano)	173,906
Taboão da Serra	182,506
Tatuí	78,312
Taubaté	210,338
Teixeira de Freitas	81,145
Teófilo Otoni	103,220
Teresina	613,767
Teresopolis	104,977
Timon	100,704
Toledo	76,125
Uberaba	229,031
Uberlândia	430,439
Umuarama	76,552
Uruguaiana	113,258
Varginha	92,645
Várzea Grande	178,119
Várzea Paulista	78,156
Viamão	159,498
Vila Velha	295,931
Vitória	265,784
Vitória da Conquista	204,295
Vitória de Santo Antão	91,236
Volta Redonda	232,058
Votorantim	86,177
Brunei (1991)	
★ Bandar Seri Begawan	21,484
Bulgaria (1998 est.)	
Burgas	194,301
Dobrich	100,902
Pleven	122,025
Plovdiv	339,744
Ruse	166,416
Sliven	105,793
★ Sofia	1,114,168
Stara Zagora	148,103
Varna	300,413
Burkina Faso (1993 est.)	
Bobo Dioulasso	300,000
Koudougou	105,000
★ Ouagadougou	690,000
Burundi (1994 est.)	
★ Bujumbura	300,000
Gitega	101,827[9]
Cambodia (1994 est.)	
★ Phnom Penh	920,000
Cameroon (1992 est.)	
Bafoussam	120,000
Bamenda	110,000[10]
Douala	1,200,000
Garoua	160,000
Maroua	140,000
★ Yaoundé	800,000
Canada (1996)	
Abbotsford	105,403
Barrie	79,191
Brampton	268,251
Brantford	84,764
Burlington	136,976
Burnaby	179,209
Calgary	768,082
Cambridge	101,429
Coquitlam	101,820
Delta	95,411
East York	107,822
Edmonton	616,306
Etobicoke	328,718
Gatineau	100,702
Gloucester	104,022
Guelph	95,821
Halifax	113,910
Hamilton	322,352
Kamloops	76,394
Kelowna	89,442
Kitchener	178,420
Laval	330,343
London	325,646
Longueuil	127,977
Markham	173,383
Mississauga	544,382
Montreal	1,016,376
Montréal-Nord	81,581
Nepean	115,100
Niagara Falls	76,917
North York	589,653
Oakville	128,405
Oshawa	134,364
★ Ottawa	323,340
Pickering	78,989
Prince George	75,150
Quebec	167,264
Regina	180,400
Richmond	148,867
Richmond Hill	101,725
Saanich	101,388
Saint Catharines	130,926
Saint-Hubert	77,042
Saint John's	101,936
Saskatoon	193,647
Sault Sainte Marie	80,054
Scarborough	558,960
Sherbrooke	76,786
Sudbury	92,059
Surrey	304,477
Sydney	114,733
Thunder Bay	113,662
Toronto	653,734
Vancouver	514,008
Vaughan	132,549
Waterloo	77,949
Windsor	197,694
Winnipeg	618,477
York	146,534
Cape Verde (1995 est.)	
★ Praia	68,000
Central African Republic (1995 est.)	
★ Bangui	553,000
Chad (1993; MU)	
Abéché	187,936
Bongor	196,713
Doba	185,461
Moundou	282,103
★ N'Djamena	530,965
Sarh	193,753
Chile (1999 est.)	
Antofagasta	243,038
Arica	178,547
Calama	121,326
Chillán	162,969
Concepción	362,589
Copiapó	114,615
Coquimbo	126,886
Iquique	159,815
La Serena	123,166
Los Angeles	109,606
Osorno	126,645
Puente Alto	363,012
Puerto Montt	128,945
Punta Arenas	120,148
Quilpué	114,617
Rancagua	202,067
San Bernardo	223,055
★ Santiago	202,010[11]
(administrative) agglomeration	4,640,635
Talca	174,858
Talcahuano	269,265
Temuco	253,451
Valdívia	122,166
★ Valparaíso (legislative)	283,489
Viña del Mar	330,736
China (1999 est.)[12]	
Acheng	234,057
Aksu	220,415
Altay	106,665
Anda	180,795
Ankang	173,450
Anlu	112,529
Anning	128,275
Anqing	356,920
Anqiu	193,258
Anshan	1,285,849
Anshun	217,215
Anyang	527,982
Baicheng	269,732
Baise	119,150
Baishan	253,631
Baiyin	258,885
Baoding	570,167
Baoji	447,105
Baoshan	100,797
Baotou	1,092,819
Bazhong	137,627
Bazhou	80,753
Bei'an	217,980
Beihai	196,256
★ Beijing (Peking)	6,633,929
Beiliu	140,015
Beining	101,273
Beipiao	202,807
Bengbu	506,239
Benxi	827,203
Bijie	101,171
Binzhou	230,174
Bole	79,953
Botou	103,337
Bozhou	253,544
Cangzhou	304,010
Cenxi	113,589
Changchun	2,072,324
Changde	384,433
Changge	117,166
Changji	192,000
Changning	134,592
Changsha	1,334,036
Changshu	264,472
Changyi	133,754
Changzhi	387,002
Changzhou	772,700
Chaohu	280,409
Chaoyang (Liaoning)	295,302
Chaoyang (Fujian)	389,558
Chaozhou	257,521
Chengde	298,895
Chengdu	2,146,126
Chenghai	166,621
Chenzhou	274,338
Chibi	158,125
Chifeng	453,946
Chongqing (Chungking)	3,193,889
Chongzhou	85,183
Chuxiong	115,887
Chuzhou	187,985
Cixi	132,588
Conghua	128,328
Da'an	153,718
Dachuan	200,785
Dafeng	153,147
Dali	175,847
Dalian	2,000,944
Dandong	578,723
Dangyang	114,885
Danjiangkou	152,396
Danyang	211,875
Danzhou	212,572
Daqing	811,154
Dashiqiao	186,201
Datong	928,293
Daye	128,561
Dehui	149,275
Dengta	85,304
Dengzhou	119,036
Dexing	104,945
Deyang	246,221
Dezhou	310,538
Dingzhou	131,992
Dongfang	78,447
Donggang	104,971
Dongguan	378,354
Dongsheng	113,436
Dongtai	231,444
Dongyang	79,241
Dongying	479,941
Dujiangyan	154,867
Dunhua	257,190
Duyun	150,950
Emeishan	124,471
Enping	164,929
Enshi	125,937
Ezhou	301,248
Fangchenggang	119,444
Fanyu	345,275
Feicheng	301,981
Fengcheng (*Guangdong*)	173,112
Fengcheng (*Jiangxi*)	221,652
Fenghua	79,755
Fengnan	121,767
Foshan	411,107
Fu'an	100,793
Fuding	79,240
Fujin	123,280
Fuqing	139,426
Fushun	1,271,113
Fuxin	682,966
Fuyang (*Anhui*)	319,816
Fuyang (*Zhejiang*)	97,439
Fuzhou	1,057,372
Gaizhou	175,467
Ganzhou	271,952
Gao'an	130,520
Gaobeidian	79,674
Gaomi	224,162
Gaoming	121,732
Gaoyao	142,335
Gaoyou	135,728
Gaozhou	204,028
Gejiu	218,921
Genhe	173,188
Gongyi	118,985
Gongzhuling	352,978
Guanghan	121,228
Guangshui	137,189
Guangyuan	257,411
Guangzhou (Canton)	3,306,277
Guichi	103,860
Guigang	290,829
Guilin	458,333
Guiping	151,341
Guixi	102,536
Guiyang	1,320,566
Gujiao	104,560
Harbin	2,586,978
Haicheng	259,725
Haikou	438,262

Major cities and national capitals (continued)

country city	population
Hailar	209,294
Hailin	242,389
Hailun	154,148
Haimen	355,232
Haining	122,973
Haiyang	95,402
Hami	205,310
Hancheng	108,702
Hanchuan	171,827
Handan	1,005,834
Hangzhou	1,346,148
Hanzhong	215,284
Hebi	276,808
Hechi	108,942
Hechuan	202,218
Hefei	1,000,655
Hegang	591,254
Heihe	112,961
Helong	135,328
Hengshui	212,516
Hengyang	584,346
Heshan	117,049
Heyuan	164,986
Heze	307,445
Hezhou	113,031
Hohhot	754,749
Honghu	201,421
Hongjiang	130,713
Hongta	110,048
Hotan	86,019
Houma	103,578
Huadian	197,759
Huadu	195,921
Huai'an	155,657
Huaibei	574,904
Huaihua	225,414
Huainan	823,395
Huaiyin	320,841
Huanggang	241,268
Huanghua	81,033
Huangshan	130,623
Huangshi	569,394
Huaying	80,107
Huazhou	183,394
Huichun	134,379
Huixian	95,070
Huiyang	192,713
Huizhou	287,178
Hulin	152,353
Huludao	447,986
Huozhou	93,324
Huzhou	296,962
Jiamusi	579,093
Ji'an (*Jilin*)	79,792
Ji'an (*Jiangxi*)	178,957
Jiande	99,004
Jiangdu	182,208
Jiangjin	222,571
Jiangmen	333,154
Jiangyan	149,706
Jiangyin	339,420
Jiangyou	221,960
Jian'ou	99,204
Jianyang (*Fujian*)	85,500
Jianyang (*Sichuan*)	161,496
Jiaohe	170,881
Jiaonan	186,424
Jiaozhou	188,192
Jiaozuo	536,021
Jiaxing	261,465
Jiayuguan	114,510
Jieshou	97,675
Jiexiu	90,118
Jieyang	204,134
Jilin	1,165,418
Jimo	149,083
Jinan	1,713,036
Jinchang	141,578
Jincheng	200,659
Jingdezhen	315,036
Jinghong	94,162
Jingjiang	136,204
Jingmen	388,780
Jingzhou	596,860
Jinhua	199,649
Jining (*Inner Mongolia*)	206,514
Jining (*Shandong*)	427,256
Jinjiang	126,102
Jinshi	99,571
Jintan	97,651
Jinzhou	658,589
Jishou	114,650
Jiujiang	361,645
Jiuquan	99,111
Jiutai	198,316
Jixi	752,840
Jiyuan	241,406
Jurong	108,555
Kaifeng	569,300
Kaili	149,939
Kaiping	188,795
Kaiyuan (*Liaoning*)	132,481
Kaiyuan (*Yunnan*)	104,329
Karamay	225,251
Kashgar (Kashi)	205,056
Korla	200,374
Kuitun	144,048
Kunming	1,350,640
Kunshan	177,003
Laiwu	382,785
Laixi	118,709
Laiyang	166,824
Laizhou	206,786
Langfang	241,984
Langzhong	112,118
Lanxi	103,792
Lanzhou	1,429,673
Laohekou	162,343
Lechang	177,572
Leiyang	163,278
Leizhou	226,310
Lengshuijiang	176,182
Leping	129,376
Leqing	103,118
Leshan	410,423
Lhasa	121,568
Lianjiang	246,638
Lianyuan	133,059
Lianyungang	447,918
Lianzhou	91,781
Liaocheng	275,271
Liaoyang	570,483
Liaoyuan	391,841
Liling	135,453
Linchuan	232,592
Linfen	257,684
Lingbao	114,053
Linghai	94,754
Lingwu	86,246
Lingyuan	141,481
Linhai	127,378
Linhe	186,234
Linjiang	114,072
Linqing	143,203
Linxia	98,593
Linxiang	92,704
Linyi	569,419
Linzhou	110,526
Lishui	93,626
Liu'an	282,880
Liupanshui	502,327
Liuyang	133,723
Liuzhou	775,823
Liyang	292,482
Longhai	101,884
Longjing	144,940
Longkou	221,823
Longyan	237,385
Loudi	222,375
Lufeng	260,804
Luoding	338,722
Luohe	306,565
Luoyang	1,002,178
Luzhou	371,843
Ma'anshan	393,174
Macheng	175,322
Manzhouli	143,711
Maoming	302,022
Meihekou	255,514
Meizhou	230,419
Mengzhou	92,469
Mianyang	396,055
Mianzhu	92,860
Miluo	90,700
Mingguang	112,715
Mishan	153,717
Mudanjiang	641,347
Muling	134,632
Nan'an	108,684
Nanchang	1,264,739
Nanchong	390,603
Nanchuan	84,374
Nanhai	381,322
Nanjing (Nanking)	2,388,915
Nankang	102,222
Nanning	984,061
Nanping	230,931
Nantong	468,215
Nanxiong	76,876
Nanyang	477,128
Nehe	128,191
Neijiang	320,777
Ning'an	143,722
Ningbo	704,819
Ningde	84,815
Ningguo	108,767
Panjin	471,729
Panshi	165,101
Panzhihua	488,911
Penglai	114,440
Pengzhou	122,074
Pingdingshan	619,694
Pingdu	198,558
Pinghu	88,554
Pingliang	124,447
Pingxiang	392,286
Pizhou	159,194
Pulandian	166,331
Puning	312,498
Putian	145,051
Puyang	289,232
Qian'an	85,845
Qianjiang	313,500
Qidong	231,611
Qilin	210,230
Qingdao	1,702,108
Qingtongxia	77,428
Qingyuan	193,284
Qingzhou	193,996
Qinhuangdao	485,143
Qinyang	81,338
Qinzhou	172,379
Qionghai	84,235
Qionglai	75,992
Qiongshan	144,979
Qiqihar (Tsitsihar)	1,115,766
Qitaihe	289,111
Qixia	115,089
Quanzhou	281,906
Qufu	157,201
Quzhou	151,122
Renqiu	158,242
Rizhao	322,190
Rongcheng	203,263
Rugao	276,028
Rui'an	164,563
Ruichang	82,510
Rushan	116,166
Ruzhou	102,691
Sanhe	108,252
Sanmenxia	189,084
Sanming	199,201
Sanshui	145,279
Sanya	161,869
Shahe	80,352
Shanghai	8,937,175
Shangqiu	317,948
Shangrao	168,263
Shangyu	116,279
Shangzhi	228,273
Shantou	831,949
Shanwei	171,380
Shaoguan	431,053
Shaowu	99,925
Shaoxing	233,954
Shaoyang	311,261
Shengyang	3,876,289
Shengzhou	79,351
Shenzhen	899,111
Shifang	82,286
Shihezi	330,535
Shijiazhuang	1,338,796
Shishi	91,301
Shishou	140,634
Shiyan	377,232
Shizuishan	313,842
Shouguang	202,067
Shuangcheng	172,936
Shuangliao	135,663
Shuangyashan	431,170
Shulan	208,723
Shunde	339,392
Shuozhou	134,645
Sihui	125,065
Siping	382,652
Songyuan	303,821
Songzi	148,183
Suihua	262,117
Suining	229,229
Suizhou	333,766
Suqian	115,368
Suzhou (*Anhui*)	325,724
Suzhou (*Jiangsu*)	845,687
Tai'an	518,117
Taicang	119,862
Taishan	355,017
Taixing	185,270
Taiyuan	1,768,530
Taizhou (*Jiangsu*)	219,968
Taizhou (*Zhejiang*)	239,271
Tangshan	1,210,842
Taonan	156,464
Tengzhou	452,009
Tianchang	167,508
Tianjin (Tientsin)	4,835,327
Tianmen	367,036
Tianshui	301,570
Tiefa	165,956
Tieli	272,841
Tieling	313,991
Tongcheng	91,188
Tongchuan	304,809
Tonghua	362,577
Tongliao	305,885
Tongling	292,721
Tongren	83,467
Tongxiang	109,976
Tongzhou	365,003
Tumen	102,191
Ulanhot	182,128
Ürümqi	1,258,457
Wafangdian	305,249
Wanning	80,764
Wanyuan	81,160
Weifang	621,125
Weihai	287,872
Weihui	98,950
Weinan	210,079
Wenchang	86,551
Wendeng	183,952
Wenling	134,074
Wenzhou	512,523
Wuchang	227,856
Wuchuan	184,812
Wudalianchi	157,547
Wugang (*Henan*)	93,599
Wugang (*Hunan*)	77,767
Wuhai	316,718
Wuhan	3,911,824
Wuhu	495,765
Wujiang	176,514
Wujin	141,495
Wuwei	181,328
Wuxi	940,858
Wuxian	176,694
Wuxue	142,136
Wuzhong	92,241
Wuzhou	253,159
Xiamen (Amoy)	593,401
Xi'an (Sian)	2,294,790
Xiangcheng	103,692
Xiangfan	597,604
Xiangtan	518,783
Xiangxiang	103,871
Xianning	249,234
Xiantao	412,434
Xianyang	460,976
Xiaogan	224,026
Xiaoshan	220,815
Xiaoyi	117,133
Xichang	174,781
Xilinhot	99,249
Xingcheng	120,431
Xinghua	199,023
Xingning	206,712
Xingping	108,491
Xingtai	387,081
Xingyi	99,550
Xinhui	269,528
Xining	604,812
Xinmi	86,938
Xinmin	123,655
Xintai	381,637
Xinxiang	583,408
Xinyang	366,304
Xinyi (*Guangdong*)	170,368
Xinyi (*Jiangsu*)	127,496
Xinyu	250,666
Xinzheng	136,980
Xinzhou	143,840
Xishan	171,316
Xuanwei	120,046
Xuanzhou	136,914
Xuchang	275,743
Xuzhou	1,044,729
Ya'an	119,320
Yakeshi	391,627
Yan'an	133,226
Yancheng	332,125
Yangchun	206,440
Yangjiang	295,672
Yangquan	447,229
Yangzhong	81,005
Yangzhou	395,048
Yanji	329,112
Yanshi	75,234
Yantai	818,646
Yanzhou	199,491
Yibin	288,039
Yichang	481,277
Yicheng	116,586
Yichun (*Heilongjiang*)	802,931
Yichun (*Jiangxi*)	198,799
Yidu	87,288
Yima	116,760
Yinchuan	469,180
Yingcheng	120,499
Yingde	205,782
Yingkou	498,300
Yingtan	110,671
Yingyang	97,621
Yining	230,429
Yiwu	93,903
Yixing	258,808
Yiyang	297,000
Yizheng	166,358
Yizhou	96,717
Yong'an	130,688
Yongcheng	118,659
Yongchuan	186,482
Yongji	76,700
Yongzhou	276,669
Yuanjiang	140,406
Yuanping	101,689
Yucheng	79,820
Yuci	243,948
Yueyang	448,249
Yuhang	152,429
Yulin (*Guangxi*)	190,418
Yulin (*Shaanxi*)	106,391
Yumen	116,194
Yuncheng	172,620
Yunfu	168,371
Yushu	171,692
Yuyao	136,464
Yuzhou	133,619
Zalantun	143,273
Zaoyang	211,295
Zaozhuang	741,421
Zengcheng	197,023
Zhangjiagang	168,546
Zhangjiajie	115,896
Zhangjiakou	660,504
Zhangqiu	207,212
Zhangshu	112,600
Zhangye	114,592
Zhangzhou	231,333
Zhanjiang	588,583
Zhaodong	227,218
Zhaoqing	311,571
Zhaotong	104,382
Zhaoyuan	172,646
Zhengzhou	1,465,069
Zhenjiang	469,977
Zhijiang	126,808
Zhongshan	390,060
Zhongxiang	224,442
Zhoukou	189,377
Zhoushan	196,368
Zhuanghe	161,223
Zhucheng	145,952
Zhuhai	371,116
Zhuji	116,116
Zhumadian	204,020
Zhuozhou	109,390
Zhuzhou	528,958
Zibo	1,458,060
Zigong	464,497
Zixing	123,747
Ziyang	145,665
Zoucheng	302,856
Zunyi	464,945
Colombia (1999 est.; MU)	
Armenia	288,977
Barrancabermeja	195,345
Barranquilla	1,226,292
Bello	340,910
Bucaramanga	520,874
Buenaventura	263,137
Buga	125,240
Cali	2,110,571
Cartagena	877,238
Cartago	130,988
Ciénaga	170,133
Cúcuta	624,215
Dos Quebradas	171,630
Duitama	110,861
Envigado	146,406
Florencia	126,680
Floridablanca	228,749
Girardot	115,004
Giron	102,325
Ibagué	421,195
Itagüí	234,712
Lorica	116,719
Magangué	147,108
Maicao	124,385
Manizales	361,965
Medellín	1,957,928
Montería	321,249
Neiva	322,076
Palmira	271,681
Pasto	378,606
Pereira	456,816
Popayán	221,413
Quibdó	114,318
Sahagún	120,738
Santa Marta	374,933
★ Santafé de Bogotá, D.C.	6,276,428
Sincelejo	228,609
Soacha	277,161
Sogamoso	143,545
Soledad	297,037

country / city	population
Tuluá	178,027
Tumaco	148,977
Tunja	118,855
Turbo	111,578
Valledupar	328,740
Villavicencio	314,213
Comoros (1995 est.)	
★ Moroni	34,168
Congo, Dem. Rep. of the (1994 est.)	
Boma	135,284
Bukavu	201,569
Butembo	109,406
Goma	109,094
Kalemi	101,309
Kananga	393,030
Kikwit	182,142
★ Kinshasa	4,655,313
Kisangani	417,517
Kolwezi	417,810
Likasi	299,118
Lubumbashi	851,381
Matadi	172,730
Mbanadaka	169,841
Mbuji-Mayi	806,475
Mwene-Ditu	137,459
Tshikapa	180,860
Uvira	115,590
Congo, Rep. of the (1992 est.)	
★ Brazzaville	937,579
Pointe-Noire	576,206
Costa Rica (1999 est.)	
★ San José	339,128[13]
Côte d'Ivoire (1995 est.)	
★ Abidjan (de facto; legislative)	2,500,000[8]
Bouaké	330,000
Daloa	123,000
Korhogo	109,445[14]
★ Yamoussoukro (de jure; administrative)	110,000
Croatia (1991)	
Osijek	129,792
Rijeka	167,964
Split	200,459
★ Zagreb	777,826[15]
Cuba (1994 est.)	
Bayamo	137,663
Camagüey	293,961
Cienfuegos	132,038
Ciego de Avila	104,060[10]
Guantánamo	207,796
★ Havana	2,241,000[3]
Holguín	242,085
Las Tunas	126,930
Manzanillo	109,471[10]
Matanzas	123,843
Pinar del Río	128,570
Santa Clara	205,400
Santiago de Cuba	440,084
Cyprus (1998 est.)	
Limassol	152,900
★ Lefkosia (Nicosia)	194,100[16]
Czech Republic (1999 est.)	
Brno	384,727
Olomouc	103,372
Ostrava	322,111
Plzen	168,422
★ Prague	1,193,270
Denmark (1999 est.; MU)	
Ålborg	160,937
Århus	283,673
★ Copenhagen	491,082
Odense	183,584
Djibouti (1995 est.)	
★ Djibouti	383,000
Dominica (1991)	
★ Roseau	15,853
Dominican Republic (1993)	
La Romana	140,204
San Francisco de Macorís	108,485
San Pedro de Macorís	124,735
Santiago	365,463
★ Santo Domingo	1,609,966[17]
East Timor (1999 est.)	
★ Dili	45,000[18]
Ecuador (1997 est.)	
Ambato	160,302
Cuenca	255,028
Duran	135,675
Eloy Alfaro	120,364[3]
Esmeraldas	117,722
Guayaquil	1,973,880
Ibarra	119,243
Loja	117,365
Machala	197,350
Manta	156,981
Milagro	119,371
Portoviejo	167,956
Quevedo	120,640
★ Quito	1,487,513
Riobamba	117,270
Santo Domingo	183,219
Egypt (1996)	
Alexandria	3,328,196
Al-ʿArīsh	100,447
Aswān	219,017
Asyūṭ	343,498
Banhā	145,792
Banī Suwayf	172,032
Bilbays	113,608
Būr Saʿīd (Port Said)	469,533
★ Cairo	6,789,479
Damanhūr	212,203
Al-Fayyūm	260,964
Al-Ismāʿīlīyah	254,477
Al-Jīzah (Giza)	2,221,868
Kafr ad-Dawwar	231,978
Kafr ash-Shaykh	124,819
Al-Maḥallah al-Kubrā	395,402
Mallawī	119,283
Al-Manṣūrah	369,621
Mīt Ghamr	101,801
Al-Minyā	201,360
Qinā	171,275
Sawhāj	170,125
Shibīn al-Kawm	159,909
Shubrā al-Khaymah	870,716
As-Suways (Suez)	417,610
Ṭanṭā	371,010
Al-Uqṣur (Luxor)	360,503
Az-Zaqāzīq	267,351
El Salvador (1992)	
Mejicanos	131,972[19]
San Miguel	127,696
★ San Salvador	415,346
Santa Ana	139,389
Soyapango	261,122[19]
Equatorial Guinea (1995 est.)	
★ Malabo (capital)	47,500
★ Bata (capital designate)	37,000
Eritrea (1995 est.)	
★ Asmara	431,000
Estonia (1999 est.)	
★ Tallinn	411,594
Tartu	100,577
Ethiopia (1994)	
★ Addis Ababa	2,112,737
Dire Dawa	164,851
Gonder	112,249
Harer (Harar)	131,139
Jima	106,842
Nazret	127,842
Faroe Islands (1999 est.)	
★ Tórshavn	16,466
Fiji (1996)	
★ Suva	77,366
Finland (2000 est.)	
Espoo	209,667
★ Helsinki	551,123
Oulu	117,670
Tampere	193,174
Turku	172,107
Vantaa	176,386
France (1999)	
Aix-en-Provence	134,222
Amiens	135,501
Angers	151,279
Argenteuil	94,019
Asnières	75,837
Aulnay-sous-Bois	80,021
Avignon	85,854
Besançon	117,304
Bordeaux	215,118
Boulogne-Billancourt	106,367
Brest	149,634
Caen	113,987
Calais	77,333
Clermont-Ferrand	137,140
Dijon	149,867
Colombes	76,757
Créteil	82,147
Grenoble	153,317
La Rochelle	76,584
Le Havre	190,651
Le Mans	146,105
Lille	182,228
Limoges	133,960
Lyon	445,257
Marseille	797,486
Metz	123,776
Montpellier	225,392
Montreuil	90,674
Mulhouse	110,359
Nancy	103,605
Nanterre	84,325
Nantes	268,695
Nice	342,738
Nîmes	133,424
Orléans	112,833
★ Paris	2,123,261
Pau	78,732
Perpignan	105,115
Poitiers	83,448
Reims	187,206
Rennes	206,229
Roubaix	96,984
Rouen	106,035
Saint-Denis	85,832
Saint-Étienne	179,755
Strasbourg	263,940
Toulon	159,389
Toulouse	390,413
Tourcoing	93,540
Tours	132,820
Versailles	85,726
Villeurbanne	124,215
Vitry-sur-Seine	78,645
French Guiana (1999)	
★ Cayenne	50,594
French Polynesia (1988)	
★ Papeete	23,555
Gabon (1993)	
★ Libreville	362,386
Gambia, The (1993)	
★ Banjul	42,407
agglomeration	270,540
Gaza Strip (1999 est.)	
★ Gaza (Ghazzah; acting administrative centre)	388,031
Jabālyah	113,901[20]
Khān Yūnus	123,175[20]
Georgia (1997 est.)	
Bat'umi (Batumi)	137,100
K'ut'aisi (Kutaisi)	240,000
Rust'avi (Rustavi)	158,000
★ T'bilisi (Tbilisi)	1,398,968[21]
Zugdidi	105,000[22]
Germany (1998 est.)	
Aachen	245,969
Arnsberg	78,591
Augsburg	256,625
Bergisch Gladbach	105,963
★ Berlin	3,425,759
Bielefeld	323,223
Bochum	395,837
Bonn	304,841
Bottrop	121,565
Brandenburg	82,460
Braunschweig	248,944
Bremen	546,968
Bremerhaven	126,915
Castrop-Rauxel	78,771
Chemnitz	259,126
Cologne (Köln)	964,311
Cottbus	118,463
Darmstadt	137,876
Delmenhorst	77,958
Dessau	88,607
Dorsten	81,058
Dortmund	594,274
Dresden	459,222
Duisburg	529,062
Düren	89,872
Düsseldorf	570,969
Erfurt	205,361
Erlangen	100,330
Essen	608,732
Esslingen (am Neckar)	89,469
Flensburg	85,547
Frankfurt am Main	643,469
Frankfurt an der Oder	77,891
Freiburg im Breisgau	200,519
Fürth	109,521
Gelsenkirchen	286,432
Gera	118,733
Gladbeck	78,675
Göttingen	127,366
Gütersloh	94,058
Hagen	209,027
Halle	268,365
Hamburg	1,704,731
Hamm	181,194
Hanau	88,160
Hannover	520,670
Heidelberg	139,941
Heilbronn	120,987
Herne	177,863
Hildesheim	105,405
Ingolstadt	113,494
Iserlohn	99,493
Jena	99,273
Kaiserslautern	101,315
Karlsruhe	276,571
Kassel	199,453
Kiel	240,516
Koblenz	109,404
Konstanz	77,486
Krefeld	245,606
Leipzig	446,491
Leverkusen	162,298
Lübeck	215,376
Lüdenscheid	81,649
Ludwigsburg	86,318
Ludwigshafen	166,159
Lünen	91,586
Magdeburg	245,509
Mainz	186,136
Mannheim	310,475
Marburg	77,050
Marl	93,642
Minden	83,619
Moers	106,704
Mönchengladbach	266,505
Mülheim an der Ruhr	175,507
Munich (München)	1,205,923
Münster	265,138
Neubrandenburg	77,312
Neumünster	81,322
Neuss	149,206
Nürnberg	489,758
Oberhausen	223,399
Offenbach am Main	116,214
Oldenburg	153,531
Osnabrück	166,653
Paderborn	131,851
Pforzheim	118,079
Potsdam	136,077
Ratingen	89,609
Recklinghausen	126,241
Regensburg	125,085
Remscheid	120,639
Reutlingen	109,882
Rheine	75,605
Rostock	212,715
Saarbrücken	186,402
Salzgitter	115,453
Schwerin	110,847
Siegen	110,847
Solingen	164,993
Stuttgart	585,274
Trier	99,691
Tübingen	81,222
Ulm	115,628
Velbert	90,098
Viersen	77,098
Villingen-Schwenningen	80,756
Wiesbaden	267,726
Wilhelmshaven	88,950
Witten	103,872
Wolfsburg	122,798
Worms	80,622
Wuppertal	376,693
Würzburg	126,392
Zwickau	101,130
Ghana (1988 est.)	
★ Accra	949,100
Kumasi	385,192
Sekondi-Takoradi	103,653
Tamale	151,069
Tema	109,975
Greece (1991)	
★ Athens	772,072
Iráklion	116,178
Kallithéa	114,233
Larissa	112,777
Pátrai (Patras)	153,344
Peristérion	137,288
Piraiévs (Piraeus)	182,671
Thessaloníki	383,967
Greenland (1999 est.)	
★ Nuuk (Godthåb)	13,169
Grenada (1991)	
★ Saint George's	4,621
Guadeloupe (1999)	
★ Basse-Terre	12,549
Guam (1995 est.)	
★ Agana	2,000
Guatemala (1995 est.; MU)	
★ Guatemala City	1,167,495
Mixco	436,668
Villa Nueva	165,567
Guernsey (1996)	
★ St. Peter Port	16,194
Guinea (1999 est.)	
★ Conakry	1,764,000
Guinea-Bissau (1999 est.)	
★ Bissau	274,000
Guyana (1999 est.)	
★ Georgetown	275,000
Haiti (1997 est.)	
Cap-Haïtien	107,026
Carrefour	306,074
Delmas	257,247
★ Port-au-Prince	917,112
Honduras (1999 est.)	
El Progreso	104,100
La Ceiba	103,400
San Pedro Sula	452,100
★ Tegucigalpa	988,400[23]
Hong Kong (2000 est.)	
★ Hong Kong	7,072,000[24]
Hungary (1999 est.)	
★ Budapest	1,838,753
Debrecen	205,032
Győr	127,275
Kecskemét	105,464
Miskolc	173,639
Nyíregyháza	112,882
Pécs	158,607
Szeged	159,133
Székesfehérvár	105,293
Iceland (1999 est.)	
★ Reykjavík	109,184
India (1991)[25]	
Abohar	107,163
Adoni	136,182
Agartala	157,358
Agra	891,790
Ahmadabad	2,876,710
Ahmadnagar	181,339
Aizawl	155,240
Ajmer	402,700
Akola	328,034
Alandur	125,244
Alappuzha (Alleppey)	174,666
Alibag	328,640
Aligarh	480,520
Allahabad	792,858
Alwar	205,086
Ambala	119,338
Ambala Sadar	90,872
Ambattur	215,424
Amravati	421,576
Amritsar	708,835
Amroha	137,061
Anand	110,266
Anantapur	174,924
Ara (Arrah)	157,082
Asansol	262,188
Avadi	183,215
Baharampur	115,144
Bahraich	135,400
Baleshwar (Balasore)	85,442
Bally	184,474
Balurghat	119,796
Bangalore	2,660,088
Bankura	114,876
Baranagar (Barahanagar)	224,821
Barasat	102,660
Barddhaman (Burdwan)	245,079
Bareilly	587,211
Barrackpore	133,265
Basirhat	101,409
Batala	86,006
Bathinda (Bhatinda)	159,042
Beawar	105,363
Belgaum	326,399
Bellary	245,391
Bhagalpur	253,225
Bharatpur	148,519
Bharuch (Broach)	133,102
Bhatpara	304,952
Bhavnagar	402,338
Bhilainagar	395,360

Major cities and national capitals (continued)

country city	population
Bhilwara	183,965
Bhimavaram	121,314
Bhind	109,755
Bhiwandi	379,070
Bhiwani	121,629
Bhopal	1,062,771
Bhubaneshwar	411,542
Bhuj	102,176
Bhusawal	145,143
Bid (Bhir)	112,434
Bidar	108,016
Bidhan Nagar	100,048
Bihar Sharif	201,323
Bijapur	186,939
Bikaner	416,289
Bilaspur	179,833
Bokaro	333,683
Brahmapur	210,418
Budaun	116,695
Bulandshahr	127,201
Burhanpur	172,710
Burnpur	174,933
Champdani	101,067
Chandannagar	120,378
Chandigarh	504,094
Chandrapur	226,105
Chennai (Madras)	3,841,396
Chhapra	136,877
Chirala	80,861
Chitradurga	87,069
Chittoor	133,462
Coimbatore	816,321
Cuddalore	144,561
Cuddapah	121,463
Cuttack	403,418
Dabgram	147,217
Damoh	95,661
Darbhanga	218,391
Davanagere	266,082
Dehra Dun	270,159
Delhi	7,206,704
Dewas	164,364
Dhanbad	151,789
Dhule (Dhulia)	278,317
Dibrugarh	120,127
Dindigul	182,447
Durg	150,645
Durgapur	425,836
Eluru	212,866
Erode	159,232
Etawah	124,072
Faizabad	124,437
Faridabad	617,717
Farrukhabad-cum-Fatehgarh	194,567
Fatehpur	117,675
Fīrozabad	215,128
Gadag-Betigeri	134,051
Gandhidham	104,585
Gandhinagar	123,359
Ganganagar	161,482
Gaya	291,675
Ghaziabad	454,156
Godhra	96,813
Gondia	109,470
Gorakhpur	505,566
Gudivada	101,656
Gulbarga	304,099
Guna	100,490
Guntakal	107,592
Guntur	471,051
Gurgaon	121,486
Guwahati (Gauhati)	584,342
Gwalior	690,765
Habra	100,223
Haldia	100,347
Haldwani-cum-Kathgodam	104,195
Halisahar	114,028
Haora (Howrah)	950,435
Hapur	146,262
Haridwar (Hardwar)	147,305
Hassan	90,803
Hathras	113,285
Hindupur	104,651
Hisar (Hissar)	172,677
Hoshiarpur	122,705
Hospet	96,322
Hubli-Dharwad	648,298
Hugli-Chunchura	151,806
Hyderabad	3,145,939
Ichalkaranji	214,950
Imphal	198,535
Indore	1,091,674
Ingraj Bazar (English Bazar)	139,204
Jabalpur	741,927
Jaipur	1,458,183
Jalandhar (Jullundur)	509,510
Jalgaon	242,193
Jalna	174,985
Jammu	225,000[26]
Jamnagar	341,637
Jamshedpur	478,950
Jaunpur	136,062
Jhansi	300,850
Jodhpur	666,279
Junagadh	130,484
Kakinada	279,980
Kalyan	1,014,557
Kamarhati	266,889
Kamthi	78,612
Kanchipuram	144,955
Kanchrapara	100,194
Kanpur	1,874,409
Karimnagar	148,583
Karnal	173,751
Katihar	135,436
Khammam	127,992
Khandwa	143,133
Kharagpur	177,989
Kochi (Cochin)	564,589
Kolhapur	406,370
Kolkata (Calcutta)	4,399,819
Kollam (Quilon)	139,852
Kota	537,371
Kottagudem	80,440
Kozhikode (Calicut)	419,831
Krishnanagar	121,110
Kukatpalle	186,963
Kulti-Barakar	108,518
Kumbakonam	139,483
Kurnool	236,800
Lalbahadur Nagar	155,514
Latur	197,408
Lucknow	1,619,115
Ludhiana	1,042,740
Machilipatnam (Masulipatam)	159,110
Madurai	940,989
Mahbubnagar	116,833
Mahesana (Mehsana)	88,201
Malegaon	342,595
Malkajgiri	127,178
Mandya	120,265
Mangalore	273,304
Mango	108,100
Mathura	226,691
Maunath Bhanjan	136,697
Medinipur (Midnapore)	125,498
Meerut	753,778
Mira-Bhayandar	175,605
Miraj	121,593
Mizapur-cum-Vindhyachal	169,336
Modinagar	101,660
Moga	108,304
Moradabad	429,214
Morbi (Morvi)	90,357
Morena	147,124
Mumbai (Bombay)	9,925,891
Munger (Monghyr)	150,112
Murwara (Katni)	163,431
Muzaffarnagar	240,609
Muzaffarpur	241,107
Mysore	480,692
Nadiad	167,051
Nagercoil	190,084
Nagpur	1,624,752
Naihati	132,701
Nanded (Nander)	275,083
Nandyal	119,813
Nashik (Nasik)	656,925
Navadwip	125,037
Navsari	126,089
Nellore	316,606
New Bombay	307,724
★ New Delhi	301,297
Neyveli	118,080
Nizamabad	241,034
Noida	146,514
North Barrackpore	100,606
North Dum Dum	149,965
Ongole	100,836
Palghat (Palakkad)	123,289
Pali	136,842
Pallavaram	111,866
Panihati	275,990
Panipat	191,212
Parbhani	190,255
Patan	96,112
Pathankot	123,930
Patiala	238,368
Patna	917,243
Pilibhit	106,605
Pimpri-Chinchwad	517,083
Pollachi	86,897
Pondicherry	203,065
Porbandar	116,671
Proddatur	133,914
Pune	1,566,651
Puri	125,199
Purnia (Purnea)	114,912
Qutubullapur	106,591
Rae Bareli	129,904
Raichur	157,551
Raiganj	151,045
Raipur	438,639
Raj Nandgaon	125,371
Rajahmundry	324,851
Rajapalaiyam	114,202
Rajkot	559,407
Ramagundam	214,384
Rampur	243,742
Ranchi	599,306
Ratlam	183,375
Raurkela Steel Township	215,509
Rewa	128,981
Rishra	102,815
Rohtak	216,096
Sagar	195,346
Saharanpur	374,945
Salem	366,712
Sambalpur	131,138
Sambhal	150,869
Sangli	193,197
Satna	156,630
Shahjahanpur	237,713
Shambajinagar (Aurangābād)	573,272
Shantipur	109,956
Shiliguri (Siliguri)	216,950
Shillong	131,719
Shimoga	179,258
Shivpuri	108,277
Sholapur (Solapur)	604,215
Shrirampur	137,028
Sikar	148,272
Silchar	115,483
Simla (Shimla)	82,054
Sirsa	112,841
Sitapur	121,842
Sonipat (Sonepat)	143,922
South Dum Dum	232,811
Srinagar	700,000[26]
Surat	1,498,817
Surendranagar	106,110
Tambaram	107,187
Tenali	143,726
Thalassery (Tellicherry)	103,579
Thane (Thana)	803,389
Thanjavur	202,013
Thiruvananthapuram (Trivandrum)	524,006
Tiruchchirappalli	387,223
Trunelveli	135,825
Tirupati	174,369
Tirupper (Tiruppur)	235,661
Tiruvannamalai	109,196
Tiruvottiyur	168,642
Titagarh	114,085
Tonk	100,079
Tumkur	138,903
Tuticorin	199,854
Udaipur	308,571
Ujjain	362,266
Ulhasnagar	369,077
Uluberia	155,172
Unnao	107,425
Uttarpara-Kotrung	101,268
Vadodara (Baroda)	1,031,346
Valparai	106,523
Varanasi (Benares)	929,270
Vellore	175,061
Veraval	93,976
Vijayawada	701,827
Vishakhapatnam	752,037
Vizianagaram	160,359
Warangal	447,657
Wardha	102,985
Yamunanagar	144,346
Yavatmal (Yeotmal)	108,578
Indonesia (1995 est.)[27]	
Ambon	249,312
Balikpapan	338,752
Banda Aceh	143,360[9]
Bandar Lampung	457,927[9]
Bandung	2,356,120
Banjarmasin	482,931
Bengkulu	146,395[9]
Binjai	127,184[9]
Blitar	112,986[9]
Bogor	285,114
Cirebon	254,406
★ Jakarta	9,112,652
Jambi	385,201
Kediri	253,760
Madiun	171,532
Magelang	123,800
Malang	716,862
Manado	332,288
Medan	1,843,919
Padang	534,474
Palembang	1,222,764
Pasuruan	133,685[9]
Pekalongan	301,504
Pekanbaru	438,638
Pematang Siantar	203,056
Pontianak	409,632
Probolinggo	120,770
Samarinda	399,175
Semarang	1,104,405
Sukabumi	125,766
Surabaya	2,663,820
Surakarta	516,594
Tanjung Balai	101,644[9]
Tanjung Karang	680,332
Tegal	289,744
Ujung Pandang	1,060,257
Yogyakarta	418,944
Iran (1996)	
Ābādān	206,073
Ahvāz	804,980
Āmol	159,092
Andīmeshk	106,923
Arāk	380,755
Ardabīl	340,386
Bābol	158,346
Bandar 'Abbās	273,578
Bandar-e Būshehr (Būshehr)	143,641
Bīrjand	127,608
Bojnūrd	134,835
Borūjerd	217,804
Būkān	120,020
Dezfūl	202,639
Emāmshahr (Shāhrūd)	104,765
Eṣfahān (Isfahan)	1,266,072
Gonbad-e Kavus	111,253
Gorgān	188,710
Hamadān	401,281
Īlām	126,346
Islāmshahr (Eslāmshahr)	265,450
Karaj	940,968[28]
Kāshān	201,372
Kermān	384,991
Kermānshāh (Bākhtarān)	692,986
Khomeynīshahr	165,888
Khorramābād	272,815
Khorramshahr	105,636
Khvoy (Khoy)	148,944
Mahābād	107,799
Malāyer	144,373
Marāgheh	132,318
Marv Dasht	103,579
Mashhad (Meshed)	1,887,405
Masjed-e Soleymān	116,882
Najafābād	178,498
Neyshābūr	158,847
Orūmīyeh	435,200
Qā'emshahr	143,286
Qarchak	142,690
Qazvīn	291,117
Qods	138,278
Qom	777,677
Rasht	417,748
Sabzevār	170,738
Sanandaj	277,808
Saqqez	115,394
Sārī	195,882
Sāveh	111,245
Shahr-e Kord	100,477
Shīrāz	1,053,025
Sīrjān	135,024
Tabrīz	1,191,043
★ Tehrān	6,758,845
Varāmīn	107,233
Yazd	326,776
Zābol	100,888
Zāhedān	419,518
Zanjān	286,295
Iraq (1987)	
Al-'Amārah	208,797
★ Baghdad	4,689,000[29, 30]
Ba'qūbah	114,516[31]
Al-Baṣrah	406,296
Al-Ḥillah	268,834
Dīwanīyah	196,519
Irbīl	485,968
Karbalā'	296,705
Karkūk	418,624
Al-Kūt	183,183
Mosul	664,221
An-Najaf	309,010
An-Nāṣirīyah	265,937
Ar-Ramādī	192,556
As-Sulaymānīyah	364,096
Ireland (1996)	
Cork	127,092[32]
★ Dublin	480,996[32]
Isle of Man (1996)	
★ Douglas	23,487
Israel (1999 est.)	
Ashdod	155,800
Bat Yam	137,000
Beersheba (Be'er Sheva')	163,700
Bene Beraq	133,900
Haifa (Ḥefa)	265,700
Ḥolon	163,100
★ Jerusalem (Yerushalayim, Al-Quds)	633,700
Netanya	154,900
Petaḥ Tiqwa	159,400
Ramat Gan	126,900
Rishon LeẔiyyon	188,200
Tel Aviv–Yafo	348,100
Italy (1998 est.)[33]	
Alessandria	90,852
Ancona	99,074
Andria	90,063[34]
Arezzo	90,907
Bari	333,550
Barletta	89,527[34]
Bergamo	117,619
Bologna	383,761
Bolzano (Bozen)	97,073
Brescia	190,518
Brindisi	94,429
Busto Arsizio	77,094[34]
Cagliari	170,786
Casoria	79,707[34]
Catania	342,275
Catanzaro	97,118
Cesena	88,487[34]
Cinisello Balsamo	76,262[34]
Como	87,059[34]
Cosenza	76,628
Ferrara	133,270
Florence (Firenze)	379,687
Foggia	155,785
Forlì	107,461
Genoa (Genova)	647,896
La Spezia	96,930
Latina	112,517
Lecce	99,372
Livorno	163,073
Lucca	85,657
Marsala	80,177[34]
Messina	262,172
Milan (Milano)	1,302,808
Modena	175,013
Monza	120,651[34]
Naples (Napoli)	1,035,835
Novara	102,404
Padua (Padova)	211,985
Palermo	688,369
Parma	167,165
Perugia	154,566
Pesaro	88,210
Pescara	117,411
Piacenza	99,078
Pisa	93,133
Pistoia	86,118
Pozzuoli	75,142[34]
Prato	169,927
Ravenna	137,721
Reggio di Calabria	180,158
Reggio nell'Emilia	139,200
Rimini	130,074
★ Rome (Roma)	2,653,245
Salerno	142,658
Sassari	121,038
Sesto San Giovanni	86,721[34]
Siracusa (Syracuse)	126,884
Taranto	210,536
Terni	108,108
Torre del Greco	101,361[34]
Trento	103,668
Treviso	81,328
Trieste	219,715
Turin (Torino)	914,818
Udine	94,823
Varese	84,187
Venice (Venezia)	293,731
Verona	254,748
Vicenza	108,947
Jamaica (1991)	
★ Kingston	103,771
agglomeration	587,798

country city	population
Japan (1995)	
Abiko	124,257
Ageo	206,090
Aizuwakamatsu	119,640
Akashi	287,606
Akiruno	75,355
Akishima	107,292
Akita	311,948
Amagasaki	488,586
Anjō	149,464
Aomori	294,167
Asahikawa	360,568
Asaka	110,789
Ashikaga	165,828
Ashiya	75,032
Atsugi	208,627
Ayase	80,680
Beppu	128,255
Chiba	856,878
Chigasaki	212,874
Chikushino	81,988
Chita	78,202
Chitose	84,866
Chōfu	198,574
Chōshi	82,180
Daitō	128,838
Ebetsu	115,495
Ebina	113,430
Fuchu	216,211
Fuji	229,187
Fujieda	124,822
Fujimi	96,972
Fujinomiya	119,536
Fujisawa	368,651
Fukaya	100,285
Fukui	255,604
Fukuoka	1,284,795
Fukushima	285,754
Fukuyama	374,517
Funabashi	540,817
Gamagōri	83,730
Gifu	407,134
Ginowan	82,862
Gotemba	81,803
Gyōda	86,170
Habikino	117,735
Hachinohe	242,654
Hachiōji	503,363
Hadano	164,722
Hakodate	298,881
Hamakita	83,810
Hamamatsu	561,606
Handa	106,452
Hannō	80,535
Higashi-Hiroshima	113,939
Higashi-Kurume	111,097
Higashi-Matsuyama	93,342
Higashi-Murayama	135,112
Higashi-Ōsaka	517,232
Higashi-Yamato	76,355
Hikone	103,508
Himeji	470,986
Hino	166,537
Hirakata	400,144
Hiratsuka	253,822
Hirosaki	177,972
Hiroshima	1,108,888
Hitachi	199,244
Hitachinaka	146,750
Hōfu	118,803
Hoya	100,260
Ibaraki	258,233
Ichihara	277,061
Ichikawa	440,555
Ichinomiya	267,362
Iida	106,772
Iizuka	83,411
Ikeda	104,293
Ikoma	106,726
Imabari	120,214
Inazawa	98,746
Iruma	144,402
Isahaya	93,058
Ise	102,632
Isehara	98,123
Isesaki	120,236
Ishinomaki	121,208
Itami	188,431
Iwaki	360,598
Iwakuni	107,386
Iwamizawa	85,125
Iwata	85,123
Iwatsuki	109,546
Izumi	157,300
Izumisano	92,583
Izumo	84,854
Joetsu	132,205
Jōyō	85,398
Kadoma	140,506
Kagoshima	546,282
Kaizuka	84,653
Kakamigahara	131,955
Kakegawa	76,839
Kakogawa	260,567
Kamagaya	99,694
Kamakura	170,329
Kameoka	92,398
Kanazawa	453,975
Kani	86,367
Kanoya	79,403
Kanuma	93,053
Karatsu	79,575
Kariya	125,305
Kashihara	121,988
Kashiwa	317,750
Kashiwara	80,303
Kashiwazaki	91,229
Kasuga	99,206
Kasugai	277,589
Kasukabe	200,121
Kawachi- Nagano	117,082
Kawagoe	323,353
Kawaguchi	448,854
Kawanishi	144,539
Kawasaki	1,202,820
Kimitsu	93,216
Kiryū	120,377
Kisarazu	123,499
Kishiwada	194,818
Kitakami	87,969
Kita-Kyūshū	1,019,598
Kitami	110,452
Kobe	1,423,792
Kochi	321,999
Kodaira	172,946
Kofu	201,124
Koganei	109,279
Kokubunji	105,786
Komaki	137,165
Komatsu	107,965
Kōnan	95,521
Kōnosu	80,354
Koriyama	326,833
Koshigaya	298,253
Kumagaya	156,429
Kumamoto	650,341
Kurashiki	422,836
Kure	209,485
Kurume	234,433
Kusatsu	101,828
Kushiro	199,323
Kuwana	103,044
Kyōto	1,463,822
Machida	360,525
Maebashi	284,788
Maizuru	94,784
Marugame	78,090
Matsubara	134,457
Matsudo	461,503
Matsue	147,416
Matsumoto	205,523
Matsusaka	122,449
Matsuyama	460,968
Mihara	83,769
Miki	78,653
Minō	127,542
Misato	133,600
Mishima	107,890
Mitaka	165,721
Mito	246,347
Miyakonojō	132,714
Miyazaki	300,068
Mobara	91,664
Moriguchi	157,306
Morioka	286,478
Munakata	76,936
Muroran	109,766
Musashino	135,051
Nabari	79,913
Nagano	358,516
Nagaoka	190,470
Nagaokakyō	78,697
Nagareyama	146,245
Nagasaki	438,635
Nagoya	2,152,184
Naha	301,890
Nara	359,218
Narashino	152,887
Narita	91,470
Neyagawa	258,443
Niigata	494,769
Niihama	127,917
Niiza	144,726
Nishinomiya	390,389
Nishio	98,766
Nobeoka	126,629
Noda	119,790
Numazu	212,241
Obihiro	171,715
Odawara	200,103
Ōgaki	149,759
Ōita	426,979
Okayama	615,757
Okazaki	322,621
Okinawa	115,336
Ōme	137,234
Ōmiya	433,755
Ōmura	79,279
Ōmuta	145,085
Ōnojō	82,903
Onomichi	93,756
Ōsaka	2,602,421
Ōta	143,057
Ōtaru	157,022
Ōtsu	276,332
Oyama	150,115
Saga	171,231
Sagamihara	570,597
Sakado	98,221
Sakai	802,993
Sakata	101,230
Sakura	162,624
Sanda	96,279
Sanjō	85,691
Sano	84,069
Sapporo	1,757,025
Sasebo	244,909
Sayama	162,240
Sendai	971,297
Seto	129,393
Settsu	87,330
Shibata	80,498
Shimada	75,029
Shimizu	240,174
Shimonoseki	259,795
Shizuoka	474,092
Sōka	217,930
Suita	342,760
Suzuka	179,800
Tachikawa	157,884
Tajimi	101,270
Takamatsu	331,004
Takaoka	173,607
Takarazuka	202,544
Takasago	97,632
Takasaki	238,133
Takatsuki	362,270
Tama	148,113
Tatebayashi	76,857
Tochigi	85,137
Toda	97,571
Tōkai	99,738
Tokorozawa	320,406
Tokushima	268,706
Tokuyama	108,671
★ Tokyo	7,967,614
Tomakomai	169,328
Tondabayashi	121,690
Toride	84,477
Tottori	146,330
Toyama	325,375
Toyohashi	352,982
Toyokawa	114,380
Toyonaka	398,908
Toyota	341,079
Tsu	163,156
Tsuchiura	132,243
Tsukuba	156,012
Tsuruoka	100,538
Tsuyama	91,170
Ube	175,116
Ueda	123,284
Uji	184,830
Urasoe	96,002
Urawa	453,300
Urayasu	123,654
Utsunomiya	435,357
Wakayama	393,885
Yachiyo	154,509
Yaizu	115,931
Yamagata	254,488
Yamaguchi	135,579
Yamato	203,933
Yamatokōriyama	95,165
Yao	276,664
Yashio	75,322
Yatsushiro	107,709
Yawata	75,779
Yokkaichi	285,779
Yokohama	3,307,136
Yokosuka	432,193
Yonago	134,762
Yonezawa	95,592
Yono	81,944
Yotsukaidō	79,495
Zama	118,159
Jersey (1996)	
★ St. Helier	27,523
Jordan (1994)	
★ Amman	969,598
Irbid	208,329
Ar-Ruṣayfah	137,247
Az-Zarqā'	350,849
Kazakhstan (1997 est.)	
Almaty (Alma-Ata)	1,064,300
Aqtaū (Aktau; Shevchenko)	156,400
Aqtöbe (Aktyubinsk)	253,100
★ Astana (Aqmola; Tselinograd)	270,400
Atyraū (Guryev)	142,700
Auliye-Ata (Dzhambul)	301,800
Ekibastuz	139,500
Kökshetaū (Kokchetav)	131,900
Oral (Uralsk)	214,700
Öskemen (Ust-Kamenogorsk)	311,100
Pavlodar	326,500
Petropavl (Petropavlovsk)	223,100
Qaraghandy (Karaganda)	452,700
Qostanay (Kustanay)	222,600
Qyzylord (Kzyl-Orda)	156,500
Rūdny	120,500
Semey (Semipalatinsk)	292,800
Shymkent (Shimkent; Chimkent)	393,400
Taldyqorghan (Taldy-Kurgan)	109,600
Temirtaū	186,800
Zhezqazghan (Zhezkazgan; Dzhezkazgan)	105,700
Kenya (1989)	
Eldoret	111,882
Kisumu	192,733
Machakos	116,293
Mombasa	461,753
★ Nairobi	1,324,570
Nakuru	163,927
Kiribati (1990)	
★ Bairiki	2,226
agglomeration	32,000[30]
Korea, North (1987 est.)	
Anju	186,000
Ch'ŏngjin	582,480[1]
Haeju	195,000
Hamhŭng-Hungnam	709,000[1]
Hŭich'ŏn	163,000
Kaesŏng	334,433[1]
Kanggye	211,000
Kimch'aek (Songjin)	179,000
Kusŏng	177,000
Namp'o	731,448[1]
★ P'yŏngyang	3,136,000[29, 30]
Sinp'o	158,000
Sinŭiju	326,011[1]
Sunch'ŏn	356,000
Tanch'ŏn	284,000
Tŏkch'ŏn	217,000
Wŏnsan	274,000
Korea, South (1995)	
Andong	188,443
Ansan	510,314
Anyang	591,106
Asan	154,663
Ch'angwŏn	481,694
Chech'ŏn	137,070
Cheju	258,511
Chinhae	125,997
Chinju	329,886
Ch'ŏnan	330,259
Ch'ŏngju	531,376
Chŏng-ŭp	139,011
Chŏnju	563,153
Ch'unch'ŏn	234,528
Ch'ungju	205,206
Hanam	115,812
Iksan (Iri)	322,685
Inch'ŏn	2,308,188
Kangnŭng	220,403
Kimch'ŏn	147,027
Kimhae	256,370
Kimje	115,427
Kŏje	147,562
Kongju	131,229
Koyang	518,282
Kumi	311,431
Kunp'o	235,233
Kunsan	266,569
Kuri	142,173
Kwangju	1,257,636
Kwangmyŏng	350,914
Kwangyang	122,052
Kyŏngju	273,968
Kyŏngsan	173,746
Masan	441,242
Miryang	121,501
Mokp'o	247,452
Naju	107,831
Namwon	103,544
Namyangju	229,060
P'ohang	508,899
Poryŏng	122,604
Puch'ŏn	779,412
Pusan	3,814,325
P'yŏngt'aek	312,927
Sach'ŏn	113,494
Sangju	124,116
★ Seoul (Sŏul)	10,231,217
Shihŭng	133,443
Sŏngnam	869,094
Sŏsan	134,746
Sunch'ŏn	249,263
Suwŏn	755,550
Taegu	2,449,420
Taejŏn	1,272,121
Tongyŏng	131,717
Ŭijŏngbu	276,111
Ŭiwang	108,788
Ulsan	967,429
Wŏnju	237,460
Yŏngch'ŏn	113,511
Yŏngju	131,097
Yŏsu	183,596
Kuwait (1995)	
As-Sālimīyah	130,215
★ Kuwait (Al-Kuwayt)	28,859
Qalīb ash-Shuyūkh	102,178
Kyrgyzstan (1999 est.)	
★ Bishkek (Frunze)	619,000[29]
Osh	218,300[3]
Laos (1995 est.)	
★ Vientiane (Viangchan)	531,800
Latvia (1999 est.)	
Daugavpils	115,450
★ Rīga	796,732
Lebanon (1994 est.)	
★ Beirut (Bayrūt)	1,100,000
Jūniyah	100,000
Sidon (Ṣaydā)	150,000
Tripoli (Ṭarābulus)	240,000
Zaḥlah	100,000
Lesotho (1996 est.)	
★ Maseru	160,100
agglomeration	373,000[30]
Liberia (1999 est.)	
★ Monrovia	479,000[29]
Libya (1988 est.)	
Banghāzi	446,250
Misrātah	121,669
★ Tripoli (Ṭarābulus)	591,062
Liechtenstein (1998 est.)	
★ Vaduz	4,975
Lithuania (2000 est.)	
Kaunas	412,614
Klaipėda	202,484
Panevėžys	133,696
Šiauliai	146,570
★ Vilnius	577,969
Luxembourg (1999 est.)	
★ Luxembourg	79,800
Macau (2000 est.)	
★ Macau	440,000
Macedonia (1994; MU)	
Bitola	108,203
Gostivar	108,181
Kumanovo	127,814
★ Skopje (Skopije)	545,228
Tetovo	172,171
Madagascar (1993)	
★ Antananarivo	1,103,304
Antsirabe	126,062
Fianarantsoa	109,248
Mahajanga	106,780
Toamasina	137,782
Malawi (1994 est.)	
★ Blantyre (executive; judicial)	446,800
★ Lilongwe (ministerial; financial; legislative)	395,500
Malaysia (1991)	
Alor Setar	125,026
George Town (Pinang)	219,376
Ipoh	382,633
Johor Baharu	328,646
Kelang (Port Kelang)	243,698
Kota Baharu	219,713
★ Kuala Lumpur	1,145,075
Kuala Terengganu	228,659
Kuantan	198,356
Kuching	147,729
Petaling Jaya	254,849

Major cities and national capitals (continued)

country / city	population
Sandakan	126,092
Selayang Baru	124,606
Seremban	182,584
Shah Alam	101,773
Sibu	126,384
Sungai Petani	115,719
Taiping	183,165
Maldives (1995)	
★ Male	62,973
Mali (1996 est.)	
★ Bamako	809,552
Ségou	106,799
Malta (1999 est.)	
★ Valletta	7,100
Marshall Is. (1999 est.)	
★ Majuro	33,000
Martinique (1999)	
★ Fort-de-France	94,049
Mauritania (1999 est.)	
★ Nouakchott	881,000
Mauritius (1997 est.)	
★ Port Louis	137,191
Mayotte (1997; MU)	
★ Mamoudzou	32,774
★ Dzaoudzi	10,796
Mexico (1995)	
Acapulco	592,528
Aguascalientes	537,523
Apatzingán	89,834
Atizapán de Zaragoza (Ciudad López Mateos)	427,192
Atlixco	79,556
Boca del Río	123,825
Campeche	178,160
Cancún	297,183
Celaya	251,724
Chalco	96,978
Chetumal	115,152
Chihuahua	613,722
Chimalhuacán	410,031
Chilpancingo	123,475
Ciudad Apodaca (Apodaca)	212,118
Ciudad del Carmen	114,360
Ciudad Madero	171,091
Ciudad Obregón	244,028
Ciudad Santa Catarina	201,233
Ciudad Valles	102,226
Ciudad Victoria	230,304
Coacalco	202,778
Coatzacoalcos	222,027
Colima	110,997
Córdoba	132,091
Cuauhtémoc	80,428
Cuautitlan Izcalli	401,119
Cuautla Morelos	128,781
Cuernavaca	311,095
Culiacán	505,518
Delicias	94,001
Durango	397,687
Ecatepec (de Morelos)	1,455,909
El Mante	81,128
Ensenada	192,550
Fresnillo	89,338
General Escobedo	174,486
Gómez Palacio	192,888
Guadalajara	1,633,053
Guadalupe	618,610
Guaymas	90,964
Hermosillo	504,009
Heroica Nogales	131,578
Huixquilucan	93,634
Iguala	98,276
Irapuato	299,604
Ixtapaluca	153,138
Jiutepec	125,148
Juárez (Ciudad Juárez)	995,770
La Paz	154,314
Lagos de Moreno	75,220
León	941,626
Los Mochis	188,349
Los Reyes la Paz	178,534
Manzanillo	80,568
Matamoros	323,794
Mazatlán	302,808
Mérida	612,261
Metepec	147,360
Mexicali	505,016
★ Mexico City	8,489,007
Minatitlán	145,795
Monclova	188,850
Monterrey	1,088,023
Morelia	512,169
Naucalpan	822,358
Navojoa	94,837
Nezahualcóyotl	1,233,681
Nicolás Romero	192,534
Nogales (Heroica Nogales)	131,578
Nuevo Laredo	273,797
Oaxaca	242,247
Orizaba	114,341
Pachuca	209,996
Piedras Negras	114,384
Poza Rica de Hidalgo	153,585
Puebla	1,157,625
Puerta Vallarta	121,844
Querétaro	469,542
Reynosa	320,458
Salamanca	135,874
Saltillo	510,131
San Cristóbal de las Casas	99,254
San Juan del Río	84,532
San Luis Potosí	586,585
San Luis Río Colorado	115,596
San Nicolás de los Garzas	487,924
San Pablo de las Salinas	126,659
San Pedro Garza García	120,868
Santa Catarina	201,233
Soledad de Graciano Sanchez	147,188
Tampico	278,933
Tapachula	163,253
Tehuacán	172,510
Tepic	254,551
Texcoco (de Mora)	89,524
Tijuana	966,097
Tlalnepantla	708,013
Tlaquepaque	434,710
Toluca	368,384
Tonala	250,058
Torreón	481,493
Tulancingo (de Bravo)	87,458
Tultilan (Buenavista)	160,596
Tuxtepec	77,467
Tuxtla Gutiérrez	378,079
Uruapan	215,449
Valle de Chalco (Xico)	286,839
Veracruz	381,190
Villahermosa	301,238
Xalapa (Jalapa) Enríquez	324,081
Zacatecas	109,109
Zamora de Hidalgo	121,181
Zapopan	850,315
Micronesia	
★ Palikir	—
Moldova (1996 est.)	
Bălţi (Beltsy)	153,500
★ Chişinău (Kishinyov)	655,000
Tighina (Bendery)	128,000
Tiraspol	187,000
Monaco (2000 est.)	
★ Monaco	31,700
Mongolia (1999 est.)	
★ Ulaanbaatar (Ulan Bator)	668,700
Morocco (1994)	
Agadir	524,564[29]
Beni-Mellal	140,212
Casablanca	2,940,623[29]
El-Jadida	119,083
Fès	771,740[29]
Kenitra	292,627[29]
Khouribga	152,090
Ksar el-Kebir	107,065
Marrakech	672,506[29]
Meknès	459,958[29]
Nador	112,450
Oujda	365,582[29]
★ Rabat	1,385,872[29]
Safi	262,276[29]
Tanger	521,735[29]
Tétouan	363,813[29]
Mozambique (1997)	
Beira	397,368
Chimoio	171,056
★ Maputo (Lourenço Marques)	966,837
Matola	424,662
Mocuba	124,650
Nacala	158,248
Nampula	303,346
Quelimane	150,116
Tete	101,984
Myanmar (Burma) (1983)	
Bassein (Pathein)	144,096
Mandalay	532,949
Monywa	106,843
Moulmein (Mawlamyine)	219,961
Pegu (Bago)	150,528
Sittwe (Akyab)	107,621
Taunggye	108,231
★ Yangôn (Rangoon)	4,101,000[29, 30]
Namibia (1997 est.)	
★ Windhoek	169,000
Nauru (1992)	
★ Yaren	672
Nepal (1993 est.; MU)	
Bhaktapur (Bhadgaon)	130,000
Biratnagar	132,000
★ Kathmandu	535,000
Lalitpur (Patan)	190,000
Netherlands, The (1999 est.)	
Almere	136,157
Amersfoort	123,367
★ Amsterdam (capital)	727,053
Apeldoorn	152,860
Arnhem	137,222
Breda	159,042
Dordrecht	119,462
Ede	101,542
Eindhoven	199,877
Emmen	105,497
Enschede	148,814
Groningen	171,193
Haarlem	148,262
Haarlemmermeer	109,377
Leiden	117,389
Maastricht	121,479
Nijmegen	151,864
Rotterdam	592,665
's-Hertogenbosch	128,009
★ The Hague (seat of government)	440,743
Tilburg	190,559
Utrecht	232,718
Zaanstad	135,126
Zoetermeer	108,899
Zwolle	104,431
Netherlands Antilles (1999 est.)	
★ Willemstad	123,000
New Caledonia (1996)	
★ Nouméa	76,293
New Zealand (1996)	
Auckland	354,532
Christchurch	315,118
Dunedin	119,612
Hamilton	109,043
Manukau	254,603
North Shore	171,494
Waitakere	154,386
★ Wellington	159,845
Nicaragua (1995)	
León	123,865
★ Managua	864,201
Niger (1988)	
Maradi	110,005
★ Niamey	391,876
Zinder	119,827
Nigeria (1996 est.)[35]	
Aba	298,900
Abeokuta	427,400
★ Abuja	423,400[3, 36]
Ado-Ekiti	359,400
Agege	105,000
Akure	162,300
Awka	111,200
Benin City	229,400
Bida	125,500
Calabar	174,400
Deba Habe	138,600
Ede	307,100
Effon-Alaiye	153,100
Ejigbo	105,900
Enugu	316,100
Epe	101,000
Gombe	107,800
Gusau	158,000
Ibadan	1,432,000
Ife	296,800
Igboho	106,800
Ijebu-Ode	156,400
Ikare	140,800
Ikerre	244,600
Ikire	123,300
Ikirun	181,400
Ikorodu	184,900
Ila	264,000
Ilawe-Ekiti	184,500
Ilegbo	101,600
Ilesha	378,400
Ilobu	199,000
Ilorin	475,800
Inisa	119,800
Ise-Ekiti	103,400
Iseyin	217,300
Iwo	362,000
Jos	206,300
Kaduna	342,200
Kano	674,100
Katsina	206,500
Kumo	148,000
Lafia	122,500
★ Lagos	1,518,000
agglomeration	12,763,000[30]
Maiduguri	320,000
Makurdi	123,100
Minna	136,900
Mushin	333,200
Offa	197,200
Ogbomosho	730,000
Oka	142,900
Ondo	173,600
Onitsha	371,900
Oshogbo	476,800
Owo	183,500
Oyo	256,400
Port Harcourt	410,000
Sapele	139,200
Shagamu	117,200
Shaki	174,500
Shomolu	147,700
Sokoto	204,900
Ugep	102,600
Warri	126,100
Zaria	379,200
Northern Mariana Is. (1990)	
★ Capital Hill[37]	1,234
Norway (1999 est.; MU)	
Bærum	100,773
Bergen	227,276
★ Oslo	502,867
Stavanger	108,019
Trondheim	147,187
Oman (1993)	
As-Sīb	155,000
Bawshar	107,500
★ Muscat	40,900
agglomeration	887,000[30]
Salālah	116,000
Pakistan (1998)	
Abbottabad	105,999[38]
Bahawalnagar	109,642
Bahawalpur	403,408[38]
Burewala	149,857
Chiniot	169,282
Chishtian Mandi	101,659
Daska	101,500
Dera Ghazi Khan	188,149
Faisalabad (Lyallpur)	1,977,246
Gojra	114,967
Gujranwala	1,124,799
Gujrat	250,121
Hafizabad	130,216
Hyderabad	1,151,274[38]
★ Islamabad	524,500
Jacobabad	137,773
Jaranwala	103,308
Jhang Sadar	292,214
Jhelum	145,847
Kamoke	150,984
Karachi	9,269,265[38]
Kasur	241,649
Khairpur	102,188
Khanewal	132,962
Khanpur	117,764
Kohat	125,271[38]
Lahore	5,063,499[38]
Larkana	270,366
Mardan	244,511[38]
Mingaora	174,469
Mirpur Khas	184,465
Multan	1,182,441[38]
Muridike	108,578
Muzaffargarh	121,641
Nawabshah	183,110
Okara	200,901
Pakpattan	107,791
Peshawar	988,055[38]
Quetta	560,307
Rahimyar Khan	228,479
Rawalpindi	1,406,214[38]
Sadiqabad	141,509
Sahiwal	207,388
Sargodha	455,360[38]
Shekhupura	271,875
Shikarpur	133,259
Sialkot	417,597[38]
Sukkur	329,176
Tando Adam	103,363
Wah	198,431[38]
Palau (1995)	
Koror	12,299
Panama (2000)	
★ Panama City	463,093
San Miguelito	291,769
Papua New Guinea (1990)	
★ Port Moresby (National Capital District)	193,242
Paraguay (1992)	
★ Asunción	500,938
Ciudad del Este	133,881
San Lorenzo	133,395
Peru (1998 est.)	
Arequipa	710,103
Ayacucho	118,960
Cajamarca	108,009
Chiclayo	469,200
Chimbote	298,800
Chincha Alta	130,000
Cusco	278,590
Huancayo	305,039
Huánuco	129,688
Ica	194,820
Iquitos	334,013
Juliaca	180,000
Lima agglomeration	7,060,600
Ate	324,799[8]
Callao	407,904[8]
Carabayllo	115,000[8]
Chorrillos	238,739[8]
Comas	434,690[8]
El Agustino	159,707[8]
Independencia	191,151[8]
La Victoría	213,239[8]
★ Lima	316,322[8]
Los Olivos	281,115[8]
Lurigancho	110,347[8]
Puente Piedra	131,000[8]
Rímac	190,836[8]
San Borja	109,233[8]
San Juan de Lurigancho	652,681[8]
San Juan de Miraflores	329,023[8]
San Martin de Porras	411,000[8]
San Miguel	126,825[8]
Santa Anita	131,519[8]
Santiago de Surro	224,866[8]
Ventanilla	105,824[8]
Villa el Salvador	296,000[8]
Villa Maria del Triunfo	301,505[8]
Piura	308,155
Pucallpa	220,866
Puno	101,578
Sullana	170,000
Tacna	215,683
Trujillo	603,657
Philippines (1995)	
Angeles	234,011
Antipolo	120,000
Bacolod	402,345
Bacoor	250,821
Bago	132,338
Baguio	222,639
Baliuag	103,054
Biñan	160,206
Binangonan	140,700
Butuan	110,000
Cagayan de Oro	320,000
Cainta	201,550
Calamba	120,000
Caloocan	1,023,159
Cebu	662,299
Cotabato	146,779
Dagupan	126,214
Dasmariñas	160,000
Davao	600,000
General Santos	200,000
Iloilo	334,539
Lapu-Lapu	173,744
Las Piñas	413,086
Lucena	177,750
Makati	484,176
Malabon	347,484
Malolos	147,414
Mandaluyong	286,870
Mandaue	194,745
★ Manila	1,654,761
Metro Manila	9,454,040
Marawi	114,389
Marikina	357,231
Muntilupa	399,846
Naga	126,972

country city	population
Navotas	229,039
Olongapo	179,754
Parañaque	391,296
Pasay	408,610
Pasig	471,075
★ Quezon City	1,989,419
San Fernando	193,025
San Juan del Monte	124,187
San Pedro	189,333
Santa Rosa	138,257
Tacloban	167,310
Tagig	381,350
Valenzuela	437,165
Zamboanga	120,000
Poland (1999 est.)	
Białystok	283,937
Bielsko-Biała	180,307
Bydgoszcz	386,855
Bytom	205,560
Chorzów	121,708
Czestochowa	257,812
Dąbrowa Górnicza	131,037
Elbląg	129,782
Gdańsk	458,988
Gdynia	253,521
Gliwice	212,164
Gorzów Wielkopolski	126,019
Grudziadz	102,434
Jastrzębie-Zdrój	102,294
Kalisz	106,641
Katowice	345,934
Kielce	212,383
Koszalin	112,375
Kraków	740,666
Legnica	109,335
Łódź	806,728
Lublin	356,251
Olsztyn	170,904
Opole	129,553
Płock	131,011
Poznań	578,235
Radom	232,262
Ruda Śląska	159,665
Rybnik	144,582
Rzeszów	162,049
Słupsk	102,370
Sosnowiec	244,102
Szczecin	416,988
Tarnów	121,494
Toruń	206,158
Tychy	133,178
Wałbrzych	136,923
★ Warsaw (Warszawa)	1,618,468
Włocławek	123,373
Wrocław	637,877
Zabrze	200,177
Zielona Góra	118,182
Portugal (1991)	
Amadora	124,337
Funchal	109,957
★ Lisbon	677,790
Porto	310,600
Puerto Rico (1998 est.; MU)	
Arecibo	102,976
Bayamón	233,797
Caguas	142,533
Carolina	190,469
Guaynabo	105,007
Mayaguez	102,222
Ponce	191,469
★ San Juan	439,427
Qatar (1993 est.)	
★ Doha	339,471
Ar-Rayyān	143,046
Réunion (1999)	
★ Saint-Denis	131,557
Romania (1997 est.)	
Arad	184,619
Bacău	209,689
Baia Mare	149,496
Botoşani	129,285
Brăila	234,648
Braşov	317,772
★ Bucharest	2,027,512
Buzău	149,080
Cluj-Napoca	332,792
Constanţa	344,876
Craiova	312,891
Drobeta-Turnu Severin	117,882
Galaţi	331,360
Iaşi	348,399
Oradea	223,288
Piatra Neamţ	125,121
Piteşti	187,181
Ploieşti	253,414
Râmnicu Vâlcea	119,340
Satu Mare	129,886
Sibiu	168,949
Suceava	118,162
Timişoara	334,098
Târgu Mureş	165,534
Russia (1997 est.)	
Abakan	166,000
Achinsk	123,000
Almetyevsk	140,000
Angarsk	268,000
Anzhero-Sudzhensk	101,000
Arkhangelsk	371,000
Armavir	166,000
Arzamas	112,000
Asbest	81,000[39]
Astrakhan	490,000
Azou	79,000[39]
Balakovo	206,000
Balashikha	135,000
Balashov	95,000[39]
Barnaul	591,000
Bataisk	91,000[39]
Belgorod	331,000
Belovo	89,000[39]
Berdsk	79,000[39]
Berezniki	183,000
Birobidzhan	81,000[39]
Biysk	226,000
Blagoveshchensk	217,000
Bratsk	255,000
Bryansk	462,000
Bugulma	90,000[39]
Chaikovsky	87,000[39]
Chapaevsk	94,000[39]
Cheboksary	454,000
Chelyabinsk	1,084,000
Cherepovets	321,000
Cherkessk	120,000
Chernogorsk	79,000[39]
Chita	320,000
Derbent	92,000[39]
Dimitrovgrad	137,000
Dzerzhinsk	282,000
Elektrostal	148,000
Elista	94,000[39]
Engels	188,000
Gatchina	80,000[39]
Glazov	106,000
Grozny (Dzhokhar)	186,000
Gubkin	80,000[39]
Hasavyurt	82,000[39]
Irkutsk	591,000
Ivanovo	469,000
Izhevsk	654,000
Kaliningrad	424,000
Kaliningrad (*Moscow oblast*)	134,000
Kaluga	347,000
Kamensk-Uralsky	194,000
Kamyshin	128,000
Kansk	108,000
Kazan	1,085,000
Kemerovo	500,000
Khabarovsk	615,000
Khimki	133,000
Kineshma	101,000
Kirov	465,000
Kirovo-Chepeck	88,000[39]
Kiselyovsk	114,000
Kislovodsk	121,000
Klin	93,000[39]
Kolomna	153,000
Kolpino	142,000
Komsomolsk-na-Amure	300,000
Kopeisk	77,000[39]
Kostroma	286,000
Kovrov	162,000
Krasnodar	650,000
Krasnogorsk	89,000[39]
Krasnoyarsk	874,000
Kropotkin	84,000[39]
Kungur	80,000[39]
Kurgan	363,000
Kursk	444,000
Kuznetsk	100,000
Kyzyl	92,000[39]
Leninsk-Kuznetsky	118,000
Lipetsk	477,000
Lisva	76,000[39]
Lyubertsy	166,000
Magadan	123,000
Magnitogorsk	424,000
Makhachkala	338,000
Maykop	166,000
Mezhdurechensk	104,000
Miass	167,000
Michurinsk	123,000
Mineralnye Vody	80,000[39]
★ Moscow	8,405,000
Murmansk	394,000
Murom	126,000
Mytishchi	153,000
Naberezhnye Chelny (Brezhnev)	522,000
Nakhodka	161,000
Nalchik	236,000
Neftekamsk	118,000
Nevinnomyssk	133,000
Nikolo-Beryozovka (Neftekamsk)	118,000
Nizhnekamsk	216,000
Nizhnevartovsk	235,000
Nizhny Novgorod (Gorky)	1,371,000
Nizhny Tagil	404,000
Noginsk	118,000
Norilsk	155,000
Novgorod	232,000
Novocheboksarsk	123,000
Novocherkassk	188,000
Novokuybyshevsk	116,000
Novokuznetsk	566,000
Novomoskovsk (*Tula oblast*)	142,000
Novorossiysk	204,000
Novoshakhtinsk	105,000
Novosibirsk	1,367,000
Novotroitsk	110,000
Novy Urengoi	96,000[39]
Noyabrsk	92,000[39]
Obninsk	110,000
Odintsovo	128,000
Oktyabrsky	111,000
Omsk	1,158,000
Orekhovo-Zuyevo	125,000
Orenburg	531,000
Orsk	274,000
Oryol	348,000
Ozersk	81,000
Penza	534,000
Perm	1,025,000
Petrodvorets	83,000[39]
Pervouralsk	136,000
Petropavlovsk-Kamchatsky	202,000
Petrozavodsk	282,000
Podolsk	198,000
Prokopyevsk	247,000
Pskov	206,000
Pyatigorsk	133,000
Ramenskoye	86,000[39]
Rostov-na-Donu	1,023,000
Rubtsovsk	167,000
Ryazan	535,000
Rybinsk (Andropov)	245,000
Saint Petersburg (Leningrad)	4,216,000
Salavat	155,000
Samara (Kuybyshev)	1,170,000
Saransk	319,000
Sarapul	108,000
Saratov	892,000
Sergiev Posad (Zagorsk)	113,000
Serov	100,000
Serpukhov	138,000
Severodvinsk	237,000
Seversk	110,000
Shadrinsk	84,000[39]
Shakhty	228,000
Shchyolkovo	107,000
Simbirsk (Ulyanovsk)	679,000
Smolensk	356,000
Sochi	359,000
Solikamsk	107,000
Stary Oskol	205,000
Stavropol	345,000
Sterlitamak	259,000
Surgut	270,000
Svobodny	79,000[39]
Syktyvkar	230,000
Syzran	179,000
Taganrog	291,000
Tambov	318,000
Tobolsk	100,000[39]
Tolyatti	712,000
Tomsk	475,000
Troitsk	88,000[39]
Tsarskoye Selo	95,000[39]
Tula	525,000
Tver (Kalinin)	458,000
Tyumen	499,000
Ufa	1,082,000
Ukhta	103,000
Ulan-Ude	370,000
Usolye-Sibirskoye	105,000
Ussuriysk	161,000
Ust-Ilimsk	109,000
Velikiye Luki	117,000
Vladikavkaz (Ordzhonikidze)	314,000
Vladimir	340,000
Vladivostok	623,000
Volgodonsk	181,000
Volgograd	1,005,000
Vologda	302,000
Volzhsky	291,000
Vorkuta	104,000
Voronezh	910,000
Voskresensk	79,000[39]
Votkinsk	103,000
Vyborg	81,000[39]
Yakutsk	194,000
Yaroslavl	625,000
Yekaterinburg (Sverdlovsk)	1,275,000
Yeisk	87,000[39]
Yelets	122,000
Yessentuki	95,000[39]
Yoshkar-Ola	251,000
Yurga	90,000[39]
Yuzhno-Sakhalinsk	181,000
Zelenodolysk	101,000
Zelenograd	201,000
Zheleznodorozhny	98,000[39]
Zheleznogorsk (*Krasnoyarsk*)	81,000[39]
Zheleznogorsk (*Kursk*)	84,000[39]
Zlatoust	200,000
Zhukovsky	98,000[39]
Rwanda (1991)	
★ Kigali	237,782
St. Kitts and Nevis (1994 est.)	
★ Basseterre	12,605
St. Lucia (1997 est.)	
★ Castries	16,187
St. Vincent and the Grenadines (1998 est.)	
★ Kingstown	16,151
Samoa (1999 est.)	
★ Apia	38,000
San Marino (1997 est.)	
★ San Marino	2,294
São Tomé and Príncipe (1991)	
★ São Tomé	43,420
Saudi Arabia (1991 est.)	
Ad-Dammām	350,000
Jiddah	1,500,000
Mecca (Makkah)	630,000
Medina (Al-Madinah)	400,000
★ Riyadh (Ar-Riyad)	3,183,000[29, 30]
Aṭ-Ṭā'if	410,000
Senegal (1998 est.)	
★ Dakar	1,999,000[29, 30]
Kaolack	200,000
Mboure	106,046[40]
Rufisque	138,837[40]
Saint-Louis	180,000
Thiès	320,000
Ziguinchor	161,680[40]
Seychelles (1993 est.)	
★ Victoria	25,000
Sierra Leone (1999 est.)	
★ Freetown	822,000[29, 30]
Singapore (2000 est.)[41]	
★ Singapore	3,278,000
Slovakia (1998 est.)	
★ Bratislava	451,395
Košice	242,170
Slovenia (1999 est.)	
★ Ljubljana	258,960
Solomon Islands (1996 est.)	
★ Honiara	43,643
Somalia (1999 est.)	
★ Baidoa (announced interim capital from August 2000)	37,000[42]
★ Mogadishu (historic capital)	1,162,000[29]
South Africa (1991)	
Alexandra	124,586
Benoni	113,501
★ Bloemfontein (de facto judicial)	126,867
Boksburg	119,890
Botshabelo	177,926
★ Cape Town (de facto legislative)	854,616
Carletonville	118,699
Daveyton	151,659
Diepmeadow	241,099
Durban	715,669
East London	102,325
Evaton	201,026
Germiston	134,005
Ibhayi	257,054
Johannesburg	712,507
Kathlehong (Katlehong)	201,785
Kempton Park	106,606
Khayelitsa	189,586
Kwamashu (Kwa Mashu)	156,679
Lekoa	217,582
Mamelodi	154,845
Manguang (Mangaung)	125,545
Mdantsane	242,823
Ntuzuma	102,310
Pietermaritzburg	156,473
Port Elizabeth	303,353
★ Pretoria (de facto executive)	525,583
Roodepoort	162,632
Sandton	101,197
Soshanguve	146,334
Soweto	596,632
Tembisa	209,238
Umlazi	299,275
Spain (1998 est.)	
Albacete	145,454
Alcalá de Henares	163,831
Alcorcón	143,970
Algeciras	101,972
Alicante (Alacant)	272,432
Almería	168,025
Badajoz	134,710
Badalona	209,606
Barakaldo	98,649
Barcelona	1,505,581
Bilbao	358,467
Burgos	161,984
Cádiz	143,129
Cartagena	175,628
Castellón de la Plana (Castelló de la Plana)	137,741
Córdoba	309,961
Coruña, A (Coruña, La)	243,134
Donostia–San Sebastián	178,229
Elche (Elx)	191,713
Fuenlabrada	167,458
Getafe	143,629
Gijón	265,491
Granada	241,471
Hospitalet de Llobregat	248,521
Huelva	139,991
Jaén	107,184
Jerez de la Frontera	181,602
Laguna, La	127,945
Leganés	173,163
León	139,809
Lleida (Lérida)	112,207
Logroño	125,617
★ Madrid	2,881,506
Málaga	528,079
Mataró	103,265
Móstoles	195,311
Murcia	349,040
Ourense (Orense)	107,965
Oviedo	199,549
Palma (de Mallorca)	319,181
Palmas de Gran Canaria, Las	352,641
Pamplona (Iruña)	171,150
Sabadell	184,859
Salamanca	158,457
Santa Coloma de Gramanet	120,958
Santa Cruz de Tenerife	211,930
Santander	184,165
Sevilla (Seville)	701,927
Tarragona	112,795
Terrassa (Tarrasa)	165,654
Valencia (València)	739,412
Valladolid	319,946
Vigo	283,110
Vitoria–Gasteiz	216,527
Zaragoza (Saragossa)	603,367
Sri Lanka (1997 est.; MU)	
★ Colombo (administrative)	800,982
Dehiwala-Mount Lavinia	220,780
Galle	123,616
Jaffna	145,600

Major cities and national capitals (continued)

county city	population
Kandy	150,532
Moratuwa	213,000
Negombo	136,850
★ Sri Jayawardenepura Kotte (legislative and judicial)	109,000[10, 43]
Sudan, The (1993)	
Juba	114,980
Kassalā	234,270
★ Khartoum (executive)	924,505
Khartoum North	879,105
Nyala	228,778
★ Omdurman (legislative)	1,267,077
Port Sudan	305,385
Al-Qaḍārif	189,384
Al-Ubayyiḍ	228,096
Wad Madanī	218,714
Wāw	116,000[44]
Suriname (1999 est.)	
★ Paramaribo	233,000[29]
Swaziland (1998 est.)	
★ Lobamba (legislative)	...
★ Lozitha (royal)	...
★ Ludzidzini (royal)	...
★ Mbabane (administrative)	60,000
Sweden (1999 est.; MU)	
Göteborg	459,593
Helsingborg	116,337
Jönköping	115,897
Linköping	131,948
Malmö	254,904
Norrköping	122,415
Örebro	122,641
★ Stockholm	736,113
Umeå	103,517
Uppsala	187,302
Västerås	124,780
Switzerland (1999 est.)	
Basel (Bâle)	168,735
★ Bern (Berne)	123,254
Geneva (Genève)	172,809
Lausanne	114,161
Zürich	336,821
Syria (1994 est.)	
Aleppo (Ḥalab)	1,591,400
★ Damascus (Dimashq)	1,549,000
Dar'ā	180,093
Dayr az-Zawr	174,085
Dūmā	131,158
Ḥamāh	229,000[42]
Al-Ḥasakah	106,000[42]
Homs (Ḥims)	644,204
Jaramānah	138,469
Latakia (al-Ladhiqiyah)	306,535
Al-Qāmishlī	151,000[42]
Ar-Raqqah	219,016
Ṭarṭūs	136,812
Taiwan (2000 est.)	
Chang-hua	227,715
Chi-lung (Keelung)	385,201
Chia-i	265,109
Chung-ho	392,176
Chung-li	318,649
Feng-shan	318,562
Fêng-yüan	161,032
Hsi-chuh	154,976
Hsin-chu	361,958
Hsin-chuang	365,048
Hsin-tien	263,603
Hua-lien	108,407
Kao-hsiung	1,475,505
Lu-chou	160,516
Nan-t'ou	104,723
Pan-ch-'iao (T'ai-pei-hsien)	523,850
Pa-te	161,700
P'ing-chen	188,344
P'ing-tung	214,727
San-chu'ung	380,084
Shu-lin	151,260
T'ai-chung	940,589
T'ai-nan	728,060
T'ai-p'ing	165,524
T'ai-tung	111,039
★ Taipei (T'ai-pei)	2,641,312
Ta-li	171,940
T'ao-yuan	316,438
T'u-ch'eng	224,897
Yung-ho	227,700
Yung-k'ang	193,005
Tajikistan (1994 est.)	
★ Dushanbe	524,000
Khujand (Khudzhand; Leninabad)	164,500[10]
Tanzania (1988)	
Arusha	134,708
★ Dar es Salaam	1,360,850
★ Dodoma (legislative)	203,833
Mbeya	152,844
Morogoro	117,760
Mwanza	223,013
Shinyanga	100,724
Tanga	187,155
Zanzibar	157,634
Thailand (1999 est.)	
★ Bangkok (Krung Thep)	5,647,799
Chiang Mai	171,594
Hat Yai	148,632[1]
Khon Kaen	131,478[10]
Nakhon Ratchasima	188,171[1]
Nakhon Sawan	108,569[10]
Nonthaburi	261,335[1]
Ubon Ratchathani	105,936[1]
Udon Thani	156,038
Togo (1999 est.)	
★ Lomé	790,000[29]
Tonga (1999 est.)	
★ Nuku'alofa	37,000
Trinidad and Tobago (1996 est.)	
★ Port-of-Spain	43,396
Tunisia (1994)	
Aryānah	152,700
Ettadhamen	149,200
Kairouan	102,600
Ṣafāqis (Sfax)	230,900
Sūsah	125,000
★ Tunis	674,100
Turkey (1997)	
Adana	1,041,509
Adıyaman	212,475
Afyon	113,510
Aksaray	101,187
Alanya	117,311
★ Ankara	2,984,099
Antakya (Hatay)	139,046
Antalya	512,086
Aydın	133,757
Balıkesir	189,987
Batman	212,726
Bismil	101,409
Bursa	1,066,559
Çorlu	123,266
Çorum	147,112
Denizli	233,651
Diyarbakır	511,640
Edirne	115,083
Elaziğ	250,534
Erzincan	102,304
Erzurum	298,735
Eskişehir	454,536
Gaziantep	712,800
Gebze	235,211
Hatay	139,046
İçel (Mersin)	501,398
İskenderun	161,728
Isparta	134,271
Istanbul	8,260,438
İzmir	2,081,556
Kahramanmaraş (Maras)	303,594
Karabük	103,806
Karaman	104,154
Kayseri	498,233
Kırıkkale	203,496
Kızıltepe	112,015
Kocaeli (İzmit)	198,200
Konya	623,333
Kütahya	162,319
Malatya	400,248
Manisa	201,340
Ordu	117,699
Osmaniye	160,854
Sakarya (Adapazarı)	183,265
Samsun	338,387
Siirt	107,067
Sivas	232,352
Sultanbeyli	144,932
Tarsus	190,184
Tekirdağ	100,557
Trabzon	182,552
Urfa (Şanlıurfa)	410,762
Uşak	124,356
Van	226,965
Viranşehir	106,363
Zonguldak	106,176
Turkmenistan (1999 est.)	
★ Ashkhabad (Ashgabat)	525,000
Chārjew (Chardzhev; Chardzhou)	189,200[3]
Dashhowuz (Dashkhovuz; Tashauz)	141,800[3]
Mary	101,000[3]
Tuvalu (1999 est.)	
★ Funafuti	6,000
Uganda (1999 est.)	
★ Kampala	1,154,000[29]
Ukraine (1998 est.)	
Alchevsk	120,900
Berdyansk	132,300
Bila Tserkva (Belaya Tserkov)	215,200
Cherkasy (Cherkassy)	310,600
Chernihiv (Chernigov)	310,800
Chernivtsi (Chernovtsy)	259,000
Dniprodzerzhynsk (Dneprodzerzhinsk)	275,000
Dnipropetrovsk (Dnepropetrovsk)	1,122,400
Donetsk	1,065,400
Horlivka (Gorlovka)	309,300
Ivano-Frankivsk (Ivano-Frankovsk)	237,400
Kam'yanets-Podilskyy (Kamenets-Podolsky)	108,000
Kerch	167,400
Kharkiv (Kharkov)	1,521,400
Kherson	358,700
Khmelnytskyy (Khmelnitsky)	260,100
★ Kiev (Kyyiv)	2,620,900
Kirovohrad	270,200
Kostyantynivka (Konstantinovka)	100,100
Kramatorsk	190,800
Krasnyy Luch	104,500
Kremenchuk (Kremenchug)	240,700
Kryvyy Rih (Krivoy Rog)	715,400
Luhansk (Voroshilovgrad)	475,300
Lutsk	217,900
Lviv (Lvov)	793,700
Lysychansk (Lisichansk)	119,000
Makiyivka (Makeyevka)	394,800
Mariupol (Zhdanov)	504,400
Melitopol	171,000
Mykolayiv (Nikolayev)	517,900
Nikopol	152,000
Odesa (Odessa)	1,027,400
Oleksandriya (Aleksandriya)	101,000
Pavlohrad	130,000
Poltava	317,300
Rivne (Rovno)	244,900
Sevastopol	356,000
Simferopol	341,000
Slov'yansk (Slavyansk)	129,600
Stakhanov	104,500
Sumy	299,800
Syeverodonetsk	129,200
Ternopil (Ternopol)	235,100
Uzhhorod	125,500
Vinnytsya (Vinnitsa)	389,100
Yenakiyeve (Yenakiyevo)	108,700
Yevpatoriya	113,500
Zaporizhzhya (Zaporozhye)	863,100
Zhytomyr (Zhitomir)	297,700
United Arab Emirates (1995 est.)	
★ Abu Dhabi (Abū Ẓaby)	398,695
Al-'Ayn	225,970
Dubai (Dubayy)	669,181
Sharjah (Ash-Shārigah)	320,095
United Kingdom (1999 est.)	
England[45]	
Barnsley	220,937
Birmingham	961,041
Blackburn with Darwen	136,612
Blackpool	151,200
Bolton	258,584
Bournemouth	160,700
Bracknell Forest	110,000
Bradford	457,344
Brighton and Hove	245,000
Bristol	399,600
Bury	176,760
Calderdale	191,585
Coventry	294,387
Darlington	101,000
Derby	235,238
Doncaster	288,854
Dudley	304,615
Gateshead	199,588
Halton	123,038
Kingston upon Hull	266,900
Kirklees	373,127
Knowsley	152,091
Leeds	680,722
Leicester	270,493
Liverpool	452,450
★ London (Greater London)	7,187,300[21, 46]
Luton	181,500
Manchester	404,861
Milton Keynes	204,415
Newcastle upon Tyne	259,541
North Tyneside	192,286
Nottingham	284,000
Oldham	216,531
Peterborough	159,900
Plymouth	255,800
Poole	139,200
Portsmouth	190,400
Reading	142,851
Rochdale	202,164
Rotherham	251,637
St. Helens	178,764
Salford	220,463
Sandwell	290,091
Sefton	289,542
Sheffield	501,202
Slough	108,000
Solihull	199,859
Southampton	214,859
Southend	172,300
South Tyneside	154,697
Stockport	284,395
Stockton-on-Tees	179,000
Stoke-on-Trent	254,300
Sunderland	289,040
Swindon	177,118
Tameside	216,431
Thurrock	132,283
Torbay	119,674
Trafford	212,731
Wakefield	310,915
Walsall	259,488
Warrington	187,000
Wigan	306,521
Windsor and Maidenhead	132,465
Wirral	330,795
Wolverhampton	242,190
York	175,925
Northern Ireland[47]	
Belfast	297,200
Derry (Londonderry)	104,700
Lisburn	106,600
Scotland[48]	
Aberdeen	213,070
Dundee	146,690
Edinburgh	450,180
Glasgow	619,680
Wales[49]	
Cardiff	315,040
Conwy	110,600
Neath Port Talbot	139,459
Newport	136,800
Rhondda, Cynon, Taff	240,117
Swansea	230,200
Wrexham	125,200
United States (1998 est.)	
Abilene (*Texas*)	108,257
Akron (*Ohio*)	215,712
Alameda (*Calif.*)	78,695
Albany (*Ga.*)	77,545
Albany (*N.Y.*)	94,305
Albuquerque (*N.M.*)	419,311
Alexandria (*Va.*)	118,300
Alhambra (*Calif.*)	84,131
Allentown (*Pa.*)	100,757
Amarillo (*Texas*)	171,207
Anaheim (*Calif.*)	295,153
Anchorage (*Alaska*)	254,982
Antioch (*Calif.*)	81,428
Ann Arbor (*Mich.*)	109,967
Arlington (*Texas*)	306,497
Arlington (*Va.*)	177,275
Arlington Heights (*Ill.*)	76,522
Arvada (*Colo.*)	97,610
Atlanta (*Ga.*)	403,819
Aurora (*Colo.*)	250,604
Aurora (*Ill.*)	124,736
Austin (*Texas*)	552,434
Bakersfield (*Calif.*)	210,284
Baltimore (*Md.*)	645,593
Baton Rouge (*La.*)	211,251
Beaumont (*Texas*)	109,841
Bellevue (*Wash.*)	104,052
Berkeley (*Calif.*)	108,101
Billings (*Mont.*)	91,750
Birmingham (*Ala.*)	252,997
Bloomington (*Minn.*)	86,186
Boise City (*Idaho*)	157,452
Boston (*Mass.*)	555,447
Boulder (*Colo.*)	90,543
Bridgeport (*Conn.*)	137,425
Brockton (*Mass.*)	93,173
Brownsville (*Texas*)	137,883
Buffalo (*N.Y.*)	300,717
Burbank (*Calif.*)	97,430
Cambridge (*Mass.*)	93,352
Camden (*N.J.*)	83,546
Canton (*Ohio*)	79,259
Cape Coral (*Fla.*)	91,180
Carrollton (*Texas*)	100,463
Carson (*Calif.*)	87,647
Cary (*N.C.*)	82,071
Cedar Rapids (*Iowa*)	114,563
Chandler (*Ariz.*)	160,329
Charleston (*S.C.*)	87,044
Charlotte (*N.C.*)	504,637
Chattanooga (*Tenn.*)	147,790
Chesapeake (*Va.*)	199,564
Chicago (*Ill.*)	2,802,079
Chula Vista (*Calif.*)	160,553
Cincinnati (*Ohio*)	336,400
Clarksville (*Tenn.*)	97,978
Clearwater (*Fla.*)	101,474
Cleveland (*Ohio*)	495,817
Clifton (*N.J.*)	76,180
Colorado Springs (*Colo.*)	344,987
Columbia (*Mo.*)	78,915
Columbia (*S.C.*)	110,840
Columbus (*Ga.*)	182,219
Columbus (*Ohio*)	670,234
Compton (*Calif.*)	92,269
Concord (*Calif.*)	117,708
Coral Springs (*Fla.*)	111,744
Corona (*Calif.*)	112,815
Corpus Christi (*Texas*)	281,453
Costa Mesa (*Calif.*)	102,348
Dallas (*Texas*)	1,075,894
Daly City (*Calif.*)	99,231
Davenport (*Iowa*)	96,842
Dayton (*Ohio*)	167,475
Dearborn (*Mich.*)	91,691
Decatur (*Ill.*)	79,972
Denver (*Colo.*)	499,055
Denton (*Texas*)	76,933
Des Moines (*Iowa*)	191,293
Detroit (*Mich.*)	970,196
Downey (*Calif.*)	93,653
Duluth (*Minn.*)	81,228
Durham (*N.C.*)	153,513
El Cajon (*Calif.*)	94,259
El Monte (*Calif.*)	111,653
El Paso (*Texas*)	615,032
Elgin (*Ill.*)	87,507
Elizabeth (*N.J.*)	110,661
Erie (*Pa.*)	102,640
Escondido (*Calif.*)	120,578
Eugene (*Ore.*)	128,240
Evansville (*Ind.*)	122,779
Everett (*Wash.*)	88,625
Fairfield (*Calif.*)	89,854
Fall River (*Mass.*)	90,654
Fargo (*N.D.*)	86,718
Farmington Hills (*Mich.*)	79,784

[1]1993 estimate. [2]Eight villages, including Fagatogo, Utilel, and Pago Pago, are collectively known as Pago Pago (1990 census pop. 10,559). [3]1995 estimate. [4]1989 census. [5]Urban Centre ("urban agglomeration") as defined by 1996 census. [6]1996 census. [7]Population cited is for New Providence Island. [8]1996 estimate. [9]1990 census. [10]1991 estimate. [11]1992 census. [12]Excludes agricultural population within city limits. [13]San Jose canton. [14]1988 census. [15]As of 1998 administrative reorganization. [16]Excludes Lefkoşa (Turkish Nicosia), whose population per 1996 census was 36,834. [17]Population of the urban area of the National District. [18]As of October. [19]Within San Salvador metropolitan area. [20]1997 census. [21]1998 estimate. [22]Includes internally displaced persons from Abkhazia. [23]Population includes Comayagüela. [24]Urban population; Hong Kong is 100% urban. [25]Cities within the 75,000–100,000 population range are limited to those cities having urban agglomerations of more than 100,000 population. [26]Estimate. [27]Populations cited are urban only within administratively defined municipalities. [28]Population of Greater Karaj. [29]Urban

county city	population
Fayetteville (*N.C.*)	77,295
Flint (*Mich.*)	131,668
Fontana (*Calif.*)	109,777
Fort Collins (*Colo.*)	108,905
Fort Lauderdale (*Fla.*)	153,728
Fort Smith (Ark.)	75,637
Fort Wayne (*Ind.*)	185,716
Fort Worth (*Texas*)	491,801
Fremont (*Calif.*)	204,298
Fresno (*Calif.*)	398,133
Fullerton (*Calif.*)	121,954
Gainesville (*Fla.*)	92,648
Garden Grove (*Calif.*)	151,264
Garland (*Texas*)	193,408
Gary (*Ind.*)	108,469
Gilbert (*Ariz.*)	88,840
Glendale (*Ariz.*)	193,482
Glendale (*Calif.*)	185,086
Grand Prairie (*Texas*)	113,329
Grand Rapids (*Mich.*)	185,437
Green Bay (*Wis.*)	97,789
Greensboro (*N.C.*)	197,910
Gresham (*Ore.*)	85,021
Hammond (*Ind.*)	78,212
Hampton (*Va.*)	136,968
Hartford (*Conn.*)	135,523
Hayward (*Calif.*)	128,872
Henderson (*Nev.*)	152,717
Hialeah (*Fla.*)	211,392
High Point (*N.C.*)	76,117
Hollywood (*Fla.*)	130,026
Honolulu (*Ha.*)	395,789
Houston (*Texas*)	1,786,691
Huntington Beach (*Calif.*)	195,316
Huntsville (*Ala.*)	175,979
Independence (*Mo.*)	116,832
Indianapolis (*Ind.*)	741,304
Inglewood (*Calif.*)	111,618
Irvine (*Calif.*)	136,446
Irving (*Texas*)	178,253
Jackson (*Miss.*)	188,419
Jacksonville (*Fla.*)	693,630
Jersey City (*N.J.*)	232,429
Joliet (*Ill.*)	92,285
Kalamazoo (*Mich.*)	76,241
Kansas City (*Kan.*)	141,297
Kansas City (*Mo.*)	441,574
Kenosha (*Wis.*)	87,849
Killeen (*Texas*)	80,720
Knoxville (*Tenn.*)	165,540
Lafayette (*La.*)	113,615
Lakewood (*Calif.*)	76,222
Lakewood (*Colo.*)	136,883
Lancaster (*Calif.*)	118,518
Lansing (*Mich.*)	127,825
Laredo (*Texas*)	175,783
Las Cruces (*N.M.*)	76,102
Las Vegas (*Nev.*)	404,288
Lawton (*Okla.*)	81,107
Lexington-Fayette (*Ky.*)	241,749
Lincoln (*Neb.*)	213,088
Little Rock (*Ark.*)	175,303
Livonia (*Mich.*)	101,358
Long Beach (*Calif.*)	430,905
Longview (*Texas*)	75,576
Los Angeles (*Calif.*)	3,597,556
Louisville (*Ky.*)	255,045
Lowell (*Mass.*)	101,075
Lubbock (*Texas*)	190,974
Lynn (*Mass.*)	81,075
McAllen (*Texas*)	106,822
Macon (*Ga.*)	114,336
Madison (*Wis.*)	209,306
Manchester (*N.H.*)	102,524
Memphis (*Tenn.*)	603,507
Mesa (*Ariz.*)	360,076
Mesquite (*Texas*)	114,632
Miami (*Fla.*)	368,624
Miami Beach (*Fla.*)	97,053
Midland (*Texas*)	99,621
Milwaukee (*Wis.*)	578,364
Minneapolis (*Minn.*)	351,731
Mission Viejo (*Calif.*)	95,440
Mobile (*Ala.*)	202,181
Modesto (*Calif.*)	182,016
Montgomery (*Ala.*)	197,014
Moreno Valley (*Calif.*)	144,613
Naperville (*Ill.*)	117,091
Nashua (*N.H.*)	82,169
Nashville-Davidson (*Tenn.*)	510,274
New Bedford (*Mass.*)	96,353
New Haven (*Conn.*)	123,189
New Orleans (*La.*)	465,538
New York City (*N.Y.*)	7,420,166
Newark (*N.J.*)	267,823
Newport News (*Va.*)	178,615
Newton (*Mass.*)	80,345
Norfolk (*Va.*)	215,215
Norman (*Okla.*)	93,019
North Las Vegas (*Nev.*)	94,218
Norwalk (*Calif.*)	97,518
Norwalk (*Conn.*)	78,064
Oakland (*Calif.*)	365,874
Oceanside (*Calif.*)	152,367
Odessa (*Texas*)	91,572
Oklahoma City (*Okla.*)	472,221
Olathe (*Kan.*)	85,035
Omaha (*Neb.*)	371,291
Ontario (*Calif.*)	147,188
Orange (*Calif.*)	123,820
Orem (*Utah*)	78,937
Orlando (*Fla.*)	181,175
Overland Park (*Kan.*)	139,378
Oxnard (*Calif.*)	154,622
Palm Bay (*Fla.*)	77,486
Palmdale (*Calif.*)	100,157
Parma (*Ohio*)	83,347
Pasadena (*Calif.*)	134,587
Pasadena (*Texas*)	133,964
Paterson (*N.J.*)	148,212
Pembroke Pines (*Fla.*)	115,361
Peoria (*Ariz.*)	87,048
Peoria (*Ill.*)	111,148
Philadelphia (*Pa.*)	1,436,287
Phoenix (*Ariz.*)	1,198,064
Pittsburgh (*Pa.*)	340,520
Plano (*Texas*)	219,486
Plantation (*Fla.*)	81,424
Pomona (*Calif.*)	135,659
Pompano Beach (*Fla.*)	75,982
Port St. Lucie (*Fla.*)	79,351
Portland (*Ore.*)	503,891
Portsmouth (*Va.*)	98,936
Providence (*R.I.*)	150,890
Provo (*Utah*)	110,419
Pueblo (*Colo.*)	107,301
Quincy (*Mass.*)	85,752
Racine (*Wis.*)	81,095
Raleigh (*N.C.*)	259,423
Rancho Cucamonga (*Calif.*)	120,047
Redding (*Calif.*)	77,944
Reno (*Nev.*)	163,334
Rialto (*Calif.*)	83,933
Richardson (*Texas*)	86,020
Richmond (*Calif.*)	93,470
Richmond (*Va.*)	194,173
Riverside (*Calif.*)	262,140
Roanoke (*Va.*)	93,749
Rochester (*Minn.*)	78,173
Rochester (*N.Y.*)	216,887
Rockford (*Ill.*)	143,656
Sacramento (*Calif.*)	404,168
St. Louis (*Mo.*)	339,316
St. Paul (*Minn.*)	257,284
St. Petersburg (*Fla.*)	236,029
Salem (*Ore.*)	126,702
Salinas (*Calif.*)	121,458
Salt Lake City (*Utah*)	174,348
San Angelo (*Texas*)	88,233
San Antonio (*Texas*)	1,114,130
San Bernardino (*Calif.*)	186,402
San Buenaventura (Ventura) (*Calif.*)	98,366
San Diego (*Calif.*)	1,220,666
San Francisco (*Calif.*)	745,774
San Jose (*Calif.*)	861,284
San Mateo (*Calif.*)	91,282
Sandy (*Utah*)	99,186
Santa Ana (*Calif.*)	305,955
Santa Barbara (*Calif.*)	86,645
Santa Clara (*Calif.*)	100,370
Santa Clarita (*Calif.*)	127,001
Santa Monica (*Calif.*)	89,522
Santa Rosa (*Calif.*)	126,891
Savannah (*Ga.*)	131,674
Scottsdale (*Ariz.*)	195,394
Seattle (*Wash.*)	536,978
Shreveport (*La.*)	188,319
Simi Valley (*Calif.*)	110,463
Sioux City (*Iowa*)	82,697
Sioux Falls (*S.D.*)	116,762
South Bend (*Ind.*)	99,417
South Gate (*Calif.*)	88,364
Southfield (*Mich.*)	75,104
Spokane (*Wash.*)	184,058
Springfield (*Ill.*)	117,098
Springfield (*Mass.*)	148,114
Springfield (*Mo.*)	142,898
Stamford (*Conn.*)	110,689
Sterling Heights (*Mich.*)	124,339
Stockton (*Calif.*)	240,143
Sunnyvale (*Calif.*)	127,444
Sunrise (*Fla.*)	80,338
Syracuse (*N.Y.*)	152,215
Tacoma (*Wash.*)	179,814
Tallahassee (*Fla.*)	136,628
Tampa (*Fla.*)	289,156
Tempe (*Ariz.*)	167,622
Thousand Oaks (*Calif.*)	117,199
Toledo (*Ohio*)	312,174
Topeka (*Kan.*)	118,977
Torrance (*Calif.*)	137,533
Trenton (*N.J.*)	84,494
Troy (*Mich.*)	79,303
Tucson (*Ariz.*)	460,466
Tulsa (*Okla.*)	381,393
Tuscaloosa (*Ala.*)	83,376
Tyler (*Texas*)	83,908
Vacaville (*Calif.*)	83,362
Vallejo (*Calif.*)	111,539
Virginia Beach (*Va.*)	432,380
Visalia (*Calif.*)	89,308
Vista (*Calif.*)	80,909
Waco (*Texas*)	108,272
Warren (*Mich.*)	142,455
Warwick (*R.I.*)	84,094
★ Washington, D.C.	523,124
Waukegan (*Ill.*)	75,999
Waterbury (*Conn.*)	105,346
West Covina (*Calif.*)	99,455
West Palm Beach (*Fla.*)	76,308
West Valley City (*Utah*)	99,372
Westland (*Mich.*)	86,227
Westminster (*Calif.*)	84,042
Westminster (*Colo.*)	95,691
Whittier (*Calif.*)	79,135
Whichita (*Kan.*)	329,211
Wichita Falls (*Texas*)	99,326
Winston-Salem (*N.C.*)	164,316
Worcester (*Mass.*)	166,535
Yonkers (*N.Y.*)	190,153
Youngstown (*Ohio*)	84,650
Uruguay (1996)	
★ Montevideo	1,378,707
Uzbekistan (1996 est.)	
Andijon (Andizhan)	319,900
Angren	132,000[1]
Bukhoro (Bukhara)	228,200
Chirchiq (Chirchik)	156,000[1]
Farghona (Fergana)	191,000[1]
Jizzakh (Dzhizak)	116,000[1]
Marghilon (Margilan)	129,000[1]
Namangan	362,300
Nawoiy (Navoi)	115,000[1]
Nukus	185,000[1]
Olmaliq (Almalyk)	116,000[1]
Qarshi (Karshi)	177,000[1]
Qŭqon (Kokand)	184,000[1]
Samarqand (Samarkand)	362,400
★ Tashkent (Toshkent)	2,137,000[21]
Urganch (Urgench)	135,000[1]
Vanuatu (1997 est.)	
★ Vila	33,700
Venezuela (2000 est.)[50]	
Acarigua	166,720
Barcelona	311,475
Barinas	228,598
Barquisimeto	875,790
Baruta	213,373
Cabimas	214,000
Calabozo	102,000
★ Caracas	1,975,787
Carúpano	121,892
Catia la Mar	118,466
Ciudad Bolívar	312,691
Ciudad Guayana (San Felix de Guayana)	704,168
Ciudad Ojeda	103,835
Coro	158,763
Cúa	101,868
Cumaná	269,428
El Límon	119,602
El Tigre	119,609
Guacara	137,816
Guanare	112,000
Guarenas	170,204
Guatire	115,264
Los Teques	183,142
Maracaibo	1,764,038
Maracay	459,007
Mariara	101,115
Maturín	283,318
Mérida	230,101
Ocumare del Tuy	101,707
Petare	520,982
Puerto Cabello	169,959
Puerto La Cruz	205,635
Punto Fijo	109,362
San Cristóbal	307,184
Santa Teresa	126,930
Turmero	226,084
Valencia	1,338,833
Valera	116,036
Vietnam (1992 est.)	
Bien Hoa	273,879[4]
Cam Pha	109,086
Cam Ranh	114,041[4]
Can Tho	215,587
Da Lat	106,409
Da Nang	382,674
Haiphong	783,133
★ Hanoi	1,073,760
Ho Chi Minh City (Saigon)	3,015,743
Hong Gai	127,484
Hue	219,149
Long Xuyen	132,681
My Tho	108,404
Nam Dinh	171,699
Nha Trang	221,331
Phan Thiet	114,236[4]
Qui Nhon	163,385
Rach Gia	141,132
Thai Nguyen	127,643
Vinh	112,455
Vung Tau	145,145
Virgin Islands (U.S.) (1990)	
★ Charlotte Amalie	12,331
West Bank (1997)	
Hebron (Al-Khalīl)	119,401
Nābulus	100,231
★ Rām Allāh (Ramallah) (acting administrative centre)	18,017
Western Sahara (1994)	
Laayoune (El Aaiún)	136,950
Yemen (1994)	
Aden	398,300
Al-Hudaydah	298,500
Al-Mukallā	122,400
Ibb	103,300
★ Ṣan'ā'	954,400
Ta'izz	317,600
Yugoslavia (2000 est.)[51]	
★ Belgrade (Beograd)	1,194,878
Kragujevac	154,489
Niš	182,583
Novi Sad	182,778
Podgorica (Titograd)	130,875
Priština	186,611
Prizren	115,711
Zambia (1990)	
Chingola	167,954
Kabwe	166,519
Kitwe	338,207
Luanshya	146,275
★ Lusaka	1,577,000[29, 30]
Mufulira	152,944
Ndola	376,311
Zimbabwe (1998 est.)	
Bulawayo	790,000
Chitungwiza	600,000
Gweru	170,000
★ Harare	1,686,000[29, 30]
Kwekwe	100,000
Mutare	165,000

agglomeration. [30]1999 estimate. [31]1985 estimate. [32]County borough. [33]Commune population. [34]1991 census. [35]Based on official Nigerian projections of 1988. [36]Federal Capital Territory. [37]Census designated place on the island of Saipan. [38]Includes cantonment(s). [39]2000 estimate. [40]1994 estimate. [41]Urban population; Singapore is 100% urban. [42]1992 estimate. [43]Population refers to Kotte only. [44]1980 estimate. [45]All cities and borough councils of England after the local government reorganization of 1995–98. [46]32 borough councils, not listed separately, together constitute London (Greater London). [47]Cities and borough council of Northern Ireland with more than 100,000 population. [48]Cities of Scotland after the local government reorganizations of 1994–96. Borough councils do not exist in Scotland. [49]Cities and boroughs in Wales with more than 100,000 population after the local government reorganization of 1994–96. [50]Projections based on 1990 census. [51]Unofficial estimate.

Language

This table presents estimated data on the principal language communities of the countries of the world. The countries, and the principal languages (occasionally, language families) represented in each, are listed alphabetically. A bullet (●) indicates those languages that are official in each country. The sum of the estimates equals the 2000 population of the country given in the "Area and population" table.

The estimates represent, so far as national data collection systems permit, the distribution of mother tongues (a mother tongue being the language spoken first and, usually, most fluently by an individual). Many countries do not collect any official data whatever on language use, and published estimates not based on census or survey data usually span a substantial range of uncertainty. The editors have adopted the best-founded distribution in the published literature (indicating uncertainty by the degree of rounding shown) but have also adjusted or interpolated using data not part of the base estimate(s). Such adjustments have not been made to account for large-scale refugee movements, as these are of a temporary nature.

A variety of approaches have been used to approximate mother-tongue distribution when census data were unavailabe. Some countries collect data on ethnic or "national" groups only; for such countries ethnic distribution often had to be assumed to conform roughly to the distribution of language communities. This approach, however, should be viewed with caution, because a minority population is not always free to educate its children in its own language and because better economic opportunities often draw minority group members into the majority-language community. For some countries, a given individual may be visible in national statistics only as a passport-holder of a foreign country, however long he may remain resident. Such persons, often guest workers, have sometimes had to be assumed to be speakers of the principal language of their home country. For other countries, the language mosaic may be so complex, the language communities so minute in size, scholarly study so inadequate, or the census base so obsolete that it was possible only to assign percentages to entire groups, or families, of related languages, despite their mutual unintelligibility (Papuan and Melanesian languages in Papua New Guinea, for instance). For some countries in the Americas, so few speakers of any single indigenous language remain that it was necessary to combine these groups as *Amerindian* so as to give a fair impression of their aggregate size within their respective countries.

No systematic attempt has been made to account for populations that may legitimately be described as bilingual, unless the country itself collects data on that basis, as does Bolivia or the Comoros, for example. Where a nonindigenous official or excolonial language constitutes a lingua franca of the country, however, speakers of the language as a second tongue are shown in italics, even though very few may speak it as a mother tongue. No comprehensive effort has been made to distinguish between dialect communities *usually* classified as belonging to the same language, though such distinctions were possible for some countries—*e.g.*, between French and Occitan (the dialect of southern France) or among the various dialects of Chinese.

In giving the names of Bantu languages, grammatical particles specific to a language's autonym (name for itself) have been omitted (the form *Rwanda* is used here, for example, rather than *kinyaRwanda* and *Tswana* instead of *seTswana*). Parenthetical alternatives are given for a number of languages that differ markedly from the name of the people speaking them (such as Kurukh, spoken by the Oraon tribes of India) or that may be combined with other groups sometimes distinguishable in national data but appearing here under the name of the largest member—*e.g.*, "Tamil (and other Indian languages)" combining data on South Asian Indian populations in Singapore. The term *creole* as used here refers to distinguishable dialectal communities related to a national, official, or former colonial language (such as the French creole that survives in Mauritius from the end of French rule in 1810).

Internet resources for further information:

- *Ethnologue* (13th ed.; Summer Institute of Linguistics) http://www.sil.org/ethnologue
- Joshua Project 2000—People's List (Christian interfaith missionary database identifying some 2,000 ethnolinguistic groups) http://www.ad2000.org/peoples/index.htm
- U.S. Census Bureau: http://www.census.gov/ftp/pub/ipc/www/idbconf.html (especially tables 57 and 59)
- Living Languages of the Americas (Summer Institute of Linguistics) http://www.sil.org/lla

Language

Major languages by country	Number of speakers
Afghanistan[1]	
Indo-Aryan languages	
Pashai	160,000
Iranian languages	
Balochi	240,000
● Dari (Persian)	
Chahar Aimak	730,000
Hazara	2,280,000
Tajik	5,280,000
Nuristani group	200,000
Pamir group	160,000
● Pashto	13,560,000
Turkic languages	
Turkmen	500,000
Uzbek	2,280,000
Other	490,000
Albania[1]	
● Albanian	3,419,000
Greek	65,000
Macedonian	5,000
Other	1,000
Algeria	
● Arabic	26,280,000
Berber	4,280,000
English	...
French	*6,000,000*
American Samoa	
● English	2,000
English (lingua franca)	*64,000*
● Samoan	59,000
Tongan	2,000
Other	2,000
Andorra[2]	
● Catalan (Andorran)	22,000
French	5,000
Portuguese	7,000
Spanish	29,000
Other	4,000
Angola[1]	
Ambo (Ovambo)	240,000
Chokwe	430,000
Herero	70,000
Kongo	1,340,000
Luchazi	240,000
Luimbe-Nkangala	550,000
Lunda	120,000
Luvale (Luena)	360,000
Mbunda	120,000
Mbundu	2,190,000
Nyaneka-Nkhumbi	550,000
Ovimbundu (Umbundu)	3,770,000
● Portuguese	*3,600,000*
Other	160,000
Antigua and Barbuda	
● English	*71,000*
English/English Creole	67,000
Other	4,000
Argentina	
Amerindian languages	110,000
Italian	650,000
● Spanish	35,860,000
Other	410,000
Armenia	
● Armenian	3,560,000
Azerbaijani (Azeri)	100,000
Other	160,000
Aruba	
● Dutch	5,000
English	9,000
Papiamento	74,000
Spanish	7,000
Other	1,000
Australia	
Aboriginal languages	51,000
Arabic	187,000
Cantonese	219,000
Dutch	46,000
● English	15,561,000
English (lingua franca)	*18,500,000*
French	44,000
German	111,000
Greek	299,000
Hungarian	30,000
Indonesian Malay	30,000
Italian	423,000
Macedonian	79,000
Maltese	51,000
Mandarin	101,000
Pilipino (Filipino)	78,000
Polish	70,000
Portuguese	27,000
Russian	35,000
Serbo-Croatian	118,000
Spanish	100,000
Turkish	49,000
Vietnamese	154,000
Other/not stated	1,303,000
Austria	
Czech	19,000
● German	7,444,000
Hungarian	34,000
Polish	19,000
Romanian	17,000
Serbo-Croatian	176,000
Slovene	30,000
Turkish	123,000
Other	230,000
Azerbaijan	
Armenian	160,000
● Azerbaijani (Azeri)	7,170,000
Lezgi (Lezgian)	180,000
Russian	240,000
Other	310,000
Bahamas, The	
● English	...
English/English Creole	260,000
French (Haitian) Creole	30,000
Bahrain[2]	
● Arabic	470,000
English	...
Other	220,000
Bangladesh[1]	
● Bengali	126,260,000
Chakma	480,000
English	*3,400,000*
Garo	120,000
Khasi	100,000
Marma (Magh)	250,000
Mro	40,000
Santhali	90,000
Tripuri	90,000
Other	1,770,000
Barbados	
Bajan (English Creole)	254,000
● English	...
Other	13,000
Belarus	
● Belarusian	6,560,000
Polish	50,000
● Russian	3,190,000
Ukrainian	130,000
Other	60,000
Belgium[2, 3]	
Arabic	160,000
● Dutch (Flemish; Netherlandic)	6,080,000
● French (Walloon)	3,350,000
● German	100,000
Italian	250,000
Spanish	50,000
Turkish	90,000
Other	180,000
Belize	
● English	128,000
English Creole (lingua franca)	*190,000*
Garifuna (Black Carib)	17,000
German	4,000
Mayan languages	24,000
Spanish	80,000
Spanish (lingua franca)	*140,000*
Benin[1]	
Adja	710,000
Aizo (Ouidah)	550,000
Bariba	550,000
Dendi	140,000
Djougou	190,000
Fon	2,540,000
● French	*600,000*
Fula (Fulani)	360,000
Somba (Ditamari)	420,000
Yoruba (Nago)	780,000
Other	150,000
Bermuda	
● English	63,000
Portuguese	*6,000*
Bhutan[1]	
Assamese	100,000
● Dzongkha (Bhutia)	330,000
Nepali (Hindi)	230,000
Bolivia	
● Aymara	270,000
Guaraní	10,000
● Quechua	680,000
● Spanish	3,480,000
Spanish-Amerindian (multilingual), of which	3,830,000
Spanish-Aymara	*1,650,000*
Spanish-Guaraní	*30,000*
Spanish-Quechua	*2,160,000*
Other	70,000
Bosnia and Herzegovina[1]	
● Bosnian	1,690,000
● Croatian	650,000
● Serbian	1,190,000
Other	310,000
Botswana[1]	
● English (lingua franca)	*630,000*
Khoekhoe (Hottentot)	39,000
Ndebele	20,000
San (Bushman)	55,000
Shona	196,000
Tswana	1,189,000
Tswana (lingua franca)	*1,260,000*
Other	77,000
Brazil[1]	
Amerindian languages	170,000
German	910,000
Italian	700,000
Japanese	630,000
● Portuguese	162,160,000
Other	1,540,000
Brunei	
Chinese	31,000
English	10,000
● Malay	153,000
Malay-Chinese	3,000
Malay-English	97,000
English-Chinese	7,000
Malay-Chinese-English	13,000
Other	18,000
Bulgaria[1]	
● Bulgarian	6,800,000
Macedonian	200,000
Romany	300,000
Turkish	770,000
Other	100,000
Burkina Faso[4]	
Dogon	40,000
French	40,000
● French (lingua franca)	*4,900,000*
Fula (Fulani)	1,150,000
Gur (Voltaic) languages	
Bwamu	260,000
Gouin (Cerma)	70,000
Grusi (Gurunsi) group	
Ko	20,000
Lyele	290,000
Nuni	140,000
Sissala	10,000
Lobi	230,000
Mossi (Moore) group	
Dagara	370,000
Gurma	680,000
Kusaal	20,000
Mossi (Moore)	6,000,000
Senufo group	
Minianka	—
Senufo	170,000
Kru languages	
Seme (Siamou)	20,000
Mande languages	
Bobo	270,000
Busansi (Bisa)	430,000
Dyula (Jula)	310,000
Marka	200,000
Samo	280,000
Tamashek (Tuareg)	110,000
Other	850,000
Burundi[1]	
● French	*560,000*
● Rundi	5,930,000
Hutu	5,000,000
Tutsi	880,000
Twa	60,000
Other[5]	120,000

Major languages by country	Number of speakers
Cambodia[1]	
Cham	290,000
Chinese	380,000
● Khmer	10,960,000
Vietnamese	680,000
Other[6]	60,000
Cameroon[1]	
Chadic languages	
Buwal	300,000
Hausa	190,000
Kotoko	170,000
Mandara (Wandala)	870,000
Masana (Masa)	610,000
● English	*7,700,000*
● French	*4,600,000*
Niger-Congo languages	
Adamawa-Ubangi languages	
Chamba	370,000
Gbaya (Baya)	190,000
Mbum	200,000
Atlantic languages	
Fula (Fulani)	1,480,000
Benue-Congo languages	
Bamileke (Medumba)-Widikum (Mogha-mo)-Bamum (Mum)	2,860,000
Basa (Bassa)	170,000
Duala	1,680,000
Fang (Pangwe)-Beti-Bulu	3,030,000
Ibibio (Efik)	20,000
Igbo	80,000
Jukun	100,000
Lundu	420,000
Maka	760,000
Tikar	1,140,000
Tiv	400,000
Wute	50,000
Saharan languages	
Kanuri	50,000
Semitic languages	
Arabic	150,000
Other	120,000
Canada	
● English	18,218,000
● French	7,158,000
English-French	116,000
English-other	269,000
French-other	39,000
English-French-other	10,000
Arabic	160,000
Chinese	772,000
Cree	83,000
Dutch	144,000
Eskimo (Inuktitut) languages	29,000
German	486,000
Greek	131,000
Italian	523,000
Pilipino (Filipino)	144,000
Polish	230,000
Portuguese	228,000
Punjābī	218,000
Spanish	230,000
Ukrainian	175,000
Vietnamese	115,000
Other	1,293,000
Cape Verde	
Crioulo (Portuguese Creole)	401,000
● Portuguese	…
Central African Republic	
Banda	820,000
● French	*900,000*
Gbaya (Baya)	830,000
Mandjia	520,000
Mbum	220,000
Ngbaka	270,000
Nzakara	60,000
● Sango (lingua franca)	*3,100,000*
Sara	230,000
Zande (Azande)	70,000
Other	500,000
Chad[1]	
● Arabic	1,040,000
Bagirmi	130,000
Fitri-Batha	390,000
● French	*2,530,000*
Fula (Fulani)	210,000
Gorane	530,000
Hadjarai	560,000
Kanem-Bornu	760,000
Lac-Iro	50,000
Mayo-Kebbi	970,000
Ouaddai	740,000
Sara	2,330,000
Tandjile	550,000
Other	180,000
Chile[1]	
Araucanian (Mapuche)	1,460,000
Aymara	80,000
Rapa Nui	35,000
● Spanish	13,640,000
China[1]	
Achang	30,000
Bulang (Blang)	90,000
Ch'iang (Qiang)	220,000
Chinese (Han)	1,159,850,000
Cantonese (Yüeh [Yue])	*50,000,000*
Hakka	*28,000,000*
Hsiang (Xiang)	*39,000,000*
Kan (Gan)	*22,000,000*
● Mandarin	*899,000,000*
Min	*39,000,000*
Wu	*83,000,000*
Ching-p'o (Jingpo)	130,000
Chuang (Zhuang)	17,230,000
Daghur (Daur)	130,000
Evenk (Ewenki)	30,000
Gelo	490,000
Hani (Woni)	1,400,000
Hui	9,570,000
Kazak	1,240,000
Korean	2,140,000
Kyrgyz	160,000
Lahu	460,000
Li	1,240,000
Lisu	640,000
Manchu	10,930,000
Maonan	80,000
Miao	8,230,000
Mongol	5,350,000
Mulam	180,000
Na-hsi (Naxi)	310,000
Nu	30,000
Pai (Bai)	1,770,000
Pumi	30,000
Puyi (Chung-chia)	2,830,000
Salar	100,000
She	700,000
Shui	380,000
Sibo (Xibe)	190,000
Tai (Dai)	1,140,000
Tajik	40,000
Tibetan	5,110,000
Tu (Monguor)	210,000
T'u-chia (Tujia)	6,350,000
Tung (Dong)	2,800,000
Tung-hsiang (Dongxiang)	420,000
Uighur	8,030,000
Wa (Va)	390,000
Yao	2,370,000
Yi	7,310,000
Other	990,000
Colombia[1]	
Amerindian languages	360,000
Arawakan	40,000
Cariban	30,000
Chibchan	180,000
Other	110,000
English Creole	50,000
● Spanish	41,880,000
Comoros	
● Arabic	…
● Comorian	434,000
Comorian-French	75,000
Comorian-Malagasy	32,000
Comorian-Arabic	10,000
Comorian-Swahili	3,000
Comorian-French-other	23,000
● French	*120,000*
Other	3,000
Congo, Dem. Rep. of the[1]	
Boa	1,220,000
Chokwe	950,000
● English	…
● French	*4,000,000*
Kongo	8,340,000
Kongo (lingua franca)	*16,000,000*
Lingala (lingua franca)	*36,000,000*
Luba	9,340,000
Lugbara	840,000
Mongo	7,000,000
Ngala and Bangi	3,000,000
Rundi	2,000,000
Rwanda	5,340,000
Swahili (lingua franca)	*25,000,000*
Teke	1,420,000
Zande (Azande)	3,170,000
Other	9,340,000
Congo, Rep. of the[1]	
Bobangi	30,000
● French	*1,500,000*
Kongo	1,460,000
Kota	30,000
Lingala (lingua franca)	…
Maka	50,000
Mbete	140,000
Mboshi	330,000
Monokutuba (lingua franca)	*1,700,000*
Punu	90,000
Sango	80,000
Teke	490,000
Other	150,000
Costa Rica	
Chibchan languages	11,000
Bribrí	7,000
Cabécar	4,000
Chinese	7,000
English Creole	73,000
● Spanish	3,553,000
Côte d'Ivoire[1]	
Akan (including Baule and Anyi)	4,800,000
● French	*8,000,000*
Gur ([Voltaic] including Senufo and Lobi)	1,870,000
Kru (including Bete)	1,680,000
Malinke (including Dyula and Bambara)	1,830,000
Southern Mande (including Dan and Guro)	1,230,000
Other (non-Ivoirian population)	4,570,000
Croatia	
● Serbo-Croatian (Croatian)	4,110,000
Other	170,000
Cuba	
● Spanish	11,148,000
Cyprus (island)[1]	
● Greek	640,000
● Turkish	190,000
Other	30,000
Czech Republic[1]	
Bulgarian	3,000
● Czech	8,338,000
German	48,000
Greek	3,000
Hungarian	20,000
Moravian	1,322,000
Polish	60,000
Romanian	1,000
Romany	33,000
Russian	5,000
Ruthenian	2,000
Silesian	44,000
Slovak	314,000
Ukrainian	8,000
Other	70,000
Denmark[2]	
Arabic	39,000
● Danish	5,050,000
English	20,000
German	26,000
South Slavic languages	39,000
Turkish	47,000
Other	119,000
Djibouti[1]	
Afar	160,000
● Arabic	50,000
● French	*70,000*
Somali	200,000
Gadaboursi	…
Issa	…
Issaq	…
Other	40,000
Dominica	
● English	…
English Creole	76,000
French Creole	*69,000*
Dominican Republic	
French (Haitian) Creole	170,000
● Spanish	8,270,000
East Timor	
Portuguese	70,000
Tetum (Tetun)	530,000
Other	270,000
Ecuador	
Quechuan (and other Amerindian languages)	890,000
● Spanish	11,760,000
Egypt[1]	
● Arabic	65,080,000
Other	790,000
El Salvador	
● Spanish	6,123,000
Equatorial Guinea[1]	
Bubi	50,000
Fang	390,000
● French	…
Krio (English Creole)	…
● Spanish	…
Other	40,000
Eritrea	
Cushitic languages	
Afar	180,000
Bilin	130,000
Hadareb (Beja)	160,000
Saho	120,000
Nilotic languages	
Kunama	110,000
Nara	90,000
Semitic languages	
Arabic (Rashaida)	10,000
Tigré	1,310,000
Tigrinya	2,030,000
Estonia[1]	
Belarusian	21,000
● Estonian	936,000
Finnish	13,000
Russian	403,000
Ukrainian	36,000
Other	26,000
Ethiopia[1]	
Afar	1,210,000
Agew (Awngi)	610,000
Amharic	18,750,000
Berta	150,000
Gedeo	550,000
Gumuz	130,000
Gurage	2,720,000
Hadya–Libida	1,090,000
Kaffa	720,000
Kambata	800,000
Kimant	200,000
Oromo (Oromifa)	20,380,000
Sidamo	2,170,000
Somali	3,990,000
Tigrinya	3,780,000
Walaita	3,900,000
Other	5,730,000
Faroe Islands	
● Danish	…
● Faroese	46,000
Fiji[1]	
● English	*170,000*
Fijian	416,000
Hindi	358,000
Other	45,000
Finland	
Finnish	4,789,000
Russian	26,000
Sami (Lapp)	2,000
Swedish	293,000
Other	68,000
France	
Arabic[7]	1,490,000
English[7]	80,000
● French[7, 8, 9]	55,100,000
Basque	*100,000*
Breton	*800,000*
Catalan (Rousillonais)	*260,000*
Corsican	*80,000*
Dutch (Flemish)	*90,000*
German (Alsatian)	*1,000,000*
Occitan	*700,000*
Italian[7]	260,000
Polish[7]	50,000
Portuguese[7]	680,000
Spanish[7]	220,000
Turkish[7]	210,000
Other[7]	750,000
French Guiana	
Amerindian languages	3,000
● French	…
French/French Creoles	155,000
Other	7,000
French Polynesia[10]	
Chinese	13,000
● French	188,000
Polynesian languages	213,000
● Tahitian	…
Other	46,000
Gabon[1]	
Fang	430,000
● French	*1,000,000*
Kota	40,000
Mbete	170,000
Mpongwe (Myene)	180,000
Punu, Sira, Nzebi	200,000
Teke	20,000
Other	160,000
Gambia, The[1]	
● English	…
Gambians	
Aku (Krio)	8,000
Atlantic languages	
Diola (Jola)	126,000
Fula (Fulani)	221,000
Manjak	22,000
Serer	33,000
Wolof	172,000
Mande languages	
Bambara	10,000
Malinke	466,000
Soninke	105,000
Other	17,000
non-Gambians	188,000
Gaza Strip	
Arabic	1,141,000
Hebrew	6,000
Georgia	
Abkhaz	90,000
Armenian	350,000
Azerbaijani (Azeri)	280,000
● Georgian (Kartuli)	3,590,000
Ossetian	120,000
Russian	450,000
Other	160,000
Germany[2]	
● German	75,060,000
Greek	360,000
Italian	610,000
Polish	280,000
South Slavic languages	1,190,000
Turkish	2,110,000
Kurdish	*400,000*
Other	2.590,000
Ghana[1]	
Akan	10,240,000
● English	*1,370,000*
Ewe	2,320,000
Ga-Adangme	1,520,000
Gurma	650,000
Hausa (lingua franca)	*11,700,000*
Mole-Dagbani (Moore)	3,090,000
Yoruba	260,000
Other	1,450,000
Greece	
● Greek	10,400,000
Turkish	100,000
Other	60,000
Greenland[2]	
● Danish	7,000
● Greenlandic	49,000
Grenada	
● English	…
English/English Creole	102,000
Guadeloupe	
● French	…
French/French Creole	407,000
Other	21,000
Guam	
● Chamorro	45,000
Chinese	2,000
Chuukese (Trukese)	2,000
● English	58,000
English (lingua franca)	*153,000*
Japanese	4,000
Korean	5,000
Palauan	2,000
Philippine languages	31,000
Other	6,000
Guatemala	
Garífuna (Black Carib)	30,000
Mayan languages	3,990,000
Cakchiquel	1,020,000
Kekchí	550,000
Mam	310,000
Quiché	1,150,000
● Spanish	7,370,000
Guernsey	
● English	64,000
Norman French	…
Guinea[1]	
Atlantic languages	
Basari-Konyagi	90,000
Fula (Fulani)	2,880,000
Kissi	450,000
Other	230,000
● French	*700,000*
Mande languages	
Kpelle	350,000
Loma	170,000
Malinke	1,730,000
Susu	820,000
Yalunka	220,000
Other	520,000
Other	10,000
Guinea-Bissau[1]	
Balante	390,000
Crioulo (Portuguese Creole)	*570,000*
Ejamat	30,000
French	*130,000*
Fula (Fulani)	280,000
Malinke	170,000
Mandyako	140,000
Mankanya	50,000
Pepel	130,000
● Portuguese	*140,000*
Other	100,000
Guyana	
Amerindian languages	
Arawakan	11,000
Cariban	17,000
● English	…
English/English Creoles	764,000

Language (continued)

Major languages by country	Number of speakers
Haiti	
● French	*1,400,000*
● Haitian (French) Creole	6,868,000
Honduras	
English Creole	12,000
Garifuna (Black Carib)	82,000
Miskito	11,000
● Spanish	6,307,000
Other	78,000
Hong Kong	
Chinese	
● Cantonese	6,014,000
Cantonese (lingua franca)	*6,500,000*
Chiu Chau	95,000
Fukien (Min)	129,000
Hakka	113,000
Putonghua (Mandarin)	75,000
Putonghua (lingua franca)	*1,230,000*
Sze Yap	27,000
● English	150,000
English (lingua franca)	*2,140,000*
Japanese	14,000
Pilipino (Filipino)	7,000
Other	163,000
Hungary	
German	40,000
● Hungarian	9,870,000
Romanian	10,000
Romany	50,000
Serbo-Croatian	20,000
Slovak	10,000
Other	20,000
Iceland[2]	
● Icelandic	268,000
Other	12,000
India	
Afro-Asiatic languages	
Arabic	30,000
Austroasiatic languages	
Ho	1,140,000
Kharia	270,000
Khasi	1,090,000
Korku	560,000
Munda	500,000
Mundari	1,030,000
Santhali	6,250,000
Savara (Sora)	330,000
Other Austroasiatic	190,000
Dravidian languages	
Gondi	2,550,000
Kannada	39,240,000
Khond	260,000
Koya	320,000
Kui	770,000
Kurukh (Oraon)	1,710,000
Malayalam	36,400,000
Tamil	63,510,000
Telugu	79,100,000
Tulu	1,860,000
Other Dravidian	660,000
English	210,000
● English (lingua franca)	*193,000,000*
Indo-Iranian (Indo-Aryan) languages	
Assamese	15,670,000
Bengali	83,390,000
Bhili (Bhilodi)	6,680,000
Barel	*560,000*
Bhilali	*560,000*
Gujarati	48,730,000
Halabi	640,000
● Hindi	404,100,000
Awadhi	*580,000*
Baghelkhandi	*1,660,000*
Bagri	*710,000*
Banjari	*1,060,000*
Bhojpuri	*27,680,000*
Bundelkhandi	*1,990,000*
Chhattisgarhi	*12,690,000*
Dhundhari	*1,160,000*
Garhwali	*2,240,000*
Harauti	*1,480,000*
Haryanvi	*430,000*
Hindi	*279,690,000*
Kangri	*590,000*
Khortha (Khotta)	*1,260,000*
Kumauni	*2,060,000*
Lamani (Banjari)	*2,460,000*
Magahi (Magadhi)	*12,660,000*
Maithili	*9,310,000*
Malvi	*3,560,000*
Mandeali	*530,000*
Marwari	*5,600,000*
Mewari	*2,530,000*
Nagpuri	*930,000*
Nimadi	*1,700,000*
Pahari	*2,610,000*
Rajasthani	*15,970,000*
Sadani (Sadri)	*1,880,000*
Surgujia	*1,250,000*

Major languages by country	Number of speakers
Surjapuri	*440,000*
Other Hindi dialects	*7,390,000*
Hindi (lingua franca)	*669,000,000*
Kashmiri	4,720,000
Khandeshi	1,170,000
Konkani	2,110,000
Lahnda	30,000
Marathi	74,860,000
Nepali (Gorkhali)	2,490,000
Oriya	33,620,000
Punjabi	28,010,000
Sanskrit	60,000
Sindhi	2,540,000
Kachchhi	*680,000*
Urdu	52,010,000
Sino-Tibetan languages	
Adi	190,000
Angami	120,000
Ao	210,000
Bodo/Boro	1,460,000
Dimasa	110,000
Garo	810,000
Karbi/Makir	440,000
Konyak	170,000
Lotha	100,000
Lushai (Mizo)	650,000
Manipuri (Meithei)	1,520,000
Miri/Mishing	470,000
Nissi/Dafla	210,000
Rabha	170,000
Sema	200,000
Tangkhul	120,000
Thado	130,000
Tripuri	830,000
Kokbarak	*620,000*
Other Sino-Tibetan languages	1,810,000
Other	5,290,000
Indonesia	
Balinese	3,480,000
Banjarese	3,660,000
Batak	4,650,000
Buginese	4,610,000
● Indonesian (Malay)	25,350,000
Javanese	82,540,000
Madurese	9,060,000
Minangkabau	4,940,000
Sundanese	33,010,000
Other	38,040,000
Iran[1]	
Armenian	300,000
Iranian languages	
Bakhtyari (Luri)	1,050,000
Balochi	1,430,000
● Farsi (Persian)	28,610,000
Farsi (lingua franca)	*51,900,000*
Gilaki	3,310,000
Kurdish	5,720,000
Luri	2,710,000
Mazandarani	2,260,000
Other	1,360,000
Semitic languages	
Arabic	1,350,000
Other	150,000
Turkic languages	
Afshari	710,000
Azerbaijani (Azeri)	10,540,000
Qashqa'i	800,000
Shahsavani	380,000
Turkish (mostly Pishagchi, Bayat, and Qajar)	450,000
Turkmen	980,000
Other	130,000
Other	460,000
Iraq[1]	
● Arabic	17,490,000
Assyrian	190,000
Azerbaijani (Azeri)	390,000
Kurdish	4,300,000
Persian	190,000
Other	130,000
Ireland	
● English	3,720,000
● Irish[11]	60,000
Irish	*1,230,000*
Isle of Man	
● English	73,000
Israel[12]	
● Arabic	1,100,000
● Hebrew	3,850,000
Russian	550,000
Other	610,000
Italy[1]	
Albanian	120,000
Catalan	30,000
French	310,000
German	310,000
Greek	40,000
● Italian	54,290,000
Rhaetian	740,000
Friulian	720,000
Ladin	20,000

Major languages by country	Number of speakers
Romany	110,000
Sardinian	1,530,000
Slovene	120,000
Other	130,000
Jamaica	
● English	...
Jamaican/English Creoles	2,460,000
Hindī and other Indian languages	50,000
Other	100,000
Japan[2]	
Ainu	15,000
Chinese	240,000
English	80,000
● Japanese	125,800,000
Korean	660,000
Philippine languages	90,000
Other	50,000
Jersey	
● English	89,000
French	...
Norman French	*6,000*
Jordan[1]	
● Arabic	4,880,000
Armenian	50,000
Kabardian (Circassian)	50,000
Kazakhstan[1]	
Azerbaijani (Azeri)	90,000
Belarusian	150,000
German	460,000
● Kazakh	6,860,000
Korean	90,000
Russian	5,180,000
Tatar	290,000
Uighur	170,000
Ukrainian	740,000
Uzbek	340,000
Other	550,000
Kenya[1]	
Bantu languages	
Bajun (Rajun)	70,000
Basuba	120,000
Embu	360,000
Gusii (Kisii)	1,870,000
Kamba	3,420,000
Kikuyu	6,340,000
Kuria	180,000
Luhya	4,200,000
Mbere	120,000
Meru	1,660,000
Nyika (Mijikenda)	1,450,000
Pokomo	80,000
Swahili	10,000
● Swahili (lingua franca)	*20,000,000*
Taita	300,000
Cushitic languages	
Oromo languages	
Boran	140,000
Gabbra	60,000
Gurreh	160,000
Orma	60,000
Somali languages	
Degodia	190,000
Ogaden	50,000
Somali	310,000
● English (lingua franca)	*2,700,000*
Nilotic languages	
Kalenjin	3,270,000
Luo	3,870,000
Masai	480,000
Sambur	150,000
Teso	260,000
Turkana	410,000
Semitic languages	
Arabic	80,000
Other	680,000
Kiribati[1]	
● English	*23,000*
Kiribati (Gilbertese)	91,000
Tuvaluan (Ellice)	500
Other	600
Korea, North[1]	
Chinese	30,000
● Korean	21,650,000
Korea, South[1]	
Chinese	50,000
● Korean	47,220,000
Kuwait	
● Arabic	1,550,000
Other	440,000
Kyrgyzstan[1]	
Azerbaijani (Azeri)	20,000
German	30,000
Kazakh	50,000
● Kyrgyz	2,920,000
● Russian	790,000
Tajik	40,000
Tatar	60,000
Ukrainian	80,000
Uzbek	690,000
Other	210,000

Major languages by country	Number of speakers
Laos[1]	
● Lao-Lum (Lao)	2,910,000
Lao-Soung (Miao [Hmong] and Man [Yao])	550,000
Lao-Tai (Tai)	710,000
Lao-Theung (Mon-Khmer)	1,260,000
Other[13]	50,000
Latvia[1]	
Belarusian	90,000
● Latvian	1,340,000
Lithuanian	30,000
Polish	50,000
Russian	780,000
Ukrainian	70,000
Other	40,000
Lebanon[1]	
● Arabic	3,330,000
Armenian	210,000
French	*860,000*
Other	40,000
Lesotho[1]	
● English	*510,000*
● Sotho	1,820,000
Zulu	320,000
Liberia[1]	
Atlantic (Mel) languages	
Gola	130,000
Kissi	130,000
● English	*630,000*
Krio (English Creole)	*2,800,000*
Kru languages	
Bassa	440,000
Belle	20,000
De (Dewoin, Dey)	10,000
Grebo	280,000
Krahn	120,000
Kru (Krumen)	230,000
Mande (Northern) languages	
Gbandi	90,000
Kpelle	610,000
Loma	180,000
Malinke (Mandingo)	160,000
Mende	20,000
Vai	110,000
Mande (Southern) languages	
Gio (Dan)	250,000
Mano	220,000
Other	160,000
Libya	
● Arabic	4,910,000
Berber	50,000
Other[14]	150,000
Liechtenstein[2]	
● German	28,000
Italian	1,000
Other	3,000
Lithuania[1]	
Belarusian	50,000
● Lithuanian	3,020,000
Polish	260,000
Russian	300,000
Ukrainian	40,000
Other	30,000
Luxembourg[2]	
Belgian	15,000
Dutch	4,000
English	5,000
French	19,000
German	11,000
Italian	20,000
Luxemburgian	278,000
Portuguese	257,000
Other	30,000
Macau	
Chinese	
● Cantonese (Yüeh [Yue])	380,000
Mandarin	5,000
Other Chinese languages	40,000
English	2,000
● Portuguese	10,000
Other	5,000
Macedonia[1]	
Albanian	467,000
● Macedonian	1,358,000
Romany	46,000
Serbo-Croatian	41,000
Turkish	81,000
Vlach	9,000
Other	39,000
Madagascar[1]	
French	*2,300,000*
Malagasy	15,340,000
Other	160,000
Malawi[1]	
Chewa (Maravi)	6,060,000
● English	*540,000*
Lomwe	1,910,000

Major languages by country	Number of speakers
Ngoni	690,000
Yao	1,370,000
Other	350,000
Malaysia	
Bajau	150,000
Chinese	1,350,000
Chinese-others	760,000
Dusun	240,000
English	120,000
English-others	260,000
English (lingua franca)	*7,100,000*
Iban	550,000
Iban-others	90,000
● Malay	10,030,000
Malay-others	3,560,000
Tamil	900,000
Tamil-others	10,000
Other	5,240,000
Maldives	
● Divehi (Maldivian)	285,000
Mali[1]	
Afro-Asiatic languages	
Berber languages	
Tamashek (Tuareg)	780,000
Semitic languages	
Arabic (Mauri)	170,000
● French	*1,100,000*
Niger-Congo languages	
Atlantic languages	
Fula (Fulani) and Tukulor	1,490,000
Dogon	430,000
Gur (Voltaic) languages	
Bwa (Bobo)	260,000
Mossi (Moore)	40,000
Senufo and Minianka	1,280,000
Mande languages	
Bambara	3,410,000
Bambara (lingua franca)	*8,500,000*
Bobo Fing	10,000
Dyula (Jula)	310,000
Malinke, Khasonke, and Wasulunka	710,000
Samo (Duun)	70,000
Soninke	940,000
Nilo-Saharan languages	
Songhai	770,000
Other	30,000
Malta[1]	
● English	13,000
English (lingua franca)	*95,000*
● Maltese	364,000
Other	5,000
Marshall Islands[2]	
● English	*51,600*
● Marshallese	50,000
Other	1,600
Martinique	
● French	...
French/French Creole	372,000
Other	13,000
Mauritania[1]	
● Arabic	...
French	*270,000*
Fula (Fulani)	30,000
Hassānīyah Arabic	2,170,000
Soninke	70,000
Tukulor	140,000
Wolof	180,000
Zenaga	30,000
Other	40,000
Mauritius	
Bhojpuri	226,000
Bhojpuri-other	25,000
Chinese	4,000
● English	2,000
French	41,000
French Creole	732,000
French Creole-other	105,000
Hindi	15,000
Marathi	8,000
Tamil	9,000
Telugu	7,000
Urdu	8,000
Other	3,000
Mayotte[15]	
● Arabic	...
Mahorais (local dialect of Comorian Swahili)	137,000
Other Comorian Swahili dialects	60,000
Malagasy	53,000
● French	66,000
Other	10,000
Mexico	
Amerindian languages	7,800,000
Amuzgo	40,000
Aztec (Nahuatl)	1,770,000
Chatino	40,000
Chinantec	160,000
Chocho	20,000

Major languages by country	Number of speakers
Chol	190,000
Chontal	50,000
Cora	20,000
Cuicatec	20,000
Huastec	180,000
Huave	20,000
Huichol	30,000
Kanjobal	20,000
Mame	20,000
Mayo	60,000
Mazahua	200,000
Mazatec	240,000
Mixe	140,000
Mixtec	570,000
Otomí	420,000
Popoluca	50,000
Purépecha (Tarasco)	140,000
Tarahumara	80,000
Tepehua	10,000
Tepehuan	30,000
Tlapanec	100,000
Tojolabal	50,000
Totonac	310,000
Trique	20,000
Tzeltal	390,000
Tzotzil	350,000
Yaqui	20,000
Yucatec (Mayan)	1,050,000
Zapotec	580,000
Zoque	70,000
Other	350,000
● Spanish	91,080,000
Spanish-Amerindian languages	*6,350,000*
Micronesia	
Chuukese (Trukese)	49,000
English	1,000
Kosraean	9,000
Mortlockese	9,000
Palauan	500
Pohnpeian	28,000
Woleaian	4,000
Yapese	7,000
Other	11,000
Moldova	
Bulgarian	70,000
Gagauz	140,000
● Romanian (Moldovan)	2,660,000
Russian	990,000
Ukrainian	370,000
Other	60,000
Monaco[2]	
English	2,000
● French	13,000
Italian	5,000
Monegasque	5,000
Other	6,000
Mongolia[1]	
Bayad	46,000
Buryat	41,000
Darhat	17,000
Dariganga	34,000
Dörbet	65,000
Dzakhchin	26,000
Kazakh	142,000
● Khalkha (Mongolian)	1,890,000
Khalkha (lingua franca)	*2,150,000*
Ould	10,000
Torgut	12,000
Tuvan (Uryankhai)	24,000
Other	94,000
Morocco	
● Arabic	18,730,000
Berber	9,510,000
French	*11,500,000*
Other	580,000
Mozambique	
Bantu languages	
Chuabo	1,200,000
Lomwe	1,450,000
Makua	5,020,000
Sena	1,340,000
Tsonga (Changana)	2,180,000
Other Bantu languages	6,300,000
● Portuguese	1,240,000
Portuguese (lingua franca)	*7,570,000*
Other	360,000
Myanmar (Burma)[1]	
● Burmese	28,780,000
Burmese (lingua franca)	*33,400,000*
Chin	910,000
Kachin (Ching-p'o)	570,000
Karen	2,600,000
Kayah	170,000
Mon	1,010,000
Rakhine (Arakanese)	1,880,000
Shan	3,530,000
Other	2,290,000
Namibia	
Afrikaans	168,000
Caprivi	83,000
● English	14,000
English (lingua franca)	*340,000*
German	16,000
Herero	142,000
Kavango (Okavango)	172,000
Nama	221,000
Ovambo (Ambo [Kwanyama])	897,000
San (Bushman)	34,000
Tswana	8,000
Other	17,000
Nauru	
Chinese	1,000
English	900
English (lingua franca)	*10,700*
Kiribati (Gilbertese)	2,100
Nauruan	6,800
Tuvaluan (Ellice)	1,000
Nepal	
Austroasiatic (Munda) languages	
Santhali	40,000
English	*7,300,000*
Indo-Aryan languages	
Bengali	40,000
Bhojpuri	1,840,000
Dhanwar	30,000
Hindi	230,000
Hindi (Awadhi dialect)	500,000
Maithili	2,930,000
● Nepali (Eastern Pahari)	12,430,000
Rajbansi	110,000
Tharu	1,330,000
Urdu	270,000
Tibeto-Burman languages	
Bhutia (Sherpa)	160,000
Chepang	30,000
Gurung	300,000
Limbu	340,000
Magar	570,000
Newari	920,000
Rai and Kiranti	590,000
Tamang	1,210,000
Thakali	10,000
Thami	20,000
Other	790,000
Netherlands, The[2]	
Arabic	130,000
● Dutch	15,228,000
Dutch and Frisian	*600,000*
Turkish	103,000
Other	435,000
Netherlands Antilles	
● Dutch	...
English	18,000
Papiamento	190,000
Other	13,000
New Caledonia[1]	
● French	72,000
Indonesian	5,000
Melanesian languages	95,000
Polynesian languages	25,000
Vietnamese	3,000
Other	11,000
New Zealand	
● English	3,338,000
English-Māori	149,000
● Māori	14,000
Other	334,000
Nicaragua	
English Creole	27,000
Misumalpan languages	
Miskito	79,000
Sumo	8,000
● Spanish	4,697,000
Other	2,000
Niger[1]	
Atlantic languages	
Fula (Fulani)	980,000
Berber languages	
Tamashek (Tuareg)	1,050,000
Chadic languages	
Hausa	5,340,000
Hausa (lingua franca)	*7,100,000*
● French	*1,500,000*
Gur (Voltaic) languages	
Gurma	30,000
Saharan languages	
Kanuri	450,000
Teda (Tubu)	40,000
Semitic languages	
Arabic	30,000
Songhai and Zerma	2,140,000
Other	20,000
Nigeria[1]	
Arabic	300,000
Bura	1,900,000
Edo	4,200,000
● English/English Creole (lingua franca)	*56,000,000*
Fula (Fulani)	13,900,000
Hausa	26,300,000
Hausa (lingua franca)	*62,000,000*
Ibibio	6,900,000
Igbo (Ibo)	22,200,000
Ijo (Ijaw)	2,200,000
Kanuri	5,100,000
Nupe	1,500,000
Tiv	2,800,000
Yoruba	26,300,000
Other	9,600,000
Northern Mariana Islands	
● Carolinian	3,400
● Chamorro	21,500
Chinese	5,100
Chuukese (Trukese)	1,700
● English	3,400
English (lingua franca)	*65,100*
Japanese	1,400
Korean	4,700
Palauan	2,500
Philippine languages	24,500
Other	3,600
Norway[2]	
Danish	18,000
English	24,000
● Norwegian	4,332,000
Swedish	13,000
Other	100,000
Oman	
● Arabic (Omani)	1,850,000
Other	560,000
Pakistan	
Balochi	4,260,000
Brahui	1,730,000
English (lingua franca)	*16,000,000*
Pashto	18,600,000
Punjabi	
Punjabi	68,190,000
Hindko	3,440,000
Sindhi	
Saraiki	13,910,000
Sindhi	16,660,000
● Urdu	10,760,000
Other	4,030,000
Palau	
Chinese	300
● English	600
English (lingua franca)	*18,700*
● Palauan	15,500
Philippine languages	1,800
Other	700
Panama	
Amerindian languages	
Bokotá	5,000
Chibchan	
Guaymí (Ngöbe Buglé)	150,000
Kuna	57,000
Teribe	3,000
Chocó	
Emberá	18,000
Wounaan	3,000
Arabic	16,000
Chinese	8,000
English	...
English Creoles	395,000
● Spanish	2,168,000
Papua New Guinea[1]	
● English	*140,000*
Melanesian languages	990,000
Motu	*160,000*
Papuan languages	3,840,000
Tok Pisin (English Creole)	*3,200,000*
Other	100,000
Paraguay	
German	50,000
● Guaraní	2,210,000
Guaraní-Spanish	2,670,000
Portuguese	170,000
● Spanish	360,000
Other	40,000
Peru	
Amerindian languages	
● Aymara	590,000
● Quechua	4,220,000
Other	180,000
● Spanish	20,470,000
Other	200,000
Philippines	
Aklanon	560,000
Bantoanon	70,000
Bicol	4,340,000
Bilaan	40,000
Bontoc	60,000
Butuanon	80,000
Cebuano	17,760,000
Chavacano	470,000
Chinese	70,000
Davaweno (Mansaka)	520,000
● English (lingua franca)	*39,700,000*
Hiligaynon	6,950,000
Ibaloi (Nabaloi)	130,000
Ibanag	280,000
Ifugao	210,000
Ilocano	7,110,000
Ilongot	110,000
Kalinga	130,000
Kankanai	290,000
Kinaray-a (Hamtikanon)	480,000
Maguindanao	1,110,000
Manobo	510,000
Maranao	970,000
Masbateño	530,000
Palawano	80,000
Pampango	2,280,000
Pangasinan	1,380,000
● Pilipino (Filipino; Tagalog)	22,350,000
Romblon	240,000
Samal	480,000
Sambal	200,000
Subanon	310,000
Surigaonon	560,000
Tau Sug	880,000
Tboli	100,000
Tinggian	70,000
Tiruray	70,000
Waray-Waray	2,910,000
Yakan	150,000
Other	1,500,000
Poland	
Belarusian	190,000
German	500,000
● Polish	37,730,000
Ukrainian	230,000
Portugal[2]	
● Portuguese	9,910,000
Other	100,000
Puerto Rico	
● English	20,000
● Spanish	2,010,000
Spanish-English	1,840,000
Other	50,000
Qatar[2]	
● Arabic	240,000
Other[16]	360,000
Réunion	
Chinese	20,000
Comorian	20,000
● French	*220,000*
French Creole	660,000
Malagasy	10,000
Tamil	*140,000*
Other	10,000
Romania	
Bulgarian	9,000
Czech	5,000
German	97,000
Hungarian	1,612,000
Polish	3,000
● Romanian	20,343,000
Romany (Tigani)	164,000
Russian	31,000
Serbo-Croatian	33,000
Slovak	18,000
Tatar	22,000
Turkish	27,000
Ukrainian	63,000
Other	5,000
Russia	
Adyghian	120,000
Armenian	360,000
Avar	530,000
Azerbaijani (Azeri)	280,000
Bashkir	970,000
Belarusian	430,000
Buryat	360,000
Chechen	880,000
Chuvash	1,370,000
Dargin	340,000
Georgian (Kartuli)	90,000
German	350,000
Ingush	210,000
Kabardian	370,000
Kalmyk	150,000
Karachay	150,000
Kazakh	560,000
Komi-Permyak	100,000
Komi-Zyryan	240,000
Kumyk	270,000
Lak	100,000
Lezgi (Lezgian)	240,000
Mari	520,000
Mordvin	730,000
Ossetian	370,000
Romanian	110,000
Romany	130,000
● Russian	126,420,000
Tabasaran	90,000
Tatar	4,690,000
Tuvan	200,000
Udmurt	500,000
Ukrainian	1,860,000
Uzbek	100,000
Yakut	360,000
Other	1,440,000
Rwanda	
● English	...
● French	*500,000*
● Rwanda	7,299,000
St. Kitts and Nevis	
● English	...
English/English Creole	39,000
St. Lucia	
● English	31,000
English/French Creole	126,000
St. Vincent and the Grenadines	
● English	...
English/English Creole	112,000
Other	1,000
Samoa	
● English	1,000
● Samoan	85,000
Samoan-English	93,000
San Marino[1]	
● Italian (Romagnolo)	26,800
São Tomé and Príncipe	
Crioulo (Portuguese Creole)	124,000
English	...
French	1,000
● Portuguese	...
Other	18,000
Saudi Arabia[1]	
● Arabic	20,920,000
Other	1,100,000
Senegal	
● French	*3,500,000*
Senegalese	
Bambara	90,000
Diola	490,000
Fula (Fulani)-Tukulor	2,170,000
Malinke (Mandingo)	370,000
Serer	1,250,000
Soninke	130,000
Wolof	4,800,000
Wolof (lingua franca)	*8,000,000*
Other	440,000
non-Senegalese	220,000
Seychelles	
English	3,000
English (lingua franca)	*29,000*
French	1,000
French (lingua franca)	*78,000*
Seselwa (French Creole)	75,000
Other	3,000
Sierra Leone[1]	
Atlantic languages	
Bullom-Sherbro	200,000
Fula (Fulani)	200,000
Kissi	120,000
Limba	440,000
Temne	1,660,000
● English	*500,000*
Krio (English Creole [lingua franca])	*4,400,000*
Mande languages	
Kono-Vai	270,000
Kuranko	180,000
Mende	1,810,000
Susu	80,000
Yalunka	180,000
Other	90,000
Singapore[1]	
Chinese	2,517,000
● English	*1,226,000*
● Malay	456,000
● Mandarin Chinese	*1,421,000*
● Tamil (and other Indian languages)	259,000
Other	43,000
Slovakia[1]	
Czech, Moravian, and Silesian	59,000
German	5,000
Hungarian	569,000
Polish	3,000
Romany	90,000
Ruthenian, Ukrainian, and Russian	35,000
● Slovak	4,626,000
Other	15,000
Slovenia	
Hungarian	9,000
Serbo-Croatian	155,000
● Slovene	1,725,000
Other	74,000

Language (continued)

Major languages by country	Number of speakers
Solomon Islands[1]	
● English	*9,000*
Melanesian languages	399,000
Papuan languages	40,000
Polynesian languages	17,000
Solomon Island Pidgin (English Creole)	*163,000*
Other	10,000
Somalia[1]	
● Arabic	...
English	...
● Somali	7,130,000
Other	120,000
South Africa	
● Afrikaans	6,220,000
● English	3,700,000
Nguni	
● Ndebele	630,000
● Swazi	1,080,000
● Xhosa	7,700,000
● Zulu	9,840,000
Sotho	
● North Sotho (Pedi)	3,950,000
● South Sotho	3,320,000
● Tswana (Western Sotho)	3,530,000
● Tsonga	1,880,000
● Venda	940,000
Other	620,000
Spain	
Basque (Euskera)	630,000
● Castilian Spanish	29,860,000
Catalan (Català)	6,770,000
Galician (Gallego)	2,560,000
Other	300,000
Sri Lanka	
English	10,000
English-Sinhala	1,060,000
English-Sinhala-Tamil	690,000
English-Tamil	220,000
● Sinhala	11,610,000
Sinhala-Tamil	1,800,000
● Tamil	3,780,000
Other	60,000
Sudan, The[1]	
● Arabic	17,320,000
Arabic (lingua franca)	*21,000,000*
Bari	860,000
Beja	2,240,000
Dinka	4,050,000
Fur	720,000
Lotuko	520,000
Nubian languages	2,840,000
Nuer	1,720,000
Shilluk	600,000
Zande (Azande)	950,000
Other	3,260,000
Suriname	
● Dutch	*110,000*
English/English Creole	*410,000*
Sranantonga	170,000
Sranantonga-other	170,000
Other (mostly Hindī, Javanese, and Saramacca)	90,000
Swaziland[1]	
● English	*50,000*
● Swazi	970,000
Zulu	20,000
Other	80,000
Sweden[2]	
Arabic	68,000
Danish	41,000
English	32,000
Finnish	209,000
German	45,000
Iranian languages	49,000
Norwegian	46,000
Polish	39,000
South Slavic languages	116,000
Spanish	56,000
● Swedish	7,937,000
Turkish	29,000
Other	197,000
Switzerland	
● French	1,380,000
● German	4,570,000
● Italian	550,000
Romansch	40,000
Other	640,000
Syria[1]	
● Arabic	14,680,000
Kurdish	1,470,000
Other	160,000
Taiwan	
Austronesian languages	
Ami	138,000
Atayal	89,000
Bunun	42,000
Paiwan	68,000
Puyuma	10,000
Rukai	11,000
Saisiyat	6,000
Tsou	7,000
Yami	4,000
Chinese languages	
Hakka	2,440,000
● Mandarin	4,460,000
Min (South Fukien)	14,800,000
Other	120,000
Tajikistan	
Russian	610,000
● Tajik (Tojik)	3,920,000
Uzbek	1,460,000
Other	310,000
Tanzania[1]	
Chaga (Chagga), Pare	1,730,000
● English	*3,800,000*
Gogo	1,390,000
Ha	1,210,000
Haya	2,080,000
Hehet	2,430,000
Iramba	1,010,000
Luguru	1,730,000
Luo	290,000
Makonde	2,080,000
Masai	350,000
Ngoni	470,000
Nyakusa	1,910,000
Nyamwesi (Sukuma)	7,450,000
Shambala	1,510,000
● Swahili	3,120,000
Swahili (lingua franca)	*32,000,000*
Tatoga	260,000
Yao	860,000
Other	5,430,000
Thailand[1]	
Chinese	7,570,000
Karen	220,000
Malay	2,270,000
Mon-Khmer languages	
Khmer	790,000
Kuy	670,000
Other	220,000
Tai languages	
Lao	16,790,000
● Thai (Siamese)	32,820,000
Other	430,000
Other	640,000
Togo[1]	
Atlantic (Mel) languages	
Fula (Fulani)	68,000
Benue-Congo languages	
Ana (Ana-Ife)	126,000
Nago	13,000
Yoruba	10,000
Chadic languages	
Hausa	14,000
● French	*2,500,000*
Gur (Voltaic) languages	
Basari	88,000
Chakossi (Akan)	59,000
Chamba	49,000
Dye (Gangam)	47,000
Gurma	170,000
Kabre	692,000
Konkomba	71,000
Kotokoli (Tem)	289,000
Moba	270,000
Mossi (Moore)	13,000
Namba (Lamba)	153,000
Naudemba (Losso)	206,000
Tamberma	28,000
Yanga	15,000
Kwa languages	
Adja (Aja)	157,000
Adele	10,000
Ahlo	9,000
Akposo	134,000
Ane (Basila)	284,000
Anlo	4,000
Anyaga	10,000
Ewe	1,164,000
Fon	50,000
Hwe	6,000
Kebu	58,000
Kpessi	4,000
Peda-Hula (Pla)	20,000
Watyi (Ouatchi)	517,000
Other	212,000
Tonga	
● English	*30,000*
● Tongan	98,000
Other	2,000
Trinidad and Tobago	
● English	...
English Creole[17]	37,000
Hindi	45,000
Trinidad English	1,208,000
● Other	3,000
Tunisia	
● Arabic	6,710,000
Arabic-French	2,520,000
Arabic-French-English	300,000
Arabic-other	10,000
Other-no Arabic	30,000
Other	30,000
Turkey[1]	
Arabic	900,000
Kurdish[18]	6,960,000
● Turkish	57,510,000
Other	300,000
Turkmenistan[1]	
Armenian	37,000
Azerbaijani (Azeri)	40,000
Balochi	40,000
Kazakh	96,000
Russian	329,000
Tatar	40,000
● Turkmen	3,745,000
Ukrainian	25,000
Uzbek	448,000
Other	85,000
Tuvalu	
English	...
Kiribati (Gilbertese)	800
Tuvaluan (Ellice)	10,000
Uganda[1]	
Bantu languages	
Amba	90,000
Ganda (Luganda)	4,220,000
Gisu (Masaba)	1,050,000
Gwere	380,000
Kiga (Chiga)	1,950,000
Konjo	510,000
Nkole (Nyankole and Hororo)	2,500,000
Nyole	320,000
Nyoro	690,000
Ruli	100,000
Rundi	140,000
Rwanda	750,000
Samia	310,000
Soga	1,920,000
Swahili (lingua franca)	*8,200,000*
Toro	680,000
Central Sudanic languages	
Lugbara	1,100,000
Madi	180,000
Ndo	230,000
● English	*2,500,000*
Nilotic languages	
Acholi	1,030,000
Alur	550,000
Kakwa	120,000
Karamojong	490,000
Kumam	160,000
Lango	1,370,000
Padhola	350,000
Sebei (Kupsabiny)	150,000
Teso	1,400,000
Other (mostly Gujarati and Hindi)	580,000
Ukraine	
Belarusian	150,000
Bulgarian	160,000
Hungarian	150,000
Polish	30,000
Romanian	330,000
Russian	16,310,000
● Ukrainian	32,110,000
Other	430,000
United Arab Emirates[2]	
● Arabic	1,270,000
Other[16]	1,750,000
United Kingdom	
● English	58,090,000
Scots-Gaelic	80,000
Welsh	570,000
Other	970,000
United States	
Amharic	40,000
Arabic	420,000
Armenian	180,000
Bengali	50,000
Cajun	40,000
Chinese (including Formosan)	1,550,000
Czech	110,000
Danish	40,000
Dutch	170,000
English	237,320,000
English (lingua franca)	*267,000,000*
Finnish	60,000
French	2,030,000
French Creole (mostly Haitian)	220,000
German	1,850,000
Greek	460,000
Gujarati	120,000
Hebrew	170,000
Hindi (including Urdu)	400,000
Hungarian	180,000
Ilocano	50,000
Italian	1,560,000
Japanese	510,000
Korean	750,000
Kru (Gullah)	80,000
Lithuanian	70,000
Malayalam	40,000
Miao (Hmong)	100,000
Mon-Khmer (mostly Cambodian)	150,000
Navajo	180,000
Norwegian	100,000
Pennsylvania Dutch	100,000
Persian	240,000
Polish	860,000
Portuguese	510,000
Punjābī	60,000
Romanian	80,000
Russian	290,000
Samoan	40,000
Serbo-Croatian	140,000
Slovak	100,000
Spanish	20,720,000
Swedish	90,000
Syriac	40,000
Tagalog	1,010,000
Tai (including Laotian)	250,000
Turkish	50,000
Ukrainian	120,000
Vietnamese	610,000
Yiddish	250,000
Other	810,000
Uruguay	
● Spanish	3,140,000
Other	140,000
Uzbekistan[1]	
Kazakh	1,010,000
Russian	1,490,000
Tajik	1,190,000
Tatar	400,000
● Uzbek	18,770,000
Other	1,910,000
Vanuatu[19]	
● Bislama (English Creole)	120,000
● English	60,000
● French	30,000
Other	2,000
Venezuela	
Amerindian languages	
Goajiro	160,000
Warrau (Warao)	20,000
Other	150,000
● Spanish	23,310,000
Other	520,000
Vietnam[1]	
Bahnar	170,000
Cham	120,000
Chinese (Hoa)	1,100,000
French	*380,000*
Hre	120,000
Jarai	300,000
Khmer	1,090,000
Koho	110,000
Man (Mien, or Yao)	580,000
Miao (Meo, or Hmong)	690,000
Mnong	80,000
Muong	1,120,000
Nung	870,000
Rade (Rhadé)	240,000
Roglai	90,000
San Chay (Cao Lan)	140,000
San Diu	120,000
Sedang	120,000
Stieng	60,000
Tai	1,280,000
Tho (Tay)	1,460,000
● Vietnamese	68,400,000
Other	160,000
Virgin Islands (U.S.)	
● English	98,000
French	3,000
Spanish	16,000
Other	3,000
West Bank[20]	
Arabic	2,010,000
Hebrew	170,000
Western Sahara	
Arabic	245,000
Yemen[1]	
● Arabic	17,400,000
Other	70,000
Yugoslavia[1]	
Albanian	1,760,000
Hungarian	350,000
Macedonian	50,000
Romanian	40,000
Romany	150,000
● Serbo-Croatian (Serbian)	8,020,000
Serbo-Croatian (lingua franca)	*10,100,000*
Slovak	70,000
Vlach	20,000
Other	200,000
Zambia[21]	
Bemba group	
Bemba	2,850,000
Bemba (lingua franca)	*5,000,000*
Bisa	110,000
Lala	230,000
Lamba	210,000
Other	400,000
● English	110,000
English (lingua franca)	*1,800,000*
Lozi (Barotse) group	
Lozi (Barotse)	610,000
Other	110,000
Mambwe group	
Lungu	70,000
Mambwe	110,000
Mwanga (Winawanga)	130,000
Other	10,000
North-Western group	
Kaonde	220,000
Lunda	190,000
Luvale (Luena)	170,000
Other	260,000
Nyanja (Maravi) group	
Chewa	550,000
Ngoni	160,000
Nsenga	410,000
Nyanja (Maravi)	750,000
Nyanja (lingua franca)	*2,500,000*
Other	60,000
Tonga (Ila-Tonga) group	
Ila	90,000
Lenje	150,000
Tonga	1,050,000
Other	120,000
Tumbuka group	
Senga	70,000
Tumbuka	280,000
Other	10,000
Other	90,000
Zimbabwe	
● English	250,000
English (lingua franca)	*5,300,000*
Ndebele (Nguni)	1,840,000
Nyanja	260,000
Shona	8,180,000
Other	810,000

[1]Figures given represent ethnolinguistic groups. [2]Data refer to nationality (usually resident aliens holding foreign passports). [3]Data are partly based on place of residence. [4]Majority of population speak Moore (language of the Mossi); Dyula is language of commerce. [5]Swahili also spoken. [6]English and French also spoken. [7]Based on "nationality" at 1982 census. [8]Includes naturalized citizens. [9]French is the universal language throughout France; traditional dialects and minority languages are retained regionally in the approximate numbers shown, however. [10]Data reflect multilingualism; 2000 population estimate is 233,000. [11]Refers to Irish speakers in Gaeltacht areas. [12]Includes the population of the Golan Heights and East Jerusalem; excludes the Israeli population in the West Bank and Gaza Strip. [13]English and French also spoken. [14]English and Italian also spoken. [15]Data reflect ability to speak the language, not mother tongue; 2000 population estimate is 156,000. [16]Mostly Pakistanis, Indians, and Iranians. [17]Spoken on Tobago only. [18]Other estimates of the Kurdish population range from 6 percent to 20–25 percent. [19]Data reflect multilingualism; 2000 population is 190,000. [20]Excludes East Jerusalem. [21]Groups are officially defined geographic divisions; elements comprising them are named by language.

Religion

The following table presents statistics on religious affiliation for each of the countries of the world. An assessment was made for each country of the available data on distribution of religious communities within the total population; the best available figures, whether originating as census data, membership figures of the churches concerned, or estimates by external analysts in the absence of reliable local data, were applied as percentages to the estimated 2000 midyear population of the country to obtain the data shown below.

Several concepts govern the nature of the available data, each useful separately but none the basis of any standard of international practice in the collection of such data. The word "affiliation" was used above to describe the nature of the relationship joining the religious bodies named and the populations shown. This term implies some sort of formal, usually documentary, connection between the religion and the individual (a baptismal certificate, a child being assigned the religion of its parents on a census form, maintenance of one's name on the tax rolls of a state religion, etc.) but says nothing about the nature of the individual's personal religious practice, in that the individual may have lapsed, never been confirmed as an adult, joined another religion, or may have joined an organization that is formally atheist.

The user of these statistics should be careful to note that not only does the nature of the affiliation (with an organized religion) differ greatly from country to country, but the social context of religious practice does also. A country in which a single religion has long been predominant will often show more than 90% of its population to be *affiliated*, while in actual fact, no more than 10% may actually *practice* that religion on a regular basis. Such a situation often leads to undercounting of minority religions (where someone [head of household, communicant, child] is counted at all), blurring of distinctions seen to be significant elsewhere (a Hindu country may not distinguish Protestant [or even Christian] denominations; a Christian country may not distinguish among its Muslim or Buddhist citizens), or double-counting in countries where an individual may conscientiously practice more than one "religion" at a time.

Until 1989 communist countries had for long consciously attempted to ignore, suppress, or render invisible religious practice within their borders. Countries with large numbers of adherents of traditional, often animist, religions and belief systems usually have little or no formal methodology for defining the nature of local religious practice. On the other hand, countries with strong missionary traditions, or good census organizations, or few religious sensitivities may have very good, detailed, and meaningful data.

The most comprehensive works available are DAVID B. BARRETT (ed.), *World Christian Encyclopedia* (1982); and PETER BRIERLEY, *World Churches Handbook* (1997).

Religion

Religious affiliation	2000 population
Afghanistan	
Sunnī Muslim	21,750,000
Shīʿī Muslim	3,880,000
other	260,000
Albania	
Muslim	2,440,000
Albanian Orthodox	250,000
Roman Catholic	180,000
other	620,000
Algeria	
Sunnī Muslim	30,410,000
Ibāḍīyah Muslim	120,000
other	20,000
American Samoa	
Congregational	27,000
Roman Catholic	13,000
other	25,000
Andorra	
Roman Catholic	58,000
other	9,000
Angola	
Roman Catholic	5,150,000
Protestant	1,490,000
African Christian	440,000
other (mostly traditional beliefs)	3,070,000
Antigua and Barbuda	
Protestant	30,000
Anglican	23,000
Roman Catholic	8,000
other	10,000
Argentina	
Roman Catholic	32,490,000
Protestant	2,780,000
Muslim	550,000
Jewish	270,000
other	940,000
Armenia	
Armenian Apostolic (Orthodox)	2,460,000
other	1,350,000
Aruba	
Roman Catholic	69,000
other	28,000
Australia	
Roman Catholic	5,180,000
Anglican	4,210,000
Uniting Church	1,440,000
Presbyterian	730,000
other Protestant	1,390,000
Orthodox	540,000
nonreligious	3,180,000
other	2,500,000
Austria	
Roman Catholic	6,070,000
Protestant (mostly Lutheran)	430,000
atheist and nonreligious	700,000
other	890,000
Azerbaijan	
Shīʿī Muslim	5,260,000
Sunnī Muslim	2,260,000
other	530,000
Bahamas, The	
Protestant	134,000
Roman Catholic	50,000
Anglican	32,000
other	79,000
Bahrain	
Shīʿī Muslim	420,000
Sunnī Muslim	140,000
other	130,000
Bangladesh	
Muslim	114,080,000
Hindu	13,580,000
other	1,530,000
Barbados	
Anglican	88,000
Protestant	80,000
Roman Catholic	12,000
other	87,000
Belarus	
Belarusian Orthodox	3,150,000
Roman Catholic	1,770,000
other	5,070,000
Belgium	
Roman Catholic	9,010,000
other	1,240,000
Belize	
Roman Catholic	146,000
Protestant	69,000
Anglican	18,000
other	20,000
Benin	
Voodoo (traditional beliefs)	3,970,000
Roman Catholic	1,340,000
Muslim	770,000
other	320,000
Bermuda	
Anglican	23,000
Methodist	10,000
Roman Catholic	9,000
other	20,000
Bhutan	
Lamaistic Buddhist	500,000
Hindu	170,000
Bolivia	
Roman Catholic	7,370,000
Protestant	750,000
other	210,000
Bosnia and Herzegovina	
Sunnī Muslim	1,650,000
Serbian Orthodox	1,150,000
Roman Catholic	690,000
other	350,000
Botswana	
African Christian	440,000
Protestant	200,000
Roman Catholic	60,000
other (mostly traditional beliefs)	860,000
Brazil	
Roman Catholic (including syncretic Afro-Catholic cults having Spiritist beliefs and rituals)	120,100,000
Evangelical Protestant	38,500,000
other	7,500,000
Brunei	
Muslim	226,000
other	110,000
Bulgaria	
Bulgarian Orthodox	3,010,000
Muslim (mostly Sunnī)	1,070,000
other	4,090,000
Burkina Faso	
Muslim	5,970,000
traditional beliefs	4,780,000
Christian	1,190,000
Burundi	
Roman Catholic	3,940,000
nonreligious	1,130,000
other (mostly Protestant)	990,000
Cambodia	
Buddhist	11,750,000
Muslim	270,000
other	350,000
Cameroon	
Roman Catholic	5,360,000
traditional beliefs	4,010,000
Muslim	3,360,000
Protestant	2,700,000
Canada	
Roman Catholic	13,900,000
Protestant	8,560,000
Anglican	2,470,000
Eastern Orthodox	440,000
Jewish	360,000
Muslim	290,000
Buddhist	180,000
Hindu	180,000
Sikh	170,000
nonreligious	3,850,000
other	370,000
Cape Verde	
Roman Catholic	385,000
Protestant	16,000
Central African Republic	
Protestant	900,000
traditional beliefs	840,000
Roman Catholic	590,000
Muslim	530,000
other	650,000
Chad	
Muslim	4,540,000
Roman Catholic	1,710,000
Protestant	1,210,000
traditional beliefs	620,000
other	350,000
Chile	
Roman Catholic	11,670,000
Evangelical Protestant	1,890,000
other	1,650,000
China	
nonreligious	656,000,000
Chinese folk-religionist	254,000,000
atheist	152,000,000
Buddhist	107,000,000
Christian	76,000,000
Muslim	18,000,000
traditional beliefs	1,000,000
Colombia	
Roman Catholic	38,900,000
other	3,400,000
Comoros	
Sunnī Muslim	574,000
Christian	4,000
Congo, Dem. Rep. of the	
Roman Catholic	21,310,000
Protestant	16,420,000
African Christian	6,950,000
traditional beliefs	5,560,000
Muslim	730,000
other	1,000,000
Congo, Rep. of the	
Roman Catholic	1,160,000
traditional beliefs	930,000
Protestant	690,000
Muslim	50,000
Costa Rica	
Roman Catholic	3,130,000
other	510,000
Côte d'Ivoire	
Muslim	6,180,000
Roman Catholic	3,320,000
traditional beliefs	2,720,000
nonreligious	2,150,000
Protestant	850,000
other	760,000
Croatia	
Roman Catholic	3,090,000
Serbian Orthodox	600,000
Sunnī Muslim	50,000
Protestant	30,000
other	510,000
Cuba	
Roman Catholic	4,400,000
Protestant	270,000
other (mostly Santeria)	6,480,000
Cyprus	
Greek Orthodox	640,000
Muslim (mostly Sunnī)	190,000
other (mostly Christian)	30,000
Czech Republic	
Roman Catholic	4,010,000
Evangelical Church of Czech Brethren	200,000
Czechoslovak Hussite	180,000
Silesian Evangelical	30,000
Eastern Orthodox	20,000
atheist and nonreligious	4,100,000
other	1,730,000
Denmark	
Evangelical Lutheran	4,620,000
other	720,000
Djibouti	
Sunnī Muslim	440,000
Christian	10,000
Dominica	
Roman Catholic	54,000
Protestant	13,000
other	10,000
Dominican Republic	
Roman Catholic	6,910,000
Protestant	540,000
other	990,000
East Timor	
Roman Catholic	610,000
Muslim	270,000
Ecuador	
Roman Catholic	11,700,000
Protestant	430,000
other	520,000
Egypt	
Sunnī Muslim	58,630,000
Coptic Orthodox[1]	6,590,000
Protestant	660,000
El Salvador	
Roman Catholic	4,790,000
Protestant	1,050,000
other	280,000
Equatorial Guinea	
Roman Catholic	440,000
other	30,000
Eritrea	
Muslim	2,870,000
Eritrean Orthodox	1,270,000
Estonia	
Estonian Orthodox	280,000
Evangelical Lutheran	200,000
other	960,000
Ethiopia	
Ethiopian Orthodox	32,220,000
other Christian	6,890,000
Muslim (mostly Sunnī)	21,120,000

Religion (continued)

Religious affiliation	2000 population
traditional beliefs	3,090,000
other	790,000
Faroe Islands	
Evangelical Lutheran	37,000
other	9,000
Fiji	
Christian (mostly Methodist and Roman Catholic)	433,000
Hindu	313,000
Muslim	64,000
other	9,000
Finland	
Evangelical Lutheran	4,410,000
other	770,000
France	
Roman Catholic	44,850,000
nonreligious	6,260,000
Muslim	3,240,000
atheist	2,000,000
Protestant	1,090,000
Jewish	610,000
other	790,000
French Guiana	
Roman Catholic	90,000
other	75,000
French Polynesia	
Protestant	117,000
Roman Catholic	92,000
other	24,000
Gabon	
Roman Catholic	600,000
traditional beliefs	230,000
Protestant	220,000
other	160,000
Gambia, The	
Muslim (mostly Sunnī)	1,300,000
other	70,000
Gaza Strip	
Muslim (mostly Sunnī)	1,130,000
other	20,000
Georgia	
Georgian Orthodox	1,840,000
Sunnī Muslim	550,000
Armenian Apostolic (Orthodox)	280,000
Russian Orthodox	130,000
other (mostly nonreligious)	2,220,000
Germany	
Protestant (mostly Evangelical Lutheran)	35,180,000
Roman Catholic	27,890,000
Muslim	1,750,000
other (mostly nonreligious)	17,390,000
Ghana	
African Christian	5,740,000
Protestant	3,920,000
traditional beliefs	3,430,000
Roman Catholic	2,870,000
Muslim	2,810,000
other	760,000
Greece	
Greek Orthodox	9,690,000
Muslim	140,000
other	730,000
Greenland	
Evangelical Lutheran	36,000
other	20,000
Grenada	
Roman Catholic	54,000
Anglican	14,000
other	34,000
Guadeloupe	
Roman Catholic	347,000
other	81,000
Guam	
Roman Catholic	116,000
Protestant	19,000
other	20,000
Guatemala	
Roman Catholic	8,650,000
Evangelical Protestant	2,480,000
other	260,000
Guernsey	
Anglican	42,000
other	22,000
Guinea	
Muslim	6,350,000
Christian	750,000
other	370,000
Guinea-Bissau	
Muslim	590,000
traditional beliefs	510,000
Christian	190,000
Guyana	
Hindu	269,000
Protestant	148,000
Roman Catholic	91,000
Muslim	71,000
Anglican	68,000
other	145,000
Haiti	
Roman Catholic	4,710,000
Protestant	1,570,000
other	590,000
Honduras	
Roman Catholic	5,630,000
Evangelical Protestant	680,000
other	180,000
Hong Kong	
Buddhist and Taoist	5,010,000
Protestant	290,000
Roman Catholic	280,000
other	1,200,000
Hungary	
Roman Catholic	6,320,000
Protestant	2,550,000
other (mostly nonreligious and atheist)	1,152,000
Iceland	
Evangelical Lutheran	250,000
other	30,000
India	
Hindu	824,000,000
Sunnī Muslim	91,000,000
Shīʿī Muslim	30,000,000
Sikh	19,000,000
Protestant	11,000,000
Roman Catholic	11,000,000
Buddhist	8,000,000
Jain	4,000,000
Zoroastrian (Parsi)	90,000
other	13,000,000
Indonesia	
Muslim	182,570,000
Protestant	12,640,000
Roman Catholic	7,490,000
Hindu	3,830,000
Buddhist	2,160,000
other	650,000
Iran	
Shīʿī Muslim	58,870,000
Sunnī Muslim	3,560,000
other	270,000
Iraq	
Shīʿī Muslim	14,170,000
Sunnī Muslim	7,820,000
other (mostly Christian)	690,000
Ireland	
Roman Catholic	3,460,000
other	320,000
Isle of Man	
Anglican	45,000
other	28,000
Israel	
Jewish[2]	4,840,000
Muslim (mostly Sunnī)	910,000
other	360,000
Italy	
Roman Catholic	47,180,000
Muslim	700,000
other (mostly nonreligious and atheist)	9,840,000
Jamaica	
Protestant	1,020,000
Roman Catholic	270,000
Anglican	100,000
other	1,230,000
Japan	
Shintoist[3]	118,100,000
Buddhist[3]	88,400,000
Christian	1,460,000
other	10,230,000
Jersey	
Anglican	55,000
Roman Catholic	21,000
other	14,000
Jordan	
Sunnī Muslim	4,810,000
Christian	170,000
Kazakhstan	
Muslim (mostly Sunnī)	7,010,000
Russian Orthodox	1,220,000
Protestant	320,000
other (mostly nonreligious)	6,360,000
Kenya	
traditional beliefs	9,190,000
Protestant	8,560,000
Roman Catholic	5,930,000
African Christian	2,490,000
Muslim	1,820,000
Anglican	1,700,000
other	650,000
Kiribati	
Roman Catholic	50,000
Congregational	35,000
other	7,000
Korea, North	
atheist and nonreligious	14,820,000
traditional beliefs	3,380,000
Ch'ŏndogyo	3,010,000
other	480,000
Korea, South	
nonreligious	23,300,000
Buddhist	10,950,000
Protestant	9,300,000
Roman Catholic	3,130,000
Confucian	220,000
Wonbulgyo	90,000
other	290,000
Kuwait	
Sunnī Muslim	890,000
Shīʿī Muslim	600,000
other Muslim	200,000
other (mostly Christian and Hindu)	290,000
Kyrgyzstan	
Muslim (mostly Sunnī)	3,430,000
Russian Orthodox	270,000
other (mostly nonreligious)	1,200,000
Laos	
Buddhist	3,180,000
traditional beliefs	1,850,000
other	470,000
Latvia	
Roman Catholic	359,000
Evangelical Lutheran	353,000
Russian Orthodox	185,000
other (mostly nonreligious)	1,518,000
Lebanon	
Shīʿī Muslim	1,220,000
Sunnī Muslim	760,000
Maronite Catholic	680,000
Druze	250,000
Greek Orthodox	210,000
Armenian Apostolic (Orthodox)	190,000
Greek Catholic (Melchite)	160,000
other	110,000
Lesotho	
Roman Catholic	840,000
traditional beliefs	640,000
Protestant	300,000
African Christian	240,000
Anglican	120,000
Liberia	
Christian	2,140,000
traditional beliefs	580,000
Muslim	440,000
Libya	
Sunnī Muslim	4,960,000
other	150,000
Liechtenstein	
Roman Catholic	26,000
other	7,000
Lithuania	
Roman Catholic	2,670,000
Russian Orthodox	90,000
other (mostly nonreligious)	940,000
Luxembourg	
Roman Catholic	418,000
other	21,000
Macau	
nonreligious	268,000
Buddhist	74,000
other	98,000
Macedonia	
Serbian (Macedonian) Orthodox	1,110,000
Sunnī Muslim	610,000
other	320,000
Madagascar	
traditional beliefs	8,060,000
Roman Catholic	3,300,000
Protestant	3,060,000
Muslim	1,090,000
Malawi	
Protestant (mostly Presbyterian)	2,130,000
Muslim	2,080,000
Roman Catholic	1,870,000
traditional beliefs	1,040,000
African Christian	1,030,000
other	2,240,000
Malaysia	
Muslim	12,300,000
Buddhist	4,020,000
Chinese folk religionist	2,700,000
Hindu	1,630,000
Christian	1,490,000
other	1,120,000
Maldives	
Sunnī Muslim	285,000
Mali	
Muslim	9,620,000
traditional beliefs	960,000
Christian	110,000
Malta	
Roman Catholic	357,000
other	25,000
Marshall Islands	
Protestant	32,000
Roman Catholic	4,000
other	16,000
Martinique	
Roman Catholic	333,000
other	52,000
Mauritania	
Sunnī Muslim	2,650,000
other	20,000
Mauritius	
Hindu	600,000
Roman Catholic	320,000
Muslim	190,000
other	70,000
Mayotte	
Sunnī Muslim	151,000
Christian	5,000
Mexico	
Roman Catholic	89,380,000
Protestant	3,780,000
other Christian	1,800,000
other (mostly nonreligious)	3,920,000
Micronesia	
Roman Catholic	48,000
Protestant	44,000
other	26,000
Moldova	
Romanian Orthodox	1,500,000
Russian (Moldovan) Orthodox	410,000
other (mostly nonreligious)	2,390,000
Monaco	
Roman Catholic	26,000
other	6,000
Mongolia	
Tantric Buddhist (Lamaist)	2,300,000
Muslim	100,000
Morocco	
Muslim (mostly Sunnī)	28,780,000
other	50,000
Mozambique	
traditional beliefs	8,980,000
Muslim	5,390,000
Roman Catholic	2,210,000
Protestant	1,750,000
other	770,000
Myanmar (Burma)	
Buddhist	37,300,000
Christian	2,050,000
Muslim	1,600,000
traditional beliefs	480,000
Hindu	210,000
other	100,000
Namibia	
Protestant (mostly Lutheran and Dutch Reformed)	910,000
Roman Catholic	293,000
African Christian	125,000
Anglican	98,000
other	345,000
Nauru	
Protestant	6,000
Roman Catholic	3,200
other	2,600
Nepal	
Hindu	21,370,000
Buddhist	1,780,000
Muslim	870,000
other	680,000
Netherlands, The	
Roman Catholic	5,080,000
Dutch Reformed Church (NHK)	2,380,000
Reformed Churches	1,270,000
Muslim	690,000
nonreligious	6,040,000
other	440,000
Netherlands Antilles	
Roman Catholic	155,000
other	55,000
New Caledonia	
Roman Catholic	129,000
Protestant	31,000
other	51,000
New Zealand	
Anglican	670,000
Roman Catholic	500,000
Presbyterian	490,000
Methodist	130,000
Baptist	60,000
Ratana	40,000
Mormon	40,000
nonreligious	950,000
other	960,000
Nicaragua	
Roman Catholic	3,510,000
Protestant	800,000
other (mostly nonreligious)	500,000
Niger	
Sunnī Muslim	8,940,000
traditional beliefs	1,110,000
other	30,000
Nigeria	
Muslim	53,000,000
traditional beliefs	23,400,000
Protestant	18,400,000
Roman Catholic	10,100,000

Religious affiliation	2000 population
African Christian	8,300,000
Anglican	6,300,000
other	3,800,000
Northern Mariana Islands	
Roman Catholic	43,000
other	29,000
Norway	
Evangelical Lutheran (Church of Norway)	3,970,000
other	520,000
Oman	
Ibāḍīyāh Muslim	1,780,000
Sunnī Muslim	340,000
Hindu	180,000
Christian	90,000
other	30,000
Pakistan	
Sunnī Muslim	106,170,000
Shīʿī Muslim	28,310,000
Christian	2,830,000
Hindu	2,550,000
other	1,700,000
Palau	
Roman Catholic	7,000
Modekne	5,000
Protestant	5,000
other	2,000
Panama	
Roman Catholic	2,260,000
Protestant	410,000
other	150,000
Papua New Guinea	
Protestant	2,960,000
Roman Catholic	1,390,000
Anglican	190,000
other	390,000
Paraguay	
Roman Catholic	4,860,000
Protestant	270,000
other	370,000
Peru	
Roman Catholic	22,880,000
Protestant	1,700,000
other (mostly nonreligious)	1,080,000
Philippines	
Roman Catholic	63,290,000
Protestant	4,140,000
Muslim	3,490,000
Aglipayan	2,010,000
Church of Christ (Iglesia ni Cristo)	1,780,000
other	1,610,000
Poland	
Roman Catholic	35,050,000
Polish Orthodox	550,000
other (mostly nonreligious)	3,050,000
Portugal	
Roman Catholic	9,220,000
other	780,000
Puerto Rico	
Roman Catholic	2,540,000
Protestant	1,110,000
other	270,000
Qatar	
Muslim (mostly Sunnī)	570,000
other	30,000
Réunion	
Roman Catholic	650,000
other (mostly Muslim)	80,000
Romania	
Romanian Orthodox	19,480,000
Roman Catholic	1,140,000
other	1,820,000
Russia	
Russian Orthodox	23,840,000
Muslim	14,600,000
Protestant	1,330,000
Jewish	600,000
other (mostly nonreligious)	105,630,000
Rwanda	
Roman Catholic	4,700,000
traditional beliefs	1,810,000
Protestant	650,000
Muslim	70,000
St. Kitts and Nevis	
Anglican	13,000
Methodist	11,000
other	15,000
St. Lucia	
Roman Catholic	124,000
other	33,000
St. Vincent and the Grenadines	
Anglican	47,000
Methodist	24,000
Roman Catholic	13,000
other	29,000
Samoa	
Mormon	46,000
Congregational	44,000
Roman Catholic	38,000
Methodist	22,000
other	29,000
San Marino	
Roman Catholic	24,000
other	3,000
São Tomé and Príncipe	
Roman Catholic	129,000
Protestant	15,000
Saudi Arabia	
Sunnī Muslim	20,550,000
Shīʿī Muslim	740,000
Christian	650,000
other	80,000
Senegal	
Sunnī Muslim	9,190,000
traditional beliefs	600,000
Christian	200,000
Seychelles	
Roman Catholic	71,000
other	11,000
Sierra Leone	
Sunnī Muslim	3,140,000
traditional beliefs	1,570,000
Christian	520,000
Singapore	
Buddhist and Taoist	1,766,000
Muslim	489,000
Protestant	287,000
Roman Catholic	135,000
Hindu	107,000
nonreligious	474,000
other	20,000
Slovakia	
Roman Catholic	3,260,000
Slovak Evangelical	330,000
atheist	520,000
other	1,290,000
Slovenia	
Roman Catholic	1,620,000
other	340,000
Solomon Islands	
Protestant	195,000
Anglican	158,000
Roman Catholic	89,000
other	24,000
Somalia	
Sunnī Muslim	7,240,000
other	10,000
South Africa[4]	
Christian	23,390,000
Protestant	11,530,000
Dutch (Afrikaans) Reformed Churches	4,140,000
other Protestant	7,390,000
Methodist	2,060,000
Presbyterian	460,000
United Congregational	440,000
Lutheran	880,000
Apostolic Faith Mission of South Africa	460,000
New Apostolic Church	170,000
other Apostolic	480,000
Baptist	280,000
Pentecostal Protestant	80,000
African Protestant Church	40,000
Full Gospel	230,000
Pentecostal	20,000
Salvation Army	40,000
Seventh-day Adventist	100,000
Swiss	50,000
Assemblies of God	170,000
other	1,450,000
Roman Catholic	2,660,000
Anglican	1,330,000
Greek Orthodox	30,000
black independent churches	7,820,000
Zion Christian Church	1,730,000
other	6,100,000
Mormon	10,000
Hindu	440,000
Muslim	380,000
Jewish	80,000
other beliefs	30,000
nonreligious	420,000
not stated	10,460,000
Spain	
Roman Catholic	26,780,000
Muslim	460,000
other (mostly nonreligious)	12,890,000
Sri Lanka	
Buddhist	13,340,000
Hindu	2,980,000
Muslim	1,450,000
Roman Catholic	1,330,000
other	150,000
Sudan, The	
Sunnī Muslim	25,610,000
traditional beliefs	5,860,000
Christian	3,190,000
other	420,000
Suriname	
Hindu	118,000
Roman Catholic	91,000
Muslim	85,000
Protestant	71,000
other	66,000
Swaziland	
Christian	720,000
other (mostly traditional beliefs)	360,000
Sweden	
Church of Sweden (Lutheran)	7,660,000
other	1,200,000
Switzerland	
Roman Catholic	3,310,000
Protestant	2,870,000
other	1,000,000
Syria	
Sunnī Muslim	12,070,000
Shīʿī Muslim	1,960,000
Christian	900,000
Druze	490,000
other	890,000
Taiwan	
nonreligious	10,590,000
Buddhist	5,060,000
Taoist	4,010,000
I Kuan Tao	980,000
Protestant	440,000
Roman Catholic	320,000
Tien Te Chiao	210,000
Tien Ti Chiao	190,000
Confucianism (Li)	150,000
Hsuan Yuan Chiao	140,000
Muslim	50,000
Shinto (Tenrikyo)	20,000
Baha'i	20,000
Tajikistan	
Sunnī Muslim	5,050,000
Shīʿī Muslim	320,000
Russian Orthodox	90,000
other (mostly nonreligious)	850,000
Tanzania	
Christian	15,530,000
Muslim	13,060,000
traditional beliefs	6,710,000
Thailand	
Buddhist	59,180,000
Muslim	2,520,000
Christian	340,000
other	380,000
Togo	
traditional beliefs	2,510,000
Roman Catholic	1,150,000
Sunnī Muslim	750,000
Protestant	600,000
Tonga	
Free Wesleyan	43,000
Roman Catholic	16,000
other	41,000
Trinidad and Tobago	
Roman Catholic	380,000
Hindu	307,000
Protestant	243,000
Anglican	141,000
Muslim	75,000
other	146,000
Tunisia	
Sunnī Muslim	9,540,000
other	50,000
Turkey	
Muslim (mostly Sunnī)	65,510,000
other	160,000
Turkmenistan	
Muslim (mostly Sunnī)	4,250,000
Russian Orthodox	120,000
other (mostly nonreligious)	520,000
Tuvalu	
Congregational	9,200
other	1,600
Uganda	
Roman Catholic	10,390,000
Anglican	9,150,000
Muslim (mostly Sunnī)	2,460,000
other	1,320,000
Ukraine	
Ukrainian Orthodox (Russian patriarchy)	9,670,000
Ukrainian Orthodox (Kiev patriarchy)	4,830,000
Ukrainian Autocephalous Orthodox	340,000
Ukrainian Catholic (Uniate)	3,480,000
Protestant	1,770,000
Roman Catholic	590,000
Jewish	430,000
other (mostly nonreligious)	28,550,000
United Arab Emirates	
Sunnī Muslim	2,420,000
Shīʿī Muslim	480,000
other	120,000
United Kingdom	
Christian	39,370,000
Anglican	25,970,000
Protestant	5,950,000
Roman Catholic	5,820,000
Eastern Orthodox	590,000
other Christian	1,040,000
Muslim	840,000
Hindu	420,000
Jewish	310,000
Sikh	240,000
other (mostly nonreligious and atheist)	18,530,000
United States	
Christian (professing)	235,742,000
Christian (affiliated)	191,828,000
Independent	78,550,000
Protestant	64,570,000
Roman Catholic	58,000,000
Eastern Orthodox	5,762,000
Anglican	2,400,000
other Christian	10,080,000
multi-affiliated Christians	–27,534,000
Christian (unaffiliated)	43,914,000
non-Christian	42,915,000
nonreligious	25,078,000
Jewish	5,621,000
Muslim	4,132,000
Buddhist	2,450,000
atheist	1,150,000
Hindu	1,032,000
New-Religionist	811,000
Baha'i	753,000
Ethnic religionist	435,000
Sikh	234,000
Chinese folk-religionist	78,000
other	1,141,000
Uruguay	
Roman Catholic	2,570,000
Protestant	150,000
other	560,000
Uzbekistan	
Muslim (mostly Sunnī)	21,790,000
Russian Orthodox	240,000
other (mostly nonreligious)	2,730,000
Vanuatu	
Presbyterian	71,000
Roman Catholic	29,000
Anglican	28,000
other	71,000
Venezuela	
Roman Catholic	22,410,000
other	1,760,000
Vietnam	
Buddhist	52,510,000
Roman Catholic	6,090,000
New-Religionist	
Cao Dai	2,770,000
Hoa Hao	1,660,000
other	15,740,000
Virgin Islands (U.S.)	
Protestant	55,000
Roman Catholic	41,000
other	25,000
West Bank	
Muslim (mostly Sunnī)	1,790,000
Jewish[5]	220,000
Christian and other	170,000
Western Sahara	
Sunnī Muslim	245,000
Yemen	
Muslim (mostly Sunnī)	17,460,000
other	20,000
Yugoslavia	
Serbian Orthodox	6,670,000
Sunnī Muslim	2,030,000
Roman Catholic	620,000
other (mostly nonreligious)	1,340,000
Zambia	
traditional beliefs	2,590,000
Protestant	2,190,000
Roman Catholic	1,620,000
other	3,180,000
Zimbabwe	
traditional beliefs	4,590,000
Protestant	2,400,000
African Christian	1,530,000
Roman Catholic	790,000
other	2,030,000

[1]Official 1986 census figure is 5.9 percent. [2]Includes the Golan Heights and East Jerusalem; excludes the West Bank and Gaza Strip. [3]Many Japanese practice both Shintoism and Buddhism. [4]Excludes the former black independent states of Bophuthatswana, Ciskei, Transkei, and Venda, in which there are about 6,040,000 Christians and 2,180,000 practicers of traditional beliefs. [5]Excludes East Jerusalem.

Vital statistics, marriage, family

This table provides some of the basic measures of the factors that influence the size, direction, and rates of population change within a country. The accuracy of these data depends on the effectiveness of each respective national system for registering vital and civil events (birth, death, marriage, etc.) and on the sophistication of the analysis that can be brought to bear upon the data so compiled.

Data on birth rates, for example, depend not only on the completeness of registration of births in a particular country but also on the conditions under which those data are collected: Do all births take place in a hospital? Are the births reported comparably in all parts of the country? Are the records of the births tabulated at a central location in a timely way with an effort to eliminate inconsistent reporting of birth events, perinatal mortality, etc.? Similar difficulties attach to death rates but with the added need to identify "cause of death." Even in a developed country such identifications are often left to nonmedical personnel, and in a developing country with, say, only one physician for every 10,000 population, there will be too few physicians to perform autopsies to assess accurately the cause of death after the fact and also too few to provide ongoing care at a level where records would permit inference about cause of death based on prior condition or diagnosis.

Calculating natural increase, which at its most basic is simply the difference between the birth and death rates, may be affected by the differing degrees of completeness of birth and death registration for a given country. The total fertility rate may be understood as the average number of children that would be borne per woman if all childbearing women lived to the end of their childbearing years and bore children at each age at the average rate for that age. Calculating a meaningful fertility rate requires analysis of changing age structure of the female population over time, changing mortality rates among mothers and their infants, and changing medical practice at births, each improvement of natural survivorship or medical support leading to greater numbers of live-born children and greater numbers of children who survive their first year (the basis for measurement of infant mortality, another basic indicator of demographic conditions and trends within a population).

As indicated above, data for causes of death are not only particularly difficult to obtain, since many countries are not well equipped to collect the data, but also difficult to assess, as their accuracy may be suspect and their meaning may be subject to varying interpretation. Take the case of a citizen of a less developed country who dies of what is clearly a lung infection: Was the death complicated by chronic malnutrition, itself complicated by a parasitic infestation, these last two together so weakening the subject that he died of an infection that he might have survived had his general health been better? Similarly, in a developed country: Someone may die from what is identified in an autopsy as a cerebrovascular accident, but if that accident occurred in a vascular system that was weakened by diabetes, what was the actual cause of death? Statistics on causes of death seek to identify the "underlying" cause (that which sets the final train of events leading to death in motion) but often must settle for the most proximate cause or symptom. Even this kind of analysis may be misleading for those charged with interpreting the data with a view to ordering health-care priorities for a particular country. The eight groups of causes of death utilized here include most, but not all, of the detailed causes classified by the World Health Organization and would not, thus, aggregate to the country's crude death rate for the same year. Among the

Vital statistics, marriage, family

country	vital rates						causes of death (rate per 100,000 population)								
	year	birth rate per 1,000 population	death rate per 1,000 population	infant mortality rate per 1,000 live births	rate of natural increase per 1,000 population	total fertility rate	year	infectious and parasitic diseases	malignant neoplasms (cancers)	endocrine and metabolic disorders	diseases of the nervous system	diseases of the circulatory system	diseases of the respiratory system	diseases of the digestive system	accidents, poisoning, and violence
Afghanistan	1998	42.4	17.4	143.6	25.0	6.0	…	…	…	…	…	…	…	…	…
Albania	1999	19.9	6.5	43.1	13.4	2.4	1993	10.8	53.8	5.1	24.1	187.0	84.5	16.5	41.7
Algeria	1999	27.0	5.5	43.8	21.5	3.3	…	…	…	…	…	…	…	…	…
American Samoa	1999	26.5	4.2	10.5	22.3	3.7	1990	16.4[4]	46.8	16.4[5]	…	131.1[6]	65.6[7]	…	58.5
Andorra	1998	10.8[8]	3.3[8]	6.4	7.5[8]	1.3[9]	…	…	…	…	…	…	…	…	…
Angola	1999	47.2	25.3	197.8	21.9	6.6	…	…	…	…	…	…	…	…	…
Antigua and Barbuda	1997	21.6	6.4	20.7	15.2	1.7	1995	10.4	96.2	57.7	13.3	242.6	42.9	19.2	37.0
Argentina	1998	18.9	7.8	19.1	11.1	2.6	1996	28.1	145.7	19.1[5]	9.7	297.3	64.8	32.5	52.2
Armenia	1999	13.5	9.0	15.0	4.5	1.7	1997	9.2	96.5	32.6	4.4	336.6	38.9	23.9	37.9
Aruba	1999	13.6	6.1	6.7	6.7	1.8	1998	26.1	118.0	29.3[5]	4.3	184.0	35.9	14.1	52.2
Australia	2000	13.0	7.6	6.0	5.4	1.8	1995	6.0	190.0	23.0	17.0	296.0	52.0	21.0	41.0
Austria	1999	9.6	9.6	4.4	0.0	1.3[13]	1997	2.5	233.5	19.9	0.5[14]	532.6	29.9	28.4	54.9
Azerbaijan	1999	21.6	9.5	81.6[13]	12.1	2.7	1995	29.7	61.9	11.8	11.3	335.3	84.9	34.3	45.9
Bahamas, The	1996	20.7	5.4	18.4	15.3	2.3	1995	13.3	85.6	36.3	0.7	160.1	26.6	14.4	40.0
Bahrain	1999	21.2	3.9	21.3	17.3	2.8	1998	5.4	37.8	22.7	4.6	85.9	22.7	13.3	14.5
Bangladesh	1999	25.7	8.9	73.3	16.8	2.9	…	…	…	…	…	…	…	…	…
Barbados	1999	14.5	8.2	16.2	6.2	1.8	1995	27.3	162.5	149.2	22.7	365.5	55.7	34.1	36.0
Belarus	1998	9.7	13.5	14.3	–3.8	1.3	1997	8.8	191.9	8.7[19]	11.5	673.9	68.7	27.5	154.5
Belgium	1999	11.1	10.2	4.8	0.9	1.6	1994	13.4	275.0	21.7	29.2	383.4	92.5	42.6	68.5
Belize	1999	30.2	5.4	27.0	24.8	3.7	1995	23.5	37.7	22.1	6.9	118.9	47.5	16.1	67.3
Benin	1999	45.4	12.4	97.8	33.0	6.4	…	…	…	…	…	…	…	…	…
Bermuda	1996	13.9	6.9	3.6	7.0	1.8[9]	1990	…	181.5	…	…	344.4	25.2	…	38.6
Bhutan	1999	36.9	9.4	60.0	27.5	5.4	…	…	…	…	…	…	…	…	…
Bolivia	2000	31.9	23.3	62.0[9]	23.3	3.8[9]	…	…	…	…	…	…	…	…	…
Bosnia and Herzegovina	1999	13.2	8.7	26.4	4.5	1.7	1989	9.9	122.6[21]	12.6	11.9	344.1	29.0	29.2	47.1
Botswana	2000	29.6	22.1	39.0[12]	7.5	3.8	…	…	…	…	…	…	…	…	…
Brazil	1999	19.5	9.1	39.3	10.4	2.2	1996	*33.5*	*65.9*	*23.3*[19]	*9*[12]	*159.1*	*56.4*	*25.9*	*75.9*
Brunei	1999	21.1	3.1	9.0	18.0	2.7	…	…	…	…	…	…	…	…	…
Bulgaria	1998	7.9	14.3	12.8	–6.4	1.2	1998	9.4	192.9	25.4	9.7	954.4	67.6	38.8	60.7
Burkina Faso	1999	45.7	17.2	110.3	28.5	6.5	…	…	…	…	…	…	…	…	…
Burundi	1999	40.8	16.6	72.3	24.2	6.3	…	…	…	…	…	…	…	…	…
Cambodia	1999	34.9	11.3	81.0	23.6	4.9	…	…	…	…	…	…	…	…	…
Cameroon	1999	36.9	11.8	72.2	25.1	4.9	…	…	…	…	…	…	…	…	…
Canada	1998	11.4	7.2	5.5[25]	4.2	1.7[9]	1997	8.3	195.6	23.7	21.9	264.8	66.8	25.4	43.5
Cape Verde	1999	30.8	7.6	55.6	23.2	4.3	…	…	…	…	…	…	…	…	…
Central African Republic	1999	38.0	18.3	103.4	19.7	5.0	….	…	…	…	…	…	…	…	…
Chad	1999	43.1	16.6	115.0	26.5	5.7	…	…	…	…	…	…	…	…	…
Chile	1999	17.7	5.5	9.9	11.7	2.2	1994	14.2	111.9	16.5	8.6	149.5	61.2	37.2	63.6
China	2000	15.4	7.0	39.0	8.4	1.8	1994[23]	15.2	117.7	17.2[19]	4.4	206.4	125.3	25.3	56.6
Colombia	1999	23.4	5.8	25.6	16.0	2.7	1994	13.7	58.3	15.2	4.6	125.3	34.3	15.7	119.5
Comoros	1999	40.2	9.8	88.8	30.4	5.4	…	…	…	…	…	…	…	…	…
Congo, Dem. Rep. of the	1999	46.4	15.0	99.5	31.4	6.5	…	…	…	…	…	…	…	…	…
Congo, Rep. of the	1999	39.0	16.3	103.2	22.7	5.1	…	…	…	…	…	…	…	…	…
Costa Rica	1998	21.8	4.2	12.6	17.6	2.6	1994	9.7	80.0	12.6	8.5	126.6	40.6	24.6	49.7
Côte d'Ivoire	1999	41.8	16.2	94.2	25.6	5.9	…	…	…	…	…	…	…	…	…
Croatia	1997	12.1	11.4	8.2	0.7	1.9[9]	1996	8.8	227.2	25.4[19]	8.0	547.4	41.4	52.1	70.7
Cuba	1998	13.6	7.0	6.4	6.6	1.6	1995	12.8	133	25.9	11.1	305.5	64.1	24.9	84.6
Cyprus	1998	13.4	8.2	7.0	5.2	2.1[17]	…	…	…	…	…	…	…	…	…
Czech Republic	1999	9.0	10.9	5.9[25]	–1.9	1.2	1998	2.6	272.1	15.0	11.6	586.7	39.9	40.4	68.1
Denmark	1999	12.3	11.0	5.1	1.3	1.7	1996	10.1	289.2	16.5	15.3	428.4	108.1	46.1	64.1

lesser causes excluded by the present classification are: benign neoplasms; nutritional disorders; anemias; mental disorders; kidney and genito-urinary diseases not classifiable under the main groups; maternal deaths (for which data *are* provided, however, in the "Health services" table); diseases of the skin and musculoskeletal systems; congenital and perinatal conditions; and general senility and other ill-defined (ill-diagnosed) conditions, a kind of "other" category.

Expectation of life is probably the most accurate single measure of the quality of life in a given society. It summarizes in a single number all of the natural and social stresses that operate upon individuals in that society. The number may range from as few as 40 years of life in the least developed countries to as much as 80 years for women in the most developed nations. The lost potential in the years separating those two numbers is prodigious, regardless of how the loss arises—wars and civil violence, poor public health services, or poor individual health practice in matters of nutrition, exercise, stress management, and so on.

Data on marriages and marriage rates probably are less meaningful in terms of international comparisons than some of the measures mentioned above because the number, timing, and kinds of social relationships that substitute for marriage depend on many kinds of social variables—income, degree of social control, heterogeneity of the society (race, class, language communities), or level of development of civil administration (if one must travel for a day or more to obtain a legal civil ceremony, one may forgo it). Nevertheless, the data for a single country say specific things about local practice in terms of the age at which a man or woman typically marries, and the overall rate will at least define the number of legal civil marriages, though it cannot say anything about other, less formal arrangements (here the figure for the legitimacy rate for children in the next section may identify some of the societies in which economics or social constraints may operate to limit the number of marriages that are actually confirmed on civil registers). The available data usually include both first marriages and remarriages after annulment, divorce, widowhood, or the like.

The data for families provide information about the average size of a family unit (individuals related by blood or civil register) and the average number of children under a specified age (set here at 15 to provide a consistent measure of social minority internationally, though legal minority depends on the laws of each country). When well-defined family data are not collected as part of a country's national census or vital statistics surveys, data for households have been substituted on the assumption that most households worldwide represent families in some conventional sense. But increasing numbers of households worldwide are composed of unrelated individuals (unmarried heterosexual couples, aged [or younger] groups sharing limited [often fixed] incomes for reasons of economy, or homosexual couples). Such arrangements do not yet represent great numbers overall. Increasing numbers of census programs, however, even in developing countries, are making more adequate provision for distinguishing these nontraditional, often nonfamily households.

Internet resources for further information:

- World Health Organization (World) http://www.who.ch/
- Pan American Health Organization (the Americas) http://www.paho.org
- National Center for Health Statistics (U.S.) http://www.cdc.gov/nchswww/nchshome.htm

expectation of life at birth (latest year)		nuptiality, family, and family planning															country
		marriages			age at marriage (latest)						families (F), households (H) (latest)						
		year	total number	rate per 1,000 population	groom (percent)			bride (percent)			families (households)		children		induced abortions		
male	female				19 and under	20–29	30 and over	19 and under	20–29	30 and over	total ('000)	size	number under age 15	percent legitimate	number	ratio per 100 live births	
47.3	46.3	...	...	...	...	...	...	...	...	...	H 2,110	H 6.2	H 2.8[1]	...	...	...	Afghanistan
68.4	74.2	1997	25,260	6.8	1.5[2]	80.4[2]	18.1[2]	24.0[2]	71.4[2]	4.6[2]	F 675	F 3.9	F 1.6	...	...	...	Albania
68.1	70.5	1996	156,870	5.6	0.7[3]	67.1[3]	32.2[3]	29.8[3]	61.4[3]	8.8[3]	H 4,102	H 7.1	H 3.0	...	...	...	Algeria
70.8	79.8	1993	325	6.1	...	...	...	...	...	...	H 7	H 7.0	H 2.7	72.0	...	...	American Samoa
80.5	86.5	1998	208	3.2	...	...	...	...	...	...	...	...	...	...	...	...	Andorra
36.9	39.3	...	...	...	...	...	...	...	...	...	...	H 5.0	...	...	...	...	Angola
69.1	74.0	1998	1,418	22.1	1.0[10]	37.4[11]	61.6	3.7[10]	52.4[11]	43.9	H 18	H 3.2	H 1.2	23.4	...	...	Antigua and Barbuda
71.4	78.4	1996	148,721	4.2	5.6	71.5	22.9	26.0	58.6	15.4	H 10,097	H 3.2	H 1.0	67.5	...	...	Argentina
62.2	71.1	1995	14,200	4.2	5.0[12]	73.8[12]	21.2[12]	39.3[12]	49.9[12]	10.8[12]	H 559	H 4.5	H 1.8	86.0	30,571	59.8	Armenia
74.8	81.7	1998	564	6.1	...	...	...	...	...	...	H 19	H 3.6	...	57.5	...	...	Aruba
76.0	81.1	1996	109,386	6.0	0.7	54.5	44.8	3.6	63.6	32.8	H 6,636	H 2.6	H 0.6	75.0	...	...	Australia
74.7	80.9	1998	39,143	4.8	1.1[15]	49.9[15]	49.0[15]	4.2[15]	62.0[15]	33.8[15]	H 3,058	H 2.6	H 0.5	70.5	...	...	Austria
58.8	67.6	1994	47,147	6.3	1.2[16]	80.4[16]	18.4[16]	24.8[16]	63.9[16]	11.3[16]	H 1,381	H 5.2	H 1.7	94.8	42,134	23.2	Azerbaijan
70.9	77.6	1996	2,628	9.3	...	14.0	86.0	—	26.1	73.9	H 74	H 3.9	...	45.7	...	...	Bahamas, The
70.6	75.5	1998	3,677	5.7	2.6[17]	65.4[17]	32.0[17]	28.0[17]	54.6[17]	17.4[17]	H 67	H 6.5	H 2.2	100.0	...	...	Bahrain
60.1	59.5	1997	1,181,000	9.7	...	...	...	...	...	...	H 19,980	H 5.6	...	...	...	...	Bangladesh
72.4	78.0	1995	3,564	13.5	0.1[18]	40.2[18]	59.7[18]	1.4[18]	53.6[18]	44.9[18]	H 67	H 3.5	H 1.5	26.9	723	19.6	Barbados
62.3	74.6	1997	69,735	6.8	5.4[15]	69.8[15]	24.8[15]	27.1[15]	53.1[15]	19.8[15]	H 2,796	H 3.6	H 0.8	87.9	174,098	181.7	Belarus
74.3	81.1	1996	50,601	5.0	0.6[17]	59.5[17]	39.9[17]	4.0[17]	66.3[17]	29.7[17]	F 3,613	F 2.7	F 0.5	88.7	...	...	Belgium
67.2	71.3	1997	1,543	6.6	6.3[17]	58.4[17]	35.3[17]	23.4[17]	51.0[17]	25.6[17]	H 42,000	H 5.3	H 2.2	40.3	990	15.1	Belize
52.0	56.2	...	...	...	...	...	...	...	...	...	...	H 5.9	...	...	...	...	Benin
74.8	78.7	1994	944	15.4	0.2[20]	37.4[20]	62.4[20]	1.5[20]	49.4[20]	49.1[20]	H 24	H 2.5	H 0.5	57.7	92	11.0	Bermuda
60.0	63.0	...	...	...	...	...	...	...	...	...	...	H 5.4	...	...	...	...	Bhutan
60.8	65.9	...	...	...	...	...	...	...	...	...	H 1,655	H 3.8	H 1.6	80.9	...	...	Bolivia
66.9	73.0	1991	27,923	6.0	2.3	74.2	23.5	28.6	58.9	12.5	H 1,203	H 3.4	H 1.1	92.6	...	...	Bosnia and Herzegovina
59.5	65.6	1986	1,638	1.5	—	33.0	67.0	5.0	69.2	25.8	H 125	H 5.7	H 2.0	28.8	17	0.1	Botswana
58.6	68.2	1995	...	4.7	7.0[12]	68.7[12]	24.3[12]	31.2[12]	54.3[12]	14.5[12]	F 39,768	F 3.9	1.2	...	...	...	Brazil
74.0	78.0	1995	1,793	6.1	10.6[22]	50.1[22]	39.3[22]	11.4[22]	54.7[22]	33.9[22]	H 45	H 5.8	H 2.0	99.6	...	...	Brunei
68.7	76.0	1996	...	4.3	3.4[17]	73.1[17]	23.5[17]	26.9[17]	60.4[17]	12.7[17]	H 2,795	H 3.0	...	74.3	97,023	134.8	Bulgaria
46.5	47.3	...	...	...	...	...	...	...	...	...	...	H 6.2	...	...	...	...	Burkina Faso
45.5	47.2	...	...	...	...	...	...	...	...	...	...	H 5.0	...	...	...	...	Burundi
53.0	60.0	...	...	...	...	...	...	...	...	...	...	H 5.6	...	...	...	...	Cambodia
54.3	55.9	...	...	...	...	...	...	...	...	...	...	H 5.7	...	...	...	...	Cameroon
74.9	81.2	1995	160,256	5.4	0.9	49.3	49.8	3.6	57.9	38.5	H 11,580	H 2.5	H 0.6	83.8	70,549	18.7	Canada
65.4	72.0	1994	1,200	3.2	...	...	...	...	...	...	F 59	F 5.1	...	28.9	...	...	Cape Verde
45.4	49.1	...	...	...	...	...	...	...	...	...	...	H 5.9	...	...	...	...	Central African Republic
46.1	51.1	...	...	...	...	...	...	...	...	...	...	H 5.0	...	...	...	...	Chad
72.2	79.0	1996	83,547	5.8	4.7	67.5	27.8	18.6	62.2	19.2	H 3,537	H 3.8	...	61.9	67	—	Chile
69.0	73.0	1994	9,290,027	7.8	...	...	...	...	...	...	H 278.6[24]	H 4.1	H 1.1	...	10,500,000	47.7	China
66.1	74.0	...	...	...	...	...	...	...	...	...	F 4,772	F 5.3	F 2.5	75.2	...	...	Colombia
57.5	61.8	...	...	...	...	...	...	...	...	...	...	H 5.6	...	...	...	...	Comoros
47.3	51.7	...	...	...	...	...	...	...	...	...	...	H 2.3	...	...	...	...	Congo, Dem. Rep. of the
44.9	50.4	...	...	...	...	...	...	...	...	...	H 326	H 4.7	H 2.0	...	...	...	Congo, Rep. of the
73.1	78.2	1997	22,422	6.5	7.1[17]	60.9[17]	32.0[17]	26.3[17]	52.0[17]	94.7[17]	H 772	H 4.1	...	50.3	...	...	Costa Rica
44.5	47.7	...	...	...	...	...	...	...	...	...	...	H 8.0	...	...	...	...	Côte d'Ivoire
69.5	77.1	1997	24,517	5.3	1.2[15]	65.2[15]	33.6[15]	13.9[15]	66.8[15]	19.3[15]	H 1,544	H 3.1	H 0.6	92.7	12,339	22.9	Croatia
73.6	78.5	1997	60,220	5.4	5.2[17]	51.8[17]	43.0[17]	18.0[17]	49.4[17]	32.6[17]	F 2,860	F 3.7	H 1.6	...	83,963	57.1	Cuba
75.0	80.0	1996	5,761	7.8	0.8	54.6	44.6	8.1	64.2	27.7	H 160	H 3.5	H 1.1	99.6	...	...	Cyprus
70.8	78.0	1997	57,086	5.6	3.7[15]	66.5[15]	29.8[15]	15.0[15]	65.8[15]	19.2[15]	H 3,557	H 2.9	...	82.2	48,086	53.2	Czech Republic
74.0	79.1	1997	34,108	6.5	0.4[17]	36.2[17]	63.4[17]	1.4[17]	47.9[17]	50.7[17]	H 2,027	H 2.2	...	53.5	17,720	53.2	Denmark

Vital statistics, marriage, family (continued)

country	vital rates						causes of death (rate per 100,000 population)								
	year	birth rate per 1,000 population	death rate per 1,000 population	infant mortality rate per 1,000 live births	rate of natural increase per 1,000 population	total fertility rate	year	infectious and parasitic diseases	malignant neoplasms (cancers)	endocrine and metabolic disorders	diseases of the nervous system	diseases of the circulatory system	diseases of the respiratory system	diseases of the digestive system	accidents, poisoning, and violence
Djibouti	1999	41.2	15.1	105.2	26.1	5.9	…	…	…	…	…	…	…	…	…
Dominica	1999	18.7	7.4	17.7	11.3	2.1	1994	23.1	125.0	59.8	9.5	237.8	38.0	21.7	28.5
Dominican Republic	1999	25.6	4.8	37.5	20.8	3.0	1985[26]	85	45	15[5]	7[14]	165	41	25	*56*
East Timor[27]	…	…	…	…	…	…	…	…	…	…	…	…	…	…	…
Ecuador	1999[1]	22.3	5.1	30.7	11.4	2.6	1995	29.7	50.8	17.5	7.2	80.8	46.0	23.1	65.1
Egypt	2000	25.4	7.8	62.3	17.6	3.2	1992	49.0	22.4	17.3	9.5	313.5	83.4	33.5	28.8
El Salvador	1999	29.4	6.4	30.2	23.0	3.4	1994[28]	42	52	9[5]	2[14]	124	36	14	135
Equatorial Guinea	1999	38.5	13.0	91.2	25.5	5.0	…	…	…	…	…	…	…	…	…
Eritrea	1999	42.5	12.5	78.2	30.0	5.9	…	…	…	…	…	…	…	…	…
Estonia	1998	8.5	13.4	9.3	–4.9	1.2	1995	13.7	221.1	8.2	13.0	771.9	42.5	36.0	198.8
Ethiopia	1999	45.3	17.5	102.8	27.8	7.1	…	…	…	…	…	…	…	…	…
Faroe Islands	1999	13.6	8.7	7.1	22.3	2.4	1992	4.3	191.3	14.9[5]	—	352.8	59.5	14.9	57.4
Fiji	1999	23.7	5.8	14.9	17.9	2.9	…	…	…	…	…	…	…	…	…
Finland	1999	11.2	9.6	4.2	1.6	1.7[13]	1995	7.7	196.6	12.5	20.1	459.7	73.6	38.0	85.8
France	1998	12.6	9.2	4.8	3.4	1.7[25]	1994	12.8	207.7	27.8	20.7	288.2	63.9	43.9	76.1
French Guiana	1999	22.9	4.7	14.5	18.2	3.2	1989	61.7	58.1	16.3	10.9	114.3	20.9	13.6	98.0
French Polynesia	1999	22.8	4.7	11.0	18.1	2.8	1994–95	14.0	104.0	14.0	10.0	123.0	47.0	17.0	52.0
Gabon	1999	27.9	13.1	83.1	14.8	3.8	…	…	…	…	…	…	…	…	…
Gambia, The	1999	42.8	13.5	80.8	29.3	5.8	…	…	…	…	…	…	…	…	…
Gaza Strip	1999	43.8	4.4	26.7	39.4	6.7	…	…	…	…	…	…	…	…	…
Georgia	1999	11.1	14.3	52.0	3.2	1.4	1990	12.7	100.8	14.6	4.3	548.4	43.3	8.5	56.1
Germany	1997	9.9	10.5	5.0[15]	–0.6	1.4	1995	7.4	260.7	34.5	18.0	525.7	66.0	51.2	48.2
Ghana	1999	30.9	10.2	58.3	20.7	4.1	…	…	…	…	…	…	…	…	…
Greece	1999	9.4	9.5	6.7	–0.1	1.3	1998	6.7	213.4	8.3	9.4	492.4	54.9	22.1	42.8
Greenland	1997	19.6	8.7	25.4[13]	10.9	2.6	1995	29.5	198.7	3.9	1.8	214.4	9.6	5.7	206.5
Grenada	1999	27.6	5.2	11.1	22.4	3.6	1987	9.6	82.8	57.3	7.4	264.3	45.6	38.2	…
Guadeloupe	1997	18.2	5.9	8.2	12.3	2.3	1996	23.8	134.8	26.2	…	183.7	32.1	31.4	68.1
Guam	1999	23.7	4.5	10.0	19.2	3.3	1994	1.4	60.0	26.5[5]	6.8	141.8	27.9	1.4	64.1
Guatemala	1999	35.6	6.8	46.2	28.8	4.7	…	…	…	…	…	…	…	…	…
Guernsey	1999	10.5	8.2	5.2	2.3	1.3	1996	5.3	282.3	15.9	15.9	441.1	150.0	49.4	24.7
Guinea	1999	40.6	17.3	126.3	23.3	5.5	…	…	…	…	…	…	…	…	…
Guinea-Bissau	1999	39.9	15.9	126.3	15.9	5.3	…	…	…	…	…	…	…	…	…
Guyana	1999	18.1	8.2	39.8	9.9	2.1	1994	38.9	33.5	45.7	10.6	212.8	44.5	27.6	59.0
Haiti	1999	32.2	15.3	98.9	16.9	4.6	…	…	…	…	…	…	…	…	…
Honduras	1999	31.0	7.1	40.8	23.9	4.0	…	…	…	…	…	…	…	…	…
Hong Kong	1999	7.5	4.8	3.2[13]	2.7	1.3	1998	14.4	160.5	7.4	3.9	126.7	99.6	21.0	21.2
Hungary	1999	9.4	14.2	9.7	–4.8	1.3	1995	7.9	322.0	20.1	11.5	721.4	63.0	115.6	111.5
Iceland	1998	15.3	6.7	3.6	8.6	2.1	1995	6.7	176.4	3.7	19.5	308.6	82.0	3.0	56.6
India	1998[30]	26.4	9.0	72.0	17.4	3.2[9]	…	…	…	…	…	…	…	…	…
Indonesia[27]	1999	23.6	6.3	43.7	16.7	2.7	…	…	…	…	…	…	…	…	…
Iran	1999	19.4	5.5	31.3	13.9	2.4	1990[32]	*34*	*61*	*12*[19]	*26*	*304*	*48*	*24*	*108*
Iraq	1999	35.4	6.4	62.5	29.0	5.0	…	…	…	…	…	…	…	…	…
Ireland	1999	14.4	8.2	5.7	6.2	1.9	1997	4.8	205.6	10.8[5]	0.2[14]	369.9	153.4	9.4	38.4
Isle of Man	1999	12.3	13.5	2.3[33]	–1.2	1.6	1998	2.8	298.4	11.1	31.8	504.3	225.2	38.7	52.5
Israel	1999	19.5	6.2	8.1	13.3	2.7	1995	10.4	148.9	23.4	11.5	278.4	26.5	23.1	35.8
Italy	1999	9.2	9.9	5.5[25]	–0.7	1.2	1995	13.3	258.2	34.7	20.3	424.3	59.1	47.0	49.0
Jamaica	1998	23.1	6.2	14.5	16.9	2.8[25]	1991	8.1	84.1	51.3	7.5	189.5	30.2	14.1	8.4
Japan	1998	10.8	6.4	3.6	4.4	1.4[25]	1997	14.6	220.4	12.4	7.0	237.7	98.0	30.0	52.4
Jersey	1999	12.0	9.3	5.8	2.7	1.6	…	…	…	…	…	…	…	…	…
Jordan	2000	26.2	2.6	33.2[13]	23.6	3.4	…	…	…	…	…	…	…	…	…
Kazakhstan	1997	14.7	10.1	33.0	4.6	1.7	1996	45.7	133.0	10.9	1.4	436.2	71.0	32.9	101.1
Kenya	1999	31.8	13.9	69.6	17.9	4.0	…	…	…	…	…	…	…	…	…
Kiribati	1999	32.9	9.2	56.8	23.7	4.4	…	…	…	…	…	…	…	…	…
Korea, North	1995–2000	18.3	15.8	82.6	2.5	2.0	…	…	…	…	…	…	…	…	…
Korea, South	1999	15.3	5.8	10.0	9.5	1.7	1997	10.8	115.4	20.2	5.1	121.5	24.4	34.4	70.6
Kuwait	1999	22.8	2.4	11.9	20.4	3.4	1997	5.4	22.7	10.6	3.1	84.6	11.0	4.7	34.8
Kyrgyzstan	1999	24.8	7.2	39.0	17.6	3.1	1996	12.6	25.7	8.3	1.5	278.5	75.0	9.8	21.4
Laos	1999	38.8	13.0	90.0	25.8	5.6	…	…	…	…	…	…	…	…	…
Latvia	1999	7.5	14.0	15.0	–6.0	1.1[13]	1998	19.5	231.8	12.2[19]	12.7	775.6	34.6	42.2	161.8
Lebanon	1999	20.5	6.5	30.4	14.0	2.1	…	…	…	…	…	…	…	…	…
Lesotho	1999	31.3	13.2	77.6	18.1	4.0	…	…	…	…	…	…	…	…	…
Liberia	1999	47.8	16.9	136.9	30.9	6.5	…	…	…	…	…	…	…	…	…
Libya	1999	27.6	3.5	24.1	31.4	3.8	…	…	…	…	…	…	…	…	…
Liechtenstein	1999	12.1	6.8	5.3	5.3	1.5	1997	23.0[12]	199.7	…	6.6[12]	613.9	29.0	22.6	146.9
Lithuania	1998	10.0	11.0	9.3	–1.0	1.4	1995	16.4	203.2	8.0	10.3	654.2	40.5	32.1	176.0
Luxembourg	1999	13.0	8.8	4.7	4.2	1.7	1995	4.6	248.5	21.7	14.9	375.1	61.5	40.2	59.0
Macau	1999	12.6	4.6	10.0	8.0	1.4	1998	10.0	77.8	3.9	1.7	117.1	39.3	11.1	23.9
Macedonia	1998	14.6	8.4	16.3	6.2	2.0[17]	1997	17.6	138.3	24.1[5]	28.0	462.8	39.5	15.9	32.4
Madagascar	2000	43.2	13.0	87.0	30.2	5.9	…	…	…	…	…	…	…	…	…
Malawi	1999	39.2	22.3	123.4	16.9	5.5	…	…	…	…	…	…	…	…	…
Malaysia	1999	24.4	4.4	11.0	20.0	3.1	1997	15.2	19.8	3.8	1.1	37.2	8.7	2.1	13.2
Maldives	1999	34.5	6.9	47.0	27.6	5.2	…	…	…	…	…	…	…	—	…
Mali	1999	49.6	19.5	125.1	30.1	6.9	…	…	…	…	…	…	…	…	…
Malta	1998	11.9	9.1	5.3	2.8	1.8[17]	1997	5.1	281.9	25.1	12.8	354.1	70.9	26.1	28.5
Marshall Islands	2000	45.2	6.4	41.0	38.8	6.6	1993[34]	169.9	68.4	…	—	155.1	105.1	63.3	36.7
Martinique	1999	16.4	6.4	8.2	10.0	1.8	1996	21.9	150.1	27.7	…	206.6	36.3	27.2	47.2
Mauritania	1999	43.7	14.3	79.6	29.4	6.4	…	…	…	…	…	…	…	…	…
Mauritius	1999	16.9	6.9	18.4	10.0	2.0	1996	12.1	56.8	24.9	0.8	291.2	34.9	21.7	46.2
Mayotte	1999	46.1	9.4	73.2	36.7	6.4	…	…	…	…	…	…	…	…	…
Mexico	1998	27.8	4.6	25.8	23.2	2.8	1995	22.0	52.9	46.9	6.7	106.8	47.1	42.1	62.4
Micronesia	1995	23.7	4.0	20.4	19.7	2.5[17]	…	…	…	…	…	…	…	…	…
Moldova	1999	12.8	12.5	43.5	0.3	1.7	1995	14.6	133.3	10.7	11.8	559.4	76.3	114.7	113.7
Monaco	1999	10.2	13.2	6.0	–3.0	1.8	…	…	…	…	…	…	…	…	…
Mongolia	1999	22.4	6.4	49.0	16.0	2.5	1994[35]	*33*	*118*	*3*	*14*	*200*	*110*	*55*	*64*
Morocco	1999	25.3	6.1	51.6	19.2	3.1	1992	10.2	14.0	12.2	4.9	35.5	9.5	7.9	19.2

expectation of life at birth (latest year) male	female	nuptiality, family, and family planning: marriages: year	total number	rate per 1,000 population	age at marriage (latest): groom (percent): 19 and under	20–29	30 and over	bride (percent): 19 and under	20–29	30 and over	families (F), households (H) (latest): families (households): total ('000)	size	children: number under age 15	percent legitimate	induced abortions: number	ratio per 100 live births	country
48.7	52.3	...	...	...	...	...	...	...	...	...	...	H 5.6	...	96.8	...	...	Djibouti
70.3	76.1	1996	230	3.1	—	37.0	63.0	2.7	56.2	41.1	H 19	H 3.6	H 2.2	24.1	...	...	Dominica
70.9	75.1	1994	14,883	2.0	...	...	...	...	...	...	H 1,804	H 3.9	...	32.8	562	0.5	Dominican Republic
...	...	...	...	...	...	...	...	...	...	...	...	...	...	...	...	...	East Timor[27]
69.5	74.9	1996	72,094	6.2	12.6	61.7	25.7	32.6	51.4	16.0	...	H 4.1	...	67.9	...	...	Ecuador
61.3	65.5	1994	451,817	3.2	3.4	58.7	37.9	11.2	77.1	11.7	H 9,733	H 4.9	H 2.1	100.0	...	...	Egypt
65.8	73.2	1994	27,761	5.1	6.6[22]	54.8[22]	38.6[22]	21.5[22]	51.4[22]	27.1[22]	H 1,092	H 4.8	...	29.4	...	...	El Salvador
52.0	56.8	...	...	...	...	...	...	...	...	...	...	H 4.5	...	...	...	...	Equatorial Guinea
53.0	57.9	1992	68	...	...	...	...	...	...	...	...	[30]	...	...	...	...	Eritrea
64.4	75.5	1998	5,430	3.7	3.2[15]	56.4[15]	40.4[15]	13.9[15]	53.9[15]	32.2[15]	H 427	H 3.1	H 0.8	47.8	16,887	127.1	Estonia
44.7	46.3	...	...	...	...	...	...	...	...	...	...	H 4.5[29]	...	...	...	...	Ethiopia
74.8	81.7	1990	203	4.3	...	...	...	...	...	...	F 14	F 3.0	F 0.9	57.5	26	3.3	Faroe Islands
65.2	70.1	1995	7,903	9.9	...	...	...	...	...	...	F 97	F 6.0	F 2.5	82.7	...	...	Fiji
73.5	80.8	1998	24,023	4.7	1.0[15]	47.1[15]	51.9[15]	3.5[15]	55.9[15]	40.6[15]	H 2,270	H 2.2	...	62.8	10,437	17.2	Finland
74.6	82.3	1997	283,984	4.8	0.2[17]	51.9[17]	47.9[17]	1.4[17]	63.2[17]	35.4[17]	H 20,899	H 2.6	H 1.0	63.9	157,886	22.2	France
72.6	79.4	1992	716	5.3	...	...	...	...	...	...	H 33	H 3.4	H 1.2	20.3	388	16.8	French Guiana
70.0	75.0	1996	1,200	5.7	...	...	...	...	...	...	H 40	H 4.3	H 1.7	40.5	...	...	French Polynesia
49.1	51.8	...	...	...	...	...	...	...	...	...	H 136	H 4.0	...	...	...	...	Gabon
50.9	54.7	...	...	...	...	...	...	...	...	...	...	H 8.3	...	...	...	...	Gambia, The
69.4	71.9	...	...	...	...	...	...	...	...	...	...	...	...	...	...	...	Gaza Strip
61.1	68.3	1996	19,253	3.7	9.1	59.4	31.5	32.7	51.2	16.1	H 1,244	H 4.1	H 1.1	82.3	43,549	77.3	Georgia
74.1	80.2	1997	422,319	5.1	0.7[15]	44.6[15]	54.7[15]	3.7[15]	56.3[15]	40.0[15]	H 37,457	H 2.2	H 0.3	82.0	97,937	12.8	Germany
56.1	59.0	...	...	...	...	...	...	...	...	...	H 2,355	H 4.9	H 2.2	...	...	...	Ghana
75.7	81.1	1998	55,489	5.3	0.9[17]	53.6[17]	45.5[17]	9.6[17]	68.9[17]	21.5[17]	H 2,990	H 3.3	H 0.7	96.7	12,289	12.1	Greece
62.9	68.5	1996	208	3.7	1.1[2]	44.6[2]	54.3[2]	2.7[2]	59.6[2]	37.7[2]	F 31	F 1.8	F 0.5	29.2	962	80.7	Greenland
62.7	66.3	1991	...	4.3	...	...	...	...	...	...	H 24	H 3.7	H 2.2	18.1	...	...	Grenada
73.3	80.1	1997	1,936	4.7	0.5[2]	51.4[2]	48.0[2]	7.2[2]	61.4[2]	31.4[2]	H 112	H 3.4	H 0.9	37.0	561	8.7	Guadeloupe
73.0	78.0	1995	1,507	10.1	3.0[22]	55.5[22]	41.5[22]	9.2[22]	59.3[22]	31.5[22]	H 31	H 4.0	H 1.3	50.1	...	...	Guam
63.8	69.2	1995	49,194	4.6	17.6	56.0[22]	26.4[18]	40.9[18]	40.3[18]	18.8[18]	H 1,806	H 5.2	...	34.8	...	...	Guatemala
76.5	82.6	1996	340	5.8	...	...	...	...	...	...	H 21	H 2.6	H 0.5	73.2	...	...	Guernsey
44.0	49.1	...	...	...	...	...	...	...	...	...	H 1,064	H 4.1	...	...	...	...	Guinea
46.4	50.9	...	...	...	...	...	...	...	...	...	H 124	H 6.9	H 2.8	11.3	...	...	Guinea-Bissau
61.3	67.6	...	...	...	...	...	...	...	...	...	H 150	H 5.1	H 2.1	...	...	...	Guyana
47.3	50.9	...	...	...	...	...	...	...	...	...	H 1,147	H 4.4	H 1.8	...	...	...	Haiti
63.2	66.3	...	...	...	...	...	...	...	...	...	H 463	H 5.7	H 2.8	...	...	...	Honduras
76.9	82.3	1999	31,300	4.6	0.9[15]	42.7[15]	56.4[15]	3.0[15]	63.5[15]	33.5[15]	H 1,840	H 3.3	...	94.5	17,600	25.2	Hong Kong
66.7	75.7	1998	45,500	4.5	3.7[15]	69.1[15]	27.2[15]	17.5[15]	64.8[15]	17.7[15]	F 3,058	F 2.9	F 0.8	77.6	76,600	72.8	Hungary
76.8	81.1	1998	1,238	5.6	0.1[15]	40.7[15]	59.2[15]	1.2[15]	55.6[15]	43.2[15]	H 85	H 2.9	H 1.3	36.0	858	19.8	Iceland
61.5	62.7	...	...	...	...	...	...	...	...	...	H 151,033	H 5.6	H 2.4	...	581,215	...	India
65.3	70.1	1992–93[31]	1,423,774	7.6	...	...	...	...	...	...	H 39,695	H 4.5	H 1.8	...	...	...	Indonesia[27]
68.1	70.7	1996	479,263	7.8	...	...	...	...	...	...	H 9,759	H 4.8	H 2.2	...	...	...	Iran
65.5	67.6	1992	144,055	7.8	...	...	...	...	...	...	H 1,873	H 8.9	H 4.1	...	...	...	Iraq
73.9	79.5	1999	18,526	4.9	0.7[12]	62.2[12]	37.1[12]	1.6[12]	74.7[12]	23.7[12]	H 541	H 3.3	H 1.3	65.5	...	...	Ireland
73.9	80.8	1998	435	6.0	0.2	39.5	60.3	1.6	45.1	53.3	H 29,377	H 2.4	...	76.1	...	...	Isle of Man
76.4	85.0	1997	32,510	5.6	3.5[12]	74.0[12]	22.5[12]	21.2[12]	68.3[12]	10.5[12]	H 1,355	H 3.7	H 1.1	98.5	16,903	14.7	Israel
75.7	82.3	1997	275,381	4.8	0.6[17]	56.2[17]	43.2[17]	4.8[17]	71.5[17]	23.7[17]	F 19,766	F 2.6	F 0.5	90.2	134,137	25.5	Italy
73.1	77.0	1996	18,708	7.4	...	...	...	...	...	...	H 554	H 4.2	H 1.4	14.9	...	...	Jamaica
77.2	83.8	1996	795,000	6.3	1.2	61.6	37.2	2.6	77.0	20.4	H 43,447	H 2.8	...	99.0	338,867	28.1	Japan
75.9	80.9	1994	542	6.4	...	...	...	...	...	...	H 29	H 2.6	H 0.4	88.1	296	28.0	Jersey
74.9	79.9	1996	102,558	6.4	4.4[17]	70.0[17]	25.6[17]	37.3[17]	54.7[17]	8.0[17]	H 11,891	H 6.1	H 3.4	...	...	...	Jordan
63.0	73.0	1996	102,558	6.4	6.0	71.5	22.5	27.9	56.5	15.6	H 3,824	H 4.0	H 1.4	86.6	193,462	76.4	Kazakhstan
47.6	49.3	...	...	...	...	...	...	...	...	...	H 1,938	H 3.4	H 2.7	...	...	...	Kenya
56.5	62.4	...	...	...	...	...	...	...	...	...	H 11	H 6.6	H 2.5	...	...	...	Kiribati
50.8	57.4	...	...	...	...	...	...	...	...	...	H 4,054	H 4.8	H 1.7	...	...	...	Korea, North
70.5	78.4	1995	320,395	7.1	0.3	67.7	32.0	1.7	86.1	12.2	H 12,961	H 3.7	H 1.0	99.5	...	...	Korea, South
75.2	76.6	1997	9,612	5.3	6.1[22]	72.2[22]	21.7[22]	35.9[22]	53.3[22]	10.8[22]	H 246	H 3.9	H 1.6	100.0	...	...	Kuwait
64.0	72.0	1995	26,866	6.0	5.4	79.0	15.6	38.1	52.0	9.9	H 856	H 4.2	H 1.9	83.2	27,111	23.1	Kyrgyzstan
53.0	55.0	...	...	...	...	...	...	...	...	...	...	H 6.0	...	...	...	...	Laos
64.1	75.5	1998	9,641	3.9	—	61.7	38.3	—	69.0	31.0	H 732	H 2.7	H 0.8	62.9	24,227	122.5	Latvia
68.6	73.4	...	...	...	...	...	...	...	...	...	H 405	H 5.3	H 2.2	...	...	...	Lebanon
51.4	54.7	...	...	...	...	...	...	...	...	...	H 330	H 4.8	H 2.0	...	...	...	Lesotho
49.2	52.1	...	...	...	...	...	...	...	...	...	H 474	H 5.0	...	...	...	...	Liberia
73.1	77.4	...	...	...	...	...	...	...	...	...	F 383	F 5.4	F 2.9	...	...	...	Libya
74.7	82.2	1998	423	13.2	—	54.5	44.5	0.0	66.3	29.2	H 8	H 3.0	H 0.7	86.0	...	...	Liechtenstein
66.5	76.9	1997	18,769	5.0	7.1[15]	68.5[15]	24.4[15]	23.0[15]	57.8[15]	19.2[15]	H 1,000	H 2.9	H 0.8	82.0	27,829	71.0	Lithuania
73.7	80.2	1997	2,007	4.8	0.9[15]	49.1[15]	50.0[15]	4.0[15]	61.6[15]	34.4[15]	H 145	H 2.6	H 0.5	82.5	...	...	Luxembourg
75.0	80.0	1998	1,451	3.4	0.6[15]	38.6[15]	60.8[15]	2.8[15]	58.0[15]	39.2[15]	H 99	H 3.5	H 0.9	99.3	...	...	Macau
70.4	74.7	1998	13,993	7.0	5.0	75.1	19.9	26.5	63.8	9.7	H 468	H 3.8	H 1.3	90.5	18,754	57.9	Macedonia
52.3	56.8	...	...	...	...	...	...	...	...	...	H 1,709	H 4.7	H 2.0	...	...	...	Madagascar
37.3	38.4	...	...	...	...	...	...	...	...	...	...	H 4.3	...	...	...	...	Malawi
71.0	75.0	...	...	...	...	...	...	...	...	...	H 3,580	H 4.9	...	...	...	...	Malaysia
66.5	70.2	1995	4,998	19.7	13.7[18]	58.2[18]	29.1[18]	...	...	...	...	H 7.2	...	...	...	...	Maldives
45.2	47.5	...	...	...	...	...	...	...	...	...	H 1,364	H 5.0	...	...	...	...	Mali
74.4	80.1	1998	2,376	6.3	2.0[15]	74.0[15]	24.0[15]	9.5[15]	76.0[15]	14.5[15]	H 76	H 3.3	H 1.2	91.8	...	...	Malta
63.7	67.4	...	...	...	...	...	...	...	...	...	H 5	H 8.7	...	...	...	...	Marshall Islands
78.9	77.2	1993	1,555	4.2	0.1[22]	46.8[22]	53.1[22]	3.3[22]	61.5[22]	35.2[22]	H 107	H 3.3	H 0.8	34.1	1,753	30.6	Martinique
48.3	52.4	...	...	...	...	...	...	...	...	...	H 246	H 5.0	...	...	...	...	Mauritania
66.7	74.5	1997	10,887	9.5	1.8[15]	56.2[15]	42.0[15]	25.8[15]	54.0[15]	20.2[15]	F 155	F 5.3	F 2.0	72.8	...	...	Mauritius
57.0	61.1	...	...	...	...	...	...	...	...	...	H 19	H 4.9	H 2.3	89.2	...	...	Mayotte
68.6	74.8	1996	670,523	6.9	14.0	65.1	20.9	32.5	54.7	12.8	H 17,152	H 5.1	H 2.0	72.5	28,734	1.0	Mexico
65.7	69.6	...	...	...	...	...	...	...	...	...	H 11	H 6.8	...	...	...	...	Micronesia
59.8	69.2	1996	26,089	6.0	8.2[17]	70.0[17]	21.8[17]	38.2[17]	45.0[17]	16.8[17]	H 1,144	H 3.4	H 1.1	89.6	44,252	78.4	Moldova
74.7	82.9	...	...	...	...	...	...	...	...	...	H 14	H 2.2	H 0.3	96.8	...	...	Monaco
65.0	68.0	1996	14,200	6.0	...	...	...	...	...	...	F 428	F 4.8	...	...	...	...	Mongolia
66.6	71.1	...	...	...	...	...	...	...	...	...	H 2,819	H 5.8	H 2.5	...	...	...	Morocco

Vital statistics, marriage, family (continued)

country	vital rates						causes of death (rate per 100,000 population)								
	year	birth rate per 1,000 population	death rate per 1,000 population	infant mortality rate per 1,000 live births	rate of natural increase per 1,000 population	total fertility rate	year	infectious and parasitic diseases	malignant neoplasms (cancers)	endocrine and metabolic disorders	diseases of the nervous system	diseases of the circulatory system	diseases of the respiratory system	diseases of the digestive system	accidents, poisoning, and violence
Mozambique	1999	38.8	22.5	140.4	16.3	5.0	...	...	...	...	...	...	...	...	...
Myanmar (Burma)	1999	20.8	9.1	71.0[17]	11.7	2.7	...	...	...	...	...	...	...	...	...
Namibia	1999	35.7	18.3	69.6	13.2	4.9	...	...	...	...	...	...	...	...	...
Nauru	1999	28.3	7.5	11.1	20.8	3.8	...	...	...	...	...	...	...	...	...
Nepal	1999	33.8	10.1	79.0	23.7	4.4	...	...	...	...	...	...	...	...	...
Netherlands, The	1999	12.7	8.9	5.0	3.8	1.6	1995	7.6	236.1	28.1	13.3	335.1	81.8	32.6	33.5
Netherlands Antilles	1997	17.0	5.9	12.2[9]	11.1	2.1[9]	1995[36]	16.7	149.0	61.7	9.9	71.6	40.8	21.4	47.6
New Caledonia	1999	20.8	5.3	6.3	15.5	2.5	1996	17.6	110.6	8.1[16]	14.6	124.2	60.3	19.6	63.7
New Zealand	1998	14.6	6.9	5.5	7.7	1.9	1996	5.6	200.7	22.1	12.3	317.2	86.4	20.9	46.7
Nicaragua	1999	29.1	5.0	35.9	24.1	3.4	1994[35]	*68*	*62*	*25*	*12*	*156*	*64*	*29*	*120*
Niger	1999	52.1	23.6	126.2	28.5	7.2	...	...	...	...	...	...	...	...	...
Nigeria	1999	40.6	13.6	74.9	27.0	5.7	...	...	...	...	...	...	...	...	...
Northern Mariana Islands	1999	21.1	2.4	11.0	18.7	1.8	1994–96	[37]	33.3	10.9[5]	—	53.3	12.6[37]	—	47.0
Norway	1998	13.2	10.0	4.0	3.2	1.8	1994	8.3	238.3	16.4	16.4	450.1	102.2	29.8	51.8
Oman	1999	38.0	4.2	24.2	33.8	6.1	...	...	...	...	...	...	...	...	...
Pakistan	1999	33.1	9.8	84.6	23.3	4.7	...	...	...	...	...	...	...	...	...
Palau	1999	20.1	7.5	17.7	12.6	2.5	1993	43.6	136.9	...	...	192.9	43.6	...	112.0
Panama	1999	20.1	5.0	21.6	15.1	2.4	1997	21.2	64.4	18.2[5]	1.3[14]	122.1	25.4	9.6	37.1
Papua New Guinea	2000	32.7	8.0	59.9	24.7	4.4	...	...	...	...	...	...	...	...	...
Paraguay	1999	31.6	4.9	32.3	26.7	4.2	1994[38]	*29*	*53*	*18*	*6*	*162*	*31*	*18*	*48*
Peru	1999	26.1	5.7	39.0	20.4	3.2	...	...	...	...	...	...	...	...	...
Philippines	2000	27.1	5.6	33.0	21.5	3.4	1996	66.7	42.9	11.0[5]	7.1	136.3	76.9	22.4	43.4
Poland	1999	9.9	9.9	8.9	0.0	1.4	1995	6.4	202.3	14.0	8.1	504.5	34.3	33.0	74.5
Portugal	1999	11.5	10.3	6.2	1.2	1.5	1995	10.2	201.7	43.9	10.0	438.9	80.2	45.7	59.8
Puerto Rico	1999	15.1	7.3	10.5[13]	7.8	1.9	1993	59.4	122.2	66.7	19.2	242.3	80.5	43.9	34.1
Qatar	1999	16.3	4.1	23.0	12.2	3.3	1992	3.4	21.4[21]	7.3[20]	2.6	59.9	7.5	3.4	36.0
Réunion	1999	22.5	5.6	8.9	16.9	2.6	1993	14.9	99.7	22.5	16.0	170.1	41.5	59.5[39]	65.3
Romania	1999	10.7	12.3	20.3	–1.6	1.4	1995	14.1	164.1	10.4	8.8	736.1	75.8	68.2	78.7
Russia	1999	9.0	13.8	18.0	–4.8	1.3	1998	19.0	203.0	11.0[12]	10.9[12]	749.0	57.0	38.0	185.0
Rwanda	1999	35.7	21.1	120.1	14.6	5.3	...	...	...	...	...	...	...	...	...
St. Kitts and Nevis	1999	19.5	10.0	18.7	9.5	2.5	1995	57.8	108.0	55.3	20.1	482.4	65.3	50.3	45.2
St. Lucia	1999	22.8	5.5	16.1	17.3	2.5	1995	20.7	98.6	79.3	13.8	226.9	29.7	21.4	50.3
St. Vincent and the Grenadines	1999	19.0	6.3	17.7	12.7	2.2	1997	36.8	90.0	56.6	14.4	228.4	42.2	28.8	—
Samoa	1999	28.1	4.9	22.0	23.2	4.0	1992[34]	3.1	11.2	9.9	3.1	24.2	9.9	6.8	2.5
San Marino	1999	11.0	7.5	6.5	3.5	1.3	1991–95	...	229.4	2.4[5]	...	324.8	10.7	...	45.2
São Tomé and Príncipe	1999	43.2	8.0	52.0	35.2	6.1	...	...	...	...	...	...	...	...	...
Saudi Arabia	2000	37.5	6.0	52.9	31.5	6.3	...	...	...	...	...	...	...	...	...
Senegal	1999	38.4	8.8	59.5	29.6	5.3	...	...	...	...	...	...	...	...	...
Seychelles	1999	18.6	6.9	18.2	11.7	1.9	1994	43.3	128.6	16.2	16.2	288.4	98.8	39.3	43.3
Sierra Leone	1999	46.2	19.9	150.8	26.3	6.1	...	...	...	...	...	...	...	...	...
Singapore	1999	13.4	4.8	5.0[40]	8.6	1.5[13]	1995	12.4	130.5	10.9	3.0	186.1	97.5	13.7	37.3
Slovakia	1999	10.2	9.7	8.3	0.7	1.3	1997	4.0	209.0	12.0	5.0	529.0	70.0	41.0	69.0
Slovenia	1998	9.0	9.6	5.2	0.6	1.3	1997	4.4	243.9	36.4	9.0	381.1	81.0	55.2	88.6
Solomon Islands	1999	35.6	4.5	26.2	31.1	5.0	...	...	...	...	...	...	...	...	...
Somalia	1999	48.2	18.7	125.8	29.5	7.3	...	...	...	...	...	...	...	...	...
South Africa	1999	22.2	13.5	57.1	8.7	2.6	1995	71.3	55.8	20.5	10.2	98.5	51.9	15.1	112.0
Spain	1998	9.2	9.1	5.2	0.1	1.1	1995	5.9	219.8	23.1	0.4	333.6	28.0	20.4	41.3
Sri Lanka	1999	17.2	6.4	17.0	10.8	2.0	...	...	...	...	...	...	...	...	...
Sudan, The	1999	39.2	10.5	71.8	28.7	5.6	...	...	...	...	...	...	...	...	...
Suriname	1999	21.7	5.7	26.0	16.0	2.5	1992[41]	*40*	*68*	*40*	*11*	*193*	*37*	*32*	*71*
Swaziland	1999	41.1	19.3	108.3	21.8	5.9	...	...	...	...	...	...	...	...	...
Sweden	1999	10.1	10.6	3.4	–0.5	1.5	1995	8.6	234.6	23.2	14.3	525.5	85.8	33.8	48.9
Switzerland	1999	10.3	8.3	3.4	2.0	1.5	1994	16.3	238.7	23.3[19]	18.1	381.5	64.2	27.1	69.3
Syria	1999	31.4	5.4	36.1	26.0	4.1	...	...	...	...	...	...	...	...	...
Taiwan	1999	12.9	5.7	7.2	7.2	1.8	1992	...	101.5	23.7[5]	...	140.1[18]	24.3[42]	18.2[42]	63.7[42]
Tajikistan	1999	30.9	6.7	55.0	24.2	4.0	1993	128.3	40.7	8.8[2, 19]	7.9[2]	222.8	158.7	20.7	181.3
Tanzania	1999	40.6	12.8	82.5	27.8	5.6	...	...	...	...	...	...	...	...	...
Thailand	2000	16.3	5.9	22.0	10.4	1.8	1994	27.6	49.0	7.5	11.0	89.8	91.4	18.4	73.8
Togo	1999	38.9	11.1	86.0	27.8	5.7	...	...	...	...	...	...	...	...	...
Tonga	1999	25.9	6.0	37.9	19.9	3.4	1992	16.3	54.9	15.2	6.1	158.5	31.5	18.3	4.1
Trinidad and Tobago	1997	14.5	7.2	17.1	7.3	1.9	1994	11.6	94.4	119.3	14.7	286.5	49.0	28.6	52.8
Tunisia	1999	18.1	5.0	31.4	13.1	2.1	...	...	...	...	...	...	...	...	...
Turkey	1999	19.3	6.0	50.7	13.3	2.2	1993[42]	24	80	9[5]	2[12]	369	19	10	33
Turkmenistan	1999	29.3	9.0	73.1	20.3	3.7	1994	75.7	55.4	11.2	7.6	337.2	150.3	7.6	60.1
Tuvalu	1998	22.6	8.6	26.2	14.0	3.1	...	...	...	...	...	...	...	...	...
Uganda	1999	48.6	18.9	95.2	29.7	7.0	...	...	...	...	...	...	...	...	...
Ukraine	1999	9.2	16.4	21.7	–7.2	1.3	1996	17.7	192.5	8.3[19]	1.2	784.5	75.3	4.9	157.2
United Arab Emirates	1999	18.0	3.6	95.2	14.4	3.6	...	...	...	...	...	...	...	...	...
United Kingdom	1999	11.9	10.4	5.8	1.5	1.7	1997	6.8	261.2	13.8	18.5	442.1	165.8	39.5	32.7
United States	1999	14.3	8.7	6.9	5.6	2.0	1997	19.6[43]	201.6	30.3	21.0	354.4	85.2	29.5	55.9
Uruguay	1999	16.8	8.8	13.5	7.8	2.3	1990	16.0	222.8	25.5	16.2	378.4	76.3	39.1	61.7
Uzbekistan	1999	26.3	7.9	71.6	18.4	3.1	1993	38.0	48.2	9.4[22]	8.9[22]	300.3	113.8	31.4	49.5
Vanuatu	1999	31.7	5.9	37.0	25.8	4.2	1994[34]	25.0	29.2	9.1	5.5	39.0	30.4	9.7	9.1
Venezuela	1999	22.3	4.9	26.5	17.4	2.6	1994	33.0	60.5	24.1	7.4	144.7	31.9	19.3	74.1
Vietnam	1999	22.0	6.3	32.2	15.7	2.6	...	...	...	...	...	...	...	...	...
Virgin Islands (U.S.)	1999	16.1	5.3	9.9	10.8	2.3	...	...	...	...	...	...	...	...	...
West Bank	1999	45.4	4.6	23.0	40.8	5.2	...	...	...	...	...	...	...	...	...
Western Sahara	1999	45.4	16.6	136.7	28.9	6.7	...	...	...	...	...	...	...	...	...
Yemen	1999	43.5	10.2	72.2	33.3	7.1	...	...	...	...	...	...	...	...	...
Yugoslavia	1997	12.4	10.6	14.3	1.8	1.7	1995	9.0	167.7[21]	23.8	10.1	573.7	40.9	28.3	42.2
Zambia	1999	42.4	22.1	93.7	20.3	5.7	...	...	...	...	...	...	...	...	...
Zimbabwe	1999	25.4	21.3	62.3	4.1	3.4	1990	64.7	28.4	4.9	9.4	40.8	39.5	12.1	44.9

[1]Excludes nomadic tribes. [2]1991. [3]1986. [4]Septicemia only. [5]Diabetes mellitus only. [6]Cerebrovascular disease and heart disease only. [7]Chronic obstructive pulmonary diseases, pneumonia, and influenza only. [8]Official government figures. [9]1999. [10]Under 21 years of age. [11]21–29 years of age. [12]1994. [13]1998. [14]Meningitis only. [15]1996. [16]1989. [17]1995. [18]1993. [19]Includes nutritional disorders. [20]1990. [21]Includes benign neoplasms (cancers). [22]1992. [23]Results based on a sample population of about 100,000. [24]Millions of households. [25]1997. [26]Projected rates based on about 60 percent of the total deaths. [27]Indonesia includes East Timor. [28]Projected rates based on about 75 percent of the total deaths. [29]Ethiopia includes Eritrea. [30]Based on a sample

expectation of life at birth (latest year)		nuptiality, family, and family planning															country
		marriages			age at marriage (latest)						families (F), households (H) (latest)						
		year	total number	rate per 1,000 population	groom (percent)			bride (percent)			families (households)		children		induced abortions		
male	female				19 and under	20–29	30 and over	19 and under	20–29	30 and over	total ('000)	size	number under age 15	percent legitimate	number	ratio per 100 live births	
39.2	37.8	...	...	...	...	...	...	...	...	...	F 1,860	F 4.4	F 2.0	73.1	...	...	Mozambique
59.0	63.0	...	...	...	...	...	...	...	...	...	...	H 5.6	...	...	...	...	Myanmar (Burma)
45.8	42.5	...	...	...	...	...	...	...	...	...	...	H 5.2	...	...	...	...	Namibia
57.0	64.1	1995	57	5.3	...	...	...	...	...	...	H 1	H 8.0	H 2.6	...	...	...	Nauru
58.0	58.0	...	...	...	...	...	...	...	...	...	H 3,345	H 5.6	H 2.3	...	...	...	Nepal
75.2	80.7	1998	87,000	5.5	0.5[15]	47.4[15]	52.1[15]	3.2[15]	60.9[15]	35.9[15]	H 6,185	H 2.3	H 0.4	82.9	22,441	11.8	Netherlands, The
72.3	76.7	1998	1,276	6.1	...	...	...	...	...	...	H 41	H 3.7	H 2.1	51.6	...	...	Netherlands Antilles
69.6	75.6	1999	934	4.5	0.1[12]	46.5[12]	53.4[12]	5.0[12]	61.2[12]	33.8[12]	H 51	H 3.8	...	36.4	...	...	New Caledonia
74.8	80.8	1996	21,506	6.0	0.8[12]	50.6[12]	48.6[12]	3.2[12]	60.8[12]	36.0[12]	H 1,178	H 2.8	H 0.7	58.0	11,460	19.3	New Zealand
66.5	70.4	1991	13,122	3.3	...	...	...	...	...	...	H 752	H 5.8	...	...	...	...	Nicaragua
41.1	40.8	...	...	...	...	...	...	...	...	...	H 1,130	H 6.3	...	...	...	...	Niger
51.7	52.1	...	...	...	...	...	...	...	...	...	H 21,283	H 4.7	...	...	...	...	Nigeria
72.0	78.4	...	...	...	...	...	...	...	...	...	H 7	H 4.6	H 1.5	51.2	...	...	Northern Mariana Islands
75.5	81.3	1996	23,172	5.3	0.4	43.5	56.1	2.1	59.1	38.8	H 1,864	H 2.3	...	51.0	13,672	22.6	Norway
69.4	73.7	...	...	...	...	...	...	...	...	...	...	H 8.0	...	...	...	...	Oman
59.9	61.5	...	...	...	...	...	...	...	...	...	...	H 6.3	...	...	...	...	Pakistan
65.2	71.5	...	...	...	...	...	...	...	...	...	...	H 4.9	...	...	...	...	Palau
72.5	78.0	1995	8,841	3.4	2.4	52.3	45.3	10.4	57.2	32.4	H 524	H 4.4	H 1.5	25.5	...	...	Panama
61.1	65.3	...	...	...	...	...	...	...	...	...	H 674	H 4.6	...	...	...	...	Papua New Guinea
71.0	76.0	1994	23,649	5.0	4.2[22]	64.8[22]	31.0[22]	30.4[22]	50.2[22]	19.4[22]	H 868	H 4.7	1.9	68.7	...	...	Paraguay
68.1	72.8	1993	90,000	4.1	...	...	...	...	...	...	H 3,099	H 5.1	...	57.8	...	...	Peru
67.0	71.0	1993	474,407	7.1	4.9	66.3	28.8	18.0	63.8	18.2	F 9,566	F 5.7	F 2.4	93.9	2,315	...	Philippines
68.9	77.4	1996	203,641	5.3	2.8	77.2	20.0	16.6	70.5	12.9	F 9,435	F 3.6	F 0.9	95.0	491	0.1	Poland
72.0	79.2	1997	63,542	6.5	3.1[15]	70.0[15]	26.9[15]	13.9[15]	68.1[15]	18.0[15]	H 3,150	H 3.1	H 0.8	85.5	...	...	Portugal
70.9	80.0	1996	32,572	8.7	8.5	53.8	37.7	19.4	49.3	31.4	H 1,005	H 3.6	H 1.0	59.6	...	...	Puerto Rico
69.7	74.6	1996	1,641	2.9	4.9	67.5	27.6	29.6	59.7	10.7	H 61	H 6.4	...	...	...	...	Qatar
69.0	76.0	1996	3,313	4.9	1.2[20]	65.2[20]	33.6[20]	12.5[20]	66.8[20]	20.7[20]	H 185	H 3.5	...	44.1	4,302	31.7	Réunion
65.8	73.8	1997	147,105	6.5	2.6[15]	76.0[15]	21.4[15]	25.4[15]	62.1[15]	12.5[15]	H 7,115	H 3.1	...	...	456,221	197.2	Romania
61.8	72.7	1995	1,074,900	7.3	6.5	64.5	29.0	28.5	47.7	23.8	H 40,426	H 3.2	H 0.8	80.4	2,766,362	202.8	Russia
38.6	40.1	...	...	...	...	...	...	...	...	...	H 1,509	H 4.7	2.3	94.9	...	...	Rwanda
66.8	72.5	...	...	...	...	...	...	...	...	...	H 12	H 3.7	H 1.4	19.2	...	...	St. Kitts and Nevis
68.5	75.9	1997	467	3.1	0.8[16]	34.4[16]	64.8[16]	3.5[16]	45.1[16]	51.4[16]	H 33	H 4.0	H 2.0	14.2	...	...	St. Lucia
70.3	73.7	1997	508	4.6	1.0[22]	37.0[22]	62.0[22]	4.8[22]	46.3[22]	48.9[22]	H 27	H 3.9	H 2.0	...	...	...	St. Vincent and the Grenadines
70.0	74.0	1997	...	4.6	0.5[18]	51.0[18]	48.5[18]	8.0[18]	65.0[18]	27.0[18]	F 20	F 7.8	F 3.8	43.5	...	...	Samoa
77.4	84.9	1996	191	7.5	0.6[16]	75.1[16]	24.3[16]	5.3[16]	85.3[16]	9.5[16]	H 9	H 2.6	H 0.4	95.2	...	...	San Marino
63.5	66.3	...	...	...	...	...	...	...	...	...	...	H 4.0	...	9.8	...	...	São Tomé and Príncipe
66.1	69.5	...	...	...	...	...	...	...	...	...	H 1,513	H 6.1	...	...	...	...	Saudi Arabia
60.2	63.4	...	...	...	...	...	...	...	...	...	...	H 8.7	...	...	...	...	Senegal
64.5	75.8	1996	875	11.4	2.0[12]	45.8[12]	42.2[12]	11.2[12]	51.5[12]	29.6[12]	H 13	H 4.8	H 1.9	27.2	387	22.8	Seychelles
42.1	47.8	...	...	...	...	...	...	...	...	...	...	H 6.6	...	...	...	...	Sierra Leone
75.0	80.0	1997	25,667	6.9	0.5	57.3	42.2	3.1	74.5	22.4	H 662	H 4.2	H 1.3	...	14,362	29.6	Singapore
69.4	77.6	1996	27,484	5.1	6.0[17]	76.2[17]	17.8[17]	27.4[17]	62.4[17]	10.2[17]	...	H 3.2	...	86.0	35,879	58.4	Slovakia
70.7	78.7	1996	7,555	3.8	0.5	63.2	36.3	5.8	72.7	21.5	H 637	H 3.1	...	70.2	10,218	54.4	Slovenia
44.7	47.9	...	...	...	...	...	...	...	...	...	H ...	H 5.8	...	...	...	...	Solomon Islands
44.7	47.9	...	...	...	...	...	...	...	...	...	...	H 4.9	...	...	...	...	Somalia
51.9	54.2	1995	148,148	3.6	0.3	39.7	60.0	2.8	54.9	42.3	H 8,688	H 4.6	...	75.9	...	...	South Africa
74.8	82.1	1996	194,635	5.0	1.2[17]	62.5[17]	36.3[17]	5.0[17]	72.8[17]	22.2[17]	F 10,665	F 3.5	...	89.5	47,832	13.1	Spain
69.1	74.1	1996	170,444	9.3	1.3	64.3	34.4	16.7	67.1	16.2	H 3,282	H 4.6	...	96.3	...	...	Sri Lanka
55.1	57.2	...	...	...	...	...	...	...	...	...	H 3,471	H 5.3	...	...	...	...	Sudan, The
68.4	73.2	1995	2,249	5.5	...	...	...	...	...	...	...	H 4.8	...	...	...	...	Suriname
40.8	43.3	...	...	...	...	...	...	...	...	...	H 122	H 5.7	...	...	1,145	...	Swaziland
76.9	82.2	1996	33,484	3.4	0.3	40.5	59.2	1.5	54.0	44.5	H 3,670	H 2.1	H 0.5	46.1	32,117	33.7	Sweden
76.5	82.5	1997	37,575	5.3	0.4[15]	43.6[15]	56.0[15]	2.8[15]	58.8[15]	38.4[15]	H 3,250	H 2.0	0.4	91.2	...	...	Switzerland
67.1	69.3	1994	115,994	8.4	...	...	...	...	...	...	F 1,151	H 6.2	F 2.4	...	...	...	Syria
73.4	79.1	1998	145,678	6.7	1.5[20]	62.3[20]	36.2[20]	6.0[20]	77.7[20]	16.3[20]	H 5,964	H 3.6	H 1.0	97.2	...	...	Taiwan
65.0	71.0	1994	38,820	6.8	10.7	80.6	8.7	49.6	45.7	4.7	H 799	H 6.1	H 2.7	93.0	35,709	22.0	Tajikistan
51.6	53.5	...	...	...	...	...	...	...	...	...	H 3,435	H 5.2	H 2.3	...	...	...	Tanzania
71.0	76.0	1995	470,751	7.9	...	...	...	...	...	...	H 15,551	H 3.8	...	...	...	...	Thailand
53.1	57.1	...	...	...	...	...	...	...	...	...	H 479	H 6.0	...	...	...	...	Togo
67.7	72.2	1994	748	7.7	16.3	63.0	20.7	5.1	65.0	29.9	F 15	F 6.3	F 2.7	80.6	...	...	Tonga
65.1	70.2	1996	7,118	5.6	4.3	54.9	40.8	20.0	52.8	27.2	H 301	H 3.8	H 1.3	...	9	—	Trinidad and Tobago
71.9	75.1	1997	57,100	6.2	...	60.5[22]	39.5[22]	24.7[22]	62.7[22]	20.2[22]	H 1,703	H 5.1	H 1.9	99.8	23,300	10.9	Tunisia
68.4	73.1	1996	486,734	7.8	5.9[17]	74.5[17]	19.6[17]	31.4[17]	58.5[17]	10.1[17]	...	H 4.5	...	...	...	...	Turkey
57.5	64.9	1993	42,106	10.7	3.0[16]	87.4[16]	9.6[16]	16.1[16]	77.1[16]	6.8[16]	H 598	H 5.6	H 2.4	96.5	39,068	31.3	Turkmenistan
62.7	65.1	...	...	...	...	...	...	...	...	...	H 1	H 6.4	H 2.2	82.2	...	...	Tuvalu
41.9	43.2	...	...	...	...	...	...	...	...	...	H 2,766	H 4.8	...	...	...	...	Uganda
60.2	71.9	1997	345,000	6.5	7.5	68.4	24.1	35.2	45.9	18.9	H 14,507	H 3.2	H 0.8	89.2	957,022	159.5	Ukraine
71.4	76.3	1995	...	2.7	...	...	...	...	...	...	H 247	H 5.3	...	...	...	...	United Arab Emirates
74.4	79.7	1995	282,900	5.5	0.8	49.1	50.1	3.6	57.4	39.0	H 29,533	H 2.4	H 1.7	63.2	167,297	22.8	United Kingdom
74.1	79.7	1996	2,324,000	8.8	4.3[20]	51.8[20]	43.9[20]	10.9[20]	55.8[20]	35.3[20]	H 96,391	H 2.6	F 1.0	70.5	1,359,145	32.0	United States
72.7	79.2	1996	17,596	5.5	6.9[22]	57.2[22]	35.9[22]	23.5[22]	51.4[22]	25.1[22]	H 863	H 3.3	H 0.9	73.8	...	...	Uruguay
60.3	67.7	1994	176,300	7.8	11.2	80.7	8.1	49.3	45.3	5.4	H 3,415	H 5.5	H 2.4	95.8	120,434	18.3	Uzbekistan
66.0	70.0	...	...	...	...	...	...	...	...	...	H 28	H 5.1	H 2.2	...	113	2.4	Vanuatu
70.0	76.2	1996	81,951	3.7	9.5	58.7	31.8	27.9	51.7	20.4	H 2,707	H 5.3	H 2.2	47.0	...	...	Venezuela
66.5	71.5	...	...	...	...	...	...	...	...	...	H 12,958[44]	H 4.8[44]	H 1.9[44]	...	...	...	Vietnam
74.0	82.1	1993	3,646	35.1	0.4	33.6	66.0	1.9	45.9	52.2	H 32	H 3.1	H 1.0	38.4	...	...	Virgin Islands (U.S.)
70.2	73.6	...	...	...	...	...	...	...	...	...	...	...	...	...	...	...	West Bank
48.0	50.6	...	...	...	...	...	...	...	...	...	...	...	...	...	...	...	Western Sahara
57.7	61.2	...	...	...	...	...	...	...	...	...	H 1,848	H 5.6	...	...	...	...	Yemen
69.9	74.7	1997	56,004	5.3	2.3[17]	64.5[17]	33.2[17]	18.7[17]	63.5[17]	17.8[17]	H 2,870	H 3.6	H 0.9	...	91,474	65.1	Yugoslavia
37.1	37.5	...	...	...	...	...	...	...	...	...	H 1,370	H 4.4	H 2.1	...	...	...	Zambia
40.3	37.4	...	...	...	...	...	...	...	...	...	H 2,166	H 4.8	1.1	95.8	...	...	Zimbabwe

registration scheme. [31]Muslims only. [32]Projected rates based on about 20 percent of the total deaths. [33]1996–98 average. [34]Registered deaths only. [35]Projected rates based on about 45 percent of the total deaths. [36]Includes Aruba. [37]Diseases of the respiratory system included in infectious and parasitic diseases. [38]Reporting areas only (constituting about 75 percent of the total population). [39]Includes all deaths associated with alcoholism. [40]2000. [41]Projected rates based on about 70 percent of the total deaths. [42]Projected rates based on about 35 percent of the total deaths. [43]Of which AIDS, 6.2. [44]Private households only.

National product and accounts

This table furnishes, for most of the countries of the world, breakdowns of (1) gross national product (GNP)—its global and per capita values, purchasing power parity (PPP), and growth rates (1990–98), (2) principal industrial and accounting components of gross domestic product (GDP), and (3) principal elements of each country's balance of payments, including international goods trade, invisibles, external public debt outstanding, and tourism payments.

Measures of national output. The two most commonly used measures of national output are GDP and GNP. Each of these measures represents an aggregate value of goods and services produced by a specific country. The GDP, the more basic of these, is a measure of the total value of goods and services produced entirely within a given country. The GNP, the more comprehensive value, is composed of both domestic production (GDP) and the net income from current (short-term) transactions with other countries. When the income received from other countries is greater than payments to them, a country's GNP is greater than its GDP. In theory, if all national accounts could be equilibrated, the global summation of GDP would equal GNP.

In the first section of the table, data are provided for the nominal and real GNP. ("Nominal" refers to value in current prices for the year indicated and is distinguished from a "real" valuation, which is one adjusted to eliminate the effect of recent inflation [most often] or, occasionally, of deflation between two given dates.) Both the total and per capita values of this product are denominated in U.S. dollars for ease of comparison, as is a new value for GNP per capita adjusted for purchasing power parity. The latter is a concept that provides a better approximation of the ability of equivalent values of two (or more) national currencies to purchase comparable quantities of goods and services in their respective domestic markets and may differ substantially from two otherwise equal GNP per capita values based solely on currency exchange rates. Beside these are given figures for average annual growth of total and per capita real GNP. GNP per capita provides a rough measure of annual national income per person, but values should be compared cautiously, as they are subject to a number of distortions, notably of exchange rate, but also of purchasing power parity and in the existence of elements of national production that do not enter the monetary economy in such a way as to be visible to fiscal authorities (*e.g.*, food, clothing, or housing produced and consumed within families or communal groups or services exchanged). For reasons of comparability, the majority of the data in this section are taken from the World Bank's *The World Bank Atlas* (annual).

The internal structure of the national product. GDP/GNP values allow comparison of the relative size of national economies, but further information is provided when these aggregates are analyzed according to their industrial sectors of origin, component kinds of expenditure, and cost components.

The distribution of GDP for ten industrial sectors, usually compiled from national sources, is aggregated into three major industrial groups:

1. The primary sector, composed of agriculture (including forestry and fishing) and mineral production (including fossil fuels).

National product and accounts

country	gross national product (GNP), 1998						origin of gross domestic product (GDP) by economic sector, 1998 (%)										
	nominal ('000,000 U.S.$)	per capita		average annual growth rates, 1990–98			primary		secondary			tertiary					other
		nominal (U.S.$)	purchasing power parity (PPP; U.S.$)	real GNP (%)	population (%)	real GNP per capita (%)	agriculture	mining	manufacturing	construction	public utilities	transp., communications	trade	financial svcs.	other svcs.	government	
Afghanistan	5,666[1]	250[1]	…	…	…	…	…	…	…	…	…	…	…	…	…	…	…
Albania	2,718	810	2,864	2.7	0.2	2.5	54	[2]	12[2]	13	[2]	3		—18—			—
Algeria	46,389	1,550	4,595	−1.0	2.6	−3.6	11	23	10	11	—		—24—			13	8
American Samoa	253[1]	4,300[1]	…	…	…	…	…	…	…	…	…	…	…	…	…	…	…
Andorra	850[3]	13,100[3]	…	…	…	…	…	…	…	…	…	…	…	…	…	…	…
Angola	4,578	380	999	−8.2	3.8	−12.0	13	45	6	6	—	—18—			—11—		1
Antigua and Barbuda	565	8,450	8,890	3.4	0.6	2.8	3	1	2	10	3	17	19	14	6	15	10
Argentina	290,261	8,030	11,728	4.2	1.5	2.7	5[3]	2[3]	20[3]	6[3]	2[3]	6[3]	14[3]	18[3]	—24[3]—		3[3]
Armenia	1,728	460	2,074	−4.7	1.0	−5.7	31	[2]	22[2]	9	[2]	5	9		—25—		−1
Aruba	1,728[4]	18,710[4]	…	…	…	…	…	…	…	…	…	…	…	…	…	…	…
Australia	387,006	20,640	21,795	2.8	1.3	1.5	3	4	13	6	2	8	10	16	33	4	1
Austria	216,697	26,830	23,145	1.5	0.6	0.9	3	1	24	7	3	8	19	18	6	10	1
Azerbaijan	3,821	480	2,168	−12.5	1.4	−13.9	20[3]	[2]	25[2, 3]	14[3]	[2]	10[3]		—31[3]—			—
Bahamas, The	3,288[3]	11,830[3]	…	…	…	…	1[6]	15[6]	17[6]	6[6]	2[6]	11[6]	11[6]	19[6]	5[6]	19[6]	−6[6]
Bahrain	4,909	7,640	11,556	1.5	3.5	−2.0	1[5]	17[5]	22[5]	6[5]	2[5]	9[5]	11[5]	18[5]	5[5]	19[5]	−10[5]
Bangladesh	44,224	350	1,407	3.2	1.9	1.3	23	1	18	7	1	10	15	11	11	2	1
Barbados	2,318	8,700	…	…	…	…	6	1	10	8	4	8	35	—17—		12	−1
Belarus	22,332	2,180	6,314	−3.7	0.0	−3.7	13	[7]	36[7]	7	4	12	12		—16—		—
Belgium	258,968	25,380	23,622	1.6	0.3	1.3	1[3]	—	21[3]	5[3]	2[3]	8[3]	12[3]	14[3]	7[3]	24[3]	6[3]
Belize	635	2,660	4,367	0.3	3.3	−3.0	18	1	13	5	2	12	15	8	6	6	14
Benin	2,252	380	857	1.8	3.3	−1.5	38[3]	[7]	9[3, 7]	4[3]	1[3]	7[3]	18[3]	9[3]	—7[3]—		7[3]
Bermuda	2,128[3]	34,950[3]	…	…	…	…	…	…	…	…	…	…	…	…	…	…	…
Bhutan	354	470	1,438	2.1	3.4	−1.3	38	2	12	11	11	8	7	5	—9—		−3
Bolivia	8,013	1,010	2,205	2.0	2.7	−0.7	15	11	18	5	1	12	9	13	6	10	—
Bosnia and Herzegovina	3,788	1,020	…	…	…	…	12	…	24	6	3	9	19	4	14	8	—
Botswana	4,795	3,070	5,796	0.9	2.9	−2.0	3	36	5	6	2	4	18	8	4	14	—
Brazil	767,568	4,630	6,460	1.7	1.6	0.1	7[3]	1[3]	19[3]	9[3]	3[3]	5[3]	7[3]	20[3]	11[3]	13[3]	5[3]
Brunei	7,209	22,280	…	…	…	…	3	[7]	37[7]	7	1	4	10	9	—33—		−4
Bulgaria	10,085	1,220	4,683	−1.8	−0.8	−1.0	19	1	17	3	4	7	7	2	—29—		11
Burkina Faso	2,575	240	866	1.1	2.7	−1.6	30	[7]	20[7]	5	1	4	12		—22—		6
Burundi	911	140	561	−5.5	−4.0	−1.5	46	1[8]	9	5	[8]	4	4	—2—		18	11
Cambodia	2,945	260	1,246	2.0	3.3	−1.3	51	—	6	7	1	4	15	5	7	3	1
Cameroon	8,736	610	1,395	−2.3	3.2	−5.5	41	5	10	4	1			—35—			4
Canada	580,872	19,170	22,814	1.1	1.2	−0.1	2	4	18	6	3	8	12	16	24	6	1
Cape Verde	499	1,200	3,192	2.5	2.8	−0.3	12	—	10	9	—	18	19	12	7	14	−1
Central African Republic	1,053	300	1,098	−0.7	2.4	−3.1	49	4	8	4	1	2	12	—6—		6	8
Chad	1,658	230	843	−1.1	3.4	−4.5	37	1	12	2	1	—24—		—9—		11	3
Chile	73,935	4,990	8,507	6.5	1.8	4.7	7	9	15	5	2	9	18	17	6	2	10
China	923,560	750	3,051	9.6	1.2	8.4	18	[2]	42[2]	7	[2]	6	8		—18—		1
Colombia	100,667	2,470	5,861	1.7	2.2	−0.5	14	4	14	5	…	8	12	—34—		9	—
Comoros	197	370	1,400	−3.1	2.9	−6.0	40	…	4	6	1	5	25	3	1	13	2
Congo, Dem. Rep. of the	5,433	110	733	−8.5	3.6	−12.1	58[5]	4[5]	6[5]	2[5]	2[5]	3[5]	17[5]	—6[5]—		1[5]	1[5]
Congo, Rep. of the	1,899	680	846	−2.6	3.2	−5.8	11[5]	33[5]	8[5]	2[5]	1[5]	12[5]	9[5]	—8[5]—		13[5]	3[5]
Costa Rica	9,771	2,770	5,812	2.0	2.3	−0.3	15	[7]	19[7]	2	3	6	21	12	8	14	—
Côte d'Ivoire	10,196	700	1,484	1.4	3.1	−1.7	28	[2]	20[2]	5	[2]	8	15	—12—		8	4
Croatia	20,786	4,620	6,698	0.5	−0.9	1.4	7	[7]	24[7]	6	3	8	12	13	—14—		13
Cuba	14,754[4]	1,330[4]	…	…	…	…	7[3]	2[3]	37[3]	5[3]	2[3]	4[3]	21[3]	2[3]	—19[3]—		2[3]
Cyprus[9]	8,983	11,920	17,599	2.7	1.4	1.3	4	—	11	8	2	9	20	19	10	14	3
Czech Republic	53,034	5,150	12,197	−0.2	−0.1	−0.1	4	[2]	32[2]	7	[2]	9	12	17	—13—		6
Denmark	175,160	33,040	23,855	2.7	0.4	2.3	4[3]	1[3]	20[3]	6[3]	2[3]	10[3]	13[3]	19[3]	6[3]	22[3]	−3[3]
Djibouti	513[4]	1,170[4]	…	…	…	…	3	—	5	8	5	17	16	10	5	20	11
Dominica	230	3,150	4,777	1.1	0.1	1.0	20	1	9	8	5	17	14	14	1	19	−8
Dominican Republic	14,629	1,770	4,337	3.4	2.1	1.3	12	2	17	12	2	12	20	9	8	8	−2
East Timor	113	130	424	…	…	…	…	…	…	…	…	…	…	…	…	…	…
Ecuador	18,450	1,520	3,003	0.8	2.4	−1.6	17[3]	15[3]	15[3]	2[3]	1[3]	9[3]	15[3]	12[3]	6[3]	7[3]	1[3]

2. The secondary sector, composed of manufacturing, construction, and public utilities.
3. The tertiary sector, which includes transportation and communications, trade (wholesale and retail), restaurants and hotels, financial services (including banking, real estate, insurance, and business services), other services (community, social, and personal), and government services.

The category "other" contains adjustments such as import duties and bank service charges that are not distributed by sector.

There are three major domestic components of GDP expenditure: private consumption (analyzed in greater detail in the "Household budgets and consumption" table), government spending, and gross domestic investment. The fourth, nondomestic, component of GDP expenditure is net foreign trade; values are given for both exports (a positive value) and imports (a negative value, representing obligations to other countries). The sum of these five percentages, excluding statistical discrepancies and rounding, should be 100% of the GDP.

Balance of payments (external account transactions). The external account records the sum (net) of all economic transactions of a current nature between one country and the rest of the world. The account shows a country's net of overseas receipts and obligations, including not only the trade of goods and merchandise but also such invisible items as services, interest and dividends, short- and long-term investments, tourism, transfers to or from overseas residents, etc. Each transaction gives rise either to a foreign claim for payment, recorded as a deficit (*e.g.*, from imports, capital outflows), or a foreign obligation to pay, recorded as a surplus (*e.g.*, from exports, capital inflows) or a domestic claim on another country. Any international transaction automatically creates a deficit in the balance of payments of one country and a surplus in that of another. Values are given in U.S. dollars for comparability.

External public debt. Because the majority of the world's countries are in the less developed bloc, and because their principal financial concern is often external debt and its service, data are given for outstanding external public and publicly guaranteed long-term debt rather than for total public debt, which is the major concern in the developed countries. For comparability, the data are given in U.S. dollars. The data presented in the table come from the World Bank's *Global Development Finance* (formerly *World Debt Tables*).

Tourist trade. Net income or expenditure from tourism (in U.S. dollars for comparability) is often a significant element in a country's balance of payments. Receipts from foreign nationals reflect payments for goods and services from foreign currency resources by tourists in the given country. Expenditures by nationals abroad are also payments for goods and services, but in this case made by the residents of the given country as tourists abroad. The majority of the data in this section are compiled by the World Tourism Organization.

gross domestic product (GDP) by type of expenditure, 1998 (%)					external public debt outstanding (long-term, disbursed only), 1998						balance of payments, 1998 (current external transactions; '000,000 U.S.$)			tourist trade, 1997 ('000,000 U.S.$)		country
consumption		gross domestic invest- ment	foreign trade		total ('000,000 U.S.$)	creditors (%)		debt service			net transfers		current balance of payments	receipts from foreign nationals	expendi- tures by nationals abroad	
private	govern- ment		exports	imports		offi- cial	private	total ('000,000 U.S.$)	repayment(%)		goods, merchan- dise	invisibles				
									princi- pal	inter- est						
...	...	...	...	...	...	...	...	...	...	...	...	...	...	...	...	Afghanistan
...	...	...	...	...	701.3	64.2	35.8	33.2	34.9	65.1	–603.6	538.5	–65.1	27	5	Albania
51	17	27	28	–23	28,469	68.2	31.8	4,587	59.0	41.0	5,700[3]	–2,200[3]	3,500[3]	20	40	Algeria
...	...	...	...	...	...	...	...	...	...	...	...	...	...	2[1]	...	American Samoa
...	...	...	...	...	...	...	...	...	...	...	...	...	...	...	...	Andorra
...	...	...	...	...	10,616	30.4	69.6	1,308	69.9	30.1	1,463.5	–3,323.1	–1,857.6	7	90	Angola
58	22	32	73	–84	...	...	...	...	...	...	–321.3	232.7	–88.6	269	26[1]	Antigua and Barbuda
71		20	10	–13	76,799	26.1	73.9	11,814	53.7	46.3	–3,117	–11,157	–14,274	5,069	2,680	Argentina
103	11	19	19	–53	564.0	100.0	—	36.2	60.5	39.5	–577.5	187.2	–390.3	7	41	Armenia
73	13	11	2		...	...	...	...	...	...	–347.2	324.0	–23.2	666	130	Aruba
59	18	24	20	–22	...	...	...	...	...	...	–5,357	–12,780	–18,137	9,022	6,129	Australia
55	20	26	44	–45	...	...	...	...	...	...	–3,654	–955	–4,609	11,073	10,124	Austria
78[3]	12[3]	38[3]	28[3]	–55[3]	307.7	98.2	1.8	11.5	23.5	76.5	–1,046.2	–318.3	–1,364.5	146[5]	70[5]	Azerbaijan
66[5]	15[5]	23[5]	54[5]	–58[5]	...	...	...	...	...	...	–1,060.5	467.0	–593.5	1,416	250	Bahamas, The
51	21	18	78	–68	...	...	...	...	...	...	–28.5	–702.9	–731.4	248[5]	124[5]	Bahrain
78	14	13	19	–23	15,804	99.4	0.6	570	70.3	29.7	–1,720.6	1,530.8	–189.8	59	170	Bangladesh
59	21	20	58	–57	387.8	69.0	31.0	76.1	61.0	39.0	–644.1	587.6	–56.5	717	74[1]	Barbados
58	20	27	60	–65	748	65.2	34.8	104	60.6	39.4	–1,358.5	496.4	–862.1	25	114	Belarus
54	21	21	76	–72	...	...	...	...	...	...	6,981	5,187	12,168	5,275	8,275	Belgium
65	17	27	52	–61	282.2	76.8	23.2	39.8	62.1	37.9	–104.7	44.9	–59.8	87	30	Belize
81	9	18	27	–35	1,469	99.7	0.3	50	58.0	42.0	–152.9[3]	–1.1[3]	–154.0[3]	31	7	Benin
...	...	...	...	...	...	...	...	...	...	...	...	...	...	478	...	Bermuda
36[1]	29[1]	44[1]	34[1]	–44[1]	119.6	100.0	—	9.2	76.1	23.9	–24.8	–21.7	–46.5	6	...	Bhutan
75	14	23	20	–32	4,307	98.9	1.1	348	60.2	39.8	–655.5	–19.7	–675.2	170	172	Bolivia
100		38	35	–73	—	—	—	—	—	—	–1,756	658	–1,098	16[1]	...	Bosnia and Herzegovina
28	29	28	56	–41	508.2	95.2	4.8	76.3	69.9	30.1	75.5	92.6	170.1	181[1]	140[1]	Botswana
64	18	21	7	–10	98,959	29.6	70.4	16,842	69.4	30.6	–6,603	–27,226	–33,829	2,595	6,583	Brazil
...	...	...	...	...	...	...	...	...	...	...	175	1,910	2,085	...	...	Brunei
72	15	14	44	–45	7,781	31.7	68.3	823	45.9	54.1	–380.7	318.9	–61.8	496	222	Bulgaria
81	10	24	15	–30	1,129	99.7	0.3	47	68.1	31.9	–258.7	468.5	209.8	39	...	Burkina Faso
96	12	3	8	–19	1,079	99.9	0.1	21	61.9	38.1	–37.1	15.9	–21.2	1	10	Burundi
96[1]	7[1]	16[1]	28[1]	–46[1]	2,102	99.9	0.1	9	44.4	55.6	–391.4	167.5	–223.9	143	12	Cambodia
71	9	18	26	–27	8,096	94.1	5.9	435	60.0	40.0	209.4	–271.4	–62.0	36[1]	105[1]	Cameroon
59	20	20	41	–40	...	...	...	...	...	...	12,625	–23,838	–11,213	8,763	11,268	Canada
68	23	40	25	–57	237.3	95.4	4.6	19.0	81.1	18.9	–185.6	127.6	–58.0	15	17	Cape Verde
84	12	14	16	–25	829.8	98.7	1.3	16.1	58.4	41.6	–8.3	–79.1	–87.4	...	...	Central African Republic
90	10	15	18	–33	1,005	98.3	1.7	23	52.2	47.8	–50.3	–155.8	–206.1	...	...	Chad
67	11	26	25	–29	4,986	42.8	57.2	1,063	41.5	58.5	–2,516	–1,623	–4,139	1,021	946	Chile
46	12	38	4		99,424	45.4	54.6	12,794	64.0	36.0	46,613	–17,288	29,325	12,074	10,166	China
68	19	20	15	–22	16,390	35.1	64.9	2,937	66.8	33.2	–2,552	–2,741	–5,293	955	958	Colombia
91[1]	15[1]	19[1]	20[1]	–45[1]	188.1	100.0	—	5.9	89.0	11.0	–35.6	40.8	5.2	26	7[5]	Comoros
81[5]	5[5]	9[5]	28[5]	–23[5]	8,949	90.5	9.5	—	—	—	830[1]	–1,375[1]	–515[1]	...	...	Congo, Dem. Rep. of the
46	16	26	67	–55	4,250	80.9	19.1	13	53.8	46.2	941.3[3]	–1,193.2[3]	–251.9[3]	3	36	Congo, Rep. of the
56	16	28	50	–50	3,047	71.3	28.7	471	65.6	34.4	–244.5	–215.8	–460.3	719	358	Costa Rica
64	11	19	44	–37	10,800	76.9	23.1	886	42.9	57.1	1,832.3	–2,144.9	–312.6	88	282	Côte d'Ivoire
59[1]	29[1]	22[1]	42[1]	–52[1]	4,910	31.6	68.4	745	63.7	36.3	–4,169.0	2,617.3	–1,555.7	2,529	521	Croatia
71[1]	24[1]	7[1]	16[1]	–18[1]	...	...	...	...	...	...	...	...	...	1,354	...	Cuba
64	19	25	44	–52	...	...	...	...	...	...	–2,425.7	1,865.1	–560.6	1,639	278	Cyprus[9]
52	19	30	60	–61	12,901	7.8	92.2	4,288	77.3	22.7	–2,595	1,203	–1,392	3,647	2,380	Czech Republic
51	26	21	35	–33	...	...	...	...	...	...	3,723	–5,776	–2,053	3,185	4,137	Denmark
79	24	15	45	–64	263.8	100.0	—	4.8	68.8	31.3	–179.7	165.3	–14.4	4[5]	4[5]	Djibouti
58[3]	21[3]	34[3]	51[3]	–63[3]	90.9	100.0	—	9.4	72.9	21.7	36.6	–19.1	17.5	40	7[1]	Dominica
75	8	26	47	–56	3,530	81.8	18.2	311	49.0	51.0	–2,616.8	2,281.1	–335.7	2,107	242	Dominican Republic
...	...	...	...	...	...	...	...	...	...	...	...	...	...	...	...	East Timor
70	12	25	25	–32	12,589	41.6	58.4	1,398	46.0	54.0	–995	–1,174	–2,169	290	227	Ecuador

National product and accounts (continued)

country	gross national product (GNP), 1998						origin of gross domestic product (GDP) by economic sector, 1998 (%)										
	nominal ('000,000 U.S.$)	per capita		average annual growth rates, 1990–98			primary		secondary			tertiary					other
		nominal (U.S.$)	purchasing power parity (PPP; U.S.$)	real GNP (%)	population (%)	real GNP per capita (%)	agriculture	mining	manufacturing	construction	public utilities	transp., communications	trade	financial svcs.	other svcs.	government	
Egypt	79,185	1,290	3,146	2.7	2.3	0.4	16[3]	[7]	27[3, 7]	5[3]	2[3]	11[3]	19[3]	6[3]	—7[3]—		7[3]
El Salvador	11,207	1,850	4,008	3.2	2.4	0.8	12	—	22	4	2	8	19	12	7	14	—
Equatorial Guinea	478	1,110	...	13.1	2.9	10.2	22	61	—	3	1	1	4	1	2	5	—
Eritrea	781	200	984	2.2	3.0	–0.8	15	—	13	11	1	9	20	4	1	17	9
Estonia	4,878	3,360	7,563	–1.4	–1.1	–0.3	6	1	14	5	3	12	18	13	14	4	10[1]
Ethiopia	6,169	100	566	2.6	2.6	0.0	46	[7]	7[7]	3	2	6	9	7	8	13	–1
Faroe Islands	976	24,620	...	...	...	...	...	...	...	...	...	...	...	...	...	...	...
Fiji	1,748	2,210	4,094	0.5	1.0	–0.5	16	3	15	5	5	14	16	14	—20—		–8
Finland	125,091	24,280	20,641	1.8	0.5	1.3	4	—	22	4	2	8	11	11	9	16	13
France	1,465,399	24,210	21,214	1.2	0.5	0.7	3[3]	1[3]	22[3]	5[3]	3[3]	6[3]	14[3, 10]	5[3]	18[3,10]	19[3]	6[3]
French Guiana	1,543[5]	10,580[5]	...	...	...	...	...	...	...	...	...	...	...	...	...	...	...
French Polynesia	4,107[4]	18,170[4]	...	...	...	...	...	...	...	...	...	...	...	...	...	...	...
Gabon	4,922	4,170	5,615	0.3	3.0	–2.7	7[3]	43[3]	6[3]	4[3]	1[3]	5[3]	8[3]	—11[3]—		9[3]	6[3]
Gambia, The	408	340	1,428	–0.5	4.0	–4.5	24	—	5	5	2	14	17	7	5	9	12
Gaza Strip	1,368[4]	1,320[4]	...	...	...	...	13	—	10	8	2	5	15	23	8	16	—
Georgia	5,281	970	3.429	–11.3	0.0	–11.3	32	[2]	13[2]	4	[2]	11	11	11	—13—		5
Germany	2,179,802	26,570	22,026	0.9	0.5	0.4	1	[2]	25[2]	5	[2]	—17—		30	—21—		1
Ghana	7,269	390	1,735	1.4	3.1	–1.7	36	5	9	9	3	4	7	4	3	10	10
Greece	123,394	11,740	13,994	1.2	0.5	0.7	14[3]	1[3]	14[3]	6[3]	2[3]	7[3]	14[3]	3[3]	11[3]	19[3]	9[3]
Greenland	1,142[3]	20,380[3]	...	...	...	...	...	...	...	...	...	...	...	...	...	...	...
Grenada	313	3,250	5,557	1.8	0.4	1.4	9[3]	1[3]	7[3]	7[3]	5[3]	24[3]	20[3]	14[3]	3[3]	16[3]	–6[3]
Guadeloupe	3,706[4, 5]	9,200[4, 5]	...	...	...	...	...	...	...	...	...	...	...	...	...	...	...
Guam	3,066[4]	18,770[4]	...	...	...	...	...	...	...	...	...	...	...	...	...	...	...
Guatemala	17,759	1,640	3,474	1.5	3.0	–1.5	23	1	14	2	3	9	25	10	6	8	–1
Guernsey[11]	1,847	29,070	...	...	...	...	...	...	...	...	...	...	...	...	...	...	...
Guinea	3,777	530	1,722	2.1	3.0	–0.9	21	16	4	9	1	6	—28—		9	4	2
Guinea-Bissau	184	160	573	–1.3	2.5	–3.8	62	[2]	9[2]	3	[2]	2	19	—1—		3	1
Guyana	661	780	3,139	10.7	0.9	9.8	29	14	9[12]	5	[12]	6	4	6	1	11	15
Haiti	3,163	410	1,379	–3.7	2.4	–6.1	30	—	7	12	1	2	13	8	5	18	4
Honduras	4,564	740	2.338	1.4	3.3	–1.9	19	2	19	5	5	5	12	17	11	6	–1
Hong Kong	158,238	23,660	20,763	2.4	2.3	0.1	—	—	6	6	3	9	23	24	—19—		10
Hungary	45,660	4,510	9,832	0.9	–0.4	1.3	6[3]	[7]	20[3, 7]	4[3]	3[3]	9[3]	10[3]	16[3]	13	6[3]	13[3]
Iceland	7,626	27,830	24,774	1.5	1.0	0.5	9[3]	—	13[3]	6[3]	3[3]	6[3]	10[3]	15[3]	5[3]	14[3]	18[3]
India	427,407	440	2,060	4.3	2.0	2.3	25	2	15	4	2	7	14	10	6	5	10
Indonesia	130,600	640	2,407	4.0	1.9	2.1	19	13	26	5	1	5	15	8	3	4	1
Iran	102,242	1,650	5,121	1.8	1.9	–0.1	20	12	16	4	2	8	17	10	2	10	–1
Iraq	11,500[1, 4]	600[1, 4]	...	...	...	...	...	...	...	...	...	...	...	...	...	...	...
Ireland	69,322	18,710	17,991	6.1	0.8	5.3	8[1]	[13]	38[1, 13]	[13]	[13]	—18[1]—		—31[1]—		5[1]	—
Isle of Man	1,210[3]	16,810[3]	...	...	...	...	2[3]	—	12[3]	7[3]	3[3]	10[3]	12[3]	59[3]	4[3]	6[3]	–15[3]
Israel	96,483	16,180	16,861	2.2	3.5	–1.3	2[3]	[2]	19[2, 3]	9	[2]	6[3]	12[3]	30[3]	—28[3]—		–6[3]
Italy	1,157,001	20,090	20,365	1.0	0.2	0.8	3[1]	4[1]	16[1]	5[1]	6[1]	6[1]	19[1]	5[1]	13[1]	22[1]	1[1]
Jamaica	4,481	1,740	3,344	0.7	1.0	–0.3	7	5	14	10	2	11	23	12	3	12	1
Japan	4,089,140	32,350	23,592	1.3	0.3	1.0	2[3]	—	24[3]	10[3]	3[3]	7[3]	12[3]	19[3]	20[3]	8[3]	–5[3]
Jersey	2,198[4, 6]	25,920[4, 6]	...	...	...	...	...	...	...	...	...	...	...	...	...	...	...
Jordan	5,252	1,150	2,615	2.1	5.2	–3.1	3	3	12	4	2	14	11	16	5	18	12
Kazakhstan	20,856	1,340	4,317	–6.3	–0.7	–5.6	8	[2]	22[2]	4	[2]	11	17	—37—			1
Kenya	10,201	350	964	0.0	3.1	–3.1	30[1]	—	10[1]	5[1]	1[1]	8[1]	19[1]	18[1]	—8[1]—		—
Kiribati	101	1,170	3,880	2.0	2.5	–0.5	12[1]	—	1[1]	3[1]	2[1]	12[1]	19[1]	6[1]	3[1]	33[1]	9[1]
Korea, North	10,359[4]	570[4]	...	...	...	...	...	...	...	...	...	...	...	...	...	...	...
Korea, South	398,825	8,600	13,286	4.9	1.1	3.8	5	—	31	10	2	7	11	20	8	8	–2
Kuwait	35,152[3]	22,110[3]	24,270[3]	...	...	...	—	31	12	3	—	6	10	14	—26—		–2
Kyrgyzstan	1,771	380	2,247	–7.7	1.0	–8.7	41	[2]	17[2]	3	[2]	2	12	—14—		3	8
Laos	1,583	320	1,683	3.8	3.0	0.8	52	—	17	3	2	6	12	3	1	3	1
Latvia	5,917	2,420	5,777	–5.0	–1.2	–3.8	8[1]	[7]	19[1, 7]	4[1]	5[1]	—51[1]—					13[1]
Lebanon	14,975	3,560	4,144	4.5	2.1	2.4	...	...	...	...	...	...	...	...	...	...	...
Lesotho	1,167	570	2,194	2.3	2.5	–0.2	12[1]	—	14[1]	18[1]	3[1]	3[1]	10[1]	8[1]	1[1]	18[1]	13[1]
Liberia	1,174[1]	490[1]	...	...	...	...	78	2	5	2	—	5	3	3	2	2	–2
Libya	29,476[1]	5,540[1]	...	...	...	...	...	...	...	...	...	...	...	...	...	...	—
Liechtenstein	714[1, 4]	23,000[1, 4]	...	...	...	...	...	...	...	...	...	...	...	...	...	...	...
Lithuania	9,411	2,540	6,283	–5.2	–0.1	–5.1	9	[7]	17[7]	8	4	9	16	9	11	6	11
Luxembourg	19,239	45,100	36,703	1.5	1.6	–0.1	1	—	17	7	1	—24—		45	—19—		–14
Macau	6,844[4]	16,060[4]	...	...	...	...	...	...	...	...	...	...	...	...	...	...	...
Macedonia	2,584	1,290	4,224	–1.4	0.8	–2.2	10	[7]	22[7]	6	3	6	13	6	—19—		15
Madagascar	3,741	260	741	–1.2	3.2	–4.4	33	[7]	—12[7]—			—42—				5	8
Malawi	2,168	210	551	0.8	3.1	–2.3	36	1	13	2	1	4	25	9	2	10	–3
Malaysia	81,311	3,670	7,699	4.8	2.8	2.0	9	8	28	4	3	8	16	13	—16—		–5
Maldives	296	1,130	3,436	4.3	3.0	1.3	16	2	7[12]	11	[12]	7	20	—29—		8	—
Mali	2,646	250	673	0.6	3.2	–2.6	44	6	9	5	—	5	—16—		7	4	4
Malta	3,807	10,100	22,901	12.6	0.9	11.7	2	[14]	19	3[14]	7	6	10	17	9	14	13
Marshall Islands	96	1,540	...	–6.8	4.2	–11.0	15[3]	—	2[3]	7[3]	2[3]	7[3]	18[3]	15[3]	—30[3]—		4[3]
Martinique	3,942[4, 5]	10,000[4, 5]	...	...	...	...	...	...	...	...	...	...	...	...	...	...	...
Mauritania	1,033	410	1,500	1.5	3.2	–1.7	22[3]	10[3]	10[3]	—9[3]—		8[3]	15[3]	—7[3]—		10[3]	9[3]
Mauritius	4,329	3,730	8,236	3.8	1.3	2.5	7	—	21	5	2	10	15	14	5	9	12
Mayotte	54[6]	600[6]	...	...	...	...	...	...	...	...	...	...	...	...	...	...	...
Mexico	368,059	3,840	7,450	0.6	2.0	–1.4	5	1	21	5	1	11	20	14	—23—		–1
Micronesia	204	1,800	...	–2.5	2.4	–4.9	19[1]	—	1[1]	1[1]	1[1]	5[1]	24[1]	3[1]	3[1]	42[1]	1[1]
Moldova	1,652	380	1,995	–8.3	–0.2	–8.1	21	[7]	17[7]	4	2	4	7	6	—12—		27
Monaco	793[1, 4]	25,000[1, 4]	...	...	...	...	...	...	...	...	...	...	...	...	...	...	...
Mongolia	995	380	1,463	–1.5	2.2	–3.7	33	[7]	24[7]	3	—	7	19	—14—			—
Morocco	34,421	1,240	3,188	0.4	2.1	–1.7	15[3]	2[3]	18[3]	5[3]	9[3]	6[3]	19[3]	—13[3]—			13[3]
Mozambique	3,478	210	740	2.6	2.6	0.0	32	—	8	8	1	11	23	—	12	3	2
Myanmar (Burma)	55,700[3, 4]	1,190[3, 4]	...	...	...	...	53	—	6	2	—	5	30	2	—2—		—
Namibia	3,217	1,940	5,280	0.8	3.0	–2.2	9[3]	12[3]	12[3]	3[3]	3[3]	4[3]	9[3]	8[3]	3[3]	23[3]	14[3]
Nauru	81[1]	7,210[1]	...	...	...	...	...	...	...	...	...	...	...	...	...	...	...
Nepal	4,889	210	1,181	2.4	2.8	–0.4	38	1	9	10	2	8	11	10	—9—		2

gross domestic product (GDP) by type of expenditure, 1998 (%)					external public debt outstanding (long-term, disbursed only), 1998						balance of payments, 1998 (current external transactions; '000,000 U.S.$)			tourist trade, 1997 ('000,000 U.S.$)		country
consumption		gross domestic invest-ment	foreign trade		total ('000,000 U.S.$)	creditors (%)		debt service			net transfers		current balance of payments	receipts from foreign nationals	expendi-tures by nationals abroad	
private	govern-ment		exports	imports		offi-cial	private	total ('000,000 U.S.$)	repayment(%) princi-pal	inter-est	goods, merchan-dise	invisibles				
74	10	22	17	–23	27,670	96.7	3.3	1,548	56.9	43.1	–10,214	7,648	–2,566	3,727	1,347	Egypt
86	10	17	23	–36	2,443	97.2	2.8	365	71.1	28.9	–1,267.0	1,182.6	–84.4	75	75	El Salvador
...	...	...	102	–173	216.5	93.1	6.9	1.5	53.3	46.7	26.5	–400.1	–373.6	...	...	Equatorial Guinea
...	...	...	...	...	144.1	100.0	—	3.6	—	100.0	–489.9	323.5	–175.4	69[1]	...	Eritrea
59	22	29	78	–88	231.3	75.1	24.9	28.2	57.8	42.2	–1,114.8	636.9	–477.9	465	118	Estonia
79	14	18	16	–26	9,618	96.4	3.6	113	57.5	42.5	–473.9	607.9	134.0	36	40	Ethiopia
...	...	...	...	...	...	...	...	...	...	...	51.6	102.4	154.0	...	...	Faroe Islands
72	18	12	67	–69	140.0	99.9	0.1	21.4	67.8	32.2	–218.1	163.5	–54.6	297	53	Fiji
39	21	19	50	–30	...	...	...	...	...	...	12,492	–5,060	7,432	1,963	2,270	Finland
54	24	19	26	–23	...	...	...	...	...	...	26,170	13,990	40,160	28,009	16,576	France
...	...	...	...	...	...	...	...	...	...	...	...	...	...	...	...	French Guiana
...	...	...	...	...	...	...	...	...	...	...	...	...	...	345	...	French Polynesia
40[3]	11[3]	26[3]	64[3]	–42[3]	3,833	96.7	3.3	254	44.1	55.9	202.5[3]	34.6[3]	237.1[3]	7[5]	173[5]	Gabon
76	17	18	51	–62	451.3	100.0	—	20.3	73.4	26.6	–69.0	52.7	–16.3	32	16	Gambia, The
...	...	...	...	...	...	...	...	...	...	...	...	...	...	...	...	Gaza Strip
...	...	...	...	...	1,311	99.8	0.2	62	37.1	62.9	–760.3	343.9	–416.4	416	228	Georgia
57	19	22	29	–27	...	...	...	...	...	...	79,040	–82,480	–3,440	16,509	46,200	Germany
77	10	25	34	–47	5,570	89.7	10.3	382	64.9	35.1	–532.8	183.0	–349.8	266	22[1]	Ghana
71	15	21	18	–25	...	...	...	...	...	...	–17,681	14,037	–3,644	3,771	1,325	Greece
...	...	...	...	...	...	...	...	...	...	...	...	...	...	...	...	Greenland
61	18	44	53	–76	113.0	94.4	5.6	6.8	70.6	29.4	–140.7[3]	99.0[3]	–41.7[3]	59	5[1]	Grenada
...	...	...	...	...	...	...	...	...	...	...	...	...	...	372	...	Guadeloupe
...	...	...	...	...	...	...	...	...	...	...	...	...	...	...	...	Guam
87	6	16	19	–27	2,990	77.8	22.2	303	59.7	40.3	–1,408.8	369.7	–1,039.1	325	119	Guatemala
...	...	...	...	...	...	...	...	...	...	...	...	...	...	...	...	Guernsey[11]
77	7	17	22	–23	3,126	99.1	0.9	138	68.5	31.5	120.9	–239.4	–118.5	6[1]	23	Guinea
100	9	11	15	–35	873.1	99.9	0.1	6.8	35.3	64.7	–25.4	–4.9	–30.3	...	...	Guinea-Bissau
43[3]	20[3]	43[3]	78[3]	–84[3]	1,369	96.2	3.8	112	46.4	53.6	–54	–44	–98	60	21[5]	Guyana
— 103 —		13	13	–29	980	100.0	—	29	48.3	51.7	–341.4	303.3	–38.1	57	37[1]	Haiti
67	10	30	44	–51	3,946	95.8	4.2	381	58.3	41.7	–323.1	–9.8	–332.9	146	62	Honduras
61	9	30	127	–127	...	...	...	...	...	...	...	...	...	9,242	...	Hong Kong
62	11	29	51	–53	15,941	14.4	85.6	4,340	77.5	22.5	–2,354	50	–2,304	2,582	1,153	Hungary
62	21	22	35	–39	...	...	...	...	...	...	–352	–115	–467	173	324	Iceland
66	13	23	12	–13	85,207	63.6	36.4	10,584	59.4	40.6	–10,752	3,849	–6,903	3,152	1,342	India
53	4	35	40	–33	66,944	63.8	36.2	7,789	61.6	38.4	18,429	–14,333	4,096	5,437	2,436	Indonesia
65	13	22	8	–8	7,679	63.8	36.2	2,552	80.8	19.2	–626	–1,271	–1,897	327	253	Iran
...	...	...	...	...	...	...	...	...	...	...	...	...	...	...	...	Iraq
51	13	24	84	–72	...	...	...	...	...	...	23,381	–22,575	806	3,189	2,223	Ireland
...	...	...	...	...	...	...	...	...	...	...	...	...	...	...	...	Isle of Man
61	30	20	32	–43	...	...	...	...	...	...	–3,226	2,558	–668	2,741	3,570	Israel
60	18	20	24	–22	...	...	...	...	...	...	35,631	–15,633	19,998	29,714	16,631	Italy
67	18	29	43	–56	3,079	76.0	24.0	459	65.7	34.3	–1,096.7	841.4	–255.3	1,131	181	Jamaica
61	10	26	11	–9	...	...	...	...	...	...	122,390	–1,690	120,700	4,326	33,041	Japan
...	...	...	...	...	...	...	...	...	...	...	...	...	...	...	...	Jersey
70	27	25	49	–70	7,388	81.5	18.5	828	48.7	51.3	–1,601.6	1,615.7	14.1	774	398	Jordan
75	11	18	32	–37	3,040	67.4	32.6	394	48.0	52.0	–750.1	–451.2	–1,201.3	...	...	Kazakhstan
74	16	17	25	–32	5,629	90.2	9.8	442	71.8	28.2	–1,015.6	652.6	–363.0	377	194	Kenya
...	...	...	...	...	...	...	...	...	...	...	–31.6[1]	29.3[1]	–2.3[1]	1[1]	4[1]	Kiribati
...	...	...	...	...	...	...	...	...	...	...	...	...	...	...	...	Korea, North
55	11	21	48	–35	57,956	22.0	78.0	6,135	45.9	54.1	41,627	–1,069	40,558	5,116	6,262	Korea, South
56	31	14	45	–47	...	...	...	...	...	...	1,900	627	2,527	188	2,558	Kuwait
88	18	16	36	–58	909.2	99.8	0.2	38.4	44.0	56.0	–220.7	–150.2	–370.9	7	4	Kyrgyzstan
...	...	...	...	...	2,373	100.0	—	24	67.7	33.3	–164.7	14.6	–150.1	73	21	Laos
64	26	23	48	–61	413.3	88.3	11.7	31.7	45.7	54.3	–1,130	417	–713	192	326	Latvia
...	...	...	...	...	3,980	20.8	79.2	255	27.1	72.9	...	...	...	1,000	...	Lebanon
116	20	46	27	–109	660.6	91.7	8.3	45.7	54.9	45.1	–672.5	392.3	–280.2	...	...	Lesotho
...	...	...	...	...	1,092	81.8	18.2	—	—	—	–118.5	76.6	–41.9	...	...	Liberia
55[3]	27[3]	12[3]	29[3]	–23[3]	...	...	...	...	...	...	471	–862	–391	...	...	Libya
...	...	...	...	...	...	...	...	...	...	...	...	...	...	...	...	Liechtenstein
63	25	24	47	–59	1,215.8	47.4	52.6	114.6	56.7	43.3	–1,518.3	220.1	–1,298.2	360	277	Lithuania
46	17	21	116	–99	...	...	...	...	...	...	–2,012	4,242	2,230	...	...	Luxembourg
40	11	18	76	–46	...	...	...	...	...	...	...	...	...	2,947	153	Macau
74	18	23	43	–58	1,944	71.7	28.3	140	39.3	60.7	–397.6	109.7	–287.9	14	27	Macedonia
89	7	12	21	–30	4,107	99.0	1.0	10.9	53.2	46.8	–154	–147	–301	73	43	Madagascar
85	14	14	30	–42	2,310	99.1	0.9	56	60.7	39.3	–93.0[1]	–0.3[1]	–92.7[1]	5[1]	...	Malawi
42	10	27	114	–93	18,158	24.8	75.2	2,130	53.1	46.9	3,876[3]	–8,668[3]	–4,792[3]	2,490	2,478	Malaysia
...	...	...	...	...	169.7	86.8	13.2	13.2	76.1	23.9	–214.0	190.8	–23.2	286	38	Maldives
70	14	24	24	–33	2,827	100.0	—	62	71.0	29.0	9.7[3]	–187.7[3]	–178.0[3]	26	42	Mali
62	20	23	88	–94	...	...	...	...	...	...	–594.0	430.3	–167.3	648	191	Malta
...	...	...	...	...	...	...	...	...	...	...	–35.8[3]	52.2[3]	16.4[3]	3	...	Marshall Islands
...	...	...	...	...	...	...	...	...	...	...	...	...	...	400	...	Martinique
69[3]	20[3]	17[3]	42[3]	–49[3]	2,214	99.0	1.0	94	65.4	34.6	40.0	37.2	77.2	...	...	Mauritania
63	12	25	67	–67	1,152	50.5	49.5	188	64.9	35.1	–266.1	299.7	33.6	485	177	Mauritius
...	...	...	...	...	...	...	...	...	...	...	...	...	...	...	...	Mayotte
68	9	24	31	–33	87,996	26.3	73.7	18,549	62.7	37.3	–7,915	–7,775	–15,690	7,595	3,892	Mexico
...	...	...	...	...	...	...	...	...	...	...	–52.0[3]	115.8[3]	63.8[3]	...	...	Micronesia
71	24	30	— –25 —		808	65.5	34.5	89	64.6	35.4	–388.4	41.,1	–347.3	4	...	Moldova
...	...	...	...	...	...	...	...	...	...	...	...	...	...	...	...	Monaco
65[3]	16[3]	23[3]	1[3]	–5[3]	633.6	95.9	4.1	31.6	78.0	22.0	–61.8	–66.7	–128.5	21[5]	20[5]	Mongolia
65	18	22	22	–26	19,325	73.6	26.4	2,702	64.0	36.0	–2,319	2,083	–236	1,449	316	Morocco
88	9	23	12	–32	5,651	99.7	0.3	62	56.5	43.5	–491.0	61.7	–429.3	...	...	Mozambique
— 89 —		12	0	–1	5,071	89.2	10.8	88	89.8	10.2	–1,283.6	829.9	–453.7	34	...	Myanmar (Burma)
55[3]	31[3]	20[3]	53[3]	–58[3]	...	...	...	...	...	...	–172.6	334.4	161.8	336	99	Namibia
...	...	...	...	...	...	...	...	...	...	...	...	...	...	...	...	Nauru
81	9	21	24	–35	2,591	98.6	1.4	80	67.5	32.5	–752.8	689.9	–62.9	116	103	Nepal

National product and accounts (continued)

country	gross national product (GNP), 1998						origin of gross domestic product (GDP) by economic sector, 1998 (%)										
	nominal ('000,000 U.S.$)	per capita		average annual growth rates, 1990–98			primary		secondary			tertiary					other
		nominal (U.S.$)	purchasing power parity (PPP; U.S.$)	real GNP (%)	population (%)	real GNP per capita (%)	agriculture	mining	manufacturing	construction	public utilities	transp., communications	trade	financial svcs.	other svcs.	government	
Netherlands, The	389,055	24,780	22,325	2.1	0.7	1.4	3	2	17	5	2	7	15	26	11	12	—
Netherlands Antilles	2,400[3,4]	11,500[3,4]	...	...	...	...	1[5]	—	7[5]	7[5]	4[5]	13[5]	25[5]	17[5]	9[5]	18[5]	–1[5]
New Caledonia	3,373[4]	16,560[4]	...	...	...	...	2[3]	4[3]	11[3]	5[3]	2[3]	7[3]	23[3]	—20[3]—		25[3]	–1[3]
New Zealand	55,356	14,600	16,084	1.4	1.4	0.0	7	1	17	3	3	11	15	22	—22—		1
Nicaragua	1,756	370	1,896	2.0	3.2	–1.2	28	2	21	5	3	5	18	7	4	8	–1
Niger	2,023	200	729	–1.2	3.9	–5.1	37[3]	4[3]	7[3]	2[3]	2[3]	6[3]	17[3]	—21[3]—			4[3]
Nigeria	36,373	300	740	0.4	3.3	–2.9	37	26	5	1	—	3	16	5	1	1	5
Northern Mariana Is.	665[4]	8,370[4]	...	...	...	...	...	...	...	...	...	...	...	...	...	...	...
Norway	152,049	34,310	26,196	3.7	0.6	3.1	2	11	12	4	2	9	10	17	5	16	12
Oman	13,808[3]	6,050[3]	...	...	...	...	2[1]	43[1]	4[1]	2[1]	1[1]	6[1]	13[1]	8[1]	8[1]	12[1]	1[1]
Pakistan	61,451	470	1,652	1.5	2.8	–1.3	24	—	15	3	4	9	15	8	7	7	8
Palau	129[4]	7,140[4]	...	...	...	...	5	—	1	8	—	16	27	12	7	22	2
Panama	8,275	2,990	4,925	2.7	2.0	0.7	8	—	10	4	4	13	21	25	6	10	–1
Papua New Guinea	4,104	890	2,205	2.1	2.6	–0.5	24	26	9	6	1	5	9	1	—13—		6
Paraguay	9,172	1,760	4,312	0.0	3.0	–3.0	28	—	14	5	6	5	23	3	10	6	—
Peru	60,491	2,440	4,180	4.0	2.0	2.0	6[3]	2[3]	19[3]	11[3]	1[3]	4[3]	16[3]	14[3]	13[3]	7[3]	7[3]
Philippines	78,938	1,050	3,725	1.5	2.6	–1.1	17	1	22	6	3	5	14	12	11	10	–1
Poland	151,285	3,910	7,543	4.4	0.2	4.2	5	3	22	8	3	6	21	15	3	13	1
Portugal	106,391	10,670	14,569	2.1	0.1	2.0	...	...	...	...	...	...	...	...	...	...	...
Puerto Rico	25,380[3]	7,010[3]	...	...	...	...	1[1]	[14]	41[1]	2[1,14]	[15]	8[1,15]	14[1]	13[1]	11[1]	11[1]	–1[1]
Qatar	7,429[3]	11,570[3]	...	...	...	...	1[3]	38[3]	7[3]	7[3]	1[3]	4[3]	8[3]	10[3]	—24[3]—		...
Réunion	2,864[4,5]	4,300[4,5]	...	...	...	...	...	...	...	...	...	...	...	...	...	...	...
Romania	30,596	1,360	5,572	–0.6	–0.4	–0.2	19[1]	[2]	34[1,2]	7[1]	[2]	9[1]	10[1]	—17[1]—			4[1]
Russia	331,776	2,260	6,180	–7.2	–0.1	–7.1	7	[2]	33[2]	8	[2]	—23—		14	9	6	—
Rwanda	1,864	230	...	–4.3	2.2	–6.5	44	—	13	7	—	4	11	—15—		7	–1
St. Kitts	253	6,190	9,790	4.9	–0.4	5.3	6[1]	—	11[1]	12[1]	2[1]	16[1]	23[1]	16[1]	4[1]	18[1]	–8[1]
St. Lucia	556	3,660	4,897	1.3	1.8	–0.5	7	—	5	6	4	15	23	15	3	13	9
St. Vincent	290	2,560	4,484	2.4	0.8	1.6	9	—	6	12	5	17	15	8	2	15	11
Samoa	181	1,070	3,854	1.1	0.8	0.3	17[3]	...	19[3]	5[3]	2[3]	11[3]	17[3]	11[3]	7[3]	9[3]	2[3]
San Marino	883[3,4]	34,330[3,4]	...	...	...	...	...	...	...	...	...	...	...	...	...	...	...
São Tomé and Príncipe	38	270	1,289	–1.0	3.0	–4.0	23[3]	—	4[3]	15[3]	—	—19[3]—		8[3]	9[3]	22[3]	—
Saudi Arabia	143,361	6,910	10,498	–2.4	3.9	–6.3	6[1]	36[1]	9[1]	9[1]	—	6[1]	7[1]	5[1]	3[1]	17[1]	2[1]
Senegal	4,683	520	1,297	0.5	3.0	–2.5	18	[7]	13[7]	5	2	12	—21—		20	9	—
Seychelles	505	6,420	10,185	1.4	1.7	–0.3	3	...	14	9	3	15	24	10	2	13	7
Sierra Leone	703	140	445	–6.0	2.8	–8.8	39[5]	17[5]	9[5]	2[5]	—	9[5]	14[5]	2[5]	2[5]	3[5]	4[5]
Singapore	95,453	30,170	25,295	6.7	2.2	4.5	—	—	24	9	2	14	19	28	—11—		–7
Slovakia	19,941	3,700	9,624	1.1	0.3	0.8	4	1	23	5	3	8	—22—		—29—		5
Slovenia	19,385	9,780	14,400	4.4	–0.1	4.5	4[3]	1[3]	25[3]	5[3]	3[3]	7[3]	13[3]	14[3]	12[3]	5[3]	11[3]
Solomon Islands	315	760	1,904	0.3	3.7	–3.4	48[1]	—	3[1]	7[1]	2[1]	6[1]	9[1]	4[1]	—21[1]—		—
Somalia	706[1]	110[1]	...	...	...	...	...	...	...	...	...	...	...	...	...	...	...
South Africa	136,868	3,310	8,296	–0.1	2.3	–2.4	4	7	19	3	3	10	13	18	—23—		—
Spain	555,244	14,100	15,960	1.7	0.2	1.5	4[1]	[2]	24[1,2]	8[1]	[2]	—59[1]—					5[1]
Sri Lanka	15,176	810	2,945	3.9	1.4	2.5	19	2	15	7	1	10	19	9	—13—		5
Sudan, The	8,224	290	1,240	3.6	2.3	1.3	41	—	9	6	1	6	20	—14—			3
Suriname	684	1,660	...	0.1	0.4	–0.3	12[1]	11[1]	13[1]	3[1]	9[1]	15[1]	12[1]	14[1]	—13[1]—		–2[1]
Swaziland	1,384	1,400	4,195	–0.1	3.6	–3.7	12	1	27	4	2	4	7	4	1	15	23
Sweden	226,454	25,580	19,848	0.6	0.5	0.1	2[1]	—	20[1]	5[1]	3[1]	6[1]	11[1]	23[1]	4[1]	19[1]	7[1]
Switzerland	284,119	39,980	26,876	–0.2	0.8	–1.0	...	...	...	...	...	...	...	...	...	...	...
Syria	15,532	1,020	2,702	1.3	3.3	–2.0	28[1]	7[1]	4[1]	4[1]	1[1]	11[1]	26[1]	5[1]	2[1]	10[1]	—
Taiwan	268,074	12,280	...	5.0	0.9	4.1	3	—	27	4	2	7	17	23	10	10	–3
Tajikistan	2,256	370	1,041	–13.4	2.0	–15.4	20	[2]	28[2]	2	[2]	—18—		—22—			10
Tanzania	7,154	220	483	0.5	3.3	–2.8	43[3]	1[3]	6[3]	4[3]	2[3]	5[3]	12[3]	12[3]	2[3]	7[3]	6[3]
Thailand	131,916	2,160	5,524	4.4	1.4	3.0	14	2	28	5	3	8	14	—26—			—
Togo	1,453	330	1,352	–0.7	3.4	–4.1	42	6	9	3	3	5	17	—8—		7	—
Tonga	173	1,750	4,187	1.2	0.4	0.8	32	—	3	5	2	7	11	10	—18—		12
Trinidad and Tobago	5,811	4,520	7,208	1.4	0.8	0.6	2	21	8	10	—	—18—		12	17	9	3
Tunisia	19,193	2,060	5,169	2.6	1.9	0.7	12	1	18	5	5	8	—24—			14	13
Turkey	200,530	3,160	6,594	2.9	1.8	1.1	17	1	19	6	2	14	20	—13—		9	–1
Turkmenistan	2,987[3]	640[3]	...	...	...	...	25	[2]	30[2]	12	[2]	10	5	—13—			5
Tuvalu	7[1]	650[1]	...	...	...	...	22[5]	2[5]	3[5]	14[5]	2[5]	4[5]	14[5]	10[5]	—28[5]—		—
Uganda	6,566	310	1,072	4.3	3.5	0.8	41[1]	—	7[1]	7[1]	1[1]	4[1]	12[1]	7[1]	5[1]	4[1]	12[1]
Ukraine	49,207	980	3,130	–11.4	–0.4	–11.0	11	[2]	25[2]	5	[2]	13	8	—25—			13
United Arab Emirates	48,673	17,870	18,871	–1.6	5.6	–7.2	2[1]	35[1]	9[1]	9[1]	1[1]	6[1]	13[1]	13[1]	2[1]	11[1]	–1[1]
United Kingdom	1,264,262	21,410	20,314	2.0	0.4	1.6	1	2	18	5	2	7	13	23	4	15	10
United States	7,902,976	29,240	29,240	2.1	1.1	1.0	2[3]	1[3]	17[3]	4[3]	3[3]	6[3]	17[3]	19[3]	20[3]	13[3]	—
Uruguay	19,960	6,070	8,541	3.5	0.8	2.7	11	—	20	4	4	10	14	21	—15—		1
Uzbekistan	22,900	950	2,044	–2.1	2.3	–4.4	26	[2]	15[2]	8	[2]	6	8	—21—			16
Vanuatu	231	1,260	2,892	–2.9	3.1	–6.0	23	—	5	5	2	7	34	7	—17—		—
Venezuela	82,096	3,530	5,706	–0.1	2.5	–2.6	5	12	16	7	2	10	18	16	9	6	–1
Vietnam	26,535	350	1,689	6.5	2.1	4.4	26	[7]	—33[7]—			4	19	7	—12—		–1
Virgin Islands (U.S.)	1,246[4,16]	11,740[4,16]	...	...	...	...	...	...	...	...	...	...	...	...	...	...	...
West Bank	2,758[4]	1,680[4]	...	...	...	...	7	[2]	17[2]	11	[2]	[17]	14	11	19[17]	10	13
Western Sahara	60[4,18]	300[4,18]	...	...	...	...	...	...	...	...	...	...	...	...	...	...	...
Yemen	4,630	280	658	–1.1	4.8	–5.9	24	17	10	4	2	7	14	6	2	14	—
Yugoslavia	18,491[4]	1,742[4]	...	...	...	...	20	[7]	36[7]	6	3	12	19	—5—			–1
Zambia	3,234	330	678	–0.9	3.1	–4.0	17	6	11	5	4	6	19	16	—9—		7
Zimbabwe	7,214	620	2,489	–0.2	2.6	–2.8	14[5]	5[5]	18[5]	2[5]	3[5]	5[5]	18[5]	9[5]	11[5]	4[5]	11[5]

consumption: private	consumption: government	gross domestic investment	foreign trade: exports	foreign trade: imports	external public debt outstanding (long-term, disbursed only), 1998: total ('000,000 U.S.$)	creditors (%): official	creditors (%): private	debt service: total ('000,000 U.S.$)	repayment(%): principal	repayment(%): interest	balance of payments, 1998 (current external transactions; '000,000 U.S.$): net transfers: goods, merchandise	net transfers: invisibles	current balance of payments	tourist trade, 1997 ('000,000 U.S.$): receipts from foreign nationals	expenditures by nationals abroad	country
gross domestic product (GDP) by type of expenditure, 1998 (%)																
59	14	20	55	–49	...	...	...	...	...	...	18,020	7,565	25,585	6,219	10,232	Netherlands, The
67[5]	28[5]	19[5]	72[5]	–85[5]	...	...	...	...	...	...	–1,064	1,008	–56	621	243	Netherlands Antilles
...	...	...	...	...	...	...	...	...	...	...	...	...	...	109[1]	...	New Caledonia
65	15	19	31	–30	...	...	...	...	...	...	914	–4,131	–3,217	2,093	1,451	New Zealand
94	14	34	36	–78	5,212	91.8	8.2	171	50.0	50.0	–804.2	197.1	–607.1	74	65	Nicaragua
82[3]	16[3]	12[3]	19[3]	–29[3]	1,149	100.0	—	21	57.1	42.9	–17.6[5]	–134.1[5]	–151.7[5]	18	24	Niger
64	14	29	32	–38	23,455	75.4	24.6	1,264	59.6	40.4	–240	–4,004	–4,244	118	1,816	Nigeria
...	...	...	...	...	...	...	...	...	...	...	...	...	...	585	...	Northern Mariana Is.
50	22	28	37	–37	...	...	...	...	...	...	1,566	–3,727	–2,161	2,216	4,496	Norway
55	24	23	37	–39	2,228	28.5	71.5	567	72.5	27.5	291	–3,261	–2,970	108	47	Oman
72	12	17	16	–17	26,061	91.2	8.8	1,990	67.1	32.9	–1,874	—	–1,874	117	364	Pakistan
...	...	...	...	...	...	...	...	...	...	...	...	...	...	22[5]	...	Palau
58	16	33	90	–97	5,413	24.3	75.7	567	47.1	52.9	–1,371.1	159.4	–1,211.7	369	164	Panama
55[5]	16[5]	18[5]	49[5]	–37[5]	1,410	94.1	5.9	169	68.0	32.0	695.0	–723.9	–28.9	68[1]	77[1]	Papua New Guinea
86	8	23	28	–45	1,593	95.7	4.3	175	60.3	39.7	–113.9	7.5	–106.4	753	195	Paraguay
72	9	24	12	–17	20,803	77.6	22.4	1,549	40.2	59.8	–2,465	–1,335	–3,800	805	485	Peru
73	13	20	51	–58	28,189	71.7	28.3	4,014	63.6	36.4	–28	1,315	1,287	2,831	1,936	Philippines
63	16	27	25	–32	35,136	77.1	22.9	2,608	55.4	44.6	–12,836	5,935	–6,901	8,679	6,900	Poland
66	20	26	28	–40	...	...	...	...	...	...	–12,277	5,027	–7,250	4,277	2,164	Portugal
...	...	...	...	...	...	...	...	...	...	...	...	...	...	2,046	869	Puerto Rico
...	...	...	...	...	...	...	...	...	...	...	...	...	...	...	...	Qatar
...	...	...	...	...	...	...	...	...	...	...	...	...	...	249	...	Réunion
76	15	18	26	–34	6,962	58.7	41.3	1,970	79.3	20.7	–2,625	–293	–2,918	526	783	Romania
58	19	15	31	–23	119,314	57.2	42.8	7,111	51.1	48.9	16,851	–15,207	1,644	6,900	10,113	Russia
94	9	16	6	–24	1,120	99.8	0.2	15	60.0	40.0	–198.1	55.1	–143.0	...	...	Rwanda
76[1]	18[1]	24[1]	44[1]	–63[1]	111.3	84.9	15.1	10.3	54.4	45.6	...	...	...	76	6	St. Kitts
69	15	19	65	–68	127.1	94.5	5.5	13.7	58.0	42.0	–201.2	160.2	–41.0	282	29[1]	St. Lucia
74	19	32	47	–72	101.4	98.6	1.4	9.5	67.4	32.6	–119.4	75.1	–44.3	70	7[1]	St. Vincent
...	...	...	...	...	154.3	100.0	—	4.2	66.7	33.3	–76.3	96.3	20.0	39	5	Samoa
66[1]	12[1]	17[1]	234[1]	–229[1]	...	...	...	...	...	...	22.6[1]	–11.9[1]	10.7[1]	...	...	San Marino
...	...	...	...	...	233.4	100.0	—	3.2	59.4	40.6	–12.1	3.6	–8.5	...	...	São Tomé and Príncipe
41	32	21	36	–31	...	...	...	...	...	...	12,238	–25,118	–12,880	...	...	Saudi Arabia
76	10	20	32	–38	3,274	99.7	0.3	228	61.4	38.6	–284.3	174.6	–109.7	153	75[5]	Senegal
51	27	37	65	–81	145.1	78.7	21.3	19.9	67.8	32.2	–187.5[3]	124.3[3]	–63.2[3]	122	30	Seychelles
81	11	4	14	–10	944	99.3	0.7	19	57.9	42.1	–126.7[5]	0.2[5]	–126.5[5]	10[1]	2[1]	Sierra Leone
39	10	33	—18—		...	...	...	...	...	...	14,678	2,936	17,614	6,843	3,224	Singapore
50	22	39	64	–75	4,452	25.0	75.0	1,286	79.1	20.9	–2,351	225	–2,126	546	439	Slovakia
56	21	25	57	–58	...	...	...	...	...	...	–774.9	771.1	–3.8	1,188	544	Slovenia
...	...	...	...	...	108.3	96.5	3.5	6.5	72.3	27.7	–18.1	26.2	8.1	7	9	Solomon Islands
...	...	...	...	...	1,886	98.1	1.9	—	—	—	...	...	...	...	...	Somalia
63	20	16	26	–25	10,627	—	100.0	2,644	71.3	28.7	2,018	–3,954	–1,936	1,995[1]	1,947	South Africa
62	16	22	29	–28	...	...	...	...	...	...	–18,707	17,101	–1,606	26,651	4,467	Spain
71	10	25	36	–42	7,649	91.1	8.9	338	63.0	37.0	–576.4	288.0	–288.4	212	180	Sri Lanka
91	4	18	6	–19	9,226	83.1	16.9	3	33.3	66.7	–1,136.5	180.0	–956.5	4	34	Sudan, The
...	...	...	...	...	...	...	...	...	...	...	123.0[5]	–50.1[5]	72.9[5]	43	3[5]	Suriname
63	25	34	76	–99	222.5	100.0	—	21.9	65.8	34.2	–150.6	143.5	–7.1	40	37	Swaziland
50	27	17	44	–38	...	...	...	...	...	...	17,632	–12,993	4,639	3,614	6,746	Sweden
60	15	21	40	–36	...	...	...	...	...	...	988	23,559	24,547	7,902	6,904	Switzerland
69	11	20	30	–31	16,328	93.1	6.9	174	55.2	44.8	–172	231	59	1,035	545	Syria
61	14	22	49	–47	...	...	...	...	...	...	10,531	–6,803	3,728	3,402	6,493[1]	Taiwan
...	...	...	...	...	706.9	91.5	8.5	62.2	76.4	23.6	–38[5]	–36[5]	–74[5]	...	...	Tajikistan
85	8	15	19	–28	6,404	96.5	3.5	194	47.4	52.6	–775.9	–180.6	–956.5	392	407	Tanzania
50	10	24	56	–40	28,113	64.7	35.3	2,293	45.3	54.7	16,234	–1,993	14,241	7,048	1,888	Thailand
81	11	14	34	–40	1,302	100.0	—	26	63.5	36.5	–31.5	–12.3	–43.8	13[5]	18[5]	Togo
...	...	...	...	...	64.1	91.1	8.9	4.7	78.7	21.3	–67.1	47.8	–19.3	13[1]	...	Tonga
62	16	26	48	–54	1,476	51.6	48.4	253	63.4	36.6	–740.8	97.3	–643.5	193	75[1]	Trinidad and Tobago
60	16	28	42	–46	9,727	74.6	25.4	1,245	61.8	38.2	–2,151	1,476	–675	1,414	160	Tunisia
67	12	24	24	–27	49,932	29.1	70.9	10,512	69.4	30.6	–14,332	16,203	1,871	8,088	1,716	Turkey
...	...	...	...	...	1,731	16.4	83.6	281	76.7	23.3	–523.0	–411.5	–934.5	74	125	Turkmenistan
...	...	...	...	...	...	...	...	...	...	...	...	...	...	0.3	...	Tuvalu
83[3]	10[3]	15[3]	12[3]	–21[3]	3,402	97.8	2.2	91	69.2	30.8	–466.9[3]	–79.1[3]	–387.8[3]	135	137	Uganda
59	23	21	40	–43	8,606	54.7	45.3	1,293	71.7	28.3	–2,584	1,288	–1,296	...	...	Ukraine
45[1]	16[1]	26[1]	77[1]	–65[1]	...	...	...	...	...	...	8,254[3]	–1,553[3]	6,701[3]	...	...	United Arab Emirates
65	18	18	27	–28	...	...	...	...	...	...	–34,010	32,910	–1,100	20,039	27,710	United Kingdom
67	15	20	11	–13	...	...	...	...	...	...	–244,970	24,410	–220,560	73,268	51,220	United States
71	14	16	22	–22	5,142	36.6	63.4	957	66.8	33.2	–761.9	361.7	–400.2	759	264	Uruguay
...	...	...	...	...	2,485	54.8	45.2	382	66.8	33.2	171	–210	–39	19	...	Uzbekistan
49[5]	27[5]	34[5]	47[5]	–57[5]	54.2	99.9	0.1	1.2	50.0	50.0	–42.5	38.0	–4.5	46	5[5]	Vanuatu
73	8	20	20	–20	26,692	17.9	82.1	4,473	57.6	42.4	2,748	–5,310	–2,562	1,086	2,381	Venezuela
71	7	29	42	–49	19,775	77.6	22.4	962	60.3	39.7	–981	–86	–1,067	...	...	Vietnam
...	...	...	...	...	...	...	...	...	...	...	...	...	...	601	...	Virgin Islands (U.S.)
...	...	...	...	...	...	...	...	...	...	...	...	...	...	...	...	West Bank
...	...	...	...	...	...	...	...	...	...	...	...	...	...	...	...	Western Sahara
61[3]	16[3]	28[3]	43[3]	–48[3]	3,590	95.0	5.0	118	61.9	38.1	–700.5	472.4	–228.1	69	81	Yemen
...	...	...	...	...	8,321	50.4	49.6	—	—	—	...	...	...	41	...	Yugoslavia
79	16	14	29	–38	5,320	97.9	2.1	183	69.9	30.1	–148	–121	–269	75	...	Zambia
70[3]	17[3]	20[3]	38[3]	–46[3]	3,341	87.2	12.8	442	69.2	30.8	79	–423	–344	230	120	Zimbabwe

[1]1996. [2]Manufacturing includes mining and public utilities. [3]1997. [4]Gross domestic product (GDP). [5]1995. [6]1994. [7]Manufacturing includes mining. [8]Mining includes public utilities. [9]Republic of Cyprus only. [10]Services includes hotels. [11]Excludes Alderney and Sark. [12]Manufacturing includes public utilities. [13]Manufacturing includes mining, construction, and public utilities. [14]Construction includes mining. [15]Transportation, communications includes public utilities. [16]1987. [17]Services includes transportation, communications. [18]1991.

Employment and labour

This table provides international comparisons of the world's national labour forces—giving their size; composition by demographic component and employment status; and structure by industry.

The table focuses on the concept of "economically active population," which the International Labour Organisation (ILO) defines as persons of all ages who are either employed or looking for work. In general, the economically active population does not include students, persons occupied solely in domestic duties, retired persons, persons living entirely on their own means, and persons wholly dependent on others. Persons engaged in illegal economic activities—smugglers, prostitutes, drug dealers, bootleggers, black marketeers, and others—also fall outside the purview of the ILO definition. Countries differ markedly in their treatment, as part of the labour force, of such groups as members of the armed forces, inmates of institutions, the unemployed (both persons seeking their first job and those previously employed), seasonal and international migrant workers, and persons engaged in informal, subsistence, or part-time economic activities. Some countries include all or most of these groups among the economically active, while others may treat the same groups as inactive.

Three principal structural comparisons of the economically active total are given in the first part of the table: (1) participation rate, or the proportion of the economically active who possess some particular characteristic, is given for women and for those of working age (usually ages 15 to 64), (2) activity rate, the proportion of the total population who *are* economically active, is given for both sexes and as a total, and (3) employment status, usually (and here) grouped as employers, self-employed, employees, family workers (usually unpaid), and others.

Each of these measures indicates certain characteristics in a given national labour market; none should be interpreted in isolation, however, as the meaning of each is influenced by a variety of factors—demographic structure and change, social or religious customs, educational opportunity, sexual differentiation in employment patterns, degree of technological development, and the like. Participation and activity rates, for example, may be high in a particular country because it possesses an older population with few children, hence a higher proportion of working age, or because, despite a young population with many below working age, the economy attracts eligible immigrant workers, themselves almost exclusively of working age. At the same time, low activity and participation rates might be characteristic of a country having a young population with poor employment possibilities or of a country with a good job market distorted by the presence of large numbers of "guest" or contract workers who are not part of the domestic labour force. An illiterate woman in a strongly sex-differentiated labour force is likely to begin and end as a family or

Employment and labour

country	year	economically active population										distribution by economic sector			
		total ('000)	participation rate (%)		activity rate (%)			employment status (%)				agriculture, forestry, fishing		manufacturing; mining, quarrying; public utilities	
			female	ages 15–64	total	male	female	employers, self-employed	employees	unpaid family workers	other	number ('000)	% of econ. active	number ('000)	% of econ. active
Afghanistan	1979	3,941	7.9	49.1	30.3	54.2	4.9	52.2	33.8	14.0	—	2,369	60.1	494	12.5
Albania	1994	1,340	47.0[3]	92.0[3, 4]	57.4[3]	60.8[3]	54.0[3]	...	...	...	...	534	39.9	84[5]	6.3[5]
Algeria	1987	5,341	9.2	44.3	23.6	42.4	4.4	16.8	61.7	2.6	18.9	725	13.6	622	11.6
American Samoa	1990	14.2	41.1	52.6[8]	30.4	34.8	25.7	2.1	92.6	0.2	5.1	0.3	2.3	4.8	33.7
Andorra	1989	25	45.6	74.3	55.1	...	...	...	...	...	...	0.3	1.2	2.7	11.0
Angola	1995	4,493	37.5	62.4[10]	40.6	51.3	30.1	...	...	...	...	3,118	69.4	509[11]	11.3[11]
Antigua and Barbuda	1991	26.8	45.6	69.7	45.1	50.9	39.6	12.1	82.8	0.7	4.4	1.0	3.9	1.9	7.3
Argentina	1995	14,345	36.7	64.5	41.5	53.5	29.9	28.0[13]	60.4[13]	5.0[13]	6.6[13]	1,201[14]	12.0[14]	2,136[14]	21.3[14]
Armenia	1996	1,584	...	75.1[16]	42.1	...	...	...	...	...	...	587	37.1	255	16.1
Aruba	1991	31.1	42.5	67.1	46.7	54.5	39.0	7.0	86.4	0.3	6.3	0.2	0.5	2.3	7.3
Australia	1998[18]	9,343	43.3	73.3[19]	49.8	56.6	43.0	12.7	78.2	0.7	8.4	442	4.7	1,311	14.0
Austria	1998[18]	3,888	43.1	70.7	48.1	56.5	40.3	9.7[20]	87.4[20]	3.0[20]	—	246	6.3	842	21.6
Azerbaijan	1998	3,744	47.8	64.4[16, 20]	47.1	50.1	44.2	...	...	...	...	1,085	29.0	367	9.8
Bahamas, The	1994	139	47.5	77.8	50.7	54.8	46.8	11.6[22]	85.1[22]	0.3[22]	3.0[22]	6.9	5.0	7.3	5.3
Bahrain	1991	226	17.5	66.8	44.6	63.5	18.5	5.1	88.5	0.1	6.3	5	2.3	33	14.6
Bangladesh	1995–96[18]	56,014	38.1	73.7	46.0	55.8	35.7	28.8	12.1	39.1	20.0	34,530	61.6	4,211	7.5
Barbados	1995[18]	137	49.5	79.9	51.8	54.6	49.1	8.8[24]	76.4[24]	0.2[24]	14.6[24]	6.3	4.6	15.6	11.4
Belarus	1999	4,542	52.4	78.2[16]	45.3	46.0	44.7	...	...	...	...	672	14.8	1,258	27.7
Belgium	1992	4,237	42.3	51.5[25]	42.2	49.8	34.9	12.7	72.4	3.4	11.5	95	2.2	788	18.6
Belize	1996	75.5	30.8	58.5[26]	34.1	47.2	21.0	26.2[20]	59.2[20]	4.9[20]	9.8[20]	18.3[13]	31.4[13]	7.0[13]	12.0[13]
Benin	1992	2,085	42.6	73.4	43.0	50.6	35.7	58.4	5.3	30.5	5.8	1,148	55.0	162	7.8
Bermuda	1995	34.1	50.0	63.5[13]	55.8	57.4	54.4	9.7[13]	84.0[13]	0.1[13]	6.2[13]	0.5	1.5	1.4	4.2
Bhutan	...	...	...	...	...	...	...	...	...	...	...	...	...	...	...
Bolivia	1992	2,530	38.2	64.0	39.4	48.7	30.4	41.2	31.5	7.1	20.2	984	38.9	281	11.1
Bosnia and Herzegovina	1990[5]	1,026	36.9	...	22.7	...	...	...	...	...	...	39	3.8	519	50.5
Botswana	1995	440	46.6	65.4	29.9	33.1	27.0	7.9	62.7	7.9	21.5	54	12.2	47	10.8
Brazil	1997	75,213	40.4	66.9	48.2	58.7	38.1	26.3[22]	62.3[22]	7.7[22]	3.7[22]	16,771	22.3	9,281	12.3
Brunei	1991	112	32.9	67.6	43.0	54.6	30.0	3.5	91.4	0.4	4.7	2.2	1.9	11.6	10.4
Bulgaria	1995	3,738	48.4[28]	68.8[28]	46.3[28]	48.7[28]	44.1[28]	8.4	75.9	0.9	14.8	783	20.9	1,003	26.8
Burkina Faso	1995	5,250	45.5	75.8[10]	50.9	56.0	45.9	...	...	...	...	4,397	83.8	298	5.7[11]
Burundi	1990	2,780	52.6	91.4	52.5	51.2	53.8	62.8	5.1	30.3	1.8	2,574	92.6	37	1.3
Cambodia	1993	4,010	55.8	86.2	43.1	39.5	46.4	...	...	...	...	2,454[14]	74.4[14]	220[11, 14]	6.7[11, 14]
Cameroon	1991	4,740	33.2	58.9[10]	40.0	53.9	26.3	60.2[22]	14.6[22]	18.0[22]	7.1[22]	2,856	60.3	628[11]	13.2[11]
Canada	1998[18]	15,631	45.3	75.4	51.0	56.3	45.9	15.8	75.5	0.4	8.3	586	3.7	2,601	16.6
Cape Verde	1990	121	37.1	64.3	35.3	46.9	24.9	24.7	53.7	2.0	19.6	29.9	24.8	6.8	5.7
Central African Republic	1988	1,187	46.8	78.3	48.2	52.2	44.3	75.3	8.0	8.1	8.6	881	74.2	31	2.6
Chad	1991	2,016	18.2	51.6[10]	35.3	56.5	14.7	...	...	...	...	1,489	73.9	149[11]	7.4[11]
Chile	1998[18]	5,852	33.4	59.9	39.3	52.8	26.0	26.4[19]	64.6[19]	3.2[19]	5.8[19]	809	13.8	1,015	17.3
China	1990	657,290	44.9	85.0	57.9	61.8	53.7	...	...	...	...	467,926	71.2	87,275	13.3
Colombia	1985	9,558	32.8	49.4[29]	34.3	46.6	22.3	...	...	...	...	2,412[14]	28.5[14]	1,231[14]	14.5[14]
Comoros	1996	252	38.9	59.2	37.2	44.8	29.3	47.6[14]	25.6[14]	—— 26.8[14] ——		189	74.7	18[11]	7.1[11]
Congo, Dem. Rep. of the	1996	14,082	35.0	47.9[10]	31.1	40.9	21.6	...	...	...	...	9,124	64.8	2,267[11]	16.1[11]
Congo, Rep. of the	1984	563	45.6	54.0	29.5	33.0	26.2	64.3	31.4	1.2	3.1	294	52.2	50	8.8
Costa Rica	1998	1,377	32.6	59.7[25]	41.2	55.8	26.7	24.0[19]	72.2[19]	3.3[19]	0.6[19]	271	19.7	231	16.8
Côte d'Ivoire	1988	4,263	32.3	66.6	39.4	52.2	26.0	...	...	...	...	2,628	61.6	100	2.3
Croatia	1991	2,040	42.9	65.2	45.3	53.9	37.4	12.7	73.7	2.0	11.6	341	16.7	571	28.0
Cuba	1988	4,570	36.1	56.9[25]	44.2	56.2	32.1	5.7[30]	94.1[30]	0.2[30]	—	791[30]	22.3[30]	668[30]	18.9[30]
Cyprus[31, 32]	1995	303	38.6	71.5	47.0	57.8	36.2	18.7[28]	73.1[28]	6.1[28]	2.1[28]	31	10.1	48	15.9
Czech Republic	1997	5,215	44.1	72.5	50.6	58.2	43.5	12.8	81.6	0.4	5.2	296	5.7	1,617	31.0
Denmark	1998	2,848	46.3	80.3	53.7	58.3	49.2	8.7	85.8	—	5.5	103	3.6	572	20.1
Djibouti	1996	396	41.4	96.3[10]	67.2	79.7	55.0	...	...	...	...	288	72.7	56[11]	14.1[11]
Dominica	1991	26.4	34.5	62.4	38.0	50.0	26.1	29.2[33]	50.6[33]	1.9[33]	18.3[33]	7.3	27.9	2.3	8.8
Dominican Republic	1981	1,915	28.9	53.6	33.9	48.1	19.7	36.5	51.3	3.3	8.9	420	22.0	243	12.7
East Timor	...	...	...	...	...	...	...	...	...	...	...	...	...	...	...
Ecuador	1990	3,360	26.4	55.7	34.8	51.5	18.3	45.7	42.5	4.4	7.4	1,036	30.8	404	12.0
Egypt	1995[18]	17,725	22.0	49.8	29.9	45.9	13.4	24.7[28]	50.0[28]	16.4[28]	9.0[28]	5,221	30.2	2,405	13.9
El Salvador	1997	2,256	36.7	61.4	38.2	50.2	27.0	31.7	48.5	7.4	12.4	607	26.9	373	16.5
Equatorial Guinea	1983	103	35.7	66.7	39.2	52.5	26.9	29.0	16.0	29.9	25.1	59.4	57.9	1.8	1.8
Eritrea	...	...	...	...	...	...	...	...	...	...	...	...	...	...	...
Estonia	1998	711	47.7	71.8[34]	48.9	54.9	43.6	4.8[19]	85.2[19]	0.8[19]	9.2[19]	61	8.6	165	23.2

traditional agricultural worker. Loss of working-age men to war, civil violence, or emigration for job opportunities may also affect the structure of a particular labour market.

The distribution of the economically active population by employment status reveals that a large percentage of economically active persons in some less developed countries falls under the heading "employers, self-employed." This occurs because the countries involved have poor, largely agrarian economies in which the average worker is a farmer who tills his own small plot of land. In countries with well-developed economies, "employees" will usually constitute the largest portion of the economically active.

Caution should be exercised when using the economically active data to make intercountry comparisons, as countries often differ in their choices of classification schemes, definitions, and coverage of groups and in their methods of collection and tabulation of data. The population base containing the economically active population, for example, may range, in developing countries, from age 9 or 10 with no upper limit to, in developed countries, age 18 or 19 upward to a usual retirement age of from 55 to 65, with sometimes a different range for each sex. Data on female labour-force participation, in particular, often lack comparability. In many less developed countries, particularly those dominated by the Islamic faith, a cultural bias favouring traditional roles for women results in the undercounting of economically active women. In other less developed countries, particularly those in which subsistence workers are deemed economically active, the role of women may be overstated.

The second major section of the table provides data on the distribution by economic (also conventionally called industrial) sector of the economically active population. The data usually include such groups as unpaid family workers, members of the armed forces, and the unemployed, the last distributed by industry as far as possible.

The categorization of industrial sectors is based on the divisions listed in the *International Standard Industrial Classification of All Economic Activities*. The "other" category includes persons whose activities were not adequately defined and the unemployed who were not distributable by industrial sector.

A substantial part of the data presented in this table is summarized from various issues of the ILO's *Year Book of Labour Statistics*, which compiles its statistics both from official publications and from information submitted directly by national census and labour authorities. The editors have supplemented and updated ILO statistical data with information from Britannica's holdings of relevant official publications and from direct correspondence with national authorities.

construction		transportation, communications		trade, hotels, restaurants		finance, real estate		public administration, defense		services		other		country
number ('000)	% of econ. active	number ('000)	% of econ. active	number ('000)	% of econ. active	number ('000)	% of econ. active	number ('000)	% of econ. active	number ('000)	% of econ. active	number ('000)	% of econ. active	
51	1.3	66	1.6	138	3.5	[1]	[1]	[1]	[1]	749[1]	19.0[1]	78[2]	2.0[2]	Afghanistan
33[5]	2.5[5]	19[5]	1.4[5]	3[5]	0.2[5]	3[5]	0.2[5]	16[5]	1.2[5]	145[5]	10.8[5]	505[6]	37.7[6]	Albania
690	12.9	216	4.1	391	7.3	143	2.7	[7]	[7]	1,180[7]	22.1[7]	1,374	25.7	Algeria
1.2	8.3	0.8	5.5	1.8	13.0	0.3	2.1	1.4	10.0	2.8	19.8	0.7[9]	5.1[9]	American Samoa
2.9	11.8	…	…	6.0	24.2	1.3	5.4	2.6	10.3	4.1	16.7	0.1	0.5	Andorra
[11]	[11]	[12]	[12]	[12]	[12]	[12]	[12]	[12]	[12]	866[12]	19.3[12]	—	—	Angola
3.1	11.6	2.4	9.0	8.5	31.9	1.5	5.4	[7]	[7]	6.4[7]	23.9[7]	1.9	7.0	Antigua and Barbuda
1,003[14]	10.0[14]	460[14]	4.6[14]	1,702[14]	17.0[14]	396[14]	3.9[14]	[7]	[7]	2,399[7, 14]	23.9[7, 14]	736[14, 15]	7.3[14, 15]	Argentina
68	4.3	24	1.5	110	6.9	[1]	[1]	[1]	[1]	350[1]	22.1[1]	190[17]	12.0[17]	Armenia
3.2	10.4	2.3	7.5	11.0	35.4	2.4	7.8	[7]	[7]	8.6[7]	27.7[7]	1.1[17]	3.5[17]	Aruba
654	7.0	567	6.1	2,279	24.4	1,310	14.0	444	4.7	1,884	20.2	454[17]	4.9[17]	Australia
341	8.8	250	6.4	844	21.7	387	9.9	256	6.6	712	18.3	12[2]	0.3[2]	Austria
150	4.0	167	4.5	772	20.6	10	0.3	[7]	[7]	618[7]	16.5[7]	574[21]	15.3[21]	Azerbaijan
11.6	8.3	11.2	8.1	44.2	31.8	12.9	9.3	10.7	7.7	29.7	21.4	4.5[23]	3.2[23]	Bahamas, The
27	11.8	14	6.1	30	13.2	17	7.6	41	18.1	43	19.0	16[17]	7.3[17]	Bahrain
1,015	1.8	2,308	4.1	6,068	10.8	213	0.4	[7]	[7]	5,092[7]	9.1[7]	2,585[17]	4.6[17]	Bangladesh
12.2	8.9	5.9	4.3	35.3	25.8	8.4	6.1	[7]	[7]	48.8[7]	35.7[7]	4.3[2]	3.1[2]	Barbados
336	7.4	332	7.3	504	11.1	[1]	[1]	[1]	[1]	1,345[1]	29.6[1]	95[9]	2.1[9]	Belarus
245	5.8	257	6.1	634	15.0	342	8.1	7	7	1,393[7]	32.9[7]	484[17]	11.4[17]	Belgium
4.1[13]	7.0[13]	2.9[13]	5.0[13]	10.0[13]	17.2[13]	1.8[13]	3.1[13]	5.4[13]	9.2[13]	6.0[13]	10.3[13]	2.8[13]	4.8[13]	Belize
52	2.5	53	2.5	433	20.7	3	0.1	[7]	[7]	165[7]	7.9[7]	71[21]	3.4[21]	Benin
1.7	5.0	2.2	6.4	10.8	31.6	5.2	15.3	[7]	[7]	12.3[7]	35.9[7]	—	—	Bermuda
…	…	…	…	…	…	…	…	…	…	…	…	…	…	Bhutan
129	5.1	117	4.6	232	9.2	54	2.1	59	2.3	350	13.8	323[15]	12.7[15]	Bolivia
75	7.3	69	6.7	131	12.8	39	3.8	[7]	[7]	155[7]	15.1[7]	—	—	Bosnia and Herzegovina
41	9.3	8	1.8	54	12.3	12	2.7	60	13.6	69	15.7	95[17]	21.6[17]	Botswana
4,583	6.1	2,759	3.7	9,223[27]	12.3[27]	1,287	1.7	[7]	[7]	25,436[7, 27]	33.8[7, 27]	5,882[9]	7.8[9]	Brazil
14.1	12.6	5.4	4.8	15.4	13.8	5.8	5.2	[7]	[7]	52.1[7]	46.6[7]	5.3[17]	4.7[17]	Brunei
188	5.0	251	6.7	357	9.5	51	1.4	76	2.0	532	14.2	497[17]	13.3[17]	Bulgaria
[11]	[11]	[12]	[12]	[12]	[12]	[12]	[12]	[12]	[12]	558[12]	10.6[12]	—	—	Burkina Faso
20	0.7	9	0.3	26	0.9	2.0	0.1	[7]	[7]	85[7]	3.1[7]	27[17]	1.0[17]	Burundi
[11]	[11]	[12]	[12]	[12]	[12]	[12]	[12]	[12]	[12]	625[12, 14]	18.9[12, 14]	—	—	Cambodia
[11]	[11]	[12]	[12]	[12]	[12]	[12]	[12]	[12]	[12]	1,256[12]	26.5[12]	—	—	Cameroon
857	5.5	1,128	7.2	3,585	22.9	2,336	14.9	820	5.2	3,252	20.8	468[2]	3.0[2]	Canada
22.7	18.8	6.1	5.1	12.7	10.6	0.8	0.7	[7]	[7]	17.4[7]	14.4[7]	24.1	20.0	Cape Verde
6	0.5	7	0.6	92	7.8	0.7	0.1	[7]	[7]	70[7]	5.9[7]	100[17]	8.5[17]	Central African Republic
[11]	[11]	[12]	[12]	[12]	[12]	[12]	[12]	[12]	[12]	377[12]	18.7[12]	—	—	Chad
533	9.1	456	7.8	1,075	18.4	437	7.5	[7]	[7]	1,478[7]	25.3[7]	47[15]	0.8[15]	Chile
11,890	1.8	11,814	1.8	25,631	3.9	8,268	1.3	[7]	[7]	34,053[7]	5.2[7]	10,434	1.6	China
242[14]	2.9[14]	353[14]	4.2[14]	1,262[14]	14.9[14]	278[14]	3.3[14]	[7]	[7]	1,998[7, 14]	23.6[7, 14]	691[14, 15]	8.2[14, 15]	Colombia
[11]	[11]	[12]	[12]	[12]	[12]	[12]	[12]	[12]	[12]	46[12]	18.2[12]	—	—	Comoros
[11]	[11]	[12]	[12]	[12]	[12]	[12]	[12]	[12]	[12]	2,691[12]	19.1[12]	—	—	Congo, Dem. Rep. of the
25	4.5	29	5.1	67	11.8	3	0.5	[7]	[7]	85[7]	15.1[7]	10	2.0	Congo, Rep. of the
89	6.5	75	5.5	267	19.4	35	2.6	[7]	[7]	385[7]	27.9[7]	23[23]	1.7[23]	Costa Rica
85	2.0	118	2.8	530	12.4	[1]	[1]	[1]	[1]	591[1]	13.9[1]	210[2]	4.9[2]	Côte d'Ivoire
93	4.5	112	5.5	223	10.9	58	2.8	104	5.1	204	10.0	329[17]	16.1[17]	Croatia
313[30]	8.8[30]	249[30]	7.0[30]	306[30]	8.6[30]	[1]	[1]	[1]	[1]	1,086[1, 30]	30.7[1, 30]	128[30]	3.6[30]	Cuba
26	8.7	19	6.2	77	25.4	23	7.6	[7]	[7]	65[7]	21.6[7]	13	4.4	Cyprus[31, 32]
501	9.6	392	7.5	871	16.7	358	6.9	328	6.3	762	14.6	90[17]	1.7[17]	Czech Republic
185	6.5	191	6.7	467	16.4	321	11.3	175	6.1	821	28.8	18[23]	0.6[23]	Denmark
[11]	[11]	[12]	[12]	[12]	[12]	[12]	[12]	[12]	[12]	52[12]	13.2[12]	—	—	Djibouti
2.8	10.7	1.2	4.6	3.7	13.9	0.8	3.1	1.5	5.8	3.4	13.1	3.2[17]	12.3[17]	Dominica
81	4.3	40	2.1	192	10.0	22	1.2	[7]	[7]	363[7]	18.9[7]	553[15]	28.9[15]	Dominican Republic
…	…	…	…	…	…	…	…	…	…	…	…	…	…	East Timor
197	5.9	131	3.9	477	14.2	81	2.4	[7]	[7]	838[7]	24.9[7]	196[15]	5.8[15]	Ecuador
984	5.7	912	5.3	1,609	9.3	286	1.7	[7]	[7]	4,000[7]	23.2[7]	1,858[23]	10.8[23]	Egypt
159	7.1	103	4.6	462	20.5	32	1.4	[7]	[7]	485[7]	21.5[7]	36[2]	1.6[2]	El Salvador
1.9	1.9	1.8	1.7	3.1	3.0	0.4	0.4	[7]	[7]	8.4[7]	8.2[7]	25.8[17]	25.2[17]	Equatorial Guinea
…	…	…	…	…	…	…	…	…	…	…	…	…	…	Eritrea
48	6.8	60	8.4	105	14.8	44	6.2	37	5.2	122	17.2	68[9]	9.6[9]	Estonia

Employment and labour (continued)

country	year	economically active population										distribution by economic sector			
		total ('000)	participation rate (%)		activity rate (%)			employment status (%)				agriculture, forestry, fishing		manufacturing; mining, quarrying; public utilities	
			female	ages 15–64	total	male	female	employers, self-employed	employees	unpaid family workers	other	number ('000)	% of econ. active	number ('000)	% of econ. active
Ethiopia	1995	24,606	41.1	72.2	43.3	50.3	36.5	58.5[35]	6.5[35]	34.0[35]	1.0[35]	21,605	87.8	419	1.7
Faroe Islands	1977	17.6	27.2	64.0	41.9	58.2	23.9	11.9	86.1	...	2.0	3.3	18.8	3.9	21.9
Fiji	1986	241	21.2	56.0	33.7	52.4	14.5	33.6	42.2	16.3	7.9	106	44.1	22	9.0
Finland	1998	2,532	47.0	73.1	49.1	53.4	45.1	11.9	75.2	0.6	12.3	154	6.1	508	20.1
France	1994[18]	25,871	44.9	67.7	44.8	50.6	39.2	10.2	77.4	—	12.4	1,048	4.1	4,432	17.4
French Guiana	1990	48.8	38.2	67.3	42.5	50.5	33.9	10.6	62.7	2.5	24.2	4.2	8.6	3.1	6.4
French Polynesia	1988	75	37.1	64.8	39.9	48.2	30.9	13.0	55.0	4.0	28.0	7.6	10.0	5.4	7.2
Gabon	1991	504	36.9	56.0[10]	43.9	53.9	30.7	...	...	...	...	338	67.1	71[11]	14.1[11]
Gambia, The	1983	326	46.3	78.2	47.3	51.1	43.6	0.5	78.0	14.3	7.1	240	73.7	9	2.9
Gaza Strip	1996	173	9.0	36.3[25]	18.0	32.0	3.2	15.7	46.8	6.7	30.8	9.0	5.2	17.0[36]	9.8[36]
Georgia	1993	1,920	...	58.1[16, 28]	35.7	...	...	...	...	...	...	562	29.3	303	15.8
Germany	1998	39,709	43.1	70.7	48.4	56.5	40.7	9.1	80.3	1.0	9.6	1,200	3.0	10,019	25.2
Ghana	1984	5,580	51.2	82.5[25]	45.4	44.9	45.8	67.7	15.7	12.2	4.4	3,311	59.3	631	11.3
Greece	1997[18]	4,294	39.2	61.3	4.8	53.0	31.5	29.9	49.2	10.7	10.2	773	18.0	680	15.8
Greenland	1976	21.4	33.4	63.5[25]	43.1	53.0	31.4	12.6	82.5	0.4	4.5	3.2	15.1	3.3	15.3
Grenada	1988	38.9	48.6	72.7[35]	39.9	42.9	37.2	16.0[30]	64.2[30]	0.8[30]	19.0[30]	5.6	14.3	3.3	8.6
Guadeloupe	1990	172	45.5	66.4	44.5	49.6	39.7	13.2	53.7	2.0	31.1	8.4	4.9	9.6	5.6
Guam	1990	66.1	37.4	75.7[8]	49.7	58.4	39.7	2.4	94.4	0.1	3.1	0.5	0.8	3.5	5.3
Guatemala	1999	3,489	22.0	55.0	31.5	48.6	14.0	32.7[33]	47.6[33]	16.2[33]	3.5[33]	1,416[33]	48.9[33]	405[33]	14.0[33]
Guernsey[38]	1996	30.7	44.7	76.4	52.3	60.1	45.1	13.0	87.0	—	—	1.9	6.2	2.5	8.2
Guinea	1983	1,823	39.4	63.5	39.1	48.7	30.1	36.2	15.6	37.6	10.6	1,424	78.1	27	1.5
Guinea-Bissau	1995	491	39.9	65.5[10]	45.8	55.9	36.0	...	...	...	...	373	76.0	20[11]	4.1[11]
Guyana	1992–93	278	34.1	61.8	38.8	51.9	26.0	14.3[14]	63.8[14]	1.9[14]	20.0[14]	50[14]	20.4[14]	41[14]	16.8[14]
Haiti	1990	2,679	40.0	64.8	41.1	50.3	32.3	59.1	16.5	10.4	14.0	1,535	57.3	178	6.6
Honduras	1998[18]	2,135	36.9	61.2[25]	36.9	49.2	25.0	40.6	48.0	11.4	—	738	34.6	380	17.8
Hong Kong	1998[18]	3,359	39.3	70.0	51.1	61.9	40.3	9.9[19]	87.4[19]	0.7[19]	1.9[19]	10	0.3	434	12.9
Hungary	1998[18]	4,011	44.4	58.4	39.3	45.8	33.4	10.6	80.3	0.7	8.4	301	7.5	1,115	27.8
Iceland	1998	152.1	47.1	86.6[8]	55.4	59.2	52.2	17.3	80.3	0.3	2.1	12.8	8.4	27.1	17.8
India	1991	314,131	28.6	60.7[25, 30]	37.5	51.6	22.3	8.8[30]	16.3[30]	3.6[30]	71.3[30]	191,341	60.9	30,423	9.7
Indonesia	1998	92,735	38.8	65.3[25]	45.4	55.8	35.0	42.7[34]	33.0[34]	17.1[34]	7.2[34]	39,415	42.5	10,756	11.6
Iran	1996–97	16,027	12.7	46.8[13]	26.7	45.8	6.9	39.7[13]	45.4[13]	2.3[13]	12.6[13]	3,205[13]	21.8[13]	2,243[13]	15.2[13]
Iraq	1988	4,127	12.0	45.3	24.7	42.3	6.1	25.4[39]	59.5[39]	11.4[39]	3.7[39]	477	11.6	439	10.6
Ireland	1997	1,539	39.1	62.7	42.0	51.6	32.6	17.4	71.1	1.1	10.4	145	9.4	314	20.4
Isle of Man	1991	33.2	42.3	73.2	47.6	56.9	38.9	15.8	80.1	—	4.1	1.2	3.7	3.9	11.6
Israel	1998[18]	2,272	44.3	53.5[25]	40.3	45.2	35.5	13.2	77.7	0.5	8.6	50	2.3	434	19.1
Italy	1994[18]	22,680	36.9	57.4	40.1	52.1	28.8	21.4	62.8	4.0	11.8	1,573	6.9	4,837	21.3
Jamaica	1998	1,129	45.6	69.3[40]	43.9	48.7	39.2	32.3	49.9	1.9	15.9	218[19]	20.0[19]	107[19]	9.8[19]
Japan	1998	67,930	40.7	72.6	53.7	65.1	42.9	11.2	79.0	5.4	4.4	3,440	5.1	14,620	21.5
Jersey	1991	47.5	43.2	66.9[25]	56.5	66.1	47.5	12.6	84.0	...	3.4	2.2	4.7	3.8	8.0
Jordan	1993	859	11.4[42]	43.2[42]	22.2	...	...	22.8[43]	67.2[43]	0.8[43]	9.2[43]	55	6.4	97	11.3
Kazakhstan	1995	6,976	...	71.8[16, 20]	40.8	...	...	...	...	...	...	1,442	20.7	1,372	19.7
Kenya	1996	12,269	38.5	63.6[10]	43.9	53.9	33.8	...	...	...	...	9,100	74.2	1,062[11]	8.7[11]
Kiribati	1990	32.6	46.4	75.6[25]	45.1	48.9	41.4	71.9	25.3	...	2.8	23.1	71.0	0.9	2.8
Korea, North	1985	9,084	46.0	75.3	44.6	48.6	40.6	...	...	...	...	3,726[24]	44.1[24]	2,790[11, 24]	33.0[11, 24]
Korea, South	1998[18]	21,390	39.8	60.7[25]	45.9	54.9	36.8	26.8	57.0	9.3	6.8	2,450	11.5	4,246	19.9
Kuwait	1997	1,217	23.5	61.5[42]	55.1	69.0	33.2	3.9[42]	94.1[42]	0.1[42]	1.9[42]	9[42]	1.3[42]	69[42]	9.4[42]
Kyrgyzstan	1998	1,705	46.1	...	37.2	41.1	33.5	...	...	...	...	831	48.7	104	6.1
Laos	1995	2,166	56.4	83.3	47.3	46.2	52.8	...	...	...	...	1,393[14]	75.7[14]	130[11, 14]	7.1[11, 14]
Latvia	1997	1,186	48.1	70.2	48.0	54.0	42.9	11.1	69.3	5.0	14.6	203	17.1	233	19.6
Lebanon	1997	1,362	21.6	49.3	34.0	55.2	14.2	...	...	...	...	132[44]	19.1[44]	131[44]	18.9[44]
Lesotho	1986	504	27.0	44.0	31.6	47.3	16.7	16.8	55.7	20.5	7.0	131	25.9	142	28.2
Liberia	1984	704	41.0	56.3	33.5	39.1	27.8	59.1	21.6	14.4	5.0	481	68.3	31	4.4
Libya	1991	1,169	9.3	37.1[10]	24.8	42.9	4.9	...	...	...	...	129	11.0	372[11]	31.8[11]
Liechtenstein	1996	16.2	40.3	71.3	52.0	63.7	40.8	6.4	90.8	0.1	2.7	0.3	2.0	4.9	30.2
Lithuania	1998	1,835	47.9	71.7[26]	49.5	54.8	44.9	14.1	69.1	0.2	16.6	317	17.2	411	22.4
Luxembourg	1991[45]	168	36.5	62.5	43.5	56.4	31.2	9.2	85.3	1.1	4.4	5	3.2	26	15.8
Macau	1998[18]	210.7	35.3	70.7[40]	50.2	58.2	43.0	8.0	85.9	1.6	4.5	0.4	0.2	44.5	21.1
Macedonia	1996	789	39.1	60.6	39.6	48.1	31.1	...	...	...	...	103	13.0	165	20.9
Madagascar	1996	5,984	38.2	58.7	39.2	48.9	29.8	...	...	...	...	4,381	73.2	926[11]	15.5[11]
Malawi	1987	3,458	51.0	89.4	43.3	43.9	42.8	4.9	16.2	77.6	1.3	2,968	85.8	114	3.3
Malaysia	1998[18]	8,884	33.5	64.4	40.1	52.0	27.5	21.1[20]	71.4[20]	7.5[20]	—	1,617	18.2	1,986	22.4
Maldives	1990	56.4	19.9	50.2	26.5	41.3	10.8	39.7	49.3	4.5	6.5	14.1	25.0	9.4	16.6
Mali	1987	3,438	37.4	67.4	44.7	57.2	32.7	35.4	5.2	57.6	1.8	2,803	81.5	191	5.6
Malta	1990	132	25.4	47.4[13]	37.2	56.1	18.7	14.1[48]	77.4[48]	...	8.5[48]	3	2.5	38	28.8
Marshall Islands	1988	11.5	30.1	54.1[28]	26.5	37.7	14.8	21.6	58.9	7.1	12.5	2.2	18.7	1.0	9.0
Martinique	1990	165	47.5	68.1	45.9	49.8	42.2	9.5	56.9	1.5	32.1	8.4	5.1	9.7	5.9
Mauritania	1995	704	23.0	44.3[10]	31.0	48.1	14.1	...	...	...	...	437	62.1	84[11]	11.9[11]
Mauritius[49]	1995	484	32.9	63.5	42.9	58.1	28.0	15.1	72.9	2.1	9.9	65	13.5	142	29.4
Mayotte	1991	27.3	29.4	56.4	28.9	39.2	17.7	12.0	42.9	7.3	37.8	3.1	11.4	1.3	4.7
Mexico	1998	39,507	33.7	65.4	41.3	56.1	27.2	30.1[20]	53.8[20]	13.6[20]	2.6[20]	7,842	19.8	7,473	18.9
Micronesia	1990	30.5	29.8[14]	60.6	30.3	...	...	2.7[14]	74.4[14]	0.1[14]	22.7[14]	12.7	41.5	1.6	5.2
Moldova	1996	1,686	...	68.7[16, 19]	39.1	...	...	...	...	...	...	711	42.2	195	11.6
Monaco	1990	12.6	39.7	...	42.0	53.2	31.8	17.4	75.1	0.3	7.2	—	0.3	2.7	21.8
Mongolia	1998	841	48.0	64.3[51]	36.7	38.8	34.6	...	...	...	...	300[20]	35.5[20]	124[20]	14.7[20]
Morocco	1982	5,999	19.7	48.9	29.3	47.1	11.6	27.1	40.5	17.6	14.8	2,352	39.2	1,016	16.9
Mozambique	1995	9,111	46.6	74.9	56.8	61.4	52.3	...	...	...	...	7,274	80.0	881[11]	9.7[11]
Myanmar (Burma)	1997–98[18]	18,337	35.3[48]	64.2[48]	40.2[48]	52.4[48]	28.2[48]	41.4[48]	27.4[48]	30.2[48]	1.0[48]	12,093	65.9	1,831	9.9
Namibia	1991	494	43.6	61.3	35.2	39.9	30.5	17.8	49.1	17.9	15.2	190	38.5	41	8.2
Nauru	1977	2.2	...	...	30.5	...	...	...	...	...	...	...	...	...	...
Nepal	1991	7,340	40.4	57.0[10]	40.0	47.8	32.2	75.8	21.4	2.3	0.4	5,962	81.2	164	2.2
Netherlands, The	1998	7,735	42.5	72.9	49.3	57.2	41.5	10.0	84.8	0.8	4.4	236	3.1	1,162	15.0
Netherlands Antilles	1992	87.8	45.1	68.6	46.3	53.1	40.1	...	...	...	...	0.5	0.6	8.4	9.6
New Caledonia	1989	66	37.5	70.7[53]	40.2	49.1	30.8	16.3	64.3	1.6	17.8	7.8	11.8	6.2	9.3
New Zealand	1998[18]	1,864	45.0	74.0	49.2	54.9	43.6	18.1[20]	73.6[20]	0.8[20]	7.5[20]	161	8.6	326	17.5
Nicaragua	1998	1,630	29.5	61.2	34.1	48.9	19.8	...	...	...	...	457[28]	31.4[28]	183[28]	12.5[28]

construction		transportation, communications		trade, hotels, restaurants		finance, real estate		public administration, defense		services		other		country
number ('000)	% of econ. active	number ('000)	% of econ. active	number ('000)	% of econ. active	number ('000)	% of econ. active	number ('000)	% of econ. active	number ('000)	% of econ. active	number ('000)	% of econ. active	
61	0.2	103	0.4	936	3.8	19	0.1	[7]	[7]	1,252[7]	5.1[7]	210[2]	0.9[2]	Ethiopia
2.0	11.1	1.9	11.1	2.1	11.9	0.3	1.9	[7]	[7]	3.5[7]	20.1[7]	0.6	3.2	Faroe Islands
12	4.9	13	5.5	26	10.8	6	2.5	[7]	[7]	37[7]	15.2[7]	20[17]	8.2[17]	Fiji
163	6.4	178	7.0	366	14.5	269	10.6	148	5.8	653	25.8	95[23]	3.8[23]	Finland
1,443	5.7	1,397	5.5	3,716	14.6	2,340	9.2	[7]	[7]	7,733[7]	30.3[7]	3,376[17]	13.2[17]	France
4.4	9.1	1.9	3.8	4.2	8.5	1.7	3.5	[7]	[7]	17.5[7]	35.9[7]	11.8[9]	24.2[9]	French Guiana
5.5	7.4	2.8	3.7	10.3	13.7	1.2	1.5	[7]	[7]	21.5[7]	28.6[7]	21.1[17]	28.0[17]	French Polynesia
[11]	[11]	[12]	[12]	[12]	[12]	[12]	[12]	[12]	[12]	95[12]	18.8[12]	—	—	Gabon
4	1.3	8	2.5	17	5.1	5	1.4	8	2.5	9	2.9	25	7.7	Gambia, The
17.8	10.3	5.7	3.3	20.8	12.0	[1]	[1]	[1]	[1]	49.3[1, 36]	28.5[1, 36]	53.3[9]	30.8[9]	Gaza Strip
125	6.5	107	5.6	117	6.1	20	1.0	49	2.6	479	24.9	158[17]	8.2[17]	Georgia
3,760	9.5	2,090	5.3	6,924	17.4	4,098	10.3	3,174	8.0	8,182	20.6	262[2]	0.7[2]	Germany
65	1.2	123	2.2	792	14.2	27	0.5	98	1.7	376	6.7	158[9]	2.8[9]	Ghana
262	6.1	264	6.1	933	21.7	268	6.2	285	6.6	593	13.8	235[23]	5.5[23]	Greece
3.1	14.6	1.8	8.6	2.7	12.6	0.3	1.6	[7]	[7]	6.3[7]	29.5[7]	0.6	2.8	Greenland
3.5	9.1	1.7	4.4	5.4	13.9	0.8	2.0	[7]	[7]	5.9[7]	15.3[7]	12.7[17]	32.5[17]	Grenada
14.0	8.1	7.0	4.0	15.0	8.7	2.8	1.6	[7]	[7]	60.8[7]	35.2[7]	54.9[17]	31.8[17]	Guadeloupe
8.0	12.1	4.5	6.8	11.5	17.5	3.9	6.0	17.7	26.7	14.5	21.9	2.0[9]	3.1[9]	Guam
114[33]	3.9[33]	72[33]	2.5[33]	375[33]	12.9[33]	38[33]	1.3[33]	[7]	[7]	417[7]	14.4[7]	60[17]	2.1[17]	Guatemala
2.7	8.7	1.3	4.1	7.0	22.9	8.2	26.6	1.9	6.2	5.0	16.2	0.2	0.8	Guernsey[38]
9	0.5	29	1.6	37	2.0	4	0.2	[7]	[7]	138[7]	7.5[7]	156	8.5	Guinea
[11]	[11]	[12]	[12]	[12]	[12]	[12]	[12]	[12]	[12]	98[12]	20.0[12]	—	—	Guinea-Bissau
7[14]	2.8[14]	9[14]	3.8[14]	15[14]	6.2[14]	3[14]	1.2[14]	30[14]	12.1[14]	29[14]	11.9[14]	61[14, 17]	24.7[14, 17]	Guyana
28	1.0	21	0.8	353	13.2	5	0.2	[7]	[7]	155[7]	5.8[7]	404[17]	15.1[17]	Haiti
111	5.2	55	2.6	440	20.6	52	2.5	[7]	[7]	359[7]	16.8[7]	—	—	Honduras
349	10.4	377	11.2	1,024	30.5	431	12.8	[7]	[7]	718[7]	21.4[7]	16[2]	0.5[2]	Hong Kong
257	6.4	315	7.9	640	16.0	258	6.4	313	7.8	747	18.6	67[23]	1.7[23]	Hungary
11.0	7.2	11.0	7.2	25.7	16.9	14.4	9.5	7.1	4.7	41.4	27.2	1.3[2]	1.1[2]	Iceland
5,543	1.8	8,108	2.6	21,296	6.8	[1]	[1]	[1]	[1]	29,312[1]	9.3[1]	28,199	9.0	India
3,522	3.8	4,154	4.5	16,814	18.1	618	0.7	[7]	[7]	12,394[7]	13.4[7]	5,063[9]	5.5[9]	Indonesia
1,372[13]	9.3[13]	762[13]	5.2[13]	1,238[13]	8.4[13]	195[13]	1.3[13]	[7]	[7]	3,518[7, 13]	23.9[7, 13]	2,203[13, 17]	14.9[13, 17]	Iran
461	11.2	266	6.4	282	6.8	42	1.0	[7]	[7]	2,160[7]	52.3[7]	—	—	Iraq
128	8.3	69	4.5	295	19.2	140	9.1	75	4.8	312	20.3	61[17]	4.0[17]	Ireland
3.4	10.3	2.4	7.3	6.1	18.4	4.4	13.1	[7]	[7]	10.4[7]	31.4[7]	1.4[9]	4.1[9]	Isle of Man
144	6.3	130	5.7	377	16.6	304	13.4	115	5.1	606	26.7	111[17]	4.9[17]	Israel
1,641	7.2	1,080	4.8	4,221	18.6	1,514	6.7	[7]	[7]	5,134[7]	22.6[7]	2,676[9]	11.8[9]	Italy
66[19]	6.1[19]	40[19]	3.7[19]	196[19]	17.9[19]	47[19]	4.3[19]	[7]	[7]	237[7, 19]	21.7[7, 19]	180[17, 19]	16.5[17, 19]	Jamaica
6,670	10.0	4,170	6.1	15,150[41]	22.3[41]	5,930	8.7	[7]	[7]	16,010[7, 41]	23.6[7, 41]	1,810[17]	2.7[17]	Japan
4.4	9.3	2.4	5.0	6.8	14.4	7.4	15.6	3.1	6.5	15.7	33.1	1.6[17]	3.4[17]	Jersey
60	7.0	58	6.7	130	15.1	25	2.9	[7]	[7]	435[7]	50.6[7]	—	—	Jordan
364	5.2	507	7.3	1,035	14.8	334	4.8	[7]	[7]	1,664[7]	23.9[7]	258[17]	3.7[17]	Kazakhstan
[11]	[11]	[12]	[12]	[12]	[12]	[12]	[12]	[12]	[12]	2,107[12]	17.2[12]	—	—	Kenya
0.3	1.0	0.9	2.8	1.3	4.1	0.4	1.4	2.1	6.5	2.3	7.0	1.1[17]	3.4[17]	Kiribati
[11]	[11]	[12]	[12]	[12]	[12]	[12]	[12]	[12]	[12]	1,939[12, 24]	22.9[12, 24]	—	—	Korea, North
1,876	8.8	1,218	5.7	5,911	27.6	1,962	9.2	752	3.5	2,713	12.7	270[15]	1.3[15]	Korea, South
115[42]	15.7[42]	38[42]	5.2[42]	83[42]	11.4[42]	22[42]	3.0[42]	[7]	[7]	384[7, 42]	52.6[7, 42]	11[2, 42]	1.5[2, 42]	Kuwait
51	3.0	75	4.4	178	10.4	15	0.9	61	3.6	258	15.2	132	7.7	Kyrgyzstan
[11]	[11]	[12]	[12]	[12]	[12]	[12]	[12]	[12]	[12]	316[12, 14]	17.2[12, 14]	—	—	Laos
69	5.8	96	8.1	198	16.7	57	4.8	67	5.6	209	17.6	55	4.6	Latvia
43[44]	6.2[44]	48[44]	7.0[44]	115[44]	16.5[44]	24[44]	3.5[44]	[7]	[7]	200[7, 44]	28.8[7, 44]	—	—	Lebanon
28	5.5	8	1.6	24	4.7	2	0.5	[7]	[7]	157[7]	31.1[7]	13	2.6	Lesotho
4	0.6	14	2.0	47	6.7	[1]	[1]	[1]	[1]	63[1]	9.0[1]	64[17]	9.1[17]	Liberia
[11]	[11]	[12]	[12]	[12]	[12]	[12]	[12]	[12]	[12]	668[12]	57.1[12]	—	—	Libya
1.1	7.0	0.5	3.2	2.4	14.8	1.3	7.8	1.0	6.4	4.1	25.4	0.6[17]	3.4[17]	Liechtenstein
128	7.0	119	6.5	302	16.4	70	3.8	82	4.4	347	18.9	61[2]	3.3[2]	Lithuania
14	8.4	11	6.3	29	17.5	15	9.2	21	12.8	31	18.7	14[21]	8.1[21]	Luxembourg
23.0	10.9	14.3	6.8	60.0	28.5	14.4	6.8	16.5	7.8	36.6	17.4	1.0	0.5	Macau
36	4.5	27	3.4	77	9.8	15	1.9	28	3.5	88	11.1	251[46]	31.9[46]	Macedonia
[11]	[11]	[12]	[12]	[12]	[12]	[12]	[12]	[12]	[12]	677[12]	11.3[12]	—	—	Madagascar
46	1.4	25	0.7	94	2.7	6	0.2	[7]	[7]	147[7]	4.3[7]	57	1.7	Malawi
746	8.4	422	4.7	1,616	18.2	426	4.8	[7]	[7]	1,788[7]	20.1[7]	284	3.2	Malaysia
3.2	5.6	5.3	9.4	8.9	15.7	1.1	1.9	[7]	[7]	11.8[7]	21.0[7]	2.7[47]	4.7[47]	Maldives
13	0.4	6	0.2	159	4.6	0.3	—	75	2.2	84	2.4	107	3.1	Mali
6	4.4	9	6.9	13	9.8	5	3.7	[7]	[7]	53[7]	40.0[7]	5[9]	3.8[9]	Malta
1.1	9.4	0.5	4.7	1.4	12.1	0.8	7.3	[7]	[7]	3.1[7]	26.4[7]	1.4[17]	12.5[17]	Marshall Islands
9.3	5.6	6.7	4.0	14.0	8.5	3.0	1.8	[7]	[7]	59.1[7]	35.8[7]	54.8[17]	33.2[17]	Martinique
[11]	[11]	[12]	[12]	[12]	[12]	[12]	[12]	[12]	[12]	183[12]	26.0[12]	—	—	Mauritania
46	9.6	29	5.9	76	15.6	14	2.8	27	5.5	62	12.8	23[2]	4.8[2]	Mauritius[49]
3.1	11.4	1.5	5.4	2.0	7.2	0.1	0.4	[7]	[7]	5.7[7]	21.0[7]	10.5[17]	38.4[17]	Mayotte
2,189	5.5	1,730	4.4	8,777	22.2	1,518	3.8	1,630	4.1	8,051	20.4	298[17]	0.8[17]	Mexico
1.8	6.1	[50]	[50]	[50]	[50]	[50]	[50]	6.3	20.8	3.7[50]	12.1[50]	4.1[9]	13.5[9]	Micronesia
55	3.3	66	3.9	271	16.1	47	2.8	30	1.8	285	16.9	26	1.5	Moldova
0.7	5.3	...	...	2.5	20.2	1.0	8.0	2.8	22.4	1.9	14.9	0.9[21]	7.1[21]	Monaco
33	3.9	38	4.4	62	7.3	[1]	[1]	[1]	[1]	123[1, 20]	14.5[1, 20]	166[20, 21]	19.7[20, 21]	Mongolia
437	7.3	141	2.3	498	8.3	[52]	[52]	533	8.9	474[52]	7.9[52]	548[2]	9.1[2]	Morocco
[11]	[11]	[12]	[12]	[12]	[12]	[12]	[12]	[12]	[12]	936[12]	10.3[12]	—	—	Mozambique
400	2.2	495	2.7	1,781	9.7	...	...	[7]	[7]	1,485[7]	8.1[7]	270	1.5	Myanmar (Burma)
19	3.8	9	1.9	38	7.7	9	1.7	[7]	[7]	6[7]	1.2[7]	183[17]	37.1[17]	Namibia
...	...	...	...	...	...	...	...	...	...	...	...	...	...	Nauru
36	0.5	51	0.7	256	3.5	20	0.3	[7]	[7]	752[7]	10.3[7]	98	1.3	Nepal
451	5.8	442	5.7	1,487	19.2	1,097	14.2	525	6.8	1,833	23.7	498[17]	6.4[17]	Netherlands, The
6.5	7.4	5.0	5.7	20.9	23.8	8.2	9.3	[7]	[7]	24.8[7]	28.2[7]	13.4[9]	15.3[9]	Netherlands Antilles
4.5	6.8	3.1	4.7	9.5	14.3	2.5	3.8	[7]	[7]	22.0[7]	33.4[7]	13.5[9]	16.0[9]	New Caledonia
120	6.5	109	5.8	398	21.3	224	12.0	[7]	[7]	493[7]	26.4[7]	33[17]	1.8[17]	New Zealand
32[28]	2.2[28]	32[28]	2.2[28]	201[28]	13.8[28]	16[28]	1.1[28]	79[28]	5.4[28]	195[28]	13.4[28]	265[9, 28]	18.2[9, 28]	Nicaragua

Employment and labour (continued)

country	year	economically active population										distribution by economic sector			
		total ('000)	participation rate (%)		activity rate (%)			employment status (%)				agriculture, forestry, fishing		manufacturing; mining, quarrying; public utilities	
			female	ages 15–64	total	male	female	employers, self-employed	employees	unpaid family workers	other	number ('000)	% of econ. active	number ('000)	% of econ. active
Niger	1988[54]	2,316	20.4	55.2	31.9	51.1	13.0	51.4	5.0	40.3	3.3	1,764	76.2	73	3.1
Nigeria	1986[18]	30,766	33.3	58.8	31.1	41.1	20.9	64.6	18.8	10.7	5.9	13,259	43.1	1,401	4.6
Northern Mariana Islands	1990	26.6	43.2	83.6[8]	61.3	66.2	55.9	1.4	96.1	0.2	2.3	0.6	2.3	6.0	22.5
Norway	1998	2,317	46.2	80.8	52.3	56.9	47.8	7.4	88.7	0.6	3.2	104	4.5	375	16.2
Oman	1993	705	9.7	60.9	34.9	54.0	8.1	5.2	91.0	0.1	3.7	64	9.1	79	11.3
Pakistan	1996–97[18]	36,407	15.2	51.0	28.7	47.0	9.0	40.6[55]	34.2[55]	19.1[55]	6.1[55]	15,148	41.6	4,222	11.6
Palau	1990	6.1	36.9	64.1[8]	40.2	47.1	32.1	2.5	89.5	0.2	7.8	0.4	7.1	0.2	3.0
Panama	1998	1,049	35.5	66.4	38.4	49.0	27.6	23.9	59.5	2.7	13.9	180	17.2	118	11.3
Papua New Guinea	1980[56]	733	39.8	35.2[10]	24.6	28.3	20.5	72.7	26.4	—	0.9	564	77.0	21	2.9
Paraguay	1982	1,039	19.7	57.5	34.3	54.8	13.6	43.1	37.7	9.2	9.9	446	42.9	129	12.4
Peru	1995	8,906	34.7	60.9	37.8	49.8	26.1	39.8[30]	41.8[30]	8.4[30]	10.0[30]	2,693[20]	32.5[20]	1,091[20]	13.2[20]
Philippines	1998[18]	31,278	37.6	67.9	41.1	51.4	30.8	36.2[19]	41.7[19]	13.7[19]	8.4[19]	11,272	36.0	2,931	9.4
Poland	1998[18]	16,197	45.7	66.1	44.4	49.5	39.5	21.3	69.0	4.5	5.2	3,045	17.7	4,272	24.9
Portugal	1998[18]	5,000	45.0	70.3	50.2	57.3	43.6	24.2	68.0	0.8	7.0	651	13.0	1,243	24.9
Puerto Rico	1998[18]	1,320	42.2	54.5	34.2	41.0	27.9	13.6[34]	85.2[34]	0.7[34]	0.6[34]	35	2.7	203	15.4
Qatar	1988	293	11.2	80.8	53.7	77.3	22.2	1.8[44]	97.7[44]	—	0.5[44]	4.5	1.6	22.0	7.5
Réunion	1990[18]	234	41.1	60.3	39.1	46.8	31.6	8.4	53.1	1.1	37.4	11	4.8	11	4.8
Romania	1998	11,577	45.6	69.0	51.4	57.1	45.9	21.1	55.9	16.7	6.3	4,411	38.1	2,950	25.5
Russia	1996	68,264	46.6	71.9[51]	46.2	52.7	40.5	...	...	...	...	10,079	14.8	15,950	23.4
Rwanda	1996	3,719	47.5	67.5[10]	45.6	48.4	42.8	...	...	...	...	3,375	90.7	133[11]	3.6[11]
St. Kitts and Nevis	1980	17.1	41.0	69.5	39.5	48.4	31.2	9.7	78.5	0.4	11.4	4.5	26.1	3.8	22.3
St. Lucia	1991	53.1	40.3	67.6	39.9	49.1	31.2	21.0[14]	55.8[14]	1.6[14]	21.6[14]	11.6	21.8	7.5	14.0
St. Vincent	1991	41.7	35.9	67.5	39.1	50.3	28.0	18.2	59.6	2.1	20.1	8.4	20.1	3.5	8.4
Samoa	1986	45.6	18.8	48.6[30]	29.0	44.5	11.6	21.1[30]	43.5[30]	35.0[30]	0.4[30]	29.0	63.6	2.4	5.4
San Marino	1998	18.5	39.6	77.9	58.4	66.6	49.2	13.9	79.3	0.2	6.6	0.2	1.4	5.8	31.2
São Tomé and Príncipe	1991	35	33.6	59.1	30.1	40.5	20.0	25.8	68.6	0.7	4.9	13.6	38.4	1.8	5.0
Saudi Arabia	1988	5,369	3.6	59.1	36.3	54.9	3.6	...	...	...	...	192	3.6	595	11.1
Senegal	1995	3,508	38.3	62.1[10]	42.2	52.0	32	...	...	...	...	2,719	77.5	259[11]	7.4[11]
Seychelles	1993[57]	28.1	...	...	38.9	...	...	...	...	...	...	2.2	7.7	4.6[11]	16.4[11]
Sierra Leone	1995	1,648	31.7	54.1[10]	36.5	50.9	22.7	...	...	...	...	964	58.5	319[11]	19.4[11]
Singapore	1998[18]	1,932	41.8	69.0	51.6	60.8	42.6	12.2	83.6	1.0	3.2	4	0.2	429	22.2
Slovakia	1998[18]	2,464	45.6	67.0	45.7	51.1	40.6	6.0	81.9	—	12.1	185	7.5	710	28.8
Slovenia	1998	982	46.3	69.1	49.6	54.5	44.7	11.5	74.7	6.1	7.6	110	11.2	332	33.8
Solomon Islands	1993[58]	29.6	25.6[44]	24.9[44, 59]	13.7[44]	19.7[44]	7.3[44]	29.6[44]	68.6[44]	—	1.8[44]	8.1	27.4	3.1	10.4
Somalia	1996	3,667	39.3	59.9[10]	38.8	47.1	29.9	...	...	...	...	2,446	66.7	417[11]	11.4[11]
South Africa[60]	1991	11,624	39.4	69.3[53]	37.5	45.5	29.5	7.0	74.8	...	18.2	1,224	10.5	2,361	20.3
Spain	1998[18]	16,265	39.2	62.6	41.6	51.9	31.8	11.9	62.4	0.9	24.7	1,286	7.9	2,965	18.2
Sri Lanka	1998	6,693	35.8	58.8[25]	43.4	55.9	30.9	24.9[34]	54.2[34]	7.8[34]	13.1[34]	2,472	36.9	1,028	15.4
Sudan, The	1983[54]	6,343	29.1	57.4	35.1	50.0	20.4	...	...	...	...	4,029	63.5	317	5.0
Suriname	1994[61]	89.8	35.1	52.3	45.2	59.4	31.4	...	...	...	...	4.8	5.3	10.7	11.9
Swaziland	1995	361	38.2	60.6	42.2	54.8	29.6	...	...	...	...	227	62.9	43[11]	11.9[11]
Sweden	1998	4,255	47.5	76.5[8]	48.0	50.9	45.1	9.5	83.6	0.4	6.5	109	2.6	849	20.0
Switzerland	1998[18, 45]	3,975	44.2	67.9[25]	55.9	63.9	48.4	12.8[19]	84.3[19]	2.9[19]	—	179	4.5	715	18.0
Syria	1998[18]	4,411	17.5	51.2	28.3	46.9	9.8	31.0[13]	49.3[13]	13.0[13]	6.7[13]	917[13]	26.3[13]	471[13]	13.5[13]
Taiwan	1996[18]	9,310	39.2	58.4[25]	43.4	51.3	35.0	21.7	67.5	8.1	2.6	918	9.9	2,471	26.5
Tajikistan	1996	1,778	46.5	63.5[16, 20]	30.3	32.5	28.2	...	...	...	...	1,026	57.7	202	11.4
Tanzania	1996	15,170	46.6	74.1[10]	49.7	53.6	45.9	...	...	...	...	11,738	77.4	725[11]	4.8[11]
Thailand	1998[18, 62]	33,352	45.1	73.6[25]	54.5	60.0	49.0	31.2[63]	40.3[63]	19.5[63]	9.1[63]	16,472	49.4	4,449	13.3
Togo	1995	1,575	35.4	57.1[10]	38.1	49.7	26.7	70.3[30]	10.4[30]	11.3[30]	8.0[30]	1,059	67.2	183[11]	11.6[11]
Tonga	1990	32.0	33.0	57.0	33.6	45.2	22.0	33.7	45.4	16.8	4.1	11.7	36.5	5.1	15.8
Trinidad and Tobago	1998	559	38.3	65.4[34]	47.1	57.2	36.6	17.2	69.1	1.6	12.1	41	7.4	88	15.8
Tunisia	1989	2,361	20.9	50.6	29.8	46.5	12.7	20.9	54.9	7.4	16.8	510	21.6	418	17.7
Turkey	1998[18]	23,415	29.0	54.8	36.6	51.4	21.5	27.6[20]	41.5[20]	27.7[20]	3.2[20]	9,601	41.0	3,852	16.5
Turkmenistan	1996	1,680	40.0	71.9[16]	36.1	43.9	28.5	...	...	...	...	746	44.4	165	9.8
Tuvalu	1991	5.9	51.3[43]	85.5	65.3	...	...	0.3[43]	22.2[43]	— 77.5[43] —		4.2	68.0	0.1	2.0
Uganda	1996	9,636	39.9	68.9[10]	44.0	53.2	34.8	...	...	...	...	7,440	77.2	637[11]	6.6[11]
Ukraine	1998	25,936	50.9	74.9	51.6	54.6	49.0	...	...	...	...	5,074	19.6	4,227	16.3
United Arab Emirates	1990	690	10.4[42]	69.0[42]	47.0[42]	67.6[42]	12.9[42]	6.8[14]	92.7[14]	0.1[14]	0.5[14]	43	6.3	94	13.6
United Kingdom	1998	28,713	44.3	76.2[20]	49.2	55.7	43.0	11.2[20]	76.7[20]	0.5[20]	11.6[20]	479	1.7	5,592	19.5
United States	1998[18]	137,674	46.3	79.4[53]	50.9	55.9	46.1	7.5	87.9	0.1	4.5	3,724	2.7	23,723	17.2
Uruguay	1998[64]	1,239	44.0	71.3	47.0	55.8	39.1	22.9[28]	72.3[28]	2.3[28]	2.5[28]	47	3.8	215	17.3
Uzbekistan	1998	8,800	...	72.3	36.7	...	...	...	...	...	...	3,467	39.4	1,114	12.7
Vanuatu	1989	67.0	46.3	85.0	47.0	49.0	44.9	...	...	...	...	49.8	74.4	1.0	1.5
Venezuela	1997[18]	9,507	35.9	67.2	41.7	53.2	30.1	30.2[20]	61.8[20]	1.7[20]	6.3[20]	940	9.9	1,430	15.0
Vietnam	1989	30,521	51.7	79.9	47.4	47.0	47.7	...	...	...	...	20,471	67.1	3,390	11.1
Virgin Islands (U.S.)	1990[18]	47.4	47.8	70.3	46.6	50.3	43.1	7.6	85.5	0.2	6.7	0.6	1.2	3.7	7.8
West Bank	1996	356.9	16.1	42.2[25]	22.7	37.7	7.4	24.5	49.0	8.1	18.5	41.3	11.6	51.8[36]	14.5[36]
Western Sahara	...	...	...	...	...	...	...	...	...	...	...	...	...	...	...
Yemen	1988	3,029	31.6	52.6	26.4	36.8	16.4	...	...	...	...	2,152	71.1	129	4.3
Yugoslavia	1996	3,182	43.4[19]	58.7[25, 34]	30.1	...	...	...	...	...	...	104	3.3	903	28.4
Zambia	1995	3,383	30.2	54.2[10]	36.0	50.9	21.5	22.9[14]	42.5[14]	3.6[14]	31.0[14]	2,256	66.7	407[11]	12.0[11]
Zimbabwe	1992	3,601	39.6	63.4	34.6	42.8	26.7	24.1	43.9	9.2	22.8	2,110[66]	64.7[66]	179[66]	5.5[66]

[1]Services includes finance, real estate and public administration, defense. [2]Unemployed, not previously employed only. [3]Includes emigrant workers (352,000). [4]Ages 15–59 (male) and 15–54 (female). [5]State sector only. [6]Includes nonagricultural private sector (241,000) and unemployed (261,000). [7]Services includes public administration, defense. [8]Ages 16–64. [9]Unemployed only. [10]Over age 10. [11]Manufacturing; mining, quarrying; public utilities includes construction. [12]Services includes transportation, communications; trade, hotels, restaurants; finance, real estate; and public administration, defense. [13]1991. [14]1980. [15]Includes unemployed, not previously employed. [16]Ages 16–59 (male) and 16–54 (female). [17]Mostly unemployed. [18]Excludes all or some classes or elements of the military. [19]1994. [20]1993. [21]Includes unemployed. [22]1990. [23]Mostly unemployed, not previously employed. [24]1982. [25]Over age 15. [26]Ages 14–64. [27]Services includes restaurants and hotels. [28]1992. [29]Over age 12. [30]1981. [31]Republic of Cyprus only. [32]1993 population economically active for Turkish Republic of Northern Cyprus is 75,947. [33]1989. [34]1995.

construction		transportation, communications		trade, hotels, restaurants		finance, real estate		public administration, defense		services		other		country
number ('000)	% of econ. active	number ('000)	% of econ. active	number ('000)	% of econ. active	number ('000)	% of econ. active	number ('000)	% of econ. active	number ('000)	% of econ. active	number ('000)	% of econ. active	
14	0.6	15	0.6	209	9.0	2	0.1	[7]	[7]	123[7]	5.3[7]	117[21]	5.0[21]	Niger
546	1.8	1,112	3.6	7,417	24.1	120	0.4	[7]	[7]	4,902[7]	15.9[7]	2,009[17]	6.5[17]	Nigeria
5.8	21.7	1.4	5.3	5.3	19.8	1.0	3.8	1.4	5.3	4.5	16.9	0.6[9]	2.3[9]	Northern Mariana Islands
145	6.3	170	7.3	411	17.7	229	9.9	152	6.6	655	28.3	75	3.2	Norway
108	15.3	25	3.5	104	14.8	17	2.5	166	23.5	111	15.8	30[23]	4.3[23]	Oman
2,330	6.4	1,971	5.4	5,021	13.8	338	0.9	[7]	[7]	5,395[7]	14.8[7]	1,982[23]	5.4[23]	Pakistan
0.9	14.2	0.4	6.6	1.1	18.7	0.2	2.9	0.8	13.7	1.6	26.1	0.5[9]	7.8[9]	Palau
72	6.9	66	6.3	232	22.1	59	5.6	74	7.0	205	19.5	43[23]	4.1[23]	Panama
22	2.9	1.7	2.4	25	3.4	4	0.6	[7]	[7]	77[7]	10.5[7]	2	0.2	Papua New Guinea
70	6.7	31	2.9	86	8.3	18	1.7	[7]	[7]	174[7]	16.8[7]	86[15]	8.3[15]	Paraguay
308[20]	3.7[20]	364[20]	4.4[20]	1,352[20]	16.3[20]	197[20]	2.4[20]	[7]	[7]	2,287[7, 20]	27.6[7, 20]	—	—	Peru
1,511	4.8	1,885	6.0	4,328[27]	13.8[27]	695	2.2	[7]	[7]	5,631[7, 27]	18.0[7, 27]	3,024[17]	9.7[17]	Philippines
1,248	7.3	1,015	5.9	2,641	15.4	866	5.0	844	4.9	2,754	16.0	511[23]	3.0[23]	Poland
539	10.8	184	3.7	953	19.1	277	5.5	309	6.2	798	16.0	45[2]	0.9[2]	Portugal
103	7.8	50	3.8	266[41]	20.2[41]	44	3.3	[7]	[7]	602[7, 41]	45.6[7, 41]	17[23]	1.3[23]	Puerto Rico
64.2	22.0	11.9	4.1	34.2	11.7	6.2	2.1	[7]	[7]	149.6[7]	51.1[7]	—	—	Qatar
17	7.1	7	3.1	18	7.7	3	1.3	[7]	[7]	79[7]	33.9[7]	87[17]	37.4[17]	Réunion
471	4.1	545	4.7	1,134	9.8	245	2.1	522	4.5	1,006	8.7	291[23]	2.5[23]	Romania
5,516	8.1	5,219	7.6	7,165	10.5	5,077	7.4	2,726	4.0	14,229	20.8	2,314	3.4	Russia
[11]	[11]	[12]	[12]	[12]	[12]	[12]	[12]	[12]	[12]	212[12]	5.7[12]	—	—	Rwanda
0.4	2.5	0.3	1.6	1.3	7.3	0.8	4.7	1.0	5.7	2.9	17.0	2.2[17]	12.8[17]	St. Kitts and Nevis
5.0	9.3	2.7	5.0	11.1	20.8	1.9	3.6	[7]	[7]	9.2[7]	17.2[7]	4.3	8.2	St. Lucia
3.5	8.5	2.3	5.5	6.5	15.7	1.4	3.4	[7]	[7]	7.7[7]	18.5[7]	8.3[9]	20.0[9]	St. Vincent
0.1	0.1	1.5	3.3	1.7	3.7	0.8	1.8	[7]	[7]	9.4[7]	20.7[7]	0.6	1.4	Samoa
1.5	8.2	0.4	1.9	2.8	15.2	1.4	7.8	2.3	12.4	2.8	15.2	1.3[21]	6.8[21]	San Marino
2.9	8.1	2.2	6.2	4.5	12.6	0.2	0.5	[7]	[7]	8.0[7]	22.5[7]	2.4	6.7	São Tomé and Príncipe
1,181	22.0	321	6.0	964	18.0	151	2.8	[7]	[7]	1,965[7]	36.6[7]	—	—	Saudi Arabia
[11]	[11]	[12]	[12]	[12]	[12]	[12]	[12]	[12]	[12]	530[12]	15.1[12]	—	—	Senegal
[11]	[11]	3.4	12.2	5.2	18.6	1.0	3.4	2.6	9.1	5.6	20.0	3.6[17]	12.6[17]	Seychelles
[11]	[11]	[12]	[12]	[12]	[12]	[12]	[12]	[12]	[12]	365[12]	22.1[12]	—	—	Sierra Leone
136	7.0	212	11.0	415	21.5	300	15.5	119	6.2	307	15.9	9[2]	0.5[2]	Singapore
222	9.0	176	7.2	368	14.9	127	5.2	162	6.6	400	16.2	113[23]	4.6[23]	Slovakia
56	5.7	53	5.4	163	16.6	68	6.9	42	4.3	134	13.6	2.3[23]	2.4[23]	Slovenia
1.0	3.3	1.7	5.8	3.4	11.5	1.1	3.9	4.3	14.6	6.8	23.1	—	—	Solomon Islands
[11]	[11]	[12]	[12]	[12]	[12]	[12]	[12]	[12]	[12]	804[12]	21.9[12]	—	—	Somalia
526	4.5	497	4.3	1,358	11.7	504	4.3	[7]	[7]	2,641[7]	22.7[7]	2,513[17]	21.6[17]	South Africa[60]
1,546	9.5	828	5.1	3,387	20.8	1,331	8.2	905	5.6	2,634	16.2	1,382[23]	8.5[23]	Spain
309	4.6	268	4.0	594	8.9	117	1.8	[7]	[7]	1,007[7]	15.0[7]	897[17]	13.4[17]	Sri Lanka
139	2.2	215	3.4	294	4.6	21	0.3	[7]	[7]	550[7]	8.7[7]	777[23]	12.3[23]	Sudan, The
4.2	4.6	5.1	5.6	11.4	12.7	3.5	3.9	[7]	[7]	35.7[7]	39.7[7]	14.6[17]	16.3[17]	Suriname
[11]	[11]	[12]	[12]	[12]	[12]	[12]	[12]	[12]	[12]	91[12]	25.2[12]	—	—	Swaziland
244	5.7	285	6.7	663	15.6	519	12.2	218	5.1	1,328	31.2	39[23]	0.9[23]	Sweden
297	7.5	244	6.1	899	22.6	572	14.4	153	3.8	791	19.9	125	3.1	Switzerland
341[13]	9.8[13]	167[13]	4.8[13]	378[13]	10.9[13]	25[13]	0.7[13]	[7]	[7]	951[7, 13]	27.3[7, 13]	235[9, 13]	6.8[9, 13]	Syria
928	10.0	472	5.1	1,976	21.2	567	6.1	324	3.5	1,412	15.2	242[9]	2.6[9]	Taiwan
68	3.8	58	3.3	69	3.9	[1]	[1]	[1]	[1]	309[1]	17.3[1]	46[9]	2.6[9]	Tajikistan
[11]	[11]	[12]	[12]	[12]	[12]	[12]	[12]	[12]	[12]	2,708[12]	17.8[12]	—	—	Tanzania
1,280	3.8	923	2.8	4,464	13.4	[1]	[1]	[1]	[1]	4,584[1]	13.7[1]	1,222[17]	3.7[17]	Thailand
[11]	[11]	[12]	[12]	[12]	[12]	[12]	[12]	[12]	[12]	331[12]	21.0[12]	—	—	Togo
1.3	3.9	1.8	5.7	2.6	8.1	1.2	3.7	[7]	[7]	7.1[7]	22.0[7]	1.3[9]	4.2[9]	Tonga
84	14.9	38	6.8	99	17.6	43	7.7	[7]	[7]	165[7]	29.6[7]	1	0.1	Trinidad and Tobago
248	10.5	96	4.1	217	9.2	15	0.7	[7]	[7]	444[7]	18.8[7]	412[17]	17.5[17]	Tunisia
1,464	6.3	996	4.3	3,075	13.1	536	2.3	[7]	[7]	3,260[7]	13.9[7]	631[2]	2.7[2]	Turkey
155	9.2	83	4.9	107	6.4	55	3.3	25	1.5	300	17.9	44	2.6	Turkmenistan
0.2	4.0	0.1	1.0	0.2	4.0	—	—	[7]	[7]	1.3[7]	22.0[7]	—	—	Tuvalu
[11]	[11]	[12]	[12]	[12]	[12]	[12]	[12]	[12]	[12]	1,559[12]	16.2[12]	—	—	Uganda
1,092	4.2	1,400	5.4	1,514	5.8	213	0.8	[7]	[7]	5,886	22.7	6,509	25.1	Ukraine
119	17.3	72	10.4	101	14.7	19	2.7	[7]	[7]	241[7]	35.0[7]	—	—	United Arab Emirates
2,037	7.1	1,846	6.4	5,695	19.8	4,085	14.2	1,612	5.6	6,857	23.9	509[23]	1.8[23]	United Kingdom
9,094	6.6	8,075	5.9	28,740[41]	20.9[41]	16,151	11.7	[7]	[7]	47,623[7, 41]	34.6[7, 41]	543[23]	0.4[23]	United States
93	7.5	71	5.7	249	20.1	77	6.2	[7]	[7]	465[7]	37.5[7]	23[2]	1.9[2]	Uruguay
841	9.6	362	4.1	715	8.1	284	3.2	[7]	[7]	1,691[7]	19.2[7]	326	3.7	Uzbekistan
1.3	1.9	1.0	1.5	2.7	4.1	0.6	1.0	[7]	[7]	7.9[7]	11.8[7]	2.6	3.8	Vanuatu
841	8.8	578	6.1	2,169	22.8	523	5.5	[7]	[7]	2,616[7]	27.5[7]	410[23]	4.3[23]	Venezuela
581	1.9	576	1.9	1,880	6.2	90	0.3	305	1.0	1,374	4.5	1,854[17]	6.1[17]	Vietnam
5.7	12.0	3.7	7.8	10.3	21.8	3.6	7.7	5.1	10.8	7.8	16.4	6.9	14.6	Virgin Islands (U.S.)
60.8	17.0	15.7	4.4	52.6	14.8	[1]	[1]	[1]	[1]	68.6[1, 36]	19.2[1, 36]	66.0[9]	18.5[9]	West Bank
...	...	...	...	...	...	...	...	...	...	...	...	...	...	Western Sahara
178	5.9	90	3.0	84	2.8	4	0.1	[7]	[7]	391[7]	12.9[7]	—	—	Yemen
130	4.1	142	4.5	557[65]	17.5[65]	77	2.4	92	2.9	356	11.2	819[9]	25.7[9]	Yugoslavia
[11]	[11]	[12]	[12]	[12]	[12]	[12]	[12]	[12]	[12]	720[12]	21.3[12]	—	—	Zambia
51[66]	1.6[66]	76[66]	2.3[66]	128[66]	3.9[66]	24[66]	0.7[66]	[7]	[7]	397[7, 66]	12.2[7, 66]	277[17, 66]	8.5[17, 66]	Zimbabwe

[35]1984. [36]Services includes public utilities. [37]Ages 15–65. [38]Excludes Alderney and Sark. [39]1977. [40]Ages 14–64. [41]Services includes hotels. [42]1988. [43]1979. [44]1986. [45]Excludes foreign border workers. [46]Includes unemployed, emigrant workers, and employees in private nonagricultural sector. [47]Includes unemployed, previously employed. [48]1983. [49]Island of Mauritius only. [50]Services includes transportation, communications; trade, hotels, restaurants; and finance, real estate. [51]Ages 15–59. [52]Services includes finance, real estate. [53]Ages 20–64. [54]Excludes nomadic population. [55]1996–97. [56]Citizens over age 10 involved in money-raising activities only. [57]Excludes domestic workers (private households), self-employed, and family workers. [58]Wage earners only. [59]Over age 14. [60]Excludes the former black independent states of Bophuthatswana, Ciskei, Transkei, and Venda. [61]Districts of Wanica and Paramaribo only. [62]August survey. [63]1994; February survey. [64]Urban areas only. [65]Includes arts and crafts and owners and employees of private shops. [66]1986–87.

Crops and livestock

This table provides comparative data for selected categories of agricultural production for the countries of the world. The data are taken mainly from the United Nations Food and Agriculture Organization's (FAO) annual *Production Yearbook* and the online FAOSTAT statistics database (http://apps.fao.org/default.htm).

The FAO depends largely on questionnaires supplied to each country for its statistics, but, where no official or semiofficial responses are returned, the FAO makes estimates, using incomplete, unofficial, or other similarly limited data. And, although the FAO provides standardized guidelines upon which many nations have organized their data collection systems and methods, persistent, often traditional, variations in standards of coverage, methodology, and reporting periods reduce the comparability of statistics that *can* be supplied on such forms. FAO data are based on calendar-year periods; that is, data for any particular crop refer to the calendar year in which the harvest (or the bulk of the harvest) occurred.

In spite of the often tragic food shortages in a number of countries in recent years, worldwide agricultural production is probably more often underreported than overreported. Many countries do not report complete domestic production. Some countries, for example, report only crops that are sold commercially and ignore subsistence crops produced for family or communal consumption, or barter; others may limit reporting to production for export only, to holdings above a certain size, or represent a sampling only.

Methodological problems attach to much smaller elements of the agricultural whole, however. The FAO's cereals statistics relate, ideally, to weight or volume of crops harvested for dry grain (excluding cereal crops used for grazing, harvested for hay, or harvested green for food, feed, or silage). Some countries, however, collect the basic data they report to the FAO on sown or cultivated areas instead and calculate production statistics from estimates of yield. Millet and sorghum, which in many European and North American countries are used primarily as livestock or poultry feed, may be reportable by such countries as animal fodder only, while elsewhere many nations use the same grains for human consumption and report them as cereals. Statistics for tropical fruits are frequently not compiled by producing countries, and coverage is not uniform, with some countries reporting only commercial fruits and others including those consumed for

Crops and livestock

country	crops															
	grains				roots and tubers[a]				pulses[b]				fruits[c]		vegetables[d]	
	production ('000 metric tons)		yield (kg/hectare)		production ('000 metric tons)		yield (kg/hectare)		production ('000 metric tons)		yield (kg/hectare)		production ('000 metric tons)		production ('000 metric tons)	
	1989–91 average	1999	1989–91 average	1999	1989–91 average	1999	1989–91 average	1999	1989–91 average	1999	1989–91 average	1999	1989–91 average	1999	1989–91 average	1999
Afghanistan	2,754	3,876	1,200	1,388	217	235	16,291	16,786	32	35	913	946	647	615	466	492
Albania	792	512	2,609	2,653	88	162	8,409	14,202	20	28	729	946	154	128	377	640
Algeria	2,482	1,540	823	815	962	996	9,173	15,353	49	37	424	431	1,055	1,478	1,782	2,841
American Samoa	...	...	...	...	2	2	3,721	3,361	...	...	...	...	1	1	—	—
Andorra	...	...	...	...	...	...	...	...	...	...	...	...	...	...	...	...
Angola	313	550	350	619	1,818	3,331	3,914	6,071	35	68	273	356	414	423	250	240
Antigua and Barbuda	—	—	1,921	1,607	—	—	5,171	4,811	...	...	...	...	9	8	2	2
Argentina	19,938	33,426	2,341	3,380	2,296	3,930	18,240	25,941	244	375	1,089	1,194	5,977	7,060	2,798	3,353
Armenia	282[1]	296	1,500[1]	1,705	365[1]	425	12,080[1]	13,690	3[1]	—	1,714[1]	452	237[1]	233	444[1]	457
Aruba	...	...	...	...	...	...	...	...	...	...	...	...	...	...	...	...
Australia	21,390	31,117	1,665	1,945	1,127	1,378	28,301	31,788	1,530	2,232	1,025	1,115	2,361	2,740	1,525	1,809
Austria	5,115	4,756	5,443	5,887	810	660	24,907	28,473	119	86	3,555	3,132	944	1,021	455	607
Azerbaijan	1,130[1]	932	1,733[1]	1,596	153[1]	334	8,179[1]	9,543	...	11	...	2,343	803[1]	390	771[1]	816
Bahamas, The	1	—	1,522	2,168	1	1	6,900	5,585	1	—	1,199	718	12	30	27	22
Bahrain	...	...	...	...	—	—	14,112	16,000	—	—	836	1,091	20	22	10	12
Bangladesh	28,032	31,832	2,530	2,791	1,643	2,100	9,744	11,015	512	513	699	769	1,331	1,405	1,332	1,571
Barbados	2	2	2,656	2,500	6	7	9,271	6,038	1	1	1,261	1,254	3	3	7	12
Belarus	6,749[1]	3,353	2,610[1]	1,556	9,623[1]	8,000	12,975[1]	11,765	235[1]	253	1,335[1]	1,193	561[1]	297	917[1]	1,192
Belgium[2]	2,236	2,378	6,094	7,163	1,838	2,700	37,421	49,091	18	16	4,062	3,926	371	806	1,479	1,719
Belize	28	46	1,640	2,055	4	4	21,838	21,765	3	5	763	956	134	293	5	5
Benin	566	1,047	860	1,170	2,102	4,219	9,354	10,735	60	109	552	719	160	190	211	341
Bermuda	...	...	...	...	1	1	20,985	20,735	...	...	...	...	—	—	3	3
Bhutan	102	112	1,062	1,097	52	56	9,910	10,750	2	2	800	800	64	64	9	10
Bolivia	882	1,164	1,416	1,507	1,219	1,292	6,192	6,950	31	28	1,079	1,010	782	1,042	374	519
Bosnia and Herzegovina	1,176[1]	438	3,230[1]	2,561	230[1]	380	4,672[1]	7,755	19[1]	17	1,086[1]	1,274	130[1]	78	533[1]	609
Botswana	60	20	308	204	7	12	5,385	7,059	17	16	556	500	11	10	16	16
Brazil	37,705	47,635	1,868	2,731	27,247	24,655	12,574	13,382	2,471	2,912	473	680	30,184	37,573	5,590	5,402
Brunei	1	—	1,793	707	1	2	3,344	4,261	...	...	...	...	5	5	8	9
Bulgaria	8,872	4,888	4,121	...	495	478	11,987	9,041	89	39	1,021	709	1,576	992	1,754	1,726
Burkina Faso	1,975	2,662	717	887	79	63	5,830	5,978	60	66	815	825	71	73	229	228
Burundi	283	265	1,299	1,310	1,429	1,479	6,843	6,937	333	262	1,014	922	1,675	1,595	210	210
Cambodia	2,591	3,850	1,431	1,915	105	111	5,366	7,351	13	11	500	420	239	314	472	460
Cameroon	892	1,236	1,182	1,138	2,070	2,449	6,293	5,669	68	101	517	674	1,846	2,188	451	567
Canada	53,016	53,776	2,467	3,083	2,903	4,204	24,683	27,018	628	3,270	1,587	2,183	751	677	1,993	1,689
Cape Verde	10	10	287	313	17	9	9,102	8,000	5	3	380	67	14	15	8	17
Central African Republic	103	157	845	1,006	816	1,019	3,551	3,562	16	29	941	1,000	196	252	60	80
Chad	665	1,400	565	698	648	626	4,812	4,559	36	74	566	650	108	115	74	101
Chile	2,997	2,168	3,862	4,061	858	1,002	14,315	16,297	128	57	1,141	1,039	2,596	4,118	1,943	2,591
China	388,969	457,038	4,208	4,881	141,227	175,627	14,976	18,831	5,589	5,357	1,364	1,881	21,729	59,530	114,949	250,341
Colombia	4,090	3,286	2,471	3,059	4,120	4,931	11,578	12,206	167	141	691	1,007	4,880	6,723	1,598	1,321
Comoros	19	21	1,289	1,338	58	69	5,230	5,818	7	11	838	947	54	62	4	6
Congo, Dem. Rep. of the	1,480	1,550	803	754	19,525	17,272	7,940	7,628	191	176	609	519	3,309	3,038	558	426
Congo, Rep. of the	26	2	885	687	724	884	6,745	7,264	9	17	792	772	168	195	42	46
Costa Rica	262	292	2,775	2,982	152	254	20,865	24,437	34	17	524	422	2,119	3,059	126	257
Côte d'Ivoire	1,239	1,832	884	1,130	4,334	4,996	5,751	5,665	8	8	667	667	1,598	1,952	450	534
Croatia	2,562[1]	2,883	4,128[1]	4,613	517[1]	729	8,085[1]	11,498	22[1]	26	1,914[1]	2,209	539[1]	565	259[1]	505
Cuba	543	551	2,383	2,240	823	684	5,099	4,803	27	16	363	314	1,402	1,265	582	409
Cyprus	107	133	1,901	2,912	187	172	22,328	23,950	2	1	967	1,343	368	283	125	153
Czech Republic	6,622[3]	7,023	4,101[3]	4,405	1,652[3]	1,460	19,261[3]	20,411	175[3]	117	2,371[3]	2,469	496[3]	505	541[3]	567
Denmark	9,211	8,695	5,887	5,887	1,394	1,477	36,010	38,865	481	388	4,303	3,632	88	85	304	308
Djibouti	—	—	1,524	1,625	...	...	...	...	...	...	...	...	...	...	22	23
Dominica	—	—	1,354	1,308	23	26	9,298	9,355	—	1	450	400	85	73	6	6
Dominican Republic	523	601	3,737	3,959	310	261	7,262	6,761	92	69	974	970	1,561	1,355	252	441
East Timor[4]	...	...	...	...	...	...	...	...	...	...	...	...	...	...	...	...
Ecuador	1,422	1,859	1,718	2,102	500	889	6,596	8,176	40	44	489	552	4,446	7,448	357	333
Egypt	12,667	19,590	5,526	7,032	1,904	2,171	21,762	23,030	423	371	2,511	2,255	4,456	6,417	9,249	13,083
El Salvador	785	925	1,840	1,936	38	92	15,090	16,189	55	72	802	956	290	226	146	136
Equatorial Guinea	...	...	...	...	77	81	2,898	2,531	...	...	...	...	16	20	...	...
Eritrea	175[3]	270	740[3]	703	109[3]	125	2,804[3]	3,205	36[3]	44	545[3]	634	4[3]	4	30[3]	28
Estonia	638[1]	485	1,665[1]	1,378	590[1]	340	13,743[1]	10,000	1[1]	11	1,452[1]	1,861	33[1]	20	75[1]	44

subsistence as well. Figures on wild fruits and berries are seldom included in national reports at all. FAO vegetable statistics include vegetables and melons grown for human consumption only. Some countries do not make this distinction in their reports, and some exclude the production of kitchen gardens and small family plots, although in certain countries, such small-scale production may account for 20 to 40 percent of total output.

Livestock statistics may be distorted by the timing of country reports. Ireland, for example, takes a livestock enumeration in December that is reported the following year and that appears low against data for otherwise comparable countries because of the slaughter and export of animals at the close of the grazing season. It balances this, however, with a June enumeration, when numbers tend to be high. Milk production as defined by the FAO includes whole fresh milk, excluding milk sucked by young animals but including amounts fed by farmers or ranchers to livestock, but national practices vary. Certain countries do not distinguish between milk cows and other cattle, so that yield per dairy cow must be estimated. Some countries do not report egg production statistics (here given of metric tons), and external estimates must be based on the numbers of chickens and reported or assumed egg-laying rates. Other countries report egg production by number, and this must be converted to weight, using conversion factors specific to the makeup by species of national poultry flocks.

Metric system units used in the table may be converted to English system units as follow:

metric tons × 1.1023 = short tons
kilograms × 2.2046 = pounds
kilograms per hectare × 0.8922 = pounds per acre.

The notes that follow, keyed by references in the table headings, provide further definitional information.

a. Includes such crops as potatoes and cassava.
b. Includes beans and peas harvested for dry grain only. Does not include green beans and green peas.
c. Excludes melons.
d. Includes melons, green beans, and green peas.
e. From milk cows only.
f. From chickens only.

livestock														country
cattle		sheep		hogs		chickens		milk[e]				eggs[f]		
stock ('000 head)		stock ('000 head)		stock ('000 head)		stock ('000 head)		production ('000 metric tons)		yield (kg/animal)		production (metric tons)		
1989–91 average	1999	1989–91 average	1999	1989–91 average	1999	1989–91 average	1999	1989–91 average	1999	1989–91 average	1999	1989–91 average	1999	
1,500	1,500	14,173	14,300	...	...	7,073	7,200	300	300	395	395	14,300	18,300	Afghanistan
657	720	1,645	1,941	183	81	4,864	4,000	403	761	1,384	1,762	15,033	20,200	Albania
1,366	1,650	17,302	18,200	5	6	73,000	105,000	595	1,040	940	1,300	120,000	120,000	Algeria
—	—	—	—	11	11	34	37	—	—	...	...	30	30	American Samoa
...	...	...	...	...	...	...	...	...	...	...	...	...	...	Andorra
3,117	3,900	240	336	802	800	6,117	6,650	151	191	483	490	3,900	4,200	Angola
16	16	13	12	2	2	87	90	6	6	936	968	173	150	Antigua and Barbuda
52,633	55,000	28,139	14,000	2,633	3,200	42,333	60,000	6,375	9,750	2,621	3,900	298,453	236,170	Argentina
522[1]	512	858[1]	575	130[1]	57	3,209[1]	2,850	394[1]	452	...	1,548	11,242[1]	18,080	Armenia
...	...	1	—	1	—	50	—	...	...	...	...	...	...	Aruba
23,086	26,710	165,046	119,600	2,617	2,680	55,991	85,000	6,514	9,822	3,945	4,906	186,667	200,000	Australia
2,546	2,172	284	384	3,762	3,810	13,738	13,950	3,344	3,256	3,805	4,549	94,284	99,411	Austria
1,726[1]	1,910	4,714[1]	5,132	84[1]	26	21,267[1]	13,200	798[1]	991	...	1,209	37,333[1]	29,400	Azerbaijan
4	1	39	6	12	6	1,733	6,000	1	1	1,000	1,000	500	1,118	Bahamas, The
14	13	21	17	...	...	553	455	19	14	2,602	1,970	2,800	2,968	Bahrain
23,173	23,400	871	1,110	...	...	90,253	138,200	741	751	206	206	56,936	130,100	Bangladesh
28	23	40	41	29	33	3,437	3,600	14	8	1,784	1,688	1,511	980	Barbados
6,216[1]	4,515	332[1]	122	4,397[1]	3,608	47,573[1]	39,000	5,660[1]	4,762	...	2,506	193,200[1]	187,700	Belarus
3,264	3,185	174	155	6,439	7,632	35,000	38,000	3,875	3,294	4,313	4,809	168,171	235,000	Belgium[2]
51	58	4	3	26	23	987	1,400	7	7	1,159	1,045	1,284	1,638	Belize
1,037	1,345	869	634	479	470	23,333	29,000	16	19	130	130	17,940	19,440	Benin
1	...	...	...	1	1	75	45	1	1	2,901	3,857	472	280	Bermuda
402	435	49	59	69	75	250	310	29	29	257	257	317	380	Bhutan
5,542	6,556	7,573	8,575	2,160	2,715	23,697	85,000	113	210	1,399	1,400	47,333	68,000	Bolivia
438[1]	350	518[1]	285	404[1]	80	5,167[1]	3,871	303[1]	210	...	1,273	17,833[1]	8,000	Bosnia and Herzegovina
2,694	2,380	317	250	16	7	2,080	3,500	113	102	350	350	1,860	3,222	Botswana
147,797	163,470	20,061	18,300	33,643	27,425	557,282	950,000	15,004	22,495	780	809	1,244,227	1,500,000	Brazil
2	2	...	...	17	5	2,254	4,929	...	...	...	...	3,083	3,750	Brunei
1,548	671	8,226	2,774	4,219	1,721	34,167	14,626	1,999	1,375	3,370	3,198	129,127	92,680	Bulgaria
3,937	4,550	5,049	6,350	510	590	17,028	21,000	101	160	156	178	15,283	17,000	Burkina Faso
431	329	352	165	92	61	4,000	4,400	33	23	350	350	3,040	3,400	Burundi
2,178	2,821	...	...	1,601	2,438	8,565	12,098	17	20	170	170	8,667	11,000	Cambodia
4,660	5,900	3,407	3,800	1,344	1,430	17,333	25,000	116	125	500	500	11,867	13,600	Cameroon
11,165	12,981	595	656	10,505	12,403	110,000	145,000	7,915	8,340	5,800	6,831	319,848	345,600	Canada
18	22	6	9	115	636	505	417	1	6	447	703	495	2,000	Cape Verde
2,589	2,992	134	201	430	622	2,772	3,900	46	60	224	261	1,314	1,404	Central African Republic
4,298	5,582	1,926	2,432	14	23	3,950	4,800	116	123	270	270	3,555	4,320	Chad
3,402	4,134	4,803	4,116	1,144	2,221	32,000	70,000	1,353	2,050	1,862	1,399	95,761	95,000	Chile
79,282	107,586	112,299	127,163	360,247	429,102	2,120,630	3,420,510	4,410	7,138	1,562	1,541	6,698,453	17,357,890	China
24,383	25,614	2,547	2,196	2,627	2,765	53,333	98,000	3,897	5,600	963	977	236,933	338,700	Colombia
47	50	13	20	...	...	392	440	4	4	500	500	632	720	Comoros
1,535	900	934	930	1,050	1,100	28,623	21,000	8	5	851	825	8,143	7,000	Congo, Dem. Rep. of the
65	75	104	115	49	45	1,650	1,900	1	1	500	500	1,170	1,140	Congo, Rep. of the
2,181	1,617	3	3	270	290	14,000	17,000	431	600	1,308	1,304	18,976	27,150	Costa Rica
1,101	1,330	1,137	1,370	361	275	24,333	29,000	18	24	150	166	12,693	16,000	Côte d'Ivoire
566[1]	439	502[1]	489	1,264[1]	1,362	11,665[1]	10,871	643[1]	635	...	2,347	51,167[1]	49,085	Croatia
4,922	4,650	385	310	2,184	2,400	27,876	13,500	1,100	650	1,866	1,250	109,506	65,700	Cuba
50	63	300	250	281	436	2,625	3,700	98	129	4,746	5,059	7,942	10,130	Cyprus
2,234[3]	1,657	205[3]	94	4,179[3]	4,001	25,574[3]	27,846	3,207[3]	2,754	...	4,173	154,226[3]	183,908	Czech Republic
2,227	1,968	103	156	9,390	11,991	15,808	18,023	4,710	4,530	6,227	6,565	82,800	77,548	Denmark
188	269	433	463	...	...	...	...	7	8	350	350	...	...	Djibouti
9	13	7	8	4	5	129	190	5	6	902	910	155	225	Dominica
2,283	1,904	115	105	543	540	31,227	42,000	345	412	1,701	1,726	38,864	52,853	Dominican Republic
...	...	...	...	...	...	...	...	...	...	...	...	...	...	East Timor[4]
4,351	5,534	1,417	2,180	2,213	2,786	51,901	64,750	1,529	1,994	2,092	2,007	51,471	60,278	Ecuador
2,771	3,150	3,310	4,400	24	29	34,555	87,000	974	1,352	689	1,079	143,817	168,500	Egypt
1,213	1,141	5	5	305	335	5,200	8,000	268	410	999	1,174	45,612	45,000	El Salvador
5	5	35	36	5	5	228	245	...	...	...	...	175	190	Equatorial Guinea
1,290[3]	1,550	1,520[3]	1,570	...	...	4,300[3]	4,600	30[3]	37	...	199	5,934[3]	6,348	Eritrea
595[1]	308	116[1]	31	588[1]	326	3,965[1]	2,636	834[1]	646	...	3,924	22,487[1]	15,160	Estonia

Crops and livestock (continued)

country	crops															
	grains				roots and tubers[a]				pulses[b]				fruits[c]		vegetables[d]	
	production ('000 metric tons)		yield (kg/hectare)		production ('000 metric tons)		yield (kg/hectare)		production ('000 metric tons)		yield (kg/hectare)		production ('000 metric tons)		production ('000 metric tons)	
	1989–91 average	1999	1989–91 average	1999	1989–91 average	1999	1989–91 average	1999	1989–91 average	1999	1989–91 average	1999	1989–91 average	1999	1989–91 average	1999
Ethiopia	7,783[3]	8,406	1,409[3]	1,132	2,000[3]	4,252	3,659[3]	7,370	978[3]	784	890[3]	800	228[3]	231	568[3]	599
Faroe Islands	...	...	...	...	1	2	13,677	13,636	...	...	...	...	...	...	...	...
Fiji	30	19	2,289	2,169	36	67	3,739	9,377	—	—	773	1,000	13	13	9	17
Finland	3,845	3,418	3,360	2,996	845	756	20,656	18,900	14	11	2,549	2,245	90	22	205	215
France	57,683	64,761	6,240	7,248	5,213	6,475	29,853	38,088	3,310	2,707	4,735	5,361	10,560	12,058	7,441	8,150
French Guiana	22	31	4,199	3,376	32	14	10,178	5,906	...	...	...	...	7	13	9	20
French Polynesia	...	...	...	...	13	16	12,273	11,923	...	...	...	...	8	7	7	6
Gabon	22	32	1,563	1,728	376	436	5,409	5,888	—	—	639	667	256	304	30	35
Gambia, The	99	144	1,076	1,112	6	6	3,000	3,000	4	4	267	267	4	4	8	8
Gaza Strip	1	1	510	529	23	35	22,624	21,875	...	...	...	...	168	137	140	158
Georgia	457[1]	766	1,823[1]	1,812	223[1]	433	10,300[1]	12,371	...	...	...	...	745[1]	568	1,205[1]	591
Germany	37,910	44,333	5,534	6,679	14,057	11,420	27,747	38,363	267	797	2,750	3,511	4,652	4,949	3,806	3,219
Ghana	1,155	1,686	1,074	1,292	5,504	12,893	7,000	10,709	18	16	102	100	1,149	2,450	416	729
Greece	5,504	4,554	3,741	3,617	1,065	902	20,131	18,950	51	41	1,511	1,593	3,987	3,614	3,965	4,181
Greenland	...	...	...	...	...	...	...	...	...	...	...	...	...	...	...	...
Grenada	—	—	1,000	1,000	4	4	5,206	5,241	1	1	1,094	1,136	24	17	2	3
Guadeloupe	...	...	...	...	20	17	9,649	10,826	—	—	577	3,833	129	159	24	23
Guam	—	—	2,000	2,000	2	2	14,904	14,903	...	...	...	...	2	2	4	5
Guatemala	1,410	1,199	1,943	1,750	61	74	4,899	5,692	119	129	848	816	838	1,245	380	523
Guernsey	...	...	...	...	...	...	...	...	...	...	...	...	...	...	...	...
Guinea	632	971	1,052	1,309	578	1,065	7,320	6,122	60	60	857	857	856	996	420	476
Guinea-Bissau	165	191	1,556	1,421	67	...	6,953	7,176	2	2	960	600	64	72	20	25
Guyana	213	603	3,115	4,086	31	42	7,045	9,900	1	2	612	593	67	40	12	9
Haiti	405	413	996	914	770	745	3,785	3,882	92	77	634	678	1,005	971	283	218
Honduras	671	562	1,409	1,172	30	36	8,836	8,629	81	53	767	479	1,404	1,350	197	273
Hong Kong	—	—	1,667	—	—	—	22,000	33,333	...	...	...	...	4	4	116	59
Hungary	14,592	11,346	5,173	4,703	1,230	1,035	16,713	18,482	347	141	2,251	2,259	2,184	1,530	2,041	1,733
Iceland	...	...	...	...	9	9	9,553	10,696	...	...	...	...	—	—	2	2
India	195,478	230,042	1,911	2,264	21,280	29,700	15,906	17,533	13,427	16,095	567	634	30,505	38,561	59,320	59,395
Indonesia[4]	51,258	58,668	3,814	3,891	19,150	18,698	11,616	12,299	455	902	1,322	1,601	6,493	7,742	4,558	5,046
Iran	12,973	13,851	1,377	1,861	2,387	3,431	17,383	21,083	398	566	584	590	7,088	11,172	7,630	14,194
Iraq	2,541	1,644	927	545	196	380	15,980	14,615	19	36	995	1,079	1,507	1,492	2,855	2,790
Ireland	1,950	2,022	6,374	7,091	577	500	25,060	27,027	8	19	4,798	4,524	24	23	235	228
Isle of Man	...	...	...	...	...	...	...	...	...	...	...	...	...	...	...	...
Israel	234	90	2,222	1,200	209	341	32,359	41,472	9	9	1,276	1,411	1,711	1,424	1,263	1,675
Italy	17,921	21,005	4,005	5,038	2,340	2,087	19,637	23,680	221	138	1,430	1,722	17,569	19,126	14,436	15,723
Jamaica	3	2	1,232	1,150	225	294	12,534	16,539	6	5	898	1,068	383	416	108	184
Japan	13,946	12,281	5,645	5,998	5,539	4,943	25,459	26,908	145	103	1,670	1,768	4,838	4,169	14,457	13,115
Jersey	...	...	...	...	...	...	...	...	...	...	...	...	...	...	...	...
Jordan	105	29	1,040	257	59	93	23,167	18,525	4	2	740	369	233	268	634	738
Kazakhstan	22,521[1]	14,248	1,040[1]	1,304	2,303[1]	1,695	9,742[1]	10,843	96[1]	16	782[1]	925	160[1]	67	1,096[1]	1,657
Kenya	2,893	2,514	1,567	1,350	1,536	2,000	8,200	7,490	219	240	312	343	888	1,018	624	662
Kiribati	...	...	...	...	7	...	7,449	8,020	...	...	...	...	5	6	4	5
Korea, North	5,955	3,957	3,784	3,127	2,543	901	13,338	8,230	325	270	922	844	1,304	1,300	4,344	3,324
Korea, South	8,412	7,699	5,891	6,554	940	1,506	21,156	22,878	45	31	1,134	1,080	2,027	2,456	9,768	10,832
Kuwait	2	3	4,568	2,535	2	36	19,476	32,458	...	...	...	...	1	10	84	134
Kyrgyzstan	1,339[1]	1,630	2,271[1]	2,629	321[1]	957	12,190[1]	14,948	...	...	...	...	97[1]	109	291[1]	485
Laos	1,433	2,199	2,269	2,890	265	184	8,011	7,931	36	15	1,870	952	130	171	87	150
Latvia	1,072[1]	783	1,739[1]	1,926	1,161[1]	796	13,147[1]	15,878	6[1]	2	1,480[1]	374	73[1]	35	256[1]	131
Lebanon	82	93	1,995	2,396	249	251	18,708	19,096	28	41	1,631	2,062	1,222	1,278	798	1,259
Lesotho	170	174	805	989	45	85	15,319	16,346	9	12	481	792	18	14	24	19
Liberia	225	210	1,032	1,293	432	370	7,327	6,807	3	3	517	500	130	142	73	76
Libya	297	251	676	768	141	209	7,704	7,085	12	19	1,113	1,362	287	376	708	882
Liechtenstein	...	...	...	...	...	...	...	...	...	...	...	...	...	—	...	...
Lithuania	2,319[1]	2,114	1,974[1]	1,990	1,316[1]	1,699	11,213[1]	14,109	30[1]	106	1,239[1]	2,034	145[1]	145	306[1]	437
Luxembourg[2]	...	...	...	...	...	...	...	...	...	...	...	...	...	...	...	...
Macau	...	...	...	...	7	...	13,394	...	1	...	...	...	—	...	1	...
Macedonia	583[1]	760	2,453[1]	3,314	127[1]	180	9,534[1]	13,587	29[1]	28	1,348[1]	2,573	342[1]	356	462[1]	524
Madagascar	2,545	2,829	1,919	1,971	3,155	3,400	6,562	6,489	59	94	876	923	790	860	328	356
Malawi	1,560	2,655	1,104	1,684	506	585	4,294	4,721	268	289	589	600	485	521	252	259
Malaysia	2,014	1,984	2,890	2,826	497	488	9,683	9,513	...	...	...	...	1,115	1,074	334	559
Maldives	—	—	1,125	4,400	7	7	5,108	4,677	—	—	633	750	9	9	20	25
Mali	2,114	2,149	879	1,069	28	41	4,772	4,128	57	120	224	416	15	51	255	351
Malta	9	6	3,517	3,000	17	32	13,181	26,667	1	1	2,341	2,667	12	19	53	59
Marshall Islands	...	...	...	...	...	...	...	...	...	...	...	...	...	...	...	...
Martinique	...	...	...	...	23	18	11,540	10,456	...	1	...	...	273	356	24	28
Mauritania	131	196	831	893	6	6	1,933	2,115	28	34	385	330	19	25	9	12
Mauritius	2	—	3,885	5,200	19	16	18,733	17,612	1	2	708	...	8	12	42	86
Mayotte	...	...	...	...	...	...	...	...	...	...	...	...	...	...	...	...
Mexico	23,553	28,651	2,350	2,843	1,302	1,631	15,957	22,483	1,290	1,396	646	719	9,216	11,498	5,925	9,343
Micronesia	...	...	...	...	...	...	...	...	...	...	...	...	...	...	...	...
Moldova	2,274[1]	2,115	3,019[1]	2,437	504[1]	329	7,989[1]	4,958	107[1]	64	1,537[1]	1,202	1,562[1]	825	689[1]	515
Monaco	...	...	...	...	...	...	...	...	...	...	...	...	...	...	...	...
Mongolia	719	172	1,104	614	128	64	10,613	7,362	3	1	708	800	—	—	41	47
Morocco	7,457	3,860	1,346	746	975	1,148	17,347	18,294	386	214	790	567	2,306	2,589	2,942	3,264
Mozambique	629	1,770	403	869	3,944	5,792	4,136	5,591	87	195	301	484	368	386	197	187
Myanmar (Burma)	14,109	17,632	2,737	2,934	214	356	8,594	9,837	432	1,851	677	865	957	1,223	2,160	3,009
Namibia	103	71	745	236	197	260	8,194	8,966	7	8	1,062	1,096	10	10	8	10
Nauru	...	...	...	...	...	...	...	...	...	...	...	...	—	—	—	—
Nepal	5,685	6,465	1,887	1,987	826	1,236	7,401	8,350	168	213	597	715	457	415	962	1,449
Netherlands, The	1,327	1,345	6,909	7,041	6,947	8,200	40,168	44,809	85	17	4,109	4,000	506	715	3,455	3,560
Netherlands Antilles	...	...	...	...	...	...	...	...	...	...	...	...	...	...	...	...
New Caledonia	1	2	1,837	3,596	21	21	6,023	5,935	—	—	393	600	4	3	4	4
New Zealand	783	910	5,028	5,549	277	553	26,817	34,387	61	58	2,262	2,974	794	988	506	973
Nicaragua	453	522	1,483	1,376	77	83	11,790	10,855	69	94	621	634	304	234	54	59

livestock														country
cattle		sheep		hogs		chickens		milk[e]				eggs[f]		
stock ('000 head)		stock ('000 head)		stock ('000 head)		stock ('000 head)		production ('000 metric tons)		yield (kg/animal)		production (metric tons)		
1989–91 average	1999	1989–91 average	1999	1989–91 average	1999	1989–91 average	1999	1989–91 average	1999	1989–91 average	1999	1989–91 average	1999	
29,575[3]	35,095	21,700[3]	22,000	20[3]	25	54,200[3]	55,400	738[3]	961	...	204	73,370[3]	75,500	Ethiopia
2	2	67	68	...	...	...	...	...	...	...	...	...	...	Faroe Islands
274	345	—	7	88	112	2,600	3,900	58	54	1,705	1,701	2,494	2,700	Fiji
1,352	1,100	59	128	1,322	1,541	5,583	5,507	2,712	2,447	5,666	6,435	72,967	62,000	Finland
21,407	20,214	11,196	10,240	12,233	16,190	198,306	240,972	26,334	24,609	4,797	5,627	903,413	1,044,000	France
15	9	4	3	9	11	202	190	—	—	...	581	250	450	French Guiana
8	7	—	—	33	33	100	150	2	1	2,207	1,905	1,347	1,800	French Polynesia
30	35	161	195	160	212	2,217	3,100	1	2	250	250	1,500	1,980	Gabon
333	360	127	190	11	14	558	680	7	7	175	175	820	585	Gambia, The
3	3	24	24	...	...	2,633	3,600	7	8	4,000	4,000	4,867	8,000	Gaza Strip
1,051[1]	1,051	1,160[1]	550	525[1]	366	15,113[1]	12,500	450[1]	660	...	1,148	12,717[1]	21,670	Georgia
20,048	14,942	3,824	2,298	33,350	26,294	116,263	103,000	30,976	28,300	4,931	5,746	989,467	860,000	Germany
1,159	1,273	2,199	2,516	495	352	9,682	17,467	23	33	130	130	12,278	18,550	Ghana
651	577	8,684	9,290	1,002	933	27,213	28,000	646	770	2,523	4,583	132,343	120,000	Greece
...	...	21	22	...	...	...	...	...	...	...	...	...	...	Greenland
4	4	11	13	3	5	260	220	1	1	...	800	920	920	Grenada
70	80	4	4	28	15	311	200	1	—	506	517	1,412	1,656	Guadeloupe
—	—	...	...	4	4	170	200	...	...	...	...	367	700	Guam
2,052	2,300	432	551	602	825	14,633	24,000	312	320	680	711	66,051	109,000	Guatemala
...	...	...	...	...	...	...	...	...	...	...	...	...	...	Guernsey
1,491	2,368	429	687	24	54	5,800	8,900	42	62	185	185	14,035	7,770	Guinea
412	520	239	280	290	340	807	850	12	13	170	170	580	648	Guinea-Bissau
138	220	129	130	42	20	2,000	11,600	19	13	840	828	8,600	6,800	Guyana
1,067	1,300	86	138	330	800	5,167	5,000	25	38	250	250	3,583	3,750	Haiti
2,412	2,061	10	14	589	700	9,436	18,000	346	674	911	1,070	27,923	45,970	Honduras
2	—	—	—	296	110	5,678	3,000	2	—	...	2,236	1,497	10	Hong Kong
1,619	873	2,050	909	7,996	1,362	50,950	30,557	2,733	2,107	4,977	5,558	253,631	188,207	Hungary
75	75	540	477	18	43	450	180	112	105	3,509	3,570	2,647	2,200	Iceland
191,897	214,877	43,706	57,600	11,193	16,005	400,000	382,500	26,333	36,000	880	1,014	1,229,333	1,732,500	India
10,390	12,239	6,008	8,151	7,231	10,069	560,093	1,000,000	335	384	1,094	1,108	383,000	406,000	Indonesia[4]
7,382	8,047	44,754	53,900	—	—	161,667	230,000	2,480	4,403	1,014	1,243	310,000	538,000	Iran
1,416	1,110	7,804	6,000	...	...	58,500	18,000	297	278	734	750	64,450	23,000	Iraq
5,923	7,093	5,523	5,624	1,125	1,801	8,697	10,991	5,376	5,365	3,849	4,201	32,733	30,000	Ireland
...	...	...	...	...	...	...	...	...	...	...	...	...	...	Isle of Man
340	300	383	340	122	163	22,733	25,340	964	1,186	8,783	8,785	104,663	86,800	Israel
8,541	7,150	11,088	10,770	9,150	8,225	133,000	106,000	10,893	11,236	3,724	5,325	686,867	783,300	Italy
382	400	2	2	192	180	7,167	9,500	51	53	1,000	1,000	25,833	28,000	Jamaica
4,772	4,658	30	16	11,673	9,879	337,667	296,250	8,169	8,480	5,825	6,704	2,446,228	2,526,000	Japan
...	...	...	...	...	...	...	...	...	...	...	...	...	...	Jersey
35	65	1,660	2,000	...	...	52,300	23,300	60	125	2,485	3,205	32,420	48,119	Jordan
9,336[1]	3,960	33,688[1]	9,000	2,610[1]	892	50,400[1]	16,900	5,327[1]	2,400	...	1,733	176,667[1]	83,700	Kazakhstan
13,583	13,392	6,447	5,800	103	110	24,667	30,000	2,297	2,320	497	510	41,440	50,400	Kenya
...	...	...	...	9	10	259	300	...	...	...	...	124	140	Kiribati
1,293	565	385	185	3,215	2,970	20,767	10,371	88	80	2,379	2,286	144,333	75,000	Korea, North
2,149	2,486	3	1	4,792	7,864	70,336	94,587	1,752	2,129	5,944	6,980	398,578	464,901	Korea, South
14	20	197	445	...	...	16,982	29,204	21	42	3,226	606	6,390	17,811	Kuwait
1,124[1]	825	8,261[1]	3,400	257[1]	80	9,867[1]	2,200	918[1]	1,065	...	2,218	22,000[1]	10,730	Kyrgyzstan
853	1,497	...	...	1,397	1,937	8,165	13,882	9	6	200	200	32,500	8,500	Laos
1,068[1]	376	154[1]	27	865[1]	403	5,397[1]	2,700	1,212[1]	797	...	4,308	25,033[1]	27,200	Latvia
65	82	222	355	46	62	21,638	31,000	94	201	2,826	3,295	55,167	42,000	Lebanon
550	510	1,450	720	62	63	967	1,700	24	24	290	290	826	1,428	Lesotho
38	36	222	210	123	120	3,800	3,500	1	1	130	130	3,904	3,600	Liberia
238	142	5,100	6,400	...	...	15,867	24,500	99	135	1,202	1,205	33,917	57,750	Libya
6	6	3	3	3	3	...	...	13	12	4,645	4,444	...	...	Liechtenstein
1,761[1]	928	52[1]	16	1,579[1]	1,168	10,860[1]	6,400	2,128[1]	1,970	...	3,385	41,167[1]	43,960	Lithuania
...	...	...	...	...	...	...	...	...	...	...	...	...	...	Luxembourg[2]
...	...	...	...	...	...	450	500	...	...	...	...	638	650	Macau
282[1]	290	2,425[1]	1,550	176[1]	197	4,458[1]	3,339	127[1]	179	...	1,864	25,653[1]	21,500	Macedonia
10,254	10,353	719	790	1,431	1,700	13,062	17,500	476	530	273	280	15,050	13,800	Madagascar
862	750	179	110	236	230	11,500	14,700	37	34	460	453	11,203	19,100	Malawi
677	713	212	162	2,577	2,961	62,377	118,000	29	38	470	481	287,400	390,000	Malaysia
...	...	...	...	...	...	...	...	...	...	...	...	...	...	Maldives
5,007	6,058	6,072	5,975	59	65	22,000	24,500	123	148	245	245	11,880	11,880	Mali
21	21	6	16	101	69	867	820	24	41	3,851	4,767	6,800	6,550	Malta
...	...	...	...	...	...	...	...	...	...	...	...	...	...	Marshall Islands
37	30	46	42	39	33	347	250	2	2	756	763	1,214	1,500	Martinique
1,350	1,395	5,067	6,200	...	...	3,800	4,100	97	102	350	350	4,250	4,930	Mauritania
34	42	7	7	12	20	2,200	4,300	25	60	2,500	1,714	4,200	5,100	Mauritius
...	...	...	...	...	...	...	...	...	...	...	...	...	...	Mayotte
32,194	30,293	5,862	5,900	15,715	13,855	240,218	420,000	6,336	8,885	992	1,326	1,066,065	1,605,358	Mexico
...	14	...	...	...	...	...	185	...	...	...	...	...	175	Micronesia
962[1]	525	1,300[1]	940	1,468[1]	807	17,767[1]	13,800	998[1]	571	...	1,996	35,833[1]	31,100	Moldova
...	...	...	...	...	...	...	...	...	...	...	...	...	...	Monaco
2,694	3,726	14,266	14,694	166	21	351	72	271	325	352	330	1,669	340	Mongolia
3,284	2,560	13,528	16,576	9	8	71,200	100,000	955	1,130	521	869	170,800	180,000	Morocco
1,373	1,310	120	124	167	178	21,833	27,000	63	60	170	170	11,333	14,000	Mozambique
9,269	10,740	275	378	2,355	3,715	23,989	39,529	422	488	245	392	35,208	69,888	Myanmar (Burma)
2,104	2,000	3,289	2,100	18	14	1,717	2,200	70	75	411	417	1,306	1,580	Namibia
...	...	...	...	3	3	5	5	...	...	...	...	16	16	Nauru
6,274	7,031	903	855	571	825	8,233	17,797	252	329	366	397	16,133	21,270	Nepal
4,918	4,184	1,663	1,465	13,747	13,418	92,050	100,000	11,198	10,895	6,040	6,852	644,480	643,800	Netherlands, The
1	1	6	7	3	2	125	135	—	—	1,278	1,250	432	510	Netherlands Antilles
122	120	3	4	37	38	317	390	4	4	600	600	1,367	2,000	New Caledonia
7,987	8,876	57,861	46,100	404	413	9,067	12,500	7,572	11,372	2,835	3,462	45,507	31,750	New Zealand
1,693	1,693	4	4	565	400	4,533	10,000	162	185	797	789	25,500	30,270	Nicaragua

Crops and livestock (continued)

country	crops															
	grains				roots and tubers[a]				pulses[b]				fruits[c]		vegetables[d]	
	production ('000 metric tons)		yield (kg/hectare)		production ('000 metric tons)		yield (kg/hectare)		production ('000 metric tons)		yield (kg/hectare)		production ('000 metric tons)		production ('000 metric tons)	
	1989–91 average	1999	1989–91 average	1999	1989–91 average	1999	1989–91 average	1999	1989–91 average	1999	1989–91 average	1999	1989–91 average	1999	1989–91 average	1999
Niger	1,902	2,822	310	375	248	268	7,689	7,530	330	649	133	170	44	48	274	286
Nigeria	18,100	23,234	1,139	1,194	34,383	63,112	10,031	9,665	1,421	2,149	734	535	6,595	8,768	5,017	6,158
Northern Mariana Islands	...	...	...	...	...	...	...	...	...	...	...	...	...	...	...	...
Norway	1,410	1,299	3,943	3,877	452	453	24,246	25,599	—	—	...	...	122	102	182	138
Oman	5	6	2,124	2,173	5	6	25,208	21,923	...	...	...	...	184	210	155	173
Pakistan	21,038	26,661	1,784	2,129	1,052	1,845	11,467	14,184	719	1,123	483	654	3,931	5,511	3,165	4,460
Palau	...	...	...	...	...	...	...	...	...	...	...	...	...	...	...	...
Panama	336	339	1,884	2,262	66	88	5,901	5,850	9	9	526	479	1,225	838	65	116
Papua New Guinea	3	10	1,761	4,170	1,254	1,202	7,224	6,986	2	2	500	522	1,076	1,178	357	378
Paraguay	859	1,598	1,844	2,394	3,471	3,582	15,074	14,310	49	80	859	843	522	526	264	295
Peru	2,003	3,379	2,492	3,113	2,302	4,443	8,112	10,619	105	193	882	1,059	1,891	3,139	910	1,853
Philippines	14,350	16,031	2,018	2,400	2,716	2,724	6,876	6,662	36	59	792	776	6,250	10,024	4,143	4,960
Poland	27,594	25,750	3,231	2,959	33,247	19,927	18,350	15,717	635	277	1,857	1,948	1,793	2,390	5,797	5,840
Portugal	1,673	1,860	2,012	2,877	1,258	1,174	10,097	13,792	69	32	300	605	2,221	1,419	2,019	2,395
Puerto Rico	—	—	7,462	4,000	28	9	6,499	11,246	2	—	569	609	258	179	43	31
Qatar	3	6	2,910	3,413	—	—	9,611	10,375	...	...	...	...	8	24	30	48
Réunion	12	17	5,590	6,724	15	9	11,006	13,043	1	1	1,429	741	46	49	45	67
Romania	18,286	15,724	3,084	3,051	3,159	3,162	10,517	11,563	149	47	889	1,222	2,295	2,147	3,215	3,745
Russia	92,890[1]	53,783	1,612[1]	1,192	36,603[1]	31,200	10,673[1]	9,600	2,880[1]	877	1,383[1]	845	2,989[1]	2,630	10,411[1]	10,985
Rwanda	299	176	1,234	823	1,631	1,439	6,275	3,841	216	149	777	583	2,912	2,955	131	124
St. Kitts and Nevis	...	...	...	...	1	1	3,688	3,029	—	—	1,000	1,000	1	1	—	1
St. Lucia	—	—	699	...	11	10	4,179	3,945	—	—	2,133	2,000	176	115	1	1
St. Vincent and the Grenadines	1	2	3,348	3,333	21	12	4,917	5,064	—	—	1,000	1,000	78	49	3	4
Samoa	...	...	...	...	41	...	5,002	6,164	...	...	...	...	51	43	1	1
San Marino	...	...	...	...	...	...	...	...	...	...	...	...	...	...	...	...
São Tomé and Príncipe	3	1	2,015	2,124	6	32	7,346	8,886	...	...	...	...	10	40	3	6
Saudi Arabia	4,214	2,440	4,177	4,147	59	331	19,157	17,330	7	8	1,832	1,861	832	1,152	1,987	2,309
Senegal	996	963	823	750	67	49	4,009	2,926	19	35	337	398	105	134	129	392
Seychelles	...	...	...	...	...	...	5,000	5,000	...	...	...	...	2	2	2	2
Sierra Leone	566	280	1,225	1,119	139	262	5,220	4,777	38	42	652	676	163	153	189	180
Singapore	...	...	...	...	—	—	13,933	10,000	...	...	...	...	1	—	8	5
Slovakia	3,494[3]	2,894	4,068[3]	3,916	566[3]	384	13,232[3]	14,329	161[3]	98	2,313[3]	2,238	285[3]	251	528[3]	566
Slovenia	486[1]	469	4,131[1]	5,108	379[1]	194	13,756[1]	19,736	7[1]	5	777[1]	1,590	255[1]	207	77[1]	82
Solomon Islands	...	5	...	...	107	131	17,595	17,023	2	3	1,175	1,296	15	16	6	7
Somalia	497	207	715	489	50	70	10,421	10,000	13	14	312	250	284	211	65	71
South Africa	12,237	9,612	1,956	2,139	1,334	1,700	16,535	22,089	135	114	1,269	1,162	3,903	4,777	1,885	2,216
Spain	19,306	17,943	2,489	2,705	5,337	3,300	19,448	24,452	238	278	755	564	13,490	14,769	10,966	11,659
Sri Lanka	2,370	2,731	2,924	3,156	547	336	8,845	8,174	50	28	780	605	743	833	578	608
Sudan, The	2,755	3,779	505	532	138	170	2,674	2,648	103	178	1,064	1,295	758	964	903	1,120
Suriname	229	181	3,770	3,606	3	5	11,900	12,000	—	—	690	727	75	84	26	24
Swaziland	127	114	1,401	1,803	9	8	1,665	1,930	5	7	569	972	144	69	13	11
Sweden	5,677	5,149	4,594	4,300	1,132	986	32,977	29,000	91	140	2,494	3,180	188	94	261	310
Switzerland	1,331	1,040	6,352	5,628	731	484	37,867	35,073	8	11	4,267	2,523	625	543	308	309
Syria	2,598	3,247	668	1,255	407	250	17,543	12,500	131	113	577	603	1,353	1,699	1,691	1,158
Taiwan	...	...	...	...	...	...	...	...	...	...	...	...	...	...	...	...
Tajikistan	256[1]	521	944[1]	1,806	151[1]	136	12,215[1]	9,067	7[1]	8	742[1]	1,804	248[1]	317	623[1]	526
Tanzania	4,142	3,977	1,390	1,261	8,167	7,947	8,824	7,801	437	423	501	560	2,094	2,066	1,099	1,158
Thailand	23,624	28,105	2,149	2,459	21,776	16,771	14,245	15,471	476	367	794	857	6,164	7,491	2,514	2,774
Togo	505	620	809	887	913	1,293	7,992	6,898	22	39	202	285	48	49	152	160
Tonga	...	...	...	...	99	92	6,551	10,008	...	...	...	...	15	13	20	7
Trinidad and Tobago	17	12	2,816	3,086	10	12	9,645	10,315	3	4	1,458	2,566	62	76	16	24
Tunisia	1,611	1,825	1,115	1,355	205	298	12,592	11,908	73	104	663	913	670	836	1,477	2,053
Turkey	28,283	30,282	2,065	2,255	4,321	5,316	22,388	25,913	1,946	1,661	885	1,006	9,117	10,389	17,963	21,777
Turkmenistan	1,038[1]	1,567	2,870[1]	1,996	32[1]	28	4,750[1]	5,620	...	7	...	1,167	158[1]	194	539[1]	336
Tuvalu	...	...	...	...	...	—	...	...	...	...	...	...	1	1	—	—
Uganda	1,597	1,977	1,483	1,422	5,360	6,369	6,335	6,382	493	448	774	531	8,384	10,050	404	529
Ukraine	37,208[1]	23,764	2,957[1]	1,995	19,129[1]	15,405	12,040[1]	10,182	2,840[1]	605	2,300[1]	1,203	2,597[1]	1,594	5,750[1]	5,746
United Arab Emirates	7	1	5,383	1,455	4	5	19,300	20,909	...	...	...	...	205	358	270	1,055
United Kingdom	22,644	22,045	6,168	7,025	6,333	7,100	35,916	39,978	750	732	3,425	3,883	514	362	3,747	3,055
United States	292,060	336,028	4,582	5,735	18,530	22,246	32,018	38,822	1,621	1,884	1,832	1,989	25,392	28,400	30,808	35,150
Uruguay	1,237	2,212	2,414	3,711	215	212	7,514	11,778	6	6	986	982	391	593	117	158
Uzbekistan	2,281[1]	4,306	1,714[1]	2,480	468[1]	650	10,083[1]	12,492	...	15	...	1,250	985[1]	1,276	3,760[1]	3,201
Vanuatu	1	1	515	539	49	65	10,072	10,000	...	...	...	...	18	20	8	10
Venezuela	1,989	2,097	2,423	3,245	682	1,096	8,686	12,940	57	34	585	719	2,579	2,535	498	1,214
Vietnam	20,013	33,146	3,060	3,977	4,758	3,923	7,432	7,354	187	245	639	686	4,009	3,972	3,625	4,829
Virgin Islands (U.S.)	...	...	...	...	...	...	...	...	...	...	...	...	—	—	...	...
West Bank	...	30	...	...	...	17	...	...	...	2	...	...	...	153	...	228
Western Sahara	...	3	...	794	...	...	...	...	...	...	...	...	...	...	...	...
Yemen	693	635	871	969	153	201	12,223	12,536	64	74	1,424	1,211	314	570	536	591
Yugoslavia	7,613[1]	8,704	3,102[1]	3,852	766[1]	991	6,928[1]	8,543	100[1]	116	1,438[1]	1,850	1,391[1]	1,165	1,045[1]	1,232
Zambia	1,467	1,057	1,569	1,391	573	912	5,388	5,223	15	15	629	500	105	99	274	261
Zimbabwe	2,391	1,987	1,488	1,044	127	202	4,792	4,844	50	49	694	757	170	190	153	145

livestock														country
cattle		sheep		hogs		chickens		milk[e]				eggs[f]		
stock ('000 head)		stock ('000 head)		stock ('000 head)		stock ('000 head)		production ('000 metric tons)		yield (kg/animal)		production (metric tons)		
1989–91 average	1999	1989–91 average	1999	1989–91 average	1999	1989–91 average	1999	1989–91 average	1999	1989–91 average	1999	1989–91 average	1999	
1,712	2,174	3,100	4,312	37	39	17,833	20,000	140	168	393	400	8,500	9,180	Niger
14,650	19,850	12,477	20,500	3,558	12,400	122,120	126,000	350	386	239	244	313,000	628,560	Nigeria
...	...	...	...	...	...	...	...	...	...	...	...	...	...	Northern Mariana Islands
959	1,042	2,202	2,399	696	690	3,663	3,240	1,944	1,833	5,757	5,744	51,046	47,700	Norway
137	148	141	160	...	...	2,500	3,200	18	19	420	420	5,850	6,300	Oman
17,677	18,000	25,703	31,300	...	...	77,767	223,000	3,525	4,708	842	1,078	210,867	285,600	Pakistan
...	...	...	...	...	...	...	...	...	...	...	...	...	...	Palau
1,401	1,400	...	...	228	252	7,668	12,549	129	157	1,162	1,309	11,117	14,000	Panama
103	86	4	6	997	1,500	2,883	3,600	—	—	...	100	2,950	3,900	Papua New Guinea
7,985	9,863	422	395	2,443	2,500	15,065	15,000	224	445	1,904	2,405	34,883	45,000	Paraguay
4,126	4,898	12,484	13,700	2,417	2,784	62,406	79,917	788	1,013	1,323	1,948	103,800	161,300	Peru
1,644	2,395	30	30	7,968	10,390	76,853	137,675	14	10	1,036	1,056	276,000	528,000	Philippines
9,875	6,555	3,934	392	20,056	18,538	58,196	50,017	15,560	12,373	3,260	4,021	410,255	420,158	Poland
1,355	1,270	5,531	5,850	2,531	2,341	19,667	28,000	1,500	1,750	3,734	4,930	85,400	110,000	Portugal
595	388	7	8	204	175	11,241	11,643	396	357	4,233	3,933	16,690	15,143	Puerto Rico
10	14	126	207	...	...	2,932	4,150	3	11	1,490	1,642	3,270	4,050	Qatar
20	27	2	2	88	89	6,916	11,000	7	14	627	964	4,117	5,400	Réunion
6,029	3,143	15,236	8,409	12,675	7,194	120,969	69,480	3,450	4,450	1,867	2,781	354,367	310,000	Romania
51,939[1]	28,637	46,998[1]	13,650	31,820[1]	17,300	582,667[1]	350,000	45,088[1]	31,800	...	2,356	2,233,333[1]	1,853,000	Russia
592	726	387	290	117	160	1,292	1,400	85	86	579	741	1,787	2,000	Rwanda
4	4	14	8	2	3	56	70	...	...	...	...	347	300	St. Kitts and Nevis
12	12	16	13	12	15	223	260	1	1	1,396	1,250	528	516	St. Lucia
6	6	13	13	10	9	205	200	1	1	1,351	1,374	627	640	St. Vincent and the Grenadines
24	26	...	...	186	179	356	350	1	1	1,000	1,000	192	200	Samoa
...	...	...	...	...	...	...	...	...	...	...	...	...	...	San Marino
4	4	2	3	3	2	124	290	—	—	...	170	175	315	São Tomé and Príncipe
195	265	6,370	8,300	...	...	76,000	130,000	274	520	6,254	7,849	113,005	132,000	Saudi Arabia
2,616	2,955	3,500	4,300	295	330	19,667	45,000	98	105	360	360	14,767	33,000	Senegal
2	1	...	...	18	18	293	540	—	—	...	6	1,760	2,100	Seychelles
333	400	271	350	50	52	5,900	6,000	17	17	250	250	6,785	6,900	Sierra Leone
—	—	—	—	300	190	2,500	2,000	...	...	...	...	16,543	16,000	Singapore
1,030[3]	705	412[3]	326	2,162[3]	1,593	13,321[3]	13,117	1,206[3]	1,073	...	4,096	79,549[3]	64,790	Slovakia
488[1]	453	23[1]	72	574[1]	592	10,420[1]	8,550	569[1]	600	...	2,961	19,712[1]	23,648	Slovenia
11	10	...	...	53	58	144	185	1	1	650	650	288	372	Solomon Islands
3,967	5,000	12,117	13,000	9	4	2,833	3,100	435	500	403	385	2,267	2,400	Somalia
12,920	13,565	32,060	28,680	1,480	1,531	46,000	60,000	2,426	2,990	2,637	2,990	213,362	334,000	South Africa
5,125	6,065	23,800	23,751	16,720	21,600	75,000	127,000	6,100	6,300	3,728	4,667	649,413	631,000	Spain
1,690	1,599	25	12	88	76	8,630	9,600	172	217	271	314	46,033	49,657	Sri Lanka
20,593	35,000	20,179	42,500	...	...	32,371	41,000	2,252	2,976	480	480	33,212	43,500	Sudan, The
91	102	9	11	29	25	7,625	2,200	17	16	1,832	2,286	3,033	3,000	Suriname
712	652	24	26	23	31	1,133	980	42	38	274	289	315	340	Swaziland
1,704	1,757	408	420	2,243	2,321	11,433	7,516	3,401	3,303	6,097	7,356	116,333	106,000	Sweden
1,845	1,615	392	490	1,793	1,420	5,912	6,720	3,892	3,827	4,954	5,315	37,833	3,940	Switzerland
786	905	14,571	15,000	1	1	14,405	21,000	782	1,120	2,314	2,635	75,133	125,650	Syria
157	...	...	...	8,813	10,509[5]	80,119	101,838[5]	204	318[5]	4,349	4,802[5]	...	...	Taiwan
1,238[1]	912	2,110[1]	1,620	49[1]	2	4,029[1]	600	472[1]	280	...	509	14,667[1]	615	Tajikistan
13,047	14,350	3,551	4,150	320	345	20,567	28,000	516	680	169	206	41,167	56,160	Tanzania
5,513	5,677	161	41	4,766	7,200	107,858	172,000	137	476	1,659	2,267	430,033	554,188	Thailand
247	223	1,164	740	617	850	6,070	7,500	8	8	225	225	5,558	6,325	Togo
11	9	...	...	94	81	221	266	—	—	...	2	287	28	Tonga
55	34	14	12	53	28	9,500	8,500	11	10	1,593	1,531	9,167	9,000	Trinidad and Tobago
626	780	5,935	6,600	6	6	39,367	37,000	393	800	1,420	1,633	52,250	80,000	Tunisia
12,037	11,185	43,195	30,238	10	5	73,181	166,273	8,183	9,000	1,352	1,597	369,080	820,000	Turkey
962[1]	880	5,793[1]	5,650	203[1]	48	6,900[1]	4,000	565[1]	875	...	1,751	14,933[1]	15,900	Turkmenistan
...	...	...	...	12	13	29	27	...	...	...	...	12	12	Tuvalu
4,777	5,700	1,350	1,970	797	960	18,667	23,000	418	499	350	350	14,933	18,100	Uganda
22,597[1]	11,722	6,658[1]	1,198	16,437[1]	10,083	180,352[1]	105,000	18,363[1]	13,200	...	2,182	664,865[1]	481,500	Ukraine
49	85	255	440	...	...	6,733	14,500	5	9	210	210	9,877	14,000	United Arab Emirates
11,980	11,423	29,241	44,656	7,519	7,284	124,076	154,180	14,976	15,023	5,206	6,157	616,334	583,674	United Kingdom
96,316	98,522	11,384	7,238	54,557	62,206	1,333,000	1,720,000	66,423	73,482	6,672	8,043	4,004,766	4,885,000	United States
9,019	10,700	25,359	15,500	217	360	7,900	13,000	1,006	1,210	1,604	1,780	21,933	37,000	Uruguay
5,273[1]	5,225	8,681[1]	8,000	524[1]	208	26,867[1]	13,935	3,622[1]	3,499	...	1,555	96,833[1]	68,300	Uzbekistan
124	151	...	...	59	62	306	320	2	3	202	203	312	280	Vanuatu
13,311	15,992	551	781	2,801	4,500	59,890	110,000	1,518	1,311	1,285	1,278	118,562	167,900	Venezuela
3,153	4,064	...	...	12,225	18,886	77,228	179,323	38	45	800	800	97,133	164,400	Vietnam
8	8	3	3	3	3	30	35	2	2	2,725	2,703	120	160	Virgin Islands (U.S.)
...	12	...	352	...	...	...	...	...	27	...	35	...	15,000	West Bank
...	...	...	29	...	...	...	...	...	...	...	...	...	...	Western Sahara
1,154	1,289	3,682	4,595	...	...	16,385	27,300	152	172	600	600	17,612	31,200	Yemen
1,925[1]	1,831	2,701[1]	2,392	3,876[1]	4,372	21,920[1]	24,322	1,841[1]	2,197	...	2,093	96,833[1]	90,600	Yugoslavia
2,845	2,273	59	120	296	324	16,033	28,000	77	62	300	300	25,653	44,800	Zambia
6,147	5,500	584	525	300	272	12,000	15,000	609	575	454	439	15,500	19,500	Zimbabwe

[1]1992–94 average. [2]Belgium includes Luxembourg. [3]1993–95 average. [4]Indonesia includes East Timor. [5]1995.

Extractive industries

Extractive industries are generally defined as those exploiting in situ natural resources and include such activities as mining, forestry, fisheries, and agriculture; the definition is often confined, however, to nonrenewable resources only. For the purposes of this table, agriculture is excluded; it is covered in the preceding table.

Extractive industries are divided here into three parts: mining, forestry, and fisheries. These major headings are each divided into two main subheadings, one that treats production and one that treats foreign trade. The production sections are presented in terms of volume except for mining, and the trade sections are presented in terms of U.S. dollars. Volume of production data usually imply output of primary (unprocessed) raw materials only, but, because of the way national statistical information is reported, the data may occasionally include some processed and manufactured materials as well, since these are often indistinguishably associated with the extractive process (sulfur from petroleum extraction, cured or treated lumber, or "processed" fish). This is also the case in the trade sections, where individual national trade nomenclatures may not distinguish some processed and manufactured goods from unprocessed raw materials.

Mining. In the absence of a single international source publication or standard of practice for reporting volume or value of mineral production, single-country sources predominantly have been used to compile mining production figures, supplemented by U.S. Bureau of Mines data, by the United Nations' *National Accounts Statistics* (annual; 2 parts), and by industry sources, especially *Mining Journal's Mining Annual Review*. Each country has its own methods of classifying mining data, which do not always accord with the principal mineral production categories adopted in this table—namely, "metals," "nonmetals," and "energy." The available data have therefore been adjusted to accord better with the definition of each group. Included in the "metal" category are all ferrous and nonferrous metallic ores, concentrates, and scrap; the "nonmetal" group includes all nonmetallic minerals (stone, clay, precious gems, etc.) except the mineral fuels; the last group, "energy," is composed predominantly of the natural hydrocarbon fuels, though it may also include manufactured gas.

The contribution (value) of each national mineral sector to its country's gross domestic product is given, as is the distribution by group of that contribution (to gross domestic product and to foreign trade), although statistics regarding the value of mineral production are less readily available in country sources than those regarding trade or volume of minerals produced. Figures for value added by mineral output, though not always available, were sought first, as they provide the most consistent standard to compare the importance of minerals both within a particular national economy and among national mineral sectors worldwide. Where value added to the gross domestic product was not available, gross value of production or sales was substituted and the exception footnoted. Figures for value of production are reported here in millions of U.S. dollars to permit comparisons to be made from country to country. Comparisons can also be made as to the relative importance of each mineral group within a given country.

Extractive industries

country	mining														
	% of GDP, 1998	mineral production (value added)					trade (value)								
		year	total ('000,000 U.S.$)	by kind (%)			year	exports				imports			
				metals[a]	non-metals[b]	energy[c]		total ('000,000 U.S.$)	by kind (%) metals[a]	non-metals[b]	energy[c]	total ('000,000 U.S.$)	by kind (%) metals[a]	non-metals[b]	energy[c]
Afghanistan	...	...	...	...	...	...	1997	0.1	—	100.0	—	...	...	...	...
Albania	...	1994[1]	81.4	46.1	0.8	53.1	1997	16.5	93.9	6.1	—	12.9	—	34.9	65.1
Algeria	23.0	1998	10,895.7	—	—	100.0	1996	8,931.6	—	0.2	99.8	22.4	—	—	100.0
American Samoa	...	1998	...	—	100.0	—	...	...	...	...	...	...	...	...	...
Andorra	...	...	...	...	...	...	...	...	...	...	...	...	...	...	...
Angola	60.9[2]	1997	3,935.1	—	7.7	92.3	1997	212.6	—	90.4	9.6	...	...	...	...
Antigua and Barbuda	1.5	1998	9.0	—	100.0	—	...	...	...	...	...	...	...	...	...
Argentina	2.4[2]	1997	7,821.8[3]	...	...	...	1997	2,429.7[4]	—	—	100.0[4]	419.5	65.2	1.6	33.2
Armenia	...	1998	...	—100.0—		—	1997	106.9	—	100.0	—	187.2	50.5	49.5	—
Aruba	...	1998	...	—	100.0	—	1997	1.4	—	100.0	—	...	...	...	...
Australia	4.4	1998	15,105.6	...	...	...	1997	17,083.6	40.1	3.6	56.3	3,181.5	3.4	9.0	87.6
Austria	0.5	1995	819.3	2.5	53.5	44.0	1997	484.0[4]	38.5[4]	61.2[4]	0.3[4]	3,055.2	16.7	10.2	73.1
Azerbaijan	...	...	...	...	...	...	1994	...	...	...	...	224.1	—	—	100.0
Bahamas, The	...	1998	...	—	100.0	—	1997	1.2	100.0	—	—	...	...	...	...
Bahrain	13.6	1998	841.2	—	1.5	98.5	1996	2,471.1[5]	0.6[5]	—	99.3[5]	2.002.2	15.8	0.6	83.7
Bangladesh	1.0	1997–98	417.6	—	47.4	52.6	1996	...	...	...	...	80.0	—	77.5	22.5
Barbados	1.0	1998	4.6[3]	—	—100.0[3]—		1997	0.1	100.0	—	—	8.3	—	43.4	56.6
Belarus	...	1998	...	—	—100.0—		1997	175.2	—	92.5	7.5	39.6	—	100.0	—
Belgium	0.3[2]	1997	617.8	—	—100.0—		1997	13,490.0	8.2	88.6	3.3	21,328.3	12.4	54.9	32.7
Belize	0.5	1998	2.5	—	100.0	—	1997	...	...	...	...	3.4	—	14.7	85.3
Benin	0.7[5]	1995	14.4[7]	—	—100.0[7]—		...	...	...	...	...	...	...	...	...
Bermuda	...	...	...	...	...	...	1997	...	...	...	...	14.0	—	100.0	—
Bhutan	2.3[2]	1997	8.5	—	—100.0—		1994	2.9	—	82.8	17.2	1.7	—	29.4	70.6
Bolivia	11.1	1998	686.1	—49.5—		50.5	1997	377.7	72.9	1.1	26.0	17.7	85.9	14.1	—
Bosnia and Herzegovina	...	...	...	...	...	...	1997	2.9	—	—	100.0	...	...	...	...
Botswana	37.6	1997–98	1,950.6	11.4[8]	88.0[8]	0.7[8]	[9]	...	...	...	...	...	...	...	...
Brazil	0.8[2]	1997	6,760.5	...	...	...	1997	3,454.5	92.4	7.6	—	5,433.9	8.2	4.4	87.4
Brunei	36.7	1998	1,777.6	—8.5—		91.5	1997	1,970.2[5]	—	—	100.0[5]	9.3	—	100.0	—
Bulgaria	1.4	1998	167.4	...	...	...	1997	120.4	37.7	62.3	—	1,166.2	13.4	3.4	83.2
Burkina Faso	...	1998	...	—100.0—		—	...	...	...	...	...	...	...	...	...
Burundi	0.6[2]	1995	6.2	...	...	...	...	...	...	...	...	...	...	...	...
Cambodia	0.3	1998	8.8	—	100.0	—	...	...	...	...	...	...	...	...	...
Cameroon	5.5	1997–98	491.5	—	—	100.0	1996	628.8	—	—	100.0	187.6	16.4	4.0	79.6
Canada	3.7	1998	21,998.8	19.4	12.0	68.6	1997	22,630.2	16.3	3.7	79.9	10,037.9	24.5	6.4	69.1
Cape Verde	0.3[8]	1994	0.9	—	100.0	—	...	...	...	...	...	...	...	...	...
Central African Republic	3.8	1998	39.8[10]	—100.0[10]—		—	1997	104.1	—	100.0	—	0.8[4]	—	100.0[4]	—
Chad	...	...	...	...	...	...	...	...	...	...	...	...	...	...	...
Chile	8.5	1998	3,555.7	—100.0—		—	1997	2,553.3	96.9	3.1	—	1,505.5	4.1	—	95.9
China	...	...	...	...	...	...	1997	5,786.1	2.5	24.5	73.0	10,446.5	32.9	5.6	61.5
Colombia	5.5[4]	1996	4,735.4	...	...	...	1997	3,363.5	0.1	4.2	95.7	86.1	20.0	80.0	—
Comoros	—	1998	...	—	100.0	—	...	...	...	...	...	...	...	...	...
Congo, Dem. Rep. of the	22.8[5]	1995	288.6	—100.0—		—	1995	302.7	—	84.5	15.5	3.4	—	100.0	—
Congo, Rep. of the	40.6[12]	1996[12]	978.8[12]	...	...	...	1995	939.5	—	0.3	99.7	5.2	—	48.1	51.9
Costa Rica	...	...	...	...	...	...	1997	5.1	100.0	—	—	123.1[4]	—	7.0[4]	93.0[4]
Côte d'Ivoire	0.2[12]	1998[12]	28.1[12]	...	...	...	1997	132.0	—	100.0	—	489.9[4]	—	3.2[4]	96.8[4]
Croatia	0.4	1998	96.9	...	...	...	1997	135.0	23.1	14.1	62.8	772.7	—	7.3	92.7
Cuba	...	...	...	...	...	...	1997	...	...	...	...	13.3	—	100.0	—
Cyprus	0.3[13]	1998[13]	25.1	—	100.0	—	1997[13]	20.6	46.6	53.4	—	167.9	—	12.9	87.1
Czech Republic	...	...	...	...	...	...	1997	651.0	23.9	11.0	65.1	2,175.5	13.0	4.1	82.9
Denmark	1.4[2]	1997	2,023.8	—	—100.0—		1997	1,193.7	15.2	6.9	77.8	1,004.3	7.7	18.6	73.7
Djibouti	—	1998	...	—	100.0	—	...	...	...	...	...	...	...	...	...
Dominica	0.9	1998	2.0	—	100.0	—	1996	0.9	—	100.0	—	1.1	—	—	100.0
Dominican Republic	2.0	1998	309.3	—100.0—		—	1994	2.7	—	100.0	—	...	...	...	...
East Timor	...	...	...	...	...	...	...	...	...	...	...	...	...	...	...
Ecuador	7.8	1997	1,560.0	—6.8[14]—		93.2[14]	1997	1,404.8	—	—	100.0	95.0	—	9.4	90.6

Since the data for value of mineral production are obtained mostly from country sources, there is some variation (from a standard calendar year) in the time periods to which the data refer. In addition, the time period for which production data are available does not always correspond with the year for which mineral trade data are available.

The Standard International Trade Classification (SITC), Revision 3, was used to determine the commodity groupings for foreign trade statistics. The actual trade data for these groups is taken largely from the United Nations' *International Trade Statistics Yearbook* (2 vol.) and national sources.

Forestry. Data for the production and trade sections of forestry are based on the Food and Agriculture Organization (FAO) of the United Nations' *Yearbook of Forest Products.* Production of roundwood (all wood obtained in removals from forests) is the principal indicator of the volume of each country's forestry sector; this total is broken down further (as percentages of the roundwood total) into its principal components: fuelwood and charcoal, and industrial roundwood. The latter group was further divided to show its principal component, sawlogs and veneer; lesser categories of industrial roundwood could not be shown for reasons of space. These included pitprops (used in mining, a principal consumer of wood) and pulpwood (used in papermaking and plastics). Value of trade in forest products is given for both imports and exports, although exports alone tend to be the significant indicator for producing countries, while imports of wood are rarely a significant fraction of the trade of most importing countries.

Fisheries. Data for nominal (live weight) catches of fish, crustaceans, mollusks, etc., in all fishing areas (marine areas and inland waters) are taken from the FAO *Yearbook of Fishery Statistics* (*Catches and Landings*). Total catch figures are given in metric tons; the catches in inland waters and marine areas are given as percentages of the total catch, as are the main kinds of catch—fish, crustaceans, and mollusks. The total catch figures exclude marine mammals, such as whales and seals; and such aquatic animal products as corals, sponges, and pearls; but include frogs, turtles, and jellyfish. The subtotals by kind of catch, however, exclude the last group, which do not belong taxonomically to the fish, crustaceans, or mollusks.

Figures for trade in fishery products (including processed products and preparations like oils, meals, and animal feeding stuffs) are taken from the FAO's *Yearbook of Fishery Statistics* (*Commodities*). Value figures for trade in fish products are given for both imports and exports.

The following notes further define the column headings:

a. Includes ferrous and nonferrous metallic ores, concentrates, and scraps, such as iron ore, bauxite and alumina, copper, zinc, gold (except unwrought or semimanufactured), lead, or uranium.

b. Includes natural fertilizers; stone, sand, and aggregate; and pearls, precious and semiprecious stones, worked and unworked.

c. Includes hydrocarbon solids, liquids, and gases.

1 cubic metre = 35.3147 cubic feet

1 metric ton = 1.1023 short tons

country	forestry, 1998						fisheries, 1997							
	production of roundwood				trade (value, '000 U.S.$)		catch (nominal)						trade (value, '000 U.S.$)	
	total ('000 cubic metres)	fuelwood, charcoal (%)	industrial roundwood (%) total	industrial roundwood (%) sawlogs, veneer	exports	imports	total ('000 metric tons)	by source (%) marine	by source (%) inland	by kind of catch (%) fish	crusta-ceans	mollusks	exports	imports
Afghanistan	8,091	78.1	21.5	10.6	303	934	1.3	—	100.0	100.0	—	—	—	...
Albania	409	84.5	15.5	15.5	4,122	16,353	1.0	82.5	17.5	82.0	1.6	16.4	5,337	2,637
Algeria	2,735	83.8	16.2	2.5	91	310,076	91.6	100.0	—	97.3	1.9	0.8	3,458	112,311
American Samoa	...	...	...	...	—	302	0.6	100.0	—	100.0	—	—	...	...
Andorra	...	...	...	...	80	6,383	—	—	100.0	100.0	—	—	...	...
Angola	6,472	83.3	16.7	1.0	1,101	4,769	136.1	95.6	4.4	100.0	—	—	5,236	10,670
Antigua and Barbuda	...	...	...	...	157	4,604	0.5	100.0	—	76.0	0.4	8.9	647	1,852
Argentina	11,428	32.7	67.3	31.3	258,821	928,128	1,351.1	99.1	0.9	76.0	0.4	23.5	1,033,589	88,094
Armenia	36	100.0	—	—	156	1,655	0.6	—	100.0	100.0	—	—	314	708
Aruba	...	...	...	...	6	7,321	0.2	100.0	—	100.0	—	—	...	1,211
Australia	22,935	11.8	88.2	44.0	745,392	1,329,819	198.3	99.1	0.9	74.7	16.4	8.9	901,925	487,078
Austria	14,033	22.6	77.4	58.2	4,051,236	2,178,143	0.5	—	100.0	99.9	0.1	—	9,549	185,306
Azerbaijan	...	...	...	...	206	28,166	5.1	—	100.0	100.0	—	—	374	259
Bahamas, The	117	—	100.0	14.5	46	27,798	10.4	100.0	—	55.1	41.4	3.4	55,760	7,300
Bahrain	—	—	—	—	31,570	31,570	10.1	100.0	—	71.3	27.8	0.9	9,652	4,996
Bangladesh	33,058	98.1	1.9	0.5	14,405	131,819	829.4	35.6	64.4	91.0	9.0	—	255,366	619
Barbados	5	—	100.0	100.0	...	49,834	2.8	100.0	—	100.0	—	—	1,540	9,553
Belarus	17,745	4.6	95.4	62.1	73,918	63,254	0.5	—	100.0	100.0	—	—	5,118	19,638
Belgium	4,315[6]	12.7[6]	87.3[6]	57.5[6]	2,810,056[6]	3,805,708[6]	30.5	98.3	1.7	94.4	3.8	1.8	436,356[6]	978,221[6]
Belize	188	67.2	32.8	32.8	3,627	4,166	1.2	100.0	—	52.4	42.5	5.1	17,934	876
Benin	5,994	94.3	5.7	0.8	2,598	3,219	43.8	24.9	75.1	86.5	13.5	—	2,125	7,228
Bermuda	...	...	...	...	...	...	0.5	100.0	—	92.3	7.7	—	...	5,677
Bhutan	1,702	97.4	2.6	1.1	156	2,159	0.3	—	100.0	100.0	—	—	...	...
Bolivia	1,989	68.1	31.9	11.7	52,573	49,002	6.0	—	100.0	100.0	—	—	131	2,916
Bosnia and Herzegovina	40	...	100.0	100.0	72,219	23,986	2.6	—	100.0	100.0	—	—	14	693
Botswana	1,673	93.8	6.2	—	...	...	2.0	—	100.0	100.0	—	—	91	4,926
Brazil	197,816	57.7	42.3	23.6	2,381,839	1,051,769	744.6	76.0	24.0	91.6	6.9	1.1	126,476	483,600
Brunei	296	26.7	73.3	69.6	22	8,550	4.5	99.6	0.4	96.5	3.1	0.4	559	99,228
Bulgaria	3,041	38.8	61.2	26.6	75,289	77,741	11.2	82.3	16.7	78.0	—	22.0	12,175	9,890
Burkina Faso	10,794	95.4	4.6	—	22	3,237	8.0	—	100.0	100.0	—	—	170	3,107
Burundi	1,799	83.9	16.1	12.3	72	843	20.3	—	100.0	100.0	—	—	153	761
Cambodia	8,008	87.0	13.0	5.1	85,417	12,925	102.8	29.0	71.0	93.3	5.5	1.2	14,300	...
Cameroon	15,172	80.4	19.6	13.3	411,482	22,576	94.0	68.1	31.9	99.5	0.5	—	1,392	23,157
Canada	191,178	2.8	97.2	79.3	24,430,930	4,113,097	963.5	96.0	4.0	76.5	13.3	9.9	2,270,730	1,129,212
Cape Verde	...	...	...	...	2,319	3,617	11.1	100.0	—	99.5	0.5	—	1,579	1,883
Central African Republic	3,518	76.4	23.6	15.0	35,645	159	12.5	—	100.0	100.0	—	—	—	352
Chad	1,919	61.3	38.7	0.7	116	1,650	85.0	—	100.0	100.0	—	—	...	...
Chile	31,670	32.7	67.3	32.6	1,273,098	280,780	5,811.6	100.0	—	97.2	0.6	1.4	1,781,812	38,506
China	291,865[11]	65.4[11]	34.6[11]	19.2[11]	1,176,905[11]	8,422,649[11]	15,722.3	85.5	14.5	74.8	6.0	18.2	5,299,484	1,796,234
Colombia	18,618	89.8	10.2	9.2	69,179	352,418	149.4	86.2	13.8	93.3	6.1	0.6	217,842	110,779
Comoros	...	...	...	...	...	2,033	12.5	100.0	—	99.8	0.2	—	—	749
Congo, Dem. Rep. of the	49,534	92.7	7.3	0.5	55,062	3,332	162.2	2.4	97.6	100.0	—	—	1,351	56,959
Congo, Rep. of the	4,314	58.5	41.5	24.5	201,410	1,463	38.1	50.1	49.9	98.5	1.5	—	1,480	13,976
Costa Rica	5,311	68.5	31.5	26.4	13,347	133,290	24.2	95.5	4.5	83.6	16.1	0.3	259,064	47,867
Côte d'Ivoire	13,283	76.3	23.7	16.9	241,070	35,832	67.3	82.1	17.9	98.6	1.4	—	230,571	136,235
Croatia	3,398	32.6	67.4	55.9	226,338	319,218	16.4	97.5	2.5	90.1	2.5	7.4	51,602	41,204
Cuba	2,756	77.8	22.2	7.0	60	24,509	77.3	98.5	1.5	83.4	10.0	6.6	...	...
Cyprus	35	23.6	76.4	53.0	3,820	107,399	2.4	97.1	2.9	91.7	0.7	7.6	2,897	31,848
Czech Republic	13,781	4.4	95.6	53.8	885,555	695,283	3.2	—	100.0	100.0	—	—	28,962	90,411
Denmark	2,129	22.8	77.2	29.2	421,938	1,940,103	1,826.9	100.0	—	94.5	0.8	4.6	2,648,497	1,520,792
Djibouti	—	—	—	—	209	3,604	0.3	100.0	—	100.0	—	—	81	860
Dominica	...	...	...	...	239	5,122	1.0	100.0	—	99.7	0.3	—	6	1,380
Dominican Republic	562	98.9	1.1	0.6	736	185,119	14.5	92.8	7.2	83.8	7.2	9.1	613	36,623
East Timor	...	...	...	...	...	...	...	...	...	...	...	...	...	...
Ecuador	11,340	47.8	52.2	45.6	99,347	221,624	549.0	100.0	—	82.3	17.7	—	1,178,913	5,495

Extractive industries (continued)

country	mining														
	% of GDP, 1998	mineral production (value added)					trade (value)								
		year	total ('000,000 U.S.$)	by kind (%)			year	exports				imports			
								total ('000,000 U.S.$)	by kind (%)			total ('000,000 U.S.$)	by kind (%)		
				metals[a]	non-metals[b]	energy[c]			metals[a]	non-metals[b]	energy[c]		metals[a]	non-metals[b]	energy[c]
Egypt	9.8[8]	1994	5,151.3	——1.0——		99.0	1997	704.6	—	5.2	94.8	381.9	40.7	19.2	40.1
El Salvador	0.4	1998	47.6	100.0	—	—	1997	...	...	...	...	151.9	—	5.4	94.6
Equatorial Guinea	61.3	1998	279.6	—	—	100.0	...	...	...	...	...	...	...	...	...
Eritrea	0.1	1998	0.5	——100.0——		—	...	...	...	...	...	...	...	...	...
Estonia	1.0	1998	54.2	—	——100.0——		1997	76.5	79.0	—	21.0	113.1	27.9	20.2	52.0
Ethiopia	0.5	1997–98	33.3	——100.0——		—	1995	...	...	...	...	68.4	—	—	100.0
Faroe Islands	0.2[4]	1996	1.7	...	...	...	...	...	...	...	...	...	...	...	...
Fiji	3.4[4]	1996	42.5	——100.0——		—	1994	0.8	100.0	—	—	5.8	—	41.4	58.6
Finland	0.2	1998	307.4	——100.0——		—	1997	295.9	64.2	33.1	2.8	3,383.4	28.5	8.5	63.1
France	0.8[5]	1995	11,521.0	4.8	14.3	81.0	1997	2,335.7	46.6	32.5	20.9	20,162.7	9.2	5.2	85.5
French Guiana	...	1998	...	——100.0——		—	...	...	...	...	...	...	...	...	...
French Polynesia	...	...	...	...	...	...	1997	191.4	—	100.0	—	...	...	...	...
Gabon	41.8[4]	1996	2,382.8	4.0	—	96.0	1996	2,621.1	2.4	—	97.6	6.7	—	50.7	49.3
Gambia, The	—	1998	...	—	100.0	—	1995	...	...	...	...	1.4	—	—	100.0
Gaza Strip	...	...	...	...	...	...	...	...	...	...	...	...	...	...	...
Georgia	...	...	...	...	...	...	...	...	...	...	...	...	...	...	...
Germany	...	...	...	...	...	...	1997	5,631.4	43.6	21.0	35.3	30,568.8	16.3	5.6	78.1
Ghana	5.2	1998	388.6	——100.0——		—	1997	225.2	—	100.0	—	56.5	100.0	—	—
Greece	0.6[2]	1997	707.9	...	...	...	1997	310.3	40.9	35.9	23.2	1,393.2	6.9	7.2	85.9
Greenland	...	...	...	...	...	...	1997	...	...	...	...	1.6	—	100.0	—
Grenada	1.4	1998	1.3	—	100.0	—	1996	...	...	...	...	2.4	—	25.0	75.0
Guadeloupe	...	1998	...	—	100.0	—	...	...	...	...	...	...	...	...	...
Guam	...	1998	...	—	100.0	—	...	...	...	...	...	...	...	...	...
Guatemala	0.6	1998	30.0	...	...	...	1997	102.9	—	6.2	93.8	172.1	—	—	100.0
Guernsey	...	...	...	...	...	...	...	...	...	...	...	...	...	...	...
Guinea	15.7	1998	645.4[16]	——100.0[16]——		—	1997	396.7	80.3	19.7	—	...	...	...	...
Guinea-Bissau	...	1998	...	—	100.0	—	...	...	...	...	...	...	...	...	...
Guyana	13.6	1998	98.0	——100.0——		—	1997	94.3	100.0	—	—	...	...	...	...
Haiti	0.2	1998	1.8	—	100.0	—	...	...	...	...	...	...	...	...	...
Honduras	1.8	1998	82.3	——100.0——		—	1997	30.6	100.0	—	—	10.1	—	—	100.0
Hong Kong	0.02	1998	39.1	—	100.0	—	1997	2,264.8	27.2	72.8	—	4,639.9	12.9	75.8	11.2
Hungary	0.4[2]	1997	181.5	15.6	26.5	57.9	1997	136.5	99.6	—	0.4	1,747.1	1.9	3.5	94.6
Iceland	...	1998	...	—	100.0	—	1997	19.7	34.0	66.0	—	50.7	68.6	21.5	9.9
India	1.0	1996–97	3,268.9	...	...	...	1997	5,168.2	13.3	86.2	0.5	10,499.3[4]	7.8[4]	31.2[4]	61.0[4]
Indonesia	12.9	1998	12,704.4	——34.7——		65.3	1997	13,660.2	12.7	0.9	86.4	2,138.5	16.9	14.5	68.6
Iran	7.2	1998–99	13,441.8	——9.1——		90.9	1995	18,525.9	1.0	0.4	98.6	1,271.4	17.5	7.5	75.0
Iraq	...	...	...	...	...	...	...	...	...	...	...	...	...	...	...
Ireland	...	...	...	...	...	...	1997	538.5	75.1	16.5	8.4	825.7	14.4	12.9	72.7
Isle of Man	...	1998	...	—	100.0	—	...	...	...	...	...	...	...	...	...
Israel	...	...	...	...	...	...	1997	6,948.8	0.5	99.5	—	7,117.3	0.2	73.3	26.5
Italy	...	...	...	...	...	...	1997	851.4	34.6	57.2	8.2	16,573.7	15.0	9.3	75.7
Jamaica	4.5	1998	310.3	97.2	2.8	...	1997	682.4	100.0	—	—	105.8	—	—	100.0
Japan	0.2[4]	1996	9,863.9	...	...	...	1997	1,315.4	44.0	56.0	—	67,595.7	12.8	5.8	81.4
Jersey	...	...	...	...	...	...	...	...	...	...	...	...	...	...	...
Jordan	3.3	1998	239.3	—	100.0	—	1997	353.6	5.0	95.0	—	416.7[5]	0.6[5]	8.8[5]	90.6[5]
Kazakhstan	...	...	...	...	...	...	1996	837.9	18.9	12.8	68.4	170.9	29.9	25.8	44.3
Kenya	0.2[5]	1995	14.1	——100.0——		—	1997	40.4	—	100.0	—	227.3[4]	—	2.6[4]	97.4[4]
Kiribati	...	...	...	...	...	...	1995	...	...	...	...	0.1	—	100.0	—
Korea, North	...	...	...	...	...	...	1997	90.6	30.8	36.9	32.3	52.7[5]	—	36.1[5]	63.9[5]
Korea, South	0.4	1998	1,141.7	...	...	...	1997	238.6	13.9	53.9	32.2	23,311.9[4]	12.8[4]	3.0[4]	84.2[4]
Kuwait	39.5[5]	1995	10,513.4	—	—	100.0	1997	14,130.4[4]	0.2[4]	—	99.8[4]	60.7	—	100.0	—
Kyrgyzstan	...	...	...	...	...	...	1996	15.8	75.9	—	24.1	118.2	2.5	4.8	92.7
Laos	0.4	1998	5.8	——100.0——		—	...	...	...	...	...	...	...	...	...
Latvia	0.5	1998	116.4	—	——100.0——		1997	32.3	85.1	—	14.9	148.9	13.7	8.1	78.2
Lebanon	...	...	...	...	...	...	1997	130.5	31.0	69.0	—	132.8	—	100.0	—
Lesotho	0.01[4]	1996	0.1	—	100.0	—	[9]	...	...	...	...	...	...	...	...
Liberia	2.4	1998	8.6	—	100.0	—	1997	15.7	100.0	—	—	14.8	—	100.0	—
Libya	25.8[4]	1996	8,441.7	—	7.1	92.9	1997	9,451.2[5]	—	—	100.0[5]	51.2	100.0	—	—
Liechtenstein	...	...	...	...	...	...	...	...	...	...	...	...	...	...	...
Lithuania	0.5	1998	49.3	—	33.9[2]	66.1[2]	1997	130.7	48.7	—	51.3	850.6	2.4	7.0	90.6
Luxembourg	0.2	1998	24.8	—	100.0	—	[6]	...	...	...	...	...	...	...	...
Macau	...	...	...	...	...	...	1997	...	...	...	...	17.3	—	20.8	79.2
Macedonia	...	...	...	...	...	...	1995	29.5	68.1	31.9	—	41.8	6.7	39.5	53.8
Madagascar	0.3[8]	1994	5.2	——100.0——		—	1997	26.6	40.6	59.4	—	79.5	—	—	100.0
Malawi	1.0[8]	1994	12.8	...	...	...	1995	...	...	...	...	5.1	—	62.7	37.3
Malaysia	7.9	1998	3,675.2[3]	...	...	...	1996	5,509.7	2.4	2.3	95.3	1,175.0	43.1	32.2	24.7
Maldives	1.6	1998	2.2	—	100.0	—	...	...	...	...	...	...	...	...	...
Mali	5.5	1998	81.7	——100.0——		—	1997	7.0	—	100.0	—	...	...	...	...
Malta	...	1998	...	—	100.0	—	1996	3.5[5]	97.9[5]	2.1[5]	—	10.2	—	100.0	—
Marshall Islands	0.3[5]	1995	0.3	—	100.0	—	...	...	...	...	...	...	...	...	...
Martinique	...	1998	...	—	100.0	—	1995	4.1	19.4	38.3	42.3	102.5	—	—	100.0
Mauritania	9.6[2]	1997	105.9	——100.0——		—	1997	301.6	100.0	—	—	...	...	...	...
Mauritius	0.1	1998	5.6	—	100.0	—	1996	56.2	—	73.8	26.2	56.2	—	73.8	26.2
Mayotte	...	...	...	...	...	...	...	...	...	...	...	...	...	...	...
Mexico	1.2	1998	5,128.4	...	...	...	1997	11,181.6	4.8	2.3	93.0	1,715.3	39.7	25.2	35.1
Micronesia	...	...	...	...	...	...	...	...	...	...	...	...	...	...	...
Moldova	...	1998	...	—	100.0	—	1997	18.7[5]	100.0[5]	—	—	147.5	—	—	100.0
Monaco	...	...	...	...	...	...	...	...	...	...	...	...	...	...	...
Mongolia	...	...	...	...	...	...	1996	254.1	90.9	9.1	—	...	...	...	...
Morocco	2.2[2]	1997	746.5	...	...	...	1997	751.1	23.6	76.4	—	1,449.6	—	11.3	88.7
Mozambique	...	...	...	...	...	...	1996	8.4	72.6	27.4	—	3.3	—	100.0	—
Myanmar (Burma)	0.4	1998–99	1,107.3	...	...	...	1997	39.0	—	100.0	—	...	...	...	...
Namibia	11.7[2]	1997	382.8	——100.0——		—	[9]	...	...	...	...	...	...	...	...
Nauru	...	1998	...	—	100.0	—	1997	151.6	—	100.0	—	...	...	...	...
Nepal	0.5	1998–99	26.8	——100.0——		—	1995	...	...	...	...	9.1	51.6	—	48.4

forestry, 1998						fisheries, 1997								country
production of roundwood				trade (value, '000 U.S.$)		catch (nominal)						trade (value, '000 U.S.$)		
total ('000 cubic metres)	fuelwood, charcoal (%)	industrial roundwood (%)		exports	imports	total ('000 metric tons)	by source (%)		by kind of catch (%)			exports	imports	
		total	sawlogs, veneer				marine	inland	fish	crusta-ceans	mollusks			
2,829	95.4	4.6	—	4,748	892,906	345.2	28.7	71.3	97.2	2.3	0.6	2,736	101,611	Egypt
5,129	88.1	11.9	8.3	5,884	59,877	10.6	73.4	26.6	71.1	25.4	3.5	34,535	5,909	El Salvador
811	55.1	44.9	44.9	54,878	972	6.1	86.0	14.0	87.3	9.3	3.3	2,878	1,419	Equatorial Guinea
2,196	100.0	...	...	...	20,798	1.0	100.0	—	99.9	0.1	—	178	5	Eritrea
6,061	25.0	75.0	28.0	390,390	122,492	123.6	98.0	2.0	96.2	3.8	—	100,026	19,649	Estonia
50,148	95.0	5.0	0.1	...	20,284	10.4	—	100.0	100.0	—	—	5	229	Ethiopia
...	...	...	...	221	4,162	329.7	100.0	—	96.1	2.9	1.0	381,542	8,820	Faroe Islands
594	6.2	93.8	93.7	30,434	8,189	27.8	84.4	15.6	75.3	2.5	20.4	47,517	19,881	Fiji
42,770	7.5	92.5	47.7	10,998,080	827,263	180.1	73.6	26.4	99.9	0.1	—	20,714	126,020	Finland
47,220	22.9	77.1	51.0	5,209,761	7,091,138	567.5	99.2	0.8	75.6	1.9	22.5	1,095,936	3,060	France
120	49.8	50.2	42.6	2,481	2,424	7.7	100.0	—	65.2	34.8	—	40,495	5,136	French Guiana
...	...	...	...	103	20,446	10.8	99.9	0.1	99.0	0.8	0.1	731	10,450	French Polynesia
5,332	48.0	52.0	52.0	202,470	4,935	44.7	77.8	22.2	95.6	4.0	0.1	6,247	8,237	Gabon
813	86.1	13.9	13.0	179	1,100	32.3	92.2	7.8	99.1	0.1	0.8	2,585	413	Gambia, The
...	...	...	...	...	...	3.8	100.0	—	92.4	4.5	3.1	...	...	Gaza Strip
...	...	...	...	11,952	5,749	2.6	100.0	—	98.4	—	1.6	312	2,885	Georgia
39,052	6.7	93.3	63.1	9,855,096	10,841,800	259.4	91.2	8.8	89.1	5.2	5.8	886,234	2,362,547	Germany
21,905	94.4	5.6	5.2	140,950	17,721	446.8	84.3	15.7	98.7	0.5	0.7	55,994	19,359	Ghana
1,692	70.7	29.3	21.3	79,693	830,094	170.5	90.6	9.4	82.6	1.9	15.6	218,062	296,429	Greece
—	—	—	—	77	7,179	120.6	100.0	—	63.8	35.2	1.0	269,524	669	Greenland
...	...	...	...	—	5,167	1.4	100.0	—	98.5	1.0	0.1	1,619	1,274	Grenada
15	98.0	2.0	2.0	145	30,639	10.5	100.0	—	94.3	1.5	4.2	266	30,393	Guadeloupe
...	...	...	...	...	...	0.2	100.0	—	94.8	5.2	—	...	...	Guam
12,995	98.5	1.5	1.2	13,522	135,444	6.9	25.7	74.3	77.5	22.2	0.2	16,215	6,270	Guatemala
...	...	...	...	...	...	[15]	[15]	[15]	[15]	[15]	[15]	...	...	Guernsey
8,650	92.5	7.5	1.6	8,857	6,291	62.4	94.2	5.8	92.3	1.5	6.2	31,051	3,622	Guinea
589	71.6	28.4	6.8	2,083	155	7.3	96.6	3.4	84.4	15.4	0.2	20,056	554	Guinea-Bissau
442	2.5	97.5	92.8	30,000	3,469	54.0	98.8	1.2	75.1	24.9	—	16,386	2,099	Guyana
6,397	96.3	3.7	3.5	...	12,236	5.3	90.6	9.4	78.6	16.1	5.3	1,238	4,099	Haiti
7,176	88.9	11.1	11.0	42,183	66,972	17.3	99.3	0.7	58.8	30.0	11.2	50,351	9,311	Honduras
21	100.0	—	—	2,508,240	3,101,116	186.0	100.0	—	89.4	3.4	7.2	577,246	2,094,229	Hong Kong
4,167	44.9	55.1	28.0	347,330	588,205	7.4	—	100.0	100.0	—	—	6,422	46,550	Hungary
—	—	—	—	648	65,695	2,205.9	100.0	—	95.7	3.6	0.7	1,360,574	32,860	Iceland
299,460	91.6	8.4	6.1	37,607	778,176	3,517.1	81.3	18.7	92.2	5.8	2.1	1,115,991	10,616	India
193,218	81.3	18.7	11.1	3,392,027	868,481	3,791.0	92.0	8.0	89.5	7.6	2.1	1,620,753	106,152	Indonesia
6,793	29.4	70.6	5.0	1,351	198,881	349.9	68.2	31.8	95.4	2.3	2.3	32,498	63,991	Iran
177	66.7	33.3	14.1	...	3,008	31.3	34.4	65.6	100.0	—	—	16	...	Iraq
2,266	3.2	96.8	59.6	221,237	732,049	292.7	98.7	1.3	88.1	4.0	7.9	341,854	126,982	Ireland
...	...	...	...	...	...	4.3	100.0	—	—	16.9	83.9	...	...	Isle of Man
124	11.3	88.7	32.3	26,151	684,764	5.2	71.6	24.8	98.6	1.3	0.2	9,800	123,282	Israel
9,550	54.3	45.7	26.9	3,442,528	8,925,404	341.0	98.0	2.0	70.3	3.7	26.0	376,930	2,568,668	Italy
343	87.5	12.5	12.1	88	72,131	8.4	93.0	7.0	83.5	3.0	13.5	25,706	50,729	Jamaica
20,093	3.9	96.1	67.5	1,453,540	11,173,660	5,916.2	98.6	1.4	79.7	2.3	17.6	889,407	15,546,350	Japan
...	...	...	...	...	...	4.2[15]	100.0[15]	—[15]	11.0[15]	49.8[15]	39.2[15]	...	...	Jersey
11	63.6	36.4	—	17,681	136,506	0.5	22.2	77.8	100.0	—	—	2,596	34,628	Jordan
315	100.0	...	...	598	48,398	31.8	—	100.0	100.0	—	—	19,.017	16,881	Kazakhstan
29,377	93.3	6.7	1.6	2,064	38,124	161.1	3.8	96.2	99.3	0.4	0.3	52,309	12,229	Kenya
...	...	...	...	...	769	31.4	100.0	—	85.3	0.7	14.0	2,002	555	Kiribati
7,000	78.6	21.4	14.3	15,192	8,781	236.5	91.5	8.5	76.1	3.8	20.1	70,843	197,595	Korea, North
1,822	21.6	78.4	26.9	1,488,235	2,079,746	2,204.0	99.7	0.3	72.3	3.1	23.7	1,376,462	1,023,599	Korea, South
...	...	...	...	392	93,985	7.8	100.0	—	81.4	18.6	—	10,043	15,860	Kuwait
42	74.5	25.5	21.9	225	9,892	0.2	—	100.0	100.0	—	—	—	487	Kyrgyzstan
4,591	85.0	15.0	12.2	41,512	2,022	26.0	—	100.0	100.0	—	—	171	1,063	Laos
10,030	28.4	71.6	44.9	585,197	85,465	105.7	99.5	0.5	99.1	0.9	—	82,019	38,122	Latvia
407	98.2	1.8	1.8	3,065	180,191	3.7	99.5	0.5	95.5	3.4	1.1	...	22,170	Lebanon
1,594	100.0	—	—	...	...	0.03	—	100.0	100.0	—	—	[9]	[9]	Lesotho
3,021	89.4	10.6	5.2	12,505	1,635	8.6	48.2	51.8	98.6	1.4	0.0	603	2,422	Liberia
651	82.3	17.7	9.7	3	46,183	33.7	98.9	—	100.0	—	—	31,169	13,734	Libya
13	30.8	69.2	69.2	...	...	—	...	...	...	...	...	[17]	[17]	Liechtenstein
4,879	24.0	76.0	49.8	171,466	118,630	20.8	90.7	9.3	91.8	8.2	—	68,709	71,096	Lithuania
[6]	[6]	[6]	[6]	[6]	[6]	—	...	...	...	...	...	[6]	[6]	Luxembourg
...	...	...	...	1,841	14,022	1.5	100.0	—	75.8	22.2	2.0	2,123	18,150	Macau
774	79.6	20.4	19.3	13,821	53,533	0.1	—	100.0	100.0	—	—	133	10,205	Macedonia
9,517	96.1	3.9	0.4	12,483	9,572	116.4	74.2	25.8	87.9	10.3	0.6	51,747	4,535	Madagascar
9,692	94.7	5.3	1.3	2,456	4,698	56.3	—	100.0	100.0	—	—	450	850	Malawi
29,297	25.8	74.2	69.0	2,515,354	746,830	1,172.9	99.7	0.3	80.7	6.9	9.0	326,692	344,655	Malaysia
...	...	...	...	14	4,220	107.8	100.0	—	99.5	—	0.3	...	...	Maldives
6,437	93.7	6.3	0.1	1,984	6,926	99.6	—	100.0	100.0	—	—	450	1,757	Mali
...	...	...	...	—	62,831	0.9	100.0	—	98.8	0.6	0.6	6,962	19,225	Malta
...	...	...	...	...	...	0.4	100.0	—	100.0	—	—	2,977	102	Marshall Islands
12	83.3	16.7	16.7	110	22,864	5.0	100.0	—	96.8	2.9	—	168	38,658	Martinique
15	60.0	40.0	6.7	339	1,680	84.0	92.9	7.1	77.3	0.5	22.2	150,808	818	Mauritania
15	44.0	56.0	39.0	423	51,115	13.7	100.0	—	97.2	0.6	2.2	45,417	44,511	Mauritius
...	...	...	...	...	...	1.5	100.0	—	100.0	—	—	3	161	Mayotte
23,866	66.8	33.2	27.3	319,124	1,480,408	1,489.0	92.4	7.6	82.4	6.5	11.0	810,260	113,593	Mexico
...	...	...	...	...	2,110	10.4	100.0	—	99.5	0.3	0.2	412	3,919	Micronesia
406	87.7	12.3	4.9	1,541	15,095	0.6	—	100.0	100.0	—	—	1,764	6,229	Moldova
...	...	...	...	...	...	0.004	100.0	—	100.0	—	—	...	...	Monaco
631	29.5	70.5	70.5	24,741	2,873	0.2	—	100.0	100.0	—	—	136	52	Mongolia
1,746	44.1	55.9	13.2	55,406	333,295	783.6	99.7	0.3	91.6	0.9	7.5	684,538	12,243	Morocco
18,018	92.8	7.2	0.7	8,580	328	42.1	72.6	27.4	78.4	20.5	1.0	36,292	8,513	Mozambique
22,430	84.6	15.4	9.4	225,490	11,843	830.3	81.0	19.0	97.4	2.6	—	90,681	3	Myanmar (Burma)
[18]	[18]	[18]	[18]	[18]	[18]	279.5	95.5	0.5	99.7	0.1	0.2	[9]	[9]	Namibia
...	...	...	...	23	205	0.4	100.0	—	100.0	—	—	...	...	Nauru
21,474	97.1	2.9	2.9	1,410	1,444	11.2	—	100.0	100.0	—	—	...	...	Nepal

Extractive industries (continued)

country	mining														
	% of GDP, 1998	mineral production (value added)					trade (value)								
		year	total ('000,000 U.S.$)	by kind (%)			year	exports				imports			
				metals[a]	non-metals[b]	energy[c]		total ('000,000 U.S.$)	by kind (%) metals[a]	non-metals[b]	energy[c]	total ('000,000 U.S.$)	by kind (%) metals[a]	non-metals[b]	energy[c]
Netherlands, The	2.7[5]	1995[3]	9,620.1[3]	...	...	...	1997	6,275.9	19.2	8.5	72.3	12,803.2	12.5	5.9	81.6
Netherlands Antilles	...	1998	...	—	100.0	—	1995	901.5	—	0.1	99.9	900.5	—	—	100.0
New Caledonia	10.7[2]	1997	352.1	100.0	—	—	1997	208.9	100.0	—	—	12.9	—	—	100.0
New Zealand	...	...	...	...	...	...	1996	110.9	31.3	0.4	68.3	854.0	21.1	13.5	65.5
Nicaragua	1.6	1998	34.0	—— 100.0 ——		—	1997	4.0	100.0	—	—	130.0	—	4.6	95.4
Niger	3.5[8]	1994	62.5	—— 100.0 ——		—	...	...	...	...	...	...	...	...	...
Nigeria	26.0	1998	33,716.8	—	0.5	99.5	1995	11,131.5	—	—	100.0	19.9	1.5	98.5	—
Northern Mariana Islands	...	...	...	...	...	...	...	...	...	...	...	...	...	...	...
Norway	10.9	1998	16,068.2	—— 1.8 ——		98.2	1997	24,255.2	0.4	1.0	98.6	1,820.3	73.2	11.3	15.5
Oman	40.6[2]	1997	6,361.2	—	0.7	99.3	1996	5,768.3	—	0.1	99.9	70.7	78.8	21.2	—
Pakistan	0.5	1997–98	301.4	...	...	...	1997	57.3	—	1.4	98.6	338.9	50.5	7.5	42.0
Palau	0.1	1998	0.1	—	100.0	—	...	...	...	...	...	...	...	...	...
Panama	0.2	1998	10.5	—— 100.0 ——		—	1996	6.7	100.0	—	—	324.5	—	—	100.0
Papua New Guinea	26.0	1998	975.2	—— 64.0 ——		36.0	1995	1,123.1	48.0	—	52.0	...	...	...	...
Paraguay	0.3	1998	29.2	—	100.0	—	1996	...	...	...	...	124.9	—	66.9	33.1
Peru	10.9	1998	2,378.8	—— 67.9[5, 20] ——		32.1[5]	1997	1,150.6	79.1	0.1	20.8	564.2	0.4	—	99.6
Philippines	0.7	1998	489.1	57.7[5]	41.3[5]	1.0[5]	1997	567.7	55.4	25.5	19.1	4,078.1	14.2	4.1	81.7
Poland	2.9	1998	4,613.0	...	...	...	1997	1,400.6[4]	7.0[4]	11.6[4]	81.4[4]	3,751.2	11.7	6.5	81.8
Portugal	0.5[5]	1995	529.3	40.2	59.6	0.2	1997	391.8	57.0	35.6	7.5	2,369.2	0.7	7.7	91.6
Puerto Rico	...	...	...	...	...	...	...	...	...	...	...	...	...	...	...
Qatar	38.1[2]	1997	3,502.7[3]	...	...	...	1995	3,000.3	—	0.1	99.9	51.3[8]	75.3[8]	24.7[8]	—
Réunion	...	1998	...	—	100.0	—	1995	0.9	100.0	—	—	15.0	—	—	100.0
Romania	3.3[8]	1994	990.9	—	16.1	83.9	1997	75.6	62.6	37.4	—	1,723.1[8]	9.7[8]	3.7[8]	86.6[8]
Russia	...	...	...	...	...	...	1997	32,522.7	5.6	1.0	93.4	560.0[5]	60.2[5]	16.9[5]	23.0[5]
Rwanda	0.06	1998	1.2	...	...	...	...	...	...	...	...	...	...	...	...
St. Kitts and Nevis	0.3[5]	1995	0.6	—	100.0	—	1997	...	...	...	...	2.1	—	33.3	66.7
St. Lucia	0.5	1998	2.6	—	100.0	—	1996	...	...	...	...	5.1	—	49.0	51.0
St. Vincent	0.3	1998	0.9	—	100.0	—	1997	1.6	—	18.8	81.3	1.6[5]	—	18.8[5]	81.3[5]
Samoa	...	...	...	...	...	...	...	...	...	...	...	...	...	...	...
San Marino	...	...	...	...	...	...	...	...	...	...	...	...	...	...	...
São Tomé and Príncipe	...	1998	—	—	100.0	—	...	...	...	...	...	...	...	...	...
Saudi Arabia	37.2[2]	1997	54,352.5	—— 1.1 ——		98.9	1997	50,116.9[2]	0.1[2]	—	99.9[2]	136.7	88.6	11.4	—
Senegal	0.2	1998	6.3	—	100.0	—	1995	55.8	7.3	92.7	—	102.6	—	13.5	86.5
Seychelles	...	1998	—	—	100.0	—	1996	...	...	...	...	0.5	—	100.0	—
Sierra Leone	16.8[23]	1994–95	117.7	—— 100.0 ——		—	1995	16.7	25.4	74.6	—	0.6	—	100.0	—
Singapore	0.02	1998	14.3	—	100.0	—	1997	787.1	31.0	41.7	27.3	8,895.9	0.7	9.0	90.3
Slovakia	0.9	1998	178.8	...	...	...	1997	68.5	28.0	72.0	—	1,106.3	8.9	4.1	87.0
Slovenia	1.0[2]	1997	182.6	...	...	...	1997	28.6	100.0	—	—	386.4	23.4	17.1	59.4
Solomon Islands	...	1998	...	—— 100.0[24] ——		—	1996	...	...	...	...	2.0	—	—	100.0
Somalia	...	...	...	...	...	...	...	...	...	...	...	...	...	...	...
South Africa	6.5	1998	8,003.2	...	...	...	1997[9]	7,936.4	23.4	51.1	25.4	3,452.8	9.7	14.3	76.0
Spain	...	...	...	...	...	...	1997	771.2	39.7	55.0	5.3	12,200.5[4]	16.5[4]	4.2[4]	79.3[4]
Sri Lanka	1.9	1998	269.4[25]	—— 100.0[25] ——		—	1995	216.5	—	100.0	—	271.1	—	40.0	60.0
Sudan, The	0.3	1998	27.4	...	...	...	1995	...	...	...	...	34.1	—	—	100.0
Suriname	10.9[4]	1996	58.9[26]	...	...	...	1997	594.7	100.0	—	—	15.9[5]	—	31.4[5]	68.6[5]
Swaziland	0.7	1998	8.9	...	...	...	[9]	...	...	...	...	...	...	...	...
Sweden	0.3[5]	1995	634.3	59.2[8]	40.8[8]	—	1997	1,127.6	83.8	11.2	5.0	4,369.9	13.4	6.2	80.4
Switzerland	...	1998	...	—	100.0	—	1997	1,931.1	15.0	85.0	—	4,056.5	3.0	69.0	28.0
Syria	6.6[8]	1994	2,594.1[7]	—	—— 100.0[7] ——		1995	2,675.5	—	1.4	98.6	21.6	—	—	100.0
Taiwan	0.3[5]	1995	791.6	—	79.6	20.4	1995	843.7	...	...	...	8,035.8	—— 35.8 ——		64.2
Tajikistan	...	...	...	...	...	...	1997	1.0	—	100.0	—	228.0[4]	—	100.0[4]	—
Tanzania	1.3	1998	111.9	...	...	...	...	...	...	...	...	...	...	...	...
Thailand	1.8[2]	1997	2,756.6	...	...	...	1997	1,334.0	9.3	74.9	15.7	5,929.7	4.7	14.2	81.1
Togo	5.8	1998	88.3	—	100.0	—	1997	145.3	—	100.0	—	...	...	...	...
Tonga	0.3[5]	1995	0.4	—	100.0	—	1995	0.1	—	100.0	—	1.3	—	46.2	53.6
Trinidad and Tobago	12.2	1998	708.6	—	—	100.0	1996	492.4	—	—	100.0	476.9	12.7	2.1	85.1
Tunisia	5.6	1998	1,456.4	—— 17.1 ——		82.9	1997	438.9	2.7	11.6	85.7	367.1	—	32.4	67.6
Turkey	1.1	1998	2,160.5	...	...	...	1997	325.8	61.7	38.3	—	5,709.8	21.0	3.3	75.7
Turkmenistan	9.7[2]	1997	204.0	—	—	100.0	1997	489.9	—	0.2	99.8	...	...	...	...
Tuvalu	0.9[5]	1995	0.1	—	100.0	—	...	...	...	...	...	...	...	...	...
Uganda	0.3[27]	1995–96	15.8	—— 100.0 ——		—	1996	...	...	...	...	11.2	—	100.0	—
Ukraine	...	...	...	...	...	...	1997	1,421.6	60.4	19.7	19.8	6,790.7	3.4	3.1	93.5
United Arab Emirates	33.4[8]	1994[3]	12,269.1[3]	...	...	...	1996	23,700.1	0.5	0.5	99.0	233.3	17.1	82.9	—
United Kingdom	1.7	1998	21,115.8	—— 8.5 ——		91.5	1997	18,681.6	5.5	32.6	61.8	16,302.2	16.2	38.7	45.1
United States	1.5[2]	1997	120,500.0	4.8	9.5	85.7	1997	13,394.6	35.4	33.2	31.4	80,065.7	5.6	12.8	81.6
Uruguay	0.2	1997	47.6	—	100.0	—	1997	...	...	...	...	229.7	—	6.4	93.6
Uzbekistan	...	...	...	...	...	...	1997	114.5	—	—	100.0	13.9	100.0	—	—
Vanuatu	...	1998	...	—	100.0	—	1994	...	...	...	...	0.5	—	—	100.0
Venezuela	12.1	1998	10,676.5	—— 6.4 ——		93.6	1997	12,510.3	1.8	—	98.2	132.3	41.5	58.5	—
Vietnam	6.2	1998	1,091.3	—— 9.4 ——		90.6	1997	103.2	1.8	—	98.8	32.1	—	100.0	—
Virgin Islands (U.S.)	...	1998	...	—	100.0	—	...	...	...	...	...	...	...	...	...
West Bank	...	...	...	...	...	...	...	...	...	...	...	...	...	...	...
Western Sahara	...	...	...	...	...	...	...	...	...	...	...	...	...	...	...
Yemen	9.8[8]	1994	1,788.2[7]	—	—— 100.0[7] ——		1995	1,424.0	—	—	100.0	208.4	—	—	100.0
Yugoslavia	9.5[8]	1994	981.7	12.0	3.1	84.9	1997	16.8	32.1	—	67.9	708.7	23.6	5.9	70.6
Zambia	6.1	1998	203.0	...	...	...	1995	12.9	—	100.0	—	1.7	100.0	—	—
Zimbabwe	6.9[8]	1994	336.1	...	...	...	1997	95.9	4.9	94.3	0.8	35.3[4]	17.8[4]	37.1[4]	45.0[4]

[1]Gross value of production (output). [2]1997. [3]Mostly crude petroleum and natural gas. [4]1996. [5]1995. [6]Belgium includes Luxembourg. [7]Mostly crude petroleum. [8]1994. [9]South Africa includes Botswana, Lesotho, Namibia, and Swaziland. [10]Mostly diamonds, some gold. [11]China includes Taiwan. [12]Petroleum sector only. [13]Republic of Cyprus only. [14]1993. [15]Jersey includes Guernsey.

forestry, 1998						fisheries, 1997								country
production of roundwood				trade (value, '000 U.S.$)		catch (nominal)						trade (value '000 U.S.$)		
total ('000 cubic metres)	fuelwood, charcoal (%)	industrial roundwood (%)		exports	imports	total ('000 metric tons)	by source (%)		by kind of catch (%)			exports	imports	
		total	sawlogs, veneer				marine	inland	fish	crusta-ceans	mollusks			
1,023	14.7	85.3	57.5	2,733,092	4,921,392	451.8	99.5	0.5	82.3	2.0	15.7	1,424,883	1,107,268	Netherlands, The
...	...	...	...	982	20,695	1.1	100.0	—	100.0	—	—	1,189	4,112	Netherlands Antilles
5	—	100.0	58.3	210	11,172	2.4	100.0	—	65.6	22.0	2.7	13,299	6,848	New Caledonia
15,324	—	100.0	40.6	1,125,686	304,811	596.0	99.8	0.2	84.1	0.8	15.0	791,546	61,008	New Zealand
4,198	94.6	5.4	5.4	18,722	15,144	16.2	92.0	8.0	61.4	38.6	—	81,246	2,277	Nicaragua
6,460	93.8	6.2	—	272	1,851	6.3	—	100.0	100.0	—	—	234	768	Niger
98,514	90.4	9.6	7.2	41,288	107,960	365.7	69.8	30.2	94.0	6.0	—	40,995	131,760	Nigeria
...	...	...	...	...	51	0.3	100.0	—	100.0	—	—	...	...	Northern Mariana Islands
7,985	3.8	96.2	52.7	1,682,379	1,134,569	2,856.0	100.0	—	98.8	1.2	—	3,401,593	562,863	Norway
...	...	...	...	632	18,696	117.5	100.0	—	94.7	0.5	4.8	67,654	5,061	Oman
33,044	93.0	7.0	5.2	...	131,926	589.7	71.6	28.4	93.2	5.4	1.4	150,760	207	Pakistan
...	...	...	...		1,123	1.4	100.0	—	98.6	1.2	0.1	934	2,070	Palau
1,098	91.1	8.9	3.4	6,534	58,088	166.6	99.9	0.1	88.5	10.6	0.9	162,399[19]	3,298[19]	Panama
8,772	63.1	36.9	34.9	123,265	10,085	43.7	69.0	31.0	95.6	3.1	—	12,010	21,958	Papua New Guinea
8,097	52.1	47.9	42.2	80,081	36,067	27.7	—	100.0	100.0	—	—	31	3,531	Paraguay
9,157	80.0	20.0	17.7	46,554	166,496	7,869.9	99.6	0.4	99.1	0.3	0.6	1,321,869	5,849	Peru
42,530	91.8	8.2	1.1	65,726	498,709	1,805.8	91.2	8.8	88.1	4.5	7.4	435,260	135,304	Philippines
23,300	6.3	93.7	45.1	876,484	1,212,815	361.9	93.9	6.1	90.9	4.5	4.5	206,128	260,685	Poland
8,978	6.1	93.9	43.1	1,392,446	1,247,652	221.9	100.0	—	99.0	1.0	—	260,077	748,230	Portugal
...	...	...	...	...	...	2.6	100.0	—	87.9	6.9	5.2	[21]	[21]	Puerto Rico
...	...	...	...	19	19,927	5.0	100.0	—	98.1	1.2	0.7	14	2,300	Qatar
36	85.9	14.1	11.6	342	69,029	5.9	100.0	—	95.1	4.9	—	16,434	44,537	Réunion
11,649	25.9	74.1	36.9	335,150	172,186	8.2	47.5	52.5	100.0	—	—	440	40,837	Romania
115,600	34.5	65.5	32.0	2,858,399	535,500	4,661.9	95.1	4.9	96.6	1.4	1.7	1,686,162	418,977	Russia
3,000	100.0	—	—	...	1,836	4.4	—	100.0	100.0	—	—	...	291	Rwanda
...	...	...	...	33	1,797	0.2	100.0	—	85.5	4.1	10.4	200[22]	538[22]	St. Kitts and Nevis
...	...	...	...	—	11,692	1.3	100.0	—	97.2	1.0	1.9	...	4,212	St. Lucia
...	...	...	...	8	18,545	1.4	99.9	0.1	99.3	—	7.2	897	835	St. Vincent
131	53.4	46.6	44.3	467	1,790	7.1	100.0	—	99.4	0.1	0.4	601	6,096	Samoa
...	...	...	...	...	...	—	—	100.0	100.0	—	—	...	...	San Marino
9	—	100.0	100.0	504	196	3.3	100.0	—	99.3	0.1	0.6	202	213	São Tomé and Príncipe
...	...	...	...	5,410	634,152	49.4	100.0	—	84.6	14.4	0.9	1,196	14,703	Saudi Arabia
4,909	84.2	15.8	0.8	91	23,707	507.0	84.1	15.9	94.8	2.0	3.2	113,292[4]	11,970[4]	Senegal
...	...	...	...	99	1,416	5.3	100.0	—	77.3	7.9	14.8	39,733	19,206	Seychelles
3,315	96.3	3.7	0.1	646	1,503	68.8	78.9	21.1	96.1	3.1	0.8	16,530	3,446	Sierra Leone
120	—	—	—	585,809	937,413	9.3	100.0	—	74.5	6.7	18.8	459,215	507,282	Singapore
5,532	7.3	92.7	39.4	303,855	226,977	1.4	—	100.0	100.0	—	—	2,175	36,697	Slovakia
2,133	25.3	74.7	46.9	399,531	296,900	2.3	88.1	11.9	98.4	—	1.6	5,120	28,548	Slovenia
872	15.8	84.2	84.2	104,578	...	62.1	100.0	—	98.5	—	0.2	103,421	113	Solomon Islands
7,955	98.7	1.3	0.4	132	257	15.7	98.1	1.9	98.3	2.4	3.0	7,349	71	Somalia
33,171[18]	44.0[18]	56.0[18]	14.4[18]	983,808[18]	435,675[18]	514.5	99.8	0.2	18.3	0.3	1.4	218,335[9]	153,335[9]	South Africa
15,631	20.5	79.5	36.7	1,611,703	4,139,459	1,143.1	99.2	0.8	80.9	2.0	17.1	1,469,278	3,083,068	Spain
10,414	93.2	6.8	0.6	2,862	81,534	240.0	89.5	10.5	95.6	4.3	0.1	75,430	78,373	Sri Lanka
9,486	77.5	22.5	1.3	121	37,559	47.0	10.6	89.4	99.9	—	0.1	95	2,639	Sudan, The
183	0.5	99.5	98.9	4,100	1,277	13.0	98.8	1.2	98.1	1.9	—	13,804	1,675	Suriname
1,494	37.5	62.5	17.4	60,000	—	0.1	—	100.0	97.8	2.2	—	[9]	[9]	Swaziland
58,100	6.5	93.5	55.1	10,020,790	1,549,809	357.4	99.4	0.6	98.6	1.0	0.4	336,574	596,381	Sweden
4,546	22.0	78.0	65.8	1,927,453	2,425,061	1.9	—	100.0	100.0	—	—	3,258[17]	360,565[17]	Switzerland
50	31.5	68.5	31.7	364	139,859	6.1	42.2	58.0	98.9	1.1	—	38	5,977	Syria
...	...	...	...	...	...	1,038.0	100.0	—	...	...	...	...	...	Taiwan
...	...	...	...	80	4,131	—	...	...	100.0	—	—	114	288	Tajikistan
39,022	94.2	5.8	0.8	3,522	10,207	357.0	14.1	85.9	99.2	0.4	0.1	21,457	373	Tanzania
36,302	92.1	7.9	0.1	727,045	863,098	2,877.6	93.6	6.4	82.5	9.3	7.5	1,351,428	481,386	Thailand
1,182	75.7	24.3	4.7	1,891	4,646	14.3	65.0	35.0	99.5	—	0.5	2,153	13,752	Togo
5	—	100.0	100.0	20	1,388	2.7	100.0	—	93.8	3.4	—	1,645	513	Tonga
60	16.7	83.3	83.3	465	72,778	15.0	100.0	—	95.2	4.8	—	10,232	6,468	Trinidad and Tobago
2,807	94.2	7.6	0.7	16,423	212,439	87.0	98.8	1.2	82.8	4.9	12.3	95,726	16,713	Tunisia
17,668	43.5	56.5	27.4	87,308	938,834	459.2	89.0	11.0	95.0	0.6	4.2	124,647	84,650	Turkey
...	...	...	...	501	3,880	8.2	—	100.0	100.0	—	—	314	105	Turkmenistan
...	...	...	...	—	323	0.4	100.0	—	100.0	—	—	391	...	Tuvalu
15,649	85.9	14.1	1.1	58	4,216	218.0	—	100.0	100.0	—	—	34,598	105	Uganda
10,052	...	...	...	132,755	235,646	373.0	98.3	1.7	96.9	1.0	2.1	154,370	34,621	Ukraine
...	...	...	...	1,718	328,207	114.4	100.0	—	99.9	0.1	—	26,568	5,923	United Arab Emirates
7,635	3.0	97.0	51.9	2,317,273	9,851,730	886.3	99.8	0.2	88.0	4.5	7.5	1,008,260	2,141,038	United Kingdom
490,618	14.3	85.7	51.1	17,727,670	24,561,880	4,983.5	99.2	0.6	83.2	5.8	10.7	2,859,619	8,143,229	United States
6,163	70.3	29.7	22.3	97,173	99,447	136.9	98.4	1.6	84.5	2.2	13.3	109,582	11,293	Uruguay
...	...	...	...	240	37,231	3.1	—	100.0	100.0	—	—	21	1,026	Uzbekistan
63	38.0	62.0	62.0	3,767	570	30.7	100.0	—	70.5	11.0	17.1	385	1,011	Vanuatu
2,038	43.9	56.1	54.8	93,544	192,665	463.2	91.2	8.8	89.2	3.9	6.9	114,524	23,672	Venezuela
36,232	87.5	12.5	6.7	34,719	141,949	1,078.7	93.7	6.3	77.8	17.8	4.4	503,555	6,431	Vietnam
...	...	...	...	...	...	0.9	100.0	—	87.7	8.0	4.2	...	...	Virgin Islands (U.S.)
...	...	...	...	...	...	...	...	...	...	...	...	...	...	West Bank
...	...	...	...	...	...	—	—	—	—	—	—	...	...	Western Sahara
—	—	—	—	166	53,798	101.2	100.0	—	92.2	0.9	6.9	10,782	1,992	Yemen
1,320	3.8	96.2	82.6	44,990	166,400	3.9	9.6	90.4	99.4	0.1	0.4	989	52,733	Yugoslavia
8,042	89.8	10.2	4.0	832	8,118	65.9	—	100.0	100.0	—	—	399	1,576	Zambia
8,378	74.7	25.3	11.0	22,055	29,244	18.1	—	100.0	100.0	—	—	3,687	18,684	Zimbabwe

[16]Mostly bauxite and diamonds. [17]Switzerland includes Liechtenstein. [18]South Africa includes Namibia. [19]Excludes the Free Zone of Colón and the Canal Zone. [20]Includes coal mining. [21]United States includes Puerto Rico. [22]Includes Anguilla. [23]1994–95. [24]Mostly gold. [25]Mostly precious and semiprecious stones. [26]Mostly bauxite. [27]1995–96.

Manufacturing industries

This table provides a summary of manufacturing activity by industrial sector for the countries of the world, providing figures for total manufacturing value added, as well as the percentage contribution of 29 major branches of manufacturing activity to the gross domestic product. U.S. dollar figures for total value added by manufacturing are given but should be used with caution because of uncertainties with respect to national accounting methods; purchasing power parities; preferential price structures and exchange rates; labour costs; and costs for material inputs influenced by " most favored" international trade agreements, barter, and the like.

Manufacturing activity is classified here according to a modification of the International Standard Industrial Classification (ISIC), revision 2, published by the United Nations. A summary of the 2-, 3-, and 4-digit ISIC codes (groups) defining these 29 sectors follows, providing definitional detail beyond that possible in the column headings.

The collection and publication of national manufacturing data is usually carried out by one of three methods: a full census of manufacturing (usually done every 5 to 10 years for a given country), a periodic survey of manufacturing (usually taken at annual or other regular intervals between censuses), and the onetime sample survey (often limited in geographic, sectoral, or size-of-enterprise coverage). The full census is, naturally, the most complete, but, since up to 10 years may elapse between such censuses, it has sometimes been necessary to substitute a survey of more recent date but less complete coverage. In addition to national sources, data published by the United Nations Industrial Development Organization (UNIDO), especially its *International Yearbook of Industrial Statistics* and *Industrial Development Global Report;* occasional publications of the International Monetary Fund (IMF); and other sources have been used.

ISIC code(s)		Products manufactured
31		Food, beverages, and tobacco
	311 + 312	food including prepared animal feeds
	313	alcoholic and nonalcoholic beverages
	314	tobacco manufactures
32		Textiles, wearing apparel, and leather goods
	321	spinning of textile fibres, weaving and finishing of textiles, knitted articles, carpets, rope, etc.
	322	wearing apparel (including leather clothing; excluding knitted articles and footwear)
	323 + 324	leather products (including footwear; excluding wearing apparel), leather substitutes, and fur products

Manufacturing industries

country	year	total manufacturing value added ('000,000 U.S.$)	(31) food (311 + 312)	beverages (313)	tobacco manufactures (314)	(32) textiles (exc. wearing apparel) (321)	wearing apparel (322)	leather and fur products (323 + 324)	(33) wood products (exc. furniture) (331)	wood furniture (332)	(34) paper, paper products (341)	printing and publishing (342)	(35) industrial chemicals (351)	paints, soaps, etc. (352 exc. 3522)	drugs and medicines (3522)
Afghanistan	1988–89[1]	435	18.3	1.9	—	8.0	0.4	16.7	—0.5—		0.9	4.9	4.8	0.2	2.7
Albania	1996[2, 3, 4]	283	34.8	7.5	10.7	—	0.9	1.4	0.5	—	—	0.2	0.1	0.4	—
Algeria	1995	4,147	15.0	3.2	4.1	2.8	2.6	1.2	1.9	0.9	2.2	0.3	0.4	—2.4—	
American Samoa	1993[5, 6]	326	99.5[7]	…	…	…	…	…	…	…	…	…	…	…	…
Andorra	1997[8]	48	1.1	6.1	2.2	—15.7—			0.9	4.4[9]	0.7	10.6	—3.4—		—
Angola	1989	319	20.0	—12.2—		—11.6—			—3.7—		—0.3—		9.1[10]	[10]	[10]
Antigua and Barbuda	1995	8.4	…	…	…	…	…	…	…	…	…	…	…	…	…
Argentina	1993[12]	29,622	16.0	6.0	6.2	4.4	2.4	2.4	1.2	1.2[9]	2.0	5.1	2.2	3.6	3.8
Armenia	1995[2,12]	322	36.8	3.7	1.3	1.9	6.1	1.1	0.4	0.3	0.1	0.8	3.9	—1.3—	
Aruba	1994	89[13]	…	…	…	…	…	…	…	…	…	…	…	…	…
Australia	1995	65,859	15.2	3.4	0.6	2.7	1.9	0.6	2.9	1.8	2.4	8.0	3.2	—4.7—	
Austria	1995[3, 5]	41,735	8.7	2.3	…	3.8	1.3	0.7	4.6	3.8[9]	4.7	4.6	…	…	2.1
Azerbaijan	1996[2, 5]	1,483	1.1	0.2	0.4	13.0	—	—	1.0	…	…	0.2	—3.2—		
Bahamas, The	1992[5]	95	7.4	38.9	—	0.3	3.6	—	—	3.5	…	10.0	…	22.0	…
Bahrain	1992	761	5.0	1.1	—	—	6.5	0.1	0.1	8.4	0.4	4.4	5.6	—	—
Bangladesh	1991–92[12, 14]	1,899	12.7	0.6	12.2	23.5	10.2	3.9	0.7	0.1	2.9	1.2	5.6	4.5	5.8
Barbados	1995	289	18.0	16.9	2.4	0.7	2.1	—	—	1.4	1.0	8.3	5.9	—4.1—	
Belarus	1994[2, 5, 15]	3,006	16.2	…	…	7.0	2.1	2.6	—5.4[16]—		—[16]—		16.3[10]	[10]	[10]
Belgium	1995	53,712	15.4	2.0	0.7	4.3	2.3	0.1	0.6	3.6	2.2	4.6	11.5	—3.8—	
Belize	1992[12]	59	45.9	7.5	3.9	—3.8—			5.5	2.7	1.1	1.5	—14.1—		
Benin	1990	59	20.6	13.1	—	3.2	5.5	6.9	3.6	5.2	—	2.5	—	—9.5—	
Bermuda	1995	170	…	…	…	…	…	…	…	…	…	…	…	…	…
Bhutan	1989[12]	21	6.0	10.1	—	—5.6—			18.1	2.7	0.4	1.0	21.5	—1.7—	
Bolivia	1995[12, 19]	910	20.9	13.5	0.6	2.6	0.6	1.5	2.6	0.5	1.6	1.9	0.5	1.1	1.8
Bosnia and Herzegovina	1991	4,021	9.1	2.6	1.7	5.9	4.5	3.3	6.3	4.2	3.9	1.4	5.5	—4.1—	
Botswana	1995	212	32.5	12.7	—	8.0	5.2	2.8	2.4	1.4	2.8	2.8	1.4	—1.4—	
Brazil	1995	277,242	13.7	1.4	1.2	4.6	2.2	2.6	0.7	0.8	3.6	2.2	8.9	—4.7—	
Brunei	1995	314	…	…	…	…	…	…	…	…	…	…	…	…	…
Bulgaria	1995[20]	5,498	9.3	3.3	3.1	5.9	3.5	3.6	1.6	1.4	1.2	2.0	2.0	—1.9—	
Burkina Faso	1995	162	47.2	15.5	1.2	13.7	1.2	4.4	—	1.2	—	1.2	0.6	—	—
Burundi	1995	117	54.7	21.4	5.1	9.4	—	—	0.9	—	—	0.9	—	—1.7—	
Cambodia	1995[12, 14]	71	—14.2—		5.9	0.7	—21.7—		—10.4[21]—		[21]	0.5	—0.3—		
Cameroon	1995–96[12]	543	19.4	21.0	2.3	10.3	0.3	—	13.0	0.1	1.9	0.5	—	—4.2—	
Canada	1995[12]	126,465	9.6	2.5	1.0	1.6	1.8	0.3	4.9	2.3[9]	10.5	5.6	5.2	3.2	1.9
Cape Verde	1990	14	33.1	0.6	26.8	…	8.0	2.0	…	…	…	9.2	…	…	…
Central African Republic	1995	36	27.0	13.5	21.6	—	—	—	13.5	2.7	…	5.4	2.7	—5.4—	
Chad	1998	200	…	…	…	…	—	—	—	—	—	—	—	…	—
Chile	1995[12, 22]	16,538	20.4	5.0	3.4	2.6	2.2	1.8	3.3	0.8	9.6	3.5	2.9	4.6	2.5
China	1996	174,971	6.9	3.1	5.2	7.1	3.1	1.9	1.6	0.5	2.3	1.2	—9.5—		2.5
Colombia	1995[12, 14]	14,781	19.9	9.6	0.5	6.4	3.3	1.4	0.6	0.5	4.6	3.8	5.9	6.0	4.6
Comoros	1996	11	…	…	—	…	…	…	…	…	—	—	—	—	—
Congo, Dem. Rep. of the	1990	808	86.7	5.4	1.9	0.6	0.2	0.6	0.1	0.2	—	0.1	0.9	—0.1—	
Congo, Rep. of the	1995	86	26.7	24.4	7.0	2.3	1.2	2.3	3.5	2.3	1.2	1.2	3.5	—4.7—	
Costa Rica	1996[5, 12]	1,381	31.6	15.0	2.6	1.8	3.3	0.8	1.3	1.2	3.7	3.4	6.6	3.9	1.6
Côte d'Ivoire	1995	1,395	17.6	4.3	6.0	10.9	2.2	0.9	5.9	0.8	0.2	0.6	5.5	—1.2—	
Croatia	1995	6,539	17.3	3.9	3.6	5.2	5.1	2.1	3.7	2.7	2.0	3.0	3.3	—8.0—	
Cuba	1995	4,077[20]	15.7	5.4	39.9	3.6	1.9	1.2	1.0	0.8	0.2	1.2	1.9	—7.8—	
Cyprus[23]	1996	1,018[12]	17.8	7.9	7.2	3.6	8.0	2.3	6.0	4.3	2.4	5.3	0.5	3.1	1.3
Czech Republic	1998[24]	12,054	—13.5—			—5.8—		0.9	—2.3—		—4.5—		—6.7—		
Denmark	1995	33,560	19.3	3.5	0.9	2.3	1.0	0.4	2.0	2.7	2.7	6.7	5.1	—7.0—	
Djibouti	1992[6]	13	—5.0—			—3.0—			—	—	—0.3—		—1.0—		
Dominica	1997[3, 5]	13	0.1	…	—	—	…	—	…	…	—	—	—	98.1	—
Dominican Republic	1990	1,298	31.9	13.8	5.2	3.5	1.2	3.0	0.2	1.5	2.9	1.7	1.6	—3.4—	
East Timor	…	…	…	…	…	…	…	…	…	…	…	…	…	…	…
Ecuador	1996[12, 14]	2,134	20.1	6.1	0.3	4.5	0.8	1.2	1.3	0.9	3.8	2.3	2.0	2.8	1.7
Egypt	1994–95[3, 27]	6,050	13.6	1.7	2.0	10.0	2.3	0.1	0.8	0.3	1.8	1.4	5.1	3.4	3.8
El Salvador	1996[12, 19, 28]	1,012	16.1	8.5	3.0	6.7	11.4	0.8	0.1	0.7	2.9	4.4	2.6	11.6	4.5
Equatorial Guinea	1990[2]	1.9	27.6	4.1	…	…	2.6	…	…	49.3	…	1.2	…	—13.8—	
Eritrea	1996[12, 14]	53	—65.7—			—2.6—		5.5	…	…	—2.2—		—12.6—		
Estonia	1996[2, 5]	2,134	26.8	6.1	…	8.4	4.3	1.4	8.0	5.8	1.6	4.5	2.5	5.5	0.8

ISIC code(s)		Products manufactured
33		Wood and wood products
	331	sawlogs, wood products (excluding furniture), cane products, and cork products
	332	wood furniture
34		Paper and paper products, printing and publishing
	341	wood pulp, paper, and paper products
	342	printing, publishing, and bookbinding
35		Chemicals and chemical, petroleum, coal, rubber, and plastic products
	351	basic industrial chemicals (including fertilizers, pesticides, and synthetic fibres)
	352 minus 3522	chemical products not elsewhere specified (including paints, varnishes, and soaps and other toiletries)
	3522	drugs and medicines
	353 + 354	refined petroleum and derivatives of petroleum and coal
	355	rubber products
	356	plastic products (excluding synthetic fibres)
36		Glass, ceramic, and nonmetallic mineral products
	361 + 362	pottery, china, glass, and glass products
	369	bricks, tiles, cement, cement products, plaster products, etc.

ISIC code(s)		Products manufactured
37		Basic metals
	371	iron and steel
	372	nonferrous basic metals and processed nickel and cobalt
38		Fabricated metal products, machinery and equipment
	381	fabricated metal products (including cutlery, hand tools, fixtures, and structural metal products)
	382 minus 3825	nonelectrical machinery and apparatus not elsewhere specified
	3825	office, computing, and accounting machinery
	383 minus 3832	electrical machinery and apparatus not elsewhere specified
	3832	radio, television, and communications equipment (including electronic parts)
	384 minus 3843	transport equipment not elsewhere specified
	3843	motor vehicles (excluding motorcycles)
	385	professional and scientific equipment; photographic and optical goods; watches and clocks
39		Other manufactured goods
	390	jewelry, musical instruments, sporting goods, artists' equipment, toys, etc.

			(36)		(37)		(38)								(39)	country
refined petroleum and products (353 + 354)	rubber products (355)	plastic products (356)	pottery, china, and glass (361 + 362)	bricks, tiles, cement, etc. (369)	iron and steel (371)	non-ferrous metals (372)	fabricated metal products (381)	nonelectrical machinery (382 exc. 3825)	office equip., computers (3825)	electrical equip. (383 exc. 3832)	radio, television (3832)	transport equip. exc. motor vehicles (384 exc. 3843)	motor vehicles (3843)	professional equip. (385)	jewelry, musical instruments (390)	
—	—	2.1	1.1		0.4	—	—	—	—	—	—	—	0.1	—	37.1	Afghanistan
18.6	0.1	0.3	—	6.8	2.6	13.1	0.6	1.0	—	0.3	—	—	—	—	0.3	Albania
3.8	0.4	0.9	1.3	9.5	15.3	0.9	12.5	1.5		5.8		8.5		1.4	1.3	Algeria
…	…	…	…	…	…	…	…	…	…	…	…	…	…	…	…	American Samoa
—	0.1	2.4	0.2	1.0	0.8		0.7	5.3		19.8		0.1	13.4	3.0	8.0	Andorra
20.0	[10]	[10]	11.3		1.9		5.0					4.7		[11]	0.3[11]	Angola
…	…	…	…	…	…	…	…	…	…	…	…	…	…	…	…	Antigua and Barbuda
9.1	0.9	3.0	1.2	2.4	2.4	0.8	4.6	5.6	0.2	2.2	1.4	0.6	7.6	0.7	0.8	Argentina
0.3	0.8	0.1	0.5	5.0	0.2	2.1	2.2	4.2		6.6		0.6		3.6	16.1	Armenia
…	…	…	…	…	…	…	…	…	…	…	…	…	…	…	…	Aruba
3.5	0.9	3.6	1.1	3.9	3.8	7.2	7.3	6.2		4.6		8.7		0.9	0.8	Australia
…	0.8	3.3	2.4	4.4	5.0	1.6	9.2	10.5	0.1	4.9	6.2	0.9	4.6	1.8	1.6	Austria
47.6	0.6	…	…	…	0.1	—	…	1.1	—	0.8	0.1	0.5	—	0.3	…	Azerbaijan
…	…	…	…	7.0	2.6	—	—	—	—	…	…	—	—	…	…	Bahamas, The
13.7	0.8	—	—	4.5	4.4	33.4	0.3	0.4		3.4	—	3.4	—	—	4.1	Bahrain
0.4	0.5	0.4	1.0	1.7	3.6	0.1	1.2	0.4	—	1.2	0.5	0.8	3.7	—	0.6	Bangladesh
—	6.6	14.9	0.7	2.8	—	—	6.9	3.8		2.4		1.0		—	0.3	Barbados
7.6	[10]	[10]	5.5		3.0		26.8								…	Belarus
1.0	0.6	5.4	2.5	2.1	4.7	1.8	7.1	7.1		7.8		7.0		0.5	1.3	Belgium
—	0.3[17]		[17]	6.2	—	—	2.0	—	—	0.1		4.2		—	1.1	Belize
—	—	—	0.5	24.6	—	—	4.8	—	—	—	—	—	—	—	—	Benin
…	…	…	…	…	…	…	…	…	…	…	…	…	…	…	…	Bermuda
…	0.7	2.2	29.0		…	…	1.0[18]								[18]	Bhutan
36.4	—	1.5	0.7	6.0	—	2.4	1.1	0.3	…	0.4	…	0.1	0.3	0.1	0.8	Bolivia
2.3	0.3	1.3	0.5	3.2	5.5	3.4	10.8	5.0		3.3		8.6		2.6	0.7	Bosnia and Herzegovina
—	0.5	0.5	—	—	—	—	2.4	0.9		0.9		1.4		—	19.8	Botswana
5.0	1.1	2.4	0.8	3.6	5.7	1.5	4.0	7.8		8.4		10.6		0.9	1.5	Brazil
…	…	…	…	…	…	…	…	…	…	…	…	…	…	…	…	Brunei
1.6[20]	0.7	0.6	3.2	2.1	18.6	3.9	5.9	6.6		5.4		5.5		—	7.2	Bulgaria
—	1.2	0.6	—	—	1.2	—	0.6	—	—	0.6		1.2		—	8.1	Burkina Faso
—	—	0.9	—	1.7	—	—	2.6	—	—	—	—	—	—	—	0.9	Burundi
…	17.4		24.6		3.8		0.5	—	—	—	—	—	—	—	0.1	Cambodia
2.4	10.7	0.6	—	2.9	—	7.5	0.6	—	—	1.1		—	—	—	1.0	Cameroon
1.6	1.4	2.2	0.8	1.7	3.5	3.3	5.5	5.3	0.7	2.1	3.9	3.6	12.2	0.5	1.5	Canada
…	…	…	…	…	…	…	…	…	…	…	…	20.1		…	0.2	Cape Verde
—	—	—	—	—	—	—	2.7	…	…	—	—	2.7		—	2.7	Central African Republic
—	—	—	—	—	—	—	—	…	—	—	—	…	—	—	…	Chad
6.0	1.0	2.8	1.0	3.5	2.4	11.5	3.7	2.2	—	1.1	0.2	0.8	0.8	0.2	0.2	Chile
3.8	1.3	2.2	7.3		6.9	2.1	3.4	8.6		5.1	4.6	6.4		1.0	2.5	China
5.2	1.2	3.2	2.3	5.3	2.4	0.4	3.4	1.9	—	2.0	0.6	0.8	2.6	0.5	1.0	Colombia
—	—	—	—	—	—	—	—	—	—	—	—	—	—	—	—	Comoros
0.1	—	—	—	0.2	…	…	0.4	0.3		0.2		0.5		—	1.5	Congo, Dem. Rep. of the
—	2.3	—	—	1.2	—	—	7.0	2.3		3.5		3.5		—	—	Congo, Rep. of the
3.0	1.7	4.3	1.2	2.7	…	0.1	2.2	1.4		1.0	3.8	1.0	0.2	…	0.2	Costa Rica
22.0	1.3	—	0.1	1.9	0.1	0.1	4.9	0.1		0.4		7.6		2.2	3.2	Côte d'Ivoire
3.2	0.3	1.6	1.5	4.0	2.6	0.9	4.5	5.7		6.9		8.2		0.4	0.3	Croatia
…	2.4	2.1	0.5	1.9	0.7	0.9	1.7	1.7		0.9		3.5		0.3	3.0	Cuba
1.2	0.4	3.5	0.4	10.2	—	—	7.3	2.7		1.2	—	0.3	0.8	0.1	2.1	Cyprus[23]
1.4	4.7		8.2		16.7[25]		[25]	11.8		9.2[26]		10.4		[26]	3.9	Czech Republic
1.5	0.4	2.9	0.7	3.6	1.0	0.3	8.1	12.9		4.9		4.7		2.9	2.6	Denmark
			0.1		0.1		13.0								77.5	Djibouti
—	—	—	—	…	—	—	…	—	—	…	—	—	—	—	…	Dominica
16.2	0.8	1.6	0.7	3.5	1.8	0.2	3.7	0.5		0.8		0.1		0.2	0.2	Dominican Republic
…	…	…	…	…	…	…	…	…	…	…	…	…	…	…	…	East Timor
32.7	1.1	3.5	1.2	5.4	1.3	0.4	2.1	1.4	—	1.4	—	0.1	1.3	—	0.4	Ecuador
17.4	0.4	1.1	0.9	10.6	1.8	2.5	3.6	7.3	0.2	3.1	0.6	1.1	2.4	0.4	0.1	Egypt
10.2	0.4	3.1	0.1	5.1	0.8	—	2.2	1.3	—	1.6	0.8	—	0.1	0.1	0.9	El Salvador
…	…	…	…	0.8	…	…	0.6	…	…	…	…	…	…	…	…	Equatorial Guinea
…	2.0		7.1		0.2[25]		[25]	0.5						0.2	1.4	Eritrea
0.3	0.1	1.5	1.4	3.3	—	—	5.4	2.7	0.5	2.4	1.2	2.1	2.0	0.8	0.8	Estonia

Manufacturing industries (continued)

country	year	total manufacturing value added ('000,000 U.S.$)	(31)			(32)			(33)		(34)		(35)		
			food	beverages	tobacco manufactures	textiles (exc. wearing apparel)	wearing apparel	leather and fur products	wood products (exc. furniture)	wood furniture	paper, paper products	printing and publishing	industrial chemicals	paints, soaps, etc.	drugs and medicines
			(311 + 312)	(313)	(314)	(321)	(322)	(323 + 324)	(331)	(332)	(341)	(342)	(351)	(352 exc. 3522)	(3522)
Ethiopia	1995–96[12, 29]	435	25.3	22.7	4.4	9.8	1.2	7.5	1.7	1.2	1.7	3.6	–0.2	3.2	0.8
Faroe Islands	1997[6]	389	95.8	—	—	—	0.1	0.1	—	—	—	—	—	—	—
Fiji	1994	160	42.6	6.1	—	—13.8—		1.3	9.7	1.9	3.8	5.1	—	3.1	—
Finland	1995	27,928	8.3	1.4	0.2	1.1	1.1	0.4	4.9	1.5[9]	22.5	6.1	3.9	1.4	1.2
France	1995	297,536	10.5	2.3	1.2	2.4	1.8	0.9	1.7	1.6	2.6	5.6	3.4	—5.6—	
French Guiana	1991[14]	45	…	…	…		—[31]—		—38.2[31]—		…	…	…	…	…
French Polynesia	1993[5]	214	—27.2—		—	…	…	—	…	…	—	—	—	…	—
Gabon	1995	243	9.1	7.0	6.2	0.8	1.7	—	18.1	2.5	0.8	1.2	4.1	—1.7—	
Gambia, The	1995[12, 19]	9.2	—65.0—		—		—8.3—		—6.2[33]—		—	4.2	8.8[10]	[10]	[10]
Gaza Strip[34]	…	…	…	…	…	…	…	…	…	…	…	…	…	…	…
Georgia	1997	503	…	…	…	…	…	…	…	…	…	…	…	…	…
Germany	1997[24]	598,758	—8.7—		2.3	1.4	0.8	0.3	1.3	[35]	2.4	4.6		—11.7—	
Ghana	1993[12, 24]	610	8.4	9.1	18.1	4.6	—0.5—		15.2	0.8	1.8	1.3	0.9	—8.9—	
Greece	1995[3, 14]	10,741	18.3	6.3	2.0	7.0	5.8	1.4	1.6	1.5[9]	3.2	3.7	2.5	—8.5—	
Greenland	1991	27	…	…	…	…	…	…	…	…	…	…	…	…	…
Grenada	1995[2, 37]	19	29.1	55.2	2.4	—	…	—	…	…	7.0	—	—	6.3	…
Guadeloupe	1995	152	…	…	…	…	…	…	…	…	…	…	…	…	…
Guam	1997[1, 5]	165		—14.8—			—[47]—		—[47]—		—	24.4		—[47]—	
Guatemala	1995	1,468	28.7	6.2	3.1	5.7	2.5	1.2	0.8	0.5	1.5	4.5	3.5	—16.4—	
Guernsey	1997[5, 6]	85	…	[38]	…	[38]	…	…	…	7.8[38]	…	18.5	…	…	…
Guinea	1996	143	…	…	…	…	…	…	…	…	…	…	…	…	…
Guinea-Bissau	1995	19	…	…	…	…	…	…	…	…	…	…	…	…	…
Guyana	1998[5, 39]	58	43.2[40]	…	…	…	…	…	…	…	…	…	—	…	…
Haiti	1996[5]	64	35.0	2.9	8.5		—19.1—		…	…	…	…			—11.4—
Honduras	1996[3, 19]	575	28.8	10.4	2.9	2.5	18.8	1.0	4.8	1.5	2.9	2.2	0.4	3.7	1.0
Hong Kong	1996	10,666	7.0	2.2	1.5	11.5	13.3	0.3	0.2	0.1	2.1	13.9		—2.7—	
Hungary	1998[2, 14]	30,856	16.2	2.1	0.7	1.9	1.8	0.8	1.4	0.9	1.9	2.1	3.2	1.8	3.0
Iceland	1995	933	47.3	2.1	—	2.1	1.5	1.1	0.2	3.6	1.2	9.7	1.0	2.2	—
India	1994–95[3, 41]	29,199	9.8	1.0	1.9	11.3	2.6	0.8	0.3	—	2.0	1.7	10.2	3.6	3.8
Indonesia	1996[3, 24]	39,847	8.4	1.0	9.5	10.3	3.5	3.2	6.3	1.1	3.4	1.8	5.6	2.0	1.5
Iran	1995	9,147	12.8	2.2	0.8	10.8	0.3	0.9	0.7	0.3	1.7	0.9	4.7	—5.4—	
Iraq	1995	567	9.9	3.4	1.2	3.5	1.2	3.5	—	0.2	3.5	1.4	9.2	—1.1—	
Ireland	1995[3, 42]	26,040	18.1	4.5	0.8	1.0	1.0	0.2	0.4	0.5[9]	1.4	12.1	13.6	4.8	5.5
Isle of Man	1996–97[3, 5]	120	—15.2—		…	…	…	…	…	…	…	…	…	…	…
Israel	1995[12, 19]	13,521	10.3	1.7	0.2	3.3	4.5	0.7	1.1	1.6	2.2	5.5	5.6	—3.3—	
Italy	1995	156,300	7.2	1.5	0.5	6.7	3.9	3.0	1.3	2.4	2.7	3.4	3.5	—6.4—	
Jamaica	1996[12, 14]	916	25.4	11.5	10.6	—6.2—		0.6	0.2	2.4	—3.9—		9.5[10]	[10]	[10]
Japan	1995	1,363,980	8.1	2.0	0.3	2.5	1.1	0.4	1.5	1.0[9]	2.8	5.7	4.1	2.9	3.3
Jersey	1991	45	…	…	…	…	…	…	…	…	…	…	…	…	…
Jordan	1995[12]	1,000	11.3	5.2	13.5	2.9	2.5	1.1	1.0	3.0[9]	2.9	3.1	7.6	2.7	4.8
Kazakhstan	1996[2, 5]	7,167	13.5	1.1	2.0	2.6	0.5	0.1	0.1	0.4	—	0.5	3.4	4.1	0.1
Kenya	1995	814	31.7	9.6	1.5	5.8	1.6	1.4	1.7	0.7	4.4	2.4	1.8	—6.6—	
Kiribati	1992	0.68	…	…	—	—	—	—	…	—	—	—	—	…	—
Korea, North	…	…	…	…	…	…	…	…	…	…	…	…	…	…	…
Korea, South	1996[19]	216,564	—7.1—		1.8	5.2	3.0	1.3	0.8	[35]	2.3	2.8		—9.2—	
Kuwait	1995[12]	3,148	4.3	1.4	—	0.7	3.7	0.1	0.7	1.5	1.0	0.7	4.7	0.7	—
Kyrgyzstan	1996[2]	408	33.9	4.7	2.7	17.3	1.7	1.5	0.3	0.5	—	0.9	—	0.1	0.1
Laos	1990[2]	66	4.5	7.4	16.3	—	5.1	0.3	40.1	5.0	—	1.2		—4.0—	
Latvia	1996[3, 5]	947	27.6	11.5	…	6.3	4.0	1.2	9.1	2.3[9]	1.0	5.4	0.1	1.5	2.2
Lebanon	1994	1,679	—25.2—		1.9	3.3	9.6	3.0	—3.4—		2.4	2.4	2.4	—	—
Lesotho	1995	134	43.3	28.4	…	10.4	3.0	2.2	…	0.7	…	1.5	…	—6.7—	
Liberia	1995	78	…	…	…	…	…	…	…	…	…	…	…	…	…
Libya	1995	857	4.3	2.2	9.4	3.7	3.3	8.5	0.3	0.2	0.3	1.0	7.0	—5.2—	
Liechtenstein	1997[5, 6, 45]	1,830		—4.2—		…	…	…	…	…	…	…			—7.8—
Lithuania	1996[2, 5]	3,590	26.9	4.2	…	7.3	6.2	1.4	2.8	2.2[9]	1.5	2.0	…	0.4	0.8
Luxembourg	1995	2,459	4.8	3.1	0.8	7.0	0.6	…	0.3	0.5	3.7	2.1	3.7	—4.8—	
Macau	1996[5, 12]	425	2.6	0.9	[47]	16.9	59.8	1.1	0.1	0.7	0.3	2.2	—	0.4	0.8
Macedonia	1996	603	19.7	4.8	7.5	5.9	8.0	3.9	0.2	2.1	0.9	4.6	5.5	—5.1—	
Madagascar	1995	127	15.0	11.8	0.8	35.4	3.1	2.4	0.8	0.8	3.9	1.6	—	—6.3—	
Malawi	1995	153	35.3	5.9	1.3	7.8	—	…	1.3	—	2.0	5.2	7.8	—9.8—	
Malaysia	1995[3]	23,810	8.4	0.8	1.2	3.0	2.0	0.2	5.7	1.5	1.8	2.8	5.7	1.9	0.3
Maldives	1997	13[48]	…	…	—	—	…	—	—	…	—	…	—	…	—
Mali	1990	96	18.4	1.2	13.1	36.5	10.3	0.1	0.1	—	0.4	0.8	0.8	—0.7—	
Malta	1996	700	7.7	7.9	1.4	1.9	9.0	2.7	0.2	4.6	1.2	6.9	0.3	2.5	1.0
Marshall Islands	1997	2.2	…	…	…	…	…	…	…	…	…	…	…	…	…
Martinique	1995	207	…	…	…	…	…	…	…	…	…	…	…	…	…
Mauritania	1993	35	—42.9—		—	—	—	—	—	—	6.0	—			—18.8—
Mauritius	1995[3, 49]	826	17.1	—7.7—		7.2	43.5	1.2	—1.6—		—1.5—			—5.2—	
Mayotte	1992	…	…	…	—	—	—	—	—	—	—	—	—	—	—
Mexico	1995	54,750	15.4	6.4	1.9	4.9	1.9	1.4	1.2	0.8	2.7	2.6	6.3	—7.3—	
Micronesia	1992	2.2[6]	[51]	…	…	…	91.0	…	…	…	…	…	…	1.6[51]	…
Moldova	1996[2, 12, 52]	862	46.2	17.9	6.2	2.9	1.9	2.0	0.8	1.9	2.1	0.6	—	0.6	0.5
Monaco	…	…	…	…	…	…	…	…	…	…	…	…	…	…	…
Mongolia	1996[12]	54	34.9	11.3	—	22.2	9.5	4.7	2.5	0.3[9]	—	2.9	—	0.8	1.7
Morocco	1996[5]	5,295	17.1	4.3	13.1	8.9	7.7	1.3	1.1	0.4	2.5	1.2	10.9	2.9	1.9
Mozambique	1996[2]	246	26.9	30.9	1.8	3.8	0.4	0.1	0.4	0.6	1.1	2.5	1.6	—5.9—	
Myanmar (Burma)	1993	858[53]	14.8	20.4	4.6	26.4	…	…	1.9	0.7	5.7	…	0.2	2.0	1.6
Namibia	1996[5]	327	21.1[54]	…	…	…	…	…	…	…	…	…	…	…	…
Nauru	1989	—	—	—	—	—	—	—	—	—	—	—	—	—	—
Nepal	1996–97[5, 12, 14]	381	13.6	9.1	12.0	25.9	6.3	1.3	1.4	0.9[9]	1.7	1.3	…	3.4	2.4
Netherlands, The	1995	56,417	14.8	4.0	5.2	2.0	0.4	0.2	1.0	0.9	3.5	8.3	8.6	—5.5—	
Netherlands Antilles	1995	157	…	…	…	…	…	…	…	…	…	…	…	…	…
New Caledonia	1992[5]	341		—15.4—		…	…	…	…	…	…	…	…	…	
New Zealand	1995	9,878	25.1	3.0	0.6	2.9	2.3	1.1	4.6	1.8	7.7	7.8	3.6	—3.1—	
Nicaragua	1997[5]	313	39.9	25.6	7.6	1.6	0.1	1.1	2.4	0.5	0.5	1.8		—3.1—	

			(36)		(37)		(38)								(39)	country
refined petroleum and products	rubber products	plastic products	pottery, china, and glass	bricks, tiles, cement, etc.	iron and steel	non-ferrous metals	fabricated metal products	nonelectrical machinery	office equip., computers	electrical equip.	radio, television	transport equip. exc. motor vehicles	motor vehicles	professional equip.	jewelry, musical instruments	
(353 + 354)	(355)	(356)	(361 + 362)	(369)	(371)	(372)	(381)	(382 exc. 3825)	(3825)	(383 exc. 3832)	(3832)	(384 exc. 3843)	(3843)	(385)	(390)	
—	1.2	1.4	0.5	7.1	3.0	—	1.9	0.2	—	—	—	—	1.8	—	—	Ethiopia
—	—	—	—	—	—	—	—	—	—	—	—	3.4	—	—	0.7	Faroe Islands
—	0.5	2.0	—	3.0[30]	[30]	—	3.2	1.2	—	—	—	0.4	1.0	—	1.2	Fiji
0.8	0.7	2.3	0.7	1.9	6.5		4.0	11.2	0.5	3.8	6.9	3.0	1.2	1.7	0.6	Finland
6.4	1.2	2.7	1.6	2.9	2.8	1.9	8.0	7.8		10.6		11.1		1.6	1.7	France
…	…	…	61.8[32]		[32]		[32]								…	French Guiana
—	…	…	…	…	—	—	35.4								…	French Polynesia
10.3	—	—	0.8	5.8	2.1	2.1	8.7	0.8		5.4		7.0		0.4	3.3	Gabon
—	[10]	[10]	—	—	1.8		4.8	0.8						—	[33]	Gambia, The
…	…	…	…	…	…	…	…	…	…	…	…	…	…	…	…	Gaza Strip[34]
…	…	…	…	…	…	…	…	…	…	…	…	…	…	…	…	Georgia
4.4	4.5		3.8		4.0		6.7	13.2	1.3	7.4	2.1	1.8	12.0	2.7	2.7[35]	Germany
8.1	0.6	2.6	4.4		0.7	8.2	3.4	0.3		1.5		0.6[36]		—	[36]	Ghana
5.2	0.3	3.2	6.3		2.8	3.9	3.6	3.2	0.1	2.2	1.7	4.0	0.6	0.3	0.6	Greece
…	…	…	…	…	…	…	…	…	…	…	…	…	…	…	…	Greenland
—	…	—	—	—	—	—	—	—	—	…	…	—	—	—	…	Grenada
…	…	…	…	…	…	…	…	…	…	…	…	…	…	…	…	Guadeloupe
—	—	—	10.3		—	—	2.6	[47]							0.6	Guam
1.1	2.5	4.0	2.5	4.8	2.7	0.1	2.5	0.8		3.4		0.3		0.2	0.4	Guatemala
…	…	…	…	…	…	…	…	8.8		…	34.3	4.0	…	…	…	Guernsey
…	…	…	…	…	…	…	…	…	…	…	…	…	…	…	…	Guinea
…	…	…	…	…	…	…	…	…	…	…	…	…	…	…	…	Guinea-Bissau
—	—	—	…	…	—	—	—	…	…	…	—	—	—	—	…	Guyana
			…	3.5	…	…	12.1	…	…	…	…	…	…	…	…	Haiti
0.2	1.1	3.3	0.1	7.5	0.5	0.2	3.6	0.7	—	0.9	0.1	—	0.2	0.1	0.7	Honduras
0.1	0.1	2.8	3.0		1.0		4.5	7.0	5.5	0.9	9.7	3.7		3.2	3.7	Hong Kong
5.8	0.8	2.7	1.1	2.1	3.0	2.2	4.1	4.8	7.3	5.1	5.9	0.7	15.0	1.1	0.4	Hungary
—	—	2.9	0.5	3.8	2.2	4.6	7.9	—	—	—	—	2.0	—	—	3.9	Iceland
5.2	1.6	1.0	0.6	3.5	9.0	2.7	2.4	6.1	0.9	5.5	3.1	3.0	4.7	0.7	0.8	India
0.2	1.9	2.0	1.7	2.3	9.3	1.2	4.2	1.4	—	3.9	3.3	5.7	4.3	0.3	0.7	Indonesia
0.7	2.1	1.6	1.7	7.7	15.2	3.6	4.5	4.0		7.8		8.3		0.7	0.4	Iran
25.2	0.5	1.4	0.7	18.2	4.1	—	4.8	2.3		4.4		0.4		—	—	Iraq
[43]	0.7	1.5	2.5		0.1	0.4	1.9	3.2	13.3	3.2	2.1	0.8	0.7	3.8	1.7[43]	Ireland
…	…	…	…	…	…	…	…	…	…	…	…	…	…	…	…	Isle of Man
2.1	0.6	5.4	0.6	3.6	1.2	0.8	12.0	3.3		22.6		5.2		1.4	1.2	Israel
2.5	1.7	2.9	1.5	4.2	3.7	1.3	7.1	13.8		8.1		7.5		2.2	1.0	Italy
9.3	[10]	[10]	5.9		[44]		14.2[44]								0.2	Jamaica
1.3	1.2	3.6	1.4	2.9	4.3	1.2	7.5	10.9	2.4	5.0	8.5	1.2	9.4	1.9	1.7	Japan
…	…	…	…	…	…	…	…	…	…	…	…	…	…	…	…	Jersey
5.4	0.2	3.1	0.1	15.7	3.0	0.9	4.5	1.9	—	1.0	1.0	—	1.2	0.2	0.4	Jordan
8.1	0.2	0.1	0.4	1.2	8.3	17.6	1.5	2.6	…	0.6	…	…	…	0.1	0.1	Kazakhstan
0.7	3.1	3.3	0.5	3.6	1.7	—	6.3	0.6		5.7		3.4		0.1	1.7	Kenya
—	—	—	—	—	—	—	…	—	—	—	—	…	—	—	…	Kiribati
…	…	…	…	…	…	…	…	…	…	…	…	…	…	…	…	Korea, North
2.9	3.8		4.6		6.3		5.5	8.5	1.2	3.7	15.1	3.1	8.6	1.1	2.2[35]	Korea, South
65.4	0.1	1.5	0.5	4.8	0.7	—	3.5	1.5	—	1.3	—	0.6	0.1	—	0.6	Kuwait
—	0.1	0.2	3.6	8.4	—	9.2	0.6	5.8	0.2	5.6	—	0.1	0.9	0.8	0.9	Kyrgyzstan
—	0.5		0.1	3.8	—	—	10.8	0.5		0.2		—	—	—	0.1	Laos
0.1	—	0.8	0.7	1.9	…	0.1	3.1	5.2	0.2	2.3	1.5	5.0	0.4	0.4	1.4	Latvia
1.6	—	3.2	12.0		4.9		8.9	2.2		2.1		1.0		—	10.5	Lebanon
…	…	…	…	0.7	…	…	3.0	…	…	…	…	…	…	…	…	Lesotho
…	…	…	…	…	…	…	…	…	…	…	…	…	…	…	…	Liberia
27.2	0.1	0.8	0.2	21.7	—	—	0.5	—	—	—	—	—	—	—	4.0	Libya
			…	…	1.0		15.3	50.0							…	Liechtenstein
18.0	0.1	0.9	1.0	2.5	0.2	—	1.4	3.3	0.1	1.8	3.3	2.0	0.2	0.6	0.6[46]	Lithuania
0.2	10.6	2.3	3.9	7.5	15.9	3.5	12.2	7.2		3.1		0.7		1.5	0.1	Luxembourg
—	[47]	0.3	—	3.0	—	—	2.0	0.3	—	3.3	—	1.2	—	—	3.7	Macau
0.4	0.1	1.2	0.8	0.6	6.2	—	5.4	1.1		9.5		4.7		0.3	1.7	Macedonia
7.9	0.8	0.8	—	2.4	—	—	3.1	—	—	2.4		0.8		—	—	Madagascar
—	0.7	3.3	—	1.3	—	—	5.9	4.6		1.3		0.7		—	5.9	Malawi
3.2	4.6	3.8	1.2	4.3	1.4	1.0	4.2	4.3	0.7	4.1	24.9	1.7	3.4	1.2	0.8	Malaysia
—	—	…	—	…	—	—	…	—	—	—	—	…	—	—	…	Maldives
0.7	0.3	0.4	—	1.3	—	—	6.2	0.5		1.7		—	6.5	—	—	Mali
—	3.2	2.4	0.4	3.3	—	—	3.8	1.0	0.3	4.4	23.6	1.1	0.1	3.8	5.3	Malta
…	…	…	…	…	…	…	…	…	…	…	…	…	…	…	…	Marshall Islands
…	…	…	…	…	…	…	…	…	…	…	…	…	…	…	…	Martinique
			—	16.8	—	—	15.5	—	—	—	—	—	—	—	—	Mauritania
—	0.3	1.6	3.9		1.0		1.6	1.6[50]		0.9		[50]		1.7	2.6	Mauritius
—	—	—	—	…	—	—	—	—	—	—	—	—	—	—	—	Mayotte
11.6	1.4	1.8	2.2	1.7	4.1	1.1	3.9	3.1		3.1		9.3		2.0	1.9	Mexico
…	…	…	…	…	…	…	…	…	…	…	…	…	…	…	7.4	Micronesia
—	—	0.3	2.6	3.7	0.1	0.1	0.8	5.0	0.1	0.5	1.3	0.2	—	0.7	0.8	Moldova
…	…	…	…	…	…	…	…	…	…	…	…	…	…	…	…	Monaco
—	—	—	0.1	5.7	–1.5	—	–0.1	0.1	—	0.3	2.0	0.3	0.4	0.7	1.0	Mongolia
…	1.0	1.5	1.4	9.3	1.1	0.3	3.9	0.8	0.5	2.1	0.8	0.3	3.0	0.2	0.1	Morocco
0.2	2.6	1.7	0.3	13.3	0.8	0.5	2.2	0.2		0.7		1.4		—	0.1	Mozambique
…	0.5	0.2	…	0.5	6.1	7.0	0.2	…	…	0.7	—	…	1.5	—	5.0	Myanmar (Burma)
…	…	…	…	…	…	…	…	…	…	…	…	…	…	…	…	Namibia
—	—	—	—	—	—	—	—	—	—	—	—	—	—	—	—	Nauru
0.2	1.3	1.7	0.1	7.2	1.6	0.1	4.8	0.1	—	2.2	0.3	—	—	—	0.5	Nepal
2.4	0.5	3.3	1.7	2.3	2.8	0.1	6.8	8.2		11.4		4.5		0.9	0.3	Netherlands, The
…	…	…	…	…	…	…	…	…	…	…	…	…	…	…	…	Netherlands Antilles
…	…	…	…	…	…	43.2	…	…	…	…	…	…	…	…	…	New Caledonia
1.5	0.7	3.6	1.3	2.1	1.8	2.3	7.7	4.8		4.4		4.4		0.4	1.3	New Zealand
4.5	0.1	…	7.4		…	…	0.7	0.3				0.2		…	…	Nicaragua

Manufacturing industries (continued)

country	year	total manufacturing value added ('000,000 U.S.$)	(31) food	beverages	tobacco manufactures	(32) textiles (exc. wearing apparel)	wearing apparel	leather and fur products	(33) wood products (exc. furniture)	wood furniture	(34) paper, paper products	printing and publishing	(35) industrial chemicals	paints, soaps, etc.	drugs and medicines
			(311 + 312)	(313)	(314)	(321)	(322)	(323 + 324)	(331)	(332)	(341)	(342)	(351)	(352 exc. 3522)	(3522)
Niger	1996[12]	9.8		23.2			1.2		0.5		35.5				21.8
Nigeria	1995	7,884	17.6	15.3	1.9	10.4	0.1	3.1	0.5	0.9	3.8	3.4	0.3	11.7	
Northern Mariana Islands	1997[1, 5]	762		0.7		[47]	91.8	—	[47]	[47]	[47]	0.7		0.3	
Norway	1995[14]	16,835		20.7		1.0	0.4	0.1	3.4	2.1[9]	6.7	9.3	6.7	1.2	2.0
Oman	1995	660	12.1	3.0	—	2.0	6.2	0.1	2.3	2.1[9]	1.3	2.4	0.9	3.5	1.3
Pakistan	1995	7,550	15.2	1.3	7.1	18.7	2.1	1.7	0.3	0.2	1.7	1.8	9.8	7.9	
Palau	1998	1.2[56]	...	...	...	...	...	...	...	...	...	...	...	...	...
Panama	1995	694	43.5	10.0	3.6	0.8	2.6	1.1	1.4	1.3	4.0	2.8	1.4	5.5	
Papua New Guinea	1989	451	48.4	13.1	4.9	—	0.4	—	11.6	2.0	1.1	2.4	1.1	1.1	
Paraguay	1995	904	30.6	10.0	0.7	7.4	0.3	5.3	18.8	1.8	0.1	4.6	0.8	0.8	
Peru	1995	7,485	14.8	13.2	0.9	8.7	0.9	0.6	0.6	0.5	1.1	3.2	3.0	7.7	
Philippines	1995[12, 14]	15,323	18.9	8.4	4.7	3.1	4.7	0.5	0.7	0.5[9]	2.0	1.4	2.5	5.2	4.0
Poland	1996	27,032	16.1		0.8	3.7	4.6	1.7	3.7	4.4[57]	2.0	4.8		8.4	
Portugal	1995[12]	20,472	7.5	2.6	4.2	8.5	6.5	3.9	3.5	1.7	4.9	4.3	2.0	1.7	1.6
Puerto Rico	1997[5]	36,427	4.0	5.7	...	0.2	1.9	0.6	...	0.1[9]	0.4	1.2	2.5	2.3	54.0
Qatar	1994	694	3.6	0.2	—	0.3	7.1	0.1	1.0	2.0	0.1	3.4	28.0	0.4	—
Réunion	1994	371	34.5	12.3	—	0.5		—	3.8		5.0[58]	6.3	...	3.7	
Romania	1995[5, 59]	9,387	18.8	8.9	0.7	4.4	6.6	1.7	3.3	3.4[9]	1.3	1.1	3.5	2.4	1.8
Russia	1995	58,394[53]	15.0	1.5	0.3	2.1	1.2	0.7	1.6	0.9	3.1	0.7	6.2	1.5	0.8
Rwanda	1990	178	29.1	18.1	11.2	...	...	...	4.4	0.9	1.0	1.3	9.0	—	—
St. Kitts and Nevis	1995[5]	21	16.0[61]	...	...	...	...	...	...	...	...	...	...	...	...
St. Lucia	1995[2, 37]	46	10.0	27.6		2.4	7.2	...	...	...	40.8	...	...	...	...
St. Vincent	1997[3]	19	...	...	...	...	...	...	...	...	...	...	...	...	...
Samoa	1995[5]	25	...	...	...	—	...	—	...	—	—	—	—	...	...
San Marino	...	...	...	...	...	...	...	...	...	...	...	...	...	...	...
São Tomé and Príncipe	1993[2]	4.6	26.3	20.7	—	—	26.3	—	15.1		—	1.2	—	6.6	—
Saudi Arabia	1995	7,461	5.8	0.5	0.3	0.4	0.1	0.1	0.1	0.5	2.2	1.0	40.4	2.3	
Senegal	1996[12]	309[62]	36.1[62]	3.9	3.9	3.2	—	0.2	0.3	0.1	1.3	1.9	21.1	6.0	3.4
Seychelles	1989	26		79.6			0.6		2.1		6.0				4.1
Sierra Leone	1993[12]	92	37.0	21.6	10.5	—	1.0	0.1	0.3	1.2	0.2	2.2			20.2
Singapore	1996[3, 14]	26,157	2.8	0.8	—	0.2	0.7	0.1	0.2	0.6[9]	1.3	4.5	1.6	3.6	4.1
Slovakia	1996	3,277	10.5[53]	2.9	...	2.4[53]	3.3	1.6	1.9	1.6[9]	4.9[53]	2.7	6.7	0.9	2.9
Slovenia	1995[12]	5,857	8.4	2.3	0.6	3.4	4.1	3.3	2.8	3.0	6.1	4.3	7.8	6.4	
Solomon Islands	1995	8.2	...	...	...	—	...	—	...	...	—	...	—	—	—
Somalia	1990	36	21.6	6.3	37.5	10.5	0.8	2.0	—	7.3	–0.6	0.3	0.4	5.1	
South Africa	1995	29,071	10.4	5.7	0.4	3.2	2.8	1.3	1.3	1.1	5.0	3.4	5.0	4.9	
Spain	1996	95,026	11.6	3.9	0.7	3.0	2.3	1.6	2.2	2.5	3.2	5.2	4.3	6.2	
Sri Lanka	1993[12, 19]	1,267	14.8	12.4	11.8	8.3	20.1	1.9	0.6	0.2	2.5	1.1	0.9	4.5	0.3
Sudan, The	1990	1,179	40.0	3.0	16.7	11.9	0.4	5.4	0.2	0.2	2.1	6.4	0.7	2.2	
Suriname	1992[2, 3, 37]	700	33.4	22.3	12.3	...	1.5	1.6	8.7	1.4	0.7	1.6	...	8.3	
Swaziland	1995[3, 5, 14]	335	27.5	42.0	...	0.4	3.0	...	1.2	0.8	17.9	1.1	—	0.2	...
Sweden	1994[3, 14]	35,125	7.2	1.2	0.5	1.0	0.2	0.1	4.9	1.1	9.8	5.8	3.9	1.8	5.4
Switzerland	1994	60,111	8.1	1.4	0.8	1.8	1.0	0.5	4.6	3.0	1.9	7.4	7.4	5.9	
Syria	1995	3,805	12.0	5.8	3.8	20.2	1.2	2.1	2.2	0.2	0.4	0.8	0.2	0.9	
Taiwan	1997	78,385	6.6		1.4	6.3	2.2	0.7	0.5	0.8	1.9	1.1	7.6	2.1	
Tajikistan	1996[2, 5]	864	26.1[53]	0.2	0.6	18.9[53]	0.5	0.1[53]	—	0.1	—	0.1[53]	4.7[53]	0.1[53]	...
Tanzania	1995	119	10.7	5.8	10.7	17.4	0.8	1.7	1.7	0.8	3.3	3.3	14.9	2.5	
Thailand	1994[12, 14]	38,122	9.3	3.9	2.9	8.0	9.4	0.6	1.3	0.4	1.7	4.6	0.9	0.7	0.7
Togo	1995[5]	59	15.3	40.7	...	16.9	—	6.8	—	—	—	1.7	10.2	...	...
Tonga	1994[2, 12]	13		45.1		1.1	1.5	2.0	1.3	[63]	[63]	5.0	—	24.9	
Trinidad and Tobago	1995	862	12.0	9.1	3.3	0.2	0.9	0.2	0.4	1.0	2.8	2.5	36.5	1.4	0.1
Tunisia	1996[12]	5,216	9.4	2.9	6.5	7.0	14.9	4.0	4.8		2.2		4.8	2.8	0.6
Turkey	1997	42,524	8.2	2.5	2.0	11.7	4.3	0.4	0.6	0.4	1.6	1.4	4.5	7.7	
Turkmenistan	1992[2, 5, 15]	801	13.3	...	...	18.9	1.2	0.4	0.3[16]		[16]		3.2[10]	[10]	[10]
Tuvalu	1995[3]	0.35	...	—	—	—	...	—	—	...	—	—	—	...	—
Uganda	1989	155	42.8	11.9	8.9	8.0	1.3	1.5	0.1	4.0	0.9	1.4	0.3	0.7	5.1
Ukraine	1996[3, 5]	27,508	24.1	3.4	0.6	1.4[53]	0.6	0.6	0.7	0.7	0.9	0.4	6.2	1.0[53]	0.8
United Arab Emirates	1993[2]	6,621		8.7			4.7		2.8		2.8				53.8
United Kingdom	1996	283,255	10.6	2.7	1.2	2.9	1.7	0.6	1.3	2.2[9]	3.1	9.2	4.6	3.8	3.1
United States	1996	1,749,662	8.2	2.0	1.5	1.9	2.2	0.3	2.4	1.6[9]	4.1	7.5	4.7	3.0	3.4
Uruguay	1996[19]	3,755	24.9	10.9	4.6	5.6	3.0	3.2	0.3	0.4	2.4	4.2	1.6	8.3	
Uzbekistan	1992[2, 5, 15]	2,147	12.6	...	...	21.4	3.1	1.9	1.3[16]		[16]		5.4[10]	[10]	[10]
Vanuatu	1994[5]	11		37.5			6.8		24.8		7.5				6.3[67]
Venezuela	1996[12, 19]	15,621	11.3	4.0	12.7	1.8	1.9	0.9	0.4	0.5	1.7	1.5	7.8	3.4	1.3
Vietnam	1997[2, 5]	12,096	32.7		4.1	10.3		4.9	5.6[68]	...	[68]	1.5		7.0	
Virgin Islands (U.S.)	1997[1, 5]	146		22.0		[47]	0.8	[47]	1.1	[47]	—	14.5			[47]
West Bank[34]	1994	314	12.9	0.1	0.5	2.8	19.2	4.7	2.5	1.3	2.2	0.5	0.4	2.0	1.0
Western Sahara	...	...	...	...	...	...	...	...	...	...	...	...	...	...	...
Yemen	1996[2, 14]	1,153		40.4			1.5		0.4		7.9				39.0
Yugoslavia	1996	4,439	20.0	6.9	1.9	4.2	2.7	2.0	1.8	1.8	1.9	5.2	2.1	9.4	
Zambia	1995	450	19.2	17.1	6.7	9.8	1.1	0.7	3.3	1.1	0.9	2.2	4.9	10.5	
Zimbabwe	1995–96[3]	1,627	14.9	13.9	4.3	9.0	3.0	2.5	2.6	1.8	2.3	3.0	3.9[77]	2.1	2.9

[1]Gross output in value of sales. [2]Gross output of production. [3]In factor values. [4]State sector only except food and beverages. [5]Complete ISIC detail is not available. [6]Value of manufactured exports. [7]Canned tuna and salmon. [8]Value of manufactured exports (excluding duty-free reexports). [9]Includes metal furniture. [10]351 includes 352, 355, and 356. [11]390 includes 385. [12]In producer's prices. [13]Estimated figure includes agriculture. [14]Establishments employing 10 or more persons. [15]Includes extraction of petroleum, natural gas, metals, and nonmetals. [16]33 includes 34. [17]355 and 356 includes 361 + 362. [18]38 includes 39. [19]Establishments employing five or more persons. [20]Excludes petroleum refining. [21]33 includes 341. [22]Establishments employing 50 or more persons. [23]Republic of Cyprus only. [24]Establishments employing 20 or more persons. [25]37 includes 381. [26]383 includes 385. [27]Private establishments employing 10 or more persons and all public establishments. [28]Excludes establishments processing coffee or cotton. [29]Establishments employing 10 or more persons and using power-driven machines. [30]369 includes 371. [31]33 includes 32. [32]36 includes 37 and 38. [33]34 includes 39. [34]West Bank includes Gaza Strip. [35]390 includes 332. [36]384 includes 390. [37]Selected industries only. [38]332 includes 313 and 321. [39]Includes public

			(36)		(37)		(38)								(39)	country
refined petroleum and products	rubber products	plastic products	pottery, china, and glass	bricks, tiles, cement, etc.	iron and steel	non-ferrous metals	fabricated metal products	nonelectrical machinery	office equip., computers	electrical equip.	radio, television	transport equip. exc. motor vehicles	motor vehicles	professional equip.	jewelry, musical instruments	
(353 + 354)	(355)	(356)	(361+ 362)	(369)	(371)	(372)	(381)	(382 exc. 3825)	(3825)	(383 exc. 3832)	(3832)	(384 exc. 3843)	(3843)	(385)	(390)	
			10.3		...	...	7.6								...	Niger
—	1.9	2.8	0.4	5.8	1.0	1.9	3.7	1.1		2.0		9.8		—	0.5	Nigeria
[47]	[47]	[47]	2.8		—	—	—	—	—	—	—	0.2		—	[47]	Northern Mariana Islands
0.8	0.2	1.7	0.8	2.4	2.7	6.5	4.3	6.6	0.3	3.4	1.8	11.0[55]	1.3	1.8	0.9	Norway
27.9	—	1.5	1.5	16.5	—	6.0	5.8	1.3	—	1.6	—	0.1	0.1	—	0.4	Oman
3.1	0.9	0.6	1.1	8.3	6.5	—	0.8	3.0		4.6		2.8		0.2	0.3	Pakistan
...	...	...	...	...	...	...	...	...	...	...	...	...	...	...	...	Palau
5.8	0.2	4.1	0.6	4.8	1.2	0.4	2.2	—	—	0.9	—	1.2	0.2	0.1	0.3	Panama
—	—	0.4	0.7	1.6	...	—	6.7	1.3		0.7		2.4		...	...	Papua New Guinea
4.3	—	1.9	0.6	3.0	—	1.3	1.2	0.2		0.1		0.7		0.1	5.5	Paraguay
18.2	0.8	2.4	1.1	4.0	2.0	6.0	3.1	1.5		1.6		2.0		0.3	1.8	Peru
10.5	1.3	1.8	1.3	3.3	3.6	1.6	1.6	0.7	1.3	3.1	7.9	0.8	3.2	0.3	0.9	Philippines
1.9	4.5		6.3		5.5		6.8	9.2	0.3	4.0	1.8	3.1	4.3	1.9	[57]	Poland
13.8	0.6	1.7	3.5	5.1	1.0	0.5	6.1	3.2	0.1	3.3	2.0	1.6	3.1	0.5	1.0	Portugal
2.3	—	1.0	1.6		0.2		1.1	7.3		2.6	5.4	—	0.3	4.2	0.4	Puerto Rico
31.5	—	0.8	—	6.7	11.4	—	2.8	—	—	0.1		0.3	—	—	0.2	Qatar
—	—	[58]	...	16.8	—	—	12.2	5.0							—	Réunion
2.2	1.4	1.0	5.3		5.6	1.3	4.2	8.5	0.2	2.9	2.2	0.9	3.4	1.4	0.9	Romania
7.3	1.4	0.5	1.1	6.0	8.8	9.3	1.8	12.5	0.5	3.2	[47]	2.1[60]	1.5	1.0	1.6	Russia
—	—	—	—	11.7	—	—	10.3	0.9		0.8		1.4		—	...	Rwanda
...	...	...	...	...	...	...	...	...	...	...	...	...	...	...	...	St. Kitts and Nevis
...	...	...	...	...	...	...	...	...	...	12.0		...	...	...	...	St. Lucia
...	...	...	...	...	...	...	...	...	...	...	...	...	...	...	...	St. Vincent
—	—	—	—	—	—	—	—	—	—	—	—	—	21.0	—	—	Samoa
...	...	...	...	...	...	...	...	...	...	...	...	...	...	...	...	San Marino
—	—	—	3.8		—	—	—	—	—	—	—	—	—	—	—	São Tomé and Príncipe
13.1	0.1	3.0	0.5	12.2	7.5	0.4	5.3	1.0		2.0		0.6		—	0.6	Saudi Arabia
3.7	—	1.6	—	7.4	—	—	4.1	0.5	—	–0.1	—	1.1	0.4	—	—	Senegal
			5.2		—	—	2.4								—	Seychelles
			3.5		...	...	2.1	...	...	...	...	...	...	...	0.1	Sierra Leone
5.5	0.3	2.5	0.5	1.5	0.4	0.1	5.9	6.7	25.6	2.9	18.9	5.7	0.3	2.1	0.5	Singapore
5.4	2.4	2.3	3.1	3.2[53]	9.0	3.6[53]	2.3	9.3[53]	0.3	3.0[53]	1.4	2.6[53]	3.6	1.7[53]	0.8[53]	Slovakia
0.4	1.6	2.4	3.7		10.2	1.6	7.3	5.9		7.9		3.9		2.0	0.7	Slovenia
—	—	—	—	—	—	—	—	—	—	—	—	...	—	—	—	Solomon Islands
1.6	—	0.5	—	3.0	—	—	1.1	—	—	—	—	0.9		—	1.7	Somalia
5.9	1.3	2.6	1.5	3.4	9.3	3.2	6.3	6.3		4.7		8.0		0.9	2.0	South Africa
1.4	1.6	3.1	1.9	5.7	5.3	1.9	8.3	7.3		5.5		11.1		1.0	1.0	Spain
1.4	4.2	1.4	1.8	2.9	1.1	0.2	1.3	0.9	0.2	1.1	0.1	1.6	0.3	—	2.1	Sri Lanka
1.3	0.8	1.2	0.1	0.5	0.1	0.7	2.6	0.1		1.2		2.1		—	0.1	Sudan, The
...	0.7	0.6	5.3		...	...	...	...	...	...	...	0.9		0.2	0.5	Suriname
...	...	0.2	0.1	0.5	...	...	2.2	2.8	...	...	...	...	0.2	...	—	Swaziland
1.2	0.7	1.4	0.7	1.6	4.8	1.3	7.7	11.9	0.8	3.1	5.6	2.7	10.5	2.8	0.3	Sweden
2.0	0.8	2.3	1.7	2.7	1.2	1.9	6.4	12.8		16.9		1.7		5.4	0.4	Switzerland
17.1	0.3	0.6	4.7	7.1	—	0.6	14.0	2.4		2.4		0.5		—	0.3	Syria
7.7	1.1	5.3	3.2		7.8		7.0	4.7		21.7		7.5		0.9	2.0	Taiwan
...	—	—	0.3	1.4[53]	...	41.6	...	0.7[53]	...	...	...	...	0.4[53]	...	1.8[53]	Tajikistan
4.1	0.8	1.7	—	5.8	1.7	2.5	4.1	0.8		1.7		3.3		—	—	Tanzania
11.5	1.7	1.2	1.0	3.7	3.0	0.4	3.2	17.4	—	2.4	3.1	1.7	3.7	0.3	1.3	Thailand
...	...	...	—	3.4	3.4	...	—	...	...	...	...	...	...	...	—	Togo
—	—	—	4.7		—	—	3.8	—	—	—	—	4.1		—	6.4[63]	Tonga
10.5	0.2	0.5	1.2	3.6	8.2	—	1.4	0.3	—	1.4	0.3	0.1	0.1	[11]	1.9[11]	Trinidad and Tobago
16.8	0.8	1.4[64]	2.5	6.9	1.5	3.0[65]	[65]	0.4		3.0	[66]	0.2	1.8	[66]	1.8[66]	Tunisia
10.0	1.9	2.9	3.0	4.0	7.2	1.1	2.9	5.8		7.5		7.8		0.4	0.2	Turkey
55.7	[10]	[10]	4.0		0.1		0.8								...	Turkmenistan
—	—	—	—	...	—	—	—	—	—	—	—	—	—	—	...	Tuvalu
—	0.2	—	—	2.5	3.0	—	4.7	0.7	—	1.3	0.5	—	0.1	—	—	Uganda
4.8	2.2	0.1	1.0	4.6	23.6	1.6	5.2	5.6	0.1	2.1[53]		2.9[53]	0.8	0.6[53]	0.1[53]	Ukraine
			8.3		8.2		9.2								1.4	United Arab Emirates
1.9	1.1	3.9	1.6	1.9	3.7		6.9	8.5	2.1	3.4	3.5	3.6	6.6	3.0	1.2	United Kingdom
1.8	1.1	3.2	0.9	1.7	2.2	1.8	6.2	8.3	2.3	3.5	7.0	4.0	6.1	5.6	1.5	United States
14.9	0.7	2.5	1.0	2.3	1.6	0.2	2.8	0.8		1.7		0.9		0.6	0.4	Uruguay
12.4	[10]	[10]	5.4		12.2		13.2								...	Uzbekistan
			[67]		11.4[25]		[25]	...	...	...	...	...	...	...	...	Vanuatu
15.8	2.2	1.6	2.3	2.9	7.0	6.1	2.7	1.7	—	1.7	0.1	0.3	5.9	0.3	0.3	Venezuela
—	2.9		10.7		7.6[25]		[25]	1.8		5.1		3.5		...	...	Vietnam
			15.0		—	—	2.3	[47]		—	—	3.4		19.8	1.9	Virgin Islands (U.S.)
—	—	2.1	0.6	26.6	0.1	—	10.6	1.3		0.4		—	0.5	0.1	7.6	West Bank[34]
...	...	...	...	...	...	...	...	...	...	...	...	...	...	...	...	Western Sahara
			7.9		2.8		—	—	—	—	—	—	—	—	—	Yemen
0.9	2.0	1.8	1.4	4.9	1.6	2.6	7.8	4.5		6.3		5.6		0.5	0.4	Yugoslavia
4.2	1.8	1.3	–0.2	3.3	1.3	—	5.3	1.1		3.3		0.7		—	0.2	Zambia
[69]	2.7	1.3	0.4	5.3	8.4	0.8	6.3	1.2		3.4	0.2	0.3	2.6	0.2	0.7	Zimbabwe

utilities. [40]Sugar and rice manufacturing only. [41]Establishments with electric power and employing 10 or more workers and all establishments employing 20 or more workers. [42]Establishments employing three or more persons. [43]390 includes 353 + 354. [44]38 includes 37. [45]Excludes exports destined for Switzerland. [46]Includes recycled waste and scrap. [47]Data withheld for reasons of confidentiality. [48]Includes public utilities. [49]Statistical breakdown is based on 89.3% of total manufacturing value added (U.S.$737,000,000); detail for some establishments employing nine or fewer employees is unavailable. [50]382 includes 384. [51]Coconut soap includes coconut oil. [52]Excludes Transdniester area and city of Tighina (Bendery). [53]Sum of available data. [54]Fish and meat processing. [55]Includes petroleum platforms (6.2% of total). [56]Includes mining. [57]332 includes 390. [58]341 includes 356. [59]State enterprises only; state enterprises account for about 80% of all industrial output. [60]Excludes shipbuilding and aircraft. [61]Refined sugar only. [62]Excludes fish processing. [63]39 includes 332 and 341. [64]Includes synthetic fibres. [65]372 includes 381. [66]390 includes 3832 and 385. [67]35 includes 36. [68]331 includes 341. [69]351 includes 353 + 354.

Energy

This table provides data about the commercial energy supplies (reserves, production, consumption, and trade) of the various countries of the world, together with data about oil pipeline networks and traffic. Many of the data and concepts used in this table are adapted from the United Nations' *Energy Statistics Yearbook*.

Electricity. Total installed electrical power capacity comprises the sum of the rated power capacities of all main and auxiliary generators in a country. "Total installed capacity" (kW) is multiplied by 8,760 hours per year to yield "Total production capacity" (kW-hr).

Production of electricity comprises the total gross production of electricity by publicly or privately owned enterprises and also that generated by industrial establishments for their own use, but usually excludes consumption by the utility itself. Measured in millions of kilowatt-hours (kW-hr), annual production of electricity ranges generally between 50% and 60% of total production capacity. The data are further analyzed by type of generation: fossil fuels, hydroelectric power, and nuclear fuel.

The great majority of the world's electrical and other energy needs are met by the burning of fossil hydrocarbon solids, liquids, and gases, either for thermal generation of electricity or in internal combustion engines. Many renewable and nontraditional sources of energy are being developed worldwide (wood, biogenic gases and liquids, tidal, wave, and wind power, geothermal and photothermal [solar] energy, and so on), but collectively these sources are still negligible in the world's total energy consumption. For this reason only hydroelectric and nuclear generation are considered here separately with fossil fuels.

Trade in electrical energy refers to the transfer of generated electrical output via an international grid. Total electricity consumption (residential and nonresidential) is equal to total electricity requirements less transformation and distribution losses.

Coal. The term coal, as used in the table, comprises all grades of anthracite, bituminous, subbituminous, and lignite that have acquired or may in the future, by reason of new technology or changed market prices, acquire an economic value. These types of coal may be differentiated according to heat content (density) and content of impurities. Most coal reserve data are based on proven recoverable reserves only, of all grades of coal. Exceptions are footnoted, with proven in-place reserves reported only when recoverable reserves are unknown. Production figures include deposits removed from both surface and underground workings as well as quantities used by the producers themselves or issued to the miners. Wastes recovered from mines or nearby preparation plants are excluded from production figures.

Natural gas. This term refers to any combustible gas (usually chiefly methane) of natural origin from underground sources. The data for production cover, to the extent possible, gas obtained from gas fields,

Energy

country	electricity													coal		
	installed capacity, 1996 ('000 kW)	production, 1996		power source, 1996			trade, 1996		consumption				reserves, latest ('000,000 metric tons)	production, 1996 ('000 metric tons)	consumption, 1996 ('000 metric tons)
		capacity ('000,000 kW-hr)	amount ('000,000 kW-hr)	fossil fuel (%)	hydro-power (%)	nuclear fuel (%)	exports ('000,000 kW-hr)	imports ('000,000 kW-hr)	amount, 1996 ('000,000 kW-hr)	per capita, 1996 (kW-hr)	residential, 1995 (%)	non-residential, 1995 (%)			
Afghanistan	494	4,327	593	34.2	65.8	—	—	110	703	34	…	…	73	4	4
Albania	1,892	16,574	5,926	6.7	93.3	—	—	200	6,126	1,801	42.9	57.1	15[1]	111	91
Algeria	6,039	52,902	20,654	99.4	0.6	—	422	146	20,378	708	49.5	50.5	47	22	1,202
American Samoa	35	307	130	100.0	—	—	—	—	130	2,321	…	…	—	—	…
Andorra	…	…	…	…	…	…	…	…	…	…	…	…	—	—	…
Angola	617	5,405	1,885	26.0	74.0	—	…	…	1,885	169	29.4	70.6	…	—	—
Antigua and Barbuda	26	228	98	100.0	—	—	—	—	98	1,485	…	…	…	…	…
Argentina	19,920	174,499	69,746	46.2	41.8	12.0	300	3,663	73,109	2,076	30.3	69.7	143	311	1,396
Armenia	3,005	26,324	6,214	37.3	25.3	37.4	3	13	6,224	1,711	…	…	…	…	5
Aruba	90	788	463	100.0	—	—	—	—	463	6,521	…	…	…	…	…
Australia	39,693	347,711	177,326	91.1	8.9	—	—	—	177,326	9,820	…	…	100,244	246,989	109,472
Austria	17,510	153,388	54,835	35.1	64.9	—	8,476	9,428	55,787	6,882	…	…	34	1,108	5,454
Azerbaijan	5,239	45,894	17,088	91.0	9.0	—	580	1,022	17,530	2,308	19.5	80.5	…	…	6
Bahamas, The	401	3,513	1,340	100.0	—	—	—	—	1,340	4,718	…	…	…	—	—
Bahrain	1,100	9,636	5,016	100.0	—	—	—	—	5,016	8,800	53.1	46.9	…	…	…
Bangladesh	3,301	28,917	12,404	94.0	6.0	—	—	—	12,404	103	26.6	73.4	1,054[1]	…	—
Barbados	142	1,244	650	100.0	—	—	—	—	650	2,490	32.7	67.3	…	—	—
Belarus	7,408	64,894	23,728	99.9	0.1	—	2,601	11,144	32,271	3,119	17.1	82.9	…	—	1,116
Belgium	14,938	130,857	76,050	41.4	1.6	57.0	5,446	9,637	80,241	7,899	…	…	410	560	12,343
Belize	35	307	152	59.9	40.1	—	—	25	177	808	89.4	10.6	…	…	…
Benin	15	131	6	100.0	—	—	—	264	270	49	68.4	31.6	…	…	…
Bermuda	146	1,279	525	100.0	—	—	—	—	525	8,203	…	…	…	—	—
Bhutan	371	3,250	1,737	0.4	99.6	—	1,480	4	261	144	…	…	…	2	23
Bolivia	995	8,716	3,216	54.2	45.8	—	3	14	3,227	425	38.4	61.6	1	—	—
Bosnia and Herzegovina	2,407	21,085	2,203	35.5	64.5	—	182	387	2,408	664	…	…	…	1,640	1,640
Botswana	[2]	[2]	[2]	[2]	[2]	[2]	[2]	[2]	[2]	[2]	41.0	59.0	3,858	[2]	[2]
Brazil	60,756	532,223	289,815	7.5	91.7	0.8	8	36,566	326,373	2,026	24.0	76.0	3,136	4,805	17,294
Brunei	475	4,161	1,575	100.0	—	—	—	—	1,575	5,250	47.2	52.8	…	—	—
Bulgaria	12,087	105,882	42,716	52.3	5.6	42.1	2,252	1,803	42,267	4,991	31.0	69.0	2,988	31,302	34,219
Burkina Faso	78	683	223	66.4	33.6	—	—	—	223	21	…	…	…	…	…
Burundi	43	377	120	1.7	98.3	—	—	29	149	24	73.7	26.3	…	…	…
Cambodia	35	307	201	62.2	37.8	—	—	—	201	20	…	…	…	—	—
Cameroon	627	5,493	2,753	3.2	96.8	—	—	—	2,753	203	…	…	…	1	1
Canada	113,612	995,241	555,712	20.8	63.4	15.8	43,839	6,183	518,056	17,455	…	…	9,505	75,871	53,247
Cape Verde	7	61	41	100.0	—	—	—	—	41	104	…	…	…	—	—
Central African Republic	43	377	104	21.2	78.8	—	—	—	104	31	…	…	4	…	…
Chad	29	254	90	100.0	—	—	—	—	90	14	…	…	…	…	…
Chile	5,971	52,306	31,278	39.9	60.1	—	—	—	31,278	2,169	29.2	70.8	1,302	1,157	3,596
China	217,067	1,901,507	1,081,310	81.4	17.4	1.2	4,500	2,100	1,078,910	891	10.8	89.2	126,215	1,397,000	1,383,170
Colombia	10,794	94,555	44,605	22.3	77.7	—	—	164	44,769	1,228	40.9	59.1	5,003	30,065	4,919
Comoros	5	44	17	88.2	11.8	—	—	—	17	27	…	…	…	…	…
Congo, Dem. Rep. of the	3,193	27,971	5,408	0.3	99.7	—	1,038	50	4,420	94	33.2	66.8	97	95	140
Congo, Rep. of the	118	1,034	438	0.7	99.3	—	—	115	553	207	52.7	47.3	…	…	…
Costa Rica	1,165	10,205	4,853	15.5	74.8	9.7[3]	44	188	4,997	1,428	45.3	54.7	…	…	…
Côte d'Ivoire	1,173	10,275	1,918	42.2	57.8	—	—	—	1,918	137	39.0	61.0	…	…	…
Croatia	3,606	31,589	10,548	31.5	68.5	—	1,630	3,960	12,878	2,861	43.2	56.8	43	66	266
Cuba	3,988	34,935	13,236	99.2	0.8	—	—	—	13,236	1,201	25.8	74.2	…	—	163
Cyprus	699	6,123	2,592	100.0	—	—	—	—	2,592	3,429	32.2	67.8	…	—	19
Czech Republic	13,852	121,344	60,977	74.8	4.1	21.1	8,814	8,811	60,974	5,948	…	…	5,668	76,223	67,216
Denmark	11,144	97,621	54,981	97.3	0.1	2.6[3]	19,181	3,782	39,582	7,558	…	…	63	—	10,948
Djibouti	85	745	185	100.0	—	—	—	—	185	300	…	…	…	…	…
Dominica	8	70	37	48.6	51.4	—	—	—	37	521	…	…	…	…	…
Dominican Republic	1,490	13,052	6,847	69.3	30.7	—	—	—	6,847	860	24.3	75.7	…	—	128
East Timor	…	…	…	…	…	—	…	…	…	…	…	…	…	…	…
Ecuador	2,908	25,474	9,260	19.0	81.0	—	—	—	9,260	792	36.7	63.3	26	…	…

petroleum fields, or coal mines that is actually collected and marketed. (Much natural gas in Middle Eastern and North African oil fields is flared [burned] because it is often not economical to capture and market it.) Manufactured gas is generally a by-product of industrial operations such as gasworks, coke ovens, and blast furnaces. It is usually burned at the point of production and rarely enters the marketplace. Production of manufactured gas is, therefore, only reported as a percentage of domestic gas consumption.

Crude petroleum. Crude petroleum is the liquid product obtained from oil wells; the term also includes shale oil, tar sand extract, and field or lease condensate. Production and consumption data in the table refer, so far as possible, to the same year so that the relationship between national production and consumption patterns can be clearly seen; both are given in barrels.

Proven reserves are that oil remaining underground in known fields whose existence has been "proved" by the evaluation of nearby producing wells or by seismic tests in sedimentary strata known to contain crude petroleum, and that is judged recoverable within the limits of present technology and economic conditions (prices). The published proven reserve figures do not necessarily reflect the true reserves of a country, because government authorities or corporations often have political or economic motives for withholding or altering such data.

The estimated exhaustion rate of petroleum reserves is an extrapolated ratio of published proven reserves to the current rate of withdrawal/production. Present world published proven reserves will last about 40 to 45 years at the present rate of withdrawal, but there are large country-to-country variations above or below the average.

Data on petroleum and refined product pipelines are provided because of the great importance to both domestic and international energy markets of this means of bringing these energy sources from their production or transportation points to refineries, intermediate consumption and distribution points, and final consumers. Their traffic may represent a very significant fraction of the total movement of goods within a country. Available data for petroleum pipelines are often incomplete and their basis varies internationally, some countries reporting only international shipments, others reporting domestic shipments of 50 kilometres or more, and so on.

For data in the hydrocarbons portions of the table (coal, natural gas, and petroleum), extensive use has been made of a variety of international sources, such as those of the United Nations, the International Energy Agency (of the Organization for Economic Cooperation and Development), the World Energy Council (in its *World Energy Resources* [triennial]); the U.S. Department of Energy (especially its *International Energy Annual*); and of various industry surveys, such as those published by the *International Petroleum Encyclopedia* and *World Oil.*

country	natural gas						crude petroleum						
	published proven reserves, 2000 ('000,000,-000 cu m)	production		consumption			reserves, 2000		production, 1996 ('000,000 barrels)	consumption, 1996 ('000,000 barrels)	refining capacity, 1998 ('000 barrels per day)	pipelines (latest)	
		natural gas, 1996 ('000,000 cu m)	manufactured gas, 1996 (% of total gas consumption)	amount, 1996 ('000,000 cu m)	residential, 1995 (%)	nonresidential, 1995 (%)	published proven ('000,000 barrels)	years to exhaust proven reserves				length (km)	traffic ('000,000 metric ton-km)
Afghanistan	100	160	…	160	…	…	…	…	—	—	—	…	…
Albania	2.8	23	…	23	13.0	87.0	165	52	3.2	3.3	26	200	…
Algeria	4,522	66,190	20.6	25,981	11.9	88.1	9,200	31	297	165	503	6,910	…
American Samoa	…	…	…	…	…	…	…	…	—	—	—	—	…
Andorra	…	…	…	…	…	…	…	…	—	—	—	—	—
Angola	46	179	11.2	179	…	…	5,412	21	258	12	39	179	…
Antigua and Barbuda	…	…	…	…	…	…	…	…	—	—	—	—	—
Argentina	687	29,693	10.6	31,883	22.9	77.1	2,753	10	288	175	653	6,990	…
Armenia	…	…	…	1,051	…	…	…	…	—	1.03	—	—	—
Aruba	…	…	…	…	…	…	…	…	—	2.3	205	—	—
Australia	1,264	31,732	21.8	20,676	…	…	2,895	19	156	206	807	3,000	…
Austria	26	1,581	12.2	8,668	…	…	86	13	6.8	61	209	777	6,701
Azerbaijan	125	6,091	1.8	6,115	…	…	1,178	18	65	65	442	1,760	1,705
Bahamas, The	…	—	—	…	…	…	…	…	—	—	—	—	—
Bahrain	110	7,008	4.7	7,008	…	…	148	12	12	83	249	72	…
Bangladesh	301	8,278	0.2	8,278	7.4	92.6	57	1,140	0.05	11	33	—	—
Barbados	0.2	29	3.0	29	62.6	37.4	3	7.5	0.4	1.6	4	—	—
Belarus	2.8	222	1.8	12,994	8.1	91.9	198	14	14	91	474	2,570	…
Belgium	—	2.5	17.2	17,274	…	…	…	…	—	231	715	1,328	1,168
Belize	…	…	…	…	…	…	…	…	—	—	—	—	—
Benin	1.2	…	…	…	…	…	8	11	0.7	…	—	—	—
Bermuda	…	…	…	…	…	…	…	…	—	—	—	—	—
Bhutan	…	…	…	…	…	…	…	…	—	—	—	—	—
Bolivia	123	3,866	16.9	1,767	0.1	99.9	132	14	9.6	8.3	48	2,380	…
Bosnia and Herzegovina	…	—	…	252	…	…	…	…	—	…	…	174	—
Botswana	…	…	[2]	…	…	…	—	…	—	[2]	—	—	—
Brazil	226	4,936	53.1	4,936	1.1	98.9	7,357	26	286	485	1,772	5,804	…
Brunei	391	9,218	1.6	1,269	3.5	96.5	1,350	23	60	0.9	9	553	…
Bulgaria	5.9	44	12.5	6,197	…	…	15	75	0.2	51	134	718	259
Burkina Faso	…	…	…	…	…	…	…	…	—	—	—	—	—
Burundi	…	…	…	…	…	…	…	…	—	—	—	—	—
Cambodia	…	…	…	…	…	…	…	…	—	—	—	—	—
Cameroon	110	—	95.6	…	…	…	400	9.5	42	8.5	35	—	—
Canada	1,809	159,020	24.0	81,683	…	…	4,931	8.3	596	490	1,873	23,564	99,908
Cape Verde	…	…	…	…	…	…	…	…	—	—	—	—	—
Central African Republic	…	…	…	…	…	…	…	…	—	—	—	—	—
Chad	…	…	…	…	…	…	…	…	—	—	—	—	—
Chile	98	2,056	33.0	1,983	12.7	87.3	150	44	3.4	63	205	1,540	…
China	1,368	20,067	49.2	20,067	11.2	88.8	24,000	21	1,152	1,157	4,347	9,630	61,200
Colombia	196	5,674	25.4	5,674	6.9	93.1	2,577	11	230	110	249	4,935	…
Comoros	…	…	…	…	…	…	…	…	—	—	—	—	—
Congo, Dem. Rep. of the	1.0	—	…	—	—	—	187	22	8.4	0.5	17	390	…
Congo, Rep. of the	91	3.4	58.1	3.4	…	…	1,506	19	78	12	21	25	…
Costa Rica	…	—	4.3	—	—	—	…	…	—	4.5	15	176	…
Côte d'Ivoire	30	—	60.0	—	—	—	100	11	9.2	31	69	—	—
Croatia	35	1,739	18.7	2,584	16.3	83.7	92	8	11	38	236	690	89
Cuba	18	43	84.3	43	3.4	96.6	284	30	9.4	44	301	—	—
Cyprus	—	—	61.2	—	—	—	…	…	—	6	27	—	—
Czech Republic	4.0	256	17.3	10,621	…	…	15	15	1.0	52	198	—	—
Denmark	96	6,537	13.8	4,185	…	…	1,069	14	78	81	135	688	2,212
Djibouti	…	…	…	…	…	…	…	…	—	—	—	—	—
Dominica	…	…	…	…	…	…	—	—	—	—	—	—	—
Dominican Republic	—	—	11.5	…	…	…	…	…	—	17	51	104	…
East Timor	…	…	…	…	…	…	…	…	…	…	…	…	…
Ecuador	104	534	28.6	534	—	—	2,115	15	137	58	176	2,158	…

Energy (continued)

country	electricity: installed capacity, 1996 ('000 kW)	production, 1996: capacity ('000,000 kW-hr)	production, 1996: amount ('000,000 kW-hr)	power source, 1996: fossil fuel (%)	power source, 1996: hydro-power (%)	power source, 1996: nuclear fuel (%)	trade, 1996: exports ('000,000 kW-hr)	trade, 1996: imports ('000,000 kW-hr)	consumption: amount, 1996 ('000,000 kW-hr)	consumption: per capita, 1996 (kW-hr)	consumption: resi-dential, 1995 (%)	consumption: non-resi-dential, 1995 (%)	coal: reserves, latest ('000,000 metric tons)	coal: pro-duction, 1996 ('000 metric tons)	coal: con-sump-tion, 1996 ('000 metric tons)
Egypt	16,617	145,565	50,660	78.0	22.0	—	—	—	50,660	801	35.4	64.6	58	—	1,876
El Salvador	980	8,585	3,452	33.0	54.5	12.5[3]	21	42	3,473	599	34.2	65.8	…	…	…
Equatorial Guinea	5	44	20	90.0	10.0	—	—	—	20	49	…	…	…	…	…
Eritrea	…	…	…	…	…	…	…	…	…	…	…	…	…	…	…
Estonia	2,699	23,643	9,103	99.9	0.1	—	1,100	240	8,243	5,604	17.7	82.3	…	14,735	16,131
Ethiopia	486	4,257	1,675	5.8	90.0	4.2[3]	—	—	1,675	27	28.8	71.2	11	—	—
Faroe Islands	92	806	180	56.1	43.3	0.6[3]	—	—	180	3,830	…	…	…	—	—
Fiji	200	1,752	545	21.1	78.9	—	—	—	545	684	25.7	74.3	…	—	22
Finland	14,479	126,836	75,868	58.7	15.6	25.7	1,706	5,367	79,529	15,515	…	…	…	—	7,704
France	109,443[4]	958,721[4]	507,582[4]	7.8[4]	13.8[4]	78.4[4]	72,428[4]	3,617[4]	438,771[4]	7,518[4]	…	…	153	8,109[4]	24,707[4]
French Guiana	165	1,445	450	100.0	—	—	—	—	450	2,941	…	…	…	…	…
French Polynesia	89	780	360	62.8	37.2	—	—	—	360	1,614	…	…	…	…	…
Gabon	310	2,716	949	23.3	76.7	—	—	—	949	858	28.1	71.9	…	…	…
Gambia, The	29	254	76	100.0	—	—	—	—	76	67	…	…	…	…	…
Gaza Strip	…	…	…	…	…	…	…	…	…	…	…	…	…	…	…
Georgia	4,558	39,928	7,195	15.0	85.0	—	280	400	7,315	1,344	…	…	…	20	230
Germany	115,443	1,011,281	544,443	65.5	4.9	29.6	42,670	37,404	539,177	6,582	…	…	74,186	240,396	264,937
Ghana	1,187	10,398	6,631	0.1	99.9	—	230	4	6,405	359	7.0	93.0	…	—	3
Greece	8,943	78,341	47,079	90.4	9.5	0.1[3]	1,314	2,664	48,429	4,617	…	…	3,307	59,781	62,894
Greenland	106	929	258	100.0	—	—	—	—	258	4,448	…	…	202	…	…
Grenada	12	105	95	100.0	—	—	—	—	95	1,033	88.1	11.9	…	…	…
Guadeloupe	388	3,399	1,015	100.0	—	—	—	—	1,015	2,355	…	…	…	…	…
Guam	302	2,646	825	100.0	—	—	—	—	825	5,392	…	…	…	…	…
Guatemala	766	6,710	3,500	33.2	66.8	—	—	—	3,500	320	34.0	66.0	…	…	…
Guernsey	…	…	…	…	…	…	…	…	…	…	…	…	…	…	…
Guinea	186	1,629	541	65.2	34.8	—	—	—	541	72	…	…	…	…	…
Guinea-Bissau	11	96	43	100.0	—	—	—	—	43	39	…	…	…	…	…
Guyana	114	999	328	98.5	1.5	—	—	14	342	408	…	…	…	…	…
Haiti	153	1,340	633	59.7	40.3	—	—	—	633	87	46.2	53.8	13[1]	…	…
Honduras	475	4,161	2,815	8.2	91.8	—	…	4	2,819	485	54.5	45.5	21[1]	…	…
Hong Kong	10,067	88,187	28,440	100.0	—	—	531	7,778	35,687	5,764	25.2	74.8	…	—	6,769
Hungary	7,012	61,425	34,217	58.0	0.6	41.4	1,276	3,473	36,414	3,624	61.3	38.7	4,917	15,190	16,044
Iceland	1,083	9,487	5,131	0.2	93.0	6.8[3]	—	—	5,131	18,934	…	…	…	—	66
India	96,803	847,994	432,339	81.1	17.0	1.9	50	1,625	433,914	459	15.1	84.9	77,103	307,803	319,233
Indonesia	21,312	186,693	73,794	81.4	15.1	3.5[3]	—	—	73,794	368	32.9	67.1	35,343	47,339	15,796
Iran	26,750	234,330	82,600	90.8	9.2	—	—	—	82,600	1,180	31.6	68.4	213	1,135	1,460
Iraq	9,500	83,220	29,660	98.0	2.0	—	—	—	29,660	1,439	…	…	…	—	—
Ireland	4,410	38,632	19,177	94.7	5.1	0.2[3]	182	53	19,048	5,360	…	…	15	1	2,831
Isle of Man	…	…	…	100.0	—	—	—	—	…	…	…	…	…	…	…
Israel	4,480	39,245	32,466	99.9	0.1	—	305	—	32,161	5,678	29.1	70.9	…	—	7,808
Italy	68,146[6]	596,959[6]	241,413[6]	78.9[6]	19.5[6]	1.6[3, 6]	760[6]	38,149[6]	278,802[6]	4,870[6]	…	…	37	296[6]	16,646[6]
Jamaica	1,182	10,354	6,038	97.9	2.1	—	—	—	6,038	2,424	14.4	85.6	…	—	64
Japan	233,737	2,047,536	1,012,145	60.9	8.8	30.3	—	—	1,012,145	8,074	…	…	905	6,496	132,621
Jersey	…	…	…	…	…	…	…	…	…	…	…	…	…	…	…
Jordan	1,260	11,038	6,058	99.6	0.4	—	—	…	6,058	1,085	27.4	72.6	…	…	…
Kazakhstan	18,960	166,090	58,657	87.5	12.5	—	12,705	19,550	65,502	3,894	10.6	89.4	25,000[1]	76,597	55,852
Kenya	809	7,087	3,745	8.9	83.3	7.8[3]	—	175	3,920	141	30.1	69.9	…	—	100
Kiribati	2	18	7	100.0	—	—	—	—	7	88	…	…	…	—	—
Korea, North	9,500	83,220	35,000	35.7	64.3	—	—	—	35,000	1,558	…	…	661	95,900	97,790
Korea, South	39,239	343,734	227,554	65.2	2.3	32.5	—	—	227,554	5,022	16.2	83.8	202	4,951	50,277
Kuwait	6,988	61,215	25,925	100.0	—	—	—	—	25,925	15,368	93.2	6.8	…	…	…
Kyrgyzstan	3,688	32,307	13,480	9.1	90.9	—	9,196	7,116	11,400	2,551	25.4	…	812[1]	410	1,018
Laos	256	2,243	1,249	3.4	96.6	—	782	50	517	103	…	…	…	1	1
Latvia	2,092	18,326	3,123	40.4	59.6	—	211	3,438	6,350	2,536	23.4	76.6	…	—	293
Lebanon	1,220	10,687	5,795	86.3	13.7	—	—	50	5,845	1,895	54.5	45.5	…	—	200
Lesotho	[2]	[2]	[2]	[2]	[2]	[2]	[2]	[2]	[2]	[2]	…	…	…	[2]	[2]
Liberia	332	2,908	488	63.1	36.9	—	—	—	488	217	…	…	…	…	…
Libya	4,600	40,296	18,300	100.0	—	—	—	—	18,300	3,272	…	…	—	—	5
Liechtenstein	[8]	[8]	[8]	[8]	[8]	[8]	[8]	[8]	[8]	[8]	…	…	…	—	[8]
Lithuania	6,335	55,495	16,789	11.8	5.2	83.0	9,341	4,182	11,630	3,120	16.2	83.8	…	…	338
Luxembourg	1,265	11,081	1,307	33.0	67.0	—	808	5,712	6,211	15,075	…	…	…	—	242
Macau	367	3,215	1,620	100.0	—	—	1	175	1,794	4,077	82.8	17.2	…	—	—
Macedonia	1,494	13,087	6,489	87.5	12.5	—	…	…	6,489	2,985	44.5	55.5	…	7,145	7,330
Madagascar	220	1,927	683	37.8	62.2	—	—	—	683	44	32.2	67.8	1,075[1]	—	14
Malawi	185	1,621	874	2.2	97.8	—	2	—	872	89	65.2	34.8	2	—	17
Malaysia	11,800	103,368	53,000	90.3	9.7	—	14	—	52,986	2,575	17.3	82.7	4	83	2,416
Maldives	25	219	63	100.0	—	—	—	—	63	240	…	…	…	…	…
Mali	114	999	335	36.7	63.3	—	—	—	335	30	…	…	—	…	…
Malta	250	2,190	1,514	100.0	—	—	—	—	1,514	4,103	29.2	70.8	…	—	310
Marshall Islands	99[10]	867[10]	…	…	…	—	—	—	…	…	…	…	…	…	…
Martinique	115	1,007	906	100.0	—	—	—	—	906	2,359	…	…	…	…	…
Mauritania	105	920	153	81.7	18.3	—	—	—	153	66	…	…	…	—	6
Mauritius	364	3,189	1,255	91.8	8.2	—	—	—	1,255	1,112	65.2	34.8	…	—	67
Mayotte	…	…	…	…	…	—	—	—	…	…	…	…	…	…	…
Mexico	44,258	387,700	162,526	72.1	19.5	8.4[3]	1,288	1,387	162,625	1,754	29.7	70.3	1,335	10,372	11,725
Micronesia	…	…	…	…	…	—	…	…	…	…	…	…	…	…	…
Moldova	1,060	9,286	6,122	94.0	6.0	—	4	1,610	7,728	1,739	…	…	…	—	1,124
Monaco	[4]	[4]	[4]	[4]	[4]	[4]	[4]	[4]	[4]	[4]	…	…	…	[4]	[4]
Mongolia	901	7,893	2,580	100.0	—	—	—	395	2,975	1,183	29.8[11]	70.2[11]	24,000[1]	5,111	4,928
Morocco	3,962	34,707	12,178	93.7	6.3	—	—	1,050	13,228	490	28.0	72.0	50	504	2,649
Mozambique	2,383	20,875	568	91.2	8.8	—	—	600	1,168	66	33.2	66.8	265	40	60
Myanmar (Burma)	1,393	12,203	4,256	61.7	38.3	—	—	—	4,256	93	43.0	57.0	3	72	78
Namibia	[2]	[2]	[2]	[2]	[2]	[2]	[2]	[2]	[2]	[2]	…	…	…	[2]	[2]
Nauru	10	88	32	100.0	—	—	—	—	32	2,909	…	…	…	…	…
Nepal	292	2,558	1,218	5.3	94.7	—	90	115	1,243	56	38.5	61.5	…	—	50

natural gas						crude petroleum							country
published proven reserves, 2000 ('000,000,000 cu m)	production		consumption			reserves, 2000		production, 1996 ('000,000 barrels)	consumption, 1996 ('000,000 barrels)	refining capacity, 1998 ('000 barrels per day)	pipelines (latest)		
	natural gas, 1996 ('000,000 cu m)	manufactured gas, 1996 (% of total gas consumption)	amount, 1996 ('000,000 cu m)	residential, 1995 (%)	nonresidential, 1995 (%)	published proven ('000,000 barrels)	years to exhaust proven reserves				length (km)	traffic ('000,000 metric ton-km)	
996	14,435	13.1	14,435	5.1	94.9	2,948	9	311	205	578	1,767	...	Egypt
—	—	14.7	—	—	—	...	...	—	5.4	20	—	—	El Salvador
37	...	...	...	...	...	12	1.9	6.3	...	—	—	—	Equatorial Guinea
...	...	...	...	...	...	...	...	...	...	18	—	—	Eritrea
...	...	...	689	8.2	91.8	—	—	—	...	...	—	—	Estonia
25	—	100.0	—	...	...	0.4	...	—	5.5	—	—	—	Ethiopia
...	...	...	...	...	...	...	...	—	—	—	—	—	Faroe Islands
...	—	—	—	—	—	...	...	—	—	—	—	—	Fiji
—	—	31.5	3,582	...	...	...	...	—	72	200	—	—	Finland
14	2,985	18.3[4]	40,549[4]	32.4[4]	67.6[4]	107	7.1	15	623[4]	1,947	7,546	22,501	France
...	...	...	...	...	...	...	...	—	—	—	—	—	French Guiana
...	...	...	...	...	...	...	...	—	—	—	—	—	French Polynesia
34	826	1.3	826	19.7	80.3	2,499	18	141	6.1	17	284	...	Gabon
...	...	...	...	...	...	...	...	—	—	—	—	—	Gambia, The
...	...	...	...	...	...	...	...	—	—	—	—	—	Gaza Strip
8.5	2.9	...	918	...	...	35	38	0.9	0.9	106	670	...	Georgia
339	24,070	15.1	111,999	...	...	357	17	21	758	2,246	7,590	13,872	Germany
24	—	94.8	—	—	—	17	8.5	2	7.3	45	—	—	Ghana
1.0	54	106.6	57	...	...	10	3.2	3.1	128	388	573	...	Greece
...	...	...	...	...	...	...	...	—	—	—	—	—	Greenland
...	...	...	...	...	...	...	...	—	—	—	—	—	Grenada
...	...	...	...	...	...	...	...	—	—	—	—	—	Guadeloupe
...	—	100.0	—	—	—	...	...	—	—	—	—	—	Guam
3.1	11	5.2	11	...	...	526	99	5.3	5.2	20	275	...	Guatemala
...	...	...	...	...	...	...	...	—	—	—	—	—	Guernsey
...	...	...	...	...	...	...	...	—	—	—	—	—	Guinea
...	...	...	...	...	...	...	...	—	—	—	—	—	Guinea-Bissau
...	...	...	...	...	...	...	...	—	—	—	—	—	Guyana
...	...	...	...	...	...	...	...	—	—	—	—	—	Haiti
—	—	...	—	—	—	...	...	—	...	14[5]	—	—	Honduras
...	—	76.0	—	—	—	...	...	—	—	—	—	—	Hong Kong
81	4,614	6.5	13,115	...	...	110	11	9.9	45	232	1,204	2,607	Hungary
...	...	...	...	...	...	...	...	—	—	—	—	—	Iceland
648	27,113	12.1	27,113	1.3	98.7	4,838	19	252	502	1,142	5,692	...	India
2,046	76,442	11.1	38,885	2.7	97.3	4,980	8.9	559	311	930	2,961	...	Indonesia
23,002	40,055	10.3	40,055	26.8	73.2	89,700	68	1,318	351	1,448	9,800	...	Iran
3,109	3,240	44.8	3,240	...	...	112,500	418	269	209	348	5,075	...	Iraq
20	2,535	2.7	2,566	...	...	—	...	—	16	67	—	—	Ireland
...	—	...	...	...	...	...	...	—	...	...	—	—	Isle of Man
0.3	13	112.7	13	—	100.0	4	133	0.03	77	220	998	...	Israel
229	20,499	12.7[6]	49,513[6]	...	...	622	17	37	550	2,446	3,851	11,348	Italy
—	—	27.9	—	—	—	...	...	—	7.8	36	10	...	Jamaica
40	2,230	40.6	63,574	...	...	59	16	3.8	1,607	5,059	406	...	Japan
...	...	...	...	...	...	...	...	—	—	—	—	—	Jersey
6.8	294[7]	68.8	—	—	—	0.9	...	...	23	90	209	...	Jordan
1,841	7,107	0.7	10,609	...	...	5,417	36	150	63	427	4,350	22,300	Kazakhstan
—	—	103.2	—	—	—	...	...	—	13	90	483	...	Kenya
...	...	...	...	...	...	...	...	—	—	—	—	—	Kiribati
...	...	...	...	...	...	...	...	—	16	71	37	...	Korea, North
—	—	33.4	12,814	...	...	...	...	—	722	2,540	455	...	Korea, South
1,492	9,098	44.4	9,098	25.0	75.0	96,500	132	731	283	886	917	...	Kuwait
5.7	26	...	1,053	...	...	40	67	0.6	0.5	10	—	—	Kyrgyzstan
...	...	...	...	...	...	...	...	—	—	—	136	...	Laos
...	—	...	938	10.5	89.5	...	...	—	...	...	1,530	...	Latvia
—	—	...	...	...	...	...	...	—	...	38	72	...	Lebanon
—	—	[2]	—	...	...	...	...	—	[2]	—	—	—	Lesotho
—	—	...	—	...	...	...	...	—	—	15	—	—	Liberia
1,314	6,392	18.9	5,192	...	...	29,500	59	504	113	348	4,826	...	Libya
—	—	[8]	[8]	...	...	...	...	—	[8]	—	—	—	Liechtenstein
—	...	11.3	2,327	9.3	90.7	12	11	1.1	28	263	105	...	Lithuania
...	—	15.4	713	...	...	...	...	—	[9]	—	48	...	Luxembourg
...	...	...	...	...	...	...	...	—	—	—	—	—	Macau
...	—	36.9	...	...	...	...	...	—	6.0	51	—	—	Macedonia
2.0	—	33.6	—	...	...	...	...	—	1.5	15	—	—	Madagascar
...	—	—	—	—	—	...	...	—	—	—	—	—	Malawi
2,313	35,268	8.4	18,885	2.5	97.5	3,900	15	258	132	474	1,307	...	Malaysia
...	...	...	...	...	...	...	...	—	—	—	—	—	Maldives
...	...	...	...	...	...	...	...	—	—	—	—	—	Mali
—	...	—	...	...	...	...	...	—	—	—	—	—	Malta
...	...	...	...	...	...	...	...	—	—	...	—	—	Marshall Islands
—	—	161.5	...	...	...	...	...	—	5.8	16	—	—	Martinique
...	...	88.4	...	...	...	...	...	—	6.9	—	—	—	Mauritania
...	...	...	...	...	...	...	...	—	—	—	—	—	Mauritius
...	...	...	...	...	...	...	...	—	—	—	—	—	Mayotte
851	28,464	24.4	30,850	...	...	28,399	27	1,034	487	1,525	38,350	...	Mexico
...	...	...	...	...	...	...	...	—	—	...	—	—	Micronesia
...	—	...	3,503	11.6	88.4	...	...	—	...	...	—	—	Moldova
...	...	[4]	[4]	...	...	...	...	—	[4]	—	—	—	Monaco
...	...	...	...	...	...	...	...	—	—	—	—	—	Mongolia
1.4	20	25.0	20	—	100.0	1.9	...	...	46	157	362	...	Morocco
57	—	—	—	...	...	...	...	—	—	...	595	...	Mozambique
283	1,576	0.6	1,576	—	...	50	18	2.8	5.3	32	1,343	...	Myanmar (Burma)
85	—	[2]	—	...	...	...	...	—	[2]	—	—	—	Namibia
...	...	...	...	...	...	...	...	—	—	—	—	—	Nauru
...	—	—	—	—	—	...	...	—	—	—	—	—	Nepal

Energy (continued)

country	electricity												coal		
	installed capacity, 1996 ('000 kW)	production, 1996		power source, 1996			trade, 1996		consumption				reserves, latest ('000,000 metric tons)	production, 1996 ('000 metric tons)	consumption, 1996 ('000 metric tons)
		capacity ('000,000 kW-hr)	amount ('000,000 kW-hr)	fossil fuel (%)	hydro-power (%)	nuclear fuel (%)	exports ('000,000 kW-hr)	imports ('000,000 kW-hr)	amount, 1996 ('000,000 kW-hr)	per capita, 1996 (kW-hr)	residential, 1995 (%)	non-residential, 1995 (%)			
Netherlands, The	19,012	166,545	85,089	94.5	0.1	5.4	699	11,288	95,678	6,143	...	...	548	—	14,996
Netherlands Antilles	220	1,927	1,482	100.0	—	—	—	—	1,482	7,600	...	...	...	...	...
New Caledonia	253	2,216	1,567	69.6	30.4	—	—	—	1,567	8,516	...	...	2	—	168
New Zealand	7,520	65,875	35,932	22.8	71.6	5.6[3]	—	—	35,932	9,976	...	...	129	3,611	2,438
Nicaragua	457	4,003	1,919	50.2	18.5	31.3[3]	10	14	1,923	454	31.5	68.5	...	...	...
Niger	63	552	177	100.0	—	—	—	196	373	39	49.2	50.8	77	173	173
Nigeria	5,881	51,518	14,820	59.5	40.5	—	...	—	14,820	129	50.1	49.9	209	50	50
Northern Mariana Islands	...	...	...	...	...	—	...	—	...	...	...	...	...	...	...
Norway	27,681	242,486	104,756	0.7	99.3	—	4,236	3,212	103,732	23,830	...	...	4	230	934
Oman	2,037	17,844	8,979	100.0	—	—	—	—	8,979	3,901	...	...	...	...	...
Pakistan	12,969	113,608	56,946	58.4	40.8	0.8	—	—	56,946	407	37.8	62.2	809	3,638	4,718
Palau	62	543	208	85.6	14.4	—	—	—	208	896	...	...	—	—	—
Panama	959	8,401	3,958	24.1	75.9	—	20	44	3,978	1,486	74.5	25.5	...	—	56
Papua New Guinea	490	4,292	1,790	72.3	27.7	—	—	—	1,790	407	28.0	72.0	...	...	1
Paraguay	6,553	57,404	48,200	0.3	99.7	—	40,262	—	7,938	1,601	58.2	41.8	...	...	...
Peru	3,845	33,682	20,038	17.5	82.5	—	—	—	20,038	837	37.7	62.3	1,168	58	302
Philippines	8,646	75,739	34,775	63.5	19.0	17.5[3]	—	—	34,775	502	27.7	72.3	289	1,109	2,589
Poland	29,469	258,148	139,790	97.2	2.8	—	7,925	4,801	136,666	3,540	15.3	84.7	46,407	200,939	173,219
Portugal	9,348	81,888	33,540	55.5	44.3	0.2	3,005	4,116	34,651	3,533	...	...	40	—	5,471
Puerto Rico	4,575	40,077	19,029	98.3	1.7	—	—	—	19,029	5,093	...	...	...	—	170
Qatar	1,445	12,658	6,340	100.0	—	—	—	—	6,340	11,362	83.7	16.3	...	...	...
Réunion	339	2,970	1,132	55.4	44.6	—	—	—	1,132	1,705	...	...	...	...	...
Romania	22,856	200,219	61,350	72.1	25.7	2.2	1,435	2,242	62,157	2,744	14.4	85.6	3,437	41,869	45,477
Russia	210,857	1,847,107	847,200	68.8	19.5	11.7	31,800	12,300	827,700	5,588	18.3	81.7	264,762	260,100	247,111
Rwanda	34	298	164	2.4	97.6	—	3	14	175	32	...	...	...	...	...
St. Kitts and Nevis	16	140	82	100.0	—	—	—	—	82	2,000	...	...	...	...	...
St. Lucia	22	193	115	100.0	—	—	—	—	115	799	...	...	...	...	...
St. Vincent and the Grenadines	14	123	66	68.2	31.8	—	—	—	66	584	...	...	...	...	...
Samoa	19	166	65	61.5	38.5	—	—	—	65	392	...	...	...	...	...
San Marino	[6]	[6]	[6]	[6]	[6]	[6]	[6]	[6]	[6]	[6]	...	...	...	[6]	[6]
São Tomé and Príncipe	6	53	15	46.7	53.3	—	—	—	15	111	...	...	...	...	...
Saudi Arabia	21,110	184,924	104,118	100.0	—	—	—	—	104,118	5,528	47.2	52.8	...	...	...
Senegal	235	2,059	1,160	100.0	—	—	—	—	1,160	136	21.2	78.8	...	...	...
Seychelles	28	245	128	100.0	—	—	—	—	128	1,730	32.0	68.0	...	...	...
Sierra Leone	126	1,104	241	100.0	—	—	—	—	241	56	...	...	...	—	—
Singapore	5,600	49,056	23,458	100.0	—	—	—	—	23,458	6,932	16.0	84.0	...	—	1
Slovakia	7,438	65,157	25,278	37.5	17.9	44.6	698	4,220	28,800	5,386	20.6	79.4	251	3,829	12,199
Slovenia	2,495	21,856	12,770	35.5	28.8	35.7	2,516	855	11,109	5,774	24.8	75.2	...	4,768	4,961
Solomon Islands	12	105	32	100.0	—	—	—	—	32	82	...	...	...	...	...
Somalia	70[5]	613[5]	259[5]	100.0[5]	—	—	—	—	259[5]	29[5]	...	...	...	...	...
South Africa	35,897[2]	314,458[2]	193,096[2]	93.1[2]	0.8[2]	6.1[2]	5,579[2]	720	188,237[2]	3,888[2]	14.1	85.9	60,994	207,488[2]	136,903[2]
Spain	45,889	401,988	172,888	43.0	23.7	33.3	5,690	6,750	173,948	4,384	...	...	1,598	27,292	41,528
Sri Lanka	1,555	13,622	4,366	25.6	74.4	—	—	—	4,366	241	22.6	77.4	...	—	—
Sudan, The	500	4,380	1,338	29.3	70.7	—	—	—	1,338	49	18.6	81.4	...	—	—
Suriname	425	3,723	1,621	20.8	79.2	—	—	—	1,621	3,752	...	...	...	—	—
Swaziland	[2]	[2]	[2]	[2]	[2]	[2]	[2]	...	[2]	[2]	...	...	1,229	[2]	[2]
Sweden	29,726	260,400	138,676	9.9	37.2	52.9	9,747	15,885	144,814	16,421	...	...	1	...	3,662
Switzerland	16,657[8]	145,915[8]	57,063[8]	3.9[8]	52.0[8]	44.1[8]	24,187[8]	23,241[8]	56,117[8]	7,735[8]	...	...	...	—	183[8]
Syria	4,430	38,807	17,278	85.2	14.8	—	—	—	17,278	1,186	34.6	65.4	...	—	—
Taiwan	23,763	208,164	124,973	63.7	7.2	29.1	—	—	111,140	5,183	21.5	78.5	109	147	...
Tajikistan	4,443	38,921	15,000	1.2	98.8	—	4,610	4,930	15,320	2,581	14.6	85.4	...	20	120
Tanzania	543	4,757	1,737	14.1	85.9	—	—	—	1,737	56	36.6	63.4	221	5	5
Thailand	18,513	162,174	91,467	92.0	8.0	—	89	805	92,183	1,570	19.7	80.3	1,101	21,477	24,826
Togo	34	298	93	93.5	6.5	—	—	315	408	97	...	...	...	...	...
Tonga	7	61	34	100.0	—	—	—	—	34	347	...	...	...	...	...
Trinidad and Tobago	1,150	10,074	4,541	100.0	—	—	—	—	4,541	3,501	26.5	73.5	...	—	—
Tunisia	1,719	15,058	7,837	99.1	0.9	—	149	163	7,851	857	26.4	73.6	—	...	2
Turkey	20,954	183,557	96,143	57.8	42.1	0.1[3]	343	270	96,070	1,555	...	...	7,879	56,329	63,106
Turkmenistan	3,950	34,602	10,100	100.0	0.0	—	3,750	950	7,300	1,757	...	...	...	...	100
Tuvalu	...	...	...	...	...	...	...	...	...	...	...	...	...	...	...
Uganda	162	1,419	793	0.9	99.1	—	115	—	678	33	...	...	...	...	...
Ukraine	54,243	475,169	181,709	66.1	6.3	27.6	13,200	11,200	179,709	3,482	...	...	...	74,800	83,800
United Arab Emirates	5,490	48,092	19,250	100.0	—	—	—	—	19,250	8,518	...	...	...	...	...
United Kingdom	73,262	641,775	347,052	71.2	1.4	27.4	37	16,714	363,729	6,232	...	...	2,756	50,197	71,056
United States	783,502	6,863,478	3,459,974	70.0	10.0	20.0	9,021	46,543	3,497,496	12,980	...	...	271,877	966,287	894,180
Uruguay	2,174	19,044	6,666	7.0	93.0	—	437	309	6,538	2,041	45.4	54.6	...	—	—
Uzbekistan	11,733	102,781	45,418	85.6	14.4	—	12,826	13,918	46,510	2,004	...	...	...	2,837	2,880
Vanuatu	11	96	30	100.0	—	—	—	—	30	172	...	...	...	...	...
Venezuela	19,975	174,981	74,968	25.3	74.7	—	151	—	74,817	3,353	21.3	78.7	460	3,486	328
Vietnam	4,587	40,182	16,320	14.1	82.1	3.8[3]	—	—	16,320	217	32.6	67.4	165	9,823	5,551
Virgin Islands (U.S.)	323	2,829	1,075	100.0	—	—	—	—	1,075	10,142	...	...	...	—	250
West Bank	...	...	...	...	...	...	...	...	...	...	...	...	...	...	...
Western Sahara	56	491	87	100.0	—	—	—	—	87	340	...	...	...	...	...
Yemen	810	7,096	2,334	100.0	—	—	—	—	2,334	149	...	...	1	...	...
Yugoslavia	11,779	103,184	38,093	70.5	29.5	—	156	—	37,937	3,685	41.4	...	18,222	38,445	38,505
Zambia	2,436	21,339	7,795	0.5	99.5	—	1,500	20	6,315	763	10.5	89.5	61	350	345
Zimbabwe	2,071	18,142	7,819	72.3	27.7	—	...	3,172	10,991	961	16.5	83.5	809	5,247	5,242

natural gas						crude petroleum							country
published proven reserves, 2000 ('000,000,000 cu m)	production		consumption			reserves, 2000		production, 1996 ('000,000 barrels)	consumption, 1996 ('000,000 barrels)	refining capacity, 1998 ('000 barrels per day)	pipelines (latest)		
	natural gas, 1996 ('000,000 cu m)	manufactured gas, 1996 (% of total gas consumption)	amount, 1996 ('000,000 cu m)	residential, 1995 (%)	nonresidential, 1995 (%)	published proven ('000,000 barrels)	years to exhaust proven reserves				length (km)	traffic ('000,000 metric ton-km)	
1,771	100,200	18.4	54,789	…	…	107	7.1	15	397	1,188	1,383	5,503	Netherlands, The
—	—	114.5	…	…	…	…	…	—	99	250	—	—	Netherlands Antilles
…	…	…	…	…	…	…	…	—	—	—	—	—	New Caledonia
69	4,781	7.0	4,780	…	…	127	7.9	16	35	98	160	…	New Zealand
—	—	67.6	—	—	—	…	…	—	4.5	19	56	…	Nicaragua
…	—	—	—	—	—	…	…	—	—	—	—	—	Niger
3,511	4,470	1.5	4,470	—	100.0	22,500	33	679	47	439	5,042	…	Nigeria
…	…	…	…	…	…	…	…	—	—	…	—	—	Northern Mariana Islands
1,172	42,714	38.5	3,713	…	…	10,787	9	1,193	109	312	53	11,019	Norway
805	4,723	1.5	4,723	…	…	5,283	16	323	27	85	1,300	…	Oman
612	17,894	1.1	17,894	19.3	80.7	208	9.9	21	51	139	1,135	…	Pakistan
—	—	—	…	…	…	—	—	—	…	…	—	—	Palau
—	—	31.9	61	—	—	…	…	—	13	60	130	…	Panama
154	83	…	83	—	—	333	11	29	0.4	—	—	—	Papua New Guinea
—	—	1.5	…	…	…	…	…	—	1.1	8	—	—	Paraguay
255	208	46.4	208	61.4	38.6	355	8.1	44	52	182	800	…	Peru
79	—	54.7	—	—	—	289	963	0.3	117	389	357	…	Philippines
145	4,810	23.7	14,160	45.0	55.0	115	48	2.4	108	382	2,280	11,932	Poland
—	—	40.7	…	…	…	…	…	—	86	304	80	…	Portugal
—	—	128.7	…	…	…	…	…	—	44	49	—	—	Puerto Rico
8,495	13,700	11.4	13,700	—	100.0	3,700	26	141	22	58	235	…	Qatar
…	…	…	…	…	…	…	…	—	…	—	—	—	Réunion
374	14,460	9.8	20,401	9.6	90.4	1,426	29	50	103	522	4,229	2,558	Romania
48,139	555,880	4.9	373,589	11.2	88.8	48,573	22	2,160	1,315	6,733	63,000	1,899,000	Russia
57	0.2	—	0.2	…	…	…	…	—	—	—	—	—	Rwanda
…	…	…	…	…	…	…	…	—	—	—	—	—	St. Kitts and Nevis
…	…	…	…	…	…	…	…	—	—	—	—	—	St. Lucia
…	…	…	…	…	…	…	…	—	—	—	—	—	St. Vincent and the Grenadines
…	…	…	…	…	…	…	…	…	…	—	—	—	Samoa
…	…	[6]	[6]	…	…	…	…	—	[6]	—	—	—	San Marino
…	…	…	…	…	…	…	…	—	—	—	—	—	São Tomé and Príncipe
5,791	41,339	48.2	41,339	…	…	263,500	90	2,935	635	1,685	6,550	…	Saudi Arabia
—	—	13.7	…	…	…	…	…	—	6.4	17	—	—	Senegal
…	…	…	…	…	…	…	…	—	—	—	—	—	Seychelles
—	…	…	…	…	…	…	…	—	1.7	10	—	—	Sierra Leone
—	—	347.7	—	—	—	…	…	—	432	1,172	—	—	Singapore
15	262	12.9	5,743	20.9	79.1	9	18	0.5	38	115	…	…	Slovakia
4	12	…	782	7.7	92.3	7	…	…	3.3	12	290	128	Slovenia
…	—	—	—	—	—	…	…	—	—	—	—	—	Solomon Islands
5.7	—	…	…	…	…	…	…	—	…	10	15	…	Somalia
22	1,840	56.6[2]	1,840	…	…	29	0.5	54	159[2]	469	2,679	…	South Africa
1.7	484	27.9	9,931	…	…	14	3.7	3.8	409	1,316	2,059	5,266	Spain
—	—	49.5	—	—	—	…	…	—	15	48	62	…	Sri Lanka
85	—	58.3	…	…	…	262	29	9.1	7.6	22	815	…	Sudan, The
—	…	…	…	…	…	74	49	1.5	1.2	—	—	—	Suriname
…	…	[2]	…	…	…	…	…	…	[2]	—	—	—	Swaziland
—	—	39.4	868	…	…	…	…	…	141	427	—	—	Sweden
—	—	14.0[8]	2,902[8]	…	…	…	…	…	39[8]	132	314	1,265	Switzerland
241	2,614	9.3	2,614	…	…	2,500	13	189	84	242	1,819	…	Syria
76	909	…	4,440	15.9	84.1	4	10	0.3	265	770	615	…	Taiwan
5.7	54	…	1,276	…	…	12	…	0.1	0.1	…	—	—	Tajikistan
28	—	100.0	—	…	…	…	…	…	4.3	15	982	…	Tanzania
355	13,274	20.9	13,274	—	100.0	296	33	8.9	221	713	67	…	Thailand
—	…	…	…	…	…	…	…	…	…	—	—	—	Togo
…	…	…	…	…	…	…	…	…	…	—	—	—	Tonga
560	7,509	6.9	7,509	1.8	98.2	605	13	47	40	160	1,051	…	Trinidad and Tobago
78	660	6.1	1,952	3.7	96.3	308	9.6	32	14	34	883	…	Tunisia
8.9	212	22.9	8,542	…	…	299	12	25	189	688	4,059	2,994	Turkey
2,860	33,991	…	10,803	…	…	546	20	28	29	237	250	…	Turkmenistan
…	…	…	…	…	…	…	…	…	…	—	—	—	Tuvalu
…	…	…	…	…	…	…	…	…	…	—	—	—	Uganda
1,121	20,433	0.4	95,502	…	…	395	13	30	98	1,085	3,930	38,402	Ukraine
6,003	36,249	17.7	29,509	…	…	97,800	126	777	77	309	830	…	United Arab Emirates
755	97,126	11.7	97,251	…	…	5,153	5.7	909	651	1,854	3,926	10,388	United Kingdom
4,645	555,653	15.5	633,866	…	…	21,034	8.9	2,345	5,335	16,423	276,000	843,586	United States
—	—	63.0	—	—	—	…	…	…	14	37	—	—	Uruguay
1,875	44,127	0.1	36,415	…	…	594	17	36	35	222	290	200	Uzbekistan
…	…	…	…	…	…	…	…	…	…	—	—	—	Vanuatu
4,035	39,411	12.4	39,411	9.1	90.9	72,600	72	1,006	371	1,187	6,850	…	Venezuela
193	7.7	…	7.7	…	…	600	9.7	62	0.3	—	150	…	Vietnam
—	—	100.7	…	…	…	…	…	…	119	545	—	—	Virgin Islands (U.S.)
…	…	…	…	…	…	…	…	…	…	—	—	—	West Bank
…	…	…	…	…	…	…	…	…	…	—	—	—	Western Sahara
479	…	100.0	…	…	…	4,000	31	128	41	120	676	—	Yemen
48	711	0.6	2,935	…	…	78	10	7.6	17	167	545	…	Yugoslavia
—	—	100.0	—	—	—	…	…	…	4.2	25	1,724	…	Zambia
…	—	89.8	—	—	—	…	…	…	…	—	212	…	Zimbabwe

[1]Estimated reserves in place. [2]South Africa includes Botswana, Lesotho, Namibia, and Swaziland. [3]Geothermally generated electricity. [4]France includes Monaco. [5]1994. [6]Italy includes San Marino. [7]1995. [8]Switzerland includes Liechtenstein. [9]Belgium includes Luxembourg. [10]1993. [11]1985.

Transportation

This table presents data on the transportation infrastructure of the various countries and dependencies of the world and on their commercial passenger and cargo traffic. Most states have roads and airports, with services corresponding to the prevailing level of economic development. A number of states, however, lack railroads or inland waterways because of either geographic constraints or lack of development capital and technical expertise. Pipelines, one of the oldest means of bulk transport if aqueducts are considered, are today among the most narrowly developed transportation modes worldwide for shipment of bulk materials. Because the principal contemporary application of pipeline technology is to facilitate the shipment of hydrocarbon liquids and gases, coverage of pipelines will be found in the "Energy" table. It is, however, also true that pipelines now find increasing application for slurries of coal or other raw materials.

While the United Nations' *Statistical Yearbook* and *Monthly Bulletin of Statistics* provide much data on infrastructure and traffic and have established basic definitions and classifications for transportation statistics, the number of countries covered is limited. Several commercial publications maintain substantial databases and publishing programs for their particular areas of interest: highway and vehicle statistics are provided by the International Road Federation's annual *World Road Statistics;* the International Union of Railway's *International Railway Statistics* and Jane's *World Railways* provide similar data for railways; Lloyd's *Register of Shipping Statistical Tables* summarizes the world's merchant marine; the *Official Airline Guide,* the International Civil Aviation Organization's *Digest of Statistics: Commercial Air Carriers,* and the International Air Transport Association's *World Air Transport Statistics* have also been used to supplement and update data collected by the UN. Because several of these agencies are commercially or insurance-oriented, their data tend to be more complete, accurate, and timely than those of intergovernmental organizations, which depend on periodic responses to questionnaires or publication of results in official sources. All of these international sources have been extensively supplemented by national statistical sources to provide additional data. Such diversity of sources, however, imposes limitations on the comparability of the statistics from country to country because the basis and completeness of data collection and the frequency and timeliness of analysis and publication may vary greatly. Data shown in italic are from 1993 or earlier.

The categories adopted in the table also have special problems of comparability. Total road length is subject to wide international variation of interpretation, as "roads" can mean anything from mere tracks to highly developed highways. Each country also has individual classifications that differ according to climate, availability of road-building materials, traffic patterns, administrative responsibility, and so on. "Paved roads," by contrast, is a much more tightly definable category, but the proportion of paved to total roads may be distorted by the less comparable total road statistics. Automobile and truck and bus fleet statistics, which are usually

Transportation

country	roads and motor vehicles (latest)								railroads (latest)					
	roads			motor vehicles			cargo		track length		traffic			
	length		paved (percent)	automobiles	trucks and buses	persons per vehicle	short ton-mi ('000,000)	metric ton-km ('000,000)	mi	km	passengers		cargo	
	mi	km									passenger-mi ('000,000)	passenger-km ('000,000)	short ton-mi ('000,000)	metric ton-km ('000,000)
Afghanistan	13,000	21,000	13	31,000	25,000	401	*1,993*	*2,910*	16	25	...	...	...	...
Albania	11,000	18,000	30	67,031	34,058	32	55	80	416	670	122.4	197.0	0.03	0.05
Algeria	63,643	102,424	69	725,000	780,000	19	*9,589*	*14,000*	2,451[2]	3,945[2]	1,135	1,826	1,465	2,139
American Samoa	*217*	*350*	*43*	4,672	199	11	...	...	—	—	—	—	—	—
Andorra	167	269	74	35,358	4,238	1.6	...	...	—	—	—	—	—	—
Angola	45,128	72,626	25	207,000	25,000	41	...	...	1,834[2]	2,952[2]	*203*	*326*	*1,178*	*1,720*
Antigua and Barbuda	155	250	...	13,588	1,342	4.3	...	...	—	—	—	—	—	—
Argentina	135,630	218,276	29	4,459,000	955,000	6.5	...	...	22,216	35,753	4,968	7,996	5,826	8,506
Armenia	5,238	8,431	100	1,300	4,460	655	328.0	478.9	516	830	52	84	218	351
Aruba	*236*	*380*	*100*	38,834	990	2.4	...	...	—	—	—	—	—	—
Australia	567,300	913,000	39	8,879,000	2,129,470	1.7	*786,643*	*1,148,480*	20,567[2, 7]	33,099[2, 7]	7,152	11,510	46,697	68,176
Austria	124,000	200,000	100	3,782,544	310,444	2.0	7,877	11,500	3,524	5,672	5,376[7]	8,652[7]	10,513[7]	15,348[7]
Azerbaijan	28,502	45,870	94	281,100	104,300	21	340	497	1,317	2,120	342	550	3,160	4,613
Bahamas, The	1,522	2,450	57	89,263	17,228	2.6	...	...	—	—	—	—	—	—
Bahrain	1,966	3,164	77	149,636	32,213	3.4	...	...	—	—	—	—	—	—
Bangladesh	126,773	204,022	12	54,784	69,394	991	...	...	1,681[2]	2,706[2]	2,333	3,754	536	782
Barbados	1,025	1,650	96	43,711	10,583	4.9	...	...	—	—	—	—	—	—
Belarus	33,186	53,407	99	1,132,843	8,867	8.9	6,209	9,065	3,410	5,488	8,021	12,909	20,984	30,636
Belgium	89,353	143,800	97	4,415,343	449,904	2.1	18,800	27,500	2,100[2]	3,380[2]	4,340	6,984	5,113	7,465
Belize	1,398	2,250	18	9,695	11,698	11	...	...	—	—	—	—	—	—
Benin	4,217	6,787	20	37,772	8,058	123	...	...	359	578	75.7	121.8	193.5	311.4
Bermuda	140	225	100	21,220	4,007	2.4	...	...	—	—	—	—	—	—
Bhutan	2,041	3,285	61	*2,590*	*1,367*	*348*	...	...	—	—	—	—	—	—
Bolivia	30,696	49,400	6	223,829	138,536	21	*1,133*	*1,654*	2,187[2]	3,519[2]	84.9	136.7	359.0	524.2
Bosnia and Herzegovina	13,574	21,846	52	96,182	10,919	30	*2,708*	*3,954*	641	1,031	19.3	31.1	63.6	92.8
Botswana	11,388	18,327	25	30,517	59,710	17	...	...	603	971	60	96	545	795
Brazil	1,230,000	1,980,000	9	12,000,000	3,160,689	10	*178,359*	*260,400*	18,578[2]	29,899[2]	9,009	14,498	93,455	136,442
Brunei	1,064	1,712	75	91,047	15,918	2.9	...	...	12[13]	19[13]	—	—	...	...
Bulgaria	23,190	37,320	92	1,730,506	251,382	4.2	331	483	4,020	6,470	3,645	5,866	5,099	7,444
Burkina Faso	7,519	12,100	16	38,220	17,980	190	...	...	386[2]	622[2]	126	202	31	45
Burundi	8,997	14,480	7	19,200	18,240	145	...	...	—	—	—	—	—	—
Cambodia	22,226	35,769	8	52,919	13,574	171	822	1,200	409	649	23.9	38.4	5.3	7.8
Cameroon	30,074	48,400	8	98,000	64,350	88	*175*	*255*	625[2]	1,006[2]	197	317	556	812
Canada	634,400	1,021,000	35	13,217,336	3,643,652	1.8	48,955	71,473	40,639	65,403	944	1,519	193,489	282,489
Cape Verde	680	1,095	78	3,280	820	94	...	...	—	—	—	—	—	—
Central African Republic	14,900	24,000	2	9,500	7,000	195	41	60	—	—	—	—	—	—
Chad	20,800	33,400	1	10,560	14,550	293	580	850	—	—	—	—	—	—
Chile	49,590	79,800	14	1,017,052	573,177	9.1	...	...	4,084	6,572	506.1	814.5	1,595	2,329
China	736,814	1,185,789	80	4,880,200	5,750,300	115	343,239	501,120	47,672	76,721	206,629	332,537	888,403	1,297,046
Colombia	71,808	115,564	12	762,000	672,000	27	*4,265*	*6,227*	*2,007*[2]	*3,230*[2]	*9.6*	*15.5*	504.3	736.2
Comoros	559	900	76	9,100	4,950	36	...	...	—	—	—	—	—	—
Congo, Dem. Rep. of the	95,708	154,027	2	787,000	60,000	55	...	...	3,193	5,138	18[14]	29[14]	121[14]	176[14]
Congo, Rep. of the	7,950	12,800	10	37,240	15,520	49	*46*	*67*	556	894	188	302	183	267
Costa Rica	22,119	35,597	17	294,083	163,428	7.6	2,103	3,070	590[2]	950[2]	3.7	5.9	45.8	66.8
Côte d'Ivoire	31,300	50,400	10	293,000	163,000	32	...	...	397[2]	639[2]	80[17]	129[17]	40[17]	58[17]
Croatia	17,299	27,840	82	932,278	114,505	4.1	322	470	1,694	2,726	610	981	1,285	1,876
Cuba	37,815	60,858	49	172,574	185,495	31	*2,482*	*3,623*	2,987	4,807	1,021	1,643	763	1,075
Cyprus	6,620	10,654	58	234,976	108,452	2.4	...	...	—	—	—	—	—	—
Czech Republic	78,234	125,905	44	3,547,745	402,353	2.6	29,513	43,088	5,860	9,430	4,791	7,710	15,347	22,406
Denmark	44,389	71,437	100	1,782,369	349,734	2.5	7,603	11,100	1,704[2]	2,743[2]	3,099	4,988	1,109	1,619
Djibouti	1,796	2,890	13	9,200	2,040	38	...	...	*66*	*106*	361	762	144	232
Dominica	485	780	50	6,581	2,825	7.8	...	...	—	—	—	—	—	—
Dominican Republic	7,829	12,600	49	224,000	151,550	21	...	...	1,083[2]	1,743[2]	...	...	...	...
East Timor	...	...	...	...	...	...	...	...	...	...	...	...	...	...
Ecuador	26,841	43,197	19	464,902	52,630	23	2,437	3,558	600[2]	966[2]	29	47	1.8	2.6

based upon registration, are relatively accurate, though some countries round off figures, and unregistered vehicles may cause substantial undercount. There is also inconsistent classification of vehicle types; in some countries a vehicle may serve variously as an automobile, a truck, or a bus, or even as all three on certain occasions. Relatively few countries collect and maintain commercial road traffic statistics.

Data on national railway systems are generally given for railway track length rather than the length of routes, which may be multitracked. Siding tracks usually are not included, but some countries fail to distinguish them. The United States data include only class 1 railways, which account for about 94 percent of total track length. Passenger traffic is usually calculated from tickets sold to fare-paying passengers. Such statistics are subject to distortion if there are large numbers of nonpaying passengers, such as military personnel, or if season tickets are sold and not all the allowed journeys are utilized. Railway cargo traffic is calculated by weight hauled multiplied by the length of the journey. Changes in freight load during the journey should be accounted for but sometimes are not, leading to discrepancies.

Merchant fleet and tonnage statistics collected by Lloyd's registry service for vessels over 100 gross tons are quite accurate. Cargo statistics, however, reflect the port and customs requirements of each country and the reporting rules of each country's merchant marine authority (although these, increasingly, reflect the recommendations of the International Maritime Organization); often, however, they are only estimates based on customs declarations and the count of vessels entered and cleared. Even when these elements are reported consistently, further uncertainties may be introduced because of ballast, bunkers, ships' stores, or transshipped goods included in the data.

Airport data are based on scheduled flights reported in the commercial *Official Airline Guide* and are both reliable and current. The comparability of civil air traffic statistics suffers from differing characteristics of the air transportation systems of different countries; data for an entire country may be two to three years behind those for a single airport.

Outside of Europe, where standardization of data on inland waterways is necessitated by the volume of international traffic, comparability of national data declines markedly. Calculations as to both the length of a country's waterway system (or route length of river, lake, and coastal traffic) and the makeup of its stock of commercially significant vessels (those for which data will be collected) are largely determined by the nature and use of the country's hydrographic net—its seasonality, relief profile, depth, access to potential markets—and inevitably differ widely from country to country. Data for coastal or island states may refer to scheduled coastwise or interisland traffic.

merchant marine (latest)				air					canals and inland waterways (latest)				country
fleet (vessels over 100 gross tons)	total dead-weight tonnage ('000)	international cargo (latest)		airports with sched-uled flights (latest)	traffic (latest)				length		cargo		
					passengers		cargo		mi	km	short ton-mi ('000,000)	metric ton-km ('000,000)	
		loaded metric tons ('000)	off-loaded metric tons ('000)		passenger-mi ('000,000)	passenger-km ('000,000)	short ton-mi ('000,000)	metric ton-km ('000,000)					
—	—	—	—	3	171.5[1]	276.0[1]	26[1]	38[1]	750	1,200	...	...	Afghanistan
24	81.0	120	2,040	1	2.2	3.5	0.15	0.22	27	43	24	35	Albania
149	1,093.4	63,110	15,700	28	1,803[3]	2,901[3]	12.5[3]	18.3[3]	...	...	...	...	Algeria
3	0.1	380	581	3	...	...	...	...	...	...	...	...	American Samoa
—	—	—	—	—	—	—	—	—	—	—	—	—	Andorra
113	123.5	23,288	1,261	17[4]	1,061[4]	1,708[4]	131.7[4]	212.0[4]	805	1,295	...	...	Angola
292	997.4	28	113	2	157	252	0.1	0.2	...	...	...	...	Antigua and Barbuda
423	1,173.1	69,372	19,536	39	3,805[5]	6,124[5]	481.4[5]	702.9[5]	6,804	10,950	19,326	28,215	Argentina
...	...	...	...	1[4]	3,453	5,557	34	49	...	...	...	...	Armenia
[6]	[6]	...	...	1	318	511	...	...	...	...	...	...	Aruba
695	3,857.3	35,664	43,360	400	45,354	72,990	1,304	1,904	5,200	8,368	31,891	46,560	Australia
26	208.5	1,479	5,766	6	6,847	11,020	181.3	264.7	222	358	1,753	2,560	Austria
69	...	...	...	3	1,025	1,650	125	183	...	...	3,112	5,008	Azerbaijan
1,061	33,081.7	5,920	5,705	22	87	140	0.32	0.455	...	...	...	...	Bahamas, The
87	192.5	13,285	3,512	1	1,762[8]	2,836[8]	81.3[8]	118.7[8]	...	...	...	...	Bahrain
301	566.8	948	10,404	8[4]	2,009	3,233	338.6	494.4	5,000	8,046	...	...	Bangladesh
37	84.0	206	538	1	93[9]	149[9]	0.8[10]	1.1[10]	...	...	...	...	Barbados
...	18,373.0	...	...	1	864	1,390	7	10	...	...	71	103	Belarus
232	218.5	360,984	367,680	2	5,356	8,620	517.9	756.2	1,269	2,043	3,819	5,575	Belgium
32	45.7	255	277	9[4]	...	...	...	...	513	825	...	...	Belize
12	0.2	339	1,738	1[4]	160.5[11]	258.3[11]	8.4[11]	13.5[11]	...	...	...	...	Benin
94	5,206.5	130	470	1	...	...	...	...	...	...	...	...	Bermuda
—	—	—	—	1[4]	29	46	...	...	—	—	—	—	Bhutan
1	15.8	...	...	14[4]	1,223	1,968	28.7	41.9	6,214	10,000	90	132	Bolivia
...	...	...	...	1	25.1	40.4	0.29	0.43	...	...	...	...	Bosnia and Herzegovina
—	—	—	—	7	35.3[12]	56.8[12]	0.1[12]	0.2[12]	...	...	...	...	Botswana
635	9,348.3	239,932	146,452	139	27,550	44,338	1,105	1,614	31,069	50,000	56,030	81,803	Brazil
51	349.7	42	1,308	1	1,742	2,803	75.0	109.5	130	209	...	...	Brunei
107	391	5,290	20,080	3	1,259	2,026	18.9	30.4	292	470	2	3	Bulgaria
—	—	—	—	2	134.9	217.2	23.4	34.2	...	...	...	...	Burkina Faso
1	0.4	35	188	1	1.2	2.0	...	...	...	...	...	...	Burundi
3	3.8	11	95	8	26.1	42.0	0.3	0.4	2,300	3,700	51	75	Cambodia
47	39.8	2,385	2,497	5	348	560	57	91	1,299	2,090	...	...	Cameroon
1,185	2,896.8	187,716	94,536	269	49,754	80,072	1,220	1,781	1,860	3,000	...	...	Canada
42	30.9	144	299	9	106	171	13.2	19.2	...	...	...	...	Cape Verde
—	—	53	126	1	139.6[12]	224.7[12]	11.2[12]	16.4[12]	500	800	185	270	Central African Republic
—	—	—	—	1	145	233	25	37	1,240	2,000	...	...	Chad
392	854.9	29,532	18,144	23	4,217	6,787	972	1,419	450	725	5,629	8,218	Chile
2,390	20,658.0	1,146,084	101,688	113	46,469	74,784	1,708	2,493	68,351	110,000	1,223,479	1,786,250	China
101	403.0	49,332	15,288	43	3,723	5,991	573	836	11,272	18,140	7,038	10,276	Colombia
6	3.6	12	107	2	1.9	3.0	...	...	...	...	...	...	Comoros
27	30.7	2,395	1,453	22	173[15]	279[15]	29[15]	42[15]	9,300	15,000	678	990	Congo, Dem. Rep. of the
22	10.8	708	533	10	139[11]	223[11]	10.5	15.3	696	1,120	...	...	Congo, Rep. of the
24	8.4	3,017	3,972	14	2,167[16]	3,487[16]	61.9[16]	90.4[16]	454	730	...	...	Costa Rica
51	98.6	4,173	7,228	5	191[18]	307[18]	30[18]	44[18]	609	980	...	...	Côte d'Ivoire
203	140.9	4,416	7,680	4	339	546	2.0	3.0	488	785	128	187	Croatia
393	924.6	8,092	15,440	14	2,202	3,543	38.5	56.2	149	240	108	158	Cuba
1,416	36,198.1	1,344	4,308	2	1,685	2,711	26	38	...	...	...	...	Cyprus
18[19]	514.1[19]	759	409	2	2,189	3,523	18.6	27.2	421	677	464	678	Czech Republic
456	7,589.1	21,060	38,292	13	3,340[20]	5,376[20]	117[20]	171[20]	259	417	1,100	1,600	Denmark
10	4.1	414	958	1	42	67	4	6	...	...	...	...	Djibouti
7	3.2	103	181	2	...	...	...	...	...	...	...	...	Dominica
28	10.4	1,668	4,182	7	9.8	15.8	7.9	11.6	...	...	...	...	Dominican Republic
...	...	...	...	...	...	...	...	...	...	...	...	...	East Timor
154	504.1	11,783	1,958	14	574	924	79	116	932	1,500	...	...	Ecuador

Transportation (continued)

country	roads and motor vehicles (latest)								railroads (latest)					
	roads			motor vehicles			cargo		track length		traffic			
	length		paved (per-cent)	auto-mobiles	trucks and buses	persons per vehicle	short ton-mi ('000,-000)	metric ton-km ('000,-000)	mi	km	passengers		cargo	
	mi	km									passen-ger-mi ('000,000)	passen-ger-km ('000,000)	short ton-mi ('000,000)	metric ton-km ('000,000)
Egypt	39,800[21]	64,000[21]	78[21]	1,354,000	496,000	33	21,600	31,500	2,989	4,810	29,821	47,992	1,600	2,336
El Salvador	6,232	10,029	20	177,488	184,859	16	...	...	349[2]	562[2]	3.0	4.8	11.8	17.3
Equatorial Guinea	1,740	2,800	13	6,500	4,000	37	...	...	—	—	—	—	—	—
Eritrea	2,491	4,010	22	5,940	...	...	...	...	43	70	...	...	...	...
Estonia	10,209	16,430	51	451,000	86,900	2.7	1,899	2,773	636	1,024	147	236	4,164	6,079
Ethiopia	12,117	19,500	15	52,012	39,936	642	...	...	486[22]	782[22]	98	157	73	106
Faroe Islands	285	458	...	12,748	3,085	2.8	...	...	—	—	—	—	—	—
Fiji	3,200	5,100	20	49,712	33,928	9.4	...	...	370[13]	595[13]	...	...	...	...
Finland	48,340	77,796	64	1,948,126	275,394	2.3	17,398	25,400	3,657[2]	5,886[2]	2,098	3,376	6,751	9,856
France	504,987	812,700	*92*	25,100,000	5,005,000	1.9	113,700	166,000	19,847[2]	31,940[2]	34,467	55,470	32,466	47,400
French Guiana	*706*	*1,137*	*40*	*29,100*	*10,600*	*3.2*	...	...	—	—	—	—	—	—
French Polynesia	549	884	44	*37,000*	*15,300*	*4.0*	...	...	—	—	—	—	—	—
Gabon	4,760	7,670	8	24,750	16,490	28	...	...	506	814	53	85	345	503
Gambia, The	1,678	2,700	35	8,640	9,000	68	...	...	—	—	—	—	—	—
Gaza Strip	...	...	...	37,061	8,105	23	...	...	—	—	—	—	—	—
Georgia	12,862	20,700	93	427,000	41,510	11	67	98	961	1,546	231	371	*1,199*	*1,750*
Germany	143,584	231,076	99	41,326,900	2,428,300	1.9	139,125	203,119	54,188	87,207	39,780	64,020	49,797	72,703
Ghana	24,000	38,700	40	90,000	45,000	133	*873*	*1,275*	*592*[2]	*953*[2]	*731.4*	*1,177*	*93.9*	*137.1*
Greece	23,777	38,265	94	2,339,421	939,923	3.2	8,797	12,844	1,537[2]	2,474[2]	940	1,513	209	306
Greenland	93	150	60	2,242	1,474	15	...	...	—	—	—	—	—	—
Grenada	646	1,040	61	*4,739*	*3,068*	*12*	...	...	—	—	—	—	—	—
Guadeloupe	2,122	3,415	*80*	*101,600*	*37,500*	*2.9*	...	...	—	—	—	—	—	—
Guam	550	885	76	79,800	34,700	1.3	...	...	—	—	—	—	—	—
Guatemala	8,140	13,100	28	102,000	97,000	51	...	...	549[2]	884[2]	10.3	16.6	58.6	85.6
Guernsey	...	...	...	36,460	7,247	1.5	...	...	—	—	—	—	—	—
Guinea	18,952	30,500	16	14,100	21,000	219	...	...	411[2]	662[2]	25.8	41.5	5.0	7.3
Guinea-Bissau	2,734	4,400	10	7,120	5,640	91	...	...	—	—	—	—	—	—
Guyana	4,952	7,970	7	24,000	9,000	22	...	...	116[15]	187[15]	...	...	...	...
Haiti	2,585	4,160	24	32,000	21,000	121	...	...	—	—	—	—	—	—
Honduras	9,073	14,602	18	81,439	170,006	22	...	...	614	988	*4.8*	*7.7*	*20.7*	*30.2*
Hong Kong	1,158	1,865	100	318,000	134,000	15	...	...	21[2]	34[2]	2,231	3,591	68	99
Hungary	116,944	188,203	43	2,297,115	333,858	3.9	527	770	8,178	13,161	5,520	8,884	5,605	8,183
Iceland	7,691	12,378	25	151,409	19,428	1.6	*318*	*464*	—	—	—	—	—	—
India	2,062,727	3,319,644	46	4,189,000	2,234,000	148	*144,000*	*210,000*	39,093[2]	62,915[2]	230,250	370,560	194,609	284,124
Indonesia	212,943	342,700	54	2,639,523	2,159,799	42	*17,000*	*25,000*	4,013[2]	6,458[2]	10,185	16,392	5,622	8,208
Iran	100,700	162,000	50	1,793,000	692,000	24	*46,750*	*68,250*	3,703[2]	5,960[2]	4,377	7,044	9,341	13,638
Iraq	29,453	47,400	86	772,986	323,906	18	...	...	1,263[2]	2,032[2]	973	1,566	1,129	1,649
Ireland	57,477	92,500	94	1,057,383	161,355	3.0	3,519	5,138	1,210[2]	1,947[2]	805	1,295	390	570
Isle of Man	500	805	58	40,168	4,925	1.6	...	...	32[2]	52[2]	...	...	...	...
Israel	9,609	15,464	100	1,273,000	294,100	3.7	...	...	379[2]	610[2]	215	346	679	992
Italy	195,334	314,360	100	31,700,000	5,127,000	1.6	95,798	139,863	12,133	19,527	43,294	69,675	17,430	25,447
Jamaica	11,800	19,000	71	156,751	61,482	12	...	...	*129*[2]	*208*[2]	*12.1*	*19.5*	*1.7*	*2.5*
Japan	713,333	1,148,000	73	48,684,000	19,402,000	1.9	209,257	305,510	16,937	27,258	249,888	402,156	17,102	24,968
Jersey	346	557	100	58,491	9,922	1.3	...	...	—	—	—	—	—	—
Jordan	4,432	7,133	100	213,874	79,153	15	*19,133*	*27,934*	421[2]	677[2]	*3.7*	*6.0*	915	1,336
Kazakhstan	78,166	125,796	83	973,323	361,920	11	4,439	6,481	8,388[2]	13,500[2]	8,078	13,000	73,631	107,500
Kenya	39,600	63,800	14	278,000	81,200	78	*134*	*196*	1,885[2]	3,034[2]	239	385	813	1,309
Kiribati	416	670	5	222	115	260	...	...	—	—	—	—	—	—
Korea, North	14,526	23,377	8	*248,000*	...	...	...	...	*5,302*	*8,533*	*2,100*	*3,400*	*6,200*	*9,100*
Korea, South	52,797	84,968	74	7,586,474	2,826,953	4.4	51,031	74,504	4,089	6,580	18,686	30,073	8,706	12,710
Kuwait	2,765	4,450	81	538,000	155,000	2.5	...	...	—	—	—	—	—	—
Kyrgyzstan	11,495	18,500	91	146,000	...	...	240	350	264	424	19	30	276	403
Laos	13,870	22,321	14	16,320	4,200	242	16	23	—	—	—	—	—	—
Latvia	34,761	55,942	38	431,816	95,329	4.7	548	800	1,499	2,413	658	1,059	8,901	12,995
Lebanon	3,951	6,359	95	1,217,000	86,640	2.6	...	...	138	222	*5.3*	*8.6*	*29*	*42*
Lesotho	3,079	4,955	18	12,610	25,000	53	...	...	1.6	2.6	...	...	...	...
Liberia	6,600	10,600	6	9,400	25,000	59	...	...	304[2]	490[2]	...	...	534[15]	860[15]
Libya	50,704	81,600	57	809,514	357,528	4.0	...	...	—	—	—	—	—	—
Liechtenstein	201	323	...	21,150	2,684	1.4	...	...	12	19	...	...	...	...
Lithuania	44,350	71,375	91	980,910	105,022	3.4	5,906	8,622	1,241[2]	1,997[2]	444	715	5,661	8,265
Luxembourg	3,206	5,160	99	244,129	27,283	1.6	*164*	*239*	170[2]	274[2]	169.1	272.2	419.8	612.9
Macau	31	50	100	45,184	6,578	8.2	...	...	—	—	—	—	—	—
Macedonia	7,154	11,513	63	288,678	24,745	6.4	829	1,210	575	925	93	150	279	408
Madagascar	30,967	49,837	17	62,000	16,460	140	*220*	*321*	*680*[2]	*1,095*[2]	*152*	*245*	*90*	*132*
Malawi	10,222	16,451	19	27,000	29,700	171	—	—	495[2]	797[2]	11.0	18.0	29.7	43.4
Malaysia	58,719	94,500	75	3,333,423	618,066	5.5	...	...	1,113	1,791	867[31]	1,396[31]	971[31]	1,417[31]
Maldives	...	...	...	1,716	586	114	...	...	—	—	—	—	—	—
Mali	9,383	15,100	12	26,190	18,240	213	...	...	398[2]	641[2]	577.6	929.6	371	542.8
Malta	1,219	1,961	94	185,247	49,520	1.6	...	...	—	—	—	—	—	—
Marshall Islands	...	...	...	1,374	262	29	...	...	—	—	—	—	—	—
Martinique	1,299	2,091	*75*	*108,300*	*32,200*	*2.6*	...	...	—	—	—	—	—	—
Mauritania	4,760	7,660	11	18,810	10,450	82	...	...	437[2]	704[2]	...	...	1,603	2,340
Mauritius	1,184	1,905	93	46,300	12,100	20	...	...	—	—	—	—	—	—
Mayotte	145	233	77	——6,553——		20	...	...	—	—	—	—	—	—
Mexico	199,824	321,586	37	8,607,000	4,426,000	7.1	113,000	165,000	16,543[2]	26,623[2]	1,118	1,800	28,578	41,723
Micronesia	*140*	*226*	*17*	...	...	...	...	...	—	—	—	—	—	—
Moldova	7,643	12,300	87	166,757	67,638	18	534	780	819	1,318	410	660	1,404	2,050
Monaco	31	50	100	21,120	2,770	1.3	...	...	1	2	...	...	...	...
Mongolia	31,000	50,000	3	39,921	31,061	33	84.4	123.2	1,128	1,815	348	560	1.3	1.9
Morocco	35,921	57,810	52	1,018,146	278,075	21	1,429	2,086	1,099[2]	1,768[2]	1,104	1,776	3,258	4,757
Mozambique	18,890	30,400	19	4,900	7,520	1,431	75	110	1,940	3,123	317	510	781	1,140
Myanmar (Burma)	17,523	28,200	12	27,000	42,000	587	*71*	*103.7*	2,458[2]	3,955[2]	2,453	3,948	674	984
Namibia	40,526	65,220	8	74,875	66,500	12	...	...	1,480	2,382	21.6	34.7	738	1,077
Nauru	19	30	79	——*1,448*——		*6.3*	...	...	3[13]	5[13]	...	...	*4.7*	*6.8*
Nepal	4,785	7,700	42	47,541	29,371	306	*984*	*1,437*	37[2]	59[2]	...	...	...	...

merchant marine (latest)				air					canals and inland waterways (latest)				country
fleet (vessels over 100 gross tons)	total dead-weight tonnage ('000)	international cargo (latest)		airports with sched-uled flights (latest)	traffic (latest)				length		cargo		
					passengers		cargo						
		loaded metric tons ('000)	off-loaded metric tons ('000)		passenger-mi ('000,000)	passenger-km ('000,000)	short ton-mi ('000,000)	metric ton-km ('000,000)	mi	km	short ton-mi ('000,000)	metric ton-km ('000,000)	
444	1,685.2	15,012	22,044	11	4,996	8,040	146	213	2,175	3,500	452	660	Egypt
15	…	221	1,023	1	1,355	2,181	10.9	16.0	…	…	…	…	El Salvador
3	6.7	110	64	1	4	7	0.7	1.0	…	…	…	…	Equatorial Guinea
…	…	…	…	2	…	…	…	…	…	…	…	…	Eritrea
234	680.4	30,024	5,784	1	103.6	166.7	0.6	0.9	199	320	0.3	0.4	Estonia
27	84.3	234	1,242	31	1,190	1,915	225	328	…	…	…	…	Ethiopia
191	59.8	223	443	1	…	…	…	…	…	…	…	…	Faroe Islands
64	60.4	568	625	13	742	1,195	51.6	75.4	126	203	…	…	Fiji
263	989.3	39,312	38,052	24	6,657	10,714	143.1	208.9	4,148	6,675	2,055	3,000	Finland
729	4,981.0	64,704	189,504	61	48,512[23]	78,073[23]	7,740[23]	11,300[23]	9,278	14,932	3,288	4,800	France
7	0.7	73	447	8	…	…	…	…	286	460	…	…	French Guiana
41	16.5	15	666	17	…	…	…	…	…	…	…	…	French Polynesia
29	30.2	12,828	212	17	452	728	68	100	994	1,600	…	…	Gabon
11	2.0	185	240	1	31	50	3	5	250	400	…	…	Gambia, The
—	—	…	…	1	…	…	…	…	—	—	…	…	Gaza Strip
54	1,108	…	…	1	78.9	127.1	0.5	0.8	…	…	12,603	18,400	Georgia
1,375	6,832.3	74,568	138,864	35	46,744	75,227	4,224	6,167	4,660	7,500	9,965	14,549	Germany
155	131.0	2,424	2,904	1	407	655	20	30	803	1,293	75	110	Ghana
1,872	45,276.6	16,464	45,024	36	5,302	8,533	81.3	118.7	50	80	585	854	Greece
82	17.2	298	288	18	104	167	0.23	0.34	…	…	…	…	Greenland
3	0.5	21	193	2	…	…	…	…	…	…	…	…	Grenada
20	4.4	349	2,285	7	…	…	…	…	…	…	…	…	Guadeloupe
5	0.1	195	1,524	1	…	…	…	…	…	…	…	…	Guam
8	0.4	2,096	3,822	2	311	500	48	70	162	260	…	…	Guatemala
—	—	…	…	2	…	…	…	…	…	…	…	…	Guernsey
23	1.7	16,760	734	1	32	52	3	5	805	1,295	…	…	Guinea
19	1.8	46	283	2	6.2	10.0	0.7	1.0	…	…	…	…	Guinea-Bissau
82	13.5	1,730	673	1	154	248	2.3	3.3	3,660	5,900	…	…	Guyana
4	0.4	170	704	2	…	…	…	…	60	100	…	…	Haiti
966	1,437.3	1,316	1,002	8	212[24]	341[24]	23[24]	33[24]	289	465	…	…	Honduras
387	11,688.6	36,132[25]	80,820[25]	1	…	…	…	…	…	…	…	…	Hong Kong
15	93.2	…	…	1	1,560	2,510	25.3	37.0	853	1,373	13	19	Hungary
394	114.9	1,162	1,733	24	2,273	3,658	50.9	74.4	…	…	58	84	Iceland
888	10,365.9	61,880	102,630	66	14,511	23,354	330.2	482.1	10,054	16,180	202,000	295,000	India
2,014	3,130.2	310,246	208,871	81	15,746	25,340	503.9	735.7	13,409	21,579	17,000	25,000	Indonesia
403	8,345.3	32,148	37,404	19	3,786	6,093	66.9	97.7	562	904	…	…	Iran
131	1,578.8	97,830	8,638	…	976	1,570	37.4	54.6	631	1,015	…	…	Iraq
189	208.6	6,367	17,637	9	4,018	6,466	88.8	129.6	435	700	…	…	Ireland
101	2,836.5	6	203	1	526.1	846.8	0.1	0.2	…	…	…	…	Isle of Man
58	723.4	12,876	20,916	7	7,547[26]	12,146[26]	765[26]	1,117[26]	…	…	…	…	Israel
1,966	7,149.5	48,252	234,120	34	18,312[27]	29,471[27]	835[27]	1,219[27]	1,500	2,400	85,681	125,092	Italy
12	16.2	8,802	5,285	4	1,038[28]	1,670[28]	20.2[28]	29.5[28]	…	…	…	…	Jamaica
6,756	17,582	124,548	754,464	73	79,512	127,963	4,641	6,776	1,100	1,770	165,589	241,756	Japan
—	—	…	…	1	…	…	…	…	…	…	…	…	Jersey
5	113.6	7,308	5,328	2	2,526	4,065	150.1	219.2	…	…	19,202	28,035	Jordan
…	…	…	…	20	1,509	2,429	162	237	2,423	3,900	223	326	Kazakhstan
29	11.6	1,596	3,228	11	1,062[29]	1,709[29]	126[29]	203[29]	…	…	…	…	Kenya
7	2.7	15	26	9	4.4	7.0	0.6	1.0	3	5	…	…	Kiribati
100	951.2	635	5,520	1	128.6	207.0	13.7	22.0	1,400	2,253	…	…	Korea, North
2,138	11,724.9	255,888	448,416	14	36,894	59,376	5,449	7,955	1,000	1,609	31,027	45,299	Korea, South
209	3,188.5	51,400	4,522	1	3,728	6,000	255.2	372.6	…	…	…	…	Kuwait
…	…	…	…	2	2,739	4,408	44.7	65.2	373	600	6	9	Kyrgyzstan
1	1.5	—	—	11	30	48	3	5	2,850	4,587	68	100	Laos
261	1,436.9	45,144	3,888	1	185	298	6	9	186	300	418	610	Latvia
163	438.2	152	1,150	1	1,174	1,889	32	46	…	…	…	…	Lebanon
—	—	—	—	1	3.9	6.2	0.4	0.6	—	—	—	—	Lesotho
1,672	97,374.0	21,653	1,608	1	4.3	7.0	0.7	1.0	…	…	…	…	Liberia
150	1,223.6	62,491	7,808	12	264[30]	425[30]	23[30]	34[30]	—	—	…	…	Libya
—	—	—	—	—	—	—	—	—	…	…	…	…	Liechtenstein
52	373.9	12,864	2,796	3	190.5	306.6	1.8	2.6	373	600	5	8	Lithuania
54	2,603.6	—	—	1	79.5	232	606.9	886.1	23	37	232	338	Luxembourg
6	0.1	755	3,935	—	—	—	—	—	…	…	…	…	Macau
…	…	…	…	2	553.5	890.7	239.2	349.2	…	…	…	…	Macedonia
85	82.1	540	984	44	519	836	20.2	29.5	…	…	…	…	Madagascar
1	0.3	…	…	5	68	110	10	14	89	144	1,683	2,457	Malawi
552	2,916.3	39,756	54,852	39	17,836	28,704	979	1,429	4,534	7,296	…	…	Malaysia
44	79.0	27	78	5	44	71	…	…	…	…	…	…	Maldives
—	—	—	—	9	140	225	23	37	1,128	1,815	18	27	Mali
889	17,073.2	309	1,781	1	1,173	1,888	7.7	11.2	…	…	…	…	Malta
35	4,182.4	29	123	25	17	28	0.003	0.005	…	…	…	…	Marshall Islands
6	1.1	960	1,584	1	…	…	…	…	…	…	…	…	Martinique
126	23.9	10,400	724	9	160.5	258.3	9.2	13.5	…	…	…	…	Mauritania
35	152.2	966	2,753	1	2,398	3,859	561.2	819.4	…	…	…	…	Mauritius
1	1.1	158	31	1	…	…	…	…	…	…	…	…	Mayotte
635	1,495.3	134,400	67,500	83	14,864	23,922	1,779	2,597	1,800	2,900	…	…	Mexico
19	9.2	…	…	4	…	…	…	…	…	…	…	…	Micronesia
…	…	…	…	1	0.1	0.2	0.7	1.0	263	424	172	251	Moldova
1	…	…	…	—	—	—	…	…	…	…	…	…	Monaco
—	—	—	—	1	326	525	33	48	247	397	0.1	0.2	Mongolia
492	586.2	24,228	27,972	11	2,789	4,489	260	380	…	…	…	…	Morocco
107	31.6	2,800	3,400	7	239	384	6	9	2,330	3,750	57	83	Mozambique
144	1,354.0	1,788	3,456	19	272	438	2.2	3.2	7,954	12,800	240	351	Myanmar (Burma)
30	5.9	1,132	644	11	470	756	16	23	…	…	…	…	Namibia
2	5.8	1,650	59	1	151[32]	243[32]	15[32]	24[32]	…	…	…	…	Nauru
—	—	—	—	24	532	856	64	93	…	…	…	…	Nepal

Transportation (continued)

country	roads and motor vehicles (latest)								railroads (latest)					
	roads			motor vehicles			cargo		track length		traffic			
	length		paved (per-cent)	auto-mobiles	trucks and buses	persons per vehicle	short ton-mi ('000,-000)	metric ton-km ('000,-000)	mi	km	passengers		cargo	
	mi	km									passen-ger-mi ('000,000)	passen-ger-km ('000,000)	short ton-mi ('000,000)	metric ton-km ('000,000)
Netherlands, The	77,379	124,530	91	5,740,000	681,000	2.4	22,535	32,900	1,737	2,795	8,756	14,091	2,139	3,123
Netherlands Antilles	367	590	51	75,105	17,753	2.2	...	...	—	—	—	—	—	—
New Caledonia	3,582	5,764	52	56,700	21,200	2.6	...	...	—	—	—	—	—	—
New Zealand	57,164	91,996	61	1,831,118	351,494	1.7	...	...	2,548[2]	4,100[2]	*285*	*458*	2,482	3,624
Nicaragua	11,200	18,000	10	73,000	61,650	33	...	...	—	—	—	—	—	—
Niger	6,276	10,100	8	38,220	15,200	169	*1,044*	*1,524*	—	—	—	—	—	—
Nigeria	38,897	62,598	19	663,000	68,300	134	...	...	*2,178*	*3,505*	*345*	*555*	*1.5*	*2.2*
Northern Mariana Islands	225	360	100	12,113	6,479	3.0	...	...	—	—	—	—	—	—
Norway	56,702	91,254	74	1,758,001	435,427	2.0	8,108	11,838	2,499[2]	4,021[2]	1,591	2,561	1,643	2,399
Oman	20,518	33,020	24	211,000	97,020	7.2	...	...	—	—	—	—	—	—
Pakistan	142,874	229,934	58	665,102	291,683	138	57,654	84,174	5,453[2]	8,775[2]	12,723	20,476	3,582	5,229
Palau	*40*	*64*	*59*	——4,271——		3.8	...	...	...	...	...	...	...	...
Panama	7,022	11,301	33	203,760	74,637	9.4	...	...	220[2]	354[2]	...	...	*0.5*	*0.7*
Papua New Guinea	*12,263*	*19,736*	*6*	13,000	32,000	93	...	...	—	—	—	—	—	—
Paraguay	18,330	29,500	10	71,000	50,000	41	...	...	274[2]	441[2]	1.9	3.0	3.8	5.5
Peru	45,836	73,766	12	557,042	359,374	26	...	...	1,238[2]	1,992[2]	106.3	171.1	582.4	850.3
Philippines	100,235	161,313	18	743,299	244,065	72	...	...	557[2]	897[2]	106.6	171.6	1.0	1.5
Poland	234,286	377,048	66	8,533,449	1,594,797	3.8	65,412	95,500	14,904	23,986	16,550	26,635	47,341	69,116
Portugal	42,708	68,732	88	2,865,000	219,696	3.2	8,162	11,917	1,909[2]	3,072[2]	2,798	4,503	1,492	2,178
Puerto Rico	8,948	14,400	100	878,000	190,000	3.5	...	...	—	—	—	—	—	—
Qatar	764	1,230	90	126,000	64,000	2.9	...	...	—	—	—	—	—	—
Réunion	1,711	2,754	*79*	190,300	44,300	3.0	...	...	—	—	—	—	—	—
Romania	95,175	153,170	51	2,408,000	409,550	8.0	15,343	22,400	7,062	11,365	11,433	18,400	19,041	27,800
Russia	354,628	570,719	79	17,631,600	4,905,900	6.5	95	138	93,800	151,000	94,635	152,300	699	1,020
Rwanda	9,528	14,900	9	13,000	17,100	188	*140*	*200*	—	—	—	—	—	—
St. Kitts and Nevis	199	320	43	*3,700*	*2,200*	*6.8*	...	...	22	36	—	—	—	—
St. Lucia	750	1,210	5	14,783	1,020	9.5	...	...	—	—	—	—	—	—
St. Vincent and the Grenadines	646	1,040	31	6,089	3,670	11	...	...	—	—	—	—	—	—
Samoa	491	790	42	1,068	1,169	74	...	...	—	—	—	—	—	—
San Marino	157	252	...	25,571	2,636	0.9	...	...	—	—	—	—	—	—
São Tomé and Príncipe	199	320	68	4,040	1,540	24	...	...	—	—	—	—	—	—
Saudi Arabia	101,000	162,000	43	1,744,000	1,192,000	6.6	57,859	84,473	864[2]	1,390[2]	86	139	559	816
Senegal	9,134	14,700	29	85,488	36,962	72	*375*	*547*	761	1,225	*128*	*206*	*476*	*695*
Seychelles	263	424	87	7,120	1,980	8.5	...	...	—	—	—	—	—	—
Sierra Leone	7,270	11,700	11	17,640	10,890	163	*36*	*53*	*52*	*84*	...	...	...	...
Singapore	1,875	3,017	97	395,226	152,480	5.8	...	...	52	83	[33]	[33]	[33]	[33]
Slovakia	10,953	17,627	...	1,135,914	100,254	4.4	2,588	3,779	2,282	3,673	1,900	3,057	8,475	12,373
Slovenia	9,228	14,851	82	764,789	59,450	2.4	1,216	1,775	746	1,201	383	616	1,953	2,852
Solomon Islands	845	1,360	3	*2,052*	*2,574*	*75*	...	...	—	—	—	—	—	—
Somalia	13,732	22,100	12	1,020	6,440	866	...	...	—	—	—	—	—	—
South Africa	205,838	331,265	41	4,004,000	1,664,000	7.4	*1,053*	*1,538*	12,626[2]	20,319[2]	*556*	*895*	65,248	95,260
Spain	215,335	346,548	99	15,297,366	3,256,009	2.1	53,973	78,799	8,252[2]	13,280[2]	9,696	15,605	6,708	9,794
Sri Lanka	61,640	99,200	40	107,000	150,160	71	21	30	909[2]	1,463[2]	2,014	3,241	73.6	107.5
Sudan, The	7,394	11,900	36	285,000	53,000	93	...	...	2,855[2]	4,595[2]	100	161	1,346	1,965
Suriname	2,815	4,530	26	46,408	19,255	6.4	...	...	187	301	...	...	...	...
Swaziland	2,367	3,810	29	31,882	32,772	17	...	...	187	301	*752*	*1,210*	*1,993*	*2,910*
Sweden	121,807	196,030	72	3,655,000	339,000	2.2	21,302	31,100	6,756	10,874	3,944	6,348	12,904	18,840
Switzerland	44,147	71,048	96	3,323,421	279,347	2.0	8,900	13,000	3,132	5,041	7,227	11,630	5,056	7,382
Syria	25,756	41,451	23	139,592	281,930	35	*1,075*	*1,570*	1,507[2]	2,425[2]	181	292	934	1,364
Taiwan	12,545	20,189	89	4,536,600	834,200	4.1	9,932	14,500	2,410	3,879	6,085	9,793	962	1,404
Tajikistan	8,500	13,700	83	680	8,190	667	*3,518*	*5,136*	295	474	77	124	1,449	2,115
Tanzania	54,805	88,200	4	23,760	115,700	229	...	...	2,218	3,569	*2,324*	*3,740*	927	1,354
Thailand	40,141	64,600	98	1,661,000	2,855,000	14	...	...	2,511[2]	4,041[2]	7,335	11,804	2,318	3,384
Togo	4,673	7,520	32	79,200	34,240	39	...	...	245[2]	395[2]	10.3	16.5	34	49
Tonga	423	680	27	1,140	780	51	...	...	—	—	—	—	—	—
Trinidad and Tobago	5,170	8,320	51	122,000	24,000	8.7	...	...	—	—	—	—	—	—
Tunisia	14,354	23,100	79	269,000	312,000	16	*678*	*990*	1,341[2]	2,158[2]	614	988	1,595	2,329
Turkey	237,610	382,397	25	3,767,162	985,320	13	95,747	139,789	5,348	8,607	3,885	6,252	5,844	8,532
Turkmenistan	8,500	13,700	83	220,000	58,200	16	*3,283*	*4,793*	1,317	2,120	1,307	2,104	4,643	6,779
Tuvalu	5	8	—	...	...	...	...	...	—	—	—	—	—	—
Uganda	16,653	26,800	8	35,361	48,430	249	...	...	771[2]	1,241[2]	17	27	162	236
Ukraine	107,111	172,378	95	4,885,691	...	...	14,063	20,532	14,021	22,564	33,865	54,500	109,878	160,419
United Arab Emirates	3,004	4,835	100	201,000	56,950	9.6	...	...	—	—	—	—	—	—
United Kingdom	229,824	369,867	100	21,681,000	2,317,000	2.5	107,500	157,000	23,518[44]	37,849[44]	18,154	29,216	1,997	2,916
United States	3,912,226	6,296,130	91	129,728,341	75,212,684	1.3	985,997	1,439,532	137,900	222,000	25,950	41,762	1,355,971	1,979,685
Uruguay	5,395	8,683	30	516,889	50,264	5.6	*500*	*730*	1,288[2]	2,073[2]	*87.4*	*140.6*	123	180
Uzbekistan	52,444	84,400	87	865,300	14,500	25	*15,037*	*21,954*	2,271	3,655	1,553	2,500	11,580	16,907
Vanuatu	665	1,070	24	4,000	2,600	27	...	...	—	—	—	—	—	—
Venezuela	59,443	95,664	36	1,505,000	542,000	11	...	...	390[2]	627[2]	93.1	149.9	37.3	54.5
Vietnam	58,000	93,300	25	——200,000——		358	1,462	2,134	1,648[2]	2,652[2]	1,668	2,685	1,007	1,470
Virgin Islands (U.S.)	532	856	100	*51,000*	*13,300*	1.7	...	...	—	—	—	—	—	—
West Bank	...	...	...	88,056	24,324	18	...	...	...	...	...	...	...	...
Western Sahara	*3,900*	*6,200*	*23*	*6,284*	*424*	*20*	...	...	—	—	—	—	—	—
Yemen	40,218	64,725	8	229,084	282,615	31	...	...	—	—	—	—	—	—
Yugoslavia	31,377	50,497	60	1,400,000	132,000	6.9	852	1,244	2,528	4,069	1,084	1,744	1,666	2,432
Zambia	24,170	38,898	18	157,000	81,000	37	...	...	787	1,266	166	267	316	462
Zimbabwe	11,395	18,338	47	323,000	32,000	31	...	...	1,714[2]	2,759[2]	253.6	408.2	3.2	4.6

[1]Ariana Afghan Airlines only. [2]Route length. [3]Air Algérie International flights only. [4]TAAG airline only. [5]Aerolineas Argentinas only. [6]Included in Netherlands Antilles. [7]Government railways only. [8]Portion of Gulf Air traffic. [9]Caribbean Airways only. [10]Caribbean Air Cargo only. [11]Air Afrique only. [12]Air Botswana only. [13]For industrial purposes only. [14]Zaire National Railways only. [15]Air Zaire only. [16]LASCA only. [17]Traffic between Ouagadougou, Burkina Faso, and Abidjan, Côte d'Ivoire. [18]Air Ivoire only. [19]Data refer to former Czechoslovakia. [20]Including SAS international and domestic traffic. [21]National roads only. [22]Includes 62 mi (100 km) of the Chemin de Fer Djibouti-Ethiopien (CDE) in Djibouti. [23]Air France and UTA only. [24]TAN and SAHSA airlines only. [25]Includes

merchant marine (latest)				air					canals and inland waterways (latest)				country
fleet (vessels over 100 gross tons)	total dead-weight tonnage ('000)	international cargo (latest)		airports with sched-uled flights (latest)	traffic (latest)				length		cargo		
		loaded metric tons ('000)	off-loaded metric tons ('000)		passengers		cargo		mi	km	short ton-mi ('000,000)	metric ton-km ('000,000)	
					passenger-mi ('000,000)	passenger-km ('000,000)	short ton-mi ('000,000)	metric ton-km ('000,000)					
399	*2,874*	91,920	305,232	6	35,591	57,279	2,646	3,863	3,135	5,046	3,493	5,100	Netherlands, The
154[33]	*1,053.6*[33]	215	517	6	*234*[34]	*377*[34]	*1.2*[34]	*1.8*[34]	…	…	…	…	Netherlands Antilles
17	*18.1*	*1,040*	*930*	11	*145*[35]	*233*[35]	*3.4*[35]	*4.9*[35]	…	…	…	…	New Caledonia
139	*279.8*	20,640	13,308	36	11,151	17,946	562	821	1,000	1,609	*1,503*	*2,195*	New Zealand
25	*1.3*	*320*	*1,629*	10	49	79	6	9	1,379	2,220	…	…	Nicaragua
—	—	—	—	6	160.5	258.3	9.3	13.5	186	300	14	20	Niger
271	*733.3*	*86,993*	*11,346*	12	509	819	1.3	1.9	5,328	8,575	…	…	Nigeria
2	*0.9*	*33*	*205*	2	…	…	…	…	…	…	…	…	Northern Mariana Islands
1,597	20,834	151,116	25,788	50	6,168[20]	9,927[20]	773[20]	1,128[20]	980	1,577	5,112	7,463	Norway
26	*11.7*	43,525	5,303	6	821[8]	1,322[8]	18[8]	27[8]	…	…	…	…	Oman
73	*513.8*	6,408	31,008	35	6,818	10,972	275	402	…	…	…	…	Pakistan
4	…	…	64	1	…	…	…	…	…	…	…	…	Palau
5,217	*79,255.6*	117,924	76,800	10	853	1,373	14.9	21.8	497	800	…	…	Panama
87	*40.9*	*2,463*	*1,784*	129	*458.8*	*738.4*	*56.4*	*82.4*	6,798	10,940	…	…	Papua New Guinea
38	*38.5*	…	…	5	134	215	13	19	1,900	3,100	…	…	Paraguay
623	*615.6*	*10,197*	*5,077*	27	1,637	2,634	172	251	5,300	8,600	…	…	Peru
1,499	*13,807.1*	16,980	52,596	21	10,484[36]	16,872[36]	323.2[36]	471.9[36]	2,000	3,219	…	…	Philippines
644	*4,314.3*	33,360	15,864	8	3,063	4,930	79	116	2,369	3,812	637	930	Poland
332	*1,129.3*	7,572	37,740	16	4,957	7,978	143.6	209.7	510	820	…	…	Portugal
13	…	…	…	7	…	…	…	…	…	…	…	…	Puerto Rico
65	*635.6*	*18,145*	*2,588*	1	1,372[8]	2,208[8]	60.3[8]	88.0[8]	…	…	…	…	Qatar
7	*33.5*	454	2,302	2	…	…	…	…	…	…	…	…	Réunion
439	*4,845.5*	11,676	18,972	12	1,446	2,327	33.8	49.4	1,071	1,724	2,473	3,610	Romania
4,543	*16,592.3*	7,092	744	75	35,100	56,500	1,370	2,000	62,800	101,000	53	77	Russia
—	—	—	—	2	1.2	2.0	…	…	…	…	…	…	Rwanda
1	*0.6*	*24*	*36*	2	…	…	…	…	…	…	…	…	St. Kitts and Nevis
7	*2.1*	138	547	2	…	…	…	…	…	…	…	…	St. Lucia
946	1,253	72	128	5	…	…	…	…	…	…	…	…	St. Vincent and the Grenadines
7	6.5	48	144	3	165	265	18	26	—	—	—	—	Samoa
—	—	—	—	—	—	—	—	—	—	—	—	—	San Marino
4	*2.3*	*16*	*45*	2	6	9	0.7	1.0	…	…	…	…	São Tomé and Príncipe
301	*1,361.7*	*214,070*	*46,437*	25	11,694	18,820	651.7	951.5	…	…	…	…	Saudi Arabia
183	*27.5*	1,396	2,894	7	139.6[30]	224.7[30]	11.2[30]	16.4[30]	557	897	…	…	Senegal
9	*3.3*	47	543	2	*389*	*626*	*48*	*70*	…	…	…	…	Seychelles
62	*18.4*	*2,310*	*589*	1	*68*[37]	*110*[37]	*1.4*[37]	*2.0*[37]	500	800	*447*	*652*	Sierra Leone
946	*14,929.2*	326,040	188,234	1	34,235	55,096	3,260	4,760	…	…	…	…	Singapore
…	…	…	…	2	143.8	231.4	0.5	0.7	107	172	1,040	1,519	Slovakia
13	*346.5*	2,460	5,952	1	421	677	2.4	3.6	…	…	12,282	17,932	Slovenia
33	*5.0*	*278*	*349*	21	29[38]	47[38]	0.9	1.3	…	…	…	…	Solomon Islands
28	*18.5*	*324*	*1,007*	1	*81*	*131*	*3.0*	*5.0*	…	…	…	…	Somalia
219	*282.5*	114,331	22,203	24	9,852[39]	15,855[39]	202[39]	295[39]	…	…	…	…	South Africa
2,190	*5,077.3*	55,752	169,848	25	32,093	51,649	3,601	5,257	649	1,045	*21,836*[40]	*31,880*[40]	Spain
66	*472.6*	9,288	16,632	1	2,640	4,248	125.0	182.5	267	430	0.7	1	Sri Lanka
16	*62.2*	*1,543*	*4,300*	3	330[41]	531[41]	14[41]	20[41]	3,300	5,310	…	…	Sudan, The
24	*15.7*	*1,595*	*1,265*	1	549[42]	883[42]	66[42]	106[42]	746	1,200	…	…	Suriname
—	—	—	—	1	30.7	49.4	0.09	0.1	—	—	—	—	Swaziland
430	2,881	61,320	75,528	48	8,853[20]	14,247[20]	201[20]	293[20]	1,275	2,052	5,891	8,600	Sweden
24	*602.8*	…	…	5	17,426	28,044	1,298	1,895	40	65	110	160	Switzerland
94	*210.4*	2,136	5,112	5	749	1,205	10.7	15.6	541	870	…	…	Syria
649	*9,241.3*	182,127	301,275	13	24,369	39,218	2,828	4,129	…	…	274	400	Taiwan
…	…	…	…	1	1,386	2,231	140	205	…	…	…	…	Tajikistan
43	*48.5*	*1,249*	*2,721*	11	114	184	2.0	2.9	…	…	…	…	Tanzania
351	*1,194.5*	42,495	74,579	25	21,338	34,340	1,042	1,522	2,300	3,701	…	…	Thailand
8	*20.6*	391	1,274	2	139.6	224.7	11.2	16.4	31	50	…	…	Togo
15	*13.7*	*15*	*104*	6	7	11	0.7	1.0	…	…	…	…	Tonga
53	*17.5*	*9,622*	*10,961*	2	1,652	2,658	182	265	…	…	…	…	Trinidad and Tobago
77	*443.3*	6,792	13,152	5	1,716	2,762	13.2	19.2	…	…	…	…	Tunisia
880	*7,114.3*	24,756	78,168	26	8,098[43]	13,033[43]	166.6[43]	243.3[43]	750	1,200	*209*	*305*	Turkey
…	…	…	…	1	970	1,562	98	143	…	…	…	…	Turkmenistan
6	*16.0*	…	…	1	…	…	…	…	…	…	…	…	Tuvalu
2	*8.6*	…	…	1	32.4	52.1	3	5	…	…	…	…	Uganda
…	…	77,004	7,116	12	1,225	1,972	30.3	44.2	2,734	4,400	3,731	5,447	Ukraine
276	*1,491.7*	*88,153*	*9,595*	6	9,714[8]	15,633[8]	1,646[8]	2,403[8]	…	…	…	…	United Arab Emirates
1,631	*4,355*	177,228	178,572	57	77,576	124,847	2,625	3,832	1,990	3,200	33,014	48,200	United Kingdom
509	18,585	392,076[45]	713,880[45]	834	540,400	869,700	14,568	21,270	25,482	41,009	355,125	518,474	United States
93	*172.5*	*710*[46]	*1,450*[46]	1	398	640	42	62	1,000	1,600	…	…	Uruguay
…	…	…	…	9	2,150	3,460	220	321	684	1,100	…	…	Uzbekistan
280	*3,259.6*	*80*	*55*	29	110.8	178.3	1.3	1.9	…	…	…	…	Vanuatu
271	*1,355.4*	*101,435*	*17,932*	20	3,600	5,800	438	639	4,400	7,100	…	…	Venezuela
230	*872.8*	*303*	*1,510*	12	2,352	3,785	70.9	103.6	11,000	17,702	1,339	1,955	Vietnam
1	…	*105.5*	*648.3*	2	…	…	…	…	…	…	…	…	Virgin Islands (U.S.)
—	—	…	…	—	—	—	—	—	…	…	…	…	West Bank
—	—	*40*	*15*	1	…	…	…	…	…	…	…	…	Western Sahara
40	*13.7*	*1,936*	*7,829*	12	735	1,183	82	119	…	…	…	…	Yemen
462[47]	*5,173.1*[47]	360	972	5	650	1,046	3,962	5,784	365	587	905	1,322	Yugoslavia
—	—	—	—	4	*192*	*308*	*6.8*	*9.9*	1,398	2,250	…	…	Zambia
—	—	—	—	7	544	875	24	35	…	…	…	…	Zimbabwe

transshipments. [26]El Al only. [27]Alitalia only. [28]Air Jamaica only. [29]Kenya Airways only. [30]International traffic only. [31]Peninsular Malaysia and Singapore. [32]Air Nauru only. [33]Includes Aruba. [34]Antillean Airlines only. [35]Air Caledonie only. [36]Philippine Air Lines only. [37]Sierra Leone Airlines international traffic only. [38]Solair only. [39]SAA only. [40]Coastal shipping only. [41]Sudan Airways only. [42]Suriname Airways only. [43]Turkish Airlines only. [44]British Railways only; excludes Northern Ireland. [45]Includes Puerto Rico. [46]Port of Montevideo only. [47]Data refer to Yugoslavia as constituted prior to 1991.

Communications

Virtually all the states of the world have a variety of communications media and services available to their citizens: book, periodical, and newspaper publishing (although only daily papers are included in this table); postal services; and telecommunication systems: radio and television broadcasting, telephones (fixed and mobile), facsimile (fax) machines, personal computers (PCs), and access to the Internet. Unfortunately, the availability of information about these services often runs behind the capabilities of the services themselves. Certain countries publish no official information; others publish data analyzed according to a variety of fiscal, calendar, religious, or other years; still others, while they possess such data almost simultaneously with the end of the business or calendar year, may not see them published except in company or parastatal reports of limited distribution. Even when such data are published in national statistical summaries, it may be only after a delay of up to several years.

The data also differ in their completeness and reliability. Figures for book production, for example, generally include all works published in separate bindings except advertising works, timetables, telephone directories, price lists, catalogs of businesses or exhibitions, musical scores, maps, atlases, and the like. The figures include government publications, school texts, theses, offprints, series works, and illustrated works, even those consisting principally of illustrations. Figures refer to works actually published during the year of survey, usually by a registered publisher, and deposited for copyright. A book is defined as a work of 49 or more pages; a work published simultaneously in more than one country is counted as having been published in each. A periodical is a publication issued at regular or stated intervals and, in Unesco's usage, directed to the general public. Newspaper statistics are especially difficult to collect and compare. Newspapers continually are founded, cease publication, merge, or change frequency of publication. Data on circulation are often incomplete, slow to be aggregated at the national level, or regarded as proprietary. In some countries no daily newspaper exists.

Post office statistics are compiled mainly from the Universal Postal Union's annual summary *Statistique des services postaux.* Postal services, unlike the other media discussed earlier, tend most often to be operated by

Communications

country	publishing (latest)							postal services				telecommunications	
	books		periodicals		daily newspapers			post offices, 1998				radio, 1997	
	number of titles	number of copies ('000)	number of titles	number of copies ('000)	number	total circulation ('000)	circulation per 1,000 persons	number	persons per office	pieces of mail handled ('000,000)	pieces handled per person	receivers (all types; '000)	receivers per 1,000 persons
Afghanistan	2,795	3,741	...	...	12	113	6	373	50,400	0.5	—	2,750	132
Albania	381	5,710	143	3,477	5	116	34	698[2]	4,840[2]	3.2	0.6	810	259
Algeria	670	...	48	803	5	1,080	38	3,223[3]	9,140[3]	736[3]	21[3]	7,100	242
American Samoa	...	...	...	...	2	5.0	93	...	...	...	...	57	929
Andorra	57	...	...	...	3	4.0	58	...	...	...	...	16	227
Angola	22	419	...	...	5	128	11	80[3]	145,000[3]	1.2	0.1	630	54
Antigua and Barbuda	...	...	...	...	1	6.0	91	16[1]	4,375[1]	...	...	36	542
Argentina	9,850	39,663	...	...	181	4,320	123	6,678[3]	5,340[3]	472[3]	11[3]	24,300	681
Armenia	396[4]	20,212[4]	44	541	11	85	23	...	...	0.7[5]	0.2[5]	850	239
Aruba	...	...	...	...	13	73	852	4	17,500	10	90	50	557
Australia	10,835	...	...	...	65	5,730	297	3,922	4,780	4,732	225	25,500	1,391
Austria	8,056[6]	...	2,481	...	17	2,382	294	2,436	3,320	3,133[3]	372[3]	6,080	751
Azerbaijan	542	2,643	49	801	6	210	28	1,673[3]	4,560[3]	12[3]	1.3[3]	175	23
Bahamas, The	...	...	...	...	3	28	100	138	2,170	61[7]	51[7]	215	739
Bahrain	40[4]	...	26	73	4	67	117	13	49,200	55	50	338	580
Bangladesh	...	...	...	...	37	1,117	9.0	9,093[3]	13,400[3]	589[3]	4.3[3]	6,150	50
Barbados	...	...	...	...	2	53	199	16	16,900	39	114	237	888
Belarus	3,809	59,073	155	3,765	10	1,899	187	3,852	2,640	709	67	3,020	292
Belgium	13,913	...	13,706	...	30	1,625	160	1,637[1]	6,200[1]	3,713	346	8,075	797
Belize	70	—	...	...	4	23.5	0.5	134[3]	1,720[3]	4.0[3]	12[3]	133	591
Benin	84[4]	42[4]	...	...	1	12	2.2	178	32,500	9.6	1.2	620	110
Bermuda	...	...	...	...	1	17	270	14[2]	4,500[2]	15[2]	240[2]	82	1,296
Bhutan	...	...	...	...	...	...	...	106[3]	17,540[3]	1.8[3]	0.7[3]	37	19
Bolivia	...	...	...	...	18	420	55	171	46,500	9.9	0.7	5,250	675
Bosnia and Herzegovina	...	...	...	...	3	518	146	210	20,050	9.8	1.6	940	267
Botswana	158[4]	...	14	177	1	40	27	180	8,720	54	26	237	154
Brazil	21,574[9]	104,397	...	...	380	6,472	55	11,713	13,800	5,223	32	71,000	434
Brunei	45[4]	56[4]	15	132	1	21	69	18	17,200	20	52	93	302
Bulgaria	4,840	20,317	772	1,740	17	2,145	253	3,303	2,500	156[2]	18[2]	4,510	537
Burkina Faso	12[4]	14[4]	37	24	4	14	1.3	85	130,000	7.3[10]	...	370	34
Burundi	...	...	...	...	1	20	3.2	28	225,000	16	1.3	440	69
Cambodia	...	...	...	...	...	...	...	56	204,000	3.2	0.2	1,340	128
Cameroon	...	...	...	...	2	91	6.7	377[3]	37,000[3]	6.1[3, 11]	0.4[3, 11]	2,270	163
Canada	19,900	...	1,400	37,108	107	4,718	158	18,607[7]	1,570[7]	10,715[8, 10]	370[8, 10]	32,300	1,067
Cape Verde	...	...	...	...	...	...	...	54	7,780	1.6	2.1	73	183
Central African Republic	...	...	...	...	3	6.0	1.8	35	99,710	...	...	283	83
Chad	...	...	...	...	1	2.0	0.2	36	201,900	13	1.0	1,670	236
Chile	2,469	4,095	417	3,450	52	1,411	99	710	20,870	343[11]	23[11]	5,180	354
China	100,951	5,945[12]	6,486	205,060	44	48,000	42	112,204	11,200	6,967[3]	5.5[3]	417,000	335
Colombia	1,481	11,314	...	...	37	1,800	49	1,354	30,200	116[3]	2.2[3]	21,000	524
Comoros	...	...	...	...	...	...	...	37	17,800	0.4	0.3	90	141
Congo, Dem. Rep. of the	64[4]	535[4]	...	...	9	124	2.7	497	98,870	...	...	18,030	376
Congo, Rep. of the	...	...	3	34	6	20	7.8	114[2]	22,720[2]	1.8[2]	0.5[2]	341	126
Costa Rica	963	...	...	...	6	320	88	134	24,900	32[3]	6.9[3]	980	261
Côte d'Ivoire	...	...	...	...	12	231	17	373	38,300	31	1.9	2,260	161
Croatia	1,718	...	352	6,357	10	515	114	1,168	3,910	299	60	1,510	337
Cuba	932	4,610	14	285	17	1,300	118	1,855	5,990	12[11]	1.1[11]	3,900	352
Cyprus	930	1,776	39	338	9	84	111	777	990	64	67	310	406
Czech Republic	10,244	...	1,168	81,387	21	2,620	256	3,369	3,050	803	72	8,270	803
Denmark	12,352	...	157	6,930	37	1,628	311	1,169	4,530	1,828[2]	335[2]	6,020	1,145
Djibouti	...	...	7	6.0	...	...	...	12	51,700	16[2]	12[2]	52	84
Dominica	...	...	...	...	...	...	...	64[7]	1,090[7]	2.9[2]	30[7]	46	647
Dominican Republic	...	...	...	...	12	416	52	239	33,900	9.8[14]	1.3[14]	1,440	178
East Timor	...	...	...	...	...	...	...	...	...	...	...	18	21
Ecuador	12[4]	19[4]	199	...	24	820	70	315	38,600	13	0.4	4,150	348
Egypt	2,215	92,353	258	2,373	17	2,400	38	7,488	8,810	317	3.3	20,500	317
El Salvador	...	...	45	774	5	278	48	289	20,900	18	1.9	2,750	465
Equatorial Guinea	...	...	...	...	1	2.0	4.9	23[7]	17,000[7]	...	...	180	428
Eritrea	106	420	...	...	...	...	...	37[1]	91,900[1]	2.3	0.5	345	100
Estonia	2,628	6,662	517	2,323	15	255	173	560	2,550	75	43	1,010	698

a single national service, to cover a country completely, and to record traffic data according to broadly similar schemes (although the details of *classes* of mail handled may differ). Some countries do not enumerate domestic traffic or may record only international traffic requiring handling charges.

Data for some kinds of telecommunications apparatus are relatively easy to collect; telephones, for example, must be installed, and service recorded so that it may be charged. But in most countries the other types of apparatus mentioned above may be purchased by anyone and used whenever desired. As a result, data on distribution and use of these types of apparatus may be collected in a variety of ways—on the basis of numbers of subscribers, licenses issued, periodic sample surveys, trade data, census or housing surveys, or private consumer surveys. Data on broadcast media refer to receivers; data on telephones to "main lines," or the lines connecting a subscriber's apparatus (fixed or mobile) to the public, switched net. Information on fax machines and PCs is estimated only, as noted above. "Users" refers to the number of people with access to computers connected to the Internet.

The *Statistical Yearbook* of Unesco contains extensive data on book, periodical, and newspaper publishing, and on radio and television broadcasting that have been collected from standardized questionnaires. The quality and recency of its data, however, depend on the completion and timely return of each questionnaire by national authorities. The commercially published annual *World Radio TV Handbook* (Andrew G. Sennitt, editor) is a valuable source of information on broadcast media and has complete and timely coverage. It depends on data received from broadcasters, but, because some do not respond, local correspondents and monitors are used in many countries, and some unconfirmed or unofficial data are included as estimates. The statistics on telecommunication apparatus and computers are derived mainly from the UN-affiliated International Telecommunication Union's *World Telecommunication Development Report* (annual).

... Not available.

— None, nil, or not applicable.

television, 1998		telephones, 1998		cellular phones, 1998		fax, 1998		personal computers, 1998		Internet users, 1998	country
receivers (all types; '000)	receivers per 1,000 persons	main lines ('000)	main lines per 1,000 persons	cellular subscriptions ('000)	subscriptions per 1,000 persons	receivers ('000)	receivers per 1,000 persons	units ('000)	units per 1,000 persons	('000)	
250[1]	12[1]	29	1.4	...	...	...	...	...	...	...	Afghanistan
430	113	116	30	5.6	1.5	14	3.6	...	...	...	Albania
3,200	106	1,477	49	18	0.6	7[1]	0.2[1]	160	5.3	2.0	Algeria
13[1]	236[1]	14	214	2.6	42	...	...	...	...	...	American Samoa
30	400	33	441	14	188	5.0	67	...	...	4.5	Andorra
170	14	72	6.0	9.8	0.8	...	...	10	0.8	2.5	Angola
31[1]	457[1]	34	468	1.3[1]	19[1]	...	...	...	...	...	Antigua and Barbuda
10,600	293	7,132	197	2,530	70	87	2.4	1,500	42	200	Argentina
840	238	556	157	7.0	2.0	0.4[1]	0.1[1]	15	4.2	4.0	Armenia
33[2]	405[2]	33[3]	367[3]	5.4	57	0.5[2]	6.9[2]	...	...	...	Aruba
13,200	705	9,540	509	5,342	285	900[3]	48[3]	7,700	411	3,000	Australia
4,200	516	3,999	491	2,030	249	285[2]	35[2]	1,900	233	1,100	Austria
1,950	254	680	89	65	8.5	2.5[2]	0.1[2]	0.4	0.1	1.0	Azerbaijan
66[1]	232[1]	106	358	8.1	27	0.5[2]	1.8[2]	...	...	...	Bahamas, The
265	413	158	245	92	143	6.7	10.4	60	93	20	Bahrain
920	7.4	378	3.0	75	0.6	4.0[2]	3.3[2]	120	1.0	1.2	Bangladesh
77	287	113	422	12	48	1.8[2]	6.8[2]	20	75	5.0	Barbados
3,300	322	2,490	243	12	1.2	19	1.9	...	...	7.5	Belarus
5,300	523	5,073	500	1,756	173	190[1]	19[1]	2,900	286	800	Belgium
42	183	32	138	3.4	15	0.5[8]	2.6[8]	30	130	10	Belize
65	11	38	6.6	6.3	1.1	1.0[1]	0.2[1]	7.0	1.2	2.0	Benin
66[1]	1,041[1]	54	840	13	196	...	...	...	...	...	Bermuda
12.5	20	10	16	—	—	1.5	2.4	2.5	3.9	...	Bhutan
930	117	535[3]	69[3]	218	27	...	...	60	7.5	17	Bolivia
385[2]	111[2]	333	91	25	6.8	...	...	...	...	...	Bosnia and Herzegovina
32	20	102	65	23	15	3.5[3]	2.3[3]	40	25	10	Botswana
45,000	278	19,987	120	7,761	48	500[3]	3.1[3]	5,000	30	2,500	Brazil
200	635	78	247	49	156	2.0[2]	7.0[2]	8.0[2]	29[2]	10	Brunei
3,400	408	2,742	329	127	15	15[2]	1.8[2]	250[2]	30[2]	150	Bulgaria
120	11	41	3.6	2.7	0.2	...	...	10	0.9	1.0	Burkina Faso
28	4.3	18	2.9	0.6	0.1	4.0[1]	0.6[1]	...	...	0.2	Burundi
96	9.0	20	1.9	61	5.7	3.0[3]	0.3[3]	9.0[3]	0.9[3]	0.7[3]	Cambodia
480	34	75[3]	5.4[3]	4.2[3]	0.3[3]	...	...	30	2.1	2.0	Cameroon
21,450[3]	715[3]	19,206	635	5,320	176	1,075	36	10,000	331	7,500	Canada
2.0	4.9	40	98	1.0	2.5	1.0[1]	2.5[1]	...	...	2.0	Cape Verde
19	5.4	9.6	2.7	0.7	0.2	0.3	0.1	3.5	1.0	0.2	Central African Republic
10	1.4	8.6	1.2	...	...	0.2	0.03	...	...	0.3	Chad
3,500	236	2,753	186	964	65	40[3]	2.7[3]	714	48	250	Chile
360,000	287	87,421	70	23,863	19.0	2,000	1.6	11,200	8.9	2,100	China
8,000	203	6,367	161	1,800	46	173	4.6	1,024	26	350	Colombia
2.0[2]	5.0[2]	6.2	9.5	...	...	0.1[2]	0.2[2]	...	...	0.1	Comoros
150[1]	3.2[1]	36[2]	0.8[2]	10[2]	0.2[2]	5.0[2]	0.1[2]	...	...	...	Congo, Dem. Rep. of the
42[2]	17[2]	22	7.9	3.4	1.2	0.1[2]	0.04[2]	...	...	0.3	Congo, Rep. of the
870	226	660	172	109	28	8.5[3]	2.3[3]	150	39	100	Costa Rica
1,000	70	170	12	91	6.4	...	...	65	4.5	10	Côte d'Ivoire
1,250	279	1,558	348	182	41	50[3]	11[3]	500	112	200	Croatia
2,660	239	388	35	4.1	0.4	0.4[13]	0.04[13]	...	...	25	Cuba
117	157	405	545	116	157	7.0[8]	11.4[8]	30[2]	46[2]	30	Cyprus
4,800	467	3,741	364	965	94	107	10	1,000	97	400	Czech Republic
3,100	585	3,496	660	1,931	364	250[2]	48[2]	2,000	377	1,000	Denmark
29	46	7.9	13	0.2	0.4	0.3[3]	0.6[3]	5.5	8.8	0.5	Djibouti
10[13]	141[13]	19[1]	252[1]	0.6	8.6	0.3[2]	4.0[2]	...	...	...	Dominica
750[1]	94[1]	764	93	256	31	2.5[2]	0.3[2]	...	...	...	Dominican Republic
...	...	...	...	...	...	...	...	...	...	...	East Timor
2,500	205	991	81	243	20	30[8]	2.6[8]	225	18	15	Ecuador
7,900	120	3,972	60	91	1.4	31[1]	0.5[1]	600	9.1	100	Egypt
800	133	482	80	106	18	...	...	...	...	30	El Salvador
37[2]	92[2]	5.6	13	0.3	0.7	0.1[2]	0.3[2]	...	...	200	Equatorial Guinea
50	14	24	6.7	...	...	0.8[2]	0.2[2]	...	...	0.3	Eritrea
720	496	498	344	247	170	13	8.7	50	34	150	Estonia

Communications (continued)

country	publishing (latest)							postal services				telecommunications	
	books		periodicals		daily newspapers			post offices, 1998				radio, 1997	
	number of titles	number of copies ('000)	number of titles	number of copies ('000)	number	total circulation ('000)	circulation per 1,000 persons	number	persons per office	pieces of mail handled ('000,000)	pieces handled per person	receivers (all types; '000)	receivers per 1,000 persons
Ethiopia	240	674	...	...	4	86	1.5	534	112,000	27	0.3	11,750	202
Faroe Islands	...	...	...	...	1	6.0	136	42[3]	1,190[3]	10[3]	161[3]	26	582
Fiji	401	2,256	...	...	1	40	50	318	2,520	40	35	500	636
Finland	13,104	...	5,711	...	56	2,332	455	1,601	3,220	1,614	305	7,770	1,498
France	34,766	1,041	2,672	120,018	117	12,700	218	17,038	3,450	26,115	436	55,300	946
French Guiana	...	...	...	...	1	2.0	7.0	...	...	...	...	104	650
French Polynesia	...	...	...	...	4	24	108	97	2,370	28	102	128	574
Gabon	...	...	...	...	2	33	30	108	11,000	5.9	2.2	208	183
Gambia, The	14[15]	10[15]	10	885	1	2.0	1.7	...	...	...	...	196	165
Gaza Strip	...	...	...	...	...	...	...	...	...	...	...	...	...
Georgia	581[4]	834[4]	...	...	9	84	111	1,190[3]	4,560[3]	1,025[7, 11]	188[7, 11]	3,020	590
Germany	71,515	...	9,010	395,036	375	25,500	311	14,500	5,650	21,105[3]	249[3]	77,800	948
Ghana	28	648	121	774	4	250	14	1,010	18,800	225	3.4	4,400	236
Greece	4,225	...	...	...	156	1,622	153	1,225	8,590	392[1, 10]	37[1, 10]	5,020	475
Greenland	...	...	...	...	2	1.0	18	75[3]	800[3]	7.8[3]	72[3]	27	483
Grenada	...	...	4	89	1[16]	4.0[16]	45[16]	58[7]	1,550[7]	...	...	57	615
Guadeloupe	...	...	...	...	1	35	81	...	...	...	...	113	258
Guam	...	...	...	...	1	26	180	...	...	...	...	221	1,400
Guatemala	...	...	...	...	7	338	33	540[7]	19,700[7]	79[7]	7.7[7]	835	79
Guernsey	...	...	...	...	...	...	...	18	3,440	10[10]	169[10]	...	...
Guinea	...	...	3	5.0	...	...	...	96	47,400	7.9	0.4	357	49
Guinea-Bissau	...	...	...	...	1	6.0	5.4	18[1]	60,600[1]	31[12, 17]	0.3[2, 17]	49	43
Guyana	42[4]	508[4]	...	...	2	42	50	85[3]	10,000[3]	4.0[3, 11]	4.7[3, 11]	420	498
Haiti	...	...	...	...	4	20	2.5	85	90,000	1.2[17]	0.2[17]	415	53
Honduras	22	80	...	...	7	320	55	435[2]	13,700[2]	35[2]	3.0[2]	2,450	410
Hong Kong	...	...	598	...	52	5,000	800	125	53,500	1,254	175	3,700[1]	586[1]
Hungary	9,193	53,194	1,203	14,927	40	1,895	189	3,236	3,120	1,046	103	7,010	690
Iceland	1,527	...	938	384	5	145	535	94[1]	2,870[1]	73[1]	254[1]	260	950
India	11,903	...	...	...	3,037	22,969	27	153,021	6,240	16,394	16	116,000	120
Indonesia	4,018[15]	8,103[15]	115	4,173	69	4,665	23	20,139	10,200	758	3.4	31,500	155
Iran	15,073	87,861	318	6,166	32	1,651	24	13,715	4,490	274	4.2	17,000	263
Iraq	...	...	...	...	4	407	20	...	...	69	2.1	4,850	229
Ireland	...	...	...	...	6	543	153	1,912	1,940	748	170	2,550	697
Isle of Man	...	...	...	...	...	...	...	36	1,940	21[1, 5]	300[1, 5]	...	...
Israel	2,310[18]	9,368[18]	...	...	34	1,650	291	664	8,990	601	95	3,070	524
Italy	35,236	278,821	9,951	80,469	74	5,985	105	13,967[3]	4,120[3]	5,850[3]	99[3]	50,500	880
Jamaica	...	...	...	...	3	158	63	688	3,690	67	19	1,215	483
Japan	56,221[4]	400,013[4]	2,926	...	122	72,705	580	24,678	5,120	25,731[3]	202[3]	120,500	956
Jersey	...	...	...	...	...	...	...	23[3]	3,650[3]	62[3]	468[3]	...	...
Jordan	511	2,673[4]	31	43	4	250	45	687	9,170	118[3]	17[3]	1,660	271
Kazakhstan	1,226	21,014	...	...	3	500	30	3,580	4,700	201[2, 10]	0.01[2, 10]	6,470	395
Kenya	300[4]	452	...	...	4	263	9.4	1,033	28,100	413	14	3,070	108
Kiribati	...	...	...	...	...	...	...	25[3]	3,200[3]	1.9[3]	1.2[3]	17	212
Korea, North	...	...	...	...	3	4,500	200	...	...	...	...	3,360	146
Korea, South	30,487[4]	142,804[4]	...	...	60	18,000	394	3,610	12,900	3,631	77	47,500	1,039
Kuwait	196[19]	6,107	...	...	8	635	376	51[3]	35,500[3]	99[8]	68[8]	1,175	678
Kyrgyzstan	351	1,980	...	...	3	67	15	914[3]	5,080[3]	39[3, 10]	8.5[3, 10]	520	119
Laos	88[4]	995[4]	...	...	3	18	4.0	106	48,700	5.2	0.9	730	145
Latvia	1,965	7,734	213	1,660	24	616	246	978	2,500	37	12	1,760	715
Lebanon	...	...	...	...	15	435	141	268[3]	11,700[3]	3.9[3]	1.2[3]	2,850	907
Lesotho	...	...	...	...	2	15	7.6	157	13,100	64	16	104	52
Liberia	...	...	...	...	6	35	16	34[1]	8,260[1]	...	...	790	329
Libya	26	2,645	...	...	4	71	14	342	15,600	39	3.5	1,350	259
Liechtenstein	...	...	...	...	2	19	606	12[1]	2,500[1]	17[13]	0.6[13]	21	658
Lithuania	3,645	14,915	269	...	19	344	92	978[3]	3,790[3]	51	11	1,900	513
Luxembourg	681	...	508	...	5	135	327	106	3,960	169	340	285	683
Macau	67	99	16	...	10	197	448	17	25,300	19	30	160	356
Macedonia	892	2,496	74	347	3	41	19	294	6,800	27	11	410	206
Madagascar	119	296	55	108	5	66	4.6	764	19,700	26	1.5	3,050	209
Malawi	117[4, 20]	9,174[4, 20]	...	...	1	25	2.6	314	34,100	44	3.4	2,600	258
Malaysia	5,843	29,040	25	996	42	3,345	163	1,382	7,490	993[5]	96[5]	9,100	434
Maldives	...	...	...	...	2	5.0	18	249[3]	1,080[3]	2.5	5.9	34	129
Mali	14[4]	28[4]	...	...	3	12	1.2	124	86,200	3.4	0.2	570	55
Malta	404	...	359	...	2	48	130	51[11]	7,450[11]	14[11]	34[11]	255	669
Marshall Islands	...	...	...	...	...	...	...	...	...	...	...	...	...
Martinique	...	...	...	...	1	30	78	...	...	...	...	82	213
Mauritania	...	...	...	...	2	1.0	0.5	61	41,500	4.2	0.5	360	146
Mauritius	80	163	62	...	6	85	76	101	11,500	63	47	420	371
Mayotte	...	...	...	...	...	...	...	...	...	...	...	50[1]	427[1]
Mexico	...	...	158	13,097	295	9,030	97	9,432	10,600	1,133	9.4	31,000	329
Micronesia	...	...	...	...	...	...	...	...	...	...	...	70[1]	667[1]
Moldova	921	2,779	76	196	4	261	59	1,276	3,430	41	8.1	3,220	736
Monaco	41	722	3	38	1	8.0	263	...	...	...	...	34	1,039
Mongolia	285[4]	959[4]	45	6,361	4	68	27	339[3]	7,050[3]	1.1[3]	0.3[3]	360	142
Morocco	918	1,836	...	...	22	704	27	1,469	18,900	240	7.7	6,640	247
Mozambique	...	3,490	...	...	2	49	2.7	353	47,900	6.8	0.1	730	40
Myanmar (Burma)	3,660	4,038	...	...	5	449	10	1,238	37,500	88[2]	1.9[2]	4,200	96
Namibia	106	...	...	...	4	30	19	115	14,400	66[10]	4.0[10]	232	143
Nauru	...	...	...	...	...	...	...	1[3]	10,000[3]	...	...	7.0	609
Nepal	...	...	...	...	29	250	11	4,156	5,260	29[1, 5]	1.4[1, 5]	840	38
Netherlands, The	34,067	...	367	19,283	38	4,753	305	2,387	6,580	7,009[21]	447[21]	15,300	980
Netherlands Antilles	...	...	...	...	6	70	334	16	12,625	...	...	217	1,031
New Caledonia	...	...	...	...	3	24	127	54	3,700	21	75	107	527
New Zealand	...	...	126	3,991	23	804	223	...	...	...	...	3,750	997
Nicaragua	...	...	...	...	4	135	30	183	26,300	8.3	1.2	1,240	265

television, 1998		telephones, 1998		cellular phones, 1998		fax, 1998		personal computers, 1998		Internet users, 1998	country
receivers (all types; '000)	receivers per 1,000 persons	main lines ('000)	main lines per 1,000 persons	cellular subscrip-tions ('000)	subscrip-tions per 1,000 persons	receivers ('000)	receivers per 1,000 persons	units ('000)	units per 1,000 persons	('000)	
340	6.0	164	2.9	...	...	2.5	0.04	35	0.6	6.0	Ethiopia
14[1]	298[1]	24	544	6.5	147	...	...	...	...	...	Faroe Islands
80	102	77	98	8.0	10	3.4	4.3	...	...	5.0	Fiji
3,300	640	2,855	553	2,947	571	198[3]	38[3]	1,800	349	1,473	Finland
36,000	603	34,000	570	11,210	188	2,800[3]	47[3]	12,400	208	3,500	France
27[1]	180[1]	46	277	...	...	...	...	...	...	...	French Guiana
42	183	53	232	11	48	3.0	13	...	...	3.0	French Polynesia
65	56	37[3]	33[3]	9.5[3]	8.3[3]	0.5[3]	0.4[3]	10	8.6	2.0	Gabon
4.0	3.2	26	21	5.0	4.1	1.1[3]	0.9[3]	4.0	3.2	2.5	Gambia, The
...	...	...	...	...	...	...	...	...	...	...	Gaza Strip
2,580	474	629	115	60	11	0.5[7]	0.1[7]	0.7	0.1	5.0	Georgia
47,590	580	46,530	567	13,925	170	6,000	73	25,000	305	7,500	Germany
1,900	99	144	7.5	22[3]	1.2[3]	5.0[2]	0.3[2]	40	2.1	6.0	Ghana
5,000	472	5,536	522	2,057	194	40[1]	3.8[1]	550	52	350	Greece
21[1]	356[1]	25	446	8.9	159	...	...	...	...	...	Greenland
32[1]	351[1]	27	298	1.4	15	0.3[2]	3.1[2]	...	...	...	Grenada
116[1]	269[1]	197	445	...	...	3.4[2]	8.1[2]	...	...	...	Guadeloupe
102[1]	667[1]	71[3]	453[3]	5.7[3]	36[3]	...	...	...	...	...	Guam
660	61	517	48	111	10	10[7]	1.0[7]	90	8.3	50	Guatemala
...	...	48	776	12	191	0.7[2]	11[2]	...	...	...	Guernsey
330	43	37	4.8	22	2.8	2.8	0.4	25	3.2	0.5	Guinea
...	...	8.1	7.0	...	...	0.5	0.4	...	...	0.3	Guinea-Bissau
55	65	60	70	1.4	1.7	...	...	20	24	2.0	Guyana
36[1]	5.0[1]	60[3]	8.0[3]	...	...	...	...	...	...	...	Haiti
590	94	250	40	35	5.6	...	...	50	8.0	18	Honduras
2,884	431	3,729	558	3,174	475	363	54	1,700	254	1,000	Hong Kong
4,500	442	3,423	336	1,070	105	180	18	600	59	300	Hungary
100	362	178	646	91	331	4.1[8]	15[8]	90	326	100	Iceland
70,000	71	21,594	22	1,195	1.2	150[3]	0.2[3]	2,700	2.7	500	India
28,000	136	5,572	27	1,066	5.2	185	0.9	1,700	8.2	300	Indonesia
10,300	157	7,355	112	390	5.9	30[7]	0.5[7]	...	...	100	Iran
1,700[1]	82[1]	675	31	...	...	...	...	...	...	...	Iraq
1,500	407	1,600	435	946	257	100[3]	27[3]	1,000	272	300	Ireland
...	...	...	...	...	...	...	...	...	...	...	Isle of Man
1,900	318	2,819	471	2,147	359	140[2]	25[2]	1,300	217	450	Israel
28,000	488	25,986	453	20,489	357	1,800[3]	31[3]	10,000	174	3,000	Italy
480	189	419[3]	166[3]	55[1]	22[1]	1.6[13]	0.6[13]	100	39	50	Jamaica
90,000	712	63,580	503	47,285	374	16,000	126	30,000	237	16,740	Japan
...	...	69	751	18	200	0.7[2]	8.0[2]	...	...	1.0[1]	Jersey
520	85	511	83	70	12	52	8.4	77	12	61	Jordan
3,890	238	1,775	108	30	1.8	1.6[3]	0.1[3]	...	...	20	Kazakhstan
640	22	288	9.9	6.8	0.2	3.8[2]	0.1[2]	100	3.4	15	Kenya
2.0[2]	25[2]	2.8	34	...	...	0.2[2]	2.5[2]	...	...	...	Kiribati
1,080[1]	48[1]	1,100	46	—	—	3.0	0.1	...	...	...	Korea, North
16,056	346	20,089	433	14,019	302	400[2]	8.6[2]	7,282	157	3,103	Korea, South
890	491	427	236	250	138	50	28	190	105	60	Kuwait
200[1]	45[1]	355	76	1.3	0.3	...	...	...	...	2.5	Kyrgyzstan
50	10	28	5.5	6.4	1.2	0.5[7]	0.1[7]	5.0[1]	1.0[1]	...	Laos
1,550	630	741	302	167	68	0.9[2]	0.3[2]	20[2]	7.9[2]	100	Latvia
1,120	351	620	194	500	157	3.0[13]	1.1[13]	125	39.2	100	Lebanon
31	15	20	9.7	9.8	4.8	0.6[2]	0.3[2]	...	...	0.2	Lesotho
60[1]	27[1]	6.4[3]	2.2[3]	...	...	...	...	...	...	0.1	Liberia
680[1]	122[1]	500	91	20	3.6	...	...	...	...	...	Libya
11[1]	342[1]	20	618	...	...	...	...	...	...	...	Liechtenstein
1,550	418	1,110	300	268	72	6.2[3]	1.7[3]	200	54	80	Lithuania
242[2]	593[2]	293	691	130	308	20	47	310	731	50	Luxembourg
123	285	174	403	75	175	6.8	16	40[2]	94[2]	30	Macau
500	250	439	220	30	15	3.0[3]	1.5[3]	...	...	20	Macedonia
340	22	47	3.0	13	0.8	...	...	25	1.6	3.0	Madagascar
26	2.5	37	3.5	10	1.0	1.3	0.1	8.0	0.8	2.0	Malawi
3,700	170	4,384	202	2,200	101	175	8.0	1,300	60	800	Malaysia
10[3]	38[3]	20	72	1.6	5.8	3.5[2]	14[2]	3.0[2]	12[2]	1.5	Maldives
130	12	27	2.5	4.5	0.4	...	...	9.0	0.8	1.0	Mali
200	521	192	499	22	59	6.0	16	100	260	20	Malta
...	...	3.7	62	0.3	5.8	...	...	...	...	...	Marshall Islands
65[1]	169[1]	172	443	55	141	20[2]	52[2]	36[2]	93[2]	...	Martinique
231	91	15	5.8	...	...	4.3	1.7	15	5.9	1.0	Mauritania
260	227	245	214	60	53	30	26	100	87	12	Mauritius
3.5[1]	30[1]	12	95	...	...	...	...	...	...	...	Mayotte
25,000	261	9,927	104	3,349	35	285[3]	3.0[3]	4,500	47	1,350	Mexico
2.0	21	9.1	80	...	...	0.5	4.7	...	...	1.0	Micronesia
1,300	297	657	150	7.0	1.6	0.7	0.2	28	6.4	11	Moldova
24[1]	727[1]	33	991	12	360	...	...	...	...	...	Monaco
152	61	96	38	5.3	2.1	6.4[3]	2.7[3]	13[3]	5.4[3]	1.2[3]	Mongolia
4,500	162	1,515	55	117	4.2	18[3]	0.6[3]	200	7.2	40	Morocco
95	5.0	75	4.0	6.7	0.4	7.2[7]	0.4[7]	40	2.1	3.5	Mozambique
3,450[2]	76[2]	229	5.2	8.5	0.2	2.3	0.05	...	...	...	Myanmar (Burma)
63	38	114	69	20	12	...	...	40	24	5.0	Namibia
...	...	1.7	150	0.8	75	...	...	...	...	...	Nauru
85	3.7	202	8.8	...	...	5.0	0.2	50	2.2	15	Nepal
8,700	552	9,337	593	3,351	213	600[3]	38[3]	5,000	318	1,600	Netherlands, The
67[1]	346[1]	76[2]	366[2]	16	75	...	...	...	...	...	Netherlands Antilles
95	461	49	239	13	63	2.2[7]	12[7]	...	...	0.5[1]	New Caledonia
1,950	512	1,868	490	790	207	65[2]	18[2]	1,100	289	600	New Zealand
310[1]	73[1]	140	30	20	4.3	...	...	35	7.5	15	Nicaragua

Communications (continued)

country	publishing (latest)							postal services				telecommunications	
	books		periodicals		daily newspapers			post offices, 1998				radio, 1997	
	number of titles	number of copies ('000)	number of titles	number of copies ('000)	number	total circulation ('000)	circulation per 1,000 persons	number	persons per office	pieces of mail handled ('000,000)	pieces handled per person	receivers (all types; '000)	receivers per 1,000 persons
Niger	5[4]	11[4]	...	...	1	2	0.2	53	190,000	3.4	0.3	680	70
Nigeria	1,314	18,800	...	...	25	2,740	27	3,971	26,800	391	2.0	23,500	226
Northern Mariana Islands	...	...	...	...	...	...	...	...	...	...	...	11[1]	190[1]
Norway	6,900[6, 18]	...	8,017	...	83	2,578	593	1,534[3]	210[3]	2,524[3]	555[3]	4,030	917
Oman	7[4]	21[4]	15	...	4	63	27	90[2]	23,700[2]	43	7.1	1,400	607
Pakistan	124	714	...	...	264	2,840	22	13,294	9,820	413	2.9	13,500	94
Palau	...	...	...	...	...	...	...	...	...	...	...	12	663
Panama	...	...	...	...	7	166	62	176	15,700	18	4.4	815	299
Papua New Guinea	122	...	...	...	2	65	15	108[22]	39,800[22]	39[22]	10[22]	410	91
Paraguay	152	...	...	...	5	213	43	326	16,000	4.6	0.5	925	182
Peru	612	1,836	...	...	74	2,000	85	963	25,800	43	1.3	6,650	273
Philippines	1,507	14,718[4]	1,570	9,468	47	5,700	82	3,023[7]	22,600[7]	3,205[1]	12[1]	11,500	161
Poland	14,104	80,306	5,260	75,358	55	4,351	113	7,836	4,930	2,503	63	20,200	522
Portugal	7,868[9]	26,942	984	10,208	27	740	75	3,712	2,660	1,201	117	3,020	306
Puerto Rico	...	...	...	...	3	475	127	...	...	...	...	2,700	714
Qatar	209[15]	2,205	11	47	5	90	161	26	20,800	20[11]	38[11]	256	450
Réunion	69	...	...	...	3	55	83	...	...	...	...	173	257
Romania	7,199	38,374	987	...	69	6,800	297	6,324	3,560	327	14	7,200	319
Russia	36,237	421,387	2,751	387,832	285	15,517	105	43,900[3]	3,350[3]	5,614[3, 5]	38[3, 5]	61,500	417
Rwanda	...	...	15	101	1	0.5	0.1	39	169,000	3.8	0.4	601	101
St. Kitts and Nevis	...	...	10	44	...	...	...	7	5,710	2.6	46	28	701
St. Lucia	...	...	...	...	...	...	...	63	2,380	2.3[10]	15[10]	111	746
St. Vincent and the Grenadines	...	...	...	...	1	1.0	9.0	41[3]	2,680[3]	...	...	77	690
Samoa	...	...	...	...	...	...	...	38	4,470	0.9	3.0	178	1,035
San Marino	...	...	15	9	3	2.0	72	10[1]	3,000[1]	...	...	16	610
São Tomé and Príncipe	...	...	...	...	...	...	...	18	7,780	0.3	0.6	38	272
Saudi Arabia	3,900[4]	14,493[4, 20]	471	...	13	1,105	59	1,421	14,200	1,246	45	6,250	321
Senegal	...	...	...	...	1	45	5.3	134	69,200	12	0.7	1,240	141
Seychelles	...	...	...	...	1	3.0	46	5	16,000	5.2	49	42	560
Sierra Leone	...	...	...	...	1	20	4.7	54[2]	83,500[2]	1.1[2]	0.1[2]	1,121	253
Singapore	...	...	...	...	8	1,095	324	939	4,120	772[3]	184[3]	2,550	744
Slovakia	3,800	6,139	424	8,725	19	989	185	1,728	3,120	518	90	3,120	581
Slovenia	3,441	6,267	784	...	7	397	206	545	3,630	387	189	805	403
Solomon Islands	...	...	...	...	...	...	...	127	3,150	4.3[2]	11[2]	57	141
Somalia	...	...	...	...	2	10	1.2	...	...	...	...	470	53
South Africa	5,418	31,349	11	2,149	17	1,288	34	2,449	17,200	2,170[5]	52[5]	13,750	355
Spain	46,330	192,019	...	...	94	3,931	99	4,093	9,620	4,565	112	13,100	331
Sri Lanka	4,115	19,650	...	...	9	530	29	4,282	4,380	463	23	3,850	211
Sudan, The	...	...	...	...	5	737	27	491	57,600	4.4[1]	0.1[1]	7,550	272
Suriname	47[4]	21[4]	...	...	4	50	116	33	12,400	...	...	300	728
Swaziland	...	...	...	...	3	24	27	60[3]	15,200[3]	21[3]	18[3]	155	168
Sweden	13,496	...	373	19,242	94	3,933	446	1,720[1]	5,140[1]	4,570[1]	503[1]	8,250	932
Switzerland	15,371	...	60	4,561	88	2,383	330	3,630[1]	1,950[1]	4,230[13]	601[13]	7,100	979
Syria	598	310[4]	30	192	8	287	20	619	25,200	19	1.0	4,150	278
Taiwan	...	...	...	...	...	4,000	188	...	...	...	...	8,620[1]	402[1]
Tajikistan	132[4]	997[4]	11	130	2	120	20	706[3]	8,570[3]	3.0[3]	0.4[3]	850	143
Tanzania	172[4]	364[4]	...	...	3	120	3.9	612	52,400	55	1.3	8,800	280
Thailand	8,142	...	1,522	...	30	3,800	65	4,265	14,300	1,315	21	13,959	234
Togo	...	...	...	...	1	15	3.6	50[3]	86,400[3]	8.3[3]	0.7[3]	940	219
Tonga	...	...	...	...	1	7.0	71	1.8[8]	55,600[8]	4.0[8]	40[8]	61	400
Trinidad and Tobago	26	30	...	...	4	156	121	245	5,220	30[2]	16[2]	680	533
Tunisia	720	6,000[20]	170	1,748	8	280	31	947[2]	9,740[2]	117[2]	12[2]	2,060	224
Turkey	6,546	...	3,554	...	57	6,845	111	16,984	3,740	1,088	16	11,300	178
Turkmenistan	450[4]	5,493[4]	...	...	...	...	...	1,673[1]	2,730[1]	27[1]	6.0[1]	1,225	289
Tuvalu	...	...	...	...	...	...	...	...	...	...	...	4.0	384
Uganda	288	2,229[18]	26	158	2	40	2.1	313	67,200	18[3]	0.5[3]	2,600	130
Ukraine	6,225	68,876	717	2,521	44	2,780	54	15,227	3,320	374	6.3	45,050	882
United Arab Emirates	293[20]	5,117[20]	80	922	7	384	170	243	11,190	182	39	820	355
United Kingdom	107,263	...	...	...	99	19,332	332	18,760	3,130	19,556	325	84,500	1,443
United States	68,175	...	11,593	...	1,520	59,990	212	38,159	7,090	197,688	729	575,000	2,116
Uruguay	934	1,970	...	...	36	950	296	942	3,490	16	6.0	1,970	603
Uzbekistan	1,003	30,914	81	684	3	75	3.0	3,044[3]	7,700[3]	12[3]	0.4[3]	10,800	465
Vanuatu	...	...	...	...	...	...	...	...	...	...	...	62	350
Venezuela	3,468[4]	7,420[4]	...	...	86	4,600	206	407	57,600	141	5.1	10,750	472
Vietnam	5,581	83,000	338	2,710	10	300	4.0	3,075	25,200	...	...	8,200	107
Virgin Islands (U.S.)	...	...	...	...	3	42	326	9[3]	2,000[3]	3.6[7, 11]	0.2[7, 11]	107	1,119
West Bank	...	...	...	...	...	...	...	...	...	...	...	...	...
Western Sahara	...	...	...	...	...	...	...	...	...	...	...	56	211
Yemen	...	...	...	...	3	230	15	265	64,400	5.5	0.1	1,050	64
Yugoslavia	5,367	16,669	395	...	18	1,128	110	1,783	5,940	242	19	3,150	296
Zambia	...	...	...	...	3	114	14	195	45,000	16	0.8	1,030	120
Zimbabwe	232	...	28	680	2	209	19	296	42,800	137	9.4	1,140	102

television, 1998		telephones, 1998		cellular phones, 1998		fax, 1998		personal computers, 1998		Internet users, 1998	country
receivers (all types; '000)	receivers per 1,000 persons	main lines ('000)	main lines per 1,000 persons	cellular subscriptions ('000)	subscriptions per 1,000 persons	receivers ('000)	receivers per 1,000 persons	units ('000)	units per 1,000 persons	('000)	
270	27	18	1.8	1.3	0.1	0.3	0.03	3.0	0.3	0.3	Niger
7,200	68	407	3.8	20	0.2	...	...	650	6.1	...	Nigeria
...	...	20[3]	400[3]	1.2[2]	25[2]	...	...	...	...	...	Northern Mariana Islands
2,600	585	2,935	660	2,107	474	220[3]	50[3]	1,660	373	1,000	Norway
132[2]	61[2]	220	92	103	43	6.4	2.7	50	21	20	Oman
2,800[2]	22[2]	2,757	19	202	1.4	268	1.8	561	3.8	62	Pakistan
...	...	...	...	...	...	...	...	...	...	...	Palau
530	192	419	151	80	29	...	...	75	27	30	Panama
40[1]	9.1[1]	47[1]	11[1]	3.0[1]	0.7[1]	0.8[7]	0.2[7]	...	...	...	Papua New Guinea
530[1]	107[1]	288	55	215	41	1.7[13]	0.4[13]	50	10	10	Paraguay
3,600	145	1,555	63	743	30	15[2]	0.6[2]	450	18	0.2	Peru
8,000	110	2,700	37	1,734	24	50	0.7	1,100	15	0.2	Philippines
16,000	413	8,812	228	1,928	50	55[2]	1.4[2]	1,700	44	1,581	Poland
5,400	542	4,117	413	3,076	309	70	7.0	810	81	600	Portugal
1,250	324	1,322[3]	345[3]	580	150	543[8]	149[8]	...	...	100	Puerto Rico
490	846	150	260	66	114	10	18	70	121	20	Qatar
123[1]	185[1]	243	356	50.3	74	1.9[2]	2.9[2]	...	...	...	Réunion
5,400	240	3,649	162	643	29	21[2]	0.9[2]	230	10	0.2	Romania
62,000	421	29,031	197	747	5.1	53	0.4	6,000	41	1,000	Russia
10[2]	1.7[2]	11	1.6	...	...	0.5[2]	0.1[2]	...	...	0.1	Rwanda
10[1]	251[1]	17[3]	438[3]	0.4	11	...	...	...	...	...	St. Kitts and Nevis
31[1]	217[1]	40	266	1.9	12	...	...	...	...	...	St. Lucia
18[1]	159[1]	21	188	0.8	6.7	...	...	...	...	...	St. Vincent and the Grenadines
9.0	52	8.5	49	3.0	17	0.5	2.9	0.9	5.2	0.4	Samoa
9.0	358	19	773	5.0	196	...	...	...	...	...	San Marino
22[1]	14[1]	3.1	22	...	...	0.2[2]	1.5[2]	...	...	...	São Tomé and Príncipe
5,300	263	2,878	143	627	31	150[2]	8.2[2]	1,000	50	20	Saudi Arabia
370	41	140	16	22	2.4	...	...	120	13	7.5	Senegal
12	157	19	248	3.8	50	0.6[1]	8.5[1]	9.5	124	2.0	Seychelles
60	13	17	3.8	...	...	2.5	0.5	...	...	5.0	Sierra Leone
1,120	354	1,778	562	1,095	346	100	32	1,450	458	750	Singapore
2,600[1]	486[1]	1,539	286	465	86	54	10	350	65	500	Slovakia
710	356	757	380	162	81	21	10	500	251	200	Slovenia
6.0	14	7.9	19	0.7	1.7	0.7	1.7	...	...	2.0	Solomon Islands
129[1]	13[1]	15[2]	1.7[2]	...	...	...	...	...	...	...	Somalia
5,450	134	5,075	125	2,500	61	150[3]	3.6[3]	2,100	52	1,266	South Africa
20,000	508	16,289	414	7,051	179	700[1]	18[1]	5,700	145	1,733	Spain
1,800	98	524	28	174	9.4	11[7]	0.6[7]	76[3]	4.1[3]	20	Sri Lanka
2,450	86	162	5.7	8.6	0.3	18	0.6	55	1.9	0.5	Sudan, The
98	236	67	162	6.0	14	0.8	1.9	...	...	7.2	Suriname
108	113	29	30	4.7	4.9	1.2[1]	1.3[1]	...	...	1.0	Swaziland
4,700	531	5,965	674	4,108	464	450[1]	51[1]	3,200	361	3,500	Sweden
3,800[3]	536[3]	4,803	674	1,672	235	207[1]	29[1]	3,000	421	1,000	Switzerland
1,060	69	1,463	95	22	1.4	22	1.4	200	13	10	Syria
7,500	342	11,500	524	4,727	216	430[7]	20[7]	3,478	159	3,011	Taiwan
1,900	316	221	37	0.4	0.1	2.0	0.3	...	...	...	Tajikistan
670	21	122	3.8	38	1.2	2.0[13]	0.1[13]	55	1.7	3.0	Tanzania
14,500	240	5,036	84	1,957	32	150[3]	2.5[3]	1,300	22	200	Thailand
80	18	31	7.1	7.5	1.7	18	4.1	30	6.8	75	Togo
2.0[2]	20[2]	7.8	79	0.3	3.1	0.2[2]	2.0[2]	...	...	—	Tonga
430	335	264	206	26	20	5.0	3.9	60	47	20	Trinidad and Tobago
970	104	752	81	39	4.2	31[3]	3.4[3]	138	15	10	Tunisia
21,000	315	16,960	254	3,506	52	108[3]	1.7[3]	1,550	23	450	Turkey
865	201	354	82	3.0	0.7	...	...	...	...	...	Turkmenistan
0.1[1]	13[1]	0.6	55	...	...	...	...	...	...	...	Tuvalu
580	28	57	2.8	30	1.4	3.0[1]	0.2[1]	40	1.9	15	Uganda
21,000	413	9,698	191	116	2.3	12[7]	0.2[7]	700	14	150	Ukraine
720	306	915	389	493	210	50[3]	21[3]	250	106	200	United Arab Emirates
38,000	644	32,829	557	14,874	252	1,992[1]	34[1]	15,500	263	8,000	United Kingdom
231,000	849	179,822	661	85,018	312	21,000[3]	78[3]	124,000	456	60,000	United States
1,750	532	824	250	196	60	11[2]	3.5[2]	300	91	230	Uruguay
6,600	278	1,537	65	27	1.1	1.8	0.1	...	...	10	Uzbekistan
2.0[1]	13[1]	5.2	28	0.2	1.2	0.6[2]	3.6[2]	...	...	...	Vanuatu
4,300	185	2,712	117	2,015	87	70[3]	3.0[3]	1,000	43	350	Venezuela
3,600	46	2,000	26	187	2.4	20[1]	0.3[1]	500	6.4	10	Vietnam
67[1]	634[1]	65	548	40[3]	14[3]	...	...	...	...	...	Virgin Islands (U.S.)
...	...	167	58	20[2]	16[2]	...	...	...	...	...	West Bank
6[1]	24[1]	...	...	...	...	...	...	...	...	...	Western Sahara
4,800	284	250	15	18	1.1	2.8[2]	0.2[2]	...	...	4.0	Yemen
2,900	273	2,319	218	240	22	20	1.9	200	19	100	Yugoslavia
1,200	137	78	8.8	5.2	0.6	1.0	0.1	60	6.8	3.0	Zambia
390	34	212[3]	19[3]	55	4.8	4.1	0.4	130	11.4	10	Zimbabwe

[1]1996. [2]1995. [3]1997. [4]First editions only. [5]Domestic and foreign-dispatched only. [6]Not including school textbooks. [7]1994. [8]1993. [9]Including reprints. [10]Domestic only. [11]Foreign-dispatched and foreign-received only. [12]Millions of copies. [13]1992. [14]1985. [15]School textbooks and government publications only. [16]1980. [17]Foreign-received only. [18]Not including government publications. [19]Government publications only. [20]School textbooks only. [21]Domestic and foreign-received only. [22]1991.

Trade: external

The following table presents comparative data on the international, or foreign, trade of the countries of the world. The table analyzes data for both imports and exports in two ways: (1) into several major commodity groups defined in accordance with the United Nations system called the Standard International Trade Classification (SITC) and (2) by direction of trade for each country with major world trading blocs and partners. These commodity groupings are defined by the SITC code numbers beneath the column headings. The single-digit numbers represent broad SITC categories (in the SITC, called "sections"); the double-digit numbers represent subcategories ("divisions") of the single-digit categories (27 is a subcategory of 2); the three-digit number is a subcategory ("group") of the double-digit (667 is a subcategory of 66). Where a plus or minus sign is used before one of these SITC numbers, the SITC category or subcategory is being added to or subtracted from the aggregate implied by the total of the preceding sections. The SITC commodity aggregations used here are listed in the table at the end of this headnote. The full SITC commodity breakdown—some 3,118 basic headings—is presented in the 1986 United Nations publication *Standard International Trade Classification, Revision 3.*

The SITC was developed by the United Nations through its Statistical Commission as an outgrowth of the need for a standard system of aggregating commodities of external trade to provide international comparability of foreign trade statistics. The United Nations Statistical Commission has defined external merchandise trade as "all goods whose movement into or out of the customs area of a country compiling the statistics adds to or subtracts from the material resources of the country." Goods passing through a country for transport only are excluded, but goods entering for reexport, or deposited (as in a bonded warehouse, or free trade area) for reimport, are included. Statistics in this table refer only to goods and exclude purely financial transactions that are covered in the "Finance" and "National product and accounts" tables. Gold for fabrication (*e.g.*, as jewelry) is included; monetary and reserve gold are excluded.

For purposes of comparability of data, total value of imports and exports is given in this table in U.S. dollars. Conversions from currencies other than U.S. dollars are determined according to the average market rates for the year for which data are supplied; these are mainly as calculated by the International Monetary Fund (IMF) or other official sources. The commodity categories are given in terms of percentages of the total value of the country's import or export trade (with the exclusions noted above). Value is based on transaction value: for imports, the value at which the goods were purchased by the importer plus the cost of transportation and insurance to the frontier of the importing country (c.i.f. [cost, insurance,

Trade: external

country	year	imports												
		total value ('000,000 U.S.$)	Standard International Trade Classification (SITC) categories (%)							direction of trade (%)				
			food and agricultural raw materials (0 + 1 + 2 − 27 − 28 + 4)	mineral ores and concentrates (27 + 28 + 667)	fuels and other energy (3)	manufactured goods				from European Union (EU)[b]	from United States	from Eastern Europe[c]	from Japan	from all other[d]
						total[a] (5 + 6 − 667 + 7 + 8 + 9)	of which chemicals and related products (5)	of which machinery and transport equipment (7)	of which other[a] (6 − 667 + 8 + 9)					
Afghanistan	1996[1]	359.0	19.9[2]		2.7	77.4[3]	—	15.2	62.2[3]	16.5[4]	1.1[4]	8.3[4]	25.3[4]	48.8[4]
Albania	1997	950.2	28.4	0.5	3.2	68.0	6.9	21.3	39.7	83.4	0.2	4.9	—	11.5
Algeria	1996	9,105.6	34.2	0.2	1.2	64.4	8.7	30.8	24.9	62.5	10.2	2.3	2.6	22.3
American Samoa	1993[6]	427.5	63.1[2]		8.1	28.8[3]	0.2	5.5	23.1[3]	0.2[7]	73.4[7]	—[7]	8.5[7]	17.9[7]
Andorra	1998	1,080.5	24.2	3.9	3.5	68.4	10.7	25.8	31.9	88.2	2.3	0.2	3.2	6.1
Angola	1994	1,432.0	33.6[2, 5]		0.3[5]	66.1[3, 5]	9.1[5]	30.1[5]	26.9[3, 5]	50.0[4]	15.6[4]	6.2[4]	1.3[4]	26.9[4]
Antigua and Barbuda	1991	245.9	17.8[2]		9.9	72.3[3]	6.2	26.8	39.3[3]	41.3[8]	29.5[8]	—[8]	—[8]	29.2[8]
Argentina	1996	23,761.6	6.8	1.4	3.6	88.2	18.5	46.0	23.7	29.0	20.0	1.2	3.1	46.8
Armenia	1997	892.0	32.8	23.5[2]		43.7[3]	12.2	13.2	18.3[3]	20.3	13.0	29.9	0.3	36.4
Aruba	1998	832.5[9]	21.7	4.1	—	74.2	10.4	36.9	26.9	12.0	72.0	—	1.9	14.1
Australia	1997	61,832.5	6.2	0.7	6.1	86.9	10.8	46.3	29.8	24.3	22.1	0.3	13.7	39.7
Austria	1996	67,283.8	8.6	1.2	5.3	84.8	10.3	37.9	36.6	70.8	4.5	8.7	2.4	13.6
Azerbaijan	1997	794.0	29.2	12.3[2]		58.6[3]	9.9	27.6	21.1[3]	13.3	0.3	34.7	—	51.8
Bahamas, The	1997	1,622.0	18.4[2]		9.2	72.4[3]	10.3	28.7	33.3[3]	2.6[10]	93.0[10]	...	...	4.4[10]
Bahrain	1996	4,092.6	12.3	5.3	40.9	41.5	5.2	15.7	20.7	18.9	6.7	0.2	3.7	70.6
Bangladesh	1996[12]	6,225.3	21.3	1.0	7.2	70.5	7.7	19.2	43.6	11.0	4.0	1.0	7.0	77.0
Barbados	1997	995.3	20.4	0.4	8.3	70.9	10.5	29.2	31.3	14.9	45.4	0.1	6.8	32.8
Belarus	1997	8,689.0	15.3	27.7[2]		57.0[3]	16.0	19.9	21.2[3]	16.5	1.6	73.9	0.5	7.5
Belgium[13]	1997	152,106.2	12.2	9.4	7.1	71.3	14.6	29.7	26.9	72.2	7.5	2.3	2.4	15.6
Belize	1997	286.1	20.1	0.2	12.9	66.8	10.1	25.6	31.2	9.2	51.7	—	1.7	37.4
Benin	1991	408.0	32.9[2]		11.6	55.5[3]	7.5	13.7	34.4[3]	30.6	4.5	0.7	2.4	61.8
Bermuda	1993	588.9	20.5	0.1[2]	5.8	73.6[3]	13.9	23.3	36.3[3]	11.6	70.2	0.2	5.4	12.5
Bhutan	1994	91.5	23.0	0.5	11.5	65.0	8.4	30.2	26.4	9.4	1.3	—	13.9	75.4[17]
Bolivia	1997	1,909.2	9.7	0.9	7.6	81.8	12.2	48.8	20.9	14.7	23.2	0.1	12.4	49.6
Bosnia and Herzegovina	1998	1,193.2	24.3[2]		5.7	70.0[3]	10.5	28.2	31.3[3]	40.5	2.3	13.7[4]	1.0[4]	42.6[4]
Botswana	1997	2,261.9	16.6	2.7	5.6	75.0	7.3	37.6	30.2	8.2	...	—	...	91.8[20]
Brazil	1997	65,074.7	11.6	1.1	11.7	75.6	15.1	42.5	18.0	26.2	23.4	1.1	5.9	43.4
Brunei	1994	1,873.7	15.1	1.7	0.4	82.8	4.6	42.3	35.8	17.9	11.3	27.9	10.1	32.8
Bulgaria	1997	4,760.5	13.8	4.1	31.3	50.7	11.3	16.0	23.4	38.3	3.8	38.2	0.8	18.9
Burkina Faso	1997	586.5	25.6[2, 5]		11.6[5]	62.8[3, 5]	18.5[5]	20.8[5]	23.5[3, 5]	46.0	4.2	3.4	5.5	40.9
Burundi	1993	204.5	13.0	0.6	12.4	74.0	14.1	21.3	38.6	45.4	1.8	0.4	9.2	43.3
Cambodia	1993	403.9	17.2[22]	...	11.7	...	6.5[22]	17.0[22]	...	9.2[4]	4.5[4]	2.5[4]	12.2[4]	71.6[4]
Cameroon	1996	1,204.3	16.2	3.2	15.7	64.9	14.6	27.6	22.7	53.4	8.5	1.8	5.0	31.3
Canada	1997	196,029.2	6.9	1.6	4.5	87.0	7.9	51.7	27.3	9.9	67.6	0.5	4.6	17.5
Cape Verde	1994	210.1	32.8	—	3.6	63.6	5.1	36.0	22.5	75.0	2.3	0.7	5.0	17.0
Central African Republic	1996	179.9	25.9	0.4	8.1	65.6	7.9	37.4	20.3	48.6	1.7	—	8.7	41.1
Chad	1995	215.2	24.7	0.5	17.9	57.0	7.2	23.8	25.9	51.3	6.5	0.4	2.4	39.5
Chile	1997	18,110.9	7.9	0.6	10.0	81.5	11.2	43.5	26.8	21.9	23.9	0.4	5.8	48.0
China	1997	142,370.4	10.1	2.8	7.3	79.8	13.4	37.0	29.4	13.5	11.5	3.3	20.4	51.4
Colombia	1997	15,378.9	13.2	0.6	3.0	83.2	17.5	38.9	26.7	18.5	35.3	1.0	6.2	39.0
Comoros	1995	62.7	37.8[22]	...	12.4	49.8	1.1[22]	7.2[22]	41.5	49.5[4]	1.6[4]	—[4]	4.8[4]	44.1[4]
Congo, Dem. Rep. of the	1992	420.0	20.0[8]		13.8[8]	66.2[8]	4.4[8]	45.5[8]	16.3[8]	57.9[4]	4.9[4]	0.8[4]	2.7[4]	33.7[4]
Congo, Rep. of the	1995	556.0	21.7	0.4	19.6	58.3	13.8	20.3	24.2	45.4	8.0	0.1	2.2	44.3
Costa Rica	1996	3,885.7	12.9	0.2	8.6	78.2	17.3	23.9	37.0	10.1	49.9	0.4	3.8	35.9
Côte d'Ivoire	1996	2,812.0	19.1	0.8	23.1	57.0	15.8	20.9	20.3	49.9	5.9	2.3	4.1	37.8
Croatia	1997	9,122.4	12.3	0.7	9.4	77.7	10.2	33.5	34.0	59.5	3.0	12.3	1.5	23.6
Cuba	1997	3,560.0	19.8[2]		33.7	46.5[3]	8.4	19.8	18.3[3]	28.7	0.3	8.9	0.6	61.6
Cyprus	1997	3,698.1	28.0	0.6	8.3	63.0	8.0	21.7	33.3	47.6	19.0	6.7	5.3	21.5
Czech Republic	1997	27,183.6	8.7	1.4	8.7	81.2	11.4	37.8	32.0	61.5	3.8	20.7	1.9	12.1
Denmark	1997	44,492.4	15.8	0.5	3.9	79.8	10.1	33.7	36.1	70.1	5.0	3.4	2.0	19.5
Djibouti	1991	214.4	38.3	0.2	9.1	52.3	6.0	15.5	30.8	46.6	3.7	0.7[4]	7.2	41.8
Dominica	1996	129.9	29.7	0.2	6.5	63.6	13.2	21.7	28.6	18.8	40.9	0.1	5.6	34.6
Dominican Republic	1994	2,626.4	13.7[25]	0.3[25]	35.2[25]	50.7[25]	11.7[25]	23.2[25]	15.9[25]	2.0[4]	37.4[4]	—[4]	1.5[4]	59.1[4]
East Timor[27]	...	...	...	...	...	...	...	...	...	...	...	...	...	...
Ecuador	1997	4,510.7	12.1	0.2	8.5	79.1	18.2	36.0	24.9	16.7	30.5	1.4	5.8	45.5

and freight] valuation); for exports, the value at which the goods were sold by the exporter, including the cost of transportation and insurance to bring the goods onto the transporting vehicle at the frontier of the exporting country (f.o.b. [free-on-board] valuation).

The largest part of the information presented here comes from the United Nations' *Commodity Trade Statistics* (microfiche format) and *International Trade Statistics Yearbook.* These sources, however, cannot always provide the most recent data for all countries listed in this table and must be supplemented by national and regional information. In some cases where the original data were only available for an alternative trade classification, an approximation has been made of the SITC commodity groupings.

The notes that follow further define the column headings.

a. Also includes any unallocated commodities.
b. EU of 15 countries (Austria, Belgium, Denmark, Finland, France, Germany, Greece, Ireland, Italy, Luxembourg, The Netherlands, Portugal, Spain, Sweden, and the United Kingdom).
c. Includes Albania, Bulgaria, Czech Republic, Hungary, Poland, Romania, Slovakia, and European republics of the former U.S.S.R. (Belarus, Estonia, Latvia, Lithuania, Moldova, Russia, and Ukraine).
d. May include value of trade shown as not available (...) in any of the four preceding columns. May include any unspecified areas or countries.

... Not available.
— None, less than 0.05%, or not applicable.
Detail may not add to 100.0 or indicated subtotals because of rounding.

SITC category codes		
0		food and live animals
1		beverages and tobacco
2		crude materials, inedible, except fuels
	27	crude fertilizers and crude minerals (excluding coal, petroleum, and precious stones)
	28	metalliferous ores and metal scrap
3		mineral fuels, lubricants, and related materials (including coal, petroleum, natural gas, and electric current)
4		animal and vegetable oils, fats, and waxes
5		chemicals and related products not elsewhere specified
6		manufactured goods classified chiefly by material
	667	pearls, precious and semiprecious stones, unworked or worked
7		machinery and transport equipment
8		miscellaneous manufactured articles
9		commodities and transactions not classified elsewhere

exports													country
total value ('000,000 U.S.$)	Standard International Trade Classification (SITC) categories (%)							direction of trade (%)					
	food and agricultural raw materials (0 + 1 + 2 − 27 − 28 + 4)	mineral ores and concentrates (27 + 28 + 667)	fuels and other energy (3)	manufactured goods: total[a] (5 + 6 − 667 + 7 + 8 + 9)	of which chemicals and related products (5)	of which machinery and transport equipment (7)	of which other[a] (6 − 667 + 8 + 9)	to European Union (EU)[b]	to United States	to Eastern Europe[c]	to Japan	to all other[d]	
166.0	—— 63.0[2, 5] ——		...	37.0[3, 5]	...	...	...	19.3[4]	3.0[4]	8.4[4]	0.6[4]	68.7[4]	Afghanistan
210.5	25.2	7.8	1.8	65.3	0.8	5.7	58.8	87.5	1.5	0.6	0.1	10.4	Albania
11,099.2	1.3	0.4	92.9	5.4	2.6	0.4	2.4	60.0	15.3	5.1	0.5	19.0	Algeria
488.2	100.0	—	—	—	—	—	—	—[5]	100.0[5]	—[5]	—[5]	—[5]	American Samoa
57.8	11.9	1.5	—	86.7	6.5	30.7	49.5	87.4	0.2	0.3	8.5	3.6	Andorra
3,002.0	0.3	3.2	96.5	—	—	—	—	22.9[4]	70.2[4]	—[4]	0.3[4]	6.6[4]	Angola
39.8	—— 4.4[2] ——		25.0	70.6[3]	7.1	30.2	33.3[3]	15.0[8]	15.4[8]	—[8]	—[8]	69.5[8]	Antigua and Barbuda
23,809.6	55.8	0.3	13.0	31.0	5.7	10.9	14.4	19.3	8.3	1.3	2.2	69.0	Argentina
233.0	12.6	—— 7.7[2] ——		79.7[3]	5.8	14.7	59.2[3]	28.5	3.0	29.5	—	38.9	Armenia
42.8[9]	23.4	2.8	—	73.7	1.9	44.9	26.9	10.2	55.1	0.1	0.1	34.5	Aruba
62,566.5	29.4	11.9	17.8	40.9	3.6	13.3	24.0	10.2	7.5	0.5	19.9	61.8	Australia
57,830.5	7.3	0.8	1.2	90.6	9.3	40.6	40.6	64.2	3.2	12.3	1.5	18.8	Austria
781.0	7.3	—— 61.7[2] ——		31.0[3]	5.3	5.3	20.4[3]	10.8	2.8	30.1	0.1	56.2	Azerbaijan
181.4	—— 58.4[2] ——		—	41.6[3]	18.9	16.8	5.9[3]	14.6	73.4	...	...	11.9	Bahamas, The
4,602.0	2.1	0.4	66.5	31.0	3.2	1.0	26.7	1.6	2.3	—	4.3	91.8[11]	Bahrain
3,538.5	12.2	—	0.3	87.5	3.0	0.6	84.0	45.3	32.9	0.8	4.2	16.7	Bangladesh
283.0	35.1	0.3	16.1	48.6	13.0	14.0	21.6	20.2	14.7	—	0.4	64.8	Barbados
7,301.0	11.9	—— 9.5[2] ——		78.6[3]	17.5	31.1	30.0[3]	6.7	1.3	80.7	0.1	11.2	Belarus
166,041.0	11.3	7.9	3.1	77.8	16.5	28.3	33.1	73.2	4.9	3.1	1.0	17.8	Belgium[13]
176.2	82.7	—	2.2	15.2	0.5	2.6	12.0	40.0	46.7	—	—	13.2	Belize
43.0	—— 63.5[2] ——		29.0	7.5[3]	1.0	2.8	3.8[3]	18.6	18.7	—	0.4	62.3	Benin
35.3	5.6[14]	3.1[14, 15]	45.6[14]	45.8[14, 16]	9.5[14]	18.5[14]	17.8[14, 16]	27.0[14]	62.3[14]	—[14]	—[14]	10.6[14]	Bermuda
66.8	30.7	3.6	25.6[18]	40.1	20.4	—	19.8	—	—	—	—	100.0[19]	Bhutan
1,272.1	38.2	22.0	8.4	31.4	1.1	1.2	29.1	24.6	20.8	0.1	0.3	54.1	Bolivia
185.3	—— 37.3[2] ——		4.3	58.4[3]	3.9	11.0	43.5[3]	35.8	2.9	1.0[4]	0.1[4]	60.2[4]	Bosnia and Herzegovina
2,923.6	3.3	75.1	—	21.7	1.5	11.9	8.3	56.9	...	—	...	43.1[21]	Botswana
52,985.9	34.5	6.5	0.6	58.3	6.3	22.6	29.4	27.5	17.8	2.4	5.8	46.6	Brazil
2,110.4	—	—	98.7	1.3	—	—	1.3	—	1.1	—	72.3	26.5	Brunei
4,760.4	18.2	2.5	7.9	71.4	18.0	11.6	41.8	44.7	2.7	17.9	0.8	33.8	Bulgaria
228.9	83.5[5]	0.5[5]	—[5]	16.0[5]	0.1[5]	1.0[5]	14.9[5]	32.5	1.5	—	1.0	64.9	Burkina Faso
68.7	85.1	—	—	14.9	1.4	—	13.4	48.4	2.0[4]	—[4]	1.0[4]	47.3[4]	Burundi
219.1[23]	88.9[24]	...	...	...	...	...	...	15.5[4]	0.5[4]	0.5[4]	37.6[4]	45.9[4]	Cambodia
1,757.9	49.5	0.1	36.2	14.3	1.1	1.1	12.1	77.4	2.3	0.2	0.8	19.3	Cameroon
214,333.4	15.4	2.1	10.2	72.2	5.7	39.0	27.4	5.1	82.5	0.3	3.7	8.5	Canada
5.0[24]	50.6	0.6	—	48.9	0.1	2.2	46.6	98.3	0.1	—	—	1.6	Cape Verde
115.1	25.4	60.1	0.2	14.3	—	7.5	6.8	95.1	—	—	—	4.8	Central African Republic
252.0	88.2[14]	—[14]	—[14]	11.9[14]	6.5[14]	3.1[14]	2.3[14]	76.6[4]	2.4[4]	0.8[4]	2.4[4]	17.7[4]	Chad
16,678.3	34.3	15.3	0.3	50.1	4.6	2.6	43.0	24.5	14.6	0.5	16.1	44.3	Chile
182,791.7	8.6	0.9	3.8	86.7	5.5	23.9	57.4	13.1	17.9	2.0	17.4	49.6	China
11,530.2	37.0	1.4	31.4	30.1	9.2	3.8	17.1	22.7	37.8	1.2	3.1	35.2	Colombia
11.4	57.9	—	—	42.1	21.0[22]	—	21.2	44.7[4]	28.1	—	—	27.2[4]	Comoros
506.0	13.1	58.5[2, 15]	11.1	17.3[3, 16]	0.2	1.2	15.9[3, 16]	58.7	15.7[4]	4.5	6.5	14.6[4]	Congo, Dem. Rep. of the
1,089.8	9.3	0.3	87.6	2.7	—	0.4	2.3	41.3	28.5	—	0.3	29.9	Congo, Rep. of the
2,881.6	69.8	0.3	0.8	29.1	6.6	4.0	18.5	29.8	39.0	1.0	1.2	28.9	Costa Rica
4,446.1	68.2[14]	0.3[2, 14, 15]	15.4[14]	16.1[3, 14, 16]	3.3[14]	2.0[14]	10.9[3, 14, 16]	62.8	7.0	3.0	0.2	27.0	Côte d'Ivoire
4,340.9	18.3	1.2	9.8	70.7	12.7	17.3	40.7	51.2	2.2	8.9	0.1	37.5	Croatia
1,850.0	82.2[14]	8.4[2, 14, 15]	4.8[14]	4.6[3, 14, 16]	2.7[14]	0.6[14]	1.3[3, 14, 16]	29.5	0.5	20.4	5.9	43.7	Cuba
1,250.2	59.7	1.6	4.4	34.2	5.4	8.8	20.0	27.1	1.1	31.5	0.1	40.1	Cyprus
22,746.4	8.0	1.0	3.8	87.2	8.2	37.6	41.4	59.9	2.6	26.6	0.4	10.5	Czech Republic
48,800.5	26.5	0.5	3.8	69.2	9.9	26.9	32.4	60.9	4.0	5.4	2.9	26.7	Denmark
17.3	32.5	—	—	67.5	0.4	8.3	58.7	62.6	0.8	—	0.9	35.7	Djibouti
51.2	48.8	1.7	—	49.5	46.3	1.1	2.1	43.5	7.3	—	0.1	49.2	Dominica
2,007.8	20.7	0.1	—	79.2[26]	2.6	11.6	65.1[26]	8.6	83.6	—	0.8	6.9	Dominican Republic
...	...	...	...	...	...	...	...	...	...	...	...	...	East Timor[27]
5,214.2	60.7	0.1	29.7	9.5	1.4	2.0	6.1	19.3	38.2	3.8	3.0	35.7	Ecuador

Trade: external (continued)

country	year	imports												
		total value ('000,000 U.S.$)	Standard International Trade Classification (SITC) categories (%)							direction of trade (%)				
			food and agricultural raw materials (0 + 1 + 2 – 27 – 28 + 4)	mineral ores and concen-trates (27 + 28 + 667)	fuels and other energy (3)	manufactured goods				from European Union (EU)[b]	from United States	from Eastern Europe[c]	from Japan	from all other[d]
						total[a] (5 + 6 – 667 + 7 + 8 + 9)	of which chemicals and related products (5)	of which machinery and transport equipment (7)	of which other[a] (6 – 667 + 8 + 9)					
Egypt	1997	13,168.5	32.2	1.7	1.8	64.2	13.1	26.9	24.2	38.2	13.1	7.9	3.4	37.5
El Salvador	1997	2,961.5	19.8	0.4	11.4	68.5	17.0	26.5	25.0	8.9	41.4	0.9	3.1	45.8
Equatorial Guinea	1990	61.6	13.5	3.4	7.7	75.4	3.9	58.2	13.3	31.5	39.9	—	0.3[4]	28.3
Eritrea	1995	423.6	— 21.3[2] —		1.9	76.8[3]	6.0	45.2	25.6[3]	27.2[29]	5.9	...	...	66.9
Estonia	1997	4,438.8	18.6	1.2	8.2	72.0	9.3	34.0	28.7	59.1	3.8	21.5	3.3	12.2
Ethiopia	1993	771.6	17.4	0.1	21.6	60.9	13.8	26.8	20.3	39.3	9.5	—	4.1	47.2
Faroe Islands	1994	238.2	30.7	0.6	11.8	56.8	8.5	19.8	28.5	67.5	1.4	3.6	2.0	25.5
Fiji	1994	830.5	15.9	0.3	11.2	72.5	7.3	30.9	34.3	3.9	14.8	0.1	8.0	73.3
Finland	1997	31,001.1	9.2	4.0	9.7	77.0	11.3	39.3	26.4	57.5	7.3	10.9	5.3	18.9
France[31]	1997	266,575.4	12.1	1.1	8.2	78.6	12.1	36.3	30.2	61.0	8.8	2.9	3.3	24.0
French Guiana	1995	783.3	18.8	0.1	5.3	75.8	8.0	42.2	25.6	76.9	3.3	0.5	1.4	17.9
French Polynesia	1994	880.7	20.4[32]	0.2[32]	5.4[32]	74.1[32]	6.4[32]	35.9[32]	31.8[32]	44.8[29]	13.9	—	4.0	37.3
Gabon	1996	898.1	19.8	0.4	3.4	76.4	10.7	39.3	26.4	68.1	10.4	0.3	6.0	15.2
Gambia, The	1995[12]	141.3	— 35.3[2] —		14.4	50.3[3]	5.6	20.3	24.5[3]	47.3	5.2	0.7	3.5	43.3
Gaza Strip	1994	339.3	...	...	...	...	...	...	...	...	...	...	...	100.0[33]
Georgia	1997	940.0	36.4	— 28.5[2] —		35.1[3]	10.2	16.7	8.2[3]	22.4	7.5	27.9	—	42.2
Germany	1997	436,458.2	11.2	1.5	7.6	79.7	8.5	34.2	37.0	53.1	7.5	8.2	4.8	26.4
Ghana	1992	2,145.4	12.5	3.1	17.4	66.9	11.1	33.6	22.2	43.6	10.2	1.4	6.6	38.2
Greece	1997	25,208.6	17.4	0.8	6.5	75.3	12.9	29.8	32.7	65.0	3.8	6.5	3.8	20.9
Greenland	1997	374.1	16.5	0.4	9.7	73.4	3.6	26.2	43.6	76.0	3.1	0.3	2.9	17.7
Grenada	1996	151.4	29.0	0.3	9.7	60.9	8.1	22.1	30.8	15.1	42.6	0.2	3.7	38.4
Guadeloupe	1995	1,901.3	22.6	0.3	5.8	71.3	9.5	32.0	29.8	77.8	3.3	0.3	2.2	16.5
Guam	1992	450.0	16.9[37]	0.1[37]	46.9[37]	36.2[37]	2.3[37]	19.1[37]	14.8[37]	...	23.4[37]	...	19.9[37]	56.6[37]
Guatemala	1997	3,852.0	15.1	0.3	10.7	73.9	17.8	30.8	25.3	9.5	41.9	1.0	3.4	44.2
Guernsey[38]	...	...	...	...	...	...	...	...	...	...	...	...	...	...
Guinea	1994	687.0	10.8	...	9.9	...	...	22.3	...	54.3[4]	8.0[4]	0.7[4]	3.8[4]	33.2[4]
Guinea-Bissau	1997	88.6	42.7	...	10.7	46.6	...	23.7	...	39.5[4]	3.4[4]	—[4]	7.9[4]	49.2[4]
Guyana	1993	483.8	9.0	...	16.7	74.3	5.1	44.5	24.7	21.9[4]	27.9[4]	0.4[4]	18.2[4]	31.6[4]
Haiti	1993[6]	226.0	— 46.6[2] —		28.4	25.1[3]	6.9	5.4	12.8	18.1[4]	57.9[4]	...	4.8[4]	19.3[4]
Honduras	1997	2,435.1	20.4	0.1	10.4	69.1	13.7	26.1	29.3	4.3	61.2	0.5	2.9	31.1
Hong Kong	1997	213,300.0	6.9	1.7	1.9	89.5	6.3	37.8	45.4	11.2	7.7	0.5	13.5	67.2
Hungary	1997	21,234.1	6.7	0.4	9.2	83.6	10.8	41.3	31.5	62.4	3.7	16.6	3.3	13.9
Iceland	1997	2,019.5	11.8	2.3	7.6	78.3	8.0	37.3	33.0	58.1	9.4	4.1	4.9	23.5
India	1997[1]	39,112.8	7.8	10.5	29.3	52.5	12.7	18.7	21.1	26.5	9.2	2.2	5.6	56.4
Indonesia	1997	41,679.8	13.5	1.6	9.9	74.9	13.8	42.0	19.1	20.0	13.1	1.1	19.8	46.0
Iran	1992	30,712.1	— 11.4[2] —		1.3	87.4[3]	9.8	50.3	27.3[3]	49.8	2.7	2.4[4]	12.0	33.1
Iraq	1990	4,833.9	— 31.5[2] —		0.4	68.1[3]	8.8	30.3	28.9[3]	45.7[4]	10.8[4]	3.0[4]	4.6[4]	35.9[4]
Ireland	1999	46,486.7	8.3	0.6	2.8	88.4	11.4	51.0	26.1	54.1	16.1	1.1	5.7	22.4
Isle of Man[38]	...	...	...	...	...	...	...	...	...	...	...	...	...	...
Israel	1997	29,022.7	8.4	18.0	7.9	65.8	9.1	32.5	24.2	51.0	18.8	1.5	3.6	25.2
Italy[39]	1997	208,317.2	15.3	1.9	8.0	74.8	12.8	30.9	31.1	60.6	5.0	5.7	2.0	26.7
Jamaica	1996	2,916.4	16.2	0.2	15.2	68.4	10.1	26.7	31.7	11.2	52.3	0.5	5.6	30.4
Japan	1997	338,842.4	19.7	3.7	18.6	58.0	6.7	24.6	26.7	13.3	22.4	1.4	—	62.9
Jersey	1980	537.1	23.9	0.4	9.3	66.5	6.5	24.8	35.2	84.9[40]	...	...	...	15.1
Jordan	1995	3,722.7	22.7	1.1	12.9	63.4	12.3	24.5	26.5	33.2	9.3	4.6	3.5	49.4
Kazakhstan	1997	4,275.0	18.1	— 16.2[2] —		65.7[3]	14.3	32.1	19.4[3]	21.6	4.7	54.5	0.7	18.5
Kenya	1998	3,301.8	17.1	0.5	17.5	65.0	15.1	31.2	18.7	32.2	7.9	1.1	7.9	51.0
Kiribati	1995	34.1	40.5	0.3	10.3	49.0	7.0	14.7	27.3	1.1	3.1	—	7.6	88.2
Korea, North	1997	1,444.0[4]	...	...	...	...	...	...	...	17.6[4]	0.2[4]	6.9[4]	13.6[4]	61.7[4]
Korea, South	1996	150,334.3	10.4	2.4	16.2	71.0	8.8	36.4	25.8	14.1	22.2	1.5	20.9	41.3
Kuwait	1996	8,373.7	16.6	0.4	0.6	82.4	7.2	41.6	33.6	32.0	16.7	1.0	12.1	38.3
Kyrgyzstan	1996	837.9	22.4	1.0	28.6	48.0	7.8	26.1	14.0	11.1	4.3	25.1	1.5	58.1
Laos	1995	587.2	— 36.8[2] —		6.1	57.1[3]	...	29.3	27.8[3]	2.0[4]	0.9	0.7[4]	11.8	84.6
Latvia	1997	2,721.0	15.2	1.2	13.6	70.0	11.9	27.3	30.8	53.2	2.3	37.1	0.3	7.1
Lebanon	1994	5,990.0	21.7	— 13.3 —		65.0	10.2	27.0	27.8	49.1[4]	9.3	4.6[4]	4.2	32.8[4]
Lesotho	1992	977.0	23.2[42]	0.4[42]	8.7[42]	67.8[42]	7.4[42]	16.7[42]	43.7[42]	4.8	...	—[4]	—[4]	95.2[43]
Liberia	1992	5,760.0[4]	— 19.8[2, 32] —		20.3[32]	59.9[3, 32]	5.6[32]	30.2[32]	24.1[3, 32]	22.6[4]	0.6[4]	0.8[4]	28.3[4]	47.7[4]
Libya	1991	5,357.5	25.7	0.3	0.4	73.7	7.6	33.8	32.2	62.6	1.3	0.9[4]	3.3	31.9
Liechtenstein	1995	906.4	3.8	0.3[2]	1.1	94.8[3]	4.6	33.9	56.3[3]	...	...	...	...	...
Lithuania	1997	5,469.6	13.7	1.5	14.4	70.4	12.1	30.7	27.6	47.7	2.4	42.7	0.2	7.0
Luxembourg	1998	10,177.5	12.0	— 7.3 —		80.7	13.2	35.3	32.2	89.1	4.4	0.1	1.5	4.9
Macau	1997	2,076.7	14.3	0.2	6.6	78.9	4.1	16.9	57.9	12.3	6.3	—	8.5	72.8
Macedonia	1996	1,626.9	19.6	1.0	9.1	70.3	10.5	22.3	37.5	38.7	4.2	13.0	1.0	43.1
Madagascar	1997	573.1	16.6	0.1	21.1	62.2	12.7	25.6	23.9	37.5	4.5	0.5	6.1	51.5
Malawi	1995	500.5	14.5	0.6	11.1	73.6	22.5	27.6	23.6	31.9	2.6	0.5	5.0	60.0
Malaysia	1996	77,923.4	6.6	1.1	2.7	89.6	6.8	59.9	22.8	14.5	15.6	0.7	24.7	44.5
Maldives	1993	191.4	31.5	2.8	12.8	52.9	7.5	22.2	23.2	7.9	1.0	0.4	3.9	86.9
Mali	1990	601.8	26.2	0.9	19.5	53.5	10.7	22.2	20.6	46.8	4.8	1.3[4]	4.3	42.9
Malta	1996	2,802.3	11.5	0.4	5.4	82.7	7.4	48.4	26.9	68.5	6.9	1.3	3.2	20.1
Marshall Islands	1995	75.1	34.5	1.0[4]	30.0	34.5	2.6	12.8	19.2	...	51.1	...	7.4	41.5
Martinique	1995	1,969.8	20.4	0.2	7.5	71.9	10.3	32.4	29.2	76.8	2.9	0.2	2.2	17.9
Mauritania	1992	600.0[4]	30.6[32]	...	7.0[32]	62.4[32]	...	51.0[32]	11.4[32]	58.4[4]	11.2[4]	1.8[4]	3.8[4]	24.7[4]
Mauritius	1996	2,276.9	19.4	1.8	7.9	70.9	7.7	21.9	41.3	33.0	2.5	0.2	4.4	59.8
Mayotte	1996	144.3	— 23.7 —		4.6	71.7	11.0	35.1	25.6	74.0[14, 46]	...	...	3.3[14]	22.7[14]
Mexico	1997	111,974.2	7.9	1.0	2.7	88.4	9.0	46.2	33.2	9.3	74.3	0.4	4.0	12.0
Micronesia	1994	129.1	— 24.7[2] —		14.3	61.0[3]	4.4	13.5	43.1[3]	...	32.9	...	32.0	35.1
Moldova	1995	840.7	10.7	1.0	45.9	42.4	9.2	15.2	17.9	13.7	1.3	80.2	0.2	4.7
Monaco[31]	...	...	...	...	...	...	...	...	...	...	...	...	...	...
Mongolia	1996	450.9	14.9	0.3	19.3	65.5	5.0	39.7	20.7	14.7	2.3	39.0	11.7	32.2
Morocco	1996	8,253.9	24.1	2.2	15.6	58.1	12.7	23.6	21.8	54.1	7.4	5.4	1.8	31.3
Mozambique	1996	782.6	23.6	0.6	11.5	64.3	8.2	32.3	23.8	27.1	4.2	—	4.0	64.7
Myanmar (Burma)	1996	1,914.0	— 8.7[2] —		4.4	86.9[3]	8.6	27.0	51.3[3]	2.6	4.9	—	22.5	69.9
Namibia	1994	1,374.3	23.8	1.1[2]	4.2	70.9[3]	7.1	31.4	32.5[3]	4.5	0.9	—	1.3	93.3[47]
Nauru	1994	31.8	87.8	...	...	12.2	...	2.8	9.3	...	...	...	...	...
Nepal	1996[12]	1,404.2	13.7	0.5	8.9	77.0	9.1	19.5	48.4	7.9	1.0	0.3	5.5	85.3

exports													country
total value ('000,000 U.S.$)	Standard International Trade Classification (SITC) categories (%)							direction of trade (%)					
	food and agricultural raw materials (0 + 1 + 2 − 27 − 28 + 4)	mineral ores and concen-trates (27 + 28 + 667)	fuels and other energy (3)	manufactured goods				to European Union (EU)[b]	to United States	to Eastern Europe[c]	to Japan	to all other[d]	
				total[a] (5 + 6 − 667 + 7 + 8 + 9)	of which chemicals and related products (5)	of which machinery and transport equipment (7)	of which other[a] (6 − 667 + 8 + 9)						
3,908.0	11.5	1.1	45.4	42.1	5.1	1.2	35.8	41.5	11.4	2.8	2.3	42.0	Egypt
1,354.0	56.0	0.1	3.3	40.6	12.3	3.7	24.6	29.6	19.2	—	1.0	50.2	El Salvador
61.7	48.6	—	—	51.4	0.1	39.8[28]	11.5	47.2	—	—	—	52.8	Equatorial Guinea
86.0	—— 59.8 ——		...	40.2	2.5	3.8	34.0	2.7[29]	...	...	...	97.3[30]	Eritrea
2,926.5	25.5	2.3	6.3	65.8	8.4	24.6	32.8	48.6	1.8	41.1	0.5	7.9	Estonia
201.7	95.3	—	4.0	0.7	0.1	—	0.6	41.6	9.2	0.3	19.0	29.9	Ethiopia
321.3	96.8	—	—	3.2	0.1	2.5	0.6	88.0	2.9	0.1	2.7	6.3	Faroe Islands
544.5	49.3	0.1	7.4	43.2	1.0	8.0	34.3	20.3	17.9	—	6.8	55.0	Fiji
40,980.1	10.2	0.7	2.4	86.8	6.2	38.8	41.8	51.5	6.9	14.9	1.9	24.9	Finland
283,345.8	14.5	0.7	2.6	82.3	12.8	41.6	27.8	62.8	6.5	3.1	1.7	25.9	France[31]
158.2	33.6	0.1	0.2	66.1	1.4	33.0	31.7	77.6	1.0	—	—	21.3	French Guiana
226.2	5.9[32]	31.3[32]	—[32]	62.8[32]	1.6[32]	38.6[32]	22.6[32]	32.7[29]	8.4	—	45.8	13.1	French Polynesia
3,145.6	13.3	2.0	82.7	1.9	0.4	0.4	1.1	11.5	64.1	0.1	2.1	22.3	Gabon
21.5	—— 78.8[2] ——		—	21.2[3]	1.6	2.5	17.1	57.1[4]	3.6[4]	—[4]	—[4]	39.3[4]	Gambia, The
49.4	...	...	...	...	...	...	...	...	...	...	...	100.0[34]	Gaza Strip
240.0	35.7	—— 21.5[2] ——		42.8[3]	10.9	7.3	24.5[3]	9.2	1.7	37.0	—	52.0	Georgia
511,942.1	5.6	0.7	1.3	92.5	12.7	49.5	30.2	54.0	8.4	9.0	2.2	26.4	Germany
1,234.4	37.7	6.2	5.4	50.6	0.2	1.2	49.3[35]	30.3	2.6	1.1	1.8	64.2[36]	Ghana
10,794.6	30.3	2.2	8.7	58.8	5.5	8.3	45.0	47.5	4.5	14.6	0.7	32.8	Greece
285.3	93.2	—	1.1	5.7	—	2.0	3.7	91.3	2.1	—	3.4	3.3	Greenland
19.8	80.5	0.1	—	19.4	2.2	3.3	14.0	38.8	21.4	—	—	39.8	Grenada
162.0	52.3	0.6	—	47.0	1.1	36.5	9.4	77.0	3.4	—	—	19.6	Guadeloupe
86.1	—— 69.5[2] ——		0.7	29.7[3]	0.7	3.8	25.2	2.3[4]	—	—	57.5	40.2	Guam
2,344.1	65.0	0.4	4.2	30.3	11.2	2.2	16.9	13.2	35.9	0.4	2.3	48.2	Guatemala
...	...	...	...	...	...	...	...	...	...	...	...	...	Guernsey[38]
625.9	12.2[22]	66.3	—	21.5	...	...	...	63.4[4]	15.1[4]	8.3[4]	1.3[4]	11.9[4]	Guinea
48.5	97.7	...	—	2.3	...	...	...	14.3[4]	—[4]	—[4]	1.4[4]	84.3[4]	Guinea-Bissau
404.0	43.5[22]	47.3[22]	—	9.2	...	...	...	35.9[4]	22.8[4]	—[4]	2.1[4]	39.2[4]	Guyana
74.3	14.1	—	—	86.0	1.7	14.0	70.3	12.4[4]	78.8[4]	—[4]	0.8[4]	8.0[4]	Haiti
1,033.3	68.3	3.0	0.2	28.6	1.5	1.9	25.2	21.1	68.0	0.2	2.7	8.1	Honduras
188,201.3	4.0	1.2	1.1	93.7	5.6	32.9	55.2	14.8	21.8	0.6	6.1	56.9	Hong Kong
19,099.2	15.5	0.8	2.3	81.5	7.6	44.9	29.0	69.9	3.1	14.4	0.5	12.2	Hungary
1,851.5	74.7	1.1	0.1	24.1	0.4	5.6	18.1	60.6	14.3	2.9	6.6	15.6	Iceland
33,468.6	21.0	15.5	1.5	62.0	9.0	8.2	44.8	25.9	19.6	3.2	6.0	45.3	India
53,443.7	16.0	3.5	24.6	55.9	3.5	8.6	43.7	15.2	13.4	0.5	23.4	47.6	Indonesia
19,868.0	7.8	1.9[2, 15]	80.9	9.3[3, 16]	0.2	0.5	8.6[3, 16]	39.8	0.8	9.9[4]	13.5	36.0	Iran
6,659.0	0.8	0.3[15]	96.8	2.1[16]	1.2	0.2	0.7[16]	26.6[4]	33.6[4]	6.8[4]	9.5[4]	23.5[4]	Iraq
70,525.1	9.9	0.8	0.3	89.0	31.8	39.3	17.9	64.6	15.4	1.5	2.9	15.6	Ireland
...	...	...	...	...	...	...	...	...	...	...	...	...	Isle of Man[38]
22,503.0	6.1	30.8	0.5	62.6	13.6	30.2	18.7	30.1	32.1	3.2	4.6	30.1	Israel
238,265.9	7.0	0.3	1.4	91.2	7.8	37.8	45.6	54.6	7.9	6.2	2.0	29.3	Italy[39]
1,386.9	23.7	49.7	0.4	26.2	3.4	2.3	20.5	31.2	37.1	1.9	2.3	27.5	Jamaica
421,053.0	1.1	0.3	0.5	98.1	6.9	69.0	22.2	15.6	28.1	0.5	—	55.7	Japan
209.2	27.6	4.3[41]	—	68.0	1.2	31.1	35.7	67.3[40]	...	...	...	32.7	Jersey
1,782.0	24.1	19.4	—	56.5	27.0	13.1	16.4	8.0	3.9	1.3	1.1	85.7	Jordan
6,366.0	12.9	—— 37.6[2] ——		49.5[3]	6.9	3.6	39.1[3]	26.8	2.2	42.2	1.7	27.1	Kazakhstan
1,916.6	64.9	2.6	8.6	23.9	6.3	0.9	16.6	31.6	3.6	0.3	0.8	63.7	Kenya
7.2	85.3	—	—	14.7	—	—	14.7	2.2	10.4	—	—	87.4	Kiribati
884.0[4]	...	...	...	...	...	...	...	10.2[4]	—[4]	3.7[4]	30.4[4]	55.7[4]	Korea, North
129,714.6	3.4	0.1	3.0	93.5	7.1	52.1	34.3	11.9	16.9	3.0	12.2	56.0	Korea, South
14,855.7	0.6	0.2	95.2	4.0	1.5	1.3	1.2	12.2[4]	10.9[4]	—[4]	19.4[4]	57.5[4]	Kuwait
507.1	39.7	2.5	15.3	42.4	12.9	9.8	19.8	3.9	3.5	32.1	0.2	60.3	Kyrgyzstan
347.9	—— 35.4[2] ——		7.0	57.5[3]	...	5.1	52.4[3]	9.7[4]	3.2	3.2[4]	0.6	83.3	Laos
1,671.7	38.0	1.9	1.1	59.1	6.7	10.5	41.9	48.9	1.4	42.0	0.3	7.5	Latvia
572.7	19.6	—— 10.5 ——		69.9	9.1	11.5	49.3	17.0[4]	3.7	4.9[4]	0.7	73.7[4]	Lebanon
109.1	14.8	1.3	—	83.9	0.5	10.2	73.2	22.7	23.0[4]	—	—	54.3[44]	Lesotho
389.0	32.4	33.7[2, 15]	2.6	31.3[3, 16]	—	26.0	5.3[3, 16]	66.8	11.4[4]	1.5	—	20.3[4]	Liberia
11,211.7	0.7	—	95.4	3.9	3.4	—	0.5	86.2	—	1.6	—	12.2	Libya
1,817.7	4.4	—[2]	0.1	95.5[3]	8.1	46.9	40.5[3]	45.7[45]	...	...	...	54.3	Liechtenstein
3,343.1	23.4	2.1	4.4	70.1	12.4	23.2	34.6	36.7	1.8	53.0	0.4	8.1	Lithuania
7,921.6	7.9	—— 1.1 ——		91.0	15.5	29.0	46.5	83.2	5.5	0.5	0.4	10.3	Luxembourg
2,282.1	2.5	—	0.4	97.1	0.9	3.9	92.2	31.2	42.5	0.1	1.0	25.2	Macau
1,147.4	24.7	2.3	0.9	72.1	6.1	7.7	58.4	42.8	6.2	8.3	0.2	42.5	Macedonia
277.8	60.7	9.6	2.9	26.9	2.1	0.7	24.0	65.8	3.8	0.5	9.0	20.9	Madagascar
433.4	90.2	—	—	9.8	0.4	2.0	7.4	47.7	13.2	3.5	5.0	30.6	Malawi
78,186.1	13.9	0.4	7.9	77.8	3.2	55.3	19.3	13.7	18.2	0.3	13.4	54.3	Malaysia
34.4	83.7	0.2	—	16.1	0.1	—	16.0	31.3	11.3	—	4.1	53.3	Maldives
330.3	98.4	—	—	1.6	—	0.9	0.8	26.0	0.6[4]	—	0.9[4]	72.5	Mali
1,747.9	3.3	0.2	2.7	93.8	2.9	60.1	30.8	57.1	13.4	1.0	2.9	25.7	Malta
23.1	71.0	—	—	29.0	—	—	29.0	...	80.0[4]	...	...	20.0[4]	Marshall Islands
241.9	62.3	1.0	17.8	18.9	2.1	13.0	3.8	78.0	2.6	—	—	19.3	Martinique
471.0	48.2	48.6[2, 15]	1.9	1.3[3, 16]	—	—	1.3[3, 16]	58.2	4.5	10.8[4]	20.4	6.1	Mauritania
1,699.4	31.8	1.9	—	66.3	0.6	0.4	65.3	77.4	13.4	—	0.6	8.5	Mauritius
8.2	21.3[24]	—[24]	—[24]	78.7[24]	78.7[24]	—[24]	—[24]	70.0[14, 46]	...	...	...	30.0[14]	Mayotte
110,047.0	7.2	0.7	10.0	82.1	3.8	54.0	24.3	3.5	84.5	0.1	0.9	10.9	Mexico
78.2	96.9	—	—	3.1	...	...	...	...	3.5	...	72.7	23.8	Micronesia
745.5	73.5	2.7	0.9	22.9	1.4	7.9	13.7	11.6	1.1	80.5	—	6.8	Moldova
...	...	...	...	...	...	...	...	...	...	...	...	...	Monaco[31]
424.3	29.9	59.9	—	10.2	0.6	7.4	7.8	13.6	0.2	63.1	0.5	22.5	Mongolia
4,741.9	35.4	11.0	1.6	52.0	20.1	2.9	28.9	61.5	3.5	1.8	6.9	26.3	Morocco
226.1	77.9	3.7	1.2	17.2	0.5	11.5	5.3	34.7	11.4	0.3	7.6	46.0	Mozambique
883.1	—— 77.3[2] ——		0.6	22.2[3]	—	1.1	21.1[3]	4.3	4.9	—	7.3	83.5	Myanmar (Burma)
1,321.4	47.0	50.1	—	2.8	...	...	...	...	3.0[4, 5]	...	—[4, 5]	97.0[4, 5]	Namibia
31.2	—	100.0	—	—	—	—	—	...	...	...	...	...	Nauru
363.7	10.8	0.1	—	89.1	1.8	0.1	87.2	42.4	28.3	0.2	0.4	28.7	Nepal

Trade: external (continued)

country	year	imports												
		total value ('000,000 U.S.$)	Standard International Trade Classification (SITC) categories (%)							direction of trade (%)				
			food and agricultural raw materials (0 + 1 + 2 – 27 – 28 + 4)	mineral ores and concen-trates (27 + 28 + 667)	fuels and other energy (3)	manufactured goods				from European Union (EU)[b]	from United States	from Eastern Europe[c]	from Japan	from all other[d]
						total[a] (5 + 6 – 667 + 7 + 8 + 9)	of which chemicals and related products (5)	of which machinery and transport equipment (7)	of which other[a] (6 – 667 + 8 + 9)					
Netherlands, The	1997	162,359.7	13.1	1.5	8.7	76.7	11.2	37.8	27.7	58.8	9.9	3.2	3.9	24.2
Netherlands Antilles	1995	1,832.5	— 12.9[2] —		55.2	31.9[3]	4.5	12.7	14.7[3]	13.1	19.9	—	1.7	65.4
New Caledonia	1997	924.2	— 20.3[2] —		11.7	68.0[3]	7.7	33.3	27.0[3]	41.9	5.3	—	4.3	48.5
New Zealand	1996	14,724.2	8.6	2.0	6.3	83.0	12.6	41.9	28.6	20.2	16.7	0.1	14.3	48.7
Nicaragua	1997	1,469.8	15.2	0.4	12.2	72.2	18.8	26.9	26.6	8.5	37.4	0.5	4.8	48.9
Niger	1991	355.3	25.7	2.1	9.4	62.7	9.6	13.6	39.5	39.6	5.1	0.3	6.6	48.4
Nigeria	1992	8,839.3	7.6	0.9	0.4	91.0	13.9	54.2	22.9	62.8	8.5	0.8[4]	6.3	21.7
Northern Mariana Islands	1991	392.2	19.3	—	20.9	59.8	2.3	22.2	35.3	...	18.2	...	16.6	65.2
Norway	1999	33,810.8	9.3	4.1	3.2	83.3	9.2	41.7	32.4	68.6	7.3	2.7	4.0	15.6
Oman	1996	4,577.8	18.2	1.6	1.0	79.2	6.7	41.5	31.0	25.3	7.5	0.2	17.2	49.8
Pakistan	1998	9,312.5	25.0	1.1	15.9	58.0	20.4	22.8	14.8	18.3	9.8	1.0	8.1	62.8
Palau	1984	25.1[49]	28.9	0.1[2]	0.9[49]	70.0[3]	4.0	24.5	41.5[3]	—	41.8	—	38.2	20.0
Panama	1996	2,779.7	11.8	0.3	15.9	72.0	13.1	30.6	28.3	7.8	37.8	0.1	6.0	48.3
Papua New Guinea	1993	1,298.6	18.8[50]	0.3[50]	6.8[50]	74.1[50]	7.0[50]	38.3[50]	28.8[50]	4.0	3.9	0.9	14.5	76.7
Paraguay	1996	3,107.4	20.9	2.8	8.1	68.2	10.6	36.4	21.2	10.2	11.2	0.2	6.6	71.8
Peru	1997	8,558.4	15.7	0.2	10.4	73.7	12.7	38.3	22.8	15.9	26.5	0.8	5.6	51.2
Philippines	1997	38,581.0	9.2	1.4	8.5	81.0	8.1	38.9	33.9	11.6	19.8	1.5	20.6	46.5
Poland	1996	37,095.0	12.7	1.6	9.2	76.5	13.2	33.0	30.3	64.0	4.4	14.7	1.6	15.2
Portugal	1997	32,964.7	15.6	0.7	8.1	75.7	9.6	35.8	30.2	75.3	3.3	1.4	2.5	17.6
Puerto Rico	1992[12]	15,387.3	17.3	0.3	10.6	71.8	25.4	21.8	24.7	4.8	68.1	0.1	3.7	23.2
Qatar	1994	1,927.4	15.8	2.7	0.6	80.8	7.0	39.7	34.2	33.9	10.6	1.4[4]	13.4	40.8
Réunion	1995	2,711.1	21.5	0.2	4.7	73.6	10.7	29.8	33.1	80.1	0.6	0.1	2.1	17.2
Romania	1997	11,279.8	7.7	2.7	18.9	70.6	9.2	26.4	35.0	52.5	4.1	20.5	1.2	21.7
Russia	1997	67,619.0	19.6	2.4[2]	2.8	75.2[3]	7.3	21.9	46.0[3]	29.0	6.0	20.8	1.5	42.7
Rwanda	1990	291.1	18.2	1.9	15.3	64.6	10.2	16.1	38.3	44.6	1.2	1.4[4]	7.7	45.1
St. Kitts and Nevis	1997	147.2	21.3	0.5	7.5	70.9	7.1	28.9	34.9	12.2	56.0	0.1	4.2	27.6
St. Lucia	1996	313.5	27.7	0.8	8.3	63.3	10.2	21.8	31.3	18.5	39.9	0.1	4.9	36.6
St. Vincent and the Grenadines	1995	134.5	25.1	0.2[2]	6.0	68.6[3]	12.9	17.8	37.9[3]	21.6	36.9	0.1	2.3	39.2
Samoa	1993	130.9	21.6	0.6[2]	8.4	69.4[3]	5.0	37.0	27.4[3]	4.3	8.3	—	15.9	71.5
San Marino[39]	1994	1,652.2	...	...	...	...	...	...	...	...	...	...	...	...
São Tomé and Príncipe	1994	30.4	21.5[22]	...	7.2	71.3	...	40.2	31.1	53.8[29]	25.0[4]	...	5.3	15.9[4]
Saudi Arabia	1996	27,765.0	18.2	0.9	0.2	80.8	9.4	35.5	35.9	34.5	21.9	1.3	7.0	35.2
Senegal	1995	1,224.5	34.7	1.1	10.0	54.2	13.9	18.1	22.2	53.4	5.7	1.8	3.7	35.3
Seychelles	1996	346.7	21.0	0.2	3.3	75.6	4.9	47.9	22.7	31.4	28.9	—	2.4	37.2
Sierra Leone	1995	136.3	— 47.9[2] —		17.4	34.8[3]	7.6	14.7	12.5[3]	48.4[4]	8.1[4]	2.8[4]	0.8[4]	39.8[4]
Singapore	1997	132,441.8	4.9	0.7	9.5	84.9	5.6	57.5	21.8	14.0	16.9	0.5	17.6	51.1
Slovakia	1997	10,264.5	9.4	1.4	11.8	77.4	11.6	32.5	33.3	39.5	3.3	46.5	1.7	8.9
Slovenia	1997	9,365.7	10.9	1.7	8.5	79.0	11.7	33.0	34.4	67.4	3.1	10.6	1.7	17.3
Solomon Islands	1997	184.5	— 17.9[2] —		8.6	73.5[3]	4.9	37.7	30.9[3]	3.4	2.1	—	14.9	79.6
Somalia	1992	228.0[4]	30.3[42]	0.2[42]	4.6[42]	64.9[42]	5.1[42]	37.1[42]	22.7[42]	27.2[4]	10.1[4]	—[4]	0.7[4]	62.0[4]
South Africa[54]	1996	26,872.4	8.4	2.6	9.5	79.5	12.1	38.1	29.3	44.2	12.9	0.4	7.8	34.7
Spain	1996	121,255.4	14.9	2.1	9.1	73.9	11.8	37.3	24.8	66.3	6.2	2.2	2.8	22.5
Sri Lanka	1995	2,833.2	15.0	3.9	7.9	73.2	9.9	19.8	43.5	18.2	3.5	0.9	10.2	67.1
Sudan, The	1996	1,072.9	18.9	0.2	19.4	61.6	15.0	25.7	20.9	25.6	8.5	6.4	5.6	53.8
Suriname	1995	582.9	14.1	0.9	11.8	73.3	14.8	35.6	22.9	24.1	42.4	—	2.1	31.4
Swaziland	1994	962.6	21.8[1]	0.4[1]	10.3[1]	67.4[1]	10.2[1]	26.7[1]	30.6[1]	7.6[1]	0.6[1]	—[1]	0.9[1]	90.9[1, 56]
Sweden	1997	62,864.7	8.9	1.4	7.2	82.5	9.7	42.9	29.8	68.1	6.2	4.1	2.7	18.9
Switzerland[57]	1997	75,900.4	7.8	3.8	4.5	83.8	15.6	31.5	36.7	77.1	8.4	2.0	2.8	9.8
Syria	1995	4,708.8	20.0	0.5	1.1	78.4	10.2	31.6	36.7	34.4	6.8	10.8	4.4	43.7
Taiwan	1999	110,931.0	7.9	1.3	7.4	83.5	11.8	49.3	22.3	13.0	17.8	1.6	27.6	40.0
Tajikistan	1997	750.0	17.4	— 56.8[2] —		25.8[3]	6.9	14.4	4.6[3]	3.6	0.4	20.6	—	75.3
Tanzania	1990	1,021.5	5.4	1.5	10.3	82.8	9.8	45.6	27.4	58.2	1.6	0.8[4]	7.7	31.8
Thailand	1997	62,461.8	7.9	1.8	9.3	80.9	9.6	46.9	24.4	13.9	13.9	1.6	25.6	45.0
Togo	1993	179.5	30.3	0.4	8.0	61.3	16.3	21.8	23.2	66.8	6.8	0.8	4.3	21.2
Tonga	1997	72.9	35.0	0.8	14.1	50.0	7.2	19.2	23.6	0.8	12.3	—	5.7	81.3
Trinidad and Tobago	1996	2,204.5	14.5	3.2	19.2	63.1	10.0	30.7	22.5	17.2	38.1	0.6	4.0	40.1
Tunisia	1997	7,947.1	14.2	1.7	8.0	76.2	8.4	29.6	38.3	72.9	4.3	2.5	2.4	17.8
Turkey	1997	48,585.1	10.1	2.9	10.4	76.7	13.0	38.2	25.4	51.2	8.9	8.9	4.2	26.8
Turkmenistan	1997	1,228.0	26.0	— 8.0[2] —		66.0[3]	12.8	34.7	18.5[3]	11.7	7.2	39.8	0.6	40.7
Tuvalu	1995	15.2	36.1[5]	0.1[2, 5]	14.6[5]	49.2[3, 5]	6.8[5]	13.9[5]	28.5[3, 5]	5.9[29]	2.0	—	1.3	90.8
Uganda	1996	816.1	14.6	1.4[2]	11.2	72.8[3]	14.3	30.5	28.0[3]	27.7	2.7	—	8.1	61.5
Ukraine	1997	17,261.6	8.1	— 47.6[2] —		44.3[3]	11.5	20.2	12.6[3]	19.6	3.8	58.5	0.9	17.3
United Arab Emirates	1992	17,410.0	11.6	0.7	1.7	86.1	5.5	35.1	45.4	33.5	8.9	0.5	16.6	40.5
United Kingdom[38]	1999	320,302.0	10.8	3.2	2.7	83.4	9.7	45.8	27.8	53.0	12.7	2.3	4.8	27.2
United States[59]	1997	898,025.6	6.9	1.6	9.2	82.3	5.7	44.8	31.8	18.1	—	1.0	13.8	67.1
Uruguay	1997	3,715.6	13.2	0.4	9.2	77.2	16.1	35.3	25.7	19.3	11.7	1.6	2.6	64.8
Uzbekistan	1995	2,892.7	19.3	— 2.7 —		78.0	9.0	43.1	25.9	17.7	1.1	36.9	1.5	42.8
Vanuatu	1994	83.3	21.1	0.2	6.8	71.8	6.1	31.8	33.8	9.5	1.4	—	9.5	79.6
Venezuela	1996	8,902.3	18.7	1.3	1.5	78.5	14.8	38.0	25.7	17.9	45.0	0.2	3.4	33.5
Vietnam	1995	8,155.4	— 12.4[2] —		11.1	76.5[3]	15.8	28.7	32.0[3]	8.1	1.6	2.5	11.2	76.5
Virgin Islands (U.S.)	1995	3,200.3	...	...	68.6[60]	...	...	...	...	...	32.7	...	...	...
West Bank[62]	1994	102.5[63]	...	...	...	...	...	...	...	...	...	...	...	...
Western Sahara	...	...	...	...	...	...	...	...	...	...	...	...	...	...
Yemen	1998	2,167.4	36.4	0.1[2]	6.4	57.1[3]	9.7	24.2	23.1[3]	27.4	5.8	0.7	3.4	62.7
Yugoslavia	1997	4,798.8	18.0	4.3	16.1	61.6	12.8	17.8	31.0	41.2	2.8	22.5	1.2	32.2
Zambia	1993	809.0	3.7[50]	1.1[2, 50]	15.2[50]	79.9[3, 50]	12.6[50]	47.0[50]	20.3[3, 50]	24.5	2.8	—	4.3	68.4
Zimbabwe	1997	3,092.3	9.1	1.0	10.2	79.7	14.8	38.8	26.1	22.9	5.5	0.7	5.6	65.4

[1]Year ending March. [2]Excluding precious stones, etc. (667). [3]Including precious stones, etc. (667). [4]Estimate. [5]1991. [6]Year ending September 30. [7]Percentage of the total excluding fish imports or the cannery (52.1% of the overall total), and government purchases (0.1%). [8]1987. [9]Excluding mineral fuels; overall totals on a balance of payments basis, f.o.b.: imports U.S.$1,518,200,000, exports U.S.$1,164,800,000. [10]Percentage of non-oil imports. [11]Includes 66.5% for special categories. [12]Year ending June 30. [13]Figures for Belgium-Luxembourg Economic Union (Luxembourg is also shown separately). [14]1992. [15]Including metals. [16]Excluding metals. [17]Includes 71.5% from India. [18]Mainly electricity. [19]Includes 92.8% to India. [20]Includes 72.2% from South Africa. [21]Includes 19.4% to Switzerland. [22]Main items only. [23]Includes 82.8% for reexports. [24]Domestic exports only. [25]1985. [26]Includes 9.1% for ferronickel. [27]East Timor is included in Indonesia. [28]Includes 38.7% for ships and boats. [29]Main countries only. [30]Includes 63.3% for Ethiopia. [31]Figures for France include Monaco. [32]1988. [33]Includes 82.4% from Israel. [34]Includes 69.2% to Israel and 25.1% to Jordan. [35]Includes 42.5% for nonmonetary gold. [36]Includes 41.5% to Switzerland. [37]1983. [38]Figures for United Kingdom include Guernsey, Isle of Man, and Jersey (data for Jersey is

exports													country
total value ('000,000 U.S.$)	Standard International Trade Classification (SITC) categories (%)							direction of trade (%)					
	food and agricultural raw materials (0 + 1 + 2 – 27 – 28 + 4)	mineral ores and concen-trates (27 + 28 + 667)	fuels and other energy (3)	manufactured goods: total[a] (5 + 6 – 667 + 7 + 8 + 9)	of which chemicals and related products (5)	of which machinery and transport equipment (7)	of which other[a] (6 – 667 + 8 + 9)	to European Union (EU)[b]	to United States	to Eastern Europe[c]	to Japan	to all other[d]	
184,433.3	19.1	0.9	7.3	72.6	15.5	32.1	25.0	77.8	3.9	3.4	1.0	13.9	Netherlands, The
1,355.8	6.9	2.0	85.1	6.0	1.0	1.7	3.3	14.3	13.9	—	0.2	71.5	Netherlands Antilles
529.4	—	39.5	—	60.5	—	—	60.5[48]	36.1[4]	11.3[4]	—[4]	29.8[4]	22.7	New Caledonia
14,354.3	61.4	0.4	2.3	36.0	7.2	8.2	20.6	16.1	9.2	1.0	15.4	58.4	New Zealand
666.7	72.2	0.6	1.0	26.2	1.5	7.5	17.2	27.3	45.8	0.9	0.7	25.4	Nicaragua
311.9	22.4	74.8	0.8	2.0	0.1	1.2	0.7	56.4	0.1	—	18.8	24.7	Niger
11,886.5	1.8	—	97.6	0.7	—	—	0.6	46.9	44.1	—	—	9.0	Nigeria
263.0	—	—	—	100.0	—	—	100.0	—	100.0	—	—	—	Northern Mariana Islands
44,917.4	10.6	0.8	51.0	37.6	6.4	12.8	18.4	73.8	7.8	0.7	2.6	13.7	Norway
7,221.9	4.0	0.4	80.4	15.2	0.5	9.4	5.4	0.8	1.0	0.4	15.2	82.5	Oman
8,498.2	15.4	0.2	0.3	84.1	0.7	1.1	82.3	30.8	21.5	0.6	3.4	43.7	Pakistan
0.5	69.1	—	—	30.9	—	—	30.9	—	8.0	—	58.8	33.2	Palau
569.2	71.6	1.2	4.9	22.3	5.1	0.3	16.9	22.9	50.3	0.1	0.8	25.9	Panama
2,624.6	26.8	19.5	30.6	23.1[51]	—	2.5	20.6[51]	12.1	4.0	—	21.4	62.5	Papua New Guinea
1,043.0	82.1	0.2	0.6	17.0	2.2	0.4	14.3	21.7	3.6	—	0.1	74.6	Paraguay
6,759.4	33.9	13.8	5.9	46.4	2.7	0.6	43.0	24.1	23.6	1.0	7.0	44.3	Peru
25,227.7	9.2	0.9	1.2	88.7	1.5	29.9	57.3	18.0	35.1	0.2	16.6	30.0	Philippines
24,393.1	13.1	1.1	6.9	79.0	7.7	23.4	47.9	66.6	2.3	20.0	0.2	10.9	Poland
22,745.7	10.6	1.6	2.3	85.4	4.4	31.6	49.4	80.1	4.8	1.1	0.7	13.3	Portugal
21,051.2	15.8	0.1	2.6	81.5	43.7	21.7	16.2	5.1	87.5	—	0.2	7.2	Puerto Rico
3,212.9	0.5	0.2	73.8	25.4	15.9	1.4	8.1	1.9[4]	2.5[4]	—[4]	55.6[4]	40.0[4]	Qatar
208.7	78.6	0.5	0.2	20.7	1.7	12.7	6.2	79.9	0.6	—	6.1	13.4	Réunion
8,431.1	10.5	0.9	6.1	82.4	7.8	14.0	60.7	56.6	3.8	10.2	0.4	28.9	Romania
87,368.0	4.9	2.5[2]	43.6	49.1[3]	5.2	5.2	38.7[3]	32.3	5.1	18.3	3.4	40.9	Russia
131.9	72.8	3.9	—	23.3[52]	—	—	23.3[52]	64.1[4]	6.1[4]	—[4]	1.9[4]	27.9[4]	Rwanda
41.1	58.2	—	—	41.8	0.2	37.2	4.4	33.7	57.4	—	4.6	4.4	St. Kitts and Nevis
79.5	72.7	—	—	27.3	0.9	5.9	20.4	67.8	14.9	—	0.3	17.0	St. Lucia
59.4	81.2	—[2]	—	18.8[3]	1.0	4.0	13.8[3]	41.0	9.4	—	0.1	49.5	St. Vincent and the Grenadines
17.5	32.7	...	...	67.3	...	...	...	—	3.2	—	—	96.8	Samoa
1,416.3	...	...	...	...	...	...	...	...	...	...	...	...	San Marino[39]
6.5	77.6[22]	...	...	...	...	...	...	88.8[29]	1.9[4]	...	0.5[4]	8.8[4]	São Tomé and Príncipe
56,509.5	0.8	0.2	88.6	10.4	6.9	1.3	2.3	15.6	16.7	—	12.3	55.4[53]	Saudi Arabia
530.8	23.9	10.5	15.1	50.5	39.5	2.5	8.5	23.8	0.6	—	0.4	75.2	Senegal
139.4	29.9	0.1	21.9	48.2	0.2	46.1	1.9	28.6	37.3	—	1.4	32.7	Seychelles
76.1	13.3	77.0	—	9.7	—	—	9.7	65.3[4]	13.3[4]	1.0[4]	1.5[4]	18.9[4]	Sierra Leone
124,988.2	4.2	0.5	7.0	88.2	5.9	65.9	16.4	14.0	18.4	0.8	7.1	59.8	Singapore
8,790.0	7.8	1.0	4.9	86.3	9.3	27.1	49.9	45.0	1.6	45.4	0.1	7.9	Slovakia
8,368.9	5.4	0.4	1.2	93.0	11.0	33.6	48.4	63.6	2.9	11.3	0.2	22.0	Slovenia
156.5	—— 96.5[2] ——		—	3.5[3]	—	—	3.5[3]	24.9	0.1	—	39.7	35.2	Solomon Islands
44.0	95.4	2.3	—	2.3	—	2.3	—	52.3	—	—	—	47.7	Somalia
29,221.0	12.1	15.3	8.7	63.9	7.3	9.0	47.5	28.2	7.7	0.5	6.9	56.7[55]	South Africa[54]
100,955.5	16.9	0.7	2.5	79.9	8.0	42.7	29.2	71.3	4.2	2.2	1.2	21.1	Spain
2,391.4	22.8	7.4	0.9	68.9	0.8	3.2	64.9	31.4	36.3	2.8	5.2	24.3	Sri Lanka
273.2	81.4	0.3	—	18.2	—	0.4	17.8	31.4	1.9	0.1	4.5	62.1	Sudan, The
482.7	18.4	63.6	2.2	15.7	—	1.1	14.7	32.0	22.0	1.2	6.0	38.8	Suriname
751.8	69.1[24]	3.3[24]	0.9[24]	26.7[24]	1.4[24]	8.3[24]	17.1[24]	19.8[24]	3.1[24]	—[24]	0.7[24]	76.4[24]	Swaziland
81,180.3	8.1	1.3	2.2	88.4	6.7	44.9	36.7	54.7	8.5	5.0	3.0	28.8	Sweden
76,150.1	3.4	2.6	0.2	93.8	27.3	31.1	35.4	59.8	10.5	2.9	4.0	22.8	Switzerland[57]
3,969.9	18.6	0.6	62.5	18.2	0.6	0.8	16.8	57.0	0.9	6.1	0.2	35.8	Syria
121,508.9	6.7	0.1	0.8	92.4	8.0	57.0	27.4	15.7	25.4	0.5	9.8	48.6	Taiwan
746.0	4.8	—— 21.5[2] ——		73.7[3]	2.6	2.4	68.8[3]	36.0	0.6	12.7	—	50.7	Tajikistan
416.1	82.0	1.0	2.0	15.1	1.0	2.2	11.8	40.5	6.8	0.7[4]	3.9	48.2	Tanzania
58,282.6	22.3	1.9	2.4	73.4	4.2	38.3	30.9	16.1	19.6	0.8	15.0	48.5	Thailand
136.0	57.7	32.8	0.3	9.2	1.2	3.4	4.6	23.6	0.1	2.9	—	73.3	Togo
10.9	92.0	0.2	—	7.8	0.8	0.1	7.0	1.6	14.6	—	48.8	35.0	Tonga
2,569.2	8.3	0.2	50.3	41.2	22.8	3.8	14.6	9.6	48.8	—	0.2	41.3	Trinidad and Tobago
5,559.4	11.7	1.2	9.1	78.0	12.5	10.8	54.7	78.4	0.7	0.4	0.2	20.3	Tunisia
26,244.8	20.8	1.2	0.7	77.2	4.0	12.7	60.5	46.7	7.7	13.6	0.5	31.5	Turkey
751.0	0.9	—— 77.8[2] ——		21.3[3]	0.6	0.2	20.5[3]	6.5	0.1	37.8	—	55.6	Turkmenistan
2.2	92.2[58]	—[58]	—[58]	7.8[58]	—[58]	—[58]	7.8[58]	9.1[29]	—	—	—	90.9	Tuvalu
665.3	82.4	—	0.6	17.0	5.5	1.5	10.1	62.5	2.3	8.3	1.5	25.5	Uganda
14,231.9	14.1	—— 9.0[2] ——		76.9[3]	13.2	13.4	50.3[3]	12.4	2.1	45.8	0.7	39.0	Ukraine
24,756.0	0.3	0.1	96.6	3.0	0.2	0.2	2.6	7.0[4]	3.2[4]	0.1[4]	35.7[4]	53.9[4]	United Arab Emirates
269,040.3	6.7	2.7	5.5	85.1	13.9	47.7	23.4	58.3	14.7	2.3	2.0	22.8	United Kingdom[38]
687,532.7	11.2	1.3	1.9	85.6	10.0	51.2	24.3	20.6	—	1.0	9.5	68.9	United States[59]
2,729.6	53.2	0.3	0.7	45.8	5.3	5.6	34.9	18.9	6.0	0.8	1.1	73.2	Uruguay
3,109.0	2.5	—— 14.8 ——		82.7	2.8	2.4	77.4	18.6	0.4	24.3	0.1	56.7	Uzbekistan
20.8	87.0	—	—	13.0	—	1.0	12.0	32.4	—	—	23.7	44.0	Vanuatu
22,674.4	2.5	0.5	82.2	14.9	3.1	2.1	9.7	8.3	61.1	0.1	0.6	29.9	Venezuela
5,448.9	—— 45.0[2] ——		22.2	32.8[3]	0.6	1.6	30.6[3]	11.9	3.1	2.5	26.8	55.7	Vietnam
3,026.3	...	...	83.3[60, 61]	...	...	...	...	...	92.7	...	...	...	Virgin Islands (U.S.)
22.6[64]	...	...	...	...	...	...	...	...	...	...	...	...	West Bank[62]
...	...	...	...	...	...	...	...	...	...	...	...	...	Western Sahara
1,497.5	5.4	0.3[2]	91.5	2.8[3]	0.4	1.2	1.2[3]	5.8	2.7	—	3.7	87.8	Yemen
2,367.8	21.0	0.3	2.0	76.7	13.0	9.5	54.1	35.4	0.7	17.0	—	46.9	Yugoslavia
920.6	—— 5.3 ——		1.7	93.0	0.4	0.8	91.8	29.8	0.4	—	13.3	56.6	Zambia
2,127.8	56.5	5.3	1.5	36.8	3.4	3.4	30.0	36.4	5.8	2.7	6.1	49.0	Zimbabwe

also shown separately). [39]Figures for Italy include San Marino. [40]United Kingdom only. [41]Including coins. [42]1986. [43]Includes 83.8% from rest of Customs Union of Southern Africa. [44]Includes 50.8% to rest of Customs Union of Southern Africa. [45]Including also Iceland and Norway. [46]France only. [47]Includes 85.0% from South Africa. [48]Includes 52.5% for ferroalloys. [49]Excluding bulk imports of fuels. [50]1990. [51]Includes 19.7% for nonmonetary gold. [52]Includes 19.8% for nonmonetary gold. [53]Includes 46.0% shown as special categories. [54]Figures for South Africa refer to the Customs Union of Southern Africa (includes South Africa, Botswana, Lesotho, Namibia, and Swaziland, also shown separately). [55]Including unspecified destinations for gold exports of 19.7%. [56]Includes 87.7% from South Africa; these imports may have had their origin from other countries. [57]Figures for Switzerland include Liechtenstein also shown separately. [58]1989. [59]Figures for United States include American Samoa, Guam, Puerto Rico, and Virgin Islands (U.S.), also shown separately. [60]1993. [61]Exports of refined petroleum to United States only. [62]Total external trade for West Bank and Gaza Strip in 1997: imports U.S.$1,860,000,000, exports U.S.$267,000,000. [63]Excluding imports from Israel (90.9% in 1987). [64]Excluding exports to Israel (70.3% in 1987).

Household budgets and consumption

This table provides international data on household income, on the consumption expenditure of households for goods and services, and on the principal object of such expenditure (in most countries), food consumption (by kind). For purposes of this compilation, income comprises pretax monetary payments and payment in kind. The first part of the table provides data on distribution of income by households and by sources of income; the second part analyzes the largest portion of income use—consumption expenditure. Such expenditure is defined as the purchase of goods and services to satisfy current wants and needs. This definition excludes income expended on taxes, debts, savings and investments, and insurance policies. The third and last part of the table focuses on food, which usually, and often by a wide margin, represents the largest share of consumer spending worldwide. The data provided include daily available calories per capita and consumption of major food groups.

For both sources of income and consumption expenditure, the primary basis of analysis for most countries is the household, an economic unit that can be as small as a single person or as large as an extended family. For some of the countries that do not compile information by household, the table provides data on personal income and personal expenditure—*i.e.*, the income and expenditure of all the individuals constituting a society's households. When no expenditure data at all is available, the table reports the weights of each major class of goods and services making up a given country's consumer (or retail) price index (CPI). The weighting of the components of the CPI usually reflects household spending patterns within the country or its principal urban or rural areas.

The data on distribution of income show, collectively for an entire country, the proportion of total income earned (occasionally, expended) by households constituting the lowest quintile and highest decile (poorest 20% and wealthiest 10%) within the country. These figures show the degree to which either group represents a disproportionate share of poverty or wealth.

The data on sources of income illuminate patterns of economic structure in the gaining of an income. They indicate, for example, that in poor, agrarian countries income often derives largely from self-employment (usually farming) or that in industrial countries, with well-developed systems of salaried employment and social welfare, income derives mainly from wages and salaries and secondarily from transfer payments (*see* note a). Because household sizes and numbers of income earners vary so greatly internationally, and because the frequency and methodology of household and CPI surveys do not permit single-year comparisons for more than a few countries at once, no summary of total *household* income or expenditure was possible. Instead, U.S. dollar figures are supplied for *per capita* private final consumption expenditure (for a single, recent year) that are more comparable internationally and refer to the same date. The figures on distribution of consumption expenditure by end use reveal patterns of personal and family use of disposable income and indicate, inter alia, that in developing countries, food may absorb 50% or more of disposable income, while in the larger household budgets of the developed countries, by contrast, food purchases may account for only 20–30% of spending. Each category of expenditure betrays similar complexities of local habit, necessity, and aspiration.

The reader should exercise caution when using these data to make intercountry comparisons. Most of the information comes from single-country surveys, which often differ markedly in their coverage of economically or demographically stratified groups, in sample design, or in the methods

Household budgets and consumption

country	income (latest)						consumption expenditure						
	percent received by		by source (percent)				per capita private final, U.S.$ (1995)	by kind or end use (percent of household or personal budget; latest)					
	lowest 20% of households	highest 10% of households	wages, salaries	self-employment	transfer payments[a]	other[b]		food[c]	housing[d]	clothing[e]	health care	energy, water	education
Afghanistan	…	…	20.7	28.0	8.2	43.1	…	33.9	3.0	…	1.1	0.7	…
Albania	…	…	53.0	4.0	11.5	31.5	680	…	…	…	…	…	…
Algeria	7.0[1]	26.8[1]	43.1	38.3	18.6	1.8	810	52.3	6.7[2]	8.6	2.8	[2]	[3]
American Samoa	…	…	…	…	…	…	1,880[4]	32.9	20.4[5]	5.2	…	…	…
Andorra	…	…	…	…	…	…	…	…	…	…	…	…	…
Angola	…	…	…	…	…	…	370	74.1[6]	10.2[2, 6]	5.5[6]	1.8[6]	[2, 6]	2.7[6]
Antigua and Barbuda	…	…	…	…	…	…	4,050	*42.9*	*23.3*	*7.5*	…	5.5	…
Argentina	*4.4*	*35.2*	53.9	31.5	1.5	12.7	6,620	40.1	9.3	8.0	7.9	9.0	2.6
Armenia	…	…	24.5	13.6[7]	5.5	56.4	360	69.6	…	17.4	…	…	…
Aruba	…	…	…	…	…	…	11,190	26.9	9.9	8.4	2.9	8.5	1.9
Australia	5.9	25.4	72.7	7.5	13.0	6.8	12,040	18.7	18.5	5.6	7.1	2.2	1.6
Austria	*10.4*	*19.3*	55.7	[8]	24.4	19.9[8]	16,020	28.1	14.5	8.5	5.8	4.0	0.4
Azerbaijan	…	…	70.2	10.8[7]	19.0	—	460	42.2	—	13.6	4.8	—	—
Bahamas, The	3.6	32.1	…	…	…	…	3,950[9]	13.8	32.8	5.9	4.4	…	5.3
Bahrain	…	…	…	…	…	…	2,240	32.4	21.2	5.9	2.3	2.2	2.3
Bangladesh	8.7[1]	28.6[1]	18.7	48.3	7.5	25.5	170[10]	63.3	8.8	5.9	1.1	8.4	1.2
Barbados	*7.0*	*44.0*[11]	…	…	…	…	4,860	45.8	16.8	5.1	3.8	5.2	[3]
Belarus	11.4[1]	20.0[1]	47.1	7.3[9]	45.6	—	610	29.0	2.7	…	…	…	…
Belgium	*9.5*[12]	*20.2*[12]	49.6	10.9	20.7	18.8	16,550	18.3	11.4	7.0	10.5	6.2	[3]
Belize	…	…	*84.1*		— *15.9* —		1,780	34.0	9.0	8.8	1.6	9.1	2.3
Benin	*8.0*	*39.0*	26.3		— 73.7 —		240	37.0	10.0	14.0	5.0	2.0	4.0
Bermuda	7.2	24.7	65.3	9.0	3.3	22.4	12,690[13]	14.6	27.7	4.9	7.6	3.3	3.8
Bhutan	…	…	…	…	…	…	170	*72.3*	…	*21.2*	…	*3.7*	…
Bolivia	5.6[12]	31.7[12]	…	…	…	…	690	46.6	7.8	5.1	2.1	4.7	0.3
Bosnia and Herzegovina	…	…	53.2	12.0	18.2	16.6	1,890[14]	44.7	1.6	8.3	3.4	7.8	[3]
Botswana	3.7	42.9	73.3	15.4	10.8	0.4	1,030	39.5[15]	11.8	5.6	2.3	2.5	4.9
Brazil	2.5[12]	47.6[12]	62.4	14.7	10.9	12.0	4,420	25.3	21.3[2]	12.9	9.1	[2]	…
Brunei	…	…	…	…	…	…	…	*45.1*	*2.6*	*6.1*	…	*2.4*	[3]
Bulgaria	8.5[1]	22.5[1]	34.7	23.6[7]	14.8	—	1,470	47.0	4.1	7.4	3.2	4.3	[3]
Burkina Faso	5.5[1]	39.5[1]	…	…	…	…	220	38.7[6]	5.1[6]	4.4[6]	5.2[6]	13.7[6]	[3]
Burundi	7.9[1]	26.6[1]	…	…	…	…	190	59.6[6]	4.4[6]	11.1[6]	…	5.8[6]	…
Cambodia	6.9[1]	33.8[1]	…	…	…	…	280	…	…	…	…	…	…
Cameroon	…	…	41.4	52.6	3.0	3.0	570	49.1	18.0[2]	7.6	8.6	[2]	…
Canada	7.5[12]	23.8[12]	57.0	13.7	20.7	8.6	11,460	13.4	24.5[2]	5.3	4.7	[2]	3.1
Cape Verde	…	…	…	…	…	…	920	60.0	8.5	2.5	0.5	4.9	[17]
Central African Republic	2.0[1]	47.7[1]	…	…	…	…	350	70.5[6]	0.6[6]	9.5[6]	1.0[6]	6.5[6]	…
Chad	*8.0*	*30.0*	…	…	…	…	170	45.3[6]	…	3.5[6]	11.9[6]	5.8[6]	…
Chile	3.5[12]	46.1[12]	— 75.1 —		12.0	12.9	2,940	27.9	15.2	22.5	…	…	…
China	5.9[12]	30.4[12]	21.6	72.2	— 6.2 —		260	49.9[15, 18]	6.8[18]	13.7[18]	2.9[18]	…	2.3[18]
Colombia	3.0[12]	46.1[12]	45.1	35.4	14.2	5.3	1,540	45.0	7.8	4.5	6.4	2.2	1.7
Comoros	…	…	*25.6*	*64.5*	*8.7*	*1.2*	350	67.3	2.3	11.6	3.2	3.8	[3]
Congo, Dem. Rep. of the	…	…	…	…	…	…	190	61.7	11.5[2]	9.7	2.6	[2]	[3]
Congo, Rep. of the	*7.0*	*43.5*	…	…	…	…	870	37.0	6.0	6.0	6.0	3.0	8.0
Costa Rica	4.0[12]	34.7[12]	61.0	22.6	9.6	6.8	1,600	39.1	12.1[2]	9.4	3.7	[2]	[3]
Côte d'Ivoire	7.1[1]	28.8[1]	44.9	49.9	— 5.2 —		480	48.0	7.8	10.0	0.7	8.5	…
Croatia	9.3[1]	21.6[1]	40.2	40.8	12.1	6.9	3,790	37.8	2.9	8.6	4.3	7.6	[3]
Cuba	…	…	57.3		— 42.7 —		1,510[9]	26.7	…	…	…	2.5	…
Cyprus	…	…	76.3	5.9	14.4	3.4	8,300	22.7	5.5	10.0	3.1	1.3	1.4
Czech Republic	10.3[12]	22.4[12]	— 66.7 —		27.6	5.7	2,620	26.7	5.5[2]	7.3	[19]	[2]	…
Denmark	9.6[12]	20.5[12]	63.3	14.6	25.9	–3.8	17,730	17.9	22.9	5.2	2.2	6.1	1.9
Djibouti	…	…	*51.6*	*36.0*	*10.5*	*1.9*	590	50.3	6.4	1.7	2.4	13.1	…
Dominica	…	…	…	…	…	…	2,110	43.1	16.1	6.5	…	5.4	…
Dominican Republic	4.3[12]	37.8[12]	*41.7*	*31.8*	*1.5*	*25.0*	1,150	46.0	10.0	3.0	8.0	5.0	3.0
East Timor	…	…	…	…	…	…	…	…	…	…	…	…	…
Ecuador	5.4[1]	33.8[1]	17.4	76.9	3.6	2.1	1,040	36.1	9.0	10.1	4.2	3.3	[17]

employed for collection, classification, and tabulation of data. Further, the reference period of the data varies greatly; while a significant portion of the data is from 1980 or later, information for some countries dates from the 1970s. This older information is typeset in italic. Finally, intercountry comparisons of annual personal consumption expenditure may be misleading because of the distortions of price and purchasing power present when converting a national currency unit into U.S. dollars.

The table's food consumption data include total daily available calories per capita (food supply), which amounts to domestic production and imports minus exports, animal feed, and nonfood uses, and a percentage breakdown of the major food groups that make up food supply.

The data for daily available calories per capita provide a measure of the nutritional adequacy of each nation's food supply. The following list, based on estimates from the United Nations Food and Agriculture Organization (FAO), indicates the regional variation in recommended daily minimum nutritional requirements, which are defined by factors such as climatic ambience, physical activity, and average body weight: Africa (2,320 calories), formerly Centrally Planned Asia (2,300 calories), Far East (2,240 calories), Latin America (2,360 calories), Near East (2,440 calories).

The breakdown of diet by food groups describes the character of a nation's food supply. A typical breakdown for a low-income country might show a diet with heavy intake of vegetable foods, such as cereals, potatoes, or cassava. In the high-income countries, a relatively larger portion of total calories derives from animal products (meat, eggs, and milk). The reader should note that these data refer to total national *supply* and often do not reflect the differences that may exist within a single country.

In compiling this table, Britannica editors rely on both numerous national reports and principal secondary sources such as the World Bank's *World Development Report* (annual), the International Labour Organisation's *Sources and Methods: Labour Statistics vol. 1 Consumer Price Indices* (3rd ed.), the UN's *Yearbook of National Accounts Statistics* (annual) and *National Accounts Statistics: Compendium of Income Distribution Statistics,* and the FAO's *Food Balance Sheets.*

The following terms further define the column headings:

a. Includes pensions, family allowances, unemployment payments, remittances from abroad, and social security and related benefits.
b. Includes interest and dividends, rents and royalties, and all other income not reported under the three preceding categories.
c. Includes alcoholic and nonalcoholic beverages and meals away from home when identifiable. Excludes tobacco except as noted.
d. Rent, maintenance of dwellings, and taxes only; excludes energy and water (heat, light, power, and water) and household durables (furniture, appliances, utensils, and household operations), shown separately.
e. Includes footwear.
f. Furniture, appliances, and utensils; usually includes expenditure on household operation.
g. Includes expenditure on cultural activities other than education.
h. May include data not shown separately in preceding categories, including meals away from home (*see* note c).
i. Represents pure fats and oils only.
j. Consists mainly of peas, beans, and lentils; spices; stimulants; alcoholic beverages (when combined with "other"); sugars and honey; and nuts and oilseeds.

transportation, communications	household durable goods[f]	recreation[g]	personal effects, other[h]	food consumption, 1998: daily available calories per capita	percent of total calories derived from: cereals	potatoes, cassava	meat, poultry	fish	eggs, milk	fruits, vegetables	fats, oils[i]	other[j]	country
…	…	…	61.3	1,716	83.4	1.1	4.1	—	2.4	2.6	3.8	2.6	Afghanistan
…	…	…	…	2,976	51.1	1.8	5.1	0.1	16.9	6.0	9.0	10.0	Albania
12.0	4.5	4.6[3]	8.5	3,020	60.3	2.2	2.7	0.3	6.1	5.1	13.8	9.5	Algeria
17.8	[5]	1.1	22.6	…	…	…	…	…	…	…	…	…	American Samoa
…	…	…	…	3,348	22.6	4.7	13.4	2.4	9.3	6.7	21.6	19.4	Andorra
3.9[6]	…	…	1.8[6]	…	…	…	…	…	…	…	…	…	Angola
10.0	…	…	*10.8*	2,450	25.8	1.0	15.8	1.7	11.3	7.9	16.4	20.2	Antigua and Barbuda
11.6	…	7.5	5.9	3,144	29.5	5.2	16.5	0.5	10.3	4.5	15.4	18.0	Argentina
…	6.6	…	28.7	2,356	52.3	6.7	5.3	0.1	7.0	6.5	11.7	10.4	Armenia
15.5	9.1	3.1	11.9	2,659	28.2	2.3	18.9	1.4	10.8	5.0	13.6	19.7	Aruba
15.1	7.0	7.5	16.7	3,190	22.7	3.2	15.5	0.8	11.8	5.3	17.0	23.5	Australia
16.3	7.8	7.1	7.5	3,531	20.7	3.1	13.8	0.6	11.4	5.5	21.5	23.4	Austria
5.1	6.5	0.7	27.1	2,191	66.6	2.7	4.6	0.1	9.7	5.1	2.8	8.4	Azerbaijan
14.8	8.9	4.9	9.2	2,546	30.1	1.4	18.8	1.1	5.9	8.6	9.3	24.9	Bahamas, The
8.5	9.8	6.4	9.0	…	…	…	…	…	…	…	…	…	Bahrain
0.9	…	…	10.4	2,050	81.6	1.3	0.8	0.9	1.5	1.1	5.6	7.2	Bangladesh
10.5	8.1	4.8[3]	—	2,978	31.6	3.9	12.6	2.3	6.6	3.4	12.8	26.8	Barbados
…	…	…	68.3	3,136	36.2	9.9	10.5	0.1	10.2	2.6	12.0	18.7	Belarus
13.4	10.6	6.8[3]	15.8	3,606	20.4	5.2	8.6	1.1	10.8	6.5	25.7	21.7	Belgium
13.7	8.0	…	9.4	2,922	34.0	1.4	6.3	0.4	7.5	9.6	10.2	30.7	Belize
14.0	5.0	…	9.0	2,571	37.5	36.9	2.2	0.7	0.8	2.6	5.3	14.0	Benin
7.3	16.6	10.8	3.4	2,921	22.8	2.6	15.7	2.7	7.8	12.4	15.2	20.8	Bermuda
…	*0.7*	…	*2.1*	…	…	…	…	…	…	…	…	…	Bhutan
17.7	9.7	2.7	3.3	2,214	40.7	6.6	11.2	0.1	3.7	8.6	11.4	17.7	Bolivia
6.0	4.1	3.5[3]	2.3	2,801	64.6	5.6	4.3	0.1	3.7	4.5	3.7	13.4	Bosnia and Herzegovina
13.1	13.8	3.1	3.4	2,159	46.9	1.8	6.3	0.5	8.9	2.5	11.6	21.6	Botswana
15.0	…	…	16.4	2,926	30.9	4.3	10.8	0.4	8.3	4.5	12.6	28.2	Brazil
17.2	*8.3*	*8.9*[3]	*9.4*	2,851	48.0	1.2	13.0	1.3	6.4	5.0	6.3	18.9	Brunei
6.6	4.0	3.0[3]	21.5	2,740	37.6	2.1	10.7	0.3	12.1	5.4	15.6	16.3	Bulgaria
18.6[6]	3.0[6]	2.3[3, 6]	9.0[6]	2,149	73.2	0.7	2.6	0.1	1.9	0.9	5.2	15.5	Burkina Faso
…	6.0[6]	…	13.1[6, 16]	1,578	16.7	30.0	1.3	0.4	0.8	10.3	1.5	39.0	Burundi
…	…	…	…	2,078	77.9	1.3	6.2	0.8	0.5	2.9	4.7	5.7	Cambodia
13.0	…	2.4	1.3	2,209	41.7	16.3	3.4	0.8	1.4	13.7	9.1	13.6	Cameroon
14.3	8.8	8.0	17.9	3,167	24.9	2.9	11.4	1.1	8.8	6.6	20.5	23.8	Canada
8.8	6.9	[17]	7.9[17]	3,099	40.3	2.5	5.8	1.5	4.9	3.1	17.6	24.2	Cape Verde
4.1[6]	0.8[6]	1.3[6]	5.7[6]	2,056	18.9	35.9	6.4	0.3	1.5	6.2	13.7	17.1	Central African Republic
…	…	…	33.5[6]	2,171	53.8	9.4	2.3	0.5	2.2	1.5	7.1	23.2	Chad
6.4	…	…	28.0	2,844	38.7	3.4	12.5	1.2	6.7	4.8	12.4	20.3	Chile
4.7[18]	5.3[18]	2.4[18]	12.0[18]	2,972	54.7	5.6	13.2	13.2	2.6	5.3	7.3	10.1	China
18.5	5.7	…	8.2	2,559	32.5	7.2	7.2	0.4	8.7	7.9	11.9	24.2	Colombia
2.2	3.0	2.5[3]	4.1	1,858	42.7	15.6	1.8	2.4	1.1	8.0	10.3	18.1	Comoros
5.9	4.8	3.8[3]	—	1,701	19.2	56.3	1.9	0.6	0.1	6.5	6.3	9.1	Congo, Dem. Rep. of the
15.0	4.0	…	15.0	2,241	25.4	37.9	3.1	2.2	1.5	6.2	11.7	11.9	Congo, Rep. of the
11.6	10.9	4.4[3]	8.8	2,781	32.9	1.9	5.3	0.5	9.5	5.0	14.1	30.9	Costa Rica
12.2	3.4	…	9.4	2,695	42.5	24.7	1.9	0.7	0.9	8.7	11.2	9.4	Côte d'Ivoire
9.3	4.5	4.1[3]	1.5	2,479	31.2	8.4	4.2	0.3	10.6	7.5	11.9	25.8	Croatia
5.4	…	…	65.4	2,473	37.3	5.3	5.3	0.8	4.9	5.1	9.6	31.7	Cuba
15.6	10.5	6.3	23.6	3,474	25.6	2.4	14.7	1.0	12.7	8.0	12.7	22.9	Cyprus
3.1	4.5	0.8[19]	52.7	3,292	27.6	4.4	10.1	0.7	9.6	4.3	17.9	25.4	Czech Republic
15.5	6.1	8.3	13.9	3,443	25.4	3.8	11.7	1.4	9.9	4.9	17.6	25.3	Denmark
…	1.5	…	24.6	2,074	51.3	0.2	4.5	0.2	4.8	1.6	17.9	19.4	Djibouti
11.6	6.0	…	11.3	2,996	23.9	9.1	10.6	1.6	8.7	12.5	6.9	26.7	Dominica
4.0	8.0	…	13.0	2,277	28.3	2.8	7.6	0.7	5.2	10.1	19.1	26.4	Dominican Republic
…	…	…	…	…	…	…	…	…	…	…	…	…	East Timor
12.8	5.5	[17]	19.0[17]	2,724	34.5	2.7	5.8	0.6	6.6	4.4	20.6	24.8	Ecuador

Household budgets and consumption (continued)

country	income (latest)						consumption expenditure						
	percent received by		by source (percent)				per capita private final, U.S.$ (1995)	by kind or end use (percent of household or personal budget; latest)					
	lowest 20% of households	highest 10% of households	wages, salaries	self-employment	transfer payments[a]	other[b]		food[c]	housing[d]	clothing[e]	health care	energy, water	education
Egypt	9.8[1]	25.0[1]	...	...	...	...	740	50.2	10.5[2]	10.9	2.7	[2]	[3]
El Salvador	*3.4*[12]	*40.5*[12]	...	...	...	...	1,520	37.0[18]	12.1[18]	6.7[18]	4.2[18]	3.6[18]	3.7[18]
Equatorial Guinea	...	...	57.0[6]	42.0[6]	—	1.0[6]	310	62.0[6]	...	10.0[6]	6.0[6]	...	...
Eritrea	...	...	...	...	...	...	170	...	...	...	...	...	...
Estonia	6.2[12]	26.2[12]	53.0	5.7	12.8	28.5	1,390	41.0	9.6	8.4	[19]	6.5	3.1
Ethiopia	7.1[1]	33.7[1]	0.2	79.5	—	20.3	87	49.0	7.0	6.0	3.0	7.0	4.0
Faroe Islands	...	...	88.3	11.7	—	—	...	40.9	11.0	8.0	...	18.9	...
Fiji	*3.7*	*37.8*	*81.5*	*9.1*	—	*9.4*	1,430[10]	34.7	15.6[2]	9.3	2.4	[2]	[3]
Finland	10.0[12]	21.6[12]	70.3	7.4	9.7	12.6	13,260	22.5	16.9	5.0	4.8	4.6	[3]
France	7.2[12]	25.1[12]	51.1	14.1	27.5	7.3	15,810	17.4	16.2	6.1	9.8	3.8	0.7
French Guiana	...	...	74.6		——25.4——		...	30.0[15]	16.1[2]	6.7	4.4	[2]	[3]
French Polynesia	...	...	61.9	18.5	16.6	3.0	4,310[20]	39.6	9.7	6.3	1.0	8.1	1.0
Gabon	*3.3*	*54.4*	...	...	...	...	4,060	...	...	...	...	...	...
Gambia, The	...	...	...	...	...	...	330	58.0[21]	5.1[21]	17.5[21]	...	5.4[21]	...
Gaza Strip	...	...	...	...	...	...	910[22]	...	...	...	...	...	...
Georgia	...	...	34.5	21.6[7]	21.7	22.0	430	38.3	...	14.8	...	0.3	...
Germany	8.2[12]	23.7[12]	57.9	[8]	21.3	20.8[8]	16,850	19.0	16.9	7.9	3.5	4.1	[3]
Ghana	8.4[1]	26.1[1]	41.6[23]	47.1[23]	—	11.3[23]	290	*57.4*	*11.5*[2]	*14.3*	*1.3*	[2]	[3]
Greece	7.5[12]	25.3[12]	34.0	22.8	17.0	26.2	8,140	29.9	14.1	6.5	3.1	3.3	0.5
Greenland	...	...	...	...	...	...	11,110	30.1	10.0	7.7	0.3	5.4	...
Grenada	...	...	...	...	...	...	1,650	40.7[15]	11.9	5.2	[24]	3.9	[3]
Guadeloupe	...	...	78.9	13.7	7.4	—	4,080[27]	31.6[15]	11.3[2]	9.3	4.6	[2]	[3]
Guam	...	...	...	...	...	...	...	*24.1*	*28.6*	*10.6*	*4.8*	...	...
Guatemala	2.1[12]	46.6[12]	...	...	...	...	1,180	64.4	16.0[2]	3.1	0.6	[2]	0.3
Guernsey	...	...	...	...	...	...	...	23.7	12.1	7.5	...	8.2	...
Guinea	6.4[1]	32.0[1]	...	...	...	...	510	*61.5*	*7.3*[2]	*7.9*	*11.1*	[2]	...
Guinea-Bissau	2.1[1]	42.4[1]	...	...	...	...	230	...	...	...	...	...	...
Guyana	4.0	40.0[11]	*73.0*	...	*6.3*	*20.7*	...	*42.5*[15]	*21.4*	*8.6*	...	*5.2*	[3]
Haiti	...	...	...	...	...	...	320	51.1[15]	4.3	8.7	2.2	...	[3]
Honduras	3.4[12]	42.1[12]	58.3	[8]	1.8	39.9[8]	450	44.4	22.4[2]	9.1	7.0	[2]	[3]
Hong Kong	...	...	...	...	...	...	13,880	15.1	15.7[2]	21.3	5.0	[2]	0.5
Hungary	8.8[12]	24.8[12]	——55.0——		19.2	5.8	4,270	38.1	5.7	7.4	1.5	6.1	0.7
Iceland	4.7	27.3	73.1	2.7	10.2	14.0	15,850	31.3	16.0	7.5	2.3	2.9	1.3
India	8.1[1]	33.5[1]	42.2	39.7	——18.1——		210	52.2	6.1[25]	10.0	2.4	4.7[25]	1.8
Indonesia	8.0[12]	30.3[12]	*42.1*	*41.5*	*2.5*	*13.9*	640	47.5[18]	20.1[2, 18]	5.5[18]	...	[2]	...
Iran	*3.8*	*41.7*	37.4[18]	30.5[18]	——32.1[18]——		1,040	42.6[15]	24.9[2]	11.8	3.9	[2]	[3]
Iraq	...	...	23.9	33.9	23.0	18.6	1,710[13]	50.2	19.9[2]	10.6	1.6	[2]	[3]
Ireland	6.7[12]	27.4[12]	58.6	13.3	19.9	8.2	9,650	30.5	7.1	7.4	3.2	6.1	2.4
Isle of Man	6.4	26.6	64.1	6.6	16.9	12.4	...	31.0	7.9	7.0	...	11.0	...
Israel	6.9[12]	26.9[12]	63.4[18, 26]	14.6[18, 26]	18.9[18, 26]	3.1[18, 26]	9,930	23.8	19.8	5.3	6.2	2.4	2.9
Italy	8.7[12]	21.8[12]	41.7	25.9	20.3	12.1	11,860	19.5	10.0	9.8	6.7	3.8	0.7
Jamaica	7.0[1]	28.9[1]	63.6	13.9	14.0	8.5	1,770	35.7	5.7	4.6	2.8	4.9	0.2
Japan	10.6[12]	21.7[12]	59.3	11.1	19.5	10.1	24,670	22.6	6.7	6.0	2.7	5.6	5.3
Jersey	...	...	...	...	...	...	...	*28.3*	*14.9*	*8.3*	...	*6.5*	...
Jordan	7.6[1]	29.8[1]	51.4	11.1	13.7	23.8	1,020	40.6	15.8	6.7	2.2	5.0	3.5
Kazakhstan	6.7[1]	26.3[1]	67.7	5.8[7]	16.9	9.6	1,290	29.6	2.6	...	...	...	...
Kenya	5.0	34.9	...	...	...	...	220	46.5	10.0	7.7	2.2	2.6	1.0
Kiribati	...	...	*69.7*	*21.4*	*6.0*	*2.9*	370[4]	50.0[15]	7.5[2, 5]	8.0	...	[2]	...
Korea, North	...	...	...	...	...	...	...	46.5[27]	0.6[27]	29.9[27]	...	3.3[27]	...
Korea, South	7.5[1]	24.3[1]	53.8	25.1	13.1	8.0	5,390	29.7	4.1	7.7	5.0	4.0	14.2
Kuwait	...	...	*53.8*	*20.8*	——*25.4*——		...	28.1[15]	15.5	8.1	0.7	9.6	[3]
Kyrgyzstan	6.3[12]	31.7[12]	67.3		——32.7——		670	33.5	2.2	...	...	...	...
Laos	9.6[1]	26.4[1]	...	...	...	...	140[9]	...	...	...	...	...	...
Latvia	7.6[12]	25.9[12]	67.0	5.4[7]	17.4	10.2	2,400	51.6	...	...	...	...	...
Lebanon	*5.0*	*45.0*	*27.9*	...	*3.0*	*69.1*	3,010	*42.8*[6]	*16.8*[6]	*8.6*[6]	*7.2*[6]	*4.5*[6]	*3.9*[6]
Lesotho	2.8[1]	43.4[1]	22.4	27.8	44.7	5.1	530	48.0[15]	10.1	16.4	...	...	...
Liberia	5.0	73.0[11]	...	...	...	...	330[9]	*34.4*[6]	*14.9*[6]	*13.8*[6]	...	*5.0*[6]	...
Libya	...	...	...	...	...	...	2,330[9]	*37.2*[15]	*32.2*[2]	*6.9*	*3.3*	[2]	[3]
Liechtenstein	...	...	...	...	...	...	...	21.3[15]	18.0	6.6	7.7	4.4	[3]
Lithuania	7.8[1]	25.6[1]	66.4	9.7	18.7	5.2	1,910	50.3	...	...	...	...	...
Luxembourg	10.0	34.0[11]	67.1	4.8	28.1	—	15,140[28]	12.8	13.7	5.9	7.3	6.1	[3]
Macau	...	...	65.0	18.1	7.0	9.9	5,480	39.2[15]	17.5	6.8	4.0	5.2	[3]
Macedonia	...	...	57.7	17.2	16.2	9.0	1,010	40.6	1.9	7.8	3.0	7.8	[3]
Madagascar	5.1[1]	36.7[1]	*58.8*[6, 29]	*14.1*[6, 29]	—	*27.1*[6, 29]	220	59.0	6.0	6.0	2.0	6.0	4.0
Malawi	*10.4*	*40.1*	83.3	6.0	—	11.7	109	30.0	4.0	9.0	4.0	5.0	10.0
Malaysia	4.5[12]	37.9[12]	...	...	...	...	2,090	28.7	10.2[2]	4.3	2.5	[2]	0.6
Maldives	...	...	...	...	...	...	270[9]	57.4	1.6	8.0	2.5	...	[3]
Mali	4.6[1]	40.4[1]	...	...	...	...	200	57.0	2.0	6.0	2.0	6.0	4.0
Malta	...	...	63.8	19.3	—	16.9	5,380	31.2	3.5	7.6	3.5	2.0	0.4
Marshall Islands	...	...	...	...	...	...	...	57.7	15.6[2, 5]	12.0	...	[2]	...
Martinique	...	...	80.0	...	...	20.0	4,840[6]	32.1[15]	10.6[2]	8.0	5.2	[2]	[3]
Mauritania	6.2[1]	29.9[1]	...	...	...	...	470	73.1	2.5	8.1	0.9	7.7	0.4
Mauritius	4.0	46.7	51.7	29.0	11.2	8.1	2,290	41.9	8.8	8.4	3.0	6.4	2.9
Mayotte	...	...	...	...	...	...	...	42.2	...	31.5	...	6.8	...
Mexico	3.6[12]	42.8[12]	61.5	29.1	7.8	1.6	2,110	36.6[15]	13.3[2]	8.4	3.4	[2]	[3]
Micronesia	...	...	51.8	23.0	2.1	23.1	...	73.5	...	...	...	...	...
Moldova	6.9[12]	25.8[12]	41.2	10.4	15.3	33.1	220	...	...	...	...	...	...
Monaco	...	...	...	...	...	...	...	...	...	...	...	...	...
Mongolia	7.3[1]	24.5[1]	72.1	9.5[7]	9.7	8.7	230	39.1	5.9[2]	23.4	0.5	[2]	2.9
Morocco	6.5[1]	30.9[1]	...	...	...	...	900	38.0	7.0	11.0	5.0	2.0	8.0
Mozambique	6.5[1]	31.7[1]	51.6		——48.4——		57	74.6	11.7	3.7	0.8	...	[3]
Myanmar (Burma)	*8.0*	*40.0*[11]	...	...	...	...	750[28]	*49.1*[6]	*10.4*[6]	*15.3*[6]	*2.4*[6]	*4.0*[6]	*5.9*[6]
Namibia	...	...	67.1	27.5	5.4	...	1,050	...	...	...	...	...	...
Nauru	...	...	...	...	...	...	...	...	...	...	...	...	...
Nepal	7.6[1]	29.8[1]	25.1	63.4	——11.5——		170	61.2	17.3	11.7	3.7	...	[3]

				food consumption, 1998									country
				daily available calories per capita	percent of total calories derived from:								
transportation, communications	household durable goods[f]	recreation[g]	personal effects, other[h]		cereals	potatoes, cassava	meat, poultry	fish	eggs, milk	fruits, vegetables	fats, oils[i]	other[j]	
4.7	5.0	3.3[3]	12.7	3,282	65.4	1.6	2.9	0.6	2.1	6.9	6.1	14.3	Egypt
10.2[18]	5.7[18]	4.3[18]	12.5[18]	2,522	53.4	1.5	2.6	0.2	6.3	3.5	7.7	24.9	El Salvador
...	...	...	22.0[6]	...	...	...	...	...	...	...	...	...	Equatorial Guinea
...	...	...	...	1,744	73.4	4.4	0.6	0.0	1.9	0.1	0.7	18.8	Eritrea
9.2	2.3	5.0[19]	15.0	3,058	38.5	5.3	8.9	1.6	12.7	4.3	13.3	15.4	Estonia
8.0	2.0	...	14.0	1,805	66.3	13.1	3.2	0.0	1.9	0.6	2.8	12.1	Ethiopia
...	6.6	...	14.6	...	...	...	...	...	...	...	...	...	Faroe Islands
13.8	9.3	4.3[3]	10.6	2,852	42.3	6.9	8.5	1.4	3.0	1.8	18.7	17.3	Fiji
14.8	6.3	9.5[3]	15.6	3,180	33.6	4.2	16.3	2.0	15.7	3.9	12.9	18.6	Finland
16.1	7.7	6.9	15.3	3,541	24.3	3.4	16.5	1.2	12.0	4.7	19.7	18.3	France
17.5	7.9	6.2[3]	11.2	2,818	32.4	7.9	13.2	2.1	7.5	7.0	10.5	19.3	French Guiana
16.4	4.4	4.0	9.5	2,924	33.6	4.0	13.3	4.4	6.1	3.0	13.6	22.1	French Polynesia
...	...	...	...	2,560	29.5	17.9	7.3	3.1	2.4	16.4	7.9	15.5	Gabon
...	...	...	14.0[21]	2,559	54.0	0.7	1.3	1.9	1.4	0.9	17.7	22.1	Gambia, The
...	...	...	...	...	...	...	...	...	...	...	...	...	Gaza Strip
...	5.9	...	40.7	2,252	60.5	4.8	4.9	0.2	7.6	4.8	3.0	14.2	Georgia
17.8	9.4	10.6[3]	10.8	3,402	22.5	4.1	11.7	0.8	10.3	5.7	21.6	23.3	Germany
3.3	*3.8*	*3.9*[3]	*4.5*	2,684	26.2	48.2	1.2	1.8	0.2	9.6	4.6	8.3	Ghana
17.5	6.9	5.2	13.0	3,630	29.1	3.5	8.9	1.2	11.8	8.6	20.0	16.8	Greece
8.0	9.2	15.5	13.8	...	...	...	...	...	...	...	...	...	Greenland
9.1	13.7	4.6[3]	10.9[24]	2,681	25.3	2.5	9.1	1.5	9.5	9.2	13.1	29.8	Grenada
20.5	9.3	4.7[3]	8.7	2,732	37.8	2.6	10.8	2.6	8.5	8.4	13.1	16.1	Guadeloupe
18.0	...	*5.1*	*8.8*	...	...	...	...	...	...	...	...	...	Guam
7.0	5.0	0.9	2.7	2,159	55.3	0.4	3.6	0.1	5.1	3.1	7.0	25.4	Guatemala
15.7	8.3	...	24.7	3,257	22.8	6.1	14.4	1.0	11.6	5.0	19.1	20.0	Guernsey
5.1	*2.9*	*4.1*	*0.1*	2,315	42.9	15.6	0.9	1.2	1.0	13.0	14.7	10.8	Guinea
...	...	...	...	2,411	61.2	7.4	4.6	0.2	1.4	4.2	13.0	8.1	Guinea-Bissau
4.8	*2.9*	*6.4*[3]	*8.2*	2,476	47.3	3.8	4.8	4.2	5.4	2.8	4.1	27.6	Guyana
7.6	9.2	5.3[3]	11.6	1,876	46.7	8.8	3.3	0.3	2.0	7.4	8.8	22.8	Haiti
3.0	8.3	2.4[3]	3.1	2,343	46.7	0.3	3.6	0.3	8.6	6.7	11.9	21.9	Honduras
8.4	17.5	8.1	8.4	3,200	27.1	1.6	20.0	3.3	5.2	4.0	19.7	19.2	Hong Kong
15.2	8.8	5.9	10.6	3,408	25.4	3.6	10.1	0.2	8.4	5.4	22.7	24.1	Hungary
14.5	7.6	9.6	7.0	3,222	20.7	3.2	14.3	3.6	14.6	4.0	13.4	26.2	Iceland
10.6	3.1	1.8	5.7	2,466	62.7	1.6	0.9	0.4	4.5	3.2	8.5	18.3	India
...	2.9[18]	...	24.0	2,850	64.6	5.8	2.2	1.3	0.6	2.3	7.8	15.4	Indonesia
5.0	6.4	1.7[3]	3.7	2,822	51.2	3.2	4.3	0.3	3.8	11.2	10.8	15.1	Iran
6.5	6.7	0.8[3]	3.7	2,419	59.4	1.2	1.4	0.1	1.9	8.0	19.5	8.6	Iraq
14.0	7.2	8.9	13.1	3,622	26.8	6.0	13.1	0.8	11.3	4.0	16.5	21.4	Ireland
14.9	5.7	...	22.5	3,257	22.8	6.1	14.4	1.0	11.6	5.0	19.1	20.0	Isle of Man
12.9	10.8	4.3	11.6	3,466	33.5	2.5	8.2	0.9	7.6	8.6	18.3	20.3	Israel
13.2	9.5	8.4	18.4	3,608	31.8	1.9	11.1	1.1	8.9	7.2	22.0	15.9	Italy
12.4	5.5	2.1	26.1	2,711	30.5	9.3	8.5	0.8	5.3	7.2	13.1	25.3	Jamaica
11.0	3.7	9.5	26.9	2,874	40.7	2.5	5.8	6.3	6.5	4.3	12.0	21.8	Japan
13.9	*7.1*	...	*21.0*	3,257	22.8	6.1	14.4	1.0	11.6	5.0	19.1	20.0	Jersey
11.2	6.1	4.0	4.9	2,791	52.7	1.1	5.1	0.2	5.4	3.9	15.3	16.3	Jordan
...	...	...	67.8	2,517	54.4	4.1	9.1	0.2	12.0	2.1	7.4	10.8	Kazakhstan
8.4	9.4	3.1	9.1	1,968	52.4	8.6	3.7	0.5	7.2	3.2	9.3	15.3	Kenya
8.0	[5]	...	26.5	2,977	34.7	8.3	4.6	4.6	1.6	4.6	7.2	34.4	Kiribati
...	3.8[27]	...	15.9	1,899	64.5	1.1	3.1	1.3	1.0	7.6	5.8	15.5	Korea, North
11.3	5.0	—— 19.0 ——		3,069	49.7	1.1	9.6	3.0	2.2	7.1	9.7	17.7	Korea, South
13.7	11.2	5.2[3]	7.9	3,059	36.8	1.9	11.2	0.5	9.8	8.4	10.2	21.2	Kuwait
...	...	...	64.3	2,535	58.3	6.7	8.7	—	13.0	2.1	3.6	7.6	Kyrgyzstan
...	...	...	...	2,175	77.7	3.8	4.4	0.7	0.5	2.2	2.3	8.5	Laos
...	...	...	54.8	2,994	32.7	8.4	6.0	0.9	12.9	3.8	15.3	20.0	Latvia
5.4[6]	*2.6*[6]	*1.9*[6]	*6.3*[6]	3,285	34.6	3.9	4.9	0.4	5.2	15.9	13.9	21.2	Lebanon
4.7	11.9	...	8.8	2,210	75.5	4.3	3.4	—	1.1	1.4	3.1	11.2	Lesotho
...	*6.1*[6]	...	*25.8*[6]	1,979	41.5	20.4	2.0	0.4	0.5	5.5	19.8	10.0	Liberia
9.4	*4.6*	*8.5*[3]	*2.5*	3,267	46.3	2.0	4.8	0.3	5.7	7.3	17.0	16.7	Libya
13.3	5.8	16.3[3]	6.6	3,222	22.1	2.3	14.8	0.8	12.5	6.1	18.7	22.7	Liechtenstein
...	...	...	49.7	3,104	45.5	7.8	8.9	0.9	6.9	5.3	10.1	14.6	Lithuania
19.1	10.8	4.2[3]	20.1	3,606	20.4	5.2	8.6	1.1	10.8	6.5	25.7	21.7	Luxembourg
8.2	3.0	8.8[3]	7.3	2,471	36.3	0.7	15.7	2.3	4.7	3.7	20.7	15.8	Macau
6.5	4.2	3.3[3]	1.8	2,938	39.7	3.3	7.0	0.3	5.2	6.9	15.7	21.8	Macedonia
4.0	1.0	...	12.0	2,001	53.0	21.1	5.5	0.7	3.1	3.8	4.4	8.3	Madagascar
10.0	3.0	...	25.0	2,226	59.0	15.8	1.3	0.4	0.5	4.2	4.0	14.7	Malawi
20.9	7.7	11.0	14.1	2,901	41.6	2.1	9.2	3.1	5.2	3.4	12.5	22.8	Malaysia
2.6	17.0	5.9[3]	5.0	2,451	43.5	3.2	1.4	13.1	4.3	5.6	5.2	23.7	Maldives
10.0	1.0	...	12.0	2,118	69.9	0.5	4.2	0.8	4.6	1.2	7.4	11.3	Mali
16.4	9.9	7.1	18.4	3,382	30.8	4.0	8.8	1.6	11.3	7.9	11.5	24.0	Malta
...	[5]	...	14.7	...	...	...	...	...	...	...	...	...	Marshall Islands
20.7	9.4	5.4[3]	8.6	2,865	30.0	4.2	12.1	2.9	8.5	11.0	8.7	22.5	Martinique
2.0	1.2	4.0	0.1	2,640	54.8	0.4	4.0	0.9	10.8	1.2	9.9	18.1	Mauritania
10.0	6.4	—	12.2	2,944	44.7	1.3	4.8	1.2	6.3	3.0	16.6	22.2	Mauritius
5.1	8.8	...	5.6	...	...	...	...	...	...	...	...	...	Mayotte
10.0	11.8	5.5[3]	11.0	3,144	46.2	0.8	8.2	0.7	6.0	4.0	11.3	22.8	Mexico
...	...	...	26.5	...	...	...	...	...	...	...	...	...	Micronesia
...	...	...	...	2,763	48.4	4.2	4.0	0.1	8.9	6.6	8.2	19.7	Moldova
...	...	...	...	3,541	24.3	3.4	16.5	1.2	6.3	3.0	16.6	22.2	Monaco
3.5	8.0	0.4	16.2	2,010	47.0	2.2	27.2	—	10.4	1.2	4.7	7.2	Mongolia
8.0	5.0	...	16.0	3,165	59.7	2.0	2.8	0.5	2.0	5.4	10.4	17.3	Morocco
...	...	1.4[3]	7.9	1,911	41.2	37.3	1.4	0.2	0.6	1.4	8.9	9.1	Mozambique
3.8[6]	*0.5*[6]	*1.1*[6]	*7.5*[6]	2,832	76.3	0.5	2.0	1.0	0.9	2.6	7.0	9.6	Myanmar (Burma)
...	...	...	...	2,107	48.6	13.9	5.6	0.6	3.4	1.9	5.1	20.9	Namibia
...	...	...	...	...	...	...	...	...	...	...	...	...	Nauru
1.2	...	2.9[3]	2.0	2,170	76.8	3.4	2.0	0.1	3.8	2.5	4.4	7.0	Nepal

Household budgets and consumption (continued)

country	income (latest)						consumption expenditure						
	percent received by		by source (percent)				per capita private final, U.S.$ (1995)	by kind or end use (percent of household or personal budget; latest)					
	lowest 20% of households	highest 10% of households	wages, salaries	self-employment	transfer payments[a]	other[b]		food[c]	housing[d]	clothing[e]	health care	energy, water	education
Netherlands, The	7.3[1]	25.1[1]	48.2	10.7	29.1	12.0	15,290	13.6	14.9	7.1	12.9	3.1	0.7
Netherlands Antilles	...	...	...	...	...	...	6,050[10]	24.4[30]	10.4[30]	8.7[30]	2.2[30]	8.3[30]	1.2[30]
New Caledonia	...	...	68.2	18.1	13.7	...	5,410[31]	25.9	23.3[2, 5]	3.5	3.2	[2]	...
New Zealand	2.7[12]	29.8[12]	65.8	9.8	15.2	9.1	10,300	20.0	19.4	4.4	2.9	3.2	1.5
Nicaragua	4.2[1]	39.8[1]	...	...	...	...	360	...	...	...	...	...	...
Niger	2.6	35.4	...	...	...	...	210	50.5	19.1[5]	7.3	...	...	...
Nigeria	4.4[1]	40.8[1]	30.2[18]	46.3[18]	0.9[18]	22.6[18]	350[32]	48.0	3.0	5.0	3.0	1.0	4.0
Northern Mariana Islands	...	...	...	...	...	...	...	49.2[15]	19.5[2, 5]	9.1	[19]	[2]	...
Norway	9.7[12]	21.8[12]	58.8	9.9	24.2	7.1	16,570	23.5	13.7	7.0	5.4	6.2	0.6
Oman	...	...	...	...	...	...	3,000	40.6	24.6	5.1	2.4	3.2	[3]
Pakistan	9.5[1]	27.6[1]	22.0	56.0	— 22.0 —		300	37.0	11.0	6.0	1.0	5.0	1.0
Palau	...	...	63.7	7.4	18.5	10.4	...	...	...	...	...	...	...
Panama	3.6[1]	35.7[1]	60.8[6]	12.8[6]	13.2[6]	13.2[6]	1,570	34.9	12.6[2]	5.1	3.5	[2]	[3]
Papua New Guinea	4.5[1]	40.5[1]	*57.3*	[8]	*1.1*	*41.6*[8]	1,140	40.9	12.5[5]	6.2	...	4.9	...
Paraguay	2.3	46.6	33.9	[8]	2.5	63.6[8]	1,590	48.7	16.4	9.7	3.4	—	1.5
Peru	4.4[12]	35.4[12]	31.2	65.1	3.7	...	1,820	44.1[15]	6.8[2]	10.1	2.7	[2]	[3]
Philippines	5.4[1]	36.6[1]	45.7	42.5	3.4	8.4	800	56.8	4.1[2]	3.9	...	[2]	...
Poland	7.7[12]	26.3[12]	34.0	4.3	20.7	41.0	1,940	41.2	2.8	10.9	8.1	1.0	[3]
Portugal	*7.3*[12]	*28.4*[12]	46.4	[8]	21.8	31.8[8]	6,860	34.8	2.0	10.3	4.5	3.0	1.4
Puerto Rico	*3.2*	*34.7*	56.3	6.4	29.5	7.8	5,640[10]	20.6	11.8[2]	7.4	11.6	[2]	3.1
Qatar	...	...	80.8	5.6	...	13.6	3,600[4]	24.5	35.1[5]	9.1	1.0	1.9	4.3
Réunion	...	...	68.9	[8]	16.0	15.1[8]	4,820[31]	22.4	11.8	7.9	2.2	2.2	[3]
Romania	8.9[12]	22.7[12]	62.6	— 37.4 —			1,570	51.1	16.4[2, 5]	15.7	1.2	[2]	[3]
Russia	4.4[1]	38.7[1]	68.5	6.4	15.7	12.1	1,180	34.8	2.7	22.3	...	...	...
Rwanda	9.7[1]	24.2[1]	10.4[33]	47.7[33]	13.9[33]	28.0[33]	130	32.1[33]	13.1[33]	9.4[33]	1.3[33]	1.2[33]	[33]
St. Kitts and Nevis	...	...	...	...	...	...	2,480[28]	*55.6*[15]	*7.6*	*7.5*	...	*6.6*	...
St. Lucia	...	...	...	...	...	...	...	49.6[15]	13.5	6.5	2.3	4.5	[3]
St. Vincent and the Grenadines	...	...	...	...	...	...	1,700	59.8	6.3	7.7	...	6.2	...
Samoa	...	...	*49.4*	*22.8*	...	*27.8*	710[1]	58.8	5.1[5]	4.2	...	5.0	...
San Marino	...	...	...	...	...	...	...	22.1	20.9[2]	8.0	2.6	[2]	[3]
São Tomé and Príncipe	...	...	...	...	...	...	270	...	...	...	...	...	...
Saudi Arabia	...	...	...	...	...	...	2,980	52.2[18, 34]	17.2[18, 34]	6.6[18, 34]	2.1[18, 34]	1.8[18, 34]	1.1[18, 34]
Senegal	6.4[1]	33.5[1]	51.6[6]	— 48.4[6] —			380	49.0	7.0	11.0	2.0	4.0	6.0
Seychelles	4.1	35.6	*77.2*	*3.8*	*3.2*	*15.8*	3,410[32]	53.9	13.6	4.2	0.4	9.1	...
Sierra Leone	*1.1*[1]	*43.6*[1]	27.9	61.6	— 10.5 —		190	63.8	5.8[2]	7.3	4.5	[2]	[3]
Singapore	5.1	33.5	81.2	16.8	— 2.0 —		11,710	18.7	10.2[2]	7.1	4.6	[2]	1.4
Slovakia	11.9[12]	18.2[12]	76.7	[8]	8.7	14.4[8]	1,580	26.8	7.6[2]	8.9	...	[2]	...
Slovenia	8.4[12]	20.7[12]	52.4	13.0	23.4	11.2	5,460	30.8	18.3	8.5	5.0	7.3	[3]
Solomon Islands	...	...	74.1	— 25.9 —			820[4]	46.8	21.9[2, 5]	5.7	[19]	[2]	...
Somalia	...	...	...	...	...	...	...	62.3[6, 15]	15.3[6]	5.6[6]	...	4.3[6]	...
South Africa	2.9[1]	45.9[1]	73.6	[8]	4.9	21.5[8]	1,970	29.3	12.6[2]	7.5	4.5	[2]	1.4
Spain	7.5[12]	25.2[12]	48.5	27.5	19.5	4.5	8,840	21.6[15]	12.6[2]	8.6	4.7	[2]	[3]
Sri Lanka	8.0[1]	28.0[1]	48.5	[8]	9.7	41.8[8]	520	48.0	1.9	10.1	1.8	3.3	0.8
Sudan, The	*4.0*	*34.6*	...	...	...	...	1,050[35]	63.6	11.5	5.3	4.1	3.8	[3]
Suriname	...	...	*74.6*	...	*3.2*	*22.2*	5,960[10]	*39.9*[6]	*4.4*[6]	*11.0*[6]	*3.6*[6]	*6.9*[6]	*2.6*[6]
Swaziland	*2.8*	*54.5*	44.4	22.2	12.2	21.2	500	33.5[15]	13.4[2]	6.0	1.8	[2]	[3]
Sweden	9.6[12]	20.1[12]	58.9	9.7	25.8	5.6	13,680	21.3	19.9	8.6	3.2	4.9	0.1
Switzerland	6.9[12]	25.2[12]	63.6	[8]	16.5	19.9[8]	26,060	27.0[15]	13.1	4.4	9.9	7.7	[3]
Syria	...	...	40.7	...	25.1	34.2	2,210	58.8[15]	16.0[2]	7.5	...	[2]	[3]
Taiwan	7.1	25.5	64.5	19.7	4.5	11.3	12,230	26.8	22.5	5.6	7.8	3.0	5.6
Tajikistan	...	...	64.3	5.6[7]	30.1	—	340	65.3	...	...	...	...	...
Tanzania	6.8[1]	30.1[1]	28.1	34.2	3.5	34.2	150	66.7	8.3	9.9	1.3	7.6	...
Thailand	6.4[1]	32.4[1]	36.4	45.0	0.9	17.7	1,540	29.0	6.3	11.6	8.0	1.7	0.5
Togo	*8.0*	*30.5*	...	...	...	...	210	42.5[6]	13.4[2, 6]	11.5[6]	5.0[6]	[2, 6]	[3, 6]
Tonga	...	...	...	...	...	...	...	49.3	10.5	5.6	0.3	2.7	...
Trinidad and Tobago	*2.6*	*33.6*	...	...	...	...	2,050	25.5[15]	21.6	10.4	[19]	...	1.5
Tunisia	5.9[1]	30.7[1]	...	...	...	...	1,260	39.0	10.7	6.0	3.0	5.1	1.8
Turkey	5.8[1]	32.3[1]	24.1	51.4	10.8	13.7	1,940	38.5	22.8[2]	9.0	2.6	[2]	1.4
Turkmenistan	6.1[1]	31.7[1]	56.6	26.0[7]	14.4	3.0	570[10]	...	...	...	...	...	...
Tuvalu	...	...	*17.9*	*76.1*	...	*6.0*	...	45.5	11.5[5]	7.5	...	...	...
Uganda	6.6[1]	31.2[1]	...	...	...	...	260	57.1[6, 15]	...	5.5[6]	...	7.3[6]	...
Ukraine	8.6[1]	26.4[1]	66.4	9.3	13.4	10.9	490	41.3	1.7	...	...	...	[3]
United Arab Emirates	...	...	...	...	...	...	7,940	24.1	23.7	9.1	1.1	1.2	3.9
United Kingdom	6.6[12]	27.3[12]	66.2	9.8	13.9	11.0	12,020	17.1	21.7	6.0	...	4.6	...
United States	5.2[12]	30.5[12]	64.4	9.0	19.3	7.3	18,840	15.4	14.9	6.9	17.0	3.5	2.2
Uruguay	5.4[12]	32.7[12]	53.5	17.0	— 29.5 —		4,140	39.9	17.6[2]	7.0	9.3	[2]	1.3
Uzbekistan	7.4[12]	25.2[12]	59.8	18.5	21.7	...	950	...	...	...	...	...	...
Vanuatu	...	...	59.0	33.7	— 7.3 —		680	30.5[15]	29.0[2, 5]	4.7	[19]	[2]	...
Venezuela	3.7[12]	37.0[12]	...	...	...	...	2,490	30.4	11.5	10.6	2.9	3.0	0.8
Vietnam	8.0[1]	29.9[1]	17.2	64.6	17.6	0.5	280	62.4	2.5	5.0	...	...	2.9
Virgin Islands (U.S.)	...	...	65.7	2.6	13.0	12.7	...	25.3[36]	*24.9*[36]	*5.4*[36]	...	*6.5*[36]	...
West Bank	...	...	...	...	...	...	1,380[22]	...	...	...	...	...	...
Western Sahara	...	...	...	...	...	...	...	...	...	...	...	...	...
Yemen	6.1[1]	30.8[1]	...	...	...	...	310	61.0[37]	13.2[37]	...	1.1[37]	6.1[37]	...
Yugoslavia	...	...	41.7	15.8	12.7	29.8	2,480[35]	51.6	1.4	7.4	5.2	8.4	[3]
Zambia	4.2[1]	39.2[1]	79.9	17.8	1.3	1.0	220	36.0	7.0	10.0	8.0	4.0	14.0
Zimbabwe	4.0[1]	46.9[1]	92.0	1.0	...	7.0	580	30.1[15]	6.5	10.3	7.1	8.9	6.0

[1]Data refer to consumption shares by fractiles of persons. [2]Housing includes energy, water. [3]Recreation includes education. [4]1988. [5]Housing includes household durable goods. [6]Capital city only. [7]Agricultural self-employment only. [8]Other includes self-employment. [9]1989. [10]1993. [11]Highest 20%. [12]Data refer to income shares by fractiles of persons. [13]1985. [14]1990. [15]Includes tobacco. [16]Includes wage taxes. [17]Personal effects, other includes education and recreation. [18]Urban areas only. [19]Recreation includes health care. [20]1984. [21]Low-income population in Banjul

transportation, communications	household durable goods[f]	recreation[g]	personal effects, other[h]	food consumption, 1998									country
				daily available calories per capita	percent of total calories derived from:								
					cereals	potatoes, cassava	meat, poultry	fish	eggs, milk	fruits, vegetables	fats, oils[i]	other[j]	
13.3	7.1	9.7	17.6	3,282	17.1	4.5	15.0	1.0	15.0	6.1	16.1	25.1	Netherlands, The
19.5[30]	10.0[30]	4.2[30]	10.1[30]	2,659	28.2	2.3	18.9	1.4	10.8	5.0	13.6	19.7	Netherlands Antilles
16.1	[5]	6.7	21.3	2,812	30.9	6.1	13.1	1.5	8.6	3.9	16.0	19.9	New Caledonia
17.1	10.9	—— 20.6 ——		3,315	22.1	4.1	15.1	1.3	11.1	7.4	16.8	22.3	New Zealand
...	...	...	...	2,208	50.4	1.3	2.4	0.1	4.3	2.7	10.9	27.9	Nicaragua
...	[5]	...	23.1	1,966	70.5	3.2	2.6	0.1	2.2	1.7	4.4	15.2	Niger
3.0	6.0	...	27.0	2,882	45.8	18.6	2.4	0.4	1.0	4.4	14.1	13.3	Nigeria
8.3	[5]	13.9[19]	—	...	...	...	...	...	...	...	...	...	Northern Mariana Islands
12.8	6.9	8.8	15.1	3,425	27.4	4.3	10.7	3.5	12.2	4.9	17.7	19.2	Norway
8.9	7.1	4.1[3]	4.0	...	...	...	...	...	...	...	...	...	Oman
13.0	5.0	...	21.0	2,447	57.0	0.9	3.1	0.2	8.5	2.9	13.2	14.3	Pakistan
...	...	...	...	...	...	...	...	...	...	...	...	...	Palau
15.1	8.4	11.7[3]	8.7	2,476	37.0	2.7	7.5	1.1	7.4	5.7	16.1	22.5	Panama
13.0	[5]	...	22.5	2,168	31.2	25.4	7.7	1.3	0.6	17.6	6.2	9.9	Papua New Guinea
4.5	6.2	2.3	7.3	2,577	27.8	13.9	11.5	0.4	7.3	4.3	16.2	18.7	Paraguay
7.3	7.5	7.6[3]	13.9	2,420	35.7	13.4	4.3	1.8	4.5	6.4	11.6	22.4	Peru
5.0	12.8	...	17.3	2,280	51.7	4.2	8.8	3.0	2.2	8.3	5.9	15.9	Philippines
8.9	8.3	15.0[3]	3.8	3,351	34.4	7.4	10.4	1.0	8.6	4.5	15.6	18.0	Poland
15.4	8.6	4.4	15.6	3,691	28.6	6.3	10.8	2.4	8.3	7.1	17.0	19.6	Portugal
11.8	11.2	7.9	14.7	...	...	...	...	...	...	...	...	...	Puerto Rico
13.0	[5]	—— 11.1 ——		...	...	...	...	...	...	...	...	...	Qatar
24.9	6.0	10.1[3]	12.5	3,308	41.4	1.7	11.9	1.5	5.2	5.0	9.8	23.5	Réunion
6.6	[5]	4.5[3]	4.5	3,263	49.5	4.5	7.4	0.1	11.3	4.5	10.5	12.2	Romania
...	9.4	...	30.8	2,835	41.3	8.0	9.0	1.6	10.3	3.4	9.6	20.6	Russia
1.7[33]	5.3[33]	0.4[33]	35.5[33]	2,035	22.4	23.1	1.1	—	1.4	25.9	5.5	—	Rwanda
4.3	*9.4*	...	*9.0*	2,766	24.9	2.6	13.6	1.9	8.6	4.6	11.6	32.1	St. Kitts and Nevis
6.3	5.8	3.2[3]	8.3	2,842	34.3	4.8	14.0	1.3	6.8	9.3	6.9	22.7	St. Lucia
3.7	6.6	...	9.7	2,554	35.2	4.3	10.4	1.1	6.1	5.2	9.6	28	St. Vincent and the Grenadines
9.0	[5]	...	17.9	...	...	...	...	...	...	...	...	...	Samoa
17.6	7.2	7.1[3]	14.5	3,608	31.8	1.9	11.1	1.1	8.9	7.2	22.0	15.9	San Marino
...	...	...	...	2,201	28.3	15.4	1.4	2.1	0.8	17.0	10.6	24.3	São Tomé and Príncipe
4.5[18, 34]	5.9[18, 34]	...	8.6[18, 34]	2,888	46.6	1.1	7.3	0.4	4.9	10.1	11.4	18.2	Saudi Arabia
5.0	2.0	...	12.0	2,277	57.5	1.0	3.7	2.8	2.4	2.0	18.7	11.9	Senegal
6.4	6.6	1.4	4.4	2,462	37.3	1.2	5.6	5.1	6.5	5.8	11.5	27.1	Seychelles
4.4	3.9	3.8[3]	4.8	2,045	53.4	10.4	1.0	1.4	0.6	2.9	17.6	12.8	Sierra Leone
13.8	8.9	13.1	23.3	...	...	...	...	...	...	...	...	...	Singapore
...	3.9	...	26.2	2,953	27.3	4.3	10.5	0.3	8.9	4.7	20.8	23.2	Slovakia
12.7	3.3	6.1[3]	8.0	2,950	35.4	3.5	11.1	0.4	12.0	5.3	15.2	17.2	Slovenia
9.9	[5]	[19]	15.7	2,130	33.3	36.3	3.1	3.7	0.6	2.7	2.9	17.4	Solomon Islands
...	...	...	12.1[6]	1,531	33.4	1.5	8.7	0.2	28.4	2.8	7.4	17.5	Somalia
16.7	10.0	6.3	11.7	2,909	53.0	2.0	7.0	0.5	4.8	2.8	11.7	18.1	South Africa
15.3	7.1	7.0[3]	23.1	3,348	22.6	4.7	13.4	2.4	9.3	6.7	21.6	19.4	Spain
17.0	3.9	2.4	10.8	2,314	51.3	2.9	0.9	1.9	3.4	4.5	2.9	32.3	Sri Lanka
1.5	5.5	0.7[3]	4.0	2,444	56.5	0.6	5.1	0.1	13.3	2.9	9.5	11.9	Sudan, The
9.5[6]	*12.3*[6]	*5.8*[6]	*4.0*[6]	2,633	41.2	2.3	7.0	1.6	4.8	6.2	12.5	24.5	Suriname
8.8	12.8	3.3[3]	20.4	2,503	48.1	1.3	6.4	—	5.2	1.8	6.2	31.0	Swaziland
15.7	6.6	10.9	8.8	3,114	25.6	3.6	10.2	1.8	14.1	5.2	18.9	20.7	Sweden
12.9	5.1	9.8[3]	10.1	3,222	22.1	2.3	14.8	0.8	12.5	6.1	18.7	22.7	Switzerland
2.4	5.8	2.1[3]	7.4	3,378	53.9	1.2	3.8	0.1	6.6	5.6	12.9	15.9	Syria
10.7	2.2	1.1	4.7	...	...	...	...	...	...	...	...	...	Taiwan
...	...	...	34.7	2,176	67.9	0.1	2.8	—	3.4	4.3	12.2	9.2	Tajikistan
4.1	1.4	0.7	—	1,999	49.0	19.5	2.6	1.1	2.2	5.4	6.8	13.6	Tanzania
12.9	10.9	4.2	14.9	2,462	47.1	1.9	6.6	2.6	2.8	5.7	6.1	27.3	Thailand
9.5[6]	4.4[6]	5.1[3, 6]	8.6[6]	2,513	50.7	29.2	2.3	1.3	0.6	1.3	7.2	7.5	Togo
5.8	10.6	0.5	14.7	...	...	...	...	...	...	...	...	...	Tonga
15.2	14.3	[17]	6.2[17]	2,711	36.8	2.8	4.5	0.9	6.8	3.8	14.6	29.9	Trinidad and Tobago
9.0	11.2	7.1	7.1	3,297	52.9	1.8	3.0	0.5	4.6	6.2	15.8	15.3	Tunisia
8.8	9.0	5.6	2.3	3,554	48.4	3.7	2.5	0.4	6.9	7.9	15.1	15.1	Turkey
...	...	...	...	2,684	57.7	0.5	7.6	0.1	8.2	3.4	16.4	6.1	Turkmenistan
10.5	[5]	...	25.0	...	...	...	...	...	...	...	...	...	Tuvalu
5.9[6]	...	...	24.2[6]	2,216	20.4	23.4	3.2	0.8	1.9	25.8	2.2	22.3	Uganda
...	6.8	6.3[3]	43.9	2,878	44.5	8.8	5.8	0.7	10.3	3.4	10.8	15.7	Ukraine
14.1	11.6	4.7	6.5	3,372	33.8	1.6	11.5	1.4	9.5	14.3	10.3	17.7	United Arab Emirates
15.1	8.0	15.9	11.6	3,257	22.8	6.1	14.4	1.0	11.6	5.0	19.1	20.0	United Kingdom
13.9	1.5	5.8	18.9	3,757	23.6	2.9	11.9	0.8	11.7	5.2	17.9	26.1	United States
10.4	6.3	3.1	5.1	2,866	28.9	3.7	19.1	0.6	12.3	4.0	11.0	20.3	Uruguay
...	...	...	...	2,564	55.8	2.1	6.9	—	9.4	4.1	15.3	6.2	Uzbekistan
13.2	[5]	12.3[19]	10.3	2,737	21.4	30.7	9.2	1.6	1.5	6.4	8.9	20.3	Vanuatu
7.1	4.5	2.7	26.4	2,358	34.9	3.1	6.6	1.7	6.5	7.3	15.2	24.7	Venezuela
...	4.6	...	22.6	2,422	70.9	4.0	7.6	1.3	0.5	3.9	3.2	8.6	Vietnam
11.7[36]	*4.3*[36]	...	*21.9*[36]	...	...	...	...	...	...	...	...	...	Virgin Islands (U.S.)
...	...	...	...	...	...	...	...	...	...	...	...	...	West Bank
...	...	...	...	...	...	...	...	...	...	...	...	...	Western Sahara
1.9[37]	3.0[37]	...	13.7[37]	2,087	68.7	1.0	2.7	0.7	1.8	3.0	8.2	13.9	Yemen
5.7	1.6	2.4[3]	16.3	2,963	29.4	2.3	16.3	0.2	11.4	6.8	17.8	15.8	Yugoslavia
5.0	1.0	...	15.0	1,950	64.9	14.5	2.7	0.8	1.3	1.5	3.4	10.9	Zambia
1.1	12.9	0.6	16.5	2,153	60.5	2.1	2.3	0.3	3.1	1.0	11.9	18.8	Zimbabwe

and Kombo St. Mary only. [22]1986. [23]Urban areas of Eastern region only. [24]Personal effects, other includes health care. [25]Housing includes water. [26]Wage earners only. [27]Workers and clerical workers only. [28]1992. [29]Malagasy households only. [30]Curaçao only. [31]1987. [32]1994. [33]Rural areas only. [34]Middle-income population only. [35]1991. [36]St. Thomas only. [37]Data refer to former Yemen Arab Republic.

Health services

The provision of health services in most countries is both a principal determinant of the quality of life and a large and growing sector of the national economy. This table summarizes the basic indicators of health personnel; hospitals, by kind and utilization; mortality rates that are most indicative of general health services; external controls on health (adequacy of food supply and availability of safe drinking water); and sources and amounts of expenditure on health care. Each datum refers more or less directly to the availability or use of a particular health service in a country, and, while each may be a representative measure at a national level, each may also conceal considerable differences in availability of the particular service to different segments of a population or regions of a country. In the United States, for example, the availability of physicians ranges from about one per 730 persons in the least well-served states to one per 260 in the best-served, with a rate of one per 150 in the national capital. In addition, even when trained personnel exist and facilities have been created, limited financial resources at the national or local level may leave facilities underserved; or lack of good transportation may prevent those most in need from reaching a clinic or hospital that could help them.

Definitions and limits of data have been made as consistent as possible in the compilation of this table. For example, despite wide variation worldwide in the nature of the qualifying or certifying process that permits an individual to represent himself as a physician, organizations such as the World Health Organization (WHO) try to maintain more specific international standards for training and qualification. International statistics presented here for "physicians" refer to persons qualified according to WHO standards and exclude traditional health practitioners, whatever the local custom with regard to the designation "doctor." Statistics for health personnel in this table uniformly include all those actually working in the health service field, whether in the actual provision of services or in teaching, administration, research, or other tasks. One group of practitioners for whom this type of guideline works less well is that of midwives, whose training and qualifications vary enormously from country to country but who must be included, as they represent, after nurses, perhaps the largest and most important category of health auxiliary worldwide. The statistics here refer to those midwives working in some kind of institutional setting (a hospital, clinic, community health-care centre, or the like) and exclude rural noninstitutional midwives and traditional birth attendants.

Hospitals also differ considerably worldwide in terms of staffing and services. In this tabulation, the term hospital refers generally to a permanent facility offering inpatient services and/or nursing care and staffed by at least one physician. Establishments offering only outpatient or custodial care are excluded. These statistics are broken down into data for general hospitals (those providing care in more than one specialty), specialized facilities (with care in only one specialty), local medical centres, and rural health-care centres; the last two generally refer to institutions that provide a more limited range of medical or nursing care, often less than full-time. Hospital data are further analyzed into three categories of administrative classification: public, private nonprofit, and private for profit. Statistics on number of beds refer to beds that are maintained and staffed on a full-time basis for a succession of inpatients to whom care is provided.

Data on hospital utilization refer to institutions defined as above. Admission and discharge, the two principal points at which statistics are normally collected, are the basis for the data on the amount and distribution of care by kind of facility. The data on numbers of patients exclude babies born during a maternal confinement but include persons who die before being discharged. The bed-occupancy and average length-of-stay statistics depend on the concept of a "patient-day," which is the annual total of daily censuses of inpatients. The bed-occupancy rate is the ratio of total patient-days to potential days based on the number of beds; the average length-of-stay rate is the ratio of total patient-days to total admissions. Bed-occu-

Health services

country	health personnel							hospitals									
	year	physicians	dentists	nurses	pharma-cists	midwives	popu-lation per physi-cian	year	number	kinds (%)				ownership (%)			hos-pital beds per 10,000 pop.
										gen-eral	spe-cial-ized	medical centres	rural	govern-ment	private non-profit	private for profit	
Afghanistan	1997	2,556	232	4,182	464	...	9,090	1988–93	...	...	...	...	...	...	...	...	3
Albania	1995	4,848	1,332	14,559	772[2]	9,936[2]	668	1993	40	...	...	...	...	100.0	—	—	31
Algeria	1996	27,650	7,837	...	3,866	...	1,015	1996[3]	186	...	...	...	...	...	...	...	12
American Samoa	1991	26	7[6]	140[6]	2[6]	1[6]	1,885	1990	1	100.0	—	—	—	100.0	—	—	27
Andorra	1998	166	35	188	59	6	434	1996	1	100.0	—	—	—	100.0	—	—	28
Angola	1997	736	...	10,942	...	411	13,228	1990	58	...	...	...	...	...	...	...	12
Antigua and Barbuda	1996	75	12	187	13	31	915	1998	3	50.0	50.0	—	—	100.0	—	—	42
Argentina	1992	88,800	21,900[8]	18,000[6]	...	...	376	1997	1,235	...	...	...	...	56.8	—43.2—		22
Armenia	1998	18,000[9]	[9]	18,258	144	1,750	292[9]	1998	183[10]	...	...	...	...	100.0	...	...	28
Aruba	1997	103	21	515	15	3	874	1999	2	50.0	—	50.0	—	100.0	—	—	32
Australia	1997–98	47,400	8,800	148,300	15,600	...	395	1996–97	1,222	...	...	...	...	61.0	—39.0—		95
Austria	1998	33,698	1,534	35,834	2,137[12]	1,056	240	1998	329	37.7	62.3	—	—	...	...	...	92
Azerbaijan	1998	28,850	2,426	62,213	2,560	10,843	274	1997	762	...	...	...	...	100.0	...	...	92
Bahamas, The	1996	419	72	648	52[4]	...	673	1997	5	60.0	20.0	20.0	—	60.0	—40.0—		38
Bahrain	1997	620	56	1,755	124	...	1,000	1994	12	58.3	42.7	—	—	75.0	16.7	8.3	30[13]
Bangladesh	1997	27,546	938	15,408	7,485[4]	13,211	4,627	1997	976	...	...	...	...	69.3	—30.7—		4
Barbados	1993	330	42	869	138[11]	377[11]	797	1995	9	66.7	33.3	—	—	80.0	—	20.0	74
Belarus	1999	39,007	4,522	47,343	3,152[12]	5,826	261	1999	276	55.4		—44.6—		100.0	...	...	68
Belgium	1998	39,420	7,360	109,187	14,597	6,602	259	1993	363	80.4	19.6	—	—	38.6	61.4	—	76
Belize	1998	155	26	404	30	230	1,542	1998	7	...	...	...	...	100.0	—	—	23
Benin	1995	312	16	1,116	85	432	17,538	1993	...	...	...	...	...	...	...	...	2
Bermuda	1996	96	22	522	29	...	639	1996	2	50.0	50.0	—	—	...	...	...	40
Bhutan	1997	101	9[4]	355[13]	5[4]	326[13]	6,128	1997	28	...	...	...	...	...	...	...	16
Bolivia	1996	4,346	444	2,062	...	...	1,747	1996	336	10.7[13]	8.9[13]	23.5[13]	56.8[13]	...	...	...	11
Bosnia and Herzegovina	1998	4,813	640	15,241	370	1,565[8]	699	1996	...	...	...	...	...	...	...	...	48
Botswana	1994	339	...	3,329	...	...	4,395	1994	30	53.3	3.3	43.3	—	...	...	...	23
Brazil	1997	205,828	137,600	67,760	51,847	...	774	1997	6,410	—100.0—		—	—	35.5	—64.5—		31
Brunei	1996	259	26	1,229	15[13]	278[13]	1,181	1995	10	90.0	—	—	10.0	90.0	—10.0—		33
Bulgaria	1998	28,823	5,324	47,434	1,230	5,923	286	1998	288	—71.2—		28.8	—	...	...	...	104
Burkina Faso	1991[14]	341	19	2,627	113	339	27,158	1993	78	—14.1—		85.9	—	100.0	—	—	5
Burundi	1996	329	9[4]	1,131	55[4]	...	16,507	1996	...	...	...	...	...	...	...	...	0.7
Cambodia	1998	3,464	210	8,608	262[11]	3,359	3,367	1988[3]	188	...	...	...	...	100.0	—	—	16
Cameroon	1996	1,031	56	5,112	206[6]	70	13,510	1988	629	—27.0—		—73.0—		72.3	—27.7—		27
Canada	1996	55,006	15,636	232,869	22,197	...	539	1989	1,079	81.8	16.6	1.6	—	95.8	—	4.2	54[10]
Cape Verde	1996	66	...	213	6	...	5,818	1996	65	8.0	—	92.0	—	100.0	—	—	15[15]
Central African Republic	1995	112	16	282	22[4]	157	28,600	1990	255	—21.1[16]—		—78.9[16]—		79.7[16]	—20.3[16]—		14[8]
Chad	1994	228	14	1,014	10	159	30,260	1994	...	...	...	...	...	...	...	...	13
Chile	1996	13,857	5,817	6,738	1,830[14]	5,369[14]	1,040	1994	198	...	...	...	...	89.4	—10.6—		31
China	1998	1,999,500[9, 17]	[9]	1,218,000	440,000	51,000	621[17]	1998	69,105	11.2	13.4	—75.4—		100.0	—	—	23
Colombia	1997	40,355	22,121	46,187	...	...	1,102	1997	1,657	...	...	...	...	...	...	...	1
Comoros	1997	64	6[4]	180	6[4]	74	7,765	1995	...	...	...	...	...	...	...	...	29
Congo, Dem. Rep. of the	1996	3,224	514	20,652	59[4]	...	14,492	1986	400	...	...	...	...	52.5	—47.5—		21
Congo, Rep. of the	1995	632	35[4]	4,663	175[4]	160	4,083	1990	...	...	...	...	...	...	...	...	33
Costa Rica	1997	5,500	1,420	3,720	1,362	...	641	1997	29	...	...	...	...	87.9	—	12.1	14
Côte d'Ivoire	1996	1,318	219[4]	4,568	135[4]	2,196	11,108	1993	...	...	...	...	...	...	...	...	5
Croatia	1998	9,766	2,802	20,216	1,940	1,407	436	1997	70	52.8	47.2	—	—	...	...	...	63
Cuba	1996	60,129	9,600	76,013	...	...	183	1993	244	...	...	...	...	100.0	—	—	65
Cyprus[18]	1997	1,725	594	2,942	668[13]	120[19]	486	1997[20]	103	71.8	22.1	—	6.1	10.0[19]	0.9[19]	89.1[19]	48
Czech Republic	1999	38,828	6,383	91,213	4,785	4,602	265	1999	365	59.2	40.8	—	—	70.7	—29.3—		67
Denmark	1995	15,175	4,605	36,944	747	1,046	345	1992	163	42.9	57.1	—	—	42.9	57.1	—	35

pancy rates may exceed 100% because stays of partial days are counted as full days.

Two measures that give health planners and policy makers an excellent indication of the level of ordinary health care are those for mortality of children under age five and for maternal mortality. The former reflects the probability of a newborn infant dying before age five. The latter refers to deaths attributable to delivery or complications of pregnancy, childbirth, the puerperium (the period immediately following birth), or abortion. A principal source for the former data was WHO's *The World Health Report* (annual) and for the latter, the UN Development Programme's *Human Development Report* (annual).

Levels of nutrition and access to safe drinking water are two of the most basic limitations imposed by the physical environment in which health-care activities take place. The nutritional data are based on reported levels of food supply (whether or not actually consumed), referred to the recommendations of the United Nations' Food and Agriculture Organization for the necessary daily intake (in calories) for a moderately active person of average size in a climate of a particular kind (fewer calories are needed in a hot climate) to remain in average *good* health. Excess intake in the many developed countries ranges to more than 40% above the minimum required to maintain health (the excess usually being construed to diminish, rather than raise, health). The range of deficiency is less dramatic numerically but far more critical to the countries in which deficiencies are chronic, because the deficiencies lead to overall poor health (raising health service needs and costs), to decreased productivity in nearly every area of national economic life, and to the loss of social and economic potential through early mortality. By "safe" water is meant only water that has no substantial quantities of chemical or biological pollutants—*i.e.*, quantities sufficient to cause "immediate" health problems. Data refer to the proportion of persons having "reasonable access" to an "adequate" supply of water within a "convenient" distance of the person's dwelling, as these concepts are interpreted locally.

The data on health care expenditure were excerpted from a joint effort by the WHO and the World Bank to create better analytical tools by which the interrelations among health policy, health care delivery systems, and human health might be examined against the more general frameworks of government operations, resource allocation, and development process. First published in the World Bank's *World Development Report 1993: Investing in Health* and, the following year, in the World Health Organization's *Global Comparative Assessments in the Health Sector* (edited by C.J.L. Murray and A.D. Lopez), the database and underlying methodology are expected to provide a continuing basis for international comparisons and policy analysis. The first two of ten volumes of the final results appeared in 1996 as *The Global Burden of Disease* and *Global Health Statistics* by the same editors.

Expenditures were tabulated for direct preventative and curative activities and for public health and public education programs having direct impact on health status—family planning, nutrition, and health education—but not more indirect programs like environmental, waste removal, or relief activities. Public, parastatal (semipublic, *e.g.*, social security institutions), international aid, and household expenditure reports and surveys were utilized to build up a comprehensive picture of national, regional, and world patterns of health care expenditures and investment that could not have been assembled from any single type of source. For reasons of space, public and parastatal are combined as the former.

Internet resources for further information:

- Most Recent Values of W.H.O. Global Health-For-All Indicators (for personnel and general indicators) http://www.who.int/htl/countrysup/countrye.htm

No comparable source exists for hospitals.

admissions or discharges					bed occupancy rate (%)	average length of stay (days)	mortality		population with access to safe water 1994–98 (%)	food supply (% of FAO requirement) 1998	total health expenditures, 1990					country
rate per 10,000 pop.	by kinds of hospital (%)						under age 5 per 1,000 live newborn 1997	maternal mortality per 100,000 live births 1990–97			as percent of GDP	per capita (U.S.$)	by source (percent)			
	general	specialized	medical centres	rural									public	private	international aid	
...	...	...	...	...	...	...	257	...	10	73[1]	...	...	...	...	...	Afghanistan
...	...	...	...	...	...	...	40	65	...	124	4.00	26	84.0	16.0	—	Albania
371	...	...	...	...	49.3[4]	5[4]	39	220	90[5]	126	6.95	149	76.9	23.0	0.1	Algeria
965	100.0	—	—	—	38.4	4	...	...	...	...	...	...	...	...	...	American Samoa
...	...	...	...	...	...	...	6	...	...	...	...	...	...	...	...	Andorra
238	...	...	...	...	44.5[7]	16[7]	292	1,500	32	82	...	...	...	...	...	Angola
64[7]	...	...	...	...	50.0[7]	8[7]	21	150	88	99	4.55	241	59.1	37.3	3.6	Antigua and Barbuda
560[3]	...	...	...	...	52.0[3]	7[3]	24	44	81	134	4.21	137	60.1	39.7	0.2	Argentina
...	...	...	...	...	...	...	30	35	...	92	4.17	152	59.8	40.2	—	Armenia
...	...	...	...	...	92.2[11]	...	...	...	...	...	...	...	...	...	...	Aruba
...	...	...	...	...	...	4.5	6	9	95	120	7.67	1,294	69.6	30.4	—	Australia
2,650	...	...	...	...	80.1	10	5	10	100[5]	134	8.38	1,711	66.4	33.6	—	Austria
...	...	...	...	...	...	...	46	37	...	86	4.27	99	61.2	38.8	—	Azerbaijan
837[3]	...	...	...	...	85.4[3]	12[3]	21	...	94	105	...	...	...	...	...	Bahamas, The
...	...	...	...	...	...	...	22	46	100[5]	...	4.62	324	63.0	36.9	0.1	Bahrain
...	...	...	...	...	...	...	109	440	95	89	3.19	6	24.8	56.7	18.5	Bangladesh
810[11]	93.5[11]	6.5[11]	—	—	88.3[11]	32[11]	12	0	100[5]	123	5.04	323	64.3	33.8	1.9	Barbados
...	...	...	...	...	...	...	27	22	100	123	3.19	157	68.7	31.3	—	Belarus
1,963	96.0	4.0	—	—	84.4	12	7	10	100[5]	137	7.50	1,449	82.5	17.5	—	Belgium
...	...	...	...	...	...	...	43	140	83	129	5.88	23	48.4	41.0	10.7	Belize
...	...	...	...	...	...	...	167	500	56	112	4.32	19	26.3	36.4	37.3	Benin
1,313	97.0	3.0	—	—	75.0	8	...	...	...	116	...	...	...	...	...	Bermuda
...	...	...	...	...	...	...	121	380	58	...	5.05	10	41.1	30.4	28.5	Bhutan
250	...	...	...	...	48.0	6	96	390	80	93	4.01	25	39.9	39.6	20.5	Bolivia
529[6, 7]	...	...	...	...	82.4[6, 7]	11[6, 7]	19	10	...	110	...	...	...	...	...	Bosnia and Herzegovina
...	...	...	...	...	93.1[6]	...	49	330	90	93	6.19	139	61.8	21.6	16.5	Botswana
740	...	...	...	...	...	6	44	220	76	122	4.20	146	65.7	33.9	0.4	Brazil
...	...	...	...	...	...	...	10	0	90[5]	127	...	...	...	...	...	Brunei
...	...	...	...	...	...	...	19	15	99[5]	110	5.36	121	81.4	18.6	—	Bulgaria
...	...	...	...	...	...	...	169	930	78[5]	91	8.46	7	9.8	17.9	72.3	Burkina Faso
...	...	...	...	...	...	...	176	1,300	52	68	3.28	30	42.4	48.3	9.3	Burundi
...	...	...	...	...	...	...	167	470	30	94	...	...	...	...	...	Cambodia
...	...	...	...	...	...	...	145	550	54	98	2.62	27	26.4	61.7	11.9	Cameroon
...	...	...	...	...	...	14	7	6	100	119	9.05	1,945	74.1	25.9	—	Canada
...	...	...	...	...	...	...	73	55	65[5]	132	6.32	64	20.7	25.5	53.7	Cape Verde
...	...	...	...	...	...	...	173	1,100	38	91	4.19	18	26.5	37.5	36.0	Central African Republic
...	...	...	...	...	...	...	198	830	54	91	6.22	12	27.6	24.7	47.7	Chad
749[3]	...	...	...	...	69.9[3]	7[3]	13	23	96	117	4.73	100	70.1	29.1	0.7	Chile
418[13]	— 60.4[13] —		— 39.6[13] —		66.9[13]	15[13]	47	60	67	126	3.51	11	58.5	40.9	0.6	China
614[6]	41.4[6]	16.7[6]	— 41.9[6] —		57.2[6]	6[6]	30	80	96	119	3.98	51	44.0	54.4	1.6	Colombia
...	...	...	...	...	...	...	93	500	53[5]	79	5.40	28	46.3	29.2	24.5	Comoros
...	...	...	...	...	...	...	207	870	42	77	2.38	5	8.5	64.8	26.7	Congo, Dem. Rep. of the
...	...	...	...	...	...	...	108	890	34	101	3.99	50	47.1	40.7	12.1	Congo, Rep. of the
958[8]	...	...	...	...	78.2[8]	6[8]	14	29	100	124	6.51	132	73.6	25.2	1.2	Costa Rica
...	...	...	...	...	...	...	150	600	42	117	3.35	28	48.7	47.9	3.4	Côte d'Ivoire
1,578	70.0	30.0	—	—	83.0	13	9	12	96	98	...	...	...	...	...	Croatia
1,376[8]	...	...	...	...	...	...	8	24	93	107	...	...	...	...	...	Cuba
522	...	...	...	...	78.9	6	9	0	100[5]	140	3.96	64	62.9	26.8	10.3	Cyprus[18]
1,982	97.6	2.4	—	—	79.0[13]	9	7	9	100[5]	133	5.94[21]	169[21]	84.9[21]	15.1[21]	—	Czech Republic
1,253	92.9	7.1	—	—	80.4	8	6	10	100	128	6.30	1,588	84.2	15.8	—	Denmark

Health services (continued)

country	health personnel							hospitals									
	year	physicians	dentists	nurses	pharma-cists	midwives	population per physician	year	number	kinds (%)				ownership (%)			hospital beds per 10,000 pop.
										general	specialized	medical centres	rural	government	private non-profit	private for profit	
Djibouti	1996	60	7	315	8	…	7,100	1993	8	—25.0—		—75.0—		100.0	…	…	27[6]
Dominica	1998	38	10	361	27[10]	…	2,000	1994	53	1.9	—	—	98.1	100.0	—	—	25
Dominican Republic	1997	17,315	1,879	8,600	372	…	464	1992[3]	723	—7.9—		—92.1—		…	…	…	12[10]
East Timor	…	…	…	…	…	…	…	…	…	…	…	…	…	…	…	…	…
Ecuador	1995	15,212	1,788	5,212	906[19]	802	753	1995	474	17.0	8.0	—75.0—		26.0	11.3	62.7	16
Egypt	1998	129,000	15,211	141,770	20,254[12]	…	490	1998	7,411	4.5	—95.5—			87.9	—12.1—		19
El Salvador	1997	6,177	5,604	12,851	…	1,940[8]	936	1993	78	…	…	…	…	61.5	1.3	37.2	17
Equatorial Guinea	1996	105	4	169	…	9	4,086	1988	…	…	…	…	…	…	…	…	29
Eritrea	1996	108	4	574	…	79	33,240	1993	10	…	…	…	…	…	…	…	9
Estonia	1998	4,471	987	9,088[22]	775	[22]	336	1998	78	…	…	…	…	87.2	—12.8—		73
Ethiopia	1988	1,466	…	3,496	364	…	30,195	1986–87	86	…	…	…	…	…	…	…	3
Faroe Islands	1995	85	40	412	10	19	529	1994	3	33.3	—	—	66.7	100.0	—	—	64
Fiji	1997	409	36	1,742	…	…	1,919	1997	25	…	…	…	…	…	…	…	23
Finland	1998	15,407	4,828	111,408	7,472	4,019	334	1994[7]	380	…	…	…	…	…	…	…	98
France	1997	177,585	39,736	291,287	58,609	12,718	330	1997	4,186	—91.6—			8.4	25.4	—74.6—		113
French Guiana	1994	213	38	495	47	40	669	1996	25	…	…	…	…	10	…	15	143
French Polynesia	1999	384	94	599	51	54[19]	599	1999	7	…	…	…	…	…	…	…	37
Gabon	1989	448	32	759	71	240	2,504	1988	27	…	…	…	…	…	…	…	51
Gambia, The	1997	43	…	155	6	102	28,791	1994	13	15.4	—	—84.6—		…	…	…	7
Gaza Strip	1993[23]	…	…	…	…	…	…	1995	6	…	…	…	…	83.3	—16.7—		9
Georgia	1998	22,236	1,800	24,174	469	1,586	229	1997	422[4]	…	…	…	…	100.0	…	…	48
Germany	1998	287,164	62,274	785,190	47,341	9,271	286	1996	2,269	…	…	…	…	49.2[19]	36.0[19]	14.8[19]	72
Ghana	1996[14]	1,117	36	12,970	67[6]	9,583	16,127	1991	121	90.9	9.1	—	—	60.3	—39.7—		16[10]
Greece	1995	40,995	10,667	30,967[10]	8,147[12]	1,837[10]	255	1996	356	49.7	50.3	—	—	…	…	…	50
Greenland	1997	83	28	528	10[8]	11	674	1990	16	6.3	—	—	93.7	100.0	—	—	75
Grenada	1996	96	14	232	47	…	582	1996[7]	3	100.0	—	—	—	100.0	—	—	35
Guadeloupe	1996	690	129	1,640	220	140	597	1995	29	…	…	…	…	44.8	—55.2—		76
Guam	1986	147	…	594[22]	…	[22]	823	1998	1	…	…	…	…	…	…	…	…
Guatemala	1997	9,812	1,367	13,247[19]	…	18,924[19]	1,072	1985	35[13]	…	…	…	…	…	…	…	11[13]
Guernsey	1993	79	…	…	…	…	804	1993	1	100.0	—	—	—	100.0	—	—	…
Guinea	1995	930	22[16]	3,983	197[8]	372	7,688	1991	38	—100.0—		…	…	100.0	—	—	5
Guinea-Bissau	1996	194	11	1,277	12[16]	148	6,015	1993	16	…	…	…	…	62.5	—37.5—		13
Guyana	1996	214	35	504	40	165	3,612	1994	30	…	…	…	…	83.3	—16.7—		30
Haiti	1996	773	95[10]	2,630	…	…	8,418	1994	49	…	…	…	…	…	…	…	10
Honduras	1997	4,896	989	6,152	975[19]	…	1,202	1994	61	…	…	…	…	47.5	—52.5—		9
Hong Kong	1999	9,580	2,052	38,320	1,368	…	714	1995	88	…	…	…	…	78.4	—21.6—		49
Hungary	1998	36,143	5,671	51,965	4,789	2,227	279	1998	167	…	…	…	…	…	…	…	83
Iceland	1998	893	288	2,370	228	235	307	1995	57	89.0	11.0	—	—	…	…	…	147
India	1998[24]	512,352	19,523[19]	449,351[19]	…	…	1,916	1998	15,067[8]	…	…	…	…	55.0[8]	—45.0[8]—		27
Indonesia	1997	31,887[9]	[9]	155,911[22]	5,440[12]	[22]	6,267[9]	1997	1,090	…	…	…	…	…	…	…	6
Iran	1997	50,770	9,427	136,030	6,816	7,387	1,195	1997	685	…	…	…	…	83.5	—16.5—		16
Iraq	1998	11,769	1,220	50,499	2,525	…	1,818	1993	185	…	…	…	…	…	…	…	14
Ireland	1998	8,114	1,712	59,021	2,882	15,228	457	1996	62[3, 7]	100.0	—	—	—	100.0	—	—	33
Isle of Man	1998	117	26	…	25[12]	…	615	1986	3	33.3	33.3	—	33.3	100.0	—	—	…
Israel	1998	22,345	6,733	35,579	3,511	1,080	260	1995	259	18.5	81.5	—	—	12.0	51.7	36.3	61
Italy	1997	318,616	37,039	280,263	58,662	…	180	1997	1,589	91.5	8.5	—	—	59.2	—40.8—		65
Jamaica	1996	421	57	1,241	52	273	5,974	1996	24	75.0	25.0	—	—	75.0	—25.0—		24
Japan	1997	240,908	85,518	960,477	194,300	23,615	525	1997	9,413	88.7	11.3	—	—	73.5	—26.5—		131
Jersey	1995	95	…	…	…	…	895	1990	6	16.7	83.3	—	—	100.0	—	—	88
Jordan	1997	7,250	2,140	12,929	3,363	861[13]	602	1994	63	…	…	…	…	42.9	—57.1—		18[25]
Kazakhstan	1998	53,207	3,783	97,824	9,903	8,456	283	1996	1,518	…	…	…	…	100.0	…	…	123
Kenya	1995	3,606	600	24,610	605[19]	…	7,575	1994	846	—35.1—		—64.9—		…	…	…	14
Kiribati	1998	26	4	208	…	…	3,385	1990	1	…	…	…	…	…	…	…	40
Korea, North	1995	64,006	…	38,792	…	12,931	337	1989	…	…	…	…	…	…	…	…	135
Korea, South	1997	62,609	15,383	133,920	45,820	8,516	735	1997	6,446	70.0	30.0	—	—	…	…	…	47
Kuwait	1997	3,419	470	8,593	633[25]	19[13]	529	1995	24	…	…	…	…	66.7	—	33.3	31
Kyrgyzstan	1998	14,355	1,307	35,768	320	3,472	332	1994	348[13]	89.1	—	10.9	—	100.0	—	—	101[13]
Laos	1996	1,208	214	5,354	…	…	1,603	1995	25	0.7[4]	—99.3[4]—			100.0	—	—	25[4]
Latvia	1998	6,900	1,064	13,445	292[10]	81	355	1998	150	51.2[10]	4.1[10]	28.8[10]	15.9[10]	97.5	2.5	—	94
Lebanon	1997	7,203	2,744	3,430	1,715	…	476	1995	153	…	…	…	…	10.5	—89.5—		22
Lesotho	1995	105	10	1,169	60[14]	914	18,524	1987	22	90.9	9.1	—	—	54.5	45.5	—	15
Liberia	1997	53	2	136	…	99	43,434	1988	92	—37.0—		—63.0—		…	…	…	…
Libya	1997	6,092	619[25]	17,136[25]	1,095[25]	…	781	1991	…	…	…	…	…	…	…	…	41
Liechtenstein	1997	41	18	…	2	…	764	1998	1	…	…	…	…	…	…	…	34
Lithuania	1999	14,578	2,316	37,448	2,143	1,611	254	1999	186	…	…	…	…	100.0	…	…	94
Luxembourg	1998	1,164	282	3,347	297	94	368	1994	34	50.0	50.0	—	—	…	…	…	109
Macau	1998	532	31	706	48	…	800	1994	30	6.7	—	93.3	—	46.7	—53.3—		22
Macedonia	1998	4,110	1,046	9,833	300	1,342	490	1994	58[25]	27.4	24.2	—48.4—		100.0	—	—	52[25]
Madagascar	1996	1,470	137	2,969	19[4]	1,471	9,351	1990	…	…	…	…	…	…	…	…	9
Malawi	1989	186	…	284	5	…	49,118	1987	395	12.2	0.8	—87.0—		59.2	—40.8—		16
Malaysia	1997	14,258	1,865	24,550	…	5,872	1,519	1997	337	…	…	…	…	35.1	—64.9—		20
Maldives	1995	100	…	281	134	461	2,533	1996	5	20.0	—	80.0	—	100.0	—	—	12
Mali	1994	419	9	1,167	57[27]	267	21,269	1987	…	…	…	…	…	…	…	…	4
Malta	1998	987	135	4,158	186	291	383	1996	7	…	…	…	…	71.4	—28.6—		57
Marshall Islands	1997	34	4	141	…	6	1,794	1997	2	100.0	—	—	—	100.0	—	—	21
Martinique	1996	680	130	1,700	230	150	547	1993	8[13]	…	…	…	…	…	…	…	56[13]
Mauritania	1995	323	47	1,461	6[8]	237	7,251	1990	16	…	…	…	…	100.0	—	—	7
Mauritius	1998	1,033	144	2,826[22]	250	[22]	1,117	1998	13	73.9[10]	17.4[10]	8.7[10]	—	60.9[10]	4.3[10]	34.8[10]	33
Mayotte	1985	9	1	51	1	2	7,427	1994	2	100.0	—	—	—	100.0	—	—	9
Mexico	1997	116,047	8,926	161,303	…	…	812	1993	1,888[25]	…	…	…	…	53.9	—46.1—		9[25]
Micronesia	1999	76	16	368	7[19]	…	1,737	1993	4	100.0	—	—	—	100.0	—	—	31
Moldova	1998	14,959	1,761	37,355	2,885	3,723	286	1996	312	…	…	…	…	100.0	…	…	125
Monaco	1997	188	22	500[13]	67[13]	11[13]	170	1997	1	100.0	—	—	—	100.0	—	—	173
Mongolia	1998	5,676	315	7,169	1,113[19]	…	411	1997	407	…	…	…	…	…	…	…	78
Morocco	1997	12,534	1,090	28,610	2,997	87[4]	2,173	1993[28]	201	48.8	—	51.2	—	100.0	—	—	10

admissions or discharges: rate per 10,000 pop.	by kinds of hospital (%): general	special-ized	medical centres	rural	bed occu-pancy rate (%)	aver-age length of stay (days)	mortality: under age 5 per 1,000 live newborn 1997	maternal mortality per 100,000 live births 1990–97	popu-lation with access to safe water 1994–98 (%)	food supply (% of FAO require-ment) 1998	total health expenditures, 1990: as percent of GDP	per capita (U.S.$)	by source (percent): public	private	inter-national aid	country
...	...	...	...	...	...	...	156	...	90[5]	89	...	...	...	...	...	Djibouti
1,026	...	...	...	...	94.6	8	20	65	96[5]	124	8.06	192	65.1	20.4	14.5	Dominica
470	...	...	...	...	...	...	53	230	79	101	3.72	38	52.7	43.3	4.0	Dominican Republic
...	...	...	...	...	...	...	...	...	...	...	...	...	...	...	...	East Timor
508	...	...	...	...	53.1	6	39	160	68	119	4.14	44	55.9	37.3	6.8	Ecuador
317	...	...	...	...	...	...	73	170	87	131	2.61	28	30.3	62.0	7.7	Egypt
...	...	...	...	...	54.9[3, 11]	6[3, 11]	36	160	66	110	5.86	58	29.7	55.6	14.7	El Salvador
...	...	...	...	...	...	...	172	...	95[5]	68	7.60	28	36.6	20.7	42.7	Equatorial Guinea
...	...	...	...	...	...	...	116	1,000	22	75	...	...	...	...	...	Eritrea
1,952	76.7[10]	21.5[10]	—	1.8[10]	75.1	10	23	50	100	120	3.62	228	53.0	47.0	—	Estonia
...	...	...	...	...	...	...	175	1,400	25	78	3.80	4	41.3	39.9	18.8	Ethiopia
...	...	...	...	...	86.4	12	...	...	...	...	...	...	...	...	...	Faroe Islands
...	...	...	...	...	...	...	24	38	77[5]	125	3.76	70	54.9	38.3	6.9	Fiji
2,322	...	...	...	...	70.9	11	4	6	100	117	7.82	2,046	83.3	16.7	—	Finland
2,128	...	...	...	...	...	...	5	10	100	141	9.40	1,869	74.2	25.8	—	France
1,714[19]	...	...	...	...	70.3[19]	8[19]	...	...	84	125	...	...	...	...	...	French Guiana
...	...	...	...	...	...	...	...	...	...	129	...	...	...	...	...	French Polynesia
...	...	...	...	...	...	...	145	500	67	109	4.10	164	52.7	40.9	6.4	Gabon
...	...	...	...	...	...	...	87	1,100	69	108	7.53	22	28.3	20.7	51.0	Gambia, The
752	...	...	...	...	74.9	3	...	...	...	...	...	...	...	...	...	Gaza Strip
...	...	...	...	...	...	...	23	60	...	88	4.45	152	62.5	37.5	—	Georgia
1,812[19]	...	...	...	...	82.8[19]	13[19]	5	8	100[5]	128	8.73	1,511	72.7	27.3	—	Germany
...	...	...	...	...	...	...	107	210	65	117	3.50	15	35.0	51.8	13.2	Ghana
1,370	81.0	19.0	—	—	66.0	9	8	10	99[5]	145	5.39	359	76.0	24.0	—	Greece
2,450	29.2	—	—	70.8	69.4	8	...	...	...	...	...	...	...	...	...	Greenland
774[8]	100.0	—	—	—	59.1[8]	7[8]	29	0	85[5]	111	5.96	133	68.8	27.8	3.5	Grenada
2,154	...	...	...	...	84.0	10	...	...	90	113	...	...	...	...	...	Guadeloupe
...	...	...	...	...	...	...	...	...	...	...	...	...	...	...	...	Guam
284	...	...	...	...	57.7	9	55	190	68	99	3.70	27	44.2	43.2	12.6	Guatemala
1,100	100.0	—	—	—	...	...	...	...	...	...	...	...	...	...	...	Guernsey
...	...	...	...	...	...	...	201	670	46	100	3.90	17	39.7	40.3	20.0	Guinea
...	...	...	...	...	...	...	220	910	43	104	8.15	16	31.3	18.9	49.8	Guinea-Bissau
...	...	...	...	...	...	...	82	180	91[5]	109	10.37	42	40.7	15.1	44.2	Guyana
...	...	...	...	...	...	...	132	1,000	37	83	6.99	27	26.3	54.8	19.0	Haiti
459[19]	...	...	...	...	...	...	45	220	78	104	4.54	52	56.7	35.7	7.7	Honduras
1,811	...	...	...	...	...	...	6	7	100[5]	143	5.69	687	19.5	80.5	0.0	Hong Kong
2,502	...	...	...	...	77.0	10	11	15	100[5]	130	5.95	185	84.4	15.6	—	Hungary
2,828[11]	94.0[11]	6.0[11]	—	—	86.5[11]	12[11]	5	6	100[5]	121	8.34	1,884	87.5	12.5	—	Iceland
...	...	...	...	...	...	...	108	440	81	112	6.00	21	20.0	78.4	1.6	India
...	...	...	...	...	...	...	60	450	74	132	2.01	12	25.6	66.7	7.7	Indonesia
...	...	...	...	...	...	...	35	37	95	117	2.54	244	56.9	43.1	0.0	Iran
645[4]	...	...	...	...	42.4[4]	4[4]	122	310	81	100	...	...	...	...	...	Iraq
1,470	100.0	—	—	—	82.2	7	7	10	100[5]	144	7.22	876	81.1	18.9	—	Ireland
...	...	...	...	...	...	...	...	...	...	...	...	...	...	...	...	Isle of Man
1,979	...	...	...	...	91.2	10	6	5	99	135	4.20	480	49.3	50.6	0.1	Israel
1,743	90.4	9.6	—	—	72.0	9	6	7	100[5]	143	7.54	1,449	77.7	22.3	—	Italy
242[3]	81.7[3]	18.3[3]	—	—	53.7	5	11	120	86	121	5.04	83	57.4	33.2	9.5	Jamaica
...	...	...	...	...	...	...	6	8	97	123	6.45	1.538	74.5	25.5	—	Japan
1,718	84.0	16.0	—	—	...	...	...	...	...	...	...	...	...	...	...	Jersey
478[3]	...	...	...	...	68.1[3]	4[3]	24	41	97	114	3.77	55	36.9	52.3	10.8	Jordan
...	...	...	...	...	...	...	44	70	93	98	4.44	154	62.3	37.7	—	Kazakhstan
...	...	...	...	...	...	...	87	370	44	85	4.33	16	40.0	37.9	22.1	Kenya
...	...	...	...	...	...	...	78[10]	...	99[5]	131	...	...	...	...	...	Kiribati
...	...	...	...	...	...	...	30	110	100	81	...	...	...	...	...	Korea, North
629[13]	97.5[13]	2.5[13]	—	—	65.5[13]	13[13]	6	20	93	131	6.61	365	40.9	58.9	0.2	Korea, South
950[3, 10]	72.2[3, 10]	27.8[3, 10]	—	—	64.9[3, 10]	7[3, 10]	13	5	100[5]	126	4.86	541	64.2	35.6	0.1	Kuwait
1,775	95.5	—	4.5	—	75.6	15	68	65	79	99	4.97	118	66.7	33.3	—	Kyrgyzstan
...	...	...	...	...	...	...	122	650	44	98	2.53	5	17.4	60.7	21.9	Laos
2,210	78.4[10]	4.6[10]	13.8[10]	3.2[10]	76.5	13	22	45	100	117	3.87	220	56.1	43.9	—	Latvia
...	...	...	...	...	...	...	37	100	94	132	...	...	...	...	...	Lebanon
221[7]	...	...	...	...	...	...	137	610	62	97	8.32	26	38.3	26.5	35.2	Lesotho
...	...	...	...	...	...	...	235	...	46	86	8.24	4	19.9	11.8	68.3	Liberia
...	...	...	...	...	...	...	25	75	97	138	...	...	...	...	...	Libya
...	...	...	...	...	...	...	7	...	100[5]	...	...	...	...	...	...	Liechtenstein
2,001[13]	...	...	...	...	74.4[13]	15[13]	24	18	100	121	3.58	159	72.0	28.0	—	Lithuania
1,941	94.6	5.4	—	—	75.0	16	7	0	100[5]	137	6.56	1,662	91.4	8.6	—	Luxembourg
329	...	...	...	...	64.4	16	...	...	...	108	...	...	...	...	...	Macau
995	67.2	6.1	—— 26.7 ——		68.5	14	23	11	...	116	...	...	...	...	...	Macedonia
...	...	...	...	...	...	...	158	490	40	88	2.56	7	29.0	49.6	21.4	Madagascar
...	...	...	...	...	...	...	215	620	47	96	4.98	11	35.0	41.7	23.3	Malawi
717[3, 6]	...	...	...	...	...	...	11	39	78	130	2.96	71	44.0	55.8	0.2	Malaysia
256[19, 26]	...	...	...	...	71.4[19, 26]	4[19, 26]	74	350	60	111	...	...	...	...	...	Maldives
...	...	...	...	...	...	...	239	580	66	90	5.19	15	24.9	46.7	28.4	Mali
...	...	...	...	...	...	...	10	...	100[5]	136	5.38	349	68.3	31.7	0.0	Malta
...	...	...	...	...	...	...	92[10]	...	82	...	...	...	...	...	...	Marshall Islands
2,092	...	...	...	...	73.7	10	...	...	94	118	...	...	...	...	...	Martinique
...	...	...	...	...	...	...	183	550	37	114	3.80	18	28.5	41.5	30.0	Mauritania
1,446[3, 10]	...	...	...	...	74.6[3, 10]	5[3, 10]	23	30	98	130	4.40	100	47.8	39.0	13.3	Mauritius
...	...	...	...	...	...	...	...	...	...	...	...	...	...	...	...	Mayotte
403[3, 8]	...	...	...	...	64.7[3, 8]	5[3, 8]	35	48	85	135	3.17	89	49.3	49.8	0.9	Mexico
...	...	...	...	...	...	...	24	...	100[5]	...	...	...	...	...	...	Micronesia
...	...	...	...	...	...	...	35	42	98	108	3.91	143	74.4	25.6	—	Moldova
...	...	...	...	...	...	...	5	...	100	140	...	...	...	...	...	Monaco
205	...	...	...	...	...	...	150	150	45	83	6.63	58	83.0	15.1	1.9	Mongolia
255	...	...	...	...	63.8	8	72	230	65	131	2.55	26	33.6	63.3	3.1	Morocco

Health services (continued)

country	health personnel							hospitals									
	year	physicians	dentists	nurses	pharmacists	midwives	population per physician	year	number	kinds (%)				ownership (%)			hospital beds per 10,000 pop.
										general	specialized	medical centres	rural	government	private non-profit	private for profit	
Mozambique	1990	387	108	3,533	353	1,139	36,320	1990	238	4.2	0.8	—95.0—		100.0	—	—	8[19]
Myanmar (Burma)	1999	12,313	871	10,820	...	9,162	3,367	1996	737	...	...	...	...	...	...	...	7
Namibia	1997	495	67	2,817	91[8]	1,954	3,388	1992	47	...	...	...	...	91.5	—8.5—		45[8]
Nauru	1995	17	...	62	...	...	624	...	...	...	...	...	...	...	...	...	...
Nepal	1997	874	45[13]	3,845	18[13]	1,621[13]	26,316	1997	74	...	...	...	...	...	...	...	2
Netherlands, The	1997	33,618	7,319	124,000[19]	2,622	1,357	462	1998	222	64.4	35.6	—	—	...	...	...	53
Netherlands Antilles	1998	339	62	1,198	42	11	617	1998	11	38.3	36.3	25.4	—	...	...	...	70
New Caledonia	1996	362	107	852	74	61	549	1996	9	12.5[4]	12.5[4]	75.0[4]	—	62.5[4]	—37.5[4]—		45
New Zealand	1997	12,399	1,467	29,000	3,634	2,114	303	1996	368	...	...	...	...	32.3	—67.7—		59
Nicaragua	1995	4,551	1,099	2,577	...	...	957	1994	56	46.4	7.1	46.4	—	...	...	...	11
Niger	1997	325	19	2,126	29[4]	511	28,560	1987	...	...	...	...	...	...	...	...	5
Nigeria	1993	21,739	1,335	80,186	6,474[11]	62,386	3,707	1985	11,588	6.6	0.5	—92.9—		81.4	—18.6—		7[13]
Northern Mariana Islands	1986	23	4	103	2	2	1,324	1988	1	100.0	—	—	—	100.0	—	—	19
Norway	1998	18,304	5,230	81,548	2,531	2,619	242	1994	...	...	...	...	...	...	...	...	51
Oman	1998	3,061	201	7,453	435	65	773	1998	62	—8.1—		—91.9—		25.8	—74.2—		36
Pakistan	1997	78,470	3,159	28,661	47,618[25]	20,869[13]	1,836	1997	5,118	—7.6[10]—		—92.4[10]—		...	...	...	6
Palau	1998	20	2	26	...	1	900	1998	1	...	...	...	...	...	...	...	37[4]
Panama	1998	3,518	784	3,203	756	...	773	1998	60	...	...	...	...	...	...	...	27
Papua New Guinea	1998	342	127	3,141	...	...	13,708	1993	...	...	...	...	...	...	...	...	34
Paraguay	1995	3,730	1,279	1,875	433	1,547	1,294	1995	...	...	...	...	...	...	...	...	14
Peru	1996	23,249	1,197	16,043	4,789	3,832	1,030	1996	472	...	...	...	...	50.2	—49.8—		13
Philippines	1996	36,375	1,668	5,663	...	13,750	1,923	1996	1,738	96.5	3.1	0.5	—	34.5	—65.5—		12
Poland	1998	91,121	17,869	215,295	20,139	25,014	424	1998	765	93.8	6.2	—	—	100	...	...	54
Portugal	1998	31,097	3,319	37,775	7,505	827	320	1993	335	43.0	18.8	38.2	—	74.3	14.7	11.0	41[13]
Puerto Rico	1989–92	6,269	902	19,666	2,111	120	558	1994	72	83.3	8.3	8.3	—	36.1	30.6	33.3	26
Qatar	1996[14]	703	117	1,612	285	...	793	1995	4	25.0	75.0	—	—	100.0	—	—	18
Réunion	1999	1,346	337	2,906	284	176	520	1998	19	85.5	—14.5—			71.0	—29.0—		39
Romania	1998	41,415	5,379	92,057	1,643	8,913	543	1995	414	...	...	...	...	99.5	—0.5—		77
Russia	1998	618,718	47,322	1,615,000	9,112	91,853	238	1998	11,200	37.4[10]	17.2[10]	—	45.4[10]	99.8	—0.2—		119
Rwanda	1989	272	7	835	25	...	24,697	1985[3]	220	—13.6—		—86.4—		100.0	—	—	9[6]
St. Kitts and Nevis	1998	50	8	274	21	...	846	1998	4	50.0	—50.0—			...	...	...	62
St. Lucia	1997	81	13	312	13	...	1,876	1998	6	25.0[11]	25.0[11]	—	50.0[11]	...	...	...	14
St. Vincent	1998	59	6	267	27[8]	...	2,075	1997	11	...	...	...	...	77.8[11]	—22.2[11]—		19
Samoa	1996	62	7	281	6[11]	65	2,919	1992	36	2.8	—	—	97.2	100.0	—	—	34
San Marino	1998	84	...	...	...	...	309	1998	...	...	...	...	...	...	...	...	58
São Tomé and Príncipe	1996	61	7	167	1[6]	39	2,147	...	...	...	...	...	...	...	...	...	...
Saudi Arabia	1997	33,110	3,191	65,821	4,189	...	602	1996	290	...	...	...	...	74.1	—25.9—		22
Senegal	1996	649	93	1,876	322	588	13,656	1996	17	...	...	...	...	...	...	...	9
Seychelles	1998	93	15	342	7	...	849	1997	7	14.3	14.3	71.4	—	100.0	—	—	54
Sierra Leone	1996	339	19	1,532	...	218	13,696	1998	219	—25.6[16]—		—74.4[16]—		...	...	...	8
Singapore	1998	5,147	914	15,570	858[25]	487[25]	615	1997	23	...	...	...	...	43.5	—56.5—		35
Slovakia	1998	19,030	2,598	38,168	1,822	2,119[13]	283	1991	111	72.1	27.9	—	—	100.0	—	—	92[13]
Slovenia	1998	4,501	1,201	3,125	887	...	440	1998	28	57.7	42.3	—	—	...	...	...	56
Solomon Islands	1997	31	...	464	...	283	13,258	1997	11	100.0	—	—	—	75.0	25.0	—	51
Somalia	1997	265	13	1,327	70	540[15]	25,034	1988	...	...	...	...	...	...	...	...	7
South Africa	1998	29,369	4,387	174,754	9,948	...	1,459	1998	704	...	...	...	...	51.1	—48.9—		34
Spain	1996	165,560	14,877	177,034	43,221	6,314	240	1994	783	57.5	18.5	—24.0—		42.5	—57.5—		40
Sri Lanka	1999	6,881	471	19,362	848	7,899	2,740	1995[3]	407	...	...	...	...	100.0	—	—	26
Sudan, The	1996	2,818	219	18,158	344	...	11,110	1986	...	...	...	...	...	...	...	...	8
Suriname	1996	305	31	631	14	40	1,373	1998	...	...	...	...	...	...	...	...	34
Swaziland	1996	149	7[4]	1,264[4]	13[4]	...	6,617	1986	24	—41.7—		—58.3—		...	...	...	...
Sweden	1997	27,511	13,446	72,625	5,953	6,351	322	1996	...	...	...	...	...	...	...	...	43
Switzerland	1998	22,965	3,470	55,387	4,373	1,884	310	1997	...	...	...	...	...	...	...	...	66
Syria	1998	22,293	11,456	29,259	8,205	6,063[13]	694	1995	294	...	...	...	...	20.5	—79.5—		12
Taiwan	1998	27,168	7,900	71,215	22,761	704	804	1998	700	...	...	...	...	13.7	—86.3—		57
Tajikistan	1998	12,291	1,125	29,597	734	3,999	498	1994	449	...	...	...	...	98.2	—1.8—		88
Tanzania	1995	1,277	218	26,536	...	13,953	24,389	1993	173[8]	...	...	...	...	...	...	...	10
Thailand	1995	14,181	2,920	54,262	5,867	9,713	4,192	1996	1,397	93.6	6.4	—	—	65.8	—34.2—		21
Togo	1995	320	29	1,252	65[8]	438	13,168	1990	...	...	...	...	...	...	...	...	16
Tonga	1997	43	9	309	...	30	2,279	1993	4	...	...	...	...	...	...	...	28
Trinidad and Tobago	1997	949	141	1,378[22]	518	[22]	1,339	1997	77	...	...	...	...	...	...	...	37
Tunisia	1997	6,464	1,200	26,409	1,570	...	1,429	1994[3]	163	—13.5—		—86.5—		100.0	—	—	18
Turkey	1998	77,375	13,428	69,701	21,486	41,181	826	1997	1,078	75.3[10]	8.8[10]	—15.9[10]—		84.3[10]	—15.7[10]—		23
Turkmenistan	1997	14,022	1,010	21,436	1,566	3,664	333	1994	368	...	...	...	...	100.0	—	—	115
Tuvalu	1999	8	1	33	...	10	1,375	1985	8	11.1	—	—	88.9	100.0	—	—	36
Uganda	1996	840[19]	42	3,897	...	2,835	22,399[19]	1989	81	...	...	...	...	...	...	...	12
Ukraine	1998	150,382	19,615	370,171	23,488	29,523	334	1997	3,400	...	...	...	...	100.0	...	...	99
United Arab Emirates	1997	4,749	644[25]	8,450[25]	2,007[25]	...	553	1996	50	...	...	...	...	72.0	—28.0—		29
United Kingdom	1998	82,803	20,216	299,010	33,759[11]	24,801[6]	716	1997	...	...	...	...	...	...	...	...	42
United States	1998	756,700	196,000	2,162,000	184,000[13]	3,000[13]	357	1998	6,097	88.0	12.0	—	—	25.3	49.2	25.5	38
Uruguay	1998	11,964	3,921	2,369	1,009	586	269	1997	118	...	...	...	...	75.4	—24.6—		35
Uzbekistan	1998	74,230	5,869	243,166	746	16,235	324	1995	192	...	...	...	...	100.0	...	...	84
Vanuatu	1997	21	3[13]	259[13]	6[13]	33[13]	8,524	1995	90	5.6	—	21.1	73.3	100.0	—	—	32
Venezuela	1997	53,818	13,000	46,305	8,571	...	423	1997	556	...	...	...	...	37.0	—63.0—		17
Vietnam	1998	36,683	...	42,797	6,500[19]	13,450	2,083	1994	12,500	...	...	...	...	...	...	...	27
Virgin Islands (U.S.)	1985	167	...	...	...	...	622	1985	...	...	...	...	...	...	...	...	49
West Bank	1993[23]	1,344	445	2,279	149	56	1,536	1995	17	...	...	...	...	52.9	—47.1—		9
Western Sahara	1994	100	...	...	24	...	2,504	...	...	...	...	...	...	...	...	...	...
Yemen	1998	3,883	245[25]	7,578[13]	613	385[10]	4,211	1998	81	...	...	...	...	...	...	...	55
Yugoslavia	1997	22,498	4,209	...	2,032	...	471	1997	...	...	...	...	...	...	...	...	55
Zambia	1995	601	26[4]	9,853	24[4]	311[4]	14,496	1987	965	8.2	0.3	19.0	72.5	80.9	19.1	—	29[19]
Zimbabwe	1995	1,522	142	14,095	411[19]	3,078	7,196	1993[3]	1,378	0.9	2.6	83.7	12.7	100.0	—	—	19[13]

[1]1997. [2]1987. [3]Government hospitals only. [4]1990. [5]Data refer to a period other than 1994–95, differ from the standard definition, or refer to only part of the country. [6]1989. [7]General hospitals only. [8]1991. [9]Physicians include dentists. [10]1994. [11]1992. [12]Number of pharmacies. [13]1995. [14]Government-employed personnel only. [15]1987. [16]1988. [17]Includes doctors of traditional Chinese medicine. [18]Republic of Cyprus only. [19]1993. [20]Excludes psychiatric hospitals. [21]Data refer to former Czechoslovakia. [22]Nurses include midwives. [23]West Bank includes Gaza Strip. [24]Registered personnel; all may

admissions or discharges: rate per 10,000 pop.	by kinds of hospital (%): general	specialized	medical centres	rural	bed occupancy rate (%)	average length of stay (days)	mortality: under age 5 per 1,000 live newborn 1997	maternal mortality per 100,000 live births 1990–97	population with access to safe water 1994–98 (%)	food supply (% of FAO requirement) 1998	total health expenditures, 1990: as percent of GDP	per capita (U.S.$)	by source (percent): public	private	international aid	country
...	...	...	...	...	...	...	209	1,100	46	82	5.86	5	21.0	25.7	53.3	Mozambique
...	...	...	...	...	...	...	114	230	60	131	...	...	...	...	...	Myanmar (Burma)
...	...	...	...	...	...	...	75	230	83	92	3.92	45	47.8	41.3	10.9	Namibia
...	...	...	...	...	...	...	30	...	...	...	...	...	...	...	...	Nauru
...	...	...	...	...	...	...	104	540	71	99	4.54	7	23.0	51.7	25.4	Nepal
1,028	96.7	3.3	—	—	70.1	10	6	7	100	122	8.03	1,501	72.6	27.4	—	Netherlands, The
...	...	...	...	...	...	...	...	...	...	110	...	...	...	...	...	Netherlands Antilles
1,165[4, 7]	...	...	...	...	84.8[4, 7]	8[4, 7]	...	...	...	123	...	...	...	...	...	New Caledonia
1,332[3]	...	...	...	...	64.0[3]	6[3]	7	15	100[5]	126	7.37	925	81.7	18.3	—	New Zealand
769	—— 76.2 ——		23.8	—	...	...	57	160	78	98	8.61	34	56.9	22.5	20.6	Nicaragua
...	...	...	...	...	...	...	285	590	61	84	4.98	16	24.5	31.3	34.1	Niger
...	...	...	...	...	...	...	187	1,000	49	122	2.72	10	36.5	57.4	6.1	Nigeria
1,550	100.0	—	—	—	54.7	4	...	...	...	...	...	...	...	...	...	Northern Mariana Islands
1,515	96.4	3.6	—	—	83.0	10	4	6	100	128	7.35	1,835	95.7	4.3	—	Norway
911	...	...	...	...	...	...	18	21	85	...	4.22	209	59.5	40.1	0.5	Oman
...	...	...	...	...	...	...	136	340	79	106	3.48	12	47.4	47.1	5.5	Pakistan
1,582	...	...	...	...	48.5	6	34	...	88	...	...	...	...	...	...	Palau
1,239	...	...	...	...	52.5	8	20	85	93	107	7.13	142	72.6	23.1	4.3	Panama
...	...	...	...	...	...	...	112	370	41	95	4.44	37	59.1	36.1	4.8	Papua New Guinea
...	...	...	...	...	...	...	33	190	60	112	2.97	35	35.1	58.2	6.7	Paraguay
...	...	...	...	...	...	...	56	270	67	103	3.21	61	56.1	41.7	2.2	Peru
538	...	...	...	...	62.1	5	46	210	85	101	2.15	16	46.7	46.4	6.9	Philippines
1,288[11]	96.0[11]	4.0[11]	—	—	72.5[11]	14[11]	11	8	100[5]	128	5.07	84	80.3	19.7	—	Poland
1,146	86.3	10.5	3.2	—	74.5	10	8	8	100[5]	151	6.99	383	61.7	38.3	—	Portugal
1,101	94.0	4.3	1.7	—	63.1	5	...	...	...	...	...	...	...	...	...	Puerto Rico
...	...	...	...	...	71.7[11, 29]	7[11, 29]	20	10	100[5]	...	4.73	630	63.0	36.9	0.0	Qatar
1,951[10]	...	...	...	...	79.8[10]	7[10]	...	...	...	146	...	...	...	...	...	Réunion
...	...	...	...	...	...	...	26	41	100[5]	123	3.87	58	61.4	38.6	—	Romania
2,320	...	...	...	...	85.0	14	22	49	...	111	3.02	159	66.8	33.2	—	Russia
85	...	...	...	...	42.8[27]	7[27]	170	1,300	66[5]	88	3.44	10	15.0	45.2	39.8	Rwanda
1,068[7, 11]	...	...	...	...	49.3[7, 11]	9[7, 11]	37	130	100[5]	114	5.99	212	58.1	27.8	14.1	St. Kitts and Nevis
890[11, 27]	...	...	...	...	...	...	29	30	85	117	7.18	169	75.6	23.0	1.4	St. Lucia
728	...	...	...	...	68.2	7	21	43	89	106	5.69	102	68.5	28.8	2.7	St. Vincent
894	70.8	—	—	29.2	32.9	5	27	...	68	...	2.94	20	6.1	54.2	39.7	Samoa
...	...	...	...	...	...	...	6	...	100[5]	...	...	...	...	...	...	San Marino
...	...	...	...	...	...	...	78	...	82	94	9.22	38	28.8	17.0	54.2	São Tomé and Príncipe
...	...	...	...	...	...	...	28	130	95	119	4.76	260	64.3	35.7	0.0	Saudi Arabia
...	...	...	...	...	...	...	124	560	81	96	3.66	29	45.1	38.0	16.9	Senegal
1,744[30]	...	...	...	...	76.4[30]	5[30]	18	...	97[5]	105	6.03	289	50.2	28.0	21.9	Seychelles
...	...	...	...	...	...	...	316	1,800	34[5]	89	2.43	4	19.6	30.9	49.5	Sierra Leone
1,127[25]	...	...	...	...	73.1[10]	8[10]	4	6	100	...	1.87	215	58.3	41.6	0.1	Singapore
1,679[13]	94.9[13]	5.1[13]	—	—	73.2[13]	14[13]	11	9	...	120	...	...	...	...	...	Slovakia
1,643	...	...	...	...	78.4	10	6	11	...	116	...	...	...	...	...	Slovenia
...	...	...	...	...	...	...	28	550	...	93	2.18	117	43.2	50.5	6.3	Solomon Islands
...	...	...	...	...	...	...	211	...	31	66	1.51	8	7.3	41.1	51.6	Somalia
...	...	...	...	...	...	...	82	230	87	119	5.56	77	57.5	42.5	0.0	South Africa
1,053	...	...	...	...	76.7[8]	12[8]	5	6	99	136	6.59	831	78.4	21.6	—	Spain
1,464[4]	...	...	...	...	...	...	19	60	57	104	3.74	18	40.4	51.1	8.6	Sri Lanka
...	...	...	...	...	...	...	115	550	73	104	3.33	34	11.0	84.5	4.5	Sudan, The
766[31]	...	...	...	...	68.8[31]	10[31]	36	110	72[5]	116	2.88	93	37.9	58.0	4.1	Suriname
...	...	...	...	...	...	...	94	230	50	108	7.22	64	43.6	22.2	34.2	Swaziland
1,906[10]	...	...	...	...	82.2[10]	8[10]	4	5	100[5]	116	8.79	2,343	89.3	10.7	—	Sweden
...	...	...	...	...	...	...	5	5	100	120	7.52	2,520	68.5	31.5	—	Switzerland
352[3, 19]	...	...	...	...	75.5[3, 19]	3[3, 19]	33	110	86	136	2.07	41	16.6	79.4	4.0	Syria
...	...	...	...	...	...	...	8	8	90	...	4.30	323	53.0	47.0	0.0	Taiwan
1,492	...	...	...	...	70.2	15	76	85	60	85	5.98	100	72.6	27.4	—	Tajikistan
...	...	...	...	...	...	...	143	530	66	86	4.73	4	14.4	31.6	54.0	Tanzania
...	...	...	...	...	...	...	38	44	81	110	4.98	72	20.4	78.7	0.9	Thailand
...	...	...	...	...	...	...	125	640	55	109	4.10	18	40.4	38.5	21.2	Togo
622[11]	...	...	...	...	56.2[11]	10[11]	23	...	95	...	6.46	63	60.3	25.0	14.8	Tonga
1,114[3, 7]	...	...	...	...	70.7[3, 7]	6[3, 7]	17	90	97	112	4.54	180	62.4	36.9	0.6	Trinidad and Tobago
...	...	...	...	...	...	...	33	70	98	126	4.91	76	63.8	33.3	3.0	Tunisia
709	...	...	...	...	...	...	45	130	92	141	3.94	76	36.2	63.3	0.5	Turkey
...	...	...	...	...	...	...	78	110	74	105	4.99	125	66.4	33.2	0.4	Turkmenistan
1,368	40.9	—	—	59.1	51.5[7]	12.2[7]	56	...	100[5]	...	2.66	472	34.0	66.0	0.1	Tuvalu
...	...	...	...	...	...	...	137	510	46	95	3.40	8	13.3	53.0	33.7	Uganda
...	...	...	...	...	...	...	23	30	97	112	3.30	131	69.7	30.3	—	Ukraine
...	...	...	...	...	...	...	10	3	97	132	2.66	472	34.0	66.0	0.1	United Arab Emirates
...	...	...	...	...	...	...	7	7	100	129	6.11	1,039	84.9	15.1	—	United Kingdom
1,180[32]	...	...	...	...	61.8[32]	6[32]	8	8	90	142	12.71	2,765	44.1	55.9	—	United States
477[3]	...	...	...	...	78.8[3]	9[3]	21	21	93	107	4.62	123	53.8	44.8	1.4	Uruguay
...	...	...	...	...	...	...	58	21	90	100	5.90	116	72.1	27.9	—	Uzbekistan
567	...	...	...	...	41.9	6	50	...	77	120	5.68	67	51.5	25.7	22.8	Vanuatu
601[3]	...	...	...	...	69.7[3]	6[3]	25	65	79	96	3.60	88	54.2	45.6	0.1	Venezuela
...	...	...	...	...	...	...	43	160	45	112	2.11	3	39.3	47.4	13.3	Vietnam
...	...	...	...	...	...	...	...	...	...	...	...	...	...	...	...	Virgin Islands (U.S.)
711	...	...	...	...	80.9	4	...	...	...	...	...	...	...	...	...	West Bank
...	...	...	...	...	...	...	...	...	...	...	...	...	...	...	...	Western Sahara
...	...	...	...	...	...	...	100	1,400	61	86	3.19	20	34.7	54.1	11.3	Yemen
1,154	...	...	...	...	72.0	12	21	10	76	117	5.11[33]	264[33]	80.4[33]	19.6[33]	—	Yugoslavia
1,249	—— 75.7 ——		—— 24.3 ——		68.5	7	202	650	38	84	3.16	17	65.4	30.6	4.1	Zambia
546	...	...	...	...	69.8	7	80	400	79	90	6.23	39	40.3	48.7	11.0	Zimbabwe

not be present and working in the country. [25]1996. [26]Central hospital only. [27]General and specialized hospitals only. [28]Public sector only. [29]Hamad General Hospital only. [30]Victoria Hospital only. [31]Paramaribo hospitals (1,213 beds) only. [32]5,037 community hospitals only. [33]Data refer to the former Socialist Federal Republic of Yugoslavia.

Social protection

This table summarizes three principal areas of social protective activity for the countries of the world: social security, crime and law enforcement, and military affairs. Because the administrative structure, financing, manning, and scope of institutions and programmed tasks in these fields vary so greatly from country to country, no well-accepted or well-documented body of statistical comparisons exists in international convention to permit objective assessment of any of these subjects, either from the perspective of a single country or internationally. The data provided within any single subject area do, however, represent the most consistent approach to problems of international comparison found in the published literature for that field.

The provision of social security programs to answer specific social needs, for example, is summarized simply in terms of the existence or nonexistence of a specific type of benefit program because of the great complexity of national programs in terms of eligibility, coverage, term, age limits, financing, payments, and so on. Activities connected with a particular type of benefit often take place at more than one governmental level, through more than one agency at the same level, or through a mixture of public and private institutions. The data shown here are summarized from the U.S. Social Security Administration's *Social Security Programs Throughout the World* (biennial). A bullet symbol (•) indicates that a country has at least one program within the defined area; in some cases it may have several. A blank space indicates that no program existed providing the benefit shown; ellipses [...] indicate that no information was available as to whether a program existed.

Data given for social security expenditure as a percentage of total central governmental expenditure are taken from the International Monetary Fund's *Government Finance Statistics Yearbook*, which provides the most comparable analytic series on the consolidated accounts of central governments, governmentally administered social security funds, and independent national agencies, all usually separate accounting entities, through which these services may be provided in a given country.

Data on the finances of social security programs are taken in large part from the International Labour Office's *The Cost of Social Security* (triennial), supplemented by national data sources.

Figures for criminal offenses known to police, usually excluding civil offenses and minor traffic violations, are taken in part from Interpol's *International Crime Statistics* (annual) and a variety of national sources. Statistics are usually based on the number of offenses reported to police, not the number of offenders apprehended or tried in courts. Attempted offenses are counted as the offense that was attempted. A person identified as having committed multiple offenses is counted only under the most serious offense. Murder refers to all acts involving the voluntary taking of life, including infanticide, but excluding abortion, or involuntary acts such as those normally classified as manslaughter. Assault includes "serious," or aggravated, assault—that involving injury, endangering life, or perpetrated with the use of a dangerous instrument. Burglary involves theft from the premises of another; although Interpol statistics are reported as "breaking and entering," national data may not always distinguish cases of forcible

Social protection

country	social security						finances										
	programs available, 1999					expenditures, 1997 (% of total central govt.)[f]	year	receipts					expenditures			
	old-age, invalidity, death[a]	sickness and maternity[b]	work injury[c]	unemployment[d]	family allowances[e]			total ('000,000 natl. cur.)	insured persons (%)	employers (%)	government (%)	other (%)	total ('000,000 natl. cur.)	benefits (%)	administration (%)	other (%)
Afghanistan	•	•	•		•	...	...	...	...	...	...	...	...	...	...	...
Albania	•	•	•	•	•	24.4	1990	967.0	—	—	88.8	11.2	1,440.0	99.5	— 0.5 —	
Algeria	•	•	•	•	•	...	1990	27,700.0	...	...	...	...	28,748.0	61.8	30.6	7.6
American Samoa	•	...	...	...	...	...	1990	...	...	...	...	...	13.0	100.0	—	—
Andorra	•	•	•			...	1993	11,832.2	...	...	...	...	7,937.2	90.2	4.6	5.2
Angola	...	...	...	...	...	...	...	...	...	...	...	...	...	...	...	...
Antigua and Barbuda	•	•				...	1983	13.0	29.2	48.7	—	22.1	4.2	66.1	33.9	—
Argentina	•	•	•	•	•	52.3	1989	1,015,837.0	28.8	45.0	16.6	9.6	989,009.0	95.0	5.0	—
Armenia	•	•	•	•	•	...	...	...	...	...	...	...	...	...	...	...
Aruba	•	...	•	...	...	[9]	1998	197.1	...	...	...	...	179.0	...	...	...
Australia	•	•	•	•	•	35.3	1998–99	...	...	...	...	1.9	41,825	99.6	0.3	—
Austria	•	•	•	•	•	42.0	1989	425,417.0	30.1	45.9	21.1	2.9	412,134.0	96.5	2.3	1.2
Azerbaijan	•	•	•	•	•	31.9	...	...	...	...	...	...	...	...	...	...
Bahamas, The	•	•	•			5.2	1989	95.9	22.9	38.5	2.1	36.5	43.5	71.1	27.2	1.7
Bahrain	•		•			3.9	1989	39.6	12.3	40.2	—	47.5	9.7	69.8	20.9	9.3
Bangladesh		•	•	•		9.8[10]	1989	73.6	12.4	37.5	2.4	47.7	34.1	94.0	6.0	—
Barbados	•	•	•	•		19.8[6, 11]	1989	191.7	38.0	40.8	1.5	19.7	149.1	93.5	5.8	0.7
Belarus	•	•	•	•	•	32.2	1986	3,199.0	—	—	93.2	6.8	3,199.0	100.0	—	—
Belgium	•	•	•	•	•	42.3[6]	1986	1,347,070.0	24.4	39.7	31.6	4.3	1,322,636.0	94.5	4.3	1.2
Belize	•	•	•			5.9	1989	15.3	8.9	53.2	—	38.0	3.9	56.7	43.3	—
Benin	•		•		•	8.7[14]	1989	3,551.9	16.8	81.4	—	1.8	4,500.9	69.3	28.1	2.6
Bermuda	•		•			...	...	...	...	...	...	...	...	...	...	...
Bhutan	...	...	...	...	...	0.5[15]	1990	...	...	...	...	...	26.0[16]	...	...	...
Bolivia	•	•	•		•	27.7	1989	346.6	29.3	47.7	11.2	11.8	340.2	84.9	14.3	0.8
Bosnia and Herzegovina	•	•	•	•	•	...	...	...	...	...	...	...	...	...	...	...
Botswana	•		•			1.1[12]	1996	—	...	...	...	...	65.0[16]	...	...	...
Brazil	•	•	•	•	•	30.4[18]	1989	71,847.0	24.4	51.0	20.0	4.6	68,957.0	61.9	18.6	19.5
Brunei	•	...	...	...	...	...	1984	...	...	...	...	...	39.5	...	...	...
Bulgaria	•	•	•	•	•	27.1	1989	6,016.8	—	71.4	28.1	0.5	6,000.1	96.6	3.3	0.1
Burkina Faso	•		•		•	0.1[19]	1989	8,816.5	15.6	62.9	—	21.5	4,975.3	69.5	30.4	0.1
Burundi	•		•		•	5.8	1989	1,991.5	31.6	47.6	—	20.8	1,563.9	74.8	16.8	8.4
Cambodia	...	...	•	...	•	...	...	...	...	...	...	...	...	...	...	...
Cameroon	•		•		•	0.7[13]	1989	41,331.8	13.1	64.8	—	22.1	41,332.0	70.6	28.8	0.6
Canada	•	•	•	•	•	42.9[13]	1989	130,306.6	9.9	15.6	64.4	10.1	115,764.2	96.9	2.5	0.6
Cape Verde	•	•	•		•	...	1989	697.7	26.5	58.5	—	15.0	316.7	82.4	16.1	1.5
Central African Republic	•		•		•	6.2[4]	1989	3,604.0	8.4	76.0	—	15.6	3,247.0	64.6	32.9	2.5
Chad	•		•		•	1.9[11, 20]	1989	1,172.8	12.6	77.6	—	9.8	634.5	43.0	51.4	5.6
Chile	•	•	•	•	•	34.5	1989	1,186,056.0	32.8	2.7	37.9	26.6	798,770.0	83.9	14.7	1.4
China	•	•	•	•		0.2	1989	57,446.2	—	99.4	—	0.6	54,654	98.4	0.6	1.0
Colombia	•	•	•		•	8.5	1989	294,438.0	24.8	56.0	0.2	19.0	257,455.0	85.5	11.5	3.0
Comoros	...	...	...	...	...	...	1983	40.7	100.0	—	—	—	54.3	17.4	62.3	20.3
Congo, Dem. Rep. of the	•		•		•	—	1986	1,238.3	28.6	60.2	—	11.2	1,044.2	27.9	72.1	—
Congo, Rep. of the	•		•		•	0.4[11, 23]	1983	15,272.8	12.1	80.2	—	7.7	7,256.7	66.6	21.3	12.1
Costa Rica	•	•	•		•	20.5	1989	36,407.3	33.2	44.4	1.2	21.2	31,049.8	89.0	4.1	6.9
Côte d'Ivoire	•		•		•	3.6[4, 11]	1989	27,288.4	19.3	75.4	—	5.3	20,593.5	100.0	—	—
Croatia	•	•	•	•	•	36.2	...	...	...	...	...	...	...	...	...	...
Cuba	•	•	•			...	1989	2,284.8	—	37.4	62.6	—	2,284.8	96.7	—	3.3
Cyprus[24]	•	•	•	•	•	24.5	1989	217.5	24.7	40.3	17.3	17.7	117.7	98.4	1.6	—
Czech Republic	•	•	•	•	•	36.2	1989[26]	132,748.0	—	3.9	96.1	—	132,748.0	99.7	0.3	—
Denmark	•	•	•	•	•	43.2[13]	1989	225,965.6	4.3	5.0	88.2	2.5	218,258.2	97.0	3.0	—
Djibouti	•	...	...	...	•	6.2[27]	1979	1,352.2	...	...	...	...	1,115.7	...	...	...
Dominica	•	•	•			1.4[11, 14]	1986	12.3	22.6	50.9	—	26.5	4.4	68.0	32.0	—
Dominican Republic	•	•	•			5.6	1986	77.9	20.1	72.9	—	6.8	74.3	75.9	24.1	—
East Timor[29]	...	...	...	...	...	...	...	...	...	...	...	...	...	...	...	...
Ecuador	•	•	•	•		1.9[3]	1988	71,286.0	37.0	50.0	—	13.0	52,032.4	86.0	14.0	—

entry. Automobile theft excludes brief use of a car without the owner's permission, "joyriding," and implies intent to deprive the owner of the vehicle permanently. Criminal offense data for certain countries refer to cases disposed of in court, rather than to complaints. Police manpower figures refer, for the most part, to full-time, paid professional staff, excluding clerical support and volunteer staff. Personnel in military service who perform police functions are presumed to be employed in their principal activity, military service.

The figures for military manpower refer to full-time, active-duty military service and exclude reserve, militia, paramilitary, and similar organizations. Because of the difficulties attached to the analysis of data on military manpower and budgets (including problems such as data withheld on national security grounds, or the publication of budgetary data specifically intended to hide actual expenditure, or the complexity of long-term financing of purchases of military matériel [how much was actually spent as opposed to what was committed, offset by nonmilitary transfers, etc.]), extensive use is made of the principal international analytic tools: publications such as those of the International Institute for Strategic Studies (*The Military Balance* and *Strategic Survey*) and the U.S. Arms Control and Disarmament Agency (*World Military Expenditures and Arms Transfers*), both annuals.

The data on military expenditures are from the sources identified above, as well as from the IMF's *Government Finance Statistics Yearbook* and country statistical publications.

The following notes further define the column headings:

a. Programs providing cash payments for *each* of the three types of long-term benefit indicated to persons (1) exceeding a specified working age (usually 50–65, often 5 years earlier for women) who are qualified by a term of covered employment, (2) partially or fully incapacitated for their usual employment by injury or illness, and (3) qualified by their status as spouse, cohabitant, or dependent minor of a qualified person who dies.
b. Programs providing cash payments (jointly, or alternatively, medical services as well) to occupationally qualified persons for *both* of the short-term benefits indicated: (1) illness and (2) maternity.
c. Programs providing cash or medical services to employment-qualified persons who become temporarily or permanently incapacitated (fully or partially) by work-related injury or illness.
d. Programs providing term-limited cash compensation (usually 40–75% of average earnings) to persons qualified by previous employment (of six months minimum, typically) for periods of involuntary unemployment.
e. Programs providing cash payments to families or mothers to mitigate the cost of raising children and to encourage the formation of larger families.
f. Includes welfare.
g. A police officer is a full-time, paid professional, performing domestic security functions. Data include administrative staff but exclude clerical employees, volunteers, and members of paramilitary groups.
h. Includes all active-duty personnel, regular and conscript, performing national security functions. Excludes reserves, paramilitary forces, border patrols, and gendarmeries.

crime and law enforcement (latest)						military protection								country
offenses reported to the police per 100,000 population					population per police officer[g]	manpower, 1999[h]		expenditure, 1997				arms trade, 1997 ('000,000 U.S.$)		
total	personal		property			total ('000)	per 1,000 population	total '000,000	per capita	% of central government expenditure	% of GDP or GNP	imports	exports	
	murder	assault	burglary	automobile theft										
…	…	…	…	…	540[1]	[2]	[2]	408[3]	24[4]	64.4[4]	9.1[4]	5	0	Afghanistan
75	30.3	5.7	9.5	14.0	550	[5]	[5]	157[6]	56[6]	11.3[6]	4.1[6]	10	0	Albania
584	1.5	19.7	11.8	8.5	840	122.0	4.1	1,750	59	12.0	3.9	480	0	Algeria
3,006	8.0	494.0	588.0	6.0	460	—	[7]	—	—	—	—	…	…	American Samoa
2,606	1.6	57.6	648.5	97.0	220	—	—	…	…	…	…	…	…	Andorra
40	10.4	7.1	…	3.7	14[8]	112.5	11.3	1,550	147	36.3	20.5	80	0	Angola
4,977	4.7	475.0	1,984.4	35.9	120	0.2	2.1	…	…	…	…	…	…	Antigua and Barbuda
606	4.5	86.9	34.7	107.9	1,270	71.0	1.9	3,700	103	6.3	1.2	70	0	Argentina
283	3.8	5.5	18.1	1.1	…	53.4	14.0	342	99	…	3.5	0	0	Armenia
5,461	1.2	180.0	451.3	202.5	…	—	[7]	—	—	—	—	…	…	Aruba
7,001	3.6	713.7	2,338.4	706.2	438	55.2	2.9	8,460	459	8.6	2.2	925	30	Australia
5,940	2.0	2.7	1,008.9	35.8	470	40.5	5.0	1,790	221	1.9	0.9	170	20	Austria
188	5.1	1.1	2.9	0.2	…	69.9	8.8	225	29	10.8	1.9	0	0	Azerbaijan
6,814	21.9	119.6	2,229.1	393.2	125	0.9	2.9	9[4]	40[4]	2.5[4]	0.5[4]	…	…	Bahamas, The
1,390	1.6	0.5	380.1	207.6	180	11.0	17.1	533	883	24.9	10.4	90	0	Bahrain
90	2.8	4.3	4.3	1.1	2,560	137.0	1.1	592	5.0	10.7	1.4	50	0	Bangladesh
3,779	7.5	168.2	966.7	70.8	280	0.6	2.3	14[12]	54[12]	2.0[12]	0.8[12]	5	0	Barbados
1,204	10.2	20.3	173.9	17.5	…	81.0	8.0	841	81	4.8	1.7	0	490	Belarus
8,478	5.3	535.8	2,031.3	376.5	640	41.8	4.1	3,690	363	3.2	1.7	240	110	Belgium
…	12.8	20.0	600.0	4.0	290	1.1	4.3	9[13]	44[13]	5.9[13]	1.6[13]	0	0	Belize
297	5.1	102.0	4.6	0.6	3,250	4.8	0.8	27	5.0	6.8	1.3	0	0	Benin
8,871	5.1	221.7	1,949.2	…	370	—	[7]	—	—	—	—	…	…	Bermuda
…	…	…	…	…	…	4.0[10]	3.1[10]	…	…	…	…	0	0	Bhutan
660	28.6	59.4	0.9	…	…	32.5	4.0	150	20	6.7	1.9	30	0	Bolivia
402	2.5	2.6	…	…	…	[17]	[17]	259	80	14.1	5.9	180	0	Bosnia and Herzegovina
8,281	12.7	431.9	1.9	73.1	750	9.0	5.8	241	168	13.4	5.1	20	0	Botswana
1,404	21.2	255.7	5.2	61.2	…	291.0	1.8	14,100	84	3.9[13]	1.8	430	30	Brazil
849.8	0.6	2.2	67.7	64.6	100	5.0	15.2	374	1,220	13.8	4.6	50	0	Brunei
1,992	7.5	2.3	532.5	97.3	…	67.0	8.2	949	114	9.2	3.0	10	120	Bulgaria
9	0.4	1.7	—	—	…	5.8	0.5	67	6	12.3	2.8	0	0	Burkina Faso
156	9.7	10.8	2.0	0.2	…	40.0	6.8	57	11	25.8	6.1	20	0	Burundi
…	…	…	…	…	1,980	104.0	8.7	126	11	25.8	4.1	10	0	Cambodia
78	0.4	1.2	1.2	5.1	1,170	13.1	0.9	240	16	17.7	3.0	10	0	Cameroon
8,453	4.3	142.3	1,155.7	547.2	8,640	60.6	2.0	7,800	257	7.1[18]	1.3	310	550	Canada
…	…	…	…	…	110	1.1	2.8	4	10	1.7	0.9	5	0	Cape Verde
135	1.6	22.8	2.7	…	2,740[1]	2.7	0.8	39	12	27.7	3.9	0	0	Central African Republic
…	…	…	…	…	990	25.4	3.1	43	6	12.6	2.7	5	0	Chad
1,349	3.5	104.9	464.6	12.9	470	93.0	6.2	2,860	196	17.8	3.9	60	0	Chile
128	0.2	5.2	45.2	6.9	1,360[21]	2,480.0	2.0	74,900	61	17.6	2.3	500	1,100	China
790	56.3	61.8	57.9	75.3	420	144.0	3.5	3,460	91	19.9	3.7	120	0	Colombia
…	…	…	…	…	960	—	[22]	…	…	…	…	…	…	Comoros
…	…	…	…	…	910	55.9	1.1	252	5.0	41.4	5.0	20	0	Congo, Dem. Rep. of the
32	1.5	4.7	0.2	0.2	870	10.0	3.6	74	28	12.3	4.1	10	0	Congo, Rep. of the
868	5.3	11.1	232.4	23.1	480	—	—	58	17	3.1	0.6	5	0	Costa Rica
67	2.5	73.1	19.5	11.9	4,640	8.4	0.5	101	7	4.0	1.1	0	0	Côte d'Ivoire
1,173	6.1	23.2	305.9	20.9	…	61.0	14.3	…	…	…	…	10	0	Croatia
…	…	…	…	…	650	60.0	5.4	720	65	…	2.3	0	0	Cuba
689	1.9	17.7	203.3	3.0	180	10.0[25]	15.0	506	680	16.2	6.1	100	0	Cyprus[24]
4,129	3.0	41.8	892.2	270.4	640[26]	58.2	5.7	1,990	193	5.8	1.9	140	90	Czech Republic
9,428	3.9	17.7	1,925.2	709.5	600	24.3	4.6	2,800	529	3.9	1.7	200	10	Denmark
252	4.2	124.2	45.0	0.5	…	8.4	18.9	20	47	11.4	4.1	0	0	Djibouti
8,846	11.9	125.1	2,019	55.3	300	[28]	[28]	…	…	…	…	…	…	Dominica
…	15.8	28.4	154.0	14.0	580	24.5	3.0	168	21	7.3	1.1	5	0	Dominican Republic
…	…	…	…	…	…	[30]	[30]	…	…	…	…	…	…	East Timor[29]
579	22.2	38.6	125.2	61.2	260	57.1	4.6	746	62	20.3	4.0	160	0	Ecuador

Social protection (continued)

country	social security: programs available, 1999: old-age, invalidity, death[a]	sickness and maternity[b]	work injury[c]	unemployment[d]	family allowances[e]	expenditures, 1997 (% of total central govt.)[f]	finances: year	receipts: total ('000,000 natl. cur.)	insured persons (%)	employers (%)	government (%)	other (%)	expenditures: total ('000,000 natl. cur.)	benefits (%)	administration (%)	other (%)
Egypt	•	•	•	•		0.5	1989	2,443.5	22.8	41.0	2.0	34.2	1,685.6	93.4	6.6	—
El Salvador	•	•	•			5.4	1989	465.3	27.1	51.7	—	21.2	368.3	78.1	21.9	—
Equatorial Guinea	•	•	•		•	…	1989	141.0	7.1	92.9	—	—	134.0	49.3	50.7	—
Eritrea	…	…	…	…	…	…	…	…	…	…	…	…	…	…	…	…
Estonia	•	•	•	•	•	32.0	…	90.1	…	…	…	…	…	…	…	…
Ethiopia	•		•			5.9[13]	1989[31]	190.9	32.8	65.3	—	1.9	153.7	98.3	1.7	—
Faroe Islands	•	…	…	…	•	…	…	…	…	…	…	…	…	…	…	…
Fiji	•		•			4.1[12]	1989	153.5	20.9	33.8	0.8	44.5	75.47	95.3	4.7	—
Finland	•	•	•	•	•	39.2	1989	118,589.0	7.7	41.1	44.0	7.2	106,235	96.3	3.7	—
France	•	•	•	•	•	39.3[32]	1989	1,700,202.0	77.7	—	20.4	1.9	1,669,096.0	95.5	3.7	0.8
French Guiana	•	…	•	…	•	…	1991	1,071.5	…	…	…	…	997.1	…	…	…
French Polynesia	•	…	•	…	•	…	1990	19,268.0	…	…	…	…	17,832.0	…	…	…
Gabon	•		•		•	…	1989	3,415.0	—	44.3	29.3	26.4	2,737.0	55.2	44.8	—
Gambia, The	•		•			3.0[3]	1982	—	…	…	…	…	5.6	…	…	…
Gaza Strip	…	…	…	…	…	—	…	…	…	…	…	…	…	…	…	…
Georgia	•	•	•	•	•	17.6	…	…	…	…	…	…	…	…	…	…
Germany	•	•	•	•	•	50.0[12]	1989[33]	522,172.0	36.9	34.3	26.1	2.7	507,604.0	97.1	2.8	0.1
Ghana	•		•			7.1[32]	1989	17,920.8	21.1	52.9	—	26.0	4,147.7	13.3	64.0	22.7
Greece	•	•	•	•	•	16.8	1989	1,314,421.0	24.9	38.4	30.8	5.9	1,349,693.0	92.5	7.5	—
Greenland	•	…	…	…	•	…	…	…	…	…	…	…	…	…	…	…
Grenada	•	•				8.6[13]	1989	24.1	20.1	60.3	3.2	16.3	13.5	93.1	6.9	—
Guadeloupe	•	…	…	…	•	…	1994	2,607.3	…	…	…	…	5,883.4	…	…	…
Guam	•	…	…	…	•	…	1989	…	…	…	…	…	7.3	…	…	…
Guatemala	•	•	•			5.2[6]	1989	348.5	29.1	54.8	—	16.1	279.7	82.7	14.6	2.7
Guernsey	•	•	•	•	•	…	1999	103,560	—— 45.0 ——		40.7	14.3	85,468	94.8	5.2	…
Guinea	•	•	•		•	…	1989	3,387.0	0.4	90.3	—	9.3	1,108.1	54.9	45.1	—
Guinea-Bissau	…	…	…	…	…	8.8[32]	1986	138.0	22.8	63.4	10.3	3.8	61.9	59.6	40.4	—
Guyana	•	•	•			3.7[11, 34]	1994	1,070.8	…	…	…	…	1,373.7	…	…	…
Haiti	•		•			5.1[11]	1977	60.5	—— 26.6 ——		69.9	3.5	52.4	92.7	7.3	—
Honduras	•	•	•			4.5[11, 14]	1986	166.2	23.9	40.8	3.3	32.0	76.8	84.6	15.4	—
Hong Kong	•	•	•	•	•	…	1998–99	…	…	…	…	…	26,939	…	…	…
Hungary	•	•	•	•	•	33.3	1994	798,000.0	—	—	—	—	737,000.0	—	—	—
Iceland	•	•	•	•	36	23.6	1997	14,799	—	—	—	—	96,094	98.2	1.8	—
India	•	•	•			…	1989	43,913.8	23.8	27.7	5.3	43.2	13,775.8	90.0	8.2	1.8
Indonesia	•		•			6.3	1989	239,477.0	50.7	49.3	—	—	181,499.0	12.3	15.8	71.9
Iran	•	•	•	•	•	14.1	1986	346,460.0	83.2	0.1	8.2	8.5	167,879.0	43.4	6.3	50.0
Iraq	•	•	•			…	1977	107.8	9.9	55.6	21.9	12.6	71.0	94.0	2.4	3.6
Ireland	•	•	•	•	•	27.1[12]	1989	4,627.5	16.3	24.8	57.7	1.2	4,612.9	95.2	4.7	0.1
Isle of Man	•	•	•	•	•	37.0[11, 38]	1985	…	…	…	…	…	14.4	…	…	…
Israel	•	•	•	•	•	24.9	1989	13,851.1	31.1	27.7	35.0	6.2	13,593.3	81.7	15.4	2.9
Italy	•	•	•	•	•	38.0[14, 39]	1989	278,383.0	16.5	51.4	30.0	2.1	100,251.0	89.3	2.0	8.7
Jamaica	•		•			…	1989	374.3	11.5	13.6	43.8	31.1	273.6	92.6	7.4	—
Japan	•	•	•	•	•	36.8[32]	1989	59,571,299.0	27.4	31.6	24.4	16.6	46,684,159.0	94.3	1.7	4.0
Jersey	•	•	•	•	•	9.5[11, 32]	1991	60.9	—— 63.8 ——		23.4	12.8	52.8	…	…	…
Jordan	•		•			17.8	1986	53.6	28.7	55.3	—	16.0	9.5	77.4	14.0	8.6
Kazakhstan	•	•	•	•	•	…	…	…	…	…	…	…	…	…	…	…
Kenya	•		•			1.0[18]	1989	4,262.0	18.2	13.7	10.0	58.1	1,857.8	53.8	46.1	0.1
Kiribati	•		•			…	…	…	…	…	…	…	…	…	…	…
Korea, North	…	…	…	…	…	…	…	…	…	…	…	…	…	…	…	…
Korea, South	•		•			10.8	1996	7,425,400.0	—	62.2	—	—	9,656,600.0	…	…	…
Kuwait	•					17.3	1989	445.8	7.1	13.2	54.3	25.4	206.5	97.0	3.0	—
Kyrgyzstan	•	•	•	•	•	15.4	…	…	…	…	…	…	…	…	…	…
Laos	…	…	•	…	…	…	…	…	…	…	…	…	…	…	…	…
Latvia	•	•	•	•	•	42.1	…	…	…	…	…	…	…	…	…	…
Lebanon	•	•	•		•	7.7	…	…	…	…	…	…	…	…	…	…
Lesotho	…	…	…	…	…	1.2[18]	1992	—	…	…	…	…	12.0[16]	…	…	…
Liberia	•		•			1.0[11, 39]	1983	2.9	—	69.0	13.8	17.2	2.6	54.4	45.6	—
Libya	•	•	•			…	1989	314.3	21.6	25.4	50.2	2.8	260.0	77.5	19.5	3.0
Liechtenstein	•	•	•	•	•	…	…	…	…	…	…	…	…	…	…	…
Lithuania	•	•	•	•		32.1	…	…	…	…	…	…	24,981.7	…	…	…
Luxembourg	•	•	•	•	•	52.3[13]	1989	72,471.8	24.2	34.6	34.4	6.8	65,214.4	97.2	2.4	0.4
Macau	•	…	…	…	•	…	1998	223.2	…	…	…	…	207.4	…	…	…
Macedonia	•	•	•	•	•	…	1996	24,482	…	…	…	…	…	…	…	…
Madagascar	•		•		•	0.9[12]	1989	15,229.0	22.2	77.8	—	—	14,542.0	81.2	18.8	—
Malawi			•			0.1[39]	1986	—	…	…	…	…	5.4	…	…	…
Malaysia	•		•			7.2	1989	7,958.7	20.7	40.2	—	39.1	2,826.5	97.0	3.0	—
Maldives	…	…	…	…	…	3.4	1990	—	…	…	…	…	7.1	…	…	…
Mali	•		•		•	3.0[11, 39]	1986	8,128.8	16.6	74.3	—	9.1	7,924.6	63.7	34.7	1.6
Malta	•	•	•	•	•	34.4	1989	82.2	26.1	31.6	42.3	—	110.7	92.5	7.5	—
Marshall Islands	•					…	…	…	…	…	…	…	…	…	…	…
Martinique	•	…	…	…	•	…	1998	3,913.1	…	…	…	…	8,429.6	…	…	…
Mauritania	•		•		•	3.7[11, 14]	1989	808.4	1.5	90.4	—	8.1	735.2	63.5	31.2	5.3
Mauritius	•		•		•	19.4	1989	1,733.5	2.9	47.9	31.7	17.5	1,072.7	95.2	3.0	1.8
Mayotte	…	…	…	…	…	…	…	…	…	…	…	…	…	…	…	…
Mexico	•	•	•			18.1	1989	16,011,795.0	20.9	54.8	12.9	11.4	14,562,293.0	79.9	15.5	4.6
Micronesia	•					…	…	…	…	…	…	…	…	…	…	…
Moldova	•	•	•	•	•	…	…	…	…	…	…	…	…	…	…	…
Monaco	•	•			•	…	…	…	…	…	…	…	…	…	…	…
Mongolia	•	•	…	…	•	23.8	1989	2,431.6	—	—	20.8	79.2	2,304.6	100.0	—	—
Morocco	•	•	•		•	7.0[12]	1989	4,660.5	20.6	47.5	12.9	19.0	3,040.7	94.8	5.0	0.2
Mozambique	•	…	…	…	…	…	1986	228.2	—	86.2	13.7	0.1	145.0	100.0	—	—
Myanmar (Burma)		•	•			2.3	1986	44.3	19.9	59.6	18.5	2.0	35.9	51.5	15.6	32.9
Namibia	•	…	…	…	…	6.8[11, 19]	…	…	…	…	…	…	…	…	…	…
Nauru	•	•	•	…	•	…	…	…	…	…	…	…	…	…	…	…
Nepal	•		•			1.5	1985	—	…	…	…	…	59.3	…	…	…

crime and law enforcement (latest)						military protection								country
offenses reported to the police per 100,000 population					population per police officer[g]	manpower, 1999[h]		expenditure, 1997				arms trade, 1997 ('000,000 U.S.$)		
total	personal		property			total ('000)	per 1,000 population	total '000,000	per capita	% of central government expenditure	% of GDP or GNP	imports	exports	
	murder	assault	burglary	automobile theft										
3,693	1.6	0.7	...	3.1	580	450.0	7.0	2,180	34	11.0	2.8	1,600	5	Egypt
...	38.8	63.7	...	148.5	1,000	24.6	4.1	101	18	6.7	0.9	10	0	El Salvador
...	...	...	...	...	190	1.3	2.9	3[12]	8[12]	5.2[12]	1.5[12]	0	0	Equatorial Guinea
...	...	...	...	...	...	182.1	45.8	65	17	18.1	7.8	90	0	Eritrea
3,145	17.1	27.6	1,468.3	144.9	...	4.8	3.3	111	77	4.5	1.5	10	0	Estonia
319	13.3	87.8	2.2	1.9	1,100[31]	352.5	5.7	117	2	7.9	1.9	0	0	Ethiopia
...	...	...	...	...	...	—	[7]	—	—	—	—	...	...	Faroe Islands
2,784	1.8	418.8	353.5	69.6	407	3.5	4.3	48	61	6.4	2.4	0	0	Fiji
14,405	0.4	35.0	1,757.0	29.5	640	31.7	6.1	1,960	381	4.3[12]	1.7	370	20	Finland
6,096	3.7	148.4	676.9	546.2	630	317.3	5.4	41,500	708	6.4	3.0	260	5,900	France
8,936	27.2	178.7	1,367.3	150.6	...	—	[7]	—	—	—	—	...	...	French Guiana
1,799	0.9	98.9	232.7	...	...	—	[7]	—	—	—	—	...	...	French Polynesia
114	1.4	17.9	2.3	7.5	1,290	4.7	3.9	91	76	7.0	2.0	0	0	Gabon
89	0.4	10.6	5.6	...	3,310	0.8	0.6	15	12	15.0	3.7	30	0	Gambia, The
4,355	...	...	...	...	...	—	—	...	...	...	...	...	...	Gaza Strip
286	4.7	99.5	21.1	0.8	...	—	—	158	31	9.6	1.4	10	0	Georgia
7,869	3.5	134.4	1,507.1	137.4	...	332.8	4.1	32,900	401	4.7	1.6	750	750	Germany
...	2.2	408.6	1.5	...	620	7.0	0.4	47	3	2.4	0.7	0	0	Ghana
3,759	3.6	67.7	418.7	163.9	380	165.7	15.7	5,530	521	13.8	4.6	850	30	Greece
9,360	18.1	845.0	1,883.5	...	340	—	[7]	—	—	—	—	...	...	Greenland
8,543	7.8	98.9	582.2	...	230	[28]	[28]	...	...	...	...	...	...	Grenada
5,793	13.2	215.2	821.5	453.9	...	—	[7]	—	—	—	—	...	...	Guadeloupe
10,080	7.9	169.3	634.2	333.6	...	—	[7]	—	—	—	—	...	...	Guam
510	27.4	77.1	27.9	58.1	670	31.4	2.8	236[12]	21[12]	15.0[12]	1.4[12]	5	0	Guatemala
...	...	...	...	...	...	—	[7]	—	—	—	—	...	...	Guernsey
18.4	0.5	0.7	0.7	0.1	1,140	9.7	1.3	54	7	8.0	1.5	30	0	Guinea
129	0.5	8.7	4.0	0.2	...	7.3	5.8	8	7	13.0	3.2	0	0	Guinea-Bissau
1,355	17.9	205.1	426.5	32.2	190	1.6	2.0	8	11	2.4	1.1	0	0	Guyana
701	...	...	...	...	400	[35]	[35]	...	...	...	...	5	0	Haiti
392	154.0	44.4	4.3	25.8	1,040	8.3	1.3[13]	52	10	5.6	1.3	10	0	Honduras
1,076	1.0	115.3	146.0	16.8	221	—	[7]	—	—	—	—	...	...	Hong Kong
5,926	4.3	80.4	932.4	46.1	237	35.0	3.5	1,320	129	4.3	1.9	100	5	Hungary
14,727	—	18.2	761.1	112.8	940	—	—	—	—	—	—	10	0	Iceland
594	4.6	...	15.6	...	820	1,173.0	1.2	10,900	11	14.3	2.8	410	90	India
60	0.8	5.1	24.8	8.0	1,119	298.0	1.4	4,810	23	13.1	2.3	410	20	Indonesia
77	0.5	47.7	...	...	...	545.6	8.8	4,730	74	11.6	3.0	850	30	Iran
197	7.1	34.7	...	...	140	429.0	19.5	1,250	59	50.8[37]	4.9	0	0	Iraq
2,279	1.8	19.1	709.6	28.6	310	11.5	3.1	744	206	3.3	1.2	30	0	Ireland
2,867	0.7	12.3	921.4	60.6	...	—	[7]	—	—	—	—	...	...	Isle of Man
5,017	2.4	463.0	1,122.3	694.1	210	173.5	29.2	9,340	1,690	20.9	9.7	1,100	370	Israel
4,214	4.4	46.4	...	537.0	680	265.5	4.6	22,700	395	4.1	2.0	430	700	Italy
1,871	37.2	511.4	135.7	7.2	430	2.8	1.1	53	20	2.4	0.9	5	0	Jamaica
1,671	1.1	15.4	187.9	28.4	480	236.3	1.9	40,800	325	6.6	1.0	2,600	20	Japan
...	...	...	...	...	...	—	[7]	—	—	—	—	...	...	Jersey
1,170	7.9	15.0	11.7	38.2	630	104.0	21.5	626	145	25.0	9.0	130	0	Jordan
815	...	...	...	...	...	65.8	4.4	699	41	4.4	1.9	140	0	Kazakhstan
484	6.4	54.1	76.9	9.7	1,500	24.2	0.8	206	7	7.2	2.1	40	0	Kenya
261	5.1	11.6	38.6	...	330	—	—	...	...	...	...	...	...	Kiribati
...	...	...	...	...	460	1,082.0	50.6	6,000	281	40.7[39]	27.5	30	70	Korea, North
1,348	2.1	54.7	6.8	...	506	672.0	14.3	15,000	327	14.6	3.4	1,100	30	Korea, South
1,346	1.5	36.4	75.9	56.7	80	15.3	8.0	2,760	1,510	26.8	7.5	2,000	0	Kuwait
987	10.4[40]	12.6	482.4	...	...	9.2	1.9	159	34	7.1	1.6	0	0	Kyrgyzstan
...	...	...	...	...	280	29.1	5.4	60	12	17.5	3.4	10	0	Laos
1,492	9.8	17.4	281.0	101.4	...	5.7	1.6	97	40	2.5	0.9	0	0	Latvia
2,713	5.3	152.8	65.9	28.6	530	67.9	19.2	465	135	8.4	3.0	40	0	Lebanon
1,885	33.9	170.6	221.5	...	1,130	2.0	0.9	32	16	6.1	2.5	0	0	Lesotho
...	...	...	...	...	1,570	[41]	[41]	...	...	...	...	0	0	Liberia
966	1.5	5.2	...	...	...	65.0	13.0	1,810	403	19.7	6.1	5	0	Libya
...	...	114.3	614.3	153.6	660	—	[42]	—	—	—	—	...	...	Liechtenstein
2,057	9.4	10.0	601.0	109.6	...	5.7	1.5	127	35	2.8	0.8	5	0	Lithuania
6,409	0.9	251.8	625.2	154.6	829	0.8	1.8	134	319	2.0[12]	0.8	60	0	Luxembourg
1,698	5.4	34.0	250.5	26.6	...	—	[7]	...	...	...	...	...	...	Macau
1,102	5.4	26.9	...	44.7	...	15.7	7.7	83	42	10.2	2.5	0	0	Macedonia
112	0.6	12.0	0.7	0.1	2,900	21.0	1.4	53	4	8.5	1.5	0	0	Madagascar
850	3.1	82.2	13.1	...	1,670	5.0	0.5	26	3	2.9	1.0	0	0	Malawi
604	3.1	25.9	155.6	20.8	760	105.0	4.6	2,090	102	9.9	2.2	725	5	Malaysia
2,353	1.9	3.3	36.1	...	35,710	—	—	...	...	...	...	...	...	Maldives
10.0	0.7	1.5	0.8	0.3	160	7.4	0.7	43	4	7.2	1.7	10	0	Mali
1,841	3.0	35.2	1,079.2	243.9	230	1.9	5.0	31	81	2.0	0.9	0	0	Malta
2,273	...	...	...	...	400	—	[43]	—	—	—	—	...	...	Marshall Islands
6,305	5.8	184.9	641.2	192.8	...	—	[7]	—	—	—	—	...	...	Martinique
225	1.8	38	2.5	9.1	710	15.7	6.0	24	10	9.8	2.3	5	0	Mauritania
3,340	4.4	10.4	109.8	...	240	—	—	12	11	1.2	0.3	10	0	Mauritius
...	...	...	...	...	...	—	[7]	—	—	—	—	...	...	Mayotte
108	7.3	30.2	...	...	...	178.8	1.8	4,290	44	6.2	1.1	130	20	Mexico
...	...	...	...	...	...	—	[43]	—	—	—	—	...	...	Micronesia
957	9.9	11.1	50.4	15.6	...	11.0	2.5	62	14	1.9	1.0	0	0	Moldova
3,337	3.3	33.3	130.0	43.3	...	—	—	...	...	...	...	...	...	Monaco
938	24.6	72.1	425.7	1.3	120	8.3	3.5	19	7	5.1	1.9	0	0	Mongolia
366	1.4	6.7	...	...	840	196.3	6.9	1,390	49	12.9	4.3	180	0	Morocco
166	4.2	9.2	45.9	...	...	[44]	[44]	73	4	9.2	2.8	0	0	Mozambique
350	2.1	18.5	0.1	0.1	650	344.0	8.3[12]	3,960	88	75.5	7.6	280	0	Myanmar (Burma)
4,062	45.2	466.8	562.6	57.7	...	9.0	5.2	90	57	7.3	2.7	5	0	Namibia
...	25.0	400.0	100.0	...	110	—	—	...	...	...	...	...	...	Nauru
9	2.7	1.1	0.8	...	1,000	46.0	1.9	42	2	5.1	0.8	0	0	Nepal

Social protection (continued)

country	social security						finances									
	programs available, 1999					expenditures, 1997 (% of total central govt.)f	year	receipts					expenditures			
	old-age, invalidity, deatha	sickness and maternityb	work injuryc	unemploymentd	family allowancese			total ('000,000 natl. cur.)	insured persons (%)	employers (%)	government (%)	other (%)	total ('000,000 natl. cur.)	benefits (%)	administration (%)	other (%)
Netherlands, The	•	•	•	•	•	37.4	1989	154,427.0	37.3	30.3	19.0	13.4	135,609.0	96.9	3.1	—
Netherlands Antilles		…	•	•	…	12.9[9, 13]	1998	317.0	100.0	—	—	—	275.0	…	…	…
New Caledonia	…	…	…	…	•	…	1987	15,834.0	…	…	…	…	14,598.0	…	…	…
New Zealand	•	•	•	•	•	39.9	1989	14,266.0	1.0	4.7	92.5	1.8	14,372.3	95.6	2.8	1.6
Nicaragua	•	•	•		•	14.9[18]	1989	647,454.8	13.5	49.1	7.6	29.8	452,038.6	82.4	17.6	—
Niger	•		•		•	1.7[46]	1989	5,634.9	9.4	90.6	—	—	3,804.2	62.5	—	37.5
Nigeria	•		•			2.5[48]	1989	54.0	50.0	50.0	—	—	22.6	42.5	57.5	—
Northern Mariana Islands	•	…	…	…	…	…	…	…	…	…	…	…	…	…	…	…
Norway	•	•	•	•	•	38.4	1989	158,105.0	18.3	31.4	46.6	3.7	131,578.2	98.7	1.3	—
Oman	•	…	•	…	…	4.3	1995	—	…	…	…	…	62.2[16]	…	…	…
Pakistan	•	•	•			0.2[11, 49]	1989	9,321.4	1.3	8.0	84.3	6.4	8,092.0	97.4	1.2	1.4
Palau	•					…	…	…	…	…	…	…	…	…	…	…
Panama	•	•	•			20.5	1989	496.7	31.0	39.5	7.1	22.4	452.8	94.0	4.8	1.2
Papua New Guinea	•		•			0.7[18]	1983	45.0	40.5	32.1	8.0	19.4	9.4	82.3	9.7	8.0
Paraguay	•	•	•			16.2[32]	1993	42,410[39]	…	…	…	…	253,341	…	…	…
Peru	•	•	•			0.2[11, 34]	1989	1,363,280.6	30.2	65.1	4.7	—	1,435,134.1	78.5	21.5	—
Philippines	•	•	•			2.5	1989	19,213.6	22.2	32.3	—	45.5	7,878.3	87.3	12.3	—
Poland	•	•	•	•	•	50.9	1989	11,572,248.0	2.1	70.2	25.1	2.6	11,452,165.0	98.8	1.2	—
Portugal	•	•	•	•	•	27.3[3]	1989	833,442.5	31.3	50.1	13.4	5.2	756,410.8	94.6	4.2	1.2
Puerto Rico	•	•	•	•	•	…	1980	…	…	…	…	…	1,041.3	100.0	—	—
Qatar	…	…	…	…	…	…	1986	80.0	—	—	100.0	—	80.0	100.0	—	—
Réunion	…	…	…	…	…	…	1998	…	…	…	…	…	13,200.0	…	…	…
Romania	•	•	•	•	•	31.0	1989	90,561.2	—	48.9	51.1	—	90,561.2	100.0	—	—
Russia	•	•	•	•	•	27.7[13]	…	…	…	…	…	…	…	…	…	…
Rwanda	•		•			2.9[37]	1989	2,350.0	23.9	39.8	—	36.3	965.8	60.8	39.2	—
St. Kitts and Nevis	•	•	•			9.4[51]	1989	14.3	…	…	…	…	7.9	…	…	…
St. Lucia	•	•	•			…	1986	14.6	28.6	28.6	—	42.8	3.4	61.4	38.6	—
St. Vincent and the Grenadines	•	•	•			6.4	1989	—	…	…	…	…	—	…	…	…
Samoa	•		•			—	…	—	…	…	…	…	—	…	…	…
San Marino	•	•	•		…	…	1983	51,673.0	12.0	48.7	36.1	3.2	46,179.0	95.7	3.7	0.6
São Tomé and Príncipe	•	•	•			…	1986	46.4	37.7	56.3	—	6.0	23.7	100.0	—	—
Saudi Arabia	•		•			…	1989	1,761.4	26.8	73.2	—	—	4,292.9	100.0	—	—
Senegal	•		•		•	2.6[11, 19]	1989	17,202.0	—	47.6	51.4	1.0	15,371.0	84.6	11.1	4.3
Seychelles	•	•	•			16.0	1983	69.1	30.1	60.2	—	9.7	42.7	69.6	4.9	25.5
Sierra Leone			•			2.3[3]	1990	…	…	…	…	…	153.00	100.00	—	—
Singapore	•	•	•			1.8	1989	7,531.9	49.1	35.3	0.1	15.6	5,045.8	78.0	0.6	21.4
Slovakia	•	•	•	•	•	29.3[54]	1998	74,205	…	…	…	…	87,916	…	…	…
Slovenia	•	•	•	•	•	…	…	…	…	…	…	…	…	…	…	…
Solomon Islands	•		•			0.7[11, 39]	1989	20.9	27.8	41.1	—	31.1	17.4	89.7	10.3	—
Somalia			•			1.7[48]	…	—	…	…	…	…	…	…	…	…
South Africa	•	•	•	•		…	1994	2,034	—	100.0	—	—	2,260.0	…	…	…
Spain	•	•	•	•	•	38.5[12]	1989	8,320,972.0	15.9	53.9	27.9	2.3	8,038,090.0	94.3	2.6	3.1
Sri Lanka	•		•		•	14.0	1989	15,399.9	22.0	24.4	29.1	24.5	5,819.0	98.5	1.3	0.2
Sudan, The	•		•			0.4[6, 11]	1989	62.0	24.9	0.5	—	74.6	14.7	37.5	62.5	—
Suriname	•	…	…	…	•	6.0[11, 49]	1989	73.0	24.7	75.3	—	—	70.6	100.0	—	—
Swaziland	•		•			0.4[32]	1986	10.7	31.4	31.4	—	37.2	3.9	45.8	54.2	—
Sweden	•	•	•	•	•	49.6	1989	446,909.7	2.8	37.9	50.8	8.5	439,997.3	93.7	3.3	3.0
Switzerland	•	•	•	•	•	50.5	1989	45,800.1	45.6	22.6	25.9	5.9	41,745.7	91.5	3.0	5.5
Syria	•		•			2.7	1989	3,147.9	30.4	60.9	…	5.6	1,455.9	95.7	4.2	0.1
Taiwan	•	•	•	•		13.8[3]	…	…	…	…	…	…	…	…	…	…
Tajikistan	•	•	•	•	•	…	…	…	…	…	…	…	…	…	…	…
Tanzania	•		•			0.5[10]	1989	3,275.8	25.9	25.9	—	48.2	2,780.7	5.8	14.1	80.1
Thailand	•	•	•			3.7	1989	654.0	—	60.2	—	39.8	260.0	88.2	11.8	—
Togo	•		•		•	6.5[11, 51]	1989	10,162.0	8.1	61.5	—	30.4	5,844.0	77.5	22.5	—
Tonga	…	…	…	…	…	0.8[19]	…	…	…	…	…	…	…	…	…	…
Trinidad and Tobago	•	•	•		•	14.3[13]	1989	584.9	12.0	24.1	39.7	24.2	438.4	85.6	11.1	3.3
Tunisia	•	•	•	•	•	16.6[12]	1989	325.3	36.9	63.1	—	—	358.3	90.0[57]	6.1[57]	3.9[57]
Turkey	•	•	•			9.0	1989	12,075,809.0	28.5	32.9	22.8	15.8	10,241,427.0	97.2	2.2	0.6
Turkmenistan	•	•	•	•	•	…	…	…	…	…	…	…	…	…	…	…
Tuvalu	•	…	…	…	…	…	1981	…	…	…	…	…	0.1	67.6	32.4	—
Uganda	•		•			2.1[11, 49]	1989	265.9	32.1	64.3	1.1	2.5	145.0	0.3	76.8	22.9
Ukraine	•	•	•	•	•	…	1989	20,350.0	—	—	—	—	20,350.0	100.0	—	—
United Arab Emirates	…	…	…	…	…	3.7	1989	182.2	17.3	6.2	0.5	76.0	182.2	100.0	…	…
United Kingdom	•	•	•	•	•	36.8	1989	92,157.0	18.1	24.9	52.9	4.1	88,294.0	93.8	3.3	2.9
United States	•		•	•		28.8	1989	804,909.0	25.5	33.9	28.8	11.8	627,653.0	95.5	3.3	1.2
Uruguay	•	•	•	•	•	62.0	1989	535,507.0	31.4	37.3	26.0	5.3	548,591.0	93.6	5.4	1.0
Uzbekistan	•	•	•	•	•	…	…	…	…	…	…	…	…	…	…	…
Vanuatu	•					0.9[11, 49]	…	—	…	…	…	…	—	…	…	…
Venezuela	•	•	•	•		6.9[49]	1986	7,457.6	21.3	40.7	12.7	25.3	6,355.7	86.1	14.9	—
Vietnam	•	•	•			…	…	…	…	…	…	…	…	…	…	…
Virgin Islands (U.S.)	•	…	…	•	•	…	…	…	…	…	…	…	…	…	…	…
West Bank	…	…	…	…	…	…	…	…	…	…	…	…	…	…	…	…
Western Sahara	…	…	…	…	…	…	…	…	…	…	…	…	…	…	…	…
Yemen	•	…	•	…	…	—	…	—	…	…	…	…	—	…	…	…
Yugoslavia	•	•	•	•	•	6.0[62]	1986[62]	2,777,651.0	63.3	32.2	3.4	1.1	2,732,679.0	90.3	1.9	7.8
Zambia	•		•			0.8	1986	179.2	28.4	28.4	—	43.2	67.7	40.6	59.4	—
Zimbabwe	•		•			3.4[6]	1983	167.0	25.9	7.6	64.2	2.3	112.2	93.7	6.2	0.1

[1]Rural areas only. [2]No national military from 1992. [3]1990. [4]1984. [5]The Albanian forces are in the process of being reestablshed. [6]1989. [7]Political dependency; defense is the responsibility of the administering country. [8]Includes civilian militia. [9]Netherlands Antilles includes Aruba. [10]1985. [11]Social security only. [12]1996. [13]1995. [14]1979. [15]1992. [16]Includes welfare. [17]About 31,000 troops of the NATO Commanded Stabilization Forces are stationed in Bosnia and Herzegovina to assure implementation of the Dayton Accords. [18]1994. [19]1991. [20]1976. [21]Local officers only. [22]Military defense is the responsibility of France. [23]1971. [24]Republic of Cyprus only. [25]National Guard only. [26]Data refer to former Czechoslovakia. [27]1981. [28]Paramilitary unit of country participating in the U.S.-sponsored Regional Security System, a defense pact among eastern Caribbean countries. [29]Indonesia includes East Timor, except where noted. [30]UN forces of about 9,300 are stationed in East Timor. [31]Ethiopia includes Eritrea. [32]1993. [33]Former West Germany. [34]1983. [35]In 1994 the military government of Haiti was replaced by a civilian administration. A national police force of about 5,300 has

crime and law enforcement (latest)						military protection								country
offenses reported to the police per 100,000 population					population per police officer[g]	manpower, 1999[h]		expenditure, 1997				arms trade, 1997 ('000,000 U.S.$)		
total	personal		property			total ('000)	per 1,000 population	total '000,000	per capita	% of central government expenditure	% of GDP or GNP	imports	exports	
	murder	assault	burglary	automobile theft										
7,808	10.9	242.8	3,100.4	239.0	510	56.4	3.6	6,840	437	6.4	1.9	460	500	Netherlands, The
5,574[45]	...	396	3,455	...	330	—	[7]	—	—	—	—	...	...	Netherlands Antilles
...	...	...	...	...	...	—	[7]	—	—	—	—	...	...	New Caledonia
13,854	3.9	546.3	2,352.9	788.6	630	9.5	2.5	766	214	3.9	1.3	100	0	New Zealand
1,069	25.6	203.8	110.7	...	90[8]	16.0	3.2	27	6	4.5	1.5	0	0	Nicaragua
99	0.9	16.6	1.0	0.7	2,350[47]	5.3	0.5	20	2	6.9	1.1	5	0	Niger
312	...	...	...	...	1,140	94.0	0.8	2,000	19	12.3	1.4	90	0	Nigeria
245	3.8	92.6	73.7	20.8	...	—	[7]	—	—	—	—	...	...	Northern Mariana Islands
10,048	1.9	59.1	95.0	487.5	660	31.0	6.9	3,250	739	4.8	2.1	250	10	Norway
280	0.8	1.9	...	...	430	43.5	17.8	1,820	795	36.4	26.1	160	0	Oman
331	7.9	21.2	10.6	11.4	720	587.0	3.9	3,380	26	24.2	5.7	600	0	Pakistan
...	...	...	323.0	...	...	—	[43]	—	—	—	—	...	...	Palau
419	2.0	11.8	25.1	77.7	180	—	—	114	42	4.8	1.4	10	0	Panama
766	8.6	66.7	63	22.0	720	4.3	0.9	63	14	4.1	1.3	0	0	Papua New Guinea
456	16.5	56.9	20.4	48.4	310	20.2	4.2	127	25	10.5	1.3	5	0	Paraguay
218	3.2	24.1	7.8	3.6	730	115.0	4.6	1,350	53	13.4	2.1	310	0	Peru
...	13.1	14.9	...	3.3	1,160	110.0	1.5	1,270	17	7.9	1.5	110	0	Philippines
2,775	2.9	84.1	918.6	158.2	370	240.7	6.2	5,600	145	5.6	2.3	150	60	Poland
653	3.1	1.8	110.8	43.8	660	49.7	5.0	2,390	241	5.9	2.4	110	10	Portugal
2,176	16.3	102.4	853.0	389.4	380	—	[7]	—	—	—	—	...	...	Puerto Rico
909	2.4	8.4	39.7	6.1	...	11.8	20.0	975	1,540	27.0	10.5	625	0	Qatar
2,097	7.8	123.1	181.3	137.9	220	—	[7]	—	—	—	—	...	...	Réunion
1,723	2.5	6.2	92.0	17.3	...	207.0	9.2	2,280	102	6.9	2.4	250	10	Romania
1,759	20.1	30.8	549.7	24.5	...	1,004.1	6.9	41,700	283	30.9	5.8	30	2,300	Russia
14,550	12,500	25.0	12.5	12.5	4,650	[50]	[50]	81	10	22.2	4.4	20	0	Rwanda
5,544	19.5	536.6	2,461.0	...	300	[28]	[28]	...	...	...	...	...	...	St. Kitts and Nevis
4,386	17.0	1,193.0	778.0	...	430	[28]	[28]	...	...	...	...	...	...	St. Lucia
3,977	10.3	986.9	...	...	250	[28]	[28]	...	...	...	...	...	...	St. Vincent and the Grenadines
...	...	...	...	...	...	—	[52]	—	—	—	—	...	...	Samoa
...	4.1	...	...	...	...	—	—	...	...	...	...	...	...	San Marino
558	4.0	...	...	...	400	—	—	—	2	1.2	0.9	0	0	São Tomé and Príncipe
149	0.5	0.2	...	45.4	280	105.5	5.0	21,100	1,050	35.8	14.5	11,600	5	Saudi Arabia
113	1.4	17.1	4.7	...	730	11.0	1.1	69	7	8.5	1.6	0	0	Senegal
4,517	2.7	698.7	1,058.9	...	120	0.2	2.5	8[4]	124[4]	7.4[4]	5.6[4]	...	...	Seychelles
...	...	...	...	...	600	[53]	[53]	48	10	33.0	5.9	0	0	Sierra Leone
991	1.0	10.9	43.6	10.9	230	73.0	22.7	5,660	1,650	19.4	5.7	400	90	Singapore
1,740	2.4	204.6	504.3	142.4	...	35.8	6.6	903	168	8.0	2.1	10	40	Slovakia
2,822	3.4	20.0	677.4	35.1	...	9.6	4.8	1,220	617	12.5	5.2	20	0	Slovenia
...	...	...	...	...	620	—	—	...	...	...	...	0	0	Solomon Islands
144	1.5	8.0	31.2	...	540	[55]	[55]	8[32]	1[32]	30.0[49]	0.9[32]	0	0	Somalia
...	...	...	...	...	870	58.0	1.3	2,320	55	5.6	1.8	20	370	South Africa
2,312	2.6	23.9	570.2	343.1	580	186.5	4.7	7,670	196	6.0	1.5	430	525	Spain
280	8.2	10.8	54.7	...	860	[56]	[56]	762	41	21.2	5.1	90	0	Sri Lanka
...	10.2	46.3	66.6	4.7	740	94.7	2.8	412	13	53.8	4.6	20	0	Sudan, The
17,819	7.6	1,824.4	...	...	...	1.8	4.2	17	41	2.6	1.2	0	0	Suriname
3,987	17.6	474.2	726.7	60.9	610	—	—	32	34	8.2	2.2	0	0	Swaziland
12,982	4.5	42.5	1,615.1	658.9	330	53.1	6.0	5,550	626	5.4	2.5	310	900	Sweden
5,406	2.6	68.5	1,172.5	1,129.9	640	3.5	0.5	3,860	533	5.8[12]	1.4	310	50	Switzerland
89	1.4	7.0	21.2	2.9	1,970	316.0	19.9	3,400	211	26.2[12]	5.6	70	0	Syria
799	8.2	...	...	124.9	720	376.0	17.1	13,100	602	23.8	4.6	9,200	20	Taiwan
317	2.5	4.6	...	...	...	7.0	1.1	113	19	10.6	1.7	0	0	Tajikistan
1,724	6.2	1.8	78.1	0.8	1,330	34.0	1.0	87	3	10.7	1.3	20	0	Tanzania
351	7.7	25.4	9.9	3.3	530	306.0	5.0	3,380	57	12.1	2.3	950	0	Thailand
11	...	...	...	...	1,970	7.0	1.4	29	6	11.6	2.0	5	0	Togo
2,100	...	...	...	...	330	—	[52]	—	—	—	—	...	...	Tonga
1,170	9.7	31.0	452.7	80.6	280	2.7	2.1	83	74	5.4	1.5	5	0	Trinidad and Tobago
1,474	2.1	169.1	72.3	10.3	340	35.0	3.7	359	39	5.3	2.0	20	0	Tunisia
426	2.7	83.6	1.2	30.4	1,570	639.0	9.9	7,790	123	14.7	4.0	1,600	10	Turkey
...	...	...	...	...	...	[58]	[58]	299	71	15.6	4.6	0	0	Turkmenistan
...	...	...	...	—	290	—	—	...	...	...	...	...	...	Tuvalu
172	8.9	35.7	15.5	6.3	1,090	[59]	[59]	268	12	23.9	4.2	30	0	Uganda
1,141	9.1	13.8	240.1	11.1	...	311.4	6.2	4,280	85	8.4	3.7	5	500	Ukraine
360	0.6	1.8	10.1	...	140	64.5	22.0	2,310	1,020	46.5	6.9	1,400	40	United Arab Emirates
9,823[60]	2.8[60]	405.2[60]	1,832.7[60]	752.9[60]	350	212.4	3.6	35,300	600	7.1	2.7	2,100	6,600	United Kingdom
5,374	9.0	430.2	1,041.8	591.2	318	1,371.5	5.0	276,000	1,030	16.3	3.3	1,600	31,800	United States
3,383	8.5	119.5	62.5	137.4	170	25.6	7.9	279	86	4.4	1.4	10	0	Uruguay
300	3.5	3.3	28.7	2.4	...	54.0	2.2[12]	1,440	63	6.1	2.5	5	70	Uzbekistan
...	...	...	...	...	450	—	—	...	...	...	...	...	...	Vanuatu
1,106	22.1	152.2	358.2	239.4	320	79.0	3.3	1,860	83	9.8	2.2	270	0	Venezuela
...	...	...	...	...	...	484.0	6.2	3,390	45	11.1	2.8	120	0	Vietnam
10,441	22.3	1,943.2	3,183.7	954	240	—	[7]	—	—	—	—	...	...	Virgin Islands (U.S.)
2,226	...	...	...	...	...	—	—	...	...	...	...	...	...	West Bank
...	...	...	...	...	...	—	[7]	—	—	—	—	...	...	Western Sahara
170[61]	...	...	...	...	1,940	66.3	3.9	411	26	17.4	8.1	110	0	Yemen
1,268	...	...	...	...	140[62]	108.7	10.1	1,200	114	55.0[3, 62]	4.9	10	0	Yugoslavia
666	9.8	9.5	153.5	9.6	540	21.6	2.3	41	4	3.9	1.1	0	0	Zambia
5,180	9.0	179.9	384.1	13.7	750	39.0	3.4	320	29	11.9	3.8	10	0	Zimbabwe

been formed and all army equipment destroyed. [36]Coverage is through the tax system. [37]1982. [38]1988–89. [39]1988. [40]Includes attempted murders. [41]As of 1998 there were about 14,000 in all armed forces. West African peacekeepers withdrew in January 1999 and the civil war resumed in some areas. [42]Military defense is the responsibility of Switzerland. [43]Military defense is the responsibility of the United States. [44]Forces are estimated between 5,100 and 6,100. [45]Curaçao only. [46]1980. [47]Includes paramilitary forces. [48]1976. [49]1986. [50]Forces are estimated between 37,000 and 47,000. [51]1987. [52]Military defense is the responsibility of New Zealand. [53]Following the civil war of May–June 1997, the armed forces were reorganized. Estimated strength is some 5,000. [54]1998. [55]Following the 1991 revolution, no national armed forces have yet been formed. [56]Forces estimated between 110,000 and 115,000. [57]1977. [58]Forces estimated between 17,000 and 19,000. [59]Forces estimated between 30,000 and 40,000. [60]England and Wales. [61]Former Yemen Arab Republic. [62]Data refer to Yugoslavia as constituted prior to 1991.

Education

This table presents international data on education analyzed to provide maximum comparability among the different educational systems in use among the nations of the world. The principal data are, naturally, numbers of schools, teachers, and students, arranged by four principal levels of education—the first (primary); general second level (secondary); vocational second level; and third level (higher). Whenever possible, data referring to preprimary education programs have been excluded from this compilation. The ratio of students to teachers is calculated for each level. These data are supplemented at each level by a figure for enrollment ratio, an indicator of each country's achieved capability to educate the total number of children potentially educable in the age group usually represented by that level. At the first and second levels this is given as a net enrollment ratio and at the third level as a gross enrollment ratio. Two additional comparative measures are given at the third level: students per 100,000 population and proportion (percentage) of adults age 25 and over who have achieved some level of higher or postsecondary education. Data in this last group are confined as far as possible to those who have completed their educations and are no longer in school. No enrollment ratio is provided for vocational training at the second level because of the great variation worldwide in the academic level at which vocational training takes place, in the need of countries to encourage or direct students into vocational programs (to support national development), and, most particularly, in the age range of students who normally constitute a national vocational system (some will be as young as 14, having just completed a primary cycle; others will be much older).

At each level of education, differences in national statistical practice, in national educational structure, public-private institutional mix, training and deployment of teachers, and timing of cycles of enrollment or completion of particular grades or standards all contribute to the problems of comparability among national educational systems.

Reporting the number of schools in a country is not simply a matter of counting permanent red-brick buildings with classrooms in them. Often the resources of a less developed country are such that temporary or outdoor facilities are all that can be afforded, while in a developed but sparsely settled country students might have to travel 80 km (50 mi) a day to find a classroom with 20 students of the same age, leading to the institution of measures such as traveling teachers, radio or televisual instruction at home under the supervision of parents, or similar systems. According to UNESCO definitions, therefore, a "school" is defined only as "a body of students . . . organized to receive instruction."

Such difficulties also limit the comparability of statistics on numbers of teachers, with the further complications that many at any level must work part-time, or that the institutions in which they work may perform a mixture of functions that do not break down into the tidy categories required by a table of this sort. In certain countries teacher training is confined to higher education, in others as a vocational form of secondary training, and so on. For purposes of this table, teacher training at the secondary level has been treated as vocational education. At the higher level, teacher training is classified as one more specialization in higher education itself.

The number of students may conceal great variation in what each country defines as a particular educational "level." Many countries do, indeed, have a primary system composed of grades 1 through 6 (or 1 through 8) that passes students on to some kind of postprimary education. But the age of intake, the ability of parents to send their children or to permit them to finish that level, or the need to withdraw the children seasonally for agricul-

Education

country	year	first level (primary)					general second level (secondary)					vocational second level[a]	
		schools	teachers[c]	students[d]	student/ teacher ratio	net enroll- ment ratio[b]	schools	teachers[c]	students[d]	student/ teacher ratio	net enroll- ment ratio[b]	schools	teachers[c]
Afghanistan	1995	2,146	21,869	1,312,197	60.0	29	…	19,085	512,815	26.9	14	…	…
Albania	1996	1,782	31,369	558,101	17.8	102	162[1]	4,147	71,391	17.2	…	259[1]	2,174
Algeria	1997	15,426	170,956	4,674,947	27.3	94	3,954	151,948	2,618,242	17.2	56	…	…
American Samoa	1996	32	524[2]	9,971	…	…	9	245[2]	3,624	…	…	1	21[2]
Andorra	1997	12	…	5,424	…	…	6	…	2,655	…	…	…	…
Angola	1992	…	31,062[1]	989,443	…	…	…	5,138[1]	199,099	…	…	…	566[1]
Antigua and Barbuda	1997	58	559	12,229	21.9	…	13	389	4,260	11.0	…	1[3]	16[3]
Argentina	1997	22,437	309,081	5,153,256	16.7	96	7,623[4]	238,791[4]	2,463,608[4]	10.3[4]	42	[4]	[4]
Armenia	1998	1,407	61,965	602,600	9.7	…	…	57,325	365,025	6.4	…	69[5]	…
Aruba	1998	33	397	8,456	21.3	…	15[4]	470[4]	7,157[4]	15.2[4]	[4]	[4]	[4]
Australia	1998	7,709	104,603	1,869,852	17.9	95	2,468	104,477	1,329,000	12.7	89	…	28,900[3]
Austria	1998	3,680	38,491	385,207	10.0	87	1,837[6]	55,337	480,200	8.7	88	981	26,248
Azerbaijan	1998	4,515	36,800	700,900	19.0	…	…	85,300	905,500	10.6	…	78	…
Bahamas, The	1997	113	1,540	34,199	22.2	98	…	1,352	27,970	20.7	86	…	…
Bahrain	1997	124[3, 8]	3,536[3, 8]	72,876	…	98	…	2,305[3, 8]	49,897	…	83	…	820[3, 8]
Bangladesh	1996	75,595	242,252[5]	17,580,000	…	64	12,858	135,217[5]	5,788,000	…	18	156	8,800
Barbados	1996	79	994	18,519	18.6	78	21	1,263	21,455	17.0	74	…	…
Belarus	1998	4,835[9]	115,300[9]	1,580,000[9]	10.9[9]	85	[9]	[9]	[9]	[9]	…	150	…
Belgium	1996	4,401	82,168[10]	742,796	…	98	1,727	115,262	737,823	6.4	88	304[11]	…
Belize	1998	247	2,015	53,118	26.4	99	30	726	11,260	15.5	29	…	…
Benin	1997	3,072	13,957	779,329	55.8	63	145[5]	5,352	146,135	27.3	…	14[5]	283[5]
Bermuda	1997	26	478	5,883	18.3	…	…	355	3,726	10.5	…	…	…
Bhutan	1994	243	1,611	60,089	37.3	…	34	544	7,299	13.4	…	8	95
Bolivia	1995	…	51,763[12]	1,538,454	24.7[12]	91	…	12,434[4, 12]	293,158[4]	17.6[4, 12]	29	…	[4]
Bosnia and Herzegovina	1991	2,205	23,369	539,875	23.1	98	238	9,030	172,063	19.1	…	…	…
Botswana	1997	714	11,454	322,268	28.1	81	274	6,772	116,076	17.1	44	50	2,618
Brazil	1998	187,497	1,460,469	35,845,742	24.5	90	17,602	380,222	6,968,531	18.3	19	…	…
Brunei	1998	184[10]	3,858[10]	58,548[10]	15.2[10]	91	38	2,636	30,956	11.7	68	9	516
Bulgaria	1999	3,011[9]	65,885[9]	887,213[9]	13.5[9]	92	[9]	[9]	[9]	[9]	74	545	20,389
Burkina Faso	1996	3,568	14,037	702,204	50.0	31	252	4,152	137,257	33.0	7	41	731
Burundi	1993	1,418	10,400	651,086	62.6	52	113[12]	2,562	55,713	21.7	5	…	…
Cambodia	1998	5,026	43,282	2,011,772	46.5	100	440[11]	16,820	302,751	18.0	…	65[11]	2,315
Cameroon	1995	6,801	40,970	1,896,722	46.3	67	…	14,917	459,068	30.8	11	…	5,885
Canada	1996	12,685	148,565	2,448,144	16.5	95	3,780	133,275	2,505,389	18.8	91	…	…
Cape Verde	1994	370[12]	2,657	78,173	29.4	100	…	438	11,808	27.0	48	…	94[14]
Central African Republic	1991	930	4,004	308,409	77.0	53	46[4]	845[4]	46,989[4]	55.6[4]	…	[4]	[4]
Chad	1996	2,660	9,395	591,493	63.0	46	153	2,468	90,100	36.5	…	18	216
Chile	1995	8,702	80,155	2,149,501	26.8	89	…	51,042	679,165	13.3	58	…	…
China	1997	628,840	5,794,000	139,954,000	24.2	101	78,642	3,587,000	60,179,000	16.8	…	14,190	598,000
Colombia	1996	48,933	193,911	4,916,934	25.4	85	7,895[4]	165,976[4]	2,323,653	…	46	[4]	[4]
Comoros	1996	327	1,508	78,527	52.1	52	…	591	21,192	35.9	…	…	…
Congo, Dem. Rep. of the	1995	14,885	121,054	5,417,506	44.8	54	4,276[4, 11]	59,325[4, 11]	1,514,323[4]	…	17	[4]	[4]
Congo, Rep. of the	1997	1,612	6,926	489,546	70.7	96	…	5,466	190,409	34.8	…	…	1,746
Costa Rica	1998	3,711	19,235	529,637	27.5	89	353	10,943	202,415	18.5	40	…	…
Côte d'Ivoire	1996	7,401	40,529	1,662,285	41.0	55	147	15,959	489,740	30.7	…	…	1,424[3]
Croatia	1998	2,127	10,365	206,121	19.9	82	1,110	19,776	266,115	13.5	66	442	13,000
Cuba	1997	9,864[16]	78,625	1,028,880	13.0	101	…	71,025	778,028	11.0	59[16]	…	27,267[16]
Cyprus[17]	1997	376	4,159	64,761	15.6	96	125[4]	5,757[4]	61,266[4]	10.6[4]	93	[4]	[4]
Czech Republic	1998	8,067[18]	83,972[18]	1,186,246[18]	14.1[18]	91	367	11,658	83,010	7.1	89	1,776	54,204
Denmark	1996	2,536[3]	33,100	336,690	10.2	99	153[3]	37,000	321,448	8.7	88	237[3]	13,100

tural work all make even even a simple enrollment figure difficult to assess in isolation. All of these difficulties are compounded when a country has instruction in more than one language or when its educational establishment is so small that higher, sometimes even secondary, education cannot take place within the country. Enrollment figures in this table may, therefore, include students enrolled outside the country.

Student-teacher ratio, however, usually provides a good measure of the ratio of trained educators to the enrolled educable. In general, at each level of education both students and teachers have been counted on the basis of full-time enrollment or employment, or full-time equivalent when country statistics permit. At the primary and secondary levels, net enrollment ratio is the ratio of the number of children within the usual age group for a particular level who are actually enrolled to the total number of children in that age group (× 100). This ratio is usually less than (occasionally, equal to) 100 and is the most accurate measure of the completeness of enrollment at that particular level. It is not always, however, the best indication of utilization of teaching staff and facilities. Utilization, provided here for higher education only, is best seen in a gross enrollment ratio, which compares total enrollment (of all ages) to the population within the normal age limits for that level. For a country with substantial adult literacy or general educational programs, the difference may be striking: typically, for a less developed country, even one with a good net enrollment ratio of 90 to 95, the gross enrollment ratio may by 20%, 25%, even 30% higher, indicating the heavy use made by the country of facilities and teachers at that level.

Literacy data provided here have been compiled as far as possible from data for the population age 15 and over for the best comparability internationally. Standards as to what constitutes literacy may also differ markedly; sometimes completion of a certain number of years of school is taken to constitute literacy; elsewhere it may mean only the ability to read or write at a minimal level testable by a census taker; in other countries studies have been undertaken to distinguish among degrees of functional literacy. When a country reports an official 100% (or near) literacy rate, it should usually be viewed with caution, as separate studies of "functional" literacy for such a country may indicate 10%, 20%, or even higher rates of inability to read, or write, effectively. Substantial use has been made of UNESCO literacy estimates, both for some of the least developed countries (where the statistical base is poorest) and for some of the most fully developed, where literacy is no longer perceived as a problem, thus no longer in need of monitoring.

Finally, the data provided for public expenditure on education are complete in that they include all levels of public expenditure (national, state, local) but are incomplete for certain countries in that they do not include data for private expenditure; in some countries this fraction of the educational establishment may be of significant size. Occasionally data for external aid to education may be included in addition to domestic expenditure.

The following notes further define the column headings:

a. Usually includes teacher training at the second level.

b. Latest.

c. Full-time.

d. Full-time; may include students registered in foreign schools.

		third level (higher)							literacy[b]				public expenditure on education (percent of GNP)[b]	country
students[d]	student/ teacher ratio	institutions	teachers[c]	students[d]	student/ teacher ratio	gross enroll- ment ratio[b]	students per 100,000 popula- tion[b]	percent of population age 25 and over with post- secondary education[b]	over age	total (%)	male (%)	female (%)		
...	...	...	...	12,800	...	2.0	165	3.0	15	36.3	51.0	20.8	2.0	Afghanistan
18,504	8.5	10[1]	2,348	34,257	14.6	12.0	1,007	...	10	91.8	95.5	88.0	3.1	Albania
...	...	...	19,910	347,410	17.4	10.9	1,236	...	15	63.3	75.1	51.3	5.1	Algeria
160[2]	7.6[2]	1	...	...	...	...	...	22.6	15	95.9	95.6	96.3	8.2	American Samoa
...	...	—	—	932	—	...	...	...	15	100.0	100.0	100.0	...	Andorra
22,401	...	1	787	6,.331	8.0	0.7	71	...	15	41.7	55.6	28.5	4.9	Angola
46[3]	2.9[3]	1	16	46	2.9	...	...	...	15	90.0	...	...	2.7	Antigua and Barbuda
[4]	[4]	1,831	117,104	936,832	8.0	38.0	3,117	12.0	15	96.9	96.9	96.9	3.5	Argentina
25,200[5]	...	15	4,420	38,500	8.7	12.0	976	...	15	98.8	99.4	98.1	2.0	Armenia
[4]	[4]	2	53	394	7.4	...	...	7.0	15	95.0	...	...	4.9	Aruba
985,000[3]	34.1[3]	92	32,663	671,853	20.6	80.0	5,552	...	15	99.5	...	...	5.5	Australia
307,548	11.7	77	20,356	232,377	11.4	48.0	2,970	6.1	15	100.0	100.0	100.0	5.4	Austria
23,500	...	23	17,900	120,870	6.6	17.0	1,516	...	15	97.3	98.9	95.9	3.0	Azerbaijan
...	...	17	160[7]	3,463[7]	21.6[7]	18.0	...	13.5	15	96.1	95.4	96.8	4.0	Bahamas, The
7,287	...	...	558	7,011	12.6	20.0	1,445	10.3	15	87.6	91.0	82.7	4.4	Bahrain
29,923[5]	16.1[5]	1,268[5]	36,000[5]	1,032,635[5]	28.7[5]	4.0	399	1.3	15	40.8	51.7	29.5	2.2	Bangladesh
...	...	4	...	6,622	...	29.0	2,602	3.3	15	97.4	98.0	96.8	7.2	Barbados
125,600	14.3	59	16,300	224,500	13.8	44.0	3,177	12.5	15	99.4	99.7	99.2	5.9	Belarus
569,041	...	151	38,014	358,214	9.4	56.0	3,494	...	15	100.0	100.0	100.0	3.1	Belgium
...	...	12	228	2,753	12.1	...	...	6.6	14	70.3	...	...	5.0	Belize
4,873[5]	17.2[5]	16[5]	962	14,085	14.6	3.0	253	1.3	15	37.5	47.8	23.6	3.2	Benin
...	...	1	...	543	...	...	...	18.4	15	96.9	96.7	97.0	3.7	Bermuda
1,822[1]	12.2[1]	2[1]	57[1]	2,055	9.1[1]	...	...	...	15	47.3	61.1	33.6	4.1	Bhutan
[4]	[4]	...	4,261[2]	109,503[2]	25.7[2]	21.0	2,154	9.9	15	85.6	92.1	79.4	4.9	Bolivia
...	...	44	2,802	37,541	13.4	...	...	...	10	85.5	96.5	76.6	...	Bosnia and Herzegovina
9,829	3.8	1	1,001	9,660	9.6	6.0	596	1.4	15	77.2	74.4	79.8	8.6	Botswana
...	...	900	173,705[13]	1,948,200[13]	11.2[13]	15.0	1,094	...	15	85.3	85.5	85.4	5.1	Brazil
2,553	4.9	4	370	2,080	5.6	7.0	518	9.4	15	91.6	94.7	88.2	2.5	Brunei
201,736	10.0	86	42,829	258,240	6.0	41.0	3,103	15.0	15	98.5	99.1	98.0	3.2	Bulgaria
9,539	13.0	9	632	9,531	15.1	0.9	83	...	15	23.0	31.2	13.1	3.6	Burkina Faso
...	...	8	556	4,256	7.6	0.8	74	0.6	15	48.1	56.3	40.5	4.0	Burundi
16,350[11]	...	9[11]	784[11]	11,652[11]	14.9[11]	1.0	98	1.0	15	65.3	79.7	53.4	2.9	Cambodia
91,779	15.6	...	1,086[12]	33,177[12]	30.5[12]	3.0	289	...	15	75.4	81.8	69.2	2.9	Cameroon
...	...	265	64,100[5]	980,251[5]	14.4[5]	88.0	5,997	21.4	15	96.6	...	...	6.9	Canada
2,289	...	...	...	...	...	...	...	...	15	73.5	84.3	65.3	4.0	Cape Verde
[4]	[4]	1	136	2,823	20.8	1.0	131	2.0	15	46.5	59.6	34.5	2.3	Central African Republic
2,926	13.5	8	288	3,446	12.0	0.6	54	...	15	53.6	66.9	40.8	1.7	Chad
...	...	...	18,084[11, 15]	367,094	...	31.0	2,546	12.3	15	95.7	95.9	95.5	3.6	Chile
9,773,000	16.3	1,020	405,000	3,174,000	7.8	6.0	473	2.0	15	85.0	92.3	77.4	2.3	China
928,474	...	266	75,568	673,353	8.9	17.0	1,768	10.4	15	91.8	91.8	91.8	4.4	Colombia
...	...	...	...	348	...	0.6	57	...	15	56.2	63.5	49.1	3.9	Comoros
[4]	[4]	...	...	52,501	...	2.0	212	1.3	15	77.3	86.6	67.7	1.0	Congo, Dem. Rep. of the
23,606	13.5	...	1,341[3]	16,602[3]	12.4[3]	7.0	582	3.0	15	80.7	87.5	74.4	6.1	Congo, Rep. of the
...	...	40[13]	...	83,106[13]	...	30.0	2,919	...	15	95.6	95.5	95.7	5.4	Costa Rica
11,037[3]	7.8[3]	...	1,657[3]	43,147[3]	26.0[3]	6.0	396	8.7	15	46.8	54.6	38.5	5.0	Côte d'Ivoire
150,792	11.6	79	6,532	90,021	13.8	28.0	1,905	6.4	15	98.3	99.4	97.3	5.3	Croatia
244,253[16]	9.0[16]	35[1]	22,967[16]	104,595	5.3[16]	12.0	1,013	5.9	15	96.4	96.5	96.4	6.7	Cuba
[4]	[4]	35	812	9,982	12.3	23.0	1,383	17.0	15	96.9	98.7	95.0	4.5	Cyprus[17]
419,843	7.7	272	18,061	203,598	11.3	24.0	1,867	8.5	15	100.0	100.0	100.0	5.1	Czech Republic
123,234	9.4	158[3]	9,600	169,783	17.7	48.0	3,189	19.6	...	100.0	100.0	100.0	8.1	Denmark

Education (continued)

country	year	first level (primary)					general second level (secondary)					vocational second level[a]	
		schools	teachers[c]	students[d]	student/ teacher ratio	net enroll- ment ratio[b]	schools	teachers[c]	students[d]	student/ teacher ratio	net enroll- ment ratio[b]	schools	teachers[c]
Djibouti	1997	81[3]	1,005[3]	33,960	...	32	26[4, 12]	628[3, 4]	11,628[4]	...	12	[4]	[4]
Dominica	1998	63	587	13,636	23.2	...	15	293	5,455	18.6	...	...	...
Dominican Republic	1995	4,001	42,135	1,462,722	34.7	81	...	10,757	240,441	22.4	22	...	1,297
East Timor	...	...	...	...	...	...	...	...	...	...	...	...	...
Ecuador	1997	17,367	74,601	1,888,172	25.3	92	...	62,630[4, 11]	765,073[4]	...	...	...	[4]
Egypt[19]	1997	18,522[16]	310,116	7,499,303	24.2	93	7,307[5, 16]	259,618	4,835,938	18.6	64	1,351[5]	138,277
El Salvador	1996	5,025	34,496	1,130,900	32.8	78	...	9,255	143,588	15.5	22	...	...
Equatorial Guinea	1994	781	1,381	75,751	54.9	...	...	466	14,511	31.1	...	...	122
Eritrea	1996	537	5,828	241,725	41.5	30	86[11]	2,031	78,902	38.8	16	4[11]	174
Estonia	1996	727	...	125,718	...	87	...	9,299	95,342	10.3	83	84	1,793
Ethiopia	1995	9,276	83,113	2,722,192	32.8	32	...	22,779	747,142	32.8	...	...	826
Faroe Islands	1995	62	554[9]	4,898	...	...	6	[9]	3,041	...	...	...	...
Fiji	1997	697[5]	5,011	142,781	28.5	99	147[5]	3,519	70,098	19.9	...	35[5]	625[2]
Finland	1997	4,392	39,966	592,500	14.8	98	454	5,766	131,900	22.9	93	467	15,063
France	1995	41,244	216,962	4,071,599	18.8	100	11,212[4]	473,673[4]	6,003,797[4]	12.7[4]	95	[4]	[4]
French Guiana	1996	78[5]	802	17,006	21.2	...	22[12]	875	13,585	15.5	...	...	210
French Polynesia	1995	278	2,949	48,160	16.3	103	38	1,745	25,541	14.6	61	...	...
Gabon	1996	1,147	4,944	250,606	50.7	...	48	2,683	72,888	27.2	...	11	412
Gambia, The	1995	250[5]	3,158[5]	113,419	33.4[5]	65	32[4, 5]	1,126[4, 5]	31,567	24.1[4, 5]	20	[4]	[4]
Gaza Strip	1997	1,118	15,903	656,353	41.3	...	...	7,634	54,692	7.2	...	...	316
Georgia	1997	3,201	16,542	293,325	17.7	77	3,139	55,817	424,465	7.6	74	...	2,146
Germany	1998	17,829	198,116	3,697,806	18.7	86	19,668	413,993	5,720,092	13.8	88	9,754	110,185
Ghana	1992	11,056	66,068	1,796,490	27.2	...	5,540	43,367	816,578	18.8	...	57[1]	422[1]
Greece	1997	8,651	46,785	652,040	13.9	90	3,044	56,899	682,201	12.0	87	682	13,783
Greenland	1999	88	975	9,341	9.6	...	3	...	1,746	...	...	...	...
Grenada	1997	58	879	23,449	26.7	...	19[3]	381[3]	7,367	19.3	...	...	...
Guadeloupe	1999	348	2,936	38,092[5]	...	...	88[4]	3,392[4]	51,366[4, 5]	13.4[4, 5]	...	[4]	[4]
Guam	1998	24	469	20,248	43.2	...	11	622	17,091	27.5	...	2	370[1]
Guatemala	1995	11,495	43,731	1,470,754	33.6	72	2,308[4]	23,807[4]	372,006[4]	15.6[4]	10	626[12]	[4]
Guernsey	1993	22[2]	236	4,697	19.9	...	8[2]	276	3,642	13.2	...	...	...
Guinea	1998	3,723	13,883	674,732	48.6	42	239	4,958	143,245	28.9	9	55[16]	1,268[16]
Guinea-Bissau	1995	...	...	100,369	...	47	...	...	7,000	...	3	...	...
Guyana	1997	420	3,461	102,000	29.5	87	...	2,150	62,043	29.5	66	...	...
Haiti	1995	10,071	30,205	1,110,398	36.8	26	1,038	...	195,418	...	22	...	...
Honduras	1999	8,768	33,431	1,111,264	33.2	90	661[3, 4]	14,539[4]	189,000[4]	13.0[4]	21	[4]	[4]
Hong Kong	1998	832	20,038	476,682	23.8	90	507	23,077	455,392	19.7	69	9	...
Hungary	1999	3,732	83,404	964,248	11.6	97	1,545	40,130	504,829	12.6	86	1,245	26,344
Iceland	1997	198	3,877	31,100	8.0	98	37	1,454	17,970	12.4	87	...	...
India	1997	598,354	1,789,733	110,393,406	61.7	...	274,944	2,738,205	65,359,339	23.9	...	...	...
Indonesia	1997	173,883	1,327,218	28,236,283	21.3	95	41,847	863,389	12,442,813	14.4	45	3,894	123,505
Iran	1997	63,101	298,755	9,238,393	31.2	90	18,445[1]	280,309	8,776,792	31.3	71	...	20,418[3]
Iraq	1996	8,145	145,455	2,903,923	20.0	76	2,635[3]	49,884	1,075,490	21.6	37	310[3]	9,903
Ireland	1997	3,254	18,968	476,632	25.1	92	440	12,694	375,518	29.6	86	324	8,305
Isle of Man	1999	33	...	6,210	...	...	5	...	4,732	...	...	...	...
Israel	1998	1,651	57,738	532,070	9.2	...	653	62,054	414,405	...	...	338	17,141[11]
Italy	1997	19,890	289,504	2,809,699	9.7	100	16,973	315,920	2,648,535	8.4	67	7,732	305,582
Jamaica	1997	788[2]	9,512	293,863	30.9	95	126[3]	8,377[3]	228,533	...	64[3]	18[3]	950[3]
Japan	1997	24,376	420,901	7,855,387	18.7	103	16,753	546,337	8,852,840	16.2	99	62	4,384
Jersey	1990	32	...	5,794	...	...	14	...	4,405	...	...	1	...
Jordan	1996	2,531	51,721	1,074,877	20.8	89	741[5]	6,309	109,906	17.4	42	54[5]	2,306
Kazakhstan	1997	8,611[16]	262,000[16]	1,342,035	...	...	...	178,900[5]	1,743,623	...	...	239	...
Kenya	1995	15,906	181,975	5,544,998	30.5	91	2,878	41,484	632,388	15.2	11	62	1,147[14]
Kiribati	1997	86	727	17,594	24.2	...	9	215	4,403	20.5	...	...	23
Korea, North	1988	4,810[13]	59,000	1,543,000	26.2	...	4,840[13]	111,000	2,468,000	22.2	...	...	...
Korea, South	1997	5,721	138,670	3,783,986	27.3	93	4,612	202,335	4,517,008	22.3	97	166	13,282
Kuwait	1997	258	9,863	142,265	14.4	62	416	19,402	213,266	11.0	61	38	793
Kyrgyzstan	1996	1,885	24,086	473,077	19.7	95	1,474[5]	38,915	498,849	12.8	...	53[5]	3,371
Laos	1997	7,896	25,831	786,335	30.4	72	750[1]	10,717	180,160	16.8	22	...	1,600[16]
Latvia	1998	638	10,883	146,653	13.5	89	380	24,112	196,148	8.1	79	123	5,470
Lebanon	1997	2,160	...	382,309	...	76	...	...	292,002	...	...	275	7,745
Lesotho	1997	1,249	7,898	374,628	47.4	70	187[3]	2,817	67,454	23.9	18	9[5]	61
Liberia	1987	...	...	...	...	...	...	...	...	...	...	...	...
Libya	1996	2,733[5]	122,020	1,333,679	10.9	96	...	17,668	170,573	9.7	62	480	...
Liechtenstein	1998	14	134	2,021	15.1	...	10[4]	198[4]	4,121[4]	20.8[4]	...	[4]	[4]
Lithuania	1997	2,292	14,093	225,071	16.0	...	...	32,172	325,480	10.1	80	104	5,078
Luxembourg	1997	...	1,844	28,232	15.3	...	...	2,673	9,463	3.5	...	...	2,904[3, 14]
Macau	1998	81	1,744	47,235	27.1	...	47	1,577	28,280	17.9	53	2	47
Macedonia	1998	1,043	13,376	256,275	19.2	94	93[4]	5,226[4]	84,059[4]	16.1[4]	51	[4]	[4]
Madagascar	1996	13,325	44,145	1,638,187	37.1	61	...	16,795	302,036	18.0	...	...	1,150
Malawi	1996	3,706	49,138	2,887,107	58.7	103	...	2,948	139,386	47.2	2	...	475
Malaysia	1997	7,084	150,681	2,870,667	19.1	102	1,460	91,659	1,767,946	19.3	...	101	5,472
Maldives	1998	228	1,992	48,895	24.5	...	...	...	15,933[2]	...	...	...	...
Mali	1998	2,511	10,853	862,875	79.5	31	307[2]	4,549[16]	166,372	...	5	...	21,731
Malta	1998	99	1,457	35,261	24.2	100	75	2,458	27,178	11.1	79	22	626
Marshall Islands	1995	103	669	13,355	20.0	...	12	144	2,400	16.7	...	...	...
Martinique	1997	273	2,603	55,569	21.3	...	76[16]	2,888	36,605	12.7	...	...	896[16]
Mauritania	1997	2,392	6,225	312,671	50.2	57	...	1,865[16]	49,221[16]	26.4[16]	...	...	202
Mauritius	1998	285	5,065	130,505	25.7	98	133	4,820	94,364	19.6	33	13	1,170[13]
Mayotte	1997	88[1]	555[11]	25,805[10]	...	...	8	246[11]	6,190	...	...	2[1]	17[1]
Mexico	1996	94,844	516,051	14,623,400	28.3	101	25,000	467,686	7,589,400	16.2	51	6,571[11]	77,347[11]
Micronesia	1995	174	...	27,281	...	...	24	...	6,898	...	...	...	...
Moldova	1997	1,700[9]	14,097	320,725	22.8	...	[9]	28,615[4]	419,256	...	...	64	[4]
Monaco	1997	8	127	1,917	15.1	...	6	192	2,416	12.6	...	4	89
Mongolia	1997	308	7,587	234,193	30.9	81	337	12,503	184,100	14.7	53	36	668
Morocco	1998	5,730	116,638	3,317,153	28.4	74	1,406	82,589	1,328,789	16.1	20	71[14]	2,951[3, 14]

		third level (higher)							literacy[b]					
students[d]	student/ teacher ratio	institutions	teachers[c]	students[d]	student/ teacher ratio	gross enroll- ment ratio[b]	students per 100,000 popula- tion[b]	percent of population age 25 and over with post- secondary education[b]	over age	total (%)	male (%)	female (%)	public expenditure on education (percent of GNP)[b]	country
[4]	[4]	1[12]	13[12]	130[18]	...	0.2	26	...	15	51.4	65.0	38.4	3.6	Djibouti
...	...	2[11]	34[11]	484[11]	14.2[11]	...	...	1.7	15	90.0	...	...	5.5	Dominica
22,795	17.6	...	9,041[15]	176,995[15]	19.6[15]	23.0	...	...	15	83.8	84.0	83.7	2.3	Dominican Republic
...	...	...	...	...	...	...	...	...	...	...	...	...	...	East Timor
[4]	...	21	12,856[1]	206,541[1]	16.1[1]	20.0	2,012	12.7	15	91.9	93.6	90.2	3.5	Ecuador
1,912,040	13.8	16[15]	38,828[5, 15]	850,051	...	20.0	1,900	4.6	15	55.3	66.6	43.7	4.8	Egypt[19]
...	...	...	5,919	112,266	19.0	18.0	1,933	6.4	15	78.7	81.6	76.1	2.5	El Salvador
2,105	17.3	...	58	578	10.0	...	164	...	15	83.2	92.5	74.5	1.7	Equatorial Guinea
4,268	24.5	1	136	3,081	22.7	1.0	95	...	...	20.0	...	...	1.8	Eritrea
16,870	9.4	37	...	40,621	...	42.0	2,956	13.7	15	99.7	99.9	99.6	7.2	Estonia
9,103	11.0	...	1,937	32,671	16.9	0.6	62	1.0	15	38.7	43.9	33.4	4.0	Ethiopia
2,090[5]	...	1[12]	20[12]	91[12]	4.6[12]	...	...	...	15	99.0	99.0	99.0	...	Faroe Islands
7,283[2]	11.6[2]	...	277[12]	7,908[12]	28.5[12]	12.0	757	4.5	15	92.9	95.0	90.9	5.4	Fiji
251,600	16.7	29	8,134	168,996	20.8	74.0	4,190	15.4	15	100.0	100.0	100.0	7.5	Finland
[4]	[4]	1,062	52,613	2,083,129	39.6	51.0	3,600	11.4	...	98.8	98.9	98.7	6.0	France
2,404	11.4	1	...	324[11]	...	...	...	6.4	15	83.0	83.6	82.3	...	French Guiana
...	...	...	...	301[2]	...	1.0	...	...	15	95.0	94.9	95.0	9.8	French Polynesia
7,664	18.6	2[2, 15]	299[2, 15]	3,000[2, 15]	10.0[2, 15]	...	650	...	15	70.8	79.8	62.2	2.9	Gabon
[4]	[4]	...	155[5]	1,591[5]	10.3[5]	2.0	148	...	15	36.5	43.8	29.6	4.9	Gambia, The
1,775	5.7	5	2,473	49,599	20.0	...	...	...	...	...	...	...	...	Gaza Strip
19,593	9.1	23	25,549	163,345	6.4	30.0	3,002	...	15	99.5	99.7	99.4	5.2	Georgia
2,838,416	25.8	296	161,383	1,813,348	11.2	47.0	2,628	...	15	100.0	100.0	100.0	4.8	Germany
13,232[1]	31.4[1]	16[1]	700[1]	9,274[1]	13.2[1]	0.6	127	...	15	70.2	79.5	61.2	4.2	Ghana
135,365	9.8	18	16,057	363,180	22.6	47.0	3,149	8.7	15	97.2	98.6	96.0	3.1	Greece
...	...	...	...	...	...	...	...	...	15	100.0	100.0	100.0	...	Greenland
...	...	1[3]	66[3]	651[3]	9.9[3]	...	...	1.5	15	85.0	...	...	4.7	Grenada
[4]	[4]	1[5]	121[5]	4,673[5]	38.6[5]	...	...	5.2	15	90.1	89.7	90.5	...	Guadeloupe
4,369	...	1	192[1]	3,533	...	...	...	39.9	15	99.0	99.0	99.0	8.5	Guam
[4]	[4]	...	...	80,228	...	8.0	755	2.2	15	68.7	76.2	61.1	1.7	Guatemala
...	...	—	—	—	—	...	...	...	15	100.0	100.0	100.0	...	Guernsey
8,151[16]	6.8[16]	2[16]	947[16]	8,151[16]	8.6[16]	1.0	108	...	15	41.1	55.1	27.0	1.9	Guinea
...	...	...	...	...	...	...	...	0.1	15	36.8	53.0	21.4	...	Guinea-Bissau
...	...	...	612	8,965	12.5	11.0	954	1.8	15	98.5	99.0	98.1	5.0	Guyana
...	...	2[20]	817[20]	12,204[20]	14.9[20]	1.0	...	0.7	15	48.6	51.0	46.5	1.5	Haiti
[4]	[4]	8	3,676[3]	56,077	...	10.0	985	3.3	15	72.2	72.5	72.0	3.6	Honduras
42,003	...	18	...	91,748	...	22.0	1,635	14.5	15	93.4	96.5	90.0	2.9	Hong Kong
362,633	13.8	89	21,351	163,164	7.6	24.0	1,926	10.1	15	99.4	99.5	99.3	4.6	Hungary
...	...	10	508	7,972	15.7	37.0	2,787	...	15	100.0	100.0	100.0	5.4	Iceland
...	...	8,407[5]	286,000[5]	5,007,000[5]	17.5[5]	7.0	642	7.3	15	55.8	68.6	42.1	3.2	India
1,767,181	14.3	1,667	180,471	2,703,886	15.0	11.0	1,167	2.3	15	87.0	91.9	82.1	1.4	Indonesia
368,218[3]	18.0[3]	...	40,477	579,070	14.3	18.0	1,599	...	15	76.9	83.7	70.0	4.0	Iran
122,939	12.4	12	11,685	232,896	19.9	12.0	...	4.1	15	58.0	70.7	45.0	4.0	Iraq
96,821	11.7	30	4,872	107,501	22.1	41.0	3,618	13.1	15	100.0	100.0	100.0	6.0	Ireland
...	...	...	...	1,128	...	...	...	...	...	...	...	...	...	Isle of Man
106,393	...	7	9,546	181,038	19.0	41.0	3,598	11.2	15	96.1	97.9	94.3	7.6	Israel
2,597,449	8.5	56[15]	48,891[15]	1,595,642[15]	32.6	47.0	3,103	3.8	15	98.5	98.9	98.1	4.9	Italy
15,898[3]	16.7[3]	15[3]	...	24,200[3]	...	8.0	803	2.7	15	86.7	82.5	90.7	7.5	Jamaica
56,294	12.8	1,243	166,051	3,136,834	18.9	41.0	3,139	20.7	15	100.0	100.0	100.0	3.6	Japan
...	...	...	...	...	...	...	...	...	15	100.0	100.0	100.0	...	Jersey
35,579	15.4	55	4,821	99,020	20.5	27.0	2,542	...	15	89.8	94.9	84.4	7.9	Jordan
177,679	...	69[3]	27,189[3]	260,043[16]	...	33.0	2,806	12.4	15	97.5	99.1	96.1	4.4	Kazakhstan
11,700[14]	10.2[4]	14[11, 15]	4,392[1, 15]	88,180[11]	...	2.0	143	...	15	82.5	89.0	76.0	6.5	Kenya
333	14.5	—	—	—	—	...	...	...	15	90.0	...	...	6.3	Kiribati
220,000	...	519[13]	27,000	390,000	14.4	...	...	...	15	95.0	...	...	...	Korea, North
745,689	56.1	742	53,300	1,469,819	27.6	68.0	5,609	21.1	15	97.8	99.2	96.4	3.7	Korea, South
3,779	4.8	1	1,691	29,509	17.5	19.0	2,247	16.4	15	82.3	84.3	79.9	5.0	Kuwait
32,005	9.5	23	3,691	49,744	13.5	12.0	1,115	...	15	97.0	98.6	95.5	5.3	Kyrgyzstan
9,400[16]	5.9[16]	9[1]	1,369	12,732	9.3	3.0	253	...	15	61.8	73.6	50.5	2.1	Laos
45,672	8.3	28	4,486	56,187	12.5	33.0	2,244	13.4	15	99.7	99.8	99.6	6.3	Latvia
55,848	7.2	20	10,444	81,588	7.8	27.0	2,712	...	15	86.1	92.3	80.4	2.5	Lebanon
678	11.1	1	574	4,614	8.0	2.0	222	...	15	83.9	73.6	93.6	8.4	Lesotho
...	...	...	472	5,095	10.8	2.0	...	...	15	53.4	69.9	36.8	5.7	Liberia
155,483	...	13	...	126,348	...	17.0	1,358	2.7	15	79.8	90.9	67.6	7.1	Libya
[4]	[4]	...	...	...	...	...	...	...	15	100.0	100.0	100.0	...	Liechtenstein
56,400	11.1	15	13,136	83,645	6.4	31.0	2,244	12.6	15	99.5	99.7	99.4	5.5	Lithuania
19,346	...	1	200[3]	957	...	10.0	...	10.8	15	100.0	100.0	100.0	4.0	Luxembourg
699	14.9	7	818	7,682	9.4	28.0	1,700	5.9	15	93.2	96.4	90.1	...	Macau
[4]	[4]	30	1,385	36,167	26.1	20.0	1,415	6.7	10	89.1	94.2	83.8	5.1	Macedonia
8,479	7.3	...	921	18,458	20.0	3.0	174	...	15	80.2	87.7	72.9	1.9	Madagascar
2,228	4.7	6	531[3]	5,561	...	0.6	58	0.4	15	60.3	74.5	46.7	5.4	Malawi
36,573	6.9	48	14,960	210,724	14.1	12.0	971	6.9	15	87.5	91.5	83.6	4.9	Malaysia
452[2]	...	—	—	—	—	...	...	1.7	15	96.3	96.3	96.4	6.4	Maldives
7,200	3.0	7	796	13,847	17.4	1.0	73	...	15	40.3	47.9	33.2	2.2	Mali
4,159	6.6	1	770	7,146	9.3	29.0	1,595	...	15	92.1	91.4	92.8	5.1	Malta
...	...	...	...	...	...	...	...	...	15	91.2	92.4	90.0	...	Marshall Islands
11,101[16]	12.4[16]	1	99[5]	3,079	45.3[5]	...	...	5.6	15	97.4	96.0	97.1	...	Martinique
2,544	12.6	4	270	8,496	31.5	4.0	374	1.3	15	39.9	50.6	29.5	5.1	Mauritania
5,496	...	3	461	6,429	13.9	6.3	594	1.9	15	84.3	87.7	81.0	4.6	Mauritius
839[11]	...	—	—	—	—	...	...	...	15	91.9	...	...	...	Mayotte
1,076,700[11]	13.9[11]	10,341	163,843	1,532,800	9.4	16.0	1,586	9.2	15	91.0	93.1	89.1	4.9	Mexico
...	...	...	...	1,461[5]	...	...	...	...	15	76.7	67.0	87.2	...	Micronesia
26,245	...	20	8,814	93,759	10.6	27.0	2,110	11.3	15	98.9	99.6	98.3	10.6	Moldova
532	6.0	1	...	112	...	...	...	...	...	...	...	...	...	Monaco
11,308	16.9	86	4,471	44,088	9.8	17.0	1,753	23.4	15	99.3	99.2	99.3	5.7	Mongolia
22,415[14]	...	68	9,667	266,507	27.5	11.0	1,132	...	15	48.9	61.9	36.0	5.3	Morocco

Education (continued)

country	year	first level (primary)					general second level (secondary)					vocational second level[a]	
		schools	teachers[c]	students[d]	student/ teacher ratio	net enroll-ment ratio[b]	schools	teachers[c]	students[d]	student/ teacher ratio	net enroll-ment ratio[b]	schools	teachers[c]
Mozambique	1997	6,025	32,670	1,899,531	57.8	40	75	1,555	51,554	33.1	8	25	565
Myanmar (Burma)	1998	35,877	167,134	5,145,400	30.8	...	2,091	56,955	1,545,600	27.1	...	103[3]	2,462[3]
Namibia	1995	933[5]	10,912[2]	368,222	32.0[2]	91	114[5]	3,943[2]	101,838[5]	...	36	17[5]	56[2]
Nauru	1995	10	138	2,207	16.0	...	4	46	...	...	...	1	...
Nepal	1996	22,218	89,378	3,447,607	38.6	...	7,582[4]	36,127[4]	1,121,335[4]	31.0[4]	...	[4]	[4]
Netherlands, The	1999	7,238	99,031[12]	1,534,000	...	100	666	89,370[12]	856,000	...	84	143	18,613[12]
Netherlands Antilles	1998	85[16]	1,111	24,061	21.7	...	21	461[16]	8,372	...	...	33	623[16]
New Caledonia	1996	279	1,622	22,942	14.1	98	46	2,021[4]	20,360	...	72	14	[4]
New Zealand	1998	2,282	23,119	445,868	19.3	100	339	15,228	224,290	14.7	90	29	5,309
Nicaragua	1997	7,224	21,020[16]	783,002	...	77	451[5]	5,990[3]	220,670[3]	36.8[3]	18	...	...
Niger	1998	3,175	11,545	482,065	41.8	24	...	3,579	97,675	27.3	6	...	215
Nigeria	1995	38,649	435,210	16,191,000	37.2	...	6,074	152,596	4,451,000	29.2	...	...	...
Northern Mariana Islands	1993	18	183	4,666	25.5	...	9[4]	152[4]	3,044[4]	20.0[4]	...	[4]	[4]
Norway	1997	3,287	39,385	487,398	12.4	100	714[4]	21,105[4]	208,280[4]	9.9[4]	97	[4]	[4]
Oman	1997	429	11,925[16]	311,955	...	69	128[1]	11,896	205,046	17.2	49	25[1]	342[5]
Pakistan	1998	158,511[10]	346,000[10]	16,642,000[10]	48.0[10]	...	25,913	259,200	5,545,000	21.4	...	673	7,546
Palau	1997	...	172	1,450	8.4	...	...	60	490	8.2	...	...	...
Panama	1997	2,866	15,058	377,898	25.1	91	417	12,450	223,155	17.9	51	...	...
Papua New Guinea	1995	2,790	13,652	525,995	38.5	...	135[1]	2,415[2]	68,818	24.1[2]	...	117[1]	878[2]
Paraguay	1996	5,928	41,713	895,777	21.5	91	804[4]	17,668	293,651[4]	...	38	[4]	...
Peru	1997	33,017	153,951	4,163,180	27.0	91	8,085[3]	106,614	1,969,501	18.5	55	2,425[3]	12,293[3]
Philippines	1997	37,645	341,183	11,902,501	34.9	101	5,880[5]	154,705[4]	4,888,246[4]	31.6[4]	59	1,261[1]	[4]
Poland	1998	19,299	322,600	4,896,400	15.2	95	1,847	39,200	757,500	19.3	85	9,320	89,900
Portugal	1996	12,884	145,462[9]	1,339,744	...	104	664	[9]	477,221	...	78	262	6,895
Puerto Rico	1986	1,542	18,359	427,582	23.3	...	395	13,612	334,661	24.6	...	52	...
Qatar	1996[8]	174	5,864	53,631	9.1	80	123[3]	3,738[3]	36,964[3]	9.9[3]	69	3	120
Réunion	1998	351	...	76,364	...	...	111[4]	6,343	96,811	15.3	...	[4]	1,120[16]
Romania	1997	13,978[18]	175,426[18]	2,546,231[18]	14.5[18]	95	1,295[21]	64,485[21]	792,788[21]	12.3[21]	73	1,692	10,942
Russia	1999	69,613[9]	1,811,000[9]	21,966,900[9]	12.1[9]	93	[9]	[9]	[9]	[9]	...	3,590	...
Rwanda	1992	1,710	18,937	1,104,902	58.3	75	...	3,413[4]	94,586[4]	27.7[4]	8	...	[4]
St. Kitts and Nevis	1998	28	320	5,928	18.5	...	9	341	4,548	13.3	...	...	...
St. Lucia	1998	84	1,160	30,536	26.3	...	17	620	11,405	18.4	...	1[11]	34[11]
St. Vincent and the Grenadines	1998	60	1,007	21,347	21.2	...	21	379	7,775	20.5	...	3	32[16]
Samoa	1995	155	1,475	35,811	24.3	96	...	...	...	...	45	...	...
San Marino	1998	14	225	1,211	5.4	...	3	148	700	4.7	...	...	44[5]
São Tomé and Príncipe	1997	69	638	21,760	34.1	...	10	415	12,280	29.6	...	...	...
Saudi Arabia	1997	11,509	175,458	2,256,185	12.9	61	7,667	115,907	1,505,072	13.0	42	...	6,133
Senegal	1997	3,530	16,567	954,758	57.6	60	359[11]	6,219	206,934	33.3	16	19[11]	182[11]
Seychelles	1999	25	656	9,868	15.0	...	13	545	7,774	14.3	...	12	218
Sierra Leone	1993	1,643	10,595	267,425	25.2	...	167	4,313	70,900	16.4	...	44	709
Singapore	1997	196	11,189	280,108	25.0	93	165	10,673	209,835	19.7	44	10	1,315
Slovakia	1998	2,482	39,535	645,941	16.3	...	198	5,849	80,116	13.7	...	365	10,104
Slovenia	1997	824	7,283	98,866	13.5	95	153	8,665	131,573	15.2	...	...	5,908
Solomon Islands	1994	520	2,514	60,493	24.1	...	23	618	7,981	12.9	...	1	...
Somalia	1990	...	...	377,000	...	10	...	...	44,000	...	3	...	...
South Africa	1996	20,863[9]	224,896	8,159,430	36.3	103	[9]	128,611[5]	3,749,449[5]	29.2[5]	58	187[5]	10,807[5]
Spain	1997	16,540[5]	163,105	2,682,894	16.4	105	25,775[4, 11]	245,118[4]	2,946,191	...	74	[4]	[4]
Sri Lanka	1998	10,947[9]	194,823[9]	4,278,124[9]	22.0[9]	...	[9]	[9]	[9]	[9]	...	36	623
Sudan, The	1997	11,158	102,987	3,000,048	24.1	54	2,578[2]	15,504	405,583	26.2	...	...	761
Suriname	1996	304	3,611	75,585	20.9	...	104	2,286	31,918	13.9	...	1	...
Swaziland	1997	529	6,094	205,829	33.8	91	165[5]	2,954[16]	57,330[16]	19.4[16]	38	5[5]	228[5]
Sweden	1997	4,936	81,800	958,972	11.7	102	641	28,305	310,000	10.9	99	...	...
Switzerland	1998	...	...	462,262	...	100	...	...	421,025	...	79	...	...
Syria	1997	10,783	114,689	2,690,205	23.5	91	2,526[3]	52,182	865,042	16.6	38	292[3]	12,479
Taiwan	1998	2,540	92,104	1,905,690	20.7	...	1,151[4]	99,411[4]	1,874,747[4]	18.9[4]	...	[4]	[4]
Tajikistan	1997	3,432	27,172	638,674	23.5	...	...	112,532	688,150	6.1	...	75[3]	...
Tanzania	1996[22]	10,892[5]	108,874	3,942,888	36.2	48	491[5]	11,689	199,093	17.0	...	40[5]	1,062
Thailand	1997	34,412[11]	445,542[11]	5,909,618	...	...	2,318[11]	107,025[11]	3,267,449	...	...	679[11]	40,116[11]
Togo	1997	3,283[16]	18,535	859,574	46.4	81	314[11]	4,736[16]	169,178	...	18	...	653
Tonga	1994	115	701	16,540	23.6	...	47	809	15,702	19.4	...	9	67[1]
Trinidad and Tobago	1997	478	7,311	181,030	24.8	88	...	5,070[4]	104,349[4]	20.6[4]	65	...	[4]
Tunisia	1997	4,428	60,101	1,450,916	24.1	98	712[3]	45,411	882,730	19.4	...	...	237[16]
Turkey	1997	47,313	217,131	6,389,060	29.4	99	11,144	143,322	3,427,715	23.9	51	4,046	75,507
Turkmenistan	1995	1,900[9]	72,900[9]	940,600[9]	12.9[9]	...	[9]	[9]	[9]	[9]	...	78	...
Tuvalu	1994	12	72[1]	1,906	...	...	2	31	345	...	...	1	10[1]
Uganda	1995[8]	8,531	76,134	2,636,409	34.6	...	...	14,447	255,158	17.7	...	...	1,788
Ukraine	1996	21,900[9]	576,000[3, 9]	7,007,000[9]	12.4[3, 9]	...	[9]	[9]	[9]	[9]	...	782	...
United Arab Emirates	1997	...	16,148	259,509	16.1	78	...	12,388[3]	178,839	12.0	71	9	249[14]
United Kingdom	1997	23,312	283,492	5,328,219	18.5	99	...	312,038	4,435,000	13.2	91	...	152,098
United States	1998	88,223[8, 9]	1,874,000	34,681,000	18.5	95	[9]	1,217,000	17,494,000	14.4	90	...	...
Uruguay	1997	2,410	16,721	348,195	20.8	93	413	19,104	192,399	10.1	...	101	...
Uzbekistan	1996	9,300[9]	413,000[9]	5,090,000[9]	12.3[9]	...	[9]	[9]	[9]	[9]	...	248	22,164[11]
Vanuatu	1992	272	852	26,267	30.8	...	...	220	4,269	19.4	17	...	...
Venezuela	1997	15,894[11]	182,192	4,262,221	23.4	84	1,621[2, 4]	43,369[4]	377,984[4]	8.7[4]	22	[4]	[4]
Vietnam	1998	13,092[5]	324,431	10,431,337	32.2	...	6,298[5]	209,500	6,642,350	31.7	...	451[5]	9,336
Virgin Islands (U.S.)	1993[8]	62	790	14,544	18.4	...	...	541[12]	12,502	17.2[12]	...	—	—
West Bank	1997	1,193[9]	15,912[9]	431,565[9]	27.1[9]	...	[9]	[9]	[9]	[9]	...	...	...
Western Sahara	1995[8]	40	925	32,257	34.9	...	13	1,267	10,541	8.3	...	...	...
Yemen	1997[14]	11,013[5]	90,478	2,699,788	29.8	...	1,224[3]	13,787	286,405	20.8	...	125[3]	369[3]
Yugoslavia	1999	4,431	52,294	864,199	16.5	69	561	27,766	367,587	13.2	62	...	...
Zambia	1996	3,907	38,528[3]	1,670,000	...	75	...	...	255,000	...	16	...	...
Zimbabwe	1996	4,659	63,718	2,493,791	39.1	...	1,536	28,354	751,349	26.5	...	25[2]	1,479[2]

		third level (higher)							literacy[b]				public expenditure on education (percent of GNP)[b]	country
students[d]	student/ teacher ratio	institutions	teachers[c]	students[d]	student/ teacher ratio	gross enroll- ment ratio[b]	students per 100,000 popula- tion[b]	percent of population age 25 and over with post- secondary education[b]	over age	total (%)	male (%)	female (%)		
12,001	21.2	3	954	7,158	7.5	0.5	40	0.1	15	43.8	59.9	28.4	4.1	Mozambique
25,374[3]	10.3[3]	51	17,089	385,300	22.5	5.0	564	2.0	15	84.7	89.0	80.6	1.2	Myanmar (Burma)
1,503[5]	...	7[5]	331[12]	11,344	...	8.0	738	4.0	15	82.1	82.9	81.2	9.1	Namibia
...	...	...	...	...	...	...	...	...	15	99.0	...	...	...	Nauru
[4]	[4]	3[2]	4,925[12]	105,694	...	5.0	501	0.6	15	41.4	59.1	21.8	3.2	Nepal
517,000	...	13	...	147,000	...	47.0	3,176	...	15	100.0	100.0	100.0	5.1	Netherlands, The
8,524	...	1	97	686	7.1	...	...	8.8	15	96.6	96.6	96.6	...	Netherlands Antilles
5,916	...	4	79	1,749	22.1	5.0	...	7.5	15	57.9	57.4	58.3	13.5	New Caledonia
105,186	19.8	7	4,973	107,837	21.7	63.0	4,508	39.1	15	100.0	100.0	100.0	7.3	New Zealand
...	...	10[5]	3,840	48,758	12.7	12.0	1,231	...	15	64.3	64.2	64.4	3.9	Nicaragua
2,145	10.0	2	355	5,569	15.7	0.7	55	...	15	15.7	23.5	8.3	2.3	Niger
...	...	31	12,103	228,000	18.8	4.0	367	...	15	64.1	72.3	56.2	0.7	Nigeria
[4]	[4]	...	...	...	...	...	...	...	15	96.3	96.9	95.6	...	Northern Mariana Islands
[4]	[4]	89	11,515	181,741	15.8	54.5	4,164	18.7	15	100.0	100.0	100.0	7.4	Norway
2,350[5]	6.9[5]	5[1]	1,162	13,251	11.4	8.0	532	...	15	71.3	80.4	61.7	4.5	Oman
95,000	12.6	984	34,078	1,052,782	30.9	3.0	291	2.5	15	43.3	57.6	27.8	2.7	Pakistan
...	...	...	...	130	...	...	...	...	15	97.6	98.3	96.6	...	Palau
...	...	14	6,409	95,341	14.9	30.0	3,024	13.2	15	91.9	92.6	91.3	5.1	Panama
9,941	12.9[2]	2[1]	...	13,663	...	3.0	318	...	15	76.0	81.7	67.7	4.7	Papua New Guinea
[4]	...	2	742[11]	42,302	...	10.0	1,049	6.6	15	93.3	94.4	92.2	4.0	Paraguay
270,576[3]	22.0[3]	886	45,443	657,586	14.2	26.0	3,268	20.6	15	89.9	94.7	85.4	2.9	Peru
[4]	[4]	975[5]	56,880[12]	2,022,106[16]	...	29.0	2,981	22.0	15	95.4	95.5	95.2	3.4	Philippines
1,599,900	17.8	246	73,300	1,091,500	14.9	25.0	1,884	7.9	15	99.8	99.8	99.8	7.5	Poland
25,234	3.7	278	16,087	319,525	19.9	39.0	3,060	7.7	15	92.2	94.8	90.0	5.8	Portugal
149,191	...	45	9,045	171,625[16]	...	...	...	28.7	15	93.8	93.7	94.0	8.2	Puerto Rico
670	5.6	1	643	8,475	13.2	27.0	1,518	13.3	15	81.3	80.5	83.2	3.4	Qatar
13,547[16]	12.1[16]	1	286	8,663	30.3	...	...	...	15	87.1	84.8	89.2	...	Réunion
351,900	32.2	102	23,477	354,488	15.1	23.0	1,817	5.6	15	98.2	99.1	97.3	3.6	Romania
1,676,000	...	913	282,400	3,597,900	12.7	43.0	2,998	14.1	15	99.4	99.8	99.2	3.5	Russia
[4]	[4]	...	646[1]	3,389[1]	5.2[1]	0.4	...	...	15	67.0	73.7	60.6	3.8	Rwanda
...	...	1[11]	51[11]	394[11]	7.7[11]	...	...	2.3	15	90.9	90.0	90.0	3.8	St. Kitts and Nevis
808[11]	23.7[11]	1	157[16]	2,760[16]	17.6[16]	...	...	3.4	15	82.0	...	...	9.8	St. Lucia
415	...	...	...	...	...	...	...	1.4	15	96.0	...	...	6.3	St. Vincent and the Grenadines
...	...	...	...	...	...	...	...	5.6	15	100.0	100.0	100.0	4.2	Samoa
455[5]	10.3[5]	...	...	...	...	...	...	...	15	99.1	99.4	98.8	...	San Marino
...	...	...	...	...	...	...	...	0.3	15	54.2	70.2	39.1	3.8	São Tomé and Príncipe
51,916	8.5	68[15]	8,998[15]	165,262[15]	18.4[15]	16.0	1,455	...	15	77.0	84.1	67.2	7.5	Saudi Arabia
7,301[11]	40.1[11]	2	965[15]	24,081[15]	25.0[15]	3.0	297	...	15	37.3	47.2	27.6	3.7	Senegal
2,002	9.2	...	...	...	...	...	...	4.6	15	84.2	82.9	85.7	7.9	Seychelles
7,756	10.9	1	257[12]	2,571[12]	10.0[12]	2.0	119	1.5	15	36.3	50.7	22.6	0.9	Sierra Leone
9,906	7.5	7	7,764	97,392	12.5	39.0	2,722	7.6	15	92.4	96.4	88.5	3.0	Singapore
116,681	11.5	18	8,544	83,942	9.8	22.0	1,903	9.5	15	100.0	100.0	100.0	5.0	Slovakia
80,885	13.7	37	3,907	51,009	13.1	38.0	2,775	10.4	15	100.0	100.0	100.0	5.7	Slovenia
...	...	...	...	...	...	...	...	...	15	54.1	62.4	44.9	3.8	Solomon Islands
10,400	...	1	549[12]	4,640[12]	...	0.5	...	...	15	24.0	36.0	14.0	0.4	Somalia
140,531[5]	13.0[5]	...	27,099[5]	617,897[5]	22.8[5]	19.0	1,664	1.5	15	85.1	85.8	84.5	8.0	South Africa
1,029,606	...	...	88,922	1,741,528	19.6	51.0	4,017	8.4	15	97.7	98.6	96.8	5.0	Spain
11,652	18.7	12	3,050	38,192	12.5	5.0	474	1.1	15	91.6	94.5	88.9	3.4	Sri Lanka
26,421	34.7	6	1,417	52,260	36.9	3.0	272	0.8	15	57.1	68.3	46.0	1.4	Sudan, The
1,462	...	1	155	1,335	8.6	...	1,124	...	15	94.2	95.9	92.6	3.5	Suriname
2,958[5]	13.0[5]	1	467	5,658	12.1	6.0	642	3.3	15	79.8	80.9	78.7	5.7	Swaziland
...	...	64	33,498[13]	275,217[13]	8.2[13]	50.0	2,972	21.0	15	100.0	100.0	100.0	8.3	Sweden
198,452	...	...	7,709[3]	151,021	...	33.0	2,066	11.5	15	100.0	100.0	100.0	5.4	Switzerland
92,622	7.4	...	4,733[3, 15]	215,734[3]	...	16.0	1,559	...	15	74.4	88.3	60.4	3.1	Syria
[4]	[4]	139	38,806	856,186	22.1	...	...	...	15	94.0	97.6	90.2	5.2	Taiwan
29,482[3]	...	10[3]	5,200[3]	76,613	...	20.0	1,864	11.7	15	99.2	99.6	98.9	2.2	Tajikistan
12,571	11.8	...	1,650	12,776	7.7	0.6	43	2.0	15	75.2	84.1	66.6	3.4	Tanzania
658,474	...	102	25,171[16]	481,936[16]	19.1[16]	22.0	2,096	5.1	15	95.6	97.2	94.0	4.6	Thailand
9,076	13.8	1	443	11,639	26.3	4.0	317	1.3	15	57.1	72.2	42.6	4.5	Togo
824	...	1	53	226[2]	...	...	...	2.8	15	92.8	92.9	92.8	4.7	Tonga
[4]	[4]	3	...	6,007	...	7.7	771	3.4	15	98.2	99.0	97.5	4.4	Trinidad and Tobago
3,839[16]	16.2[16]	...	6,641	121,787	18.3	14.0	1,330	2.8	15	70.8	81.4	60.1	7.7	Tunisia
1,333,177	17.6	863	53,805	1,222,362	22.7	21.0	1,960	10.8	15	85.2	93.6	76.7	2.2	Turkey
26,000	...	15	...	29,435[16]	...	22.0	2,072	...	15	97.7	98.8	96.6	3.9	Turkmenistan
581[12]	...	—	—	—	—	...	...	7.0	15	95.0	...	...	...	Tuvalu
36,063	20.2	...	2,006	29,343	14.6	2.0	154	0.5	15	67.3	77.7	57.1	2.6	Uganda
618,000	...	255[15]	...	922,800[15]	...	41.0	2,977	...	15	98.4	99.5	97.4	7.3	Ukraine
1,925[14]	7.7[14]	4	510[11]	17,950	...	12.0	801	...	15	76.5	75.5	79.5	1.8	United Arab Emirates
2,435,321	16.0	...	89,241	1,820,849	20.4	52.0	3,135	...	15	100.0	100.0	100.0	5.3	United Kingdom
...	...	5,758[11]	940,000	14,350,000	15.3	81.0	5,339	46.5	15	95.5	95.7	95.3	5.4	United States
58,246	...	2	7,165	62,026	8.7	30.0	2,487	10.1	15	97.8	97.4	98.2	3.3	Uruguay
240,100[13]	...	55[13]	...	272,300[13]	...	32.0	2,938	...	15	97.2	98.5	96.0	7.7	Uzbekistan
444	...	1	...	124[12]	...	...	...	...	15	52.9	57.3	47.8	4.8	Vanuatu
[4]	[4]	99[12]	36,232	717,192	19.8	28.0	2,820	11.8	15	93.0	93.3	92.7	5.2	Venezuela
179,907	19.3	104[5]	23,522	509,300	21.7	7.0	404	2.6	15	93.3	95.7	91.0	3.0	Vietnam
—	—	1	266	2,924	11.0	...	...	24.4	...	...	...	...	7.5	Virgin Islands (U.S.)
...	...	22	1,598	30,622	19.2	...	...	...	...	...	...	...	...	West Bank
1,222	...	—	...	...	...	...	...	...	...	...	...	...	...	Western Sahara
67,883	...	2	1,991[3]	65,675	...	4.0	419	...	15	46.4	67.4	25.0	7.0	Yemen
...	...	83	10,998	147,981	13.5	22.0	1,674	...	15	93.3	97.6	89.2	...	Yugoslavia
7,982[12]	...	2	640	4,470	7.0	2.0	241	1.5	15	78.0	85.2	71.2	2.2	Zambia
27,431[2]	18.5[2]	28[2]	3,581[3]	43,200[3]	12.1[3]	7.0[3]	638	4.9	15	92.7	95.5	89.9	7.1	Zimbabwe

[1]1990. [2]1992. [3]1995. [4]General second level includes vocational second level. [5]1994. [6]Includes upper primary. [7]College of the Bahamas only. [8]Public schools only. [9]First level includes general second level. [10]Includes preschool. [11]1993. [12]1991. [13]1997. [14]Excludes teacher training. [15]Universities only. [16]1996. [17]Republic of Cyprus only. [18]Includes lower secondary. [19]Data exclude 1,770 primary and 1,449 secondary schools in the Al-Azhar education system. [20]Port-au-Prince universities only. [21]Upper second level only. [22]Mainland Tanzania only.

BIBLIOGRAPHY AND SOURCES

The following list indicates the principal documentary sources used in the compilation of *Britannica World Data.* It is by no means a complete list, either for international or for national sources, but is indicative more of the range of materials to which reference has been made in preparing this compilation.

While *Britannica World Data* has long been based primarily on print sources, many rare in North American library collections, the burgeoning resources of the Internet can be accessed from any appropriately equipped personal computer (PC). At this writing, more than 100 national statistical offices had Internet sites and there were also sites for central banks, national information offices, individual ministries, and the like.

Because of the relative ease of access to these sites for PC users, uniform resource locators (URLs) for mainly official sites have been added to both country statements (at the end, in boldface) and individual Comparative National Statistics tables (at the end of the headnote) when a source providing comparable international data existed. Many sites exist that are narrower in coverage or less official and that may also serve the reader (on-line newspapers; full texts of national constitutions; business and bank sites) but space permitted the listing of only the top national and intergovernmental sites. Sites that are wholly or predominantly in a language other than English are so identified.

International Statistical Sources

Asian Development Bank. *Asian Development Outlook* (annual); *Key Indicators of Developing Member Countries of ADB* (annual).

Billboard Books. *World Radio TV Handbook* (annual).

Caribbean Development Bank. *Annual Report.*

Christian Research. *World Churches Handbook* (1997).

Comité Monétaire de la Zone Franc. *La Zone Franc: Rapport* (annual).

Commonwealth of Independent States. *Demographic Yearbook; Sodruzhestvo Nezavizimykh Gosudarstv v 19** godu; Strany-Chleny SNG: Statistichesky Yezhegodnik (Member States of the CIS: Statistical Yearbook).*

Eastern Caribbean Central Bank. *Report and Statement of Accounts* (annual).

Europa Publications Ltd. *Africa South of the Sahara* (annual); *The Europa Year Book* (2 vol.); *The Far East and Australasia* (annual); *The Middle East and North Africa* (annual).

Food and Agriculture Organization. *Food Balance Sheets; Production Yearbook; Trade Yearbook; World Census of Agriculture* (decennial); *Yearbook of Fishery Statistics* (2 vol.); *Yearbook of Forest Products.*

Her Majesty's Stationery Office. *The Commonwealth Yearbook.*

Instituts d'Émission d'Outre-Mer et des Départements d'Outre-Mer (France). *Bulletin trimestriel* (quarterly); *Rapport annuel.*

Inter-American Development Bank. *Economic and Social Progress in Latin America* (annual).

Inter-Parliamentary Union. *Chronicle of Parliamentary Elections and Developments* (annual); *World Directory of Parliaments* (annual).

International Air Transport Association. *World Air Transport Statistics* (annual).

International Bank for Reconstruction and Development/The World Bank. *Statistical Handbook 19**: States of the Former USSR* (annual); *World Bank Atlas* (annual); *Global Development Finance* (2 vol.; annual); *World Development Report* (annual).

International Civil Aviation Organization. *Civil Aviation Statistics of the World* (annual); *Digest of Statistics.*

International Institute for Strategic Studies. *The Military Balance* (annual).

International Labour Organisation. *Year Book of Labour Statistics; The Cost of Social Security: Basic Tables* (triennial).

International Monetary Fund. *Annual Report on Exchange Arrangements and Exchange Restrictions; Direction of Trade Statistics Yearbook; Government Finance Statistics Yearbook; IMF Staff Country Reports* (irreg.); *International Financial Statistics* (monthly, with yearbook).

International Road Federation. *World Road Statistics* (annual).

International Telecommunication Union. *Yearbook of Statistics: Telecommunication Services* (annual).

Jane's Publishing Co., Ltd. *Jane's World Railways* (annual).

Keesing's Worldwide LLC. *Keesing's Record of World Events* (monthly except August).

Macmillan Press Ltd. *The Statesman's Year-Book.*

Middle East Economic Digest Ltd. *Middle East Economic Digest* (semimonthly).

Mining Journal, Ltd. *Mining Annual Review* (2 vol.).

Organization for Economic Cooperation and Development. *Economic Surveys* (annual); *Financing and External Debt of Developing Countries* (annual).

Organization of Eastern Caribbean States. *Statistical Booklet* (irreg.).

Oxford University Press. *World Christian Encyclopedia* (David B. Barrett, ed. [1982]).

Pan American Health Organization. *Health Conditions in the Americas* (2 vol.; quadrennial).

PennWell Publishing Co. *International Petroleum Encyclopedia* (annual).

René Moreux et Cie. *Marchés tropicaux & Méditerranéens* (weekly).

United Nations (UN). *Demographic Yearbook; Energy Balances and Electricity Profiles* (biennial); *Industrial Commodities Statistics Yearbook; Energy Statistics Yearbook; International Trade Statistics Yearbook* (2 vol.); *Monthly Bulletin of Statistics; Population Studies* (irreg.); *National Accounts Statistics* (2 parts; annual); *Population and Vital Statistics Report* (quarterly); *Statistical Yearbook; World Population Prospects 19*** (biennial).

UN: Economic Commission for Africa. *African Socio-Economic Indicators* (annual); *African Statistical Yearbook* (2 vol. in 4 parts); *Demographic and Related Socio-Economic Data Sheets for ECA Member States* (irreg.); *Economic and Social Survey of Africa* (annual).

UN: Economic Commission for Europe. *Annual Bulletin of Housing and Building Statistics for Europe; Annual Bulletin of Transport Statistics for Europe.*

UN: Economic Commission for Latin America. *Economic Survey of Latin America and the Caribbean* (2 vol.; annual); *Statistical Yearbook for Latin America and the Caribbean.*

UN: Economic and Social Commission for Asia and the Pacific. *Statistical Indicators for Asia and the Pacific* (quarterly); *Statistical Yearbook for Asia and the Pacific.*

UN: Economic and Social Commission for Western Asia. *Demographic and Related Socio-Economic Data Sheets* (irreg.); *National Accounts Studies of the ESCWA Region* (irreg.); *The Population Situation in the ESCWA Region* (irreg.); *Prices and Financial Statistics in the ESCWA Region* (irreg.); *Statistical Abstract of the Region of the Economic and Social Commission for Western Asia* (annual).

UN: Educational, Scientific, and Cultural Organization. *Statistical Yearbook.*

United Nations Industrial Development Organization. *Industrial Development Review Series* (irreg.); *Industrial Development: Global Report* (annual); *International Yearbook of Industrial Statistics.*

United States: Central Intelligence Agency, *The World Factbook* (annual); Dept. of Commerce, *World Population Profile* (biennial); Dept. of Health and Human Services, *Social Security Programs Throughout the World* (biennial); Dept. of Interior, *Minerals Yearbook* (3 vol. in 6 parts); Dept. of State, *Background Notes* (irreg.).

World Health Organization. *World Health Statistics Annual; World Health Statistics Quarterly.*

World Tourism Organization. *Compendium of Tourism Statistics* (annual).

National Statistical Sources

Afghanistan. *Preliminary Results of the First Afghan Population Census (1979).*

Albania. *Albania: Statistical Annex* (IMF Staff Country Report [2000]); *Population and Housing Census 1989; Statistical Yearbook of Albania.*

Algeria. *Annuaire statistique; Recensement général de la population et de l'habitat, 1998; Algeria: Recent Economic Developments* (IMF Country Staff Report [2000]).

American Samoa. *American Samoa Statistical Digest* (annual); *American Samoa Economic Report; Report on the State of the Island* (U.S. Department of the Interior [annual]); *1990 Census of Population and Housing.*

Andorra. *Informe Econòmic Anual; Recull Estadístic General de la Població Andorra 90.*

Angola. *Angola—Recent Economic Developments* (IMF Staff Country Report [2000]); *Perfil estatístico de Angola* (annual).

Antigua. *Antigua and Barbuda—Statistical Annex* (IMF Staff Country Report [1999]); *Statistical Yearbook; 1991 Population and Housing Census.*

Argentina. *Anuario estadístico de la República Argentina; Censo nacional de población y vivienda, 1991; Encuesta permanente de hogares* (irreg.).

Armenia. *Recent Economic Development and Selected Issues* (IMF Staff Country Report [1999]); *Statisticheskii Yezhegodnik Armenii* (Statistical Yearbook of Armenia).

Aruba. *Statistical Yearbook; Central Bank of Aruba Bulletin* (quarterly); *Third Population and Housing Census October 6, 1991.*

Australia. *Monthly Summary of Statistics, Australia; Social Indicators* (annual); *Year Book Australia; 1996 Census of Population and Housing.*

Austria. *Grosszählung 1991* (General Census 1991). *Sozialstatistische Daten* (irreg.); *Statistisches Jahrbuch für die Republik Österreich.*

Azerbaijan. *Azerbaijan—Recent Economic Developments* (IMF Staff Country Report [2000]); *Statistical Yearbook of Azerbaijan.*

Bahamas, The. *Census of Population and Housing 1990; Statistical Abstract* (annual); *The Bahamas: Selected Issues and Statistical Appendix* (IMF Staff Country Report [1999]).

Bahrain. *Statistical Abstract* (annual); *The Population, Housing, Buildings and Establishments Census—1991.*

Bangladesh. *Bangladesh Population Census, 1991; Statistical Yearbook of Bangladesh; Bangladesh: Recent Economic Developments* (IMF Staff Country Report [2000]).

Barbados. *Barbados Economic Report* (annual); *Monthly Digest of Statistics; Barbados: Statistical Appendix* (IMF Staff Country Report [1999]).

Belarus. *Narodnoye Khozyaystvo Respubliki Belarus: Statisticheskiy Yezhegodnik* (National Economy of the Republic of Belarus: Statistical Yearbook).

Belgium. *Annuaire statistique de la Belgique; Recensement de la population et des logements au 1er mars 1991.*

Belize. *Abstract of Statistics* (annual); *Belize Economic Survey* (annual); *Belize—Statistical Appendix* (IMF Staff Country Report [2000]); *Labour Force Survey (1993); 1991 Population Census: Major Findings.*

Benin. *Annuaire statistique; Recensement général de la population et de l'habitation* (1992); *Benin—Selected Issues and Statistical Appendix* (IMF Staff Country Report [1998]).

Bermuda. *Bermuda Digest of Statistics* (annual); *Report of the Manpower Survey* (annual); *The 1991 Census of Population and Housing.*

Bhutan. *Bhutan—Statistical Annex* (IMF Staff Coun-try Report [1999]); *Statistical Yearbook of Bhutan.*

Bolivia. *Anuario estadístico; Censo nacional de población y vivienda 1992; Compendio estadístico* (annual); *Estadísticas socio-económicas* (annual); *Resumen estadístico* (annual); *Bolivia: Statistical Annex* (IMF Staff Country Report [2000]).

Bosnia and Herzegovina. *Bosnia and Herzegovina—Selected Issues and Statistical Appendix* (IMF Staff Country Report [2000]).

Botswana. *National Development Plan 7, 1991–1997; 1991 Population and Housing Census; Botswana—Selected Issues and Statistical Appendix* (IMF Staff Country Report [1999]).

Brazil. *Anuário Estatístico do Brasil; Contagem da Populacao 1996.*

Brunei. *Brunei Statistical Yearbook; Summary Tables of the Population Census 1991.*

Bulgaria. *Prebroyavaneto na naselenìeto kŭm 4.12.1985 godina* (Census of Population of Dec. 4,

1985); *Naselenie* (Population; annual); *Statisticheskii godishnik na Republika Bŭlgariya* (Statistical Yearbook of the Republic of Bulgaria).

Burkina Faso. *Annuaire Statistique; Burkina Faso—Recent Economic Developments* (IMF Staff Country Report [2000]); *Recensement général de la population du 10 au 20 decembre 1985.*

Burundi. *Annuaire statistique; Recensement général de la population, 1990; Burundi: Statistical Annex* (IMF Staff Country Report [2000]).

Cambodia. *1998 Population Census of Cambodia.*

Cameroon. *Cameroon—Statistical Appendix* (IMF Staff Country Report [2000]); *Recensement général de la population et de l'habitat 1987.*

Canada. *Canada Year Book* (biennial); *Census Canada 1996: Population.*

Cape Verde. *Boletím Anual de Estatística; Cape Verde—Recent Economic Developments* (IMF Staff Country Report [1999]); *I.º Recenseamento Geral da População e Habìtação—1990.*

Central African Republic. *Annuaire statistique; Central African Republic—Statistical Annex* (IMF Staff Country Report [2000]); *Recensement général de la population 1988.*

Chad. *Annuaire statistique; Recensement general de la population et de l'habitat 1993; Chad—Recent Economic Developments* (IMF Staff Country Report [1999]).

Chile. *Chile XVI censo nacional de población y V de vivienda, 22 de abril 1992; Compendio estadístico* (annual).

China, People's Republic of. *People's Republic of China Year-Book; Statistical Yearbook of China; 10 Percent Sampling Tabulation on the 1990 Population Census of the People's Republic of China.*

Colombia. *Colombia estadística* (annual); *Censo 93 informacion de vivienda* (1985); *Colombia: Statistical Appendix* (IMF Staff Country Report [2000]).

Comoros. *Comoros—Statistical Annex* (IMF Staff Country Report [2000]); *Recensement général de la population et de l'habitat 15 septembre 1980.*

Congo, Dem. Rep. of the (Zaire). *Annuaire statistique* (irreg.); *Recensement Scientifique de la Population du 1er juillet 1984.*

Congo, Rep. of the. *Annuaire statistique; Recensement général de la population et de l'habitat de 1984.*

Costa Rica. *Anuario estadístico; Costa Rica at a Glance* (annual); *Censo de Población 1984.*

Côte d'Ivoire. *Côte d'Ivoire—Selected Issues and Statistical Appendix* (IMF Staff Country Report [2000]); *Recensement général de la population et de l'habitat 1988.*

Croatia. *Census of Population, Households, Dwellings and Farms 31st March 1991; Statistical Yearbook.*

Cuba. *Anuario estadístico; Censo de población y viviendas, 1981.*

Cyprus. *Census of Industrial Production* (annual); *Census of Population 1992; Economic Report* (annual); *Statistical Abstract* (annual).

Czech Republic. *Statistická ročenka České Republiky* (Statistical Yearbook of the Czech Republic).

Denmark. *Folke- og boligtaellingen, 1981* (Population and Housing Census); *Statistisk årbog* (Statistical Yearbook).

Djibouti. *Annuaire statistique de Djibouti.*

Dominica. *Dominica—Statistical Annex* (IMF Staff Country Report [2000]); *Population and Housing Census 1991; Statistical Digest* (irreg.).

Dominican Republic. *Cifras Dominicanas* (irreg.); *VI Censo nacional de población y vivienda, 1981.*

Ecuador. *Serie estadística* (quinquennial); *Censo de población (V) y de vivienda (IV) 1990.*

Egypt. *Population, Housing, and Establishment Census, 1986; Statistical Yearbook.*

El Salvador. *Anuario estadístico* (irreg.); *Censos nacionales: V censo de población y IV de vivienda (1992); El Salvador en cifras* (annual); *Indicadores económicos y sociales* (annual).

Equatorial Guinea. *Censos nacionales, I de población y I de vivienda—4 al 17 de julio de 1983; Equatorial Guinea—Recent Economic Developments* (IMF Staff Country Report [1999]).

Eritrea. *Eritrea—Selected Issues* (IMF Staff Country Report [1998]).

Estonia. *Eesti Statistika Aastaraamat* (Estonia Statistical Yearbook); *Estonian Human Development Report* (annual).

Ethiopia. *1994 Population and Housing Census of Ethiopia; Ethiopia Statistical Abstract* (annual); *Ethiopia—Recent Economic Developments* (IMF Staff Country Report [1999]).

Faroe Islands. *Rigsombudsmanden på Færøerne: Beretning* (annual); *Statistical Bulletin* (annual).

Fiji. *Annual Employment Survey; Census of Industries* (annual); *Current Economic Statistics* (quarterly); *1996 Census of the Population and Housing.*

Finland. *Annual Statistics of Agriculture; Economic Survey* (annual); *Population Census 1990; Statistical Yearbook of Finland.*

France. *Annuaire statistique de la France; Données sociales* (triennial); *Recensement général de la population de 1990; Tableaux de l'Economie Française* (annual).

French Guiana. *Recensement général de la population de 1990: logements-population-emplois, 973: Guyane; Tableaux economiques regionaux: Guyane* (biennial).

French Polynesia. *Résultats du Recensement Général de la Population de la Polynésie Française, du 6 Septembre 1996; Tableaux de l'economie polynesienne* (irreg.); *Te avei'a: Bulletin d'information statistique* (monthly).

Gabon. *Situation économique, financière et sociale de la République Gabonaise* (annual); *Gabon—Statistical Annex* (IMF Staff Country Report [1997]).

Gambia, The. *Statistical Abstract* (annual?); *The Gambia—Selected Issues* (IMF Staff Country Report [2000]).

Gaza Strip. *Judaea, Samaria, and Gaza Area Statistics Quarterly; Palestinian Statistical Abstract* (annual).

Georgia. *Georgia—Recent Economic Developments and Selected Issues* (IMF Staff Country Report [2000]); *Narodnoye Khozyaystvo Gruzinskoy SSR* (National Economy of the Georgian S.S.R. [annual]).

Germany. *Statistisches Jahrbuch für die Bundesrepublik Deutschland; Volkszählung vom 25. Mai 1987* (Census of Population).

Ghana. *Ghana—Statistical Appendix* (IMF Staff Country Report [2000]); *Population Census of Ghana, 1984; Quarterly Digest of Statistics.*

Greece. *Recensement de la population et des habitations, 1991; Statistical Yearbook of Greece.*

Greenland. *Grønland* (annual); *Grønlands befolkning* (Greenland Population [annual]).

Grenada. *Abstract of Statistics* (annual); *Grenada—Statistical Appendix* (IMF Staff Country Report [2000]). *1991 Population and Housing Census.*

Guadeloupe. *Recensement général de la population de 1990: logements-population-emplois, 971: Guadeloupe; Tableaux economiques regionaux: Guadeloupe* (biennial).

Guam. *Guam Annual Economic Review; Census '90: Guam.*

Guatemala. *Anuario estadística; Censo nacional instituto nacional de estadística 1994: X Nacional de población y V de habitación.*

Guernsey. *Guernsey Census 1996; Statistical Digest* (annual); *Economic and Statistics Review* (annual).

Guinea. *Guinea—Statistical Appendix* (IMF Staff Country Report [2000]).

Guinea-Bissau. *Guinea-Bissau—Statistical Annex* (IMF Staff Country Report [1999]); *Recenseamento Geral da População e da Habitação, 1994.*

Guyana. *Bank of Guyana: Annual Report and Statement of Accounts; Guyana: Recent Economic Developments* (IMF Staff Country Report [1999]); *Guyana and Belize: Country Studies* (1993).

Haiti. *Banque de la République d'Haiti: Rapport Annuel; Haiti—Statistical Annex* (IMF Staff Country Report [1999]). *Résultats préliminaires du recensement général (Septembre 1982).*

Honduras. *Anuario estadístico; Censo nacional de población y vivienda, 1988; Honduras—Statistical Appendix* (IMF Staff Country Report [2000]); *Honduras en cifras* (annual).

Hong Kong. *Annual Digest of Statistics; Hong Kong* (annual); *Hong Kong 1991 Population Census; Hong Kong Social and Economic Trends* (biennial).

Hungary. *Statisztikai évkönyv* (Statistical Yearbook); *1990, Évi népszámlálás* (Census of Population).

Iceland. *Hagtidhindi* (monthly); *Landshagir* (Statistical Yearbook of Iceland [annual]); *Utanrikisverslun* (External Trade [annual]).

India. *Census of India, 1991; Economic Survey* (annual); *India: A Reference Annual; Statistical Abstract* (annual).

Indonesia. *Indonesia: An Official Handbook* (irreg.); *Hasil Sensus penduduk Indonesia, 1990* (Census of Population); *Statistical Yearbook of Indonesia.*

Iran. *Multi-Round Population Survey 1991; National Census of Population and Housing, October 1996; Iran Statistical Yearbook; Islamic Republic of Iran Statistical Appendix* (IMF Staff Country Report [1999]).

Iraq. *Iraq: A Country Study* (1990); *Annual Abstract of Statistics.*

Ireland. *Census of Population of Ireland, 1996; National Income and Expenditure* (annual); *Statistical Abstract* (annual).

Isle of Man. *Census Report 1996; Isle of Man Digest of Economic and Social Statistics* (annual).

Israel. *1995 Census of Population and Housing; Statistical Abstract* (annual).

Italy. *Statistica agrarie; Statistiche demografiche* (4 parts); *Statistiche dell'istruzione; Annuario statistico Italiano; 13º Censimento generale della popolazione e delle Abitazioni 20 Ottobre 1991.*

Jamaica. *Economic and Social Survey* (annual); *Statistical Abstract* (annual); *Statistical Yearbook of Jamaica.*

Japan. *Japan Statistical Yearbook; Statistical Indicators on Social Life* (annual); *1995 Population Census of Japan.*

Jersey. *Report of the Census for 1996; Statistical Digest* (annual); *An Introduction to Jersey* (irreg.).

Jordan. *Population and Housing Census 1994; Jordan—Statistical Appendix* (IMF Staff Country Report [1997]); *National Accounts* (irreg.); *Statistical Yearbook.*

Kazakhstan. *Republic of Kazakhstan: Selected Issues and Statistical Appendix* (IMF Staff Country Report [2000]); *Statistical Yearbook; Statistichesky Yezhegodnik* (Statistical Yearbook).

Kenya. *Economic Survey* (annual); *Population Census 1989; Statistical Abstract* (annual); *Kenya—Selected Issues and Statistical Appendix* (IMF Staff Country Report [1998]).

Kiribati. *Annual Abstract of Statistics; Kiribati Population Census 1990; Kiribati—Statistical Appendix* (IMF Staff Country Report [1997]).

Korea, North. *North Korea: A Country Study* (1994); *The Population of North Korea* (1990).

Korea, South. *Korea Statistical Yearbook; Social Indicators in Korea* (annual); *1995 Population and Housing Census.*

Kuwait. *Annual Statistical Abstract; General Census of Population and Housing and Buildings 1995.*

Kyrgyzstan. *Kyrgyz Republic: Selected Issues and Statistical Appendix* (IMF Staff Country Report [2000]); *Statistichesky Yezhegodnik Kyrgyzstana* (Statistical Yearbook of Kyrgyzstan).

Laos. *Lao People's Democratic Republic—Recent Economic Developments* (IMF Staff Country Report [2000]).

Latvia. *Statistical Yearbook of Latvia.*

Lebanon. *Lebanon: A Country Study* (1989).

Lesotho. *Lesotho—Statistical Annex* (IMF Staff Country Report [1998]); *Statistical Yearbook; 1986 Population Census.*

Liberia. *Economic Survey* (annual); *Liberia: Selected Issues and Statistical Appendix* (IMF Staff Country Report [2000]).

Libya. *Libya Population Census, 1973.*

Liechtenstein. *Statistisches Jahrbuch; Volkszählung, 2 Dezember 1980* (Census of Population); *Liechtenstein in Figures* (annual).

Lithuania. *Lietuvos Statistikos Metraštis* (Lithuanian Statistical Yearbook).

Luxembourg. *Annuaire statistique; Bulletin du STATEC* (monthly); *Recensement général de la population du 31 mars 1991.*

Macau. *Anuário Estatístico; XIII Recenseamento Geral da População, 1991.*

Macedonia. *Former Yugoslav Republic of Macedonia—Recent Economic Developments* (IMF Staff Country Report [2000]); *Statistical Yearbook of the Republic of Macedonia.*

Madagascar. *Madagascar—Statistical Annex* (IMF Staff Country Report [1999]); *Recensement général de la population et de l'habitat, aout 1993; Situation économique* (annual).

Malawi. *1998 Population and Housing Census; Malawi Statistical Yearbook; Malawi Yearbook; Malawi—Recent Economic Developments* (IMF Staff Country Report [1997]).

Malaysia. *Population and Housing Census of Malaysia 1991; Yearbook of Statistics.*

Maldives. *National Development Plan 1991–1993; Population and Housing Census of Maldives 1990; Statistical Year Book of Maldives.*

Mali. *Annuaire statistique du Mali; Recensement general de la population et de l'habitat (du 1er au 14 avril 1987); Mali: Selected Issues and Statistical Annex* (IMF Staff Country Report [2000]).

Malta. *Annual Abstract of Statistics; Quarterly Digest of Statistics.*

Marshall Islands. *Marshall Islands Statistical Abstract* (annual); *Report on the State of the Islands* (U.S. Department of the Interior [annual]).

Martinique. *Recensement de la population de 1990: logements-population-emplois, 972: Martinique; Tableaux economiques regionaux: Martinique* (biennial).

Mauritania. *Annuaire Statistique; Mauritania—Recent Economic Developments* (IMF Staff Country Report [1999]).

Mauritius. *Annual Digest of Statistics; 1990 Housing and Population Census of Mauritius.*

Mayotte. *Bulletin Trimestriel* (quarterly) and *Rapport Annuel* (Institut d'Emission, France); *Recensement de la population de Mayotte: août 1997.*
Mexico. *Anuario estadístico; XI Censo general de población y vivienda, 1990; Anuario estadístico de los Estados Unidos Mexicanos.*
Micronesia. *Micronesia—Recent Economic Developments* (IMF Staff Country Report [1998]); *FSM Statistical Yearbook* (annual).
Moldova. *Economic Reviews: Moldova* (IMF [irreg.]); *Republica Moldova in Cifre* (annual); *Republic of Moldova* (UNDP).
Monaco. *Recensement general de la population 1990.*
Mongolia. *Mongolian Statistical Yearbook* (annual); *Mongolia—Statistical Annex* (IMF Staff Country Report [2000]).
Morocco. *Annuaire statistique du Maroc; Recensement général de la population et de l'habitat de 1994.*
Mozambique. *Anuário Estatístico; Republic of Mozambique—Selected Issues* (IMF Staff Country Report [1998]); *II Recenseamento Geral da População e habitação, 1997.*
Myanmar (Burma). *Myanmar—Recent Economic Developments* (IMF Staff Country Report [1999]); *Report to the Pyithu Hluttaw on the Financial, Social, and Economic Conditions for 19*** (annual); *Statistical Abstract* (irreg.); *1983 Population Census.*
Namibia. *1991 Population and Housing Census; Statistical/Economic Review* (annual); *Namibia—Statistical Appendix* (IMF Staff Country Report [1999]).
Nauru. *Population Profile* (irreg.).
Nepal. *Economic Survey* (annual); *Population Monograph of Nepal* (1995); *The Seventh Plan (1985–90); Statistical Pocket Book* (irreg.); *Statistical Yearbook of Nepal.*
Netherlands, The. *Statistical Yearbook of the Netherlands; 14e Algemene volkstelling, 28 februari 1971* (14th General Population Census).
Netherlands Antilles. *Netherlands Antilles—Selected Issues* (IMF Staff Country Report [1999]); *Tweede Algemene Volks- en Woningtelling Nederlandse Antillen: toestand per 1 Februari 1992; Statistical Yearbook of the Netherlands Antilles.*
New Caledonia. *Annuaire statistique; Images de la population de la Nouvelle-Calédonie principaux resultats du recensement 1996; Tableaux bilan economique* (annual); *New Caledonia Facts and Figures* (annual).
New Zealand. *1996 New Zealand Census of Population and Dwellings; New Zealand Official Yearbook.*
Nicaragua. *Censos Nacionales 1995; Compendio Estadístico* (annual); *Nicaragua—Recent Economic Developments and Statistical Annex* (IMF Staff Country Report [1999]).
Niger. *Annuaire statistique; Niger—Statistical Annex* (IMF Staff Country Report [1997]); *2ème Recensement général de la population 1988.*
Nigeria. *Annual Abstract of Statistics; Nigeria: A Country Study* (1992); *Nigeria—Statistical Appendix* (IMF Staff Country Report [2000]).
Northern Mariana Islands. *CNMI Population Profile; Report on the State of the Islands* (U.S. Department of the Interior [annual]).
Norway. *Folke- og boligtelling 1990* (Population and Housing Census); *Industristatistikk* (annual); *Statistisk årbok* (Statistical Yearbook).
Oman. *General Census of Population, Housing, and Establishments* (1993); *Statistical Year Book.*
Pakistan. *Economic Survey* (annual); *Pakistan Statistical Yearbook; Population Census of Pakistan, 1981.*
Palau. *Statistical Year Book* (annual); *Census '90.*
Panama. *Indicadores económicos y sociales* (annual); *X censo nacional de poblacion y vivienda realizados el 14 de mayo del 2000; Panama en cifras* (annual); *Situación económica: Cuentas nacionales* (annual); *Situación económica: Industria* (annual).
Papua New Guinea. *Papua New Guinea—Statistical Appendix* (IMF Staff Country Report [1999]); *Summary of Statistics* (annual); *1990 National Population Census.*
Paraguay. *Anuario estadístico del Paraguay; Censo nacional de población y viviendas, 1992.*
Peru. *Censos nacionales; IX de población: IV de vivienda, 11 de julio de 1993; Compendio estadístico* (3 vol.; annual); *Informe estadístico* (annual).
Philippines. *Philippine Statistical Yearbook; Philippine Yearbook; 2000 Census of Population and Housing.*
Poland. *Narodowy spis powszechny 1988* (Census of Population); *Rocznik statystyczny* (Statistical Yearbook).
Portugal. *Anuário Estatístico; XIII Recenseamento Geral da População: III Recenseamento Geral da Habitação, 1991.*
Puerto Rico. *Estadísticas socioeconomicas* (annual); *Informe económico al gobernador* (Economic Report to the Governor [annual]); *1990 Census of Population and Housing* (U.S.).
Qatar. *Annual Statistical Abstract; Economic Survey of Qatar* (annual); *Qatar Year Book.*
Réunion. *Recensement général de la population de 1990: logements-population-emploi, 974; Réunion; Tableau Economique de la Réunion* (biennial).
Romania. *Anuarul statistic al României; Population and Housing Census January 7, 1992.*
Russia. *Demograficheskiy Yezhegodnik Rossii* (Demographic Yearbook of Russia; [annual]); *Rossiysky Statistichesky Yezhegodnik* (Russian Statistical Yearbook).
Rwanda. *Bulletin de Statistique: Supplement Annuel; Recensement general de la population et de l'habitat 1991; Rwanda: Recent Economic Developments* (IMF Staff Country Report [2000]).
St. Kitts and Nevis. *Annual Digest of Statistics; St. Christopher and Nevis—Recent Economic Developments* (IMF Staff Country Report [1997]).
St. Lucia. *Annual Statistical Digest; St. Lucia—Statistical Annex* (IMF Staff Country Report [1999]).
St. Vincent and the Grenadines. *Digest of Statistics* (annual); *Population and Housing Census 1991.*
Samoa (Western Samoa). *Annual Statistical Abstract; Census of Population and Housing, 1981; Seventh Development Plan 1992–1994; Samoa—Statistical Appendix* (IMF Staff Country Report [1999]).
San Marino. *Bollettino di Statistica* (quarterly); *5 Censimento generale della popolazione* (1979); *Annuario Statistico Demografico 1992–1996* (irreg.).
São Tomé and Príncipe. *1º Recenseamento Geral da População e da Habitação 1981; Sao Tome—Statistical Appendix* (IMF Staff Country Report [1998]).
Saudi Arabia. *Saudi Arabian Monetary Agency: Annual Report* (annual).
Senegal. *Recensement de la population et de l'habitat 1988; Situation économique du Senegal* (annual); *Senegal—Statistical Appendix* (IMF Staff Country Report [1999]).
Seychelles. *Statistical Abstract* (annual); *Seychelles—Statistical Annex* (IMF Staff Country Report [1998]); *National Population and Housing Census 1994.*
Sierra Leone. *Sierra Leone—Recent Economic Developments* (IMF Staff Country Report [1997]).
Singapore. *Census of Population, 1990; Singapore Yearbook; Yearbook of Statistics Singapore.*
Slovakia. *Sčítanie L'udu, Domov a Bytov 1991* (Census of Population, Housing, and Families 1991); *Statistical Yearbook of the Slovak Republic.*
Slovenia. *Statistični Letopis Republike Slovenija* (Statistical Yearbook of the Republic of Slovenia).
Solomon Islands. *Solomon Islands 1986 Population Census; Solomon Islands—Statistical Appendix* (IMF Staff Country Report [1998]).
Somalia. *Statistical Abstract* (annual).
South Africa. *The People of South Africa Population Census, 1996; South Africa: Official Yearbook of the Republic of South Africa; Stats in Brief* (annual).
Spain. *Anuario estadístico; Censo de población de 1991.*
Sri Lanka. *Census of Population and Housing, 1981; Sri Lanka Statistical Abstract* (irreg.); *Statistical Pocketbook of the Democratic Socialist Republic of Sri Lanka* (annual).
Sudan, The. *Sudan—Statistical Appendix* (IMF Staff Country Report [2000]); *Third Population Census, 1983.*
Suriname. *General Population Census 1980; Statistisch Jaarboek van Suriname; Suriname—Recent Economic Developments* (IMF Staff Country Report [1997]).
Swaziland. *Annual Statistical Bulletin; Report on the 1986 Swaziland Population Census; Swaziland—Selected Issues and Statistical Appendix* (IMF Staff Country Report [2000]).
Sweden. *Folk- och bostadsräkningen, 1990* (Population and Housing Census); *Statistisk årsbok för Sverige* (Statistical Abstract of Sweden [annual]).
Switzerland. *Recensement fédéral de la population, 1990; Statistisches Jahrbuch* (Statistical Yearbook).
Syria. *General Census of Housing and Inhabitants, 1981; Statistical Abstract* (annual).
Taiwan. *The Republic of China Yearbook; Social Indicators of the Republic of China* (annual); *Statistical Abstract* (annual); *Statistical Yearbook of the Republic of China; Taiwan Statistical Data Book* (annual); *1990 Census of Population and Housing.*
Tajikistan. *Republic of Tajikistan: Recent Economic Developments* (IMF Staff Country Report [2000]); *Narodnoye Khozyaystvo Tadzhikskoy SSR* (National Economy of the Tadzhik S.S.R. [annual]).
Tanzania. *Tanzania—Statistical Annex* (IMF Staff Country Report [2000]); *Tanzania in Figures* (annual); *Tanzania Statistical Abstract* (irreg.); *1978 Population Census.*
Thailand. *Report of the Industrial Survey, Whole Kingdom* (biennial); *Report of the Labor Force Survey: Whole Kingdom* (three issues annually); *Statistical Handbook of Thailand* (annual); *Statistical Yearbook; 1990 Population and Housing Census.*
Togo. *Annuaire statistique du Togo; Eurostat Country Profile: Togo* (1991); *Recensement général de la population et de l'habitat 1981; Togo—Selected Issues* (IMF Staff Country Report [1999]).
Tonga. *Population Census, 1986; Sixth Development Plan 1991–95; Tonga—Statistical Annex* (IMF Staff Country Report [1998]).
Trinidad and Tobago. *Central Bank of Trinidad and Tobago: Annual Economic Survey; 1990 Population and Housing Census.*
Tunisia. *Annuaire statistique de la Tunisie; Recensement général de la population et des logements, 30 mars 1984; Tunisia: Recent Economic Developments* (IMF Staff Country Report [2000]).
Turkey. *1990 Genel Nüfus Sayımı* (1990 Census of Population); *Türkiye İstatistik Yilliği* (Statistical Yearbook of Turkey).
Turkmenistan. *Turkmenistan—Recent Economic Developments* (IMF Staff Country Report [1998]); *Turkmenistan v tsifrakh* (Turkmenistan in figures [annual]).
Tuvalu. *1992–94 Medium-Term Economic Framework Programme.*
Uganda. *Uganda: A Country Study; Uganda—Selected Issues and Statistical Appendix* (IMF Staff Country Report [1998]).
Ukraine. *Statistichniy Shchorichnik Ukraini za 19*** *rik* (Statistical Yearbook of Ukraine for the year 19**); *Ukraine—Recent Economic Developments* (IMF Staff Country Report [1999]).
United Arab Emirates. *Statistical Yearbook* (Abu Dhabi).
United Kingdom. *Annual Abstract of Statistics; Britain: An Official Handbook* (annual); *Census 1991; General Household Survey* series (individual titles vary; annual).
United States. *Agricultural Statistics* (annual); *Annual Energy Review; Current Population Reports; Digest of Education Statistics* (annual); *Minerals Yearbook* (3 vol. in 6 parts); *National Transportation Statistics* (annual); *Statistical Abstract* (annual); *U.S. Exports: SIC-Based Products* (annual); *U.S. Imports: SIC-Based Products* (annual); *Vital and Health Statistics* (series 1–20); *1996 Census of Agriculture; 1992 Census of Construction Industries; 1992 Census of Manufacturing; 1992 Census of Retail Trade; 1992 Census of Service Industries; 1992 Census of Wholesale Trade; 1990 Census of Population and Housing.*
Uruguay. *Anuario estadístico; VII Censo general de poblacion III de hogares y V de viviendas, 22 de mayo de 1996; Uruguay—Statistical Annex* (IMF Staff Country Report [1999]).
Uzbekistan. *Narodnoye Khozyaystvo Respubliki Uzbekistan v 19*** *g.* (National Economy of Uzbekistan in the Year 19** [annual]); *Republic of Uzbekistan; Uzbekistan—Recent Economic Developments* (IMF Staff Country Report [2000]).
Vanuatu. *National Population Census 1989; Second National Development Plan 1987–1991* (2 vol.); *Vanuatu Statistical Yearbook.*
Venezuela. *Anuario estadístico; Censo general de la población y vivienda 1990; Encuesta de hogares por muestreo* (annual); *Encuesta industrial* (annual).
Vietnam. *Nien Giam Thong Ke* (Statistical Yearbook); *Tong Dieu Tra Dan So Viet Nam—1989 (Vietnam Population Census—1989); Vietnam—Statistical Appendix and Background Notes* (IMF Staff Country Report [2000]).
Virgin Islands of the United States. *1990 Census of Population and Housing* (U.S.).
West Bank. *Population, Housing and Establishment Census—1997; Palestinian Statistical Abstract* (annual); *West Bank and Gaza Strip; Economic Development in the Five Years Since Oslo* (IMF [irreg.]).
Western Sahara. *Recensement general de la population et de l'habitat* (1994 [Morocco]).
Yemen. *Country Presentation: Republic of Yemen* (1990); *The Yemens: Country Studies* (1986).
Yugoslavia. *Popis stanovištva, domaćinstava, stanova i poljoprivrednih gazdinstava 1991 godine* (Census of Population, Households, Housing, and Agricultural Holdings 1991); *Statistički godišnjak Jugoslavije* (Statistical Yearbook of Yugoslavia).
Zambia. *Zambia—Statistical Appendix* (IMF Staff Country Report [1999]); *1990 Census of Population, Housing, Agriculture.*
Zimbabwe. *Population Census 1992; Statistical Yearbook* (irreg.); *Zimbabwe—Statistical Appendix* (IMF Staff Country Report [1999]).

Index

This index covers both *Britannica Book of the Year* (cumulative for 10 years) and *Britannica World Data.*

Entries in dark type are titles of articles in the *Book of the Year;* **an accompanying year in dark type gives the year the reference appears, and the accompanying page number** in light type **shows where the article appears. References for previous years are preceded by the year in dark type. For example, "Education 01:**204; **00:**191; **99:**209; **98:**201; **97:**203; **96:**191; **95:**174; **94:**154; **93:**153; **92:**151**" indicates that the article "Education" appeared every year from 1992 through 2001. Other references that appear with a page number but without a year refer to references from the current yearbook.**

Indented entries in light type that follow dark-type article titles refer by page number to other places in the text where the subject of the article is discussed. Light-type entries that are not indented refer by page number to subjects that are not themselves article titles. Names of people covered in biographies and obituaries from previous years are followed by the abbreviation "(biog.)" or "(obit.)" with the year in dark type and a page number in light type, e.g., Shore, Francis Rose (obit.) **95:**84. Biographies and obituaries for the current year appear as subentries under the main entry. In cases where a person has both a biography and an obituary, the words appear as subentries under the main entry and are alphabetized accordingly, e.g.:
Assad, Hafez, al- 424, 447, 499
  biography **92:**34
  obituary **01:**100
References to illustrations are by page number and are preceded by the abbreviation *il.*

The index uses word-by-word alphabetization (treating a word as one or more characters separated by a space from the next word). Names beginning with "Mc" and "Mac" are alphabetized as "Mac"; "St." is treated as "Saint."

A

B

C

D

Entries in **boldface** are major title headings in the yearbook; numbers in **boldface** signify the yearbook edition.

F

G

Entries in **boldface** are major title headings in the yearbook; numbers in **boldface** signify the yearbook edition.

H

J

K

L

M

Entries in **boldface** are major title headings in the yearbook; numbers in **boldface** signify the yearbook edition.

O

P

Entries in **boldface** are major title headings in the yearbook; numbers in **boldface** signify the yearbook edition.

S

Entries in **boldface** are major title headings in the yearbook; numbers in **boldface** signify the yearbook edition.

U

V

W

Y

Z

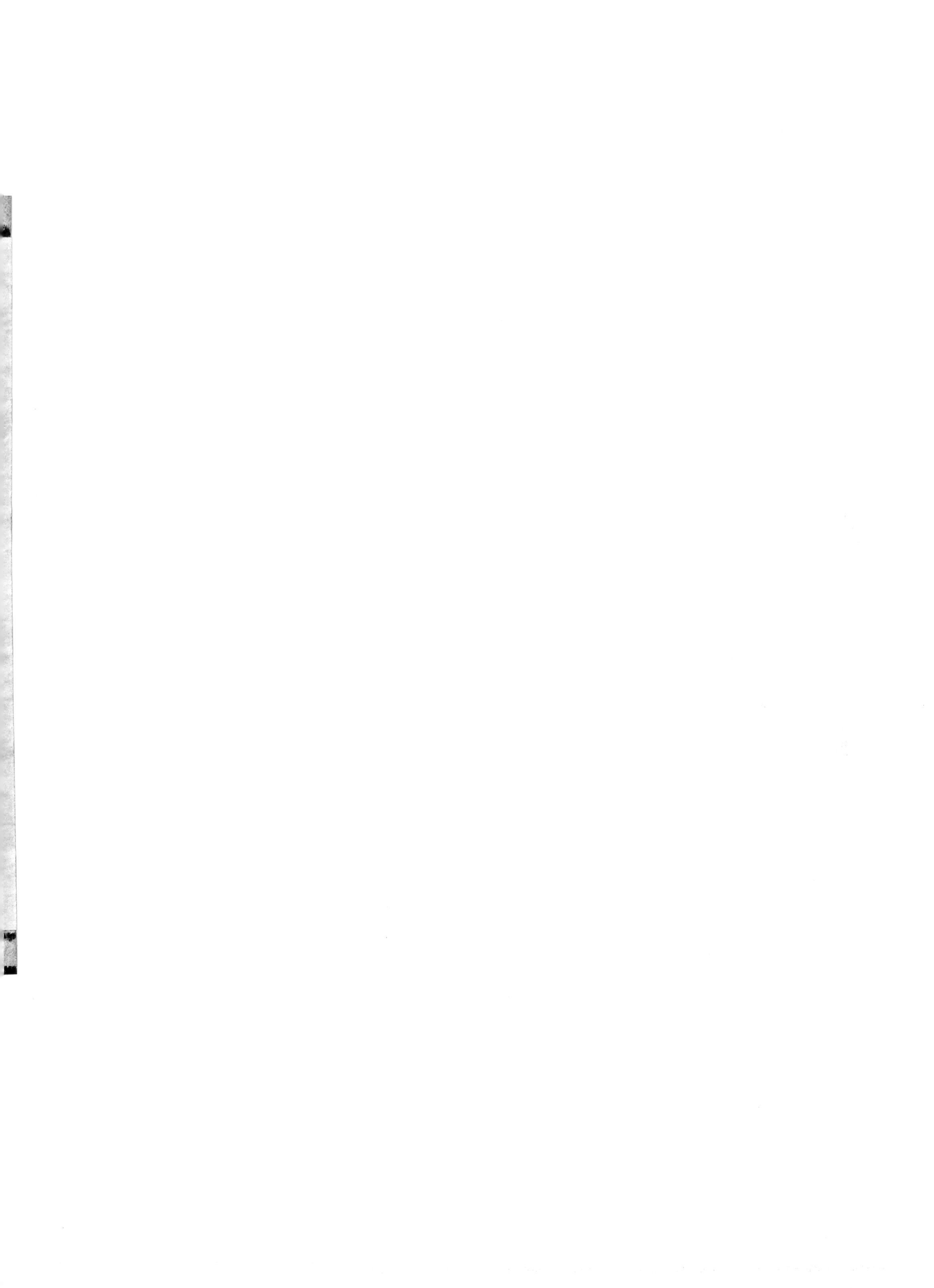